BUTTERWORTHS
DATA PROTECTION LAW
HANDBOOK

BUTTERWORTHS
DATA PROTECTION LAW HANDBOOK

Third edition

Consultant Editors
Anthony Taylor CIPP/E and Adam Gillert
Lexis®PSL Information Law team

Members of the LexisNexis® Group worldwide

United Kingdom	RELX (UK) Limited trading as LexisNexis®, 1–3 Strand, London WC2N 5JR
LNUK Global Partners	LexisNexis® encompasses authoritative legal publishing brands dating back to the 19th century including: Butterworths® in the United Kingdom, Canada and the Asia-Pacific region; Les Editions du Juris Classeur in France; and Matthew Bender® worldwide. Details of LexisNexis® locations worldwide can be found at **www.lexisnexis.com**

© 2021 RELX (UK) Ltd.
Published by LexisNexis®

This is a Butterworths® title

A CIP Catalogue record for this book is available from the British Library.

ISBN for this volume: 978 1 4743 1721 4

Printed and bound by Hobbs the Printers, Hampshire, SO40 3WX

Visit LexisNexis at www.lexisnexis.co.uk

PART 3   DATA PROTECTION: INTERNATIONAL TREATIES

PART 4   EPRIVACY – UK LAW

PART 5   EPRIVACY – EU LAW

PART 6   HUMAN RIGHTS

PART 7   KEY BREXIT TREATIES AND RELATED UK LEGISLATION

CONTENTS

This Handbook also includes key legislation concerning related laws that practitioners will often find it useful to refer to when considering data protection matters, including:

• ePrivacy
• Human rights.

Amendments are indicated using the house style of the LexisNexis® Handbook series as follows: In force repeals/revocations are indicated by an ellipsis. Insertions and in force substitutions are in square brackets. Prospective repeals/revocations or substitutions are in italics with, in the case of substitutions, the text to be substituted set out in the notes (note that this also applies to prospective substitutions that have been brought into force for some, but not all, purposes). Text that has been repealed or revoked with savings in relation to its continued application is also in italics (with details of the relevant savings or transitional provisions set out in the notes). A summary follows—

— **insertion (in force and prospective):** [text in square brackets]

— **in force substitution:** [text in square brackets]

— **prospective substitution:** *text in italics* (with new text set out in notes)

— **in force repeal or revocation:** . . . (an ellipsis)

— **prospective repeal or revocation:** *text in italics*

— **repealed/revoked with savings or transitional provisions:** *text in italics* (with details of savings, etc, set out in notes)

Commencement information is given at provision level for Acts and SIs in cases where the provision came into force on or after 1 April 2016, or where it is not yet in force for all or some purposes.

This Handbook is up-to-date to 1 April 2021, though later developments have been included where possible.

Adam Gillert, Solicitor
Lexis®PSL Information Law team

Anthony Taylor CIPP/E, Solicitor
Data Protection Officer
LexisNexis® Legal & Professional

April 2021

PREFACE

The world has been transformed since the 1980s, when the Council of Europe's Convention 108 became the first binding international instrument to seek to protect against abuses in the processing of personal data. Since that time, the quantity, variety and speed of data processing have grown dramatically, creating new industries as well as new regulatory concerns and frameworks. Enabled by ever more powerful computing and communications technology, the collection, storage, sharing, analysis, and other processing of data now pervades the operations of all sectors of the economy.

In-house counsel and general law practitioners, as well as information law specialists, need to have a good working understanding of data protection law and convenient access to the key pieces of legislation in this increasingly complex and important area of law.

On 31 December 2020, the United Kingdom General Data Protection Regulation (the UK GDPR) replaced the EU's General Data Protection Regulation (the EU GDPR) as the UK's primary general data protection law following the end of the Brexit transition period.

Important aspects of the UK GDPR regime, including permitted national derogations, are contained in the Data Protection Act 2018 (DPA 2018).

As well as being a vital part of the legislative jigsaw when advising on the UK GDPR regime, the DPA 2018 sets out:
• the regime governing the processing of personal data in connection with law enforcement
• the regime for the processing of personal data controlled by intelligence services
• the roles and powers of the Information Commissioner, and various criminal offences.

The end of the Brexit transition period, and introduction of the UK GDPR, resulted in a number of immediate changes for organisations with a UK nexus.

However, the longer-term implications of Brexit for data protection law remain to be seen. At the time of writing, a key question in the short-term remains whether (and on what terms) the EU will grant the UK an adequacy decision, which would:
• allow transfers of personal data from the European Economic Area (EEA) to the UK to continue under the EU GDPR without organisations needing to employ additional transfer mechanisms or specific derogations, and
• suspend the application of the 'Frozen GDPR' regime that applies to certain personal data further to Article 71 of the EU-UK Withdrawal Agreement.

In the longer-term it remains uncertain to what extent the UK will diverge from the key principles of the EU GDPR, and whether any UK adequacy decision granted by the EU will be revoked by the EU or successfully challenged at the Court of Justice.

What seems certain, given that three-quarters of the UK's cross-border data flows are with EU countries, is that EU data protection law will remain a key area of focus for UK organisations. This Handbook, therefore, covers both UK data protection law and also the EU GDPR regime at EEA level.

Since the last edition of this Handbook, the body of key guidance issued by the UK Information Commissioner's Office (ICO) and European Data Protection Board (EDPB) has grown considerably. EDPB guidance is directly relevant to the EU GDPR regime and is also likely to remain highly influential in relation to interpretations of the UK GDPR regime.

Therefore, this edition has been supplemented with statutory codes issued by the ICO, and guidelines issued or endorsed by the EDPB, including draft versions where final versions were not available at the time of publication.

PART 1
DATA PROTECTION – UK LAW AND STATUTORY CODES

RETAINED EUROPEAN PARLIAMENT AND COUNCIL REGULATION

(2016/679/EU)

of 27 April 2016

on the protection of natural persons with regard to the processing of personal data and on the free movement of such data [(United Kingdom General Data Protection Regulation)]

(Text with EEA relevance)

[1.1]

NOTES

Date of publication in OJ: OJ L119, 4.5.2016, p 1. The text of this Regulation incorporates the corrigendum published in OJ L127, 23.5.2018, p 2.

© European Union, 1998–2021.

Editorial Note: this Regulation became retained EU law in accordance with the European Union (Withdrawal) Act 2018, s 3, as from IP completion day, as defined in s 20 of the 2018 Act.

The words in square brackets in the title of this Regulation were substituted by the Data Protection, Privacy and Electronic Communications (Amendments etc) (EU Exit) Regulations 2019, SI 2019/419, reg 3, Sch 1, paras 1, 2.

THE EUROPEAN PARLIAMENT AND THE COUNCIL OF THE EUROPEAN UNION,

Having regard to the Treaty on the Functioning of the European Union, and in particular Article 16 thereof, Having regard to the proposal from the European Commission,

After transmission of the draft legislative act to the national parliaments,

Having regard to the opinion of the European Economic and Social Committee,[1] Having regard to the opinion of the Committee of the Regions,[2]

Acting in accordance with the ordinary legislative procedure,[3] Whereas:

(1) The protection of natural persons in relation to the processing of personal data is a fundamental right. Article 8(1) of the Charter of Fundamental Rights of the European Union (the 'Charter') and Article 16(1) of the Treaty on the Functioning of the European Union (TFEU) provide that everyone has the right to the protection of personal data concerning him or her.

(2) The principles of, and rules on the protection of natural persons with regard to the processing of their personal data should, whatever their nationality or residence, respect their fundamental rights and freedoms, in particular their right to the protection of personal data. This Regulation is intended to contribute to the accomplishment of an area of freedom, security and justice and of an economic union, to economic and social progress, to the strengthening and the convergence of the economies within the internal market, and to the well-being of natural persons.

(3) Directive 95/46/EC of the European Parliament and of the Council[4] seeks to harmonise the protection of fundamental rights and freedoms of natural persons in respect of processing activities and to ensure the free flow of personal data between Member States.

(4) The processing of personal data should be designed to serve mankind. The right to the protection of personal data is not an absolute right; it must be considered in relation to its function in society and be balanced against other fundamental rights, in accordance with the principle of proportionality. This Regulation respects all fundamental rights and observes the freedoms and principles recognised in the Charter as enshrined in the Treaties, in particular the respect for private and family life, home and communications, the protection of personal data, freedom of thought, conscience and religion, freedom of expression and information, freedom to conduct a business, the right to an effective remedy and to a fair trial, and cultural, religious and linguistic diversity.

(5) The economic and social integration resulting from the functioning of the internal market has led to a substantial increase in cross-border flows of personal data. The exchange of personal data between public and private actors, including natural persons, associations and undertakings across the Union has increased. National authorities in the Member States are being called upon by Union law to cooperate and exchange personal data so as to be able to perform their duties or carry out tasks on behalf of an authority in another Member State.

(6) Rapid technological developments and globalisation have brought new challenges for the protection of personal data. The scale of the collection and sharing of personal data has increased significantly. Technology allows both private companies and public authorities to make use of personal data on an unprecedented scale in order to pursue their activities. Natural persons increasingly make personal information available publicly and globally. Technology has transformed both the economy and social life, and should further facilitate the free flow of personal data within the Union and the transfer to third countries and international organisations, while ensuring a high level of the protection of personal data.

(7) Those developments require a strong and more coherent data protection framework in the Union, backed by strong enforcement, given the importance of creating the trust that will allow the digital economy to develop across the internal market. Natural persons should have control of their own personal data. Legal and practical certainty for natural persons, economic operators and public authorities should be enhanced.

(8) Where this Regulation provides for specifications or restrictions of its rules by Member State law, Member States may, as far as necessary for coherence and for making the national provisions comprehensible to the persons to whom they apply, incorporate elements of this Regulation into their national law.

(9) The objectives and principles of Directive 95/46/EC remain sound, but it has not prevented fragmentation in the implementation of data protection across the Union, legal uncertainty or a widespread public perception that there are significant risks to the protection of natural persons, in particular with regard to online activity. Differences in the level of protection of the rights and freedoms of natural persons, in particular the right to the protection of personal data, with regard to the processing of personal data in the Member States may prevent the free flow of personal data throughout the Union. Those differences may therefore constitute an obstacle to the pursuit of economic activities at the level of the Union, distort competition and impede authorities in the discharge of their responsibilities under Union law. Such a difference in levels of protection is due to the existence of differences in the implementation and application of Directive 95/46/EC.

(10) In order to ensure a consistent and high level of protection of natural persons and to remove the obstacles to flows of personal data within the Union, the level of protection of the rights and freedoms of natural persons with regard to the processing of such data should be equivalent in all Member States. Consistent and homogenous application of the rules for the protection of the fundamental rights and freedoms of natural persons with regard to the processing of personal data should be ensured throughout the Union. Regarding the processing of personal data for compliance with a legal obligation, for the performance of a task carried out in the public interest or in the exercise of official authority vested in the controller, Member States should be allowed to maintain or introduce national provisions to further specify the application of the rules of this Regulation. In conjunction with the general and horizontal law on data protection implementing Directive 95/46/EC, Member States have several sector-specific laws in areas that need more specific provisions. This Regulation also provides a margin of manoeuvre for Member States to specify its rules, including for the processing of special categories of personal data ('sensitive data'). To that extent, this Regulation does not exclude Member State law that sets out the circumstances for specific processing situations, including determining more precisely the conditions under which the processing of personal data is lawful.

(11) Effective protection of personal data throughout the Union requires the strengthening and setting out in detail of the rights of data subjects and the obligations of those who process and determine the processing of personal data, as well as equivalent powers for monitoring and ensuring compliance with the rules for the protection of personal data and equivalent sanctions for infringements in the Member States.

(12) Article 16(2) TFEU mandates the European Parliament and the Council to lay down the rules relating to the protection of natural persons with regard to the processing of personal data and the rules relating to the free movement of personal data.

(13) In order to ensure a consistent level of protection for natural persons throughout the Union and to prevent divergences hampering the free movement of personal data within the internal market, a Regulation is necessary to provide legal certainty and transparency for economic operators, including micro, small and medium-sized enterprises, and to provide natural persons in all Member States with the same level of legally enforceable rights and obligations and responsibilities for controllers and processors, to ensure consistent monitoring of the processing of personal data, and equivalent sanctions in all Member States as well as effective cooperation between the supervisory authorities of different Member States. The proper functioning of the internal market requires that the free movement of personal data within the Union is not restricted or prohibited for reasons connected with the protection of natural persons with regard to the processing of personal data. To take account of the specific situation of micro, small and medium-sized enterprises, this Regulation includes a derogation for organisations with fewer than 250 employees with regard to record-keeping. In addition, the Union institutions and bodies, and Member States and their supervisory authorities, are encouraged to take account of the specific needs of micro, small and medium-sized enterprises in the application of this Regulation. The notion of micro, small and medium-sized enterprises should draw from Article 2 of the Annex to Commission Recommendation 2003/361/EC.[5]

(14) The protection afforded by this Regulation should apply to natural persons, whatever their nationality or place of residence, in relation to the processing of their personal data. This Regulation does not cover the processing of personal data which concerns legal persons and in particular undertakings established as legal persons, including the name and the form of the legal person and the contact details of the legal person.

(15) In order to prevent creating a serious risk of circumvention, the protection of natural persons should be technologically neutral and should not depend on the techniques used. The protection of natural persons should apply to the processing of personal data by automated means, as well as to manual processing, if the personal data are contained or are intended to be contained in a filing system. Files or sets of files, as well as their cover pages, which are not structured according to specific criteria should not fall within the scope of this Regulation.

(16) This Regulation does not apply to issues of protection of fundamental rights and freedoms or the free flow of personal data related to activities which fall outside the scope of Union law, such as activities concerning national security. This Regulation does not apply to the processing of personal data by the Member States when carrying out activities in relation to the common foreign and security policy of the Union.

(17) Regulation (EC) No 45/2001 of the European Parliament and of the Council[6] applies to the processing of personal data by the Union institutions, bodies, offices and agencies. Regulation (EC) No 45/2001 and other Union legal acts applicable to such processing of personal data should be adapted to the principles and rules established in this Regulation and applied in the light of this Regulation. In order to provide a strong and coherent data protection framework in the Union, the necessary adaptations of Regulation (EC) No 45/2001 should follow after the adoption of this Regulation, in order to allow application at the same time as this Regulation.

(18) This Regulation does not apply to the processing of personal data by a natural person in the course of a purely personal or household activity and thus with no connection to a professional or commercial activity. Personal or household activities could include correspondence and the holding of addresses, or social networking and online activity undertaken within the context of such activities. However, this Regulation applies to controllers or processors which provide the means for processing personal data for such personal or household activities.

(19) The protection of natural persons with regard to the processing of personal data by competent authorities for the purposes of the prevention, investigation, detection or prosecution of criminal offences or the execution of criminal penalties, including the safeguarding against and the prevention of threats to public security and the free movement of such data, is the subject of a specific Union legal act. This Regulation should not, therefore, apply to processing activities for those purposes. However, personal data processed by public authorities under this Regulation should, when used for those purposes, be governed by a more specific Union legal act, namely Directive (EU) 2016/680 of the European Parliament and of the Council.[7] Member States may entrust competent authorities within the meaning of Directive (EU) 2016/680 with tasks which are not necessarily carried out for the purposes of the prevention, investigation, detection or prosecution of criminal offences or the execution of criminal penalties, including the safeguarding against and prevention of threats to public security, so that the processing of personal data for those other purposes, in so far as it is within the scope of Union law, falls within the scope of this Regulation.

With regard to the processing of personal data by those competent authorities for purposes falling within scope of this Regulation, Member States should be able to maintain or introduce more specific provisions to adapt the application of the rules of this Regulation. Such provisions may determine more precisely specific requirements for the processing of personal data by those competent authorities for those other purposes, taking into account the constitutional, organisational and administrative structure of the respective Member State. When the processing of personal data by private bodies falls within the scope of this Regulation, this Regulation should provide for the possibility for Member States under specific conditions to restrict by law certain obligations and rights when such a restriction constitutes a necessary and proportionate measure in a democratic society to safeguard specific important interests including public security and the prevention, investigation, detection or prosecution of criminal offences or the execution of criminal penalties, including the safeguarding against and the prevention of threats to public security. This is relevant for instance in the framework of anti-money laundering or the activities of forensic laboratories.

(20) While this Regulation applies, inter alia, to the activities of courts and other judicial authorities, Union or Member State law could specify the processing operations and processing procedures in relation to the processing of personal data by courts and other judicial authorities. The competence of the supervisory authorities should not cover the processing of personal data when courts are acting in their judicial capacity, in order to safeguard the independence of the judiciary in the performance of its judicial tasks, including decision-making. It should be possible to entrust supervision of such data processing operations to specific bodies within the judicial system of the Member State, which should, in particular ensure compliance with the rules of this Regulation, enhance awareness among members of the judiciary of their obligations under this Regulation and handle complaints in relation to such data processing operations.

(21) This Regulation is without prejudice to the application of Directive 2000/31/EC of the European Parliament and of the Council,[8] in particular of the liability rules of intermediary service providers in Articles 12 to 15 of that Directive. That Directive seeks to contribute to the proper functioning of the internal market by ensuring the free movement of information society services between Member States.

(22) Any processing of personal data in the context of the activities of an establishment of a controller or a processor in the Union should be carried out in accordance with this Regulation, regardless of whether the processing itself takes place within the Union. Establishment implies the effective and real exercise of activity through stable arrangements. The legal form of such arrangements, whether through a branch or a subsidiary with a legal personality, is not the determining factor in that respect.

(23) In order to ensure that natural persons are not deprived of the protection to which they are entitled under this Regulation, the processing of personal data of data subjects who are in the Union by a controller or a processor not established in the Union should be subject to this Regulation where the processing activities are related to offering goods or services to such data subjects irrespective of whether connected to a payment. In order to determine whether such a controller or processor is offering goods or services to data subjects who are in the Union, it should be ascertained whether it is apparent that the controller or processor envisages offering services to data subjects in one or more Member States in the Union. Whereas the mere accessibility of the controller's, processor's or an intermediary's website in the Union, of an email address or of other contact details, or the use of a language generally used in the third country where the controller is established, is insufficient to ascertain such intention, factors such as the use of a language or a currency generally used in one or

more Member States with the possibility of ordering goods and services in that other language, or the mentioning of customers or users who are in the Union, may make it apparent that the controller envisages offering goods or services to data subjects in the Union.

(24) The processing of personal data of data subjects who are in the Union by a controller or processor not established in the Union should also be subject to this Regulation when it is related to the monitoring of the behaviour of such data subjects in so far as their behaviour takes place within the Union. In order to determine whether a processing activity can be considered to monitor the behaviour of data subjects, it should be ascertained whether natural persons are tracked on the internet including potential subsequent use of personal data processing techniques which consist of profiling a natural person, particularly in order to take decisions concerning her or him or for analysing or predicting her or his personal preferences, behaviours and attitudes.

(25) Where Member State law applies by virtue of public international law, this Regulation should also apply to a controller not established in the Union, such as in a Member State's diplomatic mission or consular post.

(26) The principles of data protection should apply to any information concerning an identified or identifiable natural person. Personal data which have undergone pseudonymisation, which could be attributed to a natural person by the use of additional information should be considered to be information on an identifiable natural person. To determine whether a natural person is identifiable, account should be taken of all the means reasonably likely to be used, such as singling out, either by the controller or by another person to identify the natural person directly or indirectly. To ascertain whether means are reasonably likely to be used to identify the natural person, account should be taken of all objective factors, such as the costs of and the amount of time required for identification, taking into consideration the available technology at the time of the processing and technological developments. The principles of data protection should therefore not apply to anonymous information, namely information which does not relate to an identified or identifiable natural person or to personal data rendered anonymous in such a manner that the data subject is not or no longer identifiable. This Regulation does not therefore concern the processing of such anonymous information, including for statistical or research purposes.

(27) This Regulation does not apply to the personal data of deceased persons. Member States may provide for rules regarding the processing of personal data of deceased persons.

(28) The application of pseudonymisation to personal data can reduce the risks to the data subjects concerned and help controllers and processors to meet their data-protection obligations. The explicit introduction of 'pseudonymisation' in this Regulation is not intended to preclude any other measures of data protection.

(29) In order to create incentives to apply pseudonymisation when processing personal data, measures of pseudonymisation should, whilst allowing general analysis, be possible within the same controller when that controller has taken technical and organisational measures necessary to ensure, for the processing concerned, that this Regulation is implemented, and that additional information for attributing the personal data to a specific data subject is kept separately. The controller processing the personal data should indicate the authorised persons within the same controller.

(30) Natural persons may be associated with online identifiers provided by their devices, applications, tools and protocols, such as internet protocol addresses, cookie identifiers or other identifiers such as radio frequency identification tags. This may leave traces which, in particular when combined with unique identifiers and other information received by the servers, may be used to create profiles of the natural persons and identify them.

(31) Public authorities to which personal data are disclosed in accordance with a legal obligation for the exercise of their official mission, such as tax and customs authorities, financial investigation units, independent administrative authorities, or financial market authorities responsible for the regulation and supervision of securities markets should not be regarded as recipients if they receive personal data which are necessary to carry out a particular inquiry in the general interest, in accordance with Union or Member State law. The requests for disclosure sent by the public authorities should always be in writing, reasoned and occasional and should not concern the entirety of a filing system or lead to the interconnection of filing systems. The processing of personal data by those public authorities should comply with the applicable data-protection rules according to the purposes of the processing.

(32) Consent should be given by a clear affirmative act establishing a freely given, specific, informed and unambiguous indication of the data subject's agreement to the processing of personal data relating to him or her, such as by a written statement, including by electronic means, or an oral statement. This could include ticking a box when visiting an internet website, choosing technical settings for information society services or another statement or conduct which clearly indicates in this context the data subject's acceptance of the proposed processing of his or her personal data. Silence, pre-ticked boxes or inactivity should not therefore constitute consent. Consent should cover all processing activities carried out for the same purpose or purposes. When the processing has multiple purposes, consent should be given for all of them. If the data subject's consent is to be given following a request by electronic means, the request must be clear, concise and not unnecessarily disruptive to the use of the service for which it is provided.

(33) It is often not possible to fully identify the purpose of personal data processing for scientific research purposes at the time of data collection. Therefore, data subjects should be allowed to give their consent to certain areas of scientific research when in keeping with recognised ethical standards for scientific research. Data subjects should have the opportunity to give their consent only to certain areas of research or parts of research projects to the extent allowed by the intended purpose.

(34) Genetic data should be defined as personal data relating to the inherited or acquired genetic characteristics of a natural person which result from the analysis of a biological sample from the natural person in question, in particular chromosomal, deoxyribonucleic acid (DNA) or ribonucleic acid (RNA) analysis, or from the analysis of another element enabling equivalent information to be obtained.

(35) Personal data concerning health should include all data pertaining to the health status of a data subject which reveal information relating to the past, current or future physical or mental health status of the data subject. This includes information about the natural person collected in the course of the registration for, or the provision of, health care services as referred to in Directive 2011/24/EU of the European Parliament and of the Council[9] to that natural person; a number, symbol or particular assigned to a natural person to uniquely identify the natural person for health purposes; information derived from the testing or examination of a body part or bodily substance, including from genetic data and biological samples; and any information on, for example, a disease, disability, disease risk, medical history, clinical treatment or the physiological or biomedical state of the data subject independent of its source, for example from a physician or other health professional, a hospital, a medical device or an in vitro diagnostic test.

(36) The main establishment of a controller in the Union should be the place of its central administration in the Union, unless the decisions on the purposes and means of the processing of personal data are taken in another establishment of the controller in the Union, in which case that other establishment should be considered to be the main establishment. The main establishment of a controller in the Union should be determined according to objective criteria and should imply the effective and real exercise of management activities determining the main decisions as to the purposes and means of processing through stable arrangements. That criterion should not depend on whether the processing of personal data is carried out at that location. The presence and use of technical means and technologies for processing personal data or processing activities do not, in themselves, constitute a main establishment and are therefore not determining criteria for a main establishment. The main establishment of the processor should be the place of its central administration in the Union or, if it has no central administration in the Union, the place where the main processing activities take place in the Union. In cases involving both the controller and the processor, the competent lead supervisory authority should remain the supervisory authority of the Member State where the controller has its main establishment, but the supervisory authority of the processor should be considered to be a supervisory authority concerned and that supervisory authority should participate in the cooperation procedure provided for by this Regulation. In any case, the supervisory authorities of the Member State or Member States where the processor has one or more establishments should not be considered to be supervisory authorities concerned where the draft decision concerns only the controller. Where the processing is carried out by a group of undertakings, the main establishment of the controlling undertaking should be considered to be the main establishment of the group of undertakings, except where the purposes and means of processing are determined by another undertaking.

(37) A group of undertakings should cover a controlling undertaking and its controlled undertakings, whereby the controlling undertaking should be the undertaking which can exert a dominant influence over the other undertakings by virtue, for example, of ownership, financial participation or the rules which govern it or the power to have personal data protection rules implemented. An undertaking which controls the processing of personal data in undertakings affiliated to it should be regarded, together with those undertakings, as a group of undertakings.

(38) Children merit specific protection with regard to their personal data, as they may be less aware of the risks, consequences and safeguards concerned and their rights in relation to the processing of personal data. Such specific protection should, in particular, apply to the use of personal data of children for the purposes of marketing or creating personality or user profiles and the collection of personal data with regard to children when using services offered directly to a child. The consent of the holder of parental responsibility should not be necessary in the context of preventive or counselling services offered directly to a child.

(39) Any processing of personal data should be lawful and fair. It should be transparent to natural persons that personal data concerning them are collected, used, consulted or otherwise processed and to what extent the personal data are or will be processed. The principle of transparency requires that any information and communication relating to the processing of those personal data be easily accessible and easy to understand, and that clear and plain language be used. That principle concerns, in particular, information to the data subjects on the identity of the controller and the purposes of the processing and further information to ensure fair and transparent processing in respect of the natural persons concerned and their right to obtain confirmation and communication of personal data concerning them which are being processed. Natural persons should be made aware of risks, rules, safeguards and rights in relation to the processing of personal data and how to exercise their rights in relation to such processing. In particular, the specific purposes for which personal data are processed should be explicit and legitimate and determined at the time of the collection of the personal data. The personal data should be adequate, relevant and limited to what is necessary for the purposes for which they are processed. This requires, in particular, ensuring that the period for which the personal data are stored is limited to a strict minimum. Personal data should be processed only if the purpose of the processing could not reasonably be fulfilled by other means. In order to ensure that the personal data are not kept longer than necessary, time limits should be established by the controller for erasure or for a periodic review. Every reasonable step should be taken to ensure that personal data which are inaccurate are rectified or deleted. Personal data should be processed in a manner that ensures appropriate security and confidentiality of the personal data, including for preventing unauthorised access to or use of personal data and the equipment used for the processing.

(40) In order for processing to be lawful, personal data should be processed on the basis of the consent of the data subject concerned or some other legitimate basis, laid down by law, either in this Regulation or in other Union or Member State law as referred to in this Regulation, including the necessity for compliance with the legal obligation to which the controller is subject or the necessity for the performance of a contract to which the data subject is party or in order to take steps at the request of the data subject prior to entering into a contract.

(41) Where this Regulation refers to a legal basis or a legislative measure, this does not necessarily require a legislative act adopted by a parliament, without prejudice to requirements pursuant to the constitutional order of the Member State concerned. However, such a legal basis or legislative measure should be clear and precise and its application should be foreseeable to persons subject to it, in accordance with the case-law of the Court of Justice of the European Union (the 'Court of Justice') and the European Court of Human Rights.

(42) Where processing is based on the data subject's consent, the controller should be able to demonstrate that the data subject has given consent to the processing operation. In particular in the context of a written declaration on another matter, safeguards should ensure that the data subject is aware of the fact that and the extent to which consent is given. In accordance with Council Directive 93/13/EEC[10] a declaration of consent pre-formulated by the controller should be provided in an intelligible and easily accessible form, using clear and plain language and it should not contain unfair terms. For consent to be informed, the data subject should be aware at least of the identity of the controller and the purposes of the processing for which the personal data are intended. Consent should not be regarded as freely given if the data subject has no genuine or free choice or is unable to refuse or withdraw consent without detriment.

(43) In order to ensure that consent is freely given, consent should not provide a valid legal ground for the processing of personal data in a specific case where there is a clear imbalance between the data subject and the controller, in particular where the controller is a public authority and it is therefore unlikely that consent was freely given in all the circumstances of that specific situation. Consent is presumed not to be freely given if it does not allow separate consent to be given to different personal data processing operations despite it being appropriate in the individual case, or if the performance of a contract, including the provision of a service, is dependent on the consent despite such consent not being necessary for such performance.

(44) Processing should be lawful where it is necessary in the context of a contract or the intention to enter into a contract.

(45) Where processing is carried out in accordance with a legal obligation to which the controller is subject or where processing is necessary for the performance of a task carried out in the public interest or in the exercise of official authority, the processing should have a basis in Union or Member State law. This Regulation does not require a specific law for each individual processing. A law as a basis for several processing operations based on a legal obligation to which the controller is subject or where processing is necessary for the performance of a task carried out in the public interest or in the exercise of an official authority may be sufficient. It should also be for Union or Member State law to determine the purpose of processing. Furthermore, that law could specify the general conditions of this Regulation governing the lawfulness of personal data processing, establish specifications for determining the controller, the type of personal data which are subject to the processing, the data subjects concerned, the entities to which the personal data may be disclosed, the purpose limitations, the storage period and other measures to ensure lawful and fair processing. It should also be for Union or Member State law to determine whether the controller performing a task carried out in the public interest or in the exercise of official authority should be a public authority or another natural or legal person governed by public law, or, where it is in the public interest to do so, including for health purposes such as public health and social protection and the management of health care services, by private law, such as a professional association.

(46) The processing of personal data should also be regarded to be lawful where it is necessary to protect an interest which is essential for the life of the data subject or that of another natural person. Processing of personal data based on the vital interest of another natural person should in principle take place only where the processing cannot be manifestly based on another legal basis. Some types of processing may serve both important grounds of public interest and the vital interests of the data subject as for instance when processing is necessary for humanitarian purposes, including for monitoring epidemics and their spread or in situations of humanitarian emergencies, in particular in situations of natural and man-made disasters.

(47) The legitimate interests of a controller, including those of a controller to which the personal data may be disclosed, or of a third party, may provide a legal basis for processing, provided that the interests or the fundamental rights and freedoms of the data subject are not overriding, taking into consideration the reasonable expectations of data subjects based on their relationship with the controller. Such legitimate interest could exist for example where there is a relevant and appropriate relationship between the data subject and the controller in situations such as where the data subject is a client or in the service of the controller. At any rate the existence of a legitimate interest would need careful assessment including whether a data subject can reasonably expect at the time and in the context of the collection of the personal data that processing for that purpose may take place. The interests and fundamental rights of the data subject could in particular override the interest of the data controller where personal data are processed in circumstances where data subjects do not reasonably expect further processing. Given that it is for the legislator to provide by law for the legal basis for public authorities to process personal data, that legal basis should not apply to the processing by public authorities in the performance

of their tasks. The processing of personal data strictly necessary for the purposes of preventing fraud also constitutes a legitimate interest of the data controller concerned. The processing of personal data for direct marketing purposes may be regarded as carried out for a legitimate interest.

(48) Controllers that are part of a group of undertakings or institutions affiliated to a central body may have a legitimate interest in transmitting personal data within the group of undertakings for internal administrative purposes, including the processing of clients' or employees' personal data. The general principles for the transfer of personal data, within a group of undertakings, to an undertaking located in a third country remain unaffected.

(49) The processing of personal data to the extent strictly necessary and proportionate for the purposes of ensuring network and information security, i.e. the ability of a network or an information system to resist, at a given level of confidence, accidental events or unlawful or malicious actions that compromise the availability, authenticity, integrity and confidentiality of stored or transmitted personal data, and the security of the related services offered by, or accessible via, those networks and systems, by public authorities, by computer emergency response teams (CERTs), computer security incident response teams (CSIRTs), by providers of electronic communications networks and services and by providers of security technologies and services, constitutes a legitimate interest of the data controller concerned. This could, for example, include preventing unauthorised access to electronic communications networks and malicious code distribution and stopping 'denial of service' attacks and damage to computer and electronic communication systems.

(50) The processing of personal data for purposes other than those for which the personal data were initially collected should be allowed only where the processing is compatible with the purposes for which the personal data were initially collected. In such a case, no legal basis separate from that which allowed the collection of the personal data is required. If the processing is necessary for the performance of a task carried out in the public interest or in the exercise of official authority vested in the controller, ~~Union or Member State law may determine and specify the tasks and purposes for which the further~~ processing should be regarded as compatible and lawful. Further processing for archiving purposes in the public interest, scientific or historical research purposes or statistical purposes should be considered to be compatible lawful processing operations. The legal basis provided by Union or Member State law for the processing of personal data may also provide a legal basis for further processing. In order to ascertain whether a purpose of further processing is compatible with the purpose for which the personal data are initially collected, the controller, after having met all the requirements for the lawfulness of the original processing, should take into account, inter alia: any link between those purposes and the purposes of the intended further processing; the context in which the personal data have been collected, in particular the reasonable expectations of data subjects based on their relationship with the controller as to their further use; the nature of the personal data; the consequences of the intended further processing for data subjects; and the existence of appropriate safeguards in both the original and intended further processing operations.

Where the data subject has given consent or the processing is based on Union or Member State law which constitutes a necessary and proportionate measure in a democratic society to safeguard, in particular, important objectives of general public interest, the controller should be allowed to further process the personal data irrespective of the compatibility of the purposes. In any case, the application of the principles set out in this Regulation and in particular the information of the data subject on those other purposes and on his or her rights including the right to object, should be ensured. Indicating possible criminal acts or threats to public security by the controller and transmitting the relevant personal data in individual cases or in several cases relating to the same criminal act or threats to public security to a competent authority should be regarded as being in the legitimate interest pursued by the controller. However, such transmission in the legitimate interest of the controller or further processing of personal data should be prohibited if the processing is not compatible with a legal, professional or other binding obligation of secrecy.

(51) Personal data which are, by their nature, particularly sensitive in relation to fundamental rights and freedoms merit specific protection as the context of their processing could create significant risks to the fundamental rights and freedoms. Those personal data should include personal data revealing racial or ethnic origin, whereby the use of the term 'racial origin' in this Regulation does not imply an acceptance by the Union of theories which attempt to determine the existence of separate human races. The processing of photographs should not systematically be considered to be processing of special categories of personal data as they are covered by the definition of biometric data only when processed through a specific technical means allowing the unique identification or authentication of a natural person. Such personal data should not be processed, unless processing is allowed in specific cases set out in this Regulation, taking into account that Member States law may lay down specific provisions on data protection in order to adapt the application of the rules of this Regulation for compliance with a legal obligation or for the performance of a task carried out in the public interest or in the exercise of official authority vested in the controller. In addition to the specific requirements for such processing, the general principles and other rules of this Regulation should apply, in particular as regards the conditions for lawful processing. Derogations from the general prohibition for processing such special categories of personal data should be explicitly provided, inter alia, where the data subject gives his or her explicit consent or in respect of specific needs in particular where the processing is carried out in the course of legitimate activities by certain associations or foundations the purpose of which is to permit the exercise of fundamental freedoms.

(52) Derogating from the prohibition on processing special categories of personal data should also be allowed when provided for in Union or Member State law and subject to suitable safeguards, so as to protect personal data and other fundamental rights, where it is in the public interest to do so, in

particular processing personal data in the field of employment law, social protection law including pensions and for health security, monitoring and alert purposes, the prevention or control of communicable diseases and other serious threats to health. Such a derogation may be made for health purposes, including public health and the management of health-care services, especially in order to ensure the quality and cost-effectiveness of the procedures used for settling claims for benefits and services in the health insurance system, or for archiving purposes in the public interest, scientific or historical research purposes or statistical purposes. A derogation should also allow the processing of such personal data where necessary for the establishment, exercise or defence of legal claims, whether in court proceedings or in an administrative or out-of-court procedure.

(53) Special categories of personal data which merit higher protection should be processed for health-related purposes only where necessary to achieve those purposes for the benefit of natural persons and society as a whole, in particular in the context of the management of health or social care services and systems, including processing by the management and central national health authorities of such data for the purpose of quality control, management information and the general national and local supervision of the health or social care system, and ensuring continuity of health or social care and cross-border healthcare or health security, monitoring and alert purposes, or for archiving purposes in the public interest, scientific or historical research purposes or statistical purposes, based on Union or Member State law which has to meet an objective of public interest, as well as for studies conducted in the public interest in the area of public health. Therefore, this Regulation should provide for harmonised conditions for the processing of special categories of personal data concerning health, in respect of specific needs, in particular where the processing of such data is carried out for certain health-related purposes by persons subject to a legal obligation of professional secrecy. Union or Member State law should provide for specific and suitable measures so as to protect the fundamental rights and the personal data of natural persons. Member States should be allowed to maintain or introduce further conditions, including limitations, with regard to the processing of genetic data, biometric data or data concerning health. However, this should not hamper the free flow of personal data within the Union when those conditions apply to cross-border processing of such data.

(54) The processing of special categories of personal data may be necessary for reasons of public interest in the areas of public health without consent of the data subject. Such processing should be subject to suitable and specific measures so as to protect the rights and freedoms of natural persons. In that context, 'public health' should be interpreted as defined in Regulation (EC) No 1338/2008 of the European Parliament and of the Council,[11] namely all elements related to health, namely health status, including morbidity and disability, the determinants having an effect on that health status, health care needs, resources allocated to health care, the provision of, and universal access to, health care as well as health care expenditure and financing, and the causes of mortality. Such processing of data concerning health for reasons of public interest should not result in personal data being processed for other purposes by third parties such as employers or insurance and banking companies.

(55) Moreover, the processing of personal data by official authorities for the purpose of achieving the aims, laid down by constitutional law or by international public law, of officially recognised religious associations, is carried out on grounds of public interest.

(56) Where in the course of electoral activities, the operation of the democratic system in a Member State requires that political parties compile personal data on people's political opinions, the processing of such data may be permitted for reasons of public interest, provided that appropriate safeguards are established.

(57) If the personal data processed by a controller do not permit the controller to identify a natural person, the data controller should not be obliged to acquire additional information in order to identify the data subject for the sole purpose of complying with any provision of this Regulation. However, the controller should not refuse to take additional information provided by the data subject in order to support the exercise of his or her rights. Identification should include the digital identification of a data subject, for example through authentication mechanism such as the same credentials, used by the data subject to log-in to the on-line service offered by the data controller.

(58) The principle of transparency requires that any information addressed to the public or to the data subject be concise, easily accessible and easy to understand, and that clear and plain language and, additionally, where appropriate, visualisation be used. Such information could be provided in electronic form, for example, when addressed to the public, through a website. This is of particular relevance in situations where the proliferation of actors and the technological complexity of practice make it difficult for the data subject to know and understand whether, by whom and for what purpose personal data relating to him or her are being collected, such as in the case of online advertising. Given that children merit specific protection, any information and communication, where processing is addressed to a child, should be in such a clear and plain language that the child can easily understand.

(59) Modalities should be provided for facilitating the exercise of the data subject's rights under this Regulation, including mechanisms to request and, if applicable, obtain, free of charge, in particular, access to and rectification or erasure of personal data and the exercise of the right to object. The controller should also provide means for requests to be made electronically, especially where personal data are processed by electronic means. The controller should be obliged to respond to requests from the data subject without undue delay and at the latest within one month and to give reasons where the controller does not intend to comply with any such requests.

(60) The principles of fair and transparent processing require that the data subject be informed of the existence of the processing operation and its purposes. The controller should provide the data subject with any further information necessary to ensure fair and transparent processing taking into account the specific circumstances and context in which the personal data are processed. Furthermore, the data

subject should be informed of the existence of profiling and the consequences of such profiling. Where the personal data are collected from the data subject, the data subject should also be informed whether he or she is obliged to provide the personal data and of the consequences, where he or she does not provide such data. That information may be provided in combination with standardised icons in order to give in an easily visible, intelligible and clearly legible manner, a meaningful overview of the intended processing. Where the icons are presented electronically, they should be machine-readable.

(61) The information in relation to the processing of personal data relating to the data subject should be given to him or her at the time of collection from the data subject, or, where the personal data are obtained from another source, within a reasonable period, depending on the circumstances of the case. Where personal data can be legitimately disclosed to another recipient, the data subject should be informed when the personal data are first disclosed to the recipient. Where the controller intends to process the personal data for a purpose other than that for which they were collected, the controller should provide the data subject prior to that further processing with information on that other purpose and other necessary information. Where the origin of the personal data cannot be provided to the data subject because various sources have been used, general information should be provided.

(62) However, it is not necessary to impose the obligation to provide information where the data subject already possesses the information, where the recording or disclosure of the personal data is expressly laid down by law or where the provision of information to the data subject proves to be impossible or would involve a disproportionate effort. The latter could in particular be the case where processing is carried out for archiving purposes in the public interest, scientific or historical research purposes or statistical purposes. In that regard, the number of data subjects, the age of the data and any appropriate safeguards adopted should be taken into consideration.

(63) A data subject should have the right of access to personal data which have been collected concerning him or her, and to exercise that right easily and at reasonable intervals, in order to be aware of, and verify, the lawfulness of the processing. This includes the right for data subjects to have access to data concerning their health, for example the data in their medical records containing information such as diagnoses, examination results, assessments by treating physicians and any treatment or interventions provided. Every data subject should therefore have the right to know and obtain communication in particular with regard to the purposes for which the personal data are processed, where possible the period for which the personal data are processed, the recipients of the personal data, the logic involved in any automatic personal data processing and, at least when based on profiling, the consequences of such processing. Where possible, the controller should be able to provide remote access to a secure system which would provide the data subject with direct access to his or her personal data. That right should not adversely affect the rights or freedoms of others, including trade secrets or intellectual property and in particular the copyright protecting the software. However, the result of those considerations should not be a refusal to provide all information to the data subject. Where the controller processes a large quantity of information concerning the data subject, the controller should be able to request that, before the information is delivered, the data subject specify the information or processing activities to which the request relates.

(64) The controller should use all reasonable measures to verify the identity of a data subject who requests access, in particular in the context of online services and online identifiers. A controller should not retain personal data for the sole purpose of being able to react to potential requests.

(65) A data subject should have the right to have personal data concerning him or her rectified and a 'right to be forgotten' where the retention of such data infringes this Regulation or Union or Member State law to which the controller is subject. In particular, a data subject should have the right to have his or her personal data erased and no longer processed where the personal data are no longer necessary in relation to the purposes for which they are collected or otherwise processed, where a data subject has withdrawn his or her consent or objects to the processing of personal data concerning him or her, or where the processing of his or her personal data does not otherwise comply with this Regulation. That right is relevant in particular where the data subject has given his or her consent as a child and is not fully aware of the risks involved by the processing, and later wants to remove such personal data, especially on the internet. The data subject should be able to exercise that right notwithstanding the fact that he or she is no longer a child. However, the further retention of the personal data should be lawful where it is necessary, for exercising the right of freedom of expression and information, for compliance with a legal obligation, for the performance of a task carried out in the public interest or in the exercise of official authority vested in the controller, on the grounds of public interest in the area of public health, for archiving purposes in the public interest, scientific or historical research purposes or statistical purposes, or for the establishment, exercise or defence of legal claims.

(66) To strengthen the right to be forgotten in the online environment, the right to erasure should also be extended in such a way that a controller who has made the personal data public should be obliged to inform the controllers which are processing such personal data to erase any links to, or copies or replications of those personal data. In doing so, that controller should take reasonable steps, taking into account available technology and the means available to the controller, including technical measures, to inform the controllers which are processing the personal data of the data subject's request.

(67) Methods by which to restrict the processing of personal data could include, inter alia, temporarily moving the selected data to another processing system, making the selected personal data unavailable to users, or temporarily removing published data from a website. In automated filing systems, the restriction of processing should in principle be ensured by technical means in such a manner that the personal data are not subject to further processing operations and cannot be changed. The fact that the processing of personal data is restricted should be clearly indicated in the system.

(68) To further strengthen the control over his or her own data, where the processing of personal data is carried out by automated means, the data subject should also be allowed to receive personal data concerning him or her which he or she has provided to a controller in a structured, commonly used, machine-readable and interoperable format, and to transmit it to another controller. Data controllers should be encouraged to develop interoperable formats that enable data portability. That right should apply where the data subject provided the personal data on the basis of his or her consent or the processing is necessary for the performance of a contract. It should not apply where processing is based on a legal ground other than consent or contract. By its very nature, that right should not be exercised against controllers processing personal data in the exercise of their public duties. It should therefore not apply where the processing of the personal data is necessary for compliance with a legal obligation to which the controller is subject or for the performance of a task carried out in the public interest or in the exercise of an official authority vested in the controller. The data subject's right to transmit or receive personal data concerning him or her should not create an obligation for the controllers to adopt or maintain processing systems which are technically compatible. Where, in a certain set of personal data, more than one data subject is concerned, the right to receive the personal data should be without prejudice to the rights and freedoms of other data subjects in accordance with this Regulation. Furthermore, that right should not prejudice the right of the data subject to obtain the erasure of personal data and the limitations of that right as set out in this Regulation and should, in particular, not imply the erasure of personal data concerning the data subject which have been provided by him or her for the performance of a contract to the extent that and for as long as the personal data are necessary for the performance of that contract. Where technically feasible, the data subject should have the right to have the personal data transmitted directly from one controller to another.

(69) Where personal data might lawfully be processed because processing is necessary for the performance of a task carried out in the public interest or in the exercise of official authority vested in the controller, or on grounds of the legitimate interests of a controller or a third party, a data subject should, nevertheless, be entitled to object to the processing of any personal data relating to his or her particular situation. It should be for the controller to demonstrate that its compelling legitimate interest overrides the interests or the fundamental rights and freedoms of the data subject.

(70) Where personal data are processed for the purposes of direct marketing, the data subject should have the right to object to such processing, including profiling to the extent that it is related to such direct marketing, whether with regard to initial or further processing, at any time and free of charge. That right should be explicitly brought to the attention of the data subject and presented clearly and separately from any other information.

(71) The data subject should have the right not to be subject to a decision, which may include a measure, evaluating personal aspects relating to him or her which is based solely on automated processing and which produces legal effects concerning him or her or similarly significantly affects him or her, such as automatic refusal of an online credit application or e-recruiting practices without any human intervention. Such processing includes 'profiling' that consists of any form of automated processing of personal data evaluating the personal aspects relating to a natural person, in particular to analyse or predict aspects concerning the data subject's performance at work, economic situation, health, personal preferences or interests, reliability or behaviour, location or movements, where it produces legal effects concerning him or her or similarly significantly affects him or her. However, decision-making based on such processing, including profiling, should be allowed where expressly authorised by Union or Member State law to which the controller is subject, including for fraud and tax-evasion monitoring and prevention purposes conducted in accordance with the regulations, standards and recommendations of Union institutions or national oversight bodies and to ensure the security and reliability of a service provided by the controller, or necessary for the entering or performance of a contract between the data subject and a controller, or when the data subject has given his or her explicit consent. In any case, such processing should be subject to suitable safeguards, which should include specific information to the data subject and the right to obtain human intervention, to express his or her point of view, to obtain an explanation of the decision reached after such assessment and to challenge the decision. Such measure should not concern a child.

In order to ensure fair and transparent processing in respect of the data subject, taking into account the specific circumstances and context in which the personal data are processed, the controller should use appropriate mathematical or statistical procedures for the profiling, implement technical and organisational measures appropriate to ensure, in particular, that factors which result in inaccuracies in personal data are corrected and the risk of errors is minimised, secure personal data in a manner that takes account of the potential risks involved for the interests and rights of the data subject, and prevent, inter alia, discriminatory effects on natural persons on the basis of racial or ethnic origin, political opinion, religion or beliefs, trade union membership, genetic or health status or sexual orientation, or processing that results in measures having such an effect.

(72) Profiling is subject to the rules of this Regulation governing the processing of personal data, such as the legal grounds for processing or data protection principles. The European Data Protection Board established by this Regulation (the 'Board') should be able to issue guidance in that context.

(73) Restrictions concerning specific principles and the rights of information, access to and rectification or erasure of personal data, the right to data portability, the right to object, decisions based on profiling, as well as the communication of a personal data breach to a data subject and certain related obligations of the controllers may be imposed by Union or Member State law, as far as necessary and proportionate in a democratic society to safeguard public security, including the protection of human life especially in response to natural or manmade disasters, the prevention, investigation and prosecution of criminal offences or the execution of criminal penalties, including the safeguarding against and the prevention of

threats to public security, or of breaches of ethics for regulated professions, other important objectives of general public interest of the Union or of a Member State, in particular an important economic or financial interest of the Union or of a Member State, the keeping of public registers kept for reasons of general public interest, further processing of archived personal data to provide specific information related to the political behaviour under former totalitarian state regimes or the protection of the data subject or the rights and freedoms of others, including social protection, public health and humanitarian purposes. Those restrictions should be in accordance with the requirements set out in the Charter and in the European Convention for the Protection of Human Rights and Fundamental Freedoms.

(74) The responsibility and liability of the controller for any processing of personal data carried out by the controller or on the controller's behalf should be established. In particular, the controller should be obliged to implement appropriate and effective measures and be able to demonstrate the compliance of processing activities with this Regulation, including the effectiveness of the measures. Those measures should take into account the nature, scope, context and purposes of the processing and the risk to the rights and freedoms of natural persons.

(75) The risk to the rights and freedoms of natural persons, of varying likelihood and severity, may result from personal data processing which could lead to physical, material or non-material damage, in particular: where the processing may give rise to discrimination, identity theft or fraud, financial loss, damage to the reputation, loss of confidentiality of personal data protected by professional secrecy, unauthorised reversal of pseudonymisation, or any other significant economic or social disadvantage; where data subjects might be deprived of their rights and freedoms or prevented from exercising control over their personal data; where personal data are processed which reveal racial or ethnic origin, political opinions, religion or philosophical beliefs, trade union membership, and the processing of genetic data, data concerning health or data concerning sex life or criminal convictions and offences or related security measures; where personal aspects are evaluated, in particular analysing or predicting aspects concerning performance at work, economic situation, health, personal preferences or interests, reliability or behaviour, location or movements, in order to create or use personal profiles; where personal data of vulnerable natural persons, in particular of children, are processed; or where processing involves a large amount of personal data and affects a large number of data subjects.

(76) The likelihood and severity of the risk to the rights and freedoms of the data subject should be determined by reference to the nature, scope, context and purposes of the processing. Risk should be evaluated on the basis of an objective assessment, by which it is established whether data processing operations involve a risk or a high risk.

(77) Guidance on the implementation of appropriate measures and on the demonstration of compliance by the controller or the processor, especially as regards the identification of the risk related to the processing, their assessment in terms of origin, nature, likelihood and severity, and the identification of best practices to mitigate the risk, could be provided in particular by means of approved codes of conduct, approved certifications, guidelines provided by the Board or indications provided by a data protection officer. The Board may also issue guidelines on processing operations that are considered to be unlikely to result in a high risk to the rights and freedoms of natural persons and indicate what measures may be sufficient in such cases to address such risk.

(78) The protection of the rights and freedoms of natural persons with regard to the processing of personal data require that appropriate technical and organisational measures be taken to ensure that the requirements of this Regulation are met. In order to be able to demonstrate compliance with this Regulation, the controller should adopt internal policies and implement measures which meet in particular the principles of data protection by design and data protection by default. Such measures could consist, inter alia, of minimising the processing of personal data, pseudonymising personal data as soon as possible, transparency with regard to the functions and processing of personal data, enabling the data subject to monitor the data processing, enabling the controller to create and improve security features. When developing, designing, selecting and using applications, services and products that are based on the processing of personal data or process personal data to fulfil their task, producers of the products, services and applications should be encouraged to take into account the right to data protection when developing and designing such products, services and applications and, with due regard to the state of the art, to make sure that controllers and processors are able to fulfil their data protection obligations. The principles of data protection by design and by default should also be taken into consideration in the context of public tenders.

(79) The protection of the rights and freedoms of data subjects as well as the responsibility and liability of controllers and processors, also in relation to the monitoring by and measures of supervisory authorities, requires a clear allocation of the responsibilities under this Regulation, including where a controller determines the purposes and means of the processing jointly with other controllers or where a processing operation is carried out on behalf of a controller.

(80) Where a controller or a processor not established in the Union is processing personal data of data subjects who are in the Union whose processing activities are related to the offering of goods or services, irrespective of whether a payment of the data subject is required, to such data subjects in the Union, or to the monitoring of their behaviour as far as their behaviour takes place within the Union, the controller or the processor should designate a representative, unless the processing is occasional, does not include processing, on a large scale, of special categories of personal data or the processing of personal data relating to criminal convictions and offences, and is unlikely to result in a risk to the rights and freedoms of natural persons, taking into account the nature, context, scope and purposes of the processing or if the controller is a public authority or body. The representative should act on behalf of the controller or the processor and may be addressed by any supervisory authority. The representative should be explicitly designated by a written mandate of the controller or of the processor to act on its

behalf with regard to its obligations under this Regulation. The designation of such a representative does not affect the responsibility or liability of the controller or of the processor under this Regulation. Such a representative should perform its tasks according to the mandate received from the controller or processor, including cooperating with the competent supervisory authorities with regard to any action taken to ensure compliance with this Regulation. The designated representative should be subject to enforcement proceedings in the event of non-compliance by the controller or processor.

(81) To ensure compliance with the requirements of this Regulation in respect of the processing to be carried out by the processor on behalf of the controller, when entrusting a processor with processing activities, the controller should use only processors providing sufficient guarantees, in particular in terms of expert knowledge, reliability and resources, to implement technical and organisational measures which will meet the requirements of this Regulation, including for the security of processing. The adherence of the processor to an approved code of conduct or an approved certification mechanism may be used as an element to demonstrate compliance with the obligations of the controller. The carrying-out of processing by a processor should be governed by a contract or other legal act under Union or Member State law, binding the processor to the controller, setting out the subject- matter and duration of the processing, the nature and purposes of the processing, the type of personal data and categories of data subjects, taking into account the specific tasks and responsibilities of the processor in the context of the processing to be carried out and the risk to the rights and freedoms of the data subject. The controller and processor may choose to use an individual contract or standard contractual clauses which are adopted either directly by the Commission or by a supervisory authority in accordance with the consistency mechanism and then adopted by the Commission. After the completion of the processing on behalf of the controller, the processor should, at the choice of the controller, return or delete the personal data, unless there is a requirement to store the personal data under Union or Member State law to which the processor is subject.

(82) In order to demonstrate compliance with this Regulation, the controller or processor should maintain records of processing activities under its responsibility. Each controller and processor should be obliged to cooperate with the supervisory authority and make those records, on request, available to it, so that it might serve for monitoring those processing operations.

(83) In order to maintain security and to prevent processing in infringement of this Regulation, the controller or processor should evaluate the risks inherent in the processing and implement measures to mitigate those risks, such as encryption. Those measures should ensure an appropriate level of security, including confidentiality, taking into account the state of the art and the costs of implementation in relation to the risks and the nature of the personal data to be protected. In assessing data security risk, consideration should be given to the risks that are presented by personal data processing, such as accidental or unlawful destruction, loss, alteration, unauthorised disclosure of, or access to, personal data transmitted, stored or otherwise processed which may in particular lead to physical, material or non-material damage.

(84) In order to enhance compliance with this Regulation where processing operations are likely to result in a high risk to the rights and freedoms of natural persons, the controller should be responsible for the carrying-out of a data protection impact assessment to evaluate, in particular, the origin, nature, particularity and severity of that risk. The outcome of the assessment should be taken into account when determining the appropriate measures to be taken in order to demonstrate that the processing of personal data complies with this Regulation. Where a data-protection impact assessment indicates that processing operations involve a high risk which the controller cannot mitigate by appropriate measures in terms of available technology and costs of implementation, a consultation of the supervisory authority should take place prior to the processing.

(85) A personal data breach may, if not addressed in an appropriate and timely manner, result in physical, material or non-material damage to natural persons such as loss of control over their personal data or limitation of their rights, discrimination, identity theft or fraud, financial loss, unauthorised reversal of pseudonymisation, damage to reputation, loss of confidentiality of personal data protected by professional secrecy or any other significant economic or social disadvantage to the natural person concerned. Therefore, as soon as the controller becomes aware that a personal data breach has occurred, the controller should notify the personal data breach to the supervisory authority without undue delay and, where feasible, not later than 72 hours after having become aware of it, unless the controller is able to demonstrate, in accordance with the accountability principle, that the personal data breach is unlikely to result in a risk to the rights and freedoms of natural persons. Where such notification cannot be achieved within 72 hours, the reasons for the delay should accompany the notification and information may be provided in phases without undue further delay.

(86) The controller should communicate to the data subject a personal data breach, without undue delay, where that personal data breach is likely to result in a high risk to the rights and freedoms of the natural person in order to allow him or her to take the necessary precautions. The communication should describe the nature of the personal data breach as well as recommendations for the natural person concerned to mitigate potential adverse effects. Such communications to data subjects should be made as soon as reasonably feasible and in close cooperation with the supervisory authority, respecting guidance provided by it or by other relevant authorities such as law-enforcement authorities. For example, the need to mitigate an immediate risk of damage would call for prompt communication with data subjects whereas the need to implement appropriate measures against continuing or similar personal data breaches may justify more time for communication.

(87) It should be ascertained whether all appropriate technological protection and organisational measures have been implemented to establish immediately whether a personal data breach has taken place and to inform promptly the supervisory authority and the data subject. The fact that the notification

was made without undue delay should be established taking into account in particular the nature and gravity of the personal data breach and its consequences and adverse effects for the data subject. Such notification may result in an intervention of the supervisory authority in accordance with its tasks and powers laid down in this Regulation.

(88) In setting detailed rules concerning the format and procedures applicable to the notification of personal data breaches, due consideration should be given to the circumstances of that breach, including whether or not personal data had been protected by appropriate technical protection measures, effectively limiting the likelihood of identity fraud or other forms of misuse. Moreover, such rules and procedures should take into account the legitimate interests of law-enforcement authorities where early disclosure could unnecessarily hamper the investigation of the circumstances of a personal data breach.

(89) Directive 95/46/EC provided for a general obligation to notify the processing of personal data to the supervisory authorities. While that obligation produces administrative and financial burdens, it did not in all cases contribute to improving the protection of personal data. Such indiscriminate general notification obligations should therefore be abolished, and replaced by effective procedures and mechanisms which focus instead on those types of processing operations which are likely to result in a high risk to the rights and freedoms of natural persons by virtue of their nature, scope, context and purposes. Such types of processing operations may be those which in, particular, involve using new technologies, or are of a new kind and where no data protection impact assessment has been carried out before by the controller, or where they become necessary in the light of the time that has elapsed since the initial processing.

(90) In such cases, a data protection impact assessment should be carried out by the controller prior to the processing in order to assess the particular likelihood and severity of the high risk, taking into account the nature, scope, context and purposes of the processing and the sources of the risk. That impact assessment should include, in particular, the measures, safeguards and mechanisms envisaged for mitigating that risk, ensuring the protection of personal data and demonstrating compliance with this Regulation.

(91) This should in particular apply to large-scale processing operations which aim to process a considerable amount of personal data at regional, national or supranational level and which could affect a large number of data subjects and which are likely to result in a high risk, for example, on account of their sensitivity, where in accordance with the achieved state of technological knowledge a new technology is used on a large scale as well as to other processing operations which result in a high risk to the rights and freedoms of data subjects, in particular where those operations render it more difficult for data subjects to exercise their rights. A data protection impact assessment should also be made where personal data are processed for taking decisions regarding specific natural persons following any systematic and extensive evaluation of personal aspects relating to natural persons based on profiling those data or following the processing of special categories of personal data, biometric data, or data on criminal convictions and offences or related security measures. A data protection impact assessment is equally required for monitoring publicly accessible areas on a large scale, especially when using optic-electronic devices or for any other operations where the competent supervisory authority considers that the processing is likely to result in a high risk to the rights and freedoms of data subjects, in particular because they prevent data subjects from exercising a right or using a service or a contract, or because they are carried out systematically on a large scale. The processing of personal data should not be considered to be on a large scale if the processing concerns personal data from patients or clients by an individual physician, other health care professional or lawyer. In such cases, a data protection impact assessment should not be mandatory.

(92) There are circumstances under which it may be reasonable and economical for the subject of a data protection impact assessment to be broader than a single project, for example where public authorities or bodies intend to establish a common application or processing platform or where several controllers plan to introduce a common application or processing environment across an industry sector or segment or for a widely used horizontal activity.

(93) In the context of the adoption of the Member State law on which the performance of the tasks of the public authority or public body is based and which regulates the specific processing operation or set of operations in question, Member States may deem it necessary to carry out such assessment prior to the processing activities.

(94) Where a data protection impact assessment indicates that the processing would, in the absence of safeguards, security measures and mechanisms to mitigate the risk, result in a high risk to the rights and freedoms of natural persons and the controller is of the opinion that the risk cannot be mitigated by reasonable means in terms of available technologies and costs of implementation, the supervisory authority should be consulted prior to the start of processing activities. Such high risk is likely to result from certain types of processing and the extent and frequency of processing, which may result also in a realisation of damage or interference with the rights and freedoms of the natural person. The supervisory authority should respond to the request for consultation within a specified period. However, the absence of a reaction of the supervisory authority within that period should be without prejudice to any intervention of the supervisory authority in accordance with its tasks and powers laid down in this Regulation, including the power to prohibit processing operations. As part of that consultation process, the outcome of a data protection impact assessment carried out with regard to the processing at issue may be submitted to the supervisory authority, in particular the measures envisaged to mitigate the risk to the rights and freedoms of natural persons.

(95) The processor should assist the controller, where necessary and upon request, in ensuring compliance with the obligations deriving from the carrying out of data protection impact assessments and from prior consultation of the supervisory authority.

(96) A consultation of the supervisory authority should also take place in the course of the preparation of a legislative or regulatory measure which provides for the processing of personal data, in order to ensure compliance of the intended processing with this Regulation and in particular to mitigate the risk involved for the data subject.

(97) Where the processing is carried out by a public authority, except for courts or independent judicial authorities when acting in their judicial capacity, where, in the private sector, processing is carried out by a controller whose core activities consist of processing operations that require regular and systematic monitoring of the data subjects on a large scale, or where the core activities of the controller or the processor consist of processing on a large scale of special categories of personal data and data relating to criminal convictions and offences, a person with expert knowledge of data protection law and practices should assist the controller or processor to monitor internal compliance with this Regulation. In the private sector, the core activities of a controller relate to its primary activities and do not relate to the processing of personal data as ancillary activities. The necessary level of expert knowledge should be determined in particular according to the data processing operations carried out and the protection required for the personal data processed by the controller or the processor. Such data protection officers, whether or not they are an employee of the controller, should be in a position to perform their duties and tasks in an independent manner.

(98) Associations or other bodies representing categories of controllers or processors should be encouraged to draw up codes of conduct, within the limits of this Regulation, so as to facilitate the effective application of this Regulation, taking account of the specific characteristics of the processing carried out in certain sectors and the specific needs of micro, small and medium enterprises. In particular, such codes of conduct could calibrate the obligations of controllers and processors, taking into account the risk likely to result from the processing for the rights and freedoms of natural persons.

(99) When drawing up a code of conduct, or when amending or extending such a code, associations and other bodies representing categories of controllers or processors should consult relevant stakeholders, including data subjects where feasible, and have regard to submissions received and views expressed in response to such consultations.

(100) In order to enhance transparency and compliance with this Regulation, the establishment of certification mechanisms and data protection seals and marks should be encouraged, allowing data subjects to quickly assess the level of data protection of relevant products and services.

(101) Flows of personal data to and from countries outside the Union and international organisations are necessary for the expansion of international trade and international cooperation. The increase in such flows has raised new challenges and concerns with regard to the protection of personal data. However, when personal data are transferred from the Union to controllers, processors or other recipients in third countries or to international organisations, the level of protection of natural persons ensured in the Union by this Regulation should not be undermined, including in cases of onward transfers of personal data from the third country or international organisation to controllers, processors in the same or another third country or international organisation. In any event, transfers to third countries and international organisations may only be carried out in full compliance with this Regulation. A transfer could take place only if, subject to the other provisions of this Regulation, the conditions laid down in the provisions of this Regulation relating to the transfer of personal data to third countries or international organisations are complied with by the controller or processor.

(102) This Regulation is without prejudice to international agreements concluded between the Union and third countries regulating the transfer of personal data including appropriate safeguards for the data subjects. Member States may conclude international agreements which involve the transfer of personal data to third countries or international organisations, as far as such agreements do not affect this Regulation or any other provisions of Union law and include an appropriate level of protection for the fundamental rights of the data subjects.

(103) The Commission may decide with effect for the entire Union that a third country, a territory or specified sector within a third country, or an international organisation, offers an adequate level of data protection, thus providing legal certainty and uniformity throughout the Union as regards the third country or international organisation which is considered to provide such level of protection. In such cases, transfers of personal data to that third country or international organisation may take place without the need to obtain any further authorisation. The Commission may also decide, having given notice and a full statement setting out the reasons to the third country or international organisation, to revoke such a decision.

(104) In line with the fundamental values on which the Union is founded, in particular the protection of human rights, the Commission should, in its assessment of the third country, or of a territory or specified sector within a third country, take into account how a particular third country respects the rule of law, access to justice as well as international human rights norms and standards and its general and sectoral law, including legislation concerning public security, defence and national security as well as public order and criminal law. The adoption of an adequacy decision with regard to a territory or a specified sector in a third country should take into account clear and objective criteria, such as specific processing activities and the scope of applicable legal standards and legislation in force in the third country. The third country should offer guarantees ensuring an adequate level of protection essentially equivalent to that ensured within the Union, in particular where personal data are processed in one or several specific sectors. In particular, the third country should ensure effective independent data protection supervision and should provide for cooperation mechanisms with the Member States' data protection authorities, and the data subjects should be provided with effective and enforceable rights and effective administrative and judicial redress.

(105) Apart from the international commitments the third country or international organisation has entered into, the Commission should take account of obligations arising from the third country's or international organisation's participation in multilateral or regional systems in particular in relation to the protection of personal data, as well as the implementation of such obligations. In particular, the third country's accession to the Council of Europe Convention of 28 January 1981 for the Protection of Individuals with regard to the Automatic Processing of Personal Data and its Additional Protocol should be taken into account. The Commission should consult the Board when assessing the level of protection in third countries or international organisations.

(106) The Commission should monitor the functioning of decisions on the level of protection in a third country, a territory or specified sector within a third country, or an international organisation, and monitor the functioning of decisions adopted on the basis of Article 25(6) or Article 26(4) of Directive 95/46/EC. In its adequacy decisions, the Commission should provide for a periodic review mechanism of their functioning. That periodic review should be conducted in consultation with the third country or international organisation in question and take into account all relevant developments in the third country or international organisation. For the purposes of monitoring and of carrying out the periodic reviews, the Commission should take into consideration the views and findings of the European Parliament and of the Council as well as of other relevant bodies and sources. The Commission should evaluate, within a reasonable time, the functioning of the latter decisions and report any relevant findings to the Committee within the meaning of Regulation (EU) No 182/2011 of the European Parliament and of the Council[12] as established under this Regulation, to the European Parliament and to the Council.

(107) The Commission may recognise that a third country, a territory or a specified sector within a third country, or an international organisation no longer ensures an adequate level of data protection. Consequently the transfer of personal data to that third country or international organisation should be prohibited, unless the requirements in this Regulation relating to transfers subject to appropriate safeguards, including binding corporate rules, and derogations for specific situations are fulfilled. In that case, provision should be made for consultations between the Commission and such third countries or international organisations. The Commission should, in a timely manner, inform the third country or international organisation of the reasons and enter into consultations with it in order to remedy the situation.

(108) In the absence of an adequacy decision, the controller or processor should take measures to compensate for the lack of data protection in a third country by way of appropriate safeguards for the data subject. Such appropriate safeguards may consist of making use of binding corporate rules, standard data protection clauses adopted by the Commission, standard data protection clauses adopted by a supervisory authority or contractual clauses authorised by a supervisory authority. Those safeguards should ensure compliance with data protection requirements and the rights of the data subjects appropriate to processing within the Union, including the availability of enforceable data subject rights and of effective legal remedies, including to obtain effective administrative or judicial redress and to claim compensation, in the Union or in a third country. They should relate in particular to compliance with the general principles relating to personal data processing, the principles of data protection by design and by default. Transfers may also be carried out by public authorities or bodies with public authorities or bodies in third countries or with international organisations with corresponding duties or functions, including on the basis of provisions to be inserted into administrative arrangements, such as a memorandum of understanding, providing for enforceable and effective rights for data subjects. Authorisation by the competent supervisory authority should be obtained when the safeguards are provided for in administrative arrangements that are not legally binding.

(109) The possibility for the controller or processor to use standard data-protection clauses adopted by the Commission or by a supervisory authority should prevent controllers or processors neither from including the standard data-protection clauses in a wider contract, such as a contract between the processor and another processor, nor from adding other clauses or additional safeguards provided that they do not contradict, directly or indirectly, the standard contractual clauses adopted by the Commission or by a supervisory authority or prejudice the fundamental rights or freedoms of the data subjects. Controllers and processors should be encouraged to provide additional safeguards via contractual commitments that supplement standard protection clauses.

(110) A group of undertakings, or a group of enterprises engaged in a joint economic activity, should be able to make use of approved binding corporate rules for its international transfers from the Union to organisations within the same group of undertakings, or group of enterprises engaged in a joint economic activity, provided that such corporate rules include all essential principles and enforceable rights to ensure appropriate safeguards for transfers or categories of transfers of personal data.

(111) Provisions should be made for the possibility for transfers in certain circumstances where the data subject has given his or her explicit consent, where the transfer is occasional and necessary in relation to a contract or a legal claim, regardless of whether in a judicial procedure or whether in an administrative or any out-of-court procedure, including procedures before regulatory bodies. Provision should also be made for the possibility for transfers where important grounds of public interest laid down by Union or Member State law so require or where the transfer is made from a register established by law and intended for consultation by the public or persons having a legitimate interest. In the latter case, such a transfer should not involve the entirety of the personal data or entire categories of the data contained in the register and, when the register is intended for consultation by persons having a legitimate interest, the transfer should be made only at the request of those persons or, if they are to be the recipients, taking into full account the interests and fundamental rights of the data subject.

(112) Those derogations should in particular apply to data transfers required and necessary for important reasons of public interest, for example in cases of international data exchange between competition authorities, tax or customs administrations, between financial supervisory authorities, between services competent for social security matters, or for public health, for example in the case of contact tracing for contagious diseases or in order to reduce and/or eliminate doping in sport. A transfer of personal data should also be regarded as lawful where it is necessary to protect an interest which is essential for the data subject's or another person's vital interests, including physical integrity or life, if the data subject is incapable of giving consent. In the absence of an adequacy decision, Union or Member State law may, for important reasons of public interest, expressly set limits to the transfer of specific categories of data to a third country or an international organisation. Member States should notify such provisions to the Commission. Any transfer to an international humanitarian organisation of personal data of a data subject who is physically or legally incapable of giving consent, with a view to accomplishing a task incumbent under the Geneva Conventions or to complying with international humanitarian law applicable in armed conflicts, could be considered to be necessary for an important reason of public interest or because it is in the vital interest of the data subject.

(113) Transfers which can be qualified as not repetitive and that only concern a limited number of data subjects, could also be possible for the purposes of the compelling legitimate interests pursued by the controller, when those interests are not overridden by the interests or rights and freedoms of the data subject and when the controller has assessed all the circumstances surrounding the data transfer. The controller should give particular consideration to the nature of the personal data, the purpose and duration of the proposed processing operation or operations, as well as the situation in the country of origin, the third country and the country of final destination, and should provide suitable safeguards to protect fundamental rights and freedoms of natural persons with regard to the processing of their personal data. Such transfers should be possible only in residual cases where none of the other grounds for transfer are applicable. For scientific or historical research purposes or statistical purposes, the legitimate expectations of society for an increase of knowledge should be taken into consideration. The controller should inform the supervisory authority and the data subject about the transfer.

(114) In any case, where the Commission has taken no decision on the adequate level of data protection in a third country, the controller or processor should make use of solutions that provide data subjects with enforceable and effective rights as regards the processing of their data in the Union once those data have been transferred so that they will continue to benefit from fundamental rights and safeguards.

(115) Some third countries adopt laws, regulations and other legal acts which purport to directly regulate the processing activities of natural and legal persons under the jurisdiction of the Member States. This may include judgments of courts or tribunals or decisions of administrative authorities in third countries requiring a controller or processor to transfer or disclose personal data, and which are not based on an international agreement, such as a mutual legal assistance treaty, in force between the requesting third country and the Union or a Member State. The extraterritorial application of those laws, regulations and other legal acts may be in breach of international law and may impede the attainment of the protection of natural persons ensured in the Union by this Regulation. Transfers should only be allowed where the conditions of this Regulation for a transfer to third countries are met. This may be the case, inter alia, where disclosure is necessary for an important ground of public interest recognised in Union or Member State law to which the controller is subject.

(116) When personal data moves across borders outside the Union it may put at increased risk the ability of natural persons to exercise data protection rights in particular to protect themselves from the unlawful use or disclosure of that information. At the same time, supervisory authorities may find that they are unable to pursue complaints or conduct investigations relating to the activities outside their borders. Their efforts to work together in the cross-border context may also be hampered by insufficient preventative or remedial powers, inconsistent legal regimes, and practical obstacles like resource constraints. Therefore, there is a need to promote closer cooperation among data protection supervisory authorities to help them exchange information and carry out investigations with their international counterparts. For the purposes of developing international cooperation mechanisms to facilitate and provide international mutual assistance for the enforcement of legislation for the protection of personal data, the Commission and the supervisory authorities should exchange information and cooperate in activities related to the exercise of their powers with competent authorities in third countries, based on reciprocity and in accordance with this Regulation.

(117) The establishment of supervisory authorities in Member States, empowered to perform their tasks and exercise their powers with complete independence, is an essential component of the protection of natural persons with regard to the processing of their personal data. Member States should be able to establish more than one supervisory authority, to reflect their constitutional, organisational and administrative structure.

(118) The independence of supervisory authorities should not mean that the supervisory authorities cannot be subject to control or monitoring mechanisms regarding their financial expenditure or to judicial review.

(119) Where a Member State establishes several supervisory authorities, it should establish by law mechanisms for ensuring the effective participation of those supervisory authorities in the consistency mechanism. That Member State should in particular designate the supervisory authority which functions as a single contact point for the effective participation of those authorities in the mechanism, to ensure swift and smooth cooperation with other supervisory authorities, the Board and the Commission.

(120) Each supervisory authority should be provided with the financial and human resources, premises and infrastructure necessary for the effective performance of their tasks, including those related to mutual assistance and cooperation with other supervisory authorities throughout the Union. Each supervisory authority should have a separate, public annual budget, which may be part of the overall state or national budget.

(121) The general conditions for the member or members of the supervisory authority should be laid down by law in each Member State and should in particular provide that those members are to be appointed, by means of a transparent procedure, either by the parliament, government or the head of State of the Member State on the basis of a proposal from the government, a member of the government, the parliament or a chamber of the parliament, or by an independent body entrusted under Member State law. In order to ensure the independence of the supervisory authority, the member or members should act with integrity, refrain from any action that is incompatible with their duties and should not, during their term of office, engage in any incompatible occupation, whether gainful or not. The supervisory authority should have its own staff, chosen by the supervisory authority or an independent body established by Member State law, which should be subject to the exclusive direction of the member or members of the supervisory authority.

(122) Each supervisory authority should be competent on the territory of its own Member State to exercise the powers and to perform the tasks conferred on it in accordance with this Regulation. This should cover in particular the processing in the context of the activities of an establishment of the controller or processor on the territory of its own Member State, the processing of personal data carried out by public authorities or private bodies acting in the public interest, processing affecting data subjects on its territory or processing carried out by a controller or processor not established in the Union when targeting data subjects residing on its territory. This should include handling complaints lodged by a data subject, conducting investigations on the application of this Regulation and promoting public awareness of the risks, rules, safeguards and rights in relation to the processing of personal data.

(123) The supervisory authorities should monitor the application of the provisions pursuant to this Regulation and contribute to its consistent application throughout the Union, in order to protect natural persons in relation to the processing of their personal data and to facilitate the free flow of personal data within the internal market. For that purpose, the supervisory authorities should cooperate with each other and with the Commission, without the need for any agreement between Member States on the provision of mutual assistance or on such cooperation.

(124) Where the processing of personal data takes place in the context of the activities of an establishment of a controller or a processor in the Union and the controller or processor is established in more than one Member State, or where processing taking place in the context of the activities of a single establishment of a controller or processor in the Union substantially affects or is likely to substantially affect data subjects in more than one Member State, the supervisory authority for the main establishment of the controller or processor or for the single establishment of the controller or processor should act as lead authority. It should cooperate with the other authorities concerned, because the controller or processor has an establishment on the territory of their Member State, because data subjects residing on their territory are substantially affected, or because a complaint has been lodged with them. Also where a data subject not residing in that Member State has lodged a complaint, the supervisory authority with which such complaint has been lodged should also be a supervisory authority concerned. Within its tasks to issue guidelines on any question covering the application of this Regulation, the Board should be able to issue guidelines in particular on the criteria to be taken into account in order to ascertain whether the processing in question substantially affects data subjects in more than one Member State and on what constitutes a relevant and reasoned objection.

(125) The lead authority should be competent to adopt binding decisions regarding measures applying the powers conferred on it in accordance with this Regulation. In its capacity as lead authority, the supervisory authority should closely involve and coordinate the supervisory authorities concerned in the decision-making process. Where the decision is to reject the complaint by the data subject in whole or in part, that decision should be adopted by the supervisory authority with which the complaint has been lodged.

(126) The decision should be agreed jointly by the lead supervisory authority and the supervisory authorities concerned and should be directed towards the main or single establishment of the controller or processor and be binding on the controller and processor. The controller or processor should take the necessary measures to ensure compliance with this Regulation and the implementation of the decision notified by the lead supervisory authority to the main establishment of the controller or processor as regards the processing activities in the Union.

(127) Each supervisory authority not acting as the lead supervisory authority should be competent to handle local cases where the controller or processor is established in more than one Member State, but the subject matter of the specific processing concerns only processing carried out in a single Member State and involves only data subjects in that single Member State, for example, where the subject matter concerns the processing of employees' personal data in the specific employment context of a Member State. In such cases, the supervisory authority should inform the lead supervisory authority without delay about the matter. After being informed, the lead supervisory authority should decide, whether it will handle the case pursuant to the provision on cooperation between the lead supervisory authority and other supervisory authorities concerned ('one-stop-shop mechanism'), or whether the supervisory authority which informed it should handle the case at local level. When deciding whether it will handle the case, the lead supervisory authority should take into account whether there is an establishment of the controller or processor in the Member State of the supervisory authority which informed it in order to ensure effective enforcement of a decision vis-à-vis the controller or processor.

Where the lead supervisory authority decides to handle the case, the supervisory authority which informed it should have the possibility to submit a draft for a decision, of which the lead supervisory authority should take utmost account when preparing its draft decision in that one-stop-shop mechanism.

(128) The rules on the lead supervisory authority and the one-stop-shop mechanism should not apply where the processing is carried out by public authorities or private bodies in the public interest. In such cases the only supervisory authority competent to exercise the powers conferred to it in accordance with this Regulation should be the supervisory authority of the Member State where the public authority or private body is established.

(129) In order to ensure consistent monitoring and enforcement of this Regulation throughout the Union, the supervisory authorities should have in each Member State the same tasks and effective powers, including powers of investigation, corrective powers and sanctions, and authorisation and advisory powers, in particular in cases of complaints from natural persons, and without prejudice to the powers of prosecutorial authorities under Member State law, to bring infringements of this Regulation to the attention of the judicial authorities and engage in legal proceedings. Such powers should also include the power to impose a temporary or definitive limitation, including a ban, on processing. Member States may specify other tasks related to the protection of personal data under this Regulation. The powers of supervisory authorities should be exercised in accordance with appropriate procedural safeguards set out in Union and Member State law, impartially, fairly and within a reasonable time. In particular each measure should be appropriate, necessary and proportionate in view of ensuring compliance with this Regulation, taking into account the circumstances of each individual case, respect the right of every person to be heard before any individual measure which would affect him or her adversely is taken and avoid superfluous costs and excessive inconveniences for the persons concerned. Investigatory powers as regards access to premises should be exercised in accordance with specific requirements in Member State procedural law, such as the requirement to obtain a prior judicial authorisation. Each legally binding measure of the supervisory authority should be in writing, be clear and unambiguous, indicate the supervisory authority which has issued the measure, the date of issue of the measure, bear the signature of the head, or a member of the supervisory authority authorised by him or her, give the reasons for the measure, and refer to the right of an effective remedy. This should not preclude additional requirements pursuant to Member State procedural law. The adoption of a legally binding decision implies that it may give rise to judicial review in the Member State of the supervisory authority that adopted the decision.

(130) Where the supervisory authority with which the complaint has been lodged is not the lead supervisory authority, the lead supervisory authority should closely cooperate with the supervisory authority with which the complaint has been lodged in accordance with the provisions on cooperation and consistency laid down in this Regulation. In such cases, the lead supervisory authority should, when taking measures intended to produce legal effects, including the imposition of administrative fines, take utmost account of the view of the supervisory authority with which the complaint has been lodged and which should remain competent to carry out any investigation on the territory of its own Member State in liaison with the competent supervisory authority.

(131) Where another supervisory authority should act as a lead supervisory authority for the processing activities of the controller or processor but the concrete subject matter of a complaint or the possible infringement concerns only processing activities of the controller or processor in the Member State where the complaint has been lodged or the possible infringement detected and the matter does not substantially affect or is not likely to substantially affect data subjects in other Member States, the supervisory authority receiving a complaint or detecting or being informed otherwise of situations that entail possible infringements of this Regulation should seek an amicable settlement with the controller and, if this proves unsuccessful, exercise its full range of powers. This should include: specific processing carried out in the territory of the Member State of the supervisory authority or with regard to data subjects on the territory of that Member State; processing that is carried out in the context of an offer of goods or services specifically aimed at data subjects in the territory of the Member State of the supervisory authority; or processing that has to be assessed taking into account relevant legal obligations under Member State law.

(132) Awareness-raising activities by supervisory authorities addressed to the public should include specific measures directed at controllers and processors, including micro, small and medium-sized enterprises, as well as natural persons in particular in the educational context.

(133) The supervisory authorities should assist each other in performing their tasks and provide mutual assistance, so as to ensure the consistent application and enforcement of this Regulation in the internal market. A supervisory authority requesting mutual assistance may adopt a provisional measure if it receives no response to a request for mutual assistance within one month of the receipt of that request by the other supervisory authority.

(134) Each supervisory authority should, where appropriate, participate in joint operations with other supervisory authorities. The requested supervisory authority should be obliged to respond to the request within a specified time period.

(135) In order to ensure the consistent application of this Regulation throughout the Union, a consistency mechanism for cooperation between the supervisory authorities should be established. That mechanism should in particular apply where a supervisory authority intends to adopt a measure intended to produce legal effects as regards processing operations which substantially affect a significant number of data subjects in several Member States. It should also apply where any supervisory authority concerned or the Commission requests that such matter should be handled in the consistency mechanism. That mechanism should be without prejudice to any measures that the Commission may take in the exercise of its powers under the Treaties.

(136) In applying the consistency mechanism, the Board should, within a determined period of time, issue an opinion, if a majority of its members so decides or if so requested by any supervisory authority concerned or the Commission. The Board should also be empowered to adopt legally binding decisions where there are disputes between supervisory authorities. For that purpose, it should issue, in principle by a two-thirds majority of its members, legally binding decisions in clearly specified cases where there are conflicting views among supervisory authorities, in particular in the cooperation mechanism between the lead supervisory authority and supervisory authorities concerned on the merits of the case, in particular whether there is an infringement of this Regulation.

(137) There may be an urgent need to act in order to protect the rights and freedoms of data subjects, in particular when the danger exists that the enforcement of a right of a data subject could be considerably impeded. A supervisory authority should therefore be able to adopt duly justified provisional measures on its territory with a specified period of validity which should not exceed three months.

(138) The application of such mechanism should be a condition for the lawfulness of a measure intended to produce legal effects by a supervisory authority in those cases where its application is mandatory. In other cases of cross- border relevance, the cooperation mechanism between the lead supervisory authority and supervisory authorities concerned should be applied and mutual assistance and joint operations might be carried out between the supervisory authorities concerned on a bilateral or multilateral basis without triggering the consistency mechanism.

(139) In order to promote the consistent application of this Regulation, the Board should be set up as an independent body of the Union. To fulfil its objectives, the Board should have legal personality. The Board should be represented by its Chair. It should replace the Working Party on the Protection of Individuals with Regard to the Processing of Personal Data established by Directive 95/46/EC. It should consist of the head of a supervisory authority of each Member State and the European Data Protection Supervisor or their respective representatives. The Commission should participate in the Board's activities without voting rights and the European Data Protection Supervisor should have specific voting rights. The Board should contribute to the consistent application of this Regulation throughout the Union, including by advising the Commission, in particular on the level of protection in third countries or international organisations, and promoting cooperation of the supervisory authorities throughout the Union. The Board should act independently when performing its tasks.

(140) The Board should be assisted by a secretariat provided by the European Data Protection Supervisor. The staff of the European Data Protection Supervisor involved in carrying out the tasks conferred on the Board by this Regulation should perform its tasks exclusively under the instructions of, and report to, the Chair of the Board.

(141) Every data subject should have the right to lodge a complaint with a single supervisory authority, in particular in the Member State of his or her habitual residence, and the right to an effective judicial remedy in accordance with Article 47 of the Charter if the data subject considers that his or her rights under this Regulation are infringed or where the supervisory authority does not act on a complaint, partially or wholly rejects or dismisses a complaint or does not act where such action is necessary to protect the rights of the data subject. The investigation following a complaint should be carried out, subject to judicial review, to the extent that is appropriate in the specific case. The supervisory authority should inform the data subject of the progress and the outcome of the complaint within a reasonable period. If the case requires further investigation or coordination with another supervisory authority, intermediate information should be given to the data subject. In order to facilitate the submission of complaints, each supervisory authority should take measures such as providing a complaint submission form which can also be completed electronically, without excluding other means of communication.

(142) Where a data subject considers that his or her rights under this Regulation are infringed, he or she should have the right to mandate a not-for-profit body, organisation or association which is constituted in accordance with the law of a Member State, has statutory objectives which are in the public interest and is active in the field of the protection of personal data to lodge a complaint on his or her behalf with a supervisory authority, exercise the right to a judicial remedy on behalf of data subjects or, if provided for in Member State law, exercise the right to receive compensation on behalf of data subjects. A Member State may provide for such a body, organisation or association to have the right to lodge a complaint in that Member State, independently of a data subject's mandate, and the right to an effective judicial remedy where it has reasons to consider that the rights of a data subject have been infringed as a result of the processing of personal data which infringes this Regulation. That body, organisation or association may not be allowed to claim compensation on a data subject's behalf independently of the data subject's mandate.

(143) Any natural or legal person has the right to bring an action for annulment of decisions of the Board before the Court of Justice under the conditions provided for in Article 263 TFEU. As addressees of such decisions, the supervisory authorities concerned which wish to challenge them have to bring action within two months of being notified of them, in accordance with Article 263 TFEU. Where decisions of the Board are of direct and individual concern to a controller, processor or complainant, the latter may bring an action for annulment against those decisions within two months of their publication on the website of the Board, in accordance with Article 263 TFEU. Without prejudice to this right under Article 263 TFEU, each natural or legal person should have an effective judicial remedy before the competent national court against a decision of a supervisory authority which produces legal effects concerning that person. Such a decision concerns in particular the exercise of investigative, corrective and authorisation powers by the supervisory authority or the dismissal or rejection of complaints. However, the right to an effective judicial remedy does not encompass measures taken by supervisory authorities which are not legally binding, such as opinions issued by or advice provided by the supervisory authority. Proceedings against a supervisory authority should be brought before the courts of

the Member State where the supervisory authority is established and should be conducted in accordance with that Member State's procedural law. Those courts should exercise full jurisdiction, which should include jurisdiction to examine all questions of fact and law relevant to the dispute before them.

Where a complaint has been rejected or dismissed by a supervisory authority, the complainant may bring proceedings before the courts in the same Member State. In the context of judicial remedies relating to the application of this Regulation, national courts which consider a decision on the question necessary to enable them to give judgment, may, or in the case provided for in Article 267 TFEU, must, request the Court of Justice to give a preliminary ruling on the interpretation of Union law, including this Regulation. Furthermore, where a decision of a supervisory authority implementing a decision of the Board is challenged before a national court and the validity of the decision of the Board is at issue, that national court does not have the power to declare the Board's decision invalid but must refer the question of validity to the Court of Justice in accordance with Article 267 TFEU as interpreted by the Court of Justice, where it considers the decision invalid. However, a national court may not refer a question on the validity of the decision of the Board at the request of a natural or legal person which had the opportunity to bring an action for annulment of that decision, in particular if it was directly and individually concerned by that decision, but had not done so within the period laid down in Article 263 TFEU.

(144) Where a court seized of proceedings against a decision by a supervisory authority has reason to believe that proceedings concerning the same processing, such as the same subject matter as regards processing by the same controller or processor, or the same cause of action, are brought before a competent court in another Member State, it should contact that court in order to confirm the existence of such related proceedings. If related proceedings are pending before a court in another Member State, any court other than the court first seized may stay its proceedings or may, on request of one of the parties, decline jurisdiction in favour of the court first seized if that court has jurisdiction over the proceedings in question and its law permits the consolidation of such related proceedings. Proceedings are deemed to be related where they are so closely connected that it is expedient to hear and determine them together in order to avoid the risk of irreconcilable judgments resulting from separate proceedings.

(145) For proceedings against a controller or processor, the plaintiff should have the choice to bring the action before the courts of the Member States where the controller or processor has an establishment or where the data subject resides, unless the controller is a public authority of a Member State acting in the exercise of its public powers.

(146) The controller or processor should compensate any damage which a person may suffer as a result of processing that infringes this Regulation. The controller or processor should be exempt from liability if it proves that it is not in any way responsible for the damage. The concept of damage should be broadly interpreted in the light of the case-law of the Court of Justice in a manner which fully reflects the objectives of this Regulation. This is without prejudice to any claims for damage deriving from the violation of other rules in Union or Member State law. Processing that infringes this Regulation also includes processing that infringes delegated and implementing acts adopted in accordance with this Regulation and Member State law specifying rules of this Regulation. Data subjects should receive full and effective compensation for the damage they have suffered. Where controllers or processors are involved in the same processing, each controller or processor should be held liable for the entire damage. However, where they are joined to the same judicial proceedings, in accordance with Member State law, compensation may be apportioned according to the responsibility of each controller or processor for the damage caused by the processing, provided that full and effective compensation of the data subject who suffered the damage is ensured. Any controller or processor which has paid full compensation may subsequently institute recourse proceedings against other controllers or processors involved in the same processing.

(147) Where specific rules on jurisdiction are contained in this Regulation, in particular as regards proceedings seeking a judicial remedy including compensation, against a controller or processor, general jurisdiction rules such as those of Regulation (EU) No 1215/2012 of the European Parliament and of the Council[13] should not prejudice the application of such specific rules.

(148) In order to strengthen the enforcement of the rules of this Regulation, penalties including administrative fines should be imposed for any infringement of this Regulation, in addition to, or instead of appropriate measures imposed by the supervisory authority pursuant to this Regulation. In a case of a minor infringement or if the fine likely to be imposed would constitute a disproportionate burden to a natural person, a reprimand may be issued instead of a fine. Due regard should however be given to the nature, gravity and duration of the infringement, the intentional character of the infringement, actions taken to mitigate the damage suffered, degree of responsibility or any relevant previous infringements, the manner in which the infringement became known to the supervisory authority, compliance with measures ordered against the controller or processor, adherence to a code of conduct and any other aggravating or mitigating factor. The imposition of penalties including administrative fines should be subject to appropriate procedural safeguards in accordance with the general principles of Union law and the Charter, including effective judicial protection and due process.

(149) Member States should be able to lay down the rules on criminal penalties for infringements of this Regulation, including for infringements of national rules adopted pursuant to and within the limits of this Regulation. Those criminal penalties may also allow for the deprivation of the profits obtained through infringements of this Regulation. However, the imposition of criminal penalties for infringements of such national rules and of administrative penalties should not lead to a breach of the principle of *ne bis in idem*, as interpreted by the Court of Justice.

(150) In order to strengthen and harmonise administrative penalties for infringements of this Regulation, each supervisory authority should have the power to impose administrative fines. This Regulation should indicate infringements and the upper limit and criteria for setting the related administrative fines, which should be determined by the competent supervisory authority in each individual case, taking into

account all relevant circumstances of the specific situation, with due regard in particular to the nature, gravity and duration of the infringement and of its consequences and the measures taken to ensure compliance with the obligations under this Regulation and to prevent or mitigate the consequences of the infringement. Where administrative fines are imposed on an undertaking, an undertaking should be understood to be an undertaking in accordance with Articles 101 and 102 TFEU for those purposes. Where administrative fines are imposed on persons that are not an undertaking, the supervisory authority should take account of the general level of income in the Member State as well as the economic situation of the person in considering the appropriate amount of the fine. The consistency mechanism may also be used to promote a consistent application of administrative fines. It should be for the Member States to determine whether and to which extent public authorities should be subject to administrative fines. Imposing an administrative fine or giving a warning does not affect the application of other powers of the supervisory authorities or of other penalties under this Regulation.

(151) The legal systems of Denmark and Estonia do not allow for administrative fines as set out in this Regulation. The rules on administrative fines may be applied in such a manner that in Denmark the fine is imposed by competent national courts as a criminal penalty and in Estonia the fine is imposed by the supervisory authority in the framework of a misdemeanour procedure, provided that such an application of the rules in those Member States has an equivalent effect to administrative fines imposed by supervisory authorities. Therefore the competent national courts should take into account the recommendation by the supervisory authority initiating the fine. In any event, the fines imposed should be effective, proportionate and dissuasive.

(152) Where this Regulation does not harmonise administrative penalties or where necessary in other cases, for example in cases of serious infringements of this Regulation, Member States should implement a system which provides for effective, proportionate and dissuasive penalties. The nature of such penalties, criminal or administrative, should be determined by Member State law.

(153) Member States law should reconcile the rules governing freedom of expression and information, including journalistic, academic, artistic and or literary expression with the right to the protection of personal data pursuant to this Regulation. The processing of personal data solely for journalistic purposes, or for the purposes of academic, artistic or literary expression should be subject to derogations or exemptions from certain provisions of this Regulation if necessary to reconcile the right to the protection of personal data with the right to freedom of expression and information, as enshrined in Article 11 of the Charter. This should apply in particular to the processing of personal data in the audiovisual field and in news archives and press libraries. Therefore, Member States should adopt legislative measures which lay down the exemptions and derogations necessary for the purpose of balancing those fundamental rights. Member States should adopt such exemptions and derogations on general principles, the rights of the data subject, the controller and the processor, the transfer of personal data to third countries or international organisations, the independent supervisory authorities, cooperation and consistency, and specific data-processing situations. Where such exemptions or derogations differ from one Member State to another, the law of the Member State to which the controller is subject should apply. In order to take account of the importance of the right to freedom of expression in every democratic society, it is necessary to interpret notions relating to that freedom, such as journalism, broadly.

(154) This Regulation allows the principle of public access to official documents to be taken into account when applying this Regulation. Public access to official documents may be considered to be in the public interest. Personal data in documents held by a public authority or a public body should be able to be publicly disclosed by that authority or body if the disclosure is provided for by Union or Member State law to which the public authority or public body is subject. Such laws should reconcile public access to official documents and the reuse of public sector information with the right to the protection of personal data and may therefore provide for the necessary reconciliation with the right to the protection of personal data pursuant to this Regulation. The reference to public authorities and bodies should in that context include all authorities or other bodies covered by Member State law on public access to documents. Directive 2003/98/EC of the European Parliament and of the Council[14] leaves intact and in no way affects the level of protection of natural persons with regard to the processing of personal data under the provisions of Union and Member State law, and in particular does not alter the obligations and rights set out in this Regulation. In particular, that Directive should not apply to documents to which access is excluded or restricted by virtue of the access regimes on the grounds of protection of personal data, and parts of documents accessible by virtue of those regimes which contain personal data the re-use of which has been provided for by law as being incompatible with the law concerning the protection of natural persons with regard to the processing of personal data.

(155) Member State law or collective agreements, including 'works agreements', may provide for specific rules on the processing of employees' personal data in the employment context, in particular for the conditions under which personal data in the employment context may be processed on the basis of the consent of the employee, the purposes of the recruitment, the performance of the contract of employment, including discharge of obligations laid down by law or by collective agreements, management, planning and organisation of work, equality and diversity in the workplace, health and safety at work, and for the purposes of the exercise and enjoyment, on an individual or collective basis, of rights and benefits related to employment, and for the purpose of the termination of the employment relationship.

(156) The processing of personal data for archiving purposes in the public interest, scientific or historical research purposes or statistical purposes should be subject to appropriate safeguards for the rights and freedoms of the data subject pursuant to this Regulation. Those safeguards should ensure that technical and organisational measures are in place in order to ensure, in particular, the principle of data

minimisation. The further processing of personal data for archiving purposes in the public interest, scientific or historical research purposes or statistical purposes is to be carried out when the controller has assessed the feasibility to fulfil those purposes by processing data which do not permit or no longer permit the identification of data subjects, provided that appropriate safeguards exist (such as, for instance, pseudonymisation of the data). Member States should provide for appropriate safeguards for the processing of personal data for archiving purposes in the public interest, scientific or historical research purposes or statistical purposes. Member States should be authorised to provide, under specific conditions and subject to appropriate safeguards for data subjects, specifications and derogations with regard to the information requirements and rights to rectification, to erasure, to be forgotten, to restriction of processing, to data portability, and to object when processing personal data for archiving purposes in the public interest, scientific or historical research purposes or statistical purposes. The conditions and safeguards in question may entail specific procedures for data subjects to exercise those rights if this is appropriate in the light of the purposes sought by the specific processing along with technical and organisational measures aimed at minimising the processing of personal data in pursuance of the proportionality and necessity principles. The processing of personal data for scientific purposes should also comply with other relevant legislation such as on clinical trials.

(157) By coupling information from registries, researchers can obtain new knowledge of great value with regard to widespread medical conditions such as cardiovascular disease, cancer and depression. On the basis of registries, research results can be enhanced, as they draw on a larger population. Within social science, research on the basis of registries enables researchers to obtain essential knowledge about the long-term correlation of a number of social conditions such as unemployment and education with other life conditions. Research results obtained through registries provide solid, high-quality knowledge which can provide the basis for the formulation and implementation of knowledge-based policy, improve the quality of life for a number of people and improve the efficiency of social services. In order to facilitate scientific research, personal data can be processed for scientific research purposes, subject to appropriate conditions and safeguards set out in Union or Member State law.

(158) Where personal data are processed for archiving purposes, this Regulation should also apply to that processing, bearing in mind that this Regulation should not apply to deceased persons. Public authorities or public or private bodies that hold records of public interest should be services which, pursuant to Union or Member State law, have a legal obligation to acquire, preserve, appraise, arrange, describe, communicate, promote, disseminate and provide access to records of enduring value for general public interest. Member States should also be authorised to provide for the further processing of personal data for archiving purposes, for example with a view to providing specific information related to the political behaviour under former totalitarian state regimes, genocide, crimes against humanity, in particular the Holocaust, or war crimes.

(159) Where personal data are processed for scientific research purposes, this Regulation should also apply to that processing. For the purposes of this Regulation, the processing of personal data for scientific research purposes should be interpreted in a broad manner including for example technological development and demonstration, fundamental research, applied research and privately funded research. In addition, it should take into account the Union's objective under Article 179(1) TFEU of achieving a European Research Area. Scientific research purposes should also include studies conducted in the public interest in the area of public health. To meet the specificities of processing personal data for scientific research purposes, specific conditions should apply in particular as regards the publication or otherwise disclosure of personal data in the context of scientific research purposes. If the result of scientific research in particular in the health context gives reason for further measures in the interest of the data subject, the general rules of this Regulation should apply in view of those measures.

(160) Where personal data are processed for historical research purposes, this Regulation should also apply to that processing. This should also include historical research and research for genealogical purposes, bearing in mind that this Regulation should not apply to deceased persons.

(161) For the purpose of consenting to the participation in scientific research activities in clinical trials, the relevant provisions of Regulation (EU) No 536/2014 of the European Parliament and of the Council[15] should apply.

(162) Where personal data are processed for statistical purposes, this Regulation should apply to that processing. Union or Member State law should, within the limits of this Regulation, determine statistical content, control of access, specifications for the processing of personal data for statistical purposes and appropriate measures to safeguard the rights and freedoms of the data subject and for ensuring statistical confidentiality. Statistical purposes mean any operation of collection and the processing of personal data necessary for statistical surveys or for the production of statistical results. Those statistical results may further be used for different purposes, including a scientific research purpose. The statistical purpose implies that the result of processing for statistical purposes is not personal data, but aggregate data, and that this result or the personal data are not used in support of measures or decisions regarding any particular natural person.

(163) The confidential information which the Union and national statistical authorities collect for the production of official European and official national statistics should be protected. European statistics should be developed, produced and disseminated in accordance with the statistical principles as set out in Article 338(2) TFEU, while national statistics should also comply with Member State law. Regulation (EC) No 223/2009 of the European Parliament and of the Council[16] provides further specifications on statistical confidentiality for European statistics.

(164) As regards the powers of the supervisory authorities to obtain from the controller or processor access to personal data and access to their premises, Member States may adopt by law, within the limits of this Regulation, specific rules in order to safeguard the professional or other equivalent secrecy

obligations, in so far as necessary to reconcile the right to the protection of personal data with an obligation of professional secrecy. This is without prejudice to existing Member State obligations to adopt rules on professional secrecy where required by Union law.

(165) This Regulation respects and does not prejudice the status under existing constitutional law of churches and religious associations or communities in the Member States, as recognised in Article 17 TFEU.

(166) In order to fulfil the objectives of this Regulation, namely to protect the fundamental rights and freedoms of natural persons and in particular their right to the protection of personal data and to ensure the free movement of personal data within the Union, the power to adopt acts in accordance with Article 290 TFEU should be delegated to the Commission. In particular, delegated acts should be adopted in respect of criteria and requirements for certification mechanisms, information to be presented by standardised icons and procedures for providing such icons. It is of particular importance that the Commission carry out appropriate consultations during its preparatory work, including at expert level. The Commission, when preparing and drawing-up delegated acts, should ensure a simultaneous, timely and appropriate transmission of relevant documents to the European Parliament and to the Council.

(167) In order to ensure uniform conditions for the implementation of this Regulation, implementing powers should be conferred on the Commission when provided for by this Regulation. Those powers should be exercised in accordance with Regulation (EU) No 182/2011. In that context, the Commission should consider specific measures for micro, small and medium-sized enterprises.

(168) The examination procedure should be used for the adoption of implementing acts on standard contractual clauses between controllers and processors and between processors; codes of conduct; technical standards and mechanisms for certification; the adequate level of protection afforded by a third country, a territory or a specified sector within that third country, or an international organisation; standard protection clauses; formats and procedures for the exchange of information by electronic means between controllers, processors and supervisory authorities for binding corporate rules; mutual assistance; and arrangements for the exchange of information by electronic means between supervisory authorities, and between supervisory authorities and the Board.

(169) The Commission should adopt immediately applicable implementing acts where available evidence reveals that a third country, a territory or a specified sector within that third country, or an international organisation does not ensure an adequate level of protection, and imperative grounds of urgency so require.

(170) Since the objective of this Regulation, namely to ensure an equivalent level of protection of natural persons and the free flow of personal data throughout the Union, cannot be sufficiently achieved by the Member States and can rather, by reason of the scale or effects of the action, be better achieved at Union level, the Union may adopt measures, in accordance with the principle of subsidiarity as set out in Article 5 of the Treaty on European Union (TEU). In accordance with the principle of proportionality as set out in that Article, this Regulation does not go beyond what is necessary in order to achieve that objective.

(171) Directive 95/46/EC should be repealed by this Regulation. Processing already under way on the date of application of this Regulation should be brought into conformity with this Regulation within the period of two years after which this Regulation enters into force. Where processing is based on consent pursuant to Directive 95/46/EC, it is not necessary for the data subject to give his or her consent again if the manner in which the consent has been given is in line with the conditions of this Regulation, so as to allow the controller to continue such processing after the date of application of this Regulation. Commission decisions adopted and authorisations by supervisory authorities based on Directive 95/46/EC remain in force until amended, replaced or repealed.

(172) The European Data Protection Supervisor was consulted in accordance with Article 28(2) of Regulation (EC) No 45/2001 and delivered an opinion on 7 March 2012.[17]

(173) This Regulation should apply to all matters concerning the protection of fundamental rights and freedoms vis-à-vis the processing of personal data which are not subject to specific obligations with the same objective set out in Directive 2002/58/EC of the European Parliament and of the Council,[18] including the obligations on the controller and the rights of natural persons. In order to clarify the relationship between this Regulation and Directive 2002/58/EC, that Directive should be amended accordingly. Once this Regulation is adopted, Directive 2002/58/EC should be reviewed in particular in order to ensure consistency with this Regulation,

NOTES

[1]   OJ C229, 31.7.2012, p 90.

[2]   OJ C391, 18.12.2012, p 127.

[3]   Position of the European Parliament of 12 March 2014 (not yet published in the Official Journal) and position of the Council at first reading of 8 April 2016 (not yet published in the Official Journal). Position of the European Parliament of 14 April 2016.

[4]   Directive 95/46/EC of the European Parliament and of the Council of 24 October 1995 on the protection of individuals with regard to the processing of personal data and on the free movement of such data (OJ L281, 23.11.1995, p 31).

[5]   Commission Recommendation of 6 May 2003 concerning the definition of micro, small and medium‑sized enterprises (C(2003) 1422) (OJ L124, 20.5.2003, p 36).

[6]   Regulation (EC) No 45/2001 of the European Parliament and of the Council of 18 December 2000 on the protection of individuals with regard to the processing of personal data by the Community institutions and bodies and on the free movement of such data (OJ L8, 12.1.2001, p 1).

[7]   Directive (EU) 2016/680 of the European Parliament and of the Council of 27 April 2016 on the protection of natural

persons with regard to the processing of personal data by competent authorities for the purposes of prevention, investigation, detection or prosecution of criminal offences or the execution of criminal penalties, and the free movement of such data and repealing Council Framework Decision 2008/977/JHA (see page 89 of this Official Journal).

[8] Directive 2000/31/EC of the European Parliament and of the Council of 8 June 2000 on certain legal aspects of information society services, in particular electronic commerce, in the Internal Market ('Directive on electronic commerce') (OJ L178, 17.7.2000, p 1).

[9] Directive 2011/24/EU of the European Parliament and of the Council of 9 March 2011 on the application of patients' rights in crossâ€'border healthcare (OJ L88, 4.4.2011, p 45).

[10] Council Directive 93/13/EEC of 5 April 1993 on unfair terms in consumer contracts (OJ L95, 21.4.1993, p 29).

[11] Regulation (EC) No 1338/2008 of the European Parliament and of the Council of 16 December 2008 on Community statistics on public health and health and safety at work (OJ L354, 31.12.2008, p 70).

[12] Regulation (EU) No 182/2011 of the European Parliament and of the Council of 16 February 2011 laying down the rules and general principles concerning mechanisms for control by Member States of the Commission's exercise of implementing powers (OJ L55, 28.2.2011, p 13).

[13] Regulation (EU) No 1215/2012 of the European Parliament and of the Council of 12 December 2012 on jurisdiction and the recognition and enforcement of judgments in civil and commercial matters (OJ L351, 20.12.2012, p 1).

[14] Directive 2003/98/EC of the European Parliament and of the Council of 17 November 2003 on the reâ€'use of public sector information (OJ L345, 31.12.2003, p 90).

[15] Regulation (EU) No 536/2014 of the European Parliament and of the Council of 16 April 2014 on clinical trials on medicinal products for human use, and repealing Directive 2001/20/EC (OJ L158, 27.5.2014, p 1).

[16] Regulation (EC) No 223/2009 of the European Parliament and of the Council of 11 March 2009 on European statistics and repealing Regulation (EC, Euratom) No 1101/2008 of the European Parliament and of the Council on the transmission of data subject to statistical confidentiality to the Statistical Office of the European Communities, Council Regulation (EC) No 322/97 on Community Statistics, and Council Decision 89/382/EEC, Euratom establishing a Committee on the Statistical Programmes of the European Communities (OJ L87, 31.3.2009, p 164).

[17] OJ C 192, 30.6.2012, p 7.

[18] Directive 2002/58/EC of the European Parliament and of the Council of 12 July 2002 concerning the processing of personal data and the protection of privacy in the electronic communications sector (Directive on privacy and electronic communications) (OJ L201, 31.7.2002, p 37).

HAVE ADOPTED THIS REGULATION:

CHAPTER I GENERAL PROVISIONS

[1.2]
Article 1   Subject-matter and objectives
1. This Regulation lays down rules relating to the protection of natural persons with regard to the processing of personal data and rules relating to the free movement of personal data.
2. This Regulation protects fundamental rights and freedoms of natural persons and in particular their right to the protection of personal data.
3.   . . .

NOTES
Para 3: repealed by the Data Protection, Privacy and Electronic Communications (Amendments etc) (EU Exit) Regulations 2019, SI 2019/419, reg 3, Sch 1, paras 1, 3.

[1.3]
Article 2   Material scope
[1. This Regulation applies to the automated or structured processing of personal data, including—
  (a) processing in the course of an activity which, immediately before IP completion day, fell outside the scope of EU law, and
  (b) processing in the course of an activity which, immediately before IP completion day, fell within the scope of Chapter 2 of Title 5 of the Treaty on European Union (common foreign and security policy activities).
1A. This Regulation also applies to the manual unstructured processing of personal data held by an FOI public authority.]
[2. This Regulation does not apply to—
  (a) the processing of personal data by an individual in the course of a purely personal or household activity;
  (b) the processing of personal data by a competent authority for any of the law enforcement purposes (see Part 3 of the 2018 Act);
  (c) the processing of personal data to which Part 4 of the 2018 Act (intelligence services processing) applies.]
3.   . . .
4. This Regulation shall be without prejudice to the application of [the Electronic Commerce (EC Directive) Regulations 2002, in particular the provisions about mere conduits, caching and hosting (see regulations 17 to 19 of those Regulations).]
[5. In this Article—
  (a) 'the automated or structured processing of personal data' means—
      (i)   the processing of personal data wholly or partly by automated means, and
      (ii)   the processing otherwise than by automated means of personal data which forms part of a filing system or is intended to form part of a filing system;
  (b) 'the manual unstructured processing of personal data' means the processing of personal data which is not the automated or structured processing of personal data;
  (c) 'FOI public authority' has the same meaning as in Chapter 3 of Part 2 of the 2018 Act (see section 21(5) of that Act);

(d) references to personal data 'held' by an FOI public authority are to be interpreted in accordance with section 21(6) and (7) of the 2018 Act;

(e) 'competent authority' and 'law enforcement purposes' have the same meaning as in Part 3 of the 2018 Act (see sections 30 and 31 of that Act).]

NOTES

Paras 1, 1A were substituted for the original para 1, para 2 and the words in square brackets in para 4 were substituted, para 3 was repealed, and para 5 was added, by the Data Protection, Privacy and Electronic Communications (Amendments etc) (EU Exit) Regulations 2019, SI 2019/419, reg 3, Sch 1, paras 1, 4. Note that Sch 1 to the 2019 Regulations was amended by the Data Protection, Privacy and Electronic Communications (Amendments etc) (EU Exit) Regulations 2020, SI 2020/1586, reg 4, as from IP Completion Day (and the effect of the amendment has been incorporated in the text set out above).

[1.4]
Article 3   Territorial scope
1. This Regulation applies to the processing of personal data in the context of the activities of an establishment of a controller or a processor in [the United Kingdom], regardless of whether the processing takes place in [the United Kingdom] or not.
2. This Regulation applies to the [relevant] processing of personal data of data subjects who are in [the United Kingdom] by a controller or processor not established in [the United Kingdom], where the processing activities are related to:
(a) the offering of goods or services, irrespective of whether a payment of the data subject is required, to such data subjects in [the United Kingdom]; or
(b) the monitoring of their behaviour as far as their behaviour takes place within [the United Kingdom].
[2A. In paragraph 2, "relevant processing of personal data" means processing to which this Regulation applies, other than processing described in Article 2(1)(a) or (b) or (1A).]
3. This Regulation applies to the processing of personal data by a controller not established in [the United Kingdom], but in a place where [domestic law] applies by virtue of public international law.

NOTES

Paras 1, 3: words in square brackets substituted by the Data Protection, Privacy and Electronic Communications (Amendments etc) (EU Exit) Regulations 2019, SI 2019/419, reg 3, Sch 1, paras 1, 5(1), (2), (5).

Para 2: word in first pair of square brackets inserted, and other words in square brackets substituted, by SI 2019/419, reg 3, Sch 1, paras 1, 5(1), (3).

Para 2A: inserted by SI 2019/419, reg 3, Sch 1, paras 1, 5(1), (4).

[1.5]
Article 4   Definitions
For the purposes of this Regulation:
[(A1) 'the 2018 Act' means the Data Protection Act 2018;
(A2) 'domestic law' means the law of the United Kingdom or of a part of the United Kingdom;
(A3) 'the Commissioner' means the Information Commissioner (see section 114 of the 2018 Act);]
(1) "personal data" means any information relating to an identified or identifiable natural person ("data subject"); an identifiable natural person is one who can be identified, directly or indirectly, in particular by reference to an identifier such as a name, an identification number, location data, an online identifier or to one or more factors specific to the physical, physiological, genetic, mental, economic, cultural or social identity of that natural person;
(2) "processing" means any operation or set of operations which is performed on personal data or on sets of personal data, whether or not by automated means, such as collection, recording, organisation, structuring, storage, adaptation or alteration, retrieval, consultation, use, disclosure by transmission, dissemination or otherwise making available, alignment or combination, restriction, erasure or destruction;
(3) "restriction of processing" means the marking of stored personal data with the aim of limiting their processing in the future;
(4) "profiling" means any form of automated processing of personal data consisting of the use of personal data to evaluate certain personal aspects relating to a natural person, in particular to analyse or predict aspects concerning that natural person's performance at work, economic situation, health, personal preferences, interests, reliability, behaviour, location or movements;
(5) "pseudonymisation" means the processing of personal data in such a manner that the personal data can no longer be attributed to a specific data subject without the use of additional information, provided that such additional information is kept separately and is subject to technical and organisational measures to ensure that the personal data are not attributed to an identified or identifiable natural person;
(6) "filing system" means any structured set of personal data which are accessible according to specific criteria, whether centralised, decentralised or dispersed on a functional or geographical basis;
(7) "controller" means the natural or legal person, public authority, agency or other body which, alone or jointly with others, determines the purposes and means of the processing of personal data [(but see section 6 of the 2018 Act)];
(8) "processor" means a natural or legal person, public authority, agency or other body which processes personal data on behalf of the controller;
(9) "recipient" means a natural or legal person, public authority, agency or another body, to which the personal data are disclosed, whether a third party or not. However, public authorities which may receive personal data in the framework of a particular inquiry in accordance with [domestic law] shall not be regarded as recipients; the processing of those data by those public authorities shall be in compliance with the applicable data protection rules according to the purposes of the processing;
(10) "third party" means a natural or legal person, public authority, agency or body other than the data subject, controller, processor and persons who, under the direct authority of the controller or processor, are authorised to process personal data;

[(10A) 'public authority' and 'public body' are to be interpreted in accordance with section 7 of the 2018 Act and provision made under that section;]

(11) "consent of the data subject" means any freely given, specific, informed and unambiguous indication of the data subject's wishes by which he or she, by a statement or by a clear affirmative action, signifies agreement to the processing of personal data relating to him or her;

(12) "personal data breach" means a breach of security leading to the accidental or unlawful destruction, loss, alteration, unauthorised disclosure of, or access to, personal data transmitted, stored or otherwise processed;

(13) "genetic data" means personal data relating to the inherited or acquired genetic characteristics of a natural person which give unique information about the physiology or the health of that natural person and which result, in particular, from an analysis of a biological sample from the natural person in question;

(14) "biometric data" means personal data resulting from specific technical processing relating to the physical, physiological or behavioural characteristics of a natural person, which allow or confirm the unique identification of that natural person, such as facial images or dactyloscopic data;

(15) "data concerning health" means personal data related to the physical or mental health of a natural person, including the provision of health care services, which reveal information about his or her health status;

(16) . . .

(17) "representative" means a natural or legal person established in [the United Kingdom] who, designated by the controller or processor in writing pursuant to Article 27, represents the controller or processor with regard to their respective obligations under this Regulation;

(18) "enterprise" means a natural or legal person engaged in an economic activity, irrespective of its legal form, including partnerships or associations regularly engaged in an economic activity;

(19) "group of undertakings" means a controlling undertaking and its controlled undertakings;

(20) "binding corporate rules" means personal data protection policies which are adhered to by a controller or processor established [in the United Kingdom] for transfers or a set of transfers of personal data to a controller or processor in one or more third countries within a group of undertakings, or group of enterprises engaged in a joint economic activity;

(21) . . .

[(21A) 'foreign designated authority' means an authority designated for the purposes of Article 13 of the Data Protection Convention (as defined in section 3 of the 2018 Act) by a party, other than the United Kingdom, which is bound by that Convention;]

(22) . . .

(23) . . .

(24) . . .

(25) information society service means a service as defined in point (b) of Article 1(1) of Directive (EU) 2015/1535 of the European Parliament and of the Council[1] [as it has effect immediately before IP completion day];

(26) international organisation means an organisation and its subordinate bodies governed by public international law, or any other body which is set up by, or on the basis of, an agreement between two or more countries;

[(27) 'third country' means a country or territory outside the United Kingdom;

(28) references to a fundamental right or fundamental freedom (however expressed) are to a fundamental right or fundamental freedom which continues to form part of domestic law on and after IP completion day by virtue of section 4 of the European Union (Withdrawal) Act 2018, as the right or freedom is amended or otherwise modified by domestic law from time to time on or after IP completion day.]

NOTES

Paras (A1), (A2), (A3), (10A), (21A) were inserted, the words in square brackets in paras (7), (9), (17), (20) were substituted, paras (16), (21), (22)–(24) were repealed, the words in square in para (25) were inserted, and paras (27), (28) were added, by the Data Protection, Privacy and Electronic Communications (Amendments etc) (EU Exit) Regulations 2019, SI 2019/419, reg 3, Sch 1, paras 1, 6. Note that para 6 of Sch 1 to the 2019 Regulations was amended by the Data Protection, Privacy and Electronic Communications (Amendments etc) (EU Exit) Regulations 2020, SI 2020/1586, reg 4 (and the effect of the amendment has been incorporated in the text set out above).

[1] Directive (EU) 2015/1535 of the European Parliament and of the Council of 9 September 2015 laying down a procedure for the provision of information in the field of technical regulations and of rules on Information Society services (OJ L241, 17.9.2015, p 1).

CHAPTER II PRINCIPLES

[1.6]
Article 5   Principles relating to processing of personal data

1. Personal data shall be:
   (a) processed lawfully, fairly and in a transparent manner in relation to the data subject ('lawfulness, fairness and transparency');
   (b) collected for specified, explicit and legitimate purposes and not further processed in a manner that is incompatible with those purposes; further processing for archiving purposes in the public interest, scientific or historical research purposes or statistical purposes shall, in accordance with Article 89(1), not be considered to be incompatible with the initial purposes ('purpose limitation');
   (c) adequate, relevant and limited to what is necessary in relation to the purposes for which they are processed ('data minimisation');
   (d) accurate and, where necessary, kept up to date; every reasonable step must be taken to ensure that personal data that are inaccurate, having regard to the purposes for which they are processed, are erased or rectified without delay ('accuracy');
   (e) kept in a form which permits identification of data subjects for no longer than is necessary for the purposes for which the personal data are processed; personal data may be stored for longer periods insofar as the personal

data will be processed solely for archiving purposes in the public interest, scientific or historical research purposes or statistical purposes in accordance with Article 89(1) subject to implementation of the appropriate technical and organisational measures required by this Regulation in order to safeguard the rights and freedoms of the data subject ('storage limitation');

(f) processed in a manner that ensures appropriate security of the personal data, including protection against unauthorised or unlawful processing and against accidental loss, destruction or damage, using appropriate technical or organisational measures ('integrity and confidentiality').

2. The controller shall be responsible for, and be able to demonstrate compliance with, paragraph 1 ('accountability').

[1.7]
Article 6   Lawfulness of processing
1. Processing shall be lawful only if and to the extent that at least one of the following applies:

(a) the data subject has given consent to the processing of his or her personal data for one or more specific purposes;

(b) processing is necessary for the performance of a contract to which the data subject is party or in order to take steps at the request of the data subject prior to entering into a contract;

(c) processing is necessary for compliance with a legal obligation to which the controller is subject;

(d) processing is necessary in order to protect the vital interests of the data subject or of another natural person;

(e) processing is necessary for the performance of a task carried out in the public interest or in the exercise of official authority vested in the controller;

(f) processing is necessary for the purposes of the legitimate interests pursued by the controller or by a third party, except where such interests are overridden by the interests or fundamental rights and freedoms of the data subject which require protection of personal data, in particular where the data subject is a child.

Point (f) of the first subparagraph shall not apply to processing carried out by public authorities in the performance of their tasks.

2.   . . .

3. The basis for the processing referred to in point (c) and (e) of paragraph 1 shall be laid down by [domestic law]. The purpose of the processing shall be determined in that legal basis or, as regards the processing referred to in point (e) of paragraph 1, shall be necessary for the performance of a task carried out in the public interest or in the exercise of official authority vested in the controller. That legal basis may contain specific provisions to adapt the application of rules of this Regulation, inter alia: the general conditions governing the lawfulness of processing by the controller; the types of data which are subject to the processing; the data subjects concerned; the entities to, and the purposes for which, the personal data may be disclosed; the purpose limitation; storage periods; and processing operations and processing procedures, including measures to ensure lawful and fair processing such as those for other specific processing situations as provided for in Chapter IX. [The domestic law] shall meet an objective of public interest and be proportionate to the legitimate aim pursued.

4. Where the processing for a purpose other than that for which the personal data have been collected is not based on the data subject's consent or on a [domestic law] which constitutes a necessary and proportionate measure in a democratic society to safeguard [national security, defence or any of] the objectives referred to in Article 23(1), the controller shall, in order to ascertain whether processing for another purpose is compatible with the purpose for which the personal data are initially collected, take into account, inter alia:

(a) any link between the purposes for which the personal data have been collected and the purposes of the intended further processing;

(b) the context in which the personal data have been collected, in particular regarding the relationship between data subjects and the controller;

(c) the nature of the personal data, in particular whether special categories of personal data are processed, pursuant to Article 9, or whether personal data related to criminal convictions and offences are processed, pursuant to Article 10;

(d) the possible consequences of the intended further processing for data subjects;

(e) the existence of appropriate safeguards, which may include encryption or pseudonymisation.

NOTES
Para 2: repealed by the Data Protection, Privacy and Electronic Communications (Amendments etc) (EU Exit) Regulations 2019, SI 2019/419, reg 3, Sch 1, paras 1, 7(1), (2).
Para 3: words in square brackets substituted by SI 2019/419, reg 3, Sch 1, paras 1, 7(1), (3).
Para 4: words in first pair of square brackets substituted and words in second pair of square brackets inserted, by SI 2019/419, reg 3, Sch 1, paras 1, 7(1), (4).

[1.8]
Article 7   Conditions for consent
1. Where processing is based on consent, the controller shall be able to demonstrate that the data subject has consented to processing of his or her personal data.

2. If the data subject's consent is given in the context of a written declaration which also concerns other matters, the request for consent shall be presented in a manner which is clearly distinguishable from the other matters, in an intelligible and easily accessible form, using clear and plain language. Any part of such a declaration which constitutes an infringement of this Regulation shall not be binding.

3. The data subject shall have the right to withdraw his or her consent at any time. The withdrawal of consent shall not affect the lawfulness of processing based on consent before its withdrawal. Prior to giving consent, the data subject shall be informed thereof. It shall be as easy to withdraw as to give consent.

4. When assessing whether consent is freely given, utmost account shall be taken of whether, inter alia, the performance of a contract, including the provision of a service, is conditional on consent to the processing of personal data that is not necessary for the performance of that contract.

[1.9]
Article 8   Conditions applicable to child's consent in relation to information society services
1. Where point (a) of Article 6(1) applies, in relation to the offer of information society services directly to a child, the processing of the personal data of a child shall be lawful where the child is at least [13 years old]. Where the child is below the age [of 13 years], such processing shall be lawful only if and to the extent that consent is given or authorised by the holder of parental responsibility over the child.

. . .

2. The controller shall make reasonable efforts to verify in such cases that consent is given or authorised by the holder of parental responsibility over the child, taking into consideration available technology.
3. Paragraph 1 shall not affect the general contract law [as it operates in domestic law] such as the rules on the validity, formation or effect of a contract in relation to a child.
[4. In paragraph 1, the reference to information society services does not include preventive or counselling services.]

NOTES
The words in square brackets in para 1, 3 were substituted, the words omitted from para 1 were repealed, and para 4 was added, by the Data Protection, Privacy and Electronic Communications (Amendments etc) (EU Exit) Regulations 2019, SI 2019/419, reg 3, Sch 1, paras 1, 8.

[1.10]
Article 9   Processing of special categories of personal data
1. Processing of personal data revealing racial or ethnic origin, political opinions, religious or philosophical beliefs, or trade union membership, and the processing of genetic data, biometric data for the purpose of uniquely identifying a natural person, data concerning health or data concerning a natural person's sex life or sexual orientation shall be prohibited.
2. Paragraph 1 shall not apply if one of the following applies:
  (a) the data subject has given explicit consent to the processing of those personal data for one or more specified purposes, except where [domestic law provides] that the prohibition referred to in paragraph 1 may not be lifted by the data subject;
  (b) processing is necessary for the purposes of carrying out the obligations and exercising specific rights of the controller or of the data subject in the field of employment and social security and social protection law in so far as it is authorised by [domestic law] or a collective agreement pursuant [to domestic law] providing for appropriate safeguards for the fundamental rights and the interests of the data subject;
  (c) processing is necessary to protect the vital interests of the data subject or of another natural person where the data subject is physically or legally incapable of giving consent;
  (d) processing is carried out in the course of its legitimate activities with appropriate safeguards by a foundation, association or any other not-for-profit body with a political, philosophical, religious or trade union aim and on condition that the processing relates solely to the members or to former members of the body or to persons who have regular contact with it in connection with its purposes and that the personal data are not disclosed outside that body without the consent of the data subjects;
  (e) processing relates to personal data which are manifestly made public by the data subject;
  (f) processing is necessary for the establishment, exercise or defence of legal claims or whenever courts are acting in their judicial capacity;
  (g) processing is necessary for reasons of substantial public interest, on the basis of [domestic law which shall be proportionate to the aim pursued, respect the essence of the right to data protection and provide for suitable and specific measures to safeguard the fundamental rights and the interests of the data subject;
  (h) processing is necessary for the purposes of preventive or occupational medicine, for the assessment of the working capacity of the employee, medical diagnosis, the provision of health or social care or treatment or the management of health or social care systems and services on the basis of [domestic law] or pursuant to contract with a health professional and subject to the conditions and safeguards referred to in paragraph 3;
  (i) processing is necessary for reasons of public interest in the area of public health, such as protecting against serious cross-border threats to health or ensuring high standards of quality and safety of health care and of medicinal products or medical devices, on the basis of [domestic law] which provides for suitable and specific measures to safeguard the rights and freedoms of the data subject, in particular professional secrecy;
  (j) processing is necessary for archiving purposes in the public interest, scientific or historical research purposes or statistical purposes in accordance with Article 89(1) [(as supplemented by section 19 of the 2018 Act)] based on [domestic law] which shall be proportionate to the aim pursued, respect the essence of the right to data protection and provide for suitable and specific measures to safeguard the fundamental rights and the interests of the data subject.
3. Personal data referred to in paragraph 1 may be processed for the purposes referred to in point (h) of paragraph 2 when those data are processed by or under the responsibility of a professional subject to the obligation of professional secrecy under [domestic law] or rules established by national competent bodies or by another person also subject to an obligation of secrecy under [domestic law] or rules established by national competent bodies.
[3A. In paragraph 3, 'national competent bodies' means competent bodies of the United Kingdom or a part of the United Kingdom.]
4.   . . .
[5. In the 2018 Act—
  (a) section 10 makes provision about when the requirement in paragraph 2(b), (g), (h), (i) or (j) of this Article for authorisation by, or a basis in, domestic law is met;
  (b) section 11(1) makes provision about when the processing of personal data is carried out in circumstances described in paragraph 3 of this Article.]

NOTES

Para 2: the words in first pair of square brackets in sub-para (j) were inserted and all other words in square brackets were substituted, by the Data Protection, Privacy and Electronic Communications (Amendments etc) (EU Exit) Regulations 2019, SI 2019/419, reg 3, Sch 1, paras 1, 9(1)–(7).

Para 3: words in square brackets substituted by SI 2019/419, reg 3, Sch 1, paras 1, 9(1), (8).

Paras 3A, 5: inserted and added respectively, by SI 2019/419, reg 3, Sch 1, paras 1, 9(1), (9), (11).

Para 4: repealed by SI 2019/419, reg 3, Sch 1, paras 1, 9(1), (10).

[1.11]
Article 10   Processing of personal data relating to criminal convictions and offences
[1.] Processing of personal data relating to criminal convictions and offences or related security measures based on Article 6(1) shall be carried out only under the control of official authority or when the processing is authorised by [domestic law] providing for appropriate safeguards for the rights and freedoms of data subjects. Any comprehensive register of criminal convictions shall be kept only under the control of official authority.
[2. In the 2018 Act—
   (a)   section 10 makes provision about when the requirement in paragraph 1 of this Article for authorisation by domestic law is met;
   (b)   section 11(2) makes provision about the meaning of "personal data relating to criminal convictions and offences or related security measures".]

NOTES

The existing text was numbered as para 1, the words in square brackets therein were substituted and para 2 was added, by the Data Protection, Privacy and Electronic Communications (Amendments etc) (EU Exit) Regulations 2019, SI 2019/419, reg 3, Sch 1, paras 1, 10.

[1.12]
Article 11   Processing which does not require identification
1. If the purposes for which a controller processes personal data do not or do no longer require the identification of a data subject by the controller, the controller shall not be obliged to maintain, acquire or process additional information in order to identify the data subject for the sole purpose of complying with this Regulation.
2. Where, in cases referred to in paragraph 1 of this Article, the controller is able to demonstrate that it is not in a position to identify the data subject, the controller shall inform the data subject accordingly, if possible. In such cases, Articles 15 to 20 shall not apply except where the data subject, for the purpose of exercising his or her rights under those articles, provides additional information enabling his or her identification.

CHAPTER III RIGHTS OF THE DATA SUBJECT

SECTION 1 TRANSPARENCY AND MODALITIES

[1.13]
Article 12   Transparent information, communication and modalities for the exercise of the rights of the data subject
1. The controller shall take appropriate measures to provide any information referred to in Articles 13 and 14 and any communication under Articles 15 to 22 and 34 relating to processing to the data subject in a concise, transparent, intelligible and easily accessible form, using clear and plain language, in particular for any information addressed specifically to a child. The information shall be provided in writing, or by other means, including, where appropriate, by electronic means. When requested by the data subject, the information may be provided orally, provided that the identity of the data subject is proven by other means.
2. The controller shall facilitate the exercise of data subject rights under Articles 15 to 22. In the cases referred to in Article 11(2), the controller shall not refuse to act on the request of the data subject for exercising his or her rights under Articles 15 to 22, unless the controller demonstrates that it is not in a position to identify the data subject.
3. The controller shall provide information on action taken on a request under Articles 15 to 22 to the data subject without undue delay and in any event within one month of receipt of the request. That period may be extended by two further months where necessary, taking into account the complexity and number of the requests. The controller shall inform the data subject of any such extension within one month of receipt of the request, together with the reasons for the delay. Where the data subject makes the request by electronic form means, the information shall be provided by electronic means where possible, unless otherwise requested by the data subject.
4. If the controller does not take action on the request of the data subject, the controller shall inform the data subject without delay and at the latest within one month of receipt of the request of the reasons for not taking action and on the possibility of lodging a complaint with [the Commissioner] and seeking a judicial remedy.
5. Information provided under Articles 13 and 14 and any communication and any actions taken under Articles 15 to 22 and 34 shall be provided free of charge. Where requests from a data subject are manifestly unfounded or excessive, in particular because of their repetitive character, the controller may either:
   (a)   charge a reasonable fee taking into account the administrative costs of providing the information or communication or taking the action requested; or
   (b)   refuse to act on the request.
     The controller shall bear the burden of demonstrating the manifestly unfounded or excessive character of the request.
6. Without prejudice to Article 11, where the controller has reasonable doubts concerning the identity of the natural person making the request referred to in Articles 15 to 21, the controller may request the provision of additional information necessary to confirm the identity of the data subject.
[6A. The Commissioner may publish (and amend or withdraw)—
   (a)   standardised icons for use in combination with information provided to data subjects under Articles 13 and 14;

(b)   a notice stating that other persons may publish (and amend or withdraw) such icons, provided that the icons satisfy requirements specified in the notice as to the information to be presented by the icons and the procedures for providing the icons.

6B.   The Commissioner must not publish icons or a notice under paragraph 6A unless satisfied (as appropriate) that the icons give a meaningful overview of the intended processing in an easily visible, intelligible and clearly legible manner or that the notice will result in icons that do so.]

7.   [If standardised icons are published as described in paragraph 6A (and not withdrawn), the information] to be provided to data subjects pursuant to Articles 13 and 14 may be provided in combination with [the icons]. Where the icons are presented electronically they shall be machine-readable.

8.   . . .

NOTES

The words in square brackets in paras 4, 7 were substituted, paras 6A, 6B were inserted and para 8 was repealed, by the Data Protection, Privacy and Electronic Communications (Amendments etc) (EU Exit) Regulations 2019, SI 2019/419, reg 3, Sch 1, paras 1, 11.

SECTION 2 INFORMATION AND ACCESS TO PERSONAL DATA

[1.14]
Article 13   Information to be provided where personal data are collected from the data subject
1.   Where personal data relating to a data subject are collected from the data subject, the controller shall, at the time when personal data are obtained, provide the data subject with all of the following information:
(a)   the identity and the contact details of the controller and, where applicable, of the controller's representative;
(b)   the contact details of the data protection officer, where applicable;
(c)   the purposes of the processing for which the personal data are intended as well as the legal basis for the processing;
(d)   where the processing is based on point (f) of Article 6(1), the legitimate interests pursued by the controller or by a third party;
(e)   the recipients or categories of recipients of the personal data, if any;
(f)   where applicable, the fact that the controller intends to transfer personal data to a third country or international organisation and the existence or absence of [relevant adequacy regulations under section 17A of the 2018 Act], or in the case of transfers referred to in Article 46 or 47, or the second subparagraph of Article 49(1), reference to the appropriate or suitable safeguards and the means by which to obtain a copy of them or where they have been made available.
2.   In addition to the information referred to in paragraph 1, the controller shall, at the time when personal data are obtained, provide the data subject with the following further information necessary to ensure fair and transparent processing:
(a)   the period for which the personal data will be stored, or if that is not possible, the criteria used to determine that period;
(b)   the existence of the right to request from the controller access to and rectification or erasure of personal data or restriction of processing concerning the data subject or to object to processing as well as the right to data portability;
(c)   where the processing is based on point (a) of Article 6(1) or point (a) of Article 9(2), the existence of the right to withdraw consent at any time, without affecting the lawfulness of processing based on consent before its withdrawal;
(d)   the right to lodge a complaint with [the Commissioner];
(e)   whether the provision of personal data is a statutory or contractual requirement, or a requirement necessary to enter into a contract, as well as whether the data subject is obliged to provide the personal data and of the possible consequences of failure to provide such data;
(f)   the existence of automated decision-making, including profiling, referred to in Article 22(1) and (4) and, at least in those cases, meaningful information about the logic involved, as well as the significance and the envisaged consequences of such processing for the data subject.
3.   Where the controller intends to further process the personal data for a purpose other than that for which the personal data were collected, the controller shall provide the data subject prior to that further processing with information on that other purpose and with any relevant further information as referred to in paragraph 2.
4.   Paragraphs 1, 2 and 3 shall not apply where and insofar as the data subject already has the information.

NOTES

Words in square brackets in paras 1, 2 substituted by the Data Protection, Privacy and Electronic Communications (Amendments etc) (EU Exit) Regulations 2019, SI 2019/419, reg 3, Sch 1, paras 1, 12.

[1.15]
Article 14   Information to be provided where personal data have not been obtained from the data subject
1.   Where personal data have not been obtained from the data subject, the controller shall provide the data subject with the following information:
(a)   the identity and the contact details of the controller and, where applicable, of the controller's representative;
(b)   the contact details of the data protection officer, where applicable;
(c)   the purposes of the processing for which the personal data are intended as well as the legal basis for the processing;
(d)   the categories of personal data concerned;
(e)   the recipients or categories of recipients of the personal data, if any;

(f) where applicable, that the controller intends to transfer personal data to a recipient in a third country or international organisation and the existence or absence of [relevant adequacy regulations under section 17A of the 2018 Act], or in the case of transfers referred to in Article 46 or 47, or the second subparagraph of Article 49(1), reference to the appropriate or suitable safeguards and the means to obtain a copy of them or where they have been made available.

2. In addition to the information referred to in paragraph 1, the controller shall provide the data subject with the following information necessary to ensure fair and transparent processing in respect of the data subject:

(a) the period for which the personal data will be stored, or if that is not possible, the criteria used to determine that period;

(b) where the processing is based on point (f) of Article 6(1), the legitimate interests pursued by the controller or by a third party;

(c) the existence of the right to request from the controller access to and rectification or erasure of personal data or restriction of processing concerning the data subject and to object to processing as well as the right to data portability;

(d) where processing is based on point (a) of Article 6(1) or point (a) of Article 9(2), the existence of the right to withdraw consent at any time, without affecting the lawfulness of processing based on consent before its withdrawal;

(e) the right to lodge a complaint with [the Commissioner];

(f) from which source the personal data originate, and if applicable, whether it came from publicly accessible sources;

(g) the existence of automated decision-making, including profiling, referred to in Article 22(1) and (4) and, at least in those cases, meaningful information about the logic involved, as well as the significance and the envisaged consequences of such processing for the data subject.

3. The controller shall provide the information referred to in paragraphs 1 and 2:

(a) within a reasonable period after obtaining the personal data, but at the latest within one month, having regard to the specific circumstances in which the personal data are processed;

(b) if the personal data are to be used for communication with the data subject, at the latest at the time of the first communication to that data subject; or

(c) if a disclosure to another recipient is envisaged, at the latest when the personal data are first disclosed.

4. Where the controller intends to further process the personal data for a purpose other than that for which the personal data were obtained, the controller shall provide the data subject prior to that further processing with information on that other purpose and with any relevant further information as referred to in paragraph 2.

5. Paragraphs 1 to 4 shall not apply where and insofar as:

(a) the data subject already has the information;

(b) the provision of such information proves impossible or would involve a disproportionate effort, in particular for processing for archiving purposes in the public interest, scientific or historical research purposes or statistical purposes, subject to the conditions and safeguards referred to in Article 89(1) or in so far as the obligation referred to in paragraph 1 of this Article is likely to render impossible or seriously impair the achievement of the objectives of that processing. In such cases the controller shall take appropriate measures to protect the data subject's rights and freedoms and legitimate interests, including making the information publicly available;

(c) obtaining or disclosure is expressly laid down by [a provision of domestic law] which provides appropriate measures to protect the data subject's legitimate interests; or

(d) where the personal data must remain confidential subject to an obligation of professional secrecy regulated by [domestic law], including a statutory obligation of secrecy.

NOTES

Paras 1, 2, 5: words in square brackets substituted by the Data Protection, Privacy and Electronic Communications (Amendments etc) (EU Exit) Regulations 2019, SI 2019/419, reg 3, Sch 1, paras 1, 13.

[1.16]
Article 15   Right of access by the data subject

1. The data subject shall have the right to obtain from the controller confirmation as to whether or not personal data concerning him or her are being processed, and, where that is the case, access to the personal data and the following information:

(a) the purposes of the processing;

(b) the categories of personal data concerned;

(c) the recipients or categories of recipient to whom the personal data have been or will be disclosed, in particular recipients in third countries or international organisations;

(d) where possible, the envisaged period for which the personal data will be stored, or, if not possible, the criteria used to determine that period;

(e) the existence of the right to request from the controller rectification or erasure of personal data or restriction of processing of personal data concerning the data subject or to object to such processing;

(f) the right to lodge a complaint with [the Commissioner];

(g) where the personal data are not collected from the data subject, any available information as to their source;

(h) the existence of automated decision-making, including profiling, referred to in Article 22(1) and (4) and, at least in those cases, meaningful information about the logic involved, as well as the significance and the envisaged consequences of such processing for the data subject.

2. Where personal data are transferred to a third country or to an international organisation, the data subject shall have the right to be informed of the appropriate safeguards pursuant to Article 46 relating to the transfer.

3. The controller shall provide a copy of the personal data undergoing processing. For any further copies requested by the data subject, the controller may charge a reasonable fee based on administrative costs. Where the data subject makes the request by electronic means, and unless otherwise requested by the data subject, the information shall be provided in a commonly used electronic form.

4. The right to obtain a copy referred to in paragraph 3 shall not adversely affect the rights and freedoms of others.

NOTES

Para 1: words in square brackets substituted by the Data Protection, Privacy and Electronic Communications (Amendments etc) (EU Exit) Regulations 2019, SI 2019/419, reg 3, Sch 1, paras 1, 14.

SECTION 3 RECTIFICATION AND ERASURE

[1.17]
Article 16   Right to rectification
The data subject shall have the right to obtain from the controller without undue delay the rectification of inaccurate personal data concerning him or her. Taking into account the purposes of the processing, the data subject shall have the right to have incomplete personal data completed, including by means of providing a supplementary statement.

[1.18]
Article 17   Right to erasure ('right to be forgotten')
1. The data subject shall have the right to obtain from the controller the erasure of personal data concerning him or her without undue delay and the controller shall have the obligation to erase personal data without undue delay where one of the following grounds applies:
   (a) the personal data are no longer necessary in relation to the purposes for which they were collected or otherwise processed;
   (b) the data subject withdraws consent on which the processing is based according to point (a) of Article 6(1), or point (a) of Article 9(2), and where there is no other legal ground for the processing;
   (c) the data subject objects to the processing pursuant to Article 21(1) and there are no overriding legitimate grounds for the processing, or the data subject objects to the processing pursuant to Article 21(2);
   (d) the personal data have been unlawfully processed;
   (e) the personal data have to be erased for compliance with a legal obligation [under domestic law];
   (f) the personal data have been collected in relation to the offer of information society services referred to in Article 8(1).
2. Where the controller has made the personal data public and is obliged pursuant to paragraph 1 to erase the personal data, the controller, taking account of available technology and the cost of implementation, shall take reasonable steps, including technical measures, to inform controllers which are processing the personal data that the data subject has requested the erasure by such controllers of any links to, or copy or replication of, those personal data.
3. Paragraphs 1 and 2 shall not apply to the extent that processing is necessary:
   (a) for exercising the right of freedom of expression and information;
   (b) for compliance with a legal obligation which requires processing [under domestic law] or for the performance of a task carried out in the public interest or in the exercise of official authority vested in the controller;
   (c) for reasons of public interest in the area of public health in accordance with points (h) and (i) of Article 9(2) as well as Article 9(3);
   (d) for archiving purposes in the public interest, scientific or historical research purposes or statistical purposes in accordance with Article 89(1) in so far as the right referred to in paragraph 1 is likely to render impossible or seriously impair the achievement of the objectives of that processing; or
   (e) for the establishment, exercise or defence of legal claims.

NOTES

Paras 1, 3: words in square brackets substituted by the Data Protection, Privacy and Electronic Communications (Amendments etc) (EU Exit) Regulations 2019, SI 2019/419, reg 3, Sch 1, paras 1, 15.

[1.19]
Article 18   Right to restriction of processing
1. The data subject shall have the right to obtain from the controller restriction of processing where one of the following applies:
   (a) the accuracy of the personal data is contested by the data subject, for a period enabling the controller to verify the accuracy of the personal data;
   (b) the processing is unlawful and the data subject opposes the erasure of the personal data and requests the restriction of their use instead;
   (c) the controller no longer needs the personal data for the purposes of the processing, but they are required by the data subject for the establishment, exercise or defence of legal claims;
   (d) the data subject has objected to processing pursuant to Article 21(1) pending the verification whether the legitimate grounds of the controller override those of the data subject.
2. Where processing has been restricted under paragraph 1, such personal data shall, with the exception of storage, only be processed with the data subject's consent or for the establishment, exercise or defence of legal claims or for the protection of the rights of another natural or legal person or for reasons of important public interest . . . .
3. A data subject who has obtained restriction of processing pursuant to paragraph 1 shall be informed by the controller before the restriction of processing is lifted.

NOTES

Para 2: words omitted repealed by the Data Protection, Privacy and Electronic Communications (Amendments etc) (EU Exit) Regulations 2019, SI 2019/419, reg 3, Sch 1, paras 1, 16.

[1.20]
Article 19   Notification obligation regarding rectification or erasure of personal data or restriction of processing
The controller shall communicate any rectification or erasure of personal data or restriction of processing carried out in accordance with Article 16, Article 17(1) and Article 18 to each recipient to whom the personal data have been disclosed, unless this proves impossible or involves disproportionate effort. The controller shall inform the data subject about those recipients if the data subject requests it.

[1.21]
Article 20   Right to data portability
1. The data subject shall have the right to receive the personal data concerning him or her, which he or she has provided to a controller, in a structured, commonly used and machine-readable format and have the right to transmit those data to another controller without hindrance from the controller to which the personal data have been provided, where:
    (a)   the processing is based on consent pursuant to point (a) of Article 6(1) or point (a) of Article 9(2) or on a contract pursuant to point (b) of Article 6(1); and
    (b)   the processing is carried out by automated means.
2. In exercising his or her right to data portability pursuant to paragraph 1, the data subject shall have the right to have the personal data transmitted directly from one controller to another, where technically feasible.
3. The exercise of the right referred to in paragraph 1 of this Article shall be without prejudice to Article 17. That right shall not apply to processing necessary for the performance of a task carried out in the public interest or in the exercise of official authority vested in the controller.
4. The right referred to in paragraph 1 shall not adversely affect the rights and freedoms of others.

SECTION 4 RIGHT TO OBJECT AND AUTOMATED INDIVIDUAL DECISION-MAKING

[1.22]
Article 21   Right to object
1. The data subject shall have the right to object, on grounds relating to his or her particular situation, at any time to processing of personal data concerning him or her which is based on point (e) or (f) of Article 6(1), including profiling based on those provisions. The controller shall no longer process the personal data unless the controller demonstrates compelling legitimate grounds for the processing which override the interests, rights and freedoms of the data subject or for the establishment, exercise or defence of legal claims.
2. Where personal data are processed for direct marketing purposes, the data subject shall have the right to object at any time to processing of personal data concerning him or her for such marketing, which includes profiling to the extent that it is related to such direct marketing.
3. Where the data subject objects to processing for direct marketing purposes, the personal data shall no longer be processed for such purposes.
4. At the latest at the time of the first communication with the data subject, the right referred to in paragraphs 1 and 2 shall be explicitly brought to the attention of the data subject and shall be presented clearly and separately from any other information.
5. In the context of the use of information society services, . . . the data subject may exercise his or her right to object by automated means using technical specifications[, notwithstanding domestic law made before IP completion day implementing Directive 2002/58/EC of the European Parliament and of the Council of 12th July 2002 concerning the processing of personal data and the protection of privacy in the electronic communications sector].
6. Where personal data are processed for scientific or historical research purposes or statistical purposes pursuant to Article 89(1), the data subject, on grounds relating to his or her particular situation, shall have the right to object to processing of personal data concerning him or her, unless the processing is necessary for the performance of a task carried out for reasons of public interest.

NOTES
    Para 5: words omitted were repealed and words in square brackets inserted, by the Data Protection, Privacy and Electronic Communications (Amendments etc) (EU Exit) Regulations 2019, SI 2019/419, reg 3, Sch 1, paras 1, 17. Note that para 17 of Sch 1 to the 2019 Regulations was amended by the Data Protection, Privacy and Electronic Communications (Amendments etc) (EU Exit) Regulations 2020, SI 2020/1586, reg 4 (and the effect of the amendment has been incorporated in the text set out above).

[1.23]
Article 22   Automated individual decision-making, including profiling
1. The data subject shall have the right not to be subject to a decision based solely on automated processing, including profiling, which produces legal effects concerning him or her or similarly significantly affects him or her.
2. Paragraph 1 shall not apply if the decision:
    (a)   is necessary for entering into, or performance of, a contract between the data subject and a data controller;
    (b)   is [required or authorised by domestic law] which also lays down suitable measures to safeguard the data subject's rights and freedoms and legitimate interests; or
    (c)   is based on the data subject's explicit consent.
3. In the cases referred to in points (a) and (c) of paragraph 2, the data controller shall implement suitable measures to safeguard the data subject's rights and freedoms and legitimate interests, at least the right to obtain human intervention on the part of the controller, to express his or her point of view and to contest the decision.
[3A. Section 14 of the 2018 Act, and regulations under that section, make provision to safeguard data subjects' rights, freedoms and legitimate interests in cases that fall within point (b) of paragraph 2 (but not within point (a) or (c) of that paragraph).]

4. Decisions referred to in paragraph 2 shall not be based on special categories of personal data referred to in Article 9(1), unless point (a) or (g) of Article 9(2) applies and suitable measures to safeguard the data subject's rights and freedoms and legitimate interests are in place.

NOTES

The words in square brackets in para 2 were substituted and para 3A was inserted, by the Data Protection, Privacy and Electronic Communications (Amendments etc) (EU Exit) Regulations 2019, SI 2019/419, reg 3, Sch 1, paras 1, 18.

SECTION 5 RESTRICTIONS

[1.24]
Article 23   Restrictions
1. [The Secretary of State may restrict] the scope of the obligations and rights provided for in Articles 12 to 22 and Article 34, as well as Article 5 in so far as its provisions correspond to the rights and obligations provided for in Articles 12 to 22, when such a restriction respects the essence of the fundamental rights and freedoms and is a necessary and proportionate measure in a democratic society to safeguard:
  (a)   . . .
  (b)   . . .
  (c)   public security;
  (d)   the prevention, investigation, detection or prosecution of criminal offences or the execution of criminal penalties, including the safeguarding against and the prevention of threats to public security;
  (e)   other important objectives of general public interest . . . , in particular an important economic or financial interest [of the United Kingdom], including monetary, budgetary and taxation a matters, public health and social security;
  (f)   the protection of judicial independence and judicial proceedings;
  (g)   the prevention, investigation, detection and prosecution of breaches of ethics for regulated professions;
  (h)   a monitoring, inspection or regulatory function connected, even occasionally, to the exercise of official authority in the cases referred to in points (a) to (e) and (g);
  (i)   the protection of the data subject or the rights and freedoms of others;
  (j)   the enforcement of civil law claims.
2. In particular, [provision made in exercise of the power under] paragraph 1 shall contain specific provisions at least, where relevant, as to:
  (a)   the purposes of the processing or categories of processing;
  (b)   the categories of personal data;
  (c)   the scope of the restrictions introduced;
  (d)   the safeguards to prevent abuse or unlawful access or transfer;
  (e)   the specification of the controller or categories of controllers;
  (f)   the storage periods and the applicable safeguards taking into account the nature, scope and purposes of the processing or categories of processing;
  (g)   the risks to the rights and freedoms of data subjects; and
  (h)   the right of data subjects to be informed about the restriction, unless that may be prejudicial to the purpose of the restriction.
[3. The Secretary of State may exercise the power under paragraph 1 only by making regulations under section 16 of the 2018 Act.]

NOTES

Para 1: words in square brackets substituted and words omitted repealed by the Data Protection, Privacy and Electronic Communications (Amendments etc) (EU Exit) Regulations 2019, SI 2019/419, reg 3, Sch 1, paras 1, 19(1), (2).

Para 2: words in square brackets substituted by SI 2019/419, reg 3, Sch 1, paras 1, 19(1), (3).

Para 3: added by SI 2019/419, reg 3, Sch 1, paras 1, 19(1), (4).

CHAPTER IV CONTROLLER AND PROCESSOR

SECTION 1 RESPONSIBILITY OF THE CONTROLLER

[1.25]
Article 24   Responsibility of the controller
1. Taking into account the nature, scope, context and purposes of processing as well as the risks of varying likelihood and severity for the rights and freedoms of natural persons, the controller shall implement appropriate technical and organisational measures to ensure and to be able to demonstrate that processing is performed in accordance with this Regulation. Those measures shall be reviewed and updated where necessary.
2. Where proportionate in relation to processing activities, the measures referred to in paragraph 1 shall include the implementation of appropriate data protection policies by the controller.
3. Adherence to approved codes of conduct as referred to in Article 40 or approved certification mechanisms as referred to in Article 42 may be used as an element by which to demonstrate compliance with the obligations of the controller.

[1.26]
Article 25   Data protection by design and by default
1. Taking into account the state of the art, the cost of implementation and the nature, scope, context and purposes of processing as well as the risks of varying likelihood and severity for rights and freedoms of natural persons posed by the processing, the controller shall, both at the time of the determination of the means for processing and at the time

of the processing itself, implement appropriate technical and organisational measures, such as pseudonymisation, which are designed to implement data-protection principles, such as data minimisation, in an effective manner and to integrate the necessary safeguards into the processing in order to meet the requirements of this Regulation and protect the rights of data subjects.

2. The controller shall implement appropriate technical and organisational measures for ensuring that, by default, only personal data which are necessary for each specific purpose of the processing are processed. That obligation applies to the amount of personal data collected, the extent of their processing, the period of their storage and their accessibility. In particular, such measures shall ensure that by default personal data are not made accessible without the individual's intervention to an indefinite number of natural persons.

3. An approved certification mechanism pursuant to Article 42 may be used as an element to demonstrate compliance with the requirements set out in paragraphs 1 and 2 of this Article.

[1.27]
Article 26   Joint controllers

1. Where two or more controllers jointly determine the purposes and means of processing, they shall be joint controllers. They shall in a transparent manner determine their respective responsibilities for compliance with the obligations under this Regulation, in particular as regards the exercising of the rights of the data subject and their respective duties to provide the information referred to in Articles 13 and 14, by means of an arrangement between them unless, and in so far as, the respective responsibilities of the controllers are determined by [domestic law]. The arrangement may designate a contact point for data subjects.

2. The arrangement referred to in paragraph 1 shall duly reflect the respective roles and relationships of the joint controllers vis-à-vis the data subjects. The essence of the arrangement shall be made available to the data subject.

3. Irrespective of the terms of the arrangement referred to in paragraph 1, the data subject may exercise his or her rights under this Regulation in respect of and against each of the controllers.

NOTES
Para 1: words in square brackets substituted by the Data Protection, Privacy and Electronic Communications (Amendments etc) (EU Exit) Regulations 2019, SI 2019/419, reg 3, Sch 1, paras 1, 20.

[1.28]
Article 27   Representatives of controllers or processors not established in [the United Kingdom]

1. Where Article 3(2) applies, the controller or the processor shall designate in writing a representative in [the United Kingdom].

2. The obligation laid down in paragraph 1 of this Article shall not apply to:
   (a) processing which is occasional, does not include, on a large scale, processing of special categories of data as referred to in Article 9(1) or processing of personal data relating to criminal convictions and offences referred to in Article 10, and is unlikely to result in a risk to the rights and freedoms of natural persons, taking into account the nature, context, scope and purposes of the processing; or
   (b) a public authority or body.

3. . . .

4. The representative shall be mandated by the controller or processor to be addressed in addition to or instead of the controller or the processor by, in particular, [the Commissioner] and data subjects, on all issues related to processing, for the purposes of ensuring compliance with this Regulation.

5. The designation of a representative by the controller or processor shall be without prejudice to legal actions which could be initiated against the controller or the processor themselves.

NOTES
Words in square brackets in each place substituted, and para 3 repealed, by the Data Protection, Privacy and Electronic Communications (Amendments etc) (EU Exit) Regulations 2019, SI 2019/419, reg 3, Sch 1, paras 1, 21.

[1.29]
Article 28   Processor

1. Where processing is to be carried out on behalf of a controller, the controller shall use only processors providing sufficient guarantees to implement appropriate technical and organisational measures in such a manner that processing will meet the requirements of this Regulation and ensure the protection of the rights of the data subject.

2. The processor shall not engage another processor without prior specific or general written authorisation of the controller. In the case of general written authorisation, the processor shall inform the controller of any intended changes concerning the addition or replacement of other processors, thereby giving the controller the opportunity to object to such changes.

3. Processing by a processor shall be governed by a contract or other legal act under [domestic law], that is binding on the processor with regard to the controller and that sets out the subject-matter and duration of the processing, the nature and purpose of the processing, the type of personal data and categories of data subjects and the obligations and rights of the controller. That contract or other legal act shall stipulate, in particular, that the processor:
   (a) processes the personal data only on documented instructions from the controller, including with regard to transfers of personal data to a third country or an international organisation, unless required to do so by [domestic law]; in such a case, the processor shall inform the controller of that legal requirement before processing, unless that law prohibits such information on important grounds of public interest;
   (b) ensures that persons authorised to process the personal data have committed themselves to confidentiality or are under an appropriate statutory obligation of confidentiality;
   (c) takes all measures required pursuant to Article 32;
   (d) respects the conditions referred to in paragraphs 2 and 4 for engaging another processor;
   (e) taking into account the nature of the processing, assists the controller by appropriate technical and organisational measures, insofar as this is possible, for the fulfilment of the controller's obligation to respond to requests for exercising the data subject's rights laid down in Chapter III;

(f)   assists the controller in ensuring compliance with the obligations pursuant to Articles 32 to 36 taking into account the nature of processing and the information available to the processor;

(g)   at the choice of the controller, deletes or returns all the personal data to the controller after the end of the provision of services relating to processing, and deletes existing copies unless [domestic law] requires storage of the personal data;

(h)   makes available to the controller all information necessary to demonstrate compliance with the obligations laid down in this Article and allow for and contribute to audits, including inspections, conducted by the controller or another auditor mandated by the controller.

With regard to point (h) of the first subparagraph, the processor shall immediately inform the controller if, in its opinion, an instruction infringes this Regulation or [other domestic law relating to data protection].

4.   Where a processor engages another processor for carrying out specific processing activities on behalf of the controller, the same data protection obligations as set out in the contract or other legal act between the controller and the processor as referred to in paragraph 3 shall be imposed on that other processor by way of a contract or other legal act under [domestic law], in particular providing sufficient guarantees to implement appropriate technical and organisational measures in such a manner that the processing will meet the requirements of this Regulation. Where that other processor fails to fulfil its data protection obligations, the initial processor shall remain fully liable to the controller for the performance of that other processor's obligations.

5.   Adherence of a processor to an approved code of conduct as referred to in Article 40 or an approved certification mechanism as referred to in Article 42 may be used as an element by which to demonstrate sufficient guarantees as referred to in paragraphs 1 and 4 of this Article.

6.   Without prejudice to an individual contract between the controller and the processor, the contract or the other legal act referred to in paragraphs 3 and 4 of this Article may be based, in whole or in part, on standard contractual clauses referred to in [paragraph 8] of this Article, including when they are part of a certification granted to the controller or processor pursuant to Articles 42 and 43.

7.   . . .

8.   [The Commissioner] may adopt standard contractual clauses for the matters referred to in paragraph 3 and 4 of this Article   . . . .

9.   The contract or the other legal act referred to in paragraphs 3 and 4 shall be in writing, including in electronic form.

10.   Without prejudice to Articles 82, 83 and 84, if a processor infringes this Regulation by determining the purposes and means of processing, the processor shall be considered to be a controller in respect of that processing.

NOTES

The words in square brackets in paras 3, 4, 6, 8 were substituted, and para 7 and the words omitted from para 8 were repealed, by the Data Protection, Privacy and Electronic Communications (Amendments etc) (EU Exit) Regulations 2019, SI 2019/419, reg 3, Sch 1, paras 1, 22.

[1.30]
Article 29   Processing under the authority of the controller or processor
The processor and any person acting under the authority of the controller or of the processor, who has access to personal data, shall not process those data except on instructions from the controller, unless required to do so by [domestic law].

NOTES

Words in square brackets substituted by the Data Protection, Privacy and Electronic Communications (Amendments etc) (EU Exit) Regulations 2019, SI 2019/419, reg 3, Sch 1, paras 1, 23.

[1.31]
Article 30   Records of processing activities
1.   Each controller and, where applicable, the controller's representative, shall maintain a record of processing activities under its responsibility. That record shall contain all of the following information:

(a)   the name and contact details of the controller and, where applicable, the joint controller, the controller's representative and the data protection officer;

(b)   the purposes of the processing;

(c)   a description of the categories of data subjects and of the categories of personal data;

(d)   the categories of recipients to whom the personal data have been or will be disclosed including recipients in third countries or international organisations;

(e)   where applicable, transfers of personal data to a third country or an international organisation, including the identification of that third country or international organisation and, in the case of transfers referred to in the second subparagraph of Article 49(1), the documentation of suitable safeguards;

(f)   where possible, the envisaged time limits for erasure of the different categories of data;

(g)   where possible, a general description of the technical and organisational security measures referred to in Article 32(1) [or, as appropriate, the security measures referred to in section 28(3) of the 2018 Act].

2.   Each processor and, where applicable, the processor's representative shall maintain a record of all categories of processing activities carried out on behalf of a controller, containing:

(a)   the name and contact details of the processor or processors and of each controller on behalf of which the processor is acting, and, where applicable, of the controller's or the processor's representative, and the data protection officer;

(b)   the categories of processing carried out on behalf of each controller;

(c)   where applicable, transfers of personal data to a third country or an international organisation, including the identification of that third country or international organisation and, in the case of transfers referred to in the second subparagraph of Article 49(1), the documentation of suitable safeguards;

(d) where possible, a general description of the technical and organisational security measures referred to in Article 32(1) [or, as appropriate, the security measures referred to in section 28(3) of the 2018 Act].

3. The records referred to in paragraphs 1 and 2 shall be in writing, including in electronic form.

4. The controller or the processor and, where applicable, the controller's or the processor's representative, shall make the record available to [the Commissioner] on request.

5. The obligations referred to in paragraphs 1 and 2 shall not apply to an enterprise or an organisation employing fewer than 250 persons unless the processing it carries out is likely to result in a risk to the rights and freedoms of data subjects, the processing is not occasional, or the processing includes special categories of data as referred to in Article 9(1) or personal data relating to criminal convictions and offences referred to in Article 10.

NOTES

The words in square brackets in paras 1, 2 were inserted and the words in square brackets in para 4 were substituted, by the Data Protection, Privacy and Electronic Communications (Amendments etc) (EU Exit) Regulations 2019, SI 2019/419, reg 3, Sch 1, paras 1, 24.

[1.32]
Article 31   Cooperation with [the Commissioner]
The controller and the processor and, where applicable, their representatives, shall cooperate, on request, with [the Commissioner in the performance of the Commissioner's tasks].

NOTES

Words in square brackets substituted by the Data Protection, Privacy and Electronic Communications (Amendments etc) (EU Exit) Regulations 2019, SI 2019/419, reg 3, Sch 1, paras 1, 25.

SECTION 2 SECURITY OF PERSONAL DATA

[1.33]
Article 32   Security of processing
1. Taking into account the state of the art, the costs of implementation and the nature, scope, context and purposes of processing as well as the risk of varying likelihood and severity for the rights and freedoms of natural persons, the controller and the processor shall implement appropriate technical and organisational measures to ensure a level of security appropriate to the risk, including inter alia as appropriate:
(a) the pseudonymisation and encryption of personal data;
(b) the ability to ensure the ongoing confidentiality, integrity, availability and resilience of processing systems and services;
(c) the ability to restore the availability and access to personal data in a timely manner in the event of a physical or technical incident;
(d) a process for regularly testing, assessing and evaluating the effectiveness of technical and organisational measures for ensuring the security of the processing.

2. In assessing the appropriate level of security account shall be taken in particular of the risks that are presented by processing, in particular from accidental or unlawful destruction, loss, alteration, unauthorised disclosure of, or access to personal data transmitted, stored or otherwise processed.

3. Adherence to an approved code of conduct as referred to in Article 40 or an approved certification mechanism as referred to in Article 42 may be used as an element by which to demonstrate compliance with the requirements set out in paragraph 1 of this Article.

4. The controller and processor shall take steps to ensure that any natural person acting under the authority of the controller or the processor who has access to personal data does not process them except on instructions from the controller, unless he or she is required to do so by [domestic law].

NOTES

Para 4: words in square brackets substituted by the Data Protection, Privacy and Electronic Communications (Amendments etc) (EU Exit) Regulations 2019, SI 2019/419, reg 3, Sch 1, paras 1, 26.

[1.34]
Article 33   Notification of a personal data breach to [the Commissioner]
1. In the case of a personal data breach, the controller shall without undue delay and, where feasible, not later than 72 hours after having become aware of it, notify the personal data breach to [the Commissioner], unless the personal data breach is unlikely to result in a risk to the rights and freedoms of natural persons. Where [the notification under this paragraph] is not made within 72 hours, it shall be accompanied by reasons for the delay.

2. The processor shall notify the controller without undue delay after becoming aware of a personal data breach.

3. The notification referred to in paragraph 1 shall at least:
(a) describe the nature of the personal data breach including where possible, the categories and approximate number of data subjects concerned and the categories and approximate number of personal data records concerned;
(b) communicate the name and contact details of the data protection officer or other contact point where more information can be obtained;
(c) describe the likely consequences of the personal data breach;
(d) describe the measures taken or proposed to be taken by the controller to address the personal data breach, including, where appropriate, measures to mitigate its possible adverse effects.

4. Where, and in so far as, it is not possible to provide the information at the same time, the information may be provided in phases without undue further delay.

5. The controller shall document any personal data breaches, comprising the facts relating to the personal data breach, its effects and the remedial action taken. That documentation shall enable [the Commissioner] to verify compliance with this Article.

NOTES
Words in square brackets in each place substituted by the Data Protection, Privacy and Electronic Communications (Amendments etc) (EU Exit) Regulations 2019, SI 2019/419, reg 3, Sch 1, paras 1, 27.

[1.35]
Article 34　Communication of a personal data breach to the data subject

1. When the personal data breach is likely to result in a high risk to the rights and freedoms of natural persons, the controller shall communicate the personal data breach to the data subject without undue delay.

2. The communication to the data subject referred to in paragraph 1 of this Article shall describe in clear and plain language the nature of the personal data breach and contain at least the information and measures referred to in points (b), (c) and (d) of Article 33(3).

3. The communication to the data subject referred to in paragraph 1 shall not be required if any of the following conditions are met:

(a) the controller has implemented appropriate technical and organisational protection measures, and those measures were applied to the personal data affected by the personal data breach, in particular those that render the personal data unintelligible to any person who is not authorised to access it, such as encryption;

(b) the controller has taken subsequent measures which ensure that the high risk to the rights and freedoms of data subjects referred to in paragraph 1 is no longer likely to materialise;

(c) it would involve disproportionate effort. In such a case, there shall instead be a public communication or similar measure whereby the data subjects are informed in an equally effective manner.

4. If the controller has not already communicated the personal data breach to the data subject, [the Commissioner], having considered the likelihood of the personal data breach resulting in a high risk, may require it to do so or may decide that any of the conditions referred to in paragraph 3 are met.

NOTES
Para 4: words in square brackets substituted by the Data Protection, Privacy and Electronic Communications (Amendments etc) (EU Exit) Regulations 2019, SI 2019/419, reg 3, Sch 1, paras 1, 28.

SECTION 3　DATA PROTECTION IMPACT ASSESSMENT AND PRIOR CONSULTATION

[1.36]
Article 35　Data protection impact assessment

1. Where a type of processing in particular using new technologies, and taking into account the nature, scope, context and purposes of the processing, is likely to result in a high risk to the rights and freedoms of natural persons, the controller shall, prior to the processing, carry out an assessment of the impact of the envisaged processing operations on the protection of personal data. A single assessment may address a set of similar processing operations that present similar high risks.

2. The controller shall seek the advice of the data protection officer, where designated, when carrying out a data protection impact assessment.

3. A data protection impact assessment referred to in paragraph 1 shall in particular be required in the case of:

(a) a systematic and extensive evaluation of personal aspects relating to natural persons which is based on automated processing, including profiling, and on which decisions are based that produce legal effects concerning the natural person or similarly significantly affect the natural person;

(b) processing on a large scale of special categories of data referred to in Article 9(1), or of personal data relating to criminal convictions and offences referred to in Article 10; or

(c) a systematic monitoring of a publicly accessible area on a large scale.

4. [The Commissioner] shall establish and make public a list of the kind of processing operations which are subject to the requirement for a data protection impact assessment pursuant to paragraph 1. . . .

5. [The Commissioner] may also establish and make public a list of the kind of processing operations for which no data protection impact assessment is required. . . .

6. . . .

7. The assessment shall contain at least:

(a) a systematic description of the envisaged processing operations and the purposes of the processing, including, where applicable, the legitimate interest pursued by the controller;

(b) an assessment of the necessity and proportionality of the processing operations in relation to the purposes;

(c) an assessment of the risks to the rights and freedoms of data subjects referred to in paragraph 1; and

(d) the measures envisaged to address the risks, including safeguards, security measures and mechanisms to ensure the protection of personal data and to demonstrate compliance with this Regulation taking into account the rights and legitimate interests of data subjects and other persons concerned.

8. Compliance with approved codes of conduct referred to in Article 40 by the relevant controllers or processors shall be taken into due account in assessing the impact of the processing operations performed by such controllers or processors, in particular for the purposes of a data protection impact assessment.

9. Where appropriate, the controller shall seek the views of data subjects or their representatives on the intended processing, without prejudice to the protection of commercial or public interests or the security of processing operations.

[10. In the case of processing pursuant to point (c) or (e) of Article 6(1), paragraphs 1 to 7 of this Article do not apply if a data protection impact assessment has already been carried out for the processing as part of a general impact assessment required by domestic law, unless domestic law provides otherwise.]

11. Where necessary, the controller shall carry out a review to assess if processing is performed in accordance with the data protection impact assessment at least when there is a change of the risk represented by processing operations.

Part 1	Data Protection: UK Law

NOTES

In paras 4, 5 the words in square brackets were substituted and the words omitted were repealed, para 6 was repealed and para 10 was substituted, by the Data Protection, Privacy and Electronic Communications (Amendments etc) (EU Exit) Regulations 2019, SI 2019/419, reg 3, Sch 1, paras 1, 29.

[1.37]
Article 36   Prior consultation
1. The controller shall consult [the Commissioner] prior to processing where a data protection impact assessment under Article 35 indicates that the processing would result in a high risk in the absence of measures taken by the controller to mitigate the risk.
2. Where [the Commissioner] is of the opinion that the intended processing referred to in paragraph 1 would infringe this Regulation, in particular where the controller has insufficiently identified or mitigated the risk, [the Commissioner] shall, within period of up to eight weeks of receipt of the request for consultation, provide written advice to the controller and, where applicable to the processor, and may use any of its powers referred to in Article 58. That period may be extended by six weeks, taking into account the complexity of the intended processing. [The Commissioner] shall inform the controller and, where applicable, the processor, of any such extension within one month of receipt of the request for consultation together with the reasons for the delay. Those periods may be suspended until [the Commissioner has obtained information the Commissioner] has requested for the purposes of the consultation.
3. When consulting [the Commissioner] pursuant to paragraph 1, the controller shall provide [the Commissioner] with:
   (a) where applicable, the respective responsibilities of the controller, joint controllers and processors involved in the processing, in particular for processing within a group of undertakings;
   (b) the purposes and means of the intended processing;
   (c) the measures and safeguards provided to protect the rights and freedoms of data subjects pursuant to this Regulation;
   (d) where applicable, the contact details of the data protection officer;
   (e) the data protection impact assessment provided for in Article 35; and
   (f) any other information requested by [the Commissioner].
4. [The relevant authority must consult the Commissioner] during the preparation of a proposal for a legislative measure to be adopted by [Parliament, the National Assembly for Wales, the Scottish Parliament or the Northern Ireland Assembly], or of a regulatory measure based on such a legislative measure, which relates to processing.
[4A. In paragraph 4, "the relevant authority" means—
   (a) in relation to a legislative measure adopted by Parliament, or a regulatory measure based on such a legislative measure, the Secretary of State;
   (b) in relation to a legislative measure adopted by the National Assembly for Wales, or a regulatory measure based on such a legislative measure, the Welsh Ministers;
   (c) in relation to a legislative measure adopted by the Scottish Parliament, or a regulatory measure based on such a legislative measure, the Scottish Ministers;
   (d) in relation to a legislative measure adopted by the Northern Ireland Assembly, or a regulatory measure based on such a legislative measure, the relevant Northern Ireland department.]
5. . . .

NOTES

The words in square brackets in paras 1–4 were substituted, para 4A was inserted and para 5 was repealed, by the Data Protection, Privacy and Electronic Communications (Amendments etc) (EU Exit) Regulations 2019, SI 2019/419, reg 3, Sch 1, paras 1, 30.

National Assembly for Wales: as to the renaming of the National Assembly for Wales, see the note at **[1.94]**.

SECTION 4 DATA PROTECTION OFFICER

[1.38]
Article 37   Designation of the data protection officer
1. The controller and the processor shall designate a data protection officer in any case where:
   (a) the processing is carried out by a public authority or body, except for courts acting in their judicial capacity;
   (b) the core activities of the controller or the processor consist of processing operations which, by virtue of their nature, their scope and/or their purposes, require regular and systematic monitoring of data subjects on a large scale; or
   (c) the core activities of the controller or the processor consist of processing on a large scale of special categories of data pursuant to Article 9 or personal data relating to criminal convictions and offences referred to in Article 10.
2. A group of undertakings may appoint a single data protection officer provided that a data protection officer is easily accessible from each establishment.
3. Where the controller or the processor is a public authority or body, a single data protection officer may be designated for several such authorities or bodies, taking account of their organisational structure and size.
4. In cases other than those referred to in paragraph 1, the controller or processor or associations and other bodies representing categories of controllers or processors may . . . designate a data protection officer. The data protection officer may act for such associations and other bodies representing controllers or processors.
5. The data protection officer shall be designated on the basis of professional qualities and, in particular, expert knowledge of data protection law and practices and the ability to fulfil the tasks referred to in Article 39.
6. The data protection officer may be a staff member of the controller or processor, or fulfil the tasks on the basis of a service contract.

7. The controller or the processor shall publish the contact details of the data protection officer and communicate them to [the Commissioner].

NOTES

The words omitted from para 4 were repealed and the words in square brackets in para 7 were substituted, by the Data Protection, Privacy and Electronic Communications (Amendments etc) (EU Exit) Regulations 2019, SI 2019/419, reg 3, Sch 1, paras 1, 31.

[1.39]
Article 38   Position of the data protection officer
1. The controller and the processor shall ensure that the data protection officer is involved, properly and in a timely manner, in all issues which relate to the protection of personal data.
2. The controller and processor shall support the data protection officer in performing the tasks referred to in Article 39 by providing resources necessary to carry out those tasks and access to personal data and processing operations, and to maintain his or her expert knowledge.
3. The controller and processor shall ensure that the data protection officer does not receive any instructions regarding the exercise of those tasks. He or she shall not be dismissed or penalised by the controller or the processor for performing his tasks. The data protection officer shall directly report to the highest management level of the controller or the processor.
4. Data subjects may contact the data protection officer with regard to all issues related to processing of their personal data and to the exercise of their rights under this Regulation.
5. The data protection officer shall be bound by secrecy or confidentiality concerning the performance of his or her tasks, in accordance with [domestic law].
6. The data protection officer may fulfil other tasks and duties. The controller or processor shall ensure that any such tasks and duties do not result in a conflict of interests.

NOTES

Para 5: words in square brackets substituted by the Data Protection, Privacy and Electronic Communications (Amendments etc) (EU Exit) Regulations 2019, SI 2019/419, reg 3, Sch 1, paras 1, 32.

[1.40]
Article 39   Tasks of the data protection officer
1. The data protection officer shall have at least the following tasks:
   (a)   to inform and advise the controller or the processor and the employees who carry out processing of their obligations pursuant to this Regulation and to [other domestic law relating to data protection];
   (b)   to monitor compliance with this Regulation, with [other domestic law relating to data protection] and with the policies of the controller or processor in relation to the protection of personal data, including the assignment of responsibilities, awareness-raising and training of staff involved in processing operations, and the related audits;
   (c)   to provide advice where requested as regards the data protection impact assessment and monitor its performance pursuant to Article 35;
   (d)   to cooperate with [the Commissioner];
   (e)   to act as the contact point for [the Commissioner] on issues relating to processing, including the prior consultation referred to in Article 36, and to consult, where appropriate, with regard to any other matter.
2. The data protection officer shall in the performance of his or her tasks have due regard to the risk associated with processing operations, taking into account the nature, scope, context and purposes of processing.

NOTES

Para 1: words in square brackets substituted by the Data Protection, Privacy and Electronic Communications (Amendments etc) (EU Exit) Regulations 2019, SI 2019/419, reg 3, Sch 1, paras 1, 33.

SECTION 5 CODES OF CONDUCT AND CERTIFICATION

[1.41]
Article 40   Codes of conduct
1. [The Commissioner] shall encourage the drawing up of codes of conduct intended to contribute to the proper application of this Regulation, taking account of the specific features of the various processing sectors and the specific needs of micro, small and medium-sized enterprises.
2. Associations and other bodies representing categories of controllers or processors may prepare codes of conduct, or amend or extend such codes, for the purpose of specifying the application of this Regulation, such as with regard to:
   (a)   fair and transparent processing;
   (b)   the legitimate interests pursued by controllers in specific contexts;
   (c)   the collection of personal data;
   (d)   the pseudonymisation of personal data;
   (e)   the information provided to the public and to data subjects;
   (f)   the exercise of the rights of data subjects;
   (g)   the information provided to, and the protection of, children, and the manner in which the consent of the holders of parental responsibility over children is to be obtained;
   (h)   the measures and procedures referred to in Articles 24 and 25 and the measures to ensure security of processing referred to in Article 32;
   (i)   the notification of personal data breaches to [the Commissioner] and the communication of such personal data breaches to data subjects;
   (j)   the transfer of personal data to third countries or international organisations; or

(k)   out-of-court proceedings and other dispute resolution procedures for resolving disputes between controllers and data subjects with regard to processing, without prejudice to the rights of data subjects pursuant to Articles 77 and 79.

3. In addition to adherence by controllers or processors subject to this Regulation, codes of conduct approved pursuant to paragraph 5 of this Article . . . may also be adhered to by controllers or processors that are not subject to this Regulation pursuant to Article 3 in order to provide appropriate safeguards within the framework of personal data transfers to third countries or international organisations under the terms referred to in point (e) of Article 46(2). Such controllers or processors shall make binding and enforceable commitments, via contractual or other legally binding instruments, to apply those appropriate safeguards including with regard to the rights of data subjects.

4. A code of conduct referred to in paragraph 2 of this Article shall contain mechanisms which enable the body referred to in Article 41(1) to carry out the mandatory monitoring of compliance with its provisions by the controllers or processors which undertake to apply it, without prejudice to the tasks and powers of [the Commissioner].

5. Associations and other bodies referred to in paragraph 2 of this Article which intend to prepare a code of conduct or to amend or extend an existing code shall submit the draft code, amendment or extension to [the Commissioner, who] shall provide an opinion on whether the draft code, amendment or extension complies with this Regulation and shall approve that draft code, amendment or extension if [the Commissioner finds] that it provides sufficient appropriate safeguards.

6. Where the draft code, or amendment or extension is approved in accordance with paragraph 5, [the Commissioner] shall register and publish the code.

7.   . . .

8.   . . .

9.   . . .

10.   . . .

11.   . . .

NOTES

The words in square brackets in paras 1, 2,4, 5, 6 were substituted, the words omitted from para 3 were repealed and the whole of paras 7–11 were repealed, by the Data Protection, Privacy and Electronic Communications (Amendments etc) (EU Exit) Regulations 2019, SI 2019/419, reg 3, Sch 1, paras 1, 34.

[1.42]
Article 41   Monitoring of approved codes of conduct

1. Without prejudice to the tasks and powers of [the Commissioner] under Articles 57 and 58, the monitoring of compliance with a code of conduct pursuant to Article 40 may be carried out by a body which has an appropriate level of expertise in relation to the subject-matter of the code and is accredited for that purpose by [the Commissioner].

2. A body as referred to in paragraph 1 may be accredited to monitor compliance with a code of conduct where that body has:

(a)   demonstrated its independence and expertise in relation to the subject-matter of the code to the satisfaction of [the Commissioner];

(b)   established procedures which allow it to assess the eligibility of controllers and processors concerned to apply the code, to monitor their compliance with its provisions and to periodically review its operation;

(c)   established procedures and structures to handle complaints about infringements of the code or the manner in which the code has been, or is being, implemented by a controller or processor, and to make those procedures and structures transparent to data subjects and the public; and

(d)   demonstrated to the satisfaction of [the Commissioner] that its tasks and duties do not result in a conflict of interests.

3.   . . .

4. Without prejudice to the tasks and powers of [the Commissioner] and the provisions of Chapter VIII, a body as referred to in paragraph 1 of this Article shall, subject to appropriate safeguards, take appropriate action in cases of infringement of the code by a controller or processor, including suspension or exclusion of the controller or processor concerned from the code. It shall inform [the Commissioner] of such actions and the reasons for taking them.

5. [The Commissioner] shall revoke the accreditation of a body as referred to in paragraph 1 if the requirements for accreditation are not, or are no longer, met or where actions taken by the body infringe this Regulation.

6. This Article shall not apply to processing carried out by public authorities and bodies.

NOTES

The words in square brackets in paras 1, 2, 4, 5 were substituted and para 3 was repealed, by the Data Protection, Privacy and Electronic Communications (Amendments etc) (EU Exit) Regulations 2019, SI 2019/419, reg 3, Sch 1, paras 1, 35.

[1.43]
Article 42   Certification

1. [The Commissioner] shall encourage . . . the establishment of data protection certification mechanisms and of data protection seals and marks, for the purpose of demonstrating compliance with this Regulation of processing operations by controllers and processors. The specific needs of micro, small and medium-sized enterprises shall be taken into account.

2. In addition to adherence by controllers or processors subject to this Regulation, data protection certification mechanisms, seals or marks approved pursuant to paragraph 5 of this Article may be established for the purpose of demonstrating the existence of appropriate safeguards provided by controllers or processors that are not subject to this Regulation pursuant to Article 3 within the framework of personal data transfers to third countries or international organisations under the terms referred to in point (f) of Article 46(2). Such controllers or processors shall make binding and enforceable commitments, via contractual or other legally binding instruments, to apply those appropriate safeguards, including with regard to the rights of data subjects.

3. The certification shall be voluntary and available via a process that is transparent.

4. A certification pursuant to this Article does not reduce the responsibility of the controller or the processor for compliance with this Regulation and is without prejudice to the tasks and powers of [the Commissioner].

5. A certification pursuant to this Article shall be issued by the certification bodies referred to in Article 43 or by [the Commissioner], on the basis of criteria approved by [the Commissioner] pursuant to Article 58(3) . . . . Where the criteria are approved by the Board, this may result in a common certification, the European Data Protection Seal.

6. The controller or processor which submits its processing to the certification mechanism shall provide the certification body referred to in Article 43, or where applicable, [the Commissioner], with all information and access to its processing activities which are necessary to conduct the certification procedure.

7. Certification shall be issued to a controller or processor for a maximum period of three years and may be renewed, under the same conditions, provided that the relevant criteria continue to be met. Certification shall be withdrawn, as applicable, by the certification bodies referred to in Article 43 or by [the Commissioner] where the criteria for the certification are not or are no longer met.

8. [The Commissioner] shall collate all certification mechanisms and data protection seals and marks in a register and shall make them publicly available by any appropriate means.

NOTES
The words in square brackets in paras 1, 4–8 were substituted and the words omitted from paras 1, 5 were repealed, by the Data Protection, Privacy and Electronic Communications (Amendments etc) (EU Exit) Regulations 2019, SI 2019/419, reg 3, Sch 1, paras 1, 36.

[1.44]
Article 43   Certification bodies

1. Without prejudice to the tasks and powers of the [the Commissioner] under Articles 57 and 58, certification bodies which have an appropriate level of expertise in relation to data protection shall, after informing [the Commissioner] in order to allow it to exercise its powers pursuant to point (h) of Article 58(2) where necessary, issue and renew certification. [In accordance with section 17 of the 2018 Act, those certification bodies may only be] accredited by one or both of the following:

[(a)   the Commissioner;]
(b)   [the UK national accreditation body] named in accordance with Regulation (EC) No 765/2008 of the European Parliament and of the Council[1] in accordance with EN-ISO/IEC 17065/2012 and with the additional requirements established by [the Commissioner].

2. Certification bodies referred to in paragraph 1 shall be accredited in accordance with that paragraph only where they have:
(a)   demonstrated their independence and expertise in relation to the subject-matter of the certification to the satisfaction of [the Commissioner];
(b)   undertaken to respect the criteria referred to in Article 42(5) and approved by [the Commissioner] which is competent pursuant to Article 55 or 56 or by the Board pursuant to Article 63;
(c)   established procedures for the issuing, periodic review and withdrawal of data protection certification, seals and marks;
(d)   established procedures and structures to handle complaints about infringements of the certification or the manner in which the certification has been, or is being, implemented by the controller or processor, and to make those procedures and structures transparent to data subjects and the public; and
(e)   demonstrated, to the satisfaction of [the Commissioner], that their tasks and duties do not result in a conflict of interests.

3. The accreditation of certification bodies as referred to in paragraphs 1 and 2 of this Article shall take place on the basis of requirements approved by [the Commissioner]. In the case of accreditation pursuant to point (b) of paragraph 1 of this Article, those requirements shall complement those envisaged in Regulation (EC) No 765/2008 and the technical rules that describe the methods and procedures of the certification bodies.

4. The certification bodies referred to in paragraph 1 shall be responsible for the proper assessment leading to the certification or the withdrawal of such certification without prejudice to the responsibility of the controller or processor for compliance with this Regulation. The accreditation shall be issued for a maximum period of five years and may be renewed on the same conditions provided that the certification body meets the requirements set out in this Article.

5. The certification bodies referred to in paragraph 1 shall provide [the Commissioner] with the reasons for granting or withdrawing the requested certification.

6. The requirements referred to in paragraph 3 of this Article and the criteria referred to in Article 42(5) shall be made public by [the Commissioner] in an easily accessible form. . . .

7. Without prejudice to Chapter VIII, [the Commissioner or the UK national accreditation body] shall revoke an accreditation of a certification body pursuant to paragraph 1 of this Article where the conditions for the accreditation are not, or are no longer, met or where actions taken by a certification body infringe this Regulation.

8. . . .

9. . . .

NOTES
The words in square brackets in paras 1–3, 5–7 were substituted, the words omitted from para 6 were repealed and paras 8, 9 were repealed, by the Data Protection, Privacy and Electronic Communications (Amendments etc) (EU Exit) Regulations 2019, SI 2019/419, reg 3, Sch 1, paras 1, 37.

[1]   Regulation (EC) No 765/2008 of the European Parliament and of the Council of 9 July 2008 setting out the requirements for accreditation and market surveillance relating to the marketing of products and repealing Regulation (EEC) No 339/93 (OJ L218, 13.8.2008, p 30).

CHAPTER V TRANSFERS OF PERSONAL DATA TO THIRD COUNTRIES OR INTERNATIONAL ORGANISATIONS

[1.45]
Article 44   General principle for transfers
Any transfer of personal data which are undergoing processing or are intended for processing after transfer to a third country or to an international organisation shall take place only if, subject to the other provisions of this Regulation, the conditions laid down in this Chapter are complied with by the controller and processor, including for onward transfers of personal data from the third country or an international organisation to another third country or to another international organisation. All provisions in this Chapter shall be applied in order to ensure that the level of protection of natural persons guaranteed by this Regulation is not undermined.

[1.46]
Article 45   Transfers on the basis of an adequacy decision
1. A transfer of personal data to a third country or an international organisation may take place [where it is based on adequacy regulations (see section 17A of the 2018 Act)]. Such a transfer shall not require any specific authorisation.
2. When assessing the adequacy of the level of protection [for the purposes of sections 17A and 17B of the 2018 Act, the Secretary of State] shall, in particular, take account of the following elements:
   (a) the rule of law, respect for human rights and fundamental freedoms, relevant legislation, both general and sectoral, including concerning public security, defence, national security and criminal law and the access of public authorities to personal data, as well as the implementation of such legislation, data protection rules, professional rules and security measures, including rules for the onward transfer of personal data to another third country or international organisation which are complied with in that country or international organisation, case-law, as well as effective and enforceable data subject rights and effective administrative and judicial redress for the data subjects whose personal data are being transferred;
   (b) the existence and effective functioning of one or more independent supervisory authorities in the third country or to which an international organisation is subject, with responsibility for ensuring and enforcing compliance with the data protection rules, including adequate enforcement powers, for assisting and advising the data subjects in exercising their rights and for cooperation with [the Commissioner]; and
   (c) the international commitments the third country or international organisation concerned has entered into, or other obligations arising from legally binding conventions or instruments as well as from its participation in multilateral or regional systems, in particular in relation to the protection of personal data.
3–6.   . . .
7. [The amendment or revocation of regulations under section 17A of the 2018 Act] is without prejudice to transfers of personal data to the third country, a territory or one or more specified sectors within that third country, or the international organisation in question pursuant to Articles 46 to 49.
8.   . . .
9.   . . .

NOTES
    The words in square brackets in paras 1, 2, 7 were substituted, and paras 3–6, 8, 9 were repealed, by the Data Protection, Privacy and Electronic Communications (Amendments etc) (EU Exit) Regulations 2019, SI 2019/419, reg 3, Sch 1, paras 1, 38.

[1.47]
Article 46   Transfers subject to appropriate safeguards
1. In the absence of [adequacy regulations under section 17A of the 2018 Act], a controller or processor may transfer personal data to a third country or an international organisation only if the controller or processor has provided appropriate safeguards, and on condition that enforceable data subject rights and effective legal remedies for data subjects are available.
2. The appropriate safeguards referred to in paragraph 1 may be provided for, without requiring any specific authorisation from [the Commissioner], by:
   (a) a legally binding and enforceable instrument between public authorities or bodies;
   (b) binding corporate rules in accordance with Article 47;
   [(c) standard data protection clauses specified in regulations made by the Secretary of State under section 17C of the 2018 Act and for the time being in force;
   (d) standard data protection clauses specified in a document issued (and not withdrawn) by the Commissioner under section 119A of the 2018 Act and for the time being in force;]
   (e) an approved code of conduct pursuant to Article 40 together with binding and enforceable commitments of the controller or processor in the third country to apply the appropriate safeguards, including as regards data subjects' rights; or
   (f) an approved certification mechanism pursuant to Article 42 together with binding and enforceable commitments of the controller or processor in the third country to apply the appropriate safeguards, including as regards data subjects' rights.
3. [With authorisation from the Commissioner], the appropriate safeguards referred to in paragraph 1 may also be provided for, in particular, by:
   (a) contractual clauses between the controller or processor and the controller, processor or the recipient of the personal data in the third country or international organisation; or
   (b) provisions to be inserted into administrative arrangements between public authorities or bodies which include enforceable and effective data subject rights.
4.   . . .
5.   . . .

NOTES

The words in square brackets in paras 1–3 were substituted, and paras 4, 5 were repealed, by the Data Protection, Privacy and Electronic Communications (Amendments etc) (EU Exit) Regulations 2019, SI 2019/419, reg 3, Sch 1, paras 1, 39.

[1.48]
Article 47   Binding corporate rules
1. [The Commissioner] shall approve binding corporate rules . . . , provided that they:
    (a) are legally binding and apply to and are enforced by every member concerned of the group of undertakings, or group of enterprises engaged in a joint economic activity, including their employees;
    (b) expressly confer enforceable rights on data subjects with regard to the processing of their personal data; and
    (c) fulfil the requirements laid down in paragraph 2.
2. The binding corporate rules referred to in paragraph 1 shall specify at least:
    (a) the structure and contact details of the group of undertakings, or group of enterprises engaged in a joint economic activity and of each of its members;
    (b) the data transfers or set of transfers, including the categories of personal data, the type of processing and its purposes, the type of data subjects affected and the identification of the third country or countries in question;
    (c) their legally binding nature, both internally and externally;
    (d) the application of the general data protection principles, in particular purpose limitation, data minimisation, limited storage periods, data quality, data protection by design and by default, legal basis for processing, processing of special categories of personal data, measures to ensure data security, and the requirements in respect of onward transfers to bodies not bound by the binding corporate rules;
    (e) the rights of data subjects in regard to processing and the means to exercise those rights, including the right not to be subject to decisions based solely on automated processing, including profiling in accordance with Article 22, the right to lodge a complaint with [the Commissioner and before a court in accordance with Article 79 (see section 180 of the 2018 Act)], and to obtain redress and, where appropriate, compensation for a breach of the binding corporate rules;
    (f) the acceptance by the controller or processor [established in the United Kingdom] of liability for any breaches of the binding corporate rules by any member concerned [not established in the United Kingdom]; the controller or the processor shall be exempt from that liability, in whole or in part, only if it proves that that member is not responsible for the event giving rise to the damage;
    (g) how the information on the binding corporate rules, in particular on the provisions referred to in points (d), (e) and (f) of this paragraph is provided to the data subjects in addition to Articles 13 and 14;
    (h) the tasks of any data protection officer designated in accordance with Article 37 or any other person or entity in charge of the monitoring compliance with the binding corporate rules within the group of undertakings, or group of enterprises engaged in a joint economic activity, as well as monitoring training and complaint-handling;
    (i) the complaint procedures;
    (j) the mechanisms within the group of undertakings, or group of enterprises engaged in a joint economic activity for ensuring the verification of compliance with the binding corporate rules. Such mechanisms shall include data protection audits and methods for ensuring corrective actions to protect the rights of the data subject. Results of such verification should be communicated to the person or entity referred to in point (h) and to the board of the controlling undertaking of a group of undertakings, or of the group of enterprises engaged in a joint economic activity, and should be available upon request to [the Commissioner];
    (k) the mechanisms for reporting and recording changes to the rules and reporting those changes to [the Commissioner];
    (l) the cooperation mechanism with [the Commissioner] to ensure compliance by any member of the group of undertakings, or group of enterprises engaged in a joint economic activity, in particular by making available to [the Commissioner] the results of verifications of the measures referred to in point (j);
    (m) the mechanisms for reporting to [the Commissioner] any legal requirements to which a member of the group of undertakings, or group of enterprises engaged in a joint economic activity is subject in a third country which are likely to have a substantial adverse effect on the guarantees provided by the binding corporate rules; and
    (n) the appropriate data protection training to personnel having permanent or regular access to personal data.
3. . . .

NOTES

The words in square brackets in paras 1, 2 were substituted, and the words omitted from para 1 and the whole of para 3 were repealed by the Data Protection, Privacy and Electronic Communications (Amendments etc) (EU Exit) Regulations 2019, SI 2019/419, reg 3, Sch 1, paras 1, 40.

Article 48   *(Repealed by the Data Protection, Privacy and Electronic Communications (Amendments etc) (EU Exit) Regulations 2019, SI 2019/419, reg 3, Sch 1, paras 1, 41.)*

[1.49]
Article 49   Derogations for specific situations
1. In the absence of [adequacy regulations under section 17A of the 2018 Act], or of appropriate safeguards pursuant to Article 46, including binding corporate rules, a transfer or a set of transfers of personal data to a third country or an international organisation shall take place only on one of the following conditions:
    (a) the data subject has explicitly consented to the proposed transfer, after having been informed of the possible risks of such transfers for the data subject due to the absence of an adequacy decision and appropriate safeguards;

(b)   the transfer is necessary for the performance of a contract between the data subject and the controller or the implementation of pre-contractual measures taken at the data subject's request;

(c)   the transfer is necessary for the conclusion or performance of a contract concluded in the interest of the data subject between the controller and another natural or legal person;

(d)   the transfer is necessary for important reasons of public interest;

(e)   the transfer is necessary for the establishment, exercise or defence of legal claims;

(f)   the transfer is necessary in order to protect the vital interests of the data subject or of other persons, where the data subject is physically or legally incapable of giving consent;

(g)   the transfer is made from a register which according to [domestic law] is intended to provide information to the public and which is open to consultation either by the public in general or by any person who can demonstrate a legitimate interest, but only to the extent that the conditions laid down by [domestic law] for consultation are fulfilled in the particular case.

Where a transfer could not be based on a provision in Article 45 or 46, including the provisions on binding corporate rules, and none of the derogations for a specific situation referred to in the first subparagraph of this paragraph is applicable, a transfer to a third country or an international organisation may take place only if the transfer is not repetitive, concerns only a limited number of data subjects, is necessary for the purposes of compelling legitimate interests pursued by the controller which are not overridden by the interests or rights and freedoms of the data subject, and the controller has assessed all the circumstances surrounding the data transfer and has on the basis of that assessment provided suitable safeguards with regard to the protection of personal data. The controller shall inform [the Commissioner] of the transfer. The controller shall, in addition to providing the information referred to in Articles 13 and 14, inform the data subject of the transfer and on the compelling legitimate interests pursued.

2.   A transfer pursuant to point (g) of the first subparagraph of paragraph 1 shall not involve the entirety of the personal data or entire categories of the personal data contained in the register. Where the register is intended for consultation by persons having a legitimate interest, the transfer shall be made only at the request of those persons or if they are to be the recipients.

3.   Points (a), (b) and (c) of the first subparagraph of paragraph 1 and the second subparagraph thereof shall not apply to activities carried out by public authorities in the exercise of their public powers.

4.   The public interest referred to in point (d) of the first subparagraph of paragraph 1 [must be public interest that is recognised in domestic law (whether in regulations under section 18(1) of the 2018 Act or otherwise)].

5.   . . . .

[5A.   This Article and Article 46 are subject to restrictions in regulations under section 18(2) of the 2018 Act.]

6.   The controller or processor shall document the assessment as well as the suitable safeguards referred to in the second subparagraph of paragraph 1 of this Article in the records referred to in Article 30.

NOTES

The words in square brackets in paras 2, 4 were substituted, para 5 was repealed and para 5A was inserted, by the Data Protection, Privacy and Electronic Communications (Amendments etc) (EU Exit) Regulations 2019, SI 2019/419, reg 3, Sch 1, paras 1, 42.

[1.50]
Article 50   International cooperation for the protection of personal data
In relation to third countries and international organisations, [the Commissioner] shall take appropriate steps to:

(a)   develop international cooperation mechanisms to facilitate the effective enforcement of legislation for the protection of personal data;

(b)   provide international mutual assistance in the enforcement of legislation for the protection of personal data, including through notification, complaint referral, investigative assistance and information exchange, subject to appropriate safeguards for the protection of personal data and other fundamental rights and freedoms;

(c)   engage relevant stakeholders in discussion and activities aimed at furthering international cooperation in the enforcement of legislation for the protection of personal data;

(d)   promote the exchange and documentation of personal data protection legislation and practice, including on jurisdictional conflicts with third countries.

NOTES

Words in square brackets substituted by the Data Protection, Privacy and Electronic Communications (Amendments etc) (EU Exit) Regulations 2019, SI 2019/419, reg 3, Sch 1, paras 1, 43.

CHAPTER VI [THE COMMISSIONER]

NOTES

Chapter heading substituted by the Data Protection, Privacy and Electronic Communications (Amendments etc) (EU Exit) Regulations 2019, SI 2019/419, reg 3, Sch 1, paras 1, 44.

SECTION 1 INDEPENDENT STATUS

[1.51]
Article 51   [Monitoring the application of this Regulation]
1.   [The Commissioner is] responsible for monitoring the application of this Regulation, in order to protect the fundamental rights and freedoms of natural persons in relation to processing and to facilitate the free flow of personal data   . . . .

2–4.   . . . .

NOTES

The words in square brackets in the heading and para 1 were substituted, and the words omitted from para 1 and the whole of paras 2–4 were repealed, by the Data Protection, Privacy and Electronic Communications (Amendments etc) (EU Exit) Regulations 2019, SI 2019/419, reg 3, Sch 1, paras 1, 45.

[1.52]
Article 52   Independence
1. [The Commissioner] shall act with complete independence in performing . . . tasks and exercising . . .
powers in accordance with this Regulation.
2. [The Commissioner] shall, in the performance of . . . tasks and exercise of . . . powers in accordance with
this Regulation, remain free from external influence, whether direct or indirect, and shall neither seek nor take
instructions from anybody.
3. [The Commissioner] shall refrain from any action incompatible with [the Commissioner's duties] and shall not,
[while holding office], engage in any incompatible occupation, whether gainful or not.
4–6. . . .

NOTES
   The words in square brackets in paras 1–3 were substituted, and the words omitted from paras 1, 2, and the whole of
paras 4–6 were repealed, by the Data Protection, Privacy and Electronic Communications (Amendments etc) (EU Exit)
Regulations 2019, SI 2019/419, reg 3, Sch 1, paras 1, 46.

Articles 53, 54   *(Repealed by the Data Protection, Privacy and Electronic Communications (Amendments etc)*
(EU Exit) Regulations 2019, SI 2019/419, reg 3, Sch 1, paras 1, 47, 48.)

SECTION 2 [TASKS] AND POWERS

NOTES
   The word in square brackets in the section heading was substituted by the Data Protection, Privacy and
Electronic Communications (Amendments etc) (EU Exit) Regulations 2019, SI 2019/419, reg 3, Sch 1, paras 1, 49.

Articles 55, 56   *(Repealed by the Data Protection, Privacy and Electronic Communications (Amendments etc)*
(EU Exit) Regulations 2019, SI 2019/419, reg 3, Sch 1, paras 1, 50, 51.)

[1.53]
Article 57   Tasks
1. Without prejudice to other tasks set out under this Regulation, [the Commissioner must]:
   (a) monitor and enforce the application of this Regulation;
   (b) promote public awareness and understanding of the risks, rules, safeguards and rights in relation to processing.
         Activities addressed specifically to children shall receive specific attention;
   (c) advise [Parliament], the government, and other institutions and bodies on legislative and administrative
         measures relating to the protection of natural persons' rights and freedoms with regard to processing;
   (d) promote the awareness of controllers and processors of their obligations under this Regulation;
   (e) upon request, provide information to any data subject concerning the exercise of their rights under this
         Regulation and, if appropriate, cooperate with [foreign designated authorities] to that end;
   (f) handle complaints lodged by a data subject, or by a body, organisation or association in accordance with
         Article 80, and investigate, to the extent appropriate, the subject matter of the complaint and inform the
         complainant of the progress and the outcome of the investigation within a reasonable period, in particular if
         further investigation or coordination with [a foreign designated authority] is necessary;
   (g)   . . .
   (h) conduct investigations on the application of this Regulation, including on the basis of information received
         from [a foreign designated authority] or other public authority;
   (i) monitor relevant developments, insofar as they have an impact on the protection of personal data, in particular
         the development of information and communication technologies and commercial practices;
   (j) adopt standard contractual clauses referred to in Article 28(8) and [issue standard data protection
         clauses referred to] in point (d) of Article 46(2);
   (k) establish and maintain a list in relation to the requirement for data protection impact assessment pursuant to
         Article 35(4);
   (l) give advice on the processing operations referred to in Article 36(2);
   (m) encourage the drawing up of codes of conduct pursuant to Article 40(1) and provide an opinion and approve
         such codes of conduct which provide sufficient safeguards, pursuant to Article 40(5);
   (n) encourage the establishment of data protection certification mechanisms and of data protection seals and
         marks pursuant to Article 42(1), and approve the criteria of certification pursuant to Article 42(5);
   (o) where applicable, carry out a periodic review of certifications issued in accordance with Article 42(7);
   [(oa) maintain a public register of certification mechanisms and data protection seals and marks pursuant to Article
         42(8) and of controllers or processors established in third countries and certified pursuant to Article 42(7);]
   (p) draft and publish the requirements for accreditation of a body for monitoring codes of conduct pursuant to
         Article 41 and of a certification body pursuant to Article 43;
   (q) conduct the accreditation of a body for monitoring codes of conduct pursuant to Article 41 and of a
         certification body pursuant to Article 43;
   (r) authorise contractual clauses and provisions referred to in Article 46(3);
   (s) approve binding corporate rules pursuant to Article 47;
   (t)   . . .
   (u) keep internal records of infringements of this Regulation and of measures taken in accordance with Article
         58(2); and
   (v) fulfil any other tasks related to the protection of personal data.
2. [The Commissioner] shall facilitate the submission of complaints referred to in point (f) of paragraph 1 by
measures such as a complaint submission form which can also be completed electronically, without excluding other
means of communication.

3. The performance of [the Commissioner's tasks is to be] free of charge for the data subject and, where applicable, for the data protection officer.

4. Where requests are manifestly unfounded or excessive, in particular because of their repetitive character, the [Commissioner] may charge a reasonable fee based on administrative costs, or refuse to act on the request. The [Commissioner] shall bear the burden of demonstrating the manifestly unfounded or excessive character of the request.

NOTES

Para 1: the words in square brackets in the opening text and sub-paras (c), (e), (f), (h) were substituted, sub-paras (g), (t) were repealed, the words in square brackets in sub-para (j) were inserted, and para (oa) was inserted, by the Data Protection, Privacy and the Electronic Communications (Amendments etc) (EU Exit) Regulations 2019, SI 2019/419, reg 3, Sch 1, paras 1, 52(1), (2).

Paras 2–4: words in square brackets substituted by SI 2019/419, reg 3, Sch 1, paras 1, 52(1), (3)–(5).

[1.54]

Article 58   Powers

1. [The Commissioner has] all of the following investigative powers:
   (a) to order the controller and the processor, and, where applicable, the controller's or the processor's representative to provide any information it requires for the performance of its tasks;
   (b) to carry out investigations in the form of data protection audits;
   (c) to carry out a review on certifications issued pursuant to Article 42(7);
   (d) to notify the controller or the processor of an alleged infringement of this Regulation;
   (e) to obtain, from the controller and the processor, access to all personal data and to all information necessary for the performance of [the Commissioner's] tasks;
   (f) to obtain access to any premises of the controller and the processor, including to any data processing equipment and means, in accordance with [domestic law].

2. [The Commissioner has] all of the following corrective powers:
   (a) to issue warnings to a controller or processor that intended processing operations are likely to infringe provisions of this Regulation;
   (b) to issue reprimands to a controller or a processor where processing operations have infringed provisions of this Regulation;
   (c) to order the controller or the processor to comply with the data subject's requests to exercise his or her rights pursuant to this Regulation;
   (d) to order the controller or processor to bring processing operations into compliance with the provisions of this Regulation, where appropriate, in a specified manner and within a specified period;
   (e) to order the controller to communicate a personal data breach to the data subject;
   (f) to impose a temporary or definitive limitation including a ban on processing;
   (g) to order the rectification or erasure of personal data or restriction of processing pursuant to Articles 16, 17 and 18 and the notification of such actions to recipients to whom the personal data have been disclosed pursuant to Article 17(2) and Article 19;
   (h) to withdraw a certification or to order the certification body to withdraw a certification issued pursuant to Articles 42 and 43, or to order the certification body not to issue certification if the requirements for the certification are not or are no longer met;
   (i) to impose an administrative fine pursuant to Article 83, in addition to, or instead of measures referred to in this paragraph, depending on the circumstances of each individual case;
   (j) to order the suspension of data flows to a recipient in a third country or to an international organisation.

3. [The Commissioner has] all of the following authorisation and advisory powers:
   (a) to advise the controller in accordance with the prior consultation procedure referred to in Article 36;
   (b) to issue, on [the Commissioner's] own initiative or on request, opinions to [Parliament, the government or] other institutions and bodies as well as to the public on any issue related to the protection of personal data;
   (c)   . . .
   (d) to issue an opinion and approve draft codes of conduct pursuant to Article 40(5);
   (e) to accredit certification bodies pursuant to Article 43;
   (f) to issue certifications and approve criteria of certification in accordance with Article 42(5);
   (g) to adopt standard data protection clauses referred to in Article 28(8) and in point (d) of Article 46(2);
   (h) to authorise contractual clauses referred to in point (a) of Article 46(3);
   (i) to authorise administrative arrangements referred to in point (b) of Article 46(3);
   (j) to approve binding corporate rules pursuant to Article 47.

[3A. In the 2018 Act, section 115(4) to (9) provide that the Commissioner's functions under this Article are subject to certain safeguards.]

4–6.   . . .

NOTES

The words in square brackets in paras 1–3 were substituted, point (c) of para 3 was repealed, para 3A was inserted, and paras 4–6 were repealed, by the Data Protection, Privacy and Electronic Communications (Amendments etc) (EU Exit) Regulations 2019, SI 2019/419, reg 3, Sch 1, paras 1, 53.

[1.55]

Article 59   Activity reports

[The Commissioner] shall draw up an annual report on [the Commissioner's] activities, which may include a list of types of infringement notified and types of measures taken in accordance with Article 58(2). [The Commissioner must arrange for those reports to be laid before Parliament and send a copy to the Secretary of State.] They shall be made available to the public . . . .

NOTES

Words in square brackets substituted and words omitted repealed, by the Data Protection, Privacy and Electronic Communications (Amendments etc) (EU Exit) Regulations 2019, SI 2019/419, reg 3, Sch 1, paras 1, 54.

Articles 60–76   *((Chapter VII) Repealed by the Data Protection, Privacy and Electronic Communications (Amendments etc) (EU Exit) Regulations 2019, SI 2019/419, reg 3, Sch 1, paras 1, 55.)*

CHAPTER VIII REMEDIES, LIABILITY AND PENALTIES

[1.56]
Article 77   Right to lodge a complaint with [the Commissioner]
1. Without prejudice to any other administrative or judicial remedy, every data subject shall have the right to lodge a complaint with [the Commissioner] if the data subject considers that the processing of personal data relating to him or her infringes this Regulation.
2. [The Commissioner] shall inform the complainant on the progress and the outcome of the complaint including the possibility of a judicial remedy pursuant to Article 78.

NOTES

Words in square brackets substituted by the Data Protection, Privacy and Electronic Communications (Amendments etc) (EU Exit) Regulations 2019, SI 2019/419, reg 3, Sch 1, paras 1, 56.

[1.57]
Article 78   Right to an effective judicial remedy against [the Commissioner]
1. Without prejudice to any other administrative or non-judicial remedy, each natural or legal person shall have the right to an effective judicial remedy against a legally binding decision of [the Commissioner] concerning them.
2. Without prejudice to any other administrative or non-judicial remedy, each data subject shall have the right to a an effective judicial remedy where [the Commissioner] does not handle a complaint or does not inform the data subject within three months on the progress or outcome of the complaint lodged pursuant to Article 77.
3.   . . .
4.   . . .

NOTES

The words in square brackets in each place were substituted and paras 3, 4 were repealed, by the Data Protection, Privacy and Electronic Communications (Amendments etc) (EU Exit) Regulations 2019, SI 2019/419, reg 3, Sch 1, paras 1, 57.

[1.58]
Article 79   Right to an effective judicial remedy against a controller or processor
1. Without prejudice to any available administrative or non-judicial remedy, including the right to lodge a complaint with [the Commissioner] pursuant to Article 77, each data subject shall have the right to an effective judicial remedy where he or she considers that his or her rights under this Regulation have been infringed as a result of the processing of his or her personal data in non-compliance with this Regulation.
2.   . . .

NOTES

The words in square brackets in para 1 were substituted and para 2 was repealed, by the Data Protection, Privacy and Electronic Communications (Amendments etc) (EU Exit) Regulations 2019, SI 2019/419, reg 3, Sch 1, paras 1, 58.

[1.59]
Article 80   Representation of data subjects
1. The data subject shall have the right to mandate [a body or other organisation which meets the conditions in section 187(3) and (4) of the 2018 Act] to lodge the complaint on his or her behalf, to exercise the rights referred to in Articles 77, 78 and 79 on his or her behalf, and to exercise the right to receive compensation referred to in Article 82 on his or her behalf   . . . .
2. [The Secretary of State] may provide that any body, organisation or association referred to in paragraph 1 of this Article, independently of a data subject's mandate, has the right to lodge . . . a complaint with [the Commissioner] and to exercise the rights referred to in Articles 78 and 79 if it considers that the rights of a data subject under this Regulation have been infringed as a result of the processing.
[3. The Secretary of State may exercise the power under paragraph 2 of this Article only by making regulations under section 190 of the 2018 Act.]

NOTES

In paras 1, 2 the words in square brackets were substituted and the words omitted were repealed, and para 3 was added, by the Data Protection, Privacy and Electronic Communications (Amendments etc) (EU Exit) Regulations 2019, SI 2019/419, reg 3, Sch 1, paras 1, 59.

Article 81   *(Repealed by the Data Protection, Privacy and Electronic Communications (Amendments etc) (EU Exit) Regulations 2019, SI 2019/419, reg 3, Sch 1, paras 1, 60.)*

[1.60]
Article 82   Right to compensation and liability
1. Any person who has suffered material or non-material damage as a result of an infringement of this Regulation shall have the right to receive compensation from the controller or processor for the damage suffered.

2. Any controller involved in processing shall be liable for the damage caused by processing which infringes this Regulation. A processor shall be liable for the damage caused by processing only where it has not complied with obligations of this Regulation specifically directed to processors or where it has acted outside or contrary to lawful instructions of the controller.

3. A controller or processor shall be exempt from liability under paragraph 2 if it proves that it is not in any way responsible for the event giving rise to the damage.

4. Where more than one controller or processor, or both a controller and a processor, are involved in the same processing and where they are, under paragraphs 2 and 3, responsible for any damage caused by processing, each controller or processor shall be held liable for the entire damage in order to ensure effective compensation of the data subject.

5. Where a controller or processor has, in accordance with paragraph 4, paid full compensation for the damage suffered, that controller or processor shall be entitled to claim back from the other controllers or processors involved in the same processing that part of the compensation corresponding to their part of responsibility for the damage, in accordance with the conditions set out in paragraph 2.

6.   . . .

NOTES

Para 6: repealed by the Data Protection, Privacy and Electronic Communications (Amendments etc) (EU Exit) Regulations 2019, SI 2019/419, reg 3, Sch 1, paras 1, 61.

[1.61]
Article 83   General conditions for imposing administrative fines
1. [The Commissioner] shall ensure that the imposition of administrative fines pursuant to this Article in respect of infringements of this Regulation referred to in paragraphs 4, 5 and 6 shall in each individual case be effective, proportionate and dissuasive.

2. Administrative fines shall, depending on the circumstances of each individual case, be imposed in addition to, or instead of, measures referred to in points (a) to (h) and (j) of Article 58(2). When deciding whether to impose an administrative fine and deciding on the amount of the administrative fine in each individual case due regard shall be given to the following:

(a)   the nature, gravity and duration of the infringement taking into account the nature scope or purpose of the processing concerned as well as the number of data subjects affected and the level of damage suffered by them;

(b)   the intentional or negligent character of the infringement;

(c)   any action taken by the controller or processor to mitigate the damage suffered by data subjects;

(d)   the degree of responsibility of the controller or processor taking into account technical and organisational measures implemented by them pursuant to Articles 25 and 32;

(e)   any relevant previous infringements by the controller or processor;

(f)   the degree of cooperation with [the Commissioner], in order to remedy the infringement and mitigate the possible adverse effects of the infringement;

(g)   the categories of personal data affected by the infringement;

(h)   the manner in which the infringement became known to [the Commissioner], in particular whether, and if so to what extent, the controller or processor notified the infringement;

(i)   where measures referred to in Article 58(2) have previously been ordered against the controller or processor concerned with regard to the same subject-matter, compliance with those measures;

(j)   adherence to approved codes of conduct pursuant to Article 40 or approved certification mechanisms pursuant to Article 42; and

(k)   any other aggravating or mitigating factor applicable to the circumstances of the case, such as financial benefits gained, or losses avoided, directly or indirectly, from the infringement.

3. If a controller or processor intentionally or negligently, for the same or linked processing operations, infringes several provisions of this Regulation, the total amount of the administrative fine shall not exceed the amount specified for the gravest infringement.

4. Infringements of the following provisions shall, in accordance with paragraph 2, be subject to administrative fines up to [£8,700,000], or in the case of an undertaking, up to 2% of the total worldwide annual turnover of the preceding financial year, whichever is higher:

(a)   the obligations of the controller and the processor pursuant to Articles 8, 11, 25 to 39 and 42 and 43;

(b)   the obligations of the certification body pursuant to Articles 42 and 43;

(c)   the obligations of the monitoring body pursuant to Article 41(4).

5. Infringements of the following provisions shall, in accordance with paragraph 2, be subject to administrative fines up to [£17,500,000], or in the case of an undertaking, up to 4% of the total worldwide annual turnover of the preceding financial year, whichever is higher:

(a)   the basic principles for processing, including conditions for consent, pursuant to Articles 5, 6, 7 and 9;

(b)   the data subjects' rights pursuant to Articles 12 to 22;

(c)   the transfers of personal data to a recipient in a third country or an international organisation pursuant to Articles 44 to 49;

[(d)   any obligations under Part 5 or 6 of Schedule 2 to the 2018 Act or regulations made under section 16(1)(c) of the 2018 Act;]

(e)   non-compliance with an order or a temporary or definitive limitation on processing or the suspension of data flows by [the Commissioner] pursuant to Article 58(2) or failure to provide access in violation of Article 58(1).

6. Non-compliance with an order by [the Commissioner] as referred to in Article 58(2) shall, in accordance with paragraph 2 of this Article, be subject to administrative fines up to 20,000,000 EUR, or in the case of an undertaking, up to 4% of the total worldwide annual turnover of the preceding financial year, whichever is higher.

7–9. . . .
[10. In the 2018 Act, section 115(9) makes provision about the exercise of the Commissioner's functions under this Article.]

NOTES
The words in square brackets in paras 1, 2, 4–6 were substituted, paras 7–9 were repealed, and para 10 was added, by the Data Protection, Privacy and Electronic Communications (Amendments etc) (EU Exit) Regulations 2019, SI 2019/419, reg 3, Sch 1, paras 1, 62.

[1.62]
Article 84   Penalties
[Part 6 of the 2018 Act makes further provision about penalties applicable to infringements of this Regulation.]

NOTES
Words in square brackets substituted by the Data Protection, Privacy and Electronic Communications (Amendments etc) (EU Exit) Regulations 2019, SI 2019/419, reg 3, Sch 1, paras 1, 63.

CHAPTER IX PROVISIONS RELATING TO SPECIFIC PROCESSING SITUATIONS

[1.63]
Article 85   Processing and freedom of expression and information
1. . . .
2. For processing carried out for journalistic purposes or the purpose of academic artistic or literary expression, [the Secretary of State may] provide for exemptions or derogations from Chapter II (principles), Chapter III (rights of the data subject), Chapter IV (controller and processor), Chapter V (transfer of personal data to third countries or international organisations), Chapter VI ([the Commissioner]) . . . and Chapter IX (specific data processing situations) if they are necessary to reconcile the right to the protection of personal data with the freedom of expression and information.
[2A. The Secretary of State may exercise the power under paragraph 2 of this Article only by making regulations under section 16 of the 2018 Act.]
3. . . .

NOTES
Paras 1, 3 and the words omitted from para 2 were repealed, the words in square brackets in para 2 were substituted, and para 2A was inserted, by the Data Protection, Privacy and Electronic Communications (Amendments etc) (EU Exit) Regulations 2019, SI 2019/419, reg 3, Sch 1, paras 1, 64.

[1.64]
Article 86   Processing and public access to official documents
[1.] Personal data in official documents held by a public authority or a public body or a private body for the performance of a task carried out in the public interest may be disclosed by the authority or body in accordance with [domestic law] to which the public authority or body is subject in order to reconcile public access to official documents with the right to the protection of personal data pursuant to this Regulation.
[2. Chapter 3 of Part 2 of the 2018 Act makes provision about the application of this Regulation to the manual unstructured processing of personal data held by an FOI public authority (as defined in Article 2).]

NOTES
The existing text was numbered as para 1, the words in square brackets therein were substituted, and para 2 was added, by the Data Protection, Privacy and Electronic Communications (Amendments etc) (EU Exit) Regulations 2019, SI 2019/419, reg 3, Sch 1, paras 1, 65.

[1.65]
[Article 86A   Processing and national security and defence
Chapter 3 of Part 2 of the 2018 Act makes provision about the application of this Regulation where processing is carried out, or exemption from a provision of this Regulation is required, for the purposes of safeguarding national security or for defence purposes.]

NOTES
Commencement: IP completion day (as defined in the European Union (Withdrawal Agreement) Act 2020, s 39).
Inserted by the Data Protection, Privacy and Electronic Communications (Amendments etc) (EU Exit) Regulations 2019, SI 2019/419, reg 3, Sch 1, paras 1, 66.

[1.66]

Articles 87, 88   *(Repealed by the Data Protection, Privacy and Electronic Communications (Amendments etc) (EU Exit) Regulations 2019, SI 2019/419, reg 3, Sch 1, paras 1, 67, 68.)*

[1.67]
Article 89   Safeguards and derogations relating to processing for archiving purposes in the public interest, scientific or historical research purposes or statistical purposes
1. Processing for archiving purposes in the public interest, scientific or historical research purposes or statistical purposes, shall be subject to appropriate safeguards, in accordance with this Regulation, for the rights and freedoms of the data subject. Those safeguards shall ensure that technical and organisational measures are in place in particular in order to ensure respect for the principle of data minimisation. Those measures may include pseudonymisation provided that those purposes can be fulfilled in that manner. Where those purposes can be fulfilled by further processing which does not permit or no longer permits the identification of data subjects, those purposes shall be fulfilled in that manner.

[1A. In the 2018 Act, section 19 makes provision about when the requirements in paragraph 1 are satisfied.]
2–4. . . .

NOTES
Para 1A was inserted and paras 2–4 were repealed, by the Data Protection, Privacy and Electronic Communications (Amendments etc) (EU Exit) Regulations 2019, SI 2019/419, reg 3, Sch 1, paras 1, 69.

Articles 90–93   (*Articles 90, 91 and Articles 92, 93 (Chapter 10) repealed by the Data Protection, Privacy and Electronic Communications (Amendments etc) (EU Exit) Regulations 2019, SI 2019/419, reg 3, Sch 1, paras 1, 70–72.*)

CHAPTER XI FINAL PROVISIONS

[1.68]
Article 94   Repeal of Directive 95/46/EC
1. . . .
2. References to [Directive 95/46/EC of the European Parliament and of the Council of 24th October 1995 on the protection of individuals with regard to the processing of personal data and on the free movement of such data (which ceased to have effect on 25th May 2018)] shall be construed as references to this Regulation. References to the Working Party on the Protection of Individuals with regard to the Processing of Personal Data established by Article 29 of Directive 95/46/EC shall be construed as references to the European Data Protection Board established [by the EU GDPR (as defined in section 3 of the 2018 Act)].

NOTES
Para 1 was repealed and the words in square brackets in para 2 were substituted by the Data Protection, Privacy and Electronic Communications (Amendments etc) (EU Exit) Regulations 2019, SI 2019/419, reg 3, Sch 1, paras 1, 73.

[1.69]
Article 95   Relationship with Directive 2002/58/EC
This Regulation shall not impose additional obligations on natural or legal persons in relation to processing in connection with the provision of publicly available electronic communications services in public communication networks in [the United Kingdom] in relation to matters for which they are subject to specific obligations with the same objective set out in [domestic law made before IP completion day implementing Directive 2002/58/EC of the European Parliament and of the Council of 12th July 2002 concerning the processing of personal data and the protection of privacy in the electronic communications sector].

NOTES
Words in square brackets substituted by the Data Protection, Privacy and Electronic Communications (Amendments etc) (EU Exit) Regulations 2019, SI 2019/419, reg 3, Sch 1, paras 1, 74. Note that para 74 of Sch 1 to the 2019 Regulations was amended by the Data Protection, Privacy and Electronic Communications (Amendments etc) (EU Exit) Regulations 2020, SI 2020/1586, reg 4 (and the effect of the amendment has been incorporated in the text set out above).

[1.70]
Article 96   Relationship with previously concluded Agreements
International agreements involving the transfer of personal data to third countries or international organisations which were concluded by [the United Kingdom or the Commissioner] prior to 24 May 2016, and which comply with [domestic law] as applicable prior to that date, shall remain in force until amended, replaced or revoked.

NOTES
Words in square brackets substituted by the Data Protection, Privacy and Electronic Communications (Amendments etc) (EU Exit) Regulations 2019, SI 2019/419, reg 3, Sch 1, paras 1, 75.

Articles 97–99   (*Repealed by the Data Protection, Privacy and Electronic Communications (Amendments etc) (EU Exit) Regulations 2019, SI 2019/419, reg 3, Sch 1, paras 1, 76–79).*)

DATA PROTECTION ACT 2018

(2018 c 12)

An Act to make provision for the regulation of the processing of information relating to individuals; to make provision in connection with the Information Commissioner's functions under certain regulations relating to information; to make provision for a direct marketing code of practice; and for connected purposes.

[23 May 2018]

NOTES
Commencement: the commencement of this Act is provided for by s 212 at **[1.283]**. Subsection (2)(a)–(e) of that section provide that certain provisions of this Act come into force on the day on which this Act is passed (23 May 2018). Subsection (3) provides that certain specified provisions come into force on 23 July 2018. Note that sub-(2)(f) provides that "any other provision of this Act so far as it confers power to make regulations or Tribunal Procedure Rules or is otherwise necessary for enabling the exercise of such a power on or after the day on which this Act is passed" shall also come into force on 23 May 2018. Except as noted *ante*, s 212 provides that this Act shall come into force on such day as the Secretary of State may by regulations appoint (see sub-s (1) of that section).
The Data Protection Act 2018 (Commencement No 1 and Transitional and Saving Provisions) Regulations 2018, SI 2018/625 provide that most of the remaining provisions of this Act come into force on 25 May 2018 (see reg 2) and 23 July 2018 (see reg 3). The Data Protection Act 2018 (Commencement No 2) Regulations 2019, SI 2019/1188 brought ss 93, 102–105, 108 into

force on 16 September 2019. The Data Protection Act 2018 (Commencement No 3) Regulations 2019, SI 2019/1434 brought paras 211 and 227 of Sch 19 into force on 2 December 2019.

PART 3
LAW ENFORCEMENT PROCESSING

CHAPTER 1 SCOPE AND DEFINITIONS

Scope

Definitions

CHAPTER 2 PRINCIPLES

CHAPTER 3 RIGHTS OF THE DATA SUBJECT

Overview and scope

Information: controller's general duties

Data subject's right of access

Data subject's rights to rectification or erasure etc

Automated individual decision-making

Supplementary

CHAPTER 4 CONTROLLER AND PROCESSOR

Overview and scope

General obligations

Obligations relating to security

Part 1 Data Protection: UK Law

PART 1 PRELIMINARY

[1.71]

1 Overview

(1) This Act makes provision about the processing of personal data.

(2) Most processing of personal data is subject to the [UK GDPR].

(3) Part 2 supplements the [UK GDPR].

(4) Part 3 makes provision about the processing of personal data by competent authorities for law enforcement purposes . . . .

(5) Part 4 makes provision about the processing of personal data by the intelligence services.

(6) Part 5 makes provision about the Information Commissioner.

(7) Part 6 makes provision about the enforcement of the data protection legislation.

(8) Part 7 makes supplementary provision, including provision about the application of this Act to the Crown and to Parliament.

NOTES

Commencement: 23 May 2018 (see also the introductory notes to this Act preceding s 1 at **[1.71]**).

The words in square brackets in sub-ss (2), (3) were substituted and the words omitted from sub-s (4) were repealed, by the Data Protection, Privacy and Electronic Communications (Amendments etc) (EU Exit) Regulations 2019, SI 2019/419, reg 4, Sch 2, paras 1, 2.

[1.72]

2 Protection of personal data

(1) The [UK GDPR] and this Act protect individuals with regard to the processing of personal data, in particular by—

    (a) requiring personal data to be processed lawfully and fairly, on the basis of the data subject's consent or another specified basis,

    (b) conferring rights on the data subject to obtain information about the processing of personal data and to require inaccurate personal data to be rectified, and

    (c) conferring functions on the Commissioner, giving the holder of that office responsibility for monitoring and enforcing their provisions.

(2) When carrying out functions under the [UK GDPR] and this Act, the Commissioner must have regard to the importance of securing an appropriate level of protection for personal data, taking account of the interests of data subjects, controllers and others and matters of general public interest.

NOTES

Commencement: 25 May 2018 (see also the introductory notes to this Act preceding s 1 at **[1.71]**).

Words in square brackets substituted by the Data Protection, Privacy and Electronic Communications (Amendments etc) (EU Exit) Regulations 2019, SI 2019/419, reg 4, Sch 2, paras 1, 3.

[1.73]

3 Terms relating to the processing of personal data

(1) This section defines some terms used in this Act.

(2) "Personal data" means any information relating to an identified or identifiable living individual (subject to subsection (14)(c)).

(3) "Identifiable living individual" means a living individual who can be identified, directly or indirectly, in particular by reference to—

    (a) an identifier such as a name, an identification number, location data or an online identifier, or

    (b) one or more factors specific to the physical, physiological, genetic, mental, economic, cultural or social identity of the individual.

(4) "Processing", in relation to information, means an operation or set of operations which is performed on information, or on sets of information, such as—

    (a) collection, recording, organisation, structuring or storage,

    (b) adaptation or alteration,

    (c) retrieval, consultation or use,

    (d) disclosure by transmission, dissemination or otherwise making available,

    (e) alignment or combination, or

    (f) restriction, erasure or destruction,

(subject to subsection (14)(c) and sections 5(7), 29(2) and 82(3), which make provision about references to processing in the different Parts of this Act).

(5) "Data subject" means the identified or identifiable living individual to whom personal data relates.

(6) "Controller" and "processor", in relation to the processing of personal data to which . . . Part 2, Part 3 or Part 4 applies, have the same meaning as in that . . . Part (see sections 5, 6, 32 and 83 and see also subsection (14)(d)).

(7) "Filing system" means any structured set of personal data which is accessible according to specific criteria, whether held by automated means or manually and whether centralised, decentralised or dispersed on a functional or geographical basis.

(8) "The Commissioner" means the Information Commissioner (see section 114).

(9) "The data protection legislation" means—

    [(a) the UK GDPR,]

    (b) . . .

    (c) this Act,

    (d) regulations made under this Act, and

    (e) regulations made under section 2(2) of the European Communities Act 1972 which relate to [the EU GDPR] or the Law Enforcement Directive.

(10) "[The UK GDPR]" means Regulation (EU) 2016/679 of the European Parliament and of the Council of 27 April 2016 on the protection of natural persons with regard to the processing of personal data and on the free movement of such data [(United Kingdom General Data Protection Regulation), as it forms part of the law of England and Wales, Scotland and Northern Ireland by virtue of section 3 of the European Union (Withdrawal) Act 2018 (and see section 205(4))].

[(10A) "The EU GDPR" means Regulation (EU) 2016/679 of the European Parliament and of the Council of 27th April 2016 on the protection of natural persons with regard to the processing of personal data and on the free movement of such data (General Data Protection Regulation) as it has effect in EU law.]

(11) . . .

(12) "The Law Enforcement Directive" means Directive (EU) 2016/680 of the European Parliament and of the Council of 27 April 2016 on the protection of natural persons with regard to the processing of personal data by competent authorities for the purposes of the prevention, investigation, detection or prosecution of criminal offences or the execution of criminal penalties, and on the free movement of such data, and repealing Council Framework Decision 2008/977/JHA.

(13) "The Data Protection Convention" means the Convention for the Protection of Individuals with regard to Automatic Processing of Personal Data which was opened for signature on 28 January 1981, as amended up to the day on which this Act is passed.

(14) In Parts 5 to 7, except where otherwise provided—

[(a) references to the UK GDPR are to the UK GDPR read with Part 2;]

(b) . . .

(c) references to personal data, and the processing of personal data, are to personal data and processing to which . . . Part 2, Part 3 or Part 4 applies;

(d) references to a controller or processor are to a controller or processor in relation to the processing of personal data to which . . . Part 2, Part 3 or Part 4 applies.

(15) There is an index of defined expressions in section 206.

NOTES

Commencement: 23 May 2018 (see also the introductory notes to this Act preceding s 1 at **[1.71]**).

Sub-s (6): words omitted repealed by the Data Protection, Privacy and Electronic Communications (Amendments etc) (EU Exit) Regulations 2019, SI 2019/419, reg 4, Sch 2, paras 1, 4(1), (2).

Sub-ss (9), (14): words in square brackets substituted and words omitted repealed, by SI 2019/419, reg 4, Sch 2, paras 1, 4(1), (3), (7).

Sub-s (10): words in square brackets substituted by SI 2019/419, reg 4, Sch 2, paras 1, 4(1), (4).

Sub-s (10A): inserted by SI 2019/419, reg 4, Sch 2, paras 1, 4(1), (5).

Sub-s (11): repealed by SI 2019/419, reg 4, Sch 2, paras 1, 4(1), (6).

PART 2 GENERAL PROCESSING

CHAPTER 1 SCOPE AND DEFINITIONS

[1.74]

4 Processing to which this Part applies

(1) This Part is relevant to most processing of personal data.

(2) [This Part]—

(a) applies to the types of processing of personal data to which the [UK GDPR] applies by virtue of Article 2 of the [UK GDPR], and

(b) supplements, and must be read with, the [UK GDPR].

(3) . . .

NOTES

Commencement: 25 May 2018 (see also the introductory notes to this Act preceding s 1 at **[1.71]**).

The words in square brackets in sub-s (2) were substituted and sub-s (3) was repealed, by the Data Protection, Privacy and Electronic Communications (Amendments etc) (EU Exit) Regulations 2019, SI 2019/419, reg 4, Sch 2, paras 1, 5.

[1.75]

5 Definitions

(1) Terms used in . . . this Part and in the [UK GDPR] have the same meaning in [this Part as] they have in the [UK GDPR].

(2) In subsection (1), the reference to a term's meaning in the [UK GDPR] is to its meaning in the [UK GDPR] read with any provision of [this Part] which modifies the term's meaning for the purposes of the [UK GDPR].

(3) Subsection (1) is subject to any provision in [this Part] which provides expressly for the term to have a different meaning and to section 204.

(4)–(6) . . .

(7) A reference in . . . this Part to the processing of personal data is to processing to which [this Part] applies.

(8) Sections 3 and 205 include definitions of other expressions used in this Part.

NOTES

Commencement: 25 May 2018 (see also the introductory notes to this Act preceding s 1 at **[1.71]**).

Sub-ss (1)–(3), (7): words in square brackets substituted and words omitted repealed by the Data Protection, Privacy and Electronic Communications (Amendments etc) (EU Exit) Regulations 2019, SI 2019/419, reg 4, Sch 2, paras 1, 6(1)–(4), (6).

Sub-ss (4)–(6): repealed by SI 2019/419, reg 4, Sch 2, paras 1, 6(1), (5).

CHAPTER 2 [THE UK GDPR]

NOTES

Words in square brackets in the Chapter heading substituted by the Data Protection, Privacy and Electronic Communications (Amendments etc) (EU Exit) Regulations 2019, SI 2019/419, reg 4, Sch 2, paras 1, 7.

Meaning of certain terms used in the [UK GDPR]

[1.76]

6 Meaning of "controller"

(1) The definition of "controller" in Article 4(7) of the [UK GDPR] has effect subject to—

(a) subsection (2),

(b) section 209, and

(c) section 210.

(2) For the purposes of the [UK GDPR], where personal data is processed only—

(a) for purposes for which it is required by an enactment to be processed, and

(b) by means by which it is required by an enactment to be processed,

the person on whom the obligation to process the data is imposed by the enactment (or, if different, one of the enactments) is the controller.

NOTES

Commencement: 25 May 2018 (see also the introductory notes to this Act preceding s 1 at **[1.71]**).

Words in square brackets in each place, including the heading preceding this section, substituted by the Data Protection, Privacy and Electronic Communications (Amendments etc) (EU Exit) Regulations 2019, SI 2019/419, reg 4, Sch 2, paras 1, 8, 9.

[1.77]
7 Meaning of "public authority" and "public body"
(1) For the purposes of the [UK GDPR], the following (and only the following) are "public authorities" and "public bodies" . . . —
   (a) a public authority as defined by the Freedom of Information Act 2000,
   (b) a Scottish public authority as defined by the Freedom of Information (Scotland) Act 2002 (asp 13), and
   (c) an authority or body specified or described by the Secretary of State in regulations,
subject to subsections (2), (3) and (4).
(2) An authority or body that falls within subsection (1) is only a "public authority" or "public body" for the purposes of the [UK GDPR] when performing a task carried out in the public interest or in the exercise of official authority vested in it.
(3) The references in subsection (1)(a) and (b) to public authorities and Scottish public authorities as defined by the Freedom of Information Act 2000 and the Freedom of Information (Scotland) Act 2002 (asp 13) do not include any of the following that fall within those definitions—
   (a) a parish council in England;
   (b) a community council in Wales;
   (c) a community council in Scotland;
   (d) a parish meeting constituted under section 13 of the Local Government Act 1972;
   (e) a community meeting constituted under section 27 of that Act;
   (f) charter trustees constituted—
      (i) under section 246 of that Act,
      (ii) under Part 1 of the Local Government and Public Involvement in Health Act 2007, or
      (iii) by the Charter Trustees Regulations 1996 (SI 1996/263).
(4) The Secretary of State may by regulations provide that a person specified or described in the regulations that is a public authority described in subsection (1)(a) or (b) is not a "public authority" or "public body" for the purposes of the [UK GDPR].
(5) Regulations under this section are subject to the affirmative resolution procedure.

NOTES
Commencement: 25 May 2018 (see also the introductory notes to this Act preceding s 1 at **[1.71]**).
The words in square brackets in sub-ss (1), (2), (4) were substituted, and the words omitted from sub-s (1) were repealed, by the Data Protection, Privacy and Electronic Communications (Amendments etc) (EU Exit) Regulations 2019, SI 2019/419, reg 4, Sch 2, paras 1, 10.

Lawfulness of processing

[1.78]
8 Lawfulness of processing: public interest etc
In Article 6(1) of the [UK GDPR] (lawfulness of processing), the reference in point (e) to processing of personal data that is necessary for the performance of a task carried out in the public interest or in the exercise of the controller's official authority includes processing of personal data that is necessary for—
   (a) the administration of justice,
   (b) the exercise of a function of either House of Parliament,
   (c) the exercise of a function conferred on a person by an enactment or rule of law,
   (d) the exercise of a function of the Crown, a Minister of the Crown or a government department, or
   (e) an activity that supports or promotes democratic engagement.

NOTES
Commencement: 25 May 2018 (see also the introductory notes to this Act preceding s 1 at **[1.71]**).
Words in square brackets substituted by the Data Protection, Privacy and Electronic Communications (Amendments etc) (EU Exit) Regulations 2019, SI 2019/419, reg 4, Sch 2, paras 1, 11.

9 (*Repealed by the Data Protection, Privacy and Electronic Communications (Amendments etc) (EU Exit) Regulations 2019, SI 2019/419, reg 4, Sch 2, paras 1, 12.*)

Special categories of personal data

[1.79]
10 Special categories of personal data and criminal convictions etc data
(1) Subsections (2) and (3) make provision about the processing of personal data described in Article 9(1) of the [UK GDPR] (prohibition on processing of special categories of personal data) in reliance on an exception in one of the following points of Article 9(2)—
   (a) point (b) (employment, social security and social protection);
   (b) point (g) (substantial public interest);
   (c) point (h) (health and social care);
   (d) point (i) (public health);
   (e) point (j) (archiving, research and statistics).
(2) The processing meets the requirement in point (b), (h), (i) or (j) of Article 9(2) of the [UK GDPR] for authorisation by, or a basis in, the law of the United Kingdom or a part of the United Kingdom only if it meets a condition in Part 1 of Schedule 1.
(3) The processing meets the requirement in point (g) of Article 9(2) of the [UK GDPR] for a basis in the law of the United Kingdom or a part of the United Kingdom only if it meets a condition in Part 2 of Schedule 1.

(4) Subsection (5) makes provision about the processing of personal data relating to criminal convictions and offences or related security measures that is not carried out under the control of official authority.

(5) The processing meets the requirement in Article [10(1) of the UK GDPR] for authorisation by the law of the United Kingdom or a part of the United Kingdom only if it meets a condition in Part 1, 2 or 3 of Schedule 1.

(6) The Secretary of State may by regulations—

    (a) amend Schedule 1—

        (i)   by adding or varying conditions or safeguards, and

        (ii)   by omitting conditions or safeguards added by regulations under this section, and

    (b) consequentially amend this section.

(7) Regulations under this section are subject to the affirmative resolution procedure.

NOTES

Commencement: 25 May 2018 (see also the introductory notes to this Act preceding s 1 at **[1.71]**).

Sub-ss (1)–(3), (5): words in square brackets substituted by the Data Protection, Privacy and Electronic Communications (Amendments etc) (EU Exit) Regulations 2019, SI 2019/419, reg 4, Sch 2, paras 1, 13.

[1.80]

11   Special categories of personal data etc: supplementary

(1) For the purposes of Article 9(2)(h) of the [UK GDPR] (processing for health or social care purposes etc), the circumstances in which the processing of personal data is carried out subject to the conditions and safeguards referred to in Article 9(3) of the [UK GDPR] (obligation of secrecy) include circumstances in which it is carried out—

    (a) by or under the responsibility of a health professional or a social work professional, or

    (b) by another person who in the circumstances owes a duty of confidentiality under an enactment or rule of law.

(2) In Article 10 of the [UK GDPR] and section 10, references to personal data relating to criminal convictions and offences or related security measures include personal data relating to—

    (a) the alleged commission of offences by the data subject, or

    (b) proceedings for an offence committed or alleged to have been committed by the data subject or the disposal of such proceedings, including sentencing.

NOTES

Commencement: 25 May 2018 (see also the introductory notes to this Act preceding s 1 at **[1.71]**).

Sub-ss (1), (2): words in square brackets substituted by the Data Protection, Privacy and Electronic Communications (Amendments etc) (EU Exit) Regulations 2019, SI 2019/419, reg 4, Sch 2, paras 1, 14.

Rights of the data subject

[1.81]

12   Limits on fees that may be charged by controllers

(1) The Secretary of State may by regulations specify limits on the fees that a controller may charge in reliance on—

    (a) Article 12(5) of the [UK GDPR] (reasonable fees when responding to manifestly unfounded or excessive requests), or

    (b) Article 15(3) of the [UK GDPR] (reasonable fees for provision of further copies).

(2) The Secretary of State may by regulations—

    (a) require controllers of a description specified in the regulations to produce and publish guidance about the fees that they charge in reliance on those provisions, and

    (b) specify what the guidance must include.

(3) Regulations under this section are subject to the negative resolution procedure.

NOTES

Commencement: 25 May 2018 (see also the introductory notes to this Act preceding s 1 at **[1.71]**).

Sub-s (1): words in square brackets substituted by the Data Protection, Privacy and Electronic Communications (Amendments etc) (EU Exit) Regulations 2019, SI 2019/419, reg 4, Sch 2, paras 1, 15.

[1.82]

13   Obligations of credit reference agencies

(1) This section applies where a controller is a credit reference agency (within the meaning of section 145(8) of the Consumer Credit Act 1974).

(2) The controller's obligations under Article 15(1) to (3) of the [UK GDPR] (confirmation of processing, access to data and safeguards for third country transfers) are taken to apply only to personal data relating to the data subject's financial standing, unless the data subject has indicated a contrary intention.

(3) Where the controller discloses personal data in pursuance of Article 15(1) to (3) of the [UK GDPR], the disclosure must be accompanied by a statement informing the data subject of the data subject's rights under section 159 of the Consumer Credit Act 1974 (correction of wrong information).

NOTES

Commencement: 25 May 2018 (see also the introductory notes to this Act preceding s 1 at **[1.71]**).

Sub-ss (2), (3): words in square brackets substituted by the Data Protection, Privacy and Electronic Communications (Amendments etc) (EU Exit) Regulations 2019, SI 2019/419, reg 4, Sch 2, paras 1, 16.

[1.83]

14   Automated decision-making authorised by law: safeguards

(1) This section makes provision for the purposes of Article 22(2)(b) of the [UK GDPR] (exception from Article 22(1) of the [UK GDPR] for significant decisions based solely on automated processing that are [required or authorised under the law of the United Kingdom or a part of the United Kingdom] and subject to safeguards for the data subject's rights, freedoms and legitimate interests).

(2) A decision is a "significant decision" for the purposes of this section if, in relation to a data subject, it—

    (a)   produces legal effects concerning the data subject, or

    (b)   similarly significantly affects the data subject.

(3) A decision is a "qualifying significant decision" for the purposes of this section if—

    (a)   it is a significant decision in relation to a data subject,

    (b)   it is required or authorised by law, and

    (c)   it does not fall within Article 22(2)(a) or (c) of the [UK GDPR] (decisions necessary to a contract or made with the data subject's consent).

(4) Where a controller takes a qualifying significant decision in relation to a data subject based solely on automated processing—

    (a)   the controller must, as soon as reasonably practicable, notify the data subject in writing that a decision has been taken based solely on automated processing, and

    (b)   the data subject may, before the end of the period of 1 month beginning with receipt of the notification, request the controller to—

        (i)   reconsider the decision, or

        (ii)   take a new decision that is not based solely on automated processing.

(5) If a request is made to a controller under subsection (4), the controller must, within the period described in Article 12(3) of the [UK GDPR]—

    (a)   consider the request, including any information provided by the data subject that is relevant to it,

    (b)   comply with the request, and

    (c)   by notice in writing inform the data subject of—

        (i)   the steps taken to comply with the request, and

        (ii)   the outcome of complying with the request.

(6) In connection with this section, a controller has the powers and obligations under Article 12 of the [UK GDPR] (transparency, procedure for extending time for acting on request, fees, manifestly unfounded or excessive requests etc) that apply in connection with Article 22 of the [UK GDPR].

(7) The Secretary of State may by regulations make such further provision as the Secretary of State considers appropriate to provide suitable measures to safeguard a data subject's rights, freedoms and legitimate interests in connection with the taking of qualifying significant decisions based solely on automated processing.

(8) Regulations under subsection (7)—

    (a)   may amend this section, and

    (b)   are subject to the affirmative resolution procedure.

NOTES

Commencement: 25 May 2018 (see also the introductory notes to this Act preceding s 1 at **[1.71]**).

Words in square brackets in each place substituted by the Data Protection, Privacy and Electronic Communications (Amendments etc) (EU Exit) Regulations 2019, SI 2019/419, reg 4, Sch 2, paras 1, 17.

[Exemptions etc]

NOTES

Heading substituted by the Data Protection, Privacy and Electronic Communications (Amendments etc) (EU Exit) Regulations 2019, SI 2019/419, reg 4, Sch 2, paras 1, 18.

[1.84]

15   Exemptions etc

(1) Schedules 2, 3 and 4 make provision for exemptions from, and restrictions and adaptations of the application of, rules of the [UK GDPR].

(2) In Schedule 2—

    (a)   Part 1 makes provision adapting or restricting the application of rules contained in Articles 13 to 21 and 34 of the [UK GDPR] in specified circumstances [(of a kind described in] Article 6(3) and Article 23(1) of the [UK GDPR)];

    (b)   Part 2 makes provision restricting the application of rules contained in Articles 13 to 21 and 34 of the [UK GDPR] in specified circumstances [(of a kind described in] Article 23(1) of the [UK GDPR)];

    (c)   Part 3 makes provision restricting the application of Article 15 of the [UK GDPR] where this is necessary to protect the rights of others [(of a kind described in] Article 23(1) of the [UK GDPR)];

    (d)   Part 4 makes provision restricting the application of rules contained in Articles 13 to 15 of the [UK GDPR] in specified circumstances [(of a kind described in] Article 23(1) of the [UK GDPR)];

    (e)   Part 5 makes provision containing exemptions or derogations from Chapters II, III, IV [and V of the UK GDPR] for reasons relating to freedom of expression [(of a kind described in Article 85(2) of the UK GDPR)];

    (f)   Part 6 makes provision containing derogations from rights contained in Articles 15, 16, 18, 19, 20 and 21 of the [UK GDPR] for scientific or historical research purposes, statistical purposes and archiving purposes

    . . .

(3) Schedule 3 makes provision restricting the application of rules contained in Articles 13 to 21 of the [UK GDPR] to health, social work, education and child abuse data [(of a kind described in] Article 23(1) of the [UK GDPR)].

(4) Schedule 4 makes provision restricting the application of rules contained in Articles 13 to 21 of the [UK GDPR] to information the disclosure of which is prohibited or restricted by an enactment [(of a kind described in] Article 23(1) of the [UK GDPR)].

[(4A) In connection with the manual unstructured processing of personal data held by an FOI public authority, see Chapter 3 of this Part (sections 21, 24 and 25).]

(5) In connection with the safeguarding of national security and with defence, see Chapter 3 of this Part [(sections 26 to 28)].

NOTES

Commencement: 25 May 2018 (see also the introductory notes to this Act preceding s 1 at **[1.71]**).

Sub-s (4A) was inserted, all other words in square brackets were substituted, and the words omitted from sub-s (2)(f) were repealed, by the Data Protection, Privacy and Electronic Communications (Amendments etc) (EU Exit) Regulations 2019, SI 2019/419, reg 4, Sch 2, paras 1, 19.

[1.85]
16   Power to make further exemptions etc by regulations
(1) The following powers to make provision altering the application of the [UK GDPR] may be exercised by way of regulations made by the Secretary of State under this section—
   (a)   the power in Article 6(3) . . . to lay down a legal basis containing specific provisions to adapt the application of rules of the [UK GDPR] where processing is necessary for compliance with a legal obligation, for the performance of a task in the public interest or in the exercise of official authority;
   (b)   the power in Article 23(1) to make a [provision] restricting the scope of the obligations and rights mentioned in that Article where necessary and proportionate to safeguard certain objectives of general public interest;
   (c)   the power in Article 85(2) to provide for exemptions or derogations from certain Chapters of the [UK GDPR] where necessary to reconcile the protection of personal data with the freedom of expression and information.
(2) Regulations under this section may—
   (a)   amend Schedules 2 to 4—
      (i)   by adding or varying provisions, and
      (ii)   by omitting provisions added by regulations under this section, . . .
   (b)   consequentially amend section 15[, and
   (c)   consequentially amend the UK GDPR by adding, varying or omitting a reference to section 15, Schedule 2, 3 or 4, this section or regulations under this section.]
(3) Regulations under this section are subject to the affirmative resolution procedure.

NOTES
Commencement: 25 May 2018 (see also the introductory notes to this Act preceding s 1 at **[1.71]**).
Sub-s (1): words in square brackets substituted and words omitted repealed, by the Data Protection, Privacy and Electronic Communications (Amendments etc) (EU Exit) Regulations 2019, SI 2019/419, reg 4, Sch 2, paras 1, 20(1), (2).
Sub-s (2): word omitted from para (a) repealed, and para (c) inserted together with preceding word, by SI 2019/419, reg 4, Sch 2, paras 1, 20(1), (3).

[Certification]

NOTES
Heading substituted by the Data Protection, Privacy and Electronic Communications (Amendments etc) (EU Exit) Regulations 2019, SI 2019/419, reg 4, Sch 2, paras 1, 21.

[1.86]
17   Accreditation of certification providers
(1) Accreditation of a person as a certification provider is only valid when carried out by—
   (a)   the Commissioner, or
   (b)   the [UK national accreditation body].
(2) The Commissioner may only accredit a person as a certification provider where the Commissioner—
   (a)   has published a statement that the Commissioner will carry out such accreditation, and
   (b)   has not published a notice withdrawing that statement.
(3) The [UK national accreditation body] may only accredit a person as a certification provider where the Commissioner—
   (a)   has published a statement that the body may carry out such accreditation, and
   (b)   has not published a notice withdrawing that statement.
(4) The publication of a notice under subsection (2)(b) or (3)(b) does not affect the validity of any accreditation carried out before its publication.
(5) Schedule 5 makes provision about reviews of, and appeals from, a decision relating to accreditation of a person as a certification provider.
(6) The [UK national accreditation body] may charge a reasonable fee in connection with, or incidental to, the carrying out of the body's functions under this section, Schedule 5 and Article 43 of the [UK GDPR].
(7) The [UK national accreditation body] must provide the Secretary of State with such information relating to its functions under this section, Schedule 5 and Article 43 of the [UK GDPR] as the Secretary of State may reasonably require.
(8) In this section—
   "certification provider" means a person who issues certification for the purposes of Article 42 of the [UK GDPR];
   "the [UK national accreditation body]" means the [UK national accreditation body] for the purposes of Article 4(1) of Regulation (EC) No 765/2008 of the European Parliament and of the Council of 9 July 2008 setting out the requirements for accreditation and market surveillance relating to the marketing of products and repealing Regulation (EEC) No 339/93.

NOTES
Commencement: 25 May 2018 (see also the introductory notes to this Act preceding s 1 at **[1.71]**).
Words in square brackets in each place substituted by the Data Protection, Privacy and Electronic Communications (Amendments etc) (EU Exit) Regulations 2019, SI 2019/419, reg 4, Sch 2, paras 1, 22.

[1.87]
[17A   Transfers based on adequacy regulations
(1) The Secretary of State may by regulations specify any of the following which the Secretary of State considers ensures an adequate level of protection of personal data—
   (a)   a third country,

(b) a territory or one or more sectors within a third country,

(c) an international organisation, or

(d) a description of such a country, territory, sector or organisation.

(2) For the purposes of the UK GDPR and this Part of this Act, a transfer of personal data to a third country or an international organisation is based on adequacy regulations if, at the time of the transfer, regulations made under this section are in force which specify, or specify a description which includes—

(a) in the case of a third country, the country or a relevant territory or sector within the country, or

(b) in the case of an international organisation, the organisation.

(3) Regulations under this section may specify that the Secretary of State considers that an adequate level of protection of personal data is ensured only for a transfer specified or described in the regulations and, if they do so, only such a transfer may rely on those regulations for the purposes of subsection (2).

(4) Article 45(2) of the UK GDPR makes provision about the assessment of the adequacy of the level of protection for the purposes of this section and section 17B.

(5) Regulations under this section—

(a) where they relate to a third country, must specify their territorial and sectoral application;

(b) where applicable, must specify the independent supervisory authority or authorities referred to in Article 45(2)(b) of the UK GDPR.

(6) Regulations under this section may, among other things—

(a) provide that in relation to a country, territory, sector, organisation or transfer specified, or falling within a description specified, in the regulations, section 17B(1) has effect as if it required the reviews described there to be carried out at such shorter intervals as are specified in the regulations;

(b) identify a transfer of personal data by any means, including by reference to the controller or processor, the recipient, the personal data transferred or the means by which the transfer is made or by reference to relevant legislation, lists or other documents, as they have effect from time to time;

(c) confer a discretion on a person.

(7) Regulations under this section are subject to the negative resolution procedure.]

NOTES

Commencement: IP completion day (as defined in the European Union (Withdrawal Agreement) Act 2020, s 39).

Inserted, together with ss 17B, 17C, by the Data Protection, Privacy and Electronic Communications (Amendments etc) (EU Exit) Regulations 2019, SI 2019/419, reg 4, Sch 2, paras 1, 23.

[1.88]

[17B Transfers based on adequacy regulations: review etc

(1) For so long as regulations under section 17A are in force which specify, or specify a description which includes, a third country, a territory or sector within a third country or an international organisation, the Secretary of State must carry out a review of whether the country, territory, sector or organisation ensures an adequate level of protection of personal data at intervals of not more than 4 years.

(2) Each review under subsection (1) must take into account all relevant developments in the third country or international organisation.

(3) The Secretary of State must, on an ongoing basis, monitor developments in third countries and international organisations that could affect decisions to make regulations under section 17A or to amend or revoke such regulations.

(4) Where the Secretary of State becomes aware that a country, territory, sector or organisation specified, or falling within a description specified, in regulations under section 17A no longer ensures an adequate level of protection of personal data, whether as a result of a review under this section or otherwise, the Secretary of State must, to the extent necessary, amend or revoke the regulations.

(5) Where regulations under section 17A are amended or revoked in accordance with subsection (4), the Secretary of State must enter into consultations with the third country or international organisation concerned with a view to remedying the lack of an adequate level of protection.

(6) The Secretary of State must publish—

(a) a list of the third countries, territories and specified sectors within a third country and international organisations, and the descriptions of such countries, territories, sectors and organisations, which are for the time being specified in regulations under section 17A, and

(b) a list of the third countries, territories and specified sectors within a third country and international organisations, and the descriptions of such countries, territories, sectors and organisations, which have been but are no longer specified in such regulations.

(7) In the case of regulations under section 17A which specify that an adequate level of protection of personal data is ensured only for a transfer specified or described in the regulations—

(a) the duty under subsection (1) is only to carry out a review of the level of protection ensured for such a transfer, and

(b) the lists published under subsection (6) must specify or describe the relevant transfers.]

NOTES

Commencement: IP completion day (as defined in the European Union (Withdrawal Agreement) Act 2020, s 39).

Inserted as noted to s 17A at **[1.87]**.

[1.89]

[17C Standard data protection clauses

(1) The Secretary of State may by regulations specify standard data protection clauses which the Secretary of State considers provide appropriate safeguards for the purposes of transfers of personal data to a third country or an international organisation in reliance on Article 46 of the UK GDPR (and see also section 119A).

(2) The Secretary of State must keep under review the standard data protection clauses specified in regulations under this section that are for the time being in force.

(3) Regulations under this section are subject to the negative resolution procedure.]

NOTES

Commencement: IP completion day (as defined in the European Union (Withdrawal Agreement) Act 2020, s 39).
Inserted as noted to s 17A at **[1.87]**.

Transfers of personal data to third countries etc

[1.90]
18 Transfers of personal data to third countries etc[: public interest]
(1) The Secretary of State may by regulations specify, for the purposes of Article 49(1)(d) of the [UK GDPR]—
  (a) circumstances in which a transfer of personal data to a third country or international organisation is to be taken to be necessary for important reasons of public interest, and
  (b) circumstances in which a transfer of personal data to a third country or international organisation which is not required by an enactment is not to be taken to be necessary for important reasons of public interest.

(2) The Secretary of State may by regulations restrict the transfer of a category of personal data to a third country or international organisation where—
  [(a) the transfer cannot take place based on adequacy regulations (see section 17A),] and
  (b) the Secretary of State considers the restriction to be necessary for important reasons of public interest.

(3) Regulations under this section—
  (a) are subject to the made affirmative resolution procedure where the Secretary of State has made an urgency statement in respect of them;
  (b) are otherwise subject to the affirmative resolution procedure.

(4) For the purposes of this section, an urgency statement is a reasoned statement that the Secretary of State considers it desirable for the regulations to come into force without delay.

NOTES

Commencement: 25 May 2018 (see also the introductory notes to this Act preceding s 1 at **[1.71]**).

The words in square brackets in the heading were inserted and words in square brackets in sub-ss (1), (2) were substituted, by the Data Protection, Privacy and Electronic Communications (Amendments etc) (EU Exit) Regulations 2019, SI 2019/419, reg 4, Sch 2, paras 1, 24.

Specific processing situations

[1.91]
19 Processing for archiving, research and statistical purposes: safeguards
(1) This section makes provision about—
  (a) processing of personal data that is necessary for archiving purposes in the public interest,
  (b) processing of personal data that is necessary for scientific or historical research purposes, and
  (c) processing of personal data that is necessary for statistical purposes.

(2) Such processing does not satisfy the requirement in Article 89(1) of the [UK GDPR] for the processing to be subject to appropriate safeguards for the rights and freedoms of the data subject if it is likely to cause substantial damage or substantial distress to a data subject.

(3) Such processing does not satisfy that requirement if the processing is carried out for the purposes of measures or decisions with respect to a particular data subject, unless the purposes for which the processing is necessary include the purposes of approved medical research.

(4) In this section—
"approved medical research" means medical research carried out by a person who has approval to carry out that research from—
  (a) a research ethics committee recognised or established by the Health Research Authority under Chapter 2 of Part 3 of the Care Act 2014, or
  (b) a body appointed by any of the following for the purpose of assessing the ethics of research involving individuals—
    (i) the Secretary of State, the Scottish Ministers, the Welsh Ministers, or a Northern Ireland department;
    (ii) a relevant NHS body;
    (iii) United Kingdom Research and Innovation or a body that is a Research Council for the purposes of the Science and Technology Act 1965;
    (iv) an institution that is a research institution for the purposes of Chapter 4A of Part 7 of the Income Tax (Earnings and Pensions) Act 2003 (see section 457 of that Act);
"relevant NHS body" means—
  (a) an NHS trust or NHS foundation trust in England,
  (b) an NHS trust or Local Health Board in Wales,
  (c) a Health Board or Special Health Board constituted under section 2 of the National Health Service (Scotland) Act 1978,
  (d) the Common Services Agency for the Scottish Health Service, or
  (e) any of the health and social care bodies in Northern Ireland falling within paragraphs (a) to (e) of section 1(5) of the Health and Social Care (Reform) Act (Northern Ireland) 2009 (c 1 (NI)).

(5) The Secretary of State may by regulations change the meaning of "approved medical research" for the purposes of this section, including by amending subsection (4).

(6) Regulations under subsection (5) are subject to the affirmative resolution procedure.

NOTES

Commencement: 25 May 2018 (see also the introductory notes to this Act preceding s 1 at **[1.71]**).

Sub-s (2): words in square brackets substituted by the Data Protection, Privacy and Electronic Communications (Amendments etc) (EU Exit) Regulations 2019, SI 2019/419, reg 4, Sch 2, paras 1, 25.

Minor definition

[1.92]

20 Meaning of "court"

Section 5(1) (terms used in [this Part] to have the same meaning as in the [UK GDPR]) does not apply to references in [this Part] to a court and, accordingly, such references do not include a tribunal.

NOTES

Commencement: 25 May 2018 (see also the introductory notes to this Act preceding s 1 at **[1.71]**).

Words in square brackets substituted by the Data Protection, Privacy and Electronic Communications (Amendments etc) (EU Exit) Regulations 2019, SI 2019/419, reg 4, Sch 2, paras 1, 26.

CHAPTER 3 [EXEMPTIONS FOR MANUAL UNSTRUCTURED PROCESSING AND FOR NATIONAL SECURITY AND DEFENCE PURPOSES]

NOTES

Chapter heading substituted by the Data Protection, Privacy and Electronic Communications (Amendments etc) (EU Exit) Regulations 2019, SI 2019/419, reg 4, Sch 2, paras 1, 27.

[Definitions]

NOTES

Heading substituted by the Data Protection, Privacy and Electronic Communications (Amendments etc) (EU Exit) Regulations 2019, SI 2019/419 reg 4, Sch 2, paras 1, 20.

[1.93]

21 [Definitions]

(1)–(4) . . .

(5) In this Chapter, "FOI public authority" means—

    (a) a public authority as defined in the Freedom of Information Act 2000, or

    (b) a Scottish public authority as defined in the Freedom of Information (Scotland) Act 2002 (asp 13).

(6) References in this Chapter to personal data "held" by an FOI public authority are to be interpreted—

    (a) in relation to England and Wales and Northern Ireland, in accordance with section 3(2) of the Freedom of Information Act 2000, and

    (b) in relation to Scotland, in accordance with section 3(2), (4) and (5) of the Freedom of Information (Scotland) Act 2002 (asp 13),

but such references do not include information held by an intelligence service (as defined in section 82) on behalf of an FOI public authority.

(7) But personal data is not to be treated as "held" by an FOI public authority for the purposes of this Chapter, where—

    (a) section 7 of the Freedom of Information Act 2000 prevents Parts 1 to 5 of that Act from applying to the personal data, or

    (b) section 7(1) of the Freedom of Information (Scotland) Act 2002 (asp 13) prevents that Act from applying to the personal data.

NOTES

Commencement: 25 May 2018 (see also the introductory notes to this Act preceding s 1 at **[1.71]**).

The heading was substituted and sub-ss (1)–(4) were repealed by the Data Protection, Privacy and Electronic Communications (Amendments etc) (EU Exit) Regulations 2019, SI 2019/419, reg 4, Sch 2, paras 1, 29.

22, 23 *(Repealed by the Data Protection, Privacy and Electronic Communications (Amendments etc) (EU Exit) Regulations 2019, SI 2019/419, reg 4, Sch 2, paras 1, 30, 31.)*

Exemptions etc

[1.94]

24 Manual unstructured data held by FOI public authorities

(1) The provisions of [the UK GDPR] and this Act listed in subsection (2) do not apply to personal data to which [the UK GDPR] applies by virtue of [Article 2(1A)] (manual unstructured personal data held by FOI public authorities).

(2) Those provisions are—

    (a) in Chapter II of [the UK GDPR] (principles)—

        (i) Article 5(1)(a) to (c), (e) and (f) (principles relating to processing, other than the accuracy principle),

        (ii) Article 6 (lawfulness),

        (iii) Article 7 (conditions for consent),

        (iv) Article 8(1) and (2) (child's consent),

        (v) Article 9 (processing of special categories of personal data),

        (vi) Article 10 (data relating to criminal convictions etc), and

        (vii) Article 11(2) (processing not requiring identification);

    (b) in Chapter III of [the UK GDPR] (rights of the data subject)—

        (i) Article 13(1) to (3) (personal data collected from data subject: information to be provided),

        (ii) Article 14(1) to (4) (personal data collected other than from data subject: information to be provided),

      (iii)   Article 20 (right to data portability), and
      (iv)   Article 21(1) (objections to processing);
  (c)   in Chapter V of [the UK GDPR], Articles 44 to 49 (transfers of personal data to third countries or international organisations);
  [(ca) in Part 2 of this Act, sections 17A, 17B and 17C (transfers to third countries);
  (cb) in Part 5 of this Act, section 119A (standard clauses for transfers to third countries);]
  [(d) in Part 7 of this Act, sections 170 and 171 (offences relating to personal data)]
(see also paragraph 1(2) of Schedule 18).

(3) In addition, the provisions of [the UK GDPR] listed in subsection (4) do not apply to personal data to which [the UK GDPR] applies by virtue of [Article 2(1A)] where the personal data relates to appointments, removals, pay, discipline, superannuation or other personnel matters in relation to—
  (a) service in any of the armed forces of the Crown;
  (b) service in any office or employment under the Crown or under any public authority;
  (c) service in any office or employment, or under any contract for services, in respect of which power to take action, or to determine or approve the action taken, in such matters is vested in—
      (i)   Her Majesty,
      (ii)   a Minister of the Crown,
      (iii)   the National Assembly for Wales,
      (iv)   the Welsh Ministers,
      (v)   a Northern Ireland Minister (within the meaning of the Freedom of Information Act 2000), or
      (vi)   an FOI public authority.

(4) Those provisions are—
  (a) the remaining provisions of Chapters II and III (principles and rights of the data subject);
  (b) Chapter IV (controller and processor);
  (c) Chapter IX (specific processing situations).

(5) A controller is not obliged to comply with Article 15(1) to (3) of [the UK GDPR] (right of access by the data subject) in relation to personal data to which [the UK GDPR] applies by virtue of [Article 2(1A)] if—
  (a) the request under [Article 15] does not contain a description of the personal data, or
  (b) the controller estimates that the cost of complying with the request so far as relating to the personal data would exceed the appropriate maximum.

(6) Subsection (5)(b) does not remove the controller's obligation to confirm whether or not personal data concerning the data subject is being processed unless the estimated cost of complying with that obligation alone in relation to the personal data would exceed the appropriate maximum.

(7) An estimate for the purposes of this section must be made in accordance with regulations under section 12(5) of the Freedom of Information Act 2000.

(8) In subsections (5) and (6), "the appropriate maximum" means the maximum amount specified by the Secretary of State by regulations.

(9) Regulations under subsection (8) are subject to the negative resolution procedure.

NOTES

Commencement: 25 May 2018 (see also the introductory notes to this Act preceding s 1 at **[1.71]**).

Sub-ss (1), (4), (5): words in square brackets substituted by the Data Protection, Privacy and Electronic Communications (Amendments etc) (EU Exit) Regulations 2019, SI 2019/419, reg 4, Sch 2, paras 1, 32(1), (2), (4), (5).

Sub-s (2): words in square brackets in paras (a)–(c) substituted, paras (ca), (cb) inserted, and para (d) substituted, by SI 2019/419, reg 4, Sch 2, paras 1, 32(1), (3).

National Assembly for Wales: see further, in relation to the renaming of the National Assembly for Wales as the Senedd Cymru or the Welsh Parliament, the Senedd and Elections (Wales) Act 2020, s 2 (with effect from 6 May 2020). See also ss 3–9 of the 2020 Act in relation to the renaming of Acts of the National Assembly for Wales, Members of the National Assembly for Wales, etc.

[1.95]
25 Manual unstructured data used in longstanding historical research

(1) The provisions of [the UK GDPR] listed in subsection (2) do not apply to personal data to which [the UK GDPR] applies by virtue of [Article 2(1A)] (manual unstructured personal data held by FOI public authorities) at any time when—
  (a) the personal data—
      (i)   is subject to processing which was already underway immediately before 24 October 1998, and
      (ii)   is processed only for the purposes of historical research, and
  (b) the processing is not carried out—
      (i)   for the purposes of measures or decisions with respect to a particular data subject, or
      (ii)   in a way that causes, or is likely to cause, substantial damage or substantial distress to a data subject.

(2) Those provisions are—
  (a) in Chapter II . . . (principles), Article 5(1)(d) (the accuracy principle), and
  (b) in Chapter III . . . (rights of the data subject)—
      (i)   Article 16 (right to rectification), and
      (ii)   Article 17(1) and (2) (right to erasure).

(3) The exemptions in this section apply in addition to the exemptions in section 24.

NOTES

Commencement: 25 May 2018 (see also the introductory notes to this Act preceding s 1 at **[1.71]**).

The words in square brackets in sub-s (1) were substituted and the words omitted from sub-s (2) were repealed, by the Data Protection, Privacy and Electronic Communications (Amendments etc) (EU Exit) Regulations 2019, SI 2019/419, reg 4, Sch 2, paras 1, 33.

[1.96]
26   National security and defence exemption
(1)   A provision of [the UK GDPR] or this Act mentioned in subsection (2) does not apply to personal data to which [the UK GDPR] applies if exemption from the provision is required for—
  (a)   the purpose of safeguarding national security, or
  (b)   defence purposes.
(2)   The provisions are—
  (a)   Chapter II of [the UK GDPR] (principles) except for—
      (i)   Article 5(1)(a) (lawful, fair and transparent processing), so far as it requires processing of personal data to be lawful;
      (ii)   Article 6 (lawfulness of processing);
      (iii)   Article 9 (processing of special categories of personal data);
  (b)   Chapter III of [the UK GDPR] (rights of data subjects);
  (c)   in Chapter IV of [the UK GDPR]—
      (i)   Article 33 (notification of personal data breach to the Commissioner);
      (ii)   Article 34 (communication of personal data breach to the data subject);
  (d)   Chapter V of [the UK GDPR] (transfers of personal data to third countries or international organisations);
  (e)   in Chapter VI of [the UK GDPR]—
      (i)   Article 57(1)(a) and (h) (Commissioner's duties to monitor and enforce [the UK GDPR] and to conduct investigations);
      (ii)   Article 58 (investigative, corrective, authorisation and advisory powers of Commissioner);
  (f)   Chapter VIII of [the UK GDPR] (remedies, liabilities and penalties) except for—
      (i)   Article 83 (general conditions for imposing administrative fines);
      (ii)   Article 84 (penalties);
  [(fa) in Part 2 of this Act, sections 17A, 17D and 17C (transfers to third countries)]
  (g)   in Part 5 of this Act—
      (i)   in section 115 (general functions of the Commissioner), subsections (3) and (8);
      (ii)   in section 115, subsection (9), so far as it relates to Article 58(2)(i) of [the UK GDPR];
      (iii)   section 119 (inspection in accordance with international obligations);
      [(iv)   section 119A (standard clauses for transfers to third countries);]
  (h)   in Part 6 of this Act—
      (i)   sections 142 to 154 and Schedule 15 (Commissioner's notices and powers of entry and inspection);
      (ii)   sections 170 to 173 (offences relating to personal data);
  (i)   in Part 7 of this Act, section 187 (representation of data subjects).

NOTES
  Commencement: 25 May 2018 (see also the introductory notes to this Act preceding s 1 at **[1.71]**).
  The words "the UK GDPR" in each place they appear in square brackets were substituted, and in sub-s (2), paras (fa), (g)(iv) were inserted, by the Data Protection, Privacy and Electronic Communications (Amendments etc) (EU Exit) Regulations 2019, SI 2019/419, reg 4, Sch 2, paras 1, 34.

[1.97]
27   National security: certificate
(1)   Subject to subsection (3), a certificate signed by a Minister of the Crown certifying that exemption from all or any of the provisions listed in section 26(2) is, or at any time was, required in relation to any personal data for the purpose of safeguarding national security is conclusive evidence of that fact.
(2)   A certificate under subsection (1)—
  (a)   may identify the personal data to which it applies by means of a general description, and
  (b)   may be expressed to have prospective effect.
(3)   Any person directly affected by a certificate under subsection (1) may appeal to the Tribunal against the certificate.
(4)   If, on an appeal under subsection (3), the Tribunal finds that, applying the principles applied by a court on an application for judicial review, the Minister did not have reasonable grounds for issuing a certificate, the Tribunal may—
  (a)   allow the appeal, and
  (b)   quash the certificate.
(5)   Where, in any proceedings under or by virtue of [the UK GDPR] or this Act, it is claimed by a controller that a certificate under subsection (1) which identifies the personal data to which it applies by means of a general description applies to any personal data, another party to the proceedings may appeal to the Tribunal on the ground that the certificate does not apply to the personal data in question.
(6)   But, subject to any determination under subsection (7), the certificate is to be conclusively presumed so to apply.
(7)   On an appeal under subsection (5), the Tribunal may determine that the certificate does not so apply.
(8)   A document purporting to be a certificate under subsection (1) is to be—
  (a)   received in evidence, and
  (b)   deemed to be such a certificate unless the contrary is proved.
(9)   A document which purports to be certified by or on behalf of a Minister of the Crown as a true copy of a certificate issued by that Minister under subsection (1) is—
  (a)   in any legal proceedings, evidence of that certificate;
  (b)   in any legal proceedings in Scotland, sufficient evidence of that certificate.
(10) The power conferred by subsection (1) on a Minister of the Crown is exercisable only by—
  (a)   a Minister who is a member of the Cabinet, or
  (b)   the Attorney General or the Advocate General for Scotland.

NOTES
Commencement: 25 May 2018 (see also the introductory notes to this Act preceding s 1 at **[1.71]**).
Sub-s (5): words in square brackets substituted by the Data Protection, Privacy and Electronic Communications (Amendments etc) (EU Exit) Regulations 2019, SI 2019/419, reg 4, Sch 2, paras 1, 35.

[1.98]
28   National security and defence: modifications to Articles 9 and 32 of the [UK GDPR]
(1) Article 9(1) of [the UK GDPR] (prohibition on processing of special categories of personal data) does not prohibit the processing of personal data to which [the UK GDPR] applies to the extent that the processing is carried out—
  (a)   for the purpose of safeguarding national security or for defence purposes, and
  (b)   with appropriate safeguards for the rights and freedoms of data subjects.
(2) Article 32 of [the UK GDPR] (security of processing) does not apply to a controller or processor to the extent that the controller or the processor (as the case may be) is processing personal data to which [the UK GDPR] applies for—
  (a)   the purpose of safeguarding national security, or
  (b)   defence purposes.
(3) Where Article 32 of [the UK GDPR] does not apply, the controller or the processor must implement security measures appropriate to the risks arising from the processing of the personal data.
(4) For the purposes of subsection (3), where the processing of personal data is carried out wholly or partly by automated means, the controller or the processor must, following an evaluation of the risks, implement measures designed to—
  (a)   prevent unauthorised processing or unauthorised interference with the systems used in connection with the processing,
  (b)   ensure that it is possible to establish the precise details of any processing that takes place,
  (c)   ensure that any systems used in connection with the processing function properly and may, in the case of interruption, be restored, and
  (d)   ensure that stored personal data cannot be corrupted if a system used in connection with the processing malfunctions.
[(5) The functions conferred on the Commissioner in relation to the UK GDPR by Articles 57(1)(a), (d), (e), (h) and (u) and 58(1)(d) and (2)(a) to (d) of the UK GDPR (which are subject to safeguards set out in section 115) include functions in relation to subsection (3).]

NOTES
Commencement: 25 May 2018 (see also the introductory notes to this Act preceding s 1 at **[1.71]**).
The words in square brackets in the heading and in sub-ss (1)–(3) were substituted, and sub-s (5) was added, by the Data Protection, Privacy and Electronic Communications (Amendments etc) (EU Exit) Regulations 2019, SI 2019/419, reg 4, Sch 2, paras 1, 36.

PART 3   LAW ENFORCEMENT PROCESSING
CHAPTER 1   SCOPE AND DEFINITIONS
Scope

[1.99]
29   Processing to which this Part applies
(1) This Part applies to—
  (a)   the processing by a competent authority of personal data wholly or partly by automated means, and
  (b)   the processing by a competent authority otherwise than by automated means of personal data which forms part of a filing system or is intended to form part of a filing system.
(2) Any reference in this Part to the processing of personal data is to processing to which this Part applies.
(3) For the meaning of "competent authority", see section 30.

NOTES
Commencement: 25 May 2018 (see also the introductory notes to this Act preceding s 1 at **[1.71]**).

Definitions

[1.100]
30   Meaning of "competent authority"
(1) In this Part, "competent authority" means—
  (a)   a person specified or described in Schedule 7, and
  (b)   any other person if and to the extent that the person has statutory functions for any of the law enforcement purposes.
(2) But an intelligence service is not a competent authority within the meaning of this Part.
(3) The Secretary of State may by regulations amend Schedule 7—
  (a)   so as to add or remove a person or description of person;
  (b)   so as to reflect any change in the name of a person specified in the Schedule.
(4) Regulations under subsection (3) which make provision of the kind described in subsection (3)(a) may also make consequential amendments of section 73(4)(b).
(5) Regulations under subsection (3) which make provision of the kind described in subsection (3)(a), or which make provision of that kind and of the kind described in subsection (3)(b), are subject to the affirmative resolution procedure.
(6) Regulations under subsection (3) which make provision only of the kind described in subsection (3)(b) are subject to the negative resolution procedure.
(7) In this section—

"intelligence service" means—
- (a) the Security Service;
- (b) the Secret Intelligence Service;
- (c) the Government Communications Headquarters;

"statutory function" means a function under or by virtue of an enactment.

NOTES

Commencement: 25 May 2018 (see also the introductory notes to this Act preceding s 1 at **[1.71]**).

[1.101]
31 "The law enforcement purposes"

For the purposes of this Part, "the law enforcement purposes" are the purposes of the prevention, investigation, detection or prosecution of criminal offences or the execution of criminal penalties, including the safeguarding against and the prevention of threats to public security.

NOTES

Commencement: 25 May 2018 (see also the introductory notes to this Act preceding s 1 at **[1.71]**).

[1.102]
32 Meaning of "controller" and "processor"

(1) In this Part, "controller" means the competent authority which, alone or jointly with others—
- (a) determines the purposes and means of the processing of personal data, or
- (b) is the controller by virtue of subsection (2).

(2) Where personal data is processed only—
- (a) for purposes for which it is required by an enactment to be processed, and
- (b) by means by which it is required by an enactment to be processed,

the competent authority on which the obligation to process the data is imposed by the enactment (or, if different, one of the enactments) is the controller.

(3) In this Part, "processor" means any person who processes personal data on behalf of the controller (other than a person who is an employee of the controller).

NOTES

Commencement: 25 May 2018 (see also the introductory notes to this Act preceding s 1 at **[1.71]**).

[1.103]
33 Other definitions

(1) This section defines certain other expressions used in this Part.

(2) "Employee", in relation to any person, includes an individual who holds a position (whether paid or unpaid) under the direction and control of that person.

(3) "Personal data breach" means a breach of security leading to the accidental or unlawful destruction, loss, alteration, unauthorised disclosure of, or access to, personal data transmitted, stored or otherwise processed.

(4) "Profiling" means any form of automated processing of personal data consisting of the use of personal data to evaluate certain personal aspects relating to an individual, in particular to analyse or predict aspects concerning that individual's performance at work, economic situation, health, personal preferences, interests, reliability, behaviour, location or movements.

(5) "Recipient", in relation to any personal data, means any person to whom the data is disclosed, whether a third party or not, but it does not include a public authority to whom disclosure is or may be made in the framework of a particular inquiry in accordance with the law.

(6) "Restriction of processing" means the marking of stored personal data with the aim of limiting its processing for the future.

(7) "Third country" means a country or territory [outside the United Kingdom].

(8) Sections 3 and 205 include definitions of other expressions used in this Part.

NOTES

Commencement: 25 May 2018 (see also the introductory notes to this Act preceding s 1 at **[1.71]**).

Sub-s (7): words in square brackets substituted by the Data Protection, Privacy and Electronic Communications (Amendments etc) (EU Exit) Regulations 2019, SI 2019/419, reg 4, Sch 2, paras 1, 37.

CHAPTER 2 PRINCIPLES

[1.104]
34 Overview and general duty of controller

(1) This Chapter sets out the six data protection principles as follows—
- (a) section 35(1) sets out the first data protection principle (requirement that processing be lawful and fair);
- (b) section 36(1) sets out the second data protection principle (requirement that purposes of processing be specified, explicit and legitimate);
- (c) section 37 sets out the third data protection principle (requirement that personal data be adequate, relevant and not excessive);
- (d) section 38(1) sets out the fourth data protection principle (requirement that personal data be accurate and kept up to date);
- (e) section 39(1) sets out the fifth data protection principle (requirement that personal data be kept for no longer than is necessary);
- (f) section 40 sets out the sixth data protection principle (requirement that personal data be processed in a secure manner).

(2) In addition—

(a) each of sections 35, 36, 38 and 39 makes provision to supplement the principle to which it relates, and

(b) sections 41 and 42 make provision about the safeguards that apply in relation to certain types of processing.

(3) The controller in relation to personal data is responsible for, and must be able to demonstrate, compliance with this Chapter.

NOTES

Commencement: 25 May 2018 (see also the introductory notes to this Act preceding s 1 at **[1.71]**).

[1.105]
35   The first data protection principle
(1) The first data protection principle is that the processing of personal data for any of the law enforcement purposes must be lawful and fair.

(2) The processing of personal data for any of the law enforcement purposes is lawful only if and to the extent that it is based on law and either—

(a) the data subject has given consent to the processing for that purpose, or

(b) the processing is necessary for the performance of a task carried out for that purpose by a competent authority.

(3) In addition, where the processing for any of the law enforcement purposes is sensitive processing, the processing is permitted only in the two cases set out in subsections (4) and (5).

(4) The first case is where—

(a) the data subject has given consent to the processing for the law enforcement purpose as mentioned in subsection (2)(a), and

(b) at the time when the processing is carried out, the controller has an appropriate policy document in place (see section 42).

(5) The second case is where—

(a) the processing is strictly necessary for the law enforcement purpose,

(b) the processing meets at least one of the conditions in Schedule 8, and

(c) at the time when the processing is carried out, the controller has an appropriate policy document in place (see section 42).

(6) The Secretary of State may by regulations amend Schedule 8—

(a) by adding conditions;

(b) by omitting conditions added by regulations under paragraph (a).

(7) Regulations under subsection (6) are subject to the affirmative resolution procedure.

(8) In this section, "sensitive processing" means—

(a) the processing of personal data revealing racial or ethnic origin, political opinions, religious or philosophical beliefs or trade union membership;

(b) the processing of genetic data, or of biometric data, for the purpose of uniquely identifying an individual;

(c) the processing of data concerning health;

(d) the processing of data concerning an individual's sex life or sexual orientation.

NOTES

Commencement: 25 May 2018 (see also the introductory notes to this Act preceding s 1 at **[1.71]**).

[1.106]
36   The second data protection principle
(1) The second data protection principle is that—

(a) the law enforcement purpose for which personal data is collected on any occasion must be specified, explicit and legitimate, and

(b) personal data so collected must not be processed in a manner that is incompatible with the purpose for which it was collected.

(2) Paragraph (b) of the second data protection principle is subject to subsections (3) and (4).

(3) Personal data collected for a law enforcement purpose may be processed for any other law enforcement purpose (whether by the controller that collected the data or by another controller) provided that—

(a) the controller is authorised by law to process the data for the other purpose, and

(b) the processing is necessary and proportionate to that other purpose.

(4) Personal data collected for any of the law enforcement purposes may not be processed for a purpose that is not a law enforcement purpose unless the processing is authorised by law.

NOTES

Commencement: 25 May 2018 (see also the introductory notes to this Act preceding s 1 at **[1.71]**).

[1.107]
37   The third data protection principle
The third data protection principle is that personal data processed for any of the law enforcement purposes must be adequate, relevant and not excessive in relation to the purpose for which it is processed.

NOTES

Commencement: 25 May 2018 (see also the introductory notes to this Act preceding s 1 at **[1.71]**).

[1.108]
38   The fourth data protection principle
(1) The fourth data protection principle is that—

(a) personal data processed for any of the law enforcement purposes must be accurate and, where necessary, kept up to date, and

(b)   every reasonable step must be taken to ensure that personal data that is inaccurate, having regard to the law enforcement purpose for which it is processed, is erased or rectified without delay.

(2) In processing personal data for any of the law enforcement purposes, personal data based on facts must, so far as possible, be distinguished from personal data based on personal assessments.

(3) In processing personal data for any of the law enforcement purposes, a clear distinction must, where relevant and as far as possible, be made between personal data relating to different categories of data subject, such as—

(a)   persons suspected of having committed or being about to commit a criminal offence;

(b)   persons convicted of a criminal offence;

(c)   persons who are or may be victims of a criminal offence;

(d)   witnesses or other persons with information about offences.

(4) All reasonable steps must be taken to ensure that personal data which is inaccurate, incomplete or no longer up to date is not transmitted or made available for any of the law enforcement purposes.

(5) For that purpose—

(a)   the quality of personal data must be verified before it is transmitted or made available,

(b)   in all transmissions of personal data, the necessary information enabling the recipient to assess the degree of accuracy, completeness and reliability of the data and the extent to which it is up to date must be included, and

(c)   if, after personal data has been transmitted, it emerges that the data was incorrect or that the transmission was unlawful, the recipient must be notified without delay.

NOTES

Commencement: 25 May 2018 (see also the introductory notes to this Act preceding s 1 at **[1.71]**).

[1.109]
39   The fifth data protection principle

(1) The fifth data protection principle is that personal data processed for any of the law enforcement purposes must be kept for no longer than is necessary for the purpose for which it is processed.

(2) Appropriate time limits must be established for the periodic review of the need for the continued storage of personal data for any of the law enforcement purposes.

NOTES

Commencement: 25 May 2018 (see also the introductory notes to this Act preceding s 1 at **[1.71]**).

[1.110]
40   The sixth data protection principle

The sixth data protection principle is that personal data processed for any of the law enforcement purposes must be so processed in a manner that ensures appropriate security of the personal data, using appropriate technical or organisational measures (and, in this principle, "appropriate security" includes protection against unauthorised or unlawful processing and against accidental loss, destruction or damage).

NOTES

Commencement: 25 May 2018 (see also the introductory notes to this Act preceding s 1 at **[1.71]**).

[1.111]
41   Safeguards: archiving

(1) This section applies in relation to the processing of personal data for a law enforcement purpose where the processing is necessary—

(a)   for archiving purposes in the public interest,

(b)   for scientific or historical research purposes, or

(c)   for statistical purposes.

(2) The processing is not permitted if—

(a)   it is carried out for the purposes of, or in connection with, measures or decisions with respect to a particular data subject, or

(b)   it is likely to cause substantial damage or substantial distress to a data subject.

NOTES

Commencement: 25 May 2018 (see also the introductory notes to this Act preceding s 1 at **[1.71]**).

[1.112]
42   Safeguards: sensitive processing

(1) This section applies for the purposes of section 35(4) and (5) (which require a controller to have an appropriate policy document in place when carrying out sensitive processing in reliance on the consent of the data subject or, as the case may be, in reliance on a condition specified in Schedule 8).

(2) The controller has an appropriate policy document in place in relation to the sensitive processing if the controller has produced a document which—

(a)   explains the controller's procedures for securing compliance with the data protection principles (see section 34(1)) in connection with sensitive processing in reliance on the consent of the data subject or (as the case may be) in reliance on the condition in question, and

(b)   explains the controller's policies as regards the retention and erasure of personal data processed in reliance on the consent of the data subject or (as the case may be) in reliance on the condition in question, giving an indication of how long such personal data is likely to be retained.

(3) Where personal data is processed on the basis that an appropriate policy document is in place, the controller must during the relevant period—

(a)   retain the appropriate policy document,

(b)   review and (if appropriate) update it from time to time, and

(c) make it available to the Commissioner, on request, without charge.

(4) The record maintained by the controller under section 61(1) and, where the sensitive processing is carried out by a processor on behalf of the controller, the record maintained by the processor under section 61(3) must include the following information—

(a) whether the sensitive processing is carried out in reliance on the consent of the data subject or, if not, which condition in Schedule 8 is relied on,

(b) how the processing satisfies section 35 (lawfulness of processing), and

(c) whether the personal data is retained and erased in accordance with the policies described in subsection (2)(b) and, if it is not, the reasons for not following those policies.

(5) In this section, "relevant period", in relation to sensitive processing in reliance on the consent of the data subject or in reliance on a condition specified in Schedule 8, means a period which—

(a) begins when the controller starts to carry out the sensitive processing in reliance on the data subject's consent or (as the case may be) in reliance on that condition, and

(b) ends at the end of the period of 6 months beginning when the controller ceases to carry out the processing.

NOTES

Commencement: 25 May 2018 (see also the introductory notes to this Act preceding s 1 at **[1.71]**).

CHAPTER 3 RIGHTS OF THE DATA SUBJECT

Overview and scope

[1.113]
43 Overview and scope
(1) This Chapter—

(a) imposes general duties on the controller to make information available (see section 44);

(b) confers a right of access by the data subject (see section 45);

(c) confers rights on the data subject with respect to the rectification of personal data and the erasure of personal data or the restriction of its processing (see sections 46 to 48);

(d) regulates automated decision-making (see sections 49 and 50);

(e) makes supplementary provision (see sections 51 to 54).

(2) This Chapter applies only in relation to the processing of personal data for a law enforcement purpose.

(3) But sections 44 to 48 do not apply in relation to the processing of relevant personal data in the course of a criminal investigation or criminal proceedings, including proceedings for the purpose of executing a criminal penalty.

(4) In subsection (3), "relevant personal data" means personal data contained in a judicial decision or in other documents relating to the investigation or proceedings which are created by or on behalf of a court or other judicial authority.

(5) In this Chapter, "the controller", in relation to a data subject, means the controller in relation to personal data relating to the data subject.

NOTES

Commencement: 25 May 2018 (see also the introductory notes to this Act preceding s 1 at **[1.71]**).

Information: controller's general duties

[1.114]
44 Information: controller's general duties
(1) The controller must make available to data subjects the following information (whether by making the information generally available to the public or in any other way)—

(a) the identity and the contact details of the controller;

(b) where applicable, the contact details of the data protection officer (see sections 69 to 71);

(c) the purposes for which the controller processes personal data;

(d) the existence of the rights of data subjects to request from the controller—

(i) access to personal data (see section 45),

(ii) rectification of personal data (see section 46), and

(iii) erasure of personal data or the restriction of its processing (see section 47);

(e) the existence of the right to lodge a complaint with the Commissioner and the contact details of the Commissioner.

(2) The controller must also, in specific cases for the purpose of enabling the exercise of a data subject's rights under this Part, give the data subject the following—

(a) information about the legal basis for the processing;

(b) information about the period for which the personal data will be stored or, where that is not possible, about the criteria used to determine that period;

(c) where applicable, information about the categories of recipients of the personal data (including recipients in third countries or international organisations);

(d) such further information as is necessary to enable the exercise of the data subject's rights under this Part.

(3) An example of where further information may be necessary as mentioned in subsection (2)(d) is where the personal data being processed was collected without the knowledge of the data subject.

(4) The controller may restrict, wholly or partly, the provision of information to the data subject under subsection (2) to the extent that and for so long as the restriction is, having regard to the fundamental rights and legitimate interests of the data subject, a necessary and proportionate measure to—

(a) avoid obstructing an official or legal inquiry, investigation or procedure;

(b) avoid prejudicing the prevention, detection, investigation or prosecution of criminal offences or the execution of criminal penalties;

(c) protect public security;

(d)   protect national security;

(e)   protect the rights and freedoms of others.

(5) Where the provision of information to a data subject under subsection (2) is restricted, wholly or partly, the controller must inform the data subject in writing without undue delay—

(a)   that the provision of information has been restricted,

(b)   of the reasons for the restriction,

(c)   of the data subject's right to make a request to the Commissioner under section 51,

(d)   of the data subject's right to lodge a complaint with the Commissioner, and

(e)   of the data subject's right to apply to a court under section 167.

(6) Subsection (5)(a) and (b) do not apply to the extent that complying with them would undermine the purpose of the restriction.

(7) The controller must—

(a)   record the reasons for a decision to restrict (whether wholly or partly) the provision of information to a data subject under subsection (2), and

(b)   if requested to do so by the Commissioner, make the record available to the Commissioner.

NOTES

Commencement: 25 May 2018 (see also the introductory notes to this Act preceding s 1 at **[1.71]**).

Data subject's right of access

[1.115]

45   Right of access by the data subject

(1) A data subject is entitled to obtain from the controller—

(a)   confirmation as to whether or not personal data concerning him or her is being processed, and

(b)   where that is the case, access to the personal data and the information set out in subsection (2).

(2) That information is—

(a)   the purposes of and legal basis for the processing;

(b)   the categories of personal data concerned;

(c)   the recipients or categories of recipients to whom the personal data has been disclosed (including recipients or categories of recipients in third countries or international organisations);

(d)   the period for which it is envisaged that the personal data will be stored or, where that is not possible, the criteria used to determine that period;

(e)   the existence of the data subject's rights to request from the controller—

   (i)   rectification of personal data (see section 46), and

   (ii)   erasure of personal data or the restriction of its processing (see section 47);

(f)   the existence of the data subject's right to lodge a complaint with the Commissioner and the contact details of the Commissioner;

(g)   communication of the personal data undergoing processing and of any available information as to its origin.

(3) Where a data subject makes a request under subsection (1), the information to which the data subject is entitled must be provided in writing—

(a)   without undue delay, and

(b)   in any event, before the end of the applicable time period (as to which see section 54).

(4) The controller may restrict, wholly or partly, the rights conferred by subsection (1) to the extent that and for so long as the restriction is, having regard to the fundamental rights and legitimate interests of the data subject, a necessary and proportionate measure to—

(a)   avoid obstructing an official or legal inquiry, investigation or procedure;

(b)   avoid prejudicing the prevention, detection, investigation or prosecution of criminal offences or the execution of criminal penalties;

(c)   protect public security;

(d)   protect national security;

(e)   protect the rights and freedoms of others.

(5) Where the rights of a data subject under subsection (1) are restricted, wholly or partly, the controller must inform the data subject in writing without undue delay—

(a)   that the rights of the data subject have been restricted,

(b)   of the reasons for the restriction,

(c)   of the data subject's right to make a request to the Commissioner under section 51,

(d)   of the data subject's right to lodge a complaint with the Commissioner, and

(e)   of the data subject's right to apply to a court under section 167.

(6) Subsection (5)(a) and (b) do not apply to the extent that the provision of the information would undermine the purpose of the restriction.

(7) The controller must—

(a)   record the reasons for a decision to restrict (whether wholly or partly) the rights of a data subject under subsection (1), and

(b)   if requested to do so by the Commissioner, make the record available to the Commissioner.

NOTES

Commencement: 25 May 2018 (see also the introductory notes to this Act preceding s 1 at **[1.71]**).

Data subject's rights to rectification or erasure etc

[1.116]

46   Right to rectification

(1) The controller must, if so requested by a data subject, rectify without undue delay inaccurate personal data relating to the data subject.

(2) Where personal data is inaccurate because it is incomplete, the controller must, if so requested by a data subject, complete it.

(3) The duty under subsection (2) may, in appropriate cases, be fulfilled by the provision of a supplementary statement.

(4) Where the controller would be required to rectify personal data under this section but the personal data must be maintained for the purposes of evidence, the controller must (instead of rectifying the personal data) restrict its processing.

NOTES
Commencement: 25 May 2018 (see also the introductory notes to this Act preceding s 1 at **[1.71]**).

[1.117]
47 Right to erasure or restriction of processing
(1) The controller must erase personal data without undue delay where—
    (a) the processing of the personal data would infringe section 35, 36(1) to (3), 37, 38(1), 39(1), 40, 41 or 42, or
    (b) the controller has a legal obligation to erase the data.

(2) Where the controller would be required to erase personal data under subsection (1) but the personal data must be maintained for the purposes of evidence, the controller must (instead of erasing the personal data) restrict its processing.

(3) Where a data subject contests the accuracy of personal data (whether in making a request under this section or section 46 or in any other way), but it is not possible to ascertain whether it is accurate or not, the controller must restrict its processing.

(4) A data subject may request the controller to erase personal data or to restrict its processing (but the duties of the controller under this section apply whether or not such a request is made).

NOTES
Commencement: 25 May 2018 (see also the introductory notes to this Act preceding s 1 at **[1.71]**).

[1.118]
48 Rights under section 46 or 47: supplementary
(1) Where a data subject requests the rectification or erasure of personal data or the restriction of its processing, the controller must inform the data subject in writing—
    (a) whether the request has been granted, and
    (b) if it has been refused—
        (i) of the reasons for the refusal,
        (ii) of the data subject's right to make a request to the Commissioner under section 51,
        (iii) of the data subject's right to lodge a complaint with the Commissioner, and
        (iv) of the data subject's right to apply to a court under section 167.

(2) The controller must comply with the duty under subsection (1)—
    (a) without undue delay, and
    (b) in any event, before the end of the applicable time period (see section 54).

(3) The controller may restrict, wholly or partly, the provision of information to the data subject under subsection (1)(b)(i) to the extent that and for so long as the restriction is, having regard to the fundamental rights and legitimate interests of the data subject, a necessary and proportionate measure to—
    (a) avoid obstructing an official or legal inquiry, investigation or procedure;
    (b) avoid prejudicing the prevention, detection, investigation or prosecution of criminal offences or the execution of criminal penalties;
    (c) protect public security;
    (d) protect national security;
    (e) protect the rights and freedoms of others.

(4) Where the rights of a data subject under subsection (1) are restricted, wholly or partly, the controller must inform the data subject in writing without undue delay—
    (a) that the rights of the data subject have been restricted,
    (b) of the reasons for the restriction,
    (c) of the data subject's right to lodge a complaint with the Commissioner, and
    (d) of the data subject's right to apply to a court under section 167.

(5) Subsection (4)(a) and (b) do not apply to the extent that the provision of the information would undermine the purpose of the restriction.

(6) The controller must—
    (a) record the reasons for a decision to restrict (whether wholly or partly) the provision of information to a data subject under subsection (1)(b)(i), and
    (b) if requested to do so by the Commissioner, make the record available to the Commissioner.

(7) Where the controller rectifies personal data, it must notify the competent authority (if any) from which the inaccurate personal data originated.

(8) . . .

(9) Where the controller rectifies, erases or restricts the processing of personal data which has been disclosed by the controller—
    (a) the controller must notify the recipients, and
    (b) the recipients must similarly rectify, erase or restrict the processing of the personal data (so far as they retain responsibility for it).

(10) Where processing is restricted in accordance with section 47(3), the controller must inform the data subject before lifting the restriction.

NOTES

Commencement: 25 May 2018 (see also the introductory notes to this Act preceding s 1 at **[1.71]**).

Sub-s (8): repealed by the Data Protection, Privacy and Electronic Communications (Amendments etc) (EU Exit) Regulations 2019, SI 2019/419, reg 4, Sch 2, paras 1, 38.

Automated individual decision-making

[1.119]

49 Right not to be subject to automated decision-making

(1) A controller may not take a significant decision based solely on automated processing unless that decision is required or authorised by law.

(2) A decision is a "significant decision" for the purpose of this section if, in relation to a data subject, it—

    (a)   produces an adverse legal effect concerning the data subject, or

    (b)   significantly affects the data subject.

NOTES

Commencement: 25 May 2018 (see also the introductory notes to this Act preceding s 1 at **[1.71]**).

[1.120]

50 Automated decision-making authorised by law: safeguards

(1) A decision is a "qualifying significant decision" for the purposes of this section if—

    (a)   it is a significant decision in relation to a data subject, and

    (b)   it is required or authorised by law.

(2) Where a controller takes a qualifying significant decision in relation to a data subject based solely on automated processing—

    (a)   the controller must, as soon as reasonably practicable, notify the data subject in writing that a decision has been taken based solely on automated processing, and

    (b)   the data subject may, before the end of the period of 1 month beginning with receipt of the notification, request the controller to—

        (i)   reconsider the decision, or

        (ii)   take a new decision that is not based solely on automated processing.

(3) If a request is made to a controller under subsection (2), the controller must, before the end of the period of 1 month beginning with receipt of the request—

    (a)   consider the request, including any information provided by the data subject that is relevant to it,

    (b)   comply with the request, and

    (c)   by notice in writing inform the data subject of—

        (i)   the steps taken to comply with the request, and

        (ii)   the outcome of complying with the request.

(4) The Secretary of State may by regulations make such further provision as the Secretary of State considers appropriate to provide suitable measures to safeguard a data subject's rights, freedoms and legitimate interests in connection with the taking of qualifying significant decisions based solely on automated processing.

(5) Regulations under subsection (4)—

    (a)   may amend this section, and

    (b)   are subject to the affirmative resolution procedure.

(6) In this section "significant decision" has the meaning given by section 49(2).

NOTES

Commencement: 25 May 2018 (see also the introductory notes to this Act preceding s 1 at **[1.71]**).

Supplementary

[1.121]

51 Exercise of rights through the Commissioner

(1) This section applies where a controller—

    (a)   restricts under section 44(4) the information provided to the data subject under section 44(2) (duty of the controller to give the data subject additional information),

    (b)   restricts under section 45(4) the data subject's rights under section 45(1) (right of access), or

    (c)   refuses a request by the data subject for rectification under section 46 or for erasure or restriction of processing under section 47.

(2) The data subject may—

    (a)   where subsection (1)(a) or (b) applies, request the Commissioner to check that the restriction imposed by the controller was lawful;

    (b)   where subsection (1)(c) applies, request the Commissioner to check that the refusal of the data subject's request was lawful.

(3) The Commissioner must take such steps as appear to the Commissioner to be appropriate to respond to a request under subsection (2) (which may include the exercise of any of the powers conferred by sections 142 and 146).

(4) After taking those steps, the Commissioner must inform the data subject—

    (a)   where subsection (1)(a) or (b) applies, whether the Commissioner is satisfied that the restriction imposed by the controller was lawful;

    (b)   where subsection (1)(c) applies, whether the Commissioner is satisfied that the controller's refusal of the data subject's request was lawful.

(5) The Commissioner must also inform the data subject of the data subject's right to apply to a court under section 167.

(6) Where the Commissioner is not satisfied as mentioned in subsection (4)(a) or (b), the Commissioner may also inform the data subject of any further steps that the Commissioner is considering taking under Part 6.

NOTES
Commencement: 25 May 2018 (see also the introductory notes to this Act preceding s 1 at **[1.71]**).

[1.122]
52 Form of provision of information etc
(1) The controller must take reasonable steps to ensure that any information that is required by this Chapter to be provided to the data subject is provided in a concise, intelligible and easily accessible form, using clear and plain language.
(2) Subject to subsection (3), the information may be provided in any form, including electronic form.
(3) Where information is provided in response to a request by the data subject under section 45, 46, 47 or 50, the controller must provide the information in the same form as the request where it is practicable to do so.
(4) Where the controller has reasonable doubts about the identity of an individual making a request under section 45, 46 or 47, the controller may—
    (a) request the provision of additional information to enable the controller to confirm the identity, and
    (b) delay dealing with the request until the identity is confirmed.
(5) Subject to section 53, any information that is required by this Chapter to be provided to the data subject must be provided free of charge.
(6) The controller must facilitate the exercise of the rights of the data subject under sections 45 to 50.

NOTES
Commencement: 25 May 2018 (see also the introductory notes to this Act preceding s 1 at **[1.71]**).

[1.123]
53 Manifestly unfounded or excessive requests by the data subject
(1) Where a request from a data subject under section 45, 46, 47 or 50 is manifestly unfounded or excessive, the controller may—
    (a) charge a reasonable fee for dealing with the request, or
    (b) refuse to act on the request.
(2) An example of a request that may be excessive is one that merely repeats the substance of previous requests.
(3) In any proceedings where there is an issue as to whether a request under section 45, 46, 47 or 50 is manifestly unfounded or excessive, it is for the controller to show that it is.
(4) The Secretary of State may by regulations specify limits on the fees that a controller may charge in accordance with subsection (1)(a).
(5) Regulations under subsection (4) are subject to the negative resolution procedure.

NOTES
Commencement: 25 May 2018 (see also the introductory notes to this Act preceding s 1 at **[1.71]**).

[1.124]
54 Meaning of "applicable time period"
(1) This section defines "the applicable time period" for the purposes of sections 45(3)(b) and 48(2)(b).
(2) "The applicable time period" means the period of 1 month, or such longer period as may be specified in regulations, beginning with the relevant time.
(3) "The relevant time" means the latest of the following—
    (a) when the controller receives the request in question;
    (b) when the controller receives the information (if any) requested in connection with a request under section 52(4);
    (c) when the fee (if any) charged in connection with the request under section 53 is paid.
(4) The power to make regulations under subsection (2) is exercisable by the Secretary of State.
(5) Regulations under subsection (2) may not specify a period which is longer than 3 months.
(6) Regulations under subsection (2) are subject to the negative resolution procedure.

NOTES
Commencement: 25 May 2018 (see also the introductory notes to this Act preceding s 1 at **[1.71]**).

CHAPTER 4 CONTROLLER AND PROCESSOR
Overview and scope

[1.125]
55 Overview and scope
(1) This Chapter—
    (a) sets out the general obligations of controllers and processors (see sections 56 to 65);
    (b) sets out specific obligations of controllers and processors with respect to security (see section 66);
    (c) sets out specific obligations of controllers and processors with respect to personal data breaches (see sections 67 and 68);
    (d) makes provision for the designation, position and tasks of data protection officers (see sections 69 to 71).
(2) This Chapter applies only in relation to the processing of personal data for a law enforcement purpose.
(3) Where a controller is required by any provision of this Chapter to implement appropriate technical and organisational measures, the controller must (in deciding what measures are appropriate) take into account—
    (a) the latest developments in technology,
    (b) the cost of implementation,
    (c) the nature, scope, context and purposes of processing, and

(d)   the risks for the rights and freedoms of individuals arising from the processing.

NOTES

Commencement: 25 May 2018 (see also the introductory notes to this Act preceding s 1 at **[1.71]**).

General obligations

[1.126]
56   General obligations of the controller
(1)   Each controller must implement appropriate technical and organisational measures to ensure, and to be able to demonstrate, that the processing of personal data complies with the requirements of this Part.
(2)   Where proportionate in relation to the processing, the measures implemented to comply with the duty under subsection (1) must include appropriate data protection policies.
(3)   The technical and organisational measures implemented under subsection (1) must be reviewed and updated where necessary.

NOTES

Commencement: 25 May 2018 (see also the introductory notes to this Act preceding s 1 at **[1.71]**).

[1.127]
57   Data protection by design and default
(1)   Each controller must implement appropriate technical and organisational measures which are designed—
     (a)   to implement the data protection principles in an effective manner, and
     (b)   to integrate into the processing itself the safeguards necessary for that purpose.
(2)   The duty under subsection (1) applies both at the time of the determination of the means of processing the data and at the time of the processing itself.
(3)   Each controller must implement appropriate technical and organisational measures for ensuring that, by default, only personal data which is necessary for each specific purpose of the processing is processed.
(4)   The duty under subsection (3) applies to—
     (a)   the amount of personal data collected,
     (b)   the extent of its processing,
     (c)   the period of its storage, and
     (d)   its accessibility.
(5)   In particular, the measures implemented to comply with the duty under subsection (3) must ensure that, by default, personal data is not made accessible to an indefinite number of people without an individual's intervention.

NOTES

Commencement: 25 May 2018 (see also the introductory notes to this Act preceding s 1 at **[1.71]**).

[1.128]
58   Joint controllers
(1)   Where two or more competent authorities jointly determine the purposes and means of processing personal data, they are joint controllers for the purposes of this Part.
(2)   Joint controllers must, in a transparent manner, determine their respective responsibilities for compliance with this Part by means of an arrangement between them, except to the extent that those responsibilities are determined under or by virtue of an enactment.
(3)   The arrangement must designate the controller which is to be the contact point for data subjects.

NOTES

Commencement: 25 May 2018 (see also the introductory notes to this Act preceding s 1 at **[1.71]**).

[1.129]
59   Processors
(1)   This section applies to the use by a controller of a processor to carry out processing of personal data on behalf of the controller.
(2)   The controller may use only a processor who provides guarantees to implement appropriate technical and organisational measures that are sufficient to secure that the processing will—
     (a)   meet the requirements of this Part, and
     (b)   ensure the protection of the rights of the data subject.
(3)   The processor used by the controller may not engage another processor ("a sub-processor") without the prior written authorisation of the controller, which may be specific or general.
(4)   Where the controller gives a general written authorisation to a processor, the processor must inform the controller if the processor proposes to add to the number of sub-processors engaged by it or to replace any of them (so that the controller has the opportunity to object to the proposal).
(5)   The processing by the processor must be governed by a contract in writing between the controller and the processor setting out the following—
     (a)   the subject-matter and duration of the processing;
     (b)   the nature and purpose of the processing;
     (c)   the type of personal data and categories of data subjects involved;
     (d)   the obligations and rights of the controller and processor.
(6)   The contract must, in particular, provide that the processor must—
     (a)   act only on instructions from the controller,
     (b)   ensure that the persons authorised to process personal data are subject to an appropriate duty of confidentiality,
     (c)   assist the controller by any appropriate means to ensure compliance with the rights of the data subject under this Part,

(d) at the end of the provision of services by the processor to the controller—
    (i) either delete or return to the controller (at the choice of the controller) the personal data to which the services relate, and
    (ii) delete copies of the personal data unless subject to a legal obligation to store the copies,
(e) make available to the controller all information necessary to demonstrate compliance with this section, and
(f) comply with the requirements of this section for engaging sub-processors.

(7) The terms included in the contract in accordance with subsection (6)(a) must provide that the processor may transfer personal data to a third country or international organisation only if instructed by the controller to make the particular transfer.

(8) If a processor determines, in breach of this Part, the purposes and means of processing, the processor is to be treated for the purposes of this Part as a controller in respect of that processing.

NOTES
Commencement: 25 May 2018 (see also the introductory notes to this Act preceding s 1 at **[1.71]**).

[1.130]
60 Processing under the authority of the controller or processor
A processor, and any person acting under the authority of a controller or processor, who has access to personal data may not process the data except—
(a) on instructions from the controller, or
(b) to comply with a legal obligation.

NOTES
Commencement: 25 May 2018 (see also the introductory notes to this Act preceding s 1 at **[1.71]**).

[1.131]
61 Records of processing activities
(1) Each controller must maintain a record of all categories of processing activities for which the controller is responsible.
(2) The controller's record must contain the following information—
(a) the name and contact details of the controller;
(b) where applicable, the name and contact details of the joint controller;
(c) where applicable, the name and contact details of the data protection officer;
(d) the purposes of the processing;
(e) the categories of recipients to whom personal data has been or will be disclosed (including recipients in third countries or international organisations);
(f) a description of the categories of—
    (i) data subject, and
    (ii) personal data;
(g) where applicable, details of the use of profiling;
(h) where applicable, the categories of transfers of personal data to a third country or an international organisation;
(i) an indication of the legal basis for the processing operations, including transfers, for which the personal data is intended;
(j) where possible, the envisaged time limits for erasure of the different categories of personal data;
(k) where possible, a general description of the technical and organisational security measures referred to in section 66.
(3) Each processor must maintain a record of all categories of processing activities carried out on behalf of a controller.
(4) The processor's record must contain the following information—
(a) the name and contact details of the processor and of any other processors engaged by the processor in accordance with section 59(3);
(b) the name and contact details of the controller on behalf of which the processor is acting;
(c) where applicable, the name and contact details of the data protection officer;
(d) the categories of processing carried out on behalf of the controller;
(e) where applicable, details of transfers of personal data to a third country or an international organisation where explicitly instructed to do so by the controller, including the identification of that third country or international organisation;
(f) where possible, a general description of the technical and organisational security measures referred to in section 66.
(5) The controller and the processor must make the records kept under this section available to the Commissioner on request.

NOTES
Commencement: 25 May 2018 (see also the introductory notes to this Act preceding s 1 at **[1.71]**).

[1.132]
62 Logging
(1) A controller (or, where personal data is processed on behalf of the controller by a processor, the processor) must keep logs for at least the following processing operations in automated processing systems—
(a) collection;
(b) alteration;
(c) consultation;
(d) disclosure (including transfers);

 (e) combination;
 (f) erasure.
(2) The logs of consultation must make it possible to establish—
 (a) the justification for, and date and time of, the consultation, and
 (b) so far as possible, the identity of the person who consulted the data.
(3) The logs of disclosure must make it possible to establish—
 (a) the justification for, and date and time of, the disclosure, and
 (b) so far as possible—
  (i) the identity of the person who disclosed the data, and
  (ii) the identity of the recipients of the data.
(4) The logs kept under subsection (1) may be used only for one or more of the following purposes—
 (a) to verify the lawfulness of processing;
 (b) to assist with self-monitoring by the controller or (as the case may be) the processor, including the conduct of internal disciplinary proceedings;
 (c) to ensure the integrity and security of personal data;
 (d) the purposes of criminal proceedings.
(5) The controller or (as the case may be) the processor must make the logs available to the Commissioner on request.

NOTES

Commencement: 25 May 2018 (see also the introductory notes to this Act preceding s 1 at **[1.71]**).

[1.133]
63 Co-operation with the Commissioner
Each controller and each processor must co-operate, on request, with the Commissioner in the performance of the Commissioner's tasks.

NOTES

Commencement: 25 May 2018 (see also the introductory notes to this Act preceding s 1 at **[1.71]**).

[1.134]
64 Data protection impact assessment
(1) Where a type of processing is likely to result in a high risk to the rights and freedoms of individuals, the controller must, prior to the processing, carry out a data protection impact assessment.
(2) A data protection impact assessment is an assessment of the impact of the envisaged processing operations on the protection of personal data.
(3) A data protection impact assessment must include the following—
 (a) a general description of the envisaged processing operations;
 (b) an assessment of the risks to the rights and freedoms of data subjects;
 (c) the measures envisaged to address those risks;
 (d) safeguards, security measures and mechanisms to ensure the protection of personal data and to demonstrate compliance with this Part, taking into account the rights and legitimate interests of the data subjects and other persons concerned.
(4) In deciding whether a type of processing is likely to result in a high risk to the rights and freedoms of individuals, the controller must take into account the nature, scope, context and purposes of the processing.

NOTES

Commencement: 25 May 2018 (see also the introductory notes to this Act preceding s 1 at **[1.71]**).

[1.135]
65 Prior consultation with the Commissioner
(1) This section applies where a controller intends to create a filing system and process personal data forming part of it.
(2) The controller must consult the Commissioner prior to the processing if a data protection impact assessment prepared under section 64 indicates that the processing of the data would result in a high risk to the rights and freedoms of individuals (in the absence of measures to mitigate the risk).
(3) Where the controller is required to consult the Commissioner under subsection (2), the controller must give the Commissioner—
 (a) the data protection impact assessment prepared under section 64, and
 (b) any other information requested by the Commissioner to enable the Commissioner to make an assessment of the compliance of the processing with the requirements of this Part.
(4) Where the Commissioner is of the opinion that the intended processing referred to in subsection (1) would infringe any provision of this Part, the Commissioner must provide written advice to the controller and, where the controller is using a processor, to the processor.
(5) The written advice must be provided before the end of the period of 6 weeks beginning with receipt of the request for consultation by the controller or the processor.
(6) The Commissioner may extend the period of 6 weeks by a further period of 1 month, taking into account the complexity of the intended processing.
(7) If the Commissioner extends the period of 6 weeks, the Commissioner must—
 (a) inform the controller and, where applicable, the processor of any such extension before the end of the period of 1 month beginning with receipt of the request for consultation, and
 (b) provide reasons for the delay.

NOTES

Commencement: 25 May 2018 (see also the introductory notes to this Act preceding s 1 at **[1.71]**).

Obligations relating to security

[1.136]

66 Security of processing

(1) Each controller and each processor must implement appropriate technical and organisational measures to ensure a level of security appropriate to the risks arising from the processing of personal data.

(2) In the case of automated processing, each controller and each processor must, following an evaluation of the risks, implement measures designed to—

(a) prevent unauthorised processing or unauthorised interference with the systems used in connection with it,

(b) ensure that it is possible to establish the precise details of any processing that takes place,

(c) ensure that any systems used in connection with the processing function properly and may, in the case of interruption, be restored, and

(d) ensure that stored personal data cannot be corrupted if a system used in connection with the processing malfunctions.

NOTES

Commencement: 25 May 2018 (see also the introductory notes to this Act preceding s 1 at **[1.71]**).

Obligations relating to personal data breaches

[1.137]

67 Notification of a personal data breach to the Commissioner

(1) If a controller becomes aware of a personal data breach in relation to personal data for which the controller is responsible, the controller must notify the breach to the Commissioner—

(a) without undue delay, and

(b) where feasible, not later than 72 hours after becoming aware of it.

(2) Subsection (1) does not apply if the personal data breach is unlikely to result in a risk to the rights and freedoms of individuals.

(3) Where the notification to the Commissioner is not made within 72 hours, the notification must be accompanied by reasons for the delay.

(4) Subject to subsection (5), the notification must include—

(a) a description of the nature of the personal data breach including, where possible, the categories and approximate number of data subjects concerned and the categories and approximate number of personal data records concerned;

(b) the name and contact details of the data protection officer or other contact point from whom more information can be obtained;

(c) a description of the likely consequences of the personal data breach;

(d) a description of the measures taken or proposed to be taken by the controller to address the personal data breach, including, where appropriate, measures to mitigate its possible adverse effects.

(5) Where and to the extent that it is not possible to provide all the information mentioned in subsection (4) at the same time, the information may be provided in phases without undue further delay.

(6) The controller must record the following information in relation to a personal data breach—

(a) the facts relating to the breach,

(b) its effects, and

(c) the remedial action taken.

(7) The information mentioned in subsection (6) must be recorded in such a way as to enable the Commissioner to verify compliance with this section.

(8) . . .

(9) If a processor becomes aware of a personal data breach (in relation to personal data processed by the processor), the processor must notify the controller without undue delay.

NOTES

Commencement: 25 May 2018 (see also the introductory notes to this Act preceding s 1 at **[1.71]**).

Sub-s (8): repealed by the Data Protection, Privacy and Electronic Communications (Amendments etc) (EU Exit) Regulations 2019, SI 2019/419, reg 4, Sch 2, paras 1, 39.

[1.138]

68 Communication of a personal data breach to the data subject

(1) Where a personal data breach is likely to result in a high risk to the rights and freedoms of individuals, the controller must inform the data subject of the breach without undue delay.

(2) The information given to the data subject must include the following—

(a) a description of the nature of the breach;

(b) the name and contact details of the data protection officer or other contact point from whom more information can be obtained;

(c) a description of the likely consequences of the personal data breach;

(d) a description of the measures taken or proposed to be taken by the controller to address the personal data breach, including, where appropriate, measures to mitigate its possible adverse effects.

(3) The duty under subsection (1) does not apply where—

(a) the controller has implemented appropriate technological and organisational protection measures which were applied to the personal data affected by the breach,

(b) the controller has taken subsequent measures which ensure that the high risk to the rights and freedoms of data subjects referred to in subsection (1) is no longer likely to materialise, or

(c) it would involve a disproportionate effort.

(4) An example of a case which may fall within subsection (3)(a) is where measures that render personal data unintelligible to any person not authorised to access the data have been applied, such as encryption.

(5) In a case falling within subsection (3)(c) (but not within subsection (3)(a) or (b)), the information mentioned in subsection (2) must be made available to the data subject in another equally effective way, for example, by means of a public communication.

(6) Where the controller has not informed the data subject of the breach the Commissioner, on being notified under section 67 and after considering the likelihood of the breach resulting in a high risk, may—

(a) require the controller to notify the data subject of the breach, or

(b) decide that the controller is not required to do so because any of paragraphs (a) to (c) of subsection (3) applies.

(7) The controller may restrict, wholly or partly, the provision of information to the data subject under subsection (1) to the extent that and for so long as the restriction is, having regard to the fundamental rights and legitimate interests of the data subject, a necessary and proportionate measure to—

(a) avoid obstructing an official or legal inquiry, investigation or procedure;

(b) avoid prejudicing the prevention, detection, investigation or prosecution of criminal offences or the execution of criminal penalties;

(c) protect public security;

(d) protect national security;

(e) protect the rights and freedoms of others.

(8) Subsection (6) does not apply where the controller's decision not to inform the data subject of the breach was made in reliance on subsection (7).

(9) The duties in section 52(1) and (2) apply in relation to information that the controller is required to provide to the data subject under this section as they apply in relation to information that the controller is required to provide to the data subject under Chapter 3.

NOTES

Commencement: 25 May 2018 (see also the introductory notes to this Act preceding s 1 at **[1.71]**).

Data protection officers

[1.139]
69 Designation of a data protection officer
(1) The controller must designate a data protection officer, unless the controller is a court, or other judicial authority, acting in its judicial capacity.

(2) When designating a data protection officer, the controller must have regard to the professional qualities of the proposed officer, in particular—

(a) the proposed officer's expert knowledge of data protection law and practice, and

(b) the ability of the proposed officer to perform the tasks mentioned in section 71.

(3) The same person may be designated as a data protection officer by several controllers, taking account of their organisational structure and size.

(4) The controller must publish the contact details of the data protection officer and communicate these to the Commissioner.

NOTES

Commencement: 25 May 2018 (see also the introductory notes to this Act preceding s 1 at **[1.71]**).

[1.140]
70 Position of data protection officer
(1) The controller must ensure that the data protection officer is involved, properly and in a timely manner, in all issues which relate to the protection of personal data.

(2) The controller must provide the data protection officer with the necessary resources and access to personal data and processing operations to enable the data protection officer to—

(a) perform the tasks mentioned in section 71, and

(b) maintain his or her expert knowledge of data protection law and practice.

(3) The controller—

(a) must ensure that the data protection officer does not receive any instructions regarding the performance of the tasks mentioned in section 71;

(b) must ensure that the data protection officer does not perform a task or fulfil a duty other than those mentioned in this Part where such task or duty would result in a conflict of interests;

(c) must not dismiss or penalise the data protection officer for performing the tasks mentioned in section 71.

(4) A data subject may contact the data protection officer with regard to all issues relating to—

(a) the processing of that data subject's personal data, or

(b) the exercise of that data subject's rights under this Part.

(5) The data protection officer, in the performance of this role, must report to the highest management level of the controller.

NOTES

Commencement: 25 May 2018 (see also the introductory notes to this Act preceding s 1 at **[1.71]**).

[1.141]
71 Tasks of data protection officer
(1) The controller must entrust the data protection officer with at least the following tasks—

(a) informing and advising the controller, any processor engaged by the controller, and any employee of the controller who carries out processing of personal data, of that person's obligations under this Part,

(b) providing advice on the carrying out of a data protection impact assessment under section 64 and monitoring compliance with that section,

(c) co-operating with the Commissioner,

(d) acting as the contact point for the Commissioner on issues relating to processing, including in relation to the consultation mentioned in section 65, and consulting with the Commissioner, where appropriate, in relation to any other matter,

(e) monitoring compliance with policies of the controller in relation to the protection of personal data, and

(f) monitoring compliance by the controller with this Part.

(2) In relation to the policies mentioned in subsection (1)(e), the data protection officer's tasks include—

(a) assigning responsibilities under those policies,

(b) raising awareness of those policies,

(c) training staff involved in processing operations, and

(d) conducting audits required under those policies.

(3) In performing the tasks set out in subsections (1) and (2), the data protection officer must have regard to the risks associated with processing operations, taking into account the nature, scope, context and purposes of processing.

NOTES
Commencement: 25 May 2018 (see also the introductory notes to this Act preceding s 1 at **[1.71]**).

CHAPTER 5 TRANSFERS OF PERSONAL DATA TO THIRD COUNTRIES ETC
Overview and interpretation

[1.142]
72 Overview and interpretation
(1) This Chapter deals with the transfer of personal data to third countries or international organisations, as follows—

(a) sections 73 to 76 set out the general conditions that apply;

(b) section 77 sets out the special conditions that apply where the intended recipient of personal data is not a relevant authority in a third country or an international organisation;

(c) section 78 makes special provision about subsequent transfers of personal data.

(2) In this Chapter, "relevant authority", in relation to a third country, means any person based in a third country that has (in that country) functions comparable to those of a competent authority.

NOTES
Commencement: 25 May 2018 (see also the introductory notes to this Act preceding s 1 at **[1.71]**).

General principles for transfers

[1.143]
73 General principles for transfers of personal data
(1) A controller may not transfer personal data to a third country or to an international organisation unless—

(a) the three conditions set out in subsections (2) to (4) are met, and

(b) in a case where the personal data was originally transmitted or otherwise made available to the controller or another competent authority by a member State . . . , that member State, or any person based in that member State which is a competent authority for the purposes of the Law Enforcement Directive, has authorised the transfer in accordance with the law of the member State.

(2) Condition 1 is that the transfer is necessary for any of the law enforcement purposes.

(3) Condition 2 is that the transfer—

(a) is based on [adequacy regulations (see section 74A)],

(b) if not based on [adequacy regulations], is based on there being appropriate safeguards (see section 75), or

(c) if not based on [adequacy regulations] or on there being appropriate safeguards, is based on special circumstances (see section 76).

(4) Condition 3 is that—

(a) the intended recipient is a relevant authority in a third country or an international organisation that is a relevant international organisation, or

(b) in a case where the controller is a competent authority specified in any of paragraphs 5 to 17, 21, 24 to 28, 34 to 51, 54 and 56 of Schedule 7—

(i) the intended recipient is a person in a third country other than a relevant authority, and

(ii) the additional conditions in section 77 are met.

(5) Authorisation is not required as mentioned in subsection (1)(b) if—

(a) the transfer is necessary for the prevention of an immediate and serious threat either to the public security of . . . a third country or to the essential interests of a member State, and

(b) the authorisation cannot be obtained in good time.

(6) Where a transfer is made without the authorisation mentioned in subsection (1)(b), the authority in the member State which would have been responsible for deciding whether to authorise the transfer must be informed without delay.

(7) In this section, "relevant international organisation" means an international organisation that carries out functions for any of the law enforcement purposes.

NOTES
Commencement: 25 May 2018 (see also the introductory notes to this Act preceding s 1 at **[1.71]**).
The words omitted from sub-ss (1), (5) were repealed and the words in square brackets in sub-s (3) were substituted by the Data Protection, Privacy and Electronic Communications (Amendments etc) (EU Exit) Regulations 2019, SI 2019/419, reg 4, Sch 2, paras 1, 40.

74 (*Repealed by the Data Protection, Privacy and Electronic Communications (Amendments etc) (EU Exit) Regulations 2019, SI 2019/419, reg 4, Sch 2, paras 1, 41.*)

[1.144]
[74A Transfers based on adequacy regulations
(1) The Secretary of State may by regulations specify any of the following which the Secretary of State considers ensures an adequate level of protection of personal data—
  (a) a third country,
  (b) a territory or one or more sectors within a third country,
  (c) an international organisation, or
  (d) a description of such a country, territory, sector or organisation.
(2) For the purposes of this Part of this Act, a transfer of personal data to a third country or an international organisation is based on adequacy regulations if, at the time of the transfer, regulations made under this section are in force which specify, or specify a description which includes—
  (a) in the case of a third country, the country or a relevant territory or sector within the country, and
  (b) in the case of an international organisation, the organisation,
and such a transfer does not require specific authorisation.
(3) Regulations under this section may specify that the Secretary of State considers that an adequate level of protection of personal data is ensured only for a transfer specified or described in the regulations and, if they do so, only such a transfer may rely on those regulations for the purposes of subsection (2).
(4) When assessing the adequacy of the level of protection for the purposes of this section or section 74B, the Secretary of State must, in particular, take account of—
  (a) the rule of law, respect for human rights and fundamental freedoms, relevant legislation, both general and sectoral, including concerning public security, defence, national security and criminal law and the access of public authorities to personal data, as well as the implementation of such legislation, data protection rules, professional rules and security measures, including rules for the onward transfer of personal data to another third country or international organisation, which are complied with in that country or international organisation, case-law, as well as effective and enforceable data subject rights and effective administrative and judicial redress for the data subjects whose personal data is transferred,
  (b) the existence and effective functioning of one or more independent supervisory authorities in the third country or to which an international organisation is subject, with responsibility for ensuring and enforcing compliance with data protection rules, including adequate enforcement powers, for assisting and advising data subjects in exercising their rights and for cooperation with the Commissioner, and
  (c) the international commitments the third country or international organisation concerned has entered into, or other obligations arising from legally binding conventions or instruments as well as from its participation in multilateral or regional systems, in particular in relation to the protection of personal data.
(5) Regulations under this section—
  (a) where they relate to a third country, must specify their territorial and sectoral application;
  (b) where applicable, must specify the independent supervisory authority or authorities referred to in subsection (4)(b).
(6) Regulations under this section may, among other things—
  (a) provide that, in relation to a country, territory, sector, organisation or territory specified, or falling within a description specified, in the regulations, section 74B(1) has effect as if it required the reviews described there to be carried out at such shorter intervals as are specified in the regulations;
  (b) identify a transfer of personal data by any means, including by reference to the controller or processor, the recipient, the personal data transferred or the means by which the transfer is made or by reference to relevant legislation, lists or other documents, as they have effect from time to time;
  (c) confer a discretion on a person.
(7) Regulations under this section are subject to the negative resolution procedure.]

NOTES
Commencement: IP completion day (as defined in the European Union (Withdrawal Agreement) Act 2020, s 39).
Inserted, together with s 74B, by the Data Protection, Privacy and Electronic Communications (Amendments etc) (EU Exit) Regulations 2019, SI 2019/419, reg 4, Sch 2, paras 1, 42.

[1.145]
[74B Transfers based on adequacy regulations: review etc
(1) For so long as regulations under section 74A are in force which specify, or specify a description which includes, a third country, a territory or sector within a third country or an international organisation, the Secretary of State must carry out a review of whether the country, territory, sector or organisation ensures an adequate level of protection of personal data at intervals of not more than 4 years.
(2) Each review under subsection (1) must take into account all relevant developments in the third country or international organisation.
(3) The Secretary of State must, on an ongoing basis, monitor developments in third countries and international organisations that could affect decisions to make regulations under section 74A or to amend or revoke such regulations.
(4) Where the Secretary of State becomes aware that a country, territory, sector or organisation specified, or falling within a description specified, in regulations under section 74A no longer ensures an adequate level of protection of personal data, whether as a result of a review under this section or otherwise, the Secretary of State must, to the extent necessary, amend or revoke the regulations.
(5) Where regulations under section 74A are amended or revoked in accordance with subsection (4), the Secretary of State must enter into consultations with the third country or international organisation concerned with a view to remedying the lack of an adequate level of protection.

(6) The Secretary of State must publish—
  (a) a list of the third countries, territories and specified sectors within a third country and international organisations, and the descriptions of such countries, territories, sectors and organisations, which are for the time being specified in regulations under section 74A, and
  (b) a list of the third countries, territories and specified sectors within a third country and international organisations, and the descriptions of such countries, territories, sectors and organisations, which have been but are no longer specified in such regulations.
(7) In the case of regulations under section 74A which specify that an adequate level of protection of personal data is ensured only for a transfer specified or described in the regulations—
  (a) the duty under subsection (1) is only to carry out a review of the level of protection ensured for such a transfer, and
  (b) the lists published under subsection (6) must specify or describe the relevant transfers.]

NOTES

Commencement: IP completion day (as defined in the European Union (Withdrawal Agreement) Act 2020, s 39).
Inserted as noted to s 74A at **[1.144]**.

[1.146]
75   Transfers on the basis of appropriate safeguards
(1) A transfer of personal data to a third country or an international organisation is based on there being appropriate safeguards where—
  (a) a legal instrument containing appropriate safeguards for the protection of personal data binds the intended recipient of the data, or
  (b) the controller, having assessed all the circumstances surrounding transfers of that type of personal data to the third country or international organisation, concludes that appropriate safeguards exist to protect the data.
(2) The controller must inform the Commissioner about the categories of data transfers that take place in reliance on subsection (1)(b).
(3) Where a transfer of data takes place in reliance on subsection (1)—
  (a) the transfer must be documented,
  (b) the documentation must be provided to the Commissioner on request, and
  (c) the documentation must include, in particular—
    (i) the date and time of the transfer,
    (ii) the name of and any other pertinent information about the recipient,
    (iii) the justification for the transfer, and
    (iv) a description of the personal data transferred.

NOTES

Commencement: 25 May 2018 (see also the introductory notes to this Act preceding s 1 at **[1.71]**).

[1.147]
76   Transfers on the basis of special circumstances
(1) A transfer of personal data to a third country or international organisation is based on special circumstances where the transfer is necessary—
  (a) to protect the vital interests of the data subject or another person,
  (b) to safeguard the legitimate interests of the data subject,
  (c) for the prevention of an immediate and serious threat to the public security of . . . a third country,
  (d) in individual cases for any of the law enforcement purposes, or
  (e) in individual cases for a legal purpose.
(2) But subsection (1)(d) and (e) do not apply if the controller determines that fundamental rights and freedoms of the data subject override the public interest in the transfer.
(3) Where a transfer of data takes place in reliance on subsection (1)—
  (a) the transfer must be documented,
  (b) the documentation must be provided to the Commissioner on request, and
  (c) the documentation must include, in particular—
    (i) the date and time of the transfer,
    (ii) the name of and any other pertinent information about the recipient,
    (iii) the justification for the transfer, and
    (iv) a description of the personal data transferred.
(4) For the purposes of this section, a transfer is necessary for a legal purpose if—
  (a) it is necessary for the purpose of, or in connection with, any legal proceedings (including prospective legal proceedings) relating to any of the law enforcement purposes,
  (b) it is necessary for the purpose of obtaining legal advice in relation to any of the law enforcement purposes, or
  (c) it is otherwise necessary for the purposes of establishing, exercising or defending legal rights in relation to any of the law enforcement purposes.

NOTES

Commencement: 25 May 2018 (see also the introductory notes to this Act preceding s 1 at **[1.71]**).
Sub-s (1): words omitted repealed by the Data Protection, Privacy and Electronic Communications (Amendments etc) (EU Exit) Regulations 2019, SI 2019/419, reg 4, Sch 2, paras 1, 43.

Transfers to particular recipients

[1.148]
77   Transfers of personal data to persons other than relevant authorities
(1) The additional conditions referred to in section 73(4)(b)(ii) are the following four conditions.

(2) Condition 1 is that the transfer is strictly necessary in a specific case for the performance of a task of the transferring controller as provided by law for any of the law enforcement purposes.

(3) Condition 2 is that the transferring controller has determined that there are no fundamental rights and freedoms of the data subject concerned that override the public interest necessitating the transfer.

(4) Condition 3 is that the transferring controller considers that the transfer of the personal data to a relevant authority in the third country would be ineffective or inappropriate (for example, where the transfer could not be made in sufficient time to enable its purpose to be fulfilled).

(5) Condition 4 is that the transferring controller informs the intended recipient of the specific purpose or purposes for which the personal data may, so far as necessary, be processed.

(6) Where personal data is transferred to a person in a third country other than a relevant authority, the transferring controller must inform a relevant authority in that third country without undue delay of the transfer, unless this would be ineffective or inappropriate.

(7) The transferring controller must—

    (a) document any transfer to a recipient in a third country other than a relevant authority, and

    (b) inform the Commissioner about the transfer.

(8) This section does not affect the operation of any international agreement in force between [the United Kingdom] and third countries in the field of judicial co-operation in criminal matters and police co-operation.

NOTES

Commencement: 25 May 2018 (see also the introductory notes to this Act preceding s 1 at **[1.71]**).

Sub-s (8): words in square brackets substituted by the Data Protection, Privacy and Electronic Communications (Amendments etc) (EU Exit) Regulations 2019, SI 2019/419, reg 4, Sch 2, paras 1, 44.

Subsequent transfers

[1.149]

78 Subsequent transfers

(1) Where personal data is transferred in accordance with section 73, the transferring controller must make it a condition of the transfer that the data is not to be further transferred to a third country or international organisation without the authorisation of the transferring controller or another competent authority.

(2) A competent authority may give an authorisation under subsection (1) only where the further transfer is necessary for a law enforcement purpose.

(3) In deciding whether to give the authorisation, the competent authority must take into account (among any other relevant factors)—

    (a) the seriousness of the circumstances leading to the request for authorisation,

    (b) the purpose for which the personal data was originally transferred, and

    (c) the standards for the protection of personal data that apply in the third country or international organisation to which the personal data would be transferred.

(4) In a case where the personal data was originally transmitted or otherwise made available to the transferring controller or another competent authority by a member State . . . , an authorisation may not be given under subsection (1) unless that member State, or any person based in that member State which is a competent authority for the purposes of the Law Enforcement Directive, has authorised the transfer in accordance with the law of the member State.

(5) Authorisation is not required as mentioned in subsection (4) if—

    (a) the transfer is necessary for the prevention of an immediate and serious threat either to the public security of . . . a third country or to the essential interests of a member State, and

    (b) the authorisation cannot be obtained in good time.

(6) Where a transfer is made without the authorisation mentioned in subsection (4), the authority in the member State which would have been responsible for deciding whether to authorise the transfer must be informed without delay.

NOTES

Commencement: 25 May 2018 (see also the introductory notes to this Act preceding s 1 at **[1.71]**).

Sub-ss (4), (5): words omitted repealed by the Data Protection, Privacy and Electronic Communications (Amendments etc) (EU Exit) Regulations 2019, SI 2019/419, reg 4, Sch 2, paras 1, 45.

CHAPTER 6 SUPPLEMENTARY

[1.150]

79 National security: certificate

(1) A Minister of the Crown may issue a certificate certifying, for the purposes of section 44(4), 45(4), 48(3) or 68(7), that a restriction is a necessary and proportionate measure to protect national security.

(2) The certificate may—

    (a) relate to a specific restriction (described in the certificate) which a controller has imposed or is proposing to impose under section 44(4), 45(4), 48(3) or 68(7), or

    (b) identify any restriction to which it relates by means of a general description.

(3) Subject to subsection (6), a certificate issued under subsection (1) is conclusive evidence that the specific restriction or (as the case may be) any restriction falling within the general description is, or at any time was, a necessary and proportionate measure to protect national security.

(4) A certificate issued under subsection (1) may be expressed to have prospective effect.

(5) Any person directly affected by the issuing of a certificate under subsection (1) may appeal to the Tribunal against the certificate.

(6) If, on an appeal under subsection (5), the Tribunal finds that, applying the principles applied by a court on an application for judicial review, the Minister did not have reasonable grounds for issuing the certificate, the Tribunal may—

    (a) allow the appeal, and

(b) quash the certificate.

(7) Where in any proceedings under or by virtue of this Act, it is claimed by a controller that a restriction falls within a general description in a certificate issued under subsection (1), any other party to the proceedings may appeal to the Tribunal on the ground that the restriction does not fall within that description.

(8) But, subject to any determination under subsection (9), the restriction is to be conclusively presumed to fall within the general description.

(9) On an appeal under subsection (7), the Tribunal may determine that the certificate does not so apply.

(10) A document purporting to be a certificate under subsection (1) is to be—

(a) received in evidence, and

(b) deemed to be such a certificate unless the contrary is proved.

(11) A document which purports to be certified by or on behalf of a Minister of the Crown as a true copy of a certificate issued by that Minister under subsection (1) is—

(a) in any legal proceedings, evidence of that certificate, and

(b) in any legal proceedings in Scotland, sufficient evidence of that certificate.

(12) The power conferred by subsection (1) on a Minister of the Crown is exercisable only by—

(a) a Minister who is a member of the Cabinet, or

(b) the Attorney General or the Advocate General for Scotland.

(13) No power conferred by any provision of Part 6 may be exercised in relation to the imposition of—

(a) a specific restriction in a certificate under subsection (1), or

(b) a restriction falling within a general description in such a certificate.

NOTES

Commencement: 25 May 2018 (see also the introductory notes to this Act preceding s 1 at **[1.71]**).

[1.151]

80 Special processing restrictions

(1) Subsections (3) and (4) apply where, for a law enforcement purpose, a controller transmits or otherwise makes available personal data to [a non-UK recipient].

(2) In this section—

. . .

"[non-UK recipient]" means—

(a) a recipient in a third country, or

(b) an international organisation.

(3) The controller must consider whether, if the personal data had instead been transmitted or otherwise made available within the United Kingdom to another competent authority, processing of the data by the other competent authority would have been subject to any restrictions by virtue of any enactment or rule of law.

(4) Where that would be the case, the controller must inform [the non-UK recipient] that the data is transmitted or otherwise made available subject to compliance by that person with the same restrictions (which must be set out in the information given to that person).

(5)–(7) . . .

NOTES

Commencement: 25 May 2018 (see also the introductory notes to this Act preceding s 1 at **[1.71]**).

The words in square brackets in each place were substituted, the words omitted from sub-s (2) were repealed, and sub-ss (5)–(7) were repealed, by the Data Protection, Privacy and Electronic Communications (Amendments etc) (EU Exit) Regulations 2019, SI 2019/419, reg 4, Sch 2, paras 1, 46.

[1.152]

81 Reporting of infringements

(1) Each controller must implement effective mechanisms to encourage the reporting of an infringement of this Part.

(2) The mechanisms implemented under subsection (1) must provide that an infringement may be reported to any of the following persons—

(a) the controller;

(b) the Commissioner.

(3) The mechanisms implemented under subsection (1) must include—

(a) raising awareness of the protections provided by Part 4A of the Employment Rights Act 1996 and Part 5A of the Employment Rights (Northern Ireland) Order 1996 (SI 1996/1919 (NI 16)), and

(b) such other protections for a person who reports an infringement of this Part as the controller considers appropriate.

(4) A person who reports an infringement of this Part does not breach—

(a) an obligation of confidence owed by the person, or

(b) any other restriction on the disclosure of information (however imposed).

(5) Subsection (4) does not apply if or to the extent that the report includes a disclosure which is prohibited by any of Parts 1 to 7 or Chapter 1 of Part 9 of the Investigatory Powers Act 2016.

(6) Until the repeal of Part 1 of the Regulation of Investigatory Powers Act 2000 by paragraphs 45 and 54 of Schedule 10 to the Investigatory Powers Act 2016 is fully in force, subsection (5) has effect as if it included a reference to that Part.

NOTES

Commencement: 25 May 2018 (see also the introductory notes to this Act preceding s 1 at **[1.71]**).

PART 4 INTELLIGENCE SERVICES PROCESSING

CHAPTER 1 SCOPE AND DEFINITIONS

Scope

[1.153]
82 Processing to which this Part applies
(1) This Part applies to—
　(a) the processing by an intelligence service of personal data wholly or partly by automated means, and
　(b) the processing by an intelligence service otherwise than by automated means of personal data which forms part of a filing system or is intended to form part of a filing system.
(2) In this Part, "intelligence service" means—
　(a) the Security Service;
　(b) the Secret Intelligence Service;
　(c) the Government Communications Headquarters.
(3) A reference in this Part to the processing of personal data is to processing to which this Part applies.

NOTES
　Commencement: 25 May 2018 (see also the introductory notes to this Act preceding s 1 at **[1.71]**).

Definitions

[1.154]
83 Meaning of "controller" and "processor"
(1) In this Part, "controller" means the intelligence service which, alone or jointly with others—
　(a) determines the purposes and means of the processing of personal data, or
　(b) is the controller by virtue of subsection (2).
(2) Where personal data is processed only—
　(a) for purposes for which it is required by an enactment to be processed, and
　(b) by means by which it is required by an enactment to be processed,
the intelligence service on which the obligation to process the data is imposed by the enactment (or, if different, one of the enactments) is the controller.
(3) In this Part, "processor" means any person who processes personal data on behalf of the controller (other than a person who is an employee of the controller).

NOTES
　Commencement: 25 May 2018 (see also the introductory notes to this Act preceding s 1 at **[1.71]**).

[1.155]
84 Other definitions
(1) This section defines other expressions used in this Part.
(2) "Consent", in relation to the processing of personal data relating to an individual, means a freely given, specific, informed and unambiguous indication of the individual's wishes by which the individual, by a statement or by a clear affirmative action, signifies agreement to the processing of the personal data.
(3) "Employee", in relation to any person, includes an individual who holds a position (whether paid or unpaid) under the direction and control of that person.
(4) "Personal data breach" means a breach of security leading to the accidental or unlawful destruction, loss, alteration, unauthorised disclosure of, or access to, personal data transmitted, stored or otherwise processed.
(5) "Recipient", in relation to any personal data, means any person to whom the data is disclosed, whether a third party or not, but it does not include a person to whom disclosure is or may be made in the framework of a particular inquiry in accordance with the law.
(6) "Restriction of processing" means the marking of stored personal data with the aim of limiting its processing for the future.
(7) Sections 3 and 205 include definitions of other expressions used in this Part.

NOTES
　Commencement: 25 May 2018 (see also the introductory notes to this Act preceding s 1 at **[1.71]**).

CHAPTER 2 PRINCIPLES

Overview

[1.156]
85 Overview
(1) This Chapter sets out the six data protection principles as follows—
　(a) section 86 sets out the first data protection principle (requirement that processing be lawful, fair and transparent);
　(b) section 87 sets out the second data protection principle (requirement that the purposes of processing be specified, explicit and legitimate);
　(c) section 88 sets out the third data protection principle (requirement that personal data be adequate, relevant and not excessive);
　(d) section 89 sets out the fourth data protection principle (requirement that personal data be accurate and kept up to date);
　(e) section 90 sets out the fifth data protection principle (requirement that personal data be kept for no longer than is necessary);
　(f) section 91 sets out the sixth data protection principle (requirement that personal data be processed in a secure manner).

(2) Each of sections 86, 87 and 91 makes provision to supplement the principle to which it relates.

NOTES
Commencement: 25 May 2018 (see also the introductory notes to this Act preceding s 1 at **[1.71]**).

The data protection principles

[1.157]
86 The first data protection principle
(1) The first data protection principle is that the processing of personal data must be—
  (a) lawful, and
  (b) fair and transparent.
(2) The processing of personal data is lawful only if and to the extent that—
  (a) at least one of the conditions in Schedule 9 is met, and
  (b) in the case of sensitive processing, at least one of the conditions in Schedule 10 is also met.
(3) The Secretary of State may by regulations amend Schedule 10—
  (a) by adding conditions;
  (b) by omitting conditions added by regulations under paragraph (a).
(4) Regulations under subsection (3) are subject to the affirmative resolution procedure.
(5) In determining whether the processing of personal data is fair and transparent, regard is to be had to the method by which it is obtained.
(6) For the purposes of subsection (5), data is to be treated as obtained fairly and transparently if it consists of information obtained from a person who—
  (a) is authorised by an enactment to supply it, or
  (b) is required to supply it by an enactment or by an international obligation of the United Kingdom.
(7) In this section, "sensitive processing" means—
  (a) the processing of personal data revealing racial or ethnic origin, political opinions, religious or philosophical beliefs or trade union membership;
  (b) the processing of genetic data for the purpose of uniquely identifying an individual;
  (c) the processing of biometric data for the purpose of uniquely identifying an individual;
  (d) the processing of data concerning health;
  (e) the processing of data concerning an individual's sex life or sexual orientation;
  (f) the processing of personal data as to—
      (i)   the commission or alleged commission of an offence by an individual, or
      (ii) proceedings for an offence committed or alleged to have been committed by an individual, the disposal of such proceedings or the sentence of a court in such proceedings.

NOTES
Commencement: 25 May 2018 (see also the introductory notes to this Act preceding s 1 at **[1.71]**).

[1.158]
87 The second data protection principle
(1) The second data protection principle is that—
  (a) the purpose for which personal data is collected on any occasion must be specified, explicit and legitimate, and
  (b) personal data so collected must not be processed in a manner that is incompatible with the purpose for which it is collected.
(2) Paragraph (b) of the second data protection principle is subject to subsections (3) and (4).
(3) Personal data collected by a controller for one purpose may be processed for any other purpose of the controller that collected the data or any purpose of another controller provided that—
  (a) the controller is authorised by law to process the data for that purpose, and
  (b) the processing is necessary and proportionate to that other purpose.
(4) Processing of personal data is to be regarded as compatible with the purpose for which it is collected if the processing—
  (a) consists of—
      (i)   processing for archiving purposes in the public interest,
      (ii)   processing for the purposes of scientific or historical research, or
      (iii) processing for statistical purposes, and
  (b) is subject to appropriate safeguards for the rights and freedoms of the data subject.

NOTES
Commencement: 25 May 2018 (see also the introductory notes to this Act preceding s 1 at **[1.71]**).

[1.159]
88 The third data protection principle
The third data protection principle is that personal data must be adequate, relevant and not excessive in relation to the purpose for which it is processed.

NOTES
Commencement: 25 May 2018 (see also the introductory notes to this Act preceding s 1 at **[1.71]**).

[1.160]
89 The fourth data protection principle
The fourth data protection principle is that personal data undergoing processing must be accurate and, where necessary, kept up to date.

NOTES

Commencement: 25 May 2018 (see also the introductory notes to this Act preceding s 1 at **[1.71]**).

[1.161]
90   The fifth data protection principle
The fifth data protection principle is that personal data must be kept for no longer than is necessary for the purpose for which it is processed.

NOTES

Commencement: 25 May 2018 (see also the introductory notes to this Act preceding s 1 at **[1.71]**).

[1.162]
91   The sixth data protection principle
(1) The sixth data protection principle is that personal data must be processed in a manner that includes taking appropriate security measures as regards risks that arise from processing personal data.
(2) The risks referred to in subsection (1) include (but are not limited to) accidental or unauthorised access to, or destruction, loss, use, modification or disclosure of, personal data.

NOTES

Commencement: 25 May 2018 (see also the introductory notes to this Act preceding s 1 at **[1.71]**).

CHAPTER 3 RIGHTS OF THE DATA SUBJECT
Overview

[1.163]
92   Overview
(1) This Chapter sets out the rights of the data subject as follows—
   (a)   section 93 deals with the information to be made available to the data subject;
   (b)   sections 94 and 95 deal with the right of access by the data subject;
   (c)   sections 96 and 97 deal with rights in relation to automated processing;
   (d)   section 98 deals with the right to information about decision-making;
   (e)   section 99 deals with the right to object to processing;
   (f)   section 100 deals with rights to rectification and erasure of personal data.
(2) In this Chapter, "the controller", in relation to a data subject, means the controller in relation to personal data relating to the data subject.

NOTES

Commencement: 25 May 2018 (see also the introductory notes to this Act preceding s 1 at **[1.71]**).

Rights

[1.164]
93   Right to information
(1) The controller must give a data subject the following information—
   (a)   the identity and the contact details of the controller;
   (b)   the legal basis on which, and the purposes for which, the controller processes personal data;
   (c)   the categories of personal data relating to the data subject that are being processed;
   (d)   the recipients or the categories of recipients of the personal data (if applicable);
   (e)   the right to lodge a complaint with the Commissioner and the contact details of the Commissioner;
   (f)   how to exercise rights under this Chapter;
   (g)   any other information needed to secure that the personal data is processed fairly and transparently.
(2) The controller may comply with subsection (1) by making information generally available, where the controller considers it appropriate to do so.
(3) The controller is not required under subsection (1) to give a data subject information that the data subject already has.
(4) Where personal data relating to a data subject is collected by or on behalf of the controller from a person other than the data subject, the requirement in subsection (1) has effect, in relation to the personal data so collected, with the following exceptions—
   (a)   the requirement does not apply in relation to processing that is authorised by an enactment;
   (b)   the requirement does not apply in relation to the data subject if giving the information to the data subject would be impossible or involve disproportionate effort.

NOTES

Commencement: 16 September 2019 (see also the introductory notes to this Act preceding s 1 at **[1.71]**).

[1.165]
94   Right of access
(1) An individual is entitled to obtain from a controller—
   (a)   confirmation as to whether or not personal data concerning the individual is being processed, and
   (b)   where that is the case—
      (i)   communication, in intelligible form, of the personal data of which that individual is the data subject, and
      (ii)   the information set out in subsection (2).
(2) That information is—
   (a)   the purposes of and legal basis for the processing;

    (b)   the categories of personal data concerned;
    (c)   the recipients or categories of recipients to whom the personal data has been disclosed;
    (d)   the period for which the personal data is to be preserved;
    (e)   the existence of a data subject's rights to rectification and erasure of personal data (see section 100);
    (f)   the right to lodge a complaint with the Commissioner and the contact details of the Commissioner;
    (g)   any information about the origin of the personal data concerned.
(3) A controller is not obliged to provide information under this section unless the controller has received such reasonable fee as the controller may require, subject to subsection (4).
(4) The Secretary of State may by regulations—
    (a)   specify cases in which a controller may not charge a fee;
    (b)   specify the maximum amount of a fee.
(5) Where a controller—
    (a)   reasonably requires further information—
        (i)   in order that the controller be satisfied as to the identity of the individual making a request under subsection (1), or
        (ii)   to locate the information which that individual seeks, and
    (b)   has informed that individual of that requirement,
the controller is not obliged to comply with the request unless the controller is supplied with that further information.
(6) Where a controller cannot comply with the request without disclosing information relating to another individual who can be identified from that information, the controller is not obliged to comply with the request unless—
    (a)   the other individual has consented to the disclosure of the information to the individual making the request, or
    (b)   it is reasonable in all the circumstances to comply with the request without the consent of the other individual.
(7) In subsection (6), the reference to information relating to another individual includes a reference to information identifying that individual as the source of the information sought by the request.
(8) Subsection (6) is not to be construed as excusing a controller from communicating so much of the information sought by the request as can be communicated without disclosing the identity of the other individual concerned, whether by the omission of names or other identifying particulars or otherwise.
(9) In determining for the purposes of subsection (6)(b) whether it is reasonable in all the circumstances to comply with the request without the consent of the other individual concerned, regard must be had, in particular, to—
    (a)   any duty of confidentiality owed to the other individual,
    (b)   any steps taken by the controller with a view to seeking the consent of the other individual,
    (c)   whether the other individual is capable of giving consent, and
    (d)   any express refusal of consent by the other individual.
(10) Subject to subsection (6), a controller must comply with a request under subsection (1)—
    (a)   promptly, and
    (b)   in any event before the end of the applicable time period.
(11) If a court is satisfied on the application of an individual who has made a request under subsection (1) that the controller in question has failed to comply with the request in contravention of this section, the court may order the controller to comply with the request.
(12) A court may make an order under subsection (11) in relation to a joint controller whose responsibilities are determined in an arrangement under section 104 only if the controller is responsible for compliance with the obligation to which the order relates.
(13) The jurisdiction conferred on a court by this section is exercisable by the High Court or, in Scotland, by the Court of Session.
(14) In this section—
    "the applicable time period" means—
        (a)   the period of 1 month, or
        (b)   such longer period, not exceeding 3 months, as may be specified in regulations made by the Secretary of State,
    beginning with the relevant time;
    "the relevant time", in relation to a request under subsection (1), means the latest of the following—
        (a)   when the controller receives the request,
        (b)   when the fee (if any) is paid, and
        (c)   when the controller receives the information (if any) required under subsection (5) in connection with the request.
(15) Regulations under this section are subject to the negative resolution procedure.

NOTES
    Commencement: 25 May 2018 (see also the introductory notes to this Act preceding s 1 at **[1.71]**).

[1.166]
95 Right of access: supplementary
(1) The controller must comply with the obligation imposed by section 94(1)(b)(i) by supplying the data subject with a copy of the information in writing unless—
    (a)   the supply of such a copy is not possible or would involve disproportionate effort, or
    (b)   the data subject agrees otherwise;
and where any of the information referred to in section 94(1)(b)(i) is expressed in terms which are not intelligible without explanation the copy must be accompanied by an explanation of those terms.
(2) Where a controller has previously complied with a request made under section 94 by an individual, the controller is not obliged to comply with a subsequent identical or similar request under that section by that individual unless a reasonable interval has elapsed between compliance with the previous request and the making of the current request.

(3) In determining for the purposes of subsection (2) whether requests under section 94 are made at reasonable intervals, regard must be had to—

(a) the nature of the data,

(b) the purpose for which the data is processed, and

(c) the frequency with which the data is altered.

(4) The information to be supplied pursuant to a request under section 94 must be supplied by reference to the data in question at the time when the request is received, except that it may take account of any amendment or deletion made between that time and the time when the information is supplied, being an amendment or deletion that would have been made regardless of the receipt of the request.

(5) For the purposes of section 94(6) to (8), an individual can be identified from information to be disclosed to a data subject by a controller if the individual can be identified from—

(a) that information, or

(b) that and any other information that the controller reasonably believes the data subject making the request is likely to possess or obtain.

NOTES

Commencement: 25 May 2018 (see also the introductory notes to this Act preceding s 1 at **[1.71]**).

[1.167]
96   Right not to be subject to automated decision-making

(1) The controller may not take a decision significantly affecting a data subject that is based solely on automated processing of personal data relating to the data subject.

(2) Subsection (1) does not prevent such a decision being made on that basis if—

(a) the decision is required or authorised by law,

(b) the data subject has given consent to the decision being made on that basis, or

(c) the decision is a decision taken in the course of steps taken—

    (i)   for the purpose of considering whether to enter into a contract with the data subject,

    (ii)   with a view to entering into such a contract, or

    (iii)   in the course of performing such a contract.

(3) For the purposes of this section, a decision that has legal effects as regards an individual is to be regarded as significantly affecting the individual.

NOTES

Commencement: 25 May 2018 (see also the introductory notes to this Act preceding s 1 at **[1.71]**).

[1.168]
97   Right to intervene in automated decision-making

(1) This section applies where—

(a) the controller takes a decision significantly affecting a data subject that is based solely on automated processing of personal data relating to the data subject, and

(b) the decision is required or authorised by law.

(2) This section does not apply to such a decision if—

(a) the data subject has given consent to the decision being made on that basis, or

(b) the decision is a decision taken in the course of steps taken—

    (i)   for the purpose of considering whether to enter into a contract with the data subject,

    (ii)   with a view to entering into such a contract, or

    (iii)   in the course of performing such a contract.

(3) The controller must as soon as reasonably practicable notify the data subject that such a decision has been made.

(4) The data subject may, before the end of the period of 1 month beginning with receipt of the notification, request the controller—

(a) to reconsider the decision, or

(b) to take a new decision that is not based solely on automated processing.

(5) If a request is made to the controller under subsection (4), the controller must, before the end of the period of 1 month beginning with receipt of the request—

(a) consider the request, including any information provided by the data subject that is relevant to it, and

(b) by notice in writing inform the data subject of the outcome of that consideration.

(6) For the purposes of this section, a decision that has legal effects as regards an individual is to be regarded as significantly affecting the individual.

NOTES

Commencement: 25 May 2018 (see also the introductory notes to this Act preceding s 1 at **[1.71]**).

[1.169]
98   Right to information about decision-making

(1) Where—

(a) the controller processes personal data relating to a data subject, and

(b) results produced by the processing are applied to the data subject,

the data subject is entitled to obtain from the controller, on request, knowledge of the reasoning underlying the processing.

(2) Where the data subject makes a request under subsection (1), the controller must comply with the request without undue delay.

NOTES

Commencement: 25 May 2018 (see also the introductory notes to this Act preceding s 1 at **[1.71]**).

[1.170]
99 Right to object to processing
(1) A data subject is entitled at any time, by notice given to the controller, to require the controller—
  (a) not to process personal data relating to the data subject, or
  (b) not to process such data for a specified purpose or in a specified manner,
on the ground that, for specified reasons relating to the situation of the data subject, the processing in question is an unwarranted interference with the interests or rights of the data subject.
(2) Where the controller—
  (a) reasonably requires further information—
      (i)   in order that the controller be satisfied as to the identity of the individual giving notice under subsection (1), or
      (ii) to locate the data to which the notice relates, and
  (b) has informed that individual of that requirement,
the controller is not obliged to comply with the notice unless the controller is supplied with that further information.
(3) The controller must, before the end of 21 days beginning with the relevant time, give a notice to the data subject—
  (a) stating that the controller has complied or intends to comply with the notice under subsection (1), or
  (b) stating the controller's reasons for not complying with the notice to any extent and the extent (if any) to which the controller has complied or intends to comply with the notice under subsection (1).
(4) If the controller does not comply with a notice under subsection (1) to any extent, the data subject may apply to a court for an order that the controller take steps for complying with the notice.
(5) If the court is satisfied that the controller should comply with the notice (or should comply to any extent), the court may order the controller to take such steps for complying with the notice (or for complying with it to that extent) as the court thinks fit.
(6) A court may make an order under subsection (5) in relation to a joint controller whose responsibilities are determined in an arrangement under section 104 only if the controller is responsible for compliance with the obligation to which the order relates.
(7) The jurisdiction conferred on a court by this section is exercisable by the High Court or, in Scotland, by the Court of Session.
(8) In this section, "the relevant time", in relation to a notice under subsection (1), means—
  (a) when the controller receives the notice, or
  (b) if later, when the controller receives the information (if any) required under subsection (2) in connection with the notice.

NOTES
Commencement: 25 May 2018 (see also the introductory notes to this Act preceding s 1 at **[1.71]**).

[1.171]
100 Rights to rectification and erasure
(1) If a court is satisfied on the application of a data subject that personal data relating to the data subject is inaccurate, the court may order the controller to rectify that data without undue delay.
(2) If a court is satisfied on the application of a data subject that the processing of personal data relating to the data subject would infringe any of sections 86 to 91, the court may order the controller to erase that data without undue delay.
(3) If personal data relating to the data subject must be maintained for the purposes of evidence, the court may (instead of ordering the controller to rectify or erase the personal data) order the controller to restrict its processing without undue delay.
(4) If—
  (a) the data subject contests the accuracy of personal data, and
  (b) the court is satisfied that the controller is not able to ascertain whether the data is accurate or not,
the court may (instead of ordering the controller to rectify or erase the personal data) order the controller to restrict its processing without undue delay.
(5) A court may make an order under this section in relation to a joint controller whose responsibilities are determined in an arrangement under section 104 only if the controller is responsible for carrying out the rectification, erasure or restriction of processing that the court proposes to order.
(6) The jurisdiction conferred on a court by this section is exercisable by the High Court or, in Scotland, by the Court of Session.

NOTES
Commencement: 25 May 2018 (see also the introductory notes to this Act preceding s 1 at **[1.71]**).

CHAPTER 4 CONTROLLER AND PROCESSOR
Overview

[1.172]
101 Overview
This Chapter sets out—
  (a) the general obligations of controllers and processors (see sections 102 to 106);
  (b) specific obligations of controllers and processors with respect to security (see section 107);
  (c) specific obligations of controllers and processors with respect to personal data breaches (see section 108).

NOTES
Commencement: 25 May 2018 (see also the introductory notes to this Act preceding s 1 at **[1.71]**).

General obligations

[1.173]
102   General obligations of the controller
Each controller must implement appropriate measures—
  (a)   to ensure, and
  (b)   to be able to demonstrate, in particular to the Commissioner,
that the processing of personal data complies with the requirements of this Part.

NOTES
  Commencement: 16 September 2019 (see also the introductory notes to this Act preceding s 1 at **[1.71]**).

[1.174]
103   Data protection by design
(1)   Where a controller proposes that a particular type of processing of personal data be carried out by or on behalf of the controller, the controller must, prior to the processing, consider the impact of the proposed processing on the rights and freedoms of data subjects.
(2)   A controller must implement appropriate technical and organisational measures which are designed to ensure that—
  (a)   the data protection principles are implemented, and
  (b)   risks to the rights and freedoms of data subjects are minimised.

NOTES
  Commencement: 16 September 2019 (see also the introductory notes to this Act preceding s 1 at **[1.71]**).

[1.175]
104   Joint controllers
(1)   Where two or more intelligence services jointly determine the purposes and means of processing personal data, they are joint controllers for the purposes of this Part.
(2)   Joint controllers must, in a transparent manner, determine their respective responsibilities for compliance with this Part by means of an arrangement between them, except to the extent that those responsibilities are determined under or by virtue of an enactment.
(3)   The arrangement must designate the controller which is to be the contact point for data subjects.

NOTES
  Commencement: 16 September 2019 (see also the introductory notes to this Act preceding s 1 at **[1.71]**).

[1.176]
105   Processors
(1)   This section applies to the use by a controller of a processor to carry out processing of personal data on behalf of the controller.
(2)   The controller may use only a processor who undertakes—
  (a)   to implement appropriate measures that are sufficient to secure that the processing complies with this Part;
  (b)   to provide to the controller such information as is necessary for demonstrating that the processing complies with this Part.
(3)   If a processor determines, in breach of this Part, the purposes and means of processing, the processor is to be treated for the purposes of this Part as a controller in respect of that processing.

NOTES
  Commencement: 16 September 2019 (see also the introductory notes to this Act preceding s 1 at **[1.71]**).

[1.177]
106   Processing under the authority of the controller or processor
A processor, and any person acting under the authority of a controller or processor, who has access to personal data may not process the data except—
  (a)   on instructions from the controller, or
  (b)   to comply with a legal obligation.

NOTES
  Commencement: 25 May 2018 (see also the introductory notes to this Act preceding s 1 at **[1.71]**).

Obligations relating to security

[1.178]
107   Security of processing
(1)   Each controller and each processor must implement security measures appropriate to the risks arising from the processing of personal data.
(2)   In the case of automated processing, each controller and each processor must, following an evaluation of the risks, implement measures designed to—
  (a)   prevent unauthorised processing or unauthorised interference with the systems used in connection with it,
  (b)   ensure that it is possible to establish the precise details of any processing that takes place,
  (c)   ensure that any systems used in connection with the processing function properly and may, in the case of interruption, be restored, and
  (d)   ensure that stored personal data cannot be corrupted if a system used in connection with the processing malfunctions.

NOTES

Commencement: 25 May 2018 (see also the introductory notes to this Act preceding s 1 at **[1.71]**).

Obligations relating to personal data breaches

[1.179]
108 Communication of a personal data breach
(1) If a controller becomes aware of a serious personal data breach in relation to personal data for which the controller is responsible, the controller must notify the Commissioner of the breach without undue delay.
(2) Where the notification to the Commissioner is not made within 72 hours, the notification must be accompanied by reasons for the delay.
(3) Subject to subsection (4), the notification must include—
   (a) a description of the nature of the personal data breach including, where possible, the categories and approximate number of data subjects concerned and the categories and approximate number of personal data records concerned;
   (b) the name and contact details of the contact point from whom more information can be obtained;
   (c) a description of the likely consequences of the personal data breach;
   (d) a description of the measures taken or proposed to be taken by the controller to address the personal data breach, including, where appropriate, measures to mitigate its possible adverse effects.
(4) Where and to the extent that it is not possible to provide all the information mentioned in subsection (3) at the same time, the information may be provided in phases without undue further delay.
(5) If a processor becomes aware of a personal data breach (in relation to data processed by the processor), the processor must notify the controller without undue delay.
(6) Subsection (1) does not apply in relation to a personal data breach if the breach also constitutes a relevant error within the meaning given by section 231(9) of the Investigatory Powers Act 2016.
(7) For the purposes of this section, a personal data breach is serious if the breach seriously interferes with the rights and freedoms of a data subject.

NOTES

Commencement: 16 September 2019 (see also the introductory notes to this Act preceding s 1 at **[1.71]**).

CHAPTER 5 TRANSFERS OF PERSONAL DATA OUTSIDE THE UNITED KINGDOM

[1.180]
109 Transfers of personal data outside the United Kingdom
(1) A controller may not transfer personal data to—
   (a) a country or territory outside the United Kingdom, or
   (b) an international organisation,
unless the transfer falls within subsection (2).
(2) A transfer of personal data falls within this subsection if the transfer is a necessary and proportionate measure carried out—
   (a) for the purposes of the controller's statutory functions, or
   (b) for other purposes provided for, in relation to the controller, in section 2(2)(a) of the Security Service Act 1989 or section 2(2)(a) or 4(2)(a) of the Intelligence Services Act 1994.

NOTES

Commencement: 25 May 2018 (see also the introductory notes to this Act preceding s 1 at **[1.71]**).

CHAPTER 6 EXEMPTIONS

[1.181]
110 National security
(1) A provision mentioned in subsection (2) does not apply to personal data to which this Part applies if exemption from the provision is required for the purpose of safeguarding national security.
(2) The provisions are—
   (a) Chapter 2 (the data protection principles), except section 86(1)(a) and (2) and Schedules 9 and 10;
   (b) Chapter 3 (rights of data subjects);
   (c) in Chapter 4 , section 108 (communication of a personal data breach to the Commissioner);
   (d) in Part 5—
      (i) section 119 (inspection in accordance with international obligations);
      (ii) in Schedule 13 (other general functions of the Commissioner), paragraphs 1(a) and (g) and 2;
   (e) in Part 6—
      (i) sections 142 to 154 and Schedule 15 (Commissioner's notices and powers of entry and inspection);
      (ii) sections 170 to 173 (offences relating to personal data);
      (iii) sections 174 to 176 (provision relating to the special purposes).

NOTES

Commencement: 25 May 2018 (see also the introductory notes to this Act preceding s 1 at **[1.71]**).

[1.182]
111 National security: certificate
(1) Subject to subsection (3), a certificate signed by a Minister of the Crown certifying that exemption from all or any of the provisions mentioned in section 110(2) is, or at any time was, required for the purpose of safeguarding national security in respect of any personal data is conclusive evidence of that fact.
(2) A certificate under subsection (1)—

(a) may identify the personal data to which it applies by means of a general description, and

(b) may be expressed to have prospective effect.

(3) Any person directly affected by the issuing of a certificate under subsection (1) may appeal to the Tribunal against the certificate.

(4) If on an appeal under subsection (3), the Tribunal finds that, applying the principles applied by a court on an application for judicial review, the Minister did not have reasonable grounds for issuing the certificate, the Tribunal may—

(a) allow the appeal, and

(b) quash the certificate.

(5) Where, in any proceedings under or by virtue of this Act, it is claimed by a controller that a certificate under subsection (1) which identifies the personal data to which it applies by means of a general description applies to any personal data, another party to the proceedings may appeal to the Tribunal on the ground that the certificate does not apply to the personal data in question.

(6) But, subject to any determination under subsection (7), the certificate is to be conclusively presumed so to apply.

(7) On an appeal under subsection (5), the Tribunal may determine that the certificate does not so apply.

(8) A document purporting to be a certificate under subsection (1) is to be—

(a) received in evidence, and

(b) deemed to be such a certificate unless the contrary is proved.

(9) A document which purports to be certified by or on behalf of a Minister of the Crown as a true copy of a certificate issued by that Minister under subsection (1) is—

(a) in any legal proceedings, evidence of that certificate, and

(b) in any legal proceedings in Scotland, sufficient evidence of that certificate.

(10) The power conferred by subsection (1) on a Minister of the Crown is exercisable only by—

(a) a Minister who is a member of the Cabinet, or

(b) the Attorney General or the Advocate General for Scotland.

NOTES

Commencement: 25 May 2018 (see also the introductory notes to this Act preceding s 1 at **[1.71]**).

[1.183]
112 Other exemptions
Schedule 11 provides for further exemptions.

NOTES

Commencement: 25 May 2018 (see also the introductory notes to this Act preceding s 1 at **[1.71]**).

[1.184]
113 Power to make further exemptions
(1) The Secretary of State may by regulations amend Schedule 11—

(a) by adding exemptions from any provision of this Part;

(b) by omitting exemptions added by regulations under paragraph (a).

(2) Regulations under this section are subject to the affirmative resolution procedure.

NOTES

Commencement: 25 May 2018 (see also the introductory notes to this Act preceding s 1 at **[1.71]**).

PART 5 THE INFORMATION COMMISSIONER
The Commissioner

[1.185]
114 The Information Commissioner
(1) There is to continue to be an Information Commissioner.

(2) Schedule 12 makes provision about the Commissioner.

NOTES

Commencement: 25 May 2018 (see also the introductory notes to this Act preceding s 1 at **[1.71]**).

General functions

[1.186]
115 General functions under the [UK GDPR] and safeguards
(1) . . .

(2) General functions are conferred on the Commissioner by—

(a) Article 57 of the [UK GDPR] (tasks), and

(b) Article 58 of the [UK GDPR] (powers),

(and see also the Commissioner's duty under section 2 [and section 28(5)]).

(3) The Commissioner's functions in relation to the processing of personal data to which the [UK GDPR] applies include—

(a) a duty to advise Parliament, the government and other institutions and bodies on legislative and administrative measures relating to the protection of individuals' rights and freedoms with regard to the processing of personal data, and

(b) a power to issue, on the Commissioner's own initiative or on request, opinions to Parliament, the government or other institutions and bodies as well as to the public on any issue related to the protection of personal data.

(4) The Commissioner's functions under Article 58 of the [UK GDPR] are subject to the safeguards in subsections (5) to (9).

(5) The Commissioner's power under Article 58(1)(a) of the [UK GDPR] (power to require a controller or processor to provide information that the Commissioner requires for the performance of the Commissioner's tasks under the [UK GDPR]) is exercisable only by giving an information notice under section 142.

(6) The Commissioner's power under Article 58(1)(b) of the [UK GDPR] (power to carry out data protection audits) is exercisable only in accordance with section 146.

(7) The Commissioner's powers under Article 58(1)(e) and (f) of the [UK GDPR] (power to obtain information from controllers and processors and access to their premises) are exercisable only—

(a) in accordance with Schedule 15 (see section 154), or

(b) to the extent that they are exercised in conjunction with the power under Article 58(1)(b) of the [UK GDPR], in accordance with section 146.

(8) The following powers are exercisable only by giving an enforcement notice under section 149—

(a) the Commissioner's powers under Article 58(2)(c) to (g) and (j) of the [UK GDPR] (certain corrective powers);

(b) the Commissioner's powers under Article 58(2)(h) to order a certification body to withdraw, or not to issue, a certification under Articles 42 and 43 of the [UK GDPR].

(9) The Commissioner's powers under Articles 58(2)(i) and 83 of the [UK GDPR] (administrative fines) are exercisable only by giving a penalty notice under section 155.

(10) This section is without prejudice to other functions conferred on the Commissioner, whether by the [UK GDPR], this Act or otherwise.

NOTES

Commencement: 25 May 2018 (see also the introductory notes to this Act preceding s 1 at **[1.71]**).

The words "UK GDPR" in each place they appear, including the heading, were substituted, sub-s (1) was repealed, and the words in the final pair of square brackets in sub-s (2) were inserted, by the Data Protection, Privacy and Electronic Communications (Amendments etc) (EU Exit) Regulations 2019, SI 2019/419, reg 4, Sch 2, paras 1, 47.

[1.187]
116 Other general functions

[(A1) The Commissioner is responsible for monitoring the application of Part 3 of this Act, in order to protect the fundamental rights and freedoms of individuals in relation to processing by a competent authority for any of the law enforcement purposes (as defined in Part 3) and to facilitate the free flow of personal data.]

(1) The Commissioner—

(a) . . .

(b) is to continue to be the designated authority in the United Kingdom for the purposes of Article 13 of the Data Protection Convention.

(2) Schedule 13 confers general functions on the Commissioner in connection with processing to which the [UK GDPR] does not apply (and see also the Commissioner's duty under section 2).

(3) This section and Schedule 13 are without prejudice to other functions conferred on the Commissioner, whether by this Act or otherwise.

NOTES

Commencement: 25 May 2018 (see also the introductory notes to this Act preceding s 1 at **[1.71]**).

Sub-s (A1) was inserted, sub-s (1)(a) was repealed and the words in square brackets in sub-s (2) were substituted by the Data Protection, Privacy and Electronic Communications (Amendments etc) (EU Exit) Regulations 2019, SI 2019/419, reg 4, Sch 2, paras 1, 48.

[1.188]
117 Competence in relation to courts etc

Nothing in this Act [or the UK GDPR] permits or requires the Commissioner to exercise functions in relation to the processing of personal data by—

(a) an individual acting in a judicial capacity, or

(b) a court or tribunal acting in its judicial capacity,

. . .

NOTES

Commencement: 25 May 2018 (see also the introductory notes to this Act preceding s 1 at **[1.71]**).

Words in square brackets inserted and words omitted repealed, by the Data Protection, Privacy and Electronic Communications (Amendments etc) (EU Exit) Regulations 2019, SI 2019/419, reg 4, Sch 2, paras 1, 49.

International role

[1.189]
118 [Co-operation between parties to the Data Protection Convention]

(1)–(4) . . .

(5) Part 2 of Schedule 14 makes provision as to the functions to be carried out by the Commissioner for the purposes of Article 13 of the Data Protection Convention (co-operation between parties).

NOTES

Commencement: 25 May 2018 (see also the introductory notes to this Act preceding s 1 at **[1.71]**).

The section heading was substituted and sub-ss (1)–(4) were repealed, by the Data Protection, Privacy and Electronic Communications (Amendments etc) (EU Exit) Regulations 2019, SI 2019/419, reg 4, Sch 2, paras 1, 50.

[1.190]
119 Inspection of personal data in accordance with international obligations

(1) The Commissioner may inspect personal data where the inspection is necessary in order to discharge an international obligation of the United Kingdom, subject to the restriction in subsection (2).

(2) The power under subsection (1) is exercisable only if the personal data—
(a) is processed wholly or partly by automated means, or
(b) is processed otherwise than by automated means and forms part of a filing system or is intended to form part of a filing system.

(3) The power under subsection (1) includes power to inspect, operate and test equipment which is used for the processing of personal data.

(4) Before exercising the power under subsection (1), the Commissioner must by written notice inform the controller and any processor that the Commissioner intends to do so.

(5) Subsection (4) does not apply if the Commissioner considers that the case is urgent.

(6) It is an offence—
(a) intentionally to obstruct a person exercising the power under subsection (1), or
(b) to fail without reasonable excuse to give a person exercising that power any assistance the person may reasonably require.

(7) Paragraphs (c) and (d) of section 3(14) do not apply to references in this section to personal data, the processing of personal data, a controller or a processor.

NOTES

Commencement: 25 May 2018 (see also the introductory notes to this Act preceding s 1 at **[1.71]**).

[1.191]
[119A   Standard clauses for transfers to third countries etc
(1) The Commissioner may issue a document specifying standard data protection clauses which the Commissioner considers provide appropriate safeguards for the purposes of transfers of personal data to a third country or an international organisation in reliance on Article 46 of the UK GDPR (and see also section 17C).

(2) The Commissioner may issue a document that amends or withdraws a document issued under subsection (1)

(3) A document issued under this section—
(a) must specify when it comes into force,
(b) may make different provision for different purposes, and
(c) may include transitional provision or savings.

(4) Before issuing a document under this section, the Commissioner must consult the Secretary of State and such of the following as the Commissioner considers appropriate—
(a) trade associations;
(b) data subjects;
(c) persons who appear to the Commissioner to represent the interests of data subjects.

(5) After a document is issued under this section—
(a) the Commissioner must send a copy to the Secretary of State, and
(b) the Secretary of State must lay it before Parliament.

(6) If, within the 40-day period, either House of Parliament resolves not to approve the document then, with effect from the end of the day on which the resolution is passed, the document is to be treated as not having been issued under this section (so that the document, and any amendment or withdrawal made by the document, is to be disregarded for the purposes of Article 46(2)(d) of the UK GDPR).

(7) Nothing in subsection (6)—
(a) affects any transfer of personal data previously made in reliance on the document, or
(b) prevents a further document being laid before Parliament.

(8) The Commissioner must publish—
(a) a document issued under this section, and
(b) a notice identifying any document which, under subsection (6), is treated as not having been issued under this section.

(9) The Commissioner must keep under review the clauses specified in a document issued under this section for the time being in force.

(10) In this section, "the 40-day period" means—
(a) if the document is laid before both Houses of Parliament on the same day, the period of 40 days beginning with that day, or
(b) if the document is laid before the Houses of Parliament on different days, the period of 40 days beginning with the later of those days.

(11) In calculating the 40-day period, no account is to be taken of any period during which Parliament is dissolved or prorogued or during which both Houses of Parliament are adjourned for more than 4 days.

(12) In this section, "trade association" includes a body representing controllers or processors.]

NOTES

Commencement: IP completion day (as defined in the European Union (Withdrawal Agreement) Act 2020, s 39).

Inserted by the Data Protection, Privacy and Electronic Communications (Amendments etc) (EU Exit) Regulations 2019, SI 2019/419, reg 4, Sch 2, paras 1, 51.

[1.192]
120   Further international role
(1) The Commissioner must, in relation to third countries and international organisations, take appropriate steps to—
(a) develop international co-operation mechanisms to facilitate the effective enforcement of legislation for the protection of personal data;
(b) provide international mutual assistance in the enforcement of legislation for the protection of personal data, subject to appropriate safeguards for the protection of personal data and other fundamental rights and freedoms;

(c) engage relevant stakeholders in discussion and activities aimed at furthering international co-operation in the enforcement of legislation for the protection of personal data;

(d) promote the exchange and documentation of legislation and practice for the protection of personal data, including legislation and practice relating to jurisdictional conflicts with third countries.

(2) Subsection (1) applies only in connection with the processing of personal data to which the [UK GDPR] does not apply; for the equivalent duty in connection with the processing of personal data to which the [UK GDPR] applies, see Article 50 of the [UK GDPR] (international co-operation for the protection of personal data).

[(2A) The Commissioner may contribute to the activities of international organisations with data protection functions.]

(3) The Commissioner must carry out data protection functions which the Secretary of State directs the Commissioner to carry out for the purpose of enabling Her Majesty's Government in the United Kingdom to give effect to an international obligation of the United Kingdom.

(4) The Commissioner may provide an authority carrying out data protection functions under the law of a British overseas territory with assistance in carrying out those functions.

(5) The Secretary of State may direct that assistance under subsection (4) is to be provided on terms, including terms as to payment, specified or approved by the Secretary of State.

(6) In this section—

"data protection functions" means functions relating to the protection of individuals with respect to the processing of personal data;

"mutual assistance in the enforcement of legislation for the protection of personal data" includes assistance in the form of notification, complaint referral, investigative assistance and information exchange;

"third country" means a country or territory [outside the United Kingdom].

(7) Section 3(14)(c) does not apply to references to personal data and the processing of personal data in this section.

NOTES

Commencement: 25 May 2018 (see also the introductory notes to this Act preceding s 1 at **[1.71]**).

The words in square brackets in paras (2), (6) were substituted and para (2A) was inserted, by the Data Protection, Privacy and Electronic Communications (Amendments etc) (EU Exit) Regulations 2019, SI 2019/419, reg 4, Sch 2, paras 1, 52.

Codes of practice

[1.193]
121 Data-sharing code
(1) The Commissioner must prepare a code of practice which contains—
   (a) practical guidance in relation to the sharing of personal data in accordance with the requirements of the data protection legislation, and
   (b) such other guidance as the Commissioner considers appropriate to promote good practice in the sharing of personal data.
(2) Where a code under this section is in force, the Commissioner may prepare amendments of the code or a replacement code.
(3) Before preparing a code or amendments under this section, the Commissioner must consult the Secretary of State and such of the following as the Commissioner considers appropriate—
   (a) trade associations;
   (b) data subjects;
   (c) persons who appear to the Commissioner to represent the interests of data subjects.
(4) A code under this section may include transitional provision or savings.
(5) In this section—
   "good practice in the sharing of personal data" means such practice in the sharing of personal data as appears to the Commissioner to be desirable having regard to the interests of data subjects and others, including compliance with the requirements of the data protection legislation;
   "the sharing of personal data" means the disclosure of personal data by transmission, dissemination or otherwise making it available;
   "trade association" includes a body representing controllers or processors.

NOTES

Commencement: 25 May 2018 (see also the introductory notes to this Act preceding s 1 at **[1.71]**).

[1.194]
122 Direct marketing code
(1) The Commissioner must prepare a code of practice which contains—
   (a) practical guidance in relation to the carrying out of direct marketing in accordance with the requirements of the data protection legislation and the Privacy and Electronic Communications (EC Directive) Regulations 2003 (SI 2003/2426), and
   (b) such other guidance as the Commissioner considers appropriate to promote good practice in direct marketing.
(2) Where a code under this section is in force, the Commissioner may prepare amendments of the code or a replacement code.
(3) Before preparing a code or amendments under this section, the Commissioner must consult the Secretary of State and such of the following as the Commissioner considers appropriate—
   (a) trade associations;
   (b) data subjects;
   (c) persons who appear to the Commissioner to represent the interests of data subjects.
(4) A code under this section may include transitional provision or savings.
(5) In this section—

"direct marketing" means the communication (by whatever means) of advertising or marketing material which is directed to particular individuals;

"good practice in direct marketing" means such practice in direct marketing as appears to the Commissioner to be desirable having regard to the interests of data subjects and others, including compliance with the requirements mentioned in subsection (1)(a);

"trade association" includes a body representing controllers or processors.

NOTES

Commencement: 25 May 2018 (see also the introductory notes to this Act preceding s 1 at **[1.71]**).

[1.195]
123   Age-appropriate design code

(1) The Commissioner must prepare a code of practice which contains such guidance as the Commissioner considers appropriate on standards of age-appropriate design of relevant information society services which are likely to be accessed by children.

(2) Where a code under this section is in force, the Commissioner may prepare amendments of the code or a replacement code.

(3) Before preparing a code or amendments under this section, the Commissioner must consult the Secretary of State and such other persons as the Commissioner considers appropriate, including—

  (a) children,

  (b) parents,

  (c) persons who appear to the Commissioner to represent the interests of children,

  (d) child development experts, and

  (e) trade associations.

(4) In preparing a code or amendments under this section, the Commissioner must have regard—

  (a) to the fact that children have different needs at different ages, and

  (b) to the United Kingdom's obligations under the United Nations Convention on the Rights of the Child.

(5) A code under this section may include transitional provision or savings.

(6) Any transitional provision included in the first code under this section must cease to have effect before the end of the period of 12 months beginning when the code comes into force.

(7) In this section—

"age-appropriate design" means the design of services so that they are appropriate for use by, and meet the development needs of, children;

"information society services" has the same meaning as in the [UK GDPR], but does not include preventive or counselling services;

"relevant information society services" means information society services which involve the processing of personal data to which the [UK GDPR] applies;

"standards of age-appropriate design of relevant information society services" means such standards of age-appropriate design of such services as appear to the Commissioner to be desirable having regard to the best interests of children;

"trade association" includes a body representing controllers or processors;

"the United Nations Convention on the Rights of the Child" means the Convention on the Rights of the Child adopted by the General Assembly of the United Nations on 20 November 1989 (including any Protocols to that Convention which are in force in relation to the United Kingdom), subject to any reservations, objections or interpretative declarations by the United Kingdom for the time being in force.

NOTES

Commencement: 23 July 2018 (see also the introductory notes to this Act preceding s 1 at **[1.71]**).

Sub-s (7): words in square brackets substituted by the Data Protection, Privacy and Electronic Communications (Amendments etc) (EU Exit) Regulations 2019, SI 2019/419, reg 4, Sch 2, paras 1, 53.

[1.196]
124   Data protection and journalism code

(1) The Commissioner must prepare a code of practice which contains—

  (a) practical guidance in relation to the processing of personal data for the purposes of journalism in accordance with the requirements of the data protection legislation, and

  (b) such other guidance as the Commissioner considers appropriate to promote good practice in the processing of personal data for the purposes of journalism.

(2) Where a code under this section is in force, the Commissioner may prepare amendments of the code or a replacement code.

(3) Before preparing a code or amendments under this section, the Commissioner must consult such of the following as the Commissioner considers appropriate—

  (a) trade associations;

  (b) data subjects;

  (c) persons who appear to the Commissioner to represent the interests of data subjects.

(4) A code under this section may include transitional provision or savings.

(5) In this section—

"good practice in the processing of personal data for the purposes of journalism" means such practice in the processing of personal data for those purposes as appears to the Commissioner to be desirable having regard to—

  (a) the interests of data subjects and others, including compliance with the requirements of the data protection legislation, and

  (b) the special importance of the public interest in the freedom of expression and information;

"trade association" includes a body representing controllers or processors.

NOTES
Commencement: 23 July 2018 (see also the introductory notes to this Act preceding s 1 at **[1.71]**).

[1.197]
125 Approval of codes prepared under sections 121 to 124
(1) When a code is prepared under section 121, 122, 123 or 124—
  (a) the Commissioner must submit the final version to the Secretary of State, and
  (b) the Secretary of State must lay the code before Parliament.
(2) In relation to the first code under section 123—
  (a) the Commissioner must prepare the code as soon as reasonably practicable and must submit it to the Secretary of State before the end of the period of 18 months beginning when this Act is passed, and
  (b) the Secretary of State must lay it before Parliament as soon as reasonably practicable.
(3) If, within the 40-day period, either House of Parliament resolves not to approve a code prepared under section 121, 122, 123 or 124, the Commissioner must not issue the code.
(4) If no such resolution is made within that period—
  (a) the Commissioner must issue the code, and
  (b) the code comes into force at the end of the period of 21 days beginning with the day on which it is issued.
(5) If, as a result of subsection (3), there is no code in force under section 121, 122, 123 or 124, the Commissioner must prepare another version of the code.
(6) Nothing in subsection (3) prevents another version of the code being laid before Parliament.
(7) In this section, "the 40-day period" means—
  (a) if the code is laid before both Houses of Parliament on the same day, the period of 40 days beginning with that day, or
  (b) if the code is laid before the Houses of Parliament on different days, the period of 40 days beginning with the later of those days.
(8) In calculating the 40-day period, no account is to be taken of any period during which Parliament is dissolved or prorogued or during which both Houses of Parliament are adjourned for more than 4 days.
(9) This section, other than subsections (2) and (5), applies in relation to amendments prepared under section 121, 122, 123 or 124 as it applies in relation to codes prepared under those sections.

NOTES
Commencement: 23 July 2018 (see also the introductory notes to this Act preceding s 1 at **[1.71]**).

[1.198]
126 Publication and review of codes issued under section 125(4)
(1) The Commissioner must publish a code issued under section 125(4).
(2) Where an amendment of a code is issued under section 125(4), the Commissioner must publish—
  (a) the amendment, or
  (b) the code as amended by it.
(3) The Commissioner must keep under review each code issued under section 125(4) for the time being in force.
(4) Where the Commissioner becomes aware that the terms of such a code could result in a breach of an international obligation of the United Kingdom, the Commissioner must exercise the power under section 121(2), 122(2), 123(2) or 124(2) with a view to remedying the situation.

NOTES
Commencement: 23 July 2018 (see also the introductory notes to this Act preceding s 1 at **[1.71]**).

[1.199]
127 Effect of codes issued under section 125(4)
(1) A failure by a person to act in accordance with a provision of a code issued under section 125(4) does not of itself make that person liable to legal proceedings in a court or tribunal.
(2) A code issued under section 125(4), including an amendment or replacement code, is admissible in evidence in legal proceedings.
(3) In any proceedings before a court or tribunal, the court or tribunal must take into account a provision of a code issued under section 125(4) in determining a question arising in the proceedings if—
  (a) the question relates to a time when the provision was in force, and
  (b) the provision appears to the court or tribunal to be relevant to the question.
(4) Where the Commissioner is carrying out a function described in subsection (5), the Commissioner must take into account a provision of a code issued under section 125(4) in determining a question arising in connection with the carrying out of the function if—
  (a) the question relates to a time when the provision was in force, and
  (b) the provision appears to the Commissioner to be relevant to the question.
(5) Those functions are functions under—
  (a) the data protection legislation, or
  (b) the Privacy and Electronic Communications (EC Directive) Regulations 2003 (SI 2003/2426).

NOTES
Commencement: 23 July 2018 (see also the introductory notes to this Act preceding s 1 at **[1.71]**).

[1.200]
128 Other codes of practice
(1) The Secretary of State may by regulations require the Commissioner—

(a) to prepare appropriate codes of practice giving guidance as to good practice in the processing of personal data, and

(b) to make them available to such persons as the Commissioner considers appropriate.

(2) Before preparing such codes, the Commissioner must consult such of the following as the Commissioner considers appropriate—

(a) trade associations;

(b) data subjects;

(c) persons who appear to the Commissioner to represent the interests of data subjects.

(3) Regulations under this section—

(a) must describe the personal data or processing to which the code of practice is to relate, and

(b) may describe the persons or classes of person to whom it is to relate.

(4) Regulations under this section are subject to the negative resolution procedure.

(5) In this section—

"good practice in the processing of personal data" means such practice in the processing of personal data as appears to the Commissioner to be desirable having regard to the interests of data subjects and others, including compliance with the requirements of the data protection legislation;

"trade association" includes a body representing controllers or processors.

NOTES

Commencement: 25 May 2018 (see also the introductory notes to this Act preceding s 1 at **[1.71]**).

Consensual audits

[1.201]

129　Consensual audits

(1) The Commissioner's functions under Article 58(1) of the [UK GDPR] and paragraph 1 of Schedule 13 include power, with the consent of a controller or processor, to carry out an assessment of whether the controller or processor is complying with good practice in the processing of personal data.

(2) The Commissioner must inform the controller or processor of the results of such an assessment.

(3) In this section, "good practice in the processing of personal data" has the same meaning as in section 128.

NOTES

Commencement: 25 May 2018 (see also the introductory notes to this Act preceding s 1 at **[1.71]**).

Sub-s (1): words in square brackets substituted by the Data Protection, Privacy and Electronic Communications (Amendments etc) (EU Exit) Regulations 2019, SI 2019/419, reg 4, Sch 2, paras 1, 54.

Records of national security certificates

[1.202]

130　Records of national security certificates

(1) A Minister of the Crown who issues a certificate under section 27, 79 or 111 must send a copy of the certificate to the Commissioner.

(2) If the Commissioner receives a copy of a certificate under subsection (1), the Commissioner must publish a record of the certificate.

(3) The record must contain—

(a) the name of the Minister who issued the certificate,

(b) the date on which the certificate was issued, and

(c) subject to subsection (4), the text of the certificate.

(4) The Commissioner must not publish the text, or a part of the text, of the certificate if—

(a) the Minister determines that publishing the text or that part of the text—

(i) would be against the interests of national security,

(ii) would be contrary to the public interest, or

(iii) might jeopardise the safety of any person, and

(b) the Minister has notified the Commissioner of that determination.

(5) The Commissioner must keep the record of the certificate available to the public while the certificate is in force.

(6) If a Minister of the Crown revokes a certificate issued under section 27, 79 or 111, the Minister must notify the Commissioner.

NOTES

Commencement: 25 May 2018 (see also the introductory notes to this Act preceding s 1 at **[1.71]**).

Information provided to the Commissioner

[1.203]

131　Disclosure of information to the Commissioner

(1) No enactment or rule of law prohibiting or restricting the disclosure of information precludes a person from providing the Commissioner with information necessary for the discharge of the Commissioner's functions.

(2) But this section does not authorise the making of a disclosure which is prohibited by any of Parts 1 to 7 or Chapter 1 of Part 9 of the Investigatory Powers Act 2016.

(3) Until the repeal of Part 1 of the Regulation of Investigatory Powers Act 2000 by paragraphs 45 and 54 of Schedule 10 to the Investigatory Powers Act 2016 is fully in force, subsection (2) has effect as if it included a reference to that Part.

NOTES

Commencement: 25 May 2018 (see also the introductory notes to this Act preceding s 1 at **[1.71]**).

[1.204]
132 Confidentiality of information
(1) A person who is or has been the Commissioner, or a member of the Commissioner's staff or an agent of the Commissioner, must not disclose information which—
  (a) has been obtained by, or provided to, the Commissioner in the course of, or for the purposes of, the discharging of the Commissioner's functions,
  (b) relates to an identified or identifiable individual or business, and
  (c) is not available to the public from other sources at the time of the disclosure and has not previously been available to the public from other sources,
unless the disclosure is made with lawful authority.
(2) For the purposes of subsection (1), a disclosure is made with lawful authority only if and to the extent that—
  (a) the disclosure was made with the consent of the individual or of the person for the time being carrying on the business,
  (b) the information was obtained or provided as described in subsection (1)(a) for the purpose of its being made available to the public (in whatever manner),
  (c) the disclosure was made for the purposes of, and is necessary for, the discharge of one or more of the Commissioner's functions,
  (d) . . .
  (e) the disclosure was made for the purposes of criminal or civil proceedings, however arising, or
  (f) having regard to the rights, freedoms and legitimate interests of any person, the disclosure was necessary in the public interest.
(3) It is an offence for a person knowingly or recklessly to disclose information in contravention of subsection (1).

NOTES
Commencement: 25 May 2018 (see also the introductory notes to this Act preceding s 1 at **[1.71]**).
Sub-s (2): para (d) repealed by the Data Protection, Privacy and Electronic Communications (Amendments etc) (EU Exit) Regulations 2019, SI 2019/419, reg 4, Sch 2, paras 1, 55.

[1.205]
133 Guidance about privileged communications
(1) The Commissioner must produce and publish guidance about—
  (a) how the Commissioner proposes to secure that privileged communications which the Commissioner obtains or has access to in the course of carrying out the Commissioner's functions are used or disclosed only so far as necessary for carrying out those functions, and
  (b) how the Commissioner proposes to comply with restrictions and prohibitions on obtaining or having access to privileged communications which are imposed by an enactment.
(2) The Commissioner—
  (a) may alter or replace the guidance, and
  (b) must publish any altered or replacement guidance.
(3) The Commissioner must consult the Secretary of State before publishing guidance under this section (including altered or replacement guidance).
(4) The Commissioner must arrange for guidance under this section (including altered or replacement guidance) to be laid before Parliament.
(5) In this section, "privileged communications" means—
  (a) communications made—
      (i)   between a professional legal adviser and the adviser's client, and
      (ii) in connection with the giving of legal advice to the client with respect to legal obligations, liabilities or rights, and
  (b) communications made—
      (i)   between a professional legal adviser and the adviser's client or between such an adviser or client and another person,
      (ii) in connection with or in contemplation of legal proceedings, and
      (iii) for the purposes of such proceedings.
(6) In subsection (5)—
  (a) references to the client of a professional legal adviser include references to a person acting on behalf of the client, and
  (b) references to a communication include—
      (i)   a copy or other record of the communication, and
      (ii) anything enclosed with or referred to in the communication if made as described in subsection (5)(a)(ii) or in subsection (5)(b)(ii) and (iii).

NOTES
Commencement: 25 May 2018 (see also the introductory notes to this Act preceding s 1 at **[1.71]**).

Fees

[1.206]
134 Fees for services
The Commissioner may require a person other than a data subject or a data protection officer to pay a reasonable fee for a service provided to the person, or at the person's request, which the Commissioner is required or authorised to provide under the data protection legislation.

NOTES
Commencement: 25 May 2018 (see also the introductory notes to this Act preceding s 1 at **[1.71]**).

Part 1 Data Protection: UK Law

[1.207]
135 Manifestly unfounded or excessive requests by data subjects etc

(1) Where a request to the Commissioner from a data subject or a data protection officer is manifestly unfounded or excessive, the Commissioner may—

    (a) charge a reasonable fee for dealing with the request, or

    (b) refuse to act on the request.

(2) An example of a request that may be excessive is one that merely repeats the substance of previous requests.

(3) In any proceedings where there is an issue as to whether a request described in subsection (1) is manifestly unfounded or excessive, it is for the Commissioner to show that it is.

(4) Subsections (1) and (3) apply only in cases in which the Commissioner does not already have such powers and obligations under Article 57(4) of the [UK GDPR].

NOTES

Commencement: 25 May 2018 (see also the introductory notes to this Act preceding s 1 at **[1.71]**).

Sub-s (4): words in square brackets substituted by the Data Protection, Privacy and Electronic Communications (Amendments etc) (EU Exit) Regulations 2019, SI 2019/419, reg 4, Sch 2, paras 1, 56.

[1.208]
136 Guidance about fees

(1) The Commissioner must produce and publish guidance about the fees the Commissioner proposes to charge in accordance with—

    (a) section 134 or 135, or

    (b) Article 57(4) of the [UK GDPR].

(2) Before publishing the guidance, the Commissioner must consult the Secretary of State.

NOTES

Commencement: 25 May 2018 (see also the introductory notes to this Act preceding s 1 at **[1.71]**).

Sub-s (1): words in square brackets substituted by the Data Protection, Privacy and Electronic Communications (Amendments etc) (EU Exit) Regulations 2019, SI 2019/419, reg 4, Sch 2, paras 1, 57.

Charges

[1.209]
137 Charges payable to the Commissioner by controllers

(1) The Secretary of State may by regulations require controllers to pay charges of an amount specified in the regulations to the Commissioner.

(2) Regulations under subsection (1) may require a controller to pay a charge regardless of whether the Commissioner has provided, or proposes to provide, a service to the controller.

(3) Regulations under subsection (1) may—

    (a) make provision about the time or times at which, or period or periods within which, a charge must be paid;

    (b) make provision for cases in which a discounted charge is payable;

    (c) make provision for cases in which no charge is payable;

    (d) make provision for cases in which a charge which has been paid is to be refunded.

(4) In making regulations under subsection (1), the Secretary of State must have regard to the desirability of securing that the charges payable to the Commissioner under such regulations are sufficient to offset—

    (a) expenses incurred by the Commissioner in discharging the Commissioner's functions—

        (i) under the data protection legislation,

        (ii) under the Data Protection Act 1998,

        (iii) under or by virtue of sections 108 and 109 of the Digital Economy Act 2017, and

        (iv) under or by virtue of the Privacy and Electronic Communications (EC Directive) Regulations 2003 (SI 2003/2426),

    (b) any expenses of the Secretary of State in respect of the Commissioner so far as attributable to those functions,

    (c) to the extent that the Secretary of State considers appropriate, any deficit previously incurred (whether before or after the passing of this Act) in respect of the expenses mentioned in paragraph (a), and

    (d) to the extent that the Secretary of State considers appropriate, expenses incurred by the Secretary of State in respect of the inclusion of any officers or staff of the Commissioner in any scheme under section 1 of the Superannuation Act 1972 or section 1 of the Public Service Pensions Act 2013.

(5) The Secretary of State may from time to time require the Commissioner to provide information about the expenses referred to in subsection (4)(a).

(6) The Secretary of State may by regulations make provision—

    (a) requiring a controller to provide information to the Commissioner, or

    (b) enabling the Commissioner to require a controller to provide information to the Commissioner,

for either or both of the purposes mentioned in subsection (7).

(7) Those purposes are—

    (a) determining whether a charge is payable by the controller under regulations under subsection (1);

    (b) determining the amount of a charge payable by the controller.

(8) The provision that may be made under subsection (6)(a) includes provision requiring a controller to notify the Commissioner of a change in the controller's circumstances of a kind specified in the regulations.

NOTES

Commencement: 25 May 2018 (see also the introductory notes to this Act preceding s 1 at **[1.71]**).

Regulations: Data Protection (Charges and Information) (Amendment) Regulations 2019, SI 2019/478.

[1.210]
138 Regulations under section 137: supplementary
(1) Before making regulations under section 137(1) or (6), the Secretary of State must consult such representatives of persons likely to be affected by the regulations as the Secretary of State thinks appropriate (and see also section 182).
(2) The Commissioner—
  (a) must keep under review the working of regulations under section 137(1) or (6), and
  (b) may from time to time submit proposals to the Secretary of State for amendments to be made to the regulations.
(3) The Secretary of State must review the working of regulations under section 137(1) or (6)—
  (a) at the end of the period of 5 years beginning with the making of the first set of regulations under section 108 of the Digital Economy Act 2017, and
  (b) at the end of each subsequent 5 year period.
(4) Regulations under section 137(1) are subject to the negative resolution procedure if—
  (a) they only make provision increasing a charge for which provision is made by previous regulations under section 137(1) or section 108(1) of the Digital Economy Act 2017, and
  (b) they do so to take account of an increase in the retail prices index since the previous regulations were made.
(5) Subject to subsection (4), regulations under section 137(1) or (6) are subject to the affirmative resolution procedure.
(6) In subsection (4), "the retail prices index" means—
  (a) the general index of retail prices (for all items) published by the Statistics Board, or
  (b) where that index is not published for a month, any substitute index or figures published by the Board.
(7) Regulations under section 137(1) or (6) may not apply to—
  (a) Her Majesty in her private capacity,
  (b) Her Majesty in right of the Duchy of Lancaster, or
  (c) the Duke of Cornwall.

NOTES
Commencement: 25 May 2018 (see also the introductory notes to this Act preceding s 1 at **[1.71]**).

Reports etc

[1.211]
139 Reporting to Parliament
(1) The Commissioner must—
  (a) produce a general report on the carrying out of the Commissioner's functions annually,
  (b) arrange for it to be laid before Parliament, and
  (c) publish it.
(2) The report must include the annual report required under Article 59 of the [UK GDPR].
(3) The Commissioner may produce other reports relating to the carrying out of the Commissioner's functions and arrange for them to be laid before Parliament.

NOTES
Commencement: 25 May 2018 (see also the introductory notes to this Act preceding s 1 at **[1.71]**).
Sub-s (2): words in square brackets substituted by the Data Protection, Privacy and Electronic Communications (Amendments etc) (EU Exit) Regulations 2019, SI 2019/419, reg 4, Sch 2, paras 1, 58.

[1.212]
140 Publication by the Commissioner
A duty under this Act for the Commissioner to publish a document is a duty for the Commissioner to publish it, or to arrange for it to be published, in such form and manner as the Commissioner considers appropriate.

NOTES
Commencement: 25 May 2018 (see also the introductory notes to this Act preceding s 1 at **[1.71]**).

[1.213]
141 Notices from the Commissioner
(1) This section applies in relation to a notice authorised or required by this Act to be given to a person by the Commissioner.
(2) The notice may be given to an individual—
  (a) by delivering it to the individual,
  (b) by sending it to the individual by post addressed to the individual at his or her usual or last-known place of residence or business, or
  (c) by leaving it for the individual at that place.
(3) The notice may be given to a body corporate or unincorporate—
  (a) by sending it by post to the proper officer of the body at its principal office, or
  (b) by addressing it to the proper officer of the body and leaving it at that office.
(4) The notice may be given to a partnership in Scotland—
  (a) by sending it by post to the principal office of the partnership, or
  (b) by addressing it to that partnership and leaving it at that office.
(5) The notice may be given to the person by other means, including by electronic means, with the person's consent.
(6) In this section—
  "principal office", in relation to a registered company, means its registered office;
  "proper officer", in relation to any body, means the secretary or other executive officer charged with the conduct of its general affairs;

"registered company" means a company registered under the enactments relating to companies for the time being in force in the United Kingdom.

(7) This section is without prejudice to any other lawful method of giving a notice.

NOTES

Commencement: 25 May 2018 (see also the introductory notes to this Act preceding s 1 at **[1.71]**).

PART 6 ENFORCEMENT

Information notices

[1.214]
142 Information notices

(1) The Commissioner may, by written notice (an "information notice")—
  (a) require a controller or processor to provide the Commissioner with information that the Commissioner reasonably requires for the purposes of carrying out the Commissioner's functions under the data protection legislation, or
  (b) require any person to provide the Commissioner with information that the Commissioner reasonably requires for the purposes of—
    (i) investigating a suspected failure of a type described in section 149(2) or a suspected offence under this Act, or
    (ii) determining whether the processing of personal data is carried out by an individual in the course of a purely personal or household activity.

(2) An information notice must state—
  (a) whether it is given under subsection (1)(a), (b)(i) or (b)(ii), and
  (b) why the Commissioner requires the information.

(3) An information notice
  (a) may specify or describe particular information or a category of information;
  (b) may specify the form in which the information must be provided;
  (c) may specify the time at which, or the period within which, the information must be provided;
  (d) may specify the place where the information must be provided;
(but see the restrictions in subsections (5) to (7)).

(4) An information notice must provide information about—
  (a) the consequences of failure to comply with it, and
  (b) the rights under sections 162 and 164 (appeals etc).

(5) An information notice may not require a person to provide information before the end of the period within which an appeal can be brought against the notice.

(6) If an appeal is brought against an information notice, the information need not be provided pending the determination or withdrawal of the appeal.

(7) If an information notice—
  (a) states that, in the Commissioner's opinion, the information is required urgently, and
  (b) gives the Commissioner's reasons for reaching that opinion,
subsections (5) and (6) do not apply but the notice must not require the information to be provided before the end of the period of 24 hours beginning when the notice is given.

(8) The Commissioner may cancel an information notice by written notice to the person to whom it was given.

(9) In subsection (1), in relation to a person who is a controller or processor for the purposes of the [UK GDPR], the reference to a controller or processor includes a representative of a controller or processor designated under Article 27 of the [UK GDPR] (representatives of controllers or processors not established in [the United Kingdom]).

(10) Section 3(14)(c) does not apply to the reference to the processing of personal data in subsection (1)(b).

NOTES

Commencement: 25 May 2018 (see also the introductory notes to this Act preceding s 1 at **[1.71]**).

Sub-s (9): words in square brackets substituted by the Data Protection, Privacy and Electronic Communications (Amendments etc) (EU Exit) Regulations 2019, SI 2019/419, reg 4, Sch 2, paras 1, 59.

[1.215]
143 Information notices: restrictions

(1) The Commissioner may not give an information notice with respect to the processing of personal data for the special purposes unless—
  (a) a determination under section 174 with respect to the data or the processing has taken effect, or
  (b) the Commissioner—
    (i) has reasonable grounds for suspecting that such a determination could be made, and
    (ii) the information is required for the purposes of making such a determination.

(2) An information notice does not require a person to give the Commissioner information to the extent that requiring the person to do so would involve an infringement of the privileges of either House of Parliament.

(3) An information notice does not require a person to give the Commissioner information in respect of a communication which is made—
  (a) between a professional legal adviser and the adviser's client, and
  (b) in connection with the giving of legal advice to the client with respect to obligations, liabilities or rights under the data protection legislation.

(4) An information notice does not require a person to give the Commissioner information in respect of a communication which is made—
  (a) between a professional legal adviser and the adviser's client or between such an adviser or client and another person,

(b) in connection with or in contemplation of proceedings under or arising out of the data protection legislation, and

(c) for the purposes of such proceedings.

(5) In subsections (3) and (4), references to the client of a professional legal adviser include references to a person acting on behalf of the client.

(6) An information notice does not require a person to provide the Commissioner with information if doing so would, by revealing evidence of the commission of an offence expose the person to proceedings for that offence.

(7) The reference to an offence in subsection (6) does not include an offence under—

(a) this Act;

(b) section 5 of the Perjury Act 1911 (false statements made otherwise than on oath);

(c) section 44(2) of the Criminal Law (Consolidation) (Scotland) Act 1995 (false statements made otherwise than on oath);

(d) Article 10 of the Perjury (Northern Ireland) Order 1979 (SI 1979/1714 (NI 19)) (false statutory declarations and other false unsworn statements).

(8) An oral or written statement provided by a person in response to an information notice may not be used in evidence against that person on a prosecution for an offence under this Act (other than an offence under section 144) unless in the proceedings—

(a) in giving evidence the person provides information inconsistent with the statement, and

(b) evidence relating to the statement is adduced, or a question relating to it is asked, by that person or on that person's behalf.

(9) In subsection (6), in relation to an information notice given to a representative of a controller or processor designated under Article 27 of the [UK GDPR], the reference to the person providing the information being exposed to proceedings for an offence includes a reference to the controller or processor being exposed to such proceedings.

NOTES

Commencement: 25 May 2018 (see also the introductory notes to this Act preceding s 1 at **[1.71]**).

Sub-s (9): words in square brackets substituted by the Data Protection, Privacy and Electronic Communications (Amendments etc) (EU Exit) Regulations 2019, SI 2019/419, reg 4, Sch 2, paras 1, 60.

[1.216]
144 False statements made in response to information notices
It is an offence for a person, in response to an information notice—

(a) to make a statement which the person knows to be false in a material respect, or

(b) recklessly to make a statement which is false in a material respect.

NOTES

Commencement: 25 May 2018 (see also the introductory notes to this Act preceding s 1 at **[1.71]**).

[1.217]
145 Information orders
(1) This section applies if, on an application by the Commissioner, a court is satisfied that a person has failed to comply with a requirement of an information notice.

(2) The court may make an order requiring the person to provide to the Commissioner some or all of the following—

(a) information referred to in the information notice;

(b) other information which the court is satisfied the Commissioner requires, having regard to the statement included in the notice in accordance with section 142(2)(b).

(3) The order—

(a) may specify the form in which the information must be provided,

(b) must specify the time at which, or the period within which, the information must be provided, and

(c) may specify the place where the information must be provided.

NOTES

Commencement: 25 May 2018 (see also the introductory notes to this Act preceding s 1 at **[1.71]**).

Assessment notices

[1.218]
146 Assessment notices
(1) The Commissioner may by written notice (an "assessment notice") require a controller or processor to permit the Commissioner to carry out an assessment of whether the controller or processor has complied or is complying with the data protection legislation.

(2) An assessment notice may require the controller or processor to do any of the following—

(a) permit the Commissioner to enter specified premises;

(b) direct the Commissioner to documents on the premises that are of a specified description;

(c) assist the Commissioner to view information of a specified description that is capable of being viewed using equipment on the premises;

(d) comply with a request from the Commissioner for a copy (in such form as may be requested) of—

(i) the documents to which the Commissioner is directed;

(ii) the information which the Commissioner is assisted to view;

(e) direct the Commissioner to equipment or other material on the premises which is of a specified description;

(f) permit the Commissioner to inspect or examine the documents, information, equipment or material to which the Commissioner is directed or which the Commissioner is assisted to view;

(g) provide the Commissioner with an explanation of such documents, information, equipment or material;

(h) permit the Commissioner to observe the processing of personal data that takes place on the premises;

(i) make available for interview by the Commissioner a specified number of people of a specified description who process personal data on behalf of the controller, not exceeding the number who are willing to be interviewed.

(3) In subsection (2), references to the Commissioner include references to the Commissioner's officers and staff.

(4) An assessment notice must, in relation to each requirement imposed by the notice, specify the time or times at which, or period or periods within which, the requirement must be complied with (but see the restrictions in subsections (6) to (9)).

(5) An assessment notice must provide information about—
  (a) the consequences of failure to comply with it, and
  (b) the rights under sections 162 and 164 (appeals etc).

(6) An assessment notice may not require a person to do anything before the end of the period within which an appeal can be brought against the notice.

(7) If an appeal is brought against an assessment notice, the controller or processor need not comply with a requirement in the notice pending the determination or withdrawal of the appeal.

(8) If an assessment notice—
  (a) states that, in the Commissioner's opinion, it is necessary for the controller or processor to comply with a requirement in the notice urgently,
  (b) gives the Commissioner's reasons for reaching that opinion, and
  (c) does not meet the conditions in subsection (9)(a) to (d),
subsections (6) and (7) do not apply but the notice must not require the controller or processor to comply with the requirement before the end of the period of 7 days beginning when the notice is given.

(9) If an assessment notice—
  (a) states that, in the Commissioner's opinion, there are reasonable grounds for suspecting that a controller or processor has failed or is failing as described in section 149(2) or that an offence under this Act has been or is being committed,
  (b) indicates the nature of the suspected failure or offence,
  (c) does not specify domestic premises,
  (d) states that, in the Commissioner's opinion, it is necessary for the controller or processor to comply with a requirement in the notice in less than 7 days, and
  (e) gives the Commissioner's reasons for reaching that opinion,
subsections (6) and (7) do not apply.

(10) The Commissioner may cancel an assessment notice by written notice to the controller or processor to whom it was given.

(11) Where the Commissioner gives an assessment notice to a processor, the Commissioner must, so far as reasonably practicable, give a copy of the notice to each controller for whom the processor processes personal data.

(12) In this section—
  "domestic premises" means premises, or a part of premises, used as a dwelling;
  "specified" means specified in an assessment notice.

NOTES

Commencement: 25 May 2018 (see also the introductory notes to this Act preceding s 1 at **[1.71]**).

[1.219]
147 Assessment notices: restrictions

(1) An assessment notice does not require a person to do something to the extent that requiring the person to do it would involve an infringement of the privileges of either House of Parliament.

(2) An assessment notice does not have effect so far as compliance would result in the disclosure of a communication which is made—
  (a) between a professional legal adviser and the adviser's client, and
  (b) in connection with the giving of legal advice to the client with respect to obligations, liabilities or rights under the data protection legislation.

(3) An assessment notice does not have effect so far as compliance would result in the disclosure of a communication which is made—
  (a) between a professional legal adviser and the adviser's client or between such an adviser or client and another person,
  (b) in connection with or in contemplation of proceedings under or arising out of the data protection legislation, and
  (c) for the purposes of such proceedings.

(4) In subsections (2) and (3)—
  (a) references to the client of a professional legal adviser include references to a person acting on behalf of such a client, and
  (b) references to a communication include—
    (i) a copy or other record of the communication, and
    (ii) anything enclosed with or referred to in the communication if made as described in subsection (2)(b) or in subsection (3)(b) and (c).

(5) The Commissioner may not give a controller or processor an assessment notice with respect to the processing of personal data for the special purposes.

(6) The Commissioner may not give an assessment notice to—
  (a) a body specified in section 23(3) of the Freedom of Information Act 2000 (bodies dealing with security matters), or
  (b) the Office for Standards in Education, Children's Services and Skills in so far as it is a controller or processor in respect of information processed for the purposes of functions exercisable by Her Majesty's Chief Inspector of Education, Children's Services and Skills by virtue of section 5(1)(a) of the Care Standards Act 2000.

NOTES
Commencement: 25 May 2018 (see also the introductory notes to this Act preceding s 1 at **[1.71]**).

Information notices and assessment notices: destruction of documents etc

[1.220]
148 Destroying or falsifying information and documents etc
(1) This section applies where a person—
  (a) has been given an information notice requiring the person to provide the Commissioner with information, or
  (b) has been given an assessment notice requiring the person to direct the Commissioner to a document, equipment or other material or to assist the Commissioner to view information.
(2) It is an offence for the person—
  (a) to destroy or otherwise dispose of, conceal, block or (where relevant) falsify all or part of the information, document, equipment or material, or
  (b) to cause or permit the destruction, disposal, concealment, blocking or (where relevant) falsification of all or part of the information, document, equipment or material,
with the intention of preventing the Commissioner from viewing, or being provided with or directed to, all or part of the information, document, equipment or material.
(3) It is a defence for a person charged with an offence under subsection (2) to prove that the destruction, disposal, concealment, blocking or falsification would have occurred in the absence of the person being given the notice.

NOTES
Commencement: 25 May 2018 (see also the introductory notes to this Act preceding s 1 at **[1.71]**).

Enforcement notices

[1.221]
149 Enforcement notices
(1) Where the Commissioner is satisfied that a person has failed, or is failing, as described in subsection (2), (3), (4) or (5), the Commissioner may give the person a written notice (an "enforcement notice") which requires the person—
  (a) to take steps specified in the notice, or
  (b) to refrain from taking steps specified in the notice,
or both (and see also sections 150 and 151).
(2) The first type of failure is where a controller or processor has failed, or is failing, to comply with any of the following—
  (a) a provision of Chapter II of the [UK GDPR] or Chapter 2 of Part 3 or Chapter 2 of Part 4 of this Act (principles of processing);
  (b) a provision of Articles 12 to 22 of the [UK GDPR] or Part 3 or 4 of this Act conferring rights on a data subject;
  (c) a provision of Articles 25 to 39 of the [UK GDPR] or section 64 or 65 of this Act (obligations of controllers and processors);
  (d) a requirement to communicate a personal data breach to the Commissioner or a data subject under section 67, 68 or 108 of this Act;
  (e) the principles for transfers of personal data to third countries, non-Convention countries and international organisations in Articles 44 to 49 of the [UK GDPR] or in sections 73 to 78 or 109 of this Act.
(3) The second type of failure is where a monitoring body has failed, or is failing, to comply with an obligation under Article 41 of the [UK GDPR] (monitoring of approved codes of conduct).
(4) The third type of failure is where a person who is a certification provider—
  (a) does not meet the requirements for accreditation,
  (b) has failed, or is failing, to comply with an obligation under Article 42 or 43 of the [UK GDPR] (certification of controllers and processors), or
  (c) has failed, or is failing, to comply with any other provision of the [UK GDPR] (whether in the person's capacity as a certification provider or otherwise).
(5) The fourth type of failure is where a controller has failed, or is failing, to comply with regulations under section 137.
(6) An enforcement notice given in reliance on subsection (2), (3) or (5) may only impose requirements which the Commissioner considers appropriate for the purpose of remedying the failure.
(7) An enforcement notice given in reliance on subsection (4) may only impose requirements which the Commissioner considers appropriate having regard to the failure (whether or not for the purpose of remedying the failure).
(8) The Secretary of State may by regulations confer power on the Commissioner to give an enforcement notice in respect of other failures to comply with the data protection legislation.
(9) Regulations under this section—
  (a) may make provision about the giving of an enforcement notice in respect of the failure, including by amending this section and sections 150 to 152,
  (b) may make provision about the giving of an information notice, an assessment notice or a penalty notice, or about powers of entry and inspection, in connection with the failure, including by amending sections 142, 143, 146, 147 and 155 to 157 and Schedules 15 and 16, and
  (c) are subject to the affirmative resolution procedure.

NOTES
Commencement: 25 May 2018 (see also the introductory notes to this Act preceding s 1 at **[1.71]**).
Sub-ss (2)–(4): words in square brackets substituted by the Data Protection, Privacy and Electronic Communications (Amendments etc) (EU Exit) Regulations 2019, SI 2019/419, reg 4, Sch 2, paras 1, 61.

[1.222]
150   Enforcement notices: supplementary
(1) An enforcement notice must—
   (a)   state what the person has failed or is failing to do, and
   (b)   give the Commissioner's reasons for reaching that opinion.
(2) In deciding whether to give an enforcement notice in reliance on section 149(2), the Commissioner must consider whether the failure has caused or is likely to cause any person damage or distress.
(3) In relation to an enforcement notice given in reliance on section 149(2), the Commissioner's power under section 149(1)(b) to require a person to refrain from taking specified steps includes power—
   (a)   to impose a ban relating to all processing of personal data, or
   (b)   to impose a ban relating only to a specified description of processing of personal data, including by specifying one or more of the following—
      (i)   a description of personal data;
      (ii)   the purpose or manner of the processing;
      (iii) the time when the processing takes place.
(4) An enforcement notice may specify the time or times at which, or period or periods within which, a requirement imposed by the notice must be complied with (but see the restrictions in subsections (6) to (8)).
(5) An enforcement notice must provide information about—
   (a)   the consequences of failure to comply with it, and
   (b)   the rights under sections 162 and 164 (appeals etc).
(6) An enforcement notice must not specify a time for compliance with a requirement in the notice which falls before the end of the period within which an appeal can be brought against the notice.
(7) If an appeal is brought against an enforcement notice, a requirement in the notice need not be complied with pending the determination or withdrawal of the appeal.
(8) If an enforcement notice—
   (a)   states that, in the Commissioner's opinion, it is necessary for a requirement to be complied with urgently, and
   (b)   gives the Commissioner's reasons for reaching that opinion,
subsections (6) and (7) do not apply but the notice must not require the requirement to be complied with before the end of the period of 24 hours beginning when the notice is given.
(9) In this section, "specified" means specified in an enforcement notice.

NOTES
   Commencement: 25 May 2018 (see also the introductory notes to this Act preceding s 1 at **[1.71]**).

[1.223]
151   Enforcement notices: rectification and erasure of personal data etc
(1) Subsections (2) and (3) apply where an enforcement notice is given in respect of a failure by a controller or processor—
   (a)   to comply with a data protection principle relating to accuracy, or
   (b)   to comply with a data subject's request to exercise rights under Article 16, 17 or 18 of the [UK GDPR] (right to rectification, erasure or restriction on processing) or section 46, 47 or 100 of this Act.
(2) If the enforcement notice requires the controller or processor to rectify or erase inaccurate personal data, it may also require the controller or processor to rectify or erase any other data which—
   (a)   is held by the controller or processor, and
   (b)   contains an expression of opinion which appears to the Commissioner to be based on the inaccurate personal data.
(3) Where a controller or processor has accurately recorded personal data provided by the data subject or a third party but the data is inaccurate, the enforcement notice may require the controller or processor—
   (a)   to take steps specified in the notice to ensure the accuracy of the data,
   (b)   if relevant, to secure that the data indicates the data subject's view that the data is inaccurate, and
   (c)   to supplement the data with a statement of the true facts relating to the matters dealt with by the data that is approved by the Commissioner,
(as well as imposing requirements under subsection (2)).
(4) When deciding what steps it is reasonable to specify under subsection (3)(a), the Commissioner must have regard to the purpose for which the data was obtained and further processed.
(5) Subsections (6) and (7) apply where—
   (a)   an enforcement notice requires a controller or processor to rectify or erase personal data, or
   (b)   the Commissioner is satisfied that the processing of personal data which has been rectified or erased by the controller or processor involved a failure described in subsection (1).
(6) An enforcement notice may, if reasonably practicable, require the controller or processor to notify third parties to whom the data has been disclosed of the rectification or erasure.
(7) In determining whether it is reasonably practicable to require such notification, the Commissioner must have regard, in particular, to the number of people who would have to be notified.
(8) In this section, "data protection principle relating to accuracy" means the principle in—
   (a)   Article 5(1)(d) of the [UK GDPR],
   (b)   section 38(1) of this Act, or
   (c)   section 89 of this Act.

NOTES
   Commencement: 25 May 2018 (see also the introductory notes to this Act preceding s 1 at **[1.71]**).

NOTES
Sub-ss (1), (8): words in square brackets substituted by the Data Protection, Privacy and Electronic Communications (Amendments etc) (EU Exit) Regulations 2019, SI 2019/419, reg 4, Sch 2, paras 1, 62.

[1.224]
152 Enforcement notices: restrictions
(1) The Commissioner may not give a controller or processor an enforcement notice in reliance on section 149(2) with respect to the processing of personal data for the special purposes unless—
   (a) a determination under section 174 with respect to the data or the processing has taken effect, and
   (b) a court has granted leave for the notice to be given.
(2) A court must not grant leave for the purposes of subsection (1)(b) unless it is satisfied that—
   (a) the Commissioner has reason to suspect a failure described in section 149(2) which is of substantial public importance, and
   (b) the controller or processor has been given notice of the application for leave in accordance with rules of court or the case is urgent.
(3) An enforcement notice does not require a person to do something to the extent that requiring the person to do it would involve an infringement of the privileges of either House of Parliament.
(4) In the case of a joint controller in respect of the processing of personal data to which Part 3 or 4 applies whose responsibilities for compliance with that Part are determined in an arrangement under section 58 or 104, the Commissioner may only give the controller an enforcement notice in reliance on section 149(2) if the controller is responsible for compliance with the provision, requirement or principle in question.

NOTES
Commencement: 25 May 2018 (see also the introductory notes to this Act preceding s 1 at **[1.71]**).

[1.225]
153 Enforcement notices: cancellation and variation
(1) The Commissioner may cancel or vary an enforcement notice by giving written notice to the person to whom it was given.
(2) A person to whom an enforcement notice is given may apply in writing to the Commissioner for the cancellation or variation of the notice.
(3) An application under subsection (2) may be made only—
   (a) after the end of the period within which an appeal can be brought against the notice, and
   (b) on the ground that, by reason of a change of circumstances, one or more of the provisions of that notice need not be complied with in order to remedy the failure identified in the notice.

NOTES
Commencement: 25 May 2018 (see also the introductory notes to this Act preceding s 1 at **[1.71]**).

Powers of entry and inspection

[1.226]
154 Powers of entry and inspection
Schedule 15 makes provision about powers of entry and inspection.

NOTES
Commencement: 25 May 2018 (see also the introductory notes to this Act preceding s 1 at **[1.71]**).

Penalties

[1.227]
155 Penalty notices
(1) If the Commissioner is satisfied that a person—
   (a) has failed or is failing as described in section 149(2), (3), (4) or (5), or
   (b) has failed to comply with an information notice, an assessment notice or an enforcement notice,
the Commissioner may, by written notice (a "penalty notice"), require the person to pay to the Commissioner an amount in sterling specified in the notice.
(2) Subject to subsection (4), when deciding whether to give a penalty notice to a person and determining the amount of the penalty, the Commissioner must have regard to the following, so far as relevant—
   (a) to the extent that the notice concerns a matter to which the [UK GDPR] applies, the matters listed in Article 83(1) and (2) of the [UK GDPR];
   (b) to the extent that the notice concerns another matter, the matters listed in subsection (3).
(3) Those matters are—
   (a) the nature, gravity and duration of the failure;
   (b) the intentional or negligent character of the failure;
   (c) any action taken by the controller or processor to mitigate the damage or distress suffered by data subjects;
   (d) the degree of responsibility of the controller or processor, taking into account technical and organisational measures implemented by the controller or processor in accordance with section 57, 66, 103 or 107;
   (e) any relevant previous failures by the controller or processor;
   (f) the degree of co-operation with the Commissioner, in order to remedy the failure and mitigate the possible adverse effects of the failure;
   (g) the categories of personal data affected by the failure;
   (h) the manner in which the infringement became known to the Commissioner, including whether, and if so to what extent, the controller or processor notified the Commissioner of the failure;

    (i)   the extent to which the controller or processor has complied with previous enforcement notices or penalty notices;

    (j)   adherence to approved codes of conduct or certification mechanisms;

    (k)   any other aggravating or mitigating factor applicable to the case, including financial benefits gained, or losses avoided, as a result of the failure (whether directly or indirectly);

    (l)   whether the penalty would be effective, proportionate and dissuasive.

(4)   Subsections (2) and (3) do not apply in the case of a decision or determination relating to a failure described in section 149(5).

(5)   Schedule 16 makes further provision about penalty notices, including provision requiring the Commissioner to give a notice of intent to impose a penalty and provision about payment, variation, cancellation and enforcement.

(6)   The Secretary of State may by regulations—

    (a)   confer power on the Commissioner to give a penalty notice in respect of other failures to comply with the data protection legislation, and

    (b)   provide for the maximum penalty that may be imposed in relation to such failures to be either the standard maximum amount or the higher maximum amount.

(7)   Regulations under this section—

    (a)   may make provision about the giving of penalty notices in respect of the failure,

    (b)   may amend this section and sections 156 to 158, and

    (c)   are subject to the affirmative resolution procedure.

(8)   In this section, "higher maximum amount" and "standard maximum amount" have the same meaning as in section 157.

NOTES

    Commencement: 25 May 2018 (see also the introductory notes to this Act preceding s 1 at **[1.71]**).

    Sub-s (2): words in square brackets substituted by the Data Protection, Privacy and Electronic Communications (Amendments etc) (EU Exit) Regulations 2019, SI 2019/419, reg 4, Sch 2, paras 1, 63.

[1.228]

156   Penalty notices: restrictions

(1)   The Commissioner may not give a controller or processor a penalty notice in reliance on section 149(2) with respect to the processing of personal data for the special purposes unless—

    (a)   a determination under section 174 with respect to the data or the processing has taken effect, and

    (b)   a court has granted leave for the notice to be given.

(2)   A court must not grant leave for the purposes of subsection (1)(b) unless it is satisfied that—

    (a)   the Commissioner has reason to suspect a failure described in section 149(2) which is of substantial public importance, and

    (b)   the controller or processor has been given notice of the application for leave in accordance with rules of court or the case is urgent.

(3)   The Commissioner may not give a controller or processor a penalty notice with respect to the processing of personal data where the purposes and manner of the processing are determined by or on behalf of either House of Parliament.

(4)   The Commissioner may not give a penalty notice to—

    (a)   the Crown Estate Commissioners, or

    (b)   a person who is a controller by virtue of section 209(4) (controller for the Royal Household etc).

(5)   In the case of a joint controller in respect of the processing of personal data to which Part 3 or 4 applies whose responsibilities for compliance with that Part are determined in an arrangement under section 58 or 104, the Commissioner may only give the controller a penalty notice in reliance on section 149(2) if the controller is responsible for compliance with the provision, requirement or principle in question.

NOTES

    Commencement: 25 May 2018 (see also the introductory notes to this Act preceding s 1 at **[1.71]**).

[1.229]

157   Maximum amount of penalty

(1)   In relation to an infringement of a provision of the [UK GDPR], the maximum amount of the penalty that may be imposed by a penalty notice is—

    (a)   the amount specified in Article 83 of the [UK GDPR], or

    (b)   if an amount is not specified there, the standard maximum amount.

(2)   In relation to an infringement of a provision of Part 3 of this Act, the maximum amount of the penalty that may be imposed by a penalty notice is—

    (a)   in relation to a failure to comply with section 35, 36, 37, 38(1), 39(1), 40, 44, 45, 46, 47, 48, 49, 52, 53, 73, . . . 75, 76, 77 or 78, the higher maximum amount, and

    (b)   otherwise, the standard maximum amount.

(3)   In relation to an infringement of a provision of Part 4 of this Act, the maximum amount of the penalty that may be imposed by a penalty notice is—

    (a)   in relation to a failure to comply with section 86, 87, 88, 89, 90, 91, 93, 94, 100 or 109, the higher maximum amount, and

    (b)   otherwise, the standard maximum amount.

(4)   In relation to a failure to comply with an information notice, an assessment notice or an enforcement notice, the maximum amount of the penalty that may be imposed by a penalty notice is the higher maximum amount.

(5)   The "higher maximum amount" is—

    (a)   in the case of an undertaking, [£17,500,000] or 4% of the undertaking's total annual worldwide turnover in the preceding financial year, whichever is higher, or

(b) in any other case, [£17,500,000].

(6) The "standard maximum amount" is—

(a) in the case of an undertaking, [£8,700,000] or 2% of the undertaking's total annual worldwide turnover in the preceding financial year, whichever is higher, or

(b) in any other case, [£8,700,000].

(7) . . .

NOTES

Commencement: 25 May 2018 (see also the introductory notes to this Act preceding s 1 at **[1.71]**).

The words in square brackets in sub-s (1) were substituted, the figure omitted from sub-s (2) was repealed, the sums in square brackets in sub-ss (5), (6) were substituted and sub-s (7) was repealed, by the Data Protection, Privacy and Electronic Communications (Amendments etc) (EU Exit) Regulations 2019, SI 2019/419, reg 4, Sch 2, paras 1, 64.

[1.230]
158 Fixed penalties for non-compliance with charges regulations

(1) The Commissioner must produce and publish a document specifying the amount of the penalty for a failure to comply with regulations made under section 137.

(2) The Commissioner may specify different amounts for different types of failure.

(3) The maximum amount that may be specified is 150% of the highest charge payable by a controller in respect of a financial year in accordance with the regulations, disregarding any discount available under the regulations.

(4) The Commissioner—

(a) may alter or replace the document, and

(b) must publish any altered or replacement document.

(5) Before publishing a document under this section (including any altered or replacement document), the Commissioner must consult—

(a) the Secretary of State, and

(b) such other persons as the Commissioner considers appropriate.

(6) The Commissioner must arrange for a document published under this section (including any altered or replacement document) to be laid before Parliament.

NOTES

Commencement: 25 May 2018 (see also the introductory notes to this Act preceding s 1 at **[1.71]**).

[1.231]
159 Amount of penalties: supplementary

(1) For the purposes of Article 83 of the [UK GDPR] and section 157, the Secretary of State may by regulations—

(a) provide that a person of a description specified in the regulations is or is not an undertaking, and

(b) make provision about how an undertaking's turnover is to be determined.

(2) For the purposes of Article 83 of the [UK GDPR], section 157 and section 158, the Secretary of State may by regulations provide that a period is or is not a financial year.

(3) Regulations under this section are subject to the affirmative resolution procedure.

NOTES

Commencement: 25 May 2018 (see also the introductory notes to this Act preceding s 1 at **[1.71]**).

Sub-ss (1), (2): the words in square brackets were substituted by the Data Protection, Privacy and Electronic Communications (Amendments etc) (EU Exit) Regulations 2019, SI 2019/419, reg 4, Sch 2, paras 1, 65.

Guidance

[1.232]
160 Guidance about regulatory action

(1) The Commissioner must produce and publish guidance about how the Commissioner proposes to exercise the Commissioner's functions in connection with—

(a) information notices,

(b) assessment notices,

(c) enforcement notices, and

(d) penalty notices.

(2) The Commissioner may produce and publish guidance about how the Commissioner proposes to exercise the Commissioner's other functions under this Part.

(3) In relation to information notices, the guidance must include—

(a) provision specifying factors to be considered in determining the time at which, or the period within which, information is to be required to be provided;

(b) provision about the circumstances in which the Commissioner would consider it appropriate to give an information notice to a person in reliance on section 142(7) (urgent cases);

(c) provision about how the Commissioner will determine how to proceed if a person does not comply with an information notice.

(4) In relation to assessment notices, the guidance must include—

(a) provision specifying factors to be considered in determining whether to give an assessment notice to a person;

(b) provision about the circumstances in which the Commissioner would consider it appropriate to give an assessment notice in reliance on section 146(8) or (9) (urgent cases);

(c) provision specifying descriptions of documents or information that—

(i) are not to be examined or inspected in accordance with an assessment notice, or

(ii) are to be so examined or inspected only by a person of a description specified in the guidance;

(d) provision about the nature of inspections and examinations carried out in accordance with an assessment notice;

(e) provision about the nature of interviews carried out in accordance with an assessment notice;

(f) provision about the preparation, issuing and publication by the Commissioner of assessment reports in respect of controllers and processors that have been given assessment notices;

(g) provision about how the Commissioner will determine how to proceed if a person does not comply with an assessment notice.

(5) The guidance produced in accordance with subsection (4)(c) must include provisions that relate to—

(a) documents and information concerning an individual's physical or mental health;

(b) documents and information concerning the provision of social care for an individual.

(6) In relation to enforcement notices, the guidance must include—

(a) provision specifying factors to be considered in determining whether to give an enforcement notice to a person;

(b) provision about the circumstances in which the Commissioner would consider it appropriate to give an enforcement notice to a person in reliance on section 150(8) (urgent cases);

(c) provision about how the Commissioner will determine how to proceed if a person does not comply with an enforcement notice.

(7) In relation to penalty notices, the guidance must include—

(a) provision about the circumstances in which the Commissioner would consider it appropriate to issue a penalty notice;

(b) provision about the circumstances in which the Commissioner would consider it appropriate to allow a person to make oral representations about the Commissioner's intention to give the person a penalty notice;

(c) provision explaining how the Commissioner will determine the amount of penalties;

(d) provision about how the Commissioner will determine how to proceed if a person does not comply with a penalty notice.

(8) The Commissioner—

(a) may alter or replace guidance produced under this section, and

(b) must publish any altered or replacement guidance.

(9) Before producing guidance under this section (including any altered or replacement guidance), the Commissioner must consult—

(a) the Secretary of State, and

(b) such other persons as the Commissioner considers appropriate.

(10) Section 161 applies in relation to the first guidance under subsection (1).

(11) The Commissioner must arrange for other guidance under this section (including any altered or replacement guidance) to be laid before Parliament.

(12) In this section, "social care" has the same meaning as in Part 1 of the Health and Social Care Act 2008 (see section 9(3) of that Act).

NOTES

Commencement: 25 May 2018 (see also the introductory notes to this Act preceding s 1 at **[1.71]**).

[1.233]

161　Approval of first guidance about regulatory action

(1) When the first guidance is produced under section 160(1)—

(a) the Commissioner must submit the final version to the Secretary of State, and

(b) the Secretary of State must lay the guidance before Parliament.

(2) If, within the 40-day period, either House of Parliament resolves not to approve the guidance—

(a) the Commissioner must not issue the guidance, and

(b) the Commissioner must produce another version of the guidance (and this section applies to that version).

(3) If, within the 40-day period, no such resolution is made—

(a) the Commissioner must issue the guidance, and

(b) the guidance comes into force at the end of the period of 21 days beginning with the day on which it is issued.

(4) Nothing in subsection (2)(a) prevents another version of the guidance being laid before Parliament.

(5) In this section, "the 40-day period" means—

(a) if the guidance is laid before both Houses of Parliament on the same day, the period of 40 days beginning with that day, or

(b) if the guidance is laid before the Houses of Parliament on different days, the period of 40 days beginning with the later of those days.

(6) In calculating the 40-day period, no account is to be taken of any period during which Parliament is dissolved or prorogued or during which both Houses of Parliament are adjourned for more than 4 days.

NOTES

Commencement: 25 May 2018 (see also the introductory notes to this Act preceding s 1 at **[1.71]**).

Appeals etc

[1.234]

162　Rights of appeal

(1) A person who is given any of the following notices may appeal to the Tribunal—

(a) an information notice;

(b) an assessment notice;

(c) an enforcement notice;

(d) a penalty notice;

(e) a penalty variation notice.

(2) A person who is given an enforcement notice may appeal to the Tribunal against the refusal of an application under section 153 for the cancellation or variation of the notice.

(3) A person who is given a penalty notice or a penalty variation notice may appeal to the Tribunal against the amount of the penalty specified in the notice, whether or not the person appeals against the notice.

(4) Where a determination is made under section 174 in respect of the processing of personal data, the controller or processor may appeal to the Tribunal against the determination.

NOTES
Commencement: 25 May 2018 (see also the introductory notes to this Act preceding s 1 at **[1.71]**).

[1.235]
163 Determination of appeals
(1) Subsections (2) to (4) apply where a person appeals to the Tribunal under section 162(1) or (3).

(2) The Tribunal may review any determination of fact on which the notice or decision against which the appeal is brought was based.

(3) If the Tribunal considers—
  (a) that the notice or decision against which the appeal is brought is not in accordance with the law, or
  (b) to the extent that the notice or decision involved an exercise of discretion by the Commissioner, that the Commissioner ought to have exercised the discretion differently,
the Tribunal must allow the appeal or substitute another notice or decision which the Commissioner could have given or made.

(4) Otherwise, the Tribunal must dismiss the appeal.

(5) On an appeal under section 162(2), if the Tribunal considers that the enforcement notice ought to be cancelled or varied by reason of a change in circumstances, the Tribunal must cancel or vary the notice.

(6) On an appeal under section 162(4), the Tribunal may cancel the Commissioner's determination.

NOTES
Commencement: 25 May 2018 (see also the introductory notes to this Act preceding s 1 at **[1.71]**).

[1.236]
164 Applications in respect of urgent notices
(1) This section applies where an information notice, an assessment notice or an enforcement notice given to a person contains an urgency statement.

(2) The person may apply to the court for either or both of the following—
  (a) the disapplication of the urgency statement in relation to some or all of the requirements of the notice;
  (b) a change to the time at which, or the period within which, a requirement of the notice must be complied with.

(3) On an application under subsection (2), the court may do any of the following—
  (a) direct that the notice is to have effect as if it did not contain the urgency statement;
  (b) direct that the inclusion of the urgency statement is not to have effect in relation to a requirement of the notice;
  (c) vary the notice by changing the time at which, or the period within which, a requirement of the notice must be complied with;
  (d) vary the notice by making other changes required to give effect to a direction under paragraph (a) or (b) or in consequence of a variation under paragraph (c).

(4) The decision of the court on an application under this section is final.

(5) In this section, "urgency statement" means—
  (a) in relation to an information notice, a statement under section 142(7)(a),
  (b) in relation to an assessment notice, a statement under section 146(8)(a) or (9)(d), and
  (c) in relation to an enforcement notice, a statement under section 150(8)(a).

NOTES
Commencement: 25 May 2018 (see also the introductory notes to this Act preceding s 1 at **[1.71]**).

Complaints

[1.237]
165 Complaints by data subjects
(1) Articles 57(1)(f) and (2) and 77 of the [UK GDPR] (data subject's right to lodge a complaint) confer rights on data subjects to complain to the Commissioner if the data subject considers that, in connection with personal data relating to him or her, there is an infringement of the [UK GDPR].

(2) A data subject may make a complaint to the Commissioner if the data subject considers that, in connection with personal data relating to him or her, there is an infringement of Part 3 or 4 of this Act.

(3) The Commissioner must facilitate the making of complaints under subsection (2) by taking steps such as providing a complaint form which can be completed electronically and by other means.

(4) If the Commissioner receives a complaint under subsection (2), the Commissioner must—
  (a) take appropriate steps to respond to the complaint,
  (b) inform the complainant of the outcome of the complaint,
  (c) inform the complainant of the rights under section 166, and
  (d) if asked to do so by the complainant, provide the complainant with further information about how to pursue the complaint.

(5) The reference in subsection (4)(a) to taking appropriate steps in response to a complaint includes—
  (a) investigating the subject matter of the complaint, to the extent appropriate, and
  (b) informing the complainant about progress on the complaint, including about whether further investigation or co-ordination with [a] foreign designated authority is necessary.

(6) . . .

(7) In this section—
  "foreign designated authority" means an authority designated for the purposes of Article 13 of the Data Protection Convention by a party, other than the United Kingdom, which is bound by that Convention;

. . .

NOTES
Commencement: 25 May 2018 (see also the introductory notes to this Act preceding s 1 at **[1.71]**).
The words in square brackets in sub-ss (1), (5) were substituted, and sub-s (6) and the words omitted from sub-s (7) were repealed, by the Data Protection, Privacy and Electronic Communications (Amendments etc) (EU Exit) Regulations 2019, SI 2019/419, reg 4, Sch 2, paras 1, 66.

[1.238]
166 Orders to progress complaints
(1) This section applies where, after a data subject makes a complaint under section 165 or Article 77 of the [UK GDPR], the Commissioner—
  (a) fails to take appropriate steps to respond to the complaint,
  (b) fails to provide the complainant with information about progress on the complaint, or of the outcome of the complaint, before the end of the period of 3 months beginning when the Commissioner received the complaint, or
  (c) if the Commissioner's consideration of the complaint is not concluded during that period, fails to provide the complainant with such information during a subsequent period of 3 months.
(2) The Tribunal may, on an application by the data subject, make an order requiring the Commissioner—
  (a) to take appropriate steps to respond to the complaint, or
  (b) to inform the complainant of progress on the complaint, or of the outcome of the complaint, within a period specified in the order.
(3) An order under subsection (2)(a) may require the Commissioner—
  (a) to take steps specified in the order;
  (b) to conclude an investigation, or take a specified step, within a period specified in the order.
(4) Section 165(5) applies for the purposes of subsections (1)(a) and (2)(a) as it applies for the purposes of section 165(4)(a).

NOTES
Commencement: 25 May 2018 (see also the introductory notes to this Act preceding s 1 at **[1.71]**).
Sub-s (1): words in square brackets substituted by the Data Protection, Privacy and Electronic Communications (Amendments etc) (EU Exit) Regulations 2019, SI 2019/419, reg 4, Sch 2, paras 1, 67.

Remedies in the court
[1.239]
167 Compliance orders
(1) This section applies if, on an application by a data subject, a court is satisfied that there has been an infringement of the data subject's rights under the data protection legislation in contravention of that legislation.
(2) A court may make an order for the purposes of securing compliance with the data protection legislation which requires the controller in respect of the processing, or a processor acting on behalf of that controller—
  (a) to take steps specified in the order, or
  (b) to refrain from taking steps specified in the order.
(3) The order may, in relation to each step, specify the time at which, or the period within which, it must be taken.
(4) In subsection (1)—
  (a) the reference to an application by a data subject includes an application made in exercise of the right under Article 79(1) of the [UK GDPR] (right to an effective remedy against a controller or processor);
  (b) the reference to the data protection legislation does not include Part 4 of this Act or regulations made under that Part.
(5) In relation to a joint controller in respect of the processing of personal data to which Part 3 applies whose responsibilities are determined in an arrangement under section 58, a court may only make an order under this section if the controller is responsible for compliance with the provision of the data protection legislation that is contravened.

NOTES
Commencement: 25 May 2018 (see also the introductory notes to this Act preceding s 1 at **[1.71]**).
Sub-s (4): words in square brackets substituted by the Data Protection, Privacy and Electronic Communications (Amendments etc) (EU Exit) Regulations 2019, SI 2019/419, reg 4, Sch 2, paras 1, 68.

[1.240]
168 Compensation for contravention of the [UK GDPR]
(1) In Article 82 of the [UK GDPR] (right to compensation for material or non-material damage), "non-material damage" includes distress.
(2) Subsection (3) applies where—
  (a) in accordance with rules of court, proceedings under Article 82 of the [UK GDPR] are brought by a representative body on behalf of a person, and
  (b) a court orders the payment of compensation.
(3) The court may make an order providing for the compensation to be paid on behalf of the person to—
  (a) the representative body, or
  (b) such other person as the court thinks fit.

NOTES
Commencement: 25 May 2018 (see also the introductory notes to this Act preceding s 1 at **[1.71]**).
The words in square brackets in the heading and in sub-ss (1), (2) were substituted by the Data Protection, Privacy and Electronic Communications (Amendments etc) (EU Exit) Regulations 2019, SI 2019/419, reg 4, Sch 2, paras 1, 69.

[1.241]
169   Compensation for contravention of other data protection legislation
(1) A person who suffers damage by reason of a contravention of a requirement of the data protection legislation, other than the [UK GDPR], is entitled to compensation for that damage from the controller or the processor, subject to subsections (2) and (3).
(2) Under subsection (1)—
   (a) a controller involved in processing of personal data is liable for any damage caused by the processing, and
   (b) a processor involved in processing of personal data is liable for damage caused by the processing only if the processor—
      (i)   has not complied with an obligation under the data protection legislation specifically directed at processors, or
      (ii)   has acted outside, or contrary to, the controller's lawful instructions.
(3) A controller or processor is not liable as described in subsection (2) if the controller or processor proves that the controller or processor is not in any way responsible for the event giving rise to the damage.
(4) A joint controller in respect of the processing of personal data to which Part 3 or 4 applies whose responsibilities are determined in an arrangement under section 58 or 104 is only liable as described in subsection (2) if the controller is responsible for compliance with the provision of the data protection legislation that is contravened.
(5) In this section, "damage" includes financial loss and damage not involving financial loss, such as distress.

NOTES
Commencement: 25 May 2018 (see also the introductory notes to this Act preceding s 1 at **[1.71]**).
Sub-s (1): words in square brackets substituted by the Data Protection, Privacy and Electronic Communications (Amendments etc) (EU Exit) Regulations 2019, SI 2019/419, reg 4, Sch 2, paras 1, 70.

Offences relating to personal data
[1.242]
170   Unlawful obtaining etc of personal data
(1) It is an offence for a person knowingly or recklessly—
   (a) to obtain or disclose personal data without the consent of the controller,
   (b) to procure the disclosure of personal data to another person without the consent of the controller, or
   (c) after obtaining personal data, to retain it without the consent of the person who was the controller in relation to the personal data when it was obtained.
(2) It is a defence for a person charged with an offence under subsection (1) to prove that the obtaining, disclosing, procuring or retaining—
   (a) was necessary for the purposes of preventing or detecting crime,
   (b) was required or authorised by an enactment, by a rule of law or by the order of a court or tribunal, or
   (c) in the particular circumstances, was justified as being in the public interest.
(3) It is also a defence for a person charged with an offence under subsection (1) to prove that—
   (a) the person acted in the reasonable belief that the person had a legal right to do the obtaining, disclosing, procuring or retaining,
   (b) the person acted in the reasonable belief that the person would have had the consent of the controller if the controller had known about the obtaining, disclosing, procuring or retaining and the circumstances of it, or
   (c) the person acted—
      (i)   for the special purposes,
      (ii)   with a view to the publication by a person of any journalistic, academic, artistic or literary material, and
      (iii)   in the reasonable belief that in the particular circumstances the obtaining, disclosing, procuring or retaining was justified as being in the public interest.
(4) It is an offence for a person to sell personal data if the person obtained the data in circumstances in which an offence under subsection (1) was committed.
(5) It is an offence for a person to offer to sell personal data if the person—
   (a) has obtained the data in circumstances in which an offence under subsection (1) was committed, or
   (b) subsequently obtains the data in such circumstances.
(6) For the purposes of subsection (5), an advertisement indicating that personal data is or may be for sale is an offer to sell the data.
(7) In this section—
   (a) references to the consent of a controller do not include the consent of a person who is a controller by virtue of Article 28(10) of the [UK GDPR] or section 59(8) or 105(3) of this Act (processor to be treated as controller in certain circumstances);
   (b) where there is more than one controller, such references are references to the consent of one or more of them.

NOTES
Commencement: 25 May 2018 (see also the introductory notes to this Act preceding s 1 at **[1.71]**).
Sub-s (7): words in square brackets substituted by the Data Protection, Privacy and Electronic Communications (Amendments etc) (EU Exit) Regulations 2019, SI 2019/419, reg 4, Sch 2, paras 1, 71.

[1.243]
171   Re-identification of de-identified personal data
(1) It is an offence for a person knowingly or recklessly to re-identify information that is de-identified personal data without the consent of the controller responsible for de-identifying the personal data.
(2) For the purposes of this section and section 172—
   (a) personal data is "de-identified" if it has been processed in such a manner that it can no longer be attributed, without more, to a specific data subject;

(b) a person "re-identifies" information if the person takes steps which result in the information no longer being de-identified within the meaning of paragraph (a).

(3) It is a defence for a person charged with an offence under subsection (1) to prove that the re-identification—

(a) was necessary for the purposes of preventing or detecting crime,

(b) was required or authorised by an enactment, by a rule of law or by the order of a court or tribunal, or

(c) in the particular circumstances, was justified as being in the public interest.

(4) It is also a defence for a person charged with an offence under subsection (1) to prove that—

(a) the person acted in the reasonable belief that the person—

(i) is the data subject to whom the information relates,

(ii) had the consent of that data subject, or

(iii) would have had such consent if the data subject had known about the re-identification and the circumstances of it,

(b) the person acted in the reasonable belief that the person—

(i) is the controller responsible for de-identifying the personal data,

(ii) had the consent of that controller, or

(iii) would have had such consent if that controller had known about the re-identification and the circumstances of it,

(c) the person acted—

(i) for the special purposes,

(ii) with a view to the publication by a person of any journalistic, academic, artistic or literary material, and

(iii) in the reasonable belief that in the particular circumstances the re-identification was justified as being in the public interest, or

(d) the effectiveness testing conditions were met (see section 172).

(5) It is an offence for a person knowingly or recklessly to process personal data that is information that has been re-identified where the person does so

(a) without the consent of the controller responsible for de-identifying the personal data, and

(b) in circumstances in which the re-identification was an offence under subsection (1).

(6) It is a defence for a person charged with an offence under subsection (5) to prove that the processing—

(a) was necessary for the purposes of preventing or detecting crime,

(b) was required or authorised by an enactment, by a rule of law or by the order of a court or tribunal, or

(c) in the particular circumstances, was justified as being in the public interest.

(7) It is also a defence for a person charged with an offence under subsection (5) to prove that—

(a) the person acted in the reasonable belief that the processing was lawful,

(b) the person acted in the reasonable belief that the person—

(i) had the consent of the controller responsible for de-identifying the personal data, or

(ii) would have had such consent if that controller had known about the processing and the circumstances of it, or

(c) the person acted—

(i) for the special purposes,

(ii) with a view to the publication by a person of any journalistic, academic, artistic or literary material, and

(iii) in the reasonable belief that in the particular circumstances the processing was justified as being in the public interest.

(8) In this section—

(a) references to the consent of a controller do not include the consent of a person who is a controller by virtue of Article 28(10) of the [UK GDPR] or section 59(8) or 105(3) of this Act (processor to be treated as controller in certain circumstances);

(b) where there is more than one controller, such references are references to the consent of one or more of them.

NOTES

Commencement: 25 May 2018 (see also the introductory notes to this Act preceding s 1 at **[1.71]**).

Sub-s (8): words in square brackets substituted by the Data Protection, Privacy and Electronic Communications (Amendments etc) (EU Exit) Regulations 2019, SI 2019/419, reg 4, Sch 2, paras 1, 72.

[1.244]

172　Re-identification: effectiveness testing conditions

(1) For the purposes of section 171, in relation to a person who re-identifies information that is de-identified personal data, "the effectiveness testing conditions" means the conditions in subsections (2) and (3).

(2) The first condition is that the person acted—

(a) with a view to testing the effectiveness of the de-identification of personal data,

(b) without intending to cause, or threaten to cause, damage or distress to a person, and

(c) in the reasonable belief that, in the particular circumstances, re-identifying the information was justified as being in the public interest.

(3) The second condition is that the person notified the Commissioner or the controller responsible for de-identifying the personal data about the re-identification—

(a) without undue delay, and

(b) where feasible, not later than 72 hours after becoming aware of it.

(4) Where there is more than one controller responsible for de-identifying personal data, the requirement in subsection (3) is satisfied if one or more of them is notified.

NOTES

Commencement: 25 May 2018 (see also the introductory notes to this Act preceding s 1 at **[1.71]**).

[1.245]
173 Alteration etc of personal data to prevent disclosure to data subject
(1) Subsection (3) applies where—
   (a) a request has been made in exercise of a data subject access right, and
   (b) the person making the request would have been entitled to receive information in response to that request.
(2) In this section, "data subject access right" means a right under—
   (a) Article 15 of the [UK GDPR] (right of access by the data subject);
   (b) Article 20 of the [UK GDPR] (right to data portability);
   (c) section 45 of this Act (law enforcement processing: right of access by the data subject);
   (d) section 94 of this Act (intelligence services processing: right of access by the data subject).
(3) It is an offence for a person listed in subsection (4) to alter, deface, block, erase, destroy or conceal information with the intention of preventing disclosure of all or part of the information that the person making the request would have been entitled to receive.
(4) Those persons are—
   (a) the controller, and
   (b) a person who is employed by the controller, an officer of the controller or subject to the direction of the controller.
(5) It is a defence for a person charged with an offence under subsection (3) to prove that—
   (a) the alteration, defacing, blocking, erasure, destruction or concealment of the information would have occurred in the absence of a request made in exercise of a data subject access right, or
   (b) the person acted in the reasonable belief that the person making the request was not entitled to receive the information in response to the request.

NOTES
Commencement: 25 May 2018 (see also the introductory notes to this Act preceding s 1 at **[1.71]**).
Sub-s (2): words in square brackets substituted by the Data Protection, Privacy and Electronic Communications (Amendments etc) (EU Exit) Regulations 2019, SI 2019/419, reg 4, Sch 2, paras 1, 73.

The special purposes

[1.246]
174 The special purposes
(1) In this Part, "the special purposes" means one or more of the following—
   (a) the purposes of journalism;
   (b) academic purposes;
   (c) artistic purposes;
   (d) literary purposes.
(2) In this Part, "special purposes proceedings" means legal proceedings against a controller or processor which relate, wholly or partly, to personal data processed for the special purposes and which are—
   (a) proceedings under section 167 (including proceedings on an application under Article 79 of the [UK GDPR]), or
   (b) proceedings under Article 82 of the [UK GDPR] or section 169.
(3) The Commissioner may make a written determination, in relation to the processing of personal data, that—
   (a) the personal data is not being processed only for the special purposes;
   (b) the personal data is not being processed with a view to the publication by a person of journalistic, academic, artistic or literary material which has not previously been published by the controller.
(4) The Commissioner must give written notice of the determination to the controller and the processor.
(5) The notice must provide information about the rights of appeal under section 162.
(6) The determination does not take effect until one of the following conditions is satisfied—
   (a) the period for the controller or the processor to appeal against the determination has ended without an appeal having been brought, or
   (b) an appeal has been brought against the determination and—
     (i) the appeal and any further appeal in relation to the determination has been decided or has otherwise ended, and
     (ii) the time for appealing against the result of the appeal or further appeal has ended without another appeal having been brought.

NOTES
Commencement: 25 May 2018 (see also the introductory notes to this Act preceding s 1 at **[1.71]**).
Sub-s (2): words in square brackets substituted by the Data Protection, Privacy and Electronic Communications (Amendments etc) (EU Exit) Regulations 2019, SI 2019/419, reg 4, Sch 2, paras 1, 74.

[1.247]
175 Provision of assistance in special purposes proceedings
(1) An individual who is a party, or prospective party, to special purposes proceedings may apply to the Commissioner for assistance in those proceedings.
(2) As soon as reasonably practicable after receiving an application under subsection (1), the Commissioner must decide whether, and to what extent, to grant it.
(3) The Commissioner must not grant the application unless, in the Commissioner's opinion, the case involves a matter of substantial public importance.
(4) If the Commissioner decides not to provide assistance, the Commissioner must, as soon as reasonably practicable, notify the applicant of the decision, giving reasons for the decision.
(5) If the Commissioner decides to provide assistance, the Commissioner must—

(a) as soon as reasonably practicable, notify the applicant of the decision, stating the extent of the assistance to be provided, and

(b) secure that the person against whom the proceedings are, or are to be, brought is informed that the Commissioner is providing assistance.

(6) The assistance that may be provided by the Commissioner includes—

(a) paying costs in connection with the proceedings, and

(b) indemnifying the applicant in respect of liability to pay costs, expenses or damages in connection with the proceedings.

(7) In England and Wales or Northern Ireland, the recovery of expenses incurred by the Commissioner in providing an applicant with assistance under this section (as taxed or assessed in accordance with rules of court) is to constitute a first charge for the benefit of the Commissioner—

(a) on any costs which, by virtue of any judgment or order of the court, are payable to the applicant by any other person in respect of the matter in connection with which the assistance is provided, and

(b) on any sum payable to the applicant under a compromise or settlement arrived at in connection with that matter to avoid, or bring to an end, any proceedings.

(8) In Scotland, the recovery of such expenses (as taxed or assessed in accordance with rules of court) is to be paid to the Commissioner, in priority to other debts—

(a) out of any expenses which, by virtue of any judgment or order of the court, are payable to the applicant by any other person in respect of the matter in connection with which the assistance is provided, and

(b) out of any sum payable to the applicant under a compromise or settlement arrived at in connection with that matter to avoid, or bring to an end, any proceedings.

NOTES

Commencement: 25 May 2018 (see also the introductory notes to this Act preceding s 1 at **[1.71]**).

[1.248]
176 Staying special purposes proceedings
(1) In any special purposes proceedings before a court, if the controller or processor claims, or it appears to the court, that any personal data to which the proceedings relate—

(a) is being processed only for the special purposes,

(b) is being processed with a view to the publication by any person of journalistic, academic, artistic or literary material, and

(c) has not previously been published by the controller,

the court must stay or, in Scotland, sist the proceedings.

(2) In considering, for the purposes of subsection (1)(c), whether material has previously been published, publication in the immediately preceding 24 hours is to be ignored.

(3) Under subsection (1), the court must stay or sist the proceedings until either of the following conditions is met—

(a) a determination of the Commissioner under section 174 with respect to the personal data or the processing takes effect;

(b) where the proceedings were stayed or sisted on the making of a claim, the claim is withdrawn.

NOTES

Commencement: 25 May 2018 (see also the introductory notes to this Act preceding s 1 at **[1.71]**).

[1.249]
177 Guidance about how to seek redress against media organisations
(1) The Commissioner must produce and publish guidance about the steps that may be taken where an individual considers that a media organisation is failing or has failed to comply with the data protection legislation.

(2) In this section, "media organisation" means a body or other organisation whose activities consist of or include journalism.

(3) The guidance must include provision about relevant complaints procedures, including—

(a) who runs them,

(b) what can be complained about, and

(c) how to make a complaint.

(4) For the purposes of subsection (3), relevant complaints procedures include procedures for making complaints to the Commissioner, the Office of Communications, the British Broadcasting Corporation and other persons who produce or enforce codes of practice for media organisations.

(5) The guidance must also include provision about—

(a) the powers available to the Commissioner in relation to a failure to comply with the data protection legislation,

(b) when a claim in respect of such a failure may be made before a court and how to make such a claim,

(c) alternative dispute resolution procedures,

(d) the rights of bodies and other organisations to make complaints and claims on behalf of data subjects, and

(e) the Commissioner's power to provide assistance in special purpose proceedings.

(6) The Commissioner—

(a) may alter or replace the guidance, and

(b) must publish any altered or replacement guidance.

(7) The Commissioner must produce and publish the first guidance under this section before the end of the period of 1 year beginning when this Act is passed.

NOTES

Commencement: 23 July 2018 (see also the introductory notes to this Act preceding s 1 at **[1.71]**).

[1.250]
178 Review of processing of personal data for the purposes of journalism
(1) The Commissioner must—
  (a) review the extent to which, during each review period, the processing of personal data for the purposes of journalism complied with—
    (i) the data protection legislation, and
    (ii) good practice in the processing of personal data for the purposes of journalism,
  (b) prepare a report of the review, and
  (c) submit the report to the Secretary of State.
(2) In this section—
  "good practice in the processing of personal data for the purposes of journalism" has the same meaning as in section 124;
  "review period" means—
    (a) the period of 4 years beginning with the day on which Chapter 2 of Part 2 of this Act comes into force, and
    (b) each subsequent period of 5 years beginning with the day after the day on which the previous review period ended.
(3) The Commissioner must start a review under this section, in respect of a review period, within the period of 6 months beginning when the review period ends.
(4) The Commissioner must submit the report of a review under this section to the Secretary of State—
  (a) in the case of the first review, before the end of the period of 18 months beginning when the Commissioner started the review, and
  (b) in the case of each subsequent review, before the end of the period of 12 months beginning when the Commissioner started the review.
(5) The report must include consideration of the extent of compliance (as described in subsection (1)(a)) in each part of the United Kingdom.
(6) The Secretary of State must—
  (a) lay the report before Parliament, and
  (b) send a copy of the report to—
    (i) the Scottish Ministers,
    (ii) the Welsh Ministers, and
    (iii) the Executive Office in Northern Ireland.
(7) Schedule 17 makes further provision for the purposes of a review under this section.

NOTES
Commencement: 23 July 2018 (see also the introductory notes to this Act preceding s 1 at **[1.71]**).

[1.251]
179 Effectiveness of the media's dispute resolution procedures
(1) The Secretary of State must, before the end of each review period, lay before Parliament a report produced by the Secretary of State or an appropriate person on—
  (a) the use of relevant alternative dispute resolution procedures, during that period, in cases involving a failure, or alleged failure, by a relevant media organisation to comply with the data protection legislation, and
  (b) the effectiveness of those procedures in such cases.
(2) In this section—
  "appropriate person" means a person who the Secretary of State considers has appropriate experience and skills to produce a report described in subsection (1);
  "relevant alternative dispute resolution procedures" means alternative dispute resolution procedures provided by persons who produce or enforce codes of practice for relevant media organisations;
  "relevant media organisation" means a body or other organisation whose activities consist of or include journalism, other than a broadcaster;
  "review period" means—
    (a) the period of 3 years beginning when this Act is passed, and
    (b) each subsequent period of 3 years.
(3) The Secretary of State must send a copy of the report to—
  (a) the Scottish Ministers,
  (b) the Welsh Ministers, and
  (c) the Executive Office in Northern Ireland.

NOTES
Commencement: 23 July 2018 (see also the introductory notes to this Act preceding s 1 at **[1.71]**).

Jurisdiction of courts
[1.252]
180 Jurisdiction
(1) The jurisdiction conferred on a court by the provisions listed in subsection (2) is exercisable—
  (a) in England and Wales, by the High Court or the county court,
  (b) in Northern Ireland, by the High Court or a county court, and
  (c) in Scotland, by the Court of Session or the sheriff,
subject to subsections (3) and (4).
(2) Those provisions are—
  (a) section 145 (information orders);
  (b) section 152 (enforcement notices and processing for the special purposes);

(c)   section 156 (penalty notices and processing for the special purposes);
(d)   section 167 and Article 79 of the [UK GDPR] (compliance orders);
(e)   sections 168 and 169 and Article 82 of the [UK GDPR] (compensation).
(3) In relation to the processing of personal data to which Part 4 applies, the jurisdiction conferred by the provisions listed in subsection (2) is exercisable only by the High Court or, in Scotland, the Court of Session.
(4) In relation to an information notice which contains a statement under section 142(7), the jurisdiction conferred on a court by section 145 is exercisable only by the High Court or, in Scotland, the Court of Session.
(5) The jurisdiction conferred on a court by section 164 (applications in respect of urgent notices) is exercisable only by the High Court or, in Scotland, the Court of Session.

NOTES

Commencement: 25 May 2018 (see also the introductory notes to this Act preceding s 1 at **[1.71]**).

Sub-s (2): words in square brackets substituted by the Data Protection, Privacy and Electronic Communications (Amendments etc) (EU Exit) Regulations 2019, SI 2019/419, reg 4, Sch 2, paras 1, 75.

Definitions

[1.253]
181   Interpretation of Part 6
In this Part—
    "assessment notice" has the meaning given in section 146;
    "certification provider" has the meaning given in section 17;
    "enforcement notice" has the meaning given in section 149;
    "information notice" has the meaning given in section 142;
    "penalty notice" has the meaning given in section 155;
    "penalty variation notice" has the meaning given in Schedule 16;
    "representative", in relation to a controller or processor, means a person designated by the controller or processor under Article 27 of the [UK GDPR] to represent the controller or processor with regard to the controller's or processor's obligations under the [UK GDPR].

NOTES

Commencement: 25 May 2018 (see also the introductory notes to this Act preceding s 1 at **[1.71]**).

The words in square brackets in the definition "representative" were substituted by the Data Protection, Privacy and Electronic Communications (Amendments etc) (EU Exit) Regulations 2019, SI 2019/419, reg 4, Sch 2, paras 1, 76.

PART 7 SUPPLEMENTARY AND FINAL PROVISION

Regulations under this Act

[1.254]
182   Regulations and consultation
(1) Regulations under this Act are to be made by statutory instrument.
(2) Before making regulations under this Act, the Secretary of State must consult—
    (a)   the Commissioner, and
    (b)   such other persons as the Secretary of State considers appropriate.
(3) Subsection (2) does not apply to regulations made under—
    (a)   . . .
    (b)   section 30;
    (c)   section 211;
    (d)   section 212;
    (e)   section 213;
    (f)   paragraph 15 of Schedule 2.
(4) Subsection (2) does not apply to regulations made under section 18 where the Secretary of State has made an urgency statement in respect of them.
(5) Regulations under this Act may—
    (a)   make different provision for different purposes;
    (b)   include consequential, supplementary, incidental, transitional, transitory or saving provision.
(6) Where regulations under this Act are subject to "the negative resolution procedure" the statutory instrument containing the regulations is subject to annulment in pursuance of a resolution of either House of Parliament.
(7) Where regulations under this Act are subject to "the affirmative resolution procedure" the regulations may not be made unless a draft of the statutory instrument containing them has been laid before Parliament and approved by a resolution of each House of Parliament.
(8) Where regulations under this Act are subject to "the made affirmative resolution procedure"—
    (a)   the statutory instrument containing the regulations must be laid before Parliament after being made, together with the urgency statement in respect of them, and
    (b)   the regulations cease to have effect at the end of the period of 120 days beginning with the day on which the instrument is made, unless within that period the instrument is approved by a resolution of each House of Parliament.
(9) In calculating the period of 120 days, no account is to be taken of any time during which—
    (a)   Parliament is dissolved or prorogued, or
    (b)   both Houses of Parliament are adjourned for more than 4 days.
(10) Where regulations cease to have effect as a result of subsection (8), that does not—
    (a)   affect anything previously done under the regulations, or
    (b)   prevent the making of new regulations.

(11) Any provision that may be included in regulations under this Act subject to the negative resolution procedure may be made by regulations subject to the affirmative resolution procedure or the made affirmative resolution procedure.

(12) If a draft of a statutory instrument containing regulations under section 7 would, apart from this subsection, be treated for the purposes of the standing orders of either House of Parliament as a hybrid instrument, it is to proceed in that House as if it were not such an instrument.

(13) A requirement under a provision of this Act to consult may be satisfied by consultation before, as well as by consultation after, the provision comes into force.

(14) In this section, "urgency statement" has the meaning given in section 18(4).

NOTES

Commencement: 23 May 2018 (see also the introductory notes to this Act preceding s 1 at **[1.71]**).

Sub-s (3): para (a) repealed by the Data Protection, Privacy and Electronic Communications (Amendments etc) (EU Exit) Regulations 2019, SI 2019/419, reg 4, Sch 2, paras 1, 77.

Changes to the Data Protection Convention

[1.255]
183 Power to reflect changes to the Data Protection Convention

(1) The Secretary of State may by regulations make such provision as the Secretary of State considers necessary or appropriate in connection with an amendment of, or an instrument replacing, the Data Protection Convention which has effect, or is expected to have effect, in the United Kingdom.

(2) The power under subsection (1) includes power—
   (a) to amend or replace the definition of "the Data Protection Convention" in section 3;
   (b) to amend Chapter 3 of Part 2 of this Act;
   (c) to amend Part 4 of this Act;
   (d) to make provision about the functions of the Commissioner, courts or tribunals in connection with [relevant processing of personal data], including provision amending Parts 5 to 7 of this Act;
   (e) to make provision about the functions of the Commissioner in connection with the Data Protection Convention or an instrument replacing that Convention, including provision amending Parts 5 to 7 of this Act;
   (f) to consequentially amend this Act.

[(2A) In subsection (2)(d), "relevant processing of personal data" means—
   (a) processing of personal data described in Article 2(1)(a) or (b) or (1A) of the UK GDPR, and
   (b) processing of personal data to which Part 4 of this Act applies.]

(3) Regulations under this section are subject to the affirmative resolution procedure.

(4) Regulations under this section may not be made after the end of the period of 3 years beginning with the day on which this Act is passed.

NOTES

Commencement: 25 May 2018 (see also the introductory notes to this Act preceding s 1 at **[1.71]**).

The words in square brackets in sub-s (2) were substituted and sub-s (2A) was inserted, by the Data Protection, Privacy and Electronic Communications (Amendments etc) (EU Exit) Regulations 2019, SI 2019/419, reg 4, Sch 2, paras 1, 78.

Rights of the data subject

[1.256]
184 Prohibition of requirement to produce relevant records

(1) It is an offence for a person ("P1") to require another person to provide P1 with, or give P1 access to, a relevant record in connection with—
   (a) the recruitment of an employee by P1,
   (b) the continued employment of a person by P1, or
   (c) a contract for the provision of services to P1.

(2) It is an offence for a person ("P2") to require another person to provide P2 with, or give P2 access to, a relevant record if—
   (a) P2 is involved in the provision of goods, facilities or services to the public or a section of the public, and
   (b) the requirement is a condition of providing or offering to provide goods, facilities or services to the other person or to a third party.

(3) It is a defence for a person charged with an offence under subsection (1) or (2) to prove that imposing the requirement—
   (a) was required or authorised by an enactment, by a rule of law or by the order of a court or tribunal, or
   (b) in the particular circumstances, was justified as being in the public interest.

(4) The imposition of the requirement referred to in subsection (1) or (2) is not to be regarded as justified as being in the public interest on the ground that it would assist in the prevention or detection of crime, given Part 5 of the Police Act 1997 (certificates of criminal records etc).

(5) In subsections (1) and (2), the references to a person who requires another person to provide or give access to a relevant record include a person who asks another person to do so—
   (a) knowing that, in the circumstances, it would be reasonable for the other person to feel obliged to comply with the request, or
   (b) being reckless as to whether, in the circumstances, it would be reasonable for the other person to feel obliged to comply with the request,

and the references to a "requirement" in subsections (3) and (4) are to be interpreted accordingly.

(6) In this section—
   "employment" means any employment, including—
      (a) work under a contract for services or as an office-holder,

(b)   work under an apprenticeship,
(c)   work experience as part of a training course or in the course of training for employment, and
(d)   voluntary work,
and "employee" is to be interpreted accordingly;
"relevant record" has the meaning given in Schedule 18 and references to a relevant record include—
(a)   a part of such a record, and
(b)   a copy of, or of part of, such a record.

NOTES

Commencement: 25 May 2018 (see also the introductory notes to this Act preceding s 1 at **[1.71]**).

[1.257]
185   Avoidance of certain contractual terms relating to health records
(1) A term or condition of a contract is void in so far as it purports to require an individual to supply another person with a record which—
(a)   consists of the information contained in a health record, and
(b)   has been or is to be obtained by a data subject in the exercise of a data subject access right.
(2) A term or condition of a contract is also void in so far as it purports to require an individual to produce such a record to another person.
(3) The references in subsections (1) and (2) to a record include a part of a record and a copy of all or part of a record.
(4) In this section, "data subject access right" means a right under—
(a)   Article 15 of the [UK GDPR] (right of access by the data subject);
(b)   Article 20 of the [UK GDPR] (right to data portability);
(c)   section 45 of this Act (law enforcement processing: right of access by the data subject);
(d)   section 94 of this Act (intelligence services processing: right of access by the data subject).

NOTES

Commencement: 25 May 2018 (see also the introductory notes to this Act preceding s 1 at **[1.71]**).
Sub-s (4): words in square brackets substituted by the Data Protection, Privacy and Electronic Communications (Amendments etc) (EU Exit) Regulations 2019, SI 2019/419, reg 4, Sch 2, paras 1, 79.

[1.258]
186   Data subject's rights and other prohibitions and restrictions
(1) An enactment or rule of law prohibiting or restricting the disclosure of information, or authorising the withholding of information, does not remove or restrict the obligations and rights provided for in the provisions listed in subsection (2), except as provided by or under the provisions listed in subsection (3).
(2) The provisions providing obligations and rights are—
(a)   Chapter III of the [UK GDPR] (rights of the data subject),
(b)   Chapter 3 of Part 3 of this Act (law enforcement processing: rights of the data subject), and
(c)   Chapter 3 of Part 4 of this Act (intelligence services processing: rights of the data subject).
(3) The provisions providing exceptions are—
(a)   in Chapter 2 of Part 2 of this Act, sections 15 and 16 and Schedules 2, 3 and 4,
(b)   in Chapter 3 of Part 2 of this Act, sections . . . 24, 25 and 26,
(c)   in Part 3 of this Act, sections 44(4), 45(4) and 48(3), and
(d)   in Part 4 of this Act, Chapter 6.

NOTES

Commencement: 25 May 2018 (see also the introductory notes to this Act preceding s 1 at **[1.71]**).
The words in square brackets in sub-s (2) were substituted, and the figure omitted from sub-s (3) was repealed, by the Data Protection, Privacy and Electronic Communications (Amendments etc) (EU Exit) Regulations 2019, SI 2019/419, reg 4, Sch 2, paras 1, 80.

Representation of data subjects

[1.259]
187   Representation of data subjects with their authority
(1) In relation to the processing of personal data to which the [UK GDPR applies, Article 80(1) of the UK GDPR (representation of data subjects)]—
(a)   . . . enables a data subject to authorise a body or other organisation which meets the conditions set out in [subsections (3) and (4)] to exercise the data subject's rights under Articles 77, 78 and 79 of the [UK GDPR] (rights to lodge complaints and to an effective judicial remedy) on the data subject's behalf, and
(b)   [also authorises] such a body or organisation to exercise the data subject's rights under Article 82 of the [UK GDPR] (right to compensation).
(2) In relation to the processing of personal data to which the [UK GDPR] does not apply, a body or other organisation which meets the conditions in subsections (3) and (4), if authorised to do so by a data subject, may exercise some or all of the following rights of a data subject on the data subject's behalf—
(a)   rights under section 165(2) [and (4)(d)] (complaints to the Commissioner);
(b)   rights under section 166(2) (orders for the Commissioner to progress complaints);
(c)   rights under section 167(1) (compliance orders);
(d)   the right to bring judicial review proceedings against the Commissioner.
(3) The first condition is that the body or organisation, by virtue of its constitution or an enactment—
(a)   is required (after payment of outgoings) to apply the whole of its income and any capital it expends for charitable or public purposes,

(b)   is prohibited from directly or indirectly distributing amongst its members any part of its assets (otherwise than for charitable or public purposes), and

(c)   has objectives which are in the public interest.

(4)   The second condition is that the body or organisation is active in the field of protection of data subjects' rights and freedoms with regard to the protection of their personal data.

(5)   In this Act, references to a "representative body", in relation to a right of a data subject, are to a body or other organisation authorised to exercise the right on the data subject's behalf under Article 80 of the [UK GDPR] or this section.

NOTES

Commencement: 25 May 2018 (see also the introductory notes to this Act preceding s 1 at **[1.71]**).

The words in square brackets in sub-ss (1), (2), (5) were substituted, and the words omitted from sub-s (1) were repealed, by the Data Protection, Privacy and Electronic Communications (Amendments etc) (EU Exit) Regulations 2019, SI 2019/419, reg 4, Sch 2, paras 1, 81.

[1.260]
188   Representation of data subjects with their authority: collective proceedings
(1)   The Secretary of State may by regulations make provision for representative bodies to bring proceedings before a court or tribunal in England and Wales or Northern Ireland combining two or more relevant claims.

(2)   In this section, "relevant claim", in relation to a representative body, means a claim in respect of a right of a data subject which the representative body is authorised to exercise on the data subject's behalf under Article 80(1) of the [UK GDPR] or section 187.

(3)   The power under subsection (1) includes power—
(a)   to make provision about the proceedings;
(b)   to confer functions on a person, including functions involving the exercise of a discretion;
(c)   to make different provision in relation to England and Wales and in relation to Northern Ireland.

(4)   The provision mentioned in subsection (3)(a) includes provision about—
(a)   the effect of judgments and orders;
(b)   agreements to settle claims;
(c)   the assessment of the amount of compensation;
(d)   the persons to whom compensation may or must be paid, including compensation not claimed by the data subject;
(e)   costs.

(5)   Regulations under this section are subject to the negative resolution procedure.

NOTES

Commencement: 23 July 2018 (see also the introductory notes to this Act preceding s 1 at **[1.71]**).

Sub-s (2): words in square brackets substituted by the Data Protection, Privacy and Electronic Communications (Amendments etc) (EU Exit) Regulations 2019, SI 2019/419, reg 4, Sch 2, paras 1, 82.

[1.261]
189   Duty to review provision for representation of data subjects
(1)   Before the end of the review period, the Secretary of State must—
(a)   review the matters listed in subsection (2) in relation to England and Wales and Northern Ireland,
(b)   prepare a report of the review, and
(c)   lay a copy of the report before Parliament.

(2)   Those matters are—
(a)   the operation of Article 80(1) of the [UK GDPR],
(b)   the operation of section 187,
(c)   the merits of exercising the power under Article 80(2) of the [UK GDPR] (power to enable a body or other organisation which meets the conditions in Article 80(1) of [UK GDPR] to exercise some or all of a data subject's rights under Articles 77, 78 and 79 of the [UK GDPR] without being authorised to do so by the data subject),
(d)   the merits of making equivalent provision in relation to data subjects' rights under Article 82 of the [UK GDPR] (right to compensation), and
(e)   the merits of making provision for a children's rights organisation to exercise some or all of a data subject's rights under Articles 77, 78, 79 and 82 of the [UK GDPR] on behalf of a data subject who is a child, with or without being authorised to do so by the data subject.

(3)   "The review period" is the period of 30 months beginning when section 187 comes into force.

(4)   In carrying out the review, the Secretary of State must—
(a)   consider the particular needs of children separately from the needs of adults,
(b)   have regard to the fact that children have different needs at different stages of development,
(c)   carry out an analysis of the particular challenges that children face in authorising, and deciding whether to authorise, other persons to act on their behalf under Article 80(1) of the [UK GDPR] or section 187,
(d)   consider the support and advice available to children in connection with the exercise of their rights under Articles 77, 78, 79 and 82 of the [UK GDPR] by another person on their behalf and the merits of making available other support or advice, and
(e)   have regard to the United Kingdom's obligations under the United Nations Convention on the Rights of the Child.

(5)   Before preparing the report under subsection (1), the Secretary of State must consult the Commissioner and such other persons as the Secretary of State considers appropriate, including—
(a)   persons active in the field of protection of data subjects' rights and freedoms with regard to the protection of their personal data,

    (b)   children and parents,
    (c)   children's rights organisations and other persons who appear to the Secretary of State to represent the interests of children,
    (d)   child development experts, and
    (e)   trade associations.
(6) In this section—
    "children's rights organisation" means a body or other organisation which—
        (a)   is active in representing the interests of children, and
        (b)   has objectives which are in the public interest;
    "trade association" includes a body representing controllers or processors;
    "the United Nations Convention on the Rights of the Child" means the Convention on the Rights of the Child adopted by the General Assembly of the United Nations on 20 November 1989 (including any Protocols to that Convention which are in force in relation to the United Kingdom), subject to any reservations, objections or interpretative declarations by the United Kingdom for the time being in force.

NOTES

Commencement: 23 July 2018 (see also the introductory notes to this Act preceding s 1 at **[1.71]**).

Sub-ss (2), (4): words in square brackets substituted by the Data Protection, Privacy and Electronic Communications (Amendments etc) (EU Exit) Regulations 2019, SI 2019/419, reg 4, Sch 2, paras 1, 83.

[1.262]
190 Post-review powers to make provision about representation of data subjects
(1) After the report under section 189(1) is laid before Parliament, the Secretary of State may by regulations—
    (a)   exercise the powers under Article 80(2) of the [UK GDPR] in relation to England and Wales and Northern Ireland,
    (b)   make provision enabling a body or other organisation which meets the conditions in Article 80(1) of the [UK GDPR] to exercise a data subject's rights under Article 82 of the [UK GDPR] in England and Wales and Northern Ireland without being authorised to do so by the data subject, and
    (c)   make provision described in section 189(2)(e) in relation to the exercise in England and Wales and Northern Ireland of the rights of a data subject who is a child.
(2) The powers under subsection (1) include power—
    (a)   to make provision enabling a data subject to prevent a body or other organisation from exercising, or continuing to exercise, the data subject's rights;
    (b)   to make provision about proceedings before a court or tribunal where a body or organisation exercises a data subject's rights;
    (c)   to make provision for bodies or other organisations to bring proceedings before a court or tribunal combining two or more claims in respect of a right of a data subject;
    (d)   to confer functions on a person, including functions involving the exercise of a discretion;
    (e)   to amend sections 166 to 168, 180, 187, 203, 205 and 206;
    (f)   to insert new sections and Schedules into Part 6 or 7 ;
    (g)   to make different provision in relation to England and Wales and in relation to Northern Ireland.
(3) The powers under subsection (1)(a) and (b) include power to make provision in relation to data subjects who are children or data subjects who are not children or both.
(4) The provision mentioned in subsection (2)(b) and (c) includes provision about—
    (a)   the effect of judgments and orders;
    (b)   agreements to settle claims;
    (c)   the assessment of the amount of compensation;
    (d)   the persons to whom compensation may or must be paid, including compensation not claimed by the data subject;
    (e)   costs.
(5) Regulations under this section are subject to the affirmative resolution procedure.

NOTES

Commencement: 23 July 2018 (see also the introductory notes to this Act preceding s 1 at **[1.71]**).

Sub-s (1): words in square brackets substituted by the Data Protection, Privacy and Electronic Communications (Amendments etc) (EU Exit) Regulations 2019, SI 2019/419, reg 4, Sch 2, paras 1, 84.

Framework for Data Processing by Government

[1.263]
191 Framework for Data Processing by Government
(1) The Secretary of State may prepare a document, called the Framework for Data Processing by Government, which contains guidance about the processing of personal data in connection with the exercise of functions of—
    (a)   the Crown, a Minister of the Crown or a United Kingdom government department, and
    (b)   a person with functions of a public nature who is specified or described in regulations made by the Secretary of State.
(2) The document may make provision relating to all of those functions or only to particular functions or persons.
(3) The document may not make provision relating to, or to the functions of, a part of the Scottish Administration, the Welsh Government, a Northern Ireland Minister or a Northern Ireland department.
(4) The Secretary of State may from time to time prepare amendments of the document or a replacement document.
(5) Before preparing a document or amendments under this section, the Secretary of State must consult—
    (a)   the Commissioner, and
    (b)   any other person the Secretary of State considers it appropriate to consult.
(6) Regulations under subsection (1)(b) are subject to the negative resolution procedure.

(7) In this section, "Northern Ireland Minister" includes the First Minister and deputy First Minister in Northern Ireland.

NOTES
Commencement: 23 July 2018 (see also the introductory notes to this Act preceding s 1 at **[1.71]**).

[1.264]
192 Approval of the Framework
(1) Before issuing a document prepared under section 191, the Secretary of State must lay it before Parliament.
(2) If, within the 40-day period, either House of Parliament resolves not to approve the document, the Secretary of State must not issue it.
(3) If no such resolution is made within that period—
  (a) the Secretary of State must issue the document, and
  (b) the document comes into force at the end of the period of 21 days beginning with the day on which it is issued.
(4) Nothing in subsection (2) prevents another version of the document being laid before Parliament.
(5) In this section, "the 40-day period" means—
  (a) if the document is laid before both Houses of Parliament on the same day, the period of 40 days beginning with that day, or
  (b) if the document is laid before the Houses of Parliament on different days, the period of 40 days beginning with the later of those days.
(6) In calculating the 40-day period, no account is to be taken of any period during which Parliament is dissolved or prorogued or during which both Houses of Parliament are adjourned for more than 4 days.
(7) This section applies in relation to amendments prepared under section 191 as it applies in relation to a document prepared under that section.

NOTES
Commencement: 23 July 2018 (see also the introductory notes to this Act preceding s 1 at **[1.71]**).

[1.265]
193 Publication and review of the Framework
(1) The Secretary of State must publish a document issued under section 192(3).
(2) Where an amendment of a document is issued under section 192(3), the Secretary of State must publish—
  (a) the amendment, or
  (b) the document as amended by it.
(3) The Secretary of State must keep under review the document issued under section 192(3) for the time being in force.
(4) Where the Secretary of State becomes aware that the terms of such a document could result in a breach of an international obligation of the United Kingdom, the Secretary of State must exercise the power under section 191(4) with a view to remedying the situation.

NOTES
Commencement: 23 July 2018 (see also the introductory notes to this Act preceding s 1 at **[1.71]**).

[1.266]
194 Effect of the Framework
(1) When carrying out processing of personal data which is the subject of a document issued under section 192(3) which is for the time being in force, a person must have regard to the document.
(2) A failure to act in accordance with a provision of such a document does not of itself make a person liable to legal proceedings in a court or tribunal.
(3) A document issued under section 192(3), including an amendment or replacement document, is admissible in evidence in legal proceedings.
(4) In any legal proceedings before a court or tribunal, the court or tribunal must take into account a provision of any document issued under section 192(3) in determining a question arising in the proceedings if—
  (a) the question relates to a time when the provision was in force, and
  (b) the provision appears to the court or tribunal to be relevant to the question.
(5) In determining a question arising in connection with the carrying out of any of the Commissioner's functions, the Commissioner must take into account a provision of a document issued under section 192(3) if—
  (a) the question relates to a time when the provision was in force, and
  (b) the provision appears to the Commissioner to be relevant to the question.

NOTES
Commencement: 23 July 2018 (see also the introductory notes to this Act preceding s 1 at **[1.71]**).

Data-sharing: HMRC and reserve forces

195 (*Inserts the Reserve Forces Act 1996, ss 125A–125C (outside the scope of this work).*)

Offences

[1.267]
196 Penalties for offences
(1) A person who commits an offence under section 119 or 173 or paragraph 15 of Schedule 15 is liable—
  (a) on summary conviction in England and Wales, to a fine;
  (b) on summary conviction in Scotland or Northern Ireland, to a fine not exceeding level 5 on the standard scale.
(2) A person who commits an offence under section 132, 144, 148, 170, 171 or 184 is liable—

(a) on summary conviction in England and Wales, to a fine;
(b) on summary conviction in Scotland or Northern Ireland, to a fine not exceeding the statutory maximum;
(c) on conviction on indictment, to a fine.
(3) Subsections (4) and (5) apply where a person is convicted of an offence under section 170 or 184.
(4) The court by or before which the person is convicted may order a document or other material to be forfeited, destroyed or erased if—
(a) it has been used in connection with the processing of personal data, and
(b) it appears to the court to be connected with the commission of the offence,
subject to subsection (5).
(5) If a person, other than the offender, who claims to be the owner of the material, or to be otherwise interested in the material, applies to be heard by the court, the court must not make an order under subsection (4) without giving the person an opportunity to show why the order should not be made.

NOTES
Commencement: 25 May 2018 (see also the introductory notes to this Act preceding s 1 at **[1.71]**).

[1.268]
197 Prosecution
(1) In England and Wales, proceedings for an offence under this Act may be instituted only—
(a) by the Commissioner, or
(b) by or with the consent of the Director of Public Prosecutions.
(2) In Northern Ireland, proceedings for an offence under this Act may be instituted only—
(a) by the Commissioner, or
(b) by or with the consent of the Director of Public Prosecutions for Northern Ireland.
(3) Subject to subsection (4), summary proceedings for an offence under section 173 (alteration etc of personal data to prevent disclosure) may be brought within the period of 6 months beginning with the day on which the prosecutor first knew of evidence that, in the prosecutor's opinion, was sufficient to bring the proceedings.
(4) Such proceedings may not be brought after the end of the period of 3 years beginning with the day on which the offence was committed.
(5) A certificate signed by or on behalf of the prosecutor and stating the day on which the 6 month period described in subsection (3) began is conclusive evidence of that fact.
(6) A certificate purporting to be signed as described in subsection (5) is to be treated as so signed unless the contrary is proved.
(7) In relation to proceedings in Scotland, section 136(3) of the Criminal Procedure (Scotland) Act 1995 (deemed date of commencement of proceedings) applies for the purposes of this section as it applies for the purposes of that section.

NOTES
Commencement: 25 May 2018 (see also the introductory notes to this Act preceding s 1 at **[1.71]**).

[1.269]
198 Liability of directors etc
(1) Subsection (2) applies where—
(a) an offence under this Act has been committed by a body corporate, and
(b) it is proved to have been committed with the consent or connivance of or to be attributable to neglect on the part of—
   (i)   a director, manager, secretary or similar officer of the body corporate, or
   (ii)   a person who was purporting to act in such a capacity.
(2) The director, manager, secretary, officer or person, as well as the body corporate, is guilty of the offence and liable to be proceeded against and punished accordingly.
(3) Where the affairs of a body corporate are managed by its members, subsections (1) and (2) apply in relation to the acts and omissions of a member in connection with the member's management functions in relation to the body as if the member were a director of the body corporate.
(4) Subsection (5) applies where—
(a) an offence under this Act has been committed by a Scottish partnership, and
(b) the contravention in question is proved to have occurred with the consent or connivance of, or to be attributable to any neglect on the part of, a partner.
(5) The partner, as well as the partnership, is guilty of the offence and liable to be proceeded against and punished accordingly.

NOTES
Commencement: 25 May 2018 (see also the introductory notes to this Act preceding s 1 at **[1.71]**).

[1.270]
199 Recordable offences
(1) The National Police Records (Recordable Offences) Regulations 2000 (SI 2000/1139) have effect as if the offences under the following provisions were listed in the Schedule to the Regulations—
(a) section 119;
(b) section 132;
(c) section 144;
(d) section 148;
(e) section 170;
(f) section 171;
(g) section 173;

(h)   section 184;

(i)   paragraph 15 of Schedule 15.

(2) Regulations under section 27(4) of the Police and Criminal Evidence Act 1984 (recordable offences) may repeal subsection (1).

NOTES
Commencement: 25 May 2018 (see also the introductory notes to this Act preceding s 1 at **[1.71]**).

[1.271]
200   Guidance about PACE codes of practice
(1) The Commissioner must produce and publish guidance about how the Commissioner proposes to perform the duty under section 67(9) of the Police and Criminal Evidence Act 1984 (duty to have regard to codes of practice under that Act when investigating offences and charging offenders) in connection with offences under this Act.
(2) The Commissioner—
(a)   may alter or replace the guidance, and
(b)   must publish any altered or replacement guidance.
(3) The Commissioner must consult the Secretary of State before publishing guidance under this section (including any altered or replacement guidance).
(4) The Commissioner must arrange for guidance under this section (including any altered or replacement guidance) to be laid before Parliament.

NOTES
Commencement: 25 May 2018 (see also the introductory notes to this Act preceding s 1 at **[1.71]**).

The Tribunal

[1.272]
201   Disclosure of information to the Tribunal
(1) No enactment or rule of law prohibiting or restricting the disclosure of information precludes a person from providing the First-tier Tribunal or the Upper Tribunal with information necessary for the discharge of—
(a)   its functions under the data protection legislation, or
(b)   its other functions relating to the Commissioner's acts and omissions.
(2) But this section does not authorise the making of a disclosure which is prohibited by any of Parts 1 to 7 or Chapter 1 of Part 9 of the Investigatory Powers Act 2016.
(3) Until the repeal of Part 1 of the Regulation of Investigatory Powers Act 2000 by paragraphs 45 and 54 of Schedule 10 to the Investigatory Powers Act 2016 is fully in force, subsection (2) has effect as if it included a reference to that Part.

NOTES
Commencement: 25 May 2018 (see also the introductory notes to this Act preceding s 1 at **[1.71]**).

[1.273]
202   Proceedings in the First-tier Tribunal: contempt
(1) This section applies where—
(a)   a person does something, or fails to do something, in relation to proceedings before the First-tier Tribunal—
(i)   on an appeal under section 27, 79, 111 or 162, or
(ii)   for an order under section 166, and
(b)   if those proceedings were proceedings before a court having power to commit for contempt, the act or omission would constitute contempt of court.
(2) The First-tier Tribunal may certify the offence to the Upper Tribunal.
(3) Where an offence is certified under subsection (2), the Upper Tribunal may—
(a)   inquire into the matter, and
(b)   deal with the person charged with the offence in any manner in which it could deal with the person if the offence had been committed in relation to the Upper Tribunal.
(4) Before exercising the power under subsection (3)(b), the Upper Tribunal must—
(a)   hear any witness who may be produced against or on behalf of the person charged with the offence, and
(b)   hear any statement that may be offered in defence.

NOTES
Commencement: 25 May 2018 (see also the introductory notes to this Act preceding s 1 at **[1.71]**).

[1.274]
203   Tribunal Procedure Rules
(1) Tribunal Procedure Rules may make provision for regulating—
(a)   the exercise of the rights of appeal conferred by section 27, 79, 111 or 162, and
(b)   the exercise of the rights of data subjects under section 166, including their exercise by a representative body.
(2) In relation to proceedings involving the exercise of those rights, Tribunal Procedure Rules may make provision about—
(a)   securing the production of material used for the processing of personal data, and
(b)   the inspection, examination, operation and testing of equipment or material used in connection with the processing of personal data.

NOTES
Commencement: 25 May 2018 (see also the introductory notes to this Act preceding s 1 at **[1.71]**).

Interpretation

[1.275]
204 Meaning of "health professional" and "social work professional"

(1) In this Act, "health professional" means any of the following—
  (a) a registered medical practitioner;
  (b) a registered nurse or midwife;
  (c) a registered dentist within the meaning of the Dentists Act 1984 (see section 53 of that Act);
  (d) a registered dispensing optician or a registered optometrist within the meaning of the Opticians Act 1989 (see section 36 of that Act);
  (e) a registered osteopath with the meaning of the Osteopaths Act 1993 (see section 41 of that Act);
  (f) a registered chiropractor within the meaning of the Chiropractors Act 1994 (see section 43 of that Act);
  (g) a person registered as a member of a profession to which the Health . . . Professions Order 2001 (SI 2002/254) for the time being extends . . . ;
  (h) a registered pharmacist or a registered pharmacy technician within the meaning of the Pharmacy Order 2010 (SI 2010/231) (see article 3 of that Order);
  (i) a registered person within the meaning of the Pharmacy (Northern Ireland) Order 1976 (SI 1976/1213 (NI 22)) (see Article 2 of that Order);
  (j) a child psychotherapist;
  (k) a scientist employed by a health service body as head of a department.

(2) In this Act, "social work professional" means any of the following—
  [(a) a person registered as a social worker in the register maintained by Social Work England under section 39(1) of the Children and Social Work Act 2017;]
  (b) a person registered as a social worker in the register maintained by Social Care Wales under section 80 of the Regulation and Inspection of Social Care (Wales) Act 2016 (anaw 2);
  (c) a person registered as a social worker in the register maintained by the Scottish Social Services Council under section 44 of the Regulation of Care (Scotland) Act 2001 (asp 8);
  (d) a person registered as a social worker in the register maintained by the Northern Ireland Social Care Council under section 3 of the Health and Personal Social Services Act (Northern Ireland) 2001 (c 3 (NI)).

(3) In subsection (1)(a) "registered medical practitioner" includes a person who is provisionally registered under section 15 or 21 of the Medical Act 1983 and is engaged in such employment as is mentioned in subsection (3) of that section.

(4) In subsection (1)(k) "health service body" means any of the following—
  (a) the Secretary of State in relation to the exercise of functions under section 2A or 2B of, or paragraph 7C, 8 or 12 of Schedule 1 to, the National Health Service Act 2006;
  (b) a local authority in relation to the exercise of functions under section 2B or 111 of, or any of paragraphs 1 to 7B or 13 of Schedule 1 to, the National Health Service Act 2006;
  (c) a National Health Service trust first established under section 25 of the National Health Service Act 2006;
  (d) a Special Health Authority established under section 28 of the National Health Service Act 2006;
  (e) an NHS foundation trust;
  (f) the National Institute for Health and Care Excellence;
  (g) the Health and Social Care Information Centre;
  (h) a National Health Service trust first established under section 5 of the National Health Service and Community Care Act 1990;
  (i) a Local Health Board established under section 11 of the National Health Service (Wales) Act 2006;
  (j) a National Health Service trust first established under section 18 of the National Health Service (Wales) Act 2006;
  (k) a Special Health Authority established under section 22 of the National Health Service (Wales) Act 2006;
  (l) a Health Board within the meaning of the National Health Service (Scotland) Act 1978;
  (m) a Special Health Board within the meaning of the National Health Service (Scotland) Act 1978;
  (n) a National Health Service trust first established under section 12A of the National Health Service (Scotland) Act 1978;
  (o) the managers of a State Hospital provided under section 102 of the National Health Service (Scotland) Act 1978;
  (p) the Regional Health and Social Care Board established under section 7 of the Health and Social Care (Reform) Act (Northern Ireland) 2009 (c 1 (NI));
  (q) a special health and social care agency established under the Health and Personal Social Services (Special Agencies) (Northern Ireland) Order 1990 (SI 1990/247 (NI 3));
  (r) a Health and Social Care trust established under Article 10 of the Health and Personal Social Services (Northern Ireland) Order 1991 (SI 1991/194 (NI 1)).

NOTES

Commencement: 23 May 2018 (see also the introductory notes to this Act preceding s 1 at [1.71]).

The words omitted from para (g) of sub-s (1) were repealed, and para (a) of sub-s (2) was substituted, by the Data Protection Act 2018, s 211(1)(a), Sch 19, Pt 1, para 227(1), (2)(a), (b), (3).

[1.276]
205 General interpretation

(1) In this Act—
  "biometric data" means personal data resulting from specific technical processing relating to the physical, physiological or behavioural characteristics of an individual, which allows or confirms the unique identification of that individual, such as facial images or dactyloscopic data;

"data concerning health" means personal data relating to the physical or mental health of an individual, including the provision of health care services, which reveals information about his or her health status;

"enactment" includes—

(a)   an enactment passed or made after this Act,

(b)   an enactment comprised in subordinate legislation,

(c)   an enactment comprised in, or in an instrument made under, a Measure or Act of the National Assembly for Wales,

(d)   an enactment comprised in, or in an instrument made under, an Act of the Scottish Parliament, . . .

(e)   an enactment comprised in, or in an instrument made under, Northern Ireland legislation; [and

(f)   any retained direct EU legislation;]

"genetic data" means personal data relating to the inherited or acquired genetic characteristics of an individual which gives unique information about the physiology or the health of that individual and which results, in particular, from an analysis of a biological sample from the individual in question;

"government department" includes the following (except in the expression "United Kingdom government department")—

(a)   a part of the Scottish Administration;

(b)   a Northern Ireland department;

(c)   the Welsh Government;

(d)   a body or authority exercising statutory functions on behalf of the Crown;

"health record" means a record which—

(a)   consists of data concerning health, and

(b)   has been made by or on behalf of a health professional in connection with the diagnosis, care or treatment of the individual to whom the data relates;

"inaccurate", in relation to personal data, means incorrect or misleading as to any matter of fact;

"international obligation of the United Kingdom" includes—

(a)   . . .

(b)   an obligation that arises under an international agreement or arrangement to which the United Kingdom is a party;

"international organisation" means an organisation and its subordinate bodies governed by international law, or any other body which is set up by, or on the basis of, an agreement between two or more countries;

"Minister of the Crown" has the same meaning as in the Ministers of the Crown Act 1975;

"publish" means make available to the public or a section of the public (and related expressions are to be read accordingly);

"subordinate legislation" has the meaning given in the Interpretation Act 1978;

"tribunal" means any tribunal in which legal proceedings may be brought;

"the Tribunal", in relation to an application or appeal under this Act, means—

(a)   the Upper Tribunal, in any case where it is determined by or under Tribunal Procedure Rules that the Upper Tribunal is to hear the application or appeal, or

(b)   the First-tier Tribunal, in any other case.

[(1A) In this Act, references to a fundamental right or fundamental freedom (however expressed) are to a fundamental right or fundamental freedom which continues to form part of domestic law on and after IP completion day by virtue of section 4 of the European Union (Withdrawal) Act 2018, as the right or freedom is amended or otherwise modified by the law of the United Kingdom, or of a part of the United Kingdom, from time to time on or after IP completion day]

(2) References in this Act to a period expressed in hours, days, weeks, months or years are to be interpreted in accordance with Article 3 of Regulation (EEC, Euratom) No 1182/71 of the Council of 3 June 1971 determining the rules applicable to periods, dates and time limits, except in—

[(za) section 119A(10) and (11);]

(a)   section 125(4), (7) and (8);

(b)   section 161(3), (5) and (6);

(c)   section 176(2);

(d)   section 178(2);

(e)   section 182(8) and (9);

(f)   section 183(4);

(g)   section 192(3), (5) and (6);

(h)   section 197(3) and (4);

(i)   paragraph 23(4) and (5) of Schedule 1;

(j)   paragraphs 5(4) and 6(4) of Schedule 3;

(k)   Schedule 5;

(l)   paragraph 11(5) of Schedule 12;

(m)   Schedule 15;

(and the references in section 5 to terms used in   . . .   Part 2 do not include references to a period expressed in hours, days, weeks, months or years).

(3)   . . .

[(4) In the definition of "the UK GDPR" in section 3(10)—

(a)   the reference to Regulation (EU) 2016/679 as it forms part of the law of England and Wales, Scotland and Northern Ireland by virtue of section 3 of the European Union (Withdrawal) Act 2018 is to be treated as a reference to that Regulation as modified by Schedule 1 to the Data Protection, Privacy and Electronic Communications (Amendments etc) (EU Exit) Regulations 2019 ("the 2019 Regulations"), but

(b)   nothing in the definition or in paragraph (a) determines whether, where Regulation (EU) 2016/679 is modified on or after IP completion day by the law of England and Wales, Scotland or Northern Ireland (other than by Schedule 1 to the 2019 Regulations), the reference to Regulation (EU) 2016/679 is then to be read as a reference to that Regulation as modified.

(5)   Subsection (4) is not to be read as implying anything about how other references to Regulation (EU) 2016/679 or references to other retained EU law are to be interpreted.]

NOTES

Commencement: 23 May 2018 (see also the introductory notes to this Act preceding s 1 at **[1.71]**).

Sub-s (1): in the definition "enactment" the word omitted was repealed and the words in square brackets were inserted, and the words omitted from the definition "international obligation of the United Kingdom" were repealed, by the Data Protection, Privacy and Electronic Communications (Amendments etc) (EU Exit) Regulations 2019, SI 2019/419, reg 4, Sch 2, paras 1, 85(1)–(3).

Sub-ss (1A), (4), (5): inserted and added respectively, by SI 2019/419, reg 4, Sch 2, paras 1, 85(1), (4), (7).

Sub-s (2): para (za) was inserted and the words omitted were repealed, by SI 2019/419, reg 4, Sch 2, paras 1, 85(1), (5).

Sub-s (3): repealed by SI 2019/419, reg 4, Sch 2, paras 1, 85(1), (6).

Note that Sch 2, para 85 to the 2019 Regulations was amended by the Data Protection, Privacy and Electronic Communications (Amendments etc) (EU Exit) Regulations 2020, SI 2020/1586, reg 5 (and the effect of the amendment has been incorporated in the text set out above).

National Assembly for Wales: as to the renaming of the National Assembly for Wales, see the note at **[1.94]**.

[1.277]
206   Index of defined expressions

The Table below lists provisions which define or otherwise explain terms defined for this Act, for a Part of this Act or for Chapter 2 or 3 of Part 2 of this Act.

the affirmative resolution procedure	section 182
. . .	. . .
. . .	. . .
assessment notice (in Part 6)	section 181
biometric data	section 205
certification provider (in Part 6)	section 181
the Commissioner	section 3
competent authority (in Part 3)	section 30
consent (in Part 4)	section 84
controller	section 3
data concerning health	section 205
the Data Protection Convention	section 3
the data protection legislation	section 3
data subject	section 3
employee (in Parts 3 and 4)	sections 33 and 84
enactment	section 205
enforcement notice (in Part 6)	section 181
[the EU GDPR	section 3]
filing system	section 3
FOI public authority (in Chapter 3 of Part 2)	section 21
. . .	. . .
genetic data	section 205
government department	section 205
health professional	section 204
health record	section 205
identifiable living individual	section 3
inaccurate	section 205
information notice (in Part 6)	section 181
intelligence service (in Part 4)	section 82
international obligation of the United Kingdom	section 205
international organisation	section 205
the Law Enforcement Directive	section 3
the law enforcement purposes (in Part 3)	section 31
the made affirmative resolution procedure	section 182
Minister of the Crown	section 205
the negative resolution procedure	section 182

penalty notice (in Part 6)	section 181
penalty variation notice (in Part 6)	section 181
personal data	section 3
personal data breach (in Parts 3 and 4)	sections 33 and 84
processing	section 3
processor	section 3
profiling (in Part 3)	section 33
public authority (in the [UK GDPR] and Part 2)	section 7
public body (in the [UK GDPR] and Part 2)	section 7
publish	section 205
recipient (in Parts 3 and 4)	sections 33 and 84
representative (in Part 6)	section 181
representative body (in relation to a right of a data subject)	section 187
restriction of processing (in Parts 3 and 4)	sections 33 and 84
social work professional	section 204
the special purposes (in Part 6)	section 174
special purposes proceedings (in Part 6)	section 174
subordinate legislation	section 205
third country (in Part 3)	section 33
tribunal	section 205
the Tribunal	section 205
[the UK GDPR	section 3]

NOTES

Commencement: 23 May 2018 (see also the introductory notes to this Act preceding s 1 at **[1.71]**).

The entries omitted were repealed, the entries "the EU GDPR" and "the UK GDPR" were inserted and the words in square brackets in the entries "public authority" and "public body" were substituted by the Data Protection, Privacy and Electronic Communications (Amendments etc) (EU Exit) Regulations 2019, SI 2019/419, reg 4, Sch 2, paras 1, 86.

Territorial application

[1.278]

207 Territorial application of this Act

(1) This Act applies only to processing of personal data described in subsections [(1A) and (2)].

[(1A) In the case of the processing of personal data to which Part 2 (the UK GDPR) applies, it applies to the types of such processing to which the UK GDPR applies by virtue of Article 3 of the UK GDPR.]

(2) [In the case of the processing of personal data to which Part 2 does not apply, it applies where such processing is carried out] in the context of the activities of an establishment of a controller or processor in the United Kingdom, whether or not the processing takes place in the United Kingdom.

(3)   . . .

(4) [Subsections (1), (1A) and (2)] have effect subject to any provision in or made under section 120 providing for the Commissioner to carry out functions in relation to other processing of personal data.

(5) Section 3(14)(c) does not apply to the reference to the processing of personal data in subsection (2).

(6)   . . .

(7) In this section, references to a person who has an establishment in the United Kingdom include the following—

   (a) an individual who is ordinarily resident in the United Kingdom,

   (b) a body incorporated under the law of the United Kingdom or a part of the United Kingdom,

   (c) a partnership or other unincorporated association formed under the law of the United Kingdom or a part of the United Kingdom, and

   (d) a person not within paragraph (a), (b) or (c) who maintains, and carries on activities through, an office, branch or agency or other stable arrangements in the United Kingdom,

. . .

NOTES

Commencement: 25 May 2018 (see also the introductory notes to this Act preceding s 1 at **[1.71]**).

The words in square brackets in sub-ss (1), (2), (4) were substituted, sub-s (1A) was inserted, and sub-ss (3), (6) and the words omitted from sub-s (7) were repealed, by the Data Protection, Privacy and Electronic Communications (Amendments etc) (EU Exit) Regulations 2019, SI 2019/419, reg 4, Sch 2, paras 1, 87.

General

[1.279]

208 Children in Scotland

(1) Subsections (2) and (3) apply where a question falls to be determined in Scotland as to the legal capacity of a person aged under 16 to—

   (a) exercise a right conferred by the data protection legislation, or

   (b) give consent for the purposes of the data protection legislation.

(2) The person is to be taken to have that capacity where the person has a general understanding of what it means to exercise the right or give such consent.

(3) A person aged 12 or over is to be presumed to be of sufficient age and maturity to have such understanding, unless the contrary is shown.

NOTES

Commencement: 25 May 2018 (see also the introductory notes to this Act preceding s 1 at **[1.71]**).

[1.280]
209 Application to the Crown

(1) This Act binds the Crown.

(2) For the purposes of the [UK GDPR] and this Act, each government department is to be treated as a person separate from the other government departments (to the extent that is not already the case).

(3) Where government departments are not able to enter into contracts with each other, a provision of the [UK GDPR] or this Act that would require relations between them to be governed by a contract (or other binding legal act) in writing is to be treated as satisfied if the relations are the subject of a memorandum of understanding between them.

(4) Where the purposes for which and the manner in which personal data is, or is to be, processed are determined by a person acting on behalf of the Royal Household, the Duchy of Lancaster or the Duchy of Cornwall, the controller in respect of that data for the purposes of the [UK GDPR] and this Act is—

    (a) in relation to the Royal Household, the Keeper of the Privy Purse,

    (b) in relation to the Duchy of Lancaster, such person as the Chancellor of the Duchy appoints, and

    (c) in relation to the Duchy of Cornwall, such person as the Duke of Cornwall, or the possessor for the time being of the Duchy of Cornwall, appoints.

(5) Different persons may be appointed under subsection (4)(b) or (c) for different purposes.

(6) As regards criminal liability—

    (a) a government department is not liable to prosecution under this Act;

    (b) nothing in subsection (4) makes a person who is a controller by virtue of that subsection liable to prosecution under this Act;

    (c) a person in the service of the Crown is liable to prosecution under the provisions of this Act listed in subsection (7).

(7) Those provisions are—

    (a) section 119;

    (b) section 170;

    (c) section 171;

    (d) section 173;

    (e) paragraph 15 of Schedule 15.

NOTES

Commencement: 23 May 2018 (see also the introductory notes to this Act preceding s 1 at **[1.71]**).

The words in square brackets in sub-ss (2)–(4) were substituted by the Data Protection, Privacy and Electronic Communications (Amendments etc) (EU Exit) Regulations 2019, SI 2019/419, reg 4, Sch 2, paras 1, 88.

[1.281]
210 Application to Parliament

(1) Parts 1, 2 and 5 to 7 of this Act apply to the processing of personal data by or on behalf of either House of Parliament.

(2) Where the purposes for which and the manner in which personal data is, or is to be, processed are determined by or on behalf of the House of Commons, the controller in respect of that data for the purposes of the [UK GDPR] and this Act is the Corporate Officer of that House.

(3) Where the purposes for which and the manner in which personal data is, or is to be, processed are determined by or on behalf of the House of Lords, the controller in respect of that data for the purposes of the [UK GDPR] and this Act is the Corporate Officer of that House.

(4) Subsections (2) and (3) do not apply where the purposes for which and the manner in which the personal data is, or is to be, processed are determined by or on behalf of the Intelligence and Security Committee of Parliament.

(5) As regards criminal liability—

    (a) nothing in subsection (2) or (3) makes the Corporate Officer of the House of Commons or the Corporate Officer of the House of Lords liable to prosecution under this Act;

    (b) a person acting on behalf of either House of Parliament is liable to prosecution under the provisions of this Act listed in subsection (6).

(6) Those provisions are—

    (a) section 170;

    (b) section 171;

    (c) section 173;

    (d) paragraph 15 of Schedule 15.

NOTES

Commencement: 23 May 2018 (see also the introductory notes to this Act preceding s 1 at **[1.71]**).

The words in square brackets in sub-ss (2), (3) were substituted by the Data Protection, Privacy and Electronic Communications (Amendments etc) (EU Exit) Regulations 2019, SI 2019/419, reg 4, Sch 2, paras 1, 89.

[1.282]
211 Minor and consequential provision

(1) In Schedule 19—

    (a) Part 1 contains minor and consequential amendments of primary legislation;

(b) Part 2 contains minor and consequential amendments of other legislation;

(c) Part 3 contains consequential modifications of legislation;

(d) Part 4 contains supplementary provision.

(2) The Secretary of State may by regulations make provision that is consequential on any provision made by this Act.

(3) Regulations under subsection (2)—

(a) may include transitional, transitory or saving provision;

(b) may amend, repeal or revoke an enactment.

(4) The reference to an enactment in subsection (3)(b) does not include an enactment passed or made after the end of the Session in which this Act is passed.

(5) Regulations under this section that amend, repeal or revoke primary legislation are subject to the affirmative resolution procedure.

(6) Any other regulations under this section are subject to the negative resolution procedure.

(7) In this section, "primary legislation" means—

(a) an Act;

(b) an Act of the Scottish Parliament;

(c) a Measure or Act of the National Assembly for Wales;

(d) Northern Ireland legislation.

NOTES

Commencement: 25 May 2018 and 2 December 2019 (see also the introductory notes to this Act preceding s 1 at **[1.71]**).
National Assembly for Wales: as to the renaming of the National Assembly for Wales, see the note at **[1.94]**.

Final

[1.283]
212 Commencement

(1) Except as provided by subsections (2) and (3), this Act comes into force on such day as the Secretary of State may by regulations appoint.

(2) This section and the following provisions come into force on the day on which this Act is passed—

(a) sections 1 and 3;

(b) section 182;

(c) sections 204, 205 and 206;

(d) sections 209 and 210;

(e) sections 213(2), 214 and 215;

(f) any other provision of this Act so far as it confers power to make regulations or Tribunal Procedure Rules or is otherwise necessary for enabling the exercise of such a power on or after the day on which this Act is passed.

(3) The following provisions come into force at the end of the period of 2 months beginning when this Act is passed—

(a) section 124;

(b) sections 125, 126 and 127, so far as they relate to a code prepared under section 124;

(c) section 177;

(d) section 178 and Schedule 17;

(e) section 179.

(4) Regulations under this section may make different provision for different areas.

NOTES

Commencement: 23 May 2018 (see also the introductory notes to this Act preceding s 1 at **[1.71]**).
Regulations: the Data Protection Act 2018 (Commencement No 1 and Transitional and Saving Provisions) Regulations 2018, SI 2018/625; the Data Protection Act 2018 (Commencement No 2) Regulations 2019, SI 2019/1188; Data Protection Act 2018 (Commencement No 3) Regulations 2019, SI 2019/1434.

[1.284]
213 Transitional provision

(1) Schedule 20 contains transitional, transitory and saving provision.

(2) The Secretary of State may by regulations make transitional, transitory or saving provision in connection with the coming into force of any provision of this Act or with the [EU GDPR] beginning to apply, including provision amending or repealing a provision of Schedule 20.

(3) Regulations under this section that amend or repeal a provision of Schedule 20 are subject to the negative resolution procedure.

[(4) Schedule 21 contains further transitional, transitory and saving provision made in connection with the amendment of this Act and the UK GDPR by regulations under section 8 of the European Union (Withdrawal) Act 2018.]

NOTES

Commencement: 23 May 2018 (sub-s (2)); 25 May 2018 (otherwise) (see also the introductory notes to this Act preceding s 1 at **[1.71]**).
The words in square brackets in sub-s (2) were substituted and sub-s (4) was added, by the Data Protection, Privacy and Electronic Communications (Amendments etc) (EU Exit) Regulations 2019, SI 2019/419, reg 4, Sch 2, paras 1, 90.
Regulations: the Data Protection Act 2018 (Commencement No 1 and Transitional and Saving Provisions) Regulations 2018, SI 2018/625.

[1.285]
214   Extent
(1) This Act extends to England and Wales, Scotland and Northern Ireland, subject to—
  (a) subsections (2) to (5), and
  (b) paragraph 12 of Schedule 12.
(2) Section 199 extends to England and Wales only.
(3) Sections 188, 189 and 190 extend to England and Wales and Northern Ireland only.
(4) An amendment, repeal or revocation made by this Act has the same extent in the United Kingdom as the enactment amended, repealed or revoked.
(5) This subsection and the following provisions also extend to the Isle of Man—
  (a) paragraphs 332 and 434 of Schedule 19;
  (b) sections 211(1), 212(1) and 213(2), so far as relating to those paragraphs.
(6) Where there is a power to extend a part of an Act by Order in Council to any of the Channel Islands, the Isle of Man or any of the British overseas territories, the power may be exercised in relation to an amendment or repeal of that part which is made by or under this Act.

NOTES
Commencement: 23 May 2018 (see also the introductory notes to this Act preceding s 1 at **[1.71]**).
Orders: the Immigration (Isle of Man) (Amendment) Order 2019, SI 2019/562.

[1.286]
215   Short title
This Act may be cited as the Data Protection Act 2018.

NOTES
Commencement: 23 May 2018 (see also the introductory notes to this Act preceding s 1 at **[1.71]**).

SCHEDULES

SCHEDULE 1
SPECIAL CATEGORIES OF PERSONAL DATA AND CRIMINAL CONVICTIONS ETC DATA
Section 10

PART 1   CONDITIONS RELATING TO EMPLOYMENT, HEALTH AND RESEARCH ETC
Employment, social security and social protection

[1.287]
1. (1) This condition is met if—
  (a) the processing is necessary for the purposes of performing or exercising obligations or rights which are imposed or conferred by law on the controller or the data subject in connection with employment, social security or social protection, and
  (b) when the processing is carried out, the controller has an appropriate policy document in place (see paragraph 39 in Part 4 of this Schedule).
(2) See also the additional safeguards in Part 4 of this Schedule.
(3) In this paragraph—
  "social security" includes any of the branches of social security listed in Article 3(1) of Regulation (EC) No 883/2004 of the European Parliament and of the Council on the co-ordination of social security systems (as amended from time to time);
  "social protection" includes an intervention described in Article 2(b) of Regulation (EC) 458/2007 of the European Parliament and of the Council of 25 April 2007 on the European system of integrated social protection statistics (ESSPROS) [as it had effect in EU law immediately before exit day].

Health or social care purposes

2. (1) This condition is met if the processing is necessary for health or social care purposes.
(2) In this paragraph "health or social care purposes" means the purposes of—
  (a) preventive or occupational medicine,
  (b) the assessment of the working capacity of an employee,
  (c) medical diagnosis,
  (d) the provision of health care or treatment,
  (e) the provision of social care, or
  (f) the management of health care systems or services or social care systems or services.
(3) See also the conditions and safeguards in Article 9(3) of the [UK GDPR] (obligations of secrecy) and section 11(1).

Public health

3. This condition is met if the processing—
  (a) is necessary for reasons of public interest in the area of public health, and
  (b) is carried out—
    (i)   by or under the responsibility of a health professional, or
    (ii) by another person who in the circumstances owes a duty of confidentiality under an enactment or rule of law.

Research etc

4. This condition is met if the processing—

(a) is necessary for archiving purposes, scientific or historical research purposes or statistical purposes,
(b) is carried out in accordance with Article 89(1) of the [UK GDPR] (as supplemented by section 19), and
(c) is in the public interest.

NOTES

Commencement: 25 May 2018 (see also the introductory notes to this Act preceding s 1 at **[1.71]**).

The words in square brackets in paras 2(3), 4(b) were substituted by the Data Protection, Privacy and Electronic Communications (Amendments etc) (EU Exit) Regulations 2019, SI 2019/419, reg 4, Sch 2, paras 1, 91(1)–(3). Words in square brackets in the definition "social protection" in para 1(3) substituted by the UK Statistics (Amendment etc) (EU Exit) Regulations 2019, SI 2019/489, reg 3.

PART 2 SUBSTANTIAL PUBLIC INTEREST CONDITIONS

Requirement for an appropriate policy document when relying on conditions in this Part

[1.288]
5. (1) Except as otherwise provided, a condition in this Part of this Schedule is met only if, when the processing is carried out, the controller has an appropriate policy document in place (see paragraph 39 in Part 4 of this Schedule).

(2) See also the additional safeguards in Part 4 of this Schedule.

Statutory etc and government purposes

6. (1) This condition is met if the processing—
(a) is necessary for a purpose listed in sub-paragraph (2), and
(b) is necessary for reasons of substantial public interest.

(2) Those purposes are—
(a) the exercise of a function conferred on a person by an enactment or rule of law;
(b) the exercise of a function of the Crown, a Minister of the Crown or a government department.

Administration of justice and parliamentary purposes

7. This condition is met if the processing is necessary—
(a) for the administration of justice, or
(b) for the exercise of a function of either House of Parliament.

Equality of opportunity or treatment

8. (1) This condition is met if the processing—
(a) is of a specified category of personal data, and
(b) is necessary for the purposes of identifying or keeping under review the existence or absence of equality of opportunity or treatment between groups of people specified in relation to that category with a view to enabling such equality to be promoted or maintained,
subject to the exceptions in sub-paragraphs (3) to (5).

(2) In sub-paragraph (1), "specified" means specified in the following table—

Category of personal data	*Groups of people (in relation to a category of personal data)*
Personal data revealing racial or ethnic origin	People of different racial or ethnic origins
Personal data revealing religious or philosophical beliefs	People holding different religious or philosophical beliefs
Data concerning health	People with different states of physical or mental health
Personal data concerning an individual's sexual orientation	People of different sexual orientation

(3) Processing does not meet the condition in sub-paragraph (1) if it is carried out for the purposes of measures or decisions with respect to a particular data subject.

(4) Processing does not meet the condition in sub-paragraph (1) if it is likely to cause substantial damage or substantial distress to an individual.

(5) Processing does not meet the condition in sub-paragraph (1) if—
(a) an individual who is the data subject (or one of the data subjects) has given notice in writing to the controller requiring the controller not to process personal data in respect of which the individual is the data subject (and has not given notice in writing withdrawing that requirement),
(b) the notice gave the controller a reasonable period in which to stop processing such data, and
(c) that period has ended.

Racial and ethnic diversity at senior levels of organisations

9. (1) This condition is met if the processing—
(a) is of personal data revealing racial or ethnic origin,
(b) is carried out as part of a process of identifying suitable individuals to hold senior positions in a particular organisation, a type of organisation or organisations generally,
(c) is necessary for the purposes of promoting or maintaining diversity in the racial and ethnic origins of individuals who hold senior positions in the organisation or organisations, and
(d) can reasonably be carried out without the consent of the data subject,
subject to the exception in sub-paragraph (3).

(2) For the purposes of sub-paragraph (1)(d), processing can reasonably be carried out without the consent of the data subject only where—
(a) the controller cannot reasonably be expected to obtain the consent of the data subject, and
(b) the controller is not aware of the data subject withholding consent.

(3) Processing does not meet the condition in sub-paragraph (1) if it is likely to cause substantial damage or substantial distress to an individual.

(4) For the purposes of this paragraph, an individual holds a senior position in an organisation if the individual—
(a) holds a position listed in sub-paragraph (5), or
(b) does not hold such a position but is a senior manager of the organisation.

(5) Those positions are—
(a) a director, secretary or other similar officer of a body corporate;
(b) a member of a limited liability partnership;
(c) a partner in a partnership within the Partnership Act 1890, a limited partnership registered under the Limited Partnerships Act 1907 or an entity of a similar character formed under the law of a country or territory outside the United Kingdom.

(6) In this paragraph, "senior manager", in relation to an organisation, means a person who plays a significant role in—
(a) the making of decisions about how the whole or a substantial part of the organisation's activities are to be managed or organised, or
(b) the actual managing or organising of the whole or a substantial part of those activities.

(7) The reference in sub-paragraph (2)(b) to a data subject withholding consent does not include a data subject merely failing to respond to a request for consent.

Preventing or detecting unlawful acts

10. (1) This condition is met if the processing—
(a) is necessary for the purposes of the prevention or detection of an unlawful act,
(b) must be carried out without the consent of the data subject so as not to prejudice those purposes, and
(c) is necessary for reasons of substantial public interest.

(2) If the processing consists of the disclosure of personal data to a competent authority, or is carried out in preparation for such disclosure, the condition in sub-paragraph (1) is met even if, when the processing is carried out, the controller does not have an appropriate policy document in place (see paragraph 5 of this Schedule).

(3) In this paragraph—
"act" includes a failure to act;
"competent authority" has the same meaning as in Part 3 of this Act (see section 30).

Protecting the public against dishonesty etc

11. (1) This condition is met if the processing—
(a) is necessary for the exercise of a protective function,
(b) must be carried out without the consent of the data subject so as not to prejudice the exercise of that function, and
(c) is necessary for reasons of substantial public interest.

(2) In this paragraph, "protective function" means a function which is intended to protect members of the public against—
(a) dishonesty, malpractice or other seriously improper conduct,
(b) unfitness or incompetence,
(c) mismanagement in the administration of a body or association, or
(d) failures in services provided by a body or association.

Regulatory requirements relating to unlawful acts and dishonesty etc

12. (1) This condition is met if—
(a) the processing is necessary for the purposes of complying with, or assisting other persons to comply with, a regulatory requirement which involves a person taking steps to establish whether another person has—
    (i) committed an unlawful act, or
    (ii) been involved in dishonesty, malpractice or other seriously improper conduct,
(b) in the circumstances, the controller cannot reasonably be expected to obtain the consent of the data subject to the processing, and
(c) the processing is necessary for reasons of substantial public interest.

(2) In this paragraph—
"act" includes a failure to act;
"regulatory requirement" means—
    (a) a requirement imposed by legislation or by a person in exercise of a function conferred by legislation, or
    (b) a requirement forming part of generally accepted principles of good practice relating to a type of body or an activity.

Journalism etc in connection with unlawful acts and dishonesty etc

13. (1) This condition is met if—
(a) the processing consists of the disclosure of personal data for the special purposes,
(b) it is carried out in connection with a matter described in sub-paragraph (2),
(c) it is necessary for reasons of substantial public interest,
(d) it is carried out with a view to the publication of the personal data by any person, and

(e) the controller reasonably believes that publication of the personal data would be in the public interest.

(2) The matters mentioned in sub-paragraph (1)(b) are any of the following (whether alleged or established)—
  (a) the commission of an unlawful act by a person;
  (b) dishonesty, malpractice or other seriously improper conduct of a person;
  (c) unfitness or incompetence of a person;
  (d) mismanagement in the administration of a body or association;
  (e) a failure in services provided by a body or association.

(3) The condition in sub-paragraph (1) is met even if, when the processing is carried out, the controller does not have an appropriate policy document in place (see paragraph 5 of this Schedule).

(4) In this paragraph—
  "act" includes a failure to act;
  "the special purposes" means—
      (a)   the purposes of journalism;
      (b)   academic purposes;
      (c)   artistic purposes;
      (d)   literary purposes.

Preventing fraud

14. (1) This condition is met if the processing—
  (a) is necessary for the purposes of preventing fraud or a particular kind of fraud, and
  (b) consists of—
      (i)   the disclosure of personal data by a person as a member of an anti-fraud organisation,
      (ii)   the disclosure of personal data in accordance with arrangements made by an anti-fraud organisation,
             or
      (iii) the processing of personal data disclosed as described in sub-paragraph (i) or (ii).

(2) In this paragraph, "anti-fraud organisation" has the same meaning as in section 68 of the Serious Crime Act 2007.

Suspicion of terrorist financing or money laundering

15. This condition is met if the processing is necessary for the purposes of making a disclosure in good faith under either of the following—
  (a) section 21CA of the Terrorism Act 2000 (disclosures between certain entities within regulated sector in relation to suspicion of commission of terrorist financing offence or for purposes of identifying terrorist property);
  (b) section 339ZB of the Proceeds of Crime Act 2002 (disclosures within regulated sector in relation to suspicion of money laundering).

Support for individuals with a particular disability or medical condition

16. (1) This condition is met if the processing—
  (a) is carried out by a not-for-profit body which provides support to individuals with a particular disability or medical condition,
  (b) is of a type of personal data falling within sub-paragraph (2) which relates to an individual falling within sub-paragraph (3),
  (c) is necessary for the purposes of—
      (i)   raising awareness of the disability or medical condition, or
      (ii)   providing support to individuals falling within sub-paragraph (3) or enabling such individuals to provide support to each other,
  (d) can reasonably be carried out without the consent of the data subject, and
  (e) is necessary for reasons of substantial public interest.

(2) The following types of personal data fall within this sub-paragraph—
  (a) personal data revealing racial or ethnic origin;
  (b) genetic data or biometric data;
  (c) data concerning health;
  (d) personal data concerning an individual's sex life or sexual orientation.

(3) An individual falls within this sub-paragraph if the individual is or has been a member of the body mentioned in sub-paragraph (1)(a) and—
  (a) has the disability or condition mentioned there, has had that disability or condition or has a significant risk of developing that disability or condition, or
  (b) is a relative or carer of an individual who satisfies paragraph (a) of this sub-paragraph.

(4) For the purposes of sub-paragraph (1)(d), processing can reasonably be carried out without the consent of the data subject only where—
  (a) the controller cannot reasonably be expected to obtain the consent of the data subject, and
  (b) the controller is not aware of the data subject withholding consent.

(5) In this paragraph—
  "carer" means an individual who provides or intends to provide care for another individual other than—
      (a)   under or by virtue of a contract, or
      (b)   as voluntary work;
  "disability" has the same meaning as in the Equality Act 2010 (see section 6 of, and Schedule 1 to, that Act).

(6) The reference in sub-paragraph (4)(b) to a data subject withholding consent does not include a data subject merely failing to respond to a request for consent.

Counselling etc

17. (1) This condition is met if the processing—
- (a) is necessary for the provision of confidential counselling, advice or support or of another similar service provided confidentially,
- (b) is carried out without the consent of the data subject for one of the reasons listed in sub-paragraph (2), and
- (c) is necessary for reasons of substantial public interest.

(2) The reasons mentioned in sub-paragraph (1)(b) are—
- (a) in the circumstances, consent to the processing cannot be given by the data subject;
- (b) in the circumstances, the controller cannot reasonably be expected to obtain the consent of the data subject to the processing;
- (c) the processing must be carried out without the consent of the data subject because obtaining the consent of the data subject would prejudice the provision of the service mentioned in sub-paragraph (1)(a).

Safeguarding of children and of individuals at risk

18. (1) This condition is met if—
- (a) the processing is necessary for the purposes of—
    - (i) protecting an individual from neglect or physical, mental or emotional harm, or
    - (ii) protecting the physical, mental or emotional well-being of an individual,
- (b) the individual is—
    - (i) aged under 18, or
    - (ii) aged 18 or over and at risk,
- (c) the processing is carried out without the consent of the data subject for one of the reasons listed in sub-paragraph (2), and
- (d) the processing is necessary for reasons of substantial public interest,

(2) The reasons mentioned in sub-paragraph (1)(c) are—
- (a) in the circumstances, consent to the processing cannot be given by the data subject;
- (b) in the circumstances, the controller cannot reasonably be expected to obtain the consent of the data subject to the processing;
- (c) the processing must be carried out without the consent of the data subject because obtaining the consent of the data subject would prejudice the provision of the protection mentioned in sub-paragraph (1)(a).

(3) For the purposes of this paragraph, an individual aged 18 or over is "at risk" if the controller has reasonable cause to suspect that the individual—
- (a) has needs for care and support,
- (b) is experiencing, or at risk of, neglect or physical, mental or emotional harm, and
- (c) as a result of those needs is unable to protect himself or herself against the neglect or harm or the risk of it.

(4) In sub-paragraph (1)(a), the reference to the protection of an individual or of the well-being of an individual includes both protection relating to a particular individual and protection relating to a type of individual.

Safeguarding of economic well-being of certain individuals

19. (1) This condition is met if the processing—
- (a) is necessary for the purposes of protecting the economic well-being of an individual at economic risk who is aged 18 or over,
- (b) is of data concerning health,
- (c) is carried out without the consent of the data subject for one of the reasons listed in sub-paragraph (2), and
- (d) is necessary for reasons of substantial public interest.

(2) The reasons mentioned in sub-paragraph (1)(c) are—
- (a) in the circumstances, consent to the processing cannot be given by the data subject;
- (b) in the circumstances, the controller cannot reasonably be expected to obtain the consent of the data subject to the processing;
- (c) the processing must be carried out without the consent of the data subject because obtaining the consent of the data subject would prejudice the provision of the protection mentioned in sub-paragraph (1)(a).

(3) In this paragraph, "individual at economic risk" means an individual who is less able to protect his or her economic well-being by reason of physical or mental injury, illness or disability.

Insurance

20. (1) This condition is met if the processing—
- (a) is necessary for an insurance purpose,
- (b) is of personal data revealing racial or ethnic origin, religious or philosophical beliefs or trade union membership, genetic data or data concerning health, and
- (c) is necessary for reasons of substantial public interest,

subject to sub-paragraphs (2) and (3).

(2) Sub-paragraph (3) applies where—
- (a) the processing is not carried out for the purposes of measures or decisions with respect to the data subject, and
- (b) the data subject does not have and is not expected to acquire—
    - (i) rights against, or obligations in relation to, a person who is an insured person under an insurance contract to which the insurance purpose mentioned in sub-paragraph (1)(a) relates, or
    - (ii) other rights or obligations in connection with such a contract.

(3) Where this sub-paragraph applies, the processing does not meet the condition in sub-paragraph (1) unless, in addition to meeting the requirements in that sub-paragraph, it can reasonably be carried out without the consent of the data subject.

(4) For the purposes of sub-paragraph (3), processing can reasonably be carried out without the consent of the data subject only where—
- (a) the controller cannot reasonably be expected to obtain the consent of the data subject, and
- (b) the controller is not aware of the data subject withholding consent.

(5) In this paragraph—
"insurance contract" means a contract of general insurance or long-term insurance;
"insurance purpose" means—
- (a) advising on, arranging, underwriting or administering an insurance contract,
- (b) administering a claim under an insurance contract, or
- (c) exercising a right, or complying with an obligation, arising in connection with an insurance contract, including a right or obligation arising under an enactment or rule of law.

(6) The reference in sub-paragraph (4)(b) to a data subject withholding consent does not include a data subject merely failing to respond to a request for consent.

(7) Terms used in the definition of "insurance contract" in sub-paragraph (5) and also in an order made under section 22 of the Financial Services and Markets Act 2000 (regulated activities) have the same meaning in that definition as they have in that order.

Occupational pensions

21. (1) This condition is met if the processing—
- (a) is necessary for the purpose of making a determination in connection with eligibility for, or benefits payable under, an occupational pension scheme,
- (b) is of data concerning health which relates to a data subject who is the parent, grandparent, great-grandparent or sibling of a member of the scheme,
- (c) is not carried out for the purposes of measures or decisions with respect to the data subject, and
- (d) can reasonably be carried out without the consent of the data subject.

(2) For the purposes of sub-paragraph (1)(d), processing can reasonably be carried out without the consent of the data subject only where—
- (a) the controller cannot reasonably be expected to obtain the consent of the data subject, and
- (b) the controller is not aware of the data subject withholding consent.

(3) In this paragraph—
"occupational pension scheme" has the meaning given in section 1 of the Pension Schemes Act 1993;
"member", in relation to a scheme, includes an individual who is seeking to become a member of the scheme.

(4) The reference in sub-paragraph (2)(b) to a data subject withholding consent does not include a data subject merely failing to respond to a request for consent.

Political parties

22. (1) This condition is met if the processing—
- (a) is of personal data revealing political opinions,
- (b) is carried out by a person or organisation included in the register maintained under section 23 of the Political Parties, Elections and Referendums Act 2000, and
- (c) is necessary for the purposes of the person's or organisation's political activities,

subject to the exceptions in sub-paragraphs (2) and (3).

(2) Processing does not meet the condition in sub-paragraph (1) if it is likely to cause substantial damage or substantial distress to a person.

(3) Processing does not meet the condition in sub-paragraph (1) if—
- (a) an individual who is the data subject (or one of the data subjects) has given notice in writing to the controller requiring the controller not to process personal data in respect of which the individual is the data subject (and has not given notice in writing withdrawing that requirement),
- (b) the notice gave the controller a reasonable period in which to stop processing such data, and
- (c) that period has ended.

(4) In this paragraph, "political activities" include campaigning, fund-raising, political surveys and case-work.

Elected representatives responding to requests

23. (1) This condition is met if—
- (a) the processing is carried out—
  - (i) by an elected representative or a person acting with the authority of such a representative,
  - (ii) in connection with the discharge of the elected representative's functions, and
  - (iii) in response to a request by an individual that the elected representative take action on behalf of the individual, and
- (b) the processing is necessary for the purposes of, or in connection with, the action reasonably taken by the elected representative in response to that request,

subject to sub-paragraph (2).

(2) Where the request is made by an individual other than the data subject, the condition in sub-paragraph (1) is met only if the processing must be carried out without the consent of the data subject for one of the following reasons—
- (a) in the circumstances, consent to the processing cannot be given by the data subject;
- (b) in the circumstances, the elected representative cannot reasonably be expected to obtain the consent of the data subject to the processing;
- (c) obtaining the consent of the data subject would prejudice the action taken by the elected representative;
- (d) the processing is necessary in the interests of another individual and the data subject has withheld consent unreasonably.

(3) In this paragraph, "elected representative" means—
  (a) a member of the House of Commons;
  (b) a member of the National Assembly for Wales;
  (c) a member of the Scottish Parliament;
  (d) a member of the Northern Ireland Assembly;
  (e) . . .
  (f) an elected member of a local authority within the meaning of section 270(1) of the Local Government Act 1972, namely—
     (i) in England, a county council, a district council, a London borough council or a parish council;
     (ii) in Wales, a county council, a county borough council or a community council;
  (g) an elected mayor of a local authority within the meaning of Part 1A or 2 of the Local Government Act 2000;
  (h) a mayor for the area of a combined authority established under section 103 of the Local Democracy, Economic Development and Construction Act 2009;
  (i) the Mayor of London or an elected member of the London Assembly;
  (j) an elected member of—
     (i) the Common Council of the City of London, or
     (ii) the Council of the Isles of Scilly;
  (k) an elected member of a council constituted under section 2 of the Local Government etc (Scotland) Act 1994;
  (l) an elected member of a district council within the meaning of the Local Government Act (Northern Ireland) 1972 (c 9 (NI));
  (m) a police and crime commissioner.

(4) For the purposes of sub-paragraph (3), a person who is—
  (a) a member of the House of Commons immediately before Parliament is dissolved,
  (b) a member of the National Assembly for Wales immediately before that Assembly is dissolved,
  (c) a member of the Scottish Parliament immediately before that Parliament is dissolved, or
  (d) a member of the Northern Ireland Assembly immediately before that Assembly is dissolved,
is to be treated as if the person were such a member until the end of the fourth day after the day on which the subsequent general election in relation to that Parliament or Assembly is held.

(5) For the purposes of sub-paragraph (3), a person who is an elected member of the Common Council of the City of London and whose term of office comes to an end at the end of the day preceding the annual Wardmotes is to be treated as if he or she were such a member until the end of the fourth day after the day on which those Wardmotes are held.

Disclosure to elected representatives

24. (1) This condition is met if—
  (a) the processing consists of the disclosure of personal data—
     (i) to an elected representative or a person acting with the authority of such a representative, and
     (ii) in response to a communication to the controller from that representative or person which was made in response to a request from an individual,
  (b) the personal data is relevant to the subject matter of that communication, and
  (c) the disclosure is necessary for the purpose of responding to that communication,
subject to sub-paragraph (2).

(2) Where the request to the elected representative came from an individual other than the data subject, the condition in sub-paragraph (1) is met only if the disclosure must be made without the consent of the data subject for one of the following reasons—
  (a) in the circumstances, consent to the processing cannot be given by the data subject;
  (b) in the circumstances, the elected representative cannot reasonably be expected to obtain the consent of the data subject to the processing;
  (c) obtaining the consent of the data subject would prejudice the action taken by the elected representative;
  (d) the processing is necessary in the interests of another individual and the data subject has withheld consent unreasonably.

(3) In this paragraph, "elected representative" has the same meaning as in paragraph 23.

Informing elected representatives about prisoners

25. (1) This condition is met if—
  (a) the processing consists of the processing of personal data about a prisoner for the purpose of informing a member of the House of Commons, a member of the National Assembly for Wales or a member of the Scottish Parliament about the prisoner, and
  (b) the member is under an obligation not to further disclose the personal data.

(2) The references in sub-paragraph (1) to personal data about, and to informing someone about, a prisoner include personal data about, and informing someone about, arrangements for the prisoner's release.

(3) In this paragraph—
  "prison" includes a young offender institution, a remand centre, a secure training centre or a secure college;
  "prisoner" means a person detained in a prison.

Publication of legal judgments

26. This condition is met if the processing—
  (a) consists of the publication of a judgment or other decision of a court or tribunal, or
  (b) is necessary for the purposes of publishing such a judgment or decision.

Anti-doping in sport

27. (1) This condition is met if the processing is necessary—

(a) for the purposes of measures designed to eliminate doping which are undertaken by or under the responsibility of a body or association that is responsible for eliminating doping in a sport, at a sporting event or in sport generally, or

(b) for the purposes of providing information about doping, or suspected doping, to such a body or association.

(2) The reference in sub-paragraph (1)(a) to measures designed to eliminate doping includes measures designed to identify or prevent doping.

(3) If the processing consists of the disclosure of personal data to a body or association described in sub-paragraph (1)(a), or is carried out in preparation for such disclosure, the condition in sub-paragraph (1) is met even if, when the processing is carried out, the controller does not have an appropriate policy document in place (see paragraph 5 of this Schedule).

Standards of behaviour in sport

28. (1) This condition is met if the processing—
(a) is necessary for the purposes of measures designed to protect the integrity of a sport or a sporting event,
(b) must be carried out without the consent of the data subject so as not to prejudice those purposes, and
(c) is necessary for reasons of substantial public interest.

(2) In sub-paragraph (1)(a), the reference to measures designed to protect the integrity of a sport or a sporting event is a reference to measures designed to protect a sport or a sporting event against—
(a) dishonesty, malpractice or other seriously improper conduct, or
(b) failure by a person participating in the sport or event in any capacity to comply with standards of behaviour set by a body or association with responsibility for the sport or event.

NOTES

Commencement: 25 May 2018 (see also the introductory notes to this Act preceding s 1 at **[1.71]**).

Para 23: sub-para (3)(e) was repealed by the European Parliamentary Elections Etc. (Repeal, Revocation, Amendment and Saving Provisions) (United Kingdom and Gibraltar) (EU Exit) Regulations 2018, SI 2018/1310, reg 4, Sch 1, Pt 1.

Para 23: National Assembly for Wales: as to the renaming of the National Assembly for Wales, see the note at **[1.94]**.

PART 3 ADDITIONAL CONDITIONS RELATING TO CRIMINAL CONVICTIONS ETC

Consent

[1.289]
29. This condition is met if the data subject has given consent to the processing.

Protecting individual's vital interests

30. This condition is met if—
(a) the processing is necessary to protect the vital interests of an individual, and
(b) the data subject is physically or legally incapable of giving consent.

Processing by not-for-profit bodies

31. This condition is met if the processing is carried out—
(a) in the course of its legitimate activities with appropriate safeguards by a foundation, association or other not-for-profit body with a political, philosophical, religious or trade union aim, and
(b) on condition that—
    (i) the processing relates solely to the members or to former members of the body or to persons who have regular contact with it in connection with its purposes, and
    (ii) the personal data is not disclosed outside that body without the consent of the data subjects.

Personal data in the public domain

32. This condition is met if the processing relates to personal data which is manifestly made public by the data subject.

Legal claims

33. This condition is met if the processing—
(a) is necessary for the purpose of, or in connection with, any legal proceedings (including prospective legal proceedings),
(b) is necessary for the purpose of obtaining legal advice, or
(c) is otherwise necessary for the purposes of establishing, exercising or defending legal rights.

Judicial acts

34. This condition is met if the processing is necessary when a court or tribunal is acting in its judicial capacity.

Administration of accounts used in commission of indecency offences involving children

35. (1) This condition is met if—
(a) the processing is of personal data about a conviction or caution for an offence listed in sub-paragraph (2),
(b) the processing is necessary for the purpose of administering an account relating to the payment card used in the commission of the offence or cancelling that payment card, and
(c) when the processing is carried out, the controller has an appropriate policy document in place (see paragraph 39 in Part 4 of this Schedule).

(2) Those offences are an offence under—
(a) section 1 of the Protection of Children Act 1978 (indecent photographs of children),
(b) Article 3 of the Protection of Children (Northern Ireland) Order 1978 (SI 1978/1047 (NI 17)) (indecent photographs of children),
(c) section 52 of the Civic Government (Scotland) Act 1982 (indecent photographs etc of children),

(d) section 160 of the Criminal Justice Act 1988 (possession of indecent photograph of child),
(e) Article 15 of the Criminal Justice (Evidence etc) (Northern Ireland) Order 1988 (SI 1988/1847 (NI 17)) (possession of indecent photograph of child), or
(f) section 62 of the Coroners and Justice Act 2009 (possession of prohibited images of children),
or incitement to commit an offence under any of those provisions.

(3) See also the additional safeguards in Part 4 of this Schedule.

(4) In this paragraph—
"caution" means a caution given to a person in England and Wales or Northern Ireland in respect of an offence which, at the time when the caution is given, is admitted;
"conviction" has the same meaning as in the Rehabilitation of Offenders Act 1974 or the Rehabilitation of Offenders (Northern Ireland) Order 1978 (SI 1978/1908 (NI 27));
"payment card" includes a credit card, a charge card and a debit card.

Extension of conditions in Part 2 of this Schedule referring to substantial public interest

36. This condition is met if the processing would meet a condition in Part 2 of this Schedule but for an express requirement for the processing to be necessary for reasons of substantial public interest.

Extension of insurance conditions

37. This condition is met if the processing—
(a) would meet the condition in paragraph 20 in Part 2 of this Schedule (the "insurance condition"), or
(b) would meet the condition in paragraph 36 by virtue of the insurance condition,
but for the requirement for the processing to be processing of a category of personal data specified in paragraph 20(1)(b).

NOTES

Commencement: 25 May 2018 (see also the introductory notes to this Act preceding s 1 at **[1.71]**).

PART 4 APPROPRIATE POLICY DOCUMENT AND ADDITIONAL SAFEGUARDS

Application of this Part of this Schedule

[1.290]
38. This Part of this Schedule makes provision about the processing of personal data carried out in reliance on a condition in Part 1, 2 or 3 of this Schedule which requires the controller to have an appropriate policy document in place when the processing is carried out.

Requirement to have an appropriate policy document in place

39. The controller has an appropriate policy document in place in relation to the processing of personal data in reliance on a condition described in paragraph 38 if the controller has produced a document which—
(a) explains the controller's procedures for securing compliance with the principles in Article 5 of the [UK GDPR] (principles relating to processing of personal data) in connection with the processing of personal data in reliance on the condition in question, and
(b) explains the controller's policies as regards the retention and erasure of personal data processed in reliance on the condition, giving an indication of how long such personal data is likely to be retained.

Additional safeguard: retention of appropriate policy document

40. (1) Where personal data is processed in reliance on a condition described in paragraph 38, the controller must during the relevant period—
(a) retain the appropriate policy document,
(b) review and (if appropriate) update it from time to time, and
(c) make it available to the Commissioner, on request, without charge.

(2) "Relevant period", in relation to the processing of personal data in reliance on a condition described in paragraph 38, means a period which—
(a) begins when the controller starts to carry out processing of personal data in reliance on that condition, and
(b) ends at the end of the period of 6 months beginning when the controller ceases to carry out such processing.

Additional safeguard: record of processing

41. A record maintained by the controller, or the controller's representative, under Article 30 of the [UK GDPR] in respect of the processing of personal data in reliance on a condition described in paragraph 38 must include the following information—
(a) which condition is relied on,
(b) how the processing satisfies Article 6 of the [UK GDPR] (lawfulness of processing), and
(c) whether the personal data is retained and erased in accordance with the policies described in paragraph 39(b) and, if it is not, the reasons for not following those policies.

NOTES

Commencement: 25 May 2018 (see also the introductory notes to this Act preceding s 1 at **[1.71]**).

The words in square brackets in paras 39, 41 were substituted by the Data Protection, Privacy and Electronic Communications (Amendments etc) (EU Exit) Regulations 2019, SI 2019/419, reg 4, Sch 2, paras 1, 91(1), (4), (5).

SCHEDULE 2
EXEMPTIONS ETC FROM THE [UK GDPR]

Section 15

NOTES

The words in square brackets in the Schedule heading were substituted by the Data Protection, Privacy and Electronic Communications (Amendments etc) (EU Exit) Regulations 2019, SI 2019/419, reg 4, Sch 2, paras 1, 92(1), (2).

PART 1 ADAPTATIONS AND RESTRICTIONS [AS DESCRIBED IN] ARTICLES 6(3) AND 23(1)

[UK GDPR] provisions to be adapted or restricted: "the listed GDPR provisions"

[1.291]

1. In this Part of this Schedule, "the listed GDPR provisions" means—
  (a) the following provisions of the [UK GDPR] (the rights and obligations in which may be restricted by virtue of Article 23(1) of the [UK GDPR])—
    (i) Article 13(1) to (3) (personal data collected from data subject: information to be provided);
    (ii) Article 14(1) to (4) (personal data collected other than from data subject: information to be provided);
    (iii) Article 15(1) to (3) (confirmation of processing, access to data and safeguards for third country transfers);
    (iv) Article 16 (right to rectification);
    (v) Article 17(1) and (2) (right to erasure);
    (vi) Article 18(1) (restriction of processing);
    (vii) Article 19 (notification obligation regarding rectification or erasure of personal data or restriction of processing);
    (viii) Article 20(1) and (2) (right to data portability);
    (ix) Article 21(1) (objections to processing);
    (x) Article 5 (general principles) so far as its provisions correspond to the rights and obligations provided for in the provisions mentioned in sub-paragraphs (i) to (ix); and
  (b) the following provisions of the [UK GDPR] (the application of which may be adapted by virtue of Article 6(3) of the [UK GDPR])—
    (i) Article 5(1)(a) (lawful, fair and transparent processing), other than the lawfulness requirements set out in Article 6;
    (ii) Article 5(1)(b) (purpose limitation).

Crime and taxation: general

2. (1) The listed GDPR provisions and Article 34(1) and (4) of the [UK GDPR] (communication of personal data breach to the data subject) do not apply to personal data processed for any of the following purposes—
  (a) the prevention or detection of crime,
  (b) the apprehension or prosecution of offenders, or
  (c) the assessment or collection of a tax or duty or an imposition of a similar nature,
to the extent that the application of those provisions would be likely to prejudice any of the matters mentioned in paragraphs (a) to (c).

(2) Sub-paragraph (3) applies where—
  (a) personal data is processed by a person ("Controller 1") for any of the purposes mentioned in sub-paragraph (1)(a) to (c), and
  (b) another person ("Controller 2") obtains the data from Controller 1 for the purpose of discharging statutory functions and processes it for the purpose of discharging statutory functions.

(3) Controller 2 is exempt from the obligations in the following provisions of the [UK GDPR]—
  (a) Article 13(1) to (3) (personal data collected from data subject: information to be provided),
  (b) Article 14(1) to (4) (personal data collected other than from data subject: information to be provided),
  (c) Article 15(1) to (3) (confirmation of processing, access to data and safeguards for third country transfers), and
  (d) Article 5 (general principles) so far as its provisions correspond to the rights and obligations provided for in the provisions mentioned in paragraphs (a) to (c),
to the same extent that Controller 1 is exempt from those obligations by virtue of sub-paragraph (1).

Crime and taxation: risk assessment systems

3. (1) The [UK GDPR] provisions listed in sub-paragraph (3) do not apply to personal data which consists of a classification applied to the data subject as part of a risk assessment system falling within sub-paragraph (2) to the extent that the application of those provisions would prevent the system from operating effectively.

(2) A risk assessment system falls within this sub-paragraph if—
  (a) it is operated by a government department, a local authority or another authority administering housing benefit, and
  (b) it is operated for the purposes of—
    (i) the assessment or collection of a tax or duty or an imposition of a similar nature, or
    (ii) the prevention or detection of crime or apprehension or prosecution of offenders, where the offence concerned involves the unlawful use of public money or an unlawful claim for payment out of public money.

(3) The [UK GDPR] provisions referred to in sub-paragraph (1) are the following provisions of the [UK GDPR] (the rights and obligations in which may be restricted by virtue of Article 23(1) of the [UK GDPR])—
  (a) Article 13(1) to (3) (personal data collected from data subject: information to be provided);
  (b) Article 14(1) to (4) (personal data collected other than from data subject: information to be provided);
  (c) Article 15(1) to (3) (confirmation of processing, access to data and safeguards for third country transfers);

(d)   Article 5 (general principles) so far as its provisions correspond to the rights and obligations provided for in the provisions mentioned in paragraphs (a) to (c).

Immigration

4. (1) The [UK GDPR] provisions listed in sub-paragraph (2) do not apply to personal data processed for any of the following purposes—
   (a)   the maintenance of effective immigration control, or
   (b)   the investigation or detection of activities that would undermine the maintenance of effective immigration control,
to the extent that the application of those provisions would be likely to prejudice any of the matters mentioned in paragraphs (a) and (b).

(2) The [UK GDPR] provisions referred to in sub-paragraph (1) are the following provisions of the [UK GDPR] (the rights and obligations in which may be restricted by virtue of Article 23(1) of the [UK GDPR])—
   (a)   Article 13(1) to (3) (personal data collected from data subject: information to be provided);
   (b)   Article 14(1) to (4) (personal data collected other than from data subject: information to be provided);
   (c)   Article 15(1) to (3) (confirmation of processing, access to data and safeguards for third country transfers);
   (d)   Article 17(1) and (2) (right to erasure);
   (e)   Article 18(1) (restriction of processing);
   (f)   Article 21(1) (objections to processing);
   (g)   Article 5 (general principles) so far as its provisions correspond to the rights and obligations provided for in the provisions mentioned in sub-paragraphs (a) to (f).
(That is, the listed GDPR provisions other than Article 16 (right to rectification), Article 19 (notification obligation regarding rectification or erasure of personal data or restriction of processing) and Article 20(1) and (2) (right to data portability) and, subject to sub-paragraph (2)(g) of this paragraph, the provisions of Article 5 listed in paragraph 1(b).)

(3) Sub-paragraph (4) applies where—
   (a)   personal data is processed by a person ("Controller 1"), and
   (b)   another person ("Controller 2") obtains the data from Controller 1 for any of the purposes mentioned in sub-paragraph (1)(a) and (b) and processes it for any of those purposes.

(4) Controller 1 is exempt from the obligations in the following provisions of the [UK GDPR]—
   (a)   Article 13(1) to (3) (personal data collected from data subject: information to be provided),
   (b)   Article 14(1) to (4) (personal data collected other than from data subject: information to be provided),
   (c)   Article 15(1) to (3) (confirmation of processing, access to data and safeguards for third country transfers), and
   (d)   Article 5 (general principles) so far as its provisions correspond to the rights and obligations provided for in the provisions mentioned in paragraphs (a) to (c),
to the same extent that Controller 2 is exempt from those obligations by virtue of sub-paragraph (1).

Information required to be disclosed by law etc or in connection with legal proceedings

5. (1) The listed GDPR provisions do not apply to personal data consisting of information that the controller is obliged by an enactment to make available to the public, to the extent that the application of those provisions would prevent the controller from complying with that obligation.

(2) The listed GDPR provisions do not apply to personal data where disclosure of the data is required by an enactment, a rule of law or an order of a court or tribunal, to the extent that the application of those provisions would prevent the controller from making the disclosure.

(3) The listed GDPR provisions do not apply to personal data where disclosure of the data—
   (a)   is necessary for the purpose of, or in connection with, legal proceedings (including prospective legal proceedings),
   (b)   is necessary for the purpose of obtaining legal advice, or
   (c)   is otherwise necessary for the purposes of establishing, exercising or defending legal rights,
to the extent that the application of those provisions would prevent the controller from making the disclosure.

NOTES

Commencement: 25 May 2018 (see also the introductory notes to this Act preceding s 1 at **[1.71]**).

The words in square brackets in each place were substituted by the Data Protection, Privacy and Electronic Communications (Amendments etc) (EU Exit) Regulations 2019, SI 2019/419, reg 4, Sch 2, paras 1, 92(1), (3)–(8).

PART 2 RESTRICTIONS [AS DESCRIBED IN] ARTICLE 23(1): RESTRICTIONS OF RULES IN ARTICLES 13 TO 21 AND 34

[UK GDPR] provisions to be restricted: "the listed GDPR provisions"

[1.292]
6. In this Part of this Schedule, "the listed GDPR provisions" means the following provisions of the [UK GDPR] (the rights and obligations in which may be restricted by virtue of Article 23(1) of the [UK GDPR])—
   (a)   Article 13(1) to (3) (personal data collected from data subject: information to be provided);
   (b)   Article 14(1) to (4) (personal data collected other than from data subject: information to be provided);
   (c)   Article 15(1) to (3) (confirmation of processing, access to data and safeguards for third country transfers);
   (d)   Article 16 (right to rectification);
   (e)   Article 17(1) and (2) (right to erasure);
   (f)   Article 18(1) (restriction of processing);
   (g)   Article 19 (notification obligation regarding rectification or erasure of personal data or restriction of processing);
   (h)   Article 20(1) and (2) (right to data portability);
   (i)   Article 21(1) (objections to processing);

(j)   Article 5 (general principles) so far as its provisions correspond to the rights and obligations provided for in the provisions mentioned in sub-paragraphs (a) to (i).

Functions designed to protect the public etc

7. The listed GDPR provisions do not apply to personal data processed for the purposes of discharging a function that—

(a)   is designed as described in column 1 of the Table, and

(b)   meets the condition relating to the function specified in column 2 of the Table,

to the extent that the application of those provisions would be likely to prejudice the proper discharge of the function.

Table

Description of function design	Condition
1 The function is designed to protect members of the public against— (a) financial loss due to dishonesty, malpractice or other seriously improper conduct by, or the unfitness or incompetence of, persons concerned in the provision of banking, insurance, investment or other financial services or in the management of bodies corporate, or (b) financial loss due to the conduct of discharged or undischarged bankrupts.	The function is— (a) conferred on a person by an enactment, (b) a function of the Crown, a Minister of the Crown or a government department, or (c) of a public nature, and is exercised in the public interest.
2 The function is designed to protect members of the public against— (a) dishonesty, malpractice or other seriously improper conduct, or (b) unfitness or incompetence.	The function is— (a) conferred on a person by an enactment, (b) a function of the Crown, a Minister of the Crown or a government department, or (c) of a public nature, and is exercised in the public interest.
3 The function is designed— (a) to protect charities or community interest companies against misconduct or mismanagement (whether by trustees, directors or other persons) in their administration, (b) to protect the property of charities or community interest companies from loss or misapplication, or (c) to recover the property of charities or community interest companies.	The function is— (a) conferred on a person by an enactment, (b) a function of the Crown, a Minister of the Crown or a government department, or (c) of a public nature, and is exercised in the public interest.
4 The function is designed— (a) to secure the health, safety and welfare of persons at work, or (b) to protect persons other than those at work against risk to health or safety arising out of or in connection with the action of persons at work.	The function is— (a) conferred on a person by an enactment, (b) a function of the Crown, a Minister of the Crown or a government department, or (c) of a public nature, and is exercised in the public interest.
5 The function is designed to protect members of the public against— (a) maladministration by public bodies, (b) failures in services provided by public bodies, or (c) a failure of a public body to provide a service which it is a function of the body to provide.	The function is conferred by any enactment on— (a) the Parliamentary Commissioner for Administration, (b) the Commissioner for Local Administration in England, (c) the Health Service Commissioner for England, (d) the Public Services Ombudsman for Wales, (e) the Northern Ireland Public Services Ombudsman, (f) the Prison Ombudsman for Northern Ireland, or (g) the Scottish Public Services Ombudsman.
6 The function is designed— (a) to protect members of the public against conduct which may adversely affect their interests by persons carrying on a business, (b) to regulate agreements or conduct which have as their object or effect the prevention, restriction or distortion of competition in connection with any commercial activity, or (c) to regulate conduct on the part of one or more undertakings which amounts to the abuse of a dominant position in a market.	The function is conferred on the Competition and Markets Authority by an enactment.

Audit functions

8. (1) The listed GDPR provisions do not apply to personal data processed for the purposes of discharging a function listed in sub-paragraph (2) to the extent that the application of those provisions would be likely to prejudice the proper discharge of the function.

(2) The functions are any function that is conferred by an enactment on—

    (a)   the Comptroller and Auditor General;

    (b)   the Auditor General for Scotland;

    (c)   the Auditor General for Wales;

    (d)   the Comptroller and Auditor General for Northern Ireland.

Functions of the Bank of England

9. (1) The listed GDPR provisions do not apply to personal data processed for the purposes of discharging a relevant function of the Bank of England to the extent that the application of those provisions would be likely to prejudice the proper discharge of the function.

(2) "Relevant function of the Bank of England" means—

    (a)   a function discharged by the Bank acting in its capacity as a monetary authority (as defined in section 244(2)(c) and (2A) of the Banking Act 2009);

    (b)   a public function of the Bank within the meaning of section 349 of the Financial Services and Markets Act 2000;

    (c)   a function conferred on the Prudential Regulation Authority by or under the Financial Services and Markets Act 2000 or by another enactment.

Regulatory functions relating to legal services, the health service and children's services

10. (1) The listed GDPR provisions do not apply to personal data processed for the purposes of discharging a function listed in sub-paragraph (2) to the extent that the application of those provisions would be likely to prejudice the proper discharge of the function.

(2) The functions are—

    (a)   a function of the Legal Services Board;

    (b)   the function of considering a complaint under the scheme established under Part 6 of the Legal Services Act 2007 (legal complaints);

    (c)   the function of considering a complaint under—

        (i)   section 14 of the NHS Redress Act 2006,

        (ii)   section 113(1) or (2) or section 114(1) or (3) of the Health and Social Care (Community Health and Standards) Act 2003,

        (iii)   section 24D or 26 of the Children Act 1989, or

        (iv)   Part 2A of the Public Services Ombudsman (Wales) Act 2005 [or Part 3 of the Public Services Ombudsman (Wales) Act 2019];

    (d)   the function of considering a complaint or representations under Chapter 1 of Part 10 of the Social Services and Well-being (Wales) Act 2014 (anaw 4).

Regulatory functions of certain other persons

11. The listed GDPR provisions do not apply to personal data processed for the purposes of discharging a function that—

    (a)   is a function of a person described in column 1 of the Table, and

    (b)   is conferred on that person as described in column 2 of the Table,

to the extent that the application of those provisions would be likely to prejudice the proper discharge of the function.

Table

Person on whom function is conferred	**How function is conferred**
1 The Commissioner.	By or under— (a) the data protection legislation; (b) the Freedom of Information Act 2000; (c) section 244 of the Investigatory Powers Act 2016; (d) the Privacy and Electronic Communications (EC Directive) Regulations 2003 (SI 2003/2426); (e) the Environmental Information Regulations 2004 (SI 2004/3391); (f) the INSPIRE Regulations 2009 (SI 2009/3157); (g) Regulation (EU) No 910/2014 of the European Parliament and of the Council of 23 July 2014 on electronic identification and trust services for electronic transactions in the internal market and repealing Directive 1999/93/EC; (h) the Re-use of Public Sector Information Regulations 2015 (SI 2015/1415); (i) the Electronic Identification and Trust Services for Electronic Transactions Regulations 2016 (SI 2016/696).
2 The Scottish Information Commissioner.	By or under— (a) the Freedom of Information (Scotland) Act 2002 (asp 13); (b) the Environmental Information (Scotland) Regulations 2004 (SSI 2004/520); (c) the INSPIRE (Scotland) Regulations 2009 (SSI 2009/440).
3 The Pensions Ombudsman.	By or under Part 10 of the Pension Schemes Act 1993 or any corresponding legislation having equivalent effect in Northern Ireland.
4 The Board of the Pension Protection Fund.	By or under sections 206 to 208 of the Pensions Act 2004 or any corresponding legislation having equivalent effect in Northern Ireland.

Person on whom function is conferred	How function is conferred
5 The Ombudsman for the Board of the Pension Protection Fund.	By or under any of sections 209 to 218 or 286(1) of the Pensions Act 2004 or any corresponding legislation having equivalent effect in Northern Ireland.
6 The Pensions Regulator.	By an enactment.
7 The Financial Conduct Authority.	By or under the Financial Services and Markets Act 2000 or by another enactment.
8 The Financial Ombudsman.	By or under Part 16 of the Financial Services and Markets Act 2000.
9 The investigator of complaints against the financial regulators.	By or under Part 6 of the Financial Services Act 2012.
. . .	. . .
11 The monitoring officer of a relevant authority.	By or under the Local Government and Housing Act 1989.
12 The monitoring officer of a relevant Welsh authority.	By or under the Local Government Act 2000.
13 The Public Services Ombudsman for Wales.	By or under the Local Government Act 2000.
14 The Charity Commission.	By or under— (a) the Charities Act 1992; (b) the Charities Act 2006; (c) the Charities Act 2011.

12. In the Table in paragraph 11—

 . . .

  . . .

the "Financial Ombudsman" means the scheme operator within the meaning of Part 16 of the Financial Services and Markets Act 2000 (see section 225 of that Act);

the "investigator of complaints against the financial regulators" means the person appointed under section 84(1)(b) of the Financial Services Act 2012;

"relevant authority" has the same meaning as in section 5 of the Local Government and Housing Act 1989, and "monitoring officer", in relation to such an authority, means a person designated as such under that section;

"relevant Welsh authority" has the same meaning as "relevant authority" in section 49(6) of the Local Government Act 2000, and "monitoring officer", in relation to such an authority, has the same meaning as in Part 3 of that Act.

Parliamentary privilege

13. The listed GDPR provisions and Article 34(1) and (4) of the [UK GDPR] (communication of personal data breach to the data subject) do not apply to personal data where this is required for the purpose of avoiding an infringement of the privileges of either House of Parliament.

Judicial appointments, judicial independence and judicial proceedings

14. (1) The listed GDPR provisions do not apply to personal data processed for the purposes of assessing a person's suitability for judicial office or the office of Queen's Counsel.

(2) The listed GDPR provisions do not apply to personal data processed by—

 (a) an individual acting in a judicial capacity, or

 (b) a court or tribunal acting in its judicial capacity.

(3) As regards personal data not falling within sub-paragraph (1) or (2), the listed GDPR provisions do not apply to the extent that the application of those provisions would be likely to prejudice judicial independence or judicial proceedings.

Crown honours, dignities and appointments

15. (1) The listed GDPR provisions do not apply to personal data processed for the purposes of the conferring by the Crown of any honour or dignity.

(2) The listed GDPR provisions do not apply to personal data processed for the purposes of assessing a person's suitability for any of the following offices—

 (a) archbishops and diocesan and suffragan bishops in the Church of England;

 (b) deans of cathedrals of the Church of England;

 (c) deans and canons of the two Royal Peculiars;

 (d) the First and Second Church Estates Commissioners;

 (e) lord-lieutenants;

 (f) Masters of Trinity College and Churchill College, Cambridge;

 (g) the Provost of Eton;

 (h) the Poet Laureate;

 (i) the Astronomer Royal.

(3) The Secretary of State may by regulations amend the list in sub-paragraph (2) to—

 (a) remove an office, or

 (b) add an office to which appointments are made by Her Majesty.

(4) Regulations under sub-paragraph (3) are subject to the affirmative resolution procedure.

NOTES

Commencement: 25 May 2018 (see also the introductory notes to this Act preceding s 1 at **[1.71]**).

The words in square brackets in the Part heading, para 6 (and preceding heading) and para 13, were substituted by the Data Protection, Privacy and Electronic Communications (Amendments etc) (EU Exit) Regulations 2019, SI 2019/419, reg 4, Sch 2, paras 1, 92(1), (9)–(12).

The words in square brackets in para 10(2)(c)(iv) were inserted by the Public Services Ombudsman (Wales) Act 2019, s 75(3), Sch 5, Pt 2, para 28.

The words omitted from the table in para 11 were repealed, and the definitions "consumer protection officer" and "CPC Regulation" (omitted) in para 12 were repealed by the Consumer Protection (Enforcement) (Amendment etc.) (EU Exit) Regulations 2019, SI 2019/203, reg 5.

PART 3 RESTRICTION [FOR THE] PROTECTION OF RIGHTS OF OTHERS

Protection of the rights of others: general

[1.293]

16. (1) Article 15(1) to (3) of the [UK GDPR] (confirmation of processing, access to data and safeguards for third country transfers), and Article 5 of the [UK GDPR] so far as its provisions correspond to the rights and obligations provided for in Article 15(1) to (3), do not oblige a controller to disclose information to the data subject to the extent that doing so would involve disclosing information relating to another individual who can be identified from the information.

(2) Sub-paragraph (1) does not remove the controller's obligation where—
   (a) the other individual has consented to the disclosure of the information to the data subject, or
   (b) it is reasonable to disclose the information to the data subject without the consent of the other individual.

(3) In determining whether it is reasonable to disclose the information without consent, the controller must have regard to all the relevant circumstances, including—
   (a) the type of information that would be disclosed,
   (b) any duty of confidentiality owed to the other individual,
   (c) any steps taken by the controller with a view to seeking the consent of the other individual,
   (d) whether the other individual is capable of giving consent, and
   (e) any express refusal of consent by the other individual.

(4) For the purposes of this paragraph—
   (a) "information relating to another individual" includes information identifying the other individual as the source of information;
   (b) an individual can be identified from information to be provided to a data subject by a controller if the individual can be identified from—
      (i) that information, or
      (ii) that information and any other information that the controller reasonably believes the data subject is likely to possess or obtain.

Assumption of reasonableness for health workers, social workers and education workers

17. (1) For the purposes of paragraph 16(2)(b), it is to be considered reasonable for a controller to disclose information to a data subject without the consent of the other individual where—
   (a) the health data test is met,
   (b) the social work data test is met, or
   (c) the education data test is met.

(2) The health data test is met if—
   (a) the information in question is contained in a health record, and
   (b) the other individual is a health professional who has compiled or contributed to the health record or who, in his or her capacity as a health professional, has been involved in the diagnosis, care or treatment of the data subject.

(3) The social work data test is met if—
   (a) the other individual is—
      (i) a children's court officer,
      (ii) a person who is or has been employed by a person or body referred to in paragraph 8 of Schedule 3 in connection with functions exercised in relation to the information, or
      (iii) a person who has provided for reward a service that is similar to a service provided in the exercise of any relevant social services functions, and
   (b) the information relates to the other individual in an official capacity or the other individual supplied the information—
      (i) in an official capacity, or
      (ii) in a case within paragraph (a)(iii), in connection with providing the service mentioned in paragraph (a)(iii).

(4) The education data test is met if—
   (a) the other individual is an education-related worker, or
   (b) the other individual is employed by an education authority (within the meaning of the Education (Scotland) Act 1980) in pursuance of its functions relating to education and—
      (i) the information relates to the other individual in his or her capacity as such an employee, or
      (ii) the other individual supplied the information in his or her capacity as such an employee.

(5) In this paragraph—
   "children's court officer" means a person referred to in paragraph 8(1)(q), (r), (s), (t) or (u) of Schedule 3;

"education-related worker" means a person referred to in paragraph 14(4)(a) or (b) or 16(4)(a), (b) or (c) of Schedule 3 (educational records);

"relevant social services functions" means functions specified in paragraph 8(1)(a), (b), (c) or (d) of Schedule 3.

NOTES

Commencement: 25 May 2018 (see also the introductory notes to this Act preceding s 1 at **[1.71]**).

The words in square brackets in the Part heading and in para 16 were substituted by the Data Protection, Privacy and Electronic Communications (Amendments etc) (EU Exit) Regulations 2019, SI 2019/419, reg 4, Sch 2, paras 1, 92(1), (13), (14).

PART 4 RESTRICTIONS [AS DESCRIBED IN] ARTICLE 23(1): RESTRICTIONS OF RULES IN ARTICLES 13 TO 15

[UK GDPR] provisions to be restricted: "the listed GDPR provisions"

[1.294]

18. In this Part of this Schedule, "the listed GDPR provisions" means the following provisions of the [UK GDPR] (the rights and obligations in which may be restricted by virtue of Article 23(1) of the [UK GDPR])—

   (a)   Article 13(1) to (3) (personal data collected from data subject: information to be provided);

   (b)   Article 14(1) to (4) (personal data collected other than from data subject: information to be provided);

   (c)   Article 15(1) to (3) (confirmation of processing, access to data and safeguards for third country transfers);

   (d)   Article 5 (general principles) so far as its provisions correspond to the rights and obligations provided for in the provisions mentioned in sub-paragraphs (a) to (c).

Legal professional privilege

19. The listed GDPR provisions do not apply to personal data that consists of—

   (a)   information in respect of which a claim to legal professional privilege or, in Scotland, confidentiality of communications, could be maintained in legal proceedings, or

   (b)   information in respect of which a duty of confidentiality is owed by a professional legal adviser to a client of the adviser.

Self incrimination

20. (1) A person need not comply with the listed GDPR provisions to the extent that compliance would, by revealing evidence of the commission of an offence, expose the person to proceedings for that offence.

(2) The reference to an offence in sub-paragraph (1) does not include an offence under—

   (a)   this Act,

   (b)   section 5 of the Perjury Act 1911 (false statements made otherwise than on oath),

   (c)   section 44(2) of the Criminal Law (Consolidation) (Scotland) Act 1995 (false statements made otherwise than on oath), or

   (d)   Article 10 of the Perjury (Northern Ireland) Order 1979 (SI 1979/1714 (NI 19)) (false statutory declarations and other false unsworn statements).

(3) Information disclosed by any person in compliance with Article 15 of the [UK GDPR] is not admissible against the person in proceedings for an offence under this Act.

Corporate finance

21. (1) The listed GDPR provisions do not apply to personal data processed for the purposes of or in connection with a corporate finance service provided by a relevant person to the extent that either Condition A or Condition B is met.

(2) Condition A is that the application of the listed GDPR provisions would be likely to affect the price of an instrument.

(3) Condition B is that—

   (a)   the relevant person reasonably believes that the application of the listed GDPR provisions to the personal data in question could affect a decision of a person—

      (i)   whether to deal in, subscribe for or issue an instrument, or

      (ii)   whether to act in a way likely to have an effect on a business activity (such as an effect on the industrial strategy of a person, the capital structure of an undertaking or the legal or beneficial ownership of a business or asset), and

   (b)   the application of the listed GDPR provisions to that personal data would have a prejudicial effect on the orderly functioning of financial markets or the efficient allocation of capital within the economy.

(4) In this paragraph—

"corporate finance service" means a service consisting in—

      (a)   underwriting in respect of issues of, or the placing of issues of, any instrument,

      (b)   services relating to such underwriting, or

      (c)   advice to undertakings on capital structure, industrial strategy and related matters and advice and service relating to mergers and the purchase of undertakings;

"instrument" means an instrument listed in section C of Annex 1 to Directive 2004/39/EC of the European Parliament and of the Council of 21 April 2004 on markets in financial instruments, and references to an instrument include an instrument not yet in existence but which is to be or may be created;

"price" includes value;

"relevant person" means—

      (a)   a person who, by reason of a permission under Part 4A of the Financial Services and Markets Act 2000, is able to carry on a corporate finance service without contravening the general prohibition;

(b)   an EEA firm of the kind mentioned in paragraph 5(a) or (b) of Schedule 3 to that Act which has qualified for authorisation under paragraph 12 of that Schedule, and may lawfully carry on a corporate finance service;

(c)   a person who is exempt from the general prohibition in respect of any corporate finance service—
    (i)   as a result of an exemption order made under section 38(1) of that Act, or
    (ii)   by reason of section 39(1) of that Act (appointed representatives);

(d)   a person, not falling within paragraph (a), (b) or (c), who may lawfully carry on a corporate finance service without contravening the general prohibition;

(e)   a person who, in the course of employment, provides to their employer a service falling within paragraph (b) or (c) of the definition of "corporate finance service";

(f)   a partner who provides to other partners in the partnership a service falling within either of those paragraphs.

(5) In the definition of "relevant person" in sub-paragraph (4), references to "the general prohibition" are to the general prohibition within the meaning of section 19 of the Financial Services and Markets Act 2000.

Management forecasts

22. The listed GDPR provisions do not apply to personal data processed for the purposes of management forecasting or management planning in relation to a business or other activity to the extent that the application of those provisions would be likely to prejudice the conduct of the business or activity concerned.

Negotiations

23. The listed GDPR provisions do not apply to personal data that consists of records of the intentions of the controller in relation to any negotiations with the data subject to the extent that the application of those provisions would be likely to prejudice those negotiations.

Confidential references

24. The listed GDPR provisions do not apply to personal data consisting of a reference given (or to be given) in confidence for the purposes of—
    (a)   the education, training or employment (or prospective education, training or employment) of the data subject,
    (b)   the placement (or prospective placement) of the data subject as a volunteer,
    (c)   the appointment (or prospective appointment) of the data subject to any office, or
    (d)   the provision (or prospective provision) by the data subject of any service.

Exam scripts and exam marks

25. (1) The listed GDPR provisions do not apply to personal data consisting of information recorded by candidates during an exam.

(2) Where personal data consists of marks or other information processed by a controller—
    (a)   for the purposes of determining the results of an exam, or
    (b)   in consequence of the determination of the results of an exam,
the duty in Article 12(3) or (4) of the [UK GDPR] for the controller to provide information requested by the data subject within a certain time period, as it applies to Article 15 of the [UK GDPR] (confirmation of processing, access to data and safeguards for third country transfers), is modified as set out in sub-paragraph (3).

(3) Where a question arises as to whether the controller is obliged by Article 15 of the [UK GDPR] to disclose personal data, and the question arises before the day on which the exam results are announced, the controller must provide the information mentioned in Article 12(3) or (4)—
    (a)   before the end of the period of 5 months beginning when the question arises, or
    (b)   if earlier, before the end of the period of 40 days beginning with the announcement of the results.

(4) In this paragraph, "exam" means an academic, professional or other examination used for determining the knowledge, intelligence, skill or ability of a candidate and may include an exam consisting of an assessment of the candidate's performance while undertaking work or any other activity.

(5) For the purposes of this paragraph, the results of an exam are treated as announced when they are first published or, if not published, first communicated to the candidate.

NOTES

Commencement: 25 May 2018 (see also the introductory notes to this Act preceding s 1 at **[1.71]**).

The words in square brackets in the Part heading and in paras 18, 20, 25, were substituted by the Data Protection, Privacy and Electronic Communications (Amendments etc) (EU Exit) Regulations 2019, SI 2019/419, reg 4, Sch 2, paras 1, 92(1), (15)–(19).

PART 5 EXEMPTIONS ETC . . . FOR REASONS OF FREEDOM OF EXPRESSION AND INFORMATION

Journalistic, academic, artistic and literary purposes

[1.295]

26. (1) In this paragraph, "the special purposes" means one or more of the following—
    (a)   the purposes of journalism;
    (b)   academic purposes;
    (c)   artistic purposes;
    (d)   literary purposes.

(2) Sub-paragraph (3) applies to the processing of personal data carried out for the special purposes if—
    (a)   the processing is being carried out with a view to the publication by a person of journalistic, academic, artistic or literary material, and
    (b)   the controller reasonably believes that the publication of the material would be in the public interest.

(3) The listed GDPR provisions do not apply to the extent that the controller reasonably believes that the application of those provisions would be incompatible with the special purposes.

(4) In determining whether publication would be in the public interest the controller must take into account the special importance of the public interest in the freedom of expression and information.

(5) In determining whether it is reasonable to believe that publication would be in the public interest, the controller must have regard to any of the codes of practice or guidelines listed in sub-paragraph (6) that is relevant to the publication in question.

(6) The codes of practice and guidelines are—
   (a) BBC Editorial Guidelines;
   (b) Ofcom Broadcasting Code;
   (c) Editors' Code of Practice.

(7) The Secretary of State may by regulations amend the list in sub-paragraph (6).

(8) Regulations under sub-paragraph (7) are subject to the affirmative resolution procedure.

(9) For the purposes of this paragraph, the listed GDPR provisions are the following provisions of the [UK GDPR] (which may be exempted or derogated from by virtue of Article 85(2) of the [UK GDPR])—
   (a) in Chapter II of the [UK GDPR] (principles)—
       (i)   Article 5(1)(a) to (e) (principles relating to processing);
       (ii)   Article 6 (lawfulness);
       (iii) Article 7 (conditions for consent);
       (iv)   Article 8(1) and (2) (child's consent);
       (v)   Article 9 (processing of special categories of data);
       (vi)   Article 10 (data relating to criminal convictions etc);
       (vii) Article 11(2) (processing not requiring identification);
   (b) in Chapter III of the [UK GDPR] (rights of the data subject)—
       (i)   Article 13(1) to (3) (personal data collected from data subject: information to be provided);
       (ii)   Article 14(1) to (4) (personal data collected other than from data subject: information to be provided);
       (iii) Article 15(1) to (3) (confirmation of processing, access to data and safeguards for third country transfers);
       (iv)   Article 16 (right to rectification);
       (v)   Article 17(1) and (2) (right to erasure);
       (vi)   Article 18(1)(a), (b) and (d) (restriction of processing);
       (vii) Article 19 (notification obligation regarding rectification or erasure of personal data or restriction of processing);
       (viii) Article 20(1) and (2) (right to data portability);
       (ix)   Article 21(1) (objections to processing);
   (c) in Chapter IV of the [UK GDPR] (controller and processor)—
       (i)   Article 34(1) and (4) (communication of personal data breach to the data subject);
       (ii)   Article 36 (requirement for controller to consult Commissioner prior to high risk processing);
   (d) in Chapter V of the [UK GDPR] (transfers of data to third countries etc), Article 44 (general principles for transfers);
   (e)   . . .

NOTES

Commencement: 25 May 2018 (see also the introductory notes to this Act preceding s 1 at **[1.71]**).

The words omitted from the Part heading were repealed, and in para 26 the words in square brackets were substituted and the words omitted were repealed, by the Data Protection, Privacy and Electronic Communications (Amendments etc) (EU Exit) Regulations 2019, SI 2019/419, reg 4, Sch 2, paras 1, 92(1), (20), (21).

PART 6 DEROGATIONS ETC . . . FOR RESEARCH, STATISTICS AND ARCHIVING

Research and statistics

[1.296]
27. (1) The listed GDPR provisions do not apply to personal data processed for—
   (a) scientific or historical research purposes, or
   (b) statistical purposes,
to the extent that the application of those provisions would prevent or seriously impair the achievement of the purposes in question.
This is subject to [sub-paragraphs (3) and (4)].

(2) For the purposes of this paragraph, the listed GDPR provisions are the following provisions of the [UK GDPR]—
   (a) Article 15(1) to (3) (confirmation of processing, access to data and safeguards for third country transfers);
   (b) Article 16 (right to rectification);
   (c) Article 18(1) (restriction of processing);
   (d) Article 21(1) (objections to processing).

(3) The exemption in sub-paragraph (1) is available only where—
   (a) the personal data is processed in accordance with Article 89(1) of the [UK GDPR] (as supplemented by section 19), and
   (b) as regards the disapplication of Article 15(1) to (3), the results of the research or any resulting statistics are not made available in a form which identifies a data subject.

[(4) Where processing for a purpose described in sub-paragraph (1) serves at the same time another purpose, the exemption in sub-paragraph (1) is available only where the personal data is processed for a purpose referred to in that sub-paragraph.]

Archiving in the public interest

28. (1) The listed GDPR provisions do not apply to personal data processed for archiving purposes in the public interest to the extent that the application of those provisions would prevent or seriously impair the achievement of those purposes.

This is subject to [sub-paragraphs (3) and (4)].

(2) For the purposes of this paragraph, the listed GDPR provisions are the following provisions of the [UK GDPR]—

    (a)   Article 15(1) to (3) (confirmation of processing, access to data and safeguards for third country transfers);

    (b)   Article 16 (right to rectification);

    (c)   Article 18(1) (restriction of processing);

    (d)   Article 19 (notification obligation regarding rectification or erasure of personal data or restriction of processing);

    (e)   Article 20(1) (right to data portability);

    (f)   Article 21(1) (objections to processing).

(3) The exemption in sub-paragraph (1) is available only where the personal data is processed in accordance with Article 89(1) of the [UK GDPR] (as supplemented by section 19).

[(4) Where processing for a purpose described in sub-paragraph (1) serves at the same time another purpose, the exemption in sub-paragraph (1) is available only where the personal data is processed for a purpose referred to in that sub-paragraph.]

NOTES

Commencement: 25 May 2018 (see also the introductory notes to this Act preceding s 1 at **[1.71]**).

The words omitted from the Part heading were repealed, paras 27(4) and 28(4) were inserted, and all other words in square brackets were substituted, by the Data Protection, Privacy and Electronic Communications (Amendments etc) (EU Exit) Regulations 2019, SI 2019/419, reg 4, Sch 2, paras 1, 92(1), (22)–(24).

SCHEDULE 3
EXEMPTIONS ETC FROM THE [UK GDPR]: HEALTH, SOCIAL WORK, EDUCATION AND CHILD ABUSE DATA

Section 15

PART 1 [UK GDPR] PROVISIONS TO BE RESTRICTED

[1.297]

1. In this Schedule "the listed GDPR provisions" means the following provisions of the [UK GDPR] (the rights and obligations in which may be restricted by virtue of Article 23(1) of the [UK GDPR])—

    (a)   Article 13(1) to (3) (personal data collected from data subject: information to be provided);

    (b)   Article 14(1) to (4) (personal data collected other than from data subject: information to be provided);

    (c)   Article 15(1) to (3) (confirmation of processing, access to data and safeguards for third country transfers);

    (d)   Article 16 (right to rectification);

    (e)   Article 17(1) and (2) (right to erasure);

    (f)   Article 18(1) (restriction of processing);

    (g)   Article 20(1) and (2) (right to data portability);

    (h)   Article 21(1) (objections to processing);

    (i)   Article 5 (general principles) so far as its provisions correspond to the rights and obligations provided for in the provisions mentioned in sub-paragraphs (a) to (h).

NOTES

Commencement: 25 May 2018 (see also the introductory notes to this Act preceding s 1 at **[1.71]**).

The words in square brackets in each place were substituted by the Data Protection, Privacy and Electronic Communications (Amendments etc) (EU Exit) Regulations 2019, SI 2019/419, reg 4, Sch 2, paras 1, 93(1)–(4).

PART 2 HEALTH DATA

Definitions

[1.298]

2. (1) In this Part of this Schedule—

"the appropriate health professional", in relation to a question as to whether the serious harm test is met with respect to data concerning health, means—

    (a)   the health professional who is currently or was most recently responsible for the diagnosis, care or treatment of the data subject in connection with the matters to which the data relates,

    (b)   where there is more than one such health professional, the health professional who is the most suitable to provide an opinion on the question, or

    (c)   a health professional who has the necessary experience and qualifications to provide an opinion on the question, where—

        (i)   there is no health professional available falling within paragraph (a) or (b), or

        (ii)   the controller is the Secretary of State and data is processed in connection with the exercise of the functions conferred on the Secretary of State by or under the Child Support Act 1991 and the Child Support Act 1995, or the Secretary of State's functions in relation to social security or war pensions, or

        (iii)   the controller is the Department for Communities in Northern Ireland and data is processed in connection with the exercise of the functions conferred on the Department by or under the Child Support (Northern Ireland) Order 1991 (SI 1991/2628 (NI 23)) and the Child Support (Northern Ireland) Order 1995 (SI 1995/2702 (NI 13));

"war pension" has the same meaning as in section 25 of the Social Security Act 1989 (establishment and functions of war pensions committees).

(2) For the purposes of this Part of this Schedule, the "serious harm test" is met with respect to data concerning health if the application of Article 15 of the [UK GDPR] to the data would be likely to cause serious harm to the physical or mental health of the data subject or another individual.

Exemption from the listed GDPR provisions: data processed by a court

3. (1) The listed GDPR provisions do not apply to data concerning health if—
  (a) it is processed by a court,
  (b) it consists of information supplied in a report or other evidence given to the court in the course of proceedings to which rules listed in subparagraph (2) apply, and
  (c) in accordance with those rules, the data may be withheld by the court in whole or in part from the data subject.

(2) Those rules are—
  (a) the Magistrates' Courts (Children and Young Persons) Rules (Northern Ireland) 1969 (SR (NI) 1969 No 221);
  (b) the Magistrates' Courts (Children and Young Persons) Rules 1992 (SI 1992/2071 (L 17));
  (c) the Family Proceedings Rules (Northern Ireland) 1996 (SR (NI) 1996 No 322);
  (d) the Magistrates' Courts (Children (Northern Ireland) Order 1995) Rules (Northern Ireland) 1996 (SR (NI) 1996 No 323);
  (e) the Act of Sederunt (Child Care and Maintenance Rules) 1997 (SI 1997/291 (S 19));
  (f) the Sheriff Court Adoption Rules 2009;
  (g) the Family Procedure Rules 2010 (SI 2010/2955 (L 17));
  (h) the Children's Hearings (Scotland) Act 2011 (Rules of Procedure in Children's Hearings) Rules 2013 (SSI 2013/194).

Exemption from the listed GDPR provisions: data subject's expectations and wishes

4. (1) This paragraph applies where a request for data concerning health is made in exercise of a power conferred by an enactment or rule of law and—
  (a) in relation to England and Wales or Northern Ireland, the data subject is an individual aged under 18 and the person making the request has parental responsibility for the data subject,
  (b) in relation to Scotland, the data subject is an individual aged under 16 and the person making the request has parental responsibilities for the data subject, or
  (c) the data subject is incapable of managing his or her own affairs and the person making the request has been appointed by a court to manage those affairs.

(2) The listed GDPR provisions do not apply to data concerning health to the extent that complying with the request would disclose information—
  (a) which was provided by the data subject in the expectation that it would not be disclosed to the person making the request,
  (b) which was obtained as a result of any examination or investigation to which the data subject consented in the expectation that the information would not be so disclosed, or
  (c) which the data subject has expressly indicated should not be so disclosed.

(3) The exemptions under sub-paragraph (2)(a) and (b) do not apply if the data subject has expressly indicated that he or she no longer has the expectation mentioned there.

Exemption from Article 15 of the [UK GDPR]: serious harm

5. (1) Article 15(1) to (3) of the [UK GDPR] (confirmation of processing, access to data and safeguards for third country transfers) do not apply to data concerning health to the extent that the serious harm test is met with respect to the data.

(2) A controller who is not a health professional may not rely on sub-paragraph (1) to withhold data concerning health unless the controller has obtained an opinion from the person who appears to the controller to be the appropriate health professional to the effect that the serious harm test is met with respect to the data.

(3) An opinion does not count for the purposes of sub-paragraph (2) if—
  (a) it was obtained before the beginning of the relevant period, or
  (b) it was obtained during that period but it is reasonable in all the circumstances to re-consult the appropriate health professional.

(4) In this paragraph, "the relevant period" means the period of 6 months ending with the day on which the opinion would be relied on.

Restriction of Article 15 of the [UK GDPR]: prior opinion of appropriate health professional

6. (1) Article 15(1) to (3) of the [UK GDPR] (confirmation of processing, access to data and safeguards for third country transfers) do not permit the disclosure of data concerning health by a controller who is not a health professional unless the controller has obtained an opinion from the person who appears to the controller to be the appropriate health professional to the effect that the serious harm test is not met with respect to the data.

(2) Sub-paragraph (1) does not apply to the extent that the controller is satisfied that the data concerning health has already been seen by, or is within the knowledge of, the data subject.

(3) An opinion does not count for the purposes of sub-paragraph (1) if—
  (a) it was obtained before the beginning of the relevant period, or
  (b) it was obtained during that period but it is reasonable in all the circumstances to re-consult the appropriate health professional.

(4) In this paragraph, "the relevant period" means the period of 6 months ending with the day on which the opinion would be relied on.

NOTES

Commencement: 25 May 2018 (see also the introductory notes to this Act preceding s 1 at **[1.71]**).

The words in square brackets in each place were substituted by the Data Protection, Privacy and Electronic Communications (Amendments etc) (EU Exit) Regulations 2019, SI 2019/419, reg 4, Sch 2, paras 1, 93(1), (5)–(9).

PART 3 SOCIAL WORK DATA

Definitions

[1.299]

7. (1) In this Part of this Schedule—

"education data" has the meaning given by paragraph 17 of this Schedule;

"Health and Social Care trust" means a Health and Social Care trust established under the Health and Personal Social Services (Northern Ireland) Order 1991 (SI 1991/194 (NI 1));

"Principal Reporter" means the Principal Reporter appointed under the Children's Hearings (Scotland) Act 2011 (asp 1), or an officer of the Scottish Children's Reporter Administration to whom there is delegated under paragraph 10(1) of Schedule 3 to that Act any function of the Principal Reporter;

"social work data" means personal data which—

    (a)   is data to which paragraph 8 applies, but

    (b)   is not education data or data concerning health.

(2) For the purposes of this Part of this Schedule, the "serious harm test" is met with respect to social work data if the application of Article 15 of the [UK GDPR] to the data would be likely to prejudice carrying out social work, because it would be likely to cause serious harm to the physical or mental health of the data subject or another individual.

(3) In sub-paragraph (2), "carrying out social work" is to be taken to include doing any of the following—

    (a)   the exercise of any functions mentioned in paragraph 8(1)(a), (d), (f) to (j), (m), (p), (s), (t), (u), (v) or (w);

    (b)   the provision of any service mentioned in paragraph 8(1)(b), (c) or (k);

    (c)   the exercise of the functions of a body mentioned in paragraph 8(1)(e) or a person mentioned in paragraph 8(1)(q) or (r).

(4) In this Part of this Schedule, a reference to a local authority, in relation to data processed or formerly processed by it, includes a reference to the Council of the Isles of Scilly, in relation to data processed or formerly processed by the Council in connection with any functions mentioned in paragraph 8(1)(a)(ii) which are or have been conferred on the Council by an enactment.

8. (1) This paragraph applies to personal data falling within any of the following descriptions—

    (a)   data processed by a local authority—

        (i)   in connection with its social services functions (within the meaning of the Local Authority Social Services Act 1970 or the Social Services and Well-being (Wales) Act 2014 (anaw 4)) or any functions exercised by local authorities under the Social Work (Scotland) Act 1968 or referred to in section 5(1B) of that Act, or

        (ii)   in the exercise of other functions but obtained or consisting of information obtained in connection with any of the functions mentioned in sub-paragraph (i);

    (b)   data processed by the Regional Health and Social Care Board—

        (i)   in connection with the provision of social care within the meaning of section 2(5) of the Health and Social Care (Reform) Act (Northern Ireland) 2009 (c 1 (NI)), or

        (ii)   in the exercise of other functions but obtained or consisting of information obtained in connection with the provision of that care;

    (c)   data processed by a Health and Social Care trust—

        (i)   in connection with the provision of social care within the meaning of section 2(5) of the Health and Social Care (Reform) Act (Northern Ireland) 2009 (c 1 (NI)) on behalf of the Regional Health and Social Care Board by virtue of an authorisation made under Article 3(1) of the Health and Personal Social Services (Northern Ireland) Order 1994 (SI 1994/429 (NI 2)), or

        (ii)   in the exercise of other functions but obtained or consisting of information obtained in connection with the provision of that care;

    (d)   data processed by a council in the exercise of its functions under Part 2 of Schedule 9 to the Health and Social Services and Social Security Adjudications Act 1983;

    (e)   data processed by—

        (i)   a probation trust established under section 5 of the Offender Management Act 2007, or

        (ii)   the Probation Board for Northern Ireland established by the Probation Board (Northern Ireland) Order 1982 (SI 1982/713 (NI 10));

    (f)   data processed by a local authority in the exercise of its functions under section 36 of the Children Act 1989 or Chapter 2 of Part 6 of the Education Act 1996, so far as those functions relate to ensuring that children of compulsory school age (within the meaning of section 8 of the Education Act 1996) receive suitable education whether by attendance at school or otherwise;

    (g)   data processed by the Education Authority in the exercise of its functions under Article 55 of the Children (Northern Ireland) Order 1995 (SI 1995/755 (NI 2)) or Article 45 of, and Schedule 13 to, the Education and Libraries (Northern Ireland) Order 1986 (SI 1986/594 (NI 3)), so far as those functions relate to ensuring that children of compulsory school age (within the meaning of Article 46 of the Education and Libraries (Northern Ireland) Order 1986) receive efficient full-time education suitable to their age, ability and aptitude and to any special educational needs they may have, either by regular attendance at school or otherwise;

(h)   data processed by an education authority in the exercise of its functions under sections 35 to 42 of the Education (Scotland) Act 1980 so far as those functions relate to ensuring that children of school age (within the meaning of section 31 of the Education (Scotland) Act 1980) receive efficient education suitable to their age, ability and aptitude, whether by attendance at school or otherwise;

(i)   data relating to persons detained in a hospital at which high security psychiatric services are provided under section 4 of the National Health Service Act 2006 and processed by a Special Health Authority established under section 28 of that Act in the exercise of any functions similar to any social services functions of a local authority;

(j)   data relating to persons detained in special accommodation provided under Article 110 of the Mental Health (Northern Ireland) Order 1986 (SI 1986/595 (NI 4)) and processed by a Health and Social Care trust in the exercise of any functions similar to any social services functions of a local authority;

(k)   data which—
  (i)   is processed by the National Society for the Prevention of Cruelty to Children, or by any other voluntary organisation or other body designated under this paragraph by the Secretary of State or the Department of Health in Northern Ireland, and
  (ii)   appears to the Secretary of State or the Department, as the case may be, to be processed for the purposes of the provision of any service similar to a service provided in the exercise of any functions specified in paragraph (a), (b), (c) or (d);

(l)   data processed by a body mentioned in sub-paragraph (2)—
  (i)   which was obtained, or consists of information which was obtained, from an authority or body mentioned in any of paragraphs (a) to (k) or from a government department, and
  (ii)   in the case of data obtained, or consisting of information obtained, from an authority or body mentioned in any of paragraphs (a) to (k), fell within any of those paragraphs while processed by the authority or body;

(m)   data processed by a National Health Service trust first established under section 25 of the National Health Service Act 2006, section 18 of the National Health Service (Wales) Act 2006 or section 5 of the National Health Service and Community Care Act 1990 in the exercise of any functions similar to any social services functions of a local authority;

(n)   data processed by an NHS foundation trust in the exercise of any functions similar to any social services functions of a local authority;

(o)   data processed by a government department—
  (i)   which was obtained, or consists of information which was obtained, from an authority or body mentioned in any of paragraphs (a) to (n), and
  (ii)   which fell within any of those paragraphs while processed by that authority or body;

(p)   data processed for the purposes of the functions of the Secretary of State pursuant to section 82(5) of the Children Act 1989;

(q)   data processed by—
  (i)   a children's guardian appointed under Part 16 of the Family Procedure Rules 2010 (SI 2010/2955 (L 17)),
  (ii)   a guardian ad litem appointed under Article 60 of the Children (Northern Ireland) Order 1995 (SI 1995/755 (NI 2)) or Article 66 of the Adoption (Northern Ireland) Order 1987 (SI 1987/2203 (NI 22)), or
  (iii)   a safeguarder appointed under section 30(2) or 31(3) of the Children's Hearings (Scotland) Act 2011 (asp 1);

(r)   data processed by the Principal Reporter;

(s)   data processed by an officer of the Children and Family Court Advisory and Support Service for the purpose of the officer's functions under section 7 of the Children Act 1989 or Part 16 of the Family Procedure Rules 2010 (SI 2010/2955 (L 17));

(t)   data processed by the Welsh family proceedings officer for the purposes of the functions under section 7 of the Children Act 1989 or Part 16 of the Family Procedure Rules 2010;

(u)   data processed by an officer of the service appointed as guardian ad litem under Part 16 of the Family Procedure Rules 2010;

(v)   data processed by the Children and Family Court Advisory and Support Service for the purpose of its functions under section 12(1) and (2) and section 13(1), (2) and (4) of the Criminal Justice and Court Services Act 2000;

(w)   data processed by the Welsh Ministers for the purposes of their functions under section 35(1) and (2) and section 36(1), (2), (4), (5) and (6) of the Children Act 2004;

(x)   data processed for the purposes of the functions of the appropriate Minister pursuant to section 12 of the Adoption and Children Act 2002 (independent review of determinations).

(2)   The bodies referred to in sub-paragraph (1)(l) are—
  (a)   a National Health Service trust first established under section 25 of the National Health Service Act 2006 or section 18 of the National Health Service (Wales) Act 2006;
  (b)   a National Health Service trust first established under section 5 of the National Health Service and Community Care Act 1990;
  (c)   an NHS foundation trust;
  (d)   a clinical commissioning group established under section 14D of the National Health Service Act 2006;
  (e)   the National Health Service Commissioning Board;
  (f)   a Local Health Board established under section 11 of the National Health Service (Wales) Act 2006;
  (g)   a Health Board established under section 2 of the National Health Service (Scotland) Act 1978.

Exemption from the listed GDPR provisions: data processed by a court

9. (1)   The listed GDPR provisions do not apply to data that is not education data or data concerning health if—

(a) it is processed by a court,

(b) it consists of information supplied in a report or other evidence given to the court in the course of proceedings to which rules listed in subparagraph (2) apply, and

(c) in accordance with any of those rules, the data may be withheld by the court in whole or in part from the data subject.

(2) Those rules are—

(a) the Magistrates' Courts (Children and Young Persons) Rules (Northern Ireland) 1969 (SR (NI) 1969 No 221);

(b) the Magistrates' Courts (Children and Young Persons) Rules 1992 (SI 1992/2071 (L 17));

(c) the Family Proceedings Rules (Northern Ireland) 1996 (SR (NI) 1996 No 322);

(d) the Magistrates' Courts (Children (Northern Ireland) Order 1995) Rules (Northern Ireland) 1996 (SR (NI) 1996 No 323);

(e) the Act of Sederunt (Child Care and Maintenance Rules) 1997 (SI 1997/291 (S 19));

(f) the Sheriff Court Adoption Rules 2009;

(g) the Family Procedure Rules 2010 (SI 2010/2955 (L 17));

(h) the Children's Hearings (Scotland) Act 2011 (Rules of Procedure in Children's Hearings) Rules 2013 (SSI 2013/194).

Exemption from the listed GDPR provisions: data subject's expectations and wishes

10. (1) This paragraph applies where a request for social work data is made in exercise of a power conferred by an enactment or rule of law and—

(a) in relation to England and Wales or Northern Ireland, the data subject is an individual aged under 18 and the person making the request has parental responsibility for the data subject,

(b) in relation to Scotland, the data subject is an individual aged under 16 and the person making the request has parental responsibility for the data subject, or

(c) the data subject is incapable of managing his or her own affairs and the person making the request has been appointed by a court to manage those affairs.

(2) The listed GDPR provisions do not apply to social work data to the extent that complying with the request would disclose information—

(a) which was provided by the data subject in the expectation that it would not be disclosed to the person making the request,

(b) which was obtained as a result of any examination or investigation to which the data subject consented in the expectation that the information would not be so disclosed, or

(c) which the data subject has expressly indicated should not be so disclosed.

(3) The exemptions under sub-paragraph (2)(a) and (b) do not apply if the data subject has expressly indicated that he or she no longer has the expectation mentioned there.

Exemption from Article 15 of the [UK GDPR]: serious harm

11. Article 15(1) to (3) of the [UK GDPR] (confirmation of processing, access to data and safeguards for third country transfers) do not apply to social work data to the extent that the serious harm test is met with respect to the data.

Restriction of Article 15 of the [UK GDPR]: prior opinion of Principal Reporter

12. (1) This paragraph applies where—

(a) a question arises as to whether a controller who is a social work authority is obliged by Article 15(1) to (3) of the [UK GDPR] (confirmation of processing, access to data and safeguards for third country transfers) to disclose social work data, and

(b) the data—

(i) originated from or was supplied by the Principal Reporter acting in pursuance of the Principal Reporter's statutory duties, and

(ii) is not data which the data subject is entitled to receive from the Principal Reporter.

(2) The controller must inform the Principal Reporter of the fact that the question has arisen before the end of the period of 14 days beginning when the question arises.

(3) Article 15(1) to (3) of the [UK GDPR] (confirmation of processing, access to data and safeguards for third country transfers) do not permit the controller to disclose the data to the data subject unless the Principal Reporter has informed the controller that, in the opinion of the Principal Reporter, the serious harm test is not met with respect to the data.

(4) In this paragraph "social work authority" means a local authority for the purposes of the Social Work (Scotland) Act 1968.

NOTES

Commencement: 25 May 2018 (see also the introductory notes to this Act preceding s 1 at **[1.71]**).

The words in square brackets in each place were substituted by the Data Protection, Privacy and Electronic Communications (Amendments etc) (EU Exit) Regulations 2019, SI 2019/419, reg 4, Sch 2, paras 1, 93(1), (10)–(14).

PART 4 EDUCATION DATA

Educational records

[1.300]

13. In this Part of this Schedule "educational record" means a record to which paragraph 14, 15 or 16 applies.

14. (1) This paragraph applies to a record of information which—

(a) is processed by or on behalf of the proprietor of, or a teacher at, a school in England and Wales specified in sub-paragraph (3),

  (b) relates to an individual who is or has been a pupil at the school, and

  (c) originated from, or was supplied by or on behalf of, any of the persons specified in sub-paragraph (4).

(2) But this paragraph does not apply to information which is processed by a teacher solely for the teacher's own use.

(3) The schools referred to in sub-paragraph (1)(a) are—

  (a) a school maintained by a local authority;

  (b) an Academy school;

  (c) an alternative provision Academy;

  (d) an independent school that is not an Academy school or an alternative provision Academy;

  (e) a non-maintained special school.

(4) The persons referred to in sub-paragraph (1)(c) are—

  (a) an employee of the local authority which maintains the school;

  (b) in the case of—

      (i)   a voluntary aided, foundation or foundation special school (within the meaning of the School Standards and Framework Act 1998),

      (ii)   an Academy school,

      (iii) an alternative provision Academy,

      (iv) an independent school that is not an Academy school or an alternative provision Academy, or

      (v)   a non-maintained special school,

    a teacher or other employee at the school (including an educational psychologist engaged by the proprietor under a contract for services);

  (c) the pupil to whom the record relates;

  (d) a parent, as defined by section 576(1) of the Education Act 1996, of that pupil.

(5) In this paragraph—

  "independent school" has the meaning given by section 463 of the Education Act 1996;

  "local authority" has the same meaning as in that Act (see sections 579(1) and 581 of that Act);

  "non-maintained special school" has the meaning given by section 337A of that Act;

  "proprietor" has the meaning given by section 579(1) of that Act.

15. (1) This paragraph applies to a record of information which is processed—

  (a) by an education authority in Scotland, and

  (b) for the purpose of the relevant function of the authority.

(2) But this paragraph does not apply to information which is processed by a teacher solely for the teacher's own use.

(3) For the purposes of this paragraph, information processed by an education authority is processed for the purpose of the relevant function of the authority if the processing relates to the discharge of that function in respect of a person—

  (a) who is or has been a pupil in a school provided by the authority, or

  (b) who receives, or has received, further education provided by the authority.

(4) In this paragraph "the relevant function" means, in relation to each education authority, its function under section 1 of the Education (Scotland) Act 1980 and section 7(1) of the Self-Governing Schools etc (Scotland) Act 1989.

16. (1) This paragraph applies to a record of information which—

  (a) is processed by or on behalf of the Board of Governors, proprietor or trustees of, or a teacher at, a school in Northern Ireland specified in sub-paragraph (3),

  (b) relates to an individual who is or has been a pupil at the school, and

  (c) originated from, or was supplied by or on behalf of, any of the persons specified in sub-paragraph (4).

(2) But this paragraph does not apply to information which is processed by a teacher solely for the teacher's own use.

(3) The schools referred to in sub-paragraph (1)(a) are—

  (a) a grant-aided school;

  (b) an independent school.

(4) The persons referred to in sub-paragraph (1)(c) are—

  (a) a teacher at the school;

  (b) an employee of the Education Authority, other than a teacher at the school;

  (c) an employee of the Council for Catholic Maintained Schools, other than a teacher at the school;

  (d) the pupil to whom the record relates;

  (e) a parent, as defined by Article 2(2) of the Education and Libraries (Northern Ireland) Order 1986 (SI 1986/594 (NI 3)).

(5) In this paragraph, "grant-aided school", "independent school", "proprietor" and "trustees" have the same meaning as in the Education and Libraries (Northern Ireland) Order 1986 (SI 1986/594 (NI 3)).

Other definitions

17. (1) In this Part of this Schedule—

  "education authority" and "further education" have the same meaning as in the Education (Scotland) Act 1980;

  "education data" means personal data consisting of information which—

      (a)   constitutes an educational record, but

      (b)   is not data concerning health;

  "Principal Reporter" means the Principal Reporter appointed under the Children's Hearings (Scotland) Act 2011 (asp 1), or an officer of the Scottish Children's Reporter Administration to whom there is delegated under paragraph 10(1) of Schedule 3 to that Act any function of the Principal Reporter;

  "pupil" means—

    (a)   in relation to a school in England and Wales, a registered pupil within the meaning of the Education Act 1996,

    (b)   in relation to a school in Scotland, a pupil within the meaning of the Education (Scotland) Act 1980, and

    (c)   in relation to a school in Northern Ireland, a registered pupil within the meaning of the Education and Libraries (Northern Ireland) Order 1986 (SI 1986/594 (NI 3));

"school"—

    (a)   in relation to England and Wales, has the same meaning as in the Education Act 1996,

    (b)   in relation to Scotland, has the same meaning as in the Education (Scotland) Act 1980, and

    (c)   in relation to Northern Ireland, has the same meaning as in the Education and Libraries (Northern Ireland) Order 1986;

"teacher" includes—

    (a)   in Great Britain, head teacher, and

    (b)   in Northern Ireland, the principal of a school.

(2) For the purposes of this Part of this Schedule, the "serious harm test" is met with respect to education data if the application of Article 15 of the [UK GDPR] to the data would be likely to cause serious harm to the physical or mental health of the data subject or another individual.

Exemption from the listed GDPR provisions: data processed by a court

18. (1) The listed GDPR provisions do not apply to education data if—

    (a)   it is processed by a court,

    (b)   it consists of information supplied in a report or other evidence given to the court in the course of proceedings to which rules listed in subparagraph (2) apply, and

    (c)   in accordance with those rules, the data may be withheld by the court in whole or in part from the data subject.

(2) Those rules are—

    (a)   the Magistrates' Courts (Children and Young Persons) Rules (Northern Ireland) 1969 (SR (NI) 1969 No 221);

    (b)   the Magistrates' Courts (Children and Young Persons) Rules 1992 (SI 1992/2071 (L 17));

    (c)   the Family Proceedings Rules (Northern Ireland) 1996 (SR (NI) 1996 No 322);

    (d)   the Magistrates' Courts (Children (Northern Ireland) Order 1995) Rules (Northern Ireland) 1996 (SR (NI) 1996 No 323);

    (e)   the Act of Sederunt (Child Care and Maintenance Rules) 1997 (SI 1997/291 (S 19));

    (f)   the Sheriff Court Adoption Rules 2009;

    (g)   the Family Procedure Rules 2010 (SI 2010/2955 (L 17));

    (h)   the Children's Hearings (Scotland) Act 2011 (Rules of Procedure in Children's Hearings) Rules 2013 (SSI 2013/194).

Exemption from Article 15 of the [UK GDPR]: serious harm

19. Article 15(1) to (3) of the [UK GDPR] (confirmation of processing, access to data and safeguards for third country transfers) do not apply to education data to the extent that the serious harm test is met with respect to the data.

Restriction of Article 15 of the [UK GDPR]: prior opinion of Principal Reporter

20. (1) This paragraph applies where—

    (a)   a question arises as to whether a controller who is an education authority is obliged by Article 15(1) to (3) of the [UK GDPR] (confirmation of processing, access to data and safeguards for third country transfers) to disclose education data, and

    (b)   the controller believes that the data—

        (i)   originated from or was supplied by or on behalf of the Principal Reporter acting in pursuance of the Principal Reporter's statutory duties, and

        (ii)   is not data which the data subject is entitled to receive from the Principal Reporter.

(2) The controller must inform the Principal Reporter of the fact that the question has arisen before the end of the period of 14 days beginning when the question arises.

(3) Article 15(1) to (3) of the [UK GDPR] (confirmation of processing, access to data and safeguards for third country transfers) do not permit the controller to disclose the data to the data subject unless the Principal Reporter has informed the controller that, in the opinion of the Principal Reporter, the serious harm test is not met with respect to the data.

NOTES

Commencement: 25 May 2018 (see also the introductory notes to this Act preceding s 1 at **[1.71]**).

The words in square brackets in each place were substituted by the Data Protection, Privacy and Electronic Communications (Amendments etc) (EU Exit) Regulations 2019, SI 2019/419, reg 4, Sch 2, paras 1, 93(1), (15)–(19).

PART 5 CHILD ABUSE DATA

Exemption from Article 15 of the [UK GDPR]: child abuse data

[1.301]

21. (1) This paragraph applies where a request for child abuse data is made in exercise of a power conferred by an enactment or rule of law and—

    (a)   the data subject is an individual aged under 18 and the person making the request has parental responsibility for the data subject, or

    (b)   the data subject is incapable of managing his or her own affairs and the person making the request has been appointed by a court to manage those affairs.

(2) Article 15(1) to (3) of the [UK GDPR] (confirmation of processing, access to data and safeguards for third country transfers) do not apply to child abuse data to the extent that the application of that provision would not be in the best interests of the data subject.

(3) "Child abuse data" is personal data consisting of information as to whether the data subject is or has been the subject of, or may be at risk of, child abuse.

(4) For this purpose, "child abuse" includes physical injury (other than accidental injury) to, and physical and emotional neglect, ill-treatment and sexual abuse of, an individual aged under 18.

(5) This paragraph does not apply in relation to Scotland.

NOTES

Commencement: 25 May 2018 (see also the introductory notes to this Act preceding s 1 at **[1.71]**).

The words in square brackets were substituted by the Data Protection, Privacy and Electronic Communications (Amendments etc) (EU Exit) Regulations 2019, SI 2019/419, reg 4, Sch 2, paras 1, 93(1), (20), (21).

SCHEDULE 4
EXEMPTIONS ETC FROM THE [UK GDPR]: DISCLOSURE PROHIBITED OR RESTRICTED BY AN ENACTMENT

Section 15

[UK GDPR] provisions to be restricted: "the listed GDPR provisions"

[1.302]

1. In this Schedule "the listed GDPR provisions" means the following provisions of the [UK GDPR] (the rights and obligations in which may be restricted by virtue of Article 23(1) of the [UK GDPR])—
   (a) Article 15(1) to (3) (confirmation of processing, access to data and safeguards for third country transfers);
   (b) Article 5 (general principles) so far as its provisions correspond to the rights and obligations provided for in Article 15(1) to (3).

Human fertilisation and embryology information

2. The listed GDPR provisions do not apply to personal data consisting of information the disclosure of which is prohibited or restricted by any of sections 31, 31ZA to 31ZE and 33A to 33D of the Human Fertilisation and Embryology Act 1990.

Adoption records and reports

3. (1) The listed GDPR provisions do not apply to personal data consisting of information the disclosure of which is prohibited or restricted by an enactment listed in sub-paragraph (2), (3) or (4).

(2) The enactments extending to England and Wales are—
   (a) regulation 14 of the Adoption Agencies Regulations 1983 (SI 1983/1964);
   (b) regulation 41 of the Adoption Agencies Regulations 2005 (SI 2005/389);
   (c) regulation 42 of the Adoption Agencies (Wales) Regulations 2005 (SI 2005/1313 (W 95));
   (d) rules 5, 6, 9, 17, 18, 21, 22 and 53 of the Adoption Rules 1984 (SI 1984/265);
   (e) rules 24, 29, 30, 65, 72, 73, 77, 78 and 83 of the Family Procedure (Adoption) Rules 2005 (SI 2005/2795 (L 22));
   (f) in the Family Procedure Rules 2010 (SI 2010/2955 (L 17)), rules 14.6, 14.11, 14.12, 14.13, 14.14, 14.24, 16.20 (so far as it applies to a children's guardian appointed in proceedings to which Part 14 of those Rules applies), 16.32 and 16.33 (so far as it applies to a children and family reporter in proceedings to which Part 14 of those Rules applies).

(3) The enactments extending to Scotland are—
   (a) regulation 23 of the Adoption Agencies (Scotland) Regulations 1996 (SI 1996/3266 (S 254));
   (b) rule 67.3 of the Act of Sederunt (Rules of the Court of Session 1994) 1994 (SI 1994/1443 (S 69));
   (c) rules 10.3, 17.2, 21, 25, 39, 43.3, 46.2 and 47 of the Act of Sederunt (Sheriff Court Rules Amendment) (Adoption and Children (Scotland) Act 2007) 2009 (SSI 2009/284);
   (d) sections 53 and 55 of the Adoption and Children (Scotland) Act 2007 (asp 4);
   (e) regulation 28 of the Adoption Agencies (Scotland) Regulations 2009 (SSI 2009/154);
   (f) regulation 3 of the Adoption (Disclosure of Information and Medical Information about Natural Parents) (Scotland) Regulations 2009 (SSI 2009/268).

(4) The enactments extending to Northern Ireland are—
   (a) Articles 50 and 54 of the Adoption (Northern Ireland) Order 1987 (SI 1987/2203 (NI 22));
   (b) rule 53 of Order 84 of the Rules of the Court of Judicature (Northern Ireland) 1980 (SR (NI) 1980 No 346);
   (c) rules 4A.4(5), 4A.5(1), 4A.6(6), 4A.22(5) and 4C 7 of Part IVA of the Family Proceedings Rules (Northern Ireland) 1996 (SR (NI) 1996 No 322).

Statements of special educational needs

4. (1) The listed GDPR provisions do not apply to personal data consisting of information the disclosure of which is prohibited or restricted by an enactment listed in sub-paragraph (2).

(2) The enactments are—
   (a) regulation 17 of the Special Educational Needs and Disability Regulations 2014 (SI 2014/1530);
   (b) regulation 10 of the Additional Support for Learning (Co-ordinated Support Plan) (Scotland) Amendment Regulations 2005 (SSI 2005/518);
   (c) regulation 22 of the Education (Special Educational Needs) Regulations (Northern Ireland) 2005 (SR (NI) 2005 No 384).

Part 1   Data Protection: UK Law

Parental order records and reports

5. (1) The listed GDPR provisions do not apply to personal data consisting of information the disclosure of which is prohibited or restricted by an enactment listed in sub-paragraph (2), (3) or (4).

(2) The enactments extending to England and Wales are—
   (a) sections 60, 77, 78 and 79 of the Adoption and Children Act 2002, as applied with modifications by regulation 2 of and Schedule 1 to the Human Fertilisation and Embryology (Parental Orders) Regulations 2010 (SI 2010/985) in relation to parental orders made under—
      (i) section 30 of the Human Fertilisation and Embryology Act 1990, or
      (ii) section 54 of the Human Fertilisation and Embryology Act 2008;
   (b) rules made under section 144 of the Magistrates' Courts Act 1980 by virtue of section 141(1) of the Adoption and Children Act 2002, as applied with modifications by regulation 2 of and Schedule 1 to the Human Fertilisation and Embryology (Parental Orders) Regulations 2010, so far as the rules relate to—
      (i) the appointment and duties of the parental order reporter, and
      (ii) the keeping of registers and the custody, inspection and disclosure of documents and information relating to parental order proceedings or related proceedings;
   (c) rules made under section 75 of the Courts Act 2003 by virtue of section 141(1) of the Adoption and Children Act 2002, as applied with modifications by regulation 2 of Schedule 1 to the Human Fertilisation and Embryology (Parental Orders) Regulations 2010 (SI 2010/985), so far as the rules relate to—
      (i) the appointment and duties of the parental order reporter, and
      (ii) the keeping of registers and the custody, inspection and disclosure of documents and information relating to parental order proceedings or related proceedings.

(3) The enactments extending to Scotland are—
   (a) sections 53 and 55 of the Adoption and Children (Scotland) Act 2007 (asp 4), as applied with modifications by regulation 4 of and Schedule 3 to the Human Fertilisation and Embryology (Parental Orders) Regulations 2010 (SI 2010/985) in relation to parental orders made under—
      (i) section 30 of the Human Fertilisation and Embryology Act 1990, or
      (ii) section 54 of the Human Fertilisation and Embryology Act 2008;
   (b) rules 2.47 and 2.59 of the Act of Sederunt (Child Care and Maintenance Rules) 1997 (SI 1997/291 (S 19));
   (c) rules 21 and 25 of the Sheriff Court Adoption Rules 2009.

(4) The enactments extending to Northern Ireland are—
   (a) Articles 50 and 54 of the Adoption (Northern Ireland) Order 1987 (SI 1987/2203 (NI 22)), as applied with modifications by regulation 3 of and Schedule 2 to the Human Fertilisation and Embryology (Parental Orders) Regulations 2010 in respect of parental orders made under—
      (i) section 30 of the Human Fertilisation and Embryology Act 1990, or
      (ii) section 54 of the Human Fertilisation and Embryology Act 2008;
   (b) rules 4, 5 and 16 of Order 84A of the Rules of the Court of Judicature (Northern Ireland) 1980 (SR (NI) 1980 No 346);
   (c) rules 3, 4 and 15 of Order 50A of the County Court Rules (Northern Ireland) 1981 (SR (NI) 1981 No 225).

Information provided by Principal Reporter for children's hearing

6. The listed GDPR provisions do not apply to personal data consisting of information the disclosure of which is prohibited or restricted by any of the following enactments—
   (a) section 178 of the Children's Hearings (Scotland) Act 2011 (asp 1);
   (b) the Children's Hearings (Scotland) Act 2011 (Rules of Procedure in Children's Hearings) Rules 2013 (SSI 2013/194).

NOTES

Commencement: 25 May 2018 (see also the introductory notes to this Act preceding s 1 at **[1.71]**).

The words in square brackets in the Part heading and para 1 (including the preceding heading) were substituted by the Data Protection, Privacy and Electronic Communications (Amendments etc) (EU Exit) Regulations 2019, SI 2019/419, reg 4, Sch 2, paras 1, 94.

SCHEDULE 5
ACCREDITATION OF CERTIFICATION PROVIDERS: REVIEWS AND APPEALS

Section 17

Introduction

[1.303]
1. (1) This Schedule applies where—
   (a) a person ("the applicant") applies to an accreditation authority for accreditation as a certification provider, and
   (b) is dissatisfied with the decision on that application.

(2) In this Schedule—
   "accreditation authority" means—
      (a) the Commissioner, or
      (b) the [UK national accreditation body];
   "certification provider" and "[UK national accreditation body]" have the same meaning as in section 17.

Review

2. (1) The applicant may ask the accreditation authority to review the decision.

(2) The request must be made in writing before the end of the period of 28 days beginning with the day on which the person receives written notice of the accreditation authority's decision.

(3) The request must specify—

   (a) the decision to be reviewed, and

   (b) the reasons for asking for the review.

(4) The request may be accompanied by additional documents which the applicant wants the accreditation authority to take into account for the purposes of the review.

(5) If the applicant makes a request in accordance with sub-paragraphs (1) to (4), the accreditation authority must—

   (a) review the decision, and

   (b) inform the applicant of the outcome of the review in writing before the end of the period of 28 days beginning with the day on which the request for a review is received.

Right to appeal

3. (1) If the applicant is dissatisfied with the decision on the review under paragraph 2, the applicant may ask the accreditation authority to refer the decision to an appeal panel constituted in accordance with paragraph 4.

(2) The request must be made in writing before the end of the period of 3 months beginning with the day on which the person receives written notice of the decision on the review.

(3) A request must specify—

   (a) the decision to be referred to the appeal panel, and

   (b) the reasons for asking for it to be referred.

(4) The request may be accompanied by additional documents which the applicant wants the appeal panel to take into account.

(5) The applicant may discontinue an appeal at any time by giving notice in writing to the accreditation authority.

Appeal panel

4. (1) If the applicant makes a request in accordance with paragraph 3, an appeal panel must be established in accordance with this paragraph.

(2) An appeal panel must consist of a chair and at least two other members.

(3) Where the request relates to a decision of the Commissioner—

   (a) the Secretary of State may appoint one person to be a member of the appeal panel other than the chair, and

   (b) subject to paragraph (a), the Commissioner must appoint the members of the appeal panel.

(4) Where the request relates to a decision of the [UK national accreditation body]—

   (a) the Secretary of State—

      (i)   may appoint one person to be a member of the appeal panel other than the chair, or

      (ii)   may direct the Commissioner to appoint one person to be a member of the appeal panel other than the chair, and

   (b) subject to paragraph (a), the chair of the [UK national accreditation body] must appoint the members of the appeal panel.

(5) A person may not be a member of an appeal panel if the person—

   (a) has a commercial interest in the decision referred to the panel,

   (b) has had any prior involvement in any matters relating to the decision, or

   (c) is an employee or officer of the accreditation authority.

(6) The Commissioner may not be a member of an appeal panel to which a decision of the Commissioner is referred.

(7) The applicant may object to all or any of the members of the appeal panel appointed under sub-paragraph (3) or (4).

(8) If the applicant objects to a member of the appeal panel under sub-paragraph (7), the person who appointed that member must appoint a replacement.

(9) The applicant may not object to a member of the appeal panel appointed under sub-paragraph (8).

Hearing

5. (1) If the appeal panel considers it necessary, a hearing must be held at which both the applicant and the accreditation authority may be represented.

(2) Any additional documents which the applicant or the accreditation authority want the appeal panel to take into account must be submitted to the chair of the appeal panel at least 5 working days before the hearing.

(3) The appeal panel may allow experts and witnesses to give evidence at a hearing.

Decision following referral to appeal panel

6. (1) The appeal panel must, before the end of the period of 28 days beginning with the day on which the appeal panel is established in accordance with paragraph 4—

   (a) make a reasoned recommendation in writing to the accreditation authority, and

   (b) give a copy of the recommendation to the applicant.

(2) For the purposes of sub-paragraph (1), where there is an objection under paragraph 4(7), an appeal panel is not to be taken to be established in accordance with paragraph 4 until the replacement member is appointed (or, if there is more than one objection, until the last replacement member is appointed).

(3) The accreditation authority must, before the end of the period of 3 working days beginning with the day on which the authority receives the recommendation—

   (a) make a reasoned final decision in writing, and

   (b) give a copy of the decision to the applicant.

(4) Where the accreditation authority is the [UK national accreditation body], the recommendation must be given to, and the final decision must be made by, the chief executive of that body.

Meaning of "working day"

7. In this Schedule, "working day" means any day other than—
(a) Saturday or Sunday,
(b) Christmas Day or Good Friday, or
(c) a day which is a bank holiday under the Banking and Financial Dealings Act 1971 in any part of the United Kingdom.

NOTES

Commencement: 25 May 2018 (see also the introductory notes to this Act preceding s 1 at **[1.71]**).

The words in square brackets in paras 1(2), 4(4) and 6(4) were substituted by the Data Protection, Privacy and Electronic Communications (Amendments etc) (EU Exit) Regulations 2019, SI 2019/419, reg 4, Sch 2, paras 1, 95.

SCHEDULE 6

(Repealed by the Data Protection, Privacy and Electronic Communications (Amendments etc) (EU Exit) Regulations 2019, SI 2019/419, reg 4, Sch 2, paras 1, 96.)

SCHEDULE 7
COMPETENT AUTHORITIES

Section 30

[1.304]

1. Any United Kingdom government department other than a non-ministerial government department.

2. The Scottish Ministers.

3. Any Northern Ireland department.

4. The Welsh Ministers.

Chief officers of police and other policing bodies

5. The chief constable of a police force maintained under section 2 of the Police Act 1996.

6. The Commissioner of Police of the Metropolis.

7. The Commissioner of Police for the City of London.

8. The Chief Constable of the Police Service of Northern Ireland.

9. The chief constable of the Police Service of Scotland.

10. The chief constable of the British Transport Police.

11. The chief constable of the Civil Nuclear Constabulary.

12. The chief constable of the Ministry of Defence Police.

13. The Provost Marshal of the Royal Navy Police.

14. The Provost Marshal of the Royal Military Police.

15. The Provost Marshal of the Royal Air Force Police.

16. The chief officer of—
(a) a body of constables appointed under provision incorporating section 79 of the Harbours, Docks, and Piers Clauses Act 1847;
(b) a body of constables appointed under an order made under section 14 of the Harbours Act 1964;
(c) the body of constables appointed under section 154 of the Port of London Act 1968 (c xxxii).

17. A body established in accordance with a collaboration agreement under section 22A of the Police Act 1996.

18. The Director General of the Independent Office for Police Conduct.

19. The Police Investigations and Review Commissioner.

20. The Police Ombudsman for Northern Ireland.

Other authorities with investigatory functions

21. The Commissioners for Her Majesty's Revenue and Customs.

22. The Welsh Revenue Authority.

23. Revenue Scotland.

24. The Director General of the National Crime Agency.

25. The Director of the Serious Fraud Office.

26. The Director of Border Revenue.

27. The Financial Conduct Authority.

28. The Health and Safety Executive.

29. The Competition and Markets Authority.

30. The Gas and Electricity Markets Authority.

31. The Food Standards Agency.

32. Food Standards Scotland.

33. Her Majesty's Land Registry.

34. The Criminal Cases Review Commission.

35. The Scottish Criminal Cases Review Commission.

Authorities with functions relating to offender management

36. A provider of probation services (other than the Secretary of State), acting in pursuance of arrangements made under section 3(2) of the Offender Management Act 2007.

37. The Youth Justice Board for England and Wales.

38. The Parole Board for England and Wales.

39. The Parole Board for Scotland.

40. The Parole Commissioners for Northern Ireland.

41. The Probation Board for Northern Ireland.

42. The Prisoner Ombudsman for Northern Ireland.

43. A person who has entered into a contract for the running of, or part of—
  (a) a prison or young offender institution under section 84 of the Criminal Justice Act 1991, or
  (b) a secure training centre under section 7 of the Criminal Justice and Public Order Act 1994.

44. A person who has entered into a contract with the Secretary of State—
  (a) under section 80 of the Criminal Justice Act 1991 for the purposes of prisoner escort arrangements, or
  (b) under paragraph 1 of Schedule 1 to the Criminal Justice and Public Order Act 1994 for the purposes of escort arrangements.

45. A person who is, under or by virtue of any enactment, responsible for securing the electronic monitoring of an individual.

46. A youth offending team established under section 39 of the Crime and Disorder Act 1998.

Other authorities

47. The Director of Public Prosecutions.

48. The Director of Public Prosecutions for Northern Ireland.

49. The Lord Advocate.

50. A Procurator Fiscal.

51. The Director of Service Prosecutions.

52. The Information Commissioner.

53. The Scottish Information Commissioner.

54. The Scottish Courts and Tribunal Service.

55. The Crown agent.

56. A court or tribunal.

NOTES

Commencement: 25 May 2018 (see also the introductory notes to this Act preceding s 1 at **[1.71]**).

SCHEDULE 8
CONDITIONS FOR SENSITIVE PROCESSING UNDER PART 3

Section 35(5)

Statutory etc purposes

[1.305]
1. This condition is met if the processing—
  (a) is necessary for the exercise of a function conferred on a person by an enactment or rule of law, and
  (b) is necessary for reasons of substantial public interest.

Administration of justice

2. This condition is met if the processing is necessary for the administration of justice.

Protecting individual's vital interests

3. This condition is met if the processing is necessary to protect the vital interests of the data subject or of another individual.

Safeguarding of children and of individuals at risk

4. (1) This condition is met if—
  (a) the processing is necessary for the purposes of—
      (i) protecting an individual from neglect or physical, mental or emotional harm, or
      (ii) protecting the physical, mental or emotional well-being of an individual,
  (b) the individual is—
      (i) aged under 18, or
      (ii) aged 18 or over and at risk,
  (c) the processing is carried out without the consent of the data subject for one of the reasons listed in sub-paragraph (2), and
  (d) the processing is necessary for reasons of substantial public interest.

(2) The reasons mentioned in sub-paragraph (1)(c) are—

(a) in the circumstances, consent to the processing cannot be given by the data subject;

(b) in the circumstances, the controller cannot reasonably be expected to obtain the consent of the data subject to the processing;

(c) the processing must be carried out without the consent of the data subject because obtaining the consent of the data subject would prejudice the provision of the protection mentioned in sub-paragraph (1)(a).

(3) For the purposes of this paragraph, an individual aged 18 or over is "at risk" if the controller has reasonable cause to suspect that the individual—

(a) has needs for care and support,

(b) is experiencing, or at risk of, neglect or physical, mental or emotional harm, and

(c) as a result of those needs is unable to protect himself or herself against the neglect or harm or the risk of it.

(4) In sub-paragraph (1)(a), the reference to the protection of an individual or of the well-being of an individual includes both protection relating to a particular individual and protection relating to a type of individual.

Personal data already in the public domain

5. This condition is met if the processing relates to personal data which is manifestly made public by the data subject.

Legal claims

6. This condition is met if the processing—

(a) is necessary for the purpose of, or in connection with, any legal proceedings (including prospective legal proceedings),

(b) is necessary for the purpose of obtaining legal advice, or

(c) is otherwise necessary for the purposes of establishing, exercising or defending legal rights.

Judicial acts

7. This condition is met if the processing is necessary when a court or other judicial authority is acting in its judicial capacity.

Preventing fraud

8. (1) This condition is met if the processing—

(a) is necessary for the purposes of preventing fraud or a particular kind of fraud, and

(b) consists of—

    (i) the disclosure of personal data by a competent authority as a member of an anti-fraud organisation,

    (ii) the disclosure of personal data by a competent authority in accordance with arrangements made by an anti-fraud organisation, or

    (iii) the processing of personal data disclosed as described in sub-paragraph (i) or (ii).

(2) In this paragraph, "anti-fraud organisation" has the same meaning as in section 68 of the Serious Crime Act 2007.

Archiving etc

9. This condition is met if the processing is necessary—

(a) for archiving purposes in the public interest,

(b) for scientific or historical research purposes, or

(c) for statistical purposes.

NOTES

Commencement: 25 May 2018 (see also the introductory notes to this Act preceding s 1 at **[1.71]**).

SCHEDULE 9
CONDITIONS FOR PROCESSING UNDER PART 4

Section 86

[1.306]

1. The data subject has given consent to the processing.

2. The processing is necessary—

(a) for the performance of a contract to which the data subject is a party, or

(b) in order to take steps at the request of the data subject prior to entering into a contract.

3. The processing is necessary for compliance with a legal obligation to which the controller is subject, other than an obligation imposed by contract.

4. The processing is necessary in order to protect the vital interests of the data subject or of another individual.

5. The processing is necessary—

(a) for the administration of justice,

(b) for the exercise of any functions of either House of Parliament,

(c) for the exercise of any functions conferred on a person by an enactment or rule of law,

(d) for the exercise of any functions of the Crown, a Minister of the Crown or a government department, or

(e) for the exercise of any other functions of a public nature exercised in the public interest by a person.

6. (1) The processing is necessary for the purposes of legitimate interests pursued by—

(a) the controller, or

(b) the third party or parties to whom the data is disclosed.

(2) Sub-paragraph (1) does not apply where the processing is unwarranted in any particular case because of prejudice to the rights and freedoms or legitimate interests of the data subject.

(3) In this paragraph, "third party", in relation to personal data, means a person other than the data subject, the controller or a processor or other person authorised to process personal data for the controller or processor.

NOTES
Commencement: 25 May 2018 (see also the introductory notes to this Act preceding s 1 at **[1.71]**).

SCHEDULE 10
CONDITIONS FOR SENSITIVE PROCESSING UNDER PART 4

Section 86

Consent to particular processing

[1.307]

1. The data subject has given consent to the processing.

Right or obligation relating to employment

2. The processing is necessary for the purposes of exercising or performing any right or obligation which is conferred or imposed by an enactment or rule of law on the controller in connection with employment.

Vital interests of a person

3. The processing is necessary—
  (a) in order to protect the vital interests of the data subject or of another person, in a case where—
    (i) consent cannot be given by or on behalf of the data subject, or
    (ii) the controller cannot reasonably be expected to obtain the consent of the data subject, or
  (b) in order to protect the vital interests of another person, in a case where consent by or on behalf of the data subject has been unreasonably withheld.

Safeguarding of children and of individuals at risk

4. (1) This condition is met if—
  (a) the processing is necessary for the purposes of—
    (i) protecting an individual from neglect or physical, mental or emotional harm, or
    (ii) protecting the physical, mental or emotional well-being of an individual,
  (b) the individual is—
    (i) aged under 18, or
    (ii) aged 18 or over and at risk,
  (c) the processing is carried out without the consent of the data subject for one of the reasons listed in sub-paragraph (2), and
  (d) the processing is necessary for reasons of substantial public interest.

(2) The reasons mentioned in sub-paragraph (1)(c) are—
  (a) in the circumstances, consent to the processing cannot be given by the data subject;
  (b) in the circumstances, the controller cannot reasonably be expected to obtain the consent of the data subject to the processing;
  (c) the processing must be carried out without the consent of the data subject because obtaining the consent of the data subject would prejudice the provision of the protection mentioned in sub-paragraph (1)(a).

(3) For the purposes of this paragraph, an individual aged 18 or over is "at risk" if the controller has reasonable cause to suspect that the individual—
  (a) has needs for care and support,
  (b) is experiencing, or at risk of, neglect or physical, mental or emotional harm, and
  (c) as a result of those needs is unable to protect himself or herself against the neglect or harm or the risk of it.

(4) In sub-paragraph (1)(a), the reference to the protection of an individual or of the well-being of an individual includes both protection relating to a particular individual and protection relating to a type of individual.

Data already published by data subject

5. The information contained in the personal data has been made public as a result of steps deliberately taken by the data subject.

Legal proceedings etc

6. The processing—
  (a) is necessary for the purpose of, or in connection with, any legal proceedings (including prospective legal proceedings),
  (b) is necessary for the purpose of obtaining legal advice, or
  (c) is otherwise necessary for the purposes of establishing, exercising or defending legal rights.

Administration of justice, parliamentary, statutory etc and government purposes

7. The processing is necessary—
  (a) for the administration of justice,
  (b) for the exercise of any functions of either House of Parliament,
  (c) for the exercise of any functions conferred on any person by an enactment or rule of law, or
  (d) for the exercise of any functions of the Crown, a Minister of the Crown or a government department.

Medical purposes

8. (1) The processing is necessary for medical purposes and is undertaken by—
  (a) a health professional, or
  (b) a person who in the circumstances owes a duty of confidentiality which is equivalent to that which would arise if that person were a health professional.

(2) In this paragraph, "medical purposes" includes the purposes of preventative medicine, medical diagnosis, medical research, the provision of care and treatment and the management of healthcare services.

Equality

9. (1) The processing—

(a) is of sensitive personal data consisting of information as to racial or ethnic origin,

(b) is necessary for the purpose of identifying or keeping under review the existence or absence of equality of opportunity or treatment between persons of different racial or ethnic origins, with a view to enabling such equality to be promoted or maintained, and

(c) is carried out with appropriate safeguards for the rights and freedoms of data subjects.

(2) In this paragraph, "sensitive personal data" means personal data the processing of which constitutes sensitive processing (see section 86(7)).

NOTES

Commencement: 25 May 2018 (see also the introductory notes to this Act preceding s 1 at **[1.71]**).

SCHEDULE 11
OTHER EXEMPTIONS UNDER PART 4

Section 112

Preliminary

[1.308]

1. In this Schedule, "the listed provisions" means—

(a) Chapter 2 of Part 4 (the data protection principles), except section 86(1)(a) and (2) and Schedules 9 and 10;

(b) Chapter 3 of Part 4 (rights of data subjects);

(c) in Chapter 4 of Part 4, section 108 (communication of personal data breach to the Commissioner).

Crime

2. The listed provisions do not apply to personal data processed for any of the following purposes—

(a) the prevention and detection of crime, or

(b) the apprehension and prosecution of offenders,

to the extent that the application of the listed provisions would be likely to prejudice any of the matters mentioned in paragraph (a) or (b).

Information required to be disclosed by law etc or in connection with legal proceedings

3. (1) The listed provisions do not apply to personal data consisting of information that the controller is obliged by an enactment to make available to the public, to the extent that the application of the listed provisions would prevent the controller from complying with that obligation.

(2) The listed provisions do not apply to personal data where disclosure of the data is required by an enactment, a rule of law or the order of a court, to the extent that the application of the listed provisions would prevent the controller from making the disclosure.

(3) The listed provisions do not apply to personal data where disclosure of the data—

(a) is necessary for the purpose of, or in connection with, legal proceedings (including prospective legal proceedings),

(b) is necessary for the purpose of obtaining legal advice, or

(c) is otherwise necessary for the purposes of establishing, exercising or defending legal rights,

to the extent that the application of the listed provisions would prevent the controller from making the disclosure.

Parliamentary privilege

4. The listed provisions do not apply to personal data where this is required for the purpose of avoiding an infringement of the privileges of either House of Parliament.

Judicial proceedings

5. The listed provisions do not apply to personal data to the extent that the application of the listed provisions would be likely to prejudice judicial proceedings.

Crown honours and dignities

6. The listed provisions do not apply to personal data processed for the purposes of the conferring by the Crown of any honour or dignity.

Armed forces

7. The listed provisions do not apply to personal data to the extent that the application of the listed provisions would be likely to prejudice the combat effectiveness of any of the armed forces of the Crown.

Economic well-being

8. The listed provisions do not apply to personal data to the extent that the application of the listed provisions would be likely to prejudice the economic well-being of the United Kingdom.

Legal professional privilege

9. The listed provisions do not apply to personal data that consists of—

(a) information in respect of which a claim to legal professional privilege or, in Scotland, confidentiality of communications, could be maintained in legal proceedings, or

(b) information in respect of which a duty of confidentiality is owed by a professional legal adviser to a client of the adviser.

Negotiations

10. The listed provisions do not apply to personal data that consists of records of the intentions of the controller in relation to any negotiations with the data subject to the extent that the application of the listed provisions would be likely to prejudice the negotiations.

Confidential references given by the controller

11. The listed provisions do not apply to personal data consisting of a reference given (or to be given) in confidence by the controller for the purposes of—
  (a) the education, training or employment (or prospective education, training or employment) of the data subject,
  (b) the appointment (or prospective appointment) of the data subject to any office, or
  (c) the provision (or prospective provision) by the data subject of any service.

Exam scripts and marks

12. (1) The listed provisions do not apply to personal data consisting of information recorded by candidates during an exam.

(2) Where personal data consists of marks or other information processed by a controller—
  (a) for the purposes of determining the results of an exam, or
  (b) in consequence of the determination of the results of an exam,
section 94 has effect subject to sub-paragraph (3).

(3) Where the relevant time falls before the results of the exam are announced, the period mentioned in section 94(10)(b) is extended until the earlier of—
  (a) the end of the period of 5 months beginning with the relevant time, and
  (b) the end of the period of 40 days beginning with the announcement of the results.

(4) In this paragraph—
  "exam" means an academic, professional or other examination used for determining the knowledge, intelligence, skill or ability of a candidate and may include an exam consisting of an assessment of the candidate's performance while undertaking work or any other activity;
  "the relevant time" has the same meaning as in section 94.

(5) For the purposes of this paragraph, the results of an exam are treated as announced when they are first published or, if not published, first communicated to the candidate.

Research and statistics

13. (1) The listed provisions do not apply to personal data processed for—
  (a) scientific or historical research purposes, or
  (b) statistical purposes,
to the extent that the application of those provisions would prevent or seriously impair the achievement of the purposes in question.

(2) The exemption in sub-paragraph (1) is available only where—
  (a) the personal data is processed subject to appropriate safeguards for the rights and freedoms of data subjects, and
  (b) the results of the research or any resulting statistics are not made available in a form which identifies a data subject.

Archiving in the public interest

14. (1) The listed provisions do not apply to personal data processed for archiving purposes in the public interest to the extent that the application of those provisions would prevent or seriously impair the achievement of those purposes.

(2) The exemption in sub-paragraph (1) is available only where the personal data is processed subject to appropriate safeguards for the rights and freedoms of data subjects.

NOTES

Commencement: 25 May 2018 (see also the introductory notes to this Act preceding s 1 at **[1.71]**).

SCHEDULE 12
THE INFORMATION COMMISSIONER

Section 114

Status and capacity

[1.309]
1. (1) The Commissioner is to continue to be a corporation sole.

(2) The Commissioner and the Commissioner's officers and staff are not to be regarded as servants or agents of the Crown.

Appointment

2. (1) The Commissioner is to be appointed by Her Majesty by Letters Patent.

(2) No recommendation may be made to Her Majesty for the appointment of a person as the Commissioner unless the person concerned has been selected on merit on the basis of fair and open competition.

(3) The Commissioner is to hold office for such term not exceeding 7 years as may be determined at the time of the Commissioner's appointment, subject to paragraph 3.

(4) A person cannot be appointed as the Commissioner more than once.

Resignation and removal

3. (1) The Commissioner may be relieved of office by Her Majesty at the Commissioner's own request.

(2) The Commissioner may be removed from office by Her Majesty on an Address from both Houses of Parliament.

(3) No motion is to be made in either House of Parliament for such an Address unless a Minister of the Crown has presented a report to that House stating that the Minister is satisfied that one or both of the following grounds is made out—

(a) the Commissioner is guilty of serious misconduct;
(b) the Commissioner no longer fulfils the conditions required for the performance of the Commissioner's functions.

Salary etc

4. (1) The Commissioner is to be paid such salary as may be specified by a resolution of the House of Commons.

(2) There is to be paid in respect of the Commissioner such pension as may be specified by a resolution of the House of Commons.

(3) A resolution for the purposes of this paragraph may—

(a) specify the salary or pension,
(b) specify the salary or pension and provide for it to be increased by reference to such variables as may be specified in the resolution, or
(c) provide that the salary or pension is to be the same as, or calculated on the same basis as, that payable to, or in respect of, a person employed in a specified office under, or in a specified capacity in the service of, the Crown.

(4) A resolution for the purposes of this paragraph may take effect from—

(a) the date on which it is passed, or
(b) from an earlier date or later date specified in the resolution.

(5) A resolution for the purposes of this paragraph may make different provision in relation to the pension payable to, or in respect of, different holders of the office of Commissioner.

(6) A salary or pension payable under this paragraph is to be charged on and issued out of the Consolidated Fund.

(7) In this paragraph, "pension" includes an allowance or gratuity and a reference to the payment of a pension includes a reference to the making of payments towards the provision of a pension.

Officers and staff

5. (1) The Commissioner—

(a) must appoint one or more deputy commissioners, and
(b) may appoint other officers and staff.

(2) The Commissioner is to determine the remuneration and other conditions of service of people appointed under this paragraph.

(3) The Commissioner may pay pensions, allowances or gratuities to, or in respect of, people appointed under this paragraph, including pensions, allowances or gratuities paid by way of compensation in respect of loss of office or employment.

(4) The references in sub-paragraph (3) to paying pensions, allowances or gratuities includes making payments towards the provision of pensions, allowances or gratuities.

(5) In making appointments under this paragraph, the Commissioner must have regard to the principle of selection on merit on the basis of fair and open competition.

(6) The Employers' Liability (Compulsory Insurance) Act 1969 does not require insurance to be effected by the Commissioner.

Carrying out of the Commissioner's functions by officers and staff

6. (1) The functions of the Commissioner are to be carried out by the deputy commissioner or deputy commissioners if—

(a) there is a vacancy in the office of the Commissioner, or
(b) the Commissioner is for any reason unable to act.

(2) When the Commissioner appoints a second or subsequent deputy commissioner, the Commissioner must specify which deputy commissioner is to carry out which of the Commissioner's functions in the circumstances referred to in sub-paragraph (1).

(3) A function of the Commissioner may, to the extent authorised by the Commissioner, be carried out by any of the Commissioner's officers or staff.

Authentication of the seal of the Commissioner

7. The application of the seal of the Commissioner is to be authenticated by—

(a) the Commissioner's signature, or
(b) the signature of another person authorised for the purpose.

Presumption of authenticity of documents issued by the Commissioner

8. A document purporting to be an instrument issued by the Commissioner and to be—

(a) duly executed under the Commissioner's seal, or
(b) signed by or on behalf of the Commissioner,

is to be received in evidence and is to be deemed to be such an instrument unless the contrary is shown.

Money

9. The Secretary of State may make payments to the Commissioner out of money provided by Parliament.

Fees etc and other sums

10. (1) All fees, charges, penalties and other sums received by the Commissioner in carrying out the Commissioner's functions are to be paid by the Commissioner to the Secretary of State.

(2) Sub-paragraph (1) does not apply where the Secretary of State, with the consent of the Treasury, otherwise directs.

(3) Any sums received by the Secretary of State under sub-paragraph (1) are to be paid into the Consolidated Fund.

Accounts

11. (1) The Commissioner must—
   (a) keep proper accounts and other records in relation to the accounts, and
   (b) prepare in respect of each financial year a statement of account in such form as the Secretary of State may direct.

(2) The Commissioner must send a copy of the statement to the Comptroller and Auditor General—
   (a) on or before 31 August next following the end of the year to which the statement relates, or
   (b) on or before such earlier date after the end of that year as the Treasury may direct.

(3) The Comptroller and Auditor General must examine, certify and report on the statement.

(4) The Commissioner must arrange for copies of the statement and the Comptroller and Auditor General's report to be laid before Parliament.

(5) In this paragraph, "financial year" means a period of 12 months beginning with 1 April.

Scotland

12. Paragraphs 1(1), 7 and 8 do not extend to Scotland.

NOTES

Commencement: 25 May 2018 (see also the introductory notes to this Act preceding s 1 at **[1.71]**).

SCHEDULE 13
OTHER GENERAL FUNCTIONS OF THE COMMISSIONER

Section 116

General tasks

[1.310]

1. (1) The Commissioner must—
   (a) monitor and enforce Parts 3 and 4 of this Act;
   (b) promote public awareness and understanding of the risks, rules, safeguards and rights in relation to processing of personal data to which those Parts apply;
   (c) advise Parliament, the government and other institutions and bodies on legislative and administrative measures relating to the protection of individuals' rights and freedoms with regard to processing of personal data to which those Parts apply;
   (d) promote the awareness of controllers and processors of their obligations under Parts 3 and 4 of this Act;
   (e) on request, provide information to a data subject concerning the exercise of the data subject's rights under Parts 3 and 4 of this Act and, if appropriate, co-operate with . . . foreign designated authorities to provide such information;
   (f) co-operate with . . . foreign designated authorities with a view to ensuring the consistency of application and enforcement of . . . the Data Protection Convention, including by sharing information and providing mutual assistance;
   (g) conduct investigations on the application of Parts 3 and 4 of this Act, including on the basis of information received from . . . , a foreign designated authority or another public authority;
   (h) monitor relevant developments to the extent that they have an impact on the protection of personal data, including the development of information and communication technologies;
   (i) . . .

(2) Section 3(14)(c) does not apply to the reference to personal data in sub-paragraph (1)(h).

General powers

2. The Commissioner has the following investigative, corrective, authorisation and advisory powers in relation to processing of personal data to which Part 3 or 4 of this Act applies—
   (a) to notify the controller or the processor of an alleged infringement of Part 3 or 4 of this Act;
   (b) to issue warnings to a controller or processor that intended processing operations are likely to infringe provisions of Part 3 or 4 of this Act;
   (c) to issue reprimands to a controller or processor where processing operations have infringed provisions of Part 3 or 4 of this Act;
   (d) to issue, on the Commissioner's own initiative or on request, opinions to Parliament, the government or other institutions and bodies as well as to the public on any issue related to the protection of personal data.

Definitions

3. In this Schedule—
   "foreign designated authority" means an authority designated for the purposes of Article 13 of the Data Protection Convention by a party, other than the United Kingdom, which is bound by that Convention;
   . . .

NOTES

Commencement: 25 May 2018 (see also the introductory notes to this Act preceding s 1 at **[1.71]**).

The words omitted from paras 1, 3 were repealed by the Data Protection, Privacy and Electronic Communications (Amendments etc) (EU Exit) Regulations 2019, SI 2019/419, reg 4, Sch 2, paras 1, 97.

SCHEDULE 14
CO-OPERATION AND MUTUAL ASSISTANCE

Section 118

(Pt I (paras 1–5) was repealed by the Data Protection, Privacy and Electronic Communications (Amendments etc) (EU Exit) Regulations 2019, SI 2019/419, reg 4, Sch 2, paras 1, 98.)

PART 2 DATA PROTECTION CONVENTION

Co-operation between the Commissioner and foreign designated authorities

[1.311]

6. (1) The Commissioner must, at the request of a foreign designated authority—

(a) provide that authority with such information referred to in Article 13(3)(a) of the Data Protection Convention (information on law and administrative practice in the field of data protection) as is the subject of the request, and

(b) take appropriate measures in accordance with Article 13(3)(b) of the Data Protection Convention for providing that authority with information relating to the processing of personal data in the United Kingdom.

(2) The Commissioner may ask a foreign designated authority—

(a) to provide the Commissioner with information referred to in Article 13(3) of the Data Protection Convention, or

(b) to take appropriate measures to provide such information.

Assisting persons resident outside the UK with requests under Article 14 of the Convention

7. (1) This paragraph applies where a request for assistance in exercising any of the rights referred to in Article 8 of the Data Protection Convention in the United Kingdom is made by a person resident outside the United Kingdom, including where the request is forwarded to the Commissioner through the Secretary of State or a foreign designated authority.

(2) The Commissioner must take appropriate measures to assist the person to exercise those rights.

Assisting UK residents with requests under Article 8 of the Convention

8. (1) This paragraph applies where a request for assistance in exercising any of the rights referred to in Article 8 of the Data Protection Convention in a country or territory (other than the United Kingdom) specified in the request is—

(a) made by a person resident in the United Kingdom, and

(b) submitted through the Commissioner under Article 14(2) of the Convention.

(2) If the Commissioner is satisfied that the request contains all necessary particulars referred to in Article 14(3) of the Data Protection Convention, the Commissioner must send the request to the foreign designated authority in the specified country or territory.

(3) Otherwise, the Commissioner must, where practicable, notify the person making the request of the reasons why the Commissioner is not required to assist.

Restrictions on use of information

9. Where the Commissioner receives information from a foreign designated authority as a result of—

(a) a request made by the Commissioner under paragraph 6(2), or

(b) a request received by the Commissioner under paragraph 6(1) or 7,

the Commissioner may use the information only for the purposes specified in the request.

Foreign designated authority

10. In this Part of this Schedule, "foreign designated authority" means an authority designated for the purposes of Article 13 of the Data Protection Convention by a party, other than the United Kingdom, which is bound by that Data Protection Convention.

NOTES

Commencement: 25 May 2018 (see also the introductory notes to this Act preceding s 1 at **[1.71]**).

SCHEDULE 15
POWERS OF ENTRY AND INSPECTION

Section 154

Issue of warrants in connection with non-compliance and offences

[1.312]

1. (1) This paragraph applies if a judge of the High Court, a circuit judge or a District Judge (Magistrates' Courts) is satisfied by information on oath supplied by the Commissioner that—

(a) there are reasonable grounds for suspecting that—

(i) a controller or processor has failed or is failing as described in section 149(2), or

(ii) an offence under this Act has been or is being committed, and

(b) there are reasonable grounds for suspecting that evidence of the failure or of the commission of the offence is to be found on premises specified in the information or is capable of being viewed using equipment on such premises.

(2) The judge may grant a warrant to the Commissioner.

Issue of warrants in connection with assessment notices

2. (1) This paragraph applies if a judge of the High Court, a circuit judge or a District Judge (Magistrates' Courts) is satisfied by information on oath supplied by the Commissioner that a controller or processor has failed to comply with a requirement imposed by an assessment notice.

(2) The judge may, for the purpose of enabling the Commissioner to determine whether the controller or processor has complied or is complying with the data protection legislation, grant a warrant to the Commissioner in relation to premises that were specified in the assessment notice.

Restrictions on issuing warrants: processing for the special purposes

3. A judge must not issue a warrant under this Schedule in respect of personal data processed for the special purposes unless a determination under section 174 with respect to the data or the processing has taken effect.

Restrictions on issuing warrants: procedural requirements

4. (1) A judge must not issue a warrant under this Schedule unless satisfied that—
   (a) the conditions in sub-paragraphs (2) to (4) are met,
   (b) compliance with those conditions would defeat the object of entry to the premises in question, or
   (c) the Commissioner requires access to the premises in question urgently.

(2) The first condition is that the Commissioner has given 7 days' notice in writing to the occupier of the premises in question demanding access to the premises.

(3) The second condition is that—
   (a) access to the premises was demanded at a reasonable hour and was unreasonably refused, or
   (b) entry to the premises was granted but the occupier unreasonably refused to comply with a request by the Commissioner or the Commissioner's officers or staff to be allowed to do any of the things referred to in paragraph 5.

(4) The third condition is that, since the refusal, the occupier of the premises—
   (a) has been notified by the Commissioner of the application for the warrant, and
   (b) has had an opportunity to be heard by the judge on the question of whether or not the warrant should be issued.

(5) In determining whether the first condition is met, an assessment notice given to the occupier is to be disregarded.

Content of warrants

5. (1) A warrant issued under this Schedule must authorise the Commissioner or any of the Commissioner's officers or staff—
   (a) to enter the premises,
   (b) to search the premises, and
   (c) to inspect, examine, operate and test any equipment found on the premises which is used or intended to be used for the processing of personal data.

(2) A warrant issued under paragraph 1 must authorise the Commissioner or any of the Commissioner's officers or staff—
   (a) to inspect and seize any documents or other material found on the premises which may be evidence of the failure or offence mentioned in that paragraph,
   (b) to require any person on the premises to provide, in an appropriate form, a copy of information capable of being viewed using equipment on the premises which may be evidence of that failure or offence,
   (c) to require any person on the premises to provide an explanation of any document or other material found on the premises and of any information capable of being viewed using equipment on the premises, and
   (d) to require any person on the premises to provide such other information as may reasonably be required for the purpose of determining whether the controller or processor has failed or is failing as described in section 149(2).

(3) A warrant issued under paragraph 2 must authorise the Commissioner or any of the Commissioner's officers or staff—
   (a) to inspect and seize any documents or other material found on the premises which may enable the Commissioner to determine whether the controller or processor has complied or is complying with the data protection legislation,
   (b) to require any person on the premises to provide, in an appropriate form, a copy of information capable of being viewed using equipment on the premises which may enable the Commissioner to make such a determination,
   (c) to require any person on the premises to provide an explanation of any document or other material found on the premises and of any information capable of being viewed using equipment on the premises, and
   (d) to require any person on the premises to provide such other information as may reasonably be required for the purpose of determining whether the controller or processor has complied or is complying with the data protection legislation.

(4) A warrant issued under this Schedule must authorise the Commissioner or any of the Commissioner's officers or staff to do the things described in sub-paragraphs (1) to (3) at any time in the period of 7 days beginning with the day on which the warrant is issued.

(5) For the purposes of this paragraph, a copy of information is in an "appropriate form" if—
   (a) it can be taken away, and
   (b) it is visible and legible or it can readily be made visible and legible.

Copies of warrants

6. A judge who issues a warrant under this Schedule must—
   (a) issue two copies of it, and

(b)   certify them clearly as copies.

Execution of warrants: reasonable force

7. A person executing a warrant issued under this Schedule may use such reasonable force as may be necessary.

Execution of warrants: time when executed

8. A warrant issued under this Schedule may be executed only at a reasonable hour, unless it appears to the person executing it that there are grounds for suspecting that exercising it at a reasonable hour would defeat the object of the warrant.

Execution of warrants: occupier of premises

9. (1) If an occupier of the premises in respect of which a warrant is issued under this Schedule is present when the warrant is executed, the person executing the warrant must—
(a)   show the occupier the warrant, and
(b)   give the occupier a copy of it.

(2) Otherwise, a copy of the warrant must be left in a prominent place on the premises.

Execution of warrants: seizure of documents etc

10. (1) This paragraph applies where a person executing a warrant under this Schedule seizes something.

(2) The person must, on request—
(a)   give a receipt for it, and
(b)   give an occupier of the premises a copy of it.

(3) Sub-paragraph (2)(b) does not apply if the person executing the warrant considers that providing a copy would result in undue delay.

(4) Anything seized may be retained for so long as is necessary in all the circumstances.

Matters exempt from inspection and seizure: privileged communications

11. (1) The powers of inspection and seizure conferred by a warrant issued under this Schedule are not exercisable in respect of a communication which is made—
(a)   between a professional legal adviser and the adviser's client, and
(b)   in connection with the giving of legal advice to the client with respect to obligations, liabilities or rights under the data protection legislation.

(2) The powers of inspection and seizure conferred by a warrant issued under this Schedule are not exercisable in respect of a communication which is made—
(a)   between a professional legal adviser and the adviser's client or between such an adviser or client and another person,
(b)   in connection with or in contemplation of proceedings under or arising out of the data protection legislation, and
(c)   for the purposes of such proceedings.

(3) Sub-paragraphs (1) and (2) do not prevent the exercise of powers conferred by a warrant issued under this Schedule in respect of—
(a)   anything in the possession of a person other than the professional legal adviser or the adviser's client, or
(b)   anything held with the intention of furthering a criminal purpose.

(4) The references to a communication in sub-paragraphs (1) and (2) include—
(a)   a copy or other record of the communication, and
(b)   anything enclosed with or referred to in the communication if made as described in sub-paragraph (1)(b) or in sub-paragraph (2)(b) and (c).

(5) In sub-paragraphs (1) to (3), the references to the client of a professional legal adviser include a person acting on behalf of such a client.

Matters exempt from inspection and seizure: Parliamentary privilege

12. The powers of inspection and seizure conferred by a warrant issued under this Schedule are not exercisable where their exercise would involve an infringement of the privileges of either House of Parliament.

Partially exempt material

13. (1) This paragraph applies if a person in occupation of premises in respect of which a warrant is issued under this Schedule objects to the inspection or seizure of any material under the warrant on the grounds that it consists partly of matters in respect of which those powers are not exercisable.

(2) The person must, if the person executing the warrant so requests, provide that person with a copy of so much of the material as is not exempt from those powers.

Return of warrants

14. (1) Where a warrant issued under this Schedule is executed—
(a)   it must be returned to the court from which it was issued after being executed, and
(b)   the person by whom it is executed must write on the warrant a statement of the powers that have been exercised under the warrant.

(2) Where a warrant issued under this Schedule is not executed, it must be returned to the court from which it was issued within the time authorised for its execution.

Offences

15. (1) It is an offence for a person—
(a)   intentionally to obstruct a person in the execution of a warrant issued under this Schedule, or

(b) to fail without reasonable excuse to give a person executing such a warrant such assistance as the person may reasonably require for the execution of the warrant.

(2) It is an offence for a person—

(a) to make a statement in response to a requirement under paragraph 5(2)(c) or (d) or (3)(c) or (d) which the person knows to be false in a material respect, or

(b) recklessly to make a statement in response to such a requirement which is false in a material respect.

Self-incrimination

16. (1) An explanation given, or information provided, by a person in response to a requirement under paragraph 5(2)(c) or (d) or (3)(c) or (d) may only be used in evidence against that person—

(a) on a prosecution for an offence under a provision listed in sub-paragraph (2), or

(b) on a prosecution for any other offence where—

    (i) in giving evidence that person makes a statement inconsistent with that explanation or information, and

    (ii) evidence relating to that explanation or information is adduced, or a question relating to it is asked, by that person or on that person's behalf.

(2) Those provisions are—

(a) paragraph 15,

(b) section 5 of the Perjury Act 1911 (false statements made otherwise than on oath),

(c) section 44(2) of the Criminal Law (Consolidation) (Scotland) Act 1995 (false statements made otherwise than on oath), or

(d) Article 10 of the Perjury (Northern Ireland) Order 1979 (SI 1979/1714 (NI 19)) (false statutory declarations and other false unsworn statements).

Vessels, vehicles etc

17. In this Schedule—

(a) "premises" includes a vehicle, vessel or other means of transport, and

(b) references to the occupier of premises include the person in charge of a vehicle, vessel or other means of transport.

Scotland

18. In the application of this Schedule to Scotland—

(a) references to a judge of the High Court have effect as if they were references to a judge of the Court of Session,

(b) references to a circuit judge have effect as if they were references to the sheriff or the summary sheriff,

(c) references to information on oath have effect as if they were references to evidence on oath, and

(d) references to the court from which the warrant was issued have effect as if they were references to the sheriff clerk.

Northern Ireland

19. In the application of this Schedule to Northern Ireland—

(a) references to a circuit judge have effect as if they were references to a county court judge, and

(b) references to information on oath have effect as if they were references to a complaint on oath.

NOTES

Commencement: 25 May 2018 (see also the introductory notes to this Act preceding s 1 at **[1.71]**).

SCHEDULE 16
PENALTIES

Section 155

Meaning of "penalty"

[1.313]
1. In this Schedule, "penalty" means a penalty imposed by a penalty notice.

Notice of intent to impose penalty

2. (1) Before giving a person a penalty notice, the Commissioner must, by written notice (a "notice of intent") inform the person that the Commissioner intends to give a penalty notice.

(2) The Commissioner may not give a penalty notice to a person in reliance on a notice of intent after the end of the period of 6 months beginning when the notice of intent is given, subject to sub-paragraph (3).

(3) The period for giving a penalty notice to a person may be extended by agreement between the Commissioner and the person.

Contents of notice of intent

3. (1) A notice of intent must contain the following information—

(a) the name and address of the person to whom the Commissioner proposes to give a penalty notice;

(b) the reasons why the Commissioner proposes to give a penalty notice (see sub-paragraph (2));

(c) an indication of the amount of the penalty the Commissioner proposes to impose, including any aggravating or mitigating factors that the Commissioner proposes to take into account.

(2) The information required under sub-paragraph (1)(b) includes—

(a) a description of the circumstances of the failure, and

(b) where the notice is given in respect of a failure described in section 149(2), the nature of the personal data involved in the failure.

(3) A notice of intent must also—
  (a) state that the person may make written representations about the Commissioner's intention to give a penalty notice, and
  (b) specify the period within which such representations may be made.

(4) The period specified for making written representations must be a period of not less than 21 days beginning when the notice of intent is given.

(5) If the Commissioner considers that it is appropriate for the person to have an opportunity to make oral representations about the Commissioner's intention to give a penalty notice, the notice of intent must also—
  (a) state that the person may make such representations, and
  (b) specify the arrangements for making such representations and the time at which, or the period within which, they may be made.

Giving a penalty notice

4. (1) The Commissioner may not give a penalty notice before a time, or before the end of a period, specified in the notice of intent for making oral or written representations.

(2) When deciding whether to give a penalty notice to a person and determining the amount of the penalty, the Commissioner must consider any oral or written representations made by the person in accordance with the notice of intent.

Contents of penalty notice

5. (1) A penalty notice must contain the following information—
  (a) the name and address of the person to whom it is addressed;
  (b) details of the notice of intent given to the person;
  (c) whether the Commissioner received oral or written representations in accordance with the notice of intent;
  (d) the reasons why the Commissioner proposes to impose the penalty (see sub-paragraph (2));
  (e) the reasons for the amount of the penalty, including any aggravating or mitigating factors that the Commissioner has taken into account;
  (f) details of how the penalty is to be paid;
  (g) details of the rights of appeal under section 162;
  (h) details of the Commissioner's enforcement powers under this Schedule.

(2) The information required under sub-paragraph (1)(d) includes—
  (a) a description of the circumstances of the failure, and
  (b) where the notice is given in respect of a failure described in section 149(2), the nature of the personal data involved in the failure.

Period for payment of penalty

6. (1) A penalty must be paid to the Commissioner within the period specified in the penalty notice.

(2) The period specified must be a period of not less than 28 days beginning when the penalty notice is given.

Variation of penalty

7. (1) The Commissioner may vary a penalty notice by giving written notice (a "penalty variation notice") to the person to whom it was given.

(2) A penalty variation notice must specify—
  (a) the penalty notice concerned, and
  (b) how it is varied.

(3) A penalty variation notice may not—
  (a) reduce the period for payment of the penalty;
  (b) increase the amount of the penalty;
  (c) otherwise vary the penalty notice to the detriment of the person to whom it was given.

(4) If—
  (a) a penalty variation notice reduces the amount of the penalty, and
  (b) when that notice is given, an amount has already been paid that exceeds the amount of the reduced penalty,
the Commissioner must repay the excess.

Cancellation of penalty

8. (1) The Commissioner may cancel a penalty notice by giving written notice to the person to whom it was given.

(2) If a penalty notice is cancelled, the Commissioner—
  (a) may not take any further action under section 155 or this Schedule in relation to the failure to which that notice relates, and
  (b) must repay any amount that has been paid in accordance with that notice.

Enforcement of payment

9. (1) The Commissioner must not take action to recover a penalty unless—
  (a) the period specified in accordance with paragraph 6 has ended,
  (b) any appeals against the penalty notice have been decided or otherwise ended,
  (c) if the penalty notice has been varied, any appeals against the penalty variation notice have been decided or otherwise ended, and
  (d) the period for the person to whom the penalty notice was given to appeal against the penalty, and any variation of it, has ended.

(2) In England and Wales, a penalty is recoverable—
  (a) if the county court so orders, as if it were payable under an order of that court;

(b)   if the High Court so orders, as if it were payable under an order of that court.

(3) In Scotland, a penalty may be enforced in the same manner as an extract registered decree arbitral bearing a warrant for execution issued by the sheriff court of any sheriffdom in Scotland.

(4) In Northern Ireland, a penalty is recoverable—

    (a)   if a county court so orders, as if it were payable under an order of that court;

    (b)   if the High Court so orders, as if it were payable under an order of that court.

NOTES

Commencement: 25 May 2018 (see also the introductory notes to this Act preceding s 1 at **[1.71]**).

SCHEDULE 17
REVIEW OF PROCESSING OF PERSONAL DATA FOR THE PURPOSES OF JOURNALISM

Section 178

Interpretation

[1.314]

1. In this Schedule—

"relevant period" means—

    (a)   the period of 18 months beginning when the Commissioner starts the first review under section 178, and

    (b)   the period of 12 months beginning when the Commissioner starts a subsequent review under that section;

"the relevant review", in relation to a relevant period, means the review under section 178 which the Commissioner must produce a report about by the end of that period.

Information notices

2. (1) This paragraph applies where the Commissioner gives an information notice during a relevant period.

(2) If the information notice—

    (a)   states that, in the Commissioner's opinion, the information is required for the purposes of the relevant review, and

    (b)   gives the Commissioner's reasons for reaching that opinion,

subsections (5) and (6) of section 142 do not apply but the notice must not require the information to be provided before the end of the period of 24 hours beginning when the notice is given.

Assessment notices

3. (1) Sub-paragraph (2) applies where the Commissioner gives an assessment notice to a person during a relevant period.

(2) If the assessment notice—

    (a)   states that, in the Commissioner's opinion, it is necessary for the controller or processor to comply with a requirement in the notice for the purposes of the relevant review, and

    (b)   gives the Commissioner's reasons for reaching that opinion,

subsections (6) and (7) of section 146 do not apply but the notice must not require the controller or processor to comply with the requirement before the end of the period of 7 days beginning when the notice is given.

(3) During a relevant period, section 147 has effect as if for subsection (5) there were substituted—

"(5)   The Commissioner may not give a controller or processor an assessment notice with respect to the processing of personal data for the special purposes unless a determination under section 174 with respect to the data or the processing has taken effect."

Applications in respect of urgent notices

4. Section 164 applies where an information notice or assessment notice contains a statement under paragraph 2(2)(a) or 3(2)(a) as it applies where such a notice contains a statement under section 142(7)(a) or 146(8)(a).

NOTES

Commencement: 23 July 2018 (see also the introductory notes to this Act preceding s 1 at **[1.71]**).

SCHEDULE 18
RELEVANT RECORDS

Section 184

Relevant records

[1.315]

1. (1) In section 184, "relevant record" means—

    (a)   a relevant health record (see paragraph 2),

    (b)   a relevant record relating to a conviction or caution (see paragraph 3), or

    (c)   a relevant record relating to statutory functions (see paragraph 4).

(2) A record is not a "relevant record" to the extent that it relates, or is to relate, only to personal data which falls within [Article 2(1A) of the UK GDPR] (manual unstructured personal data held by FOI public authorities).

Relevant health records

2. "Relevant health record" means a health record which has been or is to be obtained by a data subject in the exercise of a data subject access right.

Relevant records relating to a conviction or caution

3. (1) "Relevant record relating to a conviction or caution" means a record which—
  (a) has been or is to be obtained by a data subject in the exercise of a data subject access right from a person listed in sub-paragraph (2), and
  (b) contains information relating to a conviction or caution.

(2) Those persons are—
  (a) the chief constable of a police force maintained under section 2 of the Police Act 1996;
  (b) the Commissioner of Police of the Metropolis;
  (c) the Commissioner of Police for the City of London;
  (d) the Chief Constable of the Police Service of Northern Ireland;
  (e) the chief constable of the Police Service of Scotland;
  (f) the Director General of the National Crime Agency;
  (g) the Secretary of State.

(3) In this paragraph—
  "caution" means a caution given to a person in England and Wales or Northern Ireland in respect of an offence which, at the time when the caution is given, is admitted;
  "conviction" has the same meaning as in the Rehabilitation of Offenders Act 1974 or the Rehabilitation of Offenders (Northern Ireland) Order 1978 (SI 1978/1908 (NI 27)).

Relevant records relating to statutory functions

4. (1) "Relevant record relating to statutory functions" means a record which—
  (a) has been or is to be obtained by a data subject in the exercise of a data subject access right from a person listed in sub-paragraph (2), and
  (b) contains information relating to a relevant function in relation to that person.

(2) Those persons are—
  (a) the Secretary of State;
  (b) the Department for Communities in Northern Ireland;
  (c) the Department of Justice in Northern Ireland;
  (d) the Scottish Ministers;
  (e) the Disclosure and Barring Service.

(3) In relation to the Secretary of State, the "relevant functions" are—
  (a) the Secretary of State's functions in relation to a person sentenced to detention under—
      (i) section 92 of the Powers of Criminal Courts (Sentencing) Act 2000,
      [(ia) section 260 of the Sentencing Code,]
      (ii) section 205(2) or 208 of the Criminal Procedure (Scotland) Act 1995, or
      (iii) Article 45 of the Criminal Justice (Children) (Northern Ireland) Order 1998 (SI 1998/1504 (NI 9));
  (b) the Secretary of State's functions in relation to a person imprisoned or detained under—
      (i) the Prison Act 1952,
      (ii) the Prisons (Scotland) Act 1989, or
      (iii) the Prison Act (Northern Ireland) 1953 (c 18 (NI));
  (c) the Secretary of State's functions under—
      (i) the Social Security Contributions and Benefits Act 1992,
      (ii) the Social Security Administration Act 1992,
      (iii) the Jobseekers Act 1995,
      (iv) Part 5 of the Police Act 1997,
      (v) Part 1 of the Welfare Reform Act 2007, or
      (vi) Part 1 of the Welfare Reform Act 2012.

(4) In relation to the Department for Communities in Northern Ireland, the "relevant functions" are its functions under—
  (a) the Social Security Contributions and Benefits (Northern Ireland) Act 1992,
  (b) the Social Security Administration (Northern Ireland) Act 1992,
  (c) the Jobseekers (Northern Ireland) Order 1995 (SI 1995/2705 (NI 15)), or
  (d) Part 1 of the Welfare Reform Act (Northern Ireland) 2007 (c 2 (NI)).

(5) In relation to the Department of Justice in Northern Ireland, the "relevant functions" are its functions under Part 5 of the Police Act 1997.

(6) In relation to the Scottish Ministers, the "relevant functions" are their functions under
  (a) Part 5 of the Police Act 1997, or
  (b) Parts 1 and 2 of the Protection of Vulnerable Groups (Scotland) Act 2007 (asp 14).

(7) In relation to the Disclosure and Barring Service, the "relevant functions" are its functions under—
  (a) Part 5 of the Police Act 1997,
  (b) the Safeguarding Vulnerable Groups Act 2006, or
  (c) the Safeguarding Vulnerable Groups (Northern Ireland) Order 2007 (SI 2007/1351 (NI 11)).

Data subject access right

5. In this Schedule, "data subject access right" means a right under—
  (a) Article 15 of the [UK GDPR] (right of access by the data subject);
  (b) Article 20 of the [UK GDPR] (right to data portability);
  (c) section 45 of this Act (law enforcement processing: right of access by the data subject);
  (d) section 94 of this Act (intelligence services processing: right of access by the data subject).

Records stating that personal data is not processed

6. For the purposes of this Schedule, a record which states that a controller is not processing personal data relating to a particular matter is to be taken to be a record containing information relating to that matter.

Power to amend

7. (1) The Secretary of State may by regulations amend this Schedule.

(2) Regulations under this paragraph are subject to the affirmative resolution procedure.

NOTES
Commencement: 25 May 2018 (see also the introductory notes to this Act preceding s 1 at **[1.71]**).
The words in square brackets in paras 1, 5 were substituted by the Data Protection, Privacy and Electronic Communications (Amendments etc) (EU Exit) Regulations 2019, SI 2019/419, reg 4, Sch 2, paras 1, 99.
In para 4, sub-para (3)(a)(ia) was inserted by the Sentencing Act 2020, s 410, Sch 24, Pt 1, para 297.

SCHEDULE 19
MINOR AND CONSEQUENTIAL AMENDMENTS

Section 211

PARTS 1 AND 2

(Part 1 of this Schedule contains amendments to primary legislation (including the repeal of the Data Protection Act 1998). Part 2 contains amendments to other legislation. In so far as relevant to this work, they have been incorporated at the appropriate place.)

PART 3 MODIFICATIONS
Introduction

[1.316]
430. (1) Unless the context otherwise requires, legislation described in sub-paragraph (2) has effect on and after the day on which this Part of this Schedule comes into force as if it were modified in accordance with this Part of this Schedule.

(2) That legislation is—
  (a) subordinate legislation made before the day on which this Part of this Schedule comes into force;
  (b) primary legislation that is passed or made before the end of the Session in which this Act is passed.

(3) In this Part of this Schedule—
  "primary legislation" has the meaning given in section 211(7);
  "references" includes any references, however expressed.

General modifications

431. (1) References to a particular provision of, or made under, the Data Protection Act 1998 have effect as references to the equivalent provision or provisions of, or made under, the data protection legislation.

(2) Other references to the Data Protection Act 1998 have effect as references to the data protection legislation.

(3) References to disclosure, use or other processing of information that is prohibited or restricted by an enactment which include disclosure, use or other processing of information that is prohibited or restricted by the Data Protection Act 1998 have effect as if they included disclosure, use or other processing of information that is prohibited or restricted by [the UK GDPR].

Specific modification of references to terms used in the Data Protection Act 1998

432. (1) References to personal data, and to the processing of such data, as defined in the Data Protection Act 1998, have effect as references to personal data, and to the processing of such data, as defined for the purposes of Parts 5 to 7 of this Act (see section 3(2), (4) and (14)).

(2) References to processing as defined in the Data Protection Act 1998, in relation to information, have effect as references to processing as defined in section 3(4).

(3) References to a data subject as defined in the Data Protection Act 1998 have effect as references to a data subject as defined in section 3(5).

(4) References to a data controller as defined in the Data Protection Act 1998 have effect as references to a controller as defined for the purposes of Parts 5 to 7 of this Act (see section 3(6) and (14)).

(5) References to the data protection principles set out in the Data Protection Act 1998 have effect as references to the principles set out in—
  (a) Article 5(1) of [the UK GDPR], and
  (b) sections 34(1) and 85(1) of this Act.

(6) References to direct marketing as defined in section 11 of the Data Protection Act 1998 have effect as references to direct marketing as defined in section 122 of this Act.

(7) References to a health professional within the meaning of section 69(1) of the Data Protection Act 1998 have effect as references to a health professional within the meaning of section 204 of this Act.

(8) References to a health record within the meaning of section 68(2) of the Data Protection Act 1998 have effect as references to a health record within the meaning of section 205 of this Act.

NOTES
Commencement: 25 May 2018 (see also the introductory notes to this Act preceding s 1 at **[1.71]**).

The words in square brackets in paras 431, 432 were substituted by the Data Protection, Privacy and Electronic Communications (Amendments etc) (EU Exit) Regulations 2019, SI 2019/419, reg 4, Sch 2, paras 1, 100.

PART 4 SUPPLEMENTARY

Definitions

[1.317]

433. Section 3(14) does not apply to this Schedule.

Provision inserted in subordinate legislation by this Schedule

434. Provision inserted into subordinate legislation by this Schedule may be amended or revoked as if it had been inserted using the power under which the subordinate legislation was originally made.

NOTES

Commencement: 25 May 2018 (see also the introductory notes to this Act preceding s 1 at **[1.71]**).

SCHEDULE 20
TRANSITIONAL PROVISION ETC

Section 213

PART 1 GENERAL

Interpretation

[1.318]

1. (1) In this Schedule—

"the 1984 Act" means the Data Protection Act 1984;

"the 1998 Act" means the Data Protection Act 1998;

"the 2014 Regulations" means the Criminal Justice and Data Protection (Protocol No 36) Regulations 2014 (SI 2014/3141);

"data controller" has the same meaning as in the 1998 Act (see section 1 of that Act);

"the old data protection principles" means the principles set out in—

    (a)   Part 1 of Schedule 1 to the 1998 Act, and

    (b)   regulation 30 of the 2014 Regulations.

(2) A provision of the 1998 Act that has effect by virtue of this Schedule is not, by virtue of that, part of the data protection legislation (as defined in section 3).

NOTES

Commencement: 25 May 2018 (see also the introductory notes to this Act preceding s 1 at **[1.71]**).

PART 2 RIGHTS OF DATA SUBJECTS

Right of access to personal data under the 1998 Act

[1.319]

2. (1) The repeal of sections 7 to 9A of the 1998 Act (right of access to personal data) does not affect the application of those sections after the relevant time in a case in which a data controller received a request under section 7 of that Act (right of access to personal data) before the relevant time.

(2) The repeal of sections 7 and 8 of the 1998 Act and the revocation of regulation 44 of the 2014 Regulations (which applies those sections with modifications) do not affect the application of those sections and that regulation after the relevant time in a case in which a UK competent authority received a request under section 7 of the 1998 Act (as applied by that regulation) before the relevant time.

(3) The revocation of the relevant regulations, or their amendment by Schedule 19 to this Act, and the repeals and revocation mentioned in sub-paragraphs (1) and (2), do not affect the application of the relevant regulations after the relevant time in a case described in those sub-paragraphs.

(4) In this paragraph—

"the relevant regulations" means—

    (a)   the Data Protection (Subject Access) (Fees and Miscellaneous Provisions) Regulations 2000 (SI 2000/191);

    (b)   regulation 4 of, and Schedule 1 to, the Consumer Credit (Credit Reference Agency) Regulations 2000 (SI 2000/290);

    (c)   regulation 3 of the Freedom of Information and Data Protection (Appropriate Limit and Fees) Regulations 2004 (SI 2004/3244);

"the relevant time" means the time when the repeal of section 7 of the 1998 Act comes into force;

"UK competent authority" has the same meaning as in Part 4 of the 2014 Regulations (see regulation 27 of those Regulations).

Right to prevent processing likely to cause damage or distress under the 1998 Act

3. (1) The repeal of section 10 of the 1998 Act (right to prevent processing likely to cause damage or distress) does not affect the application of that section after the relevant time in a case in which an individual gave notice in writing to a data controller under that section before the relevant time.

(2) In this paragraph, "the relevant time" means the time when the repeal of section 10 of the 1998 Act comes into force.

Right to prevent processing for purposes of direct marketing under the 1998 Act

4. (1) The repeal of section 11 of the 1998 Act (right to prevent processing for purposes of direct marketing) does not affect the application of that section after the relevant time in a case in which an individual gave notice in writing to a data controller under that section before the relevant time.

(2) In this paragraph, "the relevant time" means the time when the repeal of section 11 of the 1998 Act comes into force.

Automated processing under the 1998 Act

5. (1) The repeal of section 12 of the 1998 Act (rights in relation to automated decision-taking) does not affect the application of that section after the relevant time in relation to a decision taken by a person before that time if—
  (a) in taking the decision the person failed to comply with section 12(1) of the 1998 Act, or
  (b) at the relevant time—
      (i) the person had not taken all of the steps required under section 12(2) or (3) of the 1998 Act, or
      (ii) the period specified in section 12(2)(b) of the 1998 Act (for an individual to require a person to reconsider a decision) had not expired.

(2) In this paragraph, "the relevant time" means the time when the repeal of section 12 of the 1998 Act comes into force.

Compensation for contravention of the 1998 Act or Part 4 of the 2014 Regulations

6. (1) The repeal of section 13 of the 1998 Act (compensation for failure to comply with certain requirements) does not affect the application of that section after the relevant time in relation to damage or distress suffered at any time by reason of an act or omission before the relevant time.

(2) The revocation of regulation 45 of the 2014 Regulations (right to compensation) does not affect the application of that regulation after the relevant time in relation to damage or distress suffered at any time by reason of an act or omission before the relevant time.

(3) "The relevant time" means—
  (a) in sub-paragraph (1), the time when the repeal of section 13 of the 1998 Act comes into force;
  (b) in sub-paragraph (2), the time when the revocation of regulation 45 of the 2014 Regulation comes into force.

Rectification, blocking, erasure and destruction under the 1998 Act

7. (1) The repeal of section 14(1) to (3) and (6) of the 1998 Act (rectification, blocking, erasure and destruction of inaccurate personal data) does not affect the application of those provisions after the relevant time in a case in which an application was made under subsection (1) of that section before the relevant time.

(2) The repeal of section 14(4) to (6) of the 1998 Act (rectification, blocking, erasure and destruction: risk of further contravention in circumstances entitling data subject to compensation under section 13 of the 1998 Act) does not affect the application of those provisions after the relevant time in a case in which an application was made under subsection (4) of that section before the relevant time.

(3) In this paragraph, "the relevant time" means the time when the repeal of section 14 of the 1998 Act comes into force.

Jurisdiction and procedure under the 1998 Act

8. The repeal of section 15 of the 1998 Act (jurisdiction and procedure) does not affect the application of that section in connection with sections 7 to 14 of the 1998 Act as they have effect by virtue of this Schedule.

Exemptions under the 1998 Act

9. (1) The repeal of Part 4 of the 1998 Act (exemptions) does not affect the application of that Part after the relevant time in connection with a provision of Part 2 of the 1998 Act as it has effect after that time by virtue of paragraphs 2 to 7 of this Schedule.

(2) The revocation of the relevant Orders, and the repeal mentioned in sub-paragraph (1), do not affect the application of the relevant Orders after the relevant time in connection with a provision of Part 2 of the 1998 Act as it has effect as described in sub-paragraph (1).

(3) In this paragraph—
"the relevant Orders" means—
      (a) the Data Protection (Corporate Finance Exemption) Order 2000 (SI 2000/184);
      (b) the Data Protection (Subject Access Modification) (Health) Order 2000 (SI 2000/413);
      (c) the Data Protection (Subject Access Modification) (Education) Order 2000 (SI 2000/414);
      (d) the Data Protection (Subject Access Modification) (Social Work) Order 2000 (SI 2000/415);
      (e) the Data Protection (Crown Appointments) Order 2000 (SI 2000/416);
      (f) Data Protection (Miscellaneous Subject Access Exemptions) Order 2000 (SI 2000/419);
      (g) Data Protection (Designated Codes of Practice) (No 2) Order 2000 (SI 2000/1864);
"the relevant time" means the time when the repeal of the provision of Part 2 of the 1998 Act in question comes into force.

(4) As regards certificates issued under section 28(2) of the 1998 Act, see Part 5 of this Schedule.

Prohibition by this Act of requirement to produce relevant records

10. (1) In Schedule 18 to this Act, references to a record obtained in the exercise of a data subject access right include a record obtained at any time in the exercise of a right under section 7 of the 1998 Act.

(2) In section 184 of this Act, references to a "relevant record" include a record which does not fall within the definition in Schedule 18 to this Act (read with sub-paragraph (1)) but which, immediately before the relevant time, was a "relevant record" for the purposes of section 56 of the 1998 Act.

(3) In this paragraph, "the relevant time" means the time when the repeal of section 56 of the 1998 Act comes into force.

Avoidance under this Act of certain contractual terms relating to health records

11. In section 185 of this Act, references to a record obtained in the exercise of a data subject access right include a record obtained at any time in the exercise of a right under section 7 of the 1998 Act.

NOTES

Commencement: 25 May 2018 (see also the introductory notes to this Act preceding s 1 at **[1.71]**).

PART 3 THE [UK GDPR] AND PART 2 OF THIS ACT

Exemptions from the [UK GDPR]: restrictions of rules in Articles 13 to 15 of the [UK GDPR]

[1.320]
12. In paragraph 20(2) of Schedule 2 to this Act (self-incrimination), the reference to an offence under this Act includes an offence under the 1998 Act or the 1984 Act.

Manual unstructured data held by FOI public authorities

13. Until the first regulations under section 24(8) of this Act come into force, "the appropriate maximum" for the purposes of that section is—
  (a) where the controller is a public authority listed in Part 1 of Schedule 1 to the Freedom of Information Act 2000, £600, and
  (b) otherwise, £450.

NOTES

Commencement: 25 May 2018 (see also the introductory notes to this Act preceding s 1 at **[1.71]**).
  The words in square brackets in the Part heading and the heading above para 12 were substituted by the Data Protection, Privacy and Electronic Communications (Amendments etc) (EU Exit) Regulations 2019, SI 2019/419, reg 4, Sch 2, paras 1, 101(1)–(3).

PART 4 LAW ENFORCEMENT AND INTELLIGENCE SERVICES PROCESSING

Logging

[1.321]
14. (1) In relation to an automated processing system set up before 6 May 2016, subsections (1) to (3) of section 62 of this Act do not apply if and to the extent that compliance with them would involve disproportionate effort.

(2) Sub-paragraph (1) ceases to have effect at the beginning of 6 May 2023.

Regulation 50 of the 2014 Regulations (disapplication of the 1998 Act)

15. Nothing in this Schedule, read with the revocation of regulation 50 of the 2014 Regulations, has the effect of applying a provision of the 1998 Act to the processing of personal data to which Part 4 of the 2014 Regulations applies in a case in which that provision did not apply before the revocation of that regulation.

Maximum fee for data subject access requests to intelligence services

16. Until the first regulations under section 94(4)(b) of this Act come into force, the maximum amount of a fee that may be required by a controller under that section is £10.

NOTES

Commencement: 25 May 2018 (see also the introductory notes to this Act preceding s 1 at **[1.71]**).

PART 5 NATIONAL SECURITY CERTIFICATES

National security certificates: processing of personal data under the 1998 Act

[1.322]
17. (1) The repeal of section 28(2) to (12) of the 1998 Act does not affect the application of those provisions after the relevant time with respect to the processing of personal data to which the 1998 Act (including as it has effect by virtue of this Schedule) applies.

(2) A certificate issued under section 28(2) of the 1998 Act continues to have effect after the relevant time with respect to the processing of personal data to which the 1998 Act (including as it has effect by virtue of this Schedule) applies.

(3) Where a certificate continues to have effect under sub-paragraph (2) after the relevant time, it may be revoked or quashed in accordance with section 28 of the 1998 Act after the relevant time.

(4) In this paragraph, "the relevant time" means the time when the repeal of section 28 of the 1998 Act comes into force.

National security certificates: processing of personal data under the 2018 Act

18. (1) This paragraph applies to a certificate issued under section 28(2) of the 1998 Act (an "old certificate") which has effect immediately before the relevant time.

(2) If and to the extent that the old certificate provides protection with respect to personal data which corresponds to protection that could be provided by a certificate issued under section 27, 79 or 111 of this Act, the old certificate also has effect to that extent after the relevant time as if—
  (a) it were a certificate issued under one or more of sections 27, 79 and 111 (as the case may be),
  (b) it provided protection in respect of that personal data in relation to the corresponding provisions of this Act or the [UK GDPR], and
  (c) where it has effect as a certificate issued under section 79, it certified that each restriction in question is a necessary and proportionate measure to protect national security.

(3) Where an old certificate also has effect as if it were a certificate issued under one or more of sections 27, 79 and 111, that section has, or those sections have, effect accordingly in relation to the certificate.

(4) Where an old certificate has an extended effect because of sub-paragraph (2), section 130 of this Act does not apply in relation to it.

(5) An old certificate that has an extended effect because of sub-paragraph (2) provides protection only with respect to the processing of personal data that occurs during the period of 1 year beginning with the relevant time (and a Minister of the Crown may curtail that protection by wholly or partly revoking the old certificate).

(6) For the purposes of this paragraph—
   (a) a reference to the protection provided by a certificate issued under—
      (i) section 28(2) of the 1998 Act, or
      (ii) section 27, 79 or 111 of this Act,
      is a reference to the effect of the evidence that is provided by the certificate;
   (b) protection provided by a certificate under section 28(2) of the 1998 Act is to be regarded as corresponding to protection that could be provided by a certificate under section 27, 79 or 111 of this Act where, in respect of provision in the 1998 Act to which the certificate under section 28(2) relates, there is corresponding provision in this Act or the [UK GDPR] to which a certificate under section 27, 79 or 111 could relate.

(7) In this paragraph, "the relevant time" means the time when the repeal of section 28 of the 1998 Act comes into force.

[(8) In this paragraph, references to the UK GDPR do not include the EU GDPR as it was directly applicable to the United Kingdom before IP completion day (see paragraph 2 of Schedule 21).]

NOTES
Commencement: 25 May 2018 (see also the introductory notes to this Act preceding s 1 at **[1.71]**).
Para 18: the words in square brackets in sub-paras (2)(b) and (6)(b) were substituted, and sub-para (8) was added, by the Data Protection, Privacy and Electronic Communications (Amendments etc) (EU Exit) Regulations 2019, SI 2019/419, reg 4, Sch 2, paras 1, 101(1), (4). Note that Sch 2, para 101 to the 2019 Regulations was amended by the Data Protection, Privacy and Electronic Communications (Amendments etc) (EU Exit) Regulations 2020, SI 2020/1586, reg 5 (and the effect of the amendment has been incorporated in the text set out above).

PART 6 THE INFORMATION COMMISSIONER
Appointment etc
[1.323]
19. (1) On and after the relevant day, the individual who was the Commissioner immediately before that day—
   (a) continues to be the Commissioner,
   (b) is to be treated as having been appointed under Schedule 12 to this Act, and
   (c) holds office for the period—
      (i) beginning with the relevant day, and
      (ii) lasting for 7 years less a period equal to the individual's pre-commencement term.

(2) On and after the relevant day, a resolution passed by the House of Commons for the purposes of paragraph 3 of Schedule 5 to the 1998 Act (salary and pension of Commissioner), and not superseded before that day, is to be treated as having been passed for the purposes of paragraph 4 of Schedule 12 to this Act.

(3) In this paragraph—
   "pre-commencement term", in relation to an individual, means the period during which the individual was the Commissioner before the relevant day;
   "the relevant day" means the day on which Schedule 12 to this Act comes into force.

Accounts
20. (1) The repeal of paragraph 10 of Schedule 5 to the 1998 Act does not affect the duties of the Commissioner and the Comptroller and Auditor General under that paragraph in respect of the Commissioner's statement of account for the financial year beginning with 1 April 2017.

(2) The Commissioner's duty under paragraph 11 of Schedule 12 to this Act to prepare a statement of account for each financial year includes a duty to do so for the financial year beginning with 1 April 2018.

Annual report
21. (1) The repeal of section 52(1) of the 1998 Act (annual report) does not affect the Commissioner's duty under that subsection to produce a general report on the exercise of the Commissioner's functions under the 1998 Act during the period of 1 year beginning with 1 April 2017 and to lay it before Parliament.

(2) The repeal of section 49 of the Freedom of Information Act 2000 (annual report) does not affect the Commissioner's duty under that section to produce a general report on the exercise of the Commissioner's functions under that Act during the period of 1 year beginning with 1 April 2017 and to lay it before Parliament.

(3) The first report produced by the Commissioner under section 139 of this Act must relate to the period of 1 year beginning with 1 April 2018.

Fees etc received by the Commissioner
22. (1) The repeal of Schedule 5 to the 1998 Act (Information Commissioner) does not affect the application of paragraph 9 of that Schedule after the relevant time to amounts received by the Commissioner before the relevant time.

(2) In this paragraph, "the relevant time" means the time when the repeal of Schedule 5 to the 1998 Act comes into force.

23. Paragraph 10 of Schedule 12 to this Act applies only to amounts received by the Commissioner after the time when that Schedule comes into force.

Functions in connection with the Data Protection Convention

24. (1) The repeal of section 54(2) of the 1998 Act (functions to be discharged by the Commissioner for the purposes of Article 13 of the Data Protection Convention), and the revocation of the Data Protection (Functions of Designated Authority) Order 2000 (SI 2000/186), do not affect the application of articles 1 to 5 of that Order after the relevant time in relation to a request described in those articles which was made before that time.

(2) The references in paragraph 9 of Schedule 14 to this Act (Data Protection Convention: restrictions on use of information) to requests made or received by the Commissioner under paragraph 6 or 7 of that Schedule include a request made or received by the Commissioner under article 3 or 4 of the Data Protection (Functions of Designated Authority) Order 2000 (SI 2000/186).

(3) The repeal of section 54(7) of the 1998 Act (duty to notify the European Commission of certain approvals and authorisations) does not affect the application of that provision after the relevant time in relation to an approval or authorisation granted before the relevant time.

(4) In this paragraph, "the relevant time" means the time when the repeal of section 54 of the 1998 Act comes into force.

Co-operation with the European Commission: transfers of personal data outside the EEA

25. (1) The repeal of section 54(3) of the 1998 Act (co-operation by the Commissioner with the European Commission etc), and the revocation of the Data Protection (International Co-operation) Order 2000 (SI 2000/190), do not affect the application of articles 1 to 4 of that Order after the relevant time in relation to transfers that took place before the relevant time.

(2) In this paragraph—

"the relevant time" means the time when the repeal of section 54 of the 1998 Act comes into force;

"transfer" has the meaning given in article 2 of the Data Protection (International Co-operation) Order 2000 (SI 2000/190).

Charges payable to the Commissioner by controllers

26. (1) The Data Protection (Charges and Information) Regulations 2018 (SI 2018/480) have effect after the relevant time (until revoked) as if they were made under section 137 of this Act.

(2) In this paragraph, "the relevant time" means the time when section 137 of this Act comes into force.

Requests for assessment

27. (1) The repeal of section 42 of the 1998 Act (requests for assessment) does not affect the application of that section after the relevant time in a case in which the Commissioner received a request under that section before the relevant time, subject to sub-paragraph (2).

(2) The Commissioner is only required to make an assessment of acts and omissions that took place before the relevant time.

(3) In this paragraph, "the relevant time" means the time when the repeal of section 42 of the 1998 Act comes into force.

Codes of practice

28. (1) The repeal of section 52E of the 1998 Act (effect of codes of practice) does not affect the application of that section after the relevant time in relation to legal proceedings or to the exercise of the Commissioner's functions under the 1998 Act as it has effect by virtue of this Schedule.

(2) In section 52E of the 1998 Act, as it has effect by virtue of this paragraph, the references to the 1998 Act include that Act as it has effect by virtue of this Schedule.

(3) For the purposes of subsection (3) of that section, as it has effect by virtue of this paragraph, the data-sharing code and direct marketing code in force immediately before the relevant time are to be treated as having continued in force after that time.

(4) In this paragraph—

"the data-sharing code" and "the direct marketing code" mean the codes respectively prepared under sections 52A and 52AA of the 1998 Act and issued under section 52B(5) of that Act;

"the relevant time" means the time when the repeal of section 52E of the 1998 Act comes into force.

NOTES

Commencement: 25 May 2018 (see also the introductory notes to this Act preceding s 1 at **[1.71]**).

PART 7 ENFORCEMENT ETC UNDER THE 1998 ACT

Interpretation of this Part

[1.324]

29. (1) In this Part of this Schedule, references to contravention of the sixth data protection principle sections are to relevant contravention of any of sections 7, 10, 11 or 12 of the 1998 Act, as they continue to have effect by virtue of this Schedule after their repeal (and references to compliance with the sixth data protection principle sections are to be read accordingly).

(2) In sub-paragraph (1), "relevant contravention" means contravention in a manner described in paragraph 8 of Part 2 of Schedule 1 to the 1998 Act (sixth data protection principle).

Information notices

30. (1) The repeal of section 43 of the 1998 Act (information notices) does not affect the application of that section after the relevant time in a case in which—

(a) the Commissioner served a notice under that section before the relevant time (and did not cancel it before that time), or

(b) the Commissioner requires information after the relevant time for the purposes of—

    (i) responding to a request made under section 42 of the 1998 Act before that time,

    (ii) determining whether a data controller complied with the old data protection principles before that time, or

    (iii) determining whether a data controller complied with the sixth data protection principle sections after that time.

(2) In section 43 of the 1998 Act, as it has effect by virtue of this paragraph—

(a) the reference to an offence under section 47 of the 1998 Act includes an offence under section 144 of this Act, and

(b) the references to an offence under the 1998 Act include an offence under this Act.

(3) In this paragraph, "the relevant time" means the time when the repeal of section 43 of the 1998 Act comes into force.

Special information notices

31. (1) The repeal of section 44 of the 1998 Act (special information notices) does not affect the application of that section after the relevant time in a case in which—

(a) the Commissioner served a notice under that section before the relevant time (and did not cancel it before that time), or

(b) the Commissioner requires information after the relevant time for the purposes of—

    (i) responding to a request made under section 42 of the 1998 Act before that time, or

    (ii) ascertaining whether section 44(2)(a) or (b) of the 1998 Act was satisfied before that time.

(2) In section 44 of the 1998 Act, as it has effect by virtue of this paragraph—

(a) the reference to an offence under section 47 of the 1998 Act includes an offence under section 144 of this Act, and

(b) the references to an offence under the 1998 Act include an offence under this Act.

(3) In this paragraph, "the relevant time" means the time when the repeal of section 44 of the 1998 Act comes into force.

Assessment notices

32. (1) The repeal of sections 41A and 41B of the 1998 Act (assessment notices) does not affect the application of those sections after the relevant time in a case in which—

(a) the Commissioner served a notice under section 41A of the 1998 Act before the relevant time (and did not cancel it before that time), or

(b) the Commissioner considers it appropriate, after the relevant time, to investigate—

    (i) whether a data controller complied with the old data protection principles before that time, or

    (ii) whether a data controller complied with the sixth data protection principle sections after that time.

(2) The revocation of the Data Protection (Assessment Notices) (Designation of National Health Service Bodies) Order 2014 (SI 2014/3282), and the repeals mentioned in sub-paragraph (1), do not affect the application of that Order in a case described in sub-paragraph (1).

(3) Sub-paragraph (1) does not enable the Secretary of State, after the relevant time, to make an order under section 41A(2)(b) or (c) of the 1998 Act (data controllers on whom an assessment notice may be served) designating a public authority or person for the purposes of that section.

(4) Section 41A of the 1998 Act, as it has effect by virtue of sub-paragraph (1), has effect as if subsections (8) and (11) (duty to review designation orders) were omitted.

(5) The repeal of section 41C of the 1998 Act (code of practice about assessment notice) does not affect the application, after the relevant time, of the code issued under that section and in force immediately before the relevant time in relation to the exercise of the Commissioner's functions under and in connection with section 41A of the 1998 Act, as it has effect by virtue of sub-paragraph (1).

(6) In this paragraph, "the relevant time" means the time when the repeal of section 41A of the 1998 Act comes into force.

Enforcement notices

33. (1) The repeal of sections 40 and 41 of the 1998 Act (enforcement notices) does not affect the application of those sections after the relevant time in a case in which—

(a) the Commissioner served a notice under section 40 of the 1998 Act before the relevant time (and did not cancel it before that time), or

(b) the Commissioner is satisfied, after that time, that a data controller—

    (i) contravened the old data protection principles before that time, or

    (ii) contravened the sixth data protection principle sections after that time.

(2) In this paragraph, "the relevant time" means the time when the repeal of section 40 of the 1998 Act comes into force.

Determination by Commissioner as to the special purposes

34. (1) The repeal of section 45 of the 1998 Act (determination by Commissioner as to the special purposes) does not affect the application of that section after the relevant time in a case in which—

(a) the Commissioner made a determination under that section before the relevant time, or

(b) the Commissioner considers it appropriate, after the relevant time, to make a determination under that section.

(2) In this paragraph, "the relevant time" means the time when the repeal of section 45 of the 1998 Act comes into force.

Restriction on enforcement in case of processing for the special purposes

35. (1) The repeal of section 46 of the 1998 Act (restriction on enforcement in case of processing for the special purposes) does not affect the application of that section after the relevant time in relation to an enforcement notice or information notice served under the 1998 Act—

(a) before the relevant time, or

(b) after the relevant time in reliance on this Schedule.

(2) In this paragraph, "the relevant time" means the time when the repeal of section 46 of the 1998 Act comes into force.

Offences

36. (1) The repeal of sections 47, 60 and 61 of the 1998 Act (offences of failing to comply with certain notices and of providing false information etc in response to a notice) does not affect the application of those sections after the relevant time in connection with an information notice, special information notice or enforcement notice served under Part 5 of the 1998 Act—

(a) before the relevant time, or

(b) after that time in reliance on this Schedule.

(2) In this paragraph, "the relevant time" means the time when the repeal of section 47 of the 1998 Act comes into force.

Powers of entry

37. (1) The repeal of sections 50, 60 and 61 of, and Schedule 9 to, the 1998 Act (powers of entry) does not affect the application of those provisions after the relevant time in a case in which—

(a) a warrant issued under that Schedule was in force immediately before the relevant time,

(b) before the relevant time, the Commissioner supplied information on oath for the purposes of obtaining a warrant under that Schedule but that had not been considered by a circuit judge or a District Judge (Magistrates' Courts), or

(c) after the relevant time, the Commissioner supplies information on oath to a circuit judge or a District Judge (Magistrates' Courts) in respect of—

    (i) a contravention of the old data protection principles before the relevant time;

    (ii) a contravention of the sixth data protection principle sections after the relevant time;

    (iii) the commission of an offence under a provision of the 1998 Act (including as the provision has effect by virtue of this Schedule);

    (iv) a failure to comply with a requirement imposed by an assessment notice issued under section 41A the 1998 Act (including as it has effect by virtue of this Schedule).

(2) In paragraph 16 of Schedule 9 to the 1998 Act, as it has effect by virtue of this paragraph, the reference to an offence under paragraph 12 of that Schedule includes an offence under paragraph 15 of Schedule 15 to this Act.

(3) In this paragraph, "the relevant time" means the time when the repeal of Schedule 9 to the 1998 Act comes into force.

(4) Paragraphs 14 and 15 of Schedule 9 to the 1998 Act (application of that Schedule to Scotland and Northern Ireland) apply for the purposes of this paragraph as they apply for the purposes of that Schedule.

Monetary penalties

38. (1) The repeal of sections 55A, 55B, 55D and 55E of the 1998 Act (monetary penalties) does not affect the application of those provisions after the relevant time in a case in which—

(a) the Commissioner served a monetary penalty notice under section 55A of the 1998 Act before the relevant time,

(b) the Commissioner served a notice of intent under section 55B of the 1998 Act before the relevant time, or

(c) the Commissioner considers it appropriate, after the relevant time, to serve a notice mentioned in paragraph (a) or (b) in respect of—

    (i) a contravention of section 4(4) of the 1998 Act before the relevant time, or

    (ii) a contravention of the sixth data protection principle sections after the relevant time.

(2) The revocation of the relevant subordinate legislation, and the repeals mentioned in sub-paragraph (1), do not affect the application of the relevant subordinate legislation (or of provisions of the 1998 Act applied by them) after the relevant time in a case described in sub-paragraph (1).

(3) Guidance issued under section 55C of the 1998 Act (guidance about monetary penalty notices) which is in force immediately before the relevant time continues in force after that time for the purposes of the Commissioner's exercise of functions under sections 55A and 55B of the 1998 Act as they have effect by virtue of this paragraph.

(4) In this paragraph—

"the relevant subordinate legislation" means—

    (a) the Data Protection (Monetary Penalties) (Maximum Penalty and Notices) Regulations 2010 (SI 2010/31);

    (b) the Data Protection (Monetary Penalties) Order 2010 (SI 2010/910);

"the relevant time" means the time when the repeal of section 55A of the 1998 Act comes into force.

Appeals

39. (1) The repeal of sections 48 and 49 of the 1998 Act (appeals) does not affect the application of those sections after the relevant time in relation to a notice served under the 1998 Act or a determination made under section 45 of that Act—

(a) before the relevant time, or

(b) after that time in reliance on this Schedule.

(2) In this paragraph, "the relevant time" means the time when the repeal of section 48 of the 1998 Act comes into force.

Exemptions

40. (1) The repeal of section 28 of the 1998 Act (national security) does not affect the application of that section after the relevant time for the purposes of a provision of Part 5 of the 1998 Act as it has effect after that time by virtue of the preceding paragraphs of this Part of this Schedule.

(2) In this paragraph, "the relevant time" means the time when the repeal of the provision of Part 5 of the 1998 Act in question comes into force.

(3) As regards certificates issued under section 28(2) of the 1998 Act, see Part 5 of this Schedule.

Tribunal Procedure Rules

41. (1) The repeal of paragraph 7 of Schedule 6 to the 1998 Act (Tribunal Procedure Rules) does not affect the application of that paragraph, or of rules made under that paragraph, after the relevant time in relation to the exercise of rights of appeal conferred by section 28 or 48 of the 1998 Act, as they have effect by virtue of this Schedule.

(2) Part 3 of Schedule 19 to this Act does not apply for the purposes of Tribunal Procedure Rules made under paragraph 7(1)(a) of Schedule 6 to the 1998 Act as they apply, after the relevant time, in relation to the exercise of rights of appeal described in sub-paragraph (1).

(3) In this paragraph, "the relevant time" means the time when the repeal of paragraph 7 of Schedule 6 to the 1998 Act comes into force.

Obstruction etc

42. (1) The repeal of paragraph 8 of Schedule 6 to the 1998 Act (obstruction etc in proceedings before the Tribunal) does not affect the application of that paragraph after the relevant time in relation to an act or omission in relation to proceedings under the 1998 Act (including as it has effect by virtue of this Schedule).

(2) In this paragraph, "the relevant time" means the time when the repeal of paragraph 8 of Schedule 6 to the 1998 Act comes into force.

Enforcement etc under the 2014 Regulations

43. (1) The references in the preceding paragraphs of this Part of this Schedule to provisions of the 1998 Act include those provisions as applied, with modifications, by regulation 51 of the 2014 Regulations (other functions of the Commissioner).

(2) The revocation of regulation 51 of the 2014 Regulations does not affect the application of those provisions of the 1998 Act (as so applied) as described in those paragraphs.

NOTES

Commencement: 25 May 2018 (see also the introductory notes to this Act preceding s 1 at **[1.71]**).

PART 8 ENFORCEMENT ETC UNDER THIS ACT

Information notices

[1.325]
44. In section 143 of this Act—

(a) the reference to an offence under section 144 of this Act includes an offence under section 47 of the 1998 Act (including as it has effect by virtue of this Schedule), and

(b) the references to an offence under this Act include an offence under the 1998 Act (including as it has effect by virtue of this Schedule) or the 1984 Act.

Powers of entry

45. In paragraph 16 of Schedule 15 to this Act (powers of entry: self-incrimination), the reference to an offence under paragraph 15 of that Schedule includes an offence under paragraph 12 of Schedule 9 to the 1998 Act (including as it has effect by virtue of this Schedule).

Tribunal Procedure Rules

46. (1) Tribunal Procedure Rules made under paragraph 7(1)(a) of Schedule 6 to the 1998 Act (appeal rights under the 1998 Act) and in force immediately before the relevant time have effect after that time as if they were also made under section 203 of this Act.

(2) In this paragraph, "the relevant time" means the time when the repeal of paragraph 7(1)(a) of Schedule 6 to the 1998 Act comes into force.

NOTES

Commencement: 25 May 2018 (see also the introductory notes to this Act preceding s 1 at **[1.71]**).

PART 9 OTHER ENACTMENTS

Powers to disclose information to the Commissioner

[1.326]

47. (1) The following provisions (as amended by Schedule 19 to this Act) have effect after the relevant time as if the matters they refer to included a matter in respect of which the Commissioner could exercise a power conferred by a provision of Part 5 of the 1998 Act, as it has effect by virtue of this Schedule—

    (a)   section 11AA(1)(a) of the Parliamentary Commissioner Act 1967 (disclosure of information by Parliamentary Commissioner);

    (b)   sections 33A(1)(a) and 34O(1)(a) of the Local Government Act 1974 (disclosure of information by Local Commissioner);

    (c)   section 18A(1)(a) of the Health Service Commissioners Act 1993 (disclosure of information by Health Service Commissioner);

    (d)   paragraph 1 of the entry for the Information Commissioner in Schedule 5 to the Scottish Public Services Ombudsman Act 2002 (asp 11) (disclosure of information by the Ombudsman);

    (e)   section 34X(3)(a) of the Public Services Ombudsman (Wales) Act 2005 (disclosure of information by the Ombudsman);

    (f)   section 18(6)(a) of the Commissioner for Older People (Wales) Act 2006 (disclosure of information by the Commissioner);

    (g)   section 22(3)(a) of the Welsh Language (Wales) Measure 2011 (nawm 1) (disclosure of information by the Welsh Language Commissioner);

    (h)   section 49(3)(a) of the Public Services Ombudsman Act (Northern Ireland) 2016 (c 4 (NI))(disclosure of information by the Ombudsman);

    (i)   section 44(3)(a) of the Justice Act (Northern Ireland) 2016 (c 21 (NI)) (disclosure of information by the Prison Ombudsman for Northern Ireland).

(2) The following provisions (as amended by Schedule 19 to this Act) have effect after the relevant time as if the offences they refer to included an offence under any provision of the 1998 Act other than paragraph 12 of Schedule 9 to that Act (obstruction of execution of warrant)—

    (a)   section 11AA(1)(b) of the Parliamentary Commissioner Act 1967;

    (b)   sections 33A(1)(b) and 34O(1)(b) of the Local Government Act 1974;

    (c)   section 18A(1)(b) of the Health Service Commissioners Act 1993;

    (d)   paragraph 2 of the entry for the Information Commissioner in Schedule 5 to the Scottish Public Services Ombudsman Act 2002 (asp 11);

    (e)   section 34X(5) of the Public Services Ombudsman (Wales) Act 2005 (disclosure of information by the Ombudsman);

    (f)   section 18(8) of the Commissioner for Older People (Wales) Act 2006;

    (g)   section 22(5) of the Welsh Language (Wales) Measure 2011 (nawm 1);

    (h)   section 49(5) of the Public Services Ombudsman Act (Northern Ireland) 2016 (c 4 (NI));

    (i)   section 44(3)(b) of the Justice Act (Northern Ireland) 2016 (c 21 (NI)).

(3) In this paragraph, "the relevant time", in relation to a provision of a section or Schedule listed in sub-paragraph (1) or (2), means the time when the amendment of the section or Schedule by Schedule 19 to this Act comes into force.

Codes etc required to be consistent with the Commissioner's data-sharing code

48. (1) This paragraph applies in relation to the code of practice issued under each of the following provisions—

    (a)   section 19AC of the Registration Service Act 1953 (code of practice about disclosure of information by civil registration officials);

    (b)   section 43 of the Digital Economy Act 2017 (code of practice about disclosure of information to improve public service delivery);

    (c)   section 52 of that Act (code of practice about disclosure of information to reduce debt owed to the public sector);

    (d)   section 60 of that Act (code of practice about disclosure of information to combat fraud against the public sector);

    (e)   section 70 of that Act (code of practice about disclosure of information for research purposes).

(2) During the relevant period, the code of practice does not have effect to the extent that it is inconsistent with the code of practice prepared under section 121 of this Act (data-sharing code) and issued under section 125(4) of this Act (as altered or replaced from time to time).

(3) In this paragraph, "the relevant period", in relation to a code issued under a section mentioned in sub-paragraph (1), means the period—

    (a)   beginning when the amendments of that section in Schedule 19 to this Act come into force, and

    (b)   ending when the code is first reissued under that section.

49. (1) This paragraph applies in relation to the original statement published under section 45E of the Statistics and Registration Service Act 2007 (statement of principles and procedures in connection with access to information by the Statistics Board).

(2) During the relevant period, the statement does not have effect to the extent that it is inconsistent with the code of practice prepared under section 121 of this Act (data-sharing code) and issued under section 125(4) of this Act (as altered or replaced from time to time).

(3) In this paragraph, "the relevant period" means the period—

    (a)   beginning when the amendments of section 45E of the Statistics and Registration Service Act 2007 in Schedule 19 to this Act come into force, and

    (b)   ending when the first revised statement is published under that section.

Consumer Credit Act 1974

50. In section 159(1)(a) of the Consumer Credit Act 1974 (correction of wrong information) (as amended by Schedule 19 to this Act), the reference to information given under Article 15(1) to (3) of the [UK GDPR] includes information given at any time under section 7 of the 1998 Act.

Freedom of Information Act 2000

51. Paragraphs 52 to 55 make provision about the Freedom of Information Act 2000 ("the 2000 Act").

52. (1) This paragraph applies where a request for information was made to a public authority under the 2000 Act before the relevant time.

(2) To the extent that the request is dealt with after the relevant time, the amendments of sections 2 and 40 of the 2000 Act in Schedule 19 to this Act have effect for the purposes of determining whether the authority deals with the request in accordance with Part 1 of the 2000 Act.

(3) To the extent that the request was dealt with before the relevant time—
  (a) the amendments of sections 2 and 40 of the 2000 Act in Schedule 19 to this Act do not have effect for the purposes of determining whether the authority dealt with the request in accordance with Part 1 of the 2000 Act, but
  (b) the powers of the Commissioner and the Tribunal, on an application or appeal under the 2000 Act, do not include power to require the authority to take steps which it would not be required to take in order to comply with Part 1 of the 2000 Act as amended by Schedule 19 to this Act.

(4) In this paragraph—
  "public authority" has the same meaning as in the 2000 Act;
  "the relevant time" means the time when the amendments of sections 2 and 40 of the 2000 Act in Schedule 19 to this Act come into force.

53. (1) Tribunal Procedure Rules made under paragraph 7(1)(b) of Schedule 6 to the 1998 Act (appeal rights under the 2000 Act) and in force immediately before the relevant time have effect after that time as if they were also made under section 61 of the 2000 Act (as inserted by Schedule 19 to this Act).

(2) In this paragraph, "the relevant time" means the time when the repeal of paragraph 7(1)(b) of Schedule 6 to the 1998 Act comes into force.

54. (1) The repeal of paragraph 8 of Schedule 6 to the 1998 Act (obstruction etc in proceedings before the Tribunal) does not affect the application of that paragraph after the relevant time in relation to an act or omission before that time in relation to an appeal under the 2000 Act.

(2) In this paragraph, "the relevant time" means the time when the repeal of paragraph 8 of Schedule 6 to the 1998 Act comes into force.

55. (1) The amendment of section 77 of the 2000 Act in Schedule 19 to this Act (offence of altering etc record with intent to prevent disclosure: omission of reference to section 7 of the 1998 Act) does not affect the application of that section after the relevant time in relation to a case in which—
  (a) the request for information mentioned in section 77(1) of the 2000 Act was made before the relevant time, and
  (b) when the request was made, section 77(1)(b) of the 2000 Act was satisfied by virtue of section 7 of the 1998 Act.

(2) In this paragraph, "the relevant time" means the time when the repeal of section 7 of the 1998 Act comes into force.

Freedom of Information (Scotland) Act 2002

56. (1) This paragraph applies where a request for information was made to a Scottish public authority under the Freedom of Information (Scotland) Act 2002 ("the 2002 Act") before the relevant time.

(2) To the extent that the request is dealt with after the relevant time, the amendments of the 2002 Act in Schedule 19 to this Act have effect for the purposes of determining whether the authority deals with the request in accordance with Part 1 of the 2002 Act.

(3) To the extent that the request was dealt with before the relevant time—
  (a) the amendments of the 2002 Act in Schedule 19 to this Act do not have effect for the purposes of determining whether the authority dealt with the request in accordance with Part 1 of the 2002 Act, but
  (b) the powers of the Scottish Information Commissioner and the Court of Session, on an application or appeal under the 2002 Act, do not include power to require the authority to take steps which it would not be required to take in order to comply with Part 1 of the 2002 Act as amended by Schedule 19 to this Act.

(4) In this paragraph—
  "Scottish public authority" has the same meaning as in the 2002 Act;
  "the relevant time" means the time when the amendments of the 2002 Act in Schedule 19 to this Act come into force.

Access to Health Records (Northern Ireland) Order 1993 (SI 1993/1250 (NI 4))

57. Until the first regulations under Article 5(4)(a) of the Access to Health Records (Northern Ireland) Order 1993 (as amended by Schedule 19 to this Act) come into force, the maximum amount of a fee that may be required for giving access under that Article is £10.

Privacy and Electronic Communications (EC Directive) Regulations 2003 (SI 2003/2450)

58. (1) The repeal of a provision of the 1998 Act does not affect its operation for the purposes of the Privacy and Electronic Communications (EC Directive) Regulations 2003 ("the PECR 2003") (see regulations 2, 31 and 31B of, and Schedule 1 to, those Regulations).

(2) Where subordinate legislation made under a provision of the 1998 Act is in force immediately before the repeal of that provision, neither the revocation of the subordinate legislation nor the repeal of the provision of the 1998 Act affect the application of the subordinate legislation for the purposes of the PECR 2003 after that time.

(3) Part 3 of Schedule 19 to this Act (modifications) does not have effect in relation to the PECR 2003.

(4) Part 7 of this Schedule does not have effect in relation to the provisions of the 1998 Act as applied by the PECR 2003.

Health and Personal Social Services (Quality, Improvement and Regulation) (Northern Ireland) Order 2003 (SI 2003/431 (NI 9))

59. Part 3 of Schedule 19 to this Act (modifications) does not have effect in relation to the reference to an accessible record within the meaning of section 68 of the 1998 Act in Article 43 of the Health and Personal Social Services (Quality, Improvement and Regulation) (Northern Ireland) Order 2003.

Environmental Information Regulations 2004 (SI 2004/3391)

60. (1) This paragraph applies where a request for information was made to a public authority under the Environmental Information Regulations 2004 ("the 2004 Regulations") before the relevant time.

(2) To the extent that the request is dealt with after the relevant time, the amendments of the 2004 Regulations in Schedule 19 to this Act have effect for the purposes of determining whether the authority deals with the request in accordance with Parts 2 and 3 of those Regulations.

(3) To the extent that the request was dealt with before the relevant time—
  (a) the amendments of the 2004 Regulations in Schedule 19 to this Act do not have effect for the purposes of determining whether the authority dealt with the request in accordance with Parts 2 and 3 of those Regulations, but
  (b) the powers of the Commissioner and the Tribunal, on an application or appeal under the 2000 Act (as applied by the 2004 Regulations), do not include power to require the authority to take steps which it would not be required to take in order to comply with Parts 2 and 3 of those Regulations as amended by Schedule 19 to this Act.

(4) In this paragraph—
  "public authority" has the same meaning as in the 2004 Regulations;
  "the relevant time" means the time when the amendments of the 2004 Regulations in Schedule 19 to this Act come into force.

Environmental Information (Scotland) Regulations 2004 (SSI 2004/520)

61. (1) This paragraph applies where a request for information was made to a Scottish public authority under the Environmental Information (Scotland) Regulations 2004 ("the 2004 Regulations") before the relevant time.

(2) To the extent that the request is dealt with after the relevant time, the amendments of the 2004 Regulations in Schedule 19 to this Act have effect for the purposes of determining whether the authority deals with the request in accordance with those Regulations.

(3) To the extent that the request was dealt with before the relevant time—
  (a) the amendments of the 2004 Regulations in Schedule 19 to this Act do not have effect for the purposes of determining whether the authority dealt with the request in accordance with those Regulations, but
  (b) the powers of the Scottish Information Commissioner and the Court of Session, on an application or appeal under the 2002 Act (as applied by the 2004 Regulations), do not include power to require the authority to take steps which it would not be required to take in order to comply with those Regulations as amended by Schedule 19 to this Act.

(4) In this paragraph—
  "Scottish public authority" has the same meaning as in the 2004 Regulations;
  "the relevant time" means the time when the amendments of the 2004 Regulations in Schedule 19 to this Act come into force.

NOTES

Commencement: 25 May 2018 (see also the introductory notes to this Act preceding s 1 at **[1.71]**).

Para 50: the words in square brackets were substituted by the Data Protection, Privacy and Electronic Communications (Amendments etc) (EU Exit) Regulations 2019, SI 2019/419, reg 4, Sch 2, paras 1, 101(1). (5).

[SCHEDULE 21
FURTHER TRANSITIONAL PROVISION ETC

Section 213

PART 1 INTERPRETATION

[1.327]
1 The applied GDPR

In this Schedule, "the applied GDPR" means the EU GDPR as applied by Chapter 3 of Part 2 before IP completion day.]

NOTES

Commencement: IP completion day (as defined in the European Union (Withdrawal Agreement) Act 2020, s 39).

Schedule 21 was added by the Data Protection, Privacy and Electronic Communications (Amendments etc) (EU Exit) Regulations 2019, SI 2019/419, reg 4, Sch 2, paras 1, 102. Note that Sch 2, para 102 to the 2019 Regulations was amended by the Data Protection, Privacy and Electronic Communications (Amendments etc) (EU Exit) Regulations 2020, SI 2020/1586, reg 5 (and the effect of the amendment has been incorporated in the text set out above).

[PART 2 CONTINUATION OF EXISTING ACTS ETC

[1.328]

2 Merger of the directly applicable GDPR and the applied GDPR

(1) On and after IP completion day, references in an enactment to the UK GDPR (including the reference in the definition of "the data protection legislation" in section 3(9)) include—

   (a) the EU GDPR as it was directly applicable to the United Kingdom before IP completion day, read with Chapter 2 of Part 2 of this Act as it had effect before IP completion day, and

   (b) the applied GDPR, read with Chapter 3 of Part 2 of this Act as it had effect before IP completion day.

(2) On and after IP completion day, references in an enactment to, or to a provision of, Chapter 2 of Part 2 of this Act (including general references to this Act or to Part 2 of this Act) include that Chapter or that provision as applied by Chapter 3 of Part 2 of this Act as it had effect before IP completion day.

(3) Sub-paragraphs (1) and (2) have effect—

   (a) in relation to references in this Act, except as otherwise provided;

   (b) in relation to references in other enactments, unless the context otherwise requires.

3 (1) Anything done in connection with the EU GDPR as it was directly applicable to the United Kingdom before IP completion day, the applied GDPR or this Act—

   (a) if in force or effective immediately before IP completion day, continues to be in force or effective on and after IP completion day, and

   (b) if in the process of being done immediately before IP completion day, continues to be done on and after IP completion day.

(2) References in this paragraph to anything done include references to anything omitted to be done.]

NOTES

Commencement: IP completion day (as defined in the European Union (Withdrawal Agreement) Act 2020, s 39).

Added as noted to Pt 1 of this Schedule at **[1.327]**.

[PART 3 TRANSFERS TO THIRD COUNTRIES AND INTERNATIONAL ORGANISATIONS

[1.329]

4 UK GDPR: adequacy decisions and adequacy regulations

(1) On and after IP completion day, for the purposes of the UK GDPR and Part 2 of this Act, a transfer of personal data to a third country or an international organisation is based on adequacy regulations if, at the time of the transfer, paragraph 5 specifies, or specifies a description which includes—

   (a) in the case of a third country, the country or a relevant territory or sector within the country, or

   (b) in the case of an international organisation, the organisation.

(2) Sub-paragraph (1) has effect subject to provision in paragraph 5 providing that only particular transfers to the country, territory, sector or organisation may rely on a particular provision of paragraph 5 for the purposes of sub-paragraph (1).

(3) The Secretary of State may by regulations—

   (a) repeal sub-paragraphs (1) and (2) and paragraph 5;

   (b) amend paragraph 5 so as to omit a third country, territory, sector or international organisation specified, or of a description specified, in that paragraph;

   (c) amend paragraph 5 so as to replace a reference to, or description of, a third country, territory, sector or organisation with a narrower reference or description, including by specifying or describing particular transfers of personal data and making provision described in sub-paragraph (2).

(4) Regulations under this paragraph may, among other things—

   (a) identify a transfer of personal data by any means, including by reference to the controller or processor, the recipient, the personal data transferred or the means by which the transfer is made or by reference to relevant legislation, lists or other documents, as they have effect from time to time;

   (b) confer a discretion on a person.

(5) Regulations under this paragraph are subject to the negative resolution procedure.

(6) Sub-paragraphs (1) and (2) have effect in addition to section 17A(2) and (3).

5 (1) The following are specified for the purposes of paragraph 4(1)—

   (a) an EEA state;

   (b) Gibraltar;

   (c) a Union institution, body, office or agency set up by, or on the basis of, the Treaty on the European Union, the Treaty on the Functioning of the European Union or the Euratom Treaty;

   (d) an equivalent institution, body, office or agency set up by, or on the basis of, the Treaties establishing the European Economic Area;

   (e) a third country which is the subject of a decision listed in sub-paragraph (2), other than a decision that, immediately before IP completion day, had been repealed or was suspended;

   (f) a third country, territory or sector within a third country or international organisation which is the subject of an adequacy decision made by the European Commission before IP completion day on the basis of Article 45(3) of the EU GDPR, other than a decision that, immediately before IP completion day, had been repealed or was suspended.

(2) The decisions mentioned in sub-paragraph (1)(e) are the following—

   (a) Commission Decision 2000/518/EC of 26th July 2000 pursuant to Directive 95/46/EC of the European Parliament and of the Council on the adequate protection of personal data provided in Switzerland;

(b)   Commission Decision 2002/2/EC of 20th December 2001 pursuant to Directive 95/46/EC of the European Parliament and of the Council on the adequate protection of personal data provided by the Canadian Personal Information Protection and Electronic Documents Act;

(c)   Commission Decision 2003/490/EC of 30th June 2003 pursuant to Directive 95/46/EC of the European Parliament and of the Council on the adequate protection of personal data in Argentina;

(d)   Commission Decision 2003/821/EC of 21st November 2003 on the adequate protection of personal data in Guernsey;

(e)   Commission Decision 2004/411/EC of 28th April 2004 on the adequate protection of personal data in the Isle of Man;

(f)   Commission Decision 2008/393/EC of 8th May 2008 pursuant to Directive 95/46/EC of the European Parliament and of the Council on the adequate protection of personal data in Jersey;

(g)   Commission Decision 2010/146/EU of 5th March 2010 pursuant to Directive 95/46/EC of the European Parliament and of the Council on the adequate protection provided by the Faeroese Act on processing of personal data;

(h)   Commission Decision 2010/625/EU of 19th October 2010 pursuant to Directive 95/46/EC of the European Parliament and of the Council on the adequate protection of personal data in Andorra;

(i)   Commission Decision 2011/61/EU of 31st January 2011 pursuant to Directive 95/46/EC of the European Parliament and of the Council on the adequate protection of personal data by the State of Israel with regard to automated processing of personal data;

(j)   Commission Implementing Decision 2012/484/EU of 21st August 2012 pursuant to Directive 95/46/EC of the European Parliament and of the Council on the adequate protection of personal data by the Eastern Republic of Uruguay with regard to automated processing of personal data;

(k)   Commission Implementing Decision 2013/65/EU of 19th December 2012 pursuant to Directive 95/46/EC of the European Parliament and of the Council on the adequate protection of personal data by New Zealand;

(m)   Commission Implementing Decision (EU) 2019/419 of 23rd January 2019 pursuant to Regulation (EU) 2016/679 of the European Parliament and of the Council on the adequate protection of personal data by Japan under the Act on the Protection of Personal Information.

(3)   Where a decision described in sub-paragraph (1)(e) or (f) states that an adequate level of protection of personal data is ensured only for a transfer specified or described in the decision, only such a transfer may rely on that provision and that decision for the purposes of paragraph 4(1).

(4)   The references to a decision in sub-paragraphs (1)(e) and (f) and (2) are to the decision as it had effect in EU law immediately before IP completion day, subject to sub-paragraphs (5) and (6).

(5)   For the purposes of this paragraph, where a reference to legislation, a list or another document in a decision described in sub-paragraph (1)(e) or (f) is a reference to the legislation, list or document as it has effect from time to time, it is to be treated as a reference to the legislation, list or other document as it has effect at the time of the transfer.

(6)   For the purposes of this paragraph, where a decision described in sub-paragraph (1)(e) or (f) relates to—

(a)   transfers from the European Union (or the European Community) or the European Economic Area, or

(b)   transfers to which the EU GDPR applies,

it is to be treated as relating to equivalent transfers to or from the United Kingdom or transfers to which the UK GDPR applies (as appropriate).

6   (1)   In the provisions listed in sub-paragraph (2)—

(a)   references to regulations made under section 17A (other than references to making such regulations) include the provision made in paragraph 5;

(b)   references to the revocation of such regulations include the repeal of all or part of paragraph 5.

(2)   Those provisions are—

(a)   Articles 13(1)(f), 14(1)(f), 45(1) and (7), 46(1) and 49(1) of the UK GDPR;

(b)   sections 17B(1), (3), (6) and (7) and 18(2) of this Act.

7   UK GDPR: transfers subject to appropriate safeguards provided by standard data protection clauses

(1)   Subject to paragraph 8, the appropriate safeguards referred to in Article 46(1) of the UK GDPR may be provided for on and after IP completion day as described in this paragraph.

(2)   The safeguards may be provided for by any standard data protection clauses included in an arrangement which, if the arrangement had been entered into immediately before IP completion day, would have provided for the appropriate safeguards referred to in Article 46(1) of the EU GDPR by virtue of Article 46(2)(c) or (d) or (5) of the EU GDPR.

(3)   The safeguards may be provided for by a version of standard data protection clauses described in sub-paragraph (2) incorporating changes where—

(a)   all of the changes are made in consequence of the withdrawal of the United Kingdom from the EU or provision made by regulations under section 8 or 23 of the European Union (Withdrawal) Act 2018 (or both), and

(b)   none of the changes alters the effect of the clauses.

(4)   The following changes are to be treated as falling within sub-paragraph (3)(a) and (b)—

(a)   changing references to adequacy decisions made by the European Commission into references to equivalent provision made by regulations under section 17A or by or under paragraphs 4 to 6 of this Schedule;

(b)   changing references to transferring personal data outside the European Union or the European Economic Area into references to transferring personal data outside the United Kingdom.

(5)   In the case of a transfer of personal data made under arrangements entered into before IP completion day, the safeguards may be provided for on and after IP completion day by standard data protection clauses not falling within sub-paragraph (2) which—

(a)   formed part of the arrangements immediately before IP completion day, and

(b)   at that time, provided for the appropriate safeguards referred to in Article 46(1) of the EU GDPR by virtue of Article 46(2)(c) or (d) or (5) of the EU GDPR.

(6)   The Secretary of State and the Commissioner must keep the operation of this paragraph under review.

(7)   In this paragraph, "adequacy decision" means a decision made on the basis of—
(a)   Article 45(3) of the EU GDPR, or
(b)   Article 25(6) of Directive 95/46/EC of the European Parliament and of the Council of 24th October 1995 on the protection of individuals with regard to the processing of personal data and on the free movement of such data.

(8)   This paragraph has effect in addition to Article 46(2) and (3) of the UK GDPR.

8   (1)   Paragraph 7 does not apply to the extent that it has been disapplied by—
(a)   regulations made by the Secretary of State, or
(b)   a document issued by the Commissioner.

(2)   Regulations under this paragraph are subject to the negative resolution procedure.

(3)   Subsections (3) to (8) and (10) to (12) of section 119A apply in relation to a document issued by the Commissioner under this paragraph as they apply to a document issued by the Commissioner under section 119A(2).

9   UK GDPR: transfers subject to appropriate safeguards provided by binding corporate rules

(1)   The appropriate safeguards referred to in Article 46(1) of the UK GDPR may be provided for on and after IP completion day as described sub-paragraphs (2) to (4), subject to sub-paragraph (5).

(2)   The safeguards may be provided for by any binding corporate rules authorised by the Commissioner which, immediately before IP completion day, provided for the appropriate safeguards referred to in Article 46(1) of the EU GDPR by virtue of Article 46(5) of the EU GDPR.

(3)   The safeguards may be provided for by a version of binding corporate rules described in sub-paragraph (2) incorporating changes where—
(a)   all of the changes are made in consequence of the withdrawal of the United Kingdom from the EU or provision made by regulations under section 8 or 23 of the European Union (Withdrawal) Act 2018 (or both), and
(b)   none of the changes alters the effect of the rules.

(4)   The following changes are to be treated as falling within sub-paragraph (3)(a) and (b)—
(a)   changing references to adequacy decisions made by the European Commission into references to equivalent provision made by regulations under section 17A or by or under paragraphs 4 to 6 of this Schedule;
(b)   changing references to transferring personal data outside the European Union or the European Economic Area into references to transferring personal data outside the United Kingdom.

(5)   Sub-paragraphs (2) to (4) cease to apply in relation to binding corporate rules if, on or after IP completion day, the Commissioner withdraws the authorisation of the rules (or, where sub-paragraph (3) is relied on, the authorisation of the rules mentioned in sub-paragraph (2)).

(5A)   For the purposes of sub-paragraph (2), binding corporate rules which, immediately before IP completion day, provided for the appropriate safeguards referred to in Article 46(1) of the EU GDPR by virtue of Article 46(5) of the EU GDPR but which were authorised other than by the Commissioner are to be treated as authorised by the Commissioner where—
(a)   a valid notification of the rules has been made to the Commissioner,
(b)   the Commissioner has approved them, and
(c)   that approval has not been withdrawn.

(5B)   A notification is valid if it—
(a)   is made by a controller or processor established in the United Kingdom,
(b)   is made to the Commissioner before the end of the period of 6 months beginning with IP completion day, and
(c)   includes—
(i)   the name and contact details of the data protection officer or other contact point for the controller or processor, and
(i)   such other information as the Commissioner may reasonably require.

(5C)   Where a valid notification is made the Commissioner must, without undue delay—
(a)   decide whether or not to approve the rules, and
(b)   notify the controller or processor of that decision.

(6)   The Commissioner must keep the operation of this paragraph under review.

(7)   In this paragraph—
"adequacy decision" means a decision made on the basis of—
(a)   Article 45(3) of the EU GDPR, or
(b)   Article 25(6) of Directive 95/46/EC of the European Parliament and of the Council of 24th October 1995 on the protection of individuals with regard to the processing of personal data and on the free movement of such data;
"binding corporate rules" has the meaning given in Article 4(20) of the UK GDPR.

(8)   This paragraph has effect in addition to Article 46(2) and (3) of the UK GDPR.

10   Part 3 (law enforcement processing): adequacy decisions and adequacy regulations

(1)   On and after IP completion day, for the purposes of Part 3 of this Act, a transfer of personal data to a third country or an international organisation is based on adequacy regulations if, at the time of the transfer, paragraph 11 specifies, or specifies a description which includes—

(a)   in the case of a third country, the country or a relevant territory or sector within the country, or

(b)   in the case of an international organisation, the organisation.

(2)   Sub-paragraph (1) has effect subject to provision in paragraph 11 providing that only particular transfers to the country, territory, sector or organisation may rely on a particular provision of paragraph 11 for the purposes of sub-paragraph (1).

(3)   The Secretary of State may by regulations—

(a)   repeal sub-paragraphs (1) and (2) and paragraph 11;

(b)   amend paragraph 11 so as to omit a third country, territory, sector or international organisation specified, or of a description specified, in that paragraph;

(c)   amend paragraph 11 so as to replace a reference to, or description of, a third country, territory, sector or organisation with a narrower reference or description, including by specifying or describing particular transfers of personal data and by making provision described in sub-paragraph (2).

(4)   Regulations under this paragraph may, among other things—

(a)   identify a transfer of personal data by any means, including by reference to the controller or processor, the recipient, the personal data transferred or the means by which the transfer is made or by reference to relevant legislation, lists or other documents, as they have effect from time to time;

(b)   confer a discretion on a person.

(5)   Regulations under this paragraph are subject to the negative resolution procedure.

(6)   Sub-paragraphs (1) and (2) have effect in addition to section 74A(2) and (3).

11   (1)   The following are specified for the purposes of paragraph 10(1)—

(a)   an EEA state;

(aa)   Switzerland;

(b)   Gibraltar;

(c)   a third country, a territory or sector within a third country or an international organisation which is the subject of an adequacy decision made by the European Commission before IP completion day on the basis of Article 36(3) of the Law Enforcement Directive, other than a decision that, immediately before IP completion day, had been repealed or was suspended.

(2)   Where a decision described in sub-paragraph (1)(c) states that an adequate level of protection of personal data is ensured only for a transfer specified or described in the decision, only such a transfer may rely on that provision and that decision for the purposes of paragraph 10(1).

(3)   The reference to a decision in sub-paragraph (1)(c) is to the decision as it had effect in EU law immediately before IP completion day, subject to sub-paragraphs (4) and (5).

(4)   For the purposes of this paragraph, where a reference to legislation, a list or another document in a decision described in sub-paragraph (1)(c) is a reference to the legislation, list or document as it has effect from time to time, it is to be treated as a reference to the legislation, list or other document as it has effect at the time of the transfer.

(5)   For the purposes of this paragraph, where a decision described in sub-paragraph (1)(c) relates to—

(a)   transfers from the European Union (or the European Community) or the European Economic Area, or

(b)   transfers to which the Law Enforcement Directive applies,

it is to be treated as relating to equivalent transfers from the United Kingdom or transfers to which Part 3 of this Act applies (as appropriate).

12   In section 74B(1), (3), (6) and (7)—

(a)   references to regulations made under section 74A (other than references to making such regulations) include the provision made in paragraph 11;

(b)   references to the revocation of such regulations include the repeal of all or part of paragraph 11.]

NOTES

Commencement: IP completion day (as defined in the European Union (Withdrawal Agreement) Act 2020, s 39).

Added as noted to Pt 1 of this Schedule at **[1.327]**.

Note that the para 5(2) of this Schedule as inserted by the Data Protection, Privacy and Electronic Communications (Amendments etc) (EU Exit) Regulations 2019, SI 2019/419, Sch 2, para 102 originally contained a sub-paragraph (l) but that sub-paragraph was deleted from the text to be inserted by the Data Protection, Privacy and Electronic Communications (Amendments etc) (EU Exit) Regulations 2020, SI 2020/1586, reg 5.

[PART 4 REPEAL OF PROVISIONS IN CHAPTER 3 OF PART 2

[1.330]

13   Applied GDPR: power to make provision in consequence of GDPR regulations

(1)   Regulations made under section 23 before IP completion day continue in force until they are revoked, despite the repeal of that section by the Data Protection, Privacy and Electronic Communications (Amendments etc) (EU Exit) Regulations 2019.

(2)   The provisions listed in section 186(3) include regulations made under section 23 before IP completion day (and not revoked).

(3)   Sub-paragraphs (1) and (2) do not have effect so far as otherwise provided by the law of England and Wales, Scotland or Northern Ireland.

14   Applied GDPR: national security certificates

(1)   This paragraph applies to a certificate issued under section 27 of this Act which has effect immediately before IP completion day.

(2)   A reference in the certificate to a provision of the applied GDPR has effect, on and after IP completion day, as it if were a reference to the corresponding provision of the UK GDPR or this Act.]

NOTES

Commencement: IP completion day (as defined in the European Union (Withdrawal Agreement) Act 2020, s 39).
Added as noted to Pt 1 of this Schedule at **[1.327]**.

[PART 5 THE INFORMATION COMMISSIONER

[1.331]
15 Confidentiality of information
The repeal of section 132(2)(d) by the Data Protection, Privacy and Electronic Communications (Amendments etc) (EU Exit) Regulations 2019 has effect only in relation to a disclosure of information made on or after IP completion day.]

NOTES

Commencement: IP completion day (as defined in the European Union (Withdrawal Agreement) Act 2020, s 39).
Added as noted to Pt 1 of this Schedule at **[1.327]**.

[PART 6 ENFORCEMENT

[1.332]
16 GDPR: maximum amount of penalties
In relation to an infringement, before IP completion day, of a provision of the EU GDPR (as it was directly applicable to the United Kingdom) or the applied GDPR—
  (a) Article 83(5) and (6) of the UK GDPR and section 157(5)(a) and (b) of this Act have effect as if for "£17,500,000" there were substituted "20 million Euros";
  (b) Article 83(4) of the UK GDPR and section 157(6)(a) and (b) of this Act have effect as if for "£8,700,000" there were substituted "10 million Euros";
  (c) the maximum amount of a penalty in sterling must be determined by applying the spot rate of exchange set by the Bank of England on the day on which the penalty notice is given under section 155 of this Act.

17 GDPR: right to an effective remedy against the Commissioner
(1) This paragraph applies where—
  (a) proceedings are brought against a decision made by the Commissioner before IP completion day, and
  (b) the Commissioner's decision was preceded by an opinion or decision of the European Data Protection Board in accordance with the consistency mechanism referred to in Article 63 of the EU GDPR.
(2) The Commissioner must forward the Board's opinion or decision to the court or tribunal dealing with the proceedings.]

NOTES

Commencement: IP completion day (as defined in the European Union (Withdrawal Agreement) Act 2020, s 39).
Added as noted to Pt 1 of this Schedule at **[1.327]**.

DATA PROTECTION (CHARGES AND INFORMATION) REGULATIONS 2018

(SI 2018/480)

ARRANGEMENT OF REGULATIONS

NOTES

Made: 11 April 2018.
Authority: Digital Economy Act 2017, ss 108(1), (5), 110(6).
Commencement: 25 May 2018.

[1.333]
1 Citation, commencement and interpretation
(1) These Regulations may be cited as the Data Protection (Charges and Information) Regulations 2018 and come into force on 25th May 2018.
(2) In these Regulations—
    "business" includes any trade or profession;

"charge period" has the meaning given in regulation 2(6);

["data controller" means a person who is a controller for the purposes of Parts 5 to 7 of the Data Protection Act 2018 (see section 3(6) and (14) of that Act);]

"data controller's financial year" means—

    (a)   if the data controller has been in existence for less than 12 months, the period of its existence, or

    (b)   in any other case, the most recent financial year of the data controller that ended prior to the first day of the charge period in respect of which information is being provided, or a charge is being paid, pursuant to regulation 2;

"exempt processing" has the meaning given in the Schedule;

"financial year", in paragraph (b) of the definition of "data controller's financial year"—

    (a)   in relation to a company, is determined in accordance with section 390 of the Companies Act 2006,

    (b)   in relation to a limited liability partnership, is determined in accordance with section 390 of the Companies Act 2006 as applied by regulation 7 of the Limited Liability Partnerships (Accounts and Audit) (Application of Companies Act 2006) Regulations 2008, and

    (c)   in relation to any other case, means the period, covering 12 consecutive months, over which a data controller determines income and expenditure;

"member of staff" means any—

    (a)   employee,

    (b)   worker within the meaning given in section 296 of the Trade Union and Labour Relations (Consolidation) Act 1992,

    (c)   office holder, or

    (d)   partner;

"number of members of staff" means the number calculated by—

    (a)   ascertaining for each completed month of the data controller's financial year the total number of persons who have been members of staff of the data controller in that month,

    (b)   adding together the monthly totals, and

    (c)   dividing by the number of months in the data controller's financial year;

["personal data" has the same meaning as in Parts 5 to 7 of the Data Protection Act 2018 (see section 3(2) and (14) of that Act);]

"processing", in relation to personal data, means an operation or set of operations which is performed on personal data;

"public authority" means a public authority as defined by the Freedom of Information Act 2000 or a Scottish public authority as defined by the Freedom of Information (Scotland) Act 2002;

"turnover"—

    (a)   in relation to a company, has the meaning given in section 474 of the Companies Act 2006,

    (b)   in relation to a limited liability partnership, has the meaning given in section 474 of the Companies Act 2006 as applied by regulation 32 of the Limited Liability Partnerships (Accounts and Audit) (Application of Companies Act 2006) Regulations 2008, and

    (c)   in relation to any other case, means the amounts derived by the data controller from the provision of goods and services falling within the data controller's ordinary activities, after deduction of—

        (i)   trade discounts,

        (ii)   value added tax, and

        (iii)   any other taxes based on the amounts so derived.

NOTES

Commencement: 25 May 2018.

Para (2): definitions "data controller" and "personal data" inserted by the Data Protection Act 2018, s 211(1)(b), Sch 19, Pt 2, para 421.

[1.334]
2 Requirements on data controllers

(1) A data controller must comply with the requirements of this regulation unless all of the processing of personal data they undertake is exempt processing.

(2) Within the first 21 days of each charge period a data controller must pay a charge to the Information Commissioner, determined in accordance with regulation 3.

(3) Within the first 21 days of each charge period a data controller must provide to the Information Commissioner the following information, as of the first day of each charge period—

    (a)   the name and address of the data controller;

    (b)   whether the number of members of staff of the data controller is—

        (i)   less than or equal to 10,

        (ii)   greater than 10 but less than or equal to 250, or

        (iii)   greater than 250;

    (c)   whether the turnover for the data controller's financial year is—

        (i)   less than or equal to £632,000,

        (ii)   greater than £632,000 but less than or equal to £36 million, or

        (iii)   greater than £36 million; and

    (d)   whether the data controller is a public authority.

(4) Paragraph (3)(c) does not apply to a data controller that is a public authority.

(5) For the purposes of paragraph (3)(a)—

    (a)   the address of a registered company is that of its registered office, and

(b) the address of a person (other than a registered company) carrying on a business is that of the person's principal place of business in the UK.

(6) In this regulation—

"charge period" means—

    (a) for a person who is a data controller immediately before 25th May 2018 and has paid a fee pursuant to section 18(5) or 19(4) of the Data Protection Act 1998—

        (i) the period of 12 months beginning on the date which is 12 months after the date on which that fee was most recently received by the Information Commissioner, and

        (ii) each subsequent period of 12 months;

    (b) for a person who is a data controller immediately before 25th May 2018 but has not paid a fee pursuant to section 18(5) or 19(4) of the Data Protection Act 1998—

        (i) the period of 12 months beginning on 25th May 2018, and

        (ii) each subsequent period of 12 months; or

    (c) for a person who becomes a data controller on or after 25th May 2018—

        (i) the period of 12 months beginning on the date on which the person becomes a data controller, and

        (ii) each subsequent period of 12 months;

"registered company" means a company registered under the Companies Acts as defined by section 2(1) of the Companies Act 2006.

NOTES

Commencement: 25 May 2018.

[1.335]
3 Amount of charge payable under regulation 2

(1) For the purposes of regulation 2(2), the charge payable by a data controller in—

    (a) tier 1 (micro organisations), is £40;

    (b) tier 2 (small and medium organisations), is £60;

    (c) tier 3 (large organisations), is £2,900.

(2) For the purposes of this regulation, a data controller is, subject to paragraph (3)—

    (a) in tier 1 if—

        (i) it has a turnover of less than or equal to £632,000 for the data controller's financial year,

        (ii) the number of members of staff of the data controller is less than or equal to 10,

        (iii) it is a charity, or

        (iv) it is a small occupational pension scheme;

    (b) in tier 2 if it is not in tier 1 and—

        (i) it has a turnover of less than or equal to £36 million for the data controller's financial year, or

        (ii) the number of members of staff of the data controller is less than or equal to 250;

    (c) in tier 3 if it is not in tier 1 or tier 2.

(3) Paragraphs (2)(a)(i) and (2)(b)(i) are to be disregarded in relation to a public authority.

(4) For the purposes of regulation 3(2), the turnover and number of members of staff is determined on the first day of the charge period to which the charge relates.

(5) The applicable charge in paragraph (1) is reduced by £5.00 for a data controller that makes payment of the charge by direct debit.

(6) In this regulation—

"charity"—

        (i) in relation to England and Wales, has the meaning given in section 1 of the Charities Act 2011,

        (ii) in relation to Scotland, means a body entered in the Scottish Charity Register maintained under section 3 of the Charity and Trustee Investment (Scotland) Act 2005, and

        (iii) in relation to Northern Ireland, has the meaning given in section 1 of the Charities Act (Northern Ireland) 2008;

"small occupational pension scheme" has the meaning given in regulation 4 of the Occupational and Personal Pension Schemes (Consultation by Employers and Miscellaneous Amendment) Regulations 2006.

NOTES

Commencement: 25 May 2018.

[1.336]
4 Requirements in respect of partnerships

(1) In any case in which two or more persons carrying on a business in partnership are the data controllers in respect of personal data for the purposes of that business, the requirements of regulation 2 may be satisfied in respect of those persons in the name of the firm.

(2) Where the requirements of regulation 2 are satisfied in the name of a firm under paragraph (1) above—

    (a) the name to be specified for the purposes of regulation 2(3)(a) is the name of that firm, and

    (b) the address to be specified for the purposes of regulation 2(3)(a) is the address of that firm's principal place of business.

(3) For the purposes of regulations 2 and 3, references to the turnover and number of members of staff of a data controller which is a partnership are references to the turnover and number of members of staff of the firm as a whole.

NOTES
Commencement: 25 May 2018.

[1.337]
5　Requirements in respect of the governing body of, and head teacher at, any school

(1)　In any case in which a governing body of a school and a head teacher at a school are both data controllers for the purposes of that school, the requirements of regulation 2 may be satisfied in respect of that governing body and head teacher in the name of the school.

(2)　Where the requirements of regulation 2 are satisfied in the name of a school under paragraph (1) above, the name and address to be specified for the purposes of regulation 2(3)(a) are those of the school.

(3)　For the purposes of this regulation, in the definition of "number of members of staff" in regulation 1(2) any reference to a data controller is to be treated as a reference to the school.

(4)　In this regulation—
"head teacher" includes, in Northern Ireland, the principal of a school;
"school"—
　　　(a)　in relation to England and Wales, has the same meaning as in the Education Act 1996,
　　　(b)　in relation to Scotland, has the same meaning as in the Education (Scotland) Act 1980, and
　　　(c)　in relation to Northern Ireland, has the same meaning as in the Education and Libraries (Northern Ireland) Order 1986.

NOTES
Commencement: 25 May 2018.

[1.338]
6　Crown application

These Regulations bind the Crown but do not apply to—
　　(a)　Her Majesty in Her private capacity,
　　(b)　Her Majesty in right of the Duchy of Lancaster, or
　　(c)　the Duke of Cornwall.

NOTES
Commencement: 25 May 2018.

SCHEDULE
EXEMPT PROCESSING

Regulation 2(1)

Interpretation

[1.339]
1　In this Schedule—
["elected representative" has the meaning given in paragraph 23(3)(a) to (d) and (f) to (m) of Schedule 1 to the Data Protection Act 2018;]
"judge" includes—
　　　(a)　a justice of the peace (or, in Northern Ireland, a lay magistrate),
　　　(b)　a member of a tribunal, and
　　　(c)　a clerk or other officer entitled to exercise the jurisdiction of a court or tribunal;
"public register" means any register which, pursuant to a requirement imposed—
　　　(a)　by or under any enactment, or
　　　(b)　in pursuance of any international agreement,
　　　is open to public inspection or open to any inspection by any person having a legitimate interest.

Exempt processing

2　(1)　For the purposes of regulation 2(1), processing of personal data is exempt processing if it—
　　(a)　falls within one or more of the descriptions of processing set out in sub-paragraph (2), or
　　(b)　does not fall within one or more of those descriptions solely by virtue of the fact that disclosure of the personal data is made for one of the reasons set out in sub-paragraph (3).

(2)　The processing is—
　　(a)　of personal data which is not being processed wholly or partly by automated means or recorded with the intention that it should be processed wholly or partly by automated means;
　　(b)　undertaken by a data controller for the purposes of their personal, family or household affairs, including—
　　　(i)　the processing of personal data for recreational purposes, and
　　　(ii)　the capturing of images, in a public space, containing personal data;
　　(c)　for the purpose of the maintenance of a public register;
　　(d)　for the purposes of matters of administration in relation to the members of staff and volunteers of, or persons working under any contract for services provided to, the data controller;
　　(e)　for the purposes of advertising, marketing and public relations in respect of the data controller's business, activity, goods or services;
　　(f)　subject to sub-paragraph (4), for the purposes of—
　　　(i)　keeping accounts, or records of purchases, sales or other transactions,
　　　(ii)　deciding whether to accept any person as a customer or supplier, or
　　　(iii)　making financial or financial management forecasts,

in relation to any activity carried on by the data controller;

(g) carried out by a body or association which is not established or conducted for profit and which carries out the processing for the purposes of establishing or maintaining membership or support for the body or association, or providing or administering activities for individuals who are either a member of the body or association or who have regular contact with it; . . .

(h) carried out by—
 (i) a judge, or
 (ii) a person acting on the instructions, or on behalf, of a judge,
 for the purposes of exercising judicial functions including the functions of appointment, discipline, administration or leadership of judges[; or]

[(i) carried out by—
 (i) a member of the House of Lords who is entitled to receive writs of summons to attend that House, or
 (ii) a person acting on the instructions, or on behalf, of such a member,
 for the purposes of exercising the member's functions as such;

(j) carried out by—
 (i) an elected representative, or
 (ii) a person acting on the instructions, or on behalf, of such a representative,
 for the purposes of exercising the elected representative's functions as such;

(k) carried out by—
 (i) a person seeking to become (or remain) an elected representative (a "prospective representative"), or
 (ii) a person acting on the instructions, or on behalf, of a prospective representative,
 in connection with any activity which can be reasonably regarded as intended to promote or procure the election (or re-election) of the prospective representative].

(3) The disclosure is—
 (a) required by or under any enactment, by any rule of law or by the order of a court;
 (b) made for the purposes of—
 (i) the prevention or detection of crime,
 (ii) the apprehension or prosecution of offenders, or
 (iii) the assessment or collection of any tax or duty or of any imposition of a similar nature,
 and not otherwise being able to make the disclosure would be likely to prejudice any of the matters in (i) to (iii) above;
 (c) necessary—
 (i) for the purpose of, or in connection with, any legal proceedings (including prospective legal proceedings), or
 (ii) for the purposes of obtaining legal advice,
 or is otherwise necessary for the purposes of establishing, exercising or defending legal rights; or
 (d) required for the purpose of avoiding an infringement of the privileges of either House of Parliament.

(4) The processing of personal data by or obtained from a credit reference agency (within the meaning of section 145(8) of the Consumer Credit Act 1974) does not fall within the description of processing set out in sub-paragraph (2)(f).

NOTES

Commencement: 25 May 2018.

Para 1: definition "elected representative" inserted by the Data Protection (Charges and Information) (Amendment) Regulations 2019, SI 2019/478, reg 2(1), (2).

Para 2: word omitted from sub-para (2)(g) revoked and sub-para (2)(i)–(k) inserted, together with preceding word, by SI 2019/478, reg 2(1), (3).

INFORMATION COMMISSIONER'S OFFICE CODES OF PRACTICE

ICO: AGE APPROPRIATE DESIGN: A CODE OF PRACTICE FOR ONLINE SERVICES

[1.340]

NOTES

This code of practice entered into force on 2 September 2020, with a 12 month transition period. Organisations must conform with it by 2 September 2021. The latest version of the code is available at: https://ico.org.uk/for-organisations/guide-to-data-protection/key-data-protection-themes/age-appropriate-design-code/.

2 September 2020; version 2.1.115; © Information Commissioner's Office, licensed under the Open Government Licence.

TABLE OF CONTENTS

The Secretary of State laid the Age Appropriate Design Code to Parliament under section 125(1)(b) of the Data Protection Act 2018 (the Act) on 11 June 2020. The ICO issued the code on 12 August 2020 and it will come into force on 2 September 2020 with a 12 month transition period.

There is more information in the Explanatory Memorandum.

INFORMATION COMMISSIONER'S FOREWORD

[1.341]

Data sits at the heart of the digital services children use every day. From the moment a young person opens an app, plays a game or loads a website, data begins to be gathered. Who's using the service? How are they using it? How frequently? Where from? On what device?

That information may then inform techniques used to persuade young people to spend more time using services, to shape the content they are encouraged to engage with, and to tailor the advertisements they see.

For all the benefits the digital economy can offer children, we are not currently creating a safe space for them to learn, explore and play.

This statutory code of practice looks to change that, not by seeking to protect children from the digital world, but by protecting them within it.

This code is necessary.

This code will lead to changes that will help empower both adults and children.

One in five UK internet users are children, but they are using an internet that was not designed for them. In our own research conducted to inform the direction of the code, we heard children describing data practices as "nosy", "rude" and a "bit freaky".

Our recent national survey into people's biggest data protection concerns ranked children's privacy second only to cyber security. This mirrors similar sentiments in research by Ofcom and the London School of Economics.

This code will lead to changes in practices that other countries are considering too.

It is rooted in the United Nations Convention on the Rights of the Child (UNCRC) that recognises the special safeguards children need in all aspects of their life. Data protection law at the European level reflects this and provides its own additional safeguards for children.

The code is the first of its kind, but it reflects the global direction of travel with similar reform being considered in the USA, Europe and globally by the Organisation for Economic Co-operation and Development (OECD).

This code will lead to changes that UK Parliament wants.

Parliament and government ensured UK data protection laws will truly transform the way we look after children online by requiring my office to introduce this statutory code of practice.

The code delivers on that mandate and requires information society services to put the best interests of the child first when they are designing and developing apps, games, connected toys and websites that are likely to be accessed by them.

This code is achievable.

The code is not a new law but it sets standards and explains how the General Data Protection Regulation applies in the context of children using digital services. It follows a thorough consultation process that included speaking with parents, children, schools, children's campaign groups, developers, tech and gaming companies and online service providers.

Such conversations helped shape our code into effective, proportionate and achievable provisions.

Organisations should conform to the code and demonstrate that their services use children's data fairly and in compliance with data protection law.

The code is a set of 15 flexible standards – they do not ban or specifically prescribe – that provides built-in protection to allow children to explore, learn and play online by ensuring that the best interests of the child are the primary consideration when designing and developing online services.

minimum amount of personal data should be collected and retained; children's data should not usually be shared; geolocation services should be switched off by default. Nudge techniques should not be used to encourage children to provide unnecessary personal data, weaken or turn off their privacy settings. The code also addresses issues of parental control and profiling.

This code will make a difference.

Developers and those in the digital sector must act. We have allowed the maximum transition period of 12 months and will continue working with the industry.

We want coders, UX designers and system engineers to engage with these standards in their day-to-day to work and we're setting up a package of support to help.

But the next step must be a period of action and preparation. I believe companies will want to conform with the standards because they will want to demonstrate their commitment to always acting in the best interests of the child. Those companies that do not make the required changes risk regulatory action.

What's more, they risk being left behind by those organisations that are keen to conform.

A generation from now, I believe we will look back and find it peculiar that online services weren't always designed with children in mind.

When my grandchildren are grown and have children of their own, the need to keep children safer online will be as second nature as the need to ensure they eat healthily, get a good education or buckle up in the back of a car.

And while our code will never replace parental control and guidance, it will help people have greater confidence that their children can safely learn, explore and play online.

There is no doubt that change is needed. The code is an important and significant part of that change.

Elizabeth Denham CBE

EXECUTIVE SUMMARY

[1.342]
Children are being 'datafied' with companies and organisations recording many thousands of data points about them as they grow up. These can range from details about their mood and their friendships to what time they woke up and when they went to bed.

Conforming to this statutory code of practice will ensure that as an organisation providing online services likely to be accessed by children in the UK, you take into account the best interests of the child. It will help you to develop services that recognise and cater for the fact that children warrant special protection in how their personal data is used, whilst also offering plenty of opportunity to explore and develop online.

You have 12 months to implement the necessary changes from the date that the code takes effect following the Parliamentary approval process. The ICO approach to enforcement as set out in our Regulatory Action Policy will apply. That policy and this code both apply a proportionate and risk-based approach.

The United Nations Convention on the Rights of the Child (UNCRC) recognises that children need special safeguards and care in all aspects of their life. There is agreement at international level and within the UK that much more needs to be done to create a safer online space for them to learn, explore and play.

In the UK, Parliament and government have acted to ensure that our domestic data protection laws truly transform the way we safeguard our children when they access online services by requiring the Commissioner to produce this statutory code of practice. This code seeks to protect children **within** the digital world, not protect them from it.

The code sets out 15 standards of age appropriate design reflecting a risk-based approach. The focus is on providing default settings which ensures that children have the best possible access to online services whilst minimising data collection and use, by default.

It also ensures that children who choose to change their default settings get the right information, guidance and advice before they do so, and proper protection in how their data is used afterwards.

You should follow the standards as part of your approach to complying with data protection law. If you can show us that you conform to these standards then you will conform to the code. The standards are cumulative and interlinked and you must implement them all, to the extent they are relevant to your service, in order to demonstrate your conformity.

The detail below the standards provides further explanation to help you understand and implement them in practice. It is designed to help you if you aren't sure what to do, but it is not prescriptive. This should give you enough flexibility to develop services which conform to the standards in your own way, taking a proportionate and risk-based approach. It will help you to design services that comply with the General Data Protection Regulation (GDPR) and the Privacy and Electronic Communications Regulations (PECR).

ADDITIONAL RESOURCES

[1.343]
[Age appropriate design code]

NOTES
    The additional resources under this section can be found on the ICO website at: https://ico.org.uk/for-organisations/childrens-code-hub.

CODE STANDARDS

[1.344]
The standards are:

1.   Best interests of the child: The best interests of the child should be a primary consideration when you design and develop online services likely to be accessed by a child.

2.   Data protection impact assessments: Undertake a DPIA to assess and mitigate risks to the rights and freedoms of children who are likely to access your service, which arise from your data processing. Take into account differing ages, capacities and development needs and ensure that your DPIA builds in compliance with this code.

3.   Age appropriate application: Take a risk-based approach to recognising the age of individual users and ensure you effectively apply the standards in this code to child users. Either establish age with a level of certainty that is appropriate to the risks to the rights and freedoms of children that arise from your data processing, or apply the standards in this code to all your users instead.

4.   Transparency: The privacy information you provide to users, and other published terms, policies and community standards, must be concise, prominent and in clear language suited to the age of the child. Provide additional specific 'bite-sized' explanations about how you use personal data at the point that use is activated.

5.   Detrimental use of data: Do not use children's personal data in ways that have been shown to be detrimental to their wellbeing, or that go against industry codes of practice, other regulatory provisions or Government advice.

6.   Policies and community standards: Uphold your own published terms, policies and community standards (including but not limited to privacy policies, age restriction, behaviour rules and content policies).

7.   Default settings: Settings must be 'high privacy' by default (unless you can demonstrate a compelling reason for a different default setting, taking account of the best interests of the child).

8. Data minimisation: Collect and retain only the minimum amount of personal data you need to provide the elements of your service in which a child is actively and knowingly engaged. Give children separate choices over which elements they wish to activate.

9. Data sharing: Do not disclose children's data unless you can demonstrate a compelling reason to do so, taking account of the best interests of the child.

10. Geolocation: Switch geolocation options off by default (unless you can demonstrate a compelling reason for geolocation to be switched on by default, taking account of the best interests of the child). Provide an obvious sign for children when location tracking is active. Options which make a child's location visible to others must default back to 'off' at the end of each session.

11. Parental controls: If you provide parental controls, give the child age appropriate information about this. If your online service allows a parent or carer to monitor their child's online activity or track their location, provide an obvious sign to the child when they are being monitored.

12. Profiling: Switch options which use profiling 'off' by default (unless you can demonstrate a compelling reason for profiling to be on by default, taking account of the best interests of the child). Only allow profiling if you have appropriate measures in place to protect the child from any harmful effects (in particular, being fed content that is detrimental to their health or wellbeing).

13. Nudge techniques: Do not use nudge techniques to lead or encourage children to provide unnecessary personal data or weaken or turn off their privacy protections.

14. Connected toys and devices: If you provide a connected toy or device ensure you include effective tools to enable conformance to this code.

15. Online tools: Provide prominent and accessible tools to help children exercise their data protection rights and report concerns.

ABOUT THIS CODE

AT A GLANCE

[1.345]
This code explains how to ensure your online services appropriately safeguard children's personal data. You should follow the code to help you process children's data fairly. It will also enable you to design services that comply, and demonstrate you comply, with the GDPR and PECR. If you do not follow this code, you are likely to find it more difficult to demonstrate your compliance with the law, should we take regulatory action against you.
• Who is this code for?
• What is the purpose of this code?
• What is the status of this code?
• How should we use the code?

WHO IS THIS CODE FOR?

This code is for providers of information society services (ISS). It applies to you if you provide online products or services (including apps, programs, websites, games or community environments, and connected toys or devices with or without a screen) that process personal data and are likely to be accessed by children in the UK. It is not only for services aimed at children. In this code 'online service' means a relevant ISS. For more information, see the separate section on services covered by this code.

WHAT IS THE PURPOSE OF THIS CODE?

This code addresses how to design data protection safeguards into online services to ensure they are appropriate for use by, and meet the development needs of, children.

It reflects the increasing concern about the position of children in society and the modern digital world in particular. There is agreement at international level and within the UK that much more needs to be done to create a safe online space for them to learn, explore and play. This code achieves this not by seeking to protect children from the digital world, but by protecting them within it.

The UNCRC recognises that children need special safeguards and care in all aspects of their life and requires that these should be guaranteed by appropriate legal protections. European level data protection law reflects this and provides its own additional safeguards for children.

In the UK, Parliament and government have acted to ensure that our domestic data protection laws do truly transform the way we safeguard our children when they access online services by requiring the Commissioner to produce this statutory code of practice. This code delivers on Parliament and the government's intent to use data protection law to make a profound and lasting change to how we look after our children when they access online services.

It takes account of the standards and principles set out in the UNCRC, and sets out specific protections for children's personal data in compliance with the provisions of the GDPR.

If you provide relevant online services, this code will help you to comply, and demonstrate that you comply, with your data protection obligations. Conforming to the standards in this code will be a key measure of your compliance with data protection laws. Following this code will also show parents and other users of your services that you take children's privacy seriously, you can be trusted with children's data, and your services are appropriate for children to use.

How does this code take account of the rights of the child?

In preparing this code, the Commissioner is required to consider the UK's obligations under the UNCRC, and the fact that children have different needs at different ages.

The code incorporates the key principle from the UNCRC that the best interests of the child should be a primary consideration in all actions concerning children. It also aims to respect the rights and duties of parents, and the child's evolving capacity to make their own choices.

In particular, this code aims to ensure that online services use children's data in ways that support the rights of the child to:
*   freedom of expression;
*   freedom of thought, conscience and religion;
*   freedom of association;
*   privacy;
*   access information from the media (with appropriate protection from information and material
*   injurious to their well-being);
*   play and engage in recreational activities appropriate to their age; and
*   protection from economic, sexual or other forms of exploitation.

How does this code support parents?

Parents (or guardians) play a key role in protecting their children and deciding what is in their best interests. However, in the context of online services, parents and children may find it difficult to make informed choices or exercise any control over the way those services use children's data. Often the only choice in practice is to avoid online services altogether, which means the child loses the benefits of online play, interaction and development. This code therefore expects providers of these services to take responsibility for ensuring that the way their services use personal data is appropriate to the child's age, takes account of their best interests, and respects their rights; as well as supporting parents or older children in making choices (where appropriate) in the child's best interests.

How does this code support data protection compliance?

The UK data protection regime is set out in the Data Protection Act 2018 (DPA 2018) and the GDPR. This regime requires you to take a risk-based approach when you use people's data, based on certain key principles, rights and obligations.

This code supports compliance with those general principles by setting out specific protections you need to build in when designing online services likely to be accessed by children, in line with Recital 38 of the GDPR:

"Children merit specific protection with regard to their personal data, as they may be less aware of the risks, consequences and safeguards concerned and their rights in relation to the processing of personal data. Such specific protection should, in particular, apply to the use of personal data of children for the purposes of marketing or creating personality or user profiles and the collection of personal data with regard to children when using services offered directly to a child . . . "

In particular, this code sets out practical measures and safeguards to ensure processing under the GDPR can be considered 'fair' in the context of online risks to children, and will help you comply with:
*   Article 5(1)(a): the fairness, lawfulness and transparency principle;
*   Article 5(1)(b): the purpose limitation principle;
*   Article 5(1)(c): the data minimisation principle;
*   Article 5(1)(e): the storage limitation principle;
*   Article 5(2): the accountability principle;
*   Article 6: lawfulness of processing;
*   Articles 12, 13 and 14: the right to be informed;
*   Articles 15 to 20: the rights of data subjects;
*   Article 22: profiling and automated decision-making;
*   Article 25: data protection by design and by default; and
*   Article 35: data protection impact assessments (DPIAs).

It covers your use of 'inferred data' (information about a child that you don't collect directly, but that you infer from other information or from their behaviours online) as well as data you collect directly from the child.

Annex C also includes some guidance on identifying your lawful basis for processing in the context of an online service. If you rely on consent, it explains the Article 8 rule on parental consent for children under 13.

PECR also set some specific rules on the use of cookies and other technologies which rely on access to user devices, and on electronic marketing messages. This code refers to those requirements where relevant, but for full details on how to comply you should read our separate Guide to PECR.

If you need to process personal data in order to protect children from online harms, such as child sexual exploitation and abuse, then this code shouldn't prevent you from doing so. However, you need to satisfy all the usual data protection requirements before you proceed, such as ensuring that the processing is fair and proportionate to the harm you are seeking to prevent, identifying a lawful basis for processing and providing transparency information.

WHAT IS THE STATUS OF THIS CODE?

What is the legal status of the code?

This is a statutory code of practice prepared under section 123 of the DPA 2018:

"The Commissioner must prepare a code of practice which contains such guidance as the Commissioner considers appropriate on standards of age appropriate design of relevant information society services which are likely to be accessed by children."

It was laid before Parliament on 11 June 2020 and issued on 12 August 2020 under section 125 of the DPA 2018. It comes into force on 2 September 2020.

As was made clear in the Parliamentary debates when the Data Protection Bill passed through Parliament, if your online service fails to conform to a provision of this code you may find it difficult to demonstrate compliance with the law and you may invite regulatory action.

In accordance with section 127 of the DPA 2018, the Commissioner must take the code into account when considering whether an online service has complied with its data protection obligations under the GDPR or PECR. In particular, the Commissioner will take the code into account when considering questions of fairness, lawfulness, transparency and accountability under the GDPR, and in the use of her enforcement powers.

The code can also be used in evidence in court proceedings, and the courts must take its provisions into account wherever relevant.

What happens if we don't conform to the standards in this code?

If you don't conform to the standards in this code, you are likely to find it more difficult to demonstrate that your processing is fair and complies with the GDPR and PECR. If you process a child's personal data in breach of the GDPR or PECR, we can take action against you.

Tools at our disposal include assessment notices, warnings, reprimands, enforcement notices and penalty notices (administrative fines). For serious breaches of the data protection principles, we have the power to issue fines of up to €20 million (£17.5 million when the UK GDPR comes into effect) or 4% of your annual worldwide turnover, whichever is higher.

Our approach to using these powers will take account of the risks to children that arise from your data processing, and the efforts you have made to conform to the standards in this code. In cases where we find against you, we are more likely to allow you time to bring your service into compliance if you have a well-documented and reasoned case to support the approach you have taken.

Conversely, if you have not taken proper steps to conform despite clear evidence or constructive knowledge that children are likely to access your service, and clear evidence of significant risk arising from the use of children's data, we are more likely to take formal regulatory action. The established ICO approach to enforcement as set out in our Regulatory Action Policy will apply to use of children's personal data under the GDPR and consideration of this code.

For more information, see the separate section on enforcement of this code.

How is this code affected when the UK leaves the EU?

This code is based on and refers to the relevant provisions of the DPA 2018 and GDPR as they apply in the UK in November 2019, before exit day.

If the UK leaves the EU with no deal, the EU version of the GDPR will no longer be law in the UK. However, a UK version of the GDPR will be written into UK law (UK GDPR). The UK GDPR will sit alongside an amended version of the DPA 2018. Although this code is based on the provisions of the DPA 2018 and EU GDPR in effect before exit day, the key data protection principles, rights and obligations underlying this code will remain the same under the UK GDPR.

The standards in this code will therefore still apply. The Commissioner will continue to take the code into account. However, after exit day, you should read references in this code to the GDPR as references to the equivalent provision in the UK GDPR. We have also highlighted a few specific changes throughout this code where directly relevant.

If the UK agrees to leave the EU with a deal, there will be an implementation period during which the GDPR – and this code – will continue to apply in the UK in the same way as before exit day. At the end of the implementation period, the default position is the same as for a no-deal exit, and we expect this code to remain in effect.

If there are any further changes to the details of the future UK regime, the Commissioner will review the standards in this code to ensure they remain relevant and appropriate to support compliance with UK law.

What is the status of 'further reading' or other linked resources?

Any further reading or other resources which are mentioned in or linked from this code do not form part of the code. We provide links to give you helpful context and further guidance on specific issues, but there is no statutory obligation under the DPA 2018 for the Commissioner or courts to take it into account (unless it is another separate statutory code of practice).

Where we link to other ICO guidance, that guidance will inevitably reflect the Commissioner's views and inform our general approach to interpretation, compliance and enforcement.

We may also link to relevant guidance provided by the European Data Protection Board (EDPB), which is the independent body established to ensure consistency within the EU when interpreting the GDPR and taking regulatory action.

HOW SHOULD WE USE THE CODE?

The standards at the start of this code are the 15 headline 'standards of age appropriate design' that you need to implement. The main body of this code is then divided into 15 sections, each giving more detail on what the standard means, why it is important, and how you can implement it. This further explanation is designed to help you if you aren't sure what to do, but it is not prescriptive. It should give you enough flexibility to develop services which conform to the standards in your own way, taking a proportionate and risk-based approach. It will help you to design services that comply with the GDPR and PECR.

Your conformity to the code will be assessed against the 15 headline standards. However, we recommend that you read the code in full as it will help you understand how you can implement each standard properly. These standards are cumulative and interdependent - you must implement all of them, to the extent they are relevant to your service, in order to demonstrate your conformance to the code.

This code assumes familiarity with key data protection terms and concepts. We have included a glossary at the end of this code as a quick reference point for common concepts and abbreviations, but if you need an introduction to data protection – or more context and guidance on key concepts – you should refer to our separate Guide to Data Protection.

This code focuses on specific safeguards to ensure your data regime is appropriate for children who are likely to access your service, so that you process their data fairly. It is not intended as an exhaustive guide to data protection compliance. For example, it does not elaborate on your obligations on security, processors or breach reporting. You need to make sure you are aware of all of your obligations, and you should read this code alongside our other guidance. Your DPIA process should incorporate measures to comply with your data protection obligations generally, as well as conform to the specific standards in this code.

Further reading outside this code

United Nations Convention on the Rights of the Child

Guide to Data Protection

Guide to PECR

ICO Regulatory Action Policy

DP and Brexit

SERVICES COVERED BY THIS CODE

AT A GLANCE

[1.346]
This code applies to "information society services likely to be accessed by children" in the UK. This includes many apps, programs, connected toys and devices, search engines, social media platforms, streaming services, online games, news or educational websites and websites offering other goods or services to users over the internet. It is not restricted to services specifically directed at children.

IN MORE DETAIL

- What services does this code apply to?
- What do you mean by an 'information society service'?
- What types of online services are not 'relevant ISS'?
- When are services 'likely to be accessed by children'?
- Does it apply to services based outside the UK?
- What about the eCommerce Regulations 2002?

What services does this code apply to?

Section 123 of the DPA 2018 says that this code applies to:

"relevant information society services which are likely to be accessed by children."

It says that 'information society services' has the same meaning as it has in the GDPR except that it does not include 'preventive or counselling services', and that 'relevant ISS' are those which involve the processing of personal data to which the GDPR applies.

The vast majority of online services used by children are covered, although there are some limited exceptions that are discussed in more detail below. Annex A to this code provides a flowchart setting out the questions you will need to answer if you are uncertain whether your service is covered.

What do you mean by an 'information society service'?

The definition is broad and the majority of online services that children use are covered.

'Information society service' is defined as:

"any service normally provided for remuneration, at a distance, by electronic means and at the individual request of a recipient of services.

For the purposes of this definition:

(i) 'at a distance' means that the service is provided without the parties being simultaneously present;

(ii) 'by electronic means' means that the service is sent initially and received at its destination by means of electronic equipment for the processing (including digital compression) and storage of data, and entirely transmitted, conveyed and received by wire, by radio, by optical means or by other electromagnetic means;

(iii) 'at the individual request of a recipient of services' means that the service is provided through the transmission of data on individual request."

Essentially this means that most online services are ISS, including apps, programs and many websites including search engines, social media platforms, online messaging or internet based voice telephony services, online marketplaces, content streaming services (eg video, music or gaming services), online games, news or educational websites, and any websites offering other goods or services to users over the internet. Electronic services for controlling connected toys and other connected devices are also ISS.

These services are covered even if the 'remuneration' or funding of the service doesn't come directly from the end user. For example, an online gaming app or search engine that is provided free to the end user but funded via advertising still comes within the definition of an ISS. This code also covers not-for-profit apps, games and educational sites, as long as those services can be considered as 'economic activity' in a more general sense. For example, they are types of services which are typically provided on a commercial basis.

If you are a small business with a website, your website is an ISS if you sell your products online, or offer a type of service which is transacted solely or mainly via your website without you needing to spend time with the customer in person.

What types of online services are not 'relevant ISS'?

Some services provided by public authorities

If you are a public authority which provides an online public service then, as long as the type of service you offer is not typically provided on a commercial basis your service is not a relevant ISS. This is because it is not a service 'normally provided for remuneration'.

If you are a police force or other competent authority with an online service which processes personal data for law enforcement purposes, then your service isn't a relevant ISS. This is because relevant ISS are those which involve the processing of personal data 'to which the GDPR applies'. The GDPR does not apply to processing by competent law enforcement authorities for law enforcement purposes. For further information about the scope of the GDPR and how data protection law applies to processing for law enforcement purposes see our Guide to data protection.

Websites which just provide information about a real-world business or service

If your website just provides information about your real-world business, but does not allow customers to buy products online or access a specific online service, it is not an ISS. This is because the service being offered is not provided 'at a distance'. An online booking service for an in-person appointment does not qualify as an ISS.

Traditional voice telephony services

Traditional voice telephony services are not relevant ISS. This is because they are not considered to be 'delivered by electronic means'. This differs from internet based voice calling services (VOIP) which are within scope as they are delivered over the internet by electronic means.

General broadcast services

The definition of an ISS does not include broadcast services such as scheduled television or radio transmissions that are broadcast to a general audience, rather than at the request of the individual (even if the channel is broadcast over the internet).

This differs from 'on demand' services which are, by their nature, provided 'at the individual request of a recipient'.

If you provide both a general broadcast and an on demand service, then the on demand element of your service will be covered by the code.

Preventive or counselling services

This code does not apply to websites or apps specifically offering online counselling or other preventive services (such as health screenings or check-ups) to children. This is because s123 scopes out 'preventive or counselling services'. However, more general health, fitness or wellbeing apps or services are covered.

When are services 'likely to be accessed by children'?

This code applies if children are likely to use your service. A child is defined in the UNCRC and for the purposes of this code as a person under 18.

If your service is designed for and aimed specifically at under-18s then the code applies. However, the provision in section 123 of the DPA is wider than this. It also applies to services that aren't specifically aimed or targeted at children, but are nonetheless likely to be used by under-18s.

It is important to recognise that Parliament sought to use the wording 'likely to be accessed by' rather than narrower terms, to ensure that the application of the code did not exclude services that children were using in reality. This drew on experience of other online child protection regimes internationally, that only focused on services designed for children and therefore left a gap in coverage and greater risk.

We consider that for a service to be 'likely' to be accessed, the possibility of this happening needs to be more probable than not. This recognises the intention of Parliament to cover services that children use in reality, but does not extend the definition to cover all services that children could possibly access.

In practice, whether your service is likely to be accessed by children or not is likely to depend on:
*   the nature and content of the service and whether that has particular appeal for children; and
*   the way in which the service is accessed and any measures you put in place to prevent children gaining access.

You should take a common sense approach to this question. If your service is the kind of service that you would not want children to use in any case, then your focus should be on how you prevent access (in which case this code does not apply), rather than on making it child-friendly. For example, if it is an adult only, restricted, or otherwise child-inappropriate service. This code should not lead to the perverse outcome of providers of restricted services having to make their services child-friendly.

If your service is not aimed at children but is not inappropriate for them to use either, then your focus should be on assessing how appealing your service will be to them. If the nature, content or presentation of your service makes you think that children will want to use it, then you should conform to the standards in this code.

If you have an existing service and children form a substantive and identifiable user group, the 'likely to be accessed by' definition will apply.

Given the breadth of application, the ICO recognises that it will be possible to conform to this code in a risk-based and proportionate manner.

If you decide that your service is not likely to be accessed by children and that you are therefore not going to implement the code then you should document and support your reasons for your decision. You may wish to refer to market research, current evidence on user behaviour, the user base of similar or existing services and service types and testing of access restriction measures.

If you initially judge that the service is not likely to be accessed by children, but evidence later emerges that a significant number of children are in fact accessing your service, you will need to conform to the standards in this code or review your access restrictions if you do not think it is appropriate for children to use your service.

Does it apply to services based outside the UK?

This code is issued under the DPA 2018. The DPA 2018 applies to online services based in the UK.

It also applies to online services based outside the UK that have a branch, office or other 'establishment' in the UK, and process personal data in the context of the activities of that establishment.

The DPA 2018 may also apply to some other services based outside the UK even if they don't have an establishment in the UK. If the relevant establishment is outside the European Economic Area (EEA), the DPA 2018 still applies if you offer your service to users in the UK, or monitor the behaviour of users in the UK. The code applies if that service is likely to be accessed by children.

If you don't have a UK establishment, but do have an establishment elsewhere in the EEA this code does not apply (even if you offer your service to UK users, or monitor the behaviour of users in the UK).

If the code applies to your processing but, under the GDPR 'one-stop-shop' arrangements you have a lead supervisory authority other than the ICO, then we may ask them to take the code into account when considering your compliance with the GDPR and PECR. Alternatively, if we consider the case to be a 'local' case (affecting UK users only), we may take action ourselves and take the code into account.

How will this change when the UK leaves the EU?

When the UK leaves the EU (or at the end of the implementation period, if the UK leaves the EU with a deal), the UK regime will apply to services established in the EEA who are targeting UK users in the same way as to services established outside the EEA. The UK will no longer be part of the GDPR one-stop-shop system.

If you are established in the EEA and offer your service to UK users, or monitor the behaviour of users in the UK, this code will apply to you from exit day (or from the end of the implementation period if a deal is agreed).

What about the eCommerce Regulations 2002?

The eCommerce Regulations 2002 (ECR) do not exempt you from compliance with your data protection obligations. Regulation 3(1)(b) of the ECR, as amended by Schedule 19 Part 2 paragraph 288 of the DPA 2018, states that:

'Nothing in these Regulations shall apply in respect of –

    (b)   questions relating to information society services covered by the GDPR and Directive 2002/58/EC of the European Parliament and of the Council of 12th July 2002 concerning the processing of personal data and the protection of privacy in the electronic communications sector (Directive on privacy and electronic communications)'

Whilst the ECR includes a 'safe harbour' regime for certain activities that you may carry out as an 'intermediary' service provider, it is important to note that:

*   this does not remove your responsibility for data protection compliance, either in general or in relation to those activities; and
*   the provisions of the GDPR are without prejudice to this regime.

The ICO will take the safe harbour regime into account, particularly in cases of complaints and potential regulatory action arising from activities relating to those that the safe harbour regime covers.

You should assess how the legal framework applies to activities you perform in your own right, and those which you perform as an intermediary. For example, an Internet Service Provider (ISP) or Mobile Network Operator (MNO) might provide core connectivity services as an intermediary service provider whilst also providing services such as customer service Apps or corporate websites in their own right. If necessary you may need to obtain specialist legal advice.

For more information, see the section on 'Enforcement of this Code'.

Further reading outside this code

For further information on the definition of an ISS see:

Article 1(1) and Annex 1 of Directive (EU) 2015/1535 (Article 4(25) of the GDPR incorporates this definition into the GDPR) Ker-Optika v ANTSZ (CJEU case C-108/09, 2 December 2010)

McFadden v Sony (CJEU case C-484/14, 15 September 2016)

Elite Taxi v Uber (Opinion of the AG in case C-434/15, 11 May 2017)

For more information on whether the GDPR applies, see our guidance:

Introduction to Data Protection - Which regime?

For more information on the GDPR one-stop-shop principle, see the EDPB guidelines on the lead supervisory authority.

The ICO has launched a consultation on a package of support for the providers of online services likely to be accessed by children.

TRANSITIONAL ARRANGEMENTS

AT A GLANCE

[1.347]
Providers of ISS likely to be accessed by children should bring their processing in line with the standards in this code by 2 September 2021.

IN MORE DETAIL

*   When will the code take effect?
*   What should we do about our existing services?

When will the code take effect?

The code was issued on 12 August 2020.

It comes into force on 2 September 2020.

From 2 September 2021 the Commissioner must take the code into account when considering whether an online service has complied with its data protection obligations under the GDPR and PECR. The courts must also take the provision of the code into account, when relevant, from this date.

Our approach is to encourage conformance and we would encourage you to start preparing for the code taking effect sooner rather than later. In accordance with our Regulatory Action Policy, when considering any enforcement action we will take into account the efforts you have made towards conformance during the transition period, as well as the size and resources of your organisation, and the risks to children inherent in your data processing.

The code will apply to both new and existing services.

What should we do about our existing services?

We recommend that you start by reviewing your existing services to establish whether they are covered.

For services that are covered, you should already have a DPIA – but you should now review it (or conduct a new one) as soon as possible. This will give you the maximum amount of time available to you to bring your processing into line with the standards in the code. You should focus on assessing conformance with the standards in this code and identifying any additional measures necessary to conform.

You should make changes to your service as soon as possible, and in any event by 2 September 2021.

Where changes include changes to physical rather than purely online products, then you should ensure that the necessary changes are incorporated into manufacturing cycles schedules commencing after 2 September 2021. For example, if you are making changes to packaging, printed information or the physical component of a connected toy or device. You will not be required to recall or amend existing stock, or to amend manufacturing cycles that were already scheduled to commence before 2 September 2021 when this code came into force.

You should also consider how to manage any changes to the way in which your service operates with your existing users. You should think about how their online experience might change and how best to communicate and prepare them for these changes so that any impact is properly managed.

STANDARDS OF AGE APPROPRIATE DESIGN

[1.348]
Section 123 of the DPA 2018 says this code must contain:

"such guidance as the Commissioner considers appropriate on standards of age-appropriate design of relevant information society services which are likely to be accessed by children."

It defines 'standards of age-appropriate design' as:

"such standards of age-appropriate design of such services as appear to the Commissioner to be desirable having regard to the best interests of children."

The standards are not intended as technical standards, but as a set of technology-neutral design principles and practical privacy features. The focus of the code is to set a benchmark for the appropriate protection of children's personal data. Different services will require different technical solutions.

You must build the standards set out in this code into your design processes from the start, into subsequent upgrade and service development processes and into your DPIA process.

For more information on how we enforce these standards, see the separate section on enforcement of this code.

1. BEST INTERESTS OF THE CHILD

[1.349]
The best interests of the child should be a primary consideration when you design and develop online services likely to be accessed by a child.

WHAT DO YOU MEAN BY 'THE BEST INTERESTS OF THE CHILD'?

The concept of the best interests of the child comes from Article 3 of the United Nations Convention on the Rights of the Child (UNCRC):

"In all actions concerning children, whether undertaken by public or private social welfare institutions, courts of law, administrative authorities or legislative bodies, the best interests of the child shall be a primary consideration."

The UNCRC incorporates provisions aimed at supporting the child's needs for safety, health, wellbeing, family relationships, physical, psychological and emotional development, identity, freedom of expression, privacy and agency to form their own views and have them heard. Put simply, the best interests of the child are whatever is best for that individual child.

The UNCRC expressly recognises the role of parents and carers (including extended family, guardians and others with legal responsibility) in protecting and promoting the best interests of the child.

It also recognises the child's right to privacy and freedom from economic exploitation. The importance of access to information, association with others, and play in supporting the child's development. And the child's right, in line with their evolving capacities, to have a voice in matters that affect them.

The UNCRC provides a framework which balances a number of different interests and concerns, with the intention of providing whatever is best for each individual child.

The placing of the best interests of the child as a 'primary consideration' recognises that the best interests of the child have to be balanced against other interests. For example the best interests of two individual children might be in conflict, or acting solely in the best interests of one child might prejudice the rights of others. It is unlikely however that the commercial interests of an organisation will outweigh a child's right to privacy.

WHY IS THIS IMPORTANT?

This is important because the Information Commissioner is required to have regard to the United Kingdom's obligations under the UNCRC in drafting this code.

It is also important because it provides a framework to help you understand the needs of children and the rights that you have to take into account when designing online services.

Article 5(1)(a) of the GDPR says personal data shall be:

"processed lawfully, fairly and in a transparent manner in relation to the data subject ('lawfulness, fairness and transparency)"

And recital 38 to the GDPR says:

"Children merit specific protection with regard to their personal data, as they may be less aware of the risks, consequences and safeguards concerned and their rights in relation to the processing . . . "

If you consider the best interests of child users in all aspects of your design of online services, then you should be well placed to comply with the 'lawfulness, fairness and transparency' principle, and to take proper account of Recital 38.

The principle of 'the best interests of the child' is therefore both something that you specifically need to consider when designing your online service, and a theme that runs throughout the provisions of this code.

HOW CAN WE MAKE SURE THAT WE MEET THIS STANDARD?

Consider and support the rights of children

In order to implement this standard you need to consider the needs of child users and work out how you can best support those needs in the design of your online service, when you process their personal data. In doing this you should take into account the age of the user. You may need to use evidence and advice from expert third parties to help you do this.

In particular you should consider how, in your use of personal data, you can:
* keep them safe from exploitation risks, including the risks of commercial or sexual exploitation and sexual abuse;
* protect and support their health and wellbeing;
* protect and support their physical, psychological and emotional development;
* protect and support their need to develop their own views and identity;
* protect and support their right to freedom of association and play;
* support the needs of children with disabilities in line with your obligations under the relevant equality legislation for England, Scotland, Wales and Northern Ireland;
* recognise the role of parents in protecting and promoting the best interests of the child and support them in this task; and
* recognise the evolving capacity of the child to form their own view, and give due weight to that view.

Taking account of the best interests of the child does not mean that you cannot pursue your own commercial or other interests. Your commercial interests may not be incompatible with the best interests of the child, but you need to account for the best interests of the child as a primary consideration where any conflict arises.

Further reading outside this code

United Nations Convention of Rights of the Child

2. DATA PROTECTION IMPACT ASSESSMENTS

[1.350]
Undertake a DPIA to assess and mitigate risks to the rights and freedoms of children who are likely to access your service, which arise from your data processing. Take into account differing ages, capacities and development needs and ensure that your DPIA builds in compliance with this code.

WHAT DO YOU MEAN BY A 'DPIA'?

A DPIA is a defined process to help you identify and minimise the data protection risks of your service – and in particular the specific risks to children who are likely to access your service which arise from your processing of their personal data.

You should begin a DPIA early in the design of your service, before you start your processing. It should include these steps:
* Step 1: identify the need for a DPIA
* Step 2: describe the processing
* Step 3: consider consultation
* Step 4: assess necessity and proportionality
* Step 5: identify and assess risks arising from your processing
* Step 6: identify measures to mitigate the risks
* Step 7: sign off, record and integrate outcomes

The DPIA process is designed to be flexible and scalable. You can design a process that fits with your existing approach to design and development, as long as it contains these key elements, and the outcomes influence the design of your service. It does not need to be a time-consuming process in every case.

Further reading outside this code

See our detailed guidance on DPIAs

WHY ARE DPIAS IMPORTANT?

DPIAs are a key part of your accountability obligations under the GDPR, and help you adopt a 'data protection by design' approach. A good DPIA is also an effective way to assess and document your compliance with all of your data protection obligations and the provisions of this code.

The GDPR says you must do a DPIA before you begin any **type of processing** that is **likely to result in a high risk** to the rights and freedoms of individuals.

This is not about whether your service is actually high risk, but about screening for potential indicators of high risk. The nature and context of online services within the scope of this code mean they inevitably involve a type of processing likely to result in a high risk to the rights and freedoms of children.

The ICO is required by Article 35(4) of the GDPR to publish a list of processing operations that require a DPIA. This list supplements GDPR criteria and relevant European guidelines, and includes:

"the use of the personal data of children or other vulnerable individuals for marketing purposes, profiling or other automated decision-making, or if you intend to offer online services directly to children."

Online services may also trigger several other criteria indicating the need for a DPIA, including innovative technology, large-scale profiling, biometric data, and online tracking. In practice, this means that if you offer an online service likely to be accessed by children, you must do a DPIA.

However, DPIAs are not just a compliance exercise. Your DPIA should consider compliance risks, but also broader risks to the rights and freedoms of children that might arise from your processing, including the potential for any significant material, physical, psychological or social harm.

An effective DPIA allows you to identify and fix problems at an early stage, designing data protection in from the start. This can bring cost savings and broader benefits for both children and your organisation. It can reassure parents that you protect their children's interests and your service is appropriate for children to use. The consultation phase of a DPIA can also give children and parents the chance to have a say in how their data is used, help you build trust, and improve your understanding of child-specific needs, concerns and expectations. It may also help you avoid reputational damage later on.

HOW CAN WE MAKE SURE THAT WE MEET THIS STANDARD?

There is no definitive DPIA template, but you can use or adapt the template included as an annex to this code if you wish.

You must consult your Data Protection Officer (DPO) (if you have one) and, where appropriate, individuals and relevant experts. Any processors may also need to assist you.

Your DPIA must have a particular focus on the specific rights of and risks to children using your service that arise from your data processing. It should also assess and document your compliance with this code. You should build these additional elements into each stage of your DPIA, not bolt them on the end.

You need to follow the usual DPIA process set out in our separate guidance on how to conduct a DPIA, but you should build in the following specific issues at each stage.

Step 1: Identify when to do your DPIA

You must embed a DPIA into the design of any new online service that is likely to be accessed by children. You must complete your DPIA before the service is launched, and ensure the outcomes can influence your design. You should not treat a DPIA as a rubber stamp or tick-box exercise at the end of the design process.

You must also do a DPIA if you are planning to make any significant changes to the processing operations of an existing online service likely to be accessed by children.

An external change to the wider context of your service may also prompt you to review your DPIA. For example, if a new security flaw is identified, or a new public concern is raised over specific features of your service or particular risks to children.

Further reading outside this code

ICO list of processing operations that require a DPIA

European guidelines on DPIAs

Step 2: Describe the processing

You need to describe the nature, scope, context and purposes of the processing. In particular, you should include:

*   whether you are designing your service for children;
*   if not, whether children are nevertheless likely to access your service;
*   the age range of those children;
*   your plans, if any, for parental controls;

- your plans, if any, for establishing the age of your individual users;
- the intended benefits for children;
- the commercial interests (of yourself or third parties) that you have taken into account
- any profiling or automated decision-making involved;
- any geolocation elements;
- the use of any nudge techniques;
- any processing of special category data;
- any processing of inferred data;
- any current issues of public concern over online risks to children;
- any relevant industry standards or codes of practice;
- your responsibilities under the applicable equality legislation for England, Scotland, Wales and Northern Ireland; and
- any relevant guidance or research on the development needs, wellbeing or capacity of children in the relevant age range.

Step 3: Consult with children and parents

Depending on the size of your organisation, resources and the risks you have identified, you can seek and document the views of children and parents (or their representatives), and take them into account in your design.

We will expect larger organisations to do some form of consultation in most cases. For example, you could choose to get feedback from existing users, carry out a general public consultation, conduct market research, conduct user testing, or contact relevant children's rights groups for their views. This should include feedback on the child's ability to understand the ways you use their data and the information you provide. If you consider that it is not possible to do any form of consultation, or it is unnecessary or wholly disproportionate, you should record that decision in your DPIA, and be prepared to justify it to us. However, it is usually possible to carry out some form of market research or user feedback.

You should also consider seeking independent advice from experts in children's rights and developmental needs as part of this stage. This is especially important for services which:
- are specifically designed for children;
- are designed for general use but known to be widely used by children (such as games or social media sites); or
- use children's data in novel or unanticipated ways.

Step 4: Assess necessity, proportionality and compliance

You need to explain why your processing is necessary and proportionate for your service. You must also include information about how you comply with the GDPR, including:
- your lawful basis for processing (see Annex C);
- your condition for processing any special category data;
- measures to ensure accuracy, avoid bias and explain use of AI; and
- specific details of your technological security measures (eg hashing or encryption standards).

In addition, at this stage you should include an explanation of how you conform to each of the standards set out in this code.

Step 5: Identify and assess risks

You must consider the potential impact on children and any harm or damage your data processing may cause – whether physical, emotional, developmental or material. You should also specifically look at whether the processing could cause, permit or contribute to the risk of:
- physical harm;
- online grooming or other sexual exploitation;
- social anxiety, self-esteem issues, bullying or peer pressure;
- access to harmful or inappropriate content;
- misinformation or undue restriction on information;
- encouraging excessive risk-taking or unhealthy behaviour;
- undermining parental authority or responsibility;
- loss of autonomy or rights (including control over data);
- compulsive use or attention deficit disorders;
- excessive screen time;
- interrupted or inadequate sleep patterns;
- economic exploitation or unfair commercial pressure; or
- any other significant economic, social or developmental disadvantage.

You should bear in mind children's needs and maturity will differ according to their age and development stage. Annex B should help you to consider this.

To assess the level of risk, you must consider both the likelihood and the severity of any impact on children. High risk could result from either a high probability of some harm, or a lower possibility of serious harm. You should bear in mind that some children will be less resilient than others, so you should always take a precautionary approach to assessing the potential severity of harm. You may find that there is a high risk for some age ranges, even if the risk for other age ranges is lower.

Step 6: Identify measures to mitigate those risks

You must consider whether you could make any changes to your service to reduce or avoid each of the risks you have identified. As a minimum, you should implement the measures set out in this code, but you should also consider whether you can put any additional safeguards in place as part of your service design.

Transparency is important. However, you should also identify and consider measures that do not rely on children's ability or willingness to engage with your privacy information.

Step 7: Record the conclusion

If you have a DPO, you must record their independent advice on the outcome of the DPIA before making any final decisions.

You should record any additional measures you plan to take, and integrate them into the design of your service. If you identify a high risk that you are not mitigating, you must consult the ICO before you can go ahead.

It is good practice to publish your DPIA.

Further reading outside this code

See our detailed guidance on DPIAs

3. AGE APPROPRIATE APPLICATION

[1.351]

Take a risk-based approach to recognising the age of individual users and ensure you effectively apply the standards in this code to child users. Either establish age with a level of certainty that is appropriate to the risks to the rights and freedoms of children that arise from your data processing, or apply the standards in this code to all your users instead.

WHAT DO YOU MEAN BY 'AGE APPROPRIATE APPLICATION'?

This means that the age range of your audience and the different needs of children at different ages and stages of development should be at the heart of how you design your service and apply this code.

It also means you must apply this code so that all children are given an appropriate level of protection in how their personal data is used. There is flexibility for you to decide how to apply this standard in the context and circumstances of your online service. It will usually mean establishing (with a level of certainty that is appropriate to the risks to the rights and freedoms that arise from your data processing) what age range your individual users fall into, so that you can tailor the protections and safeguards you give to their personal data accordingly, by applying the standards in this code. You should use your DPIA to help you assess this.

Alternatively, if you can't or don't wish to do this, you could choose to apply the standards to all your users instead. This is so that children are afforded some protection against the risks that arise from how their personal data is used, even if you aren't sufficiently certain whether they are children or not.

WHY IS THIS IMPORTANT?

The ultimate aim of this code is to ensure that online services likely to be accessed by children are appropriate for their use and meet their development needs.

Understanding the age range of children likely to access the service – and the different needs of children at different ages and stages of development – is fundamental to the whole concept of 'age-appropriate design'.

Children are individuals, and age ranges are not a perfect guide to the interests, needs and evolving capacity of each child. However, to help you assess what is appropriate for children broadly of that age, you can use age ranges as a guide to the capacity, skills and behaviours a child might be expected to display at each stage of their development. For the purposes of this code, we have used the following age ranges and developmental stages as a guide:

- 0–5: pre-literate and early literacy
- 6–9: core primary school years
- 10–12: transition years
- 13–15: early teens
- 16–17: approaching adulthood

There is no requirement for you to design services for development stages that aren't likely to access your service, or to use these exact age ranges if you can justify why slightly different age groupings are more appropriate for your particular service.

Further information about relevant capacities, needs, skills and behaviours at each stage is set out at Annex B of this code for reference purposes, and where relevant throughout these standards.

You should also consider the needs of disabled children in line with any obligations you may have under the relevant equality legislation for England, Scotland, Wales and Northern Ireland.

The GDPR and DPA 2018 also specify that if you rely on consent for any aspects of your online service, you need to get parental authorisation for children under 13. If you do rely on consent as your lawful basis for processing personal data then these provisions have significant practical implications for you. Meeting the standards in this code should allow you to comply with these GDPR requirements in a proportionate way. See Annex C for full details.

HOW CAN WE MAKE SURE THAT WE MEET THIS STANDARD?

Consider the risks to children that arise from your data processing, and the level of certainty you have that you know the age of your users

You can implement this standard by following these steps:

• Think about the risks to children that would arise from your processing of their personal data. Your DPIA will help you to do this. You may wish to take into account factors such as: the types of data collected; the volume of data; the intrusiveness of any profiling; whether decision making or other actions follow from profiling; and whether the data is being shared with third parties. Both the ICO and the European Data Protection Board have also provided guidance on DPIAs which consider assessing risk in more detail.

• Consider how well you know your users. How certain are you that an individual user is an adult or a child? How confident are you about the age range your individual child users fall into?

• Decide whether the level of certainty you have about the age of your individual users is appropriate to the risks that arise from your data processing.

• If it is, then you can apply the rest of the standards in this code to your child users only.

• If it isn't, then decide whether you prefer to:

    • reduce the data risks inherent in your service;

    • put additional measures in place to increase your level of age confidence; or

    • apply the standards in this code to all users of your service (regardless of whether they have self-declared as an adult or a child).

HOW CAN WE ESTABLISH AGE WITH AN APPROPRIATE LEVEL OF CERTAINTY?

This code is not prescriptive about exactly what methods you should use to establish age, or what level of certainty different methods provide. This is because this will vary depending on the specifics of the techniques you use. We want to allow enough flexibility for you to use measures that suit the specifics of your individual service and that can develop over time. However you should always use a method that is appropriate to the risks that arise from your data processing.

Some of the methods you may wish to consider are listed below. This list is not exhaustive. Other measures may exist or emerge over time. In assessing whether you have chosen an appropriate method, we will take into account the products currently available in the marketplace, particularly for small businesses which don't have the resources to develop their own solutions.

• **Self-declaration** – This is where a user simply states their age but does not provide any evidence to confirm it. It may be suitable for low risk processing or when used in conjunction with other techniques. Even if you prefer to apply the standards in the code to all your users, self-declaration of age can provide a useful starting point when providing privacy information and age appropriate explanations of processing (see 'What does applying the standards to all users mean in practice?' for more detail).

• **Artificial intelligence** – It may be possible to make an estimate of a user's age by using artificial intelligence to analyse the way in which the user interacts with your service. Similarly you could use this type of profiling to check that the way a user interacts with your service is consistent with their self-declared age. This technique will typically provide a greater level of certainty about the age of users with increased use of your service. If you choose to use this technique then you need to:

    • tell users that you are going to do this upfront;

    • only collect the minimum amount of personal data that you need for this purpose; and

    • don't use any personal data you collect for this purpose for other purposes.

• **Third party age verification services** – You may choose to use a third party service to provide you with an assurance of the age of your users. Such services typically work on an 'attribute' system where you request confirmation of a particular user attribute (in this case age or age range) and the service provides you with a 'yes' or 'no' answer. This method reduces the amount of personal data you need to collect yourself and may allow you to take advantage of technological expertise and latest developments in the field. If you use a third party service you will need to carry out some due diligence checks to satisfy yourself that the level of certainty with which it confirms age is sufficient (PAS standard 1296 'Online age checking' may help you with this), and that it is compliant with data protection requirements. You should also provide your users with clear information about the service you use.

• **Account holder confirmation** - You may be able to rely upon confirmation of user age from an existing account holder who you know to be an adult. For example, if you provide a logged-in or subscription based service, you may allow the main (confirmed adult) account holder to set up child profiles, restrict further access with a password or PIN, or simply confirm the age range of additional account users.

- **Technical measures** – Technical measures which discourage false declarations of age, or identify and close under age accounts, may be useful to support or strengthen self-declaration mechanisms. Examples include neutral presentation of age declaration screens (rather than nudging towards the selection of certain ages), or preventing users from immediately resubmitting a new age if they are denied access to your service when they first self-declare their age.
- **Hard identifiers** – You can confirm age using solutions which link back to formal identify documents or 'hard identifiers' such as a passport. However, we recommend that you avoid giving users no choice but to provide hard identifiers unless the risks inherent in your processing really warrant such an approach. This is because some children do not have access to formal identity documents and may have limited parental support, making it difficult for them to access age verified services at all, even if they are age appropriate. Requiring hard identifiers may also have a disproportionate impact on the privacy of adults.

We recognise that methods of age assurance will vary depending on whether the service is used by authenticated or non-authenticated users (eg whether users are logged in) and that the risks may also vary in this context.

WHAT IF WE NEED TO COLLECT PERSONAL DATA IN ORDER TO ESTABLISH AGE?

You may be able to collect and record personal data which provides an assurance of age yourself. If so, remember that you need to comply with data protection obligations for your collection and retention of that data, including data minimisation, purpose limitation, storage limitation and security obligations.

The key to this is making sure that you only collect the minimum amount of personal data you need to give you an appropriate level of certainty about the age of your individual users, and making sure you don't use personal data collected for the purposes of establishing or estimating age in order to conform to this code for other purposes.

For example, if you use profiling to help you estimate the age of individual users so that you can apply the standards in this code, then you can use that profile information to ensure that you:
- provide age appropriate privacy information and nudges;
- provide high privacy settings for child users by default; and
- don't serve children content deemed detrimental to their health and wellbeing.

You can't however simply re-purpose that information for other purposes, such as targeting children with advertising for products you think they might like, or sending them details of 'birthday offers'. If you want to profile children for this purpose then you need their consent. See the section of this code on profiling for further detail.

We recognise there is a tension between age assurance and compliance with GDPR, as the implementation of age assurance could increase the risk of intrusive data collection. We do not require organisations to create these counter risks. However, age assurance and GDPR are compatible if privacy by design solutions are used.

Age-assurance tools are still a developing area. The Commissioner will support work to establish clear industry standards and certification schemes to assist children, parents and online services in identifying age-assurance services which comply with data protection standards.

WHAT DOES APPLYING THE STANDARDS TO ALL USERS MEAN IN PRACTICE?

If you don't have a level of certainty about the age of your users that is appropriate to the risks to children arising from your data processing, then your alternative is to apply the standards in the code to all users. This should mean that even if you don't really know how old a user is, or if a child has lied about their age, children will still receive some important protections in how their personal data is used.

However, it doesn't mean that you have to ignore any information you do have about the user's age, or that adult users have to be infantilised. It just means that all users will receive some basic protections in how their personal data is used by default.

You should apply the standards in the code in a way that recognises both the information you do have about the users age and the fact that your level of confidence in this information is inadequate to the risks inherent in your processing. For example, providing privacy information that is appropriate to the self-declared age of the user, but giving them the option to access versions written for different age groups as well.

Further reading outside this code

ICO detailed guidance on DPIAs

European guidelines on DPIAs

PAS standard 1296 Online Age Checking- code of practice

4. TRANSPARENCY

[1.352]
The privacy information you provide to users, and other published terms, policies and community standards, must be concise, prominent, and in clear language suited to the age of the child. Provide

additional specific 'bite-sized' explanations about how you use personal data at the point that use is activated.

WHAT DO YOU MEAN BY 'TRANSPARENCY'?

Transparency is about being clear, open and honest with your users about what they can expect when they access your online service.

WHY IS IT IMPORTANT?

Transparency is key to the requirement under Article 5(1) of the GDPR to process personal data:

> "lawfully, fairly and in a transparent manner in relation to the data subject ('lawfulness, fairness and transparency')"

The GDPR also contains more specific provisions about the information that you must give to data subjects when you process their personal data. These are set out at Article 13 (when you have obtained the personal data directly from the data subject) and Article 14 (when you have not obtained the personal data directly from the data subject).

Article 12 of the GDPR requires you to provide children with this information in a way in which they can access and understand it:

> "The controller shall take appropriate measures to provide any information referred to in Article 13 and 14 and any communication under Articles 15 to 22 and 34 relating to processing to the data subject in a concise, transparent, intelligible and easily accessible form, using clear and plain language, in particular for any information addressed specifically to a child. The information shall be provided in writing, or by other means, including, where appropriate, by electronic means. When requested by the data subject the information may be provided orally, provided that the identity of the data subject is proven by other means."

On a wider level transparency is also intrinsic to the fairness element of Article 5(1). If you aren't clear open and honest about the service that you provide and the rules that govern that service, then your original collection and ongoing use of the child's personal data is unlikely to be fair.

HOW CAN WE MAKE SURE THAT WE MEET THIS STANDARD?

Provide clear privacy information

Firstly you need to provide the privacy information set out in Articles 13 and 14 in a clear and prominent place on your online service. You should make this information easy to find and accessible for children and parents who seek out privacy information.

However, it is not sufficient to rely on children or their parents seeking out this privacy information.

Provide 'bite-sized' explanations at the point at which use of personal data is activated

In order to provide children with the specific protection envisaged by Recital 38 you should also provide clear information about what you do with children's personal data in more specific, 'bite-size' explanations, at the point at which the use of the personal data is activated. This is sometimes referred to as a 'just in time notice'. Depending on the age of the child and the risks inherent in the processing, you should also prompt them to speak to an adult before they activate any new use of their data, and not to proceed if they are uncertain.

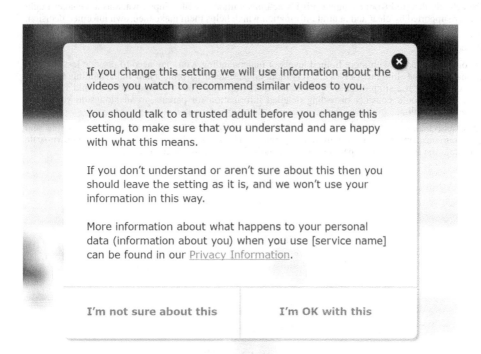

You should also consider if there are any other points in your user journey when it might be appropriate to provide bite-sized explanations to aid the child's understanding of how their personal data is being used.

Provide clear terms, policies and community standards

All other information you provide for users about your service should also be clear and accessible. This includes terms and conditions, policies and community standards.

In every case you should provide information that is accurate and does not promise protections or standards that are not routinely upheld.

This should help children or their parents make properly informed decisions about whether to provide the information required to access or sign up to your service in the first place, and to continue to use it.

If you believe that you need to draft your terms and conditions in a certain way in order to make them legally robust, then you can provide child-friendly explanations to sit alongside the legal drafting.

Present information in a child friendly way

You should present all this information in a way that is likely to appeal to the age of the child who is accessing your online service.

This may include using diagrams, cartoons, graphics, video and audio content, and gamified or interactive content that will attract and interest children, rather than relying solely on written communications.

You may use tools such as privacy dashboards, layered information, icons and symbols to aid children's understanding and to present the information in a child-friendly way. You should consider the modality of your service, and take into account user interaction patterns that do not take place in screen-based environments, as appropriate.

Dashboards should be displayed in a way that clearly identifies and differentiates between processing that is essential to the provision of your service and non-essential or optional processing that the child can choose whether to activate.

Tailor your information to the age of the child

You need to consider how you can tailor the content and presentation of the information you provide depending on the age of the user.

There may be some scenarios in which providing one, simplified, accessible to all, set of information may work. For example, if you are an online retailer which only collects the personal data needed to complete online transactions and deliver goods.

However, in many cases a-one-size-fits-all approach does not recognise that children have different needs at different stages of their development. For example, a pre-literate or primary school child might need to be actively deterred from changing privacy settings without parental input, whereas a teenager might be better supported by clear and neutral information which helps them make their own informed decision.

For more information about the developmental needs of children at different ages please see Annex B to this code.

For younger children, with more limited levels of understanding, you may need to provide less detailed information for the child themselves and rely more on parental involvement and understanding. However you should never use simplification with the aim of hiding what you are doing with the child's personal data and you should consider providing detailed information for parents, to sit alongside your child directed information.

You should make all versions of resources (including versions for parents) easily accessible and incorporate mechanisms to allow children or parents to choose which version they see, or to down-scale or up-scale the information depending on their individual level of understanding.

I don't get this – can you make it a bit easier for me?

This is a bit basic for me – can you give me some more detail?

The following table provides some recommendations. However, they are only a starting point and you are free to develop your own service specific information and user journeys which take account of the risks inherent in your service.

Depending on the size of your organisation, your number of users, and your assessment of risk you may decide to carry out user testing to make sure that the information you provide is sufficiently clear and accessible for the age range in question. You should document the results of any user testing in your DPIA to support your final conclusions and justify the presentation and content of your final resources. If you decide that user testing isn't warranted, then you should document the reasons why in your DPIA.

You should also consider any additional responsibilities you may have under the applicable equality legislation for England, Scotland, Wales and Northern Ireland.

Age range	Recommendations
0–5 Pre-literate & early literacy	Provide full privacy information as required by Articles 13 & 14 of the GDPR in a format suitable for parents.
	Provide audio or video prompts telling children to leave things as they are or get help from a parent or trusted adult if they try and change any high privacy default settings.
6–9 Core primary school years	Provide full privacy information as required by Articles 13 & 14 of the GDPR in a format suitable for parents.
	Provide cartoon, video or audio materials to sit alongside parental resources. Explain the basic concepts of online privacy within your service, the privacy settings you offer, who can see what, their information rights, how to be in control of their own information, and respecting other people's privacy. Explain the basics of your service and how it works, what they can expect from you and what you expect from them.
	Provide resources for parents to use with their children to explain privacy concepts and risks within your service. Provide resources for parents to use with their children to explain the basics of your service and how it works, what they can expect from you and what you expect from them.
	If a child attempts to change a default high privacy setting provide cartoon, video or audio materials to explain what will happen to their information and any associated risks. Tell them to leave things as they are or get help from a parent or trusted adult before they change the setting.

Age range	Recommendations
10–12 Transition years	Provide full privacy information as required by Articles 13 & 14 of the GDPR in a format suitable for parents.
	Provide full privacy information as required by Articles 13 & 14 of the GDPR in a format suitable for children within this age group. Allow children to choose between written and video/audio options. Give children the choice to upscale or downscale the information they see (to materials developed for an older or younger age group) depending on their individual needs.
	If a child attempts to change a default high privacy setting provide written, cartoon, video or audio materials to explain what will happen to their information and any associated risks. Tell them to leave things as they are or get help from a parent or trusted adult before they change the setting.
13–15 Early teens	Provide full privacy information as required by Articles 13 & 14 of the GDPR in a format suitable for this age group. Allow them to choose between written and video/audio options. Give them the choice to upscale or downscale the information they see (to materials developed for an older or younger age group) depending on their individual needs.
	If a child attempts to change a default high privacy setting provide written, video or audio materials to explain what will happen to their information and any associated risks. Prompt them to ask for help from a parent or trusted adult and not change the setting if they have any concerns or don't understand what you have told them.
	Provide full information in a format suitable for parents to sit alongside the child focused information.
16–17 Approaching adulthood	Provide full information in a format suitable for this age group. Allow them to choose between written and video/audio options. Give them the choice to upscale or downscale the information they see (to materials developed for an older or younger age group) depending on their individual needs.
	If a child in this age group attempts to change a default high privacy setting provide written, video or audio materials to explain what will happen to their information and any associated risks. Prompt them to check with an adult or other source of trusted information and not change the setting if they have any concerns or don't understand what you have told them.
	Provide full information in a format suitable for parents to sit alongside the child focused information.

Further reading outside this code

Guide to the GDPR – lawfulness, fairness and transparency

Guide to the GDPR – the right to be informed

5. DETRIMENTAL USE OF DATA

[1.353]
Do not use children's personal data in ways that have been shown to be detrimental to their wellbeing, or that go against industry codes of practice, other regulatory provisions, or Government advice.

WHAT DO YOU MEAN BY 'THE DETRIMENTAL USE OF DATA'?

We mean any use of data that is obviously detrimental to children's physical or mental health and wellbeing or that goes against industry codes of practice, other regulatory provisions or Government advice on the welfare of children.

WHY IS THIS IMPORTANT?

Article 5(1)(a) of the GDPR says that personal data must be processed lawfully, fairly and in a transparent manner in relation to the data subject, and Recital 38 that children merit specific protection with regard to the use of their personal data.

Recital 2 to the GDPR states (emphasis added):

"The principles of, and rules on the protection of natural persons with regard to the processing of their personal data should, whatever their nationality or residence, respect their fundamental rights and freedoms, in particular their right to the protection of personal data. **This Regulation is intended to contribute to . . . the well-being of natural persons**."

Recital 75 to the GDPR says that:

"The risk to the rights and freedoms of natural persons, or varying likelihood and severity may result from personal data processing which could lead to physical, material or non-material damage, in particular: . . . .where personal data of vulnerable natural persons, in particular children, are processed . . . ."

This means that you should not process children's personal data in ways that are obviously, or have been shown to be, detrimental to their health or wellbeing. To do so would not be fair.

HOW CAN WE MAKE SURE THAT WE MEET THIS STANDARD?

Keep up date with relevant recommendations and advice

As a provider of an online service likely to be accessed by children you should be aware of relevant standards and codes of practice within your industry or sector, and any provisions within them that relate to children. You should also keep up to date with Government advice on the welfare of children in the context of digital or online services. The ICO does not regulate content and is not an expert on matters of children's health and wellbeing. We will however refer to other codes of practice or regulatory advice where relevant to help us assess your conformance to this standard.

Do not process children's personal data in ways that are obviously detrimental or run counter to such advice

You should not process children's personal data in ways that run contrary to those standards, codes or advice and should take account of any age specific advice to tailor your online service to the age of the child. You should take particular care when profiling children, including making inferences based on their personal data, or processing geo-location data.

You should apply a pre-cautionary approach where this has been formally recommended despite evidence being under debate. This means you should not process children's personal data in ways that have been formally identified as requiring further research or evidence to establish whether or not they are detrimental to the health and wellbeing of children.

WHAT CODES OR ADVICE ARE LIKELY TO BE RELEVANT?

Some specific areas where there is relevant guidance, and that are likely to arise in the context of providing your online service are given below.

However, this is not an exhaustive list and you need to identify and consider anything that is relevant to your specific data processing scenario in your DPIA.

Marketing and behavioural advertising

The Committee of Advertising Practice (CAP) publishes guidance about online behavioural advertising which, in addition to providing rules applicable to all advertising, specifically covers advertising to children.

It includes rules which address:
• physical, mental or moral harm to children;
• exploiting children's credulity and applying unfair pressure;
• direct exhortation of children and undermining parental authority; and
• promotions.

It also has rules which govern or prohibit the marketing of certain products, such as high fat, salt and sugar food and drinks and alcohol, to children, and general guidance on transparency of paid-for content and product placement.

Broadcasting

Ofcom has published a code practice for broadcasters which covers the protection of under-18s in the following areas:
• the coverage of sexual and other offences in the UK involving under-18s;
• drugs, smoking, solvents and alcohol;
• violence and dangerous behaviour;
• offensive language;
• sexual material;
• nudity;
• exorcism, the occult and the paranormal; and
• the involvement of people under 18 in programmes.

The press

The Independent Press Standards Organisation (Ipso) has published The Editors' Code of Practice which includes provisions about reporting and children.

Online games

The Office for Fair Trading (OFT) has published principles for online and app-based games which includes provisions about:
• exploiting children's inexperience, vulnerability and credulity, including by aggressive commercial practices; and
• including direct exhortations to children to buy advertised products or persuade their parents or other adults to buy advertised products for them.

Strategies used to extend user engagement

Strategies used to extend user engagement, sometimes referred to as 'sticky' features can include mechanisms such as reward loops, continuous scrolling, notifications and auto-play features which encourage users to continue playing a game, watching video content or otherwise staying online.

Although there is currently no formal Government position on the effect of these mechanisms on the health and wellbeing of children, the UK Chief Medical Officers have issued a 'commentary on screen-based activities on children and young people'. This identifies a need for further research and in the meantime recommends that technology companies 'recognise a precautionary approach in developing structures and remove addictive capabilities.'

DOES THIS MEAN WE CAN'T USE FEATURES SUCH AS REWARDS, NOTIFICATIONS AND 'LIKES' WITHIN OUR SERVICE?

No, not all such features rely on the use of personal data and you may have designed your feature taking into account the needs of children and in a way that makes it easy for them to disengage without feeling pressurised or disadvantaged if they do so. However, it does mean that you need to carefully consider the impact on children if you use their personal data to support such features. You should consider both intended and unintended consequences of the data use as part of your DPIA.

Given the precautionary advice from the Chief Medical Officers, designing in data-driven features which make it difficult for children to disengage with your service is likely to breach the Article 5(1)(a) fairness principle of the GDPR. For example, features which use personal data to exploit human susceptibility to reward, anticipatory and pleasure seeking behaviours, or peer pressure.

You should:

- avoid using personal data in a way that incentivises children to stay engaged, such as offering children personalised in-game advantages (based upon your use of the individual user's personal data) in return for extended play;
- present options to continue playing or otherwise engaging with your service neutrally without suggesting that children will lose out if they don't;
- avoid features which use personal data to automatically extend use instead of requiring children to make an active choice about whether they want to spend their time in this way (data-driven autoplay features); and
- introduce mechanisms such as pause buttons which allow children to take a break at any time without losing their progress in a game, or provide age appropriate content to support conscious choices about taking breaks, such as that provided in the Chief Medical Officers' advice.

Further reading outside the code

Committee on Advertising Practice guidance

The Ofcom Broadcasting Code (with the Cross-Promotion Code and the On Demand Programme Service Rules)

The Editors' Code of Practice

OFT principles for online and app-based games

UK Chief Medical Officers' commentary on 'screen based activities and children and young people's mental health and psychosocial wellbeing: a systematic map of reviews'

6. POLICIES AND COMMUNITY STANDARDS

[1.354]
Uphold your own published terms, policies and community standards (including but not limited to privacy policies, age restriction, behaviour rules and content policies).

WHAT DO YOU MEAN BY 'UPHOLDING YOUR OWN STANDARDS'?

We mean that you need to adhere to your own published terms and conditions and policies.

We also mean that, when you set community rules and conditions of use for users of your service, you need to actively uphold or enforce those rules and conditions.

WHY IS THIS IMPORTANT?

Article 5(1) of the GDPR says that personal data shall be:

> "processed lawfully, fairly and in a transparent manner in relation to the data subject ('lawfulness, fairness and transparency')"

When children provide you with their personal data in order to join or access your service they should be able to expect the service to operate in the way that you say it will, and for you to do what you say you are going to do. If this doesn't happen then your collection of their personal data may be unfair and in breach of Article 5(1)(a).

Keeping to your own standards should also benefit you by giving children and their parents confidence that they can trust your online service with their personal data.

HOW CAN WE MAKE SURE THAT WE MEET THIS STANDARD?

To some extent this depends on the content of your published terms and conditions, policies and community standards.

However you should follow the overarching principle that you say what you do and do what you say. You should at least ensure that you do the following:

Only use personal data in accordance with your privacy policy

Article 5(1)(b) of the GDPR sets out the 'purpose limitation' principle, that personal data shall be:

"collected for specified, explicit and legitimate purposes and not further processed in a manner that is incompatible with those purposes . . . "

Articles 13 and 14 of the GDPR require you to tell data subjects what these purposes are. You do this by providing privacy information, which you may include in a privacy notice, policy or statement.

Article 5(1)(a) of the GDPR requires you to process personal data fairly and transparently.

The combined result of these provisions is that you need to use your privacy information to tell users what you will do with their personal data and why, and then make sure that you follow this through in practice.

Uphold any user behaviour policies

If you have any published rules which govern the behaviour of users of your service then you need to uphold these rules and put in place the systems that you have said you will. So if you say that you actively monitor user behaviour, or offer real time, automated, or human moderation of 'chat' functions, then you need to do so.

If you only rely on 'back end' processes, such as user reporting, to identify behaviour which breaches your policies then you need to have made that very clear in your policies or community standards. This approach also needs to be reasonable given the risks to children of different ages inherent in your service. If the risks are high then 'light touch' or 'back end only' processes to uphold your standards are unlikely to be sufficient.

If you do not have adequate systems to properly uphold your own user behaviour policies then your original collection and continued use of a child's personal data may be unfair and in breach of the GDPR.

Uphold any content or other policies

If you make commitments to users about the content or other aspects of your online service then you need to have systems to ensure that you meet those commitments.

So if you say that the content of your online service is suitable for children within a certain age range then you need to have systems to ensure that it is. If you say that you do not tolerate bullying, then you need to have adequate mechanisms to swiftly and effectively deal with bullying incidents.

Again, if your systems aren't adequate or you don't keep to your promises then your original collection and continued use of the child's personal data may be unfair and in breach of the GDPR.

If you have different policies depending on the age of your users then you need to take account of the age of the child when upholding your policies.

7. DEFAULT SETTINGS

[1.355]
Settings must be 'high privacy' by default (unless you can demonstrate a compelling reason for a different default setting, taking account of the best interests of the child).

WHAT DO YOU MEAN BY 'DEFAULT PRIVACY SETTINGS'?

Privacy settings are a practical way for you to offer children a choice over how their personal data is used and protected. You can use them whenever you collect and process children's personal data in order to 'improve' 'enhance' or 'personalise' their online experience beyond the provision of your core service.

They can cover how children's personal data is used:
- in an interpersonal sense; the extent to which their personal data is made visible or accessible to other users of your online service;
- by yourself as provider of the online service; for example using personal data to suggest in-app purchases; and
- by third parties; for example to allow third parties to promote or market products.

Default privacy settings govern the use of children's personal data if the child does not make any changes to the settings when they start using your online service.

WHY ARE THEY IMPORTANT?

Many children will just accept whatever default settings you provide and never change their privacy settings. This means that it is of the utmost importance that the defaults you set are appropriate for children and provide them with adequate protection in how their personal data is used. For children, it is not enough to allow them to activate high privacy settings, you need to provide them by default (unless you have a compelling reason to do otherwise, taking into account the best interests of the child).

They are also important because of Article 25(2) of the GDPR which provides as follows.

> "25(2) The controller shall implement appropriate technical and organisational measures for ensuring that, by default, only personal data which are necessary for each specific purpose of the processing are processed. That obligation applies to the amount of personal data collected, the extent of their processing, the period of their storage and their accessibility. In particular, such measures shall ensure that by default personal data are not made accessible without the individual's intervention to an indefinite number of natural persons."

This means that, by default, you should not:

* collect any more personal data than you need to provide each individual element of your online service; or
* make your users' personal data visible to indefinite numbers of other users of your online service.

You can also use privacy settings to support the exercise of children's data protection rights (such as the rights to object to or restrict processing). And they can give children and parents confidence in their interactions with your online service, and help them explore the implications of allowing you to use their personal data in different ways.

DO WE HAVE TO PROVIDE A PRIVACY SETTING EVERY TIME WE USE A CHILD'S PERSONAL DATA?

You should provide privacy settings (set to high privacy by default) to give children control over when and how you use their personal data whenever you can.

It is not necessary however for you to provide a privacy setting for any personal data that you have to process in order to provide your core or most basic service. This is because without this essential processing there is no core service for you to offer. In this circumstance, if the child wishes to access the core service, you cannot offer them a choice over whether their personal data is processed or not.

In order to give children control over when and how their personal data is used, you should provide privacy settings for any processing that is needed to provide additional elements of service that go beyond the core service.

We will look very carefully at any claims that a privacy setting cannot be provided because the personal data is needed to provide the core service. You should follow the spirit not just 'the letter of' the code in this respect and should take care not to abuse the concept of a core service by applying it more widely than is warranted.

See also Annex C to this code 'Lawful basis for processing' which explains the need to differentiate between core and non-core elements of your service in any case, in order to identify an appropriate lawful basis for processing as required by the GDPR.

There may also be some other limited types of processing where it is not appropriate to offer a privacy setting. For example, if you need to process a child's personal data in order to meet a legal obligation (such as a child protection requirement) or to prevent child sexual exploitation and abuse online. It is then not appropriate to offer them a choice over whether their personal data is processed for this purpose or not.

HOW CAN WE MAKE SURE THAT WE MEET THIS STANDARD?

Provide 'high privacy' default settings

If it is appropriate for you to offer a privacy setting, then your default position for each individual privacy setting should be 'high privacy'.

This means that children's personal data is only visible or accessible to other users of the service if the child amends their settings to allow this.

This also means that unless the setting is changed, your own use of the children's personal data is limited to use that is essential to the provision of the service. Any optional uses of personal data, including any uses designed to personalise the service have to be individually selected and activated by the child.

Similarly any settings which allow third parties to use personal data have to be activated by the child.

The exception to this rule is if you can demonstrate that there is a compelling reason for a different default setting taking into account the best interests of the child.

Consider the need for any further intervention at the point at which any setting is changed

Making sure that privacy settings are set to high privacy by default will in itself mitigate the risks to children, as many children will never change their privacy settings from the default position.

Similarly, providing age appropriate explanations and prompts at the point at which a child attempts to change a privacy settings, as required under the transparency standard, will mitigate risk.

However you should also consider whether to put any further measures in place when a child attempts to change a setting. This depends on your assessment of the risks inherent in the processing covered by each setting and could include further age assurance measures. You should use your DPIA to help you assess risks and identify suitable mitigation.

Allow users the option to change settings permanently or just for the current use

If a user does change their settings you should generally give them the option to do so permanently or to return to the high privacy defaults when they end the current session. You should not 'nudge' them towards taking a lower privacy option (for more information on this see the section of this code on Nudge techniques). Slightly different considerations apply for geolocation data which makes the child's location visible to others. This is covered in more detail in the section of this code on geolocation.

Ultimately you need to demonstrate that you have made it easy for a child to maintain or revert to high privacy settings if they wish to do so.

Retain user choices or high privacy defaults when software is updated

If you introduce a software update, (eg to update security measures or introduce new features), then you should retain any privacy settings that the user has applied. If it is not possible to do this (eg if a new aspect or feature to the product or service is introduced, or an existing feature is significantly changed so the previous privacy settings are no longer relevant) you should set the new setting to high privacy by default.

Allow for different user choices on multi-user devices

If you provide an online service that allows multiple users to access the service from one device, then whenever possible you should allow users to set up their own profiles with their own individual privacy settings. This means that children do not have to share an adult's privacy settings when they share the same device. Profiles could be accessed via screen-based options or using voice recognition technology for voice activated online services.

You should include clear information for the person who sets up or registers the device alerting them to the potential for the personal data of multiple users to be collected.

ARE PRIVACY SETTINGS A CONSENT MECHANISM?

For consent to be valid under the GDPR it needs to meet the following definition:

GDPR Article 4(11)
"'consent' of the data subject means any freely given, specific, informed and unambiguous indication of the data subjects wishes by which he or she, by a statement or by a clear affirmative action, signifies agreement to the processing of personal data relating to him or her"

If your settings are off by default and the user has to activate the processing by changing the default setting, then you may be able to use privacy settings as part of your mechanism for obtaining consent to your processing under the GDPR. However, you also need to meet the requirements of Article 7 of the GDPR (conditions for consent) and the age verification and parental responsibility verification requirements of Article 8 (these only allow children of 13 or over to provide their own consent), so they won't be enough on their own.

Privacy settings aren't just relevant to consent. You may also use them to give children choice over how their personal data is used if you rely on other lawful bases for processing (such as legitimate interests) which don't have any formal consent requirements.

For more information about lawful bases for processing, including consent, please see the supplementary guidance in Annex C. You may also wish to talk to your DPO if you have one.

8. DATA MINIMISATION

[1.356]
Collect and retain only the minimum amount of personal data you need to provide the elements of your service in which a child is actively and knowingly engaged. Give children separate choices over which elements they wish to activate.

WHAT DO YOU MEAN BY 'DATA MINIMISATION'?

Data minimisation means collecting the minimum amount of personal data that you need to deliver an individual element of your service. It means you cannot collect more data than you need to provide the elements of a service the child actually wants to use.

WHY IS IT IMPORTANT?

Article 5(1)(c) of the GDPR says that personal data shall be:

"adequate, relevant and limited to what is necessary in relation to the purposes for which they are processed ('data minimisation')"

Article 25 of the GDPR provides that this approach shall be applied by default to 'each specific purpose of the processing'.

It sits alongside the 'purpose limitation' principle set out at Article 5(1)(b) of the GDPR which states that the purpose for which you collect personal data must be 'specified, explicit and legitimate' and the storage limitation principle set out in Article 5(1)(e) which states that personal data should be kept 'no longer than is necessary' for the purposes for which it is processed.

HOW CAN WE MAKE SURE THAT WE MEET THIS STANDARD?

Identify what personal data you need to provide each individual element of your service

The GDPR requires you to be clear about the purposes for which you collect personal data, to only collect the minimum amount of personal data you need for those purposes and to only store that data for the minimum amount of time you need it for. This means that you need to differentiate between each individual element of your service and consider what personal data you need, and for how long, to deliver each one.

Example

You offer a music download service.

One element of your service is to allow users to search for tracks they might want to download.

Another element of your service is to provide recommendations to users based on previous searches, listens and downloads.

A further element of your service is to share what individual users are listening to with other groups of users

These are all separate elements of your overall service. The personal data that you need to provide each element will vary.

Give children choice over which elements of your service they wish to use

You should give children as much choice as possible over which elements of your service they wish to use and therefore how much personal data they need to provide.

This is particularly important for your collection of personal data in order to 'improve' 'enhance' or 'personalise' your users' online experience beyond the provision of your core service.

You should not 'bundle in' your collection of children's personal data in order to provide such enhancements with the collection of personal data you need to provide the core service, as you are effectively collecting personal data for different purposes. Neither should you bundle together several additional elements or enhancements of the service. You should give children a choice as to whether they wish their personal data to be used for each additional purpose or service enhancement. You can do this via your default privacy settings, as covered in the earlier section of this code.

Only collect personal data when the child is actively and knowingly using that element of your service

You should only collect the personal data needed to provide each element of your service when the child is actively and knowingly engaged with that element of the service.

Example:

It is acceptable to collect a child's location when they are using a maps based element of your service to help them find their way to a specified destination, and if you provide an obvious sign so that they know their location is being tracked.

It is not acceptable to continue to track their location after they have closed the map or reached their destination.

Further reading outside the code:

Guide to GDPR – data minimisation

9. DATA SHARING

[1.357]
Do not disclose children's data unless you can demonstrate a compelling reason to do so, taking account of the best interests of the child.

WHAT DO YOU MEAN BY 'DATA SHARING'?

Data sharing usually means disclosing personal data to third parties outside your organisation. It can also cover the sharing of personal data between different parts of your own organisation, or other organisations within the same group or under the same parent company.

Data sharing can be done routinely (for example the provider of an educational app routinely sharing data with the child's school) or in response to a one-off or emergency situation (for example sharing a child's personal data with the police for safeguarding reasons).

Data sharing includes making a child's personal data visible to a third party.

WHY IS IT IMPORTANT?

It is important because if you share children's personal data with third parties or with other parts of your own organisation it needs to be fair to the child to do so. Sharing children's personal data with third parties, including sharing data inferred or derived from their personal data, can expose children to risks arising from their processing of personal data, which go beyond those inherent in your own processing.

The GDPR provides that:

"5(1) Personal data shall be:

(a)   processed lawfully, fairly and in a transparent manner in relation to the data subject ('lawfulness, fairness and transparency');

(b)   collected for specified, explicit and legitimate purposes and not further processed in a manner that is incompatible with those purposes".

Articles 13 and 14 of the GDPR require you to tell data subjects who you share the personal data with (the recipients or categories of recipients of the personal data).

HOW CAN WE MAKE SURE THAT WE MEET THIS STANDARD?

Consider the best interests of the child

The best interests of the child should be a primary consideration for you whenever you contemplate sharing children's personal data.

If you have already made sure that your privacy settings are set to 'high privacy' by default, then the amount of data sharing that takes place should already be limited; with children having to actively change the default settings to allow you to share their personal data in many circumstances.

You should not share personal data if you can reasonably foresee that doing so will result in third parties using children's personal data in ways that have been shown to be detrimental to their wellbeing. You should obtain assurances from whoever you share the personal data with about this, and undertake due diligence checks as to the adequacy of their data protection practices and any further distribution of the data.

Any default settings related to data sharing should specify the purpose of the sharing and who the data will be shared with. Settings which allow general or unlimited sharing will not be compliant.

Ultimately, it is up to the person you have shared the data with to ensure they comply with the requirements of the GDPR (in their role as a data controller for the personal data they receive). However, you are responsible for ensuring that it is fair to share the personal data in the first place. You should not share personal data unless you have a compelling reason to do so, taking account of the best interests of the child.

One clear example of a compelling reason is data sharing for safeguarding purposes, preventing child sexual exploitation and abuse online, or for the purposes of preventing or detecting crimes against children such as online grooming.

An example that is unlikely to amount to a compelling reason for data sharing is selling on children's personal data for commercial re-use.

Consider the specific issues and risks raised at each stage of your DPIA

You should assess the issues and risks raised at each individual step of your DPIA process. These steps are set out and explained in the section of this code on DPIAs.

Further reading outside the code

For further reading on data sharing see our Data Sharing Code of Practice

10. GEOLOCATION

[1.358]
Switch geolocation options off by default (unless you can demonstrate a compelling reason for geolocation to be switched on by default, taking account of the best interests of the child), and provide an obvious sign for children when location tracking is active. Options which make a child's location visible to others should default back to 'off' at the end of each session.

WHAT DO YOU MEAN BY 'GEOLOCATION DATA'?

Geolocation data means data taken from a user's device which indicates the geographical location of that device, including GPS data or data about connection with local wifi equipment.

WHY IS IT IMPORTANT?

Recital 38 to the GDPR states that:

> "Children merit specific protection with regard to their personal data, as they may be less aware of the risks, consequences and safeguards concerned and their rights in relation to the processing . . . .."

The use of geolocation data in relation to children is of particular concern. This is because the ability to ascertain or track the physical location of a child carries with it the risk that the data could be misused to compromise the physical safety of that child. In short it can make children vulnerable to risks such as abduction, physical and mental abuse, sexual abuse and trafficking.

Persistent sharing of location may also mean that children have a diminished sense of their own private space which may affect the development of their sense of their own identity. It may potentially fail to respect the child's rights under the UNCRC to privacy, freedom of association, and freedom from economic exploitation, irrespective of threats to their physical safety.

SHOULD ALL GEOLOCATION SERVICES BE CONTROLLED BY A PRIVACY SETTING?

For any geolocation data you need to process in order to provide your core service, it is not appropriate to have a privacy setting (as without the processing there is no core service to provide). For example, map services may need to know the user location in order to properly display the required map or direct the user to their chosen destination.

However, you should offer children control over whether and how their personal data is used whenever you can. So any geolocation services that go over and above your core service should be subject to a privacy setting. For example, enhanced mapping services that make recommendations for places to visit based on location.

HOW CAN WE MAKE SURE THAT WE MEET THIS STANDARD?

Ensure geolocation options are off by default

Any geolocation privacy setting you do provide should be switched off by default; with children having to actively change the default setting to allow their geolocation data to be used. The exception to this is if you can demonstrate a compelling reason for a geolocation option to be switched on by default, taking into account the best interests of the child. For example you may be able to argue that metrics needed to measure demand for regional services may be sufficiently un-intrusive to be warranted (taking into account the best interests of the child).

You should also consider at what level of granularity the location needs to be tracked to provide each element of your service. Do not collect more granular detail than you actually need, and offer different settings for different levels of service if appropriate.

Make it obvious to the child that their location is being tracked

You should provide information at the point of sign-up, and each time the service is accessed that alerts the child to the use of geolocation data and prompts them to discuss this with a trusted adult if they don't understand what it means.

You should also provide a clear indication of when the child's location is and isn't being tracked (eg by use of a clear symbol visible to the user), and ensure that location tracking can't be left on inadvertently or by mistake.

Revert settings which make the child's location visible to others to 'off' after each use

You should make sure that any option which makes the child's location visible to others is subject to a privacy setting which reverts to 'off' after each session. The exception to this is if you can demonstrate that you have a compelling reason to do otherwise taking into account the best interests of the child.

WHAT ABOUT PECR?

If the geolocation data that you are processing also meets the definition of 'location data' in PECR then you should refer to our Guide to PECR for further guidance, as there are PECR specific requirements you have to meet.

Location data is defined as:

> "any data processed in an electronic communications network or by an electronic communications service indicating the geographical position of the terminal equipment of a user of a public electronic communications service, including data relating to —
>
> (f)   the latitude, longitude or altitude of the terminal equipment;
> (g)   the direction of travel of the user; or
> (h)   the time the location information was recorded".

In other words, it is information collected by a network or service about where the user's phone or other device is or was located. For example, tracing the location of a mobile phone from data collected by base stations on a mobile phone network.

The PECR rules do not generally include GPS-based location information from smartphones, tablets, sat-navs or other devices, as this data is created and collected independently of the network or service provider. Neither does it include location information collected at a purely local level (eg by wifi equipment installed by businesses offering wifi on their premises).

Further reading outside this code

Guide to PECR – location data

11. PARENTAL CONTROLS

[1.359]
If you provide parental controls, give the child age appropriate information about this. If your online service allows a parent or carer to monitor their child's online activity or track their location, provide an obvious sign to the child when they are being monitored.

WHAT DO YOU MEAN BY 'PARENTAL CONTROLS'?

Parental controls are tools which allow parents or guardians to place limits on a child's online activity and thereby mitigate the risks that the child might be exposed to. They include things such as setting time limits or bedtimes, restricting internet access to pre-approved sites only, and restricting in-app purchases. They can also be used to monitor a child's online activity or to track their physical location.

WHY ARE THEY IMPORTANT?

They are important because they can be used to support parents in protecting and promoting the best interests of their child, a role recognised by the UNCRC and discussed in the section of this code on the best interests of the child.

However they also impact on the child's right to privacy as recognised by Article 16 of the same convention and on their rights to association, play, access to information and freedom of expression. Children who are subject to persistent parental monitoring may have a diminished sense of their own private space which may affect the development of their sense of their own identity. This is particularly the case as the child matures and their expectation of privacy increases.

Article 5(1)(a) of the GDPR requires any processing of personal data related to their use to be lawful, fair and transparent.

"5(1) Personal data shall be:

(a) processed lawfully, fairly and in a transparent manner in relation to the data subject ('lawfulness, fairness and transparency');"

HOW CAN WE MAKE SURE THAT WE MEET THIS STANDARD?

Make it clear to the child if parental controls are in place and if they are being tracked or monitored

If you provide parental controls then you should provide age appropriate information so that the child knows that parental controls are in place.

If your online service allows parental monitoring or tracking of a child, you should provide age appropriate resources to explain the service to the child so that they are aware that their activity is being monitored by their parents or their location tracked. You should provide a clear and obvious sign for the child (such as a lit up icon) which lets them know when monitoring or tracking is active.

You should also provide parents with information about the child's right to privacy under the UNCRC and resources to support age appropriate discussion between parent and child.

The following table provides some guidelines on the type of information you might wish provide and how you might provide it. They are only a starting point and you are free to develop your own, service specific, user journeys that follow the principle in the headline standard.

You should also consider any additional responsibilities you may have under the applicable equality legislation for England, Scotland, Wales and Northern Ireland.

Age range	Recommendations
0-5 Pre-literate & early literacy	Provide audio or video materials for the child to explain that their parent is being told what they do online to help keep them safe.
	Provide materials for parents explaining the child's right to privacy under the UNCRC and how their expectations about this are likely to increase as they get older.
	Provide a clear and obvious sign that indicates when monitoring or tracking is active.

Age range	Recommendations
6-9 Core primary school years	Provide audio or video materials for the child to explain that their parent is being told where they are and/or what they do online to help keep them safe.
	Provide materials for parents explaining the child's right to privacy under the UNCRC and how their expectations about this are likely to increase as they get older.
	Provide resources to help parents explain the service to their child and discuss privacy with them.
	Provide a clear and obvious sign that indicates when monitoring or tracking is active.
10-12 Transition years	Provide audio or video materials for the child to explain that their parent is being told where they are and/or what they do online to help keep them safe.
	Provide materials for parents explaining the child's right to privacy under the UNCRC and how their expectations about this are likely to be increasing now they are getting older.
	Provide resources to help parents explain the service to their child and discuss privacy with them.
	Provide resources suitable for the child to use independently which explain the service and discusses privacy rights.
	Provide a clear and obvious sign that indicates when monitoring or tracking is active.
13 -15 Early teens	Provide audio, video or written materials for the child to explain how your service works and the balance between parental and child privacy rights.
	Provide materials for parents explaining the child's right to privacy under the UNCRC.
	Provide a clear and obvious sign that indicates when monitoring or tracking is active.
16-17 Approaching adulthood	Provide audio, video or written materials for the child to explain how your service works and the balance between parental and child privacy rights.
	Provide materials for parents explaining the child's right to privacy under the UNCRC.
	Provide a clear and obvious sign that indicates when monitoring or tracking is active.

12. PROFILING

[1.360]
Switch options which use profiling 'off' by default (unless you can demonstrate a compelling reason for profiling to be on by default, taking account of the best interests of the child). Only allow profiling if you have appropriate measures in place to protect the child from any harmful effects (in particular, being fed content that is detrimental to their health or wellbeing).

WHAT DO YOU MEAN BY 'PROFILING'?

Profiling is defined in the GDPR:

> "any form of automated processing of personal data consisting of the use of personal data to evaluate certain aspects relating to a natural person, in particular to analyse or predict aspects concerning that natural person's performance at work, economic situation, health, personal preferences, interests, reliability, behaviour location or movements"

Profiling can be used for a wide range of purposes. It can be used extensively in an online context to suggest or serve content to users, to determine where, when and how frequently that content should be served, to encourage users towards particular behaviours, or to identify users as belonging to particular groups. It can also be used to help establish or estimate the age of a user (as detailed in the standard on age appropriate application), or for child protection, countering terrorism, or the prevention of crime.

Profiles are usually based on a user's past online activity or browsing history. They can be created using directly collected personal data or by drawing inferences (eg preferences or characteristics inferred from associations with other users or past online choices).

Content feeds based on profiling can include advertising content, content provided by other websites, downloads, content generated by other internet users, written, audio or visual content. Profiling may also be used to suggest other users to 'connect with' or 'follow'.

WHY IS IT IMPORTANT?

Profiling is mentioned in Recital 38 to the GDPR as an area in which children merit specific protection with regard to the use of their personal data.

There are also specific rules at Article 22 of the GDPR about decisions (including profiling) which are based solely on the automated processing of personal data, and which have a legal or similarly significant effect on the data subject.

"22(1) The data subject shall have the right not to be subject to a decision based solely on automated processing, including profiling, which produces legal effects concerning him or her or similarly affects him or her"

Recital 71 to the GDPR states that such decisions 'should not concern a child'.

The lawfulness, fairness and transparency principle at Article 5(1) is also relevant because this is an area of largely 'invisible processing' in which it is difficult for children to understand how their personal data is being used, and what the consequences of that use might be.

"5(1) Personal data shall be

(a)   processed lawfully, fairly and in a transparent manner in relation to the data subject ('lawfulness, fairness and transparency')"

Some profiling may be relatively benign, for example personalisation of a 'walled garden' online environment to incorporate an animal theme in the displayed content. Other profiling, such as content feeds which gradually take the child away from their original area of interest into other less suitable content, raise much more significant concerns.

SHOULD ALL PROFILING BE CONTROLLED BY A PRIVACY SETTING?

It is important to remember that 'off by default' does not mean that profiling is not possible or banned. Following the safeguards and steps set out in this section, which could include effective consent, can enable profiling using children's data to take place, safely and fairly.

There is no point in offering a privacy setting if the profiling is essential to the provision of the core service that the child has requested. This is because if the profiling were turned off there would be no residual service left for the child to use. This concept should be interpreted narrowly, eg that it is completely intrinsic to the service.

However, whenever you can, you should offer children control over whether and how their personal data is used. So most profiling should be subject to a privacy setting. If you can provide a core or residual service without profiling, then you should provide a privacy setting for any additional aspects of your service which rely on profiling.

You should always provide a privacy setting for behavioural advertising which is used to fund a service, but is not part of the core service that the child wishes to access. Although there may be some limited examples of services where behavioural advertising is part of the core service (eg a voucher or 'money off' service), we think these will be exceptional. In most cases the funding model will be distinct from the core service and so should be subject to a privacy setting that is 'off' by default.

There may also be some other limited circumstances in which it won't be appropriate for you to offer a privacy setting over profiling. For example, if you are profiling in order to meet a legal or regulatory requirement (such as a safeguarding or child protection requirement), to prevent child sexual exploitation or abuse online or to age assure so you can properly apply the provisions of this code to child users.

HOW DOES THIS FIT WITH PECR REQUIREMENTS?

Profiling may rely on the use of cookies and similar technologies in order to store or 'remember' the information about a user's past online activity.

A cookie is a small text file that is downloaded onto 'terminal equipment' (eg a computer or smartphone) when the user accesses a website. It allows the website to recognise that user's device and store some information about the user's preferences or past actions.

PECR requires that you provide users with clear and comprehensive information about your use of cookies and obtain prior consent for any that are 'non-essential'.

So if you use cookies for the purposes of profiling you need to consider PECR rules for the setting of the cookie, and the GDPR and this code for the underlying processing of personal data (profiling) that the cookie supports or enables.

Profiling and non-essential cookies

If the cookie isn't essential to provide the service that the child wants to access, then the underlying profiling it facilitates normally needs to be subject to a privacy setting. This gives the child control over whether their personal data is used for this purpose.

You need consent for the cookie as well as a GDPR lawful basis for processing for the underlying processing (in practice this may also be consent).

Cookies, profiling, and your core services

If the cookie is essential to the provision of your core service then it is likely that the underlying profiling that the cookie enables is too. In this circumstance providing a privacy setting which allows the child to control whether their personal data is used for this purpose won't be appropriate. You need a lawful basis (other than consent) for the underlying processing (profiling) and won't need consent for the cookie.

Cookies, profiling and your non-core services

Cookies may also be essential for providing your non-core services. However, as these are optional elements of your service you firstly need to provide a privacy setting which gives the child control over whether they wish their personal data to be processed in order to access them.

If the child decides to do so, then you do not need consent for the use of the cookie – as the child is specifically requesting to access part of your service and the cookie is strictly necessary for this purpose.

You do however need a lawful basis for the underlying processing.

Cookies, profiling, and age estimation or age assurance

You may also use cookies for profiling that intends to meet the implied age verification requirements of Article 8 of the GDPR, or to age assure in order to properly apply the standards of this code. For more detail about the Article 8 requirements see Annex C Lawful bases for processing.

In this circumstance, the purpose you use the cookies for is regarded as essential for the service, as you need to do so to provide an age appropriate service and comply with the GDPR. Provided that the cookie in question is solely used for this purpose, and not for any other purpose, then the child does not need to consent to the cookie.

For more information about cookies, and when a cookie is essential and non-essential, see our guidance on Cookies and similar technologies.

HOW CAN WE MAKE SURE THAT WE MEET THIS STANDARD?

Differentiate between different types of profiling for different purposes

Because profiling can be used to serve a wide range of purposes it is particularly important to be clear about the purposes for which your service uses personal data to profile its users, and to differentiate between them. Catch-all purposes, such as 'providing a personalised service' are not specific enough.

Where it is appropriate to offer privacy settings then you should offer separate settings for each different type of profiling. It is not acceptable to bundle different types of profiling together under one privacy setting, or to bundle in profiling with processing for other purposes.

Acceptable practice:

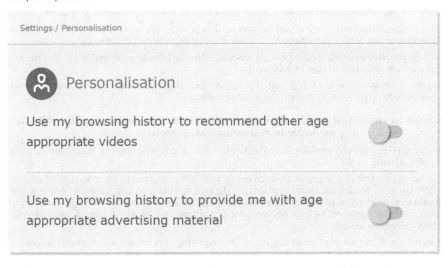

Unacceptable practice:

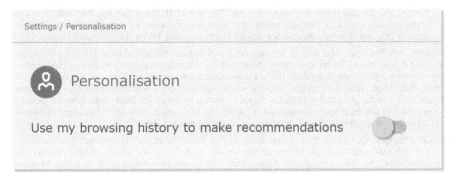

Ensure features that rely on profiling are switched off by default (unless there is a compelling reason to do otherwise)

You need to switch any options within your service which rely on profiling off by default, unless you can demonstrate a compelling reason why this should not be the case, taking account of the best interests of the child. You need to assess this in the specific circumstances of your processing.

In practice it is likely to mean that any non-essential features that rely on profiling and that you provide for commercial purposes are subject to a privacy setting which is switched off by default.

In the case of any profiling you do for the purposes of behavioural advertising, which is facilitated by cookies, this approach is supported by the comments of the EDPB. EDPB have indicated that 'legitimate interests' is unlikely to provide a valid lawful basis for processing for this purpose which means that consent is your only viable basis for processing. As valid consent has to be 'opt in', allowing such profiling 'by default' is not an option. You also need to comply with the Article 8 GDPR requirements for parental consent if the child is under the age of 13. For more information about lawful bases for processing and Article 8 requirements see Annex C.

However, you may have a compelling argument that you need to switch profiling options for other purposes on by default.

For example, it may be appropriate for profiling for the purposes of ensuring that a service is accessible to a disabled child (eg identifying that a child has an ongoing need for a subtitled, signed or other supported service) to be switched on by default.

You may be able to demonstrate that profiling for the purposes of informing news content feeds should be allowed by default, in order to recognise the rights of children to access information. Although you still need consent to set the cookies that support the profiling in accordance with PECR requirements. This is more likely to be the case if you can demonstrate that you conform with existing regulatory codes of practice which govern media content and practices (such as The Editors' Code of Practice) and have editorial control over the content that children will be shown as a result of the profiling. It is unlikely to apply if you do not have such editorial control or adhere to other regulatory controls. See also our FAQs for the news media.

Provide appropriate interventions at the point at which any profiling is activated

At the point any profiling options are turned on, you need to provide age appropriate information about what will happen to the child's personal data and any risks inherent in that processing.

You should also provide age appropriate prompts to seek assistance from an adult and not to activate the profiling if they are uncertain or don't understand.

Depending on your assessment of risk and the age of the child you may wish to make further interventions, which might include further age assurance measures.

If profiling is on ensure that you put appropriate measures in place to safeguard the child (in particular from inappropriate content)

If your online service uses any profiling then you need to take appropriate steps to make sure that this does not result in harm to the child.

In practice this means that if you profile children (using their personal data) in order to suggest content to them, then you need suitable measures in place to make sure that children aren't served content which is detrimental to their physical or mental health or wellbeing, taking into account their age. As covered in the section of this code on DPIAs, testing your algorithms should assist you in assessing the effectiveness of your measures.

Such measures could include contextual tagging, robust reporting procedures, and elements of human moderation. It could also include your own editorial controls over the content you display, including adherence to codes of conduct or other regulatory provisions (such as compliance with The Editors' Code of Practice, or the Ofcom Broadcasting Code). We recognise the importance of the rights of children to access information from the media, and the societal and developmental benefits of children being able to engage in current affairs and the world around them. We would therefore accept that adherence to editorial or broadcasting codes of conduct negate the need for providers of online news to take any additional steps in relation to news content for children. See also our FAQs for the news media.

If you are using children's personal data to automatically recommend content to them based on their past usage/browsing history then you have a responsibility for the recommendations you make. This applies even if the content itself is user generated. In data protection terms, you have a greater responsibility in this situation than if the child were to pro-actively search out such content themselves. This is because it is your processing of the personal data that serves the content to the child. Data protection law doesn't make you responsible for third party content but it does make you responsible for the content you serve to children who use your service, based on your use of their personal data.

Your general approach should be that if the content you promote or the behaviours your features encourage are obviously detrimental, or are recognised as harmful to the child, in one context (eg marketing rules, film classification, advice from official Government sources such as Chief Medical Officers' advice, PEGI ratings) then you should assume that the same type of content or behaviour is harmful in other contexts as well. Where evidence is inconclusive you should apply the same precautionary principle.

Content or behaviours that may be detrimental to children's health and wellbeing (taking into account their age) include:

- advertising or marketing content that is contrary to CAP guidelines on marketing to children;
- film or on-demand television content that is classified as unsuitable for the age group concerned;
- music content that is labelled as parental advisory or explicit;
- pornography or other adult or violent content;
- user generated content (content that is posted by other internet users) that is obviously detrimental to children's wellbeing or is formally recognised as such (eg pro-suicide, pro-self harm, pro-anorexia content. Content depicting or advocating risky or dangerous behaviour by children); and
- strategies used to extend user engagement, such as timed notifications that respond to inactivity.

Ultimately, if you believe that it is not feasible for you to put suitable measures in place, then you are not be able to profile children for the purposes of recommending online content. In this circumstance you need to make sure that children cannot change any privacy settings which allow this type of profiling.

Similarly, if you cannot put suitable measures in place to safeguard children from harms arising from profiling for other purposes (such as profiling to promote certain behaviours), you should not profile children for these purposes either.

HOW DOES THIS FIT WITH OTHER RULES ON RESTRICTING ACCESS TO CONTENT FOR CHILDREN?

You may need to take account of other rules on restricting access to content in order to ensure that you don't use children's personal data in ways that have been shown to be detrimental to their wellbeing (for more detail see the standard on detrimental use of data).

The CAP code requires that when advertising is targeted through the use of personal data, advertisers must show that they have taken reasonable steps to reduce the likelihood of those who are, or are likely to be, in a protected age category being exposed to age-restricted marketing content.

The Ofcom On Demand Programme Service Rules require providers of 'on demand' content to only make certain content ('specially restricted material') available, if it can do so in a way that ensures that those under the age of 18 will not normally be able to see or hear it.

The Audiovisual Media Services Directive 2018 (AVMSD) (if implemented in the UK) will require 'video sharing platform services' to use proportionate measures in relation to how they organise the content they share, to protect minors from content which might impair their physical, mental or moral development.

We consider that it is consistent with these provisions to only allow children's personal data to be used to determine content feeds if you can put suitable measures in place to guard against them being served content that is detrimental to their health and wellbeing

The AVMSD also requires that you should not use personal data collected or generated for the purposes of protecting minors from content which might impair their physical, mental or moral development for commercial purposes such as direct marketing, profiling and behaviourally targeted advertising.

We consider that this requirement is consistent with the purpose limitation principle of the GDPR and with our guidance in the sections of this code on age appropriate application - What if we need to collect personal data in order to establish age? It doesn't mean that services within the scope of the AVMSD can't ever process personal data for commercial purposes. It just means that you can't use personal data collected for one purpose for another. If such services wish to profile children for the purpose of behavioural advertising you will need the child's (or parent's) consent. For more information on consent see Annex C Lawful bases for processing.

We will work with other regulators as necessary where issues of regulatory consistency arise.

Further reading outside this code

The Editors' Code of Practice

The Ofcom Broadcasting Code (with the Cross-promotion Code and the on Demand Programme Service Rules)

Directive (EU) 2018/1808 amending Directive 2010/13/EU (Audiovisual Media Services Directive) and the UK government's Audiovisual Media Services Consultation Document

Age Appropriate Design Code FAQs for the news media

13. NUDGE TECHNIQUES

[1.361]
Do not use nudge techniques to lead or encourage children to provide unnecessary personal data or turn off privacy protections.

WHAT DO YOU MEAN BY 'NUDGE TECHNIQUES'?

Nudge techniques are design features which lead or encourage users to follow the designer's preferred paths in the user's decision making. For example, in the graphic below the large green 'yes' button is presented far more prominently then the small print 'no' option, with the result that the user is 'nudged' towards answering 'yes' rather than 'no' to whatever option is being presented.

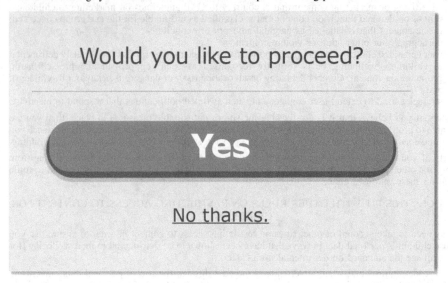

In the next example the language used to explain the outcomes of two alternatives is framed more positively for one alternative than for the other, again 'nudging' the user towards the service provider's preferred option.

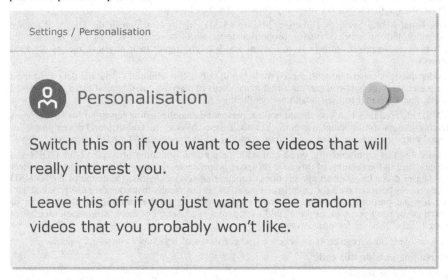

A further nudge technique involves making one option much less cumbersome or time consuming than the alternative, therefore encouraging many users to just take the easy option. For example providing a low privacy option instantly with just one 'click', and the high privacy alternative via a six click mechanism, or with a delay to accessing the service.

WHY IS THIS IMPORTANT?

Article 5(1)(a) of the GDPR says that personal data shall be:

"processed lawfully, fairly and in a transparent manner in relation to the data subject ('lawfulness, fairness and transparency')"

Recital 38 to the GDPR states that:

"Children merit specific protection with regard to their personal data, as they may be less aware of the risks, consequences and safeguards concerned and their rights in relation to the processing of personal data . . . ."

The employment of nudge techniques in the design of online services can be used to encourage users, including children, to provide an online service with more personal data than they would otherwise volunteer. Similarly it can be used to lead users, particularly children, to select less privacy-enhancing choices when personalising their privacy settings.

Using techniques based on the exploitation of human psychological bias in this way goes against the 'fairness' and 'transparency' provisions of the GDPR as well as the child specific considerations set out in Recital 38.

HOW CAN WE MAKE SURE THAT WE MEET THIS STANDARD?

Do not use nudge techniques to lead children to make poor privacy decisions

You should not use nudge techniques to lead or encourage children to activate options that mean they give you more of their personal data, or turn off privacy protections.

You should not exploit unconscious psychological processes to this end (such as associations between certain colours or imagery and positive outcomes, or human affirmation needs).

You should not use nudge techniques that might lead children to lie about their age. For example pre-selecting an older age range for them, or not allowing them the option of selecting their true age range.

Use pro-privacy nudges where appropriate

Taking into account the best interests of the child as a primary consideration, your design should support the developmental needs of the age of your child users.

Younger children, with limited levels understanding and decision making skills need more instruction based interventions, less explanation, unambiguous rules to follow and a greater level of parental support. Nudges towards high privacy options, wellbeing enhancing behaviours and parental controls and involvement should support these needs.

As children get older your focus should gradually move to supporting them in developing conscious decision making skills, providing clear explanations of functionality, risks and consequences. They will benefit from more neutral interventions that require them to think things through. Parental support may still be required but you should present this as an option alongside signposting to other resources.

Consider nudging to promote health and wellbeing

You may also wish to consider nudging children in ways that support their health and wellbeing. For example, nudging them towards supportive resources or providing tools such as pause and save buttons.

If you use personal data to support these features then you still need to make sure your processing is compliant (including having a lawful basis for processing and have providing clear privacy information), but subject to this it is likely that such processing will be fair.

The table below gives some recommendations that you might wish to apply to children of different ages. Although again you are free to develop your own, service specific, user journeys that follow the principle in the headline standard.

You should also consider any additional responsibilities you may have under the applicable equality legislation for England, Scotland, Wales and Northern Ireland.

Age range	Recommendations
0-5 Pre-literate & early literacy	Provide design architecture which is high-privacy by default. If change of default attempted nudge towards maintaining high privacy or towards parental or trusted adult involvement.
	Avoid explanations – present as rules to protect and help. Consider further interventions such as parental notifications, activation delays or disabling facility to change defaults without parental involvement, depending on the risks inherent in the processing.
	Nudge towards wellbeing enhancing behaviours (such as taking breaks).
	Provide tools to support wellbeing enhancing behaviours (such as mid-level pause and save features).
6-9 Core primary school years	Provide design architecture which is high-privacy by default. If change of default attempted nudge towards maintaining high privacy or parental or trusted adult involvement.
	Provide simple explanations of functionality and inherent risk, but continue to present as rules to protect and help.
	Consider further interventions such as parental notifications, activation delays or disabling facility to change defaults without parental involvement, depending on the risks inherent in the processing.
	Nudge towards wellbeing enhancing behaviours (such as taking breaks).
	Provide tools to support wellbeing enhancing behaviours (such as mid-level pause and save features).

Age range	Recommendations
10-12 Transition years	Provide design architecture which is high-privacy by default. If change of default attempted provide explanations of functionality and inherent risk and suggest parental or trusted adult involvement.
	Present option in ways that encourage conscious decision making.
	Consider further interventions such as parental notifications, activation delays or disabling facility to change defaults without parental involvement, depending on the risks.
	Nudge towards wellbeing enhancing behaviours (such as taking breaks).
	Provide tools to support wellbeing enhancing behaviours (such as mid-level pause and save features).
13 -15 Early teens	Provide design architecture which is high-privacy by default.
	Provide explanations of functionality and inherent risk.
	Present options in ways that encourage conscious decision making.
	Signpost towards sources of support including parents.
	Consider further interventions depending on the risks.
	Suggest wellbeing enhancing behaviours (such as taking breaks).
	Provide tools to support wellbeing enhancing behaviours (such as mid-level pause and save features).
16-17 Approaching adulthood	Provide design architecture which is high-privacy by default.
	Provide explanations of functionality and inherent risk.
	Present options in ways that encourage conscious decision making.
	Signpost towards sources of support including parents.
	Suggest wellbeing enhancing behaviours (such as taking breaks).
	Provide tools to support wellbeing enhancing behaviours (such as mid-level pause and save features).

14. CONNECTED TOYS AND DEVICES

> **[1.362]**
> If you provide a connected toy or device, ensure you include effective tools to enable conformance to this code.

WHAT DO YOU MEAN BY 'CONNECTED TOYS AND DEVICES'?

These are children's toys and other devices which are connected to the internet. They are physical products which are supported by functionality provided through an internet connection. For example:

• a talking teddy bear with a microphone that records what the child is saying and then sends this data back to your servers so that you can use it to personalise the teddy bear's responses;

• a fitness band that records the child's level of physical activity and then transmits this back to your servers so the child can then access activity reports via a fitness app; or

• a 'home hub' interactive speaker device that provides internet based services via a voice recognition service.

You need to conform to the standards in this code if you provide a toy or device which collects and personal data and transmits it via a network connection in this way. If you provide electronic toys or devices that do not connect to the internet, and only store personal data within the device itself, this code does not apply to you as you do not have access to any personal data.

WHY IS THIS IMPORTANT?

Connected toys and devices raise particular issues because their scope for collecting and processing personal data, via functions such as cameras and microphones, is considerable. They are often used by multiple people of different ages, and by very young children without adult supervision. Delivering transparency via a physical rather than a screen-based product can also be a particular challenge.

Nevertheless you still have a responsibility to meet GDPR requirements and to ensure your processing is lawful, fair and transparent as required by Article 5(1); so you need to make sure you have tools to enable you to conform with this code.

HOW CAN WE MAKE SURE THAT WE MEET THIS STANDARD?

Be clear about who is processing the personal data and what their responsibilities are

If you provide a connected toy or device then you need to be clear about who will process the personal data that it transmits via the network connection and what their data protection responsibilities are.

If you provide both the physical product and the online functionality that supports it, then you are solely responsible for ensuring compliant processing. If you outsource or 'buy in' the online functionality or 'connected' element of the device then whoever provides this aspect of the overall product will also have responsibilities. The extent of these will vary depending on whether they are a 'processor' acting only on your behalf, or a 'controller' in their own right.

However, you cannot absolve yourself of your data protection obligations by outsourcing the 'connected' element of your toy or device to someone else. If you provide a connected toy or device then you need to comply with the GDPR and follow this code, and make sure that any third parties you use to deliver your overall product do so too.

This is particularly important when you are making sure that the product incorporates adequate security measures to mitigate risks such as unauthorised access to data, or 'hacking' of the device in order to communicate with the child (eg taking over microphone capabilities) or track their location.

Anticipate and provide for use by multiple users of different ages

If you provide a connected device then you need to pay attention to the potential for it to be used by multiple users of different ages. This is particularly the case for devices such as home hub interactive speaker devices which are likely to be used by multiple household members, including children, and may also be used by visitors to the home. Similarly interactive toys are often shared or may be used by several children at once when they play together.

You can do this by a combination of:
*   making sure that the service that you provide by default (the service that would be provided, for example, to occasional visitors to a household) is suitable for use by all children; and
*   providing user profile options for people who use the device regularly (eg household members and frequent visitors to a household) to support use by adults, or to tailor the service to the age of a particular child.

Provide clear information about your use of personal data at point of purchase and on set-up

You should provide clear information indicating that the product processes personal data at the point of sale and prior to device set-up. Both the packaging of the physical product, and your product leaflet or instruction booklet (paper or digital) could carry a clear indication (such as an icon) that the product is 'connected' and processes users' personal data.

You should allow potential purchasers to view your privacy information, terms and conditions of use and other relevant information online without having to purchase and set up the device first, so that they can make an informed decision about whether or not to buy the device in the first place.

You should also have a particular focus on the tools you provide to facilitate the set-up of the connected toy or device. This is a key opportunity for you to provide information about how your service works, how personal data is used and to explain the implications of this, especially if set-up is activated using a screen-based interface. If the child's ongoing use of the device is not screen-based this is particularly important as this may limit the ways in which you can convey information to the child on an ongoing basis.

Find ways to communicate 'just in time' information

You should consider how your connected device operates and how best to communicate 'just in time' information to the child or their parent. (See the section of this code on transparency for more detail about 'just in time' notices.)

For example using auto-play audio messages, only allowing default settings to be changed via use of a support app, or facilitating interactive auto-bot 'conversations' with the user.

Avoid passive collection of personal data

You should provide features that make it clear to the child or their parent when you are collecting personal data. For example a light that switches on when the device is audio recording, filming or collecting personal data in another way.

If the device uses a stand-by or 'listening' mode (eg it listens out for the name you or the child has given to the device, or for another key word or phrase to be used, and activates data collection when that word or phrase is used) again you should provide a clear indication that listening mode is active. You should not collect personal data in listening mode.

You should provide features which allow collection or listening modes to be easily switched off on the device itself (a 'connection off' button), or via online functionality options, so that the toy or device can be used as a non-connected device so far as this is practicable.

Further reading outside the code

Guide to the GDPR –Contracts and liabilities between controllers and processors

Guide to the GDPR – Security

Department for Digital, Culture, Media & Sport: Code of Practice for consumer IOT security

15. ONLINE TOOLS

[1.363]
Provide prominent and accessible tools to help children exercise their data protection rights and report concerns.

WHAT DO YOU MEAN BY 'ONLINE TOOLS'?

Online tools are mechanisms to help children exercise their rights simply and easily when they are online. They can be used to help children exercise their right to access a copy of their personal data, or to make a complaint or exercise any of their remedial rights.

WHY IS THIS IMPORTANT?

The GDPR gives data subjects the following rights over their personal data in articles 15 to 22:
* The right of access
* The right to rectification
* The right to erasure
* The right to restrict processing
* The right to data portability
* The right to object
* Rights in relation to automated decision making and profiling

Recital 65 states that the right to erasure has particular relevance for children using online services:

" . . . that right is relevant in particular where the data subject has given his or her consent as a child and is not fully aware of the risks involved by the processing, and later wants to remove such personal data, especially on the internet . . . "

Article 12 of the GDPR provides that:

"12(1) The controller shall take appropriate measures to provide . . . . any communication under Articles 15 to 22 . . . .. relating to the data subject in a concise, transparent, intelligible and easily accessible form, using clear and plain language, in particular for any information addressed specifically to a child. The information shall be provided in writing or by other means, including where appropriate by electronic means . . . ..

(2) The controller shall facilitate the exercise of data subject rights under Articles 15 to 22 . . . .

(3) The controller shall provide information on action taken on a request under Articles 15 to 22 to the data subject without undue delay and in any event within one month of receipt of the request. That period may be extended by a further two months where necessary, taking into account the complexity and number of the requests. The controller shall inform the data subject of any such extension within one month of receipt of the request, together with the reasons for the delay. Where the data subject makes the request by electronic form means, the information shall be provided by electronic means where possible, unless otherwise requested by the data subject."

In order to comply with these provisions you need to find ways to make sure that children know about their rights and are able to easily exercise them. You have an obligation not just to allow children to exercise their rights but to help them to do so.

HOW CAN WE MAKE SURE THAT WE MEET THIS STANDARD?

In order for children to exercise their rights they firstly need to know that these rights exist and what they are.

Make your tools prominent

The tools which you provide to help children exercise their rights and report concerns to you must be easy for the child to find. You therefore need to give them prominence on your online service. You should highlight the reporting tool in your set up process and provide a clear and easily identifiable icon or other access mechanism in a prominent place on the screen display.

If your online service includes a physical product, for example a connected toy or speaker, you can include the icon on your packaging, highlighting online reporting tools as a product feature, and find ways to highlight reporting tools in a prominent way even if the product is not screen-based.

Make them age appropriate and easy to use

Your tools should be age appropriate and easy to use. You should therefore tailor them to the age of the child in question. The following table provides some guidelines. However, these are only a starting point and you are free to develop your own, service specific, user journeys that follow the principle in the headline standard.

You should also consider any additional responsibilities you may have under the applicable equality legislation for England, Scotland, Wales and Northern Ireland.

Age range	Recommendations
0-5 Pre-literate & early literacy	Provide icon(s), audio prompts or similar that even the youngest of children will recognise as meaning 'I'm not happy' or 'I need help'.
	If these buttons are pressed, or other prompts responded to, provide video or audio material prompting the child to get help from a parent or trusted adult.
	Provide online tools suitable for use by parents.
6-9 Core primary school years	Provide icon(s), audio prompts or similar that children will recognise as meaning 'I'm not happy' or 'I need help'.
	If these buttons are pressed, or other prompts responded to, provide video or audio material prompting the child to get help from a parent or trusted adult, then direct the child to your online tool.
	Provide online tools that children could use either by themselves or with the help of an adult.
10-12 Transition years	Provide icon(s), audio prompts or similar that children will recognise as meaning 'I'm not happy' or 'I need help'.
	If these buttons are pressed, or other prompts responded to, direct the child to your online tool and prompt them to get help from a parent or trusted adult if they need it.
	Provide online tools that children could use either by themselves or with the help of an adult.
13 -15 Early teens	Provide icon(s), audio prompts or similar that children will recognise as meaning 'I want to raise a concern' 'I want to access my information' or 'I need help'.
	If these buttons are pressed, or other prompts responded to, direct the child to your online tools and prompt them to get help from a parent or other trusted resource if they need it.
	Provide online tools suitable for use by the child without the help of an adult.
16-17 Approaching adulthood	Provide icon(s), audio prompts or similar that children will recognise as 'I want to raise a concern' 'I want to access my information' or 'I need help'.
	If these buttons are pressed, or other prompts responded to, direct the child to your online tools and prompt them to get help from a parent or other trusted resource if they need it.
	Provide online tools suitable for use by the child without the help of an adult.

Make your tools specific to the rights they support

You should tailor your tools to support the rights children have under the GDPR. For example:
- a 'download all my data' tool to support the right of access, and right to data portability;
- a 'delete all my data' or 'select data for deletion' tool to support the right to erasure;
- a 'stop using my data' tool to support the rights to restrict or object to processing; and
- a 'correction' tool to support the right to rectification.

Used together with privacy setting such tools should help to give children control over their personal data.

Include mechanisms for tracking progress and communicating with you

Your online tools can include ways for the child or their parent to track the progress of their complaint or request, and communicate with you about what is happening.

You should provide information about your timescales for responding to requests from children to exercise their rights, and should deal with all requests within the timescales set out at Article 12(3) of the GDPR.

You should have mechanisms for children to indicate that they think their complaint or request is urgent and why, and you should actively consider any information they provide in this respect and prioritise accordingly. You should have procedures in place to take swift action where information is provided indicating there is an ongoing safeguarding issue.

Further reading outside this code

Guide to the GDPR – individual rights

GOVERNANCE AND ACCOUNTABILITY

AT A GLANCE

[1.364]
You should put systems in place to support and demonstrate your compliance with data protection legislation and conformance to this code. These should include implementing an accountability programme, having suitable data protection policies in place, providing appropriate training for your staff and keeping proper records of your processing activities.

IN MORE DETAIL
- What do you mean by 'governance and accountability'?
- Why is it important?
- What do we need to do?
- What about certification schemes?

WHAT DO YOU MEAN BY 'GOVERNANCE AND ACCOUNTABILITY'?

Governance and accountability means having systems in place to support and demonstrate compliance with data protection legislation and this code.

WHY IS IT IMPORTANT?

It is important because it is a vehicle for you to build compliance as a long term sustainable activity across your business. It is a global concept which can work across jurisdictions and allow different approaches under different law to fit together. It is most successful when supported by Board level leadership.

Article 24(1) of the GDPR provides that:

"24(1) Taking into account the nature, scope, context and purposes of processing as well as the risks of varying likelihood and severity for the rights and freedoms of natural persons the controller shall implement appropriate technical and organisational measures to ensure and to be able to demonstrate that processing is performed in accordance with this regulation. Those measures shall be reviewed and updated where necessary."

Article 5(2) of the GDPR says that you need to be able to demonstrate your compliance with the data protection principles:

"The controller shall be responsible for, and able to demonstrate compliance with paragraph 1 (accountability)"

WHAT DO WE NEED TO DO?

Implement an accountability programme

You should implement an accountability programme to effectively address the standards in this code. This can be tailored to the size and resources or your business or organisation and the risks to children inherent in your online service. It should be driven by your DPO, if you have appointed one, and overseen by senior management at Board level if your business is structured in this way. For smaller businesses which may not have such formal structures it is still important to make sure that children's privacy is understood by key personnel and is a seen as an important business priority and key accountability measure.

You should assess and revise the programme on an ongoing basis, building in changes to reflect the changing environment of children's privacy.

You should report against the standards in this code in any internal or external accountability reports, introducing KPIs (key performance indicators) on children's privacy to support this as appropriate.

Have policies to support and demonstrate your compliance with data protection legislation

You should have policies (proportionate to the size of your organisation) that document how your organisation ensures adherence to this code and the requirements of the GDPR and PECR. For larger organisations these should include appropriate board level reporting mechanisms and mechanisms to ensure adequate resourcing of relevant projects.

In particular you should ensure that your policies cover your obligations under Article 30(1) to keep a record of your processing activities.

Train your staff in data protection

In order to meet the requirements of the GDPR, any staff involved in the design of your ISS need to understand what those requirements are and how we expect them to be met. So you should make sure that your staff receive appropriate training in data protection and are aware of the provisions of the GDPR and this code.

Keep proper records

Under Article 30(1) of the GDPR you are required to keep the following records of your processing activities:
- the name and contact details of your organisation (and where applicable, of other controllers, your representative and your DPO);
- the purposes of your processing;
- a description of the categories of individuals and categories of personal data;
- the categories of recipients of personal data;
- details of your transfers to third countries including documenting the transfer mechanism safeguards in place;

- retention schedules; and
- a description of your technical and organisational security measures.

In the context of providing an online service this rule applies to you regardless of the size of your organisation. This is because the Commissioner considers that, given the vulnerability of children and the risks inherent in them being online, any such processing is likely to result in a risk to the rights and freedoms of children.

There are templates on our website that you can use to record these details.

You should also keep a record of your DPIA. This is a key document that you can use to demonstrate that you have properly considered and mitigated risks arising from your processing of children's personal data. It should help you to demonstrate your thinking and decisions on:
- whether children are likely to access your online service;
- what ages of children are likely to access your online service; and
- what measures you have taken to comply with this code.

Be prepared to demonstrate your conformance to this code

You should be prepared to demonstrate your conformance to this code to the ICO if we ask you to do so. You can do this by firstly providing us with copies of your DPIA, relevant policies, training records, and records of processing activities. You may also need to provide evidence of how you have implemented the provisions of the code in your online service in practice. For example, by showing us your privacy notices, or explaining or demonstrating your default settings, online tools, complaint processes and approach to profiling.

WHAT ABOUT CERTIFICATION SCHEMES?

Article 42 of the GDPR provides a mechanism for the establishment of certification and data protection seal schemes by which data controllers could demonstrate their compliance with the GDPR.

This would be of particular benefit to children and their parents in making decisions about which online services to use (or allow their children to use) without having to assess the compliance and practice of the online service provider themselves.

It would also benefit you as a provider of an online service to give assurance to your customers and potential customers of your data protection compliance, thereby increasing consumer confidence in online service and brand.

As and when any such schemes become available and offer certification of adherence to this code, you will be able to use them to demonstrate your compliance in accordance with article 24(1) of the GDPR.

Further reading outside this code

Guide to the GDPR Accountability and governance

Documentation template for controllers

Documentation template for processors

ENFORCEMENT OF THIS CODE

AT A GLANCE

[1.365]
The ICO upholds information rights in the public interest. Data relating to children is afforded special protection in the GDPR and is a regulatory priority for the ICO. Conforming to the standards set out in this code will be a key measure of your compliance with data protection laws.

We will monitor conformance to this code through a series of proactive audits, will consider complaints, and take appropriate action to enforce the underlying data protection standards, subject to applicable law and in line with our Regulatory Action Policy. To ensure proportionate and effective regulation we will target our most significant powers, focusing on organisations and individuals suspected of repeated or wilful misconduct or serious failure to comply with the law. If you do not follow this code, you may find it difficult to demonstrate that your processing is fair and complies with the GDPR or PECR.

We have various powers to take action for a breach of the GDPR or PECR, including where a child's personal data has been processed in breach of relevant provisions of these laws. This includes the power to issue warnings, reprimands, stop-now orders and fines.

IN MORE DETAIL
- What is the role of the ICO?
- How will the ICO monitor compliance?
- How will the ICO deal with complaints?
- What are the ICO's enforcement powers?

WHAT IS THE ROLE OF THE ICO?

The Information Commissioner is the independent supervisory authority for data protection in the UK.

Our mission is to uphold information rights for the public in the digital age. Our vision for data protection is to increase the confidence that the public have in organisations that process personal data. We offer advice and guidance, promote good practice, monitor and investigate breach reports, monitor compliance, conduct audits and advisory visits, consider complaints, and take enforcement action where appropriate. Our enforcement powers are set out in part 6 of the DPA 2018.

Our focus is on compliance with data protection legislation in the UK. In particular, to ensure that the protections provided for children's data are adhered to.

Where the provisions of this code overlap with other regulators we will work with them to ensure a consistent and co-ordinated response.

HOW WILL THE ICO MONITOR CONFORMANCE?

Key objectives in our Regulatory Action Policy include:

"To be proactive in identifying and mitigating new or emerging risks arising from technological and societal change" and,
"To be effective, proportionate, dissuasive and consistent in our application of sanctions, targeting our most significant powers (i) for organisations and individuals suspected of repeated or wilful misconduct or serious failures to take proper steps to protect personal data, and (ii) where formal regulatory action serves as an important deterrent to those who risk non-compliance with the law."

We have also made use of children's data a regulatory priority.

We will monitor conformance to this code using the full range of measures available to us from intelligence gathering through to using our audit or assessment powers to understand an issue, through to investigation and regulatory action where appropriate and proportionate..

Our approach is to encourage conformance. Where we find issues we take fair, proportionate and timely regulatory action with a view to guaranteeing that individuals' information rights are properly protected. We will take account of the size and resources of the organisation concerned, the availability of technological solutions in the marketplace and the risks to children that are inherent in the processing. We will take a proportionate and responsible approach, focussing on areas with the potential for most harm and selecting the most suitable regulatory tool.

HOW DOES THE ICO DEAL WITH COMPLAINTS?

If someone raises a concern with us about your conformance to this code or the way you have handled a child's personal data in the context of a relevant online service, we will record and consider their complaint.

We will take this code into account, along with other relevant legislation, when considering whether you have complied with the GDPR or PECR. In particular, we will take the code into account when considering questions of fairness, lawfulness, transparency and accountability.

We will assess your initial response to the complaint, and we may contact you to ask some questions and give you a further opportunity to explain your position. We may also ask for details of your policies and procedures, your DPIA, and other relevant documentation. However, we expect you to be accountable for how you meet your obligations under GDPR and PECR, so you should make sure that when you initially respond to complaints from individuals you do so with a full and detailed explanation about how you use their personal data and how you comply.

If we consider that you have failed (or are failing) to comply with the GDPR or PECR, we have the power to take enforcement action. This may require you to take steps to bring your operations into compliance or we may decide to fine you. Or both.

WHAT ARE THE ICO'S ENFORCEMENT POWERS?

We have various powers to take action for a breach of the GDPR or PECR, including where a child's personal data is involved. We have a statutory duty to take the provisions of this code into account when enforcing the GDPR and PECR.

Without prejudice to the specifics of applicable law such as the eCommerce Regulations 2002, tools at our disposal include assessment notices, warnings, reprimands, enforcement notices and penalty notices (administrative fines). For serious breaches of the data protection principles, we have the power to issue fines of up to €20 million (or £17.5 million when the UK GDPR comes into effect) or 4% of your annual worldwide turnover, whichever is higher.

In line with our policy, we consider that the public interest in protecting children online is a significant factor weighing in the balance when considering the type of regulatory action. This means that where see harm or potential harm to children we will likely take more severe action against a company than would be the case for other types of personal data. We will nevertheless take account of the size and resources of the organisation concerned, the availability of technological solutions in the marketplace and the specific risks to children that are inherent in the processing. We will also take into account the efforts made to conform to the provision in this code.

Further reading outside this code

What we do

Make a complaint

What action can the ICO take to enforce PECR?

Regulatory Action Policy

GLOSSARY

[1.366]
This glossary is included as a quick reference point for key data protection terms and abbreviations used in this code. It includes links to further reading and other resources which do not form part of this code, but may provide useful context and more detailed guidance.

ASA	The Advertising Standards Authority. See www.asa.org.uk
CAP code	The UK Code of Non-broadcast Advertising and Direct & Promotional Marketing. See: www.asa.org.uk/codes-and-rulings/advertising-codes/non-broadcast-code.html
Child	A person under the age of 18 years, as defined in the UNCRC.
Competent authority	A public authority listed in schedule 7 of the DPA 2018, or any other organisation or person with statutory law enforcement functions. For more information, see our separate Guide to Law Enforcement Processing.
Consent	A freely given, specific, informed and unambiguous indication of the data subject's wishes by which he or she, by a statement or by clear affirmative action, signifies agreement to the processing of personal data. For more information, see our separate guidance on consent.
Controller	The person (usually an organisation) who decides how and why to collect and use the data. For more information, see our separate guidance on controllers and processors.
DPA 2018	The Data Protection Act 2018. For more information, see our separate introduction to data protection.
DPIA	Data protection impact assessment. For more information, see our separate guidance on DPIAs.
GDPR	The General Data Protection Regulation (EU) 2016/679, as amended and incorporated into UK law. For more information, see our separate Guide to Data Protection. When the UK leaves the EU (or at the end of any agreed implementation period if we leave with a deal), you should read references to the GDPR in this code as references to the UK GDPR.
ISS	Information society service, as defined in Directive (EU) 2015/1535 and incorporated into the GDPR (any service normally provided for remuneration, at a distance, by electronic means and at the individual request of a recipient).
One-stop-shop	The one-stop-shop means you can generally deal with a single European supervisory authority taking action on behalf of the other European supervisory authorities. It avoids you having to deal with regulatory and enforcement action from every supervisory authority in every EEA and EU state where individuals are affected. For more information, see EDPB guidelines on the lead supervisory authority.
PECR	The Privacy and Electronic Communications (EC Directive) Regulations 2003. For more information, see our separate Guide to PECR.
PEGI	Pan European Game Information. For more information see www.pegi.info/
Processor	A person (usually an organisation) who processes personal data on behalf of a controller. For more information, see our separate guidance on controllers and processors.
UK GDPR	The UK version of the GDPR, as amended and incorporated into UK law after the UK leaves the EU by the European Union (Withdrawal) Act 2018 and associated Exit Regulations. The government has published a Keeling Schedule for the UK GDPR which shows the planned amendments.
UNCRC	The 1989 United Nations Convention on the Rights of the Child.

ANNEX A: SERVICES COVERED BY THE CODE FLOWCHART

[1.367]
This flowchart sets out the questions you will need to answer if you are uncertain whether your online service is covered by the code.

However, as a starting point, you should note that we expect the vast majority of online services used by children to be covered, and those that aren't covered to be exceptional.

The services that fall out of scope tend to do so for fairly technical legal reasons (such as the definition of an ISS as derived from Directive EU 2015/1535), so if you think you may be out of scope then you may benefit from getting your own legal advice to support or confirm this.

Do you provide an online service or connected toy or device?	NO→	The code does not apply.
YES↓		
Does your online service process personal data?	NO→	The code does not apply.
YES↓		

Is your online service a counselling or preventive service?	YES→	The code does not apply.
NO↓		
Are you a law enforcement agency (eg police, courts) whose online service processes personal data for law enforcement purposes?	YES→	The code does not apply to any processing your online service does for law enforcement purposes. It may apply to any processing your online service does for other purposes.
NO↓		
Is your online service the kind of service which is typically provided or funded on a commercial basis (even if the funding isn't provided by the end user)?	NO→	The code does not apply.
YES↓		
Is your online service a 'general broadcast' service (a service which transmits radio or TV broadcasts to a general audience according to a set schedule or timetable)?	YES→	The code does not apply to your 'general broadcast' services. If you also provide 'on demand' broadcast services then the code may apply to these.
NO↓		
Does your online service only provide information about a 'realworld' business (without allowing customers to buy products or access specific services online)?	YES→	The code does not apply.
NO↓		
Is your service a 'traditional' voice telephony service as opposed to an internet based voice calling service or VOIP (Voice Over Internet Protocol)?	YES→	The code does not apply.
NO↓		
Is your online service likely to be accessed by children? (This will depend upon whether the content and design of your service is likely to appeal to children, and any measures you may have in place to restrict or discourage their access to your service).	NO→	The code does not apply.
YES↓		
Do you have an office, base, or other 'establishment' in the UK, and does your online service process personal data in the context of that establishment?	NO→	The code applies to your service if it meets the following criteria: • you offer your online service to UK users, or monitor the behaviour of UK users; and • (until the UK leaves the EU) you do not have an office base or other establishment elsewhere within the EEA (European Economic Area). Otherwise the code does not apply.

YES↓

The code applies to your service.

ANNEX B: AGE AND DEVELOPMENTAL STAGES

[1.368]

Children are individuals, and age ranges are not a perfect guide to the interests, needs and evolving capacity of an individual child. However, you can use age ranges as a guide to the capacity, skills and behaviours a child might be expected to display at each stage of their development, to help you assess what is appropriate for children of broadly that age.

This annex provides some guidance on key considerations relevant at different ages. This has been developed drawing on responses to the ICO's call for evidence on the age appropriate design code, ICO funded research by Sonia Livingstone at the London School of Economics and on the following sources:

- UKCCIS report Education for a connected world
- UKCCIS report Children's online activities, risks and safety
- UKCCIS guide Child Safety Online
- Children's Commissioner for England report Life in Likes
- 5Rights Foundation report Digital Childhood
- Revealing Reality report Towards a better digital future Informing the Age Appropriate Design Code

Children with disabilities may have additional needs and you should consider any additional responsibilities you may have under the applicable equality legislation for England, Scotland, Wales and Northern Ireland.

Age/Stage	Key considerations
0–5 Pre-literate & early literacy	There is relatively little evidence on the understanding of the digital environment of children in this age range, particularly for 0-3 years old. However anecdotal evidence suggests that significant numbers of children are online from the earliest of ages and that any understanding and awareness of online risks that have children within this age range is very limited.
	At age 3-5 children start to develop the ability to 'put themselves in others shoes', but are easily fooled by appearances. They are developing friendships, although peer pressure is relatively low and parental or family guidance or influence is key. They are learning to follow clear and simple rules but are unlikely to have the cognitive ability to understand or follow more nuanced rules or instructions, or to make anything but the simplest of decisions. They have limited capacity for self-control or ability to manage their own time online. They are pre-dominantly engaged in adult-guided activities, playing within 'walled' environments, or watching video streams.
	Children in this age range are less likely than older children to have their own device, although significant numbers do, and often play on their parents' devices which may or may not be set up with child specific profiles. They may use connected toys (such as talking teddies or dolls) and may also mimic parents' use of voice activated devices such as 'home hubs'.
	Children within this age range are pre-literate or in the earliest stages of literacy, so text based information is of very limited use in communicating with them
	UK children in this age range cannot provide their own consent to the processing of their personal data in the context of an online service offered directly to a child (by virtue of Article 8(1) of the GDPR and s9 of the DPA 2018). So if you wish to rely on consent as your lawful basis for processing their personal data you need parental consent.
6–9 Core primary school years	Children in this age range are more likely than younger children to have their own device (such as a tablet), although use of parents' devices is still common. They are increasingly using devices independently, with or without the benefit of child specific profiles. Connected toys are popular and they may engage enthusiastically with voice activated devices such as home hubs.
	Children in this age range often prefer online gaming and creative based activities, and video streaming services remain popular. Children may be experimenting with social media use, either through social aspects of online games, through their parents' social media accounts or by setting up their own social media accounts. They may relate to and be influenced by online vloggers, particularly those within a similar age range.
	They are likely to be absorbing messages from school about online safety and the digital environment, and be developing a basic understanding of privacy concepts and some of the more obvious online risks. They are unlikely however to have a clear understanding of the many ways in which their personal data may be used or of any less direct or obvious risks that their online behaviour may expose them to.
	The need to fit in with their peer group becomes more important so they may be more susceptible to peer pressure. However home and family still tends to be the strongest influencer. They still tend to comply with clear messages or rules from home and school, but if risks aren't explained clearly then they may fill the gap with their own explanations or come up with protective strategies that aren't as effective as they think they are.
	Literacy levels can vary considerably and ability or willingness to engage with written materials cannot be assumed.
	UK children in this age range cannot provide their own consent to the processing of their personal data in the context of an online service offered directly to a child (by virtue of Article 8(1) of the GDPR and s9 of the DPA 2018). So if you wish to rely on consent as your lawful basis for processing their personal data you need parental consent.
10–12 Transition years	This is a key age range in which children's online activity is likely to change significantly. The transition, or anticipated transition, from primary school to high school means that children are much more likely to have their own personal device (pre-dominantly smartphones).

Age/Stage	Key considerations
	There is also likely to be a shift towards use of the online environment to explore and develop self-identity and relationships, expand and stay in contact with their peer group, and 'fit in' socially. This may lead to an increased use of social networking functions or services by children within this age range, an increased susceptibility to peer pressure, branding and online 'influencers', and an increase in risk taking behaviours. Self-esteem may fall as children compare themselves to others and strive to present an acceptable version of themselves online and the 'fear of missing out' may become a concern.
	Online gaming and video and music streaming services are also popular. Children may feel pressurised into playing online games when their friends are playing, again for fear of missing out.
	Attitudes towards parental rules, authority and involvement in their online activity may vary considerably, with some children relatively accepting of this and others seeking higher levels of autonomy. However parents and family still tend to be the main source of influence for children in this age range.
	Children in this age range are moving towards more adult ways of thinking but may have limited capacity to think beyond immediate consequences, be particularly susceptible to reward based systems, and tend towards impulsive behaviours. Parental or other support therefore still tends to be needed, if not always desired. It may however need to be offered or encouraged in a less directive way than for younger children.
	Children in this age range are developing a better understanding of how the online environment operates, but are still unlikely to be aware of less obvious uses of their personal data.
	Although children in this age range are likely to have more developed literacy skills they may still prefer media such as video content instead.
	12 is the age at which, under s208 of the DPA 2018, children in Scotland are presumed (unless the contrary is shown) to be of sufficient age and maturity to have a general understanding of what it means to exercise their data protection rights. There is no such provision for children in the rest of the UK, although this may be considered a useful reference point.
	UK children in this age range cannot provide their own consent to the processing of their personal data in the context of an online service offered directly to a child (by virtue of Article 8(1) of the GDPR and s9 of the DPA 2018). So if you wish to rely on consent as your lawful basis for processing their personal data you need parental consent.
13–15 Early teens	In this age range the need for identification with their own peer group, and exploration of identity and relationships increases further and children are likely to seek greater levels of independence and autonomy. They may reject or distance themselves from the values of their parents or seek to actively flaunt parental or online rules. The use of new services that parents aren't aware of or don't use is popular as is the use of language that parents may not easily understand. However, despite this, family remains a key influence on children within this age range.
	The use of social media functions and applications is widespread although gaming and video and music streaming services are also popular. Again children may seek to emulate online 'influencers' or vloggers at this stage in their development.
	Children of this age may still look to parents to assist if they encounter problems online, but some may be reluctant to do so due to concerns about their parents' reaction to their online activity.
	Developmentally they may tend toward idealised or polarised thinking and be susceptible to negative comparison of themselves with others. They may overestimate their own ability to cope with risks and challenges arising from online behaviour and relationships and may benefit from signposting towards sources of support, including but not limited to parental support.
	Literacy skills are likely to be more developed but they may still benefit from a choice of media.
	13 is the age at which children in the UK are able to provide their own consent to processing, if you relying on consent as your lawful basis for processing in the context of offering an online service directly to a child (by virtue of Article 8(1) of the GDPR and s9 of the DPA 2018).
16–17 Approaching adulthood	By this age many children have developed reasonably robust online skills, coping strategies and resilience. However they are still developing cognitively and emotionally and should not be expected to have the same resilience, experience or appreciation of the long term consequences of their online actions as adults may have.
	Technical knowledge and capabilities may be better developed than their emotional literacy or their ability to handle complex personal relationships. Their capacity to engage in long term thinking is still developing and they may still tend towards risk taking or impulsive behaviours and be susceptible to reward based systems.

Age/Stage	Key considerations
	Parental support is more likely to be viewed as one option that they may or may not wish to use, rather than as the preferred or only option, and they expect a reasonable level of autonomy. Signposting to other sources of support in addition to parental support is important.
	By virtue of Article 8(1) of the GDPR and s9 of the DPA 2018, if you are relying on consent as your lawful basis for processing in the context of offering an online service directly to a child, UK children in this age range can provide their own consent to the processing of their personal data.

ANNEX C: LAWFUL BASIS FOR PROCESSING

[1.369]
The guidance in this annex is not linked to a specific standard in the code, but if you provide an online service to children it will help you comply with your lawfulness obligations under the GDPR and DPA 2018.

- What is a lawful basis for processing?
- Which lawful basis can we use for our 'core' processing?
- Which lawful basis can we use for 'non-core' processing?
- When do we have to get parental consent?
- What about special category data?

WHAT IS A LAWFUL BASIS FOR PROCESSING?

You must have a valid lawful basis for each of your processing activities. Article 6 of the GDPR sets out six potential lawful bases:

(a)   **Consent:** the individual has given valid consent for you to process their personal data for a specific purpose.

(b)   **Contract:** the processing is necessary to perform a contract you have with the individual, or because they have asked you to take specific steps before entering into a contract.

(c)   **Legal obligation:** the processing is necessary for you to comply with the law (not including contractual obligations).

(d)   **Vital interests:** the processing is necessary to protect someone's life.

(e)   **Public task:** the processing is necessary for you to perform a task in the public interest or for your official functions, and the task or function has a clear basis in law.

(f)   **Legitimate interests:** the processing is necessary for your legitimate interests or the legitimate interests of a third party, unless there is a good reason to protect the individual's personal data which overrides those legitimate interests – in particular where they are a child. (This cannot apply if you are a public authority performing your official tasks.)

It is up to you to decide which lawful basis for processing is most appropriate to your processing, and demonstrate that it applies. This depends on your specific purposes and on the context of the processing. In practice it is likely that you will have more than one purpose, in which case you may have more than one basis for processing.

You should consider this separately for each distinct processing activity, thinking about what you want to do with the personal data you are collecting and why, and taking into account how essential this is to the provision of your online service.

Further reading outside this code:

Lawful basis for processing

Lawful basis interactive guidance tool

WHICH LAWFUL BASIS CAN WE USE FOR OUR 'CORE' PROCESSING?

By 'core processing', we mean processing which is integral to the provision of your core service – in other words, you need to process the data in that way in order to actually deliver the elements of the service the individual has signed up for. This doesn't include processing for broader business purposes (eg for marketing, service improvement or as part of an indirect funding model).

For this type of core processing, you could consider:

- **(b) Contract:** the most obvious basis is 'necessary for performance of a contract'. However, if you want to rely on this basis, you need to be sure that the child has the legal capacity to enter into a contract. If the child is not competent to enter into the contract then the contract is voidable. If the contract is voided then this basis for processing will not be valid.

- **(f) Legitimate interests:** alternatively you can consider legitimate interests (unless you are a public authority performing your functions). If you do choose to rely on legitimate interests, you have a particular responsibility to protect children from risks that they may not fully appreciate and from consequences that they may not envisage. You must ensure their interests are adequately protected and that there are appropriate safeguards. You need to give extra weight to their interests, and you need a more compelling interest to justify any potential impact on children. Your DPIA is a useful tool to help you assess this balance.

- **(e) Public task:** if you are offering a service as part of your public functions, or performing a specific task in the public interest. You need to identify a statutory or common law basis for that function or task.

Consent is unlikely to be the most appropriate basis for processing which is necessary to deliver the core service. This is because the processing is a condition of the contract, so asking for separate consent is unnecessary and potentially confusing. It risks diluting the general concept of consent as a clear and separate choice with no strings attached, and may contribute to 'consent fatigue'. You only need consent where specifically required under another provision, such as:

- to comply with PECR rules - although you don't need consent for cookies which are strictly necessary for your service; or
- to get explicit consent for specific elements of your service that process special category data (more on this below).

Legal obligation may be relevant for some fraud prevention, child protection or safeguarding measures, if you can point to a specific legal provision or appropriate source of advice or guidance on your legal obligations.

Vital interests is unlikely to be relevant in this context. Legitimate interests is likely to be a more reliable basis for any measures you take to protect a child's health or safety.

WHICH LAWFUL BASIS CAN WE USE FOR 'NON-CORE' PROCESSING?

By 'non-core' processing, we mean processing that is not integral to the provision of your core service. This includes processing for optional elements of the service, or processing for broader business purposes such as marketing, service improvement or indirect funding models.

You should give the child (and their parent where appropriate) as much choice as you can over these elements of your processing. This includes as a minimum implementing the standards in this code on default privacy settings, data minimisation, geolocation and profiling.

For optional elements of your service which a child has specifically activated, you can consider **necessary for contract** for any processing which is objectively necessary to deliver that specific element of the service if the child has capacity to enter into a contract, in the same way as for core processing. You can also consider **legitimate interests**. However, for these to apply, you must give the child separate choices to activate each separate element of the service wherever this is functionally possible. You cannot bundle independent elements of a service together. See also the standard on data minimisation in this code.

You do not need consent under PECR cookie rules as long as the processing is strictly necessary for these extra elements of a service, and they have been requested by the child. There are advantages to using legitimate interests or contract instead of consent, to avoid repeated consent requests and 'consent fatigue'. However, you still need to conform to the standards in this code related to privacy settings and controls, even if this falls short of a full consent mechanism.

To reinforce the importance of a child's choice, or as a safeguard against a particular risk to a child's interests, you may decide to rely on **consent** for some non-core processing. If you do so then you need to ensure you use a positive opt-in method of consent which is clear, separate from your terms and conditions, separate from your privacy information, and easy to withdraw. You must also comply with Article 8 of the GDPR (as adapted by section 9 of the DPA 2018) and obtain parental consent for children under 13. More on this below. You must also still conform to all the standards in this code to the extent they are relevant to your service.

You should remember that you need GDPR-compliant consent under PECR for any relevant cookies, apps or other technologies which gain access to, or store data on, the user device, but which are not strictly necessary for the service. You should also note the opinion of the European Data Protection Board (EDPB) about processing for the purposes of online behavioural advertising. EDPB has been clear that it considers that legitimate interests will not be an appropriate lawful basis for processing for this type of online activity (which leaves consent as the only remaining viable lawful basis for processing).

If you're processing for broader business purposes and you are not caught by the cookie rules, you may still be able to consider legitimate interests, public task or legal obligation, depending on why and how you are using the data.

Further reading outside this code:

See our separate guidance on:

Consent

Contract

Legal obligation

Public task

Legitimate interests

Guide to PECR – Cookies and similar technologies

Further reading — European Data Protection Board

The European Data Protection Board (EDPB), which has replaced the Article 29 Working Party (WP29), includes representatives from the data protection authorities of each EU member state. It adopts guidelines for complying with the requirements of the GDPR.

The EDPB has published 'Opinion 5/2019 on the interplay between the ePrivacy Directive and the GDPR'. This provides useful information about how the cookie rules relate to the GDPR and re-states the positions previously taken by WP29 about when consent should be required for certain processing operations beyond the setting of cookies.

WP29 previously published 'Opinion 3/2013 on purpose limitation' and 'Opinion 6/2014 on the notion of legitimate interests'. Although this guidance was produced under the previous data protection framework, much of it applies under the GDPR.

WHEN DO WE HAVE TO GET PARENTAL CONSENT?

Article 8(1) of the GDPR (as modified by section 9 of the DPA 2018) says that if you are relying on consent as your lawful basis:

> "in relation to the offer of information society services directly to a child, the processing of the personal data of a child shall be lawful where the child is at least [13] years old. Where the child is below the age of [13] years, such processing shall be lawful only if and to the extent that consent is given or authorised by the holder of parental responsibility over the child.

This does not mean that you always have to obtain parental consent for users under 13. It only applies if you make your service available to children, and you rely on consent as your lawful basis (eg for any non-core processing, cookies or similar technologies, or processing of special category data).

If so, it says you need to make 'reasonable efforts' to obtain and verify parental consent for children under 13.

You can take available technology into account in deciding what is reasonable for the purposes of Article 8. You can also consider other circumstances, including your resources and the level of risk identified in your DPIA, but you must be able to justify your approach.

Meeting the standards in this code should also help. This is because the standards in the code work together to mitigate risks arising from the processing of children's personal data. In particular, if you conform to the standard on age appropriate application (and apply the standards to all users where you are unable to establish age with a level of confidence that is appropriate to the risks) then you are providing significant protections for children by default, even if they have lied about their age. This means that the risks that might arise from not knowing how old a user is, or from not verifying parental consent to a high standard, are reduced. Parental consent becomes only one of a number of measures in place to protect children online.

Your approach to age verification and parental consent under Article 8 should therefore be compatible with your approach to age appropriate application under this code.

If you verify age and parental authority for Article 8 purposes then you need to do so in a privacy friendly way. Collect the minimum amount of 'hard identifiers' (such as passport scans or credit card details). Remember that you need to comply with the GDPR in your processing of any personal data you collect for verification purposes, including the purpose limitation, data minimisation, storage limitation and security principles.

If you are using a third party verification service, you should use 'attribute' systems which offer a yes/no response when asked if an individual is over a given age, or if a person holds parental responsibility over the child.

If you can show that your processing is particularly low-impact and does not carry any significant risk to children, you may be able to show that self- declaration mechanisms are reasonable on their own (eg analytics cookies).

If the risks are higher then you need to either rely on more robust methods, or mitigate risks by applying the standards in this code to all users regardless of their self-declared age.

Further reading outside this code:

Detailed guidance on consent

Children and the GDPR – What are the rules about an ISS and consent?

WHAT ABOUT SPECIAL CATEGORY DATA?

If your online service processes any special category data of children, you must identify both a lawful basis under Article 6 and an additional condition for processing that data under Article 9. Special category data includes information about:
- race;
- ethnic origin;
- politics;
- religion;
- trade union membership;
- genetics;

- biometric identification (eg facial or fingerprint recognition);
- health (including data collected by fitness apps);
- sex life; or
- sexual orientation.

The most relevant Article 9 conditions are likely to be:

- **Article 9(2)(a) - explicit consent:** If you need to process special category data to provide a service to the individual, explicit consent may be available as your condition for processing that data even if it is a condition of service. However, you must be confident that you can demonstrate that consent is still freely given. In particular, that the processing is objectively necessary to perform a requested element of the service, and not bundled together with other elements of the service or included in your terms for broader business purposes.
- **Article 9(2)(d) - not-for-profit bodies:** if you are a not-for-profit body and your online service has a political, philosophical, religious or trade union aim. The child must either be a member or someone in regular contact with you for those purposes, and you must not disclose their data outside your organisation without consent. You must also comply with all the safeguards set out in this code, as well as other appropriate safeguards identified in your DPIA.
- **Article 9(2)(g) - substantial public interest:** you can rely on this condition if you can meet one of 23 specific substantial public interest conditions set out in schedule 1 of the DPA 2018. You also need an 'appropriate policy document' which briefly sets out which condition you are relying on, how you comply with the principles, and your retention and deletion policies (this can be taken from step 4 of your DPIA).

In particular, you may be able to consider the specific substantial public interest conditions in schedule 1 of the DPA 2018 for:

- statutory or government purposes (condition 6);
- preventing or detecting unlawful acts (condition 10);
- preventing fraud (condition 14); or
- safeguarding of children (condition 18)

You should review the detail of these conditions carefully. If no other specific condition is available, you must get the valid explicit consent of the child (or their parent, if the child is under 13), otherwise you cannot process special category data.

You must document and justify your condition as part of your DPIA.

Further reading outside this code

See our separate guidance on special category data

See our separate detailed guidance on consent

ANNEX D: DPIA TEMPLATE

[1.370]
This template is an example of how you can record your DPIA process and outcome for an online service likely to be accessed by children. It is adapted from our general DPIA template, and follows the process set out in our DPIA guidance and the age appropriate design code. It should be read alongside the code and DPIA guidance, and the Criteria for an acceptable DPIA set out in European guidelines.

You should start to fill out the template early in the design of your online service, or early in your development process if you are making a significant change to an existing online service likely to be accessed by children. The final outcomes should be integrated back into the design of your service.

SUBMITTING CONTROLLER DETAILS

Name of controller

Subject/title of DPIA

Name of controller contact /DPO
(delete as appropriate)

STEP 1: IDENTIFY THE NEED FOR A DPIA

Explain broadly the nature of your online service, and the current stage of design or development. You may find it helpful to refer or link to other documents. Summarise when and how you identified the need for a DPIA.

STEP 2: DESCRIBE THE PROCESSING

Describe the nature of the processing: how will you collect, use, store and delete data? What are the sources of the data? Will you be sharing data with anyone? You might find it useful to refer to a flow diagram or other way of describing data flows. What types of processing identified as likely high risk are involved? Does your service involve any profiling, automated decision-making, or geolocation elements? What are your plans (if any) for age-assurance? What are your plans (if any) for parental controls?

Describe the scope of the processing: what is the nature of the data, and does it include special category or criminal offence data? How much data will you be collecting and using? How often? How long will you keep it? How many individuals are affected? What geographical area does it cover?

Describe the context of the processing: what is the nature of your service? Are you designing it for children? If not, are children under 18 likely to access it anyway? What is the likely age range of your users? How much control will they have? Would they understand and expect you to use their data in this way? Does your service use any nudge techniques? Are there prior concerns over similar services or particular security flaws? Is your service novel in any way? What is the current state of technology in this area? Are there any current issues of public concern that you should factor in, particularly over online risks to children? Are there any relevant industry standards, codes of practice or public guidance in this area? What responsibilities do you have under the applicable equality legislation for England, Scotland, Wales and Northern Ireland. Is there any relevant guidance or research on the development needs, wellbeing or capacity of children in the relevant age range? Are you signed up to any approved code of conduct or certification scheme (once any have been approved)?

Describe the purposes of the processing: what do you want to achieve with your service? What is the intended effect on individuals? What are the benefits of the processing – for you, and more broadly? What are the specific intended benefits for children?

STEP 3: CONSULTATION PROCESS

Consider how to consult with relevant stakeholders: describe when and how you will seek individuals' views - and specifically how you will seek the views of children and parents – or justify why it's not possible to do so. Who else do you need to involve within your organisation? Do you need to ask your processors to assist? Do you plan to consult experts in children's rights and developmental needs? If not, why not? Do you plan to consult any other experts?

STEP 4: ASSESS NECESSITY AND PROPORTIONALITY

Describe compliance and proportionality measures, in particular: what is your lawful basis for processing? Does the processing actually achieve your purpose? Is there another way to achieve the same outcome? How will you prevent function creep? How will you ensure data quality and data minimisation? If you use AI, how will you avoid bias and explain its use? What information will you give individuals? How will you help to support their rights? What measures do you take to ensure processors comply? How do you safeguard any international transfers?

Describe how you comply with the age-appropriate design code: what specific measures have you taken to meet each of the standards in the code?
(1)   **Best interests of the child:**
(2)   **Data protection Impact Assessments:**
(3)   **Ageappropriate application:**
(4)   **Transparency:**
(5)   **Detrimental use of data:**
(6)   **Policies and community standards:**
(7)   **Default settings:**
(8)   **Data Minimisation:**
(9)   **Data sharing:**
(10) **Geolocation:**
(11) **Parental controls:**
(12) **Profiling:**
(13) **Nudge techniques:**
(14) **Connected toys and devices:**
(15) **Online tools:**

STEP 5: IDENTIFY AND ASSESS RISKS

Describe source of risk and nature of potential impact on individuals. Include as a minimum an assessment of particular risks to children as listed in the DPIA standard in the age appropriate design code. You may need to consider separately for different age groups.	Likelihood of harm	Severity of harm	Overall risk
	Remote, possible or probable	Minimal, significant or severe	Low, medium or high
Describe source of risk and nature of potential impact on individuals. Include as a minimum an assessment of particular risks to children as listed in the DPIA standard in the age appropriate design code. You may need to consider separately for different age groups.	Likelihood of harm	Severity of harm	Overall risk

STEP 6: IDENTIFY MEASURES TO REDUCE RISK

Identify additional measures you could take to reduce or eliminate risks identified as medium or high risk in step 5

Risk	Options to reduce or eliminate risk	Effect on risk	Residual risk	Measure approved
		Eliminated reduced accepted	Low medium high	Yes/no

STEP 7: SIGN OFF AND RECORD OUTCOMES

Item	Name/position/date	Notes
Measures approved by:		Integrate actions back into project plan, with date and responsibility for completion
Residual risks approved by:		If accepting any residual high risk, consult the ICO before going ahead
DPO advice provided:		DPO should advise on compliance, step 6 measures and whether processing can proceed
Summary of DPO advice:		
DPO advice accepted or overruled by:		If overruled, you must explain your reasons
Comments:		
Consultation responses reviewed by:		If your decision departs from individuals' views, you must explain your reasons
Comments:		
This DPIA will kept under review by:		The DPO should also review ongoing compliance with DPIA

ICO: DATA SHARING CODE OF PRACTICE

[1.371]

NOTES
This is the latest version (1.0.123) of this code published on the ICO website at https://ico.org.uk/for-organisations/data-sharing-a-code-of-practice/, on 16 April 2021. Following the end of the UK's transition out of the EU, the ICO has explained it will update this code and materials in good time for it being laid before Parliament. Subject to Parliamentary approval, the code is expected to enter into force in 2021.
© Information Commissioner's Office, licensed under the Open Government Licence.

TABLE OF CONTENTS

INFORMATION COMMISSIONER'S FOREWORD

[1.372]
In 2011 the ICO published its first Data Sharing Code; in the intervening period the type and amount of data collected by organisations has changed enormously, as has the technology used to store and share it, and even the purposes for which it is used. It is imperative that we keep up to date with these developments through this new code.

As the UK Information Commissioner, I know that data is one of modern society's greatest assets. Ready access to information and knowledge, including about individual citizens, can lead to many economic and social benefits, including greater growth, technological innovations and the delivery of more efficient and targeted services.

We have written this Data Sharing Code to give individuals, businesses and organisations the confidence to share data in a fair, safe and transparent way in this changing landscape. This code will guide practitioners through the practical steps they need to take to share data while protecting people's privacy. We hope to dispel many of the misunderstandings about data sharing along the way.

I have seen first-hand how proportionate, targeted data sharing delivered at pace between organisations in the public, private and voluntary sectors has been crucial to supporting and protecting the most vulnerable during the response to the COVID-19 pandemic. Be it through the shielding programme for vulnerable people, or sharing of health data in the Test and Trace system. On a local and national level, data sharing has been pivotal to fast, efficient and effective delivery of pandemic responses.

Utilising the data we collectively hold and allowing it to be maximised properly will have economic benefits. Data sharing that engenders trust in how personal data is being used is a driver of innovation, competition, economic growth and greater choice for consumers and citizens. This is also true in the sphere of public service delivery where efficient sharing of data can improve insights, outcomes and increase options for recipients.

This code demonstrates that the legal framework is an enabler to responsible data sharing and busts some of the myths that currently exist. But we cannot pretend that a code of practice is a panacea to solve all the challenges for data sharing. Or that targeted ICO engagement and advice will solve everything. There are other barriers to data sharing, including cultural, technical and organisational factors. Overcoming these will require more than just the ICO; it will require a collective effort from practitioners, government and the regulator.

I see the publication of this code not as a conclusion but as a milestone in this ongoing work. The ICO will continue to provide clarity and advice in how data can be shared in line with the law. This code, and the products and toolkits published alongside it, provides a gateway to good data sharing practice and the benefits we can expect from the results.

Elizabeth Denham CBE

Information Commissioner

EXECUTIVE SUMMARY

[1.373]
About this code
* This is a statutory code of practice made under section 121 of the Data Protection Act 2018.
* It is a practical guide for organisations about how to share personal data in compliance with data protection law. It aims to give you confidence to share data fairly and proportionately.

DATA PROTECTION LAW ENABLES FAIR AND PROPORTIONATE DATA SHARING
* Data protection law facilitates data sharing when you approach it in a fair and proportionate way.
* Data protection law is an enabler for fair and proportionate data sharing, rather than a blocker. It provides a framework to help you make decisions about sharing data.
* This code helps you to balance the benefits and risks and implement data sharing.
* Data sharing has benefits for society as a whole.
* Sometimes it can be more harmful not to share data.
* When considering sharing data:
  * you must comply with data protection law;
  * we recommend that you assess the risks using a Data Protection Impact Assessment (DPIA); and
  * it is good practice to have a data sharing agreement.
* When sharing data, you must follow the key principles in data protection legislation:
  * The accountability principle means that you are responsible for your compliance, and you must be able to demonstrate that compliance.
  * You must share personal data fairly and transparently.
  * You must identify at least one lawful basis for sharing data before you start any sharing.
  * You must process personal data securely, with appropriate organisational and technical measures in place.
* In your data sharing arrangement, you should have policies and procedures that allow data subjects to exercise their individual rights easily.
* You can share data in an emergency, as is necessary and proportionate. Examples of an emergency situation are the risk of serious harm to human life, or the immediate need to protect national security.

- You may share children's data if you can demonstrate a compelling reason to do so, taking account of the best interests of the child.
- The government has devised a framework for the sharing of personal data, for defined purposes across the public sector, under the Digital Economy Act 2017 (DEA).

UK EXIT FROM THE EUROPEAN UNION

- Now the UK has left the EU, the GDPR (which we refer to in this code as the EU GDPR) has been written into UK law as the UK GDPR, to sit alongside the DPA 2018.
- For the latest information and guidance on data protection and the UK's position in relation to data protection and the EU, see the ICO website.

ICO POWERS

- The ICO upholds information rights in the public interest. Our focus is to help you carry out data sharing in a compliant way. We will always use our powers in a targeted and proportionate manner, in line with our regulatory action policy.

NAVIGATING THE DATA SHARING CODE

[1.374]

A quick reference guide to help you find the content you need on each topic.

What you need to do or consider	→	Where you can find it in the data sharing code
Identify your objective in sharing the data	→	• Deciding to share data • Data sharing agreements
Be clear as to what data you are sharing	→	• Deciding to share data • Data sharing agreements
Understand the position following UK exit from the EU	→	• How is this code affected by the UK's exit from the European Union
Consider the risks and benefits of sharing and not sharing	→	• What is the purpose of this code? • The benefits of data sharing • Deciding to share data
Carry out a Data Protection Impact Assessment (DPIA)	→	• Deciding to share data
Put in place a data sharing agreement	→	• Data sharing agreements • Accountability
Ensure you follow the data protection principles	→	• Data protection principles
Check your data sharing is fair and transparent	→	• Fairness and transparency
Identify at least one lawful basis for sharing the data before you start sharing it	→	• What is our lawful basis for sharing? • Lawful basis for sharing personal data
Put in place policies and procedures that allow data subjects to exercise their individual rights easily	→	• What about access and individual rights? • The rights of individuals • Law enforcement processing
Be clear about sharing data under the law enforcement processing provisions of Part 3 DPA 2018, and sharing between the UK GDPR/Part 2 DPA 2018 and Part 3 DPA 2018	→	• Law enforcement processing: Part 3 DPA 2018; and sharing with competent authorities under the UK GDPR and Part 2 DPA 2018
Demonstrate a compelling reason if you are planning to share children's data, taking account of the best interests of the child	→	• Data sharing and children
Share data in an emergency as is necessary and proportionate. Plan ahead as far as possible	→	• Data sharing in an urgent situation or in an emergency
Document your decisions about the data sharing, evidencing your compliance with data protection law	→	• Accountability • Data sharing agreements
Put in place quality checks on the data	→	• What information governance
Arrange regular reviews of the data sharing arrangement	→	• When should we review a data sharing arrangement? • Accountability
Agree retention periods and make arrangements for secure deletion	→	• Security • Accountability

ABOUT THIS CODE

AT A GLANCE

[1.375]
This is a statutory code of practice prepared under section 121 of the Data Protection Act 2018.

It is a practical guide for organisations about how to share personal data in a way that complies with data protection law.

It aims to give you confidence to share data fairly and proportionately.

IN MORE DETAIL

What is the status of this code?

This is a statutory code of practice prepared under section 121 of the Data Protection Act 2018 (DPA 2018):

"The Commissioner must prepare a code of practice which contains—
(a)   practical guidance in relation to the sharing of personal data in accordance with the requirements of the data protection legislation, and
(b)   such other guidance as the Commissioner considers appropriate to promote good practice in the sharing of personal data."

It was laid before Parliament on [date] and issued on [date], under section 125 of the DPA 2018. It comes into force on [date].

The code contains practical guidance on how to share data fairly and lawfully, and how to meet your accountability obligations. It does not impose any additional barriers to data sharing, but will help you comply with your legal obligations under the UK GDPR and the DPA 2018.

It also contains some optional good practice recommendations, which do not have the status of legal requirements but aim to help you adopt an effective approach to data protection compliance.

In accordance with section 127 of the DPA 2018, the Commissioner must take the code into account when considering whether you have complied with your data protection obligations when sharing data. In particular, the Commissioner will take the code into account when considering questions of fairness, lawfulness, transparency and accountability under the UK GDPR or the DPA 2018 and in the use of her enforcement powers.

The code can also be used in evidence in court proceedings, and the courts must take its provisions into account wherever relevant.

FURTHER READING
Relevant provisions in the legislation - see DPA 2018 sections 121
Relevant provisions in the legislation - see DPA 2018 sections 125
Relevant provisions in the legislation - see DPA 2018 sections 127

How is the code affected by the UK's exit from the European Union?

Now the UK has left the EU, a UK version of the EU GDPR has been written into UK law as the UK GDPR to sit alongside the DPA 2018.

The EU GDPR may still apply to you if you operate in the European Economic Area (EEA) or offer goods and services to individuals or monitor the behaviour of individuals there. Rules on international transfers now apply to the flow of data to and from the EEA.

If there are any further changes to the details of the future UK regime, the Commissioner will publicise them, and will note the changes on the ICO website.

For the latest information and guidance on data protection and the UK's position regarding the EU, see the ICO website.

FURTHER READING
Relevant provisions in the legislation - see DPA 2018 section 207
International transfers
Data protection at the end of the transition period
UK Government website: "Brexit: new rules are here"

What happens if we don't comply with the code?

If you don't comply with the guidance in this code, you may find it more difficult to demonstrate that your data sharing is fair, lawful and accountable and complies with the UK GDPR or the DPA 2018.

If you process personal data in breach of this code and this results in a breach of the UK GDPR or the DPA 2018, we can take action against you.

Tools at our disposal include assessment notices, warnings, reprimands, enforcement notices and penalty notices (administrative fines). For serious breaches of the data protection principles, we have the power to issue fines of up to £17.5 million or 4% of your annual worldwide turnover, whichever is higher.

There is no penalty if you fail to adopt good practice recommendations, as long as you find another way to comply with the law.

For more information, see the section on enforcement of this code.

What is the purpose of this code?

It provides practical guidance for organisations about sharing personal data in a way that complies with data protection law. It explains the law and promotes good practice. It dispels myths and misconceptions about data sharing.

Many organisations using this code of practice will have already shared data under the former data protection regime. The code should give you the knowledge and the confidence you need to continue sharing data under the UK GDPR and the DPA 2018 and assess how to share personal data in new projects and programmes. You should use the code to help you review and, where necessary, update ongoing data sharing arrangements.

The code of practice:
* updates and reflects key changes in data protection law since the last data sharing code was published (in particular from the UK GDPR and the DPA 2018);
* explains new developments and their impact on data protection;
* references new areas for you to consider; and
* helps you to manage risks in sharing data, which are magnified if the quantity of data is large.

Who is this code for?

The code is mainly aimed at organisations that are controllers sharing personal data. In particular, it is aimed at data protection officers (DPOs) and other individuals within organisations who are responsible for data sharing matters.

Please see the sections below on joint controllers and processors.

In the code the reader is addressed by the term 'you' (and by the term 'we' in some headings that take the form of questions). It uses this terminology to refer to organisations that are sharing data or considering doing so. The code will also be helpful to controller organisations receiving shared data.

Controllers are defined under Article 4 of the UK GDPR and section 32 of the DPA 2018 as having responsibility for deciding the "purposes and means of the processing of personal data".

The code is also aimed at controllers sharing data under the law enforcement processing regime (Part 3 DPA 2018), and between the UK GDPR/Part 2 DPA 2018 and Part 3 DPA 2018. There is a separate section about this, but the code includes references to some Part 3 provisions throughout to highlight significant differences. If you are one of these controllers, you should still read the whole of this code, which distinguishes between the regimes where appropriate.

Much of the advice is applicable to public, private and social sector organisations. Some of the code is necessarily focused on sector-specific issues. However, the majority of the code applies to all data sharing, regardless of its scale and context.

Reading and understanding this code and adopting its practical recommendations will give you confidence to collect and share personal data in a way that is fair, transparent and in line with the rights and expectations of the people whose information you are sharing.

The code will help you identify what you need to consider before you share personal data and clarify when it is appropriate for you to do so.

Common misconceptions about data sharing

The code also clears up misconceptions about data sharing and barriers to sharing.

It is true that data sharing can sometimes be a complex activity. But for some organisations the perceived risks of getting it wrong - in the shape of reputational damage or enforcement action by the regulator – outweigh the benefits that can be gained from data sharing, leading to missed opportunities for innovation and improved public services.

However, data protection law is an enabler for fair and proportionate data sharing, rather than a blocker. It provides a framework to help you make decisions about sharing data.

Many of the requirements of data protection law simply place on a statutory footing the good practice that you will already have followed, or plan to follow.

The key question is often not whether you can share data, but how.

For example:

Misconception
The UK GDPR and the DPA 2018 prevent us from sharing data.
Reality
This is mistaken. Data protection law does not prevent data sharing, as long as you approach it in a fair and proportionate way. If you were able to share data lawfully under the former data protection regime, it is likely that you are able to continue to do so now. While there are some differences, the new legislation helps you to ensure you are sharing data in a way that promotes trust and transparency.

Misconception
There is little benefit to be gained from data sharing.
Reality
Data sharing brings significant benefits to your organisation, to individuals and to society at large. Done well, it helps government, public, social sector and commercial organisations to deliver modern, more efficient services which better meet people's needs and make their lives easier. It can also identify people at risk, help protect them from harm and address problems before they have a significant adverse impact.

Misconception
We can only share data with people's consent.
Reality
Most data sharing does not rely on consent as the lawful basis.
If you cannot offer a genuine choice, consent is not appropriate. Public authorities, employers and other organisations in a position of power over individuals should avoid relying on consent unless they are confident they can demonstrate it is freely given.

Misconception
We can't share data in an emergency.
Reality
You can share data in an emergency; you should do whatever is necessary and proportionate. Examples of an emergency situation are the risk of serious harm to human life, the protection of public health, or the protection of national security. Please see our section on this topic later in the code. Where possible you should plan ahead and put contingencies in place.

The benefits of data sharing

The code highlights the benefits that sharing personal data can bring to everyone: society, organisations, and individuals, whether as citizens or consumers.

Data sharing can help public bodies and other organisations to fulfil their functions and deliver modern, efficient services that make everyone's lives easier. It can help keep the vulnerable safe at times of crisis, and help to produce official statistics, research and analysis for better decision-making for the public good.

Conversely, not sharing data can mean that everyone fails to benefit from these opportunities; and in some instances the chance is missed to assist people in need, whether in urgent or longer-term situations.

Example

In the banking sector, Open Banking enables businesses to offer services to customers using their personal data.

For example, a fintech company can offer a service helping a customer to save, by automatically transferring money from their account to savings every month based on an analysis of their spending.

This use of their personal data benefits the customer by increasing their savings and reducing inconvenience for them. This all takes place within a framework that protects the customer's privacy.

It benefits the bank because it allows it to benchmark products against competitors and reach new customers more easily, and provides evidence for anti-fraud prevention checks and customer verification, which is also in the public interest.

Example

A local area set up an integrated care record to share patient records between health and social care staff. This sharing between public and social sectors resulted in:

• a more holistic picture about a patient's health;

• coordinated and safer care across the region;

• better decision-making around a patient's care; and

• patients only having to tell their story once.

Example

A private day nursery collected information about the behaviour of an adult towards a child in its care and found a concerning pattern.

The nursery shared this information with local authority safeguarding leads to protect the child and others, and to investigate the adult's behaviour.

> **Example**
>
> Several health professionals from different organisations and care businesses were involved in providing health and social care to a group of older adults. By exchanging information about recent changes in behaviour from one of the clients, they identified a pattern of evidence indicating the person might be a victim of abuse. To ensure the safeguarding of the person, they shared this information with the person's social worker for further investigation.

How should we use this code?

The code covers data sharing by controller organisations (organisations that determine how personal data is used) under two separate regimes:
- general processing under the UK GDPR, which has to be read together with Part 2 of the DPA 2018; and
- law enforcement processing under the law enforcement provisions in Part 3 of the DPA 2018.

It also covers data sharing between the two regimes.

Most data sharing is likely to be under the UK GDPR and Part 2 of the DPA 2018 because it involves sharing data that is not law enforcement or intelligence personal data, but where provisions differ we clarify this as far as possible. The main body of the code therefore applies to processing under the UK GDPR and Part 2 of the DPA 2018. There is a separate section in this code on law enforcement processing under Part 3 of the DPA 2018 that describes the differences in more detail, but controllers carrying out that type of processing should still read the whole of the code.

While the code does not cover the details of data sharing under the intelligence services regime in Part 4 of the DPA 2018, it is relevant to that regime, subject to the specific provisions of Part 4.

The code also discusses data sharing for defined purposes across the public sector under the Digital Economy Act 2017.

The code is complementary to other ICO guidance and codes of practice about data protection. It assumes knowledge of key data protection terms and concepts. While the code stands as your guide to data sharing, it does not seek to reproduce other ICO guidance, and you might need at times to refer to guidance on the ICO website or contact our helpline. The code will highlight particular instances when it would be useful for you to refer to such guidance.

In particular, you will find it helpful to use the data protection impact assessment (DPIA) process along with the code when considering sharing data. Some or all of the DPIA questions are likely to help you when you are assessing whether it is appropriate to share data, and whether it would be in compliance with the law. You can find more on DPIAs later in the code.

Another area where you will find it helpful to refer to detailed ICO guidance is in checking whether an exception, exemption or restriction applies in your circumstances, under the UK GDPR or the DPA 2018.

For instance, if an exemption applies under the DPA 2018, you may not have to comply with all the usual rights and obligations. There is a wide range of exemptions relating to matters such as crime and taxation, certain regulatory functions, journalism, research and statistics, and archiving in the public interest.

Using the code

The code is divided into sections headed by each topic, and there are links to content in the guide to Navigating the data sharing code, and throughout the code to help you find your way around it.

As stated above, you will find it helpful to refer to other information and guidance. Because the code is statutory and is not readily updatable, any hyperlinks to guidance, tools and further information from the ICO or other sources are contained in boxes headed "Further Reading". These links do not form part of the code.

To clarify any unfamiliar terms and acronyms, you may also wish to refer to the Glossary towards the end of the code.

We have used examples in the code to illustrate the law and good practice. You can find longer case studies in Annex C.

In addition to linking to sources of information outside the code (for example, links to guidance, such as on conducting a DPIA) the code contains tools for you to use:
- The guide to Navigating the data sharing code directs you to the section of the code that you need.
- Annex A is a checklist to help you decide whether or not to share data.
- Annex B contains template data sharing request and decision forms.

Further Reading

Guide to data protection
Guide to Law Enforcement Processing
Guidance on exemptions
Further resources and support are available on the ICO data sharing information hub.

Why should we use the data sharing code?

The benefits for you in adopting the recommendations in the code may include:
- greater trust in you by the public and customers, whose data you may want to share;

whether you can share the data, but with steps to mitigate the risks. ...re, the DPIA process will help not only to ensure the protection of the data, but will also help you ...additional safeguards in place to mitigate risk where needed. In turn, this will help to provide ...ance to the people whose data you are sharing.

FURTHER READING
...vant provisions in the legislation - see UK GDPR Articles 35 and 36
...vant provisions in the legislation - see UK GDPR Recitals 74-77, 84, 89-92, 94 and 95
...protection impact assessments
...iled guidance on DPIAs
...A sample template
...A checklists

...Article 29 Working Party (WP29) produced guidelines on data protection impact assessments, ...ch have been endorsed by the European Data Protection Board (EDPB). The EDPB, which replaced ...29, includes representatives from the data protection authorities of each EU member state. It adopts ...delines for complying with the requirements of the EU GDPR. Whilst EDPB guidelines are no longer ...ctly relevant to the UK regime and are not binding under the UK regime, they may still provide ...pful guidance on certain issues.

...S
...WP guidelines are produced in Part 2, see **[2.186]**.

DATA SHARING AGREEMENTS

AT A GLANCE

8]
...good practice to have a data sharing agreement.
...sharing agreements set out the purpose of the data sharing, cover what happens to the data at each ..., set standards and help all the parties involved in sharing to be clear about their roles and ...onsibilities.
...ing a data sharing agreement in place helps you to demonstrate you are meeting your accountability ...gations under the UK GDPR.

IN MORE DETAIL

Introduction

...data sharing agreement between the parties sending and receiving data can form a major part of your ...mpliance with the accountability principle, although it is not mandatory. Your organisation might use ...fferent title for a data sharing agreement, for example:
- an information sharing agreement;
- a data or information sharing protocol or contract; or
- a personal information sharing agreement.

...hatever the terminology, it is good practice to have a data sharing agreement in place. ...vernment departments and certain other public bodies (for example, regulators, law enforcement ...dies and executive agencies) may enter into a memorandum of understanding with each other that ...ludes data sharing provisions and fulfils the role of a data sharing agreement.

...owever on their own, the following do not constitute a data sharing agreement:
- a memorandum of understanding (except between government departments and certain other public bodies);
- a list of standards; or
- an addendum to a purchase agreement or to a purchase order or proposal.

What are the benefits of a data sharing agreement?

...data sharing agreement:
- helps all the parties be clear about their roles;
- sets out the purpose of the data sharing;
- covers what happens to the data at each stage; and
- sets standards.

...should help you to justify your data sharing and demonstrate that you have been mindful of, and have ...ocumented, the relevant compliance issues. A data sharing agreement provides a framework to help you ...meet the requirements of the data protection principles.

...There is no set format for a data sharing agreement; it can take a variety of forms, depending on the scale ...nd complexity of the data sharing. Since a data sharing agreement is a set of common rules that bind ...ll the organisations involved, you should draft it in clear, concise language that is easy to understand.

...Drafting and adhering to a data sharing agreement should help you to comply with the law, but it does ...not provide immunity from breaching the law or from the consequences of doing so. However, the ICO ...will take into account the existence of any relevant data sharing agreement when assessing any complai... ...we receive about your data sharing.

- an improved understanding of whether and when it is appropriate to share personal data;
- greater confidence within your organisation that you are sharing data appropriately and correctly;
- the confidence to share data in a one-off situation or in an emergency;
- a reduced reputational risk when sharing data;
- more robust, demonstrable compliance with the law; and
- better protection for individuals whose data you are sharing.

FURTHER READING
Relevant provisions in the legislation - see UK GDPR Articles 4(7) and 4(8)
Relevant provisions in the legislation - see DPA 2018 section 3(9)
Data sharing hub
For organisations
Controllers and processors

DATA SHARING COVERED BY THE CODE

AT A GLANCE

[1.376]
The code covers the sharing of personal data between organisations that are controllers. It includes when you give access to data to a third party, by whatever means. Data sharing can take place in a routine, scheduled way or on a one-off basis. When needed, you can share data in an urgent or emergency situation.

IN MORE DETAIL

Data sharing between controllers

The code focuses on the sharing of personal data between controllers, ie where separate or joint controllers determine the purposes and means of the processing of personal data, as defined in UK GDPR Article 4(7).

Sharing data with a processor is not covered by the code

If a controller asks another party to process personal data on its behalf, for the purposes of the UK GDPR the other party is a "processor", as defined in Article 4(8) of the UK GDPR. The UK GDPR draws a distinction between a controller sharing personal data with another controller, and a processor processing personal data on behalf of a controller.

Article 28 of the UK GDPR lays down requirements that must be in place between a controller and processor, in order to protect the rights of the data subject. These requirements include a written contract and guarantees about security. Under the UK GDPR a processor must only process personal data on documented instructions from the controller. A processor has its own liabilities and responsibilities both under the contract and the UK GDPR.

This type of processing arrangement is outside the scope of this code, but further information is available on the ICO website.

"Data sharing" within an organisation is not covered by the code

The code does not apply to the disclosure of data within the same organisation, where the controller is one and the same. The movement of data by one part of an organisation to another part - by the controller to itself - is not data sharing. The other obligations under data protection law obviously still apply, however.

Data sharing covered by the code

There is no formal definition of data sharing within the legislation, although the scope of this code is defined by section 121 of the DPA 2018 as "the disclosure of personal data by transmission, dissemination or otherwise making it available". This includes:
- providing personal data to a third party, by whatever means;
- receiving personal data as a joint participant in a data sharing arrangement;
- the two-way transmission of personal data; and
- providing a third party with access to personal data on or via your IT systems.

For the purposes of this code, data sharing does not include providing data access to employees or contractors, or with processors such as third-party IT processors. Please read the paragraphs later in this section on sharing data with processors.

The following examples illustrate a range of data sharing types within the scope of the code:
- a one-way or reciprocal exchange of data between organisations;
- an organisation providing another organisation with access to personal data on its IT system for a specific research purpose;
- several organisations pooling information and making it available to each other or to a third party or parties;
- data sharing on a routine, systematic basis for an established purpose;

- one-off, exceptional or ad hoc data sharing; and
- one-off data sharing in an urgent or emergency situation.

Examples of real-life data sharing activities

- a bank disclosed personal data about its employees to an anti-fraud body;
- a primary school passed details about a child showing signs of harm to the police and social services;
- the police and Border Force exchanged information about individuals thought to be involved in serious crime;
- a supermarket gave information about a customer's purchases to the police following an allegation of shoplifting;
- a secondary school provided information about its pupils to a research company for research purposes; and
- a multi-agency network group regularly exchanged information about individuals for safeguarding or social care purposes.

The code only applies to sharing personal data. Neither the UK GDPR, the DPA 2018, nor this code, applies to sharing information that does not constitute personal data. Some sharing doesn't involve personal data; for example, if an organisation is sharing information that cannot identify anyone (anonymous information; please refer to the ICO website for forthcoming guidance on anonymisation).

Example

These are two examples of data sharing, one of which is subject to the UK GDPR and the second which is not.

A travel business collects data on individual travel movements. Prior to sharing with third parties, it removes directly identifiable information such as name or address from the data. In this case, it is still personal data as it is very likely that an individual could be identified by combining the data with other available information; for example, social media accounts. This will be considered personal data under the UK GDPR.

However, if the travel business shares high-level aggregate statistics with third parties, for example: "on Fridays, for a particular journey there are 130% fewer passengers than on Tuesdays", no individual can be identified. Therefore this would qualify as anonymous information and is not personal data under the UK GDPR.

The position is different for pseudonymised data. Data which has undergone pseudonymisation is defined in the UK GDPR as data that can no longer be attributed to a data subject without the use of additional information. If you have pseudonymised the data according to the definition of the UK GDPR, such that the additional information could be used to re-identify a data subject within that data, then you must treat the pseudonymised data as personal data.

It is common to consider data sharing as falling into two main types of scenario:

- data sharing on a frequent and/or regular basis, also known as routine or 'systematic' data sharing, where the same data sets are regularly shared between the same organisations for an established purpose; and
- exceptional, one-off decisions to share data for a purpose that is ad hoc, unexpected or due to an urgent situation or an emergency.

Different approaches apply to these two scenarios, and the code reflects this. Most of the code concentrates on routine data sharing.

Routine data sharing

This is data sharing done on a regular basis in a routine, pre-planned way. It generally involves sharing data between organisations for an established purpose – perhaps with standardised data structures and values – at regular, scheduled intervals.

For example, a group of organisations might make an arrangement to share or pool their data for specific purposes, again on a frequent and/or regular basis.

If you are carrying out this type of data sharing, you should establish rules and agree procedures in advance.

Ad hoc or one-off data sharing

It is good practice to formalise your data sharing through a data sharing agreement. However in some instances you may decide, or be asked, to share data in ad hoc situations that are not covered by any routine arrangement or agreement. It is still possible to share data in this situation, but you should carefully assess the risks every time. We recommend that you make plans to cover such contingencies.

Sometimes you may have to make a decision quickly about data sharing in conditions of real urgency, or even in an emergency situation. You should not be put off from data sharing in a scenario like this; in an urgent situation you should assess the risk and do what is necessary and proportionate. Please see the section later in this code on Data sharing in an urgent situation or in an emergency.

Data pooling

Data pooling is a form of data sharing where organisations decide together to pool information they hold and make it available to each other, or to different organisations, for a specific purpose or purposes. The organisations should consider whether they are separate or joint controllers.

If the organisations are joint controllers, under Article 26 of the UK GDPR they [...] transparent arrangement setting out agreed roles and responsibilities for complyi[...] For more details, you should refer to the guidance on controllers and processor[...]

Further Reading

Contracts and liabilities between controllers and processors
Key definitions: controllers and processors
Controllers and processors
What does it mean if you are joint controllers?
Relevant provisions in the legislation – see GDPR Articles 4, 26, 28, 82 and 8[...]
Relevant provisions in the legislation – see GDPR Recitals 26, 28, 29, 30, 31, [...]
79 81, 82 and 146
Relevant provisions in the legislation – see DPA 2018 section 121

DECIDING TO SHARE DATA

[1.377]
AT A GLANCE

In addition to considering whether the data sharing achieves a benefit and is necessar[...] your overall compliance with data protection law when sharing data.

We recommend that as a first step you carry out a Data Protection Impact Assessm[...] you are not legally obliged to carry one out. Carrying out a DPIA is an example of be[...] you to build in openness and transparency.

A DPIA will help you assess the risks in your planned data sharing and determine w[...] introduce any safeguards. It will help you assess those considerations, and document t[...] help to provide reassurance to those whose data you plan to share.

IN MORE DETAIL

What do we need to consider?

We have described earlier the benefits of data sharing to society, to organisations, and t[...] and consumers.

When thinking about sharing data, as well as considering whether there is a benefit to[...] and whether it is necessary, you must consider your overall compliance with data prote[...] including fairness and transparency.

As a first step, we recommend that you carry out a Data Protection Impact Assessment [...] is an invaluable tool to help you assess any risks in your proposed data sharing, and w[...] mitigate these risks. It will help you to ensure you are sharing data fairly and transpare[...] you to consider these matters, and to document them.

In law you are required to consider doing a DPIA. However, even if you are not legally [...] one out, it is very beneficial for you to follow the DPIA process.

Do we need to do a DPIA?

We recommend that you carry out a DPIA, as it can benefit both you and the public whose[...] to share. It will help you to:

- assess any risks in your planned data sharing; and
- promote public trust in your data sharing plans.

You are obliged to carry out a DPIA for data sharing that is **likely to result in a high risk t[...]** This includes some specified types of processing.

To help you determine whether you need to carry out a DPIA, you can:

- use our screening checklists on the ICO website; and
- read the detailed guidance on DPIAs on the ICO website.

It is good practice to carry out a DPIA if you have a major project that involves disclosing p[...] or any plans for routine data sharing, even if there is no specific indicator of likely high r[...]

If you have taken into account the nature, scope, context and purposes of the sharing a[...] confident that the type of data sharing you have in mind is unlikely to result in high risk, [...] legally required to carry out a DPIA.

However, we recommend that you carry out a DPIA even where you are not legally obliged to[...] can use the DPIA process as a flexible and scalable tool to suit your project. A DPIA is a pr[...] that will help you assess the risks in any planned data sharing. A DPIA need not be a 'bolt-o[...] – you can integrate the DPIA into any risk frameworks your organisation may already have [...]

As already stated in this code, data sharing must be done in a fair and proportionate way. Using [...] to assess the risks in your proposed data sharing will help you achieve that proportionality, as th[...] will help you to fully understand:

- whether you can share the data at all; and

What should we include in a data sharing agreement?

You should address a range of questions in a data sharing agreement.

Who are the parties to the agreement?

Your agreement should state who the controllers are at every stage, including after the sharing has taken place.

What is the purpose of the data sharing initiative?

Your agreement should explain:
* the specific aims you have;
* why the data sharing is necessary to achieve those aims; and
* the benefits you hope to bring to individuals or to society more widely.

You should document this in precise terms so that all parties are absolutely clear about the purposes for which they may share or use the data.

Which other organisations will be involved in the data sharing?

Your agreement should clearly identify all the organisations that will be involved in the data sharing and should include contact details for their data protection officer (DPO) or another relevant employee who has responsibility for data sharing, and preferably for other key members of staff. It should also contain procedures for including additional organisations in the data sharing arrangement and for dealing with cases where an organisation needs to be excluded from the sharing.

Are we sharing data along with another controller?

If you are acting with another controller as joint controllers of personal data, there is a legal obligation to set out your responsibilities in a joint control arrangement, under both the UK GDPR/Part 2 of the DPA 2018 and under Part 3 of the DPA 2018. Although the code mainly focuses on data sharing between separate controllers, the provisions of a data sharing agreement could help you to put a joint control arrangement in place.

What data items are we going to share?

Your agreement should set out the types of data you are intending to share. This is sometimes known as a data specification. This may need to be detailed, because in some cases it will be appropriate to share only certain information held in a file about an individual, omitting other, more sensitive, material. In some cases it may be appropriate to attach 'permissions' to certain data items, so that only particular members of staff or staff in specific roles are allowed to access them; for example, staff who have received appropriate training.

What is our lawful basis for sharing?

You need to clearly explain your lawful basis for sharing data. The lawful basis for one organisation in a data sharing arrangement might not be the same as that for the other one.

If you are using consent as a lawful basis for disclosure, then your agreement should provide a model consent form. You should also address issues surrounding the withholding or retraction of consent.

You should also set out the legal power under which you are allowed to share the data.

Is there any special category data, sensitive data or criminal offence data?

You must document the relevant conditions for processing, as appropriate under the UK GDPR or the DPA 2018, if the data you are sharing contains special category data or criminal offence data under the UK GDPR, or there is sensitive processing within the meaning of Part 3 of the DPA 2018.

What about access and individual rights?

You should set out procedures for compliance with individual rights. This includes the right of access to information as well as the right to object and requests for rectification and erasure. You must make it clear in the agreement that all controllers remain responsible for compliance, even if you have processes setting out who should carry out particular tasks.

For example, the agreement should explain what to do when an organisation receives a request for access to shared data or other information, whether it is under the data protection legislation, or under freedom of information legislation. In particular, given data subjects can contact any controller involved in the sharing, it should make clear that one staff member (generally a DPO in the case of personal data) or organisation takes overall responsibility for ensuring that the individual can easily gain access to all their personal data that has been shared.

For joint controllers, Article 26 of the UK GDPR and section 58 of the DPA 2018 for Part 3 processing require you to state in the agreement which controller is the contact point for data subjects.

You will have to take decisions about access on a case-by-case basis.

For public authorities, the agreement should also cover the need to include certain types of information in your freedom of information publication scheme.

There are more details on individual rights under the UK GDPR/Part 2 of the DPA 2018 and under Part 3 of the DPA 2018 in the section of this code on the rights of individuals. There is also more information on Part 3 in the section in this code on law enforcement processing.

What information governance arrangements should we have?

Your agreement should also deal with the main practical problems that may arise when sharing personal data. This should ensure that all organisations involved in the sharing:

- have detailed advice about which datasets they can share, to prevent irrelevant or excessive information being disclosed;
- make sure that the data they are sharing is accurate, for example by requiring a periodic sampling exercise and data quality analysis;
- record data in the same format, abiding by open standards when applicable. The agreement could include examples showing how to record or convert particular data items, for example dates of birth;
- have common rules for the retention and deletion of shared data items, as appropriate to their nature and content, and procedures for dealing with cases where different organisations may have different statutory or professional retention or deletion rules;
- have common technical and organisational security arrangements, including the transmission of the data and procedures for dealing with any breach of the agreement in a timely manner;
- ensure their staff are properly trained and are aware of their responsibilities for any shared data they have access to;
- have procedures for dealing with access requests, complaints or queries from members of the public;
- have a timescale for assessing the ongoing effectiveness of the data sharing initiative and the agreement that governs it; and
- have procedures for dealing with the termination of the data sharing initiative, including the deletion of shared data or its return to the organisation that supplied it originally.

What further details should we include?

It is likely to be helpful for your agreement to have an appendix or annex, including:

- a summary of the key legislative and other legal provisions, for example relevant sections of the DPA 2018, any law which provides your legal power for data sharing and links to any authoritative professional guidance;
- a model form for seeking individuals' consent for data sharing, where that is the lawful basis; and
- a diagram to show how to decide whether to share data.

You may also want to consider including:

- a data sharing request form; and
- a data sharing decision form.

You can find examples of these in the Annex to this code.

When should we review a data sharing arrangement?

You should review your data sharing arrangements on a regular basis; and particularly when a change in circumstances or in the rationale for the data sharing arises. You should update your data sharing agreement to reflect any changes. If there is a significant complaint, or a security breach, this should be a trigger for you to review the arrangement.

DATA PROTECTION PRINCIPLES

[1.379]
When sharing data, you must follow the data protection principles.

As previously stated, a data sharing agreement will provide a framework to help you to do this.

There are some differences between the principles in the respective pieces of legislation:

- the UK GDPR and Part 2 of the DPA 2018 for general data processing; and
- Part 3 of the DPA 2018 for law enforcement processing.

You should refer to the detailed guidance on the ICO website.

FURTHER READING

Relevant provisions in the legislation - see UK GDPR Article 5
Relevant provisions in the legislation - see UK GDPR Recital 39
Relevant provisions in the legislation - for Law Enforcement Processing under Part 3 of the DPA 2018, see sections 34-40
The principles
Guide to Law Enforcement Processing

ACCOUNTABILITY

AT A GLANCE

[1.380]
Accountability should form an important part of the culture and business of your organisation.

The specific accountability requirements of the UK GDPR mean that you are responsible for your compliance with the UK GDPR or the DPA 2018. You must be able to demonstrate that compliance.

You should review all your accountability measures regularly.

IN MORE DETAIL

What is accountability?

Accountability is a legal requirement for data sharing; it is one of the principles applicable to general data processing under the UK GDPR. The importance of accountability cannot be overstated. To be effective, you have to embed the message of accountability in the culture and business of your organisation, from board level through to all your employees and contractors.

You must consider the risks data sharing may create, and take appropriate action. You need to ensure staff are adequately trained, assess your data processing and put data protection at the heart of your organisation. It is more than box ticking or bolt-on compliance. It is an opportunity to make data protection a part of the cultural and business fabric of your organisation. It means not only complying with the legislation, but showing it.

Accountability obligations mean that if you are involved in a data sharing arrangement, you are responsible for your compliance with the UK GDPR or DPA 2018, and you must be able to demonstrate that compliance. As part of this, and where proportionate, you must put in place a data protection policy which adopts a "data protection by design and default" approach. This will help you comply with data protection law and good practice whenever you process data.

There is a general obligation to evidence your compliance and justify your approach, so you should maintain relevant documentation and adopt additional measures as necessary. A data sharing agreement is one example of good practice to demonstrate you are meeting your accountability obligations. If you are unable to justify your approach, it is likely you will fail to meet those obligations.

Successfully embedding accountability will enhance your reputation as a business that can be trusted with personal data. The public are increasingly demanding to be shown how their data is being used and how it is being looked after. They want to know that their personal data is in safe hands, and that you have put in place mechanisms to protect their information.

For law enforcement processing, similar provisions are set out in Chapter 2 of Part 3 of the DPA 2018.

What documentation do we need to keep?

Accountability should form part of a long-term programme of compliance and sound governance within your organisation. Documentation forms one of the requirements to ensure effective accountability, and the UK GDPR is specific on this point. Under Article 30 of the UK GDPR, larger organisations are required to maintain a record of their processing activities. Even if you are not a larger organisation, you should document any data sharing you undertake, and review it regularly.

Documenting this information is a practical way of taking stock of your data sharing. Knowing what information you have, where it is, and what you do with it makes it much easier for you to comply with other aspects of the UK GDPR, such as making sure that you hold accurate and secure information. You should follow good records management practice, and for this purpose you may find it helpful to refer to the codes of practice under section 46 of the Freedom of Information Act 2000 (FOIA) and section 61 of the Freedom of Information (Scotland) Act 2002 (FOISA).

As well as any record of all aspects of the data sharing and other processing activities required under Article 30, you must keep sufficient documentation to demonstrate your compliance with the UK GDPR when sharing data, such as:
* your compliance with all data protection principles, obligations and rights;
* your record of the lawful basis for processing and the privacy information you provide;
* any records of consent; and
* records of any personal data breaches.

For data sharing that constitutes law enforcement processing under Part 3 of the DPA 2018, section 61 of the DPA 2018 sets out the records to keep, including logs of processing operations in automated processing systems.

What is the role of the data protection officer (DPO) in a data sharing arrangement?

If you have a DPO, they should be closely involved from the outset in any plans to enter into a data sharing arrangement. Some organisations may have multiple individuals with responsibility for data sharing matters, depending on the context of the data sharing and the arrangements within the organisation. Many of the references to the DPO in this code are applicable to them as well. In all cases, you should document the advice you receive from them.

DPOs play an important role while a data sharing arrangement is under way. Since there will be a number of organisations involved, each of you will have your own responsibilities for the data you share or received. Often a data sharing arrangement involves processing sensitive information. In each of the organisations, the DPO advises everyone on information governance, ensures compliance with the law, and provides advice to staff faced with decisions about data sharing. They may also be a contact point for individuals to exercise their rights.

The ICO's main contact point with an organisation is through the DPO and we are here to advise and address their concerns.

Example

An airline looked to develop its service by improving transport schedules, mitigating disruption for passengers and taking steps to improve its carbon footprint. To do this, the airline wanted to use the personal data that it held about its customers for a new purpose.

It considered the requirements of Article 6.4 of the UK GDPR and undertook a DPIA, as the processing required the combination of different datasets.

To implement some of the strategies proposed, the airline needed to provide some of the data to a partner company which had developed software to enhance customer engagement in this area. In sharing the data, the airline considered whether the partner company adhered to appropriate security measures and had a written contract covering the scope of the data sharing and processing.

In this case, the airline had implemented a 'data protection by design and default' approach. It had:

• taken appropriate measures to establish if the new processing arrangements were lawful

• been clear with the third party about the extent of the processing permitted; and

• had kept clear evidence of the steps taken to comply with the requirements of the UK GDPR.

Example

A police intelligence database on gangs in an area (the gangs database) had been shared by the police with the local authority. The council went on to share it inappropriately with a number of organisations. This constituted a data breach.

Shortly afterwards there were incidents of gang violence in the area and some victims had featured in the gangs database. Although it was not possible to establish a causal connection to the data breach, it was obvious that there was a risk of distress and harm when this type of sensitive data was not kept secure.

In this case, it was apparent that it was unfair and excessive for the council to have shared the unredacted database with a large number of people and other organisations. It should have realised that there was an obvious risk in doing so.

There is a national concern about the need to tackle gang crime, and it is widely recognised that this is a challenge for public authorities. Data sharing has an important role to play in tackling this challenge; however, it has to be carried out in compliance with the law. Data must be processed lawfully, fairly, proportionately and securely. However, data protection law is not a barrier to data sharing.

To help prevent such incidents happening, organisations processing sensitive data should have in place policies, processes and governance, as well as training for staff. Conducting a DPIA is one way an organisation can try to ensure it is complying with the law. This data sharing code also provides practical information.

Example

A health care organisation provided an out-of-hours emergency telephone service. As calls could be received about clients' welfare, it was essential that advisors had access to some personal data about the organisation's clients to carry out their role and where appropriate to share data in the public interest.

A call was taken by a new advisor late one evening from someone identifying themselves as a police officer and requesting the address of one of the organisation's clients.

The organisation had protocols to follow about sharing data to third parties, and it was mandatory that all new advisors had this training on appointment. The advisor therefore knew the procedure to follow to determine whether or not they could share this information.

FURTHER READING

Relevant provisions in the legislation - see UK GDPR Articles 5.1(b), 5.2, 6.4, 25, 28,29,30,31,32,34,35, 38, 39

Relevant provisions in the legislation - see UK GDPR Recitals 39, 81-83

Relevant provisions in the legislation - see DPA 2018 Part 3, Sections 61 and 62

Guidance on DPIAs, DPOs, documentation and accountability

ICO's Accountability Framework

Data protection by design and default

Guide to Law Enforcement Processing

Sharing personal data with law enforcement authorities

Data sharing and re-use of data by competent authorities for non-law enforcement purposes

The Lord Chancellor's code of practice on records management under section 46 FOIA

Scottish government code of practice on records management under section 61 FOISA

What happens if we have a new purpose?

Purpose limitation

FAIRNESS AND TRANSPARENCY IN DATA SHARING

AT A GLANCE

[1.381]

The gateway to getting data sharing right is always to share personal data fairly and in a transparent manner.

* You must treat individuals fairly and not use their data in ways that would have unjustified adverse effects on them.
* When you share personal data, you must ensure it is reasonable and proportionate.
* You must ensure that individuals know what is happening to their data.
* Before sharing data, you must tell individuals about what you propose to do with their personal data in a way that is accessible and easy to understand.

Fairness and transparency are fundamental to your approach to sharing data under the UK GDPR, and they are closely linked. Understanding that you are responsible for ensuring fairness and transparency will help you to ensure your general compliance with data protection law.

Fairness also forms a key part of the principles under the law enforcement provisions of Part 3 of the DPA 2018. However, the principles in Part 3 do not include transparency; this is due to the potential to prejudice an ongoing law enforcement investigation in certain circumstances. It is essential that the law enforcement agencies have the powers that they need to investigate crimes and bring offenders to justice. However, section 44 of the DPA 2018 sets out the information a controller should make available to data subjects for law enforcement processing purposes.

As part of fairness and transparency considerations, you should also bear in mind ethical factors when deciding whether to share personal data; ask yourself whether it is right to share it.

Example

Two county councils and 19 relevant partner organisations (both public and private sector) decided to share personal information in order to prevent social exclusion amongst young people who had been, or were at high risk of, disengaging from education, employment or training. By sharing information, the partner organisations aimed to co-ordinate their approach to identifying and contacting each young person to support and encourage them back into education, or into work or training.

While the partner organisations took the view that the data sharing would benefit the young people, data protection law required them to consider whether it was fundamentally fair to the young people. The organisations had to pause and consider certain questions before deciding they could go ahead with the sharing:

• Would they only be sharing data in a way that would be in line with the reasonable expectations of the individuals concerned?

• How sure were they that they would not be sharing data in a way that would adversely affect the individuals?

• Did they mislead the individuals when they collected their personal data?

The organisations also had to consider whether they had met their transparency obligations:

• Were they open and honest with the individuals as to how they would use their personal data?

• Did they tell the individuals about the proposed use of their personal data in a clear, accessible way?

The councils were not prevented by data protection law from sharing data, but had to be sure they had done so fairly and transparently by answering these questions.

FURTHER READING

Relevant provisions in the legislation - see UK GDPR Articles 5.1(a), 13, 14
Relevant provisions in the legislation - see UK GDPR Recitals 39, 58, 60-62
Relevant provisions in the legislation - see DPA 2018 Part 3 section 44
Guidance on the right to be informed
Guidance on the first principle
Guide to Law Enforcement Processing: principles
Guidance on exemptions

LAWFULNESS

AT A GLANCE

[1.382]

In order to comply with the lawfulness principle, you must ensure that your data sharing is lawful in a general sense.

This includes checking that you have a legal power to share data.

The legal power to share data is separate from the lawful basis provisions.

IN MORE DETAIL

Introduction

This section looks at the principle of lawfulness and discusses the legal constraints on you, outside data protection legislation, and the legal powers you have to share data.

Before sharing any personal data, you must consider all the legal implications. You must ensure that your data sharing is lawful in a general sense in order to comply with the lawfulness principle. For public sector bodies, this includes identifying whether you have a legal power to share data.

Compliance with the lawfulness principle is in addition to identifying a lawful basis for your data sharing. Do not confuse lawful basis with general lawfulness or legal powers that are beyond the UK GDPR/DPA. However, there is a link with the lawful bases - if you do not have a lawful basis to share data, you will be in breach of the lawfulness principle.

This might sound complex, so this section will break down the different elements you should consider.

Do we have a legal power to share data?

If you wish to share personal data with another organisation, either by a one-off disclosure or as part of a routine data sharing arrangement, you need to consider:

* what type of organisation you are, because your legal status also affects your ability to share information. In particular, it depends on whether you are within the public, private or social sector; and
* whether you have a general legal power to share information, for instance, under the law setting you up, or under your constitution. This is likely to be more relevant to public sector organisations.

What are the legal powers in the public sector?

Public sector organisations must check that they have the legal power to share data. When deciding whether you may proceed with any data sharing initiative, you should identify and document the law that is relevant to you. Even if this does not mention data sharing explicitly (and usually it doesn't) it is likely to lead you to a clearer understanding of your legal position.

Public sector organisations mostly derive their powers from sources such as the Act of Parliament or Royal Charter which set them up, or from case law, or duties under common law, or other laws regulating their activities. Government departments headed by a Minister of the Crown have common law powers to share information.

The relevant legislation probably defines your functions in terms of your purposes, the things that you must do and the powers you may exercise in order to achieve those purposes. So you should identify where the data sharing would fit, if at all, into the range of things that you are able to do. Broadly speaking, there are three ways in which you may do so:

* **Express statutory obligations**
  Occasionally, a public body is legally obliged to share particular information with a named organisation. This is only the case in highly specific circumstances.
* **Express statutory powers**
  Sometimes, a public body has an express power to share information. An express power is often designed to permit disclosure of information for certain purposes. Express statutory obligations and powers to share information are often referred to as "gateways". For example, specific gateways exist under the Digital Economy Act 2017 (DEA). Under the DEA there is a framework providing a legal gateway for data sharing for defined purposes between specified public authorities, for the public benefit. There is a separate section in this code on the DEA.
* **Implied statutory powers**
  Often, the law regulating a public body's activities is silent on the issue of data sharing. In these circumstances, it may be possible to rely on an implied power to share information derived from the express provisions of legislation. This is because express statutory powers may be taken to authorise the organisation to do other things that are reasonably incidental to those which are expressly permitted.
  Public authorities are likely to rely on the public task lawful basis in Article 6.3 of the UK GDPR. This requires the legal power to be laid down by law; however it does not need to be contained in an explicit piece of legislation, but could be a common law task, function or power. You can rely on this power to share data so long as it is sufficiently foreseeable and transparent.
  Whatever the source of your power to share information, you must check that the power covers that specific disclosure or data sharing arrangement. If it does not, you must not share the information unless, in the particular circumstances, there is an overriding public interest in a disclosure taking place.

What are the legal powers for private and social sector organisations?

The legal framework that applies to private and social sector organisations differs from that for public sector organisations. Most private and social sector organisations do not need to identify a specific power to share data. They have a general ability to share information, provided this does not breach the data protection legislation or any other law. If you are a private or social sector organisation you should check your constitutional documents, legal agreements or any other legal or regulatory requirements (such as the common law duty of confidentiality, or the Scottish law of privacy) to make sure you are complying with those requirements and that there are no restrictions that would prevent you from sharing personal data in a particular context. Big organisations with complex, larger scale processing should consider obtaining legal advice.

Private and social sector organisations should pay attention to any industry-specific regulation, guidance or UK GDPR code of conduct about handling personal data, as this might affect your ability to share information.

What is the impact of human rights law?

Public authorities must comply with the Human Rights Act 1998 (HRA) in the performance of their functions. The HRA also applies to organisations in the private sector insofar as they carry out functions of a public nature.

Where the HRA applies, organisations must not act in a way that would be incompatible with rights under the European Convention on Human Rights. Article 8 of the Convention, which gives everyone the right to respect for their private and family life, home and correspondence, is especially relevant to sharing personal data.

If you disclose or share personal data only in ways that comply with the data protection legislation, the sharing or disclosure of that information is also likely to comply with the HRA.

You should seek specialist advice if you have any concerns about human rights issues (other than the data protection elements of Article 8) regarding the disclosure or data sharing arrangement you are proposing.

Have we checked whether there are any additional legal requirements that need to be met when sharing data?

Your ability to share information may be subject to a number of legal constraints outside data protection law. There might be other considerations such as specific legal requirements that need to be met, for example:

- prohibitions on sharing;
- copyright restrictions; or
- a duty of confidence that might affect your ability to share personal data.

A duty of confidence might be stated explicitly, or it might be implied, either by the content of the information or because it was collected in circumstances where confidentiality is expected (eg medical or banking information). If you are a big organisation planning to carry out complex, larger scale processing, you should consider obtaining legal advice on your data sharing plans.

In some private sector contexts, there are legal constraints on the disclosure of personal data, other than data protection law.

Further Reading

Relevant provisions in the legislation - European Convention on Human Rights: Article 8
Lawfulness principle
Lawful basis for processing
Guide to Law Enforcement Processing
Sharing personal data with law enforcement authorities
Data sharing and re-use of data by competent authorities for non-law enforcement purposes

LAWFUL BASIS FOR SHARING PERSONAL DATA

AT A GLANCE

[1.383]
You must identify at least one lawful basis for sharing data before you start.

You must be able to show that you considered this before sharing any data, in order to satisfy the accountability principle.

What are the provisions on lawful basis?

You must identify at least one lawful basis for sharing data. The lawful bases are different for:

- general processing under the UK GDPR and Part 2 of the DPA 2018; and
- law enforcement processing under Part 3 of the DPA 2018.

At least one lawful basis must apply before you start. You must be able to show that you considered this before sharing any data, in order to satisfy the accountability principle in the UK GDPR and in Part 3 of the DPA 2018. And without at least one lawful basis for processing, any data sharing you do will be in breach of the first principle in each piece of legislation.

Example
A water company and an electricity network operator conducted a data sharing trial to share priority service data with one another. The two companies worked together to jointly identify and safeguard customers who might have found themselves in vulnerable circumstances if their services were disrupted.
Both companies previously held their own registers. The trial allowed the organisations to work together to simplify their processes and introduce a 'tell us once' style registration system. The organisations gained explicit consent from relevant customers before undertaking the trial, sharing the data manually and securely on Excel spreadsheets.
Due to the success of the trial, the two companies decided to continue the data sharing as part of their business as usual operations.

Example
A government office responsible for overseeing business competition required information about the practices of a supermarket chain and its performance in the online retail sector.

> **Example**
>
> To understand how the supermarket chain operated, the office gathered evidence about customers' online shopping habits. The data assisted the office in understanding the range and quality of online services provided by the supermarket chain, as well as its overall value.
>
> As the review formed part of a statutory function, the office was able to demonstrate that the processing was necessary in the public interest and relied on this as its lawful basis for obtaining the customer data from the supermarket chain.

> **Example**
>
> A fintech company launched a paid-for digital tool to assist consumers in handling their finances. The tool could be viewed online and via a mobile phone application. It allowed individuals to access and consider their current accounts, savings accounts, credit cards, investments and pension information in one place. The tool also analysed spending habits and assisted the consumer in developing and managing their budgets. The analysis and planning could be addressed month by month and by different categories, such as grocery shopping, utilities and eating out.
>
> For the service to function correctly, personal data needed to be shared with third-party providers. This was so the customer's experience could be personalised with third-party services and materials accessible via the tool.
>
> The fintech company relied on 'performance of a contract' as its basis for processing under Article 6 of the UK GDPR. As some of the services required the provision of sensitive personal data, explicit consent was also relied on as a condition for processing under Article 9.

FURTHER READING

Relevant provisions in the legislation - see UK GDPR Articles 6.1(c), 6.1(e), 6.1(f), 6.3, 9.2, 13.1(c), 14.1(c)

Relevant provisions in the legislation - see UK GDPR Recitals 39, 41, 45, 47-49, 50, 51

Relevant provisions in the legislation - see DPA 2018 section 7

Relevant provisions in the legislation - see DPA 2018 section 8

Relevant provisions in the legislation - see DPA 2018 section 10

Relevant provisions in the legislation - see DPA 2018 section 11

Relevant provisions in the legislation - see DPA 2018 section 35

Relevant provisions in the legislation - see DPA 2018 section 42

Relevant provisions in the legislation - see DPA 2018 Schedule 1 (paras 6 and 7)

Relevant provisions in the legislation - see DPA 2018 Schedule 8

Lawful basis for processing

Lawful basis interactive guidance tool

Legitimate interests

Legitimate interests assessment

Guide to Law Enforcement Processing

Sharing personal data with law enforcement authorities

Data sharing and re-use of data by competent authorities for non-law enforcement purposes

SECURITY

AT A GLANCE

[1.384]

Data protection law requires you to process personal data securely, with appropriate organisational and technical measures in place.

The security measures must be "appropriate" to the nature, scope, context and purpose of the processing and the risks posed to the rights and freedoms of individuals.

You must also take into account the various security measures available and the costs of implementation when determining what measures are appropriate for your circumstances.

IN MORE DETAIL

What does data protection law say about security?

Data protection law requires you to process personal data securely, with appropriate organisational and technical measures in place. The security measures must be "appropriate" to the nature, scope, context and purpose of the processing and the risks posed to the rights and freedoms of individuals.

This section applies to processing both under the UK GDPR/Part 2 of the DPA 2018 and Part 3 of the DPA 2018.

You must also take into account the various security measures available and the costs of implementation when deciding what measures are appropriate for your circumstances. The "data protection by design and default" approach described in the section on accountability will help you to consider the security measures to put in place.

As stated earlier, you should aim to build a culture of compliance and good practice throughout your organisation to help you to share data securely. This must apply from board level, through to all employees and contractors.

For more details, please see the guidance on security on the ICO website.

Are we still responsible after we've shared the data?

Organisations that you share data with take on their own legal responsibilities for the data, including its security. However you should still take reasonable steps to ensure that the data you share will continue to be protected with adequate security by the recipient organisation. You should:

*   ensure that the recipient understands the nature and sensitivity of the information;
*   take reasonable steps to be certain that security measures are in place, particularly to ensure that you have incorporated an agreed set of security standards into your data sharing agreement, where you have one; and
*   resolve any difficulties before you share the personal data in cases where you and the recipient organisation have different standards of security, different IT systems and procedures, different protective marking systems etc.

Undertaking a DPIA for any data sharing operation can be an effective means of considering these issues and implementing appropriate mitigating measures.

You should also note that in certain circumstances you are required to do a DPIA when sharing data, and we recommend that you always do so when planning to share data. Please refer to the section in this code on Deciding to share data.

FURTHER READING

Relevant provisions in the legislation - see UK GDPR Articles 5,1(f), 32, 35
Relevant provisions in the legislation - see UK GDPR Recitals 39, 83
Relevant provisions in the legislation - see DPA 2018 section 40 (law enforcement processing)
Guidance on security
Guidance on data protection by design and default
The ICO has also worked closely with the National Cyber Security Centre (NCSC) to develop a set of security outcomes that you can use to help determine what's appropriate for you. The security outcomes can also help you when considering any data sharing arrangements.

THE RIGHTS OF INDIVIDUALS

AT A GLANCE

[1.385]
In a data sharing arrangement, you must have policies and procedures that allow data subjects to exercise their individual rights easily.

There are additional requirements if your data sharing involves automated decision-making.

The position on individual rights is slightly different for law enforcement processing.

IN MORE DETAIL

What is the impact of the rights of individuals on data sharing?

In a data sharing arrangement, you must have policies and procedures that allow data subjects to exercise their individual rights.

The rights available to an individual data subject under the UK GDPR and under Part 3 of the DPA 2018 (law enforcement processing) differ in some respects. Please see the paragraph below on individual rights under Part 3 for law enforcement processing.

The UK GDPR gives individuals specific rights over their personal data. For general data processing under the UK GDPR, in summary these are:

*   the right to access personal data held about them (the right of subject access);
*   the right to be informed about how and why their data is used - and you must give them privacy information;
*   the rights to have their data rectified, erased or restricted;
*   the right to object;
*   the right to portability of their data; and
*   the right not to be subject to a decision based solely on automated processing.

There are exemptions and restrictions that can, in some circumstances, be legitimately applied to exempt or qualify the right of individuals to exercise their rights.

This section of the code does not seek to replicate existing ICO guidance on individual rights, but rather focuses on how the rights impact on data sharing. You should refer to guidance on the ICO website for more details.

How do we allow individuals to exercise their information rights in a data sharing scenario under the UK GDPR?

*   You must have policies and procedures that allow individuals to exercise their rights easily, and you must set these out in your data sharing agreement.

- If you are a joint controller, these should be set out clearly in the transparent arrangement you and your other joint controller or controllers are required to enter into under Article 26 of the UK GDPR (for law enforcement processing, it is set out in section 58 in Part 3 of the DPA 2018).
- You must provide details of how to exercise these rights in the privacy information you issue to individuals.
- You must make the exercise of individual rights as straightforward as possible. Be aware that although your DPO may be the first point of contact, individuals may contact any part of your organisation.
- Where several organisations are sharing data, it may be difficult for an individual to decide which organisation they should contact. You should make that clear in the privacy information you provide to them at the time you collect their data, as well as in any transparent arrangement made under Article 26.
- In a data sharing arrangement it is good practice to provide a single point of contact for individuals, which allows them to exercise their rights over the data that has been shared without making multiple requests to several organisations. However, they are permitted to choose to exercise their rights against any controller they wish.

Example

A social sector organisation providing childcare services held information shared from a local authority and the NHS. The Article 26 transparency arrangement set out a clear procedure that whichever organisation received a request for personal data should take a lead on providing the data and notify the other parties if necessary.

The arrangement also set out procedures for how to deal with the exercising of other individual rights.

The procedures were also provided in privacy information given to service users and contained in a data sharing agreement published on the respective organisations' websites.

What is the impact on a data sharing arrangement of requests for erasure, rectification or the restriction of processing?

Under Articles 16, 17 and 18 of the UK GDPR, data subjects have a right to request erasure, rectification of their data, or the restriction of processing of their data. As with other individual rights, it will be easier for you and for the other organisations in a data sharing arrangement if you have clear policies and procedures about how to handle such requests.

Under Article 19 of the UK GDPR, if you have shared information with other organisations you must inform them of the rectification, erasure or restriction of the personal data, unless this proves impossible or involves disproportionate effort. If asked, you must also inform the individual about those organisations that you have shared their data with.

How do we deal with complaints and queries from individuals about sharing their data?

Individual data subjects may have queries or complaints about the sharing of their personal data, particularly if they think the data is wrong or that the sharing is having an adverse effect on them.

The way you handle these queries and complaints makes a difference both to the individuals and to your organisation. It is not always a case of simply providing a response. The comments you receive might be an invaluable resource for you when you are reviewing your data sharing arrangement.

It is good practice to:
- have procedures to deal with any complaints and queries in a quick and helpful way;
- provide a single point of contact for complainants or enquirers;
- review the comments (good and bad) you receive in order to obtain a clearer understanding of public attitudes to the data sharing you carry out;
- take the opportunity to provide individuals with information about your data sharing, further to that contained in your privacy information, when answering their specific queries;
- use any significant objections, negative comments or other expressions of concern you receive when you inform people about your data sharing, to help you review your data sharing: the amount of data you share, or which organisations you share it with. You may need to decide whether the sharing can go ahead in the face of public opposition. For example, you might decide to go ahead because you are under a legal obligation to share the data; and
- consider setting up focus groups to explore individuals' concerns, if you are carrying out large-scale data sharing operations.

What do we need to do if the data sharing involves solely automated processing?

Article 22 of the UK GDPR gives data subjects additional protective rights if your data sharing arrangement involves solely automated processing:

"The data subject shall have the right not to be subject to a decision based solely on automated processing, including profiling, which produces legal effects concerning him or her or similarly significantly affects him or her."

"Solely" here means that there is no human influence on the outcome.

Example of solely automated decision-making

A bank made a decision not to grant a loan to an individual:

Example of solely automated decision-making

• based on personal data obtained about the individual from a range of sources; and

• using algorithms, rather than the decision-making input of a member of bank staff.

If your data sharing arrangement involves any automated decision-making, including profiling, you must document the specific lawful basis for that in your data protection policy.

Documenting your processing activities will help you to decide whether they constitute profiling and solely automated decision-making.

Processing involving automated processing and profiling has a high level of risk. The GDPR requires you to carry out a DPIA in respect of processing that meets the Article 22 definition, to show you have considered the risks and how you will deal with them.

The UK GDPR allows you to carry out processing falling within Article 22, so long as you can rely on one of three exceptions:
•   When the decision is necessary for a contract.
•   When the decision is authorised by domestic law.
•   When the decision is based on the individual's specific consent.

In respect of any processing that falls within Article 22 you must also:
•   give individuals specific information about the processing;
•   explain to them their rights to challenge a decision and request human intervention; and
•   ensure you have measures in place to prevent errors, bias and discrimination in your systems.

Where the processing includes profiling, you must tell individuals that they have a right under Article 21 of the UK GDPR to object to it in certain circumstances.

What do we need to do if the data sharing involves automated decision-making or profiling that does not fall within Article 22 of the UK GDPR?

If your data sharing arrangement features automated decision-making or profiling, but does not fall within Article 22, it is still good practice to tell individuals about it; this will help you to meet your transparency obligation. Think carefully about what they would expect you to do with their data.

You must still comply with UK GDPR principles, document your lawful basis and allow individuals to exercise their rights easily.

You must also tell individuals that they have a right under Article 21 of the UK GDPR to object to profiling in certain circumstances.

All automated decision-making or profiling of special category data and of children's personal data has additional protections.

What individual rights are provided by Part 3 of the DPA 2018: law enforcement processing?

The individual rights are:
•   the right to be informed;
•   the right of access;
•   the right to rectification;
•   the right to erasure or restrict processing; and
•   the right not to be subject to automated decision-making.

Certain rights under the UK GDPR, such as the right to object and the right to data portability, do not exist in Part 3 of the DPA 2018. As with the UK GDPR, there are also exemptions and restrictions that can, in some circumstances, be legitimately applied to exempt or qualify the exercise of individuals' rights.

FURTHER READING
Relevant provisions in the legislation - see UK GDPR Articles 16-19 and 22
Relevant provisions in the legislation - see DPA 2018 Part 3
Guidance on the rights of individuals
Individual rights under the law enforcement processing provisions
Guidance on exemptions

LAW ENFORCEMENT PROCESSING

AT A GLANCE
[1.386]
Most data sharing, and the bulk of this code, is covered by the general processing provisions under the UK GDPR and Part 2 of the DPA 2018. However, data sharing by a "competent authority" for specific law enforcement purposes is subject to a different regime under Part 3 of the DPA 2018 for law enforcement processing.

If you are a competent authority, it is very likely that you will also be processing personal data for general purposes under the UK GDPR/Part 2 of the DPA 2018, eg for Human Resources matters or other non-law enforcement purposes. In that instance, you should follow the general sections of the code on UK GDPR/Part 2 data sharing.

IN MORE DETAIL

Introduction

There are compelling reasons why data sharing is needed for law enforcement purposes. We are aware that sometimes organisations are hesitant about data sharing in this context. However, we emphasise that data protection law does not prevent appropriate data sharing when it is necessary to protect the public, to support ongoing policing activities, or in an emergency for example. Adhering to the provisions of the legislation and following the good practice set out in this code will help you to share data in a compliant and proportionate way.

Most data sharing, and hence the bulk of the code, is covered by the general processing provisions under Part 2 of the DPA 2018; in practice, this means referring to the UK GDPR. Data sharing by a **competent authority** for specific **law enforcement purposes** is subject to a different regime under Part 3 of the DPA 2018, which provides a separate but complementary framework. However, there are common elements to both regimes which means that data sharing processes under either Part 2 or Part 3 can be adapted, rather than having to start a new process.

Example

Requests for information made by competent authorities must be reasonable in the context of their law enforcement purpose, and the necessity for the request should be clearly explained to the organisation.

For example, the police might ask a social worker to pass on case files to them containing details of young teenagers who may be at risk of exploitation.

The social worker might feel reluctant to voluntarily disclose information to the police if the request appears excessive, or the necessity or urgency appears unjustified. The police should provide as much clarity as they can about their lines of enquiry, without prejudicing their investigation.

What is a competent authority?

A competent authority is:
* a person specified in Schedule 7 of the DPA 2018; or
* any other person if, and to the extent that, they have statutory functions to exercise public authority or public powers for the law enforcement purposes (section 30(1)(b) of the DPA 2018).

You need to check whether you are listed as a competent authority in Schedule 7 of the DPA 2018. The list includes most government departments, police chief constables, the Commissioners of HMRC, the Parole Boards and HM Land Registry.

If you are not listed in Schedule 7, you may still be a competent authority if you have a legal power to process personal data for law enforcement purposes. For example, local authorities who prosecute trading standards offences, or the Environment Agency when prosecuting environmental offences.

What are the law enforcement purposes?

This term is defined in section 31 of the DPA 2018 as:

> "the purposes of the prevention, investigation, detection, or prosecution of criminal offences or the execution of criminal penalties, including the safeguarding against and the prevention of threats to public security"

Criminal law enforcement must be the primary purpose of the processing.

Even if you are a competent authority, it is very likely that you will also be processing personal data for general purposes under the UK GDPR/Part 2 of the DPA 2018, rather than for law enforcement purposes. An example might be for Human Resources matters. In that instance, you should follow the general data sharing guidance contained elsewhere in this code; we also refer to this below.

We are a competent authority. How do we share data under Part 3 of the DPA 2018?

If you are a competent authority, and the sharing is to another competent authority for law enforcement purposes, then Part 3 should provide a framework allowing you to share data.

This differs in some ways from the general processing provisions in the UK GDPR and Part 2 of the DPA 2018. The differences, including lawful basis, are primarily because of the purpose for which you are processing the data.

In particular, there are some differences in the principles in Part 3, and processing of data described in Part 3 as "sensitive" is subject to additional safeguards, such as conditions in Schedule 8 of the DPA 2018. You can find out more about the requirements on the ICO website.

We are a competent authority. How do we share data with a controller that is not a competent authority?

Part 3 to Part 2 DPA 2018 data sharing

A common scenario here is data sharing by a competent authority (that is processing for law enforcement purposes) to a recipient where the disclosure is not for law enforcement purposes, or the recipient is not a competent authority. In practice, Part 3 DPA 2018 information may be shared with a third party or repurposed internally, and then be used for general processing purposes under the UK GDPR and Part 2 of the DPA 2018.

- Section 36(4) of the DPA 2018 allows you to do this, provided that "the processing is authorised by law".
- As a competent authority, you must determine whether any processing of such data for non-law enforcement purposes is "authorised by law". This might be, for example, statute, common law, royal prerogative or statutory code.
- The question of "authorised by law" will, in part, depend on the specific laws to which the relevant competent authority is subject. For some authorities (such as the police), you may be able to rely more heavily on common law than other organisations that are more constrained by the nature of their constitution and legal framework. These would include local authorities, which may only do those things that they are empowered to do by statute, or those that are reasonably ancillary or incidental to those powers.
- You should start by identifying the reason and the lawful basis for the sharing.
- If you are the police you should also take into account the relevant policing purposes. In the absence of a clear policing purpose, it may be that the Part 3 DPA 2018 personal data/police information should not be disclosed. See more on this below. You should then identify a relevant processing condition under the UK GDPR/Part 2 of the DPA 2018.

For the police, in the absence of an obvious statute or code of practice to provide authorisation, common law may be the natural basis to rely upon. However, as recognised by the College of Policing, common law does not provide the police with an unconditional power to engage in any activity that is not otherwise provided for by statute. It cannot be used in a way that contravenes or conflicts with any legislation, and actions based on common law must be still be compliant with the Human Rights Act 1998 and the DPA 2018.

Example

The police may provide information to the civil courts about child protection proceedings. Both the police and the court are competent authorities, but since the court proceedings are civil rather than criminal, the disclosure by the police is not in the context of law enforcement purposes. This is the case even though the reason for the police disclosing the information is to protect life, which is a policing purpose.

We are not a competent authority. How do we share data with a competent authority?

Part 2 to Part 3 DPA 2018 data sharing

If you are an organisation that does not fall within the DPA 2018 definition of a competent authority, then you can share data for law enforcement purposes with a competent authority, such as the police, in compliance with the UK GDPR and Part 2 of the DPA 2018. However, you must still have a lawful basis under Article 6 for the sharing; for example, legitimate interests. Where a request has come from a law enforcement agency under the Investigatory Powers Act 2016, the lawful basis might be legal obligation. You are also likely to need a condition for disclosing the data under Schedule 1 of the DPA 2018.

Requests for information made to you by competent authorities must be reasonable in the context of their law enforcement purpose, and they should clearly explain the necessity for the request to you.

Where necessary in the circumstances, you can also rely on the "crime and taxation" exemption from some UK GDPR provisions that is set out in DPA 2018 schedule 2, paragraph 2(1). This includes exemption from transparency obligations and most individual rights, to the extent that the application of those provisions is likely to prejudice the prevention or detection of crime.

If you are not a competent authority and are disclosing data about an individual's criminal offences and convictions (including allegations that an individual has committed an offence) you must comply with Article 10 of the UK GDPR.

In practice, this means you need to meet a relevant condition in Schedule 1 of the DPA 2018. In this scenario, the most likely condition is in Schedule 1 paragraph 10, as modified by paragraph 36: disclosures of "criminal offence" data which are necessary for the purposes of the prevention or detection of unlawful acts; and where asking for the individual's consent would prejudice those purposes.

The personal data of witnesses, victims, bystanders and other persons who are not the offender or alleged offender is not "criminal offence" data and a Schedule 1 DPA condition is not required to allow the processing and sharing of their data.

However, if the data you are sharing includes special category data, a condition under Article 9 of the UK GDPR needs to apply, together with a linked condition in Schedule 1 of the DPA 2018 in most cases (most likely Article 9.2(g) together with Schedule 1 paragraph 10 of the DPA 2018). You must be able to demonstrate that sharing the special category data is necessary for reasons of substantial public interest.

The DPA 2018 usually requires organisations to have an appropriate policy document to cover their general data processing under this condition. However, an organisation disclosing data to a competent authority in reliance on the condition in Schedule 1 paragraph 10 of the DPA 2018 does not need to have a policy document to cover that disclosure.

> **Example**
>
> A shopkeeper used CCTV, and routinely captured footage of customers in the premises. A copy of some CCTV footage was requested by a police force for an ongoing criminal investigation. The police force told the shopkeeper why they wanted it (some competent authorities may use a standard form for this).
>
> The shopkeeper was processing data under the UK GDPR and Part 2 of the DPA 2018. Assuming the shopkeeper had a lawful basis for the processing, they could give the police a copy of the footage to help with the investigation. If the footage included images of an alleged offender they could rely on Schedule 1, paragraph 10 to process the CCTV data, and enable the sharing of the relevant footage with the police to help with the investigation.
>
> The receiving police force (competent authority) was processing the information under Part 3 of the DPA 2018. This enabled them to fulfil their statutory functions.

How do we allow individuals to exercise their information rights under Part 3?

There are differences in the availability of individual rights for law enforcement processing. Certain individual rights under the UK GDPR, such as the right to object and the right to data portability, do not exist in Part 3 of the DPA 2018. There are exemptions and restrictions that can, in some circumstances, be legitimately applied to prevent individuals from exercising rights if there is a likely prejudice to the law enforcement purposes.

For further details on this, please refer to the section in this code on the rights of individuals, and to the ICO website guidance on law enforcement processing.

How do we comply with the accountability requirement under Part 3?

Section 34(2) in Part 3 of the DPA 2018 states that you are responsible for compliance. It requires you, as controller, to demonstrate that you comply with the principles.

You must put in place appropriate technical and organisational measures that ensure and demonstrate that you comply. This may include policies and procedures, including data protection by design and default.

You must also maintain relevant documentation of data processing activities.

Please also see the earlier section in this code on accountability. For more specific details on Part 3 DPA 2018, please refer to the ICO guidance on law enforcement processing.

FURTHER READING
Relevant provisions in the legislation - see UK GDPR Articles 6, 9, 10
Relevant provisions in the legislation - see UK GDPR Recitals 40, 41, 44, 45, 46, 47, 48, 49, 50, 51, 52, 53, 54, 55, 56
Relevant provisions in the legislation - see DPA 2018 section 10
Relevant provisions in the legislation - see DPA 2018 section 11(2)
Relevant provisions in the legislation - see DPA 2018 section 15
Relevant provisions in the legislation - see DPA 2018 section 30(1)(b)
Relevant provisions in the legislation - see DPA 2018 section 31
Relevant provisions in the legislation - see DPA 2018 schedule 1 (paragraphs 10 and 36)
Relevant provisions in the legislation - see DPA 2018 schedule 2 (paragraph 2)
Relevant provisions in the legislation - see DPA 2018 schedule 7
Guide to Law Enforcement Processing
Sharing personal data with law enforcement authorities
Data sharing and re-use of data by competent authorities for non-law enforcement purposes
Guide to data protection
Guidance on exemptions
Guidance on the appropriate policy document
Further resources and support are available on the ICO data sharing information hub.

DUE DILIGENCE

AT A GLANCE

[1.387]
If a merger or acquisition or other change in organisational structure means that you have to transfer data to a different or additional controller, you must consider data sharing as part of the due diligence you carry out when taking on the organisation and its obligations. This includes establishing the purposes for which the data was originally obtained, your lawful basis for sharing it, and whether these have changed following the merger or acquisition.

You must comply with the data protection principles, and document your data sharing.

Consider when and how you will inform individual data subjects about what's happening to their data. You must also ensure sound governance, accountability and security.

IN MORE DETAIL

Introduction

This section is of particular relevance to the private sector. It highlights situations such as mergers and acquisitions, or other changes in organisational structure, where you need to make good data sharing practice a priority.

How does data sharing apply to mergers and acquisitions?

Data sharing considerations may become a priority when a merger or acquisition or other change in organisational structure means that you have to transfer data to a different organisation. For example, as part of a takeover; or on insolvency, data might be sold as an asset to a different legal personality. You must take care if, as a result of the changes, there is a change in the controller of the data, or if the data is being shared with an additional controller. This is the case whether you are the sharing or recipient controller. You might be an insolvency practitioner or other adviser taking the role of controller for the time being, or advising a different controller. You need to:

- ensure that you consider the data sharing as part of the due diligence you carry out;
- follow this data sharing code;
- establish what data you are transferring;
- identify the purposes for which the data was originally obtained;
- establish your lawful basis for sharing the data;
- ensure you comply with the data processing principles - especially lawfulness, fairness and transparency to start with;
- document the data sharing;
- seek technical advice before sharing data where different systems are involved; there is a potential security risk that could result in the loss, corruption or degradation of the data; and
- consider when and how you will inform data subjects about what is happening. Under the UK GDPR you are required to keep individual data subjects informed about certain changes relating to the processing of their data, and they may have a right to object. Please see the guidance on individual rights on the ICO website. The same considerations may apply in reverse to the controller receiving the data.

How do we manage shared data following a merger or restructure or other change of controller?

On a practical level, it can be difficult to manage shared data immediately after a change of this kind, especially if you are using different databases, or you are trying to integrate different systems. It is particularly important in this period to consider the governance and accountability requirements of the UK GDPR. You must:

- check that the data records are accurate and up to date;
- ensure you document what you do with the data;
- adhere to a consistent retention policy for all records; and
- ensure appropriate security is in place.

FURTHER READING

Relevant provisions in the legislation - see UK GDPR Articles 5, 6, 7 and 21
Relevant provisions in the legislation - see UK GDPR Recitals 39, 40, 42, 43, 50, 69, 70
Guidance on individual rights under the UK GDPR

SHARING PERSONAL DATA IN DATABASES AND LISTS

AT A GLANCE

[1.388]
The transfer of databases or lists of individuals is a form of data sharing, whether for money or other consideration, and whether for profit or not.

It is your responsibility to satisfy yourself about the integrity of the data supplied to you.

You are responsible for compliance with the law for the data you receive, and you have to respond to any complaints about it.

IN MORE DETAIL

How does data sharing apply to the acquisition or transfer of databases and lists?

The transfer of databases or lists of individuals is a form of data sharing, whether for money or other consideration, and whether for profit or not. This section considers data sharing which has not resulted from organisational changes.

Examples of organisations involved in this type of data sharing may include:

- data brokers;
- credit reference agencies;
- marketing agencies;

- franchised businesses;
- separate parts of a business that operate independently from their head office;
- clubs and societies;
- charities and voluntary groups; and
- political parties.

Please note that some of these examples may involve transfers between controllers and processors and are therefore outside the scope of this code.

You will find it beneficial to follow the good practice set out in this code. The due diligence carried out by both the sharing and recipient controllers is crucial to compliance.

We will look at this from the viewpoint of the organisation receiving the database or list. The organisation sharing the data should follow a similar process.

What must we do to ensure the database or list we are receiving is being shared in compliance with the law?

It is your responsibility to satisfy yourself about the integrity of the data supplied to you. You are responsible for compliance with the law for the data you receive, and you have to respond to any complaints about it. You should make appropriate enquiries and checks, including the following:

- confirm the source of the data;
- identify the lawful basis on which it was obtained and that any conditions about that lawful basis were complied with;
- check what individuals were told at the time of handing over their data;
- verify details of how and when the data was initially collected;
- check the records of consent, if you are relying on consent;
- review a copy of the privacy information given at the time of collection of the data;
- check what information was given to individuals in accordance with Article 14 of the UK GDPR - ie privacy information that must be given when data is obtained from a source other than the data subject;
- check that the data is accurate and up to date; and
- ensure that the data you receive is not excessive or irrelevant for your needs.

It is good practice to have a written contract with the organisation supplying you with the data.

What else do we need to do?

You must tell data subjects who you are sharing their data with, and for what purposes. Under Article 13 of the UK GDPR you must give privacy information to data subjects at the same time as collecting the data from them. Under Article 14 of the UK GDPR you must give privacy information to individuals whose data has been shared with you indirectly " . . . within a reasonable period after obtaining the personal data, but at the latest within one month . . . ". There are some exceptions to these requirements; for example, you do not need to provide individuals with information they already have. It is your responsibility on receiving the data to be satisfied that this has been done.

How does data sharing interact with direct marketing?

If this form of data sharing is relevant to your data sharing arrangement you should read the ICO's detailed guidance on direct marketing.

How does data sharing interact with political campaigning?

Political parties, referendum campaigners and candidates use information about voters to help them target their campaign materials more effectively and to raise funds. They may:

- buy lists and databases from organisations such as data brokers; and
- use third parties to send out campaign materials.

This may involve data sharing. Communicating with voters, such as via social media platforms and targeting political messages, may also amount to direct marketing.

You should carry out the checks described earlier in this section in order to satisfy yourself about the integrity of the data supplied to you.

If you use a third-party organisation to send out campaign materials on your behalf using your database, you may be sharing data with that external organisation, which is either a controller or a processor. For the purposes of this code, if you are both controllers you should still be careful to check and monitor what the third party is doing. You are responsible as controller(s) for that data and for compliance with the law. You should read and follow the ICO guidance on the law about both political campaigning and direct marketing.

FURTHER READING

Relevant provisions in the legislation - see UK GDPR Articles 13 and 14

See the Direct marketing code and guidance on the ICO website www.ico.org.uk

See the Political campaigning guidance on the ICO website www.ico.org.uk

See the Guide to Privacy and Electronic Communications Regulations (PECR)

DATA SHARING AND CHILDREN

AT A GLANCE

[1.389]

If you are considering sharing children's personal data, you must take extra care.

You may share children's personal data as long as you can demonstrate a compelling reason to do so, taking account of the best interests of the child. The best interests of the child should be a primary consideration.

You should build all this into the systems and processes in your data sharing arrangement. A high level of privacy should be your default.

Sharing children's data with third parties can expose them to unintended risks if not done properly.

You should carry out a DPIA to assess and mitigate risks to the rights and freedoms of children, which arise from your data sharing.

What do we need to bear in mind when sharing children's data?

The best interests of the child should be a primary consideration. This concept comes from the United Nations Convention on the Rights of the Child (UNCRC), which declares that "In all actions concerning children, whether undertaken by public or private social welfare institutions, courts of law, administrative authorities or legislative bodies, the best interests of the child shall be a primary consideration." In essence, the best interests of the child are whatever is best for that individual child.

Things you should consider:

- You may share children's personal data as long as you have a compelling reason to do so, taking account of the best interests of the child. One clear example of a compelling reason is data sharing for safeguarding purposes; another is the importance for official national statistics of good quality information about children. However, selling on children's personal data for commercial re-use is unlikely to amount to a compelling reason for data sharing. Even if you have a compelling reason for sharing children's personal data, you must still carry out a DPIA, because children are a vulnerable group.
- Use a DPIA to assess and mitigate risks to the rights and freedoms of children, which arise from your data sharing.
- You have to balance the best interests of the child against the rights of others. For example, it is unlikely that the commercial interests of an organisation will outweigh a child's right to privacy.
- Considering the best interests of the child should form part of your compliance with the lawfulness, fairness and transparency requirements. Is it fair to share the child's data? What is the purpose of the sharing?
- Children are less aware than adults of the risks involved in having their data collected and processed, so you have a responsibility to assess the risks and put appropriate measures in place. Where appropriate, consider children's views when designing your data sharing arrangement.
- Children's vulnerability means that the risks in sharing their data may be higher than in the similar processing of adults' data.
- The privacy information you provide must be clear and presented in plain, age-appropriate language.
- You should carry out due diligence checks on the organisations with which you are planning to share data. You should consider what the organisation you are sharing the data with plans to do with it. If you can reasonably foresee that the data will be used in a way that is detrimental to the child, or otherwise unfair, then you shouldn't share.
- You should ensure that any default settings relating to data sharing specify the purpose of the sharing and who the data will be shared with. Settings which allow general or unlimited sharing are not compliant.
- Consent is not the only lawful basis to use. Other lawful bases might be more appropriate.
- If you are relying on consent, you must consider the competence of the child to give their own consent, and whether that consent is freely given (eg where there is an imbalance of power).
- You should also consider the child's competence if you are relying on the lawful basis that the sharing is necessary for the performance of a contract.
- If you (or another data controller in the data sharing arrangement) are a provider of an online service likely to be used by children then you also need to comply with the Age Appropriate Design Code.

FURTHER READING

Relevant provisions in the legislation - see UK GDPR Articles 6.1, 8, 12.1 and Recitals 38, 58, 65, 71, 75

Guide to data protection: children

Children and the UK GDPR

Age Appropriate Design Code

Children's code hub

United Nations Convention on the Rights of the Child

DATA SHARING IN AN URGENT SITUATION OR IN AN EMERGENCY

AT A GLANCE

[1.390]
In an emergency you should go ahead and share data as is necessary and proportionate.

An example of an emergency situation is the risk of serious harm to human life.

You should plan ahead for urgent or emergency situations as far as possible.

IN MORE DETAIL

Much of this code envisages that you are carrying out data sharing on a routine basis and that you have the opportunity and time to plan carefully ahead. However this might not always be the case.

What should we do in an urgent or emergency situation?

Urgent or emergency situations can arise that you may not have envisaged, and you have to deal with them on the spot.

In an emergency, you should go ahead and share data as is necessary and proportionate. Not every urgent situation is an emergency. An emergency includes:
* preventing serious physical harm to a person;
* preventing loss of human life;
* protection of public health;
* safeguarding vulnerable adults or children;
* responding to an emergency; or
* an immediate need to protect national security.

Tragedies over recent years such as the Grenfell Tower fire, individual instances of self-harm, major terrorist attacks in London and Manchester, and the crisis arising from the coronavirus pandemic have illustrated the need for joined-up public services responses where urgent or rapid data sharing can make a real difference to public health and safety. In these situations, it might be more harmful not to share data than to share it. You should factor in the risks involved in not sharing data to your service.

How can we plan ahead for data sharing in urgent or emergency situations?

In an urgent or emergency situation, you have to take decisions rapidly. Often, forward planning helps. In the same way as emergency services plan for various scenarios, you should plan ahead for your organisation and train your staff accordingly. In urgent or emergency situations, when there is less time to consider issues in detail, it can be particularly difficult to make sound judgements about whether to share information.

Likewise, there can be reasons why organisations and agencies are hesitant about the concept of sharing information when carrying out emergency planning, or about sharing it in the recovery phase of an incident, where the need to share information may appear less urgent.

The key point is that the UK GDPR and the DPA 2018 do not prevent you from sharing personal data where it is appropriate to do so. It is particularly relevant to factor into your considerations, training and procedures for this type of situation the risks involved in not sharing data.

Where possible, if you are likely to be involved in responding to emergency or critical situations, you should consider the types of data you are likely to need to share in advance. As part of this it would be useful to consider any pre-existing DPIA, and also refer to your business continuity and disaster recovery plans. As part of your planning, you should bear in mind that criminals might use a major incident or crisis as an opportunity to try to obtain personal data unlawfully. Therefore, the security measures outlined earlier in this code still remain relevant and necessary in times of urgent sharing.

All this should help you to establish what relevant data you hold, and help to prevent any delays in an emergency or crisis situation.

All types of organisations might have to face an urgent but foreseeable situation, so you should have procedures about the personal data you hold and whether, and how, you should share any of this information. As part of your accountability duty, you should document the action you took after the event, if you can't do it at the time.

> **Example**
>
> The police, the fire service and local councils met to plan for identifying and assisting vulnerable people in their area in an emergency situation such as a flood or major fire. As part of the process, they determined what type of personal data they each held and had a data sharing agreement to set out what they would share and how they would share it in an emergency.
>
> They reviewed this plan at regular scheduled intervals.

Further information

The ICO's Data protection and coronavirus information hub

DATA SHARING ACROSS THE PUBLIC SECTOR: THE DIGITAL ECONOMY ACT CODES

AT A GLANCE

[1.391]

The government has devised a framework for sharing personal data, for defined purposes across specific parts of the public sector, under the Digital Economy Act 2017 (DEA).

The aim is to improve public services through the better use of data, while ensuring privacy, clarity and consistency in how the public sector shares data.

IN MORE DETAIL

Data sharing under the Digital Economy Act 2017

The government introduced a framework for sharing personal data for defined purposes across specific parts of the public sector, under the Digital Economy Act 2017 (DEA): the DEA framework.

Its aims are to:
* ensure clarity and consistency in how the public sector shares personal data;
* improve public services through the better use of data; and
* ensure data privacy.

The government has also made it clear that you should only share data when there is a clear public benefit.

Part 5 of the DEA focuses on digital government, providing gateways that allow specified public authorities to share data with each other. Some of these gateways enable the sharing of personal data, while others allow the sharing of non-identifying data. The objectives and purposes for data sharing under the DEA powers are tightly defined.

Under the DEA you must still comply with the data protection legislation.

Part 5 of the DEA explicitly:
* states that all processing of information under the DEA powers must comply with data protection legislation; and
* prohibits the disclosure of information where it would contravene data protection legislation.

Note that although the DEA pre-dates the coming into force of the EU GDPR and of the UK GDPR, it was drafted with a view to being consistent with EU GDPR provisions, as these were already known following agreement of the EU GDPR text in 2016.

The powers to share information under Part 5 of the DEA are supplemented by statutory codes of practice (the DEA codes) which must be consistent with the Information Commissioner's data sharing code of practice "as altered or replaced from time". The DEA codes must follow the data protection principles, ensuring that sharing personal data under the DEA powers is proportionate.

For example, there is a DEA code for public authorities sharing personal data about aspects of public service delivery. Its purpose is to achieve specified public service delivery objectives:
* to assist people experiencing multiple social or economic disadvantages, or living in fuel or water poverty;
* to reduce and manage debt owed to the public sector; and
* to combat fraud against the public sector.

There are also provisions in the DEA facilitating data sharing by and with the Statistics Board to allow the production of statistics, disclosure of information by civil registration officials, disclosure of information by Revenue Authorities, and data sharing for research purposes.

The DEA does not currently cover data sharing relating to the provision of health and social care.

The DEA codes contain guidance about what data you can share and for which purpose. They include safeguards to make sure that the privacy of citizens' data is protected. The two DEA codes that cover public service delivery, debt and fraud powers, and civil registration powers, require public authorities to put in place a data sharing or information sharing agreement, and specify what the agreement must cover.

Anyone who discloses information under the DEA Part 5 powers must also "have regard" to other codes of practice issued by the Information Commissioner. This is in "so far as they apply to the information in question":
* on the identification and reduction of risks to privacy of a proposal to disclose information; and
* on the information to be provided to individuals about how information collected from them will be used.

The Framework for data processing by government

Section 191 of the DPA 2018 confers a discretionary power on the Secretary of State to publish a Framework for Data Processing by Government. The DEA framework is separate from this, but the expectation is that any government Framework will be consistent with the data sharing code and any future guidance published by government.

FURTHER READING
Relevant provisions in the legislation - Digital Economy Act 2017
Digital Economy Act Part 5 Codes of practice

ENFORCEMENT OF THIS CODE

AT A GLANCE

[1.392]
The ICO upholds information rights in the public interest. In the context of data sharing, our focus is to help you carry out data sharing in a compliant way.

We have various powers to take action for a breach of the GDPR or DPA 2018. We will always use our powers in a targeted and proportionate manner, in line with our regulatory action policy.

IN MORE DETAIL

What is the role of the ICO?

The ICO is the independent supervisory authority for data protection in the UK.

Our mission is to uphold information rights for the public in the digital age. Our vision for data protection is to increase the confidence that the public have in organisations that process personal data. We offer advice and guidance, promote good practice, monitor and investigate breach reports, monitor compliance, conduct audits and advisory visits, consider complaints and take enforcement action where appropriate. Our enforcement powers are set out in Part 6 of the DPA 2018.

We have also introduced initiatives such as the Sandbox to support organisations using personal data to develop innovative products and services.

Where the provisions of this code overlap with other regulators, we will work with them to ensure a consistent and co-ordinated response.

How does the ICO monitor compliance?

We use this code in our work to assess the compliance of controllers through our audit programme and other activities.

Our approach is to encourage compliance. Where we do find issues, we take fair, proportionate and timely regulatory action to guarantee that individuals' information rights are properly protected.

How does the ICO deal with complaints?

If someone raises a concern with us about your data sharing, we will record and consider their complaint.

We will take this code into account when considering whether you have complied with the UK GDPR or DPA 2018, particularly when considering questions of fairness, lawfulness, transparency and accountability.

We will assess your initial response to the complaint, and we may contact you to ask some questions and give you a further opportunity to explain your position. We may also ask for details of your policies and procedures, your DPIA, and other relevant documentation. We expect you to be accountable for how you meet your obligations under the legislation, so you should make sure that when you initially respond to complaints from data subjects you do so with a full and detailed explanation about how you use their personal data and how you comply.

If we consider that you have failed (or are failing) to comply with the GDPR or the DPA 2018, we have the power to take enforcement action. We may require you to take steps to bring your operations into compliance or we may decide to fine you, or both.

However, it should be noted that the ICO prefers to work with organisations to find a resolution. Organisations that recognise and take ownership for the correction of shortcomings through the development of a performance improvement plan can avoid formal enforcement action.

What are the ICO's enforcement powers?

We have various powers to take action for a breach of the UK GDPR or DPA 2018.

Tools at our disposal include assessment notices, warnings, reprimands, enforcement notices and penalty notices (administrative fines). For serious breaches of the data protection principles, we have the power to issue fines of up to £17.5 million or 4% of your annual worldwide turnover, whichever is higher.

In line with our regulatory action policy, we take a risk-based approach to enforcement. Our aim is to create an environment within which, on the one hand, data subjects are protected, while ensuring that organisations are able to operate and innovate efficiently in the digital age. We will be as robust as we need to be in upholding the law, while ensuring that enterprise is not constrained by red tape, or by concern that sanctions will be used disproportionately. The ICO focuses the use of its enforcement powers on cases involving reckless or deliberate harms, and is therefore unlikely to take enforcement action against any organisation genuinely seeking to comply with the provisions of the legislation. Nor does it seek to penalise organisations where a member of staff has made a genuine mistake when acting in good faith and in the public interest; for example in an emergency situation, or to protect someone's safety.

In an emergency situation, as previously explained, our approach will be proportionate.

These powers are set out in detail on the ICO website.

FURTHER READING
Relevant provisions in the legislation - see UK GDPR Articles 12-22
Relevant provisions in the legislation - see UK GDPR Recitals 58-72
Relevant provisions in the legislation - see DPA 2018 sections 129-165
Relevant provisions in the legislation - see DPA 2018 schedule 12
What we do
Make a complaint
Regulatory Action Policy
The Guide to the Sandbox

GLOSSARY

[1.393]
This glossary is a quick reference for key terms and abbreviations. It includes links to further reading and other resources which may provide useful context and more detailed information.

Please note, this glossary is not a substitute for reading the data sharing code, the ICO's guidance, and associated legislation.

Accountability principle	This requires organisations to be responsible for their own compliance with the UK GDPR or DPA 2018, as appropriate, and to demonstrate that compliance.
Anonymisation	The UK GDPR refers to 'Anonymous information'; information that does not relate to an individual, and is therefore is no longer 'personal data' and is not subject to the obligations of the UK GDPR. In order to determine whether data is anonymised you should take into account all the means reasonably likely to be used by a third party to directly or indirectly identify an individual. Please check the ICO website for the most up to date guidance.
Appropriate policy document	An appropriate policy document is a short document outlining your compliance measures and retention policies for special category data. The DPA 2018 says you must have one in place for almost all of the substantial public interest conditions (and also for the employment, social security and social protection condition), as a specific accountability and documentation measure.
Competent authority	A public authority to which Part 3 of the DPA 2018 applies. Competent authorities are defined as those listed in schedule 7 of the DPA 2018, and any other organisation or person with statutory law enforcement functions. For more information, see our Guide to Law Enforcement Processing.
Consent	A freely given, specific, informed and unambiguous indication of the data subject's wishes by which he or she, by a statement or by clear affirmative action, signifies agreement to the processing of personal data. For more information, see our guidance on consent.
Controller	The person (usually an organisation) who decides how and why to process data. For more information, see our guidance on controllers and processors.
Data protection by design and default	A legal obligation requiring organisations to put in place appropriate technical and organisational measures to implement the data protection principles in an effective manner and safeguard individual rights.
Data sharing	Although there is no formal definition of data sharing, the scope of the data sharing code is defined by section 121 of the DPA 2018 as "the disclosure of personal data by transmission, dissemination or otherwise making it available".
Data sharing agreements / protocols	These may be known by different names, but all set out the arrangements and a common set of rules to be adopted by the organisations involved in data sharing.
Data subject	The identified or identifiable living individual to whom personal data relates.
DEA	The Digital Economy Act 2017.
DPA; the DPA 2018	The Data Protection Act 2018, which sits alongside the UK GDPR and sets out the framework for data protection in the UK. For more information, see our guidance: About the DPA 2018.
DPIA	Data Protection Impact Assessment. This is a process to help you identify and minimise the data protection risks of a project. You must do a DPIA for processing that is **likely to result in a high risk** to individuals. For more information, see our guidance on DPIAs.
DPO	Data protection officer.

EDPB	European Data Protection Board (formerly the Article 29 Working Party). This is the independent body established by the EU GDPR to ensure consistency within the EU on interpreting the law and taking regulatory action. EDPB guidelines are no longer directly relevant to the UK regime and are not binding under the UK regime. However, they may still provide helpful guidance on certain issues.
Exemptions	The UK GDPR and the DPA 2018 set out exemptions and qualifications to some rights and obligations in some circumstances. For more details, please see our guidance on exemptions and the Guide to Law Enforcement Processing.
Freedom of information legislation	In the UK the main legislation is: Freedom of Information Act 2000 (FOIA), Freedom of Information (Scotland) Act 2002 (FOISA), Environmental Information Regulations 2004 (EIR) and the Environmental Information (Scotland) Regulations 2004.
GDPR	The General Data Protection Regulation (EU) 2016/679 (EU GDPR). Since the UK left the EU, this has been incorporated into UK data protection law as the UK GDPR, which sits alongside the DPA 2018. The EU GDPR may still apply to you if you operate in the European Economic Area (EEA), or monitor the behaviour of individuals in the EEA. For more information, see our guidance Data protection after the end of the transition period and the Guide to Data Protection.
Information Sharing Agreement (ISA)	Another name for a data sharing agreement.
Joint controllers	Where two or more controllers jointly determine the purposes and means of processing. For more information, see our guidance on controllers and processors.
Law enforcement purposes	For Part 3 of the DPA 2018, the purposes of the prevention, investigation, detection, or prosecution of criminal offences or the execution of criminal penalties, including the safeguarding against and the prevention of threats to public security. For more information, see our Guide to Law Enforcement Processing.
Part 2 DPA 2018	This supplements and tailors the UK GDPR for general data processing. For more information, see our guidance About the DPA 2018.
Part 3 DPA 2018	This sets out a separate regime for law enforcement authorities with law enforcement functions (competent authorities) when they are processing data for law enforcement purposes. For more information, see our guidance About the DPA 2018.
Part 4 DPA 2018	This sets out a separate regime for processing, as specified in Part 4, by an intelligence service or by processors acting on their behalf. An intelligence service for the purpose of Part 4 means the Security Service (MI5), the Secret Intelligence Service (commonly known as MI6), and GCHQ.
Personal data	Any information relating to an identified or identifiable natural person ('data subject'). For more information, see our guidance on What is personal data?
Privacy information	The information that organisations need to provide to individual data subjects about the collection and use of their data. For general data processing, this is specified in Articles 13 and 14 of the UK GDPR. For more details, see our guidance on the Right to be informed. For Law Enforcement Processing under Part 3 of the DPA 2018, the provisions are contained in section 44 of the DPA 2018. For more information on that, see the Guide to Law Enforcement Processing: The right to be informed.
Processing	In relation to personal data, this means any operation or set of operations which is performed on it. This includes collecting, storing, recording, using, amending, analysing, disclosing or deleting it.
Processor	A person (usually an organisation) who processes personal data on behalf of a controller. For more information, see the our guidance on controllers and processors.
Pseudonymisation	Data which has undergone pseudonymisation is defined in the UK GDPR as data that can no longer be attributed to a data subject without the use of additional information. You must ensure that the additional information is kept separately, and that appropriate technical and organisational controls are in place to ensure that re-identification of an individual is not possible. Please check the ICO website for the most up to date guidance.
Publication scheme	For public authorities covered by FOIA and FOISA, you must publish certain information proactively in a publication scheme. Guidance is available on the websites of the Information Commissioner and the Scottish Information Commissioner, respectively.
Sensitive processing	This term is used in Part 3 of the DPA 2018 in relation to law enforcement processing. It is defined in section 35(8) of the DPA 2018 as: (a) the processing of personal data revealing racial or ethnic origin, political opinions, religious or philosophical beliefs or trade union membership; (b) the processing of genetic data, or of biometric data, for the purpose of uniquely identifying an individual; (c) the processing of data concerning health; or (d) the processing of data concerning an individual's sex life or sexual orientation. This type of data processing needs greater protection. For more information, see the Guide to Law Enforcement Processing.

Special category data   This term is used about general data processing under the UK GDPR and Part 2 of the DPA 2018. It is defined in Article 9.1 of the UK GDPR as personal data revealing racial or ethnic origin, political opinions, religious or philosophical beliefs, or trade union membership, and the processing of genetic data, biometric data for the purpose of uniquely identifying a natural person, data concerning health or data concerning a natural person's sex life or sexual orientation. The processing of this type of data needs greater protection. For more information, see our guidance on Special category data.

UK GDPR   The UK version of the EU GDPR, as amended and incorporated into UK law from the end of the transition period by the European Union (Withdrawal) Act 2018 and associated Exit Regulations. The government has published a Keeling Schedule for the UK GDPR which shows the planned amendments.

WP29   Article 29 Working Party (now the European Data Protection Board).

ANNEX A: DATA SHARING CHECKLIST

[1.394]

This checklist provides a step-by-step guide to deciding whether to share personal data.

You should use it alongside the data sharing code and guidance on the ICO website ico.org.uk.

It highlights what you should consider in order to ensure that your sharing complies with the law and meets individuals' expectations.

CHECK WHETHER THE SHARING IS JUSTIFIED

Key points to consider:

- ☐ What is the sharing meant to achieve?
- ☐ Have you assessed the potential benefits and risks to individuals and/or society of sharing or not sharing?
- ☐ Is it fair to share data in this way?
- ☐ Is the sharing necessary and proportionate to the issue you are addressing?
- ☐ What is the minimum data you can share to achieve the aim?
- ☐ Could the objective be achieved without sharing personal data, or by sharing less personal data?
- ☐ What safeguards can you put in place to minimise the risks or potential adverse effects of the sharing?
- ☐ Is there an applicable exemption in the DPA 2018?

CONSIDER DOING A DATA PROTECTION IMPACT ASSESSMENT

Decide whether you need to carry out a DPIA:

- ☐ You must do a DPIA for data sharing that is likely to result in a high risk to individuals. This will depend on the nature, scope, context and purposes of the sharing. For more details on this, see the relevant section of this code and guidance on the ICO website ico.org.uk.
- ☐ For any data sharing plans, you may find it useful to follow the DPIA process as a flexible and scalable tool to suit your project.

IF YOU DECIDE TO SHARE

It is good practice to have a data sharing agreement. As well as considering the key points above, your data sharing agreement should cover the following issues. You should ensure you cover these matters in any event, whether or not you have a formal agreement in place:

- ☐ What information will you share?
- ☐ Is any of it special category data (or does it involve sensitive processing under Part 3 of the DPA 2018)? What additional safeguards will you have in place?
- ☐ How should you share the information?
You must share information securely.
You must ensure you are giving the information to the right recipient.
- ☐ What is to happen to the data at every stage?
- ☐ Who in each organisation can access the shared data? Ensure it is restricted to authorised personnel in each organisation.
- ☐ What organisation(s) will be involved? You all need to be clear about your respective roles.
- ☐ How will you comply with your transparency obligations?
- Consider what you need to tell people about sharing their data and how you will communicate that information in a way that is concise, transparent, easily accessible and uses clear and plain language.
- Consider whether you have obtained the personal data from a source other than the individual.
- Decide what arrangements need to be in place to comply with individuals' information rights. Bear in mind the differences under Part 3 of the DPA 2018, if applicable.

☐ What quality checks are appropriate to ensure the shared data is accurate and up-to-date?

☐ What technical and organisational measures are appropriate to ensure the security of the data?

☐ What common retention periods for data do you all agree to?

☐ What processes do you need to ensure secure deletion takes place?

☐ When should regularly scheduled reviews of the data sharing arrangement take place?

ACCOUNTABILITY PRINCIPLE

You must comply with the principles; this point focuses on the accountability principle:

☐ The accountability principle means that you are responsible for your compliance with the UK GDPR or DPA 2018 as appropriate and you must be able to demonstrate that compliance.

☐ You must maintain documentation for all your data sharing operations.

☐ This obligation encompasses the requirement to carry out a DPIA when appropriate.

☐ You must implement a "data protection by design and default" approach, putting in appropriate technical and organisational measures to implement data protection principles and safeguard individual rights.

☐ You must ensure that staff in your organisation who are likely to make decisions about sharing data have received the right training to do so appropriately.

DECIDE WHAT YOUR LAWFUL BASIS IS FOR SHARING THE DATA

Key points to consider:

☐ What is the nature of the data and the purpose for sharing it, as well as the scope and context?

☐ Are you relying on legitimate interests as a lawful basis? If so, you must carry out a legitimate interests assessment (LIA).

☐ Is any of the data either special category data or criminal offence data? If so, you need to identify additional conditions.

☐ For law enforcement processing under Part 3 of the DPA 2018, please refer to the references throughout the code and in particular to the Part 3 section.

CHECK WHETHER YOU HAVE THE POWER TO SHARE

Key points to consider:

☐ What type of organisation you work for. The position is different for the public and private sectors. Please refer to the data sharing code for more details.

☐ Any relevant functions or powers of your organisation.

☐ The nature of the information you have been asked to share.

☐ Whether there are any legal requirements that need to be met when sharing the data - such as copyright or a duty of confidence, or any prohibitions.

☐ Whether there is a legal obligation or other legal requirement about sharing information – such as a statutory requirement, a court order or common law.

DOCUMENT YOUR DECISION

Document your data sharing decision and your reasoning – whether or not you share the information.

If you shared information you should document:

☐ your justification for sharing;

☐ what information was shared and for what purpose;

☐ who it was shared with;

☐ when and how it was shared;

☐ whether the information was shared with or without consent, and how that was recorded;

☐ the lawful basis for processing and any additional conditions applicable;

☐ individuals' rights;

☐ Data protection impact assessment reports;

☐ compliance with any DPO advice given (where applicable);

☐ evidence of the steps you have taken to comply with the UK GDPR and the DPA 2018 as appropriate; and

☐ where you have reviewed and updated your accountability measures at appropriate intervals.

ANNEX B: DATA SHARING REQUEST FORM TEMPLATE

FOR USE BY THE ORGANISATION MAKING THE REQUEST FOR DATA SHARING
[1.395]

Name of organisation

Name and position of person requesting data

If requester is not the data protection officer (DPO) or equivalent, have they been consulted and their views considered?

Date of request

Description of data requested

Data controller relationship: ☐ Joint ☐ Separate
Will we have a data sharing agreement in place? ☐ Yes ☐ No
Purpose of sharing

Does processing involve any special category data (or sensitive processing under part 3 DPA 2018)?
☐ Yes ☐ No
Are there any specific arrangements for retention / deletion of data?

Are there any circumstances in the proposed sharing that might result in a risk to individuals?

Date(s) provision of data is required

DATA SHARING DECISION FORM TEMPLATE

FOR USE BY THE ORGANISATION TAKING THE DECISION TO SHARE DATA
[1.396]

Name of organisation receiving request to share data

Name of organisation requesting data

Name and position of person requesting data

Date request received

Description of data requested

Data controller relationship: ☐ Joint ☐ Separate
Will we have a data sharing agreement in place? ☐ Yes ☐ No
Purpose of sharing

Lawful basis for sharing – please state which

Why is sharing 'necessary'?

Are additional conditions met for special category data or criminal offence data sharing (where applicable)?

Are additional provisions met in the case of Part 3 DPA 2018 data sharing?

Which legal power for sharing applies (if relevant)?

Have you considered a DPIA?

DPIA undertaken and outcome (if applicable)

Were views of DPO (or equivalent) considered? (if DPIA not done)

Are there any specific arrangements for retention/deletion of data?

What are the security considerations?

What arrangements are there for complying with individuals' information rights?

Date(s) of requested sharing (or intervals if data is to be shared on a regular basis)

Decision on request

Reason(s) for sharing or not sharing

Decision taken by (name and position)

Signed: Dated:

ANNEX C: CASE STUDIES

FAIRNESS AND TRANSPARENCY

Supermarket providing privacy information to customers

[1.397]
A supermarket held information about its customers through its loyalty card scheme, in-store CCTV and records of payments. The company did not normally disclose any information to third parties, such as for marketing purposes. However, it would do so if the information it held was relevant to a police investigation or in response to a court order, for example.

The supermarket or the loyalty card scheme operator had to give customers privacy information that provided an explanation, in general terms, of the sorts of circumstances in which it would share information about scheme members with a third party, such as the police.

If the supermarket were to disclose information about a particular scheme member to the police, it would not need to inform the individual of the disclosure if this would prejudice crime prevention.

Sharing customer details with a credit reference agency

A mobile phone company decided to share details of customer accounts with a credit reference agency.

It had to inform customers when they opened an account that it would share information with credit reference agencies.

Credit reference agencies need to be able to link records to the correct individual, so the mobile phone company had to ensure it was collecting adequate information to distinguish between individuals; for example dates of birth.

The organisations involved had to put procedures in place to deal with complaints about the accuracy of the information they shared.

Duty to process data fairly when carrying out research using shared data

A university wanted to conduct research into the academic performance of children from deprived family backgrounds in the local area. The university wanted to identify the relevant children by finding out which ones were eligible for Pupil Premium. Therefore it decided to ask all local primary and secondary schools to share this personal data, as well as the relevant children's test results for the previous three years.

The DPA 2018 contains various provisions that are intended to facilitate the processing of personal data for research purposes. However, there is no exemption from the general duty to process the data fairly. Data about families' income levels, or eligibility for benefits, could be inferred from the Pupil Premium status of a child.

In this example, parents and their children might well have objected to the disclosure of this data because they considered it sensitive and potentially stigmatising. Data about a child's academic performance could be considered equally sensitive.

Instead the school could have identified eligible children on the researchers' behalf and contacted their parents, explaining what the research was about and what data the researchers wanted. The school might have wished to obtain parents' consent for sharing the data, but other lawful bases could have been available to it.

Alternatively, the school could have disclosed an anonymous data set, or statistical information, to the researchers.

DATA SHARING AGREEMENT: ACCOUNTABILITY

Information sharing framework in healthcare

Healthcare partners in one county decided to develop an information sharing framework to standardise their sharing processes and encourage agencies to share personal data safely. The framework helped their staff to comply with data protection law by sharing information lawfully, securely and confidentially. As a result, they were able to integrate service provision across the county and deliver better care outcomes for their residents. In a key step, partners brought together information governance leads to oversee the changes needed to develop the framework.

Main purposes of the framework were to ensure that:
* people only had to tell their story once and could expect a better service delivery;
* local people had clear guidance about how their information was shared (and in what circumstances their consent might need to be sought to share it);
* professionals had access to the information they needed, when they needed it, to support better outcomes for local people;
* good decision making was supported by an information sharing framework, providing staff with clear direction; and
* unnecessary appointments and admissions could be avoided.

The principles of the framework were to:
(a)   identify the appropriate lawful basis for information sharing;
(b)   provide the basis for security of information and the legal requirements associated with information sharing;
(c)   address the need to develop and manage the use of Information Sharing Agreements (ISAs);
(d)   encourage flows of personal data and develop good practice across integrated teams;
(e)   provide the basis for county-wide processes which would monitor and review data flows, and information sharing between partner services;
(f)   protect partner organisations from unlawful use of personal data; and
(g)   reduce the need for individuals to repeat their story when receiving an integrated service.

Key learning from the introduction of the framework
* Staff needed to be empowered to feel confident about sharing information between partners. Senior leaders needed to be visible to give staff the confidence to share patient information.
* Internal culture needed to be supportive. The culture needed to be underpinned by strong values and ethos. It was essential for a learning culture to be developed so that mistakes could be shared and learnt from, rather than brushed aside. This learning included developing formal training for all staff who were using an integrated care record, supported by the framework.
* Transparency needed to be established so that there was a collective understanding of how the data would be shared and by whom. Staff needed to have clarity around their roles and responsibilities and the benefits of sharing information.
* A need to develop a culture of appropriate sharing in plain English. Messages needed to be simplified to avoid confusion, and jargon needed to be reduced.

LAWFUL BASIS; LEGAL OBLIGATION; FAIRNESS AND TRANSPARENCY; INDIVIDUAL RIGHTS

Data sharing required by law

A local authority was required by law to participate in a nationwide anti-fraud exercise that involved disclosing personal data about its employees to an anti–fraud body. The exercise was intended to detect local authority employees who were illegally claiming benefits that they were not entitled to.

Even though the sharing was required by law, the local authority still had to inform any employees affected that data about them was going to be shared and still had to explain why this was taking place, unless this would have prejudiced proceedings.

The local authority had to say what data items were going to be shared – names, addresses and National Insurance numbers - and to provide the identity of the organisation they would be shared with.

There was no need for the local authority to seek employees' consent for the sharing because the law says the sharing could take place without consent. The local authority also had to be clear with its employees that even if they objected to the sharing, it would still take place.

The local authority had to be prepared to investigate complaints from any employees who believed they had been treated unfairly because, for example, their records had been mixed up with those of an employee with the same name.

Considerations for a healthcare data sharing agreement

Relevant parts of the NHS and social services in a region shared personal information with the region's police force to ensure that mental health service users who were in contact with the police were safeguarded and had access to appropriate specialist support.

The partner organisations had developed a data sharing agreement to support their joint mental health policy. Depending on the circumstances of each case, the lawful basis might have been consent or a task carried out in the public interest. The data sharing agreement clearly identified the various pieces of law that each partner relied on to specify their public functions and the provisions they needed to meet if relying on consent. As special category data was likely to be necessary for referrals, they also identified Article 9 conditions. The data sharing agreement reminded all parties to maintain the rights and dignity of patients, their carers and families, involving them in risk assessments wherever possible while also ensuring their safety and that of others.

FAIRNESS AND TRANSPARENCY; INDIVIDUAL RIGHTS

A data sharing arrangement in the private sector relating to the use of new software

A company specialising in both business-to-business and business-to-consumer transactions used a software-as-a-service ("SaaS") provider to manage client contact information and integrate communications into its operations. The SaaS provider automated the processes and kept all information up to date. To comply with the requirements of the UK GDPR, the company entered into a data sharing agreement with the SaaS provider.

The agreement outlined a number of obligations for the SaaS provider, such as the nature and scope of information that was to be processed and how the parties intended to implement appropriate security measures.

The company ensured its privacy information was up to date and accurately reflected the data sharing arrangement entered into with the SaaS provider. The fair processing information explained who the data was being shared with and for what purposes. The company also made use of a preference management tool, ensuring individuals were able to control non-essential elements of data sharing between the parties.

DATA SHARING AGREEMENT; ACCOUNTABILITY; INDIVIDUAL RIGHTS

Public sector bodies sharing data to provide a co-ordinated approach

Personal information was shared between two councils, their local schools and colleges, housing providers, relevant community organisations, the local job centres and careers service in order to identify young people who already had been or were currently at high risk of disengaging from education, employment or training. By sharing the information, the partner organisations were able to ensure a co-ordinated approach to providing the most appropriate support to the young person to encourage them back into education, work or training.

The partners used a data sharing agreement to set out their purpose, lawful bases and the information to be shared. The agreement included a section on how to handle data subjects' rights, and agreed shared security standards; the partners also updated their privacy notices. To quality-assure their agreement, they shared it with a regional group of data protection practitioners for feedback. A timescale was also set for the partners to regularly review the agreement to ensure it stayed up to date and fit for purpose.

DATA SHARING UNDER THE DIGITAL ECONOMY ACT 2017 POWERS

Both Companies House (CH) and Her Majesty's Revenue and Customs (HMRC) collect annual accounts from businesses. The accounts contain key corporate and financial information about the company, such as the names of company directors or financial reporting figures showing their profit and loss.

There is the opportunity, however, for the same company to file a different set of accounts to each of the two organisations. By filing inflated accounts at CH and lower figures at HMRC, they would simultaneously increase their creditworthiness with financial institutions and wider government while also reducing tax liabilities.

Until 2018, restrictions on data sharing had prevented HMRC and CH from sharing company accounts for comparison. With the introduction of the Digital Economy Act 2017, however, a permissive legal gateway was provided to share information to combat fraud.

Prior to sharing information, CH and HMRC met to draw up the governance and processes:
- They would share information as a pilot.
- Both parties designed and agreed a data specification.
- They completed a data protection impact assessment (DPIA) to ensure they considered proportionality and fair processing.
- Both parties signed an information sharing agreement.

HMRC disclosed the first set of company accounts information to CH in October 2018 – the very first transfer of data under the Digital Economy Act powers.

The pilot sought to address the fraud problem through 10 defined data analytics and compliance work streams, each one relating to a mode of behaviour indicating false account filing and fraudulent activity. For the first time, the pilot utilised qualitative analysis to access and compare key words and phrases.

Further to this, the pilot also utilised CH back-office data to uncover previously hidden links between companies, combined for the first time with HMRC intelligence.

The data sharing pilot identified around £10m of savings, with upwards of £50m potential annual savings projected if the data share was embedded as business as usual.

In addition, they identified over 3,500 sets of accounts as incorrect at Companies House, thereby improving the integrity of the data held on the register.

DATA SHARING FOR OFFICIAL STATISTICS AND ANALYSIS: MEASURING THE PAY PROGRESSION AND GEOGRAPHICAL MOBILITY OF YOUNG WORKERS

Understanding how young people enter the labour market and progress through their early careers helps to highlight disparities in opportunities and shine a light on differing experiences of being in work, incomes and social mobility. The factors that influence labour market and earnings progression, as well as the geographic mobility of workers, had been a long-standing evidence gap in official statistics and analysis.

In 2018, the Office for National Statistics (ONS) brought together data from the 2011 Census with data on earnings and benefits from the Department for Work and Pensions (DWP) and HM Revenue and Customs (HMRC), for the period 2012 to 2016. This new longitudinal study created a dataset of 28 million individual records, allowing for new analysis of how earnings had changed over this period, not previously possible using the traditional survey sources. Only anonymised data was used in the analysis and results were published at an aggregated level, so that individuals could never be identified by ONS analysts undertaking the research or in the published research outputs.

Alongside 2011 Census data on individual and household characteristics, the new dataset drew on local geography information contained in the DWP administrative dataset to produce analysis of the impact of moving home on pay and earnings progression, especially patterns of movement of young people between local authorities and how earnings growth varied depending on the geographical place of origin and different city or regional destinations. While this showed that four in five young people did not move between local authority areas over the period of the study, for those that did move, on average, young people experienced higher earnings growth. Those moving to London experienced the highest average annual growth in earnings (+22%) while those that either did not move local authority or moved elsewhere had much lower earnings growth (+7%).

Further analysis was published as experimental research on the ONS website in Young People's Earnings Progression and Geographic Mobility.

DATA SHARING ARRANGEMENT BETWEEN SECTORS TO SUPPORT FAMILIES

Sharing data between a local authority and local NHS trust to provide better early help and support to families

Families sometimes have hidden needs so don't receive the support they require from public services – or may be receiving support through one organisation for a specific issue, but have other needs too.

A council worked with an NHS trust to establish a data sharing arrangement between the council and health services to help identify children and families who would benefit from receiving co-ordinated and targeted early help for a range of issues they might be facing.

The data sharing arrangement cross-referenced NHS trust and council caseload data and identified children and families who were being supported by the trust, but not by the council's early help services. These families would then be engaged in wider support to address their needs through the Troubled Families Programme. The data would also be used to understand whether families had in fact benefitted from the support they received and to inform future commissioning of services.

Before sharing data, the two organisations worked together to put measures in place to ensure that the data would be protected and shared responsibly:

- A data protection impact assessment, led by the Head of Information Governance and data protection officer (DPO) at the NHS trust, which identified the potential risks to privacy and how those risks would be mitigated.
- An operational agreement setting out the arrangements for the exchange of data, under the overarching information sharing framework signed by the trust and the council.
- A methodology to make sure the minimum amount of data was shared.
- Privacy information.

Organisations involved: Children's public health, Health Visiting, and Child and Adolescent Mental Health Services (CAMHS); the council and local NHS trust.

DIRECT MARKETING CODE OF PRACTICE
Draft code for consultation

[1.398]

___

NOTES

The ICO launched a consultation on this draft code of practice in January 2020. An updated version is expected after this book goes to press. Draft version as available on ICO website at time of going to print, at https://ico.org.uk/media/for-organisations/documents/2021/2619043/direct-marketing-code-draft-guidance-122020.pdf. © Information Commissioner's Office, licensed under the Open Government Licence.

___

CONTENTS

FOREWORD

[1.399]

A foreword by Information Commissioner Elizabeth Denham will be included in the final version of the code.

SUMMARY

[1.400]
About this code
- This is a statutory code of practice prepared under section 122 of the Data Protection Act 2018. It provides practical guidance for those conducting direct marketing or operating within the broader direct marketing ecosystem. It explains the law and provides good practice recommendations. Following the code along with other ICO guidance will help you to comply with the GDPR and PECR.

Does this code apply to us?
- This code applies if you process personal data for direct marketing purposes.
- Direct marketing includes the promotion of aims and ideals as well as advertising goods or services. Any method of communication which is directed to particular individuals could constitute direct marketing. Direct marketing purposes include all processing activities that lead up to, enable or support the sending of direct marketing.

Planning your marketing: DP by design
- A key part of the GDPR is accountability and you must be able to demonstrate your compliance. You must consider data protection and privacy issues upfront when you are planning your direct marketing activities. Depending on your direct marketing activity you may be required to conduct a DPIA.
- Generally speaking the two lawful bases most likely to be applicable to your direct marketing purposes are consent and legitimate interests. However if PECR requires consent then in practice consent will be your lawful basis under the GDPR. If you intend to process special category data for direct marketing purposes it is likely that the only Article 9 condition available to you will be 'explicit consent'.
- In most cases it is unlikely that you will be able to make using an individual's data for direct marketing purposes a condition of your service or buying your product.
- It is important to keep personal data accurate and up to date. It should not be kept for longer than is necessary. Children's personal data requires specific protection in regard to direct marketing.

Generating leads and collecting contact details
- Transparency is a key part of the GDPR and as part of this individuals have the right to be informed about your collection and use of their personal data for direct marketing purposes.
- If you collect data directly from individuals you must provide privacy information at the time you collect their details. If you collect personal data from sources other than the individual (eg public sources or from third parties) you must provide privacy information within a reasonable period of obtaining the data and no later than one month from the date of collection. Your privacy information must be in clear and plain language and easily accessible.

- If you are considering buying or renting direct marketing lists you must ensure you have completed appropriate due diligence.

Profiling and data enrichment

- Profiling and enrichment activities must be done in a way that is fair, lawful and transparent. If you are considering using profiling or enrichment services you must ensure you have completed appropriate due diligence.
- If you are carrying out solely automated decision making, including profiling, that has legal or similarly significant effects on individuals then there are addition rules in the GDPR that you must comply with. If you want to profile people on the using their special categories of data you must have their explicit consent to do this.
- If you use non-personal data such as assumptions about the type of people who live in a particular postcode to enrich the details you hold about an individual it will become personal data.
- In most instances, buying additional contact details for your existing customers or supporters is likely to be unfair unless the individual has previously agreed to you having these extra contact details.
- You are unlikely to be able to justify tracing an individual in order to send direct marketing to their new address – such tracing takes away control from the individual to be able to choose not to tell you their new details.

Sending direct marketing messages

- No matter which method you use for sending direct marketing messages the GDPR will apply when you are processing personal data.
- The direct marketing provisions in PECR only apply to live and automated calls, electronic mail (eg text and emails) and faxes. The electronic mail 'soft opt-in' only applies to the commercial marketing of products and services, it does not apply to the promotion of aims and ideals.
- PECR may apply differently to business to business marketing depending on the type of subscriber you want to contact.
- PECR may still apply even if you ask someone else to send your electronic direct marketing messages.

Online advertising and new technologies

- Individuals may not understand how non-traditional direct marketing technologies work. Therefore it is particularly important that you are clear and transparent about what you intend to do with their personal data.
- Individuals are unlikely to understand how you target them with marketing on social media so you must be upfront about targeting individuals in this way.
- If you are planning to use cookies or similar technologies for direct marketing purposes you must provide clear and comprehensive information to the user about these and gain their consent (which must be to the GDPR standard).
- Regardless of what technology or contact method you consider, you still need to comply with the GDPR and PECR. If you are using new technologies for marketing and online advertising, it is highly likely that you require a DPIA.

Selling or sharing data

- If you are planning on selling or sharing personal data for direct marketing purposes you must ensure that it is fair and lawful to do so. You must also be transparent and tell people about the selling or sharing.

Individual rights

- As well as the right to be informed, the rights to objection, rectification, erasure and access are the most likely to be relevant in the direct marketing context.
- The right to object to direct marketing is absolute. This means if someone objects you must stop processing for direct marketing purposes (which is not limited to sending direct marketing). You should add their details to your suppression list so that you can screen any new marketing lists against it.

Exemptions

- The DPA 2018 contains a number of exemptions from particular GDPR provisions and these add to the exceptions that are already built into certain GDPR provisions. There are no exemptions that specifically apply to processing for direct marketing purposes.
- PECR contains very few exemptions. The two exemptions in Regulation 6 from the requirement to provide clear and comprehensive information and gain consent for cookies and similar technologies do not apply to online advertising, tracking technologies or social media plugins.

Enforcement of this code

- The ICO upholds information rights in the public interest. We will monitor compliance with this code through proactive audits, will consider complaints and enforce the direct marketing rules in line with our Regulatory Action Policy. Adherence to this code will be a key measure of your compliance with data protection laws. If you do not follow this code, you will find it difficult to demonstrate that your processing complies with the GDPR or PECR.

The transition period for leaving the EU ended on 31 December 2020. The GDPR has been retained in UK law as the UK GDPR, and will continue to be read alongside the Data Protection Act 2018, with technical amendments to ensure it can function in UK law.

ABOUT THIS CODE

AT A GLANCE

[1.401]
This is a statutory code of practice prepared under section 122 of the Data Protection Act 2018. It provides practical guidance for those conducting direct marketing or operating within the broader direct marketing ecosystem. It explains the law and provides good practice recommendations. Following the code along with other ICO guidance will help you to comply with the GDPR and PECR.

WHO IS THIS CODE FOR?

This code is for anyone who intends to conduct marketing that is directed to particular individuals or anyone that operates within the broader direct marketing ecosystem. For example, if you are processing for direct marketing purposes and use or offer profiling, data enrichment, or list brokering services.

You will be caught by the direct marketing rules if you are using data with the intention to market, advertise, or promote products, services, aims or ideals. For example:
- commercial businesses marketing their products and services;
- charities and third sector organisations fundraising or promoting their aims and ideals;
- political parties fundraising or canvassing for votes;
- public authorities promoting their services or objectives; or
- organisations involved in buying, selling, profiling or enriching personal data for direct marketing purposes.

This code assumes familiarity with key data protection and PECR terms and concepts. If you need an introduction to either, including key concepts – you should refer to our Guides to Data Protection and PECR.

WHAT IS THE PURPOSE OF THIS CODE?

The code helps you to comply and demonstrate that you comply with data protection and e-privacy rules when you are processing data for direct marketing purposes or conducting direct marketing campaigns.

How does this code support data protection and e-privacy compliance?

The UK data protection regime is set out in the Data Protection Act 2018 (DPA 2018) and the General Data Protection Regulation (GDPR). This regime requires you to take a risk-based approach when you use people's data, based on certain key principles.

The e-privacy rules in the UK are set out in the Privacy and Electronic Communications Regulation 2003 (PECR). This regime sets out more detailed privacy rules in the area of electronic marketing communications and cookies and similar technologies. It is broader than the GDPR in the sense that it applies even if you are not processing any personal data.

There is some overlap between the data protection and e-privacy regimes, and they use some of the same concepts and definitions – including the definition of consent. In some circumstances you will find your direct marketing is covered by both GDPR and PECR but on other occasions you may find that only one of these applies.

This code looks at both regimes and takes you through the steps to comply with the rules.

THE REGULATORY FRAMEWORK

The Commissioner regulates data protection and e-privacy laws. However there are other rules and industry standards affecting direct marketing which are regulated by other bodies.

Compliance with other regulation and industry standards can assist in you demonstrating that your processing of personal data for direct marketing purposes is lawful and fair.

Other resources outside this code

Ofcom regulates the Communications Act 2003, which covers the improper use of a public electronic communications network, including making silent or abandoned calls. Ofcom has powers to issue fines up to £2 million for persistent misuse.

The Competition and Markets Authority (CMA) and local trading standards offices enforce The Consumer Protection from Unfair Trading Regulations 2008 which prohibit a number of unfair, misleading or aggressive marketing practices, including 'making persistent and unwanted solicitations by telephone, fax, email or other remote media'.

The Advertising Standards Authority (ASA) enforces the UK Code of Non- broadcast Advertising, Sales Promotion and Direct Marketing (the CAP code). The CAP code contains rules which all advertisers, agencies and media must follow. It covers the content of advertising material, and specific rules on certain types of advertising (eg advertising to children, advertising certain types of products, or distance selling).

The Data & Marketing Association (DMA) (formally the Direct Marketing Association) publishes the DMA code, setting standards of ethical conduct and best practice in direct marketing. Compliance is mandatory for all DMA members and the code is enforced by the independent Direct Marketing Commission.

The Fundraising Regulator is the independent, non-statutory body that regulates fundraising across the charitable sector in England, Wales and Northern Ireland. It sets standards for fundraising including in its Code of fundraising practice.

You should always ensure that you are familiar with all laws and standards of conduct that apply to you.

WHAT IS THE STATUS OF THIS CODE?

What is the legal status of the code?

This is a statutory code of practice prepared under section 122 of the DPA 2018:

"(1) The Commissioner must prepare a code of practice which contains—

    (a)   practical guidance in relation to the carrying out of direct marketing in accordance with the requirements of the data protection legislation and the Privacy and Electronic Communications (EC Directive) Regulations 2003 (S.I. 2003/2426), and

    (b)   such other guidance as the Commissioner considers appropriate to promote good practice in direct marketing."

Section 122(5) of DPA 2018 states that 'good practice in direct marketing' means:

"such practice in direct marketing as appears to the Commissioner to be desirable having regard to the interests of data subjects and others, including compliance with the requirements mentioned in subsection (1)(a)"

This code was laid before parliament on **[DATE]** and issued on **[date 40 days after laid, ignoring parliamentary recess]** under section 125 of the DPA 2018. It comes into force on **[date 21 days after issue]**.

The code contains practical guidance on how to carry out direct marketing fairly and lawfully, and how to meet your accountability obligations. It does not impose any additional legal obligations that go beyond the requirements of the GDPR or PECR, but following the code will ensure you comply with those obligations. It also contains some optional good practice recommendations, which do not have the status of legal requirements but aim to help you adopt an effective approach to data protection compliance.

In accordance with section 127 of the DPA 2018, the Commissioner must take the code into account when considering whether those engaging in direct marketing purposes have complied with its obligations under the GDPR or PECR. In particular, the Commissioner will take the code into account when considering questions of fairness, lawfulness, transparency and accountability under the GDPR, and in the use of her enforcement powers.

The code can also be used in evidence in court proceedings, and the courts must take its provisions into account wherever relevant.

What happens if we do not comply with the code?

If you do not comply with the guidance in this code, you may find it more difficult to demonstrate that your processing for direct marketing purposes is fair, lawful and accountable and complies with the GDPR and PECR.

We can take action against you if you send direct marketing or process personal data for direct marketing purposes in breach of this code and this results in an infringement of the GDPR or PECR.

Tools at our disposal include assessment notices, warnings, reprimands, enforcement notices and penalty notices (administrative fines). For serious infringements of the data protection principles, we have the power to issue fines of up to €20 million or 4% of your annual worldwide turnover, whichever is higher.

There is no penalty if you fail to adopt good practice recommendations, as long as you find another way to comply with the law.

For more information see the Enforcement of this code section.

What is the status of 'further reading' or other linked resources?

Any further reading or other resources which are mentioned in or linked from this code do not form part of the code. We provide links to give you helpful context and further guidance on specific issues, but there is no statutory obligation under the DPA 2018 for the Commissioner or courts to take it into account (unless it is another of our statutory codes of practice).

However, where we link to other ICO guidance, that guidance inevitably reflects the Commissioner's views and informs our general approach to interpretation, compliance and enforcement.

We may also link to relevant guidance provided by the European Data Protection Board (EDPB), which is the independent body established to ensure consistency within the EU when interpreting the GDPR and taking regulatory action.

HOW DO WE USE THIS CODE?

The code takes a life-cycle approach to direct marketing. It starts with a section that looks at the definition of direct marketing to help you decide if this code applies to you. It then contains separate sections on planning your marketing, collecting data, delivering your marketing messages, working with others, and individuals' rights.

As well as having examples throughout, the code has a glossary of terms in its annex. Outside of this code the ICO has produced practical tools and resources, including checklists, to help you work through your compliance with the direct marketing rules.

The code is designed to reflect all of the different stages that might be involved in end-to-end marketing activities. In practice, the sections that you need to read depend on the type of activities you engage in. You may not need to read every section, but you should always start with the section on planning and DP by design.

The key recommendations of this code are highlighted in the summary section at the beginning of this code and in the 'at a glance' boxes at the start of each section – but you need to read the full section in order to understand the detail.

How should charities and not-for-profits use this code?

In general the direct marketing rules are the same for charities and not-for- profit organisations as for private and public sector organisations. Therefore you need to read all the sections of the code that relate to your activities. Where relevant, any issues that are specific to your sector are discussed along with examples.

Further reading outside this code

See our separate guidance on:

The Guide to Data protection

The Guide to PECR

DOES THE CODE APPLY TO US?

AT A GLANCE

[1.402]
This code applies if you process personal data for direct marketing purposes.

Direct marketing includes the promotion of aims and ideals as well as

advertising goods or services. Any method of communication which is

directed to particular individuals could constitute direct marketing. Direct

marketing purposes include all processing activities that lead up to, enable or support the sending of direct marketing.

WHAT IS THE DEFINITION OF DIRECT MARKETING?

The definition of direct marketing is in section 122(5) of the DPA 2018:

"'"direct marketing" means the communication (by whatever means) of advertising or marketing material which is directed to particular individuals"

This definition also applies for PECR. This is because regulation 2(2) of PECR provides that any undefined expressions have the same meaning as in the UK data protection regime (formerly the Data Protection Act 1998, now the DPA 2018).

Relevant provisions in the legislation

PECR – see Regulation 2(2)

DPA 2018 – see Schedule 19 paragraph 430 and paragraph 432(6)

WHAT ARE DIRECT MARKETING PURPOSES?

GDPR and PECR do not define the term 'direct marketing purposes', but clearly it is intended to be wider than simply sending direct marketing communications. The focus is on the purpose of the processing, not the activity. Therefore, if the ultimate aim is to send direct marketing communications, then all processing activities which lead up to, enable or support sending those communications is processing for direct marketing purposes, not just the communication itself.

Therefore, if you are processing personal data with the intention that it is used for communicating direct marketing by you or a third party you are processing for direct marketing purposes. For example, if you are collecting personal data from various sources in order to build up a profile on an individual – such as the products they buy, the services they like to use, or the causes they are likely to support – with the intention that this is used to target advertising at them, whether by you or by a third party. Other examples include:
- lead generation;
- list brokering;
- data enrichment;
- data cleansing, matching or screening;
- audience segmenting or other profiling; and
- contacting individuals to ask them for consent to direct marketing.

Disclosing the data to third parties for them to use for their own direct marketing also constitutes direct marketing purposes.

> **Example**
> A hotel sends an email to its previous guests asking them if they would like to consent to receiving its special offers and discounts. Whilst this email does not itself contain any of these discounts or offers, it is still being sent for direct marketing purposes.

Direct marketing purposes include trying to generate leads by sending mass texts, emails or automated calls or cold-calling numbers registered with the Telephone Preference Service (TPS), even if these messages do not contain any sales or promotional material. Therefore if you intend to do this you must ensure that you have complied with PECR.

WHAT IS 'ADVERTISING OR MARKETING MATERIAL'?

The DPA 2018 and PECR do not clarify what is meant by 'advertising or marketing material'. However it is interpreted widely and covers any advertising or marketing material, not just commercial marketing. For example it includes the promotion of aims and ideals as well as advertising goods or services. This wide interpretation acknowledges that unwanted, and in some cases nuisance, direct marketing is not always limited to commercial marketing.

This is a long standing interpretation which was supported by an Information Tribunal in 2006:

> **Example**
> The Scottish National Party (SNP) made a series of automated campaigning calls to selected Scottish voters in the lead-up to the 2005 general election. PECR states that automated direct marketing calls can only be made with prior consent, but the SNP claimed that the rules on direct marketing did not apply to them – only to commercial organisations. The case went to the Information Tribunal.
> In the Scottish National Party v Information Commissioner (EA/2005/0021, 15 May 2006), the Tribunal agreed that the direct marketing rules in PECR and the (now superseded) Data Protection Act 1998 covered the promotional activities of both commercial and not-for-profit organisations, and so political parties had to comply with PECR when carrying out campaigning calls.

All promotional material falls within the definition. Examples of material promoting aims and ideals could be about:
- fundraising;
- political parties or candidates; or
- the use of public services.

Often it is very obvious that a message contains advertising or marketing material but sometimes it is not as clear cut. In these circumstances the tone, content and the context of the message is likely to be important. The question is whether the communication is:
- promotional in nature – does it advertise goods or services or otherwise promote the organisation itself or its interests?; or
- more neutral and informative in nature – does it seek simply to provide information the individual needs in the context of the existing relationship?

You should think about why you want to communicate with individuals – for example to try to influence thought or behaviour, or encourage an action as this will help you in deciding if the message is direct marketing. See the section What are service messages? for further information.

WHAT TYPE OF 'COMMUNICATIONS' ARE COVERED?

The definition of direct marketing covers any means of communication, although PECR rules only apply to specific types of electronic communication (eg phone calls, emails, text messages, in-app messaging, push notifications).

Online behavioural advertising and some types of social media marketing are not classed as electronic mail under PECR but these are still direct marketing communications.

The definition is designed to be technology neutral and is therefore not limited to traditional forms of direct marketing such as telesales or mailshots, but can extend to online marketing, social networking or any other emerging channels of communication or approach.

Any background processing that takes place to enable or target those communications is also processing for direct marketing for purposes. See the section above What are direct marketing purposes? for further information.

WHAT DOES 'DIRECTED TO' MEAN?

The key element of the definition is that the marketing material must be 'directed to' particular individuals. For example:
- personally addressed post;
- calls to a particular telephone number;
- emails sent to a particular email account;
- online advertising that is targeted to a particular individual; and
- advertising on social media that is targeted to a particular individual.

Indiscriminate blanket marketing does not therefore fall within this definition of direct marketing. For example, leaflets delivered to every house in an area, magazine inserts, or adverts shown to every person who views a website.

Your marketing material is still 'directed to' particular individuals if you process their personal data behind the scenes, then remove their name from the resulting mailing. Omitting names from the marketing material you send does not stop it from being direct marketing.

WHAT IS 'SOLICITED' AND 'UNSOLICITED' MARKETING?

There is no restriction on sending 'solicited' direct marketing – that is, marketing material that the person has specifically requested. PECR rules only apply to 'unsolicited' direct marketing messages, and the GDPR does not prevent you providing information which someone has asked for. So, if someone specifically asks you to send them particular marketing material, you can do so.

Example
An individual submits an online form to a double glazing company requesting a quote. By sending this quote to the individual the company is responding to the individual's request, and so the marketing is solicited.

If someone specifically signs up to a service for the sole purpose of receiving marketing within certain defined parameters, we accept that messages sent within the parameters of that service are solicited. For example, some types of loyalty schemes or offer schemes.

If the direct marketing has not been specifically requested, it is unsolicited and the PECR rules apply. This is true even if the customer has 'opted in' to receiving marketing in general from you.

Example
When they requested the quote for double glazing, the individual also ticked a box opting in to receiving information about future home improvement offers from the company. A few months later, the company sends an email with details of a new offer.
This is unsolicited marketing, because the customer did not contact the company to specifically request information about that particular offer. However, this does not mean that the company should not have sent details of the new offer. They can do so because the individual has consented to receiving these offers.

An opt-in means that the individual is happy to receive further marketing in future, and is likely to mean that unsolicited marketing is lawful. But it is still likely to be unsolicited marketing, which means the PECR rules apply. See the section on <u>Sending direct marketing messages</u> for further information.

IS MARKET RESEARCH DIRECT MARKETING?

Market research will not constitute direct marketing if you contact individuals to conduct genuine market research (or you contract a research firm to do so). For example your purpose is to use market research to make decisions for commercial or public policy, or product development and there is no direct marketing purpose involved. However, you still need to comply with other provisions of the GDPR, and in particular ensure you process any individually identifiable research data fairly, transparently, securely and only for research purposes.

What is 'sugging'?

If your market research is for a direct marketing purpose (ie to ultimately send direct marketing communications to individuals) it will constitute direct marketing. You cannot avoid the direct marketing rules by labelling your message as a survey or market research, if you are actually trying to sell goods or services, or to collect data to help you (or others) to contact people for marketing purposes at a later date. This is sometimes referred to as 'sugging' (selling under the guise of research). If the call or message includes any promotional material, or collects data to use in future marketing exercises, the call or message is for direct marketing purposes. You must say so, and comply with the direct marketing rules.

Do not claim you are simply conducting a survey when your real purpose (or one of your purposes) is to sell goods or services, generate leads, or collect data for marketing purposes – this is likely to infringe the GDPR when you process the personal data. If you call a number registered with the TPS, sent a text or email without consent, or asked someone else to do so you may breach PECR.

Unless the individuals' contacted agreed to this and all communications comply with PECR, you must not ask market research firms you employ to:
*   promote your products (this includes asking the research firm to use your goods/services as a way to incentivise participation); or
*   give you the research data for future sales or marketing purposes.

If during a genuine market research project you discover errors in your customer database, you can use the research data to correct these errors without breaching the GDPR or PECR. This is consistent with the obligation under the GDPR accuracy principle to ensure personal data is accurate and up to date. However, you should not deliberately use market research as a method of keeping your customer database updated.

Further reading outside this code

More information on market research, including professional standards for research projects and mixed-purpose projects, is available on the <u>Market</u> Research Society (MRS) website.

WHAT ARE 'SERVICE MESSAGES'?

The term 'service message' is not used in the GDPR or PECR but it is a way of describing a communication sent to an individual for administrative or customer service purposes. For example contacting a customer to:

- remind them how to contact you in case of a problem;
- check that their details are correct; or
- update them on your terms and conditions.

In these examples there is no advertising or marketing occurring and no promotional material being transmitted.

> **Example**
> A bank makes a telephone call to a customer about the administration of their bank account. The purpose of the call is simply to advise the customer that there is a problem with one of their standing orders. Therefore the call does not constitute direct marketing.

You must be able to justify that a message is a service message and not an attempt to promote or advertise for it to fall outside of the direct marketing definition. Care must be taken over the content and tone.

In order to determine whether a communication is a service message or a direct marketing message, a key factor is likely to be the phrasing, tone and context.

If a message is actively promoting or encouraging an individual to make use of a particular service, special offer, or upgrade for example, then it is likely to be direct marketing. However if the message has a neutral tone and simply informs the individual for example of a benefit on their account then these are more likely to be viewed as a service message.

> **Example**
> An individual holds a credit card which has variable balance transfer rates. The card provider wants to email the individual to tell them that the rate is changing for a limited period. Obviously the card provider needs to tell their customer about this.
> If the card provider emails the individual simply telling them this information, then this is more likely to be viewed as a service message. However if the message actively encourages the individual to make use of the rate change offer then this is likely to fall within the definition of direct marketing as the card provider is promoting the rate in order to gain further business from the individual.

> **Example**
> A mobile network provider sends a text message to a customer that states that they are reaching their monthly data limit and advises what the data charges are under its terms and conditions if the customer exceeds the limit. Because this message is purely informative about their account, it is likely to be viewed as service message. However if, for example, the mobile network provider also uses the message to encourage the customer to take up a special offer to buy more data, then this constitutes direct marketing.

You may need to send the individual a renewal or end of contract notice. These are unlikely to constitute direct marketing if neutrally worded and not actively promoting or encouraging the individual to renew or take on a further contract with you.

However, it is important to understand that you cannot avoid the direct marketing rules by simply using a neutral tone. For example a message from a supermarket chain sent to an individual saying 'Your local supermarket stocks carrots' is clearly still promotional despite the use of a neutral tone.

If the service message has elements that are direct marketing then the marketing rules apply, even if that is not the main purpose of the message.

> **Example**
> During a call about the administration of their account the bank also decides to outline its mortgage products. Although the main purpose of the call is for administration, because the call is also being used by the bank to promote other products and services, it now falls within the definition of direct marketing.

ARE REGULATORY COMMUNICATIONS DIRECT MARKETING?

The term 'regulatory communications' is often used to describe situations where a statutory regulator asks or requires the industry it regulates to send out specific communications to consumers (in sectors such as finance, insurance, telecoms and utilities). For example about new initiatives or to promote competition in the market.

Regulators have the interests of consumers in mind when asking particular sectors to send these communications. However, it is important to remember that the direct marketing provisions of the GDPR and PECR may apply to communications that are sent to meet a regulatory objective, comply with a licence condition or meet a wider public policy initiative.

The content and context of the message is likely to determine whether it is direct marketing, regardless of the wider public policy objective behind it. If the communication actively promotes the initiative, by highlighting the benefits and encouraging consumers to participate, it will constitute direct marketing.

The normal rules apply to your proposed method of communication. You should check phone numbers against the TPS and you should not send direct marketing to people who have issued objections.

Examples of when a 'regulatory communication' might not constitute direct marketing includes information that you have been asked to inform customers about that is:

* in a neutral tone, without any encouragement or promotion;
* is given solely for the benefit of the individual; and
* is against your interests and your only motivation is to comply with a regulatory requirement (eg the regulator is requiring you to tell people that they should consider using your competitors' services).

However this always depends on a case by case basis taking into account the particular circumstances.

See the sections on What is 'advertising or marketing material'? and What are 'service messages'? for further information.

CAN PUBLIC SECTOR COMMUNICATIONS BE DIRECT MARKETING?

The public sector is also capable of carrying out promotional activities. Just because your motivation might be to fulfil your statutory functions rather than for profit or charity, you can still engage in promotional activity. If, as a public body, you use marketing or advertising methods to promote your interests, you must comply with the direct marketing rules. For example, direct marketing in the public sector can include:

* a GP sending text messages to patients inviting them to healthy eating event;
* a regulator sending out emails promoting its annual report launch;
* a local authority sending out an e-newsletter update on the work they are doing; and
* a government body sending personally addressed post promoting a health and safety campaign they are running.

This is not an exhaustive list. It is important therefore that if you are a public body planning a promotional campaign you ensure that you are compliant with the GDPR and PECR.

However not everything you send to meet a public policy initiative will be direct marketing.

Example
A regulator wants to send an email to individuals promoting their new online complaints tool.
Whilst this email is ultimately to further the regulator's statutory function it is still direct marketing, therefore they must comply with the direct marketing rules.
However if the regulator sends an email in response to an individual's query which also includes information about its complaint service, this is unlikely to be considered marketing of that complaints service. This is because the context is different and the regulator is providing important objective information in response to the individual about their right to complain.

Whether or not the messages you send constitute direct marketing is likely to depend on the context and content of the messages. For example a text message sent by a hospital to confirm an individual's appointment is not caught by PECR because it is purely a service message not a direct marketing message.

A key thing to remember is whether the message is advertising or promoting something. Often this comes down to the tone of the communication.

Example
Scenario A
A GP sends the following text message to a patient:
'Our records show you are due for x screening, please call the surgery on 12345678 to make an appointment.'
As this is neutrally worded and relates to the patient's care it is not a direct marketing message but rather a service message.
Scenario B
A GP sends the following text message to a patient:
'Our flu clinic is now open. If you would like a flu vaccination please call the surgery on 12345678 to make an appointment.'
This is more likely to be considered to be direct marketing because it does not relate to the patient's specific care but rather to a general service that is available.

See the section What are 'service messages'? for further information.

It is important to remember that you must be transparent when collecting people's details and clearly explain what you will use their data for. This applies regardless of whether the message you send contains direct marketing or not.

ARE FUNDRAISING AND CAMPAIGNING MESSAGES DIRECT MARKETING?

Yes, direct marketing is not limited to the sale of good and services, it also includes fundraising, campaigning and promotional activities. This means that the activities of not-for-profit organisations such as charities and political parties are covered by the direct marketing rules.

Examples include:

* a university contacting its alumni to ask for donations;
* a charity appeal asking individuals to become supporters or leave a legacy donation;
* a political party contacting particular individuals to seek their votes; and

- a civil society group contacting people to encourage them to write to their MP or attend a public meeting or rally.

You still need to ensure that you comply with the GDPR and PECR rules even if you are contacting existing supporters.

Further reading outside this code

See our separate guidance on:

Draft framework code of practice for the use of personal data in political campaigning

PLANNING YOUR MARKETING: DP BY DESIGN

AT A GLANCE

[1.403]
A key part of the GDPR is accountability and you must be able to demonstrate your compliance. You must consider data protection and privacy issues upfront when you are planning your direct marketing activities. Depending on your direct marketing activity you may be required to conduct a DPIA.

Generally speaking the two lawful bases most likely to be applicable to your direct marketing purposes are consent and legitimate interests. However if PECR requires consent then in practice consent will be your lawful basis under the GDPR. If you intend to process special category data for direct marketing purposes it is likely that the only Article 9 condition available to you will be 'explicit consent'.

In most cases it is unlikely that you will be able to make using an individual's data for direct marketing purposes a condition of your service or buying your product.

It is important to keep personal data accurate and up to date. It should not be kept for longer than is necessary. Children's personal data requires specific protection in regard to direct marketing.

WHY IS IT IMPORTANT TO PLAN OUR DIRECT MARKETING ACTIVITIES?

It is important to plan your direct marketing activity before you start so that you can build in data protection and PECR. It is hard to retrofit GDPR and PECR into your direct marketing activities once you have started the processing and you may find that you are infringing on the direct marketing rules by not having planned properly. This in turn may also harm your reputation and your relationship with your customers or supporters. Therefore it makes good business sense to properly plan ahead.

A key part of GDPR is accountability. You are responsible for ensuring that your direct marketing practices are compliant and you must be able to demonstrate your compliance. You are likely to need to:
- adopt data protection policies;
- take a 'data protection by design and default' approach;
- maintain documentation of your processing activities;
- have written contracts with organisations that process personal data on your behalf; and
- carry out data protection impact assessments (DPIAs) (see the section Do we need to conduct a DPIA? for more information).

You must be clear which legislation applies to your direct marketing activities so you can follow all the relevant rules. In some cases only the GDPR or only PECR will apply, but in other circumstances both may apply. For example, if you are processing personal data when sending direct marketing by electronic message or when using cookies (or similar technologies) for direct marketing purposes.

Further reading outside this code

See our separate guidance on:

Accountability and governance

WHAT IS DATA PROTECTION BY DESIGN?

The GDPR requires you to put in place appropriate technical and organisational measures to implement the data protection principles and safeguard individuals' rights. This means you must consider data protection and privacy issues upfront when you are planning your direct marketing activities. You need to as a minimum ask yourself the following questions:
- Who is your target audience? Is it particular groups of individuals, is it business contacts?
- Are you a controller or a joint controller? Do you intend to use a processor to send direct marketing on your behalf?
- How will you ensure that your direct marketing activity is lawful, fair to individuals and your purposes transparent? (lawfulness, fairness and transparency principle)
- What specified direct marketing purposes do you intend to collect this data for? (purpose limitation principle)
- What personal data is actually necessary and proportionate for your direct marketing activity? (data minimisation principle)
- How will you ensure the accuracy of the data that you are using for your direct marketing activity? (accuracy principle)
- How long will it be necessary for you to keep the data for your direct marketing purposes? (retention principle)

- How will you ensure that appropriate security measures are taken with regard to the data you want to use for direct marketing purposes? (security principle)
- Will any of the personal data be transferred overseas?
- How will you implement and support individuals' rights?

Thinking about these questions will help your direct marketing to be compliant with the GDPR.

Relevant provisions in the legislation

GDPR – see Article 25 and Recital 78

Further reading outside this code

See our separate guidance on:

Data Protection by design and default Principles

ARE WE RESPONSIBLE FOR COMPLIANCE?

In most situations it is likely to be obvious that you are the controller and have responsibility for complying with data protection. However it is common in the direct marketing context to work with third parties and this can be beneficial to you – but you do need to ensure that your collaboration with others is compliant with the GDPR and PECR.

In particular you need to be clear who in the relationship is the controller and what your responsibilities are. It is also important that any work you do with third parties is lawful, fair and transparent.

In some instances you might choose to use a processor to assist with your processing for direct marketing purposes. A processor acts on your behalf under your authority and in line with your instructions. You are the data controller in this situation.

For example, you might use a processor to screen your telephone marketing list against the TPS or to print and send your postal marketing to the people on your customer list.

If you use a processor you must comply with the GDPR rules on controllers and processors. For example you must choose a processor that provides sufficient guarantees that they implement appropriate technical and organisational measures to ensure their processing meets GDPR requirements.

The GDPR and PECR do not prevent you from conducting joint direct marketing campaigns with third parties. However you and the third party need to be clear about your responsibilities under the legislation.

You need to be clear who the controller is, if you and the other party are both processing the personal data. If you are joint controllers then you must arrange between yourselves who takes primary responsibility for complying with the GDPR – but remember that all joint controllers remain responsible for compliance with the controller obligations which means action can be taken against any of you. You need to have a transparency agreement that sets out your agreed roles and compliance responsibilities.

If you are planning electronic communications as dual branding promotion with a third party, you still need to comply with PECR even if you do not have access to the data that is used. Both you and the third party are responsible for complying with PECR.

Example
A supermarket decides to support a particular charity at Christmas and sends out a marketing email to its customers promoting the charity's work. Whilst the email is promoting the charity, it also constitutes marketing by the supermarket itself as it is promoting its values.
Although the supermarket is not passing the contact details of its customers to the charity it still needs to ensure there is appropriate consent from its customers to receive direct marketing promoting the charity. Where possible it would be good practice for the supermarket to screen against the charity's suppression list.

Relevant provisions in the legislation

GDPR – see Article 26, 28, 82, 83 and Recitals 79 and 146

Further reading outside this code

See our separate guidance on:

Controllers and processors

Contracts and liabilities between controllers and processors The Guide to PECR

DO WE NEED TO COMPLETE A DPIA?

A data protection impact assessment (DPIA) enables you to analyse your processing and help you identify and minimise the data protection risks. It is an integral part of the accountability requirements of GDPR.

DPIAs are a legal requirement for processing that is likely to be high risk. But an effective DPIA can also bring broader compliance, financial and reputational benefits, helping you demonstrate accountability and building trust and engagement with individuals.

Article 35 of the GDPR says you must do a DPIA if you plan to:
- use systematic and extensive profiling with significant effects;
- process special category or criminal offence data on a large scale; or

- systematically monitor publicly accessible places on a large scale.

The ICO has compiled a list of processing operations where a DPIA is required as these are 'likely to result in a high risk'. Many of these operations that require a DPIA are relevant to the direct marketing context:

- large scale profiling;
- data matching – eg for direct marketing;
- invisible processing – eg list brokering, online tracking by third parties, online advertising, re-use of publicly available data;
- tracking the geolocation or behaviour of individuals – eg online advertising, web and cross device tracking, tracing services (tele- matching, tele-appending), wealth profiling, loyalty schemes; and
- targeting children or other vulnerable individuals for marketing and profiling.

Some of these processing operations require a DPIA automatically. Others require a DPIA if they occur in combination with any other criterion from the European guidelines on DPIAs. There are nine of these criteria that may act as indicators of likely high risk processing.

If your direct marketing activity includes processing of a type likely to result in high risk, you must do a DPIA before you begin the processing. You therefore need to carry it out in the early stages of developing a project, prior to processing personal data. You may need to consult with the ICO and so should build in time for potential consultation to your project plan.

You do not need to submit all DPIAs to the ICO for prior consultation. However, you must consult with the ICO if your DPIA identifies a high risk and you are not able to take measures to reduce this risk.

The DPIA is a dynamic document and you should review and update it to ensure it reflects any changes to your project. The review process does not stop once processing personal data commences. You should periodically review the DPIA at suitable intervals during longer term projects to ensure it remains an accurate assessment of the processing undertaken, the risks and the mitigations in place.

Good practice recommendation

Even if there is no specific indication of likely high risk in your direct marketing activity, it is good practice to do a DPIA for any major new project involving the use of personal data.

Relevant provisions in the legislation

GDPR – see Article 35 and Recitals 84, 89, 90, 91, 92, 93, and 95

Further reading outside this code

See our separate guidance on:

DPIAs

See also:

EDPB Guidelines on Data Protection Impact Assessment (DPIA)

HOW DO WE DECIDE WHAT OUR LAWFUL BASIS IS FOR DIRECT MARKETING?

You must decide and document your lawful basis before you start processing personal data for direct marketing purposes. There are six lawful bases for processing in the GDPR. The most appropriate basis to use depends on your direct marketing activity, the context and your relationship with the individual.

It is likely to be obvious to you that certain lawful bases do not apply to your direct marketing. For example vital interests does not apply in a direct marketing context. For other lawful bases it may not be as clear.

If you have a contractual relationship with the individual you might be able to apply the contract lawful basis to your direct marketing. However it is important to remember that this lawful basis only applies to processing that is necessary for the performance of that contract. It does not apply if the processing for direct marketing purposes is necessary to maintain your business model or is included in your terms and conditions for business purposes beyond delivering the contractual service.

For example, just because you may be able to rely on the contract lawful basis to process an individual's address to supply them with goods, does not mean that you can also use this basis to send direct marketing to them or profile them based on their purchases.

If you are a public authority you might be able to use public task for your direct marketing if you can demonstrate that the processing is necessary for a specific task or function set down in law.

Generally speaking the two lawful bases that are most likely to be applicable to your direct marketing purposes are consent and legitimate interests. However it is important to remember that neither of these lawful bases are the 'easy option' and both require work.

Your choice between these two bases is likely to be affected by a number of factors including whether you want to give individuals choice and control (consent) or whether you want to take responsibility for protecting the individual's interests (legitimate interests). However, the first thing you need to consider is PECR.

PECR requires consent for some methods of sending direct marketing. If PECR requires consent, then processing personal data for electronic direct marketing purposes is unlawful under the GDPR without consent. If you have not got the necessary consent, you cannot rely on legitimate interests instead. You are not able to use legitimate interests to legitimise processing that is unlawful under other legislation.

If you have obtained consent in compliance with PECR (which must be to the GDPR standard), then in practice consent is also the appropriate lawful basis under the GDPR. Trying to apply legitimate interests when you already have GDPR-compliant consent would be an entirely unnecessary exercise, and would cause confusion for individuals.

The table below lists different methods of sending direct marketing and whether PECR requires consent:

Marketing method	Does PECR require consent?
'Live' phone calls to TPS/CPTS registered numbers	√
'Live' phone calls to those who have objected to your calls	√
'Live' phone calls where there is no TPS/CTPS registration or objection	✦
Automated phone calls	√
Emails/texts/in app/in-platform direct messaging to individuals – obtained using 'soft opt-in'	✦
Emails/texts/in-app/in platform direct messaging to individuals – without 'soft opt-in'	√
Emails/text messages to business contacts (corporate subscribers)	✦
Post	✦ (not covered by PECR)

See the section below on How does consent apply to direct marketing? for further information.

If PECR does not require consent, legitimate interests may well be appropriate. Likewise legitimate interests may be appropriate for 'solicited' marketing (ie marketing proactively requested by the individual). See the section below on How does legitimate interests apply to direct marketing? for further information.

Good practice recommendation

Get consent for all your direct marketing regardless of whether PECR requires it or not. This gives you the benefit of only having to deal with one basis for your direct marketing as well as increasing individuals' trust and control. See the section How does consent apply to direct marketing? for the requirements of consent.

In order to be accountable, if you rely on consent you must keep appropriate records of the consent and if you rely on legitimate interests you must document how it applies to your processing.

Relevant provisions in the legislation

GDPR – see Article 6(1)(a), 6(1)(b), 6(1)(e) and 6(1)(f)

Further reading outside this code

See our separate guidance on:

Lawful basis for processing Consent

Contract

Public task

Legitimate interests

The use of cookies and similar technologies

See also EDPB Guidelines 2/2019 on the processing of personal data under

Article 6(1)(b) GDPR in the context of the provision of online services to data subjects

HOW DOES CONSENT APPLY TO DIRECT MARKETING?

The consent lawful basis is about giving people choice and control over how you use their data.

The GDPR defines consent in Article 4(11) as:

> "any freely given, specific, informed and unambiguous indication of the data subject's wishes by which he or she, by a statement or by a clear affirmative action, signifies agreement to the processing of personal data relating to him or her"

Individuals can withdraw consent at any time. You must make it as easy to withdraw consent to direct marketing as it was to give it. See the section What do we do if someone withdraws their consent? for further information.

Remember you do not automatically have an individual's consent to process their personal data for direct marketing purposes just because you have a pre-existing relationship with them – for example because they are your customer, previously donated to your cause, or are one of your alumni.

> **Example**
> An individual sees a charity appeal in a newspaper and decides to donate £5 by text message. However the fact that the individual has decided to donate on this occasion (and provided their telephone number to the charity as a result) does not mean that the charity has their consent to use their details to contact them about future campaigns. The charity cannot therefore use the individual's details for direct marketing purposes.

If you want to rely on consent to process the individual's personal data for direct marketing purposes you must meet all the elements of valid consent.

Freely given

The individual must:
- have genuine choice and control over whether or not to consent to their personal data being used by you for direct marketing purposes;
- be able to refuse consent to direct marketing without detriment; and
- be able to withdraw consent at any time.

You should not coerce or unduly incentivise people to consent to direct marketing. However in the marketing context there is usually some inherent benefit to individuals if they consent to marketing, eg discounted products or access to special offers. But you must be careful not to cross the line and unfairly penalise those who refuse consent to your direct marketing.

> **Example**
> Joining a retailer's loyalty scheme comes with access to money-off vouchers. Clearly there is some incentive for people to consent to marketing. However the fact that this benefit is unavailable to those who do not sign up doesn't amount to a detriment for refusal.

You must also be careful if you make consent for marketing a condition of accessing a service or benefit. For more information see the section <u>Can we make our services conditional on the individual receiving direct marketing?</u>.

Specific and informed

Your request for consent for direct marketing must cover:
- the name of the controller who wants to rely on the consent – this includes you and any third party controllers who are relying on the consent for direct marketing;
- the purposes of the processing – you need to be specific about your direct marketing purposes;
- the types of processing activity – where possible you should provide granular consent options for each separate type of processing (eg consent to profiling to better target your marketing or different methods of sending the marketing), unless those activities are clearly interdependent – but as a minimum you must specifically cover all processing activities; and
- the right to withdraw consent at any time – we also advise you should include details of how to do so.

You must clearly explain to people in a way they can easily understand that they are consenting to direct marketing. The request for consent needs to be prominent, concise, in plain language, and separate from your privacy information or other terms and conditions.

Whilst PECR takes its definition of consent from the GDPR it also reinforces the need to be specific and informed by requiring that the consent is to 'such communications'. For example you cannot make an automated call unless that person has consented to receiving that type of communication from you.

Unambiguous indication

It must be obvious that the individual has consented to you processing their personal data for direct marketing purposes. It must be a clear, affirmative act, where the individual takes a deliberate and specific action to agree to your direct marketing purpose.

> **Example**
> An airline's privacy policy states that they send direct marketing material to individuals who buy a flight from them. In order to submit the online form, individuals must tick a box to say that they have read that policy. However confirmation that the individual has read the privacy policy does not constitute an unambiguous indication that the individual has consented to receive direct marketing. Therefore the airline is not able to rely on consent as their lawful basis.

Pre-ticked opt-in boxes are banned under the GDPR. You cannot rely on silence, inactivity or default settings – consent must be separate, freely given, unambiguous and affirmative. Failing to opt-out of direct marketing is not valid consent.

Relevant provisions in the legislation

GDPR – see Article 4(11), Article 6(1)(a), Article 7, Recital 32, 42, and 43

Further reading outside this code

See our separate guidance on:

Consent

See also:

European Data Protection Board (EDPB) Guidelines on consent

HOW DOES LEGITIMATE INTERESTS APPLY TO DIRECT MARKETING?

If you do not need consent under PECR, then you might be able to rely on legitimate interests for your direct marketing purposes if you can show the way you use people's data is proportionate, has a minimal privacy impact and is not a surprise to people or they are not likely to object to what you are doing.

The legitimate interests lawful basis is made up of a three-part test:
*   Purpose test – is there a legitimate interest behind the processing?
*   Necessity test – is the processing necessary for that purpose?
*   Balancing test – is the legitimate interest overridden by the individual's interests, rights or freedoms?

We refer to this test as a legitimate interests assessment (LIA). You must objectively consider whether legitimate interests apply to your direct marketing purposes.

Recital 47 of the GDPR says:

" . . . The processing of personal data for direct marketing purposes may be regarded as carried out for a legitimate interest."

It is important to note that the GDPR says that direct marketing **may** be a legitimate interest. It does not say that it is always a legitimate interest and it does not mean that you are automatically able to apply this lawful basis to your direct marketing. Whether you can apply it depends on the particular circumstances.

The fact that direct marketing 'may be regarded' as a legitimate interest is likely to help you demonstrate the purpose test, as long as the marketing is carried out in compliance with e-privacy laws and other legal and industry standards.

You still need to show that your processing passes the necessity and balancing tests. You may also need to be more specific about your purposes for some elements of your processing in order to show that processing is necessary and to weigh the benefits in the balancing test. For example, if you use profiling to target your marketing.

It is sometimes suggested that direct marketing is in the interests of individuals, for example if they receive money-off products or offers that are directly relevant to their needs. This is unlikely however to add much weight to your balancing test, and we recommend you focus primarily on your own interests and avoid undue focus on presumed benefits to customers unless you have very clear evidence of their preferences.

In some cases direct marketing has the potential to have a significant negative effect on the individual, depending on their personal circumstances. For example, someone known or likely to be in financial difficulties who is regularly targeted with direct marketing for high interest loans may sign up for these offers and potentially incur further debt.

When looking at the balancing test, you should also consider factors such as:
*   whether people would expect you to use their details in this way;
*   the potential nuisance factor of unwanted marketing messages; and
*   the effect your chosen method and frequency of communication might have on vulnerable individuals.

Example
A theatre wants to send details of its programme of summer performances by post to people who have attended events there in the past and have not previously objected to receiving direct marketing from it. The theatre's purpose of direct marketing to increase its revenues is a legitimate interest. The theatre considers it is necessary to process the name and address details for this purpose and that posting the programme is a proportionate way of achieving this. The theatre determines that the impact of this postal marketing on the individuals is likely to be minimal but it includes details within the mailing about how to opt-out.

Given that individuals have the absolute right to object to direct marketing, it is more difficult to pass the balancing test if you do not give individuals a clear option to opt out of direct marketing when you initially collect their details (or in your first communication, if the data was not collected directly from the individual). The lack of any proactive opportunity to opt-out in advance would arguably contribute to a loss of control over their data and act as an unnecessary barrier to exercising their data protection rights.

Other examples of when it is very difficult for you to pass the balancing test include:
*   processing for direct marketing purposes that you have not told individuals about (ie invisible processing) and they would not expect; or
*   collecting and combining vast amounts of personal data from various different sources to create personality profiles on individuals to use for direct marketing purposes.

Remember if PECR requires consent then in practice it is consent and not legitimate interests that is the appropriate lawful basis.

Relevant provisions in the legislation

GDPR – see Article 6(1)(f) and Recital 47

Further reading outside this code

See our separate guidance on:

Legitimate interests

See also:

Article 29 Working party (which has been replaced by the EDPB) Opinion 06/2014 on the notion of legitimate interests of the data controller – whilst this was written under the previous data protection framework it is still useful guidance.

CAN WE MAKE OUR SERVICES CONDITIONAL ON THE INDIVIDUAL RECEIVING DIRECT MARKETING?

In most cases it is unlikely that you can make using an individual's data for direct marketing purposes a precondition of entering into a contract to buy your product, use your services or support your cause etc.

If the direct marketing is not necessary for the performance of that service or contract then the consent will be invalid because it is not freely given.

Example

A train company has signs in its carriages saying that free wifi is available for its passengers.

In order to access the wifi the passenger is required to provide their name, email address and telephone number.

There is a notice at the bottom of the sign up process which says:

I understand that by submitting my details I am agreeing to receive marketing from the train company.

If the passenger does not tick the box they cannot access the 'free' wifi – in other words accessing the wifi is conditional on them receiving electronic direct marketing.

It is not necessary for the train company to collect these details for direct marketing purposes in order to provide the wifi, therefore the consent is not valid.

If you believe that your processing of personal data for direct marketing purposes is necessary for the service, then you may be able to rely on the contracts lawful basis. However you still need consent if you want to send certain types of electronic marketing under PECR.

If you are considering legitimate interests as your lawful basis you must be able to demonstrate how making your service conditional on direct marketing is actually necessary and proportionate and how this impacts on the individual's rights and freedoms. See the section How do we decide what our lawful basis for processing is? for further information.

There may be occasions when making direct marketing a condition of service is necessary for that service. For example, a retail loyalty scheme that is operated purely for the purposes of sending people marketing offers, is likely to be able to show that the direct marketing is necessary for that service. But you need to be upfront and clear about this purpose and ensure that the consent individuals provide when signing up meets the GDPR standard. If on the other hand your loyalty scheme allows people to collect points when they shop, which they can then redeem against future purchases, you cannot require them to consent to marketing messages in order for them to collect these points.

Relevant provisions in the legislation

GDPR – see Article 6(1)(a) and Article 7(4), Article 6(1)(b), and Article 6(1)(f)

Further reading outside this code

See our separate guidance on:

Consent guidance

CAN WE USE SPECIAL CATEGORY DATA FOR DIRECT MARKETING?

Special category data is specifically defined in the GDPR. It is recognised as more sensitive and in need of more protection (eg racial or ethnic origin, political opinions, religious beliefs, health data or sexual life). If you want to use this type of data for your direct marketing purposes you must have a special category condition from Article 9 of the GDPR as well as having an Article 6 lawful basis for the processing.

There are ten conditions for processing special category data in the GDPR itself and the DPA 2018 contains additional conditions. These conditions are narrow to cover very specific circumstances and none of them relate specifically to direct marketing. In practice the only condition available for processing special category data for direct marketing purposes is 'explicit consent'.

Therefore if you do not have the individual's explicit consent you cannot process their special category data for direct marketing purposes.

Explicit consent is not defined in the GDPR, but must meet the usual GDPR standard for consent. In particular, it must be freely given, informed, specific, affirmative (opt-in) and unambiguous, and able to be withdrawn at any time. In practice, the extra requirements for consent to be 'explicit' are likely to be that it:

- must be confirmed in a clear statement (whether oral or written), rather than by any other type of affirmative action;
- must specify the nature of the special category data; and
- should be separate from any other consents you are seeking.

Special category data can be a particular issue if you are trying to better target your direct marketing by profiling individuals. If you are profiling for direct marketing purposes on the basis of special category data, you need explicit consent for that profiling – including drawing inferences about people's likely race, ethnicity, politics, beliefs, health or sexual orientation from other data. You also need to be careful that these assumptions about people do not lead you to process inaccurate, inadequate or irrelevant personal data.

Example

A supermarket wants to promote its baby club. It decides to use its loyalty card data to predict which of its customers might be pregnant in order to send them messages about its baby club.

Because the supermarket does not have its customers explicit consent to do this, it has infringed the GDPR.

Simply holding a list of customer names will not trigger Article 9, even if those names are associated with a particular ethnicity or religion, even if those names are associated with marketing on the basis of that inference. Likewise if you could infer special category data from your customer list due to the nature of the products you sell – eg you are a company selling disability aids – this will not trigger Article 9 unless you hold specific information about the individual's condition or specifically target marketing on the inference of their health status.

Relevant provisions in the legislation

DPA 2018 – see Sections 10, 11 and Schedule 1

GDPR – see Article 9 and Article 9(2)(a), and Recital 43

Further reading outside this code

See our separate guidance on:

Special category data

Consent

HOW DO WE KEEP PERSONAL DATA WE USE FOR DIRECT MARKETING ACCURATE AND UP TO DATE?

The accuracy principle of the GDPR requires that personal data is accurate and where necessary kept up to date. This is important for direct marketing.

For example you need to accurately record:
- the data that you have been provided with eg contact details;
- the source of that data;
- which methods of direct marketing the individual has consented to;
- objections, opt-outs, withdrawals of consent; and
- people's details on suppression lists.

You need to have a process for considering challenges that individuals may make to the accuracy of the data you hold about them. Individuals have a specific right under the GDPR to have inaccurate data rectified. See the section What do we do if someone tells us their data is inaccurate? for further information.

You must take reasonable steps to ensure that personal data you hold for direct marketing purposes is not factually incorrect or misleading. It is reasonable to rely on the individual to tell you when they change address or other contact details. It may be sensible to periodically ask individuals to update their own details, but you do not need to take extreme measures to ensure people's contact details are up to date such as using tracing services. See the section Can we use data cleansing and tracing services? for further information.

Example

A retailer sends direct marketing by post to an individual. The marketing is returned to the retailer marked with the words 'no longer at this address'.

The retailer complies with the accuracy principle by making a note on the individual's record to say that the address is no longer correct.

It is important that any suppression lists you use are kept up to date. For example ensure that you use the most recent version of the TPS to screen telephone numbers t before making live direct marketing calls.

You should have a policy to periodically review and update the data you hold for direct marketing purposes.

Relevant provisions in the legislation

GDPR – see Article 5(1)(d)

Further reading outside this code

See our separate guidance on:

Accuracy

HOW LONG SHOULD WE KEEP PERSONAL DATA FOR DIRECT MARKETING PURPOSES?

The GDPR does not specify how long you should keep personal data for direct marketing purposes. However the storage limitation principle says that you must not keep it for longer than you need it.

Therefore it depends on how long you need the data for this purpose. The onus is on you to properly consider why you need to retain personal data and be able to justify why it is necessary for your direct marketing purpose to keep it.

In order to comply with the documentation requirements of the GDPR you are likely to need a policy that sets your retention periods. Also, you need to tell people how long you will store their personal data or the criteria you used to determine the period, to meet one of the requirements of the right to be informed.

You need to remember that if you are relying on consent to send direct marketing that consent does not last forever. How long consent remains valid depends on the particular circumstances including:

* the context in which it was given;
* the nature of the individual's relationship with you; and
* the individual's expectations.

PECR is also clear that consent is only 'for the time being' which implies that consent lasts as long as the circumstances remain the same. The question is whether it is still reasonable to treat it as an ongoing indication of that individual's wishes. Depending on the circumstances it is likely to be harder to rely on consent as a genuine indication of wishes as time passes.

Consent for a one-off message, or consent that is clearly only intended to cover a short period of time or a particular context, does not count as ongoing consent for all future direct marketing.

> **Example**
> A retailer collects email addresses from individuals who have specifically asked to be kept up to date about a new product launch.
> Once the product has been launched the retailer needs to consider whether it is still necessary for them to keep these email addresses given that the specific reason that these were provided has now ended. The consent that individuals gave for the product launch does not cover sending direct marketing about other products.

If you obtained an individual's consent via a third party to send direct marketing they may be happy to hear from you at the time they gave their consent. However they are unlikely to expect to start receiving your messages at a much later date. This may be different in very specific cases where the circumstances clearly indicate that the individual would expect to start receiving marketing from you at a particular time in the future. For example consent given via a third party to receive your offers on seasonal products or annually renewable insurance services.

Good practice recommendation

When sending direct marketing to new customers on the basis of consent collected by a third party we recommend that you do not rely on consent that was given more than six months ago.

Remember individuals' can withdraw their consent at any time. If the individual withdraws their consent, you must stop any of the processing for direct marketing purposes that was based on that consent. See the section What do we do if someone withdraws their consent? for further information.

Individuals can also opt-out or unsubscribe from receiving your direct marketing messages. If this happens, you cannot send any further direct marketing messages to them.

Individuals can object to you using their personal data for direct marketing. If this happens, you must stop that processing. See the section on Individual rights for more information.

If you no longer need the personal data for your direct marketing purposes you should erase (delete) or anonymise it (ie so it is no longer in a form that allows the individual to be identified).

It is important to regularly review the personal data that you hold in order to reduce the risk that it has become irrelevant, excessive or inaccurate.

Relevant provisions in the legislation

GDPR – see Article 5(1)(e), Article 13 and 14, and Article 30

Further reading outside this code

See our separate guidance on:

Storage limitation

Consent

Legitimate interests

What is personal data?

CAN WE USE CHILDREN'S PERSONAL DATA FOR DIRECT MARKETING?

You are not necessarily prevented from using children's personal data for direct marketing purposes. The normal rules apply – for example, you must be transparent, comply with all the data protection principles and you must comply with PECR, if you are sending electronic communications.

The GDPR does highlight children's personal data as requiring specific protection especially for direct marketing. Recital 38 says:

"Children merit specific protection with regard to their personal data, as they may be less aware of the risks, consequences and safeguards concerned and their rights in relation to the processing of personal data. Such specific protection should, in particular, apply to the use of personal data of children for the purposes of marketing or creating personality or user profiles and the collection of personal data with regard to children when using services offered directly to a child . . . ."

The GDPR also says that you must explain your direct marketing purposes in a way that a child understands. Recital 58 says:

" . . . Given that children merit specific protection, any information and communication, where processing is addressed to a child, should be in such a clear and plain language that the child can easily understand."

If a child gives you their personal data, such as an email address, or information about their hobbies or interests, then they may not realise that you will use it to market them, and they may not even understand what marketing is and how it works. This may lead to them receiving direct marketing that they do not want. If they are also unable to critically assess the content of the marketing then their lack of awareness of the consequences of providing their personal data may make them vulnerable in more significant ways. For example, they may be influenced to make unhealthy food choices, or to spend money on goods that they have no use for or cannot afford.

So, if you wish to use a child's personal data for direct marketing you need to think about if and how you can mitigate these risks and take into account their reduced ability to recognise and critically assess the purposes behind your processing and the potential consequences of providing their personal data to you. You should not exploit any lack of understanding or vulnerability.

Advertising standards stipulate that marketing targeted directly at or featuring children should not contain anything that is likely to result in their physical, mental or moral harm and must not exploit their credulity, loyalty, vulnerability or lack of experience. For example some adverting industry standards ban or limit direct marketing of certain types of products to services (eg gambling, high fat, salt or sugar foods in adverts aimed at children).

Whilst you are not prevented from profiling children for the purposes of direct marketing you need to take particular care if you do so to ensure that any marketing they receive as a result of your profiling complies with advertising standards and is not detrimental to their health or wellbeing.

The EDPB Guidelines on Automated Individual decision-making and Profiling state:

"Because children represent a more vulnerable group of society, organisations should, in general, refrain from profiling them for marketing purposes. Children can be particularly susceptible in the online environment and more easily influenced by behavioural advertising. For example, in online gaming, profiling can be used to target players that the algorithm considers are more likely to spend money on the game as well as providing more personalised adverts. The age and maturity of the child may affect their ability to understand the motivation behind this type of marketing or the consequences."

You should also note that the child's right to object to your processing their personal data for direct marketing also extends to any profiling that is related to that direct marketing. So if the child (or someone acting on their behalf) asks you to stop profiling for this purpose, then you must do so.

You must complete a DPIA if you intend to target children (or other vulnerable individuals) for direct marketing purposes. See the section Do we need to complete a DPIA? for further information.

Further reading outside this code

See our separate guidance on:

Children

Draft Age appropriate design code of practice

DPIAs

See also:

EDPB Guidelines on Automated Individual decision-making and Profiling

Sector specific guidance on marketing to children eg Advertising Standards Authority

GENERATING LEADS AND COLLECTING CONTACT DETAILS

AT A GLANCE

[1.404]
Transparency is a key part of the GDPR and as part of this individuals have the right to be informed about your collection and use of their personal data for direct marketing purposes.

If you collect data directly from individuals you must provide privacy information at the time you collect their details. If you collect personal data from sources other than the individual (eg public sources or from third parties) you must provide privacy information within a reasonable period of obtaining the data and no later than one month from the date of collection. Your privacy information must be in clear and plain language and easily accessible.

If you are considering buying or renting direct marketing lists you must ensure you have completed appropriate due diligence.

WHAT IS LEAD GENERATION?

There are a number of ways that you may decide to generate leads and seek contact details to use for your direct marketing purposes. For example from:

- the individuals who buy your products and services or support your cause (ie people who have a direct relationship with you);
- third parties who sell or rent lists of contact details; or
- publicly available sources.

Whichever method you wish to use, you must ensure that your processing is fair, lawful and transparent. This includes giving individuals appropriate privacy information about what you intend to do with their data.

WHAT DO WE NEED TO TELL PEOPLE IF WE COLLECT THEIR DATA DIRECTLY FROM THEM?

Transparency is a key part of the GDPR and as part of this individuals have the right to be informed about your collection and use of their personal data for direct marketing purposes.

Article 13 of the GDPR contains a list of the information that you must provide to individuals if you collect their personal data directly from them. For example you must:

- explain why you are using people's personal data (eg to send postal marketing, profile people's buying habits and interests etc);
- tell people who the third parties are that you intend to share their data with or the specific categories that they fall into if applicable;
- tell people what your retention periods are for the data that you are using for direct marketing purposes;
- say which lawful bases you are relying on for your direct marketing;
- say what the legitimate interests are if you are using legitimate interests as your lawful basis;
- tell people about the right to withdraw consent if you are relying on consent as your lawful basis;
- provide details about any solely automated decisions (including profiling) that have legal or similarly significant effects which you intend to make; and
- tell people what rights they have under the GDPR (including the right to object to your direct marketing).

You must provide this privacy information to individuals at the time you collect their details. If at later date you want to process for purposes other than those which you initially collected the data for you need to give individuals further privacy information (assuming the new purposes are fair and lawful.

See the section below <u>How do we tell people that we want to use their personal data for direct marketing?</u> for further information.

Relevant provisions in the legislation

GDPR – see Article 5(1), and Article 13

Further reading outside this code

See our separate guidance on:

Right to be informed

WHAT DO WE NEED TO TELL PEOPLE IF WE COLLECT THEIR DATA FROM OTHER SOURCES?

If you collect personal data indirectly, ie from sources other than the individual, you must still be transparent and comply with the right to be informed. Other sources could include publicly available data, third parties such as data brokers, or other organisations that you work with.

Article 14 of the GDPR contains a list of the information you must provide to individuals if you have not collected their personal data directly from them. In general these requirements are the same as when you collect the data directly from the individual but you also need to provide:

- details of the categories (types) of the individual's personal data that you have collected (eg contact details, interests, ethnicity etc); and
- the source of their personal data (eg the name of the third party, the name of the publicly available source).

You must provide privacy information to individuals within a reasonable period and at the latest within a month of obtaining their data.

If you plan to use the personal data you obtain to send direct marketing to the individual it relates to, or to disclose to someone else, the latest point at which you must provide the information is when you first communicate with the individual or disclose their data to someone else. However it is important to remember that the one month time limit still applies in these situations. For example, if you plan on disclosing an individual's personal data to someone else for direct marketing purposes two months after obtaining it, you must still provide that individual with privacy information within a month of obtaining the data.

> **Example**
> A travel company obtains a list of contact details from Company Z.
> Three weeks after obtaining the data the travel company sends out its brochure to the people on the list along with details of its privacy information which includes the types of information it holds (names and addresses) and details of the source of the individual's personal data (Company Z).

There are a number of exceptions to Article 14 requirements. The majority are unlikely to be applicable in a direct marketing context but the following may be relevant depending on the particular circumstances:
- the individual already has the information; or
- providing the information to the individual would involve a disproportionate effort.

Individual already has the information

To rely on the exception that the individual already has the information, you must be able to demonstrate and verify what information they already have. You must ensure that they have been provided with all of the information listed in Article 14 – you must provide anything that you are unsure about or that is missing.

Disproportionate effort

If you want to rely on the disproportionate effort exception, you must assess and document whether there's a proportionate balance between the effort involved for you to give privacy information and the effect of the processing on the individual. If the processing has a minor effect on the individual then your assessment might find that it's not proportionate to put significant resources into informing individuals. However the more significant the effect the processing has on the individual then, the less likely you are to be able to rely on this exception.

You are unlikely to be able to rely on disproportionate effort in situations where you are collecting personal data from various sources to build an extensive profile of an individual's interests and characteristics for direct marketing purposes. Individuals will not reasonably expect organisations to collect and use large volumes of data in this way, especially if they do not have any direct relationship with them. If individuals do not know about such extensive processing of their data they are unable to exercise their rights over it.

If you determine that providing privacy information does involve a disproportionate effort, you must record your reasoning in order to demonstrate your accountability. Even if disproportionate effort correctly applies, the GDPR still requires you to publish the privacy information (eg on your website).

> **Good practice recommendation**
> If it is relatively easy for you to inform individuals and in context it is useful to them, you should always do so, even if the effect of the processing on individuals is minor.

If you do not actively tell people about your processing it results in 'invisible processing'. Therefore you must carry out a DPIA before you start. See the section Do we need to complete a DPIA? for further information.

Further information on publicly available personal data is in the section Can we use publicly available personal data for direct marketing purposes?.

Relevant provisions in the legislation

GDPR – see Article 14

Further reading outside this code

See our separate guidance on:

Right to be informed

HOW DO WE TELL PEOPLE THAT WE WANT TO USE THEIR DATA FOR DIRECT MARKETING?

The privacy information you provide to individuals must be concise, intelligible, in clear and plain language, and easily accessible. This applies regardless of how you collect the personal data for direct marketing purposes (eg online, over the phone, in person).

You should tailor your privacy information to your audience – so think about who your customers, supporters, contacts etc are and what they are likely to understand.

You need to clearly explain the purposes for which you want to process the individual's personal data for. Vague terms such as 'marketing purposes', 'marketing services' or 'marketing insights' are not sufficiently clear. These terms are wide and potentially cover all sorts of processing for direct marketing purposes such as sending direct marketing messages, profiling or analysing individual's behaviours.

If you find it difficult to explain what you will be doing with people's personal data, or you do not want to be transparent because you think they might object to that processing, then this is a clear sign that you should rethink your intended purpose or processing.

> **Example**
> A charity wants to conduct wealth profiling of its supporters to determine their financial standing so they can target their campaigns appropriately. It includes the following statement in its privacy information:
> 'We analyse our supporters and the donations they have made. Some of the results from this analysis provide us with an indication of the likely donations we may receive in the future.'
> This statement is vague and not clear what purpose the charity is using the data for. It does not explain to supporters that the charity wants to profile their financial standing to decide who has capacity to donate more money or who might leave a legacy.
> As the statement is not sufficiently transparent any processing based on this statement infringes the GDPR.

There is no set way that you should provide your privacy information. You can consider whichever method suits the way you are collecting the data. For example, you might consider 'just in time notices' in an online context or have layered notices. The key point is that you should be upfront about your direct marketing processing.

Any unusual or unexpected processing ought to be at the forefront of any layered privacy information. For example as it is highly unlikely that your customers or supporters etc expect you to collect additional data on them from other sources, this should therefore clearly be brought to the individual's attention.

Further reading outside this code

See our separate guidance on:

Right to be informed

See also:

EDPB Guidelines on Transparency

CAN WE USE PUBLICLY AVAILABLE PERSONAL DATA FOR DIRECT MARKETING PURPOSES?

The term 'publicly available' can refer to information sourced from various places, including:
* the open version of the electoral register;
* Companies House;
* social media; and
* press articles or 'rich' lists.

You might seek personal data from publicly available sources to find new customers or supporters, or to add to the profile or data you already hold about individuals.

The GDPR does not prevent you from collecting and using personal data from publicly available sources for direct marketing purposes. However you should not assume that such data is 'fair game'. The GDPR and PECR still apply and once you have collected this data you are a controller for it and you must comply.

For example, you must meet the transparency requirements of the GDPR and provide people with privacy information (unless you are relying on an exception). See the section what do we need to tell people if we collect their data from other sources? for further information.

You must also ensure that your processing of personal data is fair, taking into account the source of the data. You must consider whether what you intend to do with the data is unexpected to individuals. For example you cannot assume that simply because an individual has put their personal data into the public domain, they are agreeing to it being used for direct marketing purposes. An individual may want as many people as possible to read their social media post but that does not mean they are agreeing to have that data collected and analysed to profile them to target your direct marketing campaigns. Likewise just because an individual's social media page has not been made private does not mean that you are free to use their personal data for direct marketing purposes.

You must also comply if you are collecting personal data from publicly available sources in order to package it up and make it available to other organisations for them to use for direct marketing purposes you still need to comply with the GDPR. This means you are required to provide privacy information about your processing to the individuals whose data you collect. You must provide this within a month of obtaining the data or before you disclose their data to others, whichever is soonest.

If you collect people's contact details from publicly available sources and then send electronic marketing you may breach PECR. See the section on Sending direct marketing messages for further information.

WHAT DO WE NEED TO CONSIDER WHEN BUYING OR RENTING DIRECT MARKETING LISTS?

Many organisations, including data brokers, offer direct marketing lists for sale, rent or on license.

It is important to remember that you are responsible for ensuring compliance with the GDPR and PECR. Simply accepting a third party's assurances that the data they are supplying is compliant is not enough. You must be able to demonstrate your compliance and be accountable

You must be very careful about using these lists and undertake proportionate due diligence.

Due diligence when buying data could include ensuring you have certain details as described below:

- **Who** compiled the data – was it the organisation you are buying it from or was it someone else?
- **Where** was the data obtained from – did it come from the individuals directly or has it come from other sources?
- **What** privacy information was used when the data was collected – what were individuals told their data would be used for?
- **When** was the personal data compiled – what date was it collected and how old is it?
- **How** was the personal data collected – what was the context and method of the collection?
- **Records** of the consent (if it is 'consented' data) – what did individuals' consent to, what were they told, were you named, when and how did they consent?
- **Evidence** that the data has been checked against opt-out lists (if claimed) – can it be demonstrated that the TPS or CTPS has been screened against and how recently?
- **How** does the seller deal with individuals' rights – do they pass on objections?

A reputable third party should be able to demonstrate to you that the data is reliable. If they cannot do this, or if you are not satisfied with their explanations, you should not use the data.

You may wish to have a written contract in place confirming the reliability of the personal data, as well as making your own checks. The contract should give reasonable control and audit powers. However it is important to remember that you are still responsible for compliance and such a contract does not remove this responsibility from you.

Your own compliance

You need to be clear how your use of the list complies with the GDPR. For example, can you can demonstrate what your lawful basis is for processing the list.

You also need to screen the lists that you obtain against your own suppression lists. This ensures you do not contact anyone who has already said they object or want to opt-out of your direct marketing (unless they have given you consent that overrides their previous objection). See the Individual rights section for further information on suppression.

Once you have obtained the data, you must comply with the right to be informed and provide people with your own transparency information detailing anything they have not already been told. See the section What do we need to tell people if we collect their data from other sources? for further information.

You also must be prepared to deal with any inaccuracies or complaints arising from your use of the data. If you receive complaints from individuals whose details came from a particular source, this might suggest that the source is unreliable and you should not use it.

Relevant provisions in the legislation GDPR – see Article 6(1)(a), and Article 14

Further reading outside this code See our separate guidance on:

Consent

The right to be informed

CAN WE ASK OUR EXISTING CUSTOMERS TO GIVE US CONTACT DETAILS OF THEIR FRIENDS AND FAMILY?

You cannot escape your GDPR and PECR obligations by asking existing customers or supporters to provide you with contact details for their friends and family to use for direct marketing purposes. In practice it is very difficult to comply with the GDPR when collecting details for direct marketing purposes in this way or to demonstrate your accountability.

For example you have no idea what the individual has told their friends and family about you processing their data and you would not be able to verify whether these contacts actually gave valid consent for you to collect their data. If you want to do this you need to very carefully plan how you will demonstrate accountability and compliance – in practice this is likely to be difficult in most circumstances.

If you use contact details collected in this manner to send electronic direct marketing you are likely to breach PECR. For example, you would not have valid consent to send direct marketing emails, texts (the soft opt-in would not apply) or to make automated calls or to override a TPS registration.

PROFILING AND DATA ENRICHMENT

AT A GLANCE

[1.405]
Profiling and enrichment activities must be done in a way that is fair, lawful and transparent. If you are considering using profiling or enrichment services you must ensure you have completed appropriate due diligence.

If you are carrying out solely automated decision making, including profiling, that has legal or similarly significant effects on individuals then there are additional rules in the GDPR that you must comply with. If you want to profile people using their special categories of data you must have their explicit consent to do this.

If you use non-personal data such as assumptions about the type of people who live in a particular postcode to enrich the details you hold about an individual it will become personal data.

In most instances, buying additional contact details for your existing customers or supporters is likely to be unfair unless the individual has previously agreed to you having these extra contact details.

You are unlikely to be able to justify tracing an individual in order to send direct marketing to their new address – such tracing takes away control from the individual to be able to choose not to tell you their new details.

WHAT DOES PROFILING AND DATA ENRICHMENT MEAN?

Profiling is where the behavioural characteristics of individuals are analysed to find out about their preferences, predict their behaviour, make decisions about them or classify them into different groups or sectors.

Data enrichment is where you find out more data on individuals to add to the profile that you already hold on them.

Profiling and data enrichment can be very useful for direct marketing and there are often clear business benefits. For example, knowing more about your customers and supporters can help you tailor your direct marketing messages in order to get better response rates.

However you must ensure that any profiling or enrichment that you do, or that you buy from third parties (such as data brokers), complies with the GDPR and, where applicable, PECR.

CAN WE USE PROFILING TO BETTER TARGET OUR DIRECT MARKETING?

Profiling is defined in Article 4(4) as:

> "any form of automated processing of personal data consisting of the use of personal data to evaluate certain personal aspects relating to a natural person, in particular to analyse or predict aspects concerning that natural person's performance at work, economic situation, health, personal preferences, interests, reliability, behaviour, location or movements."

Profiling is not necessarily restricted to facts about individuals. Profiling for direct marketing purposes often involves predictions, inferences or assumptions about individuals.

Profiling might occur in direct marketing in the following circumstances:
* analysing loyalty card data to decide what new products to suggest to a customer;
* identifying high net-worth individuals in order to send them fundraising material about legacy donations;
* predicting what products an individual might buy based on their online browsing history;
* applying assumptions about an individual's personal circumstances based on their postcode;
* combining online and offline data to build up a picture of an individual's interests; and
* segmenting customers into different categories based on perceived characteristics.

Profiling can help you to target your messages to people who are more likely to buy your product or support your cause. But it can potentially pose significant risks to the rights and freedoms of individuals because:
* they might not know it is happening or fully understand what is involved;
* it might restrict and undermine the individual's freedom to choose;
* it might perpetuate stereotypes; or
* it might cause discrimination.

You can profile aspects of an individual's personality, behaviour, interests or habits in order to use this for direct marketing purposes, but you must still comply with the direct marketing rules and where applicable the rules on automated decision-making.

You must be transparent and clearly explain to individuals what you will be doing. You also need to make sure the processing is fair and lawful as well as ensuring the personal data you hold as part of the profile is accurate and not excessive for your purpose.

It is important to remember that you cannot profile individuals on the basis of their special categories of data without their explicit consent. See the section <u>Can we use special category data for direct marketing?</u> for further information.

If explicit consent is not required and you are considering using legitimate interests as your lawful basis, you need to give careful consideration to the three-part test. It is unlikely that you will be able to apply legitimate interests for intrusive profiling for direct marketing purposes. This type of profiling is not generally in an individual's reasonable expectations and is rarely transparent enough.

Remember, if you want to engage in 'large-scale profiling' or 'wealth profiling' you are required to complete a DPIA before your start processing. See the section <u>Do we need to complete a DPIA?</u> for further information.

Solely automated decisions

Article 22 of the GDPR has rules to protect individuals if you are carrying out solely automated decision-making including profiling that has legal or similarly significant effects on individuals. The profiling that you undertake for direct marketing purposes is only caught by Article 22 if there is no human involvement and there is a legal or similarly significant effect on the individual.

Automated profiling is likely to occur in online behavioural advertising because this happens without human involvement.

Whilst the majority of direct marketing based on solely automated profiling is unlikely to have a legal or 'similarly significant effect', there could be situations where it does for example:

- profiling to target vulnerable groups or children;
- targeting individuals known to be in financial difficulty with marketing about high interest loans;
- targeting known problem gamblers with adverts for betting websites; or
- using profiling to effectively 'price-out' individuals of owning a particular product by giving them a much higher price than other people.

If Article 22 is engaged you need the individual's explicit consent to profile for direct marketing purposes.

Further reading outside this code

See our separate guidance on:

Rights related to automated decision making including profiling

See also:

EDPB Guidelines on Automated individual decision-making and Profiling

Relevant provisions in the legislation

GDPR – see Article 4(4) and Article 22

CAN WE ENRICH THE DATA WE ALREADY HOLD?

Enrichment is where you use other sources such as data brokers or publicly available data to find out more information about your customers or supporters to add to a profile on them.

Examples of enrichment include obtaining information about:

- an individual's interests and buying habits;
- customer segmentation (the type of customers you have);
- postcode data (eg assumptions or census data about the type of people who live in a certain area); and
- enriching online data with offline data (and vice versa).

It is important to remember that if non-personal data such as postcode data is added to the details you hold about the individual it will become personal data. This means that you must comply with the GDPR. For example, you must ensure that this processing is transparent, fair and lawful.

You need to be careful that the enrichment is not unfair to individuals. It is unlikely that individuals will anticipate you seeking to learn more about them using enrichment or indeed understand what enrichment is.

If you are considering enrichment you need to check what you have previously told individuals about using third parties or public sources to gather extra data to create or expand a profile on them. Likewise if the data held by the third party is personal data, you need to check what that third party told people about selling that data to you. You are not able to enrich the personal data you hold if you and the third party (where applicable) did not tell people about this.

You must have explicit consent from the individual for processing if any of the data is special category data. See the section Can we use special category data for direct marketing? for further information.

As enrichment is profiling, you should also read the section Can we use profiling to better target our direct marketing?.

CAN WE MATCH OR APPEND DATA?

Data matching or appending is where you match the data you already hold on individuals with other contact details that you did not already have. For example, buying phone numbers for your customers to add to the address details that you already hold. These additional contact details are usually obtained from third parties, such as data brokers.

In most instances, buying additional contact details for your existing

customers or supporters is likely to be unfair, unless the individual has expressly agreed.

This is likely to be true no matter how clearly you explain it in your privacy information that you might seek out further personal data about individuals from third parties. This is because it removes people's choice about what channels you can contact them on for direct marketing purposes.

Individuals use different email addresses as a way of managing their data and relationships, including as a means to limit or to manage the direct marketing they receive. By getting that information from a third party, you may be going directly against their wishes.

You cannot assume that an individual wants you to contact them by other channels or has forgotten to give you the data. Even if they had forgotten, they still would not reasonably expect you to contact them via contact details they never gave you. It must be for the individual to choose what contact details they give you.

If an individual has consented via a third party for you to have their additional contact details to use for direct marketing then you are able to match this to what you already hold about them. However you need to make sure that the consent is valid.

See the section What do we need to consider when using profiling or enrichment services? for further information.

CAN WE USE DATA CLEANSING AND TRACING SERVICES?

Some organisations such as data brokers offer data cleansing and tracing services for direct marketing purposes. For example, these services are used for:
- removing the contact details of people who are deceased from a marketing list;
- removing contact details that are out of date; and
- tracing the new addresses of individuals.

Data cleansing that removes deceased records from your database is unlikely to be a problem under the GDPR (assuming this information is accurate) because the GDPR only applies to living individuals. Likewise removing out of date contact details helps you comply with the accuracy and data minimisation principles. However tracing is very difficult to do for direct marketing purposes in a way that is compliant.

Often you may become aware that an individual's contact details are no longer correct but they have not told you of the change. For example, because your direct marketing material is being returned to sender due to the individual no longer living there, their email address is no longer valid or their phone number is no longer in service.

There is no requirement for people to tell you when they have changed contact details so that you can continue using their data for direct marketing purposes.

However in some cases individuals may express a wish for their updated contact details to be shared. For example, the individual may have moved house and made clear to a third party data source, by ticking a box or some other positive action, that they wanted the source to inform further third parties of the change of address. In this instance you are able to continue to market them at the new address (assuming your initial collection of the data at the old address was compliant). If there's no evidence of a recent expectation that their updated contact details would be shared, it is highly likely that the 'tracing' will be unfair and unlawful.

You cannot assume that an individual has simply forgotten to tell you that they have changed their details. Even if they had previously consented to your direct marketing at their old address, this consent is not transferrable to a new address that they have not given you. Likewise under PECR, consent is non transferrable – it is specific to receipt of calls or texts to a particular telephone number, or messages to a particular email address.

Tracing an individual for direct marketing purposes takes away control from people to be able to choose not to tell you their new details. Your commercial interests in continuing to market them do not outweigh this. Therefore you are unlikely to be able to justify this processing under legitimate interests.

Whilst the GDPR requires you to keep personal data up to date 'where necessary', your processing must always be fair. The actions you take to update contact details must be reasonable and proportionate. It will be difficult to justify taking intrusive steps such as tracing to keep contact details used for direct marketing up to date.

It is not necessary to trace individuals, because it is more reasonable in a direct marketing context to rely on individuals to inform you of changes to their details.

> **Example**
> A university sends fundraising newsletters by post to the last address that they held for their alumni. Some of the alumni graduated a number of years ago. A large number of the mailings are returned to the university because the address details are now incorrect.
> The university decides to use a data broker to 'cleanse' its alumni database and provide up to date address details. The university then sends its newsletters to the new addresses.
> The university has infringed the GDPR by taking this action Because it is unfair to trace individuals in these circumstances and it takes away their control. The university's legitimate interest in raising money does not outweigh the rights of the alumni to choose not to share their new address.

If you already hold other contact details for communication with the individual, you could consider using these to remind them how they can keep their details updated with you. But you must be very careful to check that this contact is fair, lawful and transparent, as well as complying with PECR (where applicable).

See the section How do we keep personal data we use for direct marketing accurate and up to date? for more information on complying with the accuracy principle.

Relevant provisions in the legislation

GDPR – see Article 5(1)(d)

Further reading outside this code

See our separate guidance on:

Accuracy

The right to be informed

WHAT DUE DILIGENCE DO WE NEED TO CONSIDER WHEN USING PROFILING OR ENRICHMENT SERVICES?

You are responsible for ensuring compliance with the GDPR and PECR. It is not enough to simply accept a third party's assurances that the data they are supplying to you is compliant. You must be able to demonstrate your compliance and be accountable.

As part of your planning stage you should do appropriate due diligence before you use profiling or enrichment services. Due diligence could include having answers to the following questions:
* what is the third party's approach to transparency – do people know that the company has their data?
* what sources of data is the third party using – is using these sources fair?
* what does the third party's DPIAs say – have they completed any?
* when was the data compiled – how old is the data?
* records of the consent (if it is 'consented' data) – what did individuals consent to, what were they told and how did they give consent?
* is any of the data special category data?

A reputable third party should be able to demonstrate to you that the data is compliant. If they cannot do this, or if you are not satisfied with their explanations, you should not use the data.

It is important to remember that before you obtain data on your customers or supporters via such services you must ensure that undertaking this activity is compliant with the GDPR. For example:
* have you told people about using profiling or enrichment services?
* have you been sufficiently transparent about this and is it fair to do this?
* what lawful basis are you relying on and do/can you meet the requirements of that basis?

Relevant provisions in the legislation

GDPR – see Article 14

SENDING DIRECT MARKETING MESSAGES

AT A GLANCE

[1.406]
No matter which method you use for sending direct marketing messages the GDPR will apply when you are processing personal data.

The direct marketing provisions in PECR only apply to live and automated calls, electronic mail (eg text and emails) and faxes. The electronic mail 'soft opt-in' only applies to the commercial marketing of products and services, it does not apply to the promotion of aims and ideals.

PECR may apply differently to business to business marketing. PECR may still apply even if you ask someone else to send your electronic direct marketing messages.

WHY DOES THE TYPE OF MESSAGE MATTER?

The methods you use to contact individuals as part of your direct marketing campaign may vary. However the GDPR rules are the same no matter what method you choose to communicate with people. For example, you still need to tell people that you are processing their data and what for, and have a lawful basis for the processing in place, prior to contacting them.

In contrast the direct marketing rules in PECR vary depending on your

chosen method of contacting individuals and can also be different if you are contacting your business contacts. The rules can also be different if you are promoting aims and ideals rather than selling products and services.

DIRECT MARKETING BY POST

Direct marketing by post is not covered by PECR. But you must still comply with the GDPR if you are processing personal data as part of your campaign.

If you conduct a mail drop addressed to 'the householder' or 'the occupier' this is unlikely to constitute direct marketing because it is not directed to a particular individual. However you cannot use this as a way to get around the GDPR. If you process an individual's data to target them with advertising, merely omitting that individual's name from the final marketing communication does not prevent the processing being for direct marketing purposes. A name on an envelope is not the sole factor when determining whether someone's personal data has been processed to allow the marketing material to be 'directed to' that particular individual.

Before you start your postal direct marketing campaign you need to consider for example:
* Do people know that you intend to use the data for direct marketing by post?
* Have you screened the contact details against your suppression list of people who have previously opted out of your direct marketing?

- Do you have a process for dealing with people who exercise their right to object to direct marketing?

> **Good practice recommendation**
> Unlike live telephone calls and faxes there is no statutory preference service for direct marketing by post where individuals can register their objection to such contact. However we recommend that you screen individual's names and addresses against the mail preference service (MPS) prior to sending out the direct marketing. You should also be aware that screening against the MPS is a requirement under some industry codes.

DIRECT MARKETING BY 'LIVE' CALLS

Direct marketing by 'live' telephone call (where there is a live person who is speaking) is covered by different provisions of PECR depending on what the call is about.

In general the PECR rules on making live marketing calls are that you:
- cannot call numbers registered with the Telephone Preference Service (TPS) or the Corporate Telephone Preference Service (CTPS) unless the subscriber has consented to your marketing calls;
- cannot call the number of a subscriber who has previously objected to your calls;
- must say who is calling (eg the name of your organisation);
- must allow your number (or an alternative contact number) to be displayed to the person receiving the call; and
- must provide your contact details or a Freephone number if asked.

In short you can call numbers that are not registered on the TPS or CTPS without the subscriber's consent, but only if there is no previous objection.

There are however specific stricter rules for direct marketing calls about claims management services and pension schemes which are dealt with below.

If you want to call a number registered with the TPS or CTPS you must have the subscriber's consent in order to override their general objection to direct marketing calls.

> **Example**
> A utility company collects an individual's contact details verbally. During the conversation the company asks the individual if they would like to receive direct marketing telephone calls from it. The individual verbally agrees to such calls.
> Assuming the consent is valid, the utility company does not need to screen this number against the TPS or their own 'do not call' lists because the individual has consented to receive such calls.

It is not enough that someone simply failed to object to past calls, or failed to take positive steps to opt-out of your calls. For example, you cannot assume that failing to click on an unsubscribe link, or not replying to an email inviting them to opt-out, is notification that they do not object. They must have taken a proactive step to 'notify' you that they wish to receive direct marketing calls from you.

> **Example**
> A travel insurance company collects contact details using an online form and provides a tick box for individuals to use if they wish to opt-out of their live direct marketing calls.
> The company screens the phone numbers of those who did not opt-out against the TPS and its own 'do not call list'. It discovers that a small percentage of these numbers are registered with the TPS or have previously told the company they do not want their calls.
> Because failing to opt-out does not constitute consent to receive live direct marketing calls, this does not override the TPS registration or objection. The travel insurance company does not make the calls to these numbers.

If someone you have called in the past subsequently registers their number with TPS or CPTS, you cannot make any more direct marketing calls to them from that point. Even if they have not specifically objected to your calls before, registering with TPS acts as a general objection which you must respect. You can only call that TPS registered number again if the subscriber has already specifically consented to receive your direct marketing calls. If so, the fact that they later register with TPS does not override that specific consent, and you may continue to call them (assuming that they do not withdraw their consent for your calls).

> **Example**
> A charity has called an individual in the past to fundraise. The individual has never specifically objected to receiving the calls nor did they specifically consent to the direct marketing calls.
> When undertaking its regular screening against the TPS the charity notices that the individual has now registered their number on the list. The charity might be confident in light of its past relationship with the individual that they would not object to further calls, however it will breach PECR if it continues to make direct marketing calls to that individual.

You also need to comply with the GDPR if you are processing personal data when making the calls. For example because you know the name of the person you are calling. See the section on Planning your marketing: DP by design for further information.

In line with the purpose limitation principle, and in order to ensure fairness, you cannot make a direct marketing call to a number that you originally collected for an entirely different purpose.

> **Example**
> A bank records information about some of the individuals who are shareholders of its corporate account customers. It collects and holds this information to comply with its duties under anti-money laundering regulations. Unless the bank has obtained their prior consent, it is unfair to use this information to make marketing calls inviting those individuals to open personal accounts with the bank.

In order to be fair to individuals you should not make calls to them which would unduly distress people or cause them other unjustified harm. Be particularly careful if you are aware that someone is elderly or vulnerable, or if the nature of the direct marketing call might cause offence or stress. You should avoid frequent redialling of unanswered numbers or making calls at antisocial hours.

You must make sufficient checks of third parties and give them clear instructions if you outsource any part of your telephone marketing campaign, such as asking someone else to screen the numbers against the TPS or to make the calls on your behalf. You still retain responsibility for complying with PECR and the GDPR. See the section on Planning your marketing: DP by design for further information.

If an individual tells you they do not want your calls anymore you must respect this and suppress their details by adding it to your 'do not call list'. See the section What are direct marketing suppression lists? for more information.

Calls management calls

The rules on live direct marketing calls about claims management services are stricter than other types of direct marketing calls (with the exception of pension scheme calls).

This means the following services in relation to making a claim:
* advice;
* financial services or assistance;
* acting on behalf of, or representing, a person;
* the referral or introduction of one person to another; or
* the making of inquiries.

The term 'claim' means a claim for compensation, restitution, repayment or any other remedy or relief in respect of loss or damage or in respect of an obligation, whether the claim is made or could be made:
* by way of legal proceedings;
* in accordance with a scheme of regulation (whether voluntary or compulsory); or
* in pursuance of a voluntary undertaking.

You can only make direct marketing calls about claims management services if the person you are calling has specifically consented to your calls. This means that unlike other types of direct marketing calls there is no need to check against the TPS or CTPS, because you must have consent. For more information on consent see the section How does consent apply to direct marketing?.

If you have consent to make these calls then you must also:
* say who is calling (eg the name of your organisation);
* allow your number (or an alternative contact number) to be displayed to the person receiving the call; and
* provide contact details or a Freephone number for your organisation if asked.

Pension scheme calls

The rules on live calls for direct marketing of pension schemes (eg occupational pensions or personal pensions) are very strict. This type of call is banned except in specific circumstances.

Regulation 21B says that direct marketing of pension schemes includes:
* marketing a product or service to be acquired using funds held, or previously held in a pension scheme;
* offering advice or another service that promotes, or promotes consideration of, withdrawing or transferring funds from a pension scheme; or
* offering advice or another service to enable the assessment of the performance of a pension scheme (including its performance in comparison with other forms of investment).

You can make live direct marketing calls about pension schemes, if you meet all the requirements of the specifically defined exception.

For the exception to apply, firstly you must be a trustee or manager of an occupational or personal pension scheme or authorised by the Financial Conduct Authority (FCA).

Secondly you must either have the individual's consent to receive the calls or your relationship with the individual must meet strict criteria, as follows:
* you have an existing client relationship with the person you are calling (this doesn't include a relationship that you have established primarily in order to allow you to make such a call);
* that person might reasonably envisage such a call from you; and
* you gave them a chance to opt-out of such calls when you collected their details and in every communication you send them.

For more information on consent see the section How does consent apply to direct marketing?.

In order for you to be fair and transparent you should say who is calling (eg the name of your organisation) and allow your number (or an alternative contact number) to be displayed to the person receiving the call. You should also provide contact details or a Freephone number for your organisation if asked.

Relevant provisions in the legislation

PECR – see Regulation 21 and Regulation 24, Regulation 21A (as inserted by section 35 of the Financial Guidance and claims Act 2018) and Regulation 21B

Further reading outside this code

See our separate guidance on:

The Guide to PECR

DIRECT MARKETING BY AUTOMATED CALLS

Direct marketing by automated telephone call is covered by Regulation 19 of PECR. These are calls made by an automated dialling system that plays a recorded message.

You can only make this type of call if you have consent. General consent for direct marketing, or even consent for live calls, is not enough. The consent must specifically cover automated calls from you.

There is no need for you to screen against the TPS or CTPS because it makes no difference whether or not a number is registered with a preference service. You cannot make that call without the subscriber's consent, even if the number is not on these lists.

PECR also requires that your automated call must:
* say who is calling (eg the name of your organisation);
* allow your number (or an alternative contact number) to be displayed to the person receiving the call; and
* provide your contact details or a Freephone number.

You also need to comply with the GDPR if you are processing personal data when making the calls. For example because you know the name of the person you are calling. See the section on Planning your marketing: DP by design for further information.

If you intend to buy a 'consented' list of telephone numbers to use for automated calls, you need to undertake appropriate due diligence. See the section What do we need to consider when buying or renting direct marketing lists? for further information.

Relevant provisions in the legislation

PECR – see Regulation 19 and Regulation 24

Further reading outside this code

See our separate guidance on:

The Guide to PECR

DIRECT MARKETING BY ELECTRONIC MAIL (INCLUDING EMAILS AND TEXTS)

Direct marketing by electronic mail is covered by Regulation 22 of PECR. Electronic mail is defined in Regulation 2 as:

> "any text, voice, sound or image message sent over a public electronic communications network which can be stored in the network or in the recipient's terminal equipment until it is collected by the recipient and includes messages sent using a short message service"

This means it covers any electronically stored messages. For example email, texts, picture or video messages, voicemail messages, in-app messages and direct messaging on social media.

Currently the most commonly used forms of electronic mail are email and text messages. However the guidance on these two types is also relevant to any form of electronic mail.

In general under PECR, direct marketing by electronic mail requires that you have the individual subscriber's consent. However there is an exception to this known as the 'soft opt-in'.

If you intend to rely on consent you must ensure that it is specific to the individual receiving that particular type of electronic mail from you (for example specific consent for emails or specific consent for text messages). If you are intending to send direct marketing text messages it is important to remember that consent to use their phone number for live or automated calls does not cover direct marketing by text message.

See the section How does consent apply to direct marketing? for further information.

Example

An individual is buying a pair of jeans from a high street retailer. At the end of the payment the shop assistant asks the individual if they would like their receipt emailed to them. The individual agrees and gives their email address.

Later that day the individual receives an email that contains an electronic receipt of their purchase.

However the following day the individual receives a further email promoting the retailer's footwear sale.

Whilst the first email was compliant because it did not contain any marketing, the second email is not. This is because the individual did not consent to their email address being used for direct marketing and no information was given to the individual about it being used for this purpose. There are also GDPR issues in terms of fairness and transparency.

Example

An individual uses their mobile phone to call a takeaway to verbally order a pizza. The takeaway advises the individual how much the order costs and how long it will take to be ready.

Shortly after the call the individual receives a text message from the takeaway thanking them for their order and telling them how to opt-out of its offers. The individual then receives multiple text messages offering discounts on pizzas.

The individual did not consent to their phone number being used to send direct marketing text messages and no information was given to the individual during the phone call about it being used for this purpose.

The takeaway is in breach of PECR by automatically opting the number into receiving direct marketing text messages.

If you want to rely on the soft opt-in instead of consent see the section on The soft opt-in for further information.

Regardless of whether you are relying on consent or the soft opt-in, you must not disguise or conceal your identity and you must provide a valid contact address or Freephone number for individuals to opt out or unsubscribe.

You must comply if an individual tells you they do not want direct marketing by electronic mail, for example if they unsubscribe or opt-out. You must make it easy for them to withdraw their consent or opt-out. See the section on Individual rights for further information.

If you intend to ask or 'instigate' someone else to send your electronic marketing, see the sections on Can we use third parties to send our direct marketing? and Can we ask individuals to send our direct marketing? for further information.

You also need to comply with the GDPR if you are processing personal data when sending the electronic mail. For example because you know the name of the person you are texting.

Because an email address identifies a unique user and distinguishes them from other users, it is personal data, therefore you also need to comply with the GDPR. For example, you must provide transparency information to people and have a lawful basis for the processing. See the section on Planning your marketing: DP by design for further information.

If you use 'tracking pixels' within your direct marketing emails then you need to be aware that:

- regulation 22 applies to the email itself; and
- if the pixel involves storing information, or accessing information stored, on the device used to read the email – such as its location, operating system, etc – then PECR's rules on cookies and similar technologies (Regulation 6) will also apply.

See the section on Online advertising and using other technologies for further information.

Further reading outside of this code

See our separate guidance on:

What is personal data?

Cookies and similar technologies

THE 'SOFT OPT-IN'

The term 'soft opt-in' is not used in PECR, but it is commonly used to describe the exception to the consent requirement of Regulation 22.

Regulation 22(3) says:

"A person may send or instigate the sending of electronic mail for the purposes of direct marketing where—

    (a)   that person has obtained the contact details of the recipient of that electronic mail in the course of the sale or negotiations for the sale of a product or service to that recipient;

    (b)   the direct marketing is in respect of that person's similar products and services only; and

    (c)   the recipient has been given a simple means of refusing (free of charge except for the costs of the transmission of the refusal) the use of his contact details for the purposes of such direct marketing, at the time that the details were initially collected, and, where he did not initially refuse the use of the details, at the time of each subsequent communication."

The soft opt-in only applies to electronic mail (eg emails and texts), it does not apply to other methods of direct marketing. If you want to use the soft opt-in you must meet all of its requirements. It breaks down into five requirements;

(1)   You obtained the contact details;

(2)   In the course of a sale or negotiation of a sale of a product or service;

(3)   Your similar products and services are being marketed;

(4)   Opportunity to refuse or opt-out given when you collected the details; and

(5)   Opportunity to refuse or opt-out given in every communication.

These requirements are described in detail below.

1) You obtained the contact details

You must have obtained the contact details directly from the individual. If the contact details were obtained by someone else then the soft opt-in does not apply.

Example

A restaurant chain is offered a list of individuals' mobile phone numbers which the third party claims are 'soft opt-in compliant'.

If the restaurant chain uses this list to send direct marketing text messages they will breach PECR. The soft opt-in does not apply because the restaurant chain did not obtain the contact details direct from the individuals. There is no such thing as a third party marketing list that is 'soft opt-in compliant'.

---

2) In the course of a sale or negotiation of a sale of a product or service

The individual does not actually need to have bought anything from you to trigger the soft opt-in. It is enough if 'negotiations for a sale' took place. This means that the individual should have actively expressed an interest in buying your products or services. For example, by requesting a quote or asking for more details of what you offer. There must be some form of express communication.

Example

A customer logs into a company's website to browse its range of products. This is not enough to constitute negotiations. But if the customer completes an online enquiry form asking for more details about a product or range of products, this could be enough.

The communication must be about buying products or services. It's not enough for the individual to send any type of query.

Example

A customer sends an online enquiry to ask if the company can order a particular product. This could constitute negotiations for a sale. But an enquiry asking if the company is going to open more branches in a particular location does not.

---

3) Your similar products and services are being marketed

You can only send electronic mail about your similar products or services. The key question is whether the individual reasonably expects direct marketing about your particular product or service. This is likely to depend on the context, including the type of business you are and the category of product.

Example

A customer buys bread and bananas online from a large supermarket chain. Afterwards they might reasonably expect emails about bread, fruit, and other groceries, but also a wide range of products including books, DVDs, kitchen equipment and other everyday goods commonly sold in supermarkets.

However, they are unlikely to expect emails about banking or insurance products sold under the supermarket brand. These products are not bought and sold in a similar context.

Because the soft opt-in applies to 'products and services' it can only apply to commercial marketing. This means that charities, political parties or other not-for-profit bodies are not able to rely on the soft opt-in for their campaigning or fundraising, even with existing supporters. In other words, you must have consent to send electronic mail promoting your aims or ideals.

4) Opportunity to refuse or opt-out given when you collected the details

You must give individuals a clear opportunity to opt-out of your direct marketing when you first collect their details. You cannot assume that individuals who engage with you are automatically happy to receive direct marketing from you in the future.

It must be simple to opt out. When first collecting a customer's details, this should be part of the same process. For example, your online forms should include a prominent opt-out box, and staff taking down details verbally should specifically offer an opt-out.

Example

An individual buys some trainers from an online shoe retailer and as part of the buying process provides their email address.

The retailer automatically adds this email address to their marketing database and the individual subsequently receives an email with a 10% discount code for their next purchase.

However these emails are not compliant with the soft opt-in. Even though the individual's email address was collected during the course of a sale and the marketing is for the retailer's similar products, the retailer did not give the individual an opportunity to opt-out of receiving direct marketing emails when it collected their details.

---

5) Opportunity to refuse or opt-out given in every communication

You must give individuals the chance to opt-out of every subsequent communication that you send.

It must be simple for individuals to change their mind and opt-out or unsubscribe. For example, in subsequent messages the individual should be able to reply directly to the message, or click a clear 'unsubscribe' link. In the case of text messages you could offer an opt-out by telling individuals to send a stop message to a short code number. This must be free of charge, apart from the cost to the individual of sending the message.

Example
A yoga studio sends its clients an email about forthcoming events. At the bottom of the email the studio provides the following information:
'If you don't want to receive these emails from us anymore please click here and we will unsubscribe you.'

Example
A hairdresser sends its clients a text message offering 30% off colour treatments. At the end of the text it says:
'To opt-out text STOP to 12345.'

Relevant provisions in the legislation

PECR – see Regulation 22(3)

Does the does the soft opt-in apply to fundraising or campaigning?

If you are fundraising or promoting aims and ideals, you need to take particular care when communicating by electronic mail. This is because the 'soft opt-in' exception only applies to commercial marketing of products or services. It does not apply to the promotion of aims and ideals eg campaigning or fundraising.

You might be able to use the soft opt-in for any commercial products or services you offer. But you are not able to send campaigning or fundraising texts or emails without specific consent, even to existing supporters.

Example
A charity has an online shop that sells various ethically sourced products. An individual buys some speciality teas from the online shop and when they provide their details they are given a clear upfront chance to opt-out of direct marketing by email.
If the individual doesn't tick the opt-out box the charity may be able to rely on the soft opt-in to send direct marketing emails about the products in its online shop (assuming the other soft opt-in criteria are met).
However the charity cannot send emails to the individual which were about fundraising because this is not covered by the soft opt-in.

BUSINESS TO BUSINESS MARKETING

Business to business (B2B) marketing is where you send direct marketing to another business or a business contact rather than to an individual in their personal capacity.

The GDPR still applies to B2B marketing if you are processing personal data. It is the PECR rules that may be different for B2B (when compared to contacting individuals). This depends on your chosen method of direct marketing and the type of business you intend to contact (ie they are a corporate subscriber).

It is important to remember that not all types of businesses are classed as corporate subscribers under PECR. Sole traders and some types of partnerships constitute individual subscribers which means they have greater protections under PECR.

The table below shows when PECR applies to business contacts:

Marketing method	Does PECR apply?
'Live' phone calls to corporate subscribers	√
'Live' phone calls to sole traders and some types of partnerships	√
Automated phone calls to corporate subscribers	√
Automated phone calls to sole traders and some types of subscribers	√
Faxes sent to corporate subscribers	√
Faxes sent to sole traders and some types of partnerships	√
Electronic mail (eg mails/text messages) to corporate subscribers	✢
Electronic mail (eg mails/text messages) to sole traders and some types of partnership	√

The PECR rules apply if you are intending to send direct marketing to your B2B contacts by live or automated call or by fax. It is important to remember, however, that some businesses (sole traders and some partnerships) register with the TPS, and others register with the CTPS. For live B2B calls, you therefore need to screen against both the TPS and the CTPS registers, as well as your own 'do not call' list. See the section Direct marketing by 'live' calls for further information.

You can send direct marketing faxes to corporate subscribers without their consent, but you cannot fax any number listed on the Fax Preference Service unless they have specifically said that they do not object to your faxes. You also cannot fax anyone who has told you not to. If you want to send marketing faxes to a sole trader you must have consent because the rules for individual subscribers are different. In practice for fax B2B marketing you need to:

* check if the business is an individual subscriber;
* screen against the Fax Preference Service;
* screen against your own do not fax lists; and
* include your name and contact address or Freephone number on all B2B direct marketing faxes.

The PECR rules on marketing by electronic mail (eg email and text messages) do not apply to corporate subscribers. This means you can send B2B direct marketing emails or texts to any corporate body. However you must still say who you are and give a valid address for the recipients to unsubscribe from your emails.

Good practice recommendation

It makes good business sense for you to keep a 'do not email or text' list of any businesses that object or opt out of your direct marketing by electronic mail, and screen any new B2B direct marketing lists against it.

Because sole traders and some partnerships are treated as individual subscribers you can only market them by electronic mail if they have specifically consented, or the 'soft opt-in' applies. See the section Direct marketing by electronic mail (including emails and texts) for further information.

If you are unsure whether the contact details belong to an individual subscriber or a corporate subscriber this puts you at risk of breaching PECR. To mitigate that risk you should treat the details as belonging to an individual subscriber and ensure that you comply with rules on electronic mail.

If you do not know the name of who you are sending direct marketing to at a business, then you are not processing personal data and the GDPR does not apply to your marketing. For example, you are sending your direct marketing by post addressed simply to 'the IT department' or your email to 'info@company. com'.

However the GDPR does apply wherever you are processing personal data. This means if you can identify an individual either directly or indirectly, the GDPR applies, even if they are acting in a professional capacity. For example, you must comply with the GDPR if you have the name and number of a business contact on file or their email address identifies them (eg initials.lastname@company.com).

If you collect an individual's contact details in their business capacity and you intend to send them direct marketing you must make them aware of this and have a lawful basis for the processing. Also if you intend to buy or sell a list of business contacts for direct marketing purposes you must ensure that the list complies with the GDPR if individuals can be identified from it. See the section What do we need to consider when buying or renting a direct marketing lists? and Selling or sharing data for further information.

Example

A business conference organiser collects the email addresses of delegates as part of the sign up process. This process does not say what the email addresses are used for and no options are given.

After the event the organiser decides they want to use the list to send emails to delegates about future events and that they also want to sell on the delegate contact list to third parties.

In terms of GDPR, no transparency information was provided to delegates about their data being sold onto other organisations. Also, the delegates were not made aware that their details would be used for direct marketing.

In terms of PECR, if any of the email addresses belong to sole traders or some types of partnership these are classed as 'individual subscribers'. As no consent was sought and the requirements of the soft opt-in were not met the organiser is in breach of PECR if they send direct marketing emails to these types of subscribers.

Assuming PECR does not require consent, in many cases it is likely that legitimate interests will be the appropriate lawful basis for processing individuals' personal data in their business capacity for direct marketing purposes. But there is no absolute rule and you need to apply the three-part test.

The GDPR does not necessarily apply to your collection of other people's hard copy business cards but this depends on what you intend to do with this information.

Example

At an industry networking event some of the attendees share their business cards which each other.

One of the attendees takes the business cards back to their organisation and places them loose into their desk drawer. At this point the GDPR does not apply to these business cards even though these have people's names on them. This is because the GDPR only applies to business cards if you intend to file them or input the details into a computer system.

One of the other attendees takes the business cards back to their organisation and adds them to their business contacts database. The GDPR applies to the personal data they have added to their marketing database therefore the organisation needs to ensure they comply with the GDPR.

Individuals have the right to object to you processing their personal data for direct marketing purposes and the right to withdraw their consent to your processing. If an individual withdraws their consent or objects, you must stop processing their personal data as part of your B2B marketing. See the section on Individual rights for further information.

Relevant provisions in the legislation

PECR – see Regulation 19, 20, 21, 21A, 21B and 23

Further reading outside of this code

See our separate guidance on:

Legitimate interests (contains a section on using legitimate interests for business to business contacts)

CAN WE USE THIRD PARTIES TO SEND OUR DIRECT MARKETING?

You might decide that you want to use the services of a third party to send your direct marketing on your behalf. You are not prevented from doing this, but you must ensure that you comply with the direct marketing rules.

Using third parties to send your direct marketing can take different forms, for example:

* you provide a third party with the contact details of your customers and ask them to do it on your behalf; or
* you ask a third party to use their own marketing lists to send your direct marketing content to individuals (sometimes known as 'hosted marketing').

Although in both these forms you are not physically sending the marketing yourself, this does not mean that you stop being responsible for compliance.

PECR applies to the 'sender', 'caller', or 'instigator' of the direct marketing message. This means that PECR may still apply even if you do not send the electronic message yourself or you do not hold the contact details that your direct marketing messages are sent to.

The term 'instigator' is not defined in PECR; however you are likely to be instigating if you encourage, incite, or ask someone else to send your direct marketing message.

Both you and the third party are responsible for complying with PECR. For example if Company A is encouraged by Company B to send its marketing emails then both companies require consent from the individual under PECR - Company A because they are the sender and Company B because they are the instigator.

In terms of responsibilities under the GDPR when using third parties to send your direct marketing, you may be joint controllers with the third party or there may be a controller/processor relationship. Whichever applies both of you have your own obligations and there are obligations around contracts and transparency arrangements, for example.

Further reading outside this code

See our separate guidance on:

The Guide to PECR

Controllers and processors

CAN WE ASK INDIVIDUALS TO SEND OUR DIRECT MARKETING?

The direct marketing rules also apply to asking individuals to send your direct marketing to their family and friends. This is often known as viral marketing or 'tell a friend' campaigns. You still need to comply even if you do not send the messages yourself, but instead instigate individuals to send or forward these.

Instigate does not necessarily mean that you have incentivised the individual to send your messages. Actively encouraging the individual to forward your direct marketing messages to their friends without actually providing a reward or benefit still means that you are instigating the sending of the message and you therefore need to comply with PECR.

Direct marketing emails and text messages require consent (the 'soft opt-in' does not apply in this situation) and you must be able to demonstrate this consent. As you have no direct contact with the people you are instigating the individual to send the direct marketing to, it is impossible for you to collect valid consent.

It is likely therefore that viral marketing and 'tell a friend' campaigns by electronic mail would breach PECR.

Example

An online retailer operates a 'refer a friend' scheme where individuals are given 10% off their orders if they participate. The individual provides their own name and email address and the retailer automatically generates an email containing its marketing for the individual to send to their friends and family.

The retailer is instigating the direct marketing therefore they have responsibility for complying with the PECR rules. Because the retailer does not have the consent of the friends and family these emails breach PECR.

However you are not responsible if the individual chooses, with no encouragement from you, to send their family or friends a link to a product from your website or details of your promotion or campaign, for example.

Relevant provisions in the legislation

PECR – see Regulation 22

ONLINE ADVERTISING AND NEW TECHNOLOGIES

AT A GLANCE

[1.407]
Individuals may not understand how non-traditional direct marketing technologies work. Therefore it is particularly important that you are clear and transparent about what you intend to do with their personal data.

Individuals are unlikely to understand how you target them with marketing on social media so you must be upfront about targeting individuals in this way.

If you are planning to use cookies or similar technologies for direct marketing purposes you must provide clear and comprehensive information to the user about these and gain their consent (which must be to the GDPR standard).

Regardless of what technology or contact method you consider, you still need to comply with the GDPR and PECR. If you are using new technologies for marketing and online advertising, it is highly likely that you require a DPIA.

WHAT DO WE NEED TO KNOW WHEN USING NEW TECHNOLOGIES FOR DIRECT MARKETING?

Using new technologies for direct marketing can be very beneficial to you in reaching new or existing customers and supporters, such as those available in the digital or online environment.

However, the tools, techniques and amount of personal data available differ substantially from traditional advertising methods. Additionally, the personal data you collect is often wider than that an individual actively provides to you. For example:

*   'observed data' – personal data you can obtain via observing how an individual uses or interacts with a technology or an online environment (eg the devices they use, the content they have generated); and
*   'inferred data' – personal data that is inferred or derived from the data provided or observed (eg inferences about the characteristics and interests of the user).

Individuals may not understand how these non-traditional marketing technologies work or how their data is used. As a result, these methods and technologies can have a greater potential impact on individual rights. It is therefore particularly important that you are clear and transparent about what you intend to do with this data and how you are processing it.

The type and volume of processing that you can undertake in the online world, and the risks associated with that processing, mean you are also highly likely to have to conduct a data protection impact assessment prior to the processing. See the section Do we need to complete a DPIA? for further information.

IS ALL ONLINE ADVERTISING COVERED BY THE DIRECT MARKETING RULES?

Whether your online advertising is covered by the direct marketing rules depends on your particular circumstances.

If your online advertising does not involve the processing of personal data – ie it is not based on any interests, behaviours or other information about individuals – then the GDPR will not apply.

For example, if the advertising is non-targeted (ie the same marketing is displayed to everyone who visits your website) or contextual (ie targeted to the content of the page rather than the identity or characteristics of the visitor) then this will not constitute direct marketing because it is not 'directed to' an individual.

However, even if your online advertising does not involve processing personal data, Regulation 6 of PECR may still apply. For example, you need to comply with Regulation 6 if you store information, or access information stored, on user devices (eg through cookies or similar technologies) – whether you do this for the purposes of online advertising or any other reason.

In the vast majority of cases, online advertising involves the use of cookies and similar technologies and therefore PECR applies. Additionally, if you engage in behavioural advertising – for example by personalising adverts on the basis of things like an individual's browsing history, purchase history or login information – this will constitute direct marketing. This is because the decision to target that particular user with a specific advert is based on what you know, or perceive to know, about the interests and characteristics of that individual and the device(s) they use.

What do we need to know if we use cookies and similar technologies for direct marketing purposes?

PECR does not have specific rules on online or behavioural advertising. However, if online behavioural advertising uses cookies or similar technologies it is covered by Regulation 6.

When we say 'cookies' we mean cookies and similar technologies. This covers any means you use to store information, or access information stored, on a user's device, including:

*   first-party and third-party advertising cookies;
*   fingerprinting techniques;

- tracking pixels and plugins, including those from third parties (such as social media platforms and ad networks/adtech providers); and
- other third party tracking technologies.

You may already use some of the above on your own website or be managing your advertising campaigns through using cookies on other organisation's websites, or both, whether through your direct relationship with that other organisation or via intermediaries.

If you are planning to use cookies for direct marketing purposes (whether or not they are targeted on the basis of those users' personal data), you need to comply with Regulation 6 by:

- providing users with clear and comprehensive information about the cookies etc that you intend to use; and
- getting their consent (which must be to the GDPR standard).

Regulation 6 contains two exemptions from these requirements, which are:

- the use of the cookie is necessary for the transmission of a communication; and
- the cookie is 'strictly necessary' for the provision of the online service the user requests (such as cookies used for authentication or security purposes).

Neither of these exemptions apply to online advertising (as well as tracking technologies and social media plugins). This means that you need to get consent from your users or subscribers for any cookie that you use for these purposes – whether the cookie is yours, or that of a third party.

You also need to explain what the cookies you use are doing as well as having valid consent. If you do not do either of these you will breach PECR. There are no alternatives to consent in PECR for the use of cookies. See the section How does consent apply to direct marketing? for further information.

As consent must be both freely given and a genuine choice, you also need to be very careful if you are considering requiring your users to 'agree' or 'accept' the setting of cookies for advertising purposes before they can access the content of your online service (this is known as a 'cookie wall').

This is because consent cannot be bundled up as a condition of a service unless it is necessary for that service. In many circumstances a cookie wall is unlikely to be appropriate as it will not demonstrate that you have valid consent.

How does the GDPR apply to online advertising?

It is clear that the GDPR applies if you are processing personal data such as an individual's name, account name or other similar information in the context of online advertising. However, even if you are targeting a particular user without knowing this sort of information, you still need to comply.

This is because you are 'singling out' a particular user and profiling them, making that user 'identified or identifiable, directly or indirectly', particularly when compared to other information you or another person may obtain or possess.

For example, this means that you must ensure that your processing is fair, lawful and transparent – this is particularly important if you are seeking to match an individual's 'online' behaviours with their 'offline' life.

Recital 58 of the GDPR specifically says online advertising is an area where it is important that you provide individuals with concise, easy to understand transparency information (additional highlighting):

> "The principle of transparency requires that any information addressed to the public or to the data subject be concise, easily accessible and easy to understand, and that clear and plain language and, additionally, where appropriate, visualisation be used. Such information could be provided in electronic form, for example, when addressed to the public, through a website. **This is of particular relevance in situations where the proliferation of actors and the technological complexity of practice make it difficult for the data subject to know and understand whether, by whom and for what purpose personal data relating to him or her are being collected, such as in the case of online advertising . . . "**

You need to have a lawful basis for your processing. In many circumstances it is likely that consent will be the most appropriate because PECR requires you to obtain consent when using cookies or similar technologies.

Also, if any of the personal data you process is special category data – for example where you target an individual because you infer that they might suffer from a particular condition on the basis that their browsing history contains medical websites – then you need an Article 9 condition in order to process that data.

Where Article 9 applies, you need to obtain the individual's explicit consent. See the section Can we use special category data for direct marketing? for further information.

Relevant provisions in the legislation

GDPR – see Recital 58 and Article 9

PECR – see Regulation 6

Further reading outside this code

See our separate guidance on:

Cookies and similar technologies Consent

See also our Update report into adtech and real time bidding

HOW DOES DIRECT MARKETING USING SOCIAL MEDIA WORK?

Social media platforms process large amounts of personal data about their users' behaviour and interactions. Generally, this falls into three main types:

- personal data users provide (eg their account profile information);
- personal data observed through use of the platform – social media platforms process personal data about how their users interact with the service, (eg their activity on the platform and the devices they use to access it, 'off platform' data collected by third-party websites that include the platform's plugins or other technolgies);
- personal data inferred or derived about the user (eg data created on the basis of data provided by individuals or observed by their use of the service). For example, social media platforms can generate 'insights' based on provided and observed data which constitute inferences about the characteristics and interests of the user.

Social media platforms may enable the targeting of individuals for direct marketing purposes based on all of the above types, alone or in combination.

It is therefore important to understand that, when you decide to use your social media presence to target direct marketing at individuals or use the platform's advertising services and technologies, many different data sources are likely to be used for this purpose. You need to be very clear about what data you will be using and why.

This type of targeted advertising on social media does not fall within the definition of electronic mail in PECR. However, if you use direct messaging on a social media platform, this is covered by Regulation 22 because this does constitute electronic mail. See the section Direct marketing by electronic mail (including emails and texts) for further information.

Can we target our customers or supporters on social media?

Social media platforms offer 'list-based' targeting tools that allow you to display direct marketing to users of the platform. This list-based targeting is where you upload personal data you already have to the platform (such as a list of email addresses). The platform then matches this data with its own user base. Any user that matches the uploaded list is then added into a group that you then target your messaging to on the platform itself.

These tools are generally known as 'audiences', although the precise term can differ depending on the platform. Examples include Facebook Custom Audiences or Linkedin Contact Targeting.

You must be transparent and clearly inform individuals about this processing so that they fully understand you will use their personal data in this way. For example, that you will use their email addresses to match them on social media for the purposes of showing them direct marketing.

You must be upfront about this processing. Individuals are unlikely to expect that this processing takes place, therefore you should not bury information about any list-based tools you use on social media within your privacy information. It is likely that consent is the appropriate lawful basis for this processing as it is difficult to see how it would meet the three-part test of the legitimate interests basis. However you will still need to ensure you also meet transparency requirements.

If an individual has objected to you using their personal data for direct marketing purposes, you cannot use their data to target them on social media, including by using list-based tools.

See the sections on Planning your marketing: DP by design, Generating leads and collecting contact details, and Profiling and data enrichment for further information.

Can we target people on social media who are similar to our customers or supporters?

Social media platforms also offer you the ability to build other audiences based on the characteristics of an original audience that you created using a list-based tool. These are commonly known as 'lookalike' audiences, although again the terminology may change depending on the platform.

These audiences generally comprise individuals that you have not previously engaged with, but who 'look like' your list-based audience (ie, they are individuals with similar interests, behaviours or characteristics to the kinds of people you already target).

When you create this sort of audience, the social media platform uses data it has about other users of its platform to find people who match the interests and behaviours of people you already target with your marketing.

Additionally, the widespread use of social media plugins and tracking pixels on other websites can result in users being added to this sort of audience. So you need to be aware that this can take place and you must demonstrate that you have considered the data protection implications.

From a data protection perspective, these activities are complex. Whilst the social media platform undertakes the majority of the processing activities, you are the organisation that instigated this processing and provided the platform with the initial dataset (ie, your original list-based audience). Therefore it is likely that both you and the platform are joint controllers for this activity.

However, you may not have any direct relationship with the individuals that are being added to this type of audience. You therefore need to be satisfied that the social media platform has taken all necessary steps to provide the appropriate transparency information to individuals. Particularly because this type of audience can change according to people's behaviour or interests.

You also need to inform individuals who have provided information to you that you intend to process their data to create these other audiences and ensure that you have a valid lawful basis.

If individuals have objected to the use of their personal data for marketing purposes, you also must not use their data for the creation of a 'lookalike' audience.

HOW ARE OTHER TECHNOLOGIES USED IN DIRECT MARKETING?

There are a number of different ways to reach individuals with direct marketing, and in some cases these are increasingly popular. This section looks briefly at some of these and other emerging methods of direct marketing. It is not designed to be an exhaustive list. Regardless of what technology or contact method you consider, you still need comply with the GDPR and PECR.

You should also remember the use of new technologies, particularly where they are used for marketing and online advertising, is highly likely to require a DPIA – see the section Do we need to complete a DPIA? for further information.

Direct marketing on subscription TV, on-demand and 'over the top' (OTT) services

We use the term 'subscription TV' to cover any service that requires the user to subscribe, whether it is free or paid for. This includes online services that deliver content over the internet instead of traditional means (known as 'over the top' or OTT services) whether or not they require a set-top box, as well as on-demand or 'catch-up' services (which may also be a feature of a wider subscription TV service). These services may be entirely subscription-based, ad-supported, transactional (where the user pays for individual pieces of content), or a combination.

In many cases subscription TV involves profiling, such as to personalise the service towards the user. This can simply involve making programme recommendations based on analysis of the content the user accesses. However, profiling can also be more extensive and can involve combining and matching personal data from other sources and the use of cross-device tracking. For example when a user accesses the service on devices like their smart TV, desktop computer or via a mobile app.

Many providers have direct marketing services that are similar to those offered by social media platforms. Such as where you can provide a list of your customers or supporters and the provider shows your advert on their service to those who are also their customer, or you ask the provider to show your adverts to their subscribers who 'look like' your customers or supporters. The data protection issues are the same as using social media to target marketing, so you need to be transparent, fair and lawful. See the section How does direct marketing using social media work? for further information.

You also need to assess whether PECR applies to your service, and take steps to comply. For example, the above type of targeted advertising on subscription TV does not fall within PECR's definition of electronic mail, so Regulation 22 does not apply. However, other PECR provisions may apply, depending on your service's circumstances.

Direct marketing using facial recognition or detection

Whilst facial recognition and detection technologies can be deployed in a number of circumstances, in the marketing context they generally involve billboards or digital screens in public spaces and retail establishments.

Facial recognition and detection involves processing biometric data. Facial recognition seeks to identify or verify a specific individual, whilst facial detection seeks to distinguish between different categories of individuals.

Biometric data is special category data when it is processed specifically 'for the purpose of uniquely identifying a natural person'. It is the end purpose of the processing which determines whether it is special category data, not whether the deployment has the technical capability to uniquely identify an individual.

It is unlikely that you will be able to use facial recognition technology to display direct marketing to specific individuals. It will be very difficult to comply with the lawfulness, fairness and transparency requirements of the GDPR when using the technology for this purpose.

Additionally, as facial recognition uses biometric data for the purposes of uniquely identifying an individual it constitutes special category data (whether this is for targeting them with direct marketing or other reasons). In order to process special category data to uniquely identify individuals for direct marketing, you must have their explicit consent under Article 9 of the GDPR (the other Article 9 conditions will not apply).

Unlike facial recognition, facial detection is not necessarily seeking to identify an individual but rather is segmenting the audience into categories – eg seeking to detect people's age, gender, facial attributes, their mood etc – and then showing them an advert based on these characteristics. Even in cases where a facial template is stored briefly and then deleted, this processing is likely to be personal data so the GDPR applies. However, categorisation does not automatically trigger Article 9. This is because it may not involve processing for the purposes of uniquely identifying an individual, but rather for the purposes of distinguishing one 'category' of people from another.

You must still be careful when using such technology and be clear about how it works and what the capabilities are. For example, a facial detection system may have the technical capability for use as a facial recognition system as well, depending on its features. Similarly, a facial detection system can still fall into Article 9 in some circumstances, such as where it stores a template to track the individual across an area covered by various screens and billboards (eg in a shopping centre). This is because it is then being used for the purposes of uniquely identifying that individual by singling them out, profiling their behaviour and taking some sort of action based on that processing. You also need to be careful of 'function creep' and remember that the GDPR requires you to only process the minimum of personal data necessary for your purpose.

Relevant provisions in the legislation

GDPR – see Article 4(14) and Article 9

Further reading outside of this code

See our guidance on

Special category data

See also EDPB Guidelines 03/2019 on processing of personal data through video devices

Direct marketing and in-game advertising

In-game advertising is where adverts are shown in computer or video games. It can take different forms such as an advert on an in-game billboard or an advert whilst the game loads; in many cases, the type of advertising used depends on the type of game in question.

Not all in-game advertising is covered by the direct marketing rules. For example, in-game advertising that is built into the game (eg 'static' in-game advertising) where all users see the same advert and that advert is not based on any characteristics of the users will not be in scope.

However, other types of in-game advertising that is more targeted at particular users (eg 'dynamic' in-game advertising) may be caught by the GDPR, particularly where it uses things like the user's location and other information such as time of the day the user plays to tailor the advertising.

You need to be transparent and fair with users so that they are aware that you will be targeting them with marketing in this way.

If you are sharing information such as the profile of the user or device information with third parties for direct marketing purposes this must also comply with the direct marketing rules.

Additionally, if your in-game advertising involves storing information, or accessing information stored, on user devices – whether these are gaming devices, PCs, mobile apps or anything else – then you also need to consider whether Regulation 6 of PECR applies.

Further reading outside of this code

See our separate guidance:

Draft Age appropriate design code

Direct marketing and mobile apps

Advertising within mobile apps generally works in the same way as on websites, with the use of technologies to connect the app to advertisers and developers. As with the web there can be many types of mobile app marketing, from display ads to video ads etc.

As with online advertising, you must comply with Regulation 6 of PECR if you use cookies and similar technologies as part of in-app marketing – whether this is for contextual or personalised advertising. This means that you must provide users with clear and comprehensive information about your use of cookies for these purposes and gain their consent. See the section What do we need to know when using new technology for direct marketing? for further information.

Even if you are not using cookies, it is likely that consent will be the appropriate lawful basis under the GDPR for any behavioural advertising or profiling that you wish to engage in for the same reasons as online advertising more generally.

It is also important to remember that consent must be separate and cannot be bundled into your terms and conditions for the use of your mobile app, unless you can demonstrate that consent for marketing is necessary for the provision of your service. See the section How does consent apply to direct marketing? for further information.

You must also be transparent and upfront about any advertising or profiling for this purpose and clearly explain what you want to use the data for.

Relevant provisions in the legislation

PECR – see Regulation 6

Further reading outside of this code

See the Article 29 Working Party (now the EDPB)

Opinion 02/2013 on apps on smart devices

Direct marketing and the use of advertising IDs

Device operating systems such as Android or iOS incorporate unique identifiers which can be used for marketing purposes. These are known as the 'Google Advertising ID' (ADID) on Android, the 'Identifier for Advertising' (IDFA) on iOS and the 'Advertising ID' on Windows 10.

Whilst often described as an 'anonymous identifier', an advertising ID forms an example of an 'online identifier' which Recital 30 of the GDPR states can be personal data.

When the advertising ID is enabled, your mobile app may access and use it for personalised advertising, similar to how online services use unique identifiers stored in cookies. App developers and ad networks can therefore link personal data they process with advertising IDs as a means of providing personalised advertising across their apps and services.

You should also note that advertising IDs can also be used in other types of online behavioural advertising, such as real-time bidding. For example, they can be included in the exchange of data that takes place in this ecosystem.

If you decide to use advertising IDs in your marketing, you need to know the specific details of how the different platforms use these identifiers, the information and controls they provide to individuals (and what you also provide), and how your use links to other advertising techniques. You also need to consider compliance with other relevant laws such as PECR.

Location-based direct marketing

Location-based marketing, sometimes known as geo-targeting, is where data is processed from a user's device that indicates the geographical location of that device, including GPS data or data about connection with local wifi equipment. This data can be used to target marketing.

If you are considering using location-based marketing techniques you must be transparent and clearly tell people about this type of tracking. You are also likely to need consent for this type of marketing as it will be difficult for you to demonstrate that you can meet the legitimate interests requirements, especially as it is unlikely to be in people's reasonable expectations that you will track their location in order to send adverts to them.

Additionally, PECR has rules on the use of location data. Regulation 14 applies to situations where a network or service collects information about the location of a user's phone or other device. For example tracing the location of a mobile phone from data collected by base stations on a mobile phone network to determine where it is or was.

However, these rules do not generally include GPS-based location information from smartphones, tablets, sat-navs or other devices, as this data is created and collected independently of the network or service provider. It also does not include location information collected at a purely local level (eg by wifi equipment installed by businesses offering wifi on their premises).

Ultimately you must be clear about whether PECR applies and comply where required.

Relevant provisions in the legislation

PECR – see Regulation 14

Further reading outside of this code

See our separate guidance:

Guide to PECR – location data

Draft Age appropriate design code

Direct marketing and connected devices

The term 'connected devices' covers 'Internet of Things' (IoT) devices like smart TVs, connected cars and wearables. It also covers broader concepts like smart cities.

It is important to note that where personal data is processed by connected devices, the GDPR applies. This is also the case if you seek to undertake direct marketing to users of connected devices.

Also, Regulation 6 of PECR generally applies to connected devices as in most cases they meet the definition of 'terminal equipment'. This means that if your marketing involves storing or accessing information from a user's connected device, you must comply with the requirements of Regulation 6.

See the section Is all online advertising covered by the direct marketing rules? for further information.

You must ensure that your processing is transparent and that you have a valid lawful basis if you want to use the data gained from connected devices for direct marketing purposes, including profiling, or you want to send advertising to users via connected devices.

If any of the data you are processing is special category data you need the user's explicit consent to process this for direct marketing purposes.

WHAT DUE DILIGENCE DO WE NEED TO DO WHEN CONSIDERING USING NEW TECHNOLOGIES FOR DIRECT MARKETING?

In most instances you will not be the developer of marketing or advertising technologies but rather you will be buying it in or using it to show your adverts. Given you are likely to have obligations under the GDPR and PECR, depending on the context, you need to undertake appropriate due diligence.

Examples of the types of due diligence you may want to consider include:

- Are you clear about the capabilities and functionality of the technology?
- Are you confident that what the product developer or provider is telling you is correct?
- Has the product developer or provider taken a data protection by design approach when developing the technology or service?
- Has the product developer or provider conducted a DPIA? (Although this may not be an obligation placed on them, it is good practice to undertake a DPIA, and this can also assist you in meeting your own requirements in this area. If the developer or provider is also your processor, they can assist you with your own DPIA.)
- Is any of the data special category data, and if so, how are the GDPR's requirements met?

You also need to have done your own DPIA where required, as well as ensuring you meet the other requirements of the GDPR and PECR.

SELLING OR SHARING DATA

AT A GLANCE

[1.408]
If you are planning on selling or sharing personal data for direct marketing purposes you must ensure that it is fair and lawful to do so. You must also be transparent and tell people about the selling or sharing.

DO WE SELL OR SHARE DATA?

There is a large trade in personal data for direct marketing purposes. A core part of the business of some organisations, such as data brokers, is selling or licensing data for direct marketing purposes. However selling data is not limited to these types of organisation. If you are contemplating selling or licensing data to other organisations you must ensure that you do so in compliance with the GDPR, and where applicable, PECR.

Sharing data for direct marketing purposes is not necessarily done for any monetary gain but is still mutually beneficial to you and the organisation you share it with. Lack of monetary exchange when you share the data does not absolve you from complying with the GDPR and PECR.

You need to be careful if you are planning on selling or sharing data for direct marketing purposes because you are responsible for ensuring that it is fair and lawful to do so.

CAN WE SELL OR SHARE DATA FOR DIRECT MARKETING PURPOSES?

You must ensure that you comply with the GDPR when selling or sharing data for direct marketing purposes.

If you obtain personal data from individuals with the intention of selling or sharing these details on, you must make it clear that you want to sell to third parties for direct marketing purposes.

Likewise if you obtain data from sources other than the individual, you must be transparent and tell people about your intention to sell or share the data. See the section on Generating leads and collecting contact details for further information.

If you are seeking to rely on an individual's consent, you must ensure that the consent was valid to sell or share their data for direct marketing purposes (eg specific, unambiguous, informed, freely given) and that you have clear records of it. You cannot infer that you have consent just because you are selling the list to organisations with similar aims or objectives to you. See the section How does consent apply to direct marketing? for more information.

Example
A charity sells its supporter database to another charity. The charity selling the list believes that its supporters would not mind being contacted by the other charity because it campaigns on the same issues.
Such an assumption does not override the GDPR. The charity should have made clear to its supporters that it wanted to sell their details to another charity and obtained their consent to do so.

You may be able to lawfully disclose data on the basis of legitimate interests. These might be your own interests, or the interests of the third party receiving the data, or a combination of the two.

Your focus is on justifying your disclosure when you carry out the three-part test. Although the third party's intentions and interests are directly relevant, your focus is on whether the disclosure itself is justified for that purpose. The third party is responsible for ensuring their own further processing is fair and lawful, including carrying out their own three-part test if they plan to rely on legitimate interests as their basis for processing.

As part of your balancing test you need to take into account the reasonable expectations of individuals when determining if legitimate interests applies to your sharing or selling of the data. For example:

Part 1   Data Protection: UK Law

- Do you have an existing relationship with the individual? If so, what is the nature of that relationship?
- Did you collect data directly from the individual?
- What did you tell individuals at the time?
- If you obtained the data from a third party, what did they tell individuals about reuse of the data by third parties for other purposes?
- How long ago was the data collected?
- Is your intended purpose and method obvious or widely understood?

You also need to look at the impact on individuals of your selling or sharing their data for direct marketing purposes. For example, will individuals have a loss of control over their data if you sell it?

As a safeguard when you first collect the details from individuals, you should include a clear, simple opt-out opportunity for people to use if they object to you sharing or selling their details to third parties.

You cannot always use legitimate interests to sell data for direct marketing purposes. For example, to sell unconsented data for email marketing.

If you want to sell a marketing list for use in telephone campaigns you should make clear to buyers whether you have pre-screened it against the TPS register, and if so on what date it was last screened.

It is important that you maintain records of how and when you collected the details and what individuals were told – this is part of your accountability requirements under the GDPR. You should be able to give buyers proper assurances about the data that you are selling and demonstrate to them that it is compliant with the GDPR and PECR.

If you receive erasure or rectification requests you may be required to pass these down the chain to the third parties who you have sold or shared the personal data with. See the Individual Rights section for further information.

Remember it is a criminal offence under the DPA 2018 to knowingly or recklessly disclose, or procure the disclosure of, personal data without the consent of the controller. This means that if you sell or offer to sell a marketing list of customers where you do not have the consent of the controller to do this, then you are committing a criminal offence.

Relevant provisions in the legislation

DPA 2018 – see section 170 (unlawful obtaining of personal data)

GDPR – see Article 6(1)(a), 6(1)(f), Article 13 and 14 and Article 30

Further reading outside this code

See our separate guidance on:

Draft data sharing code of practice

CAN WE OFFER DATA BROKING SERVICES?

Data broking services involve collecting data about individuals from a variety of sources, then combining it and selling it on to other organisations. Data broking can involve providing a variety of services for other organisations including:

- selling lists of contact details;
- selling copies of the open electoral register;
- enrichment;
- profiling;
- data matching;
- data cleansing and tracing; and
- screening services.

If you operate as a data broker you are still subject to the GDPR and the majority of the processing that you undertake is likely to be for direct marketing purposes.

In most instances data brokers do not collect the data directly from individuals or have any direct relationship with them. Data brokers instead rely on data collected from other sources such as publicly available data, third parties (eg competition websites or lifestyle survey companies), or buying data from other data brokers. Therefore it is particularly important that your processing is transparent, fair and lawful.

You need to ensure that you provide individuals with privacy information that clearly explains what you will be doing with their data, what the source of their personal data is and how they can exercise their rights including the right to object to direct marketing. You must provide this information to the individual within a month of collecting their data. See the section on Generating leads and collecting contact details for further information.

If third parties are collecting and sharing personal data with you for direct marketing purposes on the basis of consent, then you must ensure that the consent is valid (eg freely given, specific, informed, unambiguous, separate from terms and conditions etc).

Where data is shared with you for direct marketing purposes on the basis of consent, then the appropriate lawful basis for your subsequent processing for direct marketing purposes will also be consent. It is not appropriate to switch to legitimate interests for your further processing for direct marketing purposes.

Switching to legitimate interests would mean the original consent was no longer specific or informed, and misrepresented the degree of control and the nature of the relationship with the individual. This misrepresentation and the impact on the effectiveness of consent withdrawal mechanisms would cause a problem with the balancing test, meaning that it would inevitably cause the balance to be against you.

If you are considering collecting and subsequently processing using legitimate interests as your lawful basis, you need to objectively work through the three-part test (the legitimate interests assessment) prior to the processing and record the outcome. A key part of the balancing test is the reasonable expectations of individuals, and transparency will be vital. It is unlikely to be in people's reasonable expectations that you will be building extensive profiles on them in order to sell these to lots of other organisations.

Example

The European Article 29 Working Party (which has been replace by the EDPB) was of the view that consent should be required for data brokering. It stated in Opinion 03/2013 on purpose limitation:

" . . . when an organisation specifically wants to analyse or predict the personal preferences, behaviour and attitudes of individual customers, which will subsequently inform 'measures or decisions' that are taken with regard to those customers . . . free, specific, informed and unambiguous 'opt-in' consent would almost always be required, otherwise further use cannot be considered compatible. Importantly, such consent should be required, for example, for tracking and profiling for purposes of direct marketing, behavioural advertisement, data-brokering, location-based advertising or tracking-based digital market research."

The Working Party reiterated this view in its Opinion 06/2014 on the notion of legitimate interests of the data controller. Whilst both of these Opinions relate to the old data protection regime this view is still relevant.

See the sections How does consent apply to direct marketing? and How does legitimate interests apply to direct marketing? for further information.

Remember that you must have the individual's explicit consent if any of the personal data that you are processing is special category data or inferred special category data.

You must have a process in place to deal with individuals' rights including how you will notify the third parties that you have disclosed the data to when an individual has exercised a particular right. See the section on Individual rights for further information.

Further reading outside this code

See our separate guidance on:

Legitimate interests

See also:

Article 29 Working party (which has been replaced by the EDPB)

Opinion 03/2013 on purpose limitation

Opinion 06/2014 on the notion of legitimate interests of the data controller

(whilst written under the previous data protection framework these are still relevant guidance).

INDIVIDUAL RIGHTS

AT A GLANCE

[1.409]

As well as the right to be informed, the rights to objection, rectification, erasure and access are the most likely to be relevant in the direct marketing context.

The right to object to direct marketing is absolute. This means if someone objects you must stop processing for direct marketing purposes (which is not limited to sending direct marketing). You should add their details to your suppression list so that you can screen any new marketing lists against it.

WHAT RIGHTS DO INDIVIDUALS HAVE?

Individuals have a number of rights under the GDPR, including the right to:
- object;
- rectification;
- erasure;
- access;
- restriction; and
- data portability.

Some of these rights are very relevant in the direct marketing context. Two of them – the right to restriction and the right to data portability – are less likely to be relevant. However it is still important to be aware that these are available for individuals to use. Our Guide to GDPR contains further details on these two rights, if you need to know more.

The rights to objection, rectification, erasure and access are discussed in further detail in this section of the code.

Individuals also have the right to be informed – see the Generating leads and collecting contact details section for further information. In addition there are rights about automated decision making. See the section Can we use profiling to better target our direct marketing? for further information.

Relevant provisions in the legislation

GDPR – see Articles 13 and 14, Article 22, Article 15, Article 16, Article 17, Article 18, Article 20, and Article 21

Further reading outside this code

See our separate guidance on:

Individual rights

Right to restrict processing

Right to data portability

WHAT DO WE DO IF SOMEONE OBJECTS TO OUR DIRECT MARKETING?

Individuals have the right to object to your processing of their personal data for direct marketing purposes. Article 21(2) says:

"Where personal data are processed for direct marketing purposes, the data subject shall have the right to object at any time to processing of personal data concerning him or her for such marketing, which includes profiling to the extent that it is related to such direct marketing."

This is an absolute right. If someone objects, you must stop processing their personal data for these purposes. There are no exemptions or grounds for you to refuse the objection.

This right covers any processing that is for direct marketing **purposes** which includes profiling – it is not limited to sending direct marketing. This means that you must stop using their data for any direct marketing purposes. For example, using people's data to create direct marketing insights into particular geographical location or disclosing the data to third parties for direct marketing purposes.

You must make individuals aware of their right to object to processing for direct marketing purposes. Article 21(4) says this must be 'at the latest' at the time of your first communication with them. This right must be explicitly brought to the individual's attention, presented clearly and separately from other matters, and in plain language. It is also important to remember that the right to be informed (Articles 13 and 14) requires you to tell people of their right to object when you collect their details. See the section on Generating leads and collecting contact details for further information.

Individuals can exercise their objection right at any time. This means they can object straight away or in advance of you using their data for direct marketing purposes. It may also be possible for an individual to object via a third party opt-out service.

Good practice recommendation
Provide mechanisms for individuals to easily object to your direct marketing at the time you collect their details (where this is not already required or where you are not relying on consent to process).
This is supported by the EDPB Profiling Guidelines which say:
"In line with Article 12(2) controllers who collect personal data from individuals with the aim of using it for direct marketing purposes should, at the moment of collection, consider offering data subjects an easy way to indicate that they do not wish their personal data to be used for direct marketing purposes, rather than requiring them to exercise their right to object at a later occasion." (footnote 31)

It must be free of charge for individuals to object. The GDPR does not specify how a valid objection should be made and there is no form of words that individuals must use. This also means that an individual could object verbally as well as in writing, and the objection could be made to any part of your organisation. You need to have a process in place to recognise and deal with objections to processing for direct marketing purposes.

If you have any reasonable doubts over the individual's identity, you can ask them for further information, but only what is necessary for you to action their objection. For example you may need to confirm what their email address or phone number is, in order to stop processing these details for direct marketing purposes.

Whilst you must comply with an objection to your direct marketing, this does not automatically mean that you need to erase the individual's personal data. In most cases it is preferable to suppress their details. See the sections on What are direct marketing suppression lists? and What do we do if someone asks us to erase their data? for further information.

An individual's most recent indication of their wishes about the receipt of your direct marketing is the most important. It is possible for an individual to change their mind about objecting to your direct marketing. For example, if an individual specifically withdraws their objection or in the future actively solicits direct marketing from you, then this would override their original objection. However failing to opt-out of your direct marketing at a later date (for example if you are using the electronic mail soft opt-in) does not override an individual's previous Article 21(2) objection.

Relevant provisions in the legislation

GDPR – see Article 21(2), 21(3), 21(4) and Recital 70, and Article 12, Article 13(2)(b) and Article 14(2)(c)

Further reading outside this code

See our separate guidance on:

Right to object

See also:

EDPB Guidelines on Automated individual decision-making and Profiling

WHAT DO WE DO IF SOMEONE OPTS OUT OF OUR DIRECT MARKETING?

If someone opts out of your direct marketing, you must stop processing their data for the direct marketing purposes that the opt-out covers.

For example, if you are relying on the soft opt-in to send direct marketing emails to an individual and they use the 'unsubscribe' link within your email, you cannot send them any further marketing emails.

An opt-out of receiving direct marketing, such as the individual placing a tick in an opt-out box, has the same effect on your ability to use that method of contact as if the individual had issued an objection to direct marketing on that channel. This is because the individual is making it clear that they do not wish to be marketed to. However unlike an Article 21(2) objection, an opt- out is more likely to cover a specific method of contact or a particular direct marketing activity rather than being a general objection to all direct marketing purposes.

WHAT DO WE DO IF SOMEONE WITHDRAWS THEIR CONSENT?

The GDPR gives people a specific right to withdraw their consent. They can choose to use this right at any time and it must be as easy for them to withdraw consent as it was to give it.

If an individual withdraws consent for their data to be used for direct marketing purposes, you must stop the processing that the consent covers immediately or as soon as possible. Whilst the withdrawal does not affect the lawfulness of your processing up to that point, you can no longer rely on consent as your lawful basis for direct marketing purposes.

You cannot swap from consent to another lawful basis for this processing at the point the individual withdraws consent. Even if you could originally have relied on a different lawful basis, once you choose to rely on consent you are handing control to the individual. It is inherently unfair to tell people they have a choice, but then continue the processing after they withdraw their consent.

This means that when an individual withdraws consent for you to use their data for direct marketing purposes, you cannot swap to legitimate interests in order to try to justify continuing the processing.

PECR refers to consent being given 'for the time being'. Therefore individuals can change their mind and decide that they no longer wish to consent to your electronic direct marketing communications.

The GDPR does not prevent a third party acting on behalf of an individual to withdraw their consent, but you need to be satisfied that the third party has the authority to do so. This leaves the door open for sectoral opt-out registers or other broader shared opt-out mechanisms, which could help individuals regain control they might feel they have lost. It might also help to demonstrate that consent is as easy to withdraw as it was to give.

> **Example**
> The Fundraising Regulator has set up the Fundraising Preference Service (FPS). The FPS operates as a mechanism to withdraw consent to charity fundraising. If an individual wishes to stop receiving marketing from particular charities, they can use the FPS to withdraw consent from those specific charities

Relevant provisions in the legislation

GDPR – see Article 7(3)

Further reading outside this code

See our separate guidance on:

Consent

WHAT ARE DIRECT MARKETING SUPPRESSION LISTS?

Direct marketing suppression lists are a list of people who have told you that they do not want to receive direct marketing from you (eg by issuing an objection or unsubscribing). When someone tells you they do not want direct marketing from you, you should add them to your suppression list. Doing this, rather than simply deleting all record of the individual, means that you can screen any new direct marketing lists against it. This ensures that you do not send direct marketing to anyone who has asked you not to.

Suppression involves retaining just enough information about people to ensure that in future you respect their preference not to either receive direct marketing or have their data processed for direct marketing purposes.

Direct marketing suppression lists is not a concept in the GDPR or PECR, but if you do not use a suppression list you risk infringing the legislation by processing people's data for direct marketing purposes despite them having told you not to.

The GPDR does not prevent you from placing an individual onto a suppression list when they have objected to you processing their personal data for direct marketing purposes. The keeping of such a list is not in itself for direct marketing purposes, but in order to comply with your statutory obligations – so you will not infringe on the right to object by keeping one.

In fact in order to comply with the right to object it will be necessary for you to keep a suppression list to ensure that individuals' wishes and rights are complied with, so they do not receive direct marketing material from you in future or so that their data is not subsequently used for direct marketing purposes. Likewise if an individual has opted-out or told you not to send them electronic direct marketing messages you will breach PECR if you contact them again, therefore maintaining the suppression list is necessary to ensure that you comply.

The appropriate lawful basis for you to keep the minimum amount of an individual's data on a suppression list is likely to be 'necessary for compliance with a legal obligation' (Article 6(1)(c)).

You do need to clearly mark the data so that it is not processed for the direct marketing purposes the individual has objected to.

Example

An individual whose phone number is not on the TPS receives a live direct marketing call from a motor company. The individual asks the company not to call them again. In response the motor company simply deletes the individual's phone number.

A few months later the motor company buys in a list of telephone numbers that have been screened against the TPS. This list includes the individual's number because it is not registered on the TPS. The motor company makes a further direct marketing call to the individual.

The motor company has breached PECR by calling the individual's number.

If the company had placed the number on a suppression list rather than simply deleting it, the breach would have been prevented. This is because screening the bought in list against the suppression list would have identified that there was an objection to receiving direct marketing calls on that number.

The TPS and CTPS registers are also types of suppression lists, and so too is the Mail Preference Service although this is not a statutory one, where individuals or organisations have actively registered an objection to receiving certain types of direct marketing.

You should not confuse direct marketing suppression lists which are used to record an individual's direct marketing objection with a screening list that you have decided to use to screen out certain people because they do not fit the particular direct marketing campaign that you or a third party are running.

Example

A lender decides they only want to send direct marketing to customers who have balances above a certain level. It screens out anyone with a balance that does not meet that threshold and creates a list of those people above it so it can use this again in future.

This is not a direct marketing suppression list because it is unrelated to an individual's wishes.

Relevant provisions in the legislation

GDPR – see Article 6(1)(c)

Further reading outside this code

See our separate guidance on:

Legal obligation

WHAT DO WE DO IF SOMEONE TELLS US THEIR DATA IS INACCURATE?

Individuals have the right to have inaccurate personal data rectified, or completed if it is incomplete – this is known as the right to rectification. They can do this verbally or in writing and you have one calendar month to respond to them.

Example

An individual regularly receives direct marketing from a travel company about cycling and walking holidays as they previously opted-in for information on these types of holidays. However the individual subsequently starts receiving direct marketing from the same company about holidays for the over 60's.

Because the individual is not over 60 (they are in fact in their 30's) they decide to contact the travel company and ask it to correct the inaccurate data about their age. The travel company corrects the data so it no longer indicates that the individual is over 60.

This right links to the accuracy principle. See the section How do we keep personal data we use for direct marketing accurate and up to date? for more information on accuracy.

If you are required to rectify the personal data, you may need to inform each recipient you have disclosed the data to, unless this proves impossible or involves disproportionate effort. If the individual asks you about who you have disclosed their data to, you need to tell them.

Example

A data broker receives a rectification request from an individual. The data broker corrects the incorrect data that it holds about the individual. It also informs the two organisations that it had sold the incorrect data to about the inaccuracy.

Relevant provisions in the legislation

GDPR – see Article 5(1)(d), Article 16, Article 19

Further reading outside this code

See our separate guidance on:

Right to rectification

WHAT DO WE DO IF SOMEONE ASKS US TO ERASE THEIR DATA?

Individuals have the right to have their personal data erased (also known as 'the right to be forgotten'). This can include personal data processed for direct marketing purposes. They can do this verbally or in writing and you have one month to respond to them.

This right is not absolute, it only applies in certain circumstances as listed in Article 17(1). The most relevant ones in a direct marketing context are likely to be if:

- you are relying on consent to process and the individual withdraws their consent;
- the personal data is no longer necessary for your direct marketing purpose; or
- the individual exercises their right to object to you processing their data for direct marketing purposes.

You must comply with the request if you receive an erasure request and any of the circumstances listed in Article 17(1) apply. There is an exception to this requirement, but you must be able to demonstrate that the processing is necessary for one of the reasons listed in Article 17(3). However these are narrow and are likely to be difficult to apply in the direct marketing context.

You do not need to automatically treat a withdrawal of consent or an objection to direct marketing as an erasure request. However in practice if someone withdraws their consent you no longer have a basis upon which to process for that purpose. So you are likely to need to erase that data (unless you need to keep a small amount for another purpose, such as a suppression list). Likewise if someone objects to the processing of their personal data for direct marketing purposes, you must stop that processing. Similarly, this is likely to mean that you may need to erase the data (unless you need a small amount for a suppression list).

Because we do not consider that a suppression list is processed for direct marketing purposes there would not be an automatic right to have the suppression list erased. Even if the right to erasure did arise, it is likely that you could show that Article 17(3)(b) applies because the processing of the suppression list to ensure that their wishes and rights are complied with is necessary for compliance with a legal obligation (ie the legal obligation not to use personal data for direct marketing purposes where someone has asked you not to). See the section What are direct marketing suppression lists? for further information.

> **Example**
> An individual contacts a company to issue an objection to direct marketing and at the same time asks it to delete their data. The company stops using the individual's data for direct marketing and erases all of it, apart from a small amount which it keeps on its suppression list. This prevents it from using the individual's personal data for direct marketing purposes in the future.

There may be circumstances where reasons other than the right to erasure mean in practice that you need to delete or erase personal data. For example, if the circumstances change and you no longer have a lawful basis for processing the personal data, you discover that you hold excessive personal data, or the deletion is in line with your retention periods.

If you are required to erase personal data, you may need to inform each recipient you have disclosed the data to, unless this proves impossible or involves disproportionate effort. If the individual asks you about who you have disclosed their data to, you need to tell them.

Relevant provisions in the legislation

GDPR – see Article 17 and Recitals 65 and 66, and Article 19

Further reading outside this code

See our separate guidance on:

Right to erasure

WHAT DO WE DO IF SOMEONE ASKS US FOR ACCESS TO THEIR DATA?

Individuals have the right of access to a copy of the personal data that you hold about them, which includes their data that you process for direct marketing purposes. Depending on what data you hold, this could include their contact details, online credentials, purchase history, or profile including any assumptions, categories or segments you have assigned to them (eg based on their location or behaviour).

Individuals can request access (which is commonly known as a 'subject access request') verbally or in writing. There are no set words that they must use to exercise this right but it must be clear that they are asking for their own personal data. You have one month to respond and in most cases you cannot charge a fee to deal with a subject access request.

Individuals are also entitled to other supplementary information about your processing of their personal data, however this largely corresponds to the information that you should provide in your privacy notice.

There are exemptions to this right, but whether any of these apply depends on the particular circumstances. See the section on Exemptions for further information.

Relevant provisions in the legislation

GDPR – see Article 15 and Recitals 63 and 64

Further reading outside this code

See our separate guidance on:

Right of access

EXEMPTIONS

AT A GLANCE

[1.410]

The DPA 2018 contains a number of exemptions from particular GDPR provisions and these add to the exceptions that are already built into certain GDPR provisions. There are no exemptions that specifically apply to processing for direct marketing purposes.

PECR contains very few exemptions. The two exemptions in Regulation 6 from the requirement to provide clear and comprehensive information and gain consent for cookies and similar technologies do not apply to online advertising, tracking technologies or social media plugins.

WHAT ARE EXEMPTIONS?

If an exemption applies it means that you do not have to comply with the particular provision that the exemption discharges you from.

The DPA 2018 contains a number of exemptions from particular GDPR provisions. These add to and complement a number of exceptions already built-in to certain GDPR provisions. PECR also contain some limited exemptions.

You should consider exemptions on a case-by-case basis. You must be able to justify why you are relying on an exemption and ensure that you document this.

ARE THERE ANY PECR EXEMPTIONS THAT APPLY TO DIRECT MARKETING?

PECR contains very few exemptions and none generally apply to the rules on using electronic communications for sending direct marketing.

As discussed earlier in this code, Regulation 6 contains two exemptions to the requirement to provide clear and comprehensive information and gain consent for cookies and similar technologies. However neither of these exemptions apply for online advertising, tracking technologies and social media plugins. See the section Is all online advertising covered by the direct marketing rules? for further information.

Regulation 29 contains a law and crime exemption for 'communications providers', ie someone who provides or operates an electronic communications network or electronic communications service. It exempts communications providers from any of the rules in PECR if complying with that particular rule would breach a provision of another law. For example this exemption could be relevant if another law required a communications provider to send electronic direct marketing emails to individual subscribers.

If you are not a communications provider, you cannot use this exemption. So even if there is a law requiring you to send direct marketing, you must still comply with the PECR rules on sending electronic communications.

Relevant provisions in the legislation

PECR – see Regulation 6 and Regulation 29

Further reading outside this code

See our separate guidance on:

PECR exemptions

ARE THERE ANY DATA PROTECTION EXEMPTIONS THAT APPLY TO DIRECT MARKETING?

The DPA 2018 sets out a number of exemptions from some of the GDPR rights and provisions. Whether or not you can rely on an exemption generally depends on why you are processing the personal data.

Some exemptions apply simply because you have a particular purpose. Others only apply to the extent that complying with the GDPR would be likely to prejudice your purpose, or prevent or seriously impair you from processing personal data in a way that is required or necessary for your purpose.

The exemptions cover specific areas such as:
- crime, law and public protection;
- regulation, parliament and the judiciary;
- journalism, research and archiving;
- health, social work, education and child abuse;

- finance, management and negotiations;
- references and exams; and
- subject access requests where you hold information about other people.

There are no exemptions in the DPA 2018 that specifically apply to processing for direct marketing purposes. As previously discussed in the Individual rights section of this code, the right to object to direct marketing is absolute which means that you cannot exempt yourself from complying with such an objection.

Some of the provisions in the GDPR contain exceptions which set out when its requirements do not apply. In the case of Article 14, there are a number of exceptions to providing privacy information if the personal data has not been collected from the individual. See the section What do we need to tell people if we collect their data from other sources? for further information.

Relevant provisions in the legislation

DPA 2018 – see Schedules 2 to 4

GDPR – see Article 14(5)

Further reading outside this code

See our separate guidance on:

Exemptions guidance

ENFORCEMENT OF THIS CODE

AT A GLANCE

[1.411]
The ICO upholds information rights in the public interest. We will monitor compliance with this code through proactive audits, will consider complaints and enforce the direct marketing rules in line with our Regulatory Action Policy. Adherence to this code will be a key measure of your compliance with data protection laws. If you do not follow this code, you will find it difficult to demonstrate that your processing complies with the GDPR or PECR.

WHAT IS THE ROLE OF THE ICO?

The Information Commissioner is the independent supervisory authority for data protection in the UK.

Our mission is to uphold information rights for the public in the digital age. Our vision for data protection is to increase the confidence that the public have in organisations that process personal data. We offer advice and guidance, promote good practice, monitor and investigate breach reports, monitor compliance, conduct audits and advisory visits, consider complaints, and take enforcement action where appropriate. Our enforcement powers are set out in part 6 of the DPA 2018.

Our focus is on compliance with data protection legislation in the UK. In particular, to ensure that the direct marketing rules are adhered to.

Where the provisions of this code overlap with other regulators we will work with them to ensure a consistent and co-ordinated response.

HOW WILL THE ICO MONITOR COMPLIANCE?

We will monitor compliance with this code using the full range of measures available to us from intelligence gathering, using our audit or assessment powers to understand an issue, through to investigation and fining where necessary.

Our approach is to encourage compliance. Where we find issues we take fair, proportionate and timely regulatory action with a view to guaranteeing that individuals' information rights are properly protected.

HOW WILL THE ICO DEAL WITH COMPLAINTS?

If someone raises a concern with us about your compliance with this code or the way you have handled personal data or sent electronic messages in the context of direct marketing, we will record and consider it.

We will take this code into account when considering whether you have complied with the GDPR or PECR. In particular, when considering questions of fairness, lawfulness, transparency and accountability.

We will assess your initial response to the complaint, and we may contact you to ask some questions and give you a further opportunity to explain your position. We may also ask for details of your policies and procedures, your DPIA, and other relevant documentation. However, we expect you to be accountable for how you meet your obligations under GDPR and PECR, so you should make sure that when you initially respond to complaints from individuals you do so with a full and detailed explanation about how you use their personal data and how you comply.

If we consider that you have failed (or are failing) to comply with the GDPR or PECR, we have the power to take enforcement action. This may require you to take steps to bring your operations into compliance or we may decide to fine you. Or both.

WHAT ARE THE ICO'S ENFORCEMENT POWERS?

We have various powers to take action for a breach of the GDPR or PECR. We have a statutory duty to take the provisions of this code into account when enforcing the GDPR and PECR.

Tools at our disposal for data protection infringements include:
* assessment notices;
* warnings;
* reprimands;
* enforcement notices; and
* penalty notices (administrative fines).

For serious infringements of the data protection principles, we have the power to issue fines of up to €20 million or 4% of your annual worldwide turnover, whichever is higher.

We have several ways of taking action to change the behaviour of anyone who breaches PECR. These include criminal prosecution, non-criminal enforcement and audit. The Information Commissioner can also serve a monetary penalty notice imposing a fine of up to £500,000 which can be issued against the organisation or its directors. These powers are not mutually exclusive. We will use them in combination where justified by the circumstances.

Relevant provisions in the legislation

DPA 2018 – see Part 6 Enforcement

Further reading outside this code

See our separate guidance on:

What we do

Make a complaint

Regulatory Action Policy

ANNEX A: GLOSSARY

GLOSSARY OF TERMS

[1.412]
This glossary is included as a quick reference for key data protection and PECR terms and abbreviations used in this code.

Consent	Any freely given, specific, informed and unambiguous indication of the data subject's wishes by which he or she, by a statement or by a clear affirmative action, signifies agreement to the processing of personal data relating to him or her.
Controller	The natural or legal person, public authority, agency or other body which, alone or jointly with others, determines the purposes and means of the processing of personal data.
Corporate subscriber	Corporate body with separate legal status - includes companies, limited liability partnerships, Scottish partnerships, and some government bodies.
CTPS	Corporate telephone preference service
DPA 2018	Data Protection Act 2018
DPIA	Data protection impact assessment
EDPB	European Data Protection Board (formally the Article 29 Working Party)
Electronic mail	Any text, voice, sound or image message sent over a public electronic communications network which can be stored in the network or in the recipient's terminal equipment until it is collected by the recipient and includes messages sent using a short message service.
GDPR	General Data Protection Regulation
Individual subscriber	Individual customers (including sole traders) and other organisations (eg other types of partnership).
Joint controller	Where two or more controllers jointly determine the purposes and means of processing.
PECR	Privacy and Electronic Communications Regulations 2003
Personal data	Any information relating to an identified or identifiable natural person ('data subject'); an identifiable natural person is one who can be identified, directly or indirectly, in particular by reference to an identifier such as a name, an identification number, location data, an online identifier or to one or more factors specific to the physical, physiological, genetic, mental, economic, cultural or social identity of that natural person.
Processor	A natural or legal person, public authority, agency or other body which processes personal data on behalf of the controller.

Profiling	Any form of automated processing of personal data consisting of the use of personal data to evaluate certain personal aspects relating to a natural person, in particular to analyse or predict aspects concerning that natural person's performance at work, economic situation, health, personal preferences, interests, reliability, behaviour, location or movements.
Special category data	Personal data revealing racial or ethnic origin, political opinions, religious or philosophical beliefs, or trade union membership, and the processing of genetic data, biometric data for the purpose of uniquely identifying a natural person, data concerning health or data concerning a natural person's sex life or sexual orientation.
Subscriber	A person who is party to a contract with a provider of public electronic communications services for the supply of such services.
TPS	Telephone preference service
User	Any individual using a public electronic communications service.

PART 2
DATA PROTECTION – EU LAW AND EDPB EU GDPR GUIDELINES AND RECOMMENDATIONS

EUROPEAN PARLIAMENT AND COUNCIL REGULATION

(2016/679/EU)

of 27 April 2016

on the protection of natural persons with regard to the processing of personal data and on the free movement of such data, and repealing Directive 95/46/EC (General Data Protection Regulation)

(Text with EEA relevance)

[2.1]

NOTES

Date of publication in OJ: OJ L119, 4.5.2016, p 1. The text of this Regulation incorporates the corrigendum published in OJ L127, 23.5.2018, p 2.

© European Union, 1998–2021.

THE EUROPEAN PARLIAMENT AND THE COUNCIL OF THE EUROPEAN UNION,

Having regard to the Treaty on the Functioning of the European Union, and in particular Article 16 thereof, Having regard to the proposal from the European Commission,

After transmission of the draft legislative act to the national parliaments,

Having regard to the opinion of the European Economic and Social Committee,[1] Having regard to the opinion of the Committee of the Regions,[2]

Acting in accordance with the ordinary legislative procedure,[3] Whereas:

(1) The protection of natural persons in relation to the processing of personal data is a fundamental right. Article 8(1) of the Charter of Fundamental Rights of the European Union (the 'Charter') and Article 16(1) of the Treaty on the Functioning of the European Union (TFEU) provide that everyone has the right to the protection of personal data concerning him or her.

(2) The principles of, and rules on the protection of natural persons with regard to the processing of their personal data should, whatever their nationality or residence, respect their fundamental rights and freedoms, in particular their right to the protection of personal data. This Regulation is intended to contribute to the accomplishment of an area of freedom, security and justice and of an economic union, to economic and social progress, to the strengthening and the convergence of the economies within the internal market, and to the well-being of natural persons.

(3) Directive 95/46/EC of the European Parliament and of the Council[4] seeks to harmonise the protection of fundamental rights and freedoms of natural persons in respect of processing activities and to ensure the free flow of personal data between Member States.

(4) The processing of personal data should be designed to serve mankind. The right to the protection of personal data is not an absolute right; it must be considered in relation to its function in society and be balanced against other fundamental rights, in accordance with the principle of proportionality. This Regulation respects all fundamental rights and observes the freedoms and principles recognised in the Charter as enshrined in the Treaties, in particular the respect for private and family life, home and communications, the protection of personal data, freedom of thought, conscience and religion, freedom of expression and information, freedom to conduct a business, the right to an effective remedy and to a fair trial, and cultural, religious and linguistic diversity.

(5) The economic and social integration resulting from the functioning of the internal market has led to a substantial increase in cross-border flows of personal data. The exchange of personal data between public and private actors, including natural persons, associations and undertakings across the Union has increased. National authorities in the Member States are being called upon by Union law to cooperate and exchange personal data so as to be able to perform their duties or carry out tasks on behalf of an authority in another Member State.

(6) Rapid technological developments and globalisation have brought new challenges for the protection of personal data. The scale of the collection and sharing of personal data has increased significantly. Technology allows both private companies and public authorities to make use of personal data on an unprecedented scale in order to pursue their activities. Natural persons increasingly make personal information available publicly and globally. Technology has transformed both the economy and social life, and should further facilitate the free flow of personal data within the Union and the transfer to third countries and international organisations, while ensuring a high level of the protection of personal data.

(7) Those developments require a strong and more coherent data protection framework in the Union, backed by strong enforcement, given the importance of creating the trust that will allow the digital economy to develop across the internal market. Natural persons should have control of their own personal data. Legal and practical certainty for natural persons, economic operators and public authorities should be enhanced.

(8) Where this Regulation provides for specifications or restrictions of its rules by Member State law, Member States may, as far as necessary for coherence and for making the national provisions comprehensible to the persons to whom they apply, incorporate elements of this Regulation into their national law.

(9) The objectives and principles of Directive 95/46/EC remain sound, but it has not prevented fragmentation in the implementation of data protection across the Union, legal uncertainty or a widespread public perception that there are significant risks to the protection of natural persons, in

particular with regard to online activity. Differences in the level of protection of the rights and freedoms of natural persons, in particular the right to the protection of personal data, with regard to the processing of personal data in the Member States may prevent the free flow of personal data throughout the Union. Those differences may therefore constitute an obstacle to the pursuit of economic activities at the level of the Union, distort competition and impede authorities in the discharge of their responsibilities under Union law. Such a difference in levels of protection is due to the existence of differences in the implementation and application of Directive 95/46/EC.

(10) In order to ensure a consistent and high level of protection of natural persons and to remove the obstacles to flows of personal data within the Union, the level of protection of the rights and freedoms of natural persons with regard to the processing of such data should be equivalent in all Member States. Consistent and homogenous application of the rules for the protection of the fundamental rights and freedoms of natural persons with regard to the processing of personal data should be ensured throughout the Union. Regarding the processing of personal data for compliance with a legal obligation, for the performance of a task carried out in the public interest or in the exercise of official authority vested in the controller, Member States should be allowed to maintain or introduce national provisions to further specify the application of the rules of this Regulation. In conjunction with the general and horizontal law on data protection implementing Directive 95/46/EC, Member States have several sector-specific laws in areas that need more specific provisions. This Regulation also provides a margin of manoeuvre for Member States to specify its rules, including for the processing of special categories of personal data ('sensitive data'). To that extent, this Regulation does not exclude Member State law that sets out the circumstances for specific processing situations, including determining more precisely the conditions under which the processing of personal data is lawful.

(11) Effective protection of personal data throughout the Union requires the strengthening and setting out in detail of the rights of data subjects and the obligations of those who process and determine the processing of personal data, as well as equivalent powers for monitoring and ensuring compliance with the rules for the protection of personal data and equivalent sanctions for infringements in the Member States.

(12) Article 16(2) TFEU mandates the European Parliament and the Council to lay down the rules relating to the protection of natural persons with regard to the processing of personal data and the rules relating to the free movement of personal data.

(13) In order to ensure a consistent level of protection for natural persons throughout the Union and to prevent divergences hampering the free movement of personal data within the internal market, a Regulation is necessary to provide legal certainty and transparency for economic operators, including micro, small and medium-sized enterprises, and to provide natural persons in all Member States with the same level of legally enforceable rights and obligations and responsibilities for controllers and processors, to ensure consistent monitoring of the processing of personal data, and equivalent sanctions in all Member States as well as effective cooperation between the supervisory authorities of different Member States. The proper functioning of the internal market requires that the free movement of personal data within the Union is not restricted or prohibited for reasons connected with the protection of natural persons with regard to the processing of personal data. To take account of the specific situation of micro, small and medium-sized enterprises, this Regulation includes a derogation for organisations with fewer than 250 employees with regard to record-keeping. In addition, the Union institutions and bodies, and Member States and their supervisory authorities, are encouraged to take account of the specific needs of micro, small and medium-sized enterprises in the application of this Regulation. The notion of micro, small and medium-sized enterprises should draw from Article 2 of the Annex to Commission Recommendation 2003/361/EC.[5]

(14) The protection afforded by this Regulation should apply to natural persons, whatever their nationality or place of residence, in relation to the processing of their personal data. This Regulation does not cover the processing of personal data which concerns legal persons and in particular undertakings established as legal persons, including the name and the form of the legal person and the contact details of the legal person.

(15) In order to prevent creating a serious risk of circumvention, the protection of natural persons should be technologically neutral and should not depend on the techniques used. The protection of natural persons should apply to the processing of personal data by automated means, as well as to manual processing, if the personal data are contained or are intended to be contained in a filing system. Files or sets of files, as well as their cover pages, which are not structured according to specific criteria should not fall within the scope of this Regulation.

(16) This Regulation does not apply to issues of protection of fundamental rights and freedoms or the free flow of personal data related to activities which fall outside the scope of Union law, such as activities concerning national security. This Regulation does not apply to the processing of personal data by the Member States when carrying out activities in relation to the common foreign and security policy of the Union.

(17) Regulation (EC) No 45/2001 of the European Parliament and of the Council[6] applies to the processing of personal data by the Union institutions, bodies, offices and agencies. Regulation (EC) No 45/2001 and other Union legal acts applicable to such processing of personal data should be adapted to the principles and rules established in this Regulation and applied in the light of this Regulation. In order to provide a strong and coherent data protection framework in the Union, the necessary adaptations of Regulation (EC) No 45/2001 should follow after the adoption of this Regulation, in order to allow application at the same time as this Regulation.

(18) This Regulation does not apply to the processing of personal data by a natural person in the course of a purely personal or household activity and thus with no connection to a professional or commercial activity. Personal or household activities could include correspondence and the holding of addresses, or social networking and online activity undertaken within the context of such activities. However, this Regulation applies to controllers or processors which provide the means for processing personal data for such personal or household activities.

(19) The protection of natural persons with regard to the processing of personal data by competent authorities for the purposes of the prevention, investigation, detection or prosecution of criminal offences or the execution of criminal penalties, including the safeguarding against and the prevention of threats to public security and the free movement of such data, is the subject of a specific Union legal act. This Regulation should not, therefore, apply to processing activities for those purposes. However, personal data processed by public authorities under this Regulation should, when used for those purposes, be governed by a more specific Union legal act, namely Directive (EU) 2016/680 of the European Parliament and of the Council.[7] Member States may entrust competent authorities within the meaning of Directive (EU) 2016/680 with tasks which are not necessarily carried out for the purposes of the prevention, investigation, detection or prosecution of criminal offences or the execution of criminal penalties, including the safeguarding against and prevention of threats to public security, so that the processing of personal data for those other purposes, in so far as it is within the scope of Union law, falls within the scope of this Regulation.

With regard to the processing of personal data by those competent authorities for purposes falling within scope of this Regulation, Member States should be able to maintain or introduce more specific provisions to adapt the application of the rules of this Regulation. Such provisions may determine more precisely specific requirements for the processing of personal data by those competent authorities for those other purposes, taking into account the constitutional, organisational and administrative structure of the respective Member State. When the processing of personal data by private bodies falls within the scope of this Regulation, this Regulation should provide for the possibility for Member States under specific conditions to restrict by law certain obligations and rights when such a restriction constitutes a necessary and proportionate measure in a democratic society to safeguard specific important interests including public security and the prevention, investigation, detection or prosecution of criminal offences or the execution of criminal penalties, including the safeguarding against and the prevention of threats to public security. This is relevant for instance in the framework of anti-money laundering or the activities of forensic laboratories.

(20) While this Regulation applies, inter alia, to the activities of courts and other judicial authorities, Union or Member State law could specify the processing operations and processing procedures in relation to the processing of personal data by courts and other judicial authorities. The competence of the supervisory authorities should not cover the processing of personal data when courts are acting in their judicial capacity, in order to safeguard the independence of the judiciary in the performance of its judicial tasks, including decision-making. It should be possible to entrust supervision of such data processing operations to specific bodies within the judicial system of the Member State, which should, in particular ensure compliance with the rules of this Regulation, enhance awareness among members of the judiciary of their obligations under this Regulation and handle complaints in relation to such data processing operations.

(21) This Regulation is without prejudice to the application of Directive 2000/31/EC of the European Parliament and of the Council,[8] in particular of the liability rules of intermediary service providers in Articles 12 to 15 of that Directive. That Directive seeks to contribute to the proper functioning of the internal market by ensuring the free movement of information society services between Member States.

(22) Any processing of personal data in the context of the activities of an establishment of a controller or a processor in the Union should be carried out in accordance with this Regulation, regardless of whether the processing itself takes place within the Union. Establishment implies the effective and real exercise of activity through stable arrangements. The legal form of such arrangements, whether through a branch or a subsidiary with a legal personality, is not the determining factor in that respect.

(23) In order to ensure that natural persons are not deprived of the protection to which they are entitled under this Regulation, the processing of personal data of data subjects who are in the Union by a controller or a processor not established in the Union should be subject to this Regulation where the processing activities are related to offering goods or services to such data subjects irrespective of whether connected to a payment. In order to determine whether such a controller or processor is offering goods or services to data subjects who are in the Union, it should be ascertained whether it is apparent that the controller or processor envisages offering services to data subjects in one or more Member States in the Union. Whereas the mere accessibility of the controller's, processor's or an intermediary's website in the Union, of an email address or of other contact details, or the use of a language generally used in the third country where the controller is established, is insufficient to ascertain such intention, factors such as the use of a language or a currency generally used in one or more Member States with the possibility of ordering goods and services in that other language, or the mentioning of customers or users who are in the Union, may make it apparent that the controller envisages offering goods or services to data subjects in the Union.

(24) The processing of personal data of data subjects who are in the Union by a controller or processor not established in the Union should also be subject to this Regulation when it is related to the monitoring of the behaviour of such data subjects in so far as their behaviour takes place within the Union. In order to determine whether a processing activity can be considered to monitor the behaviour of data

subjects, it should be ascertained whether natural persons are tracked on the internet including potential subsequent use of personal data processing techniques which consist of profiling a natural person, particularly in order to take decisions concerning her or him or for analysing or predicting her or his personal preferences, behaviours and attitudes.

(25) Where Member State law applies by virtue of public international law, this Regulation should also apply to a controller not established in the Union, such as in a Member State's diplomatic mission or consular post.

(26) The principles of data protection should apply to any information concerning an identified or identifiable natural person. Personal data which have undergone pseudonymisation, which could be attributed to a natural person by the use of additional information should be considered to be information on an identifiable natural person. To determine whether a natural person is identifiable, account should be taken of all the means reasonably likely to be used, such as singling out, either by the controller or by another person to identify the natural person directly or indirectly. To ascertain whether means are reasonably likely to be used to identify the natural person, account should be taken of all objective factors, such as the costs of and the amount of time required for identification, taking into consideration the available technology at the time of the processing and technological developments. The principles of data protection should therefore not apply to anonymous information, namely information which does not relate to an identified or identifiable natural person or to personal data rendered anonymous in such a manner that the data subject is not or no longer identifiable. This Regulation does not therefore concern the processing of such anonymous information, including for statistical or research purposes.

(27) This Regulation does not apply to the personal data of deceased persons. Member States may provide for rules regarding the processing of personal data of deceased persons.

(28) The application of pseudonymisation to personal data can reduce the risks to the data subjects concerned and help controllers and processors to meet their data-protection obligations. The explicit introduction of 'pseudonymisation' in this Regulation is not intended to preclude any other measures of data protection.

(29) In order to create incentives to apply pseudonymisation when processing personal data, measures of pseudonymisation should, whilst allowing general analysis, be possible within the same controller when that controller has taken technical and organisational measures necessary to ensure, for the processing concerned, that this Regulation is implemented, and that additional information for attributing the personal data to a specific data subject is kept separately. The controller processing the personal data should indicate the authorised persons within the same controller.

(30) Natural persons may be associated with online identifiers provided by their devices, applications, tools and protocols, such as internet protocol addresses, cookie identifiers or other identifiers such as radio frequency identification tags. This may leave traces which, in particular when combined with unique identifiers and other information received by the servers, may be used to create profiles of the natural persons and identify them.

(31) Public authorities to which personal data are disclosed in accordance with a legal obligation for the exercise of their official mission, such as tax and customs authorities, financial investigation units, independent administrative authorities, or financial market authorities responsible for the regulation and supervision of securities markets should not be regarded as recipients if they receive personal data which are necessary to carry out a particular inquiry in the general interest, in accordance with Union or Member State law. The requests for disclosure sent by the public authorities should always be in writing, reasoned and occasional and should not concern the entirety of a filing system or lead to the interconnection of filing systems. The processing of personal data by those public authorities should comply with the applicable data-protection rules according to the purposes of the processing.

(32) Consent should be given by a clear affirmative act establishing a freely given, specific, informed and unambiguous indication of the data subject's agreement to the processing of personal data relating to him or her, such as by a written statement, including by electronic means, or an oral statement. This could include ticking a box when visiting an internet website, choosing technical settings for information society services or another statement or conduct which clearly indicates in this context the data subject's acceptance of the proposed processing of his or her personal data. Silence, pre-ticked boxes or inactivity should not therefore constitute consent. Consent should cover all processing activities carried out for the same purpose or purposes. When the processing has multiple purposes, consent should be given for all of them. If the data subject's consent is to be given following a request by electronic means, the request must be clear, concise and not unnecessarily disruptive to the use of the service for which it is provided.

(33) It is often not possible to fully identify the purpose of personal data processing for scientific research purposes at the time of data collection. Therefore, data subjects should be allowed to give their consent to certain areas of scientific research when in keeping with recognised ethical standards for scientific research. Data subjects should have the opportunity to give their consent only to certain areas of research or parts of research projects to the extent allowed by the intended purpose.

(34) Genetic data should be defined as personal data relating to the inherited or acquired genetic characteristics of a natural person which result from the analysis of a biological sample from the natural person in question, in particular chromosomal, deoxyribonucleic acid (DNA) or ribonucleic acid (RNA) analysis, or from the analysis of another element enabling equivalent information to be obtained.

(35) Personal data concerning health should include all data pertaining to the health status of a data subject which reveal information relating to the past, current or future physical or mental health status of the data subject. This includes information about the natural person collected in the course of the

registration for, or the provision of, health care services as referred to in Directive 2011/24/EU of the European Parliament and of the Council[9] to that natural person; a number, symbol or particular assigned to a natural person to uniquely identify the natural person for health purposes; information derived from the testing or examination of a body part or bodily substance, including from genetic data and biological samples; and any information on, for example, a disease, disability, disease risk, medical history, clinical treatment or the physiological or biomedical state of the data subject independent of its source, for example from a physician or other health professional, a hospital, a medical device or an in vitro diagnostic test.

(36) The main establishment of a controller in the Union should be the place of its central administration in the Union, unless the decisions on the purposes and means of the processing of personal data are taken in another establishment of the controller in the Union, in which case that other establishment should be considered to be the main establishment. The main establishment of a controller in the Union should be determined according to objective criteria and should imply the effective and real exercise of management activities determining the main decisions as to the purposes and means of processing through stable arrangements. That criterion should not depend on whether the processing of personal data is carried out at that location. The presence and use of technical means and technologies for processing personal data or processing activities do not, in themselves, constitute a main establishment and are therefore not determining criteria for a main establishment. The main establishment of the processor should be the place of its central administration in the Union or, if it has no central administration in the Union, the place where the main processing activities take place in the Union. In cases involving both the controller and the processor, the competent lead supervisory authority should remain the supervisory authority of the Member State where the controller has its main establishment, but the supervisory authority of the processor should be considered to be a supervisory authority concerned and that supervisory authority should participate in the cooperation procedure provided for by this Regulation. In any case, the supervisory authorities of the Member State or Member States where the processor has one or more establishments should not be considered to be supervisory authorities concerned where the draft decision concerns only the controller. Where the processing is carried out by a group of undertakings, the main establishment of the controlling undertaking should be considered to be the main establishment of the group of undertakings, except where the purposes and means of processing are determined by another undertaking.

(37) A group of undertakings should cover a controlling undertaking and its controlled undertakings, whereby the controlling undertaking should be the undertaking which can exert a dominant influence over the other undertakings by virtue, for example, of ownership, financial participation or the rules which govern it or the power to have personal data protection rules implemented. An undertaking which controls the processing of personal data in undertakings affiliated to it should be regarded, together with those undertakings, as a group of undertakings.

(38) Children merit specific protection with regard to their personal data, as they may be less aware of the risks, consequences and safeguards concerned and their rights in relation to the processing of personal data. Such specific protection should, in particular, apply to the use of personal data of children for the purposes of marketing or creating personality or user profiles and the collection of personal data with regard to children when using services offered directly to a child. The consent of the holder of parental responsibility should not be necessary in the context of preventive or counselling services offered directly to a child.

(39) Any processing of personal data should be lawful and fair. It should be transparent to natural persons that personal data concerning them are collected, used, consulted or otherwise processed and to what extent the personal data are or will be processed. The principle of transparency requires that any information and communication relating to the processing of those personal data be easily accessible and easy to understand, and that clear and plain language be used. That principle concerns, in particular, information to the data subjects on the identity of the controller and the purposes of the processing and further information to ensure fair and transparent processing in respect of the natural persons concerned and their right to obtain confirmation and communication of personal data concerning them which are being processed. Natural persons should be made aware of risks, rules, safeguards and rights in relation to the processing of personal data and how to exercise their rights in relation to such processing. In particular, the specific purposes for which personal data are processed should be explicit and legitimate and determined at the time of the collection of the personal data. The personal data should be adequate, relevant and limited to what is necessary for the purposes for which they are processed. This requires, in particular, ensuring that the period for which the personal data are stored is limited to a strict minimum. Personal data should be processed only if the purpose of the processing could not reasonably be fulfilled by other means. In order to ensure that the personal data are not kept longer than necessary, time limits should be established by the controller for erasure or for a periodic review. Every reasonable step should be taken to ensure that personal data which are inaccurate are rectified or deleted. Personal data should be processed in a manner that ensures appropriate security and confidentiality of the personal data, including for preventing unauthorised access to or use of personal data and the equipment used for the processing.

(40) In order for processing to be lawful, personal data should be processed on the basis of the consent of the data subject concerned or some other legitimate basis, laid down by law, either in this Regulation or in other Union or Member State law as referred to in this Regulation, including the necessity for compliance with the legal obligation to which the controller is subject or the necessity for the performance of a contract to which the data subject is party or in order to take steps at the request of the data subject prior to entering into a contract.

(41) Where this Regulation refers to a legal basis or a legislative measure, this does not necessarily require a legislative act adopted by a parliament, without prejudice to requirements pursuant to the constitutional order of the Member State concerned. However, such a legal basis or legislative measure should be clear and precise and its application should be foreseeable to persons subject to it, in accordance with the case-law of the Court of Justice of the European Union (the 'Court of Justice') and the European Court of Human Rights.

(42) Where processing is based on the data subject's consent, the controller should be able to demonstrate that the data subject has given consent to the processing operation. In particular in the context of a written declaration on another matter, safeguards should ensure that the data subject is aware of the fact that and the extent to which consent is given. In accordance with Council Directive 93/13/EEC[10] a declaration of consent pre-formulated by the controller should be provided in an intelligible and easily accessible form, using clear and plain language and it should not contain unfair terms. For consent to be informed, the data subject should be aware at least of the identity of the controller and the purposes of the processing for which the personal data are intended. Consent should not be regarded as freely given if the data subject has no genuine or free choice or is unable to refuse or withdraw consent without detriment.

(43) In order to ensure that consent is freely given, consent should not provide a valid legal ground for the processing of personal data in a specific case where there is a clear imbalance between the data subject and the controller, in particular where the controller is a public authority and it is therefore unlikely that consent was freely given in all the circumstances of that specific situation. Consent is presumed not to be freely given if it does not allow separate consent to be given to different personal data processing operations despite it being appropriate in the individual case, or if the performance of a contract, including the provision of a service, is dependent on the consent despite such consent not being necessary for such performance.

(44) Processing should be lawful where it is necessary in the context of a contract or the intention to enter into a contract.

(45) Where processing is carried out in accordance with a legal obligation to which the controller is subject or where processing is necessary for the performance of a task carried out in the public interest or in the exercise of official authority, the processing should have a basis in Union or Member State law. This Regulation does not require a specific law for each individual processing. A law as a basis for several processing operations based on a legal obligation to which the controller is subject or where processing is necessary for the performance of a task carried out in the public interest or in the exercise of an official authority may be sufficient. It should also be for Union or Member State law to determine the purpose of processing. Furthermore, that law could specify the general conditions of this Regulation governing the lawfulness of personal data processing, establish specifications for determining the controller, the type of personal data which are subject to the processing, the data subjects concerned, the entities to which the personal data may be disclosed, the purpose limitations, the storage period and other measures to ensure lawful and fair processing. It should also be for Union or Member State law to determine whether the controller performing a task carried out in the public interest or in the exercise of official authority should be a public authority or another natural or legal person governed by public law, or, where it is in the public interest to do so, including for health purposes such as public health and social protection and the management of health care services, by private law, such as a professional association.

(46) The processing of personal data should also be regarded to be lawful where it is necessary to protect an interest which is essential for the life of the data subject or that of another natural person. Processing of personal data based on the vital interest of another natural person should in principle take place only where the processing cannot be manifestly based on another legal basis. Some types of processing may serve both important grounds of public interest and the vital interests of the data subject as for instance when processing is necessary for humanitarian purposes, including for monitoring epidemics and their spread or in situations of humanitarian emergencies, in particular in situations of natural and man-made disasters.

(47) The legitimate interests of a controller, including those of a controller to which the personal data may be disclosed, or of a third party, may provide a legal basis for processing, provided that the interests or the fundamental rights and freedoms of the data subject are not overriding, taking into consideration the reasonable expectations of data subjects based on their relationship with the controller. Such legitimate interest could exist for example where there is a relevant and appropriate relationship between the data subject and the controller in situations such as where the data subject is a client or in the service of the controller. At any rate the existence of a legitimate interest would need careful assessment including whether a data subject can reasonably expect at the time and in the context of the collection of the personal data that processing for that purpose may take place. The interests and fundamental rights of the data subject could in particular override the interest of the data controller where personal data are processed in circumstances where data subjects do not reasonably expect further processing. Given that it is for the legislator to provide by law for the legal basis for public authorities to process personal data, that legal basis should not apply to the processing by public authorities in the performance of their tasks. The processing of personal data strictly necessary for the purposes of preventing fraud also constitutes a legitimate interest of the data controller concerned. The processing of personal data for direct marketing purposes may be regarded as carried out for a legitimate interest.

(48) Controllers that are part of a group of undertakings or institutions affiliated to a central body may have a legitimate interest in transmitting personal data within the group of undertakings for internal administrative purposes, including the processing of clients' or employees' personal data. The general principles for the transfer of personal data, within a group of undertakings, to an undertaking located in a third country remain unaffected.

(49) The processing of personal data to the extent strictly necessary and proportionate for the purposes of ensuring network and information security, i.e. the ability of a network or an information system to resist, at a given level of confidence, accidental events or unlawful or malicious actions that compromise the availability, authenticity, integrity and confidentiality of stored or transmitted personal data, and the security of the related services offered by, or accessible via, those networks and systems, by public authorities, by computer emergency response teams (CERTs), computer security incident response teams (CSIRTs), by providers of electronic communications networks and services and by providers of security technologies and services, constitutes a legitimate interest of the data controller concerned. This could, for example, include preventing unauthorised access to electronic communications networks and malicious code distribution and stopping 'denial of service' attacks and damage to computer and electronic communication systems.

(50) The processing of personal data for purposes other than those for which the personal data were initially collected should be allowed only where the processing is compatible with the purposes for which the personal data were initially collected. In such a case, no legal basis separate from that which allowed the collection of the personal data is required. If the processing is necessary for the performance of a task carried out in the public interest or in the exercise of official authority vested in the controller, Union or Member State law may determine and specify the tasks and purposes for which the further processing should be regarded as compatible and lawful. Further processing for archiving purposes in the public interest, scientific or historical research purposes or statistical purposes should be considered to be compatible lawful processing operations. The legal basis provided by Union or Member State law for the processing of personal data may also provide a legal basis for further processing. In order to ascertain whether a purpose of further processing is compatible with the purpose for which the personal data are initially collected, the controller, after having met all the requirements for the lawfulness of the original processing, should take into account, inter alia: any link between those purposes and the purposes of the intended further processing; the context in which the personal data have been collected, in particular the reasonable expectations of data subjects based on their relationship with the controller as to their further use; the nature of the personal data; the consequences of the intended further processing for data subjects; and the existence of appropriate safeguards in both the original and intended further processing operations.

Where the data subject has given consent or the processing is based on Union or Member State law which constitutes a necessary and proportionate measure in a democratic society to safeguard, in particular, important objectives of general public interest, the controller should be allowed to further process the personal data irrespective of the compatibility of the purposes. In any case, the application of the principles set out in this Regulation and in particular the information of the data subject on those other purposes and on his or her rights including the right to object, should be ensured. Indicating possible criminal acts or threats to public security by the controller and transmitting the relevant personal data in individual cases or in several cases relating to the same criminal act or threats to public security to a competent authority should be regarded as being in the legitimate interest pursued by the controller. However, such transmission in the legitimate interest of the controller or further processing of personal data should be prohibited if the processing is not compatible with a legal, professional or other binding obligation of secrecy.

(51) Personal data which are, by their nature, particularly sensitive in relation to fundamental rights and freedoms merit specific protection as the context of their processing could create significant risks to the fundamental rights and freedoms. Those personal data should include personal data revealing racial or ethnic origin, whereby the use of the term 'racial origin' in this Regulation does not imply an acceptance by the Union of theories which attempt to determine the existence of separate human races. The processing of photographs should not systematically be considered to be processing of special categories of personal data as they are covered by the definition of biometric data only when processed through a specific technical means allowing the unique identification or authentication of a natural person. Such personal data should not be processed, unless processing is allowed in specific cases set out in this Regulation, taking into account that Member States law may lay down specific provisions on data protection in order to adapt the application of the rules of this Regulation for compliance with a legal obligation or for the performance of a task carried out in the public interest or in the exercise of official authority vested in the controller. In addition to the specific requirements for such processing, the general principles and other rules of this Regulation should apply, in particular as regards the conditions for lawful processing. Derogations from the general prohibition for processing such special categories of personal data should be explicitly provided, inter alia, where the data subject gives his or her explicit consent or in respect of specific needs in particular where the processing is carried out in the course of legitimate activities by certain associations or foundations the purpose of which is to permit the exercise of fundamental freedoms.

(52) Derogating from the prohibition on processing special categories of personal data should also be allowed when provided for in Union or Member State law and subject to suitable safeguards, so as to protect personal data and other fundamental rights, where it is in the public interest to do so, in particular processing personal data in the field of employment law, social protection law including pensions and for health security, monitoring and alert purposes, the prevention or control of communicable diseases and other serious threats to health. Such a derogation may be made for health

purposes, including public health and the management of health-care services, especially in order to ensure the quality and cost-effectiveness of the procedures used for settling claims for benefits and services in the health insurance system, or for archiving purposes in the public interest, scientific or historical research purposes or statistical purposes. A derogation should also allow the processing of such personal data where necessary for the establishment, exercise or defence of legal claims, whether in court proceedings or in an administrative or out-of-court procedure.

(53) Special categories of personal data which merit higher protection should be processed for health-related purposes only where necessary to achieve those purposes for the benefit of natural persons and society as a whole, in particular in the context of the management of health or social care services and systems, including processing by the management and central national health authorities of such data for the purpose of quality control, management information and the general national and local supervision of the health or social care system, and ensuring continuity of health or social care and cross-border healthcare or health security, monitoring and alert purposes, or for archiving purposes in the public interest, scientific or historical research purposes or statistical purposes, based on Union or Member State law which has to meet an objective of public interest, as well as for studies conducted in the public interest in the area of public health. Therefore, this Regulation should provide for harmonised conditions for the processing of special categories of personal data concerning health, in respect of specific needs, in particular where the processing of such data is carried out for certain health-related purposes by persons subject to a legal obligation of professional secrecy. Union or Member State law should provide for specific and suitable measures so as to protect the fundamental rights and the personal data of natural persons. Member States should be allowed to maintain or introduce further conditions, including limitations, with regard to the processing of genetic data, biometric data or data concerning health. However, this should not hamper the free flow of personal data within the Union when those conditions apply to cross-border processing of such data.

(54) The processing of special categories of personal data may be necessary for reasons of public interest in the areas of public health without consent of the data subject. Such processing should be subject to suitable and specific measures so as to protect the rights and freedoms of natural persons. In that context, 'public health' should be interpreted as defined in Regulation (EC) No 1338/2008 of the European Parliament and of the Council,[11] namely all elements related to health, namely health status, including morbidity and disability, the determinants having an effect on that health status, health care needs, resources allocated to health care, the provision of, and universal access to, health care as well as health care expenditure and financing, and the causes of mortality. Such processing of data concerning health for reasons of public interest should not result in personal data being processed for other purposes by third parties such as employers or insurance and banking companies.

(55) Moreover, the processing of personal data by official authorities for the purpose of achieving the aims, laid down by constitutional law or by international public law, of officially recognised religious associations, is carried out on grounds of public interest.

(56) Where in the course of electoral activities, the operation of the democratic system in a Member State requires that political parties compile personal data on people's political opinions, the processing of such data may be permitted for reasons of public interest, provided that appropriate safeguards are established.

(57) If the personal data processed by a controller do not permit the controller to identify a natural person, the data controller should not be obliged to acquire additional information in order to identify the data subject for the sole purpose of complying with any provision of this Regulation. However, the controller should not refuse to take additional information provided by the data subject in order to support the exercise of his or her rights. Identification should include the digital identification of a data subject, for example through authentication mechanism such as the same credentials, used by the data subject to log-in to the on-line service offered by the data controller.

(58) The principle of transparency requires that any information addressed to the public or to the data subject be concise, easily accessible and easy to understand, and that clear and plain language and, additionally, where appropriate, visualisation be used. Such information could be provided in electronic form, for example, when addressed to the public, through a website. This is of particular relevance in situations where the proliferation of actors and the technological complexity of practice make it difficult for the data subject to know and understand whether, by whom and for what purpose personal data relating to him or her are being collected, such as in the case of online advertising. Given that children merit specific protection, any information and communication, where processing is addressed to a child, should be in such a clear and plain language that the child can easily understand.

(59) Modalities should be provided for facilitating the exercise of the data subject's rights under this Regulation, including mechanisms to request and, if applicable, obtain, free of charge, in particular, access to and rectification or erasure of personal data and the exercise of the right to object. The controller should also provide means for requests to be made electronically, especially where personal data are processed by electronic means. The controller should be obliged to respond to requests from the data subject without undue delay and at the latest within one month and to give reasons where the controller does not intend to comply with any such requests.

(60) The principles of fair and transparent processing require that the data subject be informed of the existence of the processing operation and its purposes. The controller should provide the data subject with any further information necessary to ensure fair and transparent processing taking into account the specific circumstances and context in which the personal data are processed. Furthermore, the data subject should be informed of the existence of profiling and the consequences of such profiling. Where the personal data are collected from the data subject, the data subject should also be informed whether he or she is obliged to provide the personal data and of the consequences, where he or she does not

provide such data. That information may be provided in combination with standardised icons in order to give in an easily visible, intelligible and clearly legible manner, a meaningful overview of the intended processing. Where the icons are presented electronically, they should be machine-readable.

(61) The information in relation to the processing of personal data relating to the data subject should be given to him or her at the time of collection from the data subject, or, where the personal data are obtained from another source, within a reasonable period, depending on the circumstances of the case. Where personal data can be legitimately disclosed to another recipient, the data subject should be informed when the personal data are first disclosed to the recipient. Where the controller intends to process the personal data for a purpose other than that for which they were collected, the controller should provide the data subject prior to that further processing with information on that other purpose and other necessary information. Where the origin of the personal data cannot be provided to the data subject because various sources have been used, general information should be provided.

(62) However, it is not necessary to impose the obligation to provide information where the data subject already possesses the information, where the recording or disclosure of the personal data is expressly laid down by law or where the provision of information to the data subject proves to be impossible or would involve a disproportionate effort. The latter could in particular be the case where processing is carried out for archiving purposes in the public interest, scientific or historical research purposes or statistical purposes. In that regard, the number of data subjects, the age of the data and any appropriate safeguards adopted should be taken into consideration.

(63) A data subject should have the right of access to personal data which have been collected concerning him or her, and to exercise that right easily and at reasonable intervals, in order to be aware of, and verify, the lawfulness of the processing. This includes the right for data subjects to have access to data concerning their health, for example the data in their medical records containing information such as diagnoses, examination results, assessments by treating physicians and any treatment or interventions provided. Every data subject should therefore have the right to know and obtain communication in particular with regard to the purposes for which the personal data are processed, where possible the period for which the personal data are processed, the recipients of the personal data, the logic involved in any automatic personal data processing and, at least when based on profiling, the consequences of such processing. Where possible, the controller should be able to provide remote access to a secure system which would provide the data subject with direct access to his or her personal data. That right should not adversely affect the rights or freedoms of others, including trade secrets or intellectual property and in particular the copyright protecting the software. However, the result of those considerations should not be a refusal to provide all information to the data subject. Where the controller processes a large quantity of information concerning the data subject, the controller should be able to request that, before the information is delivered, the data subject specify the information or processing activities to which the request relates.

(64) The controller should use all reasonable measures to verify the identity of a data subject who requests access, in particular in the context of online services and online identifiers. A controller should not retain personal data for the sole purpose of being able to react to potential requests.

(65) A data subject should have the right to have personal data concerning him or her rectified and a 'right to be forgotten' where the retention of such data infringes this Regulation or Union or Member State law to which the controller is subject. In particular, a data subject should have the right to have his or her personal data erased and no longer processed where the personal data are no longer necessary in relation to the purposes for which they are collected or otherwise processed, where a data subject has withdrawn his or her consent or objects to the processing of personal data concerning him or her, or where the processing of his or her personal data does not otherwise comply with this Regulation. That right is relevant in particular where the data subject has given his or her consent as a child and is not fully aware of the risks involved by the processing, and later wants to remove such personal data, especially on the internet. The data subject should be able to exercise that right notwithstanding the fact that he or she is no longer a child. However, the further retention of the personal data should be lawful where it is necessary, for exercising the right of freedom of expression and information, for compliance with a legal obligation, for the performance of a task carried out in the public interest or in the exercise of official authority vested in the controller, on the grounds of public interest in the area of public health, for archiving purposes in the public interest, scientific or historical research purposes or statistical purposes, or for the establishment, exercise or defence of legal claims.

(66) To strengthen the right to be forgotten in the online environment, the right to erasure should also be extended in such a way that a controller who has made the personal data public should be obliged to inform the controllers which are processing such personal data to erase any links to, or copies or replications of those personal data. In doing so, that controller should take reasonable steps, taking into account available technology and the means available to the controller, including technical measures, to inform the controllers which are processing the personal data of the data subject's request.

(67) Methods by which to restrict the processing of personal data could include, inter alia, temporarily moving the selected data to another processing system, making the selected personal data unavailable to users, or temporarily removing published data from a website. In automated filing systems, the restriction of processing should in principle be ensured by technical means in such a manner that the personal data are not subject to further processing operations and cannot be changed. The fact that the processing of personal data is restricted should be clearly indicated in the system.

(68) To further strengthen the control over his or her own data, where the processing of personal data is carried out by automated means, the data subject should also be allowed to receive personal data concerning him or her which he or she has provided to a controller in a structured, commonly used, machine-readable and interoperable format, and to transmit it to another controller. Data controllers

should be encouraged to develop interoperable formats that enable data portability. That right should apply where the data subject provided the personal data on the basis of his or her consent or the processing is necessary for the performance of a contract. It should not apply where processing is based on a legal ground other than consent or contract. By its very nature, that right should not be exercised against controllers processing personal data in the exercise of their public duties. It should therefore not apply where the processing of the personal data is necessary for compliance with a legal obligation to which the controller is subject or for the performance of a task carried out in the public interest or in the exercise of an official authority vested in the controller. The data subject's right to transmit or receive personal data concerning him or her should not create an obligation for the controllers to adopt or maintain processing systems which are technically compatible. Where, in a certain set of personal data, more than one data subject is concerned, the right to receive the personal data should be without prejudice to the rights and freedoms of other data subjects in accordance with this Regulation. Furthermore, that right should not prejudice the right of the data subject to obtain the erasure of personal data and the limitations of that right as set out in this Regulation and should, in particular, not imply the erasure of personal data concerning the data subject which have been provided by him or her for the performance of a contract to the extent that and for as long as the personal data are necessary for the performance of that contract. Where technically feasible, the data subject should have the right to have the personal data transmitted directly from one controller to another.

(69) Where personal data might lawfully be processed because processing is necessary for the performance of a task carried out in the public interest or in the exercise of official authority vested in the controller, or on grounds of the legitimate interests of a controller or a third party, a data subject should, nevertheless, be entitled to object to the processing of any personal data relating to his or her particular situation. It should be for the controller to demonstrate that its compelling legitimate interest overrides the interests or the fundamental rights and freedoms of the data subject.

(70) Where personal data are processed for the purposes of direct marketing, the data subject should have the right to object to such processing, including profiling to the extent that it is related to such direct marketing, whether with regard to initial or further processing, at any time and free of charge. That right should be explicitly brought to the attention of the data subject and presented clearly and separately from any other information.

(71) The data subject should have the right not to be subject to a decision, which may include a measure, evaluating personal aspects relating to him or her which is based solely on automated processing and which produces legal effects concerning him or her or similarly significantly affects him or her, such as automatic refusal of an online credit application or e-recruiting practices without any human intervention. Such processing includes 'profiling' that consists of any form of automated processing of personal data evaluating the personal aspects relating to a natural person, in particular to analyse or predict aspects concerning the data subject's performance at work, economic situation, health, personal preferences or interests, reliability or behaviour, location or movements, where it produces legal effects concerning him or her or similarly significantly affects him or her. However, decision-making based on such processing, including profiling, should be allowed where expressly authorised by Union or Member State law to which the controller is subject, including for fraud and tax-evasion monitoring and prevention purposes conducted in accordance with the regulations, standards and recommendations of Union institutions or national oversight bodies and to ensure the security and reliability of a service provided by the controller, or necessary for the entering or performance of a contract between the data subject and a controller, or when the data subject has given his or her explicit consent. In any case, such processing should be subject to suitable safeguards, which should include specific information to the data subject and the right to obtain human intervention, to express his or her point of view, to obtain an explanation of the decision reached after such assessment and to challenge the decision. Such measure should not concern a child.

In order to ensure fair and transparent processing in respect of the data subject, taking into account the specific circumstances and context in which the personal data are processed, the controller should use appropriate mathematical or statistical procedures for the profiling, implement technical and organisational measures appropriate to ensure, in particular, that factors which result in inaccuracies in personal data are corrected and the risk of errors is minimised, secure personal data in a manner that takes account of the potential risks involved for the interests and rights of the data subject, and prevent, inter alia, discriminatory effects on natural persons on the basis of racial or ethnic origin, political opinion, religion or beliefs, trade union membership, genetic or health status or sexual orientation, or processing that results in measures having such an effect.

(72) Profiling is subject to the rules of this Regulation governing the processing of personal data, such as the legal grounds for processing or data protection principles. The European Data Protection Board established by this Regulation (the 'Board') should be able to issue guidance in that context.

(73) Restrictions concerning specific principles and the rights of information, access to and rectification or erasure of personal data, the right to data portability, the right to object, decisions based on profiling, as well as the communication of a personal data breach to a data subject and certain related obligations of the controllers may be imposed by Union or Member State law, as far as necessary and proportionate in a democratic society to safeguard public security, including the protection of human life especially in response to natural or manmade disasters, the prevention, investigation and prosecution of criminal offences or the execution of criminal penalties, including the safeguarding against and the prevention of threats to public security, or of breaches of ethics for regulated professions, other important objectives of general public interest of the Union or of a Member State, in particular an important economic or financial interest of the Union or of a Member State, the keeping of public registers kept for reasons of general public interest, further processing of archived personal data to provide specific information

related to the political behaviour under former totalitarian state regimes or the protection of the data subject or the rights and freedoms of others, including social protection, public health and humanitarian purposes. Those restrictions should be in accordance with the requirements set out in the Charter and in the European Convention for the Protection of Human Rights and Fundamental Freedoms.

(74) The responsibility and liability of the controller for any processing of personal data carried out by the controller or on the controller's behalf should be established. In particular, the controller should be obliged to implement appropriate and effective measures and be able to demonstrate the compliance of processing activities with this Regulation, including the effectiveness of the measures. Those measures should take into account the nature, scope, context and purposes of the processing and the risk to the rights and freedoms of natural persons.

(75) The risk to the rights and freedoms of natural persons, of varying likelihood and severity, may result from personal data processing which could lead to physical, material or non-material damage, in particular: where the processing may give rise to discrimination, identity theft or fraud, financial loss, damage to the reputation, loss of confidentiality of personal data protected by professional secrecy, unauthorised reversal of pseudonymisation, or any other significant economic or social disadvantage; where data subjects might be deprived of their rights and freedoms or prevented from exercising control over their personal data; where personal data are processed which reveal racial or ethnic origin, political opinions, religion or philosophical beliefs, trade union membership, and the processing of genetic data, data concerning health or data concerning sex life or criminal convictions and offences or related security measures; where personal aspects are evaluated, in particular analysing or predicting aspects concerning performance at work, economic situation, health, personal preferences or interests, reliability or behaviour, location or movements, in order to create or use personal profiles; where personal data of vulnerable natural persons, in particular of children, are processed; or where processing involves a large amount of personal data and affects a large number of data subjects.

(76) The likelihood and severity of the risk to the rights and freedoms of the data subject should be determined by reference to the nature, scope, context and purposes of the processing. Risk should be evaluated on the basis of an objective assessment, by which it is established whether data processing operations involve a risk or a high risk.

(77) Guidance on the implementation of appropriate measures and on the demonstration of compliance by the controller or the processor, especially as regards the identification of the risk related to the processing, their assessment in terms of origin, nature, likelihood and severity, and the identification of best practices to mitigate the risk, could be provided in particular by means of approved codes of conduct, approved certifications, guidelines provided by the Board or indications provided by a data protection officer. The Board may also issue guidelines on processing operations that are considered to be unlikely to result in a high risk to the rights and freedoms of natural persons and indicate what measures may be sufficient in such cases to address such risk.

(78) The protection of the rights and freedoms of natural persons with regard to the processing of personal data require that appropriate technical and organisational measures be taken to ensure that the requirements of this Regulation are met. In order to be able to demonstrate compliance with this Regulation, the controller should adopt internal policies and implement measures which meet in particular the principles of data protection by design and data protection by default. Such measures could consist, inter alia, of minimising the processing of personal data, pseudonymising personal data as soon as possible, transparency with regard to the functions and processing of personal data, enabling the data subject to monitor the data processing, enabling the controller to create and improve security features. When developing, designing, selecting and using applications, services and products that are based on the processing of personal data or process personal data to fulfil their task, producers of the products, services and applications should be encouraged to take into account the right to data protection when developing and designing such products, services and applications and, with due regard to the state of the art, to make sure that controllers and processors are able to fulfil their data protection obligations. The principles of data protection by design and by default should also be taken into consideration in the context of public tenders.

(79) The protection of the rights and freedoms of data subjects as well as the responsibility and liability of controllers and processors, also in relation to the monitoring by and measures of supervisory authorities, requires a clear allocation of the responsibilities under this Regulation, including where a controller determines the purposes and means of the processing jointly with other controllers or where a processing operation is carried out on behalf of a controller.

(80) Where a controller or a processor not established in the Union is processing personal data of data subjects who are in the Union whose processing activities are related to the offering of goods or services, irrespective of whether a payment of the data subject is required, to such data subjects in the Union, or to the monitoring of their behaviour as far as their behaviour takes place within the Union, the controller or the processor should designate a representative, unless the processing is occasional, does not include processing, on a large scale, of special categories of personal data or the processing of personal data relating to criminal convictions and offences, and is unlikely to result in a risk to the rights and freedoms of natural persons, taking into account the nature, context, scope and purposes of the processing or if the controller is a public authority or body. The representative should act on behalf of the controller or the processor and may be addressed by any supervisory authority. The representative should be explicitly designated by a written mandate of the controller or of the processor to act on its behalf with regard to its obligations under this Regulation. The designation of such a representative does not affect the responsibility or liability of the controller or of the processor under this Regulation. Such a representative should perform its tasks according to the mandate received from the controller or

processor, including cooperating with the competent supervisory authorities with regard to any action taken to ensure compliance with this Regulation. The designated representative should be subject to enforcement proceedings in the event of non-compliance by the controller or processor.

(81) To ensure compliance with the requirements of this Regulation in respect of the processing to be carried out by the processor on behalf of the controller, when entrusting a processor with processing activities, the controller should use only processors providing sufficient guarantees, in particular in terms of expert knowledge, reliability and resources, to implement technical and organisational measures which will meet the requirements of this Regulation, including for the security of processing. The adherence of the processor to an approved code of conduct or an approved certification mechanism may be used as an element to demonstrate compliance with the obligations of the controller. The carrying-out of processing by a processor should be governed by a contract or other legal act under Union or Member State law, binding the processor to the controller, setting out the subject- matter and duration of the processing, the nature and purposes of the processing, the type of personal data and categories of data subjects, taking into account the specific tasks and responsibilities of the processor in the context of the processing to be carried out and the risk to the rights and freedoms of the data subject. The controller and processor may choose to use an individual contract or standard contractual clauses which are adopted either directly by the Commission or by a supervisory authority in accordance with the consistency mechanism and then adopted by the Commission. After the completion of the processing on behalf of the controller, the processor should, at the choice of the controller, return or delete the personal data, unless there is a requirement to store the personal data under Union or Member State law to which the processor is subject.

(82) In order to demonstrate compliance with this Regulation, the controller or processor should maintain records of processing activities under its responsibility. Each controller and processor should be obliged to cooperate with the supervisory authority and make those records, on request, available to it, so that it might serve for monitoring those processing operations.

(83) In order to maintain security and to prevent processing in infringement of this Regulation, the controller or processor should evaluate the risks inherent in the processing and implement measures to mitigate those risks, such as encryption. Those measures should ensure an appropriate level of security, including confidentiality, taking into account the state of the art and the costs of implementation in relation to the risks and the nature of the personal data to be protected. In assessing data security risk, consideration should be given to the risks that are presented by personal data processing, such as accidental or unlawful destruction, loss, alteration, unauthorised disclosure of, or access to, personal data transmitted, stored or otherwise processed which may in particular lead to physical, material or non-material damage.

(84) In order to enhance compliance with this Regulation where processing operations are likely to result in a high risk to the rights and freedoms of natural persons, the controller should be responsible for the carrying-out of a data protection impact assessment to evaluate, in particular, the origin, nature, particularity and severity of that risk. The outcome of the assessment should be taken into account when determining the appropriate measures to be taken in order to demonstrate that the processing of personal data complies with this Regulation. Where a data-protection impact assessment indicates that processing operations involve a high risk which the controller cannot mitigate by appropriate measures in terms of available technology and costs of implementation, a consultation of the supervisory authority should take place prior to the processing.

(85) A personal data breach may, if not addressed in an appropriate and timely manner, result in physical, material or non-material damage to natural persons such as loss of control over their personal data or limitation of their rights, discrimination, identity theft or fraud, financial loss, unauthorised reversal of pseudonymisation, damage to reputation, loss of confidentiality of personal data protected by professional secrecy or any other significant economic or social disadvantage to the natural person concerned. Therefore, as soon as the controller becomes aware that a personal data breach has occurred, the controller should notify the personal data breach to the supervisory authority without undue delay and, where feasible, not later than 72 hours after having become aware of it, unless the controller is able to demonstrate, in accordance with the accountability principle, that the personal data breach is unlikely to result in a risk to the rights and freedoms of natural persons. Where such notification cannot be achieved within 72 hours, the reasons for the delay should accompany the notification and information may be provided in phases without undue further delay.

(86) The controller should communicate to the data subject a personal data breach, without undue delay, where that personal data breach is likely to result in a high risk to the rights and freedoms of the natural person in order to allow him or her to take the necessary precautions. The communication should describe the nature of the personal data breach as well as recommendations for the natural person concerned to mitigate potential adverse effects. Such communications to data subjects should be made as soon as reasonably feasible and in close cooperation with the supervisory authority, respecting guidance provided by it or by other relevant authorities such as law-enforcement authorities. For example, the need to mitigate an immediate risk of damage would call for prompt communication with data subjects whereas the need to implement appropriate measures against continuing or similar personal data breaches may justify more time for communication.

(87) It should be ascertained whether all appropriate technological protection and organisational measures have been implemented to establish immediately whether a personal data breach has taken place and to inform promptly the supervisory authority and the data subject. The fact that the notification

was made without undue delay should be established taking into account in particular the nature and gravity of the personal data breach and its consequences and adverse effects for the data subject. Such notification may result in an intervention of the supervisory authority in accordance with its tasks and powers laid down in this Regulation.

(88) In setting detailed rules concerning the format and procedures applicable to the notification of personal data breaches, due consideration should be given to the circumstances of that breach, including whether or not personal data had been protected by appropriate technical protection measures, effectively limiting the likelihood of identity fraud or other forms of misuse. Moreover, such rules and procedures should take into account the legitimate interests of law-enforcement authorities where early disclosure could unnecessarily hamper the investigation of the circumstances of a personal data breach.

(89) Directive 95/46/EC provided for a general obligation to notify the processing of personal data to the supervisory authorities. While that obligation produces administrative and financial burdens, it did not in all cases contribute to improving the protection of personal data. Such indiscriminate general notification obligations should therefore be abolished, and replaced by effective procedures and mechanisms which focus instead on those types of processing operations which are likely to result in a high risk to the rights and freedoms of natural persons by virtue of their nature, scope, context and purposes. Such types of processing operations may be those which in, particular, involve using new technologies, or are of a new kind and where no data protection impact assessment has been carried out before by the controller, or where they become necessary in the light of the time that has elapsed since the initial processing.

(90) In such cases, a data protection impact assessment should be carried out by the controller prior to the processing in order to assess the particular likelihood and severity of the high risk, taking into account the nature, scope, context and purposes of the processing and the sources of the risk. That impact assessment should include, in particular, the measures, safeguards and mechanisms envisaged for mitigating that risk, ensuring the protection of personal data and demonstrating compliance with this Regulation.

(91) This should in particular apply to large-scale processing operations which aim to process a considerable amount of personal data at regional, national or supranational level and which could affect a large number of data subjects and which are likely to result in a high risk, for example, on account of their sensitivity, where in accordance with the achieved state of technological knowledge a new technology is used on a large scale as well as to other processing operations which result in a high risk to the rights and freedoms of data subjects, in particular where those operations render it more difficult for data subjects to exercise their rights. A data protection impact assessment should also be made where personal data are processed for taking decisions regarding specific natural persons following any systematic and extensive evaluation of personal aspects relating to natural persons based on profiling those data or following the processing of special categories of personal data, biometric data, or data on criminal convictions and offences or related security measures. A data protection impact assessment is equally required for monitoring publicly accessible areas on a large scale, especially when using optic-electronic devices or for any other operations where the competent supervisory authority considers that the processing is likely to result in a high risk to the rights and freedoms of data subjects, in particular because they prevent data subjects from exercising a right or using a service or a contract, or because they are carried out systematically on a large scale. The processing of personal data should not be considered to be on a large scale if the processing concerns personal data from patients or clients by an individual physician, other health care professional or lawyer. In such cases, a data protection impact assessment should not be mandatory.

(92) There are circumstances under which it may be reasonable and economical for the subject of a data protection impact assessment to be broader than a single project, for example where public authorities or bodies intend to establish a common application or processing platform or where several controllers plan to introduce a common application or processing environment across an industry sector or segment or for a widely used horizontal activity.

(93) In the context of the adoption of the Member State law on which the performance of the tasks of the public authority or public body is based and which regulates the specific processing operation or set of operations in question, Member States may deem it necessary to carry out such assessment prior to the processing activities.

(94) Where a data protection impact assessment indicates that the processing would, in the absence of safeguards, security measures and mechanisms to mitigate the risk, result in a high risk to the rights and freedoms of natural persons and the controller is of the opinion that the risk cannot be mitigated by reasonable means in terms of available technologies and costs of implementation, the supervisory authority should be consulted prior to the start of processing activities. Such high risk is likely to result from certain types of processing and the extent and frequency of processing, which may result also in a realisation of damage or interference with the rights and freedoms of the natural person. The supervisory authority should respond to the request for consultation within a specified period. However, the absence of a reaction of the supervisory authority within that period should be without prejudice to any intervention of the supervisory authority in accordance with its tasks and powers laid down in this Regulation, including the power to prohibit processing operations. As part of that consultation process, the outcome of a data protection impact assessment carried out with regard to the processing at issue may be submitted to the supervisory authority, in particular the measures envisaged to mitigate the risk to the rights and freedoms of natural persons.

(95) The processor should assist the controller, where necessary and upon request, in ensuring compliance with the obligations deriving from the carrying out of data protection impact assessments and from prior consultation of the supervisory authority.

(96) A consultation of the supervisory authority should also take place in the course of the preparation of a legislative or regulatory measure which provides for the processing of personal data, in order to ensure compliance of the intended processing with this Regulation and in particular to mitigate the risk involved for the data subject.

(97) Where the processing is carried out by a public authority, except for courts or independent judicial authorities when acting in their judicial capacity, where, in the private sector, processing is carried out by a controller whose core activities consist of processing operations that require regular and systematic monitoring of the data subjects on a large scale, or where the core activities of the controller or the processor consist of processing on a large scale of special categories of personal data and data relating to criminal convictions and offences, a person with expert knowledge of data protection law and practices should assist the controller or processor to monitor internal compliance with this Regulation. In the private sector, the core activities of a controller relate to its primary activities and do not relate to the processing of personal data as ancillary activities. The necessary level of expert knowledge should be determined in particular according to the data processing operations carried out and the protection required for the personal data processed by the controller or the processor. Such data protection officers, whether or not they are an employee of the controller, should be in a position to perform their duties and tasks in an independent manner.

(98) Associations or other bodies representing categories of controllers or processors should be encouraged to draw up codes of conduct, within the limits of this Regulation, so as to facilitate the effective application of this Regulation, taking account of the specific characteristics of the processing carried out in certain sectors and the specific needs of micro, small and medium enterprises. In particular, such codes of conduct could calibrate the obligations of controllers and processors, taking into account the risk likely to result from the processing for the rights and freedoms of natural persons.

(99) When drawing up a code of conduct, or when amending or extending such a code, associations and other bodies representing categories of controllers or processors should consult relevant stakeholders, including data subjects where feasible, and have regard to submissions received and views expressed in response to such consultations.

(100) In order to enhance transparency and compliance with this Regulation, the establishment of certification mechanisms and data protection seals and marks should be encouraged, allowing data subjects to quickly assess the level of data protection of relevant products and services.

(101) Flows of personal data to and from countries outside the Union and international organisations are necessary for the expansion of international trade and international cooperation. The increase in such flows has raised new challenges and concerns with regard to the protection of personal data. However, when personal data are transferred from the Union to controllers, processors or other recipients in third countries or to international organisations, the level of protection of natural persons ensured in the Union by this Regulation should not be undermined, including in cases of onward transfers of personal data from the third country or international organisation to controllers, processors in the same or another third country or international organisation. In any event, transfers to third countries and international organisations may only be carried out in full compliance with this Regulation. A transfer could take place only if, subject to the other provisions of this Regulation, the conditions laid down in the provisions of this Regulation relating to the transfer of personal data to third countries or international organisations are complied with by the controller or processor.

(102) This Regulation is without prejudice to international agreements concluded between the Union and third countries regulating the transfer of personal data including appropriate safeguards for the data subjects. Member States may conclude international agreements which involve the transfer of personal data to third countries or international organisations, as far as such agreements do not affect this Regulation or any other provisions of Union law and include an appropriate level of protection for the fundamental rights of the data subjects.

(103) The Commission may decide with effect for the entire Union that a third country, a territory or specified sector within a third country, or an international organisation, offers an adequate level of data protection, thus providing legal certainty and uniformity throughout the Union as regards the third country or international organisation which is considered to provide such level of protection. In such cases, transfers of personal data to that third country or international organisation may take place without the need to obtain any further authorisation. The Commission may also decide, having given notice and a full statement setting out the reasons to the third country or international organisation, to revoke such a decision.

(104) In line with the fundamental values on which the Union is founded, in particular the protection of human rights, the Commission should, in its assessment of the third country, or of a territory or specified sector within a third country, take into account how a particular third country respects the rule of law, access to justice as well as international human rights norms and standards and its general and sectoral law, including legislation concerning public security, defence and national security as well as public order and criminal law. The adoption of an adequacy decision with regard to a territory or a specified sector in a third country should take into account clear and objective criteria, such as specific processing activities and the scope of applicable legal standards and legislation in force in the third country. The third country should offer guarantees ensuring an adequate level of protection essentially equivalent to that ensured within the Union, in particular where personal data are processed in one or several specific sectors. In particular, the third country should ensure effective independent data protection supervision and should provide for cooperation mechanisms with the Member States' data protection authorities, and the data subjects should be provided with effective and enforceable rights and effective administrative and judicial redress.

(105) Apart from the international commitments the third country or international organisation has entered into, the Commission should take account of obligations arising from the third country's or international organisation's participation in multilateral or regional systems in particular in relation to the protection of personal data, as well as the implementation of such obligations. In particular, the third country's accession to the Council of Europe Convention of 28 January 1981 for the Protection of Individuals with regard to the Automatic Processing of Personal Data and its Additional Protocol should be taken into account. The Commission should consult the Board when assessing the level of protection in third countries or international organisations.

(106) The Commission should monitor the functioning of decisions on the level of protection in a third country, a territory or specified sector within a third country, or an international organisation, and monitor the functioning of decisions adopted on the basis of Article 25(6) or Article 26(4) of Directive 95/46/EC. In its adequacy decisions, the Commission should provide for a periodic review mechanism of their functioning. That periodic review should be conducted in consultation with the third country or international organisation in question and take into account all relevant developments in the third country or international organisation. For the purposes of monitoring and of carrying out the periodic reviews, the Commission should take into consideration the views and findings of the European Parliament and of the Council as well as of other relevant bodies and sources. The Commission should evaluate, within a reasonable time, the functioning of the latter decisions and report any relevant findings to the Committee within the meaning of Regulation (EU) No 182/2011 of the European Parliament and of the Council[12] as established under this Regulation, to the European Parliament and to the Council.

(107) The Commission may recognise that a third country, a territory or a specified sector within a third country, or an international organisation no longer ensures an adequate level of data protection. Consequently the transfer of personal data to that third country or international organisation should be prohibited, unless the requirements in this Regulation relating to transfers subject to appropriate safeguards, including binding corporate rules, and derogations for specific situations are fulfilled. In that case, provision should be made for consultations between the Commission and such third countries or international organisations. The Commission should, in a timely manner, inform the third country or international organisation of the reasons and enter into consultations with it in order to remedy the situation.

(108) In the absence of an adequacy decision, the controller or processor should take measures to compensate for the lack of data protection in a third country by way of appropriate safeguards for the data subject. Such appropriate safeguards may consist of making use of binding corporate rules, standard data protection clauses adopted by the Commission, standard data protection clauses adopted by a supervisory authority or contractual clauses authorised by a supervisory authority. Those safeguards should ensure compliance with data protection requirements and the rights of the data subjects appropriate to processing within the Union, including the availability of enforceable data subject rights and of effective legal remedies, including to obtain effective administrative or judicial redress and to claim compensation, in the Union or in a third country. They should relate in particular to compliance with the general principles relating to personal data processing, the principles of data protection by design and by default. Transfers may also be carried out by public authorities or bodies with public authorities or bodies in third countries or with international organisations with corresponding duties or functions, including on the basis of provisions to be inserted into administrative arrangements, such as a memorandum of understanding, providing for enforceable and effective rights for data subjects. Authorisation by the competent supervisory authority should be obtained when the safeguards are provided for in administrative arrangements that are not legally binding.

(109) The possibility for the controller or processor to use standard data-protection clauses adopted by the Commission or by a supervisory authority should prevent controllers or processors neither from including the standard data-protection clauses in a wider contract, such as a contract between the processor and another processor, nor from adding other clauses or additional safeguards provided that they do not contradict, directly or indirectly, the standard contractual clauses adopted by the Commission or by a supervisory authority or prejudice the fundamental rights or freedoms of the data subjects. Controllers and processors should be encouraged to provide additional safeguards via contractual commitments that supplement standard protection clauses.

(110) A group of undertakings, or a group of enterprises engaged in a joint economic activity, should be able to make use of approved binding corporate rules for its international transfers from the Union to organisations within the same group of undertakings, or group of enterprises engaged in a joint economic activity, provided that such corporate rules include all essential principles and enforceable rights to ensure appropriate safeguards for transfers or categories of transfers of personal data.

(111) Provisions should be made for the possibility for transfers in certain circumstances where the data subject has given his or her explicit consent, where the transfer is occasional and necessary in relation to a contract or a legal claim, regardless of whether in a judicial procedure or whether in an administrative or any out-of-court procedure, including procedures before regulatory bodies. Provision should also be made for the possibility for transfers where important grounds of public interest laid down by Union or Member State law so require or where the transfer is made from a register established by law and intended for consultation by the public or persons having a legitimate interest. In the latter case, such a transfer should not involve the entirety of the personal data or entire categories of the data contained in the register and, when the register is intended for consultation by persons having a legitimate interest, the transfer should be made only at the request of those persons or, if they are to be the recipients, taking into full account the interests and fundamental rights of the data subject.

(112) Those derogations should in particular apply to data transfers required and necessary for important reasons of public interest, for example in cases of international data exchange between competition authorities, tax or customs administrations, between financial supervisory authorities, between services competent for social security matters, or for public health, for example in the case of contact tracing for contagious diseases or in order to reduce and/or eliminate doping in sport. A transfer of personal data should also be regarded as lawful where it is necessary to protect an interest which is essential for the data subject's or another person's vital interests, including physical integrity or life, if the data subject is incapable of giving consent. In the absence of an adequacy decision, Union or Member State law may, for important reasons of public interest, expressly set limits to the transfer of specific categories of data to a third country or an international organisation. Member States should notify such provisions to the Commission. Any transfer to an international humanitarian organisation of personal data of a data subject who is physically or legally incapable of giving consent, with a view to accomplishing a task incumbent under the Geneva Conventions or to complying with international humanitarian law applicable in armed conflicts, could be considered to be necessary for an important reason of public interest or because it is in the vital interest of the data subject.

(113) Transfers which can be qualified as not repetitive and that only concern a limited number of data subjects, could also be possible for the purposes of the compelling legitimate interests pursued by the controller, when those interests are not overridden by the interests or rights and freedoms of the data subject and when the controller has assessed all the circumstances surrounding the data transfer. The controller should give particular consideration to the nature of the personal data, the purpose and duration of the proposed processing operation or operations, as well as the situation in the country of origin, the third country and the country of final destination, and should provide suitable safeguards to protect fundamental rights and freedoms of natural persons with regard to the processing of their personal data. Such transfers should be possible only in residual cases where none of the other grounds for transfer are applicable. For scientific or historical research purposes or statistical purposes, the legitimate expectations of society for an increase of knowledge should be taken into consideration. The controller should inform the supervisory authority and the data subject about the transfer.

(114) In any case, where the Commission has taken no decision on the adequate level of data protection in a third country, the controller or processor should make use of solutions that provide data subjects with enforceable and effective rights as regards the processing of their data in the Union once those data have been transferred so that they will continue to benefit from fundamental rights and safeguards.

(115) Some third countries adopt laws, regulations and other legal acts which purport to directly regulate the processing activities of natural and legal persons under the jurisdiction of the Member States. This may include judgments of courts or tribunals or decisions of administrative authorities in third countries requiring a controller or processor to transfer or disclose personal data, and which are not based on an international agreement, such as a mutual legal assistance treaty, in force between the requesting third country and the Union or a Member State. The extraterritorial application of those laws, regulations and other legal acts may be in breach of international law and may impede the attainment of the protection of natural persons ensured in the Union by this Regulation. Transfers should only be allowed where the conditions of this Regulation for a transfer to third countries are met. This may be the case, inter alia, where disclosure is necessary for an important ground of public interest recognised in Union or Member State law to which the controller is subject.

(116) When personal data moves across borders outside the Union it may put at increased risk the ability of natural persons to exercise data protection rights in particular to protect themselves from the unlawful use or disclosure of that information. At the same time, supervisory authorities may find that they are unable to pursue complaints or conduct investigations relating to the activities outside their borders. Their efforts to work together in the cross-border context may also be hampered by insufficient preventative or remedial powers, inconsistent legal regimes, and practical obstacles like resource constraints. Therefore, there is a need to promote closer cooperation among data protection supervisory authorities to help them exchange information and carry out investigations with their international counterparts. For the purposes of developing international cooperation mechanisms to facilitate and provide international mutual assistance for the enforcement of legislation for the protection of personal data, the Commission and the supervisory authorities should exchange information and cooperate in activities related to the exercise of their powers with competent authorities in third countries, based on reciprocity and in accordance with this Regulation.

(117) The establishment of supervisory authorities in Member States, empowered to perform their tasks and exercise their powers with complete independence, is an essential component of the protection of natural persons with regard to the processing of their personal data. Member States should be able to establish more than one supervisory authority, to reflect their constitutional, organisational and administrative structure.

(118) The independence of supervisory authorities should not mean that the supervisory authorities cannot be subject to control or monitoring mechanisms regarding their financial expenditure or to judicial review.

(119) Where a Member State establishes several supervisory authorities, it should establish by law mechanisms for ensuring the effective participation of those supervisory authorities in the consistency mechanism. That Member State should in particular designate the supervisory authority which functions as a single contact point for the effective participation of those authorities in the mechanism, to ensure swift and smooth cooperation with other supervisory authorities, the Board and the Commission.

(120) Each supervisory authority should be provided with the financial and human resources, premises and infrastructure necessary for the effective performance of their tasks, including those related to mutual assistance and cooperation with other supervisory authorities throughout the Union. Each supervisory authority should have a separate, public annual budget, which may be part of the overall state or national budget.

(121) The general conditions for the member or members of the supervisory authority should be laid down by law in each Member State and should in particular provide that those members are to be appointed, by means of a transparent procedure, either by the parliament, government or the head of State of the Member State on the basis of a proposal from the government, a member of the government, the parliament or a chamber of the parliament, or by an independent body entrusted under Member State law. In order to ensure the independence of the supervisory authority, the member or members should act with integrity, refrain from any action that is incompatible with their duties and should not, during their term of office, engage in any incompatible occupation, whether gainful or not. The supervisory authority should have its own staff, chosen by the supervisory authority or an independent body established by Member State law, which should be subject to the exclusive direction of the member or members of the supervisory authority.

(122) Each supervisory authority should be competent on the territory of its own Member State to exercise the powers and to perform the tasks conferred on it in accordance with this Regulation. This should cover in particular the processing in the context of the activities of an establishment of the controller or processor on the territory of its own Member State, the processing of personal data carried out by public authorities or private bodies acting in the public interest, processing affecting data subjects on its territory or processing carried out by a controller or processor not established in the Union when targeting data subjects residing on its territory. This should include handling complaints lodged by a data subject, conducting investigations on the application of this Regulation and promoting public awareness of the risks, rules, safeguards and rights in relation to the processing of personal data.

(123) The supervisory authorities should monitor the application of the provisions pursuant to this Regulation and contribute to its consistent application throughout the Union, in order to protect natural persons in relation to the processing of their personal data and to facilitate the free flow of personal data within the internal market. For that purpose, the supervisory authorities should cooperate with each other and with the Commission, without the need for any agreement between Member States on the provision of mutual assistance or on such cooperation.

(124) Where the processing of personal data takes place in the context of the activities of an establishment of a controller or a processor in the Union and the controller or processor is established in more than one Member State, or where processing taking place in the context of the activities of a single establishment of a controller or processor in the Union substantially affects or is likely to substantially affect data subjects in more than one Member State, the supervisory authority for the main establishment of the controller or processor or for the single establishment of the controller or processor should act as lead authority. It should cooperate with the other authorities concerned, because the controller or processor has an establishment on the territory of their Member State, because data subjects residing on their territory are substantially affected, or because a complaint has been lodged with them. Also where a data subject not residing in that Member State has lodged a complaint, the supervisory authority with which such complaint has been lodged should also be a supervisory authority concerned. Within its tasks to issue guidelines on any question covering the application of this Regulation, the Board should be able to issue guidelines in particular on the criteria to be taken into account in order to ascertain whether the processing in question substantially affects data subjects in more than one Member State and on what constitutes a relevant and reasoned objection.

(125) The lead authority should be competent to adopt binding decisions regarding measures applying the powers conferred on it in accordance with this Regulation. In its capacity as lead authority, the supervisory authority should closely involve and coordinate the supervisory authorities concerned in the decision-making process. Where the decision is to reject the complaint by the data subject in whole or in part, that decision should be adopted by the supervisory authority with which the complaint has been lodged.

(126) The decision should be agreed jointly by the lead supervisory authority and the supervisory authorities concerned and should be directed towards the main or single establishment of the controller or processor and be binding on the controller and processor. The controller or processor should take the necessary measures to ensure compliance with this Regulation and the implementation of the decision notified by the lead supervisory authority to the main establishment of the controller or processor as regards the processing activities in the Union.

(127) Each supervisory authority not acting as the lead supervisory authority should be competent to handle local cases where the controller or processor is established in more than one Member State, but the subject matter of the specific processing concerns only processing carried out in a single Member State and involves only data subjects in that single Member State, for example, where the subject matter concerns the processing of employees' personal data in the specific employment context of a Member State. In such cases, the supervisory authority should inform the lead supervisory authority without delay about the matter. After being informed, the lead supervisory authority should decide, whether it will handle the case pursuant to the provision on cooperation between the lead supervisory authority and other supervisory authorities concerned ('one-stop-shop mechanism'), or whether the supervisory authority which informed it should handle the case at local level. When deciding whether it will handle the case, the lead supervisory authority should take into account whether there is an establishment of the controller or processor in the Member State of the supervisory authority which informed it in order to ensure effective enforcement of a decision vis-à-vis the controller or processor.

Where the lead supervisory authority decides to handle the case, the supervisory authority which informed it should have the possibility to submit a draft for a decision, of which the lead supervisory authority should take utmost account when preparing its draft decision in that one-stop-shop mechanism.

(128) The rules on the lead supervisory authority and the one-stop-shop mechanism should not apply where the processing is carried out by public authorities or private bodies in the public interest. In such cases the only supervisory authority competent to exercise the powers conferred to it in accordance with this Regulation should be the supervisory authority of the Member State where the public authority or private body is established.

(129) In order to ensure consistent monitoring and enforcement of this Regulation throughout the Union, the supervisory authorities should have in each Member State the same tasks and effective powers, including powers of investigation, corrective powers and sanctions, and authorisation and advisory powers, in particular in cases of complaints from natural persons, and without prejudice to the powers of prosecutorial authorities under Member State law, to bring infringements of this Regulation to the attention of the judicial authorities and engage in legal proceedings. Such powers should also include the power to impose a temporary or definitive limitation, including a ban, on processing. Member States may specify other tasks related to the protection of personal data under this Regulation. The powers of supervisory authorities should be exercised in accordance with appropriate procedural safeguards set out in Union and Member State law, impartially, fairly and within a reasonable time. In particular each measure should be appropriate, necessary and proportionate in view of ensuring compliance with this Regulation, taking into account the circumstances of each individual case, respect the right of every person to be heard before any individual measure which would affect him or her adversely is taken and avoid superfluous costs and excessive inconveniences for the persons concerned. Investigatory powers as regards access to premises should be exercised in accordance with specific requirements in Member State procedural law, such as the requirement to obtain a prior judicial authorisation. Each legally binding measure of the supervisory authority should be in writing, be clear and unambiguous, indicate the supervisory authority which has issued the measure, the date of issue of the measure, bear the signature of the head, or a member of the supervisory authority authorised by him or her, give the reasons for the measure, and refer to the right of an effective remedy. This should not preclude additional requirements pursuant to Member State procedural law. The adoption of a legally binding decision implies that it may give rise to judicial review in the Member State of the supervisory authority that adopted the decision.

(130) Where the supervisory authority with which the complaint has been lodged is not the lead supervisory authority, the lead supervisory authority should closely cooperate with the supervisory authority with which the complaint has been lodged in accordance with the provisions on cooperation and consistency laid down in this Regulation. In such cases, the lead supervisory authority should, when taking measures intended to produce legal effects, including the imposition of administrative fines, take utmost account of the view of the supervisory authority with which the complaint has been lodged and which should remain competent to carry out any investigation on the territory of its own Member State in liaison with the competent supervisory authority.

(131) Where another supervisory authority should act as a lead supervisory authority for the processing activities of the controller or processor but the concrete subject matter of a complaint or the possible infringement concerns only processing activities of the controller or processor in the Member State where the complaint has been lodged or the possible infringement detected and the matter does not substantially affect or is not likely to substantially affect data subjects in other Member States, the supervisory authority receiving a complaint or detecting or being informed otherwise of situations that entail possible infringements of this Regulation should seek an amicable settlement with the controller and, if this proves unsuccessful, exercise its full range of powers. This should include: specific processing carried out in the territory of the Member State of the supervisory authority or with regard to data subjects on the territory of that Member State; processing that is carried out in the context of an offer of goods or services specifically aimed at data subjects in the territory of the Member State of the supervisory authority; or processing that has to be assessed taking into account relevant legal obligations under Member State law.

(132) Awareness-raising activities by supervisory authorities addressed to the public should include specific measures directed at controllers and processors, including micro, small and medium-sized enterprises, as well as natural persons in particular in the educational context.

(133) The supervisory authorities should assist each other in performing their tasks and provide mutual assistance, so as to ensure the consistent application and enforcement of this Regulation in the internal market. A supervisory authority requesting mutual assistance may adopt a provisional measure if it receives no response to a request for mutual assistance within one month of the receipt of that request by the other supervisory authority.

(134) Each supervisory authority should, where appropriate, participate in joint operations with other supervisory authorities. The requested supervisory authority should be obliged to respond to the request within a specified time period.

(135) In order to ensure the consistent application of this Regulation throughout the Union, a consistency mechanism for cooperation between the supervisory authorities should be established. That mechanism should in particular apply where a supervisory authority intends to adopt a measure intended to produce legal effects as regards processing operations which substantially affect a significant number of data subjects in several Member States. It should also apply where any supervisory authority concerned or the Commission requests that such matter should be handled in the consistency mechanism. That mechanism should be without prejudice to any measures that the Commission may take in the exercise of its powers under the Treaties.

(136) In applying the consistency mechanism, the Board should, within a determined period of time, issue an opinion, if a majority of its members so decides or if so requested by any supervisory authority concerned or the Commission. The Board should also be empowered to adopt legally binding decisions where there are disputes between supervisory authorities. For that purpose, it should issue, in principle by a two-thirds majority of its members, legally binding decisions in clearly specified cases where there are conflicting views among supervisory authorities, in particular in the cooperation mechanism between the lead supervisory authority and supervisory authorities concerned on the merits of the case, in particular whether there is an infringement of this Regulation.

(137) There may be an urgent need to act in order to protect the rights and freedoms of data subjects, in particular when the danger exists that the enforcement of a right of a data subject could be considerably impeded. A supervisory authority should therefore be able to adopt duly justified provisional measures on its territory with a specified period of validity which should not exceed three months.

(138) The application of such mechanism should be a condition for the lawfulness of a measure intended to produce legal effects by a supervisory authority in those cases where its application is mandatory. In other cases of cross- border relevance, the cooperation mechanism between the lead supervisory authority and supervisory authorities concerned should be applied and mutual assistance and joint operations might be carried out between the supervisory authorities concerned on a bilateral or multilateral basis without triggering the consistency mechanism.

(139) In order to promote the consistent application of this Regulation, the Board should be set up as an independent body of the Union. To fulfil its objectives, the Board should have legal personality. The Board should be represented by its Chair. It should replace the Working Party on the Protection of Individuals with Regard to the Processing of Personal Data established by Directive 95/46/EC. It should consist of the head of a supervisory authority of each Member State and the European Data Protection Supervisor or their respective representatives. The Commission should participate in the Board's activities without voting rights and the European Data Protection Supervisor should have specific voting rights. The Board should contribute to the consistent application of this Regulation throughout the Union, including by advising the Commission, in particular on the level of protection in third countries or international organisations, and promoting cooperation of the supervisory authorities throughout the Union. The Board should act independently when performing its tasks.

(140) The Board should be assisted by a secretariat provided by the European Data Protection Supervisor. The staff of the European Data Protection Supervisor involved in carrying out the tasks conferred on the Board by this Regulation should perform its tasks exclusively under the instructions of, and report to, the Chair of the Board.

(141) Every data subject should have the right to lodge a complaint with a single supervisory authority, in particular in the Member State of his or her habitual residence, and the right to an effective judicial remedy in accordance with Article 47 of the Charter if the data subject considers that his or her rights under this Regulation are infringed or where the supervisory authority does not act on a complaint, partially or wholly rejects or dismisses a complaint or does not act where such action is necessary to protect the rights of the data subject. The investigation following a complaint should be carried out, subject to judicial review, to the extent that is appropriate in the specific case. The supervisory authority should inform the data subject of the progress and the outcome of the complaint within a reasonable period. If the case requires further investigation or coordination with another supervisory authority, intermediate information should be given to the data subject. In order to facilitate the submission of complaints, each supervisory authority should take measures such as providing a complaint submission form which can also be completed electronically, without excluding other means of communication.

(142) Where a data subject considers that his or her rights under this Regulation are infringed, he or she should have the right to mandate a not-for-profit body, organisation or association which is constituted in accordance with the law of a Member State, has statutory objectives which are in the public interest and is active in the field of the protection of personal data to lodge a complaint on his or her behalf with a supervisory authority, exercise the right to a judicial remedy on behalf of data subjects or, if provided for in Member State law, exercise the right to receive compensation on behalf of data subjects. A Member State may provide for such a body, organisation or association to have the right to lodge a complaint in that Member State, independently of a data subject's mandate, and the right to an effective judicial remedy where it has reasons to consider that the rights of a data subject have been infringed as a result of the processing of personal data which infringes this Regulation. That body, organisation or association may not be allowed to claim compensation on a data subject's behalf independently of the data subject's mandate.

(143) Any natural or legal person has the right to bring an action for annulment of decisions of the Board before the Court of Justice under the conditions provided for in Article 263 TFEU. As addressees of such decisions, the supervisory authorities concerned which wish to challenge them have to bring action within two months of being notified of them, in accordance with Article 263 TFEU. Where decisions of the Board are of direct and individual concern to a controller, processor or complainant, the latter may bring an action for annulment against those decisions within two months of their publication on the website of the Board, in accordance with Article 263 TFEU. Without prejudice to this right under Article 263 TFEU, each natural or legal person should have an effective judicial remedy before the competent national court against a decision of a supervisory authority which produces legal effects concerning that person. Such a decision concerns in particular the exercise of investigative, corrective and authorisation powers by the supervisory authority or the dismissal or rejection of complaints. However, the right to an effective judicial remedy does not encompass measures taken by supervisory authorities which are not legally binding, such as opinions issued by or advice provided by the supervisory authority. Proceedings against a supervisory authority should be brought before the courts of

the Member State where the supervisory authority is established and should be conducted in accordance with that Member State's procedural law. Those courts should exercise full jurisdiction, which should include jurisdiction to examine all questions of fact and law relevant to the dispute before them.

Where a complaint has been rejected or dismissed by a supervisory authority, the complainant may bring proceedings before the courts in the same Member State. In the context of judicial remedies relating to the application of this Regulation, national courts which consider a decision on the question necessary to enable them to give judgment, may, or in the case provided for in Article 267 TFEU, must, request the Court of Justice to give a preliminary ruling on the interpretation of Union law, including this Regulation. Furthermore, where a decision of a supervisory authority implementing a decision of the Board is challenged before a national court and the validity of the decision of the Board is at issue, that national court does not have the power to declare the Board's decision invalid but must refer the question of validity to the Court of Justice in accordance with Article 267 TFEU as interpreted by the Court of Justice, where it considers the decision invalid. However, a national court may not refer a question on the validity of the decision of the Board at the request of a natural or legal person which had the opportunity to bring an action for annulment of that decision, in particular if it was directly and individually concerned by that decision, but had not done so within the period laid down in Article 263 TFEU.

(144) Where a court seized of proceedings against a decision by a supervisory authority has reason to believe that proceedings concerning the same processing, such as the same subject matter as regards processing by the same controller or processor, or the same cause of action, are brought before a competent court in another Member State, it should contact that court in order to confirm the existence of such related proceedings. If related proceedings are pending before a court in another Member State, any court other than the court first seized may stay its proceedings or may, on request of one of the parties, decline jurisdiction in favour of the court first seized if that court has jurisdiction over the proceedings in question and its law permits the consolidation of such related proceedings. Proceedings are deemed to be related where they are so closely connected that it is expedient to hear and determine them together in order to avoid the risk of irreconcilable judgments resulting from separate proceedings.

(145) For proceedings against a controller or processor, the plaintiff should have the choice to bring the action before the courts of the Member States where the controller or processor has an establishment or where the data subject resides, unless the controller is a public authority of a Member State acting in the exercise of its public powers.

(146) The controller or processor should compensate any damage which a person may suffer as a result of processing that infringes this Regulation. The controller or processor should be exempt from liability if it proves that it is not in any way responsible for the damage. The concept of damage should be broadly interpreted in the light of the case-law of the Court of Justice in a manner which fully reflects the objectives of this Regulation. This is without prejudice to any claims for damage deriving from the violation of other rules in Union or Member State law. Processing that infringes this Regulation also includes processing that infringes delegated and implementing acts adopted in accordance with this Regulation and Member State law specifying rules of this Regulation. Data subjects should receive full and effective compensation for the damage they have suffered. Where controllers or processors are involved in the same processing, each controller or processor should be held liable for the entire damage. However, where they are joined to the same judicial proceedings, in accordance with Member State law, compensation may be apportioned according to the responsibility of each controller or processor for the damage caused by the processing, provided that full and effective compensation of the data subject who suffered the damage is ensured. Any controller or processor which has paid full compensation may subsequently institute recourse proceedings against other controllers or processors involved in the same processing.

(147) Where specific rules on jurisdiction are contained in this Regulation, in particular as regards proceedings seeking a judicial remedy including compensation, against a controller or processor, general jurisdiction rules such as those of Regulation (EU) No 1215/2012 of the European Parliament and of the Council[13] should not prejudice the application of such specific rules.

(148) In order to strengthen the enforcement of the rules of this Regulation, penalties including administrative fines should be imposed for any infringement of this Regulation, in addition to, or instead of appropriate measures imposed by the supervisory authority pursuant to this Regulation. In a case of a minor infringement or if the fine likely to be imposed would constitute a disproportionate burden to a natural person, a reprimand may be issued instead of a fine. Due regard should however be given to the nature, gravity and duration of the infringement, the intentional character of the infringement, actions taken to mitigate the damage suffered, degree of responsibility or any relevant previous infringements, the manner in which the infringement became known to the supervisory authority, compliance with measures ordered against the controller or processor, adherence to a code of conduct and any other aggravating or mitigating factor. The imposition of penalties including administrative fines should be subject to appropriate procedural safeguards in accordance with the general principles of Union law and the Charter, including effective judicial protection and due process.

(149) Member States should be able to lay down the rules on criminal penalties for infringements of this Regulation, including for infringements of national rules adopted pursuant to and within the limits of this Regulation. Those criminal penalties may also allow for the deprivation of the profits obtained through infringements of this Regulation. However, the imposition of criminal penalties for infringements of such national rules and of administrative penalties should not lead to a breach of the principle of *ne bis in idem*, as interpreted by the Court of Justice.

(150) In order to strengthen and harmonise administrative penalties for infringements of this Regulation, each supervisory authority should have the power to impose administrative fines. This Regulation should indicate infringements and the upper limit and criteria for setting the related administrative fines, which should be determined by the competent supervisory authority in each individual case, taking into

account all relevant circumstances of the specific situation, with due regard in particular to the nature, gravity and duration of the infringement and of its consequences and the measures taken to ensure compliance with the obligations under this Regulation and to prevent or mitigate the consequences of the infringement. Where administrative fines are imposed on an undertaking, an undertaking should be understood to be an undertaking in accordance with Articles 101 and 102 TFEU for those purposes. Where administrative fines are imposed on persons that are not an undertaking, the supervisory authority should take account of the general level of income in the Member State as well as the economic situation of the person in considering the appropriate amount of the fine. The consistency mechanism may also be used to promote a consistent application of administrative fines. It should be for the Member States to determine whether and to which extent public authorities should be subject to administrative fines. Imposing an administrative fine or giving a warning does not affect the application of other powers of the supervisory authorities or of other penalties under this Regulation.

(151) The legal systems of Denmark and Estonia do not allow for administrative fines as set out in this Regulation. The rules on administrative fines may be applied in such a manner that in Denmark the fine is imposed by competent national courts as a criminal penalty and in Estonia the fine is imposed by the supervisory authority in the framework of a misdemeanour procedure, provided that such an application of the rules in those Member States has an equivalent effect to administrative fines imposed by supervisory authorities. Therefore the competent national courts should take into account the recommendation by the supervisory authority initiating the fine. In any event, the fines imposed should be effective, proportionate and dissuasive.

(152) Where this Regulation does not harmonise administrative penalties or where necessary in other cases, for example in cases of serious infringements of this Regulation, Member States should implement a system which provides for effective, proportionate and dissuasive penalties. The nature of such penalties, criminal or administrative, should be determined by Member State law.

(153) Member States law should reconcile the rules governing freedom of expression and information, including journalistic, academic, artistic and or literary expression with the right to the protection of personal data pursuant to this Regulation. The processing of personal data solely for journalistic purposes, or for the purposes of academic, artistic or literary expression should be subject to derogations or exemptions from certain provisions of this Regulation if necessary to reconcile the right to the protection of personal data with the right to freedom of expression and information, as enshrined in Article 11 of the Charter. This should apply in particular to the processing of personal data in the audiovisual field and in news archives and press libraries. Therefore, Member States should adopt legislative measures which lay down the exemptions and derogations necessary for the purpose of balancing those fundamental rights. Member States should adopt such exemptions and derogations on general principles, the rights of the data subject, the controller and the processor, the transfer of personal data to third countries or international organisations, the independent supervisory authorities, cooperation and consistency, and specific data-processing situations. Where such exemptions or derogations differ from one Member State to another, the law of the Member State to which the controller is subject should apply. In order to take account of the importance of the right to freedom of expression in every democratic society, it is necessary to interpret notions relating to that freedom, such as journalism, broadly.

(154) This Regulation allows the principle of public access to official documents to be taken into account when applying this Regulation. Public access to official documents may be considered to be in the public interest. Personal data in documents held by a public authority or a public body should be able to be publicly disclosed by that authority or body if the disclosure is provided for by Union or Member State law to which the public authority or public body is subject. Such laws should reconcile public access to official documents and the reuse of public sector information with the right to the protection of personal data and may therefore provide for the necessary reconciliation with the right to the protection of personal data pursuant to this Regulation. The reference to public authorities and bodies should in that context include all authorities or other bodies covered by Member State law on public access to documents. Directive 2003/98/EC of the European Parliament and of the Council[14] leaves intact and in no way affects the level of protection of natural persons with regard to the processing of personal data under the provisions of Union and Member State law, and in particular does not alter the obligations and rights set out in this Regulation. In particular, that Directive should not apply to documents to which access is excluded or restricted by virtue of the access regimes on the grounds of protection of personal data, and parts of documents accessible by virtue of those regimes which contain personal data the re-use of which has been provided for by law as being incompatible with the law concerning the protection of natural persons with regard to the processing of personal data.

(155) Member State law or collective agreements, including 'works agreements', may provide for specific rules on the processing of employees' personal data in the employment context, in particular for the conditions under which personal data in the employment context may be processed on the basis of the consent of the employee, the purposes of the recruitment, the performance of the contract of employment, including discharge of obligations laid down by law or by collective agreements, management, planning and organisation of work, equality and diversity in the workplace, health and safety at work, and for the purposes of the exercise and enjoyment, on an individual or collective basis, of rights and benefits related to employment, and for the purpose of the termination of the employment relationship.

(156) The processing of personal data for archiving purposes in the public interest, scientific or historical research purposes or statistical purposes should be subject to appropriate safeguards for the rights and freedoms of the data subject pursuant to this Regulation. Those safeguards should ensure that technical and organisational measures are in place in order to ensure, in particular, the principle of data

minimisation. The further processing of personal data for archiving purposes in the public interest, scientific or historical research purposes or statistical purposes is to be carried out when the controller has assessed the feasibility to fulfil those purposes by processing data which do not permit or no longer permit the identification of data subjects, provided that appropriate safeguards exist (such as, for instance, pseudonymisation of the data). Member States should provide for appropriate safeguards for the processing of personal data for archiving purposes in the public interest, scientific or historical research purposes or statistical purposes. Member States should be authorised to provide, under specific conditions and subject to appropriate safeguards for data subjects, specifications and derogations with regard to the information requirements and rights to rectification, to erasure, to be forgotten, to restriction of processing, to data portability, and to object when processing personal data for archiving purposes in the public interest, scientific or historical research purposes or statistical purposes. The conditions and safeguards in question may entail specific procedures for data subjects to exercise those rights if this is appropriate in the light of the purposes sought by the specific processing along with technical and organisational measures aimed at minimising the processing of personal data in pursuance of the proportionality and necessity principles. The processing of personal data for scientific purposes should also comply with other relevant legislation such as on clinical trials.

(157) By coupling information from registries, researchers can obtain new knowledge of great value with regard to widespread medical conditions such as cardiovascular disease, cancer and depression. On the basis of registries, research results can be enhanced, as they draw on a larger population. Within social science, research on the basis of registries enables researchers to obtain essential knowledge about the long-term correlation of a number of social conditions such as unemployment and education with other life conditions. Research results obtained through registries provide solid, high-quality knowledge which can provide the basis for the formulation and implementation of knowledge-based policy, improve the quality of life for a number of people and improve the efficiency of social services. In order to facilitate scientific research, personal data can be processed for scientific research purposes, subject to appropriate conditions and safeguards set out in Union or Member State law.

(158) Where personal data are processed for archiving purposes, this Regulation should also apply to that processing, bearing in mind that this Regulation should not apply to deceased persons. Public authorities or public or private bodies that hold records of public interest should be services which, pursuant to Union or Member State law, have a legal obligation to acquire, preserve, appraise, arrange, describe, communicate, promote, disseminate and provide access to records of enduring value for general public interest. Member States should also be authorised to provide for the further processing of personal data for archiving purposes, for example with a view to providing specific information related to the political behaviour under former totalitarian state regimes, genocide, crimes against humanity, in particular the Holocaust, or war crimes.

(159) Where personal data are processed for scientific research purposes, this Regulation should also apply to that processing. For the purposes of this Regulation, the processing of personal data for scientific research purposes should be interpreted in a broad manner including for example technological development and demonstration, fundamental research, applied research and privately funded research. In addition, it should take into account the Union's objective under Article 179(1) TFEU of achieving a European Research Area. Scientific research purposes should also include studies conducted in the public interest in the area of public health. To meet the specificities of processing personal data for scientific research purposes, specific conditions should apply in particular as regards the publication or otherwise disclosure of personal data in the context of scientific research purposes. If the result of scientific research in particular in the health context gives reason for further measures in the interest of the data subject, the general rules of this Regulation should apply in view of those measures.

(160) Where personal data are processed for historical research purposes, this Regulation should also apply to that processing. This should also include historical research and research for genealogical purposes, bearing in mind that this Regulation should not apply to deceased persons.

(161) For the purpose of consenting to the participation in scientific research activities in clinical trials, the relevant provisions of Regulation (EU) No 536/2014 of the European Parliament and of the Council[15] should apply.

(162) Where personal data are processed for statistical purposes, this Regulation should apply to that processing. Union or Member State law should, within the limits of this Regulation, determine statistical content, control of access, specifications for the processing of personal data for statistical purposes and appropriate measures to safeguard the rights and freedoms of the data subject and for ensuring statistical confidentiality. Statistical purposes mean any operation of collection and the processing of personal data necessary for statistical surveys or for the production of statistical results. Those statistical results may further be used for different purposes, including a scientific research purpose. The statistical purpose implies that the result of processing for statistical purposes is not personal data, but aggregate data, and that this result or the personal data are not used in support of measures or decisions regarding any particular natural person.

(163) The confidential information which the Union and national statistical authorities collect for the production of official European and official national statistics should be protected. European statistics should be developed, produced and disseminated in accordance with the statistical principles as set out in Article 338(2) TFEU, while national statistics should also comply with Member State law. Regulation (EC) No 223/2009 of the European Parliament and of the Council[16] provides further specifications on statistical confidentiality for European statistics.

(164) As regards the powers of the supervisory authorities to obtain from the controller or processor access to personal data and access to their premises, Member States may adopt by law, within the limits of this Regulation, specific rules in order to safeguard the professional or other equivalent secrecy

obligations, in so far as necessary to reconcile the right to the protection of personal data with an obligation of professional secrecy. This is without prejudice to existing Member State obligations to adopt rules on professional secrecy where required by Union law.

(165) This Regulation respects and does not prejudice the status under existing constitutional law of churches and religious associations or communities in the Member States, as recognised in Article 17 TFEU.

(166) In order to fulfil the objectives of this Regulation, namely to protect the fundamental rights and freedoms of natural persons and in particular their right to the protection of personal data and to ensure the free movement of personal data within the Union, the power to adopt acts in accordance with Article 290 TFEU should be delegated to the Commission. In particular, delegated acts should be adopted in respect of criteria and requirements for certification mechanisms, information to be presented by standardised icons and procedures for providing such icons. It is of particular importance that the Commission carry out appropriate consultations during its preparatory work, including at expert level. The Commission, when preparing and drawing-up delegated acts, should ensure a simultaneous, timely and appropriate transmission of relevant documents to the European Parliament and to the Council.

(167) In order to ensure uniform conditions for the implementation of this Regulation, implementing powers should be conferred on the Commission when provided for by this Regulation. Those powers should be exercised in accordance with Regulation (EU) No 182/2011. In that context, the Commission should consider specific measures for micro, small and medium-sized enterprises.

(168) The examination procedure should be used for the adoption of implementing acts on standard contractual clauses between controllers and processors and between processors; codes of conduct; technical standards and mechanisms for certification; the adequate level of protection afforded by a third country, a territory or a specified sector within that third country, or an international organisation; standard protection clauses; formats and procedures for the exchange of information by electronic means between controllers, processors and supervisory authorities for binding corporate rules; mutual assistance; and arrangements for the exchange of information by electronic means between supervisory authorities, and between supervisory authorities and the Board.

(169) The Commission should adopt immediately applicable implementing acts where available evidence reveals that a third country, a territory or a specified sector within that third country, or an international organisation does not ensure an adequate level of protection, and imperative grounds of urgency so require.

(170) Since the objective of this Regulation, namely to ensure an equivalent level of protection of natural persons and the free flow of personal data throughout the Union, cannot be sufficiently achieved by the Member States and can rather, by reason of the scale or effects of the action, be better achieved at Union level, the Union may adopt measures, in accordance with the principle of subsidiarity as set out in Article 5 of the Treaty on European Union (TEU). In accordance with the principle of proportionality as set out in that Article, this Regulation does not go beyond what is necessary in order to achieve that objective.

(171) Directive 95/46/EC should be repealed by this Regulation. Processing already under way on the date of application of this Regulation should be brought into conformity with this Regulation within the period of two years after which this Regulation enters into force. Where processing is based on consent pursuant to Directive 95/46/EC, it is not necessary for the data subject to give his or her consent again if the manner in which the consent has been given is in line with the conditions of this Regulation, so as to allow the controller to continue such processing after the date of application of this Regulation. Commission decisions adopted and authorisations by supervisory authorities based on Directive 95/46/EC remain in force until amended, replaced or repealed.

(172) The European Data Protection Supervisor was consulted in accordance with Article 28(2) of Regulation (EC) No 45/2001 and delivered an opinion on 7 March 2012.[17]

(173) This Regulation should apply to all matters concerning the protection of fundamental rights and freedoms vis-à-vis the processing of personal data which are not subject to specific obligations with the same objective set out in Directive 2002/58/EC of the European Parliament and of the Council,[18] including the obligations on the controller and the rights of natural persons. In order to clarify the relationship between this Regulation and Directive 2002/58/EC, that Directive should be amended accordingly. Once this Regulation is adopted, Directive 2002/58/EC should be reviewed in particular in order to ensure consistency with this Regulation,

NOTES

[1]　　OJ C229, 31.7.2012, p 90.

[2]　　OJ C391, 18.12.2012, p 127.

[3]　　Position of the European Parliament of 12 March 2014 (not yet published in the Official Journal) and position of the Council at first reading of 8 April 2016 (not yet published in the Official Journal). Position of the European Parliament of 14 April 2016.

[4]　　Directive 95/46/EC of the European Parliament and of the Council of 24 October 1995 on the protection of individuals with regard to the processing of personal data and on the free movement of such data (OJ L281, 23.11.1995, p 31).

[5]　　Commission Recommendation of 6 May 2003 concerning the definition of micro, small and medium‒'sized enterprises (C(2003) 1422) (OJ L124, 20.5.2003, p 36).

[6]　　Regulation (EC) No 45/2001 of the European Parliament and of the Council of 18 December 2000 on the protection of individuals with regard to the processing of personal data by the Community institutions and bodies and on the free movement of such data (OJ L8, 12.1.2001, p 1).

[7]　　Directive (EU) 2016/680 of the European Parliament and of the Council of 27 April 2016 on the protection of natural

persons with regard to the processing of personal data by competent authorities for the purposes of prevention, investigation, detection or prosecution of criminal offences or the execution of criminal penalties, and the free movement of such data and repealing Council Framework Decision 2008/977/JHA (see page 89 of this Official Journal).

8   Directive 2000/31/EC of the European Parliament and of the Council of 8 June 2000 on certain legal aspects of information society services, in particular electronic commerce, in the Internal Market ('Directive on electronic commerce') (OJ L178, 17.7.2000, p 1).

9   Directive 2011/24/EU of the European Parliament and of the Council of 9 March 2011 on the application of patients' rights in crossâ€'border healthcare (OJ L88, 4.4.2011, p 45).

10   Council Directive 93/13/EEC of 5 April 1993 on unfair terms in consumer contracts (OJ L95, 21.4.1993, p 29).

11   Regulation (EC) No 1338/2008 of the European Parliament and of the Council of 16 December 2008 on Community statistics on public health and health and safety at work (OJ L354, 31.12.2008, p 70).

12   Regulation (EU) No 182/2011 of the European Parliament and of the Council of 16 February 2011 laying down the rules and general principles concerning mechanisms for control by Member States of the Commission's exercise of implementing powers (OJ L55, 28.2.2011, p 13).

13   Regulation (EU) No 1215/2012 of the European Parliament and of the Council of 12 December 2012 on jurisdiction and the recognition and enforcement of judgments in civil and commercial matters (OJ L351, 20.12.2012, p 1).

14   Directive 2003/98/EC of the European Parliament and of the Council of 17 November 2003 on the reâ€'use of public sector information (OJ L345, 31.12.2003, p 90).

15   Regulation (EU) No 536/2014 of the European Parliament and of the Council of 16 April 2014 on clinical trials on medicinal products for human use, and repealing Directive 2001/20/EC (OJ L158, 27.5.2014, p 1).

16   Regulation (EC) No 223/2009 of the European Parliament and of the Council of 11 March 2009 on European statistics and repealing Regulation (EC, Euratom) No 1101/2008 of the European Parliament and of the Council on the transmission of data subject to statistical confidentiality to the Statistical Office of the European Communities, Council Regulation (EC) No 322/97 on Community Statistics, and Council Decision 89/382/EEC, Euratom establishing a Committee on the Statistical Programmes of the European Communities (OJ L87, 31.3.2009, p 164).

17   OJ C 192, 30.6.2012, p 7.

18   Directive 2002/58/EC of the European Parliament and of the Council of 12 July 2002 concerning the processing of personal data and the protection of privacy in the electronic communications sector (Directive on privacy and electronic communications) (OJ L201, 31.7.2002, p 37).

HAVE ADOPTED THIS REGULATION:

CHAPTER I GENERAL PROVISIONS

[2.2]
Article 1   Subject-matter and objectives
1. This Regulation lays down rules relating to the protection of natural persons with regard to the processing of personal data and rules relating to the free movement of personal data.
2. This Regulation protects fundamental rights and freedoms of natural persons and in particular their right to the protection of personal data.
3. The free movement of personal data within the Union shall be neither restricted nor prohibited for reasons connected with the protection of natural persons with regard to the processing of personal data.

[2.3]
Article 2   Material scope
1. This Regulation applies to the processing of personal data wholly or partly by automated means and to the processing other than by automated means of personal data which form part of a filing system or are intended to form part of a filing system.
2. This Regulation does not apply to the processing of personal data:
    (a) in the course of an activity which falls outside the scope of Union law;
    (b) by the Member States when carrying out activities which fall within the scope of Chapter 2 of Title V of the TEU;
    (c) by a natural person in the course of a purely personal or household activity;
    (d) by competent authorities for the purposes of the prevention, investigation, detection or prosecution of criminal offences or the execution of criminal penalties, including the safeguarding against and the prevention of threats to public security.
3. For the processing of personal data by the Union institutions, bodies, offices and agencies, Regulation (EC) No 45/2001 applies. Regulation (EC) No 45/2001 and other Union legal acts applicable to such processing of personal data shall be adapted to the principles and rules of this Regulation in accordance with Article 98.
4. This Regulation shall be without prejudice to the application of Directive 2000/31/EC, in particular of the liability rules of intermediary service providers in Articles 12 to 15 of that Directive.

[2.4]
Article 3   Territorial scope
1. This Regulation applies to the processing of personal data in the context of the activities of an establishment of a controller or a processor in the Union, regardless of whether the processing takes place in the Union or not.
2. This Regulation applies to the processing of personal data of data subjects who are in the Union by a controller or processor not established in the Union, where the processing activities are related to:
    (a) the offering of goods or services, irrespective of whether a payment of the data subject is required, to such data subjects in the Union; or
    (b) the monitoring of their behaviour as far as their behaviour takes place within the Union.
3. This Regulation applies to the processing of personal data by a controller not established in the Union, but in a place where Member State law applies by virtue of public international law.

[2.5]
Article 4   Definitions

For the purposes of this Regulation:

(1) "personal data" means any information relating to an identified or identifiable natural person ("data subject"); an identifiable natural person is one who can be identified, directly or indirectly, in particular by reference to an identifier such as a name, an identification number, location data, an online identifier or to one or more factors specific to the physical, physiological, genetic, mental, economic, cultural or social identity of that natural person;

(2) "processing" means any operation or set of operations which is performed on personal data or on sets of personal data, whether or not by automated means, such as collection, recording, organisation, structuring, storage, adaptation or alteration, retrieval, consultation, use, disclosure by transmission, dissemination or otherwise making available, alignment or combination, restriction, erasure or destruction;

(3) "restriction of processing" means the marking of stored personal data with the aim of limiting their processing in the future;

(4) "profiling" means any form of automated processing of personal data consisting of the use of personal data to evaluate certain personal aspects relating to a natural person, in particular to analyse or predict aspects concerning that natural person's performance at work, economic situation, health, personal preferences, interests, reliability, behaviour, location or movements;

(5) "pseudonymisation" means the processing of personal data in such a manner that the personal data can no longer be attributed to a specific data subject without the use of additional information, provided that such additional information is kept separately and is subject to technical and organisational measures to ensure that the personal data are not attributed to an identified or identifiable natural person;

(6) "filing system" means any structured set of personal data which are accessible according to specific criteria, whether centralised, decentralised or dispersed on a functional or geographical basis;

(7) "controller" means the natural or legal person, public authority, agency or other body which, alone or jointly with others, determines the purposes and means of the processing of personal data; where the purposes and means of such processing are determined by Union or Member State law, the controller or the specific criteria for its nomination may be provided for by Union or Member State law;

(8) "processor" means a natural or legal person, public authority, agency or other body which processes personal data on behalf of the controller;

(9) "recipient" means a natural or legal person, public authority, agency or another body, to which the personal data are disclosed, whether a third party or not. However, public authorities which may receive personal data in the framework of a particular inquiry in accordance with Union or Member State law shall not be regarded as recipients; the processing of those data by those public authorities shall be in compliance with the applicable data protection rules according to the purposes of the processing;

(10) "third party" means a natural or legal person, public authority, agency or body other than the data subject, controller, processor and persons who, under the direct authority of the controller or processor, are authorised to process personal data;

(11) "consent of the data subject" means any freely given, specific, informed and unambiguous indication of the data subject's wishes by which he or she, by a statement or by a clear affirmative action, signifies agreement to the processing of personal data relating to him or her;

(12) "personal data breach" means a breach of security leading to the accidental or unlawful destruction, loss, alteration, unauthorised disclosure of, or access to, personal data transmitted, stored or otherwise processed;

(13) "genetic data" means personal data relating to the inherited or acquired genetic characteristics of a natural person which give unique information about the physiology or the health of that natural person and which result, in particular, from an analysis of a biological sample from the natural person in question;

(14) "biometric data" means personal data resulting from specific technical processing relating to the physical, physiological or behavioural characteristics of a natural person, which allow or confirm the unique identification of that natural person, such as facial images or dactyloscopic data;

(15) "data concerning health" means personal data related to the physical or mental health of a natural person, including the provision of health care services, which reveal information about his or her health status;

(16) "main establishment" means:

  (a) as regards a controller with establishments in more than one Member State, the place of its central administration in the Union, unless the decisions on the purposes and means of the processing of personal data are taken in another establishment of the controller in the Union and the latter establishment has the power to have such decisions implemented, in which case the establishment having taken such decisions is to be considered to be the main establishment;

  (b) as regards a processor with establishments in more than one Member State, the place of its central administration in the Union, or, if the processor has no central administration in the Union, the establishment of the processor in the Union where the main processing activities in the context of the activities of an establishment of the processor take place to the extent that the processor is subject to specific obligations under this Regulation;

(17) "representative" means a natural or legal person established in the Union who, designated by the controller or processor in writing pursuant to Article 27, represents the controller or processor with regard to their respective obligations under this Regulation;

(18) "enterprise" means a natural or legal person engaged in an economic activity, irrespective of its legal form, including partnerships or associations regularly engaged in an economic activity;

(19) "group of undertakings" means a controlling undertaking and its controlled undertakings;

(20) "binding corporate rules" means personal data protection policies which are adhered to by a controller or processor established on the territory of a Member State for transfers or a set of transfers of personal data to a controller or processor in one or more third countries within a group of undertakings, or group of enterprises engaged in a joint economic activity;

Part 2   Data Protection: EU Law etc

(21) "supervisory authority" means an independent public authority which is established by a Member State pursuant to Article 51;

(22) "supervisory authority concerned" means a supervisory authority which is concerned by the processing of personal data because:

    (a) the controller or processor is established on the territory of the Member State of that supervisory authority;

    (b) data subjects residing in the Member State of that supervisory authority are substantially affected or likely to be substantially affected by the processing; or

    (c) a complaint has been lodged with that supervisory authority;

(23) "cross-border processing" means either:

    (a) processing of personal data which takes place in the context of the activities of establishments in more than one Member State of a controller or processor in the Union where the controller or processor is established in more than one Member State; or

    (b) processing of personal data which takes place in the context of the activities of a single establishment of a controller or processor in the Union but which substantially affects or is likely to substantially affect data subjects in more than one Member State.

(24) "relevant and reasoned objection" means an objection to a draft decision as to whether there is an infringement of this Regulation, or whether envisaged action in relation to the controller or processor complies with this Regulation, which clearly demonstrates the significance of the risks posed by the draft decision as regards the fundamental rights and freedoms of data subjects and, where applicable, the free flow of personal data within the Union;

(25) information society service means a service as defined in point (b) of Article 1(1) of Directive (EU) 2015/1535 of the European Parliament and of the Council;[1]

(26) international organisation means an organisation and its subordinate bodies governed by public international law, or any other body which is set up by, or on the basis of, an agreement between two or more countries.

NOTES

[1]   Directive (EU) 2015/1535 of the European Parliament and of the Council of 9 September 2015 laying down a procedure for the provision of information in the field of technical regulations and of rules on Information Society services (OJ L241, 17.9.2015, p 1).

CHAPTER II PRINCIPLES

[2.6]
Article 5   Principles relating to processing of personal data

1. Personal data shall be:

    (a) processed lawfully, fairly and in a transparent manner in relation to the data subject ('lawfulness, fairness and transparency');

    (b) collected for specified, explicit and legitimate purposes and not further processed in a manner that is incompatible with those purposes; further processing for archiving purposes in the public interest, scientific or historical research purposes or statistical purposes shall, in accordance with Article 89(1), not be considered to be incompatible with the initial purposes ('purpose limitation');

    (c) adequate, relevant and limited to what is necessary in relation to the purposes for which they are processed ('data minimisation');

    (d) accurate and, where necessary, kept up to date; every reasonable step must be taken to ensure that personal data that are inaccurate, having regard to the purposes for which they are processed, are erased or rectified without delay ('accuracy');

    (e) kept in a form which permits identification of data subjects for no longer than is necessary for the purposes for which the personal data are processed; personal data may be stored for longer periods insofar as the personal data will be processed solely for archiving purposes in the public interest, scientific or historical research purposes or statistical purposes in accordance with Article 89(1) subject to implementation of the appropriate technical and organisational measures required by this Regulation in order to safeguard the rights and freedoms of the data subject ('storage limitation');

    (f) processed in a manner that ensures appropriate security of the personal data, including protection against unauthorised or unlawful processing and against accidental loss, destruction or damage, using appropriate technical or organisational measures ('integrity and confidentiality').

2. The controller shall be responsible for, and be able to demonstrate compliance with, paragraph 1 ('accountability').

[2.7]
Article 6   Lawfulness of processing

1. Processing shall be lawful only if and to the extent that at least one of the following applies:

    (a) the data subject has given consent to the processing of his or her personal data for one or more specific purposes;

    (b) processing is necessary for the performance of a contract to which the data subject is party or in order to take steps at the request of the data subject prior to entering into a contract;

    (c) processing is necessary for compliance with a legal obligation to which the controller is subject;

    (d) processing is necessary in order to protect the vital interests of the data subject or of another natural person;

    (e) processing is necessary for the performance of a task carried out in the public interest or in the exercise of official authority vested in the controller;

    (f) processing is necessary for the purposes of the legitimate interests pursued by the controller or by a third party, except where such interests are overridden by the interests or fundamental rights and freedoms of the data subject which require protection of personal data, in particular where the data subject is a child.

Point (f) of the first subparagraph shall not apply to processing carried out by public authorities in the performance of their tasks.

2. Member States may maintain or introduce more specific provisions to adapt the application of the rules of this Regulation with regard to processing for compliance with points (c) and (e) of paragraph 1 by determining more precisely specific requirements for the processing and other measures to ensure lawful and fair processing including for other specific processing situations as provided for in Chapter IX.

3. The basis for the processing referred to in point (c) and (e) of paragraph 1 shall be laid down by:

   (a) Union law; or
   (b) Member State law to which the controller is subject.

The purpose of the processing shall be determined in that legal basis or, as regards the processing referred to in point (e) of paragraph 1, shall be necessary for the performance of a task carried out in the public interest or in the exercise of official authority vested in the controller. That legal basis may contain specific provisions to adapt the application of rules of this Regulation, inter alia: the general conditions governing the lawfulness of processing by the controller; the types of data which are subject to the processing; the data subjects concerned; the entities to, and the purposes for which, the personal data may be disclosed; the purpose limitation; storage periods; and processing operations and processing procedures, including measures to ensure lawful and fair processing such as those for other specific processing situations as provided for in Chapter IX. The Union or the Member State law shall meet an objective of public interest and be proportionate to the legitimate aim pursued.

4. Where the processing for a purpose other than that for which the personal data have been collected is not based on the data subject's consent or on a Union or Member State law which constitutes a necessary and proportionate measure in a democratic society to safeguard the objectives referred to in Article 23(1), the controller shall, in order to ascertain whether processing for another purpose is compatible with the purpose for which the personal data are initially collected, take into account, inter alia:

   (a) any link between the purposes for which the personal data have been collected and the purposes of the intended further processing;
   (b) the context in which the personal data have been collected, in particular regarding the relationship between data subjects and the controller;
   (c) the nature of the personal data, in particular whether special categories of personal data are processed, pursuant to Article 9, or whether personal data related to criminal convictions and offences are processed, pursuant to Article 10;
   (d) the possible consequences of the intended further processing for data subjects;
   (e) the existence of appropriate safeguards, which may include encryption or pseudonymisation.

[2.8]
Article 7   Conditions for consent

1. Where processing is based on consent, the controller shall be able to demonstrate that the data subject has consented to processing of his or her personal data.

2. If the data subject's consent is given in the context of a written declaration which also concerns other matters, the request for consent shall be presented in a manner which is clearly distinguishable from the other matters, in an intelligible and easily accessible form, using clear and plain language. Any part of such a declaration which constitutes an infringement of this Regulation shall not be binding.

3. The data subject shall have the right to withdraw his or her consent at any time. The withdrawal of consent shall not affect the lawfulness of processing based on consent before its withdrawal. Prior to giving consent, the data subject shall be informed thereof. It shall be as easy to withdraw as to give consent.

4. When assessing whether consent is freely given, utmost account shall be taken of whether, inter alia, the performance of a contract, including the provision of a service, is conditional on consent to the processing of personal data that is not necessary for the performance of that contract.

[2.9]
Article 8   Conditions applicable to child's consent in relation to information society services

1. Where point (a) of Article 6(1) applies, in relation to the offer of information society services directly to a child, the processing of the personal data of a child shall be lawful where the child is at least 16 years old. Where the child is below the age of 16 years, such processing shall be lawful only if and to the extent that consent is given or authorised by the holder of parental responsibility over the child.

   Member States may provide by law for a lower age for those purposes provided that such lower age is not below 13 years.

2. The controller shall make reasonable efforts to verify in such cases that consent is given or authorised by the holder of parental responsibility over the child, taking into consideration available technology.

3. Paragraph 1 shall not affect the general contract law of Member States such as the rules on the validity, formation or effect of a contract in relation to a child.

[2.10]
Article 9   Processing of special categories of personal data

1. Processing of personal data revealing racial or ethnic origin, political opinions, religious or philosophical beliefs, or trade union membership, and the processing of genetic data, biometric data for the purpose of uniquely identifying a natural person, data concerning health or data concerning a natural person's sex life or sexual orientation shall be prohibited.

2. Paragraph 1 shall not apply if one of the following applies:

   (a) the data subject has given explicit consent to the processing of those personal data for one or more specified purposes, except where Union or Member State law provide that the prohibition referred to in paragraph 1 may not be lifted by the data subject;
   (b) processing is necessary for the purposes of carrying out the obligations and exercising specific rights of the controller or of the data subject in the field of employment and social security and social protection law in so far as it is authorised by Union or Member State law or a collective agreement pursuant to Member State law providing for appropriate safeguards for the fundamental rights and the interests of the data subject;

(c) processing is necessary to protect the vital interests of the data subject or of another natural person where the data subject is physically or legally incapable of giving consent;

(d) processing is carried out in the course of its legitimate activities with appropriate safeguards by a foundation, association or any other not-for-profit body with a political, philosophical, religious or trade union aim and on condition that the processing relates solely to the members or to former members of the body or to persons who have regular contact with it in connection with its purposes and that the personal data are not disclosed outside that body without the consent of the data subjects;

(e) processing relates to personal data which are manifestly made public by the data subject;

(f) processing is necessary for the establishment, exercise or defence of legal claims or whenever courts are acting in their judicial capacity;

(g) processing is necessary for reasons of substantial public interest, on the basis of Union or Member State law which shall be proportionate to the aim pursued, respect the essence of the right to data protection and provide for suitable and specific measures to safeguard the fundamental rights and the interests of the data subject;

(h) processing is necessary for the purposes of preventive or occupational medicine, for the assessment of the working capacity of the employee, medical diagnosis, the provision of health or social care or treatment or the management of health or social care systems and services on the basis of Union or Member State law or pursuant to contract with a health professional and subject to the conditions and safeguards referred to in paragraph 3;

(i) processing is necessary for reasons of public interest in the area of public health, such as protecting against serious cross-border threats to health or ensuring high standards of quality and safety of health care and of medicinal products or medical devices, on the basis of Union or Member State law which provides for suitable and specific measures to safeguard the rights and freedoms of the data subject, in particular professional secrecy;

(j) processing is necessary for archiving purposes in the public interest, scientific or historical research purposes or statistical purposes in accordance with Article 89(1) based on Union or Member State law which shall be proportionate to the aim pursued, respect the essence of the right to data protection and provide for suitable and specific measures to safeguard the fundamental rights and the interests of the data subject.

3. Personal data referred to in paragraph 1 may be processed for the purposes referred to in point (h) of paragraph 2 when those data are processed by or under the responsibility of a professional subject to the obligation of professional secrecy under Union or Member State law or rules established by national competent bodies or by another person also subject to an obligation of secrecy under Union or Member State law or rules established by national competent bodies.

4. Member States may maintain or introduce further conditions, including limitations, with regard to the processing of genetic data, biometric data or data concerning health.

[2.11]
Article 10   Processing of personal data relating to criminal convictions and offences
Processing of personal data relating to criminal convictions and offences or related security measures based on Article 6(1) shall be carried out only under the control of official authority or when the processing is authorised by Union or Member State law providing for appropriate safeguards for the rights and freedoms of data subjects. Any comprehensive register of criminal convictions shall be kept only under the control of official authority.

[2.12]
Article 11   Processing which does not require identification
1. If the purposes for which a controller processes personal data do not or do no longer require the identification of a data subject by the controller, the controller shall not be obliged to maintain, acquire or process additional information in order to identify the data subject for the sole purpose of complying with this Regulation.

2. Where, in cases referred to in paragraph 1 of this Article, the controller is able to demonstrate that it is not in a position to identify the data subject, the controller shall inform the data subject accordingly, if possible. In such cases, Articles 15 to 20 shall not apply except where the data subject, for the purpose of exercising his or her rights under those articles, provides additional information enabling his or her identification.

CHAPTER III RIGHTS OF THE DATA SUBJECT
SECTION 1 TRANSPARENCY AND MODALITIES

[2.13]
Article 12   Transparent information, communication and modalities for the exercise of the rights of the data subject
1. The controller shall take appropriate measures to provide any information referred to in Articles 13 and 14 and any communication under Articles 15 to 22 and 34 relating to processing to the data subject in a concise, transparent, intelligible and easily accessible form, using clear and plain language, in particular for any information addressed specifically to a child. The information shall be provided in writing, or by other means, including, where appropriate, by electronic means. When requested by the data subject, the information may be provided orally, provided that the identity of the data subject is proven by other means.

2. The controller shall facilitate the exercise of data subject rights under Articles 15 to 22. In the cases referred to in Article 11(2), the controller shall not refuse to act on the request of the data subject for exercising his or her rights under Articles 15 to 22, unless the controller demonstrates that it is not in a position to identify the data subject.

3. The controller shall provide information on action taken on a request under Articles 15 to 22 to the data subject without undue delay and in any event within one month of receipt of the request. That period may be extended by two further months where necessary, taking into account the complexity and number of the requests. The controller shall inform the data subject of any such extension within one month of receipt of the request, together with the reasons for the delay. Where the data subject makes the request by electronic form means, the information shall be provided by electronic means where possible, unless otherwise requested by the data subject.

4. If the controller does not take action on the request of the data subject, the controller shall inform the data subject without delay and at the latest within one month of receipt of the request of the reasons for not taking action and on the possibility of lodging a complaint with a supervisory authority and seeking a judicial remedy.

5. Information provided under Articles 13 and 14 and any communication and any actions taken under Articles 15 to 22 and 34 shall be provided free of charge. Where requests from a data subject are manifestly unfounded or excessive, in particular because of their repetitive character, the controller may either:

   (a) charge a reasonable fee taking into account the administrative costs of providing the information or communication or taking the action requested; or

   (b) refuse to act on the request.

     The controller shall bear the burden of demonstrating the manifestly unfounded or excessive character of the request.

6. Without prejudice to Article 11, where the controller has reasonable doubts concerning the identity of the natural person making the request referred to in Articles 15 to 21, the controller may request the provision of additional information necessary to confirm the identity of the data subject.

7. The information to be provided to data subjects pursuant to Articles 13 and 14 may be provided in combination with standardised icons in order to give in an easily visible, intelligible and clearly legible manner a meaningful overview of the intended processing. Where the icons are presented electronically they shall be machine-readable.

8. The Commission shall be empowered to adopt delegated acts in accordance with Article 92 for the purpose of determining the information to be presented by the icons and the procedures for providing standardised icons.

SECTION 2 INFORMATION AND ACCESS TO PERSONAL DATA

[2.14]

Article 13   **Information to be provided where personal data are collected from the data subject**

1. Where personal data relating to a data subject are collected from the data subject, the controller shall, at the time when personal data are obtained, provide the data subject with all of the following information:

   (a) the identity and the contact details of the controller and, where applicable, of the controller's representative;

   (b) the contact details of the data protection officer, where applicable;

   (c) the purposes of the processing for which the personal data are intended as well as the legal basis for the processing;

   (d) where the processing is based on point (f) of Article 6(1), the legitimate interests pursued by the controller or by a third party;

   (e) the recipients or categories of recipients of the personal data, if any;

   (f) where applicable, the fact that the controller intends to transfer personal data to a third country or international organisation and the existence or absence of an adequacy decision by the Commission, or in the case of transfers referred to in Article 46 or 47, or the second subparagraph of Article 49(1), reference to the appropriate or suitable safeguards and the means by which to obtain a copy of them or where they have been made available.

2. In addition to the information referred to in paragraph 1, the controller shall, at the time when personal data are obtained, provide the data subject with the following further information necessary to ensure fair and transparent processing:

   (a) the period for which the personal data will be stored, or if that is not possible, the criteria used to determine that period;

   (b) the existence of the right to request from the controller access to and rectification or erasure of personal data or restriction of processing concerning the data subject or to object to processing as well as the right to data portability;

   (c) where the processing is based on point (a) of Article 6(1) or point (a) of Article 9(2), the existence of the right to withdraw consent at any time, without affecting the lawfulness of processing based on consent before its withdrawal;

   (d) the right to lodge a complaint with a supervisory authority;

   (e) whether the provision of personal data is a statutory or contractual requirement, or a requirement necessary to enter into a contract, as well as whether the data subject is obliged to provide the personal data and of the possible consequences of failure to provide such data;

   (f) the existence of automated decision-making, including profiling, referred to in Article 22(1) and (4) and, at least in those cases, meaningful information about the logic involved, as well as the significance and the envisaged consequences of such processing for the data subject.

3. Where the controller intends to further process the personal data for a purpose other than that for which the personal data were collected, the controller shall provide the data subject prior to that further processing with information on that other purpose and with any relevant further information as referred to in paragraph 2.

4. Paragraphs 1, 2 and 3 shall not apply where and insofar as the data subject already has the information.

[2.15]

Article 14   **Information to be provided where personal data have not been obtained from the data subject**

1. Where personal data have not been obtained from the data subject, the controller shall provide the data subject with the following information:

   (a) the identity and the contact details of the controller and, where applicable, of the controller's representative;

   (b) the contact details of the data protection officer, where applicable;

   (c) the purposes of the processing for which the personal data are intended as well as the legal basis for the processing;

   (d) the categories of personal data concerned;

   (e) the recipients or categories of recipients of the personal data, if any;

(f) where applicable, that the controller intends to transfer personal data to a recipient in a third country or international organisation and the existence or absence of an adequacy decision by the Commission, or in the case of transfers referred to in Article 46 or 47, or the second subparagraph of Article 49(1), reference to the appropriate or suitable safeguards and the means to obtain a copy of them or where they have been made available.

2. In addition to the information referred to in paragraph 1, the controller shall provide the data subject with the following information necessary to ensure fair and transparent processing in respect of the data subject:

(a) the period for which the personal data will be stored, or if that is not possible, the criteria used to determine that period;

(b) where the processing is based on point (f) of Article 6(1), the legitimate interests pursued by the controller or by a third party;

(c) the existence of the right to request from the controller access to and rectification or erasure of personal data or restriction of processing concerning the data subject and to object to processing as well as the right to data portability;

(d) where processing is based on point (a) of Article 6(1) or point (a) of Article 9(2), the existence of the right to withdraw consent at any time, without affecting the lawfulness of processing based on consent before its withdrawal;

(e) the right to lodge a complaint with a supervisory authority;

(f) from which source the personal data originate, and if applicable, whether it came from publicly accessible sources;

(g) the existence of automated decision-making, including profiling, referred to in Article 22(1) and (4) and, at least in those cases, meaningful information about the logic involved, as well as the significance and the envisaged consequences of such processing for the data subject.

3. The controller shall provide the information referred to in paragraphs 1 and 2:

(a) within a reasonable period after obtaining the personal data, but at the latest within one month, having regard to the specific circumstances in which the personal data are processed;

(b) if the personal data are to be used for communication with the data subject, at the latest at the time of the first communication to that data subject; or

(c) if a disclosure to another recipient is envisaged, at the latest when the personal data are first disclosed.

4. Where the controller intends to further process the personal data for a purpose other than that for which the personal data were obtained, the controller shall provide the data subject prior to that further processing with information on that other purpose and with any relevant further information as referred to in paragraph 2.

5. Paragraphs 1 to 4 shall not apply where and insofar as:

(a) the data subject already has the information;

(b) the provision of such information proves impossible or would involve a disproportionate effort, in particular for processing for archiving purposes in the public interest, scientific or historical research purposes or statistical purposes, subject to the conditions and safeguards referred to in Article 89(1) or in so far as the obligation referred to in paragraph 1 of this Article is likely to render impossible or seriously impair the achievement of the objectives of that processing. In such cases the controller shall take appropriate measures to protect the data subject's rights and freedoms and legitimate interests, including making the information publicly available;

(c) obtaining or disclosure is expressly laid down by Union or Member State law to which the controller is subject and which provides appropriate measures to protect the data subject's legitimate interests; or

(d) where the personal data must remain confidential subject to an obligation of professional secrecy regulated by Union or Member State law, including a statutory obligation of secrecy.

[2.16]
Article 15   Right of access by the data subject

1. The data subject shall have the right to obtain from the controller confirmation as to whether or not personal data concerning him or her are being processed, and, where that is the case, access to the personal data and the following information:

(a) the purposes of the processing;

(b) the categories of personal data concerned;

(c) the recipients or categories of recipient to whom the personal data have been or will be disclosed, in particular recipients in third countries or international organisations;

(d) where possible, the envisaged period for which the personal data will be stored, or, if not possible, the criteria used to determine that period;

(e) the existence of the right to request from the controller rectification or erasure of personal data or restriction of processing of personal data concerning the data subject or to object to such processing;

(f) the right to lodge a complaint with a supervisory authority;

(g) where the personal data are not collected from the data subject, any available information as to their source;

(h) the existence of automated decision-making, including profiling, referred to in Article 22(1) and (4) and, at least in those cases, meaningful information about the logic involved, as well as the significance and the envisaged consequences of such processing for the data subject.

2. Where personal data are transferred to a third country or to an international organisation, the data subject shall have the right to be informed of the appropriate safeguards pursuant to Article 46 relating to the transfer.

3. The controller shall provide a copy of the personal data undergoing processing. For any further copies requested by the data subject, the controller may charge a reasonable fee based on administrative costs. Where the data subject makes the request by electronic means, and unless otherwise requested by the data subject, the information shall be provided in a commonly used electronic form.

4. The right to obtain a copy referred to in paragraph 3 shall not adversely affect the rights and freedoms of others.

SECTION 3 RECTIFICATION AND ERASURE

[2.17]
Article 16   Right to rectification
The data subject shall have the right to obtain from the controller without undue delay the rectification of inaccurate personal data concerning him or her. Taking into account the purposes of the processing, the data subject shall have the right to have incomplete personal data completed, including by means of providing a supplementary statement.

[2.18]
Article 17   Right to erasure ('right to be forgotten')
1. The data subject shall have the right to obtain from the controller the erasure of personal data concerning him or her without undue delay and the controller shall have the obligation to erase personal data without undue delay where one of the following grounds applies:
    (a) the personal data are no longer necessary in relation to the purposes for which they were collected or otherwise processed;
    (b) the data subject withdraws consent on which the processing is based according to point (a) of Article 6(1), or point (a) of Article 9(2), and where there is no other legal ground for the processing;
    (c) the data subject objects to the processing pursuant to Article 21(1) and there are no overriding legitimate grounds for the processing, or the data subject objects to the processing pursuant to Article 21(2);
    (d) the personal data have been unlawfully processed;
    (e) the personal data have to be erased for compliance with a legal obligation in Union or Member State law to which the controller is subject;
    (f) the personal data have been collected in relation to the offer of information society services referred to in Article 8(1).
2. Where the controller has made the personal data public and is obliged pursuant to paragraph 1 to erase the personal data, the controller, taking account of available technology and the cost of implementation, shall take reasonable steps, including technical measures, to inform controllers which are processing the personal data that the data subject has requested the erasure by such controllers of any links to, or copy or replication of, those personal data.
3. Paragraphs 1 and 2 shall not apply to the extent that processing is necessary:
    (a) for exercising the right of freedom of expression and information;
    (b) for compliance with a legal obligation which requires processing by Union or Member State law to which the controller is subject or for the performance of a task carried out in the public interest or in the exercise of official authority vested in the controller;
    (c) for reasons of public interest in the area of public health in accordance with points (h) and (i) of Article 9(2) as well as Article 9(3);
    (d) for archiving purposes in the public interest, scientific or historical research purposes or statistical purposes in accordance with Article 89(1) in so far as the right referred to in paragraph 1 is likely to render impossible or seriously impair the achievement of the objectives of that processing; or
    (e) for the establishment, exercise or defence of legal claims.

[2.19]
Article 18   Right to restriction of processing
1. The data subject shall have the right to obtain from the controller restriction of processing where one of the following applies:
    (a) the accuracy of the personal data is contested by the data subject, for a period enabling the controller to verify the accuracy of the personal data;
    (b) the processing is unlawful and the data subject opposes the erasure of the personal data and requests the restriction of their use instead;
    (c) the controller no longer needs the personal data for the purposes of the processing, but they are required by the data subject for the establishment, exercise or defence of legal claims;
    (d) the data subject has objected to processing pursuant to Article 21(1) pending the verification whether the legitimate grounds of the controller override those of the data subject.
2. Where processing has been restricted under paragraph 1, such personal data shall, with the exception of storage, only be processed with the data subject's consent or for the establishment, exercise or defence of legal claims or for the protection of the rights of another natural or legal person or for reasons of important public interest of the Union or of a Member State.
3. A data subject who has obtained restriction of processing pursuant to paragraph 1 shall be informed by the controller before the restriction of processing is lifted.

[2.20]
Article 19   Notification obligation regarding rectification or erasure of personal data or restriction of processing
The controller shall communicate any rectification or erasure of personal data or restriction of processing carried out in accordance with Article 16, Article 17(1) and Article 18 to each recipient to whom the personal data have been disclosed, unless this proves impossible or involves disproportionate effort. The controller shall inform the data subject about those recipients if the data subject requests it.

[2.21]
Article 20   Right to data portability
1. The data subject shall have the right to receive the personal data concerning him or her, which he or she has provided to a controller, in a structured, commonly used and machine-readable format and have the right to transmit those data to another controller without hindrance from the controller to which the personal data have been provided, where:

(a) the processing is based on consent pursuant to point (a) of Article 6(1) or point (a) of Article 9(2) or on a contract pursuant to point (b) of Article 6(1); and

(b) the processing is carried out by automated means.

2. In exercising his or her right to data portability pursuant to paragraph 1, the data subject shall have the right to have the personal data transmitted directly from one controller to another, where technically feasible.

3. The exercise of the right referred to in paragraph 1 of this Article shall be without prejudice to Article 17. That right shall not apply to processing necessary for the performance of a task carried out in the public interest or in the exercise of official authority vested in the controller.

4. The right referred to in paragraph 1 shall not adversely affect the rights and freedoms of others.

SECTION 4 RIGHT TO OBJECT AND AUTOMATED INDIVIDUAL DECISION-MAKING

[2.22]
Article 21   Right to object

1. The data subject shall have the right to object, on grounds relating to his or her particular situation, at any time to processing of personal data concerning him or her which is based on point (e) or (f) of Article 6(1), including profiling based on those provisions. The controller shall no longer process the personal data unless the controller demonstrates compelling legitimate grounds for the processing which override the interests, rights and freedoms of the data subject or for the establishment, exercise or defence of legal claims.

2. Where personal data are processed for direct marketing purposes, the data subject shall have the right to object at any time to processing of personal data concerning him or her for such marketing, which includes profiling to the extent that it is related to such direct marketing.

3. Where the data subject objects to processing for direct marketing purposes, the personal data shall no longer be processed for such purposes.

4. At the latest at the time of the first communication with the data subject, the right referred to in paragraphs 1 and 2 shall be explicitly brought to the attention of the data subject and shall be presented clearly and separately from any other information.

5. In the context of the use of information society services, and notwithstanding Directive 2002/58/EC, the data subject may exercise his or her right to object by automated means using technical specifications.

6. Where personal data are processed for scientific or historical research purposes or statistical purposes pursuant to Article 89(1), the data subject, on grounds relating to his or her particular situation, shall have the right to object to processing of personal data concerning him or her, unless the processing is necessary for the performance of a task carried out for reasons of public interest.

[2.23]
Article 22   Automated individual decision-making, including profiling

1. The data subject shall have the right not to be subject to a decision based solely on automated processing, including profiling, which produces legal effects concerning him or her or similarly significantly affects him or her.

2. Paragraph 1 shall not apply if the decision:

(a) is necessary for entering into, or performance of, a contract between the data subject and a data controller;

(b) is authorised by Union or Member State law to which the controller is subject and which also lays down suitable measures to safeguard the data subject's rights and freedoms and legitimate interests; or

(c) is based on the data subject's explicit consent.

3. In the cases referred to in points (a) and (c) of paragraph 2, the data controller shall implement suitable measures to safeguard the data subject's rights and freedoms and legitimate interests, at least the right to obtain human intervention on the part of the controller, to express his or her point of view and to contest the decision.

4. Decisions referred to in paragraph 2 shall not be based on special categories of personal data referred to in Article 9(1), unless point (a) or (g) of Article 9(2) applies and suitable measures to safeguard the data subject's rights and freedoms and legitimate interests are in place.

SECTION 5 RESTRICTIONS

[2.24]
Article 23   Restrictions

1. Union or Member State law to which the data controller or processor is subject may restrict by way of a legislative measure the scope of the obligations and rights provided for in Articles 12 to 22 and Article 34, as well as Article 5 in so far as its provisions correspond to the rights and obligations provided for in Articles 12 to 22, when such a restriction respects the essence of the fundamental rights and freedoms and is a necessary and proportionate measure in a democratic society to safeguard:

(a) national security;

(b) defence;

(c) public security;

(d) the prevention, investigation, detection or prosecution of criminal offences or the execution of criminal penalties, including the safeguarding against and the prevention of threats to public security;

(e) other important objectives of general public interest of the Union or of a Member State, in particular an important economic or financial interest of the Union or of a Member State, including monetary, budgetary and taxation a matters, public health and social security;

(f) the protection of judicial independence and judicial proceedings;

(g) the prevention, investigation, detection and prosecution of breaches of ethics for regulated professions;

(h) a monitoring, inspection or regulatory function connected, even occasionally, to the exercise of official authority in the cases referred to in points (a) to (e) and (g);

(i) the protection of the data subject or the rights and freedoms of others;

(j) the enforcement of civil law claims.

2. In particular, any legislative measure referred to in paragraph 1 shall contain specific provisions at least, where relevant, as to:

(a) the purposes of the processing or categories of processing;

(b) the categories of personal data;

(c) the scope of the restrictions introduced;

(d) the safeguards to prevent abuse or unlawful access or transfer;

(e) the specification of the controller or categories of controllers;

(f) the storage periods and the applicable safeguards taking into account the nature, scope and purposes of the processing or categories of processing;

(g) the risks to the rights and freedoms of data subjects; and

(h) the right of data subjects to be informed about the restriction, unless that may be prejudicial to the purpose of the restriction.

CHAPTER IV CONTROLLER AND PROCESSOR

SECTION 1 RESPONSIBILITY OF THE CONTROLLER

[2.25]
Article 24   Responsibility of the controller

1. Taking into account the nature, scope, context and purposes of processing as well as the risks of varying likelihood and severity for the rights and freedoms of natural persons, the controller shall implement appropriate technical and organisational measures to ensure and to be able to demonstrate that processing is performed in accordance with this Regulation. Those measures shall be reviewed and updated where necessary.

2. Where proportionate in relation to processing activities, the measures referred to in paragraph 1 shall include the implementation of appropriate data protection policies by the controller.

3. Adherence to approved codes of conduct as referred to in Article 40 or approved certification mechanisms as referred to in Article 42 may be used as an element by which to demonstrate compliance with the obligations of the controller.

[2.26]
Article 25   Data protection by design and by default

1. Taking into account the state of the art, the cost of implementation and the nature, scope, context and purposes of processing as well as the risks of varying likelihood and severity for rights and freedoms of natural persons posed by the processing, the controller shall, both at the time of the determination of the means for processing and at the time of the processing itself, implement appropriate technical and organisational measures, such as pseudonymisation, which are designed to implement data-protection principles, such as data minimisation, in an effective manner and to integrate the necessary safeguards into the processing in order to meet the requirements of this Regulation and protect the rights of data subjects.

2. The controller shall implement appropriate technical and organisational measures for ensuring that, by default, only personal data which are necessary for each specific purpose of the processing are processed. That obligation applies to the amount of personal data collected, the extent of their processing, the period of their storage and their accessibility. In particular, such measures shall ensure that by default personal data are not made accessible without the individual's intervention to an indefinite number of natural persons.

3. An approved certification mechanism pursuant to Article 42 may be used as an element to demonstrate compliance with the requirements set out in paragraphs 1 and 2 of this Article.

[2.27]
Article 26   Joint controllers

1. Where two or more controllers jointly determine the purposes and means of processing, they shall be joint controllers. They shall in a transparent manner determine their respective responsibilities for compliance with the obligations under this Regulation, in particular as regards the exercising of the rights of the data subject and their respective duties to provide the information referred to in Articles 13 and 14, by means of an arrangement between them unless, and in so far as, the respective responsibilities of the controllers are determined by Union or Member State law to which the controllers are subject. The arrangement may designate a contact point for data subjects.

2. The arrangement referred to in paragraph 1 shall duly reflect the respective roles and relationships of the joint controllers vis-à-vis the data subjects. The essence of the arrangement shall be made available to the data subject.

3. Irrespective of the terms of the arrangement referred to in paragraph 1, the data subject may exercise his or her rights under this Regulation in respect of and against each of the controllers.

[2.28]
Article 27   Representatives of controllers or processors not established in the Union

1. Where Article 3(2) applies, the controller or the processor shall designate in writing a representative in the Union.

2. The obligation laid down in paragraph 1 of this Article shall not apply to:

(a) processing which is occasional, does not include, on a large scale, processing of special categories of data as referred to in Article 9(1) or processing of personal data relating to criminal convictions and offences referred to in Article 10, and is unlikely to result in a risk to the rights and freedoms of natural persons, taking into account the nature, context, scope and purposes of the processing; or

(b) a public authority or body.

3. The representative shall be established in one of the Member States where the data subjects, whose personal data are processed in relation to the offering of goods or services to them, or whose behaviour is monitored, are.

4. The representative shall be mandated by the controller or processor to be addressed in addition to or instead of the controller or the processor by, in particular, supervisory authorities and data subjects, on all issues related to processing, for the purposes of ensuring compliance with this Regulation.

5. The designation of a representative by the controller or processor shall be without prejudice to legal actions which could be initiated against the controller or the processor themselves.

[2.29]
Article 28   Processor
1. Where processing is to be carried out on behalf of a controller, the controller shall use only processors providing sufficient guarantees to implement appropriate technical and organisational measures in such a manner that processing will meet the requirements of this Regulation and ensure the protection of the rights of the data subject.
2. The processor shall not engage another processor without prior specific or general written authorisation of the controller. In the case of general written authorisation, the processor shall inform the controller of any intended changes concerning the addition or replacement of other processors, thereby giving the controller the opportunity to object to such changes.
3. Processing by a processor shall be governed by a contract or other legal act under Union or Member State law, that is binding on the processor with regard to the controller and that sets out the subject-matter and duration of the processing, the nature and purpose of the processing, the type of personal data and categories of data subjects and the obligations and rights of the controller. That contract or other legal act shall stipulate, in particular, that the processor:

(a) processes the personal data only on documented instructions from the controller, including with regard to transfers of personal data to a third country or an international organisation, unless required to do so by Union or Member State law to which the processor is subject; in such a case, the processor shall inform the controller of that legal requirement before processing, unless that law prohibits such information on important grounds of public interest;

(b) ensures that persons authorised to process the personal data have committed themselves to confidentiality or are under an appropriate statutory obligation of confidentiality;

(c) takes all measures required pursuant to Article 32;

(d) respects the conditions referred to in paragraphs 2 and 4 for engaging another processor;

(e) taking into account the nature of the processing, assists the controller by appropriate technical and organisational measures, insofar as this is possible, for the fulfilment of the controller's obligation to respond to requests for exercising the data subject's rights laid down in Chapter III;

(f) assists the controller in ensuring compliance with the obligations pursuant to Articles 32 to 36 taking into account the nature of processing and the information available to the processor;

(g) at the choice of the controller, deletes or returns all the personal data to the controller after the end of the provision of services relating to processing, and deletes existing copies unless Union or Member State law requires storage of the personal data;

(h) makes available to the controller all information necessary to demonstrate compliance with the obligations laid down in this Article and allow for and contribute to audits, including inspections, conducted by the controller or another auditor mandated by the controller.

With regard to point (h) of the first subparagraph, the processor shall immediately inform the controller if, in its opinion, an instruction infringes this Regulation or other Union or Member State data protection provisions.
4. Where a processor engages another processor for carrying out specific processing activities on behalf of the controller, the same data protection obligations as set out in the contract or other legal act between the controller and the processor as referred to in paragraph 3 shall be imposed on that other processor by way of a contract or other legal act under Union or Member State law, in particular providing sufficient guarantees to implement appropriate technical and organisational measures in such a manner that the processing will meet the requirements of this Regulation. Where that other processor fails to fulfil its data protection obligations, the initial processor shall remain fully liable to the controller for the performance of that other processor's obligations.
5. Adherence of a processor to an approved code of conduct as referred to in Article 40 or an approved certification mechanism as referred to in Article 42 may be used as an element by which to demonstrate sufficient guarantees as referred to in paragraphs 1 and 4 of this Article.
6. Without prejudice to an individual contract between the controller and the processor, the contract or the other legal act referred to in paragraphs 3 and 4 of this Article may be based, in whole or in part, on standard contractual clauses referred to in paragraphs 7 and 8 of this Article, including when they are part of a certification granted to the controller or processor pursuant to Articles 42 and 43.
7. The Commission may lay down standard contractual clauses for the matters referred to in paragraph 3 and 4 of this Article and in accordance with the examination procedure referred to in Article 93(2).
8. A supervisory authority may adopt standard contractual clauses for the matters referred to in paragraph 3 and 4 of this Article and in accordance with the consistency mechanism referred to in Article 63.
9. The contract or the other legal act referred to in paragraphs 3 and 4 shall be in writing, including in electronic form.
10. Without prejudice to Articles 82, 83 and 84, if a processor infringes this Regulation by determining the purposes and means of processing, the processor shall be considered to be a controller in respect of that processing.

[2.30]
Article 29   Processing under the authority of the controller or processor
The processor and any person acting under the authority of the controller or of the processor, who has access to personal data, shall not process those data except on instructions from the controller, unless required to do so by Union or Member State law.

[2.31]
Article 30   Records of processing activities
1. Each controller and, where applicable, the controller's representative, shall maintain a record of processing activities under its responsibility. That record shall contain all of the following information:

(a) the name and contact details of the controller and, where applicable, the joint controller, the controller's representative and the data protection officer;

(b) the purposes of the processing;
(c) a description of the categories of data subjects and of the categories of personal data;
(d) the categories of recipients to whom the personal data have been or will be disclosed including recipients in third countries or international organisations;
(e) where applicable, transfers of personal data to a third country or an international organisation, including the identification of that third country or international organisation and, in the case of transfers referred to in the second subparagraph of Article 49(1), the documentation of suitable safeguards;
(f) where possible, the envisaged time limits for erasure of the different categories of data;
(g) where possible, a general description of the technical and organisational security measures referred to in Article 32(1).

2. Each processor and, where applicable, the processor's representative shall maintain a record of all categories of processing activities carried out on behalf of a controller, containing:
(a) the name and contact details of the processor or processors and of each controller on behalf of which the processor is acting, and, where applicable, of the controller's or the processor's representative, and the data protection officer;
(b) the categories of processing carried out on behalf of each controller;
(c) where applicable, transfers of personal data to a third country or an international organisation, including the identification of that third country or international organisation and, in the case of transfers referred to in the second subparagraph of Article 49(1), the documentation of suitable safeguards;
(d) where possible, a general description of the technical and organisational security measures referred to in Article 32(1).

3. The records referred to in paragraphs 1 and 2 shall be in writing, including in electronic form.

4. The controller or the processor and, where applicable, the controller's or the processor's representative, shall make the record available to the supervisory authority on request.

5. The obligations referred to in paragraphs 1 and 2 shall not apply to an enterprise or an organisation employing fewer than 250 persons unless the processing it carries out is likely to result in a risk to the rights and freedoms of data subjects, the processing is not occasional, or the processing includes special categories of data as referred to in Article 9(1) or personal data relating to criminal convictions and offences referred to in Article 10.

[2.32]
Article 31   Cooperation with the supervisory authority
The controller and the processor and, where applicable, their representatives, shall cooperate, on request, with the supervisory authority in the performance of its tasks.

SECTION 2 SECURITY OF PERSONAL DATA

[2.33]
Article 32   Security of processing
1. Taking into account the state of the art, the costs of implementation and the nature, scope, context and purposes of processing as well as the risk of varying likelihood and severity for the rights and freedoms of natural persons, the controller and the processor shall implement appropriate technical and organisational measures to ensure a level of security appropriate to the risk, including inter alia as appropriate:
(a) the pseudonymisation and encryption of personal data;
(b) the ability to ensure the ongoing confidentiality, integrity, availability and resilience of processing systems and services;
(c) the ability to restore the availability and access to personal data in a timely manner in the event of a physical or technical incident;
(d) a process for regularly testing, assessing and evaluating the effectiveness of technical and organisational measures for ensuring the security of the processing.

2. In assessing the appropriate level of security account shall be taken in particular of the risks that are presented by processing, in particular from accidental or unlawful destruction, loss, alteration, unauthorised disclosure of, or access to personal data transmitted, stored or otherwise processed.

3. Adherence to an approved code of conduct as referred to in Article 40 or an approved certification mechanism as referred to in Article 42 may be used as an element by which to demonstrate compliance with the requirements set out in paragraph 1 of this Article.

4. The controller and processor shall take steps to ensure that any natural person acting under the authority of the controller or the processor who has access to personal data does not process them except on instructions from the controller, unless he or she is required to do so by Union or Member State law.

[2.34]
Article 33   Notification of a personal data breach to the supervisory authority
1. In the case of a personal data breach, the controller shall without undue delay and, where feasible, not later than 72 hours after having become aware of it, notify the personal data breach to the supervisory authority competent in accordance with Article 55, unless the personal data breach is unlikely to result in a risk to the rights and freedoms of natural persons. Where the notification to the supervisory authority is not made within 72 hours, it shall be accompanied by reasons for the delay.

2. The processor shall notify the controller without undue delay after becoming aware of a personal data breach.

3. The notification referred to in paragraph 1 shall at least:
(a) describe the nature of the personal data breach including where possible, the categories and approximate number of data subjects concerned and the categories and approximate number of personal data records concerned;
(b) communicate the name and contact details of the data protection officer or other contact point where more information can be obtained;
(c) describe the likely consequences of the personal data breach;

    (d) describe the measures taken or proposed to be taken by the controller to address the personal data breach, including, where appropriate, measures to mitigate its possible adverse effects.

4. Where, and in so far as, it is not possible to provide the information at the same time, the information may be provided in phases without undue further delay.

5. The controller shall document any personal data breaches, comprising the facts relating to the personal data breach, its effects and the remedial action taken. That documentation shall enable the supervisory authority to verify compliance with this Article.

[2.35]
Article 34   Communication of a personal data breach to the data subject

1. When the personal data breach is likely to result in a high risk to the rights and freedoms of natural persons, the controller shall communicate the personal data breach to the data subject without undue delay.

2. The communication to the data subject referred to in paragraph 1 of this Article shall describe in clear and plain language the nature of the personal data breach and contain at least the information and measures referred to in points (b), (c) and (d) of Article 33(3).

3. The communication to the data subject referred to in paragraph 1 shall not be required if any of the following conditions are met:

    (a) the controller has implemented appropriate technical and organisational protection measures, and those measures were applied to the personal data affected by the personal data breach, in particular those that render the personal data unintelligible to any person who is not authorised to access it, such as encryption;

    (b) the controller has taken subsequent measures which ensure that the high risk to the rights and freedoms of data subjects referred to in paragraph 1 is no longer likely to materialise;

    (c) it would involve disproportionate effort. In such a case, there shall instead be a public communication or similar measure whereby the data subjects are informed in an equally effective manner.

4. If the controller has not already communicated the personal data breach to the data subject, the supervisory authority, having considered the likelihood of the personal data breach resulting in a high risk, may require it to do so or may decide that any of the conditions referred to in paragraph 3 are met.

SECTION 3 DATA PROTECTION IMPACT ASSESSMENT AND PRIOR CONSULTATION

[2.36]
Article 35   Data protection impact assessment

1. Where a type of processing in particular using new technologies, and taking into account the nature, scope, context and purposes of the processing, is likely to result in a high risk to the rights and freedoms of natural persons, the controller shall, prior to the processing, carry out an assessment of the impact of the envisaged processing operations on the protection of personal data. A single assessment may address a set of similar processing operations that present similar high risks.

2. The controller shall seek the advice of the data protection officer, where designated, when carrying out a data protection impact assessment.

3. A data protection impact assessment referred to in paragraph 1 shall in particular be required in the case of:

    (a) a systematic and extensive evaluation of personal aspects relating to natural persons which is based on automated processing, including profiling, and on which decisions are based that produce legal effects concerning the natural person or similarly significantly affect the natural person;

    (b) processing on a large scale of special categories of data referred to in Article 9(1), or of personal data relating to criminal convictions and offences referred to in Article 10; or

    (c) a systematic monitoring of a publicly accessible area on a large scale.

4. The supervisory authority shall establish and make public a list of the kind of processing operations which are subject to the requirement for a data protection impact assessment pursuant to paragraph 1. The supervisory authority shall communicate those lists to the Board referred to in Article 68.

5. The supervisory authority may also establish and make public a list of the kind of processing operations for which no data protection impact assessment is required. The supervisory authority shall communicate those lists to the Board.

6. Prior to the adoption of the lists referred to in paragraphs 4 and 5, the competent supervisory authority shall apply the consistency mechanism referred to in Article 63 where such lists involve processing activities which are related to the offering of goods or services to data subjects or to the monitoring of their behaviour in several Member States, or may substantially affect the free movement of personal data within the Union.

7. The assessment shall contain at least:

    (a) a systematic description of the envisaged processing operations and the purposes of the processing, including, where applicable, the legitimate interest pursued by the controller;

    (b) an assessment of the necessity and proportionality of the processing operations in relation to the purposes;

    (c) an assessment of the risks to the rights and freedoms of data subjects referred to in paragraph 1; and

    (d) the measures envisaged to address the risks, including safeguards, security measures and mechanisms to ensure the protection of personal data and to demonstrate compliance with this Regulation taking into account the rights and legitimate interests of data subjects and other persons concerned.

8. Compliance with approved codes of conduct referred to in Article 40 by the relevant controllers or processors shall be taken into due account in assessing the impact of the processing operations performed by such controllers or processors, in particular for the purposes of a data protection impact assessment.

9. Where appropriate, the controller shall seek the views of data subjects or their representatives on the intended processing, without prejudice to the protection of commercial or public interests or the security of processing operations.

10. Where processing pursuant to point (c) or (e) of Article 6(1) has a legal basis in Union law or in the law of the Member State to which the controller is subject, that law regulates the specific processing operation or set of operations in question, and a data protection impact assessment has already been carried out as part of a general impact assessment in the context of the adoption of that legal basis, paragraphs 1 to 7 shall not apply unless Member States deem it to be necessary to carry out such an assessment prior to processing activities.

11. Where necessary, the controller shall carry out a review to assess if processing is performed in accordance with the data protection impact assessment at least when there is a change of the risk represented by processing operations.

[2.37]
Article 36   Prior consultation

1. The controller shall consult the supervisory authority prior to processing where a data protection impact assessment under Article 35 indicates that the processing would result in a high risk in the absence of measures taken by the controller to mitigate the risk.

2. Where the supervisory authority is of the opinion that the intended processing referred to in paragraph 1 would infringe this Regulation, in particular where the controller has insufficiently identified or mitigated the risk, the supervisory authority shall, within period of up to eight weeks of receipt of the request for consultation, provide written advice to the controller and, where applicable to the processor, and may use any of its powers referred to in Article 58. That period may be extended by six weeks, taking into account the complexity of the intended processing. The supervisory authority shall inform the controller and, where applicable, the processor, of any such extension within one month of receipt of the request for consultation together with the reasons for the delay. Those periods may be suspended until the supervisory authority has obtained information it has requested for the purposes of the consultation.

3. When consulting the supervisory authority pursuant to paragraph 1, the controller shall provide the supervisory authority with:

    (a) where applicable, the respective responsibilities of the controller, joint controllers and processors involved in the processing, in particular for processing within a group of undertakings;

    (b) the purposes and means of the intended processing;

    (c) the measures and safeguards provided to protect the rights and freedoms of data subjects pursuant to this Regulation;

    (d) where applicable, the contact details of the data protection officer;

    (e) the data protection impact assessment provided for in Article 35; and

    (f) any other information requested by the supervisory authority.

4. Member States shall consult the supervisory authority during the preparation of a proposal for a legislative measure to be adopted by a national parliament, or of a regulatory measure based on such a legislative measure, which relates to processing.

5. Notwithstanding paragraph 1, Member State law may require controllers to consult with, and obtain prior authorisation from, the supervisory authority in relation to processing by a controller for the performance of a task carried out by the controller in the public interest, including processing in relation to social protection and public health.

SECTION 4 DATA PROTECTION OFFICER

[2.38]
Article 37   Designation of the data protection officer

1. The controller and the processor shall designate a data protection officer in any case where:

    (a) the processing is carried out by a public authority or body, except for courts acting in their judicial capacity;

    (b) the core activities of the controller or the processor consist of processing operations which, by virtue of their nature, their scope and/or their purposes, require regular and systematic monitoring of data subjects on a large scale; or

    (c) the core activities of the controller or the processor consist of processing on a large scale of special categories of data pursuant to Article 9 or personal data relating to criminal convictions and offences referred to in Article 10.

2. A group of undertakings may appoint a single data protection officer provided that a data protection officer is easily accessible from each establishment.

3. Where the controller or the processor is a public authority or body, a single data protection officer may be designated for several such authorities or bodies, taking account of their organisational structure and size.

4. In cases other than those referred to in paragraph 1, the controller or processor or associations and other bodies representing categories of controllers or processors may or, where required by Union or Member State law shall, designate a data protection officer. The data protection officer may act for such associations and other bodies representing controllers or processors.

5. The data protection officer shall be designated on the basis of professional qualities and, in particular, expert knowledge of data protection law and practices and the ability to fulfil the tasks referred to in Article 39.

6. The data protection officer may be a staff member of the controller or processor, or fulfil the tasks on the basis of a service contract.

7. The controller or the processor shall publish the contact details of the data protection officer and communicate them to the supervisory authority.

[2.39]
Article 38   Position of the data protection officer

1. The controller and the processor shall ensure that the data protection officer is involved, properly and in a timely manner, in all issues which relate to the protection of personal data.

2. The controller and processor shall support the data protection officer in performing the tasks referred to in Article 39 by providing resources necessary to carry out those tasks and access to personal data and processing operations, and to maintain his or her expert knowledge.

3. The controller and processor shall ensure that the data protection officer does not receive any instructions regarding the exercise of those tasks. He or she shall not be dismissed or penalised by the controller or the processor for performing his tasks. The data protection officer shall directly report to the highest management level of the controller or the processor.

4. Data subjects may contact the data protection officer with regard to all issues related to processing of their personal data and to the exercise of their rights under this Regulation.

5. The data protection officer shall be bound by secrecy or confidentiality concerning the performance of his or her tasks, in accordance with Union or Member State law.

6. The data protection officer may fulfil other tasks and duties. The controller or processor shall ensure that any such tasks and duties do not result in a conflict of interests.

[2.40]
Article 39   Tasks of the data protection officer
1. The data protection officer shall have at least the following tasks:
   (a)   to inform and advise the controller or the processor and the employees who carry out processing of their obligations pursuant to this Regulation and to other Union or Member State data protection provisions;
   (b)   to monitor compliance with this Regulation, with other Union or Member State data protection provisions and with the policies of the controller or processor in relation to the protection of personal data, including the assignment of responsibilities, awareness-raising and training of staff involved in processing operations, and the related audits;
   (c)   to provide advice where requested as regards the data protection impact assessment and monitor its performance pursuant to Article 35;
   (d)   to cooperate with the supervisory authority;
   (e)   to act as the contact point for the supervisory authority on issues relating to processing, including the prior consultation referred to in Article 36, and to consult, where appropriate, with regard to any other matter.
2. The data protection officer shall in the performance of his or her tasks have due regard to the risk associated with processing operations, taking into account the nature, scope, context and purposes of processing.

SECTION 5 CODES OF CONDUCT AND CERTIFICATION

[2.41]
Article 40   Codes of conduct
1. The Member States, the supervisory authorities, the Board and the Commission shall encourage the drawing up of codes of conduct intended to contribute to the proper application of this Regulation, taking account of the specific features of the various processing sectors and the specific needs of micro, small and medium-sized enterprises.

2. Associations and other bodies representing categories of controllers or processors may prepare codes of conduct, or amend or extend such codes, for the purpose of specifying the application of this Regulation, such as with regard to:
   (a)   fair and transparent processing;
   (b)   the legitimate interests pursued by controllers in specific contexts;
   (c)   the collection of personal data;
   (d)   the pseudonymisation of personal data;
   (e)   the information provided to the public and to data subjects;
   (f)   the exercise of the rights of data subjects;
   (g)   the information provided to, and the protection of, children, and the manner in which the consent of the holders of parental responsibility over children is to be obtained;
   (h)   the measures and procedures referred to in Articles 24 and 25 and the measures to ensure security of processing referred to in Article 32;
   (i)   the notification of personal data breaches to supervisory authorities and the communication of such personal data breaches to data subjects;
   (j)   the transfer of personal data to third countries or international organisations; or
   (k)   out-of-court proceedings and other dispute resolution procedures for resolving disputes between controllers and data subjects with regard to processing, without prejudice to the rights of data subjects pursuant to Articles 77 and 79.
3. In addition to adherence by controllers or processors subject to this Regulation, codes of conduct approved pursuant to paragraph 5 of this Article and having general validity pursuant to paragraph 9 of this Article may also be adhered to by controllers or processors that are not subject to this Regulation pursuant to Article 3 in order to provide appropriate safeguards within the framework of personal data transfers to third countries or international organisations under the terms referred to in point (e) of Article 46(2). Such controllers or processors shall make binding and enforceable commitments, via contractual or other legally binding instruments, to apply those appropriate safeguards including with regard to the rights of data subjects.

4. A code of conduct referred to in paragraph 2 of this Article shall contain mechanisms which enable the body referred to in Article 41(1) to carry out the mandatory monitoring of compliance with its provisions by the controllers or processors which undertake to apply it, without prejudice to the tasks and powers of supervisory authorities competent pursuant to Article 55 or 56.

5. Associations and other bodies referred to in paragraph 2 of this Article which intend to prepare a code of conduct or to amend or extend an existing code shall submit the draft code, amendment or extension to the supervisory authority which is competent pursuant to Article 55. The supervisory authority shall provide an opinion on whether the draft code, amendment or extension complies with this Regulation and shall approve that draft code, amendment or extension if it finds that it provides sufficient appropriate safeguards.

6. Where the draft code, or amendment or extension is approved in accordance with paragraph 5, and where the code of conduct concerned does not relate to processing activities in several Member States, the supervisory authority shall register and publish the code.

7. Where a draft code of conduct relates to processing activities in several Member States, the supervisory authority which is competent pursuant to Article 55 shall, before approving the draft code, amendment or extension, submit it in the procedure referred to in Article 63 to the Board which shall provide an opinion on whether the draft code, amendment or extension complies with this Regulation or, in the situation referred to in paragraph 3 of this Article, provides appropriate safeguards.

8. Where the opinion referred to in paragraph 7 confirms that the draft code, amendment or extension complies with this Regulation, or, in the situation referred to in paragraph 3, provides appropriate safeguards, the Board shall submit its opinion to the Commission.

9. The Commission may, by way of implementing acts, decide that the approved code of conduct, amendment or extension submitted to it pursuant to paragraph 8 of this Article have general validity within the Union. Those implementing acts shall be adopted in accordance with the examination procedure set out in Article 93(2).

10. The Commission shall ensure appropriate publicity for the approved codes which have been decided as having general validity in accordance with paragraph 9.

11. The Board shall collate all approved codes of conduct, amendments and extensions in a register and shall make them publicly available by way of appropriate means.

[2.42]
Article 41   Monitoring of approved codes of conduct

1. Without prejudice to the tasks and powers of the competent supervisory authority under Articles 57 and 58, the monitoring of compliance with a code of conduct pursuant to Article 40 may be carried out by a body which has an appropriate level of expertise in relation to the subject-matter of the code and is accredited for that purpose by the competent supervisory authority.

2. A body as referred to in paragraph 1 may be accredited to monitor compliance with a code of conduct where that body has:

(a) demonstrated its independence and expertise in relation to the subject-matter of the code to the satisfaction of the competent supervisory authority;

(b) established procedures which allow it to assess the eligibility of controllers and processors concerned to apply the code, to monitor their compliance with its provisions and to periodically review its operation;

(c) established procedures and structures to handle complaints about infringements of the code or the manner in which the code has been, or is being, implemented by a controller or processor, and to make those procedures and structures transparent to data subjects and the public; and

(d) demonstrated to the satisfaction of the competent supervisory authority that its tasks and duties do not result in a conflict of interests.

3. The competent supervisory authority shall submit the draft requirements for accreditation of a body as referred to in paragraph 1 of this Article to the Board pursuant to the consistency mechanism referred to in Article 63.

4. Without prejudice to the tasks and powers of the competent supervisory authority and the provisions of Chapter VIII, a body as referred to in paragraph 1 of this Article shall, subject to appropriate safeguards, take appropriate action in cases of infringement of the code by a controller or processor, including suspension or exclusion of the controller or processor concerned from the code. It shall inform the competent supervisory authority of such actions and the reasons for taking them.

5. The competent supervisory authority shall revoke the accreditation of a body as referred to in paragraph 1 if the requirements for accreditation are not, or are no longer, met or where actions taken by the body infringe this Regulation.

6. This Article shall not apply to processing carried out by public authorities and bodies.

[2.43]
Article 42   Certification

1. The Member States, the supervisory authorities, the Board and the Commission shall encourage, in particular at Union level, the establishment of data protection certification mechanisms and of data protection seals and marks, for the purpose of demonstrating compliance with this Regulation of processing operations by controllers and processors. The specific needs of micro, small and medium-sized enterprises shall be taken into account.

2. In addition to adherence by controllers or processors subject to this Regulation, data protection certification mechanisms, seals or marks approved pursuant to paragraph 5 of this Article may be established for the purpose of demonstrating the existence of appropriate safeguards provided by controllers or processors that are not subject to this Regulation pursuant to Article 3 within the framework of personal data transfers to third countries or international organisations under the terms referred to in point (f) of Article 46(2). Such controllers or processors shall make binding and enforceable commitments, via contractual or other legally binding instruments, to apply those appropriate safeguards, including with regard to the rights of data subjects.

3. The certification shall be voluntary and available via a process that is transparent.

4. A certification pursuant to this Article does not reduce the responsibility of the controller or the processor for compliance with this Regulation and is without prejudice to the tasks and powers of the supervisory authorities which are competent pursuant to Article 55 or 56.

5. A certification pursuant to this Article shall be issued by the certification bodies referred to in Article 43 or by the competent supervisory authority, on the basis of criteria approved by that competent supervisory authority pursuant to Article 58(3) or by the Board pursuant to Article 63. Where the criteria are approved by the Board, this may result in a common certification, the European Data Protection Seal.

6. The controller or processor which submits its processing to the certification mechanism shall provide the certification body referred to in Article 43, or where applicable, the competent supervisory authority, with all information and access to its processing activities which are necessary to conduct the certification procedure.

7. Certification shall be issued to a controller or processor for a maximum period of three years and may be renewed, under the same conditions, provided that the relevant criteria continue to be met. Certification shall be withdrawn, as applicable, by the certification bodies referred to in Article 43 or by the competent supervisory authority where the criteria for the certification are not or are no longer met.

8. The Board shall collate all certification mechanisms and data protection seals and marks in a register and shall make them publicly available by any appropriate means.

[2.44]
Article 43   Certification bodies
1. Without prejudice to the tasks and powers of the competent supervisory authority under Articles 57 and 58, certification bodies which have an appropriate level of expertise in relation to data protection shall, after informing the supervisory authority in order to allow it to exercise its powers pursuant to point (h) of Article 58(2) where necessary, issue and renew certification. Member States shall ensure that those certification bodies are accredited by one or both of the following:
  (a)   the supervisory authority which is competent pursuant to Article 55 or 56;
  (b)   the national accreditation body named in accordance with Regulation (EC) No 765/2008 of the European Parliament and of the Council[1] in accordance with EN-ISO/IEC 17065/2012 and with the additional requirements established by the supervisory authority which is competent pursuant to Article 55 or 56.
2. Certification bodies referred to in paragraph 1 shall be accredited in accordance with that paragraph only where they have:
  (a)   demonstrated their independence and expertise in relation to the subject-matter of the certification to the satisfaction of the competent supervisory authority;
  (b)   undertaken to respect the criteria referred to in Article 42(5) and approved by the supervisory authority which is competent pursuant to Article 55 or 56 or by the Board pursuant to Article 63;
  (c)   established procedures for the issuing, periodic review and withdrawal of data protection certification, seals and marks;
  (d)   established procedures and structures to handle complaints about infringements of the certification or the manner in which the certification has been, or is being, implemented by the controller or processor, and to make those procedures and structures transparent to data subjects and the public; and
  (e)   demonstrated, to the satisfaction of the competent supervisory authority, that their tasks and duties do not result in a conflict of interests.
3. The accreditation of certification bodies as referred to in paragraphs 1 and 2 of this Article shall take place on the basis of requirements approved by the supervisory authority which is competent pursuant to Article 55 or 56 or by the Board pursuant to Article 63. In the case of accreditation pursuant to point (b) of paragraph 1 of this Article, those requirements shall complement those envisaged in Regulation (EC) No 765/2008 and the technical rules that describe the methods and procedures of the certification bodies.
4. The certification bodies referred to in paragraph 1 shall be responsible for the proper assessment leading to the certification or the withdrawal of such certification without prejudice to the responsibility of the controller or processor for compliance with this Regulation. The accreditation shall be issued for a maximum period of five years and may be renewed on the same conditions provided that the certification body meets the requirements set out in this Article.
5. The certification bodies referred to in paragraph 1 shall provide the competent supervisory authorities with the reasons for granting or withdrawing the requested certification.
6. The requirements referred to in paragraph 3 of this Article and the criteria referred to in Article 42(5) shall be made public by the supervisory authority in an easily accessible form. The supervisory authorities shall also transmit those requirements and criteria to the Board.
7. Without prejudice to Chapter VIII, the competent supervisory authority or the national accreditation body shall revoke an accreditation of a certification body pursuant to paragraph 1 of this Article where the conditions for the accreditation are not, or are no longer, met or where actions taken by a certification body infringe this Regulation.
8. The Commission shall be empowered to adopt delegated acts in accordance with Article 92 for the purpose of specifying the requirements to be taken into account for the data protection certification mechanisms referred to in Article 42(1).
9. The Commission may adopt implementing acts laying down technical standards for certification mechanisms and data protection seals and marks, and mechanisms to promote and recognise those certification mechanisms, seals and marks. Those implementing acts shall be adopted in accordance with the examination procedure referred to in Article 93(2).

NOTES
  [1]   Regulation (EC) No 765/2008 of the European Parliament and of the Council of 9 July 2008 setting out the requirements for accreditation and market surveillance relating to the marketing of products and repealing Regulation (EEC) No 339/93 (OJ L218, 13.8.2008, p 30).

CHAPTER V TRANSFERS OF PERSONAL DATA TO THIRD COUNTRIES OR INTERNATIONAL ORGANISATIONS

[2.45]
Article 44   General principle for transfers
Any transfer of personal data which are undergoing processing or are intended for processing after transfer to a third country or to an international organisation shall take place only if, subject to the other provisions of this Regulation, the conditions laid down in this Chapter are complied with by the controller and processor, including for onward transfers of personal data from the third country or an international organisation to another third country or to another international organisation. All provisions in this Chapter shall be applied in order to ensure that the level of protection of natural persons guaranteed by this Regulation is not undermined.

[2.46]
Article 45   Transfers on the basis of an adequacy decision
1. A transfer of personal data to a third country or an international organisation may take place where the Commission has decided that the third country, a territory or one or more specified sectors within that third country, or the international organisation in question ensures an adequate level of protection. Such a transfer shall not require any specific authorisation.

2. When assessing the adequacy of the level of protection, the Commission shall, in particular, take account of the following elements:
  (a) the rule of law, respect for human rights and fundamental freedoms, relevant legislation, both general and sectoral, including concerning public security, defence, national security and criminal law and the access of public authorities to personal data, as well as the implementation of such legislation, data protection rules, professional rules and security measures, including rules for the onward transfer of personal data to another third country or international organisation which are complied with in that country or international organisation, case-law, as well as effective and enforceable data subject rights and effective administrative and judicial redress for the data subjects whose personal data are being transferred;
  (b) the existence and effective functioning of one or more independent supervisory authorities in the third country or to which an international organisation is subject, with responsibility for ensuring and enforcing compliance with the data protection rules, including adequate enforcement powers, for assisting and advising the data subjects in exercising their rights and for cooperation with the supervisory authorities of the Member States; and
  (c) the international commitments the third country or international organisation concerned has entered into, or other obligations arising from legally binding conventions or instruments as well as from its participation in multilateral or regional systems, in particular in relation to the protection of personal data.

3. The Commission, after assessing the adequacy of the level of protection, may decide, by means of implementing act, that a third country, a territory or one or more specified sectors within a third country, or an international organisation ensures an adequate level of protection within the meaning of paragraph 2 of this Article. The implementing act shall provide for a mechanism for a periodic review, at least every four years, which shall take into account all relevant developments in the third country or international organisation. The implementing act shall specify its territorial and sectoral application and, where applicable, identify the supervisory authority or authorities referred to in point (b) of paragraph 2 of this Article. The implementing act shall be adopted in accordance with the examination procedure referred to in Article 93(2).

4. The Commission shall, on an ongoing basis, monitor developments in third countries and international organisations that could affect the functioning of decisions adopted pursuant to paragraph 3 of this Article and decisions adopted on the basis of Article 25(6) of Directive 95/46/EC.

5. The Commission shall, where available information reveals, in particular following the review referred to in paragraph 3 of this Article, that a third country, a territory or one or more specified sectors within a third country, or an international organisation no longer ensures an adequate level of protection within the meaning of paragraph 2 of this Article, to the extent necessary, repeal, amend or suspend the decision referred to in paragraph 3 of this Article by means of implementing acts without retroactive effect. Those implementing acts shall be adopted in accordance with the examination procedure referred to in Article 93(2).

On duly justified imperative grounds of urgency, the Commission shall adopt immediately applicable implementing acts in accordance with the procedure referred to in Article 93(3).

6. The Commission shall enter into consultations with the third country or international organisation with a view to remedying the situation giving rise to the decision made pursuant to paragraph 5.

7. A decision pursuant to paragraph 5 of this Article is without prejudice to transfers of personal data to the third country, a territory or one or more specified sectors within that third country, or the international organisation in question pursuant to Articles 46 to 49.

8. The Commission shall publish in the Official Journal of the European Union and on its website a list of the third countries, territories and specified sectors within a third country and international organisations for which it has decided that an adequate level of protection is or is no longer ensured.

9. Decisions adopted by the Commission on the basis of Article 25(6) of Directive 95/46/EC shall remain in force until amended, replaced or repealed by a Commission Decision adopted in accordance with paragraph 3 or 5 of this Article.

[2.47]
Article 46   Transfers subject to appropriate safeguards
1. In the absence of a decision pursuant to Article 45(3), a controller or processor may transfer personal data to a third country or an international organisation only if the controller or processor has provided appropriate safeguards, and on condition that enforceable data subject rights and effective legal remedies for data subjects are available.

2. The appropriate safeguards referred to in paragraph 1 may be provided for, without requiring any specific authorisation from a supervisory authority, by:
  (a) a legally binding and enforceable instrument between public authorities or bodies;
  (b) binding corporate rules in accordance with Article 47;
  (c) standard data protection clauses adopted by the Commission in accordance with the examination procedure referred to in Article 93(2);
  (d) standard data protection clauses adopted by a supervisory authority and approved by the Commission pursuant to the examination procedure referred to in Article 93(2);
  (e) an approved code of conduct pursuant to Article 40 together with binding and enforceable commitments of the controller or processor in the third country to apply the appropriate safeguards, including as regards data subjects' rights; or

(f)   an approved certification mechanism pursuant to Article 42 together with binding and enforceable commitments of the controller or processor in the third country to apply the appropriate safeguards, including as regards data subjects' rights.

3. Subject to the authorisation from the competent supervisory authority, the appropriate safeguards referred to in paragraph 1 may also be provided for, in particular, by:

(a)   contractual clauses between the controller or processor and the controller, processor or the recipient of the personal data in the third country or international organisation; or

(b)   provisions to be inserted into administrative arrangements between public authorities or bodies which include enforceable and effective data subject rights.

4. The supervisory authority shall apply the consistency mechanism referred to in Article 63 in the cases referred to in paragraph 3 of this Article.

5. Authorisations by a Member State or supervisory authority on the basis of Article 26(2) of Directive 95/46/EC shall remain valid until amended, replaced or repealed, if necessary, by that supervisory authority. Decisions adopted by the Commission on the basis of Article 26(4) of Directive 95/46/EC shall remain in force until amended, replaced or repealed, if necessary, by a Commission Decision adopted in accordance with paragraph 2 of this Article.

[2.48]
Article 47   Binding corporate rules
1. The competent supervisory authority shall approve binding corporate rules in accordance with the consistency mechanism set out in Article 63, provided that they:

(a)   are legally binding and apply to and are enforced by every member concerned of the group of undertakings, or group of enterprises engaged in a joint economic activity, including their employees;

(b)   expressly confer enforceable rights on data subjects with regard to the processing of their personal data; and

(c)   fulfil the requirements laid down in paragraph 2.

2. The binding corporate rules referred to in paragraph 1 shall specify at least:

(a)   the structure and contact details of the group of undertakings, or group of enterprises engaged in a joint economic activity and of each of its members;

(b)   the data transfers or set of transfers, including the categories of personal data, the type of processing and its purposes, the type of data subjects affected and the identification of the third country or countries in question;

(c)   their legally binding nature, both internally and externally;

(d)   the application of the general data protection principles, in particular purpose limitation, data minimisation, limited storage periods, data quality, data protection by design and by default, legal basis for processing, processing of special categories of personal data, measures to ensure data security, and the requirements in respect of onward transfers to bodies not bound by the binding corporate rules;

(e)   the rights of data subjects in regard to processing and the means to exercise those rights, including the right not to be subject to decisions based solely on automated processing, including profiling in accordance with Article 22, the right to lodge a complaint with the competent supervisory authority and before the competent courts of the Member States in accordance with Article 79, and to obtain redress and, where appropriate, compensation for a breach of the binding corporate rules;

(f)   the acceptance by the controller or processor established on the territory of a Member State of liability for any breaches of the binding corporate rules by any member concerned not established in the Union; the controller or the processor shall be exempt from that liability, in whole or in part, only if it proves that that member is not responsible for the event giving rise to the damage;

(g)   how the information on the binding corporate rules, in particular on the provisions referred to in points (d), (e) and (f) of this paragraph is provided to the data subjects in addition to Articles 13 and 14;

(h)   the tasks of any data protection officer designated in accordance with Article 37 or any other person or entity in charge of the monitoring compliance with the binding corporate rules within the group of undertakings, or group of enterprises engaged in a joint economic activity, as well as monitoring training and complaint-handling;

(i)   the complaint procedures;

(j)   the mechanisms within the group of undertakings, or group of enterprises engaged in a joint economic activity for ensuring the verification of compliance with the binding corporate rules. Such mechanisms shall include data protection audits and methods for ensuring corrective actions to protect the rights of the data subject. Results of such verification should be communicated to the person or entity referred to in point (h) and to the board of the controlling undertaking of a group of undertakings, or of the group of enterprises engaged in a joint economic activity, and should be available upon request to the competent supervisory authority;

(k)   the mechanisms for reporting and recording changes to the rules and reporting those changes to the supervisory authority;

(l)   the cooperation mechanism with the supervisory authority to ensure compliance by any member of the group of undertakings, or group of enterprises engaged in a joint economic activity, in particular by making available to the supervisory authority the results of verifications of the measures referred to in point (j);

(m)   the mechanisms for reporting to the competent supervisory authority any legal requirements to which a member of the group of undertakings, or group of enterprises engaged in a joint economic activity is subject in a third country which are likely to have a substantial adverse effect on the guarantees provided by the binding corporate rules; and

(n)   the appropriate data protection training to personnel having permanent or regular access to personal data.

3. The Commission may specify the format and procedures for the exchange of information between controllers, processors and supervisory authorities for binding corporate rules within the meaning of this Article. Those implementing acts shall be adopted in accordance with the examination procedure set out in Article 93(2).

[2.49]
Article 48   Transfers or disclosures not authorised by Union law
Any judgment of a court or tribunal and any decision of an administrative authority of a third country requiring a controller or processor to transfer or disclose personal data may only be recognised or enforceable in any manner if based on an international agreement, such as a mutual legal assistance treaty, in force between the requesting third country and the Union or a Member State, without prejudice to other grounds for transfer pursuant to this Chapter.

[2.50]
Article 49   Derogations for specific situations
1. In the absence of an adequacy decision pursuant to Article 45(3), or of appropriate safeguards pursuant to Article 46, including binding corporate rules, a transfer or a set of transfers of personal data to a third country or an international organisation shall take place only on one of the following conditions:
  (a)   the data subject has explicitly consented to the proposed transfer, after having been informed of the possible risks of such transfers for the data subject due to the absence of an adequacy decision and appropriate safeguards;
  (b)   the transfer is necessary for the performance of a contract between the data subject and the controller or the implementation of pre-contractual measures taken at the data subject's request;
  (c)   the transfer is necessary for the conclusion or performance of a contract concluded in the interest of the data subject between the controller and another natural or legal person;
  (d)   the transfer is necessary for important reasons of public interest;
  (e)   the transfer is necessary for the establishment, exercise or defence of legal claims;
  (f)   the transfer is necessary in order to protect the vital interests of the data subject or of other persons, where the data subject is physically or legally incapable of giving consent;
  (g)   the transfer is made from a register which according to Union or Member State law is intended to provide information to the public and which is open to consultation either by the public in general or by any person who can demonstrate a legitimate interest, but only to the extent that the conditions laid down by Union or Member State law for consultation are fulfilled in the particular case.
Where a transfer could not be based on a provision in Article 45 or 46, including the provisions on binding corporate rules, and none of the derogations for a specific situation referred to in the first subparagraph of this paragraph is applicable, a transfer to a third country or an international organisation may take place only if the transfer is not repetitive, concerns only a limited number of data subjects, is necessary for the purposes of compelling legitimate interests pursued by the controller which are not overridden by the interests or rights and freedoms of the data subject, and the controller has assessed all the circumstances surrounding the data transfer and has on the basis of that assessment provided suitable safeguards with regard to the protection of personal data. The controller shall inform the supervisory authority of the transfer. The controller shall, in addition to providing the information referred to in Articles 13 and 14, inform the data subject of the transfer and on the compelling legitimate interests pursued.
2. A transfer pursuant to point (g) of the first subparagraph of paragraph 1 shall not involve the entirety of the personal data or entire categories of the personal data contained in the register. Where the register is intended for consultation by persons having a legitimate interest, the transfer shall be made only at the request of those persons or if they are to be the recipients.
3. Points (a), (b) and (c) of the first subparagraph of paragraph 1 and the second subparagraph thereof shall not apply to activities carried out by public authorities in the exercise of their public powers.
4. The public interest referred to in point (d) of the first subparagraph of paragraph 1 shall be recognised in Union law or in the law of the Member State to which the controller is subject.
5. In the absence of an adequacy decision, Union or Member State law may, for important reasons of public interest, expressly set limits to the transfer of specific categories of personal data to a third country or an international organisation. Member States shall notify such provisions to the Commission.
6. The controller or processor shall document the assessment as well as the suitable safeguards referred to in the second subparagraph of paragraph 1 of this Article in the records referred to in Article 30.

[2.51]
Article 50   International cooperation for the protection of personal data
In relation to third countries and international organisations, the Commission and supervisory authorities shall take appropriate steps to:
  (a)   develop international cooperation mechanisms to facilitate the effective enforcement of legislation for the protection of personal data;
  (b)   provide international mutual assistance in the enforcement of legislation for the protection of personal data, including through notification, complaint referral, investigative assistance and information exchange, subject to appropriate safeguards for the protection of personal data and other fundamental rights and freedoms;
  (c)   engage relevant stakeholders in discussion and activities aimed at furthering international cooperation in the enforcement of legislation for the protection of personal data;
  (d)   promote the exchange and documentation of personal data protection legislation and practice, including on jurisdictional conflicts with third countries.

CHAPTER VI INDEPENDENT SUPERVISORY AUTHORITIES
SECTION 1 INDEPENDENT STATUS

[2.52]
Article 51   Supervisory authority
1. Each Member State shall provide for one or more independent public authorities to be responsible for monitoring the application of this Regulation, in order to protect the fundamental rights and freedoms of natural persons in relation to processing and to facilitate the free flow of personal data within the Union ('supervisory authority').

Part 2   Data Protection: EU Law etc

2. Each supervisory authority shall contribute to the consistent application of this Regulation throughout the Union. For that purpose, the supervisory authorities shall cooperate with each other and the Commission in accordance with Chapter VII.

3. Where more than one supervisory authority is established in a Member State, that Member State shall designate the supervisory authority which is to represent those authorities in the Board and shall set out the mechanism to ensure compliance by the other authorities with the rules relating to the consistency mechanism referred to in Article 63.

4. Each Member State shall notify to the Commission the provisions of its law which it adopts pursuant to this Chapter, by 25 May 2018 and, without delay, any subsequent amendment affecting them.

[2.53]
Article 52   Independence

1. Each supervisory authority shall act with complete independence in performing its tasks and exercising its powers in accordance with this Regulation.

2. The member or members of each supervisory authority shall, in the performance of their tasks and exercise of their powers in accordance with this Regulation, remain free from external influence, whether direct or indirect, and shall neither seek nor take instructions from anybody.

3. Member or members of each supervisory authority shall refrain from any action incompatible with their duties and shall not, during their term of office, engage in any incompatible occupation, whether gainful or not.

4. Each Member State shall ensure that each supervisory authority is provided with the human, technical and financial resources, premises and infrastructure necessary for the effective performance of its tasks and exercise of its powers, including those to be carried out in the context of mutual assistance, cooperation and participation in the Board.

5. Each Member State shall ensure that each supervisory authority chooses and has its own staff which shall be subject to the exclusive direction of the member or members of the supervisory authority concerned.

6. Each Member State shall ensure that each supervisory authority is subject to financial control which does not affect its independence and that it has separate, public annual budgets, which may be part of the overall state or national budget.

[2.54]
Article 53   General conditions for the members of the supervisory authority

1. Member States shall provide for each member of their supervisory authorities to be appointed by means of a transparent procedure by:
   — their parliament;
   — their government;
   — their head of State; or
   — an independent body entrusted with the appointment under Member State law.

2. Each member shall have the qualifications, experience and skills, in particular in the area of the protection of personal data, required to perform its duties and exercise its powers.

3. The duties of a member shall end in the event of the expiry of the term of office, resignation or compulsory retirement, in accordance with the law of the Member State concerned.

4. A member shall be dismissed only in cases of serious misconduct or if the member no longer fulfils the conditions required for the performance of the duties.

[2.55]
Article 54   Rules on the establishment of the supervisory authority

1. Each Member State shall provide by law for all of the following:
   (a) the establishment of each supervisory authority;
   (b) the qualifications and eligibility conditions required to be appointed as member of each supervisory authority;
   (c) the rules and procedures for the appointment of the member or members of each supervisory authority;
   (d) the duration of the term of the member or members of each supervisory authority of no less than four years, except for the first appointment after 24 May 2016, part of which may take place for a shorter period where that is necessary to protect the independence of the supervisory authority by means of a staggered appointment procedure;
   (e) whether and, if so, for how many terms the member or members of each supervisory authority is eligible for reappointment;
   (f) the conditions governing the obligations of the member or members and staff of each supervisory authority, prohibitions on actions, occupations and benefits incompatible therewith during and after the term of office and rules governing the cessation of employment.

2. The member or members and the staff of each supervisory authority shall, in accordance with Union or Member State law, be subject to a duty of professional secrecy both during and after their term of office, with regard to any confidential information which has come to their knowledge in the course of the performance of their tasks or exercise of their powers. During their term of office, that duty of professional secrecy shall in particular apply to reporting by natural persons of infringements of this Regulation.

SECTION 2 COMPETENCE, TASKS AND POWERS

[2.56]
Article 55   Competence

1. Each supervisory authority shall be competent for the performance of the tasks assigned to and the exercise of the powers conferred on it in accordance with this Regulation on the territory of its own Member State.

2. Where processing is carried out by public authorities or private bodies acting on the basis of point (c) or (e) of Article 6(1), the supervisory authority of the Member State concerned shall be competent. In such cases Article 56 does not apply.

3. Supervisory authorities shall not be competent to supervise processing operations of courts acting in their judicial capacity.

[2.57]
Article 56   Competence of the lead supervisory authority
1. Without prejudice to Article 55, the supervisory authority of the main establishment or of the single establishment of the controller or processor shall be competent to act as lead supervisory authority for the cross-border processing carried out by that controller or processor in accordance with the procedure provided in Article 60.
2. By derogation from paragraph 1, each supervisory authority shall be competent to handle a complaint lodged with it or a possible infringement of this Regulation, if the subject matter relates only to an establishment in its Member State or substantially affects data subjects only in its Member State.
3. In the cases referred to in paragraph 2 of this Article, the supervisory authority shall inform the lead supervisory authority without delay on that matter. Within a period of three weeks after being informed the lead supervisory authority shall decide whether or not it will handle the case in accordance with the procedure provided in Article 60, taking into account whether or not there is an establishment of the controller or processor in the Member State of which the supervisory authority informed it.
4. Where the lead supervisory authority decides to handle the case, the procedure provided in Article 60 shall apply. The supervisory authority which informed the lead supervisory authority may submit to the lead supervisory authority a draft for a decision. The lead supervisory authority shall take utmost account of that draft when preparing the draft decision referred to in Article 60(3).
5. Where the lead supervisory authority decides not to handle the case, the supervisory authority which informed the lead supervisory authority shall handle it according to Articles 61 and 62.
6. The lead supervisory authority shall be the sole interlocutor of the controller or processor for the cross-border processing carried out by that controller or processor.

[2.58]
Article 57   Tasks
1. Without prejudice to other tasks set out under this Regulation, each supervisory authority shall on its territory:
   (a)   monitor and enforce the application of this Regulation;
   (b)   promote public awareness and understanding of the risks, rules, safeguards and rights in relation to processing. Activities addressed specifically to children shall receive specific attention;
   (c)   advise, in accordance with Member State law, the national parliament, the government, and other institutions and bodies on legislative and administrative measures relating to the protection of natural persons' rights and freedoms with regard to processing;
   (d)   promote the awareness of controllers and processors of their obligations under this Regulation;
   (e)   upon request, provide information to any data subject concerning the exercise of their rights under this Regulation and, if appropriate, cooperate with the supervisory authorities in other Member States to that end;
   (f)   handle complaints lodged by a data subject, or by a body, organisation or association in accordance with Article 80, and investigate, to the extent appropriate, the subject matter of the complaint and inform the complainant of the progress and the outcome of the investigation within a reasonable period, in particular if further investigation or coordination with another supervisory authority is necessary;
   (g)   cooperate with, including sharing information and provide mutual assistance to, other supervisory authorities with a view to ensuring the consistency of application and enforcement of this Regulation;
   (h)   conduct investigations on the application of this Regulation, including on the basis of information received from another supervisory authority or other public authority;
   (i)   monitor relevant developments, insofar as they have an impact on the protection of personal data, in particular the development of information and communication technologies and commercial practices;
   (j)   adopt standard contractual clauses referred to in Article 28(8) and in point (d) of Article 46(2);
   (k)   establish and maintain a list in relation to the requirement for data protection impact assessment pursuant to Article 35(4);
   (l)   give advice on the processing operations referred to in Article 36(2);
   (m)   encourage the drawing up of codes of conduct pursuant to Article 40(1) and provide an opinion and approve such codes of conduct which provide sufficient safeguards, pursuant to Article 40(5);
   (n)   encourage the establishment of data protection certification mechanisms and of data protection seals and marks pursuant to Article 42(1), and approve the criteria of certification pursuant to Article 42(5);
   (o)   where applicable, carry out a periodic review of certifications issued in accordance with Article 42(7);
   (p)   draft and publish the requirements for accreditation of a body for monitoring codes of conduct pursuant to Article 41 and of a certification body pursuant to Article 43;
   (q)   conduct the accreditation of a body for monitoring codes of conduct pursuant to Article 41 and of a certification body pursuant to Article 43;
   (r)   authorise contractual clauses and provisions referred to in Article 46(3);
   (s)   approve binding corporate rules pursuant to Article 47;
   (t)   contribute to the activities of the Board;
   (u)   keep internal records of infringements of this Regulation and of measures taken in accordance with Article 58(2); and
   (v)   fulfil any other tasks related to the protection of personal data.
2. Each supervisory authority shall facilitate the submission of complaints referred to in point (f) of paragraph 1 by measures such as a complaint submission form which can also be completed electronically, without excluding other means of communication.
3. The performance of the tasks of each supervisory authority shall be free of charge for the data subject and, where applicable, for the data protection officer.

4. Where requests are manifestly unfounded or excessive, in particular because of their repetitive character, the supervisory authority may charge a reasonable fee based on administrative costs, or refuse to act on the request. The supervisory authority shall bear the burden of demonstrating the manifestly unfounded or excessive character of the request.

[2.59]
Article 58   Powers
1. Each supervisory authority shall have all of the following investigative powers:
   (a) to order the controller and the processor, and, where applicable, the controller's or the processor's representative to provide any information it requires for the performance of its tasks;
   (b) to carry out investigations in the form of data protection audits;
   (c) to carry out a review on certifications issued pursuant to Article 42(7);
   (d) to notify the controller or the processor of an alleged infringement of this Regulation;
   (e) to obtain, from the controller and the processor, access to all personal data and to all information necessary for the performance of its tasks;
   (f) to obtain access to any premises of the controller and the processor, including to any data processing equipment and means, in accordance with Union or Member State procedural law.
2. Each supervisory authority shall have all of the following corrective powers:
   (a) to issue warnings to a controller or processor that intended processing operations are likely to infringe provisions of this Regulation;
   (b) to issue reprimands to a controller or a processor where processing operations have infringed provisions of this Regulation;
   (c) to order the controller or the processor to comply with the data subject's requests to exercise his or her rights pursuant to this Regulation;
   (d) to order the controller or processor to bring processing operations into compliance with the provisions of this Regulation, where appropriate, in a specified manner and within a specified period;
   (e) to order the controller to communicate a personal data breach to the data subject;
   (f) to impose a temporary or definitive limitation including a ban on processing;
   (g) to order the rectification or erasure of personal data or restriction of processing pursuant to Articles 16, 17 and 18 and the notification of such actions to recipients to whom the personal data have been disclosed pursuant to Article 17(2) and Article 19;
   (h) to withdraw a certification or to order the certification body to withdraw a certification issued pursuant to Articles 42 and 43, or to order the certification body not to issue certification if the requirements for the certification are not or are no longer met;
   (i) to impose an administrative fine pursuant to Article 83, in addition to, or instead of measures referred to in this paragraph, depending on the circumstances of each individual case;
   (j) to order the suspension of data flows to a recipient in a third country or to an international organisation.
3. Each supervisory authority shall have all of the following authorisation and advisory powers:
   (a) to advise the controller in accordance with the prior consultation procedure referred to in Article 36;
   (b) to issue, on its own initiative or on request, opinions to the national parliament, the Member State government or, in accordance with Member State law, to other institutions and bodies as well as to the public on any issue related to the protection of personal data;
   (c) to authorise processing referred to in Article 36(5), if the law of the Member State requires such prior authorisation;
   (d) to issue an opinion and approve draft codes of conduct pursuant to Article 40(5);
   (e) to accredit certification bodies pursuant to Article 43;
   (f) to issue certifications and approve criteria of certification in accordance with Article 42(5);
   (g) to adopt standard data protection clauses referred to in Article 28(8) and in point (d) of Article 46(2);
   (h) to authorise contractual clauses referred to in point (a) of Article 46(3);
   (i) to authorise administrative arrangements referred to in point (b) of Article 46(3);
   (j) to approve binding corporate rules pursuant to Article 47.
4. The exercise of the powers conferred on the supervisory authority pursuant to this Article shall be subject to appropriate safeguards, including effective judicial remedy and due process, set out in Union and Member State law in accordance with the Charter.
5. Each Member State shall provide by law that its supervisory authority shall have the power to bring infringements of this Regulation to the attention of the judicial authorities and where appropriate, to commence or engage otherwise in legal proceedings, in order to enforce the provisions of this Regulation.
6. Each Member State may provide by law that its supervisory authority shall have additional powers to those referred to in paragraphs 1, 2 and 3. The exercise of those powers shall not impair the effective operation of Chapter VII.

[2.60]
Article 59   Activity reports
Each supervisory authority shall draw up an annual report on its activities, which may include a list of types of infringement notified and types of measures taken in accordance with Article 58(2). Those reports shall be transmitted to the national parliament, the government and other authorities as designated by Member State law. They shall be made available to the public, to the Commission and to the Board.

CHAPTER VII COOPERATION AND CONSISTENCY

SECTION 1 COOPERATION

[2.61]

Article 60   Cooperation between the lead supervisory authority and the other supervisory authorities concerned

1. The lead supervisory authority shall cooperate with the other supervisory authorities concerned in accordance with this Article in an endeavour to reach consensus. The lead supervisory authority and the supervisory authorities concerned shall exchange all relevant information with each other.

2. The lead supervisory authority may request at any time other supervisory authorities concerned to provide mutual assistance pursuant to Article 61 and may conduct joint operations pursuant to Article 62, in particular for carrying out investigations or for monitoring the implementation of a measure concerning a controller or processor established in another Member State.

3. The lead supervisory authority shall, without delay, communicate the relevant information on the matter to the other supervisory authorities concerned. It shall without delay submit a draft decision to the other supervisory authorities concerned for their opinion and take due account of their views.

4. Where any of the other supervisory authorities concerned within a period of four weeks after having been consulted in accordance with paragraph 3 of this Article, expresses a relevant and reasoned objection to the draft decision, the lead supervisory authority shall, if it does not follow the relevant and reasoned objection or is of the opinion that the objection is not relevant or reasoned, submit the matter to the consistency mechanism referred to in Article 63.

5. Where the lead supervisory authority intends to follow the relevant and reasoned objection made, it shall submit to the other supervisory authorities concerned a revised draft decision for their opinion. That revised draft decision shall be subject to the procedure referred to in paragraph 4 within a period of two weeks.

6. Where none of the other supervisory authorities concerned has objected to the draft decision submitted by the lead supervisory authority within the period referred to in paragraphs 4 and 5, the lead supervisory authority and the supervisory authorities concerned shall be deemed to be in agreement with that draft decision and shall be bound by it.

7. The lead supervisory authority shall adopt and notify the decision to the main establishment or single establishment of the controller or processor, as the case may be and inform the other supervisory authorities concerned and the Board of the decision in question, including a summary of the relevant facts and grounds. The supervisory authority with which a complaint has been lodged shall inform the complainant on the decision.

8. By derogation from paragraph 7, where a complaint is dismissed or rejected, the supervisory authority with which the complaint was lodged shall adopt the decision and notify it to the complainant and shall inform the controller thereof.

9. Where the lead supervisory authority and the supervisory authorities concerned agree to dismiss or reject parts of a complaint and to act on other parts of that complaint, a separate decision shall be adopted for each of those parts of the matter. The lead supervisory authority shall adopt the decision for the part concerning actions in relation to the controller, shall notify it to the main establishment or single establishment of the controller or processor on the territory of its Member State and shall inform the complainant thereof, while the supervisory authority of the complainant shall adopt the decision for the part concerning dismissal or rejection of that complaint, and shall notify it to that complainant and shall inform the controller or processor thereof.

10. After being notified of the decision of the lead supervisory authority pursuant to paragraphs 7 and 9, the controller or processor shall take the necessary measures to ensure compliance with the decision as regards processing activities in the context of all its establishments in the Union. The controller or processor shall notify the measures taken for complying with the decision to the lead supervisory authority, which shall inform the other supervisory authorities concerned.

11. Where, in exceptional circumstances, a supervisory authority concerned has reasons to consider that there is an urgent need to act in order to protect the interests of data subjects, the urgency procedure referred to in Article 66 shall apply.

12. The lead supervisory authority and the other supervisory authorities concerned shall supply the information required under this Article to each other by electronic means, using a standardised format.

[2.62]

Article 61   Mutual assistance

1. Supervisory authorities shall provide each other with relevant information and mutual assistance in order to implement and apply this Regulation in a consistent manner, and shall put in place measures for effective cooperation with one another. Mutual assistance shall cover, in particular, information requests and supervisory measures, such as requests to carry out prior authorisations and consultations, inspections and investigations.

2. Each supervisory authority shall take all appropriate measures required to reply to a request of another supervisory authority without undue delay and no later than one month after receiving the request. Such measures may include, in particular, the transmission of relevant information on the conduct of an investigation.

3. Requests for assistance shall contain all the necessary information, including the purpose of and reasons for the request. Information exchanged shall be used only for the purpose for which it was requested.

4. The requested supervisory authority shall not refuse to comply with the request unless:

(a) it is not competent for the subject-matter of the request or for the measures it is requested to execute; or

(b) compliance with the request would infringe this Regulation or Union or Member State law to which the supervisory authority receiving the request is subject.

5. The requested supervisory authority shall inform the requesting supervisory authority of the results or, as the case may be, of the progress of the measures taken in order to respond to the request. The requested supervisory authority shall provide reasons for any refusal to comply with a request pursuant to paragraph 4.

6. Requested supervisory authorities shall, as a rule, supply the information requested by other supervisory authorities by electronic means, using a standardised format.

7. Requested supervisory authorities shall not charge a fee for any action taken by them pursuant to a request for mutual assistance. Supervisory authorities may agree on rules to indemnify each other for specific expenditure arising from the provision of mutual assistance in exceptional circumstances.

8. Where a supervisory authority does not provide the information referred to in paragraph 5 of this Article within one month of receiving the request of another supervisory authority, the requesting supervisory authority may adopt a provisional measure on the territory of its Member State in accordance with Article 55(1). In that case, the urgent need to act under Article 66(1) shall be presumed to be met and require an urgent binding decision from the Board pursuant to Article 66(2).

9. The Commission may, by means of implementing acts, specify the format and procedures for mutual assistance referred to in this Article and the arrangements for the exchange of information by electronic means between supervisory authorities, and between supervisory authorities and the Board, in particular the standardised format referred to in paragraph 6 of this Article. Those implementing acts shall be adopted in accordance with the examination procedure referred to in Article 93(2).

[2.63]
Article 62   Joint operations of supervisory authorities
1. The supervisory authorities shall, where appropriate, conduct joint operations including joint investigations and joint enforcement measures in which members or staff of the supervisory authorities of other Member States are involved.

2. Where the controller or processor has establishments in several Member States or where a significant number of data subjects in more than one Member State are likely to be substantially affected by processing operations, a supervisory authority of each of those Member States shall have the right to participate in joint operations. The supervisory authority which is competent pursuant to Article 56(1) or (4) shall invite the supervisory authority of each of those Member States to take part in the joint operations and shall respond without delay to the request of a supervisory authority to participate.

3. A supervisory authority may, in accordance with Member State law, and with the seconding supervisory authority's authorisation, confer powers, including investigative powers on the seconding supervisory authority's members or staff involved in joint operations or, in so far as the law of the Member State of the host supervisory authority permits, allow the seconding supervisory authority's members or staff to exercise their investigative powers in accordance with the law of the Member State of the seconding supervisory authority. Such investigative powers may be exercised only under the guidance and in the presence of members or staff of the host supervisory authority. The seconding supervisory authority's members or staff shall be subject to the Member State law of the host supervisory authority.

4. Where, in accordance with paragraph 1, staff of a seconding supervisory authority operate in another Member State, the Member State of the host supervisory authority shall assume responsibility for their actions, including liability, for any damage caused by them during their operations, in accordance with the law of the Member State in whose territory they are operating.

5. The Member State in whose territory the damage was caused shall make good such damage under the conditions applicable to damage caused by its own staff. The Member State of the seconding supervisory authority whose staff has caused damage to any person in the territory of another Member State shall reimburse that other Member State in full any sums it has paid to the persons entitled on their behalf.

6. Without prejudice to the exercise of its rights vis-à-vis third parties and with the exception of paragraph 5, each Member State shall refrain, in the case provided for in paragraph 1, from requesting reimbursement from another Member State in relation to damage referred to in paragraph 4.

7. Where a joint operation is intended and a supervisory authority does not, within one month, comply with the obligation laid down in the second sentence of paragraph 2 of this Article, the other supervisory authorities may adopt a provisional measure on the territory of its Member State in accordance with Article 55. In that case, the urgent need to act under Article 66(1) shall be presumed to be met and require an opinion or an urgent binding decision from the Board pursuant to Article 66(2).

SECTION 2 CONSISTENCY

[2.64]
Article 63   Consistency mechanism
In order to contribute to the consistent application of this Regulation throughout the Union, the supervisory authorities shall cooperate with each other and, where relevant, with the Commission, through the consistency mechanism as set out in this Section.

[2.65]
Article 64   Opinion of the Board
1. The Board shall issue an opinion where a competent supervisory authority intends to adopt any of the measures below. To that end, the competent supervisory authority shall communicate the draft decision to the Board, when it:
   (a) aims to adopt a list of the processing operations subject to the requirement for a data protection impact assessment pursuant to Article 35(4);
   (b) concerns a matter pursuant to Article 40(7) whether a draft code of conduct or an amendment or extension to a code of conduct complies with this Regulation;
   (c) aims to approve the requirements for accreditation of a body pursuant to Article 41(3), of a certification body pursuant to Article 43(3) or the criteria for certification referred to in Article 42(5);
   (d) aims to determine standard data protection clauses referred to in point (d) of Article 46(2) and in Article 28(8);
   (e) aims to authorise contractual clauses referred to in point (a) of Article 46(3); or
   (f) aims to approve binding corporate rules within the meaning of Article 47.

2. Any supervisory authority, the Chair of the Board or the Commission may request that any matter of general application or producing effects in more than one Member State be examined by the Board with a view to obtaining an opinion, in particular where a competent supervisory authority does not comply with the obligations for mutual assistance in accordance with Article 61 or for joint operations in accordance with Article 62.

3. In the cases referred to in paragraphs 1 and 2, the Board shall issue an opinion on the matter submitted to it provided that it has not already issued an opinion on the same matter. That opinion shall be adopted within eight weeks by simple majority of the members of the Board. That period may be extended by a further six weeks, taking into account the complexity of the subject matter. Regarding the draft decision referred to in paragraph 1 circulated to the members of the Board in accordance with paragraph 5, a member which has not objected within a reasonable period indicated by the Chair, shall be deemed to be in agreement with the draft decision.

4. Supervisory authorities and the Commission shall, without undue delay, communicate by electronic means to the Board, using a standardised format any relevant information, including as the case may be a summary of the facts, the draft decision, the grounds which make the enactment of such measure necessary, and the views of other supervisory authorities concerned.

5. The Chair of the Board shall, without undue, delay inform by electronic means:

   (a) the members of the Board and the Commission of any relevant information which has been communicated to it using a standardised format. The secretariat of the Board shall, where necessary, provide translations of relevant information; and

   (b) the supervisory authority referred to, as the case may be, in paragraphs 1 and 2, and the Commission of the opinion and make it public.

6. The competent supervisory authority referred to in paragraph 1 shall not adopt its draft decision referred to in paragraph 1 within the period referred to in paragraph 3.

7. The competent supervisory authority referred to in paragraph 1 shall take utmost account of the opinion of the Board and shall, within two weeks after receiving the opinion, communicate to the Chair of the Board by electronic means whether it will maintain or amend its draft decision and, if any, the amended draft decision, using a standardised format.

8. Where the competent supervisory authority referred to in paragraph 1 informs the Chair of the Board within the period referred to in paragraph 7 of this Article that it does not intend to follow the opinion of the Board, in whole or in part, providing the relevant grounds, Article 65(1) shall apply.

[2.66]
Article 65　　Dispute resolution by the Board

1. In order to ensure the correct and consistent application of this Regulation in individual cases, the Board shall adopt a binding decision in the following cases:

   (a) where, in a case referred to in Article 60(4), a supervisory authority concerned has raised a relevant and reasoned objection to a draft decision of the lead supervisory authority and the lead supervisory authority has not followed the objection or has rejected such an objection as being not relevant or reasoned. The binding decision shall concern all the matters which are the subject of the relevant and reasoned objection, in particular whether there is an infringement of this Regulation;

   (b) where there are conflicting views on which of the supervisory authorities concerned is competent for the main establishment;

   (c) where a competent supervisory authority does not request the opinion of the Board in the cases referred to in Article 64(1), or does not follow the opinion of the Board issued under Article 64. In that case, any supervisory authority concerned or the Commission may communicate the matter to the Board.

2. The decision referred to in paragraph 1 shall be adopted within one month from the referral of the subject-matter by a two-thirds majority of the members of the Board. That period may be extended by a further month on account of the complexity of the subject-matter. The decision referred to in paragraph 1 shall be reasoned and addressed to the lead supervisory authority and all the supervisory authorities concerned and binding on them.

3. Where the Board has been unable to adopt a decision within the periods referred to in paragraph 2, it shall adopt its decision within two weeks following the expiration of the second month referred to in paragraph 2 by a simple majority of the members of the Board. Where the members of the Board are split, the decision shall by adopted by the vote of its Chair.

4. The supervisory authorities concerned shall not adopt a decision on the subject matter submitted to the Board under paragraph 1 during the periods referred to in paragraphs 2 and 3.

5. The Chair of the Board shall notify, without undue delay, the decision referred to in paragraph 1 to the supervisory authorities concerned. It shall inform the Commission thereof. The decision shall be published on the website of the Board without delay after the supervisory authority has notified the final decision referred to in paragraph 6.

6. The lead supervisory authority or, as the case may be, the supervisory authority with which the complaint has been lodged shall adopt its final decision on the basis of the decision referred to in paragraph 1 of this Article, without undue delay and at the latest by one month after the Board has notified its decision. The lead supervisory authority or, as the case may be, the supervisory authority with which the complaint has been lodged, shall inform the Board of the date when its final decision is notified respectively to the controller or the processor and to the data subject. The final decision of the supervisory authorities concerned shall be adopted under the terms of Article 60(7), (8) and (9). The final decision shall refer to the decision referred to in paragraph 1 of this Article and shall specify that the decision referred to in that paragraph will be published on the website of the Board in accordance with paragraph 5 of this Article. The final decision shall attach the decision referred to in paragraph 1 of this Article.

[2.67]
Article 66　　Urgency procedure

1. In exceptional circumstances, where a supervisory authority concerned considers that there is an urgent need to act in order to protect the rights and freedoms of data subjects, it may, by way of derogation from the consistency mechanism referred to in Articles 63, 64 and 65 or the procedure referred to in Article 60, immediately adopt

provisional measures intended to produce legal effects on its own territory with a specified period of validity which shall not exceed three months. The supervisory authority shall, without delay, communicate those measures and the reasons for adopting them to the other supervisory authorities concerned, to the Board and to the Commission.

2. Where a supervisory authority has taken a measure pursuant to paragraph 1 and considers that final measures need urgently be adopted, it may request an urgent opinion or an urgent binding decision from the Board, giving reasons for requesting such opinion or decision.

3. Any supervisory authority may request an urgent opinion or an urgent binding decision, as the case may be, from the Board where a competent supervisory authority has not taken an appropriate measure in a situation where there is an urgent need to act, in order to protect the rights and freedoms of data subjects, giving reasons for requesting such opinion or decision, including for the urgent need to act.

4. By derogation from Article 64(3) and Article 65(2), an urgent opinion or an urgent binding decision referred to in paragraphs 2 and 3 of this Article shall be adopted within two weeks by simple majority of the members of the Board.

[2.68]
Article 67   Exchange of information
The Commission may adopt implementing acts of general scope in order to specify the arrangements for the exchange of information by electronic means between supervisory authorities, and between supervisory authorities and the Board, in particular the standardised format referred to in Article 64.

Those implementing acts shall be adopted in accordance with the examination procedure referred to in Article 93(2).

SECTION 3 EUROPEAN DATA PROTECTION BOARD

[2.69]
Article 68   European Data Protection Board
1. The European Data Protection Board (the 'Board') is hereby established as a body of the Union and shall have legal personality.

2. The Board shall be represented by its Chair.

3. The Board shall be composed of the head of one supervisory authority of each Member State and of the European Data Protection Supervisor, or their respective representatives.

4. Where in a Member State more than one supervisory authority is responsible for monitoring the application of the provisions pursuant to this Regulation, a joint representative shall be appointed in accordance with that Member State's law.

5. The Commission shall have the right to participate in the activities and meetings of the Board without voting right. The Commission shall designate a representative. The Chair of the Board shall communicate to the Commission the activities of the Board.

6. In the cases referred to in Article 65, the European Data Protection Supervisor shall have voting rights only on decisions which concern principles and rules applicable to the Union institutions, bodies, offices and agencies which correspond in substance to those of this Regulation.

[2.70]
Article 69   Independence
1. The Board shall act independently when performing its tasks or exercising its powers pursuant to Articles 70 and 71.

2. Without prejudice to requests by the Commission referred to in Article 70(1) and (2), the Board shall, in the performance of its tasks or the exercise of its powers, neither seek nor take instructions from anybody.

[2.71]
Article 70   Tasks of the Board
1. The Board shall ensure the consistent application of this Regulation. To that end, the Board shall, on its own initiative or, where relevant, at the request of the Commission, in particular:
    (a) monitor and ensure the correct application of this Regulation in the cases provided for in Articles 64 and 65 without prejudice to the tasks of national supervisory authorities;
    (b) advise the Commission on any issue related to the protection of personal data in the Union, including on any proposed amendment of this Regulation;
    (c) advise the Commission on the format and procedures for the exchange of information between controllers, processors and supervisory authorities for binding corporate rules;
    (d) issue guidelines, recommendations, and best practices on procedures for erasing links, copies or replications of personal data from publicly available communication services as referred to in Article 17(2);
    (e) examine, on its own initiative, on request of one of its members or on request of the Commission, any question covering the application of this Regulation and issue guidelines, recommendations and best practices in order to encourage consistent application of this Regulation;
    (f) issue guidelines, recommendations and best practices in accordance with point (e) of this paragraph for further specifying the criteria and conditions for decisions based on profiling pursuant to Article 22(2);
    (g) issue guidelines, recommendations and best practices in accordance with point (e) of this paragraph for establishing the personal data breaches and determining the undue delay referred to in Article 33(1) and (2) and for the particular circumstances in which a controller or a processor is required to notify the personal data breach;
    (h) issue guidelines, recommendations and best practices in accordance with point (e) of this paragraph as to the circumstances in which a personal data breach is likely to result in a high risk to the rights and freedoms of the natural persons referred to in Article 34(1).
    (i) issue guidelines, recommendations and best practices in accordance with point (e) of this paragraph for the purpose of further specifying the criteria and requirements for personal data transfers based on binding

corporate rules adhered to by controllers and binding corporate rules adhered to by processors and on further necessary requirements to ensure the protection of personal data of the data subjects concerned referred to in Article 47;

(j)   issue guidelines, recommendations and best practices in accordance with point (e) of this paragraph for the purpose of further specifying the criteria and requirements for the personal data transfers on the basis of Article 49(1);

(k)   draw up guidelines for supervisory authorities concerning the application of measures referred to in Article 58(1), (2) and (3) and the setting of administrative fines pursuant to Article 83;

(l)   review the practical application of the guidelines, recommendations and best practices;

(m)   issue guidelines, recommendations and best practices in accordance with point (e) of this paragraph for establishing common procedures for reporting by natural persons of infringements of this Regulation pursuant to Article 54(2);

(n)   encourage the drawing-up of codes of conduct and the establishment of data protection certification mechanisms and data protection seals and marks pursuant to Articles 40 and 42;

(o)   approve the criteria of certification pursuant to Article 42(5) and maintain a public register of certification mechanisms and data protection seals and marks pursuant to Article 42(8) and of the certified controllers or processors established in third countries pursuant to Article 42(7);

(p)   approve the requirements referred to in Article 43(3) with a view to the accreditation of certification bodies referred to in Article 43;

(q)   provide the Commission with an opinion on the certification requirements referred to in Article 43(8);

(r)   provide the Commission with an opinion on the icons referred to in Article 12(7);

(s)   provide the Commission with an opinion for the assessment of the adequacy of the level of protection in a third country or international organisation, including for the assessment whether a third country, a territory or one or more specified sectors within that third country, or an international organisation no longer ensures an adequate level of protection. To that end, the Commission shall provide the Board with all necessary documentation, including correspondence with the government of the third country, with regard to that third country, territory or specified sector, or with the international organisation.

(t)   issue opinions on draft decisions of supervisory authorities pursuant to the consistency mechanism referred to in Article 64(1), on matters submitted pursuant to Article 64(2) and to issue binding decisions pursuant to Article 65, including in cases referred to in Article 66;

(u)   promote the cooperation and the effective bilateral and multilateral exchange of information and best practices between the supervisory authorities;

(v)   promote common training programmes and facilitate personnel exchanges between the supervisory authorities and, where appropriate, with the supervisory authorities of third countries or with international organisations;

(w)   promote the exchange of knowledge and documentation on data protection legislation and practice with data protection supervisory authorities worldwide.

(x)   issue opinions on codes of conduct drawn up at Union level pursuant to Article 40(9); and

(y)   maintain a publicly accessible electronic register of decisions taken by supervisory authorities and courts on issues handled in the consistency mechanism.

2. Where the Commission requests advice from the Board, it may indicate a time limit, taking into account the urgency of the matter.

3. The Board shall forward its opinions, guidelines, recommendations, and best practices to the Commission and to the committee referred to in Article 93 and make them public.

4. The Board shall, where appropriate, consult interested parties and give them the opportunity to comment within a reasonable period. The Board shall, without prejudice to Article 76, make the results of the consultation procedure publicly available.

[2.72]
Article 71   Reports
1. The Board shall draw up an annual report regarding the protection of natural persons with regard to processing in the Union and, where relevant, in third countries and international organisations. The report shall be made public and be transmitted to the European Parliament, to the Council and to the Commission.

2. The annual report shall include a review of the practical application of the guidelines, recommendations and best practices referred to in point (l) of Article 70(1) as well as of the binding decisions referred to in Article 65.

[2.73]
Article 72   Procedure
1. The Board shall take decisions by a simple majority of its members, unless otherwise provided for in this Regulation.

2. The Board shall adopt its own rules of procedure by a two-thirds majority of its members and organise its own operational arrangements.

[2.74]
Article 73   Chair
1. The Board shall elect a chair and two deputy chairs from amongst its members by simple majority.

2. The term of office of the Chair and of the deputy chairs shall be five years and be renewable once.

[2.75]
Article 74   Tasks of the Chair
1. The Chair shall have the following tasks:
(a)   to convene the meetings of the Board and prepare its agenda;

(b)   to notify decisions adopted by the Board pursuant to Article 65 to the lead supervisory authority and the supervisory authorities concerned;

(c) to ensure the timely performance of the tasks of the Board, in particular in relation to the consistency mechanism referred to in Article 63.

2. The Board shall lay down the allocation of tasks between the Chair and the deputy chairs in its rules of procedure.

[2.76]
Article 75   Secretariat
1. The Board shall have a secretariat, which shall be provided by the European Data Protection Supervisor.
2. The secretariat shall perform its tasks exclusively under the instructions of the Chair of the Board.
3. The staff of the European Data Protection Supervisor involved in carrying out the tasks conferred on the Board by this Regulation shall be subject to separate reporting lines from the staff involved in carrying out tasks conferred on the European Data Protection Supervisor.
4. Where appropriate, the Board and the European Data Protection Supervisor shall establish and publish a Memorandum of Understanding implementing this Article, determining the terms of their cooperation, and applicable to the staff of the European Data Protection Supervisor involved in carrying out the tasks conferred on the Board by this Regulation.
5. The secretariat shall provide analytical, administrative and logistical support to the Board.
6. The secretariat shall be responsible in particular for:
    (a) the day-to-day business of the Board;
    (b) communication between the members of the Board, its Chair and the Commission;
    (c) communication with other institutions and the public;
    (d) the use of electronic means for the internal and external communication;
    (e) the translation of relevant information;
    (f) the preparation and follow-up of the meetings of the Board;
    (g) the preparation, drafting and publication of opinions, decisions on the settlement of disputes between supervisory authorities and other texts adopted by the Board.

[2.77]
Article 76   Confidentiality
1. The discussions of the Board shall be confidential where the Board deems it necessary, as provided for in its rules of procedure.
2. Access to documents submitted to members of the Board, experts and representatives of third parties shall be governed by Regulation (EC) No 1049/2001 of the European Parliament and of the Council.

CHAPTER VIII REMEDIES, LIABILITY AND PENALTIES

[2.78]
Article 77   Right to lodge a complaint with a supervisory authority
1. Without prejudice to any other administrative or judicial remedy, every data subject shall have the right to lodge a complaint with a supervisory authority, in particular in the Member State of his or her habitual residence, place of work or place of the alleged infringement if the data subject considers that the processing of personal data relating to him or her infringes this Regulation.
2. The supervisory authority with which the complaint has been lodged shall inform the complainant on the progress and the outcome of the complaint including the possibility of a judicial remedy pursuant to Article 78.

[2.79]
Article 78   Right to an effective judicial remedy against a supervisory authority
1. Without prejudice to any other administrative or non-judicial remedy, each natural or legal person shall have the right to an effective judicial remedy against a legally binding decision of a supervisory authority concerning them.
2. Without prejudice to any other administrative or non-judicial remedy, each data subject shall have the right to a an effective judicial remedy where the supervisory authority which is competent pursuant to Articles 55 and 56 does not handle a complaint or does not inform the data subject within three months on the progress or outcome of the complaint lodged pursuant to Article 77.
3. Proceedings against a supervisory authority shall be brought before the courts of the Member State where the supervisory authority is established.
4. Where proceedings are brought against a decision of a supervisory authority which was preceded by an opinion or a decision of the Board in the consistency mechanism, the supervisory authority shall forward that opinion or decision to the court.

[2.80]
Article 79   Right to an effective judicial remedy against a controller or processor
1. Without prejudice to any available administrative or non-judicial remedy, including the right to lodge a complaint with a supervisory authority pursuant to Article 77, each data subject shall have the right to an effective judicial remedy where he or she considers that his or her rights under this Regulation have been infringed as a result of the processing of his or her personal data in non-compliance with this Regulation.
2. Proceedings against a controller or a processor shall be brought before the courts of the Member State where the controller or processor has an establishment. Alternatively, such proceedings may be brought before the courts of the Member State where the data subject has his or her habitual residence, unless the controller or processor is a public authority of a Member State acting in the exercise of its public powers.

[2.81]
Article 80   Representation of data subjects
1. The data subject shall have the right to mandate a not-for-profit body, organisation or association which has been properly constituted in accordance with the law of a Member State, has statutory objectives which are in the public interest, and is active in the field of the protection of data subjects' rights and freedoms with regard to the protection

of their personal data to lodge the complaint on his or her behalf, to exercise the rights referred to in Articles 77, 78 and 79 on his or her behalf, and to exercise the right to receive compensation referred to in Article 82 on his or her behalf where provided for by Member State law.

2. Member States may provide that any body, organisation or association referred to in paragraph 1 of this Article, independently of a data subject's mandate, has the right to lodge, in that Member State, a complaint with the supervisory authority which is competent pursuant to Article 77 and to exercise the rights referred to in Articles 78 and 79 if it considers that the rights of a data subject under this Regulation have been infringed as a result of the processing.

[2.82]
Article 81   Suspension of proceedings
1. Where a competent court of a Member State has information on proceedings, concerning the same subject matter as regards processing by the same controller or processor, that are pending in a court in another Member State, it shall contact that court in the other Member State to confirm the existence of such proceedings.
2. Where proceedings concerning the same subject matter as regards processing of the same controller or processor are pending in a court in another Member State, any competent court other than the court first seized may suspend its proceedings.
3. Where those proceedings are pending at first instance, any court other than the court first seized may also, on the application of one of the parties, decline jurisdiction if the court first seized has jurisdiction over the actions in question and its law permits the consolidation thereof.

[2.83]
Article 82   Right to compensation and liability
1. Any person who has suffered material or non-material damage as a result of an infringement of this Regulation shall have the right to receive compensation from the controller or processor for the damage suffered.
2. Any controller involved in processing shall be liable for the damage caused by processing which infringes this Regulation. A processor shall be liable for the damage caused by processing only where it has not complied with obligations of this Regulation specifically directed to processors or where it has acted outside or contrary to lawful instructions of the controller.
3. A controller or processor shall be exempt from liability under paragraph 2 if it proves that it is not in any way responsible for the event giving rise to the damage.
4. Where more than one controller or processor, or both a controller and a processor, are involved in the same processing and where they are, under paragraphs 2 and 3, responsible for any damage caused by processing, each controller or processor shall be held liable for the entire damage in order to ensure effective compensation of the data subject.
5. Where a controller or processor has, in accordance with paragraph 4, paid full compensation for the damage suffered, that controller or processor shall be entitled to claim back from the other controllers or processors involved in the same processing that part of the compensation corresponding to their part of responsibility for the damage, in accordance with the conditions set out in paragraph 2.
6. Court proceedings for exercising the right to receive compensation shall be brought before the courts competent under the law of the Member State referred to in Article 79(2).

[2.84]
Article 83   General conditions for imposing administrative fines
1. Each supervisory authority shall ensure that the imposition of administrative fines pursuant to this Article in respect of infringements of this Regulation referred to in paragraphs 4, 5 and 6 shall in each individual case be effective, proportionate and dissuasive.
2. Administrative fines shall, depending on the circumstances of each individual case, be imposed in addition to, or instead of, measures referred to in points (a) to (h) and (j) of Article 58(2). When deciding whether to impose an administrative fine and deciding on the amount of the administrative fine in each individual case due regard shall be given to the following:
(a)   the nature, gravity and duration of the infringement taking into account the nature scope or purpose of the processing concerned as well as the number of data subjects affected and the level of damage suffered by them;
(b)   the intentional or negligent character of the infringement;
(c)   any action taken by the controller or processor to mitigate the damage suffered by data subjects;
(d)   the degree of responsibility of the controller or processor taking into account technical and organisational measures implemented by them pursuant to Articles 25 and 32;
(e)   any relevant previous infringements by the controller or processor;
(f)   the degree of cooperation with the supervisory authority, in order to remedy the infringement and mitigate the possible adverse effects of the infringement;
(g)   the categories of personal data affected by the infringement;
(h)   the manner in which the infringement became known to the supervisory authority, in particular whether, and if so to what extent, the controller or processor notified the infringement;
(i)   where measures referred to in Article 58(2) have previously been ordered against the controller or processor concerned with regard to the same subject-matter, compliance with those measures;
(j)   adherence to approved codes of conduct pursuant to Article 40 or approved certification mechanisms pursuant to Article 42; and
(k)   any other aggravating or mitigating factor applicable to the circumstances of the case, such as financial benefits gained, or losses avoided, directly or indirectly, from the infringement.
3. If a controller or processor intentionally or negligently, for the same or linked processing operations, infringes several provisions of this Regulation, the total amount of the administrative fine shall not exceed the amount specified for the gravest infringement.

Part 2   Data Protection: EU Law etc

4. Infringements of the following provisions shall, in accordance with paragraph 2, be subject to administrative fines up to 10,000,000 EUR, or in the case of an undertaking, up to 2% of the total worldwide annual turnover of the preceding financial year, whichever is higher:

   (a)   the obligations of the controller and the processor pursuant to Articles 8, 11, 25 to 39 and 42 and 43;
   (b)   the obligations of the certification body pursuant to Articles 42 and 43;
   (c)   the obligations of the monitoring body pursuant to Article 41(4).

5. Infringements of the following provisions shall, in accordance with paragraph 2, be subject to administrative fines up to 20,000,000 EUR, or in the case of an undertaking, up to 4% of the total worldwide annual turnover of the preceding financial year, whichever is higher:

   (a)   the basic principles for processing, including conditions for consent, pursuant to Articles 5, 6, 7 and 9;
   (b)   the data subjects' rights pursuant to Articles 12 to 22;
   (c)   the transfers of personal data to a recipient in a third country or an international organisation pursuant to Articles 44 to 49;
   (d)   any obligations pursuant to Member State law adopted under Chapter IX;
   (e)   non-compliance with an order or a temporary or definitive limitation on processing or the suspension of data flows by the supervisory authority pursuant to Article 58(2) or failure to provide access in violation of Article 58(1).

6. Non-compliance with an order by the supervisory authority as referred to in Article 58(2) shall, in accordance with paragraph 2 of this Article, be subject to administrative fines up to 20,000,000 EUR, or in the case of an undertaking, up to 4% of the total worldwide annual turnover of the preceding financial year, whichever is higher.

7. Without prejudice to the corrective powers of supervisory authorities pursuant to Article 58(2), each Member State may lay down the rules on whether and to what extent administrative fines may be imposed on public authorities and bodies established in that Member State.

8. The exercise by the supervisory authority of its powers under this Article shall be subject to appropriate procedural safeguards in accordance with Union and Member State law, including effective judicial remedy and due process.

9. Where the legal system of the Member State does not provide for administrative fines, this Article may be applied in such a manner that the fine is initiated by the competent supervisory authority and imposed by competent national courts, while ensuring that those legal remedies are effective and have an equivalent effect to the administrative fines imposed by supervisory authorities. In any event, the fines imposed shall be effective, proportionate and dissuasive. Those Member States shall notify to the Commission the provisions of their laws which they adopt pursuant to this paragraph by 25 May 2018 and, without delay, any subsequent amendment law or amendment affecting them.

[2.85]
Article 84   Penalties

1. Member States shall lay down the rules on other penalties applicable to infringements of this Regulation in particular for infringements which are not subject to administrative fines pursuant to Article 83, and shall take all measures necessary to ensure that they are implemented. Such penalties shall be effective, proportionate and dissuasive.

2. Each Member State shall notify to the Commission the provisions of its law which it adopts pursuant to paragraph 1, by 25 May 2018 and, without delay, any subsequent amendment affecting them.

CHAPTER IX PROVISIONS RELATING TO SPECIFIC PROCESSING SITUATIONS

[2.86]
Article 85   Processing and freedom of expression and information

1. Member States shall by law reconcile the right to the protection of personal data pursuant to this Regulation with the right to freedom of expression and information, including processing for journalistic purposes and the purposes of academic, artistic or literary expression.

2. For processing carried out for journalistic purposes or the purpose of academic artistic or literary expression, Member States shall provide for exemptions or derogations from Chapter II (principles), Chapter III (rights of the data subject), Chapter IV (controller and processor), Chapter V (transfer of personal data to third countries or international organisations), Chapter VI (independent supervisory authorities), Chapter VII (cooperation and consistency) and Chapter IX (specific data processing situations) if they are necessary to reconcile the right to the protection of personal data with the freedom of expression and information.

3. Each Member State shall notify to the Commission the provisions of its law which it has adopted pursuant to paragraph 2 and, without delay, any subsequent amendment law or amendment affecting them.

[2.87]
Article 86   Processing and public access to official documents

Personal data in official documents held by a public authority or a public body or a private body for the performance of a task carried out in the public interest may be disclosed by the authority or body in accordance with Union or Member State law to which the public authority or body is subject in order to reconcile public access to official documents with the right to the protection of personal data pursuant to this Regulation.

[2.88]
Article 87   Processing of the national identification number

Member States may further determine the specific conditions for the processing of a national identification number or any other identifier of general application. In that case the national identification number or any other identifier of general application shall be used only under appropriate safeguards for the rights and freedoms of the data subject pursuant to this Regulation.

[2.89]
Article 88   Processing in the context of employment
1. Member States may, by law or by collective agreements, provide for more specific rules to ensure the protection of the rights and freedoms in respect of the processing of employees' personal data in the employment context, in particular for the purposes of the recruitment, the performance of the contract of employment, including discharge of obligations laid down by law or by collective agreements, management, planning and organisation of work, equality and diversity in the workplace, health and safety at work, protection of employer's or customer's property and for the purposes of the exercise and enjoyment, on an individual or collective basis, of rights and benefits related to employment, and for the purpose of the termination of the employment relationship.
2. Those rules shall include suitable and specific measures to safeguard the data subject's human dignity, legitimate interests and fundamental rights, with particular regard to the transparency of processing, the transfer of personal data within a group of undertakings, or a group of enterprises engaged in a joint economic activity and monitoring systems at the work place.
3. Each Member State shall notify to the Commission those provisions of its law which it adopts pursuant to paragraph 1, by 25 May 2018 and, without delay, any subsequent amendment affecting them.

[2.90]
Article 89   Safeguards and derogations relating to processing for archiving purposes in the public interest, scientific or historical research purposes or statistical purposes
1. Processing for archiving purposes in the public interest, scientific or historical research purposes or statistical purposes, shall be subject to appropriate safeguards, in accordance with this Regulation, for the rights and freedoms of the data subject. Those safeguards shall ensure that technical and organisational measures are in place in particular in order to ensure respect for the principle of data minimisation. Those measures may include pseudonymisation provided that those purposes can be fulfilled in that manner. Where those purposes can be fulfilled by further processing which does not permit or no longer permits the identification of data subjects, those purposes shall be fulfilled in that manner.
2. Where personal data are processed for scientific or historical research purposes or statistical purposes, Union or Member State law may provide for derogations from the rights referred to in Articles 15, 16, 18 and 21 subject to the conditions and safeguards referred to in paragraph 1 of this Article in so far as such rights are likely to render impossible or seriously impair the achievement of the specific purposes, and such derogations are necessary for the fulfilment of those purposes.
3. Where personal data are processed for archiving purposes in the public interest, Union or Member State law may provide for derogations from the rights referred to in Articles 15, 16, 18, 19, 20 and 21 subject to the conditions and safeguards referred to in paragraph 1 of this Article in so far as such rights are likely to render impossible or seriously impair the achievement of the specific purposes, and such derogations are necessary for the fulfilment of those purposes.
4. Where processing referred to in paragraphs 2 and 3 serves at the same time another purpose, the derogations shall apply only to processing for the purposes referred to in those paragraphs.

[2.91]
Article 90   Obligations of secrecy
1. Member States may adopt specific rules to set out the powers of the supervisory authorities laid down in points (e) and (f) of Article 58(1) in relation to controllers or processors that are subject, under Union or Member State law or rules established by national competent bodies, to an obligation of professional secrecy or other equivalent obligations of secrecy where this is necessary and proportionate to reconcile the right of the protection of personal data with the obligation of secrecy. Those rules shall apply only with regard to personal data which the controller or processor has received as a result of or has obtained in an activity covered by that obligation of secrecy.
2. Each Member State shall notify to the Commission the rules adopted pursuant to paragraph 1, by 25 May 2018 and, without delay, any subsequent amendment affecting them.

[2.92]
Article 91   Existing data protection rules of churches and religious associations
1. Where in a Member State, churches and religious associations or communities apply, at the time of entry into force of this Regulation, comprehensive rules relating to the protection of natural persons with regard to processing, such rules may continue to apply, provided that they are brought into line with this Regulation.
2. Churches and religious associations which apply comprehensive rules in accordance with paragraph 1 of this Article shall be subject to the supervision of an independent supervisory authority, which may be specific, provided that it fulfils the conditions laid down in Chapter VI of this Regulation.

CHAPTER X DELEGATED ACTS AND IMPLEMENTING ACTS

[2.93]
Article 92   Exercise of the delegation
1. The power to adopt delegated acts is conferred on the Commission subject to the conditions laid down in this Article.
2. The delegation of power referred to in Article 12(8) and Article 43(8) shall be conferred on the Commission for an indeterminate period of time from 24 May 2016.
3. The delegation of power referred to in Article 12(8) and Article 43(8) may be revoked at any time by the European Parliament or by the Council. A decision of revocation shall put an end to the delegation of power specified in that decision. It shall take effect the day following that of its publication in the Official Journal of the European Union or at a later date specified therein. It shall not affect the validity of any delegated acts already in force.
4. As soon as it adopts a delegated act, the Commission shall notify it simultaneously to the European Parliament and to the Council.

5. A delegated act adopted pursuant to Article 12(8) and Article 43(8) shall enter into force only if no objection has been expressed by either the European Parliament or the Council within a period of three months of notification of that act to the European Parliament and the Council or if, before the expiry of that period, the European Parliament and the Council have both informed the Commission that they will not object. That period shall be extended by three months at the initiative of the European Parliament or of the Council.

[2.94]
Article 93   Committee procedure
1. The Commission shall be assisted by a committee. That committee shall be a committee within the meaning of Regulation (EU) No 182/2011.
2. Where reference is made to this paragraph, Article 5 of Regulation (EU) No 182/2011 shall apply.
3. Where reference is made to this paragraph, Article 8 of Regulation (EU) No 182/2011, in conjunction with Article 5 thereof, shall apply.

CHAPTER XI FINAL PROVISIONS

[2.95]
Article 94   Repeal of Directive 95/46/EC
1. Directive 95/46/EC is repealed with effect from 25 May 2018.
2. References to the repealed Directive shall be construed as references to this Regulation. References to the Working Party on the Protection of Individuals with regard to the Processing of Personal Data established by Article 29 of Directive 95/46/EC shall be construed as references to the European Data Protection Board established by this Regulation.

[2.96]
Article 95   Relationship with Directive 2002/58/EC
This Regulation shall not impose additional obligations on natural or legal persons in relation to processing in connection with the provision of publicly available electronic communications services in public communication networks in the Union in relation to matters for which they are subject to specific obligations with the same objective set out in Directive 2002/58/EC.

[2.97]
Article 96   Relationship with previously concluded Agreements
International agreements involving the transfer of personal data to third countries or international organisations which were concluded by Member States prior to 24 May 2016, and which comply with Union law as applicable prior to that date, shall remain in force until amended, replaced or revoked.

[2.98]
Article 97   Commission reports
1. By 25 May 2020 and every four years thereafter, the Commission shall submit a report on the evaluation and review of this Regulation to the European Parliament and to the Council. The reports shall be made public.
2. In the context of the evaluations and reviews referred to in paragraph 1, the Commission shall examine, in particular, the application and functioning of:
    (a) Chapter V on the transfer of personal data to third countries or international organisations with particular regard to decisions adopted pursuant to Article 45(3) of this Regulation and decisions adopted on the basis of Article 25(6) of Directive 95/46/EC;
    (b) Chapter VII on cooperation and consistency.
3. For the purpose of paragraph 1, the Commission may request information from Member States and supervisory authorities.
4. In carrying out the evaluations and reviews referred to in paragraphs 1 and 2, the Commission shall take into account the positions and findings of the European Parliament, of the Council, and of other relevant bodies or sources.
5. The Commission shall, if necessary, submit appropriate proposals to amend this Regulation, in particular taking into account of developments in information technology and in the light of the state of progress in the information society.

[2.99]
Article 98   Review of other Union legal acts on data protection
The Commission shall, if appropriate, submit legislative proposals with a view to amending other Union legal acts on the protection of personal data, in order to ensure uniform and consistent protection of natural persons with regard to processing. This shall in particular concern the rules relating to the protection of natural persons with regard to processing by Union institutions, bodies, offices and agencies and on the free movement of such data.

[2.100]
Article 99   Entry into force and application
1. This Regulation shall enter into force on the twentieth day following that of its publication in the *Official Journal of the European Union*.
2. It shall apply from 25 May 2018.
    This Regulation shall be binding in its entirety and directly applicable in all Member States.

DIRECTIVE OF THE EUROPEAN PARLIAMENT AND OF THE COUNCIL

(2016/680/EU)

of 27 April 2016

on the protection of natural persons with regard to the processing of personal data by competent authorities for the purposes of the prevention, investigation, detection or prosecution of criminal offences or the execution of criminal penalties, and on the free movement of such data, and repealing Council Framework Decision 2008/977/JHA

[2.101]

NOTES

Date of publication in OJ: L119, 4.5.2016, p 89. The text of this Directive incorporates the corrigendum published in OJ L127, 23.5.2018, p 6.

© European Union, 1998–2019.

THE EUROPEAN PARLIAMENT AND THE COUNCIL OF THE EUROPEAN UNION,

Having regard to the Treaty on the Functioning of the European Union, and in particular Article 16(2) thereof,

Having regard to the proposal from the European Commission,

After transmission of the draft legislative act to the national parliaments,

Having regard to the opinion of the Committee of the Regions,[1]

Acting in accordance with the ordinary legislative procedure,[2]

Whereas:

(1) The protection of natural persons in relation to the processing of personal data is a fundamental right. Article 8(1) of the Charter of Fundamental Rights of the European Union ('the Charter') and Article 16(1) of the Treaty on the Functioning of the European Union (TFEU) provide that everyone has the right to the protection of personal data concerning him or her.

(2) The principles of, and rules on the protection of natural persons with regard to the processing of their personal data should, whatever their nationality or residence, respect their fundamental rights and freedoms, in particular their right to the protection of personal data. This Directive is intended to contribute to the accomplishment of an area of freedom, security and justice.

(3) Rapid technological developments and globalisation have brought new challenges for the protection of personal data. The scale of the collection and sharing of personal data has increased significantly. Technology allows personal data to be processed on an unprecedented scale in order to pursue activities such as the prevention, investigation, detection or prosecution of criminal offences or the execution of criminal penalties.

(4) The free flow of personal data between competent authorities for the purposes of the prevention, investigation, detection or prosecution of criminal offences or the execution of criminal penalties, including the safeguarding against and the prevention of threats to public security within the Union and the transfer of such personal data to third countries and international organisations, should be facilitated while ensuring a high level of protection of personal data. Those developments require the building of a strong and more coherent framework for the protection of personal data in the Union, backed by strong enforcement.

(5) Directive 95/46/EC of the European Parliament and of the Council[3] applies to all processing of personal data in Member States in both the public and the private sectors. However, it does not apply to the processing of personal data in the course of an activity which falls outside the scope of Community law, such as activities in the areas of judicial cooperation in criminal matters and police cooperation.

(6) Council Framework Decision 2008/977/JHA[4] applies in the areas of judicial cooperation in criminal matters and police cooperation. The scope of application of that Framework Decision is limited to the processing of personal data transmitted or made available between Member States.

(7) Ensuring a consistent and high level of protection of the personal data of natural persons and facilitating the exchange of personal data between competent authorities of Members States is crucial in order to ensure effective judicial cooperation in criminal matters and police cooperation. To that end, the level of protection of the rights and freedoms of natural persons with regard to the processing of personal data by competent authorities for the purposes of the prevention, investigation, detection or prosecution of criminal offences or the execution of criminal penalties, including the safeguarding against and the prevention of threats to public security, should be equivalent in all Member States. Effective protection of personal data throughout the Union requires the strengthening of the rights of data subjects and of the obligations of those who process personal data, as well as equivalent powers for monitoring and ensuring compliance with the rules for the protection of personal data in the Member States.

(8) Article 16(2) TFEU mandates the European Parliament and the Council to lay down the rules relating to the protection of natural person s with regard to the processing of personal data and the rules relating to the free movement of personal data.

(9) On that basis, Regulation (EU) 2016/679 of the European Parliament and of the Council[5] lays down general rules to protect natural persons in relation to the processing of personal data and to ensure the free movement of personal data within the Union.

(10) In Declaration No 21 on the protection of personal data in the fields of judicial cooperation in criminal matters and police cooperation, annexed to the final act of the intergovernmental conference which adopted the Treaty of Lisbon, the conference acknowledged that specific rules on the protection of personal data and the free movement of personal data in the fields of judicial cooperation in criminal matters and police cooperation based on Article 16 TFEU may prove necessary because of the specific nature of those fields.

(11)   It is therefore appropriate for those fields to be addressed by a directive that lays down the specific rules relating to the protection of natural persons with regard to the processing of personal data by competent authorities for the purposes of the prevention, investigation, detection or prosecution of criminal offences or the execution of criminal penalties, including the safeguarding against and the prevention of threats to public security, respecting the specific nature of those activities. Such competent authorities may include not only public authorities such as the judicial authorities, the police or other law-enforcement authorities but also any other body or entity entrusted by Member State law to exercise public authority and public powers for the purposes of this Directive. Where such a body or entity processes personal data for purposes other than for the purposes of this Directive, Regulation (EU) 2016/679 applies. Regulation (EU) 2016/679 therefore applies in cases where a body or entity collects personal data for other purposes and further processes those personal data in order to comply with a legal obligation to which it is subject. For example, for the purposes of investigation detection or prosecution of criminal offences financial institutions retain certain personal data which are processed by them, and provide those personal data only to the competent national authorities in specific cases and in accordance with Member State law. A body or entity which processes personal data on behalf of such authorities within the scope of this Directive should be bound by a contract or other legal act and by the provisions applicable to processors pursuant to this Directive, while the application of Regulation (EU) 2016/679 remains unaffected for the processing of personal data by the processor outside the scope of this Directive.

(12)   The activities carried out by the police or other law-enforcement authorities are focused mainly on the prevention, investigation, detection or prosecution of criminal offences, including police activities without prior knowledge if an incident is a criminal offence or not. Such activities can also include the exercise of authority by taking coercive measures such as police activities at demonstrations, major sporting events and riots. They also include maintaining law and order as a task conferred on the police or other law-enforcement authorities where necessary to safeguard against and prevent threats to public security and to fundamental interests of the society protected by law which may lead to a criminal offence. Member States may entrust competent authorities with other tasks which are not necessarily carried out for the purposes of the prevention, investigation, detection or prosecution of criminal offences, including the safeguarding against and the prevention of threats to public security, so that the processing of personal data for those other purposes, in so far as it is within the scope of Union law, falls within the scope of Regulation (EU) 2016/679.

(13)   A criminal offence within the meaning of this Directive should be an autonomous concept of Union law as interpreted by the Court of Justice of the European Union (the 'Court of Justice').

(14)   Since this Directive should not apply to the processing of personal data in the course of an activity which falls outside the scope of Union law, activities concerning national security, activities of agencies or units dealing with national security issues and the processing of personal data by the Member States when carrying out activities which fall within the scope of Chapter 2 of Title V of the Treaty on European Union (TEU) should not be considered to be activities falling within the scope of this Directive.

(15)   In order to ensure the same level of protection for natural persons through legally enforceable rights throughout the Union and to prevent divergences hampering the exchange of personal data between competent authorities, this Directive should provide for harmonised rules for the protection and the free movement of personal data processed for the purposes of the prevention, investigation, detection or prosecution of criminal offences or the execution of criminal penalties, including the safeguarding against and the prevention of threats to public security. The approximation of Member States' laws should not result in any lessening of the personal data protection they afford but should, on the contrary, seek to ensure a high level of protection within the Union. Member States should not be precluded from providing higher safeguards than those established in this Directive for the protection of the rights and freedoms of the data subject with regard to the processing of personal data by competent authorities.

(16)   This Directive is without prejudice to the principle of public access to official documents. Under Regulation (EU) 2016/679 personal data in official documents held by a public authority or a public or private body for the performance of a task carried out in the public interest may be disclosed by that authority or body in accordance with Union or Member State law to which the public authority or body is subject in order to reconcile public access to official documents with the right to the protection of personal data.

(17)   The protection afforded by this Directive should apply to natural persons, whatever their nationality or place of residence, in relation to the processing of their personal data.

(18)   In order to prevent creating a serious risk of circumvention, the protection of natural persons should be technologically neutral and should not depend on the techniques used. The protection of natural persons should apply to the processing of personal data by automated means, as well as to manual processing, if the personal data are contained or are intended to be contained in a filing system. Files or sets of files, as well as their cover pages, which are not structured according to specific criteria should not fall within the scope of this Directive.

(19)   Regulation (EC) No 45/2001 of the European Parliament and of the Council[6] applies to the processing of personal data by the Union institutions, bodies, offices and agencies. Regulation (EC) No 45/2001 and other Union legal acts applicable to such processing of personal data should be adapted to the principles and rules established in Regulation (EU) 2016/679.

(20)   This Directive does not preclude Member States from specifying processing operations and processing procedures in national rules on criminal procedures in relation to the processing of personal data by courts and other judicial authorities, in particular as regards personal data contained in a judicial decision or in records in relation to criminal proceedings.

(21)   The principles of data protection should apply to any information concerning an identified or identifiable natural person. To determine whether a natural person is identifiable, account should be taken of all the means reasonably likely to be used, such as singling out, either by the controller or by another person to identify the natural person directly or indirectly. To ascertain whether means are reasonably likely to be used to identify the natural person, account should be taken of all objective factors, such as the costs of and the amount of time required for identification, taking into consideration the available technology at the time of the processing and technological developments. The principles of data protection should therefore not apply to anonymous information, namely information which does not

relate to an identified or identifiable natural person or to personal data rendered anonymous in such a manner that the data subject is no longer identifiable.

(22) Public authorities to which personal data are disclosed in accordance with a legal obligation for the exercise of their official mission, such as tax and customs authorities, financial investigation units, independent administrative authorities, or financial market authorities responsible for the regulation and supervision of securities markets should not be regarded as recipients if they receive personal data which are necessary to carry out a particular inquiry in the general interest, in accordance with Union or Member State law. The requests for disclosure sent by the public authorities should always be in writing, reasoned and occasional and should not concern the entirety of a filing system or lead to the interconnection of filing systems. The processing of personal data by those public authorities should comply with the applicable data protection rules according to the purposes of the processing.

(23) Genetic data should be defined as personal data relating to the inherited or acquired genetic characteristics of a natural person which give unique information about the physiology or health of that natural person and which result from the analysis of a biological sample from the natural person in question, in particular chromosomal, deoxyribonucleic acid (DNA) or ribonucleic acid (RNA) analysis, or from the analysis of another element enabling equivalent information to be obtained. Considering the complexity and sensitivity of genetic information, there is a great risk of misuse and re-use for various purposes by the controller. Any discrimination based on genetic features should in principle be prohibited.

(24) Personal data concerning health should include all data pertaining to the health status of a data subject which reveal information relating to the past, current or future physical or mental health status of the data subject. This includes information about the natural person collected in the course of the registration for, or the provision of, health care services as referred to in Directive 2011/24/EU of the European Parliament and of the Council[7] to that natural person; a number, symbol or particular assigned to a natural person to uniquely identify the natural person for health purposes; information derived from the testing or examination of a body part or bodily substance, including from genetic data and biological samples; and any information on, for example, a disease, disability, disease risk, medical history, clinical treatment or the physiological or biomedical state of the data subject independent of its source, for example from a physician or other health professional, a hospital, a medical device or an in vitro diagnostic test.

(25) All Member States are affiliated to the International Criminal Police Organisation (Interpol). To fulfil its mission, Interpol receives, stores and circulates personal data to assist competent authorities in preventing and combating international crime. It is therefore appropriate to strengthen cooperation between the Union and Interpol by promoting an efficient exchange of personal data whilst ensuring respect for fundamental rights and freedoms regarding the automatic processing of personal data. Where personal data are transferred from the Union to Interpol, and to countries which have delegated members to Interpol, this Directive, in particular the provisions on international transfers, should apply. This Directive should be without prejudice to the specific rules laid down in Council Common Position 2005/69/JHA[8] and Council Decision 2007/533/JHA.[9]

(26) Any processing of personal data must be lawful, fair and transparent in relation to the natural persons concerned, and only processed for specific purposes laid down by law. This does not in itself prevent the law-enforcement authorities from carrying out activities such as covert investigations or video surveillance. Such activities can be done for the purposes of the prevention, investigation, detection or prosecution of criminal offences or the execution of criminal penalties, including the safeguarding against and the prevention of threats to public security, as long as they are laid down by law and constitute a necessary and proportionate measure in a democratic society with due regard for the legitimate interests of the natural person concerned. The data protection principle of fair processing is a distinct notion from the right to a fair trial as defined in Article 47 of the Charter and in Article 6 of the European Convention for the Protection of Human Rights and Fundamental Freedoms (ECHR). Natural persons should be made aware of risks, rules, safeguards and rights in relation to the processing of their personal data and how to exercise their rights in relation to the processing. In particular, the specific purposes for which the personal data are processed should be explicit and legitimate and determined at the time of the collection of the personal data. The personal data should be adequate and relevant for the purposes for which they are processed. It should, in particular, be ensured that the personal data collected are not excessive and not kept longer than is necessary for the purpose for which they are processed. Personal data should be processed only if the purpose of the processing could not reasonably be fulfilled by other means. In order to ensure that the data are not kept longer than necessary, time limits should be established by the controller for erasure or for a periodic review. Member States should lay down appropriate safeguards for personal data stored for longer periods for archiving in the public interest, scientific, statistical or historical use.

(27) For the prevention, investigation and prosecution of criminal offences, it is necessary for competent authorities to process personal data collected in the context of the prevention, investigation, detection or prosecution of specific criminal offences beyond that context in order to develop an understanding of criminal activities and to make links between different criminal offences detected.

(28) In order to maintain security in relation to processing and to prevent processing in infringement of this Directive, personal data should be processed in a manner that ensures an appropriate level of security and confidentiality, including by preventing unauthorised access to or use of personal data and the equipment used for the processing, and that takes into account available state of the art and technology, the costs of implementation in relation to the risks and the nature of the personal data to be protected.

(29) Personal data should be collected for specified, explicit and legitimate purposes within the scope of this Directive and should not be processed for purposes incompatible with the purposes of the prevention, investigation, detection or prosecution of criminal offences or the execution of criminal penalties, including the safeguarding against and the prevention of threats to public security. If personal data are processed by the same or another controller for a purpose within the scope of this Directive other than that for which it has been collected, such processing should be permitted under the condition that such processing is authorised in accordance with applicable legal provisions and is necessary for and proportionate to that other purpose.

(30) The principle of accuracy of data should be applied while taking account of the nature and purpose of the processing concerned. In particular in judicial proceedings, statements containing personal data are based on the

subjective perception of natural persons and are not always verifiable. Consequently, the requirement of accuracy should not appertain to the accuracy of a statement but merely to the fact that a specific statement has been made.

(31)   It is inherent to the processing of personal data in the areas of judicial cooperation in criminal matters and police cooperation that personal data relating to different categories of data subjects are processed. Therefore, a clear distinction should, where applicable and as far as possible, be made between personal data of different categories of data subjects such as: suspects; persons convicted of a criminal offence; victims and other parties, such as witnesses; persons possessing relevant information or contacts; and associates of suspects and convicted criminals. This should not prevent the application of the right of presumption of innocence as guaranteed by the Charter and by the ECHR, as interpreted in the case-law of the Court of Justice and by the European Court of Human Rights respectively.

(32)   The competent authorities should ensure that personal data which are inaccurate, incomplete or no longer up to date are not transmitted or made available. In order to ensure the protection of natural persons, the accuracy, completeness or the extent to which the personal data are up to date and the reliability of the personal data transmitted or made available, the competent authorities should, as far as possible, add necessary information in all transmissions of personal data.

(33)   Where this Directive refers to Member State law, a legal basis or a legislative measure, this does not necessarily require a legislative act adopted by a parliament, without prejudice to requirements pursuant to the constitutional order of the Member State concerned. However, such a Member State law, legal basis or legislative measure should be clear and precise and its application foreseeable for those subject to it, as required by the case-law of the Court of Justice and the European Court of Human Rights. Member State law regulating the processing of personal data within the scope of this Directive should specify at least the objectives, the personal data to be processed, the purposes of the processing and procedures for preserving the integrity and confidentiality of personal data and procedures for its destruction, thus providing sufficient guarantees against the risk of abuse and arbitrariness.

(34)   The processing of personal data by competent authorities for the purposes of the prevention, investigation, detection or prosecution of criminal offences or the execution of criminal penalties, including the safeguarding against and the prevention of threats to public security, should cover any operation or set of operations which are performed upon personal data or sets of personal data for those purposes, whether by automated means or otherwise, such as collection, recording, organisation, structuring, storage, adaptation or alteration, retrieval, consultation, use, alignment or combination, restriction of processing, erasure or destruction. In particular, the rules of this Directive should apply to the transmission of personal data for the purposes of this Directive to a recipient not subject to this Directive. Such a recipient should encompass a natural or legal person, public authority, agency or any other body to which personal data are lawfully disclosed by the competent authority. Where personal data were initially collected by a competent authority for one of the purposes of this Directive, Regulation (EU) 2016/679 should apply to the processing of those data for purposes other than the purposes of this Directive where such processing is authorised by Union or Member State law. In particular, the rules of Regulation (EU) 2016/679 should apply to the transmission of personal data for purposes outside the scope of this Directive. For the processing of personal data by a recipient that is not a competent authority or that is not acting as such within the meaning of this Directive and to which personal data are lawfully disclosed by a competent authority, Regulation (EU) 2016/679 should apply. While implementing this Directive, Member States should also be able to further specify the application of the rules of Regulation (EU) 2016/679, subject to the conditions set out therein.

(35)   In order to be lawful, the processing of personal data under this Directive should be necessary for the performance of a task carried out in the public interest by a competent authority based on Union or Member State law for the purposes of the prevention, investigation, detection or prosecution of criminal offences or the execution of criminal penalties, including the safeguarding against and the prevention of threats to public security. Those activities should cover the protection of vital interests of the data subject. The performance of the tasks of preventing, investigating, detecting or prosecuting criminal offences institutionally conferred by law to the competent authorities allows them to require or order natural persons to comply with requests made. In such a case, the consent of the data subject, as defined in Regulation (EU) 2016/679, should not provide a legal ground for processing personal data by competent authorities. Where the data subject is required to comply with a legal obligation, the data subject has no genuine and free choice, so that the reaction of the data subject could not be considered to be a freely given indication of his or her wishes. This should not preclude Member States from providing, by law, that the data subject may agree to the processing of his or her personal data for the purposes of this Directive, such as DNA tests in criminal investigations or the monitoring of his or her location with electronic tags for the execution of criminal penalties.

(36)   Member States should provide that where Union or Member State law applicable to the transmitting competent authority provides for specific conditions applicable in specific circumstances to the processing of personal data, such as the use of handling codes, the transmitting competent authority should inform the recipient of such personal data of those conditions and the requirement to respect them. Such conditions could, for example, include a prohibition against transmitting the personal data further to others, or using them for purposes other than those for which they were transmitted to the recipient, or informing the data subject in the case of a limitation of the right of information without the prior approval of the transmitting competent authority. Those obligations should also apply to transfers by the transmitting competent authority to recipients in third countries or international organisations. Member States should ensure that the transmitting competent authority does not apply such conditions to recipients in other Member States or to agencies, offices and bodies established pursuant to Chapters 4 and 5 of Title V of the TFEU other than those applicable to similar data transmissions within the Member State of that competent authority.

(37)   Personal data which are, by their nature, particularly sensitive in relation to fundamental rights and freedoms merit specific protection as the context of their processing could create significant risks to the fundamental rights and freedoms. Those personal data should include personal data revealing racial or ethnic origin, whereby the use of the term 'racial origin' in this Directive does not imply an acceptance by the Union of theories which attempt to determine the existence of separate human races. Such personal data should not be processed, unless processing is subject to appropriate safeguards for the rights and freedoms of the data subject laid down by law and is allowed in cases authorised by law; where not already authorised by such a law, the processing is necessary to protect the vital interests of the data subject or of another person; or the processing relates to data which are manifestly made public by the data

subject. Appropriate safeguards for the rights and freedoms of the data subject could include the possibility to collect those data only in connection with other data on the natural person concerned, the possibility to secure the data collected adequately, stricter rules on the access of staff of the competent authority to the data and the prohibition of transmission of those data. The processing of such data should also be allowed by law where the data subject has explicitly agreed to the processing that is particularly intrusive to him or her. However, the consent of the data subject should not provide in itself a legal ground for processing such sensitive personal data by competent authorities.

(38)   The data subject should have the right not to be subject to a decision evaluating personal aspects relating to him or her which is based solely on automated processing and which produces adverse legal effects concerning, or significantly affects, him or her. In any case, such processing should be subject to suitable safeguards, including the provision of specific information to the data subject and the right to obtain human intervention, in particular to express his or her point of view, to obtain an explanation of the decision reached after such assessment or to challenge the decision. Profiling that results in discrimination against natural persons on the basis of personal data which are by their nature particularly sensitive in relation to fundamental rights and freedoms should be prohibited under the conditions laid down in Articles 21 and 52 of the Charter.

(39)   In order to enable him or her to exercise his or her rights, any information to the data subject should be easily accessible, including on the website of the controller, and easy to understand, using clear and plain language. Such information should be adapted to the needs of vulnerable persons such as children.

(40)   Modalities should be provided for facilitating the exercise of the data subject's rights under the provisions adopted pursuant to this Directive, including mechanisms to request and, if applicable, obtain, free of charge, in particular, access to and rectification or erasure of personal data and restriction of processing. The controller should be obliged to respond to requests of the data subject without undue delay, unless the controller applies limitations to data subject rights in accordance with this Directive. Moreover, if requests are manifestly unfounded or excessive, such as where the data subject unreasonably and repetitiously requests information or where the data subject abuses his or her right to receive information, for example, by providing false or misleading information when making the request, the controller should be able to charge a reasonable fee or refuse to act on the request.

(41)   Where the controller requests the provision of additional information necessary to confirm the identity of the data subject, that information should be processed only for that specific purpose and should not be stored for longer than needed for that purpose.

(42)   At least the following information should be made available to the data subject: the identity of the controller, the existence of the processing operation, the purposes of the processing, the right to lodge a complaint and the existence of the right to request from the controller access to and rectification or erasure of personal data or restriction of processing. This could take place on the website of the competent authority. In addition, in specific cases and in order to enable the exercise of his or her rights, the data subject should be informed of the legal basis for the processing and of how long the data will be stored, in so far as such further information is necessary, taking into account the specific circumstances in which the data are processed, to guarantee fair processing in respect of the data subject.

(43)   A natural person should have the right of access to data which has been collected concerning him or her, and to exercise this right easily and at reasonable intervals, in order to be aware of and verify the lawfulness of the processing. Every data subject should therefore have the right to know, and obtain communications about, the purposes for which the data are processed, the period during which the data are processed and the recipients of the data, including those in third countries. Where such communications include information as to the origin of the personal data, the information should not reveal the identity of natural persons, in particular confidential sources. For that right to be complied with, it is sufficient that the data subject be in possession of a full summary of those data in an intelligible form, that is to say a form which allows that data subject to become aware of those data and to verify that they are accurate and processed in accordance with this Directive, so that it is possible for him or her to exercise the rights conferred on him or her by this Directive. Such a summary could be provided in the form of a copy of the personal data undergoing processing.

(44)   Member States should be able to adopt legislative measures delaying, restricting or omitting the information to data subjects or restricting, wholly or partly, the access to their personal data to the extent that and as long as such a measure constitutes a necessary and proportionate measure in a democratic society with due regard for the fundamental rights and the legitimate interests of the natural person concerned, to avoid obstructing official or legal inquiries, investigations or procedures, to avoid prejudicing the prevention, investigation, detection or prosecution of criminal offences or the execution of criminal penalties, to protect public security or national security, or to protect the rights and freedoms of others. The controller should assess, by way of a concrete and individual examination of each case, whether the right of access should be partially or completely restricted.

(45)   Any refusal or restriction of access should in principle be set out in writing to the data subject and include the factual or legal reasons on which the decision is based.

(46)   Any restriction of the rights of the data subject must comply with the Charter and with the ECHR, as interpreted in the case-law of the Court of Justice and by the European Court of Human Rights respectively, and in particular respect the essence of those rights and freedoms.

(47)   A natural person should have the right to have inaccurate personal data concerning him or her rectified, in particular where it relates to facts, and the right to erasure where the processing of such data infringes this Directive. However, the right to rectification should not affect, for example, the content of a witness testimony. A natural person should also have the right to restriction of processing where he or she contests the accuracy of personal data and its accuracy or inaccuracy cannot be ascertained or where the personal data have to be maintained for purpose of evidence. In particular, instead of erasing personal data, processing should be restricted if in a specific case there are reasonable grounds to believe that erasure could affect the legitimate interests of the data subject. In such a case, restricted data should be processed only for the purpose which prevented their erasure. Methods to restrict the processing of personal data could include, inter alia, moving the selected data to another processing system, for example for archiving purposes, or making the selected data unavailable. In automated filing systems the restriction of processing should in principle be ensured by technical means. The fact that the processing of personal data is restricted should be indicated in the system in such a manner that it is clear that the processing of the personal data is restricted. Such rectification

or erasure of personal data or restriction of processing should be communicated to recipients to whom the data have been disclosed and to the competent authorities from which the inaccurate data originated. The controllers should also abstain from further dissemination of such data.

(48)   Where the controller denies a data subject his or her right to information, access to or rectification or erasure of personal data or restriction of processing, the data subject should have the right to request that the national supervisory authority verify the lawfulness of the processing. The data subject should be informed of that right. Where the supervisory authority acts on behalf of the data subject, the data subject should be informed by the supervisory authority at least that all necessary verifications or reviews by the supervisory authority have taken place. The supervisory authority should also inform the data subject of the right to seek a judicial remedy.

(49)   Where the personal data are processed in the course of a criminal investigation and court proceedings in criminal matters, Member States should be able to provide that the exercise the right to information, access to and rectification or erasure of personal data and restriction of processing is carried out in accordance with national rules on judicial proceedings.

(50)   The responsibility and liability of the controller for any processing of personal data carried out by the controller or on the controller's behalf should be established. In particular, the controller should be obliged to implement appropriate and effective measures and should be able to demonstrate that processing activities are in compliance with this Directive. Such measures should take into account the nature, scope, context and purposes of the processing and the risk to the rights and freedoms of natural persons. The measures taken by the controller should include drawing up and implementing specific safeguards in respect of the treatment of personal data of vulnerable natural persons, such as children.

(51)   The risk to the rights and freedoms of natural persons, of varying likelihood and severity, may result from data processing which could lead to physical, material or non-material damage, in particular: where the processing may give rise to discrimination, identity theft or fraud, financial loss, damage to the reputation, loss of confidentiality of data protected by professional secrecy, unauthorised reversal of pseudonymisation or any other significant economic or social disadvantage; where data subjects might be deprived of their rights and freedoms or from exercising control over their personal data; where personal data are processed which reveal racial or ethnic origin, political opinions, religion or philosophical beliefs or trade union membership; where genetic data or biometric data are processed in order to uniquely identify a person or where data concerning health or data concerning sex life and sexual orientation or criminal convictions and offences or related security measures are processed; where personal aspects are evaluated, in particular analysing and predicting aspects concerning performance at work, economic situation, health, personal preferences or interests, reliability or behaviour, location or movements, in order to create or use personal profiles; where personal data of vulnerable natural persons, in particular children, are processed; or where processing involves a large amount of personal data and affects a large number of data subjects.

(52)   The likelihood and severity of the risk should be determined by reference to the nature, scope, context and purposes of the processing. Risk should be evaluated on the basis of an objective assessment, through which it is established whether data-processing operations involve a high risk. A high risk is a particular risk of prejudice to the rights and freedoms of data subjects.

(53)   The protection of the rights and freedoms of natural persons with regard to the processing of personal data requires that appropriate technical and organisational measures are taken, to ensure that the requirements of this Directive are met. The implementation of such measures should not depend solely on economic considerations. In order to be able to demonstrate compliance with this Directive, the controller should adopt internal policies and implement measures which adhere in particular to the principles of data protection by design and data protection by default. Where the controller has carried out a data protection impact assessment pursuant to this Directive, the results should be taken into account when developing those measures and procedures. The measures could consist, inter alia, of the use of pseudonymisation, as early as possible. The use of pseudonymisation for the purposes of this Directive can serve as a tool that could facilitate, in particular, the free flow of personal data within the area of freedom, security and justice.

(54)   The protection of the rights and freedoms of data subjects as well as the responsibility and liability of controllers and processors, also in relation to the monitoring by and measures of supervisory authorities, requires a clear attribution of the responsibilities set out in this Directive, including where a controller determines the purposes and means of the processing jointly with other controllers or where a processing operation is carried out on behalf of a controller.

(55)   The carrying-out of processing by a processor should be governed by a legal act including a contract binding the processor to the controller and stipulating, in particular, that the processor should act only on instructions from the controller. The processor should take into account the principle of data protection by design and by default.

(56)   In order to demonstrate compliance with this Directive, the controller or processor should maintain records regarding all categories of processing activities under its responsibility. Each controller and processor should be obliged to cooperate with the supervisory authority and make those records available to it on request, so that they might serve for monitoring those processing operations. The controller or the processor processing personal data in non-automated processing systems should have in place effective methods of demonstrating the lawfulness of the processing, of enabling self-monitoring and of ensuring data integrity and data security, such as logs or other forms of records.

(57)   Logs should be kept at least for operations in automated processing systems such as collection, alteration, consultation, disclosure including transfers, combination or erasure. The identification of the person who consulted or disclosed personal data should be logged and from that identification it should be possible to establish the justification for the processing operations. The logs should solely be used for the verification of the lawfulness of the processing, self-monitoring, for ensuring data integrity and data security and criminal proceedings. Self-monitoring also includes internal disciplinary proceedings of competent authorities.

(58)   A data protection impact assessment should be carried out by the controller where the processing operations are likely to result in a high risk to the rights and freedoms of data subjects by virtue of their nature, scope or purposes,

which should include, in particular, the measures, safeguards and mechanisms envisaged to ensure the protection of personal data and to demonstrate compliance with this Directive. Impact assessments should cover relevant systems and processes of processing operations, but not individual cases.

(59)   In order to ensure effective protection of the rights and freedoms of data subjects, the controller or processor should consult the supervisory authority, in certain cases, prior to the processing.

(60)   In order to maintain security and to prevent processing that infringes this Directive, the controller or processor should evaluate the risks inherent in the processing and should implement measures to mitigate those risks, such as encryption. Such measures should ensure an appropriate level of security, including confidentiality and take into account the state of the art, the costs of implementation in relation to the risk and the nature of the personal data to be protected. In assessing data security risks, consideration should be given to the risks that are presented by data processing, such as the accidental or unlawful destruction, loss, alteration or unauthorised disclosure of or access to personal data transmitted, stored or otherwise processed, which may, in particular, lead to physical, material or non-material damage. The controller and processor should ensure that the processing of personal data is not carried out by unauthorised persons.

(61)   A personal data breach may, if not addressed in an appropriate and timely manner, result in physical, material or non-material damage to natural persons such as loss of control over their personal data or limitation of their rights, discrimination, identity theft or fraud, financial loss, unauthorised reversal of pseudonymisation, damage to reputation, loss of confidentiality of personal data protected by professional secrecy or any other significant economic or social disadvantage to the natural person concerned. Therefore, as soon as the controller becomes aware that a personal data breach has occurred, the controller should notify the personal data breach to the supervisory authority without undue delay and, where feasible, not later than 72 hours after having become aware of it, unless the controller is able to demonstrate, in accordance with the accountability principle, that the personal data breach is unlikely to result in a risk to the rights and freedoms of natural persons. Where such notification cannot be achieved within 72 hours, the reasons for the delay should accompany the notification and information may be provided in phases without undue further delay.

(62)   Natural persons should be informed without undue delay where the personal data breach is likely to result in a high risk to the rights and freedoms of natural persons, in order to allow them to take the necessary precautions. The communication should describe the nature of the personal data breach and include recommendations for the natural person concerned to mitigate potential adverse effects. Communication to data subjects should be made as soon as reasonably feasible, in close cooperation with the supervisory authority, and respecting guidance provided by it or other relevant authorities. For example, the need to mitigate an immediate risk of damage would call for a prompt communication to data subjects, whereas the need to implement appropriate measures against continuing or similar data breaches may justify more time for the communication. Where avoiding obstruction of official or legal inquiries, investigations or procedures, avoiding prejudice to the prevention, detection, investigation or prosecution of criminal offences or the execution of criminal penalties, protecting public security, protecting national security or protecting the rights and freedoms of others cannot be achieved by delaying or restricting the communication of a personal data breach to the natural person concerned, such communication could, in exceptional circumstances, be omitted.

(63)   The controller should designate a person who would assist it in monitoring internal compliance with the provisions adopted pursuant to this Directive, except where a Member State decides to exempt courts and other independent judicial authorities when acting in their judicial capacity. That person could be a member of the existing staff of the controller who received special training in data protection law and practice in order to acquire expert knowledge in that field. The necessary level of expert knowledge should be determined, in particular, according to the data processing carried out and the protection required for the personal data processed by the controller. His or her task could be carried out on a part-time or full-time basis. A data protection officer may be appointed jointly by several controllers, taking into account their organisational structure and size, for example in the case of shared resources in central units. That person can also be appointed to different positions within the structure of the relevant controllers. That person should help the controller and the employees processing personal data by informing and advising them on compliance with their relevant data protection obligations. Such data protection officers should be in a position to perform their duties and tasks in an independent manner in accordance with Member State law.

(64)   Member States should ensure that a transfer to a third country or to an international organisation takes place only if necessary for the prevention, investigation, detection or prosecution of criminal offences or the execution of criminal penalties, including the safeguarding against and the prevention of threats to public security, and that the controller in the third country or international organisation is an authority competent within the meaning of this Directive. A transfer should be carried out only by competent authorities acting as controllers, except where processors are explicitly instructed to transfer on behalf of controllers. Such a transfer may take place in cases where the Commission has decided that the third country or international organisation in question ensures an adequate level of protection, where appropriate safeguards have been provided, or where derogations for specific situations apply. Where personal data are transferred from the Union to controllers, to processors or to other recipients in third countries or international organisations, the level of protection of natural persons provided for in the Union by this Directive should not be undermined, including in cases of onward transfers of personal data from the third country or international organisation to controllers or processors in the same or in another third country or international organisation.

(65)   Where personal data are transferred from a Member State to third countries or international organisations, such a transfer should, in principle, take place only after the Member State from which the data were obtained has given its authorisation to the transfer. The interests of efficient law-enforcement cooperation require that where the nature of a threat to the public security of a Member State or a third country or to the essential interests of a Member State is so immediate as to render it impossible to obtain prior authorisation in good time, the competent authority should be able to transfer the relevant personal data to the third country or international organisation concerned without such a prior authorisation. Member States should provide that any specific conditions concerning the transfer should be communicated to third countries or international organisations. Onward transfers of personal data should be subject to prior authorisation by the competent authority that carried out the original transfer. When deciding on a request for the

authorisation of an onward transfer, the competent authority that carried out the original transfer should take due account of all relevant factors, including the seriousness of the criminal offence, the specific conditions subject to which, and the purpose for which, the data was originally transferred, the nature and conditions of the execution of the criminal penalty, and the level of personal data protection in the third country or an international organisation to which personal data are onward transferred. The competent authority that carried out the original transfer should also be able to subject the onward transfer to specific conditions. Such specific conditions can be described, for example, in handling codes.

(66)   The Commission should be able to decide with effect for the entire Union that certain third countries, a territory or one or more specified sectors within a third country, or an international organisation, offer an adequate level of data protection, thus providing legal certainty and uniformity throughout the Union as regards the third countries or international organisations which are considered to provide such a level of protection. In such cases, transfers of personal data to those countries should be able to take place without the need to obtain any specific authorisation, except where another Member State from which the data were obtained has to give its authorisation to the transfer.

(67)   In line with the fundamental values on which the Union is founded, in particular the protection of human rights, the Commission should, in its assessment of the third country, or of a territory or specified sector within a third country, take into account how a particular third country respects the rule of law, access to justice as well as international human rights norms and standards and its general and sectoral law, including legislation concerning public security, defence and national security, as well as public order and criminal law. The adoption of an adequacy decision with regard to a territory or a specified sector in a third country should take into account clear and objective criteria, such as specific processing activities and the scope of applicable legal standards and legislation in force in the third country. The third country should offer guarantees ensuring an adequate level of protection essentially equivalent to that ensured within the Union, in particular where data are processed in one or several specific sectors. In particular, the third country should ensure effective independent data protection supervision and provide for cooperation mechanisms with the Member States' data protection authorities, and the data subjects should be provided with effective and enforceable rights and effective administrative and judicial redress.

(68)   Apart from the international commitments the third country or international organisation has entered into, the Commission should also take account of obligations arising from the third country's or international organisation's participation in multilateral or regional systems, in particular in relation to the protection of personal data, as well as the implementation of such obligations. In particular the third country's accession to the Council of Europe Convention of 28 January 1981 for the Protection of Individuals with regard to the Automatic Processing of Personal Data and its Additional Protocol should be taken into account. The Commission should consult with the European Data Protection Board established by Regulation (EU) 2016/679 (the 'Board') when assessing the level of protection in third countries or international organisations. The Commission should also take into account any relevant Commission adequacy decision adopted in accordance with Article 45 of Regulation (EU) 2016/679.

(69)   The Commission should monitor the functioning of decisions on the level of protection in a third country, a territory or a specified sector within a third country, or an international organisation. In its adequacy decisions, the Commission should provide for a periodic review mechanism of their functioning. That periodic review should be undertaken in consultation with the third country or international organisation in question and should take into account all relevant developments in the third country or international organisation.

(70)   The Commission should also be able to recognise that a third country, a territory or a specified sector within a third country, or an international organisation, no longer ensures an adequate level of data protection. Consequently, the transfer of personal data to that third country or international organisation should be prohibited unless the requirements in this Directive relating to transfers subject to appropriate safeguards and derogations for specific situations are fulfilled. Provision should be made for procedures for consultations between the Commission and such third countries or international organisations. The Commission should, in a timely manner, inform the third country or international organisation of the reasons and enter into consultations with it in order to remedy the situation.

(71)   Transfers not based on such an adequacy decision should be allowed only where appropriate safeguards have been provided in a legally binding instrument which ensures the protection of personal data or where the controller has assessed all the circumstances surrounding the data transfer and, on the basis of that assessment, considers that appropriate safeguards with regard to the protection of personal data exist. Such legally binding instruments could, for example, be legally binding bilateral agreements which have been concluded by the Member States and implemented in their legal order and which could be enforced by their data subjects, ensuring compliance with data protection requirements and the rights of the data subjects, including the right to obtain effective administrative or judicial redress. The controller should be able to take into account cooperation agreements concluded between Europol or Eurojust and third countries which allow for the exchange of personal data when carrying out the assessment of all the circumstances surrounding the data transfer. The controller should be able to also take into account the fact that the transfer of personal data will be subject to confidentiality obligations and the principle of specificity, ensuring that the data will not be processed for other purposes than for the purposes of the transfer. In addition, the controller should take into account that the personal data will not be used to request, hand down or execute a death penalty or any form of cruel and inhuman treatment. While those conditions could be considered to be appropriate safeguards allowing the transfer of data, the controller should be able to require additional safeguards.

(72)   Where no adequacy decision or appropriate safeguards exist, a transfer or a category of transfers could take place only in specific situations, if necessary to protect the vital interests of the data subject or another person, or to safeguard legitimate interests of the data subject where the law of the Member State transferring the personal data so provides; for the prevention of an immediate and serious threat to the public security of a Member State or a third country; in an individual case for the purposes of the prevention, investigation, detection or prosecution of criminal offences or the execution of criminal penalties, including the safeguarding against and the prevention of threats to public security; or in an individual case for the establishment, exercise or defence of legal claims. Those derogations should be interpreted restrictively and should not allow frequent, massive and structural transfers of personal data, or large-scale transfers of data, but should be limited to data strictly necessary. Such transfers should be documented and should be made available to the supervisory authority on request in order to monitor the lawfulness of the transfer.

(73)   Competent authorities of Member States apply bilateral or multilateral international agreements in force, concluded with third countries in the field of judicial cooperation in criminal matters and police cooperation, for the exchange of relevant information to allow them to perform their legally assigned tasks. In principle, this takes place through, or at least with, the cooperation of the authorities competent in the third countries concerned for the purposes of this Directive, sometimes even in the absence of a bilateral or multilateral international agreement. However, in specific individual cases, the regular procedures requiring contacting such an authority in the third country may be ineffective or inappropriate, in particular because the transfer could not be carried out in a timely manner, or because that authority in the third country does not respect the rule of law or international human rights norms and standards, so that competent authorities of Member States could decide to transfer personal data directly to recipients established in those third countries. This may be the case where there is an urgent need to transfer personal data to save the life of a person who is in danger of becoming a victim of a criminal offence or in the interest of preventing an imminent perpetration of a crime, including terrorism. Even if such a transfer between competent authorities and recipients established in third countries should take place only in specific individual cases, this Directive should provide for conditions to regulate such cases. Those provisions should not be considered to be derogations from any existing bilateral or multilateral international agreements in the field of judicial cooperation in criminal matters and police cooperation. Those rules should apply in addition to the other rules of this Directive, in particular those on the lawfulness of processing and Chapter V.

(74)   Where personal data move across borders it may put at increased risk the ability of natural persons to exercise data protection rights to protect themselves from the unlawful use or disclosure of those data. At the same time, supervisory authorities may find that they are unable to pursue complaints or conduct investigations relating to the activities outside their borders. Their efforts to work together in the cross-border context may also be hampered by insufficient preventative or remedial powers and inconsistent legal regimes. Therefore, there is a need to promote closer cooperation among data protection supervisory authorities to help them exchange information with their foreign counterparts.

(75)   The establishment in Member States of supervisory authorities that are able to exercise their functions with complete independence is an essential component of the protection of natural persons with regard to the processing of their personal data. The supervisory authorities should monitor the application of the provisions adopted pursuant to this Directive and should contribute to their consistent application throughout the Union in order to protect natural persons with regard to the processing of their personal data. To that end, the supervisory authorities should cooperate with each other and with the Commission.

(76)   Member States may entrust a supervisory authority already established under Regulation (EU) 2016/679 with the responsibility for the tasks to be performed by the national supervisory authorities to be established under this Directive.

(77)   Member States should be allowed to establish more than one supervisory authority to reflect their constitutional, organisational and administrative structure. Each supervisory authority should be provided with the financial and human resources, premises and infrastructure, which are necessary for the effective performance of their tasks, including for the tasks related to mutual assistance and cooperation with other supervisory authorities throughout the Union. Each supervisory authority should have a separate, public annual budget, which may be part of the overall state or national budget.

(78)   Supervisory authorities should be subject to independent control or monitoring mechanisms regarding their financial expenditure, provided that such financial control does not affect their independence.

(79)   The general conditions for the member or members of the supervisory authority should be laid down by Member State law and should in particular provide that those members should be either appointed by the parliament or the government or the head of State of the Member State based on a proposal from the government or a member of the government, or the parliament or its chamber, or by an independent body entrusted by Member State law with the appointment by means of a transparent procedure. In order to ensure the independence of the supervisory authority, the member or members should act with integrity, should refrain from any action incompatible with their duties and should not, during their term of office, engage in any incompatible occupation, whether gainful or not. In order to ensure the independence of the supervisory authority, the staff should be chosen by the supervisory authority which may include an intervention by an independent body entrusted by Member State law.

(80)   While this Directive applies also to the activities of national courts and other judicial authorities, the competence of the supervisory authorities should not cover the processing of personal data where courts are acting in their judicial capacity, in order to safeguard the independence of judges in the performance of their judicial tasks. That exemption should be limited to judicial activities in court cases and not apply to other activities where judges might be involved in accordance with Member State law. Member States should also be able to provide that the competence of the supervisory authority does not cover the processing of personal data of other independent judicial authorities when acting in their judicial capacity, for example public prosecutor's office. In any event, the compliance with the rules of this Directive by the courts and other independent judicial authorities is always subject to independent supervision in accordance with Article 8(3) of the Charter.

(81)   Each supervisory authority should handle complaints lodged by any data subject and should investigate the matter or transmit it to the competent supervisory authority. The investigation following a complaint should be carried out, subject to judicial review, to the extent that is appropriate in the specific case. The supervisory authority should inform the data subject of the progress and the outcome of the complaint within a reasonable period. If the case requires further investigation or coordination with another supervisory authority, intermediate information should be provided to the data subject.

(82)   In order to ensure effective, reliable and consistent monitoring of compliance with and enforcement of this Directive throughout the Union pursuant to the TFEU as interpreted by the Court of Justice, the supervisory authorities should have in each Member State the same tasks and effective powers, including investigative, corrective, and advisory powers which constitute necessary means to perform their tasks. However, their powers should not interfere with specific rules for criminal proceedings, including investigation and prosecution of criminal offences, or the independence of the judiciary. Without prejudice to the powers of prosecutorial authorities under Member State law,

supervisory authorities should also have the power to bring infringements of this Directive to the attention of the judicial authorities or to engage in legal proceedings. The powers of supervisory authorities should be exercised in accordance with appropriate procedural safeguards laid down by Union and Member State law, impartially, fairly and within a reasonable time. In particular each measure should be appropriate, necessary and proportionate in view of ensuring compliance with this Directive, taking into account the circumstances of each individual case, respect the right of every person to be heard before any individual measure that would adversely affect the person concerned is taken, and avoiding superfluous costs and excessive inconvenience to the person concerned. Investigative powers as regards access to premises should be exercised in accordance with specific requirements in Member State law, such as the requirement to obtain a prior judicial authorisation. The adoption of a legally binding decision should be subject to judicial review in the Member State of the supervisory authority that adopted the decision.

(83) The supervisory authorities should assist one another in performing their tasks and provide mutual assistance, so as to ensure the consistent application and enforcement of the provisions adopted pursuant to this Directive.

(84) The Board should contribute to the consistent application of this Directive throughout the Union, including advising the Commission and promoting the cooperation of the supervisory authorities throughout the Union.

(85) Every data subject should have the right to lodge a complaint with a single supervisory authority and to an effective judicial remedy in accordance with Article 47 of the Charter where the data subject considers that his or her rights under provisions adopted pursuant to this Directive are infringed or where the supervisory authority does not act on a complaint, partially or wholly rejects or dismisses a complaint or does not act where such action is necessary to protect the rights of the data subject. The investigation following a complaint should be carried out, subject to judicial review, to the extent that is appropriate in the specific case. The competent supervisory authority should inform the data subject of the progress and the outcome of the complaint within a reasonable period. If the case requires further investigation or coordination with another supervisory authority, intermediate information should be provided to the data subject. In order to facilitate the submission of complaints, each supervisory authority should take measures such as providing a complaint submission form which can also be completed electronically, without excluding other means of communication.

(86) Each natural or legal person should have the right to an effective judicial remedy before the competent national court against a decision of a supervisory authority which produces legal effects concerning that person. Such a decision concerns in particular the exercise of investigative, corrective and authorisation powers by the supervisory authority or the dismissal or rejection of complaints. However, that right does not encompass other measures of supervisory authorities which are not legally binding, such as opinions issued by or advice provided by the supervisory authority. Proceedings against a supervisory authority should be brought before the courts of the Member State where the supervisory authority is established and should be conducted in accordance with Member State law. Those courts should exercise full jurisdiction which should include jurisdiction to examine all questions of fact and law relevant to the dispute before it.

(87) Where a data subject considers that his or her rights under this Directive are infringed, he or she should have the right to mandate a body which aims to protect the rights and interests of data subjects in relation to the protection of their personal data and is constituted according to Member State law to lodge a complaint on his or her behalf with a supervisory authority and to exercise the right to a judicial remedy. The right of representation of data subjects should be without prejudice to Member State procedural law which may require mandatory representation of data subjects by a lawyer, as defined in Council Directive 77/249/EEC,[10] before national courts.

(88) Any damage which a person may suffer as a result of processing that infringes the provisions adopted pursuant to this Directive should be compensated by the controller or any other authority competent under Member State law. The concept of damage should be broadly interpreted in the light of the case-law of the Court of Justice in a manner which fully reflects the objectives of this Directive. This is without prejudice to any claims for damage deriving from the violation of other rules in Union or Member State law. When reference is made to processing that is unlawful or that infringes the provisions adopted pursuant to this Directive it also covers processing that infringes implementing acts adopted pursuant to this Directive. Data subjects should receive full and effective compensation for the damage that they have suffered.

(89) Penalties should be imposed on any natural or legal person, whether governed by private or public law, who infringes this Directive. Member States should ensure that the penalties are effective, proportionate and dissuasive and should take all measures to implement the penalties.

(90) In order to ensure uniform conditions for the implementation of this Directive, implementing powers should be conferred on the Commission with regard to the adequate level of protection afforded by a third country, a territory or a specified sector within a third country, or an international organisation and the format and procedures for mutual assistance and the arrangements for the exchange of information by electronic means between supervisory authorities, and between supervisory authorities and the Board. Those powers should be exercised in accordance with Regulation (EU) No 182/2011 of the European Parliament and of the Council.[11]

(91) The examination procedure should be used for the adoption of implementing acts on the adequate level of protection afforded by a third country, a territory or a specified sector within a third country, or an international organisation and on the format and procedures for mutual assistance and the arrangements for the exchange of information by electronic means between supervisory authorities, and between supervisory authorities and the Board, given that those acts are of a general scope.

(92) The Commission should adopt immediately applicable implementing acts where, in duly justified cases relating to a third country, a territory or a specified sector within a third country, or an international organisation which no longer ensure an adequate level of protection, imperative grounds of urgency so require.

(93) Since the objectives of this Directive, namely to protect the fundamental rights and freedoms of natural persons and in particular their right to the protection of personal data and to ensure the free exchange of personal data by competent authorities within the Union, cannot be sufficiently achieved by the Member States and can rather, by reason of the scale or effects of the action, be better achieved at Union level, the Union may adopt measures, in accordance with the principle of subsidiarity as set out in Article 5 of the TEU. In accordance with the principle of

proportionality as set out in that Article, this Directive does not go beyond what is necessary in order to achieve those objectives

(94) Specific provisions of acts of the Union adopted in the field of judicial cooperation in criminal matters and police cooperation which were adopted prior to the date of the adoption of this Directive, regulating the processing of personal data between Member States or the access of designated authorities of Member States to information systems established pursuant to the Treaties, should remain unaffected, such as, for example, the specific provisions concerning the protection of personal data applied pursuant to Council Decision 2008/615/JHA,[12] or Article 23 of the Convention on Mutual Assistance in Criminal Matters between the Member States of the European Union.[13] Since Article 8 of the Charter and Article 16 TFEU require that the fundamental right to the protection of personal data be ensured in a consistent manner throughout the Union, the Commission should evaluate the situation with regard to the relationship between this Directive and the acts adopted prior to the date of adoption of this Directive regulating the processing of personal data between Member States or the access of designated authorities of Member States to information systems established pursuant to the Treaties, in order to assess the need for alignment of those specific provisions with this Directive. Where appropriate, the Commission should make proposals with a view to ensuring consistent legal rules relating to the processing of personal data.

(95) In order to ensure a comprehensive and consistent protection of personal data in the Union, international agreements which were concluded by Member States prior to the date of entry into force of this Directive and which comply with the relevant Union law applicable prior to that date should remain in force until amended, replaced or revoked.

(96) Member States should be allowed a period of not more than two years from the date of entry into force of this Directive to transpose it. Processing already under way on that date should be brought into conformity with this Directive within the period of two years after which this Directive enters into force. However, where such processing complies with the Union law applicable prior to the date of entry into force of this Directive, the requirements of this Directive concerning the prior consultation of the supervisory authority should not apply to the processing operations already under way on that date given that those requirements, by their very nature, are to be met prior to the processing. Where Member States use the longer implementation period expiring seven years after the date of entry into force of this Directive for meeting the logging obligations for automated processing systems set up prior to that date, the controller or the processor should have in place effective methods for demonstrating the lawfulness of the data processing, for enabling self-monitoring and for ensuring data integrity and data security, such as logs or other forms of records.

(97) This Directive is without prejudice to the rules on combating the sexual abuse and sexual exploitation of children and child pornography as laid down in Directive 2011/93/EU of the European Parliament and of the Council.[14]

(98) Framework Decision 2008/977/JHA should therefore be repealed.

(99) In accordance with Article 6a of Protocol No 21 on the position of the United Kingdom and Ireland in respect of the area of freedom, security and justice, as annexed to the TEU and to the TFEU, the United Kingdom and Ireland are not bound by the rules laid down in this Directive which relate to the processing of personal data by the Member States when carrying out activities which fall within the scope of Chapter 4 or Chapter 5 of Title V of Part Three of the TFEU where the United Kingdom and Ireland are not bound by the rules governing the forms of judicial cooperation in criminal matters or police cooperation which require compliance with the provisions laid down on the basis of Article 16 TFEU.

(100) In accordance with Articles 2 and 2a of Protocol No 22 on the position of Denmark, as annexed to the TEU and to the TFEU, Denmark is not bound by the rules laid down in this Directive or subject to their application which relate to the processing of personal data by the Member States when carrying out activities which fall within the scope of Chapter 4 or Chapter 5 of Title V of Part Three of the TFEU. Given that this Directive builds upon the Schengen *acquis*, under Title V of Part Three of the TFEU, Denmark, in accordance with Article 4 of that Protocol, is to decide within six months after adoption of this Directive whether it will implement it in its national law.

(101) As regards Iceland and Norway, this Directive constitutes a development of provisions of the Schengen *acquis*, as provided for by the Agreement concluded by the Council of the European Union and the Republic of Iceland and the Kingdom of Norway concerning the association of those two States with the implementation, application and development of the Schengen *acquis*.[15]

(102) As regards Switzerland, this Directive constitutes a development of provisions of the Schengen *acquis*, as provided for by the Agreement between the European Union, the European Community and the Swiss Confederation concerning the association of the Swiss Confederation with the implementation, application and development of the Schengen *acquis*.[16]

(103) As regards Liechtenstein, this Directive constitutes a development of provisions of the Schengen *acquis*, as provided for by the Protocol between the European Union, the European Community, the Swiss Confederation and the Principality of Liechtenstein on the accession of the Principality of Liechtenstein to the Agreement between the European Union, the European Community and the Swiss Confederation on the Swiss Confederation's association with the implementation, application and development of the Schengen *acquis*.[17]

(104) This Directive respects the fundamental rights and observes the principles recognised in the Charter as enshrined in the TFEU, in particular the right to respect for private and family life, the right to the protection of personal data, the right to an effective remedy and to a fair trial. Limitations placed on those rights are in accordance with Article 52(1) of the Charter as they are necessary to meet objectives of general interest recognised by the Union or the need to protect the rights and freedoms of others.

(105) In accordance with the Joint Political Declaration of 28 September 2011 of Member States and the Commission on explanatory documents, Member States have undertaken to accompany, in justified cases, the notification of their transposition measures with one or more documents explaining the relationship between the components of a directive and the corresponding parts of national transposition measures. With regard to this Directive, the legislator considers the transmission of such documents to be justified.

(106) The European Data Protection Supervisor was consulted in accordance with Article 28(2) of Regulation

(EC) No 45/2001 and delivered an opinion on 7 March 2012.[18]

(107) This Directive should not preclude Member States from implementing the exercise of the rights of data subjects on information, access to and rectification or erasure of personal data and restriction of processing in the course of criminal proceedings, and their possible restrictions thereto, in national rules on criminal procedure,

NOTES

[1] OJ C391, 18.12.2012, p 127.

[2] Position of the European Parliament of 12 March 2014 (not yet published in the Official Journal) and position of the Council at first reading of 8 April 2016 (not yet published in the Official Journal). Position of the European Parliament of 14 April 2016.

[3] Directive 95/46/EC of the European Parliament and of the Council of 24 October 1995 on the protection of individuals with regard to the processing of personal data and on the free movement of such data (OJ L281, 23.11.1995, p 31).

[4] Council Framework Decision 2008/977/JHA of 27 November 2008 on the protection of personal data processed in the framework of police and judicial cooperation in criminal matters (OJ L350, 30.12.2008, p 60).

[5] Regulation (EU) 2016/679 of the European Parliament and of the Council of 27 April 2016 on the protection of natural persons with regard to the processing of personal data and on the free movement of such data and repealing Directive 95/46/EC (General Data Protection Regulation) (see page 1 of this Official Journal).

[6] Regulation (EC) No 45/2001 of the European Parliament and of the Council of 18 December 2000 on the protection of individuals with regard to the processing of personal data by the Community institutions and bodies and on the free movement of such data (OJ L8, 12.1.2001, p 1).

[7] Directive 2011/24/EU of the European Parliament and of the Council of 9 March 2011 on the application of patients' rights in cross-border healthcare (OJ L88, 4.4.2011, p 45).

[8] Council Common Position 2005/69/JHA of 24 January 2005 on exchanging certain data with Interpol (OJ L27, 29.1.2005, p 61).

[9] Council Decision 2007/533/JHA of 12 June 2007 on the establishment, operation and use of the second generation Schengen Information System (SIS II) (OJ L205, 7.8.2007, p 63).

[10] Council Directive 77/249/EEC of 22 March 1977 to facilitate the effective exercise by lawyers of freedom to provide services (OJ L78, 26.3.1977, p 17).

[11] Regulation (EU) No 182/2011 of the European Parliament and of the Council of 16 February 2011 laying down the rules and general principles concerning mechanisms for control by the Member States of the Commission's exercise of implementing powers (OJ L55, 28.2.2011, p 13).

[12] Council Decision 2008/615/JHA of 23 June 2008 on the stepping up of cross-border cooperation, particularly in combating terrorism and cross-border crime (OJ L210, 6.8.2008, p 1).

[13] Council Act of 29 May 2000 establishing in accordance with Article 34 of the Treaty on European Union the Convention on Mutual Assistance in Criminal Matters between the Member States of the European Union (OJ C197, 12.7.2000, p 1).

[14] Directive 2011/93/EU of the European Parliament and of the Council of 13 December 2011 on combating the sexual abuse and sexual exploitation of children and child pornography, and replacing Council Framework Decision 2004/68/JHA (OJ L335, 17.12.2011, p 1).

[15] OJ L176, 10.7.1999, p 36.

[16] OJ L53, 27.2.2008, p 52.

[17] OJ L160, 18.6.2011, p 21.

[18] OJ C192, 30.6.2012, p 7.

HAVE ADOPTED THIS DIRECTIVE:

CHAPTER I GENERAL PROVISIONS

[2.102]
Article 1 Subject-matter and objectives
1. This Directive lays down the rules relating to the protection of natural persons with regard to the processing of personal data by competent authorities for the purposes of the prevention, investigation, detection or prosecution of criminal offences or the execution of criminal penalties, including the safeguarding against and the prevention of threats to public security.
2. In accordance with this Directive, Member States shall:
   (a) protect the fundamental rights and freedoms of natural persons and in particular their right to the protection of personal data; and
   (b) ensure that the exchange of personal data by competent authorities within the Union, where such exchange is required by Union or Member State law, is neither restricted nor prohibited for reasons connected with the protection of natural persons with regard to the processing of personal data.
3. This Directive shall not preclude Member States from providing higher safeguards than those established in this Directive for the protection of the rights and freedoms of the data subject with regard to the processing of personal data by competent authorities.

[2.103]
Article 2 Scope
1. This Directive applies to the processing of personal data by competent authorities for the purposes set out in Article 1(1).
2. This Directive applies to the processing of personal data wholly or partly by automated means, and to the processing other than by automated means of personal data which form part of a filing system or are intended to form part of a filing system.
3. This Directive does not apply to the processing of personal data:
   (a) in the course of an activity which falls outside the scope of Union law;
   (b) by the Union institutions, bodies, offices and agencies.

[2.104]
Article 3   Definitions
For the purposes of this Directive:
(1) 'personal data' means any information relating to an identified or identifiable natural person ('data subject'); an identifiable natural person is one who can be identified, directly or indirectly, in particular by reference to an identifier such as a name, an identification number, location data, an online identifier or to one or more factors specific to the physical, physiological, genetic, mental, economic, cultural or social identity of that natural person;

(2) 'processing' means any operation or set of operations which is performed on personal data or on sets of personal data, whether or not by automated means, such as collection, recording, organisation, structuring, storage, adaptation or alteration, retrieval, consultation, use, disclosure by transmission, dissemination or otherwise making available, alignment or combination, restriction, erasure or destruction;

(3) 'restriction of processing' means the marking of stored personal data with the aim of limiting their processing in the future;

(4) 'profiling' means any form of automated processing of personal data consisting of the use of personal data to evaluate certain personal aspects relating to a natural person, in particular to analyse or predict aspects concerning that natural person's performance at work, economic situation, health, personal preferences, interests, reliability, behaviour, location or movements;

(5) 'pseudonymisation' means the processing of personal data in such a manner that the personal data can no longer be attributed to a specific data subject without the use of additional information, provided that such additional information is kept separately and is subject to technical and organisational measures to ensure that the personal data are not attributed to an identified or identifiable natural person;

(6) 'filing system' means any structured set of personal data which are accessible according to specific criteria, whether centralised, decentralised or dispersed on a functional or geographical basis;

(7) 'competent authority' means:
    (a) any public authority competent for the prevention, investigation, detection or prosecution of criminal offences or the execution of criminal penalties, including the safeguarding against and the prevention of threats to public security; or
    (b) any other body or entity entrusted by Member State law to exercise public authority and public powers for the purposes of the prevention, investigation, detection or prosecution of criminal offences or the execution of criminal penalties, including the safeguarding against and the prevention of threats to public security;

(8) 'controller' means the competent authority which, alone or jointly with others, determines the purposes and means of the processing of personal data; where the purposes and means of such processing are determined by Union or Member State law, the controller or the specific criteria for its nomination may be provided for by Union or Member State law;

(9) 'processor' means a natural or legal person, public authority, agency or other body which processes personal data on behalf of the controller;

(10) 'recipient' means a natural or legal person, public authority, agency or another body, to which the personal data are disclosed, whether a third party or not. However, public authorities which may receive personal data in the framework of a particular inquiry in accordance with Member State law shall not be regarded as recipients; the processing of those data by those public authorities shall be in compliance with the applicable data protection rules according to the purposes of the processing;

(11) 'personal data breach' means a breach of security leading to the accidental or unlawful destruction, loss, alteration, unauthorised disclosure of, or access to, personal data transmitted, stored or otherwise processed;

(12) 'genetic data' means personal data, relating to the inherited or acquired genetic characteristics of a natural person which give unique information about the physiology or the health of that natural person and which result, in particular, from an analysis of a biological sample from the natural person in question;

(13) 'biometric data' means personal data resulting from specific technical processing relating to the physical, physiological or behavioural characteristics of a natural person, which allow or confirm the unique identification of that natural person, such as facial images or dactyloscopic data;

(14) 'data concerning health' means personal data related to the physical or mental health of a natural person, including the provision of health care services, which reveal information about his or her health status;

(15) 'supervisory authority' means an independent public authority which is established by a Member State pursuant to Article 41;

(16) 'international organisation' means an organisation and its subordinate bodies governed by public international law, or any other body which is set up by, or on the basis of, an agreement between two or more countries.

CHAPTER II PRINCIPLES

[2.105]
Article 4   Principles relating to processing of personal data
1. Member States shall provide for personal data to be:
(a) processed lawfully and fairly;
(b) collected for specified, explicit and legitimate purposes and not processed in a manner that is incompatible with those purposes;
(c) adequate, relevant and not excessive in relation to the purposes for which they are processed;
(d) accurate and, where necessary, kept up to date; every reasonable step must be taken to ensure that personal data that are inaccurate, having regard to the purposes for which they are processed, are erased or rectified without delay;
(e) kept in a form which permits identification of data subjects for no longer than is necessary for the purposes for which they are processed;

(f) processed in a manner that ensures appropriate security of the personal data, including protection against unauthorised or unlawful processing and against accidental loss, destruction or damage, using appropriate technical or organisational measures.

2. Processing by the same or another controller for any of the purposes set out in Article 1(1) other than that for which the personal data are collected shall be permitted in so far as:

(a) the controller is authorised to process such personal data for such a purpose in accordance with Union or Member State law; and

(b) processing is necessary and proportionate to that other purpose in accordance with Union or Member State law.

3. Processing by the same or another controller may include archiving in the public interest, scientific, statistical or historical use, for the purposes set out in Article 1(1), subject to appropriate safeguards for the rights and freedoms of data subjects.

4. The controller shall be responsible for, and be able to demonstrate compliance with, paragraphs 1, 2 and 3.

[2.106]
Article 5 Time-limits for storage and review
Member States shall provide for appropriate time limits to be established for the erasure of personal data or for a periodic review of the need for the storage of personal data. Procedural measures shall ensure that those time limits are observed.

[2.107]
Article 6 Distinction between different categories of data subject
Member States shall provide for the controller, where applicable and as far as possible, to make a clear distinction between personal data of different categories of data subjects, such as:

(a) persons with regard to whom there are serious grounds for believing that they have committed or are about to commit a criminal offence;

(b) persons convicted of a criminal offence;

(c) victims of a criminal offence or persons with regard to whom certain facts give rise to reasons for believing that he or she could be the victim of a criminal offence; and

(d) other parties to a criminal offence, such as persons who might be called on to testify in investigations in connection with criminal offences or subsequent criminal proceedings, persons who can provide information on criminal offences, or contacts or associates of one of the persons referred to in points (a) and (b).

[2.108]
Article 7 Distinction between personal data and verification of quality of personal data
1. Member States shall provide for personal data based on facts to be distinguished, as far as possible, from personal data based on personal assessments.

2. Member States shall provide for the competent authorities to take all reasonable steps to ensure that personal data which are inaccurate, incomplete or no longer up to date are not transmitted or made available. To that end, each competent authority shall, as far as practicable, verify the quality of personal data before they are transmitted or made available. As far as possible, in all transmissions of personal data, necessary information enabling the receiving competent authority to assess the degree of accuracy, completeness and reliability of personal data, and the extent to which they are up to date shall be added.

3. If it emerges that incorrect personal data have been transmitted or personal data have been unlawfully transmitted, the recipient shall be notified without delay. In such a case, the personal data shall be rectified or erased or processing shall be restricted in accordance with Article 16.

[2.109]
Article 8 Lawfulness of processing
1. Member States shall provide for processing to be lawful only if and to the extent that processing is necessary for the performance of a task carried out by a competent authority for the purposes set out in Article 1(1) and that it is based on Union or Member State law.

2. Member State law regulating processing within the scope of this Directive shall specify at least the objectives of processing, the personal data to be processed and the purposes of the processing.

[2.110]
Article 9 Specific processing conditions
1. Personal data collected by competent authorities for the purposes set out in Article 1(1) shall not be processed for purposes other than those set out in Article 1(1) unless such processing is authorised by Union or Member State law. Where personal data are processed for such other purposes, Regulation (EU) 2016/679 shall apply unless the processing is carried out in an activity which falls outside the scope of Union law.

2. Where competent authorities are entrusted by Member State law with the performance of tasks other than those performed for the purposes set out in Article 1(1), Regulation (EU) 2016/679 shall apply to processing for such purposes, including for archiving purposes in the public interest, scientific or historical research purposes or statistical purposes, unless the processing is carried out in an activity which falls outside the scope of Union law.

3. Member States shall, where Union or Member State law applicable to the transmitting competent authority provides specific conditions for processing, provide for the transmitting competent authority to inform the recipient of such personal data of those conditions and the requirement to comply with them.

4. Member States shall provide for the transmitting competent authority not to apply conditions pursuant to paragraph 3 to recipients in other Member States or to agencies, offices and bodies established pursuant to Chapters 4 and 5 of Title V of the TFEU other than those applicable to similar transmissions of data within the Member State of the transmitting competent authority.

[2.111]
Article 10   Processing of special categories of personal data
Processing of personal data revealing racial or ethnic origin, political opinions, religious or philosophical beliefs, or trade union membership, and the processing of genetic data, biometric data for the purpose of uniquely identifying a natural person, data concerning health or data concerning a natural person's sex life or sexual orientation shall be allowed only where strictly necessary, subject to appropriate safeguards for the rights and freedoms of the data subject, and only:
- (a)   where authorised by Union or Member State law;
- (b)   to protect the vital interests of the data subject or of another natural person; or
- (c)   where such processing relates to data which are manifestly made public by the data subject.

[2.112]
Article 11   Automated individual decision-making
1.   Member States shall provide for a decision based solely on automated processing, including profiling, which produces an adverse legal effect concerning the data subject or significantly affects him or her, to be prohibited unless authorised by Union or Member State law to which the controller is subject and which provides appropriate safeguards for the rights and freedoms of the data subject, at least the right to obtain human intervention on the part of the controller.
2.   Decisions referred to in paragraph 1 of this Article shall not be based on special categories of personal data referred to in Article 10, unless suitable measures to safeguard the data subject's rights and freedoms and legitimate interests are in place.
3.   Profiling that results in discrimination against natural persons on the basis of special categories of personal data referred to in Article 10 shall be prohibited, in accordance with Union law.

CHAPTER III RIGHTS OF THE DATA SUBJECT

[2.113]
Article 12   Communication and modalities for exercising the rights of the data subject
1.   Member States shall provide for the controller to take reasonable steps to provide any information referred to in Article 13 and make any communication with regard to Articles 11, 14 to 18 and 31 relating to processing to the data subject in a concise, intelligible and easily accessible form, using clear and plain language. The information shall be provided by any appropriate means, including by electronic means. As a general rule, the controller shall provide the information in the same form as the request.
2.   Member States shall provide for the controller to facilitate the exercise of the rights of the data subject under Articles 11 and 14 to 18.
3.   Member States shall provide for the controller to inform the data subject in writing about the follow up to his or her request without undue delay.
4.   Member States shall provide for the information provided under Article 13 and any communication made or action taken pursuant to Articles 11, 14 to 18 and 31 to be provided free of charge. Where requests from a data subject are manifestly unfounded or excessive, in particular because of their repetitive character, the controller may either:
The controller shall bear the burden of demonstrating the manifestly unfounded or excessive character of the request.
5.   Where the controller has reasonable doubts concerning the identity of the natural person making a request referred to in Article 14 or 16, the controller may request the provision of additional information necessary to confirm the identity of the data subject.

[2.114]
Article 13   Information to be made available or given to the data subject
1.   Member States shall provide for the controller to make available to the data subject at least the following information:
- (a)   the identity and the contact details of the controller;
- (b)   the contact details of the data protection officer, where applicable;
- (c)   the purposes of the processing for which the personal data are intended;
- (d)   the right to lodge a complaint with a supervisory authority and the contact details of the supervisory authority;
- (e)   the existence of the right to request from the controller access to and rectification or erasure of personal data and restriction of processing of the personal data concerning the data subject.
2.   In addition to the information referred to in paragraph 1, Member States shall provide by law for the controller to give to the data subject, in specific cases, the following further information to enable the exercise of his or her rights:
- (a)   the legal basis for the processing;
- (b)   the period for which the personal data will be stored, or, where that is not possible, the criteria used to determine that period;
- (c)   where applicable, the categories of recipients of the personal data, including in third countries or international organisations;
- (d)   where necessary, further information, in particular where the personal data are collected without the knowledge of the data subject.
3.   Member States may adopt legislative measures delaying, restricting or omitting the provision of the information to the data subject pursuant to paragraph 2 to the extent that, and for as long as, such a measure constitutes a necessary and proportionate measure in a democratic society with due regard for the fundamental rights and the legitimate interests of the natural person concerned, in order to:
- (a)   avoid obstructing official or legal inquiries, investigations or procedures;
- (b)   avoid prejudicing the prevention, detection, investigation or prosecution of criminal offences or the execution of criminal penalties;
- (c)   protect public security;
- (d)   protect national security;
- (e)   protect the rights and freedoms of others.

4. Member States may adopt legislative measures in order to determine categories of processing which may wholly or partly fall under any of the points listed in paragraph 3.

[2.115]
Article 14   Right of access by the data subject
Subject to Article 15, Member States shall provide for the right of the data subject to obtain from the controller confirmation as to whether or not personal data concerning him or her are being processed, and, where that is the case, access to the personal data and the following information:
  (a)   the purposes of and legal basis for the processing;
  (b)   the categories of personal data concerned;
  (c)   the recipients or categories of recipients to whom the personal data have been disclosed, in particular recipients in third countries or international organisations;
  (d)   where possible, the envisaged period for which the personal data will be stored, or, if not possible, the criteria used to determine that period;
  (e)   the existence of the right to request from the controller rectification or erasure of personal data or restriction of processing of personal data concerning the data subject;
  (f)   the right to lodge a complaint with the supervisory authority and the contact details of the supervisory authority;
  (g)   communication of the personal data undergoing processing and of any available information as to their origin.

[2.116]
Article 15   Limitations to the right of access
1. Member States may adopt legislative measures restricting, wholly or partly, the data subject's right of access to the extent that, and for as long as such a partial or complete restriction constitutes a necessary and proportionate measure in a democratic society with due regard for the fundamental rights and legitimate interests of the natural person concerned, in order to:
  (a)   avoid obstructing official or legal inquiries, investigations or procedures;
  (b)   avoid prejudicing the prevention, detection, investigation or prosecution of criminal offences or the execution of criminal penalties;
  (c)   protect public security;
  (d)   protect national security;
  (e)   protect the rights and freedoms of others.
2. Member States may adopt legislative measures in order to determine categories of processing which may wholly or partly fall under points (a) to (e) of paragraph 1.
3. In the cases referred to in paragraphs 1 and 2, Member States shall provide for the controller to inform the data subject, without undue delay, in writing of any refusal or restriction of access and of the reasons for the refusal or the restriction. Such information may be omitted where the provision thereof would undermine a purpose under paragraph 1. Member States shall provide for the controller to inform the data subject of the possibility of lodging a complaint with a supervisory authority or seeking a judicial remedy.
4. Member States shall provide for the controller to document the factual or legal reasons on which the decision is based. That information shall be made available to the supervisory authorities.

[2.117]
Article 16   Right to rectification or erasure of personal data and restriction of processing
1. Member States shall provide for the right of the data subject to obtain from the controller without undue delay the rectification of inaccurate personal data relating to him or her. Taking into account the purposes of the processing, Member States shall provide for the data subject to have the right to have incomplete personal data completed, including by means of providing a supplementary statement.
2. Member States shall require the controller to erase personal data without undue delay and provide for the right of the data subject to obtain from the controller the erasure of personal data concerning him or her without undue delay where processing infringes the provisions adopted pursuant to Article 4, 8 or 10, or where personal data must be erased in order to comply with a legal obligation to which the controller is subject.
3. Instead of erasure, the controller shall restrict processing where:
  (a)   the accuracy of the personal data is contested by the data subject and their accuracy or inaccuracy cannot be ascertained; or
  (b)   the personal data must be maintained for the purposes of evidence.
Where processing is restricted pursuant to point (a) of the first subparagraph, the controller shall inform the data subject before lifting the restriction of processing.
4. Member States shall provide for the controller to inform the data subject in writing of any refusal of rectification or erasure of personal data or restriction of processing and of the reasons for the refusal. Member States may adopt legislative measures restricting, wholly or partly, the obligation to provide such information to the extent that such a restriction constitutes a necessary and proportionate measure in a democratic society with due regard for the fundamental rights and legitimate interests of the natural person concerned in order to:
  (a)   avoid obstructing official or legal inquiries, investigations or procedures;
  (b)   avoid prejudicing the prevention, detection, investigation or prosecution of criminal offences or the execution of criminal penalties;
  (c)   protect public security;
  (d)   protect national security;
  (e)   protect the rights and freedoms of others.
Member States shall provide for the controller to inform the data subject of the possibility of lodging a complaint with a supervisory authority or seeking a judicial remedy.
5. Member States shall provide for the controller to communicate the rectification of inaccurate personal data to the competent authority from which the inaccurate personal data originate.

6. Member States shall, where personal data has been rectified or erased or processing has been restricted pursuant to paragraphs 1, 2 and 3, provide for the controller to notify the recipients and that the recipients shall rectify or erase the personal data or restrict processing of the personal data under their responsibility.

[2.118]
Article 17   Exercise of rights by the data subject and verification by the supervisory authority
1. In the cases referred to in Article 13(3), Article 15(3) and Article 16(4) Member States shall adopt measures providing that the rights of the data subject may also be exercised through the competent supervisory authority.
2. Member States shall provide for the controller to inform the data subject of the possibility of exercising his or her rights through the supervisory authority pursuant to paragraph 1.
3. Where the right referred to in paragraph 1 is exercised, the supervisory authority shall inform the data subject at least that all necessary verifications or a review by the supervisory authority have taken place. The supervisory authority shall also inform the data subject of his or her right to seek a judicial remedy.

[2.119]
Article 18   Rights of the data subject in criminal investigations and proceedings
Member States may provide for the exercise of the rights referred to in Articles 13, 14 and 16 to be carried out in accordance with Member State law where the personal data are contained in a judicial decision or record or case file processed in the course of criminal investigations and proceedings.

CHAPTER IV CONTROLLER AND PROCESSOR

SECTION 1 GENERAL OBLIGATIONS

[2.120]
Article 19   Obligations of the controller
1. Member States shall provide for the controller, taking into account the nature, scope, context and purposes of processing as well as the risks of varying likelihood and severity for the rights and freedoms of natural persons, to implement appropriate technical and organisational measures to ensure and to be able to demonstrate that processing is performed in accordance with this Directive. Those measures shall be reviewed and updated where necessary.
2. Where proportionate in relation to the processing activities, the measures referred to in paragraph 1 shall include the implementation of appropriate data protection policies by the controller.

[2.121]
Article 20   Data protection by design and by default
1. Member States shall provide for the controller, taking into account the state of the art, the cost of implementation and the nature, scope, context and purposes of processing, as well as the risks of varying likelihood and severity for rights and freedoms of natural persons posed by the processing, both at the time of the determination of the means for processing and at the time of the processing itself, to implement appropriate technical and organisational measures, such as pseudonymisation, which are designed to implement data protection principles, such as data minimisation, in an effective manner and to integrate the necessary safeguards into the processing, in order to meet the requirements of this Directive and protect the rights of data subjects.
2. Member States shall provide for the controller to implement appropriate technical and organisational measures ensuring that, by default, only personal data which are necessary for each specific purpose of the processing are processed. That obligation applies to the amount of personal data collected, the extent of their processing, the period of their storage and their accessibility. In particular, such measures shall ensure that by default personal data are not made accessible without the individual's intervention to an indefinite number of natural persons.

[2.122]
Article 21   Joint controllers
1. Member States shall, where two or more controllers jointly determine the purposes and means of processing, provide for them to be joint controllers. They shall, in a transparent manner, determine their respective responsibilities for compliance with this Directive, in particular as regards the exercise of the rights of the data subject and their respective duties to provide the information referred to in Article 13, by means of an arrangement between them unless, and in so far as, the respective responsibilities of the controllers are determined by Union or Member State law to which the controllers are subject. The arrangement shall designate the contact point for data subjects. Member States may designate which of the joint controllers can act as a single contact point for data subjects to exercise their rights.
2. Irrespective of the terms of the arrangement referred to in paragraph 1, Member States may provide for the data subject to exercise his or her rights under the provisions adopted pursuant to this Directive in respect of and against each of the controllers.

[2.123]
Article 22   Processor
1. Member States shall, where processing is to be carried out on behalf of a controller, provide for the controller to use only processors providing sufficient guarantees to implement appropriate technical and organisational measures in such a manner that the processing will meet the requirements of this Directive and ensure the protection of the rights of the data subject.
2. Member States shall provide for the processor not to engage another processor without prior specific or general written authorisation by the controller. In the case of general written authorisation, the processor shall inform the controller of any intended changes concerning the addition or replacement of other processors, thereby giving the controller the opportunity to object to such changes.

3. Member States shall provide for the processing by a processor to be governed by a contract or other legal act under Union or Member State law, that is binding on the processor with regard to the controller and that sets out the subject-matter and duration of the processing, the nature and purpose of the processing, the type of personal data and categories of data subjects and the obligations and rights of the controller. That contract or other legal act shall stipulate, in particular, that the processor:
(a) acts only on instructions from the controller;
(b) ensures that persons authorised to process the personal data have committed themselves to confidentiality or are under an appropriate statutory obligation of confidentiality;
(c) assists the controller by any appropriate means to ensure compliance with the provisions on the data subject's rights;
(d) at the choice of the controller, deletes or returns all the personal data to the controller after the end of the provision of data processing services, and deletes existing copies unless Union or Member State law requires storage of the personal data;
(e) makes available to the controller all information necessary to demonstrate compliance with this Article;
(f) complies with the conditions referred to in paragraphs 2 and 3 for engaging another processor.
4. The contract or the other legal act referred to in paragraph 3 shall be in writing, including in an electronic form.
5. If a processor determines, in infringement of this Directive, the purposes and means of processing, that processor shall be considered to be a controller in respect of that processing.

[2.124]
Article 23   Processing under the authority of the controller or processor
Member States shall provide for the processor and any person acting under the authority of the controller or of the processor, who has access to personal data, not to process those data except on instructions from the controller, unless required to do so by Union or Member State law.

[2.125]
Article 24   Records of processing activities
1. Member States shall provide for controllers to maintain a record of all categories of processing activities under their responsibility. That record shall contain all of the following information:
(a) the name and contact details of the controller and, where applicable, the joint controller and the data protection officer;
(b) the purposes of the processing;
(c) the categories of recipients to whom the personal data have been or will be disclosed including recipients in third countries or international organisations;
(d) a description of the categories of data subject and of the categories of personal data;
(e) where applicable, the use of profiling;
(f) where applicable, the categories of transfers of personal data to a third country or an international organisation;
(g) an indication of the legal basis for the processing operation, including transfers, for which the personal data are intended;
(h) where possible, the envisaged time limits for erasure of the different categories of personal data;
(i) where possible, a general description of the technical and organisational security measures referred to in Article 29(1).
2. Member States shall provide for each processor to maintain a record of all categories of processing activities carried out on behalf of a controller, containing:
(a) the name and contact details of the processor or processors, of each controller on behalf of which the processor is acting and, where applicable, the data protection officer;
(b) the categories of processing carried out on behalf of each controller;
(c) where applicable, transfers of personal data to a third country or an international organisation where explicitly instructed to do so by the controller, including the identification of that third country or international organisation;
(d) where possible, a general description of the technical and organisational security measures referred to in Article 29(1).
3. The records referred to in paragraphs 1 and 2 shall be in writing, including in electronic form.
The controller and the processor shall make those records available to the supervisory authority on request.

[2.126]
Article 25   Logging
1. Member States shall provide for logs to be kept for at least the following processing operations in automated processing systems: collection, alteration, consultation, disclosure including transfers, combination and erasure. The logs of consultation and disclosure shall make it possible to establish the justification, date and time of such operations and, as far as possible, the identification of the person who consulted or disclosed personal data, and the identity of the recipients of such personal data.
2. The logs shall be used solely for verification of the lawfulness of processing, self-monitoring, ensuring the integrity and security of the personal data, and for criminal proceedings.
3. The controller and the processor shall make the logs available to the supervisory authority on request.

[2.127]
Article 26   Cooperation with the supervisory authority
Member States shall provide for the controller and the processor to cooperate, on request, with the supervisory authority in the performance of its tasks on request.

[2.128]
Article 27   Data protection impact assessment
1. Where a type of processing, in particular, using new technologies, and taking into account the nature, scope, context and purposes of the processing is likely to result in a high risk to the rights and freedoms of natural persons, Member States shall provide for the controller to carry out, prior to the processing, an assessment of the impact of the envisaged processing operations on the protection of personal data.
2. The assessment referred to in paragraph 1 shall contain at least a general description of the envisaged processing operations, an assessment of the risks to the rights and freedoms of data subjects, the measures envisaged to address those risks, safeguards, security measures and mechanisms to ensure the protection of personal data and to demonstrate compliance with this Directive, taking into account the rights and legitimate interests of the data subjects and other persons concerned.

[2.129]
Article 28   Prior consultation of the supervisory authority
1. Member States shall provide for the controller or processor to consult the supervisory authority prior to processing which will form part of a new filing system to be created, where:
   (a) a data protection impact assessment as provided for in Article 27 indicates that the processing would result in a high risk in the absence of measures taken by the controller to mitigate the risk; or
   (b) the type of processing, in particular, where using new technologies, mechanisms or procedures, involves a high risk to the rights and freedoms of data subjects.
2. Member States shall provide for the supervisory authority to be consulted during the preparation of a proposal for a legislative measure to be adopted by a national parliament or of a regulatory measure based on such a legislative measure, which relates to processing.
3. Member States shall provide that the supervisory authority may establish a list of the processing operations which are subject to prior consultation pursuant to paragraph 1.
4. Member States shall provide for the controller to provide the supervisory authority with the data protection impact assessment pursuant to Article 27 and, on request, with any other information to allow the supervisory authority to make an assessment of the compliance of the processing and in particular of the risks for the protection of personal data of the data subject and of the related safeguards.
5. Member States shall, where the supervisory authority is of the opinion that the intended processing referred to in paragraph 1 of this Article would infringe the provisions adopted pursuant to this Directive, in particular where the controller has insufficiently identified or mitigated the risk, provide for the supervisory authority to provide, within a period of up to six weeks of receipt of the request for consultation, written advice to the controller and, where applicable, to the processor, and may use any of its powers referred to in Article 47. That period may be extended by a month, taking into account the complexity of the intended processing. The supervisory authority shall inform the controller and, where applicable, the processor of any such extension within one month of receipt of the request for consultation, together with the reasons for the delay.

SECTION 2 SECURITY OF PERSONAL DATA

[2.130]
Article 29   Security of processing
1. Member States shall provide for the controller and the processor, taking into account the state of the art, the costs of implementation and the nature, scope, context and purposes of the processing as well as the risk of varying likelihood and severity for the rights and freedoms of natural persons, to implement appropriate technical and organisational measures to ensure a level of security appropriate to the risk, in particular as regards the processing of special categories of personal data referred to in Article 10.
2. In respect of automated processing, each Member State shall provide for the controller or processor, following an evaluation of the risks, to implement measures designed to:
   (a) deny unauthorised persons access to processing equipment used for processing ('equipment access control');
   (b) prevent the unauthorised reading, copying, modification or removal of data media ('data media control');
   (c) prevent the unauthorised input of personal data and the unauthorised inspection, modification or deletion of stored personal data ('storage control');
   (d) prevent the use of automated processing systems by unauthorised persons using data communication equipment ('user control');
   (e) ensure that persons authorised to use an automated processing system have access only to the personal data covered by their access authorisation ('data access control');
   (f) ensure that it is possible to verify and establish the bodies to which personal data have been or may be transmitted or made available using data communication equipment ('communication control');
   (g) ensure that it is subsequently possible to verify and establish which personal data have been input into automated processing systems and when and by whom the personal data were input ('input control');
   (h) prevent the unauthorised reading, copying, modification or deletion of personal data during transfers of personal data or during transportation of data media ('transport control');
   (i) ensure that installed systems may, in the case of interruption, be restored ('recovery');
   (j) ensure that the functions of the system perform, that the appearance of faults in the functions is reported ('reliability') and that stored personal data cannot be corrupted by means of a malfunctioning of the system ('integrity').

Part 2   Data Protection: EU Law etc

[2.131]
Article 30   Notification of a personal data breach to the supervisory authority
1. Member States shall, in the case of a personal data breach, provide for the controller to notify without undue delay and, where feasible, not later than 72 hours after having become aware of it, the personal data breach to the supervisory authority, unless the personal data breach is unlikely to result in a risk to the rights and freedoms of natural persons. Where the notification to the supervisory authority is not made within 72 hours, it shall be accompanied by reasons for the delay.
2. The processor shall notify the controller without undue delay after becoming aware of a personal data breach.
3. The notification referred to in paragraph 1 shall at least:
(a) describe the nature of the personal data breach including, where possible, the categories and approximate number of data subjects concerned and the categories and approximate number of personal data records concerned;
(b) communicate the name and contact details of the data protection officer or other contact point where more information can be obtained;
(c) describe the likely consequences of the personal data breach;
(d) describe the measures taken or proposed to be taken by the controller to address the personal data breach, including, where appropriate, measures to mitigate its possible adverse effects.
4. Where, and in so far as, it is not possible to provide the information at the same time, the information may be provided in phases without undue further delay.
5. Member States shall provide for the controller to document any personal data breaches referred to in paragraph 1, comprising the facts relating to the personal data breach, its effects and the remedial action taken. That documentation shall enable the supervisory authority to verify compliance with this Article.
6. Member States shall, where the personal data breach involves personal data that have been transmitted by or to the controller of another Member State, provide for the information referred to in paragraph 3 to be communicated to the controller of that Member State without undue delay.

[2.132]
Article 31   Communication of a personal data breach to the data subject
1. Member States shall, where the personal data breach is likely to result in a high risk to the rights and freedoms of natural persons, provide for the controller to communicate the personal data breach to the data subject without undue delay.
2. The communication to the data subject referred to in paragraph 1 of this Article shall describe in clear and plain language the nature of the personal data breach and shall contain at least the information and measures referred to in points (b), (c) and (d) of Article 30(3).
3. The communication to the data subject referred to in paragraph 1 shall not be required if any of the following conditions are met:
(a) the controller has implemented appropriate technological and organisational protection measures, and those measures were applied to the personal data affected by the personal data breach, in particular those that render the personal data unintelligible to any person who is not authorised to access it, such as encryption;
(b) the controller has taken subsequent measures which ensure that the high risk to the rights and freedoms of data subjects referred to in paragraph 1 is no longer likely to materialise;
(c) it would involve a disproportionate effort. In such a case, there shall instead be a public communication or a similar measure whereby the data subjects are informed in an equally effective manner.
4. If the controller has not already communicated the personal data breach to the data subject, the supervisory authority, having considered the likelihood of the personal data breach resulting in a high risk, may require it to do so, or may decide that any of the conditions referred to in paragraph 3 are met.
5. The communication to the data subject referred to in paragraph 1 of this Article may be delayed, restricted or omitted subject to the conditions and on the grounds referred to in Article 13(3).

SECTION 3 DATA PROTECTION OFFICER

[2.133]
Article 32   Designation of the data protection officer
1. Member States shall provide for the controller to designate a data protection officer. Member States may exempt courts and other independent judicial authorities when acting in their judicial capacity from that obligation.
2. The data protection officer shall be designated on the basis of his or her professional qualities and, in particular, his or her expert knowledge of data protection law and practice and ability to fulfil the tasks referred to in Article 34.
3. A single data protection officer may be designated for several competent authorities, taking account of their organisational structure and size.
4. Member States shall provide for the controller to publish the contact details of the data protection officer and communicate them to the supervisory authority.

[2.134]
Article 33   Position of the data protection officer
1. Member States shall provide for the controller to ensure that the data protection officer is involved, properly and in a timely manner, in all issues which relate to the protection of personal data.
2. The controller shall support the data protection officer in performing the tasks referred to in Article 34 by providing resources necessary to carry out those tasks and access to personal data and processing operations, and to maintain his or her expert knowledge.

[2.135]
Article 34   Tasks of the data protection officer
Member States shall provide for the controller to entrust the data protection officer at least with the following tasks:

(a) to inform and advise the controller and the employees who carry out processing of their obligations pursuant to this Directive and to other Union or Member State data protection provisions;
(b) to monitor compliance with this Directive, with other Union or Member State data protection provisions and with the policies of the controller in relation to the protection of personal data, including the assignment of responsibilities, awareness-raising and training of staff involved in processing operations, and the related audits;
(c) to provide advice where requested as regards the data protection impact assessment and monitor its performance pursuant to Article 27;
(d) to cooperate with the supervisory authority;
(e) to act as the contact point for the supervisory authority on issues relating to processing, including the prior consultation referred to in Article 28, and to consult, where appropriate, with regard to any other matter.

CHAPTER V TRANSFERS OF PERSONAL DATA TO THIRD COUNTRIES OR INTERNATIONAL ORGANISATIONS

[2.136]
Article 35 General principles for transfers of personal data
1. Member States shall provide for any transfer by competent authorities of personal data which are undergoing processing or are intended for processing after transfer to a third country or to an international organisation including for onward transfers to another third country or international organisation to take place, subject to compliance with the national provisions adopted pursuant to other provisions of this Directive, only where the conditions laid down in this Chapter are met, namely:
(a) the transfer is necessary for the purposes set out in Article 1(1);
(b) the personal data are transferred to a controller in a third country or international organisation that is an authority competent for the purposes referred to in Article 1(1);
(c) where personal data are transmitted or made available from another Member State, that Member State has given its prior authorisation to the transfer in accordance with its national law;
(d) the Commission has adopted an adequacy decision pursuant to Article 36, or, in the absence of such a decision, appropriate safeguards have been provided or exist pursuant to Article 37, or, in the absence of an adequacy decision pursuant to Article 36 and of appropriate safeguards in accordance with Article 37, derogations for specific situations apply pursuant to Article 38; and
(e) in the case of an onward transfer to another third country or international organisation, the competent authority that carried out the original transfer or another competent authority of the same Member State authorises the onward transfer, after taking into due account all relevant factors, including the seriousness of the criminal offence, the purpose for which the personal data was originally transferred and the level of personal data protection in the third country or an international organisation to which personal data are onward transferred.
2. Member States shall provide for transfers without the prior authorisation by another Member State in accordance with point (c) of paragraph 1 to be permitted only if the transfer of the personal data is necessary for the prevention of an immediate and serious threat to public security of a Member State or a third country or to essential interests of a Member State and the prior authorisation cannot be obtained in good time. The authority responsible for giving prior authorisation shall be informed without delay.
3. All provisions in this Chapter shall be applied in order to ensure that the level of protection of natural persons ensured by this Directive is not undermined.

[2.137]
Article 36 Transfers on the basis of an adequacy decision
1. Member States shall provide that a transfer of personal data to a third country or an international organisation may take place where the Commission has decided that the third country, a territory or one or more specified sectors within that third country, or the international organisation in question ensures an adequate level of protection. Such a transfer shall not require any specific authorisation.
2. When assessing the adequacy of the level of protection, the Commission shall, in particular, take account of the following elements:
(a) the rule of law, respect for human rights and fundamental freedoms, relevant legislation, both general and sectoral, including concerning public security, defence, national security and criminal law and the access of public authorities to personal data, as well as the implementation of such legislation, data protection rules, professional rules and security measures, including rules for the onward transfer of personal data to another third country or international organisation, which are complied with in that country or international organisation, case-law, as well as effective and enforceable data subject rights and effective administrative and judicial redress for the data subjects whose personal data are transferred;
(b) the existence and effective functioning of one or more independent supervisory authorities in the third country or to which an international organisation is subject, with responsibility for ensuring and enforcing compliance with data protection rules, including adequate enforcement powers, for assisting and advising data subjects in exercising their rights and for cooperation with the supervisory authorities of the Member States; and
(c) the international commitments the third country or international organisation concerned has entered into, or other obligations arising from legally binding conventions or instruments as well as from its participation in multilateral or regional systems, in particular in relation to the protection of personal data.
3. The Commission, after assessing the adequacy of the level of protection, may decide, by means of implementing act, that a third country, a territory or one or more specified sectors within a third country, or an international organisation ensures an adequate level of protection within the meaning of paragraph 2 of this Article. The implementing act shall provide a mechanism for periodic review, at least every four years, which shall take into

account all relevant developments in the third country or international organisation. The implementing act shall specify its territorial and sectoral application and, where applicable, identify the supervisory authority or authorities referred to in point (b) of paragraph 2 of this Article. The implementing act shall be adopted in accordance with the examination procedure referred to in Article 58(2).

4. The Commission shall, on an ongoing basis, monitor developments in third countries and international organisations that could affect the functioning of decisions adopted pursuant to paragraph 3.

5. The Commission shall, where available information reveals, in particular following the review referred to in paragraph 3 of this Article, that a third country, a territory or one or more specified sectors within a third country, or an international organisation no longer ensures an adequate level of protection within the meaning of paragraph 2 of this Article, to the extent necessary, repeal, amend or suspend the decision referred to in paragraph 3 of this Article by means of implementing acts without retro-active effect. Those implementing acts shall be adopted in accordance with the examination procedure referred to in Article 58(2).

On duly justified imperative grounds of urgency, the Commission shall adopt immediately applicable implementing acts in accordance with the procedure referred to in Article 58(3).

6. The Commission shall enter into consultations with the third country or international organisation with a view to remedying the situation giving rise to the decision made pursuant to paragraph 5.

7. Member States shall provide for a decision pursuant to paragraph 5 to be without prejudice to transfers of personal data to the third country, the territory or one or more specified sectors within that third country, or the inter national organisation in question pursuant to Articles 37 and 38.

8. The Commission shall publish in the *Official Journal of the European Union* and on its website a list of the third countries, territories and specified sectors within a third country and international organisations for which it has decided that an adequate level of protection is or is no longer ensured.

[2.138]
Article 37   Transfers subject to appropriate safeguards
1. In the absence of a decision pursuant to Article 36(3), Member States shall provide that a transfer of personal data to a third country or an international organisation may take place where:
   (a) appropriate safeguards with regard to the protection of personal data are provided for in a legally binding instrument; or
   (b) the controller has assessed all the circumstances surrounding the transfer of personal data and concludes that appropriate safeguards exist with regard to the protection of personal data.
2. The controller shall inform the supervisory authority about categories of transfers under point (b) of paragraph 1.
3. When a transfer is based on point (b) of paragraph 1, such a transfer shall be documented and the documentation shall be made available to the supervisory authority on request, including the date and time of the transfer, information about the receiving competent authority, the justification for the transfer and the personal data transferred.

[2.139]
Article 38   Derogations for specific situations
1. In the absence of an adequacy decision pursuant to Article 36, or of appropriate safeguards pursuant to Article 37, Member States shall provide that a transfer or a category of transfers of personal data to a third country or an international organisation may take place only on the condition that the transfer is necessary:
   (a) in order to protect the vital interests of the data subject or another person;
   (b) to safeguard legitimate interests of the data subject, where the law of the Member State transferring the personal data so provides;
   (c) for the prevention of an immediate and serious threat to public security of a Member State or a third country;
   (d) in individual cases for the purposes set out in Article 1(1); or
   (e) in an individual case for the establishment, exercise or defence of legal claims relating to the purposes set out in Article 1(1).
2. Personal data shall not be transferred if the transferring competent authority determines that fundamental rights and freedoms of the data subject concerned override the public interest in the transfer set out in points (d) and (e) of paragraph 1.
3. Where a transfer is based on paragraph 1, such a transfer shall be documented and the documentation shall be made available to the supervisory authority on request, including the date and time of the transfer, information about the receiving competent authority, the justification for the transfer and the personal data transferred.

[2.140]
Article 39   Transfers of personal data to recipients established in third countries
1. By way of derogation from point (b) of Article 35(1) and without prejudice to any international agreement referred to in paragraph 2 of this Article, Union or Member State law may provide for the competent authorities referred to in point (7)(a) of Article 3, in individual and specific cases, to transfer personal data directly to recipients established in third countries only if the other provisions of this Directive are complied with and all of the following conditions are fulfilled:
   (a) the transfer is strictly necessary for the performance of a task of the transferring competent authority as provided for by Union or Member State law for the purposes set out in Article 1(1);
   (b) the transferring competent authority determines that no fundamental rights and freedoms of the data subject concerned override the public interest necessitating the transfer in the case at hand;
   (c) the transferring competent authority considers that the transfer to an authority that is competent for the purposes referred to in Article 1(1) in the third country is ineffective or inappropriate, in particular because the transfer cannot be achieved in good time;
   (d) the authority that is competent for the purposes referred to in Article 1(1) in the third country is informed without undue delay, unless this is ineffective or inappropriate;
   (e) the transferring competent authority informs the recipient of the specified purpose or purposes for which the personal data are only to be processed by the latter provided that such processing is necessary.

2. An international agreement referred to in paragraph 1 shall be any bilateral or multilateral international agreement in force between Member States and third countries in the field of judicial cooperation in criminal matters and police cooperation.

3. The transferring competent authority shall inform the supervisory authority about transfers under this Article.

4. Where a transfer is based on paragraph 1, such a transfer shall be documented.

[2.141]
Article 40   International cooperation for the protection of personal data
In relation to third countries and international organisations, the Commission and Member States shall take appropriate steps to:
- (a) develop international cooperation mechanisms to facilitate the effective enforcement of legislation for the protection of personal data;
- (b) provide international mutual assistance in the enforcement of legislation for the protection of personal data, including through notification, complaint referral, investigative assistance and information exchange, subject to appropriate safeguards for the protection of personal data and other fundamental rights and freedoms;
- (c) engage relevant stakeholders in discussion and activities aimed at furthering international cooperation in the enforcement of legislation for the protection of personal data;
- (d) promote the exchange and documentation of personal data protection legislation and practice, including on jurisdictional conflicts with third countries.

CHAPTER VI INDEPENDENT SUPERVISORY AUTHORITIES

SECTION 1 INDEPENDENT STATUS

[2.142]
Article 41   Supervisory authority
1. Each Member State shall provide for one or more independent public authorities to be responsible for monitoring the application of this Directive, in order to protect the fundamental rights and freedoms of natural persons in relation to processing and to facilitate the free flow of personal data within the Union ('supervisory authority').

2. Each supervisory authority shall contribute to the consistent application of this Directive throughout the Union. For that purpose, the supervisory authorities shall cooperate with each other and with the Commission in accordance with Chapter VII.

3. Member States may provide for a supervisory authority established under Regulation (EU) 2016/679 to be the supervisory authority referred to in this Directive and to assume responsibility for the tasks of the supervisory authority to be established under paragraph 1 of this Article.

4. Where more than one supervisory authority is established in a Member State, that Member State shall designate the supervisory authority which are to represent those authorities in the Board referred to in Article 51.

[2.143]
Article 42   Independence
1. Each Member State shall provide for each supervisory authority to act with complete independence in performing its tasks and exercising its powers in accordance with this Directive.

2. Member States shall provide for the member or members of their supervisory authorities in the performance of their tasks and exercise of their powers in accordance with this Directive, to remain free from external influence, whether direct or indirect, and that they shall neither seek nor take instructions from anybody.

3. Members of Member States' supervisory authorities shall refrain from any action incompatible with their duties and shall not, during their term of office, engage in any incompatible occupation, whether gainful or not.

4. Each Member State shall ensure that each supervisory authority is provided with the human, technical and financial resources, premises and infrastructure necessary for the effective performance of its tasks and exercise of its powers, including those to be carried out in the context of mutual assistance, cooperation and participation in the Board.

5. Each Member State shall ensure that each supervisory authority chooses and has its own staff which shall be subject to the exclusive direction of the member or members of the supervisory authority concerned.

6. Each Member State shall ensure that each supervisory authority is subject to financial control which does not affect its independence and that it has separate, public annual budgets, which may be part of the overall state or national budget.

[2.144]
Article 43   General conditions for the members of the supervisory authority
1. Member States shall provide for each member of their supervisory authorities to be appointed by means of a transparent procedure by:
- – their parliament;
- – their government;
- – their head of State; or
- – an independent body entrusted with the appointment under Member State law.

2. Each member shall have the qualifications, experience and skills, in particular in the area of the protection of personal data, required to perform their duties and exercise their powers.

3. The duties of a member shall end in the event of the expiry of the term of office, resignation or compulsory retirement, in accordance with the law of the Member State concerned.

4. A member shall be dismissed only in cases of serious misconduct or if the member no longer fulfils the conditions required for the performance of the duties.

[2.145]
Article 44   Rules on the establishment of the supervisory authority
1. Each Member State shall provide by law for all of the following:

(a) the establishment of each supervisory authority;
(b) the qualifications and eligibility conditions required to be appointed as a member of each supervisory authority;
(c) the rules and procedures for the appointment of the member or members of each supervisory authority;
(d) the duration of the term of the member or members of each supervisory authority of not less than four years, except for the first appointment after 6 May 2016, part of which may take place for a shorter period where that is necessary to protect the independence of the supervisory authority by means of a staggered appointment procedure;
(e) whether and, if so, for how many terms the member or members of each supervisory authority is eligible for reappointment;
(f) the conditions governing the obligations of the member or members and staff of each supervisory authority, prohibitions on actions, occupations and benefits incompatible therewith during and after the term of office and rules governing the cessation of employment.

2. The member or members and the staff of each supervisory authority shall, in accordance with Union or Member State law, be subject to a duty of professional secrecy both during and after their term of office, with regard to any confidential information which has come to their knowledge in the course of the performance of their tasks or the exercise of their powers. During their term of office, that duty of professional secrecy shall in particular apply to reporting by natural persons of infringements of this Directive.

SECTION 2 COMPETENCE, TASKS AND POWERS

[2.146]
Article 45   Competence
1. Each Member State shall provide for each supervisory authority to be competent for the performance of the tasks assigned to, and for the exercise of the powers conferred on, it in accordance with this Directive on the territory of its own Member State.
2. Each Member State shall provide for each supervisory authority not to be competent for the supervision of processing operations of courts when acting in their judicial capacity. Member States may provide for their supervisory authority not to be competent to supervise processing operations of other independent judicial authorities when acting in their judicial capacity.

[2.147]
Article 46   Tasks
1. Each Member State shall provide, on its territory, for each supervisory authority to:
(a) monitor and enforce the application of the provisions adopted pursuant to this Directive and its implementing measures;
(b) promote public awareness and understanding of the risks, rules, safeguards and rights in relation to processing;
(c) advise, in accordance with Member State law, the national parliament, the government and other institutions and bodies on legislative and administrative measures relating to the protection of natural persons' rights and freedoms with regard to processing;
(d) promote the awareness of controllers and processors of their obligations under this Directive;
(e) upon request, provide information to any data subject concerning the exercise of their rights under this Directive and, if appropriate, cooperate with the supervisory authorities in other Member States to that end;
(f) deal with complaints lodged by a data subject, or by a body, organisation or association in accordance with Article 55, and investigate, to the extent appropriate, the subject-matter of the complaint and inform the complainant of the progress and the outcome of the investigation within a reasonable period, in particular if further investigation or coordination with another supervisory authority is necessary;
(g) check the lawfulness of processing pursuant to Article 17, and inform the data subject within a reasonable period of the outcome of the check pursuant to paragraph 3 of that Article or of the reasons why the check has not been carried out;
(h) cooperate with, including by sharing information, and provide mutual assistance to other supervisory authorities, with a view to ensuring the consistency of application and enforcement of this Directive;
(i) conduct investigations on the application of this Directive, including on the basis of information received from another supervisory authority or other public authority;
(j) monitor relevant developments insofar as they have an impact on the protection of personal data, in particular the development of information and communication technologies;
(k) provide advice on the processing operations referred to in Article 28; and
(l) contribute to the activities of the Board.

2. Each supervisory authority shall facilitate the submission of complaints referred to in point (f) of paragraph 1 by measures such as providing a complaint submission form which can also be completed electronically, without excluding other means of communication.
3. The performance of the tasks of each supervisory authority shall be free of charge for the data subject and for the data protection officer.
4. Where a request is manifestly unfounded or excessive, in particular because it is repetitive, the supervisory authority may charge a reasonable fee based on its administrative costs, or may refuse to act on the request. The supervisory authority shall bear the burden of demonstrating that the request is manifestly unfounded or excessive.

[2.148]
Article 47   Powers
1. Each Member State shall provide by law for each supervisory authority to have effective investigative powers. Those powers shall include at least the power to obtain from the controller and the processor access to all personal data that are being processed and to all information necessary for the performance of its tasks.

2. Each Member State shall provide by law for each supervisory authority to have effective corrective powers such as, for example:
  (a) to issue warnings to a controller or processor that intended processing operations are likely to infringe the provisions adopted pursuant to this Directive;
  (b) to order the controller or processor to bring processing operations into compliance with the provisions adopted pursuant to this Directive, where appropriate, in a specified manner and within a specified period, in particular by ordering the rectification or erasure of personal data or restriction of processing pursuant to Article 16;
  (c) to impose a temporary or definitive limitation, including a ban, on processing.
3. Each Member State shall provide by law for each supervisory authority to have effective advisory powers to advise the controller in accordance with the prior consultation procedure referred to in Article 28 and to issue, on its own initiative or on request, opinions to its national parliament and its government or, in accordance with its national law, to other institutions and bodies as well as to the public on any issue related to the protection of personal data.
4. The exercise of the powers conferred on the supervisory authority pursuant to this Article shall be subject to appropriate safeguards, including effective judicial remedy and due process, as set out in Union and Member State law in accordance with the Charter.
5. Each Member State shall provide by law for each supervisory authority to have the power to bring infringements of provisions adopted pursuant to this Directive to the attention of judicial authorities and, where appropriate, to commence or otherwise engage in legal proceedings, in order to enforce the provisions adopted pursuant to this Directive.

[2.149]
Article 48   Reporting of infringements
Member States shall provide for competent authorities to put in place effective mechanisms to encourage confidential reporting of infringements of this Directive.

[2.150]
Article 49   Activity reports
Each supervisory authority shall draw up an annual report on its activities, which may include a list of types of infringement notified and types of penalties imposed. Those reports shall be transmitted to the national parliament, the government and other authorities as designated by Member State law. They shall be made available to the public, the Commission and the Board.

CHAPTER VII COOPERATION

[2.151]
Article 50   Mutual assistance
1. Each Member State shall provide for their supervisory authorities to provide each other with relevant information and mutual assistance in order to implement and apply this Directive in a consistent manner, and to put in place measures for effective cooperation with one another. Mutual assistance shall cover, in particular, information requests and supervisory measures, such as requests to carry out consultations, inspections and investigations.
2. Each Member States shall provide for each supervisory authority to take all appropriate measures required to reply to a request of another supervisory authority without undue delay and no later than one month after receiving the request. Such measures may include, in particular, the transmission of relevant information on the conduct of an investigation.
3. Requests for assistance shall contain all the necessary information, including the purpose of and reasons for the request. Information exchanged shall be used only for the purpose for which it was requested.
4. The requested supervisory authority shall not refuse to comply with the request unless:
  (a) it is not competent for the subject-matter of the request or for the measures it is requested to execute; or
  (b) compliance with the request would infringe this Directive or Union or Member State law to which the supervisory authority receiving the request is subject.
5. The requested supervisory authority shall inform the requesting supervisory authority of the results or, as the case may be, of the progress of the measures taken in order to respond to the request. The requested supervisory authority shall provide reasons for any refusal to comply with a request pursuant to paragraph 4.
6. Requested supervisory authorities shall, as a rule, supply the information requested by other supervisory authorities by electronic means, using a standardised format.
7. Requested supervisory authorities shall not charge a fee for any action taken by them pursuant to a request for mutual assistance. Supervisory authorities may agree on rules to indemnify each other for specific expenditure arising from the provision of mutual assistance in exceptional circumstances.
8. The Commission may, by means of implementing acts, specify the format and procedures for mutual assistance referred to in this Article and the arrangements for the exchange of information by electronic means between supervisory authorities, and between supervisory authorities and the Board. Those implementing acts shall be adopted in accordance with the examination procedure referred to in Article 58(2).

[2.152]
Article 51   Tasks of the Board
1. The Board established by Regulation (EU) 2016/679 shall perform all of the following tasks in relation to processing within the scope of this Directive:
  (a) advise the Commission on any issue related to the protection of personal data in the Union, including on any proposed amendment of this Directive;
  (b) examine, on its own initiative, on request of one of its members or on request of the Commission, any question covering the application of this Directive and issue guidelines, recommendations and best practices in order to encourage consistent application of this Directive;
  (c) draw up guidelines for supervisory authorities concerning the application of measures referred to in Article 47(1) and (3);

(d) issue guidelines, recommendations and best practices in accordance with point (b) of this subparagraph for establishing personal data breaches and determining the undue delay referred to in Article 30(1) and (2) and for the particular circumstances in which a controller or a processor is required to notify the personal data breach;

(e) issue guidelines, recommendations and best practices in accordance with point (b) of this subparagraph as to the circumstances in which a personal data breach is likely to result in a high risk to the rights and freedoms of natural persons as referred to in Article 31(1);

(f) review the practical application of the guidelines, recommendations and best practices;

(g) provide the Commission with an opinion for the assessment of the adequacy of the level of protection in a third country, a territory or one or more specified sectors within a third country, or an international organisation, including for the assessment whether such a third country, territory, specified sector, or international organisation no longer ensures an adequate level of protection;

(h) promote the cooperation and the effective bilateral and multilateral exchange of information and best practices between the supervisory authorities;

(i) promote common training programmes and facilitate personnel exchanges between the supervisory authorities and, where appropriate, with the supervisory authorities of third countries or with international organisations;

(j) promote the exchange of knowledge and documentation on data protection law and practice with data protection supervisory authorities worldwide.

With regard to point (g) of the first subparagraph, the Commission shall provide the Board with all necessary documentation, including correspondence with the government of the third country, with the territory or specified sector within that third country, or with the international organisation.

2. Where the Commission requests advice from the Board, it may indicate a time limit, taking into account the urgency of the matter.

3. The Board shall forward its opinions, guidelines, recommendations and best practices to the Commission and to the committee referred to in Article 58(1) and make them public.

4. The Commission shall inform the Board of the action it has taken following opinions, guidelines, recommendations and best practices issued by the Board.

CHAPTER VIII REMEDIES, LIABILITY AND PENALTIES

[2.153]
Article 52 Right to lodge a complaint with a supervisory authority
1. Without prejudice to any other administrative or judicial remedy, Member States shall provide for every data subject to have the right to lodge a complaint with a single supervisory authority, if the data subject considers that the processing of personal data relating to him or her infringes provisions adopted pursuant to this Directive.

2. Member States shall provide for the supervisory authority with which the complaint has been lodged to transmit it to the competent supervisory authority, without undue delay if the complaint is not lodged with the supervisory authority that is competent pursuant to Article 45(1). The data subject shall be informed about the transmission.

3. Member States shall provide for the supervisory authority with which the complaint has been lodged to provide further assistance on request of the data subject.

4. The data subject shall be informed by the competent supervisory authority of the progress and the outcome of the complaint, including of the possibility of a judicial remedy pursuant to Article 53.

[2.154]
Article 53 Right to an effective judicial remedy against a supervisory authority
1. Without prejudice to any other administrative or non-judicial remedy, Member States shall provide for the right of a natural or legal person to an effective judicial remedy against a legally binding decision of a supervisory authority concerning them.

2. Without prejudice to any other administrative or non-judicial remedy, each data subject shall have the right to an effective judicial remedy where the supervisory authority which is competent pursuant to Article 45(1) does not handle a complaint or does not inform the data subject within three months of the progress or outcome of the complaint lodged pursuant to Article 52.

3. Member States shall provide for proceedings against a supervisory authority to be brought before the courts of the Member State where the supervisory authority is established.

[2.155]
Article 54 Right to an effective judicial remedy against a controller or processor
Without prejudice to any available administrative or non-judicial remedy, including the right to lodge a complaint with a supervisory authority pursuant to Article 52, Member States shall provide for the right of a data subject to an effective judicial remedy where he or she considers that his or her rights laid down in provisions adopted pursuant to this Directive have been infringed as a result of the processing of his or her personal data in non-compliance with those provisions.

[2.156]
Article 55 Representation of data subjects
Member States shall, in accordance with Member State procedural law, provide for the data subject to have the right to mandate a not-for-profit body, organisation or association which has been properly constituted in accordance with Member State law, has statutory objectives which are in the public interest and is active in the field of protection of data subject's rights and freedoms with regard to the protection of their personal data to lodge the complaint on his or her behalf and to exercise the rights referred to in Articles 52, 53 and 54 on his or her behalf.

[2.157]
Article 56   Right to compensation
Member States shall provide for any person who has suffered material or non-material damage as a result of an unlawful processing operation or of any act infringing national provisions adopted pursuant to this Directive to have the right to receive compensation for the damage suffered from the controller or any other authority competent under Member State law.

[2.158]
Article 57   Penalties
Member States shall lay down the rules on penalties applicable to infringements of the provisions adopted pursuant to this Directive and shall take all measures necessary to ensure that they are implemented. The penalties provided for shall be effective, proportionate and dissuasive.

CHAPTER IX IMPLEMENTING ACTS

[2.159]
Article 58   Committee procedure
1. The Commission shall be assisted by the committee established by Article 93 of Regulation (EU) 2016/679. That committee shall be a committee within the meaning of Regulation (EU) No 182/2011.
   2.   Where reference is made to this paragraph, Article 5 of Regulation (EU) No 182/2011 shall apply.
   3.   Where reference is made to this paragraph, Article 8 of Regulation (EU) No 182/2011, in conjunction with Article 5 thereof, shall apply.

CHAPTER X FINAL PROVISIONS

[2.160]
Article 59   Repeal of Framework Decision 2008/977/JHA
1. Framework Decision 2008/977/JHA is repealed with effect from 6 May 2018.
2. References to the repealed Decision referred to in paragraph 1 shall be construed as references to this Directive.

[2.161]
Article 60   Union legal acts already in force
The specific provisions for the protection of personal data in Union legal acts that entered into force on or before 6 May 2016 in the field of judicial cooperation in criminal matters and police cooperation, which regulate processing between Member States and the access of designated authorities of Member States to information systems established pursuant to the Treaties within the scope of this Directive, shall remain unaffected.

[2.162]
Article 61   Relationship with previously concluded international agreements in the field of judicial cooperation in criminal matters and police cooperation
International agreements involving the transfer of personal data to third countries or international organisations which were concluded by Member States prior to 6 May 2016 and which comply with Union law as applicable prior to that date shall remain in force until amended, replaced or revoked.

[2.163]
Article 62   Commission reports
1. By 6 May 2022, and every four years thereafter, the Commission shall submit a report on the evaluation and review of this Directive to the European Parliament and to the Council. The reports shall be made public.
2. In the context of the evaluations and reviews referred to in paragraph 1, the Commission shall examine, in particular, the application and functioning of Chapter V on the transfer of personal data to third countries or international organisations with particular regard to decisions adopted pursuant to Article 36(3) and Article 39.
3. For the purposes of paragraphs 1 and 2, the Commission may request information from Member States and supervisory authorities.
4. In carrying out the evaluations and reviews referred to in paragraphs 1 and 2, the Commission shall take into account the positions and findings of the European Parliament, of the Council and of other relevant bodies or sources.
5. The Commission shall, if necessary, submit appropriate proposals with a view to amending this Directive, in particular taking account of developments in information technology and in the light of the state of progress in the information society.
6. By 6 May 2019, the Commission shall review other legal acts adopted by the Union which regulate processing by the competent authorities for the purposes set out in Article 1(1) including those referred to in Article 60, in order to assess the need to align them with this Directive and to make, where appropriate, the necessary proposals to amend those acts to ensure a consistent approach to the protection of personal data within the scope of this Directive.

[2.164]
Article 63   Transposition
1. Member States shall adopt and publish, by 6 May 2018, the laws, regulations and administrative provisions necessary to comply with this Directive. They shall forthwith notify to the Commission the text of those provisions. They shall apply those provisions from 6 May 2018.
When Member States adopt those provisions, they shall contain a reference to this Directive or shall be accompanied by such a reference on the occasion of their official publication. Member States shall determine how such reference is to be made.
2. By way of derogation from paragraph 1, a Member State may provide, exceptionally, where it involves disproportionate effort, for automated processing systems set up before 6 May 2016 to be brought into conformity with Article 25(1) by 6 May 2023.

3. By way of derogation from paragraphs 1 and 2 of this Article, a Member State may, in exceptional circumstances, bring an automated processing system as referred to in paragraph 2 of this Article into conformity with Article 25(1) within a specified period after the period referred to in paragraph 2 of this Article, if it would otherwise cause serious difficulties for the operation of that particular automated processing system. The Member State concerned shall notify the Commission of the grounds for those serious difficulties and the grounds for the specified period within which it shall bring that particular automated processing system into conformity with Article 25(1). The specified period shall in any event not be later than 6 May 2026.

4. Member States shall communicate to the Commission the text of the main provisions of national law which they adopt in the field covered by this Directive.

[2.165]
Article 64 Entry into force
This Directive shall enter into force on the day following that of its publication in the *Official Journal of the European Union*.

[2.166]
Article 65 Addressees
This Directive is addressed to the Member States.

EDPB: ARTICLE 29 DATA PROTECTION WORKING PARTY GUIDELINES

WORKING PARTY 29 POSITION PAPER ON THE DEROGATIONS FROM THE OBLIGATION TO MAINTAIN RECORDS OF PROCESSING ACTIVITIES PURSUANT TO ARTICLE 30(5) GDPR

[2.167]

NOTES
  This document was originally issued by the Article 29 Working Party but subsequently endorsed by the EDPB during its first plenary meeting.
  © European Data Protection Board.

The Working Party 29 has examined the obligation, under Article 30 of the GDPR, for controllers and processors to maintain a record of processing activities. This paper sets out the WP29's position on the derogation from this obligation.

Recital 13 of the GDPR says:

> 'To take account of the specific situation of micro, small and medium-sized enterprises, this Regulation includes a derogation for organisations with fewer than 250 employees with regard to record-keeping'.

Article 30(5) gives effect to Recital 13. It says that the obligation to keep a record of processing activities does not apply 'to an enterprise or an organisation employing fewer than 250 persons unless the processing it carries out is likely to result in a risk to the rights and freedoms of data subjects, the processing is not occasional, or the processing includes special categories of data as referred to in Article 9(1) or personal data relating to criminal convictions and offences referred to in Article 10.'

Some clarifications on the interpretation of this provision appear necessary, as shown by the high number of requests coming from companies and received in the last few months by national Supervisory Authorities.

The derogation provided by Article 30(5) is not absolute. There are three types of processing to which it does not apply. These are:
• Processing that is likely to result in a risk to the rights and freedoms of data subjects.
• Processing that is not occasional.
• Processing that includes special categories of data or personal data relating to criminal convictions and offences.

The WP29 underlines that the wording of Article 30(5) is clear in providing that the three types of processing to which the derogation does not apply are alternative ("or") and the occurrence of any one of them alone triggers the obligation to maintain the record of processing activities.

Therefore, although endowed with less than 250 employees, data controllers or processors who find themselves in the position of either carrying out processing likely to result in a risk (not just a high risk) to the rights of the data subjects, or processing personal data on a non-occasional basis, or processing special categories of data under Article 9(1) or data relating to criminal convictions under Article 10 are obliged to maintain the record of processing activities.

However, such organisations need only maintain records of processing activities for the types of processing mentioned by Article 30(5).

For example, a small organisation is likely to regularly process data regarding its employees. As a result, such processing cannot be considered "occasional" and must therefore be included in the record of processing activities.[1] Other processing activities which are in fact "occasional", however, do not need to be included in the record of processing activities, provided they are unlikely to result in a risk to the right and freedoms of data subjects and do not involve special categories of data or personal data relating to criminal convictions and offences.

The WP29 highlights that the record of processing activities is a very useful means to support an analysis of the implications of any processing whether existing or planned. The record facilitates the factual assessment of the risk of the processing activities performed by a controller or processor on individuals' rights, and the identification and implementation of appropriate security measures to safeguard personal data – both key components of the principle of accountability contained in the GDPR.

For many micro, small and medium-sized organisations, maintaining a record of processing activities is unlikely to constitute a particularly heavy burden. However, the WP29 recognises that Article 30 represents a new administrative requirement for controllers and processors, and therefore encourages national Supervisory Authorities to support SMEs by providing tools to facilitate the set up and management of records of processing activities. For example, a Supervisory Authority might make available on its website a simplified model that can be used by SMEs to keep records of processing activities not covered by the derogation in Article 30(5).

NOTES

[1] The WP29 considers that a processing activity can only be considered as "occasional" if it is not carried out regularly, and occurs outside the regular course of business or activity of the controller or processor. See WP29 Guidelines on Article 49 of Regulation 2016/679 (WP262).

ARTICLE 29 DATA PROTECTION WORKING PARTY: GUIDELINES ON THE RIGHT TO DATA PORTABILITY
16/EN
WP 242 rev.01

Adopted on 13 December 2016

As last Revised and adopted on 5 April 2017

[2.168]

NOTES

This document was originally issued by the Article 29 Working Party but subsequently endorsed by the EDPB during its first plenary meeting.

© European Data Protection Board.

TABLE OF CONTENTS

EXECUTIVE SUMMARY

[2.169]

Article 20 of the GDPR creates a new right to data portability, which is closely related to the right of access but differs from it in many ways. It allows for data subjects to receive the personal data that they have provided to a controller, in a structured, commonly used and machine-readable format, and to transmit those data to another data controller. The purpose of this new right is to empower the data subject and give him/her more control over the personal data concerning him or her.

Since it allows the direct transmission of personal data from one data controller to another, the right to data portability is also an important tool that will support the free flow of personal data in the EU and foster competition between controllers. It will facilitate switching between different service providers, and will therefore foster the development of new services in the context of the digital single market strategy.

This opinion provides guidance on the way to interpret and implement the right to data portability as introduced by the GDPR. It aims at discussing the right to data portability and its scope. It clarifies the conditions under which this new right applies taking into account the legal basis of the data processing (either the data subject's consent or the necessity to perform a contract) and the fact that this right is

Part 2 Data Protection: EU Law etc

limited to personal data provided by the data subject. The opinion also provides concrete examples and criteria to explain the circumstances in which this right applies. In this regard, WP29 considers that the right to data portability covers data provided knowingly and actively by the data subject as well as the personal data generated by his or her activity. This new right cannot be undermined and limited to the personal information directly communicated by the data subject, for example, on an online form.

As a good practice, data controllers should start developing the means that will contribute to answer data portability requests, such as download tools and Application Programming Interfaces. They should guarantee that personal data are transmitted in a structured, commonly used and machine-readable format, and they should be encouraged to ensure the interoperability of the data format provided in the exercise of a data portability request.

The opinion also helps data controllers to clearly understand their respective obligations and recommends best practices and tools that support compliance with the right to data portability. Finally, the opinion recommends that industry stakeholders and trade associations work together on a common set of interoperable standards and formats to deliver the requirements of the right to data portability.

I. INTRODUCTION

[2.170]
Article 20 of the General Data Protection Regulation (GDPR) introduces a new right of data portability. This right allows for data subjects to receive the personal data that they have provided to a data controller, in a structured, commonly used and machine-readable format, and to transmit those data to another data controller without hindrance. This right, which applies subject to certain conditions, supports user choice, user control and user empowerment.

Individuals making use of their right of access under the Data Protection Directive 95/46/EC were constrained by the format chosen by the data controller when providing the requested information. **The new right to data portability aims to empower data subjects regarding their own personal data, as it facilitates their ability to move, copy or transmit personal data easily from one IT environment to another** (whether to their own systems, the systems of trusted third parties or those of new data controllers).

By affirming individuals' personal rights and control over the personal data concerning them, data portability also represents an opportunity to "re-balance" the relationship between data subjects and data controllers[1].

Whilst the right to personal data portability may also enhance competition between services (by facilitating service switching), the GDPR is regulating personal data and not competition. In particular, article 20 does not limit portable data to those which are necessary or useful for switching services[2].

Although data portability is a new right, other types of portability already exist or are being discussed in other areas of legislation (e.g. in the contexts of contract termination, communication services roaming and trans-border access to services[3]). Some synergies and even benefits to individuals may emerge between the different types of portability if they are provided in a combined approach, even though analogies should be treated cautiously.

This Opinion provides guidance to data controllers so that they can update their practices, processes and policies, and clarifies the meaning of data portability in order to enable data subjects to efficiently use their new right.

NOTES

[1]   The primary aim of data portability is enhancing individual's control over their personal data and making sure they play an active role in the data ecosystem.

[2]   For example, this right may allow banks to provide additional services, under the user's control, using personal data initially collected as part of an energy supply service.

[3]   See European Commission agenda for a digital single market: https://ec.europa.eu/digital-agenda/en/digital-single-market, in particular, the first policy pillar "Better online access to digital goods and services".

II. WHAT ARE THE MAIN ELEMENTS OF DATA PORTABILITY?

[2.171]
The GDPR defines the right of data portability in Article 20 (1) as follows:

The data subject shall have the right to receive the personal data concerning him or her, which he or she has provided to a controller, in a structured, commonly used and machine-readable format and have the right to transmit those data to another controller without hindrance from the controller to which the data have been provided [. . .]

A RIGHT TO RECEIVE PERSONAL DATA

Firstly, data portability is a **right of the data subject to receive a subset of the personal data** processed by a data controller concerning him or her, and to store those data for further personal use. Such storage can be on a private device or on a private cloud, without necessarily transmitting the data to another data controller.

In this regard, data portability complements the right of access. One specificity of data portability lies in the fact that it offers an easy way for data subjects to manage and reuse personal data themselves. These data should be received "*in a structured, commonly used and machine-readable format*". For example, a data subject might be interested in retrieving his current playlist (or a history of listened tracks) from a music streaming service, to find out how many times he listened to specific tracks, or to check which music he wants to purchase or listen to on another platform. Similarly, he may also want to retrieve his contact list from his webmail application, for example, to build a wedding list, or get information about purchases using different loyalty cards, or to assess his or her carbon footprint[4].

A RIGHT TO TRANSMIT PERSONAL DATA FROM ONE DATA CONTROLLER TO AN-OTHER DATA CONTROLLER

Secondly, Article 20(1) provides data subjects with the **right to transmit personal data from one data controller to another data controller** "without hindrance". Data can also be transmitted directly from one data controller to another on request of the data subject and where it is technically feasible (Article 20(2)). In this respect, recital 68 encourages data controllers to develop interoperable formats that enable data portability[5] but without creating an obligation for controllers to adopt or maintain processing systems which are technically compatible[6]. The GDPR does, however, prohibit controllers from establishing barriers to the transmission.

In essence, this element of data portability provides the ability for data subjects not just to obtain and reuse, but also to transmit the data they have provided to another service provider (either within the same business sector or in a different one). In addition to providing consumer empowerment by preventing "lock-in", the right to data portability is expected to foster opportunities for innovation and sharing of personal data between data controllers in a safe and secure manner, under the data subject's control[7]. Data portability can promote the controlled and limited sharing by users of personal data between organisations and thus enrich services and customer experiences[8]. Data portability may facilitate transmission and reuse of personal data concerning users among the various services they are interested in.

CONTROLLERSHIP

Data portability guarantees the right to receive personal data and to process them, according to the data subject's wishes[9].

Data controllers answering data portability requests, under the conditions set forth in Article 20, are not responsible for the processing handled by the data subject or by another company receiving personal data. They act on behalf of the data subject, including when the personal data are directly transmitted to another data controller. In this respect, the data controller is not responsible for compliance of the receiving data controller with data protection law, considering that it is not the sending data controller that chooses the recipient. At the same time the controller should set safeguards to ensure they genuinely act on the data subject's behalf. For example, they can establish procedures to ensure that the type of personal data transmitted are indeed those that the data subject wants to transmit. This could be done by obtaining confirmation from the data subject either before transmission or earlier on when the original consent for processing is given or the contract is finalised.

Data controllers answering a data portability request have no specific obligation to check and verify the quality of the data before transmitting it. Of course, these data should already be accurate, and up to date, according to the principles stated in Art 5(1) of the GDPR. Moreover, data portability does not impose an obligation on the data controller to retain personal data for longer than is necessary or beyond any specified retention period[10]. Importantly, there is no additional requirement to retain data beyond the otherwise applicable retention periods, simply to serve any potential future data portability request.

Where the personal data requested are processed by a data processor, the contract concluded in accordance with Article 28 of the GDPR must include the obligation to assist "the controller by appropriate technical and organisational measures, (. . .) to respond to requests for exercising the data subject's rights". The data controller should therefore implement specific procedures in cooperation with its data processors to answer data portability requests. In case of a joint controllership, a contract should allocate clearly the responsibilities between each data controller regarding the processing of data portability requests.

In addition, a receiving data controller[11] is responsible for ensuring that the portable data provided are relevant and not excessive with regard to the new data processing. For example, in the case of a data portability request made to a webmail service, where the request is used by the data subject to obtain emails and send them to a secured archive platform, the new data controller does not need to process the contact details of the data subject's correspondents. If this information is not relevant with regard to the purpose of the new processing, it should not be kept and processed. In any case, receiving data controllers are not obliged to accept and process personal data transmitted following a data portability request. Similarly, where a data subject requests the transmission of details of his or her bank transactions to a service that assists in managing his or her budget, the receiving data controller does not need to accept all the data, or to retain all the details of the transactions once they have been labelled for the purposes of the new service. In other words, the data accepted and retained should only be that which is necessary and relevant to the service being provided by the receiving data controller.

A "receiving" organization becomes a new data controller regarding these personal data and must respect the principles stated in Article 5 of the GDPR. Therefore, the "new" receiving data controller must clearly and directly state the purpose of the new processing before any request for transmission of the portable data in accordance with the transparency requirements set out in Article 14[12]. As for any other data processing performed under its responsibility, the data controller should apply the principles laid down in Article 5, such as lawfulness, fairness and transparency, purpose limitation, data minimization, accuracy, integrity and confidentiality, storage limitation and accountability[13].

Data controllers holding personal data should be prepared to facilitate their data subject's right to data portability. Data controllers can also choose to accept data from a data subject, but are not obliged to.

DATA PORTABILITY VS. OTHER RIGHTS OF DATA SUBJECTS

When an individual exercises his or her right to data portability he or she does so without prejudice to any other right (as is the case with any other rights in the GDPR). A data subject can continue to use and benefit from the data controller's service even after a data portability operation. Data portability does not automatically trigger the erasure of the data[14] from the systems of the data controller, and does not affect the original retention period applying to the data which have been transmitted. The data subject can exercise his or her rights as long as the data controller is still processing the data.

Equally, if the data subject wants to exercise his or her right to erasure ("right to be forgotten" under Article 17), data portability cannot be used by a data controller as a way of delaying or refusing such erasure.

Should a data subject discover that personal data requested under the right to data portability does not fully address his or her request, any further request for personal data under a right of access should be fully complied with, in accordance with Article 15 of the GDPR.

Furthermore, where a specific European or Member State law in another field also provides for some form of portability of the data concerned, the conditions laid down in these specific laws must also be taken into account when satisfying a data portability request under the GDPR. First, if it is clear from the request made by the data subject that his or her intention is not to exercise rights under the GDPR, but rather, to exercise rights under sectorial legislation only, then the GDPR's data portability provisions will not apply to this request[15]. If, on the other hand, the request is aimed at portability under the GDPR, the existence of such specific legislation does not override the general application of the data portability principle to any data controller, as provided by the GDPR. Instead, it must be assessed, on a case by case basis, how, if at all, such specific legislation may affect the right to data portability.

NOTES

4   In these cases, the processing performed on the data by the data subject can either fall within the scope of household activities, when all the processing is performed under the sole control of the data subject, or it can be handled by another party, on the data subject's behalf. In the latter case, the other party should be considered as data controller, even for the sole purpose of personal data storage, and must comply with the principles and obligations laid down in the GDPR.

5   See also section V.

6   As a consequence, special attention should be paid to the format of the transmitted data, so as to guarantee that the data can be re-used, with little effort, by the data subject or another data controller. See also section V.

7   See several experimental applications in Europe, for example MiData in the United Kingdom, MesInfos / SelfData by FING in France.

8   The so-called quantified self and IoT industries have shown the benefit (and risks) of linking personal data from different aspects of an individual's life such as fitness, activity and calorie intake to deliver a more complete picture of an individual's life in a single file.

9   The right to data portability is not limited to personal data that are useful and relevant for similar services provided by competitors of the data controller.

10   In the example above, if the data controller does not retain a record of songs played by a user then this personal data cannot be included within a data portability request.

11   i.e. that receives personal data following a data portability request made by the data subject to another data controller.

12   In addition, the new data controller should not process personal data, which are not relevant, and the processing must be limited to what is necessary for the new purposes, even if the personal data are part of a more global data-set transmitted through a portability process. Personal data, which are not necessary to achieve the purpose of the new processing, should be deleted as soon as possible.

13   Once received by the data controller, the personal data sent as part of the right to data portability can be considered as "provided by" the data subject and be re-transmitted according to the right to data portability, to the extent that the other conditions applicable to this right (ie. the legal basis of the processing, . . .) are met.

14   as stated in Article 17 of the GDPR

III. WHEN DOES DATA PORTABILITY APPLY?

WHICH PROCESSING OPERATIONS ARE COVERED BY THE RIGHT TO DATA PORTABILITY?

[2.172]
Compliance with the GDPR requires data controllers to have a clear legal basis for the processing of personal data.

In accordance with Article 20(1)(a) of the GDPR, **in order to fall under the scope of data** portability, processing operations must be based:

–   either on the data subject's consent (pursuant to Article 6(1)(a), or pursuant to Article 9(2)(a) when it comes to special categories of personal data);

–   or, on a contract to which the data subject is a party pursuant to Article 6(1)(b).

As an example, the titles of books purchased by an individual from an online bookstore, or the songs listened to via a music streaming service are examples of personal data that are generally within the scope of data portability, because they are processed on the basis of the performance of a contract to which the data subject is a party.

The GDPR does not establish a general right to data portability for cases where the processing of personal data is not based on consent or contract[16]. For example, there is no obligation for financial institutions to answer a data portability request concerning personal data processed as part of their obligations obligation to prevent and detect money laundering and other financial crimes; equally, data portability does not cover professional contact details processed in a business to business relationship in cases where the processing is neither based on the consent of the data subject nor on a contract to which he or she is a party.

When it comes to employees' data, the right to data portability typically applies only if the processing is based on a contract to which the data subject is a party. In many cases, consent will not be considered freely given in this context, due to the imbalance of power between the employer and employee[17]. Some HR processings instead are based on the legal ground of legitimate interest, or are necessary for compliance with specific legal obligations in the field of employment. In practice, the right to data portability in an HR context will undoubtedly concern some processing operations (such as pay and compensation services, internal recruitment) but in many other situations a case by case approach will be needed to verify whether all conditions applying to the right to data portability are met.

Finally, the right to data portability only applies if the data processing is "carried out by automated means", and therefore does not cover most paper files.

WHAT PERSONAL DATA MUST BE INCLUDED?

Pursuant to Article 20(1), to be within the scope of the right to data portability, data must be:
- personal data concerning him or her, and
- which he or she has *provided* to a data controller.

Article 20(4) also states that compliance with this right shall not adversely affect the rights and freedoms of others.

First condition: personal data concerning the data subject

Only personal data is in scope of a data portability request. Therefore, any data that is anonymous[18] or does not concern the data subject, will not be in scope. However, pseudonymous data that can be clearly linked to a data subject (e.g. by him or her providing the respective identifier, cf. Article 11 (2)) is within the scope.

In many circumstances, data controllers will process information that contains the personal data of several data subjects. Where this is the case, data controllers should not take an overly restrictive interpretation of the sentence "personal data concerning the data subject". As an example, telephone, interpersonal messaging or VoIP records may include (in the subscriber's account history) details of third parties involved in incoming and outgoing calls. Although records will therefore contain personal data concerning multiple people, subscribers should be able to have these records provided to them in response to data portability requests, because the records are (also) concerning the data subject. However, where such records are then transmitted to a new data controller, this new data controller should not process them for any purpose which would adversely affect the rights and freedoms of the third-parties (see below: third condition).

Second condition: data provided by the data subject

The second condition narrows the scope to data "provided by" the data subject.

There are many examples of personal data, which will be knowingly and actively "provided by" the data subject such as account data (e.g. mailing address, user name, age) submitted via online forms. Nevertheless, data "provided by" the data subject also result from the observation of his activity. As a consequence, the WP29 considers that to give its full value to this new right, "provided by" should also include the personal data that are observed from the activities of users such as raw data processed by a smart meter or other types of connected objects[19], activity logs, history of website usage or search activities.

This latter category of data does not include data that are created by the data controller (using the data observed or directly provided as input) such as a user profile created by analysis of the raw smart metering data collected.

A distinction can be made between different categories of data, depending on their origin, to determine if they are covered by the right to data portability. The following categories can be qualified as "provided by the data subject":
- **Data actively and knowingly provided by the data subject** (for example, mailing address, user name, age, etc.)
- **Observed data provided by the data subject by virtue of the use of the service or the device**. They may for example include a person's search history, traffic data and location data. It may also include other raw data such as the heartbeat tracked by a wearable device.

In contrast, inferred data and derived data are created by the data controller on the basis of the data "provided by the data subject". For example, the outcome of an assessment regarding the health of a user or the profile created in the context of risk management and financial regulations (e.g. to assign a credit score or comply with anti-money laundering rules) cannot in themselves be considered as "provided by" the data subject. Even though such data may be part of a profile kept by a data controller and are inferred or derived from the analysis of data provided by the data subject (through his actions for example), these data will typically not be considered as "provided by the data subject" and thus will not be within scope of this new right[20].

In general, given the policy objectives of the right to data portability, the term "provided by the data subject" must be interpreted broadly, and should exclude "inferred data" and "derived data", which include personal data that are created by a service provider (for example, algorithmic results). A data controller can exclude those inferred data but should include all other personal data provided by the data subject through technical means provided by the controller[21].

Thus, the term "provided by" includes personal data that relate to the data subject activity or result from the observation of an individual's behaviour, but does not include data resulting from subsequent analysis of that behaviour. By contrast, any personal data which have been created by the data controller as part of the data processing, e.g. by a personalisation or recommendation process, by user categorisation or profiling are data which are derived or inferred from the personal data provided by the data subject, and are not covered by the right to data portability.

Third condition: the right to data portability shall not adversely affect the rights and freedoms of others

With respect to personal data concerning other data subjects:

The third condition is intended to avoid the retrieval and transmission of data containing the personal data of other (non-consenting) data subjects to a new data controller in cases where these data are likely to be processed in a way that would adversely affect the rights and freedoms of the other data subjects (Article 20(4) of the GDPR)[22].

Such an adverse effect would occur, for instance, if the transmission of data from one data controller to another, would prevent third parties from exercising their rights as data subjects under the GDPR (such as the rights to information, access, etc).

The data subject initiating the transmission of his or her data to another data controller, either gives consent to the new data controller for processing or enters into a contract with that controller. Where personal data of third parties are included in the data set another legal basis for the processing must be identified. For example, a legitimate interest may be pursued by the data controller under Article 6(1)(f), in particular when the purpose of the data controller is to provide a service to the data subject that allows the latter to process personal data for a purely personal or household activity. The processing operations initiated by the data subject in the context of personal activity that concern and potentially impact third parties remain under his or her responsibility, to the extent that such processing is not, in any manner, decided by the data controller.

For example, a webmail service may allow the creation of a directory of a data subject's contacts, friends, relatives, family and broader environment. Since these data relate to (and are created by) the identifiable individual that wishes to exercise his right to data portability, data controllers should transmit the entire directory of incoming and outgoing e-mails to that data subject.

Similarly, a data subject's bank account can contain personal data relating to the transactions not just of the account holder but also those of other individuals (e.g., if they have transferred money to the account holder). The rights and freedoms of those third parties are unlikely to be adversely affected by the transmission of the bank account information to the account holder once a portability request is made—provided that in both examples the data are used for the same purpose (i.e., a contact address only used by the data subject or a history of the data subject's bank account.

Conversely, the rights and freedoms of third parties will not be respected if the new data controller uses the personal data for other purposes, e.g. if the receiving data controller uses personal data of other individuals within the data subject's contact directory for marketing purposes.

Therefore, to prevent adverse effects on the third parties involved, the processing of such personal data by another controller is allowed only to the extent that the data are kept under the sole control of the requesting user and is only managed for purely personal or household needs. A receiving 'new' data controller (to whom the data can be transmitted at the request of the user) may not use the transmitted third party data for his own purposes e.g. to propose marketing products and services to those other third party data subjects. For example, this information should not be used to enrich the profile of the third party data subject and rebuild his social environment, without his knowledge and consent[23]. Neither can it be used to retrieve information about such third parties and create specific profiles, even if their personal data are already held by the data controller. Otherwise, such processing is likely to be unlawful and unfair, especially if the third parties concerned are not informed and cannot exercise their rights as data subjects.

Furthermore, it is a leading practice for all data controllers (both the "sending" and "receiving" parties) to implement tools to enable data subjects to select the relevant data they wish to receive and transmit and exclude, where relevant, data of other individuals. This will further assist in reducing the risks for third parties whose personal data may be ported.

Additionally, the data controllers should implement consent mechanisms for other data subjects involved, to ease data transmission for those cases where such parties are willing to consent, e.g. if they also want to move their data to some other data controller. Such a situation might arise, for example, with social networks, but it is up to data controllers to decide on the leading practice to follow.

With respect to data covered by intellectual property and trade secrets:

The rights and freedoms of others are mentioned in Article 20(4). While not directly related to portability, this can be understood as "including trade secrets or intellectual property and in particular the copyright protecting the software. However, even though these rights should be considered before answering a data portability request, "the result of those considerations should not be a refusal to provide all information to the data subject". Furthermore, the data controller should not reject a data portability request on the basis of the infringement of another contractual right (for example, an outstanding debt, or a trade conflict with the data subject).

The right to data portability is not a right for an individual to misuse the information in a way that could be qualified as an unfair practice or that would constitute a violation of intellectual property rights.

A potential business risk cannot, however, in and of itself serve as the basis for a refusal to answer the portability request and data controllers can transmit the personal data provided by data subjects in a form that does not release information covered by trade secrets or intellectual property rights.

NOTES

15   For example, if the data subject's request aims specifically at providing access to his banking account history to an account information service provider, for the purposes stated in the Payment Services Directive 2 (PSD2) such access should be granted according to the provisions of this directive.

16   See recital 68 and Article 20(3) of the GDPR. Article 20(3) and Recital 68 provide that data portability does not apply when the data processing is necessary for the performance of a task carried out in the public interest or in the exercise of official authority vested in the data controller, or when a data controller is exercising its public duties or complying with a legal obligation. Therefore, there is no obligation for data controllers to provide for portability in these cases. However, it is a good practice to develop processes to automatically answer portability requests, by following the principles governing the right to data portability. An example of this would be a government service providing easy downloading of past personal income tax filings. For data portability as a good practice in case of processing based on the legal ground of necessity for a legitimate interest and for existing voluntary schemes, see pages 47 & 48 of WP29 Opinion 6/2014 on legitimate interests (WP217).

17   As the WP29 outlined in its Opinion 8/2001 of 13 September 2001 (WP48).

18   http://ec.europa.eu/justice/data-protection/article-29/documentation/opinion-recommendation/files/2014/wp216_en.pdf

19   By being able to retrieve the data resulting from observation of his or her activity, the data subject will also be able to get a better view of the implementation choices made by data controller as to the scope of observed data and will be in a better situation to choose what data he or she is willing to provide to get a similar service, and be aware of the extent to which his or her right to privacy is respected.

20   Nevertheless, the data subject can still use his or her "right to obtain from the controller confirmation as to whether or not personal data concerning him or her are being processed, and, where that is the case, access to the personal data" as well as information about "the existence of automated decision-making, including profiling, referred to in Article 22(1) and (4) and, at least in those cases, meaningful information about the logic involved, as well as the significance and the envisaged consequences of such processing for the data subject", according to Article 15 of the GDPR (which refers to the right of access).

21   This includes all data observed about the data subject during the activities for the purpose of which the data are collected, such as a transaction history or access log. Data collected through the tracking and recording of the data subject (such as an app recording heartbeat or technology used to track browsing behaviour) should also be considered as "provided by" him or her even if the data are not actively or consciously transmitted.

22   Recital 68 provides that "where, in a certain set of personal data, more than one data subject is concerned, the right to receive the personal data should be without prejudice to the rights and freedoms of other data subjects in accordance with this Regulation."

23   A social networking service should not enrich the profile of its members by using personal data transmitted by a data subject as part of his right to data portability, without respecting the principle of transparency and also making sure they rely on an appropriate legal basis regarding this specific processing.

IV. HOW DO THE GENERAL RULES GOVERNING THE EXERCISE OF DATA SUBJECT RIGHTS APPLY TO DATA PORTABILITY?

WHAT PRIOR INFORMATION SHOULD BE PROVIDED TO THE DATA SUBJECT?

[2.173]

In order to comply with the new right to data portability, data controllers must inform data subjects of the existence of the new right to portability. Where the personal data concerned are directly collected from the data subject, this must happen "at the time where personal data are obtained". If the personal data have not been obtained from the data subject, the data controller must provide the information as required by Articles 13(2)(b) and 14(2)(c).

"Where the personal data have not been obtained from the data subject", Article 14(3) requires the information to be provided within a reasonable time not exceeding one month after obtaining the data, during first communication with the data subject, or when disclosure is made to third parties[24].

When providing the required information data controllers must ensure that they distinguish the right to data portability from other rights. Therefore, WP29 recommends in particular that data controllers clearly explain the difference between the types of data that a data subject can receive through the rights of subject access and data portability.

In addition, the Working Party recommends that data controllers always include information about the right to data portability before data subjects close any account they may have. This allows users to take stock of their personal data, and to easily transmit the data to their own device or to another provider before a contract is terminated.

Finally, as leading practice for "receiving" data controllers, the WP29 recommends that data subjects are provided with complete information about the nature of personal data which are relevant for the performance of their services. In addition to underpinning fair processing, this allows users to limit the risks for third parties, and also any other unnecessary duplication of personal data even where no other data subjects are involved.

HOW CAN THE DATA CONTROLLER IDENTIFY THE DATA SUBJECT BEFORE ANSWERING HIS REQUEST?

There are no prescriptive requirements to be found in the GDPR on how to authenticate the data subject. Nevertheless, Article 12(2) of the GDPR states that the data controller shall not refuse to act on request of a data subject for exercising his or her rights (including the right to data portability) unless it is processing personal data for a purpose that does not require the identification of a data subject and it can demonstrate that it is not able to identify the data subject. However, as per Article 11(2), in such circumstances the data subject can provide more information to enable his or her identification. Additionally, Article 12(6) provides that where a data controller has reasonable doubts about the identity of a data subject, it can request further information to confirm the data subject's identity. Where a data subject provides additional information enabling his or her identification, the data controller shall not refuse to act on the request. Where information and data collected online is linked to pseudonyms or unique identifiers, data controllers can implement appropriate procedures enabling an individual to make a data portability request and receive the data relating to him or her. In any case, data controllers must implement an authentication procedure in order to strongly ascertain the identity of the data subject requesting his or her personal data or more generally exercising the rights granted by the GDPR.

These procedures often already exist. The data subjects are often already authenticated by the data controller before entering into a contract or collecting his or her consent to the processing. As a consequence, the personal data used to register the individual concerned by the processing can also be used as evidence to authenticate the data subject for portability purposes[25].

While in these cases, the data subjects' prior identification may require a request for proof of their legal identity, such verification may not be relevant to assess the link between the data and the individual concerned, since such a link is not related with the official or legal identity. In essence, the ability for the data controller to request additional information to assess one's identity cannot lead to excessive demands and to the collection of personal data which are not relevant or necessary to strengthen the link between the individual and the personal data requested.

In many cases, such authentication procedures are already in place. For example, usernames and passwords are often used to allow individuals to access their data in their email accounts, social networking accounts, and accounts used for various other services, some of which individuals chose to use without revealing their full name and identity.

If the size of data requested by the data subject makes transmission via the internet problematic, rather than potentially allowing for an extended time period of a maximum of three months to comply with the request[26], the data controller may also need to consider alternative means of providing the data such as using streaming or saving to a CD, DVD or other physical media or allowing for the personal data to be transmitted directly to another data controller (as per Article 20(2) of the GDPR where technically feasible).

WHAT IS THE TIME LIMIT IMPOSED TO ANSWER A PORTABILITY REQUEST?

Article 12(3) requires that the data controller provides "information on action taken" to the data subject "without undue delay" and in any event "within one month of receipt of the request". This one month period can be extended to a maximum of three months for complex cases, provided that the data subject has been informed about the reasons for such delay within one month of the original request.

Data controllers operating information society services are likely to be better equipped to be able to comply with requests within a very short time period. To meet user expectations, it is a good practice to define the timeframe in which a data portability request can typically be answered and communicate this to data subjects.

Data controllers who refuse to answer a portability request shall, pursuant to Article 12(4), inform the data subject "the reasons for not taking action and on the possibility of lodging a complaint with a supervisory authority and seeking a judicial remedy", no later than one month after receiving the request.

Data controllers must respect the obligation to respond within the given terms, even if it concerns a refusal. In other words, the data controller cannot remain silent when it is asked to answer a data portability request.

IN WHICH CASES CAN A DATA PORTABILITY REQUEST BE REJECTED OR A FEE CHARGED?

Article 12 prohibits the data controller from charging a fee for the provision of the personal data, unless the data controller can demonstrate that the requests are manifestly unfounded or excessive, "in particular because of their repetitive character". For information society services that specialise in automated processing of personal data, implementing automated systems such as Application Programming Interfaces (APIs)[27] can facilitate the exchanges with the data subject, hence lessen the potential burden resulting from repetitive requests. Therefore, there should be very few cases where the data controller would be able to justify a refusal to deliver the requested information, even regarding multiple data portability requests.

In addition, the overall cost of the processes created to answer data portability requests should not be taken into account to determine the excessiveness of a request. In fact, Article 12 of the GDPR focuses on the requests made by one data subject and not on the total number of requests received by a data controller. As a result, the overall system implementation costs should neither be charged to the data subjects, nor be used to justify a refusal to answer portability requests.

NOTES

[24]   Article 12 requires that data controllers provide "any communications [. . .] in a concise, transparent, intelligible, and easily assessable form, using clear and plain language, in particular for any information addressed specifically to a child."

[25]   For example, when the data processing is linked to a user account, providing the relevant login and password might be sufficient to identify the data subject.

[26]   Article 12(3): "The controller shall provide information on action taken on a request".

[27]   Application Programming Interface (API) means the interfaces of applications or web services made available by data controllers so that other systems or applications can link and work with their systems.

V. HOW MUST THE PORTABLE DATA BE PROVIDED?

WHAT ARE THE EXPECTED MEANS THE DATA CONTROLLER SHOULD IMPLEMENT FOR DATA PROVISION?

[2.174]

Article 20(1) of the GDPR provides that data subjects have the right to transmit the data to another controller without hindrance from the controller to which the personal data have been provided.

Such hindrance can be characterised as any legal, technical or financial obstacles placed by data controller in order to refrain or slow down access, transmission or reuse by the data subject or by another data controller. For example, such hindrance could be: fees asked for delivering data, lack of interoperability or access to a data format or API or the provided format, excessive delay or complexity to retrieve the full dataset, deliberate obfuscation of the dataset, or specific and undue or excessive sectorial standardization or accreditation demands[28].

Article 20(2) also places obligations on data controllers for transmitting the portable data directly to other data controllers "when technically feasible".

The technical feasibility of transmission from data controller to data controller, under the control of the data subject, should be assessed on a case by case basis. Recital 68 further clarifies the limits of what is "technically feasible", indicating that "it should not create an obligation for the controllers to adopt or maintain processing systems which are technically compatible".

Data controllers are expected to transmit personal data in an interoperable format, although this does not place obligations on other data controllers to support these formats. Direct transmission from one data controller to another could therefore occur when communication between two systems is possible, in a secured way[29], and when the receiving system is technically in a position to receive the incoming data. If technical impediments prohibit direct transmission, the data controller shall explain those impediments to the data subjects, as his decision will otherwise be similar in its effect to a refusal to take action on a data subject's request (Article 12(4)).

On a technical level, data controllers should explore and assess two different and complimentary paths for making portable data available to the data subjects or to other data controllers:
–   a direct transmission of the overall dataset of portable data (or several extracts of parts of the global dataset);
–   an automated tool that allows extraction of relevant data.

The second way may be preferred by data controllers in cases involving of complex and large data sets, as it allows for the extraction of any part of the data-set that is relevant for the data subject in the context of his or her request, may help minimising risk, and possibly allows for use of data synchronisation mechanisms[30] (e.g. in the context of a regular communication between data controllers). It may be a better way to ensure compliance for the "new" data controller, and would constitute good practice in the reduction of privacy risks on the part of the initial data controller.

These two different and possibly complementary ways of providing relevant portable data could be implemented by making data available through various means such as, for example, secured messaging, an SFTP server, a secured WebAPI or WebPortal. Data subjects should be enabled to make use of a personal data store, personal information management system[31] or other kinds of trusted third-parties, to hold and store the personal data and grant permission to data controllers to access and process the personal data as required.

WHAT IS THE EXPECTED DATA FORMAT?

The GDPR places requirements on data controllers to provide the personal data requested by the individual in a format, which supports re-use. Specifically, Article 20(1) of the GDPR states that the personal data must be provided "in a structured, commonly used and machine-readable format". Recital 68 provides a further clarification that this format should be interoperable, a term that is defined[32] in the EU as:

> *the ability of disparate and diverse organisations to interact towards mutually beneficial and agreed common goals, involving the sharing of information and knowledge between the organisations, through the business processes they support, by means of the exchange of data between their respective ICT systems.*

The terms "structured", "commonly used" and "machine-readable" are a set of minimal requirements that should facilitate the interoperability of the data format provided by the data controller. In that way, "structured, commonly used and machine readable" are specifications for the means, whereas interoperability is the desired outcome.

Recital 21 of Directive 2013/37/EU[33],[34] defines "machine readable" as:

> *a file format structured so that software applications can easily identify, recognize and extract specific data, including individual statements of fact, and their internal structure. Data encoded in files that are structured in a machine-readable format are machine-readable data. Machine-readable formats can be open or proprietary; they can be formal standards or not. Documents encoded in a file format that limits automatic processing, because the data cannot, or cannot easily, be extracted from them, should not be considered to be in a machine-readable format. Member States should where appropriate encourage the use of open, machine-readable formats.*

Given the wide range of potential data types that could be processed by a data controller, the GDPR does not impose specific recommendations on the format of the personal data to be provided. The most appropriate format will differ across sectors and adequate formats may already exist, and should always be chosen to achieve the purpose of being interpretable and affording the data subject with a large degree of data portability. As such, formats that are subject to costly licensing constraints would not be considered an adequate approach.

Recital 68 clarifies that "*The data subject's right to transmit or receive personal data concerning him or her should not create an obligation for the controllers to adopt or maintain processing systems which are technically compatible.*" **Thus, portability aims to produce interoperable systems, not compatible systems**[35].

Personal data are expected to be provided in formats that have a high level of abstraction from any internal or proprietary format. As such, data portability implies an additional layer of data processing by data controllers, in order to extract data from the platform and filter out personal data outside the scope of portability, such as inferred data or data related to security of systems. In this way, data controllers are encouraged to identify beforehand data which are within the scope of portability in their own systems. This additional data processing will be considered as ancillary to the main data processing, since it is not performed to achieve a new purpose defined by the data controller.

Where no formats are in common use for a given industry or given context, **data controllers should provide personal data using commonly used open formats (e.g. XML, JSON, CSV, . . .) along with useful metadata at the best possible level of granularity,** while maintaining a high level of abstraction. As such, suitable metadata should be used in order to accurately describe the meaning of exchanged information. This metadata should be enough to make the function and reuse of the data possible but, of course, without revealing trade secrets. It is unlikely therefore that providing an individual with PDF versions of an email inbox would be sufficiently structured or descriptive to allow the inbox data to be easily re-used. Instead, the e-mail data should be provided in a format which preserves all the metadata, to allow the effective re-use of the data. As such, when selecting a data format in which to provide the personal data, the data controller should consider how this format would impact or hinder the individual's right to re-use the data. In cases where a data controller is able to provide choices to the data subject regarding the preferred format of the personal data a clear explanation of the impact of the choice should be provided. However, processing additional metadata for the sole purpose that they might be needed or wanted to answer a data portability request poses no legitimate ground for such processing.

WP29 strongly encourages cooperation between industry stakeholders and trade associations to work together on a common set of interoperable standards and formats to deliver the requirements of the right to data portability. This challenge has also been addressed by the European Interoperability Framework (EIF) which has created an agreed approach to interoperability for organizations that wish to jointly deliver public services. Within its scope of applicability, the framework specifies a set of common elements such as vocabulary, concepts, principles, policies, guidelines, recommendations, standards, specifications and practices[36].

HOW TO DEAL WITH A LARGE OR COMPLEX PERSONAL DATA COLLECTION?

The GDPR does not explain how to address the challenge of responding where a large data collection, a complex data structure or other technical issues arise that might create difficulties for data controllers or data subjects.

However, in all cases, it is crucial that the individual is in a position to fully understand the definition, schema and structure of the personal data that could be provided by the data controller. For instance, data could first be provided in a summarised form using dashboards allowing the data subject to port subsets of the personal data rather than the entirety. The data controller should provide an overview "in a concise, transparent, intelligible and easily accessible form, using clear and plain language" (see Article 12(1)) of the GDPR) in such a way that data subject should always have clear information of what data to download or transmit to another data controller in relation to a given purpose. For example, data subjects should be in a position to use software applications to easily identify, recognize and process specific data from it.

As referenced above, a practical way by which a data controller can answer requests for data portability may be by offering an appropriately secured and documented API. This may enable individuals to make requests of the data controller for their personal data via their own or third-party software or grant permission for others to so do on their behalf (including another data controller) as specified in Article 20(2) of the GDPR. By granting access to data via an externally accessible API, it may also be possible to offer a more sophisticated access system that enables individuals to make subsequent requests for data, either as a full download or as a delta function containing only changes since the last download, without these additional requests being onerous on the data controller.

HOW CAN PORTABLE DATA BE SECURED?

In general, data controllers should guarantee the "appropriate security of the personal data, including protection against unauthorised or unlawful processing and against accidental loss, destruction or damage, using appropriate technical or organisational measures" according to Article 5(1)(f) of the GDPR.

However, the transmission of personal data to the data subject may also raise some security issues:

How can data controllers ensure that personal data are securely delivered to the right person?

As data portability aims to get personal data out of the information system of the data controller, the transmission may become a possible source of risk regarding those data (in particular of data breaches during the transmission). The data controller is responsible for taking all the security measures needed to ensure not only that personal data is securely transmitted (by the use of end-to-end or data encryption) to the right destination (by the use of strong authentication measures), but also continuing to protect the personal data that remains in their systems, as well as transparent procedures for dealing with possible data breaches[37]. As such, data controllers should assess the specific risks linked with data portability and take appropriate risks mitigation measures.

Such risk mitigation measures could include: if the data subject already needs to be authenticated, using additional authentication information, such as a shared secret, or another factor of authentication, such as a onetime password; suspending or freezing the transmission if there is suspicion that the account has been compromised; in cases of a direct transmission from a data controller to another data controller, authentication by mandate, such as token-based authentications, should be used.

Such security measures must not be obstructive in nature and must not prevent users from exercising their rights, e.g. by imposing additional costs.

How to help users in securing the storage of their personal data in their own systems?

By retrieving their personal data from an online service, there is always the risk that users may store them in less secured systems than the one provided by the service. The data subject requesting the data is responsible for identifying the right measures in order to secure personal data in his own system. However, he should be made aware of this in order to take steps to protect the information he has received. As an example of leading practice data controllers may also recommend appropriate format(s), encryption tools and other security measures to help the data subject in achieving this goal.

* * *

Done in Brussels, on 13 December 2016

For the Working Party,

The Chairwoman

Isabelle FALQUE-PIERROTIN

As last revised and adopted on 05 April 2017

For the Working Party

The Chairwoman

Isabelle FALQUE-PIERROTIN

NOTES

28 Some legitimate obstacles might arise, as the ones, which are related to the rights and freedoms of others mentioned in Article 20(4), or the ones that relate to the security of the controllers' own systems. It shall be the responsibility of the data controller to justify why such obstacles would be legitimate and why they do not constitute a hindrance in the meaning of Article 20(1).

29 Through an authenticated communication with the necessary level of data encryption.

30 Synchronisation mechanism can help reaching the general obligations under Article 5 obligation of the GDPR, which provides that "personal data shall be (. . .) accurate and, where necessary, kept up to date"

31 On personal information management systems (PIMS), see, for example, EDPS Opinion 9/2016, available at https://secure.

edps.europa.eu/EDPSWEB/webdav/site/mySite/shared/Documents/Consultation/Opinions/2016/
16-10-20_PIMS_opinion_EN.pdf

³² Article 2 of Decision No 922/2009/EC of the European Parliament and of the Council of 16 September 2009 on interoperability solutions for European public administrations (ISA) OJ L 260, 03.10.2009, p. 20

³³ Amending Directive 2003/98/EC on the re-use of public sector information.

³⁴ The EU glossary (http://eur-lex.europa.eu/eli-register/glossary.html) provides further clarification on expectations related to the concepts used in this guideline, such as *machine-readable, interoperability, open format, standard, metadata.*

³⁵ ISO/IEC 2382-01 defines interoperability as follows: "The capability to communicate, execute programs, or transfer data among various functional units in a manner that requires the user to have little or no knowledge of the unique characteristics of those units."

³⁶ Source : http://ec.europa.eu/isa/documents/isa_annex_ii_eif_en.pdf

³⁷ In conformance to the Directive (EU) 2016/1148 concerning measures for a high common level of security of network and information systems across the Union

ARTICLE 29 DATA PROTECTION WORKING PARTY: GUIDELINES ON DATA PROTECTION OFFICERS ('DPOS')

16/EN
WP 243 rev.01

Adopted on 13 December 2016

As last Revised and Adopted on 5 April 2017

[2.175]

NOTES

This document was originally issued by the Article 29 Working Party but subsequently endorsed by the EDPB during its first plenary meeting.

© European Data Protection Board.

TABLE OF CONTENTS

1 INTRODUCTION

[2.176]

The General Data Protection Regulation ('GDPR'),[1] due to come into effect on 25 May 2018, provides a modernised, accountability-based compliance framework for data protection in Europe. Data Protection Officers ('DPO's) will be at the heart of this new legal framework for many organisations, facilitating compliance with the provisions of the GDPR.

Under the GDPR, it is mandatory for certain controllers and processors to designate a DPO.[2] This will be the case for all public authorities and bodies (irrespective of what data they process), and for other organisations that - as a core activity - monitor individuals systematically and on a large scale, or that process special categories of personal data on a large scale.

Even when the GDPR does not specifically require the appointment of a DPO, organisations may sometimes find it useful to designate a DPO on a voluntary basis. The Article 29 Data Protection Working Party ('WP29') encourages these voluntary efforts.

The concept of DPO is not new. Although Directive 95/46/EC[3] did not require any organisation to appoint a DPO, the practice of appointing a DPO has nevertheless developed in several Member States over the years.

Before the adoption of the GDPR, the WP29 argued that the DPO is a cornerstone of accountability and that appointing a DPO can facilitate compliance and furthermore, become a competitive advantage for businesses.[4] In addition to facilitating compliance through the implementation of accountability tools (such as facilitating data protection impact assessments and carrying out or facilitating audits), DPOs act as intermediaries between relevant stakeholders (e.g. supervisory authorities, data subjects, and business units within an organisation).

DPOs are not personally responsible in case of non-compliance with the GDPR. The GDPR makes it clear that it is the controller or the processor who is required to ensure and to be able to demonstrate that the processing is performed in accordance with its provisions (Article 24(1)). Data protection compliance is a responsibility of the controller or the processor.

The controller or the processor also has a crucial role in enabling the effective performance of the DPO's tasks. Appointing a DPO is a first step but DPOs must also be given sufficient autonomy and resources to carry out their tasks effectively.

The GDPR recognises the DPO as a key player in the new data governance system and lays down conditions for his or her appointment, position and tasks. The aim of these guidelines is to clarify the relevant provisions in the GDPR in order to help controllers and processors to comply with the law, but also to assist DPOs in their role. The guidelines also provide best practice recommendations, building on the experience gained in some EU Member States. The WP29 will monitor the implementation of these guidelines and may complement them with further details as appropriate.

NOTES

1   Regulation (EU) 2016/679 of the European Parliament and of the Council of 27 April 2016 on the protection of natural persons with regard to the processing of personal data and on the free movement of such data, and repealing Directive 95/46/EC (General Data Protection Regulation), (OJ L 119, 4.5.2016). The GDPR is relevant for the EEA and will apply after its incorporation into the EEA Agreement.

2   The appointment of a DPO is also mandatory for competent authorities under Article 32 of Directive (EU) 2016/680 of the European Parliament and of the Council of 27 April 2016 on the protection of natural persons with regard to the processing of personal data by competent authorities for the purposes of the prevention, investigation, detection or prosecution of criminal offences or the execution of criminal penalties, and on the free movement of such data, and repealing Council Framework Decision 2008/977/JHA (OJ L 119, 4.5.2016, p. 89–131), and national implementing legislation. While these guidelines focus on DPOs under the GDPR, the guidance is also relevant regarding DPOs under Directive 2016/680, with respect to their similar provisions.

3   Directive 95/46/EC of the European Parliament and of the Council of 24 October 1995 on the protection of individuals with regard to the processing of personal data and on the free movement of such data (OJ L 281, 23.11.1995, p. 31).

4   See http://ec.europa.eu/justice/data-protection/article-29/documentation/other-document/ files/2015/20150617_appendix_core_issues_plenary_en.pdf

2 DESIGNATION OF A DPO

2.1. MANDATORY DESIGNATION

[2.177]
Article 37(1) of the GDPR requires the designation of a DPO in three specific cases:[5]
(a)   where the processing is carried out by a public authority or body;[6]
(b)   where the core activities of the controller or the processor consist of processing operations, which require regular and systematic monitoring of data subjects on a large scale; or
(c)   where the core activities of the controller or the processor consist of processing on a large scale of special categories of data[7] or[8] personal data relating to criminal convictions and offences.[9]

In the following subsections, the WP29 provides guidance with regard to the criteria and terminology used in Article 37(1).

Unless it is obvious that an organisation is not required to designate a DPO, the WP29 recommends that controllers and processors document the internal analysis carried out to determine whether or not a DPO is to be appointed, in order to be able to demonstrate that the relevant factors have been taken into account properly.[10] This analysis is part of the documentation under the accountability principle. It may be required by the supervisory authority and should be updated when necessary, for example if the controllers or the processors undertake new activities or provide new services that might fall within the cases listed in Article 37(1).

When an organisation designates a DPO on a voluntary basis, the requirements under Articles 37 to 39 will apply to his or her designation, position and tasks as if the designation had been mandatory.

Nothing prevents an organisation, which is not legally required to designate a DPO and does not wish to designate a DPO on a voluntary basis to nevertheless employ staff or outside consultants with tasks relating to the protection of personal data. In this case it is important to ensure that there is no confusion regarding their title, status, position and tasks. Therefore, it should be made clear, in any communications within the company, as well as with data protection authorities, data subjects, and the public at large, that the title of this individual or consultant is not a data protection officer (DPO).[11]

The DPO, whether mandatory or voluntary, is designated for all the processing operations carried out by the controller or the processor.

2.1.1 'Public authority or body'

The GDPR does not define what constitutes a '*public authority or body*'. The WP29 considers that such a notion is to be determined under national law. Accordingly, public authorities and bodies include national, regional and local authorities, but the concept, under the applicable national laws, typically also includes a range of other bodies governed by public law.[12] In such cases, the designation of a DPO is mandatory.

A public task may be carried out, and public authority may be exercised[13] not only by public authorities or bodies but also by other natural or legal persons governed by public or private law, in sectors such as, according to national regulation of each Member State, public transport services, water and energy supply, road infrastructure, public service broadcasting, public housing or disciplinary bodies for regulated professions.

In these cases, data subjects may be in a very similar situation to when their data are processed by a public authority or body. In particular, data can be processed for similar purposes and individuals often have similarly little or no choice over whether and how their data will be processed and may thus require the additional protection that the designation of a DPO can bring.

Even though there is no obligation in such cases, the WP29 recommends, as a good practice, that private organisations carrying out public tasks or exercising public authority designate a DPO. Such a DPO's activity covers all processing operations carried out, including those that are not related to the performance of a public task or exercise of official duty (e.g. the management of an employee database).

2.1.2 'Core activities'

Article 37(1)(b) and (c) of the GDPR refers to the '*core activities of the controller or processor*'. Recital 97 specifies that the core activities of a controller relate to '*primary activities and do not relate to the processing of personal data as ancillary activities*'. 'Core activities' can be considered as the key operations necessary to achieve the controller's or processor's goals.

However, 'core activities' should not be interpreted as excluding activities where the processing of data forms an inextricable part of the controller's or processor's activity. For example, the core activity of a hospital is to provide health care. However, a hospital could not provide healthcare safely and effectively without processing health data, such as patients' health records. Therefore, processing these data should be considered to be one of any hospital's core activities and hospitals must therefore designate DPOs.

As another example, a private security company carries out the surveillance of a number of private shopping centres and public spaces. Surveillance is the core activity of the company, which in turn is inextricably linked to the processing of personal data. Therefore, this company must also designate a DPO.

On the other hand, all organisations carry out certain activities, for example, paying their employees or having standard IT support activities. These are examples of necessary support functions for the organisation's core activity or main business. Even though these activities are necessary or essential, they are usually considered ancillary functions rather than the core activity.

2.1.3 'Large scale'

Article 37(1)(b) and (c) requires that the processing of personal data be carried out on a large scale in order for the designation of a DPO to be triggered. The GDPR does not define what constitutes large-scale processing, though recital 91 provides some guidance.[14]

Indeed, it is not possible to give a precise number either with regard to the amount of data processed or the number of individuals concerned, which would be applicable in all situations. This does not exclude the possibility, however, that over time, a standard practice may develop for identifying in more specific and/or quantitative terms what constitutes '*large scale*' in respect of certain types of common processing activities. The WP29 also plans to contribute to this development, by way of sharing and publicising examples of the relevant thresholds for the designation of a DPO.

In any event, the WP29 recommends that the following factors, in particular, be considered when determining whether the processing is carried out on a large scale:
*   The number of data subjects concerned - either as a specific number or as a proportion of the relevant population
*   The volume of data and/or the range of different data items being processed
*   The duration, or permanence, of the data processing activity
*   The geographical extent of the processing activity

Examples of large-scale processing include:
*   processing of patient data in the regular course of business by a hospital
*   processing of travel data of individuals using a city's public transport system (e.g. tracking via travel cards)
*   processing of real time geo-location data of customers of an international fast food chain for statistical purposes by a processor specialised in providing these services
*   processing of customer data in the regular course of business by an insurance company or a bank
*   processing of personal data for behavioural advertising by a search engine
*   processing of data (content, traffic, location) by telephone or internet service providers

Examples that do not constitute large-scale processing include:
*   processing of patient data by an individual physician
*   processing of personal data relating to criminal convictions and offences by an individual lawyer

2.1.4 'Regular and systematic monitoring'

The notion of regular and systematic monitoring of data subjects is not defined in the GDPR, but the concept of '*monitoring of the behaviour of data subjects*' is mentioned in recital 24[15] and clearly includes all forms of tracking and profiling on the internet, including for the purposes of behavioural advertising.

However, the notion of monitoring is not restricted to the online environment and online tracking should only be considered as one example of monitoring the behaviour of data subjects.[16]

WP29 interprets 'regular' as meaning one or more of the following:
*   Ongoing or occurring at particular intervals for a particular period
*   Recurring or repeated at fixed times
*   Constantly or periodically taking place

WP29 interprets 'systematic' as meaning one or more of the following:
*   Occurring according to a system

- Pre-arranged, organised or methodical
- Taking place as part of a general plan for data collection
- Carried out as part of a strategy

Examples of activities that may constitute a regular and systematic monitoring of data subjects: operating a telecommunications network; providing telecommunications services; email retargeting; data-driven marketing activities; profiling and scoring for purposes of risk assessment (e.g. for purposes of credit scoring, establishment of insurance premiums, fraud prevention, detection of money-laundering); location tracking, for example, by mobile apps; loyalty programs; behavioural advertising; monitoring of wellness, fitness and health data via wearable devices; closed circuit television; connected devices e.g. smart meters, smart cars, home automation, etc.

2.1.5 Special categories of data and data relating to criminal convictions and offences

Article 37(1)(c) addresses the processing of special categories of data pursuant to Article 9, and personal data relating to criminal convictions and offences set out in Article 10. Although the provision uses the word 'and', there is no policy reason for the two criteria having to be applied simultaneously. The text should therefore be read to say 'or'.

2.2. DPO OF THE PROCESSOR

Article 37 applies to both controllers[17] and processors[18] with respect to the designation of a DPO. Depending on who fulfils the criteria on mandatory designation, in some cases only the controller or only the processor, in other cases both the controller and its processor are required to appoint a DPO (who should then cooperate with each other).

It is important to highlight that even if the controller fulfils the criteria for mandatory designation its processor is not necessarily required to appoint a DPO. This may, however, be a good practice.

Examples:
- A small family business active in the distribution of household appliances in a single town uses the services of a processor whose core activity is to provide website analytics services and assistance with targeted advertising and marketing. The activities of the family business and its customers do not generate processing of data on a 'large scale', considering the small number of customers and the relatively limited activities. However, the activities of the processor, having many customers like this small enterprise, taken together, are carrying out large-scale processing. The processor must therefore designate a DPO under Article 37(1)(b). At the same time, the family business itself is not under an obligation to designate a DPO.
- A medium-size tile manufacturing company subcontracts its occupational health services to an external processor, which has a large number of similar clients. The processor shall designate a DPO under Article 37(1)(c) provided that the processing is on a large scale. However, the manufacturer is not necessarily under an obligation to designate a DPO.

The DPO designated by a processor also oversees activities carried out by the processor organisation when acting as a data controller in its own right (e.g. HR, IT, logistics).

2.3. DESIGNATION OF A SINGLE DPO FOR SEVERAL ORGANISATIONS

Article 37(2) allows a group of undertakings to designate a single DPO provided that he or she is '*easily accessible from each establishment*'. The notion of accessibility refers to the tasks of the DPO as a contact point with respect to data subjects[19], the supervisory authority[20] but also internally within the organisation, considering that one of the tasks of the DPO is '*to inform and advise the controller and the processor and the employees who carry out processing of their obligations pursuant to this Regulation*'.[21]

In order to ensure that the DPO, whether internal or external, is accessible it is important to make sure that their contact details are available in accordance with the requirements of the GDPR.[22]

He or she, with the help of a team if necessary, must be in a position to efficiently communicate with data subjects[23] and cooperate[24] with the supervisory authorities concerned. This also means that this communication must take place in the language or languages used by the supervisory authorities and the data subjects concerned. The availability of a DPO (whether physically on the same premises as employees, via a hotline or other secure means of communication) is essential to ensure that data subjects will be able to contact the DPO.

According to Article 37(3), a single DPO may be designated for several public authorities or bodies, taking account of their organisational structure and size. The same considerations with regard to resources and communication apply. Given that the DPO is in charge of a variety of tasks, the controller or the processor must ensure that a single DPO, with the help of a team if necessary, can perform these efficiently despite being designated for several public authorities and bodies.

2.4. ACCESSIBILITY AND LOCALISATION OF THE DPO

According to Section 4 of the GDPR, the accessibility of the DPO should be effective.

To ensure that the DPO is accessible, the WP29 recommends that the DPO be located within the European Union, whether or not the controller or the processor is established in the European Union.

However, it cannot be excluded that, in some situations where the controller or the processor has no establishment within the European Union[25], a DPO may be able to carry out his or her activities more effectively if located outside the EU.

Part 2   Data Protection: EU Law etc

2.5. EXPERTISE AND SKILLS OF THE DPO

Article 37(5) provides that the DPO '*shall be designated on the basis of professional qualities and, in particular, expert knowledge of data protection law and practices and the ability to fulfil the tasks referred to in Article 39*'. Recital 97 provides that the necessary level of expert knowledge should be determined according to the data processing operations carried out and the protection required for the personal data being processed.

- **Level of expertise**
  The required level of expertise is not strictly defined but it must be commensurate with the sensitivity, complexity and amount of data an organisation processes. For example, where a data processing activity is particularly complex, or where a large amount of sensitive data is involved, the DPO may need a higher level of expertise and support. There is also a difference depending on whether the organisation systematically transfers personal data outside the European Union or whether such transfers are occasional. The DPO should thus be chosen carefully, with due regard to the data protection issues that arise within the organisation.
- **Professional qualities**
  Although Article 37(5) does not specify the professional qualities that should be considered when designating the DPO, it is a relevant element that DPOs must have expertise in national and European data protection laws and practices and an in-depth understanding of the GDPR. It is also helpful if the supervisory authorities promote adequate and regular training for DPOs.
  Knowledge of the business sector and of the organisation of the controller is useful. The DPO should also have a good understanding of the processing operations carried out, as well as the information systems, and data security and data protection needs of the controller.
  In the case of a public authority or body, the DPO should also have a sound knowledge of the administrative rules and procedures of the organisation.
- **Ability to fulfil its tasks**
  Ability to fulfil the tasks incumbent on the DPO should be interpreted as both referring to their personal qualities and knowledge, but also to their position within the organisation. Personal qualities should include for instance integrity and high professional ethics; the DPO's primary concern should be enabling compliance with the GDPR. The DPO plays a key role in fostering a data protection culture within the organisation and helps to implement essential elements of the GDPR, such as the principles of data processing[26], data subjects' rights[27], data protection by design and by default[28], records of processing activities[29], security of processing[30], and notification and communication of data breaches.[31]
- **DPO on the basis of a service contract**
  The function of the DPO can also be exercised on the basis of a service contract concluded with an individual or an organisation outside the controller's/processor's organisation. In this latter case, it is essential that each member of the organisation exercising the functions of a DPO fulfils all applicable requirements of Section 4 of the GDPR (e.g., it is essential that no one has a conflict of interests). It is equally important that each such member be protected by the provisions of the GDPR (e.g. no unfair termination of service contract for activities as DPO but also no unfair dismissal of any individual member of the organisation carrying out the DPO tasks). At the same time, individual skills and strengths can be combined so that several individuals, working in a team, may more efficiently serve their clients.
  For the sake of legal clarity and good organisation and to prevent conflicts of interests for the team members, it is recommended to have a clear allocation of tasks within the DPO team and to assign a single individual as a lead contact and person 'in charge' for each client. It would generally also be useful to specify these points in the service contract.

2.6. PUBLICATION AND COMMUNICATION OF THE DPO'S CONTACT DETAILS

Article 37(7) of the GDPR requires the controller or the processor:
- to publish the contact details of the DPO and
- to communicate the contact details of the DPO to the relevant supervisory authorities.

The objective of these requirements is to ensure that data subjects (both inside and outside of the organisation) and the supervisory authorities can easily and directly contact the DPO without having to contact another part of the organisation. Confidentiality is equally important: for example, employees may be reluctant to complain to the DPO if the confidentiality of their communications is not guaranteed.

The DPO is bound by secrecy or confidentiality concerning the performance of his or her tasks, in accordance with Union or Member State law (Article 38(5)).

The contact details of the DPO should include information allowing data subjects and the supervisory authorities to reach the DPO in an easy way (a postal address, a dedicated telephone number, and/or a dedicated e-mail address). When appropriate, for purposes of communications with the public, other means of communications could also be provided, for example, a dedicated hotline, or a dedicated contact form addressed to the DPO on the organisation's website.

Article 37(7) does not require that the published contact details should include the name of the DPO. Whilst it may be a good practice to do so, it is for the controller or the processor and the DPO to decide whether this is necessary or helpful in the particular circumstances.[32]

However, communication of the name of the DPO to the supervisory authority is essential in order for the DPO to serve as contact point between the organisation and the supervisory authority (Article 39(1)(e).

As a matter of good practice, the WP29 also recommends that an organisation informs its employees of the name and contact details of the DPO. For example, the name and contact details of the DPO could be published internally on organisation's intranet, internal telephone directory, and organisational charts.

NOTES

5   Note that under Article 37(4), Union or Member State law may require the designation of DPOs in other situations as well.

6   Except for courts acting in their judicial capacity. See Article 32 of Directive (EU) 2016/680.

7   Pursuant to Article 9 these include personal data revealing racial or ethnic origin, political opinions, religious or philosophical beliefs, or trade union membership, and the processing of genetic data, biometric data for the purpose of uniquely identifying a natural person, data concerning health or data concerning a natural person's sex life or sexual orientation.

8   Article 37(1)(c) uses the word '*and*'. See Section 2.1.5 below for explanation on the use of '*or*' instead of '*and.*'

9   Article 10.

10   See Article 24(1).

11   This is also relevant for chief privacy officers ('CPO's) or other privacy professionals already in place today in some companies, who may not always meet the GDPR criteria, for instance, in terms of available resources or guarantees for independence, and, if they do not, they cannot be considered and referred to as DPOs.

12   See, e.g. the definition of '*public sector body*' and '*body governed by public law*' in Article 2(1) and (2) of Directive 2003/98/EC of the European Parliament and of the Council of 17 November 2003 on the re-use of public-sector information (OJ L 345, 31.12.2003, p. 90).

13   Article 6(1)(e).

14   According to the recital, '*large-scale processing operations which aim to process a considerable amount of personal data at regional, national or supranational level and which could affect a large number of data subjects and which are likely to result in a high risk*' would be included, in particular. On the other hand, the recital specifically provides that '*the processing of personal data should not be considered to be on a large scale if the processing concerns personal data from patients or clients by an individual physician, other health care professional or lawyer*'. It is important to consider that while the recital provides examples at the extremes of the scale (processing by an individual physician versus processing of data of a whole country or across Europe); there is a large grey zone in between these extremes. In addition, it should be borne in mind that this recital refers to data protection impact assessments. This implies that some elements might be specific to that context and do not necessarily apply to the designation of DPOs in the exact same way.

15   '*In order to determine whether a processing activity can be considered to monitor the behaviour of data subjects, it should be ascertained whether natural persons are tracked on the internet including potential subsequent use of personal data processing techniques which consist of profiling a natural person, particularly in order to take decisions concerning her or him or for analysing or predicting her or his personal preferences, behaviours and attitudes*'.

16   Note that Recital 24 focuses on the extra-territorial application of the GDPR. In addition, there is also a difference between the wording '*monitoring of their behaviour*' (Article 3(2)(b)) and '*regular and systematic monitoring of data subjects*' (Article 37(1)(b)) which could therefore be seen as constituting a different notion.

17   The controller is defined by Article 4(7) as the person or body, which determines the purposes and means of the processing.

18   The processor is defined by Article 4(8) as the person or body, which processes data on behalf of the controller.

19   Article 38(4): '*data subjects may contact the data protection officer with regard to all issues related to processing of their personal data and to the exercise of their rights under this regulation*'.

20   Article 39(1)(e): '*act as a contact point for the supervisory authority on issues relating to processing, including the prior consultation referred to in Article 36 and to consult, where appropriate, with regard to any other matter*'.

21   Article 39(1)(a).

22   See also Section 2.6 below.

23   Article 12(1): '*The controller shall take appropriate measures to provide any information referred to in Articles 13 and 14 and any communication under Articles 15 to 22 and 34 relating to processing to the data subject in a concise, transparent, intelligible and easily accessible form, using clear and plain language, in particular for any information addressed specifically to a child.*'

24   Article 39(1)(d) : '*to cooperate with the supervisory authority*'

25   See Article 3 of the GDPR on the territorial scope.

26   Chapter II.

27   Chapter III.

28   Article 25.

29   Article 30.

30   Article 32.

31   Articles 33 and 34.

32   It is notable that Article 33(3)(b), which describes information that must be provided to the supervisory authority and to the data subjects in case of a personal data breach, unlike Article 37(7), specifically also requires the name (and not only the contact details) of the DPO to be communicated.

3 POSITION OF THE DPO

3.1. INVOLVEMENT OF THE DPO IN ALL ISSUES RELATING TO THE PROTECTION OF PERSONAL DATA

[2.178]
Article 38 of the GDPR provides that the controller and the processor shall ensure that the DPO is '*involved, properly and in a timely manner, in all issues which relate to the protection of personal data*'.

It is crucial that the DPO, or his/her team, is involved from the earliest stage possible in all issues relating to data protection. In relation to data protection impact assessments, the GDPR explicitly provides for the early involvement of the DPO and specifies that the controller shall seek the advice of the DPO when carrying out such impact assessments.[33] Ensuring that the DPO is informed and consulted at the outset will facilitate compliance with the GDPR, promote a privacy by design approach and should therefore be standard procedure within the organisation's governance. In addition, it is important that the DPO be seen as a discussion partner within the organisation and that he or she be part of the relevant working groups dealing with data processing activities within the organisation.

Consequently, the organisation should ensure, for example, that:
- The DPO is invited to participate regularly in meetings of senior and middle management.
- His or her presence is recommended where decisions with data protection implications are taken. All relevant information must be passed on to the DPO in a timely manner in order to allow him or her to provide adequate advice.
- The opinion of the DPO must always be given due weight. In case of disagreement, the WP29 recommends, as good practice, to document the reasons for not following the DPO's advice.
- The DPO must be promptly consulted once a data breach or another incident has occurred.

Where appropriate, the controller or processor could develop data protection guidelines or programmes that set out when the DPO must be consulted.

3.2. NECESSARY RESOURCES

Article 38(2) of the GDPR requires the organisation to support its DPO by *'providing resources necessary to carry out [their] tasks and access to personal data and processing operations, and to maintain his or her expert knowledge'*. The following items, in particular, are to be considered:
- Active support of the DPO's function by senior management (such as at board level).
- Sufficient time for DPOs to fulfil their duties. This is particularly important where an internal DPO is appointed on a part-time basis or where the external DPO carries out data protection in addition to other duties. Otherwise, conflicting priorities could result in the DPO's duties being neglected. Having sufficient time to devote to DPO tasks is paramount. It is a good practice to establish a percentage of time for the DPO function where it is not performed on a full-time basis. It is also good practice to determine the time needed to carry out the function, the appropriate level of priority for DPO duties, and for the DPO (or the organisation) to draw up a work plan.
- Adequate support in terms of financial resources, infrastructure (premises, facilities, equipment) and staff where appropriate.
- Official communication of the designation of the DPO to all staff to ensure that their existence and function are known within the organisation.
- Necessary access to other services, such as Human Resources, legal, IT, security, etc., so that DPOs can receive essential support, input and information from those other services.
- Continuous training. DPOs must be given the opportunity to stay up to date with regard to developments within the field of data protection. The aim should be to constantly increase the level of expertise of DPOs and they should be encouraged to participate in training courses on data protection and other forms of professional development, such as participation in privacy fora, workshops, etc.
- Given the size and structure of the organisation, it may be necessary to set up a DPO team (a DPO and his/her staff). In such cases, the internal structure of the team and the tasks and responsibilities of each of its members should be clearly drawn up. Similarly, when the function of the DPO is exercised by an external service provider, a team of individuals working for that entity may effectively carry out the tasks of a DPO as a team, under the responsibility of a designated lead contact for the client.

In general, the more complex and/or sensitive the processing operations, the more resources must be given to the DPO. The data protection function must be effective and sufficiently well-resourced in relation to the data processing being carried out.

3.3. INSTRUCTIONS AND 'PERFORMING THEIR DUTIES AND TASKS IN AN INDEPENDENT MANNER'

Article 38(3) establishes some basic guarantees to help ensure that DPOs are able to perform their tasks with a sufficient degree of autonomy within their organisation. In particular, controllers/processors are required to ensure that the DPO *'does not receive any instructions regarding the exercise of [his or her] tasks.'* Recital 97 adds that DPOs, *'whether or not they are an employee of the controller, should be in a position to perform their duties and tasks in an independent manner'*.

This means that, in fulfilling their tasks under Article 39, DPOs must not be instructed how to deal with a matter, for example, what result should be achieved, how to investigate a complaint or whether to consult the supervisory authority. Furthermore, they must not be instructed to take a certain view of an issue related to data protection law, for example, a particular interpretation of the law.

The autonomy of DPOs does not, however, mean that they have decision-making powers extending beyond their tasks pursuant to Article 39.

The controller or processor remains responsible for compliance with data protection law and must be able to demonstrate compliance.[34] If the controller or processor makes decisions that are incompatible with the GDPR and the DPO's advice, the DPO should be given the possibility to make his or her dissenting opinion clear to the highest management level and to those making the decisions. In this respect, Article 38(3) provides that the DPO *'shall directly report to the highest management level of the controller or the processor'*. Such direct reporting ensures that senior management (e.g. board of directors) is aware of the DPO's advice and recommendations as part of the DPO's mission to inform and advise the controller or the processor. Another example of direct reporting is the drafting of an annual report of the DPO's activities provided to the highest management level.

3.4. DISMISSAL OR PENALTY FOR PERFORMING DPO TASKS

Article 38(3) requires that DPOs should '*not be dismissed or penalised by the controller or the processor for performing [their] tasks*'.

This requirement strengthens the autonomy of DPOs and helps ensure that they act independently and enjoy sufficient protection in performing their data protection tasks.

Penalties are only prohibited under the GDPR if they are imposed as a result of the DPO carrying out his or her duties as a DPO. For example, a DPO may consider that a particular processing is likely to result in a high risk and advise the controller or the processor to carry out a data protection impact assessment but the controller or the processor does not agree with the DPO's assessment. In such a situation, the DPO cannot be dismissed for providing this advice.

Penalties may take a variety of forms and may be direct or indirect. They could consist, for example, of absence or delay of promotion; prevention from career advancement; denial from benefits that other employees receive. It is not necessary that these penalties be actually carried out, a mere threat is sufficient as long as they are used to penalise the DPO on grounds related to his/her DPO activities.

As a normal management rule and as it would be the case for any other employee or contractor under, and subject to, applicable national contract or labour and criminal law, a DPO could still be dismissed legitimately for reasons other than for performing his or her tasks as a DPO (for instance, in case of theft, physical, psychological or sexual harassment or similar gross misconduct).

In this context it should be noted that the GDPR does not specify how and when a DPO can be dismissed or replaced by another person. However, the more stable a DPO's contract is, and the more guarantees exist against unfair dismissal, the more likely they will be able to act in an independent manner. Therefore, the WP29 would welcome efforts by organisations to this effect.

3.5. CONFLICT OF INTERESTS

Article 38(6) allows DPOs to '*fulfil other tasks and duties*'. It requires, however, that the organisation ensure that '*any such tasks and duties do not result in a conflict of interests*'.

The absence of conflict of interests is closely linked to the requirement to act in an independent manner. Although DPOs are allowed to have other functions, they can only be entrusted with other tasks and duties provided that these do not give rise to conflicts of interests. This entails in particular that the DPO cannot hold a position within the organisation that leads him or her to determine the purposes and the means of the processing of personal data. Due to the specific organisational structure in each organisation, this has to be considered case by case.

As a rule of thumb, conflicting positions within the organisation may include senior management positions (such as chief executive, chief operating, chief financial, chief medical officer, head of marketing department, head of Human Resources or head of IT departments) but also other roles lower down in the organisational structure if such positions or roles lead to the determination of purposes and means of processing. In addition, a conflict of interests may also arise for example if an external DPO is asked to represent the controller or processor before the Courts in cases involving data protection issues.

Depending on the activities, size and structure of the organisation, it can be good practice for controllers or processors:

- to identify the positions which would be incompatible with the function of DPO
- to draw up internal rules to this effect in order to avoid conflicts of interests
- to include a more general explanation about conflicts of interests
- to declare that their DPO has no conflict of interests with regard to its function as a DPO, as a way of raising awareness of this requirement
- to include safeguards in the internal rules of the organisation and to ensure that the vacancy notice for the position of DPO or the service contract is sufficiently precise and detailed in order to avoid a conflict of interests. In this context, it should also be borne in mind that conflicts of interests may take various forms depending on whether the DPO is recruited internally or externally

NOTES

[33]   Article 35(2).
[34]   Article 5(2).

4 TASKS OF THE DPO

4.1. MONITORING COMPLIANCE WITH THE GDPR

[2.179]

Article 39(1)(b) entrusts DPOs, among other duties, with the duty to monitor compliance with the GDPR. Recital 97 further specifies that DPO '*should assist the controller or the processor to monitor internal compliance with this Regulation*'.

As part of these duties to monitor compliance, DPOs may, in particular:
*   collect information to identify processing activities
*   analyse and check the compliance of processing activities
*   inform, advise and issue recommendations to the controller or the processor

Monitoring of compliance does not mean that it is the DPO who is personally responsible where there is an instance of non-compliance. The GDPR makes it clear that it is the controller, not the DPO, who is required to '*implement appropriate technical and organisational measures to ensure and to be able to demonstrate that processing is performed in accordance with this Regulation*' (Article 24(1)). Data protection compliance is a corporate responsibility of the data controller, not of the DPO.

4.2. ROLE OF THE DPO IN A DATA PROTECTION IMPACT ASSESSMENT

According to Article 35(1), it is the task of the controller, not of the DPO, to carry out, when necessary, a data protection impact assessment ('DPIA'). However, the DPO can play a very important and useful role in assisting the controller. Following the principle of data protection by design, Article 35(2) specifically requires that the controller '*shall seek advice*' of the DPO when carrying out a DPIA. Article 39(1)(c), in turn, tasks the DPO with the duty to '*provide advice where requested as regards the [DPIA] and monitor its performance pursuant to Article 35*'.

The WP29 recommends that the controller should seek the advice of the DPO, on the following issues, amongst others[35]:
*   whether or not to carry out a DPIA
*   what methodology to follow when carrying out a DPIA
*   whether to carry out the DPIA in-house or whether to outsource it
*   what safeguards (including technical and organisational measures) to apply to mitigate any risks to the rights and interests of the data subjects
*   whether or not the data protection impact assessment has been correctly carried out and whether its conclusions (whether or not to go ahead with the processing and what safeguards to apply) are in compliance with the GDPR

If the controller disagrees with the advice provided by the DPO, the DPIA documentation should specifically justify in writing why the advice has not been taken into account[36].

The WP29 further recommends that the controller clearly outline, for example in the DPO's contract, but also in information provided to employees, management (and other stakeholders, where relevant), the precise tasks of the DPO and their scope, in particular with respect to carrying out the DPIA.

4.3. COOPERATING WITH THE SUPERVISORY AUTHORITY AND ACTING AS A CONTACT POINT

According to Article 39(1)(d) and (e), the DPO should '*cooperate with the supervisory authority*' and '*act as a contact point for the supervisory authority on issues relating to processing, including the prior consultation referred to in Article 36, and to consult, where appropriate, with regard to any other matter*'.

These tasks refer to the role of 'facilitator' of the DPO mentioned in the introduction to these Guidelines. The DPO acts as a contact point to facilitate access by the supervisory authority to the documents and information for the performance of the tasks mentioned in Article 57, as well as for the exercise of its investigative, corrective, authorisation, and advisory powers mentioned in Article 58. As already mentioned, the DPO is bound by secrecy or confidentiality concerning the performance of his or her tasks, in accordance with Union or Member State law (Article 38(5)). However, the obligation of secrecy/confidentiality does not prohibit the DPO from contacting and seeking advice from the supervisory authority. Article 39(1)(e) provides that the DPO can consult the supervisory authority on any other matter, where appropriate.

4.4. RISK-BASED APPROACH

Article 39(2) requires that the DPO '*have due regard to the risk associated with the processing operations, taking into account the nature, scope, context and purposes of processing*'.

This article recalls a general and common sense principle, which may be relevant for many aspects of a DPO's day-to-day work. In essence, it requires DPOs to prioritise their activities and focus their efforts on issues that present higher data protection risks. This does not mean that they should neglect monitoring compliance of data processing operations that have comparatively lower level of risks, but it does indicate that they should focus, primarily, on the higher-risk areas.

This selective and pragmatic approach should help DPOs advise the controller what methodology to use when carrying out a DPIA, which areas should be subject to an internal or external data protection audit, which internal training activities to provide to staff or management responsible for data processing activities, and which processing operations to devote more of his or her time and resources to.

4.5. ROLE OF THE DPO IN RECORD-KEEPING

Under Article 30(1) and (2), it is the controller or the processor, not the DPO, who is required to '*maintain a record of processing operations under its responsibility*' or '*maintain a record of all categories of processing activities carried out on behalf of a controller*'.

In practice, DPOs often create inventories and hold a register of processing operations based on information provided to them by the various departments in their organisation responsible for the processing of personal data. This practice has been established under many current national laws and under the data protection rules applicable to the EU institutions and bodies.[37]

Article 39(1) provides for a list of tasks that the DPO must have as a minimum. Therefore, nothing prevents the controller or the processor from assigning the DPO with the task of maintaining the record of processing operations under the responsibility of the controller or the processor. Such a record should be considered as one of the tools enabling the DPO to perform its tasks of monitoring compliance, informing and advising the controller or the processor.

In any event, the record required to be kept under Article 30 should also be seen as a tool allowing the controller and the supervisory authority, upon request, to have an overview of all the personal data processing activities an organisation is carrying out. It is thus a prerequisite for compliance, and as such, an effective accountability measure.

NOTES

35   Article 39(1) mentions the tasks of the DPO and indicates that the DPO shall have '*at least*' the following tasks. Therefore, nothing prevents the controller from assigning the DPO other tasks than those explicitly mentioned in Article 39(1), or specifying those tasks in more detail.

36   Article 24(1) provides that '*taking into account the nature, scope, context and purposes of processing as well as the risks of varying likelihood and severity for the rights and freedoms of natural persons, the controller shall implement appropriate technical and organisational measures to ensure **and to be able to demonstrate** that processing is performed in accordance with this Regulation. Those measures shall be reviewed and updated where necessary*'.

37   Article 24(1)(d), Regulation (EC) 45/2001.

5 ANNEX - DPO GUIDELINES: WHAT YOU NEED TO KNOW

[2.180]

The objective of this annex is to answer, in a simplified and easy-to-read format, some of the key questions that organisations may have regarding the new requirements under the General Data Protection Regulation (GDPR) to appoint a DPO.

DESIGNATION OF THE DPO

1 Which organisations must appoint a DPO?

The designation of a DPO is an obligation:
*   if the processing is carried out by a public authority or body (irrespective of what data is being processed)
*   if the core activities of the controller or the processor consist of processing operations, which require regular and systematic monitoring of data subjects on a large scale
*   if the core activities of the controller or the processor consist of processing on a large scale of special categories of data or personal data relating to criminal convictions and offences

Note that Union or Member State law may require the designation of DPOs in other situations as well. Finally, even if the designation of a DPO is not mandatory, organisations may sometimes find it useful to designate a DPO on a voluntary basis. The Article 29 Data Protection Working Party ('WP29') encourages these voluntary efforts. When an organisation designates a DPO on a voluntary basis, the same requirements will apply to his or her designation, position and tasks as if the designation had been mandatory.

Source: Article 37(1) of the GDPR

2 What does 'core activities' mean?

'Core activities' can be considered as the key operations to achieve the controller's or processor's objectives. These also include all activities where the processing of data forms as inextricable part of the controller's or processor's activity. For example, processing health data, such as patient's health records, should be considered as one of any hospital's core activities and hospitals must therefore designate DPOs.

On the other hand, all organisations carry out certain supporting activities, for example, paying their employees or having standard IT support activities. These are examples of necessary support functions for the organisation's core activity or main business. Even though these activities are necessary or essential, they are usually considered ancillary functions rather than the core activity.

Source: Article 37(1)(b) and (c) of the GDPR

3 What does 'large scale' mean?

The GDPR does not define what constitutes large-scale processing. The WP29 recommends that the following factors, in particular, be considered when determining whether the processing is carried out on a large scale:
*   the number of data subjects concerned - either as a specific number or as a proportion of the relevant population
*   the volume of data and/or the range of different data items being processed
*   the duration, or permanence, of the data processing activity
*   the geographical extent of the processing activity

Examples of large scale processing include:
* processing of patient data in the regular course of business by a hospital
* processing of travel data of individuals using a city's public transport system (e.g. tracking via travel cards)
* processing of real time geo-location data of customers of an international fast food chain for statistical purposes by a processor specialised in these activities
* processing of customer data in the regular course of business by an insurance company or a bank
* processing of personal data for behavioural advertising by a search engine
* processing of data (content, traffic, location) by telephone or internet service providers

Examples that do not constitute large-scale processing include:
* processing of patient data by an individual physician
* processing of personal data relating to criminal convictions and offences by an individual lawyer

Source: Article 37(1)(b) and (c) of the GDPR

4 What does 'regular and systematic monitoring' mean?

The notion of regular and systematic monitoring of data subjects is not defined in the GDPR, but clearly includes all forms of tracking and profiling on the internet, including for the purposes of behavioural advertising. However, the notion of monitoring is not restricted to the online environment.

Examples of activities that may constitute a regular and systematic monitoring of data subjects: operating a telecommunications network; providing telecommunications services; email retargeting; data-driven marketing activities; profiling and scoring for purposes of risk assessment (e.g. for purposes of credit scoring, establishment of insurance premiums, fraud prevention, detection of money-laundering); location tracking, for example, by mobile apps; loyalty programs; behavioural advertising; monitoring of wellness, fitness and health data via wearable devices; closed circuit television; connected devices e.g. smart meters, smart cars, home automation, etc.

WP29 interprets 'regular' as meaning one or more of the following:
* ongoing or occurring at particular intervals for a particular period
* recurring or repeated at fixed times
* constantly or periodically taking place

WP29 interprets 'systematic' as meaning one or more of the following:
* occurring according to a system
* pre-arranged, organised or methodical
* taking place as part of a general plan for data collection
* carried out as part of a strategy

Source: Article 37(1)(b) of the GDPR

5 Can organisations appoint a DPO jointly? If so, under what conditions?

Yes. A group of undertakings may designate a single DPO provided that he or she is '*easily accessible from each establishment*'. The notion of accessibility refers to the tasks of the DPO as a contact point with respect to data subjects, the supervisory authority and also internally within the organisation. In order to ensure that the DPO is accessible, whether internal or external, it is important to make sure that their contact details are available. The DPO, with the help of a team if necessary, must be in a position to efficiently communicate with data subjects and cooperate with the supervisory authorities concerned. This means that this communication must take place in the language or languages used by the supervisory authorities and the data subjects concerned. The availability of a DPO (whether physically on the same premises as employees, via a hotline or other secure means of communication) is essential to ensure that data subjects will be able to contact the DPO.

A single DPO may be designated for several public authorities or bodies, taking account of their organisational structure and size. The same considerations with regard to resources and communication apply. Given that the DPO is in charge of a variety of tasks, the controller or the processor must ensure that a single DPO, with the help of a team if necessary, can perform these efficiently despite being designated for several public authorities and bodies.

Source: Article 37(2) and (3) of the GDPR

6 Where should the DPO be located?

To ensure that the DPO is accessible, the WP29 recommends that the DPO be located within the European Union, whether or not the controller or the processor is established in the European Union. However, it cannot be excluded that, in some situations where the controller or the processor has no establishment within the European Union, a DPO may be able to carry out his or her activities more effectively if located outside the EU.

7 Is it possible to appoint an external DPO?

Yes. The DPO may be a staff member of the controller or the processor (internal DPO) or fulfil the tasks on the basis of a service contract. This means that the DPO can be external, and in this case, his/her function can be exercised based on a service contract concluded with an individual or an organisation.

When the function of the DPO is exercised by an external service provider, a team of individuals working for that entity may effectively carry out the DPO tasks as a team, under the responsibility of a designated lead contact and 'person in charge' of the client. In this case, it is essential that each member of the external organisation exercising the functions of a DPO fulfils all applicable requirements of the GDPR.

For the sake of legal clarity and good organisation and to prevent conflicts of interests for the team members, the Guidelines recommend to have, in the service contract, a clear allocation of tasks within the external DPO team and to assign a single individual as a lead contact and person 'in charge' of the client.

Source: Article 37(6) of the GDPR

8 What are the professional qualities that the DPO should have?

The DPO shall be designated on the basis of professional qualities and, in particular, expert knowledge of data protection law and practices and the ability to fulfil his or her tasks.

The necessary level of expert knowledge should be determined according to the data processing operations carried out and the protection required for the personal data being processed. For example, where a data processing activity is particularly complex, or where a large amount of sensitive data is involved, the DPO may need a higher level of expertise and support.

Relevant skills and expertise include:
* expertise in national and European data protection laws and practices including an in-depth understanding of the GDPR
* understanding of the processing operations carried out
* understanding of information technologies and data security
* knowledge of the business sector and the organisation
* ability to promote a data protection culture within the organisation

Source: Article 37(5) of the GDPR

POSITION OF THE DPO

9 What resources should be provided to the DPO by the controller or the processor?

The DPO must have the resources necessary to be able to carry out his or her tasks.

Depending on the nature of the processing operations and the activities and size of the organisation, the following resources should be provided to the DPO:
* active support of the DPO's function by senior management
* sufficient time for DPOs to fulfil their tasks
* adequate support in terms of financial resources, infrastructure (premises, facilities, equipment) and staff where appropriate
* official communication of the designation of the DPO to all staff
* access to other services within the organisation so that DPOs can receive essential support, input or information from those other services
* continuous training

10 What are the safeguards to enable the DPO to perform her/his tasks in an independent manner? What does 'conflict of interests' mean?

Several safeguards exist in order to enable the DPO to act in an independent manner:
* no instructions by the controllers or the processors regarding the exercise of the DPO's tasks
* no dismissal or penalty by the controller for the performance of the DPO's tasks
* no conflict of interest with possible other tasks and duties

The other tasks and duties of a DPO must not result in a conflict of interests. This means, first, that the DPO cannot hold a position within the organisation that leads him or her to determine the purposes and the means of the processing of personal data. Due to the specific organisational structure in each organisation, this has to be considered case by case.

As a rule of thumb, conflicting positions within the organisation may include senior management positions (such as chief executive, chief operating, chief financial, chief medical officer, head of marketing department, head of Human Resources or head of IT departments) but also other roles lower down in the organisational structure if such positions or roles lead to the determination of purposes and means of processing. In addition, a conflict of interests may also arise for example if an external DPO is asked to represent the controller or processor before the Courts in cases involving data protection issues.

Source: Article 38(3) and 38(6) of the GDPR

TASKS OF THE DPO

11 What does 'monitoring compliance' mean?

As part of these duties to monitor compliance, DPOs may, in particular:
* collect information to identify processing activities
* analyse and check the compliance of processing activities
* inform, advise and issue recommendations to the controller or the processor

Source: Article 39(1)(b) of the GDPR

12 Is the DPO personally responsible for non-compliance with data protection requirements?

No. DPOs are not personally responsible for non-compliance with data protection requirements. It is the controller or the processor who is required to ensure and to be able to demonstrate that processing is performed in accordance with this Regulation. Data protection compliance is the responsibility of the controller or the processor.

13 What is the role of the DPO with respect to data protection impact assessments and records of processing activities?

As far as the data protection impact assessment is concerned, the controller or the processor should seek the advice of the DPO, on the following issues, amongst others:

- whether or not to carry out a DPIA
- what methodology to follow when carrying out a DPIA
- whether to carry out the DPIA in-house or whether to outsource it
- what safeguards (including technical and organisational measures) to apply to mitigate any risks to the rights and interests of the data subjects
- whether or not the data protection impact assessment has been correctly carried out and whether its conclusions (whether or not to go ahead with the processing and what safeguards to apply) are in compliance with data protection requirements

As far as the records of processing activities are concerned, it is the controller or the processor, not the DPO, who is required to maintain records of processing operations. However, nothing prevents the controller or the processor from assigning the DPO with the task of maintaining the records of processing operations under the responsibility of the controller or the processor. Such records should be considered as one of the tools enabling the DPO to perform its tasks of monitoring compliance, informing and advising the controller or the processor.

Source: Article 39(1)(c) and Article 30 of the GDPR

Done in Brussels, on 13 December 2016

For the Working Party,

The Chairwoman

Isabelle FALQUE-PIERROTIN

As last revised and adopted on 05 April 2017

For the Working Party

The Chairwoman

Isabelle FALQUE-PIERROTIN

ARTICLE 29 DATA PROTECTION WORKING PARTY: GUIDELINES FOR IDENTIFYING A CONTROLLER OR PROCESSOR'S LEAD SUPERVISORY AUTHORITY
16/EN
WP 244 rev.01
Adopted on 13 December 2016

As last Revised and Adopted on 5 April 2017

[2.181]

NOTES
This document was originally issued by the Article 29 Working Party but subsequently endorsed by the EDPB during its first plenary meeting.
© European Data Protection Board.

TABLE OF CONTENTS

1. IDENTIFYING A LEAD SUPERVISORY AUTHORITY: THE KEY CONCEPTS.

1.1 'CROSS-BORDER PROCESSING OF PERSONAL DATA'.

[2.182]
Identifying a lead supervisory authority is only relevant where a controller or processor is carrying out

the cross-border processing of personal data. Article 4(23) of the General Data Protection Regulation (GDPR) defines 'cross-border processing' as either the:

—   *processing of personal data which takes place in the context of the activities of establishments in more than one Member State of a controller or processor in the Union where the controller or processor is established in more than one Member State; or the*

—   *processing of personal data which takes place in the context of the activities of a single establishment of a controller or processor in the Union but which substantially affects or is likely to substantially affect data subjects in more than one Member State.*

This means that where an organisation has establishments in France and Romania, for example, and the processing of personal data takes place in the context of their activities, then this will constitute cross-border processing.

Alternatively, the organisation may only carry out processing activity in the context of its establishment in France. However, if the activity substantially affects – or is likely to substantially affect - data subjects in France and Romania then this will also constitute cross-border processing.

1.1.1 'Substantially affects'.

The GDPR does not define 'substantially' or 'affects'. The intention of the wording was to ensure that not all processing activity, with any effect and that takes place within the context of a single establishment, falls within the definition of 'cross-border processing'.

The most relevant ordinary English meanings of 'substantial' include; 'of ample or considerable amount or size; sizeable, fairly large', or 'having solid worth or value, of real significance; solid; weighty, important' (Oxford English Dictionary).

The most relevant meaning of the verb 'affect' is 'to influence' or 'to make a material impression on'. The related noun -'effect'- means, amongst other things, 'a result or a consequence' (Oxford English Dictionary). This suggests that for data processing to affect someone it must have some form of impact on them. Processing that does not have a substantial effect on individuals does not fall within the second part of the definition of 'cross-border processing'. However, it would fall within the first part of the definition where the processing of personal data takes place in the context of the activities of establishments in more than one Member State of a controller or processor in the Union, where the controller or processor is established in more than one Member State.

Processing can be brought within the second part of the definition if there is the likelihood of a substantial effect, not just an actual substantial effect. Note that 'likely to' does not mean that there is a remote possibility of a substantial effect. The substantial effect must be more likely than not. On the other hand, it also means that individuals do not have to be actually affected: the likelihood of a substantial effect is sufficient to bring the processing within the definition of 'cross-border processing'.

The fact that a data processing operation may involve the processing of a number – even a large number – of individuals' personal data, in a number of Member States, does not necessarily mean that the processing has, or is likely to have, a substantial effect. Processing that does not have a substantial effect does not constitute cross-border processing for the purposes of the second part of the definition, regardless of how many individuals it affects.

Supervisory Authorities will interpret 'substantially affects' on a case by case basis. We will take into account the context of the processing, the type of data, the purpose of the processing and factors such as whether the processing:

•   causes, or is likely to cause, damage, loss or distress to individuals;

•   has, or is likely to have, an actual effect in terms of limiting rights or denying an opportunity;

•   affects, or is likely to affect individuals' health, well-being or peace of mind;

•   affects, or is likely to affect, individuals' financial or economic status or circumstances;

•   leaves individuals open to discrimination or unfair treatment;

•   involves the analysis of the special categories of personal or other intrusive data, particularly the personal data of children;

•   causes, or is likely to cause individuals to change their behaviour in a significant way;

•   has unlikely, unanticipated or unwanted consequences for individuals;

•   creates embarrassment or other negative outcomes, including reputational damage; or

•   involves the processing of a wide range of personal data.

Ultimately, the test of 'substantial effect' is intended to ensure that supervisory authorities are only required to co-operate formally through the GDPR's consistency mechanism *"where a supervisory authority intends to adopt a measure intended to produce legal effects as regards processing operations which substantially affect a significant number of data subjects in several Member States". (Recital 135)*

1.2 LEAD SUPERVISORY AUTHORITY.

Put simply, a 'lead supervisory authority' is the authority with the primary responsibility for dealing with a cross-border data processing activity, for example when a data subject makes a complaint about the processing of his or her personal data.

The lead supervisory authority will coordinate any investigation, involving other 'concerned' supervisory authorities.

Identifying the lead supervisory authority depends on determining the location of the controller's 'main establishment' or 'single establishment' in the EU. Article 56 of the GDPR says that:

– the supervisory authority of the main establishment or of the single establishment of the controller or processor shall be competent to act as lead supervisory authority for the cross-border processing carried out by that controller or processor in accordance with the [cooperation] procedure provided in Article 60.

1.3 MAIN ESTABLISHMENT.

Article 4(16) of the GDPR states that 'main establishment' means:

– as regards a controller with establishments in more than one Member State, the place of its **central administration** in the Union, unless the **decisions on the purposes and means** of the processing of personal data are taken in another establishment of the controller in the Union and the latter establishment has the **power to have such decisions implemented**, in which case the establishment having taken such decisions is to be considered to be the main establishment;

– as regards a processor with establishments in more than one Member State, the place of its central administration in the Union, or, if the processor has no central administration in the Union, the establishment of the processor in the Union where the main processing activities in the context of the activities of an establishment of the processor take place to the extent that the processor is subject to specific obligations under this Regulation;

2. STEPS TO IDENTIFY THE LEAD SUPERVISORY AUTHORITY

2.1 IDENTIFY THE 'MAIN ESTABLISHMENT' FOR CONTROLLERS

[2.183]

In order to establish where the main establishment is, it is firstly necessary to identify the central administration of the data controller in the EU, if any.[1] The approach implied in the GDPR is that the central administration in the EU is the place where decisions about the purposes and means of the processing of personal data are taken and this place has the power to have such decisions implemented.

The essence of the lead authority principle in the GDPR is that the supervision of cross-border processing should be led by only one supervisory authority in the EU. In cases where decisions relating to different cross-border processing activities are taken within the EU central administration, there will be a single lead supervisory authority for the various data processing activities carried out by the multinational company. However, there may be cases where an establishment other than the place of central administration makes autonomous decisions concerning the purposes and means of a specific processing activity. This means that there can be situations where more than one lead authority can be identified, i.e. in cases where a multinational company decides to have separate decision making centres, in different countries, for different processing activities.

It is worth recalling, that where a multinational company centralises all the decisions relating to the purposes and means of processing activities in one of its establishments in the EU (and that establishment has the power to implement such decisions), only one lead supervisory authority will be identified for the multinational.

In these situations it will be essential for companies to identify precisely where the decisions on purpose and means of processing are taken. Correct identification of the main establishment is in the interests of controllers and processors because it provides clarity in terms of which supervisory authority they have to deal with in respect of their various compliance duties under the GDPR. These may include, where relevant, designating a data protection officer or consulting for a risky processing activity that the controller cannot mitigate by reasonable means. The relevant provisions of the GDPR are intended to make these compliance tasks manageable.

The examples below illustrate this:

Example 1: A food retailer has its headquarters (i.e. its 'place of central administration') in Rotterdam, Netherlands. It has establishments in various other EU countries, which are in contact with individuals there. All establishments make use of the same software to process consumers' personal data for marketing purposes. All the decisions about the purposes and means of the processing of consumers' personal data for marketing purposes are taken within its Rotterdam headquarters. This means that the company's lead supervisory authority for this cross border processing activity is the Netherlands supervisory authority.

Example 2: A bank has its corporate headquarters in Frankfurt, and all[2] its banking processing activities are organised from there, but its insurance department is located in Vienna. If the establishment in Vienna has the power to decide on all insurance data processing activity and to implement these decisions for the whole EU, then as foreseen in Art 4(16) of the GDPR, the Austrian supervisory authority would be the lead authority in respect of the cross border processing of personal data for insurance purposes, and the German authorities (Hessen supervisory authority) would supervise the processing of personal data for banking purposes, wherever the clients are located.[3]

2.1.1 Criteria for identifying a controller's main establishment in cases where it is not the place of its central administration in the EU.

Recital 36 of the GDPR is useful in clarifying the main factor that shall be used to determine a controller's main establishment if the criterion of the central administration does not apply. This involves identifying where the effective and real exercise of management activities, that determine the main decisions as to the purposes and means of processing through stable arrangements, takes place. Recital 36 also clarifies that "the presence and use of technical means and technologies for processing personal data or processing activities do not, in themselves, constitute a main establishment and are therefore not determining criteria for a main establishment".

The data controller itself identifies where its main establishment is and therefore which supervisory authority is its lead authority. However, this can be challenged by the respective supervisory authority concerned afterwards.

The factors below are useful for determining the location of a controller's main establishment, according to the terms of the GDPR, in cases where it is not the location of its central administration in the EU.
* Where are decisions about the purposes and means of the processing given final 'sign off'?
* Where are decisions about business activities that involve data processing made?
* Where does the power to have decisions implemented effectively lie?
* Where is the Director (or Directors) with overall management responsibility for the cross border processing located?
* Where is the controller or processor registered as a company, if in a single territory?

Note that this is not an exhaustive list. Other factors may be relevant depending on the controller or processing activity in question. If a supervisory authority has reasons to doubt that the establishment identified by the controller is in reality the main establishment for the purposes of the GDPR, it can – of course – require the controller to provide the additional information necessary for it to prove where its main establishment is located.

2.1.2 Groups of undertakings

Where processing is carried out by a group of undertakings that has its headquarters in the EU, the establishment of the undertaking with overall control is presumed to be the decision-making centre relating to the processing of personal data, and will therefore be considered to be the main establishment for the group, except where decisions about the purposes and means of processing are taken by another establishment. The parent, or operational headquarters of the group of undertakings in the EU, is likely to be the main establishment, because that would be the place of its central administration.

The reference in the definition to the place of a controller's central administration works well for organisations that have a centralised decision-making headquarters and branch-type structure. In such cases it is clear that the power to make decisions about cross-border data processing, and to have them carried out, lies within the company's headquarters. In such cases, determining the location of the main establishment – and therefore which supervisory authority is the lead supervisory authority - is straightforward. However, the decision system of group of companies could be more complex, giving independent making powers relating to cross border processing to different establishments. The criteria set out above should help groups of undertakings to identify their main establishment.

2.1.3 Joint data controllers

The GDPR does not specifically deal with the issue of designating a lead authority where two or more controllers established in the EU jointly determine the purposes and means of processing – i.e. joint controllers. Article 26(1) and Recital 79 make it clear that in joint controller situations, the controllers shall in a transparent manner determine their respective responsibilities for compliance with their obligations under the Regulation. In order, therefore, to benefit from the one-stop-shop principle, the joint controllers should designate (among the establishments where decisions are taken) which establishment of the joint controllers will have the power to implement decisions about the processing with respect to all joint controllers. This establishment will then be considered to be the main establishment for the processing carried out in the joint controller situation. The arrangement of the joint controllers is without prejudice to the liability rules provided in the GDPR, in particular in Article 82(4).

2.2 BORDERLINE CASES

There will be borderline and complex situations where it is difficult to identify the main establishment or to determine where decisions about data processing are taken. This might be the case where there is cross-border processing activity and the controller is established in several Member States, but there is no central administration in the EU and none of the EU establishments are taking decisions about the processing (i.e. decisions are taken exclusively outside of the EU).

In the case above, the company carrying out cross border processing may be keen to be regulated by a lead authority to benefit from the one-stop-shop principle. However, the GDPR does not provide a solution for situations like this. In these circumstances, the company should designate the establishment that has the authority to implement decisions about the processing activity and to take liability for the processing, including having sufficient assets, as its main establishment. If the company does not designate a main establishment in this way, it will not be possible to designate a lead authority. Supervisory authorities will always be able to investigate further where this is appropriate.

The GDPR does not permit 'forum shopping'. If a company claims to have its main establishment in one Member State, but no effective and real exercise of management activity or decision making over the processing of personal data takes place there, the relevant supervisory authorities (or ultimately EDPB) will decide which supervisory authority is the 'lead', using objective criteria and looking at the evidence. The process of determining where the main establishment is may require active inquiry and co-operation by the supervisory authorities. Conclusions cannot be based solely on statements by the organisation under review. The burden of proof ultimately falls on controllers and processors to demonstrate to the relevant supervisory authorities where the relevant processing decisions are taken and where there is the power to implement such decisions. Effective records of data processing activity would help both organisations and supervisory authorities to determine the lead authority. The lead supervisory authority, or concerned authorities, can rebut the controller's analysis based on an objective examination of the relevant facts, requesting further information where required.

In some cases the relevant supervisory authorities will ask the controller to provide clear evidence, in line with any EDPB guidelines, of where its main establishment is, or where decisions about a particular data processing activity are taken. This evidence will be given due weight and the supervisory authorities involved will co-operate to decide which one of them will take the lead in investigations. Such cases will only be referred to the EDPB for a decision under Article 65(1)(b) where supervisory authorities have conflicting views in terms of identifying the lead supervisory authority. However, in most cases, we expect that the relevant supervisory authorities will be able to agree a mutually satisfactory course of action.

2.3 PROCESSOR

The GDPR also offers the one-stop-shop system for the benefit of data processors that are subject to GDPR and have establishments in more than one Member State.

Article 4(16)(b) of the GDPR states that the processor's main establishment will be the place of the central administration of the processor in the EU or, if there is no central administration in the EU, the establishment in the EU where the main processing (processor) activities take place.

However, according to Recital 36, in cases involving both controller and processor, the competent lead supervisory authority should be the lead supervisory authority for the controller. In this situation, the supervisory authority of the processor will be a 'supervisory authority concerned' and should participate in the cooperation procedure. This rule will only apply where the controller is established in the EU. In cases when controllers are subject to the GDPR on the basis of Art 3(2), they will not be subject to the one-stop-shop mechanism. A processor may provide services to multiple controllers located in different Member States – for example, a large cloud-service provider. In such cases, the lead supervisory authority will be the supervisory authority that is competent to act as lead for the controller. In effect, this means a processor may have to deal with multiple supervisory authorities.

NOTES

1 The GDPR is relevant for the EEA and will apply after its incorporation into the EEA Agreement. The GDPR is currently under scrutiny for incorporation, see http://www.efta.int/eea-lex/32016R0679

2 In the context of processing personal data for banking purposes, we recognise that are many different processing activities involved in this. However, to simplify matters, we address all of them as a single purpose. The same is true of processing done for insurance purposes.

3 It should be recalled also that the GDPR provides for the possibility of local oversight in specific cases. See Recital (127): *"Each supervisory authority* **not acting as the lead** *supervisory authority* **should be competent to handle local cases** *where the controller or processor is established in more than one Member State, but the subject matter of the specific processing concerns* **only processing carried out in a single Member State and involves only data subjects in that single Member State**, *for example, where the subject matter concerns the processing of employees' personal data in the specific employment context of a Member State." This principle means that the supervision of HR data connected to local employment context could fall to several supervisory authorities.*

---

3. OTHER RELEVANT ISSUES

3.1 THE ROLE OF THE 'SUPERVISORY AUTHORITY CONCERNED'

[2.184]
GDPR Article 4(22) says that the:

> '*supervisory authority concerned' means a supervisory authority which is concerned by the processing of personal data because: (a) the controller or processor is established on the territory of the Member State of that supervisory authority; (b) data subjects residing in the Member State of that supervisory authority are substantially affected or likely to be substantially affected by the processing; or (c) a complaint has been lodged with that supervisory authority.*

The concept of a concerned supervisory authority is meant to ensure that the 'lead authority' model does not prevent other supervisory authorities having a say in how a matter is dealt with when, for example, individuals residing outside the lead authority's jurisdiction are substantially affected by a data processing activity. In terms of factor (a) above, the same considerations as for identifying a lead authority apply. Note that in (b) the data subject must merely reside in the Member State in question; he or she does not have to be a citizen of that state. It will generally be easy – in (c) to determine – as a matter of fact – whether a particular supervisory authority has received a complaint.

Article 56, paragraphs (2) and (5) of the GDPR provide for a concerned supervisory authority to take a role in dealing with a case without being the lead supervisory authority. When a lead supervisory authority decides not to handle a case, the concerned supervisory authority that informed the lead shall handle it. This is in accordance with the procedures in Article 61 (Mutual assistance) and Article 62 (Joint operations of supervisory authorities) of the GDPR. This might be the case where a marketing company with its main establishment in Paris launches a product that only affects data subjects residing in Portugal. In such a case the French and Portuguese supervisory authorities might agree that it is appropriate for the Portuguese supervisory authority to take the lead in dealing with the matter. Supervisory authorities may request that data controllers provide input in terms of clarifying their corporate arrangements. Given that the processing activity has a purely local effect – i.e. on individuals in Portugal – the French and Portuguese supervisory authorities have the discretion to decide which supervisory authority should deal with the matter – in accordance with Recital 127.

The GDPR requires lead and concerned supervisory authorities to co-operate, with due respect for each other's views, to ensure a matter is investigated and resolved to each authority's satisfaction – and with an effective remedy for data subjects. Supervisory authorities should endeavour to reach a mutually acceptable course of action. The formal consistency mechanism should only be invoked where co-operation does not reach a mutually acceptable outcome.

The mutual acceptance of decisions can apply to substantive conclusions, but also to the course of action decided upon, including enforcement activity (e.g. full investigation or an investigation with limited scope). It can also apply to a decision not to handle a case in accordance with GDPR, for example because of a formal policy of prioritisation, or because there are other concerned authorities as described above.

The development of consensus and good will between supervisory authorities is essential to the success of the GDPR's cooperation and consistency process.

3.2 LOCAL PROCESSING.

Local data processing activity does not fall within the GDPR's cooperation and consistency provisions. Supervisory authorities will respect each other's competence to deal with local data processing activity on a local basis. Processing carried out by public authorities will always be dealt with on a 'local' basis too.

3.3 COMPANIES NOT ESTABLISHED WITHIN THE EU.

The GDPR's cooperation and consistency mechanism only applies to controllers with an establishment, or establishments, within the European Union. If the company does not have an establishment in the EU, the mere presence of a representative in a Member State does not trigger the one-stop-shop system. This means that controllers without any establishment in the EU must deal with local supervisory authorities in every Member State they are active in, through their local representative.

Done in Brussels, on 13 December 2016

For the Working Party,

The Chairwoman

Isabelle FALQUE-PIERROTIN

As last revised and adopted on 05 April 2017

For the Working Party

The Chairwoman

Isabelle FALQUE-PIERROTIN

ANNEX - QUESTIONS TO GUIDE THE IDENTIFICATION OF THE LEAD SUPERVISORY AUTHORITY

1. IS THE CONTROLLER OR PROCESSOR CARRYING OUT THE CROSS-BORDER PROCESSING OF PERSONAL DATA?

[2.185]
(a)   Yes, if:
  * the controller or processor is established in more than one Member State and
  * the processing of personal data takes place in the context of the activities of establishments in more than one Member State.

  In this case, go to section 2.

(b)   Yes, if:
  * the processing of personal data takes place in the context of the activities of a data controller or processor's single establishment in the Union, but:
  * substantially affects or is likely to substantially affect individuals in more than one Member State.

  In this case, the lead authority is the authority for the controller or processor's single establishment in a single Member State. This must – by logic - be the controller or processor's main establishment because it is its only establishment.

2. HOW TO IDENTIFY THE 'LEAD SUPERVISORY AUTHORITY'

(a)   In a case involving only a controller:
  (i)   Identify the controller's place of central administration in the EU;
  (ii)   The supervisory authority of the country where the place of central administration is located is the controller's lead authority.
           However:
  (iii)   If decisions on the purposes and means of the processing are taken in another establishment in the EU, and that establishment has the power to implement those decisions, then the lead authority is the one located in the country where this establishment is.

(b)   In a case involving a controller and a processor:

(i)   Check if the controller is established in the EU and subject to the one-stop-shop system. If so,

(ii)   Identify the lead supervisory authority of the controller. This authority will also be the lead supervisory authority for the processor.

(iii)   The (non-lead) supervisory authority competent for the processor will be a 'concerned authority' – see 3 below.

(c)   In a case involving only a processor:

     (i)   Identify the processor's place of central administration in the EU;

     (ii)   If the processor has no central administration in the EU, identify the establishment in the EU where the main processing activities of the processor take place.

(d)   In a case involving joint controllers:

     (i)   Check if the joint controllers are established in the EU.

     (ii)   Designate among the establishments where decisions on the purposes and means of the processing are taken the establishment which has the power to implement these decisions with respect to all joint controllers. This establishment will then be considered to be the main establishment for the processing carried out by the joint controllers. The lead authority is the one located in the country where this establishment is.

3. ARE THERE ANY 'CONCERNED SUPERVISORY AUTHORITIES'?

An authority is a 'concerned authority':

- when the controller or processor has an establishment on its territory, or:
- when data subjects on its territory are substantially affected or likely to be substantially affected by the processing, or:
- when a complaint is received by a particular authority.

ARTICLE 29 DATA PROTECTION WORKING PARTY: GUIDELINES ON DATA PROTECTION IMPACT ASSESSMENT (DPIA) AND DETERMINING WHETHER PROCESSING IS "LIKELY TO RESULT IN A HIGH RISK" FOR THE PURPOSES OF REGULATION 2016/679
17/EN
WP 248 rev.01
Adopted on 4 April 2017

As last Revised and Adopted on 4 October 2017

[2.186]

NOTES

This document was originally issued by the Article 29 Working Party but subsequently endorsed by the EDPB during its first plenary meeting.

© European Data Protection Board.

TABLE OF CONTENTS

I. INTRODUCTION

[2.187]
Regulation 2016/679[1] (GDPR) will apply from 25 May 2018. Article 35 of the GDPR introduces the concept of a Data Protection Impact Assessment (DPIA[2]), as does Directive 2016/680[3].

A DPIA is a process designed to describe the processing, assess its necessity and proportionality and help manage the risks to the rights and freedoms of natural persons resulting from the processing of personal data[4] by assessing them and determining the measures to address them. DPIAs are important tools for accountability, as they help controllers not only to comply with requirements of the GDPR, but also to demonstrate that appropriate measures have been taken to ensure compliance with the Regulation (see also article 24)[5]. In other words, **a DPIA is a process for building and demonstrating compliance**.

Under the GDPR, non-compliance with DPIA requirements can lead to fines imposed by the competent supervisory authority. Failure to carry out a DPIA when the processing is subject to a DPIA (Article 35(1) and (3)-(4)), carrying out a DPIA in an incorrect way (Article 35(2) and (7) to (9)), or failing to consult the competent supervisory authority where required (Article 36(3)(e)), can result in an administrative fine of up to 10M€, or in the case of an undertaking, up to 2 % of the total worldwide annual turnover of the preceding financial year, whichever is higher.

NOTES

1   Regulation (EU) 2016/679 of the European Parliament and of the Council of 27 April 2016 on the protection of natural persons with regard to the processing of personal data and on the free movement of such data, and repealing Directive 95/46/EC (General Data Protection Regulation).

2   The term "Privacy Impact Assessment" (PIA) is often used in other contexts to refer to the same concept.

3   Article 27 of the Directive (EU) 2016/680 of the European Parliament and of the Council of 27 April 2016 on the protection of natural persons with regard to the processing of personal data by competent authorities for the purposes of the prevention, investigation, detection or prosecution of criminal offences or the execution of criminal penalties, and on the free movement of such data, also states that a privacy impact assessment is needed for "*the processing is likely to result in a high risk to the rights and freedoms of natural persons*".

4   The GDPR does not formally define the concept of a DPIA as such, but
    –   its minimal content is specified by Article 35(7) as follows:
        •   "*(a) a systematic description of the envisaged processing operations and the purposes of the processing, including, where applicable, the legitimate interest pursued by the controller;*
        •   *(b) an assessment of the necessity and proportionality of the processing operations in relation to the purposes;*
        •   *(c) an assessment of the risks to the rights and freedoms of data subjects referred to in paragraph 1; and*
        •   *(d) the measures envisaged to address the risks, including safeguards, security measures and mechanisms to ensure the protection of personal data and to demonstrate compliance with this Regulation taking into account the rights and legitimate interests of data subjects and other persons concerned*";
    –   its meaning and role is clarified by recital 84 as follows: "*In order to enhance compliance with this Regulation where processing operations are likely to result in a high risk to the rights and freedoms of natural persons, the controller should be responsible for the carrying-out of a data protection impact assessment to evaluate, in particular, the origin, nature, particularity and severity of that risk*".

5   See also recital 84: "*The outcome of the assessment should be taken into account when determining the appropriate measures to be taken in order to demonstrate that the processing of personal data complies with this Regulation*".

II. SCOPE OF THE GUIDELINES

[2.188]
These Guidelines take account of:
–   the Article 29 Data Protection Working Party (WP29) Statement 14/EN WP 218[6];
–   the WP29 Guidelines on Data Protection Officer 16/EN WP 243[7];
–   the WP29 Opinion on Purpose limitation 13/EN WP 203[8];
–   international standards[9].

In line with the risk-based approach embodied by the GDPR, carrying out a DPIA is not mandatory for every processing operation. A DPIA is only required when the processing is "*likely to result in a high risk to the rights and freedoms of natural persons*" (Article 35(1)). In order to ensure a consistent interpretation of the circumstances in which a DPIA is mandatory (Article 35(3)), the present guidelines firstly aim to clarify this notion and provide criteria for the lists to be adopted by Data Protection Authorities (DPAs) under Article 35(4).

According to Article 70(1)(e), the European Data Protection Board (EDPB) will be able to issue guidelines, recommendations and best practices in order to encourage a consistent application of the GDPR. The purpose of this document is to anticipate such future work of the EDPB and therefore is to clarify the relevant provisions of the GDPR in order to help controllers to comply with the law and to provide legal certainty for controllers who are required to carry out a DPIA.

These Guidelines also seek to promote the development of:
–   a common European Union list of processing operations for which a DPIA is mandatory (Article 35(4));
–   a common EU list of processing operations for which a DPIA is not necessary (Article 35(5));
–   common criteria on the methodology for carrying out a DPIA (Article 35(5));
–   common criteria for specifying when the supervisory authority shall be consulted (Article 36(1));
–   recommendations, where possible, building on the experience gained in EU Member States.

NOTES

6   WP29 Statement 14/EN WP 218 on the role of a risk-based approach to data protection legal frameworks adopted on 30 May 2014.
    http://ec.europa.eu/justice/data-protection/article-29/documentation/opinion-recommendation/
    files/2014/wp218_en.pdf?wb48617274=72C54532

7   WP29 Guidelines on Data Protection Officer 16/EN WP 243 Adopted on 13 December 2016.
    http://ec.europa.eu/information_society/newsroom/image/document/2016-51/wp243_en_40855.
    pdf?wb48617274=CD63BD9A

8   WP29 Opinion 03/2013 on purpose limitation 13/EN WP 203 Adopted on 2 April 2013.
    http://ec.europa.eu/justice/data-protection/article-29/documentation/opinion-recommendation/
    files/2013/wp203_en.pdf?wb48617274=39E0E409

9   e.g. ISO 31000:2009, *Risk management — Principles and guidelines*, International Organization for Standardization (ISO) ; ISO/IEC 29134 (project), *Information technology – Security techniques – Privacy impact assessment – Guidelines*, International Organization for Standardization (ISO).

III. DPIA: THE REGULATION EXPLAINED

[2.189]
The GDPR requires controllers to implement appropriate measures to ensure and be able to demonstrate

compliance with the GDPR, taking into account among others the "the risks of varying likelihood and severity for the rights and freedoms of natural persons" (article 24 (1)). The obligation for controllers to conduct a DPIA in certain circumstances should be understood against the background of their general obligation to appropriately manage risks[10] presented by the processing of personal data.

A "risk" is a scenario describing an event and its consequences, estimated in terms of severity and likelihood. "Risk management", on the other hand, can be defined as the coordinated activities to direct and control an organization with regard to risk.

Article 35 refers to a likely high risk "to the rights and freedoms of individuals". As indicated in the Article 29 Data Protection Working Party Statement on the role of a risk-based approach in data protection legal frameworks, the reference to "the rights and freedoms" of data subjects primarily concerns the rights to data protection and privacy but may also involve other fundamental rights such as freedom of speech, freedom of thought, freedom of movement, prohibition of discrimination, right to liberty, conscience and religion.

In line with the risk-based approach embodied by the GDPR, carrying out a DPIA is not mandatory for every processing operation. Instead, a DPIA is only required where a type of processing is "likely to result in a high risk to the rights and freedoms of natural persons" (Article 35(1)). The mere fact that the conditions triggering the obligation to carry out DPIA have not been met does not, however, diminish controllers' general obligation to implement measures to appropriately manage risks for the rights and freedoms of data subjects. In practice, this means that controllers must continuously assess the risks created by their processing activities in order to identify when a type of processing is "likely to result in a high risk to the rights and freedoms of natural persons".

The following figure illustrates the basic principles related to the DPIA in the GDPR:

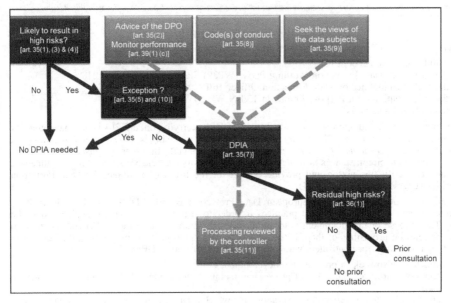

A. WHAT DOES A DPIA ADDRESS? A SINGLE PROCESSING OPERATION OR A SET OF SIMILAR PROCESSING OPERATIONS.

A DPIA may concern a single data processing operation. However, Article 35(1) states that "*a single assessment may address a set of similar processing operations that present similar high risks*". Recital 92 adds that "*there are circumstances under which it may be reasonable and economical for the subject of a data protection impact assessment to be broader than a single project, for example where public authorities or bodies intend to establish a common application or processing platform or where several controllers plan to introduce a common application or processing environment across an industry sector or segment or for a widely used horizontal activity*".

A single DPIA could be used to assess multiple processing operations that are similar in terms of nature, scope, context, purpose, and risks. Indeed, DPIAs aim at systematically studying new situations that could lead to high risks on the rights and freedoms of natural persons, and there is no need to carry out a DPIA in cases (i.e. processing operations performed in a specific context and for a specific purpose) that have already been studied. This might be the case where similar technology is used to collect the same sort of data for the same purposes. For example, a group of municipal authorities that are each setting up a similar CCTV system could carry out a single DPIA covering the processing by these separate controllers, or a railway operator (single controller) could cover video surveillance in all its train stations with one DPIA. This may also be applicable to similar processing operations implemented by various data controllers. In those cases, a reference DPIA should be shared or made publicly accessible, measures described in the DPIA must be implemented, and a justification for conducting a single DPIA has to be provided.

When the processing operation involves joint controllers, they need to define their respective obligations precisely. Their DPIA should set out which party is responsible for the various measures designed to treat risks and to protect the rights and freedoms of the data subjects. Each data controller should express his needs and share useful information without either compromising secrets (e.g.: protection of trade secrets, intellectual property, confidential business information) or disclosing vulnerabilities.

A DPIA can also be useful for assessing the data protection impact of a technology product, for example a piece of hardware or software, where this is likely to be used by different data controllers to carry out different processing operations. Of course, the data controller deploying the product remains obliged to carry out its own DPIA with regard to the specific implementation, but this can be informed by a DPIA prepared by the product provider, if appropriate. An example could be the relationship between manufacturers of smart meters and utility companies. Each product provider or processor should share useful information without neither compromising secrets nor leading to security risks by disclosing vulnerabilities.

B. WHICH PROCESSING OPERATIONS ARE SUBJECT TO A DPIA? APART FROM EXCEPTIONS, WHERE THEY ARE *"LIKELY TO RESULT IN A HIGH RISK"*.

This section describes when a DPIA is mandatory, and when it is not necessary to carry out a DPIA.

Unless the processing operation meets an exception (III.B.a), a DPIA has to be carried out where a processing operation is *"likely to result in a high risk"* **(III.B.b).**

a) When is a DPIA mandatory? When processing is *"likely to result in a high risk"*.

The GDPR does not require a DPIA to be carried out for every processing operation which may result in risks for the rights and freedoms of natural persons. The carrying out of a DPIA is only mandatory where processing is *"likely to result in a high risk to the rights and freedoms of natural persons"* (Article 35(1), illustrated by Article 35(3) and complemented by Article 35(4)). It is particularly relevant when a new data processing technology is being introduced[11].

In cases where it is not clear whether a DPIA is required, the WP29 recommends that a DPIA is carried out nonetheless as a DPIA is a useful tool to help controllers comply with data protection law.

Even though a DPIA could be required in other circumstances, Article 35(3) provides some examples when a processing operation is *"likely to result in high risks"*:

- *"(a) a systematic and extensive evaluation of personal aspects relating to natural persons which is based on automated processing, including profiling, and on which decisions are based that produce legal effects concerning the natural person or similarly significantly affect the natural person[12];*
- *(b) processing on a large scale of special categories of data referred to in Article 9(1), or of personal data relating to criminal convictions and offences referred to in Article 10[13]; or*
- *(c) a systematic monitoring of a publicly accessible area on a large scale".*

As the words *"in particular"* in the introductory sentence of Article 35(3) GDPR indicate, this is meant as a non-exhaustive list. There may be "high risk" processing operations that are not captured by this list, but yet pose similarly high risks. Those processing operations should also be subject to DPIAs. For this reason, the criteria developed below sometimes go beyond a simple explanation of what should be understood by the three examples given in Article 35(3) GDPR.

In order to provide a more concrete set of processing operations that require a DPIA due to their inherent high risk, taking into account the particular elements of Articles 35(1) and 35(3)(a) to (c), the list to be adopted at the national level under article 35(4) and recitals 71, 75 and 91, and other GDPR references to *"likely to result in a high risk"* processing operations[14], the following nine criteria should be considered.

(1) Evaluation or scoring, including profiling and predicting, especially from *"aspects concerning the data subject's performance at work, economic situation, health, personal preferences or interests, reliability or behavior, location or movements"* (recitals 71 and 91). Examples of this could include a financial institution that screens its customers against a credit reference database or against an anti-money laundering and counter-terrorist financing (AML/CTF) or fraud database, or a biotechnology company offering genetic tests directly to consumers in order to assess and predict the disease/health risks, or a company building behavioural or marketing profiles based on usage or navigation on its website.

(2) Automated-decision making with legal or similar significant effect: processing that aims at taking decisions on data subjects producing *"legal effects concerning the natural person"* or which *"similarly significantly affects the natural person"* (Article 35(3)(a)). For example, the processing may lead to the exclusion or discrimination against individuals. Processing with little or no effect on individuals does not match this specific criterion. Further explanations on these notions will be provided in the upcoming WP29 Guidelines on Profiling.

(3) Systematic monitoring: processing used to observe, monitor or control data subjects, including data collected through networks or *"a systematic monitoring of a publicly accessible area"* (Article 35(3)(c))[15]. This type of monitoring is a criterion because the personal data may be collected in circumstances where data subjects may not be aware of who is collecting their data and how they will be used. Additionally, it may be impossible for individuals to avoid being subject to such processing in public (or publicly accessible) space(s).

(4) Sensitive data or data of a highly personal nature: this includes special categories of personal data as defined in Article 9 (for example information about individuals' political opinions), as well as personal data relating to criminal convictions or offences as defined in Article 10. An example

would be a general hospital keeping patients' medical records or a private investigator keeping offenders' details. Beyond these provisions of the GDPR, some categories of data can be considered as increasing the possible risk to the rights and freedoms of individuals. These personal data are considered as sensitive (as this term is commonly understood) because they are linked to household and private activities (such as electronic communications whose confidentiality should be protected), or because they impact the exercise of a fundamental right (such as location data whose collection questions the freedom of movement) or because their violation clearly involves serious impacts in the data subject's daily life (such as financial data that might be used for payment fraud). In this regard, whether the data has already been made publicly available by the data subject or by third parties may be relevant. The fact that personal data is publicly available may be considered as a factor in the assessment if the data was expected to be further used for certain purposes. This criterion may also include data such as personal documents, emails, diaries, notes from e-readers equipped with note-taking features, and very personal information contained in life-logging applications.

(5) Data processed on a large scale: the GDPR does not define what constitutes large-scale, though recital 91 provides some guidance. In any event, the WP29 recommends that the following factors, in particular, be considered when determining whether the processing is carried out on a large scale[16]:

    (a)   the number of data subjects concerned, either as a specific number or as a proportion of the relevant population;

    (b)   the volume of data and/or the range of different data items being processed;

    (c)   the duration, or permanence, of the data processing activity;

    (d)   the geographical extent of the processing activity.

(6) Matching or combining datasets, for example originating from two or more data processing operations performed for different purposes and/or by different data controllers in a way that would exceed the reasonable expectations of the data subject[17].

(7) Data concerning vulnerable data subjects (recital 75): the processing of this type of data is a criterion because of the increased power imbalance between the data subjects and the data controller, meaning the individuals may be unable to easily consent to, or oppose, the processing of their data, or exercise their rights. Vulnerable data subjects may include children (they can be considered as not able to knowingly and thoughtfully oppose or consent to the processing of their data), employees , more vulnerable segments of the population requiring special protection (mentally ill persons, asylum seekers, or the elderly, patients, *etc.*), and in any case where an imbalance in the relationship between the position of the data subject and the controller can be identified.

(8) Innovative use or applying new technological or organisational solutions, like combining use of finger print and face recognition for improved physical access control, *etc.* The GDPR makes it clear (Article 35(1) and recitals 89 and 91) that the use of a new technology, defined in "*accordance with the achieved state of technological knowledge*" (recital 91), can trigger the need to carry out a DPIA. This is because the use of such technology can involve novel forms of data collection and usage, possibly with a high risk to individuals' rights and freedoms. Indeed, the personal and social consequences of the deployment of a new technology may be unknown. A DPIA will help the data controller to understand and to treat such risks. For example, certain "Internet of Things" applications could have a significant impact on individuals' daily lives and privacy; and therefore require a DPIA.

(9) When the processing in itself "*prevents data subjects from exercising a right or using a service or a contract*" (Article 22 and recital 91). This includes processing operations that aims at allowing, modifying or refusing data subjects' access to a service or entry into a contract. An example of this is where a bank screens its customers against a credit reference database in order to decide whether to offer them a loan.

In most cases, a data controller can consider that a processing meeting two criteria would require a DPIA to be carried out. In general, the WP29 considers that the more criteria are met by the processing, the more likely it is to present a high risk to the rights and freedoms of data subjects, and therefore to require a DPIA, regardless of the measures which the controller envisages to adopt.

However, in some cases, **a data controller can consider that a processing meeting only one of these criteria requires a DPIA.**

The following examples illustrate how the criteria should be used to assess whether a particular processing operation requires a DPIA:

Examples of processing	Possible Relevant criteria	DPIA likely to be required?
A hospital processing its patients' genetic and health data (hospital information system).	- Sensitive data or data of a highly personal nature. - Data concerning vulnerable data subjects. - Data processed on a large-scale.	Yes
The use of a camera system to monitor driving behavior on highways. The controller envisages to use an intelligent video analysis system to single out cars and automatically recognize license plates.	- Systematic monitoring. - Innovative use or applying technological or organisational solutions.	
A company systematically monitoring its employees' activities, including the monitoring of the employees' work station, internet activity, *etc*.	- Systematic monitoring. - Data concerning vulnerable data subjects.	
The gathering of public social media data for generating profiles.	- Evaluation or scoring. - Data processed on a large scale. - Matching or combining of datasets. - Sensitive data or data of a highly personal nature:	
An institution creating a national level credit rating or fraud database.	- Evaluation or scoring. - Automated decision making with legal or similar significant effect. - Prevents data subject from exercising a right or using a service or a contract. - Sensitive data or data of a highly personal nature:	
Storage for archiving purpose of pseudonymised personal sensitive data concerning vulnerable data subjects of research projects or clinical trials	- Sensitive data. - Data concerning vulnerable data subjects. - Prevents data subjects from exercising a right or using a service or a contract.	
A processing of "personal data from patients or clients by an individual physician, other health care professional or lawyer" (Recital 91).	- Sensitive data or data of a highly personal nature. - Data concerning vulnerable data subjects.	No
An online magazine using a mailing list to send a generic daily digest to its subscribers.	- Data processed on a large scale.	
An e-commerce website displaying adverts for vintage car parts involving limited profiling based on items viewed or purchased on its own website.	- Evaluation or scoring.	

Conversely, a processing operation may correspond to the above mentioned cases and still be considered by the controller not to be "likely to result in a high risk". In such cases the controller should justify and document the reasons for not carrying out a DPIA, and include/record the views of the data protection officer.

In addition, as part of the accountability principle, every data controller "*shall maintain a record of processing activities under its responsibility*" including inter alia the purposes of processing, a description of the categories of data and recipients of the data and "*where possible, a general description of the technical and organisational security measures referred to in Article 32(1)*" (Article 30(1)) and must assess whether a high risk is likely, even if they ultimately decide not to carry out a DPIA.

Note: supervisory authorities are required to establish, make public and communicate a list of the processing operations that require a DPIA to the European Data Protection Board (EDPB) (Article 35(4))[18]. The criteria set out above can help supervisory authorities to constitute such a list, with more specific content added in time if appropriate. For example, the processing of any type of biometric data or that of children could also be considered as relevant for the development of a list pursuant to article 35(4).

b) When isn't a DPIA required? When the processing is not "*likely to result in a high risk*", or a similar DPIA exists, or it has been authorized prior to May 2018, or it has a legal basis, or it is in the list of processing operations for which a DPIA is not required.

WP29 considers that a DPIA is not required in the following cases:
– **where the processing is not "*likely to result in a high risk to the rights and freedoms of natural persons*"** (Article 35(1));
– **when the nature, scope, context and purposes of the processing are very similar to the processing for which DPIA have been carried out**. In such cases, results of DPIA for similar processing can be used (Article 35(1)[19]);

–   when the processing operations have been checked by a supervisory authority before May 2018 in specific conditions that have not changed[20] (see III.C);

–   **where a processing operation,** pursuant to point (c) or (e) of article 6(1), **has a legal basis** in EU or Member State law, where the law regulates the specific processing operation **and where a DPIA has already been carried out** as part of the establishment of that legal basis (Article 35(10))[21], except if a Member state has stated it to be necessary to carry out a DPIA prior processing activities;

–   **where the processing is included on the optional list (established by the supervisory authority) of processing operations** for which no DPIA is required (Article 35(5)). Such a list may contain processing activities that comply with the conditions specified by this authority, in particular through guidelines, specific decisions or authorizations, compliance rules, *etc.* (e.g. in France, authorizations, exemptions, simplified rules, compliance packs . . .). In such cases, and subject to re-assessment by the competent supervisory authority, a DPIA is not required, but only if the processing falls strictly within the scope of the relevant procedure mentioned in the list and continues to comply fully with all the relevant requirements of the GDPR.

C. WHAT ABOUT ALREADY EXISTING PROCESSING OPERATIONS? DPIAS ARE REQUIRED IN SOME CIRCUMSTANCES.

The requirement to carry out a DPIA applies to existing processing operations likely to result in a high risk to the rights and freedoms of natural persons and for which there has been a change of the risks, taking into account the nature, scope, context and purposes of the processing.

A DPIA is not needed for processing operations that have been checked by a supervisory authority or the data protection official, in accordance with Article 20 of Directive 95/46/EC, and that are performed in a way that has not changed since the prior checking. Indeed, *"Commission decisions adopted and authorisations by supervisory authorities based on Directive 95/46/EC remain in force until amended, replaced or repealed"* (recital 171).

Conversely, this means that any data processing whose conditions of implementation (scope, purpose, personal data collected, identity of the data controllers or recipients, data retention period, technical and organisational measures, etc.) have changed since the prior checking performed by the supervisory authority or the data protection official and which are likely to result in a high risk should be subject to a DPIA.

Moreover, a DPIA could be required after a change of the risks resulting from the processing operations[22], for example because a new technology has come into use or because personal data is being used for a different purpose. Data processing operations can evolve quickly and new vulnerabilities can arise. Therefore, it should be noted that the revision of a DPIA is not only useful for continuous improvement, but also critical to maintain the level of data protection in a changing environment over time. A DPIA may also become necessary because the organisational or societal context for the processing activity has changed, for example because the effects of certain automated decisions have become more significant, or new categories of data subjects become vulnerable to discrimination. Each of these examples could be an element that leads to a change of the risk resulting from processing activity concerned.

Conversely, certain changes could lower the risk as well. For example, a processing operation could evolve so that decisions are no longer automated or if a monitoring activity is no longer systematic. In that case, the review of the risk analysis made can show that the performance of a DPIA is no longer required.

As a matter of good practice, **a DPIA should be continuously reviewed and regularly re-assessed.** Therefore, even if a DPIA is not required on 25 May 2018, it will be necessary, at the appropriate time, for the controller to conduct such a DPIA as part of its general accountability obligations.

D. HOW TO CARRY OUT A DPIA?

a) At what moment should a DPIA be carried out? Prior to the processing.

The DPIA should be carried out *"prior to the processing"* **(Articles 35(1) and 35(10), recitals 90 and 93)[23]. This is consistent with data protection by design and by default principles (Article 25 and recital 78). The DPIA should be seen as a tool for helping decision-making concerning the processing.**

The DPIA should be started as early as is practicable in the design of the processing operation even if some of the processing operations are still unknown. Updating the DPIA throughout the lifecycle project will ensure that data protection and privacy are considered and will encourage the creation of solutions which promote compliance. It can also be necessary to repeat individual steps of the assessment as the development process progresses because the selection of certain technical or organizational measures may affect the severity or likelihood of the risks posed by the processing.

The fact that the DPIA may need to be updated once the processing has actually started is not a valid reason for postponing or not carrying out a DPIA. The DPIA is an on-going process, especially where a processing operation is dynamic and subject to ongoing change. **Carrying out a DPIA is a continual process, not a one-time exercise**.

b) Who is obliged to carry out the DPIA? The controller, with the DPO and processors.

The controller is responsible for ensuring that the DPIA is carried out (Article 35(2)). Carrying out the DPIA may be done by someone else, inside or outside the organization, but the controller remains ultimately accountable for that task.

The controller must also seek the advice of the Data Protection Officer (DPO), where designated (Article 35(2)) and this advice, and the decisions taken by the controller, should be documented within the DPIA. The DPO should also monitor the performance of the DPIA (Article 39(1)(c)). Further guidance is provided in the WP29 Guidelines on Data Protection Officer 16/EN WP 243.

If the processing is wholly or partly performed by a data processor, **the processor should assist the controller in carrying out the DPIA** and provide any necessary information (in line with Article 28(3)(f)).

The controller must *"seek the views of data subjects or their representatives"* (Article 35(9)), *"where appropriate"*. The WP29 considers that:

– those views could be sought through a variety of means, depending on the context (e.g. a generic study related to the purpose and means of the processing operation, a question to the staff representatives, or usual surveys sent to the data controller's future customers) ensuring that the controller has a lawful basis for processing any personal data involved in seeking such views. Although it should be noted that consent to processing is obviously not a way for seeking the views of the data subjects;
– if the data controller's final decision differs from the views of the data subjects, its reasons for going ahead or not should be documented;
– the controller should also document its justification for not seeking the views of data subjects, if it decides that this is not appropriate, for example if doing so would compromise the confidentiality of companies' business plans, or would be disproportionate or impracticable.

Finally, it is good practice to define and document other specific roles and responsibilities, depending on internal policy, processes and rules, e.g.:

– where specific business units may propose to carry out a DPIA, those units should then provide input to the DPIA and should be involved in the DPIA validation process;
– where appropriate, it is recommended to seek the advice from independent experts of different professions[24] (lawyers, IT experts, security experts, sociologists, ethics, *etc.*).
– the roles and responsibilities of the processors must be contractually defined; and the DPIA must be carried out with the processor's help, taking into account the nature of the processing and the information available to the processor (Article 28(3)(f));
– the Chief Information Security Officer (CISO), if appointed, as well as the DPO, could suggest that the controller carries out a DPIA on a specific processing operation, and should help the stakeholders on the methodology, help to evaluate the quality of the risk assessment and whether the residual risk is acceptable, and to develop knowledge specific to the data controller context;
– the Chief Information Security Officer (CISO), if appointed, and/or the IT department, should provide assistance to the controller, and could propose to carry out a DPIA on a specific processing operation, depending on security or operational needs.

c) What is the methodology to carry out a DPIA? Different methodologies but common criteria.

The GDPR sets out the minimum features of a DPIA (Article 35(7), and recitals 84 and 90):
– *"a description of the envisaged processing operations and the purposes of the processing"*;
– *"an assessment of the necessity and proportionality of the processing"*;
– *"an assessment of the risks to the rights and freedoms of data subjects"*;
– *"the measures envisaged to:*
  • *"address the risks"*;
  • *"demonstrate compliance with this Regulation"*.

The following figure illustrates the generic iterative process for carrying out a DPIA[25]:

Part 2 Data Protection: EU Law etc

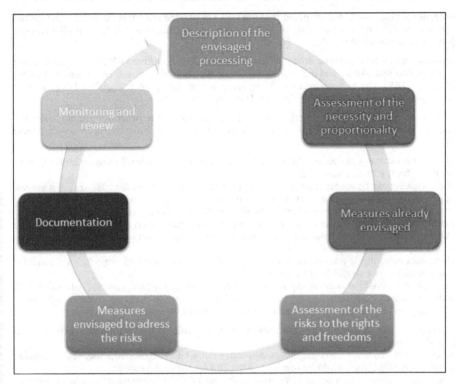

Compliance with a code of conduct (Article 40) has to be taken into account (Article 35(8)) when assessing the impact of a data processing operation. This can be useful to demonstrate that adequate measures have been chosen or put in place, provided that the code of conduct is appropriate to the processing operation. Certifications, seals and marks for the purpose of demonstrating compliance with the GDPR of processing operations by controllers and processors (Article 42), as well as Binding Corporate Rules (BCR), should be taken into account as well.

All the relevant requirements set out in the GDPR provide a broad, generic framework for designing and carrying out a DPIA. The practical implementation of a DPIA will depend on the requirements set out in the GDPR which may be supplemented with more detailed practical guidance. The DPIA implementation is therefore scalable. This means that even a small data controller can design and implement a DPIA that is suitable for their processing operations.

Recital 90 of the GDPR outlines a number of components of the DPIA which overlap with well-defined components of risk management (e.g. ISO 31000[26]). In risk management terms, a DPIA aims at "managing risks" to the rights and freedoms of natural persons, using the following processes, by:

– establishing the context: "*taking into account the nature, scope, context and purposes of the processing and the sources of the risk*";
– assessing the risks: "*assess the particular likelihood and severity of the high risk*";
– treating the risks: "*mitigating that risk*" and "*ensuring the protection of personal data*", and "*demonstrating compliance with this Regulation*".

Note: the DPIA under the GDPR is a tool for managing risks to the rights of the data subjects, and thus takes their perspective, as is the case in certain fields (e.g. societal security). Conversely, risk management in other fields (e.g. information security) is focused on the organization.

The GDPR provides data controllers with flexibility to determine the precise structure and form of the DPIA in order to allow for this to fit with existing working practices. There are a number of different established processes within the EU and worldwide which take account of the components described in recital 90. However, whatever its form, a DPIA must be a genuine assessment of risks, allowing controllers to take measures to address them.

Different methodologies (see Annex 1 for examples of data protection and privacy impact assessment methodologies) could be used to assist in the implementation of the basic requirements set out in the GDPR. In order to allow these different approaches to exist, whilst allowing controllers to comply with the GDPR, common criteria have been identified (see Annex 2). They clarify the basic requirements of the Regulation, but provide enough scope for different forms of implementation. These criteria can be used to show that a particular DPIA methodology meets the standards required by the GDPR. **It is up to the data controller to choose a methodology, but this methodology should be compliant with the criteria provided in Annex 2**.

The WP29 encourages the development of sector-specific DPIA frameworks. This is because they can draw on specific sectorial knowledge, meaning the DPIA can address the specifics of a particular type of processing operation (e.g.: particular types of data, corporate assets, potential impacts, threats, measures). This means the DPIA can address the issues that arise in a particular economic sector, or when using particular technologies or carrying out particular types of processing operation.

Finally, where necessary, *"the controller shall carry out a review to assess if processing is performed in accordance with the data protection impact assessment at least when there is a change of the risk represented by processing operation"* (Article 35(11)[27]).

d) Is there an obligation to publish the DPIA? No, but publishing a summary could foster trust, and the full DPIA must be communicated to the supervisory authority in case of prior consultation or if requested by the DPA.

Publishing a DPIA is not a legal requirement of the GDPR, it is the controller's decision to do so. However, controllers should consider publishing at least parts, such as a summary or a conclusion of their DPIA.

The purpose of such a process would be to help foster trust in the controller's processing operations, and demonstrate accountability and transparency. It is particularly good practice to publish a DPIA where members of the public are affected by the processing operation. This could particularly be the case where a public authority carries out a DPIA.

The published DPIA does not need to contain the whole assessment, especially when the DPIA could present specific information concerning security risks for the data controller or give away trade secrets or commercially sensitive information. In these circumstances, the published version could consist of just a summary of the DPIA's main findings, or even just a statement that a DPIA has been carried out.

Moreover, where a DPIA reveals high residual risks, the data controller will be required to seek prior consultation for the processing from the supervisory authority (Article 36(1)). As part of this, the DPIA must be fully provided (Article 36(3)(e)). The supervisory authority may provide its advice[28], and will not compromise trade secrets or reveal security vulnerabilities, subject to the principles applicable in each Member State on public access to official documents.

E. WHEN SHALL THE SUPERVISORY AUTHORITY BE CONSULTED?
WHEN THE RESIDUAL RISKS ARE HIGH.

As explained above:
- a DPIA is required when a processing operation *"is likely to result in a high risk to the rights and freedoms of natural person"* (Article 35(1), see III.B.a). As an example, the processing of health data on a large scale is considered as likely to result in a high risk, and requires a DPIA;
- then, it is the responsibility of the data controller to assess the risks to the rights and freedoms of data subjects and to identify the measures[29] envisaged to reduce those risks to an acceptable level and to demonstrate compliance with the GDPR (Article 35(7), see III.C.c). An example could be for the storage of personal data on laptop computers the use of appropriate technical and organisational security measures (effective full disk encryption, robust key management, appropriate access control, secured backups, *etc.*) in addition to existing policies (notice, consent, right of access, right to object, *etc.*).

In the laptop example above, if the risks have been considered as sufficiently reduced by the data controller and following the reading of Article 36(1) and recitals 84 and 94, the processing can proceed without consultation with the supervisory authority. It is in cases where the identified risks cannot be sufficiently addressed by the data controller (i.e. the residual risks remains high) that the data controller must consult the supervisory authority.

An example of an unacceptable high residual risk includes instances where the data subjects may encounter significant, or even irreversible, consequences, which they may not overcome (e.g.: an illegitimate access to data leading to a threat on the life of the data subjects, a layoff, a financial jeopardy) and/or when it seems obvious that the risk will occur (e.g.: by not being able to reduce the number of people accessing the data because of its sharing, use or distribution modes, or when a well-known vulnerability is not patched).

Whenever the data controller cannot find sufficient measures to reduce the risks to an acceptable level (i.e. the residual risks are still high), consultation with the supervisory authority is required[30].

Moreover, the controller will have to consult the supervisory authority whenever Member State law requires controllers to consult with, and/or obtain prior authorisation from, the supervisory authority in relation to processing by a controller for the performance of a task carried out by the controller in the public interest, including processing in relation to social protection and public health (Article 36(5)).

It should however be stated that regardless of whether or not consultation with the supervisory is required based on the level of residual risk then the obligations of retaining a record of the DPIA and updating the DPIA in due course remain.

NOTES

[10] It has to be stressed that in order to manage the risks to the rights and freedoms of natural persons, the risks have to identified, analyzed, estimated, evaluated, treated (e.g. mitigated . . .), and reviewed regularly. Controllers cannot escape their responsibility by covering risks under insurance policies.

[11] See recitals 89, 91 and Article 35(1) and (3) for further examples.

[12] See recital 71: *"in particular analysing or predicting aspects concerning performance at work, economic situation,*

health, personal preferences or interests, reliability or behaviour, location or movements, in order to create or use personal profiles".

13 See recital 75: "*where personal data are processed which reveal racial or ethnic origin, political opinions, religion or philosophical beliefs, trade union membership, and the processing of genetic data, data concerning health or data concerning sex life or criminal convictions and offences or related security measures*".

14 See e.g. recitals 75, 76, 92, 116.

15 The WP29 interprets "*systematic*" as meaning one or more of the following (see the WP29 Guidelines on Data Protection Officer 16/EN WP 243):
    – occurring according to a system;
    – pre-arranged, organised or methodical;
    – taking place as part of a general plan for data collection;
    – carried out as part of a strategy.
    The WP29 interprets "*publicly accessible area*" as being any place open to any member of the public, for example a piazza, a shopping centre, a street, a market place, a train station or a public library.

16 See the WP29 Guidelines on Data Protection Officer 16/EN WP 243.

17 See explanation in the WP29 Opinion on Purpose limitation 13/EN WP 203, p.24.

18 In that context, "*the competent supervisory authority shall apply the consistency mechanism referred to in Article 63 where such lists involve processing activities which are related to the offering of goods or services to data subjects or to the monitoring of their behaviour in several Member States, or may substantially affect the free movement of personal data within the Union*" (Article 35(6)).

19 "*A single assessment may address a set of similar processing operations that present similar high risks*".

20 "*Commission decisions adopted and authorisations by supervisory authorities based on Directive 95/46/EC remain in force until amended, replaced or repealed*" (recital 171).

21 When a DPIA is carried out at the stage of the elaboration of the legislation providing a legal basis for a processing, it is likely to require a review before entry into operations, as the adopted legislation may differ from the proposal in ways that affect privacy and data protection issues. Moreover, there may not be sufficient technical details available regarding the actual processing at the time of adoption of the legislation, even if it was accompanied by a DPIA. In such cases, it may still be necessary to carry out a specific DPIA prior to carrying out the actual processing activities.

22 In terms of the context, the data collected, purposes, functionalities, personal data processed, recipients, data combinations, risks (supporting assets, risk sources, potential impacts, threats, etc.), security measures and international transfers.

23 Except when it is an already existing processing that has been prior checked by the Supervisory Authority, in which case the DPIA should be carried out before undergoing significant changes.

24 *Recommendations for a privacy impact assessment framework for the European Union, Deliverable D3:* http://www.piafproject.eu/ref/PIAF_D3_final.pdf.

25 It should be underlined that the process depicted here is iterative: in practice, it is likely that each of the stages is revisited multiple times before the DPIA can be completed.

26 Risk management processes: communication and consultation, establishing the context, risk assessment, risk treatment, monitoring and review (see terms and definitions, and table of content, in the ISO 31000 preview: https://www.iso.org/obp/ui/#iso:std:iso:31000:ed-1:v1:en).

27 Article 35(10) explicitly excludes only the application of article 35 paragraphs 1 to 7.

28 Written advice to the controller is only necessary when the supervisory authority is of the opinion that the intended processing is not in line with the regulation as per Article 36(2).

29 Including taking account of existing guidance from EDPB and supervisory authorities and taking account of the state of the art and the costs of implementation as prescribed by Article 35(1).

30 Note: "*pseudonymization and encryption of personal data*" (as well as data minimization, oversight mechanisms, etc.) are not necessarily appropriate measures. They are only examples. Appropriate measures depend on the context and the risks, specific to the processing operations.

IV. CONCLUSIONS AND RECOMMENDATIONS

[2.190]
DPIAs are a useful way for data controllers to implement data processing systems that comply with the GDPR and can be mandatory for some types of processing operations. They are scalable and can take different forms, but the GDPR sets out the basic requirements of an effective DPIA. Data controllers should see the carrying out of a DPIA as a useful and positive activity that aids legal compliance.

Article 24(1) sets out the basic responsibility of the controller in terms of complying with the GDPR: "*taking into account the nature, scope, context and purposes of processing as well as the risks of varying likelihood and severity for the rights and freedoms of natural persons, the controller shall implement appropriate technical and organisational measures to ensure and to be able to demonstrate that processing is performed in accordance with this Regulation. Those measures shall be reviewed and updated where necessary*".

The DPIA is a key part of complying with the Regulation where high risk data processing is planned or is taking place. This means that data controllers should use the criteria set out in this document to determine whether or not a DPIA has to be carried out. Internal data controller policy could extend this list beyond the GDPR's legal requirements. This should result in greater trust and confidence of data subjects and other data controllers.

Where a likely high risk processing is planned, the data controller must:
– choose a DPIA methodology (examples given in Annex 1) that satisfies the criteria in Annex 2, or specify and implement a systematic DPIA process that:
    • is compliant with the criteria in Annex 2;

- • is integrated into existing design, development, change, risk and operational review processes in accordance with internal processes, context and culture;
- • involves the appropriate interested parties and clearly define their responsibilities (controller, DPO, data subjects or their representatives, business, technical services, processors, information security officer, *etc.*);
- – provide the DPIA report to the competent supervisory authority when required to do so;
- – consult the supervisory authority when they have failed to determine sufficient measures to mitigate the high risks;
- – periodically review the DPIA and the processing it assesses, at least when there is a change of the risk posed by processing the operation;
- – document the decisions taken.

ANNEX 1 – EXAMPLES OF EXISTING EU DPIA FRAMEWORKS

[2.191]
The GDPR does not specify which DPIA process must be followed but instead allows for data controllers to introduce a framework which complements their existing working practices provided it takes account of the components described in Article 35(7). Such a framework can be bespoke to the data controller or common across a particular industry. Previously published frameworks developed by EU DPAs and EU sector-specific frameworks include (but are not limited to):

Examples of EU generic frameworks:
- – DE: Standard Data Protection Model, V.1.0 – Trial version, 2016[31].
  https://www.datenschutzzentrum.de/uploads/SDM-Methodology_V1_EN1.pdf
- – ES: *Guía para una Evaluación de Impacto en la Protección de Datos Personales (EIPD)*, Agencia española de protección de datos (AGPD), 2014.
  https://www.agpd.es/portalwebAGPD/canaldocumentacion/publicaciones/common/Guias/Guia_EIPD.pdf
- – FR: Privacy Impact Assessment (PIA), Commission nationale de l'informatique et des libertés (CNIL), 2015.
  https://www.cnil.fr/fr/node/15798
- – UK: *Conducting privacy impact assessments code of practice*, Information Commissioner's Office (ICO), 2014.
  https://ico.org.uk/media/for-organisations/documents/1595/pia-code-of-practice.pdf

Examples of EU sector-specific frameworks:
- – Privacy and Data Protection Impact Assessment Framework for RFID Applications[32].
  http://ec.europa.eu/justice/data-protection/article-29/documentation/opinion-recommendation/files/2011/wp180_annex_en.pdf
- – Data Protection Impact Assessment Template for Smart Grid and Smart Metering systems[33]
  http://ec.europa.eu/energy/sites/ener/files/documents/2014_dpia_smart_grids_forces.pdf

An international standard will also provide guidelines for methodologies used for carrying out a DPIA (ISO/IEC 29134[34]).

NOTES
[31] Unanimously and affirmatively acknowledged (under abstention of Bavaria) by the 92. Conference of the Independent Data Protection Authorities of the Bund and the Länder in Kühlungsborn on 9-10 November 2016.
[32] See also :
- – Commission Recommendation of 12 May 2009 on the implementation of privacy and data protection principles in applications supported by radio- frequency identification.
  https://ec.europa.eu/digital-single-market/en/news/commission-recommendation-12-may-2009-implementation-privacy-and-data-protection-principles
- – Opinion 9/2011 on the revised Industry Proposal for a Privacy and Data Protection Impact Assessment Framework for RFID Applications.
  http://ec.europa.eu/justice/data-protection/article-29/documentation/opinion-recommendation/files/2011/wp180_en.pdf
[33] See also the Opinion 07/2013 on the Data Protection Impact Assessment Template for Smart Grid and Smart Metering Systems ('DPIA Template') prepared by Expert Group 2 of the Commission's Smart Grid Task Force. http://ec.europa.eu/justice/data-protection/article-29/documentation/opinion-recommendation/files/2013/wp209_en.pdf
[34] ISO/IEC 29134 (project), *Information technology – Security techniques – Privacy impact assessment – Guidelines*, International Organization for Standardization (ISO).

ANNEX 2 – CRITERIA FOR AN ACCEPTABLE DPIA

[2.192]
The WP29 proposes the following criteria which data controllers can use to assess whether or not a DPIA, or a methodology to carry out a DPIA, is sufficiently comprehensive to comply with the GDPR:
- • a systematic description of the processing is provided (Article 35(7)(a)):
  - • nature, scope, context and purposes of the processing are taken into account (recital 90);
  - • personal data, recipients and period for which the personal data will be stored are recorded;
  - • a functional description of the processing operation is provided;
  - • the assets on which personal data rely (hardware, software, networks, people, paper or paper transmission channels) are identified;

Part 2   Data Protection: EU Law etc

- compliance with approved codes of conduct is taken into account (Article 35(8));
- necessity and proportionality are assessed (Article 35(7)(b)):
    - measures envisaged to comply with the Regulation are determined (Article 35(7)(d) and recital 90), taking into account:
        - measures contributing to the proportionality and the necessity of the processing on the basis of:
            - specified, explicit and legitimate purpose(s) (Article 5(1)(b));
            - lawfulness of processing (Article 6);
            - adequate, relevant and limited to what is necessary data (Article 5(1)(c));
            - limited storage duration (Article 5(1)(e));
        - measures contributing to the rights of the data subjects:
            - information provided to the data subject (Articles 12, 13 and 14);
            - right of access and to data portability (Articles 15 and 20);
            - right to rectification and to erasure (Articles 16, 17 and 19);
            - right to object and to restriction of processing (Article 18, 19 and 21);
            - relationships with processors (Article 28);
            - safeguards surrounding international transfer(s) (Chapter V);
            - prior consultation (Article 36).
- risks to the rights and freedoms of data subjects are managed (Article 35(7)(c)):
    - origin, nature, particularity and severity of the risks are appreciated (cf. recital 84) or, more specifically, for each risk (illegitimate access, undesired modification, and disappearance of data) from the perspective of the data subjects:
        - risks sources are taken into account (recital 90);
        - potential impacts to the rights and freedoms of data subjects are identified in case of events including illegitimate access, undesired modification and disappearance of data;
        - threats that could lead to illegitimate access, undesired modification and disappearance of data are identified;
        - likelihood and severity are estimated (recital 90);
    - measures envisaged to treat those risks are determined (Article 35(7)(d) and recital 90);
- interested parties are involved:
    - the advice of the DPO is sought (Article 35(2));
    - the views of data subjects or their representatives are sought, where appropriate (Article 35(9)).

ARTICLE 29 DATA PROTECTION WORKING PARTY: GUIDELINES ON PERSONAL DATA BREACH NOTIFICATION UNDER REGULATION 2016/679
18/EN
WP 250 rev.01
Adopted on 3 October 2017

As last Revised and Adopted on 6 February 2018

[2.193]

NOTES

This document was originally issued by the Article 29 Working Party but subsequently endorsed by the EDPB during its first plenary meeting.

© European Data Protection Board.

TABLE OF CONTENTS

INTRODUCTION

[2.194]

The General Data Protection Regulation (the GDPR) introduces the requirement for a personal data breach (henceforth "breach") to be notified to the competent national supervisory authority[1] (or in the case of a cross-border breach, to the lead authority) and, in certain cases, to communicate the breach to the individuals whose personal data have been affected by the breach.

Obligations to notify in cases of breaches presently exist for certain organisations, such as providers of publicly-available electronic communications services (as specified in Directive 2009/136/EC and

Regulation (EU) No 611/2013)[2]. There are also some EU Member States that already have their own national breach notification obligation. This may include the obligation to notify breaches involving categories of controllers in addition to providers of publicly available electronic communication services (for example in Germany and Italy), or an obligation to report all breaches involving personal data (such as in the Netherlands). Other Member States may have relevant Codes of Practice (for example, in Ireland[3]). Whilst a number of EU data protection authorities currently encourage controllers to report breaches, the Data Protection Directive 95/46/EC[4], which the GDPR replaces, does not contain a specific breach notification obligation and therefore such a requirement will be new for many organisations. The GDPR now makes notification mandatory for all controllers unless a breach is unlikely to result in a risk to the rights and freedoms of individuals[5]. Processors also have an important role to play and they must notify any breach to their controller[6].

The Article 29 Working Party (WP29) considers that the new notification requirement has a number of benefits. When notifying the supervisory authority, controllers can obtain advice on whether the affected individuals need to be informed. Indeed, the supervisory authority may order the controller to inform those individuals about the breach[7]. Communicating a breach to individuals allows the controller to provide information on the risks presented as a result of the breach and the steps those individuals can take to protect themselves from its potential consequences. The focus of any breach response plan should be on protecting individuals and their personal data. Consequently, breach notification should be seen as a tool enhancing compliance in relation to the protection of personal data. At the same time, it should be noted that failure to report a breach to either an individual or a supervisory authority may mean that under Article 83 a possible sanction is applicable to the controller.

Controllers and processors are therefore encouraged to plan in advance and put in place processes to be able to detect and promptly contain a breach, to assess the risk to individuals[8], and then to determine whether it is necessary to notify the competent supervisory authority, and to communicate the breach to the individuals concerned when necessary. Notification to the supervisory authority should form a part of that incident response plan.

The GDPR contains provisions on when a breach needs to be notified, and to whom, as well as what information should be provided as part of the notification. Information required for the notification can be provided in phases, but in any event controllers should act on any breach in a timely manner.

In its Opinion 03/2014 on personal data breach notification[9], WP29 provided guidance to controllers in order to help them to decide whether to notify data subjects in case of a breach. The opinion considered the obligation of providers of electronic communications regarding Directive 2002/58/EC and provided examples from multiple sectors, in the context of the then draft GDPR, and presented good practices for all controllers.

The current Guidelines explain the mandatory breach notification and communication requirements of the GDPR and some of the steps controllers and processors can take to meet these new obligations. They also give examples of various types of breaches and who would need to be notified in different scenarios.

NOTES

[1]   See Article 4(21) of the GDPR

[2]   See http://eur-lex.europa.eu/legal-content/EN/TXT/?uri=celex:32009L0136 and http://eur-lex.europa.eu/legal-content/EN/TXT/?uri=CELEX%3A32013R0611

[3]   See https://www.dataprotection.ie/docs/Data_Security_Breach_Code_of_Practice/1082.htm

[4]   See http://eur-lex.europa.eu/legal-content/EN/TXT/?uri=celex:31995L0046

[5]   The rights enshrined in the Charter of Fundamental Rights of the EU, available at http://eur-lex.europa.eu/legal-content/EN/TXT/?uri=CELEX:12012P/TXT

[6]   See Article 33(2). This is similar in concept to Article 5 of Regulation (EU) No 611/2013 which states that a provider that is contracted to deliver part of an electronic communications service (without having a direct contractual relationship with subscribers) is obliged to notify the contracting provider in the event of a personal data breach.

[7]   See Articles 34(4) and 58(2)(e)

[8]   This can be ensured under the monitoring and review requirement of a DPIA, which is required for processing operations likely to result in a high risk to the rights and freedoms of natural persons (Article 35(1) and (11).

[9]   See Opinion 03/2014 on Personal Data Breach Notification http://ec.europa.eu/justice/data-protection/article-29/documentation/opinion-recommendation/files/2014/wp213_en.pdf

I. PERSONAL DATA BREACH NOTIFICATION UNDER THE GDPR

A. BASIC SECURITY CONSIDERATIONS

[2.195]
One of the requirements of the GDPR is that, by using appropriate technical and organisational measures, personal data shall be processed in a manner to ensure the appropriate security of the personal data, including protection against unauthorised or unlawful processing and against accidental loss, destruction or damage[10].

Accordingly, the GDPR requires both controllers and processors to have in place appropriate technical and organisational measures to ensure a level of security appropriate to the risk posed to the personal data being processed. They should take into account the state of the art, the costs of implementation and the nature, the scope, context and purposes of processing, as well as the risk of varying likelihood and severity for the rights and freedoms of natural persons[11]. Also, the GDPR requires all appropriate technological protection an organisational measures to be in place to establish immediately whether a breach has taken place, which then determines whether the notification obligation is engaged[12].

Consequently, a key element of any data security policy is being able, where possible, to prevent a breach and, where it nevertheless occurs, to react to it in a timely manner.

B. WHAT IS A PERSONAL DATA BREACH?

1. Definition

As part of any attempt to address a breach the controller should first be able to recognise one. The GDPR defines a "personal data breach" in Article 4(12) as:

> "a breach of security leading to the accidental or unlawful destruction, loss, alteration, unauthorised disclosure of, or access to, personal data transmitted, stored or otherwise processed."

What is meant by "destruction" of personal data should be quite clear: this is where the data no longer exists, or no longer exists in a form that is of any use to the controller. "Damage" should also be relatively clear: this is where personal data has been altered, corrupted, or is no longer complete. In terms of "loss" of personal data, this should be interpreted as the data may still exist, but the controller has lost control or access to it, or no longer has it in its possession. Finally, unauthorised or unlawful processing may include disclosure of personal data to (or access by) recipients who are not authorised to receive (or access) the data, or any other form of processing which violates the GDPR.

> **Example**
>
> An example of loss of personal data can include where a device containing a copy of a controller's customer database has been lost or stolen. A further example of loss may be where the only copy of a set of personal data has been encrypted by ransomware, or has been encrypted by the controller using a key that is no longer in its possession.

What should be clear is that a breach is a type of security incident. However, as indicated by Article 4(12), the GDPR only applies where there is a breach of personal data. The consequence of such a breach is that the controller will be unable to ensure compliance with the principles relating to the processing of personal data as outlined in Article 5 of the GDPR. This highlights the difference between a security incident and a personal data breach – in essence, whilst all personal data breaches are security incidents, not all security incidents are necessarily personal data breaches[13].

The potential adverse effects of a breach on individuals are considered below.

2. Types of personal data breaches

In its Opinion 03/2014 on breach notification, WP29 explained that breaches can be categorised according to the following three well-known information security principles[14]:
* "Confidentiality breach" - where there is an unauthorised or accidental disclosure of, or access to, personal data.
* "Integrity breach" - where there is an unauthorised or accidental alteration of personal data.
* "Availability breach" - where there is an accidental or unauthorised loss of access[15] to, or destruction of, personal data.

It should also be noted that, depending on the circumstances, a breach can concern confidentiality, integrity and availability of personal data at the same time, as well as any combination of these.

Whereas determining if there has been a breach of confidentiality or integrity is relatively clear, whether there has been an availability breach may be less obvious. A breach will always be regarded as an availability breach when there has been a permanent loss of, or destruction of, personal data.

> **Example**
>
> Examples of a loss of availability include where data has been deleted either accidentally or by an unauthorised person, or, in the example of securely encrypted data, the decryption key has been lost. In the event that the controller cannot restore access to the data, for example, from a backup, then this is regarded as a permanent loss of availability.
>
> A loss of availability may also occur where there has been significant disruption to the normal service of an organisation, for example, experiencing a power failure or denial of service attack, rendering personal data unavailable.

The question may be asked whether a temporary loss of availability of personal data should be considered as a breach and, if so, one which needs to be notified. Article 32 of the GDPR, "security of processing," explains that when implementing technical and organisational measures to ensure a level of security appropriate to the risk, consideration should be given, amongst other things, to "the ability to ensure the ongoing confidentiality, integrity, availability and resilience of processing systems and services," and "the ability to restore the availability and access to personal data in a timely manner in the event of a physical or technical incident".

Therefore, a security incident resulting in personal data being made unavailable for a period of time is also a type of breach, as the lack of access to the data can have a significant impact on the rights and freedoms of natural persons. To be clear, where personal data is unavailable due to planned system maintenance being carried out this is not a 'breach of security' as defined in Article 4(12).

As with a permanent loss or destruction of personal data (or indeed any other type of breach), a breach involving the temporary loss of availability should be documented in accordance with Article 33(5). This assists the controller in demonstrating accountability to the supervisory authority, which may ask to see those records[16]. However, depending on the circumstances of the breach, it may or may not require notification to the supervisory authority and communication to affected individuals. The controller will need to assess the likelihood and severity of the impact on the rights and freedoms of natural persons as a result of the lack of availability of personal data. In accordance with Article 33, the controller will need to notify unless the breach is unlikely to result in a risk to individuals' rights and freedoms. Of course, this will need to be assessed on a case-by-case basis.

Examples

In the context of a hospital, if critical medical data about patients are unavailable, even temporarily, this could present a risk to individuals' rights and freedoms; for example, operations may be cancelled and lives put at risk.

Conversely, in the case of a media company's systems being unavailable for several hours (e.g. due to a power outage), if that company is then prevented from sending newsletters to its subscribers, this is unlikely to present a risk to individuals' rights and freedoms.

It should be noted that although a loss of availability of a controller's systems might be only temporary and may not have an impact on individuals, it is important for the controller to consider all possible consequences of a breach, as it may still require notification for other reasons.

Example

Infection by ransomware (malicious software which encrypts the controller's data until a ransom is paid) could lead to a temporary loss of availability if the data can be restored from backup. However, a network intrusion still occurred, and notification could be required if the incident is qualified as confidentiality breach (i.e. personal data is accessed by the attacker) and this presents a risk to the rights and freedoms of individuals.

---

3. The possible consequences of a personal data breach

A breach can potentially have a range of significant adverse effects on individuals, which can result in physical, material, or non-material damage. The GDPR explains that this can include loss of control over their personal data, limitation of their rights, discrimination, identity theft or fraud, financial loss, unauthorised reversal of pseudonymisation, damage to reputation, and loss of confidentiality of personal data protected by professional secrecy. It can also include any other significant economic or social disadvantage to those individuals[17].

Accordingly, the GDPR requires the controller to notify a breach to the competent supervisory authority, unless it is unlikely to result in a risk of such adverse effects taking place. Where there is a likely high risk of these adverse effects occurring, the GDPR requires the controller to communicate the breach to the affected individuals as soon as is reasonably feasible[18].

The importance of being able to identify a breach, to assess the risk to individuals, and then notify if required, is emphasised in Recital 87 of the GDPR:

"It should be ascertained whether all appropriate technological protection and organisational measures have been implemented to establish immediately whether a personal data breach has taken place and to inform promptly the supervisory authority and the data subject. The fact that the notification was made without undue delay should be established taking into account in particular the nature and gravity of the personal data breach and its consequences and adverse effects for the data subject. Such notification may result in an intervention of the supervisory authority in accordance with its tasks and powers laid down in this Regulation."

Further guidelines on assessing the risk of adverse effects to individuals are considered in section IV.

If controllers fail to notify either the supervisory authority or data subjects of a data breach or both even though the requirements of Articles 33 and/or 34 are fulfilled, then the supervisory authority is presented with a choice that must include consideration of all of the corrective measures at its disposal, which would include consideration of the imposition of the appropriate administrative fine[19], either accompanying a corrective measure under Article 58(2) or on its own. Where an administrative fine is chosen, its value can be up to 10,000,000 EUR or up to 2 % if the total worldwide annual turnover of an undertaking under Article 83(4)(a) of the GDPR. It is also important to bear in mind that in some cases, the failure to notify a breach could reveal either an absence of existing security measures or an inadequacy of the existing security measures. The WP29 guidelines on administrative fines state: "The occurrence of several different infringements committed together in any particular single case means that the supervisory authority is able to apply the administrative fines at a level which is effective, proportionate and dissuasive within the limit of the gravest infringement". In that case, the supervisory authority will also have the possibility to issue sanctions for failure to notify or communicate the breach (Articles 33 and 34) on the one hand, and absence of (adequate) security measures (Article 32) on the other hand, as they are two separate infringements.

NOTES

[10] See Articles 5(1)(f) and 32.

[11] Article 32; see also Recital 83

[12] See Recital 87

[13] It should be noted that a security incident is not limited to threat models where an attack is made on an organisation from an external source, but includes incidents from internal processing that breach security principles.

[14] See Opinion 03/2014

[15] It is well established that "access" is fundamentally part of "availability". See, for example, NIST SP800-53rev4, which defines "availability" as: "Ensuring timely and reliable access to and use of information," available at http://nvlpubs.nist. gov/nistpubs/SpecialPublications/NIST.SP.800-53r4.pdf. CNSSI-4009 also refers to: " Timely, reliable access to data and information services for authorized users." See https://rmf.org/wp-content/uploads/2017/10/CNSSI-4009.pdf. ISO/IEC 27000:2016 also defines "availability" as "Property of being accessible and usable upon demand by an authorized entity": https://www.iso.org/obp/ui/#iso:std:iso-iec:27000:ed-4:v1:en

[16] See Article 33(5)

[17] See also Recitals 85 and 75

[18] See also Recital 86.

[19] For further details, please see WP29 Guidelines on the application and setting of administrative fines, available here: http://ec.europa.eu/newsroom/just/document.cfm?doc_id=47889

II. ARTICLE 33 – NOTIFICATION TO THE SUPERVISORY AUTHORITY

A. WHEN TO NOTIFY

1. Article 33 requirements

[2.196]
Article 33(1) provides that:

"In the case of a personal data breach, the controller shall without undue delay and, where feasible, not later than 72 hours after having become aware of it, notify the personal data breach to the supervisory authority competent in accordance with Article 55, unless the personal data breach is unlikely to result in a risk to the rights and freedoms of natural persons. Where the notification to the supervisory authority is not made within 72 hours, it shall be accompanied by reasons for the delay."

Recital 87 states[20]:

"It should be ascertained whether all appropriate technological protection and organisational measures have been implemented to establish immediately whether a personal data breach has taken place and to inform promptly the supervisory authority and the data subject. The fact that the notification was made without undue delay should be established taking into account in particular the nature and gravity of the personal data breach and its consequences and adverse effects for the data subject. Such notification may result in an intervention of the supervisory authority in accordance with its tasks and powers laid down in this Regulation."

2. When does a controller become "aware"?

As detailed above, the GDPR requires that, in the case of a breach, the controller shall notify the breach without undue delay and, where feasible, not later than 72 hours after having become aware of it. This may raise the question of when a controller can be considered to have become "aware" of a breach. WP29 considers that a controller should be regarded as having become "aware" when that controller has a reasonable degree of certainty that a security incident has occurred that has led to personal data being compromised.

However, as indicated earlier, the GDPR requires the controller to implement all appropriate technical protection and organisational measures to establish immediately whether a breach has taken place and to inform promptly the supervisory authority and the data subjects. It also states that the fact that the notification was made without undue delay should be established taking into account in particular the nature and gravity of the breach and its consequences and adverse effects for the data subject[21]. This puts an obligation on the controller to ensure that they will be "aware" of any breaches in a timely manner so that they can take appropriate action.

When, exactly, a controller can be considered to be "aware" of a particular breach will depend on the circumstances of the specific breach. In some cases, it will be relatively clear from the outset that there has been a breach, whereas in others, it may take some time to establish if personal data have been compromised. However, the emphasis should be on prompt action to investigate an incident to determine whether personal data have indeed been breached, and if so, to take remedial action and notify if required.

Examples

(1)   In the case of a loss of a USB key with unencrypted personal data it is often not possible to ascertain whether unauthorised persons gained access to that data. Nevertheless, even though the controller may not be able to establish if a confidentiality breach has taken place, such a case has to be notified as there is a reasonable degree of certainty that an availability breach has occurred; the controller would become "aware" when it realised the USB key had been lost.

(2)   A third party informs a controller that they have accidentally received the personal data of one of its customers and provides evidence of the unauthorised disclosure. As the controller has been presented with clear evidence of a confidentiality breach then there can be no doubt that it has become "aware".

(3)   A controller detects that there has been a possible intrusion into its network. The controller checks its systems to establish whether personal data held on that system has been compromised and confirms this is the case. Once again, as the controller now has clear evidence of a breach there can be no doubt that it has become "aware".

(4)   A cybercriminal contacts the controller after having hacked its system in order to ask for a ransom. In that case, after checking its system to confirm it has been attacked the controller has clear evidence that a breach has occurred and there is no doubt that it has become aware.

After first being informed of a potential breach by an individual, a media organisation, or another source, or when it has itself detected a security incident, the controller may undertake a short period of investigation in order to establish whether or not a breach has in fact occurred. During this period of investigation the controller may not be regarded as being "aware". However, it is expected that the initial investigation should begin as soon as possible and establish with a reasonable degree of certainty whether a breach has taken place; a more detailed investigation can then follow.

Once the controller has become aware, a notifiable breach must be notified without undue delay, and where feasible, not later than 72 hours. During this period, the controller should assess the likely risk to individuals in order to determine whether the requirement for notification has been triggered, as well as the action(s) needed to address the breach. However, a controller may already have an initial assessment of the potential risk that could result from a breach as part of a data protection impact assessment (DPIA)[22] made prior to carrying out the processing operation concerned. However, the DPIA may be more generalised in comparison to the specific circumstances of any actual breach, and so in any event an additional assessment taking into account those circumstances will need to be made. For more detail on assessing risk, see section IV.

In most cases these preliminary actions should be completed soon after the initial alert (i.e. when the controller or processor suspects there has been a security incident which may involve personal data.) – it should take longer than this only in exceptional cases.

Example

An individual informs the controller that they have received an email impersonating the controller which contains personal data relating to his (actual) use of the controller's service, suggesting that the security of the controller has been compromised. The controller conducts a short period of investigation and identifies an intrusion into their network and evidence of unauthorised access to personal data. The controller would now be considered as "aware" and notification to the supervisory authority is required unless this is unlikely to present a risk to the rights and freedoms of individuals. The controller will need to take appropriate remedial action to address the breach.

The controller should therefore have internal processes in place to be able to detect and address a breach. For example, for finding some irregularities in data processing the controller or processor may use certain technical measures such as data flow and log analysers, from which is possible to define events and alerts by correlating any log data[23]. It is important that when a breach is detected it is reported upwards to the appropriate level of management so it can be addressed and, if required, notified in accordance with Article 33 and, if necessary, Article 34. Such measures and reporting mechanisms could be detailed in the controller's incident response plans and/or governance arrangements. These will help the controller to plan effectively and determine who has operational responsibility within the organisation for managing a breach and how or whether to escalate an incident as appropriate.

The controller should also have in place arrangements with any processors the controller uses, which themselves have an obligation to notify the controller in the event of a breach (see below).

Whilst it is the responsibility of controllers and processors to put in place suitable measures to be able to prevent, react and address a breach, there are some practical steps that should be taken in all cases.

- Information concerning all security-related events should be directed towards a responsible person or persons with the task of addressing incidents, establishing the existence of a breach and assessing risk.
- Risk to individuals as a result of a breach should then be assessed (likelihood of no risk, risk or high risk), with relevant sections of the organisation being informed.
- Notification to the supervisory authority, and potentially communication of the breach to the affected individuals should be made, if required.
- At the same time, the controller should act to contain and recover the breach.
- Documentation of the breach should take place as it develops.

Accordingly, it should be clear that there is an obligation on the controller to act on any initial alert and establish whether or not a breach has, in fact, occurred. This brief period allows for some investigation, and for the controller to gather evidence and other relevant details. However, once the controller has established with a reasonable degree of certainty that a breach has occurred, if the conditions in Article 33(1) have been met, it must then notify the supervisory authority without undue delay and, where feasible, not later than 72 hours[24]. If a controller fails to act in a timely manner and it becomes apparent that a breach did occur, this could be considered as a failure to notify in accordance with Article 33.

Article 32 makes clear that the controller and processor should have appropriate technical and organisational measures in place to ensure an appropriate level of security of personal data: the ability to detect, address, and report a breach in a timely manner should be seen as essential elements of these measures.

3. Joint controllers

Article 26 concerns joint controllers and specifies that joint controllers shall determine their respective responsibilities for compliance with the GDPR[25]. This will include determining which party will have responsibility for complying with the obligations under Articles 33 and 34. WP29 recommends that the contractual arrangements between joint controllers include provisions that determine which controller will take the lead on, or be responsible for, compliance with the GDPR's breach notification obligations.

4. Processor obligations

The controller retains overall responsibility for the protection of personal data, but the processor has an important role to play to enable the controller to comply with its obligations; and this includes breach notification. Indeed, Article 28(3) specifies that the processing by a processor shall be governed by a contract or other legal act. Article 28(3)(f) states that the contract or other legal act shall stipulate that the processor "assists the controller in ensuring compliance with the obligations pursuant to Articles 32 to 36 taking into account the nature of processing and the information available to the processor".

Article 33(2) makes it clear that if a processor is used by a controller and the processor becomes aware of a breach of the personal data it is processing on behalf of the controller, it must notify the controller "without undue delay". It should be noted that the processor does not need to first assess the likelihood of risk arising from a breach before notifying the controller; it is the controller that must make this assessment on becoming aware of the breach. The processor just needs to establish whether a breach has occurred and then notify the controller. The controller uses the processor to achieve its purposes; therefore, in principle, the controller should be considered as "aware" once the processor has informed it of the breach. The obligation on the processor to notify its controller allows the controller to address the breach and to determine whether or not it is required to notify the supervisory authority in accordance with Article 33(1) and the affected individuals in accordance with Article 34(1). The controller might also want to investigate the breach, as the processor might not be in a position to know all the relevant facts relating to the matter, for example, if a copy or backup of personal data destroyed or lost by the processor is still held by the controller. This may affect whether the controller would then need to notify.

The GDPR does not provide an explicit time limit within which the processor must alert the controller, except that it must do so "without undue delay". Therefore, WP29 recommends the processor promptly notifies the controller, with further information about the breach provided in phases as more details become available. This is important in order to help the controller to meet the requirement of notification to the supervisory authority within 72 hours.

As is explained above, the contract between the controller and processor should specify how the requirements expressed in Article 33(2) should be met in addition to other provisions in the GDPR. This can include requirements for early notification by the processor that in turn support the controller's obligations to report to the supervisory authority within 72 hours.

Where the processor provides services to multiple controllers that are all affected by the same incident, the processor will have to report details of the incident to each controller.

A processor could make a notification on behalf of the controller, if the controller has given the processor the proper authorisation and this is part of the contractual arrangements between controller and processor. Such notification must be made in accordance with Article 33 and 34. However, it is important to note that the legal responsibility to notify remains with the controller.

B. PROVIDING INFORMATION TO THE SUPERVISORY AUTHORITY

1. Information to be provided

When a controller notifies a breach to the supervisory authority, Article 33(3) states that, at the minimum, it should:

"(a) describe the nature of the personal data breach including where possible, the categories and approximate number of data subjects concerned and the categories and approximate number of personal data records concerned;

(b) communicate the name and contact details of the data protection officer or other contact point where more information can be obtained;

(c) describe the likely consequences of the personal data breach;

(d) describe the measures taken or proposed to be taken by the controller to address the personal data breach, including, where appropriate, measures to mitigate its possible adverse effects."

The GDPR does not define categories of data subjects or personal data records. However, WP29 suggests categories of data subjects to refer to the various types of individuals whose personal data has been affected by a breach: depending on the descriptors used, this could include, amongst others, children and other vulnerable groups, people with disabilities, employees or customers. Similarly, categories of personal data records can refer to the different types of records that the controller may process, such as health data, educational records, social care information, financial details, bank account numbers, passport numbers and so on.

Recital 85 makes it clear that one of the purposes of notification is limiting damage to individuals. Accordingly, if the types of data subjects or the types of personal data indicate a risk of particular damage occurring as a result of a breach (e.g. identity theft, fraud, financial loss, threat to professional secrecy), then it is important the notification indicates these categories. In this way, it is linked to the requirement of describing the likely consequences of the breach.

Where precise information is not available (e.g. exact number of data subjects affected) this should not be a barrier to timely breach notification. The GDPR allows for approximations to be made in the number of individuals affected and the number of personal data records concerned. The focus should be directed towards addressing the adverse effects of the breach rather than providing precise figures.

Thus, when it has become clear that here has been a breach, but the extent of it is not yet known, a notification in phases (see below) is a safe way to meet the notification obligations.

Article 33(3) states that the controller "shall at least" provide this information with a notification, so a controller can, if necessary, choose to provide further details. Different types of breaches (confidentiality, integrity or availability) might require further information to be provided to fully explain the circumstances of each case.

Example

As part of its notification to the supervisory authority, a controller may find it useful to name its processor if it is at the root cause of a breach, particularly if this has led to an incident affecting the personal data records of many other controllers that use the same processor.

In any event, the supervisory authority may request further details as part of its investigation into a breach.

2. Notification in phases

Depending on the nature of a breach, further investigation by the controller may be necessary to establish all of the relevant facts relating to the incident. Article 33(4) therefore states:

"Where, and in so far as, it is not possible to provide the information at the same time, the information may be provided in phases without undue further delay."

This means that the GDPR recognises that controllers will not always have all of the necessary information concerning a breach within 72 hours of becoming aware of it, as full and comprehensive details of the incident may not always be available during this initial period. As such, it allows for a notification in phases. It is more likely this will be the case for more complex breaches, such as some types of cyber security incidents where, for example, an in-depth forensic investigation may be necessary to fully establish the nature of the breach and the extent to which personal data have been compromised. Consequently, in many cases the controller will have to do more investigation and follow-up with additional information at a later point. This is permissible, providing the controller gives reasons for the delay, in accordance with Article 33(1). WP29 recommends that when the controller first notifies the supervisory authority, the controller should also inform the supervisory authority if the controller does not yet have all the required information and will provide more details later on. The supervisory authority should agree how and when additional information should be provided. This does not prevent the controller from providing further information at any other stage, if it becomes aware of additional relevant details about the breach that need to be provided to the supervisory authority.

The focus of the notification requirement is to encourage controllers to act promptly on a breach, contain it and, if possible, recover the compromised personal data, and to seek relevant advice from the supervisory authority. Notifying the supervisory authority within the first 72 hours can allow the controller to make sure that decisions about notifying or not notifying individuals are correct.

However, the purpose of notifying the supervisory authority is not solely to obtain guidance on whether to notify the affected individuals. It will be obvious in some cases that, due to the nature of the breach and the severity of the risk, the controller will need to notify the affected individuals without delay. For example, if there is an immediate threat of identity theft, or if special categories of personal data[26] are disclosed online, the controller should act without undue delay to contain the breach and to communicate it to the individuals concerned (see section III). In exceptional circumstances, this might even take place before notifying the supervisory authority. More generally, notification of the supervisory authority may not serve as a justification for failure to communicate the breach to the data subject where it is required.

It should also be clear that after making an initial notification, a controller could update the supervisory authority if a follow-up investigation uncovers evidence that the security incident was contained and no breach actually occurred. This information could then be added to the information already given to the supervisory authority and the incident recorded accordingly as not being a breach. There is no penalty for reporting an incident that ultimately transpires not to be a breach.

Example

A controller notifies the supervisory authority within 72 hours of detecting a breach that it has lost a USB key containing a copy of the personal data of some of its customers. The USB key is later found misfiled within the controller's premises and recovered. The controller updates the supervisory authority and requests the notification be amended.

It should be noted that a phased approach to notification is already the case under the existing obligations of Directive 2002/58/EC, Regulation 611/2013 and other self-reported incidents.

3. Delayed notifications

Article 33(1) makes it clear that where notification to the supervisory authority is not made within 72 hours, it shall be accompanied by reasons for the delay. This, along with the concept of notification in phases, recognises that a controller may not always be able to notify a breach within that time period, and that a delayed notification may be permissible.

Such a scenario might take place where, for example, a controller experiences multiple, similar confidentiality breaches over a short period of time, affecting large numbers of data subjects in the same way. A controller could become aware of a breach and, whilst beginning its investigation, and before notification, detect further similar breaches, which have different causes. Depending on the circumstances, it may take the controller some time to establish the extent of the breaches and, rather than notify each breach individually, the controller instead organises a meaningful notification that represents several very similar breaches, with possible different causes. This could lead to notification to the supervisory authority being delayed by more than 72 hours after the controller first becomes aware of these breaches.

Strictly speaking, each individual breach is a reportable incident. However, to avoid being overly burdensome, the controller may be able to submit a "bundled" notification representing all these breaches, provided that they concern the same type of personal data breached in the same way, over a relatively short space of time. If a series of breaches take place that concern different types of personal data, breached in different ways, then notification should proceed in the normal way, with each breach being reported in accordance with Article 33.

Whilst the GDPR allows for delayed notifications to an extent, this should not be seen as something that regularly takes place. It is worth pointing out that bundled notifications can also be made for multiple similar breaches reported within 72 hours.

C. CROSS-BORDER BREACHES AND BREACHES AT NON-EU ESTABLISHMENTS

1. Cross-border breaches

Where there is cross-border processing[27] of personal data, a breach may affect data subjects in more than one Member State. Article 33(1) makes it clear that when a breach has occurred, the controller should notify the supervisory authority competent in accordance with Article 55 of the GDPR[28].

Article 55(1) says that:

> "Each supervisory authority shall be competent for the performance of the tasks assigned to and the exercise of the powers conferred on it in accordance with this Regulation on the territory of its own Member State."

However, Article 56(1) states:

> "Without prejudice to Article 55, the supervisory authority of the main establishment or of the single establishment of the controller or processor shall be competent to act as lead supervisory authority for the cross-border processing carried out by that controller or processor in accordance with the procedure provided in Article 60."

Furthermore, Article 56(6) states:

> "The lead supervisory authority shall be the sole interlocutor of the controller or processor for the cross-border processing carried out by that controller or processor."

This means that whenever a breach takes place in the context of cross border processing and notification is required, the controller will need to notify the lead supervisory authority[29]. Therefore, when drafting its breach response plan, a controller must make an assessment as to which supervisory authority is the lead supervisory authority that it will need to notify[30]. This will allow the controller to respond promptly to a breach and to meet its obligations in respect of Article 33. It should be clear that in the event of a breach involving cross-border processing, notification must be made to the lead supervisory authority, which is not necessarily where the affected data subjects are located, or indeed where the breach has taken place. When notifying the lead authority, the controller should indicate, where appropriate, whether the breach involves establishments located in other Member States, and in which Member States data subjects are likely to have been affected by the breach. If the controller has any doubt as to the identity of the lead supervisory authority then it should, at a minimum, notify the local supervisory authority where the breach has taken place.

2. Breaches at non-EU establishments

Article 3 concerns the territorial scope of the GDPR, including when it applies to the processing of personal data by a controller or processor that is not established in the EU. In particular, Article 3(2) states[31]:

> "This Regulation applies to the processing of personal data of data subjects who are in the Union by a controller or processor not established in the Union, where the processing activities are related to:
> (a)   the offering of goods or services, irrespective of whether a payment of the data subject is required, to such data subjects in the Union; or
> (b)   the monitoring of their behaviour as far as their behaviour takes place within the Union."

Article 3(3) is also relevant and states[32]:

> "This Regulation applies to the processing of personal data by a controller not established in the Union, but in a place where Member State law applies by virtue of public international law."

Where a controller not established in the EU is subject to Article 3(2) or Article 3(3) and experiences a breach, it is therefore still bound by the notification obligations under Articles 33 and 34. Article 27 requires a controller (and processor) to designate a representative in the EU where Article 3(2) applies. In such cases, WP29 recommends that notification should be made to the supervisory authority in the Member State where the controller's representative in the EU is established[33]. Similarly, where a processor is subject to Article 3(2), it will be bound by the obligations on processors, of particular relevance here, the duty to notify a breach to the controller under Article 33(2).

D. CONDITIONS WHERE NOTIFICATION IS NOT REQUIRED

Article 33(1) makes it clear that breaches that are "unlikely to result in a risk to the rights and freedoms of natural persons" do not require notification to the supervisory authority. An example might be where personal data are already publically available and a disclosure of such data does not constitute a likely risk to the individual. This is in contrast to existing breach notification requirements for providers of publically available electronic communications services in Directive 2009/136/EC that state all relevant breaches have to be notified to the competent authority.

In its Opinion 03/2014 on breach notification[34], WP29 explained that a confidentiality breach of personal data that were encrypted with a state of the art algorithm is still a personal data breach, and has to be notified. However, if the confidentiality of the key is intact – i.e., the key was not compromised in any security breach, and was generated so that it cannot be ascertained by available technical means by any person who is not authorised to access it – then the data are in principle unintelligible. Thus, the breach is unlikely to adversely affect individuals and therefore would not require communication to those individuals[35]. However, even where data is encrypted, a loss or alteration can have negative consequences for data subjects where the controller has no adequate backups. In that instance communication to data subjects would be required, even if the data itself was subject to adequate encryption measures.

WP29 also explained this would similarly be the case if personal data, such as passwords, were securely hashed and salted, the hashed value was calculated with a state of the art cryptographic keyed hash function, the key used to hash the data was not compromised in any breach, and the key used to hash the data has been generated in a way that it cannot be ascertained by available technological means by any person who is not authorised to access it.

Consequently, if personal data have been made essentially unintelligible to unauthorised parties and where the data are a copy or a backup exists, a confidentiality breach involving properly encrypted personal data may not need to be notified to the supervisory authority. This is because such a breach is unlikely to pose a risk to individuals' rights and freedoms. This of course means that the individual would not need to be informed either as there is likely no high risk. However, it should be borne in mind that while notification may initially not be required if there is no likely risk to the rights and freedoms of individuals, this may change over time and the risk would have to be re-evaluated. For example, if the key is subsequently found to be compromised, or a vulnerability in the encryption software is exposed, then notification may still be required.

Furthermore, it should be noted that if there is a breach where there are no backups of the encrypted personal data then there will have been an availability breach, which could pose risks to individuals and therefore may require notification. Similarly, where a breach occurs involving the loss of encrypted data, even if a backup of the personal data exists this may still be a reportable breach, depending on the length of time taken to restore the data from that backup and the effect that lack of availability has on individuals. As Article 32(1)(c) states, an important factor of security is the "the ability to restore the availability and access to personal data in a timely manner in the event of a physical or technical incident".

Example

A breach that would not require notification to the supervisory authority would be the loss of a securely encrypted mobile device, utilised by the controller and its staff. Provided the encryption key remains within the secure possession of the controller and this is not the sole copy of the personal data then the personal data would be inaccessible to an attacker. This means the breach is unlikely to result in a risk to the rights and freedoms of the data subjects in question. If it later becomes evident that the encryption key was compromised or that the encryption software or algorithm is vulnerable, then the risk to the rights and freedoms of natural persons will change and thus notification may now be required.

However, a failure to comply with Article 33 will exist where a controller does not notify the supervisory authority in a situation where the data has not actually been securely encrypted. Therefore, when selecting encryption software controllers should carefully weigh the quality and the proper implementation of the encryption offered, understand what level of protection it actually provides and whether this is appropriate to the risks presented. Controllers should also be familiar with the specifics of how their encryption product functions. For instance, a device may be encrypted once it is switched off, but not while it is in stand-by mode. Some products using encryption have "default keys" that need to be changed by each customer to be effective. The encryption may also be considered currently adequate by security experts, but may become outdated in a few years' time, meaning it is questionable whether the data would be sufficiently encrypted by that product and provide an appropriate level of protection.

NOTES

[20] Recital 85 is also important here.

[21] See Recital 87

[22] See WP29 Guidelines on DPIAs here: http://ec.europa.eu/newsroom/document.cfm?doc_id=44137

[23] It should be noted that log data facilitating auditability of, e.g., storage, modifications or erasure of data may also qualify as personal data relating to the person who initiated the respective processing operation.

[24] See Regulation No 1182/71 determining the rules applicable to periods, dates and time limits, available at: http://eur-lex.europa.eu/legal-content/EN/TXT/HTML/?uri=CELEX:31971R1182&from=EN

[25] See also Recital 79.

[26] See Article 9.

[27] See Article 4(23)

[28] See also Recital 122.

29   See WP29 Guidelines for identifying a controller or processor's lead supervisory authority, available at http://ec.europa. eu/newsroom/document.cfm?doc_id=44102

30   A list of contact details for all European national data protection authorities can be found at: http://ec.europa.eu/justice/ data-protection/bodies/authorities/index_en.htm

31   See also Recitals 23 and 24

32   See also Recital 25

33   See Recital 80 and Article 27

34   WP29, Opinion 03/2014 on breach notification, http://ec.europa.eu/justice/data-protection/article-29/documentation/ opinion-recommendation/files/2014/wp213_en.pdf

35   See also Article 4(1) and (2) of Regulation 611/2013.

III. ARTICLE 34 – COMMUNICATION TO THE DATA SUBJECT

A. INFORMING INDIVIDUALS

[2.197]
In certain cases, as well as notifying the supervisory authority, the controller is also required to communicate a breach to the affected individuals.

Article 34(1) states:

> "When the personal data breach is likely to result in a high risk to the rights and freedoms of natural persons, the controller shall communicate the personal data breach to the data subject without undue delay."

Controllers should recall that notification to the supervisory authority is mandatory unless there is unlikely to be a risk to the rights and freedoms of individuals as a result of a breach. In addition, where there is likely a high risk to the rights and freedoms of individuals as the result of a breach, individuals must also be informed. The threshold for communicating a breach to individuals is therefore higher than for notifying supervisory authorities and not all breaches will therefore be required to be communicated to individuals, thus protecting them from unnecessary notification fatigue.

The GDPR states that communication of a breach to individuals should be made "without undue delay," which means as soon as possible. The main objective of notification to individuals is to provide specific information about steps they should take to protect themselves[36]. As noted above, depending on the nature of the breach and the risk posed, timely communication will help individuals to take steps to protect themselves from any negative consequences of the breach.

Annex B of these Guidelines provides a non-exhaustive list of examples of when a breach may be likely to result in high risk to individuals and consequently instances when a controller will have to notify a breach to those affected.

B. INFORMATION TO BE PROVIDED

When notifying individuals, Article 34(2) specifies that:

> "The communication to the data subject referred to in paragraph 1 of this Article shall describe in clear and plain language the nature of the personal data breach and contain at least the information and measures referred to in points (b), (c) and (d) of Article 33(3)."

According to this provision, the controller should at least provide the following information:
- a description of the nature of the breach;
- the name and contact details of the data protection officer or other contact point;
- a description of the likely consequences of the breach; and
- a description of the measures taken or proposed to be taken by the controller to address the breach, including, where appropriate, measures to mitigate its possible adverse effects.

As an example of the measures taken to address the breach and to mitigate its possible adverse effects, the controller could state that, after having notified the breach to the relevant supervisory authority, the controller has received advice on managing the breach and lessening its impact. The controller should also, where appropriate, provide specific advice to individuals to protect themselves from possible adverse consequences of the breach, such as resetting passwords in the case where their access credentials have been compromised. Again, a controller can choose to provide information in addition to what is required here.

C. CONTACTING INDIVIDUALS

In principle, the relevant breach should be communicated to the affected data subjects directly, unless doing so would involve a disproportionate effort. In such a case, there shall instead be a public communication or similar measure whereby the data subjects are informed in an equally effective manner (Article 34(3)c).

Dedicated messages should be used when communicating a breach to data subjects and they should not be sent with other information, such as regular updates, newsletters, or standard messages. This helps to make the communication of the breach to be clear and transparent.

Examples of transparent communication methods include direct messaging (e.g. email, SMS, direct message), prominent website banners or notification, postal communications and prominent advertisements in print media. A notification solely confined within a press release or corporate blog would not be an effective means of communicating a breach to an individual. WP29 recommends that controllers should choose a means that maximizes the chance of properly communicating information to all affected individuals. Depending on the circumstances, this may mean the controller employs several methods of communication, as opposed to using a single contact channel.

Controllers may also need to ensure that the communication is accessible in appropriate alternative formats and relevant languages to ensure individuals are able to understand the information being provided to them. For example, when communicating a breach to an individual, the language used during the previous normal course of business with the recipient will generally be appropriate. However, if the breach affects data subjects who the controller has not previously interacted with, or particularly those who reside in a different Member State or other non-EU country from where the controller is established, communication in the local national language could be acceptable, taking into account the resource required. The key is to help data subjects understand the nature of the breach and steps they can take to protect themselves.

Controllers are best placed to determine the most appropriate contact channel to communicate a breach to individuals, particularly if they interact with their customers on a frequent basis. However, clearly a controller should be wary of using a contact channel compromised by the breach as this channel could also be used by attackers impersonating the controller.

At the same time, Recital 86 explains that:

> "Such communications to data subjects should be made as soon as reasonably feasible and in close cooperation with the supervisory authority, respecting guidance provided by it or by other relevant authorities such as law-enforcement authorities. For example, the need to mitigate an immediate risk of damage would call for prompt communication with data subjects whereas the need to implement appropriate measures against continuing or similar personal data breaches may justify more time for communication."

Controllers might therefore wish to contact and consult the supervisory authority not only to seek advice about informing data subjects about a breach in accordance with Article 34, but also on the appropriate messages to be sent to, and the most appropriate way to contact, individuals.

Linked to this is the advice given in Recital 88 that notification of a breach should "take into account the legitimate interests of law-enforcement authorities where early disclosure could unnecessarily hamper the investigation of the circumstances of a personal data breach". This may mean that in certain circumstances, where justified, and on the advice of law-enforcement authorities, the controller may delay communicating the breach to the affected individuals until such time as it would not prejudice such investigations. However, data subjects would still need to be promptly informed after this time.

Whenever it is not possible for the controller to communicate a breach to an individual because there is insufficient data stored to contact the individual, in that particular circumstance the controller should inform the individual as soon as it is reasonably feasible to do so (e.g. when an individual exercises their Article 15 right to access personal data and provides the controller with necessary additional information to contact them).

D. CONDITIONS WHERE COMMUNICATION IS NOT REQUIRED

Article 34(3) states three conditions that, if met, do not require notification to individuals in the event of a breach. These are:

* The controller has applied appropriate technical and organisational measures to protect personal data prior to the breach, in particular those measures that render personal data unintelligible to any person who is not authorised to access it. This could, for example, include protecting personal data with state-of-the-art encryption, or by tokenization.
* Immediately following a breach, the controller has taken steps to ensure that the high risk posed to individuals' rights and freedoms is no longer likely to materialise. For example, depending on the circumstances of the case, the controller may have immediately identified and taken action against the individual who has accessed personal data before they were able to do anything with it. Due regard still needs to be given to the possible consequences of any breach of confidentiality, again, depending on the nature of the data concerned.
* It would involve disproportionate effort[37] to contact individuals, perhaps where their contact details have been lost as a result of the breach or are not known in the first place. For example, the warehouse of a statistical office has flooded and the documents containing personal data were stored only in paper form. Instead, the controller must make a public communication or take a similar measure, whereby the individuals are informed in an equally effective manner. In the case of disproportionate effort, technical arrangements could also be envisaged to make information about the breach available on demand, which could prove useful to those individuals who may be affected by a breach, but the controller cannot otherwise contact.

In accordance with the accountability principle controllers should be able to demonstrate to the supervisory authority that they meet one or more of these conditions[38]. It should be borne in mind that while notification may initially not be required if there is no risk to the rights and freedoms of natural persons, this may change over time and the risk would have to be re-evaluated.

If a controller decides not to communicate a breach to the individual, Article 34(4) explains that the supervisory authority can require it to do so, if it considers the breach is likely to result in a high risk to individuals. Alternatively, it may consider that the conditions in Article 34(3) have been met in which case notification to individuals is not required. If the supervisory authority determines that the decision not to notify data subjects is not well founded, it may consider employing its available powers and sanctions.

NOTES

[36]   See also Recital 86.

[37]   See WP29 Guidelines on transparency, which will consider the issue of disproportionate effort, available at http://ec.europa.eu/newsroom/just/document.cfm?doc_id=48850

[38]   See Article 5(2)

IV. ASSESSING RISK AND HIGH RISK

A. RISK AS A TRIGGER FOR NOTIFICATION

[2.198]
Although the GDPR introduces the obligation to notify a breach, it is not a requirement to do so in all circumstances:
- Notification to the competent supervisory authority is required unless a breach is unlikely to result in a risk to the rights and freedoms of individuals.
- Communication of a breach to the individual is only triggered where it is likely to result in a high risk to their rights and freedoms.

This means that immediately upon becoming aware of a breach, it is vitally important that the controller should not only seek to contain the incident but it should also assess the risk that could result from it. There are two important reasons for this: firstly, knowing the likelihood and the potential severity of the impact on the individual will help the controller to take effective steps to contain and address the breach; secondly, it will help it to determine whether notification is required to the supervisory authority and, if necessary, to the individuals concerned.

As explained above, notification of a breach is required unless it is unlikely to result in a risk to the rights and freedoms of individuals, and the key trigger requiring communication of a breach to data subjects is where it is likely to result in a *high* risk to the rights and freedoms of individuals. This risk exists when the breach may lead to physical, material or non-material damage for the individuals whose data have been breached. Examples of such damage are discrimination, identity theft or fraud, financial loss and damage to reputation. When the breach involves personal data that reveals racial or ethnic origin, political opinion, religion or philosophical beliefs, or trade union membership, or includes genetic data, data concerning health or data concerning sex life, or criminal convictions and offences or related security measures, such damage should be considered likely to occur[39].

B. FACTORS TO CONSIDER WHEN ASSESSING RISK

Recitals 75 and 76 of the GDPR suggest that generally when assessing risk, consideration should be given to both the likelihood and severity of the risk to the rights and freedoms of data subjects. It further states that risk should be evaluated on the basis of an objective assessment.

It should be noted that assessing the risk to people's rights and freedoms as a result of a breach has a different focus to the risk considered in a DPIA[40]. The DPIA considers both the risks of the data processing being carried out as planned, and the risks in case of a breach. When considering a potential breach, it looks in general terms at the likelihood of this occurring, and the damage to the data subject that might ensue; in other words, it is an assessment of a hypothetical event. With an actual breach, the event has already occurred, and so the focus is wholly about the resulting risk of the impact of the breach on individuals.

Example

A DPIA suggests that the proposed use of a particular security software product to protect personal data is a suitable measure to ensure a level of security appropriate to the risk the processing would otherwise present to individuals. However, if a vulnerability becomes subsequently known, this would change the software's suitability to contain the risk to the personal data protected and so it would need to be re-assessed as part of an ongoing DPIA.

A vulnerability in the product is later exploited and a breach occurs. The controller should assess the specific circumstances of the breach, the data affected, and the potential level of impact on individuals, as well as how likely this risk will materialise.

Accordingly, when assessing the risk to individuals as a result of a breach, the controller should consider the specific circumstances of the breach, including the severity of the potential impact and the likelihood of this occurring. WP29 therefore recommends the assessment should take into account the following criteria[41]:

- The type of breach
  The type of breach that has occurred may affect the level of risk presented to individuals. For example, a confidentiality breach whereby medical information has been disclosed to unauthorised parties may have a different set of consequences for an individual to a breach where an individual's medical details have been lost, and are no longer available.
- The nature, sensitivity, and volume of personal data
  Of course, when assessing risk, a key factor is the type and sensitivity of personal data that has been compromised by the breach. Usually, the more sensitive the data, the higher the risk of harm will be to the people affected, but consideration should also be given to other personal data that may already be available about the data subject. For example, the disclosure of the name and address of an individual in ordinary circumstances is unlikely to cause substantial damage. However, if the name and address of an adoptive parent is disclosed to a birth parent, the consequences could be very severe for both the adoptive parent and child.
  Breaches involving health data, identity documents, or financial data such as credit card details, can all cause harm on their own, but if used together they could be used for identity theft. A combination of personal data is typically more sensitive than a single piece of personal data.
  Some types of personal data may seem at first relatively innocuous, however, what that data may reveal about the affected individual should be carefully considered. A list of customers accepting regular deliveries may not be particularly sensitive, but the same data about customers who have requested that their deliveries be stopped while on holiday would be useful information to criminals.
  Similarly, a small amount of highly sensitive personal data can have a high impact on an individual, and a large range of details can reveal a greater range of information about that individual. Also, a breach affecting large volumes of personal data about many data subjects can have an effect on a corresponding large number of individuals.
- Ease of identification of individuals
  An important factor to consider is how easy it will be for a party who has access to compromised personal data to identify specific individuals, or match the data with other information to identify individuals. Depending on the circumstances, identification could be possible directly from the personal data breached with no special research needed to discover the individual's identity, or it may be extremely difficult to match personal data to a particular individual, but it could still be possible under certain conditions. Identification may be directly or indirectly possible from the breached data, but it may also depend on the specific context of the breach, and public availability of related personal details. This may be more relevant for confidentiality and availability breaches.
  As stated above, personal data protected by an appropriate level of encryption will be unintelligible to unauthorised persons without the decryption key. Additionally, appropriately-implemented pseudonymisation (defined in Article 4(5) as "the processing of personal data in such a manner that the personal data can no longer be attributed to a specific data subject without the use of additional information, provided that such additional information is kept separately and is subject to technical and organisational measures to ensure that the personal data are not attributed to an identified or identifiable natural person") can also reduce the likelihood of individuals being identified in the event of a breach. However, pseudonymisation techniques alone cannot be regarded as making the data unintelligible.
- Severity of consequences for individuals.
  Depending on the nature of the personal data involved in a breach, for example, special categories of data, the potential damage to individuals that could result can be especially severe, in particular where the breach could result in identity theft or fraud, physical harm, psychological distress, humiliation or damage to reputation. If the breach concerns personal data about vulnerable individuals, they could be placed at greater risk of harm.
  Whether the controller is aware that personal data is in the hands of people whose intentions are unknown or possibly malicious can have a bearing on the level of potential risk. There may be a confidentiality breach, whereby personal data is disclosed to a third party, as defined in Article 4(10), or other recipient in error. This may occur, for example, where personal data is sent accidentally to the wrong department of an organisation, or to a commonly used supplier organisation. The controller may request the recipient to either return or securely destroy the data it has received. In both cases, given that the controller has an ongoing relationship with them, and it may be aware of their procedures, history and other relevant details, the recipient may be considered "trusted". In other words, the controller may have a level of assurance with the recipient so that it can reasonably expect that party not to read or access the data sent in error, and to comply with its instructions to return it. Even if the data has been accessed, the controller could

still possibly trust the recipient not to take any further action with it and to return the data to the controller promptly and to co-operate with its recovery. In such cases, this may be factored into the risk assessment the controller carries out following the breach – the fact that the recipient is trusted may eradicate the severity of the consequences of the breach but does not mean that a breach has not occurred. However, this in turn may remove the likelihood of risk to individuals, thus no longer requiring notification to the supervisory authority, or to the affected individuals. Again, this will depend on case-by-case basis. Nevertheless, the controller still has to keep information concerning the breach as part of the general duty to maintain records of breaches (see section V, below).

Consideration should also be given to the permanence of the consequences for individuals, where the impact may be viewed as greater if the effects are long-term.

- Special characteristics of the individual

  A breach may affect personal data concerning children or other vulnerable individuals, who may be placed at greater risk of danger as a result. There may be other factors about the individual that may affect the level of impact of the breach on them.

- Special characteristics of the data controller

  The nature and role of the controller and its activities may affect the level of risk to individuals as a result of a breach. For example, a medical organisation will process special categories of personal data, meaning that there is a greater threat to individuals if their personal data is breached, compared with a mailing list of a newspaper.

- The number of affected individuals

  A breach may affect only one or a few individuals or several thousand, if not many more. Generally, the higher the number of individuals affected, the greater the impact of a breach can have. However, a breach can have a severe impact on even one individual, depending on the nature of the personal data and the context in which it has been compromised. Again, the key is to consider the likelihood and severity of the impact on those affected.

- General points

  Therefore, when assessing the risk that is likely to result from a breach, the controller should consider a combination of the severity of the potential impact on the rights and freedoms of individuals and the likelihood of these occurring. Clearly, where the consequences of a breach are more severe, the risk is higher and similarly where the likelihood of these occurring is greater, the risk is also heightened. If in doubt, the controller should err on the side of caution and notify. Annex B provides some useful examples of different types of breaches involving risk or high risk to individuals.

  The European Union Agency for Network and Information Security (ENISA) has produced recommendations for a methodology of assessing the severity of a breach, which controllers and processors may find useful when designing their breach management response plan[42].

NOTES

[39] See Recital 75 and Recital 85.

[40] See WP Guidelines on DPIAs here: http://ec.europa.eu/newsroom/document.cfm?doc_id=44137

[41] Article 3.2 of Regulation 611/2013 provides guidance the factors that should be taken into consideration in relation to the notification of breaches in the electronic communication services sector, which may be useful in the context of notification under the GDPR. See http://eur-lex.europa.eu/LexUriServ/LexUriServ.do?uri=OJ:L:2013: 173:0002:0008:en:PDF

[42] ENISA, Recommendations for a methodology of the assessment of severity of personal data breaches, https://www.enisa.europa.eu/publications/dbn-severity

V. ACCOUNTABILITY AND RECORD KEEPING

A. DOCUMENTING BREACHES

[2.199]
Regardless of whether or not a breach needs to be notified to the supervisory authority, the controller must keep documentation of all breaches, as Article 33(5) explains:

> "The controller shall document any personal data breaches, comprising the facts relating to the personal data breach, its effects and the remedial action taken. That documentation shall enable the supervisory authority to verify compliance with this Article."

This is linked to the accountability principle of the GDPR, contained in Article 5(2). The purpose of recording non-notifiable breaches, as well notifiable breaches, also relates to the controller's obligations under Article 24, and the supervisory authority can request to see these records. Controllers are therefore encouraged to establish an internal register of breaches, regardless of whether they are required to notify or not[43].

Whilst it is up to the controller to determine what method and structure to use when documenting a breach, in terms of recordable information there are key elements that should be included in all cases. As is required by Article 33(5), the controller needs to record details concerning the breach, which should include its causes, what took place and the personal data affected. It should also include the effects and consequences of the breach, along with the remedial action taken by the controller.

The GDPR does not specify a retention period for such documentation. Where such records contain personal data, it will be incumbent on the controller to determine the appropriate period of retention in accordance with the principles in relation to the processing of personal data[44] and to meet a lawful basis for processing[45]. It will need to retain documentation in accordance with Article 33(5) insofar as it may be called to provide evidence of compliance with that Article, or with the accountability principle more generally, to the supervisory authority. Clearly, if the records themselves contain no personal data then the storage limitation principle[46] of the GDPR does not apply.

In addition to these details, WP29 recommends that the controller also document its reasoning for the decisions taken in response to a breach. In particular, if a breach is not notified, a justification for that decision should be documented. This should include reasons why the controller considers the breach is unlikely to result in a risk to the rights and freedoms of individuals[47]. Alternatively, if the controller considers that any of the conditions in Article 34(3) are met, then it should be able to provide appropriate evidence that this is the case.

Where the controller does notify a breach to the supervisory authority, but the notification is delayed, the controller must be able to provide reasons for that delay; documentation relating to this could help to demonstrate that the delay in reporting is justified and not excessive.

Where the controller communicates a breach to the affected individuals, it should be transparent about the breach and communicate in an effective and timely manner. Accordingly, it would help the controller to demonstrate accountability and compliance by retaining evidence of such communication.

To aid compliance with Articles 33 and 34, it would be advantageous to both controllers and processors to have a documented notification procedure in place, setting out the process to follow once a breach has been detected, including how to contain, manage and recover the incident, as well as assessing risk, and notifying the breach. In this regard, to show compliance with GDPR it might also be useful to demonstrate that employees have been informed about the existence of such procedures and mechanisms and that they know how to react to breaches.

It should be noted that failure to properly document a breach can lead to the supervisory authority exercising its powers under Article 58 and, or imposing an administrative fine in accordance with Article 83.

B. ROLE OF THE DATA PROTECTION OFFICER

A controller or processor may have a Data Protection Officer (DPO)[48], either as required by Article 37, or voluntarily as a matter of good practice. Article 39 of the GDPR sets a number of mandatory tasks for the DPO, but does not prevent further tasks being allocated by the controller, if appropriate.

Of particular relevance to breach notification, the mandatory tasks of the DPO includes, amongst other duties, providing data protection advice and information to the controller or processor, monitoring compliance with the GDPR, and providing advice in relation to DPIAs. The DPO must also cooperate with the supervisory authority and act as a contact point for the supervisory authority and for data subjects. It should also be noted that, when notifying the breach to the supervisory authority, Article 33(3)(b) requires the controller to provide the name and contact details of its DPO, or other contact point.

In terms of documenting breaches, the controller or processor may wish to obtain the opinion of its DPO as to the structure, the setting up and the administration of this documentation. The DPO could also be additionally tasked with maintaining such records.

These factors mean that the DPO should play an key role in assisting the prevention of or preparation for a breach by providing advice and monitoring compliance, as well as during a breach (i.e. when notifying the supervisory authority), and during any subsequent investigation by the supervisory authority. In this light, WP29 recommends that the DPO is promptly informed about the existence of a breach and is involved throughout the breach management and notification process.

NOTES
43   The controller may choose to document breaches as part of if its record of processing activities which is maintained pursuant to article 30. A separate register is not required, provided the information relevant to the breach is clearly identifiable as such and can be extracted upon request.
44   See Article 5
45   See Article 6 and also Article 9.
46   See Article 5(1)(e).
47   See Recital 85
48   See WP Guidelines on DPOs here: http://ec.europa.eu/newsroom/just/item-detail.cfm?item_id=50083

VI. NOTIFICATION OBLIGATIONS UNDER OTHER LEGAL INSTRUMENTS
[2.200]
In addition to, and separate from, the notification and communication of breaches under the GDPR, controllers should also be aware of any requirement to notify security incidents under other associated legislation that may apply to them and whether this may also require them to notify the supervisory authority of a personal data breach at the same time. Such requirements can vary between Member States, but examples of notification requirements in other legal instruments, and how these inter-relate with the GDPR, include the following:
- Regulation (EU) 910/2014 on electronic identification and trust services for electronic transactions in the internal market (eIDAS Regulation)[49].

Article 19(2) of the eIDAS Regulation requires trust service providers to notify their supervisory body of a breach of security or loss of integrity that has a significant impact on the trust service provided or on the personal data maintained therein. Where applicable—i.e., where such a breach or loss is also a personal data breach under the GDPR—the trust service provider should also notify the supervisory authority.

- Directive (EU) 2016/1148 concerning measures for a high common level of security of network and information systems across the Union (NIS Directive)[50].

  Articles 14 and 16 of the NIS Directive require operators of essential services and digital service providers to notify security incidents to their competent authority. As recognised by Recital 63 of NIS[51], security incidents can often include a compromise of personal data. Whilst NIS requires competent authorities and supervisory authorities to co-operate and exchange information that context, it remains the case that where such incidents are, or become, personal data breaches under the GDPR, those operators and/or providers would be required to notify the supervisory authority separately from the incident notification requirements of NIS.

Example

A cloud service provider notifying a breach under the NIS Directive may also need to notify a controller, if this includes a personal data breach. Similarly, a trust service provider notifying under eIDAS may also be required to notify the relevant data protection authority in the event of a breach.

- Directive 2009/136/EC (the Citizens' Rights Directive) and Regulation 611/2013 (the Breach Notification Regulation).

  Providers of publicly available electronic communication services within the context of Directive 2002/58/EC[52] must notify breaches to the competent national authorities.

  Controllers should also be aware of any additional legal, medical, or professional notification duties under other applicable regimes.

NOTES

[49]   See http://eur-lex.europa.eu/legal-content/EN/TXT/?uri=uriserv%3AOJ.L_.2014.257.01.0073.01.ENG

[50]   See http://eur-lex.europa.eu/legal-content/EN/TXT/?uri=uriserv:OJ.L_.2016.194.01.0001.01.ENG

[51]   Recital 63: *"Personal data are in many cases compromised as a result of incidents. In this context, competent authorities and data protection authorities should cooperate and exchange information on all relevant matters to tackle any personal data breaches resulting from incidents."*

[52]   On 10 January 2017, the European Commission proposed a Regulation on Privacy and Electronic Communications which will replace Directive 2009/136/EC and remove notification requirements. However, until this proposal is approved by the European Parliament the existing notification requirement remains in force, see https://ec.europa.eu/digital-single-market/en/news/proposal-regulation-privacy-and-electronic-communications

Part 2   Data Protection: EU Law etc

VII. ANNEX

A.   Flowchart showing notification requirements

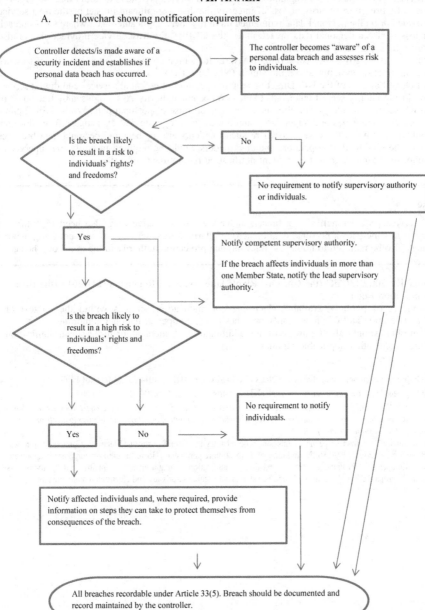

B. EXAMPLES OF PERSONAL DATA BREACHES AND WHO TO NOTIFY

[2.201]

The following non-exhaustive examples will assist controllers in determining whether they need to notify in different personal data breach scenarios. These examples may also help to distinguish between risk and high risk to the rights and freedoms of individuals.

Example	Notify the supervisory authority?	Notify the data subject?	Notes/ recommendations
i. A controller stored a backup of an archive of personal data encrypted on a USB key. The key is stolen during a break-in.	No.	No.	As long as the data are encrypted with a state of the art algorithm, backups of the data exist the unique key is not compromised, and the data can be restored in good time, this may not be a reportable breach. However if it is later compromised, notification is required.
ii. A controller maintains an online service. As a result of a cyber attack on that service, personal data of individuals are exfiltrated. The controller has customers in a single Member State.	Yes, report to the supervisory authority if there are likely consequences to individuals.	Yes, report to individuals depending on the nature of the personal data affected and if the severity of the likely consequences to individuals is high.	
iii. A brief power outage lasting several minutes at a controller's call centre meaning customers are unable to call the controller and access their records.	No.	No	This is not a notifiable breach, but still a recordable incident under Article 33(5). Appropriate records should be maintained by the controller.
iv. A controller suffers a ransomware attack which results in all data being encrypted. No back-ups are available and the data cannot be restored. On investigation, it becomes clear that the ransomware's only functionality was to encrypt the data, and that there was no other malware present in the system.	Yes, report to the supervisory authority, if there are likely consequences to individuals as this is a loss of availability.	Yes, report to individuals, depending on the nature of the personal data affected and the possible effect of the lack of availability of the data, as well as other likely consequences.	If there was a backup available and data could be restored in good time, this would not need to be reported to the supervisory authority or to individuals as there would have been no permanent loss of availability or confidentiality. However, if the supervisory authority became aware of the incident by other means, it may consider an investigation to assess compliance with the broader security requirements of Article 32.
v. An individual phones a bank's call centre to report a data breach. The individual has received a monthly statement for someone else. The controller undertakes a short investigation (i.e. completed within 24 hours) and establishes with a reasonable confidence that a personal data breach has occurred and whether it has a systemic flaw that may mean other individuals are or might be affected.	Yes.	Only the individuals affected are notified if there is high risk and it is clear that others were not affected.	If, after further investigation, it is identified that more individuals are affected, an update to the supervisory authority must be made and the controller takes the additional step of notifying other individuals if there is high risk to them.

Example	Notify the supervisory authority?	Notify the data subject?	Notes/ recommendations
vi. A controller operates an online marketplace and has customers in multiple Member States. The marketplace suffers a cyber-attack and usernames, passwords and purchase history are published online by the attacker.	Yes, report to lead supervisory authority if involves cross-border processing.	Yes, as could lead to high risk.	The controller should take action, e.g. by forcing password resets of the affected accounts, as well as other steps to mitigate the risk. The controller should also consider any other notification obligations, e.g. under the NIS Directive as a digital service provider.
vii. A website hosting company acting as a data processor identifies an error in the code which controls user authorisation. The effect of the flaw means that any user can access the account details of any other user.	As the processor, the website hosting company must notify its affected clients (the controllers) without undue delay. Assuming that the website hosting company has conducted its own investigation the affected controllers should be reasonably confident as to whether each has suffered a breach and therefore is likely to be considered as having "become aware" once they have been notified by the hosting company (the processor). The controller then must notify the supervisory authority.	If there is likely no high risk to the individuals they do not need to be notified.	The website hosting company (processor) must consider any other notification obligations (e.g. under the NIS Directive as a digital service provider). If there is no evidence of this vulnerability being exploited with any of its controllers a notifiable breach may not have occurred but it is likely to be recordable or be a matter of non-compliance under Article 32.
viii. Medical records in a hospital are unavailable for the period of 30 hours due to a cyber-attack.	Yes, the hospital is obliged to notify as high-risk to patient's well-being and privacy may occur.	Yes, report to the affected individuals.	
ix. Personal data of a large number of students are mistakenly sent to the wrong mailing list with 1000+ recipients.	Yes, report to supervisory authority.	Yes, report to individuals depending on the scope and type of personal data involved and the severity of possible consequences.	
x. A direct marketing e-mail is sent to recipients in the "to:" or "cc:" fields, thereby enabling each recipient to see the email address of other recipients.	Yes, notifying the supervisory authority may be obligatory if a large number of individuals are affected, if sensitive data are revealed (e.g. a mailing list of a psychotherapist) or if other factors present high risks (e.g. the mail contains the initial passwords).	Yes, report to individuals depending on the scope and type of personal data involved and the severity of possible consequences.	Notification may not be necessary if no sensitive data is revealed and if only a minor number of email addresses are revealed.

ARTICLE 29 DATA PROTECTION WORKING PARTY: GUIDELINES ON AUTOMATED INDIVIDUAL DECISION-MAKING AND PROFILING FOR THE PURPOSES OF REGULATION 2016/679
17/EN
WP 251 rev.01
Adopted on 3 October 2017

As last Revised and Adopted on 6 February 2018

[2.202]

NOTES

This document was originally issued by the Article 29 Working Party but subsequently endorsed by the EDPB during its first plenary meeting.

© European Data Protection Board.

TABLE OF CONTENTS

I. INTRODUCTION

[2.203]

The General Data Protection Regulation (the GDPR), specifically addresses profiling and automated individual decision-making, including profiling.[1]

Profiling and automated decision-making are used in an increasing number of sectors, both private and public. Banking and finance, healthcare, taxation, insurance, marketing and advertising are just a few examples of the fields where profiling is being carried out more regularly to aid decision-making.

Advances in technology and the capabilities of big data analytics, artificial intelligence and machine learning have made it easier to create profiles and make automated decisions with the potential to significantly impact individuals' rights and freedoms.

The widespread availability of personal data on the internet and from Internet of Things (IoT) devices, and the ability to find correlations and create links, can allow aspects of an individual's personality or behaviour, interests and habits to be determined, analysed and predicted.

Profiling and automated decision-making can be useful for individuals and organisations, delivering benefits such as:
- increased efficiencies; and
- resource savings.

They have many commercial applications, for example, they can be used to better segment markets and tailor services and products to align with individual needs. Medicine, education, healthcare and transportation can also all benefit from these processes.

However, profiling and automated decision-making can pose significant risks for individuals' rights and freedoms which require appropriate safeguards.

These processes can be opaque. Individuals might not know that they are being profiled or understand what is involved.

Profiling can perpetuate existing stereotypes and social segregation. It can also lock a person into a specific category and restrict them to their suggested preferences. This can undermine their freedom to choose, for example, certain products or services such as books, music or newsfeeds. In some cases, profiling can lead to inaccurate predictions. In other cases it can lead to denial of services and goods and unjustified discrimination.

The GDPR introduces new provisions to address the risks arising from profiling and automated decision-making, notably, but not limited to, privacy. The purpose of these guidelines is to clarify those provisions.

This document covers:
- Definitions of profiling and automated decision-making and the GDPR approach to these in general – **CHAPTER II**
- General provisions on profiling and automated decision-making – **CHAPTER III**
- Specific provisions on solely automated decision-making defined in Article 22 - **CHAPTER IV**

- Children and profiling – **CHAPTER V**
- Data protection impact assessments and data protection officers– **CHAPTER VI**

The Annexes provide best practice recommendations, building on the experience gained in EU Member States.

The Article 29 Data Protection Working Party (WP29) will monitor the implementation of these guidelines and may complement them with further details as appropriate.

NOTES

1   Regulation (EU) 2016/679 of the European Parliament and of the Council of 27 April 2016 on the protection of natural persons with regard to the processing of personal data and on the free movement of such data, and repealing Directive 95/46/EC. Profiling and automated individual decision-making are also covered by Directive (EU) 2016/680 of the European Parliament and of the Council of 27 April 2016 on the protection of natural persons with regard to the processing of personal data by competent authorities for the purposes of the prevention, investigation, detection or prosecution of criminal offences or the execution of criminal penalties, and on the free movement of such data. While these guidelines focus on profiling and automated individual decision-making under the GDPR, the guidance is also relevant regarding the two topics under Directive 2016/680, with respect to their similar provisions. The analysis of specific features of profiling and automated individual decision-making under Directive 2016/680 is not included in these guidelines, since guidance in this respect is provided by the Opinion WP258 "Opinion on some key issues of the Law Enforcement Directive (EU 2016/680)", adopted by WP29 on 29 November 2017 This Opinion covers automated individual decision-making and profiling in the context of law enforcement data processing at pages 11-14 and is available at: http://ec.europa.eu/newsroom/article29/item-detail.cfm?item_id=610178

II. DEFINITIONS

[2.204]
The GDPR introduces provisions to ensure that profiling and automated individual decision-making (whether or not this includes profiling) are not used in ways that have an unjustified impact on individuals' rights; for example:
- specific transparency and fairness requirements;
- greater accountability obligations;
- specified legal bases for the processing;
- rights for individuals to oppose profiling and specifically profiling for marketing; and
- if certain conditions are met, the need to carry out a data protection impact assessment.

The GDPR does not just focus on the decisions made as a result of automated processing or profiling. It applies to the collection of data for the creation of profiles, as well as the application of those profiles to individuals.

A. PROFILING

The GDPR defines profiling in Article 4(4) as:

> any form of automated processing of personal data consisting of the use of personal data to evaluate certain personal aspects relating to a natural person, in particular to analyse or predict aspects concerning that natural person's performance at work, economic situation, health, personal preferences, interests, reliability, behaviour, location or movements;

Profiling is composed of three elements:
- it has to be an *automated* form of processing;
- it has to be carried out on *personal data*; and
- the objective of the profiling must be *to evaluate personal aspects* about a natural person.

Article 4(4) refers to 'any form of automated processing' rather than 'solely' automated processing (referred to in Article 22). Profiling has to involve some form of automated processing – although human involvement does not necessarily take the activity out of the definition.

Profiling is a procedure which may involve a series of statistical deductions. It is often used to make predictions about people, using data from various sources to infer something about an individual, based on the qualities of others who appear statistically similar.

The GDPR says that profiling is automated processing of personal data for evaluating personal aspects, in particular to analyse or make predictions about individuals. The use of the word 'evaluating' suggests that profiling involves some form of assessment or judgement about a person.

A simple classification of individuals based on known characteristics such as their age, sex, and height does not necessarily lead to profiling. This will depend on the purpose of the classification.

For instance, a business may wish to classify its customers according to their age or gender for statistical purposes and to acquire an aggregated overview of its clients without making any predictions or drawing any conclusion about an individual. In this case, the purpose is not assessing individual characteristics and is therefore not profiling.

The GDPR is inspired by but is not identical to the definition of profiling in the Council of Europe Recommendation CM/Rec (2010)13[2] (the Recommendation), as the Recommendation excludes processing that does not include inference. Nevertheless the Recommendation usefully explains that profiling may involve three distinct stages:

- data collection;
- automated analysis to identify correlations;
- applying the correlation to an individual to identify characteristics of present or future behaviour.

Controllers carrying out profiling will need to ensure they meet the GDPR requirements in respect of all of the above stages.

Broadly speaking, profiling means gathering information about an individual (or group of individuals) and evaluating their characteristics or behaviour patterns in order to place them into a certain category or group, in particular to analyse and/or make predictions about, for example, their:

- ability to perform a task;
- interests; or
- likely behaviour.

Example

A data broker collects data from different public and private sources, either on behalf of its clients or for its own purposes. The data broker compiles the data to develop profiles on the individuals and places them into segments. It sells this information to companies who wish to improve the targeting of their goods and services. The data broker carries out profiling by placing a person into a certain category according to their interests.

Whether or not there is automated decision-making as defined in Article 22(1) will depend upon the circumstances.

D. AUTOMATED DECISION-MAKING

Automated decision-making has a different scope and may partially overlap with or result from profiling. Solely automated decision-making is the ability to make decisions by technological means without human involvement. Automated decisions can be based on any type of data, for example:

- data provided directly by the individuals concerned (such as responses to a questionnaire);
- data observed about the individuals (such as location data collected via an application);
- derived or inferred data such as a profile of the individual that has already been created (e.g. a credit score).

Automated decisions can be made with or without profiling; profiling can take place without making automated decisions. However, profiling and automated decision-making are not necessarily separate activities. Something that starts off as a simple automated decision-making process could become one based on profiling, depending upon how the data is used.

Example

Imposing speeding fines purely on the basis of evidence from speed cameras is an automated decision-making process that does not necessarily involve profiling.

It would, however, become a decision based on profiling if the driving habits of the individual were monitored over time, and, for example, the amount of fine imposed is the outcome of an assessment involving other factors, such as whether the speeding is a repeat offence or whether the driver has had other recent traffic violations.

Decisions that are not solely automated might also include profiling. For example, before granting a mortgage, a bank may consider the credit score of the borrower, with additional meaningful intervention carried out by humans before any decision is applied to an individual.

C. HOW THE GDPR ADDRESSES THE CONCEPTS

There are potentially three ways in which profiling may be used:
(i)   general profiling;
(ii)   decision-making based on profiling; and
(iii)   *solely* automated decision-making, including profiling, which produces legal effects or similarly significantly affects the data subject (Article 22[1]).

The difference between (ii) and (iii) is best demonstrated by the following two examples where an individual applies for a loan online:

- a human decides whether to agree the loan based on a profile produced by purely automated means(ii);
- an algorithm decides whether the loan is agreed and the decision is automatically delivered to the individual, without any prior and meaningful assessment by a human (iii).

Controllers can carry out profiling and automated decision-making as long as they can meet all the principles and have a lawful basis for the processing. Additional safeguards and restrictions apply in the case of solely automated decision-making, including profiling, defined in Article 22(1).

Chapter III of these guidelines explains the GDPR provisions for *all* profiling and automated individual decision-making. This includes decision-making processes that are *not* solely automated.

Chapter IV of these guidelines explains the specific provisions that *only* apply to solely automated individual decision-making, including profiling.³ A general prohibition on this type of processing exists to reflect the potential risks to individuals' rights and freedoms.

NOTES

² Council of Europe. The protection of individuals with regard to automatic processing of personal data in the context of profiling. Recommendation CM/Rec(2010)13 and explanatory memorandum. Council of Europe 23 November 2010. https://www.coe.int/t/dghl/standardsetting/cdcj/CDCJ%20Recommendations/CMRec(2010)13E_Profiling.pdf. Accessed 24 April 2017

³ As defined in Article 22(1) of the GDPR.

III. GENERAL PROVISIONS ON PROFILING AND AUTOMATED DECISION-MAKING

[2.205]

This overview of the provisions applies to all profiling and automated decision-making. Additional specific provisions set out in Chapter IV apply if the processing meets the definition in Article 22(1).

A. DATA PROTECTION PRINCIPLES

The principles are relevant for all profiling and automated decision-making involving personal data.⁴ To aid compliance, controllers should consider the following key areas:

1. Article 5(1)(a) - Lawful, fair and transparent

Transparency of processing⁵ is a fundamental requirement of the GDPR.

The process of profiling is often invisible to the data subject. It works by creating derived or inferred data about individuals – 'new' personal data that has not been provided directly by the data subjects themselves. Individuals have differing levels of comprehension and may find it challenging to understand the complex techniques involved in profiling and automated decision-making processes.

Under Article 12.1 the controller must provide data subjects with concise, transparent, intelligible and easily accessible information about the processing of their personal data.⁶

For data collected directly from the data subject this should be provided at the time of collection (Article 13); for indirectly obtained data the information should be provided within the timescales set out in Article 14(3).

Example

Some insurers offer insurance rates and services based on an individual's driving behaviour. Elements taken into account in these cases could include the distance travelled, the time spent driving and the journey undertaken as well as predictions based on other data collected by the sensors in a (smart) car. The data collected is used for profiling to identify bad driving behaviour (such as fast acceleration, sudden braking, and speeding). This information can be cross-referenced with other sources (for example the weather, traffic, type of road) to better understand the driver's behaviour.

The controller must ensure that they have a lawful basis for this type of processing. The controller must also provide the data subject with information about the collected data, and, if appropriate, the existence of automated decision-making referred to in Article 22(1) and (4), the logic involved, and the significance and envisaged consequences of such processing.

The specific requirements surrounding information and access to personal data are discussed in Chapters III (section D) and IV (section E).

Processing also has to be fair, as well as transparent.

Profiling may be unfair and create discrimination, for example by denying people access to employment opportunities, credit or insurance, or targeting them with excessively risky or costly financial products. The following example, which would not meet the requirements of Article 5(1)(a), illustrates how unfair profiling can lead to some consumers being offered less attractive deals than others.

Example

A data broker sells consumer profiles to financial companies without consumer permission or knowledge of the underlying data. The profiles define consumers into categories (carrying titles such as "Rural and Barely Making It," "Ethnic Second-City Strugglers," "Tough Start: Young Single Parents,") or "score" them, focusing on consumers' financial vulnerability. The financial companies offer these consumers payday loans and other "non-traditional" financial services (high-cost loans and other financially risky products).[7]

2. Article 5(1)(b) Further processing and purpose limitation

Profiling can involve the use of personal data that was originally collected for something else.

Example

Some mobile applications provide location services allowing the user to find nearby restaurants offering discounts. However, the data collected is also used to build a profile on the data subject for marketing purposes - to identify their food preferences, or lifestyle in general. The data subject expects their data will be used to find restaurants, but not to receive adverts for pizza delivery just because the app has identified that they arrive home late. This further use of the location data may not be compatible with the purposes for which it was collected in the first place, and may thus require the consent of the individual concerned.[8]

Whether this additional processing is compatible with the original purposes for which the data were collected will depend upon a range of factors[9], including what information the controller initially provided to the data subject. These factors are reflected in the GDPR[10] and summarised below:

- the relationship between the purposes for which the data have been collected and the purposes of further processing;
- the context in which the data were collected and the reasonable expectations of the data subjects as to their further use;
- the nature of the data;
- the impact of the further processing on the data subjects; and
- the safeguards applied by the controller to ensure fair processing and to prevent any undue impact on the data subjects.

3. Article 5(1)(c) Data minimisation

The business opportunities created by profiling, cheaper storage costs and the ability to process large amounts of information can encourage organisations to collect more personal data than they actually need, in case it proves useful in the future. Controllers must make sure they are complying with the data minimisation principle, as well as the requirements of the purpose limitation and storage limitation principles.

Controllers should be able to clearly explain and justify the need to collect and hold personal data, or consider using aggregated, anonymised or (when this provides sufficient protection) pseudonymised data for profiling.

4. Article 5(1)(d) Accuracy

Controllers should consider accuracy at all stages of the profiling process, specifically when:

- collecting data;
- analysing data;
- building a profile for an individual; or
- applying a profile to make a decision affecting the individual.

If the data used in an automated decision-making or profiling process is inaccurate, any resultant decision or profile will be flawed. Decisions may be made on the basis of outdated data or the incorrect interpretation of external data. Inaccuracies may lead to inappropriate predictions or statements about, for example, someone's health, credit or insurance risk.

Even if raw data is recorded accurately, the dataset may not be fully representative or the analytics may contain hidden bias.

Controllers need to introduce robust measures to verify and ensure on an ongoing basis that data re-used or obtained indirectly is accurate and up to date. This reinforces the importance of providing clear information about the personal data being processed, so that the data subject can correct any inaccuracies and improve the quality of the data.

5. Article 5(1)(e) Storage limitation

Machine-learning algorithms are designed to process large volumes of information and build correlations that allow organisations to build up very comprehensive, intimate profiles of individuals. Whilst there can be advantages to retaining data in the case of profiling, since there will be more data for the algorithm to learn from, controllers must comply with the data minimisation principle when they collect personal data and ensure that they retain those personal data for no longer than is necessary for and proportionate to the purposes for which the personal data are processed

The controller's retention policy should take into account the individuals' rights and freedoms in line with the requirements of Article 5(1)(e).

The controller should also make sure that the data remains updated throughout the retention period to reduce the risk of inaccuracies.[11]

B. LAWFUL BASES FOR PROCESSING

Automated decision-making defined in Article 22(1) is only permitted if one of the exceptions described in Chapter IV (sections C and D) applies. The following lawful bases for processing are relevant for all other automated individual decision-making and profiling.

1. Article 6(1)(a) consent

Consent as a basis for processing generally is addressed in the WP29 Guidelines on consent.[12] Explicit consent is one of the exceptions from the prohibition on automated decision-making and profiling defined in Article 22(1).

Profiling can be opaque. Often it relies upon data that is derived or inferred from other data, rather than data directly provided by the data subject.

Controllers seeking to rely upon consent as a basis for profiling will need to show that data subjects understand exactly what they are consenting to, and remember that consent is not always an appropriate basis for the processing.[13] In all cases, data subjects should have enough relevant information about the envisaged use and consequences of the processing to ensure that any consent they provide represents an informed choice.

2. Article 6(1)(b) – necessary for the performance of a contract

Controllers may wish to use profiling and automated decision-making processes because they:
- potentially allow for greater consistency or fairness in the decision making process (e.g. by reducing the potential for human error, discrimination and abuse of power);
- reduce the risk of customers failing to meet payments for goods or services (for example by using credit referencing); or
- enable them to deliver decisions within a shorter time frame and improve efficiency .

Regardless of the above, these considerations alone are not sufficient to show that this type of processing is *necessary* under Article 6(1)(b) for the performance of a contract. As described in the WP29 Opinion on legitimate interest[14], necessity should be interpreted narrowly.

The following is an example of profiling that would *not* meet the Article 6(1)(b) basis for processing.

Example

A user buys some items from an on-line retailer. In order to fulfil the contract, the retailer must process the user's credit card information for payment purposes and the user's address to deliver the goods. Completion of the contract is not dependent upon building a profile of the user's tastes and lifestyle choices based on his or her visits to the website. Even if profiling is specifically mentioned in the small print of the contract, this fact alone does not make it 'necessary' for the performance of the contract.

---

3. Article 6(1)(c) – necessary for compliance with a legal obligation

There may be instances where there will be a legal obligation[15] to carry out profiling – for example in connection with fraud prevention or money laundering. The WP29 Opinion on legitimate interests[16] provides useful information about this basis for processing, including the safeguards to be applied.

4. Article 6(1)(d) – necessary to protect vital interests

This covers situations where the processing is necessary to protect an interest which is essential for the life of the data subject or that of another natural person.

Certain types of processing may serve important public interest grounds as well as the vital interests of the data subject. Examples of this may include profiling necessary to develop models that predict the spread of life-threatening diseases or in situations of humanitarian emergencies. In these cases, however, and in principle, the controller can only rely on vital interest grounds if no other legal basis for the processing is available.[17] If the processing involves special category personal data the controller would also need to ensure that they meet the requirements of Article 9(2)(c).

5. Article 6(1)(e) – necessary for the performance of a task carried out in the public interest or exercise of official authority

Article 6(1)(e) might be an appropriate basis for public sector profiling in certain circumstances. The task or function must have a clear basis in law.

6. Article 6(1)(f) – necessary for the legitimate interests[18] pursued by the controller or by a third party

Profiling is allowed if it is necessary for the purposes of the legitimate interests[19] pursued by the controller or by a third party. However, Article 6(1)(f) does not automatically apply just because the controller or third party has a legitimate interest. The controller must carry out a balancing exercise to assess whether their interests are overridden by the data subject's interests or fundamental rights and freedoms.

The following are particularly relevant:
- the level of detail of the profile (a data subject profiled within a broadly described cohort such as 'people with an interest in English literature', or segmented and targeted on a granular level);
- the comprehensiveness of the profile (whether the profile only describes a small aspect of the data subject, or paints a more comprehensive picture);
- the impact of the profiling (the effects on the data subject); and
- the safeguards aimed at ensuring fairness, non-discrimination and accuracy in the profiling process.

Although the WP29 opinion on legitimate interests[20] is based on Article 7 of the data protection Directive 95/46/EC (the Directive), it contains examples that are still useful and relevant for controllers carrying out profiling. It also suggests it would be difficult for controllers to justify using legitimate interests as a lawful basis for intrusive profiling and tracking practices for marketing or advertising purposes, for example those that involve tracking individuals across multiple websites, locations, devices, services or data-brokering.

The controller should also consider the future use or combination of profiles when assessing the validity of processing under Article 6(1)(f).

C. ARTICLE 9 – SPECIAL CATEGORIES OF DATA

Controllers can only process special category personal data if they can meet one of the conditions set out in Article 9(2), as well as a condition from Article 6. This includes special category data derived or inferred from profiling activity.

Profiling can create special category data by inference from data which is not special category data in its own right but becomes so when combined with other data. For example, it may be possible to infer someone's state of health from the records of their food shopping combined with data on the quality and energy content of foods.

Correlations may be discovered that indicate something about individuals' health, political convictions, religious beliefs or sexual orientation, as demonstrated by the following example:

Example

One study[21] combined Facebook 'likes' with limited survey information and found that researchers accurately predicted a male user's sexual orientation 88% of the time; a user's ethnic origin 95% of the time; and whether a user was Christian or Muslim 82% of the time.

If sensitive preferences and characteristics are inferred from profiling, the controller should make sure that:
- the processing is not incompatible with the original purpose;
- they have identified a lawful basis for the processing of the special category data; and
- they inform the data subject about the processing.

Automated decision-making as defined in Article 22(1) that is based on special categories of data is covered in Chapter IV (section D).

D. RIGHTS OF THE DATA SUBJECT[22]

The GDPR introduces stronger rights for data subjects and creates new obligations for controllers.

In the context of profiling these rights are actionable against the controller creating the profile and the controller making an automated decision about a data subject (with or without human intervention), if these entities are not the same.

Example

A data broker undertakes profiling of personal data. In line with their Article 13 and 14 obligations the data broker should inform the individual about the processing, including whether they intend to share the profile with any other organisations. The data broker should also present separately details of the right to object under Article 21(1).

The data broker shares the profile with another company. This company uses the profile to send the individual direct marketing.

The company should inform the individual (Article 14(1)(c)) about the purposes for using this profile, and from what source they obtained the information (14(2)(f)). The company must also advise the data subject about their right to object to processing, including profiling, for direct marketing purposes (Article 21(2)).

The data broker and the company should allow the data subject the right to access the information used (Article 15) to correct any erroneous information (Article 16), and in certain circumstances erase the profile or personal data used to create it (Article 17). The data subject should also be given information about their profile, for example in which 'segments' or 'categories' they are placed.[23]

If the company uses the profile as part of a solely automated decision-making process with legal or similarly significant effects on the data subject, the company is the controller subject to the Article 22

---

provisions. (This does not exclude the data broker from Article 22 if the processing meets the relevant threshold.)

1. Articles 13 and 14 – Right to be informed

Given the core principle of transparency underpinning the GDPR, controllers must ensure they explain clearly and simply to individuals how the profiling or automated decision-making process works.

In particular, where the processing involves profiling-based decision making (irrespective of whether it is caught by Article 22 provisions), then the fact that the processing is for the purposes of both (a) profiling and (b) making a decision based on the profile generated, must be made clear to the data subject.[24]

Recital 60 states that giving information about profiling is part of the controller's transparency obligations under Article 5(1)(a). The data subject has a right *to be informed* by the controller about and, in certain circumstances, a right *to object to* 'profiling', *regardless* of whether solely automated individual decision-making based on profiling takes place.

Further guidance on transparency in general is available in the WP29 Guidelines on transparency under the GDPR[25].

2. Article 15 – Right of access

Article 15 gives the data subject the right to obtain details of any personal data used for profiling, including the categories of data used to construct a profile.

In addition to general information about the processing, pursuant to Article 15(3), the controller has a duty to make available the data used as input to create the profile as well as access to information on the profile and details of which segments the data subject has been placed into.

This differs from the right to data portability under Article 20 where the controller only needs to communicate the data provided by the data subject or observed by the controller and not the profile itself.[26]

Recital 63 provides some protection for controllers concerned about revealing trade secrets or intellectual property, which may be particularly relevant in relation to profiling. It says that the right of access 'should not adversely affect the rights or freedoms of others, including trade secrets or intellectual property and in particular the copyright protecting the software'. However, controllers cannot rely on the protection of their trade secrets as an excuse to deny access or refuse to provide information to the data subject.

Recital 63 also specifies that 'where possible, the controller should be able to provide remote access to a secure system which would provide the data subject with direct access to his or her personal data.'

3. Article 16 - Right to rectification, Article 17 Right to erasure and Article 18 Right to restriction of processing

Profiling can involve an element of prediction, which increases the risk of inaccuracy. The input data may be inaccurate or irrelevant, or taken out of context. There may be something wrong with the algorithm used to identify correlations.

The Article 16 right to rectification might apply where, for example, an individual is placed into a category that says something about their ability to perform a task, and that profile is based on incorrect information. Individuals may wish to challenge the accuracy of the data used and any grouping or category that has been applied to them.

The rights to rectification and erasure[27] apply to both the 'input personal data' (the personal data used to create the profile) and the 'output data' (the profile itself or 'score' assigned to the person).

Article 16 also provides a right for the data subject to complement the personal data with additional information.

Example

A local surgery's computer system places an individual into a group that is most likely to get heart disease. This 'profile' is not necessarily inaccurate even if he or she never suffers from heart disease.

The profile merely states that he or she is more likely to get it. That may be factually correct as a matter of statistics.

Nevertheless, the data subject has the right, taking into account the purpose of the processing, to provide a supplementary statement. In the above scenario, this could be based, for example, on a more advanced medical computer system (and statistical model) factoring in additional data and carrying out more detailed examinations than the one at the local surgery with more limited capabilities.

The right to restrict processing (Article 18) will apply to any stage of the profiling process.

4. Article 21 – Right to object

The controller has to bring details of the right to object under Article 21(1) and (2) *explicitly* to the data subject's attention, and present it clearly and separately from other information (Article 21(4)).

Under Article 21(1) the data subject can object to processing (including profiling), on grounds relating to his or her particular situation. Controllers are specifically required to provide for this right in all cases where processing is based on Article 6(1)(e) or (f).

Once the data subject exercises this right, the controller must interrupt[28] (or avoid starting) the profiling process unless it can demonstrate compelling legitimate grounds that override the interests, rights and freedoms of the data subject. The controller may also have to erase the relevant personal data.[29]

The GDPR does not provide any explanation of what would be considered compelling legitimate grounds.[30] It may be the case that, for example, the profiling is beneficial for society at large (or the wider community) and not just the business interests of the controller, such as profiling to predict the spread of contagious diseases.

The controller would need to:
- consider the importance of the profiling to their particular objective;
- consider the impact of the profiling on the data subject's interest, rights and freedoms – this should be limited to the minimum necessary to meet the objective; and
- carry out a balancing exercise.

There must always be a balancing exercise between the competing interests of the controller and the basis for the data subject's objection (which may be for personal, social or professional reasons). Unlike in the Directive 95/46/EC, the burden of proof to show compelling legitimate grounds lies with the controller rather than the data subject.

It is clear from the wording of Article 21 that the balancing test is different from that found in Article 6(1)(f). In other words, it is not sufficient for a controller to just demonstrate that their earlier legitimate interest analysis was correct. This balancing test requires the legitimate interest to be compelling, implying a higher threshold for overriding objections.

Article 21(2) grants an *unconditional right* for the data subject to object to the processing of their personal data for direct marketing purposes, including profiling to the extent that it is related to such direct marketing.[31] This means that there is no need for any balancing of interests; the controller must respect the individual's wishes without questioning the reasons for the objection. Recital 70 provides additional context to this right and says that it may be exercised at any time and free of charge.

NOTES

4   GDPR – Recital 72 "Profiling is subject to the rules of this Regulation governing the processing of personal data, such as the legal grounds for processing or data protection principles."

5   The WP29 Guidelines on transparency cover transparency generally in more detail Article 29 Data Protection Working Party. Guidelines on transparency under Regulation 2016/679 WP260, 28 November 2017 http://ec.europa.eu/newsroom/just/document.cfm?doc_id=48850, Accessed 18 December 2017.

6   Office of the Australian Information Commissioner. Consultation draft: Guide to big data and the Australian Privacy Principles, 05/2016 says: "Privacy notices have to communicate information handling practices clearly and simply, but also comprehensively and with enough specificity to be meaningful. *The very technology that leads to greater collection of personal information also presents the opportunity for more dynamic, multi-layered and user centric privacy notices.*" https://www.oaic.gov.au/engage-with-us/consultations/guide-to-big-data-and-the-australian-privacy-principles   / consultation-draft-guide-to-big-data-and-the-australian-privacy-principles. Accessed 24 April 2017

7   This example is taken from: United States Senate, Committee on Commerce, Science, and Transportation. A Review of the Data Broker Industry: Collection, Use, and Sale of Consumer Data for Marketing Purposes, Staff Report for Chairman Rockefeller, December 18, 2013. https://www.commerce.senate.gov/public/_cache/files/0d2b3642-6221 -4888-a631-08f2f255b577/AE5D72CBE7F44F5BFC846BECE22C875B.12.18. 13-senate-commerce-committee-report-on-data-broker-industry.pdf. See page ii of the Executive Summary and 12 of the main body of the document in particular. Accessed 21 July 2017

8   Note that the provisions of the future ePrivacy Regulation may also apply.

9   Highlighted in the Article 29 Data Protection Working Party. Opinion 03/2013 on purpose limitation,2 April 2013. http://ec.europa.eu/justice/data-protection/article-29/documentation/opinion-recommendation/files/2013/wp203_en.pdf.   Accessed 24 April 2017

10   GDPR Article 6(4)

11   Norwegian Data Protection Authority. The Great Data Race – How commercial utilisation of personal data challenges privacy, Report, November 2015. Datatilsynet https://www.datatilsynet.no/English/Publications/The-Great-Data-Race/ Accessed 24 April 2017

12   Article 29 Data Protection Working Party. Guidelines on Consent under Regulation 2016/679 WP259, 28 November 2017, http://ec.europa.eu/newsroom/just/document.cfm?doc_id=48849. Accessed 18 December 2017

13   Ibid

14   Opinion 06/2014 on the notion of legitimate interests of the data controller under Article 7 of Directive 95/46/EC. European Commission, 9 April 2014. http://ec.europa.eu/justice/data-protection/article-29/documentation/opinion-recommendation/files/2014/wp217_en.pdf. Accessed 24 April 2017

15   GDPR Recitals 41 and 45

16   Page 19 Article 29 Data Protection Working Party. Opinion 06/2014 on the notion of legitimate interests of the data controller under Article 7 of Directive 95/46/EC. European Commission, 9 April 2014. http://ec.europa.eu/justice/data-protection/article-29/documentation/opinion-recommendation/files/2014/wp217_en.pdf. Accessed 24 April 2017

17   GDPR Recital 46

18   Legitimate interests listed in GDPR Recital 47 include processing for direct marketing purposes and processing strictly necessary for the purposes of preventing fraud.

19   The controller's "legitimate interest" cannot render profiling lawful if the processing falls within the Article 22(1) definition.

[20]   Article 29 Data Protection Working Party. Opinion 06/2014 on the notion of legitimate interests of the data controller under Article 7 of Directive 95/46/EC. European Commission, 9 April 2014, Page 47, examples on pages 59 and 60 http://ec.europa.eu/justice/data-protection/article-29/documentation/opinion-recommendation/files/2014/wp217_en.pdf.   Accessed 24 April 2017

[21]   Michael Kosinski, David Stilwell and Thore Graepel. Private traits and attributes are predictable from digital records of human behaviour. Proceedings of the National Academy of Sciences of the United States of America, http://www.pnas.org/content/110/15/5802.full.pdf. Accessed 29 March 2017

[22]   This Section is relevant for both profiling and automated decision-making. For automated decision making under Article 22, please note that there are also additional requirements as described in Chapter IV.

[23]   The Norwegian Data Protection Authority. The Great Data Race -How commercial utilisation of personal data challenges privacy. Report, November 2015. https://www.datatilsynet.no/English/Publications/The-Great-Data-Race/ Accessed 24 April 2017

[24]   GDPR – Article 13(1)(c) and Article 14(1)(c). Article 13(2)(f) and 14(2)(g) require the controller to inform the data subject about the existence of automated decision-making, including profiling, described in Article 22(1) and (4). This is explained further in Chapter IV.

[25]   Article 29 Data Protection Working Party. Guidelines on transparency under Regulation 2016/679 WP260, 28 November 2017 http://ec.europa.eu/newsroom/just/document.cfm?doc_id=48850, Accessed 18 December 2017

[26]   Page 9, WP29 Guidelines on the Right to data portability, WP242 http://ec.europa.eu/newsroom/document.cfm?doc_id=45685. Accessed 8 January 2018

[27]   GDPR – Article 17

[28]   GDPR- Article 18(1)(d)

[29]   GDPR – Article 17(1)(c)

[30]   See explanation on legitimacy, Article 29 Data Protection Working Party Opinion 06/2014 on the notion of legitimate interests of the data controller under Article 7 of Directive 95/46/EC. 9 April 2014. Page 24 - 26 http://ec.europa.eu/justice/data-protection/article-29/documentation/opinion-recommendation/files/2014/wp217_en.pdf . Accessed 24 April 2017

[31]   In line with Article 12(2) controllers who collect personal data from individuals with the aim of using it for direct marketing purposes should, at the moment of collection, consider offering data subjects an easy way to indicate that they do not wish their personal data to be used for direct marketing purposes, rather than requiring them to exercise their right to object at a later occasion.

IV. SPECIFIC PROVISIONS ON SOLELY AUTOMATED DECISION-MAKING AS DEFINED IN ARTICLE 22

[2.206]
Article 22(1) says

> The data subject shall have the right not to be subject to a decision *based solely* on automated processing, including profiling, which produces *legal effects* concerning him or her or *similarly significantly affects him or her.*

The term "right" in the provision does not mean that Article 22(1) applies only when actively invoked by the data subject. Article 22(1) establishes a general prohibition for decision-making based solely on automated processing. This prohibition applies whether or not the data subject takes an action regarding the processing of their personal data.

In summary, Article 22 provides that:
(i)   as a rule, there is a general prohibition on fully automated individual decision-making, including profiling that has a legal or similarly significant effect;
(ii)   there are exceptions to the rule;
(iii)   where one of these exceptions applies, there must be measures in place to safeguard the data subject's rights and freedoms and legitimate interests[32].

This interpretation reinforces the idea of the data subject having control over their personal data, which is in line with the fundamental principles of the GDPR. Interpreting Article 22 as a prohibition rather than a right to be invoked means that individuals are automatically protected from the potential effects this type of processing may have. The wording of the Article suggests that this is the intention and is supported by Recital 71 which says:

> However, decision-making based on such processing, including profiling, **should be allowed** where expressly authorised by Union or Member State law . . . ., or necessary for the entering or performance of a contract . . . ., or when the data subject has given his or her explicit consent

This implies that processing under Article 22(1) is not allowed generally.[33]

However the Article 22(1) prohibition only applies in specific circumstances when a decision based solely on automated processing, including profiling, has a legal effect on or similarly significantly affects someone, as explained further in the guidelines. Even in these cases there are defined exceptions which allow such processing to take place.

The required safeguarding measures, discussed in more detail below, include the right to be informed (addressed in Articles 13 and 14 – specifically meaningful information about the logic involved, as well as the significance and envisaged consequences for the data subject), and safeguards, such as the right to obtain human intervention and the right to challenge the decision (addressed in Article 22(3)).

Any processing likely to result in a high risk to data subjects requires the controller to carry out a Data Protection Impact Assessment (DPIA).[34] As well as addressing any other risks connected with the processing, a DPIA can be particularly useful for controllers who are unsure whether their proposed activities will fall within the Article 22(1) definition, and, if allowed by an identified exception, what safeguarding measures must be applied.

A. 'DECISION BASED SOLELY ON AUTOMATED PROCESSING'

Article 22(1) refers to decisions 'based solely' on automated processing. This means that there is no human involvement in the decision process.

Example

An automated process produces what is in effect a recommendation concerning a data subject. If a human being reviews and takes account of other factors in making the final decision, that decision would not be 'based solely' on automated processing.

The controller cannot avoid the Article 22 provisions by fabricating human involvement. For example, if someone routinely applies automatically generated profiles to individuals without any actual influence on the result, this would still be a decision based solely on automated processing.

To qualify as human involvement, the controller must ensure that any oversight of the decision is meaningful, rather than just a token gesture. It should be carried out by someone who has the authority and competence to change the decision. As part of the analysis, they should consider all the relevant data.

As part of their DPIA, the controller should identify and record the degree of any human involvement in the decision-making process and at what stage this takes place.

B. 'LEGAL' OR 'SIMILARLY SIGNIFICANT' EFFECTS

The GDPR recognises that automated decision-making, including profiling can have serious consequences for individuals. The GDPR does not define 'legal' or 'similarly significant' however the wording makes it clear that only serious impactful effects will be covered by Article 22.

'Decision producing legal effects'

A legal effect requires that the decision, which is based on solely automated processing, affects someone's legal rights, such as the freedom to associate with others, vote in an election, or take legal action. A legal effect may also be something that affects a person's legal status or their rights under a contract. Examples of this type of effect include automated decisions about an individual that result in:
* cancellation of a contract;
* entitlement to or denial of a particular social benefit granted by law, such as child or housing benefit;
* refused admission to a country or denial of citizenship.

'Similarly significantly affects him or her'

Even if a decision-making process does not have an effect on people's legal rights it could still fall within the scope of Article 22 if it produces an effect that is equivalent or similarly significant in its impact.

In other words, even where there is no change in their legal rights or obligations, the data subject could still be impacted sufficiently to require the protections under this provision. The GDPR introduces the word 'similarly' (not present in Article 15 of Directive 95/46/EC) to the phrase 'significantly affects'. Therefore the threshold for *significance* must be similar to that of a decision producing a legal effect.

Recital 71 provides the following typical examples: 'automatic refusal of an online credit application' or 'e-recruiting practices without any human intervention'.

For data processing to significantly affect someone the effects of the processing must be sufficiently great or important to be worthy of attention. In other words, the decision must have the potential to:
* significantly affect the circumstances, behaviour or choices of the individuals concerned;
* have a prolonged or permanent impact on the data subject; or
* at its most extreme, lead to the exclusion or discrimination of individuals.

It is difficult to be precise about what would be considered sufficiently significant to meet the threshold, although the following decisions could fall into this category:
* decisions that affect someone's financial circumstances, such as their eligibility to credit;
* decisions that affect someone's access to health services;
* decisions that deny someone an employment opportunity or put them at a serious disadvantage;
* decisions that affect someone's access to education, for example university admissions.

This bring us also to the issue of online advertising, which increasingly relies on automated tools and involves solely automated individual decision-making. As well as complying with the general provisions of the GDPR, covered in Chapter III, the provisions of the proposed ePrivacy Regulation may also be relevant. Furthermore, children require enhanced protection, as will be discussed below in Chapter V.

In many typical cases the decision to present targeted advertising based on profiling will not have a similarly significant effect on individuals, for example an advertisement for a mainstream online fashion outlet based on a simple demographic profile: 'women in the Brussels region aged between 25 and 35 who are likely to be interested in fashion and certain clothing items'.

However it is possible that it may do, depending upon the particular characteristics of the case, including:
- the intrusiveness of the profiling process, including the tracking of individuals across different websites, devices and services;
- the expectations and wishes of the individuals concerned;
- the way the advert is delivered; or
- using knowledge of the vulnerabilities of the data subjects targeted.

Processing that might have little impact on individuals generally may in fact have a significant effect for certain groups of society, such as minority groups or vulnerable adults. For example, someone known or likely to be in financial difficulties who is regularly targeted with adverts for high interest loans may sign up for these offers and potentially incur further debt.

Automated decision-making that results in differential pricing based on personal data or personal characteristics could also have a significant effect if, for example, prohibitively high prices effectively bar someone from certain goods or services.

Similarly significant effects could also be triggered by the actions of individuals other than the one to which the automated decision relates. An illustration of this is given below.

Example

Hypothetically, a credit card company might reduce a customer's card limit, based not on that customer's own repayment history, but on non-traditional credit criteria, such as an analysis of other customers living in the same area who shop at the same stores.

This could mean that someone is deprived of opportunities based on the actions of others.

In a different context using these types of characteristics might have the advantage of extending credit to those without a conventional credit history, who would otherwise have been denied.

C. EXCEPTIONS FROM THE PROHIBITION

Article 22(1) sets out a general prohibition on solely automated individual decision-making with legal or similarly significant effects, as described above.

This means that the controller should not undertake the processing described in Article 22(1) unless one of the following Article 22(2) exceptions applies - where the decision is:

(a)   necessary for the performance of or entering into a contract;
(b)   authorised by Union or Member State law to which the controller is subject and which also lays down suitable measures to safeguard the data subject's rights and freedoms and legitimate interests; or
(c)   based on the data subject's explicit consent.

Where the decision-making involves special categories of data defined in Article 9(1) the controller must also ensure that they can meet the requirements of Article 22(4).

1. Performance of a contract

Controllers may wish to use solely automated decision-making processes for contractual purposes because they believe it is the most appropriate way to achieve the objective. Routine human involvement can sometimes be impractical or impossible due to the sheer quantity of data being processed.

The controller must be able to show that this type of processing is necessary, taking into account whether a less privacy-intrusive method could be adopted.[35] If other effective and less intrusive means to achieve the same goal exist, then it would not be 'necessary'.

Automated decision-making described in Article 22(1) may also be necessary for pre-contractual processing.

Example

A business advertises an open position. As working for the business in question is popular, the business receives tens of thousands of applications. Due to the exceptionally high volume of applications, the business may find that it is not practically possible to identify fitting candidates without first using fully automated means to sift out irrelevant applications. In this case, automated decision-making may be necessary in order to make a short list of possible candidates, with the intention of entering into a contract with a data subject.

Chapter III (Section B) provides more information on contracts as a lawful basis for processing.

2. Authorised by Union or Member State law

Automated decision-making including profiling could potentially take place under 22(2)(b) if Union or Member State law authorised its use. The relevant law must also lay down suitable measures to safeguard the data subject's rights and freedoms and legitimate interests.

Recital 71 says that this could include the use of automated decision-making defined in Article 22(1) for monitoring and preventing fraud and tax-evasion, or to ensure the security and reliability of a service provided by the controller.

3. Explicit consent

Article 22 requires *explicit* consent. Processing that falls within the definition of Article 22(1) poses significant data protection risks and a high level of individual control over personal data is therefore deemed appropriate.

'Explicit consent' is not defined in the GDPR. The WP29 guidelines on consent[36] provide guidance on how this should be interpreted.

Chapter III (Section B) provides more information on consent generally.

D. SPECIAL CATEGORIES OF PERSONAL DATA – ARTICLE 22(4)

Automated decision-making (described in Article 22(1)) that involves special categories of personal data is only allowed under the following cumulative conditions (Article 22(4)):
*   there is an applicable Article 22(2) exemption; and
*   point (a) or (g) of Article 9(2) applies.

9(2)(a) - the explicit consent of the data subject; or

9(2)(g) - processing necessary for reasons of substantial public interest, on the basis of Union or Member State law which shall be proportionate to the aim pursued, respect the essence of the right to data protection and provide for suitable and specific measures to safeguard the fundamental rights and interests of the data subject.

In both of the above cases, the controller must put in place suitable measures to safeguard the data subject's rights and freedoms and legitimate interests.

E. RIGHTS OF THE DATA SUBJECT[37]

1. Articles 13(2)(f) and 14(2)(g) - Right to be informed

Given the potential risks and interference that profiling caught by Article 22 poses to the rights of data subjects, data controllers should be particularly mindful of their transparency obligations.

Articles 13(2)(f) and 14(2)(g) require controllers to provide specific, easily accessible information about automated decision-making, based solely on automated processing, including profiling, that produces legal or similarly significant effects.[38]

If the controller is making automated decisions as described in Article 22(1), they must:
*   tell the data subject that they are engaging in this type of activity;
*   provide meaningful information about the logic involved; and
*   explain the significance and envisaged consequences of the processing.

Providing this information will also help controllers ensure they are meeting some of the required safeguards referred to in Article 22(3) and Recital 71.

If the automated decision-making and profiling does not meet the Article 22(1) definition it is nevertheless good practice to provide the above information. In any event the controller must provide sufficient information to the data subject to make the processing fair,[39] and meet all the other information requirements of Articles 13 and 14.

Meaningful information about the 'logic involved'

The growth and complexity of machine-learning can make it challenging to understand how an automated decision-making process or profiling works.

The controller should find simple ways to tell the data subject about the rationale behind, or the criteria relied on in reaching the decision. The GDPR requires the controller to provide meaningful information about the logic involved, not necessarily a complex explanation of the algorithms used or disclosure of the full algorithm.[40] The information provided should, however, be sufficiently comprehensive for the data subject to understand the reasons for the decision.

Example

A controller uses credit scoring to assess and reject an individual's loan application. The score may have been provided by a credit reference agency, or calculated directly based on information held by the controller.

Regardless of the source (and information on the source must be provided to the data subject under Article 14 (2)(f) where the personal data have not been obtained from the data subject), if the controller is reliant upon this score it must be able to explain it and the rationale, to the data subject.

The controller explains that this process helps them make fair and responsible lending decisions. It provides details of the main characteristics considered in reaching the decision, the source of this information and the relevance. This may include, for example:
- the information provided by the data subject on the application form;
- information about previous account conduct , including any payment arrears; and
- official public records information such as fraud record information and insolvency records.

The controller also includes information to advise the data subject that the credit scoring methods used are regularly tested to ensure they remain fair, effective and unbiased.

The controller provides contact details for the data subject to request that any declined decision is reconsidered, in line with the provisions of Article 22(3).

'Significance' and 'envisaged consequences'

This term suggests that information must be provided about intended or future processing, and how the automated decision-making might affect the data subject.[41] In order to make this information meaningful and understandable, real, tangible examples of the type of possible effects should be given.

In a digital context, controllers might be able to use additional tools to help illustrate such effects.

Example

An insurance company uses an automated decision making process to set motor insurance premiums based on monitoring customers' driving behaviour. To illustrate the significance and envisaged consequences of the processing it explains that dangerous driving may result in higher insurance payments and provides an app comparing fictional drivers, including one with dangerous driving habits such as fast acceleration and last-minute braking.

It uses graphics to give tips on how to improve these habits and consequently how to lower insurance premiums.

Controllers can use similar visual techniques to explain how a past decision has been made.

---

2. Article 15(1)(h) - Right of access

Article 15(1)(h) entitles data subjects to have the same information about solely automated decision-making, including profiling, as required under Articles 13(2)(f) and 14(2)(g), namely:
- the existence of automated decision making, including profiling;
- meaningful information about the logic involved; and
- the significance and envisaged consequences of such processing for the data subject.

The controller should have already given the data subject this information in line with their Article 13 obligations.[42]

Article 15(1)(h) says that the controller should provide the data subject with information about the *envisaged consequences* of the processing, rather than an explanation of a *particular* decision. Recital 63 clarifies this by stating that every data subject should have the right of access to obtain 'communication' about automatic data processing, including the logic involved, and *at least* when based on profiling, the consequences of such processing,

By exercising their Article 15 rights, the data subject can become aware of a decision made concerning him or her, including one based on profiling.

The controller should provide the data subject with general information (notably, on factors taken into account for the decision-making process, and on their respective 'weight' on an aggregate level) which is also useful for him or her to challenge the decision.

F. ESTABLISHING APPROPRIATE SAFEGUARDS

If the basis for processing is 22(2)(a) or 22(2)(c), Article 22(3) requires controllers to implement suitable measures to safeguard data subjects' rights freedoms and legitimate interests. Under Article 22(2)(b) the Member or Union State law that authorises the processing must also incorporate appropriate safeguarding measures.

Such measures should include as a minimum a way for the data subject to obtain human intervention, express their point of view, and contest the decision.

Human intervention is a key element. Any review must be carried out by someone who has the appropriate authority and capability to change the decision. The reviewer should undertake a thorough assessment of all the relevant data, including any additional information provided by the data subject.

Recital 71 highlights that *in any case* suitable safeguards should also include:

.. specific information to the data subject and the right . . . . to obtain an explanation of the decision reached after such assessment and to challenge the decision.

The controller must provide a simple way for the data subject to exercise these rights.

This emphasises the need for transparency about the processing. The data subject will only be able to challenge a decision or express their view if they fully understand how it has been made and on what basis. Transparency requirements are discussed in Chapter IV (section E).

Errors or bias in collected or shared data or an error or bias in the automated decision-making process can result in:

- incorrect classifications; and
- assessments based on imprecise projections; that
- impact negatively on individuals.

Controllers should carry out frequent assessments on the data sets they process to check for any bias, and develop ways to address any prejudicial elements, including any over-reliance on correlations.

Systems that audit algorithms and regular reviews of the accuracy and relevance of automated decision-making including profiling are other useful measures.

Controllers should introduce appropriate procedures and measures to prevent errors, inaccuracies[43] or discrimination on the basis of special category data. These measures should be used on a cyclical basis; not only at the design stage, but also continuously, as the profiling is applied to individuals. The outcome of such testing should feed back into the system design.

Further examples of appropriate safeguards can be found in the Recommendations section

---

NOTES

[32]   Recital 71 says that such processing should be "subject to suitable safeguards, which should include specific information to the data subject and the right to obtain human intervention, to express his or her point of view, to obtain an explanation of the decision reached after such assessment and to challenge the decision."

[33]   Further comments on the interpretation of Article 22 as a prohibition can be found in Annex 2.

[34]   Article 29 Data Protection Working Party. Guidelines on Data Protection Impact Assessment (DPIA) and determining whether processing is "likely to result in a high risk" for the purposes of Regulation 2016/679. 4 April 2017. European Commission. http://ec.europa.eu/newsroom/document.cfm?doc_id=44137 Accessed 24 April 2017.

[35]   Buttarelli, Giovanni. Assessing the necessity of measures that limit the fundamental right to the protection of personal data. AToolkit European Data Protection Supervisor, 11 April 2017, https://edps.europa.eu/sites/edp/files/publication/17-04-11_necessity_toolkit_en_0.pdf Accessed 24 April 2017

[36]   Article 29 Data Protection Working Party. Guidelines on Consent under Regulation 2016/679 WP259. 28 November 2017, http://ec.europa.eu/newsroom/just/document.cfm?doc_id=48849. Accessed 18 December 2017

[37]   GDPR Article 12 provides for the modalities applicable for the exercise of the data subject's rights

[38]   Referred to in Article 22(1) and (4).The WP Guidelines on transparency cover the general information requirements set out in Articles 13 and 14.

[39]   GDPR Recital 60 "The controller should provide the data subject with any further information necessary to ensure fair and transparent processing taking into account the specific circumstances and context in which the personal data are processed. Furthermore the data subject should be informed of the existence of profiling and the consequences of such profiling."

[40]   Complexity is no excuse for failing to provide information to the data subject. Recital 58 states that the principle of transparency is "of particular relevance in situations where the proliferation of actors and the technological complexity of practice makes it difficult for the data subject to know and understand whether, by whom and for what purpose personal data relating to him are being collected, such as in the case of online advertising".

[41]   Council of Europe. Draft Explanatory Report on the modernised version of CoE Convention 108, paragraph 75: "Data subjects should be entitled to know the reasoning underlying the processing of their data, including the consequences of such a reasoning, which led to any resulting conclusions, in particular in cases involving the use of algorithms for automated-decision making including profiling. For instance in the case of credit scoring, they should be entitled to know the logic underpinning the processing of their data and resulting in a 'yes' or 'no' decision, and not simply information on the decision itself. Without an understanding of these elements there could be no effective exercise of other essential safeguards such as the right to object and the right to complain to a competent authority." https://rm.coe.int/CoERMPublicCommonSearchServices/DisplayDCTMContent?documentId=09000016806b6ec2. Accessed 24 April 2017

[42]   GDPR Article 12(3) clarifies the timescales for providing this information

[43]   GDPR Recital 71 says that:

"In order to ensure fair and transparent processing in respect of the data subject, taking into account the specific circumstances and context in which the personal data are processed, the controller should use appropriate mathematical or statistical procedures for the profiling, implement technical and organisational measures appropriate to ensure, in particular, that factors which result in inaccuracies in personal data are corrected and the risk of errors is minimised, ..."

V. CHILDREN AND PROFILING

[2.207]
The GDPR creates additional obligations for data controllers when they are processing children's personal data.

Article 22 itself makes no distinction as to whether the processing concerns adults or children. However, recital 71 says that solely automated decision-making, including profiling, with legal or similarly significant effects should not apply to children.[44] Given that this wording is not reflected in the Article itself, WP29 does not consider that this represents an absolute prohibition on this type of processing in relation to children. However, in the light of this recital, WP29 recommends that, as a rule, controllers should not rely upon the exceptions in Article 22(2) to justify it.

There may nevertheless be some circumstances in which it is necessary for controllers to carry out solely automated decision-making, including profiling, with legal or similarly significant effects in relation to children, for example to protect their welfare. If so, the processing may be carried out on the basis of the exceptions in Article 22(2)(a), (b) or (c) as appropriate.

In those cases there must be suitable safeguards in place, as required by Article 22(2)(b) and 22(3), and they must therefore be appropriate for children. The controller must ensure that these safeguards are effective in protecting the rights, freedoms and legitimate interests of the children whose data they are processing.

The need for particular protection for children is reflected in recital 38, which says:

> Children merit specific protection with regard to their personal data, as they may be less aware of the risks, consequences and safeguards concerned and their rights in relation to the processing of personal data. Such specific protection should, in particular, apply to the use of personal data of children for the purposes *of marketing or creating personality or user profiles and the collection of personal data with regard to children when using services offered directly to a child.*

Article 22 does not prevent controllers from making solely automated decisions about children, if the decision will not have a legal or similarly significant effect on the child. However, solely automated decision making which influences a child's choices and behaviour could potentially have a legal or similarly significant effect on them, depending upon the nature of the choices and behaviours in question.

Because children represent a more vulnerable group of society, organisations should, in general, refrain from profiling them for marketing purposes.[45] Children can be particularly susceptible in the online environment and more easily influenced by behavioural advertising. For example, in online gaming, profiling can be used to target players that the algorithm considers are more likely to spend money on the game as well as providing more personalised adverts. The age and maturity of the child may affect their ability to understand the motivation behind this type of marketing or the consequences.[46]

Article 40(2)(g) explicitly refers to the preparation of codes of conduct incorporating safeguards for children; it may also be possible to develop existing codes.[47]

NOTES

[44] Recital 71 – "such measure should not concern a child".

[45] The WP29 Opinion 02/2013 on apps on smart devices (WP202), adopted on 27 February 2013, under the specific section 3.10 on Children, specifies at page 26 that "data controllers should not process children's data for behavioural advertising purposes, neither directly nor indirectly, since this will be outside of the scope of the child's understanding and therefore exceed the boundaries of lawful processing".

[46] An EU study on the impact of marketing through social media, online games and mobile applications on children's behaviour found that marketing practices have clear impacts on children's behaviour. This study was based on children aged between 6 and 12 years.

[47] One example of a code of conduct dealing with marketing to children is that produced by FEDMA Code of conduct, explanatory memorandum, available at: http://www.oecd.org/sti/ieconomy/2091875.pdf Accessed 15 May 2017. See, in particular: "6.2 Marketers targeting children, or for whom children are likely to constitute a section of their audience, should not exploit children's credulity, loyalty, vulnerability or lack of experience.; 6.8.5 Marketers should not make a child's access to a website contingent on the collection of detailed personal information. In, particular, special incentives such as prize offers and games should not be used to entice children to divulge detailed personal information."

VI. DATA PROTECTION IMPACT ASSESSMENTS (DPIA) AND DATA PROTECTION OFFICER (DPO)

[2.208]
Accountability is an important area and an explicit requirement under the GDPR.[48]

As a key accountability tool, a DPIA enables the controller to assess the risks involved in automated decision-making, including profiling. It is a way of showing that suitable measures have been put in place to address those risks and demonstrate compliance with the GDPR.

Article 35(3)(a) highlights the need for the controller to carry out a DPIA in the case of:

> *a systematic and extensive evaluation* of personal aspects relating to natural persons which is *based on* automated processing, including profiling, and on which decisions are based that produce legal effects concerning the natural person or similarly significantly affect the natural person;

Article 35(3)(a) refers to evaluations including profiling and decisions that are 'based' on automated processing, rather than 'solely' automated processing. We take this to mean that Article 35(3)(a) will apply in the case of decision-making including profiling with legal or similarly significant effects that is *not* wholly automated, as well as solely automated decision-making defined in Article 22(1).

If the controller envisages a 'model' where it takes *solely* automated decisions having a *high impact* on individuals based on *profiles* made about them and it *cannot* rely on the individual's consent, on a contract with the individual or on a law authorising this, the controller should not proceed.

The controller can still envisage a 'model' of decision-making based on profiling, by significantly increasing the level of human intervention so that the model is *no longer a fully automated decision making process*, although the processing could still present risks to individuals' fundamental rights and freedoms. If so the controller must ensure that they can address these risks and meet the requirements described in Chapter III of these Guidelines.

A DPIA can also be a useful way for the controller to identify what measures they will introduce to address the data protection risks involved with the processing. Such measures[49] could include:
- informing the data subject about the existence of and the logic involved in the automated decision-making process;
- explaining the significance and envisaged consequences of the processing for the data subject;
- providing the data subject with the means to oppose the decision; and
- allowing the data subject to express their point of view.

Other profiling activities may warrant a DPIA, depending upon the specifics of the case. Controllers may wish to consult the WP29 guidelines on DPIAs[50] for further information and to help determine the need to carry out a DPIA.

An additional accountability requirement is the designation of a DPO, where the profiling and/or the automated decision-making is a core activity of the controller and requires regular and systematic monitoring of data subjects on a large scale (Article 37(1)(b).[51]

NOTES

[48]   As required by the GDPR Article 5(2)

[49]   Mirroring the requirements in Article 13(2)(f), Article 14(2)(g) and Article 22(3)

[50]   Article 29 Data Protection Working Party. Guidelines on Data Protection Impact Assessment (DPIA) and determining whether processing is "likely to result in a high risk" for the purposes of Regulation 2016/679. 4 April 2017.. http://ec.europa.eu/newsroom/document.cfm?doc_id=44137 Accessed 24 April 2017.

[51]   Article 29 Data Protection Working Party. Guidelines on Data Protection Officer (DPOs). 5 April 2017; http://ec.europa.eu/newsroom/article29/item-detail.cfm?item_id=612048 Accessed 22 January 2018

ANNEX 1 - GOOD PRACTICE RECOMMENDATIONS

[2.209]
The following good practice recommendations will assist data controllers in meeting the requirements of the GDPR provisions on profiling and automated decision making.[52]

Article	Issue	Recommendation
5(1)(a),12, 13, 14	Right to have information	Controllers should consult the WP29 Guidelines on transparency WP260 for general transparency requirements.
		In addition to the general requirements, when the controller is processing data as defined in Article 22, they must provide meaningful information about the logic involved.
		Instead of providing a complex mathematical explanation about how algorithms or machine-learning work, the controller should consider using clear and comprehensive ways to deliver the information to the data subject, for example: • the categories of data that have been or will be used in the profiling or decision-making process; • why these categories are considered pertinent • how any profile used in the automated decision-making process is built, including any statistics used in the analysis; • why this profile is relevant to the automated decision-making process; and • how it is used for a decision concerning the data subject.

Article	Issue	Recommendation
		Such information will generally be more relevant to the data subject and contribute to the transparency of the processing.
		Controllers may wish to consider visualisation and interactive techniques to aid algorithmic transparency[53].
6(1)(a)	Consent as a basis for processing	If controllers are relying upon consent as a basis for processing they should consult the WP29 Guidelines on consent WP259.
15	Right of access	Controllers may want to consider implementing a mechanism for data subjects to check their profile, including details of the information and sources used to develop it.
16	Right to rectification	Controllers providing data subjects with access to their profile in connection with their Article 15 rights should allow them the opportunity to update or amend any inaccuracies in the data or profile. This can also help them meet their Article 5(1)(d) obligations. Controllers could consider introducing online preference management tools such as a privacy dashboard. This gives data subjects the option of managing what is happening to their information across a number of different services – allowing them to alter settings, update their personal details, and review or edit their profile to correct any inaccuracies.
21(1) and (2)	Right to object	The right to object in Article 21(1) and (2) has to be explicitly brought to the attention of the data subject and presented clearly and separately from other information (Article 21(4). Controllers need to ensure that this right is prominently displayed on their website or in any relevant documentation and not hidden away within any other terms and conditions.
22 and Recital 71	Appropriate safeguards	The following list, though not exhaustive, provides some good practice suggestions for controllers to consider when making solely automated decisions, including profiling(defined in Article 22(1)): <ul><li>regular quality assurance checks of their systems to make sure that individuals are being treated fairly and not discriminated against, whether on the basis of special categories of personal data or otherwise;</li><li>algorithmic auditing – testing the algorithms used and developed by machine learning systems to prove that they are actually performing as intended, and not producing discriminatory, erroneous or unjustified results;</li><li>for independent 'third party' auditing (where decision-making based on profiling has a high impact on individuals), provide the auditor with all necessary information about how the algorithm or machine learning system works;</li><li>obtaining contractual assurances for third party algorithms that auditing and testing has been carried out and the algorithm is compliant with agreed standards;</li><li>specific measures for data minimisation to incorporate clear retention periods for profiles and for any personal data used when creating or applying the profiles;</li><li>using anonymisation or pseudonymisation techniques in the context of profiling;</li><li>ways to allow the data subject to express his or her point of view and contest the decision; and,</li><li>a mechanism for human intervention in defined cases, for example providing a link to an appeals process at the point the automated decision is delivered to the data subject, with agreed timescales for the review and a named contact point for any queries .</li></ul> Controllers can also explore options such as: <ul><li>certification mechanisms for processing operations;</li><li>codes of conduct for auditing processes involving machine learning;</li><li>ethical review boards to assess the potential harms and benefits to society of particular applications for profiling.</li></ul>

NOTES

52   Controllers also need to ensure they have robust procedures in place to ensure that they can meet their obligations under Articles 15 – 22 in the timescales provided for by the GDPR.

53   Information Commissioner's Office – Big data, artificial intelligence, machine learning and data protection version 2.0, 03/2017. Page 87, paragraph 194, March 2017. https://ico.org.uk/media/for-organisations/documents/2013559/

big-data-ai-ml-and-data-protection.pdf Accessed 24 April 2017

[2.210]
ANNEX 2 – KEY GDPR PROVISIONS

KEY GDPR PROVISIONS THAT REFERENCE GENERAL PROFILING AND AUTOMATED DECISION-MAKING

Article	Recital	Comments
3(2)(b)	24	The monitoring of data subjects' behaviour as far as their behaviour takes place within the Union. Recital 24 " . . . .tracked on the internet . . . . . . use of personal data processing techniques which consist of profiling a natural person, *particularly in order to take decisions* concerning her or him or for analysing or predicting her or his personal preferences, behaviours or attitudes".
4(4)	30	**Article 4(4)** definition of profiling **Recital 30** "online identifiers . . . ., such as Internet Protocol addresses, cookie identifiers or other identifiers such as radio frequency identification tags . . . may leave traces which, in particular when combined with unique identifiers and other information received by the servers, *may be used to create profiles of the natural persons and identify them.*"
5 and 6	72	**Recital 72**: "Profiling is subject to the rules of this Regulation governing the processing of personal data, such as the legal grounds for processing (**Article 6**) or data protection principles (**Article 5**)."
8	38	Use of children's personal data for profiling. **Recital 38:** "Children merit specific protection . . . .. in particular, . . . to the use of personal data of children for the purposes of . . . .creating personality or user profiles."
13 and 14	60	Right to be informed. **Recital 60**: "Furthermore, the data subject *shall be informed of the existence of profiling and the consequences of such profiling.*"
15	63	Right of access. **Recital 63:** "right to know and obtain communication . . . ..with regard to the purposes for which the personal data are processed, ...and, *at least* when based on profiling, the consequences of such profiling".
21(1)(2) and (3)	70	Right to object to profiling. **Recital 70** " . . . the right to object to such processing, including profiling to the extent that it is related to such direct marketing."
23	73	**Recital 73**: "Restrictions concerning specific principles and concerning . . . . . . .the right to object and decisions based on profiling . . . . . . .may be imposed by Union or Member State law as far as necessary and proportionate in a democratic society . . . " to safeguard specific objectives of general public interest.
35(3)(a)	91	A DPIA is required in the case of "a systematic and extensive evaluation of personal aspects relating to natural persons which is *based* on automated processing, including profiling, and on which decisions are based that produce legal effects concerning the natural person or similarly significantly affect the natural person;" **Covers decision-making including profiling that is not solely automated.**

KEY GDPR PROVISIONS THAT REFERENCE AUTOMATED DECISION-MAKING AS DEFINED IN ARTICLE 22

Article	Recital	Comments
13(2)(f) and 14(2)(g)	61	Right to be informed about: • the existence of automated decision-making under **A22(1)** and **(4)**; • meaningful information about the logic involved; • significance and envisaged consequences of such processing.

Article	Recital	Comments
15(h)		Specific access rights to information about the existence of solely automated decision-making, including profiling.
22(1)	71	Prohibition on decision-making based solely on automated processing, including profiling, which produces legal/similarly significant effects. In addition to the explanation provided in the main body of the guidelines, the following points expand on the rationale for reading Article 22 as a prohibition: • Although Chapter III is about the rights of the data subject, the provisions in Articles 12 - 22 are not exclusively concerned with the *active* exercise of rights. Some of the rights are *passive*; they do not all relate to situations where the data subject takes an action i.e. makes a request or a complaint or a demand of some sort. Articles 15-18 and Articles 20-21 are about the data subject actively exercising their rights, but Articles 13 & 14 concern duties which the data controller has to fulfil, without any active involvement from the data subject. So the inclusion of Article 22 in that chapter does not in itself mean that it is a right to object; • Article 12(2) talks about the exercise of 'data subject rights under Articles 15 to 22; but this does not mean that Article 22(1) itself has to be interpreted as a right. There *is* an active right in A22, but it is part of the safeguards which have to be applied in those cases where automated decision making is allowed (Articles 22(2)(a-c)) - the right to obtain human intervention, express his or her point of view and to contest the decision. It only applies in those cases, because carrying out the processing described in Article 22(1) on other bases is prohibited; • Article 22 is found in a section of the GDPR called "Right to object **and** automated individual decision-making", implying that Article 22 is *not* a right to object like Article 21. This is further emphasised by the lack in Article 22 of an equivalently explicit information duty as that found in Article 21(4); • If Article 22 were to be interpreted as a right to object, the exception in Article 22(2)(c) would not make much sense. The exception states that automated decision-making can still take place if the data subject has given explicit consent (see below). This would be contradictory as a data subject cannot object and consent to the same processing; • An objection would mean that human intervention must take place. Article 22(2)(a) and (c) exceptions override the main rule in Article 22(1), but only as long as human intervention is available to the data subject, as specified in Article 22(3). Since the data subject (by objecting) has already requested human intervention, Article 22(2)(a) and (c) would automatically be circumvented in every case, thus rendering them meaningless in effect. **Recital 71**: " . . . Such processing includes 'profiling' that consists of any form of automated processing of personal data evaluating the personal aspects relating to a natural person, in particular to analyse or predict aspects concerning the data subject's performance at work, economic situation, health, personal preferences or interests, reliability or behaviour, location or movements" . . . . *"Such measure should not concern a child"*
22(2)(a-c)	71	**Article 22(2)** lifts the prohibition for processing based on **(a)** the performance of or entering into a contract, **(b)** Union or Member state law, or **(c)** explicit consent. **Recital 71** provides further context on **22(2)(b)** and says that processing described in **A22(1)**: "should be allowed where expressly authorised by Union or Member State law to which the controller is subject, including for fraud and tax-evasion monitoring and prevention purposes conducted in accordance with the regulations, standards and recommendations of Union institutions or national oversight bodies and to ensure the security and reliability of a service provided by the controller . . . "
22(3)	71	**Article 22 (3) and Recital 71** also specify that even in the cases referred to in **22(2)(a)** and **(c)** the processing should be subject to suitable safeguards. Recital 71: "which should include specific information to the data subject and the right to obtain human intervention, to express his or her point of view, to obtain an explanation of the decision reached after such assessment and to challenge the decision. Such measure should not concern a child."

Article	Recital	Comments
23	73	**Recital 73:** "Restrictions concerning specific principles and concerning . . . . .the right to object and decisions based on profiling . . . . .may be imposed by Union or Member State law as far as necessary and proportionate in a democratic society . . . " to safeguard specific objectives of general public interest.
35(3)(a)	91	Requirement to carry out a DPIA.
47(2)(e)		Binding corporate rules referred to in **47(1)** should specify at least " . . . . .the right not to be subject to decisions based solely on automated processing, including profiling in accordance with **Article 22**..."

ANNEX 3 - FURTHER READING

[2.211]
These Guidelines take account of the following:
- WP29 Advice paper on essential elements of a definition and a provision on profiling within the EU General Data Protection Regulation, adopted 13 May 2013;
- WP29 Opinion 2/2010 on online behavioural advertising, WP171;
- WP29 Opinion 03/2013 on Purpose limitation, WP 203;
- WP29 Opinion 06/2014 on the Notion of legitimate interests of the data controller under Article 7 of Directive 95/46/EC, WP217
- WP29 Statement on the role of a risk-based approach to data protection legal frameworks, WP218;
- WP29 Opinion 8/2014 on the Recent Developments on the Internet of Things, WP223;
- WP29 Guidelines on Data Protection Officers (DPOs), WP243;
- WP29 Guidelines on identifying a controller or processor's lead supervisory authority WP244;
- WP29 Guidelines on consent, WP259
- WP29 Guidelines on transparency, WP260
- Council of Europe. Recommendation CM/Rec(2010)13 on the protection of individuals with regard to automatic processing of personal data in the context of profiling;
- Council of Europe. Guidelines on the protection of individuals with regard to the processing of personal data in a world of Big Data, 01/2017
- Information Commissioner's Office – Big data, artificial intelligence, machine learning and data protection version 2.0, 03/2017
- Office of the Australian Commissioner - Consultation draft: Guide to big data and the Australian Privacy Principles, 05/2016
- European Data Protection Supervisor (EDPS) Opinion 7/2015 – Meeting the challenges of big data, 19 November 2015
- Datatilsynet – Big Data – privacy principles under pressure 09/2013
- Council of Europe. Convention for the protection of individuals with regard to automatic processing of personal data - Draft explanatory report on the modernised version of CoE Convention 108, August 2016
- Datatilsynet – The Great Data Race – How commercial utilisation of personal data challenges privacy. Report, November 2015
- European Data Protection Supervisor – Assessing the necessity of measures that limit the fundamental right to the protection of personal data: A Toolkit
- Joint Committee of the European Supervisory Authorities. Joint Committee Discussion Paper on the use of Big Data by financial institutions 2016-86. https://www.esma.europa.eu/sites/default/files/library/jc-2016-86_discussion_paper_big_data.pdf.
- Commission de la protection de la vie privée. Big Data Rapport https://www.privacycommission. be/sites/privacycommission/files/documents/Big%20Data%20voor%20MindMap%2022-02-17%20fr.pdf.
- United States Senate, Committee on Commerce, Science, and Transportation. A Review of the Data Broker Industry: Collection, Use, and Sale of Consumer Data for Marketing Purposes, Staff Report for Chairman Rockefeller, December 18, 2013. https://www.commerce.senate.gov/public/_cache/files/0d2b3642-6221-4888-a631-08f2f255b577/AE5D72CBE7F44F5BFC846BECE22C875B.12.18.13-senate-commerce-committee-report-on-data-broker-industry.pdf
- Lilian Edwards & Michael Veale. Slave to the Algorithm? Why a 'Right to an Explanation' is probably not the remedy you are looking for. Research paper, posted 24 May 2017. https://papers.ssrn.com/sol3/papers.cfm?abstract_id=2972855
- NYTimes.com. Showing the Algorithms behind New York City Services. https://mobile.nytimes.com/2017/08/24/nyregion/showing-the-algorithms-behind-new-york-city-services.html?referer=https://t.co/6uUVVjOIXx?amp=1. Accessed 24 August 2017
- Council of Europe. Recommendation CM/REC(2018)x of the Committee of Ministers to Member States on Guidelines to promote, protect and fulfil children's rights in the digital environment (revised draft, 25 July 2017). https://www.coe.int/en/web/children/-/call-for- consultation-

guidelines-for-member-states-to-promote-protect-and-fulfil-children-s-rights-in-the-digital
-environment?inheritRedirect=true&redirect=%2Fen%2Fweb%2Fchildren. Accessed 31 August
2017

– Unicef. Privacy, protection of personal information and reputation rights. Discussion paper series:
Children's Rights and Business in a Digital World. https://www.unicef.org/csr/files/
UNICEF_CRB_Digital_World_Series_PRIVACY.pdf. Accessed 31 August 2017

– House of Lords. Growing up with the internet. Select Committee on Communications, 2nd Report
of Sessions 2016 – 17. https://publications.parliament.uk/pa/ld201617/ldselect/ldcomuni/130/
13002.htm. Accessed 31 August 2017

– Sandra Wachter, Brent Mittelstadt and Luciano Floridi. Why a right to explanation of automated
decision-making does not exist in the General Data Protection Regulation, 28 December 2016.
https://www.turing.ac.uk/research_projects/data-ethics-group-deg/ . Accessed 13 December 2017

– Sandra Wachter, Brent Mittelstadt and Chris Russell. Counterfactual explanations Without Opening
the Black Box: Automated Decisions and the GDPR, 6 October 2017. https://papers.ssrn.com/sol3/
papers.cfm?abstract_id=3063289. Accessed 13 December 2017

– Australian Government. Better Practice Guide, Automated Assistance in Administrative
Decision-Making. Six steps methodology, plus summary of checklist points Part 7 February 2007.
https://www.oaic.gov.au/images/documents/migrated/migrated/betterpracticeguide.pdf. Accessed
9 January 2018

ARTICLE 29 DATA PROTECTION WORKING PARTY: GUIDELINES ON THE APPLICATION AND SETTING OF ADMINISTRATIVE FINES FOR THE PURPOSES OF THE REGULATION 2016/679

17/EN
WP 253

Adopted on 3 October 2017

[2.212]

NOTES
This document was originally issued by the Article 29 Working Party but subsequently endorsed by the EDPB during its first plenary meeting.
© European Data Protection Board.

TABLE OF CONTENTS

I. INTRODUCTION

[2.213]
The EU has completed a comprehensive reform of data protection regulation in Europe. The reform rests on several pillars (key components): coherent rules, simplified procedures, coordinated actions, user involvement, more effective information and stronger enforcement powers.

Data controllers and data processors have increased responsibilities to ensure that personal data of the individuals is protected effectively. Supervisory authorities have powers to ensure that the principles of the General Data Protection Regulation (hereafter 'the Regulation') as well as the rights of the individuals concerned are upheld according to the wording and the spirit of the Regulation.

Consistent enforcement of the data protection rules is central to a harmonized data protection regime. Administrative fines are a central element in the new enforcement regime introduced by the Regulation, being a powerful part of the enforcement toolbox of the supervisory authorities together with the other measures provided by article 58.

This document is intended for use by the supervisory authorities to ensure better application and enforcement of the Regulation and expresses their common understanding of the provisions of article 83 of the Regulation as well as its interplay with articles 58 and 70 and their corresponding recitals.

In particular, according to article 70, (1)(e), the European Data Protection Board (hereafter 'EDPB') is empowered to issue guidelines, recommendations and best practices in order to encourage consistent application of this Regulation and article 70, (1), (k) specifies the provision for guidelines concerning the setting of administrative fines.

These guidelines are not exhaustive, neither will they provide explanations about the differences between administrative, civil or criminal law systems when imposing administrative sanctions in general.

In order to achieve a consistent approach to the imposition of the administrative fines, which adequately reflects all of the principles in these guidelines, the EDPB has agreed on a common understanding of the assessment criteria in article 83 (2) of the Regulation and therefore the EDPB and individual supervisory authorities agree on using this Guideline as a common approach.

II. PRINCIPLES

[2.214]
Once an infringement of the Regulation has been established based on the assessment of the facts of the case, the competent supervisory authority must identify the most appropriate corrective measure(s) in order to address the infringement. The provisions of article 58 (2) b-j[1] indicate which tools the supervisory authorities may employ in order to address non-compliance from a controller or a processor. When using these powers, the supervisory authorities must observe the following principles:

1. INFRINGEMENT OF THE REGULATION SHOULD LEAD TO THE IMPOSITION OF "EQUIVALENT SANCTIONS".

The concept of "equivalence" is central in determining the extent of the obligations of the supervisory authorities to ensure consistency in their use of corrective powers according to article 58 (2) in general, and the application of administrative fines in particular[2].

*In order to ensure a consistent and high level of protection of natural persons and to remove the obstacles to flows of personal data within the Union, **the level of protection should be equivalent** in all Member States (recital 10). Recital 11 elaborates the fact that an equivalent level of protection of personal data throughout the Union requires, amongst others, "equivalent powers for monitoring and ensuring compliance with the rules for the protection of personal data and equivalent sanctions for infringements in the Member States.". Further more, equivalent sanctions in all Member States as well as effective cooperation between supervisory authorities of different Member States is seen as a way "to prevent divergences hampering the free movement of personal data within the internal market", in line with recital 13 of the Regulation.*

The Regulation sets a stronger basis than Directive 95/46/EC for a greater level of consistency as the Regulation is directly applicable in the Member States. While supervisory authorities operate with "complete independence" (article 52) with respect to national governments, controllers or processors, they are required to cooperate *"with a view to ensuring the consistency of application and enforcement of this Regulation"* (article 57, (1),(g)).

The Regulation calls for a greater consistency than the Directive 95/46 when imposing sanctions. In cross border cases, consistency shall be achieved primarily through the cooperation (one –stop-shop) mechanism and to some extent through the consistency mechanism set forth by the new Regulation.

In national cases covered by the Regulation, the supervisory authorities will apply these guidelines in the spirit of cooperation according to article 57, 1 (g) and article 63, with a view to ensuring the consistency of application and enforcement of the Regulation. Although supervisory authorities remain independent in their choice of the corrective measures presented in Article 58 (2), it should be avoided that different corrective measures are chosen by the supervisory authorities in similar cases.

The same principle applies when such corrective measures are imposed in the form of fines.

2. LIKE ALL CORRECTIVE MEASURES CHOSEN BY THE SUPERVISORY AUTHORITIES, ADMINISTRATIVE FINES SHOULD BE "EFFECTIVE, PROPORTIONATE AND DISSUASIVE".

Like all corrective measures in general, administrative fines should adequately respond to the nature, gravity and consequences of the breach, and supervisory authorities must assess all the facts of the case in a manner that is consistent and objectively justified. The assessment of what is effective, proportional and dissuasive in each case will have to also reflect the objective pursued by the corrective measure chosen, that is either to reestablish compliance with the rules, or to punish unlawful behavior (or both).

Supervisory authorities should identify a corrective measure that is *"effective, proportionate and dissuasive"* (art. 83 (1)), both in national cases (article 55) and in cases involving cross- border processing of personal data (as defined in article 4 (23)).

These guidelines recognize that national legislation may set additional requirements on the enforcement procedure to be followed by the supervisory authorities. This may for example include address notifications, form, deadlines for making representations, appeal, enforcement, payment[3].

Such requirements should however not hinder in practice the achievement of effectiveness, proportionality or dissuasiveness.

A more precise determination of effectiveness, proportionality or dissuasiveness will be generated by emerging practice within supervisory authorities (on data protection, as well as lessons learned from other regulatory sectors) as well as case-law when interpreting these principles.

In order to impose fines that are effective, proportionate and dissuasive, the supervisory authority shall use for the definition of the notion of an undertaking as provided for by the CJEU for the purposes of the application of Article 101 and 102 TFEU, namely that the concept of an undertaking **is understood to mean** an economic unit, which may be formed by the parent company and all involved subsidiaries. In accordance with EU law and case-law[4], an undertaking must be understood to be the economic unit, which engages in commercial/economic activities, regardless of the legal person involved (Recital 150).

3. THE COMPETENT SUPERVISORY AUTHORITY WILL MAKE AN ASSESSMENT "IN EACH INDIVIDUAL CASE".

Administrative fines may be imposed in response to a wide range of infringements. Article 83 of the Regulation provides a harmonized approach to breaches of obligations expressly listed in paras (4)-(6). Member State law may extend the application of article 83 to public authorities and bodies established in that Member State. Additionally, Member State law may allow for or even mandate the imposition of a fine for infringement of other provisions than those mentioned in article 83 (4)-(6).

The Regulation requires assessment of each case individually[5]. Article 83 (2) is the starting point for such an individual assessment. The paragraph states *"when deciding whether to impose an administrative fine, and deciding on the amount of the administrative fine in each individual case due regard shall be given to the following . . . "* Accordingly, and also in the light of Recital 148[6] the supervisory authority has the responsibility of choosing the most appropriate measure(s). In the cases mentioned in Article 83 (4) – (6), this choice **must** include consideration of all of the corrective measures, which would include consideration of the imposition of the appropriate administrative fine, either accompanying a corrective measure under Article 58(2) or on its own.

Fines are an important tool that supervisory authorities should use in appropriate circumstances. The supervisory authorities are encouraged to use a considered and balanced approach in their use of corrective measures, in order to achieve both an effective and dissuasive as well as a proportionate reaction to the breach. The point is not to qualify the fines as last resort, nor to shy away from issuing fines, but on the other hand not to use them in such a way which would devalue their effectiveness as a tool.

The EDPB, when competent according to article 65 of the Regulation, will issue a binding decision on disputes between authorities relating in particular to the determination of the existence of an infringement. When the relevant and reasoned objection raises the issue of the compliance of the corrective measure with the GDPR, the decision of EDPB will also discuss how the principles of effectiveness, proportionality and deterrence are observed in the administrative fine proposed in the draft decision of the competent supervisory authority . EDPB guidance on the application of article 65 of the Regulation will follow separately for further detail on the type of decision to be taken by the EDPB.

4. A HARMONIZED APPROACH TO ADMINISTRATIVE FINES IN THE FIELD OF DATA PROTECTION REQUIRES ACTIVE PARTICIPATION AND INFORMATION EXCHANGE AMONG SUPERVISORY AUTHORITIES

These guidelines acknowledge that fining powers represent for some national supervisory authorities a novelty in the field of data protection, raising numerous issues in terms of resources, organization and procedure. Notably, the decisions in which the supervisory authorities exercise the fining powers conferred to them will be subject to appeal before national courts.

Supervisory authorities shall cooperate with each other and where relevant, with the European Commission through the cooperation mechanisms as set out in the Regulation in order to support formal and informal information exchanges, such as through regular workshops. This cooperation would focus on their experience and practice in the application of the fining powers to ultimately achieve greater consistency.

This proactive information sharing, in addition to emerging case law on the use of these powers, may lead to the principles or the particular details of these guidelines being revisited.

NOTES

[1] Article 58 (2) a provides that warnings may be issued when "processing operations are likely to infringe provisions of the Regulation". In other words, in the case covered by the provision the infringement of the Regulation has not occurred yet.

[2] Even where the legal systems in some EU countries do not allow for the imposition of administrative fines as set out in the Regulation, such an application of the rules in those Member States needs to have an equivalent effect to administrative fines imposed by supervisory authorities (recital 151). The Courts are bound by the Regulation but they are not bound by these guidelines of the EDPB.

[3] As an example, the constitutional framework and draft data protection legislation of Ireland, provides that a formal decision is reached on the fact of the infringement itself, which is communicated to the relevant parties, before an assessment of the scale of the sanction(s). The decision on the fact of the infringement itself cannot be revisited during the assessment of the scale of the sanction(s).

[4] The ECJ case law definition is: «the concept of an undertaking encompasses every entity engaged in an economic activity regardless of the legal status of the entity and the way in which it is financed" (Case Höfner and Elsner, para 21, ECLI:EU:C:1991:161). An undertaking «must be understood as designating an economic unit even if in law that economic unit consists of several persons, natural or legal» (Case Confederación Española de Empresarios de Estaciones de Servicio [para 40, ECLI:EU:C:2006:784).

[5] Further to the application of article 83 criteria there are other provisions to bolster the foundation of this approach such as:
    – recital 141 *"the investigation following a complaint should be carried out, subject to judicial review, to the extent that is appropriate in the specific case."*
    – recital 129 *"The powers of supervisory authorities should be exercised in accordance with appropriate procedural safeguards set out in Union and Member State law, impartially, fairly and within a reasonable time. In particular each measure should be appropriate, necessary and proportionate in view of ensuring compliance with this Regulation, taking into account the circumstances of each individual case . . . ".*
    – article 57(1)(f) *"handle complaints lodged by a data subject, or by a body, organisation or association in accordance with article 8, and investigate to the extent appropriate, the subject matter of the complaint."*

6   *"In order to strengthen the enforcement of the rules of this Regulation, penalties including administrative fines should be imposed for any infringement of this Regulation, in addition to, or instead of appropriate measures imposed by the supervisory authority pursuant to this Regulation. In a case of a minor infringement or if the fine likely to be imposed would constitute a disproportionate burden to a natural person, a reprimand may be issued instead of a fine. Due regard should however be given to the nature, gravity and duration of the infringement, the intentional character of the infringement, actions taken to mitigate the damage suffered, degree of responsibility or any relevant previous infringements, the manner in which the infringement became known to the supervisory authority, compliance with measures ordered against the controller or processor, adherence to a code of conduct and any other aggravating or mitigating factor. The imposition of penalties including administrative fines should be subject to appropriate procedural safeguards in accordance with the general principles of Union law and the Charter, including effective judicial protection and due process".*

III. ASSESSMENT CRITERIA IN ARTICLE 83 (2)

[2.215]

Article 83 (2) provides a list of criteria the supervisory authorities are expected to use in the assessment both of whether a fine should be imposed and of the amount of the fine. This does not recommend a repeated assessment of the same criteria, but an assessment that takes into account all the circumstances of each individual case, as provided by article 83[7].

The conclusions reached in the first stage of the assessment may be used in the second part concerning the amount of the fine, thereby avoiding the need to assess using the same criteria twice.

This section provides guidance for the supervisory authorities of how to interpret the individual facts of the case in the light of the criteria in article 83 (2).

(A) THE NATURE, GRAVITY AND DURATION OF THE INFRINGEMENT

Almost all of the obligations of the controllers and processors according to the Regulation are categorised according to their **nature** in the provisions of article 83(4) – (6) . The Regulation, in setting up two different maximum amounts of administrative fine (10/20 million Euros), already indicates that a breach of some provisions of the Regulation may be more serious than for other provisions. However the competent supervisory authority, by assessing the facts of the case in light of the general criteria provided in article 83 (2), may decide that in the particular case there is a higher or a more reduced need to react with a corrective measure in the form of a fine. Where a fine has been chosen as the one or one of several appropriate corrective measure(s), the tiering system of the Regulation (article 83 (4)- 83 (6)) will be applied in order to identify the maximum fine that can be imposed according to the nature of the infringement in question.

Recital 148 introduces the notion of "minor infringements". Such infringements may constitute breaches of one or several of the Regulation's provisions listed in article 83 (4) or (5). The assessment of the criteria in article 83 (2) may however lead the supervisory authority to believe that in the concrete circumstances of the case, the breach for example, does not pose a significant risk to the rights of the data subjects concerned and does not affect the essence of the obligation in question. In such cases, the fine may (but not always) be replaced by a reprimand.

Recital 148 does not contain an obligation for the supervisory authority to always replace a fine by a reprimand in the case of a minor infringement (*"a reprimand may be issued instead of a fine"*), but rather a possibility that is at hand, following a concrete assessment of all the circumstances of the case.

Recital 148 opens up the same possibility to replace a fine by a reprimand , where the data controller is a natural person and the fine likely to be imposed would constitute a disproportionate burden. The starting point is that the supervisory authority has to assess whether, considering the circumstances of the case at hand, the imposition of a fine is required. If it finds in favour of imposing a fine, then the supervisory authority must also assess whether the fine to be imposed would constitute a disproportionate burden to a natural person.

Specific infringements are not given a specific price tag in the Regulation, only a cap (maximum amount). This can be indicative of a relative lower degree of gravity for a breach of obligations listed in article 83(4), compared with those set out in article 83(5). The effective, proportionate and dissuasive reaction to a breach of article 83(5) will however depend on the circumstances of the case.

It should be noticed that breaches of the Regulation, which by their nature might fall into the category of "up to 10 million Euros or up to 2% of total annual worldwide turnover" as set out in article 83 (4), might end up qualifying for a higher tier (Euro 20 million) category in certain circumstances. This would be likely to be the case where such breaches have previously been addressed in an order from the supervisory authority, an order[8] which the controller or processor failed to comply with[9] (article 83 (6)). The provisions of the national law may in practice have an impact on this assessment[10]. The nature of the infringement, but also *"the scope, purpose of the processing concerned as well as the number of data subjects affected and the level of damage suffered by them"*, will be indicative of the **gravity** of the infringement. The occurrence of several different infringements committed together in any particular single case means that the supervisory authority is able to apply the administrative fines at a level which is effective, proportionate and dissuasive within the limit of the gravest infringement. Therefore, if an infringement of article 8 and article 12 has been discovered, then the supervisory authority may be able to apply the corrective measures as set out in article 83(5) which correspond to the category of the gravest infringement, namely article 12. More detail at this stage is beyond the scope of this particular guideline (as detailed calculation work would be the focus of a potential subsequent stage of this guideline).

The factors below should be assessed in combination eg. the number of data subjects together with the possible impact on them.

The number of data subjects involved should be assessed, in order to identify whether this is an isolated event or symptomatic of a more systemic breach or lack of adequate routines in place. This is not to say that isolated events should not be enforceable, as an isolated event could still affect a lot of data subjects. This will, depending on the circumstances of the case, be relative to, for example, the total number of registrants in the database in question, the number of users of a service, the number of customers, or in relation to the population of the country, as appropriate.

The purpose of the processing must also be assessed. The WP 29 opinion on "purpose limitation"[11] previously analysed the two main building blocks of this principle in data protection law: purpose specification and compatible use. When assessing the purpose of the processing in the context of article 83 (2), the supervisory authorities should look into the extent to which the processing upholds the two key components of this principle[12]. In certain situations, the supervisory authority might find it necessary to factor in a deeper analysis of the purpose of the processing in itself in the analysis of article 83 (2).

If the data subjects have suffered **damage**, the level of the damage has to be taken into consideration. Processing of personal data may generate risks for the rights and freedoms of the individual, as illustrated by recital 75:

> *"The risk to the rights and freedoms of natural persons, of varying likelihood and severity, may result from personal data processing which could lead to physical, material or non- material damage, in particular: where the processing may give rise to discrimination, identity theft or fraud, financial loss, damage to the reputation, loss of confidentiality of personal data protected by professional secrecy, unauthorised reversal of pseudonymisation, or any other significant economic or social disadvantage; where data subjects might be deprived of their rights and freedoms or prevented from exercising control over their personal data; where personal data are processed which reveal racial or ethnic origin, political opinions, religion or philosophical beliefs, trade union membership, and the processing of genetic data, data concerning health or data concerning sex life or criminal convictions and offences or related security measures; where personal aspects are evaluated, in particular analysing or predicting aspects concerning performance at work, economic situation, health, personal preferences or interests, reliability or behaviour, location or movements, in order to create or use personal profiles; where personal data of vulnerable natural persons, in particular of children, are processed; or where processing involves a large amount of personal data and affects a large number of data subjects."*

If damages have been or are likely to be suffered due to the infringement of the Regulation then the supervisory authority should take this into account in its choice of corrective measure, although the supervisory authority itself is not competent to award the specific compensation for the damage suffered.

The imposition of a fine is not dependent on the ability of the supervisory authority to establish a causal link between the breach and the material loss (see for example article 83 (6)).

Duration of the infringement may be illustrative of, for example:
(a)   wilful conduct on the data controller's part, or
(b)   failure to take appropriate preventive measures, or
(c)   inability to put in place the required technical and organisational measures.

(B) THE INTENTIONAL OR NEGLIGENT CHARACTER OF THE INFRINGEMENT

In general, "intent" includes both knowledge and wilfulness in relation to the characteristics of an offence, whereas "unintentional" means that there was no intention to cause the infringement although the controller/processor breached the duty of care which is required in the law.

It is generally admitted that intentional breaches, demonstrating contempt for the provisions of the law, are more severe than unintentional ones and therefore may be more likely to warrant the application of an administrative fine. The relevant conclusions about wilfulness or negligence will be drawn on the basis of identifying objective elements of conduct gathered from the facts of the case. In addition, emergent case law and practice in the field of data protection under the application of the Regulation will be illustrative of circumstances indicating clearer thresholds for assessing whether a breach was intentional.

Circumstances indicative of intentional breaches might be unlawful processing authorised explicitly by the top management hierarchy of the controller, or in spite of advice from the data protection officer or in disregard for existing policies, for example obtaining and processing data about employees at a competitor with an intention to discredit that competitor in the market.

Other examples here might be:
•   amending personal data to give a misleading (positive) impression about whether targets have been met – we have seen this in the context of targets for hospital waiting times
•   the trade of personal data for marketing purpose ie selling data as 'opted in' without checking/disregarding data subjects' views about how their data should be used

Other circumstances, such as failure to read and abide by existing policies, human error, failure to check for personal data in information published, failure to apply technical updates in a timely manner, failure to adopt policies (rather than simply failure to apply them)may be indicative of negligence.

Enterprises should be responsible for adopting structures and resources adequate to the nature and complexity of their business. As such, controllers and processors cannot legitimise breaches of data protection law by claiming a shortage of resources. Routines and documentation of processing activities follow a risk-based approach according to the Regulation.

There are grey areas which will affect decision-making in relation to whether or not to impose a corrective measure and the authority may need to do more extensive investigation to ascertain the facts of the case and to ensure that all specific circumstances of each individual case were sufficiently taken into account.

(C) ANY ACTION TAKEN BY THE CONTROLLER OR PROCESSOR TO MITIGATE THE DAMAGE SUFFERED BY DATA SUBJECTS;

The data controllers and processors have an obligation to implement technical and organisational measures to ensure a level of security appropriate to the risk, to carry out data protection impact assessments and mitigate risks arising form the processing of personal data to the rights and freedoms of the individuals. However, when a breach occurs and the data subject has suffered damage, the responsible party should do whatever they can do in order to reduce the consequences of the breach for the individual(s) concerned. Such responsible behaviour (or the lack of it) would be taken into account by the supervisory authority in their choice of corrective measure(s) as well as in the calculation of the sanction to be imposed in the specific case.

Although aggravating and mitigating factors are particularly suited to fine-tune the amount of a fine to the particular circumstances of the case, their role in the choice of appropriate corrective measure should not be underestimated. In cases where the assessment based on other criteria leaves the supervisory authority in doubt about the appropriateness of an administrative fine, as a standalone corrective measure, or in combination with other measures in article 58, such aggravating or attenuating circumstances may help to choose the appropriate measures by tipping the balance in favour of what proves more effective, proportionate and dissuasive in the given case.

This provision acts as an assessment of the degree of responsibility of the controller after the infringement has occurred. It may cover cases where the controller/processor has clearly not taken a reckless/ negligent approach but where they have done all they can to correct their actions when they became aware of the infringement.

Regulatory experience from SAs under the 95/46/EC Directive has previously shown that it can be appropriate to show some degree of flexibility to those data controllers/processors who have admitted to their infringement and taken responsibility to correct or limit the impact of their actions. This might include examples such as (although this would not lead to a more flexible approach in every case):
- contacting other controllers/processors who may have been involved in an extension of the processing e.g. if there has been a piece of data mistakenly shared with third parties.
- timely action taken by the data controller/processor to stop the infringement from continuing or expanding to a level or phase which would have had a far more serious impact than it did.

(D) THE DEGREE OF RESPONSIBILITY OF THE CONTROLLER OR PROCESSOR TAKING INTO ACCOUNT TECHNICAL AND ORGANISATIONAL MEASURES IMPLEMENTED BY THEM PURSUANT TO ARTICLES 25 AND 32;

The Regulation has introduced a far greater level of accountability of the data controller in comparison with the EC Data Protection Directive 95/46/EC.

The degree of responsibility of the controller or processor assessed against the backdrop of applying an appropriate corrective measure may include:
- Has the controller implemented technical measures that follow the principles of data protection by design or by default (article 25)?
- Has the controller implemented organisational measures that give effect to the principles of data protection by design and by default (article 25) at all levels of the organisation?
- Has the controller/processor implemented an appropriate level of security (article 32)?
- Are the relevant data protection routines/policies known and applied at the appropriate level of management in the organisation? (Article 24).

Article 25 and article 32 of the Regulation require that the controllers "*take into account the state of the art, the cost of implementation and the nature, scope, context, and purposes of the processing, as well as the risks of varying likelihood and severity for rights and freedoms for the natural persons posed by the processing*". Rather than being an obligation of goal, these provisions introduce obligations of means, that is, the controller must make the necessary assessments and reach the appropriate conclusions. The question that the supervisory authority must then answer is to what extent the controller "*did what it could be expected to do*" given the nature, the purposes or the size of the processing, seen in light of the obligations imposed on them by the Regulation.

In this assessment, due account should be taken of any "best practice" procedures or methods where these exist and apply. Industry standards, as well as codes of conduct in the respective field or profession are important to take into account. Codes of practice might give an indication as to what is common practice in the field and an indication of the level of knowledge about different means to address typical security issues associated with the processing.

While best practice should be the ideal to pursue in general, the special circumstances of each individual case must be taken into account when making the assessment of the degree of responsibility.

(E) ANY RELEVANT PREVIOUS INFRINGEMENTS BY THE CONTROLLER OR PROCESSOR;

This criterion is meant to assess the track record of the entity committing the infringement. Supervisory authorities should consider that the scope of the assessment here can be quite wide because any type of breach of the Regulation, though different in nature to the one being investigated now by the supervisory authority might be "relevant" for the assessment, as it could be indicative of a general level of insufficient knowledge or disregard for the data protection rules.

The supervisory authority should assess:
* Has the controller/processor committed the same infringement earlier?
* Has the controller/ processor committed an infringement of the Regulation in the same manner? (for example as a consequence of insufficient knowledge of existing routines in the organisation, or as a consequence of inappropriate risk assessment, not being responsive to requests from the data subject in a timely manner, unjustified delay in responding to requests and so on).

(F) THE DEGREE OF COOPERATION WITH THE SUPERVISORY AUTHORITY, IN ORDER TO REMEDY THE INFRINGEMENT AND MITIGATE THE POSSIBLE ADVERSE EFFECTS OF THE INFRINGEMENT;

Article 83 (2) provides that the degree of cooperation may be given "due regard" when deciding whether to impose an administrative fine and in deciding on the amount of the fine. The Regulation does not give a precise answer to the question how to take into account the efforts of the controllers or the processors to remedy an infringement already established by the supervisory authority. Moreover, it is clear that the criteria would usually be applied when calculating the amount of the fine to be imposed.

However, where intervention of the controller has had the effect that negative consequences on the rights of the individuals did not produce or had a more limited impact than they could have otherwise done, this could also be taken into account in the choice of corrective measure that is proportionate in the individual case.

One example of a case where cooperation with the supervisory authority might be relevant to consider might be:
* Has the entity responded in a particular manner to the supervisory authority's requests during the investigation phase in that specific case which has significantly limited the impact on individuals' rights as a result?

This said, it would not be appropriate to give additional regard to cooperation that is already required by law for example, the entity is in any case required to allow the supervisory authority access to premises for audits/inspections.

(G) THE CATEGORIES OF THE PERSONAL DATA AFFECTED BY THE INFRINGEMENT;

Some examples of key questions that the supervisory authority may find it necessary to answer here, if appropriate to the case, are:
* Does the infringement concern processing of special categories of data set out in articles 9 or 10 of the Regulation?
* Is the data directly identifiable/ indirectly identifiable?
* Does the processing involve data whose dissemination would cause immediate damage/distress to the individual (which falls outside the category of article 9 or 10)?
* Is the data directly available without technical protections, or is it encrypted[13]?

(H) THE MANNER IN WHICH THE INFRINGEMENT BECAME KNOWN TO THE SUPERVISORY AUTHORITY, IN PARTICULAR WHETHER, AND IF SO TO WHAT EXTENT, THE CONTROLLER OR PROCESSOR NOTIFIED THE INFRINGEMENT;

A supervisory authority might become aware about the infringement as a result of investigation, complaints, articles in the press, anonymous tips or notification by the data controller. The controller has an obligation according to the Regulation to notify the supervisory authority about personal data breaches. Where the controller merely fulfils this obligation, compliance with the obligation cannot be interpreted as an attenuating/ mitigating factor. Similarly, a data controller/processor who acted carelessly without notifying, or at least not notifying all of the details of the infringement due to a failure to adequately assess the extent of the infringement may also be considered by the supervisory authority to merit a more serious penalty i.e. it is unlikely to be classified as a minor infringement.

(I) WHERE MEASURES REFERRED TO IN ARTICLE 58(2) HAVE PREVIOUSLY BEEN ORDERED AGAINST THE CONTROLLER OR PROCESSOR CONCERNED WITH REGARD TO THE SAME SUBJECT-MATTER, COMPLIANCE WITH THOSE MEASURES;

A controller or processor may already be on the supervisory authority's radar for monitoring their compliance after a previous infringement and contacts with the DPO where they exist are likely to have been extensive. Therefore, the supervisory authority will take into account the previous contacts.

As opposed to the criteria in (e), this assessment criteria only seeks to remind supervisory authorities to refer to measures that they themselves have previously issued to the same controller or processors "*with regard to the same subject matter*".

(J) ADHERENCE TO APPROVED CODES OF CONDUCT PURSUANT TO ARTICLE 40 OR APPROVED CERTIFICATION MECHANISMS PURSUANT TO ARTICLE 42;

Supervisory authorities have a duty to *"monitor and enforce the application of this Regulation,* (article 57 1 (a))". Adherence to approved codes of conduct may be used by the controller or processor as an way to demonstrate compliance, according to articles 24 (3), 28 (5) or 32 (3).

In case of a breach of one of the provisions of the Regulation, adherence to an approved code of conduct might be indicative of how comprehensive the need is to intervene with an effective, proportionate, dissuasive administrative fine or other corrective measure from the supervisory authority. Approved codes of conduct will, according to article 40 (4) contain *"mechanisms which enable the (monitoring) body to carry out mandatory monitoring of compliance with its provisions"*.

Where the controller or processor has adhered to an approved code of conduct, the supervisory authority may be satisfied that the code community in charge of administering the code takes the appropriate action themselves against their member, for example through the monitoring and enforcement schemes of the code of conduct itself. Therefore, the supervisory authority might consider that such measures are effective, proportionate or dissuasive enough in that particular case without the need for imposing additional measures from the supervisory authority itself. Certain forms of sanctioning non-compliant behaviour may be made through the monitoring scheme, according to article 41 (2) c and 42 (4), including suspension or exclusion of the controller or processor concerned from the code community. Nevertheless, the powers of the monitoring body are *"without prejudice to the tasks and powers of the competent supervisory authority"*, which means that the supervisory authority is not under an obligation to take into account previously imposed sanctions pertaining to the self-regulatory scheme.

Non-compliance with self-regulatory measures could also reveal the controller's/processor's negligence or intentional behaviour of non-compliance.

(K) ANY OTHER AGGRAVATING OR MITIGATING FACTOR APPLICABLE TO THE CIRCUMSTANCES OF THE CASE, SUCH AS FINANCIAL BENEFITS GAINED, OR LOSSES AVOIDED, DIRECTLY OR INDIRECTLY, FROM THE INFRINGEMENT.

The provision itself gives examples of which other elements might be taken into account when deciding the appropriateness of an administrative fine for an infringement of the provisions mentioned in Article 83(4–6).

Information about profit obtained as a result of a breach may be particularly important for the supervisory authorities as economic gain from the infringement cannot be compensated through measures that do not have a pecuniary component. As such, the fact that the controller had profited from the infringement of the Regulation may constitute a strong indication that a fine should be imposed.

NOTES

7   The assessment of the sanction to be applied may come separately after the assessment of whether there has been an infringement due to national procedural rules arising from constitutional requirements in some countries. Therefore, this may limit the content and the amount of detail in a draft decision issued by lead supervisory authority in such countries.

8   The orders, provided in article 58 (2) are:
   • to order the controller or the processor to comply with the data subject's requests to exercise his or her rights pursuant to this Regulation;
   • to order the controller or processor to bring processing operations into compliance with the provisions of this Regulation, where appropriate, in a specified manner and within a specified period;
   • to order the controller to communicate a personal data breach to the data subject;
   • to impose a temporary or definitive limitation including a ban on processing
   • to order the rectification or erasure of personal data or restriction of processing pursuant to Articles 16, 17 and 18 and the notification of such actions to recipients to whom the personal data have been disclosed pursuant to Article 17(2) and Article 19;
   • to order the certification body to withdraw a certification issued pursuant to Articles 42 and 43, or to order the certification body not to issue certification if the requirements for the certification are not or are no longer met;
   • to order the suspension of data flows to a recipient in a third country or to an international organisation.

9   Application of article 83(6) necessarily must take into account national law on procedure. National law determines how an order is issued, how it is notified, from which point it takes effect, whether there is a grace period to work on compliance. Notably, the effect of an appeal on the enforceability of an order should be taken into account.

10   Statutory provisions of limitation may have the effect that a previous order of the supervisory authority may no longer be taken in to consideration due to the amount of time that has lapsed since that previous order was issued. In some jurisdictions, rules require that after the prescription period has passed with respect to an order, no fine may be imposed for non-compliance with that order under article 83(6). It will be up to each supervisory authority in each jurisdiction to determine how such impacts will affect them.

11   WP 203, Opinion 03/2013 on purpose limitation, available at: http://ec.europa.eu/justice/dataprotection/article-29/documentation/opinion-recommendation/files/2013/wp203_en.pdf

12   See also Wp 217, opinion 6/2014 on the notion of legitimate interest of the data controller under article 7, page 24, on the question: "What makes an interest "legitimate" or "illegitimate"?"

13   It shouldn't always be considered 'a bonus' mitigating factor that the breach only concerns indirectly identifiable or even pseudonymous/encrypted data. For those breaches, an overall assessment of the other criteria might give a moderate or strong indication that a fine should be imposed.

IV. CONCLUSION

[2.216]

Reflections on the questions such as those provided in the previous section will help supervisory authorities identify, from the relevant facts of the case, those criteria which are most useful in reaching a decision on whether to impose an appropriate administrative fine in addition to or instead of other measures under Article 58. Taking into account the context provided by such assessment, the supervisory authority will identify the most effective, proportionate and dissuasive corrective measure to respond to the breach.

Article 58 provides some guidance as to which measures a supervisory authority might choose, as the corrective measures in themselves are different in nature and suited primarily for achieving different purposes. Some of the measures in article 58 may even be possible to cumulate, therefore achieving a regulatory action comprising more than one corrective measure.

It is not always necessary to supplement the measure through the use of another corrective measure. For example: The effectiveness and dissuasiveness of the intervention by the supervisory authority with its due consideration of what is proportionate to that specific case may be achieved through the fine alone.

In essence, authorities need to restore compliance through all of the corrective measures available to them. Supervisory authorities will also be required to choose the most appropriate channel for pursuing regulatory action. For example, this could include penal sanctions (where these are available at national level).

The practice of applying administrative fines consistently across the European Union is an evolving art. Actions should be taken by supervisory authorities working together to improve consistency on an ongoing basis. This can be achieved through regular exchanges through case-handling workshops or other events which allow the comparison of cases from the sub-national, national and cross-border levels. The creation of a permanent sub-group attached to a relevant part of the EDPB is recommended to support this ongoing activity.

ARTICLE 29 DATA PROTECTION WORKING PARTY: ADEQUACY REFERENTIAL
18/EN
WP 254 rev.01
Adopted on 28 November 2017

As last Revised and Adopted on 6 February 2018

[2.217]

NOTES

This document was originally issued by the Article 29 Working Party but subsequently endorsed by the EDPB during its first plenary meeting.

© European Data Protection Board.

TABLE OF CONTENTS

INTRODUCTION

[2.218]

The Working Party of EU Data Protection Authorities[1] (the WP29) has previously published a Working Document on transfers of personal data to third countries (WP12)[2]. With the replacement of the Directive by the EU General Data Protection Regulation (GDPR)[3], WP29 is revisiting WP12, its earlier guidance, to update it in the context of the new legislation and recent case law of the European Court of Justice (CJEU)[4].

This working document seeks to update Chapter One of WP12 relating to the central question of adequate level of data protection in a third country, a territory or one or more specified sectors within that third country or in an international organization (hereafter: "third countries or international organizations"). This document will be continuously reviewed and if necessary updated in the coming years, based on the practical experience gained through the application of the GDPR. Chapters 2 (*Applying the approach to countries that have ratified Convention 108*) and 3 (*Applying the approach to industry self-regulation*) of the WP12 document should be updated at a later stage.

This working paper is focused solely on adequacy decisions, which are implementing acts[5] of the European Commission, according to article 45 of the GDPR. Other aspects of transfers of personal data to third countries and international organizations will be examined in following working papers that will be published separately (BCRs, derogations).

This document aims to provide guidance to the European Commission and the WP29 under the GDPR for the assessment of the level of data protection in third countries and international organizations by establishing the core data protection principles that have to be present in a third country legal framework or an international organization in order to ensure essential equivalence with the EU framework. In addition, it may guide third countries and international organizations interested in obtaining adequacy. However, the principles set out in this working document are not addressed directly to data controllers or data processors.

The present document consists of 4 Chapters:

Chapter 1: Some broad information in relation to the concept on adequacy

Chapter 2: Procedural aspects for adequacy findings under the GDPR

Chapter 3: General Data Protection Principles. This chapter includes the core general data protection principles to ensure that the level of data protection in a third country or international organization is essentially equivalent to the one established by the EU legislation.

Chapter 4: Essential guarantees for law enforcement and national security access to limit the interferences to fundamental rights. This Chapter includes the essential guarantees for law enforcement and national security access following the CJEU Schrems judgment in 2015 and based on the Essential Guarantees WP29 working document adopted in 2016.

NOTES

1   As established under Article 29 of the EU Data Protection Directive 95/46/EC
2   WP12, 'Working Document: Transfers of personal data to third countries : Applying Articles 25 and 26 of the EU data protection directive' adopted by the Working Part on 24 July 1998.
3   Regulation (EU) 2016/679 of the European Parliament and of the Council of 27 April 2016 on the protection of natural persons with regard to the processing of personal data and on the free movement of such data, and repealing Directive 95/46/EC (General Data Protection Regulation) (Text with EEA relevance)
4   Including Case C-362/14, Maximillian Schrems v Data Protection Commissioner, 6 October 2015
5   See relevant articles 45(3) and 93(2) of the GDPR for further information on the implementing acts

CHAPTER 1: SOME BROAD INFORMATION IN RELATION TO THE CONCEPT OF ADEQUACY

[2.219]
Article 45, paragraph (1) of the GDPR sets out the principle that data transfers to a third country or international organization shall only take place if the third country, territory or one or more specified sectors within that third country or the international organization in question, ensures an adequate level of protection.

This concept of "adequate level of protection" which already existed under Directive 95/46, has been further developed by the CJEU. At this point it is important to recall the standard set by the CJEU in Schrems, namely that while the "*level of protection*" in the third country must be "essentially equivalent" to that guaranteed in the EU, "*the means to which that third country has recourse, in this connection, for the purpose of such a level of protection may differ from those employed within the [EU]*"[6]. Therefore, the objective is not to mirror point by point the European legislation, but to establish the essential – core requirements of that legislation.

The purpose of adequacy decisions by the European Commission is to formally confirm with binding effects on Member States[7] that the level of data protection in a third country or an international organization is essentially equivalent to the level of data protection in the European Union[8]. Adequacy can be achieved through a combination of rights for the data subjects and obligations on those who process data, or who exercise control over such processing and supervision by independent bodies. However, data protection rules are only effective if they are enforceable and followed in practice. It is therefore necessary to consider not only the content of rules applicable to personal data transferred to a third country or an international organization, but also the system in place to ensure the effectiveness of such rules. Efficient enforcement mechanisms are of paramount importance to the effectiveness of data protection rules.

Article 45, paragraph (2) of the GDPR, establishes the elements that the European Commission shall take into account when assessing the adequacy of the level of protection in a third country or international organization.

For example, the Commission shall take into consideration the rule of law, respect for human rights and fundamental freedoms, relevant legislation, the existence and effective functioning of one or more independent supervisory authorities and the international commitments the third country or international organization has entered into.

It is therefore clear that any meaningful analysis of adequate protection must comprise the two basic elements: the content of the rules applicable and the means for ensuring their effective application. It is upon the European Commission to verify – on a regular basis - that the rules in place are effective in practice.

The 'core' of data protection 'content' principles and 'procedural/enforcement' requirements, which could be seen as a minimum requirement for protection to be adequate, are derived from the EU Charter of Fundamental Rights and the GDPR. In addition, consideration should also be given to other international agreements on data protection, e.g. Convention 108.[9]

Attention must also be paid to the legal framework for the access of public authorities to personal data. Further guidance on this is provided in Working paper 237 (i.e. the Essential Guarantees document)[10] on safeguards in the context of surveillance.

General provisions regarding data protection and privacy in the third country are not sufficient. On the contrary, specific provisions addressing concrete needs for practically relevant aspects of the right to data protection must be included in the third country's or international organization's legal framework. These provisions have to be enforceable.

NOTES
6   Case C-362/14, Maximillian Schrems v Data Protection Commissioner, 6 October 2015 (§§ 73, 74);
7   Article 288 (2) TFEU
8   Case C-362/14, Maximillian Schrems v Data Protection Commissioner, 6 October 2015 (§§ 52);
9   Recital 105 of the GDPR
10   Working Document 01/2016 on the justification of interferences with the fundamental rights to privacy and data protection through surveillance measures when transferring personal data (European Essential Guarantees), 16/EN WP 237, 13 April 2016

CHAPTER 2: PROCEDURAL ASPECTS FOR ADEQUACY FINDINGS UNDER THE GDPR

[2.220]
For the EDPB to fulfil its task in advising the European Commission according to Article 70(1)(s) of the GDPR the EDPB should be provided with relevant documentation, including relevant correspondence and the findings made by the European Commission. Where the legal framework is complex, this should include any report prepared on the data protection level of the third country or international organization. In any case, the information provided by the European Commission should be exhaustive and put the EDPB in a position to make an own assessment regarding the level of data protection in the third country. The EDPB will provide an opinion on the European Commission's findings in due time and, identify insufficiencies in the adequacy framework, if any. The EDPB will also endeavour to propose alterations or amendments to address possible insufficiencies.

According to Article 45 (4) of the GDPR it is upon the European Commission to monitor – on an ongoing basis - developments that could affect the functioning of an adequacy decision.

Article 45 (3) of the GDPR provides that a periodic review must take place at least every four years. This is, however, a general time frame which must be adjusted to each third country or international organization with an adequacy decision. Depending on the particular circumstances at hand, a shorter review cycle could be warranted. Also, incidents or other information about or changes in the legal framework in the third country or international organization in question might trigger the need for a review ahead of schedule. It also appears to be appropriate to have a first review of an entirely new adequacy decision rather soon and gradually adjust the review cycle depending on the outcome.

Given the mandate to provide the European Commission with an opinion on whether the third country, a territory or one or more specified sectors in this third country or an international organization, no longer ensures an adequate level of protection, the EDPB must, in due time, receive meaningful information regarding the monitoring of the relevant developments in that third country or international organization by the EU Commission. Hence, the EDPB should be kept informed of any review process and review mission in the third country or to the international organization. The EDPB would appreciate to be invited to participate in these review processes and missions.

It should also be noted that according to article 45 (5) of the GDPR the European Commission has the right to repeal, amend or suspend existing adequacy decisions. The procedure to repeal, amend or suspend should consequently involve the EDPB by requesting its opinion pursuant art. 70(1)(s).

Furthermore, as now recognized in article 58 (5) of the GDPR and according to the CJEU's Schrems ruling, data protection authorities must be able to engage in legal proceedings if they find a claim by a person against an adequacy decision well founded: *"It is incumbent upon the national legislature to provide for legal remedies enabling the national supervisory authority concerned to put forward the objections which it considers well founded before the national courts in order for them, if they share its doubts as to the validity of the Commission decision, to make a reference for a preliminary ruling for the purpose of examination of the decision's validity"*[11].

NOTES
11   Case C-362/14, Maximillian Schrems v Data Protection Commissioner, 6 October 2015 (§ 65)

CHAPTER 3: GENERAL DATA PROTECTION PRINCIPLES TO ENSURE THAT THE LEVEL OF PROTECTION IN A THIRD COUNTRY, TERRITORY OR ONE OR MORE SPECIFIED SECTORS WITHIN THAT THIRD COUNTRY OR INTERNATIONAL ORGANIZATION IS ESSENTIALLY EQUIVALENT TO THE ONE GUARANTEED BY THE EU LEGISLATION

[2.221]
A third country's or international organisation's system must contain the following basic content and procedural/enforcement data protection principles and mechanisms:

A. CONTENT PRINCIPLES:

1) Concepts

Basic data protection concepts and/or principles should exist. These do not have to mirror the GDPR terminology but should reflect and be consistent with the concepts enshrined in the European data protection law. By way of example, the GDPR includes the following important concepts: "personal data", "processing of personal data", "data controller", "data processor", "recipient" and "sensitive data".

2) Grounds for lawful and fair processing for legitimate purposes

Data must be processed in a lawful, fair and legitimate manner.

The legitimate bases, under which personal data may be lawfully, fairly and legitimately processed should be set out in a sufficiently clear manner. The European framework acknowledges several such legitimate grounds including for example, provisions in national law, the consent of the data subject, performance of a contract or legitimate interest of the data controller or of a third party which does not override the interests of the individual.

3) The purpose limitation principle

Data should be processed for a specific purpose and subsequently used only insofar as this is not incompatible with the purpose of the processing.

4) The data quality and proportionality principle

Data should be accurate and, where necessary, kept up to date. The data should be adequate, relevant and not excessive in relation to the purposes for which they are processed.

5) Data Retention principle

Data should, as a general rule, be kept for no longer than is necessary for the purposes for which the personal data is processed.

6) The security and confidentiality principle

Any entity processing personal data should ensure that the data are processed in a manner that ensures security of the personal data, including protection against unauthorized or unlawful processing and against accidental loss, destruction or damage, using appropriate technical or organisational measures. The level of the security should take into consideration the state of the art and the related costs.

7) The transparency principle

Each individual should be informed of all the main elements of the processing of his/her personal data in a clear, easily accessible, concise, transparent and intelligible form. Such information should include the purpose of the processing, the identity of the data controller, the rights made available to him/her and other information insofar as this is necessary to ensure fairness. Under certain conditions, some exceptions to this right for information can exist, such as for example, to safeguard criminal investigations, national security, judicial independence and judicial proceedings or other important objectives of general public interest as is the case with Article 23 of the GDPR.

8) The right of access, rectification, erasure and objection

The data subject should have the right to obtain confirmation about whether or not data processing concerning him / her is taking place as well as access his/her data, including obtaining a copy of all data relating to him/her that are processed.

The data subject should have the right to obtain rectification of his/her data as appropriate, for specified reasons, for example, where they are shown to be inaccurate or incomplete and erasure of his/her personal data when for example their processing is no longer necessary or unlawful.

The data subject should also have the right to object on compelling legitimate grounds relating to his/her particular situation, at any time, to the processing of his/her data under specific conditions established in the third country legal framework. In the GDPR, for example, such conditions include when the processing is necessary for the performance of a task carried out in the public interest or when it is necessary for the exercise of official authority vested in the controller or when the processing is necessary for the purposes of the legitimate interests pursued by the data controller or a third party.

The exercise of those rights should not be excessively cumbersome for the data subject. Possible restrictions to these rights could exist for example to safeguard criminal investigations, national security, judicial independence and judicial proceedings or other important objectives of general public interest as is the case with Article 23 of the GDPR.

9) Restrictions on onward transfers

Further transfers of the personal data by the initial recipient of the original data transfer should be permitted only where the further recipient (i.e. the recipient of the onward transfer) is also subject to rules (including contractual rules) affording an adequate level of protection and following the relevant instructions when processing data on the behalf of the data controller. The level of protection of natural persons whose data is transferred must not be undermined by the onward transfer. The initial recipient of the data transferred from the EU shall be liable to ensure that appropriate safeguards are provided for onward transfers of data in the absence of an adequacy decision. Such onward transfers of data should only take place for limited and specified purposes and as long as there is a legal ground for that processing.

B. EXAMPLES OF ADDITIONAL CONTENT PRINCIPLES TO BE APPLIED TO SPECIFIC TYPES OF PROCESSING:

1) Special categories of data

Specific safeguards should exist where 'special categories of data are involved[12]. These categories should reflect those enshrined in Article 9 and 10 of the GDPR. This protection should be put in place, through more demanding requirements for the data processing such as for example, that the data subject gives his/her explicit consent for the processing or through additional security measures.

2) Direct marketing

Where data are processed for the purposes of direct marketing, the data subject should be able to object without any charge from having his/her data processed for such purposes at any time.

3) Automated decision making and profiling

Decisions based solely on automated processing (automated individual decision-making), including profiling, which produce legal effects or significantly affect the data subject, can take place only under certain conditions established in the third country legal framework. In the European framework, such conditions include, for example, the need to obtain the explicit consent of the data subject or the necessity of such a decision for the conclusion of a contract. If the decision does not comply with such conditions as laid down in the third country legal framework, the data subject should have the right not to be subject to it. The law of the third country should, in any case, provide for necessary safeguards, including the right to be informed about the specific reasons underlying the decision and the logic involved, to correct inaccurate or incomplete information, and to contest the decision where it has been adopted on an incorrect factual basis.

C. PROCEDURAL AND ENFORCEMENT MECHANISMS:

Although the means to which the third country has recourse for the purpose of ensuring an adequate level of protection may differ from those employed within the European Union[13], a system consistent with the European one must be characterized by the existence of the following elements:

1) Competent Independent Supervisory Authority

One or more independent supervisory authorities, tasked with monitoring, ensuring and enforcing compliance with data protection and privacy provisions in the third country should exist. The supervisory authority shall act with complete independence and impartiality in performing its duties and exercising its powers and in doing so shall neither seek nor accept instructions. In that context, the supervisory authority should have all the necessary and available powers and missions to ensure compliance with data protection rights and promote awareness. Consideration should also be given to the staff and budget of the supervisory authority. The supervisory authority shall also be able, on its own initiative, to conduct investigations.

2) The data protection system must ensure a good level of compliance

A third country system should ensure a high degree of accountability and of awareness among data controllers and those processing personal data on their behalf of their obligations, tasks and responsibilities, and among data subjects of their rights and the means of exercising them. The existence of effective and dissuasive sanctions can play an important role in ensuring respect for rules, as of course can systems of direct verification by authorities, auditors, or independent data protection officials.

3) Accountability

A third country data protection framework should oblige data controllers and/or those processing personal data on their behalf to comply with it and to be able to demonstrate such compliance in particular to the competent supervisory authority. Such measures may include for example data protection impact assessments, the keeping of records or log files of data processing activities for an appropriate period of time, the designation of a data protection officer or data protection by design and by default.

4) The data protection system must provide support and help to individual data subjects in the exercise of their rights and appropriate redress mechanisms

The individual should be able to pursue legal remedies to enforce his/her rights rapidly and effectively, and without prohibitive cost, as well as to ensure compliance. To do so there must be in place supervision mechanisms allowing for independent investigation of complaints and enabling any infringements of the right to data protection and respect for private life to be identified and punished in practice.

Where rules are not complied with, the data subject should be provided as well with effective administrative and judicial redress, including for compensation for damages as a result of the unlawful processing of his/her personal data. This is a key element which must involve a system of independent adjudication or arbitration which allows compensation to be paid and sanctions imposed where appropriate.

NOTES
12   Such special categories are also known as "sensitive data" in recital 10 of the GDPR.
13   Case C-362/14, Maximillian Schrems v Data Protection Commissioner, 6 October 2015, para. 74.

CHAPTER 4: ESSENTIAL GUARANTEES IN THIRD COUNTRIES FOR LAW ENFORCEMENT AND NATIONAL SECURITY ACCESS TO LIMIT INTERFERENCES TO FUNDAMENTAL RIGHTS

[2.222]
When assessing the adequacy of the level of protection, under Art 45(2)(a) the Commission is required to take into account "*relevant legislation, both general and sectoral, including concerning public security, defence, national security and criminal law and the access of public authorities to personal data as well as the implementation of such legislation . . .* ".

The CJEU in Schrems, noted that the "*term 'adequate level of protection' must be understood as requiring the third country in fact to ensure, by reason of its domestic law or its international commitments, a level of protection of fundamental rights and freedoms that is essentially equivalent to that guaranteed within the European Union by virtue of Directive 95/46 read in the light of the Charter*". Even though the means to which that third country has recourse, in this connection, may differ from those employed within the European Union, those means must nevertheless prove, in practice, effective[14].

In this context, the court also noted critically that the previous Safe Harbor decision did "*not contain any finding regarding the existence, in the United States, of rules adopted by the State intended to limit any interference with the fundamental rights of the persons whose data is transferred from the European Union to the United States, interference which the State entities of that country would be authorized to engage in when they pursue legitimate objectives, such as national security.*"

The WP29 has identified in the opinion WP237, adopted on 13 April 2016, essential guarantees reflecting the jurisprudence of the CJEU and the ECHR in the field of surveillance. While the recommendations detailed in WP237 remain valid and should be taken into account when assessing the adequacy of a third country in the field of surveillance, the application of these guarantees may differ in the fields of law enforcement and national security access to data. Still those four guarantees need to be respected for access to data, whether for national security purposes or for law enforcement purposes, by all third countries in order to be considered adequate:

(1)   **Processing should be based on clear, precise and accessible rules (legal basis)**
(2)   **Necessity and proportionality with regards to legitimate objectives pursued need to be demonstrated**
(3)   **The processing has to be subject to independent oversight**
(4)   **Effective remedies need to be available to the individuals**

Part 2   Data Protection: EU Law etc

ARTICLE 29 DATA PROTECTION WORKING PARTY: WORKING DOCUMENT SETTING UP A TABLE WITH THE ELEMENTS AND PRINCIPLES TO BE FOUND IN BINDING CORPORATE RULES

18/EN
WP 256 rev.01

Adopted on 28 November 2017

As last Revised and Adopted on 6 February 2018

[2.223]

NOTES

This document was originally issued by the Article 29 Working Party but subsequently endorsed by the EDPB during its first plenary meeting.

© European Data Protection Board.

INTRODUCTION

[2.224]

In order to facilitate the use of Binding Corporate Rules for Controllers (BCR-C) by a corporate group or a group of enterprises engaged in a joint economic activity for international transfers from organisations established in the EU to organisations within the same group established outside the EU, the Article 29 Working Party (WP29) has amended the Working Document 153 (which was adopted in 2008) setting up a table with the elements and principles to be found in Binding Corporate Rules in order to reflect the requirements referring to BCRs now expressly set out by the Regulation (EU) 2016/679 of the European Parliament and of the Council of 27 April 2016 on the protection of natural persons with regard to the processing of personal data and on the free movement of such data, and repealing Directive 95/46/EC (General Data Protection Regulation / GDPR)[1].

It should be recalled that BCR-Controllers are suitable for framing transfers of personal data from Controllers established in the EU to other Controllers or to Processors (established outside the EU) within the same group, whereas BCR-Processors (BCR-P) apply to data received from a Controller (established in the EU) which is not a member of the group and then processed by the concerned group members as Processors and/or Sub-processors. Hence the obligations set out in the BCR-C apply in relation to entities within the same group acting as controllers and to entities acting as 'internal' processors. As for this very last case, it is worth recalling that a contract or other legal act under Union or Member State law, binding on the processor with regard to the controller and which comprise all requirements as set out in Art. 28.3 GDPR, should be signed with all internal and external subcontractors/processors (e.g. Service Agreement or other instruments meeting the same requirements)[2]. Indeed, the obligations set forth in the BCR-C apply to entities of the group receiving personal data as ('internal') processors to the extent that this does not lead to a contradiction with the Service Agreement (i.e. the Processors members of the group processing on behalf of Controllers members of the group shall primarily abide by this contract).

Taking into account that Article 47.2 GDPR sets forth a minimum set of elements to be inserted within Binding Corporate Rules, this amended table is meant to:
- Adjust the wording of the previous referential so as to keep it in line with Article 47 GDPR,
- Clarify the necessary content of BCRs as stated in Article 47 (taking into account documents WP 74[3] & WP 108[4] adopted by the WP29 within the framework of the directive 95/46/EC),
- Make the distinction between what must be included in BCRs and what must be presented to the competent Supervisory Authority in the BCRs application (document WP 133[5]),
- Give the principles the corresponding text references in Article 47 GDPR, and
- Provide explanations/comments on the principles one by one.

Article 47 GDPR is clearly modelled on the Working documents relating to BCRs adopted by the WP29. However, it specifies some new elements that need to be taken into account when updating already existing BCRs or adopting new sets of BCRs so as to ensure their compatibility with the new framework established by the GDPR.

1.1 NEW ELEMENTS

In this perspective, the WP29 would like to draw attention in particular to the following elements:
- ***right to lodge a complaint***: Data subjects should be given the right to bring their claim, as they choose, either before the Supervisory Authority ('SA') in the Member State of his habitual residence, place of work or place of the alleged infringement (pursuant to Art. 77 GDPR) or before the competent court of the EU Member States (choice for the data subject to act before the courts where the data exporter has an establishment or where the data subject has his or her habitual residence (Article 79 GDPR);
- ***Transparency***: All data subjects benefitting from the third party beneficiary rights should in particular be provided with information as stipulated in Articles 13 and 14 GDPR and information on their rights in regard to processing and the means to exercise those rights, the clause relating to liability and the clauses relating to the data protection principles;

- *Scope of application*: The BCRs shall specify the structure and contact details of the group of undertakings or group of enterprises engaged in a joint economic activity and of each of its members (GDPR Art. 47.2.a). The BCRs must also specify its material scope, for instance the data transfers or set of transfers, including the categories of personal data, the type of processing and its purposes, the types of data subjects affected and the identification of the third country or countries (GDPR Art. 47.2.b);
- *Data Protection principles*: Along with the principles of transparency, fairness, purpose limitation, data quality, security, the BCRs should also explain the other principles referred to in Article 47.2.d – such as, in particular, the principles of lawfulness, data minimisation, limited storage periods, guarantees when processing special categories of personal data, the requirements in respect of onward transfers to bodies not bound by the binding corporate rules;
- *Accountability*: Every entity acting as data controller shall be responsible for and able to demonstrate compliance with the BCRs (GDPR Art. 5.2);
- *Third country legislation*: The BCRs should contain a commitment that where any legal requirement a member of the group of undertakings or group of enterprises engaged in a joint economic activity is subject to in a third country is likely to have a substantial adverse effect on the guarantees provided by the BCRs, the problem will be reported to the competent supervisory authority (unless otherwise prohibited, such as a prohibition under criminal law to preserve the confidentiality of a law enforcement investigation). This includes any legally binding request for disclosure of personal data by a law enforcement authority or state security body.

1.2 AMENDMENTS OF ALREADY ADOPTED BCRS

While in accordance with article 46-5 of the GDPR, authorisations by a Member State or supervisory authority made on the basis of Article 26(2) of Directive 95/46/EC will remain valid until amended, replaced or repealed, if necessary, by that supervisory authority, groups with approved BCRs should, in preparing to the GDPR, bring their BCRs in line with GDPR requirements.

This document aims also to assist those groups with approved BCRs in implementing the relevant changes to bring them in line with the GDPR. To this end, these groups are invited to notify the relevant changes to their BCRs as part of their obligation (under 5.1 of WP153) to all group members and to the DPAs via the Lead DPA under their annual update as of 25 May 2018. Such updated BCRs can be used without having to apply for a new authorization or approval.

Taking into account the above, the DPAs reserve their right to exercise their powers under article 46-5 of the GDPR.

Part 2   Data Protection: EU Law etc

Criteria for approval of BCRs	In the BCRs	In the application form	Texts of reference	Comments	References to application/BCRs[6]
1 - BINDING NATURE					
INTERNALLY					
1.1 The duty to respect the BCRs	YES	YES	GDPR Art. 47.1.a and 47.2.c	The BCRs must be legally binding and shall contain a clear duty for each participating member of the Group of undertakings or group of enterprises engaged in a joint economic activity ('BCR member') including their employees to respect the BCRs.	
1.2 An explanation of how the rules are made binding on the BCR members of the group and also the employees	NO	YES	GDPR Art. 47.1.a and 47.2.c	The Group will have to explain in its application form how the rules are made binding : i) For each participating company/entity in the group by one or more of: - Intra-group agreement, - Unilateral undertakings (this is only possible if the BCR member taking responsibility and liability is located in a Member State that recognizes Unilateral undertakings as binding and if this BCR member is legally able to bind the other members subject to BCRs), - Other means (only if the group demonstrates how the binding character of the BCRs is achieved) ii) On employees by one or more of: - Individual and separate agreement(s)/undertaking with sanctions, - Clause in employment contract with a description of applicable sanctions, - Internal policies with sanctions, or - Collective agreements with sanctions - Other means (but the group must properly explain how the BCRs are made binding on the employees)	
EXTERNALLY					
1.3 The creation of third-party beneficiary rights for data subjects. Including the possibility to lodge a complaint before the competent SA and before the courts	YES	YES	GDPR Art. 47.1.b, and 47.2.c, 47.2.e	The BCRs must expressly confer rights on data subjects to enforce the rules as third-party beneficiaries. Data subjects must at least be able to enforce the following elements of the BCRs:	

Criteria for approval of BCRs	In the BCRs	In the application form	Texts of reference	Comments	References to application/BCRs[6]
				- Data protection principles (Art. 47.2.d and Section 6.1 of this referential),	
				- Transparency and easy access to BCRs (Art. 47.2.g and Section 6.1, Section 1.7 of this referential),	
				- Rights of access, rectification, erasure, restriction, objection to processing, right not to be subject to decisions based solely on automated processing, including profiling (GDPR Art. 47.2.e and Art. 15, 16, 17,18, 21, 22),	
				- National legislation preventing respect of BCRs (Art. 47.2.m and Section 6.3 of this referential)	
				- Right to complain through the internal complaint mechanism of the companies (Art. 47.1.i and Section 2.2 of this referential),	
				- Cooperation duties with Supervisory Authorities (Art. 47.2.k and 1, Section 3.1 of this referential),	
				- Liability and jurisdiction provisions (Art. 47.2.e and f, Section 1.3, 1.4 of this referential). In particular, the BCRs must confer the right to lodge a complaint with the competent supervisory authority (choice before the SA in the Member State of his habitual residence, place of work or place of the alleged infringement, pursuant to art. 77 GDPR) and before the competent court of the EU Member States (choice for the data subject to act before the courts where the controller or processor has an establishment or where the data subject has his or her habitual residence pursuant to Article 79 GDPR).	
				The BCRs should expressly confer to the data subjects the right to judicial remedies and the right to obtain redress and, where appropriate, compensation in case of any breach of one of the enforceable elements of the BCRs as enumerated above (see Articles 77 – 82 GDPR).	
				Companies should ensure that all those rights are covered by the third party beneficiary clause of their BCRs by, for example, making a reference to the clauses/sections/parts of their BCRs where these rights are regulated or by listing them all in the said third party beneficiary clause.	
				These rights do not extend to those elements of the BCRs pertaining to internal mechanisms implemented within entities such as detail of training, audit programmes, compliance network, and mechanism for updating of the rules.	

Part 2   Data Protection: EU Law etc

Criteria for approval of BCRs	In the BCRs	In the application form	Texts of reference	Comments	References to application/BCRs[6]
1.4 The EU headquarters, EU member with delegated data protection responsibilities or the data exporter accepts liability for paying compensation and to remedy breaches of the BCRs.	YES	YES	GDPR Art. 47.2.f	The BCRs must contain a duty for the EU headquarters, or the EU BCR member with delegated responsibilities to accept responsibility for and to agree to take the necessary action to remedy the acts of other members outside of the EU bound by the BCRs and to pay compensation for any material or non-material damages resulting from the violation of the BCRs by BCR members. The BCRs must also state that, if a BCR member outside the EU violates the BCRs, the courts or other competent authorities in the EU will have jurisdiction and the data subject will have the rights and remedies against the BCR member that has accepted responsibility and liability as if the violation had been caused by them in the Member State in which they are based instead of the BCR member outside the EU. Another option, in particular if it is not possible for a group with particular corporate structures to impose on a specific entity to take all the responsibility for any breach of BCRs outside of the EU, it may provide that every BCR member exporting data out of the EU on the basis of the BCR will be liable for any breaches of the BCRs by the BCR member established outside the EU which received the data from this EU BCR member.	
1.5 The company has sufficient assets.	NO	YES	[WP 74 point 5.5.2. §2 (page 18) + WP108 point 5.17. (page 6)]	The application form must contain a confirmation that any BCR member that has accepted liability for the acts of other members bound by the BCRs outside of the EU has sufficient assets to pay compensation for damages resulting from the breach of the BCRs.	
1.6 The burden of proof lies with the company not the individual.	YES	YES	GDPR Art. 47.2.f	BCRs must state that the BCR member that has accepted liability will also have the burden of proof to demonstrate that the BCR member outside the EU is not liable for any violation of the rules which has resulted in the data subject claiming damages. If the BCR member that has accepted liability can prove that the BCR member outside the EU is not responsible for the event giving rise to the damage, it may discharge itself from any responsibility.	

Criteria for approval of BCRs	In the BCRs	In the application form	Texts of reference	Comments	References to application/BCRs[6]
1.7 Transparency and easy access to BCRs for data subjects	YES	NO	GDPR Art. 47.2.g	BCRs must contain the commitment that all data subjects benefiting from the third party beneficiary rights should be provided with the information as required by Articles 13 and 14 GDPR, information on their third party beneficiary rights with regard to the processing of their personal data and on the means to exercise those rights, the clause relating to the liability and the clauses relating to the data protection principles. The information should be provided in full and a summary will not be sufficient .. The BCRs must contain the right for every data subject to have an easy access to them. For instance, the BCRs may state that at least the parts of the BCRs on which information to the data subjects is mandatory (as described in the previous paragraph) will be published on the internet or on the intranet (when data subjects are only the company staff having access to the intranet).	
2 - EFFECTIVENESS					
2.1 The existence of a suitable training programme	YES	YES	GDPR 47.2.n	The BCRs must state that appropriate training on the BCRs will be provided to personnel that have permanent or regular access to personal data, who are involved in the collection of data or in the development of tools used to process personal data. The Supervisory Authorities evaluating the BCRs may ask for examples and explanations of the training programme during the application procedure. The training programme should be specified in the application.	
2.2 The existence of a complaint handling process for the BCRs	YES	YES	GDPR 47.2.i and 12.3	An internal complaints handling process must be set up in the BCRs to ensure that any data subject should be able to exercise his/her rights and complain about any BCR member. - The complaints must be dealt with, without undue delay and in any event within one month, by a clearly identified department or person with an appropriate level of independence in the exercise of his/her functions. Taking into account the complexity and number of the requests, that one month period may be extended at maximum by two further months, in which case the data subject should be informed accordingly. The application form must explain how data subjects will be informed about the practical steps of the complaint system, in particular: - Where to complain,	

Criteria for approval of BCRs	In the BCRs	In the application form	Texts of reference	Comments	References to application/BCRs[6]
				- In what form, - Delays for the reply on the complaint, - Consequences in case of rejection of the complaint, - Consequences in case the complaint is considered as justified, - Consequences if the data subject is not satisfied by the replies (right to lodge a claim before the Court and a complaint before the Supervisory Authority).	
2.3 The existence of an audit programme covering the BCRs	YES	YES	GDPR Art. 47.2.j and l and Art. 38.3,	The BCRs must create a duty for the group to have data protection audits on regular basis (by either internal or external accredited auditors) or on specific request from the privacy officer/function (or any other competent function in the organization) to ensure verification of compliance with the BCRs. The BCRs must state that the audit programme covers all aspects of the BCRs including methods of ensuring that corrective actions will take place. Moreover, the BCRs must state that the result will be communicated to the privacy officer/function and to the relevant board of the controlling undertaking of a group or of the group of enterprises engaged in a joint economic activity. Where appropriate, the result may be communicated to the ultimate parent's board. The BCRs must state that Supervisory Authorities can have access to the results of the audit upon request and give the SAs the authority/power to carry out a data protection audit of any BCR member if required. The application form will contain a description of the audit system. For instance : - Which entity (department within the group) decides on the audit plan/programme, - Which entity will conduct the audit, - Time of the audit (regularly or on specific request from the appropriate Privacy function.)	

Criteria for approval of BCRs	In the BCRs	In the application form	Texts of reference	Comments	References to application/BCRs[6]
				- Coverage of the audit (for instance, applications, IT systems, databases that process Personal Data, or onward transfers, decisions taken as regards mandatory requirement under national laws that conflicts with the BCRs, review of the contractual terms used for the transfers out of the Group (to controllers or processors of data), corrective actions, . . .) - Which entity will receive the results of the audits	
2.4 The creation of a network of data protection officers (DPO) or appropriate staff for monitoring compliance with the rules.	YES	NO	GDPR Art. 47.2.h and Art. 38.3	A commitment to designate a DPO where required in line with article 37 of the GDPR or any other person or entity (such as a chief privacy officer) with responsibility to monitor compliance with the BCRs enjoying the highest management support for the fulfilling of this task. The DPO or the other privacy professionals can be assisted by a team, a network of local DPOs or local contacts as appropriate. The DPO shall directly report to the highest management level (GDPR Art. 38-3). The BCRs should include a brief description of the internal structure, role, position and tasks of the DPO or similar function and the network created to ensure compliance with the rules. For example, that the DPO or chief privacy officer informs and advises the highest management, deals with Supervisory Authorities' investigations, monitors and annually reports on compliance at a global level, and that local DPOs or local contacts can be in charge of handling local complaints from data subjects, reporting major privacy issues to the DPO, monitoring training and compliance at a local level.	
3 - COOPERATION DUTY					
3.1 A duty to cooperate with SAs	YES	YES	GDPR Art. 47. 2.l	The BCRs should contain a clear duty for all BCR members to co-operate with, to accept to be audited by the Supervisory Authorities and to comply with the advice of these Supervisory Authorities on any issue related to those rules.	
4 - DESCRIPTION OF PROCESSING AND DATA FLOWS					

Criteria for approval of BCRs	In the BCRs	In the application form	Texts of reference	Comments	References to application/BCRs[6]
4.1 A description of the material scope of the BCRs (nature of data transferred, type of data subjects, countries)	YES	YES	GDPR Art. 47.2.b	The BCRs must specify their material scope and therefore contain a general description of the transfers so as to allow the Supervisory Authorities to assess that the processing carried out in third countries is compliant. The BCRs must in particular, specify the data transfers or set of transfers, including the nature and categories of personal data, the type of processing and its purposes, the types of data subjects affected (data related to employees, customers, suppliers and other third parties as part of its respective regular business activities) and the identification of the third country or countries.	
4.2 A statement of the geographical scope of the BCRs	YES	YES	GDPR art 47.2.a	The BCRs shall specify the structure and contact details of the group of undertakings or group of enterprises engaged in a joint economic activity and of each of its Members. The BCRs should indicate if they apply to: i) All personal data transferred from the European Union within the group OR, ii) All processing of personal data within the group	
5 - MECHANISMS FOR REPORTING AND RECORDING CHANGES					
5.1 A process for updating the BCRs	YES	YES	GDPR Art. 47.2.k	The BCRs can be modified (for instance to take into account modifications of the regulatory environment or the company structure) but they should impose a duty to report changes without undue delay to all BCR members and to the relevant Supervisory Authorities, via the competent Supervisory Authority. Updates to the BCRs or to the list of the Members of the BCRs are possible without having to re-apply for an approval providing that: i) An identified person or team/department keeps a fully updated list of the BCR members and keeps track of and record any updates to the rules and provide the necessary information to the data subjects or Supervisory Authorities upon request. ii) No transfer is made to a new BCR member until the new BCR member is effectively bound by the BCRs and can deliver compliance.	

Criteria for approval of BCRs	In the BCRs	In the application form	Texts of reference	Comments	References to application/BCRs[6]
				iii) Any changes to the BCRs or to the list of BCR members should be reported once a year to the relevant SAs, via the competent SA with a brief explanation of the reasons justifying the update.	
				iv) Where a modification would possibly affect the level of the protection offered by the BCRs or significantly affect the BCRs (i.e. changes to the binding character), it must be promptly communicated to the relevant Supervisory Authorities, via the competent SA.	
6 - DATA PROTECTION SAFEGUARDS					
6.1.1 A description of the data protection principles including the rules on transfers or onward transfers out of the EU.	YES	YES	GDPR art. 47.2.d	The BCRs should explicitly include the following principles to be observed by the company: i. Transparency, fairness and lawfulness (GDPR Art. 5.1.a, 6, 9, 10, 13 and 14) ii. Purpose limitation (GDPR Art.5.1.b) iii. Data minimisation and accuracy (GDPR Art. 5.1.c and d) iv. Limited storage periods (GDPR Art. 5.1.e) v. Processing of special categories of personal data vi. Security (GDPR Art. 5.f and 32) including the obligation to enter into contracts with all internal and external subcontractors/processors which comprise all requirements as set out in Art. 28.3 GDPR and as well the duty to notify without undue delay any personal data breaches to the EU headquarters or the EU BCR member with delegated data protection responsibilities and the other relevant Privacy Officer/Function and data subjects where the personal data breach is likely to result in a high risk to their rights and freedoms . Furthermore, any personal data breaches should be documented (comprising the facts relating to the personal data breach, its effects and the remedial action taken) and the documentation should be made available to the supervisory authority on request (GDPR Art. 33 and 34).	

Criteria for approval of BCRs	In the BCRs	In the application form	Texts of reference	Comments	References to application/BCRs[6]
				vii. Restriction on transfers and onward transfers to processors and controllers which are not part of the group (BCR members that are controllers can transfer data to processors/controllers out of the group that are located outside of the EU provided that adequate protection is provided according to Articles 45, 46, 47 48 GDPR, or that a derogation according to 49 GDPR applies)	
				The wording and definitions of the BCRs key principles should be consistent with the wording and definitions of the GDPR.	
6.1.2 Accountability and other tools	YES	YES	GDPR Art. 47.2.d and Art. 30	Every entity acting as data controller shall be responsible for and able to demonstrate compliance with the BCRs (GDPR Art. 5.2 and 24).	
				In order to demonstrate compliance, BCR members need to maintain a record of all categories of processing activities carried out in line with the requirements as set out in Art. 30.1 GDPR. This record should be maintained in writing, including in electronic form, and should be made available to the supervisory authority on request.	
				In order to enhance compliance and when required, data protection impact assessments should be carried out for processing operations that are likely to result in a high risk to the rights and freedoms of natural persons (GDPR Art. 35). Where a data protection impact assessment under Article 35 indicates that the processing would result in a high risk in the absence of measures taken by the controller to mitigate the risk, the competent supervisory authority, prior to processing, should be consulted (GDPR Art. 36).	
				Appropriate technical and organisational measures should be implemented which are designed to implement data protection principles and to facilitate compliance with the requirements set up by the BCRs in practice (data protection by design and by default (GDPR Art. 25)	
6.2 The list of entities bound by BCRs	YES	YES	GDPR 47.2.a	BCR shall contain a list of the entities bound by the BCRs including contact details.	

Criteria for approval of BCRs	In the BCRs	In the application form	Texts of reference	Comments	References to application/BCRs[6]
6.3 The need to be transparent where national legislation prevents the group from complying with the BCRs	YES	NO	GDPR Art. 47.2.m	A clear commitment that where a BCR member has reasons to believe that the legislation applicable to him prevents the company from fulfilling its obligations under the rules, he will promptly inform the EU headquarters or the EU BCR member with delegated data protection responsibilities and the other relevant Privacy Officer/Function (except where prohibited by a law enforcement authority, such as prohibition under criminal law to preserve the confidentiality of a law enforcement investigation). In addition, the BCRs should contain a commitment that where any legal requirement a BCR member is subject to in a third country is likely to have a substantial adverse effect on the guarantees provided by the BCRs, the problem should be reported to the competent SA. This includes any legally binding request for disclosure of the personal data by a law enforcement authority or state security body. In such a case, the competent SA should be clearly informed about the request, including information about the data requested, the requesting body, and the legal basis for the disclosure (unless otherwise prohibited, such as a prohibition under criminal law to preserve the confidentiality of a law enforcement investigation). If in specific cases the suspension and/or notification are prohibited, the BCRs shall provide that the requested BCR member will use its best efforts to obtain the right to waive this prohibition in order to communicate as much information as it can and as soon as possible, and be able to demonstrate that it did so. If, in the above cases, despite having used its best efforts, the requested BCR member is not in a position to notify the competent SAs, it must commit in the BCRs to annually providing general information on the requests it received to the competent SAs (e.g. number of applications for disclosure, type of data requested, requester if possible, etc.). In any case, the BCRs must state that transfers of personal data by a BCR member of the group to any public authority cannot be massive, disproportionate and indiscriminate in a manner that would go beyond what is necessary in a democratic society.	
6.4 A statement about the relationship between national laws and BCRs	YES	NO	N/A	BCRs shall specify the relationship between the BCRs and the relevant applicable law.	

Part 2   Data Protection: EU Law etc

Criteria for approval of BCRs	In the BCRs	In the application form	Texts of reference	Comments	References to application/BCRs[6]
				The BCRs shall state that, where the local legislation, for instance EU legislation, requires a higher level of protection for personal data it will take precedence over the BCRs. In any event personal data shall be processed in accordance to the applicable law as provided by the Article 5 of the GDPR and the relevant local legislation.	

NOTES

1 Text with EEA relevance.
2 Art. 28.3 requires, among others, for each controller-to-processor relationship a specification, by way of contract or other legal act, of the subject-matter, the duration, the nature and purposes of the processing, the type of personal data and categories of data subjects and the obligations and rights of the controller. A generic description included in the BCRs regarding the categories of data, data subjects etc. would not be sufficient in this regard.
3 Working Document WP 74: Transfers of personal data to third countries: Applying Article 26 (2) of the EU Data Protection Directive to Binding Corporate Rules for International Data Transfers, adopted on June 3, 2003, http://ec.europa.eu/justice_home/fsj/privacy/workinggroup/wpdocs/2003_en.htm
4 Working Document WP 108: Establishing a model checklist application for approval of Binding Corporate Rules, adopted on April 14, 2005, http://ec.europa.eu/justice_home/fsj/privacy/workinggroup/wpdocs/2005_en.htm
5 Working Document WP 133: Recommendation 1/2007 on the Standard Application for Approval of Binding Corporate Rules for the Transfer of Personal Data, adopted on January 10, 2007, http://ec.europa.eu/justice/data-protection/article-29/documentation/opinion-recommendation/files/2007/wp133_en.doc
6 To be completed by applicant.

ARTICLE 29 DATA PROTECTION WORKING PARTY: WORKING DOCUMENT SETTING UP A TABLE WITH THE ELEMENTS AND PRINCIPLES TO BE FOUND IN PROCESSOR BINDING CORPORATE RULES
18/EN
WP 257 rev.01
Adopted on 28 November 2017

As last Revised and Adopted on 6 February 2018

[2.225]

NOTES

This document was originally issued by the Article 29 Working Party but subsequently endorsed by the EDPB during its first plenary meeting.

© European Data Protection Board.

INTRODUCTION

[2.226]

In order to facilitate the use of Binding Corporate Rules for Processors (BCR-P) by a corporate group or a group of enterprises engaged in a joint economic activity for international transfers from organisations established in the EU to organisations within the same group established outside the EU, the Article 29 Working Party (WP29) has amended the Working Document 195 (which was adopted in 2012) setting up a table with the elements and principles to be found in Binding Corporate Rules in order to reflect the requirements referring to BCRs now expressly set out in Regulation (EU) 2016/679 of the European Parliament and of the Council of 27 April 2016 on the protection of natural persons with regard to the processing of personal data and on the free movement of such data, and repealing Directive 95/46/EC (General Data Protection Regulation / GDPR).

It should be recalled that BCR-P apply to data received from a controller established in the EU which is not a member of the group and then processed by the group members as processors and/or sub processors; whereas BCRs for Controllers (BCR-C) are suitable for framing transfers of personal data from controllers established in the EU to other controllers or to processors established outside the EU within the same group. Hence the obligations set out in the BCR-P apply in relation to third party personal data that are processed by a member of the group as a processor according to the instructions from a non-group controller.

According to Article 28.3 of the GDPR, a contract or another legal act under Union or Member State law that is binding on the processor with regard to the controller must be implemented between the controller and the processor. Such a contract or other legal act will be referred here as the "service agreement"..

Taking into account that Article 47.2 of the GDPR lists a minimum set of elements to be contained within a BCR, this amended table is meant to:
–   Adjust the wording of the previous referential so as to bring it in line with Article 47 GDPR,
–   Clarify the necessary content of a BCR as stated in Article 47 and in document WP 204[1] adopted by the WP29 within the framework of the Directive 95/46/EC,
–   Make the distinction between what must be included in BCRs and what must be presented to the competent Supervisory Authority in the BCRs application (document WP 195a[2]), and
–   Provide explanations/comments on each of the requirements.

Article 47 of the GDPR is clearly modelled on the Working documents relating to BCRs adopted by the WP29. However, it specifies some new elements that need to be taken into account when updating already existing approved BCRs or adopting new sets of BCRs so as to ensure their compatibility with the new framework established by the GDPR.

1. NEW ELEMENTS

In this perspective, the WP29 would like to draw attention in particular to the following elements:
–   ***Scope of application***: The BCRs shall specify the structure and contact details of the group of undertakings or group of enterprises engaged in a joint economic activity and of each of its members (Art. 47.2.a GDPR). The BCRs must also provide its material scope, for instance the data transfers or set of transfers, including the categories of personal data, the type of processing and its purposes, the types of data subjects affected and the identification of the third country or countries (Art. 47.2.b GDPR);
–   ***Third party beneficiary rights***: Data subjects should be able to enforce the BCRs as third party beneficiaries directly against the processor where the requirements at stake are specifically directed to processors in accordance with the GDPR (Art. 28, 29, 79 GDPR);
–   ***Right to lodge a complaint***: Data subjects should be given the right to bring their claim, at their choice, either before the Supervisory Authority ('SA') in the Member State of his habitual residence, place of work or place of the alleged infringement (Art.77 GDPR) or before the competent court of the EU Member States (choice for the data subject to act before the courts where the data exporter has an establishment or where the data subject has his or her habitual residence (Article 79 GDPR);

– **Data Protection principles**: Along with the obligations arising from principles of transparency, fairness, lawfulness, purpose limitation, data quality, security, the BCRs should also explain how other requirements, such as, in particular, in relation to data subjects rights, sub-processing and onward transfers to entities not bound by the BCRs will be observed by the processor;

– **Accountability**: Processors will have an obligation to make available to the controller all information necessary to demonstrate compliance with their obligations including through audits and inspections conducted by the Controller or an auditor mandated by the Controller (Art. 28-3-h GDPR);

– **Service Agreement**: The Service Agreement between the Controller and the Processor must contain all required elements as provided by Article 28 of the GDPR.

2. AMENDMENTS OF ALREADY ADOPTED BCRS

While in accordance with article 46-5 of the GDPR, authorisations by a Member State or supervisory authority made on the basis of Article 26(2) of Directive 95/46/EC will remain valid until amended, replaced or repealed, if necessary, by that supervisory authority, groups with approved BCRs should, in preparing to the GDPR, bring their BCRs in line with GDPR requirements.

This document aims also to assist those groups with approved BCRs in implementing the relevant changes to bring them in line with the GDPR. To this end, these groups are invited to notify the relevant changes to their BCRs as part of their obligation (under 5.1 of WP195) to all group members and to the DPAs via the Lead DPA under their annual update as of 25 May 2018. Such updated BCRs can be used without having to apply for a new authorization or approval from the DPAs.

Taking into account the above, the DPAs reserve their right to exercise their powers under article 46-5 of the GDPR.

Criteria for approval of BCRs	In the BCRs	In the application form	Comments	References to application/ BCRs
1 - BINDING NATURE				
INTERNALLY				
1.1 The duty to respect the BCRs	YES	YES	The BCRs must be legally binding and shall contain a clear duty for each participating member of the Group of undertakings or group of enterprises engaged in a joint economic activity ("BCR member") including their employees to respect the BCRs. The BCRs shall also expressly state that each Member including their employees shall respect the instructions from the controller regarding the data processing and the security and confidentiality measures as provided in the Service Agreement (Art. 28, 29 and 32 of the GDPR).	
1.2 An explanation of how the rules are made binding on the members of the group and also the employees	NO	YES	The Group will have to explain in its application form how the rules are made binding: i) For each BCR member by one or more of: – Intra-group agreement, – Unilateral undertakings (this is only possible if the BCR member taking responsibility and liability is located in a Member State that recognizes Unilateral undertakings as binding and if this BCR member is legally able to bind the other BCR members), or – Other means (only if the group demonstrates how bindingness is achieved). ii) On employees by one or more of: – Individual and separate agreement/undertaking with sanctions, or Clause in employment contract with sanctions, or – Internal policies with sanctions, or – Collective agreements with sanctions, or – Other means (but the group must properly explain how the BCRs are made binding on the employees).	
EXTERNALLY				

Criteria for approval of BCRs	In the BCRs	In the application form	Comments	References to application/ BCRs
1.3 The creation of third-party ben-eficiary rights for data subjects, including the possibility to lodge a complaint before the competent Supervisory Authorities and before the Courts	YES	YES	i) Rights which are directly enforceable against the processor The BCRs must grant rights to data subjects to enforce the BCRs as third party benefi-ciaries directly against the processor where the requirements at stake are specifically directed to processors in accordance with the GDPR. In this regard, data subjects shall at least be able to enforce the following elements of the BCRs directly against the processor: – Duty to respect the instructions from the controller regarding the data processing including for data transfers to third countries (Art. 28.3.a, 28.3.g., 29 GDPR and section 1.1, 6.1.ii and 6.1.iv of this referential), – Duty to implement appropriate technical and organizational security measures (Art. 28.3.c and 32 GDPR and section 6.1.iv of this referential) and duty to notify any personal data breach to the controller (Art. 33.2 GDPR and section 6.1.iv of this referential), – Duty to respect the conditions when engaging a sub-processor either within or outside the Group (Art. 28.2, 28.3.d . 28.4, 45, 46, 47 GDPR, section 6.1.vi and 6.1.vii of this referential), – Duty to cooperate with and assist the controller in complying and demonstrating compliance with the law such as for answering requests from data subjects in rela-tion to their rights (Art. 28.3.e, 28.3.f, 28.3.h and sections 3.2, 6.1.i, 6.1.iii, 6.1.iv, 6.1. v and 6.1. 2 of this referential) – Easy access to BCRs (Art.47.2.g GDPR and section 1.8 of this referential) – Right to complain through internal complaint mechanisms (Art.47.2.i and sec-tion 2.2 of this referential). – Duty to cooperate with the supervisory authority (Art. 31, 47.2.l of GDPR and section 3.1 of this referential) – Liability, compensation and jurisdiction provisions (Art.47.2.e, 79, 82 GDPR and sections 1.3, 1.5 and 1.7 of this referential). – National legislation preventing respect of BCRs (Art.47.2.m and section 6.3 of this referential) ii) Rights which are enforceable against the processor in case the data subject is not able to bring a claim against the controller:	

Criteria for approval of BCRs	In the BCRs	In the application form	Comments	References to application/ BCRs
			The BCRs must expressly confer rights to data subjects to enforce the BCRs as third-party beneficiaries in case the data subject is not able to bring a claim against the data controller; because the data controller has factually disappeared or ceased to exist in law or has become insolvent, unless any successor entity has assumed the entire legal obligations of the data controller by contract of by operation of law, in which case the data subject can enforce its rights against such entity.	
			In such a case, data subjects shall at least be able to enforce against the processor the following sections set out in this referential: 1.1, 1.3, 1.5, 1.7, 1.8, 2.2, 3.1, 3.2, 6.1, 6.2, 6.3	
			The data subjects' rights as mentioned under i) and ii) shall cover the judicial remedies for any breach of the third party beneficiary rights guaranteed and the right to obtain redress and where appropriate receive compensation for any damage (material harm but also any distress).	
			In particular, data subjects shall be entitled to lodge a complaint before the competent supervisory authority (choice between the supervisory authority of the EU Member State of his/her habitual residence, place of work or place of alleged infringement) and before the competent court of the EU Member State (choice for the data subject to act before the courts where the controller or processor has an establishment or where the data subject has his or her habitual residence pursuant to Article 79 of the GDPR).	
			Where the processor and the controller involved in the same processing are found responsible for any damage caused by such processing, the data subject shall be entitled to receive compensation for the entire damage directly from the processor (Art. 82.4 GDPR)	
1.4. Responsibility towards the Controller	YES	YES	The BCRs shall be made binding towards the Controller through a specific reference to it in the Service Agreement which shall comply with art 28 of the GDPR. Moreover, the BCR must state that the Controller shall have the right to enforce the BCR against any BCR member for breaches they caused, and, moreover, against the BCR member referred under point 1.5 in case of a breach of the BCRs or of the Service Agreement by BCR members established outside of EU or of a breach of the written agreement referred under 6.1.vii, by any external sub-processor established outside of the EU.	

Criteria for approval of BCRs	In the BCRs	In the application form	Comments	References to application/ BCRs
1.5 The company accepts liability for paying compensation and to remedy breaches of the BCRs.	YES	YES	The BCRs must contain a duty for the EU headquarters of the Processor or the EU BCR member of the Processor with delegated data protection responsibilities or the EU exporter Processor (e.g. the EU party contracting with the controller) to accept responsibility for and to agree to take the necessary action to remedy the acts of other BCR members established outside of EU or breaches caused by external sub-processor established outside of EU and to pay compensation for any damages resulting from a violation of the BCRs.	
			This BCR member will accept liability as if the violation had taken place by him in the Member State in which he is based instead of the BCR member outside the EU or the external sub-processor established outside of EU. This BCR member may not rely on a breach by a sub-processor (internal or external of the group) of its obligations in order to avoid its own liabilities.	
			If it is not possible for some groups with particular corporate structures to impose all the responsibility for any type of breach of the BCRs outside of the EU on a specific entity, another option may consist of stating that each and every BCR member exporting data out of the EU will be liable for any breaches of the BCR by the sub-processors (internal or external of the group) established outside the EU which received the data from this EU BCR member.	
1.6 The company has sufficient assets.	NO	YES	The application form must contain a confirmation that any BCR member that has accepted liability for the acts of other BCR members outside of EU and/or for any external sub-processor established outside of EU has sufficient assets to pay compensation for damages resulting from the breach of the BCRs.	
1.7 The burden of proof lies with the company not the individual.	YES	YES	The BCRs must state that the BCR member that has accepted liability will have the burden of proof to demonstrate that the BCR member outside the EU or the external sub-processor is not liable for any violation of the rules which has resulted in the data subject claiming damages	
			The BCRs must also state that where the Controller can demonstrate that it suffered damage and establish facts which show it is likely that the damage has occurred because of the breach of BCRs, it will be for the BCR member of the group that accepted liability to prove that the BCR member outside of the EU or the external sub-processor was not responsible for the breach of the BCRs giving rise to those damages or that no such breach took place	
			If the entity that has accepted liability can prove that the BCR member outside the EU is not responsible for the act, it may discharge itself from any responsibility/liability.	

Criteria for approval of BCRs	In the BCRs	In the application form	Comments	References to application/ BCRs
1.8 There is easy access to BCRs for data subjects and in particular easy access to the information about third party beneficiary rights for the data subject that benefit from them.	YES	NO	Access for the Controller: The Service Agreement will ensure that the BCRs are part of the contract. BCRs will be annexed to the Service Agreement or a reference to it will be made with a possibility of electronic access. Access for Data Subjects: BCRs must contain the commitment that all data subjects benefiting from the third party beneficiary rights should, in particular, be provided with the information on their third party beneficiary rights with regard to the processing of their personal data and on the means to exercise those rights. The BCRs must stipulate the right for every data subject to have easy access to them. Relevant parts of the BCRs shall be published on the website of the Processor Group or other appropriate means in a way easily accessible to data subjects or at least a document including all (and not a summary of) the information relating to points 1.1, 1.3, 1.4, 1.6, 1.7, 2.2, 3.1, 3.2, 4.1, 4.2, 6.1, 6.2, 6.3 of this referential.	
2 – EFFECTIVENESS				
2.1 The existence of a suitable training programme	YES	YES	The BCRs must state that appropriate training on the BCRs will be provided to personnel that have permanent or regular access to personal data who are involved in the collection of personal data or in the development of tools used to process personal data. The Supervisory Authorities evaluating the BCRs may ask for some examples and explanation of the training programme during the application procedure and the training programme shall be specified in the application.	
2.2 The existence of a complaint handling process for the BCRs	YES	YES	The BCRs shall contain a commitment from the Processor Group to create a specific contact point for data subjects. All BCR members shall have the duty to communicate a claim or request without undue delay to the Controller without obligation to handle it, (except if it has been agreed otherwise with the Controller). The BCRs shall contain a commitment for the Processor to handle complaints from data subjects where the Controller has disappeared factually or has ceased to exist in law or became insolvent. In all cases where the processor handles complaints, these shall be dealt without undue delay and in any event within one month by a clearly identified department or person who has an appropriate level of independence in the exercise of his/her functions. Taking into account the complexity and number of the requests, that period may be extended by two further months at the utmost, in which case the data subject should be informed accordingly.	

Part 2   Data Protection: EU Law etc

Criteria for approval of BCRs	In the BCRs	In the application form	Comments	References to application/ BCRs
			The application form must explain how data subjects will be informed about the practical steps of the complaint system, in particular: – where to complain, – in what form, – delays for the reply on the complaint, – consequences in case of rejection of the complaint – consequences in case the complaint is considered as justified – consequences if the data subject is not satisfied by the replies (right to lodge a claim before the Court/Supervisory Authority)	
2.3 The existence of an audit programme covering the BCRs	YES	YES	The BCRs must create a duty for the group to have data protection audits on regular basis (by either internal or external accredited auditors) or on specific request from the privacy officer/function (or any other competent function in the organization) to ensure the verification of compliance with the BCRs. The BCRs must state that the audit programme covers all aspects of the BCRs including methods of ensuring that corrective actions will take place. Moreover, the BCRs must state that the result will be communicated to the privacy officer/function and to the relevant board of the controlling undertaking of a group or of the group of enterprises engaged in a joint economic activity but also will be made accessible to the Controller. Where appropriate, the result may be communicated to the ultimate parent's board. The BCRs must state that the Supervisory Authorities competent for the Controller can have access to the results of the audit upon request and give the Supervisory Authorities the authority/power to carry out a data protection audit of any BCR member if required. Any processor or sub-processor processing the personal data on behalf of a particular controller will accept, at the request of that controller, to submit their data processing facilities for audit of the processing activities relating to that controller which shall be carried out by the controller or an inspection body composed of independent members and in possession of the required professional qualifications, bound by a duty of confidentiality, selected by the data controller, where applicable, in agreement with the Supervisory Authority. The application form will contain a description of the audit system. For instance: – Which entity (department within the group) decides on the audit plan/programme,	

Criteria for approval of BCRs	In the BCRs	In the application form	Comments	References to application/BCRs
			– Which entity will conduct the audit,	
			– Time of the audit (regularly or on specific request from the appropriate Privacy function.)	
			– Coverage of the audit (for instance, applications, IT systems, databases that process Personal Data, or onward transfers, decisions taken as regards mandatory requirement under national laws that conflicts with the BCRs, review of the contractual terms used for the transfers out of the Group (to controllers or processors of data), corrective actions, . . .)	
			– Which entity will receive the results of the audits.	
2.4 The creation of a network of data protection officers (DPO) or appropriate staff for monitoring compliance with the rules	YES	NO	A commitment to appoint a DPO where required in line with article 37 of the GDPR or any other person or entity (such as a chief privacy officer) with responsibility to monitor compliance with the BCRs. This person/entity shall enjoy the highest management support in exercising this function.	
			The DPO or other person/entity as mentioned, respectively, can be assisted, in exercising this function, by a team/a network of local DPOs or local contacts as appropriate. The DPO shall directly report to the highest management level (GDPR Art. 38.3).	
			A brief description of the internal structure, role, position and tasks of the DPO or similar function, as mentioned, and the team/network created to ensure compliance with the rules. For example, that the DPO or chief Privacy Officer informs and advises the highest management, deals with Supervisory Authorities' investigations, monitors and annually reports on BCRs compliance at a global level, and that local DPOs or local contacts are in charge of reporting major privacy issues to the DPO or chief privacy officer, monitoring training and compliance at a local level.	
3 – COOPERATION DUTY				
3.1 A duty to cooperate with Supervisory Authorities	YES	YES	The BCRs shall contain a clear duty for all BCR members to cooperate with and to accept to be audited by the Supervisory Authorities competent for the relevant controller and to comply with the advice of these Supervisory Authorities on any issue related to those rules.	
3.2 A duty to cooperate with the Controller	YES	YES	The BCRs shall contain a clear duty for any processor or sub-processor to co-operate and assist the Controller to comply with data protection law (such as its duty to respect the data subject rights or to handle their complaints, or to be in a position to reply to investigation or inquiry from Supervisory Authorities). This shall be done in a reasonable time and to the extent reasonably possible.	

Criteria for approval of BCRs	In the BCRs	In the application form	Comments	References to application/ BCRs
4 – DESCRIPTION OF PROCESS- ING AND DATA FLOWS				
4.1 A description of the transfers and material scope covered by the BCRs	YES	YES	The BCRs shall contain a list of BCR members, i.e. entities that are bound by the BCRs (see also point 6.2) The Processor submitting a BCR shall give a general description to the Supervisory Authority of the material scope of the BCRs (expected nature of the data transferred, categories of personal data, types of data subjects concerned by the transfers, antici- pated types of processing and its purposes.	
4.2 A statement of the geographical scope of the BCRs (nature of data, type of data subjects, countries)	YES	YES	The BCRs shall specify the structure and contact details of the group of undertakings or group of enterprises engaged in a joint economic activity and of each of the BCR members. The BCRs shall indicate that it is up to the Controller to apply the BCRs to: i) All personal data processed for processor activities and that are submitted to EU law (for instance, data has been transferred from the European Union), OR; ii) All processing of data processed for processor activities within the group whatever the origin of the data.	
5 – MECHANISMS FOR REPORT- ING AND RECORDING CHANGES				
5.1 A process for updating the BCRs	YES	YES	The BCRs can be modified (for instance to take into account modifications of the regulatory environment or the company structure) but they shall impose a duty to re- port changes to all BCR members, and to the relevant Supervisory Authorities, via the competent Supervisory Authorities and to the controller. Where a change affects the processing conditions, the information should be given to the controller in such a timely fashion that the controller has the possibility to object to the change or to terminate the contract before the modification is made (for in- stance, on any intended changes concerning the addition or replacement of subcontrac- tors, before the data are communicated to the new sub-processor). Updates to the BCRs or to the list of the BCR members are possible without having to re-apply for an approval providing that:	

Criteria for approval of BCRs	In the BCRs	In the application form	Comments	References to application/ BCRs
			i) An identified person or team/department keeps a fully updated list of the BCR members and of the sub-processors involved in the data processing activities for the controller which shall be made accessible to the data controller, data subject and Supervisory Authorities.	
			ii) This person will keep track of and record any updates to the rules and provide the necessary information systematically to the data controller and upon request to Supervisory Authorities upon request.	
			iii) No transfer is made to a new BCR member until the new BCR member is effectively bound by the BCR and can deliver compliance.	
			iv) Any changes to the BCRs or to the list of BCR members shall be reported once a year to the relevant Supervisory Authorities, via the competent Supervisory Authority with a brief explanation of the reasons justifying the update.	
			v) Where a modification would affect the level of the protection offered by the BCRs or significantly affect the BCRs (i.e. changes in the bindingness), it must be promptly communicated to the relevant Supervisory Authorities via the competent Supervisory Authority.	
6 - DATA PROTECTION SAFE-GUARDS				
6.1 A description of the privacy principles including the rules on transfers or onward transfers outside of the EU	YES	YES	The BCRs shall include the following principles to be observed by any BCR member: i) Transparency, fairness, and lawfulness: Processors and sub-processors will have a general duty to help and assist the controller to comply with the law (for instance, to be transparent about sub-processor activities in order to allow the controller to correctly inform the data subject);	

Criteria for approval of BCRs	In the BCRs	In the application form	Comments	References to application/ BCRs
			ii) Purpose limitation: duty to process the personal data only on behalf of the controller and in compliance with its documented instructions including with regard to transfers of personal data to a third country, unless required to do so by Union or Member State law to which the processor is subject. In such a case, the processor shall inform the controller of that legal requirement before processing takes place, unless that law prohibits such information on important grounds of public interest (Art. 28-3-a of the GDPR). In other cases, if the processor cannot provide such compliance for whatever reasons, it agrees to inform promptly the data controller of its inability to comply, in which case the controller is entitled to suspend the transfer of data and/or terminate the contract. On the termination of the provision of services related to the data processing, the processors and sub-processors shall, at the choice of the controller, delete or return all the personal data transferred to the controller and delete the copies thereof and certify to the controller that it has done so, unless legislation imposed upon them requires storage of the personal data transferred. In that case, the processors and the sub-processors will inform the controller and warrant that it will guarantee the confidentiality of the personal data transferred and will not actively process the personal data transferred anymore. iii) Data quality: Processors and sub-processors will have a general duty to help and assist the controller to comply with the law, in particular: – Processors and sub-processors will execute any necessary measures when asked by the Controller, in order to have the data updated, corrected or deleted. Processors and sub-processors will inform each BCR member to whom the data have been disclosed of any rectification, or deletion of data. – Processors and sub-processors will execute any necessary measures, when asked by the Controller, in order to have the data deleted or anonymised from the moment the identification form is not necessary anymore. Processor and sub-processors will communicate to each entity to whom the data have been disclosed of any deletion or anonymisation of data.	

Criteria for approval of BCRs	In the BCRs	In the application form	Comments	References to application/ BCRs
			iv) <u>Security</u>: Processors and sub-processors will have a duty to implement all appropriate technical and organizational measures to ensure a level of security appropriate to the risks presented by the processing as provided by Article 32 of the GDPR. Processors and sub-processors will also have a duty to assist the Controller in ensuring compliance with the obligations as set out in Articles 32 to 36 of the GDPR taking into account the nature of processing and information available to the processor (Art.28-3-f of the GDPR). Processors and sub-processors must implement technical and organisational measures which at least meet the requirements of the data controller's applicable law and any existing particular measures specified in the Service Agreement. Processors shall inform the Controller without undue delay after becoming aware of any personal data breach. In addition, sub-processors shall have the duty to inform the Processor and the Controller without undue delay after becoming aware of any personal data breach. v) Data subject rights: Processors and sub-processors will execute any appropriate technical and organizational measures, insofar as this is possible, when asked by the controller, for the fulfilment of the controller's obligations to respond to requests for exercising the data subjects rights as set out in Chapter III of the GDPR (Art. 28-3-e of the GDPR) including by communicating any useful information in order to help the controller to comply with the duty to respect the rights of the data subjects. Processor and sub-processors will transmit to the controller any data subject request without answering it unless he is authorised to do so. vi) Sub-processing within the Group: data may be sub-processed by other BCR members bound by the BCRs only with the prior informed specific or general written authorization of the controller[3]. The Service Agreement will specify if a general prior authorization given at the beginning of the service would be sufficient or if a specific authorization will be required for each new sub-processor. If a general authorization is given, the controller should be informed by the processor of any intended changes concerning the addition or replacement of a sub-processor in such a timely fashion that the controller has the possibility to object to the change or to terminate the contract before the data are communicated to the new sub-processor. vii) Onward transfers to external sub-processors: Data may sub processed by non-members of the BCRs only with the prior informed specific or general written authorization of the controller[4]. If a general authorization is given, the controller should be informed by the processor of any intended changes concerning the addition or replacement of sub-processors in such a timely fashion that the controller has the possibility to object to the change or to terminate the contract before the data are communicated to the new sub-processor.	

Criteria for approval of BCRs	In the BCRs	In the application form	Comments	References to application/ BCRs
			Where the BCR member bound by the BCRs subcontracts its obligations under the Service Agreement, with the authorization of the controller, it shall do so only by way of a contract or other legal act under Union or Member State law with the sub-processor which provides that adequate protection is provided as set out in Articles 28, 29, 32, 45, 46, 47 of the GDPR and which ensures that the same data protection obligations as set out in the Service Agreement between the controller and the processor and sections 1.3, 1.4, 3 and 6 of this referential are imposed on the sub-processor, in particular providing sufficient guarantees to implement appropriate technical and organization measures in such a manner that the processing will meet the requirements of the GDPR (Art. 28-4 of the GDPR).	
6.1.2 Accountability *and other tools*	YES	YES	Processors will have a duty to make available to the controller all information necessary to demonstrate compliance with their obligations as provided by Article 28-3-h of the GDPR and allow for and contribute to audits, including inspections conducted by the controller or another auditor mandated by the controller. In addition, the processor shall immediately inform the controller if in its opinion, an instruction infringes the GDPR or other Union or Member State data protection provisions. In order to demonstrate compliance with the BCRs, BCR members need to maintain a record of all categories of processing activities carried out on behalf of each controller in line with the requirements as set out in Art. 30.2 GDPR. This record should be maintained in writing, including in electronic form and should be made available to the supervisory authority on request (Art.30.3 and 30.4 GDPR) The BCR members shall also assist the controller in implementing appropriate technical and organisational measures to comply with data protection principles and facilitate compliance with the requirements set up by the BCRs in practice such as data protection by design and by default (Art. 25 and 47.2.d GDPR)	
6.2 The list of entities bound by BCRs	YES	YES	BCR shall contain a list of the entities bound by the BCRs including contact details.	
6.3 The need to be transparent where national legislation prevents the group from complying with the BCRs	YES	NO	A clear commitment that where a BCR member has reasons to believe that the existing or future legislation applicable to it may prevent it from fulfilling the instructions received from the controller or its obligations under the BCRs or Service Agreement, it will promptly notify this to the controller which is entitled to suspend the transfer of data and/or terminate the contract, to the EU headquarter processor or EU member with delegated data protection responsibilities or the other relevant Privacy Officer/function, but also to the Supervisory Authority competent for the controller and the Supervisory authority competent for the processor.	

Criteria for approval of BCRs	In the BCRs	In the application form	Comments	References to application/ BCRs
			Any legally binding request for disclosure of the personal data by a law enforcement authority or state security body shall be communicated to the controller unless otherwise prohibited (such as a prohibition under criminal law to preserve the confidentiality of a law enforcement investigation). In any case, the request for disclosure should be put on hold and the Supervisory Authority competent for the controller and the competent Supervisory Authority for the processor should be clearly informed about the request, including information about the data requested, the requesting body and the legal basis for disclosure (unless otherwise prohibited).	
			If in specific cases the suspension and/or notification are prohibited, the BCRs shall provide that the requested BCR member will use its best efforts to obtain the right to waive this prohibition in order to communicate as much information as it can and as soon as possible, and be able to demonstrate that it did so.	
			If, in the above cases, despite having used its best efforts, the requested BCR member is not in a position to notify the competent SAs, it must commit in the BCRs to annually provide general information on the requests it received to the competent SAs (e.g. number of applications for disclosure, type of data requested, requester if possible, etc.).	
			In any case, the BCRs must state that transfers of personal data by a BCR member of the group to any public authority cannot be massive, disproportionate and indiscriminate in a manner that would go beyond what is necessary in a democratic society	
6.4 A statement about the relationship between national laws and BCRs	YES	NO	BCRs shall specify the relationship between the BCRs and the relevant applicable law.	
			The BCRs shall state that, where the local legislation, for instance EU legislation, requires a higher level of protection for personal data it will take precedence over the BCRs.	
			In any event data shall be processed in accordance with the applicable law.	

NOTES

1   Working Document WP204: Explanatory Document on the Processor Binding Corporate Rules, as last revised and adopted on 22 May 2015

2   Working Document WP 195a: Recommendation 1/2012 on the Standard Application form for Approval of Binding Corporate Rules for the Transfer of Personal Data for Processing Activities, adopted on 17 September 2012

3   Information on the main elements (parties, countries, security, guarantees in case of international transfers, with a possibility to get a copy of the contracts used). The detailed information, for instance relating to the name of the sub-processors could be provided e.g. in a public digital register.

4   Information on the main elements (parties, countries, security, guarantees in case of international transfers, with a possibility to get a copy of the contracts used). The detailed information, for instance relating to the name of the sub-processors could be provided e.g. in a public digital register.

II. COMMITMENTS TO BE TAKEN IN THE SERVICE LEVEL AGREEMENT

[2.227]
The BCRs for Processors shall unambiguously be linked to the Service Level Agreement signed with each Client. To that extent, it is important to make sure in the Service Level Agreement, which must contain all required elements provided by Article 28 of the GDPR, that:

–   BCRs will be made enforceable for the Controller (Client) through a specific reference to it in the SLA (as an annex).

–   The Controller shall commit that if the transfer involves special categories of data the Data Subject has been informed or will be informed before the transfer that his data could be transmitted to a third country not providing adequate protection;

–   The Controller shall also commit to inform the data subject about the existence of processors based outside of EU and of the BCRs. The Controller shall make available to the Data Subjects upon request a copy of the BCRs and of the service agreement (without any sensitive and confidential commercial information);

–   Clear confidentiality and security measures are described or referred with an electronic link;

–   A clear description of the instructions and the data processing;

–   The service agreement will specify if data may be sub-processed inside of the Group or outside of the group and will specify if the prior authorization to it expressed by the controller is general or needs to be given specifically for each new sub-processing activities.

ARTICLE 29 WORKING PARTY GUIDELINES ON TRANSPARENCY UNDER REGULATION 2016/679
17/EN
WP 260 rev.01

Adopted on 29 November 2017

As last Revised and Adopted on 11 April 2018

[2.228]

NOTES

This document was originally issued by the Article 29 Working Party but subsequently endorsed by the EDPB during its first plenary meeting.

© European Data Protection Board.

TABLE OF CONTENTS

INTRODUCTION

[2.229]
1. These guidelines provide practical guidance and interpretative assistance from the Article 29 Working Party (WP29) on the new obligation of transparency concerning the processing of personal data under the General Data Protection Regulation[1] (the "**GDPR**"). Transparency is an overarching obligation under the GDPR applying to three central areas: (1) the provision of information to data subjects related to fair processing; (2) how data controllers communicate with data subjects in relation to their rights under the GDPR; and (3) how data controllers facilitate the exercise by data subjects of their rights[2].

Insofar as compliance with transparency is required in relation to data processing under Directive (EU) 2016/680[3], these guidelines also apply to the interpretation of that principle.[4] These guidelines are, like all WP29 guidelines, intended to be generally applicable and relevant to controllers irrespective of the sectoral, industry or regulatory specifications particular to any given data controller. As such, these guidelines cannot address the nuances and many variables which may arise in the context of the transparency obligations of a specific sector, industry or regulated area. However, these guidelines are intended to enable controllers to understand, at a high level, WP29's interpretation of what the transparency obligations entail in practice and to indicate the approach which WP29 considers controllers should take to being transparent while embedding fairness and accountability into their transparency measures.

2.   Transparency is a long established feature of the law of the EU[5]. It is about engendering trust in the processes which affect the citizen by enabling them to understand, and if necessary, challenge those processes. It is also an expression of the principle of fairness in relation to the processing of personal data expressed in Article 8 of the Charter of Fundamental Rights of the European Union. Under the GDPR (Article 5(1)(a)[6]), in addition to the requirements that data must be processed lawfully and fairly, transparency is now included as a fundamental aspect of these principles.[7] Transparency is intrinsically linked to fairness and the new principle of accountability under the GDPR. It also follows from Article 5.2 that the controller must always be able to demonstrate that personal data are processed in a transparent manner in relation to the data subject.[8] Connected to this, the accountability principle requires transparency of processing operations in order that data controllers are able to demonstrate compliance with their obligations under the GDPR[9].

3.   In accordance with Recital 171 of the GDPR, where processing is already under way prior to 25 May 2018, a data controller should ensure that it is compliant with its transparency obligations as of 25 May 2018 (along with all other obligations under the GDPR). This means that prior to 25 May 2018, data controllers should revisit all information provided to data subjects on processing of their personal data (for example in privacy statements/ notices etc.) to ensure that they adhere to the requirements in relation to transparency which are discussed in these guidelines. Where changes or additions are made to such information, controllers should make it clear to data subjects that these changes have been effected in order to comply with the GDPR. WP29 recommends that such changes or additions be actively brought to the attention of data subjects but at a minimum controllers should make this information publicly available (e.g. on their website). However, if the changes or additions are material or substantive, then in line with paragraphs 29 to 32 below, such changes should be actively brought to the attention of the data subject.

4.   Transparency, when adhered to by data controllers, empowers data subjects to hold data controllers and processors accountable and to exercise control over their personal data by, for example, providing or withdrawing informed consent and actioning their data subject rights[10]. The concept of transparency in the GDPR is user-centric rather than legalistic and is realised by way of specific practical requirements on data controllers and processors in a number of articles. The practical (information) requirements are outlined in Articles 12 - 14 of the GDPR. However, the quality, accessibility and comprehensibility of the information is as important as the actual content of the transparency information, which must be provided to data subjects.

5.   The transparency requirements in the GDPR apply irrespective of the legal basis for processing and throughout the life cycle of processing. This is clear from Article 12 which provides that transparency applies at the following stages of the data processing cycle:

* before or at the start of the data processing cycle, i.e. when the personal data is being collected either from the data subject or otherwise obtained;
* throughout the whole processing period, i.e. when communicating with data subjects about their rights; and
* at specific points while processing is ongoing, for example when data breaches occur or in the case of material changes to the processing.

NOTES

[1]   Regulation (EU) 2016/679 of the European Parliament and of the Council of 27 April 2016 on the protection of natural persons with regard to the processing of personal data and on the free movement of such data, and repealing Directive 95/46/EC.

[2]   These guidelines set out general principles in relation to the exercise of data subjects' rights rather than considering specific modalities for each of the individual data subject rights under the GDPR.

[3]   Directive (EU) 2016/680 of the European Parliament and of the Council of 27 April 2016 on the protection of natural persons with regard to the processing of personal data by competent authorities for the purposes of the prevention, investigation, detection or prosecution of criminal offences or the execution of criminal penalties, and on the free movement of such data, and repealing Council Framework Decision 2008/977/JHA

[4]   While transparency is not one of the principles relating to processing of personal data set out in Article 4 of Directive (EU) 2016/680, Recital 26 states that any processing of personal data must be "lawful, fair and transparent" in relation to the natural persons concerned.

[5]   Article 1 of the TEU refers to decisions being taken "*as openly as possible and as close to the citizen as possible*"; Article 11(2) states that "*The institutions shall maintain an open, transparent and regular dialogue with representative associations and civil society*"; and Article 15 of the TFEU refers amongst other things to citizens of the Union having a right of access to documents of Union institutions, bodies, offices and agencies and the requirements of those Union institutions, bodies, offices and agencies to ensure that their proceedings are transparent.

[6]   "Personal data shall be processed lawfully, fairly and in a transparent manner in relation to the data subject".

[7]   In Directive 95/46/EC, transparency was only alluded to in Recital 38 by way of a requirement for processing of data to be fair, but not expressly referenced in the equivalent Article 6(1)(a).

8   Article 5.2 of the GDPR obliges a data controller to demonstrate transparency (together with the five other principles relating to data processing set out in Article 5.1) under the principle of accountability.

9   The obligation upon data controllers to implement technical and organisational measures to ensure and be able to demonstrate that processing is performed in accordance with the GDPR is set out in Article 24.1.

10   See, for example, the Opinion of Advocate General Cruz Villalon (9 July 2015) in the Bara case (Case C-201/14) at paragraph 74: "*the requirement to inform the data subjects about the processing of their personal data, which guarantees transparency of all processing, is all the more important since it affects the exercise by the data subjects of their right of access to the data being processed, referred to in Article 12 of Directive 95/46, and their right to object to the processing of those data, set out in Article 14 of that directive*".

THE MEANING OF TRANSPARENCY

[2.230]
6.   Transparency is not defined in the GDPR. Recital 39 of the GDPR is informative as to the meaning and effect of the principle of transparency in the context of data processing:

> "*It should be transparent to natural persons that personal data concerning them are collected, used, consulted or otherwise processed and to what extent the personal data are or will be processed. The principle of transparency requires that any information and communication relating to the processing of those personal data be easily accessible and easy to understand, and that clear and plain language be used. That principle concerns, in particular, information to the data subjects on the identity of the controller and the purposes of the processing and further information to ensure fair and transparent processing in respect of the natural persons concerned and their right to obtain confirmation and communication of personal data concerning them which are being processed . . . *"

ELEMENTS OF TRANSPARENCY UNDER THE GDPR

[2.231]
7.   The key articles in relation to transparency in the GDPR, as they apply to the rights of the data subject, are found in Chapter III (Rights of the Data Subject). Article 12 sets out the general rules which apply to: the provision of information to data subjects (under Articles 13–14); communications with data subjects concerning the exercise of their rights (under Articles 15–22); and communications in relation to data breaches (Article 34). In particular Article 12 requires that the information or communication in question must comply with the following rules:
- it must be concise, transparent, intelligible and easily accessible (Article 12.1);
- clear and plain language must be used (Article 12.1);
- the requirement for clear and plain language is of particular importance when providing information to children (Article 12.1);
- it must be in writing "*or by other means, including where appropriate, by electronic means*" (Article 12.1);
- where requested by the data subject it may be provided orally (Article 12.1) ; and
- it generally must be provided free of charge (Article 12.5).

"CONCISE, TRANSPARENT, INTELLIGIBLE AND EASILY ACCESSIBLE"

8.   The requirement that the provision of information to, and communication with, data subjects is done in a "concise and transparent" manner means that data controllers should present the information/ communication efficiently and succinctly in order to avoid information fatigue. This information should be clearly differentiated from other non-privacy related information such as contractual provisions or general terms of use. In an online context, the use of a layered privacy statement/ notice will enable a data subject to navigate to the particular section of the privacy statement/ notice which they want to immediately access rather than having to scroll through large amounts of text searching for particular issues.

9.   The requirement that information is "intelligible" means that it should be understood by an average member of the intended audience. Intelligibility is closely linked to the requirement to use clear and plain language. An accountable data controller will have knowledge about the people they collect information about and it can use this knowledge to determine what that audience would likely understand. For example, a controller collecting the personal data of working professionals can assume its audience has a higher level of understanding than a controller that obtains the personal data of children. If controllers are uncertain about the level of intelligibility and transparency of the information and effectiveness of user interfaces/ notices/ policies etc., they can test these, for example, through mechanisms such as user panels, readability testing, formal and informal interactions and dialogue with industry groups, consumer advocacy groups and regulatory bodies, where appropriate, amongst other things.

10.   A central consideration of the principle of transparency outlined in these provisions is that the data subject should be able to determine in advance what the scope and consequences of the processing entails and that they should not be taken by surprise at a later point about the ways in which their personal data has been used. This is also an important aspect of the principle of fairness under Article 5.1 of the GDPR and indeed is linked to Recital 39 which states that "*[n]atural persons should be made aware of risks, rules, safeguards and rights in relation to the processing of personal data . . . *" In particular, for complex, technical or unexpected data processing, WP29's position is that, as well as providing the prescribed information under Articles 13 and 14 (dealt with later in these guidelines), controllers should also separately spell out in unambiguous language what the most important consequences of the processing will be: in other words, what kind of effect will the specific processing described in a privacy statement/ notice actually have on a data subject? In accordance with the principle of accountability and in line with Recital 39, data controllers should assess whether there are particular risks for natural persons involved in this type of processing which should be brought to the attention of data subjects. This can help to provide an overview of the types of processing that could have the highest impact on the fundamental rights and freedoms of data subjects in relation to the protection of their personal data.

11. The "easily accessible" element means that the data subject should not have to seek out the information; it should be immediately apparent to them where and how this information can be accessed, for example by providing it directly to them, by linking them to it, by clearly signposting it or as an answer to a natural language question (for example in an online layered privacy statement/ notice, in FAQs, by way of contextual pop-ups which activate when a data subject fills in an online form, or in an interactive digital context through a chatbot interface, etc. These mechanisms are further considered below, including at paragraphs 33 to 40).

Example

Every organisation that maintains a website should publish a privacy statement/ notice on the website. A direct link to this privacy statement/ notice should be clearly visible on each page of this website under a commonly used term (such as "Privacy", "Privacy Policy" or "Data Protection Notice"). Positioning or colour schemes that make a text or link less noticeable, or hard to find on a webpage, are not considered easily accessible.

For apps, the necessary information should also be made available from an online store prior to download. Once the app is installed, the information still needs to be easily accessible from within the app. One way to meet this requirement is to ensure that the information is never more than "two taps away" (e.g. by including a "Privacy"/ "Data Protection" option in the menu functionality of the app). Additionally, the privacy information in question should be specific to the particular app and should not merely be the generic privacy policy of the company that owns the app or makes it available to the public.

WP29 recommends as a best practice that at the point of collection of the personal data in an online context a link to the privacy statement/ notice is provided or that this information is made available on the same page on which the personal data is collected.

"CLEAR AND PLAIN LANGUAGE"

12. With written information (and where written information is delivered orally, or by audio/ audiovisual methods, including for vision-impaired data subjects), best practices for clear writing should be followed.[11] A similar language requirement (for "plain, intelligible language") has previously been used by the EU legislator[12] and is also explicitly referred to in the context of consent in Recital 42 of the GDPR[13]. The requirement for clear and plain language means that information should be provided in as simple a manner as possible, avoiding complex sentence and language structures. The information should be concrete and definitive; it should not be phrased in abstract or ambivalent terms or leave room for different interpretations. In particular the purposes of, and legal basis for, processing the personal data should be clear.

Poor Practice Examples

The following phrases are not sufficiently clear as to the purposes of processing:
- *"We may use your personal data to develop new services"* (as it is unclear what the "services" are or how the data will help develop them);
- *"We may use your personal data for research purposes* (as it is unclear what kind of "research" this refers to); and
- *"We may use your personal data to offer personalised services"* (as it is unclear what the "personalisation" entails).

Good Practice Examples[14]
- *"We will retain your shopping history and use details of the products you have previously purchased to make suggestions to you for other products which we believe you will also be interested in"* (it is clear that what types of data will be processed, that the data subject will be subject to targeted advertisements for products and that their data will be used to enable this);
- *"We will retain and evaluate information on your recent visits to our website and how you move around different sections of our website for analytics purposes to understand how people use our website so that we can make it more intuitive"* (it is clear what type of data will be processed and the type of analysis which the controller is going to undertake); and

> • *"We will keep a record of the articles on our website that you have clicked on and use that information to target advertising on this website to you that is relevant to your interests, which we have identified based on articles you have read"* (it is clear what the personalisation entails and how the interests attributed to the data subject have been identified).

13. Language qualifiers such as "may", "might", "some", "often" and "possible" should also be avoided. Where data controllers opt to use indefinite language, they should be able, in accordance with the principle of accountability, to demonstrate why the use of such language could not be avoided and how it does not undermine the fairness of processing. Paragraphs and sentences should be well structured, utilising bullets and indents to signal hierarchical relationships. Writing should be in the active instead of the passive form and excess nouns should be avoided. The information provided to a data subject should not contain overly legalistic, technical or specialist language or terminology. Where the information is translated into one or more other languages, the data controller should ensure that all the translations are accurate and that the phraseology and syntax makes sense in the second language(s) so that the translated text does not have to be deciphered or re-interpreted. (A translation in one or more other languages should be provided where the controller targets[15] data subjects speaking those languages.)

PROVIDING INFORMATION TO CHILDREN AND OTHER VULNERABLE PEOPLE

14. Where a data controller is targeting children[16] or is, or should be, aware that their goods/ services are particularly utilised by children (including where the controller is relying on the consent of the child)[17], it should ensure that the vocabulary, tone and style of the language used is appropriate to and resonates with children so that the child addressee of the information recognises that the message/ information is being directed at them.[18] A useful example of child-centred language used as an alternative to the original legal language can be found in the "UN Convention on the Rights of the Child in Child Friendly Language".[19]

15. WP29's position is that transparency is a free-standing right which applies as much to children as it does to adults. WP29 emphasises in particular that children do not lose their rights as data subjects to transparency simply because consent has been given/ authorised by the holder of parental responsibility in a situation to which Article 8 of the GDPR applies. While such consent will, in many cases, be given or authorised on a once-off basis by the holder of parental responsibility, a child (like any other data subject) has an ongoing right to transparency throughout the continuum of their engagement with a data controller. This is consistent with Article 13 of the UN Convention on the Rights of the Child which states that a child has a right to freedom of expression which includes the right to seek, receive and impart information and ideas of all kinds.[20] It is important to point out that, while providing for consent to be given on behalf of a child when under a particular age,[21] Article 8 *does not provide* for transparency measures to be directed at the holder of parental responsibility who gives such consent. Therefore, data controllers have an obligation in accordance with the specific mentions of transparency measures addressed to children in Article 12.1 (supported by Recitals 38 and 58) to ensure that where they target children or are aware that their goods or services are particularly utilised by children of a literate age, that any information and communication should be conveyed in clear and plain language or in a medium that children can easily understand. For the avoidance of doubt however, WP29 recognises that with very young or pre-literate children, transparency measures may also be addressed to holders of parental responsibility given that such children will, in most cases, be unlikely to understand even the most basic written or non-written messages concerning transparency.

16. Equally, if a data controller is aware that their goods/ services are availed of by (or targeted at) other vulnerable members of society, including people with disabilities or people who may have difficulties accessing information, the vulnerabilities of such data subjects should be taken into account by the data controller in its assessment of how to ensure that it complies with its transparency obligations in relation to such data subjects.[22] This relates to the need for a data controller to assess its audience's likely level of understanding, as discussed above at paragraph 9.

"IN WRITING OR BY OTHER MEANS"

17. Under Article 12.1, the default position for the provision of information to, or communications with, data subjects is that the information is in writing.[23] (Article 12.7 also provides for information to be provided in combination with standardised icons and this issue is considered in the section on visualisation tools at paragraphs 49 to 53). However, the GDPR also allows for other, unspecified "means" including electronic means to be used. WP29's position with regard to written electronic means is that where a data controller maintains (or operates, in part or in full, through) a website, WP29 recommends the use of layered privacy statements/ notices, which allow website visitors to navigate to particular aspects of the relevant privacy statement/ notice that are of most interest to them (see more on layered privacy statements/ notices at paragraph 35 to 37).[24] However, the entirety of the information addressed to data subjects should also be available to them in one single place or one complete document (whether in a digital or paper format) which can be easily accessed by a data subject should they wish to consult the entirety of the information addressed to them. Importantly, the use of a layered approach is not confined only to written electronic means for providing information to data subjects. As discussed at paragraphs 35 to 36 and 38 below, a layered approach to the provision of information to data subjects may also be utilised by employing a combination of *methods* to ensure transparency in relation to processing.

18. Of course, the use of digital layered privacy statements/ notices is not the only written electronic means that can be deployed by controllers. Other electronic means include "just- in-time" contextual pop-up notices, 3D touch or hover-over notices, and privacy dashboards. Non-written electronic means which may be used *in addition* to a layered privacy statement/ notice might include videos and smartphone or IoT voice alerts.[25] "Other means", which are not necessarily electronic, might include, for example, cartoons, infographics or flowcharts. Where transparency information is directed at children specifically, controllers should consider what types of measures may be particularly accessible to children (e.g. these might be comics/ cartoons, pictograms, animations, etc. amongst other measures).

19. It is critical that the method(s) chosen to provide the information is/are appropriate to the particular circumstances, i.e. the manner in which the data controller and data subject interact or the manner in which the data subject's information is collected. For example, only providing the information in electronic written format, such as in an online privacy statement/ notice may not be appropriate/ workable where a device that captures personal data does not have a screen (e.g. IoT devices/ smart devices) to access the website/ display such written information. In such cases, appropriate alternative *additional* means should be considered, for example providing the privacy statement/ notice in hard copy instruction manuals or providing the URL website address (i.e. the specific page on the website) at which the online privacy statement/ notice can be found in the hard copy instructions or in the packaging. Audio (oral) delivery of the information could also be additionally provided if the screenless device has audio capabilities. WP29 has previously made recommendations around transparency and provision of information to data subjects in its Opinion on Recent Developments in the Internet of Things[26] (such as the use of QR codes printed on internet of things objects, so that when scanned, the QR code will display the required transparency information). These recommendations remain applicable under the GDPR.

"..THE INFORMATION MAY BE PROVIDED ORALLY"

20. Article 12.1 specifically contemplates that information may be provided orally to a data subject on request, provided that their identity is proven by other means. In other words, the means employed should be more than reliance on a mere assertion by the individual that they are a specific named person and the means should enable the controller to verify a data subject's identity with sufficient assurance. The requirement to verify the identity of the data subject before providing information orally only applies to information relating to the exercise by a specific data subject of their rights under Articles 15 to 22 and 34. This precondition to the provision of oral information cannot apply to the provision of general privacy information as outlined in Articles 13 and 14, since information required under Articles 13 and 14 must also be made accessible to *future* users/ customers (whose identity a data controller would not be in a position to verify). Hence, information to be provided under Articles 13 and 14 may be provided by oral means without the controller requiring a data subject's identity to be proven.

21. The oral provision of information required under Articles 13 and 14 does not necessarily mean oral information provided on a person-to-person basis (i.e. in person or by telephone). Automated oral information may be provided in addition to written means. For example, this may apply in the context of persons who are visually impaired when interacting with information society service providers, or in the context of screenless smart devices, as referred to above at paragraph 19. Where a data controller has chosen to provide information to a data subject orally, or a data subject requests the provision of oral information or communications, WP29's position is that the data controller should allow the data subject to re-listen to pre-recorded messages. This is imperative where the request for oral information relates to visually impaired data subjects or other data subjects who may have difficulty in accessing or understanding information in written format. The data controller should also ensure that it has a record of, and can demonstrate (for the purposes of complying with the accountability requirement): (i) the request for the information by oral means, (ii) the method by which the data subject's identity was verified (where applicable – see above at paragraph 20) and (iii) the fact that information was provided to the data subject.

"FREE OF CHARGE"

22. Under Article 12.5,[27] data controllers cannot generally charge data subjects for the provision of information under Articles 13 and 14, or for communications and actions taken under Articles 15 - 22 (on the rights of data subjects) and Article 34 (communication of personal data breaches to data subjects).[28] This aspect of transparency also means that any information provided under the transparency requirements cannot be made conditional upon financial transactions, for example the payment for, or purchase of, services or goods.[29]

NOTES

[11]   See How to Write Clearly by the European Commission (2011), to be found at: https://publications.europa.eu/en/publication-detail/-/publication/c2dab20c-0414-408d-87b5-dd3c6e5dd9a5.

[12]   Article 5 of Council Directive 93/13/EEC of 5 April 1993 on unfair terms in consumer contracts

[13]   Recital 42 states that a declaration of consent pre-formulated by a data controller should be provided in an intelligible and easily accessible form, using clear and plain language and it should not contain unfair terms.

[14]   The requirement for transparency exists entirely independently of the requirement upon data controllers to ensure that there is an appropriate legal basis for the processing under Article 6.

[15]   For example, where the controller operates a website in the language in question and/or offers specific country options and/or facilitates the payment for goods or services in the currency of a particular member state then these may be indicative of a data controller targeting data subjects of a particular member state.

[16]   The term "child" is not defined under the GDPR, however WP29 recognises that, in accordance with the UN Convention on the Rights of the Child, which all EU Member States have ratified, a child is a person under the age of 18 years.

[17]   i.e. children of 16 years or older (or, where in accordance with Article 8.1 of the GDPR Member State national law has set the age of consent at a specific age between 13 and 16 years for children to consent to an offer for the provision of information society services, children who meet that national age of consent).

Part 2   Data Protection: EU Law etc

18   Recital 38 states that "Children merit special protection with regard to their personal data as they may be less aware of the risks, consequences and safeguards concerned and their rights in relation to the processing of personal data". Recital 58 states that "Given that children merit specific protection, any information and communication, where processing is addressed to a child, should be in such a clear and plain language that the child can easily understand".

19   https://www.unicef.org/rightsite/files/uncrcchildfriendlylanguage.pdf

20   Article 13 of the UN Convention on the Rights of the Child states that: "The child shall have the right to freedom of expression; this right shall include freedom to seek, receive and impart information and ideas of all kinds, regardless of frontiers, either orally, in writing or in print, in the form of art, or through any other media of the child's choice."

21   See footnote 17 above.

22   For example, the UN Convention on the Rights of Persons with Disabilities requires that appropriate forms of assistance and support are provided to persons with disabilities to ensure their access to information.

23   Article 12.1 refers to "language" and states that the information shall be provided in writing, or by other means, including, where appropriate, by electronic means.

24   The WP29's recognition of the benefits of layered notices has already been noted in Opinion 10/2004 on More Harmonised Information Provisions and Opinion 02/2013 on apps on smart devices.

25   These examples of electronic means are indicative only and data controllers may develop new innovative methods to comply with Article 12.

26   WP29 Opinion 8/2014 adopted on 16 September 2014

27   This states that "Information provided under Articles 13 and 14 and any communication and any actions taken under Articles 15 to 22 and 34 shall be provided free of charge."

28   However, under Article 12.5 the controller may charge a reasonable fee where, for example, a request by a data subject in relation to the information under Article 13 and 14 or the rights under Articles 15 - 22 or Article 34 is excessive or manifestly unfounded. (Separately, in relation to the right of access under Article 15.3 a controller may charge a reasonable fee based on administrative costs for any further copy of the personal data which is requested by a data subject).

29   By way of illustration, if a data subject's personal data is being collected in connection with a purchase, the information which is required to be provided under Article 13 should be provided prior to payment being made and at the point at which the information is being collected, rather than after the transaction has been concluded. Equally though, where free services are being provided to the data subject, the Article 13 information must be provided prior to, rather than after, sign-up given that Article 13.1 requires the provision of the information "at the time when the personal data are obtained".

INFORMATION TO BE PROVIDED TO THE DATA SUBJECT – ARTICLES 13 & 14

CONTENT

[2.232]
23.   The GDPR lists the categories of information that must be provided to a data subject in relation to the processing of their personal data where it is collected from the data subject (Article 13) or obtained from another source (Article 14). The **table in the Annex** to these guidelines summarises the categories of information that must be provided under Articles 13 and 14. It also considers the nature, scope and content of these requirements. For clarity, WP29's position is that there is no difference between the status of the information to be provided under sub-article 1 and 2 of Articles 13 and 14 respectively. All of the information across these sub-articles is of equal importance and must be provided to the data subject.

"APPROPRIATE MEASURES"

24.   As well as content, the form and manner in which the information required under Articles 13 and 14 should be provided to the data subject is also important. The notice containing such information is frequently referred to as a data protection notice, privacy notice, privacy policy, privacy statement or fair processing notice. The GDPR does not prescribe the format or modality by which such information should be provided to the data subject but does make it clear that it is the data controller's responsibility to take "appropriate measures" in relation to the provision of the required information for transparency purposes. This means that the data controller should take into account all of the circumstances of the data collection and processing when deciding upon the appropriate modality and format of the information provision. In particular, appropriate measures will need to be assessed in light of the product/ service user experience. This means taking account of the device used (if applicable), the nature of the user interfaces/ interactions with the data controller (the user "journey") and the limitations that those factors entail. As noted above at paragraph 17, WP29 recommends that where a data controller has an online presence, an online layered privacy statement/ notice should be provided.

25.   In order to help identify the most appropriate modality for providing the information, in advance of "going live", data controllers may wish to trial different modalities by way of user testing (e.g. hall tests, or other standardised tests of readability or accessibility) to seek feedback on how accessible, understandable and easy to use the proposed measure is for users. (See also further comments above on other mechanisms for carrying out user testing at paragraph 9). Documenting this approach should also assist data controllers with their accountability obligations by demonstrating how the tool/ approach chosen to convey the information is the most appropriate in the circumstances.

TIMING FOR PROVISION OF INFORMATION

26.   Articles 13 and 14 set out information which must be provided to the data subject at the commencement phase of the processing cycle[30]. Article 13 applies to the scenario where the data is collected from the data subject. This includes personal data that:

*   a data subject consciously provides to a data controller (e.g. when completing an online form); or

- a data controller collects from a data subject by observation (e.g. using automated data capturing devices or data capturing software such as cameras, network equipment, Wi-Fi tracking, RFID or other types of sensors).

Article 14 applies in the scenario where the data have not been obtained from the data subject. This includes personal data which a data controller has obtained from sources such as:
- third party data controllers;
- publicly available sources;
- data brokers; or
- other data subjects.

27.   As regards timing of the provision of this information, providing it in a timely manner is a vital element of the transparency obligation and the obligation to process data fairly. Where Article 13 applies, under Article 13.1 the information must be provided *"at the time when personal data are obtained"*. In the case of indirectly obtained personal data under Article 14, the timeframes within which the required information must be provided to the data subject are set out in Article 14.3 (a) to (c) as follows:
- The general requirement is that the information must be provided within a "reasonable period" after obtaining the personal data and no later than one month, *"having regard to the specific circumstances in which the personal data are processed"* (Article 14.3(a)).
- The general one-month time limit in Article 14.3(a) may be further curtailed under Article 14.3(b),[31] which provides for a situation where the data are being used for communication with the data subject. In such a case, the information must be provided at the latest at the time of the first communication with the data subject. If the first communication occurs prior to the one-month time limit after obtaining the personal data, then the information must be provided *at the latest* at the time of the first communication with the data subject notwithstanding that one month from the point of obtaining the data has not expired. If the first communication with a data subject occurs more than one month after obtaining the personal data then Article 14.3(a) continues to apply, so that the Article 14 Information must be provided to the data subject at the latest within one month after it was obtained.
- The general one-month time limit in Article 14.3(a) can also be curtailed under Article 14.3(c)[32] which provides for a situation where the data are being disclosed to another recipient (whether a third party or not)[33]. In such a case, the information must be provided at the latest at the time of the first disclosure. In this scenario, if the disclosure occurs prior to the one-month time limit, then the information must be provided *at the latest* at the time of that first disclosure, notwithstanding that one month from the point of obtaining the data has not expired. Similar to the position with Article 14.3(b), if any disclosure of the personal data occurs more than one month after obtaining the personal data, then Article 14.3(a) again continues to apply, so that the Article 14 information must be provided to the data subject at the latest within one month after it was obtained.

28.   Therefore, in any case, the maximum time limit within which Article 14 information must be provided to a data subject is one month. However, the principles of fairness and accountability under the GDPR require data controllers to always consider the reasonable expectations of data subjects, the effect that the processing may have on them and their ability to exercise their rights in relation to that processing, when deciding at what point to provide the Article 14 information. Accountability requires controllers to demonstrate the rationale for their decision and justify why the information was provided at the time it was. In practice, it may be difficult to meet these requirements when providing information at the 'last moment'. In this regard, Recital 39 stipulates, amongst other things, that data subjects should be *"made aware of the risks, rules, safeguards and rights in relation to the processing of personal data and how to exercise their rights in relation to such processing"*. Recital 60 also refers to the requirement that the data subject be informed of the existence of the processing operation and its purposes in the context of the principles of fair and transparent processing. For all of these reasons, WP29's position is that, wherever possible, data controllers should, in accordance with the principle of fairness, provide the information to data subjects well in advance of the stipulated time limits. Further comments on the appropriateness of the timeframe between notifying data subjects of the processing operations and such processing operations actually taking effect are set out in paragraphs 30 to 31 and 48.

CHANGES TO ARTICLE 13 AND ARTICLE 14 INFORMATION

29.   Being accountable as regards transparency applies not only at the point of collection of personal data but throughout the processing life cycle, irrespective of the information or communication being conveyed. This is the case, for example, when changing the contents of existing privacy statements/ notices. The controller should adhere to the same principles when communicating both the initial privacy statement/ notice and any subsequent substantive or material changes to this statement/ notice. Factors which controllers should consider in assessing what is a substantive or material change include the impact on data subjects (including their ability to exercise their rights), and how unexpected/ surprising the change would be to data subjects. Changes to a privacy statement/ notice that should always be communicated to data subjects include inter alia: a change in processing purpose; a change to the identity of the controller; or a change as to how data subjects can exercise their rights in relation to the processing. Conversely, an example of changes to a privacy statement/ notice which are not considered by WP29 to be substantive or material include corrections of misspellings, or stylistic/ grammatical flaws. Since most existing customers or users will only glance over communications of changes to privacy statements/ notices, the controller should take all measures necessary to ensure that these changes are communicated in such a way that ensures that most recipients will actually notice them. This means, for example, that a notification of changes should always be communicated by way of an appropriate modality (e.g. email, hard copy letter, pop-up on a webpage or other modality which will effectively bring the changes to the attention of the data subject) specifically devoted to those changes (e.g. not together with direct marketing content), with such a communication meeting the Article 12 requirements of being concise, transparent, intelligible, easily accessible and using clear and plain language. References in the privacy statement/ notice to the effect that the data subject should regularly check the privacy statement/notice for changes or updates are considered not only insufficient but also unfair in the context of Article 5.1(a). Further guidance in relation to the timing for notification of changes to data subjects is considered below at paragraph 30 to 31.

TIMING OF NOTIFICATION OF CHANGES TO ARTICLE 13 AND ARTICLE 14 INFORMATION

30. The GDPR is silent on the timing requirements (and indeed the methods) that apply for notifications of changes to information that has previously been provided to a data subject under Article 13 or 14 (excluding an intended further purpose for processing, in which case information on that further purpose must be notified prior to the commencement of that further processing as per Articles 13.3 and 14.4 – see below at paragraph 45). However, as noted above in the context of the timing for the provision of Article 14 information, the data controller must again have regard to the fairness and accountability principles in terms of any reasonable expectations of the data subject, or the potential impact of those changes upon the data subject. If the change to the information is indicative of a fundamental change to the nature of the processing (e.g. enlargement of the categories of recipients or introduction of transfers to a third country) or a change which may not be fundamental in terms of the processing operation but which may be relevant to and impact upon the data subject, then that information should be provided to the data subject well in advance of the change actually taking effect and the method used to bring the changes to the data subject's attention should be explicit and effective. This is to ensure the data subject does not "miss" the change and to allow the data subject a reasonable timeframe for them to (a) consider the nature and impact of the change and (b) exercise their rights under the GDPR in relation to the change (e.g. to withdraw consent or to object to the processing).

31. Data controllers should carefully consider the circumstances and context of each situation where an update to transparency information is required, including the potential impact of the changes upon the data subject and the modality used to communicate the changes, and be able to demonstrate how the timeframe between notification of the changes and the change taking effect satisfies the principle of fairness to the data subject. Further, WP29's position is that, consistent with the principle of fairness, when notifying such changes to data subjects, a data controller should also explain what will be the likely impact of those changes on data subjects. However, compliance with transparency requirements does not "whitewash" a situation where the changes to the processing are so significant that the processing becomes completely different in nature to what it was before. WP29 emphasises that all of the other rules in the GDPR, including those relating to incompatible further processing, continue to apply irrespective of compliance with the transparency obligations.

32. Additionally, even when transparency information (e.g. contained in a privacy statement/ notice) does not materially change, it is likely that data subjects who have been using a service for a significant period of time will not recall the information provided to them at the outset under Articles 13 and/or 14. WP29 recommends that controllers facilitate data subjects to have continuing easy access to the information to re-acquaint themselves with the scope of the data processing. In accordance with the accountability principle, controllers should also consider whether, and at what intervals, it is appropriate for them to provide express reminders to data subjects as to the fact of the privacy statement/ notice and where they can find it.

MODALITIES - FORMAT OF INFORMATION PROVISION

33. Both Articles 13 and 14 refer to the obligation on the data controller to "*provide the data subject with all of the following information . . . *" The operative word here is "provide". This means that the data controller must take active steps to furnish the information in question to the data subject or to actively direct the data subject to the location of it (e.g. by way of a direct link, use of a QR code, etc.). The data subject must not have to actively search for information covered by these articles amongst other information, such as terms and conditions of use of a website or app. The example at paragraph 11 illustrates this point. As noted above at paragraph 17, WP29 recommends that the entirety of the information addressed to data subjects should also be available to them in one single place or one complete document (e.g. whether in a digital form on a website or in paper format) which can be easily accessed should they wish to consult the entirety of the information.

34. There is an inherent tension in the GDPR between the requirements on the one hand to provide the comprehensive information to data subjects which is required under the GDPR, and on the other hand do so in a form that is concise, transparent, intelligible and easily accessible. As such, and bearing in mind the fundamental principles of accountability and fairness, controllers must undertake their own analysis of the nature, circumstances, scope and context of the processing of personal data which they carry out and decide, within the legal requirements of the GDPR and taking account of the recommendations in these Guidelines particularly at paragraph 36 below, how to prioritise information which must be provided to data subjects and what are the appropriate levels of detail and methods for conveying the information.

LAYERED APPROACH IN A DIGITAL ENVIRONMENT AND LAYERED PRIVACY STATEMENTS/ NOTICES

35. In the digital context, in light of the volume of information which is required to be provided to the data subject, a layered approach may be followed by data controllers where they opt to use a combination of methods to ensure transparency. WP29 recommends in particular that layered privacy statements/ notices should be used to link to the various categories of information which must be provided to the data subject, rather than displaying all such information in a single notice on the screen, in order to avoid information fatigue. Layered privacy statements/ notices can help resolve the tension between completeness and understanding, notably by allowing users to navigate directly to the section of the statement/ notice that they wish to read. It should be noted that layered privacy statements/ notices are not merely nested pages that require several clicks to get to the relevant information. The design and layout of the first layer of the privacy statement/ notice should be such that the data subject has a clear overview of the information available to them on the processing of their personal data and where/ how they can find that detailed information within the layers of the privacy statement/ notice. It is also important that the information contained within the different layers of a layered notice is consistent and that the layers do not provide conflicting information.

36.   As regards the content of the first modality used by a controller to inform data subjects in a layered approach (in other words the primary way in which the controller first engages with a data subject), or the content of the first layer of a layered privacy statement/ notice, WP29 recommends that the first layer/ modality should include the details of the purposes of processing, the identity of controller and a description of the data subject's rights. (Furthermore this information should be directly brought to the attention of a data subject at the time of collection of the personal data e.g. displayed as a data subject fills in an online form.) The importance of providing this information upfront arises in particular from Recital 39.[34] While controllers must be able to demonstrate accountability as to what further information they decide to prioritise, WP29's position is that, in line with the fairness principle, in addition to the information detailed above in this paragraph, the first layer/ modality should also contain information on the processing which has the most impact on the data subject and processing which could surprise them. Therefore, the data subject should be able to understand from information contained in the first layer/ modality what the consequences of the processing in question will be for the data subject (see also above at paragraph 10).

37.   In a digital context, aside from providing an online layered privacy statement/ notice, data controllers may also choose to use *additional* transparency tools (see further examples considered below) which provide tailored information to the individual data subject which is specific to the position of the individual data subject concerned and the goods/ services which that data subject is availing of. It should be noted however that while WP29 recommends the use of online layered privacy statements/ notices, this recommendation does not exclude the development and use of other innovative methods of compliance with transparency requirements.

LAYERED APPROACH IN A NON-DIGITAL ENVIRONMENT

38.   A layered approach to the provision of transparency information to data subjects can also be deployed in an offline/ non-digital context (i.e. a real-world environment such as person-to- person engagement or telephone communications) where multiple modalities may be deployed by data controllers to facilitate the provision of information. (See also paragraphs 33 to 37 and 39 to 40 in relation to different modalities for providing the information.) This approach should not be confused with the separate issue of layered privacy statements/ notices. Whatever the formats that are used in this layered approach, WP29 recommends that the first "layer" (in other words the primary way in which the controller first engages with the data subject) should generally convey the most important information (as referred to at paragraph 36 above), namely the details of the purposes of processing, the identity of controller and the existence of the rights of the data subject, together with information on the greatest impact of processing or processing which could surprise the data subject. For example, where the first point of contact with a data subject is by telephone, this information could be provided during the telephone call with the data subject and they could be provided with the balance of the information required under Article 13/ 14 by way of further, different means, such as by sending a copy of the privacy policy by email and/ or sending the data subject a link to the controller's layered online privacy statement/ notice.

"PUSH" AND "PULL" NOTICES

39.   Another possible way of providing transparency information is through the use of "push" and "pull" notices. Push notices involve the provision of "just-in-time" transparency information notices while "pull" notices facilitate access to information by methods such as permission management, privacy dashboards and "learn more" tutorials. These allow for a more user- centric transparency experience for the data subject.
- A privacy dashboard is a single point from which data subjects can view 'privacy information' and manage their privacy preferences by allowing or preventing their data from being used in certain ways by the service in question. This is particularly useful when the same service is used by data subjects on a variety of different devices as it gives them access to and control over their personal data no matter how they use the service. Allowing data subjects to manually adjust their privacy settings via a privacy dashboard can also make it easier for a privacy statement/ notice to be personalised by reflecting only the types of processing occurring for that particular data subject. Incorporating a privacy dashboard into the existing architecture of a service (e.g. by using the same design and branding as the rest of the service) is preferable because it will ensure that access and use of it will be intuitive and may help to encourage users to engage with this information, in the same way that they would with other aspects of the service. This can be an effective way of demonstrating that 'privacy information' is a necessary and integral part of a service rather than a lengthy list of legalese.

- A just-in-time notice is used to provide specific 'privacy information' in an ad hoc manner, as and when it is most relevant for the data subject to read. This method is useful for providing information at various points throughout the process of data collection; it helps to spread the provision of information into easily digestible chunks and reduces the reliance on a single privacy statement/ notice containing information that is difficult to understand out of context. For example, if a data subject purchases a product online, brief explanatory information can be provided in pop-ups accompanying relevant fields of text. The information next to a field requesting the data subject's telephone number could explain for example that this data is only being collected for the purposes of contact regarding the purchase and that it will only be disclosed to the delivery service.

OTHER TYPES OF "APPROPRIATE MEASURES"

40. Given the very high level of internet access in the EU and the fact that data subjects can go online at any time, from multiple locations and different devices, as stated above, WP29's position is that an "appropriate measure" for providing transparency information in the case of data controllers who maintain a digital/ online presence, is to do so through an electronic privacy statement/ notice. However, based on the circumstances of the data collection and processing, a data controller may need to additionally (or alternatively where the data controller does not have any digital/online presence) use other modalities and formats to provide the information. Other possible ways to convey the information to the data subject arising from the following different personal data environments may include the following modes applicable to the relevant environment which are listed below. As noted previously, a layered approach may be followed by controllers where they opt to use a combination of such methods while ensuring that the most important information (see paragraph 36 and 38) is always conveyed in the first modality used to communicate with the data subject.

(a)   Hard copy/ paper environment, for example when entering into contracts by postal means: written explanations, leaflets, information in contractual documentation, cartoons, infographics or flowcharts;

(b)   Telephonic environment: oral explanations by a real person to allow interaction and questions to be answered or automated or pre-recorded information with options to hear further more detailed information;

(c)   Screenless smart technology/ IoT environment such as Wi-Fi tracking analytics: icons, QR codes, voice alerts, written details incorporated into paper set-up instructions, videos incorporated into digital set-up instructions, written information on the smart device, messages sent by SMS or email, visible boards containing the information, public signage or public information campaigns;

(d)   Person to person environment, such as responding to opinion polls, registering in person for a service: oral explanations or written explanations provided in hard or soft copy format;

(e)   "Real-life" environment with CCTV/ drone recording: visible boards containing the information, public signage, public information campaigns or newspaper/ media notices.

INFORMATION ON PROFILING AND AUTOMATED DECISION-MAKING

41. Information on the existence of automated decision-making, including profiling, as referred to in Articles 22.1 and 22.4, together with meaningful information about the logic involved and the significant and envisaged consequences of the processing for the data subject, forms part of the obligatory information which must be provided to a data subject under Articles 13.2(f) and 14.2(g). WP29 has produced guidelines on automated individual decision-making and profiling[35] which should be referred to for further guidance on how transparency should be given effect in the particular circumstances of profiling. It should be noted that, aside from the specific transparency requirements applicable to automated decision-making under Articles 13.2(f) and 14.2(g), the comments in these guidelines relating to the importance of informing data subjects as to the consequences of processing of their personal data, and the general principle that data subjects should not be taken by surprise by the processing of their personal data, equally apply to profiling generally (not just profiling which is captured by Article 22[36]), as a type of processing.[37]

OTHER ISSUES – RISKS, RULES AND SAFEGUARDS

42. Recital 39 of the GDPR also refers to the provision of certain information which is not explicitly covered by Articles 13 and Article 14 (see recital text above at paragraph 28). The reference in this recital to making data subjects aware of the risks, rules and safeguards in relation to the processing of personal data is connected to a number of other issues. These include data protection impact assessments (DPIAs). As set out in the WP29 Guidelines on DPIAs,[38] data controllers may consider publication of the DPIA (or part of it), as a way of fostering trust in the processing operations and demonstrating transparency and accountability, although such publication is not obligatory. Furthermore, adherence to a code of conduct (provided for under Article 40) may go towards demonstrating transparency, as codes of conduct may be drawn up for the purpose of specifying the application of the GDPR with regard to: fair and transparent processing; information provided to the public and to data subjects; and information provided to, and the protection of, children, amongst other issues.

43. Another relevant issue relating to transparency is data protection by design and by default (as required under Article 25). These principles require data controllers to build data protection considerations into their processing operations and systems from the ground up, rather than taking account of data protection as a last-minute compliance issue. Recital 78 refers to data controllers implementing measures that meet the requirements of data protection by design and by default including measures consisting of transparency with regard to the functions and processing of personal data.

44. Separately, the issue of joint controllers is also related to making data subjects aware of the risks, rules and safeguards. Article 26.1 requires joint controllers to determine their respective responsibilities for complying with obligations under the GDPR in a transparent manner, in particular with regard to the exercise by data subjects of their rights and the duties to provide the information under Articles 13 and 14. Article 26.2 requires that the essence of the arrangement between the data controllers must be made available to the data subject. In other words, it must be completely clear to a data a subject as to which data controller he or she can approach where they intend to exercise one or more of their rights under the GDPR.[39]

NOTES

[30]   Pursuant to the principles of fairness and purpose limitation, the organisation which collects the personal data from the data subject should always specify the purposes of the processing at the time of collection. If the purpose includes the creation of inferred personal data, the intended purpose of creating and further processing such inferred personal data, as well as the categories of the inferred data processed, must always be communicated to the data subject at the time of collection, or prior to the further processing for a new purpose in compliance with Article 13.3 or Article 14.4.

[31]   The use of the words "*if the personal data are to be used for..*" in Article 14.3(b) indicates a specification to the general position with regard to the maximum time limit set out in Article 14.3(a) but does not replace it.

[32]   The use of the words "*if a disclosure to anther recipient is envisaged...*" in Article 14.3(c) likewise indicates a specification to the general position with regard to the maximum time limit set out in Article 14.3(a) but does not replace it.

[33]   Article 4.9 defines "recipient" and clarifies that a recipient to whom personal data are disclosed does not have to be a third party. Therefore, a recipient may be a data controller, joint controller or processor.

[34]   Recital 39 states, on the principle of transparency, that "That principle concerns, in particular, information to the data subjects on the identity of the controller and the purposes of the processing and further information to ensure fair and transparent processing in respect of natural persons concerned and their right to obtain confirmation and communication of personal data concerning them which are being processed."

[35]   Guidelines on Automated individual decision-making and Profiling for the purposes of Regulation 2016/679, WP 251

[36]   This applies to decision-making based solely on automated processing, including profiling, which produces legal effects concerning the data subject or similarly significantly affects him or her.

[37]   Recital 60, which is relevant here, states that "Furthermore, the data subject should be informed of the existence of profiling and the consequences of such profiling".

[38]   Guidelines on Data Protection Impact Assessment (DPIA) and determining whether processing is "likely to result in a high risk" for the purposes of Regulation 2016/679, WP 248 rev.1

[39]   Under Article 26.3, irrespective of the terms of the arrangement between joint data controllers under Article 26.1, a data subject may exercise his or her rights under the GDPR in respect of and against each of the joint data controllers.

INFORMATION RELATED TO FURTHER PROCESSING

[2.233]

45. Both Articles 13 and Article 14 contain a provision[40] that requires a data controller to inform a data subject if it intends to further process their personal data for a purpose other than that for which it was collected/ obtained. If so, "*the controller shall provide the data subject prior to that further processing with information on that other purpose and with any relevant further information as referred to in paragraph 2*". These provisions specifically give effect to the principle in Article 5.1(b) that personal data shall be collected for specified, explicit and legitimate purposes, and further processing in a manner that is *incompatible* with these purposes is prohibited.[41] The second part of Article 5.1(b) states that further processing for archiving purposes in the public interest, scientific or historical research purposes or for statistical purposes, shall, in accordance with Article 89.1, not be considered to be incompatible with the initial purposes. Where personal data are further processed for purposes that are *compatible* with the original purposes (Article 6.4 informs this issue[42]), Articles 13.3 and 14.4 apply. The requirements in these articles to inform a data subject about further processing promotes the position in the GDPR that a data subject should reasonably expect that at the time and in the context of the collection of personal data that processing for a particular purpose may take place.[43] In other words, a data subject should not be taken by surprise at the purpose of processing of their personal data.

46. Articles 13.3 and 14.4, insofar as they refer to the provision of "*any relevant further information as referred to in paragraph 2*", may be interpreted at first glance as leaving some element of appreciation to the data controller as to the extent of and the particular categories of information from the relevant sub-paragraph 2 (i.e. Article 13.2 or 14.2 as applicable) that should be provided to the data subject. (Recital 61 refers to this as "*other necessary information*".) However the default position is that all such information set out in that sub- article should be provided to the data subject unless one or more categories of the information does not exist or is not applicable.

47. WP29 recommends that, in order to be transparent, fair and accountable, controllers should consider making information available to data subjects in their privacy statement/ notice on the compatibility analysis carried out under Article 6.4[44] where a legal basis other than consent or national/ EU law is relied on for the new processing purpose. (In other words, an explanation as to how the processing for the other purpose(s) is compatible with the original purpose). This is to allow data subjects the opportunity to consider the compatibility of the further processing and the safeguards provided and to decide whether to exercise their rights e.g. the right to restriction of processing or the right to object to processing, amongst others.[45] Where controllers choose not to include such information in a privacy notice/ statement, WP29 recommends that they make it clear to data subjects that they can obtain the information on request.

48. Connected to the exercise of data subject rights is the issue of timing. As emphasised above, the provision of information in a timely manner is a vital element of the transparency requirements under

Articles 13 and 14 and is inherently linked to the concept of fair processing. Information in relation to *further processing* must be provided "prior to that further processing". WP29's position is that a reasonable period should occur between the notification and the processing commencing rather than an immediate start to the processing upon notification being received by the data subject. This gives data subjects the practical benefits of the principle of transparency, allowing them a meaningful opportunity to consider (and potentially exercise their rights in relation to) the further processing. What is a reasonable period will depend on the particular circumstances. The principle of fairness requires that the more intrusive (or less expected) the further processing, the longer the period should be. Equally, the principle of accountability requires that data controllers be able to demonstrate how the determinations they have made as regards the timing for the provision of this information are justified in the circumstances and how the timing overall is fair to data subjects. (See also the previous comments in relation to ascertaining reasonable timeframes above at paragraphs 30 to 32.)

NOTES

40   At Articles 13.3 and 14.4, which are expressed in identical terms, apart from the word "collected", which is used in Article 13, and which is replaced with the word "obtained" in Article 14.

41   See, for example on this principle, Recitals 47, 50, 61, 156, 158; Articles 6.4 and 89

42   Article 6.4 sets out, in non-exhaustive fashion, the factors which are to be taken into account in ascertaining whether processing for another purpose is compatible with the purpose for which the personal data are initially collected, namely: the link between the purposes; the context in which the personal data have been collected; the nature of the personal data (in particular whether special categories of personal data or personal data relating to criminal offences and convictions are included); the possible consequences of the intended further processing for data subjects; and the existence of appropriate safeguards.

43   Recitals 47 and 50

44   Also referenced in Recital 50

45   As referenced in Recital 63, this will enable a data subject to exercise the right of access in order to be aware of and to verify the lawfulness of the processing.

VISUALISATION TOOLS

[2.234]
49. Importantly, the principle of transparency in the GDPR is not limited to being effected simply through language communications (whether written or oral). The GDPR provides for visualisation tools (referencing in particular, icons, certification mechanisms, and data protection seals and marks) where appropriate. Recital 58[46] indicates that the accessibility of information addressed to the public or to data subjects is especially important in the online environment.[47]

ICONS

50. Recital 60 makes provision for information to be provided to a data subject "in combination" with standardised icons, thus allowing for a multi-layered approach. However, the use of icons should not simply replace information necessary for the exercise of a data subject's rights nor should they be used as a substitute to compliance with the data controller's obligations under Articles 13 and 14. Article 12.7 provides for the use of such icons stating that:

> "The information to be provided to data subjects pursuant to Articles 13 and 14 may be provided in combination with standardised icons in order to give in an easily visible, intelligible and clearly legible manner a meaningful overview of the intended processing. Where icons are presented electronically they shall be machine-readable".

51. As Article 12.7 states that "*Where the icons are presented electronically, they shall be machine-readable*", this suggests that there may be situations where icons are not presented electronically,[48] for example icons on physical paperwork, IoT devices or IoT device packaging, notices in public places about Wi-Fi tracking, QR codes and CCTV notices.

52. Clearly, the purpose of using icons is to enhance transparency for data subjects by potentially reducing the need for vast amounts of written information to be presented to a data subject. However, the utility of icons to effectively convey information required under Articles 13 and 14 to data subjects is dependent upon the standardisation of symbols/ images to be universally used and recognised across the EU as shorthand for that information. In this regard, the GDPR assigns responsibility for the development of a code of icons to the Commission but ultimately the European Data Protection Board may, either at the request of the Commission or of its own accord, provide the Commission with an opinion on such icons.[49] WP29 recognises that, in line with Recital 166, the development of a code of icons should be centred upon an evidence-based approach and in advance of any such standardisation it will be necessary for extensive research to be conducted in conjunction with industry and the wider public as to the efficacy of icons in this context.

CERTIFICATION MECHANISMS, SEALS AND MARKS

53. Aside from the use of standardised icons, the GDPR (Article 42) also provides for the use of data protection certification mechanisms, data protection seals and marks for the purpose of demonstrating compliance with the GDPR of processing operations by data controllers and processors and enhancing transparency for data subjects.[50] WP29 will be issuing guidelines on certification mechanisms in due course.

NOTES

46   "Such information could be provided in electronic form, for example, when addressed to the public, through a website. This is of particular relevance in situations where the proliferation of actors and the technological complexity of practice

make it difficult for the data subject to know and understand whether, by whom and for what purpose personal data relating to him or her are being collected, such as in the case of online advertising."

[47]   In this context, controllers should take into account visually impaired data subjects (e.g. red-green colour blindness).

[48]   There is no definition of "machine-readable" in the GDPR but Recital 21 of Directive 2013/37/EU17 defines "machine readable" as:

> "*a file format structured so that software applications can easily identify, recognize and extract specific data, including individual statements of fact, and their internal structure. Data encoded in files that are structured in a machine-readable format are machine-readable data. Machine-readable formats can be open or proprietary; they can be formal standards or not. Documents encoded in a file format that limits automatic processing, because the data cannot, or cannot easily, be extracted from them, should not be considered to be in a machine-readable format. Member States should where appropriate encourage the use of open, machine-readable formats.*"

[49]   Article 12.8 provides that the Commission is empowered to adopt delegated acts under Article 92 for the purpose of determining the information to be presented by the icons and the information for providing standardised icons. Recital 166 (which deals with delegated acts of the Commission in general) is instructive, providing that the Commission must carry out appropriate consultations during its preparatory work, including at expert level. However, the European Data Protection Board (EDPB) also has an important consultative role to play in relation to the standardisation of icons as Article 70.1(r) states that the EDPB shall on its own initiative or, where relevant, at the request of the Commission, provide the Commission with an opinion on icons.

[50]   See the reference in Recital 100

EXERCISE OF DATA SUBJECTS' RIGHTS

[2.235]

54. Transparency places a triple obligation upon data controllers insofar as the rights of data subjects under the GDPR are concerned, as they must:[51]

- provide information to data subjects on their rights[52] (as required under Articles 13.2(b) and 14.2(c));
- comply with the principle of transparency (i.e. relating to the quality of the communications as set out in Article 12.1) when communicating with data subjects in relation to their rights under Articles 15 to 22 and 34; and
- facilitate the exercise of data subjects' rights under Articles 15 to 22.

55. The GDPR requirements in relation to the exercise of these rights and the nature of the information required are designed to *meaningfully position* data subjects so that they can vindicate their rights and hold data controllers accountable for the processing of their personal data. Recital 59 emphasises that "*modalities should be provided for facilitating the exercise of the data subject's rights*" and that the data controller should "*also provide means for requests to be made electronically, especially where personal data are processed by electronic means*". The modality provided by a data controller for data subjects to exercise their rights should be appropriate to the context and the nature of the relationship and interactions between the controller and a data subject. To this end, a data controller may wish to provide one or more different modalities for the exercise of rights that are reflective of the different ways in which data subjects interact with that data controller.

Example

A health service provider uses an electronic form on its website, and paper forms in the receptions of its health clinics, to facilitate the submission of access requests for personal data both online and in person. While it provides these modalities, the health service still accepts access requests submitted in other ways (such as by letter and by email) and provides a dedicated point of contact (which can be accessed by email and by telephone) to help data subjects with the exercise of their rights.

NOTES

[51]   Under the Transparency and Modalities section of the GDPR on Data Subject Rights (Section 1, Chapter III, namely Article 12)

[52]   Access, rectification, erasure, restriction on processing, object to processing, portability

EXCEPTIONS TO THE OBLIGATION TO PROVIDE INFORMATION

ARTICLE 13 EXCEPTIONS

[2.236]

56. The only exception to a data controller's Article 13 obligations where it has collected personal data directly from a data subject occurs "*where and insofar as, the data subject already has the information*".[53] The principle of accountability requires that data controllers demonstrate (and document) what information the data subject already has, how and when they received it and that no changes have since occurred to that information that would render it out of date. Further, the use of the phrase "insofar as" in Article 13.4 makes it clear that even if the data subject has previously been provided with certain categories from the inventory of information set out in Article 13, there is still an obligation on the data controller to supplement that information in order to ensure that the data subject now has a complete set of the information listed in Articles 13.1 and 13.2. The following is a best practice example concerning the limited manner in which the Article 13.4 exception should be construed.

Example

An individual signs up to an online email service and receives all of the required Article 13.1 and 13.2 information at the point of sign-up. Six months later the data subject activates a connected instant message functionality through the email service provider and provides their mobile telephone number to do so. The service provider gives the data subject certain Article 13.1 and 13.2 information about the processing of the telephone number (e.g. purposes and legal basis for processing, recipients, retention period) but does not provide other information that the individual already has from 6 months ago and which has not since changed (e.g. the identity and contact details of the controller and the data protection officer, information on data subject rights and the right to complain to the relevant supervisory authority). As a matter of best practice however, the complete suite of information should be provided to the data subject again but the data subject also should be able to easily tell what information amongst it is new. The new processing for the purposes of the instant messaging service may affect the data subject in a way which would prompt them to seek to exercise a right they may have forgotten about, having been informed six months prior. Providing all the information again helps to ensure the data subject remains well informed about how their data is being used and their rights.

ARTICLE 14 EXCEPTIONS

57. Article 14 carves out a much broader set of exceptions to the information obligation on a data controller where personal data has not been obtained from the data subject. These exceptions should, as a general rule, be interpreted and applied narrowly. In addition to the circumstances where the data subject already has the information in question (Article 14.5(a)), Article 14.5 also allows for the following exceptions:
- The provision of such information is impossible or would involve a disproportionate effort, in particular for processing for archiving purposes in the public interest, scientific or historical research purposes or statistical purposes, or where it would make the achievement of the objectives of the processing impossible or seriously impair them;
- The data controller is subject to a national law or EU law requirement to obtain or disclose the personal data and that the law provides appropriate protections for the data subject's legitimate interests ; or
- An obligation of professional secrecy (including a statutory obligation of secrecy) which is regulated by national or EU law means the personal data must remain confidential.

PROVES IMPOSSIBLE, DISPROPORTIONATE EFFORT AND SERIOUS IMPAIRMENT OF OBJECTIVES

58. Article 14.5(b) allows for 3 separate situations where the obligation to provide the information set out in Articles 14.1, 14.2 and 14.4 is lifted:
(i)   Where it proves impossible (in particular for archiving, scientific/ historical research or statistical purposes);
(ii)   Where it would involve a disproportionate effort (in particular for archiving, scientific/ historical research or statistical purposes); or
(iii)   Where providing the information required under Article 14.1 would make the achievement of the objectives of the processing impossible or seriously impair them.

"PROVES IMPOSSIBLE"

59. The situation where it "proves impossible" under Article 14.5(b) to provide the information is an all or nothing situation because something is either impossible or it is not; there are no degrees of impossibility. Thus if a data controller seeks to rely on this exemption it must demonstrate the factors that actually *prevent it* from providing the information in question to data subjects. If, after a certain period of time, the factors that caused the "impossibility" no longer exist and it becomes possible to provide the information to data subjects then the data controller should immediately do so. In practice, there will be very few situations in which a data controller can demonstrate that it is actually impossible to provide the information to data subjects. The following example demonstrates this.

Example

A data subject registers for a post-paid online subscription service. After registration, the data controller collects credit data from a credit-reporting agency on the data subject in order to decide whether to provide the service. The controller's protocol is to inform data subjects of the collection of this credit data within three days of collection, pursuant to Article 14.3(a). However, the data subject's address and phone number is not registered in public registries (the data subject is in fact living abroad). The data subject did not leave an email address when registering for the service or the email address is invalid. The controller finds that it has no means to directly contact the data subject. In this case, however, the controller may give information about collection of credit reporting data on its website, prior to registration. In this case, it would not be impossible to provide information pursuant to Article 14.

IMPOSSIBILITY OF PROVIDING THE SOURCE OF THE DATA

60. Recital 61 states that *"where the origin of the personal data cannot be provided to the data subject because various sources have been used, general information should be provided"*. The lifting of the requirement to provide data subjects with information on the source of their personal data applies only where this is not possible because different pieces of personal data relating to the same data subject cannot be attributed to a particular source. For example, the mere fact that a database comprising the personal data of multiple data subjects has been compiled by a data controller using more than one source is not enough to lift this requirement if it is possible (although time consuming or burdensome) to identify the source from which the personal data of individual data subjects derived. Given the requirements of data protection by design and by default,[54] transparency mechanisms should be built into processing systems from the ground up so that all sources of personal data received into an organisation can be tracked and traced back to their source at any point in the data processing life cycle (see paragraph 43 above).

"DISPROPORTIONATE EFFORT"

61. Under Article 14.5(b), as with the "proves impossible" situation, "disproportionate effort" may also apply, in particular, for processing *"for archiving purposes in the public interest, scientific or historical research purposes or statistical purposes, subject to the safeguards referred to in Article 89(1)"*. Recital 62 also references these objectives as cases where the provision of information to the data subject would involve a disproportionate effort and states that in this regard, the number of data subjects, the age of the data and any appropriate safeguards adopted should be taken into consideration. Given the emphasis in Recital 62 and Article 14.5(b) on archiving research and statistical purposes with regard to the application of this exemption, WP29's position is that this exception should not be *routinely* relied upon by data controllers who are not processing personal data for the purposes of archiving in the public interest, for scientific or historical research purposes or statistical purposes. WP29 emphasises the fact that where these are the purposes pursued, the conditions set out in Article 89.1 must still be complied with and the provision of the information must constitute a disproportionate effort.

62. In determining what may constitute either impossibility or disproportionate effort under Article 14.5(b), it is relevant that there are no comparable exemptions under Article 13 (where personal data is collected from a data subject). The only difference between an Article 13 and an Article 14 situation is that in the latter, the personal data is not collected from the data subject. It therefore follows that impossibility or disproportionate effort typically arises by virtue of circumstances which do not apply if the personal data is collected from the data subject. In other words, the impossibility or disproportionate effort must be directly connected to the fact that the personal data was obtained other than from the data subject.

Example

A large metropolitan hospital requires all patients for day procedures, longer-term admissions and appointments to fill in a Patient Information Form which seeks the details of two next-of-kin (data subjects). Given the very large volume of patients passing through the hospital on a daily basis, it would involve disproportionate effort on the part of the hospital to provide all persons who have been listed as next-of-kin on forms filled in by patients each day with the information required under Article 14.

---

63. The factors referred to above in Recital 62 (number of data subjects, the age of the data and any appropriate safeguards adopted) may be indicative of the types of issues that contribute to a data controller having to use disproportionate effort to notify a data subject of the relevant Article 14 information.

Example

Historical researchers seeking to trace lineage based on surnames indirectly obtain a large dataset relating to 20,000 data subjects. However, the dataset was collected 50 years ago, has not been updated since, and does not contain any contact details. Given the size of the database and more particularly, the age of the data, it would involve disproportionate effort for the researchers to try to trace the data subjects individually in order to provide them with Article 14 information.

---

64. Where a data controller seeks to rely on the exception in Article 14.5(b) on the basis that provision of the information would involve a disproportionate effort, it should carry out a balancing exercise to assess the effort involved for the data controller to provide the information to the data subject against the impact and effects on the data subject if he or she was not provided with the information. This assessment should be documented by the data controller in accordance with its accountability obligations. In such a case, Article 14.5(b) specifies that the controller must take appropriate measures to protect the data subject's rights, freedoms and legitimate interests. This applies equally where a controller determines that the provision of the information proves impossible, or would likely render impossible or seriously impair the achievement of the objectives of the processing. One appropriate measure, as specified in Article 14.5(b), that controllers must always take is to make the information publicly available. A controller can do this in a number of ways, for instance by putting the information on its website, or by proactively advertising the information in a newspaper or on posters on its premises. Other appropriate measures, in addition to making the information publicly available, will depend on the circumstances of the processing, but may include: undertaking a data protection impact assessment; applying pseudonymisation techniques to the data; minimising the data collected and the storage period; and implementing technical and organisational measures to ensure a high level of security. Furthermore, there may be situations where a data controller is processing personal data which does not require the identification of a data subject (for example with pseudonymised data). In such cases, Article 11.1 may also be relevant as it states that a data controller shall not be obliged to maintain, acquire or process additional information in order to identify the data subject for the sole purposes of complying with the GDPR.

SERIOUS IMPAIRMENT OF OBJECTIVES

65. The final situation covered by Article 14.5(b) is where a data controller's provision of the information to a data subject under Article 14.1 is likely to make impossible or seriously impair the achievement of the processing objectives. To rely on this exception, data controllers must demonstrate that the provision of the information set out in Article 14.1 alone would nullify the objectives of the processing. Notably, reliance on this aspect of Article 14.5(b) pre-supposes that the data processing satisfies all of the principles set out in Article 5 and that most importantly, in all of the circumstances, the processing of the personal data is fair and that it has a legal basis.

Example

Bank A is subject to a mandatory requirement under anti-money laundering legislation to report suspicious activity relating to accounts held with it to the relevant financial law enforcement authority. Bank A receives information from Bank B (in another Member State) that an account holder has instructed it to transfer money to another account held with Bank A which appears suspicious. Bank A passes this data concerning its account holder and the suspicious activities to the relevant financial law enforcement authority. The anti-money laundering legislation in question makes it a criminal offence for a reporting bank to "tip off" the account holder that they may be subject to regulatory investigations. In this situation, Article 14.5(b) applies because providing the data subject (the account holder with Bank A) with Article 14 information on the processing of account holder's personal data received from Bank B would seriously impair the objectives of the legislation, which includes the prevention of "tip-offs". However, general information should be provided to all account holders with Bank A when an account is opened that their personal data may be processed for anti-money laundering purposes.

OBTAINING OR DISCLOSING IS EXPRESSLY LAID DOWN IN LAW

66. Article 14.5(c) allows for a lifting of the information requirements in Articles 14.1, 14.2 and 14.4 insofar as the obtaining or disclosure of personal data "*is expressly laid down by Union or Member State law to which the controller is subject*". This exemption is conditional upon the law in question providing "*appropriate measures to protect the data subject's legitimate interests*". Such a law must directly address the data controller and the obtaining or disclosure in question should be mandatory upon the data controller. Accordingly, the data controller must be able to demonstrate how the law in question applies to them and requires them to either obtain or disclose the personal data in question. While it is for Union or Member State law to frame the law such that it provides "*appropriate measures to protect the data subject's legitimate interests*", the data controller should ensure (and be able to demonstrate) that its obtaining or disclosure of personal data complies with those measures. Furthermore, the data controller should make it clear to data subjects that it obtains or discloses personal data in accordance with the law in question, unless there is a legal prohibition preventing the data controller from doing so. This is in line with Recital 41 of the GDPR, which states that a legal basis or legislative measure should be clear and precise, and its application should be foreseeable to persons subject to it, in accordance with the case law of the Court of Justice of the EU and the European Court of Human Rights. However, Article 14.5(c) will not apply where the data controller is under an obligation to obtain data *directly from a data subject*, in which case Article 13 will apply. In that case, the only exemption under the GDPR exempting the controller from providing the data subject with information on the processing will be that under Article 13.4 (i.e. where and insofar as the data subject already has the information). However, as referred to below at paragraph 68, at a national level, Member States may also legislate, in accordance with Article 23, for further specific restrictions to the right to transparency under Article 12 and to information under Articles 13 and 14.

Example

A tax authority is subject to a mandatory requirement under national law to obtain the details of employees' salaries from their employers. The personal data is not obtained from the data subjects and therefore the tax authority is subject to the requirements of Article 14. As the obtaining of the personal data by the tax authority from employers is expressly laid down by law, the information requirements in Article 14 do not apply to the tax authority in this instance.

CONFIDENTIALITY BY VIRTUE OF A SECRECY OBLIGATION

67. Article 14.5(d) provides for an exemption to the information requirement upon data controllers where the personal data *"must remain confidential subject to an obligation of professional secrecy regulated by Union or Member State law, including a statutory obligation of secrecy"*. Where a data controller seeks to rely on this exemption, it must be able to demonstrate that it has appropriately identified such an exemption and to show how the professional secrecy obligation directly addresses the data controller such that it prohibits the data controller from providing all of the information set out in Articles 14.1, 14.2 and 14.4 to the data subject.

Example

A medical practitioner (data controller) is under a professional obligation of secrecy in relation to his patients' medical information. A patient (in respect of whom the obligation of professional secrecy applies) provides the medical practitioner with information about her health relating to a genetic condition, which a number of her close relatives also have. The patient also provides the medical practitioner with certain personal data of her relatives (data subjects) who have the same condition. The medical practitioner is not required to provide those relatives with Article 14 information as the exemption in Article 14.5(d) applies. If the medical practitioner were to provide the Article 14 information to the relatives, the obligation of professional secrecy, which he owes to his patient, would be violated.

NOTES
53   Article 13.4
54   Article 25

RESTRICTIONS ON DATA SUBJECT RIGHTS

[2.237]
68. Article 23 provides for Member States (or the EU) to legislate for further restrictions on the scope of the data subject rights in relation to transparency and the substantive data subject rights[55] where such measures respect the essence of the fundamental rights and freedoms and are necessary and proportionate to safeguard one or more of the ten objectives set out in Article 23.1(a) to (j). Where such national measures lessen either the specific data subject rights or the general transparency obligations, which would otherwise apply to data controllers under the GDPR, the data controller should be able to demonstrate how the national provision applies to them. As set out in Article 23.2(h), the legislative measure must contain a provision as to the right of the data subject to be informed about a restriction on their rights, unless so informing them may be prejudicial to the purpose of the restriction. Consistent with this, and in line with principle of fairness, the data controller should also inform data subjects that they are relying on (or will rely on, in the event of a particular data subject right being exercised) such *a national legislative restriction* to the exercise of data subject rights, or to the transparency obligation, unless doing so would be prejudicial to the purpose of the legislative restriction. As such, transparency requires data controllers to provide adequate upfront information to data subjects about their rights and any particular caveats to those rights which the controller may seek to rely on, so that the data subject is not taken by surprise at a purported restriction of a particular right when they later attempt to exercise it against the controller. In relation to pseudonymisation and data minimisation, and insofar as data controllers may purport to rely on Article 11 of the GDPR, WP29 has previously confirmed in Opinion 3/ 2017[56] that Article 11 of the GDPR should be interpreted as a way of enforcing genuine data minimisation without hindering the exercise of data subject rights, and that the exercise of data subject rights must be made possible with the help of additional information provided by the data subject.

69. Additionally, Article 85 requires Member States, by law, to reconcile data protection with the right to freedom of expression and information. This requires, amongst other things, that Member States provide for appropriate exemptions or derogations from certain provisions of the GDPR (including from the transparency requirements under Articles 12 - 14) for processing carried out for journalistic, academic, artistic or literary expression purposes, if they are necessary to reconcile the two rights.

NOTES
55   As set out in Articles 12 to 22 and 34, and in Article 5 insofar as its provisions correspond to the rights and obligations provided for in Articles 12 to 22.
56   Opinion 03/2017 on Processing personal data in the context of Cooperative Intelligent Transport Systems (C-ITS) – see paragraph 4.2

TRANSPARENCY AND DATA BREACHES

[2.238]
70. WP29 has produced separate Guidelines on Data Breaches[57] but for the purposes of these guidelines, a data controller's obligations in relation to communication of data breaches to a data subject must take full account of the transparency requirements set out in Article 12.[58] The communication of

a data breach must satisfy the same requirements, detailed above (in particular for the use of clear and plain language), that apply to any other communication with a data subject in relation to their rights or in connection with conveying information under Articles 13 and 14.

NOTES

57   Guidelines on Personal data breach notification under Regulation 2016/679, WP 250

58   This is made clear by Article 12.1 which specifically refers to " . . . any communication under Articles 15 to 22 **and 34** relating to processing to the data subject..." [emphasis added].

ANNEX

[2.239]

Information that must be provided to a data subject under Article 13 or Article 14

Required Information Type	Relevant article (if personal data collected directly from data subject)	Relevant article (if personal data not obtained from the data subject)	WP29 comments on information requirement
The identity and contact details of the controller and, where applicable, their representative[59]	Article 13.1(a)	Article 14.1(a)	This information should allow for easy identification of the controller and preferably allow for different forms of communications with the data controller (e.g. phone number, email, postal address, etc.)
Contact details for the data protection officer, where applicable	Article	13.1(6)	Article 14.1(6) See WP29 Guidelines on Data Protection Officers[60]
The purposes and legal basis for the processing	Article	13.1(c)	Article 14.1(c) In addition to setting out the purposes of the processing for which the personal data is intended, the relevant legal basis relied upon under Article 6 must be specified. In the case of special categories of personal data, the relevant provision of Article 9 (and where relevant, the applicable Union or Member State law under which the data is processed) should be specified. Where, pursuant to Article 10, personal data relating to criminal convictions and offences or related security measures based on Article 6.1 is processed, where applicable the relevant Union or Member State law under which the processing is carried out should be specified.
Where legitimate interests (Article 6.1(f)) is the legal basis for the processing, the legitimate interests pursued by the data controller or a third party	Article 13.1(d)	Article 14.2(b)	The specific interest in question must be identified for the benefit of the data subject. As a matter of best practice, the controller can also provide the data subject with the information from the *balancing test*, which must be carried out to allow reliance on Article 6.1(f) as a lawful basis for processing, in advance of any collection of data subjects' personal data. To avoid information fatigue, this can be included within a layered privacy statement/ notice (see paragraph 35). In any case, the WP29 position is that information to the data subject should make it clear that they can obtain information on the balancing test upon request. This is essential for effective transparency where data subjects have doubts as to whether the balancing test has been carried out fairly or they wish to file a complaint with a supervisory authority. Categories of personal data concerned Not required Article 14.1(d) This information is required in an Article 14 scenario because the personal data has not been obtained from the data subject, who therefore lacks an awareness of which categories of their personal data the data controller has obtained.
Categories of personal data concerned	Not required	Article 14.1(d)	This information is required in an Article 14 scenario because the personal data has not been obtained from the data subject, who therefore lacks an awareness of which categories of their personal data the data controller has obtained.

Required Information Type	Relevant article (if personal data collected directly from data subject)	Relevant article (if personal data not obtained from the data subject)	WP29 comments on information requirement
Recipients[61] (or categories of recipients) of the personal data	Article 13.1(e)	Article 14.1(e)	The term "recipient" is defined in Article 4.9 as "*a natural or legal person, public authority, agency or another body, to which the personal data are disclosed, **whether a third party or not**" [emphasis added]. As such, a recipient does not have to be a third party. Therefore, other data controllers, joint controllers and processors to whom data is transferred or disclosed are covered by the term "recipient" and information on such recipients should be provided in addition to information on third party recipients. The actual (named) recipients of the personal data, or the categories of recipients, must be provided. In accordance with the principle of fairness, controllers must provide information on the recipients that is most meaningful for data subjects. In practice, this will generally be the named recipients, so that data subjects know exactly who has their personal data. If controllers opt to provide the categories of recipients, the information should be as specific as possible by indicating the type of recipient (i.e. by reference to the activities it carries out), the industry, sector and subsector and the location of the recipients.*
Details of transfers to third countries, the fact of same and the details of the relevant safeguards[62] (including the existence or absence of a Commission adequacy decision[63]) and the means to obtain a copy of them or where they have been made available	Article 13.1(f)	Article 14.1(f)	The relevant GDPR article permitting the transfer and the corresponding mechanism (e.g. adequacy decision under Article 45/ binding corporate rules under Article 47/ standard data protection clauses under Article 46.2/ derogations and safeguards under Article 49 etc.) should be specified. Information on where and how the relevant document may be accessed or obtained should also be provided e.g. by providing a link to the mechanism used. In accordance with the principle of fairness, the information provided on transfers to third countries should be as meaningful as possible to data subjects; this will generally mean that the third countries be named.
The storage period (or if not possible, criteria used to determine that period)	Article 13.2(a)	Article 14.2(a)	This is linked to the data minimisation requirement in Article 5.1(c) and storage limitation requirement in Article 5.1(e). The storage period (or criteria to determine it) may be dictated by factors such as statutory requirements or industry guidelines but should be phrased in a way that allows the data subject to assess, on the basis of his or her own situation, what the retention period will be for specific data/ purposes. It is not sufficient for the data controller to generically state that personal data will be kept as long as necessary for the legitimate purposes of the processing. Where relevant, the different storage periods should be stipulated for different categories of personal data and/or different processing purposes, including where appropriate, archiving periods.
The rights of the data subject to: • access; • rectification; • erasure; • restriction on processing; • objection to processing and • portability.	Article 13.2(b)	Article 14.2(c)	This information should be specific to the processing scenario and include a summary of what the right involves and how the data subject can take steps to exercise it and any limitations on the right (see paragraph 68 above). In particular, the right to object to processing must be explicitly brought to the data subject's attention at the latest at the time of first communication with the data subject and must be presented clearly and separately from any other information.[64] In relation to the right to portability, see WP29 Guidelines on the right to data portability.[65]
Where processing is based on consent (or explicit consent), the right to withdraw consent at any time	Article 13.2(c)	Article 14.2(d)	This information should include how consent may be withdrawn, taking into account that it should be as easy for a data subject to withdraw consent as to give it.[66]

Required Information Type	Relevant article (if personal data collected directly from data subject)	Relevant article (if personal data not obtained from the data subject)	WP29 comments on information requirement
The right to lodge a complaint with a supervisory authority	Article 13.2(d)	Article 14.2(e)	This information should explain that, in accordance with Article 77, a data subject has the right to lodge a complaint with a supervisory authority, in particular in the Member State of his or her habitual residence, place of work or of an alleged infringement of the GDPR.
Whether there is a statutory or contractual requirement to provide the information or whether it is necessary to enter into a contract or whether there is an obligation to provide the information and the possible consequences of failure.	Article 13.2(e)	Not required	For example in an employment context, it may be a contractual requirement to provide certain information to a current or prospective employer. Online forms should clearly identify which fields are "required", which are not, and what will be the consequences of not filling in the required fields.
The source from which the personal data originate, and if applicable, whether it came from a publicly accessible source	Not required	Article 14.2(f)	The specific source of the data should be provided unless it is not possible to do so – see further guidance at paragraph 60. If the specific source is not named then information provided should include: the nature of the sources (i.e. publicly/ privately held sources) and the types of organisation/ industry/ sector.
The existence of automated decision-making including profiling and, if applicable, meaningful information about the logic used and the significance and envisaged consequences of such processing for the data subject	Article 13.2(f)	Article 14.2(g)	See WP29 Guidelines on automated individual decision-making and Profiling.[67]

NOTES

[59] As defined by Article 4.17 of the GDPR (and referenced in Recital 80), "representative" means a natural or legal person established in the EU who is designated by the controller or processor in writing under Article 27 and represents the controller or processor with regard to their respective obligations under the GDPR. This obligation applies where, in accordance with Article 3.2, the controller or processor is not established in the EU but processes the personal data of data subjects who are in the EU, and the processing relates to the offer of goods or services to, or monitoring of the behaviour of, data subjects in the EU.

[60] Guidelines on Data Protection Officers, WP243 rev.01, last revised and adopted on 5 April 2017

[61] As defined by Article 4.9 of the GDPR and referenced in Recital 31

[62] As set out in Article 46.2 and 46.3

[63] In accordance with Article 45

[64] Article 21.4 and Recital 70 (which applies in the case of direct marketing)

[65] Guidelines on the right to data portability, WP 242 rev.01, last revised and adopted on 5 April 2017

[66] Article 7.3

[67] Guidelines on Automated individual decision-making and Profiling for the purposes of Regulation 2016/679, WP 251

ARTICLE 29 DATA PROTECTION WORKING PARTY: WORKING DOCUMENT SETTING FORTH A CO-OPERATION PROCEDURE FOR THE APPROVAL OF "BINDING CORPORATE RULES" FOR CONTROLLERS AND PROCESSORS UNDER THE GDPR

17/EN
WP 263 rev.01

Adopted on 11 April 2018

[2.240]

NOTES

This document was originally issued by the Article 29 Working Party but subsequently endorsed by the EDPB during its first plenary meeting.

© European Data Protection Board.

TABLE OF CONTENTS

INTRODUCTION

[2.241]

The procedure for approving binding corporate rules (BCRs) for controllers and processors is laid out by provisions contained in Articles 47.1, 63, 64 and (only if necessary) 65 of the Regulation (EU) 2016/679 (GDPR).

As a result, binding corporate rules are to be approved by the competent supervisory authority[1] in the relevant jurisdiction in accordance with the consistency mechanism set out in Article 63, under which the European Data Protection Board (EDPB) will issue a non-binding opinion on the draft decision submitted by the competent Supervisory Authority (Article 64 GDPR).

As the group applying for approval of its BCRs may have entities in more than one Member State, this procedure may involve a number of concerned Supervisory Authorities (SAs)[2], e.g. in those countries from where the transfers are to take place. However, the GDPR does not lay down specific rules for the cooperation phase which should take place among the concerned SAs in advance of referral to the EDPB. It also does not set out specific rules for identifying the competent SA – which will act as Lead Authority for the BCRs ('BCR Lead')[3]. The role of such BCR Lead includes acting as a single point of contact with the applicant organization or group during the approval process and managing the application procedure in its cooperation phase.

The aim of this document is to update the WP 107 and identify smooth and effective cooperation procedures in line with the GDPR whilst taking full advantage of the previous fruitful experience of the Data Protection Authorities in dealing with the approval of BCRs.

This document will be reviewed and if necessary updated, based on the practical experience gained through the application of the GDPR.

NOTES

[1] Article 57.1.s GDPR states that "without prejudice to other tasks set out under this Regulation, each supervisory authority shall on its territory [. . .] approve binding corporate rules pursuant to Article 47" and Article 58.3.j GDPR according to which each supervisory authority shall have the "authorisation and advisory powers [. . .] to approve binding corporate rules pursuant to Article 47".

[2] Pursuant to Article 4(22)(a) and (b), a 'supervisory authority concerned' means a supervisory authority which is concerned by the processing of personal data because the controller or processor is established on the territory of the Member State of that supervisory authority or because "data subjects residing in the Member State of that supervisory authority are substantially affected or likely to be substantially affected by the processing". As for the BCRs approval procedure, the concerned SAs are the SAs in the countries from where the transfers are to take place as specified by the applicants or, in case of BCR-P, all SAs (since a processor established in a Member State may provide services to controllers in several – potentially all – Member States).

[3] The "BCR Lead" is generally distinct from the "OSS Lead" considering that BCR transfers will not as a rule meet the definition/criteria of a cross-border processing operation. However, there could be cases in which the same SA could be the BCR Lead and the OSS Lead. This might e.g. be the case if a transfer performed by one establishment substantially affects data subjects in more than one MS (i.e. if personal data are first sent from member states A, B and C to the controller's establishment in member state A, and subsequently transferred by this establishment in A to a third country or, in case of BCR-P, where the processor carries out the same transfers for all their clients in the different member states). In any case, the BCR approval procedure would be the specific one settled by Article 64 GDPR.

1. IDENTIFICATION OF THE BCR LEAD SUPERVISORY AUTHORITY

[2.242]

1.1   A group of undertakings, or group of enterprises engaged in a joint economic activity ('Group'), interested in submitting draft binding corporate rules (BCRs) for the approval of the competent Authority according to Articles 47, 63 and 64 GDPR should propose a SA as the BCR Lead. The decision as to which SA should act as BCR Lead is based upon the criteria contained in this document (see next paragraph). It is for the organisation to justify the reasons why a given SA should be considered as the BCR Lead.

1.2   An applicant Group should justify the proposal of the BCR Lead on the basis of relevant criteria such as:
(a)   the location(s) of the Group's European headquarters;
(b)   the location of the company within the Group with delegated data protection responsibilities[4];
(c)   the location of the company which is best placed (in terms of management function, administrative burden, etc.) to deal with the application and to enforce the binding corporate rules in the Group;
(d)   the place where most decisions in terms of the purposes and the means of the processing (i.e. transfer) are taken; and
(e)   the member state within the EU from which most or all transfers outside the EEA will take place.

1.3   Particular attention will be given to factor described under 1.2 (a) above.

1.4   These are not formal criteria. The SA to which the application is sent (as prospective BCR Lead SA) will exercise its discretion in deciding whether it is in fact the most appropriate lead SA and, in any event, the SAs among themselves may decide to allocate the application to a SA other than the one to which the Group applied (see next paragraph), in particular if it would be possible and worth for speeding up the procedure (e.g. taking into account the workload of the originally requested SA).

1.5   The applicant should also provide the proposed BCR Lead (the entry point) with all appropriate information (both on paper and electronically to facilitate further distribution) which justifies its proposal, *inter alia*, the nature and general structure of the processing activities in the EU with particular attention to the place/s where decisions are made, the location and nature of affiliates in the EU, the number of employees or persons concerned, the means and purposes of the processing, the places from where the transfers to third countries do take place and the third countries to which those data are transferred.

NOTES
4   According to Article 47.2.f GDPR, there should always be an EU based member of the group established on the territory of a Member State accepting liability for any breaches of the binding corporate rules by any member concerned not established in the Union. If the headquarters of the group were somewhere else, the headquarters should delegate these responsibilities to a member based in the EU.

2. COOPERATION PROCEDURE FOR THE APPROVAL OF BCRS

[2.243]
2.1   The proposed BCR Lead will forward the information received as to why that SA has been selected by the company to be the lead authority for the BCRs to all SAs concerned[5] with an indication of whether or not it agrees to be the BCR Lead. If the entry point agrees to be the lead authority, the other concerned SAs will be asked, under Article 57.1.g GDPR, to raise any objections within two weeks (period extendable to two additional weeks if requested by any SA concerned). Silence is deemed as consent. In the event that the entry point is of the view that it should not act as the BCR Lead, it should explain the reasons for its decision as well as its recommendations (if any) as to which other SA would be the appropriate lead authority. The SAs concerned will endeavor to reach a decision within one month from the date that the papers were first circulated.

2.2   Once a decision on the BCR Lead has been made, the latter will start the discussions with the applicant and review the draft BCR documents. In order to foster a more consistent approach, it will send, under Article 57.1.g GDPR, a first revised draft of the BCRs and the related documents to one or two SAs (depending on the number of Member States from whose territories the transfers will take place)[6] which will act as co-reviewers and will help the BCR Lead in the assessment. In case there is no response from a SA acting as co-reviewer within one month from the date the draft and the related documents were sent to it (deadline extendable under justified circumstances), that SA will be deemed to have agreed with them. There may need to be several different drafts or exchanges between the applicant and the relevant SAs before a satisfactory draft is produced.

2.3   The result of these discussions should be a "consolidated draft" sent by the applicant to the BCR Lead which will circulate it among all concerned SAs[7] under Article 57.1.g GDPR for comments. According to this procedure, the period for comments on the consolidated draft will not exceed one month. A concerned SA which has not presented a reasoned objection within this period shall be deemed to be in agreement with the consolidated draft.

2.4   The BCR Lead will send any further comments on the "consolidated draft" to the applicant and may resume discussions, if necessary. If the lead authority is of the view that the applicant is in a position to address satisfactorily all comments received, it will invite the applicant to send a "final draft" to it.

2.5   Pursuant to Article 64.1 and 64.4 GDPR, the BCR Lead will submit the draft decision to the EDPB on the 'final draft' of the BCRs along with all relevant information, documentation and the views of the concerned SAs. The EDPB will adopt an opinion on the matter in accordance with Article 64.3 GDPR and its Rules of Procedure.

2.6   Where the opinion handed down by the EDPB under Article 64.3 endorses the draft decision on the draft BCRs in the form submitted, the BCR Lead will adopt its decision approving the draft BCRs.

2.7   Where the opinion handed down by the EDPB according to Article 64.3 requires any amendment to the draft BCRs, the BCR Lead will communicate to the Chair of the Board within the two-week period set out in Article 64.7 whether it intends to maintain its draft decision (i.e. not to follow the opinion of the EDPB) or whether it intends to amend it in accordance with the EDPB opinion[8]. In the first case, pursuant to Article 64.8 GDPR, Article 65.1 GDPR shall apply[9]. If the BCR Lead communicates to the Chair of the Board that it intends to amend its draft decision in accordance with the EDPB opinion, the BCR Lead will contact the applicant immediately in order to request the amendments to the draft BCRs to be made in accordance with the EDPB opinion so that the draft BCRs can be finalized. When the draft BCRs have been finalized in accordance with the EDPB opinion, the BCR Lead will amend its initial draft decision accordingly, notify the EDPB pursuant Article 64.7 of its amended decision and approve the BCR.

2.8   Once the BCR Lead approves the BCRs, it will inform and send a copy of them to all the concerned SAs. In accordance with Article 46.2.b GDPR, the approved 'binding corporate rules' will provide for the appropriate safeguards referred to in paragraph 46.1 without requiring any specific authorisation from the other concerned supervisory authorities.

2.9   Translations: as a general rule and without prejudice to other translations where necessary or required by law, all documents including the consolidated draft of the BCRs should be provided by the applicant in the language of the BCR Lead and also in English when possible in accordance with national law. The final draft and the approved BCRs must be translated by the applicant into the languages of those SAs concerned[10].

2.10   Once the BCRs have been approved, the BCR Lead, according to WP 256 and 257, points 5.1, will inform the concerned SAs of any updates to the BCRs or to the list of BCR members as provided by the applicant. In case the group extended the scope of the BCRs to an additional EU member state (because of the establishment of a new BCR member in this EU member state), the SA of this member state will then be deemed to be a new concerned SA as for point 2.8.

NOTES

[5]   See above footnote n. 2.

[6]   As a rule, the BCR Lead will consult 2 co-reviewers whenever 14 Member States or more are concerned by transfers. Under this threshold it is possible to have one or two co-reviewers depending on the specific case and the availability of SAs.

[7]   See above footnote n. 2.

[8]   According to Article 64.5, the Chair of the Board will, without undue delay, inform by electronic means the members of the Board and the Commission of this information.

[9]   In particular, in accordance with Article 65.1.c., "in order to ensure the correct and consistent application of this Regulation in individual cases, the Board shall adopt a binding decision in the following cases: [. . .] (c) where a competent supervisory authority [. . .] does not follow the opinion of the Board issued under Article 64. In that case, any supervisory authority concerned or the Commission may communicate the matter to the Board".

[10]   See also on this WP 256 and 257, Sections 1.7 according to which "The BCRs must contain the right for every data subject to have an easy access to them".

ARTICLE 29 DATA PROTECTION WORKING PARTY: RECOMMENDATION ON THE STANDARD APPLICATION FOR APPROVAL OF CONTROLLER BINDING CORPORATE RULES FOR THE TRANSFER OF PERSONAL DATA
17/EN
WP264
Adopted on 11 April 2018

[2.244]

NOTES

This document was originally issued by the Article 29 Working Party but subsequently endorsed by the EDPB during its first plenary meeting.

© European Data Protection Board.

TABLE OF CONTENTS

STANDARD APPLICATION FOR APPROVAL OF CONTROLLER BINDING CORPORATE RULES FOR THE TRANSFER OF PERSONAL DATA[1]

INTRODUCTION AND INSTRUCTIONS

[2.245]

The General Data Protection Regulation (EU) 2016/679 ('GDPR') allows personal data to be transferred outside the EEA only when the third country provides an "adequate level of protection" for the data (Art. 45) or when the controller adduces adequate safeguards with respect to the protection of privacy (Art. 46). Binding Corporate Rules (BCRs) are one of the ways in which such adequate safeguards (Art. 47) may be demonstrated by a group of undertakings, or group of enterprises engaged in a joint economic activity.

According to Article 64 GDPR, the use of BCRs as appropriate safeguards for international data transfers from the EEA requires the approval of the competent supervisory authority in accordance with the consistency mechanism set out in Article 63 without requiring any specific authorisation from a supervisory authority (Article 46.2.b GDPR). The following form is for use by companies seeking approval of BCRs. The form is based on papers previously issued by the Article 29 Working Party of European data protection authorities (the "Working Party"), and in particular WP133, and it is intended to help applicants demonstrate how to meet the requirements set out in Article 47 GDPR and WP 256.

GENERAL INSTRUCTIONS

- Only a single copy of the form need be filled out and submitted to the Supervisory Authority ('SA') you consider to be the lead authority for the BCRs ('BCR lead') in accordance with Article 47.1 and 64 GDPR and WP 263; this form may be used in all EEA Member States.
- Please fill out all entries and submit the form to the SA you consider to be the BCR lead.
- You may attach additional pages or annexes if there is insufficient space to complete your responses.
- You may indicate any responses or materials that is in your opinion commercially sensitive and should be kept confidential but, in any case, be aware that the relevant document will be shared among the concerned SAs and the European Data Protection Board (EDPB) which, under Article 64, has to issue its opinion on the approval draft decision of your BCRs. Requests by third parties for disclosure of such information, will, however, be handled by each supervisory authority involved in accordance with national legislation.
- The footnotes in the application form indicate the relevant provisions of the Article 47 GDPR and Working Party papers WP 256 and specific Sections of WP 74 and WP 108, which contain further clarification of the questions still valid under the framework of the GDPR.
- Once you have submitted the form, the SA you approached will circulate Part 1 of the form to all the 'concerned supervisory authorities'[2] in order to determine who should be the BCR Lead;
- You will be informed by the SA you approached which SA has finally been appointed by all SAs concerned to act as BCR Lead;
- As a rule, the BCR Lead will seek the cooperation of two other SAs concerned (SAs co-reviewers) in order to assess the BCRs in the light of Article 47 and WP 256[3];
- Once revised, in accordance with Article 64 GDPR, the BCR Lead will circulate the remainder of the form including your BCRs to all the other supervisory authorities concerned in order to collect their views to be sent to European Data Protection Board (EDPB) along with the draft opinion on the BCRs.

Part 1 Applicant Information

Section 1: Structure and Contact Details of the Applicant and of the Group of group of undertakings, or group of enterprises engaged in a joint economic activity ('Group')

- If the Group has its headquarters in the EEA the form should be filled out and submitted by that EEA entity.
- If the Group has its headquarters outside the EEA, then the Group should appoint a Group entity located inside the EEA – preferably established in the country of the presumptive BCR Lead - as the Group member with "delegated data protection responsibilities". This is the entity which should then submit the application on behalf of the Group.
- Contact Details of the Responsible Party for Queries:
  - Please indicate a responsible party to whom queries may be addressed concerning the application.
  - This party need not be located in the EEA, although this might be advisable for practical reasons.
  - You may indicate a function rather than a specific person.

Section 2: Short description of data flows
- The applicant should also give a brief description of the scope and nature of the data flows from the EEA for which approval is sought.

Section 3: Determination of the BCRs Lead
- In accordance with Article 64 GDPR, the BCR Lead is the authority in charge of coordinating the approval of your BCRs which then could be considered to be appropriate safeguards in the countries within the EEA which you have named in your application as the origin of transfers of personal data by Group members to third countries, without requiring any specific authorisation for the use of the BCR from the other supervisory authorities concerned.
  - Before you approach one SA as the presumptive BCR Lead you should examine the factors listed in Section 1 of WP 263 (still the same already enlisted in Sections 3.3 and 3.4. of WP 108). Based on these factors you should explain in Part 1.3 of your application

which SA should be the BCR Lead. The SAs are not obligated to accept the choice that you make if they believe that another SA is more suitable to be BCR Lead, in particular if it would be worth for speeding up the procedure (e.g. taking into account the workload of the originally requested SA).

Part 2 Background Paper

Section 4: Binding Nature of the Binding Corporate Rules

- In order for the BCRs to be approved for the transfer of personal data, they must be shown to have legally binding effect both internally (between the Group entities, and on employees and subcontractors) and externally (for the benefit of individuals whose personal data is processed by the Group) in accordance with national legislation. These questions elicit the information necessary to determine if your BCRs have such binding effect.
- Your application will need to make clear that the burden of proof with regard to an alleged breach of the rules will rest with one member of the Group established on the territory of a Member State (e.g. the member at the origin of the transfer or the European headquarters or that part of the organisation with delegated data protection responsibilities), regardless of where the claim originates.
- Regulators in some sectors (such as the financial services industry) may prohibit an entity of the Group in one country from assuming liability for another Group entity in another country. If this is the case for your application, please provide details about this situation in the subsection "Legal claims or actions" and explain any other mechanisms your Group has implemented to ensure that an aggrieved individual can obtain recourse against the Group in the EEA.

Section 5: Effectiveness

- Effectiveness (verification of compliance) may be demonstrated by a variety of mechanisms typically implemented by companies, such as a regular audit programme, corporate governance activities, compliance departments, etc. Please respond to the questions on effectiveness based on the verification mechanisms used in your group.
- You will need to confirm that you will permit the concerned SAs in the EEA to audit your compliance.

Section 6: Cooperation with SAs

- Section 6 focuses on cooperation with SAs. You have to specify how your BCRs deal with the cooperation with SAs.

Section 7: Description of Processing and Data Flows

- In order for the SAs to assess whether your BCRs provide adequate safeguards for the transfers of data in accordance with Article 47 GDPR, it is essential that you describe data flows within your Group in a complete yet understandable fashion.

Section 8: Mechanisms for Reporting and Recording Changes

- Both the SAs and the Group entities must be informed without undue delay about any changes to the BCRs. In particular, changes that significantly affect data protection compliance (e.g. will be detrimental to data subject rights), and not to mere administrative changes (unless they impact the BCRs - e.g. changes to the bindingness) must be promptly communicated to the concerned Supervisory Authorities, via the competent SA under Article 64 (i.e. BCR Lead)[4]. In this section, please describe the mechanisms your Group has implemented for reporting and recording such changes.
- The obligation to report changes applies only to the text of the BCRs themselves, and not to any supporting documentation, unless a change to such documentation would significantly affect compliance with the BCRs.

Section 9: Data Protection Safeguards

- In this Section please provide details of how your BCRs address the core data protection safeguards that are necessary to provide an adequate level of protection for the data that are transferred.

Annex 1: Copy of the Formal Binding Corporate Rules

- Please attach a copy of your BCRs. These need not necessarily be contained within one document and your BCRs may comprise a number of documents. In the latter case please clearly specify the legal relationship between these documents (e.g. general rules – more detailed rules for a specific area like HRM or CRM).
- You do not need to attach all ancillary documentation at this stage, this may be submitted separately after discussions with the BCR Lead.

NOTES

1.   This questionnaire takes also into account the draft standard application form for approval of Binding Corporate Rules drawn up by the ICC.

2.   Pursuant to Article 4(22)(a) and (b), a 'supervisory authority concerned' means a supervisory authority which is concerned by the processing of personal data because the controller or processor is established on the territory of the Member State of that supervisory authority or because "data subjects residing in the Member State of that supervisory

authority are substantially affected or likely to be substantially affected by the processing". As for the BCRs approval procedure, the concerned SAs are the SAs in the countries from where the transfers are to take place as specified by the applicants or, in case of BCR-P, all SAs (since a processor established in a Member State may provide services to controllers in several – potentially all – Member States).

3   As a rule, the BCR Lead will consult 2 co-reviewers whenever 14 Member States are concerned by transfers. Under this threshold it is possible to have one or two co-reviewers depending on the specific case and the availability of SAs.

4   See WP 155, Q 14.

STANDARD APPLICATION FOR APPROVAL OF BINDING CORPORATE RULES

PART 1: APPLICANT INFORMATION

1. Structure and contact details of the group of undertakings or group of enterprises engaged in a joint economic activity (The Group)

[2.246]

Name of the Group and location of its headquarters:

Does the Group have its headquarters in the EEA?

☐ Yes

☐ No

Name and location of the applicant:

Identification number (if any):

Legal nature of the applicant (corporation, partnership, etc.):

Description of position of the applicant within the Group:

(e.g. headquarters of the Group in the EEA, or, if the Group does not have its headquarters in the EEA, the member of the Group inside the EEA with delegated data protection responsibilities)

Name and/or function of contact person (note: the contact person may change, you may indicate a function rather than the name of a specific person):

Address:

Country:

Phone number: Fax: E-Mail:

EEA Member States from which BCRs will be used:

---

2. Short description of processing and data flows[5]

Please, indicate the following:

–   Nature of the data covered by BCRs, and in particular, if they apply to one category of data or to more than one category, the type of processing and its purposes, the types of data subjects affected ((for instance data related to employees, customers, suppliers and other third parties as part of its respective regular business activities, . . .)

–   Do the BCRs only apply to transfers from the EEA, or do they apply to all transfers between members of the group?

–   Please specify from which country most of the data are transferred outside the EEA:

| – | Extent of the transfers within the Group that are covered by the BCRs; including a description and the contact details of any Group members in the EEA or outside EEA to which personal data may be transferred |

3. Determination of the lead supervisory authority ('BCR Lead')[6]

Please explain which should be the BCR Lead, based on the following criteria:
– Location of the Group's EEA Headquarters

– If the Group is not headquartered in the EEA, the location in the EEA of the Group entity with delegated data protection responsibilities

– The location of the company which is best placed (in terms of management function, administrative burden, etc.) to deal with the application and to enforce the binding corporate rules in the Group

– Country where most of the decisions in terms of the purposes and the means of the data processing are taken

– EEA Member States from which most of the transfers outside the EEA will take place

PART 2 BACKGROUND PAPER[7]

4. Binding Nature of the Binding Corporate Rules (BCRs)

Internal Binding Nature[8]

Binding within the entities of the Group[9]

How are the BCRs made binding upon the members of the Group?

☐ Measures or rules that are legally binding on all members of the Group

☐ Contracts or intra-group agreement between the members of the Group

☐ Unilateral declarations or undertakings made or given by the parent company which are binding on the other members of the Group (this is only possible if the BCR member taking responsibility and liability is located in a Member State that recognizes Unilateral undertakings as binding and if this BCR member is legally able to bind the other members subject to BCRs)

☐ Other means (only if the group demonstrates how the binding character of the BCRs is achieved), please specify

Please explain how the mechanisms you indicated above are legally binding on the members of the Group in the sense that they can be enforced by other members of the Group (esp. headquarters):

Does the internally binding effect of your BCRs extend to the whole Group? (If some Group members should be exempted, specify how and why)

Binding upon the employees[10]

Your Group may take some or all of the following steps to ensure that the BCRs are binding on employees, but there may be other steps. Please, give details below.
– Work employment contract

– Collective agreements (approved by workers committee/another body)

– Employees must sign or attest to have read the BCRs or related ethics guidelines in which the BCRs are incorporated

- BCRs have been incorporated in relevant company policies

- Other means (but the group must properly explain how the BCRs are made binding on employees)

- Disciplinary sanctions for failing to comply with relevant company policies, including dismissal for violation

Please provide a summary supported by extracts from policies and procedures or confidentiality agreements as appropriate to explain how the BCRs are binding upon employees.

Binding upon subcontractors processing the data[11]

What steps have you taken to require subcontractors to apply protections to the processing of personal data (e.g., through the use of obligations in your contracts with them)? Please specify:

How do such contracts or other legal acts under Union or Member State law address the consequences of non-compliance?

Please specify the sanctions imposed on subcontractors for failure to comply

Externally binding nature[12]

How are the rules binding externally for the benefit of individuals (third party beneficiary rights) or how do you intend to create such rights? For example you might have created some third party beneficiary rights in contracts or unilateral declarations[13].

Legal claim or actions

Explain how you meet the obligations according to the requirement of Articles 47.2.e, 77 and 79, 82 GDPR[14]

Please confirm that the controller established on the territory of a Member State (e.g. the European headquarters of the Group, or that part of the Group with delegated data protection responsibilities in the EEA), has made appropriate arrangements to enable itself or the member of the Group at the origin of the transfer payment of compensation for any damages resulting from the breach, by any part of the Group, of the BCRs and explain how this is ensured.

Please confirm that the burden of proof with regard to an alleged breach of the rules will rest with the member of the Group at the origin of the transfer or the European headquarters or that part of the organisation in the EEA with delegated data protection responsibilities, regardless of where the claim originates.

5. Effectiveness[15]

It is important to show how the BCRs in place within your organization are brought to life in practise, in particular in non EEA countries where data will be transferred on the basis of the BCRs, as this will be significant in assessing the adequacy of the safeguards.

Training and awareness raising (employees)

– Special training programs

– Employees are tested on BCRs and data protection

– BCRs are communicated to all employees on paper or online

– Review and approval by senior officers of the company

– How are employees trained to identify the data protection implications of their work, i.e. to identify that the relevant privacy policies are applicable to their activities and to react accordingly? (This applies whether these employees are or not based in the EEA)

Internal complaint handling[16]

Do the BCRs contain an internal complaint handling system to enforce compliance?

Please describe the system for handling complaints:

Verification of compliance

What verification mechanisms does your Group have in place to audit each member's compliance with your BCRs? (e.g., an audit programme, compliance programme, etc)? Please specify:

Please explain how your verification or compliance programme functions within the Group (e.g., information as to the recipients of any audit reports and their position within the structure of the Group).

Do the BCRs provide for the use of:
– Data Protection Officer?
– internal auditors?
– external auditors?
– a combination of both internal and external auditors?

– verification by an internal compliance department?

Do your BCRs mention if the verification mechanisms are clearly set out in . . .
– a document containing your data protection standards
– other internal procedure documents and audits?

Network of data protection officers (DPO) or appropriate staff[17]

Please confirm that a network of DPOs or appropriate staff (such as a network of privacy officers) is appointed with top management support to oversee and ensure compliance with the BCR for Processors:

Please explain how your network of DPOs or privacy officers functions:
– Internal structure:

– Role and responsibilities:

---

6. Cooperation with SAs[18]

Please, specify how your BCRs deal with the issues of cooperation with SAs:

Do you confirm that you will permit the concerned SAs to audit your compliance?

Do you confirm that the Group as a whole and each of the companies of the Group will abide by the advice of the concerned Supervisory authority relating to the interpretation and the application of your BCRs?

---

7. Description of processing and data flows[19]

Please indicate the following:
– Nature of the data covered by the BCRs, e.g. HR data, and in particular, if they apply to one category of data or to more than one category

– What is the nature of the personal data being transferred?

– In broad terms where do the data flow to and from?

– What are the type of processing and the purposes for which the data covered by the BCRs are transferred to third countries and of the processing that is carried out after the transfers?

– Extent of the transfers within the Group that are covered by the BCRs, including a description and contact details of any Group members in the EEA or outside the EEA to which personal data may be transferred

Do the BCRs only apply to transfers from the EEA, or do they apply to all transfers between members of the Group? Please specify:

8. Mechanisms for reporting and recording changes[20]

Please, confirm and explain how your BCRs allow for informing other parts of the Group and the concerned SAs, via the competent SA under Article 64 (i.e. the BCR Lead), of any changes to the BCRs and/or the list of BCR members (summary):

Please confirm that you have put in place a system to record any changes to your BCRs.

9. Data protection safeguards[21]

Please, specify with reference to your BCRs how and where the following issues are addressed with supporting documentation where appropriate:
– Transparency and fairness and lawfulness

– Purpose limitation

– Data minimisation and accuracy

– Limited storage periods

– Processing of special categories of personal data

– Security (including the obligation to enter into contracts with all internal and external subcontractors/processors which comprise all requirements as set out in Art. 28.3 GDPR and as well the duty to notify without undue delay any personal data breaches to the EU headquarters or the EU BCR member with delegated data protection responsibilities and the other relevant Privacy Officer/Function and data subjects where the personal data breach is likely to result in a high risk to their rights and freedoms)

– Restrictions on onward transfers

– Other (e.g. protection of children, etc.)

10. Accountability and other tools[22]

– Please confirm and specify how BCR members will be responsible for and able to demonstrate compliance with the BCRs

– Please confirm that the BCR members will maintain a record of all categories of processing activities carried out on behalf of each controller in line with the requirements as set out in Art. 30.1 GDPR.

– Please confirm that data protection impact assessments will be carried out for processing operations that are likely to result in a high risk to the rights and freedoms of natural persons (GDPR Art. 35) and that where a data protection impact assessment under Article 35 indicates that the processing would result in a high risk in the absence of measures taken by the controller to mitigate the risk, the competent supervisory authority, prior to processing, should be consulted (GDPR Art. 36)

- Please confirm and specify which appropriate technical and organisational measures will be implemented to comply with data protection principles and facilitate compliance with the requirements set up by the BCRs in practice (e.g. data protection by design and by default, GDPR Art. 25)

Please provide supporting documents where appropriate with respect to the information requested above

NOTES

5   See Article 47.2. a and b and Section 4.1. WP 256.
6   See Part. 1 WP 263.
7   Working Document setting up a table with the elements and principles to be found in Binding Corporate Rules, WP 256, adopted on 6 February 2018.
8   See GDPR Art. 47.1.a and 47.2.c and Section 1.2 WP 256. See, also, general considerations in Section 3.3.1. WP74 and in Section 5 WP108.
9   See Section 5.3 WP108.
10 See Article 47.1.a and Section 1.2 WP 256 and Section 5.8 WP108.
11 See Art. 28.3 GDPR and Section 5.10 WP108.
12 See 47.1.b and 47.2.c and e GDPR and Section 1.3 WP 256. See also general considerations in Section 3.3.2 WP74.
13 Data subjects must at least be able to enforce the following elements of the BCRs:
    - Data protection principles (Art. 47.2.d and Section 6.1 WP 256),
    - Transparency and easy access to BCRs (Art. 47.2.g and Section 6.1, Section 1.7 WP 256),
    - Rights of access, rectification, erasure, restriction, objection to processing, right not to be subject to decisions based solely on automated processing, including profiling (GDPR Art. 47.2.e and Art. 15, 16, 17,18, 21, 22),
    - National legislation preventing respect of BCRs (Art. 47.2.m and Section 6.3 of this referential),
    - Right to complain through the internal complaint mechanism of the companies (Art. 47.1.i and Section 2.2 WP 256),
    - Cooperation duties with Data Protection Authority (Art. 47.2.k and l, Section 3.1 WP 256),
    - Liability and jurisdiction provisions (Art. 47.2.e and f, Section 1.3, 1.4 WP 256).
    Furthermore, you must be fully aware of the fact that according to civil law of some jurisdictions unilateral declarations or unilateral undertakings do not have a binding effect. In the lack of a specific legislative provision on bindingness of such declarations, only a contract with third party beneficiary clauses between the members of the Group may give proof of bindingness.
14 See also Section 1.3. WP 256: the BCRs must confer the right to lodge a complaint with the competent supervisory authority (choice before the SA in the Member State of his habitual residence, place of work or place of the alleged infringement, pursuant to art. 77 GDPR) and before the competent court of the EU Member States (choice for the data subject to act before the courts where the controller or processor has an establishment or where the data subject has his or her habitual residence pursuant to Article 79 GDPR).
15 See Articles 47.2.j and 47.2.l and Art. 38.3 GDPR and Section 2.3 WP 256. See also general considerations in Section 5.2 WP74 and Section 6 WP108.
16 See Articles 47.2.i and 12.3 GDPR and Section 2.2 WP 256. See also Section 5.3 WP74.
17 See Section 2.4 WP 256.
18 See Article 47.2.l GDPR and Section 3.1 WP 256 and Section 5.4 WP 74.
19 See Article 47.2.b GDPR and Section 4.1 WP 256 and Section 7 WP 108.
20 See Article 47.2.k GDPR and Section 5.1. WP 256.
21 See Article 47.2.d GDPR and Section 6.1. WP 256.
22 See Section 6.1.2 WP 256

ANNEX 1: COPY OF THE FORMAL BINDING CORPORATE RULES

[2.247]
Please attach a copy of your BCRs. Note that this does not include any ancillary documentation that you would like to submit (e.g. specific privacy policies and rules).

ARTICLE 29 DATA PROTECTION WORKING PARTY: RECOMMENDATION ON THE STANDARD APPLICATION FORM FOR APPROVAL OF PROCESSOR BINDING CORPORATE RULES FOR THE TRANSFER OF PERSONAL DATA
17/EN
WP 265
Adopted on 11 April 2018

[2.248]

NOTES
This document was originally issued by the Article 29 Working Party but subsequently endorsed by the EDPB during its first plenary meeting.
© European Data Protection Board.

STANDARD APPLICATION FOR APPROVAL OF BINDING CORPORATE RULES FOR PROCESSORS

PART 1: APPLICANT INFORMATION

[2.249]

1. Structure and contact details of the group of undertakings or group of enterprises engaged in a joint economic activity (The Group)
Name of the Group and location of its headquarters (ultimate parent company):
Does the Group have its headquarters in the EEA? ☐ Yes ☐ No
Name and location of the applicant:
Identification number (if any): ***
Legal nature of the applicant (corporation, partnership, etc.):
Description of position of the applicant within the Group: (e.g. headquarters of the Group in the EEA, or, if the Group does not have its headquarters in the EEA, the member of the Group inside the EEA with delegated data protection responsibilities)
Name and/or function of contact person (note: the contact person may change, you may indicate a function rather than the name of a specific person):
Address:
Country:
Phone number: *** Fax:*** E-Mail: ***
EEA Member States from which BCRs for Processors will be used:

2. Short description of processing and data flows
Please, indicate the following:
– Expected nature of the data covered by BCR, and in particular, if they apply to one category of data or to more than one category, types of data subjects concerned, (for instance human resources, customers, . . .), anticipated types of processing and its purposes
– Anticipated purposes of data transfers for processing activities
– Do the BCR only apply to transfers from the EEA, or do they apply to all transfers for processing activities between members of the Group?
– Please specify from which country most of the data are transferred outside the EEA for processing activities:
– Extent of the transfers within the Group that are covered by the BCR; including a description and contact details of any Group members in the EEA or outside EEA to which personal data may be transferred for processing activities

3. Determination of the lead supervisory authority (BCR Lead)
Please explain which should be the BCR Lead, based on the following criteria:
– Location of the Group's EEA headquarters
– If the Group is not headquartered in the EEA, the location in the EEA of the Group entity with delegated data protection responsibilities
– The location of the company which is best placed (in terms of management function, administrative burden, etc.) to deal with the application and to enforce the binding corporate rules in the Group
– EEA Member States from which most of the transfers outside the EEA will take place

Part 2 Data Protection: EU Law etc

PART 2: BACKGROUND PAPER[1]

4. Binding nature of the binding corporate rules (BCR) for processors

Internal binding nature[2]

Binding within the entities of the Group acting as internal subprocessors[3]

How are the BCR for processors made binding upon the members of the Group? ☐ Measures or rules that are legally binding on all members of the Group ☐ Contracts or intra-group agreements between the members of the Group ☐ Unilateral declarations or undertakings made or given by the parent company which are binding on the other members of the Group (that is only possible if the BCR member taking responsibility and liability is located in a Member State that recognizes Unilateral declarations or undertakings as binding and if this BCR member is legally able to bind the other members subject to BCRs); ☐ Other means (only if the Group demonstrates how the binding character of the BCRs is achieved), please specify
Please explain how the mechanisms you indicated above are legally binding on the members of the Group in the sense that they can be enforced by other members of the Group (esp. headquarters): Does the internally binding effect of your BCR for Processors extend to the whole Group? (If some Group members should be exempted, specify how and why) Please confirm that any use of subprocessors (internal) is only done after prior information to data controllers and with their prior written consent

Binding upon the employees[4]

Your Group may take some or all of the following steps to ensure that the BCR for Processors are binding on employees, but there may be other steps. Please, give details below.
Individual and separate agreement/undertaking with sanctions Work employment contract with sanctions Collective agreements (approved by workers committee/another body) with sanctions Employees must sign or attest to have read the BCR for Processors or related ethics guidelines in which the BCR for Processors are incorporated BCR for Processors have been incorporated in relevant company policies with sanctions Disciplinary sanctions for failing to comply with relevant company policies, including dismissal for violation Other means (but the group must properly explain how the BCRs are made binding on employees)
Please provide a summary supported by extracts from policies and procedures or confidentiality agreements as appropriate to explain how the BCR for Processors are binding upon employees.

Externally binding nature

Binding upon external subprocessors processing the data

Please confirm that a written contract or other legal act under Union or Member State law is put in place with external subprocessors which states that adequate protection is provided according to Articles 28, 29, 32, 45, 46, 47 of the GDPR and which ensures that the external subprocessors will have to respect the same data protection obligations as are imposed on the Group members according to the Service Agreements concluded with data controllers and Sections 1.3, 1.4, 3 and 6 of WP257[5].
How do such contracts or other legal acts under Union or Member State law address the consequences of non compliance? Please specify the sanctions imposed on subprocessors for failure to comply
Please confirm that any use of subprocessors (external) is only done after prior informed specific or general written authorization of the data controller[6]
Please confirm that subprocessors accept to submit their data processing facilities for audit, at the request of a data controller, of the processing activities relating to that controller[7]. Please describe the system.

How are the rules binding externally for the benefit of individuals (third party beneficiary rights) or how do you intend to create such rights? For example you might have created some third party beneficiary rights in contracts or unilateral declarations[8].

Please provide a summary supported by extracts from the agreement signed with data controllers as appropriate to explain how the BCR for Processors are made binding towards data controllers[9]

Please confirm that data controllers' rights shall cover the judicial remedies and the right to receive compensation

Legal claim or actions

Explain how you meet the obligations according to the requirements of Article 47.2.e, 77, 79, 82, as further specified in paragraph 1.3 of WP257[10]

Please confirm that the controller established on the territory of a Member State (e.g. EEA headquarters of the Group, the Group member of the Processor with delegated data protection responsibilities in the EEA or the EEA exporter processor (e.g., the EEA contracting party with the controller), has made appropriate arrangements to enable itself to remedy the acts and to pay compensation, for any damages suffered either by a data subject or a data controller, resulting from the breach, by any member of the Group or by any external subprocessor, of the BCR for Processors and explain how this is ensured.

Please confirm that the burden of proof with regard to an alleged breach of the rules caused either by a Group member or by an external subprocessor will rest with the member of the Group in the EU that have accepted to endorse liability for breaches caused by non EEA members of the group or by subprocessors, regardless of where the claim originates.

Easy access to BCR for Processors[11]

Please confirm that your BCR for Processors are annexed to the Service Agreements signed with data controllers, or that reference to it is made with a possibility of electronic access:

Please confirm that your BCR for Processors are published on the website of the Group of processor in a way easily accessible to data subjects, or at least that a document is published and contains all the information as required in Section 1.8 of WP257:

5. Effectiveness[12]

It is important to show how the BCR for Processors in place within your Group are brought to life in practice, in particular in non EEA countries where data will be transferred for processing activities on the basis of the BCR for Processors, as this will be significant in assessing the adequacy of the safeguards.

Training and awareness raising (employees)[13]

— Special training programs

— Employees are tested on BCR for Processors and data protection

— BCR for Processors are communicated to all employees on paper or online

— Review and approval by senior officers of the company

— How are employees trained to identify the data protection implications of their work, i.e. to identify that the relevant privacy policies are applicable to their activities and to react accordingly? (This applies whether these employees are or not based in the EEA)

Part 2   Data Protection: EU Law etc

Internal complaint handling[14]

Do the BCR for Processors contain an internal complaint handling system to (i) communicate claims or requests without delay to data controllers, and to (ii) handle complaints instead of a data controller when the latter has disappeared factually, has ceased to exist in law or became insolvent, or when it has been agreed with a data controller that the Group will handle claims and requests from data subjects? Please describe the system for handling complaints:

Verification of compliance[15]

What verification mechanisms do your Group have in place to audit each Group members' compliance with your BCR for Processors? (e.g., an audit programme, compliance programme, etc)? Please specify:
Please explain how your verification or compliance programme functions within the Group (e.g., information as to the recipients of any audit reports and their position within the structure of the Group).
Do the BCR for Processors provide for the use of: —Data Protection Officer? —Data Protection Officer? —internal auditors? —external auditors? —a combination of both internal and external auditors? —verification by an internal compliance department?
Do your BCR for Processors mention if the verification mechanisms are clearly set out in . . . —a document containing your data protection standards —other internal procedure documents and audits?

Network of data protection officers (DPO) or appropriate staff[16]

Please confirm that a network of DPOs or appropriate staff (such as a network of privacy officers) is appointed with top management support to oversee and ensure compliance with the BCR for Processors:
Please explain how your network of DPOs or privacy officers functions: —Internal structure: —Role and responsibilities:

6. Cooperation with SAs[17]

Please, specify how your BCR for Processors deal with the issues of cooperation with SAs:
Do you confirm that you will permit the relevant SAs to audit your compliance?
Do you confirm that the Group as a whole and each members of the Group will abide by the advice of the relevant Supervisory authorities relating to the interpretation and the application of your BCR for Processors?

7. Cooperation with data controllers[18]

Please specify how your BCR for Processors deal with the duty of cooperation with data controllers?
Do you confirm that you will submit your data processing facilities to data controller (or to an inspection body composed of independent members, selected by the data controller) which requested it for audits of the processing activities relating to them?

8. Description of processing and data flows[19]

Please indicate the following:

— Expected nature of the data covered by the BCR for Processors, e.g. HR data, and in particular, if they apply to one category of data or to more than one category

–What is the nature of the personal data being transferred for processing activities?

–In broad terms what is the extent of the flow of data?

— Purposes for which the data covered by the BCR for Processors are transferred to third countries and type of processing

— Extent of the transfers within the Group that are covered by the BCR for Processors, including a description and contact details of any Group members in the EEA or outside the EEA to which personal data may be transferred for processing activities

Do the BCR only apply to transfers for processing activities from the EEA, or do they apply to all transfers for processing activities between members of the Group? Please specify:

8. Mechanisms for reporting and recording changes[20]

Please confirm and explain how your BCR for Processors allow for informing other parts of the Group, the concerned Supervisory Authorities via the competent SA under Article 64 (i.e. the BCR Lead) and data controllers of any changes to the BCR for Processors and/or the list of BCR members (summary):

Please confirm that you have put in place a system to record any changes to your BCR for Processors,

Please confirm that where a change affects the processing conditions, data controllers are informed in a timely fashion that data controllers have the possibility to object to the changes or terminate the contract before the modification is made

9. Data protection safeguards[21]

Please, specify with reference to your BCR for Processors how and where the following issues are addressed with supporting documentation where appropriate:

—Transparency, fairness and lawfulness (e.g., general duty to help and assist the controller)

—Purpose limitation (e.g., duty to process personal data only on behalf of data controllers and in compliance with their instructions and to return the data to the data controller at the end of the contract)

—Data quality (e.g., general duty to help and assist the controller)

—Security

—Data subjects' rights (e.g., general duty to help and assist the controller)

—Subprocessing within the Group

—Restrictions on onward transfers to external subprocessors

—Other (e.g. protection of children, etc.)

10. Accountability and other tools[22]

—Please confirm and specify how BCR members will make available to the controller all information necessary to demonstrate compliance with their obligations as provided by Article 28-3-h (including through audits, and information of the controller if an instruction infringes the GDPR or other Union or Member State data protection provisions)

—Please confirm that the BCR members will maintain a record of all categories of processing activities carried out on behalf of each controller as provided by Article 30-2 GDPR

—Please specify how BCR members will assist the controller in implementing appropriate technical and organisational measures to comply with data protection principles and facilitate compliance with requirements set out by BCRs in practice (e.g. data protection by design, data protection by default)

Please provide supporting documents where appropriate with respect to the information requested above

NOTES

1   Working Document setting up a table with the elements and principles to be found in Processor Binding Corporate Rules, WP257, adopted on 6 February 2018.
2   See Section 1.1 and 1.2 WP 257
3   See Section 1.2 (i) WP 257
4   See Section 1.2 (ii) WP257
5   See Section 6.1 (vii) WP257
6   See Section 6.1 (vii) WP257
7   See Section 2.3 WP 257
8   You must be fully aware of the fact that according to civil law of some jurisdictions (e.g. Italy or Spain) unilateral declarations or unilateral undertakings do not have a binding effect. In the absence of a specific legislative provision on bindingness of such declarations, only a contract with third party beneficiary clauses between the members of the Group may give proof of bindingness.
9   See Section 1.4 WP 257
10 1.3 WP 257 provides that the BCRs must grant rights to data subjects to enforce BCRs as third party beneficiaries against the processor either when the requirements at stake are specifically directed to processors in accordance with the GDPR or in case the data subject is not able to bring a claim against the data controller because the data controller has factually disappeared or ceased to exist in law or has become insolvent, unless any successor entity has assumed the entire legal obligations of the data controller by contract of by operation of law, in which case the data subject can enforce its rights against such entity.
11 See Section 1.8 WP257
12 See Section 2 WP257
13 See Section 2.1 WP257
14 See Section 2.2 WP257
15 See Section 2.3 WP 257
16 See Section 2.4 WP 257
17 See Section 3.1 WP257
18 See Section 3.2 WP 257
19 See Section 4.1 WP257
20 See Section 5.1 WP257
21 See Section 6 of WP257
22 See Section 6.1.2 WP257

ANNEX 1: COPY OF THE FORMAL BINDING CORPORATE RULES FOR PROCESSORS

[2.250]
Please attach a copy of your BCR for Processors. Note that this does not include any ancillary documentation that you would like to submit (e.g. specific privacy policies and rules).

EDPB GUIDELINES AND RECOMMENDATIONS

NOTES

Recommendations 1/2021 and 1/2019 have not been included on the basis that they focus on a niche area of the Data Protection Law Enforcement Directive or data protection law for EU institutions that are unlikely to be of interest to readers.

EUROPEAN DATA PROTECTION BOARD: GUIDELINES 1/2018 ON CERTIFICATION AND IDENTIFYING CERTIFICATION CRITERIA IN ACCORDANCE WITH ARTICLES 42 AND 43 OF THE REGULATION
Version 3.0
4 June 2019

[2.251]

NOTES

In April 2021 the EDPB published an addendum to these Guidelines 1/2018 for feedback (Guidance on certification criteria assessment (Addendum to Guidelines 1/2018 on certification and identifying certification criteria in accordance with Articles 42 and 43 of the Regulation)). The aim of that additional guidance is to refine elements from EDPB Guidelines 1/2018 for helping: (a) stakeholders involved in the drafting of certification criteria; and (b) supervisory authorities and the EDPB to provide consistent evaluations. That further guidance has not been reproduced in this book but is available on the EDPB website.
© European Data Protection Board.

VERSION HISTORY

Version 3.0: 4 June 2019: Inclusion of Annex 2 (version 2.0 of Annex 2 adopted on 4 June 2019 after public consultation)

Version 2.1: 9 April 2019: Adoption of a corrigendum to the Guidelines (paragraph 45)

Version 2.0: 23 January 2019: Adoption of the Guidelines after public consultation - On the same date Annex 2 (version 1.0) was adopted for public consultation

Version 1.0: 25 May 2018: Adoption of the Guidelines for publication consultation

TABLE OF CONTENTS

Part 2   Data Protection: EU Law etc

THE EUROPEAN DATA PROTECTION BOARD

Having regard to Article 70 (1e) of the Regulation 2016/679/EU of the European Parliament and of the Council of 27 April 2016 on the protection of natural persons with regard to the processing of personal data and on the free movement of such data, and repealing Directive 95/46/EC (hereinafter "GDPR"),

Having regard to the EEA Agreement and in particular to Annex XI and Protocol 37 thereof, as amended by the Decision of the EEA joint Committee No 154/2018 of 6 July 2018,

Having regard to Article 12 and Article 22 of its Rules of Procedure of 25 May 2018,

Having considered the results of the public consultation on the guidelines that took place between 30 May 2018 and 12 July 2018, and on Annex 2 that took place between 15 February and 29 March 2019, as per Article 70 (4) of the GDPR

HAS ADOPTED THE FOLLOWING GUIDELINES

1 INTRODUCTION

[2.252]
1. The General Data Protection Regulation (Regulation 2016/279, 'the GDPR', or 'the Regulation'), provides a modernised, accountability and fundamental rights compliance framework for data protection in Europe. A range of measures that facilitate compliance with the provisions of the GDPR are central to this new framework. These include mandatory requirements in specific circumstances (including the appointment of Data Protection Officers and carrying out data protection impact assessments) and voluntary measures such as codes of conduct and certification mechanisms.

2. Before the adoption of the GDPR, the Article 29 Working Party established that certification could play an important role in the accountability framework for data protection.[1] In order for certification to provide reliable evidence of data protection compliance, clear rules setting forth requirements for the provision of certification should be in place.[2] Article 42 of the GDPR provides the legal basis for the development of such rules.

3. Article 42(1) of the GDPR provides that:

> "The Member States, the supervisory authorities, the [European Data Protection] Board and the European Commission shall encourage, in particular at the Union level, the establishment of data protection certification mechanisms and of data protection seals and marks, for the purpose of demonstrating compliance with this Regulation of processing operations by controllers and processors. The specific needs of micro, small and medium-sized enterprises shall be taken into account".

4. Certification mechanisms[3] can improve transparency for data subjects, but also in business-to-business relations, for example between controllers and processors. Recital 100 of the GDPR states that the establishment of certification mechanisms can enhance transparency and compliance with the Regulation and allow data subjects to assess the level of data protection of relevant products and services.[4]

5. The GDPR does not introduce a right to or an obligation of certification for controllers and processors; as per Article 42(3), certification is a voluntary process to assist in demonstrating compliance with the GDPR. Member States and supervisory authorities are called to encourage the establishment of certification mechanisms and will determine the stakeholder engagement in the certification process and lifecycle.

6. Furthermore, the adherence to approved certification mechanisms is a factor supervisory authorities must consider as an aggravating or mitigating factor when deciding to impose an administrative fine and when deciding on the amount of the fine (Article 83.2(j)).[5]

1.1 SCOPE OF THE GUIDELINES

7. These guidelines are limited in scope; they are not a procedural manual for certification in accordance with the GDPR. The primary aim of these guidelines is to identify overarching requirements and criteria that may be relevant to all types of certification mechanisms issued in accordance with Articles 42 and 43 of the GDPR. To this end, the guidelines:
* explore the rationale for certification as an accountability tool;
* explain the key concepts of the certification provisions in Articles 42 and 43; and
* explain the scope of what can be certified under Articles 42 and 43 and the purpose of certification;
* facilitate that the outcome of certification is meaningful, unambiguous, as reproducible as possible and comparable regardless of the certifier (comparability).

8. The GDPR allows for a number of ways for Member States and supervisory authorities to implement Articles 42 and 43. The guidelines provide advice on the interpretation and implementation of the provisions in Articles 42 and 43 and will help Member States, supervisory authorities and national accreditation bodies establish a more consistent, harmonised approach for the implementation of certification mechanisms in accordance with the GDPR.

9. The advice contained in the guidelines will be relevant for:
* competent supervisory authorities and the European Data Protection Board ('the EDPB') when approving certification criteria under Article 42(5), Article 58(3)(f) and Article 70(1)(o);
* certification bodies when drafting and revising certification criteria prior to submission to the competent supervisory authority for approval as per Article 42(5);
* the EDPB when approving a European Data Protection Seal under Articles 42(5) and 70(1)(o);
* supervisory authorities, when drafting their own certification criteria;
* the European Commission, which is empowered to adopt delegated acts for the purpose of specifying the requirements to be taken into account for certification mechanisms under Article 43(8);
* the EDPB when providing the European Commission with an opinion on the certification requirements in accordance with Article 70(1)(q) and Article 43(8);
* national accreditation bodies, which will need to take into account certification criteria with a view to the accreditation of certification bodies in accordance with EN-ISO/IEC 17065/2012 and the additional requirements in accordance with Article 43; and
* controllers and processors when defining their own GDPR compliance strategy and considering certification as a means to demonstrate compliance.

10. The EDPB will publish separate guidelines to address the identification of criteria to approve certification mechanisms as transfer tools to third countries or international organisations in accordance with Article 42(2).

1.2 THE PURPOSE OF CERTIFICATION UNDER THE GDPR

11. Article 42(1) provides that certification mechanisms shall be established "for the purpose of demonstrating compliance with this Regulation of processing operations by controllers and processors".

12. The GDPR exemplifies the context in which approved certification mechanisms may be used as an element to demonstrate compliance with obligations of the controllers and processors concerning:
* the implementation and demonstration of appropriate technical and organisational measures as referred in Articles 24(1),(3), 25, and 32(1), (3);
* sufficient guarantees (processor to controller) as referred to in paragraphs 1 and (sub-processor to processor) 4 of Article 28(5).

13. Since certification does not prove compliance in and of itself but rather forms an element that can be used to demonstrate compliance, it should be produced in a transparent manner. Demonstration of compliance requires supporting documentation, specifically written reports which not only repeat but describe how the criteria are met and if not initially met, describe the corrections and corrective actions and their appropriateness, thus providing the reasons for granting and maintaining the certification. This includes the outline of the individual decision for granting, renewing, or withdrawing of a certificate. It should provide the reasons, arguments, and proofs resulting from the application of criteria and the conclusions, judgments, or inferences from facts or premises collected during certification.

1.3 KEY CONCEPTS

14. The following section explores the key concepts in Articles 42 and 43. This analysis develops an understanding of basic terms and the scope of certification under the GDPR.

1.3.1 Interpretation of "certification"

15. The GDPR does not define "certification". The International Standards Organisation (ISO) provides a universal definition of certification as "the provision by an independent body of written assurance (a certificate) that the product, service or system in question meets specific requirements." Certification is also known as "third party conformity assessment" and certification bodies can also be referred to as "conformity assessment bodies" (CABs). In EN-ISO/IEC 17000:2004 - Conformity assessment -- Vocabulary and general principles (to which ISO17065 refers) - certification is defined in the following terms: "third party attestation . . . related to products, processes, and services".

16. Attestation is an 'issue of a statement, based on a decision following review, that fulfilment of specific requirements has been demonstrated' (section 5.2, ISO 17000:2004).

17. In the context of certification under Articles 42 and 43 of the GDPR, certification shall refer to third party attestation related to processing operations by controllers and processors.

1.3.2 Certification mechanisms, seals and marks

18. The GDPR does not define "certification mechanisms, seals or marks" – and uses the terms collectively. A certificate is a statement of conformity. A seal or mark can be used to signify the successful completion of the certification procedure. A seal or mark commonly refers to a logo or symbol whose presence (in addition to a certificate) indicates that the object of certification has been independently assessed in a certification procedure and conforms to specified requirements, stated in normative documents such as regulations, standards or technical specifications. These requirements in the context of certification under the GDPR are set out in the additional requirements that supplement the rules for accreditation of certification bodies in EN-ISO/IEC 17065/2012 and the certification criteria approved by the competent supervisory authority or the Board. A certificate, seal or mark under the GDPR can only be issued following the independent assessment of evidence by an accredited certification body or competent supervisory authority, stating that the certification criteria have been satisfied.

19. The table provides a generic example of a certification process.

Submission of application by controller or processor	Formal Check by CB	Assessment Pre-Evaluation	Assessment Evaluation on ToE	Assessment Evaluation on results	Information to CSA	Certification	Monitoring	Renewal of certification
Is the description of the target of evaluation (ToE) anambiguous and complete including interfaces?	Can the ToE description be accepted?	What are the applicable criteria?	Does the ToE meet the criteria?	Are all relevant criteria specified reflecting the ToE?	Have the reasons for granting or withdrawing certification been provided?	Can the certificate be awarded?	Does the ToE continue to meet the criteria	Does the processing still meet the certification criteria?
Can access to the ToE processing activities be granted?	Are all documents complete and up-to-date?	What are the applicable evaluation methods?	Is the documentation of the ToE correct?	Has the evaluation been sufficiently documented?		Are the reports ready for publishing?	Is the certificate/ seal / trust mark used correctly?	Have areas of development been satisfactorily addressed?
Art. 42(6)	Art. 43(4)	Art. 43(4)	Art. 42(5), Art. 43(4)	Art. 43(4)	Art. 43(1), 43(5)	Art. 43(1); Art. 42(7)	Art. 42(7)	Art. 42(7)

NOTES

1   Article 29 Working Party, Opinion 3/2010 on the principle of accountability, WP173, 13 July 2010, paragraphs 69-71.

2   Article 29 Working Party Opinion 3/2010 on the principle of accountability (WP173), paragraph 69.

3   These guidelines will refer to certification mechanisms and data protection seals and marks collectively as 'certification mechanisms', see section 1.3.2.

4   Recital 100 states that the establishment of certification mechanisms should be encouraged to 'enhance transparency and compliance with the Regulation, allowing data subjects to quickly assess the level of data protection of relevant products and services'.

5   See Article 29 Working Party, Guidelines on the application and setting of administrative fines for the purposes of the Regulation 2016/679 (WP 253).

2 THE ROLE OF THE SUPERVISORY AUTHORITIES

[2.253]

20. Article 42(5) provides that certification shall be issued by an accredited certification body or by a competent supervisory authority. The GDPR does not make the issuance of certifications a mandatory task of the supervisory authorities. Instead, the GDPR allows for a number of different models. For example, a supervisory authority may decide for one or more of the following options:

- issue certification itself, in respect of its own certification scheme;
- issue certification itself, in respect of its own certification scheme, but delegate whole or part of the assessment process to third parties;
- create its own certification scheme, and entrust certification bodies with the certification procedure which issue the certification; and
- encourage the market to develop certification mechanisms.

21. A supervisory authority will also have to consider its role in the light of the decisions made at the national level concerning accreditation mechanisms – in particular if the supervisory authority itself is empowered to accredit certification bodies under Article 43(1) GDPR. Thus each supervisory authority will determine which approach to take in order to pursue the broad intent of certification under the GDPR. This will be determined in the context of not only the tasks and powers in Articles 57 and 58, but also in accounting for certification as a factor to be taken into account in determining administrative fines, and more generally as a means of demonstrating compliance.

2.1 SUPERVISORY AUTHORITY AS CERTIFICATION BODY

22. Where a supervisory authority chooses to conduct certification, it will have to carefully assess its role with respect to its assigned tasks under the GDPR. Its role should be transparent in the exercise of its functions. It will need to give consideration specifically to the separation of powers relating to investigations and enforcement in order to avoid any potential conflicts of interest.

23. When acting as a certification body a supervisory authority will have to ensure the proper set up of a certification mechanism and develop its own or adopt certification criteria. In addition, every supervisory authority which issues certifications has the task to periodically review them (Article 57(1)(o)) and the power to withdraw them where the requirements for certification are not or no longer met (Article 58(2)(h)). To meet these requirements, it is useful to set up a certification procedure and process requirements, and, if not stipulated otherwise e.g. by national law, put in place a legally enforceable agreement for the provision of certification activities with the individual applicant organisation. It should be ensured that this certification agreement requires the applicant to comply at least with the certification criteria including necessary arrangements to conduct the evaluation, monitoring adherence to the criteria, and periodic review including access to information and/or premises, documentation and publication of reports and results, and investigation of complaints. Further, it is expected that a supervisory authority will follow the requirements in the guidelines for accreditation of certification bodies in addition to the requirements pursuant to Article 43(2).

2.2 SUPERVISORY AUTHORITY'S FURTHER TASKS REGARDING CERTIFICATION

24. In Member States where certification bodies become active, the supervisory authority has the power and task irrespective of its own activities:
- to assess a certification scheme's criteria and make a draft decision (Article 42(5));
- to communicate to the Board the draft decision when it intends to approve the criteria for certification (Article 64(1)(c), 64(7)) and consider the Board's opinion (Article 64(1)(c) and 70(1)(t));
- to approve the criteria for certification (Article 58(3)(f)) before accreditation and certification can take place (Article 42(5) and 43(2)(b));
- to publish the certification criteria (Article 43(6);
- to act as competent authority for EU wide certification schemes, which may result in an EDPB approved European Data Protection Seals (Articles 42(5) and Article 70(1)(o); and
- to order a certification body (a) not to issue certification or (b) to withdraw certification where the requirements for certification (certification procedures or criteria) are not or are no longer met (Article 58(2)(h).

25. The GPDR tasks the supervisory authority with approving certification criteria but not with developing criteria. In order to approve certification criteria under Article 42(5), a supervisory authority should have a clear understanding of what to expect, specifically in terms of scope and content for demonstrating compliance with the GDPR and with regard to its task to monitor and enforce the application of the regulation. The annex provides guidance to ensure a harmonized approach when assessing criteria for the purpose of approval.

26. Article 43(1) requires certification bodies to inform their supervisory authority before issuing or renewing certifications to allow the competent supervisory authority to exercise its corrective powers under point (h) of Article 58(2). Additionally, Article 43(5) also requires certification bodies to provide the competent supervisory authority with the reasons for granting or withdrawing the requested certification. Although the GDPR allows for supervisory authorities to determine how to receive, acknowledge, review and deal with this information operationally (for example, this could include technological solutions to enable reporting by certification bodies), a process and criteria to process the information and reports provided on each successful certification project by the certification body according to Article 43(1) may be put in place. On the basis of this information, the supervisory authority can exercise its power to order the certification body to withdraw or not issue a certification (Article 58(2)(h)) and to monitor and enforce the application of the requirements and criteria of certification under the GDPR (Article 57(1)(a) and 58(2)(h)). This will support a harmonized approach and comparability in certification by different certification bodies and that information about an organisation's certification status is known by supervisory authorities.

3 THE ROLE OF A CERTIFICATION BODY

[2.254]
27. A certification body's role is to issue, review, renew, and withdraw certifications (Article 42(5), (7)) on the basis of a certification mechanism and approved criteria (Article 43(1)). This requires the certification body or a certification scheme owner to determine and set up certification criteria and certification procedures, including procedures for monitoring of adherence, reviewing, handling complaints, and withdrawal. The certification criteria are reviewed as part of the accreditation process, which considers the rules and procedures under which certifications, seals, or marks are issued (Article 43(2)(c)).

28. The existence of a certification mechanism and certification criteria are necessary for the certification body to achieve accreditation under Article 43. A major impact on what a certification body does arises from the scope and type of certification criteria which have an impact on the certification procedures and vice versa. Specific criteria may for example require specific methods of evaluation, such as on-site inspections and code review. These procedures are mandatory for accreditation and are further explained in the guidelines on accreditation.

29. The certification body is required by the GDPR to provide supervisory authorities with information, especially on individual certifications, which is necessary to monitor the application of the certification mechanism (Article 42(7), 43(5), 58(2)(h)).

4 THE APPROVAL OF CERTIFICATION CRITERIA

[2.255]

30. The certification criteria form an integral part of any certification mechanism. Consequently, the GDPR requires the approval of certification criteria of a certification mechanism by the competent supervisory authority (Articles 42(5) and 43(2)(b)). Or in the case of a European Data Protection Seal, certification criteria is approved by the EDPB (Articles 42(5) and 70(1)(o)). Both routes for approval of certification criteria are explained below.

31. The EDPB recognizes the following purposes for approval of certification criteria:
- to properly reflect the requirements and principles concerning the protection of natural persons with regard to the processing of personal data laid down in Regulation (EU) 2016/679; and
- to contribute to the consistent application of the GDPR.

32. Approval is granted on the basis of the GDPR requirement that the certification mechanism enables controllers and processors to demonstrate compliance with the GDPR is fully reflected in the certification criteria.

4.1 APPROVAL OF CRITERIA BY THE COMPETENT SUPERVISORY AUTHORITY

33. Certification criteria must be approved by the competent supervisory authority prior or during the accreditation process for a certification body. Approval is also required for updated or additional schemes or sets of criteria under ISO 17065 by the same certification body, prior to their use of the amended certification mechanisms (Articles 42(5) and 43(2)(b)). Supervisory authorities shall treat all requests for approval of certification criteria in a fair and non-discriminatory way, according to a publicly available procedure specifying the general conditions to be met and the description of the approval process.

34. A certification body can only issue certification in a particular Member State in accordance with the criteria approved by the supervisory authority in that Member State. In other words, certification criteria need to be approved by the competent supervisory authority where the certification body aims to offer certification and obtains the accreditation. See the section below for European wide certification schemes.

4.2 APPROVAL OF CRITERIA BY EDPB FOR THE EUROPEAN DATA PROTECTION SEAL

35. A certification body can also issue certification in accordance with criteria approved by the EDPB for a European Data Protection Seal. Certification criteria approved by the EDPB pursuant to Article 63 may result in a European Data Protection Seal (Article 42(5)). In light of existing certification and accreditation conventions, the EDPB acknowledges that it is desirable to avoid fragmentation of the data protection certification market. It notes that Article 42(1) provides that Member States, supervisory authorities, the Board and the Commission shall encourage the establishment of certification mechanisms, in particular at Union level.

4.2.1 Application for approval

36. The application for approval of criteria pursuant to Article 42(5) and 70(1)(o), by the EDPB must be submitted through a competent supervisory authority and should state the intention of the scheme owner, candidate or accredited certification body to offer the criteria in a certification mechanism addressing controllers and processors in all Member States. The competent supervisory authority will provide a draft to the EDPB when it considers that the criteria could be approved by the EDPB.

37. The choice of where to submit an application for approval of criteria will be based on the certification scheme owners or the certification bodies headquarters.

38. If a certification body submits an application, it would normally be in the process of applying for accreditation or already accredited by either the competent supervisory authority or the national accreditation body of its Member State. Where the certification body is already accredited for a GDPR certification mechanism, this may help streamline the approvals process.

4.2.2 European Data Protection Seal criteria

39. The EDPB will co-ordinate the assessment process and approve the European Data Protection Seal criteria as required. The assessment will address such areas as: the criteria's scope and the ability to serve as a common certification. Where the criteria are approved by the EDPB, the competent supervisory authority for the EU headquarters of the certification body is expected to handle complaints about the mechanism itself and inform the other supervisory authorities. This supervisory authority is also competent to take measures against the certification body. As the case may be, the competent supervisory authority will notify the other supervisory authorities and the EDPB.

40. Certification criteria addressing a common certification are subject to EU-wide demands and should provide a specific mechanism to cope with these demands. European certification mechanisms must be intended for use in all Member States. Based on Article 42(5) the mechanism for a European Data Protection Seal as well as its criteria needs to be customisable in a way as to take into account national sector specific regulations where applicable, e. g., for data processing in schools and shall envisage a European-wide application.

41. Example: An international School offering schooling to data subjects in the Union is based in Member State "A". The school wishes to certify its online application process with an EU-wide certification scheme to earn a European Data Protection Seal. This school aims to apply for certification of processing operations offered by a certification body established in Member State "B" on the basis of a European Data Protection Seal. The Seal criteria designed and documented in the relevant mechanism must be able to take into account the regulations for schools applicable in Member State "A". The criteria should also require the school's online application process to provide information and take account of the applicable Member State data protection requirements that may differ in other Member States An example is sets of personal data to be submitted for application purposes, e.g. kindergarten grades or test results, differing retention periods, collection or processing of financial or biometric data, further processing limitations.

* High level criteria for approval of a European Data Protection Seal mechanism include:
  * criteria approved by the Board;
  * application across jurisdictions reflecting where appropriate national legal requirements and sector specific regulations;
* harmonised criteria which are customisable to reflect national requirements;
  * description of the certification mechanism specifying;
  * the certification agreements, recognizing pan-European requirements;
  * procedures to ensure and provide solutions for national variance and ensure the Seal helps demonstrate GDPR compliance; and
  * the language of the reports addressing all affected supervisory authorities.

42. The annex also contains advice on the European Data Protection Seal criteria.

4.2.3 Role of accreditation

43. As noted in 4.2.1, when criteria are identified as being suitable for common certification, and have been approved as such by the Board pursuant to Article 42(5), then certification bodies may be accredited to conduct certification under these criteria at Union level.

44. Schemes that are intended only to be offered only in particular Member States will not be candidates of EU Seals. Accreditation for the scope of a European Data Protection Seal will require accreditation in the Member State of the headquarters of the certification body intending to operate the scheme, i.e. responsible for issuing certifications and managing the certification activities of its entities and subsidiaries in other Member States. Where other establishments or offices manage and perform certifications autonomously, each of these establishments or offices will require separate accreditation in the Member State where they are based. In other words, accreditation is necessary only in the Member State of the headquarters of the certification body when only the headquarters issue the certificates. By contrast, when other establishments of the certification body also issue certificates, these establishments need to be accredited as well.

45. Consequently, if a certification body has not been accredited to certify under the European Data Protection Seal, then the EDPB approved criteria cannot be used and the Seal cannot be offered.

5 THE DEVELOPMENT OF CERTIFICATION CRITERIA

[2.256]
46. The GDPR established the framework for the development of certification criteria. Whereas fundamental requirements concerning the procedure of certification are addressed in Articles 42 and 43 while also providing essential criteria for certification procedures, the basis for certification criteria must be derived from the GDPR principles and rules and help to provide assurance that they are fulfilled.

47. The development of certification criteria should focus on verifiability, significance, and suitability of certification criteria to demonstrate compliance with the Regulation. The certification criteria should be formulated in such a way that they are clear and comprehensible and that they allow practical application.

48. When drafting certification criteria the following compliance aspects in support of the assessment of the processing operation, inter alia, shall be taken into account, where applicable:
* the lawfulness of processing pursuant to Article 6;
* the principles of data processing pursuant to Article 5;
* the data subjects' rights pursuant to Articles 12-23;
* the obligation to notify data breaches pursuant to Article 33;
* the obligation of data protection by design and by default, pursuant to Article 25;
* whether a data protection impact assessment, pursuant to Article 35(7)(d) has been conducted, if applicable; and
* the technical and organisational measures put in place pursuant to Article 32.

49. The extent to which these considerations are reflected in the criteria may vary depending on the scope of certification which may include the type of processing operation(s) and the area (e.g. health sector) of certification.

5.1 WHAT CAN BE CERTIFIED UNDER THE GDPR?

50. The EDPB considers that the GDPR provides a broad scope for what can be certified under the GDPR, as long as the focus is on helping demonstrate compliance with this Regulation of processing operations by controllers and processors (Article 42.1).

51. When assessing a processing operation, the following three core components must be considered, where applicable:
(1) personal data (material scope of the GDPR);
(2) technical systems - the infrastructure, such as hardware and software, used to process the personal data; and

(3)   processes and procedures related to the processing operation(s).

52. Each component used in processing operations must be subject to assessment against the set criteria. At least four different significant factors can be of influence: 1) the organisation and legal structure of the controller or processor; 2) the department, environment and people involved in the processing operation(s); 3) the technical description of the elements to be assessed; and finally 4) the IT infrastructure supporting the processing operation including operating systems, virtual systems, databases, authentication and authorization systems, routers and firewalls, storage systems, communication infrastructure or Internet access and associated technical measures.

53. All three core components are relevant for the design of certification procedures and criteria. Depending on the object of certification the extent to which they are taken into account may vary. For example, in some cases, some components can be disregarded if they are judged not relevant to the object of the certification.

54. To further specify what may be certified under the GDPR, the GDPR contains additional guidance. It follows from Article 42.7 that certifications under the GDPR are issued only to data controllers and data processors, which rule out for instance the certification of data protection officers. Art. 43(1)(b) refers to ISO 17065 which provides for the accreditation of certification bodies assessing the conformity of products, services and processes. A processing operation or a set of operations may result in a product or service in the terminology of ISO 17065 and such can be subject of certification. For instance, the processing of employee data for the purpose of salary payment or leave management is a set of operations within the meaning of the GDPR and can result in a product, process or a service in the terminology of ISO.

55. On the basis of these considerations, the EDPB considers that the scope of certification under the GDPR is directed to processing operations or sets of operations. These may comprise of governance processes in the sense of organisational measures, hence as integral parts of a processing operation (e.g. the governance process established for complaints handling as part of the processing of employee data for the purpose of salary payment).

56. In order to assess the compliance of the processing operation with the certification criteria, a use case must be provided. For example, compliance of the use of a technical infrastructure deployed in a processing operation depends on the categories of data it is designed to process. Organisational measures depend on the categories and amount of data and the technical infrastructure used for processing, taking into account the nature, scope, content and purposes of the processing as well as the risks to the rights and freedoms of the data subjects.

57. Moreover, it must be kept in mind that IT applications can differ widely even though serving the same processing purposes. Therefore, this must be considered when defining the scope of the certification mechanisms and drafting the certification criteria, i.e. the scope of certification and criteria should not be so narrow as to exclude IT applications designed differently.

5.2 DETERMINING THE OBJECT OF CERTIFICATION

58. The scope of a certification mechanism is to be distinguished from the object - also called the target of evaluation (ToE) - in individual certification projects under a certification mechanism. A certification mechanism can define its scope either generally or in relation to a specific type or area of processing operations and can thus already identify the objects of certification that fall within the scope of the certification mechanism (e.g. secure storage and protection of personal data contained in a digital vault). At any instance, a reliable, meaningful assessment of conformity can take place only if the individual object of a certification project is described precisely. It must be described clearly which processing operations are included in the object of certification and then the core components, i.e. which data, processes and technical infrastructure, will be assessed and which will not. In doing so, the interfaces to other processes must always be considered and described as well. Clearly, what is not known cannot be part of the assessment and thus cannot be certified. In any case, the individual object of certification must be meaningful with respect to the message or claim made on/by the certification and should not mislead the user, customer or consumer.

59. [Example 1]

A bank offers to its customers a website for the purpose of online banking. In the framework of this service, there is the possibility to make transfers, buy shares, initiate standing orders and manage the account. The bank wishes to certify the following under a data protection certification mechanism with a general scope based on generic criteria:
(a)   Secure log-in
       Secure log-in is a processing operation which is understandable for the end user and which is relevant from a data protection perspective since it plays an important part in ensuring the security of personal data involved. Therefore, this processing operation is necessary for secure log-in and can thus constitute a meaningful ToE if the certificate states clearly that only the log-in processing operation is certified.
(b)   Web front-end
       Whilst the web front-end can be relevant from a data protection perspective it is not understandable by the end user and therefore cannot be a meaningful ToE. Moreover, it is not clear to the user which services on the website and thus which processing operations are covered by the certification.
(c)   Online banking

The web front end together with the back-end are processing operations provided within the online banking service which can be meaningful to the user. In this context, both must be included in the ToE. Whereas processing operations that are not directly connected to the provision of the online banking service, such as processing operations for the purpose of prevention of money laundering, can be excluded from the ToE.

However, the online-banking services offered by the bank via its website may also include other services which in turn require their own processing operations. In this context, other services may include, for example, the offering of an insurance product. Since this additional service is not directly connected with the purpose of providing online banking services, it can be excluded from the ToE. If this additional service (insurance) is excluded from the ToE, the interfaces for this service integrated on the website are part of the ToE and must therefore be described in order to clearly distinguish between the services. Such a description is necessary to identify and evaluate possible data flows between the two services.

60. [Example 2]

A bank offers to its customers a service allowing them to aggregate the information related to different accounts and credit cards from several banks (account aggregation). The bank wishes to have its service certified under the GDPR. The competent supervisory authority has approved a specific set of certification criteria focusing on this type of activity. The scope of the certification mechanism only addresses the following compliance aspects:

* user authentication; and
* acceptable ways to obtain the data to be aggregated from other banks/services.

Since the scope of this certification mechanism defines the ToE by itself, it is not possible to meaningfully narrow down the ToE under the proposed scope and certify only specific features or a single processing activity. In this scenario, a ToE must equal a specific scope.

5.3 EVALUATION METHODS AND METHODOLOGY OF ASSESSMENT

61. A conformity assessment to help demonstrate compliance of processing operations requires identifying and determining the methods for evaluation and the methodology of assessment. It matters whether the information for the assessment is collected from documentation only (which would not be sufficient in itself) or whether it is actively collected on site and by direct or indirect access. The way in which information is collected has consequences for the significance of certification and should therefore be defined and described.

Procedures for the issuance and periodic review of certifications should include specifications to identify the appropriate level of evaluation (depth and granularity) to meet the certification criteria and should include the provision of:

* information about and specification of the applied assessment methods and findings collected e.g. during on site audits or from documentation,
* evaluation methods focusing on the processing operations (data, systems, processes) and the purpose of processing,
* identification of the categories of data, the protection needs and whether processors or third parties are involved,
* identification of roles and existence of an access control mechanism defined around roles and responsibilities.

62. The depth of evaluation has an impact on the significance and value of the certification. By reducing the depth of evaluation for pragmatic purposes or to reduce the costs, the significance of a data protection certification will be diminished. Decisions on the granularity of the evaluation on the other hand, may exceed the financial capabilities of the applicant and often the capability of evaluators and auditors, too. For purposes of demonstrating compliance it may not always be crucial to reach a very detailed analysis of the IT systems used to remain meaningful.

5.4 DOCUMENTATION OF ASSESSMENT

63. Certification documentation should be thorough and comprehensive. A lack of documentation means that a proper assessment cannot take place. The essential function of certification documentation is that it provides for transparency in the evaluation process under the certification mechanism. Documentation delivers answers to questions concerning the requirements set out by law. Certification mechanisms should provide for a standardized documentation methodology. Thereafter evaluation will allow comparison of the certification documentation with the actual status on-site and against the certification criteria.

64. Comprehensive documentation of what has been certified and the methodology used serves transparency. Pursuant to Article 43(2)(c), certification mechanisms should establish procedures that allow the review of certifications. In order to allow the supervisory authority to assess whether and to what extent the certification can be acknowledged in formal investigations, detailed documentation may be the most appropriate means to communicate. The documentation produced during evaluation should therefore focus on three main aspects:

* consistency and coherence of evaluation methods executed;
* evaluation methods directed to demonstrate compliance of the certification object with the certification criteria and thus with the Regulation; and
* that the results of evaluation have been validated by an independent and impartial certification body.

5.5 DOCUMENTATION OF RESULTS

65. Recital 100 provides information on the objectives pursued with the introduction of certification. "In order to enhance transparency and compliance with this Regulation, the establishment of certification mechanisms and data protection seals and marks should be encouraged, allowing data subjects to quickly assess the level of data protection of relevant products and services."

66. To enhance transparency the documentation and communication of results play an important role. Certification bodies using certification mechanisms, seals or marks directed towards the data subjects (in their roles as consumers or customers) should provide easily accessible, intelligible and meaningful information about the certified processing operation(s). This public information should include at least the

- description of the ToE;
- reference to the approved criteria applied to the specific ToE;
- the methodology for the evaluation of the criteria (on-site evaluation, documentation, etc.); and
- the duration of the validity of the certificate; and
- should allow comparability of results for supervisory authorities and the public.

6 GUIDANCE FOR DEFINING CERTIFICATION CRITERIA

[2.257]

67. Certification criteria are an integral part of a certification mechanism. The certification procedure includes the requirements of how, by whom, to what extent and the granularity of the assessment which shall take place in individual certification projects concerning a specific object or target of evaluation (ToE). The certification criteria provide the nominal requirements against which the actual processing operation defined in the ToE is assessed. These guidelines for defining certification criteria provide generic advice that will facilitate the assessment of certification criteria for the purpose of approval.

- The following general considerations should be taken into account when approving or defining certification criteria, Certification criteria should:
- be uniform and verifiable,
- auditable in order to facilitate the evaluation of processing operations under the GDPR, by specifying in particular, the objectives and the implementing guidance for achieving those objectives;
- be relevant with respect to the targeted audience (e.g. B2B and business to customer (B2C);
- take into account and where appropriate be inter-operable with other standards (such as ISO standards, national level standards); and
- be flexible and scalable for application to different types and sizes of organisations including micro, small and medium sized enterprises in accordance with Article 42(1) and the risk-based approach in accordance with Recital 77.

68. A small local company, such as a retailer, will usually carry out less complex processing operations than a large multinational retailer. While the requirements for the lawfulness of the processing operations are the same, the scope of data processing and its complexity must be taken into account; it follows that there is a need for certification mechanisms and their criteria to be scalable according to the processing activity in question.

6.1 EXISTING STANDARDS

69. Certification bodies will need to consider how specific criteria take existing relevant instruments, such as Codes of Conducts, technical standards or national regulatory and legal initiatives into account. Ideally, criteria will be interoperable with existing standards that can help a controller or processor meet their obligations under the GDPR. However, while industry standards often focus on the protection and security of the organisation against threats, the GDPR is directed at the protection of fundamental rights of natural persons. This different perspective must be taken into account when designing criteria or approving criteria or certification mechanisms based on industry standards.

6.2 DEFINING CRITERIA

70. Certification criteria must correspond to the certification statement (message or claim) of a certification mechanism or scheme and match the expectations it raises. The name of a certification mechanism may already identify the scope of application and will have consequences for the determination of criteria.

71. [Example 3]

A mechanism called "HealthPrivacyMark" should limit its scope to the health sector. The seal name raises the expectation that data protection requirements in connection with health data have been examined. Accordingly, the criteria of this mechanism must be adequate for assessing data protection requirements in this sector.

72. [Example 4]

A mechanism that relates to the certification of processing operations comprising governance systems in data processing should identify criteria that allow for the recognition and assessment of governance processes and its supporting technical and organisational measures.

73. [Example 5]

The criteria for a mechanism that relates to cloud computing needs to take account of the special technical requirements necessary for the use of cloud-based services. For instance, if servers are used outside the EU, the criteria must consider the conditions laid down in Chapter V of the GDPR with respect to data transfers to third-countries.

74. Criteria designed to fit different ToEs in different sectors and/or Member States should: allow an application to different scenarios; allow identification of the adequate measures to fit small, medium, or large processing operations and reflect the risks of varying likelihood and severity to the rights and freedoms of natural persons in line with the GDPR. Consequently, the certification procedures (e.g. for documentation, testing, or evaluation method and depth) complementing the criteria must respond to these needs and allow and have rules in place, for example to apply the relevant criteria in individual certification projects. Criteria must facilitate an assessment as to whether sufficient guarantees for the implementation of appropriate technical and organisational measures have been provided.

6.3 LIFETIME OF CERTIFICATION CRITERIA

75. Even though certification criteria must be reliable over time they should not be carved in stone. They shall be subject to revision for instance where:
- the legal framework is amended;
- terms and provisions are interpreted by judgments of the European Court of Justice; or
- the technical state of the art has evolved.

For the European Data Protection Board

The Chair

(Andrea Jelinek)

ANNEX 1: TASKS AND POWERS OF SUPERVISORY AUTHORITIES IN RELATION TO CERTIFICATION IN ACCORDANCE WITH THE GDPR

[2.258]

	Provisions	Requirements
Tasks	Article 43(6)	Requires the supervisory authority to make public the criteria referred to in Article 42(5) in an easily accessible form and transmit them to the Board.
	Article 57(1)(n)	Requires the supervisory authority to approve certification criteria pursuant to Article 42(5).
	Article 57(1)(o)	Provides that where appropriate (i.e. where it issues certification), it shall carry out a periodic review of certification issued in accordance with Article 42(7).
	Article 64(1)(c)	Requires the supervisory authority to communicate the draft decision to the Board, when it aims to approve the criteria for certification referred to in Article 42(5).
Powers	Article 58(1)(c)	Provides that the supervisory authority has the power to carry out reviews of certification pursuant to Article 42(7);
	Article 58(2)(h)	Provides that the supervisory authority has the power to withdraw or order the certification body to withdraw certification or order the certification body not to issue certification.
	Article 58(3)(e)	Provides that the supervisory authority has the power to accredit certification bodies
	Article 58(3)(f)	Provides that the supervisory authority has the power to issue certification and approve certification criteria.
	Article 58(3)(e)	Provides that the supervisory authority has the power to accredit certification bodies.
	Article 58(3)(f)	Provides that the supervisory authority has the power to issue certification and approve certification criteria.

ANNEX 2

1 INTRODUCTION

[2.259]

Annex 2 provides guidance for review and assessment of certification criteria pursuant to Article 42(5). It identifies topics that a data protection supervisory authority and the EDPB will consider and apply for the purpose of approval of certification criteria of a certification mechanism. The questions should be considered by certification bodies and scheme owners who wish to draft and present criteria for approval. The list is not exhaustive, but presents the minimum topics to be considered. Not all questions will be applicable; however they should be considered when drafting criteria and reasoning may be needed to explain why criteria do not cover specific aspects. Some questions are repeated, as they are from different perspectives. This guidance should be considered in accordance with the legal requirements provided by the GDPR and, where applicable, by national legislation.

2 SCOPE OF THE CERTIFICATION MECHANISM AND TARGET OF EVALUATION (TOE)

(a) Is the scope of the certification mechanism (for which the data protection criteria shall be used) clearly described?

(b) Is the scope of the certification mechanism meaningful to its addressed audience and not misleading?

- *Example: A "Trusted Company Seal" suggests that the processing activities of an entire company have been audited, even though only specified processing operations, e.g. the online payment process, are actually subject to certification. The scope is therefore misleading.*

(c)   Does the scope of the certification mechanism reflect all relevant aspects of the processing operations?

- *Example: A "Privacy Health Mark" must include all evaluation data concerning health in order to address requirements pursuant to Article 9.*

(d)   Does the scope of the certification mechanism allow meaningful data protection certification taking into account the nature, the content, the risk of the related processing operations?

- *Example: If the scope of the certification mechanism focuses only on specific aspects of processing operations, such as the collection of data, but not on the further processing operations, such as processing for the purpose of creating advertising profiles or the management of data subject's rights, would not be meaningful for data subjects.*

(e)   Does the scope of the certification mechanism cover personal data processing in the relevant country of application or does it address cross border processing and/or transfers?

(f)   Do the certification criteria sufficiently describe how the ToE should be defined?

- *Example: A "Privacy Seal" offering a general scope only requiring "a specification of the processing subject to certification" would not provide clear enough guidance on how to set and describe a ToE.*
- *Example: A (specific) scope, "The Privacy Vault Seal", addressing secure storage should describe in detail the requirements to meet this scope in its criteria, e.g. definition of vault, system requirements, mandatory technical and organisational measures (TOMs). In that case the scope can clearly define the ToE.*

  (1)   Do the criteria require the ToE to include an identification of all relevant processing operations, Illustration of data flows and a determination of the ToE's area of application?

  - *Example: A certification mechanism offers certification of processing operations of controllers under the GDPR without specifying further the area of application (general scope). The criteria used by the mechanism requires the applicant controller to determine the targeted processing operation (ToE) in terms of data types, systems and processes deployed.*

  (2)   Do the criteria require from the applicant to make clear where the processing that is subject to evaluation starts and ends? Do the criteria require the ToE to include interfaces where interdependent processing operations are not included as part of the ToE? And is this satisfactorily justified?

  - *Example: A ToE describing in sufficient detail the processing operation of a web based service such as including the registration of users, the provision of service, invoicing, logging of IP-addresses, interfaces to users and to third parties and excluding server hosting (yet including processing and TOM agreements).*

(g)   Do the criteria guarantee that the (individual) ToEs are understandable to its audience, including data subjects where relevant?

3 GENERAL REQUIREMENTS

(a)   Are all relevant terms used in the criteria catalogue (i.e. the full set of certification criteria) identified, explained and described?

(b)   Are all normative references identified?

(c)   Do the criteria include the definition of data protection responsibilities, procedures and processing covered by the scope of the certification mechanism?

4 PROCESSING OPERATION, ARTICLE 42(1)

With respect to the scope of the certification mechanism (general or specific), are all relevant components of the processing operations (data, systems, and processes) addressed by the criteria?

(a)   Do criteria require identification of the valid legal bases of processing with respect to the ToE?

(b)   With respect to the ToE, do the criteria recognize the relevant phases of processing and the whole life-cycle of data including the deletion and or anonymisation?

(c)   With respect to the ToE, do the criteria require data portability?

(d)   With respect to the ToE, do the criteria allow identifying and reflecting special types of processing operations, e.g. automated decision making, profiling?

(e)   With respect to the ToE, do the criteria allow identifying special categories of data?

(f)   Do the criteria allow and require assessing the risk of the individual processing operations and the protection needs for the rights and freedoms of data subjects?

(g)   Do the criteria allow and require adequate account of the risks to the rights and freedoms of natural persons?

. . .

5 LAWFULNESS OF PROCESSING

(a)   Do the criteria require checking the lawfulness of processing for individual processing operations with respect to purpose and necessity of processing?

(b)   Do the criteria require checking all the requirements of a legal basis for individual processing operations?

6 PRINCIPLES, ARTICLE 5

(a)   Do the criteria adequately address all data protection principles pursuant to Article 5?
(b)   Do the criteria require demonstration of data minimisation for the individual ToE?

. . .

7 GENERAL OBLIGATIONS OF CONTROLLERS AND PROCESSORS

(a)   Do the criteria require proof of contractual agreements between processors and controllers?
(b)   Are controller processor agreements subject to evaluation?
(c)   Do the criteria reflect the obligations of the controller pursuant to Chapter IV?
(d)   Do the criteria require proof of review and updating of technical and organisational measures implemented by the controller pursuant to Article 24(1)?
(e)   Do the criteria check that the organisation has assessed if a Data Protection Officer (DPO) should be appointed as required by Article 37? Where relevant does the DPO meet the requirements under Articles 37 to 39?
(f)   Do the criteria check that records of processing of activities are required in accordance with Article 30(5) and appropriately address Article 30 requirements?

8 RIGHTS OF THE DATA SUBJECTS

(a)   Do the criteria adequately address data subject's right to information and require respective measures to be put in place?
(b)   Do the criteria require that data subjects are granted adequate or even greater access and control of their data including data portability?
(c)   Do criteria require measures put in place providing for the possibility to intervene in the processing operation in order to guarantee data subjects' rights and allow corrections, erasure or restrictions?

. . .

9 RISKS FOR THE RIGHTS AND FREEDOMS OF NATURAL PERSONS

(a)   Do the criteria allow and require assessing the risk to the rights and freedoms of natural persons?
(b)   Do the criteria provide or require a recognized risk assessment methodology? If appropriate, is it commensurate?
(c)   Do the criteria allow and require assessing the impact of the envisaged processing operations for the rights and freedoms of natural persons?
(d)   Do the criteria, require prior consultation concerning the remaining risks that could not be mitigated, based on the results of the Data Protection Impact Assessment (DPIA)?

10 TECHNICAL AND ORGANISATIONAL MEASURES GUARANTEEING PROTECTION

(a)   Do criteria require the application of technical and organisational measures providing for confidentiality of processing operations?
(b)   Do criteria require the application of technical and organisational measures providing for integrity of processing operations?
(c)   Do criteria require the application of technical and organisational measures providing for availability of processing operations?
(d)   Do criteria require the application of measures providing for transparency of processing operations with respect to
(e)   Accountability?
(f)   Data subjects rights?
(g)   Assessment of individual processing operations, e.g. for algorithmic transparency?
(h)   Do criteria require the application of technical and organisational measures guaranteeing data subjects' rights, e.g. the ability to provide information, or to data portability?
(i)   Do criteria require the application of technical and organisational measures providing for the ability to intervene into the processing operation in order to guarantee data subjects right and allow corrections, erasure or restrictions?
(j)   Do criteria require the application of measures providing for the ability to intervene into the processing operation in order to patch or check the system or the process?
(k)   Do criteria require the application of technical and organisational measures to ensure data minimisation, for example, unlinking or separation of the data from the data subject, anonymisation or pseudonymisation or isolation of data systems?
(l)   Do criteria require technical measures to implement data protection by default?
(m)   Do criteria require technical and organisational measures implementing data protection by design, e.g. a data protection management system to demonstrate, inform, control and enforce data protection requirements?
(n)   Do criteria require technical and organisational measures implementing appropriate periodic training and education for the personnel having permanent or regular access to personal data?
(o)   Do criteria require reviewing measures?
(p)   Do criteria require self-assessment/ internal audit?
(q)   Do criteria require measure to ensure that personal data breach notification duties are carried out in due time and scope?

(r)   Do criteria require incident management procedures to be in place and verified?
(s)   Do criteria require monitoring of evolving privacy and technology issues and updating of the scheme as required?

. . .

11 OTHER SPECIAL DATA PROTECTION FRIENDLY FEATURES

(a)   Do the criteria require the implementation of data protection enhancing techniques? This could include criteria that require enhanced data protection by eliminating or reducing personal data and/or the data protection risk.
   •   *Example: Criteria requiring enhanced unlinkability by using user-centric identity management such as attribute –based credentials (ABC) over organisation-centric identity management would reflect a data protection enhancing technique.*
(b)   Do the criteria require the implementation of enhanced data subjects controls to facilitate self-determination and choice?
   . . .

12 CRITERIA FOR THE PURPOSE OF DEMONSTRATING THE EXISTENCE OF APPROPRIATE SAFEGUARDS FOR TRANSFER OF PERSONAL DATA

Criteria will be addressed in forthcoming guidelines on Article 42(2).

13 ADDITIONAL CRITERIA FOR A EUROPEAN DATA PROTECTION SEAL

(a)   Do the criteria envisage covering all Member States?
(b)   Are the criteria able to take into account Member State data protection law or scenarios?
(c)   Do the criteria require an evaluation of the individual ToE with respect to sector specific Member State data protection law?
(d)   Do the criteria require the controller or processor to provide information to data subjects and interested parties in the languages of Member States
(e)   On the processing/ToE?
(f)   Documentation of the processing/ToE?
(g)   The results of the evaluation?

. . .

14 OVERALL EVALUATION OF CRITERIA

(a)   Do the criteria fully cover the scope of the certification mechanism (i.e. comprehensive criteria) to provide sufficient guarantees so that the certification can be trusted?
   •   *Example: If the scope of the certification mechanism focuses on health processing operations, a high level of data protection should be guaranteed by defining criteria that ensure, for instance, an in-depth assessment and the application of privacy-by-design and privacy-by-default principles.*
(b)   Are the criteria commensurate with the size of the processing operation being addressed by the scope of the certification mechanism, the sensitivity of information and the risk of processing?
(c)   Are the criteria likely to improve data protection compliance of controllers and processors?
(d)   Will data subjects benefit in respect of their information rights, including explaining desired outcomes to data subjects?

EUROPEAN DATA PROTECTION BOARD: GUIDELINES 2/2018 ON DEROGATIONS OF ARTICLE 49 UNDER REGULATION 2016/679

Adopted on 25 May 2018

[2.260]

NOTES
© European Data Protection Board.

TABLE OF CONTENTS

THE EUROPEAN DATA PROTECTION BOARD

Having regard to Article 70 (1j) and (1e) of the Regulation 2016/679/EU of the European Parliament and of the Council of 27 April 2016 on the protection of natural persons with regard to the processing of personal data and on the free movement of such data, and repealing Directive 95/46/EC,

HAS ADOPTED FOLLOWING GUIDELINES:

1. GENERAL

[2.261]
This document seeks to provide guidance as to the application of Article 49 of the General Data Protection Regulation (GDPR)[1] on derogations in the context of transfers of personal data to third countries.

The document builds on the previous work[2] done by the Working Party of EU Data Protection Authorities established under Article 29 of the Data Protection Directive (the WP29) which is taken over by the European Data Protection Board (EDPB) regarding central questions raised by the application of derogations in the context of transfers of personal data to third countries. This document will be reviewed and if necessary updated, based on the practical experience gained through the application of the GDPR.

When applying Article 49 one must bear in mind that according to Article 44 the data exporter transferring personal data to third countries or international organizations must also meet the conditions of the other provisions of the GDPR. Each processing activity must comply with the relevant data protection provisions, in particular with Articles 5 and 6. Hence, a two-step test must be applied: first, a legal basis must apply to the data processing as such together with all relevant provisions of the GDPR; and as a second step, the provisions of Chapter V must be complied with.

Article 49(1) states that in the absence of an adequacy decision or of appropriate safeguards, a transfer or a set of transfers of personal data to a third country or an international organization shall take place only under certain conditions. At the same time, Article 44 requires all provisions in Chapter V to be applied in such a way as to ensure that the level of protection of natural persons guaranteed by the GDPR is not undermined. This also implies that recourse to the derogations of Article 49 should never lead to a situation where fundamental rights might be breached.[3]

The WP29, as predecessor of the EDPB, has long advocated as best practice a layered approach[4] to transfers of considering first whether the third country provides an adequate level of protection and ensuring that the exported data will be safeguarded in the third country. If the level of protection is not adequate in light of all the circumstances, the data exporter should consider providing adequate safeguards. Hence, data exporters should first endeavor possibilities to frame the transfer with one of the mechanisms included in Articles 45 and 46 GDPR, and only in their absence use the derogations provided in Article 49(1).

Therefore, derogations under Article 49 are exemptions from the general principle that personal data may only be transferred to third countries if an adequate level of protection is provided for in the third country or if appropriate safeguards have been adduced and the data subjects enjoy enforceable and effective rights in order to continue to benefit from their fundamental rights and safeguards.[5] Due to this fact and in accordance with the principles inherent in European law,[6] the derogations must be interpreted restrictively so that the exception does not become the rule.[7] This is also supported by the wording of the title of Article 49 which states that derogations are to be used for specific situations ("Derogations for specific situations").

When considering transferring personal data to third countries or international organizations, data exporters should therefore favour solutions that provide data subjects with a guarantee that they will continue to benefit from the fundamental rights and safeguards to which they are entitled as regards processing of their data once this data has been transferred. As derogations do not provide adequate protection or appropriate safeguards for the personal data transferred and as transfers based on a derogation are not required to have any kind of prior authorisation from the supervisory authorities, transferring personal data to third countries on the basis of derogations leads to increased risks for the rights and freedoms of the data subjects concerned.

Data exporters should also be aware that, in the absence of an adequacy decision, Union or Member State law may, for important reasons of public interest, expressly limit transfers of specific categories of personal data to a third country or an international organization (Article 49(5)).

OCCASIONAL AND NOT REPETITIVE TRANSFERS

The EDPB notes that the term "occasional" is used in recital 111 and the term "not repetitive" is used in the "compelling legitimate interests" derogation under Article 49 par. 1 §2. These terms indicate that such transfers may happen more than once, but not regularly, and would occur outside the regular course of actions, for example, under random, unknown circumstances and within arbitrary time intervals. For example, a data transfer that occurs regularly within a stable relationship between the data exporter and a certain data importer can basically be deemed as systematic and repeated and can therefore not be considered occasional or not-repetitive. Besides, a transfer will for example generally be considered to be non-occasional or repetitive when the data importer is granted direct access to a database (e.g. via an interface to an IT-application) on a general basis.

Recital 111 differentiates among the derogations by expressly stating that the "contract" and the "legal claims" derogations (Article 49(1) subpar. 1 (b), (c) and (e)) shall be limited to "occasional" transfers, while such limitation is absent from the "explicit consent derogation", the "important reasons of public interest derogation", the "vital interests derogation" and the "register derogation" pursuant to Article 49(1) subpar. 1 (a), (d), (f) and, respectively, (g).

Nonetheless, it has to be highlighted that even those derogations which are not expressly limited to "occasional" or "not repetitive" transfers have to be interpreted in a way which does not contradict the very nature of the derogations as being exceptions from the rule that personal data may not be transferred to a third country unless the country provides for an adequate level of data protection or, alternatively, appropriate safeguards are put in place.[8]

NECESSITY TEST

One overarching condition for the use of several derogations is that the data transfer has to be "necessary" for a certain purpose. The necessity test should be applied to assess the possible use of the derogations of Articles 49 (1)(b), (c), (d), (e) and (f). This test requires an evaluation by the data exporter in the EU of whether a transfer of personal data can be considered necessary for the specific purpose of the derogation to be used. For more information on the specific application of the necessity test in each of the concerned derogations, please refer to the relevant sections below.

ARTICLE 48 IN RELATION TO DEROGATIONS

The GDPR introduces a new provision in Article 48 that needs to be taken into account when considering transfers of personal data. Article 48 and the corresponding recital 115 provide that decisions from third country authorities, courts or tribunals are not in themselves legitimate grounds for data transfers to third countries. Therefore, a transfer in response to a decision from third country authorities is in any case only lawful, if in line with the conditions set out in Chapter V.[9]

In situations where there is an international agreement, such as a mutual legal assistance treaty (MLAT), EU companies should generally refuse direct requests and refer the requesting third country authority to existing MLAT or agreement.

This understanding also closely follows Article 44, which sets an overarching principle applying to all provisions of Chapter V, in order to ensure that the level of protection of natural persons guaranteed by the GDPR is not undermined.

NOTES

1. REGULATION (EU) 2016/679 OF THE EUROPEAN PARLIAMENT AND OF THE COUNCIL of 27 April 2016 on the protection of natural persons with regard to the processing of personal data and on the free movement of such data, and repealing Directive 95/46/EC (General Data Protection Regulation).
2. Article 29 Working Party, Working Document on a common interpretation of Article 26(1) of Directive 95/46/EC of 24 October 1995, November 25,2005 (WP114)
3. Article 29 Working Party, WP 114, p.9, and Article 29 Working Party Working Document on surveillance of electronic communications for intelligence and national security purposes (WP228), p.39.
4. Article 29 Working Party, WP114, p.9
5. Recital 114
6. Article 29 Working Party, WP114, p.7
7. See already Article 29 Working Party, WP114, pg. 7. The European Court of Justice repeatedly underlined that "the protection of the fundamental right to respect for private life at EU level requires that derogations from and limitations on the protection of personal data should apply only in so far as is strictly necessary" (judgments of 16 December 2008, Satakunnan Markkinapörssi and Satamedia, C 73/07, paragraph 56; of 9 November 2010, Volker und Markus Schecke and Eifert, C 92/09 and C 93/09, paragraph 77; the Digital Rights judgment, paragraph 52, and of 6 October 2015, Schrems, C 362/14, paragraph 92, and of 21 December 2016, Tele2 Sverige AB, C 203/15, paragraph 96). See also report on the Additional Protocol to Convention 108 on the control authorities and cross border flows of data, Article 2(2)(a), p.6 accessible at https://www.coe.int/en/web/conventions/full-list/-/conventions/treaty/181.1)
8. [No text provided for this footnote in original document]
9. See Recital 115 sentence 4

2. SPECIFIC INTERPRETATION OF THE PROVISIONS OF ARTICLE 49

2.1 THE DATA SUBJECT HAS EXPLICITLY CONSENTED TO THE PROPOSED TRANSFER, AFTER HAVING BEEN INFORMED OF THE POSSIBLE RISKS OF SUCH TRANSFERS FOR THE DATA SUBJECT DUE TO THE ABSENCE OF AN ADEQUACY DECISION AND APPROPRIATE SAFEGUARDS - ARTICLE (49(1)(A))

[2.262]
The general conditions for consent to be considered as valid are defined in Articles 4 (11)[10] and 7 of the GDPR[11]. The WP29 provides guidance on these general conditions for consent in a separate document, which is endorsed by the EDPB.[12] These conditions also apply to consent in the context of Article 49(1)(a). However, there are specific, additional elements required for consent to be considered a valid legal ground for international data transfers to third countries and international organizations as provided for in Article 49(1)(a), and this document will focus on them.

Therefore, this section (1) of the present guidelines shall be read in conjunction with the WP29 guidelines on consent, endorsed by the EDPB, which provide a more detailed analysis on the interpretation of the general conditions and criteria of consent under the GDPR.[13] It should also be noted that, according to Article 49(3), public authorities are not able to rely on this derogation in the exercise of their public powers.

Article 49(1)(a) states that a transfer of personal data to a third country or an international organization may be made in the absence of an adequacy decision pursuant to Article 45(3), or of appropriate safeguards pursuant to Article 46, including binding corporate rules, on the condition that '*the data subject has explicitly consented to the proposed transfer, after having been informed of the possible risks of such transfers for the data subject due to the absence of an adequacy decision and appropriate safeguards'.*

2.1.1 Consent must be explicit

According to Article 4 (11) of the GDPR, any consent should be freely given, specific, informed and unambiguous. On this very last condition, Article 49(1)(a) is stricter as it requires "explicit" consent. This is also a new requirement in comparison to Article 26 (1)(a) of Directive 95/46/EC, which only required "unambiguous" consent. The GDPR requires explicit consent in situations where particular data protection risks may emerge, and so, a high individual level of control over personal data is required, as is the case for the processing of special category data (Article 9 (2)(a)) and automated decisions (Article 22 (2)(c)). Such particular risks also appear in the context of international data transfers.

For further guidance on the requirement of explicit consent, and for the other applicable requirements needed for consent to be considered valid, please refer to the WP29's Guidelines on Consent which are endorsed by the EDPB.[14]

2.1.2 Consent must be specific for the particular data transfer/set of transfers

One of the requirements of valid consent is that it must be specific. In order to constitute a valid ground for a data transfer pursuant to Article 49(1)(a), hence, consent needs to be specifically given for the particular data transfer or set of transfers.

The element "specific" in the definition of consent intends to ensure a degree of user control and transparency for the data subject. This element is also closely linked with the requirement that consent should be "informed".

Since consent must be specific, it is sometimes impossible to obtain the data subject's prior consent for a future transfer at the time of the collection of the data, e.g. if the occurrence and specific circumstances of a transfer are not known at the time consent is requested, the impact on the data subject cannot be assessed. As an example, an EU company collects its customers' data for a specific purpose (delivery of goods) without considering transferring this data, at that time, to a third party outside the EU. However, some years later, the same company is acquired by a non-EU company which wishes to transfer the personal data of its customers to another company outside the EU. In order for this transfer to be valid on the grounds of the consent derogation, the data subject should give his/her consent for this specific transfer at the time when the transfer is envisaged. Therefore, the consent provided at the time of the collection of the data by the EU company for delivery purposes is not sufficient to justify the use of this derogation for the transfer of the personal data outside the EU which is envisaged later.

Therefore, the data exporter must make sure to obtain specific consent before the transfer is put in place even if this occurs after the collection of the data has been made. This requirement is also related to the necessity for consent to be informed. It is possible to obtain the specific consent of a data subject prior to the transfer and at the time of the collection of the personal data as long as this specific transfer is made known to the data subject and the circumstances of the transfer do not change after the specific consent has been given by the data subject. Therefore the data exporter must make sure that the requirements set out in section 1.3 below are also complied with.

2.1.3 Consent must be informed[15] particularly as to the possible risks of the transfer

This condition is particularly important since it reinforces and further specifies the general requirement of "informed" consent as applicable to any consent and laid down in Art. 4 (11).[16] As such, the general requirement of "informed" consent, requires, in the case of consent as a lawful basis pursuant to Article 6(1)(a) for a data transfer, that the data subject is properly informed in advance of the specific circumstances of the transfer, (i.e. the data controller's identity, the purpose of the transfer, the type of data, the existence of the right to withdraw consent, the identity or the categories of recipients).[17]

In addition to this general requirement of "informed" consent, where personal data are transferred to a third country under Article 49(1)(a), this provision requires data subjects to be also informed of the specific risks resulting from the fact that their data will be transferred to a country that does not provide adequate protection and that no adequate safeguards aimed at providing protection for the data are being implemented. The provision of this information is essential in order to enable the data subject to consent with full knowledge of these specific facts of the transfer and therefore if it is not supplied, the derogation will not apply.

The information provided to data subjects in order to obtain consent for the transfer of their personal data to third parties established in third countries should also specify all data recipients or categories of recipients, all countries to which the personal data are being transferred to, that the consent is the lawful ground for the transfer, and that the third country to which the data will be transferred does not provide for an adequate level of data protection based on a European Commission decision.[18] In addition, as mentioned above, information has to be given as to the possible risks for the data subject arising from the absence of adequate protection in the third country and the absence of appropriate safeguards. Such notice, which could be standardized, should include for example information that in the third country there might not be a supervisory authority and/or data processing principles and/or data subject rights might not be provided for in the third country.

In the specific case where a transfer is performed after the collection of personal data from the data subject has been made, the data exporter should inform the data subject of the transfer and of its risks before it takes place so as to collect his explicit consent to the "proposed" transfer.

As shown by the analysis above, the GDPR sets a high threshold for the use the derogation of consent. This high threshold, combined with the fact that the consent provided by a data subject can be withdrawn at any time, means that consent might prove not to be a feasible long term solution for transfers to third countries.

2.2 TRANSFER NECESSARY FOR THE PERFORMANCE OF A CONTRACT BETWEEN THE DATA SUBJECT AND THE CONTROLLER OR FOR THE IMPLEMENTATION OF PRECONTRACTUAL MEASURES TAKEN AT THE DATA SUBJECT'S REQUEST (49(1)(B))

In view of recital 111, data transfers on the grounds of this derogation may take place "*where the transfer is **occasional** and **necessary** in relation to a contract (. . .)*"[19]

In general, although the derogations relating to the performance of a contract may appear to be potentially rather broad, they are being limited by the criterions of **"necessity"** and of **"occasional transfers"**.

Necessity of the data transfer

The **"necessity test"**[20] limits the number of cases in which recourse can be made to Article 49(1)(b).[21] It requires a close and substantial connection between the data transfer and the purposes of the contract.

This derogation cannot be used for example when a corporate group has, for business purposes, centralized its payment and human resources management functions for all its staff in a third country as there is no direct and objective link between the performance of the employment contract and such transfer.[22] Other grounds for transfer as provided for in Chapter V such as standard contractual clauses or binding corporate rules may, however, be suitable for the particular transfer.

On the other hand, the transfer by travel agents of personal data concerning their individual clients to hotels or to other commercial partners that would be called upon in the organization of these clients' stay abroad can be deemed necessary for the purposes of the contract entered into by the travel agent and the client, since, in this case, there is a sufficient close and substantial connection between the data transfer and the purposes of the contract (organization of clients' travel).

This derogation cannot be applied to transfers of additional information not necessary for the performance of the contract or, respectively, for the implementation of precontractual measures requested by the data subject[23]; for additional data other tools would hence be required.

Occasional transfers

Personal data may only be transferred under this derogation when this transfer is occasional.[24] It would have to be established on a case by case basis whether data transfers or a data transfer would be determined as "*occasional*" or "*non-occasional*".

A transfer here may be deemed occasional for example if personal data of a sales manager, who in the context of his/her employment contract travels to different clients in third countries, are to be sent to those clients in order to arrange the meetings. A transfer could also be considered as occasional if a bank in the EU transfers personal data to a bank in a third country in order to execute a client's request for making a payment, as long as this transfer does not occur in the framework of a stable cooperation relationship between the two banks.

On the contrary, transfers would not qualify as "occasional" in a case where a multi-national company organises trainings in a training centre in a third country and systematically transfers the personal data of those employees that attend a training course (e.g. data such as name and job title, but potentially also dietary requirements or mobility restrictions). Data transfers regularly occurring within a stable relationship would be deemed as systematic and repeated, hence exceeding an "occasional" charac-ter. Consequently, in this case many data transfers within a business relationship may not be based on Article 49(1)(b).

According to Article 49(1)(3), this derogation cannot apply to activities carried out by public authorities in the exercise of their public powers.

2.3 TRANSFER NECESSARY FOR THE CONCLUSION OR PERFORMANCE OF A CONTRACT CONCLUDED IN THE INTEREST OF THE DATA SUBJECT BETWEEN THE CONTROLLER AND ANOTHER NATURAL OR LEGAL PERSON - (49(1)(C))

The interpretation of this provision is necessarily similar to that of Article 49(1)(b); namely, that a transfer of data to a third country or an international organization in the absence of an adequacy decision pursuant to Article 45(3), or of appropriate safeguards pursuant to Article 46, can only be deemed to fall under the derogation of Article 49(1)(c), if it can be considered to be "*necessary for the conclusion or performance of a contract between the data controller and another natural or legal person, in the interest of the data subject*".

Aside from being necessary, recital 111 indicates that, data transfers may only take place "*where the transfer is **occasional** and **necessary** in relation to a contract (...)*" Therefore, apart from the "necessity test", personal data here as well may only be transferred under this derogation only when the transfer is occasional.

Necessity of the data transfer and conclusion of the contract in the interest of the data subject

Where an organization has, for business purposes, outsourced activities such as payroll management to service providers outside the EU, this derogation will not provide a basis for data transfers for such purposes, since no close and substantial link between the transfer and a contract concluded in the data subject's interest can be established even if the end purpose of the transfer is the management of the pay of the employee.[25] Other transfer tools provided in Chapter V may provide a more suitable basis for such transfers such as standard contractual clauses or binding corporate rules.

Occasional transfers

Moreover, personal data may only be transferred under this derogation, when the transfer is occasional as it is the case under the derogation of Article 49(1)(b). Therefore, in order to assess whether such transfer is occasional, the same test has to be carried out[26].

Finally, according to Article 49(1)(3), this derogation cannot apply to activities carried out by public authorities in the exercise of their public powers.[27]

2.4 TRANSFER IS NECESSARY FOR IMPORTANT REASONS OF PUBLIC INTEREST - (49(1)(D))

This derogation, usually referred to as the "important public interest derogation", is very similar to the provision contained in Directive 95/46/EC[28] under Article 26 (1)(d), which provides that a transfer shall take place only where it is necessary or legally required on important public interest grounds.

According to Article 49(4), only public interests recognized in Union law or in the law of the Member State to which the controller is subject can lead to the application of this derogation.

However, for the application of this derogation, it is not sufficient that the data transfer is requested (for example by a third country authority) for an investigation which serves a public interest of a third country which, in an abstract sense, also exists in EU or Member State law. Where for example a third country authority requires a data transfer for an investigation aimed at combatting terrorism, the mere existence of EU or member state legislation also aimed at combatting terrorism is not as such a sufficient trigger to apply Article 49(1)(d) to such transfer. Rather, as emphasized by the WP29, predecessor of the EDPB, in previous statements,[29] the derogation only applies when it can also be deduced from EU law or the law of the member state to which the controller is subject that such data transfers are allowed for important public interest purposes including in the spirit of reciprocity for international cooperation. The existence of an international agreement or convention which recognises a certain objective and provides for international cooperation to foster that objective can be an indicator when assessing the existence of a public interest pursuant to Article 49(1)(d), as long as the EU or the Member States are a party to that agreement or convention.

Although mainly focused to be used by public authorities, Article 49(1)(d) may also be relied upon by private entities. This is supported by some of the examples enumerated in recital 112 which mention both transfers by public authorities and private entities[30].

As such, the essential requirement for the applicability of this derogation is the finding of an important public interest and not the nature of the organization (public, private or international organization) that transfers and/or receives the data.

Recitals 111 and 112 indicate that this derogation is not limited to data transfers that are "occasional"[31]. Yet, this does not mean that data transfers on the basis of the important public interest derogation under Article 49(1)(d) can take place on a large scale and in a systematic manner. Rather, the general principle needs to be respected according to which the derogations as set out in Article 49 shall not become "the rule" in practice, but need to be restricted to specific situations and each data exporter needs to ensure that the transfer meets the strict necessity test.[32]

Where transfers are made in the usual course of business or practice, the EDPB strongly encourages all data exporters (in particular public bodies[33]) to frame these by putting in place appropriate safeguards in accordance with Article 46 rather than relying on the derogation as per Article 49(1)(d).

2.5 TRANSFER IS NECESSARY FOR THE ESTABLISHMENT, EXERCISE OR DEFENSE OF LEGAL CLAIMS - (49(1)(E))

Establishment, exercise or defense of legal claims

Under Article 49(1)(e), transfers may take place when "*the transfer is necessary for the establishment, exercise or defense of legal claims*". Recital 111 states that a transfer can be made where it is "*occasional and necessary in relation to a contract or a legal claim, regardless of whether in a judicial procedure or whether in an administrative or any out-of-court procedure, including procedures before regulatory bodies*". This covers a range of activities for example, in the context of a criminal or administrative investigation in a third country (e.g. anti-trust law, corruption, insider trading or similar situations), where the derogation may apply to a transfer of data for the purpose of defending oneself or for obtaining a reduction or waiver of a fine legally foreseen e.g. in anti-trust investigations. As well, data transfers for the purpose of formal pre-trial discovery procedures in civil litigation may fall under this derogation. It can also cover actions by the data exporter to institute procedures in a third country for example commencing litigation or seeking approval for a merger. The derogation cannot be used to justify the transfer of personal data on the grounds of the mere possibility that legal proceedings or formal procedures may be brought in the future.

This derogation can apply to activities carried out by public authorities in the exercise of their public powers (Article 49(3)).

The combination of the terms "legal claim" and "procedure" implies that the relevant procedure must have a basis in law, including a formal, legally defined process, but is not necessarily limited to judicial or administrative procedures ("or any out of court procedure"). As a transfer needs to be made in a procedure, a close link is necessary between a data transfer and a specific procedure regarding the situation in question. The abstract applicability of a certain type of procedure would not be sufficient.

Data controllers and data processors need to be aware that national law may also contain so-called "blocking statutes", prohibiting them from or restricting them in transferring personal data to foreign courts or possibly other foreign official bodies.

Necessity of the data transfer

A data transfer in question may only take place when it is **necessary** for the establishment, exercise or defense of the legal claim in question. This *"necessity test"* requires a close and substantial connection between the data in question and the specific establishment, exercise or defense of the legal position.[34] The mere interest of third country authorities or possible "good will" to be obtained from the third country authority as such would not be sufficient.

Whilst there may be a temptation for a data exporter to transfer all possibly relevant personal data in response to a request or for instituting legal procedures, this would not be in line with this derogation or with the GDPR more generally as this (in the principle of data minimization) emphasizes the need for personal data to be adequate, relevant and limited to what is necessary in relation to the purposes for which they are processed.

In relation to litigation proceedings the WP29, predecessor of the EDPB, has already set out a layered approach to the question of whether the personal data should be transferred, including the application of this principle. As a first step, there should be a careful assessment of whether anonymized data would be sufficient in the particular case. If this is not the case, then transfer of pseudonymized data could be considered. If it is necessary to send personal data to a third country, its relevance to the particular matter should be assessed before the transfer – so only a set of personal data that is actually necessary is transferred and disclosed.

Occasional transfer

Such transfers should only be made if they are occasional. For information on the definition of occasional transfers please see the relevant section on "occasional and "non-repetitive" transfers.[35] Data exporters would need to carefully assess each specific case.

2.6 TRANSFER NECESSARY IN ORDER TO PROTECT THE VITAL INTERESTS OF THE DATA SUBJECT OR OF OTHER PERSONS, WHERE THE DATA SUBJECT IS PHYSICALLY OR LEGALLY INCAPABLE OF GIVING CONSENT – (49 (1)(F))

The derogation of Article 49(1)(f) obviously applies when data is transferred in the event of a medical emergency and where it is considered that such transfer is directly necessary in order to give the medical care required.

Thus, for example, it must be legally possible to transfer data (including certain personal data) if the data subject, whilst outside the EU, is unconscious and in need of urgent medical care, and only a exporter (e.g. his usual doctor), established in an EU Member State, is able to supply these data. In such cases the law assumes that the imminent risk of serious harm to the data subject outweighs data protection concerns.

The transfer must relate to the individual interest of the data subject or to that of another person's and, when it bears on health data, it must be necessary for an essential diagnosis. Accordingly, this derogation cannot be used to justify transferring personal medical data outside the EU if the purpose of the transfer is not to treat the particular case of the data subject or that of another person's but, for example, to carry out general medical research that will not yield results until sometime in the future.

Indeed, the GDPR does not restrict the use of this derogation to the physical integrity of a person but also leaves room for example to consider the cases where the mental integrity of a person should be protected. In this case, the person concerned would also be incapable - physically or legally - of providing his/her consent for the transfer of his/her personal data. In addition, the concerned individual whose personal data are the subject of the transfer specifically must not be able to give his/her consent – physically or legally - to this transfer.

However, whenever the data subject has the ability to make a valid decision, and his/her consent can be solicited, then this derogation cannot apply.

For example, where the personal data is required to prevent eviction from a property, this would not fall under this derogation as, even though housing be considered as a vital interest, the person concerned can provide his/her consent for the transfer of his/her data.

This ability to make a valid decision can depend on physical, mental but also legal incapability. A legal incapability can encompass, without prejudice to national representation mechanisms, for example, the case of a minor. This legal incapability has to be proved, depending on the case, through either a medical certificate showing the mental incapability of the person concerned or through a governmental document confirming the legal situation of the person concerned.

Data transfers to an international humanitarian organization, necessary to fulfil a task under the Geneva Conventions or to comply with international humanitarian law applicable in armed conflict may also fall under Article 49(1)(f), see recital 112. Again, in such cases the data subject needs to be physically or legally incapable of giving consent.

The transfer of personal data after the occurrence of natural disasters and in the context of sharing of personal information with entities and persons for the purpose of rescue and retrieval operations (for example, relatives of disaster victims as well as with government and emergency services), can be justified under this derogation. Such unexpected events (floods, earthquakes, hurricanes etc.) can warrant the urgent transfer of certain personal data to learn for example, the location and status of victims. In such situations it is considered that the data subject concerned is unable to provide his/her consent for the transfer of his/her data.

2.7. TRANSFER MADE FROM A PUBLIC REGISTER – (49(1)(G) AND 49(2))

Article 49(1)(g) and Article 49(2) allow the transfer of personal data from registers under certain conditions. A register in general is defined as a *"(written) record containing regular entries of items or details"* or as *"an* official list or record of names or items »[36], where in the context of Article 49, a register could be in written or electronic form.

The register in question must, according to Union or Member State law, be intended to provide information to the public. Therefore, private registers (those in the responsibility of private bodies) are outside of the scope of this derogation (for example private registers through which credit-worthiness is appraised.

The register must be open to consultation by either:
(a)   the public in general or
(b)   any person who can demonstrate a legitimate interest.

These could be, for example: registers of companies, registers of associations, registers of criminal convictions, (land) title registers or public vehicle registers.

In addition to the general requirements regarding the set-up of the registers themselves, transfers from these registers may only take place if and to the extent that, in each specific case, the conditions for consultation that are set forth by Union or Member State law are fulfilled (regarding these general conditions, see Article 49(1)(g).

Data controllers and data processors wishing to transfer personal data under this derogation need to be aware that a transfer cannot include the entirety of the personal data or entire categories of the personal data contained in the register (Article 49(2)). Where a transfer is made from a register established by law and where it is to be consulted by persons having a legitimate interest, the transfer can only be made at the request of those persons or if they are recipients, taking into account of the data subjects' interests and fundamental rights[37]. On a case by case basis, data exporters, in assessing whether the transfer is appropriate, would always have to consider the interests and rights of the data subject.

Further use of personal data from such registers as stated above may only take place in compliance with applicable data protection law.

This derogation can also apply to activities carried out by public authorities in the exercise of their public powers (Article 49(3)).

2.8. COMPELLING LEGITIMATE INTERESTS – (49 (1) § 2)

Article 49(1) § 2 introduces a new derogation which was not previously included in the Directive. Under a number of specific, expressly enumerated conditions, personal data can be transferred if it is necessary for the purposes of compelling legitimate interests pursued by the data exporter.

This derogation is envisaged by the law as a last resort, as it will only apply where *"a transfer could not be based on a provision in Article 45 or 46, including the provisions on binding corporate rules, and none of the derogations for a specific situation is applicable"*.[38]

This layered approach to considering the use of derogations as a basis for transfers requires consideration of whether it is possible to use a transfer tool provided in Article 45 or 46 or one of the specific derogations set out in Article 49(1) § 1, before resorting to the derogation of Article 49(1) §2. This can only be used in residual cases according to recital 113 and is dependent on a significant number of conditions expressly laid down by law. In line with the principle of accountability enshrined in the GDPR[39] the data exporter must be therefore able to demonstrate that it was neither possible to frame the data transfer by appropriate safeguards pursuant to Article 46 nor to apply one of the derogations as contained in Article 49(1) § 1.

This implies that the data exporter can demonstrate serious attempts in this regard, taking into account the circumstances of the data transfer. This may for example and depending on the case, include demonstrating verification of whether the data transfer can be performed on the basis of the data subjects' explicit consent to the transfer under Article 49(1)(a). However, in some circumstances the use of other tools might not be practically possible. For example, some types of appropriate safeguards pursuant to Article 46 may not be a realistic option for a data exporter that is a small or medium-sized company.[40] This may also be the case for example, where the data importer has expressly refused to enter into a data transfer contract on the basis of standard data protection clauses (Article 46 (2)(c)) and no other option is available (including, depending on the case, the choice of a different "data importer") – see also the paragraph below on 'compelling' legitimate interest.

Compelling legitimate interests of the controller

According to the wording of the derogation, the transfer must be necessary for the purposes of pursuing compelling legitimate interests of the data controller which are not overridden by the interests or rights and freedoms of the data subject. Consideration of the interests of a data exporter in its capacity as data processor or of the data importer are not relevant.

Moreover, only interests that can be recognized as "compelling" are relevant and this considerably limits the scope of the application of the derogation as not all conceivable "legitimate interests" under Article 6 (1)(f) will apply here. Rather a certain higher threshold will apply, requiring the compelling legitimate interest to be essential for the data controller. For example, this might be the case if a data controller is compelled to transfer the personal data in order to protect its organization or systems from serious immediate harm or from a severe penalty which would seriously affect its business.

Not repetitive

According to its express wording, Article 49(1) § 2 can only apply to a transfer that is not repetitive[41].

Limited number of data subjects

Additionally, the transfer must only concern a limited number of data subjects. No absolute threshold has been set as this will depend on the context but the number must be appropriately small taking into consideration the type of transfer in question.

In a practical context, the notion "limited number of data subjects" is dependent on the actual case in hand. For example, if a data controller needs to transfer personal data to detect a unique and serious security incident in order to protect its organization, the question here would be how many employees' data the data controller would have to transfer in order to achieve this compelling legitimate interest.

As such, in order for the derogation to apply, this transfer should not apply to all the employees of the data controller but rather to a certain confined few.

Balancing the "compelling legitimate interests of the controller" against the "interests or rights and freedoms of the data subject" on the basis of an assessment of all circumstances surrounding the data transfer and providing for suitable safeguards

As a further requirement, a balancing test between the data exporter's (compelling) legitimate interest pursued and the interests or rights and freedoms of the data subject has to be performed. In this regard, the law expressly requires the data exporter to assess all circumstances of the data transfer in question and, based on this assessment, to provide "suitable safeguards" regarding the protection of the data transferred. This requirement highlights the special role that safeguards may play in reducing the undue impact of the data transfer on the data subjects and thereby in possibly influencing the balance of rights and interests to the extent that the data controller's interests will not be overridden.[42]

As to the interests, rights and freedoms of the data subject which need to be taken into consideration, the possible negative effects, i.e. the risks of the data transfer on any type of (legitimate) interest of the data subject have to be carefully forecasted and assessed, by taking into consideration their likelihood and severity.[43] In this regard, in particular any possible damage (physical and material, but also non-material as e.g. relating to a loss of reputation) needs to be taken into consideration[44]. When assessing these risks and what could under the given circumstances possibly be considered as "suitable safeguards" for the rights and freedoms of the data subject, the data exporter needs to particularly take into account the nature of the data, the purpose and duration of the processing as well as the situation in the country of origin, the third country and, if any, the country of final destination of the transfer.[45]

Furthermore, the law requires the data exporter to apply additional measures as safeguards in order to minimize the identified risks caused by the data transfer for the data subject.[46] This is set up by the law as a mandatory requirement, so it can be followed that in the absence of additional safeguards, the controller's interests in the transfer will in any case be overridden by the interests or rights and freedoms of the data subject.[47] As to the nature of such safeguards, it is not possible to set up general requirements applicable to all cases in this regard, but these will rather very much depend on the specific data transfer in question. Safeguards might include, depending on the case, for example measures aimed at ensuring deletion of the data as soon as possible after the transfer, or limiting the purposes for which the data may be processed following the transfer. Particular attention should be paid to whether it may be sufficient to transfer pseudonymized or encrypted data.[48] Moreover, technical and organizational measures aimed at ensuring that the transferred data cannot be used for other purposes than those strictly foreseen by the data exporter should be examined.

Information of the supervisory authority

The duty to inform the supervisory authority does not mean that the transfer needs to be authorized by the supervisory authority, but rather it serves as an additional safeguard by enabling the supervisory authority to assess the data transfer (if it considers it appropriate) as to its possible impact on the rights and freedoms of the data subjects affected. As part of its compliance with the accountability principle, it is recommended that the data exporter records all relevant aspects of the data transfer e.g. the compelling legitimate interest pursued, the "competing" interests of the individual, the nature of the data transferred and the purpose of the transfer.

Providing information of the transfer and the compelling legitimate interests pursued to the data subject

The data controller must inform the data subject of the transfer and of the compelling legitimate interests pursued. This information must be provided in addition to that required to be provided under to Articles 13 and 14 of the GDPR.

For the European Data Protection Board

The Chair

(Andrea Jelinek)

NOTES

[10] According to Article 4(11) of the GDPR, 'consent' of the data subject means any freely given, specific, informed and unambiguous indication of the data subject's wishes by which he or she, by a statement or by a clear affirmative action, signifies agreement to the processing of personal data relating to him or her.

[11] Also recitals 32, 33, 42 and 43 give further guidance on consent

[12] See Article 29 Working Party Guidelines on Consent under Regulation 2016/679 (WP259)

[13] Idem

[14] Idem

[15] The general transparency requirements of Articles 13 and 14 of the GDPR should also be complied with. For more information see Guidelines on transparency under Regulation 2016/679 (WP 260)

[16] See Article 29 Working Party Guidelines on Consent under Regulation 2016/679 (WP259)

[17] Idem, page 13

[18] The last mentioned requirement also stems from the duty to inform the data subjects (Article 13(1)(f), Article 14(1)(e))

[19] The criterion of "occasional" transfers is found in recital 111 and applies to the derogations of Article 49(1)(b), (c) and (e).

[20] See also Article 29 Working Party Opinion 06/2014 on the notion of legitimate interests of the data controller under Article 7 of Directive 95/46/EC (WP 217)

[21] The "necessity" requirement also can be found in the derogations set forth in Article 49(1)(c) to (f).

[22] In addition it will not be seen as being occasional (see below).

[23] More generally, all derogations of Article 49(1)(b) to (f) only allow that the data which are necessary for the purpose of the transfer may be transferred.

[24] As to the general definition of the term « occasional » see page 4

[25] In addition it will not be seen as being occasional (see below).

[26] As to the general definition of the term "occasional" please see page 4

[27] For more information please refer to section 1, page 5 above.

[28] DIRECTIVE 95/46/EC OF THE EUROPEAN PARLIAMENT AND OF THE COUNCIL, of 24 October 1995 on the protection of individuals with regard to the processing of personal data and on the free movement of such data

[29] Article 29 Working Party Opinion 10/2006 on the processing of personal data by the Society for Worldwide Interbank Financial Telecommunication (SWIFT)(WP128), p. 25

[30] "*international data exchange between competition authorities, tax or customs administrations, between financial supervisory authorities, between services competent for social security matters, or for public health, for example in the case of contact tracing for contagious diseases or in order to reduce and/or eliminate doping in sport.*"

[31] As to the general definition of the term « occasional » see page 4

[32] See also page 3

[33] For example financial supervisory authorities exchanging data in the context of international transfers of personal data for administrative cooperation purposes

[34] Recital 111: "necessary in relation to a contract or a legal claim."

[35] Page 4

[36] Merriam Webster Dictionary, https://www.merriam-webster.com/dictionary/register (22.01.2018); Oxford Dictionary https://en.oxforddictionaries.com/definition/register (22.01.2018).

[37] Recital 111 of the GDPR

[38] Article 49(1) § 2 GDPR

[39] Article 5 (2) and Article 24 (1)

[40] For example binding corporate rules may often not be a feasible option for small and medium-sized enterprises due to the considerable administrative investments they imply.

[41] For more information on the term « not repetitive » see page 4

[42] The important role of safeguards in the context of balancing the interests of the data controller and the data subjects has already been highlighted by the Article 29 Working Party in WP 217, p. 31.

[43] See Recital 75: "*The risk to the rights and freedoms of natural persons, of varying likelihood and severity (. . .)*"

[44] See Recital 75: "*The risk to the rights and freedoms of natural persons, of varying likelihood and severity, may result from personal data processing which could lead to physical, material or non-material damage.*"

[45] Recital 113

[46] While in the context of an "ordinary" balancing test foreseen by the law such (additional) measures might not be necessary in each case (see Article 29 Working Party Working document on Draft Ad hoc contractual clauses "EU data processor to non-EU sub-processor" (WP 214), p. 41), the wording of Art. 49 (1) § 2 suggests that additional measures are mandatory in order the data transfer to comply with the "balancing test" and therefore to be feasible under this derogation.

[47] While in the context of an "ordinary" balancing test foreseen by the law such (additional) measures might not be necessary

in each case (see Article 29 Working Party Opinion 06/2014 on the notion of legitimate interests of the data controller under Article 7 of Directive 95/46/EC, WP 217, p. 41), the wording of Art. 49 (1) § 2 suggests that additional measures are mandatory in order the data transfer to comply with the "balancing test" and therefore to be feasible under this derogation.

[48]   For other examples of possible safeguards see Article 29 Working Party Working document on Draft Ad hoc contractual clauses "EU data processor to non-EU sub-processor" (WP 214), p. 41-43

EUROPEAN DATA PROTECTION BOARD: GUIDELINES 3/2018 ON THE TERRITORIAL SCOPE OF THE GDPR (ARTICLE 3)
Version 2.1
12 November 2019

[2.263]

NOTES
© European Data Protection Board.

VERSION HISTORY

Version 2.1: 07 January 2020: Formatting change

Version 2.0: 12 November 2019: Adoption of the Guidelines after public consultation

Version 1.0. 16 November 2018: Adoption of the Guidelines for publication consultation

TABLE OF CONTENTS

THE EUROPEAN DATA PROTECTION BOARD

Having regard to Article 70 (1)(e) of the Regulation 2016/679/EU of the European Parliament and of the Council of 27 April 2016 on the protection of natural persons with regard to the processing of personal data and on the free movement of such data, and repealing Directive 95/46/EC.

HAS ADOPTED THE FOLLOWING GUIDELINES:

INTRODUCTION

[2.264]
The territorial scope of General Data Protection Regulation[1] (the GDPR or the Regulation) is determined by Article 3 of the Regulation and represents a significant evolution of the EU data protection law compared to the framework defined by Directive 95/46/EC[2]. In part, the GDPR confirms choices made by the EU legislator and the Court of Justice of the European Union (CJEU) in the context of Directive 95/46/EC. However, important new elements have been introduced. Most importantly, the main objective of Article 4 of the Directive was to define which Member State's national law is applicable, whereas Article 3 of the GDPR defines the territorial scope of a directly applicable text. Moreover, while Article 4 of the Directive made reference to the 'use of equipment' in the Union's territory as a basis for bringing controllers who were "not established on Community territory" within the scope of EU data protection law, such a reference does not appear in Article 3 of the GDPR.

Article 3 of the GDPR reflects the legislator's intention to ensure comprehensive protection of the rights of data subjects in the EU and to establish, in terms of data protection requirement, a level playing field for companies active on the EU markets, in a context of worldwide data flows.

Article 3 of the GDPR defines the territorial scope of the Regulation on the basis of two main criteria: the "establishment" criterion, as per Article 3(1), and the "targeting" criterion as per Article 3(2). Where one of these two criteria is met, the relevant provisions of the GDPR will apply to relevant processing of personal data by the controller or processor concerned. In addition, Article 3(3) confirms the application of the GDPR to the processing where Member State law applies by virtue of public international law.

Through a common interpretation by data protection authorities in the EU, these guidelines seek to ensure a consistent application of the GDPR when assessing whether particular processing by a controller or a processor falls within the scope of the new EU legal framework. In these guidelines, the EDPB sets out and clarifies the criteria for determining the application of the territorial scope of the GDPR. Such a common interpretation is also essential for controllers and processors, both within and outside the EU, so that they may assess whether they need to comply with the GDPR for a given processing activity.

As controllers or processors not established in the EU but engaging in processing activities falling within Article 3(2) are required to designate a representative in the Union, these guidelines will also provide clarification on the process for the designation of this representative under Article 27 and its responsibilities and obligations.

As a general principle, the EDPB asserts that where the processing of personal data falls within the territorial scope of the GDPR, all provisions of the Regulation apply to such processing. These guidelines will specify the various scenarios that may arise, depending on the type of processing activities, the entity carrying out these processing activities or the location of such entities, and will detail the provisions applicable to each situation. It is therefore essential that controllers and processors, especially those offering goods and services at international level, undertake a careful and *in concreto* assessment of their processing activities, in order to determine whether the related processing of personal data falls under the scope of the GDPR.

The EDPB underlines that the application of Article 3 aims at determining whether a particular processing activity, rather than a person (legal or natural), falls within the scope of the GDPR. Consequently, certain processing of personal data by a controller or processor might fall within the scope of the Regulation, while other processing of personal data by that same controller or processor might not, depending on the processing activity.

These guidelines, initially adopted by the EDPB on 16 November, have been submitted to a public consultation from 23rd November 2018 to 18th January 2019 and have been updated taking into account the contributions and feedback received.

1 APPLICATION OF THE ESTABLISHMENT CRITERION - ART 3(1)

[2.265]
Article 3(1) of the GDPR provides that the *"Regulation applies to the processing of personal data in the context of the activities of an establishment of a controller or a processor in the Union, regardless of whether the processing takes place in the Union or not."*

Article 3(1) GDPR makes reference not only to an establishment of a controller, but also to an establishment of a processor. As a result, the processing of personal data by a processor may also be subject to EU law by virtue of the processor having an establishment located within the EU.

Article 3(1) ensures that the GDPR applies to the processing by a controller or processor carried out in the context of the activities of an establishment of that controller or processor in the Union, regardless of the actual place of the processing. The EDPB therefore recommends a threefold approach in determining whether or not the processing of personal data falls within the scope of the GDPR pursuant to Article 3(1).

The following sections clarify the application of the establishment criterion, first by considering the definition of an 'establishment' in the EU within the meaning of EU data protection law, second by looking at what is meant by 'processing in the context of the activities of an establishment in the Union', and lastly by confirming that the GDPR will apply regardless of whether the processing carried out in the context of the activities of this establishment takes place in the Union or not.

A) "AN ESTABLISHMENT IN THE UNION"

Before considering what is meant by "an establishment in the Union" it is first necessary to identify who is the controller or processor for a given processing activity. According to the definition in Article 4(7) of the GDPR, controller means "the natural or legal person, public authority, agency or other body which, alone or jointly with others, determines the purposes and means of the processing of personal data". A processor, according to Article 4(8) of the GDPR, is "a natural or legal person, public authority, agency or other body which processes personal data on behalf of the controller". As established by relevant CJEU case law and previous WP29 opinion[3], the determination of whether an entity is a controller or processor for the purposes of EU data protection law is a key element in the assessment of the application of the GDPR to the personal data processing in question.

While the notion of "main establishment" is defined in Article 4(16), the GDPR does not provide a definition of "establishment" for the purpose of Article 3[4]. However, Recital 22[5] clarifies that an *"[e]stablishment implies the effective and real exercise of activities through stable arrangements. The legal form of such arrangements, whether through a branch or a subsidiary with a legal personality, is not the determining factor in that respect."*

This wording is identical to that found in Recital 19 of Directive 95/46/EC, to which reference has been made in several CJEU rulings broadening the interpretation of the term "establishment", departing from a formalistic approach whereby undertakings are established solely in the place where they are registered[6]. Indeed, the CJEU ruled that the notion of establishment extends to any real and effective activity — even a minimal one — exercised through stable arrangements[7]. In order to determine whether an entity based outside the Union has an establishment in a Member State, both the degree of stability of the arrangements and the effective exercise of activities in that Member State must be considered in the light of the specific nature of the economic activities and the provision of services concerned. This is particularly true for undertakings offering services exclusively over the Internet[8].

The threshold for "stable arrangement[9]" can actually be quite low when the centre of activities of a controller concerns the provision of services online. As a result, in some circumstances, the presence of one single employee or agent of a non-EU entity in the Union may be sufficient to constitute a stable arrangement (amounting to an 'establishment' for the purposes of Art 3(1)) if that employee or agent acts with a sufficient degree of stability. Conversely, when an employee is based in the EU but the processing is not being carried out in the context of the activities of the EU-based employee in the Union (i.e. the processing relates to activities of the controller outside the EU), the mere presence of an employee in the EU will not result in that processing falling within the scope of the GDPR. In other words, the mere presence of an employee in the EU is not as such sufficient to trigger the application of the GDPR, since for the processing in question to fall within the scope of the GDPR, it must also be carried out in the context of the activities of the EU-based employee.

The fact that the non-EU entity responsible for the data processing does not have a branch or subsidiary in a Member State does not preclude it from having an establishment there within the meaning of EU data protection law. Although the notion of establishment is broad, it is not without limits. It is not possible to conclude that the non-EU entity has an establishment in the Union merely because the undertaking's website is accessible in the Union[10].

Example 1: A car manufacturing company with headquarters in the US has a fully-owned branch office located in Brussels overseeing all its operations in Europe, including marketing and advertisement.

The Belgian branch can be considered to be a stable arrangement, which exercises real and effective activities in light of the nature of the economic activity carried out by the car manufacturing company. As such, the Belgian branch could therefore be considered as an establishment in the Union, within the meaning of the GDPR.

Once it is concluded that a controller or processor is established in the EU, an *in concreto* analysis should then follow to determine whether the processing in question is carried out in the context of the activities of this establishment, in order to determine whether Article 3(1) applies. If a controller or processor established outside the Union exercises "a real and effective activity - even a minimal one" - through "stable arrangements", regardless of its legal form (e.g. subsidiary, branch, office . . .), in the territory of a Member State, this controller or processor can be considered to have an establishment in that Member State[11]. It is therefore important to consider whether the processing of personal data takes place "in the context of the activities of" such an establishment as highlighted in Recital 22.

B) PROCESSING OF PERSONAL DATA CARRIED OUT "IN THE CONTEXT OF THE ACTIVITIES OF" AN ESTABLISHMENT

Article 3(1) confirms that it is not necessary that the processing in question is carried out "by" the relevant EU establishment itself; the controller or processor will be subject to obligations under the GDPR whenever the processing is carried out "in the context of the activities" of its relevant establishment in the Union. The EDPB recommends that determining whether processing is being carried out in the context of an establishment of the controller or processor in the Union for the purposes of Article 3(1) should be carried out on a case-by-case basis and based on an analysis *in concreto*. Each scenario must be assessed on its own merits, taking into account the specific facts of the case.

The EDPB considers that, for the purpose of Article 3(1), the meaning of "*processing in the context of the activities of an establishment of a controller or a processor*" is to be understood in light of the relevant case law. On the one hand, with a view to fulfilling the objective of ensuring effective and complete protection, the meaning of "in the context of the activities of an establishment" cannot be interpreted restrictively[12]. On the other hand, the existence of an establishment within the meaning of the GDPR should not be interpreted too broadly to conclude that the existence of any presence in the EU with even the remotest links to the data processing activities of a non-EU entity will be sufficient to bring this processing within the scope of EU data protection law. Some commercial activity carried out by a non-EU entity within a Member State may indeed be so far removed from the processing of personal data by this entity that the existence of the commercial activity in the EU would not be sufficient to bring the data processing by the non-EU entity within the scope of EU data protection law[13].

Consideration of the following two factors may help to determine whether the processing is being carried out by a controller or processor in the context of its establishment in the Union

i) *Relationship between a data controller or processor outside the Union and its local establishment in the Union*

The data processing activities of a data controller or processor established outside the EU may be inextricably linked to the activities of a local establishment in a Member State, and thereby may trigger the applicability of EU law, even if that local establishment is not actually taking any role in the data processing itself[14]. If a case by case analysis on the facts shows that there is an inextricable link between the processing of personal data carried out by a non-EU controller or processor and the activities of an EU establishment, EU law will apply to that processing by the non-EU entity, whether or not the EU establishment plays a role in that processing of data[15].

ii) *Revenue raising in the Union*

Revenue-raising in the EU by a local establishment, to the extent that such activities can be considered as "inextricably linked" to the processing of personal data taking place outside the EU and individuals in the EU, may be indicative of processing by a non-EU controller or processor being carried out "in the context of the activities of the EU establishment", and may be sufficient to result in the application of EU law to such processing[16].

The EDPB recommends that non-EU organisations undertake an assessment of their processing activities, first by determining whether personal data are being processed, and secondly by identifying potential links between the activity for which the data is being processed and the activities of any presence of the organisation in the Union. If such a link is identified, the nature of this link will be key in determining whether the GDPR applies to the processing in question, and must be assessed inter alia against the two elements listed above.

Example 2: An e-commerce website is operated by a company based in China. The personal data processing activities of the company are exclusively carried out in China. The Chinese company has established a European office in Berlin in order to lead and implement commercial prospection and marketing campaigns towards EU markets.

In this case, it can be considered that the activities of the European office in Berlin are inextricably linked to the processing of personal data carried out by the Chinese e-commerce website, insofar as the commercial prospection and marketing campaign towards EU markets notably serve to make the service offered by the e-commerce website profitable. The processing of personal data by the Chinese company in relation to EU sales is indeed inextricably linked to the activities of the European office in Berlin relating to commercial prospection and marketing campaign towards EU market. The processing of personal data by the Chinese company in connection with EU sales can therefore be considered as carried out in the context of the activities of the European office, as an establishment in the Union. This processing activity by the Chinese company will therefore be subject to the provisions of the GDPR as per its Article 3(1)".

Example 3: A hotel and resort chain in South Africa offers package deals through its website, available in English, German, French and Spanish. The company does not have any office, representation or stable arrangement in the EU.

In this case, in the absence of any representation or stable arrangement of the hotel and resort chain within the territory of the Union, it appears that no entity linked to this data controller in South Africa can qualify as an establishment in the EU within the meaning of the GDPR. Therefore the processing at stake cannot be subject to the provisions of the GDPR, as per Article 3(1).

However, it must be analysed in concreto whether the processing carried out by this data controller established outside the EU can be subject to the GDPR, as per Article 3(2).

C) APPLICATION OF THE GDPR TO THE ESTABLISHMENT OF A CONTROLLER OR A PROCESSOR IN THE UNION, REGARDLESS OF WHETHER THE PROCESSING TAKES PLACE IN THE UNION OR NOT

As per Article 3(1), the processing of personal data in the context of the activities of an establishment of a controller or a processor in the Union triggers the application of the GDPR and the related obligations for the data controller or processor concerned.

The text of the GDPR specifies that the Regulation applies to processing in the context of the activities of an establishment in the EU *"regardless of whether the processing takes place in the Union or not"*. It is the presence, through an establishment, of a data controller or processor in the EU and the fact that a processing takes place in the context of the activities of this establishment that trigger the application of the GDPR to its processing activities. The place of processing is therefore not relevant in determining whether or not the processing, carried out in the context of the activities of an EU establishment, falls within the scope of the GDPR.

Example 4: A French company has developed a car-sharing application exclusively addressed to customers in Morocco, Algeria and Tunisia. The service is only available in those three countries but all personal data processing activities are carried out by the data controller in France.

While the collection of personal data takes place in non-EU countries, the subsequent processing of personal data in this case is carried out in the context of the activities of an establishment of a data controller in the Union. Therefore, even though processing relates to personal data of data subjects who are not in the Union, the provisions of the GDPR will apply to the processing carried out by the French company, as per Article 3(1).

Example 5: A pharmaceutical company with headquarters in Stockholm has located all its personal data processing activities with regards to its clinical trial data in its branch based in Singapore.

In this case, while the processing activities are taking place in Singapore, that processing is carried out in the context of the activities of the pharmaceutical company in Stockholm i.e. of a data controller established in the Union. The provisions of the GDPR therefore apply to such processing, as per Article 3(1).

In determining the territorial scope of the GDPR, geographical location will be important under Article 3(1) with regard to the place of establishment of:
–   the controller or processor itself (is it established inside or outside the Union?);
–   any business presence of a non-EU controller or processor (does it have an establishment in the Union?)

However, geographical location is not important for the purposes of Article 3(1) with regard to the place in which processing is carried out, or with regard to the location of the data subjects in question.

The text of Article 3(1) does not restrict the application of the GDPR to the processing of personal data of individuals who are in the Union. The EDPB therefore considers that any personal data processing in the context of the activities of an establishment of a controller or processor in the Union would fall under the scope of the GDPR, regardless of the location or the nationality of the data subject whose personal data are being processed. This approach is supported by Recital 14 of the GDPR which states that *"[t]he protection afforded by this Regulation should apply to natural persons, whatever their nationality or place of residence, in relation to the processing of their personal data."*

D) APPLICATION OF THE ESTABLISHMENT CRITERION TO CONTROLLER AND PROCESSOR

As far as processing activities falling under the scope of Article 3(1) are concerned, the EDPB considers that such provisions apply to controllers and processors whose processing activities are carried out in the context of the activities of their respective establishment in the EU. While acknowledging that the requirements for establishing the relationship between a controller and a processor[17] does not vary depending on the geographical location of the establishment of a controller or processor, the EDPB takes the view that when it comes to the identification of the different obligations triggered by the applicability of the GDPR as per Article 3(1), the processing by each entity must be considered separately.

The GDPR envisages different and dedicated provisions or obligations applying to data controllers and processors, and as such, should a data controller or processor be subject to the GDPR as per Article 3(1), the related obligations would apply to them respectively and separately. In this context, the EDPB notably deems that a processor in the EU should not be considered to be an establishment of a data controller within the meaning of Article 3(1) merely by virtue of its status as processor on behalf of a controller.

The existence of a relationship between a controller and a processor does not necessarily trigger the application of the GDPR to both, should one of these two entities not be established in the Union.

An organisation processing personal data on behalf of, and on instructions from, another organisation (the client company) will be acting as processor for the client company (the controller). Where a processor is established in the Union, it will be required to comply with the obligations imposed on processors by the GDPR (the 'GDPR processor obligations'). If the controller instructing the processor is also located in the Union, that controller will be required to comply with the obligations imposed on controllers by the GDPR (the 'GDPR controller obligations'). Processing activity which, when carried out by a controller, falls within the scope of the GDPR by virtue of Art 3(1) will not fall outside the scope of the Regulation simply because the controller instructs a processor not established in the Union to carry out that processing on its behalf.

i) Processing by a controller established in the EU instructing a processor not established in the Union

Where a controller subject to GDPR chooses to use a processor located outside the Union for a given processing activity, it will still be necessary for the controller to ensure by contract or other legal act that the processor processes the data in accordance with the GDPR. Article 28(3) provides that the processing by a processor shall be governed by a contract or other legal act. The controller will therefore need to ensure that it puts in place a contract with the processor addressing all the requirements set out in Article 28(3). In addition, it is likely that, in order to ensure that it has complied with its obligations under Article 28(1) – to use only a processor providing sufficient guarantees to implement measures in such a manner that processing will meet the requirements of the Regulation and protect the rights of data subjects – the controller may need to consider imposing, by contract, the obligations placed by the GDPR on processors subject to it. That is to say, the controller would have to ensure that the processor not subject to the GDPR complies with the obligations, governed by a contract or other legal act under Union or Member State law, referred to Article 28(3).

The processor located outside the Union will therefore become indirectly subject to some obligations imposed by controllers subject to the GDPR by virtue of contractual arrangements under Article 28. Moreover, provisions of Chapter V of the GDPR may apply.

Example 6: A Finnish research institute conducts research regarding the Sami people. The institute launches a project that only concerns Sami people in Russia. For this project the institute uses a processor based in Canada.

The Finnish controller has a duty to only use processors that provide sufficient guarantees to implement appropriate measures in such manner that processing will meet the requirement of the

GDPR and ensure the protection of data subjects' rights. The Finnish controller needs to enter into a data processing agreement with the Canadian processor, and the processor's duties will be stipulated in that legal act.

ii) Processing in the context of the activities of an establishment of a processor in the Union

Whilst case law provides us with a clear understanding of the effect of processing being carried out in the context of the activities of an EU establishment of the controller, the effect of processing being carried out in the context of the activities of an EU establishment of a processor is less clear.

The EDPB emphasises that it is important to consider the establishment of the controller and processor separately when determining whether each party is of itself 'established in the Union'.

The first question is whether the controller itself has an establishment in the Union, and is processing in the context of the activities of that establishment. Assuming the controller is not considered to be processing in the context of its own establishment in the Union, that controller will not be subject to GDPR controller obligations by virtue of Article 3(1) (although it may still be caught by Article 3(2)). Unless other factors are at play, the processor's EU establishment will not be considered to be an establishment in respect of the controller.

The separate question then arises of whether the processor is processing in the context of its establishment in the Union. If so, the processor will be subject to GDPR processor obligations under Article 3(1). However, this does not cause the non-EU controller to become subject to the GDPR controller obligations. That is to say, a "non-EU" controller (as described above) will not become subject to the GDPR simply because it chooses to use a processor in the Union.

By instructing a processor in the Union, the controller not subject to GDPR is not carrying out processing "in the context of the activities of the processor in the Union". The processing is carried out in the context of the controller's own activities; the processor is merely providing a processing service[18] which is not "inextricably linked" to the activities of the controller. As stated above, in the case of a data processor established in the Union and carrying out processing on behalf of a data controller established outside the Union and not subject to the GDPR as per Article 3(2), the EDPB considers that the processing activities of the data controller would not be deemed as falling under the territorial scope of the GDPR merely because it is processed on its behalf by a processor established in the Union. However, even though the data controller is not established in the Union and is not subject to the provisions of the GDPR as per Article 3(2), the data processor, as it is established in the Union, will be subject to the relevant provisions of the GDPR as per Article 3(1).

Example 7: A Mexican retail company enters into a contract with a processor established in Spain for the processing of personal data relating to the Mexican company's clients. The Mexican company offers and directs its services exclusively to the Mexican market and its processing concerns exclusively data subjects located outside the Union.

In this case, the Mexican retail company does not target persons on the territory of the Union through the offering of goods or services, nor it does monitor the behaviour of person on the territory of the Union. The processing by the data controller, established outside the Union, is therefore not subject to the GDPR as per Article 3(2).

The provisions of the GDPR do not apply to the data controller by virtue of Art 3(1) as it is not processing personal data in the context of the activities of an establishment in the Union. The data processor is established in Spain and therefore its processing will fall within the scope of the GDPR by virtue of Art 3(1). The processor will be required to comply with the processor obligations imposed by the regulation for any processing carried out in the context of its activities.

When it comes to a data processor established in the Union carrying out processing on behalf of a data controller with no establishment in the Union for the purposes of the processing activity and which does not fall under the territorial scope of the GDPR as per Article 3(2), the processor will be subject to the following relevant GDPR provisions directly applicable to data processors:

- The obligations imposed on processors under Article 28 (2), (3), (4), (5) and (6), on the duty to enter into a data processing agreement, with the exception of those relating to the assistance to the data controller in complying with its (the controller's) own obligations under the GDPR.
- The processor and any person acting under the authority of the controller or of the processor, who has access to personal data, shall not process those data except on instructions from the controller, unless required to do so by Union or Member State law, as per Article 29 and Article 32(4).
- Where applicable, the processor shall maintain a record of all categories of processing carried out on behalf of a controller, as per Article 30(2).
- Where applicable, the processor shall, upon request, cooperate with the supervisory authority in the performance of its tasks, as per Article 31.
- The processor shall implement technical and organisational measures to ensure a level of security appropriate to the risk, as per Article 32.
- The processor shall notify the controller without undue delay after becoming aware of a personal data breach, as per Article 33.

– Where applicable, the processor shall designate a data protection officer as per Articles 37 and 38.
– The provisions on transfers of personal data to third countries or international organisations, as per Chapter V.

In addition, since such processing would be carried out in the context of the activities of an establishment of a processor in the Union, the EDPB recalls that the processor will have to ensure its processing remains lawful with regards to other obligations under EU or national law. Article 28(3) also specifies that *"the processor shall immediately inform the controller if, in its opinion, an instruction infringes this Regulation or other Union or Member State data protection provisions."*

In line with the positions taken previously by the Article 29 Working Party, the EDPB takes the view that the Union territory cannot be used as a "data haven", for instance when a processing activity entails inadmissible ethical issues[19], and that certain legal obligations beyond the application of EU data protection law, in particular European and national rules with regard to public order, will in any case have to be respected by any data processor established in the Union, regardless of the location of the data controller. This consideration also takes into account the fact that by implementing EU law, provisions resulting from the GDPR and related national laws, are subject to the Charter of Fundamental Rights of the Union[20]. However, this does not impose additional obligations on controllers outside the Union in respect of processing not falling under the territorial scope of the GDPR.

NOTES

[1]   Regulation (EU) 2016/679 of the European Parliament and of the Council of 27 April 2016 on the protection of natural persons with regard to the processing of personal data and on the free movement of such data, and repealing Directive 95/46/EC (General Data Protection Regulation).

[2]   Directive 95/46/EC of the European Parliament and of the Council of 24 October 1995 on the protection of individuals with regard to the processing of personal data and on the free movement of such data.

[3]   G 29 WP169 - Opinion 1/2010 on the concepts of "controller" and "processor", adopted on 16th February 2010 and under revision by the EDPB.

[4]   The definition of "main establishment" is mainly relevant for the purpose of determining the competence of the supervisory authorities concerned according to Article 56 GDPR. See the WP29 Guidelines for identifying a controller or processor's lead supervisory authority (16/EN WP 244 rev.01) - endorsed by the EDPB.

[5]   Recital 22 of the GDPR: *"Any processing of personal data in the context of the activities of an establishment of a controller or a processor in the Union should be carried out in accordance with this Regulation, regardless of whether the processing itself takes place within the Union. Establishment implies the effective and real exercise of activity through stable arrangements. The legal form of such arrangements, whether through a branch or a subsidiary with a legal personality, is not the determining factor in that respect."*

[6]   See in particular *Google Spain SL, Google Inc. v AEPD, Mario Costeja González (C-131/12), Weltimmo v NAIH (C-230/14), Verein für Konsumenteninformation v Amazon EU (C-191/15)* and *Wirtschaftsakademie Schleswig-Holstein (C-210/16)*.

[7]   *Weltimmo*, paragraph 31.

[8]   *Weltimmo*, paragraph 29.

[9]   *Weltimmo*, paragraph 31.

[10] CJEU, Verein für Konsumenteninformation v. Amazon EU Sarl, Case C-191/15, 28 July 2016, paragraph 76 (hereafter "Verein für Konsumenteninformation").

[11] See in particular para 29 of the Weltimmo judgment, which emphasizes a flexible definition of the concept of 'establishment' and clarifies that 'the degree of stability of the arrangements and the effective exercise of activities in that other Member State must be interpreted in the light of the specific nature of the economic activities and the provision of services concerned.'

[12] *Weltimmo*, paragraph 25 and Google Spain, paragraph 53.

[13] G29 WP 179 update - Update of Opinion 8/2010 on applicable law in light of the CJEU judgment in Google Spain, 16th December 2015

[14] CJEU, Google Spain, Case C-131/12

[15] G29 WP 179 update - Update of Opinion 8/2010 on applicable law in light of the CJEU judgment in Google Spain, 16th December 2015

[16] This may potentially be the case, for example, for any foreign operator with a sales office or some other presence in the EU, even if that office has no role in the actual data processing, in particular where the processing takes place in the context of the sales activity in the EU and the activities of the establishment are aimed at the inhabitants of the Member States in which the establishment is located (WP179 update).

[17] In accordance with Article 28, the EDPB recalls that processing activities by a processor on behalf of a controller shall be governed by a contract or other legal act under Union or Member State law, that is binding on the processor with regard to the controller, and that controllers shall only use processors providing sufficient guarantees to implement appropriate measures in such manner that processing will meet the requirement of the GDPR and ensure the protection of data subjects' rights.

[18] The offering of a processing service in this context cannot be considered either as an offer of a service to data subjects in the Union.

[19] G29 WP169 - Opinion 1/2010 on the concepts of "controller" and "processor", adopted on 16th February 2010 and under revision by the EDPB.

[20] Charter of Fundamental Right of the European Union, 2012/C 326/02.

2 APPLICATION OF THE TARGETING CRITERION – ART 3(2)

[2.266]
The absence of an establishment in the Union does not necessarily mean that processing activities by a data controller or processor established in a third country will be excluded from the scope of the GDPR,

since Article 3(2) sets out the circumstances in which the GDPR applies to a controller or processor not established in the Union, depending on their processing activities.

In this context, the EDPB confirms that in the absence of an establishment in the Union, a controller or processor cannot benefit from the one-stop shop mechanism provided for in Article 56 of the GDPR. Indeed, the GDPR's cooperation and consistency mechanism only applies to controllers and processors with an establishment, or establishments, within the European Union[21].

While the present guidelines aim to clarify the territorial scope of the GDPR, the EDPB also wish to stress that controllers and processors will also need to take into account other applicable texts, such as for instance EU or Member States' sectorial legislation and national laws. Several provisions of the GDPR indeed allow Member States to introduce additional conditions and to define a specific data protection framework at national level in certain areas or in relation to specific processing situations.

Controllers and processors must therefore ensure that they are aware of, and comply with, these additional conditions and frameworks which may vary from one Member State to the other. Such variations in the data protection provisions applicable in each Member State are particularly notable in relation to the provisions of Article 8 (providing that the age at which children may give valid consent in relation to the processing of their data by information society services may vary between 13 and 16), of Article 9 (in relation to the processing of special categories of data), Article 23 (restrictions) or concerning the provisions contained in Chapter IX of the GDPR (freedom of expression and information; public access to official documents; national identification number; employment context; processing for archiving purposes in the public interest, scientific or historical research purposes or statistical purposes; secrecy; churches and religious associations).

Article 3(2) of the GDPR provides that "*this Regulation applies to the processing of personal data of data subjects who are in the Union by a controller or processor not established in the Union, where the processing activities are related to: (a) the offering of goods or services, irrespective of whether a payment of the data subject is required, to such data subjects in the Union; or (b) the monitoring of their behaviour as far as their behaviour takes place within the Union.*"

The application of the "targeting criterion" towards data subjects who are in the Union, as per Article 3(2), can be triggered by processing activities carried out by a controller or processor not established in the Union which relate to two distinct and alternative types of activities provided that these processing activities relate to data subjects that are in the Union.. In addition to being applicable only to processing by a controller or processor not established in the Union, the targeting criterion largely focuses on what the "processing activities" are "related to", which is to be considered on a case-by-case basis.

The EDPB stresses that a controller or processor may be subject to the GDPR in relation to some of its processing activities but not subject to the GDPR in relation to other processing activities. The determining element to the territorial application of the GDPR as per Article 3(2) lies in the consideration of the processing activities in question.

In assessing the conditions for the application of the targeting criterion, the EDPB therefore recommends a twofold approach, in order to determine first that the processing relates to personal data of data subjects who are in the Union, and second whether processing relates to the offering of goods or services or to the monitoring of data subjects' behaviour in the Union.

A) DATA SUBJECTS IN THE UNION

The wording of Article 3(2) refers to "*personal data of data subjects who are in the Union*". The application of the targeting criterion is therefore not limited by the citizenship, residence or other type of legal status of the data subject whose personal data are being processed. Recital 14 confirms this interpretation and states that "*[t]he protection afforded by this Regulation should apply to natural persons, whatever their nationality or place of residence, in relation to the processing of their personal data*".

This provision of the GDPR reflects EU primary law which also lays down a broad scope for the protection of personal data, not limited to EU citizens, with Article 8 of the Charter of Fundamental Rights providing that the right to the protection of personal data is not limited but is for "everyone"[22].

While the location of the data subject in the territory of the Union is a determining factor for the application of the targeting criterion as per Article 3(2), the EDPB considers that the nationality or legal status of a data subject who is in the Union cannot limit or restrict the territorial scope of the Regulation.

The requirement that the data subject be located in the Union must be assessed at the moment when the relevant trigger activity takes place, i.e. at the moment of offering of goods or services or the moment when the behaviour is being monitored, regardless of the duration of the offer made or monitoring undertaken.

The EDPB considers however that, in relation to processing activities related to the offer of services, the provision is aimed at activities that intentionally, rather than inadvertently or incidentally, target individuals in the EU. Consequently, if the processing relates to a service that is only offered to individuals outside the EU but the service is not withdrawn when such individuals enter the EU, the related processing will not be subject to the GDPR. In this case the processing is not related to the intentional targeting of individuals in the EU but relates to the targeting of individuals outside the EU which will continue whether they remain outside the EU or whether they visit the Union.

Example 8: An Australian company offers a mobile news and video content service, based on users' preferences and interest. Users can receive daily or weekly updates. The service is offered exclusively to users located in Australia, who must provide an Australian phone number when subscribing.

An Australian subscriber of the service travels to Germany on holiday and continues using the service.

Although the Australian subscriber will be using the service while in the EU, the service is not 'targeting' individuals in the Union, but targets only individuals in Australia, and so the processing of personal data by the Australian company does not fall within the scope of the GDPR.

Example 9: A start-up established in the USA, without any business presence or establishment in the EU, provides a city-mapping application for tourists. The application processes personal data concerning the location of customers using the app (the data subjects) once they start using the application in the city they visit, in order to offer targeted advertisement for places to visits, restaurant, bars and hotels. The application is available for tourists while they visit New York, San Francisco, Toronto, Paris and Rome.

The US start-up, via its city mapping application, is specifically targeting individuals in the Union (namely in Paris and Rome) through offering its services to them when they are in the Union. The processing of the EU-located data subjects' personal data in connection with the offering of the service falls within the scope of the GDPR as per Article 3(2)a. Furthermore, by processing data subject's location data in order to offer targeted advertisement on the basis of their location, the processing activities also relate to the monitoring of behaviour of individuals in the Union. The US start-up processing therefore also falls within the scope of the GDPR as per Article 3(2)b.

The EDPB also wishes to underline that the fact of processing personal data of an individual in the Union alone is not sufficient to trigger the application of the GDPR to processing activities of a controller or processor not established in the Union. The element of "targeting" individuals in the EU, either by offering goods or services to them or by monitoring their behaviour (as further clarified below), must always be present in addition.

Example 10: A U.S. citizen is travelling through Europe during his holidays. While in Europe, he downloads and uses a news app that is offered by a U.S. company. The app is exclusively directed at the U.S. market, evident by the app terms of use and the indication of US Dollar as the sole currency available for payment. The collection of the U.S. tourist's personal data via the app by the U.S. company is not subject to the GDPR.

Moreover, it should be noted that the processing of personal data of EU citizens or residents that takes place in a third country does not trigger the application of the GDPR, as long as the processing is not related to a specific offer directed at individuals in the EU or to a monitoring of their behaviour in the Union.

Example 11: A bank in Taiwan has customers that are residing in Taiwan but hold German citizenship. The bank is active only in Taiwan; its activities are not directed at the EU market. The bank's processing of the personal data of its German customers is not subject to the GDPR.

Example 12: The Canadian immigration authority processes personal data of EU citizens when entering the Canadian territory for the purpose of examining their visa application. This processing is not subject to the GDPR.

B) OFFERING OF GOODS OR SERVICES, IRRESPECTIVE OF WHETHER A PAYMENT OF THE DATA SUBJECT IS REQUIRED, TO DATA SUBJECTS IN THE UNION

The first activity triggering the application of Article 3(2) is the "offering of goods or services", a concept which has been further addressed by EU law and case law, which should be taken into account when applying the targeting criterion. The offering of services also includes the offering of information society services, defined in point (b) of Article 1(1) of Directive (EU) 2015/1535[23] as "any Information Society service, that is to say, any service normally provided for remuneration, at a distance, by electronic means and at the individual request of a recipient of services".

Article 3(2)(a) specifies that the targeting criterion concerning the offering of goods or services applies irrespective of whether a payment by the data subject is required. Whether the activity of a controller or processor not established in the Union is to be considered as an offer of a good or a service is not therefore dependent whether payment is made in exchange for the goods or services provided[24].

Example 13: A US company, without any establishment in the EU, processes personal data of its employees that were on a temporary business trip to France, Belgium and the Netherlands for human resources purposes, in particular to proceed with the reimbursement of their accommodation expenses and the payment of their daily allowance, which vary depending on the country they are in.

In this situation, while the processing activity is specifically connected to persons on the territory of the Union (i.e. employees who are temporarily in France, Belgium and the Netherlands) it does not relate to an offer of a service to those individuals, but rather is part of the processing necessary for the employer to fulfil its contractual obligation and human resources duties related to the individual's employment. The processing activity does not relate to an offer of service and is therefore not subject to the provision of the GDPR as per Article 3(2)a.

Another key element to be assessed in determining whether the Article 3(2)(a) targeting criterion can be met is whether the offer of goods or services is directed at a person in the Union, or in other words, whether the conduct on the part of the controller, which determines the means and purposes of processing, demonstrates its intention to offer goods or a services to a data subject located in the Union. Recital 23 of the GDPR indeed clarifies that *"in order to determine whether such a controller or processor is offering goods or services to data subjects who are in the Union, it should be ascertained whether it is apparent that the controller or processor envisages offering services to data subjects in one or more Member States in the Union."*

The recital further specifies that *"whereas the mere accessibility of the controller's, processor's or an intermediary's website in the Union, of an email address or of other contact details, or the use of a language generally used in the third country where the controller is established, is insufficient to ascertain such intention, factors such as the use of a language or a currency generally used in one or more Member States with the possibility of ordering goods and services in that other language, or the mentioning of customers or users who are in the Union, may make it apparent that the controller envisages offering goods or services to data subjects in the Union."*

The elements listed in Recital 23 echo and are in line with the CJEU case law based on Council Regulation 44/2001[25] on jurisdiction and the recognition and enforcement of judgments in civil and commercial matters, and in particular its Article 15(1)(c). In *Pammer v Reederei Karl Schlüter GmbH & Co and Hotel Alpenhof v Heller* (Joined cases C-585/08 and C-144/09), the Court was asked to clarify what it means to "direct activity" within the meaning of Article 15(1)(c) of Regulation 44/2001 (Brussels I). The CJEU held that, in order to determine whether a trader can be considered to be "directing" its activity to the Member State of the consumer's domicile, within the meaning of Article 15(1)(c) of Brussels I, the trader must have manifested its intention to establish commercial relations with such consumers. In this context, the CJEU considered evidence able to demonstrate that the trader was envisaging doing business with consumers domiciled in a Member State.

While the notion of "directing an activity" differs from the "offering of goods or services", the EDPB deems this case law in *Pammer v Reederei Karl Schlüter GmbH & Co and Hotel Alpenhof v Heller (Joined cases C-585/08 and C-144/09)*[26] might be of assistance when considering whether goods or services are offered to a data subject in the Union. When taking into account the specific facts of the case, the following factors could therefore *inter alia* be taken into consideration, possibly in combination with one another:

–   The EU or at least one Member State is designated by name with reference to the good or service offered;
–   The data controller or processor pays a search engine operator for an internet referencing service in order to facilitate access to its site by consumers in the Union; or the controller or processor has launched marketing and advertisement campaigns directed at an EU country audience
–   The international nature of the activity at issue, such as certain tourist activities;
–   The mention of dedicated addresses or phone numbers to be reached from an EU country;
–   The use of a top-level domain name other than that of the third country in which the controller or processor is established, for example ".de", or the use of neutral top-level domain names such as ".eu";
–   The description of travel instructions from one or more other EU Member States to the place where the service is provided;
–   The mention of an international clientele composed of customers domiciled in various EU Member States, in particular by presentation of accounts written by such customers;
–   The use of a language or a currency other than that generally used in the trader's country, especially a language or currency of one or more EU Member states;
–   The data controller offers the delivery of goods in EU Member States.

As already mentioned, several of the elements listed above, if taken alone may not amount to a clear indication of the intention of a data controller to offer goods or services to data subjects in the Union, however, they should each be taken into account in any in concreto analysis in order to determine whether the combination of factors relating to the data controller's commercial activities can together be considered as an offer of goods or services directed at data subjects in the Union.

It is however important to recall that Recital 23 confirms that the mere accessibility of the controller's, processor's or an intermediary's website in the Union, the mention on the website of its e-mail or geographical address, or of its telephone number without an international code, does not, of itself, provide sufficient evidence to demonstrate the controller or processor's intention to offer goods or a services to a data subject located in the Union. In this context, the EDPB recalls that when goods or services are inadvertently or incidentally provided to a person on the territory of the Union, the related processing of personal data would not fall within the territorial scope of the GDPR.

Example 14: A website, based and managed in Turkey, offers services for the creation, editing, printing and shipping of personalised family photo albums. The website is available in English, French, Dutch and German and payments can be made in Euros. The website indicates that photo albums can only be delivered by post mail in France, Benelux countries and Germany.

In this case, it is clear that the creation, editing and printing of personalised family photo albums constitute a service within the meaning of EU law. The fact that the website is available in four languages of the EU and that photo albums can be delivered by post in six EU Member States demonstrates that there is an intention on the part of the Turkish website to offer its services to individuals in the Union.

As a consequence, it is clear that the processing carried out by the Turkish website, as a data controller, relates to the offering of a service to data subjects in the Union and is therefore subject to the obligations and provisions of the GDPR, as per its Article 3(2)(a).

In accordance with Article 27, the data controller will have to designate a representative in the Union.

Example 15: A private company based in Monaco processes personal data of its employees for the purposes of salary payment. A large number of the company's employees are French and Italian residents.

In this case, while the processing carried out by the company relates to data subjects in France and Italy, it does not takes place in the context of an offer of goods or services. Indeed human resources management, including salary payment by a third-country company cannot be considered as an offer of service within the meaning of Art 3(2)a. The processing at stake does not relate to the offer of goods or services to data subjects in the Union (nor to the monitoring of behaviour) and, as a consequence, is not subject to the provisions of the GDPR, as per Article 3.

This assessment is without prejudice to the applicable law of the third country concerned.

Example 16: A Swiss University in Zurich is launching its Master degree selection process, by making available an online platform where candidates can upload their CV and cover letter, together with their contact details. The selection process is open to any student with a sufficient level of German and English and holding a Bachelor degree. The University does not specifically advertise to students in EU Universities, and only takes payment in Swiss currency.

As there is no distinction or specification for students from the Union in the application and selection process for this Master degree, it cannot be established that the Swiss University has the intention to target students from a particular EU member states. The sufficient level of German and English is a general requirement that applies to any applicant whether a Swiss resident, a person in the Union or a student from a third country. Without other factors to indicate the specific targeting of students in EU member states, it therefore cannot be established that the processing in question relates to the offer of an education service to data subject in the Union, and such processing will therefore not be subject to the GDPR provisions.

The Swiss University also offers summer courses in international relations and specifically advertises this offer in German and Austrian universities in order to maximise the courses' attendance. In this case, there is a clear intention from the Swiss University to offer such service to data subjects who are in the Union, and the GDPR will apply to the related processing activities.

C) MONITORING OF DATA SUBJECTS' BEHAVIOUR

The second type of activity triggering the application of Article 3(2) is the monitoring of data subject behaviour as far as their behaviour takes place within the Union.

Recital 24 clarifies that "[t]he processing of personal data of data subjects who are in the Union by a controller or processor not established in the Union should also be subject to this Regulation when it is related to the monitoring of the behaviour of such data subjects in so far as their behaviour takes place within the Union."

For Article 3(2)(b) to trigger the application of the GDPR, the behaviour monitored must first relate to a data subject in the Union and, as a cumulative criterion, the monitored behaviour must take place within the territory of the Union.

The nature of the processing activity which can be considered as behavioural monitoring is further specified in Recital 24 which states that "*in order to determine whether a processing activity can be considered to monitor the behaviour of data subjects, it should be ascertained whether natural persons are tracked on the internet including potential subsequent use of personal data processing techniques which consist of profiling a natural person, particularly in order to take decisions concerning her or him or for analysing or predicting her or his personal preferences, behaviours and attitudes.*" While Recital 24 exclusively relates to the monitoring of a behaviour through the tracking of a person on the internet, the EDPB considers that tracking through other types of network or technology involving personal data processing should also be taken into account in determining whether a processing activity amounts to a behavioural monitoring, for example through wearable and other smart devices.

As opposed to the provision of Article 3(2)(a), neither Article 3(2)(b) nor Recital 24 expressly introduce a necessary degree of "intention to target" on the part of the data controller or processor to determine whether the monitoring activity would trigger the application of the GDPR to the processing activities. However, the use of the word "monitoring" implies that the controller has a specific purpose in mind for the collection and subsequent reuse of the relevant data about an individual's behaviour within the EU. The EDPB does not consider that any online collection or analysis of personal data of individuals in the EU would automatically count as "monitoring". It will be necessary to consider the controller's purpose for processing the data and, in particular, any subsequent behavioural analysis or profiling techniques involving that data. The EDPB takes into account the wording of Recital 24, which indicates that to determine whether processing involves monitoring of a data subject behaviour, the tracking of natural persons on the Internet, including the potential subsequent use of profiling techniques, is a key consideration.

The application of Article 3(2)(b) where a data controller or processor monitors the behaviour of data subjects who are in the Union could therefore encompass a broad range of monitoring activities, including in particular:

–   Behavioural advertisement
–   Geo-localisation activities, in particular for marketing purposes
–   Online tracking through the use of cookies or other tracking techniques such as fingerprinting
–   Personalised diet and health analytics services online
–   CCTV
–   Market surveys and other behavioural studies based on individual profiles
–   Monitoring or regular reporting on an individual's health status

---

Example 17: A retail consultancy company established in the US provides advice on retail layout to a shopping centre in France, based on an analysis of customers' movements throughout the centre collected through Wi-Fi tracking.

The analysis of a customers' movements within the centre through Wi-Fi tracking will amount to the monitoring of individuals' behaviour. In this case, the data subjects' behaviour takes place in the Union since the shopping centre is located in France. The consultancy company, as a data controller, is therefore subject to the GDPR in respect of the processing of this data for this purpose as per its Article 3(2)(b).

In accordance with Article 27, the data controller will have to designate a representative in the Union.

Example 18: An app developer established in Canada with no establishment in the Union monitors the behaviour of data subject in the Union and is therefore subject to the GDPR, as per Article 3(2)b. The developer uses a processor established in the US for the app optimisation and maintenance purposes.

In relation to this processing, the Canadian controller has the duty to only use appropriate processors and to ensure that its obligations under the GDPR are reflected in the contract or legal act governing the relation with its processor in the US, pursuant to Article 28.

D) PROCESSOR NOT ESTABLISHED IN THE UNION

Processing activities which are "related" to the targeting activity which triggered the application of Article 3(2) fall within the territorial scope of the GDPR. The EDPB considers that there needs to be a connection between the processing activity and the offering of good or service, but both processing by a controller and a processor are relevant and to be taken into account.

When it comes to a data processor not established in the Union, in order to determine whether its processing may be subject to the GDPR as per Article 3(2), it is necessary to look at whether the processing activities by the processor "are related" to the targeting activities of the controller.

The EDPB considers that, where processing activities by a controller relates to the offering of goods or services or to the monitoring of individuals' behaviour in the Union ('targeting'), any processor instructed to carry out that processing activity on behalf of the controller will fall within the scope of the GDPR by virtue of Art 3(2) in respect of that processing.

The 'Targeting' character of a processing activity is linked to its purposes and means; a decision to target individuals in the Union can only be made by an entity acting as a controller. Such interpretation does not rule out the possibility that the processor may actively take part in processing activities related to carrying out the targeting criteria (i.e. the processor offers goods or services or carries out monitoring actions on behalf of, and on instruction from, the controller).

The EDPB therefore considers that the focus should be on the connection between the processing activities carried out by the processor and the targeting activity undertaken by a data controller.

Example 19: A Brazilian company sells food ingredients and local recipes online, making this offer of good available to persons in the Union, by advertising these products and offering the delivery in the France, Spain and Portugal. In this context, the company instructs a data processor also established in Brazil to develop special offers to customers in France, Spain and Portugal on the basis of their previous orders and to carry out the related data processing.

Processing activities by the processor, under the instruction of the data controller, are related to the offer of good to data subject in the Union. Furthermore, by developing these customized offers, the data processor directly monitors data subjects in the EU. Processing by the processor are therefore subject to the GDPR, as per Article 3(2).

Example 20: A US company has developed a health and lifestyle app, allowing users to record with the US company their personal indicators (sleep time, weight, blood pressure, heartbeat, etc . . .). The app then provide users with daily advice on food and sport recommendations. The processing is carried out by the US data controller. The app is made available to, and is used by, individuals in the Union. For the purpose of data storage, the US company uses a processor established in the US (cloud service provider)

To the extent that the US company is monitoring the behaviour of individuals in the EU, in operating the health and lifestyle app it will be 'targeting' individuals in the EU and its processing of the personal data of individuals in the EU will fall within the scope of the GDPR under Art 3(2).

In carrying out the processing on instructions from, and on behalf of, the US company the cloud provider/processor is carrying out a processing activity 'relating to' the targeting of individuals in the EU by its controller. This processing activity by the processor on behalf of its controller falls within the scope of the GDPR under Art 3(2).

Example 21: A Turkish company offers cultural package travels in the Middle East with tour guides speaking English, French and Spanish. The package travels are notably advertised and offered through a website available in the three languages, allowing for online booking and payment in Euros and GBP. For marketing and commercial prospection purposes, the company instructs a data processor, a call center, established in Tunisia to contact former customers in Ireland, France, Belgium and Spain in order to get feedback on their previous travels and inform them about new offers and destinations.

The controller is 'targeting' by offering its services to individuals in the EU and its processing will fall within the scope of Art 3(2).

The processing activities of the Tunisian processor, which promotes the controllers' services towards individuals in the EU, is also related to the offer of services by the controller and therefore falls within the scope of Art 3(2). Furthermore, in this specific case, the Tunisian processor actively takes part in processing activities related to carrying out the targeting criteria, by offering services on behalf of, and on instruction from, the Turkish controller.

E) INTERACTION WITH OTHER GDPR PROVISIONS AND OTHER LEGISLATIONS

The EDPB will also further assess the interplay between the application of the territorial scope of the GDPR as per Article 3 and the provisions on international data transfers as per Chapter V. Additional guidance may be issued in this regard, should this be necessary.

Controllers or processors not established in the EU will be required to comply with their own third country national laws in relation to the processing of personal data. However, where such processing relates to the targeting of individuals in the Union as per Article 3(2) the controller will, in addition to being subject to its country's national law, be required to comply with the GDPR. This would be the case regardless of whether the processing is carried out in compliance with a legal obligation in the third country or simply as a matter of choice by the controller.

NOTES

21   G29 WP244 rev.1, 13th December 2016, Guidelines for identifying a controller or processor's lead supervisory authority - endorsed by the EDPB.

22   Charter of Fundamental Right of the European Union, Article 8(1), « Everyone has the right to the protection of personal data concerning him or her".

23   Directive (EU) 2015/1535 of the European Parliament and of the Council of 9 September 2015 laying down a procedure for the provision of information in the field of technical regulations and of rules on Information Society services.

24   See, in particular, CJEU, C-352/85, Bond van Adverteerders and Others vs. The Netherlands State, 26 April 1988, par. 16), and CJEU, C-109/92, Wirth [1993] Racc. I-6447, par. 15.

25   Council Regulation (EC) No 44/2001 of 22 December 2000 on jurisdiction and the recognition and enforcement of judgments in civil and commercial matters.

26   It is all the more relevant that, under Article 6 of Regulation (EC) No 593/2008 of the European Parliament and of the Council of 17 June 2008 on the law applicable to contractual obligations (Rome I), in absence of choice of law, this criterion of "directing activity" to the country of the consumer's habitual residence is taken into account to designate the law of the consumer's habitual residence as the law applicable to the contract.

3 PROCESSING IN A PLACE WHERE MEMBER STATE LAW APPLIES BY VIRTUE OF PUBLIC INTERNATIONAL LAW

[2.267]

Article 3(3) provides that *"[t]his Regulation applies to the processing of personal data by a controller not established in the Union, but in a place where Member State law applies by virtue of public international law". This provision is expanded upon in Recital 25 which states that "[w]here Member State law applies by virtue of public international law, this Regulation should also apply to a controller not established in the Union, such as in a Member State's diplomatic mission or consular post."*

The EDPB therefore considers that the GDPR applies to personal data processing carried out by EU Member States' embassies and consulates located outside the EU as such processing falls within the scope of the GDPR by virtue of Article 3(3).. A Member State's diplomatic or consular post, as a data controller or processor, would then be subject to all relevant provisions of the GDPR, including when it comes to the rights of the data subject, the general obligations related to controller and processor and the transfers of personal data to third countries or international organisations.

Example 22: The Dutch consulate in Kingston, Jamaica, opens an online application process for the recruitment of local staff in order to support its administration.

While the Dutch consulate in Kingston, Jamaica, is not established in the Union, the fact that it is a consular post of an EU country where Member State law applies by virtue of public international law renders the GDPR applicable to its processing of personal data, as per Article 3(3).

Example 23: A German cruise ship travelling in international waters is processing data of the guests on board for the purpose of tailoring the in-cruise entertainment offer.

While the ship is located outside the Union, in international waters, the fact that it is German-registered cruise ship means that by virtue of public international law the GDPR shall be applicable to its processing of personal data, as per Article 3(3).

Though not related to the application of Article 3(3), a different situation is the one where, by virtue of international law, certain entities, bodies or organisations established in the Union benefit from privileges and immunities such as those laid down in the Vienna Convention on Diplomatic Relations of 1961[27], the Vienna Convention on Consular Relations of 1963 or headquarter agreements concluded between international organisations and their host countries in the Union. In this regard, the EDPB recalls that the application of the GDPR is without prejudice to the provisions of international law, such as the ones governing the privileges and immunities of non-EU diplomatic missions and consular posts, as well as international organisations. At the same time, it is important to recall that any controller or processor that falls within the scope of the GDPR for a given processing activity and that exchanges personal data with such entities, bodies and organisations have to comply with the GDPR, including where applicable its rules on transfers to third countries or international organisations.

NOTES

27   http://legal.un.org/ilc/texts/instruments/english/conventions/9_1_1961.pdf

4 REPRESENTATIVE OF CONTROLLERS OR PROCESSORS NOT ESTABLISHED IN THE UNION

[2.268]

Data controllers or processors subject to the GDPR as per its Article 3(2) are under the obligation to designate a representative in the Union. A controller or processor not established in the Union but subject to the GDPR failing to designate a representative in the Union would therefore be in breach of the Regulation.

This provision is not entirely new since Directive 95/46/EC already provided for a similar obligation. Under the Directive, this provision concerned controllers not established on Community territory that, for purposes of processing personal data, made use of equipment, automated or otherwise, situated on the territory of a Member State. The GDPR imposes an obligation to designate a representative in the Union to any controller or processor falling under the scope of Article 3(2), unless they meet the exemption criteria as per Article 27(2). In order to facilitate the application of this specific provision, the EDPB deems it necessary to provide further guidance on the designation process, establishment obligations and responsibilities of the representative in the Union as per Article 27.

It is worth noting that a controller or processor not established in the Union who has designated in writing a representative in the Union, in accordance with article 27 of the GDPR, does not fall within the scope of article 3(1), meaning that the presence of the representative within the Union does not constitute an "establishment" of a controller or processor by virtue of article 3(1).

A) DESIGNATION OF A REPRESENTATIVE

Recital 80 clarifies that *"[t]he representative should be explicitly designated by a written mandate of the controller or of the processor to act on its behalf with regard to its obligations under this Regulation. The designation of such a representative does not affect the responsibility or liability of the controller or of the processor under this Regulation. Such a representative should perform its tasks according to the mandate received from the controller or processor, including cooperating with the competent supervisory authorities with regard to any action taken to ensure compliance with this Regulation."*

The written mandate referred to in Recital 80 shall therefore govern the relations and obligations between the representative in the Union and the data controller or processor established outside the Union, while not affecting the responsibility or liability of the controller or processor. The representative in the Union may be a natural or a legal person established in the Union able to represent a data controller or processor established outside the Union with regard to their respective obligations under the GDPR.

In practice, the function of representative in the Union can be exercised based on a service contract concluded with an individual or an organisation, and can therefore be assumed by a wide range of commercial and non-commercial entities, such as law firms, consultancies, private companies, etc . . . provided that such entities are established in the Union. One representative can also act on behalf of several non-EU controllers and processors.

When the function of representative is assumed by a company or any other type of organisation, it is recommended that a single individual be assigned as a lead contact and person "in charge" for each controller or processor represented. It would generally also be useful to specify these points in the service contract.

In line with the GDPR, the EDPB confirms that, when several processing activities of a controller or processor fall within the scope of Article 3(2) GDPR (and none of the exceptions of Article 27(2) GDPR apply), that controller or processor is not expected to designate several representatives for each separate processing activity falling within the scope of article 3(2).The EDPB does not consider the function of representative in the Union as compatible with the role of an external data protection officer ("DPO") which would be established in the Union. Article 38(3) establishes some basic guarantees to help ensure that DPOs are able to perform their tasks with a sufficient degree of autonomy within their organisation. In particular, controllers or processors are required to ensure that the DPO *"does not receive any instructions regarding the exercise of [his or her] tasks"*. Recital 97 adds that DPOs, *"whether or not they are an employee of the controller, should be in a position to perform their duties and tasks in an independent manner"*[28]. Such requirement for a sufficient degree of autonomy and independence of a data protection officer does not appear to be compatible with the function of representative in the Union. The representative is indeed subject to a mandate by a controller or processor and will be acting on its behalf and therefore under its direct instruction[29]. The representative is mandated by the controller or processor it represents, and therefore acting on its behalf in exercising its task, and such a role cannot be compatible with the carrying out of duties and tasks of the data protection officer in an independent manner.

Furthermore, and to complement its interpretation, the EDPB recalls the position already taken by the WP29 stressing that *"a conflict of interests may also arise for example if an external DPO is asked to represent the controller or processor before the Courts in cases involving data protection issues"*[30].

Similarly, given the possible conflict of obligation and interests in cases of enforcement proceedings, the EDPB does not consider the function of a data controller representative in the Union as compatible with the role of data processor for that same data controller, in particular when it comes to compliance with their respective responsibilities and compliance.

While the GDPR does not impose any obligation on the data controller or the representative itself to notify the designation of the latter to a supervisory authority, the EDPB recalls that, in accordance with Articles 13(1)a and 14(1)a, as part of their information obligations, controllers shall provide data subjects information as to the identity of their representative in the Union. This information shall for example be included in the [privacy notice and] upfront information provided to data subjects at the moment of data collection. A controller not established in the Union but falling under Article 3(2) and failing to inform data subjects who are in the Union of the identity of its representative would be in breach of its transparency obligations as per the GDPR. Such information should furthermore be easily accessible to supervisory authorities in order to facilitate the establishment of a contact for cooperation needs.

Example 24: The website referred to in example 12, based and managed in Turkey, offers services for the creation, edition, printing and shipping of personalised family photo albums. The website is available in English, French, Dutch and German and payments can be made in Euros or Sterling. The website indicates that photo albums can only be delivered by post mail in the France, Benelux countries and Germany. This website being subject to the GDPR, as per its Article 3(2)(a), the data controller must designate a representative in the Union.

The representative must be established in one of the Member States where the service offered is available, in this case either in France, Belgium, Netherlands, Luxembourg or Germany. The name and contact details of the data controller and its representative in the Union must be part of the information made available online to data subjects once they start using the service by creating their photo album. It must also appear in the website general privacy notice.

B) EXEMPTIONS FROM THE DESIGNATION OBLIGATION[31]

While the application of Article 3(2) triggers the obligation to designate a representative in the Union for controllers or processors established outside the Union, Article 27(2) foresees derogation from the mandatory designation of a representative in the Union, in two distinct cases:
*   processing is "occasional, does not include, on a large scale, processing of special categories of data as referred to in Article 9(1) or processing of personal data relating to criminal convictions and offences referred to in Article 10", and such processing "is unlikely to result in a risk to the rights and freedoms of natural persons, taking into account the nature, context, scope and purposes of the processing".

In line with positions taken previously by the Article 29 Working Party, the EPDB considers that a processing activity can only be considered as "occasional" if it is not carried out regularly, and occurs outside the regular course of business or activity of the controller or processor[32].

Furthermore, while the GDPR does not define what constitutes large-scale processing, the WP29 has previously recommended in its guidelines WP243 on data protection officers (DPOs) that the following factors, in particular, be considered when determining whether the processing is carried out on a large scale: the number of data subjects concerned - either as a specific number or as a proportion of the relevant population; the volume of data and/or the range of different data items being processed; the duration, or permanence, of the data processing activity; the geographical extent of the processing activity[33].

Finally, the EDPB highlights that the exemption from the designation obligation as per Article 27 refers to processing "unlikely to result in a risk to the rights and freedoms of natural persons"[34], thus not limiting the exemption to processing unlikely to result in a high risk to the rights and freedoms of data subjects. In line with Recital 75, when assessing the risk to the rights and freedom of data subjects, considerations should be given to both the likelihood and severity of the risk.

Or
*   processing is carried out "by a public authority or body".

The qualification as a "public authority or body" for an entity established outside the Union will need to be assessed by supervisory authorities *in concreto* and on a case by case basis[35]. The EDPB notes that, given the nature of their tasks and missions, cases where a public authority or body in a third country would be offering goods or services to data subject in the Union, or would monitor their behaviour taking place within the Union, are likely to be limited.

C) ESTABLISHMENT IN ONE OF THE MEMBER STATES WHERE THE DATA SUBJECTS WHOSE PERSONAL DATA ARE PROCESSED

Article 27(3) foresees that "the representative shall be established in one of the Member States where the data subjects, whose personal data are processed in relation to the offering of goods or services to them, or whose behaviour is monitored, are". In cases where a significant proportion of data subjects whose personal data are processed are located in one particular Member State, the EDPB recommends, as a good practice, that the representative is established in that same Member State. However, the representative must remain easily accessible for data subjects in Member States where it is not established and where the services or goods are being offered or where the behaviour is being monitored.

The EDPB confirms that the criterion for the establishment of the representative in the Union is the location of data subjects whose personal data are being processed. The place of processing, even by a processor established in another Member State, is here not a relevant factor for determining the location of the establishment of the representative.

Example 25: An Indian pharmaceutical company, with neither business presence nor establishment in the Union and subject to the GDPR as per Article 3(2), sponsors clinical trials carried out by investigators (hospitals) in Belgium, Luxembourg and the Netherlands. The majority of patients participating to the clinical trials are situated in Belgium.

The Indian pharmaceutical company, as a data controller, shall designate a representative in the Union established in one of the three Member States where patients, as data subjects, are participating in the clinical trial (Belgium, Luxembourg or the Netherlands). Since most patients are Belgian residents, it is recommended that the representative is established in Belgium. Should this be the case, the representative in Belgium should however be easily accessible to data subjects and supervisory authorities in the Netherlands and Luxembourg.

In this specific case, the representative in the Union could be the legal representative of the sponsor in the Union, as per Article 74 of Regulation (EU) 536/2014 on clinical trials, provided that it does not act as a data processor on behalf of the clinical trial sponsor, that it is established in one of the three Member States, and that both functions are governed by and exercised in compliance with each legal framework.

D) OBLIGATIONS AND RESPONSIBILITIES OF THE REPRESENTATIVE

The representative in the Union acts on behalf of the controller or processor it represents with regard to the controller or processor's obligations under the GDPR. This implies notably the obligations relating to the exercise of data subject rights, and in this regard and as already stated, the identity and contact details of the representative must be provided to data subjects in accordance with articles 13 and 14. While not itself responsible for complying with data subject rights, the representative must facilitate the communication between data subjects and the controller or processor represented, in order to make the exercise of data subjects' rights are effective.

As per Article 30, the controller or processor's representative shall in particular maintain a record of processing activities under the responsibility of the controller or processor. The EDPB considers that, while the maintenance of this record is an obligation imposed on both the controller or processor and the representative, the controller or processor not established in the Union is responsible for the primary content and update of the record and must simultaneously provide its representative with all accurate and updated information so that the record can also be kept and made available by the representative at all time At the same time, it is the representative's own responsibility to be able to provide it in line with Article 27, e.g. when being addressed by a supervisory authority according to Art. 27(4).

As clarified by recital 80, the representative should also perform its tasks according to the mandate received from the controller or processor, including cooperating with the competent supervisory authorities with regard to any action taken to ensure compliance with this Regulation. In practice, this means that a supervisory authority would contact the representative in connection with any matter relating to the compliance obligations of a controller or processor established outside the Union, and the representative shall be able to facilitate any informational or procedural exchange between a requesting supervisory authority and a controller or processor established outside the Union.

With the help of a team if necessary, the representative in the Union must therefore be in a position to efficiently communicate with data subjects and cooperate with the supervisory authorities concerned. This means that this communication should in principle take place in the language or languages used by the supervisory authorities and the data subjects concerned or, should this result in a disproportionate effort, that other means and techniques shall be used by the representative in order to ensure the effectiveness of communication. The availability of a representative is therefore essential in order to ensure that data subjects and supervisory authorities will be able to establish contact easily with the non-EU controller or processor. In line with Recital 80 and Article 27(5), the designation of a representative in the Union does not affect the responsibility and liability of the controller or of the processor under the GDPR and shall be without prejudice to legal actions which could be initiated against the controller or the processor themselves. The GDPR does not establish a substitutive liability of the representative in place of the controller or processor it represents in the Union.

It should however be noted that the concept of the representative was introduced precisely with the aim of facilitating the liaison with and ensuring effective enforcement of the GDPR against controllers or processors that fall under Article 3(2) of the GDPR. To this end, it was the intention to enable supervisory authorities to initiate enforcement proceedings through the representative designated by the controllers or processors not established in the Union. This includes the possibility for supervisory authorities to address corrective measures or administrative fines and penalties imposed on the controller or processor not established in the Union to the representative, in accordance with articles 58(2) and 83 of the GDPR. The possibility to hold a representative directly liable is however limited to its direct obligations referred to in articles 30 and article 58(1) a of the GDPR

The EDPB furthermore highlights that article 50 of the GDPR notably aims at facilitating the enforcement of legislation in relation to third countries and international organisation, and that the development of further international cooperation mechanisms in this regard is currently being considered.

NOTES

28   WP29 Guidelines on Data Protection Officers ('DPOs'), WP 243 rev.01 - endorsed by the EDPB.

29   An external DPO also acting as representative in the Union could not for example be in a situation where he is instructed, as a representative, to communicate to a data subject a decision or measure taken by the controller or processor which he or she, as a DPO, had deemed uncompliant with the provisions of the GDPR and advised against.

30   WP29 Guidelines on Data Protection Officers ('DPOs'), WP 243 rev.01 - endorsed by the EDPB.

31   Part of the criteria and interpretation laid down in G29 WP243 rev.1 (Data Protection Officer) - endorsed by the EDPB can be used as a basis for the exemptions to the designation obligation.

32   WP29 position paper on the derogations from the obligation to maintain records of processing activities pursuant to Article 30(5) GDPR.

33   WP29 guidelines on data protections officers (DPOs), adopted on 13th December 2016, as last revised on 5th April 2017, WP 243 rev.01 - endorsed by the EDPB.

34   Article 27(2)(a) GDPR.

35   The GDPR does not define what constitutes a 'public authority or body'. The EDPB considers that such a notion is to be determined under national law. Accordingly, public authorities and bodies include national, regional and local authorities, but the concept, under the applicable national laws, typically also includes a range of other bodies governed by public law.

EUROPEAN DATA PROTECTION BOARD: GUIDELINES 4/2018 ON THE ACCREDITATION OF CERTIFICATION BODIES UNDER ARTICLE 43 OF THE GENERAL DATA PROTECTION REGULATION (2016/679)
Version 3.0
4 June 2019

[2.269]

NOTES
© European Data Protection Board.

VERSION HISTORY

Version 3.0: 4 June 2019: Inclusion of Annex 1 (version 2.0 of Annex 1 adopted on 4 June 2019 after public consultation)

Version 2.0: 4 December 2018: Adoption of the Guidelines after public consultation - On the same date Annex 1 (version 1.0) was adopted for public consultation

Version 1.0: 6 February 2018: Adoption of the Guidelines by the Article 29 Working Party (version for publication consultation). This version has been endorsed by the EDPB on 25 May 2018

TABLE OF CONTENTS

THE EUROPEAN DATA PROTECTION BOARD

Having regard to Article 70 (1)(e) of the Regulation 2016/679/EU of the European Parliament and of the Council of 27 April 2016 on the protection of natural persons with regard to the processing of personal data and on the free movement of such data, and repealing Directive 95/46/EC,

Having considered the results of the public consultation on the guidelines that took place in February 2018 and on the annex that took place between 14 December 2018 and 1 February 2019, as per Article 70 (4) of the GDPR

HAS ADOPTED THE FOLLOWING GUIDELINES

1 INTRODUCTION

[2.270]
1. The General Data Protection Regulation (Regulation (EU) 2016/679) ('the GDPR'), which comes into effect on 25 May 2018, provides a modernised, accountability and fundamental rights based compliance framework for data protection in Europe. A range of measures to facilitate compliance with the provisions of the GDPR are central to this new framework. These include mandatory requirements in specific circumstances (including the appointment of Data Protection Officers and carrying out data protection impact assessments) and voluntary measures such as codes of conduct and certification mechanisms.

2. As part of establishing certification mechanisms and data protection seals and marks, Article 43(1) of the GDPR requires Member States ensure that certification bodies issuing certification under Article

42(1) are accredited by either or both, the competent supervisory authority or the national accreditation body. If accreditation is carried out by the national accreditation body in accordance with ISO/IEC 17065/2012, the additional requirements established by the competent supervisory authority must also be applied.

3. Meaningful certification mechanisms can enhance compliance with the GDPR and transparency for data subjects and in business to business (B2B) relations, for example between controllers and processors. Data controllers and processors will benefit from an independent third-party attestation for the purpose of demonstrating compliance of their processing operations.[1]

4. In this context, the European Data Protection Board (EDPB)recognizes that it is necessary to provide guidelines in relation to accreditation. The particular value and purpose of accreditation lies in the fact that it provides an authoritative statement of the competence of certification bodies that allows the generation of trust in the certification mechanism.

5. The aim of the guidelines is to provide guidance on how to interpret and implement the provisions of Article 43 of the GDPR. In particular, they aim to help Member States, supervisory authorities and national accreditation bodies establish a consistent, harmonised baseline for the accreditation of certification bodies that issue certification in accordance with the GDPR.

NOTES
[1] Recital 100 of the GDPR states that the establishment of certification mechanisms can enhance transparency and compliance with the Regulation and allow data subjects to assess the level of data protection of relevant products and services.

2 SCOPE OF THE GUIDELINES

[2.271]
6. These guidelines.
- set out the purpose of accreditation in the context of the GDPR;
- explain the routes that are available to accredit certification bodies in accordance with Article 43(1), and identify key issues to consider;
- provide a framework for establishing additional accreditation requirements when the accreditation is handled by the national accreditation body; and
- provide a framework for establishing accreditation requirements, when the accreditation is handled by the supervisory authority.

7. The guidelines do not constitute a procedural manual for the accreditation of certification bodies in accordance with the GDPR. They do not develop a new technical standard for the accreditation of certification bodies for the purposes of the GDPR.

8. The guidelines are addressed to:
- Member States, who must ensure that certification bodies are accredited by the supervisory authority and/or the national accreditation body;
- national accreditation bodies that conduct the accreditation of certification bodies under Article 43(1)(b);
- the competent supervisory authority specifying 'additional requirements' to those in ISO/IEC 17065/2012[2] when the accreditation is carried out by the national accreditation body under Article 43(1)(b);
- the EDPB when issuing an opinion on and approving competent supervisory authority accreditation requirements pursuant to Articles 43(3), 70(1)(p) and 64(1)(c);
- the competent supervisory authority specifying the accreditation requirements when accreditation is carried out by the supervisory authority under Article 43(1)(a);
- other stakeholders such as prospective certification bodies or certification scheme owners providing for certification criteria and procedures[3].

9. Definitions

10. The following definitions seek to promote a common understanding of the basic elements of the accreditation process. They should be considered as points of reference and they do not raise any claim to be unassailable. These definitions are based on existing regulatory frameworks and standards, especially on the relevant provisions of GDPR and ISO/IEC 17065/2012.

11. For the purposes of these guidelines the following definitions shall apply:

12. *'accreditation'* of certification bodies see section 3 on interpretation of accreditation for the purposes of Article 43 of the GDPR;

13. *'additional requirements'* means the requirements established by the supervisory authority which is competent and against which an accreditation is performed[4];

14. *'certification'* shall mean the assessment and impartial, third party attestation[5] that the fulfilment of certification criteria has been demonstrated;

15. *'certification body'* shall mean a third –party conformity assessment[6] body[7] operating a certification mechanisms[8];

16. *'certification scheme'* shall mean a certification system related to specified products, processes and services to which the same specified requirements, specific rules and procedures apply;[9]

17. *'criteria'* or certification criteria shall mean the criteria against which a certification (conformity assessment)is performed;[10]

18. 'national accreditation body' shall mean the sole body in a Member State named in accordance with Regulation (EC) No 765/2008 of the European Parliament and the Council that performs accreditation with authority derived from the State[11].

NOTES

[2] International Organization for Standardization: Conformity assessment -- Requirements for bodies certifying products, processes and services.

[3] Scheme owner is an identifiable organisation which has set up certification criteria and the requirements against which conformity is to be assessed. The accreditation is of the organisation that carries out assessments (Article 43.4) against the certification scheme requirements and issues the certificates (i.e. the certification body, also known as conformity assessment body). The organisation carrying out the assessments could be the same organisation that has developed and owns the scheme, but there could be arrangements where one organisation owns the scheme, and another (or more than one other) performs the assessments.

[4] Article 43(1), (3) and (6).

[5] Note that according to ISO 17000, third-party attestation (certification) is "applicable to all objects of conformity assessment" (5.5) "except for conformity assessment bodies themselves, to which accreditation is applicable" (5.6).

[6] Third-party conformity assessment activity is performed by an organisation that is independent of the person or organization that provides the object, and of user interests in that object, cf. ISO 17000, 2.4.

[7] See ISO 17000, 2.5: "body that performs conformity assessment services"; ISO 17011: "body that performs conformity assessment services and that can be the object of accreditation"; ISO 17065, 3.12.

[8] Article 42.1, 42.5 GDPR.

[9] See 3.9 in conjunction with Annex B of ISO 17065.

[10] See Article 42(5).

[11] See Article 2.11 765/2008/EC.

3 INTERPRETATION OF 'ACCREDITATION' FOR THE PURPOSES OF ARTICLE 43 OF THE GDPR

[2.272]
19. The GDPR does not define 'accreditation'. Article 2 (10) of Regulation (EC) No 765/2008, which lays down general requirements for accreditations, defines accreditation as

20. "an attestation by a national accreditation body that a conformity assessment body meets the requirements set by harmonised standards and, where applicable, any additional requirements including those set out in relevant sectoral schemes, to carry out a specific conformity assessment activity "

21. Pursuant to ISO/IEC 17011

22. "accreditation refers to third-party attestation related to a conformity assessment body conveying formal demonstration of its competence to carry out specific conformity assessment tasks."

23. Article 43(1) provides:

24. "Without prejudice to the tasks and powers of the competent supervisory authority under Articles 57 and 58, certification bodies which have an appropriate level of expertise in relation to data protection shall, after informing the supervisory authority in order to allow it to exercise its powers pursuant to point (h) of Article 58(2) where necessary, issue and renew certification. Member States shall ensure that those certification bodies are accredited by one or both of the following:
(a)   the supervisory authority which is competent pursuant to Article 55 or 56;
(b)   the national accreditation body named in accordance with Regulation (EC) No 765/2008 of the European Parliament and of the Council in accordance with ISO/IEC 17065/2012 and with the additional requirements established by the supervisory authority which is competent pursuant to Article 55 or 56."

25. In respect of the GDPR, the accreditation requirements will be guided by:
•   ISO/IEC 17065/2012 and the 'additional requirements' established by the supervisory authority which is competent in accordance with Article 43 (1)(b), when the accreditation is carried out by the national accreditation body and by the supervisory authority, when it carries out the accreditation itself.

26. In both cases the consolidated requirements must cover the requirements mentioned in Article 43(2).

27. The EDPB acknowledges that the purpose of accreditation is to provide an authoritative statement of the competence of a body to perform certification (conformity assessment activities)[12]. Accreditation in terms of the GDPR shall be understood to mean the following:

28. an attestation[13] by a national accreditation body and/or by a supervisory authority, that a certification body[14] is qualified to carry out certification pursuant to Article 42 and 43 GDPR, taking into account ISO/IEC 17065/2012 and the additional requirements established by the supervisory authority and or by the Board.

NOTES

[12] Cf. Recital 15 765/2008/EC.

[13] Cf. Article 2.10 Regulation (EC) 765/2008 of the European Parliament and of the Council of 9 July 2008 setting out the requirements for accreditation and market surveillance relating to the marketing of products.

[14] Cf. with the definition of the term "accreditation" pursuant to ISO 17011.

4 ACCREDITATION IN ACCORDANCE WITH ARTICLE 43(1) GDPR

[2.273]

29. Article 43(1) recognises that there are several options for the accreditation of certification bodies. The GDPR requires supervisory authorities and Members States to define the process for the accreditation of certification bodies. This section sets out the routes for accreditation provided in Article 43.

4.1 ROLE FOR MEMBER STATES

30. Article 43(1) requires Member States *to ensure* that certification bodies are accredited, but allows each Member State to determine who should be responsible to conduct the assessment leading to accreditation. On the basis of Article 43(1), three options are available; accreditation is conducted:

(1)   solely by the supervisory authority, on the basis of its own requirements;

(2)   solely by the national accreditation body named in accordance with Regulation (EC) 765/2008 and on the basis of ISO/IEC 17065/2012 and with additional requirements established by the competent supervisory authority; or

(3)   by both the supervisory authority and the national accreditation body (and in accordance with all requirements listed in 2 above).

31. It is for the individual Member State to decide whether the national accreditation body or the supervisory authority or both together will carry out these accreditation activities but in any case it should ensure that adequate resources are provided[15].

4.2 INTERACTION WITH REGULATION (EC) 765/2008

32. The EDPB notes that Article 2(11) of Regulation (EC) No 765/2008 defines a national accreditation body as "the *sole* body in a Member State that performs accreditation with authority derived from the State".

33. Article 2(11) could be seen as inconsistent with Article 43(1) of the GDPR, which allows accreditation by a body other than the national accreditation body of the Member State. The EDPB considers that the intention of the EU legislation has been to derogate from the general principle that the accreditation be conducted exclusively by the national accreditation authority, by giving supervisory authorities the same power as regards the accreditation of certification bodies. Hence Article 43(1) is lex specialis vis-a-vis Article 2(11) of Regulation 765/2008.

4.3 THE ROLE OF THE NATIONAL ACCREDITATION BODY

34. Article 43(1)(b) provides that the national accreditation body will accredit certification bodies in accordance with ISO/IEC 17065/2012 and the additional requirements established by the competent supervisory authority.

35. For clarity, the EDPB notes that the specific reference to 'to point (b) of paragraph 1 Article 43(3) implies that 'those requirements' points to the 'additional requirements' established by the competent supervisory authority under Article 43(1)(b) and the requirements set out in Article 43(2).

36. In the process of accreditation, the national accreditation bodies shall apply the additional requirements to be provided by the supervisory authorities.

37. A certification body with existing accreditation on the basis of ISO/IEC 17065/2012 for non-GDPR related certification schemes that wishes to extend the scope of its accreditation to cover certification issued in accordance with the GDPR will need to meet the additional requirements established by the supervisory authority if accreditation is handled by the national accreditation body. If accreditation for certification under the GDPR is only offered by the competent supervisory authority, a certification body applying for accreditation will have to meet the requirements set by the respective supervisory authority.

4.4 THE ROLE OF THE SUPERVISORY AUTHORITY

38. The EDPB notes that Article 57(1)(q) provides that the supervisory authority *shall* conduct the accreditation of a certification body pursuant to Article 43 as a 'supervisory authority task' pursuant to Article 57 and Article 58(3)(e) provides that the supervisory authority has the authorisation and advisory power to accredit certification bodies pursuant to Article 43. The wording of Article 43(1) provides some flexibility and the supervisory authority's accreditation function should be read as a task only where appropriate. Member State law may be used to clarify this point. Yet, in the process of accreditation by a national accreditation body the certification body is required by Article 43(2)(a) to demonstrate their independence and expertise to the satisfaction of the competent supervisory authority in relation to the subject-matter of the certification mechanism it offers.[16]

39. If a Member State stipulates that the certification bodies are to be accredited by the supervisory authority, the supervisory authority should establish accreditation requirements including, but not limited to the requirements detailed in Article 43(2). In comparison to the obligations relating to the accreditation of certification bodies by national accreditation bodies, Article 43 provides less instruction about the requirements for accreditation when the supervisory authority conducts the accreditation itself. In the interests of contributing to a harmonised approach to accreditation, the accreditation criteria used by the supervisory authority should be guided by ISO/IEC 17065 and should be complemented by the additional requirements a supervisory authority establishes pursuant to Article 43(1)(b). The EDPB notes that Article 43(2)(a)-(e) reflect and specify requirements of ISO 17065. which will contribute to consistency.

40. If a Member State stipulates that the certification bodies are to be accredited by the national accreditation bodies, the supervisory authority should establish additional requirements complementing the existing accreditation conventions envisaged in Regulation (EC) 765/2008 (where Articles 3-14 relate to the organisation and operation of accreditation of conformity assessment bodies) and the technical rules that describe the methods and procedures of the certification bodies. In light of this, Regulation (EC) 765/2008 provides further guidance: Article 2(10) defines accreditation and refers to 'harmonized standards' and 'any additional requirements including those set out in relevant sectoral schemes'. It follows that the additional requirements established by the supervisory authority should include specific requirements and be focused on facilitating the assessment, amongst others, of the independence and level of data protection expertise of certification bodies, for example, their ability to evaluate and certify personal data processing operations by controllers and processors pursuant to Article 42.(1). This includes competence required for sectoral schemes, and with regard to the protection of fundamental rights and freedoms of natural persons and in particular their right to the protection of personal data.[17] The annex to these guidelines can help inform competent supervisory authorities when establishing the 'additional requirements' in accordance with Articles 43(1)(b) and 43(3).

41. Article 43(6) provides that "[t]he requirements referred to in paragraph 3 of this Article and the certification criteria referred to in Article 42(5) shall be made public by the supervisory authority in an easily accessible form". Therefore, to ensure transparency, all criteria and requirements approved by a supervisory authority shall be published. In terms of quality and trust in the certification bodies, it would be desirable, if all the requirements for accreditation were readily available to the public.

4.5 SUPERVISORY AUTHORITY ACTING AS CERTIFICATION BODY

42. Article 42(5) provides that a supervisory authority may issue certifications, but the GDPR does not require it to be accredited to meet the requirements under Regulation (EC) 765/2008. The EDPB notes that Article 43(1)(a) and specifically Article 58(2)(h), 3(a, e-f) empower supervisory authorities to perform both accreditation and certification, and at the same time provide advice, and, where applicable, withdraw certifications, or order certification bodies to not issue certifications.

43. There may be situations where the separation of accreditation and certification roles and duties is appropriate or required, for example, if a supervisory authority and other certification bodies co-exist in a Member State and both issue the same range of certifications. Supervisory authorities should therefore take sufficient organisational measures to separate the tasks under the GDPR to anchor and facilitate certification mechanisms while taking precautions to avoid conflicts of interest that may arise from these tasks. Additionally, Member States and supervisory authorities should keep in mind the harmonised European level when formulating national law and procedures relating to accreditation and certification in accordance with the GDPR.

4.6 ACCREDITATION REQUIREMENTS

44. The annex to these guidelines provides guidance on how to identify additional accreditation requirements. It identifies the relevant provisions in the GDPR and suggests requirements that supervisory authorities and national accreditation bodies should consider to ensure compliance with the GDPR.

45. As established above, where certification bodies are accredited by the national accreditation body pursuant to regulation (EC) 765/2008, ISO/IEC 17065/2012 will be the relevant accreditation standard complemented by the additional requirements established by the supervisory authority. Article 43(2) reflects generic provisions of ISO/IEC 17065/2012 in the light of fundamental rights protection under the GDPR. The framework in the annex uses Article 43(2) and ISO/IEC 17065/2012 as a basis for the identification of requirements plus further criteria relating to the assessment of the data protection expertise of certification bodies and their ability to respect the rights and freedoms of natural persons with respect to the processing of personal data as enshrined in the GDPR. The EDPB notes that it is especially focused on ensuring that certification bodies have an appropriate level of data protection expertise in accordance with Article 43(1).

46. The additional accreditation requirements established by the supervisory authority will apply to all certification bodies requesting accreditation. The accreditation body will evaluate whether that certification body is competent to carry out the certification activity in line with the additional requirements and the subject-matter of certification. There shall be references specific sectors or areas of certification for which the certification body is accredited.

47. The EDPB also notes that the special expertise in the field of data protection is also required in addition to ISO/IEC 17065/2012 requirements, if other, external bodies, such as laboratories or auditors, perform parts or components of certification activities on behalf of an accredited certification body. In these cases, accreditation of these external bodies under the GDPR itself is not possible. However, in order to ensure the suitability of these bodies for their activity on behalf of the accredited certification bodies, it is necessary for the accredited certification body to ensure that the data protection expertise required for the accredited body must also be in place and demonstrated with the external body with respect to the relevant activity performed.

48. The framework for identifying the additional accreditation requirements as presented in the annex to these guidelines does not constitute a procedural manual for the accreditation process performed by the national accreditation body or the supervisory authority. It provides guidance on structure and methodology and thus a toolbox to the supervisory authorities to identify the additional requirements for accreditation.

NOTES
¹⁵ See Article 4(9) of Regulation (EC) 765/2008.
¹⁶ The additional requirements established by the supervisory authority pursuant to Article 43(1)(b) should specify

requirements for independence and expertise. See also Annex 1 of the guidelines.
¹⁷ Article 1(2) GDPR.

¹⁷   Article 1(2) GDPR.

ANNEX 1

[2.274]
Annex 1 provides guidance for the specification of "additional" accreditation requirements with respect to ISO/IEC 17065/2012 and in accordance with Articles 43(1)(b) and 43(3) GDPR.

This Annex sets out suggested requirements that a data protection supervisory authority shall draft and that apply during the accreditation of a certification body by the National Accreditation Body or by the competent supervisory authority.¹⁸ These additional requirements are to be communicated to the European Data Protection Board before approval pursuant to Article 64(1)(c).

This Annex should be read in conjunction with ISO/IEC 17065/2012. Section numbers used here correspond to those used in ISO/IEC 17065/2012. Where supervisory authorities perform accreditation pursuant to Article 43(1)(a), good practice would be to follow this approach where practical. This will support EU harmonised accreditation.

Notwithstanding the following guidance or the absence of guidance on any item of ISO/IEC 17065/2012, the competent supervisory authority can formulate further additional requirements concerning these items if in accordance with the national law.

0 PREFIX

[This section is for any agreed Terms of cooperation, if applicable, between the National Accreditation Body and the data protection supervisory authority, e.g. who should be responsible to receive applications or how to organise the acknowledgment of approved criteria as part of the accreditation process.]

1 SCOPE¹⁹

The scope of ISO/IEC 17065/2012 shall be applied in accordance with the GDPR. The guidelines on accreditation and certification provide further information. The scope of a certification mechanism (for example, certification of cloud service processing operations) should be taken into account in the assessment by the NAB and the competent supervisory authority during the accreditation process, particularly with respect to criteria, expertise and evaluation methodology. The broad scope of ISO/IEC 17065/2012 covering products, processes and services should not lower or override the requirements of the GDPR, e.g. a governance mechanism cannot be the only element of a certification mechanism, as the certification must include processing of personal data, i.e. the processing operations. Pursuant to Article 42(1), GDPR certification is only applicable to the processing operations of controllers and processors.

2 NORMATIVE REFERENCE

GDPR has precedence over ISO/IEC 17065/2012. If in the additional requirements or by certification mechanism, reference is made to other ISO standards, they shall be interpreted in line with the requirements set out in the GDPR.

3 TERMS AND DEFINITIONS

In the context of this Annex, the terms and definitions of the guidelines on accreditation (WP 261) and certification (EDPB 1/2018) shall apply and have precedence over ISO definitions.

4 GENERAL REQUIREMENTS FOR ACCREDITATION

4.1 Legal and contractual matters

4.1.1 Legal responsibility

A certification body should be able to demonstrate (at all times) to the NAB or CSA that they have up to date procedures that demonstrate compliance with the legal responsibilities set out in the terms of accreditation, including the additional requirements in respect of the application of Regulation 2016/679/EC. Note that, as the certification body is a data controller/processor itself, it shall be able to demonstrate evidence of Regulation 2016/679/EC compliant procedures and measures specifically for controlling and handling of client organisation's personal data as part of the certification process.

The CSA may decide to add further requirements and procedures to check certification bodies GDPR compliance prior to accreditation.

4.1.2 Certification agreement ("CA")

The minimum requirements for a certification agreement shall be supplemented by the following points:

The certification body shall demonstrate in addition to the requirements of ISO/IEC 17065/2012 that its certification agreements:
(1)   require the applicant to always comply with both the general certification requirements within the meaning of 4.1.2.2 lit. a ISO/IEC 17065/2012 and the criteria approved by the competent supervisory authority or the EDPB in accordance with Article 43 (2)(b) and Article 42(5);

(2)   require the applicant to allow full transparency to the competent supervisory authority with respect to the certification procedure including contractually confidential matters related to data protection compliance pursuant to Articles 42(7) and 58(1)(c);

(3)   do not reduce the responsibility of the applicant for compliance with Regulation 2016/679/EC and is without prejudice to the tasks and powers of the supervisory authorities which is competent in line with Article 42(5);

(4)   require the applicant to provide the certification body with all information and access to its processing activities which are necessary to conduct the certification procedure pursuant to Article 42(6);

(5)   require the applicant to comply with applicable deadlines and procedures. The certification agreement must stipulate that deadlines and procedures resulting, for example, from the certification program or other regulations must be observed and adhered to;

(6)   with respect to 4.1.2.2 lit. c No. 1 ISO/IEC 17065/2012 set out the rules of validity, renewal, and withdrawal pursuant to Articles 42(7) and 43(4) including rules setting appropriate intervals for re-evaluation or review (regularity) in line with Article 42(7);

(7)   allow the certification body to disclose all information necessary for granting certification pursuant to Articles 42(8) and 43(5);

(8)   include rules on the necessary precautions for the investigation of complaints within the meaning of 4.1.2.2 lit. c No. 2, additionally, lit. j, shall also contain explicit statements on the structure and the procedure for complaint management in accordance with Article. 43(2)(d);

(9)   in addition to the minimum requirements referred to in 4.1.2.2 ISO/IEC 17065/2012, if the consequences of withdrawal or suspension of accreditation for the certification body impact on the client, in that case the consequences for the customer should all also be addressed

(10)   require the applicant to inform the certification body in the event of significant changes in its actual or legal situation and in its products, processes and services concerned by the certification.

4.1.3 Use of data protection seals and marks

Certificates, seals and marks shall only be used in compliance with Article 42 and 43 and the guidelines on accreditation and certification.

4.2 Management of impartiality

The accreditation body shall ensure that in addition to the requirement in 4.2. ISO/IEC 17065/2012

(1)   the certification body comply with the additional requirements of the competent supervisory authority (pursuant to Article 43(1)(b))

    (a)   in line with Article 43(2)(a) provide separate evidence of its independence. This applies in particular to evidence concerning the financing of the certification body in so far as it concerns the assurance of impartiality;

    (b)   its tasks and obligations do not lead to a conflict of interest pursuant to Article 43(2)(e);

(2)   the certification body has no relevant connection with the customer it assesses.

4.3 Liability and financing

The accreditation body shall in addition to the requirement in 4.3.1 ISO/IEC 17065/2012 ensure on a regular basis that the certification body has appropriate measures (e.g. insurance or reserves) to cover its liabilities in the geographical regions in which it operates.

4.4 Non-discriminatory conditions

Additional requirements may be formulated by the supervisory authority if in accordance with the national law.

4.5 Confidentiality

Additional requirements may be formulated by the supervisory authority if in accordance with the national law.

4.6 Publicly available information

The accreditation body shall in addition to the requirement in 4.6 ISO/IEC 17065/2012 require from the certification body that at minimum

(1)   all versions (current and previous) of the approved criteria used within the meaning of Article 42(5) are published and easily publicly available as well as all certification procedures, generally stating the respective period of validity;

(2)   information about complaints handling procedures and appeals are made public pursuant to Article 43(2)(d).

5 STRUCTURAL REQUIREMENTS, ARTICLE 43(4) ["PROPER" ASSESSMENT]

5.1 Organisational structure and top management

Additional requirements may be formulated by the supervisory authority.

5.2 Mechanisms for safeguarding impartiality

Additional requirements may be formulated by the supervisory authority.

6 RESOURCE REQUIREMENTS

6.1 Certification body personnel

The accreditation body shall in addition to the requirement in section 6 ISO/IEC 17065/2012 ensure for each certification body that its personnel:

(1) has demonstrated appropriate and ongoing expertise (knowledge and experience) with regard to data protection pursuant to Article 43(1);

(2) has independence and ongoing expertise with regard to the object of certification pursuant to Article 43(2)(a) and do not have a conflict of interest pursuant to Article 43(2)(e);

(3) undertakes to respect the criteria referred to in Article 42(5) pursuant to Article 43(2)(b);

(4) has relevant and appropriate knowledge about and experience in applying data protection legislation;

(5) has relevant and appropriate knowledge about and experience in technical and organisational data protection measures as relevant.

(6) is able to demonstrate experience in the fields mentioned in the additional requirements 6.1.1, 6.1.4, and 6.1.5, specifically

For personnel with technical expertise:

• Have obtained a qualification in a relevant area of technical expertise to at least EQF[20] level 6 or a recognised protected title (e.g. Dipl. Ing.) in the relevant regulated profession or have significant professional experience.

• *Personnel responsible for certification decisions* require significant professional experience in identifying and implementing data protection measures.

• *Personnel responsible for evaluations* require professional experience in technical data protection and knowledge and experience in comparable procedure (e.g. certifications/audits), and registered as applicable.

Personnel shall demonstrate they maintain domain specific knowledge in technical and audit skills through continuous professional development.

For personnel with legal expertise:

• Legal studies at a EU or state-recognised university for at least eight semesters including the academic degree Master (LL.M.) or equivalent, or significant professional experience.

• *Personnel responsible for certification decisions* shall demonstrate significant professional experience in data protection law and be registered as required by the Member State.

• *Personnel responsible for evaluations* shall demonstrate at least two years of professional experience in data protection law and knowledge and experience in comparable procedures (e.g. certifications/audits), and when required by the Member State be registered.

  • Personnel shall demonstrate they maintain domain specific knowledge in technical and audit skills through continuous professional development.

6.2 Resources for evaluation

Additional requirements may be formulated by the supervisory authority if in accordance with the national law.

7 PROCESS REQUIREMENTS, ARTICLE 43(2)(C),(D)

7.1 General

The accreditation body shall in addition to the requirement in section 7.1 ISO/IEC 17065/2012 be required to ensure the following:

(1) Certification bodies comply with the additional requirements of the competent supervisory authority (pursuant to Article 43(1)(b)) when submitting the application in order that tasks and obligations do not lead to a conflict of interests pursuant to Article 43(2)(b);

(2) Notify the relevant CSAs before a certification body starts operating an approved European Data Protection Seal in a new Member State from a satellite office.

7.2 Application

In addition to item 7.2 of ISO/IEC 17065/2012, it should be required that

(1) the object of certification (Target of Evaluation, ToE) must be described in detail in the application. This also includes interfaces and transfers to other systems and organizations, protocols and other assurances;

(2) the application shall specify whether processors are used, and when processors are the applicant, their responsibilities and tasks shall be described, and the application shall contain the relevant controller/processor contract(s).

7.3 Application Review

In addition to item 7.3 of ISO/IEC 17065/2012, it should be required that

(1) binding evaluation methods with respect to the Target of Evaluation (ToE) shall be laid down in the certification agreement;

(2) the assessment in 7.3(e) of whether there is sufficient expertise takes into account both technical and legal expertise in data protection to an appropriate extent.

7.4 Evaluation

In addition to item 7.4 of ISO/IEC 17065/2012, certification mechanisms shall describe sufficient evaluation methods for assessing the compliance of the processing operation(s) with the certification criteria, including for example where applicable:

(1)   a method for assessing the necessity and proportionality of processing operations in relation to their purpose and the data subjects concerned;

(2)   a method for evaluating the coverage, composition and assessment of all risks considered by controller and processor with regard to the legal consequences pursuant to Articles 30, 32 and 35 and 36 GDPR, and with regard to the definition of technical and organisational measures pursuant to Articles 24, 25 and 32 GDPR, insofar as the aforementioned Articles apply to the object of certification, and

(3)   a method for assessing the remedies, including guarantees, safeguards and procedures to ensure the protection of personal data in the context of the processing to be attributed to the object of certification and to demonstrate that the legal requirements as set out in the criteria are met; and

(4)   documentation of methods and findings.

The certification body should be required to ensure that these evaluation methods are standardized and generally applicable. This means that comparable evaluation methods are used for comparable ToEs. Any deviation from this procedure shall be justified by the certification body.

In addition to item 7.4.2 of ISO/IEC 17065/2012, it should be allowed that the evaluation is carried out by external experts who have been recognized by the certification body.

In addition to item 7.4.5 of ISO/IEC 17065/2012, it should be required that data protection certification in accordance with Articles 42 and 43 GDPR, which already covers part of the object of certification, may be included in a current certification. However, it will not be sufficient to completely replace (partial) evaluations. The certification body shall be obliged to check the compliance with the criteria. Recognition shall in any way require the availability of a complete evaluation report or information enabling an evaluation of the previous certification activity and its results. A certification statement or similar certification certificates should not be considered sufficient to replace a report.

In addition to item 7.4.6 of ISO/IEC 17065/2012, it should be required that the certification body shall set out in detail in its certification mechanism how the information required in item 7.4.6 informs the customer (certification applicant) about nonconformities from a certification mechanism. In this context, at least the nature and timing of such information should be defined.

In addition to item 7.4.9 of ISO/IEC 17065/2012, it should be required that documentation be made fully accessible to the data protection supervisory authority upon request.

7.5 Review

In addition to item 7.5 of ISO/IEC 17065/2012, procedures for the granting, regular review and revocation of the respective certifications pursuant to Article 43(2) and 43(3) are required.

7.6 Certification decision

In addition to point 7.6.1 of ISO/IEC 17065/2012, the certification body should be required to set out in detail in its procedures how its independence and responsibility with regard to individual certification decisions are ensured.

7.7 Certification documentation

In addition to item 7.7.1.e of ISO/IEC 17065/2012 and in accordance with Article 42(7) GDPR, it should be required that the period of validity of certifications shall not exceed three years.

In addition to item 7.7.1.e of ISO/IEC 17065/2012, it should be required that the period of the intended monitoring within the meaning of section 7.9 will also be documented.

In addition to item 7.7.1.f of ISO/IEC 17065/2012, the certification body should be required to name the object of certification in the certification documentation (stating the version status or similar characteristics, if applicable).

7.8 Directory of certified products

In addition to item 7.8 of ISO/IEC 17065/2012, the certification body should be required to keep the information on certified products, processes and services available internally and publicly available. The certification body will provide to the public an executive summary of the evaluation report. The aim of this executive summary is to help with transparency around what has been certified and how it was assessed. It will explain such things as:

(a)   the scope of the certification and a meaningful description of the object of certification (ToE),

(b)   the respective certification criteria (including version or functional status),

(c)   the evaluation methods and tests conducted and

(d)   the result(s).

In addition to item 7.8 of ISO/IEC 17065/2012 and pursuant to Article 43(5) GDPR, the certification body shall inform the competent supervisory authorities of the reasons for granting or revoking the requested certification.

7.9 Surveillance

In addition to points 7.9.1, 7.9.2 and 7.9.3 of ISO/IEC 17065/2012, and according to Article 43(2)(c) GDPR, it should be required that regular monitoring measures are obligatory to maintain certification during the monitoring period.

7.10 Changes affecting certification

In addition to points 7.10.1 and 7.10.2 of EN ISO/IEC 17065/2012, changes affecting certification to be considered by the certification body shall include: amendments to data protection legislation, the adoption of delegated acts of the European Commission in accordance with Articles 43(8) and 43(9), decisions of the European Data Protection Board and court decisions related to data protection. The change procedures to be agreed here could include such things as: transition periods, approvals process with competent supervisory authority, reassessment of the relevant object of certification and appropriate measures to revoke the certification if the certified processing operation is no longer in compliance with the updated criteria.

7.11 Termination, reduction, suspension or withdrawal of certification

In addition to chapter 7.11.1 of ISO/IEC 17065/2012, the certification body should be required to inform the competent supervisory authority and the NAB where relevant immediately in writing about measures taken and about continuation, restrictions, suspension and withdrawal of certification.

According to Article 58(2)(h), the certification body shall be required to accept decisions and orders from the competent supervisory authority to withdraw or not to issue certification to a customer (applicant) if the requirement for certification are not or no longer met.

7.12 Records

The certification body should be required to keep all documentation complete, comprehensible, up-to-date and fit to audit.

7.13 Complaints and appeals, Article 43(2)(d)

In addition to item 7.13.1 of ISO/IEC 17065/2012, the certification body should be required to define,
(a)		who can file complaints or objections,
(b)		who processes them on the part of the certification body,
(c)		which verifications take place in this context; and
(d)		the possibilities for consultation of interested parties.

In addition to item 7.13.2 of ISO/IEC 17065/2012, the certification body should be required to define,
(a)		how and to whom such confirmation must be given,
(b)		the time limits for this; and
(c)		which processes are to be initiated afterwards.

In addition to item 7.13.1 of ISO/IEC 17065/2012, the certification body must define how separation between certification activities and the handling of appeals and complaints is ensured.

8 MANAGEMENT SYSTEM REQUIREMENTS

A general requirement of the management system according to chapter 8 of ISO/IEC 17065/2012 is that the implementation of all requirements from the previous chapters within the scope of the application of the certification mechanism by the accredited certification body is documented, evaluated, controlled and monitored independently.

The basic principle of management is to define a system according to which its goals are set effectively and efficiently, specifically: the implementation of the certification services - by means of suitable specifications. This requires transparency and verifiability of the implementation of the accreditation requirements by the certification body and its permanent compliance.

To this end, the management system must specify a methodology for achieving and controlling these requirements in compliance with data protection regulations and for continuously checking them with the accredited body itself.

These management principles and their documented implementation must be transparent and be disclosed by the accredited certification body pursuant in the accreditation procedure pursuant to Article 58 and thereafter at the request of the data protection supervisory authority at any time during an investigation in the form of data protection reviews pursuant to Art. 58(1)(b) or a review of the certifications issued in accordance with Article 42(7) pursuant to Article 58(1)(c).

In particular, the accredited certification body must make public permanently and continuously which certifications were carried out on which basis (or certification mechanisms or schemes), how long the certifications are valid under which framework and conditions (recital 100).

8.1 General management system requirements

The competent supervisory authority may specify and add further additional requirements if in accordance with the national law.

8.2 Management system documentation

The competent supervisory authority may specify and add further additional requirements if in accordance with the national law.

8.3 Control of documents

The competent supervisory authority may specify and add further additional requirements if in accordance with the national law.

8.4 Control of records

The competent supervisory authority may specify and add further additional requirements if in accordance with the national law.

8.5 Management Review

The competent supervisory authority may specify and add further additional requirements if in accordance with the national law.

8.6 Internal audits

The competent supervisory authority may specify and add further additional requirements if in accordance with the national law.

8.7 Corrective actions

The competent supervisory authority may specify and add further additional requirements if in accordance with the national law.

8.8 Preventive actions

The competent supervisory authority may specify and add further additional requirements if in accordance with the national law.

9 FURTHER ADDITIONAL REQUIREMENTS[21]

9.1 Updating of evaluation methods

The certification body shall establish procedures to guide the updating of evaluation methods for application in the context of the evaluation under point 7.4. The update must take place in the course of changes in the legal framework, the relevant risk(s), the state of the art and the implementation costs of technical and organisational measures.

9.2 Maintaining expertise

Certification bodies shall establish procedures to ensure the training of their employees with a view to updating their skills, taking into account the developments listed in point 9.1.

9.3 Responsibilities and competencies

9.3.1 Communication between CB and its customers

Procedures shall be in place for implementing appropriate procedures and communication structures between the certification body and its customer. This shall include
(1)   Maintaining documentation of tasks and responsibilities by the accredited certification body, for the purpose of
    (a)   Information requests, or
    (b)   To enable contact in the event of a complaint about a certification.
(2)   Maintaining an application process for the purpose of
    (a)   Information on the status of an application;
    (b)   Evaluations by the competent supervisory authority with respect to
        (i)   Feedback;
        (ii)   Decisions by the competent supervisory authority.

9.3.2 Documentation of evaluation activities

Additional requirements may be formulated by the supervisory authority.

9.3.3 Management of complaint handling

A complaint handling shall be established as an integral part of the management system, which shall in particular implement the requirements of points 4.1.2.2 lit. c), 4.1.2.2 lit. j), 4.6 lit. d) and 7.13 ISO/IEC 17065/2012.

Relevant complaint and objections should be shared with the competent supervisory authority.

9.3.4 Management of withdrawal

The procedures in the event of suspension or withdrawal of the accreditation shall be integrated into the management system of the certification body including notifications of customers.

NOTES

18   For information about the approvals process for certification criteria please see section 4 of the certification guidelines.
19   Numbering refers to ISO/IEC 17065/2012.
20   See qualification framework comparison tool at https://ec.europa.eu/ploteus/en/compare?
21   The competent supervisory authority may specify and add further additional requirements if in accordance with national law.

EUROPEAN DATA PROTECTION BOARD: GUIDELINES 1/2019 ON CODES OF CONDUCT AND MONITORING BODIES UNDER REGULATION 2016/679
Version 2.0
4 June 2019

[2.275]

NOTES

© European Data Protection Board.

VERSION HISTORY

Version 2.0: 4 June 2019: Adoption of the Guidelines after public consultation

Version 1.0: 12 February 2019: Adoption of the Guidelines for publication consultation

TABLE OF CONTENTS

THE EUROPEAN DATA PROTECTION BOARD

Having regard to Article 70(1)(n) and Articles 40 and 41 of the Regulation 2016/679/EU of the European Parliament and of the Council of 27 April 2016 on the protection of natural persons with regard to the processing of personal data and on the free movement of such data, and repealing Directive 95/46/EC (hereinafter "GDPR"),

Having regard to the EEA Agreement and in particular to Annex XI and Protocol 37 thereof, as amended by the Decision of the EEA joint Committee No 154/2018 of 6 July 2018,

Having regard to Article 12 and Article 22 of its Rules of Procedure of 25 May 2018,

HAS ADOPTED THE FOLLOWING OPINION:

1 INTRODUCTION

[2.276]
1. Regulation 2016/679[1] ("the GDPR") came into effect on 25 May 2018. One of the main objectives

of the GDPR is to provide a consistent level of data protection throughout the European Union and to prevent divergences hampering the free movement of personal data within the internal market.[2] The GDPR also introduces the principle of accountability, which places the onus on data controllers to be responsible for, and be able to demonstrate compliance with the Regulation.[3] The provisions under Articles 40 and 41 of the GDPR in respect of codes of conduct ("codes") represent a practical, potentially cost effective and meaningful method to achieve greater levels of consistency of protection for data protection rights. Codes can act as a mechanism to demonstrate compliance with the GDPR.[4] Notably, they can help to bridge the harmonisation gaps that may exist between Member States in their application of data protection law.[5] They also provide an opportunity for particular sectors to reflect upon common data processing activities and to agree to bespoke and practical data protection rules, which will meet the needs of the sector as well as the requirements of the GDPR.[6]

2. Member States, Supervisory Authorities, the European Data Protection Board ("the Board") and the European Commission ("the Commission") are obliged to encourage the drawing up of codes to contribute to the proper application of the Regulation.[7] These guidelines will support and facilitate "code owners" in drafting, amending or extending codes.

1.1 SCOPE OF THESE GUIDELINES

3. The aim of these guidelines is to provide practical guidance and interpretative assistance in relation to the application of Articles 40 and 41 of the GDPR. They are intended to help clarify the procedures and the rules involved in the submission, approval and publication of codes at both a National and European level. They intend to set out the minimum criteria required by a Competent Supervisory Authority ("CompSA") before accepting to carry out an in depth review and evaluation of a code.[8] Further, they intend to set out the factors relating to the content to be taken into account when evaluating whether a particular code provides and contributes to the proper and effective application[9] of the GDPR. Finally, they intend to set out the requirements for the effective monitoring of compliance with a code.[10]

4. These guidelines should also act as a clear framework for all CompSAs, the Board and the Commission to evaluate codes in a consistent manner and to streamline the procedures involved in the assessment process. This framework should also provide greater transparency, ensuring that code owners who intend to seek approval for a code are fully conversant with the process and understand the formal requirements and the appropriate thresholds required for approval.

5. Guidance on codes of conduct as a tool for transfers of data as per Article 40(3) of the GDPR will be considered in separate guidelines to be issued by the EDPB.

6. All codes previously approved[11] will need to be reviewed and re-evaluated in line with the requirements of the GDPR and then resubmitted for approval as per the requirements of Articles 40 and 41 and as per the procedures outlined in this document.

NOTES

1   The General Data Protection Regulation (EU) 2016/679 of the European Parliament and of the Council of 27 April 2016 on the protection of natural persons with regard to the processing of personal data and on the free movement of such data, and repealing Directive 95/46/EC.
2   See Recital 13 of the GDPR.
3   See Article 5(2) of the GDPR.
4   See for example Articles 24(3) and 28(5) and 32(3). A code of conduct may also be used by data processors to demonstrate sufficient guarantees that their processing is compliant with the GDPR (See Article 28(5)).
5   See Recitals 77, 81, 98, 99, 148, 168 and Articles 24, 28, 35, 40, 41, 46, 57, 64, 70 of the GDPR. This is particularly the case where a code relates to processing activities in several Member States.
6   Codes do not necessarily need to be confined or limited to a specific sector. For example, a code could apply to separate sectors who have a common processing activity which share the same processing characteristics and needs. Where a code is cross-sectoral in its application, more than one monitoring body may be appointed under that code. However, where this is the case the code should make it absolutely clear as to the scope of that monitoring body's functions, in other words by specifying the sectors in respect of which each monitoring body will perform its functions under Article 41 and the oversight mechanisms available to each monitoring body. In this regard, the relevant sections of these guidelines which set out the responsibilities, obligations and accreditation requirements in relation to monitoring bodies apply individually to each such monitoring body appointed under the code.
7   Article 40(1) of the GDPR.
8   See Article 40(5), Article 55(1) and Recital 122 of the GDPR.
9   See Article 40(1) and Recital 98 of the GDPR.
10 See for example Article 41(2) and 41(3) of the GDPR.
11 By either National Data Supervisory authorities or the Article 29 Working Party prior to the GDPR and these guidelines.

2 DEFINITIONS

[2.277]

'*Accreditation*' refers to the ascertainment that the proposed monitoring body meets the requirements set out in Article 41 of the GDPR to carry out the monitoring of compliance with a code of conduct. This check is undertaken by the supervisory authority where the code is submitted for approval (Article 41(1)). The accreditation of a monitoring body applies only for a specific code.[12]

'*Code Owners*' refers to associations or other bodies who draw up and submit their code[13] and they will have an appropriate legal status as required by the code and in line with national law. 'CompSA' refers to the Supervisory Authority which is competent as per Article 55 of the GDPR. 'Monitoring body' refers to a body/committee or a number of bodies/committees (internal or external to the code owners[14]) who carry out a monitoring function to ascertain and assure that the code is complied with as per Article 41.

'*Concerned SAs*' shall have the same meaning as per Article 4(22) of the GDPR

'*National code*' refers to a code which covers processing activities contained in one Member State.

'*Transnational code*' refers to a code which covers processing activities in more than one Member State.

NOTES

¹² However, a monitoring body may be accredited for more than one code provided it satisfies the requirements for accreditation.

¹³ As per Recital 98 of the GDPR.

¹⁴ See also Paragraphs 64–67 below.

3 WHAT ARE CODES?

[2.278]

7.   GDPR codes are voluntary accountability tools which set out specific data protection rules for categories of controllers and processors. They can be a useful and effective accountability tool, providing a detailed description of what is the most appropriate, legal and ethical set of behaviours of a sector. From a data protection viewpoint, codes can therefore operate as a rulebook for controllers and processors who design and implement GDPR compliant data processing activities which give operational meaning to the principles of data protection set out in European and National law.

8.   Trade associations or bodies representing a sector can create codes to help their sector comply with the GDPR in an efficient and potentially cost effective way. As provided by the non-exhaustive list contained in Article 40(2) of the GDPR, codes of conduct may notably cover topics such as:

- fair and transparent processing;
- legitimate interests pursued by controllers in specific contexts;
- the collection of personal data; the pseudonymisation of personal data;
- the information provided to individuals and the exercise of individuals' rights;
- the information provided to and the protection of children (including mechanisms for obtaining parental consent);
- technical and organisational measures, including data protection by design and by default and security measures;
- breach notification;
- data transfers outside the EU; or
- dispute resolution procedures.

9.   The GDPR in repealing the Data Protection Directive (95/46/EC) provides more specific and detailed provisions around codes, the requirements which need to be met and the procedures involved in attaining approval, as well as their registration, publication and promotion once approved. Those provisions, in conjunction with these guidelines, will help encourage code owners to have a direct input into the establishment of data protection standards and rules for their processing sectors.

10.   It is important to note that codes are one of a number of voluntary tools that can be used from a suite of data protection accountability tools which the GDPR offers, such as Data Protection Impact Assessments (DPIAs)¹⁵ and Certification.¹⁶ They are a mechanism which can be used to assist organisations in demonstrating their compliance with the GDPR.¹⁷

NOTES

¹⁵ Codes of Conduct and Certification are voluntary accountability tools, whereas a DPIA will be mandatory in certain circumstances. For further information on other accountability tools please see the general guidance webpage of the EDPB (www.edpb.europa.eu).

¹⁶ See Article 42 of the GDPR and note the EDPB Guidelines 1/2018 on certification and identifying certification criteria in accordance with Articles 42 and 43 of the GDPR.

¹⁷ Adherence to a code does not, of itself, guarantee compliance with the GDPR or immunity for controllers/processors from sanctions or liabilities provided under the GDPR.

4 WHAT ARE THE BENEFITS OF CODES?

[2.279]

11.   Codes represent an opportunity to establish a set of rules which contribute to the proper application of the GDPR in a practical, transparent and potentially cost effective manner that takes on board the nuances for a particular sector and/or its processing activities. In this regard codes can be drawn up for controllers and processors taking account of the specific characteristics of processing carried out in certain sectors and the specific needs of micro, small and medium enterprises.¹⁸ They have the potential to be an especially important and beneficial tool for both SMEs and micro enterprise businesses¹⁹ by providing a mechanism which allows them to achieve data protection compliance in a more cost effective way.

> For example, micro enterprises involved in similar health research activities could come together via their relevant associations and collectively develop a code in respect of their collection and processing of health data rather than attempting to carry out such comprehensive data protection analysis on their own. Codes will also benefit supervisory authorities by allowing them to gain a better understanding and insight of the data processing activities of a specific profession, industry or other sector.

12.   Codes can help controllers and processors to comply with the GDPR by governing areas such as fair and transparent processing, legitimate interests, security and data protection by design and default measures and controller obligations. Codes are accessible to all processing sectors and can be drafted in as narrow or as wide-ranging a manner as is befitting that particular sector[20], provided that the code contributes to the proper and effective application of the GDPR.[21]

For example, approval could be sought for a set of rules in respect of how a specific charitable sector would ensure its processing arrangements were fair and transparent. Alternatively, the specific charitable sector could decide to draft a code, which incorporates and properly applies a multitude of different provisions under the GDPR to cover all their processing activities, from the lawful basis for the collection of personal data to the notification of personal data breaches.

---

13. Codes can provide a degree of co-regulation and they could decrease the level of reliance that controllers and processors may sometimes place upon data protection supervisory authorities to provide more granular guidance for their specific processing activities.

14. Codes can provide a degree of autonomy and control for controllers and processors to formulate and agree best practice rules for their given sectors. They can provide an opportunity to consolidate best practice processing operations in specific fields. They can also become a vital resource that businesses can rely upon to address critical issues in their processing procedures and to achieve better data protection compliance.

15. Codes can provide much needed confidence and legal certainty by providing practical solutions to problems identified by particular sectors in relation to common processing activities. They encourage the development of a collective and consistent approach to the data processing needs of a particular sector.

16. Codes can be an effective tool to earn the trust and confidence of data subjects. They can address a variety of issues, many of which may arise from concerns of the general public or even perceived concerns from within the sector itself, and as such constitute a tool for enhancing transparency towards individuals regarding the processing of their personal data.

For example, in the context of processing health data for research purposes, concerns over the appropriate measures to be adopted in order to promote compliance with the rules applying to the processing of sensitive health information could be allayed by the existence of an approved and detailed code. Such a code could outline in a fair and transparent manner the following:

- the relevant safeguards to be applied regarding the information to be provided to data subjects;
- relevant safeguards to be applied in respect of the data collected from third parties;
- communication or dissemination of the data;
- the criteria to be implemented to ensure respect for the principle of data minimisation;
- the specific security measures;
- appropriate retention schedules; and
- the mechanisms to manage the data as a result of the exercise of data subjects' rights (As per Articles 32 and 89 of the GDPR)

---

17. Codes may also provide to be a significant and useful mechanism in the area of international transfers. New provisions in the GDPR allow third parties to agree to adhere to approved codes in order to satisfy legal requirements to provide appropriate safeguards in relation to international transfers of personal data to third countries.[22] Additionally, approved codes of this nature may result in the promotion and cultivation of the level of protection which the GDPR provides to the wider international community while also permitting sustainable legally compliant international transfers of personal data. They may also serve as a mechanism which further develops and fosters data subject trust and confidence in the processing of data outside of the European Economic Area.[23]

18. Approved codes have the potential to act as effective accountability tools for both processors and controllers. As outlined in Recital 77 and Article 24(3) of the GDPR, adherence to an approved code of conduct is envisaged, amongst others, as an appropriate method for a data controller or processor to demonstrate compliance with regard to specific parts or principles of the Regulation or the Regulation as a whole.[24] Adherence to an approved code of conduct will also be a factor taken into consideration by supervisory authorities when evaluating specific features of data processing such as the security aspects[25], assessing the impact of processing under a DPIA[26] or when imposing an administrative fine.[27] In case of a breach of one of the provisions of the Regulation, adherence to an approved code of conduct might be indicative of how comprehensive the need is to intervene with an effective, proportionate, dissuasive administrative fine or other corrective measure from the supervisory authority.[28]

NOTES

[18] See Recital 98 of the GDPR in respect of Article 40(1). For example, a code could be appropriately scaled to meet the requirement of micro organisations in addition to small and medium enterprises.

[19] Article 40(1) of the GDPR in particular identifies codes as a solution to address the needs of such enterprises.

[20] Article 40(2) of the GDPR refers to codes being prepared by representative organisations of 'categories of controllers and processors'. Therefore this could include cross sector codes where practical provided the representativeness criteria is met.

[21] A narrowly focused code must make it sufficiently clear to data subjects (and to the satisfaction of a CompSA) that controllers/processors adhering to the code does not necessarily ensure compliance with all of the legislation. An appropriate safeguard in this instance could be to ensure adequate transparency regarding the limited scope of the code to those signed up to the code and data subjects.

5 ADMISSIBILITY OF A DRAFT CODE[29]

[2.280]
19.   There are a number of conditions to be met before a CompSA would be in a position to undertake to fully assess and review a code for the purposes of Article 40(5) of the GDPR. They aim to facilitate an efficient evaluation of any draft code. The following criteria apply:

5.1 EXPLANATORY STATEMENT AND SUPPORTING DOCUMENTATION

20.   Every draft code which is submitted for approval must contain a clear and concise explanatory statement, which provides details as to the purpose of the code, the scope of the code[30] and how it will facilitate the effective application of this Regulation.[31] This will assist in expediting the process and in providing the requisite clarity to accompany a submission. The submission must also include supporting documentation, where relevant, to underpin the draft code and explanatory statement.[32]

5.2 REPRESENTATIVE

21.   A code must be submitted by an association/consortium of associations or other bodies representing categories of controllers or processors (code owners) in accordance with Article 40(2). A non-exhaustive list of example of possible code owners would include: trade and representative associations, sectoral organisations, academic organisations and interest groups.

22.   The code owners must demonstrate to the CompSA that they are an effective representative body and that they are capable of understanding the needs of their members and clearly defining the processing activity or sector to which the code is intended to apply. Depending on the definition and parameters of the sector concerned, representativeness can be derived amongst others from the following elements:
•   Number or percentage of potential code members from the relevant controllers or processors in that sector;
•   Experience of the representative body with regard to the sector and processing activities concerning the code.

5.3 PROCESSING SCOPE

23.   The draft code must have a defined scope that clearly and precisely determines the processing operations (or characteristics of the processing) of personal data covered by it, as well as the categories of controllers or processors it governs. This will include the processing issues that the code seeks to address and provide practical solutions.

5.4 TERRITORIAL SCOPE

24.   The draft code must specify whether it is a national or transnational code and provide details in relation to territorial scope, identifying all relevant jurisdictions to which it intends to apply. For any transnational codes (as well as amended or extended transnational codes), a list of concerned SAs must be included. **APPENDIX 1** outlines the distinction between national and transnational codes.

5.5 SUBMISSION TO A COMPSA

25.   The code owners must ensure that the supervisory authority chosen to review a draft code is competent in accordance with Article 55 of the GDPR.[33] **APPENDIX 2** provides further information which may assist code owners in choosing a CompSA for a transnational code.

5.6 OVERSIGHT OF MECHANISMS

26.   The draft code must propose mechanisms that allow for the monitoring of compliance with its provisions by stakeholders who undertake to apply it.[34] This applies to both public and non-public sector codes.

5.7 MONITORING BODY

27.   A draft code which involves processing activities of private, non-public authorities or bodies must also identify a monitoring body and contain mechanisms which enable that body to carry out its functions as per Article 41 of the GDPR.[35] The identified monitoring body or bodies must have the appropriate standing to meet the requirements of being fully accountable in their role.[36] To this end, the monitoring body or bodies have to be accredited by the CompSA according to Article 41(1) of the GDPR.[37]

5.8 CONSULTATION

28.   A draft code must contain information as to the extent of consultation carried out. Recital 99 of the GDPR indicates when drafting a code (or amending/extending) a consultation should take place with the relevant stakeholders including data subjects, where feasible. As such, code owners should confirm and demonstrate that an appropriate level of consultation has taken place with the relevant stakeholders when submitting the code for approval. Where relevant, this will include information about other codes of conduct that potential code members may be subject to and reflect how their code complements other codes. This should also outline the level and nature of consultation which took place with their members, other stakeholders and data subjects or associations/bodies representing them.[38] In practice, a consultation is highly recommended with the members forming part of the organisation or body acting as the code owner and also taking into account the processing activity with the clients of such members. Where no consultation has been carried out with regard to relevant and specific stakeholders due to the lack of feasibility, it will be a matter for the code owner to explain this position.

5.9 NATIONAL LEGISLATION

29. Code owners must provide confirmation that the draft code is in compliance with relevant national legislation, in particular, where the code involves a sector which is governed by specific provisions set out in national law or it concerns processing operations that have to be assessed, taking into account specific requirements and relevant legal obligations under national law.

5.10 LANGUAGE

30. Code owners should comply with the language requirements of the CompSA to whom they will submit their code. In general, a code should be submitted in the language of the CompSA of that Member State.[39] For transnational codes, the code should be submitted in the language of the CompSA and also in English.[40]

5.11 CHECKLIST

31. Ultimately, it will be a matter for the chosen CompSA to determine whether the draft code goes to the next stage of evaluation i.e. a CompSA undertakes to carry out a full assessment of the content in line with Articles 40 and 41 of the GDPR and the procedures detailed below. The Checklist outlined in **APPENDIX 3** should be used to reference documentation submitted to a CompSA and to help frame the submission of the draft code.

NOTES

[29] This also applies for all codes (national and transnational) as well as amended or extended codes.

[30] The following non-exhaustive categories may apply: identification of members, processing activity, data subjects, types of data, jurisdictions, concerned SAs (Article 4(22) of the GDPR).

[31] This document provides an opportunity for code owners to demonstrate the rationale and basis for approval of their code. It provides a platform for code owners to outline the appropriateness of safeguards proposed and to demonstrate that proposed mechanisms are fit for purpose.

[32] Examples could include a consultation summary, membership information or research that demonstrates a need for the code.

[33] Article 55 of the GDPR states that each supervisory authority is competent for the performance of the tasks assigned to and the exercise of the powers conferred on it in accordance with the Regulation on the territory of its own Member State. Also see Recital 122 of the GDPR.

[34] See Article 40(4) of the GDPR.

[35] A code involving the public sector will still need to contain suitable mechanisms to monitor the code.

[36] As per Article 83(4)(c) of the GDPR infringements in relation to the obligations of a monitoring body shall be subject to an administrative fine.

[37] See section below entitled 'Accreditation Requirements for Monitoring Bodies' on page 24.

[38] For instance, codes owners could outline how they assessed the submissions received following consultation.

[39] Some Member States may have national legislation which requires a draft code to be submitted in their national language, and it is recommended that code owners explore this issue with the relevant CompSA in advance of formally submitting their draft code for approval.

[40] English is the working language of the EDPB as per Section 23 Rules of Procedure of the EDPB.

---

6 CRITERIA FOR APPROVING CODES

[2.281]
32. Code owners will need to be able to demonstrate how their code will contribute to the proper application of the GDPR, taking account of the specific features of the various processing sectors as well as the specific requirements and obligations of the controllers or processors to whom it relates. There are a number of aspects to this overarching requirement. Code owners should be able to demonstrate that their draft code:

- meets a particular need of that sector or processing activity,
- facilitates the application of the GDPR,
- specifies the application of the GPDR,
- provides sufficient safeguards[41], and
- provides effective mechanisms for monitoring compliance with a code.

6.1 MEETS A PARTICULAR NEED

33. Code owners are required to demonstrate a need for the establishment of a code. As such a code must address data protection issues which arise for a particular sector or processing activity.

> For example, the sector of information systems for the detection of consumer credit risks may identify a need to formulate a code which provides sufficient safeguards and mechanisms to ensure that the data collected are relevant, accurate and are used exclusively for the specific and legitimate purpose of protecting credit. Similarly, the health research sector may identify a need to formulate a code which provides consistency in approach by setting out standards to adequately meet explicit consent and accompanying accountability requirements under the GDPR.

34. Code owners should be able to explain and set out the problems the code seeks to address and substantiate how the solutions the code offers will be effective and beneficial not only for their members but also for data subjects.

6.2 FACILITATES THE EFFECTIVE APPLICATION OF THE GDPR

35. As per recital 98 of the GDPR, a code, in order to attain approval, will require code owners to be able demonstrate that their code facilitates the effective application of the GDPR. In this regard, a code will need to clearly stipulate its sector-specific application of the GDPR and identify and address such specific needs of a sector.[42]

> For example, providing a list of definitions that are specific to the sector as well as an adequate focus on topics that are particularly relevant to the sector are ways to facilitate the effective application of the GDPR. Using sector-specific terminology to detail the implementation of the requirements of the GDPR in the sector may also improve the clear understanding of the rules by the industry and thus facilitate the effective application of the GDPR. A code should fully take into account the likely risks involved with a particular sector processing activity and appropriately calibrate the related obligations of controllers or processors to whom it applies in light of those risks in that specific sector i.e. providing examples of acceptable terms and conditions in relation to the use of personal data in direct marketing. In terms of format, the content of the code should also be presented in a way that facilitates its understanding, practical use and effective application of the GDPR.

6.3 SPECIFIES THE APPLICATION OF THE GDPR

36. Codes will need to specify the practical application of the GDPR and accurately reflect the nature of the processing activity or sector. They should be able to provide clear industry specific improvements in terms of compliance with data protection law. Codes will need to set out realistic and attainable standards for all their members, and they will need to be of a necessary quality and internal consistency to provide sufficient added value.[43] In other words, a draft code will need to be adequately focused on particular data protection areas[44] and issues in the specific sector to which it applies and it will need to provide sufficiently clear and effective solutions to address those areas and issues.[45]

37. A code should not just re-state the GDPR.[46] Instead, it should aim to codify how the GDPR shall apply in a specific, practical and precise manner. The agreed standards and rules will need to be unambiguous, concrete, attainable and enforceable (testable). Setting out distinct rules in the particular field is an acceptable method by which a code can add value. Using terminology that is unique and relevant to the industry and providing concrete case scenarios or specific examples of 'best practice'[47] may help to meet this requirement.[48]

38. Outlining plans to promote the approved code so individuals are informed of its existence and contents may also assist in reaching the standard of "specifying the application of the GDPR". It is vital that codes are able to provide operational meaning to the principles of data protection as articulated in Article 5 of the GDPR. It is also vital that codes properly take into account relevant opinions and positions published or endorsed by the Board to that particular sector or processing activity.[49] For example, codes containing specifications with regard to processing activities, might also facilitate the identification of adequate legal grounds for these processing activities in the Member States to which they intend to apply.

6.4 PROVIDES SUFFICIENT SAFEGUARDS

39. A code should also meet the requirements of Article 40(5). Approval will only be forthcoming when it is determined that a draft code provides sufficient appropriate safeguards.[50] Codes owners will need to appropriately satisfy a CompSA that their code contains suitable and effective safeguards to mitigate the risk around data processing and the rights and freedoms of individuals.[51] It will be a matter for the code owners to provide clear evidence showing that their code will meet these requirements.

> For example, in 'high risk' processing activities such as the large scale processing of children's or health data, profiling or systematic monitoring, it would be expected that the code would contain more

demanding requirements upon controllers and processors to reflect an adequate level of protection. Additionally, code owners may benefit from carrying out a more extensive consultation as per Recital 99 of the GDPR to underpin a code involving the processing of such high risk areas.

6.5 PROVIDES MECHANISMS WHICH WILL ALLOW FOR EFFECTIVE OVERSIGHT

40. As per Article 40(4) of the GDPR, a code requires the implementation of suitable mechanisms to ensure that those rules are appropriately monitored and that efficient and meaningful enforcement measures are put in place to ensure full compliance. A code specifically needs to identify and propose structures and procedures which provide for effective monitoring and enforcement of infringements. A draft code will also need to identify an appropriate body which has at its disposal mechanisms to enable that body to provide for the effective monitoring of compliance with the code. Mechanisms may include regular audit and reporting requirements, clear and transparent complaint handling and dispute resolution procedures, concrete sanctions and remedies in cases of violations of the code, as well as policies for reporting breaches of its provisions.

41. A draft code will be required to have a monitoring body where it involves processing carried out by non-public authorities and bodies. In essence, a code must not only consider the contents of rules applicable to that sector's processing activity, but it must also implement monitoring mechanisms which will ensure the effective application of those rules. A draft code could successfully propose a number of different monitoring mechanisms where there are multiple monitoring bodies to carry out effective oversight. However, all proposed monitoring mechanisms as to how to give effect to adequate monitoring of a code will need to be clear, suitable, attainable, efficient and enforceable (testable). Code owners will need to set out the rationale and demonstrate why their proposals for monitoring are appropriate and operationally feasible.[52]

NOTES

[41] For example, 'high risk' sectors, such as processing children's or health data would be expected to contain more robust and stringent safeguards, given the sensitivity of the personal data in question.

[42] See Article 40(1) of the GDPR.

[43] This standard was first applied in WP 13 DG XV D/5004/98 adopted on 10th September 1998.

[44] Such as those listed in Article 40(2) of the GDPR.

[45] This requirement reflects the previous position of the WP 29 as outlined in Working Document on Codes WP 13 DG XV D/5004/98 adopted on 10th September 1998.

[46] Providing restatements of data protection law was a regular feature of unsuccessful draft codes which were submitted for approval to WP 29.

[47] And 'unacceptable practices'.

[48] A code should avoid, where possible, being overly legalistic.

[49] They will also need to fully take on board relevant National and European jurisprudence.

[50] See Recital 98 of the GDPR.

[51] Safeguards may also apply to monitoring bodies and their capabilities in carrying out their role in an effective manner.

[52] The Article 29 Working Party document "Judging industry self-regulation: when does it make a meaningful contribution to the level of data protection in a third country?" WP7 adopted 14 January 1998 is also an informative document providing further insight into assessing the value of a code and the general grounds required for it to be effective. It is recommended that this document is also considered (where relevant) when formulating a code.

---

7 SUBMISSION, ADMISSIBILITY AND APPROVAL[53] (NATIONAL CODE)

7.1 SUBMISSION

[2.282]
42. Code owners should formally submit their draft Code in either an electronic or written (printed/hard copy) format to the CompSA.[54] The CompSA will revert to the code owners acknowledging receipt of the submission, and proceed to carry out a review as to whether the draft code meets the admissibility criteria as set out above[55] before proceeding to carry out a full evaluation of its contents.

7.2 ADMISSIBILITY OF A CODE

43. If the draft Code is not accepted on the basis of failing to meet the criteria for admissibility[56] the CompSA will respond to the code owners in writing outlining the basis for its decision. The process would come to an end on this basis and a new submission would be required to be made by the code owners.[57]

44. If the draft code meets the criteria set out above, the CompSA should write to the code owners with confirmation that it will proceed to the next stage of the process and assess the draft code's content in accordance with the relevant procedures provided under national law.

7.3 APPROVAL

45. Unless a specific timeline is prescribed under national law, the CompSA should draft an opinion within a reasonable period of time and it should keep the draft owners regularly updated on the process and indicative timelines. The opinion should outline the basis for its decision in line with the criteria for approval as outlined above.[58]

46. If the decision made by the CompSA is to refuse approval, then the process will be completed and it will be a matter for the code owners to assess the findings of the opinion and reconsider the draft code on that basis. It would also be necessary for the code owners to formally re-submit an updated draft code at a later stage, if they choose to do so.

47. If the CompSA approves a draft code, it will be necessary for it to register and publish the code (via its website and/or other appropriate methods of communication).[59] Article 40(11) also requires the Board to make publicly available all approved codes.

NOTES

[53] Including amending and extending codes previously approved.

[54] Obviously such an authority will be the National SA for the members to whom the code applies. It is also important that code owners clearly stipulate to the CompSA that they are formally submitting a draft Code for approval and that they clearly indicate the jurisdictional scope of the code. Also please note Appendix 1 in relation to the distinction between national and transnational codes.

[55] See also Appendix 3 checklist.

[56] *Ibid*

[57] It is worth noting that refusal at this stage of the approval process will most likely be based on general or procedural preliminary requirements rather than substantive or core issues associated with the provisions of the draft code.

[58] By doing so the CompSA can provide helpful feedback to code owners if they choose to review, amend and resubmit a draft code at a future date.

[59] As per Article 40(6) of the GDPR.

8 SUBMISSION, ADMISSIBILITY AND APPROVAL[60] (TRANSNATIONAL CODE)

8.1 SUBMISSION

[2.283]
48. Code owners should formally submit their draft code in either an electronic or written format to a CompSA which will act as the principal authority for the approval of the code.[61] The CompSA will revert to the code owners acknowledging receipt of the documentation and proceed to carry out a review as to whether the draft code meets the requirements as set out above[62] before proceeding to carry out a full evaluation of its contents. The CompSA will immediately notify all other supervisory authorities of the submission of a code and provide the salient details which will allow for ease of identification and reference. All supervisory authorities should confirm by return whether they are concerned SAs as per Article 4(22)(a) and (b) of the GDPR.[63]

8.2 ADMISSIBILITY OF A CODE

49. If the draft code is not accepted on the basis of failing to meet the admissibility criteria set out above, the CompSA will write to the code owners outlining the basis for its decision. The process will come to an end on this basis and a new submission would be required to be made by the code owners.[64] The CompSA will also issue a notification updating all concerned SAs of the position.

50. If the draft code is accepted by the CompSA on the basis of meeting the admissibility criteria, the CompSA should write to the code owners with confirmation that they will proceed to the next stage of the process and assess the draft code's content. This will trigger the following informal cooperation procedure in respect of assessing the code for approval.

8.3 COOPERATION

51. The CompSA will issue a notification updating all SAs[65] of the position, identifying concerned SAs and they will make a request seeking, on a voluntary basis, a maximum of two co-reviewers to assist with the substantive assessment of the draft code. The appointment of co-reviewers will be made on a first come basis.[66] The role of co-reviewers will be to assist the CompSA in assessing the draft code. Once the co-reviewers are confirmed, comments from them on the content of the code should be provided within thirty days from their confirmation as co-reviewers. These comments will then be considered by the CompSA when carrying out its assessment for approval. As per Article 40(7) of the GDPR, the CompSA will make the final determination as to whether the draft decision should be submitted to the Board as per Articles 63 and 64 of the GDPR.[67]

52. The CompSA should aim to arrive at a decision within a reasonable period of time, and it should keep the code owners regularly updated on the progress and indicative timelines. It should outline the basis for its decision (to refuse or to approve a code) in line with the general grounds for approval and communicate that decision in a timely manner to the code owners.

8.4 REFUSAL

53. If the decision made by the CompSA is to refuse referring a draft code to the Board the process will come to an end and it will be a matter for the code owners to analyse the findings of the decision and reconsider revising their draft code. It would also be necessary for the code owners to resubmit the code for an approval at a later stage, if they choose to do so. The CompSA should also notify all concerned SAs of its position and reasons for refusing to approve a code.

8.5 PREPARATION FOR SUBMISSION TO THE BOARD

54. If the CompSA aims to approve the draft code, before submission to the EDPB, the CompSA will circulate its draft approval to all concerned SAs. All concerned SAs will have 30 days to respond and any significant issues could be brought to the relevant EDPB subgroup for discussion. If the concerned SAs do not respond, the code will proceed to the next stage of the process.

8.6 THE BOARD

55. If the decision is to refer the matter to the Board as per Article 40(7) of the GDPR. The CompSA will communicate that decision to all supervisory authorities as per the consistency mechanisms procedure.[68] The CompSA will also refer the matter to the Board in line with its rules of procedure and Article 40(7) of the GDPR.

56. Under Article 64 the Board shall issue an opinion pertaining to matters outlined in Article 40(7) of the GDPR.[69] The Rules of Procedure of the Board together with the provisions of Article 64 will apply to the Board and the CompSA when conducting an assessment and communicating a decision on the approval of transnational codes.

8.7 APPROVAL

57. The opinion of the Board will be communicated to the CompSA as per Article 64(5) of the GDPR and it will be a matter for the CompSA as to whether it will maintain or amend its draft decision as per Article 40(5).[70] An Opinion of the Board may also be submitted to the Commission pursuant to Article 40(8) and the Board, under Article 40(11), will collate all approved transnational codes and make them publicly available.

NOTES

[60] Including amending and extending codes previously approved.

[61] This should be read in the context of the procedure outlined below.

[62] See also Appendix 3 checklist.

[63] This is important as it is envisaged that co-reviewers of the draft code would be supervisory authorities which are concerned by the processing of personal data because the controller or processor is established on the territory of the Member State of that supervisory authority or because "data subjects residing in the Member State of that supervisory authority are substantially affected or likely to be substantially affected by the processing".

[64] It is worth noting that refusal at this stage of the approval process will most likely be based on general or procedural preliminary requirements rather than substantive or core issues associated with the provision of the draft code.

[65] Concerned SAs should be identifiable from the scope of the draft code.

[66] This request will remain open for ten working days. While co-reviewers are being identified, the CompSA will proceed with the assessment. As a rule, the CompSA will consult two co-reviewers whenever 14 Member States or more are concerned by the code. Under this threshold it is possible to have one or two co-reviewers depending on the specific case.

[67] This can only occur where the CompSA aims to approve the draft code. See Article 40(7) and Article 64(1).

[68] See Article 64(4) of the GDPR according to which the views of other supervisory authorities concerned should be presented along with the draft CompSA decision.

[69] See task of Board as per Article 70 (1)(x) of the GDPR.

[70] See Article 64(7) and note the procedures invoked if a CompSA disagrees with the Board's opinion as per Article 64(8) of the GDPR.

9 ENGAGEMENT

[2.284]
58. It is important to note that the assessment process should not serve as an opportunity to further consult on the provisions of the submitted code with the CompSA. The CompSA is tasked, under Article 40(5), to provide an opinion on whether the draft code complies with the GDPR.[71] As such, the communication envisaged between the CompSA and the code owners during this stage of the process will be primarily for the purposes of clarification and to assist in carrying out an evaluation under Article 40 and 41. It is anticipated that code owners will liaise, as appropriate, with supervisory authorities in advance of submitting their draft code for approval. In principle, the approval stage of the process should not invite further consultation by the code owners on particular provisions in the draft code nor should it allow for an extended assessment whereby amendments are continually submitted to the CompSA. It is also imperative that code owners are available to provide answers on points of clarification in respect of their draft code and that they are capable of doing so within a reasonable period of time. It is important that the code owners are prepared and organised to address queries in an efficient and able manner. It is recommended that a single or dedicated point of contact is provided to the CompSA. It will be at the discretion of the CompSA as to whether it needs further information before making its decision on the draft code and it will also have discretion to determine the manner of any communication between the parties. For the purposes of continuity, the CompSA will also remain as the principal point of contact during the entire approval process for transnational codes.

NOTES

[71] The CompSA may also advise and, where relevant, make recommendations to code owners in relation to the content and format of its draft code.

10 THE ROLE OF THE COMMISSION

[2.285]
59. The Commission may decide by way of an implementing Act that an approved transnational code will have general validity within the Union and shall ensure appropriate publicity if it were to do so.[72]

NOTES

[72] See Article 40(9) and Article 40(10). Such a decision would also permit controllers and processors that are not subject to the GPDR to make binding and enforceable commitments regarding a validated code (See Article 40(3)). This would

allow data transfers to third countries or international organisations on the basis that appropriate safeguards are in place and rights and effective legal remedies are available for data subjects (See also Article 46(1) and 46(2)(e)).

11 MONITORING OF A CODE

[2.286]

60. In order for a code (national or transnational) to be approved, a monitoring body (or bodies), must be identified as part of the code and accredited by the CompSA as being capable of effectively monitoring the code.[73] The CompSA will submit its draft requirements for accreditation of a monitoring body to the Board pursuant to the consistency mechanism referred to in Article 63 of the GDPR. Once approved by the Board the requirements can then be applied by the CompSA to accredit a monitoring body.

61. The GDPR does not define the term 'accreditation'. However, Article 41(2) of the GDPR outlines general requirements for the accreditation of the monitoring body. There are a number of requirements which should be met in order to satisfy the CompSA to accredit a monitoring body. Code owners will need to explain and demonstrate how their proposed monitoring body meets the requirements set out in Article 41(2) to obtain accreditation.

62. The GDPR provides flexibility around the type and structure of a monitoring body to be accredited under Article 41. Code owners may decide to use external or internal monitoring bodies provided that in both cases the relevant body meets the accreditation requirements of Article 41(2) as outlined in the eight requirements listed below.

NOTES
[73] GDPR Article 41 (1). Also note that Article 41 does not apply to public authorities or bodies.

12 ACCREDITATION REQUIREMENTS FOR MONITORING BODIES

12.1 INDEPENDENCE

[2.287]

63. The code owners will need to demonstrate that the body concerned is appropriately independent in relation to its impartiality of function from the code members and the profession, industry or sector to which the code applies. Independence could be evidenced through a number of areas such as the monitoring body's funding, appointment of members/staff, decision making process and more generally in terms of its organisational structure. These are considered in more detail below.

64. There are two main models of monitoring which could be used by code owners for fulfilling the monitoring body requirements: external and internal monitoring body. There is some flexibility within these two types of monitoring approaches and different versions could be proposed which are appropriate given the context for the code. Examples of internal monitoring bodies could include an *ad hoc* internal committee or a separate, independent department within the code owner. It will be for the code owners to explain the risk management approach with regard to its impartiality and independence.

65. For instance, where an internal monitoring body is proposed, there should be separate staff and management, accountability and function from other areas of the organisation. This may be achieved in a number of ways, for example, the use of effective organisational and information barriers and separate reporting management structures for the association and monitoring body. Similar to a data protection officer, the monitoring body should be able to act free from instructions and shall be protected from any sort of sanctions or interference (whether direct or indirect) as a consequence of the fulfilment of its task.

66. Independence could require that an external counsel or other party having participated in the drafting of the code of conduct, would need to demonstrate that there were appropriate safeguards in place to sufficiently mitigate a risk of independence or a conflict of interest. The monitoring body would need to provide evidence as to the appropriateness of the mechanisms which would satisfactorily identify and mitigate such risks.[74] A monitoring body will need to identify risks to its impartiality on an ongoing basis, such as its activities or from its relationships. If a risk to impartiality is identified, the monitoring body should demonstrate how it removes or minimises such risk and uses an appropriate mechanism for safeguarding impartiality.

67. Independence could also be demonstrated by showing full autonomy for the management of the budget and other resources, in particular in cases where the monitoring body is internal. A monitoring body would also need to be able to act independently in its choice and application of sanctions against a controller or processor adhering to the code. In essence, the body - either internal or external - will need to act independently from code owners and members within the scope of the code in performing its tasks and exercising its powers.

12.2 CONFLICT OF INTEREST[75]

68. It will need to be demonstrated that the exercise of the monitoring body's tasks and duties do not result in a conflict of interests. As such, code owners will need to demonstrate that the proposed monitoring body will refrain from any action that is incompatible with its tasks and duties and that safeguards are put in place to ensure that will not engage with an incompatible occupation. Similarly, the monitoring body must remain free from external influence, whether direct or indirect, and shall neither seek nor take instructions from any person, organisation or association. The body should have its own staff which are chosen by them or some other body independent of the code and it should be subject to the exclusive direction of those bodies only. In the case of an internal monitoring body, it shall be protected from any sort of sanctions or interference (whether direct or indirect) by the code owner, other relevant bodies,[76] or members of the code as a consequence of the fulfilment of its tasks.

12.3 EXPERTISE

69. The code owners will need to be able to demonstrate that the monitoring body has the requisite level of expertise to carry out its role in an effective manner. As such, the submission will need to include details as to the knowledge and experience of the body in respect of data protection law as well as of the particular sector or processing activity. For example, being able to point to previous experience of acting in a monitoring capacity for a particular sector may assist in meeting this requirement. Furthermore, an in-depth understanding of data protection issues and expert knowledge of the specific processing activities which are the subject matter of the code will be welcomed. The staff of the proposed monitoring body should also have appropriate operational experience and training for carrying out the monitoring of compliance such as in the field of auditing, monitoring, or quality assurance activities.

12.4 ESTABLISHED PROCEDURES AND STRUCTURES

70. A monitoring body will also need to have appropriate governance structures and procedures which allow it to adequately:
- assess for eligibility of controllers and processors to apply the code;
- to monitor compliance with its provisions; and
- to carry out reviews of the code's operation.

71. Comprehensive vetting procedures should be drafted which adequately assess the eligibility of controllers and processors to sign up to and comply with the code. It should also ensure that the provisions of the code are capable of being met by the controllers and processors.

72. Procedures and structures to actively and effectively monitor compliance by members of the code will be required. These could include random or unannounced audits, annual inspections, regular reporting and the use of questionnaires.[77] The monitoring procedures can be designed in different ways as long as they take into account factors such as the risks raised by the data processing in scope of the code, complaints received or specific incidents and the number of members of the code etc. Consideration could be given to the publication of audit reports as well as to the findings of periodic reporting from controllers and processors within the scope of the code.

73. Code owners will also need to demonstrate that the proposed monitoring body have adequate resources and staffing to carry out its tasks in an appropriate manner. Resources should be proportionate to the expected number and size of code members, as well as the complexity or degree of risk of the relevant data processing.

12.5 TRANSPARENT COMPLAINTS HANDLING

74. A monitoring body will need to establish effective procedures and structures which can deal with complaints handling in an impartial and transparent manner. As such, it needs to have a publicly accessible complaints handling process which is sufficiently resourced to manage complaints and to ensure that decisions of the body are made publicly available.

> For example, evidence of a complaints handling procedure could be a described process to receive, evaluate, track, record and resolve complaints. This could be outlined in publicly available guidance for the code so that a complainant can understand and follow the complaints process. Furthermore, the independence of such processes could be assisted by separate operational staff and management functions in the monitoring body.

75. Monitoring bodies should also have effective procedures to ensure compliance with the code by controllers or processors. An example would be to give the monitoring body powers to suspend or exclude a controller or processor from the code when it acts outside the terms of the code (i.e. corrective measures).

76. If a code member breaks the rules of the code, the monitoring body is obliged to take immediate suitable measures. The aim of suitable corrective measures will be to stop the infringement and to avoid future recurrence. Such remedial actions and sanctions could include such measures ranging from training to issuing a warning, report to the Board of the member, a formal notice requiring the implementation of specific actions within a specified deadline, temporary suspension of the member from the code until remedial action is taken to the definitive exclusion of such member from the code. These measures could be publicised by the monitoring body, especially where there are serious infringements of the code.

77. Where required, the monitoring body should be able to inform the code member, the code owner, the CompSA and all concerned SAs about the measures taken and its justification without undue delay.[78] Moreover, in the case where a Lead Supervisory Authority (LSA)[79] for a transnational code member is identifiable, the monitoring body should also appropriately inform the LSA as to its actions.

12.6 COMMUNICATION WITH THE COMPETENT SUPERVISORY AUTHORITY

78. A proposed monitoring body framework needs to allow for the effective communication of any actions carried out by a monitoring body to the CompSA and other supervisory authorities in respect of the code. This could include decisions concerning the actions taken in cases of infringement of the code by a code member, providing periodic reports on the code, or providing review or audit findings of the code.[80]

79. In addition, it will need to ensure that the supervisory authority is not prejudiced or impeded in its role. For example, a code which proposes that its members can unilaterally approve, withdraw or suspend a monitoring body without any notification and agreement with the CompSA would be in contravention of Article 41(5) of the GDPR.

12.7 REVIEW MECHANISMS

80. A code will need to set out appropriate review mechanisms to ensure that the code remains relevant and continues to contribute to the proper application of the GDPR. Review mechanisms should also be put in place to adapt to any changes in the application and interpretation of the law or where there are new technological developments which may have an impact upon the data processing carried out by its members or the provisions of the code.

12.8 LEGAL STATUS

81. The proposed monitoring body (whether internal or external) and related governance structures will need to be formulated in such a manner whereby the code owners can demonstrate that the monitoring body has the appropriate standing to carry out its role under Article 41(4) and is capable of being fined as per Article 83(4)(c) of the GDPR.

NOTES
⁷⁴ The context for the code will determine the approach to take. For example, a proposal where there is an adequate separation of duties, whereby the monitoring body personnel did not write, pilot or test the code may suffice.
⁷⁵ Impartiality of function, i.e. the ability to act autonomously.
⁷⁶ Bodies who represent categories of controllers or processors.
⁷⁷ This could also help prevent a situation whereby members are monitored repeatedly while others are not.
⁷⁸ If the monitoring is carried out by a body outside the association/body that submits the code of conduct, the code owner should also be informed.
⁷⁹ Pursuant to Art. 56 of the GDPR.
⁸⁰ See Article 41(4).

13 APPROVED CODES

[2.288]
82. Clearly the nature and content of the code will determine the roles of the relevant stakeholders in terms of ensuring compliance with the code and the GDPR. However, the CompSA will continue to have a role in ensuring the code remains fit for purpose.

83. The CompSA will therefore work closely with the monitoring body in terms of the reporting requirements arising from the code. The monitoring body will act as the lead contact and coordinator in terms of any issues which may arise in relation to the code.

84. The CompSA would also approve any further amendments or extensions to the code and accredit any new monitoring bodies.⁸¹ As per Article 40(5) of the GDPR, any amendment or extension of an existing code will also have to be submitted a CompSA in line with the procedures outlined in this document.

NOTES
⁸¹ Amendments requiring approval, for example, could include adding a new code rule, but not updating a reference to the name of an organisation, or other minor changes that do not impact on the operation of the code.

14 REVOCATION OF A MONITORING BODY

[2.289]
85. When a monitoring body does not comply with applicable provisions of the GDPR, a CompSA will also have the powers to revoke the accreditation of a monitoring body under Article 41(5).⁸² It is important that the code owner sets out in the Code suitable provisions to address a revocation scenario.

86. However, the consequences of revoking the accreditation of the sole monitoring body for a code may result in the suspension, or permanent withdrawal, of that code due to the loss of the required compliance monitoring. This may adversely affect the reputation or business interests of code members, and may result in a reduction of trust of data subjects or other stakeholders.

87. Where circumstances permit, revocation should only take place after the CompSA has given the monitoring body the opportunity to urgently address issues or make improvements as appropriate within an agreed timescale. In cases which involve transnational codes, the CompSA should, before agreeing to setting parameters with the monitoring body to address the issues raised, liaise with concerned SAs on the matter. The decision to revoke a monitoring body should also be communicated to all concerned SAs and the Board (for the purposes of Article 40(11)).

NOTES
⁸² For transnational codes, it is also essential that the CompSA should ensure that all concerned SAs will be aware of taking such an action. Similarly, for such codes, a concerned SA should also inform the CompSA in cases where a data controller (who is supposed to adopt the code) is found to be non-compliant with it, since this finding may raise concerns on the effectiveness of the monitoring body and the code.

15 PUBLIC SECTOR CODES

[2.290]
88. Article 41(6) of the GDPR provides that the monitoring of approved codes of conduct will not apply

to processing carried out by public authorities or bodies.[83] In essence, this provision removes the requirement for an accredited body to monitor a code. This exemption does not in any way dilute the requirement for the implementation of effective mechanisms to monitor a code. This could be achieved by adapting existing audit requirements to include monitoring of the code.

For the European Data Protection Board

The Chair

(Andrea Jelinek)

NOTES

83 The classification of public sector authorities or bodies is a matter for each member state to determine.

APPENDIX 1 - DISTINCTION BETWEEN NATIONAL AND TRANSNATIONAL CODES

[2.291]
A transnational code refers to a code which relates to processing activities in more than one Member State. As such, a transnational code may relate to processing activities carried out by a multiplicity of controllers or processors in several Member States without necessarily amounting to 'cross-border processing' as defined in Article 4(23) of the GDPR.

Therefore, where a code of conduct adopted by a national association in one Member State covers processing activities by its members in several Member States, it will qualify as a transnational code.

Whereas if an association with a code approved at national level is joined by an international member that conducts cross-border processing, that member could only claim the benefit of the approved code for processing activities in the Member State which approved the code.[84] Mechanisms would need to be put in place to ensure that there is adequate transparency as regards the effective territorial scope of the code.

NOTES

84 However, using the same example, it would also be open to the code owners to consider extending the scope of the code and to seek approval for a transnational code.

APPENDIX 2 - CHOOSING A COMPSA

[2.292]
Code owners may have a choice regarding the identification of a CompSA for the purposes of seeking approval of their transnational draft code.[85] The GDPR does not set out specific rules for identifying the CompSA who is most appropriate to carry out an assessment of a draft code. Nevertheless, to assist code owners in identifying the most appropriate CompSA, to evaluate their code, some of the factors which could be taken into account may include the following[86]:

- The location of the largest density of the processing activity or sector;
- The location of the largest density of data subjects affected by the processing activity or sector;
- The location of the code owner's headquarters;
- The location of the proposed monitoring body's headquarters; or
- The initiatives developed by a supervisory authority in a specific field[87];

Whilst these factors are not prescriptive criteria, the decision of choosing a CompSA is important and should be prudently considered.[88] The CompSA role includes, *inter alia*, acting as a single point of contact with the code owners during the approval process, managing the application procedure in its cooperation phase, accrediting the monitoring body (if relevant) and acting as the supervisory lead in ensuring that an approved code is being monitored effectively.

NOTES

85 See Article 55 in conjunction with Recital 122 of the GDPR.
86 This list is non-exhaustive and non-hierarchical.
87 For example, a Supervisory Authority may have published a detailed and significant policy paper which directly relates to the processing activity which is the subject matter of the code.
88 A submission for approval of a draft code cannot be refused by a CompSA on the basis that none (or only some) of the non-exhaustive list of criteria outlined in Appendix 2 are met. It can only be refused on the basis of not meeting the criteria outlined in the Section entitled 'Admissibility of a Draft Code'.

APPENDIX 3 - CHECKLIST FOR SUBMISSION

[2.293]
Before submitting a draft code to the competent supervisory authority it is important that you ensure the following (where relevant) have been submitted/set out and are appropriately signposted within the documentation:

(1)   Have you provided an explanatory statement and all relevant supporting documentation? (Paragraph 20)
(2)   Are you an association or other body representing categories of controllers or processors? (Paragraph 21)
(3)   Have you provided details in your submission to substantiate that you are an effective representative body that is capable of understanding the needs of your members? (Paragraph 22)
(4)   Have you clearly defined the processing activity or sector and the processing problems to which the code is intended to address? (Paragraph 23)

(5)   Have you identified the territorial scope of your code and included a list of all concerned SAs (where relevant)? (Paragraph 24)

(6)   Have you provided details to justify the identification of the CompSA? (Paragraph 25)

(7)   Have you included mechanisms that allow for the effective monitoring of compliance of the code? (Paragraph 26)

(8)   Have you identified a monitoring body and explained how it will fulfil the code monitoring requirements? (Paragraph 27)

(9)   Have you included information as to the extent of consultation carried out in developing the code? (Paragraph 28)

(10)   Have you provided confirmation that the draft code is compliant with Member State law(s) (where relevant)? (Paragraph 29)

(11)   Have you met the language requirements? (Paragraph 30)

Does your submission include sufficient details to demonstrate the proper application of the GDPR? (Paragraphs 32 – 41)

APPENDIX 4 – TRANSNATIONAL CODE FLOW CHART

[2.294]

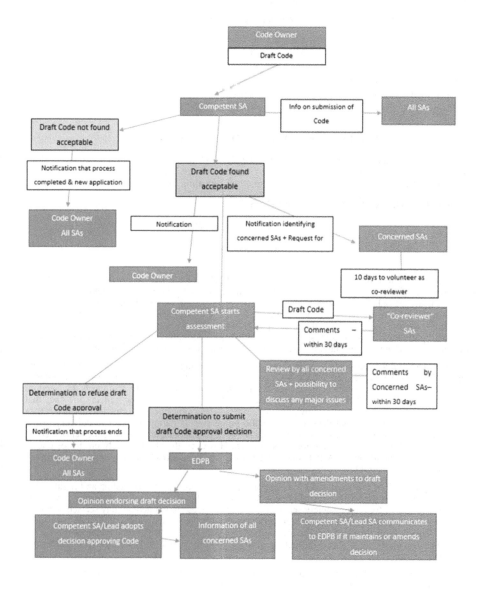

EUROPEAN DATA PROTECTION BOARD: GUIDELINES 2/2019 ON THE PROCESSING OF PERSONAL DATA UNDER ARTICLE 6(1)(B) GDPR IN THE CONTEXT OF THE PROVISION OF ONLINE SERVICES TO DATA SUBJECTS

Version 2.0

8 October 2019

[2.295]

NOTES

© European Data Protection Board.

VERSION HISTORY

Version 2.0: 8 October 2019: Adoption of the Guidelines after public consultation

Version 1.0: 9 April 2019: Adoption of the Guidelines for publication consultation

TABLE OF CONTENTS

THE EUROPEAN DATA PROTECTION BOARD

Having regard to Article 70(1)e of Regulation 2016/679/EU of the European Parliament and of the Council of 27 April 2016 on the protection of natural persons with regard to the processing of personal data and on the free movement of such data, and repealing Directive 95/46/EC,

HAS ADOPTED THE FOLLOWING GUIDELINES

1 PART 1 – INTRODUCTION

1.1 BACKGROUND

[2.296]

1. Pursuant to Article 8 of the Charter of Fundamental Rights of the European Union, personal data must be processed fairly for specified purposes and on the basis of a legitimate basis laid down by law. In this regard, Article 6(1) of the General Data Protection Regulation[1] (GDPR) specifies that processing shall be lawful only on the basis of one of six specified conditions set out in Article 6(1)(a) to (f). Identifying the appropriate legal basis that corresponds to the objective and essence of the processing is of essential importance. Controllers must, *inter alia*, take into account the impact on data subjects' rights when identifying the appropriate lawful basis in order to respect the principle of fairness.

2. Article 6(1)(b) GDPR provides a lawful basis for the processing of personal data to the extent that "processing is necessary for the performance of a contract to which the data subject is party or in order to take steps at the request of the data subject prior to entering into a contract".[2] This supports the freedom to conduct a business, which is guaranteed by Article 16 of the Charter, and reflects the fact that sometimes the contractual obligations towards the data subject cannot be performed without the data subject providing certain personal data. If the specific processing is part and parcel of delivery of the requested service, it is in the interests of both parties to process that data, as otherwise the service could not be provided and the contract could not be performed. However, the ability to rely on this or one of the other legal bases mentioned in Article 6(1) does not exempt the controller from compliance with the other requirements of the GDPR.

3. Articles 56 and 57 of the Treaty on the Functioning of the European Union define and regulate the freedom to provide services within the European Union. Specific EU legislative measures have been adopted in respect of 'information society services'.[3] These services are defined as "any service normally provided for remuneration, at a distance, by electronic means and at the individual request of a recipient of services." This definition extends to services that are not paid for directly by the persons who receive them,[4] such as online services funded through advertising. 'Online services' as used in these guidelines refers to 'information society services'.

4. The development of EU law reflects the central importance of online services in modern society. The proliferation of always-on mobile internet and the widespread availability of connected devices have enabled the development of online services in fields such as social media, e-commerce, internet search, communication, and travel. While some of these services are funded by user payments, others are provided without monetary payment by the consumer, instead financed by the sale of online advertising services allowing for targeting of data subjects. Tracking of user behaviour for the purposes of such advertising is often carried out in ways the user is often not aware of,[5] and it may not be immediately obvious from the nature of the service provided, which makes it almost impossible in practice for the data subject to exercise an informed choice over the use of their data.

5. Against this background, the European Data Protection Board[6] (EDPB) considers it appropriate to provide guidance on the applicability of Article 6(1)(b) to processing of personal data in the context of online services, in order to ensure that this lawful basis is only relied upon where appropriate.

6. The Article 29 Working Party (WP29) has previously expressed views on the contractual necessity basis under Directive 95/46/EC in its opinion on the notion of legitimate interests of the data controller.[7] Generally, that guidance remains relevant to Article 6(1)(b) and the GDPR.

1.2 SCOPE OF THESE GUIDELINES

7. These guidelines are concerned with the applicability of Article 6(1)(b) to processing of personal data in the context of contracts for online services, irrespective of how the services are financed. The guidelines will outline the elements of lawful processing under Article 6(1)(b) GDPR and consider the concept of 'necessity' as it applies to 'necessary for the performance of a contract'.

8. Data protection rules govern important aspects of how online services interact with their users, however, other rules apply as well. Regulation of online services involves cross-functional responsibilities in the fields of, *inter alia*, consumer protection law, and competition law. Considerations regarding these fields of law are beyond the scope of these guidelines.

9. Although Article 6(1)(b) can only apply in a contractual context, these guidelines do not express a view on the validity of contracts for online services generally, as this is outside the competence of the EDPB. Nonetheless, contracts and contractual terms must comply with the requirements of contract laws and, as the case may be for consumer contracts, consumer protection laws in order for processing based on those terms to be considered fair and lawful.

10. Some general observations on data protection principles are included below, but not all data protection issues that may arise when processing under Article 6(1)(b) will be elaborated on. Controllers must always ensure that they comply with the data protection principles set out in Article 5 and all other requirements of the GDPR and, where applicable, the ePrivacy legislation.

NOTES

[1]   Regulation (EU) 2016/679 of the European Parliament and of the Council of 27 April 2016 on the protection of natural persons with regard to the processing of personal data and on the free movement of such data, and repealing Directive 95/46/EC (General Data Protection Regulation).

[2]   See also recital 44.

[3]   See for example Directive (EU) 2015/1535 of the European Parliament and of the Council, and Article 8 GDPR.

[4]   See Recital 18 of Directive 2000/31/EC of the European Parliament and of the Council of 8 June 2000 on certain legal aspects of information society services, in particular electronic commerce, in the Internal Market.

[5]   In this regard, controllers need to fulfil the transparency obligations set out in the GDPR.

[6]   Established under Article 68 GDPR.

[7]   Article 29 Working Party Opinion 06/2014 on the notion of legitimate interests of the data controller under Article 7 of Directive 95/46/EC (WP217). See in particular pages 11, 16, 17, 18 and 55.

2 PART 2 - ANALYSIS OF ARTICLE 6(1)(B)

2.1 GENERAL OBSERVATIONS

[2.297]
11. The lawful basis for processing on the basis of Article 6(1)(b) needs to be considered in the context of the GDPR as a whole, the objectives set out in Article 1, and alongside controllers' duty to process personal data in compliance with the data protection principles pursuant to Article 5. This includes processing personal data in a fair and transparent manner and in line with the purpose limitation and data minimisation obligations.

12. Article 5(1)(a) GDPR provides that personal data must be processed lawfully, fairly and transparently in relation to the data subject. The principle of fairness includes, inter alia, recognising the reasonable expectations[8] of the data subjects, considering possible adverse consequences processing may have on them, and having regard to the relationship and potential effects of imbalance between them and the controller.

13. As mentioned, as a matter of lawfulness, contracts for online services must be valid under the applicable contract law. An example of a relevant factor is whether the data subject is a child. In such a case (and aside from complying with the requirements of the GDPR, including the 'specific protections' which apply to children),[9] the controller must ensure that it complies with the relevant national laws on the capacity of children to enter into contracts. Furthermore, to ensure compliance with the fairness and lawfulness principles, the controller needs to satisfy other legal requirements. For example, for consumer contracts, Directive 93/13/EEC on unfair terms in consumer contracts (the "Unfair Contract Terms Directive") may be applicable.[10] Article 6(1)(b) is not limited to contracts governed by the law of an EEA member state.[11]

14. Article 5(1)(b) of the GDPR provides for the purpose limitation principle, which requires that personal data must be collected for specified, explicit, and legitimate purposes and not further processed in a manner that is incompatible with those purposes.

15. Article 5(1)(c) provides for data minimisation as a principle, i.e. processing as little data as possible in order to achieve the purpose. This assessment complements the necessity assessments pursuant to Article 6(1)(b) to (f).

16. Both purpose limitation and data minimisation principles are particularly relevant in contracts for online services, which typically are not negotiated on an individual basis. Technological advancements make it possible for controllers to easily collect and process more personal data than ever before. As a result, there is an acute risk that data controllers may seek to include general processing terms in contracts in order to maximise the possible collection and uses of data, without adequately specifying those purposes or considering data minimisation obligations. WP29 has previously stated:

> *The purpose of the collection must be clearly and specifically identified: it must be detailed enough to determine what kind of processing is and is not included within the specified purpose, and to allow that compliance with the law can be assessed and data protection safeguards applied. For these reasons, a purpose that is vague or general, such as for instance 'improving users' experience', 'marketing purposes', 'IT-security purposes' or 'future research' will - without more detail - usually not meet the criteria of being 'specific'.[2]*

2.2 INTERACTION OF ARTICLE 6(1)(B) WITH OTHER LAWFUL BASES FOR PROCESSING

17. Where processing is not considered 'necessary for the performance of a contract', i.e. when a requested service can be provided without the specific processing taking place, the EDPB recognises that another lawful basis may be applicable, provided the relevant conditions are met. In particular, in some circumstances it may be more appropriate to rely on freely given consent under Article 6(1)(a). In other instances, Article 6(1)(f) may provide a more appropriate lawful basis for processing. The legal basis must be identified at the outset of processing, and information given to data subjects in line with Articles 13 and 14 must specify the legal basis.

18. It is possible that another lawful basis than Article 6(1)(b) may better match the objective and context of the processing operation in question. The identification of the appropriate lawful basis is tied to principles of fairness and purpose limitation.[13]

19. The WP29 guidelines on consent also clarify that where "a controller seeks to process personal data that are in fact necessary for the performance of a contract, then consent is not the appropriate lawful basis". Conversely, the EDPB considers that where processing is not in fact necessary for the performance of a contract, such processing can take place only if it relies on another appropriate legal basis.[14]

20. In line with their transparency obligations, controllers should make sure to avoid any confusion as to what the applicable legal basis is. This is particularly relevant where the appropriate legal basis is Article 6(1)(b) and a contract regarding online services is entered into by data subjects. Depending on the circumstances, data subjects may erroneously get the impression that they are giving their consent in line with Article 6(1)(a) when signing a contract or accepting terms of service. At the same time, a controller might erroneously assume that the signature of a contract corresponds to a consent in the sense of article 6(1)(a). These are entirely different concepts. It is important to distinguish between accepting terms of service to conclude a contract and giving consent within the meaning of Article 6(1)(a), as these concepts have different requirements and legal consequences.

21. In relation to the processing of special categories of personal data, in the guidelines on consent, WP29 has also observed that:

> *Article 9(2) does not recognize 'necessary for the performance of a contract' as an exception to the general prohibition to process special categories of data. Therefore controllers and Member States that deal with this situation should explore the specific exceptions in Article 9(2) subparagraphs (b) to (j). Should none of the exceptions (b) to (j) apply, obtaining explicit consent in accordance with the conditions for valid consent in the GDPR remains the only possible lawful exception to process such data.[15]*

2.3 SCOPE OF ARTICLE 6(1)(B)

22. Article 6(1)(b) applies where either of two conditions are met: the processing in question must be objectively necessary for the performance of a contract with a data subject, or the processing must be objectively necessary in order to take pre-contractual steps at the request of a data subject.

2.4 NECESSITY

23. Necessity of processing is a prerequisite for both parts of Article 6(1)(b). At the outset, it is important to note that the concept of what is 'necessary for the performance of a contract' is not simply an assessment of what is permitted by or written into the terms of a contract. The concept of necessity has an independent meaning in European Union law, which must reflect the objectives of data protection law.[16] Therefore, it also involves consideration of the fundamental right to privacy and protection of personal data,[17] as well as the requirements of data protection principles including, notably, the fairness principle.

24. The starting point is to identify the purpose for the processing, and in the context of a contractual relationship, there may be a variety of purposes for processing. Those purposes must be clearly specified and communicated to the data subject, in line with the controller's purpose limitation and transparency obligations.

25. Assessing what is 'necessary' involves a combined, fact-based assessment of the processing "for the objective pursued and of whether it is less intrusive compared to other options for achieving the same goal".[18] If there are realistic, less intrusive alternatives, the processing is not 'necessary'.[19] Article 6(1)(b) will not cover processing which is useful but not objectively necessary for performing the contractual service or for taking relevant pre-contractual steps at the request of the data subject, even if it is necessary for the controller's other business purposes.

2.5 NECESSARY FOR PERFORMANCE OF A CONTRACT WITH THE DATA SUBJECT

26. A controller can rely on the first option of Article 6(1)(b) to process personal data when it can, in line with its accountability obligations under Article 5(2), establish both that the processing takes place in the context of a valid contract with the data subject and that processing is necessary in order that the *particular contract* with the data subject can be performed. Where controllers cannot demonstrate that (a) a contract exists, (b) the contract is valid pursuant to applicable national contract laws, and (c) that the processing is objectively necessary for the performance of the contract, the controller should consider another legal basis for processing.

27. Merely referencing or mentioning data processing in a contract is not enough to bring the processing in question within the scope of Article 6(1)(b). On the other hand, processing may be objectively necessary even if not specifically mentioned in the contract. In any case, the controller must meet its transparency obligations. Where a controller seeks to establish that the processing is based on the performance of a contract with the data subject, it is important to assess what is *objectively necessary* to perform the contract. 'Necessary for performance' clearly requires something more than a contractual clause. This is also clear in light of Article 7(4). Albeit this provision only regards validity of consent, it illustratively makes a distinction between processing activities necessary for the performance of a contract, and *clauses* making the service conditional on certain processing activities that are not in fact necessary for the performance of the contract.

28. In this regard, the EDPB endorses the guidance previously adopted by WP29 on the equivalent provision under the previous Directive that 'necessary for the performance of a contract with the data subject':

> . . . *must be interpreted strictly and does not cover situations where the processing is not genuinely necessary for the performance of a contract, but rather unilaterally imposed on the data subject by the controller. Also the fact that some processing is covered by a contract does not automatically mean that the processing is necessary for its performance. [. . .] Even if these processing activities are specifically mentioned in the small print of the contract, this fact alone does not make them 'necessary' for the performance of the contract.*[20]

29. The EDPB also recalls the same WP29 guidance stating:

> *There is a clear connection here between the assessment of necessity and compliance with the purpose limitation principle. It is important to determine the exact rationale of the contract, i.e. its substance and fundamental objective, as it is against this that it will be tested whether the data processing is necessary for its performance.*[21]

30. When assessing whether Article 6(1)(b) is an appropriate legal basis for processing in the context of an online contractual service, regard should be given to the particular aim, purpose, or objective of the service. For applicability of Article 6(1)(b), it is required that the processing is *objectively necessary* for a purpose that is integral to the delivery of that contractual service to the data subject. Not excluded is processing of payment details for the purpose of charging for the service. The controller should be able to demonstrate how the main subject-matter of the *specific contract with the data subject* cannot, as a matter of fact, be performed if the specific processing of the *personal data in question* does not occur. The important issue here is the nexus between the personal data and processing operations concerned, and the performance or non-performance of the service provided under the contract.

31. Contracts for digital services may incorporate express terms that impose additional conditions about advertising, payments or cookies, amongst other things. A contract cannot artificially expand the categories of personal data or types of processing operation that the controller needs to carry out for the performance of the contract within the meaning of Article 6(1)(b).

32. The controller should be able to justify the necessity of its processing by reference to the fundamental and mutually understood contractual purpose. This depends not just on the controller's perspective, but also a reasonable data subject's perspective when entering into the contract, and whether the contract can still be considered to be 'performed' without the processing in question. Although the controller may consider that the processing is necessary for the contractual purpose, it is important that they examine carefully the perspective of an average data subject in order to ensure that there is a genuine mutual understanding on the contractual purpose.

33. In order to carry out the assessment of whether Article 6(1)(b) is applicable, the following questions can be of guidance:
- What is the nature of the service being provided to the data subject? What are its distinguishing characteristics?
- What is the exact rationale of the contract (i.e. its substance and fundamental object)?
- What are the essential elements of the contract?
- What are the mutual perspectives and expectations of the parties to the contract? How is the service promoted or advertised to the data subject? Would an ordinary user of the service reasonably expect that, considering the nature of the service, the envisaged processing will take place in order to perform the contract to which they are a party?

34. If the assessment of what is 'necessary for the performance of a contract', which must be conducted prior to the commencement of processing, shows that the intended processing goes beyond what is objectively necessary for the performance of a contract, this does not render such future processing unlawful per se. As already mentioned, Article 6 makes clear that other lawful bases are potentially available prior to the initiation of the processing.[22]

35. If, over the lifespan of a service, new technology is introduced that changes how personal data are processed, or the service otherwise evolves, the criteria above need to be assessed anew to determine if any new or altered processing operations can be based on Article 6(1)(b).

Example 1

A data subject buys items from an online retailer. The data subject wants to pay by credit card and for the products to be delivered to their home address. In order to fulfil the contract, the retailer must process the data subject's credit card information and billing address for payment purposes and the data subject's home address for delivery. Thus, Article 6(1)(b) is applicable as a legal basis for these processing activities.

However, if the customer has opted for shipment to a pick-up point, the processing of the data subject's home address is no longer necessary for the performance of the purchase contract. Any processing of the data subject's address in this context will require a different legal basis than Article 6(1)(b).

Example 2

The same online retailer wishes to build profiles of the user's tastes and lifestyle choices based on their visits to the website. Completion of the purchase contract is not dependent upon building such profiles. Even if profiling is specifically mentioned in the contract, this fact alone does not make it 'necessary' for the performance of the contract. If the on-line retailer wants to carry out such profiling, it needs to rely on a different legal basis.

---

36. Within the boundaries of contractual law, and if applicable, consumer law, controllers are free to design their business, services and contracts. In some cases, a controller may wish to bundle several separate services or elements of a service with different fundamental purposes, features or rationale into one contract. This may create a 'take it or leave it' situation for data subjects who may only be interested in one of the services.

37. As a matter of data protection law, controllers need to take into account that the processing activities foreseen must have an appropriate legal basis. Where the contract consists of several separate services or elements of a service that can in fact reasonably be performed independently of one another, the question arises to which extent Article 6(1)(b) can serve as a legal basis. The applicability of Article 6(1)(b) should be assessed in the context of each of those services *separately*, looking at what is objectively necessary to perform each of the individual services which the data subject has actively requested or signed up for. This assessment may reveal that certain processing activities are not necessary for the individual services requested by the data subject, but rather necessary for the controller's wider business model. In that case, Article 6(1)(b) will not be a legal basis for those activities. However, other legal bases may be available for that processing, such as Article 6(1)(a) or (f), provided that the relevant criteria are met. Therefore, the assessment of the applicability of Article 6(1)(b) does not affect the legality of the contract or the bundling of services as such.

38. As WP29 has previously observed, the legal basis only applies to what is necessary for the *performance* of a contract.[23] As such, it does not automatically apply to all further actions triggered by non-compliance or to all other incidents in the execution of a contract. However, certain actions can be reasonably foreseen and necessary within a normal contractual relationship, such as sending formal reminders about outstanding payments or correcting errors or delays in the performance of the contract. Article 6(1)(b) may cover processing of personal data which is necessary in relation to such actions.

Example 3

A company sells products online. A customer contacts the company because the colour of the product purchased is different from what was agreed upon. The processing of personal data of the customer for the purpose of rectifying this issue can be based on Article 6(1)(b).

---

39. Contractual warranty may be part of performing a contract, and thus storing certain data for a specified retention time after exchange of goods/services/payment has been finalised for the purpose of warranties may be necessary for the performance of a contract.

2.6 TERMINATION OF CONTRACT

40. A controller needs to identify the appropriate legal basis for the envisaged processing operations before the processing commences. Where Article 6(1)(b) is the basis for some or all processing activities, the controller should anticipate what happens if that contract is terminated.[24]

41. Where the processing of personal data is based on Article 6(1)(b) and the contract is terminated in full, then as a general rule, the processing of that data will no longer be necessary for the performance of that contract and thus the controller will need to stop processing. The data subject might have provided their personal data in the context of a contractual relationship trusting that the data would only be processed as a necessary part of that relationship. Hence, it is generally unfair to swap to a new legal basis when the original basis ceases to exist.

42. When a contract is terminated, this may entail some administration, such as returning goods or payment. The associated processing may be based on Article 6(1)(b).

43. Article 17(1)(a) provides that personal data shall be erased when they are no longer necessary in relation to the purposes for which they were collected. Nonetheless, this does not apply if processing is necessary for certain specific purposes, including compliance with a legal obligation pursuant to Article 17(3)(b), or the establishment, exercise or defence of legal claims, pursuant to Article 17(3)(e). In practice, if controllers see a general need to keep records for legal purposes, they need to identify a legal basis for this at the outset of processing, and they need to communicate clearly from the start for how long they plan to retain records for these legal purposes after the termination of a contract. If they do so, they do not need to delete the data upon the termination of the contract.

44. In any case, it may be that several processing operations with separate purposes and legal bases were identified at the outset of processing. As long as those other processing operations remain lawful and the controller communicated clearly about those operations at the commencement of processing in line with the transparency obligations of the GDPR, it will still be possible to process personal data about the data subject for those separate purposes after the contract has been terminated.

Example 4

An online service provides a subscription service that can be cancelled at any time. When a contract for the service is concluded, the controller provides information to the data subject on the processing of personal data.

The controller explains, *inter alia*, that as long as the contract is in place, it will process data about the use of the service to issue invoices. The applicable legal basis is Article 6(1)(b) as the processing for invoicing purposes can be considered to be objectively necessary for the performance of the contract. However, when the contract is terminated and assuming there are no pending, relevant legal claims or legal requirements to retain the data, the usage history will be deleted.

Furthermore, the controller informs data subjects that it has a legal obligation in national law to retain certain personal data for accounting purposes for a specified number of years. The appropriate legal basis is Article 6(1)(c), and retention will take place even if the contract is terminated.

2.7 NECESSARY FOR TAKING STEPS PRIOR TO ENTERING INTO A CONTRACT

45. The second option of Article 6(1)(b) applies where *processing is necessary in order to take steps at the request of the data subject prior to entering into a contract*. This provision reflects the fact that preliminary processing of personal data may be necessary before entering into a contract in order to facilitate the actual entering into that contract.

46. At the time of processing, it may not be clear whether a contract will actually be entered into. The second option of Article 6(1)(b) may nonetheless apply as long as the data subject makes the request in the context of *potentially* entering into a contract and the processing in question is necessary to take the steps requested. In line with this, where a data subject contacts the controller to enquire about the details of the controller's service offerings, the processing of the data subject's personal data for the purpose of responding to the enquiry can be based on Article 6(1)(b).

47. In any case, this provision would not cover unsolicited marketing or other processing which is carried out solely on the initiative of the data controller, or at the request of a third party.

Example 5

A data subject provides their postal code to see if a particular service provider operates in their area. This can be regarded as processing necessary to take steps at the request of the data subject prior to entering into a contract pursuant to Article 6(1)(b).

Example 6

In some cases, financial institutions have a duty to identify their customers pursuant to national laws. In line with this, before entering into a contract with data subjects, a bank requests to see their identity documents. In this case, the identification is necessary for a legal obligation on behalf of the bank rather than to take steps at the data subject's request. Therefore, the appropriate legal basis is not Article 6(1)(b), but Article 6(1)(c).

NOTES

[8] Some personal data are expected to be private or only processed in certain ways, and data processing should not be surprising to the data subject. In the GDPR, the concept of 'reasonable expectations' is specifically referenced in recitals 47 and 50 in relation to Article 6(1)(f) and (4).

⁹ See Recital 38, which refers to children meriting specific protection with regard to their personal data as they may be less aware of the risks, consequences and safeguards concerned and their rights in relation to the processing of personal data.

¹⁰ A contractual term that has not been individually negotiated is unfair under the Unfair Contract Terms Directive "if, contrary to the requirement of good faith, it causes a significant imbalance in the parties' rights and obligations arising under the contract, to the detriment of the consumer". Like the transparency obligation in the GDPR, the Unfair Contract Terms Directive mandates the use of plain, intelligible language. Processing of personal data that is based on what is deemed to be an unfair term under the Unfair Contract Terms Directive, will generally not be consistent with the requirement under Article 5(1)(a) GDPR that processing is lawful and fair.

¹¹ The GDPR applies to certain controllers outside the EEA; see Article 3 GDPR.

¹² Article 29 Working Party Opinion 03/2013 on purpose limitation (WP203), page 15–16.

¹³ When controllers set out to identify the appropriate legal basis in line with the fairness principle, this will be difficult to achieve if they have not first clearly identified the purposes of processing, or if processing personal data goes beyond what is necessary for the specified purposes.

¹⁴ For more information on implications in relation to Article 9, see Article 29 Working Party Guidelines on consent under Regulation 2016/679 (WP259), endorsed by the EDPB, pages 19–20.

¹⁵ Article 29 Working Party Guidelines on consent under Regulation 2016/679 (WP259), endorsed by the EDPB, page 19.

¹⁶ The CJEU stated in *Huber* that "what is at issue is a concept [necessity] which has its own independent meaning in Community law and which must be interpreted in a manner which fully reflects the objective of that Directive, [Directive 95/46], as laid down in Article 1(1) thereof". CJEU, Case C-524/06, *Heinz Huber v Bundesrepublik Deutschland*, 18 December 2008, para. 52.

¹⁷ See Articles 7 and 8 of the Charter of Fundamental Rights of the European Union

¹⁸ See EDPS Toolkit: Assessing the Necessity of Measures that limit the fundamental right to the protection of personal data, page 5.

¹⁹ In *Schecke*, the CJEU held that, when examining the necessity of processing personal data, the legislature needed to take into account alternative, less intrusive measures. CJEU, Joined Cases C-92/09 and C-93/09, *Volker und Markus Schecke GbR and Hartmut Eifert v Land Hessen*, 9. November 2010. This was repeated by the CJEU in the *Rigas* case where it held that "As regards the condition relating to the necessity of processing personal data, it should be borne in mind that derogations and limitations in relation to the protection of personal data must apply only in so far as is strictly necessary". CJEU, Case C-13/16, *Valsts policijas Rigas regiona parvaldes Kartibas policijas parvalde v Rigas pašvaldibas SIA 'Rigas satiksme'*, para. 30. A strict necessary test is required for any limitations on the exercise of the rights to privacy and to personal data protection with regard to the processing of personal data, see EDPS Toolkit: Assessing the Necessity of Measures that limit the fundamental right to the protection of personal data, page 7.

²⁰ Article 29 Working Party Opinion 06/2014 on the notion of legitimate interests of the data controller under Article 7 of Directive 95/46/EC (WP217), page 16–17.

²¹ Ibid., page 17.

²² See Article 29 Working Party Guidelines on consent under Regulation 2016/679 (WP259), endorsed by the EDPB, page 31, in which it is stated that: "Under the GDPR, it is not possible to swap between one lawful basis and another."

²³ Article 29 Working Party Opinion 06/2014 on the notion of legitimate interests of the data controller under Article 7 of Directive 95/46/EC (WP217) page 17–18.

²⁴ If a contract is subsequently invalidated, it will impact the lawfulness (as understood in Article 5(1)(a)) of continued processing. However, it does not automatically imply that the choice of Article 6(1)(b) as the legal basis was incorrect.

3 PART 3 – APPLICABILITY OF ARTICLE 6(1)(B) IN SPECIFIC SITUATIONS

3.1 PROCESSING FOR 'SERVICE IMPROVEMENT'[25]

[2.298]
48. Online services often collect detailed information on how users engage with their service. In most cases, collection of organisational metrics relating to a service or details of user engagement, cannot be regarded as necessary for the provision of the service as the service could be delivered in the absence of processing such personal data. Nevertheless, a service provider may be able to rely on alternative lawful bases for this processing, such as legitimate interest or consent.

49. The EDPB does not consider that Article 6(1)(b) would generally be an appropriate lawful basis for processing for the purposes of improving a service or developing new functions within an existing service. In most cases, a user enters into a contract to avail of an existing service. While the possibility of improvements and modifications to a service may routinely be included in contractual terms, such processing usually cannot be regarded as being objectively necessary for the performance of the contract with the user.

3.2 PROCESSING FOR 'FRAUD PREVENTION'

50. As WP29 has previously noted,[26] processing for fraud prevention purposes may involve monitoring and profiling customers. In the view of the EDPB, such processing is likely to go beyond what is objectively necessary for the performance of a contract with a data subject. However, the processing of personal data strictly necessary for the purposes of preventing fraud may constitute a legitimate interest of the data controller[27] and could thus be considered lawful, if the specific requirements of Article 6(1)(f)(legitimate interests) are met by the data controller. In addition Article 6(1)(c) (legal obligation) could also provide a lawful basis for such processing of data.

3.3 PROCESSING FOR ONLINE BEHAVIOURAL ADVERTISING

51. Online behavioural advertising, and associated tracking and profiling of data subjects, is often used to finance online services. WP29 has previously stated its view on such processing, stating:

[contractual necessity] is not a suitable legal ground for building a profile of the user's tastes and lifestyle choices based on his clickstream on a website and the items purchased. This is because the data controller has not been contracted to carry out profiling, but rather to deliver particular goods and services, for example.[28]

52.   As a general rule, processing of personal data for behavioural advertising is not necessary for the performance of a contract for online services. Normally, it would be hard to argue that the contract had not been performed because there were no behavioural ads. This is all the more supported by the fact that data subjects have the absolute right under Article 21 to object to processing of their data for direct marketing purposes.

53.   Further to this, Article 6(1)(b) cannot provide a lawful basis for online behavioural advertising simply because such advertising indirectly funds the provision of the service. Although such processing may support the delivery of a service, this in itself is not sufficient to establish that it is necessary for the performance of the contract at issue. The controller would need to consider the factors outlined in paragraph 33.

54.   Considering that data protection is a fundamental right guaranteed by Article 8 of the Charter of Fundamental Rights, and taking into account that one of the main purposes of the GDPR is to provide data subjects with control over information relating to them, personal data cannot be considered as a tradeable commodity. Even if the data subject can agree to the processing of personal data,[29] they cannot trade away their fundamental rights through this agreement.[30]

55.   The EDPB also notes that, in line with ePrivacy requirements and the existing WP29 opinion on behavioural advertising,[31] and Working Document 02/2013 providing guidance on obtaining consent for cookies,[32] controllers must obtain data subjects' prior consent to place the cookies necessary to engage in behavioural advertising.

56.   The EDPB also notes that tracking and profiling of users may be carried out for the purpose of identifying groups of individuals with similar characteristics, to enable targeting advertising to similar audiences. Such processing cannot be carried out on the basis of Article 6(1)(b), as it cannot be said to be objectively necessary for the performance of the contract with the user to track and compare users' characteristics and behaviour for purposes which relate to advertising to other individuals.[33]

3.4 PROCESSING FOR PERSONALISATION OF CONTENT[34]

57.   The EDPB acknowledges that personalisation of content may (but does not always) constitute an intrinsic and expected element of certain online services, and therefore may be regarded as necessary for the performance of the contract with the service user in some cases. Whether such processing can be regarded as an intrinsic aspect of an online service, will depend on the nature of the service provided, the expectations of the average data subject in light not only of the terms of service but also the way the service is promoted to users, and whether the service can be provided without personalisation. Where personalisation of content is not objectively necessary for the purpose of the underlying contract, for example where personalised content delivery is intended to increase user engagement with a service but is not an integral part of using the service, data controllers should consider an alternative lawful basis where applicable.

Example 7

An online hotel search engine monitors past bookings of users in order to create a profile of their typical expenditure. This profile is subsequently used to recommend particular hotels to the user when returning search results. In this case, profiling of user's past behaviour and financial data would not be objectively necessary for the performance of a contract, i.e. the provision of hospitality services based on particular search criteria provided by the user. Therefore, Article 6(1)(b) would not be applicable to this processing activity.

Example 8

An online marketplace allows potential buyers to browse for and purchase products. The marketplace wishes to display personalised product suggestions based on which listings the potential buyers have previously viewed on the platform in order to increase interactivity. This personalisation it is not objectively necessary to provide the marketplace service. Thus, such processing of personal data cannot rely on Article 6(1)(b) as a legal basis.

NOTES

[25]   Online services may also need to take into account Directive (EU) 2019/770 of the European Parliament and of the Council of 20 May 2019 on certain aspects concerning contracts for the supply of digital content and digital services (OJ L 136, 22.05.2019, p. 1), which will apply as from 1 January 2022.

[26]   Article 29 Working Party Opinion 06/2014 on the notion of legitimate interests of the data controller under Article 7 of Directive 95/46/EC (WP217), page 17.

[27]   See Recital 47, sixth sentence.

[28]   Article 29 Working Party Opinion 06/2014 on the notion of legitimate interests of the data controller under Article 7 of Directive 95/46/EC (WP217), page 17.

29   See Directive (EU) 2019/770 of the European Parliament and of the Council of 20 May 2019 on certain aspects concerning contracts for the supply of digital content and digital services.

30   Besides the fact that the use of personal data is regulated by the GDPR, there are additional reasons why processing of personal data is conceptually different from monetary payments. For example, money is countable, meaning that prices can be compared in a competitive market, and monetary payments can normally only be made with the data subject's involvement. Furthermore, personal data can be exploited by several services at the same time. Once control over one's personal data has been lost, that control may not necessarily be regained.

31   Article 29 Working Party Opinion 2/2010 on online behavioural advertising (WP171).

32   Article 29 Working Party Working Document 02/2013 providing guidance on obtaining consent for cookies (WP208).

33   See also Article 29 Working Party Guidelines on Automated individual decision-making and Profiling for the purposes of Regulation 2016/679 (WP251rev.01), endorsed by the EDPB, page 13.

34   Online services may also need to take into account Directive (EU) 2019/770 of the European Parliament and of the Council of 20 May 2019 on certain aspects concerning contracts for the supply of digital content and digital services (OJ L 136, 22.05.2019, p. 1), which will apply as from 1 January 2022.

EUROPEAN DATA PROTECTION BOARD: GUIDELINES 3/2019 ON PROCESSING OF PERSONAL DATA THROUGH VIDEO DEVICES
Version 2.0

Adopted on 29 January 2020

[2.299]

NOTES
© European Data Protection Board.

VERSION HISTORY

Version 2.1: 26 February 2020: Amending material mistake

Version 2.0: 29 January 2020: Adoption of the Guidelines after public consultation

Version 1.0: 10 July 2019: Adoption of the Guidelines for public consultation

TABLE OF CONTENTS

THE EUROPEAN DATA PROTECTION BOARD

Having regard to Article 70 (1e) of the Regulation 2016/679/EU of the European Parliament and of the Council of 27 April 2016 on the protection of natural persons with regard to the processing of personal data and on the free movement of such data, and repealing Directive 95/46/EC, (hereinafter "GDPR"),

Having regard to the EEA Agreement and in particular to Annex XI and Protocol 37 thereof, as amended by the Decision of the EEA joint Committee No 154/2018 of 6 July 2018[1],

Having regard to Article 12 and Article 22 of its Rules of Procedure,

HAS ADOPTED THE FOLLOWING GUIDELINES

NOTES
1   References to "Member States" made throughout this opinion should be understood as references to "EEA Member States".

1 INTRODUCTION

[2.300]
1.   The intensive use of video devices has an impact on citizen's behaviour. Significant implementation

of such tools in many spheres of the individuals' life will put an additional pressure on the individual to prevent the detection of what might be perceived as anomalies. De facto, these technologies may limit the possibilities of anonymous movement and anonymous use of services and generally limit the possibility of remaining unnoticed. Data protection implications are massive.

2. While individuals might be comfortable with video surveillance set up for a certain security purpose for example, guarantees must be taken to avoid any misuse for totally different and – to the data subject – unexpected purposes (e.g. marketing purpose, employee performance monitoring etc.). In addition, many tools are now implemented to exploit the images captured and turn traditional cameras into smart cameras. The amount of data generated by the video, combined with these tools and techniques increase the risks of secondary use (whether related or not to the purpose originally assigned to the system) or even the risks of misuse. The general principles in GDPR (Article 5), should always be carefully considered when dealing with video surveillance.

3. Video surveillance systems in many ways change the way professionals from the private and public sector interact in private or public places for the purpose of enhancing security, obtaining audience analysis, delivering personalized advertising, etc. Video surveillance has become high performing through the growing implementation of intelligent video analysis. These techniques can be more intrusive (e.g. complex biometric technologies) or less intrusive (e.g. simple counting algorithms). Remaining anonymous and preserving one's privacy is in general increasingly difficult. The data protection issues raised in each situation may differ, so will the legal analysis when using one or the other of these technologies.

4. In addition to privacy issues, there are also risks related to possible malfunctions of these devices and the biases they may induce. Researchers report that software used for facial identification, recognition, or analysis performs differently based on the age, gender, and ethnicity of the person it's identifying.

Algorithms would perform based on different demographics, thus, bias in facial recognition threatens to reinforce the prejudices of society. That is why data controllers must also ensure that biometric data processing deriving from video surveillance be subject to regular assessment of its relevance and sufficiency of guarantees provided.

5. Video surveillance is not by default a necessity when there are other means to achieve the underlying purpose. Otherwise we risk a change in cultural norms leading to the acceptance of lack of privacy as the general outset.

6. These guidelines aim at giving guidance on how to apply the GDPR in relation to processing personal data through video devices. The examples are not exhaustive, the general reasoning can be applied to all potential areas of use.

2 SCOPE OF APPLICATION[2]

2.1 PERSONAL DATA

[2.301]
7. Systematic automated monitoring of a specific space by optical or audio-visual means, mostly for property protection purposes, or to protect individual's life and health, has become a significant phenomenon of our days. This activity brings about collection and retention of pictorial or audio-visual information on all persons entering the monitored space that are identifiable on basis of their looks or other specific elements. Identity of these persons may be established on grounds of these details. It also enables further processing of personal data as to the persons' presence and behaviour in the given space. The potential risk of misuse of these data grows in relation to the dimension of the monitored space as well as to the number of persons frequenting the space. This fact is reflected by the General Data Protection Regulation in the Article 35 (3)(c) which requires the carrying out of a data protection impact assessment in case of a systematic monitoring of a publicly accessible area on a large scale, as well as in Article 37 (1)(b) which requires processors to designate a data protection officer, if the processing operation by its nature entails regular and systematic monitoring of data subjects.

8. However, the Regulation does not apply to processing of data that has no reference to a person, e.g. if an individual cannot be identified, directly or indirectly.

---

9. <u>Example</u>: The GDPR is not applicable for fake cameras (i.e. any camera that is not functioning as a camera and thereby is not processing any personal data). *However, in some Member States it might be subject to other legislation.*

<u>Example</u>: Recordings from a high altitude only fall under the scope of the GDPR if under the circumstances the data processed can be related to a specific person.

<u>Example</u>: A video camera is integrated in a car for providing parking assistance. If the camera is constructed or adjusted in such a way that it does not collect any information relating to a natural person (such as licence plates or information which could identify passers-by) the GDPR does not apply.

2.2 APPLICATION OF THE LAW ENFORCEMENT DIRECTIVE, LED (EU2016/680)

10. Notably processing of personal data by competent authorities for the purposes of prevention, investigation, detection or prosecution of criminal offences or the execution of criminal penalties, including the safeguarding against and the prevention of threats to public security, falls under the directive EU2016/680.

2.3 HOUSEHOLD EXEMPTION

11. Pursuant to Article 2 (2)(c), the processing of personal data by a natural person in the course of a purely personal or household activity, which can also include online activity, is out of the scope of the GDPR.[3]

12. This provision – the so-called household exemption – in the context of video surveillance must be narrowly construed. Hence, as considered by the European Court of Justice, the so called "household exemption" must *"be interpreted as relating only to activities which are carried out in the course of private or family life of individuals, which is clearly not the case with the processing of personal data consisting in publication on the internet so that those data are made accessible to an indefinite number of people"*.[4] Furthermore, if a video surveillance system, to the extent it involves the constant recording and storage of personal data and covers, *"even partially, a public space and is accordingly directed outwards from the private setting of the person processing the data in that manner, it cannot be regarded as an activity which is a purely 'personal or household' activity for the purposes of the second indent of Article 3(2) of Directive 95/46"*[5].

13. What regards video devices operated inside a private person's premises, it may fall under the household exemption. It will depend on several factors, which all have to be considered in order to reach a conclusion. Besides the above mentioned elements identified by ECJ rulings, the user of video surveillance at home needs to look at whether he has some kind of personal relationship with the data subject, whether the scale or frequency of the surveillance suggests some kind of professional activity on his side, and of the surveillance's potential adverse impact on the data subjects. The presence of any single one of the aforementioned elements does not necessarily suggest that the processing is outside the scope of the household exemption, an overall assessment is needed for that determination.

---

14. Example: A tourist is recording videos both through his mobile phone and through a camcorder to document his holidays. He shows the footage to friends and family but does not make it accessible for an indefinite number of people. This would fall under the household exemption.

Example: A downhill mountain biker wants to record her descent with an actioncam. She is riding in a remote area and only plans to use the recordings for her personal entertainment at home. This would fall under the household exemption even if to some extent personal data is processed.

Example: Somebody is monitoring and recording his own garden. The property is fenced and only the controller himself and his family are entering the garden on a regular basis. This would fall under the household exemption, provided that the video surveillance does not extend even partially to a public space or neighbouring property.

NOTES

2 The EDPB notes that where the GDPR so allows, specific requirements in national legislation might apply.

3 See also Recital 18.

4 European Court of Justice, Judgment in Case C-101/01, *Bodil Lindqvist case*, 6th November 2003, para 47.

5 European Court of Justice, Judgment in Case C-212/13, *František Ryneš v Úřad pro ochranu osobních údajů*, 11 December 2014, para. 33.

---

3 LAWFULNESS OF PROCESSING

[2.302]
15. Before use, the purposes of processing have to be specified in detail (Article 5 (1)(b)). Video surveillance can serve many purposes, e.g. supporting the protection of property and other assets, supporting the protection of life and physical integrity of individuals, collecting evidence for civil claims.[6] These monitoring purposes should be documented in writing (Article 5 (2)) and need to be specified for every surveillance camera in use. Cameras that are used for the same purpose by a single controller can be documented together. Furthermore, data subjects must be informed of the purpose(s) of the processing in accordance with Article 13 (*see section 7, Transparency and information obligations*). Video surveillance based on the mere purpose of "safety" or "for your safety" is not sufficiently specific (Article 5 (1)(b)). It is furthermore contrary to the principle that personal data shall be processed lawfully, fairly and in a transparent manner in relation to the data subject (see Article 5 (1)(a)).

16. In principle, every legal ground under Article 6 (1) can provide a legal basis for processing video surveillance data. For example, Article 6 (1)(c) applies where national law stipulates an obligation to carry out video surveillance.[7] However in practice, the provisions most likely to be used are
• Article 6 (1)(f) (legitimate interest),
• Article 6 (1)(e) (necessity to perform a task carried out in the public interest or in the exercise of official authority).
In rather exceptional cases Article 6 (1)(a) (consent) might be used as a legal basis by the controller.

3.1 LEGITIMATE INTEREST, ARTICLE 6 (1)(F)

17. The legal assessment of Article 6 (1)(f) should be based on the following criteria in compliance with Recital 47.

3.1.1 Existence of legitimate interests

18. Video surveillance is lawful if it is necessary in order to meet the purpose of a legitimate interest pursued by a controller or a third party, unless such interests are overridden by the data subject's interests or fundamental rights and freedoms (Article 6 (1)(f)). Legitimate interests pursued by a controller or a third party can be legal[8], economic or non-material interests.[9] However, the controller should consider that if the data subject objects to the surveillance in accordance with Article 21 the controller can only proceed with the video surveillance of that data subject if it is a compelling legitimate interest which overrides the interests, rights and freedoms of the data subject or for the establishment, exercise or defence of legal claims.

19.   Given a real and hazardous situation, the purpose to protect property against burglary, theft or vandalism can constitute a legitimate interest for video surveillance.

20.   The legitimate interest needs to be of real existence and has to be a present issue (i.e. it must not be fictional or speculative)[10]. A real-life situation of distress needs to be at hand – such as damages or serious incidents in the past – before starting the surveillance. In light of the principle of accountability, controllers would be well advised to document relevant incidents (date, manner, financial loss) and related criminal charges. Those documented incidents can be a strong evidence for the existence of a legitimate interest. The existence of a legitimate interest as well as the necessity of the monitoring should be reassessed in periodic intervals (e. g. once a year, depending on the circumstances).

---

21.   Example: A shop owner wants to open a new shop and wants to install a video surveillance system to prevent vandalism. He can show, by presenting statistics, that there is a high expectation of vandalism in the near neighbourhood. Also, experience from neighbouring shops is useful. It is not necessary that a damage to the controller in question must have occurred. As long as damages in the neighbourhood suggest a danger or similar, and thus can be an indication of a legitimate interest. It is however not sufficient to present national or general crime statistic without analysing the area in question or the dangers for this specific shop.

---

22.   Imminent danger situations may constitute a legitimate interest, such as banks or shops selling precious goods (e.g. jewellers), or areas that are known to be typical crime scenes for property offences (e. g. petrol stations).

23.   The GDPR also clearly states that public authorities cannot rely their processing on the grounds of legitimate interest, as long as they are carrying out their tasks, Article 6 (1) sentence 2.

3.1.2 Necessity of processing

24.   Personal data should be adequate, relevant and limited to what is necessary in relation to the purposes for which they are processed ('data minimisation'), see Article 5 (1)(c). Before installing a video-surveillance system the controller should always critically examine if this measure is firstly suitable to attain the desired goal, and secondly adequate and necessary for its purposes. Video surveillance measures should only be chosen if the purpose of the processing could not reasonably be fulfilled by other means which are less intrusive to the fundamental rights and freedoms of the data subject.

25.   Given the situation that a controller wants to prevent property related crimes, instead of installing a video surveillance system the controller could also take alternative security measures such as fencing the property, installing regular patrols of security personnel, using gatekeepers, providing better lighting, installing security locks, tamper-proof windows and doors or applying anti-graffiti coating or foils to walls. Those measures can be as effective as video surveillance systems against burglary, theft and vandalism. The controller has to assess on a case-by-case basis whether such measures can be a reasonable solution.

26.   Before operating a camera system, the controller is obliged to assess where and when video surveillance measures are strictly necessary. Usually a surveillance system operating at night-time as well as outside the regular working hours will meet the needs of the controller to prevent any dangers to his property.

27.   In general, the necessity to use video surveillance to protect the controllers' premises ends at the property boundaries.[11] However, there are cases where the surveillance of the property is not sufficient for an effective protection. In some individual cases it might be necessary to exceed the video surveillance to the immediate surroundings of the premises. In this context, the controller should consider physical and technical means, for example blocking out or pixelating not relevant areas.

---

28.   Example: A bookshop wants to protect its premises against vandalism. In general, cameras should only be filming the premises itself because it is not necessary to watch neighbouring premises or public areas in the surrounding of the bookshop premises for that purpose.

---

29.   Questions concerning the processing's necessity also arise regarding the way evidence is preserved. In some cases it might be necessary to use black box solutions where the footage is automatically deleted after a certain storage period and only accessed in case of an incident. In other situations, it might not be necessary to record the video material at all but more appropriate to use real-time monitoring instead. The decision between black box solutions and real-time monitoring should also be based on the purpose pursued. If for example the purpose of video surveillance is the preservation of evidence, real-time methods are usually not suitable. Sometimes real-time monitoring may also be more intrusive than

storing and automatically deleting material after a limited timeframe (e. g. if someone is constantly viewing the monitor it might be more intrusive than if there is no monitor at all and material is directly stored in a black box). The data minimisation principle must be regarded in this context (Article 5 (1)(c)). It should also be kept in mind that it might be possible that the controller could use security personnel instead of video surveillance that are able to react and intervene immediately.

3.1.3 Balancing of interests

30. Presuming that video surveillance is necessary to protect the legitimate interests of a controller, a video surveillance system may only be put in operation, if the legitimate interests of the controller or those of a third party (e.g. protection of property or physical integrity) are not overridden by the interests or fundamental rights and freedoms of the data subject. The controller needs to consider 1) to what extent the monitoring affects interests, fundamental rights and freedoms of individuals and 2) if this causes violations or negative consequences with regard to the data subject's rights. In fact, balancing the interests is mandatory. Fundamental rights and freedoms on one hand and the controller's legitimate interests on the other hand have to be evaluated and balanced carefully.

---

31. Example: A private parking company has documented reoccurring problems with thefts in the cars parked. The parking area is an open space and can be easily accessed by anyone, but is clearly marked with signs and road blockers surrounding the space. The parking company have a legitimate interest (preventing thefts in the customers' cars) to monitor the area during the time of day that they are experiencing problems. Data subjects are monitored in a limited timeframe, they are not in the area for recreational purposes and it is also in their own interest that thefts are prevented. The interest of the data subjects not to be monitored is in this case overridden by the controller's legitimate interest.

Example: A restaurant decides to install video cameras in the restrooms to control the tidiness of the sanitary facilities. In this case the rights of the data subjects clearly overrides the interest of the controller, therefore cameras cannot be installed there.

3.1.3.1 Making case-by-case decisions

32. As the balancing of interests is mandatory according to the regulation, the decision has to be made on a case-by-case basis (see Article 6 (1)(f)). Referencing abstract situations or comparing similar cases to one another is insufficient. The controller has to evaluate the risks of the intrusion of the data subject's rights; here the decisive criterion is the intensity of intervention for the rights and freedoms of the individual.

33. Intensity can inter alia be defined by the type of information that is gathered (information content), the scope (information density, spatial and geographical extent), the number of data subjects concerned, either as a specific number or as a proportion of the relevant population, the situation in question, the actual interests of the group of data subjects, alternative means, as well as by the nature and scope of the data assessment.

34. Important balancing factors can be the size of the area, which is under surveillance and the amount of data subjects under surveillance. The use of video surveillance in a remote area (e. g. to watch wildlife or to protect critical infrastructure such as a privately owned radio antenna) has to be assessed differently than video surveillance in a pedestrian zone or a shopping mall.

---

35. Example: If a dash cam is installed (e. g. for the purpose of collecting evidence in case of an accident), it is important to ensure that this camera is not constantly recording traffic, as well as persons who are near a road. Otherwise the interest in having video recordings as evidence in the more theoretical case of a road accident cannot justify this serious interference with data subjects' rights.[11]

3.1.3.2 Data subjects' reasonable expectations

36. According to Recital 47, the existence of a legitimate interest needs careful assessment. Here the reasonable expectations of the data subject at the time and in the context of the processing of its personal data have to be included. Concerning systematic monitoring, the relationship between data subject and controller may vary significantly and may affect what reasonable expectations the data subject might have. The interpretation of the concept of reasonable expectations should not only be based on the subjective expectations in question. Rather, the decisive criterion has to be if an objective third party could reasonably expect and conclude to be subject to monitoring in this specific situation.

37. For instance, an employee in his/her workplace is in most cases not likely expecting to be monitored by his or her employer.[12] Furthermore, monitoring is not to be expected in one's private garden, in living areas, or in examination and treatment rooms. In the same vein, it is not reasonable to expect monitoring in sanitary or sauna facilities – monitoring such areas is an intense intrusion into the rights of the data subject. The reasonable expectations of data subjects are that no video surveillance will take place in those areas. On the other hand, the customer of a bank might expect that he/she is monitored inside the bank or by the ATM.

38. Data subjects can also expect to be free of monitoring within publicly accessible areas especially if those areas are typically used for recovery, regeneration, and leisure activities as well as in places where individuals stay and/or communicate, such as sitting areas, tables in restaurants, parks, cinemas and fitness facilities. Here the interests or rights and freedoms of the data subject will often override the controller's legitimate interests.

---

39.   Example: In toilets data subjects expect not to be monitored. Video surveillance for example to prevent accidents is not proportional.

---

40.   Signs informing the data subject about the video surveillance have no relevance when determining what a data subject objectively can expect. This means that e.g. a shop owner cannot rely on customers *objectively* having reasonable expectations to be monitored just because a sign informs the individual at the entrance about the surveillance.

3.2 NECESSITY TO PERFORM A TASK CARRIED OUT IN THE PUBLIC INTEREST OR IN THE EXERCISE OF OFFICIAL AUTHORITY VESTED IN THE CONTROLLER, ARTICLE 6(1)(E)

41.   Personal data could be processed through video surveillance under Article 6 (1)(e) if it is necessary to perform a task carried out in the public interest or in the exercise of official authority.[13] It may be that the exercise of official authority does not allow for such processing, but other legislative bases such as "health and safety" for the protection of visitors and employees may provide limited scope for processing, while still having regard for GDPR obligations and data subject rights.

42.   Member States may maintain or introduce specific national legislation for video surveillance to adapt the application of the rules of the GDPR by determining more precisely specific requirements for processing as long as it is in accordance with the principles laid down by the GDPR (e.g. storage limitation, proportionality).

3.3 CONSENT, ARTICLE 6 (1)(A)

43.   Consent has to be freely given, specific, informed and unambiguous as described in the guidelines on consent.[14]

44.   Regarding systematic monitoring, the data subject's consent can only serve as a legal basis in accordance with Article 7 (see Recital 43) in exceptional cases. It is in the surveillance's nature that this technology monitors an unknown number of people at once. The controller will hardly be able to prove that the data subject has given consent prior to processing of its personal data (Article 7 (1)). Assumed that the data subject withdraws its consent it will be difficult for the controller to prove that personal data is no longer processed (Article 7 (3)).

---

45.   Example: Athletes may request monitoring during individual exercises in order to analyse their techniques and performance. On the other hand, where a sports club takes the initiative to monitor a whole team for the same purpose, consent will often not be valid, as the individual athletes may feel pressured into giving consent so that their refusal of consent does not adversely affect teammates.

---

46.   If the controller wishes to rely on consent it is his duty to make sure that every data subject who enters the area which is under video surveillance has given her or his consent. This consent has to meet the conditions of Article 7. Entering a marked monitored area (e.g. people are invited to go through a specific hallway or gate to enter a monitored area), does not constitute a statement or a clear affirmative action needed for consent, unless it meets the criteria of Article 4 and 7 as described in the guidelines on consent.[15]

47.   Given the imbalance of power between employers and employees, in most cases employers should not rely on consent when processing personal data, as it is unlikely to be freely given. The guidelines on consent should be taken into consideration in this context.

48.   Member State law or collective agreements, including 'works agreements', may provide for specific rules on the processing of employees' personal data in the employment context (see Article 88).

NOTES

 6   Rules on collecting evidence for civil claims varies in Member States.
 7   These guidelines do not analyse or go into details of national law that might differ between Member States.
 8   European Court of Justice, Judgment in Case C-13/16, *Rigas satiksme* case, 4 may 2017
 9   see WP217, Article 29 Working Party.
10   see WP217, Article 29 Working Party, p. 24 seq. See also ECJ Case C-708/18 p.44
11   This might also be subject to national legislation in some Member States.
12   See also: Article 29 Working Party, Opinion 2/2017 on data processing at work, WP249, adopted on 8 June 2017.
13   The basis for the processing referred shall be laid down by Union law or Member State law» and «shall be necessary for the performance of a task carried out in the public interest or in the exercise of official authority vested in the controller (Article 6 (3)).
14   Article 29 Working Party (Art. 29 WP) „Guidelines on consent under Regulation 2016/679" (WP 259 rev. 01). - endorsed by the EDPB
15   Article 29 Working Party (Art. 29 WP) „Guidelines on consent under Regulation 2016/679" (WP 259) - endorsed by the

EDPB - which should be taken in account.

4 DISCLOSURE OF VIDEO FOOTAGE TO THIRD PARTIES

[2.303]
49. In principle, the general regulations of the GDPR apply to the disclosure of video recordings to third parties.

4.1 DISCLOSURE OF VIDEO FOOTAGE TO THIRD PARTIES IN GENERAL

50. Disclosure is defined in Article 4 (2) as transmission (e.g. individual communication), dissemination (e.g. publishing online) or otherwise making available. Third parties are defined in Article 4 (10). Where disclosure is made to third countries or international organisations, the special provisions of Article 44 et seq. also apply.

51. Any disclosure of personal data is a separate kind of processing of personal data for which the controller needs to have a legal basis in Article 6.

---

52. Example: A controller who wishes to upload a recording to the Internet needs to rely on a legal basis for that processing, for instance by obtaining consent from the data subject according to Article 6 (1)(a).

---

53. The transmission of video footage to third parties for the purpose other than that for which the data has been collected is possible under the rules of Article 6 (4).

---

54. Example: Video surveillance of a barrier (at a parking lot) is installed for the purpose of resolving damages. A damage occurs and the recording is transferred to a lawyer to pursue a case. In this case the purpose for recording is the same as the one for transferring.

Example: Video surveillance of a barrier (at a parking lot) is installed for the purpose of resolving damages. The recording is published online for pure amusement reasons. In this case the purpose has changed and is not compatible with the initial purpose. It would furthermore be problematic to identify a legal basis for that processing (publishing).

---

55. A third party recipient will have to make its own legal analysis, in particular identifying its legal basis under Article 6 for his processing (e.g. receiving the material).

4.2 DISCLOSURE OF VIDEO FOOTAGE TO LAW ENFORCEMENT AGENCIES

56. The disclosure of video recordings to law enforcement agencies is also an independent process, which requires a separate justification for the controller.

57. According to Article 6 (1)(c), processing is legal if it is necessary for compliance with a legal obligation to which the controller is subject. Although the applicable police law is an affair under the sole control of the Member States, there are most likely general rules that regulate the transfer of evidence to law enforcement agencies in every Member State. The processing of the controller handing over the data is regulated by the GDPR. If national legislation requires the controller to cooperate with law enforcement (e. g. investigation), the legal basis for handing over the data is legal obligation under Article 6 (1)(c).

58. The purpose limitation in Article 6 (4) is then often unproblematic, since the disclosure explicitly goes back to Member State law. A consideration of the special requirements for a change of purpose in the sense of lit. a - e is therefore not necessary.

---

59. Example: A shop owner records footage at its entrance. The footage shows a person stealing another person's wallet. The police asks the controller to hand over the material in order to assist in their investigation. In that case the shop owner would use the legal basis under Article 6 (1)(c) (legal obligation) read in conjunction with the relevant national law for the transfer processing.

---

60. Example: A camera is installed in a shop for security reasons. The shop owner believes he has recorded something suspicious in his footage and decides to send the material to the police (without any indication that there is an ongoing investigation of some kind). In this case the shop owner has to assess whether the conditions under, in most cases, Article 6 (1)(f) are met. This is usually the case if the shop owner has a reasonable suspicion of that a crime has been committed.

---

61. The processing of the personal data by the law enforcement agencies themselves does not follow the GDPR (see Article 2 (2)(d)), but follows instead the Law Enforcement Directive (EU2016/680).

5 PROCESSING OF SPECIAL CATEGORIES OF DATA

[2.304]

62. Video surveillance systems usually collect massive amounts of personal data which may reveal data of a highly personal nature and even special categories of data. Indeed, apparently non-significant data originally collected through video can be used to infer other information to achieve a different purpose (e.g. to map an individual's habits). However, video surveillance is not always considered to be processing of special categories of personal data.

---

63.   Example: Video footage showing a data subject wearing glasses or using a wheel chair are not per se considered to be special categories of personal data.

---

64. However, if the video footage is processed to deduce special categories of data Article 9 applies.

---

65.   Example: Political opinions could for example be deduced from images showing identifiable data subjects taking part in an event, engaging in a strike, etc. This would fall under Article 9.

Example: A hospital installing a video camera in order to monitor a patient's health condition would be considered as processing of special categories of personal data (Article 9).

---

66. In general, as a principle, whenever installing a video surveillance system careful consideration should be given to the data minimization principle. Hence, even in cases where Article 9 (1) does not apply, the data controller should always try to minimize the risk of capturing footage revealing other sensitive data (beyond Article 9), regardless of the aim.

---

67.   Example: Video surveillance capturing a church does not per se fall under Article 9. However, the controller has to conduct an especially careful assessment under Article 6 (1)(f) taken into account the nature of the data as well as the risk of capturing other sensitive data (beyond Article 9) when assessing the interests of the data subject.

---

68. If a video surveillance system is used in order to process special categories of data, the data controller must identify both an exception for processing special categories of data under Article 9 (i.e. an exemption from the general rule that one should not process special categories of data) and a legal basis under Article 6.

69. For instance, Article 9 (2)(c) ("[. . .] *processing is necessary to protect the vital interests of the data subject or of another natural person* [. . .]") could – in theory and exceptionally – be used, but the data controller would have to justify it as an absolute necessity to safeguard the vital interests of a person and prove that this "[. . .] data subject *is physically or legally incapable of giving his consent.*". In addition, the data controller won't be allowed to use the system for any other reason.

70. It is important to note here that every exemption listed in Article 9 is not likely to be usable to justify processing of special categories of data through video surveillance. More specifically, data controllers processing those data in the context of video surveillance cannot rely on Article 9 (2)(e), which allows processing that relates to personal data that are manifestly made public by the data subject. The mere fact of entering into the range of the camera does not imply that the data subject intends to make public special categories of data relating to him or her.

71. Furthermore, processing of special categories of data requires a heightened and continued vigilance to certain obligations; for example high level of security and data protection impact assessment where necessary.

---

72.   Example: An employer must not use video surveillance recordings showing a demonstration in order to identify strikers.

5.1 GENERAL CONSIDERATIONS WHEN PROCESSING BIOMETRIC DATA

73. The use of biometric data and in particular facial recognition entail heightened risks for data subjects' rights. It is crucial that recourse to such technologies takes place with due respect to the principles of lawfulness, necessity, proportionality and data minimisation as set forth in the GDPR. Whereas the use of these technologies can be perceived as particularly effective, controllers should first of all assess the impact on fundamental rights and freedoms and consider less intrusive means to achieve their legitimate purpose of the processing.

74. To qualify as biometric data as defined in the GDPR, processing of raw data, such as the physical, physiological or behavioural characteristics of a natural person, must imply a measurement of this characteristics. Since biometric data is the result of such measurements, the GDPR states in its Article 4.14 that it is "[. . .] *resulting from specific technical processing relating to the physical, physiological or behavioural characteristics of a natural person, which allow or confirm the unique identification of* *that natural person [. . .]*'. The video footage of an individual cannot however in itself be considered as biometric data under Article 9, if it has not been specifically technically processed in order to contribute to the identification of an individual.[16]

75. In order for it to be considered as processing of special categories of personal data (Article 9) it requires that biometric data is processed "for the purpose of uniquely identifying a natural person".

76. To sum up, in light of Article 4.14 and 9, three criteria must be considered:
- **Nature of data :** data relating to physical, physiological or behavioural characteristics of a natural person,
- **Means and way of processing :** data "resulting from a specific technical processing",
- **Purpose of processing:** data must be used for the purpose of uniquely identifying a natural person.

77. The use of video surveillance including biometric recognition functionality installed by private entities for their own purposes (e.g. marketing, statistical, or even security) will, in most cases, require explicit consent from all data subjects (Article 9 (2)(a)), however another suitable exception in Article 9 could also be applicable.

---

78 Example: To improve its service a private company replaces passenger identification check points within an airport (luggage drop-off, boarding) with video surveillance systems that use facial recognition techniques to verify the identity of the passengers that have chosen to consent to such a procedure. Since the processing falls under Article 9, the passengers, who will have previously given their explicit and informed consent, will have to enlist themselves at for example an automatic terminal in order to create and register their facial template associated with their boarding pass and identity. The check points with facial recognition need to be clearly separated, e. g. the system must be installed within a gantry so that the biometric templates of non-consenting person will not be captured. Only the passengers, who will have previously given their consent and proceeded with their enrolment, will use the gantry equipped with the biometric system.

Example: A controller manages access to his building using a facial recognition method. People can only use this way of access if they have given their explicitly informed consent (according to Article 9 (2)(a)) beforehand. However, in order to ensure that no one who has not previously given his or her consent is captured, the facial recognition method should be triggered by the data subject himself, for instance by pushing a button. To ensure the lawfulness of the processing, the controller must always offer an alternative way to access the building, without biometric processing, such as badges or keys.

---

79. In this type of cases, where biometric templates are generated, controllers shall ensure that once a match or no-match result has been obtained, all the intermediate templates made on the fly (with the explicit and informed consent of the data subject) in order to be compared to the ones created by the data subjects at the time of the enlistment, are immediately and securely deleted. The templates created for the enlistment should only be retained for the realisation of the purpose of the processing and should not be stored or archived.

80. However, when the purpose of the processing is for example to distinguish one category of people from another but not to uniquely identify anyone the processing does not fall under Article 9.

---

81. Example: A shop owner would like to customize its advertisement based on gender and age characteristics of the customer captured by a video surveillance system. If that system does not generate biometric templates in order to uniquely identify persons but instead just detects those physical characteristics in order to classify the person then the processing would not fall under Article 9 (as long as no other types of special categories of data are being processed).

---

82. However, Article 9 applies if the controller stores biometric data (most commonly through templates that are created by the extraction of key features from the raw form of biometric data (e.g. facial measurements from an image)) in order to uniquely identify a person. If a controller wishes to detect a data subject re-entering the area or entering another area (for example in order to project continued customized advertisement), the purpose would then be to uniquely identify a natural person, meaning that the operation would from the start fall under Article 9. This could be the case if a controller stores generated templates to provide further tailored advertisement on several billboards throughout different locations inside the shop. Since the system is using physical characteristics to detect specific individuals coming back in the range of the camera (like the visitors of a shopping mall) and tracking them, it would constitute a biometric identification method because it is aimed at recognition through the use of specific technical processing.

---

83. Example: A shop owner has installed a facial recognition system inside his shop in order to customize its advertisement towards individuals. The data controller has to obtain the explicit and informed consent of all data subjects before using this biometric system and delivering tailored advertisement. The system would be unlawful if it captures visitors or passers-by who have not consented to the creation of their biometric template, even if their template is deleted within the shortest possible period. Indeed, these temporary templates constitute biometric data processed in order to uniquely identify a person who may not want to receive targeted advertisement.

84. The EDPB observes that some biometric systems are installed in uncontrolled environments[17], which means that the system involves capturing on the fly the faces of any individual passing in the range of the camera, including persons who have not consented to the biometric device, and thereby creating biometric templates. These templates are compared to the ones created of data subjects having given their prior consent during an enlistment process (i.e. a biometric devise user) in order for the data controller to recognise whether the person is a biometric device user or not. In this case, the system is often designed to discriminate the individuals it wants to recognize from a database from those who are not enlisted. Since the purpose is to uniquely identify natural persons, an exception under Article 9 (2) GDPR is still needed for <u>anyone</u> captured by the camera.

---

85.   Example: A hotel uses video surveillance to automatically alert the hotel manager that a VIP has arrived when the face of the guest is recognized. These VIPs have priory given their explicit consent to the use of facial recognition before being recorded in a database established for that purpose. These processing systems of biometric data would be unlawful unless all other guests monitored (in order to identify the VIPs) have consented to the processing according to Article 9 (2)(a) GDPR.

Example: A controller installs a video surveillance system with facial recognition at the entrance of the concert hall he manages. The controller must set up clearly separated entrances; one with a biometric system and one without (where you instead for example scan a ticket). The entrances equipped with biometric devices, must be installed and made accessible in a way that prevents the system from capturing biometric templates of non-consenting spectators.

---

86.   Finally, when the consent is required by Article 9 GDPR, the data controller shall not condition the access to its services to the acceptance of the biometric processing. In other words and notably when the biometric processing is used for authentication purpose, the data controller must offer an alternative solution that does not involve biometric processing – without restraints or additional cost for the data subject. This alternative solution is also needed for persons who do not meet the constraints of the biometric device (enrolment or reading of the biometric data impossible, disability situation making it difficult to use, etc.) and in anticipation of unavailability of the biometric device (such as a malfunction of the device), a "back-up solution" must be implemented to ensure continuity of the proposed service, limited however to exceptional use. In exceptional cases, there might be a situation where processing biometric data is the core activity of a service provided by contract, e.g. a museum that sets up an exhibition to demonstrate the use of a facial recognition device, in which case the data subject will not be able to reject the processing of biometric data should they wish to participate in the exhibition. In such case the consent required under Article 9 is still valid if the requirements in Article 7 are met.

5.2 SUGGESTED MEASURES TO MINIMIZE THE RISKS WHEN PROCESSING BIOMETRIC DATA

87.   In compliance with the data minimization principle, data controllers must ensure that data extracted from a digital image to build a template will not be excessive and will only contain the information required for the specified purpose, thereby avoiding any possible further processing. Measures should be put in place to guarantee that templates cannot be transferred across biometric systems.

88.   Identification and authentication/verification are likely to require the storage of the template for use in a later comparison. The data controller must consider the most appropriate location for storage of the data. In an environment under control (delimited hallways or checkpoints), templates shall be stored on an individual device kept by the user and under his or her sole control (in a smartphone or the id card) or – when needed for specific purposes and in presence of objective needs – stored in a centralized database in an encrypted form with a key/secret solely in the hands of the person to prevent unauthorised access to the template or storage location. If the data controller cannot avoid having access to the templates, he must take appropriate steps to ensure the security of the data stored. This may include encrypting the template using a cryptographic algorithm.

89.   In any case, the controller shall take all necessary precautions to preserve the availability, integrity and confidentiality of the data processed. To this end, the controller shall notably take the following measures: compartmentalize data during transmission and storage, store biometric templates and raw data or identity data on distinct databases, encrypt biometric data, notably biometric templates, and define a policy for encryption and key management, integrate an organisational and technical measure for fraud detection, associate an integrity code with the data (for example signature or hash) and prohibit any external access to the biometric data. Such measures will need to evolve with the advancement of technologies.

90.   Besides, data controllers should proceed to the deletion of raw data (face images, speech signals, the gait, etc.) and ensure the effectiveness of this deletion. If there is no longer a lawful basis for the processing, the raw data has to be deleted. Indeed, insofar as biometric templates derives from such data, one can consider that the constitution of databases could represent an equal if not even bigger threat (because it may not always be easy to read a biometric template without the knowledge of how it was programmed, whereas raw data will be the building blocks of any template). In case the data controller would need to keep such data, noise-additive methods (such as watermarking) must be explored, which would render the creation of the template ineffective. The controller must also delete biometric data and templates in the event of unauthorized access to the read-comparison terminal or storage server and delete any data not useful for further processing at the end of the biometric device's life.

NOTES

16   Recital 51 GDPR supports this analysis, stating that "[. . .] *The processing of photographs should not systematically be considered to be processing of special categories of personal data as they are covered by the definition of biometric data only when processed through a specific technical means allowing the unique identification or authentication of a natural person. [. . .]*".

17   It means that the biometric device is located in a space open to the public and is able to work on anyone passing by, as opposed to the biometric systems in controlled environments that can be used only by consenting person's participation.

6 RIGHTS OF THE DATA SUBJECT

[2.305]
91.   Due to the character of data processing when using video surveillance some data subject's rights under GDPR serves further clarification. This chapter is however not exhaustive, all rights under the GDPR applies to processing of personal data through video surveillance.

6.1 RIGHT TO ACCESS

92.   A data subject has the right to obtain confirmation from the controller as to whether or not their personal data are being processed. For video surveillance this means that if no data is stored or transferred in any way then once the real-time monitoring moment has passed the controller could only give the information that no personal data is any longer being processed (besides the general information obligations under Article 13, see *section 7 – Transparency and information obligations*). If however data is still being processed at the time of the request (i.e. if the data is stored or continuously processed in any other way), the data subject should receive access and information in accordance with Article 15.

93.   There are however, a number of limitations that may in some cases apply in relation to the right to access.
•   Article 15 (4) GDPR, adversely affect the rights of others

94.   Given that any number of data subjects may be recorded in the same sequence of video surveillance a screening would then cause additional processing of personal data of other data subjects. If the data subject wishes to receive a copy of the material (article 15 (3)), this could adversely affect the rights and freedoms of other data subject in the material. To prevent that effect the controller should therefore take into consideration that due to the intrusive nature of the video footage the controller should not in some cases hand out video footage where other data subjects can be identified. The protection of the rights of third parties should however not be used as an excuse to prevent legitimate claims of access by individuals, the controller should in those cases implement technical measures to fulfil the access request (for example, image-editing such as masking or scrambling).However, controllers are not obliged to implement such technical measures if they can otherwise ensure that they are able to react upon a request under Article 15 within the timeframe stipulated by Article 12 (3).
•   Article 11 (2) GDPR, controller is unable to identify the data subject

95.   If the video footage is not searchable for personal data, (i.e. the controller would likely have to go through a large amount of stored material in order to find the data subject in question) the controller may be unable to identify the data subject.

96.   For these reasons the data subject should (besides identifying themselves including with identification document or in person) in its request to the controller, specify when – within a reasonable timeframe in proportion to the amount of data subjects recorded – he or she entered the monitored area. The controller should notify the data subject beforehand on what information is needed in order for the controller to comply with the request. If the controller is able to demonstrate that it is not in a position to identify the data subject, the controller must inform the data subject accordingly, if possible. In such a situation, in its response to the data subject the controller should inform about the exact area for the monitoring, verification of cameras that were in use etc. so that the data subject will have the full understanding of what personal data of him/her may have been processed.

---

97.   Example: If a data subject is requesting a copy of his or her personal data processed through video surveillance at the entrance of a shopping mall with 30 000 visitors per day, the data subject should specify when he or she passed the monitored area within approximately a one-hour-timeframe. If the controller still processes the material a copy of the video footage should be provided. If other data subjects can be identified in the same material then that part of the material should be anonymised (for example by blurring the copy or parts thereof) before giving the copy to the data subject that filed the request.

Example: If the controller is automatically erasing all footage for example within 2 days, the controller is not able to supply footage to the data subject after those 2 days. If the controller receives a request after those 2 days the data subject should be informed accordingly.

•   Article 12 GDPR, excessive requests
98.   In case of excessive or manifestly unfounded requests from a data subject, the controller may either charge a reasonable fee in accordance with Article 12 (5)(a) GDPR, or refuse to act on the request (Article 12 (5)(b) GDPR). The controller needs to be able to demonstrate the manifestly unfounded or excessive character of the request.

6.2 RIGHT TO ERASURE AND RIGHT TO OBJECT

6.2.1 Right to erasure (Right to be forgotten)

99. If the controller continues to process personal data beyond real-time monitoring (e.g. storing) the data subject may request for the personal data to be erased under Article 17 GDPR.

100. Upon a request, the controller is obliged to erase the personal data without undue delay if one of the circumstances listed under Article 17 (1) GDPR applies (and none of the exceptions listed under Article 17 (3) GDPR does). That includes the obligation to erase personal data when they are no longer needed for the purpose for which they were initially stored, or when the processing is unlawful (see also *Section 8 – Storage periods and obligation to erasure*). Furthermore, depending on the legal basis of processing, personal data should be erased:
- for consent whenever the consent is withdrawn (and there is no other legal basis for the processing)
- for *legitimate interest*:
  - whenever the data subject exercises the right to object (see *Section 6.2.2*) and there are no overriding compelling legitimate grounds for the processing, or
  - in case of direct marketing (including profiling) whenever the data subject objects to the processing.

101. If the controller has made the video footage public (e.g. broadcasting or streaming online), reasonable steps need to be taken in order to inform other controllers (that are now processing the personal data in question) of the request pursuant to Article 17 (2) GDPR. The reasonable steps should include technical measures, taking into account available technology and the cost of implementation. To the extent possible, the controller should notify – upon erasure of personal data – anyone to which the personal data previously have been disclosed, in accordance with Article 19 GDPR.

102. Besides the controller's obligation to erase personal data upon the data subject's request, the controller is obliged under the general principles of the GDPR to limit the personal data stored (see *Section 8*).

103. For video surveillance it is worth noticing that by for instance blurring the picture with no retroactive ability to recover the personal data that the picture previously contained, the personal data are considered erased in accordance with GDPR.

---

104. Example: A convenience store is having trouble with vandalism in particular on its exterior and is therefore using video surveillance outside of their entrance in direct connection to the walls. A passer-by requests to have his personal data erased from that very moment. The controller is obliged to respond to the request without undue delay and at the latest within one month. Since the footage in question does no longer meet the purpose for which it was initially stored (no vandalism occurred during the time the data subject passed by), there is at the time of the request, no legitimate interest to store the data that would override the interests of the data subjects. The controller needs to erase the personal data.

6.2.2 Right to object

105. For video surveillance based on *legitimate interest* (Article 6 (1)(f) GDPR) or for the necessity when carrying out a task in the *public interest* (Article 6 (1)(e) GDPR) the data subject has the right – at any time – to object, on grounds relating to his or her particular situation, to the processing in accordance with Article 21 GDPR. Unless the controller demonstrates compelling legitimate grounds that overrides the rights and interests of the data subject, the processing of data of the individual who objected must then stop. The controller should be obliged to respond to requests from the data subject without undue delay and at the latest within one month.

106. In the context of video surveillance this objection could be made either when entering, during the time in, or after leaving, the monitored area. In practice this means that unless the controller has compelling legitimate grounds, monitoring an area where natural persons could be identified is only lawful if either
(1) the controller is able to immediately stop the camera from processing personal data when requested, or
(2) the monitored area is in such detail restricted so that the controller can assure the approval from the data subject prior to entering the area and it is not an area that the data subject as a citizen is entitled to access.

107. These guidelines do not aim to identify what is considered a *compelling* legitimate interest (Article 21 GDPR).

108. When using video surveillance for direct marketing purposes, the data subject has the right to object to the processing on a discretionary basis as the right to object is absolute in that context (Article 21 (2) and (3) GDPR).

---

109. Example: A company is experiencing difficulties with security breaches in their public entrance and is using video surveillance on the grounds of legitimate interest, with the purpose to catch those unlawfully entering. A visitor objects to the processing of his or her data through the video surveillance

> system on grounds relating to his or her particular situation. The company however in this case rejects the request with the explanation that the footage stored is needed due to an ongoing internal investigation, thereby having compelling legitimate grounds to continue processing the personal data.

7 TRANSPARENCY AND INFORMATION OBLIGATIONS[18]

[2.306]
110. It has long been inherent in European data protection law that data subjects should be aware of the fact that video surveillance is in operation. They should be informed in a detailed manner as to the places monitored.[19] Under the GDPR the general transparency and information obligations are set out in Article 12 GDPR and following. Article 29 Working Party's "Guidelines on transparency under Regulation 2016/679 (WP260)" which were endorsed by the EDPB on May 25th 2018 provide further details. In line with WP260 par. 26, it is Article 13 GDPR, which is applicable if personal data are collected "[. . .] from a data subject by observation (e.g. using automated data capturing devices or data capturing software such as cameras [. . .].".

111. In light of the volume of information, which is required to be provided to the data subject, a layered approach may be followed by data controllers where they opt to use a combination of methods to ensure transparency (WP260, par. 35; WP89, par. 22). Regarding video surveillance the most important information should be displayed on the warning sign itself (first layer) while the further mandatory details may be provided by other means (second layer).

7.1 FIRST LAYER INFORMATION (WARNING SIGN)

112. The first layer concerns the primary way in which the controller first engages with the data subject. At this stage, controllers may use a warning sign showing the relevant information. The displayed information may be provided in combination with an icon in order to give, in an easily visible, intelligible and clearly readable manner, a meaningful overview of the intended processing (Article 12 (7) GDPR). The format of the information should be adjusted to the individual location (WP89 par. 22).

7.1.1 Positioning of the warning sign

113. The information should be positioned in such a way that the data subject can easily recognize the circumstances of the surveillance before entering the monitored area (approximately at eye level). It is not necessary to reveal the position of the camera as long as there is no doubt as to which areas are subject to monitoring and the context of surveillance is clarified unambiguously (WP 89, par. 22). The data subject must be able to estimate which area is captured by a camera so that he or she is able to avoid surveillance or adapt his or her behaviour if necessary.

7.1.2 Content of the first layer

114. The first layer information (warning sign) should generally convey the most important information, e.g. the details of the purposes of processing, the identity of controller and the existence of the rights of the data subject, together with information on the greatest impacts of the processing.[20] This can include for example the legitimate interests pursued by the controller (or by a third party) and contact details of the data protection officer (if applicable). It also has to refer to the more detailed second layer of information and where and how to find it.

115. In addition the sign should also contain any information that could surprise the data subject (WP260, par. 38). That could for example be transmissions to third parties, particularly if they are located outside the EU, and the storage period. If this information is not indicated, the data subject should be able to trust that there is solely a live monitoring (without any data recording or transmission to third parties).

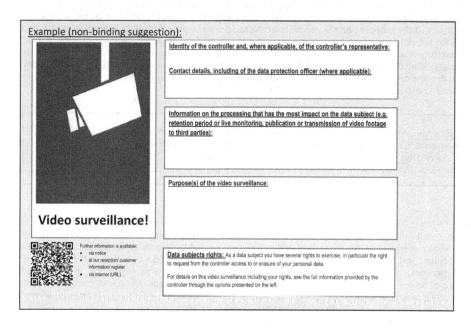

Example (non-binding suggestion):

Video surveillance!

Identity of the controller and, where applicable, of the controller's representative:

Contact details, including of the data protection officer (where applicable):

Information on the processing that has the most impact on the data subject (e.g. retention period or live monitoring, publication or transmission of video footage to third parties):

Purpose(s) of the video surveillance:

Further information is available:
• via notice
• at our reception/ customer information/ register
• via internet (URL)...

Data subjects rights: As a data subject you have several rights to exercise, in particular the right to request from the controller access to or erasure of your personal data.

For details on this video surveillance including your rights, see the full information provided by the controller through the options presented on the left.

7.2 SECOND LAYER INFORMATION

117. The second layer information must also be made available at a place easily accessible to the data subject, for example as a complete information sheet available at a central location (e.g. information desk, reception or cashier) or displayed on an easy accessible poster. As mentioned above, the first layer warning sign has to refer clearly to the second layer information. In addition, it is best if the first layer information refers to a digital source (e.g. QR-code or a website address) of the second layer. However, the information should also be easily available non-digitally. It should be possible to access the second layer information without entering the surveyed area, especially if the information is provided digitally (this can be achieved for example by a link). Other appropriate means could be a phone number that can be called. However the information is provided, it must contain all that is mandatory under Article 13 GDPR.

118. In addition to these options, and also to make them more effective, the EDPB promotes the use of technological means to provide information to data subjects. This may include for instance; geolocating cameras and including information in mapping apps or websites so that individuals can easily, on the one hand, identify and specify the video sources related to the exercise of their rights, and on the other hand, obtain more detailed information on the processing operation.

119. Example: A shop owner is monitoring his shop. To comply with Article 13 it is sufficient to place a warning sign at an easy visible point at the entrance of his shop, which contains the first layer information. In addition, he has to provide an information sheet containing the second layer information at the cashier or any other central and easy accessible location in his shop.

NOTES
18   Specific requirements in national legislation might apply.
19   See WP89, Opinion 4/2004 on the Processing of Personal Data by means of Video Surveillance by Article 29 Working Party).
20   See WP260, par. 38.

8 STORAGE PERIODS AND OBLIGATION TO ERASURE

[2.307]
120. Personal data may not be stored longer than what is necessary for the purposes for which the personal data is processed (Article 5 (1)(c) and (e) GDPR). In some Member States, there may be specific provisions for storage periods with regards to video surveillance in accordance with Article 6 (2) GDPR.

121. Whether the personal data is necessary to store or not should be controlled within a narrow timeline. In general, legitimate purposes for video surveillance are often property protection or preservation of evidence. Usually damages that occurred can be recognized within one or two days. To facilitate the demonstration of compliance with the data protection framework it is in the controller's interest to make organisational arrangements in advance (e. g. nominate, if necessary, a representative for screening and securing video material). Taking into consideration the principles of Article 5 (1)(c) and (e) GDPR, namely data minimization and storage limitation, the personal data should in most cases (e.g. for the purpose of detecting vandalism) be erased, ideally automatically, after a few days. The longer the storage period set (especially when beyond 72 hours), the more argumentation for the legitimacy of the purpose and the necessity of storage has to be provided. If the controller uses video surveillance not only for monitoring its premises but also intends to store the data, the controller must assure that the storage is actually necessary in order to achieve the purpose. If so, the storage period needs to be clearly defined and individually set for each particular purpose. It is the controller's responsibility to define the retention period in accordance with the principles of necessity and proportionality and to demonstrate compliance with the provisions of the GDPR.

---

122. Example: An owner of a small shop would normally take notice of any vandalism the same day. In consequence, a regular storage period of 24 hours is sufficient. Closed weekends or longer holidays might however be reasons for a longer storage period. If a damage is detected he may also need to store the video footage a longer period in order to take legal action against the offender.

---

9 TECHNICAL AND ORGANISATIONAL MEASURES

[2.308]
123. As stated in Article 32 (1) GDPR, processing of personal data during video surveillance must not only be legally permissible but controllers and processors must also adequately secure it. Implemented **organizational and technical measures** must be **proportional to the risks to rights and freedoms of natural persons**, resulting from accidental or unlawful destruction, loss, alteration, unauthorized disclosure or access to video surveillance data. According to Article 24 and 25 GDPR, controllers need to implement technical and organisational measures also in order to safeguard all data-protection principles during processing, and to establish means for data subjects to exercise their rights as defined in Articles 15-22 GDPR. Data controllers should adopt internal framework and policies that ensure this implementation both at the time of the determination of the means for processing and at the time of the processing itself, including the performance of data protection impact assessments when needed.

9.1 OVERVIEW OF VIDEO SURVEILLANCE SYSTEM

124. A video surveillance system (VSS)[21] consists of analogue and digital devices as well as software for the purpose of capturing images of a scene, handling the images and displaying them to an operator. Its components are grouped into the following categories:
- Video environment: image capture, interconnections and image handling:
  - the purpose of image capture is the generation of an image of the real world in such format that it can be used by the rest of the system,
  - interconnections describe all transmission of data within the video environment, i.e. connections and communications. Examples of connections are cables, digital networks, and wireless transmissions. Communications describe all video and control data signals, which could be digital or analogue,
  - image handling includes analysis, storage and presentation of an image or a sequence of images.
- From the system management perspective, a VSS has the following logical functions:
  - data management and activity management, which includes handling operator commands and system generated activities (alarm procedures, alerting operators),
  - interfaces to other systems might include connection to other security (access control, fire alarm) and non-security systems (building management systems, automatic license plate recognition).
- VSS security consists of system and data confidentiality, integrity and availability:
  - system security includes physical security of all system components and control of access to the VSS,
  - data security includes prevention of loss or manipulation of data.

125. *Figure 1- video surveillance system*

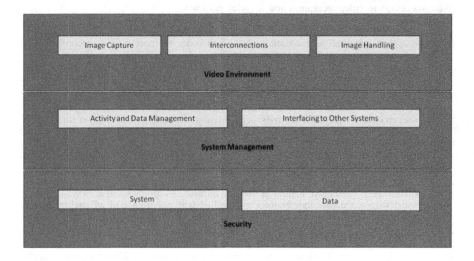

Figure 1- video surveillance system

Part 2   Data Protection: EU Law etc

9.2 DATA PROTECTION BY DESIGN AND BY DEFAULT

126. As stated in Article 25 GDPR, controllers need to implement appropriate data protection technical and organisational measures as soon as they plan for video surveillance – before they start the collection and processing of video footage. These principles emphasize the need for built-in privacy enhancing technologies, default settings that minimise the data processing, and the provision of the necessary tools that enable the highest possible protection of personal data[22].

127. Controllers should build data protection and privacy safeguards not only into the design specifications of the technology but also into organisational practices. When it comes to organisational practices, the controller should adopt an appropriate management framework, establish and enforce policies and procedures related to video surveillance. From the technical point of view, system specification and design should include requirements for processing personal data in accordance with principles stated in Article 5 GDPR (lawfulness of processing, purpose and data limitation, data minimisation by default in the sense of Article 25 (2) GDPR, integrity and confidentiality, accountability etc.). In case a controller plans to acquire a commercial video surveillance system, the controller needs to include these requirements in the purchase specification. The controller needs to ensure compliance with these requirements applying them to all components of the system and to all data processed by it, during their entire lifecycle.

9.3 CONCRETE EXAMPLES OF RELEVANT MEASURES

128. Most of the measures that can be used to secure video surveillance, especially when digital equipment and software are used, will not differ from those used in other IT systems. However, regardless of the solution selected, the controller must adequately protect all components of a video surveillance system and data under all stages, i.e. during storage (data at rest), transmission (data in transit) and processing (data in use). For this, it is necessary that controllers and processors combine organisational and technical measures.

129. When selecting technical solutions, the controller should consider privacy-friendly technologies also because they enhance security. Examples of such technologies are systems that allow masking or scrambling areas that are not relevant for the surveillance, or the editing out of images of third persons, when providing video footage to data subjects.[23] On the other hand, the selected solutions should not provide functions that are not necessary (e.g., unlimited movement of cameras, zoom capability, radio transmission, analysis and audio recordings). Functions provided, but not necessary, must be deactivated.

130. There is a lot of literature available on this subject, including international standards and technical specifications on the physical security of multimedia systems[24], and the security of general IT systems[25]. Therefore, this section provides only a high-level overview of this topic.

9.3.1 Organisational measures

131. Apart from a potential DPIA needed (see *Section 10*), controllers should consider the following topics when they create their own video surveillance policies and procedures:
*   Who is responsible for management and operation of the video surveillance system.
*   Purpose and scope of the video surveillance project.
*   Appropriate and prohibited use (where and when video surveillance is allowed and where and when it is not; e.g. use of hidden cameras and audio in addition to video recording)[26].
*   Transparency measures as referred to in *Section 7 (Transparency and information obligations)*.
*   How video is recorded and for what duration, including archival storage of video recordings related to security incidents.

- Who must undergo relevant training and when.
- Who has access to video recordings and for what purposes.
- Operational procedures (e.g. by whom and from where video surveillance is monitored, what to do in case of a data breach incident).
- What procedures external parties need to follow in order to request video recordings, and procedures for denying or granting such requests.
- Procedures for VSS procurement, installation and maintenance.
- Incident management and recovery procedures.

9.3.2 Technical measures

132. **System security** means **physical security** of all system components, and system integrity i.e. **protection against and resilience under intentional and unintentional interference with its normal operations** and **access control**. Data security means **confidentiality** (data is accessible only to those who are granted access), **integrity** (prevention against data loss or manipulation) and **availability** (data can be accessed when it is required).

133. **Physical security** is a vital part of data protection and the first line of defence, because it protect VSS equipment from theft, vandalism, natural disaster, manmade catastrophes and accidental damage (e.g. from electrical surges, extreme temperatures and spilled coffee). In case of an analogue based systems, physical security plays the main role in their protection.

134. **System and data security**, i.e. protection against intentional and unintentional interference with its normal operations may include:
- Protection of the entire VSS infrastructure (including remote cameras, cabling and power supply) against physical tampering and theft.
- Protection of footage transmission with communication channels secure against interception
- Data encryption.
- Use of hardware and software based solutions such as firewalls, antivirus or intrusion detection systems against cyber attacks.
- Detection of failures of components, software and interconnections.
- Means to restore availability and access to the system in the event of a physical or technical incident.

135. **Access control** ensures that only authorized people can access the system and data, while others are prevented from doing it. Measures that support physical and logical access control include:
- Ensuring that all premises where monitoring by video surveillance is done and where video footage is stored are secured against unsupervised access by third parties.
- Positioning monitors in such a way (especially when they are in open areas, like a reception) so that only authorized operators can view them.
- Procedures for granting, changing and revoking physical and logical access are defined and enforced.
- Methods and means of user authentication and authorization including e.g. passwords length and change frequency are implemented.
- User performed actions (both to the system and data) are recorded and regularly reviewed.
- Monitoring and detection of access failures is done continuously and identified weaknesses are addressed as soon as possible.

NOTES
[21] GDPR does not provide a definition for it, a technical description can for example be found in EN 62676-1-1:2014 Video surveillance systems for use in security applications – Part 1-1: Video system requirements.
[22] WP 168, Opinion on the "The Future of Privacy", joint contribution by the Article 29 Data Protection Working Party and the Working Party on Police and Justice to the Consultation of the European Commission on the legal framework for the fundamental right to protection of personal data (adopted on 01 December 2009).
[23] The use of such technologies may even be mandatory in some cases in order to comply with Article 5 (1)(c). In any case they can serve as best practice examples.
[24] IEC TS 62045 — Multimedia security - Guideline for privacy protection of equipment and systems in and out of use.
[25] ISO/IEC 27000 — Information security management systems series.
[26] This may depend on national laws and sector regulations.

10 DATA PROTECTION IMPACT ASSESSMENT

[2.309]
136. According to Article 35 (1) GDPR controllers are required to conduct data protection impact assessments (DPIA) when a type of data processing is likely to result in a high risk to the rights and freedoms of natural persons. Article 35 (3)(c) GDPR stipulates that controllers are required to carry out data protection impact assessments if the processing constitutes a systematic monitoring of a publicly accessible area on a large scale. Moreover, according to Article 35 (3)(b) GDPR a data protection impact assessment is also required when the controller intends to process special categories of data on a large scale.

137. The Guidelines on Data Protection Impact Assessment[27] provide further advice, and more detailed examples relevant to video surveillance (e.g. concerning the "use of a camera system to monitor driving behaviour on highways"). Article 35 (4) GDPR requires that each supervisory authority publish a list of the kind of processing operations that are subject to mandatory DPIA within their country. These lists can usually be found on the authorities' websites. Given the typical purposes of video surveillance (protection of people and property, detection, prevention and control of offences, collection of evidence and biometric identification of suspects), it is reasonable to assume that many cases of video surveillance will require a DPIA. Therefore, data controllers should carefully consult these documents in order to determine whether such an assessment is required and conduct it if necessary. The outcome of the performed DPIA should determine the controller's choice of implemented data protection measures.

138.　It is also important to note that if the results of the DPIA indicate that processing would result in a high risk despite security measures planned by the controller, then it will be necessary to consult the relevant supervisory authority prior to the processing. Details on prior consultations can be found in Article 36.

For the European Data Protection Board

The Chair

(Andrea Jelinek)

NOTES
　27　　WP248 rev.01, Guidelines on Data Protection Impact Assessment (DPIA) and determining whether processing is "likely to result in a high risk" for the purposes of Regulation 2016/679. - endorsed by the EDPB

EUROPEAN DATA PROTECTION BOARD: GUIDELINES 4/2019 ON ARTICLE 25 DATA PROTECTION BY DESIGN AND BY DEFAULT
Version 2.0
Adopted on 20 October 2020

[2.310]

NOTES
　© European Data Protection Board.

VERSION HISTORY

Version 1.0: 13 November 2019: Adoption of the Guidelines for public consultation

Version 2.0: 20 October 2020: Adoption of the Guidelines by the EDPB after public consultation

TABLE OF CONTENTS

THE EUROPEAN DATA PROTECTION BOARD

Having regard to Article 70 (1e) of the Regulation 2016/679/EU of the European Parliament and of the Council of 27 April 2016 on the protection of natural persons with regard to the processing of personal data and on the free movement of such data, and repealing Directive 95/46/EC], (hereinafter "GDPR"),

Having regard to the EEA Agreement and in particular to Annex XI and Protocol 37 thereof, as amended by the Decision of the EEA joint Committee No 154/2018 of 6 July 2018,

Having regard to Article 12 and Article 22 of its Rules of Procedure,

HAS ADOPTED THE FOLLOWING GUIDELINES

Executive summary

In an increasingly digital world, adherence to Data Protection by Design and by Default requirements plays a crucial part in promoting privacy and data protection in society. It is therefore essential that controllers take this responsibility seriously and implement the GDPR obligations when designing processing operations.

These Guidelines give general guidance on the obligation of Data Protection by Design and by Default (henceforth "DPbDD") set forth in Article 25 in the GDPR. DPbDD is an obligation for all controllers, irrespective of size and varying complexity of processing. To be able to implement the requirements of DPbDD, it is crucial that the controller understands the data protection principles and the data subject's rights and freedoms.

The core obligation is the implementation of appropriate measures and necessary safeguards that provide *effective implementation of the data protection* principles and, consequentially, *data subjects' rights and freedoms by design and by default*. Article 25 prescribes both design and default elements that should be taken into account. Those elements, will be further elaborated in these Guidelines.

Article 25(1) stipulates that controllers should consider DPbDD early on when they plan a new processing operation. Controllers shall implement DPbDD *before* processing, and also *continually* at the time of processing, by regularly reviewing the effectiveness of the chosen measures and safeguards. DPbDD also applies to existing systems that are processing personal data.

The Guidelines also contain guidance on how to effectively implement the data protection principles in Article 5, listing key design and default elements as well as practical cases for illustration. The controller should consider the appropriateness of the suggested measures in the context of the particular processing in question.

The EDPB provides recommendations on how controllers, processors and producers can cooperate to achieve DPbDD. It encourages the controllers in industry, processors, and producers to use DPbDD as a means to achieve a competitive advantage when marketing their products towards controllers and data subjects. It also encourages all controllers to make use of certifications and codes of conduct.

1 SCOPE

[2.311]
1. The Guidelines focus on controllers' implementation of DPbDD based on the obligation in Article 25 of the GDPR.[1] Other actors, such as processors and producers of products, services and applications (henceforth "producers"), who are not directly addressed in Article 25, may also find these Guidelines useful in creating GDPR compliant products and services that enable controllers to fulfil their data protection obligations.[2] Recital 78 of the GDPR adds that DPbDD should be taken into consideration in the context of public tenders. Despite all controllers having the duty to integrate DPbDD into their processing activities, this provision fosters the adoption of the data protection principles, where public administrations should lead by example. The controller is responsible for the fulfilment of the DPbDD obligations for the processing carried out by their processors and sub-processors, they should therefore take this into account when contracting with these parties.

2. The requirement described in Article 25 is for controllers to have data protection designed into the processing of personal data and as a default setting and this applies throughout the processing lifecycle. DPbDD is also a requirement for processing systems pre-existing before the GDPR entered into force. Controllers must have the processing consistently updated in line with the GDPR. For more information on how to maintain an existing system in line with DPbDD, see subchapter 2.1.4 of these Guidelines. The core of the provision is to ensure *appropriate* and *effective* data protection both by *design* and by *default*, which means that controllers should be able to demonstrate that they have the appropriate measures and safeguards in the processing to ensure that the data protection principles and the rights and freedoms of data subjects are effective.

3. Chapter 2 of the Guidelines focuses on an interpretation of the requirements set forth by Article 25 and explores the legal obligations introduced by the provision. Examples on how to apply DPbDD in the context of specific data protection principles are provided in Chapter 3.

4. The Guidelines address the possibility to establish a certification mechanism to demonstrate compliance with Article 25 in Chapter 4, as well as how the Article may be enforced by supervisory authorities in Chapter 5. Finally, the Guidelines provide stakeholders with further recommendations on how to successfully implement DPbDD. The EDPB recognizes the challenges for small and medium enterprises (henceforth "SMEs") to fully comply with the obligations of DPbDD, and provides additional recommendations specifically to SMEs in Chapter 6.

NOTES
[1] The interpretations provided herein equally apply to Article 20 of Directive (EU) 2016/680, and Article 27 of Regulation 2018/1725.
[2] Recital 78 GDPR clearly states this need: *"When developing, designing, selecting and using applications, services and products that are based on the processing of personal data or process personal data to fulfil their task, producers of the products, services and applications should be encouraged to take into account the right to data protection when developing and designing such products, services and applications and, with due regard to the "state of the art", to make sure that controllers and processors are able to fulfil their data protection obligations".*

2 ANALYSIS OF ARTICLE 25(1) AND (2) DATA PROTECTION BY DESIGN AND BY DEFAULT

[2.312]
5. The aim of this Chapter is to explore and provide guidance on the requirements to data protection by design in Article 25(1) and to data protection by default in Article 25(2) respectively. Data protection by design and data protection by default are complementary concepts, which mutually reinforce each other. Data subjects will benefit more from data protection by default if data protection by design is concurrently implemented – and vice versa.

6. DPbDD is a requirement for all controllers, including small businesses and multinational companies alike. That being the case, the complexity of implementing DPbDD may vary based on the individual processing operation. Regardless of the size however, in all cases, positive benefits for controller and data subject can be achieved by implementing DPbDD.

2.1 ARTICLE 25(1): DATA PROTECTION BY DESIGN

2.1.1 Controller's obligation to implement appropriate technical and organisational measures and necessary safeguards into the processing

7. In line with Article 25(1) the controller shall implement *appropriate* technical and organisational *measures* which are designed to implement the data protection principles and to integrate the *necessary safeguards* into the processing in order to meet the requirements and protect the rights and freedoms of data subjects. Both appropriate measures and necessary safeguards are meant to serve the same purpose of protecting the rights of data subjects and ensuring that the protection of their personal data is built into the processing.

8. *Technical and organizational measures* and necessary *safeguards* can be understood in a broad sense as any method or means that a controller may employ in the processing. Being *appropriate* means that the measures and necessary safeguards should be suited to achieve the intended purpose, i.e. they must implement the data protection principles *effectively*[3]. The requirement to appropriateness is thus closely related to the requirement of effectiveness.

9. A technical or organisational measure and safeguard can be anything from the use of advanced technical solutions to the basic training of personnel. Examples that may be suitable, depending on the context and risks associated with the processing in question, includes pseudonymization of personal data[4]; storing personal data available in a structured, commonly machine readable format; enabling data subjects to intervene in the processing, providing information about the storage of personal data; having malware detection systems; training employees about basic "cyber hygiene"; establishing privacy and information security management systems, obligating processors contractually to implement specific data minimisation practices, etc.

10. Standards, best practices and codes of conduct that are recognized by associations and other bodies representing categories of controllers can be helpful in determining appropriate measures. However, the controller must verify the appropriateness of the measures for the particular processing in question.

2.1.2 Designed to implement the data protection principles in an effective manner and protecting data subjects' rights and freedoms

11. The *data protection principles* are in Article 5 (henceforth "the principles"), the *data subjects' rights and freedoms* are the fundamental rights and freedoms of natural persons, and in particular their right to the protection of personal data, whose protection is named in Article 1(2) as the objective of the GDPR (henceforth "the rights")[5]. Their precise formulation can be found in the EU Charter of Fundamental Rights. It is essential for the controller to have an understanding of the meaning of *the principles* and *the rights* as the basis for the protection offered by the GDPR, specifically by the DPbDD obligation.

12. When implementing the appropriate technical and organisational measures, it is with respect to the effective implementation of each of the aforementioned principles and the ensuing protection of rights that the measures and safeguards should be designed.

Addressing effectiveness

13. Effectiveness is at the heart of the concept of data protection by design. The requirement to implement the principles in an effective manner means that controllers must implement the necessary measures and safeguards to protect these principles, in order to secure the rights of data subjects. Each implemented measure should produce the intended results for the processing foreseen by the controller. This observation has two consequences.

14. First, it means that Article 25 does not require the implementation of any specific technical and organizational measures, rather that the chosen measures and safeguards should be specific to the implementation of data protection principles into the particular processing in question. In doing so, the measures and safeguards should be designed to be robust and the controller should be able to implement further measures in order to scale to any increase in risk[6]. Whether or not measures are effective will therefore depend on the context of the processing in question and an assessment of certain elements that should be taken into account when determining the means of processing. The aforementioned elements will be addressed below in subchapter 2.1.3.

15. Second, controllers should be able to demonstrate that the principles have been maintained.

16. The implemented measures and safeguards should achieve the desired effect in terms of data protection, and the controller should have documentation of the implemented technical and organizational measures.[7] To do so, the controller may determine appropriate key performance indicators (KPI) to demonstrate the effectiveness. A KPI is a measurable value chosen by the controller that demonstrates how effectively the controller achieves their data protection objective. KPIs may be *quantitative*, such as the percentage of false positives or false negatives, reduction of complaints, reduction of response time when data subjects exercise their rights; or *qualitative*, such as evaluations of performance, use of grading scales, or expert assessments. Alternatively to KPIs, controllers may be able to demonstrate the effective implementation of the principles by providing the rationale behind their assessment of the effectiveness of the chosen measures and safeguards.

Part 2   Data Protection: EU Law etc

2.1.3 Elements to take into account

17. Article 25 (1) lists elements that the controller has to take into account when determining the measures of a specific processing operation. In the following, we will provide guidance on how to apply these elements in the design process, which includes design of the default settings. These elements all contribute to determine whether a measure is appropriate to effectively implement the principles. Thus, each of these elements is not a goal in and of themselves, but are factors to be considered together to reach the objective.

2.1.3.1 "state of the art"

18. The concept of "state of the art" is present in various EU acquis, e.g. environmental protection and product safety. In the GDPR, reference to the "state of the art"[8] is made not only in Article 32, for security measures,[910] but also in Article 25, thus extending this benchmark to all technical and organisational measures embedded in the processing.

19. In the context of Article 25, the reference to "state of the art" imposes an obligation on controllers, when determining the appropriate technical and organisational measures, **to take account of the current progress in technology** that is available in the market. The requirement is for controllers to have knowledge of, and stay up to date on technological advances; how technology can present data protection risks or opportunities to the processing operation; and how to implement and update the measures and safeguards that *secure effective implementation* of the principles and rights of data subjects taking into account the evolving technological landscape.

20. The "state of the art" is a dynamic concept that cannot be statically defined at a fixed point in time, but should be assessed *continuously* in the context of technological progress. In the face of technological advancements, a controller could find that a measure that once provided an adequate level of protection no longer does. Neglecting to keep up to date with technological changes could therefore result in a lack of compliance with Article 25.

21. The "state of the art" criterion does not only apply to technological measures, but also to organisational ones. Lack of appropriate organisational measures can lower or even completely undermine the effectiveness of a chosen technology. Examples of organisational measures can be adoption of internal policies; up-to date training on technology, security and data protection; and IT security governance and management policies.

22. Existing and recognized frameworks, standards, certifications, codes of conduct, etc. in different fields may play a role in indicating the current "state of the art" within the given field of use. Where such standards exist and provide a high level of protection for the data subject in compliance with – or go beyond – legal requirements, controllers should take them into account in the design and implementation of data protection measures.

2.1.3.2 "cost of implementation"

23. The controller may take the cost of implementation into account when choosing and applying appropriate technical and organisational measures and necessary safeguards that effectively implement the principles in order to protect the rights of data subjects. The cost refers to resources in general, including time and human resources.

24. The cost element does not require the controller to spend a disproportionate amount of resources when alternative, less resource demanding, yet effective measures exist. However, the cost of implementation is a factor to be considered to implement data protection by design rather than a ground to not implement it.

25. Thus, the chosen measures shall ensure that the processing activity foreseen by the controller does not process personal data in violation of the principles, independent of cost. Controllers should be able to manage the overall costs to be able to effectively implement all of the principles and, consequentially, protect the rights.

2.1.3.3 "nature, scope, context and purpose of processing"

26. Controllers must take into consideration the nature, scope, context and purpose of processing when determining needed measures.

27. These factors should be interpreted consistently with their role in other provisions of the GDPR, such as Articles 24, 32 and 35, with the aim of designing data protection principles into the processing.

28. In short, the concept of **nature** can be understood as the inherent[11] characteristics of the processing. The **scope** refers to the size and range of the processing. The **context** relates to the circumstances of the processing, which may influence the expectations of the data subject, while the purpose pertains to the aims of the processing.

2.1.3.4 "risks of varying likelihood and severity for rights and freedoms of natural persons posed by the processing"

29. The GDPR adopts a coherent risk based approach in many of its provisions, in Articles 24, 25, 32 and 35, with a view to identifying appropriate technical and organisational measures to protect individuals, their personal data and complying with the requirements of the GDPR. The assets to protect are always the same (the individuals, via the protection of their personal data), against the same risks (to individuals' rights), taking into account the same conditions (nature, scope, context and purposes of processing).

30. When performing the risk analysis for compliance with Articles 25, the controller has to identify the risks to the rights of data subjects that a violation of the principles presents, and determine their likelihood and severity in order to implement measures to effectively mitigate the identified risks. A systematic and thorough evaluation of the processing is crucial when doing risk assessments. For example, a controller assesses the particular risks associated with a lack of freely given consent, which constitutes a violation of the lawfulness principle, in the course of the processing of personal data of children and young people under 18 as a vulnerable group, in a case where no other legal ground exists, and implements appropriate measures to address and effectively mitigate the identified risks associated with this group of data subjects.

31. The "EDPB Guidelines on Data Protection Impact Assessment (DPIA)",[12] which focus on determining whether a processing operation is likely to result in a high risk to the data subject or not, also provide guidance on how to assess data protection risks and how to carry out a data protection risk assessment. These Guidelines may also be useful during the risk assessment in all the articles mentioned above, including Article 25.

32. The risk based approach does not exclude the use of baselines, best practices and standards. These might provide a useful toolbox for controllers to tackle similar risks in similar situations (nature, scope, context and purpose of processing). Nevertheless, the obligation in Article 25 (as well as Articles 24, 32 and 35(7)(c)) to take into account "*risks of varying likelihood and severity for rights and freedoms of natural persons posed by the processing*" remains. Therefore, controllers, although supported by such tools, must always carry out a data protection risk assessment on a case by case basis for the processing activity at hand and verify the effectiveness of the appropriate measures and safeguards proposed. A DPIA, or an update to an existing DPIA, may then additionally be required.

2.1.4 Time aspect

2.1.4.1 At the time of the determination of the means for processing

33. Data protection by design shall be implemented "*at the time of determination of the means for processing*".

34. The "*means for processing*" range from the general to the detailed design elements of the processing, including the architecture, procedures, protocols, layout and appearance.

35. The "*time of determination of the means for processing*" refers to the period of time when the controller is deciding how the processing will be conducted and the manner in which the processing will occur and the mechanisms which will be used to conduct such processing. It's in the process of making such decisions that the controller must assess the appropriate measures and safeguards to effectively implement the principles and rights of data subjects into the processing, and take into account elements such as the state of the art, cost of implementation, nature, scope, context and purpose, and risks. This includes the time of procuring and implementing data processing software, hardware, and services.

36. Early consideration of DPbDD is crucial for a successful implementation of the principles and protection of the rights of the data subjects. Moreover, from a cost-benefit perspective, it is also in controllers' interest to take DPbDD into account sooner rather than later, as it could be challenging and costly to make later changes to plans that have already been made and processing operations that have already been designed.

2.1.4.2 At the time of the processing itself (maintenance and review of data protection requirements)

37. Once the processing has started the controller has a continued obligation to maintain DPbDD, i.e. the continued effective implementation of the principles in order to protect the rights, staying up to date on the state of the art, reassessing the level of risk, etc. The nature, scope and context of processing operations, as well as the risk may change over the course of processing, which means that the controller must re-evaluate their processing operations through regular reviews and assessments of the effectiveness of their chosen measures and safeguards.

38. The obligation to maintain, review and update, as necessary, the processing operation also applies to pre-existing systems. This means that legacy systems designed before the GDPR entered into force are required to undergo reviews and maintenance to ensure the implementation of measures and safeguards that implement the principles and rights of data subjects in an effective manner, as outlined in these Guidelines.

39. This obligation also extends to any processing carried out by means of data processors. Processors' operations should be regularly reviewed and assessed by the controllers to ensure that they enable continuous compliance with the principles and allow the data controller to fulfil its obligations in this respect.

2.2 ARTICLE 25(2): DATA PROTECTION BY DEFAULT

2.2.1 By default, only personal data which are necessary for each specific purpose of the processing are processed

40. A "default", as commonly defined in computer science, refers to the pre-existing or preselected value of a configurable setting that is assigned to a software application, computer program or device. Such settings are also called "presets" or "factory presets", especially for electronic devices.

41. Hence, the term "by default" when processing personal data, refers to making choices regarding configuration values or processing options that are set or prescribed in a processing system, such as a software application, service or device, or a manual processing procedure that affect the amount of personal data collected, the extent of their processing, the period of their storage and their accessibility.

42. The controller should choose and be accountable for implementing default processing settings and options in a way that only processing that is strictly necessary to achieve the set, lawful purpose is carried out by default. Here, controllers should rely on their assessment of the necessity of the processing with regards to the legal grounds of Article 6(1). This means that by default, the controller shall not collect more data than is necessary, they shall not process the data collected more than is necessary for their purposes, nor shall they store the data for longer than necessary. The basic requirement is that data protection is built into the processing by default.

43. The controller is required to predetermine for which specified, explicit and legitimate purposes the personal data is collected and processed.[13] The measures must by default be appropriate to ensure that only personal data which are necessary for each specific purpose of processing are being processed. The EDPS "Guidelines to assess necessity and proportionality of measures that limit the right to data protection of personal data" can be useful also to decide which data is necessary to process in order to achieve a specific purpose.[14] [15] [16]

44. If the controller uses third party software or off-the-shelf software, the controller should carry out a risk assessment of the product and make sure that functions that do not have a legal basis or are not compatible with the intended purposes of processing are switched off.

45. The same considerations apply to organisational measures supporting processing operations. They should be designed to process, at the outset, only the minimum amount of personal data necessary for the specific operations. This should be particularly considered when allocating data access to staff with different roles and different access needs.

46. Appropriate "technical and organisational measures" in the context of data protection by default is thus understood in the same way as discussed above in subchapter 2.1.1, but applied specifically to implementing the principle of data minimisation.

47. The aforementioned obligation to only process personal data which are necessary for each specific purpose applies to the following elements.

2.2.2 Dimensions of the data minimisation obligation

48. Article 25 (2) lists the dimensions of the data minimisation obligation for default processing, by stating that the obligation applies to the amount of personal data collected, the extent of their processing, the period of their storage and their accessibility.

2.2.2.1 *"amount of personal data collected"*

49. Controllers should consider both the volume of personal data, as well as the types, categories and level of detail of personal data required for the processing purposes. Their design choices should take into account the increased risks to the principles of integrity and confidentiality, data minimisation and storage limitation when collecting large amounts of detailed personal data, and compare it to the reduction in risks when collecting smaller amounts and/or less detailed information about data subjects. In any case, the default setting shall not include collection of personal data that is not necessary for the specific processing purpose. In other words, if certain categories of personal data are unnecessary or if detailed data isn't needed because less granular data is sufficient, then any surplus personal data shall not be collected.

50. The same default requirements apply to services independent of what platform or device in use, only the necessary personal data for the given purpose can be collected.

2.2.2.2 *"the extent of their processing"*

51. Processing[17] operations performed on personal data shall be limited to what is necessary. Many processing operations may contribute to a processing purpose. Nevertheless, the fact that certain personal data is necessary to fulfil a purpose does not mean that all types of, and frequencies of, processing operations may be carried out on the data. Controllers should also be careful not to extend the boundaries of "compatible purposes" of Article 6(4), and have in mind what processing will be within the reasonable expectations of data subjects.

2.2.2.3 *"the period of their storage"*

52. Personal data collected shall not be stored if it is not necessary for the purpose of the processing and there is no other compatible purpose and legal ground according to Article 6(4). Any retention should be objectively justifiable as necessary by the data controller in accordance with the accountability principle.

53. The controller shall limit the retention period to what is necessary for the purpose. If personal data is no longer necessary for the purpose of the processing, then it shall by default be deleted or anonymized. The length of the period of retention will therefore depend on the purpose of the processing in question. This obligation is directly related to the principle of storage limitation in Article 5(1)(e), and shall be implemented by default, i.e. the controller should have systematic procedures for data deletion or anonymization embedded in the processing.

54. Anonymization[18] of personal data is an alternative to deletion, provided that all the relevant contextual elements are taken into account and the likelihood and severity of the risk, including the risk of re- identification, are regularly assessed.[19]

2.2.2.4 "their accessibility"

55. The controller should limit who has access and which types of access to personal data based on an assessment of necessity, and also make sure that personal data is in fact accessible to those who need it when necessary, for example in critical situations. Access controls should be observed for the whole data flow during the processing.

56. Article 25(2) further states that personal data shall not be made accessible, without the individual's intervention, to an indefinite number of natural persons. The controller shall by default limit accessibility and give the data subject the possibility to intervene before publishing or otherwise making available personal data about the data subject to an indefinite number of natural persons.

57. Making personal data available to an indefinite number of persons may result in even further dissemination of the data than initially intended. This is particularly relevant in the context of the Internet and search engines. This means that controllers should by default give data subjects an opportunity to intervene before personal data is made available on the open Internet. This is particularly important when it comes to children and vulnerable groups.

58. Depending on the legal grounds for processing, the opportunity to intervene could vary based on the context of the processing. For example, to ask for consent to make the personal data publicly accessible, or to have privacy settings so that data subjects themselves can control public access.

59. Even in the event that personal data is made available publicly with the permission and understanding of a data subject, it does not mean that any other controller with access to the personal data may freely process it themselves for their own purposes – they must have their own legal basis.[20]

NOTES

3   "Effectiveness" is addressed below in subchapter 2.1.2.

4   Defined in Article 4(5) GDPR.

5   See Recital 4 of the GDPR.

6   "Fundamental principles applicable to the controllers (i.e. legitimacy, data minimisation, purpose limitation, transparency, data integrity, data accuracy) should remain the same, whatever the processing and the risks for the data subjects. However, due regard to the nature and scope of such processing have always been an integral part of the application of those principles, so that they are inherently scalable." Article 29 Working Party. "Statement on the role of a risk-based approach in data protection legal frameworks". WP 218, 30 May 2014, p. 3. ec.europa.eu/justice/article-29/documentation/opinion-recommendation/files/2014/wp218_en.pdf

7   See Recitals 74 and 78.

8   See German Federal Constitutional Court's "Kalkar" decision in 1978: https://germanlawarchive.iuscomp.org/?p=67 may provide the foundation for a methodology for an objective definition of the concept. On that basis, the "state of the art" technology level would be identified between the "existing scientific knowledge and research" technology level and the more established "generally accepted rules of technology". The "state of the art" can hence be identified as the technology level of a service or technology or product that exists in the market and is most effective in achieving the objectives identified.

9   https://www.enisa.europa.eu/news/enisa-news/what-is-state-of-the-art-in-it-security

10   www.teletrust.de/en/publikationen/broschueren/state-of-the-art-in-it-security/

11   Examples are special categories personal data, automatic decision-making, skewed power relations, unpredictable processing, difficulties for the data subject to exercise the rights, etc.

12   Article 29 Working Party "Guidelines on Data Protection Impact Assessment (DPIA) and determining whether processing is "likely to result in a high risk" for the purposes of Regulation 2016/679". WP 248 rev.01, 4 October 2017. ec.europa.eu/newsroom/document.cfm?doc_id=47711 - endorsed by the EDPB.

13   Art. 5(1)(b), (c), (d), (e) GDPR.

14   EDPS. "Guidelines on assessing the necessity and proportionality of measures that limit the right to data protection". 25 February 2019. edps.europa.eu/sites/edp/files/publication/19-02- 25_proportionality_guidelines_en.pdf

15   See also EDPS. "Assessing the necessity of measures that limit the fundamental right to the protection of personal data: A Toolkit" https://edps.europa.eu/data-protection/our-work/publications/papers/necessitytoolkit_en

16   For more information on necessity, see Article 29 Working Party. "Opinion 06/2014 on the notion of legitimate interests of the data controller under Article 7 of Directive 95/46/EC". WP 217, 9 April 2014. ec.europa.eu/justice/article-29/documentation/opinion-recommendation/files/2014/wp217_en.pdf

17   According to Art. 4(2) GDPR, this includes collection, recording, organisation, structuring, storage, adaptation or alteration, retrieval, consultation, use, disclosure by transmission, dissemination or otherwise making available, alignment or combination, restriction, erasure or destruction.

18   Article 29 Working Party. "Opinion 05/2014 on Anonymisation Techniques". WP 216, 10 April 2014. ec.europa.eu/justice/article-29/documentation/opinion-recommendation/files/2014/wp216_en.pdf

19   Please see Art. 4(1) GDPR, Recital 26 GDPR, Article 29 Working Party "Opinion 05/2014 on Anonymisation Techniques". Please also see the subsection on "storage limitation" in section 3 of this document, referring to the need for the controller to ensure the effectiveness of the implemented anonymisation technique(s).

20   See Case of Satakunnan Markkinapörssi Oy and Satamedia Oy v. Finland no. 931/13.

3 IMPLEMENTING DATA PROTECTION PRINCIPLES IN THE PROCESSING OF PERSONAL DATA USING DATA PROTECTION BY DESIGN AND BY DEFAULT

[2.313]

60. In all stages of design of the processing activities, including procurement, tenders, outsourcing, development, support, maintenance, testing, storage, deletion, etc., the controller should take into account and consider the various elements of DPbDD which will be illustrated by examples in this chapter in the context of implementation of the principles.[21] [22] [23]

61. Controllers need to implement the principles to achieve DPbDD. These principles include: transparency, lawfulness, fairness, purpose limitation, data minimisation, accuracy, storage limitation, integrity and confidentiality, and accountability. These principles are outlined in Article 5 and Recital 39 of the GDPR. To have a complete understanding of how to implement DPbDD, the importance of understanding the meaning of each of the principles is emphasised.

62. When presenting examples of how to operationalize DPbDD we have made lists of **key DPbDD elements** for each of the principles. The examples, while highlighting the specific data protection principle in question, may overlap with other closely related principles as well. The EDPB underlines that the key elements and the examples presented hereunder are neither exhaustive nor binding, but are meant as guiding elements for each of the principles. Controllers need to assess how to guarantee compliance with the principles in the context of the concrete processing operation in question.

63. While this section focuses on the implementation of the principles, the controller should also implement *appropriate* and *effective* ways to protect data subjects' rights, also according to Chapter III in the GDPR where this is not already mandated by the principles themselves.

64. The accountability principle is overarching: it requires the controller to be responsible choosing the necessary technical and organisational measures.

3.1 TRANSPARENCY[24]

65. The controller must be clear and open with the data subject about how they will collect, use and share personal data. Transparency is about enabling data subjects to understand, and if necessary, make use of their rights in Articles 15 to 22. The principle is embedded in Articles 12, 13, 14 and 34. Measures and safeguards put in place to support the principle of transparency should also support the implementation of these Articles.

66. Key design and default elements for the principle of transparency may include:
- Clarity – Information shall be in clear and plain language, concise and intelligible.
- Semantics – Communication should have a clear meaning to the audience in question.
- Accessibility - Information shall be easily accessible for the data subject.
- Contextual – Information should be provided at the relevant time and in the appropriate form.
- Relevance – Information should be relevant and applicable to the specific data subject.
- Universal design – Information shall be accessible to all data subjects, include use of machine readable languages to facilitate and automate readability and clarity.
- Comprehensible – Data subjects should have a fair understanding of what they can expect with regards to the processing of their personal data, particularly when the data subjects are children or other vulnerable groups.
- Multi-channel – Information should be provided in different channels and media, not only the textual, to increase the probability for the information to effectively reach the data subject.
- Layered – The information should be layered in a manner that resolves the tension between completeness and understanding, while accounting for data subjects' reasonable expectations.

Example[25]

A controller is designing a privacy policy on their website in order to comply with the requirements of transparency. The privacy policy should not contain a lengthy bulk of information that is difficult for the average data subject to penetrate and understand. It shall be written in clear and concise language and make it easy for the user of the website to understand how their personal data is processed. The controller therefore provides information in a layered manner, where the most important points are highlighted. More detailed information is made easily available. Drop-down menus and links to other pages are provided to further explain the various items, and concepts used in the policy. The controller also makes sure that the information is provided in a multi-channel manner, providing video clips to explain the most important points of the written information. Synergy between the various pages is vital to ensure that the layered approach does not heighten confusion, rather reduce it.

The privacy policy should not be difficult for data subjects to access. The privacy policy is thus made available and visible on all web-pages of the site in question, so that the data subject is always only one click away from accessing the information. The information provided is also designed in accordance with the best practices and standards of universal design to make it accessible to all.

Moreover, necessary information should also be provided in the right context, at the appropriate time. Since the controller carries out many processing operations using the data collected on the website, a general privacy policy on the website alone is not sufficient for the controller to meet the requirements of transparency. The controller therefore designs an information flow, presenting the data subject with relevant information within the appropriate contexts using e.g. informational snippets or pop-ups. For example, when asking the data subject to enter personal data, the controller informs the data subject of how the personal data will be processed and why that personal data is necessary for the processing.

3.2 LAWFULNESS

67. The controller must identify a valid legal basis for the processing of personal data. Measures and safeguards should support the requirement to make sure that the whole processing lifecycle is in line with the relevant legal grounds of processing.

68. Key design and default elements for lawfulness may include:
- Relevance – The correct legal basis shall be applied to the processing.
- Differentiation[26] – The legal basis used for each processing activity shall be differentiated.
- Specified purpose – The appropriate legal basis must be clearly connected to the specific purpose of processing.[27]
- Necessity– Processing must be necessary and unconditional for the purpose to be lawful.
- Autonomy – The data subject should be granted the highest degree of autonomy as possible with respect to control over personal data within the frames of the legal basis.
- Gaining consent – consent must be freely given, specific, informed and unambiguous.[28] Particular consideration should be given to the capacity of children and young people to provide informed consent.
- Consent withdrawal – Where consent is the legal basis, the processing should facilitate withdrawal of consent. Withdrawal shall be as easy as giving consent. If not, then the consent mechanism of the controller does not comply with the GDPR.[29]
- Balancing of interests – Where legitimate interests is the legal basis, the controller must carry out a weighted balancing of interest, giving particular consideration to the power imbalance, specifically children under the age of 18 and other vulnerable groups. There shall be measures and safeguards to mitigate the negative impact on the data subjects.
- Predetermination – The legal basis shall be established before the processing takes place.
- Cessation – If the legal basis ceases to apply, the processing shall cease accordingly.
- Adjust – If there is a valid change of legal basis for the processing, the actual processing must be adjusted in accordance with the new legal basis.[30]
- Allocation of responsibility – Whenever joint controllership is envisaged, the parties must apportion in a clear and transparent way their respective responsibilities vis-à-vis the data subject, and design the measures of the processing in accordance with this allocation.

Example

A bank plans to offer a service to improve efficiency in the management of loan applications. The idea behind the service is that the bank, by requesting permission from the customer, is able to retrieve data about the customer directly from the public tax authorities. This example does not consider processing of personal data from other sources.

Obtaining personal data about the data subject's financial situation is necessary in order to take steps at the request of the data subject prior to entering into a loan contract.[31] However, gathering personal data directly from the tax administration is not considered necessary, because the customer is able to enter into a contract by providing the information from the tax administration him or herself. Although the bank may have a legitimate interest in acquiring the documentation from the tax authorities directly, for example to ensure efficiency in the loan processing, giving banks such direct access to the personal data of applicants presents a risks related to the use or potential misuse of access rights

When implementing the principle of lawfulness, the controller realizes that in this context, they cannot use the "necessary for contract" basis for the part of the processing that involves gathering personal data directly from the tax authorities. The fact that this specific processing presents a risk of the data subject becoming less involved in the processing of their data is also a relevant factor in assessing the lawfulness of the processing itself. The bank concludes that this part of the processing has to rely on another legal basis of processing. In the particular Member State where the controller is located, there are national laws that permits the bank to gather information from the public tax authorities directly, where the data subject consents to this beforehand.

The bank therefore presents information about the processing on the online application platform in such a manner that makes it easy for data subjects to understand what processing is mandatory and what is optional. The processing options, by default, do not allow retrieval of data directly from other sources than the data subject herself, and the option for direct information retrieval is presented in a manner that does not deter the data subject from abstaining. Any consent given to collect data directly from other controllers is a temporary right of access to a specific set of information.

Any given consent is processed electronically in a documentable manner, and data subjects are presented with an easy way of controlling what they have consented to and to withdraw their consent.

The controller has assessed these DPbDD requirements beforehand and includes all of these criteria in their requirements specification for the tender to procure the platform. The controller is aware that if they do not include the DPbDD requirements in the tender, it may either be too late or a very costly process to implement data protection afterwards.

3.3 FAIRNESS

69. Fairness is an overarching principle which requires that personal data should not be processed in a way that is unjustifiably detrimental, unlawfully discriminatory, unexpected or misleading to the data subject. Measures and safeguards implementing the principle of fairness also support the rights and freedoms of data subjects, specifically the right to information (transparency), the right to intervene (access, erasure, data portability, rectify) and the right to limit the processing (right not to be subject to automated individual decision-making and non-discrimination of data subjects in such processes).

70. Key design and default fairness elements may include:
* Autonomy – Data subjects should be granted the highest degree of autonomy possible to determine the use made of their personal data, as well as over the scope and conditions of that use or processing.
* Interaction – Data subjects must be able to communicate and exercise their rights in respect of the personal data processed by the controller.
* Expectation – Processing should correspond with data subjects' reasonable expectations.
* Non-discrimination – The controller shall not unfairly discriminate against data subjects.
* Non-exploitation – The controller should not exploit the needs or vulnerabilities of data subjects.
* Consumer choice – The controller should not "lock in" their users in an unfair manner. Whenever a service processing personal data is proprietary, it may create a lock-in to the service, which may not be fair, if it impairs the data subjects' possibility to exercise their right of data portability in accordance with Article 20.
* Power balance – Power balance should be a key objective of the controller-data subject relationship. Power imbalances should be avoided. When this is not possible, they should be recognised and accounted for with suitable countermeasures.
* No risk transfer – Controllers should not transfer the risks of the enterprise to the data subjects.
* No deception – Data processing information and options should be provided in an objective and neutral way, avoiding any deceptive or manipulative language or design.
* Respect rights – The controller must respect the fundamental rights of data subjects and implement appropriate measures and safeguards and not impinge on those rights unless expressly justified by law.
* Ethical – The controller should see the processing's wider impact on individuals' rights and dignity.
* Truthful – The controller must make available information about how they process personal data, they should act as they declare they will and not mislead the data subjects.
* Human intervention – The controller must incorporate *qualified* human intervention that is capable of uncovering biases that machines may create in accordance with the right to not be subject to automated individual decision making in Article 22.[32]
* Fair algorithms – Regularly assess whether algorithms are functioning in line with the purposes and adjust the algorithms to mitigate uncovered biases and ensure fairness in the processing. Data subjects should be informed about the functioning of the processing of personal data based on algorithms that analyse or make predictions about them, such as work performance, economic situation, health, personal preferences, reliability or behaviour, location or movements.[33]

Example 1
A controller operates a search engine that processes mostly user-generated personal data. The controller benefits from having large amounts of personal data and being able to use that personal data for targeted advertisements. The controller therefore wishes to influence data subjects to allow more extensive collection and use of their personal data. Consent is to be collected by presenting processing options to the data subject.

When implementing the fairness principle, taking into account the nature, scope, context and purpose of the processing, the controller realizes that they cannot present the options in a way that nudges the data subject in the direction of allowing the controller to collect more personal data than if the options were presented in an equal and neutral way. This means that they cannot present the processing options in such a manner that makes it difficult for data subjects to abstain from sharing their data, or make it difficult for the data subjects to adjust their privacy settings and limit the processing. These are examples of dark patterns, which are contrary to the spirit of Article 25. The default options for the processing should not be invasive, and the choice for further processing should be presented in a manner that does not pressure the data subject to give consent. Therefore, the controller presents the options to consent or abstain as two equally visible choices, accurately representing the ramifications of each choice to the data subject.

Example 2

Another controller processes personal data for the provision of a streaming service where users may choose between a regular subscription of standard quality and a premium subscription with higher quality. As part of the premium subscription, subscribers get prioritized customer service.

With regard to the fairness principle, the prioritized customer service granted to premium subscribers cannot discriminate the regular subscribers' access to exercise their rights according to the GDPR Article 12. This means that although the premium subscribers get prioritized service, such prioritization cannot result in a lack of appropriate measures to respond to request from regular subscribers without undue delay and in any event within one month of receipt of the requests.

Prioritized customers may pay to get better service, but all data subjects shall have equal and indiscriminate access to enforce their rights and freedoms as required under Article 12.

3.4 PURPOSE LIMITATION[34]

71. The controller must collect data for specified, explicit, and legitimate purposes, and not further process the data in a manner that is incompatible with the purposes for which they were collected.[35] The design of the processing should therefore be shaped by what is necessary to achieve the purposes. If any further processing is to take place, the controller must first make sure that this processing has purposes compatible with the original ones and design such processing accordingly. Whether a new purpose is compatible or not, shall be assessed according to the criteria in Article 6(4).

72. Key design and default purpose limitation elements may include:
* Predetermination – The legitimate purposes shall be determined before the design of the processing.
* Specificity – The purposes shall be specified and explicit as to why personal data is being processed.
* Purpose orientation – The purpose of processing should guide the design of the processing and set processing boundaries.
* Necessity – The purpose determines what personal data is necessary for the processing.
* Compatibility – Any new purpose must be compatible with the original purpose for which the data was collected and guide relevant changes in design.
* Limit further processing – The controller should not connect datasets or perform any further processing for new incompatible purposes.
* Limitations of reuse – The controller should use technical measures, including hashing and encryption, to limit the possibility of repurposing personal data. The controller should also have organisational measures, such as policies and contractual obligations, which limit reuse of personal data.
* Review – The controller should regularly review whether the processing is necessary for the purposes for which the data was collected and test the design against purpose limitation.

Example

The controller processes personal data about its customers. The purpose of the processing is to fulfil a contract, i.e. to be able to deliver goods to the correct address and obtain payment. The personal data stored is the purchase history, name, address, e-mail address and telephone number.

The controller is considering buying a Customer Relationship Management (CRM) product that gathers all the customer data about sales, marketing and customer service in one place. The product gives the opportunity of storing all phone calls, activities, documents, emails and marketing campaigns to get a 360-degree view of the customer. Moreover, the CRM is capable of automatically analysing the customers' purchasing power by using public information. The purpose of the analysis is to better target advertising activities. Those activities do not form part of the original lawful purpose of the processing.

To be in line with the principle of purpose limitation, the controller requires the provider of the product to map the different processing activities that use personal data to the purposes relevant for the controller.

After receiving the results of the mapping, the controller assesses whether the new marketing purpose and the targeted advertisement purpose are compatible with the original purposes defined when the data was collected, and whether there is a sufficient legal basis for the respective processing. If the assessment does not return a positive answer, the controller shall not proceed to use the respective functionalities. Alternatively, the controller could choose to forego the assessment and simply not make use of the described functionalities of the product.

3.5 DATA MINIMISATION

73. Only personal data that is adequate, relevant and limited to what is **necessary** for the purpose shall be processed.[36] As a result, the controller has to predetermine which features and parameters of processing systems and their supporting functions are permissible. Data minimisation substantiates and operationalises the principle of necessity. In the further processing, the controller should periodically consider whether processed personal data is still adequate, relevant and necessary, or if the data shall be deleted or anonymized.

74. Controllers should first of all determine whether they even need to process personal data for their relevant purposes. The controller should verify whether the relevant purposes can be achieved by processing less personal data, or having less detailed or aggregated personal data or without having to process personal data at all[37]. Such verification should take place before any processing takes place, but could also be carried out at any point during the processing lifecycle. This is also consistent with Article 11.

75. Minimising can also refer to the degree of identification. If the purpose of the processing does not require the final set of data to refer to an identified or identifiable individual (such as in statistics), but the initial processing does (e.g. before data aggregation), then the controller shall delete or anonymize personal data as soon as identification is no longer needed. Or, if continued identification is needed for other processing activities, personal data should be pseudonymized to mitigate risks for the data subjects' rights.

76. Key design and default data minimisation elements may include:
* Data avoidance – Avoid processing personal data altogether when this is possible for the relevant purpose.
* Limitation – Limit the amount of personal data collected to what is necessary for the purpose
* Access limitation – Shape the data processing in a way that a minimal number of people need access to personal data to perform their duties, and limit access accordingly.
* Relevance – Personal data should be relevant to the processing in question, and the controller should be able to demonstrate this relevance.
* Necessity – Each personal data category shall be necessary for the specified purposes and should only be processed if it is not possible to fulfil the purpose by other means.
* Aggregation – Use aggregated data when possible.
* Pseudonymization – Pseudonymize personal data as soon as it is no longer necessary to have directly identifiable personal data, and store identification keys separately.
* Anonymization and deletion – Where personal data is not, or no longer necessary for the purpose, personal data shall be anonymized or deleted.
* Data flow – The data flow should be made efficient enough to not create more copies than necessary.
* "State of the art" – The controller should apply up to date and appropriate technologies for data avoidance and minimisation.

Example 1

A bookshop wants to add to their revenue by selling their books online. The bookshop owner wants to set up a standardised form for the ordering process. To ensure customers fill out all the wanted information the bookshop owner makes all of the fields in the form mandatory (if you don't fill out all the fields the customer can't place the order). The webshop owner initially uses a standard contact form, which asks information including the customer's date of birth, phone number and home address. However, not all the fields in the form are necessary for the purpose of buying and delivering the books. In this particular case, if the data subject pays for the product up front, the data subject's date of birth and phone number are not necessary for the purchase of the product. This means that these cannot be required fields in the web form to order the product, unless the controller can clearly demonstrate that it is otherwise necessary, and why the fields are necessary. Moreover, there are situations where an address will not be necessary. For example, when ordering an eBook the customer can download the product directly to their device.

The webshop owner therefore decides to make two web forms: one for ordering books, with a field for the customer's address and one web form for ordering eBooks without a field for the customer's address.

Example 2

A public transportation company wishes to gather statistical information based on travellers' routes. This is useful for the purposes of making proper choices on changes in public transport schedules and proper routings of the trains. The passengers have to pass their ticket through a reader every time they enter or exit a means of transport. Having carried out a risk assessment related to the rights and freedoms of passengers' regarding the collection of passengers' travel routes, the controller establishes that it is possible to identify the passengers in circumstances where they live or work in scarcely populated areas, based on single route identification thanks to the ticket identifier. Therefore, since it is not necessary for the purpose of optimizing the public transport schedules and routings of the trains, the controller does not store the ticket identifier. Once the trip is over, the controller only stores the individual travel routes so as to not be able to identify trips connected to a single ticket, but only retains information about separate travel routes.

In cases where there can still be a risk of identifying a person solely by their public transportation travel route the controller implements statistical measures to reduce the risk, such as cutting the beginning and the end of the route.

Example 3

A courier aims at assessing the effectiveness of its deliveries in terms of delivery times, workload scheduling and fuel consumption. In order to reach this goal, the courier has to process a number of personal data relating to both employees (drivers) and customers (addresses, items to be delivered, etc.). This processing operation entails risks of both monitoring employees, which requires specific legal safeguards, and tracking customers' habits through the knowledge of the delivered items over time. These risks can be significantly reduced with appropriate pseudonymization of employees and customers. In particular if pseudonymization keys are frequently rotated and macro areas are considered instead of detailed addresses, an effective data minimisation is pursued, and the controller can solely focus on the delivery process and on the purpose of resource optimization, without crossing the threshold of monitoring individuals' (customers' or employees') behaviours.

Example 4

A hospital is collecting data about its patients in a hospital information system (electronic health record). Hospital staff needs to access patient files to inform their decisions regarding care for and treatment of the patients, and for the documentation of all diagnostic, care and treatment actions taken. By default, access is granted to only those members of the medical staff who are assigned to the treatment of the respective patient in the speciality department she or he is assigned to. The group of people with access to a patient's file is enlarged if other departments or diagnostic units are involved in the treatment. After the patient is discharged, and billing is completed, access is reduced to a small group of employees per speciality department who answer requests for medical information or a consultation made or asked for by other medical service providers upon authorization by the respective patient.

3.6 ACCURACY

77. Personal data shall be accurate and kept up to date, and every reasonable step shall be taken to ensure that personal data that is inaccurate, having regard to the purposes for which they are processed, are erased or rectified without delay.[38]

78. The requirements should be seen in relation to the risks and consequences of the concrete use of data. Inaccurate personal data could be a risk to the data subjects' rights and freedoms, for example when leading to a faulty diagnosis or wrongful treatment of a health protocol, or an incorrect image of a person can lead to decisions being made on the wrong basis either manually, using automated decision-making, or through artificial intelligence.

79. Key design and default accuracy elements may include:
*   Data source – Sources of personal data should be reliable in terms of data accuracy.
*   Degree of accuracy – Each personal data element should be as accurate as necessary for the specified purposes.
*   Measurably accurate - Reduce the number of false positives/negatives, for example biases in automated decisions and artificial intelligence.
*   Verification – Depending on the nature of the data, in relation to how often it may change, the controller should verify the correctness of personal data with the data subject before and at different stages of the processing (e.g. to age requirements).
*   Erasure/rectification – The controller shall erase or rectify inaccurate data without delay. The controller shall in particular facilitate this where the data subjects are or were children and later want to remove such personal data.[39]
*   Error propagation avoidance – Controllers should mitigate the effect of an accumulated error in the processing chain.
*   Access – Data subjects should be given information about and effective access to personal data in accordance with the GDPR articles 12 to 15 in order to control accuracy and rectify as needed.
*   Continued accuracy – Personal data should be accurate at all stages of the processing, tests of accuracy should be carried out at critical steps.
*   Up to date – Personal data shall be updated if necessary for the purpose.
*   Data design – Use of technological and organisational design features to decrease inaccuracy, for example present concise predetermined choices instead of free text fields.

Example 1

An insurance company wishes to use artificial intelligence (AI) to profile customers buying insurance as a basis for their decision making when calculating the insurance risk. When determining how their AI solutions should be developed, they are determining the means of processing and shall consider data protection by design when choosing an AI application from a vendor and when deciding on how to train the AI.

When determining how to train the AI, the controller should have accurate data to achieve precise results. Therefore, the controller should ensure that the data used to train the AI is accurate.

Granted that they have a valid legal basis to train the AI using personal data from a large subset of their existing customers, the controller chooses a pool of customers that is representative of the population to also avoid bias.

The customer data is then collected from the respective data handling system, including data on the type of insurance, for example health insurance, home insurance, travel insurance, etc. as well as data from public registries they have lawful access to. All data are pseudonymized prior to transfer to the system dedicated to the training of the AI model.

To ensure that the data used for AI training is as accurate as possible, the controller only collects data from data sources with correct and up-to date information.

The insurance company tests whether the AI is reliable and provides non-discriminatory results both during its development and finally before the product is released. When the AI is fully trained and operative, the insurance company uses the results to support the insurance risk assessments, yet without solely relying on the AI to decide whether to grant insurance, unless the decision is made in accordance with the exceptions in Article 22 (2) GDPR.

The insurance company will also regularly review the results from the AI, to maintain the reliability and when necessary adjust the algorithm.

Example 2

The controller is a health institution looking to find methods to ensure the integrity and accuracy of personal data in their client registers.

In situations where two persons arrive at the institution at the same time and receive the same treatment, there is a risk of mistaking them if the only parameter to distinguish them is by name. To ensure accuracy, the controller needs a unique identifier for each person, and therefore more information than just the name of the client.

The institution uses several systems containing personal information of clients, and needs to ensure that the information related to the client is correct, accurate and consistent in all the systems at any point in time. The institution has identified several risks that may arise if information is changed in one system but not in the others.

The controller decides to mitigate the risk by using a hashing technique that can be used to ensure integrity of data in the treatment journal. Immutable cryptographic time stamps are created for treatment journal records and the client associated with them so that any changes can be recognized, correlated and traced if required.

3.7 STORAGE LIMITATION

80. The controller must ensure that personal data is kept in a form which permits identification of data subjects for no longer than is necessary for the purposes for which the personal data is processed.[40]

It is vital that the controller knows exactly what personal data the company processes and why. The purpose of the processing shall be the main criterion to decide in how long personal data shall be stored.

81. Measures and safeguards that implement the principle of storage limitation shall complement the rights and freedoms of the data subjects, specifically, the right to erasure and the right to object.

82. Key design and default storage limitation elements may include:
* Deletion and anonymization – The controller should have clear internal procedures and functionalities for deletion and/or anonymization.
* Effectiveness of anonymization/deletion – The controller shall make sure that it is not possible to re-identify anonymized data or recover deleted data, and should test whether this is possible.
* Automation – Deletion of certain personal data should be automated
* Storage criteria – The controller shall determine what data and length of storage is necessary for the purpose.
* Justification – The controller shall be able to justify why the period of storage is necessary for the purpose and the personal data in question, and be able to disclose the rationale behind, and legal grounds for the retention period.
* Enforcement of retention policies – The controller should enforce internal retention policies and conduct tests of whether the organization practices its policies.
* Backups/logs – Controllers shall determine what personal data and length of storage is necessary for back-ups and logs.

- Data flow – Controllers should beware of the flow of personal data, and the storage of any copies thereof, and seek to limit their "temporary" storage.

Example

The controller collects personal data where the purpose of the processing is to administer a membership of the data subject. The personal data shall be deleted when the membership is terminated and there is no legal basis for further storage of the data.

The controller first draws up an internal procedure for data retention and deletion. According to this, employees shall manually delete personal data after the retention period ends. The employee follows the procedure to regularly delete and correct data from any devices, from backups, logs, e-mails and other relevant storage media.

To make deletion more effective, and less error-prone, the controller then implements an automatic system instead, in order to delete data automatically, reliably and more regularly. The system is configured to follow the given procedure for data deletion which then occurs at a predefined regular interval to remove personal data from all of the company's storage media. The controller reviews and tests the retention procedure regularly and ensures that it concurs with the up-to-date retention policy.

3.8 INTEGRITY AND CONFIDENTIALITY

83.   The principle of integrity and confidentiality includes protection against unauthorised or unlawful processing and against accidental loss, destruction or damage, using appropriate technical or organisational measures. The security of personal data requires appropriate measures designed to prevent and manage data breach incidents; to guarantee the proper execution of data processing tasks, and compliance with the other principles; and to facilitate the effective exercise of individuals' rights.

84.   Recital 78 states that one of the DPbDD measures could consist of enabling the controller to "*create and improve security features*". Along with other DPbDD measures, Recital 78 suggests a responsibility on the controllers to continually assess whether it is using the appropriate means of processing at all times and to assess whether the chosen measures actually counter the existing vulnerabilities. Furthermore, controllers should conduct regular reviews of the information security measures that surround and protect personal data, and the procedure for handling data breaches.

85.   Key design and default integrity and confidentiality elements may include:
- Information security management system (ISMS) – Have an operative means of managing policies and procedures for information security.
- Risk analysis – Assess the risks against the security of personal data by considering the impact on individuals' rights and counter identified risks. For use in risk assessment; develop and maintain a comprehensive, systematic and realistic "threat modelling" and an attack surface analysis of the designed software to reduce attack vectors and opportunities to exploit weak points and vulnerabilities.
- Security by design – Consider security requirements as early as possible in the system design and development and continuously integrate and perform relevant tests.
- Maintenance – Regular review and test software, hardware, systems and services, etc. to uncover vulnerabilities of the systems supporting the processing.
- Access control management – Only the authorized personnel who need to should have access to the personal data necessary for their processing tasks, and the controller should differentiate between access privileges of authorized personnel.
  - Access limitation (agents) – Shape the data processing in a way that a minimal number of people need access to personal data to perform their duties, and limit access accordingly.
  - Access limitation (content) – In the context of each processing operation, limit access to only those attributes per data set that are needed to perform that operation.
    Moreover, limit access to data pertaining to those data subjects who are in the remit of the respective employee.
  - Access segregation – Shape the data processing in a way that no individual needs comprehensive access to all data collected about a data subject, much less all personal data of a particular category of data subjects.
- Secure transfers – Transfers shall be secured against unauthorized and accidental access and changes.
- Secure storage – Data storage shall be secure from unauthorized access and changes. There should be procedures to assess the risk of centralized or decentralized storage, and what categories of personal data this applies to. Some data may need additional security measures than others or isolation from others.
- Pseudonymization – Personal data and back-ups/logs should be pseudonymized as a security measure to minimise risks of potential data breaches, for example using hashing or encryption.
- Backups/logs – Keep back-ups and logs to the extent necessary for information security, use audit trails and event monitoring as a routine security control. These shall be protected from unauthorised and accidental access and change and reviewed regularly and incidents should be handled promptly.
- Disaster recovery/ business continuity – Address information system disaster recovery and business continuity requirements to restore the availability of personal data following up major incidents.

- Protection according to risk – All categories of personal data should be protected with measures adequate with respect to the risk of a security breach. Data presenting special risks should, when possible, be kept separated from the rest of the personal data.
- Security incident response management – Have in place routines, procedures and resources to detect, contain, handle, report and learn from data breaches.
- Incident management – Controller should have processes in place to handle breaches and incidents, in order to make the processing system more robust. This includes notification procedures, such as management of notification (to the supervisory authority) and information (to data subjects).

Example

A controller wants to extract large quantities of personal data from a medical database containing electronic (patient) health records to a dedicated database server in the company in order to process the extracted data for quality assurance purposes. The company has assessed the risk for routing the extracts to a server that is accessible to all of the company's employees as likely to be high for data subjects' rights and freedoms. Since there is only one department in the company who needs to process the patient data extracts, the controller decides to restrict access to the dedicated server to employees in that department. Moreover, to further reduce risk, the data will be pseudonymized before they are transferred.

To regulate access and mitigate possible damage from malware, the company decides to segregate the network, and establish access controls to the server. In addition, they put up security monitoring and an intrusion detection and prevention system and isolates it from routine use. An automated auditing system is put in place to monitor access and changes. Reporting and automated alerts are generated from this when certain events related to usage are configured. The controller will ensure that users only have access on a need to know basis and with the appropriate access level. Inappropriate use can be quickly and easily detected.

Some of the extracts have to be compared with new extracts, and therefore are required to be stored for three months. The controller decides to put them into separate databases on the same server, and use both transparent and column-level encryption to store them. Keys for column data decryption are stored in dedicated security modules that can only be used by authorized personnel, but not extracted.

Handling upcoming incidents makes the system more robust, and reliable. The data controller understands that preventative and effective measures and safeguards should be built into all personal data processing it undertakes now and in the future, and that doing so may help prevent future such data breach incidents.

The controller establishes these security measures both to ensure accuracy, integrity and confidentiality, but also to prevent malware spread by cyber-attacks and to make the solution robust. Having robust security measures contributes to build trust with the data subjects.

3.9 ACCOUNTABILITY[41]

86. The principle of accountability states that the controller shall be responsible for, and be able to demonstrate compliance with all of the abovementioned principles.

87. The controller needs to be able to demonstrate compliance with the principles. In doing so, the controller may demonstrate the effects of the measures taken to protect the data subjects' rights, and why the measures are considered to be appropriate and effective. For example, demonstrating why a measure is appropriate to ensure the principle of storage limitation in an effective manner.

88. To be able to process personal data responsibly, the controller should have both the knowledge of and the ability to implement data protection. This entails that the controller should understand their data protection obligations of the GDPR and be able to comply with these obligations.

NOTES

[21] More examples can be found in Norwegian Data Protection Authority. "Software Development with Data Protection by Design and by Default". 28 November 2017. www.datatilsynet.no/en/about-privacy/virksomhetenes-plikter/innebygd-personvern/data-protection-by-design-and-by-default/?id=7729

[22] https://www.cnil.fr/en/cnil-publishes-gdpr-guide-developers

[23] https://www.aepd.es/sites/default/files/2019-12/guia-privacidad-desde-diseno_en.pdf

[24] Elaboration on how to understand the concept of transparency can be found in Article 29 Working Party. "Guidelines on transparency under Regulation 2016/679". WP 260 rev.01, 11 April 2018. ec.europa.eu/newsroom/article29/document.cfm?action=display&doc_id=51025 - endorsed by the EDPB

[25] The French Data Protection Authority has published several examples illustrating best practices in informing users as well as other transparency principles: https://design.cnil.fr/en/.

[26] EDPB. "Guidelines 2/2019 on the processing of personal data under Article 6(1)(b) GDPR in the context of the provision of online services to data subjects". Version 2.0, 8 October 2019. edpb.europa.eu/sites/edpb/files/files/file1/edpb_guidelines-art_6-1-b-adopted_after_public_consultation_en.pdf

[27] See section on purpose limitation below.

[28] See Guidelines 05/2020 on consent under Regulation 2016/679. https://edpb.europa.eu/our-work-tools/our-documents/guidelines/guidelines-052020-consent-under-regulation-2016679_en

29   See Guidelines 05/2020 on consent under Regulation 2016/679, p. 24. https://edpb.europa.eu/our-work-tools/our-documents/guidelines/guidelines-052020-consent-under-regulation-2016679_en

30   If the original legal basis is consent, see Guidelines 05/2020 on consent under Regulation 2016/679. https://edpb.europa.eu/our-work-tools/our-documents/guidelines/guidelines-052020-consent-under-regulation-2016679_en

31   See Article 6(1)(b) GDPR.

32   See Guidelines on Automated individual decision-making and Profiling for the purposes of Regulation 2016/679. https://ec.europa.eu/newsroom/article29/document.cfm?action=display&doc_id=49826

33   See Recital 71 GDPR.

34   The Article 29 Working Party provided guidance for the understanding of the principle of purpose limitation under Directive 95/46/EC. Although the Opinion is not adopted by the EDPB, it may still be relevant as the wording of the principle is the same under the GDPR. Article 29 Working Party. "Opinion 03/2013 on purpose limitation". WP 203, 2 April 2013. ec.europa.eu/justice/article-29/documentation/opinion-recommendation/files/2013/wp203_en.pdf

35   Art. 5(1)(b) GDPR.

36   Art. 5(1)(c) GDPR.

37   Recital 39 GDPR so states: " . . . Personal data should be processed only if the purpose of the processing could not reasonably be fulfilled by other means."

38   Art. 5(1)(d) GDPR.

39   Cf. Recital 65.

40   Art. 5(1)(c) GDPR.

41   See Recital 74, where controllers are required to demonstrate the effectiveness of their measures.

4 ARTICLE 25(3) CERTIFICATION

[2.314]

89. According to Article 25(3), certification pursuant to Article 42 may be used as an element to demonstrate compliance with DPbDD. Conversely, documents demonstrating compliance with DPbDD may also be useful in a certification process. This means that where a processing operation by a controller or a processor has been certified as per Article 42, supervisory authorities shall take this into account in their assessment of compliance with the GDPR, specifically with regards to DPbDD.

90. When a processing operation by a controller or processor is certified according to Article 42, the elements that contribute to demonstrating compliance with Article 25(1) and (2) are the design processes, i.e. the process of determining the means of processing, the governance and the technical and organizational measures to implement the data protection principles The data protection certification criteria are determined by the certification bodies or certification scheme owners and then approved by the competent supervisory authority or by the EDPB. For further information about certification mechanisms, we refer the reader to the EDPB Guideline on Certification[42] and other relevant guidance, as published on the EDPB website.

91. Even where a processing operation is awarded a certification in accordance with Article 42, the controller still has the responsibility to continuously monitor and improve compliance with the DPbDD-criteria of Article 25.

NOTES
42   EDPB. "Guidelines 1/2018 on certification and identifying certification criteria in accordance with Articles 42 and 43 of the Regulation". Version 3.0, 4 June 2019. edpb.europa.eu/sites/edpb/files/files/file1/edpb_guidelines_201801_v3.0_certificationcriteria_annex2_en.pdf

5 ENFORCEMENT OF ARTICLE 25 AND CONSEQUENCES

[2.315]

92. Supervisory authorities may assess compliance with Article 25 according to the procedures listed in Article 58. The corrective powers are specified in Article 58(2) and include the issuance of warnings, reprimands, orders to comply with data subjects' rights, limitations on or ban of processing, administrative fines, etc.

93. DPbDD is further a factor in determining the level of monetary sanctions for breaches of the GDPR, see Article 83(4).[43] [44]

NOTES
43   Article 83(2)(d) GDPR stipulates that in determining the imposition of fines for breach of the GDPR *"due regard" shall be taken of "the degree of responsibility of the controller or processor taking into account technical and organisational measures implemented by them pursuant to Articles 25 and 32".*

44   More information on fines can be found in Article 29 Working Party. "Guidelines on application and setting of administrative fines for the purposes of the Regulation 2016/679". WP 253, 3 October 2017. ec.europa.eu/newsroom/just/document.cfm?doc_id=47889 - endorsed by the EDPB.

6 RECOMMENDATIONS

[2.316]

94. Although not directly addressed in Article 25, processors and producers are also recognized as key enablers for DPbDD, they should be aware that controllers are required to only process personal data with systems and technologies that have built-in data protection.

95. When processing on behalf of controllers, or providing solutions to controllers, processors and producers should use their expertise to build trust and guide their customers, including SMEs, in designing /procuring solutions that embed data protection into the processing. This means in turn that the design of products and services should facilitate controllers' needs.

96. It should be kept in mind when implementing Article 25 that the main design objective is the *effective implementation* of the principles and protection of the rights of data subjects into the appropriate measures of the processing. In order to facilitate and enhance the adoption of DPbDD, we make the following recommendations to controllers as well as producers and processors:

- Controllers should think of data protection from the *initial stages* of planning a processing operation, even before the time of determination of the means of processing.
- Where the controller has a Data Protection Officer (DPO), the EDPB encourages the active involvement of the DPO to integrate DPbDD in the procurement and development procedures, as well as in the whole processing life-cycle.
- A processing operation may be *certified*. The ability to get a processing operation certified provides an added value to a controller when choosing between different processing software, hardware, services and/or systems from producers or processors. Therefore, producers should strive to demonstrate DPbDD in the life-cycle of their development of a processing solution. A certification seal may also guide data subjects in their choice between different goods and services. Having the ability to get a processing certified can serve as a competitive advantage for producers, processors and controllers, and even enhances data subjects' trust in the processing of their personal data. If no certification is offered, controllers should seek to have other *guarantees* that producers or processors comply with the requirements of DPbDD.
- Controllers, processors and producers, should consider their obligations to provide children under 18 and other vulnerable groups with specific protection in complying with DPbDD.
- Producers and processors should seek to facilitate DPbDD implementation in order to support the controller's ability to comply with Article 25 obligations. Controllers, on the other hand, should not choose producers or processors who do not offer systems enabling or supporting the controller to comply with Article 25, because controllers will be held accountable for the lack of implementation thereof.
- Producers and processors should play an active role in ensuring that the criteria for the "state of the art" are met, and notify controllers of any changes to the "state of the art" that may affect the effectiveness of the measures they have in place. Controllers should include this requirement as a contractual clause to make sure they are kept up to date.
- The EDPB recommends controllers to require that producers and processors demonstrate how their hardware, software, services or systems enable the controller to comply with the requirements to accountability in accordance with DPbDD, for example by using key performance indicators to demonstrate the effectiveness of the measures and safeguards at implementing the principles and rights.
- The EDPB emphasizes the need for a harmonized approach to implement principles and rights in an effective manner and encourages associations or bodies preparing codes of conduct in accordance with Article 40 to also incorporate sector-specific guidance on DPbDD.
- Controllers should be fair to data subjects and transparent on how they assess and demonstrate effective DPbDD implementation, in the same manner as controllers demonstrate compliance with the GDPR under the principle of accountability.
- Privacy-enhancing technologies (PETs) that have reached the state-of-the-art maturity can be employed as a measure in accordance with the DPbDD requirements if appropriate in a risk based approach. PETs in themselves do not necessarily cover the obligations of Article 25. Controllers shall assess whether the measure is appropriate and effective in implementing the data protection principles and the rights of data subjects.
- Existing legacy systems are under the same DPbDD-obligations as new systems. If legacy systems do not already comply with DPbDD, and changes cannot be made to comply with the obligations, then the legacy system simply does not meet GDPR-obligations and cannot be used to process personal data.
- Article 25 does not lower the threshold of requirements for SMEs. The following points may facilitate SMEs' compliance with Article 25:
  - Do early risk assessments
  - Start with small processing – then scale its scope and sophistication later
  - Look for producer and processor guarantees of DPbDD, such as certification and adherence to code of conducts
  - Use partners with a good track record
  - Talk with DPAs
  - Read guidance from DPAs and the EDPB
  - Adhere to codes of conduct where available
  - Get professional help and advice

For the European Data Protection Board

The Chair

(Andrea Jelinek)

EUROPEAN DATA PROTECTION BOARD:
GUIDELINES 5/2019 ON THE CRITERIA OF THE RIGHT TO BE FORGOTTEN IN THE SEARCH ENGINES CASES UNDER THE GDPR (PART 1)
Version 2.0
Adopted on 7 July 2020

[2.317]

NOTES
  © European Data Protection Board.

VERSION HISTORY

Version 2.0: 7 July 2020: Adoption of the Guidelines after public consultation

Version 1.1: 17 February 2020: Minor corrections

Version 1.0: 2 December 2019: Adoption of the Guidelines for public consultation

TABLE OF CONTENTS

THE EUROPEAN DATA PROTECTION BOARD

Having regard to Article 70 (1)(e) of the Regulation 2016/679/EU of the European Parliament and of the Council of 27 April 2016 on the protection of natural persons with regard to the processing of personal data and on the free movement of such data, and repealing Directive 95/46/EC, (hereinafter "GDPR"),

Having regard to the EEA Agreement and in particular to Annex XI and Protocol 37 thereof, as amended by the Decision of the EEA joint Committee No 154/2018 of 6 July 2018[1],

Having regard to Article 12 and Article 22 of its Rules of Procedure,

HAS ADOPTED THE FOLLOWING GUIDELINES

NOTES
  [1]	References to "Member States" made throughout these guidelines should be understood as references to "EEA Member States".

INTRODUCTION

[2.318]
1.   Following the Costeja judgment of the Court of Justice of the European Union ("CJEU") of the 13th of May 2014[2], a data subject may request the provider of an online search engine ("search engine provider")[3], to erase one or more links to web pages from the list of results displayed following a search made on the basis of his or her name.

2.   According to Google's Transparency Report[4], the percentage of URLs that Google has not delisted has not increased over the past 5 years since that judgement. However, further to the CJEU judgement, data subjects seem to be more aware of their right to lodge a complaint for refusals of their delisting requests since Supervisory Authorities have observed an increase in the number of complaints regarding the refusal by search engine providers to delist links.

3.   The European Data Protection Board (the "**EDPB**"), in accordance with its Action Plan, is developing guidelines in respect of Article 17 of the General Data Protection Regulation ("**GDPR**"). Until those guidelines are finalised, Supervisory Authorities must continue to handle and investigate, to the extent possible, complaints from data subjects and in a timely manner as possible.

4.   Accordingly, this document aims to interpret the Right to be Forgotten in the search engines cases in light of the provisions of Article 17 GDPR (the "**Right to request delisting**"). Indeed, the Right to be Forgotten has been especially enacted under Article 17 GDPR to take into account the Right to request delisting established in the Costeja judgement.

5.   Nonetheless, as under the Directive 95/46/EC of 24 October 1995 (the "**Directive**") and as stated by the CJEU in its aforementioned Costeja judgement[5], the Right to request delisting implies two rights

(Right to Object and Right to Erasure GDPR). Indeed, the application of Article 21 is expressly foreseen as the third ground for the Right to erasure. As a result, both Article 17 and Article 21 GDPR can serve as a legal basis for delisting requests. The right to object and the right to obtain erasure were already granted under the Directive. Nonetheless, as it will be addressed, the wording of the GDPR requires an adjustment of the interpretation of these rights.

6. As a preliminary point, it should be noted that, while Article 17 GDPR is applicable to all data controllers, this paper focuses solely on processing by search engine providers and delisting requests submitted by data subjects.

7. There are some considerations when applying Article 17 GDPR in respect of a search engine provider's data processing. In this regard, it is necessary to state that the processing of personal data carried out in the context of the activity of the search engine provider must be distinguished from processing that is carried out by the publishers of the third-party websites such as media outlets that provide online newspaper content[6].

8. If a data subject obtains the delisting of a particular content, this will result in the deletion of that specific content from the list of search results concerning the data subject when the search is, as a main rule, based on his or her name. This content will however still be available using other search criteria.

9. Delisting requests do not result in the personal data being completely erased. Indeed, the personal data will neither be erased from the source website nor from the index and cache of the search engine provider. For example, a data subject may seek the delisting of personal data from a search engine's index which have originated from a media outlet, such as a newspaper article. In this instance, the link to the personal data may be delisted from the search engine's index; however, the article in question will still remain within the control of the media outlet and may remain publicly available and accessible, even if no longer visible in search results based on queries that include in principle the data subject's name.

10. Nevertheless, search engine providers are not exempt in a general manner from the duty to fully erase. In some exceptional cases, they will need to carry out actual and full erasure in their indexes or caches. For example, in the event that search engine providers would stop respecting robots.txt requests implemented by the original publisher, they would actually have a duty to fully erase the URL to the content, as opposed to delist which is mainly based on data subject's name.

11. This paper is divided into two topics. The first topic concerns the grounds a data subject can rely on for a delisting request sent to a search engine provider pursuant to Article 17.1 GDPR. The second topic concerns the exceptions to the Right to request delisting according to Article 17.3 GDPR. This paper will be supplemented by an appendix dedicated to the assessment of criteria for handling complaints for refusals of delisting.

12. This paper does not address Article 17.2[7] GDPR. Indeed, this Article requires data controllers who have made the personal data public to inform controllers who have then reused those personal data through links, copies or replications. Such obligation of information does not apply to search engine providers when they find information containing personal data published or placed on the internet by third parties, index it automatically, store it temporarily and make it available to internet users according to a particular order of preference[8]. In addition, it does not require search engine providers, who have received a data subject's delisting request, to inform the third party which made public that information on the internet. Such obligation seeks to give greater responsibility to original controllers and try to prevent from multiplying data subjects' initiatives. In this regard, the statement by the Article 29 Working Party, saying that search engine providers *"should not as a general practice inform the webmasters of the pages affected by de-listing of the fact that some webpages cannot be acceded from the search engine in response to specific queries"* because *"such communication has no legal basis under EU data protection law"*[9] remains valid. It is also planned to have separate specific guidelines in respect of Article 17.2 GDPR.

1 THE GROUNDS OF THE RIGHT TO REQUEST DELISTING UNDER GDPR

[2.319]
13. The Right to request delisting as provided by Article 17 GDPR does not change the findings of the Costeja judgement, in which the CJEU held that a request for delisting was based on the Right to rectification/erasure and on the Right to object, pursuant to Article 12 and Article 14 of the Directive respectively.

14. Article 17.1 sets out a general principle to erase the data in the six following cases:
(a)   the personal data are no longer necessary in relation to the purposes for which they were collected or otherwise processed *(Article 17.1.a)*;
(b)   the data subject withdraws consent on which the processing is based *(Article 17.1.b)*;
(c)   the data subject exercised his or her Right to object to processing of his or her personal data pursuant to Article 21.1 and 21.2 GDPR;
(d)   the personal data have been unlawfully processed *(Article 17.1.d)*;
(e)   the erasure is compliant with a legal obligation *(Article 17.1.e)*;
(f)   the personal data have been collected in relation to the offer of information society services to a minor *(Article 17.1.f which refers to Article 8.1)*.

15. While all the grounds of Article 17 are theoretically applicable when it comes to delisting, in practice, some will be rarely or never used, such as in case of withdrawal of consent (see ground 2 below).

16. A data subject could however make a delisting request to a search engine provider based on more than one ground. For example, a data subject could request delisting because he or she considers it no longer necessary that his or her personal data are processed by the search engine (Article 17.1.a) and also exercise his or her Right to object to the processing pursuant to Article 21.1 GDPR (Article 17.1.c).

17.   In order for Supervisory Authorities to assess complaints regarding a search engine provider who has refused to erase a particular search result pursuant to Article 17 GDPR, Supervisory Authorities should establish whether the content to which an URL is referring to should be delisted or not. They should thus, in their analysis of the substance of the complaint, take into account the nature of the content made available by the publishers of the third-party websites.

1.1 GROUND 1: THE RIGHT TO REQUEST DELISTING WHEN THE PERSONAL DATA ARE NO LONGER NECESSARY IN RELATION TO THE SEARCH ENGINE PROVIDER'S PROCESSING (ARTICLE 17.1.A)

18.   According to Article 17.1.a GDPR, a data subject may request a search engine provider, following a search carried out as a general rule on the basis of his or her name, to delist content from its search results, where the data subject's personal data returned in those search results are no longer necessary in relation to the purposes of the processing by the search engine.

19.   This provision enables a data subject to request the delisting of personal information concerning him or her that have been made accessible for longer than it is necessary for the search engine provider's processing. Yet, this processing is notably carried out for the purposes of making information more easily accessible for internet users. Within the context of the Right to request delisting, the balance between the protection of privacy and the interests of Internet users in accessing the information must be undertaken. In particular, it must be assessed whether or not, over the course of time, the personal data have become out-of-date or have not been updated.

20.   For example, a data subject may exercise his or her Right to request delisting pursuant to Article 17.1.a when:
- information about him or her held by a company has been removed from the public register;
- a link to a firm's website contains his or her contact details although he or she is no longer working in that firm;
- information has to be published on the Internet for a number of years to meet a legal obligation and remained online longer than the time limit specified by the legislation.

21.   As demonstrated by the examples, a data subject may notably request the delisting of a content where the personal information are obviously inaccurate due to the course of time, or outdated. Such an assessment will incidentally be dependent on the purposes of the original processing. Consequently, the original retention periods of personal data, when available, should also be considered by Supervisory Authorities when they conduct their analysis of delisting requests pursuant to Article 17.1.a GDPR.

1.2 GROUND 2: THE RIGHT TO REQUEST DELISTING WHEN THE DATA SUBJECT WITHDRAWS CONSENT WHERE THE LEGAL BASIS FOR THE PROCESSING IS PURSUANT TO ARTICLE 6.1.A OR ARTICLE 9.2.A GDPR AND WHERE THERE IS NO OTHER LEGAL BASIS FOR THE PROCESSING (ARTICLE 17.1.B)

22.   According to Article 17.1.b GDPR, a data subject may obtain the erasure of personal data concerning him or her where he or she withdraws consent for the processing.

23.   In case of delisting, it would mean that the search engine provider would have utilised the consent of the data subject as lawful basis for its processing. Article 17.1 GDPR indeed raises the question of the lawful basis for processing relied upon by a search engine provider for the purpose of returning search engine results including personal data.

24.   For that reason, it appears unlikely that a delisting request would be submitted by a data subject on the basis that he or she wishes to withdraw consent because the controller to whom the data subject gave his or her consent is the web publisher, not the search engine operator that indexes the data. This interpretation has been endorsed by the CJEU in its judgement C-136-17 of 24 September 2019 (the "**Google 2 judgment**").[10] The Court indicates that *"(. . .) the consent must be 'specific' and must therefore relate specifically to the processing carried out in connection with the activity of the search engine (. . .). In practice, it is scarcely conceivable (. . .) that the operator of a search engine will seek the express consent of data subjects before processing personal data concerning them for the purposes of his referencing activity. In any event, (. . .) the mere fact that a person makes a request for de-referencing means, in principle, at least at the time of making the request, that he or she no longer consents to the processing carried out by the operator of the search engine."*

25.   Nonetheless, in the event where a data subject would have withdrawn his or her consent for the use of his or her data on a particular web page, the original publisher of that web page should inform search engine providers who have indexed that data pursuant to Article 17.2 GDPR. The data subject would thus still be entitled to obtain the delisting of personal data concerning him or her but according to Article 17.1.c in such case.

1.3 GROUND 3: THE RIGHT TO REQUEST DELISTING WHEN THE DATA SUBJECT HAS EXERCISED HIS OR HER RIGHT TO OBJECT TO THE PROCESSING OF HIS OR HER PERSONAL DATA (ARTICLE 17.1.C)

26.   Pursuant to Article 17.1.c GDPR, a data subject can obtain from the search engine provider the erasure of personal data concerning him or her where he or she objects to the processing according to Article 21.1 GDPR and where there are no overriding legitimate grounds for the processing by the data controller.

27.   The Right to object affords stronger safeguards to data subjects since it does not restrict the grounds according to which data subjects may request delisting as under Article 17.1 GDPR.

28. The Right to object to the processing was provided for by Article 14 of the Directive[11] and constituted a ground to request the delisting since the Costeja judgement. However, the differences in the wording of Article 21 GDPR and Article 14 of the Directive suggest that there may also be differences in their application.

29. Under the Directive, the data subject had to base his or her request *"on compelling legitimate grounds relating to his [or her] particular situation"*. In respect of the GDPR, a data subject can object to a processing *"on grounds relating to his or her particular situation"*. He or she thus no longer has to demonstrate *"compelling legitimate grounds"*.

30. The GDPR therefore changes the burden of proof, providing a presumption in favour of the data subject by obliging on the contrary the controller to demonstrate *"compelling legitimate grounds for the processing"* (Article 21.1). As a result, when a search engine provider receives a request to delist based on the data subject's particular situation, it must now erase the personal data, pursuant to Article 17.1.c GDPR, unless it can demonstrate *"overriding legitimate grounds"* for the listing of the specific search result, which read in conjunction with Article 21.1 are *"compelling legitimate grounds (. . .) which override the interests, rights and freedoms of the data subject"*. *The search engine provider can establish any "overriding legitimate grounds", including any exemption provided for under Article 17.3 GDPR. Nonetheless, if the search engine provider fails to demonstrate the existence of overriding legitimate grounds, the data subject is entitled to obtain the delisting pursuant to Article 17.1.c GDPR. As a matter of fact, delisting requests now imply to make the balance between the reasons related to the particular situation of the data subject and the compelling legitimate grounds of the search engine provider. The balance between the protection of privacy and the interests of Internet users in accessing to the information as ruled by the CJEU in the Costeja judgement can be relevant to conduct such assessment, as well as the balance operated by the European Court of Human Rights (ECHR) in press matters.*

31. Therefore, the criteria of delisting developed by the Article 29 Working Party in guidelines on the implementation of the Court of Justice of the European Union judgment on "Google Spain and Inc v. Agencia Española de Protección de Datos (AEPD) and Mario Costeja González" C-131/12 can still be used by search engine providers and Supervisory Authorities to assess a delisting request based on the Right to object (Article 17.1.c GDPR).

32. In this regard, the *"particular situation"* of the data subject will underlie the delisting request (for example, a search result creates detriment for a data subject when applying for jobs, or undermines his or her reputation in personal life) and will be taken into account when undertaking the balance between personal rights and right to information, in addition to the classic criteria for handling delisting requests, such as:

• he or she does not play a role in public life;
• the information at stake is not related to his or her professional life but affects his or her privacy;
• the information constitutes hate speech, slander, libel or similar offences in the area of expression against him or her pursuant to a court order;
• the data appears to be a verified fact but is factually inaccurate;
• the data relates to a relatively minor criminal offence that happened a long time ago and causes prejudice to the data subject.

33. Nonetheless, these criteria won't have to be examined in the absence of proof of compelling legitimate grounds to refuse the request.

1.4 GROUND 4: THE RIGHT TO REQUEST DELISTING WHEN THE PERSONAL DATA HAVE BEEN UNLAWFULLY PROCESSED (ARTICLE 17.1.D)

34. According to Article 17.1.d GDPR, a data subject may request the erasure of personal data concerning him or her in the instance where they have been unlawfully processed.

35. The notion of unlawful processing shall first be interpreted in view of Article 6 GDPR dedicated to lawfulness of processing. Other principles established under the GDPR (such as principles of Article 5 GDPR or of other provisions of Chapter II) may serve such interpretation.

36. This notion shall secondly be interpreted broadly, as the infringement of a legal provision other than the GDPR. Such interpretation must be conducted objectively by Supervisory Authorities, according to national laws or to a court decision. For instance, a delisting request shall be granted in the event where the listing of personal information has been expressly prohibited by a court order.

In cases where a search engine provider is not able to demonstrate a legal basis for its processing, a delisting request may fall under the scope of art 17.1.d GDPR, as the processing of personal data in such cases must be considered unlawful. Nonetheless, it must be reminded that in case of unlawfulness of the original processing, the data subject remains entitled to request delisting under Article 17.1.c GDPR.

1.5 GROUND 5: THE RIGHT TO REQUEST DELISTING WHEN THE PERSONAL DATA HAVE TO BE ERASED FOR COMPLIANCE WITH A LEGAL OBLIGATION (ARTICLE 17.1.E)

37. According to Article 17.1.e GDPR, a data subject may request a search engine provider to delist one or more search results if the personal data need to be erased in compliance with a legal obligation in Union or Member State Law to which the search engine provider is subject.

38. Compliance with a legal obligation may result from an injunction, an express request by national or EU law for being under a "legal obligation to erase" or the mere breach by the search engine provider of the retention period. For illustrative purposes, the retention period of data is set by a text but would not be complied with (but this hypothesis mainly concerns public files). This case could maybe encompass the hypothesis of non-anonymized or identifying data available in open data.

1.6 GROUND 6: THE RIGHT TO REQUEST DELISTING WHEN THE PERSONAL DATA HAVE BEEN COLLECTED IN RELATION TO THE OFFER OF INFORMATION SOCIETY SERVICES (ISS) TO A CHILD (ARTICLE 17.1.F)

39. According to Article 17.1.f GDPR, a data subject may request a search engine provider to delist one or more results if personal data have been collected in relation to the offer of ISS to a child referred to in Article 8.1 GDPR.

40. The Article covers the direct provision of ISS and no other types of processing. The GDPR does not define ISS; rather, it refers to existing definitions in EU law[12]. There are some difficulties in interpretation as Recital 18 of Directive 2000/31/CE of the European Parliament and of the Council of June 8, 2000 provides a definition both broad and ambiguous of the notion of *"the direct provision of information society services"*. It mainly indicates that these services *"span a wide range of economic activities which take place on-line"*, but specifies that they are not restricted to *"services giving rise to on-line contracting but also, in so far as they represent an economic activity, extend to services which are not remunerated by those who receive them, such as those offering on-line information or commercial communications, or those providing tools allowing for search, access and retrieval of data"*, outlining the criteria of economic activity.

41. It stems from the above that search engine providers' activities are likely to fall within the scope of direct provision of ISS. Nonetheless, search engine providers do not question whether the personal data they are indexing concern or not a child. Yet, in view of their specific responsibilities, and subject to the application of Article 17.3 GDPR, they would have to delist a content relating to a child pursuant to Article 17.1.c GDPR, acknowledging that being a child is a valid "ground relating to a particular situation" (Article 21 GDPR) and that *"children merit specific protection with regard to their personal data"* (Recital 38 GDPR). In such case, the context of the collection of personal data by the original controller must be considered. In particular, the date of the beginning of the processing by the original website must be taken into account when a data subject requests the delisting of a content.

NOTES

2   CJEU, Case C-131/12, Google Spain SL and Google Inc. v Agencia Española de Protección de Datos (AEPD) and Mario Costeja González, judgment of 13 May 2014.

3   including web archives such as archive.org

4   https://transparencyreport.google.com/eu-privacy/overview?hl=en

5   CJEU, Case C-131/12, judgment of 13 May 2014, paragraph 88: *"Article 12(b) and subparagraph (a) of the first paragraph of Article 14 of Directive 95/46 are to be interpreted as meaning that, in order to comply with the rights laid down in those provisions and in so far as the conditions laid down by those provisions are in fact satisfied, the operator of a search engine is obliged to remove from the list of results displayed following a search made on the basis of a person's name links to web pages, published by third parties and containing information relating to that person, also in a case where that name or information is not erased beforehand or simultaneously from those web pages, and even, as the case may be, when its publication in itself on those pages is lawful"*.

6   CJEU, Case C 131/12, judgment of 13 May 2014; European Court of Human Rights (ECHR), "M.L. and W.W. vs Germany", 28 June 2018.

7   Regulation 2016/679 (GDPR), Article 17.2: *"Where the controller has made the personal data public and is obliged pursuant to paragraph 1 to erase the personal data, the controller, taking account of available technology and the cost of implementation, shall take reasonable steps, including technical measures, to inform controllers which are processing the personal data that the data subject has requested the erasure by such controllers of any links to, or copy or replication of, those data."*

8   See CJEU, Case C-136/17, *GC and Others v CNIL*, judgment of 24 September 2019, paragraph 35 and Case C-131/12, judgment of 13 May 2014, paragraph 41.

9   Article 29 Data Protection Working Party, "Guidelines on the implementation of the Court of Justice of the European Union judgment on "Google Spain and inc v. Agencia Española de Protección de Datos (AEPD) and Mario Costeja González" C- 131/12, WP 225, 26 November 2014, p. 23.

10   CJEU, Case C-136/17, *Commission nationale de l'informatique et des libertés (CNIL) v. Google LLC*, judgment of 24 September 2019.

11   Directive 95/46/CE, Article 14: *"Member States shall grant the data subject the right: (a) at least in the cases referred to in Article 7 (e) and (f), to object at any time on compelling legitimate grounds relating to his particular situation to the processing of data relating to him, save where otherwise provided by national legislation. Where there is a justified objection, the processing instigated by the controller may no longer involve those data"*

12   Specifically, Article 1(1)(b) of Directive (EU) 2015/1535 of the European Parliament and of the Council of 9 September 2015 laying down a procedure for the provision of information in the field of technical regulations and of rules on Information Society services (codification).

2 THE EXCEPTIONS TO THE RIGHT TO REQUEST DELISTING UNDER ARTICLE 17.3

[2.320]

42. Article 17.3 GDPR states that paragraphs 1 and 2 of Article 17 GDPR will not apply when processing is necessary:

(a)   for exercising the right of freedom of expression and information *(Article 17.3.a)*;

(b)   for compliance with a legal obligation that requires processing by Union or Member State law to which the controller is subject or for the performance of a task carried out in the public interest or in the exercise of official authority vested in the controller *(Article 17.3.b)*;

(c)   for reasons of public interest in the area of public health in accordance with points (h) and (i) of Article 9.2 as well as Article 9.3 *(Article 17.3.c)*;

(d)   for archiving purposes in the public interest, scientific or historical research purposes, or statistical purposes in accordance with Article 89 (1) in so far as the right referred to in paragraph 1 is likely to render impossible or seriously impair the achievement of the objectives of that processing *(Article 17.3.d)*; or

(e)   for the establishment, exercise or defense of legal claims *(Article 17.3.e)*.

43.   This part aims to demonstrate that most of the exceptions under Article 17.3 GDPR do not appear suitable in case of a delisting request. Such inadequacy pleads in favour of the application of Article 21 GDPR for delisting requests. In any event, it must be remembered that exceptions provided for under Article 17.3 GDPR can be invoked as compelling legitimate grounds pursuant to Article 17.1.c GDPR.

2.1 PROCESSING IS NECESSARY FOR EXERCISING THE RIGHT OF FREEDOM OF EXPRESSION AND INFORMATION

44.   This exemption to the application of Article 17.1 GDPR must be interpreted and applied in the context of the characteristics that define erasure. Article 17.1 GDPR is described as a clear and unconditional mandate addressed to controllers. If the conditions set forth in Article 17.1 GDPR are met, the controller shall *"have the obligation to delete personal data without undue delay"*. Nonetheless, this is not an absolute right. The exemptions of Article 17.3 GDPR identify cases in which this obligation does not apply.

45.   However, the balance between protecting the rights of interested parties and freedom of expression, including free access to information, is an intrinsic part of Article 17 GDPR.

46.   The CJEU recognised in the Costeja judgement and repeated recently in the Google 2 judgment that the processing carried out by a search engine provider can significantly affect the fundamental rights to privacy and data protection law when the search is performed using the name of a data subject.

47.   When weighing up the rights and freedoms of data subjects and the interests of Internet users in accessing the information through the search engine provider, the Court understood that *"Whilst it is true that the data subject's rights are protected by those articles also override, as a general rule, that interest of internet users, that balance may however depend, in specific cases, on the nature of the information in question and its sensitivity for the data subject's private life and on the interest of the public in having that information, an interest which may vary, in particular, according to the role played by the data subject in public life."*[13]

48.   The Court also considered that the rights of the data subjects will prevail, in general[14], on the interest of Internet users in accessing information through the search engine provider. However, it identified several factors that may influence such determination. Among them include: the nature of the information or its sensitivity, and especially the interest of Internet users in accessing information, an interest that can vary depending on the role played by the interested party in public life.

49.   The analysis of the delisting by the Court implies that, when assessing requests for delisting, the decision on the maintenance or blocking of the search results by a search engine provider necessarily has to consider what would be the impact of a delisting decision on the access to information by Internet users[15]. This impact does not necessarily entail the rejection of a delisting request. As confirmed by the Court, such interference with the fundamental rights of the data subject has to be justified by the preponderant interest of the general public in having access to the information in question.

50.   The Court also distinguished between the legitimacy that a web publisher can have to disseminate information against the legitimacy of the search engine provider. The Court recognised that the activity of a web publisher can be undertaken exclusively for the purposes of journalism, in which case the web publisher would benefit from the exemptions that Member States could establish in these cases on the basis of Article 9 of the Directive (currently , Article 85.2 GDPR). In this regard, in the judgment *"M.L. and W.W. vs Germany"* of June 28th, 2018, the ECHR indicates that the balancing of the interests at issue may lead to different results depending on the request at stake (distinguishing (i) a request for erasure brought against the original publisher whose activity is at the heart of what freedom of expression aims to protect from (ii) a request brought against the search engine whose first interest is not to publish the original information on the data subject but notably to enable identifying any available information on this person and thus establishing his or her profile).

51.   Those considerations should be assessed in respect of Article 17 GDPR complaints as in those decisions, the rights of the data subjects that have requested the delisting must be weighed with the interests of Internet users to access the information.

52.   As explained by the CJEU in its Google 2 judgment, Article 17.3.a GDPR is *"an expression of the fact that the right to protection of personal data is not an absolute right but (. . .) must be considered in relation to its function in society and be balanced against other fundamental rights, in accordance with the principle of proportionality".*[16] It *"expressly lays down the requirement to strike a balance between the fundamental rights to privacy and protection of personal data guaranteed by Articles 7 and 8 of the Charter, on the one hand, and the fundamental right of freedom of information guaranteed by Article 11 of the Charter, on the other."*[17]

53.   The Court concludes that *"where the operator of a search engine has received a request for de-referencing relating to a link to a web page on which personal data falling within the special categories (. . .), the operator must, on the basis of all the relevant factors of the particular case and taking into* account the seriousness of the interference with the data subject's fundamental rights to privacy and protection of personal data laid down in Articles 7 and 8 of the Charter, ascertain, having regard to the reasons of substantial public interest (. . .), whether the inclusion of that link in the list of results displayed following a search on the basis of the data subject's name is strictly necessary for protecting the freedom of information of internet users potentially interested in accessing that web page by means of such a search, protected by Article 11 of the Charter."[18]

54. To conclude, depending on the circumstances of the case, search engine providers may refuse to delist a content in the event where they can demonstrate that its inclusion in the list of results is strictly necessary for protecting the freedom of information of internet users.

2.2 PROCESSING IS NECESSARY FOR COMPLIANCE WITH A LEGAL OBLIGATION TO WHICH THE CONTROLLER IS SUBJECT OR FOR THE PERFORMANCE OF A TASK CARRIED OUT IN THE PUBLIC INTEREST OR IN THE EXERCISE OF OFFICIAL AUTHORITY VESTED IN THE CONTROLLER

55. The content of this exemption makes it difficult to apply to the activity of search engine providers and it may have influence on the decisions of delisting certain results, as the processing of data by search engine providers is based, in principle, on the legitimate interest of the search engine provider.

2.2.1 Legal obligation

56. It is difficult to imagine the existence of legal provisions that oblige search engine providers to disseminate certain information. This is a consequence of the type of activity they develop. Search engine providers do not produce or present information.

57. Therefore, it seems unlikely that Member State law includes obligations for search engine providers to publish some type of information, instead of setting the obligation for that publication to be carried out in other web pages that will then be linked by search engine providers.

58. This assessment may also be extended to the possibility that Union or Member State law enables a public authority to take decisions that oblige search engine providers to publish information directly, and not through the URL links to the web page where that information is contained.

59. If there are cases in which the law of a Member State establishes the obligation for the search engine providers to publish decisions or documents containing personal information, or which authorises public authorities to demand such publication, the exemption contained in Article 17.3.b GDPR should be applied.

60. This application must take into account the terms in which it is established, that is, that the maintenance of the information in questions is necessary to meet the legal obligation of publication. For example, that a legal obligation, or the decision of an authority legally entitled to adopt it, may include a time limit to the publication, or expressly stated purposes that may have been reached within a certain time period. In these cases, if the request for delisting occurs having exceeded these time limits, it should be considered that the exemption is no longer applicable.

61. On the contrary, it is frequent that Member State law provides for the publication on web pages of information containing personal data. That legal obligation to publish or maintain the published information cannot be considered as covered by the exemption contained in Article 17.3.b GDPR, since it is not directed to the search engine provider, but to the web publishers whose content is linked by the search engine provider's index. Therefore, the search engine provider cannot invoke the existence of the obligation to reject a request for delisting.

62. However, the legal obligation of publication addressed to other web publishers should be taken into consideration when establishing the balance between the rights of data subjects and the interest of the Internet users in accessing the information. The fact that information must be published online by legal mandate, or following the decision of an authority legally entitled to adopt it, is indicative of an interest in the public being able to access that information.

63. That presumption of existence of a prevalent interest of the public does not operate in the same way in respect of the originating web pages compared to the results index of a search engine provider. Although the legal obligation to publish information on a certain web site may lead to the conclusion that this information should not be deleted from that web page, the decision regarding the results offered by the search engine provider when the name of a data subject is generally used as search term may be different.

64. The assessment of the request for delisting in these cases should not assume that the existence of the legal obligation of publication necessarily implies that, to the extent that this obligation is imposed on the original web publishers, it is not possible to accept the delisting by the search engine provider.

65. The decision should be taken, as is the general rule, by balancing the rights of the data subject and the interest of the Internet users to access this information through the search engine provider.

2.2.2 Performance of a task carried out in public interest or in the exercise of official authority

66. Search engine providers are not public authorities and therefore do not exercise public powers by themselves.

67. However, they could exercise those powers if they were attributed by the law of a Member State or of the Union. In the same way that they could carry out missions of public interest if their activity was considered necessary to satisfy that public interest in accordance with national legislation[19].

68. Given the characteristics of search engine providers, it is unlikely that Member States will grant them public powers or consider that their activity or part of it is necessary for the achievement of a legally established public interest.

69. If, in spite of that, there is a case in which the law of the Member States grants search engines public powers or links their activity to the achievement of a public interest, they could avail of the exemption provided for in Article 17.3.b GDPR. The considerations previously made on the cases in which the law of a Member State had established a legal obligation to process information for search engine providers are also valid in this case.

70. To decide not to follow a delisting request for reasons related to this exemption, it is necessary to determine whether the maintenance of the information in the search engine results is necessary for the achievement of the public interest pursued or for the exercise of the powers of attorney.

71. On the other hand, the legal definition of powers or public interest would be carried out by a Member State, and if the search engine rejects a request for delisting on the basis of this exemption, it must also be understood that it does so because it considers that its activity is necessary to achieve public interests. The search engine provider should, in that event, provide reasons why it considers its activity to be carried out in the public interest. Without such an explanation, the denial to follow a data subject's delisting request does not have the possibility of relying on the exemption.

72. Consequently, it would also be the Supervisory Authority of the Member State whose law is applicable that will have to deal with a potential complaint pursuant to Article 55.2 GDPR.

2.3 REASONS OF PUBLIC INTEREST IN THE AREA OF PUBLIC HEALTH

73. This exemption is a specific case based on the fact that processing is necessary for the performance of a public interest.

74. In this case, the public interest is limited to the area of public health, but, as with the public interest in any other area, the lawful basis for the processing must be established in Union law or Member State law.

75. From the point of view of the application of this exemption in the context of the activity of the search engine provider, the same conclusions as stated above can be reached. It does not seem likely that the law of a Member State or of the Union can establish a relationship between the activity of the search engine provider and the maintenance of information or of a category of information in the results of the search engine provider with the achievement of purposes of public interest in respect of public health.

76. This conclusion is more evident if one takes into account that the effect of delisting is only that some results are deleted from the results page that is obtained when mainly a name is entered as a search criterion. But the information is not deleted from the search engine providers' indexes and can be retrieved using other search terms.

77. It is, therefore, difficult to imagine that keeping those results visible when searches are mainly made on the basis of a data subject's name can be considered, in general, as something necessary for reasons of public interest in the area of public health.

78. The criteria on the applicability of national standards and the identification of the Supervisory Authority that must deal with possible claims in a case relating to Article 17 GDPR that was rejected using this exemption have been discussed above.

2.4 ARCHIVING PURPOSES IN THE PUBLIC INTEREST, SCIENTIFIC OR HISTORICAL RESEARCH PURPOSES, OR STATISTICAL PURPOSES IN ACCORDANCE WITH ARTICLE 89(1) IN SO FAR AS THE RIGHT REFERRED TO IN PARAGRAPH 1 IS LIKELY TO RENDER IMPOSSIBLE OR SERIOUSLY IMPAIR THE ACHIEVEMENT OF THE OBJECTIVES OF THAT PROCESSING

79. In this scenario, the search engine provider must be able to demonstrate that the delisting of a certain content on the results page is a serious obstacle or completely prevents the achievement of scientific or historical research purposes or statistical purposes.

80. It should be understood that these purposes must be objectively pursued by the search engine provider. The possibility that the suppression of results could significantly affect research purposes or statistical purposes pursued by users of the search engine provider's service is not relevant for the application of this exemption. Those purposes, if they exist, should be taken into consideration when establishing a balance between the rights of the data subject and the interests of the Internet users in accessing the information through the search engine provider.

81. It must also be noted that these purposes may be objectively pursued by the search engine provider, without a link between in principle the name of the data subject and the search results being necessary.

2.5 ESTABLISHMENT, EXERCISE OR DEFENCE OF LEGAL CLAIMS

82. In principle, it is very unlikely that search engine providers can use this exemption to reject Article 17 GDPR delisting requests.

83. It must be further emphasised that a delisting request supposes the suppression of certain results from the search results page provided by the search engine provider when the name of a data subject is normally used as search criteria. The information remains accessible using other search terms.

NOTES
13   CJEU, C-131/12, judgment of 13 May 2014, paragraph 81; CJEU, C-136/17, judgment of 24 September 2019, paragraph 66.
14   CJEU, Case C-131/12, judgment of 13 May 2014, paragraph 99; CJEU, Case C-136/17, judgment of 24 September 2019, paragraph 53.
15   CJEU, Case C-136/17, judgment of 24 September 2019, paragraph 56 et seq.
16   CJEU, Case C-136/17, judgment of 24 September 2019, paragraph 57.
17   CJEU, Case C-136/17, judgment of 24 September 2019, paragraph 59.
18   CJEU, Case C-136/17, judgment of 24 September 2019, paragraph 69.
19   GDPR, Article 6.3: "The basis for the processing referred to in point (c) and (e) of paragraph 1 shall be laid down by:
     (a)   Union law; or
     (b)   Member State law to which the controller is subject (. . .)"

EUROPEAN DATA PROTECTION BOARD: GUIDELINES 1/2020 ON PROCESSING PERSONAL DATA IN THE CONTEXT OF CONNECTED VEHICLES AND MOBILITY RELATED APPLICATIONS VERSION 2.0

Adopted on 9 March 2021

[2.321]

NOTES

VERSION HISTORY

Version 2.0: 9 March 2021: Adoption of the Guidelines after public consultation

Version 1.0: 28 January 2020: Adoption of the Guidelines for public consultation

TABLE OF CONTENTS

THE EUROPEAN DATA PROTECTION BOARD

Having regard to Article 70 (1)(e) of the Regulation 2016/679/EU of the European Parliament and of the Council of 27 April 2016 on the protection of natural persons with regard to the processing of personal data and on the free movement of such data, and repealing Directive 95/46/EC, (hereinafter "GDPR"),

Having regard to the EEA Agreement and in particular to Annex XI and Protocol 37 thereof, as amended by the Decision of the EEA joint Committee No 154/2018 of 6 July 2018[1],

Having regard to Article 12 and Article 22 of its Rules of Procedure,

HAS ADOPTED THE FOLLOWING GUIDELINES

1   References to "Member States" made throughout this document should be understood as references to "EEA Member States".

1 INTRODUCTION

[2.322]
1.   Symbol of the 20th century economy, the automobile is one of the mass consumer products that has impacted society as a whole. Commonly associated with the notion of freedom, cars are often considered as more than just a means of transportation. Indeed, they represent a private area in which people can enjoy a form of autonomy of decision, without encountering any external interferences. Today, as connected vehicles move into the mainstream, such a vision no longer corresponds to the reality. In-vehicle connectivity is rapidly expanding from luxury models and premium brands to high-volume midmarket models, and vehicles are becoming massive data hubs. Not only vehicles, but drivers and passengers are also becoming more and more connected. As a matter of fact, many models launched over the past few years on the market integrate sensors and connected on-board equipment, which may collect

and record, among other things, the engine performance, the driving habits, the locations visited, and potentially even the driver's eye movements, his or her pulse, or biometric data for the purpose of uniquely identifying a natural person.[2]

2. Such data processing is taking place in a complex ecosystem, which is not limited to the traditional players of the automotive industry, but is also shaped by the emergence of new players belonging to the digital economy. These new players may offer infotainment services such as online music, road condition and traffic information, or provide driving assistance systems and services, such as autopilot software, vehicle condition updates, usage-based insurance or dynamic mapping. Moreover, since vehicles are connected via electronic communication networks, road infrastructure managers and telecommunications operators involved in this process also play an important role with respect to the potential processing operations applied to the drivers' and passengers' personal data.

3. In addition, connected vehicles are generating increasing amounts of data, most of which can be considered personal data since they will relate to drivers or passengers. Even if the data collected by a connected car are not directly linked to a name, but to technical aspects and features of the vehicle, it will concern the driver or the passengers of the car. As an illustration, data relating to the driving style or the distance covered, data relating to the wear and tear on vehicle parts, location data or data collected by cameras may concern driver behaviour as well as information about other people who could be inside or data subjects that pass by. Such technical data are produced by a natural person, and permit his/her direct or indirect identification, by the data controller or by another person. The vehicle can be considered as a terminal that can be used by different users. Therefore, as for a personal computer, this potential plurality of users does not affect the personal nature of the data.

4. In 2016, the Fédération Internationale de l'Automobile (FIA) ran a campaign across Europe called "My Car My Data" to get a sentiment on what Europeans think about connected cars.[3] While it showed the high interest of drivers for connectivity, it also highlighted the vigilance that must be exercised with regard to the use of the data produced by vehicles as well as the importance of complying with personal data protection legislation. Thus, the challenge is, for each stakeholder, to incorporate the "protection of personal data" dimension from the product design phase, and to ensure that car users enjoy transparency and control in relation to their data in accordance with recital 78 GDPR. Such an approach helps to strengthen user confidence, and thus the long-term development of those technologies.

1.1 RELATED WORKS

5. Connected vehicles have become a substantial subject for regulators over the last decade, with a major increase in the last couple of years. Various works have thus been published at the national and international levels concerning the security and privacy of connected vehicles. Those regulations and initiatives aim at complementing the existing data protection and privacy frameworks with sector specific rules or providing guidance to professionals.

1.1.1 European-level and international initiatives

6. Since 31 March 2018, a 112-based eCall in-vehicle system is mandatory on all new types of M1 and N1 vehicles (passenger cars and light duty vehicles).[4,5] In 2006, the Article 29 Working Party had already adopted a working document on data protection and privacy implications in eCall initiative.[6] In addition, as previously discussed, the Article 29 Working Party also adopted an opinion in October 2017 regarding the processing of personal data in the context of Cooperative Intelligent Transport Systems (C-ITS).

7. In January 2017, the European Union Agency for Network and Information Security (ENISA) published a study focused on cyber security and resilience of smart cars listing the sensitive assets as well as the corresponding threats, risks, mitigation factors and possible security measures to implement.[7] In September 2017, the International Conference of Data Protection and Privacy Commissioners (ICDPPC) adopted a resolution on connected vehicles.[8] Finally, in April 2018, the International Working Group on Data Protection in Telecommunications (IWGDPT), also adopted a working paper on connected vehicles.[9]

1.1.2 National initiatives of European Data Protection Board (EDPB) members

8. In January 2016, the Conference of the German Federal and State Data Protection Authorities and the German Association of the Automotive Industry (VDA) published a common declaration on the principles of data protection in connected and not-connected vehicles.[10] In August 2017, the UK Centre for Connected and Autonomous Vehicles (CCAV) released a guide stating principles of cyber security for connected and automated vehicles in order to raise awareness on the matter within the automotive sector.[11] In October 2017, the French data protection authority, the Commission Nationale de l'Informatique et des Libertés (CNIL), released a compliance package for connected cars in order to provide assistance to stakeholders on how to integrate data protection by design and by default, enabling data subjects to have effective control over their data.[12]

1.2 APPLICABLE LAW

9. The relevant EU legal framework is the GDPR. It applies in any case where data processing in the context of connected vehicles involves processing personal data of individuals.

10. Additionally to the GDPR, directive 2002/58/EC as revised by 2009/136/EC (hereinafter – "ePrivacy directive"), **sets a specific standard for all actors that wish to store or access information stored in the terminal equipment of a subscriber or user in the European Economic Area (EEA).**

11. Indeed, if most of the ePrivacy directive provisions (art. 6, art. 9, etc.) only apply to providers of publicly available electronic communication services and providers of public communication networks, art. 5(3) ePrivacy directive is a general provision. It does not only apply to electronic communication services but also to every entity, private or public, that places on or reads information from a terminal equipment without regard to the nature of the data being stored or accessed.

12.   Regarding the notion of *"terminal equipment"*, the definition is given by directive 2008/63/CE[13]. Art. 1 (a) defines the terminal equipment as an *"equipment directly or indirectly connected to the interface of a public telecommunications network to send, process or receive information; in either case (direct or indirect), the connection may be made by wire, optical fibre or electromagnetically; a connection is indirect if equipment is placed between the terminal and the interface of the network; (b) satellite earth station equipment"*.

13.   As a result, provided that the aforementioned criteria are met, the connected vehicle and device connected to it should be considered as a *"terminal equipment"* (just like a computer, a smartphone or a smart TV) and provisions of art. 5(3) ePrivacy directive apply where relevant.

14.   As outlined by the EDPB in its opinion 5/2019 on the interplay between the ePrivacy directive and the GDPR,[14] art. 5(3) ePrivacy directive provides that, as a rule, and subject to the exceptions to that rule mentioned in paragraph 17 below, prior consent is required for the storing of information, or the gaining of access to information already stored, in the terminal equipment of a subscriber or user. To the extent that the information stored in the end-user's device constitutes personal data, art. 5(3) ePrivacy directive shall take precedence over art. 6 GDPR with regards to the activity of storing or gaining access to this information.[15] Any processing operations of personal data following the aforementioned processing operations, including processing personal data obtained by accessing information in the terminal equipment, must have a legal basis under art. 6 GDPR in order to be lawful.[16]

15.   Since the controller, when seeking consent for the storing or gaining of access to information pursuant to art. 5(3) ePrivacy directive, will have to inform the data subject about all the purposes of the processing – including any processing following the aforementioned operations (meaning the "subsequent processing") – consent under art. 6 GDPR will generally be the most adequate legal basis to cover the processing of personal data following such operations (as far as the purpose of the following processing is comprehended by the data subject's consent, see paragraphs 53-54 below). Hence, consent will likely constitute the legal basis both for the storing and gaining of access to information already stored and the subsequent processing of personal data[17]. Indeed, when assessing compliance with art. 6 GDPR, one should take into account that the processing as a whole involves specific activities for which the EU legislature has sought to provide additional protection.[18] Moreover, controllers must take into account the impact on data subjects' rights when identifying the appropriate lawful basis in order to respect the principle of fairness.[19] The bottom line is that art. 6 GDPR cannot be relied upon by controllers in order to lower the additional protection provided by art. 5(3) ePrivacy directive.

16.   The EDPB recalls that the notion of consent in the ePrivacy directive remains the notion of consent in the GDPR and must meet all the requirements of the consent as provided by art. 4(11) and 7 GDPR.

17.   However, while consent is the principle, art. 5(3) ePrivacy directive allows the storing of information or the gaining of access to information that is already stored in the terminal equipment to be exempted from the requirement of informed consent, if it satisfies one of the following criteria:
- **Exemption 1:** for the sole purpose of carrying out the transmission of a communication over an electronic communications network;
- **Exemption 2:** when it is strictly necessary in order for the provider of an information society service explicitly requested by the subscriber or user to provide the service.

18.   In such cases, the processing of personal data including personal data obtained by accessing information in the terminal equipment is based on one of the legal bases as provided by art. 6 GDPR. For example, consent is not needed when data processing is necessary to provide GPS navigation services requested by the data subject when such services can be qualified as information society services.

1.3 SCOPE

19.   The EDPB would like to point out that these guidelines are intended to facilitate compliance of the processing of personal data carried out by a wide range of stakeholders working in this environment. However, they are not intended to cover all use cases possible in this context or to provide guidance for every possible specific situation.

20.   The scope of this document focuses in particular on the personal data processing in relation to the non-professional use of connected vehicles by data subjects: e.g., drivers, passengers, vehicle owners, other road users, etc. More specifically, it deals with the personal data: (i) processed inside the vehicle, (ii) exchanged between the vehicle and personal devices connected to it (e.g., the user's smartphone) or (iii) collected locally in the vehicle and exported to external entities (e.g., vehicle manufacturers, infrastructure managers, insurance companies, car repairers) for further processing.

21.   The connected vehicle definition has to be understood as a broad concept in this document. It can be defined as a vehicle equipped with many electronic control units (ECU) that are linked together via an in-vehicle network as well as connectivity facilities allowing it to share information with other devices both inside and outside the vehicle. As such, data can be exchanged between the vehicle and personal devices connected to it, for instance allowing the mirroring of mobile applications to the car's in-dash information and entertainment unit. Also, the development of standalone mobile applications, meaning independent of the vehicle (for example, relying on the sole use of the smart phone) to assist drivers is included in the scope of this document since they contribute to the vehicle's connectivity capacities even though they may not effectively rely on the transmission of data with the vehicle *per se*. Applications for connected vehicles are multiple and diverse and can include[20]:

22. *Mobility management:* functions that allow drivers to reach a destination quickly, and in a cost-efficient manner, by providing timely information about GPS navigation, potentially dangerous environmental conditions (e.g., icy roads), traffic congestion or road construction work, parking lot or garage assistance, optimised fuel consumption or road pricing.

23. *Vehicle management:* functions that are supposed to aid drivers in reducing operating costs and improving ease of use, such as notification of vehicle condition and service reminders, transfer of usage data (e.g., for vehicle repair services), customised *"Pay As/How You Drive"* insurances, remote operations (e.g., heating system) or profile configurations (e.g., seat position).

24. *Road safety:* functions that warn the driver of external hazards and internal responses, such as collision protection, hazard warnings, lane departure warnings, driver drowsiness detection, emergency call (eCall) or crash investigation "black-boxes" (event data recorder).

25. *Entertainment:* functions providing information to and involving the entertainment of the driver and passengers, such as smart phone interfaces (hands free phone calls, voice generated text messages), WLAN hot spots, music, video, Internet, social media, mobile office or "smart home" services.

26. *Driver assistance:* functions involving partially or fully automated driving, such as operational assistance or autopilot in heavy traffic, in parking, or on highways.

27. *Well-being:* functions monitoring the driver's comfort, ability and fitness to drive such as fatigue detection or medical assistance.

28. Hence, vehicles can be natively connected or not and personal data can be collected through several means, including: (i) vehicle sensors, (ii) telematics boxes or (iii) mobile applications (e.g. accessed from a device belonging to a driver). In order to fall within the scope of this document, mobile applications need to be related to the environment of driving. For example, GPS navigation applications are in-scope. Applications whose functionalities only suggest places of interest (restaurants, historic monument, etc.) to drivers fall, however, outside the scope of these guidelines.

29. Much of the data that is generated by a connected vehicle relate to a natural person that is identified or identifiable and thus constitute personal data. For instance, data include directly identifiable data (e.g., the driver's complete identity), as well as indirectly identifiable data such as the details of journeys made, the vehicle usage data (e.g., data relating to driving style or the distance covered), or the vehicle's technical data (e.g., data relating to the wear and tear on vehicle parts), which, by cross-referencing with other files and especially the vehicle identification number (VIN), can be related to a natural person. Personal data in connected vehicles can also include metadata, such as vehicle maintenance status. In other words, any data that can be associated with a natural person therefore fall into the scope of this document.

30. The connected vehicle ecosystem covers a wide spectrum of stakeholders. This ecosystem more precisely includes traditional actors of the automotive industry as well as emerging players from the digital industry. Hence, these guidelines are directed towards vehicle manufacturers, equipment manufacturers and automotive suppliers, car repairers, automobile dealerships, vehicle service providers, fleet managers, motor insurance companies, entertainment providers, telecommunication operators, road infrastructure managers and public authorities as well as data subjects. The EDPB underlines that the categories of data subjects will differ from one service to another (e.g., drivers, owners, passengers, etc.). This is a non-exhaustive list as the ecosystem entails a wide variety of services, including services for which a direct authentication or identification is needed and services for which this is not needed.

31. Some data processing performed by natural persons within the vehicle fall within *"the course of a purely personal or household activity"* and are consequently out of the scope of the GDPR[21]. In particular, this concerns the use of personal data within the vehicles by the sole data subjects who provided such data into the vehicle's dashboard. However, the EDPB recalls that according to its recital 18 the GDPR *"applies to controllers or processors which provide the means for processing personal data for such personal or household activities"*.

1.3.1 Out of scope of this document

32. Employers providing company cars to members of their staff might want to monitor their employee's actions (e.g., in order to ensure the safety of the employee, goods or vehicles, to allocate resources, to track and bill a service or to check working time). Data processing carried out by employers in this context raises specific considerations to the employment context, which might be regulated by labour laws at the national level that cannot be detailed in these guidelines[22].

33. While the data processing in the context of commercial vehicles used for professional purposes (such as public transport) and shared transport and MaaS solution may raise specific considerations which fall out of the scope of these general guidelines, many of the principles and recommendations set out here will also be applicable to those types of processing.

34. Connected vehicles being radio-enabled systems, they are subject to passive tracking such as Wi-Fi or Bluetooth tracking. In that sense they do not differ from other connected devices and fall in the scope of the ePrivacy directive which is currently being revised. This therefore excludes also large-scale tracking of Wi-Fi equipped vehicles[23] by a dense network of bystanders who use common smartphone location services. These routinely report all visible Wi-Fi networks to central servers. Since built-in Wi-Fi can be considered a secondary vehicle identifier[24], this risks a systematic ongoing collection of complete vehicle movement profiles.

35. Vehicles are increasingly equipped with image recording devices (e.g., car parking camera systems or dashcams). Since this deals with the issue of filming public places, which requires an assessment of the relevant legislative framework which is specific to each Member State, this data processing is out of the scope of these guidelines.

36.   The processing of data enabling Cooperative Intelligent Transport Systems (C-ITS) – as defined in the directive 2010/40/EU[25] has been dealt with in a specific opinion by the Article 29 Working Party[26]. While the definition of the C-ITS concept in the directive does not bear any technical specifications, the Article 29 Working Party focuses in its opinion on short- range communications, i.e. that do not involve the intervention of a network operator. More specifically, it provides analysis for specific use cases built for initial deployment and committed to assess at a later stage the new issues that will be undoubtedly raised when higher level of automation will be implemented. Since the data protection implications in the context of C-ITS are very specific (unprecedented amounts of location data, continuous broadcasting of personal data, exchange of data between vehicles and other road infrastructural facilities, etc.) and that it is still being discussed at the European level, the processing of personal data in that context is not covered by these guidelines.

37.   Finally, this document does not aim to address all possible issues and questions raised by connected vehicles and can therefore not be considered as exhaustive.

1.4 DEFINITIONS

38.   The **processing** of personal data encompasses any operation that involves personal data such as collection, recording, organisation, structuring, storage, adaptation or alteration, retrieval, consultation, use, disclosure by transmission, dissemination or otherwise making available, alignment or combination, restriction, erasure or destruction, etc.[27]

39.   The **data subject** is the natural person to whom the data covered by the processing relate. In the context of connected vehicles, it can, in particular, be the driver (main or occasional), the passenger, or the owner of the vehicle.[28]

40.   The **data controller** is the person who determines the purposes and means of processing that take place in connected vehicles.[29] Data controllers can include service providers that process vehicle data to send the driver traffic-information, eco-driving messages or alerts regarding the functioning of the vehicle, insurance companies offering "Pay As You Drive" contracts, or vehicle manufacturers gathering data on the wear and tear affecting the vehicle's parts to improve its quality. Pursuant to art. 26 GDPR, two or more controllers can jointly determine the purposes and means of the processing and thus be considered as joint controllers. In this case, they have to clearly define their respective obligations, especially as regards the exercising of the rights of data subjects and the provision of information as referred to in art. 13 and 14 GDPR.

41.   The **data processor** is any person who processes personal data for and on behalf of the data controller.[30] The data processor collects and processes data on instruction from the data controller, without using those data for its own purposes. As an example, in a number of cases, equipment manufacturers and automotive suppliers may process data on behalf of vehicle manufacturers (which does not imply they cannot be a data controller for other purposes). In addition to requiring data processors to implement appropriate technical and organisational measures in order to guarantee a security level that is adapted to risk, art. 28 GDPR sets out data processors' obligations.

42.   The **recipient** means a natural or legal person, public authority, agency or another body, to which the personal data are disclosed, whether a third party or not.[31] As an example, a commercial partner of the service provider that receives from the service provider personal data generated from the vehicle is a recipient of personal data. Whether they act as a new data controller or as a data processor, they shall comply with all the obligations imposed by the GDPR.

43.   However, public authorities which may receive personal data in the framework of a particular inquiry in accordance with Union or Member State law shall not be regarded as recipients[32]; the processing of those data by those public authorities shall be in compliance with the applicable data protection rules according to the purposes of the processing. As an example, law enforcement authorities are authorised third parties when they request personal data as part of an investigation in accordance with European Union or Member State law.

1.5 PRIVACY AND DATA PROTECTION RISKS

44.   Article 29 Working Party has already expressed several concerns about Internet of Things (IoT) systems that can also apply to connected vehicles.[33] The issues relating to data security and control already stressed regarding IoT are even more sensitive in the context of connected vehicles, since it entails road safety concerns – and can impact the physical integrity of the driver – in an environment traditionally perceived as isolated and protected from external interferences.

45.   Also, connected vehicles raises significant data protection and privacy concerns regarding the processing of location data as its increasingly intrusive nature can put a strain on the current possibilities to remain anonymous. The EDPB wants to place particular emphasis and raise stakeholders' awareness to the fact that the use of location technologies requires the implementation of specific safeguards in order to prevent surveillance of individuals and misuse of the data.

1.5.1 Lack of control and information asymmetry

46.   Vehicle drivers and passengers may not always be adequately informed about the processing of data taking place in or through a connected vehicle. The information may be given only to the vehicle owner, who may not be the driver, and may also not be provided in a timely fashion. Thus, there is a risk that there are insufficient functionalities or options offered to exercise the control necessary for affected individuals to avail themselves of their data protection and privacy rights. This point is of importance since, during their lifetime, vehicles may belong to more than one owner either because they are sold or because they are being leased rather than purchased.

47. Also, communication in the vehicle can be triggered automatically as well as by default, without the individual being aware of it. In the absence of the possibility to effectively control how the vehicle and its connected equipment interact, it is bound to become extraordinarily difficult for the user to control the flow of data. It will be even more difficult to control its subsequent use, and thereby prevent potential function creep.

1.5.2 Quality of the user's consent

48. The EDPB underlines that, when the data processing is based on consent, all elements of valid consent have to be met which means that consent shall be free, specific and informed and constitutes an unambiguous indication of the data subject's wishes as interpreted in EDPB guidelines on consent.[34] Data controllers need to pay careful attention to the modalities of obtaining valid consent from different participants, such as car owners or car users. Such consent must be provided separately, for specific purposes and may not be bundled with the contract to buy or lease a new car. Consent must be as easily withdrawn as it is given.

49. The same has to be applied when consent is required to comply with the ePrivacy directive, for example if there is a storing of information or the gaining of access to information already stored in the vehicle as required in certain cases by art. 5(3) of the ePrivacy directive. Indeed, as outlined above, consent in this context has to be interpreted in light of the GDPR.

50. In many cases, the user may not be aware of the data processing carried out in his/her vehicle. Such lack of information constitutes a significant barrier to demonstrating valid consent under the GDPR, as the consent must be informed. In such circumstances, consent cannot be relied upon as a legal basis for the corresponding data processing under the GDPR.

51. Classic mechanisms used to obtain individuals' consent may be difficult to apply in the context of connected vehicles, resulting in a "low-quality" consent based on a lack of information or in the factual impossibility to provide fine-tuned consent in line with the preferences expressed by individuals. In practice, consent might also be difficult to obtain for drivers and passengers who are not related to the vehicle's owner in the case of second- hand, leased, rented or borrowed vehicles.

52. When the ePrivacy directive does not require the data subject consent, the controller nonetheless has the responsibility of choosing the legal basis under art. 6 GDPR that is most appropriate to the case for the processing of personal data.

1.5.3 Further processing of personal data

53. When data is collected on the basis of consent as required by art. 5(3) of the ePrivacy directive or on one of the exemptions of art. 5(3), and subsequently processed in accordance with art. 6 GDPR, it can only be further processed either if the controller seeks additional consent for this other purpose or if the data controller can demonstrate that it is based on a Union or Member State law to safeguard the objectives referred to in art. 23 (1) GDPR[35]. The EDPB considers that further processing on the basis of a compatibility test according to art. 6(4) GDPR is not possible in such cases, since it would undermine the data protection standard of the ePrivacy directive. Indeed, consent, where required under the ePrivacy directive, needs to be specific and informed, meaning that data subjects must be aware of each data processing purpose and entitled to refuse specific ones[36]. Considering that further processing on the basis of a compatibility test according to art. 6(4) of the GDPR is possible would circumvent the very principle of the consent requirements set forth by the current directive.

54. The EDPB recalls that the initial consent will never legitimise further processing as consent needs to be informed and specific to be valid.

55. For instance, telemetry data, which is collected during use of the vehicle for maintenance purposes may not be disclosed to motor insurance companies without the users consent for the purpose of creating driver profiles to offer driving behaviour-based insurance policies.

56. Furthermore, data collected by connected vehicles may be processed by law enforcement authorities to detect speeding or other infractions if and when the specific conditions in the law enforcement directive are fulfilled. In this case, such data will be considered as relating to criminal convictions and offences under the conditions laid down by art. 10 GDPR and any applicable national legislation. Manufacturers may provide the law enforcement authorities with such data if the specific conditions for such processing are fulfilled. The EDPB points out that processing of personal data for the sole purpose of fulfilling requests made by law enforcement authorities does not constitute a specified, explicit and legitimate purpose within the meaning of art. 5(1)(b) GDPR. When law enforcement authorities are authorized by law, they could be third parties within the meaning of art. 4(10) GDPR, in this case manufacturers would be entitled to provide them with any data at their disposal subject to compliance with the relevant legal framework in each Member State.

1.5.4 Excessive data collection

57. With the ever-increasing number of sensors being deployed in connected vehicles there is a very high risk of excessive data collection compared to what is necessary to achieve the purpose.

58. The development of new functionalities and more specifically those based on machine learning algorithms may require a large amount of data collected over a long period of time.

1.5.5 Security of personal data

59. The plurality of functionalities, services and interfaces (e.g., web, USB, RFID, Wi-Fi) offered by connected vehicles increases the attack surface and thus the number of potential vulnerabilities through which personal data could be compromised. Unlike most IoT devices, connected vehicles are critical systems where a security breach may endanger the life of its users and people around. The importance of addressing the risk of hackers attempting to exploit connected vehicles' vulnerabilities is thus heightened.

60. In addition, personal data stored on vehicles and/or at external locations (e.g., in cloud computing infrastructures) must be adequately secured against unauthorized access. For instance, during maintenance, a vehicle has to be handed to a technician who will require access to some of the vehicle's technical data. While the technician needs to have access to the technical data, there is a possibility that the technician could attempt to access all the data stored in the vehicle.

NOTES

[2]   Infographic "Data and the connected car" by the Future of Privacy Forum; https://fpf.org/wpcontent/uploads/2017/06/2017_0627-FPF-Connected-Car-Infographic-Version-1.0.pdf

[3]   Campaign "My Car My Data"; http://www.mycarmydata.eu/.

[4]   The interoperable EU-wide eCall; https://ec.europa.eu/transport/themes/its/road/action_plan/ecall_en.

[5]   Decision No 585/2014/EU of the European Parliament and of the Council of 15 May 2014 on the deployment of the interoperable EU-wide eCall service Text with EEA relevance; https://eur-lex.europa.eu/legalcontent/EN/TXT/PDF/?uri=CELEX:32014D0585.

[6]   Working document on data protection and privacy implications in eCall initiative; http://ec.europa.eu/justice/article-29/documentation/opinion-recommendation/files/2006/wp125_en.pdf.

[7]   Cyber security and resilience of smart cars; https://www.enisa.europa.eu/publications/cyber-security-andresilience-of-smart-cars.

[8]   Resolution on data protection in automated and connected vehicles; https://edps.europa.eu/sites/edp/files/publication/resolution-on-data-protection-in-automated-andconnected-vehicles_en_1.pdf.

[9]   Working paper on connected vehicles; https://www.datenschutz-berlin.de/infothek-undservice/veroeffentlichungen/working-paper/.

[10]   Data protection aspects of using connected and non-connected vehicles; https://www.lda.bayern.de/media/dsk_joint_statement_vda.pdf.

[11]   Principles of cyber security for connected and automated vehicles; https://www.gov.uk/government/publications/principles-of-cyber-security-for-connected-and-automatedvehicles.

[12]   Compliance package for a responsible use of data in connected cars; https://www.cnil.fr/en/connectedvehicles-compliance-package-responsible-use-data.

[13]   Commission Directive 2008/63/EC of 20 June 2008 on competition in the markets in telecommunications terminal equipment (Codified version) (Text with EEA relevance); https://eur-lex.europa.eu/legalcontent/EN/ALL/?uri=CELEX%3A32008L0063.

[14]   European Data Protection Board, Opinion 5/2019 on the interplay between the ePrivacy Directive and the GDPR, in particular regarding the competence, tasks and powers of data protection authorities, adopted on 12 March 2019 (hereinafter - "Opinion 5/2019"), paragraph 40.

[15]   Ibid, paragraph 40.

[16]   Ibid, paragraph 41.

[17]   Consent required by art. 5(3) of the "ePrivacy" directive and consent needed as a legal basis for the processing of data (art. 6 GDPR) for the same specific purpose can be collected at the same time (for example, by checking a box clearly indicating what the data subject is consenting to).

[18]   Opinion 5/2019, paragraph 41.

[19]   European Data Protection Board, Guidelines 2/2019 on the processing of personal data under Article 6(1)(b) GDPR in the context of the provision of online services to data subjects, Version 2.0, 8 October 2019, paragraph 1.

[20]   PwC Strategy 2014. "In the fast lane. The bright future of connected cars": https://www.strategyand.pwc.com/media/file/Strategyand_In-the-Fast-Lane.pdf.

[21]   See GDPR, Article 2(2)(c).

[22]   The Article 29 Working Party elaborated on this in its WP249 Opinion 2/2017 on data processing at work;https://ec.europa.eu/newsroom/article29/item-detail.cfm?item_id=610169.

[23]   See for details: https://www.datenschutzzentrum.de/artikel/1269-Location-Services-can-Systematically-Track-Vehicles-with-WiFi-Access-Points-at-Large-Scale.html.

[24]   Markus Ullmann, Tobias Franz, and Gerd Nolden, Vehicle Identification Based on Secondary Vehicle Identifier -- Analysis, and Measurements, in Proceedings, VEHICULAR 2017, The Sixth International Conference on Advances in Vehicular Systems, Technologies and Applications, Nice, France, July 23 to 27, 2017, p. 32-37.

[25]   Directive 2010/40/EU of 7 July 2020 on the framework for the deployment of Intelligent Transport Systems in the field of road transport and for interfaces with other modes of transport; https://eur-lex.europa.eu/legalcontent/EN/TXT/PDF/?uri=CELEX:32010L0040.

[26]   Article 29 Working Party - Opinion 03/2017 on Processing personal data in the context of Cooperative Intelligent Transport Systems (C-ITS); http://ec.europa.eu/newsroom/article29/itemdetail.cfm?item_id=610171.

[27]   See GDPR, Article 4 (2).

[28]   See GDPR, Article 4 (1).

[29]   See GDPR, Article 4 (7) and the European Data Protection Board, Guidelines 07/2020 on the concepts of controller and processor in the GDPR (hereinafter - "Guidelines 07/2020").

[30]   See GDPR, Article 4 (8) and the Guidelines 07/2020.

[31]   See GDPR, Article 4 (9) and the Guidelines 07/2020.

[32]   GDPR, Article 4 (9) and Recital 31.

[33]   Article 29 Working Party – Opinion 8/2014 on the Recent Developments on the Internet of Things; https://ec.europa.eu/justice/article-29/documentation/opinion-recommendation/files/2014/wp223_en.pdf.

Part 2   Data Protection: EU Law etc

[34]   European Data Protection Board, Guidelines 05/2020 on consent under Regulation 2016/679, Version 1.1, 4 May 2020 (hereinafter - "Guidelines 05/2020").
[35]   See also European Data Protection Board, Guidelines 10/2020 on restrictions under Article 23 GDPR.
[36]   Guidelines 05/2020, sections 3.2 and 3.3.

2 GENERAL RECOMMENDATIONS

[2.323]
61. In order to mitigate the risks for data subjects identified above, the following general recommendations should be followed by vehicle and equipment manufacturers, service providers or any other stakeholder who may act as data controller or data processor in relation to connected vehicles.

2.1 CATEGORIES OF DATA

62. As noted in the introduction, most data associated with connected vehicles will be considered personal data to the extent that it is possible to link it to one or more identifiable individuals. This includes technical data concerning the vehicle's movements (e.g., speed, distance travelled) as well concerning the vehicle's condition (e.g., engine coolant temperature, engine RPM, tyre pressure). Certain data generated by connected vehicles may also warrant special attention given their sensitivity and/or potential impact on the rights and interests of data subjects. At present, the EDPB has identified three categories of personal data warranting special attention, by vehicle and equipment manufacturers, service providers and other data controllers: location data, biometric data (and any special category of data as defined in art. 9 GDPR) and data that could reveal offences or traffic violations.

2.1.1 Location data

63. When collecting personal data, vehicle and equipment manufacturers, service providers and other data controllers should keep in mind that location data are particularly revealing of the life habits of data subjects. The journeys carried out are very characteristic in that they enable one to infer the place of work and of residence, as well as a driver's centres of interest (leisure), and may possibly reveal sensitive information such as religion through the place of worship, or sexual orientation through the places visited. Accordingly, the vehicle and equipment manufacturer, service provider and other data controller should be particularly vigilant not to collect location data except if doing so is absolutely necessary for the purpose of processing. As an example, when the processing consists in detecting the vehicle's movement, the gyroscope is sufficient to fulfil that function, without there being a need to collect location data.

64. In general, collecting location data is also subject to compliance with the following principles:
–   adequate configuration of the frequency of access to, and of the level of detail of, location data collected relative to the purpose of processing. For example, a weather application should not be able to access the vehicle's location every second, even with the consent of the data subject;
–   providing accurate information on the purpose of processing (e.g., is location history stored? If so, what is its purpose?);
–   when the processing is based on consent, obtaining valid (free, specific and informed) consent that is distinct from the general conditions of sale or use, for example on the on-board computer;
–   activating location only when the user launches a functionality that requires the vehicle's location to be known, and not by default and continuously when the car is started;
–   informing the user that location has been activated, in particular by using icons (e.g., an arrow that moves across the screen);
–   the option to deactivate location at any time;
–   defining a limited storage period.

2.1.2 Biometric data

65. In the context of connected vehicles, biometric data used for the purpose of uniquely identifying a natural person may be processed, within the remit of art. 9 GDPR and the national exceptions, among other things, to enable access to a vehicle, to authenticate the driver/owner, and/or to enable access to a driver's profile settings and preferences. When considering the use of biometric data, guaranteeing the data subject full control over his or her data involves, on the one hand, providing for the existence of a non-biometric alternative (e.g., using a physical key or a code) without additional constraint (that is, the use of biometrics should not be mandatory), and, on the other hand, storing and comparing the biometric template in encrypted form only on a local basis, with biometric data not being processed by an external reading/comparison terminal.

66. In the case of biometric data[37], it is important to ensure that the biometric authentication solution is sufficiently reliable, in particular by complying with the following principles:
–   the adjustment of the biometric solution used (e.g., the rate of false positives and false negatives) is adapted to the security level of the required access control;
–   the biometric solution used is based on a sensor that is resistant to attacks (such as the use of a flat-printed print for fingerprint recognition);
–   the number of authentication attempts is limited;
–   the biometric template/model is stored in the vehicle, in an encrypted form using a cryptographic algorithm and key management that comply with the state of the art;
–   the raw data used to make up the biometric template and for user authentication are processed in real time without ever being stored, even locally.

2.1.3 Data revealing criminal offenses or other infractions

67. In order to process data that relate to potential criminal offences within the meaning of art. 10 GDPR, the EDPB recommends to resort to the local processing of the data where the data subject has full control over the processing in question (see discussion on local processing in section 2.4). Indeed – except for some exceptions (see the case study on accidentology studies presented below in section 3.3) – external processing of data revealing criminal offences or other infractions is forbidden. Thus, according to the sensitivity of the data, strong security measures such as those described in section 2.7 must be put in place in order to offer protection against the illegitimate access, modification and deletion of those data.

68. Indeed, some categories of personal data from connected vehicles could reveal that a criminal offence or other infraction has been or is being committed ("offence-related data") and therefore be subject to special restrictions (e.g., data indicating that the vehicle crossed a white line, the instantaneous speed of a vehicle combined with precise location data). Notably, in the event that such data would be processed by the competent national authorities for the purposes of criminal investigation and prosecution of criminal offence, the safeguards provided for in art. 10 GDPR would apply.

2.2 PURPOSES

69. Personal data may be processed for a wide variety of purposes in relation to connected vehicles, including driver safety, insurance, efficient transportation, entertainment or information services. In accordance with the GDPR, data controllers must ensure that their purposes are "specified, explicit and legitimate", not further processed in a way incompatible with those purposes and that there is a valid legal basis for the processing as required in art. 5 GDPR. Some concrete examples of purposes that may be pursued by data controllers operating in the context of connected vehicles are discussed in Part III of these guidelines, along with specific recommendations for each type of processing.

2.3 RELEVANCE AND DATA MINIMISATION

70. To comply with the data minimization principle[38], vehicle and equipment manufacturers, service providers and other data controllers should pay special attention to the categories of data they need from a connected vehicle, as they shall only collect personal data that are relevant and necessary for the processing. For instance, location data are particularly intrusive and can reveal many life habits of the data subjects. Accordingly, industry participants should be particularly vigilant not to collect location data except if doing so is absolutely necessary for the purpose of processing (see discussion on location data above, in section 2.1).

2.4 DATA PROTECTION BY DESIGN AND BY DEFAULT

71. Taking into account the volume and diversity of personal data produced by connected vehicles, the EDPB notes that data controllers are required to ensure that technologies deployed in the context of connected vehicles are configured to respect the privacy of individuals by applying the obligations of data protection by design and by default as required by art. 25 GDPR. Technologies should be designed to minimize the collection of personal data, provide privacy-protective default settings and ensure that data subjects are well informed and have the option to easily modify configurations associated with their personal data. Specific guidance on how manufacturers and service providers can comply with data protection by design and by default could be beneficial for the industry and third party application providers.

72. Certain general practices, described below, can also help mitigate the risks to the rights and freedoms of natural persons associated with connected vehicles[39].

2.4.1 Local processing of personal data

73. In general, vehicle and equipment manufacturers, service providers and other data controllers should, wherever possible, use processes that do not involve personal data or transferring personal data outside of the vehicle (i.e., the data is processed internally). The nature of connected vehicles however does present risks, such as the possibility of attacks on local processing by outside actors or local data being leaked by selling parts of the vehicle. Therefore, adequate attention and security measures should be taken into account to ensure that local processing shall remain local. This scenario offers the advantage of guaranteeing to the user the sole and full control of his/her personal data and, as such, it presents, "by design", less privacy risks especially by prohibiting any data processing by stakeholders without the data subject knowledge. It also enables the processing of sensitive data such as biometric data or data relating to criminal offenses or other infractions, as well as detailed location data which otherwise would be subject to stricter rules (see below). In the same vein, it presents fewer cybersecurity risks and involves little latency, which makes it particularly suited to automated driving-assistance functions. Some examples of this type of solution could include:

–   eco-driving applications that process data in the vehicle in order to display eco-driving advice in real time on the on-board screen;

–   applications that involve a transfer of personal data to a device such as a smartphone under the user's full control (via, for example, Bluetooth or Wi-Fi), and where the vehicle's data are not transmitted to the application providers or the vehicle manufacturers; this would include, for instance, coupling of smartphones to use the car's display, multimedia systems, microphone (or other sensors) for phone calls, etc., to the extent that the data collected remain under the control of the data subject and is exclusively used to provide the service he or she has requested;

- in-vehicle safety enhancing applications such as those that provide audible signals or vibrations of the steering wheel when a driver overtakes a car without indicating or straying over white lines or which provides alerts as to the state of the vehicle (e.g., an alert on the wear and tear affecting brake pads);
- applications for unlocking, starting, and/or activating certain vehicle commands using the driver's biometric data that is stored within the vehicle (such as a face or voice models or fingerprint minutiae).

74. Applications such as the above involve processing carried out for the performance of purely personal activities by a natural person (i.e., without the transfer of personal data to a data controller or data processor). Therefore, in accordance with art. 2(2) GDPR, **these applications fall outside the scope of the GDPR.**

75. However, if the GDPR does not apply to the processing of personal data by a natural person in the course of a purely personal or household activity, it does apply to controllers or processors, which provide the means for processing personal data for such personal or household activities (car manufacturers, service provider, etc.) in accordance with recital 18 GDPR. Hence, when they are acting as data controller or data processor, they must develop secure in-car application and with due respect to the principle of privacy by design and by default. In any case, according to recital 78 GDPR, *"When developing, designing, selecting and using applications, services and products that are based on the processing of personal data or process personal data to fulfil their task, producers of the products, services and applications should be encouraged to take into account the right to data protection when developing and designing such products, services and applications and, with due regard to the state of the art, to make sure that controllers and processors are able to fulfil their data protection obligations".*[40] One the one hand, it will enhance the development of user-centric services and, on the other hand, it will facilitate and secure any further uses in the future which could fall back within the scope of the GDPR. More specifically, the EDPB recommends developing a secure in-car application platform, physically divided from safety relevant car functions so that the access to car data does not depend on unnecessary external cloud capabilities.

76. Local data processing should be considered by car manufacturers and service providers, whenever possible, to mitigate the potential risks of cloud processing, as they are underlined in the opinion on Cloud Computing released by the Article 29 Working Party.[41]

77. In general users should be able to control how their data are collected and processed in the vehicle:
- information regarding the processing must be provided in the driver's language (manual, settings, etc.);
- the EDPB recommends that only data strictly necessary for the functioning of the vehicle are processed by default. Data subjects should have the possibility to activate or deactivate the data processing for each other purpose and controller/processor and have the possibility to delete the data concerned, taking into account the purpose and the legal basis of the data processing ;
- data should not be transmitted to any third parties (i.e., the user has sole access to the data);
- data should be retained only for as long as is necessary for the provision of the service or otherwise required by Union or Member State law;
- data subjects should be able to delete permanently any personal data before the vehicles are put up for sale;
- data subjects should, where feasible, have a direct access to the data generated by these applications.

78. Finally, while it may not always be possible to resort to local data processing for every use- case, "hybrid processing" can often be put in place. For instance, in the context of usage- based insurance, personal data regarding driving behaviour (such as the force exerted on the brake pedal, mileage driven, etc.) could either be processed inside the vehicle or by the telematics service provider on behalf of the insurance company (the data controller) to generate numerical scores that are transferred to the insurance company on a defined basis (e.g. on a monthly basis). In this way, the insurance company does not gain access to the raw behavioural data but only to the aggregate score that is the result of the processing. This ensures that principles of data minimization are satisfied by design. This also means that users must have the ability to exercise their right when data are stored by other parties: for example, a user should have the ability to delete data stored in the systems of a car maintenance shop or dealership under the conditions of art.17 GDPR.

2.4.2 Anonymization and pseudonymisation

79. If the transmission of personal data outside the vehicle is envisaged, consideration should be given to anonymize them before being transmitted. When anonymising the controller should take into account all processing involved which could potentially lead to re- identification of data, such as the transmission of locally anonymised data. The EDPB recalls that the principles of data protection do not apply to anonymous information, namely information which does not relate to an identified or identifiable natural person or to personal data rendered anonymous in such a manner that the data subject is not or no longer identifiable[42]. Once a dataset is truly anonymised and individuals are no longer identifiable, European data protection law no longer applies. As a consequence, anonymisation, where relevant, may be a good strategy to keep the benefits and to mitigate the risks in relation to connected vehicles.

80. As detailed in the opinion by the Article 29 Working Party on anonymization techniques, various methods can be used – sometimes in combination – in order to reach data anonymisation.[43]

81. Other techniques such as pseudonymisation[44] can help minimize the risks generated by the data processing, taking into account that in most cases, directly identifiable data are not necessary to achieve the purpose of the processing. Pseudonymisation, if reinforced by security safeguards, improves the protection of personal data by reducing the risks of misuse. Pseudonymisation is reversible, unlike anonymisation, and pseudonymised data are considered as personal data subject to the GDPR.

2.4.3 Data protection impact assessments

82. Given the scale and sensitivity of the personal data that can be generated *via* connected vehicles; it is likely that processing – particularly in situations where personal data are processed outside of the vehicle - will often result in a high risk to the rights and freedoms of individuals. Where this is the case, industry participants will be required to perform a data protection impact assessment (DPIA) to identify and mitigate the risks as detailed in art. 35 and 36 GDPR. Even in the cases where a DPIA is not required, it is a best practice to conduct one as early as possible in the design process. This will allow industry participants to factor the results of this analysis into their design choices prior to the roll-out of new technologies.

2.5 INFORMATION

83. Prior to the processing of personal data, the data subject shall be informed of the identity of the data controller (e.g., the vehicle and equipment manufacturer or service provider), the purpose of processing, the data recipients, the period for which data will be stored, and the data subject's rights under the GDPR[45].

84. In addition, the vehicle and equipment manufacturer, service provider or other data controller should also provide the data subject with the following information, in clear, simple, and easily-accessible terms:

–   the contact details of the data protection officer;
–   the purposes of the processing for which the personal data are intended as well as the legal basis for the processing;
–   the explicit mention of the legitimate interests pursued by the data controller or by a third party, when such legitimate interests constitute the legal basis for processing;
–   the recipients or categories of recipients of the personal data, if any;
–   the period for which the personal data will be stored, or if that is not possible, the criteria used to determine that period;
–   the existence of the right to request from the controller access to and rectification or erasure of personal data or restriction of processing concerning the data subject or to object to processing as well as the right to data portability;
–   the existence of the right to withdraw consent at any time without affecting the lawfulness of processing based on consent before its withdrawal where the processing is based on consent;
–   where applicable, the fact that the controller intends to transfer personal data to a third country or international organisation and safeguards used to transfer them;
–   whether the provision of personal data is a statutory or contractual requirement, or a requirement necessary to enter into a contract, as well as whether the data subject is obliged to provide the personal data and of the possible consequences of failure to provide such data;
–   the existence of automated decision-making, including profiling that produces legal effects concerning the data subject or similarly significantly affects the data subject, and meaningful information about the logic involved, as well as the significance and the envisaged consequences of such processing for the data subject. This could particularly be the case in relation to the provision of usage-based insurance to individuals;
–   the right to lodge a complaint with a supervisory authority;
–   information about further processing;
–   In case of joint data controllership, clear and complete information about the responsibilities of each data controller.

85. In some cases, personal data is not collected directly from the individual concerned. For instance, a vehicle and equipment manufacturer may rely on a dealer to collect information about the owner of the vehicle in order to offer an emergency road side assistance service. When data have not been collected directly, the vehicle and equipment manufacturer, service provider or other data controller shall, in addition to the information mentioned above, also indicate the categories of personal data concerned, the source from which the personal data originate, and, if applicable, whether those data came from publicly accessible sources. That information must be provided by the controller within a reasonable period after obtaining the data, and **no later than the first of the following dates** in accordance with art. 14 (3) GDPR: (i) one month after the data are obtained, having regard to the specific circumstances in which the personal data are processed, (ii) upon first communication with the data subject, or (iii) if those data are transmitted to a third party, before the transmission of the data.

86. New information may also need to be provided to data subjects when they are taken care of by new data controller. A roadside assistance service that interacts with connected vehicles can be provided by different data controllers depending in which country or region the assistance is required. New data controllers should provide data subjects with the required information when data subjects cross borders and services that interact with connected vehicles are provided by new data controllers.

87. The information directed to the data subjects may be provided in layers[46], i.e. by separating two levels of information: on the one hand, first-level information, which is the most important for the data subjects, and, on the other hand, information that presumably is of interest at a later stage. The essential first-level information includes, in addition to the identity of the data controller, the purpose of the processing and a description of the data subject's rights, as well as any additional information on the processing which has the most impact on the data subject and processing which could surprise them. The EDPB recommends that, in the context of connected vehicles, the data subject should be made aware of all the recipients in the first layer of information. As stated in the WP29 guidelines on transparency, controllers should provide information on the recipients that is most meaningful for data subjects. In practice, this will generally be the named recipients, so that data subjects know exactly who has their personal data. If controllers cannot provide the names of the recipients, the information should be as specific as possible by indicating the type of recipient (i.e. by reference to the activities it carries out), the industry, sector and sub-sector, and the location of the recipients.

88. The data subjects may be informed by concise and easily understandable clauses in the contract of sale of the vehicle, in the contract for the provision of services, and/or in any written medium, by using distinct documents (e.g., the vehicle's maintenance record book or manual) or the on-board computer.

89. Standardised icons could be used in addition to the information necessary, as required under art. 13 and 14 GDPR, to enhance transparency by potentially reducing the need for vast amounts of written information to be presented to a data subject. It should be visible in vehicles in order to provide, in relation to the planned processing, a good overview that is understandable, and clearly legible. The EDPB emphasises the importance of standardising those icons, so that the user finds the same symbols regardless of the make or model of the vehicle. For example, when certain types of data are being collected, such as location, the vehicles could have a clear signal on-board (such as a light inside the vehicle) to inform passengers about data collection.

2.6 RIGHTS OF THE DATA SUBJECT

90. Vehicle and equipment manufacturers, service providers and other data controllers should facilitate data subjects' control over their data during the entire processing period, through the implementation of specific tools providing an effective way to exercise their rights, in particular their right of access, rectification, erasure, their right to restrict the processing and, depending on the legal basis of the processing, their right to data portability and their right to object.

91. To facilitate settings modifications, a profile management system should be implemented in order to store the preferences of known drivers and help them to change easily their privacy settings anytime. The profile management system should centralize every data setting for each data processing, especially to facilitate the access, deletion, removal and portability of personal data from vehicle systems at the request of the data subject. Drivers should be enabled to stop the collection of certain types of data, temporarily or permanently, at any moment, unless there is a specific legal ground that the controller can rely on to continue the collection of specific data. In case of a contract that provides a personalized offer based on driving behaviour this may mean that the user as a result should be reverted to the standard conditions of that contract. These features should be implemented inside the vehicle, although it could also be provided to data subjects through additional means (e.g., dedicated application). Furthermore, in order to allow data subjects to quickly and easily remove personal data that can be stored on the car's dashboard (for example, GPS navigation history, web browsing, etc.), the EDPB recommends that manufacturers provide a simple functionality (such as a delete button).

92. The sale of a connected vehicle and the ensuing change of ownership should also trigger the deletion of any personal data, which is no longer needed for the previous specified purposes and the data subject should be able to exercise his or her right to portability.

2.7 SECURITY

93. Vehicle and equipment manufacturers, service providers and other data controllers should put in place measures that guarantee the security and confidentiality of processed data and take all useful precautions to prevent control being taken by an unauthorised person. In particular, industry participants should consider adopting the following measures:
- encrypting the communication channels by means of a state-of-the-art algorithm;
- putting in place an encryption-key management system that is unique to each vehicle, not to each model;
- when stored remotely, encrypting data by means of state-of-the-art algorithms;
- regularly renewing encryption keys;
- protecting encryptions keys from any disclosure;
- authenticating data-receiving devices;
- ensuring data integrity (e.g., by hashing);
- make access to personal data subject to reliable user authentication techniques (password, electronic certificate, etc.);

94. Concerning more specifically vehicle manufacturers, the EDPB recommends the implementation of the following security measures:
- partitioning the vehicle's vital functions from those always relying on telecommunication capacities (e.g., "infotainment");
- implementing technical measures that enable vehicle manufacturers to rapidly patch security vulnerabilities during the entire lifespan of the vehicle;
- for the vehicle's vital functions, give priority as much as possible to using secure means of communications that are specifically dedicated to transportation;
- setting up an alarm system in case of attack on the vehicle's systems, with the possibility of operating in downgraded mode[47];
- storing a log history of any access to the vehicle's information system, e.g. going back six months as a maximum period, in order to enable the origin of any potential attack to be understood and periodically carry out a review of the logged information to detect possible anomalies.

95. These general recommendations should be completed by specific requirements taking into account the characteristics and purpose of each data processing.

2.8 TRANSMITTING PERSONAL DATA TO THIRD PARTIES

96. In principle, only the data controller and the data subject have access to the data generated by a connected vehicle. However, the data controller may transmit personal data to a commercial partner (recipient), to the extent that such transmission lawfully relies on one of the legal bases stated in art. 6 GDPR.

97. In view of the possible sensitivity of the vehicle-usage data (e.g., journeys made, driving style), the EDPB recommends that the data subject's consent be systematically obtained before their data are transmitted to a commercial partner acting as a data controller (e.g., by ticking a box that is not pre-ticked, or, where technically possible, by using a physical or logical device that the person can access from the vehicle). The commercial partner in turn becomes responsible for the data that it receives, and is subject to all the provisions of the GDPR.

98. The vehicle manufacturer, service provider or other data controller can transmit personal data to a data processor selected to play a part in providing the service to the data subject, provided the data processor shall not use those data for its own purpose. Data controllers and data processors shall draw up a contract or other legal document specifying the obligations of each party and setting out the provisions of art. 28 GDPR.

2.9 TRANSFER OF PERSONAL DATA OUTSIDE THE EU/EEA

99. When personal data is transferred outside the European Economic Area, special safeguards are foreseen to ensure that the protection travels with the data.

100. As a consequence, the data controller may transfer personal data to a recipient only to the extent that such transfer is in accordance with the requirements laid down in Chapter V GDPR.

2.10 USE OF IN-VEHICLE WI-FI TECHNOLOGIES

101. Advances in cellular technology have made it possible to easily use the Internet on the road. While it is possible to get Wi-Fi connectivity in a vehicle through a smartphone hotspot or a dedicated device (OBD-II dongle, wireless modem or router, etc.), most manufacturers offer nowadays models that include a built-in cellular data connection and are also capable of creating Wi-Fi networks. Depending on the case, various aspects must be considered:
–   The Wi-Fi connectivity is offered as a service by a road professional, such as a taxi driver for its customers. In this case, the professional or his/her company might be considered as an internet service provider (ISP), hence be subject to specific obligations and restrictions regarding the processing of his / her clients' personal data.
–   The Wi-Fi connectivity is put in place for the sole use of the driver (at the exclusion of the driver and his/her passengers). In this case, the processing of personal data is considered to be purely personal or household activity in accordance with art. 2(2)(c) and recital 18 GDPR.

102. In general, the proliferation of Internet connection interfaces via Wi-Fi poses greater risks to the privacy of individuals. Indeed, through their vehicles, users become continuous broadcasters, and can therefore be identified and tracked. In order to prevent tracking, easy to operate opt-out options ensuring the service set identifier (SSID) of the on-board Wi-Fi network is not collected should therefore be put in place by the vehicle and equipment manufacturers.

NOTES

37   The prohibition principle set out in article 9.1 GDPR only relates to *"biometric data for the purpose of uniquely identifying a natural person"*.
38   GDPR, Article 5(1)(c).
39   See as well European Data Protection Board, Guidelines 4/2019 on Article 25 Data Protection by Design and by Default, Version 2.0, adopted on 20 October 2020 (hereinafter - "Guidelines 4/2019").
40   For more recommendations on privacy by design and privacy by default see also Guidelines 4/2019.
41   Article 29 Working Party – Opinion 5/2012 on Cloud Computing; https://ec.europa.eu/justice/article-29/documentation/opinion-recommendation/files/2012/wp196_en.pdf.
42   See GDPR, Article 4 (1) and Recital 26.
43   WP29 - Opinion 05/2014 on Anonymisation Techniques; https://ec.europa.eu/justice/article-29/documentation/opinion-recommendation/files/2014/wp216_en.pdf.
44   GDPR, Article 4 (5). Enisa report on December 03, 2019: https://www.enisa.europa.eu/publications/pseudonymisation-techniques-and-best-practices.
45   GDPR, Article 5 (1)(a) and 13. See also Article 29 Working Party, Guidelines on Transparency under Regulation 2016/679 (wp260rev.01), endorsed by the EDPB.
46   See Article 29 Working Party, Guidelines on Transparency under Regulation 2016/679 (wp260rev.01), endorsed by the EDPB.
47   Downgraded mode is a vehicle operating mode ensuring that the functions essential for the safe operation of the vehicle (i.e., minimum safety requirements) would be guaranteed, even if other less important functionalities would be deactivated (e.g., the operation of the geo-guidance device can be considered as nonessential, as opposed to the braking system).

3 CASE STUDIES

[2.324]
103. This section addresses five specific examples of processing in the context of connected vehicles,

which correspond to scenarios likely to be encountered by stakeholders in the sector. The examples cover data processing that requires calculating power which cannot be mobilised locally in the vehicle, and/or the sending of personal data to a third party to carry out further analysis or to provide further functionality remotely. For each type of processing, this document specifies the intended purposes, the categories of data collected, the retention period of such data, the rights of data subjects, the security measures to be implemented, and the recipients of the information. In the case some of these fields are not described in the following, the general recommendations described in the previous part apply.

104.   The examples chosen are non-exhaustive and are meant to be indicative of the variety of types of processing, legal bases, actors, etc. that might be engaged in the context of connected vehicles.

3.1 PROVISION OF A SERVICE BY A THIRD PARTY

105.   Data subjects may contract with a service provider in order to obtain added-value services relating to their vehicle. For example, a data subject may enter into a usage-based insurance contract that offers reduced insurance premiums for less driving ("Pay As You Drive") or good driving behaviour ("Pay How You Drive") and which necessitates monitoring of driving habits by the insurance company. A data subject could also contract with a company that offers roadside assistance in the event of a breakdown and which entails the transmission of the vehicle's location to the company or with a service provider in order to receive messages or alerts relating to the vehicle's functioning (e.g., an alert on the state of brake wear, or a reminder of the technical-inspection date).

3.1.1 Usage-based insurance

106.   "Pay as you drive" is a type of usage-based insurance that tracks the driver's mileage and/or driving habits to differentiate and reward "safe" drivers by giving them lower premiums. The insurer will require the driver to install a built-in telematics service, a mobile application or activate a built-in module from manufacturing that tracks the miles covered and/or the driving behaviour (braking pattern, rapid acceleration, etc.) of the policy holder. The information gathered by the telematic device will be used to assign the driver scores in order to analyse what risks he/she may pose to the insurance company.

107.   As usage-based insurance requires consent under art. 5(3) of the ePrivacy directive, the EDPB outlines that the policy holder must have the choice to subscribe to a non-usage-based insurance policy. Otherwise, consent would not be considered freely given, as the performance of the contract would be conditional on the consent. Further, art. 7(3) GDPR requires that a data subject must have the right to withdraw consent.

3.1.1.1 Legal basis

108.   When the data is collected through a publicly available electronic communication service (for example via the SIM card contained in the telematics device), consent will be needed in order to gain access to information that is already stored in the vehicle as provided by art. 5(3) ePrivacy directive. Indeed, none of the exemptions provided by those provisions can apply in this context: the processing is not for the sole purpose of carrying out the transmission of a communication over an electronic communications network nor does it relate to an information society service explicitly requested by the subscriber or user. Consent could be collected at the time of the conclusion of the contract.

109.   As regards the processing of personal data following the storage or access to the end-user's terminal equipment, the insurance company can rely on art. 6(1)(b) GDPR in this specific context provided it can establish both that the processing takes place in the context of a valid contract with the data subject and that processing is necessary in order that the particular contract with the data subject can be performed. Insofar as the processing is objectively necessary for the performance of the contract with the data subject, the EDPB considers that reliance upon art. 6(1)(b) GDPR would not have the effect of lowering the additional protection provided by art. 5(3) of the ePrivacy directive in this specific instance. That legal basis is materialised by the data subject signing a contract with the insurance company.

3.1.1.2 Data collected

110.   There is two types of personal data to be considered:
–   **commercial and transactional data**: data subject's identifying information, transaction- related data, data relating to means of payment, etc.;
–   **usage data**: personal data generated by the vehicle, driving habits, location, etc.

111.   The EDPB recommends that, as far as possible, and given that there is a risk that the data collected via the telematics-box could be misused to create a precise profile of the driver's movements, raw data regarding driving behaviour should be either processed:
–   inside the vehicle in telematics boxes or in the user's smartphone so that the insurer only accesses the results data (e.g., a score relating to driving habits), not detailed raw data (see section 2.1);
–   or by the telematics service provider on behalf of the controller (the insurance company) to generate numerical scores that are transferred to the insurance company on a defined basis. In this case, raw data and data directly relating to the identity of the driver must be separated. This means that the telematics service provider receives the real-time data, but does not know the names, licence plates, etc. of the policy holders. On the other hand, the insurer knows the names of policyholders, but only receives the scores and the total kilometres and not the raw data used to produce such scores.

112.   Moreover, it has to be noted that if only the mileage is necessary for the performance of the contract, location data shall not be collected.

3.1.1.3 Retention period

113. In the context of data processing taking place for the performance of a contract (i.e. provision of a service), it is important to distinguish between two types of data before defining their respective retention periods:

– **commercial and transactional data:** those data can be retained in an active database for the full duration of the contract. At the end of the contract, they can be archived physically (on a separate medium: DVD, etc.) or logically (by authorisation management) in the event of possible litigation. Thereafter, at the end of the statutory limitation periods, the data shall be deleted or anonymised;

– **usage data:** usage data can be classified as raw data and aggregated data. As stated above, if possible, data controllers or processors should not process raw data. If it is necessary, raw data should be kept only as long as they are required to elaborate the aggregated data and to check the validity of that aggregation process. Aggregated data should be kept as long as it is necessary for the provision of the service or otherwise requested by a Union or Member State law.

3.1.1.4 Information and rights of data subjects

114. Prior to the processing of personal data, the data subject shall be informed according to art. 13 GDPR, in a transparent and understandable way. In particular, he or she must be informed of the period for which the personal data will be stored, or if that is not possible, the criteria used to determine that period. In this last case, the EDPB recommends to adopt a pedagogic approach to emphasize the difference between raw data and the score produced on this basis, stressing, when it is the case, that the insurer will only collect the result of the score where appropriate.

115. Where data are not processed inside the vehicle but by a telematics provider on behalf of the controller (the insurance company), the information could usefully mention that, in this case, the provider will not have access to data directly relating to the identity of the driver (such as names, licence plates, etc.) Also, considering the importance of informing data subjects as to the consequences of processing of their personal data and the fact that data subjects should not be taken by surprise by the processing of their personal data, the EDPB recommends that data subject should be informed of the existence of profiling and the consequences of such profiling even if it does not involve any automated decision-making as referred to in art. 22 GDPR.

116. Regarding the right of data subjects, they shall be specifically informed of the available means to exercise his or her right of access, rectification, restriction and erasure. Since raw data collected in this context are provided by the data subject (through specific forms or through his or her activity) and processed on the basis of art. 6(1)(b) GDPR (performance of a contract), the data subject is entitled to exercise his or her right to data portability. As emphasized in the guidelines on the right to data portability, the EDPB strongly recommends "that data controllers clearly explain the difference between the types of data that a data subject can receive through the rights of subject access and data portability".[48]

117. The information can be provided when the contract is signed.

3.1.1.5 Recipient:

118. The EDPB recommends that, as far as possible, the vehicle's usage data should be processed directly in telematics boxes, so that the insurer only accesses the results data (e.g. a score), not detailed raw data.

119. If a telematics service provider collects the data on behalf of the controller (the insurance company) to generate numerical scores, it does not need to know the identity of the driver (such as names, licence plates, etc.) of the policy holders.

3.1.1.6 Security:

120. General recommendations apply. See section 2.7.

3.1.2 Renting and booking a parking space

121. The owner of a parking place may want to rent it. For this, he/she lists a spot and sets a price for it on a web application. Then, once the parking spot is listed, the application notifies the owner when a driver wants to book it. The driver can select a destination and check for available parking spots based on multiple criteria. After the approval of the owner, the transaction is confirmed and the service provider handles the payment transaction then uses navigation to drive to the location.

3.1.2.1 Legal basis

122. When the data is collected through a publicly available electronic communication, art. 5(3) of the ePrivacy directive applies.

123. Because this is an information society service, art. 5(3) of the ePrivacy directive does not require consent for gaining access to information that is already stored in the vehicle when such a service is explicitly requested by the subscriber.

124. For the processing of personal data and only for data necessary for the performance of the contract to which the data subject is party, art. 6(1)(b) GDPR will be the legal basis.

3.1.2.2 Data collected

125. Data processed includes the driver contact details (name, email, telephone number, vehicle type (e.g. car, truck, motorcycle), license plate number, parking period, payment details (e.g. credit card info) as well as navigation data.

3.1.2.3 Retention period

126. Data should be retained only as long as it is necessary to fulfil the parking contract or otherwise as provided by Union or Member State law. After that data is either anonymised or deleted.

3.1.2.4 Information and rights of data subjects

127. Prior to the processing of personal data, the data subject should be informed according to art. 13 GDPR, in a transparent and understandable way.

128. The data subject should be specifically informed of the available means to exercise his or her right of access, rectification, restriction and erasure. Since the data collected in this context are provided by the data subject (through specific forms or through his or her activity) and processed on the basis of art. 6(1)(b) GDPR (performance of a contract), the data subject is entitled to exercise his or her right to data portability. As emphasized in the guidelines on the right to data portability, the EDPB strongly recommends *"that data controllers clearly explain the difference between the types of data that a data subject can receive through the rights of subject access and data portability".*

3.1.2.5 Recipient:

129. In principle, only the data controller and the data processor have access to the data.

3.1.2.6 Security:

130. General recommendations apply. See section 2.7.

3.2 ECALL

131. In the event of a serious accident in the European Union, the vehicle automatically triggers an eCall to 112, the EU-wide emergency number (see section 1.1 for further details) which allows an ambulance to be sent the place of the accident promptly according to Regulation (EU) 2015/758 of 29 April 2015 concerning type-approval requirements for the deployment of the eCall in-vehicle system based on the 112 service, and amending Directive 2007/46/EC (hereinafter – "Regulation (EU) 2015/758").

132. Indeed, the eCall generator installed inside the vehicle, which enables transmission via a public mobile wireless communications network initiates an emergency call, which is either triggered automatically by vehicle sensors or manually by the vehicle occupants only in the event of an accident. In addition to activation of the audio channel, the second event triggered automatically as a result of an accident consists in generating the Minimum Set of Data (MSD) and sending it to the public safety answering point (PSAP).

3.2.1 Legal basis

133. Regarding the application of the ePrivacy directive, two provisions have to be considered:
–   art. 9 regarding location data other than traffic data which only applies to electronic communication services;
–   art. 5(3) for the gaining access to information stored in the generator installed inside the vehicle.

134. Despite the fact that, in principle, those provisions require the consent of the data subject, Regulation (EU) 2015/758 constitutes a legal obligation to which the data controller is subject (the data subject has no genuine or free choice and will be unable to refuse the processing of his/her data). Hence, Regulation (EU) 2015/758 overrides the need of the driver's consent for the processing of location data and the MSD.[49]

135. The legal basis of the processing of those data will be compliance with a legal obligation as provided for in art. 6(1)(c) GDPR (i.e., Regulation (EU) 2015/758).

3.2.2 Data collected

136. Regulation (EU) 2015/578 provides that data sent by the 112-based eCall in-vehicle system shall include only the minimum information as referred to in the standard EN 15722:2015 'Intelligent transport systems — eSafety — eCall minimum set of data (MSD)' including:
–   the indication if eCall has been manually or automatically triggered;
–   the vehicle type;
–   the vehicle identification number (VIN);
–   the propulsion type of the vehicle;
–   the timestamp of the initial data message generation within the current eCall incident event;
–   the last known vehicle latitude and longitude position determined at the latest moment possible before message generation;
–   the vehicle's last known real direction of travel determined at the latest moment possible before message generation (only the last three locations of the vehicle).

3.2.3 Retention period

137. Regulation (EU) 2015/758 stipulates that data shall not be retained for longer than is needed for processing emergency situations. Those data shall be completely deleted when they are no longer needed for that purpose. Furthermore, in the internal memory of the eCall system, data shall be automatically and constantly deleted. Only the vehicle's last three positions can be stored, insofar as it is strictly necessary to specify the current position of the vehicle and the direction of travel at the time of the event.

3.2.4 Information and rights of data subjects

138. Art. 6 of the Regulation (EU) 2015/758 stipulates that manufacturers shall provide clear and complete information on data processing done using the eCall system. This information shall be provided in the owner's manual separately for the 112-based eCall in-vehicle system and any third-party service supported eCall systems prior to the use of the system. It includes:

- the reference to the legal basis for the processing;
- the fact that the 112-based eCall in-vehicle system is activated by default;
- the arrangements for data processing that the 112-based eCall in-vehicle system performs;
- the specific purpose of the eCall processing, which shall be limited to the emergency situations referred to in the first subparagraph of Art. 5(2) Regulation (EU) 2015/758;
- the types of data collected and processed and the recipients of that data;
- the time limit for the retention of data in the 112-based eCall in-vehicle system;
- the fact that there is no constant tracking of the vehicle;
- the arrangements for exercising data subjects' rights as well as the contact service responsible for handling access requests;
- any necessary additional information regarding traceability, tracking and processing of personal data in relation to the provision of a third-party service (TPS) eCall and/or other added value services, which shall be subject to explicit consent by the owner and in compliance with the GDPR. Particular account shall be taken of the fact that differences may exist between the data processing carried out through the 112-based eCall in-vehicle system and the TPS eCall in-vehicle systems or other added value services.

139. Furthermore, the service provider shall also provide the data subjects with information in accordance with art. 13 GDPR in a transparent and understandable way. In particular, he or she must be informed of the purposes of the processing for which the personal data are intended as well as the fact that the processing of personal data is based on a legal obligation to which the controller is subject.

140. In addition, taking into account the nature of the processing, the information about the recipients or categories of recipients of the personal data should be clear and the data subjects should be informed that the data are not be available outside the 112-based eCall in-vehicle system to any entities before the eCall is triggered.

141. Regarding rights of data subjects, it has to be noted that since the processing is based on a legal obligation, the right to object and the right to portability will not apply.

3.2.5 Recipient:

142. The data shall not be available outside the 112-based eCall in-vehicle system to any entities before the eCall is triggered.

143. When it is triggered (either manually by vehicle occupants or automatically as soon as an in-vehicle sensor detects a serious collision), the eCall system establishes a voice connection with the relevant PSAP and the MSD is sent to the PSAP operator.

144. Furthermore, data transmitted via the 112-based eCall in-vehicle system and processed by the PSAPs can be transferred to the emergency service and service partners referred to in Decision No 585/2014/EU only in the event of incidents related to eCalls and under the conditions set out in that Decision and are used exclusively for the attainment of the objectives of that Decision. Data processed by the PSAPs through the 112-based eCall in-vehicle system are not transferred to any other third parties without the explicit prior consent of the data subject.

3.2.6 Security

145. Regulation (EU) 2015/758 stipulates the requirements to incorporate into the eCall system technologies that strengthen the protection of privacy, in order to offer users the appropriate level of protection of privacy, as well as the guarantees needed to prevent surveillance and abusive uses. In addition, manufacturers should ensure that the eCall system based on the number 112, as well as any other system providing an eCall that is handled by third-party services or an added-value service, are so designed that it is impossible for personal data to be exchanged between those systems.

146. Regarding PSAPs, Member States should ensure that personal data are protected against misuse, including unlawful access, alteration or loss, and that protocols concerning personal data storage, retention duration, processing and protection are established at the appropriate level and properly observed.

3.3 ACCIDENTOLOGY STUDIES

147. Data subjects may voluntarily agree to take part in accidentology studies aimed at better understanding the causes of road accidents and more generally scientific purposes.

3.3.1 Legal basis

148. When the data are collected through a public electronic communication service, the data controller will have to collect the consent of the data subject for the gaining of access to information that is already stored in the vehicle as provided by art. 5(3) of the ePrivacy directive. Indeed, none of the exemptions provided by those provisions can apply in this context: the processing is not for the sole purpose of carrying out the transmission of a communication over an electronic communications network nor does it relate to an information society service explicitly requested by the subscriber or user.

149. Regarding the processing of personal data and taking into account the variety and amount of personal data needed for accidentology studies, the EDPB recommends the processing to be based on the prior consent of the data subject according to art. 6 GDPR. Such prior consent must be provided on a specific form, through which the data subject volunteers to take part to the study and have his or her personal data processed for that purpose. Consent shall be an expression of the free, specific, and informed will of the person whose data are being processed (e.g., ticking a box that is not pre-ticked, or configuring the onboard computer to activate a function in the vehicle). Such consent must be provided separately, for specific purposes, may not be bundled with the contract to buy or lease a new car and the consent must be as easily withdrawn as it is given. Withdrawal of consent shall lead to the processing being stopped. The data shall then be deleted from the active database, or anonymised.

150. Consent required by art. 5(3) of the ePrivacy directive and consent needed as a legal basis for the processing of data can be collected at the same time (for example by checking a box clearly indicating what the data subject is consenting to).

151. It has to be noted that, depending on the conditions of the processing (nature of the data controller, etc.), another legal basis can be lawfully chosen as long as it does not lower the additional protection provided by art. 5(3) ePrivacy directive (see paragraph 15). If the processing is based on another legal basis such as the performance of a task carried out in the public interest (art. 6(1)(e) GDPR), the EDPB recommends that the data subjects are included in the study on a voluntary basis.

3.3.2 Data collected

152. The data controller shall only collect personal data that are strictly necessary for the processing.

153. There are two types of data to be considered:
– **data relating to participants and vehicles**;
– **technical data from vehicles** (instantaneous speed, etc.).

154. Scientific research linked to accidentology justifies the collection of the instantaneous speed, including by legal persons who do not administer a public service in the strict sense.

155. Indeed, as noted above, the EDPB considers that instantaneous speed collected in the context of an accidentology study is not offence-related data by destination (i.e., it is not being collected for the purpose of investigating or prosecuting an offence), which justifies its collection by legal persons who do not administer a public service in the strict sense.

3.3.3 Retention period

156. It is important to distinguish between two types of data. First, the data relating to participants and vehicles can be retained for the duration of the study. Second, the technical data from vehicles should be retained for as short as possible for the purpose. In this regard, five years from the end date of the study appears to be a reasonable period. At the end of that period, the data shall be deleted or anonymised.

3.3.4 Information and rights of data subjects

157. Prior to the processing of personal data, the data subject shall be informed according to art. 13 GDPR, in a transparent and understandable way. In particular, in the case of collecting instantaneous speed, the data subjects should be specifically informed of the data collection. Since the data processing is based on consent, the data subject must be specifically informed of the existence of the right to withdraw consent at any time, without affecting the lawfulness of processing based on consent before its withdrawal. Moreover, because the data collected in this context are provided by the data subject (through specific forms or through his or her activity) and processed on the basis of art. 6(1)(a) GDPR (consent), the data subject is entitled to exercise his or her right to data portability. As emphasized in the guidelines on the right to data portability, the EDPB strongly recommends "that data controllers clearly explain the difference between the types of data that a data subject can receive through the rights of subject access and data portability". Consequently, the data controller should provide an easy way to withdraw his consent, freely and at any time, as well as develop tools to be able to answer data portability requests.

158. That information can be given upon signing the form to agree to take part in the accidentology study.

3.3.5 Recipient

159. In principle, only the data controller and the data processor have access to the data.

3.3.6 Security

160. As noted above, the security measures put in place shall be adapted to the level of data sensitivity. For instance, if instantaneous speed (or any other data related to criminal convictions and offences) is collected as part of the accidentology study, the EDPB strongly recommends putting in place strong security measures, such as:
– implementing pseudonymisation measures (e.g., secret-key hashing of data like the surname/first name of the data subject and the serial number);

–   storing data relating to instantaneous speed and to location in separate databases (e.g., using a state-of-the-art encryption mechanism with distinct keys and approval mechanisms);

–   and/or deleting location data as soon as the reference event or sequence is qualified (e.g., the type of road, day/night), and the storage of directly-identifying data in a separate database that can only be accessed by a small number of people.

3.4 TACKLE AUTO THEFT

161.   Data subjects may wish, in the case of theft, to attempt to find their vehicle using location. Using location data is limited to the strict needs of the investigation and to the case assessment by the competent legal authorities.

3.4.1 Legal basis

162.   When the data is collected through a publicly available electronic communication service, art. 5(3) of the ePrivacy directive applies.

163.   Because this is an information society service, art. 5(3) of the ePrivacy directive does not require consent for gaining access to information that is already stored in the vehicle when such a service is explicitly requested by the subscriber.

164.   Regarding the processing of personal data, the legal basis for processing the location data will be the consent of the vehicle's owner, or, if applicable, the performance of a contract (only for data necessary for the performance of the contract to which the vehicle's owner is party).

165.   Consent shall be an expression of the free, specific, and informed will of the person whose data are being processed (e.g. ticking a box that is not pre-ticked, or configuring the on- board computer to activate a function in the vehicle). Freedom to give consent involves the option of withdrawing consent at any time, of which the data subject should be expressly informed. Withdrawal of consent shall lead to the processing being stopped. The data should then be deleted from the active database, anonymised, or archived.

3.4.2 Data collected

166.   Location data can only be transmitted as of the declaration of theft, and cannot be collected continuously the rest of the time.

3.4.3 Retention period

167.   Location data can only be retained for the period during which the case is assessed by the competent legal authorities, or until the end of a procedure to dispel doubt that does not end with confirmation of the theft of the vehicle.

3.4.4 Information of the data subjects

168.   Prior to the processing of personal data, the data subject should be informed according to art. 13 GDPR, in a transparent and understandable way. More specifically, the EDPB recommends that the data controller emphasizes that there is no constant tracking of the vehicle and that location data can only be collected and transmitted as of the declaration of theft. Moreover, the controller must provide the data subject with information relating to the fact that only approved officers of the remote-surveillance platform and legally approved authorities have access to the data.

169.   Regarding the rights of the data subjects, when the data processing is based on consent, the data subject should be specifically informed of the existence of the right to withdraw consent at any time, without affecting the lawfulness of processing based on consent before its withdrawal. Besides, when the data collected in this context are provided by them (through specific forms or through his or her activity) and processed on the basis of art. 6(1)(a) (consent) or art. 6(1)(b) GDPR (performance of a contract), the data subject is entitled to exercise his or her right to data portability. As emphasized in the guidelines on the right to data portability, the EDPB strongly recommends "that data controllers clearly explain the difference between the types of data that a data subject can receive through the rights of subject access and data portability".

170.   Consequently, the data controller should provide an easy way to withdraw his consent (only when consent is the legal basis), freely and at any time, as well as develop tools to be able to answer data portability requests.

171.   The information can be provided when the contract is signed.

3.4.5 Recipients

172.   In the event of a theft declaration, location data can be passed on the (i) approved officers of the remote-surveillance platform, and (ii) to the legally approved authorities.

3.4.6 Security

173.   General recommendations apply. See section 2.7

NOTES

[48]   Article 29 Working Party, Guidelines on the right to data portability under Regulation 2016/676, WP242 rev.01, endorsed by EDPB, p. 13.

Part 2   Data Protection: EU Law etc

EUROPEAN DATA PROTECTION BOARD: GUIDELINES 2/2020 ON ARTICLES 46(2)(A) AND 46(3)(B) OF REGULATION 2016/679 FOR TRANSFERS OF PERSONAL DATA BETWEEN EEA AND NON-EEA PUBLIC AUTHORITIES AND BODIES
Version 2.0
Adopted on 15 December 2020

[2.325]

NOTES
© European Data Protection Board.

VERSION HISTORY

Version 2.0: 15 December 2020 — Adoption of the Guidelines after public consultation

Version 1.0: 18 February 2020 — Adoption of the Guidelines for public consultation

TABLE OF CONTENTS

THE EUROPEAN DATA PROTECTION BOARD

Having regard to Article 70 (1e) of the Regulation 2016/679/EU of the European Parliament and of the Council of 27 April 2016 on the protection of natural persons with regard to the processing of personal data and on the free movement of such data, and repealing Directive 95/46/EC, (hereinafter "GDPR"),

Having regard to the EEA Agreement and in particular to Annex XI and Protocol 37 thereof, as amended by the Decision of the EEA joint Committee No 154/2018 of 6 July 2018[1],

Having regard to Article 12 and Article 22 of its Rules of Procedure,

HAS ADOPTED THE FOLLOWING GUIDELINES

1   References to "Member States" made throughout these guidelines should be understood as references to "EEA Member States".

1 GENERAL

1.1 PURPOSE

[2.326]
1.   This document seeks to provide guidance as to the application of Articles 46 (2)(a) and 46 (3)(b) of the General Data Protection Regulation (GDPR) on transfers of personal data from EEA public authorities or bodies (hereafter "public bodies") to public bodies in third countries or to international organisations, to the extent that these are not covered by an adequacy finding adopted by the European Commission[2]. Public bodies may choose to use these mechanisms, which the GDPR considers more appropriate to their situation, but are also free to rely on other relevant tools providing for appropriate safeguards in accordance with Article 46 GDPR.

2.   The guidelines are intended to give an indication as to the expectations of the European Data Protection Board (EDPB) on the safeguards required to be put in place by a legally binding and enforceable instrument between public bodies pursuant to Article 46 (2)(a) GDPR or, subject to authorisation from the competent supervisory authority (SA), by provisions to be inserted into administrative arrangements between public bodies pursuant to Article 46 (3)(b) GDPR.[3] The EDPB strongly recommends parties to use the guidelines as a reference at an early stage when envisaging concluding or amending such instruments or arrangements.[4]

3.   The guidelines are to be read in conjunction with other previous work done by the EDPB (including endorsed documents by its predecessor, the Article 29 Working Party[5] ("WP29")) on the central questions of territorial scope and transfers of personal data to third countries[6]. The guidelines will be reviewed and if necessary updated, based on the practical experience gained from the application of the GDPR.

4.   The present guidelines cover international data transfers between public bodies occurring for various administrative cooperation purposes falling within the scope of the GDPR. As a consequence and in accordance with Article 2 (2) of the GDPR, they do not cover transfers in the area of public security, defence or state security. In addition, they do not deal with data processing and transfers by competent authorities for criminal law enforcement purposes, since this is governed by a separate specific instrument, the law enforcement Directive[7]. Finally, the guidelines only focus on transfers between public bodies and do not cover transfers of personal data from a public body to a private entity or from a private entity to a public body.

1.2 GENERAL RULES APPLICABLE TO INTERNATIONAL TRANSFERS

5.   According to Article 44 of the GDPR the data exporter transferring personal data to third countries or international organisations must, in addition to complying with Chapter V of the GDPR, also meet the conditions of the other provisions of the GDPR. In particular, each processing activity must comply with the data protection principles in Article 5 GDPR, be lawful in accordance with Article 6 GDPR and comply with Article 9 GDPR in case of special categories of data. Hence, a two-step test must be applied: first, a legal basis must apply to the data processing as such together with all relevant provisions of the GDPR; and as a second step, the provisions of Chapter V of the GDPR must be complied with.

6.   The GDPR specifies in its Article 46 that *"in the absence of a decision pursuant to Article 45(3), a controller or processor may transfer personal data to a third country or an international organisation only if the controller or processor has provided appropriate safeguards, and on condition that enforceable data subject rights and effective legal remedies for data subjects are available"*. Such appropriate safeguards may be provided for by a legally binding and enforceable instrument between public bodies (Article 46 (2)(a) GDPR) or, subject to authorisation from the competent SA, by provisions to be inserted into administrative arrangements between public bodies which include enforceable and effective data subject rights (Article 46 (3)(b) GDPR). As clarified by the Court of Justice of the European Union (CJEU), such appropriate safeguards must be capable of ensuring that data subjects whose personal data are transferred are afforded a level of protection essentially equivalent to that which is guaranteed within the EEA.[8]

7.   Aside from this solution and in its absence, Article 49 of the GDPR also offers a limited number of specific situations in which international data transfers may take place when there is no adequacy finding by the European Commission[9]. In particular, one exemption covers transfers necessary for important reasons of public interest recognised in Union law or in the law of the Member State to which the controller is subject, including in the spirit of reciprocity of international cooperation[10]. However, as explained in previous guidance issued by the EDPB, the derogations provided by Article 49 GDPR must be interpreted restrictively and mainly relate to processing activities that are occasional and non-repetitive[11].

1.3 DEFINITION OF A PUBLIC AUTHORITY OR BODY

8.   The GDPR does not define what constitutes a 'public authority or body'. The EDPB considers that this notion is broad enough to cover both public bodies in third countries and international organisations.[12] With respect to public bodies in third countries, the notion is to be determined under domestic law. Accordingly, public bodies include government authorities at different levels (e.g. national, regional and local authorities), but may also include other bodies governed by public law (e.g. executive agencies, universities, hospitals, etc.).[13] In accordance with Article 4 (26) GDPR, 'international organisation' refers to an organisation and its subordinate bodies governed by public international law, or any other body which is set up by, or on the basis of, an agreement between two countries.

9.   The EDPB recalls that the application of the GDPR is without prejudice to the provisions of international law, such as the ones governing the privileges and immunities of international organisations. At the same time, it is important to recall that any EEA public body transferring data to international organisations has to comply with the GDPR rules on transfers to third countries or international organisations.[14]

NOTES

[2]   For example Japanese public bodies, which are not covered by the Japan Adequacy Decision as it only covers private sector organisations.

[3]   These guidelines use the term "international agreements" to refer to legally binding and enforceable instruments pursuant to Article 46(2)(a) GDPR and to administrative arrangements pursuant to Article 46(3)(b) GDPR.

[4]   Art. 96 GDPR states that agreements that were concluded prior to 24 May 2016 shall remain in force until amended, replaced or revoked.

[5]   The Working Party of EU Data Protection Authorities established under Article 29 of the Data Protection Directive 95/46/EC.

[6]   See Article 29 Working Party, Adequacy Referential (WP254 rev.01, endorsed by the EDPB on 25 May 2018), EDPB Guidelines 2/2018 on derogations of Article 49 under Regulation 2016/679 and EDPB Guidelines 3/2018 on the territorial scope of the GDPR (Article 3).

[7]   Directive (EU) 2016/680 of 27 April 2016 on the protection of natural persons with regard to the processing of personal data by competent authorities for the purposes of the prevention, investigation, detection or prosecution of criminal offences or the execution of criminal penalties, and on the free movement of such data.

8　　Court of Justice of the European Union, Case C-311/18, Data Protection Commissioner v. Facebook Ireland and Maximillian Schrems ("Schrems II"), para. 96.

9　　For further information on Article 49 and its interplay with Article 46 in general, please see EDPB Guidelines 2/2018 on derogations of Article 49 under Regulation 2016/679.

10　　See EDPB Guidelines 2/2018 on derogations of Article 49 under Regulation 2016/679, page 10.

11　　See EDPB Guidelines on derogations of Article 49 under Regulation 2016/679, page 5.

12　　See also recital 108 of the GDPR.

13　　See, e.g. the definition of 'public sector body' and 'body governed by public law' in Article 2 (1) and (2) of Directive 2003/98/EC of the European Parliament and of the Council of 17 November 2003 on the re-use of public-sector information (OJ L 345, 31.12.2003, page 90).

14　　See EDPB Guidelines 3/2018 on the territorial scope of the GDPR, p. 23.

2 GENERAL RECOMMENDATIONS FOR THE APPROPRIATE SAFEGUARDS UNDER BOTH ARTICLES 46(2)(A) AND 46(3)(B) GDPR

[2.327]

10.　Unlike Article 26 (2) of the 95/46/EC Directive, Article 46 of the GDPR provides for additional appropriate safeguards as tools for transfers between public bodies:

(i)　　a legally binding and enforceable instrument, Article 46 (2)(a) GDPR or

(ii)　　provisions to be inserted into administrative arrangements, Article 46 (3)(b) GDPR.

These instruments and arrangements may be of bilateral or multilateral nature.

11.　The following section provides some general recommendations to help ensure that legally binding instruments or administrative arrangements (hereinafter "international agreements") between public bodies are in compliance with the GDPR.

12.　Although Article 46 and recital 108 of the GDPR do not provide specific indications on the guarantees to be included in such international agreements, taking into account Article 44 of the GPDR[15] and the recent CJEU case law[16] the EDPB hereby has elaborated a list of minimum safeguards to be included in international agreements between public bodies falling under Articles 46 (2)(a) or 46 (3)(b) GDPR. These safeguards aim to ensure that the level of protection of natural persons under the GDPR is not undermined when their personal data is transferred outside of the EEA and that data subjects are afforded a level of protection essentially equivalent to that guaranteed within the EU by the GDPR.[17]

13.　In accordance with the recent CJEU case law[18], it is the responsibility of the transferring public body in a Member State, if needed with the help of the receiving public body, to assess whether the level of protection required by EU law is respected in the third country, in order to determine whether the list of safeguards included in the international agreement can be complied with in practice, taking into account the possible interference created by the third country legislation with compliance with these safeguards.

14.　In this respect, it should also be noted that, to ensure the safeguards listed in these guidelines, international agreements can build on already existing elements in the national law of a third country or the internal rules/regulatory framework of an international organisation.

2.1 PURPOSE AND SCOPE

15.　International agreements should define their scope and their purposes should be explicitly and specifically determined. In addition, they should clearly state the categories of personal data affected and the type of processing of the personal data which is transferred and processed under the agreement.

2.2 DEFINITIONS

16.　International agreements should contain definitions of the basic personal data concepts and rights in line with the GDPR relevant to the agreement in question. By way of example, such agreements should, if referenced, include the following important definitions: "personal data", "processing of personal data", "data controller", "data processor", "recipient" and "sensitive data".

2.3 DATA PROTECTION PRINCIPLES

17.　International agreements shall contain specific wording requiring that the core data protection principles are ensured by both parties.

2.3.1 Purpose limitation principle

18.　International agreements need to specify the purposes for which personal data is to be transferred and processed including compatible purposes for further processing, as well as to ensure that the data will not be further processed for incompatible purposes. Compatible purposes may include storing for archiving purposes in the public interest, as well as processing for scientific or historical research purposes or statistical purposes. It is recommended, for better clarity, that the specific purposes for the processing and transferring of the data are listed in the international agreement itself.

19.　To avoid any risk of a "function creep", such agreements should also specify that transferred data cannot be used for any purpose other than those expressly mentioned in the agreement, except as set out in the paragraph below.

20.　If both parties to the international agreement wish to allow the receiving public body to make another compatible use of the transmitted personal data, further use by the receiving public body shall only be permitted if compatible with the original one and previously notified to the transferring public body which may oppose for specific reasons.

2.3.2 Data accuracy and minimisation principles

21. The international agreement must specify that the data transferred and further processed must be adequate, relevant and limited to what is necessary in relation to the purposes for which they are transmitted and further processed.

22. In practice, this data minimisation principle is important to avoid the transfer of personal data when they are inadequate or excessive.

23. Moreover, data should be accurate and up to date, having regard to the purposes for which they are processed. An international agreement must therefore provide that the transferring party will ensure that the personal data transferred under the agreement is accurate and, where applicable, up to date. In addition, the agreement should provide that, if one of the parties becomes aware that inaccurate or out of date data has been transmitted or is being processed, it must notify the other party without delay. Finally, the agreement should ensure that, where it is confirmed that data transmitted or being processed is inaccurate, each party processing the data shall take every reasonable step to rectify or erase the information.

2.3.3 Storage limitation principle

24. Parties must ensure that the international agreement contains a data retention clause. This clause should specify in particular that personal data shall not be retained indefinitely but shall be kept in a form which permits identification of data subjects only for the time necessary for the purpose for which it was transferred and subsequently processed. That may include storing it for as long as necessary for archiving purposes in the public interest, scientific or historical research purposes or statistical purposes, provided that appropriate technical and organisational measures are put in place to safeguard the rights and freedoms of the data subjects, such as additional technical measures (e.g. security measures pseudonymisation) and access restrictions. When a maximum retention period is not already set in national legislation or the internal rules/regulatory framework of an international organisation, a maximum retention period should be set in the text of the agreement.

2.3.4 Security and confidentiality of data

25. The parties should commit to ensure the security and the confidentiality of the personal data processing and transfers they carry out. In particular, the parties should commit to having in place appropriate technical and organisational measures to protect personal data against accidental or unlawful access, destruction, loss, alteration, or unauthorised disclosure. These measures may include, for example, encryption including in transit, pseudonymisation, marking information as personal data transferred from the EEA, restricting who has access to personal data, providing secure storage of personal data, or implementing policies designed to ensure personal data are kept secure and confidential. The level of security should take into consideration the risks, the state of the art and the related costs.

26. The international agreement may furthermore specify that, if one of the parties becomes aware of a personal data breach, it will inform the other party (ies) as soon as possible and use reasonable and appropriate means to remedy the personal data breach and minimise the potential adverse effects, including by communicating to the data subject a personal data breach, without undue delay, where that personal data breach is likely to result in a high risk to the rights and freedoms of the natural person.

It is recommended that the notification timeline for a personal data breach as well as the procedures for communication to the data subject are defined in the international agreement.

2.4 RIGHTS OF THE DATA SUBJECTS

27. The international agreement must ensure enforceable and effective data subject rights as specified in article 46 (1) and recital 108 of the GDPR.

28. The rights available to the data subjects, including the specific commitments taken by the parties to provide for such rights, should be listed in the agreement. To be effective, the international agreement must provide for mechanisms that ensure their application in practice. Moreover, any breach of data subject rights must carry an appropriate remedy.

2.4.1 Right to Transparency

29. Parties must ensure that the international agreement contains clear wording describing the transparency obligations of the parties.

30. Such obligations should include on the one hand, a general information notice with, as a minimum, information on how and why the public bodies may process and transfer personal data, the relevant tool used for the transfer, the entities to which such data may be transferred, the rights available to data subjects and applicable restrictions, available redress mechanisms and contact details for submitting a dispute or claim.

31. However, it is important to recall that, for the transferring public body, a general information notice on the website of the public body concerned will not suffice. Individual information to data subjects should be made by the transferring public body in accordance with the notification requirements of Articles 13 and 14 GDPR[19]. The international agreement can also provide for some exceptions to such individual information. These exceptions are limited and should be in line with the ones provided under Article 14 (5) GDPR, for example where the data subject already has the information or where the provision of such information proves impossible or would involve a disproportionate effort.

32. The parties must commit to make the international agreement available to data subjects on request and to make the international agreement or the relevant provisions providing for appropriate safeguards publicly available on their website. To the extent necessary to protect sensitive or other confidential information, the text of the international agreement may be redacted prior to sharing a copy or making it publicly available. Where necessary to allow the data subject to understand the content of the international agreement, the parties must provide a meaningful summary thereof.

2.4.2 Rights of access, to rectification, erasure, restriction of processing and to object

33. The international agreement should safeguard the data subject's right to obtain information about and access to all personal data relating to him/her that are processed, the right to rectification, erasure and restriction of processing and where relevant the right to oppose to the data processing on grounds relating to his or her particular situation.

34. As regards the right of access, the international agreement should specify that individuals shall have the right vis-à-vis the receiving public body to obtain confirmation as to whether or not personal data concerning him/her is being processed, and if that is the case, access to that data; as well as to specific information concerning the processing, including the purpose of the processing, the categories of personal data concerned, the recipients to whom personal data is disclosed, the envisaged storage period and redress possibilities.

35. The agreement should furthermore specify when these rights can be invoked and include the modalities on how the data subjects can exercise these rights before both parties as well as on how the parties will respond to such requests. For example, with respect to deletion, the international agreement could state that data is to be deleted when the information has been processed unlawfully or is no longer necessary for the purpose of processing. Moreover, the international agreement should stipulate that the parties will respond in a reasonable and timely manner to requests from data subjects. The international agreement could also state that the parties may take appropriate steps, such as charging reasonable fees to cover administrative costs where requests from a data subject are manifestly unfounded or excessive, in particular because of their repetitive character.

36. The international agreement should also allot an obligation of the transferring public body to provide information to the data subject, once his/her personal data have been transferred, on the action taken on his/her request under the rights provided for by the international agreement without undue delay by setting an appropriate time limit (e.g. one month). Finally, information should be provided to the data subject, if the parties do not take action on the request of the data subject, without delay by setting an appropriate time limit (e.g. within one month of receipt of the request), of the reasons for not taking action and on the possibility of lodging a complaint and of seeking a judicial remedy.

37. The international agreement can also provide for exceptions to these rights. For example, exceptions to the right of access and deletion such as the ones provided under Article 15 (4) and 17 (3) GDPR could be provided. Similarly, exceptions to individual rights could be foreseen where personal data is processed for scientific or historical research purposes, statistical purposes, or archiving purposes, in so far as such rights would be likely to render impossible or seriously impair the achievement of these specific purposes, and provided that appropriate safeguards are put in place (e.g. technical and organisational measures, including pseudonymisation). Finally, the agreement may provide that the parties may decline to act on a request that is manifestly unfounded or excessive.

2.4.3 Automated individual decision-making

38. If relevant to the agreement in question, international agreements should as a general principle contain a clause stating that the receiving public body will not take a decision based solely on automated individual decision-making, including profiling, producing legal effects concerning the data subject in question or similarly affecting this data subject. Where the purpose of the transfer includes the possibility for the receiving public body to take decisions solely on automated processing in the sense of Article 22 GDPR, this should only take place under certain conditions set forth in the international agreement, such as the need to obtain the explicit consent of the data subject. If the decision does not comply with such conditions, the data subject should have the right not to be subject to it. Where it allows automated individual decision-making, the international agreement should, in any case, provide for necessary safeguards, including the right to be informed about the specific reasons underlying the decision and the logic involved, to correct inaccurate or incomplete information, and to contest the decision and obtain human intervention.

2.4.4 Right to Redress

39. The safeguarded data subject rights have to be enforceable and effective. Therefore, the data subject must have access to redress. Different examples of ways to offer redress mechanisms are indicated below under sections 2.7 and 3.

2.4.5 Restrictions to the Rights of the data subjects

40. The international agreement can also provide for restrictions to the rights of data subjects. These restrictions should be in line with the restrictions envisaged by Article 23 GDPR. Such a restriction has to be a necessary and proportionate measure in a democratic society to safeguard important objectives of public interest, in line with the ones listed in Article 23(1) GDPR, including the rights and freedom of others, national security, defence or the prevention, investigation, detection or prosecution of criminal offences. It needs to be provided by law or, in the case of international organisations, the applicable internal rules/regulatory framework, and shall continue only for as long as the reason for the restriction continues to exist.

2.5 RESTRICTIONS ON ONWARD TRANSFERS AND SHARING OF DATA (INCLUDING DISCLOSURE AND GOVERNMENT ACCESS)

41. Onward transfers by the receiving public body or international organisation to recipients not bound by the agreement should, as a rule, be specifically excluded by the international agreement. Depending on the subject matter and the particular circumstances at hand, the parties may find it necessary to allow onward transfers. In this case, under the condition that the purpose limitation principle is respected[20], the international agreement should foresee that such onward transfers can only take place if the transferring public body has given its prior and express authorisation and the receiving third parties commit to respect the same data protection principles and safeguards as included in the international agreement. This should include a commitment to provide to data subjects the same data protection rights and guarantees as provided in the international agreement in order to ensure that the level of protection will not be diminished if data are onward transferred.

42. As a rule, the same safeguards as for onward transfers should apply to sharing of personal data within the same country, i.e. the international agreement shall exclude this onward sharing and exemptions should in general only be allowed if the transferring public body has given its prior and express authorization and the receiving third parties commit to respect the same data protection principles and safeguards as included in the international agreement.

43. It is recommended that before requesting the express authorisation of the transferring public body the receiving public body or international organisation provides sufficient information on the type of personal data that it intends to transfer/share, the reasons and purposes for which it considers it to be necessary to transfer/share the personal data as well as, in case of onward transfers, the countries or international organisations to which it intends to onward transfer personal data so as to be able to assess the third country legislation or, in the case of international organisations, the applicable internal rules/regulatory framework.

44. In cases where it is necessary to allow sharing of personal data with a third party in the same country of the receiving public body or another international organisation, the sharing could be allowed in specific circumstances either with prior and express authorization of the transferring public body or as long as there is a binding commitment from the receiving third party to respect the principles and guarantees included in the international agreement.

45. In addition, the international agreement could specify exceptional circumstances in which onward sharing could take place without prior authorisation or the abovementioned commitments in line with the derogations listed in Article 49 of the GDPR, for example when this specific sharing would be necessary in order to protect the vital interests of the data subject or other persons or necessary for the establishment, exercise or defence of legal claims. Such exceptional circumstances could also arise if the onward sharing is required under the law of the receiving party, as necessary for directly related investigations/ court proceedings.

46. In the cases mentioned in the paragraph above, the international agreement should clearly state the specific and exceptional circumstances under which such data sharing is allowed. The receiving public body or international organisation should also be obliged to notify the transferring public body prior to the sharing and include information about the data shared, the receiving third party and the legal basis for the sharing. In its turn the transferring public body should keep a record of such notifications from the receiving public body or international organisation and provide its SA with this information upon request. Where providing such notification prior to the sharing will impinge on confidentiality obligations provided for by law, e.g. to preserve the confidentiality of an investigation, the specific information should be provided as soon as possible after the sharing. In such a case, general information on the type of requests received over a specified period of time, including information about the categories of data requested, the requesting body and the legal basis for disclosure, should be provided to the transferring body at regular intervals.

47. In all of the above scenarios, the international agreement should only allow disclosures of personal data to other public authorities in the third country of the receiving public body that do not go beyond what is necessary and proportionate in a democratic society to safeguard important objectives of public interest in line with the ones listed in Article 23 (1) GDPR and in accordance with the jurisprudence of the CJEU. In order to assess a possible access by third country public authorities for surveillance purposes, the transferring public authority should take into account the elements recalled in the four European Essential Guarantees[21]. These include the availability of an effective remedy for data subjects in the third country of the receiving public body if their personal data is accessed by public authorities.[22] In case of transfers to international organisations, any such access must be in compliance with international law and without prejudice in particular to the privileges and immunities of the international organisation.

48. Depending on the case at hand, it may be useful to require to include an annex to the international agreement enumerating the laws governing onward sharing with other public bodies including for surveillance purposes in the destination country. Any changes to this annex should be notified to the transferring party within a set period of time.

2.6 SENSITIVE DATA

49. If an international agreement provides for the transfer of sensitive personal data within the meaning of Article 9 (1) of the GDPR, additional safeguards addressing the specific risks, to be implemented by the receiving public body or international organisation, should be included. These could, for example, include restrictions as access restrictions, restrictions of the purposes for which the information may be

Part 2 Data Protection: EU Law etc

processed, restrictions on onward transfers, etc. or specific safeguards, e.g. additional security measures, requiring specialized training for staff allowed to access the information.

2.7 REDRESS MECHANISMS

50. In order to guarantee enforceable and effective data subjects rights the international agreement must provide for a system that enables data subjects to continue to benefit from redress mechanisms after their data has been transferred to a non EEA country or an international organisation. These redress mechanisms must provide recourse for individuals who are affected by non-compliance with the provisions of the chosen instrument and thus the possibility for data subjects whose personal data have been transferred from the EEA to lodge complaints regarding such non-compliance and to have these complaints resolved. In particular, the data subject must be ensured an effective route to complain to the public bodies that are parties to the international agreement and (either directly or after having addressed the relevant party) to an independent oversight mechanism. Moreover, a judicial remedy should, in principle, be available.

51. First, the receiving public body should commit to put in place a mechanism to effectively and timely handle and resolve complaints from data subjects concerning compliance with the agreed data protection safeguards. Moreover, data subjects should be provided with the possibility to obtain effective administrative redress before an independent oversight body, including, where available, an independent data protection authority[23].

52. Second, the agreement should allow for a judicial remedy including compensation for damages - both material and non-material - as a result of the unlawful processing of the personal data. If there is no possibility to ensure effective judicial redress, for example due to restrictions in the domestic law or the specific status of the receiving public body, e.g. international organisations, the international agreement must provide for alternative safeguards. Those alternative safeguards must offer the data subject guarantees essentially equivalent to those required by Article 47 of the Charter of Fundamental Rights of the European Union (EU Charter)[24].

53. In that case, the international agreement could create a structure which enables the data subject to enforce its rights outside the courts, for example through quasi-judicial, binding mechanisms such as arbitration or alternative dispute resolution mechanisms such as mediation, which would guarantee an independent review and bind the receiving public body[25]. Moreover, the public body transferring the personal data could commit to be liable for compensation of damages through unlawful processing of the personal data which are testified by the independent review. Exceptionally, other, equally independent and effective redress mechanisms could be put in place by the agreement, for instance effective redress mechanisms implemented by international organisations.

54. For all of the abovementioned redress mechanisms, the international agreement should contain an obligation for the parties to inform each other of the outcome of the proceedings, in particular if a complaint of an individual is dismissed or not resolved.

55. The redress mechanism must be combined with the possibility for the transferring public body to suspend or terminate the transfer of personal data under the international agreement where the parties do not succeed in resolving a dispute amicably until it considers that the issue has been satisfactorily addressed by the receiving public body. Such a suspension or termination, if carried out, must be accompanied by a commitment from the receiving public body to return or delete the personal data. The transferring public body must notify the suspension or termination to the competent national SA.

2.8 SUPERVISION MECHANISMS

56. In order to make sure that all obligations created under the international agreement are fulfilled, the international agreement must provide for independent supervision monitoring the proper application of the agreement and interferences with the rights provided under the agreement.

57. First, the agreement should provide for internal supervision ensuring compliance with the agreement. Each party to the agreement should conduct periodic internal checks of the procedures put in place and of the effective application of the safeguards provided in the agreement. The periodic internal checks should also verify any changes in legislation that would prevent the party (ies) to comply with the data protection principles and safeguards included in the international agreement. Moreover, it could be provided that a party to the agreement can also request from another party to the agreement to conduct such a review. The international agreement must require that the parties must respond to inquiries from the other party concerning the effective implementation of the safeguards in the agreement. Each party conducting a review should communicate the results of the checks to the other party (ies) to the agreement. Ideally, such communication should also be made to the independent oversight mechanism governing the agreement.

58. In addition, the international agreement must include the obligation that a party informs the other party without delay if it is unable to effectively implement the safeguards in the agreement for any reason. For this case the international agreement must foresee the possibility for the transferring public body to suspend or terminate the transfer of personal data under the international agreement to the receiving public body until such time as the receiving public body informs the transferring public body that it is again able to act consistent with the safeguards. The transferring body must notify the change of situation as well as the suspension of transfers or termination of the agreement to the competent national SA.

59. Secondly, the agreement must provide for independent supervision in charge of ensuring that the parties comply with the provisions set out in the agreement. This follows directly from the EU Charter[26] and the European Convention of Human Rights (ECHR)[27] in accordance with the jurisprudence of the European Court of Human Rights (ECtHR) and in the terms established in primary law[28] as well as the corresponding case law.

60. The CJEU, has, since 2015[29], reiterated the necessity of having an independent redress and supervision mechanism.[30] Likewise, the ECtHR has frequently highlighted in its rulings that any interference with the right to respect for private life as enshrined in Article 8 ECHR needs to be subject to an effective, independent and impartial oversight system[31].

61. The agreement could, for example, invoke oversight by a competent supervisory authority, if there is one in the country of the public body receiving the EEA personal data, even if the GDPR does not specify that the competent supervisory authority needs to be the external oversight body. Moreover, the agreement could include the voluntary commitment of the receiving party to cooperate with the EEA SAs.

62. In the absence of a supervisory authority specifically in charge with the supervision of data protection law in the third country or at the international organisation, the need for an independent, effective and impartial supervisory oversight mechanism needs to be fulfilled by other means. The type of independent supervision mechanism put in place may depend on the case at hand.

63. The agreement could, for example, refer to existing oversight bodies in the third country other than a supervisory authority in the area of data protection. In addition, if no external independent oversight can be ensured from a structural or institutional point of view, e.g. because of the privileges and immunities of certain international organisations, oversight could be guaranteed through functionally autonomous mechanisms. The latter must be a body that, while not external itself, carries out its functions independently, i.e. free from instructions, with sufficient human, technical and financial resources, etc. The receiving party shall be bound by the decisions of the oversight body.

2.9 TERMINATION CLAUSE

64. The international agreement should envisage that any personal data transferred from the EEA pursuant to the international agreement prior to its effective termination shall continue to be processed in accordance with the provisions of the international agreement.

NOTES

15   Article 44 of the GDPR states: *"All provisions of this Chapter shall be applied in order to ensure that the level of protection of natural persons guaranteed by this Regulation is not undermined."*

16   CJEU, July 16, 2020, Judgment in case C-311/18, Data Protection Commissioner v Facebook Ireland Ltd and Maximillian Schrems ("Schrems II").

17   CJEU, July 16, 2020, Judgment in case C-311/18, Data Protection Commissioner v Facebook Ireland Ltd and Maximillian Schrems ("Schrems II"), para 105.

18   Idem.

19   See EDPB Guidelines on transparency under Regulation 2016/679, WP 260 rev.01, pages 13 to 22.

20   See above under 2.3.1.

21   See EDPB Recommendations 02/2020 on the European Essential Guarantees for surveillance measures.

22   See EDPB Recommendations 02/2020, Guarantee D, p. 13 and seq.

23   See also section 2.8 on supervision mechanism.

24   CJEU, July 16,2020, Judgment in case C-311/18, Data Protection Commissioner v Facebook Ireland Ltd and Maximillian Schrems ("Schrems II"), paras 96, 186 and seq.

25   CJEU, October 6, 2015, Judgment in case C-362/14, Maximillian Schrems v Data Protection Commissioner ("Schrems"), paras 41 and 95; ECJ July 16,2020, Judgment in case C-311/18, Data Protection Commissioner v Facebook Ireland Ltd and Maximillian Schrems ("Schrems II"), paras 186,187,189, 195 and seq.

26   Articles 7, 8 and 47 of the EU Charter.

27   Article 8 ECHR.

28   Article 6 Lisbon Treaty

"1.*The Union recognises the rights, freedoms and principles set out in the Charter of Fundamental Rights of the European Union of 7 December 2000, as adapted at Strasbourg, on 12 December 2007, which shall have the same legal value as the Treaties.*

The provisions of the Charter shall not extend in any way the competences of the Union as defined in the Treaties.

The rights, freedoms and principles in the Charter shall be interpreted in accordance with the general provisions in Title VII of the Charter governing its interpretation and application and with due regard to the explanations referred to in the Charter, that set out the sources of those provisions.

2. The Union shall accede to the European Convention for the Protection of Human Rights and Fundamental Freedoms. Such accession shall not affect the Union's competences as defined in the Treaties.

3. Fundamental rights, as guaranteed by the European Convention for the Protection of Human Rights and Fundamental Freedoms and as they result from the constitutional traditions common to the Member States, shall constitute general principles of the Union's law."

29   CJEU, October 6, 2015, Judgment in case C-362/14, Maximillian Schrems v Data Protection Commissioner ("Schrems"), paras 41 and 95.

30   CJEU, July 27, 2017, Opinion 1/15 on the agreement envisaged between the European Union and Canada on the transfer of Passenger Name Record data, 26 July 2017, para. 228 and seq.; CJEU, 30 April 2019, Opinion 1/17 on the Comprehensive Economic and Trade agreement between Canada and the European Union, para. 190 and seq.

31   ECtHR, September 6, 1978, Klass, v. Germany, para. 55 and 56. The requirement stemming from the ECtHR also apply to any interference with Articles 7 and 8 of the EU Charter since, according to Article 52 (3) EU Charter, the meaning

and scope of these fundamental rights shall be the same as those laid down by Article 8 ECHR.

3 SPECIFIC INFORMATION ON ARTICLE 46 GDPR

3.1 SPECIFIC INFORMATION ON LEGALLY BINDING AND ENFORCEABLE INSTRUMENTS - ARTICLE 46(2)(A) GDPR

[2.328]
65. Article 46 (2)(a) GDPR allows EEA public bodies to base transfers to public bodies in a third country or an international organisation on instruments concluded between them without obtaining prior authorisation from a SA. Such instruments have to be legally binding and enforceable. Therefore, international treaties, public-law treaties or self-executing administrative agreements may be used under this provision.

66. Any legally binding and enforceable instrument should encompass the core set of data protection principles and data subject rights as required by the GDPR.

67. The parties are obliged to commit themselves to putting sufficient data protection safeguards for transferring data into place. As a consequence, the agreement should also set out the way in which the receiving public body will apply the core set of basic data protection principles and data subject rights to all transferred personal data in order to ensure that the level of protection of natural persons under the GDPR is not undermined.

68. If there is no possibility to ensure effective judicial redress in legally binding and enforceable instruments so that alternative redress mechanism have to be agreed upon, EEA public bodies should consult the competent SA before concluding these instruments.

69. Even if the form of the instrument is not decisive as long as it is legally binding and enforceable, the EDPB considers that the best option would be to incorporate detailed data protection clauses directly within the instrument. If, however, this solution is not feasible due to the particular circumstances, the EDPB strongly recommends incorporating at least a general clause setting out the data protection principles directly within the text of the instrument and inserting the more detailed provisions and safeguards in an annex to the instrument.

3.2 SPECIFIC INFORMATION ON ADMINISTRATIVE ARRANGEMENTS - ARTICLE 46(3)(B) GDPR

70. The GDPR in its Article 46 (3)(b) also provides for alternative instruments in the form of administrative arrangements, e.g. Memorandum of Understanding "MOU", providing protection through the commitments taken by both parties in order to bring their common arrangement into force.

71. In this respect, Article 46 (1) and recital 108 of the GDPR specify that these arrangements have to ensure enforceable data subject rights and effective legal remedies. Where safeguards are provided for in administrative arrangements that are not legally binding, authorisation by the competent SA has to be obtained.

72. It should be carefully assessed whether or not to make use of non-legally binding administrative arrangements to provide safeguards in the public sector, in view of the purpose of the processing and the nature of the data at hand. If data protection rights and redress for EEA individuals are not provided for in the domestic law of the third country or the internal rules/regulatory framework of the international organisation, preference should be given to concluding a legally binding agreement. Irrespective of the type of instrument adopted, the measures in place have to be effective to ensure the appropriate implementation, enforcement and supervision.

73. In administrative arrangements specific steps have to be taken to ensure effective individual rights, redress and oversight. In particular, to ensure effective and enforceable rights, a non-binding instrument should contain assurances from the public body receiving the EEA personal data that individual rights are fully provided by its domestic law and can be exercised by EEA individuals under the same conditions as is the case for citizens and residents of the concerned third country. The same applies if administrative and judicial redress is available to EEA individuals in the domestic legal framework of the receiving public body. Similarly, international organisations should provide assurances about individual rights provided by their internal rules, as well as the available redress mechanisms.

74. If this is not the case, individual rights should be guaranteed by specific commitments from the parties, combined with procedural mechanisms to ensure their effectiveness and provide redress to the individual. These specific commitments and procedural mechanisms must make it possible, in practice, to ensure compliance with the level of protection essentially equivalent to that guaranteed within the EU by the GDPR. Such procedural mechanisms may, for example, include commitments of the parties to inform each other of requests from EEA individuals and to settle disputes or claims in a timely fashion.

75. In addition, in case such disputes or claims cannot be resolved in an amicable way between the parties themselves, independent and effective redress to the individual must be provided by alternative mechanisms, for example through a possibility for the individual to have recourse to an alternative dispute resolution mechanism, such as arbitration or mediation. Such alternative dispute resolution mechanism must be binding[32].

76. Depending on the case at hand, a combination of all or some of the above measures should be provided for in the administrative agreement in order to ensure effective redress. Other measures not included in these guidelines could also be acceptable as long as they provide for independent and effective redress.

77. Each administrative arrangement developed in accordance with Article 46 (3)(b) GDPR will be examined by the competent SA on a case by case basis, followed by the relevant EDPB procedure, if applicable. The competent SA will base its examination on the general recommendations set out in these guidelines, but might also ask for more guarantees depending on the specific case.

NOTES

> 32   CJEU, July 16, 2020, Judgment in case C-311/18, Data Protection Commissioner v Facebook Ireland Ltd and Maximillian Schrems ("Schrems II"), paras 189, 196 and seq.

4 PROCEDURAL QUESTIONS

[2.329]

78. Administrative arrangements established under Article 46 (3)(b) GDPR will be examined on a case-by-case basis due to the requirements for an authorisation by the competent SA which, according to Article 46 (4) GDPR shall apply the consistency mechanism pursuant to Article 64 (2) GDPR. When integrating alternative redress mechanisms in binding and enforceable instruments pursuant to Article 46 (2)(a) GDPR, the EDPB recommends also seeking advice from the competent SA. The EDPB strongly advises to consult the competent SA at an early stage.

For the European Data Protection Board

The Chair

(Andrea Jelinek)

EUROPEAN DATA PROTECTION BOARD: GUIDELINES 3/2020 ON THE PROCESSING OF DATA CONCERNING HEALTH FOR THE PURPOSE OF SCIENTIFIC RESEARCH IN THE CONTEXT OF THE COVID-19 OUTBREAK

Adopted on 21 April 2020

[2.330]

NOTES

VERSION HISTORY

Version 1.1: 30 April 2020 — Minor corrections

Version 1.0: 21 April 2020 — Adoption of the Guidelines

TABLE OF CONTENTS

THE EUROPEAN DATA PROTECTION BOARD

Having regard to Article 70(1)(e) of the Regulation 2016/679/EU of the European Parliament and of the Council of 27 April 2016 on the protection of natural persons with regard to the processing of personal data and on the free movement of such data, and repealing Directive 95/46/EC, (hereinafter "GDPR"),

Having regard to the EEA Agreement and in particular to Annex XI and Protocol 37 thereof, as amended by the Decision of the EEA joint Committee No 154/2018 of 6 July 2018,

Having regard to Article 12 and Article 22 of its Rules of Procedure,

HAS ADOPTED THE FOLLOWING GUIDELINES

1 INTRODUCTION

[2.331]

1. Due to the COVID-19 pandemic, there are currently great scientific research efforts in the fight against the SARS-CoV-2 in order to produce research results as fast as possible.

2. At the same time, legal questions concerning the use of health data pursuant to Article 4 (15) GDPR for such research purposes keep arising. The present guidelines aim to shed light on the most urgent of these questions such as the legal basis, the implementation of adequate safeguards for such processing of health data and the exercise of the data subject rights.

3. Please note that the development of a further and more detailed guidance for the processing of health data for the purpose of scientific research is part of the annual work plan of the EDPB. Also, please note that the current guidelines do not revolve around the processing of personal data for epidemiological surveillance.

2 APPLICATION OF THE GDPR

[2.332]
4. Data protection rules (such as the GDPR) do not hinder measures taken in the fight against the COVID-19 pandemic.[1] The GDPR is a broad piece of legislation and provides for several provisions that allow to handle the processing of personal data for the purpose of scientific research connected to the COVID-19 pandemic in compliance with the fundamental rights to privacy and personal data protection.[2] The GDPR also foresees a specific derogation to the prohibition of processing of certain special categories of personal data, such as health data, where it is necessary for these purposes of scientific research.[3]

5. Fundamental Rights of the EU must be applied when processing health data for the purpose of scientific research connected to the COVID-19 pandemic. Neither the Data Protection Rules nor the Freedom of Science pursuant to Article 13 of the Charter of Fundamental Rights of the EU have precedence over the other. Rather, these rights and freedoms must be carefully assessed and balanced, resulting in an outcome which respects the essence of both.

NOTES
[1]   See the Statement of the EDPB from 19.3.2020 on the general processing of personal data in the context of the COVID-19 outbreak, available at https://edpb.europa.eu/our-work-tools/our-documents/other/statement-processing-personal-data-context-covid-19-outbreak_en.
[2]   See for example Article 5(1)(b) and (e), Article 14(5)(b) and Article 17(3)(d) GDPR.
[3]   See for example Article 9(2)(j) and Article 89(2) GDPR.

3 DEFINITIONS

[2.333]
6. It is important to understand which processing operations benefit from the special regime foreseen in the GDPR and elaborated on in the present guidelines. Therefore, the terms "data concerning health", "processing for the purpose of scientific research" as well as "further processing" (also referred to as "primary and secondary usage of health data") must be defined.

3.1 "DATA CONCERNING HEALTH"

7. According to Article 4(15) GDPR, "data concerning health" means *"personal data related to the physical or mental health of a natural person, including the provision of health care services, which reveal information about his or her health status"*. As indicated by Recital 53, data concerning health deserves higher protection, as the use of such sensitive data may have significant adverse impacts for data subjects. In the light of this and the relevant jurisprudence of the European Court of Justice("ECJ"),[4] the term "data concerning health" must be given a wide interpretation.

8. Data concerning health can be derived from different sources, for example:
(1)   Information collected by a health care provider in a patient record (such as medical history and results of examinations and treatments).
(2)   Information that becomes health data by cross referencing with other data thus revealing the state of health or health risks (such as the assumption that a person has a higher risk of suffering heart attacks based on the high blood pressure measured over a certain period of time).
(3)   Information from a "self check" survey, where data subjects answer questions related to their health (such as stating symptoms).
(4)   Information that becomes health data because of its usage in a specific context (such as information regarding a recent trip to or presence in a region affected with COVID-19 processed by a medical professional to make a diagnosis).

3.2 "PROCESSING FOR THE PURPOSE OF SCIENTIFIC RESEARCH"

9. Article 4 GDPR does not entail an explicit definition of "processing for the purpose of scientific research". As indicated by Recital 159, *"the term processing of personal data for scientific research purposes should be interpreted in a broad manner including for example technological development and demonstration, fundamental research, applied research and privately funded research. In addition,it should take into account the Union's objective under Article 179 (1) TFEU of achieving a European Research Area. Scientific research purposes should also include studies conducted in the public interest in the area of public health."*

10. The former Article 29-Working-Party has already pointed out that the term may not be stretched beyond its common meaning though and understands that "scientific research" in this context means *"a research project set up in accordance with relevant sector-related methodological and ethical standards, in conformity with good practice"*.[5]

3.3 "FURTHER PROCESSING

11.   Finally, when talking about "processing of health data for the purpose of scientific research", there are two types of data usages:

(1)   Research on personal (health) data which consists in the use of data directly collected for the purpose of scientific studies ("primary use").

(2)   Research on personal (health) data which consists of the further processing of data initially collected for another purpose ("secondary use").

12.   Example 1: For conducting a clinical trial on individuals suspected to be infected with SARS-CoV-2, health data are collected and questionnaires are used. This is a case of "primary use" of health data as defined above.

13.   Example 2: A data subject has consulted a health care provider as a patient regarding symptoms of the SARS-CoV-2. If health data recorded by the health care provider is being used for scientific research purposes later on, this usage is classified as further processing of health data (secondary use) that has been collected for another initial purpose.

14.   The distinction between scientific research based on primary or secondary usage of health data will become particularly important when talking about the legal basis for the processing, the information obligations and the purpose limitation principle pursuant to Article 5 (1)(b) GDPR as outlined below.

NOTES

⁴   See for example, regarding the Directive 95/46/EC, ECJ 6.11.2003, C-101/01 (Lindqvist) paragraph 50.

⁵   See the Guidelines on Consent under Regulation 2016/679 of the former Article 29 Working-Party from 10.04.2018, WP259   rev.01,   17EN,   page   27   (endorsed   by   the   EDPB).   Available   at https://ec.europa.eu/newsroom/article29/item-detail.cfm?item_id=623051.

4 LEGAL BASIS FOR THE PROCESSING

[2.334]
15.   All processing of personal data concerning health must comply with the principles relating to processing set out in Article 5 GDPR and with one of the legal grounds and the specific derogations listed respectively in Article 6 and Article 9 GDPR for the lawful processing of this special category of personal data.⁶

16.   Legal bases and applicable derogations for processing health data for the purpose of scientific research are provided for respectively in Article 6 and Article 9. In the following section, the rules concerning consent and respective national legislation are addressed. It has to be noted that there is no ranking between the legal bases stipulated in the GDPR.

4.1 CONSENT

17.   The consent of the data subject, collected pursuant to Article 6(1)(a) and Article 9(2)(a) GDPR, may provide a legal basis for the processing of data concerning health in the COVID-19 context.

18.   However, it has to be noted that all the conditions for explicit consent, particularly those found in Article 4(11), Article 6(1)(a), Article 7 and Article 9(2)(a) GDPR, must be fulfilled. Notably, consent must be freely given, specific, informed, and unambiguous, and it must be made by way of a statement or "clear affirmative action".

19.   As stated in Recital 43, consent cannot be considered freely given if there is a clear imbalance between the data subject and the controller. It is therefore important that a data subject is not pressured and does not suffer from disadvantages if they decide not to give consent. The EDPB has already addressed consent in the context of clinical trials.⁷ Further guidance, particularly on the topic of explicit consent, can be found in the consent guidelines of the former Article 29-Working-Party.⁸

20.   Example: A survey is conducted as part of a non-interventional study on a given population, researching symptoms and the progress of a disease. For the processing of such health data, there searchers may seek the consent of the data subject under the conditions as stipulated in Article 7 GDPR.

21.   In the view of the EDPB, the example above is *not* considered a case of "clear imbalance of power" as mentioned in Recital 43 and the data subject should be able to give the consent to the researchers.⁹ In the example, the data subjects are not in a situation of whatsoever dependency with the researchers that could inappropriately influence the exercise of their free will and it is also clear that it will have no adverse consequences if they refuse to give their consent.

22.   However, researchers should be aware that if consent is used as the lawful basis for processing, there must be a possibility for individuals to withdraw that consent at any time pursuant to Article 7 (3)GDPR. If consent is withdrawn, all data processing operations that were based on consent remain lawful in accordance with the GDPR, but the controller shall stop the processing actions concerned and if there is no other lawful basis justifying the retention for further processing, the data should be deleted by the controller.¹⁰

4.2 NATIONAL LEGISLATIONS

23.   Article 6 (1) e or 6 (1) f GDPR in combination with the enacted derogations under Article 9 (2)(j) or Article 9 (2)(i) GDPR can provide a legal basis for the processing of personal (health) data for scientific research. In the context of clinical trial this has already been clarified by the Board.¹¹

24.   Example: A large population based study conducted on medical charts of COVID-19 patients.

25. As outlined above, the EU as well as the national legislator of each Member State may enact specific laws pursuant to Article 9 (2)(j) or Article 9 (2)(i) GDPR to provide a legal basis for the processing of health data for the purpose of scientific research. Therefore, the conditions and the extent for such processing *vary* depending on the enacted laws of the particular Member State.

26. As stipulated in Article 9(2)(i) GDPR, such laws shall provide *"for suitable and specific measures to safeguard the rights and freedoms of the data subject, in particular professional secrecy"*. As similarly stipulated in Article 9(2)(j) GDPR, such enacted laws *"shall be proportionate to the aim pursued, respect the essence of the right to data protection and provide for suitable and specific measures to safeguard the fundamental rights and the interests of the data subject"*.

27. Furthermore, such enacted laws must be interpreted in the light of the principles pursuant to Article 5 GDPR and in consideration of the jurisprudence of the ECJ. In particular, derogations and limitations in relation to the protection of data provided in Article 9(2)(j) and Article 89 GDPR must apply only in so far as is strictly necessary.[12]

NOTES

6   See for example, regarding the Directive 95/46/EC ECJ 13.5.2014, C-131/12 (Google Spain), paragraph 71.
7   See Opinion 3/2019 of the EDPB from 23.1.2019 on concerning the Questions and Answers on the interplay between the Clinical Trials Regulation (CTR) and the General Data Protection regulation (GDPR), available at https://edpb.europa.eu/our-work-tools/our-documents/avis-art-70/opinion-32019-concerning-questions-and-answers-interplay_en.
8   Guidelines on Consent under Regulation 2016/679 of the former Article 29 Working-Party from 10.04.2018, WP259 rev.01, 17EN, page 18 (endorsed by the EDPB).
9   Assuming that the data subject has not been pressured or threatened with disadvantages when not giving his or her consent.
10   See Article17 (1)(b) and (3) GDPR.
11   See Opinion 3/2019 of the EDPB from 23.1.2019, page 7.
12   See for example, regarding the Directive 95/46/EC ECJ 14.2.2019, C-345/17 (Buivids) paragraph 64.

5 DATA PROTECTION PRINCIPLES

[2.335]

28. The principles relating to processing of personal data pursuant to Article 5 GDPR shall be respected by the controller and processor, especially considering that a great amount of personal data may be processed for the purpose of scientific research. Considering the context of the present guidelines, the most important aspects of these principles are addressed in the following.

5.1 TRANSPARENCY AND INFORMATION TO DATA SUBJECTS

29. The principle of transparency means that personal data shall be processed fairly and in a transparent manner in relation to the data subject. This principle is strongly connected with the information obligations pursuant to Article 13 or Article 14 GDPR.

30. In general, a data subject must be individually informed of the existence of the processing operation and that personal (health) data is being processed for scientific purposes. The information delivered should contain all the elements stated in Article 13 or Article 14 GDPR.

31. It has to be noted that researchers often process health data that they have not obtained directly from the data subject, for instance using data from patient records or data from patients in other countries. Therefore, Article 14 GDPR, which covers information obligations where personal data is not collected directly from the data subject, will be the focus of this section.

5.1.1 When must the data subject be informed?

32. When personal data have not been obtained from the data subject, Article 14(3)(a) GDPR stipulates that the controller shall provide the information *"within a reasonable period after obtaining the personal data, but at the latest within one month, having regard to the specific circumstances in which the personal data are processed"*.

33. In the current context, it has to be particularly noted that according to Article 14(4) GDPR, where *"the controller intends to further process the personal data for a purpose other than that for which the personal data were obtained, the controller shall provide the data subject prior to that further processing with information on that other purpose"*.

34. In the case of the further processing of data for scientific purposes and taking into account the sensitivity of the data processed, an appropriate safeguard according to Article 89(1) is to deliver the information to the data subject within a reasonable period of time before the implementation of the new research project. This allows the data subject to become aware of the research project and enables the possibility to exercise his/her rights beforehand.

5.1.2 Exemptions

35. However, Article (14)(5) GDPR stipulates four exemptions of the information obligation. In the current context, the exemption pursuant to Article (14)(5 (b) ("proves impossible or would involve a disproportionate effort") and (c) ("obtaining or disclosure is expressly laid down by Union or Member State law") GDPR are of particular relevance, especially for the information obligation pursuant to Article 14(4) GDPR.

5.1.2.1 Proves impossible

36. In its Guidelines regarding the principle of Transparency,[13] the former Article 29-Working-Party has already pointed out that *"the situation where it "proves impossible" under Article 14(5)(b) to provide* the information is an all or nothing situation because something is either impossible or it is not; there are no degrees of impossibility. Thus, if a data controller seeks to rely on this exemption it must demonstrate the factors that actually prevent it from providing the information in question to data subjects. If, after a certain period of time, the factors that caused the "impossibility" no longer exist and it becomes possible to provide the information to data subjects then the data controller should immediately do so. In practice, there will be very few situations in which a data controller can demonstrate that it is actually impossible to provide the information to data subjects."

5.1.2.2 Disproportionate effort

37. In determining what constitutes disproportionate effort, Recital 62 refers to the number of data subjects, the age of the data and appropriate safeguards in place as possible indicative factors. In the Transparency Guidelines mentioned above,[14] it is recommended that the controller should therefore carry out a balancing exercise to assess the effort involved to provide the information to data subjects against the impact and effects on the data subject if they are not provided with the information.

38.   Example: A large number of data subjects where there is no available contact information could be considered as a disproportionate effort to provide the information.

5.1.2.3 Serious impairment of objectives

39. To rely on this exception, data controllers must demonstrate that the provision of the information set out in Article 14 (1) *per se* would render impossible or seriously impair the achievement of the objectives of the processing.

40. In a case where the exemption of Article (14)(5)(b) GDPR applies, *"the controller shall take appropriate measures to protect the data subject's rights and freedoms and legitimate interests, including making the information publicly available".*

5.1.2.4 Obtaining or disclosure is expressly laid down by Union or Member State law

41. Article 14(5)(c) GDPR allows for a derogation of the information requirements in Articles 14(1), (2) and (4) insofar as the obtaining or disclosure of personal data *"is expressly laid down by Union orMember State law to which the controller is subject".* This exemption is conditional upon the law in question providing *"appropriate measures to protect the data subject's legitimate interests".* As stated in the above mentioned Transparency Guidelines,[15] such law must directly address the data controller and the obtaining or disclosure in question should be mandatory upon the data controller. When relying on this exemption, the EDPB recalls that the data controller must be able to demonstrate how the law in question applies to them and requires them to either obtain or disclose the personal data in question.

5.2 PURPOSE LIMITATION AND PRESUMPTION OF COMPATIBILITY

42. As a general rule, data shall be *"collected for specified, explicit and legitimate purposes and not further processed in a manner that is incompatible with those purposes"* pursuant to Article 5(1)(b) GDPR.

43. However the "compatibility presumption" provided by Article 5(1)(b) GDPR states that *"further processing for [. . .] scientific research purposes [. . .] shall, in accordance with Article 89 (1), not be considered to be incompatible with the initial purposes".* This topic, due to its horizontal and complex nature, will be considered in more detail in the planned EDPB guidelines on the processing of health data for the purpose of scientific research.

44. Article 89 (1) GDPR stipulates that the processing of data for research purposes *"shall be subject to appropriate safeguards"* and that those *"safeguards shall ensure that technical and organisational measures are in place in particular in order to ensure respect for the principle of data minimisation- .Those measures may include pseudonymisation provided that those purposes can be fulfilled in that manner".*

45. The requirements of Article 89(1) GDPR emphasise the importance of the data minimisation principle and the principle of integrity and confidentiality as well as the principle of data protection by design and by default (see below).[16] Consequently, considering the sensitive nature of health data and the risks when re-using health data for the purpose of scientific research, strong measures must be taken in order to ensure an appropriate level of security as required by Article 32(1) GDPR.

5.3 DATA MINIMISATION AND STORAGE LIMITATION

46. In scientific research, data minimisation can be achieved through the requirement of specifying there search questions and assessing the type and amount of data necessary to properly answer these research questions. Which data is needed depends on the purpose of the research even when there search has an explorative nature and should always comply with the purpose limitation principle pursuant to Article 5 (1)(b) GDPR. It has to be noted that the data has to be anonymised where it is possible to perform the scientific research with anonymised data.

47. In addition, proportionate storage periods shall be set. As stipulated by Article 5(1)(e) GDPR *"personal data may be stored for longer periods insofar as the personal data will be processed solely for archiving [. . .] scientific purposes [. . .] in accordance with Article 89(1) subject to implementation of the appropriate technical and organisational measures required by this Regulation in order to safeguard the rights and freedoms of the data subject"*

48. In order to define storage periods (timelines), criteria such as the length and the purpose of there search should be taken into account. It has to be noted that national provisions may stipulate rules concerning the storage period as well.

5.4 INTEGRITY AND CONFIDENTIALITY

49. As mentioned above, sensitive data such as health data merit higher protection as their processing is likelier to lead to negative impacts for data subjects. This consideration especially applies in the COVID-19 outbreak as the foreseeable re-use of health data for scientific purposes leads to an increase in the number and type of entities processing such data.

50. It has to be noted that the principle of integrity and confidentiality must be read in conjunction with the requirements of Article 32 (1) GDPR and Article 89 (1) GDPR. The cited provisions must be fully complied with. Therefore, considering the high risks as outlined above, appropriate technical and organisational up-to-date measures must be implemented to ensure a sufficient level of security.

51. Such measures should *at least* consist of pseudonymisation,[17] encryption, non-disclosure agreement sand strict access role distribution, access role restrictions as well as access logs. It has to be noted that national provisions may stipulate concrete technical requirements or other safeguards such as adherence to professional secrecy rules.

52. Furthermore, a data protection impact assessment pursuant to Article 35 GDPR must be carried out when such processing is *"likely to result in a high risk to the rights and freedoms of natural persons"* pursuant to Article 35 (1) GDPR. The lists pursuant to Article 35(4) and (5) GDPR shall be taken into account.

53. At this point, the EDPB emphasises the importance of data protection officers. Where applicable, data protection officers should be consulted on processing of health data for the purpose of scientific research in the context of the COVID-19 outbreak.

54. Finally, the adopted measures to protect data (including during transfers) should be properly documented in the record of processing activities.

NOTES
13 See the Guidelines on transparency under Regulation 2016/679 of the former Article-29 Working-Party from 11.4.2018, WP260 rev.01, 17/EN, page 29 (endorsed by the EDPB). Available at https://ec.europa.eu/newsroom/article29/item-detail. cfm?item_id=622227.
14 Guidelines on transparency under Regulation 2016/679 of the former Article-29 Working-Party from 11.4.2018, WP260 rev.01, 17/EN, page 31 (endorsed by the EDPB).
15 Guidelines on transparency under Regulation 2016/679 of the former Article-29 Working-Party from 11.4.2018, WP260 rev.01, 17/EN, page 32 (endorsed by the EDPB).
16 Also see the Guidelines 4/2019 of the EDPB from 13.11.2019 on Data Protection by Design and by Default (version for public consultation), available at https://edpb.europa.eu/our-work-tools/public-consultations-art-704/2019/ guidelines-42019-article-25-data-protection-design_en
17 It has to be noted that personal (health data) that has been pseudonymised is still regarded as "personal data" pursuant to Article 4 (1) GDPR and must not be confused with "anonymised data" where it is no longer possible for anyone to refer back to individual data subjects. See for example Recital 28.

6 EXERCISE OF THE RIGHTS OF DATA SUBJECTS

[2.336]
55. In principle, situations as the current COVID-19 outbreak do not suspend or restrict the possibility of data subjects to exercise their rights pursuant to Article 12 to 22 GDPR. However, Article 89 (2) GDPR allows the national legislator to restrict (some) of the data subject's rights as set in Chapter 3 of the regulation. Because of this, the restrictions of the rights of data subjects *may vary* depending on the enacted laws of the particular Member State.

56. Furthermore, some restrictions of the rights of data subjects can be based directly on the Regulation, such as the access right restriction pursuant to Article 15(4) GDPR and the restriction of the right to erasure pursuant to Article 17 (3)(d) GDPR. The information obligation exemptions pursuant to Article14(5) GDPR have already been addressed above.

57. It has to be noted that, in the light of the jurisprudence of the ECJ, all restrictions of the rights of data subjects must apply only in so far as it is strictly necessary.[18]

NOTES
18 See for example, regarding the Directive 95/46/EC ECJ 14.2.2019, C–345/17 (Buivids) paragraph 64.

7 INTERNATIONAL DATA TRANSFERS FOR SCIENTIFIC RESEARCH PURPOSES

[2.337]
58. Within the context of research and specifically in the context of the COVID-19 pandemic, there will probably be a need for international cooperation that may also imply international transfers of health data for the purpose of scientific research outside of the EEA.

59. When personal data is transferred to a non-EEA country or international organisation, in addition to complying with the rules set out in GDPR,[19] especially its Articles 5 (data protection principles), Article 6 (lawfulness) and Article 9 (special categories of data),[20] the data exporter shall also comply with Chapter V (data transfers).[21]

60. In addition to the regular transparency requirement as mentioned on page 7 of the present guidelines, a duty rests on the data exporter to inform data subjects that it intends to transfer personal data to a third country or international organisation. This includes information about the existence or absence of an adequacy decision by the European Commission, or whether the transfer is based on a suitable safeguard from Article 46 or on a derogation of Article 49(1). This duty exists irrespective of whether the personal data was obtained directly from the data subject or not.

61. In general, when considering how to address such conditions for transfers of personal data to third countries or international organisations, data exporters should assess the risks to the rights and the freedoms of data subjects of each transfer[22] and favour solutions that guarantee data subjects the continuous protection of their fundamental rights and safeguards as regards the processing of their data, even after it has been transferred. This will be the case for transfers to countries having an adequate level of protection,[23] or in case of use of one of the appropriate safeguards included in Article 46 GDPR,[24] ensuring that enforceable rights and effective legal remedies are available for data subjects.

62. In the absence of an adequacy decision pursuant to Article 45(3) GDPR or appropriate safeguards pursuant to Article 46 GDPR, Article 49 GDPR envisages certain specific situations under which transfers of personal data can take place as an exception. The derogations enshrined in Article 49 GDPR are thus exemptions from the general rule and, therefore, must be interpreted restrictively, and on a case-by-case basis.[25] Applied to the current COVID-19 crisis, those addressed in Article 49(1)(d) ("transfer necessary for important reasons of public interest") and (a) ("explicit consent") may apply.

63. The COVID-19 pandemic causes an exceptional sanitary crisis of an unprecedented nature and scale. In this context, the EDPB considers that the fight against COVID-19 has been recognised by the EU and most of its Member States as an important public interest,[26] which may require urgent action in the field of scientific research (for example to identify treatments and/or develop vaccines), and may also involve transfers to third countries or international organisations.[27]

64. Not only public authorities, but also private entities playing a role in pursuing such public interest (for example, a university's research institute cooperating on the development of a vaccine in the context of an international partnership) could, under the current pandemic context, rely upon the derogation mentioned above.

65. In addition, in certain situations, in particular where transfers are performed by private entities for the purpose of medical research aiming at fighting the COVID-19 pandemic,[28] such transfers of personal data could alternatively take place on the basis of the explicit consent of the data subjects.[29]

66. Public authorities and private entities may, under the current pandemic context, when it is not possible to rely on an adequacy decision pursuant to Article 45(3) or on appropriate safeguards pursuant to Article 46, rely upon the applicable derogations mentioned above, mainly as a temporary measure due to the urgency of the medical situation globally.

67. Indeed, if the nature of the COVID-19 crisis may justify the use of the applicable derogations for initial transfers carried out for the purpose of research in this context, repetitive transfers of data to third countries part of a long lasting research project in this regard would need to be framed with appropriate safeguards in accordance with Article 46 GDPR.[30]

68. Finally, it has to be noted that any such transfers will need to take into consideration on a case-by-case basis the respective roles (controller, processor, joint controller) and related obligations of the actors involved (sponsor, investigator) in order to identify the appropriate measures for framing the transfer.

NOTES

[19] Article 44 GDPR.

[20] See sections 4 to 6 of the present Guidelines.

[21] See the Guidelines 2/018 of the EDPB from 25.5.2018 on derogations of Article 49 under Regulation 2016/679, page 3, on the two-step test, available at https://edpb.europa.eu/our-work-tools/our-documents/smjernice/guidelines-22018-derogations-article-49-under-regulation_en.

[22] International Data Transfers may be a risk factor to consider when performing a DPIA as referred to in page 10 of the present guidelines.

[23] The list of countries recognised adequate by the European Commission is available at https://ec.europa.eu/info/law/law-topic/data-protection/international-dimension-data-protection/adequacy-decisions_en

[24] For example standard data protection clauses pursuant to Article 46(2)(c) or (d) GDPR, ad hoc contractual clauses pursuant to Article 46 (3)(a) GDPR) or administrative arrangements pursuant to Article 46 (3)(b) GDPR.

[25] See Guidelines 2/2018, page 3.

[26] Article 168 of the Treaty on the Functioning of the European Union recognises a high level of human health protection as an important objective that should be ensured in the implementation of all Union policies and activities. On this basis, Union action supports national policies to improve public health, including in combatting against major health scourges and serious cross-border threats to health, e.g. by promoting research into their causes, transmission and prevention. Similarly, Recitals 46 and 112 of the GDPR refer to processing carried out in the context of the fight against epidemics as an example of processing serving important grounds of public interest. In the context of the COVID-19 pandemic, the EU has adopted a series of measures in a broad range of areas (e.g. funding of healthcare systems, support to cross-border patients and deployment of medical staff, financial assistance to the most deprived, transport, medical devices etc.) premised on the understanding that the EU is facing a major public health emergency requiring an urgent response.

[27] The EDPB underlines that the GDPR, in its Recital 112, refers to the international data exchange between services competent for public health purposes as an example of the application of this derogation.

[28] In accordance with Article 49(3) GDPR, consent cannot be used for activities carried out by public authorities in the exercise of their public powers.

[29] See EDPB Guidelines 2/2018, section 2.1.

[30] See EDPB Guidelines 2/2018, page 5.

8 SUMMARY

[2.338]
69. The key findings of these guidelines are:
(1)   The GDPR provides special rules for the processing of health data for the purpose of scientific research that are also applicable in the context of the COVID-19 pandemic.
(2)   The national legislator of each Member State may enact specific laws pursuant to Article (9)(2)(i) and (j) GDPR to enable the processing of health data for scientific research purposes. The processing of health data for the purpose of scientific research must also be covered by one of the legal bases in Article 6(1) GDPR. Therefore, the conditions and the extent for such processing varies depending on the enacted laws of the particular member state.
(3)   All enacted laws based on Article(9)(2)(i) and (j) GDPR must be interpreted in the light of the principles pursuant to Article 5 GDPR and in consideration of the jurisprudence of the ECJ. In particular, derogations and limitations in relation to the protection of data provided in Article 9(2)(j) and Article 89(2) GDPR must apply only in so far as is strictly necessary.
(4)   Considering the processing risks in the context of the COVID-19 outbreak, high emphasise must be put on compliance with Article 5(1)(f), Article 32(1) and Article 89(1) GDPR. There must be an assessment if a DPIA pursuant to Article 35 GDPR has to be carried out.
(5)   Storage periods (timelines) shall be set and must be proportionate. In order to define such storage periods, criteria such as the length and the purpose of the research should be taken into account. National provisions may stipulate rules concerning the storage period as well and must therefore be considered.
(6)   In principle, situations as the current COVID-19 outbreak do not suspend or restrict the possibility of data subjects to exercise their rights pursuant to Article 12 to 22 GDPR. However, Article 89 (2) GDPR allows the national legislator to restrict (some) of the data subject's rights as set in Chapter 3 of the GDPR. Because of this, the restrictions of the rights of data subjects *may vary* depending on the enacted laws of the particular Member State.
(7)   With respect to international transfers, in the absence of an adequacy decision pursuant to Article 45 (3) GDPR or appropriate safeguards pursuant to Article 46 GDPR, public authorities and private entities may rely upon the applicable derogations pursuant to Article 49 GDPR. However, the derogations of Article 49 GDPR do have exceptional character only.

For the European Data Protection Board

The Chair

(Andrea Jelinek)

EUROPEAN DATA PROTECTION BOARD: GUIDELINES 4/2020 ON THE USE OF LOCATION DATA AND CONTACT TRACING TOOLS IN THE CONTEXT OF THE COVID-19 OUTBREAK
Adopted on 21 April 2020

[2.339]

NOTES
© European Data Protection Board.

TABLE OF CONTENTS

THE EUROPEAN DATA PROTECTION BOARD

Having regard to Article 70(1)(e) of the Regulation 2016/679/EU of the European Parliament and of the Council of 27 April 2016 on the protection of natural persons with regard to the processing of personal data and on the free movement of such data, and repealing Directive 95/46/EC (hereinafter "GDPR"),

Having regard to the EEA Agreement and in particular to Annex XI and Protocol 37 thereof, as amended by the Decision of the EEA joint Committee No 154/2018 of 6 July 2018[1],

Having regard to Article 12 and Article 22 of its Rules of Procedure,

HAS ADOPTED THE FOLLOWING GUIDELINES

1 INTRODUCTION & CONTEXT

[2.340]
1   Governments and private actors are turning toward the use of data driven solutions as part of the response to the COVID-19 pandemic, raising numerous privacy concerns.

2   The EDPB underlines that the data protection legal framework was designed to be flexible and as such, is able to achieve both an efficient response in limiting the pandemic and protecting fundamental human rights and freedoms.

3   The EDPB firmly believes that, when processing of personal data is necessary for managing the COVID-19 pandemic, data protection is indispensable to build trust, create the conditions for social acceptability of any solution, and thereby guarantee the effectiveness of these measures. Because the virus knows no borders, it seems preferable to develop a common European approach in response to the current crisis, or at least put in place an interoperable framework.

4   The EDPB generally considers that data and technology used to help fight COVID-19 should be used to empower, rather than to control, stigmatise, or repress individuals. Furthermore, while data and technology can be important tools, they have intrinsic limitations and can merely leverage the effectiveness of other public health measures. The general principles of effectiveness, necessity, and proportionality must guide any measure adopted by Member States or EU institutions that involve processing of personal data to fight COVID-19.

5   These guidelines clarify the conditions and principles for the proportionate use of location data and contact tracing tools, for two specific purposes:
*   using location data to support the response to the pandemic by modelling the spread of the virus so as to assess the overall effectiveness of confinement measures ;
*   contact tracing, which aims to notify individuals of the fact that they have been in close proximity of someone who is eventually confirmed to be a carrier of the virus, in order to break the contamination chains as early as possible.

6   The efficiency of the contribution of contact tracing applications to the management of the pandemic depends on many factors (e.g., percentage of people who would need to install it; definition of a "contact" in terms of closeness and duration.). Moreover, such applications need to be part of a comprehensive public health strategy to fight the pandemic, including, inter alia, testing and subsequent manual contact tracing for the purpose of doubt removal. Their deployment should be accompanied by supporting measures to ensure that the information provided to the users is contextualized, and that alerts can be of use to the public health system. Otherwise, these applications might not reach their full impact.

7   The EDPB emphasises that the GDPR and Directive 2002/58/EC (the "ePrivacy Directive") both contain specific rules allowing for the use of anonymous or personal data to support public authorities and other actors at national and EU levels in monitoring and containing the spread of the SARS-CoV-2 virus[2].

8   In this regard, the EDPB has already taken position on the fact that the use of contact tracing applications should be voluntary and should not rely on tracing individual movements but rather on proximity information regarding users.[3]

NOTES
[1]   References to "Member States" made throughout this document should be understood as references to "EEA Member States".
[2]   See the previous statement of the EDPB on the COVID 19 outbreak.
[3]   https://edpb.europa.eu/sites/edpb/files/files/file1/edpbletterecadvisecodiv-appguidance_final.pdf

2 USE OF LOCATION DATA

2.1 SOURCES OF LOCATION DATA

[2.341]
9   There are two principal sources of location data available for modelling the spread of the virus and the overall effectiveness of confinement measures:
*   location data collected by electronic communication service providers (such as mobile telecommunication operators) in the course of the provision of their service ; and
*   location data collected by information society service providers' applications whose functionality requires the use of such data (e.g., navigation, transportation services, etc.).

10   The EDPB recalls that location data[4] collected from electronic communication providers may only be processed within the remits of articles 6 and 9 of the ePrivacy Directive. This means that these data can only be transmitted to authorities or other third parties if they have been anonymised by the provider or, for data indicating the geographic position of the terminal equipment of a user, which are not traffic data, with the prior consent of the users[5].

11   Regarding information, including location data, collected directly from the terminal equipment, art. 5(3) of the "ePrivacy" directive applies. Hence, the storing of information on the user's device or gaining access to the information already stored is allowed only if (i) the user has given consent[6] or (ii) the storage and/or access is strictly necessary for the information society service explicitly requested by the user.

12   Derogations to the rights and obligations provided for in the "ePrivacy" Directive are however possible pursuant to Art. 15, when they constitute a necessary, appropriate and proportionate measure within a democratic society for certain objectives[7].

13   As for the re-use of location data collected by an information society service provider for modelling purposes (e.g., through the operating system or some previously installed application) additional conditions must be met. Indeed, when data have been collected in compliance with Art. 5(3) of the ePrivacy Directive, they can only be further processed with the additional consent of the data subject or on the basis of a Union or Member State law which constitutes a necessary and proportionate measure in a democratic society to safeguard the objectives referred to in Art. 23 (1) GDPR.[8]

2.2 FOCUS ON THE USE OF ANONYMISED LOCATION DATA

14 The EDPB emphasises that when it comes to using location data, preference should always be given to the processing of anonymised data rather than personal data.

15 Anonymisation refers to the use of a set of techniques in order to remove the ability to link the data with an identified or identifiable natural person against any "reasonable" effort. This "reasonability test" must take into account both objective aspects (time, technical means) and contextual elements that may vary case by case (rarity of a phenomenon including population density, nature and volume of data). If the data fails to pass this test, then it has not been anonymised and therefore remains in the scope of the GDPR.

16 Evaluating the robustness of anonymisation relies on three criteria: (i) singling-out (isolating an individual in a larger group based on the data); (ii) linkability (linking together two records concerning the same individual); and (iii) inference (deducing, with significant probability, unknown information about an individual).

17 The concept of anonymisation is prone to being misunderstood and is often mistaken for pseudonymisation. While anonymisation allows using the data without any restriction, pseudonymised data are still in the scope of the GDPR.

18 Many options for effective anonymisation exist[9], but with a caveat. Data cannot be anonymised on their own, meaning that only datasets as a whole may or may not be made anonymous. In this sense, any intervention on a single data pattern (by means of encryption, or any other mathematical transformations) can at best be considered a pseudonymisation.

19 Anonymisation processes and re-identification attacks are active fields of research. It is crucial for any controller implementing anonymisation solutions to monitor recent developments in this field, especially concerning location data (originating from telecom operators and/or information society services) which are known to be notoriously difficult to anonymise.

20 Indeed, a large body of research has shown[10] that *location data thought to be anonymised* may in fact not be. Mobility traces of individuals are inherently highly correlated and unique. Therefore, they can be vulnerable to re-identification attempts under certain circumstances.

21 A single data pattern tracing the location of an individual over a significant period of time cannot be fully anonymised. This assessment may still hold true if the precision of the recorded geographical coordinates is not sufficiently lowered, or if details of the track are removed and even if only the location of places where the data subject stays for substantial amounts of time are retained. This also holds for location data that is poorly aggregated.

22 To achieve anonymisation, location data must be carefully processed in order to meet the reasonability test. In this sense, such a processing includes considering location datasets as a whole, as well as processing data from a reasonably large set of individuals using available robust anonymisation techniques, provided that they are adequately and effectively implemented.

23 Lastly, given the complexity of anonymisation processes, transparency regarding the anonymisation methodology is highly encouraged.

NOTES

4   See Art. 2(c) of the ePrivacy Directive.
5   See Art 6 and 9 of the ePrivacy Directive.
6   The notion of consent in the ePrivacy directive remains the notion of consent in the GDPR and must meet all the requirements of the consent as provided by art. 4(11) and 7 GDPR
7   For the interpretation of article 15 of the "ePrivacy" Directive, see also, CJEU Judgment of 29 January 2008 in case C-275/06, Productores de Música de España (Promusicae) v. Telefónica de España SAU.
8   See section 1.5.3 of the guidelines 1/2020 on processing personal data in the context of connected vehicles.
9   (de Montjoye et al., 2018) "On the privacy-conscientious use of mobile phone data"
10   (de Montjoye et al., 2013) "Unique in the Crowd: The privacy bounds of human mobility" and (Pyrgelis et al., 2017) "Knock Knock, Who's There? Membership Inference on Aggregate Location Data"

3 CONTACT TRACING APPLICATIONS

3.1 GENERAL LEGAL ANALYSIS

[2.342]
24 The systematic and large scale monitoring of location and/or contacts between natural persons is a grave intrusion into their privacy. It can only be legitimised by relying on a voluntary adoption by the users for each of the respective purposes. This would imply, in particular, that individuals who decide not to or cannot use such applications should not suffer from any disadvantage at all.

25 To ensure accountability, the controller of any contact tracing application should be clearly defined. The EDPB considers that the national health authorities could be the controllers[11] for such application; other controllers may also be envisaged. In any cases, if the deployment of contact tracing apps involves different actors their roles and responsibilities must be clearly established from the outset and be explained to the users.

26   In addition, with regard to the principle of purpose limitation, the purposes must be specific enough to exclude further processing for purposes unrelated to the management of the COVID-19 health crisis (e.g., commercial or law enforcement purposes). Once the objective has been clearly defined, it will be necessary to ensure that the use of personal data is adequate, necessary and proportionate.

27   In the context of a contact tracing application, careful consideration should be given to the principle of data minimisation and data protection by design and by default:

* contact tracing apps do not require tracking the location of individual users. Instead, proximity data should be used;
* as contact tracing applications can function without direct identification of individuals, appropriate measures should be put in place to prevent re-identification;
* the collected information should reside on the terminal equipment of the user and only the relevant information should be collected when absolutely necessary.

28   Regarding the lawfulness of the processing, the EDPB notes that contact tracing applications involve storage and/or access to information already stored in the terminal, which are subject to Art. 5(3) of the "ePrivacy" Directive. If those operations are strictly necessary in order for the provider of the application to provide the service explicitly requested by the user the processing would not require his/her consent. For operations that are not strictly necessary, the provider would need to seek the consent of the user.

29   Furthermore, the EDPB notes that the mere fact that the use of contact-tracing applications takes place on a voluntary basis does not mean that the processing of personal data will necessarily be based on consent. When public authorities provide a service based on a mandate assigned by and in line with requirements laid down by law, it appears that the most relevant legal basis for the processing is the necessity for the performance of a task in the public interest, i.e. Art. 6(1)(e) GDPR.

30   Article 6(3) GDPR clarifies that the basis for the processing referred to in article 6(1)(e) shall be laid down by Union or Members State law to which the controller is subject. The purpose of the processing shall be determined in that legal basis or, as regards the processing referred to in point (e) of paragraph 1, shall be necessary for the performance of a task carried out in the public interest or in the exercise of official authority vested in the controller.[12]

31   The legal basis or legislative measure that provides the lawful basis for the use of contact tracing applications should, however, incorporate meaningful safeguards including a reference to the voluntary nature of the application. A clear specification of purpose and explicit limitations concerning the further use of personal data should be included, as well as a clear identification of the controller(s) involved. The categories of data as well as the entities to (and purposes for which, the personal data may be disclosed) should also be identified. Depending on the level of interference, additional safeguards should be incorporated, taking into account the nature, scope and purposes of the processing. Finally, the EDPB also recommends including, as soon as practicable, the criteria to determine when the application shall be dismantled and which entity shall be responsible and accountable for making that determination.

32   However, if the data processing is based on another legal basis, such as consent (Art. 6(1)(a))[13] for example, the controller will have to ensure that the strict requirements for such legal basis to be valid are met.

33   Moreover, the use of an application to fight the COVID-19 pandemic might lead to the collection of health data (for example the status of an infected person). Processing of such data is allowed when such processing is necessary for reasons of public interest in the area of public health, meeting the conditions of art. 9(2)(i) GDPR[14] or for health care purposes as described in Art. 9(2)(h) GDPR[15]. Depending on the legal basis, it might also be based on explicit consent (Art. 9(2)(a) GDPR).

34   In accordance with the initial purpose, Article 9(2)(j) GDPR also allows for health data to be processed when necessary for scientific research purposes or statistical purposes.

35   The current health crisis should not be used as an opportunity to establish disproportionate data retention mandates. Storage limitation should consider the true needs and the medical relevance (this may include epidemiology-motivated considerations like the incubation period, etc.) and personal data should be kept only for the duration of the COVID-19 crisis. Afterwards, as a general rule, all personal data should be erased or anonymised.

36   It is the EDPB's understanding that such apps cannot replace, but only support, manual contact tracing performed by qualified public health personnel, who can sort out whether close contacts are likely to result in virus transmission or not (e.g., when interacting with someone protected by adequate equipment - cashiers, etc. -- or not). The EDPB underlines that procedures and processes including respective algorithms implemented by the contact tracing apps should work under the strict supervision of qualified personnel in order to limit the occurrence of any false positives and negatives. In particular, the task of providing advice on next steps should not be based solely on automated processing.

37   In order to ensure their fairness, accountability and, more broadly, their compliance with the law, algorithms must be auditable and should be regularly reviewed by independent experts. The application's source code should be made publicly available for the widest possible scrutiny.

38   False positives will always occur to a certain degree. As the identification of an infection risk probably can have a high impact on individuals, such as remaining in self isolation until tested negative, the ability to correct data and/or subsequent analysis results is a necessity. This, of course, should only apply to scenarios and implementations where data is processed and/or stored in a way where such correction is technically feasible and where the adverse effects mentioned above are likely to happen.

Part 2   Data Protection: EU Law etc

39   Finally the EDPB considers that a data protection impact assessment (DPIA) must be carried out before implementing such tool as the processing is considered likely high risk (health data, anticipated large-scale adoption, systematic monitoring, use of new technological solution)[16]. The EDPB strongly recommends the publication of DPIAs.

3.2 RECOMMENDATIONS AND FUNCTIONAL REQUIREMENTS

40   According to the principle of data minimization, among other measures of Data Protection by Design and by Default[17], the data processed should be reduced to the strict minimum. The application should not collect unrelated or not needed information, which may include civil status, communication identifiers, equipment directory items, messages, call logs, location data, device identifiers, etc.

41   Data broadcasted by applications must only include some unique and pseudonymous identifiers, generated by and specific to the application. Those identifiers must be renewed regularly, at a frequency compatible with the purpose of containing the spread of the virus, and sufficient to limit the risk of identification and of physical tracking of individuals.

42   Implementations for contact tracing can follow a centralized or a decentralized approach[18]. Both should be considered viable options, provided that adequate security measures are in place, each being accompanied by a set of advantages and disadvantages. Thus, the conceptual phase of app development should always include thorough consideration of both concepts carefully weighing up the respective effects on data protection /privacy and the possible impacts on individuals rights.

43   Any server involved in the contact tracing system must only collect the contact history or the pseudonymous identifiers of a user diagnosed as infected as the result of a proper assessment made by health authorities and of a voluntary action of the user. Alternately, the server must keep a list of pseudonymous identifiers of infected users or their contact history only for the time to inform potentially infected users of their exposure, and should not try to identify potentially infected users.

44   Putting in place a global contact tracing methodology including both applications and manual tracing may require additional information to be processed in some cases. In this context, this additional information should remain on the user terminal and only be processed when strictly necessary and with his prior and specific consent.

45   State-of-the-art cryptographic techniques must be implemented to secure the data stored in servers and applications, exchanges between applications and the remote server. Mutual authentication between the application and the server must also be performed.

46   The reporting of users as COVID-19 infected on the application must be subject to proper authorization, for example through a single-use code tied to a pseudonymous identity of the infected person and linked to a test station or health care professional. If confirmation cannot be obtained in a secure manner, no data processing should take place that presumes the validity of the user's status.

47   The controller, in collaboration with the public authorities, have to clearly and explicitly inform about the link to download the official national contact tracing app in order to mitigate the risk that individuals use a third-party app.

NOTES

[11]   See also European Commission "Guidance on Apps supporting the fight against COVID 19 pandemic in relation to data protection" Brussels, 16.4.2020 C(2020) 2523 final.

[12]   See Recital (41).

[13]   Controllers (especially public authorities) must pay special attention to the fact that consent should not be regarded as freely given if the individual has no genuine choice to refuse or withdraw its consent without detriment.

[14]   The processing must be based on Union or Member State law which provides for suitable and specific measures to safeguard the rights and freedoms of the data subject, in particular professional secrecy.

[15]   See Article 9(2)(h) GDPR

[16]   See WP29 guidelines (adopted by the EDPB) on Data Protection Impact Assessment (DPIA) and determining whether processing is "likely to result in a high risk" for the purposes of Regulation 2016/679.

[17]   See EDPB Guidelines 4/2019 on Article 25 Data Protection by Design and by Default

[18]   In general, the decentralised solution is more in line with the minimisation principle

4 CONCLUSION

[2.343]

48   The world is facing a significant public health crisis that requires strong responses, which will have an impact beyond this emergency. Automated data processing and digital technologies can be key components in the fight against COVID-19. However, one should be wary of the "ratchet effect". It is our responsibility to ensure that every measure taken in these extraordinary circumstances are necessary, limited in time, of minimal extent and subject to periodic and genuine review as well as to scientific evaluation.

49   The EDPB underlines that one should not have to choose between an efficient response to the current crisis and the protection of our fundamental rights: we can achieve both, and moreover data protection principles can play a very important role in the fight against the virus. European data protection law allows for the responsible use of personal data for health management purposes, while also ensuring that individual rights and freedoms are not eroded in the process.

For the European Data Protection Board

The Chair

(Andrea Jelinek)

ANNEX – CONTACT TRACING APPLICATIONS ANALYSIS GUIDE

0. DISCLAIMER

[2.344]
The following guidance is neither prescriptive nor exhaustive, and its sole purpose of this guide is to provide general guidance to designers and implementers of contact tracing applications. Other solutions than the ones described here can be used and can be lawful as long as they comply with the relevant legal framework (i.e. GDPR and the "ePrivacy" Directive).

It must also be noted that this guide is of a general nature. Consequently, the recommendations and obligations contained in this document must not be seen as exhaustive. Any assessment must be carried out on a case-by-case basis, and specific applications may require additional measures not included in this guide.

1. SUMMARY

In many Member States stakeholders are considering the use of contact tracing* applications to help the population discover whether they have been in contact with a person infected with SARS-Cov-2*.

The conditions under which such applications would contribute effectively to the management of the pandemic are not yet established. And these conditions would need to be established prior to any implementation of such an app. Yet, it is relevant to provide guidelines bringing relevant information to development teams upstream, so that the protection of personal data can be guaranteed from the early design stage.

It must be noted that this guide is of a general nature. Consequently, the recommendations and obligations contained in this document must not be seen as exhaustive. Any assessment must be carried out on a case-by-case basis, and specific applications may require additional measures not included in this guide. The purpose of this guide is to provide general guidance to designers and implementers of contact tracing applications.

Some criteria might go beyond the strict requirements stemming from the data protection framework. They aim at ensuring the highest level of transparency, in order to favour social acceptance of such contact tracing applications.

To this end, publishers of contact tracing applications should take into account the following criteria:
- The use of such an application must be strictly voluntary. It may not condition the access to any rights guaranteed by law. Individuals must have full control over their data at all times, and should be able to choose freely to use such an application.
- Contact tracing applications are likely to result in a high risk to the rights and freedoms of natural persons and to require a data protection impact assessment to be conducted prior to their deployment.
- Information on the proximity between users of the application can be obtained without locating them. This kind of application does not need, and, hence, should not involve the use of location data.
- When a user is diagnosed infected with the SARS-Cov-2 virus, only the persons with whom the user has been in close contact within the epidemiologically relevant retention period for contact tracing, should be informed.
- The operation of this type of application might require, depending on the architecture that is chosen, the use of a centralised server. In such a case and in accordance with the principles of data minimisation and data protection by design, the data processed by the centralised server should be limited to the bare minimum:
    - When a user is diagnosed as infected, information regarding its previous close contacts or the identifiers broadcasted by the user's application can be collected, only with the user's agreement. A verification method needs to be established that allows asserting that the person is indeed infected without identifying the user. Technically this could be achieved by alerting contacts only following the intervention of a healthcare professional, for example by using a special one-time code.
    - The information stored on the central server should neither allow the controller to identify users diagnosed as infected or having been in contact with those users, nor should it allow the inference of contact patterns not needed for the determination of relevant contacts.
- The operation of this type of application requires to broadcast data that is read by devices of other users and listening to these broadcasts:
    - It is sufficient to exchange pseudonymous identifiers between users' mobile equipment (computers, tablets, connected watches, etc.), for example by broadcasting them (e.g. via the Bluetooth Low Energy technology).
    - Identifiers must be generated using state-of-the-art cryptographic processes.
    - Identifiers must be renewed on a regular basis to reduce the risk of physical tracking and linkage attacks.
- This type of application must be secured to guarantee safe technical processes. In particular:
    - The application should not convey to the users information that allows them to infer the identity or the diagnosis of others. The central server must neither identify users, nor infer information about them.

Part 2   Data Protection: EU Law etc

Disclaimer: the above principles are related to the claimed purpose of *contact tracing* applications, and to this purpose only, which only aim to automatically inform people potentially exposed to the virus (without having to identify them).The operators of the application and its infrastructure may be controlled by the competent supervisory authority. Following all or part of these guidelines is not necessarily sufficient to ensure a full compliance to the data protection framework.

2. DEFINITIONS

Contact	For a contact tracing application, a contact is a user who has participated in an interaction with a user confirmed to be a carrier of the virus, and whose duration and distance induce a risk of significant exposure to the virus infection. Parameters for duration of exposure and distance between people must be estimated by the health authorities and can be set in the application.
Location data	It refers to all data processed in an electronic communications network or by an electronic communications service indicating the geographical position of the terminal equipment of a user of a publicly available electronic communications service (as defined in the e-Privacy Directive), as well as data from potential other sources, relating to:
	• the latitude, longitude or altitude of the terminal equipment;
	• the direction of travel of the user; or
	• the time the location information was recorded.
Interaction	In the context of the contact tracing application, an interaction is defined as the exchange of information between two devices located in close proximity to each other (in space and time), within the range of the communication technology used (e.g. Bluetooth). This definition excludes the location of the two users of the interaction.
Virus carrier	In this document, we consider virus carriers to be users who have been tested positive for the virus and who have received an official diagnosis from physicians or health centres.
Contact tracing	People who have been in close contact (according to criteria to be defined by epidemiologists) with an individual infected with the virus run a significant risk of also being infected and of infecting others in turn. Contact tracing is a disease control methodology that lists all people who have been in close proximity to a carrier of the virus so as to check whether they are at risk of infection and take the appropriate sanitary measures towards them.

3. GENERAL

GEN-1	The application must be a complementary tool to traditional contact tracing techniques (notably interviews with infected persons), i.e. be part of a wider public health program. It must be used only up until the point manual contact tracing techniques can manage alone the amount of new infections.
GEN-2	At the latest when "return to normal" is decided by the competent public authorities, a procedure must be put in place to stop the collection of identifiers (global deactivation of the application, instructions to uninstall the application, automatic uninstallation, etc.) and to activate the deletion of all collected data from all databases (mobile applications and servers).
GEN-3	The source code of the application and of its backend must be open, and the technical specifications must be made public, so that any concerned party can audit the code, and where relevant - contribute to improving the code, correcting possible bugs and ensuring transparency in the processing of personal data.
GEN-4	The stages of deployment of the application must make it possible to progressively validate its effectiveness from a public health point of view. An evaluation protocol, specifying indicators allowing to measure the effectiveness of the application, must be defined upstream for this purpose.

4. PURPOSES

PUR-1	The application must pursue the sole purpose of contact tracing so that people potentially exposed to the SARS-Cov-2 virus can be alerted and taken care of. It must not be used for another purpose.
PUR-2	The application must not be diverted from its primary use for the purpose of monitoring compliance with quarantine or confinement measures and/or social distancing.
PUR-3	The application must not be used to draw conclusions on the location of the users based on their interaction and/or any other means.

5. FUNCTIONAL CONSIDERATIONS

FUNC-1	The application must provide a functionality enabling users to be informed that they have been potentially exposed to the virus, this information being based on proximity to an infected user within a window of X days prior to the positive screening test (the X value being defined by the health authorities).

FUNC-2	The application should provide recommendations to users identified as having being potentially exposed to the virus. It should relay instructions regarding the measures they should follow, and they should allow the user to request advises. In such cases, a human intervention would be mandatory.
FUNC-3	The algorithm measuring the risk of infection by taking into account factors of distance and time and thus determining when a contact has to be recorded in the contact tracing list, must be securely tune-able to take into account the most recent knowledge on the spread of the virus.
FUNC-4	**Users must be informed in case they have been exposed to the virus**, or must regularly obtain information on whether or not they have been exposed to the virus, within the incubation period of the virus.
FUNC-5	The application should be interoperable with other applications developed across EU Member States, so that users travelling across different Member States can be efficiently notified.

6. DATA

DATA-1	The application must be able to broadcast and receive data via proximity communication technologies like Bluetooth Low Energy so that contact tracing can be carried out.
DATA-2	This broadcast data must include cryptographically strong pseudo-random identifiers, generated by and specific to the application.
DATA-3	The risk of collision between pseudo-random identifiers should be sufficiently low.
DATA-4	Pseudo-random identifiers must be renewed regularly, at a frequency sufficient to limit the risk of re-identification, physical tracking or linkage of individuals, by anyone including central server operators, other application users or malicious third parties. These identifiers must be generated by the user's application, possibly based on a seed provided by the central server.
DATA-5	According to the data minimisation principle, the application must not collect data other than what is strictly necessary for the purpose of contact tracing
DATA-6	The application must not collect location data for the purpose of contact tracing. Location data can be processed for the sole purpose of allowing the application to interact with similar applications in other countries and should be limited in precision to what is strictly necessary for this sole purpose.
DATA-7	The application should not collect health data in addition to those that are strictly necessary for the purposes of the app, except on an optional basis and for the sole purpose of assisting in the decision making process of informing the user.
DATA-8	Users must be informed of all personal data that will be collected. This data should be collected only with the user authorization.

7. TECHNICAL PROPERTIES

TECH-1	The application should available technologies such as use proximity communication technology (e.g. Bluetooth Low Energy) to detect users in the vicinity of the device running the application.
TECH-2	The application should keep the history of a user's contacts in the equipment, for a predefined limited period of time.
TECH-3	The application may rely on a central server to implement some of its functionalities.
TECH-4	The application must be based on an architecture relying as much as possible on users' devices.
TECH-5	At the initiative of users reported as infected by the virus and after confirmation of their status by an appropriately certified health professional, their contact history or their own identifiers should be transmitted to the central server.

8. SECURITY

SEC-1	A mechanism must verify the status of users who report as SARS-CoV-2positive in the application, for example by providing a single-use code linked to a test station or health care professional. If confirmation cannot be obtained in a secure manner, data must not be processed.
SEC-2	The data sent to the central server must be transmitted over a secure channel. The use of notification services provided by OS platform providers should be carefully assessed, and should not lead to disclosing any data to third parties.
SEC-3	Requests must not be vulnerable to tampering by a malicious user
SEC-4	State-of-the-art cryptographic techniques must be implemented to secure exchanges between the application and the server and between applications and as a general rule to protect the information stored in the applications and on the server. Examples of techniques that can be used include for example : symmetric and asymmetric encryption, hash functions, private membership test, private set intersection, Bloom filters, private information retrieval, homomorphic encryption, etc.
SEC-5	The central server must not keep network connection identifiers (e.g., IP addresses) of any users including those who have been positively diagnosed and who transmitted their contacts history or their own identifiers.

Part 2   Data Protection: EU Law etc

SEC-6	In order to avoid impersonation or the creation of fake users, the server must authenticate the application.
SEC-7	The application must authenticate the central server.
SEC-8	The server functionalities should be protected from replay attacks.
SEC-9	The information transmitted by the central server must be signed in order to authenticate its origin and integrity.
SEC-10	Access to all data stored in the central server and not publicly available must be restricted to authorised persons only.
SEC-11	The device's permission manager at the operating system level must only request the permissions necessary to access and use when necessary the communication modules, to store the data in the terminal, and to exchange information with the central server.

9. PROTECTION OF PERSONAL DATA AND PRIVACY OF NATURAL PERSONS

Reminder: the following guidelines concern an application whose sole purpose is contact tracing.

PRIV-1	Data exchanges must be respectful of the users' privacy (and notably respect the principle of data minimisation).
PRIV-2	The application must not allow users to be directly identified when using the application.
PRIV-3	The application must not allow users' movements to be traced.
PRIV-4	The use of the application should not allow users to learn anything about other users (and notably whether they are virus carriers or not).
PRIV-5	Trust in the central server must be limited. The management of the central server must follow clearly defined governance rules and include all necessary measures to ensure its security. The localization of the central server should allow an effective supervision by the competent supervisory authority.
PRIV-6	A Data Protection Impact Assessment must be carried out and should be made public.
PRIV-7	The application should only reveal to the user whether they have been exposed to the virus, and, if possible without revealing information about other users, the number of times and dates of exposure.
PRIV-8	The information conveyed by the application must not allow users to identify users carrying the virus, nor their movements.
PRIV-9	The information conveyed by the application must not allow health authorities to identify potentially exposed users without their agreement.
PRIV-10	Requests made by the applications to the central server must not reveal anything about the virus carrier.
PRIV-11	Requests made by the applications to the central server must not reveal any unnecessary information about the user, except, possibly, and only when necessary, for their pseudonymous identifiers and their contact list.
PRIV-12	Linkage attacks must not be possible.
PRIV-13	Users must be able to exercise their rights via the application.
PRIV-14	Deletion of the application must result in the deletion of all locally collected data.
PRIV-15	The application should only collect data transmitted by instances of the application or interoperable equivalent applications. No data relating to other applications and/or proximity communication devices shall be collected.
PRIV-16	In order to avoid re-identification by the central server, proxy servers should be implemented. The purpose of these *non-colluding servers is to* mix the identifiers of several users (both those of virus carriers and those sent by requesters) before sharing them with the central server, so as to prevent the central server from knowing the identifiers (such as IP addresses) of users.
PRIV-17	The application and the server must be carefully developed and configured in order not to collect any unnecessary data (e.g., no identifiers should be included in the server logs, etc.) and in order to avoid the use of any third party SDK collecting data for other purposes.

Most contact tracing applications currently being discussed follow basically two approaches when a user is declared infected: they can either send to a server the history of proximity contacts they have obtained through scanning, or they can send the list of their own identifiers that were broadcasted. The following principles are declined according to these two approaches. While these approaches are discussed here, that does not mean other approaches are not possible or even preferable, for example approaches that implement some form of E2E encryption or apply other security or privacy enhancing technologies.

9.1. Principles that apply only when the application sends to the server a list of contacts:

CON-1	The central server must collect the contact history of users reported as positive to COVID-19 as a result of voluntary action on their part.
CON-2	The central server must not maintain nor circulate a list of the pseudonymous identifiers of users carrying the virus.

CON-3	Contact history stored on the central server must be deleted once users are notified of their proximity with a positively diagnosed person.
CON-4	Except when the user detected as positive shares his contact history with the central server or when the user makes a request to the server to find out his potential exposure to the virus, no data must leave the user's equipment.
CON-5	Any identifier included in the local history must be deleted after X days from its collection (the X value being defined by the health authorities).
CON-6	Contact histories submitted by distinct users should not further be processed e.g. cross-correlated to build global proximity maps.
CON-7	Data in server logs must be minimised and must comply with data protection requirements

9.2. Principles that apply only when the application sends to a server a list of its own identifiers:

ID-1	The central server must collect the identifiers broadcast by the application of users reported as positive to COVID-19, as a result of voluntary action on their part.
ID-2	The central server must not maintain nor circulate the contact history of users carrying the virus.
ID-3	Identifiers stored on the central server must be deleted once they were distributed to the other applications.
ID-4	Except when the user detected as positive shares his identifiers with the central server, no data must leave the user's equipment or when the user makes a request to the server to find his potential exposure to the virus, no data must leave the user's equipment.
ID-5	Data in server logs must be minimised and must comply with data protection requirements

EUROPEAN DATA PROTECTION BOARD: GUIDELINES 5/2020 ON CONSENT UNDER REGULATION 2016/679
Version 1.1
Adopted on 4 May 2020

[2.345]

NOTES
© European Data Protection Board.

VERSION HISTORY

Version 1.1: 13 May 2020 — Formatting corrections

Version 1.0: 4 May 2020 — Adoption of the Guidelines

TABLE OF CONTENTS

THE EUROPEAN DATA PROTECTION BOARD

Having regard to Article 70 (1)(e) of the Regulation 2016/679/EU of the European Parliament and of the Council of 27 April 2016 on the protection of natural persons with regard to the processing of personal data and on the free movement of such data, and repealing Directive 95/46/EC, (hereinafter "GDPR"),

Having regard to the EEA Agreement and in particular to Annex XI and Protocol 37 thereof, as amended by the Decision of the EEA joint Committee No 154/2018 of 6 July 2018[1],

Having regard to Article 12 and Article 22 of its Rules of Procedure,

Having regard to the Article 29 Working Party Guidelines on consent under Regulation 2016/679, WP259 rev.01,

HAS ADOPTED THE FOLLOWING GUIDELINES

[1] References to "Member States" made throughout this document should be understood as references to "EEA Member States".

0 PREFACE

[2.346]
On 10 April 2018 the Article 29 Working Party adopted its Guidelines on consent under Regulation 2016/679 (WP259.01), which were endorsed by the European Data Protection Board (hereinafter "EDPB") at its first Plenary meeting. This document is a slightly updated version of those Guidelines. Any reference to the WP29 Guidelines on consent (WP259 rev.01) should from now on be interpreted as a reference to these guidelines.

The EDPB has noticed that there was a need for further clarifications, specifically regarding two questions:
(1) 1 The validity of consent provided by the data subject when interacting with so-called "cookie walls";
(2) 2 The example 16 on scrolling and consent.

The paragraphs concerning these two issues have been revised and updated, while the rest of the document was left unchanged, except for editorial changes. The revision concerns, more specifically:
• Section on Conditionality (paragraphs 38 - 41).
• Section on Unambiguous indication of wishes (paragraph 86)

1 INTRODUCTION

[2.347]
1. These Guidelines provide a thorough analysis of the notion of consent in Regulation 2016/679, the General Data Protection Regulation (hereafter: GDPR). The concept of consent as used in the Data Protection Directive (hereafter: Directive 95/46/EC) and in the e-Privacy Directive to date, has evolved. The GDPR provides further clarification and specification of the requirements for obtaining and demonstrating valid consent. These Guidelines focus on these changes, providing practical guidance to ensure compliance with the GDPR and building upon the Article 29 Working Party Opinion 15/2011 on consent. The obligation is on controllers to innovate to find new solutions that operate within the parameters of the law and better support the protection of personal data and the interests of data subjects.

2. Consent remains one of six lawful bases to process personal data, as listed in Article 6 of the GDPR.[2] When initiating activities that involve processing of personal data, a controller must always take time to consider what would be the appropriate lawful ground for the envisaged processing.

3. Generally, consent can only be an appropriate lawful basis if a data subject is offered control and is offered a genuine choice with regard to accepting or declining the terms offered or declining them without detriment. When asking for consent, a controller has the duty to assess whether it will meet all the requirements to obtain valid consent. If obtained in full compliance with the GDPR, consent is a tool that gives data subjects control over whether or not personal data concerning them will be processed. If not, the data subject's control becomes illusory and consent will be an invalid basis for processing, rendering the processing activity unlawful.[3]

4. The existing Article 29 Working Party (WP29) Opinions on consent[4] remain relevant, where consistent with the new legal framework, as the GDPR codifies existing WP29 guidance and general good practice and most of the key elements of consent remain the same under the GDPR. Therefore, in this document, the EDPB expands upon and completes earlier Article 29 Working Party Opinions on specific topics that include reference to consent under Directive 95/46/EC, rather than replacing them.

5. As the WP29 stated in its Opinion 15/2011 on the definition on consent, inviting people to accept a data processing operation should be subject to rigorous requirements, since it concerns the fundamental rights of data subjects and the controller wishes to engage in a processing operation that would be unlawful without the data subject's consent.[5] The crucial role of consent is underlined by Articles 7 and 8 of the Charter of Fundamental Rights of the European Union. Furthermore, obtaining consent also does not negate or in any way diminish the controller's obligations to observe the principles of processing enshrined in the GDPR, especially Article 5 of the GDPR with regard to fairness, necessity and proportionality, as well as data quality. Even if the processing of personal data is based on consent of the data subject, this would not legitimise collection of data, which is not necessary in relation to a specified purpose of processing and be fundamentally unfair.[6]

6. Meanwhile, the EDPB is aware of the review of the ePrivacy Directive (2002/58/EC). The notion of consent in the draft ePrivacy Regulation remains linked to the notion of consent in the GDPR.[7] Organisations are likely to need consent under the ePrivacy instrument for most online marketing messages or marketing calls, and online tracking methods including by the use of cookies or apps or other software. The EDPB has already provided recommendations and guidance to the European legislator on the Proposal for a Regulation on ePrivacy.[8]

7. With regard to the existing e-Privacy Directive, the EDPB notes that references to the repealed Directive 95/46/EC shall be construed as references to the GDPR.[9] This also applies to references to consent in the current Directive 2002/58/EC, as the ePrivacy Regulation will not (yet) be in force from

25 May 2018. According to Article 95 GDPR, additional obligations in relation to processing in connection with the provision of publicly available electronic communications services in public communication networks shall not be imposed insofar the e-Privacy Directive imposes specific obligations with the same objective. The EDPB notes that the requirements for consent under the GDPR are not considered to be an 'additional obligation', but rather as preconditions for lawful processing. Therefore, the GDPR conditions for obtaining valid consent are applicable in situations falling within the scope of the e-Privacy Directive.

NOTES

2   Article 9 GDPR provides a list of possible exemptions to the ban on processing special categories of data. One of the exemptions listed is the situation where the data subject provides explicit consent to the use of this data.

3   See also Article 29 Working Party Opinion 15/2011 on the definition of consent (WP 187), pp. 6-8, and/or Opinion 06/2014 on the notion of legitimate interests of the data controller under Article 7 of Directive 95/46/EC (WP 217), pp. 9, 10, 13 and 14.

4   Most notably, Opinion 15/2011 on the definition of consent (WP 187).

5   Opinion 15/2011, page on the definition of consent (WP 187), p. 8.

6   See also Opinion 15/2011 on the definition of consent (WP 187), and Article 5 GDPR.

7   According to Article 9 of the proposed ePrivacy Regulation, the definition of and the conditions for consent provided for in Articles 4(11) and Article 7 of the GDPR apply.

8   See EDPB statement on ePrivacy - 25/05/2018 and EDPB Statement 3/2019 on an ePrivacy regulation.

9   See Article 94 GDPR.

2 CONSENT IN ARTICLE 4(11) OF THE GDPR

[2.348]

8.   Article 4(11) of the GDPR defines consent as: *"any freely given, specific, informed and unambiguous indication of the data subject's wishes by which he or she, by a statement or by a clear affirmative action, signifies agreement to the processing of personal data relating to him or her."*

9.   The basic concept of consent remains similar to that under the Directive 95/46/EC and consent is one of the lawful grounds on which personal data processing has to be based, pursuant to Article 6 of the GDPR.[10] Besides the amended definition in Article 4(11), the GDPR provides additional guidance in Article 7 and in recitals 32, 33, 42, and 43 as to how the controller must act to comply with the main elements of the consent requirement.

10.   Finally, the inclusion of specific provisions and recitals on the withdrawal of consent confirms that consent should be a reversible decision and that there remains a degree of control on the side of the data subject.

NOTES

10   Consent was defined in Directive 95/46/EC as *"any freely given specific and informed indication of his wishes by which the data subject signifies his agreement to personal data relating to him being processed"* which must be *'unambiguously given'* in order to make the processing of personal data legitimate (Article 7(a) of Directive 95/46/EC)). See WP29 Opinion 15/2011 on the definition of consent (WP 187) for examples on the appropriateness of consent as lawful basis. In this Opinion, WP29 has provided guidance to distinguish where consent is an appropriate lawful basis from those where relying on the legitimate interest ground (perhaps with an opportunity to opt out) is sufficient or a contractual relation would be recommended. See also WP29 Opinion 06/2014, paragraph III.1.2, p. 14 and further. Explicit consent is also one of the exemptions to the prohibition on the processing of special categories of data: See Article 9 GDPR.

3 ELEMENTS OF VALID CONSENT

[2.349]

11.   Article 4(11) of the GDPR stipulates that consent of the data subject means any:

- freely given,
- specific,
- informed and
- unambiguous indication of the data subject's wishes by which he or she, by a statement or by a clear affirmative action, signifies agreement to the processing of personal data relating to him or her.

12.   In the sections below, it is analysed to what extent the wording of Article 4(11) requires controllers to change their consent requests/forms, in order to ensure compliance with the GDPR.[11]

3.1 FREE / FREELY GIVEN[12]

13.   The element "free" implies real choice and control for data subjects. As a general rule, the GDPR prescribes that if the data subject has no real choice, feels compelled to consent or will endure negative consequences if they do not consent, then consent will not be valid.[13] If consent is bundled up as a non-negotiable part of terms and conditions it is presumed not to have been freely given. Accordingly, consent will not be considered to be free if the data subject is unable to refuse or withdraw his or her consent without detriment.[14] The notion of imbalance between the controller and the data subject is also taken into consideration by the GDPR.

14.   When assessing whether consent is freely given, one should also take into account the specific situation of tying consent into contracts or the provision of a service as described in Article 7(4). Article 7(4) has been drafted in a non-exhaustive fashion by the words "inter alia", meaning that there may be a range of other situations, which are caught by this provision. In general terms, any element of inappropriate pressure or influence upon the data subject (which may be manifested in many different ways) which prevents a data subject from exercising their free will, shall render the consent invalid.

---

15. Example 1: A mobile app for photo editing asks its users to have their GPS localisation activated for the use of its services. The app also tells its users it will use the collected data for behavioural advertising purposes. Neither geolocalisation or online behavioural advertising are necessary for the provision of the photo editing service and go beyond the delivery of the core service provided. Since users cannot use the app without consenting to these purposes, the consent cannot be considered as being freely given.

3.1.1 Imbalance of power

16. Recital 43[15] clearly indicates that it is unlikely that **public authorities** can rely on consent for processing as whenever the controller is a public authority, there is often a clear imbalance of power in the relationship between the controller and the data subject. It is also clear in most cases that the data subject will have no realistic alternatives to accepting the processing (terms) of this controller. The EDPB considers that there are other lawful bases that are, in principle, more appropriate to the activity of public authorities.[16]

17. Without prejudice to these general considerations, the use of consent as a lawful basis for data processing by public authorities is not totally excluded under the legal framework of the GDPR. The following examples show that the use of consent can be appropriate under certain circumstances.

---

18. Example 2: A local municipality is planning road maintenance works. As the road works may disrupt traffic for a long time, the municipality offers its citizens the opportunity to subscribe to an email list to receive updates on the progress of the works and on expected delays. The municipality makes clear that there is no obligation to participate and asks for consent to use email addresses for this (exclusive) purpose. Citizens that do not consent will not miss out on any core service of the municipality or the exercise of any right, so they are able to give or refuse their consent to this use of data freely. All information on the road works will also be available on the municipality's website.

---

19. Example 3: An individual who owns land needs certain permits from both her local municipality and from the provincial government under which the municipality resides. Both public bodies require the same information for issuing their permit, but are not accessing each other's databases. Therefore, both ask for the same information and the land owner sends out her details to both public bodies. The municipality and the provincial authority ask for her consent to merge the files, to avoid duplicate procedures and correspondence. Both public bodies ensure that this is optional and that the permit requests will still be processed separately if she decides not to consent to the merger of her data. The land owner is able to give consent to the authorities for the purpose of merging the files freely.

---

20. Example 4: A public school asks students for consent to use their photographs in a printed student magazine. Consent in these situations would be a genuine choice as long as students will not be denied education or services and could refuse the use of these photographs without any detriment.[17]

---

21. An imbalance of power also occurs in the **employment** context.[18] Given the dependency that results from the employer/employee relationship, it is unlikely that the data subject is able to deny his/her employer consent to data processing without experiencing the fear or real risk of detrimental effects as a result of a refusal. It is unlikely that an employee would be able to respond freely to a request for consent from his/her employer to, for example, activate monitoring systems such as camera observation in a workplace, or to fill out assessment forms, without feeling any pressure to consent.[19] Therefore, the EDPB deems it problematic for employers to process personal data of current or future employees on the basis of consent as it is unlikely to be freely given. For the majority of such data processing at work, the lawful basis cannot and should not be the consent of the employees (Article 6(1)(a)) due to the nature of the relationship between employer and employee.[20]

22. However, this does not mean that employers can never rely on consent as a lawful basis for processing. There may be situations when it is possible for the employer to demonstrate that consent actually is freely given. Given the imbalance of power between an employer and its staff members, employees can only give free consent in exceptional circumstances, when it will have no adverse consequences at all whether or not they give consent.[21]

---

23. Example 5: A film crew is going to be filming in a certain part of an office. The employer asks all the employees who sit in that area for their consent to be filmed, as they may appear in the background of the video. Those who do not want to be filmed are not penalised in any way but instead are given equivalent desks elsewhere in the building for the duration of the filming.

24. Imbalances of power are not limited to public authorities and employers, they may also occur in other situations. As highlighted by the WP29 in several Opinions, consent can only be valid if the data subject is able to exercise a real choice, and there is no risk of deception, intimidation, coercion or significant negative consequences (e.g. substantial extra costs) if he/she does not consent. Consent will not be free in cases where there is any element of compulsion, pressure or inability to exercise free will.

3.1.2 Conditionality

25. To assess whether consent is freely given, Article 7(4) GDPR plays an important role.[22]

26. Article 7(4) GDPR indicates that, inter alia, the situation of "bundling" consent with acceptance of terms or conditions, or "tying" the provision of a contract or a service to a request for consent to process personal data that are not necessary for the performance of that contract or service, is considered highly undesirable. If consent is given in this situation, it is presumed to be not freely given (recital 43). Article 7(4) seeks to ensure that the purpose of personal data processing is not disguised nor bundled with the provision of a contract of a service for which these personal data are not necessary. In doing so, the GDPR ensures that the processing of personal data for which consent is sought cannot become directly or indirectly the counter-performance of a contract. The two lawful bases for the lawful processing of personal data, i.e. consent and contract cannot be merged and blurred.

27. Compulsion to agree with the use of personal data additional to what is strictly necessary limits data subject's choices and stands in the way of free consent. As data protection law is aiming at the protection of fundamental rights, an individual's control over their personal data is essential and there is a strong presumption that consent to the processing of personal data that is unnecessary, cannot be seen as a mandatory consideration in exchange for the performance of a contract or the provision of a service.

28. Hence, whenever a request for consent is tied to the performance of a contract by the controller, a data subject that does not wish to make his/her personal data available for processing by the controller runs the risk to be denied services they have requested.

29. To assess whether such a situation of bundling or tying occurs, it is important to determine what the scope of the contract is and what data would be necessary for the performance of that contract.

30. According to Opinion 06/2014 of WP29, the term "necessary for the performance of a contract" needs to be interpreted strictly. The processing must be necessary to fulfil the contract with each individual data subject. This may include, for example, processing the address of the data subject so that goods purchased online can be delivered, or processing credit card details in order to facilitate payment. In the employment context, this ground may allow, for example, the processing of salary information and bank account details so that wages can be paid.[23] There needs to be a direct and objective link between the processing of the data and the purpose of the execution of the contract.

31. If a controller seeks to process personal data that are in fact necessary for the performance of a contract, then consent is not the appropriate lawful basis.[24]

32. Article 7(4) is only relevant where the requested data are **not** necessary for the performance of the contract, (including the provision of a service), and the performance of that contract is made conditional on the obtaining of these data on the basis of consent. Conversely, if processing **is** necessary to perform the contract (including to provide a service), then Article 7(4) does not apply.

---

33. Example 6: A bank asks customers for consent to allow third parties to use their payment details for direct marketing purposes. This processing activity is not necessary for the performance of the contract with the customer and the delivery of ordinary bank account services. If the customer's refusal to consent to this processing purpose would lead to the denial of banking services, closure of the bank account, or, depending on the case, an increase of the fee, consent cannot be freely given.

---

34. The choice of the legislator to highlight conditionality, amongst others, as a presumption of a lack of freedom to consent, demonstrates that the occurrence of conditionality must be carefully scrutinized. The term "utmost account" in Article 7(4) suggests that special caution is needed from the controller when a contract (which could include the provision of a service) has a request for consent to process personal data tied to it.

35. As the wording of Article 7(4) is not construed in an absolute manner, there might be very limited space for cases where this conditionality would not render the consent invalid. However, the word "presumed" in Recital 43 clearly indicates that such cases will be highly exceptional.

36. In any event, the burden of proof in Article 7(4) is on the controller.[25] This specific rule reflects the general principle of accountability, which runs throughout the GDPR. However, when Article 7(4) applies, it will be more difficult for the controller to prove that consent was given freely by the data subject.[26]

37. The controller could argue that his organisation offers data subjects genuine choice if they were able to choose between a service that includes consenting to the use of personal data for additional purposes on the one hand, and an equivalent service offered by the same controller that does not involve consenting to data use for additional purposes on the other hand. As long as there is a possibility to have the contract performed or the contracted service delivered by this controller without consenting to the other or additional data use in question, this means there is no longer a conditional service. However, both services need to be genuinely equivalent.

38.   The EDPB considers that consent cannot be considered as freely given if a controller argues that a choice exists between its service that includes consenting to the use of personal data for additional purposes on the one hand, and an equivalent service offered by a different controller on the other hand. In such a case, the freedom of choice would be made dependent on what other market players do and whether an individual data subject would find the other controller's services genuinely equivalent. It would furthermore imply an obligation for controllers to monitor market developments to ensure the continued validity of consent for their data processing activities, as a competitor may alter its service at a later stage. Hence, using this argument means a consent relying on an alternative option offered by a third party fails to comply with the GDPR, meaning that a service provider cannot prevent data subjects from accessing a service on the basis that they do not consent.

39.   In order for consent to be freely given, access to services and functionalities must not be made conditional on the consent of a user to the storing of information, or gaining of access to information already stored, in the terminal equipment of a user (so called cookie walls)[27].

---

40.   Example 6a: A website provider puts into place a script that will block content from being visible except for a request to accept cookies and the information about which cookies are being set and for what purposes data will be processed. There is no possibility to access the content without clicking on the "Accept cookies" button. Since the data subject is not presented with a genuine choice, its consent is not freely given.

41.   This does not constitute valid consent, as the provision of the service relies on the data subject clicking the "Accept cookies" button. It is not presented with a genuine choice.

3.1.3 Granularity

42.   A service may involve multiple processing operations for more than one purpose. In such cases, the data subjects should be free to choose which purpose they accept, rather than having to consent to a bundle of processing purposes. In a given case, several consents may be warranted to start offering a service, pursuant to the GDPR.

43.   Recital 43 clarifies that consent is presumed not to be freely given if the process/procedure for obtaining consent does not allow data subjects to give separate consent for personal data processing operations respectively (e.g. only for some processing operations and not for others) despite it being appropriate in the individual case. Recital 32 states, *"Consent should cover all processing activities carried out for the same purpose or purposes. When the processing has multiple purposes, consent should be given for all of them"*.

44.   If the controller has conflated several purposes for processing and has not attempted to seek separate consent for each purpose, there is a lack of freedom. This granularity is closely related to the need of consent to be specific, as discussed in section 3.2 further below. When data processing is done in pursuit of several purposes, the solution to comply with the conditions for valid consent lies in granularity, i.e. the separation of these purposes and obtaining consent for each purpose.

---

45.   Example 7: Within the same consent request a retailer asks its customers for consent to use their data to send them marketing by email and also to share their details with other companies within their group. This consent is not granular as there is no separate consents for these two separate purposes, therefore the consent will not be valid. In this case, a specific consent should be collected to send the contact details to commercial partners. Such specific consent will be deemed valid for each partner (see also section 3.3.1), whose identity has been provided to the data subject at the time of the collection of his or her consent, insofar as it is sent to them for the same purpose (in this example: a marketing purpose).

3.1.4 Detriment

46.   The controller needs to demonstrate that it is possible to refuse or withdraw consent without detriment (recital 42). For example, the controller needs to prove that withdrawing consent does not lead to any costs for the data subject and thus no clear disadvantage for those withdrawing consent.

47.   Other examples of detriment are deception, intimidation, coercion or significant negative consequences if a data subject does not consent. The controller should be able to prove that the data subject had a free or genuine choice about whether to consent and that it was possible to withdraw consent without detriment.

48.   If a controller is able to show that a service includes the possibility to withdraw consent without any negative consequences e.g. without the performance of the service being downgraded to the detriment of the user, this may serve to show that the consent was given freely. The GDPR does not preclude all incentives but the onus would be on the controller to demonstrate that consent was still freely given in all the circumstances.

---

49. Example 8: When downloading a lifestyle mobile app, the app asks for consent to access the phone's accelerometer. This is not necessary for the app to work, but it is useful for the controller who wishes to learn more about the movements and activity levels of its users. When the user later revokes that consent, she finds out that the app now only works to a limited extent. This is an example of detriment as meant in Recital 42, which means that consent was never validly obtained (and thus, the controller needs to delete all personal data about users' movements collected this way).

---

50. Example 9: A data subject subscribes to a fashion retailer's newsletter with general discounts. The retailer asks the data subject for consent to collect more data on shopping preferences to tailor the offers to his or her preferences based on shopping history or a questionnaire that is voluntary to fill out. When the data subject later revokes consent, he or she will receive non-personalised fashion discounts again. This does not amount to detriment as only the permissible incentive was lost.

---

51. Example 10: A fashion magazine offers readers access to buy new make-up products before the official launch.

52. The products will shortly be made available for sale, but readers of this magazine are offered an exclusive preview of these products. In order to enjoy this benefit, people must give their postal address and agree to subscription on the mailing list of the magazine. The postal address is necessary for shipping and the mailing list is used for sending commercial offers for products such as cosmetics or t-shirts year round.

53. The company explains that the data on the mailing list will only be used for sending merchandise and paper advertising by the magazine itself and is not to be shared with any other organisation.

54. In case the reader does not want to disclose their address for this reason, there is no detriment, as the products will be available to them anyway.

3.2 SPECIFIC

55. Article 6(1)(a) confirms that the consent of the data subject must be given in relation to "one or more specific" purposes and that a data subject has a choice in relation to each of them.[28] The requirement that consent must be *'specific'* aims to ensure a degree of user control and transparency for the data subject. This requirement has not been changed by the GDPR and remains closely linked to the requirement of 'informed' consent. At the same time, it must be interpreted in line with the requirement for 'granularity' to obtain 'free' consent.[29] In sum, to comply with the element of 'specific' the controller must apply:
(i)   Purpose specification as a safeguard against function creep,
(ii)   Granularity in consent requests, and
(iii) Clear separation of information related to obtaining consent for data processing activities from information about other matters.

56.   Ad. (i): Pursuant to Article 5(1)(b) GDPR, obtaining valid consent is always preceded by the determination of a specific, explicit and legitimate purpose for the intended processing activity.[30] The need for specific consent in combination with the notion of purpose limitation in Article 5(1)(b) functions as a safeguard against the gradual widening or blurring of purposes for which data is processed, after a data subject has agreed to the initial collection of the data. This phenomenon, also known as function creep, is a risk for data subjects, as it may result in unanticipated use of personal data by the controller or by third parties and in loss of data subject control.

57. If the controller is relying on Article 6(1)(a), data subjects must always give consent for a specific processing purpose.[31] In line with the concept of *purpose limitation*, Article 5(1)(b) and recital 32, consent may cover different operations, as long as these operations serve the same purpose. It goes without saying that specific consent can only be obtained when data subjects are specifically informed about the intended purposes of data use concerning them.

58. Notwithstanding the provisions on compatibility of purposes, consent must be specific to the purpose. Data subjects will give their consent with the understanding that they are in control and their data will only be processed for those specified purposes. If a controller processes data based on consent and wishes to process the data for another purpose, too, that controller needs to seek additional consent for this other purpose unless there is another lawful basis, which better reflects the situation.

---

59. Example 11: A cable TV network collects subscribers' personal data, based on their consent, to present them with personal suggestions for new movies they might be interested in based on their viewing habits. After a while, the TV network decides it would like to enable third parties to send (or display) targeted advertising on the basis of the subscriber's viewing habits. Given this new purpose, new consent is needed.

60. Ad. (ii): Consent mechanisms must not only be granular to meet the requirement of 'free', but also to meet the element of 'specific'. This means, a controller that seeks consent for various different purposes should provide a separate opt-in for each purpose, to allow users to give specific consent for specific purposes.

61. Ad. (iii): Lastly, controllers should provide specific information with each separate consent request about the data that are processed for each purpose, in order to make data subjects aware of the impact of the different choices they have. Thus, data subjects are enabled to give specific consent. This issue overlaps with the requirement that controllers must provide clear information, as discussed in paragraph 3.3. below.

3.3 INFORMED

62. The GDPR reinforces the requirement that consent must be informed. Based on Article 5 of the GDPR, the requirement for transparency is one of the fundamental principles, closely related to the principles of fairness and lawfulness. Providing information to data subjects prior to obtaining their consent is essential in order to enable them to make informed decisions, understand what they are agreeing to, and for example exercise their right to withdraw their consent. If the controller does not provide accessible information, user control becomes illusory and consent will be an invalid basis for processing.

63. The consequence of not complying with the requirements for informed consent is that consent will be invalid and the controller may be in breach of Article 6 of the GDPR.

3.3.1 Minimum content requirements for consent to be 'informed'

64. For consent to be informed, it is necessary to inform the data subject of certain elements that are crucial to make a choice. Therefore, the EDPB is of the opinion that at least the following information is required for obtaining valid consent:
(i)   the controller's identity,[32]
(ii)   the purpose of each of the processing operations for which consent is sought,[33]
(iii)   what (type of) data will be collected and used,[34]
(iv)   the existence of the right to withdraw consent,[35]
(v)   information about the use of the data for automated decision-making in accordance with Article 22 (2)(c)[36] where relevant, and
(vi)   on the possible risks of data transfers due to absence of an adequacy decision and of appropriate safeguards as described in Article 46.[37]

65. With regard to item (i) and (iii), the EDPB notes that in a case where the consent sought is to be relied upon by multiple (joint) controllers or if the data is to be transferred to or processed by other controllers who wish to rely on the original consent, these organisations should all be named. Processors do not need to be named as part of the consent requirements, although to comply with Articles 13 and 14 of the GDPR, controllers will need to provide a full list of recipients or categories of recipients including processors. To conclude, the EDPB notes that depending on the circumstances and context of a case, more information may be needed to allow the data subject to genuinely understand the processing operations at hand.

3.3.2 How to provide information

66. The GDPR does not prescribe the form or shape in which information must be provided in order to fulfil the requirement of informed consent. This means valid information may be presented in various ways, such as written or oral statements, or audio or video messages. However, the GDPR puts several requirements for informed consent in place, predominantly in Article 7(2) and Recital 32. This leads to a higher standard for the clarity and accessibility of the information.

67. When seeking consent, controllers should ensure that they use clear and plain language in all cases. This means a message should be easily understandable for the average person and not only for lawyers. Controllers cannot use long privacy policies that are difficult to understand or statements full of legal jargon. Consent must be clear and distinguishable from other matters and provided in an intelligible and easily accessible form. This requirement essentially means that information relevant for making informed decisions on whether or not to consent may not be hidden in general terms and conditions.[38]

68. A controller must ensure that consent is provided on the basis of information that allows the data subjects to easily identify who the controller is and to understand what they are agreeing to. The controller must clearly describe the purpose for data processing for which consent is requested.[39]

69. Other specific guidance on the accessibility has been provided in the WP29 guidelines on transparency. If consent is to be given by electronic means, the request must be clear and concise. Layered and granular information can be an appropriate way to deal with the two-fold obligation of being precise and complete on the one hand and understandable on the other hand.

70. A controller must assess what kind of audience it is that provides personal data to their organisation. For example, in case the targeted audience includes data subjects that are underage, the controller is expected to make sure information is understandable for minors.[40] After identifying their audience, controllers must determine what information they should provide and, subsequently how they will present the information to data subjects.

71.   Article 7(2) addresses pre-formulated written declarations of consent, which also concern other matters. When consent is requested as part of a (paper) contract, the request for consent should be clearly distinguishable from the other matters. If the paper contract includes many aspects that are unrelated to the question of consent to the use of personal data, the issue of consent should be dealt with in a way that clearly stands out, or in a separate document. Likewise, if consent is requested by electronic means, the consent request has to be separate and distinct, it cannot simply be a paragraph within terms and conditions, pursuant to Recital 32.[41] To accommodate for small screens or situations with restricted room for information, a layered way of presenting information can be considered, where appropriate, to avoid excessive disturbance of user experience or product design.

72.   A controller that relies on consent of the data subject must also deal with the separate information duties laid down in Articles 13 and 14 in order to be compliant with the GDPR. In practice, compliance with the information duties and compliance with the requirement of informed consent may lead to an integrated approach in many cases. However, this section is written in the understanding that valid "informed" consent can exist, even when not all elements of Articles 13 and/or 14 are mentioned in the process of obtaining consent (these points should of course be mentioned in other places, such as the privacy notice of a company). WP29 has issued separate guidelines on the requirement of transparency.

---

73.   Example 12: Company X is a controller that received complaints that it is unclear to data subjects for what purposes of data use they are asked to consent to. The company sees the need to verify whether its information in the consent request is understandable for data subjects. X organises voluntary test panels of specific categories of its customers and presents new updates of its consent information to these test audiences before communicating it externally. The selection of the panel respects the principle of independence and is made on the basis of standards ensuring a representative, non-biased outcome. The panel receives a questionnaire and indicates what they understood of the information and how they would score it in terms of understandable and relevant information. The controller continues testing until the panels indicate that the information is understandable. X draws up a report of the test and keeps this available for future reference. This example shows a possible way for X to demonstrate that data subjects were receiving clear information before consenting to personal data processing by X.

---

74.   Example 13: A company engages in data processing on the basis of consent. The company uses a layered privacy notice that includes a consent request. The company discloses all basic details of the controller and the data processing activities envisaged.[42] However, the company does not indicate how their data protection officer can be contacted in the first information layer of the notice. For the purposes of having a valid lawful basis as meant in Article 6, this controller obtained valid "informed" consent, even when the contact details of the data protection officer have not been communicated to the data subject (in the first information layer), pursuant to Article 13(1)(b) or 14(1)(b) GDPR.

3.4 UNAMBIGUOUS INDICATION OF WISHES

75.   The GDPR is clear that consent requires a statement from the data subject or a clear affirmative act, which means that it must always be given through an active motion or declaration. It must be obvious that the data subject has consented to the particular processing.

76.   Article 2(h) of Directive 95/46/EC described consent as an "indication of wishes by which the data subject signifies his agreement to personal data relating to him being processed". Article 4(11) GDPR builds on this definition, by clarifying that valid consent requires an *unambiguous* indication by means of a *statement or by a clear affirmative action*, in line with previous guidance issued by the WP29.

77.   A "clear affirmative act" means that the data subject must have taken a deliberate action to consent to the particular processing.[43] Recital 32 sets out additional guidance on this. Consent can be collected through a written or (a recorded) oral statement, including by electronic means.

78.   Perhaps the most literal way to fulfil the criterion of a "written statement" is to make sure a data subject writes in a letter or types an email to the controller explaining what exactly he/she agrees to. However, this is often not realistic. Written statements can come in many shapes and sizes that could be compliant with the GDPR.

79.   Without prejudice to existing (national) contract law, consent can be obtained through a recorded oral statement, although due note must be taken of the information available to the data subject, prior to the indication of consent. The use of pre-ticked opt-in boxes is invalid under the GDPR. Silence or inactivity on the part of the data subject, as well as merely proceeding with a service cannot be regarded as an active indication of choice.

---

80.   Example 14: When installing software, the application asks the data subject for consent to use non-anonymised crash reports to improve the software. A layered privacy notice providing the necessary information accompanies the request for consent. By actively ticking the optional box stating, "I consent", the user is able to validly perform a 'clear affirmative act' to consent to the processing.

81. A controller must also beware that consent cannot be obtained through the same motion as agreeing to a contract or accepting general terms and conditions of a service. Blanket acceptance of general terms and conditions cannot be seen as a clear affirmative action to consent to the use of personal data. The GDPR does not allow controllers to offer pre-ticked boxes or opt-out constructions that require an intervention from the data subject to prevent agreement (for example 'opt-out boxes').[44]

82. When consent is to be given following a request by electronic means, the request for consent should not be *unnecessarily* disruptive to the use of the service for which the consent is provided.[45] An active affirmative motion by which the data subject indicates consent can be necessary when a less infringing or disturbing modus would result in ambiguity. Thus, it may be necessary that a consent request interrupts the use experience to some extent to make that request effective.

83. However, within the requirements of the GDPR, controllers have the liberty to develop a consent flow that suits their organisation. In this regard, physical motions can be qualified as a clear affirmative action in compliance with the GDPR.

84. Controllers should design consent mechanisms in ways that are clear to data subjects. Controllers must avoid ambiguity and must ensure that the action by which consent is given can be distinguished from other actions. Therefore, merely continuing the ordinary use of a website is not conduct from which one can infer an indication of wishes by the data subject to signify his or her agreement to a proposed processing operation.

---

85. Example 15: Swiping a bar on a screen, waiving in front of a smart camera, turning a smartphone around clockwise, or in a figure eight motion may be options to indicate agreement, as long as clear information is provided, and it is clear that the motion in question signifies agreement to a specific request (e.g. if you swipe this bar to the left, you agree to the use of information X for purpose Y. Repeat the motion to confirm."). The controller must be able to demonstrate that consent was obtained this way and data subjects must be able to withdraw consent as easily as it was given.

---

86. Example 16: Based on recital 32, actions such as scrolling or swiping through a webpage or similar user activity will not under any circumstances satisfy the requirement of a clear and affirmative action: such actions may be difficult to distinguish from other activity or interaction by a user and therefore determining that an unambiguous consent has been obtained will also not be possible. Furthermore, in such a case, it will be difficult to provide a way for the user to withdraw consent in a manner that is as easy as granting it.

---

87. In the digital context, many services need personal data to function, hence, data subjects receive multiple consent requests that need answers through clicks and swipes every day. This may result in a certain degree of click fatigue: when encountered too many times, the actual warning effect of consent mechanisms is diminishing.

88. This results in a situation where consent questions are no longer read. This is a particular risk to data subjects, as, typically, consent is asked for actions that are in principle unlawful without their consent. The GDPR places upon controllers the obligation to develop ways to tackle this issue.

89. An often-mentioned example to do this in the online context is to obtain consent of Internet users via their browser settings. Such settings should be developed in line with the conditions for valid consent in the GDPR, as for instance that the consent shall be granular for each of the envisaged purposes and that the information to be provided, should name the controllers.

90. In any event, consent must always be obtained before the controller starts processing personal data for which consent is needed. WP29 has consistently held in its opinions that consent should be given prior to the processing activity.[46] Although the GDPR does not literally prescribe in Article 4(11) that consent must be given prior to the processing activity, this is clearly implied. The heading of Article 6(1) and the wording "has given" in Article 6(1)(a) support this interpretation. It follows logically from Article 6 and Recital 40 that a valid lawful basis must be present before starting a data processing. Therefore, consent should be given prior to the processing activity. In principle, it can be sufficient to ask for a data subject's consent once. However, controllers do need to obtain a new and specific consent if purposes for data processing change after consent was obtained or if an additional purpose is envisaged.

NOTES

[11] For guidance with regard to ongoing processing activities based on consent in Directive 95/46, see chapter 7 of this document and recital 171 of the GDPR.

[12] In several opinions, the Article 29 Working Party has explored the limits of consent in situations where it cannot be freely given. This was notably the case in its Opinion 15/2011 on the definition of consent (WP 187), Working Document on the processing of personal data relating to health in electronic health records (WP 131), Opinion 8/2001 on the processing of personal data in the employment context (WP48), and Second opinion 4/2009 on processing of data by the World Anti-Doping Agency (WADA) (International Standard for the Protection of Privacy and Personal Information, on related provisions of the WADA Code and on other privacy issues in the context of the fight against doping in sport by WADA and (national) anti-doping organizations (WP 162).

13   See Opinion 15/2011 on the definition of consent (WP187), p. 12.

14   See Recitals 42, 43 GDPR and WP29 Opinion 15/2011 on the definition of consent, adopted on 13 July 2011, (WP 187), p. 12.

15   Recital 43 GDPR states: *"In order to ensure that consent is freely given, consent should not provide a valid legal ground for the processing of personal data in a specific case where there is a clear imbalance between the data subject and the controller, in particular where the controller is a public authority and it is therefore unlikely that consent was freely given in all the circumstances of that specific situation. (. . .)".*

16   See Article 6 GDPR, notably paragraphs (1c) and (1e).

17   For the purposes of this example, a public school means a publically funded school or any educational facility that qualifies as a public authority or body by national law.

18   See also Article 88 GDPR, where the need for protection of the specific interests of employees is emphasised and a possibility for derogations in Member State law is created. See also Recital 155.

19   See Opinion 15/2011 on the definition of consent (WP 187), pp. 12-14, Opinion 8/2001 on the processing of personal data in the employment context (WP 48), Chapter 10, Working document on the surveillance of electronic communications in the workplace (WP 55), paragraph 4.2 and Opinion 2/2017 on data processing at work (WP 249), paragraph 6.2.

20   See Opinion 2/2017 on data processing at work, page 6-7.

21   See also Opinion 2/2017 on data processing at work (WP249), paragraph 6.2.

22   Article 7(4) GDPR: *"When assessing whether consent is freely given, utmost account shall be taken of whether, inter alia, the performance of a contract, including the provision of a service, is conditional on consent to the processing of personal data that is not necessary for the performance of that contract."* See also Recital 43 GDPR, that states: *"[. . .] Consent is presumed not to be freely given if it does not allow separate consent to be given to different personal data processing operations despite it being appropriate in the individual case, or if the performance of a contract, including the provision of a service, is dependent on the consent, despite such consent not being necessary for such performance."*

23   For more information and examples, see Opinion 06/2014 on the notion of legitimate interest of the data controller under Article 7 of Directive 95/46/EC, adopted by WP29 on 9 April 2014, p. 16-17. (WP 217).

24   The appropriate lawful basis could then be Article 6(1)(b) (contract).

25   See also Article 7(1) GDPR, which states that the controller needs to demonstrate that the data subject's agreement was freely given.

26   To some extent, the introduction of this paragraph is a codification of existing WP29 guidance. As described in Opinion 15/2011, when a data subject is in a situation of dependence on the data controller – due to the nature of the relationship or to special circumstances – there may be a strong presumption that freedom to consent is limited in such contexts (e.g. in an employment relationship or if the collection of data is performed by a public authority). With Article 7(4) in force, it will be more difficult for the controller to prove that consent was given freely by the data subject. See: Article 29 Working Party Opinion 15/2011 on the definition of consent (WP 187), pp. 12-17.

27   As clarified above, the GDPR conditions for obtaining valid consent are applicable in situations falling within the scope of the e-Privacy Directive.

28   Further guidance on the determination of 'purposes' can be found in Opinion 3/2013 on purpose limitation (WP 203).

29   Recital 43 GDPR states that separate consent for different processing operations will be needed wherever appropriate. Granular consent options should be provided to allow data subjects to consent separately to separate purposes.

30   See WP 29 Opinion 3/2013 on purpose limitation (WP 203), p. 16, : *"For these reasons, a purpose that is vague or general, such as for instance 'improving users' experience', 'marketing purposes', 'IT-security purposes' or 'future research' will - without more detail - usually not meet the criteria of being 'specific'."*

31   This is consistent with WP29 Opinion 15/2011 on the definition of consent (WP 187), for example on p. 17.

32   See also Recital 42 GDPR: *" [. . .]For consent to be informed, the data subject should be aware at least of the identity of the controller and the purposes of the processing for which the personal data are intended.[. . .]."*

33   Again, see Recital 42 GDPR.

34   See also WP29 Opinion 15/2011 on the definition of consent (WP 187) pp.19-20.

35   See Article 7(3) GDPR.

36   See also WP29 Guidelines on Automated individual decision-making and Profiling for the purposes of Regulation 2016/679 (WP251), paragraph IV.B, p. 20 onwards.

37   Pursuant to Article 49(1)(a), specific information is required about the absence of safeguards described in Article 46, when explicit consent is sought. See also WP29 Opinion 15/2011 on the definition of consent (WP 187)p. 19.

38   The declaration of consent must be named as such. Drafting, such as "I know that . . . " does not meet the requirement of clear language.

39   See Articles 4(11) and 7(2) GDPR.

40   See also Recital 58 regarding information understandable for children.

41   See also Recital 42 and Directive 93/13/EC, notably Article 5 (plain intelligible language and in case of doubt, the interpretation will be in favour of consumer) and Article 6 (invalidity of unfair terms, contract continues to exist without these terms only if still sensible, otherwise the whole contract is invalid).

42   Note that when the identity of the controller or the purpose of the processing is not apparent from the first information layer of the layered privacy notice (and are located in further sub-layers), it will be difficult for the data controller to demonstrate that the data subject has given informed consent, unless the data controller can show that the data subject in question accessed that information prior to giving consent.

43   See Commission Staff Working Paper, Impact Assessment, Annex 2, p. 20 and also pp. 105-106: *"As also pointed out in the opinion adopted by WP29 on consent, it seems essential to clarify that valid consent requires the use of mechanisms that leave no doubt of the data subject's intention to consent, while making clear that – in the context of the on-line environment – the use of default options which the data subject is required to modify in order to reject the processing ('consent based on silence') does not in itself constitute unambiguous consent. This would give individuals more control over their own data, whenever processing is based on his/her consent. As regards impact on data controllers, this would not have a major impact as it solely clarifies and better spells out the implications of the current Directive in relation to the conditions for a valid and meaningful consent from the data subject. In particular, to the*

extent that 'explicit' consent would clarify – by replacing "unambiguous" – the modalities and quality of consent and that it is not intended to extend the cases and situations where (explicit) consent should be used as a ground for processing, the impact of this measure on data controllers is not expected to be major."

44   See Article 7(2). See also Working Document 02/2013 on obtaining consent for cookies (WP 208), pp. 3-6.
45   See Recital 32 GDPR.
46   WP29 has consistently held this position since Opinion 15/2011 on the definition of consent (WP 187), pp. 30- 31.

4 OBTAINING EXPLICIT CONSENT

[2.350]
91.   Explicit consent is required in certain situations where serious data protection risk emerge, hence, where a high level of individual control over personal data is deemed appropriate. Under the GDPR, explicit consent plays a role in Article 9 on the processing of special categories of data, the provisions on data transfers to third countries or international organisations in the absence of adequate safeguards in Article 49[47], and in Article 22 on automated individual decision-making, including profiling.[48]

92.   The GDPR prescribes that a "statement or clear affirmative action" is a prerequisite for 'regular' consent. As the 'regular' consent requirement in the GDPR is already raised to a higher standard compared to the consent requirement in Directive 95/46/EC, it needs to be clarified what extra efforts a controller should undertake in order to obtain the *explicit* consent of a data subject in line with the GDPR.

93.   The term *explicit* refers to the way consent is expressed by the data subject. It means that the data subject must give an express statement of consent. An obvious way to make sure consent is explicit would be to expressly confirm consent in a written statement. Where appropriate, the controller could make sure the written statement is signed by the data subject, in order to remove all possible doubt and potential lack of evidence in the future.[49]

94.   However, such a signed statement is not the only way to obtain explicit consent and, it cannot be said that the GDPR prescribes written and signed statements in all circumstances that require valid explicit consent. For example, in the digital or online context, a data subject may be able to issue the required statement by filling in an electronic form, by sending an email, by uploading a scanned document carrying the signature of the data subject, or by using an electronic signature. In theory, the use of oral statements can also be sufficiently express to obtain valid explicit consent, however, it may be difficult to prove for the controller that all conditions for valid explicit consent were met when the statement was recorded.

95.   An organisation may also obtain explicit consent through a telephone conversation, provided that the information about the choice is fair, intelligible and clear, and it asks for a specific confirmation from the data subject (e.g. pressing a button or providing oral confirmation).

---

96.   Example 17: A data controller may also obtain explicit consent from a visitor to its website by offering an explicit consent screen that contains Yes and No check boxes, provided that the text clearly indicates the consent, for instance "I, hereby, consent to the processing of my data", and not for instance, "It is clear to me that my data will be processed". It goes without saying that the conditions for informed consent as well as the other conditions for obtaining valid consent should be met.

---

97.   Example 18: A clinic for cosmetic surgery seeks explicit consent from a patient to transfer his medical record to an expert whose second opinion is asked on the condition of the patient. The medical record is a digital file. Given the specific nature of the information concerned, the clinic asks for an electronic signature of the data subject to obtain valid explicit consent and to be able to demonstrate that explicit consent was obtained.[50]

---

98.   Two stage verification of consent can also be a way to make sure explicit consent is valid. For example, a data subject receives an email notifying them of the controller's intent to process a record containing medical data. The controller explains in the email that he asks for consent for the use of a specific set of information for a specific purpose. If the data subjects agrees to the use of this data, the controller asks him or her for an email reply containing the statement 'I agree'. After the reply is sent, the data subject receives a verification link that must be clicked, or an SMS message with a verification code, to confirm agreement.

99.   Article 9(2) does not recognize "necessary for the performance of a contract" as an exception to the general prohibition to process special categories of data. Therefore, controllers and Member States that deal with this situation should explore the specific exceptions in Article 9(2) subparagraphs (b) to (j). Should none of the exceptions (b) to (j) apply, obtaining explicit consent in accordance with the conditions for valid consent in the GDPR remains the only possible lawful exception to process such data.

---

100.   Example 19: An airline company, Holiday Airways, offers an assisted travelling service for passengers that cannot travel unassisted, for example due to a disability. A customer books a flight from Amsterdam to Budapest and requests travel assistance to be able to board the plane. Holiday

Airways requires her to provide information on her health condition to be able to arrange the appropriate services for her (hence, there are many possibilities e.g. wheelchair on the arrival gate, or an assistant travelling with her from A to B.) Holiday Airways asks for explicit consent to process the health data of this customer for the purpose of arranging the requested travel assistance. -The data processed on the basis of consent should be necessary for the requested service. Moreover, flights to Budapest remain available without travel assistance. Please note that since that data are necessary for the provision of the requested service, Article 7 (4) does not apply.

---

101.   Example 20: A successful company is specialised in providing custom-made ski- and snowboard goggles, and other types of customised eyewear for outdoors sports. The idea is that people could wear these without their own glasses on. The company receives orders at a central point and delivers products from a single location all across the EU.

---

102.   In order to be able to provide its customised products to customers who are short-sighted, this controller requests consent for the use of information on customers' eye condition. Customers provide the necessary health data, such as their prescription data online when they place their order. Without this, it is not possible to provide the requested customized eyewear. The company also offers series of goggles with standardized correctional values. Customers that do not wish to share health data could opt for the standard versions. Therefore, an explicit consent under Article 9 is required and consent can be considered to be freely given.

NOTES

   47   According to Article 49(1)(a) GDPR, explicit consent can lift the ban on data transfers to countries without adequate
         levels of data protection law. Also note Working document on a common interpretation of Article 26(1) of Directive
         95/46/EC of 24 October 1995 (WP 114), p. 11, where WP29 has indicated that consent for data transfers that occur
         periodically or on an on-going basis is inappropriate.
   48   In Article 22, the GDPR introduces provisions to protect data subjects against decision-making based solely on
         automated processing, including profiling. Decisions made on this basis are allowed under certain legal condi-
         tions. Consent plays a key role in this protection mechanism, as Article 22(2)(c) GDPR makes clear that a controller may
         proceed with automated decision making, including profiling, that may significantly affect the individual, with the data
         subject's explicit consent. WP29 have produced separate guidelines on this issue: WP29 Guidelines on Automated
         decision-making and Profiling for the purposes of Regulation 2016/679, 3 October 2017 (WP 251).
   49   See also WP29 Opinion 15/2011, on the definition of consent (WP 187), p. 25.
   50   This example is without prejudice to EU Regulation (EU) No 910/2014 of the European Parliament and of the Council
         of 23 July 2014 on electronic identification and trust services for electronic transactions in the internal market.

---

5 ADDITIONAL CONDITIONS FOR OBTAINING VALID CONSENT

[2.351]
103.   The GDPR introduces requirements for controllers to make additional arrangements to ensure they obtain, and maintain and are able to demonstrate, valid consent. Article 7 of the GDPR sets out these additional conditions for valid consent, with specific provisions on keeping records of consent and the right to easily withdraw consent. Article 7 also applies to consent referred to in other articles of GDPR, e.g. Articles 8 and 9. Guidance on the additional requirement to demonstrate valid consent and on withdrawal of consent is provided below.

5.1 DEMONSTRATE CONSENT

104.   In Article 7(1), the GDPR clearly outlines the explicit obligation of the controller to demonstrate a data subject's consent. The burden of proof will be on the controller, according to Article 7(1).

105.   Recital 42 states: *"Where processing is based on the data subject's consent, the controller should be able to demonstrate that the data subject has given consent to the processing operation."*

106.   Controllers are free to develop methods to comply with this provision in a way that is fitting in their daily operations. At the same time, the duty to demonstrate that valid consent has been obtained by a controller, should not in itself lead to excessive amounts of additional data processing. This means that controllers should have enough data to show a link to the processing (to show consent was obtained) but they shouldn't be collecting any more information than necessary.

107.   It is up to the controller to prove that valid consent was obtained from the data subject. The GDPR does not prescribe exactly how this must be done. However, the controller must be able to prove that a data subject in a given case has consented. As long as a data processing activity in question lasts, the obligation to demonstrate consent exists. After the processing activity ends, proof of consent should be kept no longer then strictly necessary for compliance with a legal obligation or for the establishment, exercise or defence of legal claims, in accordance with Article 17(3)(b) and (e).

108.   For instance, the controller may keep a record of consent statements received, so he can show how consent was obtained, when consent was obtained and the information provided to the data subject at the time shall be demonstrable. The controller shall also be able to show that the data subject was informed and the controller's workflow met all relevant criteria for a valid consent. The rationale behind this obligation in the GDPR is that controllers must be accountable with regard to obtaining valid consent from data subjects and the consent mechanisms they have put in place. For example, in an online context,

Part 2   Data Protection: EU Law etc

a controller could retain information on the session in which consent was expressed, together with documentation of the consent workflow at the time of the session, and a copy of the information that was presented to the data subject at that time. It would not be sufficient to merely refer to a correct configuration of the respective website.

---

109. Example 21: A hospital sets up a scientific research programme, called project X, for which dental records of real patients are necessary. Participants are recruited via telephone calls to patients that voluntarily agreed to be on a list of candidates that may be approached for this purpose. The controller seeks explicit consent from the data subjects for the use of their dental record. Consent is obtained during a phone call by recording an oral statement of the data subject in which the data subject confirms that they agree to the use of their data for the purposes of project X.

---

110. There is no specific time limit in the GDPR for how long consent will last. How long consent lasts will depend on the context, the scope of the original consent and the expectations of the data subject. If the processing operations change or evolve considerably then the original consent is no longer valid. If this is the case, then new consent needs to be obtained.

111. The EDPB recommends as a best practice that consent should be refreshed at appropriate intervals. Providing all the information again helps to ensure the data subject remains well informed about how their data is being used and how to exercise their rights.[51]

5.2 WITHDRAWAL OF CONSENT

112. Withdrawal of consent is given a prominent place in the GDPR. The provisions and recitals on withdrawal of consent in the GDPR can be regarded as codification of the existing interpretation of this matter in WP29 Opinions.[52]

113. Article 7(3) of the GDPR prescribes that the controller must ensure that consent can be withdrawn by the data subject as easy as giving consent and at any given time. The GDPR does not say that giving and withdrawing consent must always be done through the same action.

114. However, when consent is obtained via electronic means through only one mouse-click, swipe, or keystroke, data subjects must, in practice, be able to withdraw that consent equally as easily. Where consent is obtained through use of a service-specific user interface (for example, via a website, an app, a log-on account, the interface of an IoT device or by e-mail), there is no doubt a data subject must be able to withdraw consent via the same electronic interface, as switching to another interface for the sole reason of withdrawing consent would require undue effort. Furthermore, the data subject should be able to withdraw his/her consent without detriment. This means, inter alia, that a controller must make withdrawal of consent possible free of charge or without lowering service levels.[53]

---

115. Example 22: A music festival sells tickets through an online ticket agent. With each online ticket sale, consent is requested in order to use contact details for marketing purposes. To indicate consent for this purpose, customers can select either No or Yes. The controller informs customers that they have the possibility to withdraw consent. To do this, they could contact a call centre on business days between 8am and 5pm, free of charge. The controller in this example does not comply with article 7(3) of the GDPR. Withdrawing consent in this case requires a telephone call during business hours, this is more burdensome than the one mouse-click needed for giving consent through the online ticket vendor, which is open 24/7.

---

116. The requirement of an easy withdrawal is described as a necessary aspect of valid consent in the GDPR. If the withdrawal right does not meet the GDPR requirements, then the consent mechanism of the controller does not comply with the GDPR. As mentioned in section 3.1 on the condition of informed consent, the controller must inform the data subject of the right to withdraw consent prior to actually giving consent, pursuant to Article 7(3) of the GDPR. Additionally, the controller must as part of the transparency obligation inform the data subjects on how to exercise their rights.[54]

117. As a general rule, if consent is withdrawn, all data processing operations that were based on consent and took place before the withdrawal of consent - and in accordance with the GDPR - remain lawful, however, the controller must stop the processing actions concerned. If there is no other lawful basis justifying the processing (e.g. further storage) of the data, they should be deleted by the controller.[55]

118. As mentioned earlier in these guidelines, it is very important that controllers assess the purposes for which data is actually processed and the lawful grounds on which it is based prior to collecting the data. Often companies need personal data for several purposes, and the processing is based on more than one lawful basis, e.g. customer data may be based on contract and consent. Hence, a withdrawal of consent does not mean a controller must erase data that are processed for a purpose that is based on the performance of the contract with the data subject. Controllers should therefore be clear from the outset about which purpose applies to each element of data and which lawful basis is being relied upon.

119. Controllers have an obligation to delete data that was processed on the basis of consent once that consent is withdrawn, assuming that there is no other purpose justifying the continued retention.[56] Besides this situation, covered in Article 17 (1)(b), an individual data subject may request erasure of other data concerning him that is processed on another lawful basis, e.g. on the basis of Article

6(1)(b).[57] Controllers are obliged to assess whether continued processing of the data in question is appropriate, even in the absence of an erasure request by the data subject.[58]

120. In cases where the data subject withdraws his/her consent and the controller wishes to continue to process the personal data on another lawful basis, they cannot silently migrate from consent (which is withdrawn) to this other lawful basis. Any change in the lawful basis for processing must be notified to a data subject in accordance with the information requirements in Articles 13 and 14 and under the general principle of transparency.

NOTES

[51]   See Article 29 Working Party guidelines on transparency under Regulation 2016/679 WP260 rev.01 - endorsed by the EDPB.

[52]   WP29 has discussed this subject in their Opinion on consent (see Opinion 15/2011 on the definition of consent (WP 187), pp. 9, 13, 20, 27 and 32-33) and, inter alia, their Opinion on the use of location data. (see Opinion 5/2005 on the use of location data with a view to providing value-added services (WP 115), p. 7).

[53]   See also opinion WP29 Opinion 4/2010 on the European code of conduct of FEDMA for the use of personal data in direct marketing (WP 174) and the Opinion on the use of location data with a view to providing valueadded services (WP 115).

[54]   Recital 39 GDPR, which refers to Articles 13 and 14 of that Regulation, states that *"natural persons should be made aware of risks, rules, safeguards and rights in relation to the processing of personal data and how to exercise their rights in relation to such processing.*

[55]   See Article 17(1)(b) and (3) GDPR.

[56]   In that case, the other purpose justifying the processing must have its own separate legal basis. This does not mean the controller can swap from consent to another lawful basis, see section 6 below.

[57]   See Article 17, including exceptions that may apply, and Recital 65 GDPR.

[58]   See also Article 5 (1)(e) GDPR.

6 INTERACTION BETWEEN CONSENT AND OTHER LAWFUL GROUNDS IN ARTICLE 6 GDPR

[2.352]
121. Article 6 sets the conditions for a lawful personal data processing and describes six lawful bases on which a controller can rely. The application of one of these six bases must be established prior to the processing activity and in relation to a specific purpose.[59]

122. It is important to note here that if a controller chooses to rely on consent for any part of the processing, they must be prepared to respect that choice and stop that part of the processing if an individual withdraws consent. Sending out the message that data will be processed on the basis of consent, while actually some other lawful basis is relied on, would be fundamentally unfair to individuals.

123. In other words, the controller cannot swap from consent to other lawful bases. For example, it is not allowed to retrospectively utilise the legitimate interest basis in order to justify processing, where problems have been encountered with the validity of consent. Because of the requirement to disclose the lawful basis, which the controller is relying upon at the time of collection of personal data, controllers must have decided in advance of collection what the applicable lawful basis is.

NOTES

[59]   Pursuant to Articles 13 (1)(c) and/or 14(1)(c), the controller must inform the data subject thereof.

7 SPECIFIC AREAS OF CONCERN IN THE GDPR

7.1 CHILDREN (ARTICLE 8)

[2.353]
124. Compared to the current directive, the GDPR creates an additional layer of protection where personal data of vulnerable natural persons, especially children, are processed. Article 8 introduces additional obligations to ensure an enhanced level of data protection of children in relation to information society services. The reasons for the enhanced protection are specified in Recital 38: " *[. . .] they may be less aware of the risks, consequences and safeguards concerned and their rights in relation to the processing of personal data [. . .]*" Recital 38 also states that *"Such specific protection should, in particular, apply to the use of personal data of children for the purposes of marketing or creating personality or user profiles and the collection of personal data with regard to children when using services offered directly to a child."* The words 'in particular' indicate that the specific protection is not confined to marketing or profiling but includes the wider 'collection of personal data with regard to children'.

125. Article 8(1) states that where consent applies, in relation to the offer of information society services directly to a child, the processing of the personal data of a child shall be lawful where the child is at least 16 years old. Where the child is below the age of 16 years, such processing shall be lawful only if and to the extent that consent is given or authorised by the holder of parental responsibility over the child.[60] Regarding the age limit of valid consent the GDPR provides flexibility, Member States can provide by law a lower age, but this age cannot be below 13 years.

126. As mentioned in section 3.1. on informed consent, the information shall be understandable to the audience addressed by the controller, paying particular attention to the position of children. In order to obtain "informed consent" from a child, the controller must explain in language that is clear and plain for children how it intends to process the data it collects.[61] If it is the parent that is supposed to consent, then a set of information may be required that allows adults to make an informed decision.

127. It is clear from the foregoing that Article 8 shall only apply when the following conditions are met:
* The processing is related to the offer of information society services directly to a child.[62],[63]
* The processing is based on consent.

7.1.1 Information society service

128. To determine the scope of the term 'information society service" in the GDPR, reference is made in Article 4(25) GDPR to Directive 2015/1535.

129. While assessing the scope of this definition, the EDPB also refers to case law of the ECJ.[64] The ECJ held that *information society services* cover contracts and other services that are concluded or transmitted on-line. Where a service has two economically independent components, one being the online component, such as the offer and the acceptance of an offer in the context of the conclusion of a contract or the information relating to products or services, including marketing activities, this component is defined as an information society service, the other component being the physical delivery or distribution of goods is not covered by the notion of an information society service. The online delivery of a service would fall within the scope of the term *information society service* in Article 8 GDPR.

7.1.2 Offered directly to a child

130. The inclusion of the wording 'offered directly to a child' indicates that Article 8 is intended to apply to some, not all information society services. In this respect, if an information society service provider makes it clear to potential users that it is only offering its service to persons aged 18 or over, and this is not undermined by other evidence (such as the content of the site or marketing plans) then the service will not be considered to be 'offered directly to a child' and Article 8 will not apply.

7.1.3 Age

131. The GDPR specifies that *"Member States may provide by law for a lower age for those purposes provided that such lower age is not below 13 years."* The controller must be aware of those different national laws, by taking into account the public targeted by its services. In particular, it should be noted that a controller providing a cross-border service cannot always rely on complying with only the law of the Member State in which it has its main establishment but may need to comply with the respective national laws of each Member State in which it offers the information society service(s). This depends on whether a Member State chooses to use the place of main establishment of the controller as a point of reference in its national law, or the residence of the data subject. First of all the Member States shall consider the best interests of the child during making their choice. The Working Group encourages the Member States to search for a harmonized solution in this matter.

132. When providing information society services to children on the basis of consent, controllers will be expected to make reasonable efforts to verify that the user is over the age of digital consent, and these measures should be proportionate to the nature and risks of the processing activities.

133. If the users state that they are over the age of digital consent then the controller can carry out appropriate checks to verify that this statement is true. Although the need to undertake reasonable efforts to verify age is not explicit in the GDPR it is implicitly required, for if a child gives consent while not old enough to provide valid consent on their own behalf, then this will render the processing of data unlawful.

134. If the user states that he/she is below the age of digital consent then the controller can accept this statement without further checks, but will need to go on to obtain parental authorisation and verify that the person providing that consent is a holder of parental responsibility.

135. Age verification should not lead to excessive data processing. The mechanism chosen to verify the age of a data subject should involve an assessment of the risk of the proposed processing. In some low-risk situations, it may be appropriate to require a new subscriber to a service to disclose their year of birth or to fill out a form stating they are (not) a minor.[65] If doubts arise, the controller should review their age verification mechanisms in a given case and consider whether alternative checks are required.[66]

7.1.4 Children's consent and parental responsibility

136. Regarding the authorisation of a holder of parental responsibility, the GDPR does not specify practical ways to gather the parent's consent or to establish that someone is entitled to perform this action.[67] Therefore, the EDPB recommends the adoption of a proportionate approach, in line with Article 8(2) GDPR and Article 5(1)(c) GDPR (data minimisation). A proportionate approach may be to focus on obtaining a limited amount of information, such as contact details of a parent or guardian.

137. What is reasonable, both in terms of verifying that a user is old enough to provide their own consent, and in terms of verifying that a person providing consent on behalf of a child is a holder of parental responsibility, may depend upon the risks inherent in the processing as well as the available technology. In low-risk cases, verification of parental responsibility via email may be sufficient. Conversely, in high-risk cases, it may be appropriate to ask for more proof, so that the controller is able to verify and retain the information pursuant to Article 7(1) GDPR.[68] Trusted third party verification services may offer solutions, which minimise the amount of personal data the controller has to process itself.

---

138.   Example 23: An online gaming platform wants to make sure underage customers only subscribe to its services with the consent of their parents or guardians. The controller follows these steps:

139.   Step 1: ask the user to state whether they are under or over the age of 16 (or alternative age of digital consent) If the user states that they are under the age of digital consent:

140.   Step 2: service informs the child that a parent or guardian needs to consent or authorise the processing before the service is provided to the child. The user is requested to disclose the email address of a parent or guardian.

141.   Step 3: service contacts the parent or guardian and obtains their consent via email for processing and take reasonable steps to confirm that the adult has parental responsibility.

142.   Step 4: in case of complaints, the platform takes additional steps to verify the age of the subscriber.

143.   If the platform has met the other consent requirements, the platform can comply with the additional criteria of Article 8 GDPR by following these steps.

---

144.   The example shows that the controller can put itself in a position to show that reasonable efforts have been made to ensure that valid consent has been obtained, in relation to the services provided to a child. Article 8(2) particularly adds that *"The controller shall make reasonable efforts to verify that consent is given or authorised by the holder of parental responsibility over the child, taking into consideration available technology."*

145.   It is up to the controller to determine what measures are appropriate in a specific case. As a general rule, controllers should avoid verification solutions which themselves involve excessive collection of personal data.

146.   The EDPB acknowledges that there may be cases where verification is challenging (for example where children providing their own consent have not yet established an 'identity footprint', or where parental responsibility is not easily checked. This can be taken into account when deciding what efforts are reasonable, but controllers will also be expected to keep their processes and the available technology under constant review.

147.   With regard to the data subject's autonomy to consent to the processing of their personal data and have full control over the processing, consent by a holder of parental responsibility or authorized by a holder of parental responsibility for the processing of personal data of children can be confirmed, modified or withdrawn, once the data subject reaches the age of digital consent.

148.   In practice, this means that if the child does not take any action, consent given by a holder of parental responsibility or authorized by a holder of parental responsibility for the processing of personal data given prior to the age of digital consent, will remain a valid ground for processing.

149.   After reaching the age of digital consent, the child will have the possibility to withdraw the consent himself, in line with Article 7(3). In accordance with the principles of fairness and accountability, the controller must inform the child about this possibility.[69]

150.   It is important to point out that in accordance with Recital 38, consent by a parent or guardian is not required in the context of preventive or counselling services offered directly to a child. For example the provision of child protection services offered online to a child by means of an online chat service do not require prior parental authorisation.

151.   Finally, the GDPR states that the rules concerning parental authorization requirements vis-à-vis minors shall not interfere with "the general contract law of Member States such as the rules on the validity, formation or effect of a contract in relation to a child". Therefore, the requirements for valid consent for the use of data about children are part of a legal framework that must be regarded as separate from national contract law. Therefore, this guidance paper does not deal with the question whether it is lawful for a minor to conclude online contracts. Both legal regimes may apply simultaneously, and, the scope of the GDPR does not include harmonization of national provisions of contract law.

152.   [empty]

7.2 SCIENTIFIC RESEARCH

153.   The definition of scientific research purposes has substantial ramifications for the range of data processing activities a controller may undertake. The term *'scientific research'* is not defined in the GDPR. Recital 159 states *"(. . .) For the purposes of this Regulation, the processing of personal data for scientific research purposes should be interpreted in a broad manner. (. . .)"*, however the EDPB considers the notion may not be stretched beyond its common meaning and understands that *'scientific research'* in this context means a research project set up in accordance with relevant sector-related methodological and ethical standards, in conformity with good practice.

154.   When consent is the legal basis for conducting research in accordance with the GDPR, this consent for the use of personal data should be distinguished from other consent requirements that serve as an ethical standard or procedural obligation. An example of such a procedural obligation, where the processing is based not on consent but on another legal basis, is to be found in the Clinical Trials Regulation. In the context of data protection law, the latter form of consent could be considered as an additional safeguard.[70] At the same time, the GDPR does not restrict the application of Article 6 to consent alone, with regard to processing data for research purposes. As long as appropriate safeguards are in place, such as the requirements under Article 89(1), and the processing is fair, lawful, transparent and accords with data minimisation standards and individual rights, other lawful bases such as Article 6(1)(e) or (f) may be available.[71] This also applies to special categories of data pursuant to the derogation of Article 9(2)(j).[72]

155. Recital 33 seems to bring some flexibility to the degree of specification and granularity of consent in the context of scientific research. Recital 33 states: *"It is often not possible to fully identify the purpose of personal data processing for scientific research purposes at the time of data collection. Therefore, data subjects should be allowed to give their consent to certain areas of scientific research when in keeping with recognised ethical standards for scientific research. Data subjects should have the opportunity to give their consent only to certain areas of research or parts of research projects to the extent allowed by the intended purpose."*

156. First, it should be noted that Recital 33 does not disapply the obligations with regard to the requirement of specific consent. This means that, in principle, scientific research projects can only include personal data on the basis of consent if they have a well-described purpose. For the cases where purposes for data processing within a scientific research project cannot be specified at the outset, Recital 33 allows as an exception that the purpose may be described at a more general level.

157. Considering the strict conditions stated by Article 9 GDPR regarding the processing of special categories of data, the EDPB notes that when special categories of data are processed on the basis of explicit consent, applying the flexible approach of Recital 33 will be subject to a stricter interpretation and requires a high degree of scrutiny.

158. When regarded as a whole, the GDPR cannot be interpreted to allow for a controller to navigate around the key principle of specifying purposes for which consent of the data subject is asked.

159. When research purposes cannot be fully specified, a controller must seek other ways to ensure the essence of the consent requirements are served best, for example, to allow data subjects to consent for a research purpose in more general terms and for specific stages of a research project that are already known to take place at the outset. As the research advances, consent for subsequent steps in the project can be obtained before that next stage begins. Yet, such a consent should still be in line with the applicable ethical standards for scientific research.

160. Moreover, the controller may apply further safeguards in such cases. Article 89(1), for example, highlights the need for safeguards in data processing activities for scientific or historical or statistical purposes. These purposes *"shall be subject to appropriate safeguards, in accordance with this regulation, for the rights and freedoms of data subject."* Data minimization, anonymisation and data security are mentioned as possible safeguards.[73] Anonymisation is the preferred solution as soon as the purpose of the research can be achieved without the processing of personal data.

161. Transparency is an additional safeguard when the circumstances of the research do not allow for a specific consent. A lack of purpose specification may be offset by information on the development of the purpose being provided regularly by controllers as the research project progresses so that, over time, the consent will be as specific as possible. When doing so, the data subject has at least a basic understanding of the state of play, allowing him/her to assess whether or not to use, for example, the right to withdraw consent pursuant to Article 7(3).[74]

162. Also, having a comprehensive research plan available for data subjects to take note of, before they consent could help to compensate a lack of purpose specification.[75] This research plan should specify the research questions and working methods envisaged as clearly as possible. The research plan could also contribute to compliance with Article 7(1), as controllers need to show what information was available to data subjects at the time of consent in order to be able to demonstrate that consent is valid.

163. It is important to recall that where consent is being used as the lawful basis for processing there must be a possibility for a data subject to withdraw that consent. The EDPB notes that withdrawal of consent could undermine types scientific research that require data that can be linked to individuals, however the GDPR is clear that consent can be withdrawn and controllers must act upon this – there is no exemption to this requirement for scientific research. If a controller receives a withdrawal request, it must in principle delete the personal data straight away if it wishes to continue to use the data for the purposes of the research.[76]

7.3 DATA SUBJECT'S RIGHTS

164. If a data processing activity is based on a data subject's consent, this will affect that individual's rights. Data subjects may have the right to data portability (Article 20) when processing is based on consent. At the same time, the right to object (Article 21) does not apply when processing is based on consent, although the right to withdraw consent at any time may provide a similar outcome.

165. Articles 16 to 20 of the GDPR indicate that (when data processing is based on consent), data subjects have the right to erasure when consent has been withdrawn and the rights to restriction, rectification and access.[77]

NOTES

[60] Without prejudice to the possibility of Member State law to derogate from the age limit, see Article 8(1).

[61] Recital 58 GDPR re-affirms this obligation, in stating that, where appropriate, a controller should make sure the information provided is understandable for children.

[62] According to Article 4(25) GDPR an information society service means a service as defined in point (b) of Article 1(1)

of Directive 2015/1535: *"(b) 'service' means any Information Society service, that is to say, any service normally provided for remuneration, at a distance, by electronic means and at the individual request of a recipient of services. For the purposes of this definition: (i) 'at a distance' means that the service is provided without the parties being simultaneously present; (ii) 'by electronic means' means that the service is sent initially and received at its destination by means of electronic equipment for the processing (including digital compression) and storage of data, and entirely transmitted, conveyed and received by wire, by radio, by optical means or by other electromagnetic means; (iii) 'at the individual request of a recipient of services' means that the service is provided through the transmission of data on individual request."* An indicative list of services not covered by this definition is set out in Annex I of the said Directive. See also Recital 18 of Directive 2000/31.

[63] According to the UN Convention on the Protection of the Child, Article 1, *"[. . .] a child means every human being below the age of eighteen years unless under the law applicable to the child, majority is attained earlier,"* see United Nations, General Assembly Resolution 44/25 of 20 November 1989 (Convention on the Rights of the Child).

[64] See European Court of Justice, 2 December 2010 Case C-108/09, *(Ker-Optika)*, paragraphs 22 and 28. In relation to 'composite services', the EDPB also refers to Case C-434/15 *(Asociacion Profesional Elite Taxi v Uber Systems Spain SL)*, para 40, which states that an information society service forming an integral part of an overall service whose main component is not an information society service (in this case a transport service), must not be qualified as 'an information society service'.

[65] Although this may not be a watertight solution in all cases, it is an example to deal with this provision

[66] See WP29 Opinion 5/2009 on social networking services (WP 163).

[67] WP 29 notes that it not always the case that the holder of parental responsibility is the natural parent of the child and that parental responsibility can be held by multiple parties which may include legal as well as natural persons.

[68] For example, a parent or guardian could be asked to make a payment of €0,01 to the controller via a bank transaction, including a brief confirmation in the description line of the transaction that the bank account holder is a holder of parental responsibility over the user. Where appropriate, an alternative method of verification should be provided to prevent undue discriminatory treatment of persons that do not have a bank account.

[69] Also, data subjects should be aware of the right to be forgotten as laid down in Article 17, which is in particular relevant for consent given when the data subject was still a child, see recital 63

[70] See also Recital 161 of the GDPR.

[71] Article 6(1)(c) may also be applicable for parts of the processing operations specifically required by law, such as gathering reliable and robust data following the protocol as approved by the Member State under the Clinical Trial Regulation.

[72] Specific testing of medicinal products may take place on the basis of an EU or national law pursuant to Article 9(2)(i).

[73] See for example Recital 156. The processing of personal data for scientific purposes should also comply with other relevant legislation such as on clinical trials, see Recital 156, mentioning Regulation (EU) No 536/2014 of the European Parliament and of the Council of 16 April 2014 on clinical trials on medicinal products for human use. See also WP29 Opinion 15/2011 on the definition of consent (WP 187), p. 7: *"Moreover, obtaining consent does not negate the controller's obligations under Article 6 with regard to fairness, necessity and proportionality, as well as data quality. For instance, even if the processing of personal data is based on the consent of the user, this would not legitimise the collection of data which is excessive in relation to a particular purpose."* [. . .] *As a principle, consent should not be seen as an exemption from the other data protection principles, but as a safeguard. It is primarily a ground for lawfulness, and it does not waive the application of other principles."*

[74] Other transparency measures may also be relevant. When controllers engage in data processing for scientific purposes, while full information cannot be provided at the outset, they could designate a specific contact person for data subjects to address with questions.

[75] Such a possibility can be found in Article 14(1) of the current Personal Data Act of Finland (Henkilötietolaki, 523/1999).

[76] See also WP29 Opinion 05/2014 on "Anonymisation Techniques" (WP216).

[77] In cases where certain data processing activities are restricted in accordance with Article 18, GDPR, consent of the data subject may be needed to lift restrictions.

8 CONSENT OBTAINED UNDER DIRECTIVE 95/46/EC

[2.354]

166. Controllers that currently process data on the basis of consent in compliance with national data protection law are not automatically required to completely refresh all existing consent relations with data subjects in preparation for the GDPR. Consent, which has been obtained, to date continues to be valid in so far as it is in line with the conditions laid down in the GDPR.

167. It is important for controllers to review current work processes and records in detail, before 25 May 2018, to be sure existing consents meet the GDPR standard (see Recital 171 of the GDPR[78]). In practice, the GDPR raises the bar with regard to implementing consent mechanisms and introduces several new requirements that require controllers to alter consent mechanisms, rather than rewriting privacy policies alone.[79]

168. For example, as the GDPR requires that a controller must be able to demonstrate that valid consent was obtained, all presumed consents of which no references are kept will automatically be below the consent standard of the GDPR and will need to be renewed. Likewise as the GDPR requires a "statement or a clear affirmative action", all presumed consents that were based on a more implied form of action by the data subject (e.g. a pre-ticked opt-in box) will also not be apt to the GDPR standard of consent.

169. Furthermore, to be able to demonstrate that consent was obtained or to allow for more granular indications of the data subject's wishes, operations and IT systems may need revision. Also, mechanisms for data subjects to withdraw their consent easily must be available and information about how to withdraw consent must be provided. If existing procedures for obtaining and managing consent do not meet the GDPR's standards, controllers will need to obtain fresh GDPR compliant consent.

170. On the other hand, as not all elements named in Articles 13 and 14 must always be present as a condition for informed consent, the extended information obligations under the GDPR do not necessarily oppose the continuity of consent, which has been granted before the GDPR enters into force (see page 15 above). Under Directive 95/46/EC, there was no requirement to inform data subjects of the basis upon which the processing was being conducted.

171. If a controller finds that the consent previously obtained under the old legislation will not meet the standard of GDPR consent, then controllers must undertake action to comply with these standards, for example by refreshing consent in a GDPR-compliant way. Under the GDPR, it is not possible to swap between one lawful basis and another. If a controller is unable to renew consent in a compliant way and is also unable –as a one off situation- to make the transition to GDPR compliance by basing data processing on a different lawful basis while ensuring that continued processing is fair and accounted for, the processing activities must be stopped. In any event, the controller needs to observe the principles of lawful, fair and transparent processing.

NOTES

78   Recital 171 GDPR states: *"Directive 95/46/EC should be repealed by this Regulation. Processing already under way on the date of application of this Regulation should be brought into conformity with this Regulation within the period of two years after which this Regulation enters into force. Where processing is based on consent pursuant to Directive 95/46/EC, it is not necessary for the data subject to give his or her consent again if the manner in which the consent has been given is in line with the conditions of this Regulation, so as to allow the controller to continue such processing after the date of application of this Regulation. Commission decisions adopted and authorisations by supervisory authorities based on Directive 95/46/EC remain in force until amended, replaced or repealed."*

79   As indicated in the introduction, the GDPR provides further clarification and specification of the requirements for obtaining and demonstrating valid consent. Many of the new requirements build upon Opinion 15/2011 on consent.

EUROPEAN DATA PROTECTION BOARD: GUIDELINES 6/2020 ON THE INTERPLAY OF THE SECOND PAYMENT SERVICES DIRECTIVE AND THE GDPR
Version 2.0
Adopted on 15 December 2020

[2.355]

NOTES

© European Data Protection Board.

VERSION HISTORY

Version 2.0: 15.12.2020 — Adoption of the Guidelines after public consultation

Version 1.0: 17.07.2020 — Adoption of the Guidelines for publication consultation

TABLE OF CONTENTS

THE EUROPEAN DATA PROTECTION BOARD

Having regard to Article 70 (1)(e) of Regulation 2016/679/EU of the European Parliament and of the Council of 27 April 2016 on the protection of natural persons with regard to the processing of personal data and on the free movement of such data, and repealing Directive 95/46/EC, (hereinafter "GDPR"),

Having regard to the EEA Agreement and in particular to Annex XI and Protocol 37 thereof, as amended by the Decision of the EEA joint Committee No 154/2018 of 6 July 2018[1],

Having regard to Article 12 and Article 22 of its Rules of Procedure,

Whereas:

(1)   The General Data Protection Regulation provides for a consistent set of rules for the processing of personal data throughout the EU.

(2)   The second Payment Services Directive (Directive 2015/2366/EU of the European Parliament and of the Council of 23 December 2015, hereinafter "PSD2") repeals Directive 2007/64/EC and provides new rules to ensure legal certainty for consumers, merchants and companies within the payment chain and modernizing the legal framework for the market for payment services[2]. Member States had to transpose the PSD2 into their national law before the 13 January 2018.

(3)   An important feature of the PSD2 is the introduction of a legal framework for new payment initiation services and account information services. The PSD2 allows these new payment service providers to obtain access to payment accounts of data subjects for the purposes of providing the said services.

(4)   With regard to data protection, in accordance with Article 94 (1) of the PSD2, any processing of personal data, including the provision of information about the processing, for the purposes of the PSD2, shall be carried out in accordance with the GDPR[3] and with Regulation (EU) No 2018/1725.

(5)   Recital 89 of the PSD2 states that where personal data is processed for the purposes of the PSD2, the precise purpose of the processing should be specified, the applicable legal basis should be named, the relevant security requirements laid down in the GDPR must be implemented, and the principles of necessity, proportionality, purpose limitation and proportionate data retention periods respected. Also, data protection by design and data protection by default should be embedded in all data processing systems developed and used within the framework of the PSD2[4].

(6)   Recital 93 of the PSD2 states that the payment initiation service providers and the account information service providers on the one hand and the account servicing payment service provider on the other, should observe the necessary data protection and security requirements established by, or referred to in, this Directive or included in the regulatory technical standards.

HAS ADOPTED THE FOLLOWING GUIDELINES

[1]   References to "Member States" made throughout this document should be understood as references to "EEA Member States".

[2]   Recital 6 PSD2.

[3]   As PSD2 predates the GDPR, it still refers to Directive 95/46. Article 94 GDPR states that references to the repealed Directive 95/46 shall be construed as references to the GDPR.

[4]   Recital 89, PSD2.

1. INTRODUCTION

[2.356]
1.   The second Payment Services Directive (hereinafter "PSD2") has introduced a number of novelties in the payment services field. While it creates new opportunities for consumers and enhances transparency in such field, the application of the PSD2 raises certain questions and concerns in respect of the need that the data subjects remain in full control of their personal data. The General Data Protection Regulation (hereinafter "GDPR") applies to the processing of personal data including processing activities carried out in the context of payment services as defined by the PSD2[5]. Thus, controllers acting in the field covered by the PSD2 must always ensure compliance with the requirements of the GDPR, including the principles of data protection set out in Article 5 of the GDPR, as well as the relevant provisions of the ePrivacy Directive[6]. While the PSD2[7] and the Regulatory Technical Standards for strong customer authentication and common and secure open standards of communication (hereinafter "RTS"[8]) contain certain provisions relating to data protection and security, uncertainty has arisen about the interpretation of these provisions as well as the interplay between the general data protection framework and the PSD2.

2.   On July 5 2018, the EDPB issued a letter regarding the PSD2, in which the EDPB provided clarifications on questions concerning the protection of personal data in relation to the PSD2, in particular on the processing of personal data of non-contracting parties (so called 'silent party data') by account information service providers (hereinafter "AISPs") and payment initiation service providers (hereinafter "PISPs"), the procedures with regard to giving and withdrawing consent, the RTS and the cooperation between account servicing payment services providers (hereinafter "ASPSPs") in relation to security measures. Whereas the preparatory work of these guidelines involved the collection of inputs from stakeholders, both in writing and at a stakeholder event, in order to identify the most pressing challenges.

3.   These guidelines aim to provide further guidance on data protection aspects in the context of the PSD2, in particular on the relationship between relevant provisions on the GDPR and the PSD2. The main focus of these guidelines is on the processing of personal data by AISPs and PISPs. As such, this document addresses conditions for granting access to payment account information by ASPSPs and for the processing of personal data by PISPs and AISPs, including the requirements and safeguards in relation to the processing of personal data by PISPs and AISPs for purposes other than the initial purposes for which the data have been collected, especially when they have been collected in the context of the provision of an account information service[9]. This document also addresses different notions of explicit consent under the PSD2 and the GDPR, the processing of 'silent party data', the processing of special categories of personal data by PISPs and AISPs, the application of the main data protection principles set forth by the GDPR, including data minimisation, transparency, accountability and security measures. The PSD2 involves cross-functional responsibilities in the fields of, inter alia, consumer protection and competition law. Considerations regarding these fields of law are beyond the scope of these guidelines.

4.   To facilitate the reading of the guidelines the main definitions used in this document are provided below.

1.1 DEFINITIONS

'Account Information Service Provider' ('AISP')' refers to the provider of an online service to provide consolidated information on one or more payment accounts held by the payment service user with either another payment service provider or with more than one payment service provider;

'*Account Servicing Payment Service Provider*' ('*ASPSP*') refers to a payment service provider providing and maintaining a payment account for a payer;

'*Data minimisation*' is a principle of data protection, according to which personal data shall be adequate, relevant and limited to what is necessary in relation to the purposes for which they are processed;

'*Payer*' refers to a natural or legal person who holds a payment account and allows a payment order from that payment account, or, where there is no payment account, a natural or legal person who gives a payment order;

'*Payee*' refers to a natural or legal person who is the intended recipient of funds, which have been the subject of a payment transaction;

'*Payment account*' means an account held in the name of one or more payment service users, which is used for the execution of payment transactions;

'*Payment Initiation Service Provider*' ('*PISP*') refers to the provider of a service to initiate a payment order at the request of the payment service user with respect to a payment account held at another payment service provider;

'*Payment service provider*' refers to a means a body referred to in Article 1(1) of the PSD2[10] or a natural or legal person benefiting from an exemption pursuant to Article 32 or 33 of the PSD2;

'*Payment service user*' *means a natural or legal person making use of a payment service in the capacity of payer, payee, or both;*

'*Personal data*' *means any information relating to an identified or identifiable natural person ('data subject'); an identifiable natural person is one who can be identified, directly or indirectly, in particular by reference to an identifier such as a name, an identification number, location data, an online identifier or to one or more factors specific to the physical, physiological, genetic, mental, economic, cultural or social identity of that natural person;*

'*Data protection by design*' refers to technical and organizational measures embedded into a product or service, which are designed to implement data-protection principles, in an effective manner and to integrate the necessary safeguards into the processing in order to meet the requirements of the GDPR and protect the rights of data subjects;

'*Data protection by default*' refers to appropriate technical and organisational measures implemented in a product or service which ensure that, by default, only personal data which are necessary for each specific purpose of the processing are processed;

'*RTS*' refers to the Commission Delegated Regulation (EU) 2018/389 of 27 November 2017 supplementing Directive (EU) 2015/2366 of the European Parliament and of the Council with regard to regulatory technical standards for strong customer authentication and common and secure open standards of communication;

'*Third Party Providers*' ('*TPP*') refers to both PISPs and AISPs.

1.2 SERVICES UNDER THE PSD2

5. The PSD2 introduces two new kinds of payment service (providers): PISPs and AISPs. Annex 1 of the PSD2 contains the eight payment services that are covered by the PSD2.

6. PISPs provide services to initiate payment orders at the request of the payment service user with respect to a user's payment account held at another payment service provider[1f]. A PISP can request an ASPSP (usually a bank) to initiate a transaction on behalf of the payment service user. The (payment service) user can be a natural person (data subject) or a legal person.

7. AISPs provide online services for consolidated information on one or more payment accounts held by the payment service user either with another payment service provider or with more than one payment service provider[12]. According to recital 28 PSD2, the payment service user is able to have an overall view of its financial situation immediately at any given moment.

8. When it comes to account information services, there could be several different types of services offered, with the emphasis on different features and purposes. For example, some providers may offer users services such as budget planning and monitoring spending. The processing of personal data in the context of these services is covered by the PSD2. Services that entail creditworthiness assessments of the payment service user or audit services performed on the basis of the collection of information via an account information service fall outside of the scope of the PSD2 and therefore fall under the GDPR. Furthermore, accounts other than payment accounts (e.g. savings, investments) are not covered by the PSD2 either. In any case, the GDPR is the applicable legal framework for the processing of personal data.

Example 1:

HappyPayments is a company that offers an online service consisting of the provision of information on one or more payment accounts through a mobile app in order to provide financial oversight (an Account Information Service). With this service the payment service user can see at a glance the balances and recent transactions in two or more payment accounts at different banks. It also offers, when a payment service user chooses to do so, a categorisation of spending and income according to different typologies (salary, leisure, energy, mortgage, etc.), thus helping the payment service user with

> financial planning. Within this app, HappyPayments also offers a service to initiate payments directly from the users designated payment account(s) (a Payment Initiation Service).

9. In order to provide those services, the PSD2 regulates the legal conditions under which PISPs and AISPs can access payment accounts to provide a service to the payment service user.

10. Articles 66 (1) and 67 (1) PSD2 determine that the access and the use of payment and account information services are rights of the payment service user. This means that the payment service user should remain entirely free with regard to the exercise of such right and cannot be forced to make use of this right.

11. Access to payment accounts and the use of payment account information is partly regulated in Articles 66 and 67 PSD2, which contain safeguards regarding the protection of (personal) data. Article 66 (3)(f) PSD2 states that the PISP shall not request from the payment service user any data other than those necessary to provide the payment initiation service, and Article 66 (3)(g) PSD2 provides that PISPs shall not use, access or store any data for purposes other than for performing the payment initiation service explicitly requested by the payment service user. Furthermore, Article 67 (2)(d) PSD2 limits the access of AISPs to the information from designated payment accounts and associated payment transactions, whereas Article 67 (2)(f) PSD2 states that AISPs shall not use, access or store any data for purposes other than for performing the account information service explicitly requested by the payment service user, in accordance with data protection rules. The latter emphasises that, within the context of the account information services, personal data can only be collected for specified, explicit and legitimate purposes. An AISP should therefore make explicit in the contract for what specific purposes personal account information data are going to be processed for, in the context of the account information service it provides. The contract should be lawful, fair and transparent under Article 5 of the GDPR and also comply with other consumer protection laws.

12. Depending on specific circumstances, payment service providers could be a controller or processor under the GDPR. In these guidelines, 'controllers' are those payment service providers who, alone or jointly with others, determine the purposes and means of the processing of personal data. More guidance on this can be found in the EDPB Guidelines 07/2020 on the concepts of controller and processor in the GDPR.

NOTES

5   Art. 1 (1) GDPR.

6   Directive 2002/58/EC of the European Parliament and of the Council of 12 July 2002 concerning the processing of personal data and the protection of privacy in the electronic communications sector (Directive on privacy and electronic communications); OJ L 201, 31/07/2002 P. 0037 - 0047.

7   Art. 94 PSD etc.

8   Commission Delegated Regulation (EU) 2018/389 of 27 November 2017 supplementing Directive (EU) 2015/2366 of the European Parliament and of the Council with regard to regulatory technical standards for strong customer authentication and common and secure open standards of communication (Text with EEA relevance.); C/2017/7782; OJ L 69, 13.3.2018, p. 23–43; available at https://eur-lex.europa.eu/legalcontent/ EN/TXT/PDF/?uri=CELEX:32018R0389&from=EN.

9   An account information service is an online service to provide consolidated information on one or more payment accounts held by the payment service user either with another payment service provider or with more than one payment service provider.

10   Art. 1 (1) PSD2 states that the PSD2 establishes the rules in accordance with which Member States shall distinguish between the following categories of *payment service provider*:

    (a)   credit institutions as defined in point (1) of Art. 4(1) of Regulation (EU) No 575/2013 of the European Parliament and of the Council (1), including branches thereof within the meaning of point (17) Art. 4(1) of that Regulation where such branches are located in the Union, whether the head offices of those branches are located within the Union or, in accordance with Art. 47 of Directive 2013/36/EU and with national law, outside the Union;

    (b)   electronic money institutions within the meaning of point (1) of Art. 2 of Directive 2009/110/EC, including, in accordance with Art. 8 of that Directive and with national law, branches thereof, where such branches are located within the Union and their head offices are located outside the Union, in as far as the payment services provided by those branches are linked to the issuance of electronic money;

    (c)   post office giro institutions which are entitled under national law to provide payment services;

    (d)   payment institutions;

    (e)   the ECB and national central banks when not acting in their capacity as monetary authority or other public authorities;

    (f)   Member States or their regional or local authorities when not acting in their capacity as public authorities.

11   Art. 4 (15) PSD2.

12   Art. 4 (16) PSD2.

---

2 LAWFUL GROUNDS AND FURTHER PROCESSING UNDER THE PSD2

2.1 LAWFUL GROUNDS FOR PROCESSING

[2.357]

13. Under the GDPR, controllers must have a legal basis in order to process personal data. Article 6 (1) of the GDPR constitutes an exhaustive and restrictive list of six legal bases for processing of personal data under the GDPR[13]. It is up to the controller to define the appropriate legal basis and ensure that all conditions for this legal basis are met. Determining which basis is valid and most appropriate in a specific situation depends on the circumstances under which the processing takes place, including the purpose of the processing and relationship between the controller and the data subject.

Part 2   Data Protection: EU Law etc

2.2 ARTICLE 6(1)(B) OF THE GDPR (PROCESSING IS NECESSARY FOR THE PERFORMANCE OF A CONTRACT)

14. Payment services are provided on a contractual basis between the payment services user and the payment services provider. As stated in recital 87 of the PSD2, *"[t]his Directive should concern only contractual obligations and responsibilities between the payment service user and the payment service provider."* In terms of the GDPR, the main legal basis for the processing of personal data for the provision of payment services is Article 6(1)(b) of the GDPR, meaning that the processing is necessary for the performance of a contract to which the data subject is party or in order to take steps at the request of the data subject prior to entering into a contract.

15. The payment services under the PSD2 are defined in annex 1 of the PSD2. The provision of these services as defined by the PSD2 is a requirement for the establishment of a contract in which parties have access to payment account data of the payment service user. These payment service providers also have to be licenced operators. In relation to payment initiation services and account information services under the PSD2, contracts may incorporate terms that also impose conditions about additional services that are not regulated by the PSD2. The *EDPB Guidelines 2/2019 on the processing of personal data under Article 6(1)(b) GDPR in the context of the provision of online services to data subjects* make clear that controllers have to assess what processing of personal data is objectively necessary to perform the contract. These Guidelines point out that the justification of the necessity is dependent on the nature of the service, the mutual perspectives and expectations of the parties to the contract, the rationale of the contract and the essential elements of the contract.

16. The EDPB guidelines 2/2019 also make clear that, in light of Article 7(4) of the GDPR, a distinction is made between processing activities necessary for the performance of a contract and terms making the service conditional on certain processing activities that are not in fact necessary for the performance of the contract. 'Necessary for performance' clearly requires something more than a contractual condition[14]. The controller should be able to demonstrate how the main object of the specific contract with the data subject cannot, as a matter of fact, be performed if the specific processing of the personal data in question does not occur. Merely referencing or mentioning data processing in a contract is not enough to bring the processing in question within the scope of Article 6(1)(b) of the GDPR.

17. Article 5 (1)(b) of the GDPR provides for the purpose limitation principle, which requires that personal data must be collected for specified, explicit, and legitimate purposes and not further processed in a manner that is incompatible with those purposes. When assessing whether Article 6(1)(b) is an appropriate legal basis for an online (payment) service, regard should be given to the particular aim, purpose, or objective of the service[15]. The purposes of the processing must be clearly specified and communicated to the data subject, in line with the controller's purpose limitation and transparency obligations. Assessing what is 'necessary' involves a combined, fact based assessment of the processing "for the objective pursued and of whether it is less intrusive compared to other options for achieving the same goal". Article 6(1)(b) does not cover processing which is useful but not objectively necessary for performing the contractual service or for taking relevant pre-contractual steps at the request of the data subject, even if it is necessary for the controller's other business purposes[16].

18. The EDPB Guidelines 2/2019 make clear that contracts cannot artificially expand the categories of personal data or types of processing operation that the controller needs to carry out for the performance of the contract within the meaning of Article 6(1)(b)[17]. These Guidelines also address cases in which 'take it or leave it' situations may be created for data subjects who may only be interested in one of the services. This could happen when a controller wishes to bundle several separate services or elements of a service with different fundamental purposes, features or rationale into one contract. Where the contract consists of several separate services or elements of a service that can in fact reasonably be performed independently of one another, the applicability of Article 6(1)(b) should be assessed in the context of each of those services separately, looking at what is objectively necessary to perform each of the individual services which the data subject has actively requested or signed up for[18].

19. In line with the abovementioned Guidelines, controllers have to assess what is objectively necessary for the performance of the contract. Where controllers cannot demonstrate that the processing of the personal payment account data is objectively necessary for the provision of each of these services separately, Article 6 (1)(b) of the GDPR is not a valid legal ground for processing. In these cases, the controller should consider another legal basis for processing.

2.3 FRAUD PREVENTION

20. Article 94 (1) PSD2 states that Member States shall permit processing of personal data by payment systems and payment service providers when necessary to safeguard the prevention, investigation and detection of payment fraud. The processing of personal data strictly necessary for the purposes of preventing fraud could constitute a legitimate interest of the payment service provider concerned, provided that such interests are not overridden by the interests or fundamental rights and freedoms of the data subject[19]. Processing activities for the purpose of fraud prevention should be based on a careful case by case evaluation by the controller, in accordance with the accountability principle. In addition, to prevent fraud, controllers may also be subject to specific legal obligations that necessitate the processing of personal data.

2.4 FURTHER PROCESSING (AISP AND PISP)

21. Article 6 (4) of the GDPR determines the conditions for the processing of personal data for a purpose other than that for which the personal data have been collected. More specifically, such further processing may take place, where it is based on a Union or Member State law, which constitutes a necessary and proportionate measure in a democratic society to safeguard the objectives referred to in Article 23(1), where the data subject has given their consent or where the processing for a purpose other than that for which the personal data were collected is compatible with the initial purpose.

22.   Articles 66 (3)(g) and 67 (2)(f) of the PSD2 have to be taken into careful consideration. As mentioned above, Article 66 (3)(g) of the PSD2 states that the PISP shall not use, access or store any data for purposes other than for the provision of the payment initiation service as explicitly requested by the payer. Article 67 (2)(f) of the PSD2 states that the AISP shall not use, access or store any data for purposes other than for performing the account information service explicitly requested by the payment service user, in accordance with data protection rules.

23.   Consequently, Article 66(3)(g) and Article 67 (2)(f) of the PSD2 considerably restrict the possibilities for processing for other purposes, meaning that the processing for another purpose is not allowed, unless the data subject has given consent pursuant to Article 6(1)(a) of the GDPR or the processing is laid down by Union law or Member State law to which the controller is subject, pursuant to Article 6 (4) of the GDPR. Where the processing for a purpose other than that for which the personal data have been collected is not based on the data subject's consent or on a Union or Member State law, the restrictions laid down in Article 66(3)(g) and Article 67(2)(f) of the PSD2 make clear that any other purpose is not compatible with the purpose for which the personal data are initially collected. The compatibility test of Article 6(4) GDPR cannot result in a legal basis for processing.

24.   Article 6 (4) of the GDPR allows for further processing based on Union or Member State law. For example, all PISPs and AISPs are obliged entities under Article 3 (2)(a) Directive (EU) 2015/849 of the European Parliament and of the Council of 20 May 2015 on the prevention of the use of the financial system for the purposes of money laundering or terrorist financing of the anti-money laundering directive. These obliged entities are therefore compelled to apply the customer due diligence measures as specified in the directive. The personal data processed in connection with a PSD2 service are, therefore, further processed based on at least one legal obligation resting on the service provider[20].

25.   As mentioned in paragraph 20, Article 6 (4) of the GDPR indicates that the processing for a purpose other than that for which the personal data have been collected could be based on the data subject's consent, if all the conditions for consent under the GDPR are met. As set out above, the controller needs to demonstrate that it is possible to refuse or withdraw consent without detriment (recital 42 of the GDPR).

2.5 LAWFUL GROUND FOR GRANTING ACCESS TO THE ACCOUNT (ASPSPS)

26.   As mentioned in paragraph 10, payment service users can exercise their right to make use of payment initiation and account information services. The obligations imposed on the Member States in Articles 66(1) and 67(1) of the PSD2 should be implemented in national law in order to guarantee the effective application of the right of the payment service user to benefit from the aforementioned payment services. The effective application of such rights would not be possible without the existence of a corresponding obligation on the ASPSP, typically a bank, to grant the payment service provider access to the account under the condition that it has fulfilled all requirements to get access to the account of the payment service user. Furthermore, Articles 66(5) and 67(4) of the PSD2 state clearly that the provision of payment initiation services and of account information services shall not be dependent on the existence of a contractual relationship between the PISP/AISP and the ASPSP.

27.   The processing of personal data by the ASPSP consisting of granting access to the personal data requested by the PISP and AISP in order to perform their payment service to the payment service user is based on a legal obligation. In order to achieve the objectives of the PSD2, ASPSPs must provide the personal data for the PISPs' and AISPs' services, which is a necessary condition for PISPs and AISPs to provide their services and thus ensure the rights provided for in Articles 66(1) and 67(1) of the PSD2. Therefore, the applicable legal ground in this case is Article 6 (1)(c) of the GDPR.

28.   As the GDPR has specified that processing based on a legal obligation should be clearly laid down by Union or Member State law (see Article 6 (3) of the GDPR), the obligation for ASPSPs to grant access should stem from the national law transposing the PSD2.

NOTES

13   According to Article 6 processing shall be lawful only if and to the extent that at least one of the following applies:

    (a)   the data subject has given consent to the processing of his or her personal data for one or more specific purposes;

    (b)   processing is necessary for the performance of a contract to which the data subject is party or in order to take steps at the request of the data subject prior to entering into a contract;

    (c)   processing is necessary for compliance with a legal obligation to which the controller is subject;

    (d)   processing is necessary in order to protect the vital interests of the data subject or of another natural person;

    (e)   processing is necessary for the performance of a task carried out in the public interest or in the exercise of official authority vested in the controller;

    (f)   processing is necessary for the purposes of the legitimate interests pursued by the controller or by a third party, except where such interests are overridden by the interests or fundamental rights and freedoms of the data subject which require protection of personal data, in particular where the data subject is a child.

14   Guidelines 2/2019 on the processing of personal data under Article 6(1)(b) GDPR in the context of the provision of online services to data subjects, EDPB, page 8.

15   Idem.

16   Idem, page 7.

17   Idem, page 10.

18   Idem, page 11.

[19]   Recital 47 GDPR.
[20]   Note that a thorough examination of the question whether the anti-money laundering directive meets the standard of Art. 6 (4) GDPR falls outside of the scope of this document.

3 EXPLICIT CONSENT

3.1 CONSENT UNDER THE GDPR

[2.358]
29.   Under the GDPR, consent serves as one of the six legal grounds for the lawfulness of processing of personal data. Article 4 (11) of the GDPR defines consent as "any freely given, specific, informed and unambiguous indication of the data subject's wishes by which he or she, by a statement or by a clear affirmative action, signifies agreement to the processing of personal data relating to him or her". These four conditions, freely given, specific, informed, and unambiguous, are essential for the validity of consent. According to the EDPB Guidelines 05/2020 on consent under Regulation 2016/679, consent can only be an appropriate lawful basis if a data subject is offered control and a genuine choice with regard to accepting or declining the terms offered or declining them without detriment. When asking for consent, a controller has the duty to assess whether it will meet all the requirements to obtain valid consent. If obtained in full compliance with the GDPR, consent is a tool that gives data subjects control over whether or not personal data concerning them will be processed. If not, the data subject's control becomes illusory and consent will be an invalid legal basis for processing, rendering the processing activity unlawful[21].

30.   The GDPR also contains further safeguards in Article 7, which sets out that the data controller must be in a position to demonstrate that there had been valid consent at the time of processing. Also, the request for consent must be presented in a manner which is clearly distinguishable from the other matters, in an intelligible and easily accessible form, using clear and plain language. Furthermore, the data subject must be informed of the right to withdraw consent at any time, in just as simple a way as it was to grant consent.

31.   According to Article 9 GDPR, consent is one of the exceptions from the general prohibition for processing special categories of personal data. However, in such case the data subject's consent must be 'explicit'[22].

32.   According to the EDPB Guidelines 05/2020 on consent under Regulation 2016/679, explicit consent under the GDPR refers to the way consent is expressed by the data subject. It means that the data subject should give an express statement of consent for specific processing purpose(s). An obvious way to make sure consent is explicit would be to expressly confirm consent in a written statement. Where appropriate, the controller could make sure the written statement is signed by the data subject, in order to remove all possible doubt and potential lack of evidence in the future.

33.   Under no circumstances can consent be inferred from potentially ambiguous statements or actions. A controller must also beware that consent cannot be obtained through the same motion as agreeing to a contract or accepting general terms and conditions of a service.

3.2 CONSENT UNDER THE PSD2

34.   The EDPB notes that the legal framework regarding explicit consent is complex, since both the PSD2 and the GDPR include the concept of 'explicit consent'. This leads to the question whether "explicit consent" as mentioned in Article 94 (2) PSD2 should be interpreted in the same way as explicit consent under the GDPR.

3.2.1 Explicit consent under Article 94 (2) PSD2

35.   The PSD2 includes a number of specific rules concerning the processing of personal data, in particular in Article 94 (1) of the PSD2, which determines that the processing of personal data for the purposes of the PSD2 must comply with EU data protection law. Furthermore, Article 94 (2) of the PSD2 sets out that payment service providers shall only access, process and retain personal data necessary for the provision of their payment services, with the explicit consent of the payment service user. Pursuant to Article 33 (2) of the PSD2, this requirement of the explicit consent of the payment service user does not apply to AISPs. However, Article 67 (2)(a) of the PSD2 still provides for explicit consent for AISPs for the provision of the service.

36.   As mentioned above, the list of lawful bases for processing under the GDPR is exhaustive. As mentioned in paragraph 14, the legal basis for the processing of personal data for the provision of payment services is, in principle, Article 6(1)(b) of the GDPR, meaning that the processing is necessary for the performance of a contract to which the data subject is party or in order to take steps at the request of the data subject prior to entering into a contract. From that, it follows that Article 94 (2) of the PSD2 cannot be regarded as an additional legal basis for processing of personal data. The EDPB considers that, in view of the foregoing, this paragraph should be interpreted, on the one hand, in coherence with the applicable data protection legal framework and, on the other hand, in a way that preserves its useful effect. Explicit consent under Article 94(2) PSD2 should therefore be regarded as an additional requirement of a contractual nature[23] in relation to the access to and subsequently processing and storage of personal data for the purpose of providing payment services and is therefore not the same as (explicit) consent under the GDPR.

37.   "Explicit consent" referred to in Article 94 (2) PSD2 is a contractual consent. This implies that Article 94 (2) PSD2 should be interpreted in the sense that when entering a contract with a payment service provider under the PSD2, data subjects must be made fully aware of the specific categories of personal data that will be processed. Further, they have to be made aware of the specific (payment service) purpose for which their personal data will be processed and have to explicitly agree to these clauses. Such clauses should be clearly distinguishable from the other matters dealt with in the contract and would need to be explicitly accepted by the data subject.

38. Central to the notion of "explicit consent" under Article 94 (2) of the PSD2 is the gaining of access to personal data to subsequently process and store these data for the purpose of providing payment services. This implies that the payment service[24] provider is not yet processing the personal data, but needs access to personal data that have been processed under the responsibility of any other controller. If a payment service user enters into a contract with, for example, a payment initiation service provider, this provider needs to obtain access to personal data of the payment service user that is being processed under the responsibility of the account servicing payment service provider. The object of the explicit consent under Article 94 (2) PSD2 is the permission to obtain access to those personal data, to be able to process and store these personal data that are necessary for the purpose of providing the payment service. If explicit consent is given by the data subject, the account servicing payment service provider is obliged to give access to the indicated personal data.

39. Although the consent of Article 94 (2) of the PSD2 is not a legal ground for the processing of personal data, this consent is specifically related to personal data and data protection, and ensures transparency and a degree of control for the payment service user[25]. While the PSD2 does not specify the substantive conditions for consent under Article 94 (2) PSD2, it should, as stated above, be understood in coherence with the applicable data protection legal framework and in a way that preserves its useful effect.

40. With regard to the information to be provided by controllers and the requirement of transparency, Article 29 Working Party Guidelines on Transparency specifies that a *"A central consideration of the principle of transparency outlined in these provisions is that the data subject should be able to determine in advance what the scope and consequences of the processing entails and that they should not be taken by surprise at a later point about the ways in which their personal data has been used"[26].*

41. Furthermore, as required by the principle of purpose limitation, personal data must be collected for specified, explicit and legitimate purposes (Article 5 (1)(b) of the GDPR). Where personal data are collected for more than one purpose, *"controllers should avoid identifying only one broad purpose in order to justify various further processing activities which are in fact only remotely related to the actual initial purpose"[27].* The EDPB has highlighted, most recently in the context of contracts for online services, the risk of inclusion of general processing terms in contracts and has stated that the purpose of the collection should be clearly and specifically identified: it should be detailed enough to determine what kind of processing is and is not included within the specified purpose, and to allow that compliance with the law can be assessed and data protection safeguards applied[28].

42. When considered in the context of the additional requirement of explicit consent pursuant to Article 94(2) of the PSD2, this entails that controllers must provide data subjects with specific and explicit information about the specific purposes identified by the controller for which their personal data are accessed, processed and retained. In line with Article 94(2) of the PSD2, the data subjects must explicitly accept these specific purposes.

43. Furthermore, as set out above in paragraph 10, the EDPB highlights that the payment service user must be able to choose whether or not to use the service and cannot be forced to do so. Therefore, the consent under Article 94 (2) of the PSD2 also has to be a freely given consent.

3.3 CONCLUSION

44. Explicit consent under the PSD2 is different from (explicit) consent under the GDPR. Explicit consent under Article 94 (2) of the PSD2 is an additional requirement of a contractual nature. When a payment service provider needs access to personal data for the provision of a payment service, explicit consent in line with Article 94 (2) of the PSD2 of the payment service user is needed.

NOTES
21   Guidelines 05/2020 on consent under Regulation 2016/679, EDPB, para. 3.
22   See also Opinion 15/2011 on the definition of consent (WP 187), pp. 6-8, and/or Opinion 06/2014 on the notion of legitimate interests of the data controller under Article 7 of Directive 95/46/EC (WP 217), pp. 9, 10, 13 and 14.
23   Letter of the EDPB regarding the PSD2 directive, 5 July 2018, page 4.
24   This applies to services 1 to 7 of Annex 1 of the PSD2.
25   Art. 94 (2) PSD2 falls under Chapter 4 'Data protection'.
26   Article 29 Working Party, Guidelines on transparency under Regulation 2016/679, paragraph 10 (adopted on 11 April 2018) - endorsed by the EDPB.
27   Article 29 Working Party Opinion 03/2013 on purpose limitation (WP203), page 16.
28   Guidelines 2/2019 on the processing of personal data under Article 6(1)(b) GDPR in the context of the provision of online services to data subjects, paragraph 16 (public consultation version) and Article 29 Working Party Opinion 03/2013 on purpose limitation (WP203), page 15–16.

4 THE PROCESSING OF SILENT PARTY DATA

4.1 SILENT PARTY DATA

[2.359]
45. A data protection issue that needs careful consideration, is the processing of so called 'silent party

data'. In the context of this document, silent party data are personal data concerning a data subject who is not the user of a specific payment service provider, but whose personal data are processed by that specific payment service provider for the performance of a contract between the provider and the payment service user. This is for example the case where a payment service user, data subject A, makes use of the services of an AISP, and data subject B has made a series of payment transactions to the payment account of data subject A. In this case, data subject B is regarded as the 'silent party' and the personal data (such as the account number of data subject B and the amount of money that was involved in these transactions) relating to data subject B, is regarded as 'silent party data'.

4.2 THE LEGITIMATE INTEREST OF THE CONTROLLER

46. Article 5 (1)(b) GDPR requires that personal data are only collected for specified, explicit and legitimate purposes and may not be further processed in a manner that is incompatible with those purposes. In addition, the GDPR requires that any processing of personal data must be both necessary as well as proportionate and in line with the data protection principles, such as those of purpose limitation and data minimisation.

47. The GDPR may allow for the processing of silent party data when this processing is necessary for purposes of the legitimate interests pursued by a controller or by a third party (Article 6 (1)(f) GDPR). However, such processing can only take place when the legitimate interest of the controller is not "overridden by the interests or fundamental rights and freedoms of the data subject which require protection of personal data".

48. A lawful basis for the processing of silent party data by PISPs and AISPs - in the context of the provision of payment services under the PSD2 - could thus be the legitimate interest of a controller or a third party to perform the contract with the payment service user. The necessity to process personal data of the silent party is limited and determined by the reasonable expectations of these data subjects. In the context of providing payment services that are covered by the PSD2, effective and appropriate measures have to be established to safeguard that the interests or fundamental rights and freedoms of the silent parties are not overridden, and to ensure that the reasonable expectations of these data subjects regarding the processing of their personal data are respected. In this respect, the controller (AISP or PISP) has to establish the necessary safeguards for the processing in order to protect the rights of data subjects. This includes technical measures to ensure that silent party data are not processed for a purpose other than the purpose for which the personal data were originally collected by PISPs and AISPs. If feasible, also encryption or other techniques should be applied to achieve an appropriate level of security and data minimisation.

4.3 FURTHER PROCESSING OF PERSONAL DATA OF THE SILENT PARTY

49. As stated under paragraph 29, personal data processed in connection with a payment service regulated by the PSD2, could be further processed based on legal obligations resting on the service provider. These legal obligations could concern personal data of the silent party.

50. With regard to further processing of silent party data on the basis of legitimate interest, the EDPB is of the opinion that these data cannot be used for a purpose other than that for which the personal data have been collected, other on the basis of EU or Member State law. Consent of the silent party is legally not feasible, because in order to obtain consent, personal data of the silent party would have to be collected or processed, for which no legal ground can be found under Article 6 GDPR. The compatibility test of Article 6.4 of the GDPR cannot offer a ground for the processing for other purposes (e.g. direct marketing activities) either. The rights and freedoms of these silent party data subjects will not be respected if the new data controller uses the personal data for other purposes, taking into account the context in which the personal data have been collected, especially the absence of any relationship with the data subjects that are silent parties[29]; the absence of any connection between any other purpose and the purpose for which the personal data were initially collected (i.e. the fact that PSPs only need the silent party data in order to perform a contract with the other contracting party); the nature of the personal data involved[30], the circumstance that data subjects are not in a position to reasonably expect any further processing or to even be aware which controller may be processing their personal data and given the legal restrictions on processing set out in Article 66 (3)(g) and Article 67 (2)(f) of PSD2.

NOTES

29 Recital 87 of PSD2 states that PSD2 only concerns 'contractual obligations and responsibilities between the payment service user and the payment service provider'. Silent Party Data therefore do not fall under the scope of PSD2.

30 Particular care should be taken when processing financial personal data, as the processing can be considered as increasing the possible risk to the rights and freedoms of individuals, according to the Guidelines on Data Protection Impact Assessment (DPIA).

5 THE PROCESSING OF SPECIAL CATEGORIES OF PERSONAL DATA UNDER THE PSD2

5.1 SPECIAL CATEGORIES OF PERSONAL DATA

[2.360]
51. Article 9 (1) GDPR prohibits the processing of "personal data revealing racial or ethnic origin, political opinions, religious or philosophical beliefs, or trade union membership, and the processing of genetic data, biometric data for the purpose of uniquely identifying a natural person, data concerning health or data concerning a natural person's sex life or sexual orientation".

52. It should be emphasised that in some Member States, electronic payments are already ubiquitous, and are favoured by many people over cash in their day to day transactions. At the same time, financial transactions can reveal sensitive information about an individual data subject, including those related to special categories of personal data. For example, depending on the transaction details, political opinions and religious beliefs may be revealed by donations made to political parties or organisations, churches or parishes. Trade union membership may be revealed by the deduction of an annual membership fee from a person's bank account. Personal data concerning health may be gathered from analysing medical bills paid by a data subject to a medical professional (for instance a psychiatrist). Finally, information on certain purchases may reveal information concerning a person's sex life or sexual orientation. As shown by these examples, even single transactions can contain special categories of personal data. Moreover, account information services might rely on profiling as defined by article 4 (4) of the GDPR. As previously stated in the Working Party 29 Guidelines on Automated individual decision-making and Profiling for the purposes of Regulation 2016/679, as endorsed by the EDPB , "profiling can create special category of data by inference from data which is not special category of data in its own right, but becomes so when combined with other data."[31] This means that, through the sum of financial transactions, different kinds of behavioural patterns can be revealed, which may include special categories of personal data. Therefore, the chances are considerable that a service provider processing information on financial transactions of data subjects also processes special categories of personal data.

53. With regard to the term 'sensitive payment data', the EDPB notes the following. The definition of sensitive payment data in the PSD2 differs considerably from the way the term 'sensitive personal data' is commonly used within the context of the GDPR and data protection (law). Where the PSD2 defines 'sensitive payment data' as 'data, including personalized security credentials which can be used to carry out fraud', the GDPR emphasises the need for specific protection of special categories of personal data which under Article 9 of the GDPR are, by their nature, particularly sensitive in relation to fundamental rights and freedoms, such as special categories of personal data[32]. In this regard it is recommended to at least map out and categorize precisely what kind of personal data will be processed. Most probably a Data Protection Impact Assessment (DPIA) will be required in accordance with article 35 GDPR, which will help in this mapping exercise. More guidance on DPIAs can be found in the Working Party 29 Guidelines on Data Protection Impact Assessment (DPIA) and determining whether processing is "likely to result in a high risk" for the purposes of Regulation 2016/679, as endorsed by the EDPB.

5.2 POSSIBLE DEROGATIONS

54. The prohibition of Article 9 GDPR is not absolute. In particular, whereas derogations of paragraphs (b)-(f) and (h)-(j) of Article 9 (2) GDPR are manifestly not applicable to the processing of personal data in the PSD2 context, the following two derogations in Article 9 (2) GDPR could be considered:

(a)   The prohibition does not apply if the data subject has given explicit consent to the processing of those personal data for one or more specified purposes (Article 9 (2)(a) GDPR).

(b)   The prohibition does not apply if the processing is necessary for reasons of substantial public interest, on the basis of Union or Member State law which shall be proportionate to the aim pursued, respect the essence of the right to data protection and provide for suitable and specific measures to safeguard the fundamental rights and the interests of the data subject (Article 9 (2)(g) GDPR).

(c)   It should be pointed out that the list of derogations in Article 9 (2) GDPR is exhaustive. The possibility that special categories of personal data are included in the personal data processed for the provision of any of the services falling under the PSD2 must be recognised by the service provider. As the prohibition of Article 9 (1) GDPR is applicable to these service providers, they must ensure that one of the exceptions in Article 9 (2) GDPR is applicable to them. It should be emphasised that where the service provider cannot show that one of the derogations is met, the prohibition of article 9 (1) is applicable.

55. It should be pointed out that the list of derogations in Article 9 (2) GDPR is exhaustive. The possibility that special categories of personal data are included in the personal data processed for the provision of any of the services falling under the PSD2 must be recognised by the service provider. As the prohibition of Article 9 (1) GDPR is applicable to these service providers, they must ensure that one of the exceptions in Article 9 (2) GDPR is applicable to them. It should be emphasised that where the service provider cannot show that one of the derogations is met, the prohibition of article 9 (1) is applicable.

5.3 SUBSTANTIAL PUBLIC INTEREST

56. Payments services may process special categories personal data for reasons of substantial public interest, but only when all the conditions of Article 9 (2)(g) of the GDPR are met. This means that the processing of the special categories of personal data has to be addressed in a specific derogation to article 9 (1) GDPR in Union or Member State law. This provision will have to address the proportionality in relation to the pursued aim of the processing and contain suitable and specific measures to safeguard the fundamental rights and the interests of the data subject. Furthermore, this provision under Union or Member State law will have to respect the essence of the right to data protection. Finally, the processing of the special categories of data must also be demonstrated to be necessary for the reason of the substantial public interest, including interests of systemic importance. Only when all of these conditions are fully met, this derogation could be made applicable to designated types of payment services.

5.4 EXPLICIT CONSENT

57. In cases where the derogation of article 9 (2)(g) GDPR does not apply, obtaining explicit consent in accordance with the conditions for valid consent in the GDPR, seems to remain the only possible lawful derogation to process special categories of personal data by TPPs. The EDPB Guidelines 05/2020 on consent under Regulation 2016/679 states[33] that: "Article 9(2) does not recognize "necessary for the performance of a contract" as an exception to the general prohibition to process special categories of data. Therefore, controllers and Member States that deal with this situation should explore the specific exceptions in Article 9(2) subparagraphs (b) to (j). When service providers rely on Article 9 (2)(a) GDPR, they must ensure that they have been granted explicit consent before commencing the processing." Explicit consent as set out in Article 9 (2)(a) GDPR must meet all the requirements of the GDPR.

5.5 NO SUITABLE DEROGATION

58. As noted above, where the service provider cannot show that one of the derogations is met, the prohibition of Article 9 (1) is applicable. In this case technical measures could be put in place to prevent the processing of special categories of personal data, for instance by preventing the processing of certain data points. In this respect, payment service providers may explore the technical possibilities to exclude special categories of personal data and allow a selected access which would prevent the processing of special categories of personal data related to silent parties by TPPs.

NOTES

[31] Article 29 Data Protection Working Party, Guidelines on Automated individual decision-making and Profiling for the purposes of Regulation 2016/679, WP251rev.01, page 15.

[32] For example, in recital 10 of the GDPR, special categories of personal data are being referred to as 'sensitive data'.

[33] Guidelines 05/2020 on consent under Regulation 2016/679, EDPB, para. 99

---

6 DATA MINIMISATION, SECURITY, TRANSPARENCY, ACCOUNTABILITY AND PROFILING

6.1 DATA MINIMISATION AND DATA PROTECTION BY DESIGN AND DEFAULT

[2.361]
59. The principle of data minimisation is enshrined in Article 5 (1)(c) GDPR: "Personal data shall be [. . .] adequate, relevant and limited to what is necessary in relation to the purposes for which they are processed". Essentially, under the principle of data minimisation, controllers should process no more personal data than what is necessary in order to achieve the specific purpose in question. As pointed out in Chapter 2, the amount and the kind of personal data necessary to provide the payment service is determined by the objective and mutually understood contractual purpose[34]. Data minimisation is applicable to every processing (e.g. every collection of or access to and request of personal data). The EDPB Guidelines 4/2019 on Article 25 Data Protection by Design and by Default (DPbDD), state that 'processors and technology providers are also recognised as key enablers for DPbDD, they should also be aware that controllers are required to only process personal data with systems and technologies that have built-in data protection[36].'

60. Article 25 of the GDPR contains the obligations to apply data protection by design and by default. These obligations are of particular importance to the principle of data minimisation. This Article determines that controllers shall, both at the time of the determination of the means for processing and at the time of the processing itself, implement appropriate technical and organisational measures, which are designed to implement data protection principles in an effective manner and to integrate the necessary safeguards into the processing in order to meet the requirements of the GDPR and protect the rights of data subjects. The controller shall implement appropriate technical and organisational measures for ensuring that, by default, only personal data which are necessary for each specific purpose of the processing are processed. That obligation applies to the amount of personal data collected, the extent of their processing, the period of their storage and their accessibility. These measures may include encryption, pseudonymisation and other technical measures.

61. When the obligation of article 25 of the GDPR is applied, the state of the art, the cost of implementation and the nature, scope, context and purposes of processing as well as the risks of varying likelihood and severity for rights and freedoms of natural persons posed by the processing are the elements that have to be taken into account. Further clarifications about this obligation are given in the abovementioned EDPB Guidelines 4/2019 on Article 25 Data Protection by Design and by Default.

6.2 DATA MINIMISATION MEASURES

62. The TPP accessing payment account data in order to provide the requested services must also take the principle of data minimisation into account and must only collect personal data necessary to provide the specific payment services requested by the payment service user. As a principle, the access to the personal data should be limited to what is necessary for the provision of payment services. As has been shown in Chapter 2, the PSD2 requires ASPSPs to share payment service user information on request of the payment service user, when the payment service user wishes to use a payment initiation service or an account information service.

63. When not all payment account data are necessary for the provision of the contract, a selection of the relevant data categories should be made by the AISP before the data are collected. For instance, data categories that may not be necessary may include the identity of the silent party and the transaction characteristics. Also, unless required by Member State or EU law, the IBAN of the silent party's bank account may not need to be displayed.

64. In this respect, the possible application of technical measures that enable or support TPPs in their obligation to access and retrieve only the personal data necessary for the provision of their services could be considered, as part of the implementation of appropriate data protection policies, in line with article 24 (2) GDPR. In this respect, the EDPB recommends the usage of digital tools in order to support AISPs in their obligation to only collect personal data that are necessary for the purposes for which they are processed. For instance, when a service provider does not need the transaction characteristics (in the description field of the transaction records) for the provision of their service, a digital selection tool could function as a means for TPPs to exclude this field from the overall processing operations by the TPP.

Example 2:

HappyPayments, our Account Information Service provider from example 1, wants to ensure that it only processes the personal payment account data which its users are interested in. To seek access to more payment account data would not be necessary for the provision of the service. Therefore, it allows the users to select the specific types of information they are interested in.

User A wants an overview of its spending for the last two months. Thus, it asks for its two banking accounts, held with two different ASPSPs, the information on all transactions of the last two months, the transaction amount, the date of execution and the recipient's name, and ticks the corresponding boxes in HappyPayments' user interface.

HappyPayments then commences to request from the respective ASPSPs only the information corresponding to the fields set by User A and only for the period of the last two months. Information such as the "communication" of the transfer or even the IBAN are not requested, as User A did not ask for this information.

To allow HappyPayments to comply with its data minimisation obligations, the ASPSPs allow HappyPayments to request specific fields for a range of dates.

---

65. It should also be noted in this regard that under the PSD2, ASPSPs are only allowed to provide access to payment account information. There is no legal basis under the PSD2 to provide access with regard to personal data contained in other accounts, such as savings, mortgages or investment accounts. Accordingly, under the PSD2, technical measures have to be implemented to ensure that access is limited to the necessary payment account information.

66. Besides collecting as little data as possible, the service provider also has to implement limited retention periods. Personal data should not be stored by the service provider for a period longer than is necessary in relation to the purposes requested by the payment service user.

67. If the contract between the data subject and the AISP requires the transmission of personal data to third parties, then only those personal data that are necessary for the execution of the contract can be transmitted. Data subjects should also be specifically informed about the transmission and the personal data that are going to be transmitted to this third party.

6.3 SECURITY

68. The EDPB already highlighted that the violation of financial personal data *"clearly involves serious impacts in the data subject's daily life"* and quotes the risks of payment fraud as an example[36].

69. Where a data breach involves financial data, the data subject may be exposed to considerable risks. Depending on the information that is leaked, data subjects may be exposed to a risk of identity theft, of theft of the funds in their accounts and other assets. Furthermore, there is the possibility that the exposure of transaction data is related to considerable privacy risks, as transaction data may contain references to all aspects of a data subject's private life. At the same time, financial data are obviously valuable to criminals and therefore an attractive target.

70. As controllers, payment service providers are obligated to take adequate measures to protect the personal data of data subjects (Article 24 (1) GDPR). The higher the risks associated with the processing activity carried out by the controller, the higher the security standards that need to be applied. As the processing of financial data is connected to a variety of severe risks, the security measures should be accordingly high.

71. Service providers should be held to high standards, including strong customer authentication mechanisms and high security standards for the technical equipment[37]. Other procedures, such as vetting processors for security standards and implementing procedures against unauthorised access, are also important.

6.4 TRANSPARENCY AND ACCOUNTABILITY

72. Transparency and accountability are two fundamental principles of the GDPR.

73. With regard to transparency (Article 5 (1)(a) of the GDPR), Article 12 of the GDPR specifies that controllers shall take appropriate measures to provide any information referred to in Articles 13 and 14 GDPR. Furthermore, it requires that the information or communication about the processing of personal data must be concise, transparent, intelligible and easily accessible. The information must be in clear and plain language and in writing "or by other means, including where appropriate, by electronic means". The Article 29 Working Party 'Guidelines on transparency under Regulation 2016/679', as endorsed by the EDPB, offers specific guidance for compliance with the principle of transparency in digital environments.

74. According to the abovementioned Guidelines on transparency under Regulation 2016/679, Article 11 GDPR should be interpreted as a way of enforcing genuine data minimisation without hindering the exercise of data subject rights, and that the exercise of data subject rights should be made possible with the help of additional information provided by the data subject. There may be situations where a data controller is processing personal data which does not require the identification of a data subject (for example with pseudonymised data). In such cases, Article 11.1 may also be relevant as it states that a data controller shall not be obliged to maintain, acquire or process additional information in order to identify the data subject for the sole purposes of complying with the GDPR.

75. For the services under the PSD2, Article 13 GDPR is applicable for the personal data collected from the data subject and Article 14 is applicable where personal data have not been obtained from the data subject.

76. In particular, the data subject has to be informed about the period for which the personal data will be stored, or if that is not possible, the criteria used to determine that period, and where applicable, the legitimate interests pursued by the controller or by a possible third party. Where processing is based on consent as referred to in Article 6(1)(a) GDPR or explicit consent as referred to in Article 9(2)(a) GDPR, the data subject has to be informed of the existence of the right to withdraw consent at any time.

77. The controller shall provide the information to the data subject, having regard to the specific circumstances in which the personal data are processed. If the personal data are to be used for communication with the data subject[38], which will probably will be the case for AISPs, the information has to be provided at the latest at the time of the first communication to that data subject. If personal data are to be disclosed to another recipient, the information has to be provided at the latest when the personal data are first disclosed.

78. With regard to online payment services, the abovementioned Guidelines clarify that a layered approach may be followed by data controllers where they opt to use a combination of methods to ensure transparency. It is in particularly recommended that layered privacy statements/ notices should be used to link to the various categories of information which must be provided to the data subject, rather than displaying all such information in a single notice on a screen, in order to avoid information fatigue, and at the same time ensuring the effectiveness of the information.

79. The abovementioned Guidelines also clarify that controllers may choose to use additional tools to provide information to the individual data subject, such as privacy dashboards. A privacy dashboard is a single point from which data subjects can view 'privacy information' and manage their privacy preferences by allowing or preventing their data from being used in certain ways by the controller in question[39]. A privacy dashboard could provide an overview of the TPPs that have obtained the data subjects explicit consent, and could also offer relevant information on the nature and amount of personal data that has been accessed by TPPs. In principle, an ASPSP may offer the user the possibility to withdraw a specific explicit PSD2 consent[40] through the overview, which would result in a denial of access to their payment accounts to one or more TPPs. The user could also request an ASPSP to deny access to their payment account(s) to one or more particular TPPs[41], as it is the right of the user to (not) make use of an account information service. If privacy dashboards are used in order to give or withdraw an explicit consent, they should be designed and applied lawfully and in particular prevent creating obstacles to the TPPs right to provide services in accordance with the PSD2. In this respect and in accordance with the applicable provisions under the PSD2, a TPP has the possibility to obtain explicit consent from the user again after this consent has been withdrawn.

80. The accountability principles requires the controller to lay down appropriate technical and organisational measures to ensure and to be able to demonstrate that processing is performed in accordance with the GDPR, in particular with the main data protection principles provided for by Article 5 (1). Those measures should take into account the nature, scope, context and purposes of the processing and the risk to the rights and freedoms of natural persons, and must be reviewed and updated when necessary[42].

6.5 PROFILING

81. The processing of personal data by payment service providers may entail 'profiling' as referred to in Article 4 (4) of the GDPR. For example, AISPs could rely on automated processing of personal data in order to evaluate certain personal aspects relating to a natural person. A data subject's personal financial situation could be evaluated, depending on the specifics of the service. Account information services, to be provided as requested by users, may involve an extensive evaluation of personal payment account data.

82. The controller also has to be transparent to the data subject on the existence of automated decision-making, including profiling. In those cases, the controller has to provide meaningful information about the logic involved, as well as the significance and the envisaged consequences of such processing for the data subject (Article 13(2)(f) and Article 14 (2)(g) and recital 60)[43]. Likewise, under Article 15 of the GDPR the data subject has the right to request and obtain information from the controller about the existence of automated decision-making, including profiling, the logic involved and the consequences for the data subject, and, in certain circumstances, a right to object to profiling, regardless of whether solely automated individual decision-making based on profiling takes place[44].

83. Furthermore, what is also relevant in this context is the right of the data subject not to be subject to a decision based solely on automated processing, including profiling, which produces legal effects concerning him or her or similarly significantly affecting him or her, provided for by Article 22 of GDPR. This norm also includes, in certain circumstances, the need for data controllers to implement suitable measures to safeguard the data subject's rights such as specific information to the data subject, the right to obtain human intervention in the decision making and to express his or her point of view and contest the decision. As also stated in recital 71 of GDPR this means, inter alia, that data subjects have the right not to be subject to a decision, such as automatic refusal of an online credit application without any human intervention[45].

84. Automated decision-making, including profiling that involves special categories of personal data is only allowed under the cumulative conditions of Article 22(4) GDPR:
– there is an applicable Article 22(2) exemption;
– and paragraph (a) or (g) of Article 9(2) GDPR applies. In both cases, the controller shall put in place suitable measures to safeguard the data subject's rights and freedoms and legitimate interests[46].

85. The requirements for further processing, as stated in these guidelines, should also be observed. The clarifications and instructions on automated individual decision-making and profiling given by the Working Party 29 Guidelines on Automated individual decision-making and Profiling for the purposes of Regulation 2016/679, as endorsed by the EDPB, are fully relevant in the context of payment services and should therefore be duly considered.

For the European Data Protection Board

The Chair

(Andrea Jelinek)

NOTES
[34] Guidelines 2/2019 on the processing of personal data under Article 6(1)(b) GDPR in the context of the provision of online services to data subjects, EDPB, para 32
[35] Guidelines 4/2019 on Article 25 Data Protection by Design and by Default, page 29.
[36] Article 29 Working Party Guidelines on Data Protection Impact Assessment (DPIA) and determining whether processing is "likely to result in a high risk" for the purposes of Regulation 2016/679, WP248 rev.01 - endorsed by the EDPB.
[37] See the RTS.
[38] Art. 14 (3)(b) of the GDPR.
[39] According to the Article 29 Working Party Guidelines on transparency under Regulation 2016/679 - endorsed by the EDPB, privacy dashboards are particularly useful when the same service is used by data subjects on a variety of different devices as they give them access to and control over their personal data no matter how they use the service. Allowing data subjects to manually adjust their privacy settings via a privacy dashboard can also make it easier for a privacy statement/ notice to be personalised by reflecting only the types of processing occurring for that particular data subject.
[40] See for example the 'explicit consent' mentioned in Article 67 (2)(a) of the PSD2.
[41] See also EBA/OP/2020/10, paragraph 45.
[42] Art. 5(2) and Art. 24 GDPR.
[43] Guidelines on transparency under Regulation 2016/679, WP 260 rev.01 - endorsed by the EDPB
[44] Article 29 Working Party Guidelines on Automated individual decision-making and Profiling for the purposes of Regulation 2016/679, WP251rev.01.
[45] Recital 71 GDPR.
[46] Article 29 Working Party Guidelines on Automated individual decision-making and Profiling for the purposes of Regulation 2016/679, WP251rev.01, page 24.

EUROPEAN DATA PROTECTION BOARD: GUIDELINES 7/2020 ON THE CONCEPTS OF CONTROLLER AND PROCESSOR IN THE GDPR: VERSION FOR PUBLIC CONSULTATION
Version 1.0

Adopted on 02 September 2020

[2.362]

NOTES
 This document has been published for public consultation. A subsequent version of this document is expected to be adopted by the EDPB following publication of this book
 © European Data Protection Board.

TABLE OF CONTENTS

THE EUROPEAN DATA PROTECTION BOARD

Having regard to Article 70(1e) of the Regulation 2016/679/EU of the European Parliament and of the Council of 27 April 2016 on the protection of natural persons with regard to the processing of personal data and on the free movement of such data, and repealing Directive 95/46/EC, (hereinafter "GDPR" or "the Regulation"),

Having regard to the EEA Agreement and in particular to Annex XI and Protocol 37 thereof, as amended by the Decision of the EEA joint Committee No 154/2018 of 6 July 2018[1],

Having regard to Article 12 and Article 22 of its Rules of Procedure,

Whereas the preparatory work of these guidelines involved the collection of inputs from stakeholders, both in writing and at a stakeholder event, in order to identify the most pressing challenges;

HAS ADOPTED THE FOLLOWING GUIDELINES

[1] References to "Member States" made throughout this document should be understood as references to "EEA Member States".

EXECUTIVE SUMMARY

[2.363]

The concepts of controller, joint controller and processor play a crucial role in the application of the General Data Protection Regulation 2016/679 (GDPR), since they determine who shall be responsible for compliance with different data protection rules, and how data subjects can exercise their rights in practice. The precise meaning of these concepts and the criteria for their correct interpretation must be sufficiently clear and consistent throughout the European Economic Area (EEA).

The concepts of controller, joint controller and processor are *functional* concepts in that they aim to allocate responsibilities according to the actual roles of the parties and *autonomous* concepts in the sense that they should be interpreted mainly according to EU data protection law.

CONTROLLER

In principle, there is no limitation as to the type of entity that may assume the role of a controller but in practice it is usually the organisation as such, and not an individual within the organisation (such as the CEO, an employee or a member of the board), that acts as a controller.

A controller is a body that *decides* certain key elements of the processing. Controllership may be defined by law or may stem from an analysis of the factual elements or circumstances of the case. Certain processing activities can be seen as naturally attached to the role of an entity (an employer to employees, a publisher to subscribers or an association to its members). In many cases, the terms of a contract can help identify the controller, although they are not decisive in all circumstances.

A controller determines the purposes and means of the processing, i.e. the *why* and *how* of the processing. The controller must decide on both purposes and means. However, some more practical aspects of implementation ("non-essential means") can be left to the processor. It is not necessary that the controller actually has access to the data that is being processed to be qualified as a controller.

JOINT CONTROLLERS

The qualification as joint controllers may arise where more than one actor is involved in the processing. The GDPR introduces specific rules for joint controllers and sets a framework to govern their relationship. The overarching criterion for joint controllership to exist is the joint participation of two or more entities in the determination of the purposes and means of a processing operation. Joint participation can take the form of a *common decision* taken by two or more entities or result from *converging decisions* by two or more entities, where the decisions complement each other and are necessary for the processing to take place in such a manner that they have a tangible impact on the determination of the purposes and means of the processing. An important criterion is that the processing would not be possible without both parties' participation in the sense that the processing by each party is inseparable, i.e. inextricably linked. The joint participation needs to include the determination of purposes on the one hand and the determination of means on the other hand.

PROCESSOR

A processor is a natural or legal person, public authority, agency or another body, which processes personal data on behalf of the controller. Two basic conditions for qualifying as processor exist: that it is a separate entity in relation to the controller and that it processes personal data on the controller's behalf.

The processor must not process the data otherwise than according to the controller's instructions. The controller's instructions may still leave a certain degree of discretion about how to best serve the controller's interests, allowing the processor to choose the most suitable technical and organisational means. A processor infringes the GDPR, however, if it goes beyond the controller's instructions and starts to determine its own purposes and means of the processing. The processor will then be considered a controller in respect of that processing and may be subject to sanctions for going beyond the controller's instructions.

RELATIONSHIP BETWEEN CONTROLLER AND PROCESSOR

A controller must only use processors providing sufficient guarantees to implement appropriate technical and organisational measures so that the processing meets the requirements of the GDPR. Elements to be taken into account could be the processor's expert knowledge (e.g. technical expertise with regard to security measures and data breaches); the processor's reliability; the processor's resources and the processor's adherence to an approved code of conduct or certification mechanism.

Any processing of personal data by a processor must be governed by a contract or other legal act which shall be in writing, including in electronic form, and be binding. The controller and the processor may choose to negotiate their own contract including all the compulsory elements or to rely, in whole or in part, on standard contractual clauses.

The GDPR lists the elements that have to be set out in the processing agreement. The processing agreement should not, however, merely restate the provisions of the GDPR; rather, it should include more specific, concrete information as to how the requirements will be met and which level of security is required for the personal data processing that is the object of the processing agreement.

RELATIONSHIP AMONG JOINT CONTROLLERS

Joint controllers shall in a transparent manner determine and agree on their respective responsibilities for compliance with the obligations under the GDPR. The determination of their respective responsibilities must in particular regard the exercise of data subjects' rights and the duties to provide information. In addition to this, the distribution of responsibilities should cover other controller obligations such as regarding the general data protection principles, legal basis, security measures, data breach notification obligation, data protection impact assessments, the use of processors, third country transfers and contacts with data subjects and supervisory authorities.

Each joint controller has the duty to ensure that they have a legal basis for the processing and that the data are not further processed in a manner that is incompatible with the purposes for which they were originally collected by the controller sharing the data.

The legal form of the arrangement among joint controllers is not specified by the GDPR. For the sake of legal certainty, and in order to provide for transparency and accountability, the EDPB recommends that such arrangement be made in the form of a binding document such as a contract or other legal binding act under EU or Member State law to which the controllers are subject.

The arrangement shall duly reflect the respective roles and relationships of the joint controllers vis-à-vis the data subjects and the essence of the arrangement shall be made available to the data subject.

Irrespective of the terms of the arrangement, data subjects may exercise their rights in respect of and against each of the joint controllers. Supervisory authorities are not bound by the terms of the arrangement whether on the issue of the qualification of the parties as joint controllers or the designated contact point.

INTRODUCTION

[2.364]
1.   This document seeks to provide guidance on the concepts of controller and processor based on the GDPR's rules on definitions in Article 4 and the provisions on obligations in chapter IV. The main aim is to clarify the meaning of the concepts and to clarify the different roles and the distribution of responsibilities between these actors.

2.   The concept of controller and its interaction with the concept of processor play a crucial role in the application of the GDPR, since they determine who shall be responsible for compliance with different data protection rules, and how data subjects can exercise their rights in practice. The GDPR explicitly introduces the accountability principle, i.e. the controller shall be responsible for, and be able to demonstrate compliance with, the principles relating to processing of personal data in Article 5. Moreover, the GDPR also introduces more specific rules on the use of processor(s) and some of the provisions on personal data processing are addressed -not only to controllers -but also to processors.

3.   It is therefore of paramount importance that the precise meaning of these concepts and the criteria for their correct use are sufficiently clear and shared throughout the European Union and the EEA.

4.   The Article 29 Working Party issued guidance on the concepts of controller/processor in its opinion 1/2010 (WP169)[2] in order to provide clarifications and concrete examples with respect to these concepts. Since the entry into force of the GDPR, many questions have been raised regarding to what extent the GDPR brought changes to the concepts of controller and processor and their respective roles. Questions were raised in particular to the substance and implications of the concept of joint controllership (e.g. as laid down in Article 26 GDPR) and to the specific obligations for processors laid down in Chapter IV (e.g. as laid down in Article 28 GDPR). Therefore, and as the EDPB recognizes that the concrete application of the concepts needs further clarification, the EDPB now deems it necessary to give more developed and specific guidance in order to ensure a consistent and harmonised approach throughout the EU and the EEA. The present guidelines replace the previous opinion of Working Party 29 on these concepts (WP169).

5.   In part I, these guidelines discuss the definitions of the different concepts of controller, joint controllers, processor and third party/recipient. In part II, further guidance is provided on the consequences that are attached to the different roles of controller, joint controllers and processor.

2   Article 29 Working Party Opinion 1/2010 on the concepts of "controller" and "processor" adopted on 16 February 2010, 264/10/EN, WP 169

PART I – CONCEPTS

1 GENERAL OBSERVATIONS

[2.365]

6. The GDPR, in Article 5(2), explicitly introduces the accountability principle which means that:
–   the controller shall be *responsible for the compliance* with the principles set out in Article 5(1) GDPR; and that
–   the controller shall be able to *demonstrate compliance* with the principles set out in Article 5(1) GDPR.

This principle has been described in an opinion by the Article 29 WP[3] and will not be discussed in detail here.

7. The aim of incorporating the accountability principle into the GDPR and making it a central principle was to emphasize that data controllers must implement appropriate and effective measures and be able to demonstrate compliance.[4]

8. The accountability principle has been further elaborated in Article 24, which states that the controller shall implement appropriate technical and organisational measures to ensure and to be able **to demonstrate** that processing is performed in accordance with the GDPR. Such measures shall be reviewed and updated if necessary. The accountability principle is also reflected in Article 28, which lays down the controller's obligations when engaging a processor.

9. The accountability principle is directly addressed to the controller. However, some of the more specific rules are addressed to both controllers and processors, such as the rules on supervisory authorities' powers in Article 58. Both controllers and processors can be fined in case of non-compliance with the obligations of the GDPR that are relevant to them and both are directly accountable towards supervisory authorities by virtue of the obligations to maintain and provide appropriate documentation upon request, co-operate in case of an investigation and abide by administrative orders. At the same time, it should be recalled that processors must always comply with, and act only on, instructions from the controller.

10. The accountability principle, together with the other, more specific rules on how to comply with the GDPR and the distribution of responsibility, therefore makes it necessary to define the different roles of several actors involved in a personal data processing activity.

11. A general observation regarding the concepts of controller and processor in the GDPR is that they have not changed compared to the Directive 95/46/EC and that overall, the criteria for how to attribute the different roles remain the same.

12. The concepts of controller and processor are *functional* concepts: they aim to allocate responsibilities according to the actual roles of the parties.[5] This implies that the legal status of an actor as either a "controller" or a "processor" must in principle be determined by its actual activities in a specific situation, rather than upon the formal designation of an actor as being either a "controller" or "processor" (e.g. in a contract).[6]

13. The concepts of controller and processor are also *autonomous* concepts in the sense that, although external legal sources can help identifying who is a controller, it should be interpreted mainly according to EU data protection law. The concept of controller should not be prejudiced by other -sometimes colliding or overlapping -concepts in other fields of law, such as the creator or the right holder in intellectual property rights or competition law.

14. As the underlying objective of attributing the role of controller is to ensure accountability and the effective and comprehensive protection of the personal data, the concept of 'controller' should be interpreted in a sufficiently broad way so as to ensure full effect of EU data protection law, to avoid lacunae and to prevent possible circumvention of the rules.

2 DEFINITION OF CONTROLLER

2.1 Definition of controller

[2.366]

15. A controller is defined by Article 4(7) GDPR as

"the natural or legal person, public authority, agency or other body which, alone or jointly with others, determines the purposes and means of the processing of personal data; where the purposes and means of such processing are determined by Union or Member State law, the controller or the specific criteria for its nomination may be provided for by Union or Member State law".

16. The definition of controller contains five main building blocks, which will be analysed separately for the purposes of these Guidelines. They are the following:
*   "the natural or legal person, public authority, agency or other body"
*   "determines"
*   "alone or jointly with others"

- "the purposes and means"
- "of the processing of personal data".

2.1.1 "Natural or legal person, public authority, agency or other body"

17. The first building block relates to the type of entity that can be a controller. Under the GDPR, a controller can be "*a natural or legal person, public authority, agency or other body*". This means that, in principle, there is no limitation as to the type of entity that may assume the role of a controller. It might be an organisation, but it might also be an individual or a group of individuals.[7] In practice, however, it is usually the organisation as such, and not an individual within the organisation (such as the CEO, an employee or a member of the board), that acts as a controller within the meaning of the GDPR. As far as data processing within a company group is concerned, special attention must be paid to the question of whether an establishment acts as a controller or processor, e.g. when processing data on behalf of the parent company.

18. Sometimes, companies and public bodies appoint a specific person responsible for the implementation of the processing operations. Even if a specific natural person is appointed to ensure compliance with data protection rules, this person will not be the controller but will act on behalf of the legal entity (company or public body) which will be ultimately responsible in case of infringement of the rules in its capacity as controller.

2.1.2 "Determines"

19. The second building block of the controller concept refers to the controller's *influence* over the processing, by virtue of an *exercise of decision-making power*. A controller is a body that *decides* certain key elements about the processing. This controllership may be defined by law or may stem from an analysis of the factual elements or circumstances of the case. One should look at the specific processing operations in question and understand who determines them, by first considering the following questions: "*why is this processing taking place?*" and "*who decided that the processing should take place for a particular purpose?*".

Circumstances giving rise to control

20. Having said that the concept of controller is a functional concept, it is therefore based on a **factual rather than a formal analysis**. In order to facilitate the analysis, certain rules of thumb and practical presumptions may be used to guide and simplify the process. In most situations, the "determining body" can be easily and clearly identified by reference to certain legal and/or factual circumstances from which "influence" normally can be inferred, unless other elements indicate the contrary. Two categories of situations can be distinguished: (1) control stemming from *legal provisions*; and (2) control stemming from *factual influence*.

1) Control stemming from legal provisions

21. There are cases where control can be inferred from explicit legal competence e.g., when the controller or the specific criteria for its nomination are designated by national or Union law. Indeed, Article 4(7) states that "*where the purposes and means of such processing are determined by Union or Member State law, the controller or the specific criteria for its nomination may be provided for by Union or Member State law.*" Where the controller has been specifically identified by law this will be determinative for establishing who is acting as controller. This presupposes that the legislator has designated as controller the entity that has a genuine ability to exercise control. In some countries, the national law provides that public authorities are responsible for processing of personal data within the context of their duties.

22. However, more commonly, rather than directly appointing the controller or setting out the criteria for its appointment, the law will establish a task or impose a duty on someone to collect and process certain data. In those cases, the purpose of the processing is often determined by the law. The controller will normally be the one designated by law for the realization of this purpose, this public task. For example, this would be the case where an entity which is entrusted with certain public tasks (e.g., social security) which cannot be fulfilled without collecting at least some personal data, sets up a database or register in order to fulfil those public tasks. In that case, the law, albeit indirectly, sets out who is the controller. More generally, the law may also impose an obligation on either public or private entities to retain or provide certain data. These entities would then normally be considered as controllers with respect to the processing that is necessary to execute this obligation.

Example: Legal provisions

The national law in Country A lays down an obligation for municipal authorities to provide social welfare benefits such as monthly payments to citizens depending on their financial situation. In order to carry out these payments, the municipal authority must collect and process data about the applicants' financial circumstances. Even though the law does not explicitly state that the municipal authorities are controllers for this processing, this follows implicitly from the legal provisions.

---

2) Control stemming from factual influence

23. In the absence of control arising from legal provisions, the qualification of a party as controller must be established on the basis of an assessment of the factual circumstances surrounding the processing. All relevant factual circumstances must be taken into account in order to reach a conclusion as to whether a particular entity exercises a determinative influence with respect to the processing of personal data in question.

24. The need for factual assessment also means that the role of a controller does not stem from the nature of an entity that is processing data but from its concrete activities in a specific context. In other words, the same entity may act at the same time as controller for certain processing operations and as processor for others, and the qualification as controller or processor has to be assessed with regard to each specific data processing activity.

25. In practice, certain processing activities can be considered as naturally attached to the role or activities of an entity ultimately entailing responsibilities from a data protection point of view. This can be due to more general legal provisions or an established legal practice in different areas (civil law, commercial law, labour law etc.). In this case, existing traditional roles and professional expertise that normally imply a certain responsibility will help in identifying the controller, for example an employer in relation to processing personal data about his employees, a publisher processing personal data about its subscribers, or an association processing personal data about its members or contributors. When an entity engages in processing of personal data as part of its interactions with its own employees, customers or members, it will generally be the one who factually can determine the purpose and means around the processing and is therefore acting as a controller within the meaning of the GDPR.

Example: Law firms

The company ABC hires a law firm to represent it in a dispute. In order to carry out this task, the law firm needs to process personal data related to the case. The reasons for processing the personal data is the law firm's mandate to represent the client in court. This mandate however is not specifically targeted to personal data processing. The law firm acts with a significant degree of independence, for example in deciding what information to use and how to use it, and there are no instructions from the client company regarding the personal data processing. The processing that the law firm carries out in order to fulfil the task as legal representative for the company is therefore linked to the functional role of the law firm so that it is to be regarded as controller for this processing.

---

26. In many cases, an assessment of the contractual terms between the different parties involved can facilitate the determination of which party (or parties) is acting as controller. Even if a contract is silent as to who is the controller, it may contain sufficient elements to infer who exercises a decision-making role with respect to the purposes and means of the processing. It may also be that the contract contains an explicit statement as to the identity of the controller. If there is no reason to doubt that this accurately reflects the reality, there is nothing against following the terms of the contract. However, the terms of a contract are not decisive in all circumstances, as this would simply allow parties to allocate responsibility as they see fit. It is not possible either to become a controller or to escape controller obligations simply by shaping the contract in a certain way where the factual circumstances say something else.

27. If one party in fact decides why and how personal data are processed that party will be a controller even if a contract says that it is a processor. Similarly, it is not because a commercial contract uses the term "subcontractor" that an entity shall be considered a processor from the perspective of data protection law.[8]

28. In line with the factual approach, the word "determines" means that the entity that actually exerts influence on the purposes and means of the processing is the controller. Normally, a processor agreement establishes who the determining party (controller) and the instructed party (processor) are. Even if the processor offers a service that is preliminary defined in a specific way, the controller has to be presented with a detailed description of the service and must make the final decision to actively approve the way the processing is carried out and to be able to request changes if necessary. Furthermore, the processor cannot at a later stage change the essential elements of the processing without the approval of the controller.

2.1.3 "Alone or jointly with others"

29. Article 4(7) recognizes that the "purposes and means" of the processing might be determined by more than one actor. It states that the controller is the actor who "alone or jointly with others" determines the purposes and means of the processing. This means that several different entities may act as controllers for the same processing, with each of them then being subject to the applicable data protection provisions. Correspondingly, an organisation can still be a controller even if it does not make all the decisions as to purposes and means. The criteria for joint controllership and the extent to which two or more actors jointly exercise control may take different forms, as clarified later on.[9]

2.1.4 "Purposes and means"

30. The fourth building block of the controller definition refers to the object of the controller's influence, namely the "purposes and means" of the processing. It represents the substantive part of the controller concept: what a party should determine in order to qualify as controller.

31. Dictionaries define "purpose" as "an anticipated outcome that is intended or that guides your planned actions" and "means" as "how a result is obtained or an end is achieved".

32. The GDPR establishes that data must be collected for specified, explicit and legitimate purposes and not further processed in a way incompatible with those purposes. Determination of the "purposes" of the processing and the "means" to achieve them is therefore particularly important.

33. Determining the purposes and the means amounts to deciding respectively the "why" and the "how" of the processing:[10] given a particular processing operation, the controller is the actor who has determined why the processing is taking place (i.e., "to what end"; or "what for") and *how* this objective shall be reached (i.e. which means shall be employed to attain the objective). A natural or legal person who exerts such influence over the processing of personal data, thereby participates in the determination of the purposes and means of that processing in accordance with the definition in Article 4(7) GDPR.[11]

34. The controller must decide on both purpose and means of the processing as described below. As a result, the controller cannot settle with only determining the purpose. It must also make decisions about the means of the processing. Conversely, the party acting as processor can never determine the purpose of the processing.

35. In practice, if a controller engages a processor to carry out the processing on its behalf, it often means that the processor shall be able to make certain decisions of its own on how to carry out the processing. The EDPB recognizes that some margin of manoeuvre may exist for the processor also to be able to make some decisions in relation to the processing. In this perspective, there is a need to provide guidance about which **level of influence** on the "why" and the "how" should entail the qualification of an entity as a controller and to what extent a processor may make decisions of its own.

36. When one entity clearly determines purposes and means, entrusting another entity with processing activities that amount to the execution of its detailed instructions, the situation is straightforward, and there is no doubt that the second entity should be regarded as a processor, whereas the first entity is the controller.

Essential vs. non-essential means

37. The question is where to draw the line between decisions that are reserved to the controller and decisions that can be left to the discretion of the processor. Decisions on the purpose of the processing are clearly always for the controller to make.

38. As regards the determination of means a distinction can be made between essential and non-essential means. "Essential means" are closely linked to the purpose and the scope of the processing and are traditionally and inherently reserved to the controller. Examples of essential means are the type of personal data which are processed (*"which data shall be processed?"*), the duration of the processing (*"for how long shall they be processed?"*), the categories of recipients (*"who shall have access to them?"*) and the categories of data subjects (*"whose personal data are being processed?"*). "Non-essential means" concern more practical aspects of implementation, such as the choice for a particular type of hard-or software or the detailed security measures which may be left to the processor to decide on.

Example: Payroll administration
Employer A hires another company to administer the payment of salaries to its employees. Employer A gives clear instructions on who to pay, what amounts, by what date, by which bank, how long the data shall be stored, what data should be disclosed to the tax authority etc. In this case, the processing of data is carried out for Company A's purpose to pay salaries to its employees and the payroll administrator may not use the data for any purpose of its own. The way in which the payroll administrator should carry out the processing is in essence clearly and tightly defined. Nevertheless, the payroll administrator may decide on certain detailed matters around the processing such as which software to use, how to distribute access within its own organisation etc. This does not alter its role as processor as long as the administrator does not go against or beyond the instructions given by Company A.

Example: Bank payments
As part of the instructions from Employer A, the payroll administration transmits information to Bank B so that they can carry out the actual payment to the employees of Employer A. This activity includes processing of personal data by Bank B which it carries out for the purpose of performing banking activity. Within this activity, the bank decides independently from Employer A on which data that have to be processed to provide the service, for how long the data must be stored etc. Employer A cannot have any influence on the purpose and means of Bank B's processing of data. Bank B is therefore to be seen as a controller for this processing and the transmission of personal data from the payroll administration is to be regarded as a disclosure of information between two controllers, from Employer A to Bank B.

Example: Accountants
Employer A also hires Accounting firm C to carry out audits of their bookkeeping and therefore transfers data about financial transactions (including personal data) to C. Accounting firm C processes these data without detailed instructions from A. Accounting firm C decides itself, in accordance with legal provisions regulating the tasks of the auditing activities carried out by C, that the data it collects will only be processed for the purpose of auditing A and it determines what data it needs to have, which categories of persons that need to be registered, how long the data shall be kept and what technical means to use. Under these circumstances, Accounting firm C is to be regarded as a controller of its own when performing its auditing services for A. However, this assessment may be different depending on the level of instructions from A. In a situation where the law does not lay down specific obligations for the accounting firm and the client company provides very detailed instructions on the processing, the accounting firm would indeed be acting as a processor. A distinction could be made between a situation where the processing is -in accordance with the laws regulating this profession -done as part of the accounting firm's core activity and where the processing is a more limited, ancillary task that is carried out as part of the client company's activity.

Part 2   Data Protection: EU Law etc

Example: Hosting services
Employer A hires hosting service H to store encrypted data on H's servers. The hosting service H does not determine whether the data it hosts are personal data nor does it process data in any other way than storing it on its servers. As storage is one example of a personal data processing activity, the hosting service H is processing personal data on employer A's behalf and is therefore a processor. Employer A must provide the necessary instructions to H on, for example, which technical and organisational security measures are required and a data processing agreement according to Article 28 must be concluded. H must assist A in ensuring that the necessary security measures are taken and notify it in case of any personal data breach.

---

39. Even though decisions on non-essential means can be left to the processor, the controller must still stipulate certain elements in the processor agreement, such as – in relation to the security requirement, e.g. an instruction to take all measures required pursuant to Article 32 of the GDPR. The agreement must also state that the processor shall assist the controller in ensuring compliance with, for example, Article 32. In any event, the controller remains responsible for the implementation of appropriate technical and organisational measures to ensure and be able to demonstrate that the processing is performed in accordance with the Regulation (Article 24). In doing so, the controller must take into account the nature, scope, context and purposes of the processing as well as the risks for rights and freedoms of natural persons. For this reason, the controller must be fully informed about the means that are used so that it can take an informed decision in this regard. In order for the controller to be able to demonstrate the lawfulness of the processing, it is advisable to document at the minimum necessary technical and organisational measures in the contract or other legally binding instrument between the controller and the processor.

2.1.5 "Of the processing of personal data"

40. The purposes and means determined by the controller must relate to the "processing of personal data". Article 4(2) GDPR defines the processing of personal data as "*any operation or set of operations which is performed on personal data or on sets of personal data*". As a result, the concept of a controller can be linked either to a single processing operation or to a set of operations. In practice, this may mean that the control exercised by a particular entity may extend to the entirety of processing at issue but may also be limited to a particular stage in the processing.[12]

41. Anyone who decides to process data must consider whether this includes personal data and, if so, what the obligations are according to the GDPR. An actor will be considered a "controller" even if it does not deliberately target personal data as such or has wrongfully assessed that it does not process personal data.

42. It is not necessary that the controller actually has access to the data that is being processed[13]. Someone who outsources a processing activity and in doing so, has a determinative influence on the purpose and (essential) means of the processing (e.g. by adjusting parameters of a service in such a way that it influences whose personal data shall be processed), is to be regarded as controller even though he or she will never have actual access to the data.

Example: Market research
Company ABC wishes to understand which types of consumers are most likely to be interested in its products and contracts a service provider, XYZ, to obtain the relevant information.
Company ABC instructs XYZ on what type of information it is interested in and provides a list of questions to be asked to those participating in the market research.
Company ABC receives only statistical information (e.g., identifying consumer trends per region) from XYZ and does not have access to the personal data itself. Nevertheless, Company ABC decided that the processing should take place, the processing is carried out for its purpose and its activity and it has provided XYZ with detailed instructions on what information to collect. Company ABC is therefore still to be considered a controller with respect of the processing of personal data that takes place in order to deliver the information it has requested. XYZ may only process the data for the purpose given by Company ABC and according to its detailed instructions and is therefore to be regarded as processor.

---

3 DEFINITION OF JOINT CONTROLLERS

3.1 Definition of joint controllers

[2.367]
43. The qualification as joint controllers may arise where more than one actor is involved in the processing.

44. While the concept is not new and already existed under Directive 95/46/EC, the GDPR, in its Article 26, introduces specific rules for joint controllers and sets a framework to govern their relationship. In addition, the Court of Justice of the European Union (CJEU) in recent rulings has brought clarifications on this concept and its implications[14].

45. As further elaborated in Part II, section 2, the qualification of joint controllers will mainly have consequences in terms of allocation of obligations for compliance with data protection rules and in particular with respect to the rights of individuals.

46. In this perspective, the following section aims to provide guidance on the concept of joint controllers in accordance with the GDPR and the CJEU case law to assist entities in determining where they may be acting as joint controllers and applying the concept in practice.

3.2 Existence of joint controllership

3.2.1 General considerations

47. The definition of a controller in Article 4 (7) GDPR forms the starting point for determining joint controllership. The considerations in this section are thus directly related to and supplement the considerations in the section on the concept of controller. As a consequence, the assessment of joint controllership should mirror the assessment of "single" control developed above.

48. Article 26 GDPR, which reflects the definition in Article 4 (7) GDPR, provides that *"[w]here two or more controllers jointly determine the purposes and means of processing, they shall be joint controllers."* In broad terms, joint controllership exists with regard to a specific processing activity when different parties determine *jointly* the purpose and means of this processing activity. Therefore, assessing the existence of joint controllers requires examining whether the determination of purposes and means that characterize a controller are decided by more than one party. "Jointly" must be interpreted as meaning "together with" or "not alone", in different forms and combinations, as explained below.

49. The assessment of joint controllership should be carried out on a factual, rather than a formal, analysis of the actual influence on the purposes and means of the processing. All existing or envisaged arrangements should be checked against the factual circumstances regarding the relationship between the parties. A merely formal criterion would not be sufficient for at least two reasons: in some cases, the formal appointment of a joint controller -laid down for example by law or in a contract -would be absent; in other cases, it may be that the formal appointment does not reflect the reality of the arrangements, by formally entrusting the role of controller to an entity which actually is not in the position to "determine" the purposes and means of the processing.

50. Not all processing operations involving several entities give rise to joint controllership. The overarching criterion for joint controllership to exist is the **joint participation of two or more entities in the determination of the purposes and means** of a processing operation. More specifically, joint participation needs to include the determination of purposes on the one hand and the determination of means on the other hand. If each of these elements are determined by all entities concerned, they should be considered as joint controllers of the processing at issue.

3.2.2 Assessment of joint participation

51. Joint participation in the determination of purposes and means implies that more than one entity have a decisive influence over whether and how the processing takes place. In practice, joint participation can take several different forms. For example, joint participation can take the form of a **common decision** taken by two or more entities or result from **converging decisions** by two or more entities regarding the purposes and essential means.

52. Joint participation through a *common decision* means deciding together and involves a common intention in accordance with the most common understanding of the term "jointly" referred to in Article 26 of the GDPR.

53. The situation of joint participation through *converging decisions* results more particularly from the case law of the CJEU on the concept of joint controllers. Decisions can be considered as converging on purposes and means **if they complement each other and are necessary for the processing to take place in such manner that they have a tangible impact on the determination of the purposes and means of the processing**. As such, an important criterion to identify converging decisions in this context **is whether the processing would not be possible without both parties' participation in the sense that the processing by each party is inseparable, i.e. inextricably linked.** The situation of joint controllers acting on the basis of converging decisions should however be distinguished from the case of a processor, since the latter – while participating in the performance of a processing – does not process the data for its own purposes but carries out the processing on behalf of the controller.

54. The fact that one of the parties does not have access to personal data processed is not sufficient to exclude joint controllership[15]. For example, in *Jehovah's Witnesses*, the CJEU considered that a religious community must be considered a controller, jointly with its members who engage in preaching, of the processing of personal data carried out by the latter in the context of door-to-door preaching.[16] The CJEU considered that it was not necessary that the community had access to the data in question, or to establish that that community had given its members written guidelines or instructions in relation to the data processing.[17] The community participated in the determination of purposes and means by organising and coordinating the activities of its members, which helped to achieve the objective of the Jehovah's Witnesses community.[18] In addition, the community had knowledge on a general level of the fact that such processing was carried out in order to spread its faith.[19]

55. It is also important to underline, as clarified by the CJEU, that an entity will be considered as joint controller with the other(s) only in respect of those operations for which it determines, jointly with others, the means and the purposes of the processing. If one of these entities decides alone the purposes and means of operations that precede or are subsequent in the chain of processing, this entity must be considered as the sole controller of this preceding or subsequent operation[20].

56. The existence of joint responsibility does not necessarily imply equal responsibility of the various operators involved in the processing of personal data. On the contrary, the CJEU has clarified that those operators may be involved at different stages of that processing and to different degrees so that the level of responsibility of each of them must be assessed with regard to all the relevant circumstances of the particular case.

3.2.2.1 Jointly determined purpose(s)

57.   Joint controllership exists when entities involved in the same processing operation process such data for jointly defined purposes. This will be the case if the entities involved process the data for the same, or common, purposes.

58.   In addition, when the entities do not have the same purpose for the processing, joint controllership may also, in light of the CJEU case law, be established when the entities involved pursue purposes which are closely linked or complementary. Such may be the case, for example, when there is a mutual benefit arising from the same processing operation, provided that each of the entities involved participates in the determination of the purposes and means of the relevant processing operation. In *Fashion ID*, for example, the CJEU clarified that a website operator participates in the determination of the purposes (and means) of the processing by embedding a social plug-in on a website in order to optimize the publicity of its goods by making them more visible on the social network. The CJEU considered that the processing operations at issue were performed in the economic interests of both the website operator and the provider of the social plug-in.[21]

59.   Likewise, as noted by the CJEU in *Wirtschaftsakademie*, the processing of personal data through statistics of visitors to a fan page is intended to enable Facebook to improve its system of advertising transmitted via its network and to enable the administrator of the fan page to obtain statistics to manage the promotion of its activity.[22] Each entity in this case pursues its own interest but both parties participate in the determination of the purposes (and means) of the processing of personal data as regards the visitors to the fan page.[23]

60.   In this respect, it is important to highlight that the mere existence of a mutual benefit (for ex. commercial) arising from a processing activity does not give rise to joint controllership. If the entity involved in the processing does not pursue any purpose(s) of its own in relation to the processing activity, but is merely being paid for services rendered, it is acting as a processor rather than as a joint controller.

3.2.2.2 Jointly determined means

61.   Joint controllership also requires that two or more entities have exerted influence over the means of the processing. This does not mean that, for joint controllership to exist, each entity involved needs in all cases to determine all of the means. Indeed, as clarified by the CJEU, different entities may be involved at different stages of that processing and to different degrees. Different joint controllers may therefore define the means of the processing to a different extent, depending on who is effectively in a position to do so.

62.   It may also be the case that one of the entities involved provides the means of the processing and makes it available for personal data processing activities by other entities. The entity who decides to make use of those means so that personal data can be processed for a particular purpose also participates in the determination of the means of the processing.

63.   This scenario can notably arise in case of platforms, standardised tools, or other infrastructure allowing the parties to process the same personal data and which have been set up in a certain way by one of the parties to be used by others that can also decide how to set it up[24]. The use of an already existing technical system does not exclude joint controllership when users of the system can decide on the processing of personal data to be performed in this context.

64.   As an example of this, the CJEU held in *Wirtschaftsakademie* that the administrator of a fan page hosted on Facebook, by defining parameters based on its target audience and the objectives of managing and promoting its activities, must be regarded as taking part in the determination of the means of the processing of personal data related to the visitors of its fan page.

65.   Furthermore, the choice made by an entity to use for its own purposes a tool or other system developed by another entity, allowing the processing of personal data, will likely amount to a joint decision on the means of that processing by those entities. This follows from the Fashion ID case where the CJEU concluded, that by embedding on its website the Facebook Like button made available by Facebook to website operators, Fashion ID has exerted a decisive influence in respect of the operations involving the collection and transmission of the personal data of the visitors of its website to Facebook and had thus jointly determined with Facebook the means of that processing[25].

66.   It is important to underline **that the use of a common data processing system or infrastructure will not in all cases lead to qualify the parties involved as joint controllers,** in particular where the processing they carry out is separable and could be performed by one party without intervention from the other or where the provider is a processor in the absence of any purpose of its own (the existence of a mere commercial benefit for the parties involved is not sufficient to qualify as a purpose of processing).

Example: Travel agency
A travel agency sends personal data of its customers to the airline and a chain of hotels, with a view to making reservations for a travel package. The airline and the hotel confirm the availability of the seats and rooms requested. The travel agency issues the travel documents and vouchers for its customers. Each of the actors processes the data for carrying out their own activities and using their own means. In this case, the travel agency, the airline and the hotel are three different data controllers processing the data for their own purposes and there is no joint controllership.
The travel agency, the hotel chain and the airline then decide to participate jointly in setting up an internet-based common platform for the common purpose of providing package travel deals. They agree on the essential means to be used, such as which data will be stored, how reservations will be allocated and confirmed, and who can have access to the information stored. Furthermore, they decide to share the data of their customers in order to carry out joint marketing actions. In this case, the travel agency, the airline and the hotel chain, jointly determine why and how personal data of their respective customers are processed and will therefore be joint controllers with regard to the processing operations relating to the common internet-based booking platform and the joint marketing actions. However, each of them would still retain sole control with regard to other processing activities outside the internet-based common platform.

Example: Research project by institutes
Several research institutes decide to participate in a specific joint research project and to use to that end the existing platform of one of the institutes involved in the project. Each institute feeds personal data it holds into the platform for the purpose of the joint research and uses the data provided by others through the platform for carrying out the research. In this case, all institutes qualify as joint controllers for the personal data processing that is done by storing and disclosing information from this platform since they have decided together the purpose of the processing and the means to be used (the existing platform). Each of the institutes however is a separate controller for any other processing that may be carried out outside the platform for their respective purposes.

Example: Marketing operation
Companies A and B have launched a co-branded product C and wish to organise an event to promote this product. To that end, they decide to share data from their respective clients and prospects database and decide on the list of invitees to the event on this basis. They also agree on the modalities for sending the invitations to the event, how to collect feedback during the event and follow-up marketing actions. Companies A and B can be considered as joint controllers for the processing of personal data related to the organisation of the promotional event as they decide together on the jointly defined purpose and essential means of the data processing in this context.

Example: Clinical Trials
A health care provider (the investigator) and a university (the sponsor) decide to launch together a clinical trial with the same purpose. They collaborate together to the drafting of the study protocol (i.e. purpose, methodology/design of the study, data to be collected, subject exclusion/inclusion criteria, database reuse (where relevant) etc.). They may be considered as joint controllers, for this clinical trial as they jointly determine and agree on the same purpose and the essential means of the processing. The collection of personal data from the medical record of the patient for the purpose of research is to be distinguished from the storage and use of the same data for the purpose of patient care, for which the health care provider remains the controller.
In the event that the investigator does not participate to the drafting of the protocol (he just accepts the protocol already elaborated by the sponsor), and the protocol is only designed by the sponsor, the investigator should be considered as a processor and the sponsor as the controller for this clinical trial.

Example: Headhunters
Company X helps Company Y in recruiting new staff with its famous value-added service "global matchz". Company X looks for suitable candidates both among the CVs received directly by Company Y and those it already has in its own database. Such database is created and managed by Company X on its own. This ensures that Company X enhances the matching between job offers and job seekers, thus increasing its revenues. Even though they have not formally taken a decision together, Companies X and Y jointly participate to the processing with the purpose of finding suitable candidates based on converging decisions: the decision to create and manage the service "global matchz" for Company X and the decision of Company Y to enrich the database with the CVs it directly receives. Such decisions complement each other, are inseparable and necessary for the processing of finding suitable candidates to take place. Therefore, in this particular case they should be considered as joint controllers of such processing. However, Company X is the sole controller of the processing necessary to manage its database and Company Y is the sole controller of the subsequent hiring processing for its own purpose (organisation of interviews, conclusion of the contract and management of HR data).

3.2.3 Situations where there is no joint controllership

67. The fact that several actors are involved in the same processing does not mean that they are necessarily acting as joint controllers of such processing. Not all kind of partnerships, cooperation or collaboration imply qualification of joint controllers as such qualification requires a case-by-case analysis of each processing at stake and the precise role of each entity with respect to each processing. The cases below provide non-exhaustive examples of situations where there is no joint controllership.

68. For example, the exchange of the same data or set of data between two entities without jointly determined purposes or jointly determined means of processing should be considered as a transmission of data between separate controllers.

Example: Transmission of employee data to tax authorities
A company collects and processes personal data of its employees with the purpose of managing salaries, health insurances, etc. A law imposes an obligation on the company to send all data concerning salaries to the tax authorities, with a view to reinforce fiscal control.
In this case, even though both the company and the tax authorities process the same data concerning salaries, the lack of jointly determined purposes and means with regard to this data processing will result in qualifying the two entities as two separate data controllers.

---

69. Joint controllership may also be excluded in a situation where several entities use a shared database or a common infrastructure, if each entity independently determines its own purposes.

Example: Marketing operations in a group of companies using a shared database:
A group of companies uses the same database for the management of clients and prospects. Such database is hosted on the servers of the mother company who is therefore a processor of the companies with respect to the storage of the data. Each entity of the group enters the data of its own clients and prospects and processes such data for its own purposes only. Also, each entity decides independently on the access, the retention periods, the correction or deletion of their clients and prospects' data. They cannot access or use each other's data. The mere fact that these companies use a shared group database does not as such entail joint controllership. Under these circumstances, each company is thus a separate controller.

Example: Independent controllers when using a shared infrastructure
Company XYZ hosts a database and makes it available to other companies to process and host personal data about their employees. Company XYZ is a processor in relation to the processing and storage of other companies' employees as these operations are performed on behalf and according to the instructions of these other companies. In addition, the other companies process the data without any involvement from Company XYZ and for purposes which are not in any way shared by Company XYZ.

---

70. Also, there can be situations where various actors successively process the same personal data in a chain of operations, each of these actors having an independent purpose and independent means in their part of the chain. In the absence of joint participation in the determination of the purposes and means of the same processing operation or set of operations, joint controllership has to be excluded and the various actors must be regarded as successive independent controllers.

Example: Statistical analysis for a task of public interest
A public authority (Authority A) has the legal task of making relevant analysis and statistics on how the country's employment rate develops. To do that, many other public entities are legally bound to disclose specific data to Authority A. Authority A decides to use a specific system to process the data, including collection. This also means that the other units are obligated to use the system for their disclosure of data. In this case, without prejudice to any attribution of roles by law, Authority A will be the only controller of the processing for the purpose of analysis and statistics of the employment rate processed in the system, because Authority A determines the purpose for the processing, and has decided how the processing will be organised. Of course, the other public entities, as controllers for their own processing activities, are responsible for ensuring the accuracy of the data they previously processed, which they then disclose to Authority A.

---

4 DEFINITION OF PROCESSOR

[2.368]
71. A processor is defined in Article 4 (8) as a natural or legal person, public authority, agency or another body, which processes personal data on behalf of the controller. Similar to the definition of controller, the definition of processor envisages a broad range of actors - it can be "*a natural or legal person, public authority, agency or other body*". This means that there is in principle no limitation as to which type of actor might assume the role of a processor. It might be an organisation, but it might also be an individual.

72. The GDPR lays down obligations directly applicable specifically to processors as further specified in Part II section 1 of these guidelines. A processor can be held liable or fined in case of failure to comply with such obligations or in case it acts outside or contrary to the lawful instructions of the controller.

73. Processing of personal data can involve multiple processors. For example, a controller may itself choose to directly engage multiple processors, by involving different processors at separate stages of the processing (multiple processors). A controller might also decide to engage one processor, who in turn -with the authorisation of the controller -engages one or more other processors ("sub processor(s)"). The processing activity entrusted to the processor may be limited to a very specific task or context or may be more general and extended.

74. Two basic conditions for qualifying as processor are:
(a)   being *a separate entity* in relation to the controller and
(b)   processing personal data *on the controller's behalf*.

75. A separate entity means that the controller decides to delegate all or part of the processing activities to an external organisation. Within a group of companies, one company can be a processor to another company acting as controller, as both companies are separate entities. On the other hand, a department within a company cannot generally be a processor to another department within the same entity.

76. If the controller decides to process data itself, using its own resources within its organisation, for example through its own staff, this is not a processor situation. Employees and other persons that are acting under the direct authority of the controller, such as temporarily employed staff, are not to be seen as processors since they will process personal data as a part of the controller's entity. In accordance with Article 29, they are also bound by the controller's instructions.

77. *Processing personal data on the controller's behalf* firstly requires that the separate entity processes personal data for the benefit of the controller. In Article 4(2), processing is defined as a concept including a wide array of operations ranging from collection, storage and consultation to use, dissemination or otherwise making available and destruction. In practice, this means that all imaginable handling of personal data constitutes processing.

78. Secondly, the processing must be done on behalf of a controller but otherwise than under its direct authority or control. Acting "on behalf of" means serving someone else's interest and recalls the legal concept of "delegation". In the case of data protection law, a processor is called to implement the instructions given by the controller at least with regard to the purpose of the processing and the essential elements of the means. The lawfulness of the processing according to Article 6, and if relevant Article 9, of the Regulation will be derived from the controller's activity and the processor must not process the data otherwise than according to the controller's instructions. Even so, as described above, the controller's instructions may still leave a certain degree of discretion about how to best serve the controller's interests, allowing the processor to choose the most suitable technical and organisational means.[26]

79. Acting "on behalf of" also means that the processor may not carry out processing for its own purpose(s). As provided in Article 28(10), a processor infringes the GDPR by going beyond the controller's instructions and starting to determine its own purposes and means of processing. The processor will be considered a controller in respect of that processing and may be subject to sanctions for going beyond the controller's instructions.

Example. Service provider referred to as data processor but acting as controller
Service provider MarketinZ provides promotional advertisement and direct marketing services to various companies. Company GoodProductZ concludes a contract with MarketinZ, according to which the latter company provides commercial advertising for GoodProductZ customers and is referred to as data processor. However, MarketinZ decides to use GoodProducts customer database also for other purposes than advertising for GoodProducts, such as developing their own business activity. The decision to add an additional purpose to the one for which the personal data were transferred converts MarketinZ into a data controller for this set of processing operations and their processing for this purpose would constitute an infringement of the GDPR.

---

80. The EDPB recalls that not every service provider that processes personal data in the course of delivering a service is a "processor" within the meaning of the GDPR. The role of a processor does not stem from the nature of an entity that is processing data but from its concrete activities in a specific context. The nature of the service will determine whether the processing activity amounts to processing of personal data on behalf of the controller within the meaning of the GDPR. In practice, where the provided service is not specifically targeted at processing personal data or where such processing does not constitute a key element of the service, the service provider may be in a position to independently determine the purposes and means of that processing which is required in order to provide the service. In that situation, the service provider is to be seen as a separate controller and not as a processor.[27] A case-by-case analysis remains necessary, however, in order to ascertain the degree of influence each entity effectively has in determining the purposes and means of the processing.

Example: Taxi service
A taxi service offers an online platform which allows companies to book a taxi to transport employees or guests to and from the airport. When booking a taxi, Company ABC specifies the name of the employee that should be picked up from the airport so the driver can confirm the employee's identity at the moment of pick-up. In this case, the taxi service processes personal data of the employee as part of its service to Company ABC, but the processing as such is not the target of the service. The taxi service has designed the online booking platform as part of developing its own business activity to provide transportation services, without any instructions from Company ABC. The taxi service also independently determines the categories of data it collects and how long it retains. The taxi service therefore acts as a controller in its own right, notwithstanding the fact that the processing takes places following a request for service from Company ABC.

---

81. The EDPB notes that a service provider may still be acting as a processor even if the processing of personal data is not the main or primary object of the service, provided that the customer of the service still determines the purposes and means of the processing in practice. When considering whether or not to entrust the processing of personal data to a particular service provider, controllers should carefully assess whether the service provider in question allows them to exercise a sufficient degree of control, taking into account the nature, scope, context and purposes of processing as well as the potential risks for data subjects.

Example: Call center
Company X outsources its client support to Company Y who provides a call center in order to help Company X's clients with their questions. The client support service means that Company Y has to have access to Company X client data bases. Company Y can only access data in order to provide the support that Company X has procured and they cannot process data for any other purposes than the ones stated by Company X. Company Y is to be seen as a personal data processor and a processor agreement must be concluded between Company X and Y.

Example: General IT support
Company Z hires an IT service provider to perform general support on its IT systems which include a vast amount of personal data. The access to personal data is not the main object of the support service but it is inevitable that the IT service provider systematically has access to personal data when performing the service. Company Z therefore concludes that the IT service provider -being a separate company and inevitably being required to process personal data even though this is not the main objective of the service – is to be regarded as a processor. A processor agreement is therefore concluded with the IT service provider.

Example: IT-consultant fixing a software bug
Company ABC hires an IT-specialist from another company to fix a bug in a software that is being used by the company. The IT-consultant is not hired to process personal data, and Company ABC determines that any access to personal data will be purely incidental and therefore very limited in practice. ABC therefore concludes that the IT-specialist is not a processor (nor a controller in its own right) and that Company ABC will take appropriate measures according to Article 32 of the GDPR in order to prevent the IT-consultant from processing personal data in an unauthorised manner.

---

82. As stated above, nothing prevents the processor from offering a preliminary defined service but the controller must make the final decision to actively approve the way the processing is carried out and/or to be able to request changes if necessary.

Example: Cloud service provider
A municipality has decided to use a cloud service provider for handling information in its school and education services. The cloud service provides messaging services, video conferences, storage of documents, calendar management, word processing etc. and will entail processing of personal data about school children and teachers. The cloud service provider has offered a standardized service that is offered worldwide. The municipality however must make sure that the agreement in place complies with Article 28(3) of the GDPR, that the personal data of which it is controller are processed for the municipality's purposes only. It must also make sure that their specific instructions on storage periods, deletion of data etc. are respected by the cloud service provider regardless of what is generally offered in the standardized service.

---

5 DEFINITION OF THIRD PARTY/RECIPIENT

[2.369]
83. The Regulation not only defines the concepts of controller and processor but also the concepts of recipient and third party. As opposed to the concepts of controller and processor, the Regulation does not lay down specific obligations or responsibilities for recipients and third parties. These can be said to be relative concepts in the sense that they describe a relation to a controller or processor from a specific perspective, e.g. a controller or processor discloses data to a recipient. A recipient of personal data and a third party may well simultaneously be regarded as a controller or processor from other perspectives. For example, entities that are to be seen as recipients or third parties from one perspective, are controllers for the processing for which they determine the purpose and means.

Third party

84. Article 4(10) defines a "*third party*" as a natural or legal person, public authority, agency or body other than
- the data subject,
- the controller,
- the processor and
- persons who, under the direct authority of the controller or processor, are authorised to process personal data.

85. The definition generally corresponds to the previous definition of "*third party*" in Directive 95/46/EC.

86. Whereas the terms "*personal data*", "*data subject*", "*controller*" and "*processor*" are defined in the Regulation, the concept of "*persons who, under the direct authority of the controller or processor, are authorised to process personal data*" is not. It is, however, generally understood as referring to persons that belong to the legal entity of the controller or processor (an employee or a role highly comparable to that of employees, e.g. interim staff provided via a temporary employment agency) but only insofar as they are authorized to process personal data. An employee etc. who obtains access to data that he or she is not authorised to access and for other purposes than that of the employer does not fall within this category. Instead, this employee should be considered as a third party vis-à-vis the processing undertaken by the employer. Insofar as the employee processes personal data for his or her own purposes, distinct from those of his or her employer, he or she will then be considered a controller and take on all the resulting consequences and liabilities in terms of personal data processing.[28]

87. A third party thus refers to someone who, in the specific situation at hand, is not a data subject, a controller, a processor or an employee. For example, the controller may hire a processor and instruct it to transfer personal data to a third party. This third party will then be considered a controller in its own right for the processing that it carries out for its own purposes. It should be noted that, within a group of companies, a company other than the controller or the processor is a third party, even though it belongs to the same group as the company who acts as controller or processor.

Example: Cleaning services

Company A concludes a contract with a cleaning service company to clean its offices. The cleaners are not supposed to access or otherwise process personal data. Even though they may occasionally come across such data when moving around in the office, they can carry out their task without accessing data and they are contractually prohibited to access or otherwise process personal data that Company A keeps as controller. The cleaners are not employed by Company A nor are they seen as being under the direct authority of that company. There is no intention to engage the cleaning service company or its employees to process personal data on Company A's behalf. The cleaning service company and its employees are therefore to be seen as a third party and the controller must make sure that there are adequate security measures to prevent that they have access to data and lay down a confidentiality duty in case they should accidentally come across personal data.

Example: Company groups – parent company and subsidiaries

Companies X and Y form part of the Group Z. Companies X and Y both process data about their respective employees for employee administration purposes. At one point, the parent company ZZ decides to request employee data from all subsidiaries in order to produce group wide statistics. When transferring data from companies X and Y to ZZ, the latter is to be regarded as a third party regardless of the fact that all companies are part of the same group. Company ZZ will be regarded as controller for its processing of the data for statistical purposes.

Recipient

88. Article 4(9) defines a "*recipient*" as a natural or legal person, public authority, agency or another body, to which the personal data are disclosed, whether a third party or not. Public authorities are however not to be seen as recipients when they receive personal data in the framework of a particular inquiry in accordance with Union or Member State law (e.g. tax and customs authorities, financial investigation units etc.)[29]

89. The definition generally corresponds to the previous definition of "*recipient*" in Directive 95/46/EC.

90. The definition covers anyone who receives personal data, whether they are a third party or not. For example, when a controller sends personal data to another entity, either a processor or a third party, this entity is a recipient. A third party recipient shall be considered a controller for any processing that it carries out for its own purpose(s) after it receives the data.

Example: Disclosure of data between companies

The travel agency ExploreMore arranges travels on request from its individual customers. Within this service, they send the customers' personal data to airlines, hotels and organisations of excursions in order for them to carry out their respective services. ExploreMore, the hotels, airlines and excursion providers are each to be seen as controllers for the processing that they carry out within their respective services. There is no controller-processor relation. However, the airlines, hotels and excursion providers are to be seen as recipients when receiving the personal data from ExploreMore.

NOTES

³   Article 29 Working Party Opinion 3/2010 on the principle of accountability adopted on 13 July 2010, 00062/10/EN WP 173.

⁴   Recital 74 GDPR

⁵   Article 29 Working Party Opinion 1/2010, WP 169, p. 9.

⁶   See also the Opinion of Advocate General Mengozzi, in *Jehovah's witnesses*, C-25/17, ECLI:EU:C:2018:57, paragraph 68 ("*For the purposes of determining the 'controller' within the meaning of Directive 95/46, I am inclined to consider [. . . .] that excessive formalism would make it easy to circumvent the provisions of Directive 95/46 and that, consequently, it is necessary to rely upon a more factual than formal analysis [. . .].*")

⁷   For example, in its Judgment in *Jehovah's witnesses*, C-25/17, ECLI:EU:C:2018:551, paragraph 75, the CJEU considered that a religious community of Jehovah's witnesses acted as a controller, jointly with its individual members. Judgment in *Jehovah's witnesses*, C-25/17, ECLI:EU:C:2018:551, paragraph 75.

⁸   See e.g., Article 29 Data Protection Working Party, Opinion 10/2006 on the processing of personal data by the Society for Worldwide Interbank Financial Telecommunication (SWIFT), 22 November 2006, WP128, p. 11.

⁹   See section 3, p.15

¹⁰ See also the Opinion of Advocate General Bot in *Wirtschaftsakademie*, C-210/16, ECLI:EU:C:2017:796, paragraph 46.

¹¹ Judgment in *Jehovah's witnesses*, C-25/17, ECLI:EU:C:2018:551, paragraph 68.

¹² Judgment in Fashion ID, C-40/17, ECLI:EU:C:2019:629, paragraph 74: "*(A)s the Advocate General noted, [. . . -] it appears that a natural or legal person may be a controller, within the meaning of Article 2(d) of Directive 95/46, jointly with others only in respect of operations involving the processing of personal data for which it determines jointly the purposes and means. By contrast, [. . .] that natural or legal person cannot be considered to be a controller, within the meaning of that provision, in the context of operations that precede or are subsequent in the overall chain of processing for which that person does not determine either the purposes or the means*".

¹³ Judgment in *Wirtschaftsakademie*, C-201/16, ECLI :EU :C :2018 :388, paragraph 38.

¹⁴ See in particular, *Unabhängiges Landeszentrum für Datenschutz Schleswig-Holstein v Wirtschaftsakademie*, (C-210/16), *Tietosuojavaltuutettu v Jehovan todistajat — uskonnollinen yhdyskunta* (C-25/17), Fashion ID GmbH & Co. KG v Verbraucherzentrale NRW eV (C-40/17). To be noted that while these judgments were issued by the CJUE on the interpretation of the concept of joint controllers under Directive 95/46/CE, they remain valid in the context of the GDPR, given that the elements determining this concept under the GDPR remain the same as under the Directive.

¹⁵ Judgment in *Wirtschaftsakademie*, C-210/16, ECLI:EU:C:2018:388, paragraph 38.

¹⁶ Judgment in Jehovah's witnesses, C-25/17, ECLI:EU:C:2018:551, paragraph 75.

¹⁷ Ibid.

¹⁸ Ibid, paragraph 71.

19 Ibid.

20 Judgment in *Fashion ID*, C-40/17, ECLI:EU:2018:1039, paragraph 74 "*By contrast, and without prejudice to any civil liability provided for in national law in this respect, that natural or legal person cannot be considered to be a controller, within the meaning of that provision, in the context of operations that precede or are subsequent in the overall chain of processing for which that person does not determine either the purposes or the means*".

21 Judgment in *Fashion ID*, C-40/17, ECLI:EU:2018:1039, paragraph 80.

22 Judgment in *Wirtschaftsakademie*, C-210/16, ECLI:EU:C:2018:388, paragraph 34.

23 Judgment in Wirtschaftsakademie, C-210/16, ECLI:EU:C:2018:388, paragraph 39.

24 The provider of the system can be a joint controller if the criteria mentioned above are met, i.e. if the provider participates in the determination of purposes and means. Otherwise, the provider should be considered as a processor.

25 Judgment in Fashion ID, C-40/17, ECLI:EU:2018:1039, paragraphs 77-79.

26 See section 2.1.4 describing the distinction between essential and non-essential means.

27 See also Recital 81 of the GDPR, which refers to "entrusting a processor processing activities", indicating that the processing activity as such is an important part of the decision of the controller to ask a processor to process personal data on its behalf.

28 The employer (as original controller) could nevertheless retain some responsibility in case the new processing occurred because of a lack of adequate security measures.

29 See also Recital 31 of the GDPR

PART II – CONSEQUENCES OF ATTRIBUTING DIFFERENT ROLES

1 RELATIONSHIP BETWEEN CONTROLLER AND PROCESSOR

[2.370]
91. A distinct new feature in the GDPR are the provisions that impose obligations directly upon processors. For example, a processor must ensure that persons authorised to process the personal data have committed themselves to confidentiality (Article 28(3)); a processor must maintain a record of all categories of processing activities (Article 30(2)) and must implement appropriate technical and organisational measures (Article 32). A processor must also designate a data protection officer under certain conditions (Article 37) and has a duty to notify the controller without undue delay after becoming aware of a personal data breach (Article 33(2)). Furthermore, the rules on transfers of data to third countries (Chapter V) apply to processors as well as controllers. In this regard, the EDPB considers that Article 28(3) GDPR imposes direct obligations upon processors, including the duty to assist the controller in ensuring compliance.

1.1 Choice of the processor

92. The controller has the **duty to use "only processors providing sufficient guarantees** to implement appropriate technical and organisational measures", so that processing meets the requirements of the GDPR -including for the security of processing -and ensures the protection of data subject rights.[30] The controller is therefore responsible for assessing the sufficiency of the guarantees provided by the processor and should be able to prove that it has taken all of the elements provided in the GDPR into serious consideration.

93. The guarantees "provided" by the processor are actually those that the processor is able to **demonstrate to the satisfaction of the controller**, as those are the only ones that can effectively be taken into account by the controller when assessing compliance with its obligations. Often this will require an exchange of relevant documentation (e.g. privacy policy, terms of service, record of processing activities, records management policy, information security policy, reports of external audits, recognised international certifications, like ISO 27000 series).

94. The controller's assessment of whether the guarantees are sufficient is a form of risk assessment, which will greatly depend on the type of processing entrusted to the processor and needs to be made on a case-by-case basis, taking into account the nature, scope, context and purposes of processing as well as the risks for the rights and freedoms of natural persons.

95. The following elements[31] should be taken into account by the controller in order to assess the sufficiency of the guarantees: the processor's **expert knowledge** (e.g. technical expertise with regard to security measures and data breaches); the processor's **reliability**; the processor's **resources**. The reputation of the processor on the market may also be a relevant factor for controllers to consider.

96. Furthermore, the adherence to an approved code of conduct or certification mechanism can be used as an element by which sufficient guarantees can be demonstrated.[32] The processors are therefore advised to inform the controller as to this circumstance, as well as to any change in such adherence.

97. The obligation to use only processors "providing sufficient guarantees" contained in Article 28(1) GDPR is a continuous obligation. It does not end at the moment where the controller and processor conclude a contract or other legal act. Rather the controller should, at appropriate intervals, verify the processor's guarantees, including through audits and inspections where appropriate.[33]

1.2 Form of the contract or other legal act

98. Any processing of personal data by a processor must be governed by a contract or other legal act under EU or Member State law between the controller and the processor, as required by Article 28(3) GDPR.

99. Such legal act must be in **writing, including in electronic form**.[34] Therefore, non-written agreements (regardless of how thorough or effective they are) cannot be considered sufficient to meet the requirements laid down by Article 28 GDPR. To avoid any difficulties in demonstrating that the contract or other legal act is actually in force, the EDPB recommends ensuring that the necessary signatures are included in the legal act.

100. Furthermore, the contract or the other legal act under Union or Member State law must be **binding on the processor** with regard to the controller, i.e. it must establish obligations on the processor that are binding as a matter of EU or Member State law. Also it must set out the obligations of the controller. In most cases, there will be a contract, but the Regulation also refers to "other legal act", such as a national law (primary or secondary) or other legal instrument. If the legal act does not include all the minimum required content, it must be supplemented with a contract or another legal act that includes the missing elements.

101. Since the Regulation establishes a clear obligation to enter into a written contract, where no other relevant legal act is in force, the absence thereof is an infringement of the GDPR.[35] Both the controller and processor are responsible for ensuring that there is a contract or other legal act to govern the processing.[36] Subject to the provisions of Article 3 of the GDPR, the competent supervisory authority will be able to direct an administrative fine against both the controller and the processor, taking into account the circumstances of each individual case. Contracts that have been entered into before the date of application of the GDPR should have been updated in light of Article 28(3). The absence of such update, in order to bring a previously existing contract in line with the requirements of the GDPR, constitutes an infringement of Article 28(3).

102. In order to comply with the duty to enter into a contract, **the controller and the processor may choose to negotiate their own contract** including all the compulsory elements **or to rely, in whole or in part, on standard contractual clauses in relation to obligations under Article 28.**[37]

103. A set of standard contractual clauses (SCCs) may be, alternatively, adopted by the Commission[38] or adopted by a supervisory authority, in accordance with the consistency mechanism.[39] These clauses could be part of a certification granted to the controller or processor pursuant to Articles 42 or 43.[40]

104. The EDPB would like to clarify that there is no obligation for controllers and processors to enter into a contract based on SCCs, nor is it to be necessarily preferred over negotiating an individual contract. Both options are viable for the purposes of compliance with data protection law, depending on the specific circumstances, as long as they meet the Article 28(3) requirements.

105. If the parties wish to take advantage of standard contractual clauses, the data protection clauses of their agreement must be the same as those of the SCCs. The SCCs will often leave some blank spaces to be filled in or options to be selected by the parties. Also, the SCCs will generally be embedded in a larger agreement describing the object of the contract, its financial conditions, and other agreed clauses: it will be possible for the parties to add additional clauses (e.g. applicable law and jurisdiction) as long as they do not contradict, directly or indirectly, the SCCs[41] and they do not undermine the protection afforded by the GDPR and EU or Member State data protection laws.

106. Contracts between controllers and processors may sometimes be drafted unilaterally by one of the parties. Which party or parties that draft the contract may depend on several factors, including: the parties' position in the market and contractual power, their technical expertise, as well as access to legal services. For instance, some service providers tend to set up standard terms and conditions, which include data processing agreements.

107. The fact that the contract and its detailed terms of business are prepared by the service provider rather than by the controller is not in itself problematic and is not in itself a sufficient basis to conclude that the service provider should be considered as a controller. Also, the imbalance in the contractual power of a small data controller with respect to big service providers should not be considered as a justification for the controller to accept clauses and terms of contracts which are not in compliance with data protection law, nor can it discharge the controller from its data protection obligations. The controller must evaluate the terms and in so far as it freely accepts them and makes use of the service, it has also accepted full responsibility for compliance with the GDPR. Any proposed modification, by a processor, of data processing agreements included in standard terms and conditions should be directly notified to and approved by the controller. The mere publication of these modifications on the processor's website is not compliant with Article 28.

1.3 Content of the contract or other legal act

108. Before focusing on each of the detailed requirements set out by the GDPR as to the content of the contract or other legal act, some general remarks are necessary.

109. While the elements laid down by Article 28 of the Regulation constitute the core content of the agreement, the contract should be a way for the controller and the processor to further clarify how such core elements are going to be implemented with detailed instructions. Therefore, **the processing agreement should not merely restate the provisions of the GDPR**: rather, it should include more specific, concrete information as to how the requirements will be met and which level of security is required for the personal data processing that is the object of the processing agreement. Far from being a pro-forma exercise, the negotiation and stipulation of the contract are a chance to specify details regarding the processing.[42] Indeed, the "protection of the rights and freedoms of data subjects as well as the responsibility and liability of controllers and processors [. . .] requires a clear allocation of the responsibilities" under the GDPR.[43]

110. At the same time, the contract should **take into account** *"the specific tasks and responsibilities of the processor in the context of the processing to be carried out and the risk to the rights and* *freedoms of the data subject".*[44] Generally speaking, the contract between the parties should be drafted in light of the specific data processing activity. For instance, there is no need to impose particularly stringent protections and procedures on a processor entrusted with a processing activity from which only minor risks arise: while each processor must comply with the requirements set out by the Regulation, the measures and procedures should be tailored to the specific situation. In any event, all elements of Article 28(3) must be covered by the contract. At the same time, the contract should include some elements that may help the processor in understanding the risks to the rights and freedoms of data subjects arising from the processing: because the activity is performed on behalf of the controller, often the controller has a deeper understanding of the risks that the processing entails since the controller is aware of the circumstances in which the processing is embedded.

111. Moving on to the **required content** of the contract or other legal act, EDPB interprets Article 28(3) in a way that it needs to set out:

*   the **subject-matter** of the processing (for instance, video surveillance recordings of people entering and leaving a high-security facility). While the subject matter of the processing is a broad concept, it needs to be formulated with enough specifications so that it is clear what the main object of the processing is;
*   the **duration**[45] of the processing: the exact period of time, or the criteria used to determine it, should be specified; for instance, reference could be made to the duration of the processing agreement;
*   the **nature** of the processing: the type of operations performed as part of the processing (for instance: "filming", "recording", "archiving of images", . . .) and purpose of the processing (for instance: detecting unlawful entry). This description should be as comprehensive as possible, depending on the specific processing activity, so as to allow external parties (e.g. supervisory authorities) to understand the content and the risks of the processing entrusted to the processor.
*   the **type of personal data**: this should be specified in the most detailed manner as possible (for instance: video images of individuals as they enter and leave the facility). It would not be adequate merely to specify that it is "personal data pursuant to Article 4(1) GDPR" or "special categories of personal data pursuant to Article 9". In case of special categories of data, the contract or legal act should at least specify which types of data are concerned, for example, "information regarding health records", or "information as to whether the data subject is a member of a trade union";
*   the **categories of data subjects**: this, too, should be indicated in a quite specific way (for instance: "visitors", "employees", delivery services etc.);
*   the **obligations and rights of the controller**: the rights of the controller are further dealt with in the following sections (e.g. with respect to the right of the controller to perform inspections and audits). As regards the obligations of the controller, examples include the controller's obligation to provide the processor with the data mentioned in the contract, to provide and document, in writing, any instruction bearing on the processing of data by the processor, to ensure, before and throughout the processing, compliance with the obligations set out in the GDPR on the processor's part, to supervise the processing, including by conducting audits and inspections with the processor.

112. While the GDPR lists elements that always need to be included in the agreement, other relevant information may need to be included, depending on the context and the risks of the processing as well as any additional applicable requirement.

1.3.1 The processor must only process data on documented instructions from the controller (Art. 28(3)(a) GDPR)

113. The need to specify this obligation stems from the fact that the processor processes data on behalf of the controller. Controllers must provide its processors with instructions related to each processing activity. Such instructions can include permissible and unacceptable handling of personal data, more detailed procedures, ways of securing data, etc. The processor shall not go beyond what is instructed by the controller.

114. When a processor processes data outside or beyond the controller's instructions, and this amounts to a decision determining the purposes and means of processing, the processor will be in breach of its obligations and will even be considered a controller in respect of that processing in accordance with Article 28(10) (see section 1.5 below).

115. Because such instructions must be **documented**, it is recommended to include a procedure and a template for giving further instructions in an annex to the contract or other legal act. Alternatively, they can be provided in any written form (e.g. e-mail), as long as it is possible to keep records of such instructions. In any event, to avoid any difficulties in demonstrating that the controller's instructions have been duly documented, the EDPB recommends keeping such instructions together with the contract or other legal act.

116. The duty for the processor to refrain from any processing activity not based on the controller's instructions also applies to **transfers** of personal data to a third country or international organisation. The contract should specify the requirements for transfers to third countries or international organisations, taking into account the provisions of Chapter V of the GDPR.

117. The EDPB recommends that controller pay due attention to this specific point especially when the processor is going to delegate some processing activities to other processors, and when the processor has divisions or units located in third countries. If the instructions by the controller do not allow for transfers or disclosures to third countries, the processor will not be allowed to assign the processing to a sub-processor in a third country, nor will he be allowed to have the data processed in one of his non-EU divisions.

118. A processor may process data other than on documented instructions of the controller **when the processor is required to process and/or transfer personal data on the basis of EU law or Member State law to which the processor is subject.** This provision further reveals the importance of carefully negotiating and drafting data processing agreements, as, for example, legal advice may need to be sought by either party as to the existence of any such legal requirement. This needs to be done in a timely fashion, as the processor has an obligation to inform the controller of such requirement before starting the processing. Only when that same (EU or Member State) law forbids the processor to inform the controller on "important grounds of public interest", there is no such information obligation. In any case, any transfer or disclosure may only take place if authorised by Union law, including in accordance with Article 48 of the GDPR.

1.3.2 The processor must ensure that persons authorised to process the personal data have committed themselves to confidentiality or are under an appropriate statutory obligation of confidentiality (Art. 28(3)(b) GDPR)

119. The contract must say that the processor needs to ensure that anyone it allows to process the personal data is committed to confidentiality. This may occur either via a specific contractual agreement, or due to statutory obligations already in place.

120. The broad concept of "persons authorised to process the personal data" includes employees and temporary workers. Generally speaking, the processor should make the personal data available only to the employees who actually need them to perform tasks for which processor was hired by the controller.

121. The commitment or obligation of confidentiality must be "appropriate", i.e. it must effectively forbid the authorised person from disclosing any confidential information without authorisation, and it must be sufficiently broad so as to encompass all the personal data processed on behalf of the controller as well as the details concerning the relationship.

1.3.3 The processor must take all the measures required pursuant to Article 32 (Art. 28(3)(c) GDPR)

122. Article 32 requires the controller and the processor to implement appropriate technical and organisational security measures. While this obligation is already directly imposed on the processor whose processing operations fall within the scope of the GDPR, the duty to take all measures required pursuant to Article 32 still needs to be reflected in the contract concerning the processing activities entrusted by the controller.

123. As indicated earlier, the processing contract should not merely restate the provisions of the GDPR. The contract needs to include or reference information as to the security measures to be adopted, **an obligation on the processor to obtain the controller's approval before making changes**, and a regular review of the security measures so as to ensure their appropriateness with regard to risks, which may evolve over time. The degree of detail of the information as to the security measures to be included in the contract must be such as to enable the controller to assess the appropriateness of the measures pursuant to Article 32(1) GDPR. Moreover, the description is also necessary in order to enable the controller to comply with its accountability duty pursuant to Article 5(2) and Article 24 GDPR as regards the security measures imposed on the processor. A corresponding obligation of the processor to assist the controller and to make available all information necessary to demonstrate compliance can be inferred from Art. 28.3 (f) and (h) GDPR.

124. The level of instructions provided by the controller to the processor as to the measures to be implemented will depend on the specific circumstances. In some cases, the controller may provide a clear and detailed description of the security measures to be implemented. In other cases, the controller may describe the minimum security objectives to be achieved, while requesting the processor to propose implementation of specific security measures. In any event, the controller must provide the processor with a description of the processing activities and security objectives (based on the controller's risk assessment), as well as approve the measures proposed by the processor. This could be included in an annex to the contract. The controller exercises its decision-making power over the main features of the security measures, be it by explicitly listing the measures or by approving those proposed by the processor.

1.3.4 The processor must respect the conditions referred to in Article 28(2) and 28(4) for engaging another processor (Art. 28(3)(d) GDPR).

125. The agreement must specify that the processor may not engage another processor without the controller's prior written authorisation and whether this authorisation will be specific or general. In case of general authorisation, the processor has to inform the controller of any change of sub-processors under a written authorisation, and give the controller the opportunity to object. It is recommended that the contract set out the process for this. It should be noted that the processor's duty to inform the controller of any change of sub-processors implies that the processor actively indicates or flags such changes toward the controller.[46] Also, where specific authorisation is required, the contract should set out the process for obtaining such authorisation.

126. When the processor engages another processor, a contract must be put in place between them, imposing the same data protection obligations as those imposed on the original processor or these obligations must be imposed by another legal act under Union or Member State law. This includes the obligation under Article 28(3)(h) to allow for and contribute to audits by the controller or another auditor mandated by the controller.[47] The processor is liable to the controller for the other processors' compliance with data protection obligations (for further details on the recommended content of the agreement see section 1.6 below).

1.3.5 The processor must assist the controller for the fulfilment of its obligation to respond to requests for exercising the data subject's rights (Article 28(3)(e) GDPR).

127. While ensuring that data subjects requests are dealt with is up to the controller, the contract must stipulate that the processor has an obligation to provide assistance "by appropriate technical and organisational measures, insofar as this is possible". The nature of this assistance may vary greatly "taking into account the nature of the processing" and depending on the type of activity entrusted to the processor. The details concerning the assistance to be provided by the processor should be included in the contract or in an annex thereto.

128. While the assistance may simply consist in promptly forwarding any request received, in some circumstances the processor will be given more specific, technical duties, especially when it is in the position of extracting and managing the personal data.

129. It is crucial to bear in mind that, although the practical management of individual requests can be outsourced to the processor, the controller bears the responsibility for complying with such requests. Therefore, the assessment as to whether requests by data subjects are admissible and/or the requirements set by the GDPR are met should be performed by the controller, either on a case-by-case basis or through clear instructions provided to the processor in the contract before the start of the processing. Also, the deadlines set out by Chapter III cannot be extended by the controller based on the fact that the necessary information must be provided by the processor.

1.3.6 The processor must assist the controller in ensuring compliance with the obligations pursuant to Articles 32 to 36 (Art. 28(3)(f) GDPR).

130. It is necessary for the contract to avoid merely restating these duties of assistance: **the agreement should contain details as to how the processor is asked to help the controller meet the listed obligations**. For example, procedures and template forms may be added in the annexes to the agreement, allowing the processor to provide the controller with all the necessary information.

131. The type and degree of assistance to be provided by the processor may vary widely "*taking into account the nature of processing and the information available to the processor*". The controller must adequately inform the processor as to the risk involved in the processing and as to any other circumstance that may help the processor meet its duty.

132. Moving on to the specific obligations, the processor has, first, a duty to assist the controller in meeting the obligation to adopt adequate technical and organisational measures to ensure security of processing.[48] While this may overlap, to some extent, with the requirement that the processor itself adopts adequate security measures, where the processing operations of the processor fall within the scope of the GDPR, they remain two distinct obligations, since one refers to the processor's own measures and the other refers to the controller's.

133. Secondly, the processor must assist the controller in meeting the obligation to notify personal data breaches to the supervisory authority and to data subjects. The processor must notify the controller whenever it discovers a personal data breach affecting the processor's or a sub-processor's facilities / IT systems and help the controller in obtaining the information that need to be stated in the report to the supervisory authority.[49] The GDPR requires that the controller notify a breach without undue delay in order to minimize the harm for individuals and to maximize the possibility to address the breach in an adequate manner. Thus, the processor's notification to the data controller should also take place without undue delay.[50] The EDPB recommends that there is a specific time frame of notification (e.g. number of hours) and the point of contact for such notifications be provided in the contract.[51] The contract should finally specify how the processor shall notify the controller in case of a breach.

134. Furthermore, the processor must also assist the controller in carrying out data protection impact assessments when required, and in consulting the supervisory authority when the outcome reveals that there is a high risk that cannot be mitigated.

135. The duty of assistance does not consist in a shift of responsibility, as those obligations are imposed on the controller. For instance, although the data protection impact assessment can in practice be carried out by a processor, the controller remains accountable for the duty to carry out the assessment[52] and the processor is only required to assist the controller "where necessary and upon request."[53] As a result, the controller is the one that must take the initiative to perform the data protection impact assessment, not the processor.

1.3.7 On termination of the processing activities, the processor must, at the choice of the controller, delete or return all the personal data to the controller and delete existing copies (Art. 28(3)(g) GDPR).

136. The contractual terms are meant to ensure that the personal data are subject to appropriate protection after the end of the "provision of services related to the processing": it is therefore up to the controller to decide what the processor should do with regard to the personal data.

137. The controller can decide at the beginning whether personal data shall be deleted or returned by specifying it in the contract, through a written communication to be timely sent to the processor. The contract or other legal act should reflect the possibility for the data controller to change the choice made before the end of the provision of services related to the processing. The contract should specify the process for providing such instructions.

138. If the controller chooses that the personal data be deleted, the processor should ensure that the deletion is performed in a secure manner, also in order to comply with Article 32 GDPR. The processor should confirm to the controller that the deletion has been completed within an agreed timescale and in an agreed manner.

139. The processor must delete all existing copies of the data, unless EU or Member State law requires further storage. If the processor or controller is aware of any such legal requirement, it should inform the other party as soon as possible.

1.3.8 The processor must make available to the controller all information necessary to demonstrate compliance with the obligations laid down in Article 28 and allow for and contribute to audits, including inspections, conducted by the controller or another auditor mandated by the controller (Art. 28(3)(h) GDPR).

140. The contract shall include details on how often and how the flow of information between the processor and the controller should take place so that the controller is fully informed as to the details of the processing. For instance, the relevant portions of the processor's records of processing activities may be shared with the controller. The processor should provide all information on how the processing activity will be carried out on behalf of the controller. Such information should include information on the functioning of the systems used, security measures, retention of data, data location, transfers of data, access to data and recipients of data, sub-processors used, etc.

141. Further details shall also be set out in the contract regarding the ability to carry out and the duty to contribute to inspections and audits by the controller or another auditor mandated by the controller. The parties should cooperate in good faith and assess whether and when there is a need to perform audits on the processor's premises. Likewise, specific procedures should be established regarding the processor's and the controller's inspection of sub-processors (see section 1.6 below).

1.4 Instructions infringing data protection law

142. According to Article 28(3), the processor must immediately inform the controller if, in its opinion, an instruction infringes the GDPR or other Union or Member State data protection provisions.

143. Indeed, the processor has a duty to comply with the controller's instructions, but it also has a general obligation to comply with the law. An instruction that infringes data protection law seems to cause a conflict between the aforementioned two obligations.

144. Once informed that one of its instructions may be in breach of data protection law, the controller will have to assess the situation and determine whether the instruction actually violates data protection law.

145. The EDPB recommends the parties to negotiate and agree in the contract the consequences of the notification of an infringing instruction sent by the processor and in case of inaction from the controller in this context. One example would be to insert a clause on the termination of the contract if the controller persists with an unlawful instruction.

1.5 Processor determining purposes and means of processing

146. If the processor infringes the Regulation by determining the purposes and means of processing, it shall be considered as a controller in respect of that processing (Article 28(10) GDPR).

1.6 Sub-processors

147. Data processing activities are often carried out by a great number of actors, and the chains of subcontracting are becoming increasingly complex. The GDPR introduces specific obligations that are triggered when a processor intends to engage another player, thereby adding another link to the chain.

148. Although the chain may be quite long, the controller retains its pivotal role in determining the purpose and means of processing. Article 28(2) GDPR stipulates that the processor shall not engage another processor without prior specific or general written authorisation of the controller. In the case of general written authorisation, the processor must inform the controller of any intended changes concerning the addition or replacement of other processors, thereby giving the controller the opportunity to object to such changes. In both cases, the processor must obtain the controller's authorisation in writing before any personal data processing is entrusted to the sub-processor. In order to make the assessment and the decision whether to authorise subcontracting, a list of intended sub-processors (including per each: their locations, what they will be doing and proof of what safeguards have been implemented) will have to be provided to the data controller by the processor[54].

149. The prior written authorisation may be specific, i.e. referring to a specific sub-processor for a specific processing activity and at a specific time, or general. This should be specified in the contract or other legal act that governs the processing.

150. In cases where the controller decides to accept certain sub-processors at the time of the signature of the contract, a list of approved sub-processors should be included in the contract or an annex thereto. The list should then be kept up to date, in accordance with the general or specific authorisation given by the controller.

151. If the controller chooses to give its **specific authorisation**, it should specify in writing which sub-processor and what processing activity it refers to. Any subsequent change will need to be further authorised by the controller before it is put in place. If the processor's request for a specific authorisation is not answered to within the set timeframe, it should be held as denied. The controller should make its decision to grant or withhold authorisation taking into account its obligation to only use processors providing "sufficient guarantees" (see section 1.1 above).

152. Alternatively, the controller may provide its **general authorisation** to the use of sub-processors (in the contract, including a list with such sub-processors in an annex thereto), which should be supplemented with criteria to guide the processor's choice (e.g., guarantees in terms of technical and organisational measures, expert knowledge, reliability and resources)[55]. In this scenario, the processor needs to inform the controller in due time of any intended addition or replacement of sub-processor(s) so as to provide the controller with the opportunity to object.

153. Therefore, the main difference between the specific authorisation and the general authorisation scenarios lies in the meaning given to the controller's silence: in the general authorisation situation, the controller's failure to object within the set timeframe can be interpreted as authorisation.

154. In both scenarios, the contract should include details as to the timeframe for the controller's approval or objection and as to how the parties intend to communicate regarding this topic (e.g. templates). Such timeframe needs to be reasonable in light of the type of processing, the complexity of the activities entrusted to the processor (and the sub-processors) and the relationship between the parties.

155. Regardless of the criteria suggested by the controller to choose providers, the processor remains fully liable to the controller for the performance of the sub-processors' obligations (Article 28(4) GDPR).

156. Furthermore, when a processor intends to employ an (authorised) sub-processor, it must enter into a contract with it that imposes the same obligations as those imposed on the first processor by the controller or the obligations must be imposed by another legal act under EU or Member State law. The whole chain of processing activities needs to be regulated by written agreements.

157. Imposing the "same" obligations should be construed in a functional rather than in a formal way: it is not necessary for the contract to include exactly the same words as those used in the contract between the controller and the processor, but it should ensure that the obligations in substance are the same. This also means that if the processor entrusts the sub-processor with a specific part of the processing, to which some of the obligations cannot apply, such obligations should not be included "by default" in the contract with the sub-processor, as this would only generate uncertainty.

2 CONSEQUENCES OF JOINT CONTROLLERSHIP

2.1 Determining in a transparent manner the respective responsibilities of joint controllers for compliance with the obligations under the GDPR

[2.371]
158. Article 26(1) of the GDPR provides that joint controllers shall in a transparent manner determine and agree on their respective responsibilities for compliance with the obligations under the Regulation.

159. Joint controllers thus need to set "who does what" by deciding between themselves who will have to carry out which tasks in order to make sure that the processing complies with the applicable obligations under the GDPR in relation to the joint processing at stake. In other words, a distribution of responsibilities for compliance is to be made as resulting from the use of the term "*respective*" in Article 26(1).

160. The objective of these rules is to ensure that where multiple actors are involved, especially in complex data processing environments, responsibility for compliance with data protection rules is clearly allocated in order to avoid that the protection of personal data is reduced, or that a negative conflict of competence lead to loopholes whereby some obligations are not complied with by any of the parties involved in the processing. It should be made clear here that all responsibilities have to be allocated according to the factual circumstances in order to achieve an operative agreement.

161. More specifically, Article 26(1) specifies that the determination of their respective responsibilities (i.e. tasks) for compliance with the obligations under the GDPR is to be carried out by joint controllers "*in particular*" as regards the exercising of the rights of the data subject and the duties to provide information referred in Articles 13 and 14, unless and in so far as the respective responsibilities of the controllers are determined by Union or Member State law to which the controllers are subject.

162. It is clear from this provision that joint controllers need to define who respectively will be in charge of answering to requests when data subjects exercise their rights granted by the GDPR and of providing information to them as required by Articles 13 and 14 of the GDPR. However, the use of the terms "*in particular*" indicates that the obligations subject to the allocation of responsibilities for compliance by each party involved as referred in this provision are non-exhaustive. It follows that the distribution of the responsibilities for compliance among joint controllers is not limited to the topics referred in Article 26(1) but extends to other controller's obligations under the GDPR. Indeed, joint controllers need to ensure that the whole joint processing fully complies with the GDPR.

163. In this perspective, the compliance measures and related obligations joint controllers should consider when determining their respective responsibilities, in addition to those specifically referred in Article 26(1), include amongst others without limitation:
* Implementation of general data protection principles (Article 5)
* Legal basis of the processing[56] (Article 6)

- Security measures (Article 32)
- Notification of a personal data breach to the supervisory authority and to the data subject[57] (Articles 33 and 34)
- Data Protection Impact Assessments (Articles 35 and 36)[58]
- The use of a processor (Article 28)
- Transfers of data to third countries (Chapter V)
- Organisation of contact with data subjects and supervisory authorities

164. Other topics that could be considered depending on the processing at stake and the intention of the parties are for instance the limitations on the use of personal data for another purpose by one of the joint controllers. In this respect, both controllers always have a duty to ensure that they both have a legal basis for the processing. Sometimes, in the context of joint controllership, personal data are shared by one controller to another. As a matter of accountability, each controller has the duty to ensure that the data are not further processed in a manner that is incompatible with the purposes for which they were originally collected by the controller sharing the data.[59]

165. Joint controllers can have a certain degree of flexibility in distributing and allocating obligations among them as long as they ensure full compliance with the GDPR with respect of the given processing. The allocation should take into account factors such as, who is competent and in a position to effectively ensure data subject's rights as well as to comply with the relevant obligations under the GDPR. The EDPB recommends documenting the relevant factors and the internal analysis carried out in order to allocate the different obligations. This analysis is part of the documentation under the accountability principle.

166. The obligations do not need to be equally distributed among the joint controllers. In this respect, the CJEU has recently stated that *"the existence of joint responsibility does not necessarily imply equal responsibility of the various operators involved in the processing of personal data"*[60].

167. However, there may be cases where not all of the obligations can be distributed and all joint controllers may need to comply with the same requirements arising from the GDPR, taking into account the nature and context of the joint processing. For instance, joint controllers using shared data processing tools or systems both need to ensure compliance with notably the purpose limitation principle and implement appropriate measures to ensure the security of personal data processed under the shared tools.

168. Another example is the requirement for each joint controller to maintain a record of processing activities or to designate a Data Protection Officer (DPO) if the conditions of Article 37(1) are met. Such requirements are not related to the joint processing but are applicable to them as controllers.

2.2 Allocation of responsibilities needs to be done by way of an arrangement

2.2.1 Form of the arrangement

169. Article 26(1) of the GDPR provides as a new obligation for joint controllers that they should determine their respective responsibilities *"by means of an arrangement between them"*. The legal form of such arrangement is not specified by the GDPR. Therefore, joint controllers are free to agree on the form of the arrangement.

170. In addition, the arrangement on the allocation of responsibilities is binding upon each of the joint controllers. They each agree and commit *vis-à-vis* each other on being responsible for complying with the respective obligations stated in their arrangement as their responsibility.

171. Therefore, for the sake of legal certainty, even if there is no legal requirement in the GDPR for a contract or other legal act, the EDPB recommends that such arrangement be made in the form of a binding document such as a contract or other legal binding act under EU or Member State law to which the controllers are subject. This would provide certainty and could be used to evidence transparency and accountability. Indeed, in case of non-compliance with the agreed allocation provided in the arrangement, its binding nature allows one controller to seek the liability of the other for what was stated in the agreement as falling under its responsibility. Also, in line with the accountability principle, the use of a contract or other legal act will allow joint controllers to demonstrate that they comply with the obligations imposed upon them by the GDPR.

172. The way responsibilities, i.e. the tasks, are allocated between each joint controller has to be stated in a clear and plain language in the arrangement[61]. This requirement is important as it ensures legal certainty and avoid possible conflicts not only in the relation between the joint controllers but also vis-à-vis the data subjects and the data protection authorities.

173. To better frame the allocation of responsibilities between the parties, the EDPB recommends that the arrangement also provide general information on the joint processing by notably specifying the subject matter and purpose of the processing, the type of personal data, and the categories of data subjects.

2.2.2. Obligations towards data subjects

174. The GDPR provides several obligations of joint controllers towards data subjects:

The arrangement shall duly reflect the respective roles and relationships of the joint controllers *vis-à-vis* the data subjects

175. As a complement to what is explained above in section 2.1 of the present guidelines, it is important that the joint controllers clarify in the arrangement their respective role, *"in particular"* as regards the

Part 2   Data Protection: EU Law etc

exercise of the rights of the data subject and their duties to provide the information referred to in Articles 13 and 14. Article 26 of the GDPR stresses the importance of these specific obligations. The joint controllers must therefore organise and agree on how and by whom the information will be provided and how and by whom the answers to the data subject's requests will be provided. Irrespective of the content of the arrangement on this specific point, the data subject may contact either of the joint controllers to exercise his or her rights in accordance with Article 26(3) as further explained below.

176. The way these obligations are organised in the arrangement should "*duly*", i.e. accurately, reflect the reality of the underlying joint processing. For example, if only one of the joint controllers communicates with the data subjects for the purpose of the joint processing, such controller could be in a better position to inform the data subjects and possibly to answer their requests.

The essence of the arrangement shall be made available to the data subject

177. This provision is aimed to ensure that the data subject is aware of the "*essence of the arrangement*". For example, it must be completely clear to a data subject which data controller serves as a point of contact for the exercise of data subject rights (notwithstanding the fact that he or she can exercise his or her rights in respect of and against each joint controller). The obligation to make the essence of the arrangement available to data subjects is important in case of joint controllership in order for the data subject to know which of the controllers is responsible for what.

178. What should be covered by the notion of "*essence of the arrangement*" is not specified by the GDPR. The EDPB recommends that the essence cover at least all the elements of the information referred to in Articles 13 and 14 that should already be accessible to the data subject, and for each of these elements, the arrangement should specify which joint controller is responsible for ensuring compliance with these elements. The essence of the arrangement must also indicate the contact point, if designated.

179. The way such information shall be made available to the data subject is not specified. Contrary to other provisions of the GDPR (such as Article 30(4) for the record of processing or Article 40(11) for the register of approved codes of conduct), Article 26 does not indicate that the availability should be "*upon request*" nor "*publicly available by way of appropriate means*". Therefore, it is up to the joint controllers to decide the most effective way to make the essence of the arrangement available to the data subjects (e.g. together with the information in Article 13 or 14, in the privacy policy or upon request to the data protection officer, if any, or to the contact point that may have been designated). Joint controllers should respectively ensure that the information is provided in a consistent manner.

The arrangement may designate a contact point for data subjects

180. Article 26(1) provides the possibility for joint controllers to designate in the arrangement a contact point for data subjects. Such designation is not mandatory.

181. Being informed of a single way to contact possible multiple joint controllers enables data subjects to know who they can contact with regard to all issues related to the processing of their personal data. In addition, it allows multiple joint controllers to coordinate in a more efficient manner their relations and communications *vis-à-vis* data subjects.

182. For these reasons, in order to facilitate the exercise of data subjects' rights under the GDPR, the EDPB recommends joint controllers to designate such contact point.

183. The contact point can be the DPO, if any, the representative in the Union (for joint controllers not established in the Union) or any other contact point where information can be obtained.

Irrespective of the terms of the arrangement, data subjects may exercise their rights in respect of and against each of the joint controllers.

184. Under Article 26(3), a data subject is not bound by the terms of the arrangement and may exercise his or her rights under the GDPR in respect of and against each of the joint data controllers.

185. For example, in case of joint controllers established in different Member States, or if only one of the joint controllers is established in the Union, the data subject may contact, at his or her choice, either the controller established in the Member State of his or her habitual residence or place of work, or the controller established elsewhere in the EU or in the EEA.

186. Even if the arrangement and the available essence of it indicate a contact point to receive and handle all data subjects' requests, the data subjects themselves may still choose otherwise.

187. Therefore, it is important that joint controllers organise in advance in their arrangement how they will manage answers to requests they could receive from data subjects. In this respect, it is recommended that joint controllers communicate to the other controllers in charge or to the designated contact point, the requests received in order to be effectively handled. Requiring data subjects to contact the designated contact point or the controller in charge would impose an excessive burden on the data subject that would be contrary to the objective of facilitating the exercise of their rights under the GDPR.

2.3 Obligations towards data protection authorities

188. Joint controllers should organise in the arrangement the way they will communicate with the competent supervisory data protection authorities. Such communication could cover possible consultation under Article 36 of the GDPR, notification of a personal data breach, designation of a data protection officer.

189.   It should be recalled that data protection authorities are not bound by the terms of the arrangement whether on the issue of the qualification of the parties as joint controllers or the designated contact point. Therefore, the authorities can contact any of the joint controllers to exercise their powers under Article 58 with respect to the joint processing.

NOTES

30   Article 28(1) and Recital 81 GDPR.

31   Recital 81 GDPR.

32   Article 28(5) and Recital 81 GDPR.

33   See also Article 28(3)h GDPR.

34   Article 28(9) GDPR.

35   The presence (or absence) of a written arrangement, however, is not decisive for the existence of a controller processor relationship. Where there is reason to believe that the contract does not correspond with reality in terms of actual control, the agreement may be set aside. Conversely, a controller-processor relationship might still be held to exist in absence of a written processing agreement. This would, however, imply a violation of Article 28(3) GDPR. Moreover, in certain circumstances, the absence of a clear definition of the relationship between the controller and the processor may raise the problem of the lack of legal basis on which every processing should be based, e.g. in respect of the communication of data between the controller and the alleged processor.

36   Article 28(3) is not only applicable to controllers. In the situation where only the processor is subject to the territorial scope of the GDPR, the obligation shall only be directly applicable to the processor, see also EDPB Guidelines 3/2018 on the territorial scope of the GDPR, p. 12.

37   Article 28(6) GDPR. The EDPB recalls that standard contractual clauses for the purposes of compliance with Article 28 GDPR are not the same as standard contractual clauses referred to in Article 46(2). While the former further stipulate and clarify how the provisions of Article 28(3) and (4) will be fulfilled, the latter provide appropriate safeguards in case of transfer of personal data to a third country or an international organisation in the absence of an adequacy decision pursuant to Article 45(3).

38   Article 28(7) GDPR.

39   Article 28(8) GDPR. The Register for Decisions taken by supervisory authorities and courts on issues handled in the consistency mechanism, including standard contractual clauses for the purposes of compliance with art. 28 GDPR, can be accessed here: https://edpb.europa.eu/our-work-tools/consistency-findings/register-fordecisions

40   Article 28(6) GDPR.

41   The EDPB recalls that the same degree of flexibility is allowed when the parties choose to use SCCs as appropriate safeguard for transfers to third countries pursuant to Article 46(2)(c) or Article 46(2)(d) GDPR. Recital 109 GDPR clarifies that *"The possibility for the controller or processor to use standard data-protection clauses adopted by the Commission or by a supervisory authority should prevent controllers or processors neither from including the standard data-protection clauses in a wider contract, such as a contract between the processor and another processor, nor from adding other clauses or additional safeguards provided that they do not contradict, directly or indirectly, the standard contractual clauses [. . .] or prejudice the fundamental rights or freedoms of the data subjects. Controllers and processors should be encouraged to provide additional safeguards via contractual commitments that supplement standard protection clauses"*.

42   See also EDPB Opinion 14/2019 on the draft Standard Contractual Clauses submitted by the DK SA (Article 28(8) GDPR), p. 5.

43   Recital 79 GDPR.

44   Recital 81 GDPR.

45   The duration of the processing is not necessarily equivalent to the duration of the agreement (there may be legal obligations to keep the data longer or shorter).

46   In this regard it is, by contrast, e.g. not sufficient for the processor to merely provide the controller with a generalized access to a list of the sub-processors which might be updated from time to time, without pointing to each new sub-processor envisaged. In other words, the processor must actively inform the controller of any change to the list (i.e. in particular of each new envisaged sub-processor).

47   See also EDP Opinion 14/2019 on the draft Standard Contractual Clauses submitted by the DK SA (Article 28(8) GDPR), 9 July 2019, at paragraph 44.

48   Article 32 GDPR.

49   Article 33(3) GDPR.

50   For more information, see the Guidelines on Personal data breach notification under Regulation 2016/679, WP250rev.01, 6 February 2018, p. 13-14.

51   See also EDP Opinion 14/2019 on the draft Standard Contractual Clauses submitted by the DK SA (Article 28(8) GDPR), 9 July 2019, at paragraph 40.

52   Article 29 Data Protection Working Party, Guidelines on Data Protection Impact Assessment (DPIA) and determining whether processing is "likely to result in a high risk" for the purposes of Regulation 2016/679, WP 248 rev.01, p. 14

53   Recital 95 GDPR.

54   This information is needed, so that the controller can comply with the accountability principle in Article 24 and with provisions of Articles 28(1), 32 and Chapter V of the GDPR.

55   This duty of the controller stems from the accountability principle in Article 24 and from the obligation to comply with provisions of Articles 28(1), 32 and Chapter V of the GDPR.

56   Although the GDPR does not preclude joint controllers to use different legal basis for different processing operations they carry out, it is recommended to use, whenever possible, the same legal basis for a particular purpose.

57   Please also see EDPB guidelines on Personal data breach notification under Regulation 2016/679, WP250.rev.01 which provide that joint controllership will include *"determining which party will have responsibility for complying with the obligations under Articles 33 and 34. WP29 recommends that the contractual arrangements between joint controllers include provisions that determine which controller will take the lead on, or be responsible for, compliance with the GDPR's breach notification obligations"*(p.13).

58   Please also see EDPB guidelines on DPIAs, WP248.rev01 which provide the following: *"When the processing operation involves joint controllers, they need to define their respective obligations precisely. Their DPIA should set out which party*

is responsible for the various measures designed to treat risks and to protect the rights and freedoms of the data subjects. Each data controller should express his needs and share useful information without either compromising secrets (e.g.: protection of trade secrets, intellectual property, confidential business information) or disclosing vulnerabilities" (p.7).

[59] Each disclosure by a controller requires a lawful basis and assessment of compatibility, regardless of whether the recipient is a separate controller or a joint controller. In other words, the existence of a joint controller relationship does not automatically mean that the joint controller receiving the data can also lawfully process the data for additional purposes which are beyond the scope of joint control.

[60] Judgment in *Wirtschaftsakademie*, C-210/16, ECLI:EU:C:2018:388, paragraph 43.

[61] As stated in recital 79 of the GDPR *"(. . .) the responsibility and liability of controllers and processors, also in relation to the monitoring by and measures of supervisory authorities, requires a clear allocation of the responsibilities under this Regulation, including where a controller determines the purposes and means of the processing jointly with other controllers".*

ANNEX I – FLOWCHART FOR APPLYING THE CONCEPTS OF CONTROLLER, PROCESSOR AND JOINT CONTROLLERS IN PRACTICE

Note: in order to properly assess the role of each entity involved, one must first identify the specific personal data processing at stake and its exact purpose. If multiple entities are involved, it is necessary to assess whether the purposes and means are determined jointly, leading to joint controllership.

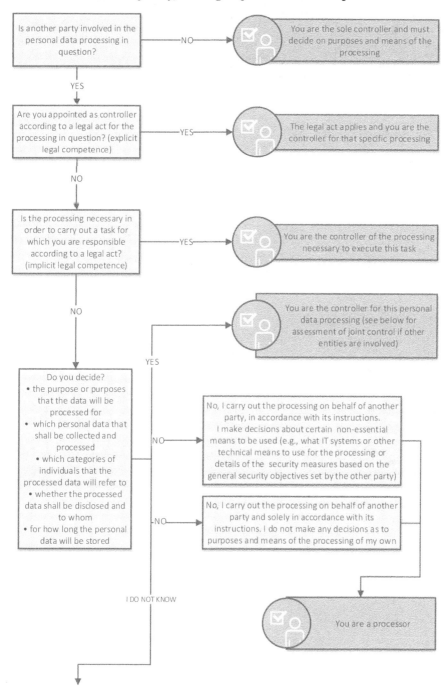

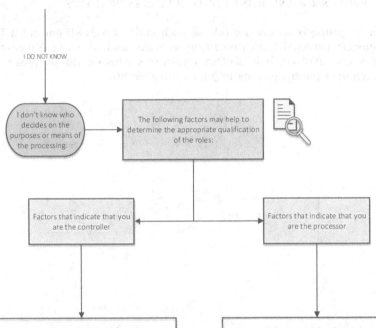

I DO NOT KNOW

I don't know who decides on the purposes or means of the processing. :

The following factors may help to determine the appropriate qualification of the roles:

Factors that indicate that you are the controller

Factors that indicate that you are the processor

• You obtain a benefit from, or have an interest in, the processing (other than the mere payment for services received from another controller)

• You make decisions about the individuals concerned as part of or as a result of the processing (e.g. the data subjects are your employees)

• The processing activities can be considered as naturally attached to the role or activities of your entity (e.g. due to traditional roles or professional expertise) which entails responsibilities from a data protection point of view

• The processing refers to your relation with the data subjects as employees, customers, members etc.

• You have complete autonomy in deciding how the personal data is processed

• You have entrusted the processing of personal data to an external organisation to process the personal data on your behalf

• You process the personal data for another party's purposes and in accordance with its documented instructions - you do not have a purpose of your own for the processing.

• Another party monitors your processing activities in order to ensure that you comply with instructions and terms of contract.

• You do not pursue your own purpose in the processing other than your own business interest to provide services.

• You have been engaged for carrying out specific processing activities by someone who in turn has been engaged to process data on another party's behalf and on this party's documented instructions (you are a sub-processor)

Joint controllership – If you are the controller and other parties are involved in the personal data processing:

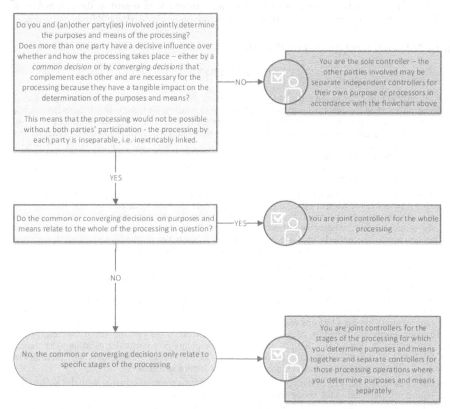

EUROPEAN DATA PROTECTION BOARD: GUIDELINES 8/2020 ON THE TARGETING OF SOCIAL MEDIA USERS
Version 2.0

Adopted on 13 April 2021

[2.372]

NOTES

© European Data Protection Board.

VERSION TABLE

Version 2.0: 13 April 2021 — Adoption of the Guidelines after public consultation

Version 1.0: 2 September 2020 — Adoption of the Guidelines for publication consultation

TABLE OF CONTENTS

THE EUROPEAN DATA PROTECTION BOARD

Having regard to Article 70(1)(e) of Regulation 2016/679/EU of the European Parliament and of the Council of 27 April 2016 on the protection of natural persons with regard to the processing of personal data and on the free movement of such data, and repealing Directive 95/46/EC.

HAS ADOPTED THE FOLLOWING GUIDELINES

1 INTRODUCTION

[2.373]

1. A significant development in the online environment over the past decade has been the rise of social media. More and more individuals use social media to stay in touch with family and friends, to engage in professional networking or to connect around shared interests and ideas. For the purposes of these guidelines, social media are understood as online platforms that enable the development of networks and communities of users, among which information and content is shared.[1] Key characteristics of social media include the ability for individuals to register in order to create "accounts" or "profiles" for themselves, to interact with one another by sharing user-generated or other content and to develop connections and networks with other users.[2]

2. As part of their business model, many social media providers offer targeting services. Targeting services make it possible for natural or legal persons ("targeters") to communicate specific messages to the users of social media in order to advance commercial, political, or other interests.[3] A distinguishing characteristic of targeting is the perceived fit between the person or group being targeted and the message that is being delivered. The underlying assumption is that the better the fit, the higher the reception rate (conversion) and thus the more effective the targeting campaign (return on investment).

3. Mechanisms to target social media users have increased in sophistication over time. Organisations now have the ability to target individuals on the basis of a wide range of criteria. Such criteria may have been developed on the basis of personal data which users have actively provided or shared, such as their relationship status. Increasingly, however, targeting criteria are also developed on the basis of personal data which has been observed or inferred, either by the social media provider or by third parties, and collected (aggregated) by the platform or by other actors (e.g., data brokers) to support ad-targeting options. In other words, the targeting of social media users involves not just the act of "selecting" the individuals or groups of individuals that are the intended recipients of a particular message (the 'target audience'), but rather it involves an entire process carried out by a set of stakeholders which results in the delivery of specific messages to individuals with social media accounts.[4]

4. The combination and analysis of data originating from different sources, together with the potentially sensitive nature of personal data processed in the context of social media[5], creates risks to the fundamental rights and freedoms of individuals. From a data protection perspective, many risks relate to the possible lack of transparency and user control. For the individuals concerned, the underlying processing of personal data which results in the delivery of a targeted message is often opaque. Moreover, it may involve unanticipated or undesired uses of personal data, which raise questions not only concerning data protection law, but also in relation to other fundamental rights and freedoms. Recently, social media targeting has gained increased public interest and regulatory scrutiny in the context of democratic decision making and electoral processes.[6]

NOTES

[1] Additional functions provided by social media may include, for example, personalization, application integration, social plug-ins, user authentication, analytics and publishing. Social media functions may be a standalone offering of controllers or they may be integrated as part of a wider service offering.

[2] In addition to "traditional" social media platforms, other examples of social media include: dating platforms where registered users present themselves to find partners they can date in real life; platforms where registered users can upload their own videos, comment on and link to other's videos; or computer games where registered users may play together in groups, exchange information or share their experiences and successes within the game.

[3] Targeting has been defined as "the act of directing or aiming something at a particular group of people" and "the act of attempting to appeal to a person or group or to influence them in some way". https://www.collinsdictionary.com/dictionary/english/targeting.

[4] The messages delivered typically consist of images and text, but may also involve video and/or audio formats.

[5] Personal data processed in the context of social media may constitute 'special categories of personal data' pursuant to Article 9 GDPR, relate to vulnerable individuals, or otherwise be of a highly personal nature. See also Article 29 Data Protection Working Party, Guidelines on Data Protection Impact Assessment (DPIA) and determining whether processing is "likely to result in a high risk" for the purposes of Regulation 2016/679, WP 248 rev. 01, p. 9.

2 SCOPE

[2.374]

5. Targeting of social media users may involve a variety of different actors which, for the purposes of these guidelines, shall be divided into four groups: social media providers, their users, targeters and other actors which may be involved in the targeting process. The importance of correctly identifying the roles and responsibilities of the various actors has recently been highlighted with the judgments in *Wirtschaftsakademie* and *Fashion ID* of the Court of Justice of the European Union (CJEU).[7] Both judgments demonstrate that the interaction between social media providers and other actors may give rise to joint responsibilities under EU data protection law.

6. Taking into account the case law of the CJEU, as well as the provisions of the GDPR regarding joint controllers and accountability, the present guidelines offer guidance concerning the targeting of social media users, in particular as regards the responsibilities of targeters and social media providers. Where joint responsibility exists, the guidelines will seek to clarify what the distribution of responsibilities might look like between targeters and social media providers on the basis of practical examples[8].

7. The main aim of these guidelines is therefore to clarify the roles and responsibilities among the social media provider and the targeter. In order to do so, the guidelines also identify the potential risks for the rights and freedoms of individuals (section 3), the main actors and their roles (section 4), and tackle the application of key data protection requirements (such as lawfulness and transparency, DPIA, etc.) as well as key elements of arrangements between social media providers and the targeters.

8 Nevertheless, the scope of these Guidelines covers the relationships between the registered users of a social network, its providers, as well as the targeters. Thorough analysis, of scenarios, such as individuals that are not-registered with social media providers does not fall under the scope of the present guidelines.

NOTES

   [6]   See, for example: https://edpb.europa.eu/sites/edpb/files/files/file1/edpb-2019-03-13-statement-onelections_en.pdf; https://ico.org.uk/about-the-ico/news-and-events/news-and-blogs/2018/07/ findingsrecommendations-and-actions-from-ico-investigation-into-data-analytics-in-political-campaigns/; https://ec. europa.eu/commission/sites/beta-political/files/soteu2018-data-protection-law-electoral-guidance- 638_en.pdf; https:// www.personuvernd.is/information-in-english/greinar/nr/2880.

   [7]   CJEU, Judgment in *Wirtschaftsakademie*, 5 June 2018, C-210/16, ECLI:EU:C:2018:388; CJEU, Judgment in *Fashion ID*, 29 July 2019, C-40/17, ECLI:EU:C:2019:629.

   [8]   The present guidance is without prejudice to the EDPB Guidelines 07/2020 on the concepts of controller and processor under the GDPR adopted on 02 September 2020, concerning the distribution of responsibilities in other contexts.

3 RISKS TO THE RIGHTS AND FREEDOMS OF USERS POSED BY THE PROCESSING OF PERSONAL DATA

[2.375]

9. The GDPR underlines the importance of properly evaluating and mitigating any risks to the rights and freedoms of individuals resulting from the processing of personal data.[9] The mechanisms that can be used to target social media users, as well as the underlying processing activities that enable targeting, may pose significant risks. These guidelines do not seek to provide an exhaustive list of the possible risks to the rights and freedoms of individuals. Nonetheless, the EDPB considers it important to point out certain types of risks and to provide a number of examples how they may manifest themselves.

10. Targeting of social media users may involve uses of personal data that go against or beyond individuals' reasonable expectations and thereby infringes applicable data protection principles and rules. For example, where a social media platform combines personal data from third-party sources with data disclosed by the users of its platform, this may result in personal data being used beyond their initial purpose and in ways the individual could not reasonably anticipate. The profiling activities that are connected to targeting might involve an inference of interests or other characteristics, which the individual had not actively disclosed, thereby undermining the individual's ability to exercise control over his or her personal data.[10] Moreover, a lack of transparency regarding the role of the different actors and the processing operations involved may undermine, complicate or hinder the exercise of data subject rights.

11. A second type of risk concerns the possibility of discrimination and exclusion. Targeting of social media users may involve criteria that, directly or indirectly, have discriminatory effects relating to an individual's racial or ethnic origin, health status or sexual orientation, or other protected qualities of the individual concerned. For example, the use of such criteria in the context of advertising related to job offers, housing or credit (loans, mortgages) may reduce the visibility of opportunities to persons within certain groups of individuals. The potential for discrimination in targeting arises from the ability for advertisers to leverage the extensive quantity and variety of personal data (e.g. demographics, behavioural data and interests) that social media platforms gather about their users.[11] Recent research suggests that the potential for discriminatory effects exists also without using criteria that are directly linked to special categories of personal data in the sense of Article 9 of the GDPR.[12]

12. A second category of risk relates to potential possible manipulation of users. Targeting mechanisms are, by definition, used in order to influence the behaviour and choices of individuals, whether it be in terms of their purchasing decisions as consumers or in terms of their political decisions as citizens engaged in civic life.[13] Certain targeting approaches may however go so far as to undermine individual autonomy and freedom, (e.g. by delivering individualized messages designed to exploit or even accentuate certain vulnerabilities, personal values or concerns). For example, an analysis of content shared through social media can reveal information about the emotional state (e.g. through an analysis of the use of certain key words). Such information could be used to target the individual with specific messages and at specific moments to which he or she is expected to be more receptive, thereby surreptitiously influencing his or her thought process, emotions and behaviour.[14]

13. Mechanisms to target social media users can also be used to unduly influence individuals when it comes to political discourse and democratic electoral processes.[15] While 'traditional' offline political campaigning intends to influence voters' behaviour via messages that are generally available and retrievable (verifiable), the available online targeting mechanisms enable political parties and campaigns to target individual voters with tailored messages, specific to the particular needs, interests and values of the target audience.[16] Such targeting might even involve disinformation or messages that individuals find particularly distressing, and are therefore (more) likely to stimulate a certain emotion or reaction by them.

When polarising or untruthful (disinformation) messages are targeted at specific individuals, with no or limited contextualisation or exposure to other viewpoints, the use of targeting mechanisms can have the effect of undermining the democratic electoral process.[17]

14. In the same vein, the use of algorithms to determine which information is displayed to which individuals may adversely affect the likelihood of access to diversified sources of information in relation to a particular subject matter. This may in turn have negative consequences for the pluralism of public debate and access to information.[18] Targeting mechanisms can be used to augment the visibility of certain messages, while giving less prominence to others. The potential adverse impact may be felt at two levels. On the one hand, there are risks related to so-called 'filter-bubbles' where people are exposed to 'more-of-the-same' information and encounter fewer opinions, resulting in increased political and ideological polarisation.[19] On the other hand, targeting mechanisms may also create risks of "information overload", whereby individuals cannot make an informed decision because they have too much information and cannot tell if it is reliable.

15. The collection of personal data by social media providers may not be limited to the activities performed by individuals on the social media platform itself. The targeting of social media users on the basis of information concerning their browsing behaviour or other activities outside the social media platform can give individuals the feeling that their behaviour is systematically being monitored. This may have a chilling effect on freedom of expression, including access to information.[20] Such effects may be exacerbated if targeting is also based on the analysis of content shared by social media users. If private messages, posts and comments are subject to analysis for commercial or political use, this may also give rise to self-censorship.

16. The potential adverse impact of targeting may be considerably greater where vulnerable categories of individuals are concerned, such as children. Targeting can influence the shaping of children's personal preferences and interests, ultimately affecting their autonomy and their right to development. Recital 38 of the GDPR indicates that specific protection should apply to the use of personal data of children for the purposes of marketing or creating personality or user profiles and the collection of personal data with regard to children when using services offered directly to a child.[21]

17. The use of social media in the EU is widespread as 54% of people aged 16-74 participated in social networks in 2019. Besides, this participation rate has steadily increased over the years.[22] The EDPB recognizes that the increase in concentration in the markets of social media and targeting may also increase risks to the rights and freedoms of a substantial number of individuals. For example, certain social media providers may be able to combine, either alone or in connection with other companies, a higher quantity and diversity of personal data. This ability, in turn, may increase the ability to offer more advanced targeting campaigns. This aspect is relevant from both a data protection (more in-depth profiling of the persons concerned) and competition law viewpoint (the unrivalled insight capabilities provided by the platform may make it an *'unavoidable trading partner'* for online marketers). The degree of market and informational power, in turn, as the EDPB has recognised, *"has the potential to threaten the level of data protection and freedom enjoyed by consumers of digital services".[23]*

18. The likelihood and severity of the aforementioned risks will depend, inter alia, on the nature of the targeting mechanism and how and for which exact purpose(s) it is used. Elements which may affect the likelihood and severity of risks in the context of the targeting of social media users will be discussed in greater detail in section 7.

NOTES

[9]   According to Article 24 of the GDPR, the controller shall implement appropriate technical and organizational measures to ensure and be able to demonstrate that processing is performed in accordance with the GDPR, "taking into account the nature, scope, context and purposes of processing as well as the risks of varying likelihood and severity for the rights and freedoms of natural persons". See also Article 29 Working Party, Guidelines on Data Protection Impact Assessment (DPIA) and determining whether processing is "likely to result in a high risk" for the purposes of Regulation 2016/679, WP248 rev. 01, 4 October 2017.

[10] See also European Data Protection Supervisor, EDPS Opinion on online manipulation, Opinion 3/2018, 19 March 2018, p. 15 (*"The concern of using data from profiles for different purposes through algorithms is that the data loses its original context. Repurposing of data is likely to affect a person's informational self-determination, further reduce the control of data subjects' over their data, thus affecting the trust in digital environments and services."*).

[11] T. Speicher a.o., Potential for Discrimination in Online Targeted Advertising, Proceedings of the 1st Conference on Fairness, Accountability and Transparency, *Proceedings of Machine Learning Research* PMLR 81:5-19, 2018, http://proceedings.mlr.press/v81/speicher18a.html.

[12] Idem.

[13] European Data Protection Supervisor, Opinion 3/2018, p. 18.

[14] See 'Experimental evidence of massive-scale emotional contagion through social networks', Adam D. I. Kramer, Jamie E. Guillory, and Jeffrey T. Hancock, PNAS June 17, 2014 111 (24) 8788-8790; first published June 2, 2014 https://doi.org/10.1073/pnas.1320040111, available at:https://www.pnas.org/content/111/24/8788 Adam D. I. Kramer Core Data Science Team, Facebook, Inc., Menlo Park, CA 94025.

[15] See also European Data Protection Board, Statement 2/2019 on the use of personal data in the course of political campaigns, 13 March 2019, p. 1.

[16] Information Commissioner's Office (ICO), *Democracy disrupted? Personal information and political influence*, 10 July 2018, p. 14.

[17] See also European Commission, Commission Guidance on the application of Union data protection law in the electoral context, A contribution from the European Commission to the Leaders' meeting in Salzburg on 19-20 September 2018. See also L.M. Neudert and N.M. Marchal, Polarisation and the use of technology in political campaigns and communication, European Parliamentary Research Service, 2019, p. 22-24.

[18] See also European Parliament resolution of 3 May 2018 on media pluralism and media freedom in the European Union.

19   European Data Protection Supervisor, Opinion 3/2018, p. 7.
20   European Data Protection Supervisor, Opinion 3/2018, p. 9 and Committee of experts on media pluralism and transparency of media ownership (MSI-MED), Internet and Electoral Campaigns, Study on the use of internet in electoral campaigns, Council of Europe study DGI(2017)11, April 2018, p. 19-21.
21   See also Article 29 Data Protection Working Party, Guidelines on Automated individual decision-making and Profiling for the purposes of Regulation 2016/679, 6 February 2018, WP251rev.01, p. 29.
22   https://ec.europa.eu/eurostat/en/web/products-eurostat-news/-/edn-20200630-2.
23   Statement of the EDPB on the data protection impacts of economic concentration, available at: https://edpb.europa.eu/sites/edpb/files/files/file1/edpb_statement_economic_concentration_en.pdf

4 ACTORS AND ROLES

4.1 USERS

[2.376]
19.   Individuals make use of social media in different capacities and for different purposes (e.g. to stay in touch with friends, to exchange information about shared interests, or to seek out employment opportunities). The term "user" is typically used to refer to individuals who are registered with the service, i.e. those who have an "account" or "profile". Many social media services can, however, also be accessed by individuals without having registered (i.e. without creating an account or profile).[24] Such individuals are typically not able to make use of all of the same features or services offered to individuals who have registered with the social media provider. Both users and non-registered individuals may be considered "data subjects" within the meaning of Article 4(1) GDPR insofar as the individual is directly or indirectly identified or identifiable.[25]

20.   Whether or not individuals are expected to register with a real name or use a nickname or pseudonym may vary according to the social media service in question. It will generally still be possible, however, to target (or otherwise single out) the user in question even in the absence of a real name policy, as most types of targeting do not rely on user names but other types of personal data such as interests, sociographic data, behaviour or other identifiers. Social media providers often encourage their users to reveal "real world" data, such as telephone numbers.[26] Finally, it is worth noting that social media providers may also enable targeting of individuals who do not have an account with the social media provider.[27]

4.2 SOCIAL MEDIA PROVIDERS

21.   Social media providers offer an online service that enables the development of networks and communities of users, among which information and content is shared. Social media services are typically offered through web browsers or dedicated apps, often after having requested the user to provide a set of personal data to constitute the user's "account" or "profile". They also often offer users associated account "controls", to enable them to access and control the personal data processed in the context of the use of their account.

22.   The social media provider determines the functionalities of the service. This in turn involves a determination of which data are processed, for which purpose, under which terms, as well as how personal data shall be processed. This allows for the provision of the social media service but also likely the provision of services, such as targeting, that can benefit business partners operating on the social media platform or in conjunction with it.

23.   The social media provider has the opportunity to gather large amounts of personal data relating to users' and individuals' that are not registered with social media providers behaviour and interactions, which enables it to obtain considerable insights into the users' socio-demographic characteristics, interests and preferences. It is important to note that the 'insights' based on user activity often involve inferred or derived personal data. For example, where a user interacts with certain content (e.g. by "liking" a post on social media, or watching video content), this action can be recorded by the social media provider, and an inference might be made that the user in question enjoyed the content he or she interacted with.

24.   Social media providers increasingly gather data not only from activities on the platform itself, but also from activities undertaken 'off-platform', combining data from multiple sources, online and offline, in order to generate further insights. The data can be combined with personal data that individuals actively disclose to the social media provider (e.g. a username, e-mail address, location, and phone number), alongside data which is "assigned" to them by the platform (such as unique identifiers).

4.3 TARGETERS

25.   These guidelines use the term "targeter" to designate natural or legal persons that use social media services in order to direct specific messages at a set of social media users on the basis of specific parameters or criteria.[28] What sets targeters apart from other users of social media is that they select their messages and/or their intended audience according to the perceived characteristics, interests or preferences of the individuals concerned, a practice which is sometimes also referred to as "microtargeting".[29] Targeters can engage in targeting to advance commercial, political, or other interests. Typical examples include brands who use social media to advertise their products including to increase brand awareness. Political parties also increasingly make use of social media as part of their campaigning strategy. Charities and other non-profit organisations also use social media to target messages at potential contributors or to develop communities.

26.   It is important to note that social media users can be targeted in different ways. For example, targeting might occur not only through displaying personalized advertisement (e.g. through a "banner"

Part 2   Data Protection: EU Law etc

shown on the top or side of a webpage), but - as far as it is happening within the social media platform - also through display in a user's "feed", "timeline" or "story", where the advertising content appears alongside user-generated content. Targeting may also involve the creation of content hosted by the social media provider (e.g. via a dedicated "page" or other social media presence) or elsewhere (i.e. on third-party websites). Targeters may have their own websites and apps, where they can integrate specific social media business tools or features such as social plugins or logins or by using the application programming interfaces (APIs) or software development kits (SDKs) offered by social media providers.

4.4 OTHER RELEVANT ACTORS

27. Targeters may directly use targeting mechanisms offered by social media providers or enlist the services of other actors, such as marketing service providers, ad networks, ad exchanges, demand-side and supply-side platforms, data management providers (DMPs) and data analytics companies. These actors are part of the complex and evolving online advertising ecosystem (which is sometimes known as "adtech") that collects and processes data relating to individuals (including social media users) by, for example, tracking their activities across websites and apps.[30]

28. Data brokers and data management providers are also relevant actors playing an important role in the targeting of social media users. Data brokers and DMPs differentiate themselves from other adtech companies to the extent that they not only process data collected by means of tracking technologies, but also by means of data collected from other sources, that can include both online and offline sources. In other words, data brokers and DMPs aggregate data collected from a wide variety of sources, which they then might sell to other stakeholders involved in the targeting process.[30]

29. While each of the other actors mentioned above can play an important role in targeting of social media users, the focus of the current guidelines is on the distribution of roles and data protection obligations of social media providers and targeters. Analogous considerations may apply, however, to the other actors involved in the online advertising ecosystem, depending on the role of each actor in the targeting process.

4.5 ROLES AND RESPONSIBILITIES

30. In order to clarify the respective roles and responsibilities of social media providers and targeters, it is important to take account of the relevant case law of the CJEU. The judgments in *Wirtschaftsakademie* (C-210/16), *Jehovah's Witnesses* (C-25/17) and *Fashion ID* (C-40/17) are particularly relevant here.

31. The starting point of the analysis is the legal definition of controller. According to Article 4(7) GDPR, a "'controller'" means *"the natural or legal person [. . .] which, alone or jointly with others, determines the purposes and means of the processing of personal data"*.

32. In *Wirtschaftsakademie*, the CJEU decided that the administrator of a so-called "fan page" on Facebook must be regarded as taking part in the determination of the purposes and means of the processing of personal data. According to the submissions made to the CJEU, the creation of a fan page involves the *definition of parameters* by the administrator, which has an *influence* on the processing of personal data for the purpose of *producing statistics* based on visits to the fan page.[32] Using the filters provided by Facebook, the administrator can define the criteria in accordance with which the statistics are to be drawn up, and even designate the categories of persons whose personal data is to be made use of by Facebook:

> *"In particular, the administrator of the fan page can ask for — and thereby request the processing of — demographic data relating to its target audience, including trends in terms of age, sex, relationship and occupation, information on the lifestyles and centers of interest of the target audience and information on the purchases and online purchasing habits of visitors to its page, the categories of goods and services that appeal the most, and geographical data which tell the fan page administrator where to make special offers and where to organise events, and more generally enable it to target best the information it offers."*

33. As the definition of parameters depends inter alia on the administrator's target audience *"and the objectives of managing and promoting its activities"*, the administrator also participates in determining the purposes of the processing of personal data.[33] The administrator was therefore categorised as a controller jointly responsible for the processing of personal data of the visitors of its 'page', together with the social media provider.

34. As further developed in section 9 of the present guidelines, controllers may be involved at different stages of the processing of personal data and to different degrees. In such circumstances, the level of responsibility of each of them must be assessed with regard to all the relevant circumstances of the particular case:

> *"[T]he existence of joint responsibility does not necessarily imply equal responsibility of the various operators involved in the processing of personal data. On the contrary, those operators may be involved at different stages of that processing of personal data and to different degrees, so that the level of responsibility of each of them must be assessed with regard to all the relevant circumstances of the particular case."*[34]

35. While concluding that the administrator of a page acts as a controller, jointly with Facebook, the CJEU also noted that in the present case, Facebook must be regarded as primarily determining the purposes and means of processing the personal data of users of Facebook and persons visiting the fan pages hosted on Facebook.[35]

36. In *Fashion ID*, the CJEU decided that a website operator can be a considered a controller when it embeds a Facebook social plugin on its website that causes the browser of a visitor to transmit personal data of the visitor to Facebook.[36] The qualification of the website operator as controller is, however, limited to the operation or set of operations in respect of which it actually determines the purposes and means. In this particular case, the CJEU considered that the website operator is only capable of determining, jointly with Facebook, the purposes and means of the collection and disclosure by transmission of the personal data of visitors to its website. As a result, the CJEU ruled that, for what concerns the embedding of a social plug-in within a website, the liability of the website operator is:

> "limited to the operation or set of operations involving the processing of personal data in respect of which it actually determines the purposes and means, that is to say, the collection and disclosure by transmission of the data at issue."[37]

37. The CJEU considered that the website operator was not a controller for subsequent[38] operations involving the processing of personal data carried out by Facebook after their transmission to the latter, as the website operator was not in a position to determine the purposes and means of those operations by virtue of embedding the social plug-in:

> "*By contrast, in the light of that information, it seems, at the outset, impossible that Fashion ID determines the purposes and means of subsequent operations involving the processing of personal data carried out by Facebook Ireland after their transmission to the latter, meaning that Fashion ID cannot be considered to be a controller in respect of those operations [. . .]*".[39]

38. In case of joint controllership, pursuant to Article 26(1) GDPR, controllers are required to put in place an arrangement which, in a transparent manner, determines their respective responsibilities for compliance with the GDPR, in particular as regards the exercising of the rights of the data subject and their respective duties to provide the information referred to in Articles 13 and 14 GDPR.

39. The following sections clarify, by way of specific examples, the roles of targeters and social media providers in relation to different targeting mechanisms. Specific considerations are given in particular as to how the requirements of lawfulness and purpose limitation apply in this context. Next, the requirements concerning transparency, data protection impact assessments and the processing of special categories of data are analysed. Finally, the Guidelines address the obligation for joint controllers to put in place an appropriate arrangement pursuant to Article 26 GDPR, taking into account the degree of responsibility of the targeter and of the social media provider.

NOTES

[24]   The personal data and profiling information maintained by social media providers in relation to non-registered users are sometimes referred to as "shadow profiles".

[25]   See also recital (26) ("singling out"). See also Article 29 Data Protection Working Party, Opinion 4/2007 on the concept of personal data, 20 June 2007, WP 136, p. 12 and following.

[26]   In some cases, social media providers ask for additional documentation to further verify the data provided, for example by requesting users to upload their ID cards or similar documentation.

[27]   Such targeting may be rendered possible on the basis of online identifiers provided by their devices, applications, tools and protocols, such as internet protocol addresses, cookie identifiers or other identifiers. This may leave traces which, in particular when combined with unique identifiers and other information received by the servers, may be used to create profiles of the natural persons and identify them. See also recital (30) GDPR. Based on this recognition, targeted ads may be displayed on a website the individual visits.

[28]   Processing of personal data by a natural person in the course of a purely personal or household activity does not fall under the material scope of the GDPR (Art. 2(2)(c)).

[29]   Simply sharing information on a social media page which is intended for the public at large (e.g. information about opening hours) without prior selection of the intended audience would not be considered as « targeting » for the purposes of these guidelines.

[30]   On the description of the different actors, see WP29, Opinion 2/2010 on behavioural advertisement, at page 5. The Opinion is available at: https://ec.europa.eu/justice/Article-29/documentation/opinion-recommendation/files/2010/wp171_en.pdf

[31]   See Consumer Policy Research Centre, "*A day in the life of data*", available at: http://cprc.org.au/publication/research-report-a-day-in-the-life-of-data/

[32]   Judgment in *Wirtschaftsakademie*, C-210/16, paragraph 36.

[33]   Judgment in *Wirtschaftsakademie*, C-210/16, paragraph 39.

[34]   Judgment in *Wirtschaftsakademie*, C-210/16, paragraph 43; Judgment in *Jehovah's Witnesses*, C-25/17, paragraph 66 and Judgment in *Fashion ID*, C-40/17, paragraph 70.

[35]   Judgment in *Wirtschaftsakademie*, C-210/16, paragraph 30.

[36]   Judgment in *Fashion ID*, C-40/17, paragraph 75 and following and paragraph 107.

[37]   Judgment in *Fashion ID*, C-40/17, paragraph 107.

[38]   Subsequent processing is any processing operation or set of processing operations which follows (i.e. takes place after) the data collection. In Fashion ID, the term is used to refer to processing operations carried out by Facebook after their transmission and for which Fashion ID should not be considered as a joint controller (because it does not effectively participate in determining the purposes and means of those processing).

     Subsequent processing for a purpose other than that for which the personal data have been collected is only permissible insofar as Article 6(4) GDPR relating to further processing is complied with. For example, if an online retailer collects data relating to an individual's home address, a subsequent processing would consist in the storage or later deletion of this information. However, if this online retailer later decides to process this personal data to enrich the profile of the data subject for targeting purposes, this would amount to further processing within the meaning of Article 6(4) GDPR as it involves processing for a purpose other than that for which they were initially collected.

[39]   Judgment in *Fashion ID*, C-40/17, paragraph 76.

Part 2   Data Protection: EU Law etc

5 ANALYSIS OF DIFFERENT TARGETING MECHANISMS

5.1 OVERVIEW

[2.377]

40. Social media users may be targeted on the basis of provided, observed or inferred data, as well as a combination thereof:

(a) **Targeting individuals on the basis of provided data** – "Provided data" refers to information actively provided by the data subject to the social media provider and/or the targeter.[40] For example:

- A social media user might indicate his or her age in the description of his or her user profile. The social media provider, in turn, might enable targeting on the basis of this criterion.

- A targeter might use information provided by the data subject to the targeter in order to target that individual specifically, for example by means of customer data (such as an email address list), to be matched with data already held on the social media platform, leading to all those users who match being targeted with advertising[41].

(b) **Targeting on the basis of observed data** – Targeting of social media users can also take place on the basis of observed data.[42] Observed data are data provided by the data subject by virtue of using a service or device.[43] For example, a particular social media user might be targeted on the basis of:

- his or her activity on the social media platform itself (for instance the content that the user has shared, consulted or liked);

- the use of devices on which the social media's application is executed (for instance GPS coordinates, mobile telephone number);

- data obtained by a third-party application developer by using the application programming interfaces (APIs) or software development kits (SDKs) offered by social media providers;

- data collected through third-party websites that have incorporated social plugins or pixels;

- data collected through other third parties (e.g. parties with whom the data subject has interacted, purchased a product, subscribed to loyalty cards, . . .); or

- data collected through services offered by companies owned or operated by the social media provider.

(c) **Targeting on the basis of inferred data** – "Inferred data" or "derived data" are created by the data controller on the basis of the data provided by the data subject or as observed by the controller.[44] For example, a social media provider or a targeter might infer that an individual is likely to be interested in a certain activity or product on the basis of his or her web browsing behaviour and/or network connections.

5.2 TARGETING ON THE BASIS OF PROVIDED DATA

5.2.1 Data provided by the user to the social media provider

41. Individuals may actively disclose a great deal of information about themselves when making use of social media. The creation of a social media account (or "profile") involves disclosure of a number of attributes, which may include name, date of birth, gender, place of residence, language, etc. Depending on the nature of the social media platform, users may include additional information such as relationship status, interests or current employment. Personal data provided by social media users can be used by the social media provider to develop criteria, which enables the targeter to address specific messages at the users of the social media.

> Example 1 :
>
> Company X sells gentlemen's shoes and wishes to promote a sale of its winter collection. For its advertising campaign, it wishes to target men between the age of 30 and 45 who have indicated that they are single in their social media profile. It uses the corresponding targeting criteria offered by the social media provider as parameters to identify the target audience to whom its advertisement should be displayed. Moreover, the targeter indicates that the advertisement should be displayed to social media users while they are using the social media service between the hours of 5pm and 8pm. To enable targeting of social media users on the basis of specific criteria, the social media provider has previously determined which types of personal data shall be used in order to develop the targeting criteria and which targeting criteria shall be offered. The social media provider also communicates certain statistical information once the advertisements has been displayed to the targeter (e.g. to report on the demographic composition of individuals that interacted with the advertisement).

A. Roles

42. In Example 1, both the targeter and the social media provider participate in determining the purpose and means of the processing personal data. This results in the display of the advertisement to the target audience.

43. As far as the determination of *purpose* is concerned, Company X and the social media provider jointly determine the purpose of the processing, which is to display a specific advertisement to a set of individuals (in this case social media users) who make up the target audience, by choosing available targeting criteria associated with these users in order to reach a likely interested audience and to provide them more relevant advertisement content. Moreover, there is also mutual benefit arising from the same processing operation, which is an additional indicator that the purposes pursued by given Company X and the social media provider are inextricably be linked.[45]

44. As far as the determination of *means* is concerned, the targeter and the social media provider jointly determine the means, which results in the targeting. The targeter participates in the determination of the means by choosing to use the services offered by the social media provider[46], and by requesting it to target an audience based on certain criteria (i.e. age range, relationship status, timing of display).[47] In doing so, the targeter defines the criteria in accordance with which the targeting takes place and designates the categories of persons whose personal data is to be made use of. The social media provider, on the other hand, has decided to process personal data of its users in such a manner to develop the targeting criteria, which it makes available to the targeter.[48] In order to do so, the social media provider has made certain decisions regarding the essential means of the processing, such as which categories of data shall be processed, which targeting criteria shall be offered and who shall have access (to what types of) personal data that is processed in the context of a particular targeting campaign.[49]

45. For the sake of completeness, the EDPB notes that the social media provider does not qualify as a processor as defined in Article 4(8) GDPR.[50] In Example 1, the targeting criteria, as developed by the social media provider on the basis of user's' personal data can be used by the social media provider for future processing operations, which demonstrates that the later cannot qualify as a processor. Moreover, the social media provider does not appear to exclusively process the data on behalf of Company X and in accordance with its instructions.

46. The joint control among the targeter and social media provider only extends to those processing operations for which they effectively co-determine the purposes and means. It extends to the processing of personal data resulting from the selection of the relevant targeting criteria and the display of the advertisement to the target audience. It also covers the processing of personal data undertaken by the social media provider to report to the targeter about the results of the targeting campaign. The joint control does not, however, extend to operations involving the processing of personal data at other stages occurring before the selection of the relevant targeting criteria or after the targeting and reporting has been completed (e.g. the development of new targeting criteria by the social media provider on the basis of completed targeting campaigns) and in which the targeter has not participated in determining the purposes and means, likewise the social media provider, in principle, does not participate in phase of planning a targeting campaign prior to the moment where the targeter makes contact with the social media provider".[51]

47. The above analysis remains the same even if the targeter only specifies the parameters of its intended audience and does not have access to the personal data of the users that are affected. Indeed, joint responsibility of several actors for the same processing does not require each of them to have access to the personal data concerned.[52] The EDPB recalls that actual access to personal data is not a prerequisite for joint responsibility.[53]

B. Legal basis

As joint controllers, both parties (the social media provider and the targeter) must be able to demonstrate the existence of a legal basis (Article 6 GDPR) to justify the processing of personal data for which each of the joint controllers is responsible. The EDPB recalls that no specific hierarchy is made between the different lawful basis of the GDPR: the controller needs to ensure that the selected lawful basis matches the objective and context of the processing operation in question. The identification of the appropriate lawful basis is tied to principles of fairness and purpose limitation.[54]

49. Generally speaking, there are two legal bases which could justify the processing that supports the targeting of social media users: data subject's consent (Article 6(1)(a) GDPR) or legitimate interests (Article 6(1)(f) GDPR). A controller must always consider what the appropriate legal basis is under the given circumstances. In respect to the social media providers Article 6(1)b GDPR cannot provide a lawful basis for online advertising simply because such advertising indirectly funds the provision of their service.[55] The same applies to the targeter as targeting of social media users cannot be considered as an intrinsic aspect of any services or necessary to perform a contract with the user.[56] While personalisation of content may, in certain circumstances, constitute an intrinsic and expected element of certain online services[57], Article 6 (1) b GDPR in the context of targeting of social media users is hardly applicable, as illustrated in the examples of these Guidelines.[58]

50. For what concerns the legitimate interest lawful basis, the EDPB recalls that in Fashion ID, the CJEU reiterated that in order for a processing to rely on the legitimate interest, three cumulative conditions should be met, namely[59] (i) the pursuit of a legitimate interest by the data controller or by the third party or parties to whom the data are disclosed, (ii) the need to process personal data for the purposes of the legitimate interests pursued, and (iii) the condition that the fundamental rights and freedoms of the data subject whose data require protection do not take precedence. The CJEU also specified that in a situation of joint controllership "*it is necessary that each of those controllers should pursue a legitimate interest [. . .] through those processing operations in order for those operations to be justified in respect of each of them*".[60]

51. With regard to Example 1, the targeter might consider its legitimate interest to be the economic interest of having an increased publicity for its goods through social media targeting. The social media provider could consider that its legitimate interest consists of making the social media service profitable by selling advertising space. Whether the targeter and the social media provider can rely upon Article 6(1)(f) GDPR as legal basis depends on whether all three cumulative conditions are met, as recently reiterated by the CJEU. Even if the targeter and the social media provider consider their economic interests to be legitimate, it does not necessarily mean that they will be able to actually rely on Article 6(1)(f) GDPR.

52. The second part of the balancing test entails that the joint controllers will need to establish that the processing is necessary to achieve those legitimate interests. "Necessary" requires a connection between the processing and the interests pursued. The 'necessity' requirement is particularly relevant in the context of the application of Article 6(1)f, in order to ensure that processing of data based on legitimate interests does not lead to an unduly broad interpretation of the necessity to process data. As in other cases, this means that it should be considered whether other less invasive means are available to serve the same end.[61]

53. The third step in assessing whether the targeter and the social media provider can rely upon Article 6(1)(f) GDPR as legal basis for the processing of personal data, is the balancing exercise necessary to determine whether the legitimate interest at stake is overridden by the data subject's interests or fundamental rights and freedoms.[62]

54. The EDPB recalls that in cases where a controller envisages to rely on legitimate interest, the duties of transparency and the right to object require careful consideration. Data subjects should be given the opportunity to object to the processing of their data for targeted purposes before the processing is initiated. Users of social media should not only be provided with the possibility to object to the display of targeted advertising when accessing the platform, but also be provided with controls that ensure the underlying processing of his or her personal data for the targeting purpose no longer takes place after he or she has objected.

55. The targeter seeking to rely on legitimate interest should, for its part, make it easy for individuals to express a prior objection to its use of social media for targeting purposes. However, insofar as the targeter does not have any direct interaction with the data subject, the targeter should at least ensure that the social media platform provide the data subject with means to efficiently express their right to prior objection. As joint controllers, the targeter and social media provider should clarify how the individuals' right to object (as well as other rights) will be accommodated in the context of the joint arrangement (see section 6). If the balancing exercise points out that data subject's interests or fundamental rights and freedoms override the legitimate interest of the social media provider and the targeter, the use of Article 6(1)(f) is not possible.

56. For what concerns the consent lawful basis, the controller needs to keep in mind that there are clearly situations in which the processing would not be lawful without the valid consent of the individuals concerned (Article 6(1)(a) GDPR). For example, the WP29 has previously considered that it would be difficult for controllers to justify using legitimate interests as a legal basis for intrusive profiling and tracking practices for marketing or advertising purposes, for example those that involve tracking individuals across multiple websites, locations, devices, services or data-brokering.[63]

57. To be valid, the consent collected for the processing needs to fulfil the conditions laid out in Articles 4(11) and 7 GDPR. Generally speaking, consent can only be an appropriate legal basis if a data subject is offered control and genuine choice. If consent is bundled up as a non-negotiable part of terms and conditions, it is presumed not to have been freely given. Consent must also be specific, informed and unambiguous and the data subject must be able to refuse or withdraw consent without detriment.[64]

58. Consent (Article 6(1)(a) GDPR) could be envisaged, provided that all the requirements for valid consent are met. The EDPB recalls that obtaining consent also does not negate or in any way diminish the controller's obligations to observe the principles of processing enshrined in the GDPR, especially Article 5 with regard to fairness, necessity and proportionality, as well as data quality. Even if the processing of personal data is based on consent of the data subject, this would not legitimize targeting which is disproportionate or unfair.[65]

59. Finally, the EDPB is of the opinion that the processing of personal data described in the Example 1 cannot be justified on the basis of Article 6(1)(b) by neither the social platform nor the targeter.[66]

5.2.2 Data provided by the user of the social media platform to the targeter

60. Targeting can also involve data provided by the data subject to the targeter, who then uses the data collected in order to target the data subject on social media. For example, "list-based" targeting occurs where a targeter uploads pre-existing lists of personal data (such as e-mail addresses or phone numbers) for the social media provider to match against the information on the platform. In this case, the social media provider compares the data uploaded by the targeter with user data that it already possesses, and any users that match are added to or excluded from the target audience (that is, the 'cluster' of persons to which the advertisement will be displayed on the social media platform). The social media provider may also allow the targeter to 'check' the list prior to finalising it, meaning that some processing takes place even before the audience has been created.

Example 2 :

Ms. Jones contacts Bank X to set up an appointment regarding a possible mortgage because she is buying a house. She contacts the bank via e-mail to set up the appointment. Following the appointment, Ms. Jones decides not to become a customer of the bank. The bank has nevertheless added the e-mail address of Ms. Jones to its customer e-mail database. Then, the bank uses its e-mail database, by allowing the social media provider to 'matching' the list of e-mail addresses it holds with those held by the social media platform, in order to target the individuals concerned with the full range of financial services on the social media platform.

Example 3:

Mr. Lopez has been a customer at Bank X for almost a year. When he became a customer, he provided an e-mail address and was informed by Bank X, at the moment of collection, that: (a) his e-mail address would be used for advertising of offers linked to the bank services that he is already using; and (b) he may object to this processing at any time. The bank has added his e-mail address to its customer email database. Afterwards, the bank uses its e-mail database to target its customers on the social media platform with the full range of financial services it has on offer.[67]

A. Roles

61. In these examples, the targeter, i.e. the bank, acts as a controller because it determines the purposes and means of the processing by actively collecting, processing and transmitting the personal data of the individuals concerned to the social media provider for advertising purposes. The social media provider, in turn, acts as a controller because it has taken the decision to use personal data acquired from the social media user (i.e. the e-mail address provided when setting up his or her account) in order to enable the targeter to display advertising to an audience of specific individuals.

62. Joint controllership exists in relation to the processing operations for which the social media provider and the targeter jointly determine the purposes and means, in this case, uploading unique identifiers related to the intended audience, matching, selection of targeting criteria and subsequent display of the advertisement, as well as any reporting relating to the targeting campaign.[68]

63. In both examples the bank acts as the sole controller regarding the initial collection of the email address of Ms. Jones and Mr. Lopez respectively. The social media provider does not participate in any way to determine the means and purposes of this collection. The joint control begins with the transmission of the personal data and the simultaneous collection of it by the social media provider. It continues throughout the display of the targeted advertisement ends (in most of the cases) when a subsequent reporting phase is completed. In some cases, joint controllership can be further extended, even until the deletion of the data phase insofar as the targeter still continues to participate in the determination of purposes and means.

64. The reason why the bank acts as sole controller when collecting the e-mail address from Ms. Jones and Mr. Lopez respectively, is because the collection of data occurs prior to (and is not inextricably linked to) the targeting campaign. Therefore, in this case one must distinguish between the initial set of processing operations for which only the bank is a controller and a subsequent processing for which joint control exists. The responsibility of the bank does not extend to operations occurring after the targeting and reporting has been completed and in which the targeter has not participated in the purposes and means and for which the social media provider acts as the sole controller.

B. Legal basis

65. In Example 2, Article 6(1)f GDPR does not provide an appropriate legal basis to justify the processing in this case, taking into account the context in which the personal data was provided. Indeed, Ms. Jones contacted the bank for the sole purpose of setting up an appointment, following which she communicated her intention not to make use of the services offered by the bank. Hence, one can consider that there is no reasonable expectation by Ms. Jones that her personal data shall be used for targeting purposes ('re-targeting'). Moreover, a compatibility test under Article 6(4) GDPR will lead to the outcome that this processing is not compatible with the purpose for which the personal data are initially collected.

66. In Example 3, the targeter might be able to rely on legitimate interest to justify the processing, taking into account inter alia that Mr. Lopez was: (a) informed of the fact that his e-mail address may be used for purposes of advertising via social media for services linked to the one used by the data subject; (b) the advertisement relates to services similar to those for Mr. Lopez is already a customer, and (c) Mr. Lopez was given the ability to object prior to the processing, at the moment where the personal data were collected by the bank. However, the EDPB would like to clarify that the fulfilment of information duties as per Articles 13 and 14 GDPR and the weighing of interests to be performed according to Article 6 (1)(f) GDPR are two different sets of obligations. Therefore, the mere fulfilment of information duties according to Articles 13 and 14 GDPR is not a transparency measure to be taken into consideration for the weighing of interests according to Article 6 (1)(f) of GDPR.

5.3 TARGETING ON THE BASIS OF OBSERVED DATA

67. There are several ways in which social media providers may be able to observe the behaviour of their users. For example, observation is possible through the social media service itself or may also be possible on external websites by virtue of social plug-ins or pixels.

Example 4: Pixel-based targeting

Mr Schmidt is browsing online in order to purchase a backpack. He visits the website "BestBags.com", views a number of items, but decides not to make a purchase. The operator of "BestBags.com" wishes to target social media users who have visited their website without making a purchase. To this end, it integrates a so-called "tracking pixel"[69] on its website, which is made available by the social media provider. After leaving the website of BestBags.com and logging into his social media account, Mr Schmidt begins to see advertisement for the backpacks he was considering when browsing BestBags.com.

Example 5: Geo-targeting

Mrs. Michu has installed the application of a social media provider on her smartphone. She is walking around Paris during her holidays. The social media provider collects information regarding Mrs Michu's whereabouts via the GPS functionalities of her smartphone on an ongoing basis[70], using the permissions that have been granted to the social media provider when the application was installed. Mrs Michu is staying at a hotel that is located next to a pizzeria. The pizzeria uses the geo-targeting functionality offered by the social media provider to target individuals who are within 1km of its premises for the first time in the last 6 months. When opening the social media provider's application on her smartphone, Mrs Michu sees an advertisement from the pizzeria, decides that she is hungry and buys a pizza via its website.

Example 6:

Mrs Ghorbani creates an account on a social media platform. During the process of registration she is asked if she consents to the processing of her personal data to see targeted advertisement on her social media page, on the basis of data she directly provides to the social media provider (such as her age, sex and location), as well as on the basis of her activity on other websites outside of the social media platform using cookies. She is informed that this data will be collected via social media plug-ins or tracking pixels, the processes are clearly described to her, as well as the fact that targeting involves other entities who are jointly responsible for ensuring compliance with the GDPR. It is also explained to her that she can withdraw her consent at any time, and she is provided with a link to the privacy policy. Because Mrs Ghorbani is interested in seeing targeted advertisement on her social media page, she gives her consent. No advertising cookies are placed or collected until Mrs Ghorbani expresses here consent.

Later on, she visits the website "Thelatesthotnews.com" that has a social media button integrated on it. A small but clearly visible banner appears on the right edge of the screen, asking Mrs Ghorbani to consent to the transmission of her personal data to the social media provider using cookies and social media plug-ins. The website operator undertook technical measures so that no personal data is transferred to the social media platform until she gives her consent.

5.3.1 Roles

68. In Example 4, both the targeter and the social media provider participate in determining the purposes and means of the processing of personal data, which results in the display of the advertisement to Mr. Schmidt.

69. As far as the determination of purpose is concerned, Bestbags.com and the social media provider jointly determine the purpose of the processing, which is to display a specific advertisement on the social media platform to the individuals who make up the target audience. By embedding the pixel into its website, Bestbags.com exerts a decisive influence over the means of the processing. The collection and transmission of the personal data of visitors of the website to the social media provider would not have occurred without the embedding of that pixel. The social media provider, on the other hand, has developed and offers the software code (pixel) that leads to the automatic collection, transmission and evaluation for marketing purposes of personal data to the social media provider. As a result, joint controllership exists in relation to the collection of personal data and its transmission by way of pixels, as well as in relation to the matching and subsequent display of the advertisement to Mr Schmidt on the social platform, and for any reporting relating to the targeting campaign. Joint controllership also exists, for similar reasons, in Example 6.

70. In Example 5, the pizzeria exercises a decisive influence over the processing of personal data by defining the parameters of the ad targeting in accordance with its business needs (for instance, opening hours of the pizzeria and geo-location of persons close to the pizzeria in this time-slot), and therefore must be regarded as taking part in the determination of the purposes and means of the data processing. The social media provider, on the other hand, has collected the information regarding Mrs. Michu's location (via GPS) for its purpose of enabling such location-based targeted advertising. As a result, joint control exists between the targeter and the social platform in relation to the collection and analysis of Mrs. Michu's location, as well as the display of the advertisement, in order to target her (as a person appearing within 1km of the pizzeria for the first time in the last 6 months) with the ad.

5.3.2 Legal basis

71. First of all, because Examples 4, 5 and 6 involve the use of cookies, requirements resulting from Article 5(3) of the ePrivacy Directive need to be taken into account.

72. In this regard, it should be noted that Article 5(3) of the ePrivacy Directive requires that users are provided with clear and comprehensive information, inter alia about the purposes of the processing, prior to giving their consent[71], subject to very narrow exceptions[72]. Clear and comprehensive information implies that a user is in a position to be able to determine easily the consequences of any consent he or she might give and ensure that the consent given is well informed.[73] As a result, the controller will have to inform data subjects about all the relevant purposes of the processing – including any subsequent processing of the personal data obtained by accessing information in the terminal equipment.

73. To be valid, the consent collected for the implementation of tracking technologies needs to fulfil the conditions laid out in Article 7 GDPR.[74] For instance, consent is not validly constituted if the use of cookies is permitted by way of a checkbox pre-ticked by the service provider, which the user must deselect to refuse his or her consent.[75] Based on recital 32, actions such as scrolling or swiping through a webpage or similar user activity will not under any circumstances satisfy the requirement of a clear and affirmative action: such actions may be difficult to distinguish from other activity or interaction by a user and therefore determining that an unambiguous consent has been obtained will also not be possible. Furthermore, in such a case, it will be difficult to provide a way for the user to withdraw consent in a manner that is as easy as granting it.[76]

74. Any (joint) controller seeking to rely on consent as a legal basis is responsible for ensuring that valid consent is obtained. In *Fashion ID*, the CJEU emphasized the importance of ensuring the efficient and timely protection of the data subject rights, and that consent should not be given only to the joint controller that is involved later in the processing. Valid consent must be obtained prior to the processing, which implies that (joint) controllers need to assess when and how information should be provided and consent should be obtained. In other words, the question as to which of the joint controllers should be in charge of collecting the consent comes down to determining which of them is involved first with the data subject. In example 6, as the placement of cookies and processing of personal data occurs at the moment of account creation, the social media provider must collect her valid consent before the placement of advertisement cookies.

75. The EDPB also recalls that in a case where the consent sought is to be relied upon by multiple (joint) controllers or if the data is to be transferred to or processed by other controllers who wish to rely on the original consent, these organisations should all be named.[77] Insofar as not all joint controllers are known at the moment when the social media provider seeks the consent, the latter will necessarily need to be complemented by further information and consent collected by the website operator embedding the social media plugin (i.e. *Thelatesthotnews.com* in Example 6).

76. The EDPB emphasizes that the consent that should be collected by the website operator for the transmission of personal data triggered by its website (by embedding a social plug-in) relates only to the operation or set of operations involving the processing of personal data in respect of which the operator actually determines the purposes and means[78]. The collection of consent by a website operator, i.e. "Thelatesthotnews.com" in Example 6 for instance, does not negate or in any way diminish the obligation of the social media provider to ensure the data subject has provided a valid consent for the processing for which it is responsible as a joint controller[79], as well as for any subsequent or further processing it carries out for which the website operator does not jointly determine the purposes and means (e.g. subsequent profiling operations for targeting purposes).

77. In addition, any subsequent processing of personal data, including personal data obtained by cookies, social plug-ins or pixels, must also have a legal basis under Article 6 of the GDPR in order to be lawful.[80] For what concerns the legal basis of the processing in Examples 4, 5, and 6, the EDPB considers that legitimate interest cannot act as an appropriate legal basis, as the targeting relies on the monitoring of individuals' behaviour across websites and locations using tracking technologies.[81]

78. Therefore, in such circumstances, the appropriate legal basis for any subsequent processing under Article 6 GDPR is also likely to be the consent of the data subject. Indeed, when assessing compliance with Article 6 GDPR, one should take into account that the processing as a whole involves specific activities for which the EU legislature has sought to provide additional protection.[82] Moreover, controllers must take into account the impact on data subjects' rights when identifying the appropriate legal basis in order to respect the principle of fairness.[83]

5.4 TARGETING ON THE BASIS OF INFERRED DATA

79. Inferred data refers to data which is created by the controller on the basis of the data provided by the data subject (regardless of whether these data were observed or actively provided by the data subject, or a combination thereof).[84] Inferences about data subjects can be made both by the social media provider and the targeter.

80. For example, by virtue of monitoring the behaviour of its users over a long period of time, both on and off the social media (e.g. pages visited, time spent on each page, number of reconnections to that page, words searched, hyperlinks followed, "likes" given), the social media provider may be able to infer information regarding the interests and other characteristics of the user of the social media. In the same vein, a targeter might also be able to infer data about specific individuals and use that knowledge when targeting him or her to display ads on his or her social media page.

Example 7:

Mrs Delucca often "likes" photos posted by the Art Gallery "Beautifulart" by impressionist painter Pataolito on its social media page. Museum Z is looking to attract individuals who are interested in impressionist paintings in light of its upcoming exhibition. Museum Z uses the following targeting criteria offered by the social media provider: "interested in impressionism", gender, age and place of residence. Mrs Delucca subsequently receives targeted advertisement by Museum Z related to the upcoming exhibition of Museum Z on her social media page.

Example 8:

Mr Leon has indicated on his social media page that he is interested in sports. He has downloaded an application on his mobile phone to follow the latest results of his favorite sport games, has set on his browser the page www.livesportsresults.com as his homepage on his laptop, often uses his desktop computer at work to search for the latest sports results on the internet. He also visits a number of online gambling websites. The social media provider tracks Mr Leon' online activity across his multiple devices, i.e. his laptop, his cell mobile phone, and his desktop computer. Based on this activity and all the information provided by Mr Leon, the social media provider infers that he will be interested in online betting. In addition, the social media platform has developed targeting criteria enabling companies to target people who are likely to be impulsive and have a lower income. The online betting company "bestpaydayloans" wishes to target users that are interested in betting and that are likely to be betting heavily. It therefore selects the criteria offered by the social media provider to target the audience to whom its advertisement should be displayed.

5.4.1 Roles

81. For what concerns the determination of the roles of the different actors, the EDPB notes the following: in Example 7, joint controllership exists between Museum Z and the social media provider concerning the processing of personal data for the purposes of targeted advertising, taking into account the collection of these data via the 'like'-functionality on the social media platform, and the 'analysis' undertaken by the social media provider in order to offer the targeting criterion ("interested in impressionism") to the targeter fitting the purpose of finally displaying the advertisement.[85]

82. In Example 8, joint control exists between "bestpaydayloans" and the social media provider in relation to the processing operations jointly determined, in this case the selection of targeting criteria and subsequent display of the advertisement, as well as any reporting relating to the targeting campaign.

5.4.2 Legal basis

83. Targeting of social media users on the basis of inferred data for advertising purposes typically involves profiling[86]. The WP29 has previously clarified that according to the GDPR, profiling is an automated processing of personal data which aims at evaluating personal aspects, in particular to analyse or make predictions about individuals, adding that *"[t]he use of the word 'evaluating' suggests that profiling involves some form of assessment or judgement about a person"*.[87] Profiling may be lawful by reference to any of the legal grounds in Article 6(1) GDPR, subject to the validity of this legal basis.

84. In Example 7, Article 5(3) of the ePrivacy Directive is applicable, insofar as the display of the advertisement on Mrs. Delucca's page related to the painter Pataolito requires a read/write operation to match this "like" with information previously held on her by the social media provider. Consent will therefore be required for these operations.

85. For what concerns Example 8, the EDPB recalls that in the case of automated decision-making which produces legal effects or similarly significantly affects the data subject, as set out in Article 22 GDPR data controllers may rely on the following exceptions:
- explicit consent of a data subject;
- the necessity of the automated decision-making for entering into, or performance of, a contract; or
- authorisation by Union or Member State law to which the controller is subject.

86. WP29 has already stated that *"In many typical cases the decision to present targeted advertising based on profiling will not have a similarly significant effect on individuals (. . .). However, it is possible that it may do, depending upon the particular characteristics of the case, including:*
- *the intrusiveness of the profiling process, including the tracking of individuals across different websites, devices and services;*
- *the expectations and wishes of the individuals concerned;*
- *the way the advert is delivered; or*
- *using knowledge of the vulnerabilities of the data subjects targeted."*[88]

87. Where the profiling undertaken by the social media provider is likely to have a "similarly significant [effect]" on a data subject, Article 22 shall be applicable. An assessment as to whether targeting will "similarly significantly [effect]" a data subject will need to be conducted by the controller (or joint controllers, as the case may be) in each instance with reference to the specific facts of the targeting.

88. In such circumstances as described in Example 8, the display of online betting advertisements may fall under the scope of Article 22 GDPR (targeting financially vulnerable persons that are interested in online betting which have the potential to significantly and adversely affect his financial situation). Therefore, in accordance with Article 22, explicit consent would be required. Furthermore, the use of tracking techniques triggers the applicability of Article 5(3) of the ePrivacy Directive, resulting in a requirement of prior consent. Finally, the EDPB recalls that for the processing to be lawful, the controller must conduct a case-by-case assessment, and that obtaining consent does not reduce other obligations to observe the requirements of fairness, necessity, proportionality and data quality, as stated in Article 5 GDPR.

NOTES

[40] Article 29 Data Protection Working Party, Guidelines on the right to data portability, WP 242 rev.01, 5 April 2017, p. 10.

[41] See for example the decision by the Higher Administrative Court of Bavaria h (Germany), Beschluss v. 26.09.2018, 5CS 18.1157, www.gesetze-bayern.de/Content/Document/Y-300-Z-BECKRS-B-2018-N-25018.

[42] In its Opinion 2/2010 on online behavioural advertising the WP29 noted that *"there are two main approaches to building user profiles: i) Predictive profiles are established by inference from observing individual and collective user behaviour over time, particularly by monitoring visited pages and ads viewed or clicked on. ii) Explicit profiles are created from personal data that data subjects themselves provide to a web service, such as by registering"* (Article 29 Data Protection Working Party, Opinion 2/2010 on online behavioural advertising, WP 171, p. 7).

[43] Article 29 Data Protection Working Party, Guidelines on the right to data portability, WP 242 rev.01, 5 April 2017, p. 10.

[44] *Idem.*

[45] See EDPB Guidelines 7/2020 on concepts of the controller and the processor in the GDPR, ("In addition, when the entities do not have the same purpose for the processing, joint controllership may also, in light of the CJEU case law, be established when the entities involved pursue purposes which are closely linked or complementary. Such may be the case, for example, when there is a mutual benefit arising from the same processing operation, provided that each of the entities involved participates in the determination of the purposes and means of the relevant processing operation").

[46] See EDPB Guidelines 7/2020 on concepts of the controller and the processor in the GDPR, ("Furthermore, the choice made by an entity to use for its own purposes a tool or other system developed by another entity, allowing the processing of personal data, will likely amount to a joint decision on the means of that processing by those entities. This follows from the Fashion ID case where the CJEU concluded, that by embedding on its website the Facebook Like button made available by Facebook to website operators, Fashion ID has exerted a decisive influence in respect of the operations involving the collection and transmission of the personal data of the visitors of its website to Facebook and had thus jointly determined with Facebook the means of that processing").

[47] See in this respect *Wirtschaftsakademie*, C-210/16, para. 39 - ECLI:EU:C:2018:388.

[48] See in the same vein also *Fashion ID*, C-40/17, para. 80: *"those processing operations are performed in the economic interests of both Fashion ID and Facebook Ireland, for whom the fact that it can use those data for its own commercial purposes is the consideration for the benefit to Fashion ID"*.

[49] See Opinion 1/2010.

[50] See EDPB Guidelines 7/2020 on concepts of the controller and the processor in the GDPR.

[51] See also Judgment in *Fashion ID*, C-40/17, para. 74 (*"[a] natural or legal person cannot be considered to be a controller, within the meaning of that provision, in the context of operations that precede or are subsequent in the overall chain of processing for which that person does not determine either the purposes or the means"*) and paragraph 101.

[52] Judgment in *Wirtschaftsakademie*, C-210/16, para. 38 - ECLI:EU:C:2018:388; Judgment in *Jehovah's Witnesses*, C-25/17, para. 69 - ECLI:EU:C:2018:551.

[53] CJEU Judgment 10 July 2018 (C-25/17, para. 68 to 72).

[54] See paragraph 18, Guidelines 2/2019 on the processing of personal data under Article 6(1)(b) GDPR in the context of the provision of online services to data subjects, Version 2.0, 8 October 2019, available at https://edpb.europa.eu/sites/edpb/files/files/file1/edpb_guidelines-art_6-1-badopted_after_public_consultation_en.pdf

[55] See para. 52, 53, Guidelines 2/2019 on the processing of personal data under Article 6(1)(b) GDPR) in the context of the provision of online services to data subjects, Version 2.0, 8 October 2019, available at https://edpb.europa.eu/sites/edpb/files/files/file1/edpb_guidelines-art_6-1-b- adopted_after_public_consultation_en.pdf.

[56] There would be a lack of necessity if the targeter were to switch to social media providers despite a direct contractual relationship with its customer and thus the possibility of direct advertising.

[57] See p. 15, Guidelines 2/2019 on the processing of personal data under Article 6(1)(b) GDPR in the context of the provision of online services to data subjects, Version 2.0, 8 October 2019, available at https://edpb.europa.eu/sites/edpb/files/files/file1/edpb_guidelines-art_6-1-badopted_ after_public_consultation_en.pdf

[58] Guidelines 2/2019 on the processing of personal data under Article 6(1)(b) GDPR in the context of the provision of online services to data subjects, para 57.

[59] CJEU, Judgment in *Fashion ID*, 29 July 2019, C-40/17, para. 95 - ECLI:EU:C:2019:629.

[60] Idem, para 97.

[61] Article 29 Working Party Opinion 06/2014 on the concept of legitimate interests of the data controller under Article 7 of Directive 95/46/EC, WP217, 9 April 2014, p. 29.

[62] When assessing the impact on the interests, fundamental rights and freedoms of the individual concerned, the following considerations are particularly relevant in the context of targeting directed to users of social media (i) the purposes of the targeting, (ii) the level of detail of the targeting criteria used (e.g., a broadly described cohort such as 'people with an interest in English literature', or more detailed criteria to allow segmentation and targeting on a more granular level), (iii) the type (and combination) of targeting criteria used (i.e. whether the targeting only focuses on a small aspect of the data subject, or is more comprehensive in nature), and (iv) the nature (sensitivity), volume and source of the data used in order to develop the targeting criteria. See Article 29 Working Party Opinion 06/2014 on the concept of legitimate interests of the data controller under Article 7 of Directive 95/46/EC, WP217, 9 April 2014 https://ec.europa.eu/justice/article-29/documentation/opinionrecommendation/files/2014/wp217_en.pdf

[63] Article 29 Working Party, Opinion on profiling and automated decision making, WP 251, rev. 01, p. 15, see also Article 29 WP, Opinion on legitimate interest, p. 32 and 48: « Overall, there is an imbalance between the company's legitimate interest and the protection of users' fundamental rights and Article 7(f) should not be relied on as a legal ground for processing. Article 7(a) would be a more appropriate ground to be used, provided that the conditions for a valid consent are met ».

[64] See Article 29 Working Party, Guidelines on consent under Regulation 2016/679, WP259 rev.01.

[65] See Article 29 Working Party, Guidelines on consent under Regulation 2016/679, WP259 rev.01, p. 3-4.

[66] See Guidelines 2/2019 on the processing of personal data under Article 6(1)(b) GDPR in the context of the provision of online services to data subjects, Version 2.0, 8 October 2019, available at https://edpb.europa.eu/sites/edpb/files/files/file1/edpb_guidelines-art_6-1-badopted_after_public_consultation_en.pdf

[67] In situations where e-mail addresses are used for direct marketing purposes controllers must also take into account the provisions of Article 13 ePrivacy Directive.

[68] The determination of purposes and means of the processing of the targeter and social media provider is similar (albeit not identical) to Example 1. By uploading the list of email addresses and setting the additional targeting criteria, the targeter defines the criteria in accordance with which the targeting takes place and designates the categories of persons whose personal data is to be made use of. The social media provider likewise makes a determination as to whose personal data shall be processed, by allowing which categories of data shall be processed, which targeting criteria shall be offered and who shall have access (to what types of) personal data that is processed in the context of a particular targeting campaign. The shared purpose underlying these processing operations resembles the purpose identified in Example 1, namely the display a specific advertisement to a set of individuals (in this case: social media users) who make up the target audience.

[69] Tracking pixels are comprised of small snippets of code that are integrated into the website of the targeter. When an individual accesses the targeter's website in their browser, the browser automatically sends a request to the social media provider's server to obtain the tracking pixel. Once the tracking pixel is downloaded, the social media provider is typically able to monitor the user's session (i.e. the individual's behaviour on the website(s) in question). The observed data can be used in order for example to add a social media user to a particular target audience.

[70] A social media provider may also be able to determine the whereabouts of their users on the basis of other data points, including IP address and WiFi information from mobile devices, or the user-derived data (e.g. if they place information about their location on the platform in a post).

[71] Court of Justice of the European Union, Judgment in Planet 49 Gmbh, Case C-673/17, paragraph 73.

[72] See Opinion 5/2019 on the interplay between the ePrivacy Directive and the GDPR, in particular regarding the competence, tasks and powers of data protection authorities. See also Court of Justice of the European Union, Judgment in Fashion ID, C-40/17, paragraphs 89-91.

[73] *Idem*, paragraph 74.

[74] EDPB Guidelines 05/2020 on consent under Regulation 2016/679, Version 1.1, p. 6.

[75] Court of Justice of the European Union, Judgement in Planet 49, C-637/17, paragraph 57.

[76] EDPB Guidelines 05/2020 on consent under Regulation 2016/679, Version 1.1, p. 19.

[77] EDPB Guidelines 05/2020 on consent under Regulation 2016/679, Version 1.1, p. 16, paragraph 65.

[78] Judgment in *Fashion ID*, 29 July 2019, C-40/17, ECLI:EU:C:2019:629, paragraphs 100-101.

[79] This is all the more the case insofar as that for most targeting tools, it is the social media that carries out the read/write

Part 2   Data Protection: EU Law etc

operations on the terminal of the user, because it collects the personal data for the purpose of targeted advertisement. Therefore, the social media provider is responsible for ensuring that valid consent is obtained.

[80] Opinion 5/2019 on the interplay between the ePrivacy Directive and the GDPR, in particular regarding the competence, tasks and powers of data protection authorities, paragraph 41.

[81] Article 29 Working Party, Opinion on profiling and automated decision making, WP 251, rev. 01, p. 15, see also Article 29 WP, Opinion on legitimate interest, p. 32 and 48: «Overall, there is an imbalance between the company's legitimate interest and the protection of users' fundamental rights and Article 7(f) should not be relied on as a legal ground for processing. Article 7(a) would be a more appropriate ground to be used, provided that the conditions for a valid consent are met».

[82] Opinion 5/2019 on the interplay between the ePrivacy Directive and the GDPR, in particular regarding the competence, tasks and powers of data protection authorities, paragraph 41.

[83] European Data Protection Board, Guidelines 2/2019 on the processing of personal data under Article 6(1)(b) GDPR in the context of the provision of online services to data subjects, Version 2.0, 8 October 2019, paragraph 1.

[84] See also Article 29 Data Protection Working Party, Guidelines on the right to data portability, WP 242 rev.01, 5 April 2017, p. 10.

[85] As regards social media pages, joint controllership may also exist in relation to statistical information provided by the social media provider to the page administrator: see CJEU C-210/16, *Wirtschaftsakademie*.

[86] The EDPB notes that profiling may have occurred in previous examples as well.

[87] Guidelines on Automated individual decision-making and Profiling for the purposes of Regulation 2016/679, WP251rev. 01, p. 7.

[88] Guidelines on Automated individual decision-making and Profiling for the purposes of Regulation 2016/679, WP251rev. 01, p. 22.

6 TRANSPARENCY AND RIGHT OF ACCESS

[2.378]
89. Article 5(1)(a) GDPR states that personal data shall be processed lawfully, fairly and in a transparent manner in relation to the data subject. Article 5(1)(b) GDPR also states that personal data shall be collected for specified, explicit and legitimate purposes. Articles 12, 13 and 14 GDPR contain specific provisions on the transparency obligations of the data controller. Finally, recital 39 states that "*it should be transparent to natural persons that personal data concerning them are collected, used, consulted or otherwise processed and to what extent the personal data are or will be processed*".[89]

90. Information presented to data subjects in respect of the way in which their personal data are processed, should be, in all cases, concise, transparent, in an intelligible and easily accessible form, using clear and plain language.

91. The EDPB recalls that the mere use of the word "advertising" would not be enough to inform the users that their activity is being monitored for the purpose of targeted advertising. It should be made transparent to individuals what types of processing activities are carried out and what this means for the data subject in practice. Data subjects should be informed in an easily understandable language if a profile will be built based on their online behaviour on the platform or on the targeter's website, respectively, by the social platform and by the targeter, providing information to the users on the types of personal data collected to build such profiles and ultimately allow targeting and behavioural advertising by targeters.[90] Users should be provided with the relevant information directly on the screen, interactively and, where appropriate or necessary, through layered notices.[91]

6.1 ESSENCE OF THE ARRANGEMENT AND INFORMATION TO PROVIDE (ARTICLE 26 (2) GDPR)

92. According to Article 26(1) GDPR, joint controllers "*shall in a transparent manner determine their respective responsibilities for compliance with the obligations under this Regulation, in particular as regards the exercising of the rights of the data subject and their respective duties to provide the information referred to in Articles 13 and 14, by means of an arrangement between them unless, and in so far as, the respective responsibilities of the controllers are determined by Union or Member State law to which the controllers are subject. The arrangement may designate a contact point for data subjects*".

93. A further expression of the transparency principle is the obligation to make the essence of the joint controllership arrangement available to the data subject according to Article 26 (2) GDPR. Indeed, Article 26 GDPR requires joint controllers to take appropriate measures to ensure that data subjects are made aware of the allocation of responsibilities.

94. As a matter of principle, the information provided to the data subject must cover all aspects of the data processing operation(s) for which the joint controllers are jointly responsible. Indeed, the data subject is entitled to receive all information (including regarding envisaged subsequent processing where there is joint controllership) at the outset, so that the information is fair and appropriate. More precisely, this joint arrangement needs to ensure that the data subject will be provided information required by Articles 13 and 14 GDPR, including on their shared or closely linked purposes, storage periods, transmission to third parties etc., which need to be communicated to the data subject upon collection of the data or before the processing starts. The arrangement needs to make it clear where the responsibilities lie in this regard. To meet these requirements, such arrangement must contain (or reference) clear and comprehensive information in respect of the processing to which it relates with explanations, where appropriate, on the various phases and actors of the processing.[92]

95. Although both joint controllers are subject to the duty to inform where there is joint responsibility, they can mutually agree that one of them shall be tasked with providing the initial information to data subjects, especially in cases where only one of the controllers interacts with the users prior to processing, for example on its website[93]. This exchange of information to provide to the data subject should be an integral part of the joint arrangement (e.g. an appendix). In case one of the joint controllers does not have all information in detail because, for example, it does not know the exact technical execution of the processing activities, the other joint controller shall provide all necessary information to enable him to provide the data subject with full information in accordance with Articles 13 and 14 GDPR.

96.   The EDPB notes that controllers are not directly responsible for providing the information required by Articles 13 and 14 GDPR in relation to further processing operations that do not fall under the scope of joint controllership. Therefore, the targeter is not directly responsible for providing the information relating to any further processing which will be carried out by the social media platform.[94]

97.   However, the EDPB emphasizes that the joint controller who intends to further use the personal data has specific obligations of information for this further processing where there is no joint responsibility, according to Article 14(4) of the GDPR, as well as obligations of compatibility of the further processing under Article 6(4).For example, the targeter and social media provider could agree that the targeter will provide certain information on behalf of the social media provider. The social media provider, however, remains ultimately responsible for ensuring that the data subject has been provided with the relevant information in relation to all the processing activities under its control.

> In Example 3 (Mr. Lopez being targeted for advertisement for Bank X on his social media page following the upload by the Bank of his email address to the social media provider), the Bank needs to inform Mr. Lopez that his email address will be used for advertising, via the social media provider, of offers linked to the bank services. Any further processing by the social media provider must be lawful and compatible with the purposes for which the Bank collected the data.
>
> In addition, to the extent that the social media provider intends to further process Mr. Lopez's email for another purpose, it must ensure that Mr. Lopez is provided with the information required by Article 14(4) GDPR prior to doing so.
>
> The social media provider and the Bank may agree that the Bank will provide Mr. Lopez with the relevant information on behalf of the social media provider. Even if that is the case, however, the social media provider remains ultimately responsible for ensuring that the data subject has been provided with the relevant information in relation to all the processing activities for which it is (alone) responsible. This obligation would not apply if Mr. Lopez has already been informed by the Bank of this processing, according to Article 14(5)(a) GDPR.
>
> These transparency obligations are to be considered without prejudice of the specific obligations applicable to legal basis considerations.

98.   Each joint controller is responsible for ensuring that the essence of the arrangement is made available to the data subject. In practice, the essence of the arrangement should be directly available on the platform, referred to in its privacy policy, and also made directly accessible by a link, for example, in the targeter's page on the social media platform or in links such as "why am I seeing this ad?".

6.2 RIGHT OF ACCESS (ARTICLE 15)

99.   Data controllers must enable users to easily and fully exercise their data subjects' rights. An easy-to-use and efficient tool should be available for the data subject to ensure the easy exercise of all of their rights, at any time, in particular the right to erasure, to object, and the right of access pursuant to Article 15 GDPR.[95] The following paragraphs focus on how and by whom the right of access should be accommodated in the context of targeting of social media users.[96]

100.   In general, to fulfill the requirements of Article 15 (1) GDPR and to ensure full transparency, controllers may want to consider implementing a mechanism for data subjects to check their profile, including details of the information and sources used to develop it. The data subject should be able to learn the identity of the targeter, and controllers should facilitate access to information regarding the targeting, including the targeting criteria that were used, as well as the other information required by Article 15 GDPR.[97]

101.   As regards the kind of access to be provided to data subjects, recital 63 advises that "*[w]here possible, the controller should be able to provide remote access to a secure system which would provide the data subject with direct access to his or her personal data.*" The specific features of social media providers - the online environment, the existence of a user account - suggest the possibility to easily grant the data subject with remote access to the personal data concerning him or her in accordance with Article 15(1), (2) GDPR. Remote access in this case can be regarded as the most "appropriate measure" in the sense of Article 12(1) GDPR, also taking into account the fact that this is a typical situation "where the proliferation of actors and the technological complexity of practice make it difficult for the data subject to know and understand whether, by whom and for what purpose personal data relating to him or her are being collected" (see recital 58, which explicitly adds "online advertising" as concrete example). In addition, if requested, social media users who have been targeted should also be given a copy of the personal data relating to them in accordance with Article 15(3) GDPR.

102.   According to Article 15(1)(c) GDPR, the user shall have access in particular to information on "*the recipients or categories of recipients to whom the personal data have been or will be disclosed, in particular recipients in third countries or international organisations*". According to Article 4(9), the term "recipient" refers to a natural or legal person, public authority, agency or another body, to which the personal data are disclosed, whether they are a third party or not. A targeter will not necessarily be a "recipient" of the personal data (see Example 1), as the personal data might not be disclosed to it, but it will receive statistics of the targeted customers in aggregated or anonymised form, e.g. as part of its campaign, or in a performance review of the same. Nevertheless, to the extent that the targeter acts as a joint controller, it must be identified as such to the social media user.

103. Although Article 15 GDPR is not explicitly identified in Article 26(1) GDPR, the wording of this Article refers to all "responsibilities for compliance" under GDPR, which includes Article 15 GDPR.

104. In order to enable data subjects to exercise their rights in an effective and easily accessible way, the arrangement between the social media provider and the targeter may designate a single point of contact for data subjects. Joint controllers are in principle free to determine amongst themselves who should be in charge of responding to and complying with data subject requests, but they cannot exclude the possibility for the data subject to exercise his or her rights in respect of and against each of them (Article 26 (3) of the GDPR). Hence, targeters and social media providers must ensure that a suitable mechanism is in place to allow the data subjects to obtain access to his or her personal data in a user-friendly manner (including the targeting criteria used) and all information required by Article 15 of the GDPR.

NOTES

89 See also Article 29 Working Party, Guidelines on transparency under Regulation 2016/679, WP260 rev.01, 11 April 2018, https://ec.europa.eu/newsroom/Article29/item-detail.cfm?item_id=622227

90 Ref. to EDPB Guidelines on transparency under Regulation 2016/679.

91 Article 29 Working Party, Guidelines on consent under Regulation 2016/679, WP259 rev. 01., para 24, 35.

92 Opinion 1/2010 on the concepts of "controller" and "processor", WP 169, p. 28.

93 CJEU *Fashion ID*, para 102, 105.

94 As clarified in the EDPB Guidelines 7/2020 on concepts of the controller and processor in the GDPR, each controller's duty, to ensure that the data are not further processed in a manner that is incompatible with the purposes for which they were originally collected by the controller sharing the data. It should be good practice that the controller that intends to process personal data for further purposes provides sufficient means to the other controller that transmits personal data to ascertain that there is indeed a legal basis, which would likely be consent, and data subjects have been properly informed as this would enable the targeter to ensure that the transfer to the social media provider is lawful.

95 Article 15(1), (2) GDPR detail the information to be given to the data subject asking for access to her data. Article 15 (3), (4) GDPR regulate the right to obtain a copy.

96 See EDPB, Guidelines on transparency under Regulation 2016/679, p. 35.

97 For further details regarding information pursuant to Art. 15 GPDR in the context of profiling, see Art. 29 Data Protection Working Party, WP 251rev.01, p. 17 for ("Article 15 gives the data subject the right to obtain details of any personal data used for profiling, including the categories of data used to construct a profile. In addition to general information about the processing, pursuant to Article 15(3), the controller has a duty to make available the data used as input to create the profile as well as access to information on the profile and details of which segments the data subject has been placed into"). It is important that such information should be tailored to the particular situation of the data subject, complementing any information already given under Articles 1 and 14.

7 DATA PROTECTION IMPACT ASSESSMENTS (DPIA)

[2.379]
105. In principle, prior to initiating the envisaged targeting operations, both joint controllers should check the list of processing operations "likely to result in a high risk" adopted at national level under Article 35(4) and recitals (71), (75) and (91) GDPR to determine if the designated targeting matches any of the types of processing operations subject to the requirement to conduct a DPIA. To assess whether the envisaged targeting operations are "likely to result in a high risk" and whether a DPIA is required, the criteria identified in the guidelines on DPIA should also be taken into account[98], as well as the lists that supervisory authorities have established of the kind of processing operations which are subject to the requirement for a data protection impact assessment (pursuant to Article 35(4)).

106. In some cases, the nature of the product or service advertised, the content of the message or the way the advert is delivered might produce effects on individuals whose impact has to be further assessed. This might be the case, for example, with products which are targeted at vulnerable people. Additional risks may emerge depending on the purposes of the advertising campaign and its intrusiveness, or if the targeting involves the processing of observed, inferred or derived personal data.

107. In addition to the obligations specifically referred to in Article 26(1) GDPR, joint controllers should also consider other obligations when determining their respective obligations. As stated in the EDPB guidelines on DPIAs "When the processing operation involves joint controllers, they need to define their respective obligations precisely".

108. As a consequence, both joint controllers need to assess whether a DPIA is necessary. If a DPIA is necessary, they are both responsible for fulfilling this obligation. The EDPB recalls that the DPIA should tackle the entire processing of personal data, which means that in principle both joint controllers need to take part in the realization of the DPIA. In this context, both controllers need to ensure that they have a sufficient level of information on the processing to carry out the required DPIA.[99] This implies that "each data controller should express his needs and share useful information without either compromising secrets (e.g.: protection of trade secrets, intellectual property, confidential business information) or disclosing vulnerabilities".[100]

109. In practice, it is possible that joint controllers decide that one of them shall be tasked with carrying out the DPIA as such. This should then be specified in the joint arrangement, without prejudice to the existence of joint responsibility as such. It may indeed be that one of the controllers is better placed to assess certain processing operations. For example, this controller may, depending on the context, be the one with a higher degree of control and knowledge of the targeting process in particular on the back-end of the deployed system, or on the means of the processing.

110. Every DPIA must include measures envisaged to address the risks, including safeguards, security measures and mechanisms to ensure the protection of personal data, and to demonstrate compliance with the GDPR taking into account the rights and legitimate interests of data subjects and other persons concerned. If the identified risks cannot be sufficiently addressed (i.e. the residual risks remain high), the joint controllers are each responsible for ensuring a prior consultation with the relevant supervisory authorities. If the targeting would infringe the GDPR, in particular because the risks have insufficiently been identified or mitigated, the targeting should not take place.

Example 9:

The political party "Letschangetheworld" wishes to encourage social media users to vote for a particular political candidate in the upcoming elections. They wish to target elderly people living in rural areas of the country, who regularly go to church, and who have not travelled abroad in the past 2 years.

---

111. There is joint controllership between the social media platform and the political party, for the matching of the profile and the display of the targeted advertisement. The assessment of whether a DPIA is required needs to be carried out both by the Letschangetheworld political party and the social media platform. Indeed, in this example, they both have sufficient knowledge on the criteria that are being used to target the individuals in order to see that the processing is likely to result in a high risk.

112. If a DPIA is necessary, the joint arrangement should address the question of how the controllers should carry it and ensure that a relevant exchange of knowledge takes place. In this example, it may be that the social media platform is better placed to assess certain processing operations, insofar as the political party merely selects general targeting criteria.

NOTES

[98]   See EDPB Guidelines on Data Protection Impact Assessment (DPIA) and determining whether processing is "likely to result in a high risk" for the purposes of Regulation 2016/679, wp248rev.0.

[99]   The EDPB reiterates that a DPIA is not required when the nature, scope, context and purposes of the processing are very similar to the processing for which DPIA have been carried out. In such cases, results of DPIA for similar processing can be used, see Article 29 Data Protection Working Party, Guidelines on Data Protection Impact Assessment (DPIA) and determining whether processing is "likely to result in a high risk" for the purposes of Regulation.2016/679, WP 248 rev.01, p. 12.

[100]   Idem, page 8.

8 SPECIAL CATEGORIES OF DATA

8.1 WHAT CONSTITUTES A SPECIAL CATEGORY OF DATA

[2.380]

113. The GDPR provides specific protection for personal data that are particularly sensitive in relation to individuals' fundamental rights and freedoms. Such data are defined in Article 9 GDPR as special categories of personal data and include data about an individual's health, racial or ethnic origin, biometry, religious or philosophical belief, political opinion, trade union membership, sex life or sexual orientation.

114. Controllers may only process special categories of data if they can meet one of the conditions set out in Article 9(2) GDPR, such as having obtained the data subject's explicit consent or the data have been manifestly made public by the data subject. In addition to the conditions in Article 9 GDPR, processing of special categories of data must rely on a legal basis laid down in Article 6 GDPR and be carried out in accordance with the fundamental principles set out in Article 5 GDPR.

115. Furthermore, the processing of special categories of personal data is relevant when assessing appropriate measures according to Articles 24, 25, 28 and 32 GDPR, but also to determine whether a DPIA must be carried out according to Article 35 GDPR, and whether a data protection officer must be appointed under Article 37 GDPR.

116. In the context of social media and targeting, it is necessary to determine whether the processing of personal data involves "special categories of data" and if such data are processed by the social media provider, the targeter or both. If special categories of personal data are processed, it must be determined whether and under what conditions the social media provider and the targeter can lawfully process such data.

117. If the social media provider processes the special category of data for targeting purposes, it must find a legal basis for the processing in Article 6 GDPR and rely on an exemption in Article 9(2) GDPR, such as explicit consent according to Article 9(2)(a) GDPR. If a targeter engages a social media provider and requests that the social media provider targets users based on this special category of data, the targeter will be jointly responsible with the social media provider for the processing of the special category data.

118. The following legal analysis will explore different situations when such processing may take place and their legal implications.

8.1.1 Explicit special categories of data

119. At times, personal data being processed clearly falls within the definition of special categories of data, e.g. in case of a direct statement about a person being member of a certain political party or religious association.

Example 10:

Ms. Flora states explicitly in her social media profile that she is a member of the GreenestPlanet political Party. The environmental organisation "Long live the Earth" wants to target social media users that are members of the GreenestPlanet political party in order to address targeted messages to them.

---

120. In Example 10, the social media provider and the environmental organisation are acting as joint controllers.[101] Insofar as the environmental organisation requests the social media provider to target users based on their political opinion, both controllers contribute to the processing of special categories of data as defined by Article 9 GDPR. Processing of these data are in principle prohibited according to Article 9(1). Both the social media provider and the environmental organisation must therefore be able to rely on one of the exemptions in Article 9(2) for their processing. In addition to that, they must also both have a legal basis according to Article 6. Out of the exemptions in Article 9(2), it appears that the only applicable exemptions in this situation would be to obtain the data subject's explicit consent, under Article 9(2)(a) GDPR, or the exemption that Ms. Flora manifestly made the personal data public, under Article 9 (2)(e) GDPR.

8.1.2 Inferred and combined special categories of data

121. Assumptions or inferences regarding special category data, for instance that a person is likely to vote for a certain party after visiting a page preaching liberal opinions, would also constitute a special category of personal data. Likewise, as previously stated by the EDPB, *"profiling can create special category of data by inference from data which is not special category of data in its own right, but becomes so when combined with other data. For example, it may be possible to infer someone's state of health from the records of their food shopping combined with data on the quality and energy content of foods".*[102]

122. For instance, the processing of a mere statement, or a single piece of location data or similar, which reveals that a user has (either once or on a few occasions) visited a place typically visited by people with certain religious beliefs will generally not in and of itself be considered as processing of special categories of data. However, it may be considered as processing of special categories of data if these data are combined with other data or because of the context in which the data are processed or the purposes for which they are being used.

> **Example 11:**
> The profile on Mr. Novak's social media account only reveals general information such as his name and domicile, but a status update reveals that he has visited the City Church frequently where he attended a religious service. Later on, the City Church wants to target its visitors with religious messages in order to encourage Christian people to join the congregation. In such circumstances, the use of personal data in Mr. Novak's status update for such a targeting purposes amounts to the processing of special categories of personal data.

123. If a social media provider or a targeter uses observed data to categorise users as having certain religious, philosophical or political beliefs - regardless of whether the categorization is correct/true or not - this categorisation of the user must obviously be seen as processing of special category of personal data in this context. As long as the categorisation enables targeting based on special category data, it does not matter how the category is labelled.

> **Example 12:**
> Mr. Sifuentes provides information in his social media profile in the shape of regular status updates, check-ins, etc., which indicate that he regularly takes part in activities arranged by the "Mind, Body and Spirit Movement". Even though no explicit statement on philosophical belief is provided, all updates, likes, check-ins and similar data provided by the user when collated, strongly indicate that Mr. Sifuentes has a certain philosophical belief.

> **Example 13:**
> A social media provider uses information actively provided by Ms. Allgrove on her social media profile page about her age, interests and address and combines it with observed data about the websites visited by her and her "likes" on the social media platform. The social media provider uses the data to infer that Ms. Allgrove is a supporter of left-wing liberal politics and places her in the "interested in left wing liberal politics" targeting category, and makes this category available to targeters for targeted advertising.

124. In Example 12, the vast information and the absence of measures to prevent targeting based on special category data implies that a processing of special categories of data is taking place. However, the mere fact that a social media provider processes large amounts of data which potentially could be used to infer special categories of data does not automatically mean that the processing falls under Article 9 GDPR. Article 9 will not be triggered if the social media provider's processing does not result in inference of special categories of data and the social media provider has taken measures to prevent that such data can be inferred or used for targeting. In any case, processing of a large amount of personal data about users may entail specific risks for the rights and freedoms of natural persons, which have to be addressed by implementing appropriate security measures, as prescribed under Article 32 GDPR, and also by taking into account the outcome of the DPIA to be performed pursuant to Article 35 GDPR.

125. In Example 13, the offering as well as use of the targeting category "interested in left wing liberal politics" amounts to processing of special categories of data, as this category could easily be used as a proxy to target individuals who have left wing liberal political beliefs. By assigning an inferred political opinion to a user, the social media provider processes special categories of data. For the purpose of Article 9 GDPR, it is not relevant whether the user in fact is a supporter of left-wing liberal politics. Nor is it relevant that the targeting category is named "interested in . . . " and not "supporter of . . . ", since the user is placed in the targeting category based on inferred political interests.

Example 14:

Mr. Svenson takes a career aptitude test developed, containing a psychological evaluation, by the company "YourPerfectJob" which is made available on a social media platform and makes use of the Application Programming Interface (API) provided by the social media provider. YourPerfectJob collects data about Mr. Svenson's education, employment status, age, hobbies, posts, email-address and connections. YourPerfectJob obtains the data through the API in accordance with the "permissions" granted by Mr. Svenson through his social media account. The stated purpose of the application is to predict what would be the best career path for a specific user.

Without the knowledge or approval of the social media provider, YourPerfectJob uses this information to infer a number of personal aspects, including his personality traits, psychological profile and political beliefs. YourPerfectJob later decides to use this information to target Mr. Svenson on behalf of a political party, using of the email-based targeting feature of the social media provider, without adding any other targeting criteria offered by the social media provider.

In Example 14, the targeter processes special categories of personal data, whereas the social media provider does not. Indeed, the assessment and identification of Mr. Svenson's political belief occurs without the involvement of the social media provider.[103] In addition to triggering the general prohibition of Article 9 GDPR, the targeting mentioned in Example 14 also constitutes an infringement of the requirements concerning fairness, transparency and purpose limitation. Indeed, Mr. Svenson is not properly informed of the fact that the personal relating to him will be processed for political targeting, which in addition, does not seem compatible with a career aptitude test.

126. While processing activities of the social media provider in Example 14 do not amount to processing of special categories of data within the meaning of Article 9 GDPR, the social media provider is responsible for integrating the necessary safeguards into the processing in order to meet the requirements of the GDPR and protect the rights of data subjects in accordance with Article 24 and 25 GDPR.

8.2 THE ARTICLE 9(2) EXCEPTION OF SPECIAL CATEGORIES OF DATA MADE MANIFESTLY PUBLIC

127. Article 9(2)(e) of the GDPR allows processing of special category of data in cases where the data have been manifestly made public by the data subject. The word "manifestly" implies that there must be a high threshold for relying on this exemption. The EDPB notes that the presence of a single element may not always be sufficient to establish that the data have been "manifestly" made public by the data subject. In practice, a combination of the following or other elements may need to be considered for controllers to demonstrate that the data subject has clearly manifested the intention to make the data public, and a case-by-case assessment is needed. The following elements may be relevant to help inform this assessment:

(i)   the default settings of the social media platform (i.e. whether the data subject took a specific action to change these default private settings into public ones); or

(ii)   the nature of the social media platform (i.e. whether this platform is intrinsically linked with the idea of connecting with close acquaintances of the data subject or creating intimate relations (such as online dating platforms), or if it is meant to provide a wider scope of interpersonal relations, such as professional relations, or microblogging, media sharing, social platforms to share online reviews, etc.; or

(iii)   the accessibility of the page where the sensitive data is published (i.e. whether the information is publicly accessible or if, for instance, the creation of an account is necessary before accessing the information); or

(iv)   the visibility of the information where the data subject is informed of the public nature of the information that they publish (i.e. whether there is for example a continuous banner on the page, or whether the button for publishing informs the data subject that the information will be made public . . .); or

128. The EDPB notes that the presence of a single element may not always be sufficient to establish that the data have been "manifestly" made public by the data subject. In practice, a combination of these or other elements may need to be considered for controllers to demonstrate that the data subject has clearly manifested the intention to make the data public.

Example 15:

Mr Jansen has opened an account on a microblogging social media platform. While completing his profile, he indicated that he is homosexual. Being a conservative, he chose to join conservative groups, knowing that he has been informed while subscribing that the messages he exchanges on the platform are public. A conservative political party wishes to target people who share the same political affiliations and sexual orientation as Mr Jansen using the social media targeting tools.

129. Because members' sexual orientation is by default "private" and that Mr. Jansen has not taken any step to make it public, it cannot be considered as having been manifestly made public. In addition, the data relating to his political affiliation has not been made manifestly public, despite of (i) the nature of the microblogging social media platform, which is meant to share information with the wide public, and (ii) the fact that he has been informed of the public nature of the messages he publishes on the forums. In addition, although he has joined public forums relating to conservatism, he cannot be targeted on the basis of this sensitive data, because it is the social media platform that makes a deduction on Mr

Janssen's political affiliation, and it was not the specific intention of the data subject to make this data manifestly public, all the more that this deduction may turn out to be false. He cannot therefore be targeted on the basis of political affiliation data. In other words, the circumstances in each specific case have to be taken into account when assessing whether the data have manifestly been made public by the data subject.[104]

NOTES

[101]   See the analysis in chapter 5.2.1.

[102]   Article 29 Data Protection Working Party, Guidelines on Automated individual decision-making and Profiling for the purposes of Regulation 2016/679, WP251rev.01, page 15.

[103]   In Example 14, there is no joint controllership between the social media provider and YourPerfectJob at the moment of collection of personal data, because they do not jointly determine the purposes of the collection and subsequent or further processing of personal data for the purposes of Yourperfectjob at this stage of the processing. The EDPB would like to recall that the analysis on the roles and responsibilities needs to be done on a case by case basis, and that the conclusion on this specific example is without prejudice of any further work that can be carried out by the EDPB on APIs. The situation would of course be different if the social media provider, in addition to making the personal data available, also participated in the determination of purpose pursued by YourPerfectJob. In any event, joint controllership still exists between the targeter and the social media provider as regards the use of list-based targeting.

[104]   The WP29 clarified in its Opinion on some key issues of the Law Enforcement Directive (WP 258, 29/11/2017, p. 10) that the expression "manifestly made public by the data subject" has to be interpreted to imply that the data subject was aware that the respective data will be publicly available which means to everyone, including authorities"; therefore, "[i]n case of doubt, a narrow interpretation should be applied . . . "

9 JOINT CONTROLLERSHIP AND RESPONSIBILITY

9.1 JOINT CONTROLLER ARRANGEMENT AND DETERMINATION OF RESPONSIBILITIES (ART. 26 GDPR)

[2.381]
130. Article 26 (1) GDPR requires joint controllers to determine – in a transparent manner – their respective responsibilities for compliance with the obligations of the GDPR in an arrangement, including, as explained above, the requirements for transparency.

131. In terms of scope, the EDPB considers that the arrangement between targeters and social media providers should encompass all processing operations for which they are jointly responsible (i.e. which are under their joint control). By concluding an arrangement that is only superficial and incomplete, targeters and social media providers would be in breach of non-compliance with their obligations under Article 26 of the GDPR.

> For instance, in Example 4 the arrangement should cover the entire processing of personal data where there is joint controllership, i.e. from the collection of personal data in the context of the visit by Mr. Schmidt of the website "BestBags.com" with a tracking pixel, to the display of the advertisement on his social media page, as well as any eventual reporting relating to the targeting campaign.

132. In order to develop a comprehensive arrangement, both the social media provider and the targeter must be aware of and have sufficiently detailed information regarding the specific data processing operations taking place. The arrangement between the targeter and the social media provider should therefore contain (or refer to) all necessary information to enable both parties to comply with their obligations under the GDPR, including their duty to comply with the principles under Article 5(1) GDPR and their duty to demonstrate their compliance according to Article 5(2) GDPR.

133. If, for example, the controller is considering to rely on Article 6(1)(f) GDPR as a legal basis, it is necessary, among other things, to know the extent of the data processing in order to be able to assess whether the interest of the controller(s) are overridden by the interests or fundamental rights and freedoms of the data subjects. Without sufficient information concerning the processing, such an assessment cannot be performed. The importance of including or referencing the necessary information in the context of a joint arrangement cannot be overstated, especially in situations where one of the parties almost exclusive has the knowledge and access to the information necessary for both parties to comply with the GDPR.

> For instance, in Example 1, when Company X is assessing whether it can rely on the legitimate interest as a legal basis to target men between the age of 30 and 45 and who have indicated that they are single, it is necessary that it has access to sufficient information concerning the processing carried out by the social media platform, including for instance for what concerns the additional measures (such as the right to prior objection) put into place by the latter, to ensure that legitimate interests are not overridden by the data subject's interests or fundamental rights and freedoms.

134. In order to ensure that the rights of the data subject can be accommodated effectively, the EDPB takes the view that the purpose of the processing and the corresponding legal basis should be also reflected in the joint arrangement between targeters and social media providers who are joint controllers. Although the GDPR does not preclude joint controllers to use different legal basis for different processing operations they carry out, it is recommended to use, whenever possible, the same legal basis for a particular targeting tool and for a particular purpose. Indeed, if each stage of the processing is processed on a different legal basis, this would render the exercise of rights impracticable for the data subject (e.g. for one stage there would be a right to data portability, for another there would be a right to object).

135. As controllers the targeter and the social media provider are both responsible for ensuring that the principle of purpose limitation is complied with and should therefore incorporate appropriate provisions to that end within the joint arrangement.

> For example, if the targeter wishes to use personal data provided to it by the data subject in order to target on social media, it must take appropriate measures to ensure that the data provided shall not be further used by the social media provider in a manner that is incompatible with those purposes, unless the valid consent of the data subject has been obtained pursuant to Article 6(4) of the GDPR.
>
> In Example 3, the Bank X should ensure that there are appropriate provisions in the joint arrangement with the social media platform that Mr. Lopez' email address is not used for other purposes that advertising of offers linked to the bank services that he is already using without Mr. Lopez' consent.
>
> Likewise, the social media provider must ensure that use of data for targeting purposes by the targeters is in compliance with the principles of purpose limitation, transparency and lawfulness.

136. Other obligations that should be considered by the targeter and social media provider in the context of their joint arrangement include: other general data protection principles contained in Article 5 GDPR, security of processing, data protection by design and by default, notifications and communications of personal data breaches, data protection impact assessments, the use of processors and transfers to third countries.

> For instance, in Example 13, the joint arrangement should address the question of which of the controllers should carry a DPIA and ensure that a relevant exchange of knowledge takes place. In other words, the political party "Letschangetheworld" should ensure that it has a sufficient level of information, for instance on the security measures put into place by the social media platform, when a DPIA is carried out.

137. Finally, the joint arrangement between the social media provider and the targeter must contain specific information about how the obligations under the GDPR shall be fulfilled in practice. If there is no clarity as to the manner in which the obligations are to be fulfilled, in particular in relation to data subject rights, both the targeter and the social media provider will be considered as acting in violation of Article 26(1) GDPR. Moreover, in such cases, both (joint) controllers will not have implemented appropriate technical and organisational measures to ensure and to be able to demonstrate that processing is performed in accordance with the GDPR and therefore will have breached their obligations under Articles 5(2) and 24.

9.2 LEVELS OF RESPONSIBILITY

138. The EDPB observes that targeters who wish to use targeting tools provided by a social media provider may be confronted with the need to adhere to pre-defined arrangements, without any possibility to negotiate or make modifications ('take it or leave it' conditions). The EDPB considers that such a situation does not negate the joint responsibility of the social media provider and the targeter and cannot serve to exempt either party from its obligations under the GDPR. Both parties to the joint arrangement are also bound to ensure that the allocation of responsibilities duly reflects their respective roles and relationships vis-à-vis data the subjects in a practical, truthful and transparent manner.

139. It is important to stress that an arrangement pursuant to Article 26 GDPR cannot override the legal obligations incumbent upon a (joint) controller. While joint controllers shall, in accordance with Article 26 GDPR *"determine their respective responsibilities for compliance"* with the GDPR, each controller remains, as a matter of principle, responsible for the compliance of processing. This means that each controller is – *inter alia* – responsible for compliance with the principles set out under Article 5(1) GDPR, including the principle of lawfulness established under Article 5(1)(a) GDPR.

140. However, the degree of responsibility of the targeter and of the social media provider in relation to specific obligations may vary. In *Wirtschaftsakademie*, the CJEU noted that *"the existence of joint responsibility does not necessarily imply equal responsibility of the various operators involved in the processing of personal data. [. . .] those operators may be involved at different stages of that processing of personal data and to different degrees, so that the level of responsibility of each of them must be assessed with regard to all the relevant circumstances of the particular case"*.[105]

141. In other words, although joint controllers are both responsible for complying with the obligations under the GDPR, and although the data subject may exercise his or her rights as against each of the controllers, their level of responsibility must be assessed on their actual role in the processing. In *Google Spain*, the CJEU clarified that a controller must ensure, *"within the framework of its responsibilities, powers and capabilities"*, that the processing of personal data meets the requirements of EU data protection law.[106]

142. When it comes to assessing the level of responsibility of targeters and social media providers, several factors may be relevant, such as the ability to influence the processing on a practical level, as well as the actual or constructive knowledge of each of the joint controllers. It is also important to be clear at what stage of the processing and to what extent or degree the targeter and the social media provider are responsible for the processing.[107]

In Example 1, Company X sets up an advertising campaign so that users corresponding to specific targeting criteria may be shown advertisements for the company on the social media platform. However, although it sets the parameters for the advertising campaign, it does not collect or have access to any personal data, nor does it have any direct contact with the data subject. Each of these elements may be relevant when assessing the level (or "degree") or responsibility of the targeter and social media provider in case a violation of the GDPR is established (e.g. in case of lack of transparency towards the data subject or failure to ensure lawfulness of processing). As indicated earlier, notwithstanding, both parties are obliged to undertake appropriate measures in order to meet the requirements of the GDPR and protect the rights of data subjects against unlawful forms of processing.

In Example 3, which involved list-based targeting, the situation is slightly different than Example 1. In Example 3, the bank initially collected the personal data and shared it with the social media provider for targeting purposes. In that case, the targeter has voluntarily caused the collection and transmission stage of the data processing. Each of these elements should be taken into account when assessing the level of responsibility of each actor and should be duly reflected in the terms of the joint arrangement.

Similarly, in Example 4, in case of pixel-based targeting, it should be taken into account that the website operator enables the transmission of personal data to the social media provider. It is indeed the website "BestBags-.com" that integrates a tracking pixel on its website so that it can target Mr Schmidt, although he has decided not to make a purchase[108]. The website is therefore actively involved in the collection and transmission of the data. As a joint controller, however, the social media provider is also under an obligation to undertake appropriate measures to meet the requirements of the GDPR and protect the rights of data subjects against unlawful forms of processing. In this case, if the data subject's consent is sought, the joint controllers should agree upon the way in which consent is collected in practice.

143. When it comes to assessing the level of responsibility of social media provider, the EDPB observes that several targeting mechanisms rely on profiling and/or other processing activities previously undertaken by the social media provider. It is the social media provider who decides to process personal data of its users in such a manner to develop the targeting criteria which it makes available to targeters. In order to do so, the social media provider has independently made certain decisions regarding the processing, such as which categories of data shall be processed, which targeting criteria shall be offered and who shall have access (to what types of) personal data that is processed in the context of a particular targeting campaign. Such processing activities must also comply with the GDPR, prior to the offering of any targeting services.

144. The examples mentioned in the preceding paragraphs indicate the importance of clearly allocating responsibilities in the joint controller arrangement between social media providers and targeters. Even though the terms of the arrangement should in any case mirror the level of responsibility of each actor, a comprehensive arrangement which duly reflects the role and capabilities of each party is necessary not only to comply with Article 26 of the GDPR, but also for complying with other rules and principles of the GDPR.

145. Finally, the EDPB notes that insofar as the terms of the joint arrangement between the social media provider and the targeter do not bind supervisory authorities, supervisory authorities may exercise their competences and powers in relation to either joint controller, as long as the joint controller in question is subject to the competence of that supervisory authority.

NOTES

[105] CJEU judgment of 05 June 2018, Wirtschaftsakademie, C-210/16, para. 43.

[106] See also CJEU, C-131/12, Google Spain ("responsibilities, powers and capabilities").

[107] The EDPB considers that in a variety of cases an assessment based on the criteria mentioned above (e.g. the data used to establish the targeting criteria, the matching of the data subject, the collection of consent) will likely lead to the outcome that it is the social media provider that has more factual influence on the processing and therefore has a higher degree of responsibility, depending on the specific targeting mechanism being used.

[108] In addition, as BestBags.com has integrated the social media tracking pixel on its website, it is also responsible for complying with the ePrivacy Directive requirements regarding this tool, which, given that the pixel also facilitates the processing of personal data, is also of importance when determining the level of responsibility.

EUROPEAN DATA PROTECTION BOARD: GUIDELINES 9/2020 ON RELEVANT AND REASONED OBJECTION UNDER REGULATION 2016/679

Version 2.0

Adopted on 9 March 2021

[2.382]

NOTES
© European Data Protection Board.

VERSION TABLE

Version 1.0: 8 October 2020 — Adoption of the Guidelines for publication consultation

Version 2.0: 9 March 2021 — Adoption of the Guidelines after public consultation

TABLE OF CONTENTS

THE EUROPEAN DATA PROTECTION BOARD

Having regard to Article 70(1)(e) of the Regulation 2016/679/EU of the European Parliament and of the Council of 27 April 2016 on the protection of natural persons with regard to the processing of personal data and on the free movement of such data, and repealing Directive 95/46/EC (hereinafter "GDPR"),

Having regard to the EEA Agreement and in particular to Annex XI and Protocol 37 thereof, as amended by the Decision of the EEA joint Committee No 154/2018 of 6 July 2018[1],

Having regard to Article 12 and Article 22 of its Rules of Procedure,

HAS ADOPTED THE FOLLOWING GUIDELINES

1 GENERAL

[2.383]

1. Within the cooperation mechanism set out by the GDPR, the supervisory authorities ("SAs") have a duty to "exchange all relevant information with each other" and cooperate "in an endeavour to reach consensus"[2]. This duty of cooperation applies to every stage of the procedure, starting with the inception of the case and extending to the whole decision-making process. The achievement of an agreement on the outcome of the case is therefore the ultimate goal of the whole procedure established by Article 60 GDPR. In the situations in which no consensus is reached among the SAs, Article 65 GDPR entrusts the EDPB with the power to adopt binding decisions. However, the exchange of information and the consultation among the Lead Supervisory Authority ("LSA") and the Concerned Supervisory Authorities ("CSAs") often enables an agreement to be reached at the early stages of the case.

2. According to Article 60(3) and (4) GDPR, the LSA is required to submit a draft decision to the CSAs, which then may raise a relevant and reasoned objection within a specific timeframe (four weeks)[3]. Upon receipt of a relevant and reasoned objection, the LSA has two options open to it. If it does not follow the relevant and reasoned objection or is of the opinion that the objection is not reasoned or relevant, it shall submit the matter to the Board within the consistency mechanism. If the LSA, on the contrary, follows the objection and issues the revised draft decision, the CSAs may express a relevant and reasoned objection on the revised draft decision within a period of two weeks.

3. When the LSA does not follow an objection or rejects it as not relevant or reasoned and therefore submits the matter to the Board according to Article 65(1)(a) GDPR, it then becomes incumbent upon the Board to adopt a binding decision on whether the objection is "relevant and reasoned" and if so, on all the matters which are the subject of the objection.

4. Therefore, one of the key elements signifying the absence of consensus between the LSA and the CSAs, is the concept of "relevant and reasoned objection". This document seeks to provide guidance with respect to this concept and aims at establishing a common understanding of the notion of the terms "relevant and reasoned", including what should be considered when assessing whether an objection "clearly demonstrates the significance of the risks posed by the draft decision" (Article 4(24) GDPR).

5. Article 4(24) GDPR defines "relevant and reasoned objection" as an *objection to a draft decision as to whether there is an infringement of this Regulation, or whether envisaged action in relation to the*

controller or processor complies with this Regulation, which clearly demonstrates the significance of the risks posed by the draft decision as regards the fundamental rights and freedoms of data subjects and, where applicable, the free flow of personal data within the Union".

6. This concept serves as a **threshold** in situations where CSAs aim to object to a (revised) draft decision to be adopted by the LSA under Article 60 GDPR. As the unfamiliarity surrounding "what constitutes relevant and reasoned objection" has the potential to create misunderstandings and inconsistent applications by the supervisory authorities, the EU legislator suggested that the EDPB should issue guidelines on this concept (end of Recital 124 GDPR).

7. In order to meet the threshold set by Article 4(24) GDPR, a submission by a CSA should in principle explicitly mention each element of the definition in relation to each specific objection. Therefore, **the objection aims, first of all, at pointing out how and why, according to the CSA, the draft decision does not appropriately address the situation of infringement of the GDPR, and/or does not envision appropriate action towards the controller or processor in the light of the demonstration of the risks that such draft decision, if left unchanged, would entail for the rights and freedoms of data subjects and for the free flow of personal data in the Union, where applicable.**. An objection submitted by a CSA should indicate each part of the draft decision that is considered deficient, erroneous or lacking some necessary elements, either by referring to specific articles/paragraphs or by other clear indications, and showing why such issues are to be deemed "relevant" as further explained below. The proposals for amendments put forward by the objection should aim to remedy these potential errors.

8. Indeed, the **degree of detail of the objection and the depth of the analysis included therein may be affected by the degree of detail in the content of the draft decision and by the degree of involvement of the CSA** in the process leading to the draft decision issued by the LSA. Therefore, the standard of "relevant and reasoned objection" is grounded on the assumption that the LSA's obligation to exchange all relevant information[4] is complied with, allowing the CSA(s) to have an in-depth understanding of the case and therefore to submit a solid and well-reasoned objection. To this end, the need for each legally binding measure of SAs to "give the reasons for the measure" (see Recital 129 GDPR) should also be kept in mind. The degree of involvement of the CSA by the LSA in the process leading to the draft decision, if it leads to an insufficient knowledge of all the aspects of the case, can therefore be considered as an element to determine the degree of detail of the relevant and reasoned objection in a more flexible way.

9. The EDPB would first like to emphasise that the focus of all SAs involved (LSA and CSAs) should be on eliminating any deficiencies in the consensus-finding process in such a way that a consensual draft decision is the result. Whilst acknowledging that raising an objection is not the most preferable tool to remedy an insufficient degree of cooperation in the preceding stages of the one-stop-shop proceeding, the EDPB nevertheless acknowledges that it is an option open to CSAs. This would be a last resort to also remedy (alleged) deficiencies in terms of CSA's involvement by the LSA in the process that should have led to a consensus-based draft decision, including as regards the legal reasoning and the scope of the investigations carried out by the LSA in respect of the case at hand.

10. The GDPR requires the CSA to justify its position on the LSA's draft decision by submitting an objection that is "relevant" and "reasoned". It is crucial to bear in mind that the two requirements, "reasoned" and "relevant", are to be deemed **cumulative**, i.e. both of them have to be met[5]. Consequently, Article 60(4) requires the LSA to submit the matter to the EDPB consistency mechanism when it is of the opinion that the objection does not meet at least one of the two elements[6].

11. The EDPB strongly advises the SAs to raise their objections and exchange information through the information and communication system set up for the exchange of information among SAs[7]. They should be clearly marked as such by using the specific dedicated functions and tools.

NOTES

1   References to "Member States" made throughout this document should be understood as references to "EEA Member States".
2   Regulation 2016/679, hereinafter "GDPR", Article 60(1).
3   It is possible for the CSAs to withdraw objections previously raised.
4   As per Article 60(1) GDPR.
5   See the wording of Art. 60 (4).
6   Pursuant to Article 60(4) GDPR the lead supervisory authority shall also submit the matter to the consistency mechanism referred to in Article 63 if it does not follow the relevant and reasoned objection.
7   See the EDPB Rules of Procedure.

2 CONDITIONS FOR A "RELEVANT AND REASONED" OBJECTION

2.1 "RELEVANT"

[2.384]
12. In order for the objection to be considered as "relevant", there must be a **direct connection between the objection and the substance of the draft decision at issue**[8]. More specifically, the objection needs to **concern either whether there is an infringement of the GDPR or whether the envisaged action in relation to the controller or processor complies with the GDPR.**

13. Consequently, the objection raised fulfils the criterion of being "relevant" when, if followed, it would entail a change leading **to a different conclusion** as to whether there is an infringement of the GDPR or as to whether the envisaged action in relation to the controller or processor, as proposed by the LSA, complies with the GDPR. There must always be a link between the content of the objection and such potential different conclusion as further explained below. While it is possible for the objection to signal a disagreement on both elements, the existence of only one of them would be sufficient to meet the conditions for a relevant objection.

14.   An objection should only be considered relevant if it relates to the specific legal and factual content of the LSA's draft decision. Raising abstract or broad concerns or remarks cannot be considered relevant in this context. Likewise, minor disagreements on the wording or regarding the legal reasoning that do not relate to the possible existence of the infringement nor to the compliance of envisaged action in relation to the controller or processor with the GDPR should not be regarded as relevant.

15.   The reasoning underlying the conclusions reached by the LSA in the draft decision can be subject to an objection, but only insofar as such reasoning is linked with the conclusion as to whether there is an infringement, whether the infringement of the GDPR has been correctly identified, or is linked with the compliance of the envisaged action with the GDPR, and to the extent that the whole Article 4(24) threshold as described in this document is met.

2.2 "REASONED"

16.   In order for the objection to be "reasoned"[9], it needs to include clarifications and arguments as to **why an amendment of the decision is proposed** (i.e. the legal / factual mistakes of the LSA's draft decision). It also needs to demonstrate **how the change would lead to a different conclusion** as to whether there is an infringement of the GDPR or whether the envisaged action in relation to the controller or processor complies with the GDPR.

17.   The CSA should provide sound and substantiated reasoning for its objection, in particular, by elaborating on **legal arguments** (relying on EU law and/or relevant national law, and including e.g. legal provisions, case law, guidelines) **or factual elements**, where applicable. The CSA should present the fact(s) allegedly leading to a different conclusion regarding the infringement of the GDPR by the controller/processor, or the aspect of the draft decision that, in their view, is deficient/erroneous.

18.   Moreover, an objection is "reasoned" insofar as it is able to **"clearly demonstrate" the significance of the risks posed by the draft decision** as described in section 3.2 below. To this end, the objection must put forward arguments or justifications concerning the consequences of issuing the decision without the changes proposed in the objection, and how such consequences would pose significant risks for data subjects' fundamental rights and freedoms and, where applicable, for the free flow of personal data within the Union.

19.   In order for an objection to be adequately reasoned, it should be **coherent, clear, precise and detailed in explaining the reasons for objection**. It should set forth, clearly and precisely, the **essential elements** on which the CSA based its assessment, and the **link between the envisaged consequences of the draft decision** (if it was to be issued as it is) **and the significance of the anticipated risks for data subjects' fundamental rights and freedoms and, where applicable, for the free flow of personal data within the Union**. Moreover, the CSA should **clearly indicate which parts of the draft decision they disagree with**. In cases where the objection is based on the opinion that the LSA failed to fully investigate an important fact of the case, or an additional violation of the GDPR, it would be sufficient for the CSA to present such arguments in a conclusive and substantiated manner.

20.   The CSA(s) must provide all the information (facts, documents, legal arguments) on which they are relying so as to effectively present their argument. This is fundamental in order to delimit the scope of the (potential) dispute. This means that, **in principle, the CSA should aim to provide a relevant and reasoned objection in one single submission** supported by all the factual and legal arguments as described above. However, **within the deadline set forth by Article 60(4) GDPR, the CSA can provide additional information related to and supporting the objection raised, bearing in mind the need to comply with the "relevant and reasoned" requirements**.

> **Example 1**: The CSA submits a formal objection, but a few days later provides the LSA with additional information through the information and communication system regarding the facts of the case. Such information may only be taken into consideration by the LSA insofar as it is provided within the deadline set forth by Article 60(4) GDPR.
>
> If the additional information amounts to a new objection, it needs to meet the "relevant and reasoned" requirements described in this section and the CSA should submit the facts, documents and legal arguments supporting the additional information.

21.   If possible, as a good practice, the objection should include **a new wording proposal** for the LSA to consider, which in the opinion of the CSA allows remedying the alleged shortcomings in the draft decision. This may serve to clarify the objection better in the relevant context.

NOTES

 8   The Oxford English Dictionary defines "relevant" as "bearing on or connected with the matter in hand; closely relating to the subject or point at issue; pertinent to a specified thing" ("relevant, adj." OED Online, Oxford University Press, June 2020, www.oed.com/view/Entry/161893. Accessed 24 July 2020).

 9   The Oxford English Dictionary defines "reasoned" as "characterised by or based on reasoning; carefully studied" ("reasoned, adj.2." OED Online, Oxford University Press, June 2020, www.oed.com/view/Entry/159078. Accessed 24 July 2020).

3 SUBSTANCE OF THE OBJECTION

[2.385]

22.   The subject matter of the objection may refer to whether there is an infringement of the GDPR and/or to whether the envisaged action in relation of the controller or the processor complies with the GDPR. The type of content will depend on the LSA's draft decision at stake and on the circumstances of the case.

23. Additionally, the CSA's objection will have to clearly demonstrate the significance of the risks posed by the draft decision as regards the fundamental rights and freedoms of data subjects and, where applicable, the free flow of personal data within the Union. The existence of an infringement and/or the non-compliance of the envisaged action with the GDPR should be assessed in light of the significance of the risks that the draft decision, if left unchanged, poses to the rights and freedoms of data subjects and, if relevant, the free flow of personal data.

3.1 EXISTENCE OF AN INFRINGEMENT OF THE GDPR AND/OR COMPLIANCE OF THE ENVISAGED ACTION WITH THE GDPR

3.1.1 Existence of an infringement of the GDPR

24. In the first case, the substance of the objection will amount to a disagreement between the CSA and the LSA as to whether, in the facts at issue, the activities and processing operations carried out by the controller or processor led to infringement(s) of the GDPR or not, and to which infringement(s) specifically.

25. In this context, the term "infringement" should be interpreted as "an infringement of a given provision of the GDPR". Therefore, the CSA's objections to the draft decision must be justified and motivated through reference to evidence and facts as exchanged between the LSA and the CSAs (the 'relevant information' referred to in Article 60 GDPR). These requirements should apply to each specific infringement and to each specific provision in question.

> **Example 2**: The draft decision states that the controller infringed Articles 6, 7, and 14 GDPR. The CSA disagrees on whether there is an infringement of Article 7 and 14 and considers that there is an additional infringement of Article 13 GDPR.
>
> **Example 3**: The CSA argues that LSA did not take into consideration the fact that the household exemption is not applicable to some of the processing operations conducted by a controller and involving the use of CCTV, hence that there is no infringement of the GDPR. In order to justify its objection, the CSA refers to Article 2(2)(c) GDPR, EDPB Guidelines 3/2019 on processing of personal data through video devices, and CJEU case C-212/13 Ryneš.

26. An objection as to whether there is an infringement of the GDPR may also include a disagreement as to the conclusions to be drawn from the findings of the investigation. For instance, the objection may state that the findings amount to the infringement of a provision of the GDPR other than (and/or in addition to) those already analysed by the LSA's draft decision. However, this is less likely to happen when the obligation for the LSA to cooperate with the CSAs and exchange all relevant information in accordance with Article 60(1) has been duly complied with in the time preceding the issuance of the draft decision.

27. In some circumstances, an objection could go as far as identifying gaps in the draft decision justifying the need for further investigation by the LSA. For instance, if the investigation carried out by the LSA unjustifiably fails to cover some of the issues raised by the complainant or resulting from an infringement reported by a CSA, a relevant and reasoned objection may be raised based on the failure of the LSA to properly handle the complaint and to safeguard the rights of the data subject. In this regard, a distinction must be made between, on one hand, own-volition inquiries and, on the other hand, investigations triggered by complaints or by reports on potential infringements shared by the CSAs. In procedures based on a complaint or on an infringement reported by a CSA, the scope of the procedure (i.e. those aspects of data processing which are potentially the subject of a violation) should be defined by the content of the complaint or of the report shared by the CSA: in other words, it should be defined by the aspects addressed by the complaint or report. In own-volition inquiries, the LSA and CSAs should seek consensus regarding the scope of the procedure (i.e. the aspects of data processing under scrutiny) prior to initiating the procedure formally. The same applies in cases where a SA dealing with a complaint or report by another SA takes the view that an own-volition inquiry is also necessary to deal with systematic compliance issues going beyond the specific complaint or report.

28. As mentioned above, raising an objection should only be considered as a last resort to remedy an allegedly insufficient involvement of the CSA(s) in the preceding stages of the process. The system designed by the legislator suggests that consensus on the scope of the investigation should be reached at an earlier stage by the competent SAs.

29. The insufficient factual information or description of the case at stake, or the absence or insufficiency of assessment or reasoning (with the consequence that the conclusion of the LSA in the draft decision is not adequately supported by the assessment carried out and the evidence presented, as required in Article 58 GDPR), can also be a matter of objection linked to the existence of an infringement. This is upon the conditions that the whole threshold set forth by Article 4(24) GDPR is met and it is possible that there can be a link between such allegedly insufficient analysis and the finding of an infringement / the envisaged action.

30. It is possible for a relevant and reasoned objection to raise issues concerning procedural aspects to the extent that they amount to situations in which the LSA allegedly disregarded procedural requirements imposed by the GDPR and this affects the conclusion reached in the draft decision.

Example 4: The SA of Member State YY is competent to act as LSA for the cross-border processing carried out by the controller CC whose main establishment is in YY. The competent SA of Member State XX informs the LSA (YY) of a complaint lodged with the XX SA substantially affecting data subjects only in XX, pursuant to Article 56(2) and (3) GDPR. The LSA decides to handle the case.

The XX SA decides to submit to the LSA a draft for a decision pursuant to Article 56(4) GDPR. The LSA prepares a draft decision pursuant to Article 60(3) GDPR and submits it to the CSA. The XX SA is of the opinion that the LSA failed to comply with its obligation to take utmost account of the draft submitted by XX SA when preparing its draft decision, pursuant to Article 56(4) GDPR as it does not provide reasoning why it is deviating from the draft for a decision provided by the XX SA.

Subsequently, the XX SA's raises a relevant and reasoned objection in which it puts forward arguments specifying the different conclusion that the draft decision would have reached if the LSA had followed its draft for a decision, in terms of establishing an infringement or determining the actions envisaged vis-à-vis the controller, and with a view to avoiding the demonstrated risks posed to data subject's fundamental rights and freedoms, and, where applicable to the free flow of personal data within the Union.

31.   An objection pursuant to Article 60(4) and Article 65(1)(a) GDPR is without prejudice to the provision of Article 65(1)(b) GDPR. Therefore, a disagreement on the competence of the SA acting as LSA to issue a decision in a specific case should not be raised through an objection pursuant to Article 60(4) GDPR, and falls outside the scope of Article 4(24) GDPR. Unlike the objection pursuant to Article 60(4) GDPR, the EDPB considers the procedure pursuant to Article 65(1)(b) GDPR to be applicable at any stage.

3.1.2 Compliance with the GDPR of the action envisaged in the draft decision in relation to the controller or processor with the GDPR

32.   In this second scenario, the substance of the relevant and reasoned objection amounts to a disagreement regarding the particular corrective measure proposed by the LSA or other action envisaged in the draft decision.

33.   More specifically, the relevant and reasoned objection should explain why the action foreseen in the draft decision is not in line with the GDPR. To this end, the CSA must clearly set out factual elements and/or legal arguments underlying the different assessment of the situation, by indicating which action would be appropriate for the LSA to undertake and include in the final decision.

Example 5: The controller disclosed sensitive medical data of the complainant to a third party without a legal basis. In the draft decision, the LSA proposed to issue a reprimand, while the CSA provides factual elements showing that the controller is facing broad and systemic issues in its compliance with the GDPR (e.g. it regularly discloses its clients' data to third parties without a legal basis). Therefore it proposes that an order to bring the processing operations into compliance, a temporary ban on the data processing, or a fine should be imposed.

Example 6: Due to a mistake of one of its employees, the controller published the name, last name and telephone numbers of all its 100.000 clients on its website. These personal data were publicly accessible for two days. As the controller reacted as soon as possible, the mistake was reported, and all the clients were individually informed, the LSA planned to simply issue a reprimand. One CSA however considers that, due to the large scale of the data breach and its possible impact/risk on the private life of the clients, the imposition of a fine would be required.

34.   As enshrined in the last sentence of Article 65 (1)(a) GDPR, the binding decision of the EDPB shall concern all the matters which are the subject of the objection, in particular in case of an infringement. Recital 150 sentence 5 GDPR states that the consistency mechanism may also be used to promote a consistent application of administrative fines. Therefore, it is possible that the objection challenges the elements relied upon to calculate the amount of the fine. If the assessment of the EDPB within this context identifies shortcomings in the reasoning leading to the imposition of the fine at stake, the LSA will be instructed to re-assess the fine and remedy the identified shortcomings. The EDPB's assessment on this matter should be based on common EDPB standards stemming from Article 83(1) and (2) GDPR and the Guidelines on the calculation of administrative fines.

Example 7: The CSA considers that the level of the fine envisaged by the LSA in the draft decision is not effective, proportionate or dissuasive, as required by Article 83(1) GDPR, taking into account the facts of the case.

3.2 SIGNIFICANCE OF THE RISKS POSED BY THE DRAFT DECISION AS REGARDS THE FUNDAMENTAL RIGHTS AND FREEDOMS OF DATA SUBJECTS AND, WHERE APPLICABLE, THE FREE FLOW OF PERSONAL DATA WITHIN THE UNION

3.2.1 Meaning of "significance of the risks"

35.   It is important to bear in mind that the goal of the work carried out by SAs is that of protecting the fundamental rights and freedoms of data subjects and facilitating the free flow of personal data within the Union (Articles 4(24) and Article 51 and Recital 123 GDPR).

36.   **The obligation to demonstrate the significance of the risks posed by the draft decision (e.g. by the measures provided for therein, or by the absence of corrective measures, etc.) for the rights and freedoms of data subjects and, where applicable, for the free flow of data within the Union lies on the CSA**. The possibility for CSAs to provide such a demonstration will also rely on the degree of detail of the draft decision itself and of the initial provision of information by the LSA, as highlighted above in paragraph 8.

37. "Risk" is mentioned in numerous sections of the GDPR, and previous EDPB guidelines[10] define it as "a scenario describing an event and its consequences, estimated in terms of severity and likelihood". Article 4(24) GDPR refers to the need to demonstrate the "significance" of the risks posed by the draft decision, that is, to show the implications the draft decision would have for the protected values. The CSA will need to do so by advancing sufficient arguments to explicitly show that such risks are substantial and plausible, for the fundamental rights and freedoms of data subjects and, where applicable, for the free flow of data in the Union. The demonstration of the significance of the risks cannot be implied from the legal and/or factual arguments provided by the CSA, but it has to be explicitly identified and elaborated in the objection.

38. It should be emphasised that while a relevant and reasoned objection needs to always clearly demonstrate the significance of the risks posed by the draft decision as regards the fundamental rights and freedoms of data subjects (see Section 3.2.2 below), the demonstration of the risks posed to the free flow of personal data within the European Union is only requested "where applicable" (see below Section 3.2.3).

3.2.2 Risks to fundamental rights and freedoms of data subjects

39. The issue at stake concerns the impact the draft decision, as a whole, would have on the data subjects' fundamental rights and freedoms. This may concern the findings the LSA made as to whether the controller or processor infringed the GDPR, and/or the imposition of corrective measures.

40. The approach to be used when assessing the risk posed by the draft decision is not the same as the one applied by a controller in carrying out a data protection impact assessment ("DPIA") to establish the risk of an intended processing operation. Indeed, the subject matter of the assessment is totally different: namely, the effects produced by the conclusions drawn by the LSA as set out in its draft decision regarding whether an infringement has been committed or not. The conclusions of the LSA may entail taking certain measures (the 'envisaged action'). As said, it is by having regard to the draft decision as a whole that such risks are to be demonstrated by the CSA.

41. Recital 129 GDPR clarifies that *"[t]he powers of supervisory authorities should be exercised in accordance with appropriate procedural safeguards set out in Union and Member State law, impartially, fairly and within a reasonable time" and that "each measure should be appropriate, necessary and proportionate in view of ensuring compliance with this Regulation, taking into account the circumstances of each individual case, respect the right of every person to be heard before any individual measure which would affect him or her adversely is taken and avoid superfluous costs and excessive inconveniences for the persons concerned"*.

42. Therefore, the evaluation of the risks posed by the draft decision to the fundamental rights and freedoms of data subjects can rely, *inter alia*, on the appropriateness, necessity, and proportionality of the measures envisaged (or not envisaged) therein as based on the findings related to the existence of an infringement and the possible remedial actions set forth by the controller or processor.

43. Additionally, the risks at stake may refer to the impact of the draft decision on the fundamental rights and freedoms of the data subjects whose personal data are processed by the controller or processor, but also to the impact on the rights and freedoms of data subjects whose personal data might be processed in the future and to the possible reduction of future infringements of the GDPR, where the facts of the case support it.

Example 8: The LSA's draft decision concluded that the principle of data minimisation enshrined in Article 5(1)(c) GDPR was not breached by the controller. The CSA brings factual elements and legal arguments in its objection showing that the processing activity carried out by the controller had actually resulted in a breach of Article 5(1)(c) GDPR, and arguing that a reprimand should be issued against the controller. In order to demonstrate the significance of the risks for the fundamental rights and freedoms of data subjects, the CSA argues that the absence of a reprimand for the violation of a fundamental principle would set a dangerous precedent, by failing to signal the need for a correction of the organisation's data processing activities, and would endanger the data subjects whose personal data are and will be processed by the controller.

3.2.3 Risks to the free flow of personal data within the Union

44. Where the objection also refers to these particular risks, the CSA will need to clarify why it is deemed to be "applicable". Additionally, an objection demonstrating risks posed to the free flow of personal data, but not to the rights and freedoms of data subjects, will not be considered as meeting the threshold set by Article 4(24) GDPR.

45. The need to avoid restricting or prohibiting the free movement of personal data for reasons connected with the protection of natural persons with regard to the processing of personal data is explicitly recalled by the GDPR[11], which aims to introduce harmonised data protection rules across the EU and enable the free flow of personal data within the Union, while ensuring a high level of protection of natural persons' fundamental rights and freedoms, in particular their right to protection of their personal data.

46. The risks to the free flow of personal data within the Union may be created by any measures, including decisions of national SAs, which introduce unjustified limitations regarding data storage (e.g. provisions which oblige a controller to store certain information in a particular Member State) and/or the free flow of personal data between Member States (e.g. through suspension of data flows or imposition of temporary or definitive limitation including a ban on processing).

47.   Likewise, the free flow of personal data within the Union may be at risk when expectations are set (or requirements imposed) on how controllers fulfil their obligations under the GDPR, namely in such a way that the actions expected from the controllers become tied to a specific region in the EU (e.g. through specific qualifications requirements).

48.   Additionally, the free flow of personal data within the Union may also be hampered if unjustifiably different decisions are issued by SAs in situations that are identical or similar (e.g. in terms of sector or type of processing), as a lack of uniformity would endanger the EU level playing field and create contradictory situations within the EU, and a risk of forum shopping. Account should be taken in this respect of national specificities as permitted by the GDPR with regard to certain sectors such as health care, journalism or archives.

NOTES
10   See e.g. WP 248 rev.01 Guidelines on Data Protection Impact Assessment (DPIA) and determining whether processing is "likely to result in a high risk" for the purposes of Regulation 2016/67.
11   GDPR, Article 1(3).

EUROPEAN DATA PROTECTION BOARD: RECOMMENDATIONS 1/2020 ON MEASURES THAT SUPPLEMENT TRANSFER TOOLS TO ENSURE COMPLIANCE WITH THE EU LEVEL OF PROTECTION OF PERSONAL DATA: VERSION FOR PUBLIC CONSULTATION

Adopted on 10 November 2020

[2.386]

NOTES
This document has been published for public consultation. A subsequent version of this document is expected to be adopted by the EDPB following publication of this book
© European Data Protection Board.

TABLE OF CONTENTS

EXECUTIVE SUMMARY

The EU General Data Protection Regulation (GDPR) was adopted to serve a dual-purpose: facilitating the free flow of personal data within the European Union, while preserving the fundamental rights and freedoms of individuals, in particular their right to the protection of personal data.

In its recent judgment C-311/18 (Schrems II) the Court of Justice of the European Union (CJEU) reminds us that the protection granted to personal data in the European Economic Area (EEA) must travel with the data wherever it goes. Transferring personal data to third countries cannot be a means to undermine or water down the protection it is afforded in the EEA. The Court also asserts this by clarifying that the level of protection in third countries does not need to be identical to that guaranteed within the EEA but essentially equivalent. The Court also upholds the validity of standard contractual clauses, as a transfer tool that may serve to ensure contractually an essentially equivalent level of protection for data transferred to third countries.

Standard contractual clauses and other transfer tools mentioned under Article 46 GDPR do not operate in a vacuum. The Court states that controllers or processors, acting as exporters, are responsible for verifying, on a case-by-case basis and, where appropriate, in collaboration with the importer in the third country, if the law or practice of the third country impinges on the effectiveness of the appropriate safeguards contained in the Article 46 GDPR transfer tools. In those cases, the Court still leaves open the possibility for exporters to implement supplementary measures that fill these gaps in the protection and bring it up to the level required by EU law. The Court does not specify which measures these could be. However, the Court underlines that exporters will need to identify them on a case-by-case basis. This is in line with the principle of accountability of Article 5.2 GDPR, which requires controllers to be responsible for, and be able to demonstrate compliance with the GDPR principles relating to processing of personal data.

To help exporters (be they controllers or processors, private entities or public bodies, processing personal data within the scope of application of the GDPR) with the complex task of assessing third countries and

Part 2   Data Protection: EU Law etc

identifying appropriate supplementary measures where needed, the European Data Protection Board (EDPB) has adopted these recommendations. These recommendations provide exporters with a series of steps to follow, potential sources of information, and some examples of supplementary measures that could be put in place.

As a **first step**, the EDPB advises you, exporters, to **know your transfers**. Mapping all transfers of personal data to third countries can be a difficult exercise. Being aware of where the personal data goes is however necessary to ensure that it is afforded an essentially equivalent level of protection wherever it is processed. You must also verify that the data you transfer is adequate, relevant and limited to what is necessary in relation to the purposes for which it is transferred to and processed in the third country.

A **second** step is to **verify the transfer tool your transfer relies on**, amongst those listed under Chapter V GDPR. If the European Commission has already declared the country, region or sector to which you are transferring the data as adequate, through one of its adequacy decisions under Article 45 GDPR or under the previous Directive 95/46 as long as the decision is still in force, you will not need to take any further steps, other than monitoring that the adequacy decision remains valid. In the absence of an adequacy decision, you need to rely on one of the transfer tools listed under Articles 46 GDPR for transfers that are regular and repetitive. Only in some cases of occasional and non-repetitive transfers you may be able to rely on one of the derogations provided for in Article 49 GDPR, if you meet the conditions.

A **third step** is to **assess** if there is anything in **the law or practice of the third country** that may impinge on the effectiveness of the appropriate safeguards of the transfer tools you are relying on, in the context of your specific transfer. Your assessment should be primarily focused on third country legislation that is relevant to your transfer and the Article 46 GDPR transfer tool you are relying on and that may undermine its level of protection. For evaluating the elements to be taken into account when assessing the law of a third country dealing with access to data by public authorities for the purpose of surveillance, please refer to the EDPB European Essential Guarantees recommendations. In particular, this should be carefully considered when the legislation governing the access to data by public authorities is ambiguous or not publicly available. In the absence of legislation governing the circumstances in which public authorities may access personal data, if you still wish to proceed with the transfer, you should look into other relevant and objective factors, and not rely on subjective factors such as the likelihood of public authorities' access to your data in a manner not in line with EU standards. You should conduct this assessment with due diligence and document it thoroughly, as you will be held accountable to the decision you may take on that basis.

A **fourth step** is **to identify and adopt supplementary measures** that are necessary to bring the level of protection of the data transferred up to the EU standard of essential equivalence. This step is only necessary if your assessment reveals that the third country legislation impinges on the effectiveness of the Article 46 GDPR transfer tool you are relying on or you intend to rely on in the context of your transfer. These recommendations contain (in annex 2) a non-exhaustive list of examples of supplementary measures with some of the conditions they would require to be effective. As is the case for the appropriate safeguards contained in the Article 46 transfer tools, some supplementary measures may be effective in some countries, but not necessarily in others. You will be responsible for assessing their effectiveness in the context of the transfer, and in light of the third country law and the transfer tool you are relying on and you will be held accountable for the decision you take. This might also require you to combine several supplementary measures. You may ultimately find that no supplementary measure can ensure an essentially equivalent level of protection for your specific transfer. In those cases where no supplementary measure is suitable, you must avoid, suspend or terminate the transfer to avoid compromising the level of protection of the personal data. You should also conduct this assessment of supplementary measures with due diligence and document it.

A **fifth step** is to **take** any **formal procedural steps** the adoption of your supplementary measure may require, depending on the Article 46 GDPR transfer tool you are relying on. These recommendations specify these formalities. You may need to consult your competent supervisory authorities on some of them.

The **sixth and final step** will be for you to re-evaluate at appropriate intervals the level of protection afforded to the data you transfer to third countries and to monitor if there have been or there will be any developments that may affect it. The principle of accountability requires continuous vigilance of the level of protection of personal data.

Supervisory authorities will continue exercising their mandate to monitor the application of the GDPR and enforce it. Supervisory authorities will pay due consideration to the actions exporters take to ensure that the data they transfer is afforded an essentially equivalent level of protection. As the Court recalls, supervisory authorities will suspend or prohibit data transfers in those cases where, following an investigation or complaint, they find that an essentially equivalent level of protection cannot be ensured.

Supervisory authorities will continue developing guidance for exporters and coordinating their actions in the EDPB to ensure consistency in the application of EU data protection law.

THE EUROPEAN DATA PROTECTION BOARD

Having regard to Article 70(1)(e) of the Regulation 2016/679/EU of the European Parliament and of the Council of 27 April 2016 on the protection of natural persons with regard to the processing of personal data and on the free movement of such data, and repealing Directive 95/46/EC (hereinafter "GDPR"),

Having regard to the European Economic Area (EEA) Agreement and in particular to Annex XI and Protocol 37 thereof, as amended by the Decision of the EEA joint Committee No 154/2018 of 6 July 2018[1],

Having regard to Article 12 and Article 22 of its Rules of Procedure,

Whereas:

(1) The Court of Justice of the European Union (CJEU) concludes in its judgment of 16 July 2020 *Data Protection Commissioner v. Facebook Ireland LTD, Maximillian Schrems*, C-311/18 that Article 46 (1) and 46 (2)(c) of the GDPR must be interpreted as meaning that the appropriate safeguards, enforceable rights and effective legal remedies required by those provisions must ensure that data subjects whose personal data are transferred to a third country pursuant to standard data protection clauses are afforded a level of protection essentially equivalent to that guaranteed within the European Union by that regulation, read in the light of the Charter of the Fundamental Rights of the European Union.[2]

(2) As underlined by the Court, a level of protection of natural persons essentially equivalent to that guaranteed within the European Union by the GDPR, read in the light of the Charter, must be guaranteed irrespective of the provision of Chapter V on the basis of which a transfer of personal data to a third country is carried out. The provisions of Chapter V intend to ensure the continuity of that high level of protection where personal data is transferred to a third country.[3]

(3) Recital 108 and Article 46 (1) GDPR provide that in the absence of an EU adequacy decision, a controller or processor should take measures to compensate for the lack of data protection in a third country by way of appropriate safeguards for the data subject. A controller or processor may provide appropriate safeguards, without requiring any specific authorisation from a supervisory authority, through its use of one of the transfer tools listed under Article 46 (2) GDPR, such as standard data protection clauses.

(4) The Court clarifies that the standard data protection clauses adopted by the Commission are solely intended to provide contractual guarantees that apply uniformly in all third countries to controllers and processors established in the European Union. Due to their contractual nature, standard data protection clauses cannot bind the public authorities of third countries, since they are not party to the contract. Consequently, data exporters may need to supplement the guarantees contained in those standard data protection clauses with supplementary measures to ensure compliance with the level of protection required under EU law in a particular third country. The Court refers to recital 109 of the GDPR, which mentions this possibility and encourages controllers and processors to use it.[4]

(5) The Court stated that it is above all, for data exporter to verify, on a case-by-case basis and, where appropriate, in collaboration with the importer of the data, whether the law of the third country of destination ensures an essentially equivalent level of protection, under EU law, of personal data transferred pursuant to standard data protection clauses, by providing, where necessary, supplementary measures to those offered by those clauses.[5]

(6) If the controller or a processor established in the European Union is not able to take appropriate supplementary measures to guarantee an essentially equivalent level of protection under EU law, the controller or processor or, failing that, the competent supervisory authority, are required to suspend or end the transfer of personal data to the third country concerned.[6]

(7) The GDPR or the Court do not define or specify the "additional safeguards", "additional measures" or "supplementary measures" to the safeguards of the transfer tools listed under Article 46.2 of the GDPR that controllers and processors may adopt to ensure compliance with the level of protection required under EU law in a particular third country.

(8) The EDPB has decided, on its own initiative, to examine this question and to provide controllers and processors, acting as exporters, with recommendations on the process they may follow to identify and adopt supplementary measures. These recommendations aim at providing a methodology for the exporters to determine whether and which additional measures would need to be put in place for their transfers. It is the primary responsibility of exporters to ensure that the data transferred is afforded in the third country of a level of protection essentially equivalent to that guaranteed within the EU. With these recommendations, the EDPB seeks to encourage consistent application of the GDPR and the Court's ruling, pursuant to the EDPB's mandate[7]

HAS ADOPTED THE FOLLOWING RECOMMENDATION:

NOTES

[1] References to "Member States" made throughout this document should be understood as references to "EEA Member States".

[2] CJEU judgment of 16 July 2020, *Data Protection Commissioner v Facebook Ireland Ltd, Maximillian Schrems, (hereinafter* C-311/18 (Schrems II)), second finding.

[3] C-311/18 (Schrems II), paragraphs 92 and 93.

[4] C-311/18 (Schrems II), paragraphs 132 and 133.

⁵   C-311/18 (Schrems II), paragraph 134.
⁶   C-311/18 (Schrems II), paragraphs 135.
⁷   Article 70.1.e GDPR.

1 ACCOUNTABILITY IN DATA TRANSFERS

[2.387]
1. EU primary law considers the right to data protection as a fundamental right.[8] Accordingly, the right to data protection is afforded a high level of protection and limitations may only be made if they are provided for by law, respect the essence of its right, are proportionate, necessary and genuinely meet objectives of general interest recognised by the Union or the need to protect the rights and freedoms of others.[9] The right to the protection of personal data is not an absolute right; it must be considered in relation to its function in society and be balanced against other fundamental rights, in accordance with the principle of proportionality.[10]

2. An essentially equivalent level of protection to that guaranteed within the EU must accompany the data when it travels to third countries outside the EEA to ensure that the level of protection guaranteed by the GDPR is not undermined.

3. The right to data protection has an active nature. It requires exporters and importers (whether they are controllers and/or processors) to go beyond an acknowledgement or passive compliance with this right.[11] Controllers and processors must seek to comply with the right to data protection in an active and continuous manner by implementing legal, technical and organisational measures that ensure its effectiveness. Controllers and processors must also be able to demonstrate these efforts to data subjects, the general public and data protection supervisory authorities. This is the so called principle of accountability.[12]

4. The principle of accountability, which is necessary to ensure the effective application of the level of protection conferred by the GDPR also applies to data transfers to third countries[13] since they are a form of data processing in themselves.[14] As the Court underlined in its judgment, a level of protection essentially equivalent to that guaranteed within the European Union by the GDPR read in the light of the Charter must be guaranteed irrespective of the provision of that chapter on the basis of which a transfer of personal data to a third country is carried out.[15]

5. In the Schrems II judgment, the Court emphasizes the responsibilities of exporters and importers to ensure that the processing of personal data has been and will continue to be carried out in compliance with the level of protection set by EU data protection law and to suspend the transfer and/or terminate the contract where the importer of the data is not, or is no longer, able to comply with standard data protection clauses incorporated in the relevant contract between the exporter and the importer.[16] The controller or processor acting as exporter must ensure that the importers collaborate with the exporter, where appropriate, in its performance of these responsibilities, by keeping it informed, for instance, of any development affecting the level of protection of the personal data received in the importer's country.[17] These responsibilities are an application of the GDPR principle of accountability to the data transfers.[18]

NOTES
⁸   Article 8(1) Charter of Fundamental Rights and Article 16 (1) TFEU, preamble 1, Article 1 (2) GDPR.
⁹   Article 52(1) of the EU Charter of Fundamental Rights.
¹⁰ Recital 4 of the GDPR and C-507/17 Google LLC, successor in law to Google Inc. v. Commission nationale de l'informatique et des libertés (CNIL), paragraph 60.
¹¹ C-92/09 and C-93/02, Volker und Markus Schecke GbR v. Land Hessen, Opinion of Advocate General Sharpston, 17 June 2010, paragraph 71.
¹² Article 5.2 and Article 28.3 (h) GDPR.
¹³ Article 44 and recital 101 GDPR, as well as Article 47(2)(d) GDPR.
¹⁴ CJEU judgment of 6 October 2015, *Maximillian Schrems v Data Protection Commissioner, (hereinafter* C-362/14 (Schrems I)), paragraph 45.
¹⁵ C-311/18 (Schrems II), paragraph 92 and 93.
¹⁶ C-311/18 (Schrems II), paragraphs 134, 135, 139, 140, 141, 142.
¹⁷ C-311/18 (Schrems II), paragraphs 134.
¹⁸ Article 5 (2) and Article 28 (3)(h) GDPR.

2 ROADMAP: APPLYING THE PRINCIPLE OF ACCOUNTABILITY TO DATA TRANSFERS IN PRACTICE

[2.388]
6. What follows is a roadmap of the steps to take in order to find out if you (the data exporter) need to put in place supplementary measures to be able to legally transfer data outside the EEA. "You" in this document means the controller or processor acting as data exporter, processing personal data within the scope of application of the GDPR – including processing by private entities and public bodies when transferring data to private bodies.[19] As for transfers of personal data carried out between public bodies, specific guidance is provided for in the *Guidelines 2/2020 on Articles 46 (2)(a) and 46 (3)(b) of Regulation 2016/679 for transfers of personal data between EEA and non-EEA public authorities and bodies.*[20]

7. You will need to document appropriately this assessment and the supplementary measures you select and implement and make such documentation available to the competent supervisory authority upon request.[21]

2.1 STEP 1: KNOW YOUR TRANSFERS

8. To know what may be required for you (the data exporter) to be able to continue with or to conduct new transfers of personal data[22], the first step is to ensure that you are fully aware of your transfers (know your transfers). Recording and mapping all transfers can be a complex exercise for entities engaging into multiple, diverse and regular transfers with third countries and using a series of processors and sub-processors. Knowing your transfers is an essential first step to fulfil your obligations under the principle of accountability.

9. To gain full awareness of your transfers, you can build on the records of processing activities that you may be obliged to maintain as controller or processor under Article 30 GDPR.[23] Previous actions to fulfil obligations to inform data subjects under Articles 13.1.f and 14.1.f GPDR about your transfers of their personal data to third countries may also assist you.[24]

10. When mapping transfers, do not forget to also take into account onward transfers, for instance whether your processors outside the EEA transfer the personal data you entrusted to them to a sub-processor in another third country or in the same third country[25].

11. In line with the GDPR principle of "data minimisation",[26] you must verify that the data you transfer is adequate, relevant and limited to what is necessary in relation to the purposes for which it is transferred to and processed in the third country.

12. These activities must be carried out before any transfer is made and updated prior to resuming transfers after suspension of data transfer operations: you must know where the personal data you exported may be located or processed by the importers (map of destinations).

13. Keep in mind that remote access from a third country (for example in support situations) and/or storage in a cloud situated outside the EEA, is also considered to be a transfer.[27] More specifically, if you are using an international cloud infrastructure you must assess if your data will be transferred to third countries and where, unless the cloud provider clearly states in its contract that the data will not be processed at all in third countries.

2.2 STEP 2: IDENTIFY THE TRANSFER TOOLS YOU ARE RELYING ON

14. A second step you must take is to identify the transfer tools you are relying on amongst those Chapter V GDPR lists and envisages.

Adequacy decisions

15. The European Commission may recognise through its **adequacy decisions** relating to some or all of the third countries to which you are transferring personal data that they offer an adequate level of protection for personal data.[28]

16. The effect of such an adequacy decision is that personal data can flow from the EEA to that third country without any Article 46 GDPR transfer tool being necessary.

17. Adequacy decisions may cover a country as a whole or be limited to a part of it. Adequacy decisions may cover all data transfers to a country or be limited to some types of transfers (e.g. in one sector).[29]

18. The European Commission publishes the list of its adequacy decisions on its website.[30]

19. If you transfer personal data to third countries, regions or sectors covered by a Commission adequacy decision (to the extent applicable), **you do not need to take any further steps as described in these recommendations**.[31] However, you must still monitor if adequacy decisions relevant to your transfers are revoked or invalidated.[32]

20. However, adequacy decisions do not prevent data subjects from filing a complaint. Nor do they prevent supervisory authorities from bringing a case before a national court if they have doubts about the validity of a decision, so that a national court can make a reference for a preliminary ruling to the CJEU for the purpose of examining that validity.[33]

> Example: An EU citizen, Mr. Schrems, filed a complaint on June 2013 with the Irish Data Protection Commission (DPC) and asked this supervisory authority to prohibit or suspend the transfer of his personal data from Facebook Ireland to the United States, as he considered that the law and practice of the United States did not ensure adequate protection of the personal data held in its territory against the surveillance activities that were engaged in there by the public authorities. The DPC rejected the complaint, on the ground, in particular, that in Decision 2000/520 the European Commission considered that, under the 'safe harbour' scheme, the United States ensured an adequate level of protection of the personal data transferred (the Safe Harbour Decision). Mr. Schrems challenged the decision of the DPC and the Irish High Court referred a question on the validity of Decision 2000/520 to the Court of Justice of the European Union (CJEU). The CJEU subsequently decided to invalidate the Commission Decision 2000/520 on the adequacy of the protection provided by the safe harbour privacy principles.[34]

Article 46 GDPR transfer tools

21. Article 46 GDPR lists a series of transfer tools containing "*appropriate safeguards*" that exporters may use to transfer personal data to third countries in the absence of adequacy decisions The main types of Article 46 GDPR transfer tools are:
- standard data protection clauses (SCCs);
- binding corporate rules (BCRs);

Part 2   Data Protection: EU Law etc

–   codes of conduct;
–   certification mechanisms;
–   ad hoc contractual clauses.

22.   Whatever Article 46 GDPR transfer tool you choose, you must ensure that, overall, the transferred personal data will have the benefit of an essentially equivalent level of protection.

23.   Article 46 GDPR transfer tools mainly contain appropriate safeguards of a contractual nature that may be applied to transfers to all third countries. The situation in the third country to which you are transferring data may still require that you supplement these transfer tools and the safeguards they contain with additional measures ("supplementary measures") to ensure an essentially equivalent level of protection.[35]

Derogations

24.   Besides adequacy decisions and Article 46 GDPR transfer tools, the GDPR contains a third avenue allowing transfers of personal data in certain situations. Subject to specific conditions, you may still be able to transfer personal data based on a derogation listed in Article 49 GDPR.

25.   Article 49 GDPR has an exceptional nature. The derogations it contains must be interpreted restrictively and mainly relate to processing activities that are occasional and non-repetitive. The EDPB has issued its Guidelines 2/2018 on derogations of Article 49 under Regulation 2016/679.[36]

26.   Before relying on an Article 49 GDPR derogation, you must check whether your transfer meets the strict conditions this provision sets forth for each of them.

***

27.   If your transfer can neither be legally based on an adequacy decision, nor on an Article 49 derogation, you need to continue with step 3.

2.3 STEP 3: ASSESS WHETHER THE ARTICLE 46 GDPR TRANSFER TOOL YOU ARE RELY-
       ING ON IS EFFECTIVE IN LIGHT OF ALL CIRCUMSTANCES OF THE TRANSFER

28.   Selecting an Article 46 GDPR transfer tool may not be enough. The transfer tool must ensure that the level of protection guaranteed by the GDPR is not undermined by the transfer.[37] In other words, your transfer tool must be effective in practice.

29.   Effective means that the transferred personal data is afforded a level of protection in the third country that is essentially equivalent to that are guaranteed in the EEA.[38] This is not the case if the data importer is prevented from complying with their obligations under the chosen Article 46 GDPR transfer tool due to the third country's legislation and practices applicable to the transfer.

30.   Therefore, you must assess, where appropriate in collaboration with the importer, if there is anything in the law or practice of the third country that may impinge on the effectiveness of the appropriate safeguards of the Article 46 GDPR transfer tool you are relying on, in the context of your specific transfer. Where appropriate, your data importer should provide you with the relevant sources and information relating to the third country in which it is established and the laws applicable to the transfer. You may also refer to other sources of information, such as the ones listed non-exhaustively in Annex 3.[39]

31.   Your assessment should take into consideration all the actors participating in the transfer (e.g. controllers, processors and sub-processors processing data in the third country), as identified in the mapping exercise of transfers. The more controllers, processors or importers involved, the more complex your assessment will be. You will also need to factor into this assessment any onward transfer that may occur.

32.   To this end, you will need to look into the characteristics of each of your transfers and determine how the domestic legal order of the country to which data is transferred (or onward transferred) applies to these transfers.

33.   The applicable legal context will depend on the circumstances of the transfer, in particular:
–   Purposes for which the data are transferred and processed (e.g. marketing, HR, storage, IT support, clinical trials);
–   Types of entities involved in the processing (public/private; controller/processor);
–   Sector in which the transfer occurs (e.g. adtech, telecommunication, financial, etc);
–   Categories of personal data transferred (e.g. personal data relating to children may fall within the scope of specific legislation in the third country);
–   Whether the data will be stored in the third country or whether there is only remote access to data stored within the EU/EEA;
–   Format of the data to be transferred (i.e. in plain text/ pseudonymised or encrypted[40]);
–   Possibility that the data may be subject to onward transfers from the third country to another third country.[41]

34.   Among the applicable laws, you will have to assess if any impinge on the commitments contained in the Article 46 GDPR transfer tool you have chosen. You should verify if commitments enabling data subjects to exercise their rights in the context of international transfers (such as access, correction and deletion requests for transferred data) can be effectively applied in practice and are not thwarted by law in the third country of destination.

35.   You will need to assess relevant rules of a general nature insofar as they have an impact on the effective application of the safeguards contained in the Article 46 GDPR transfer tool and the fundamental rights of individuals (in particular, the right of redress afforded to the data subject in case of access by third country public authorities to the transferred data).

36. You should in any case pay specific attention to any relevant laws, in particular laws laying down requirements to disclose personal data to public authorities or granting such public authorities powers of access to personal data (for instance for criminal law enforcement, regulatory supervision and national security purposes). If these requirements or powers are limited to what is necessary and proportionate in a democratic society,[42] they may not impinge on the commitments contained in the Article 46 GDPR transfer tool you are relying on.

37. EU standards, such as Articles 47 and 52 of the EU Charter of Fundamental Rights, must be used as a reference to assess whether such access by public authorities is limited to what is necessary and proportionate in a democratic society and whether data subjects are afforded effective redress.

38. In carrying out this assessment, different aspects of the legal system of that third country, e.g. the elements listed in Article 45(2) GDPR, are also be relevant.[43] For example, the rule of law situation in a third country may be relevant to assess the effectiveness of available mechanisms for individuals to obtain (judicial) redress against unlawful government access to personal data. The existence of a comprehensive data protection law or an independent data protection authority, as well as adherence to international instruments providing for data protection safeguards, may contribute to ensuring the proportionality of government interference.[44]

***

39. The EDPB European Essential Guarantees (EEG) recommendations provide elements which have to be assessed to determine whether the legal framework governing access to personal data by public authorities in a third country, being national security agencies or law enforcement authorities, can be regarded as a justifiable interference (and therefore as not impinging on the commitments taken in the art 46 GDPR transfer tool) or not. In particular, this should be carefully considered when the legislation governing the access to data by public authorities is ambiguous or not publicly available.

40. Applied to the situation of data transfers based on Article 46 transfer tools, the EDPB European Essential Guarantees recommendations can guide the data exporter and data importer in assessing whether such powers unjustifiably interfere with the data importer's obligations to ensure essential equivalence.

41. The lack of an essentially equivalent level of protection will be especially evident where the legislation or practice of the third country relevant to your transfer does not meet the requirements of the European Essential Guarantees.

42. Your assessment must be based first and foremost on legislation publicly available. However, in some situations this will not suffice because the legislation in the third countries may be lacking. In this case, if you still wish to envisage the transfer, you should look into other relevant and objective factors[45], and not rely on subjective ones such as the likelihood of public authorities' access to your data in a manner not in line with EU standards. You should conduct this assessment with due diligence and document it thoroughly, as you will be held accountable to the decision you may take on that basis.[46]

43. You may complete your assessment with information obtained from other sources[47], such as:
– Elements demonstrating that a third country authority will seek to access the data with or without the data importer's knowledge, in light of reported precedents, legislation and practice;
– Elements demonstrating that a third country authority will be able to access the data through the data importer or through direct interception of the communication channel in light of reported precedents, legal powers, and technical, financial, and human resources at its disposal.

44. Your assessment may ultimately reveal that the Article 46 GDPR transfer tool you rely on, and the appropriate safeguards it contains:
– Effectively ensures that the transferred personal data is afforded a level of protection in the third country that is essentially equivalent to that guaranteed within the EEA. The third country's legislation and practices applicable to the transfer put the data importer in a position to comply with its obligations under the chosen transfer tool. You should re-evaluate at appropriate intervals, or when significant changes come to light (see step 6).
– Does not effectively ensure an essentially equivalent level of protection. The data importer cannot comply with its obligations, owing to the third country's legislation and/or practices applicable to the transfer. The CJEU underlined that where Article 46 GDPR transfer tools fall short, it is the responsibility of the data exporter to either put in place effective supplementary measures or to not transfer personal data.[48]

> The CJEU held, for example, that Section 702 of the U.S. FISA does not respect the minimum safeguards resulting from the principle of proportionality under EU law and cannot be regarded as limited to what is strictly necessary. This means that the level of protection of the programs authorised by 702 FISA is not essentially equivalent to the safeguards required under EU law. As a consequence, if the data importer or any further recipient to which the data importer may disclose the data falls under 702 FISA[49], SCCs or other Article 46 GDPR transfer tools may only be relied upon for such transfer if additional supplementary technical measures make access to the data transferred impossible or ineffective.

2.4 STEP 4: ADOPT SUPPLEMENTARY MEASURES

45. If your assessment under step 3 has revealed that your Article 46 GDPR transfer tool is not effective, then you will need to consider, where appropriate in collaboration with the importer, if supplementary measures exist, which, when added to the safeguards contained in transfer tools, could ensure that the data transferred is afforded in the third country a level of protection essentially equivalent to that guaranteed within the EU.[50] "Supplementary measures" are by definition supplementary to the safeguards the Article 46 GDPR transfer tool already provides.[51]

46. You must identify on a case-by-case basis which supplementary measures could be effective for a set of transfers to a specific third country when using a specific Article 46 GDPR transfer tool. You will be able to build on your previous assessments under steps (1, 2 and 3 above) and check against their findings the potential effectiveness of the supplementary measures in guaranteeing the required level of protection.

47. In principle, supplementary measures may have a contractual, technical or organisational nature. Combining diverse measures in a way that they support and build on each other may enhance the level of protection and may therefore contribute to reaching EU standards.

48. Contractual and organisational measures alone will generally not overcome access to personal data by public authorities of the third country (where this unjustifiably interferes with the data importer's obligations to ensure essential equivalence). Indeed there will be situations where only technical measures might impede or render ineffective access by public authorities in third countries to personal data, in particular for surveillance purposes.[52] In such situations, contractual or organisational measures may complement technical measures and strengthen the overall level of protection of data, e.g. by creating obstacles for attempts from public authorities to access data in a manner not compliant with EU standards.

49. You may, in collaboration with the data importer where appropriate, look at the following (non-exhaustive) list of factors to identify which supplementary measures would be most effective in protecting the data transferred:
- Format of the data to be transferred (i.e. in plain text/pseudonymised or encrypted);
- Nature of the data;
- Length and complexity of data processing workflow, number of actors involved in the processing, and the relationship between them (e.g. do the transfers involve multiple controllers or both controllers and processors, or involvement of processors which will transfer the data from you to your data importer (considering the relevant provisions applicable to them under the legislation of the third country of destination));[53]
- Possibility that the data may be subject to onward transfers, within the same third country or even to other third countries (e.g. involvement of sub-processors of the data importer[54]).

Examples of supplementary measures

50. Some examples of technical, contractual and organisational measures that could be considered may be found in the non-exhaustive lists described in the Annex 2.

***

51. If you have put in place effective supplementary measures, which combined with your chosen Article 46 GDPR transfer tool reach a level of protection that is now essentially equivalent to the level of protection guaranteed within the EEA: your transfers may go ahead.

52. Where you are not able to find or implement effective supplementary measures that ensure that the transferred personal data enjoys an essentially equivalent level of protection,[55] you must not start transferring personal data to the third country concerned on the basis of the Article 46 GDPR transfer tool you are relying on. If you are already conducting transfers, you are required to suspend or end the transfer of personal data.[56] Pursuant to the safeguards contained in the Article 46 GDPR transfer tool you are relying on, the data that you have already transferred to that third country and the copies thereof should be returned to you or destroyed in their entirety by the importer.[57]

> Example: the law of the third country prohibits the supplementary measures you have identified (e.g. prohibits the use of encryption) or otherwise prevents their effectiveness. You must not start transferring personal data to this country, or you must stop ongoing existing transfers to this country.

53. If you decide to continue with the transfer notwithstanding the fact that the importer is unable to comply with the commitments taken in the Article 46 GDPR transfer tool, you should notify the competent supervisory authority in accordance with the specific provisions inserted in the relevant Article 46 GDPR transfer tool.[58] The competent supervisory authority will suspend or prohibit data transfers in those cases where it finds that an essentially equivalent level of protection cannot be ensured.[59]

54. The competent supervisory authority may impose any other corrective measure (e.g. a fine) if, despite the fact that you cannot demonstrate an essentially equivalent level of protection in the third country, you start or continue the transfer.

2.5 STEP 5: PROCEDURAL STEPS IF YOU HAVE IDENTIFIED EFFECTIVE SUPPLEMENTARY MEASURES

55. The procedural steps you may have to take in case you have identified effective supplementary measures to be put in place may differ depending on the Article 46 GDPR transfer tool you are using or you envisage to use.

2.5.1 Standard data protection clauses ("SCCs") (Art. 46(2)(c) and (d) GDPR)

56. When you intend to put in place supplementary measures in addition to SCCs, there is no need for you to request an authorisation from the competent SA to add these kind of clauses or additional safeguards as long as the identified supplementary measures do not contradict, directly or indirectly, the SCCs and are sufficient to ensure that the level of protection guaranteed by the GDPR is not undermined.[60] The data exporter and importer need to ensure that additional clauses cannot be construed in any way to restrict the rights and obligations in the SCCs or in any other way to lower the level of data protection. You should be able to demonstrate this, including the unambiguity of all clauses, according to the accountability principle and your obligation to provide for a sufficient level of data protection. The competent supervisory authorities have the power to review these supplementary clauses where required (e.g. in case of complaint or own-volition inquiry).

57. Where you intend to modify the standard data protection clauses themselves or where the supplementary measures added 'contradict' directly or indirectly the SCCs, you are no longer deemed to be relying on standard contractual clauses[61] and must seek an authorisation with the competent supervisory authority in accordance with Article 46(3)(a) GDPR.

2.5.2 BCRs (Art. 46(2)(b) GDPR)

58. The reasoning put forward by the Schrems II judgment also applies to other transfer instruments pursuant to Article 46(2) GDPR since all of these instruments are basically of contractual nature, so the guarantees foreseen and the commitments taken by the parties therein cannot bind third country public authorities.[62]

59. The Schrems II judgement is relevant for transfers of personal data on the basis of BCRs, since third countries laws may affect the protection provided by such instruments. The precise impact of the Schrems II judgment on BCRs is still under discussion. The EDPB will provide more details as soon as possible as to whether any additional commitments may need to be included in the BCRs in the WP256/257 referentials.[63]

60. The Court highlighted that it is the responsibility of the data exporter and the data importer to assess whether the level of protection required by EU law is respected in the third country concerned in order to determine if the guarantees provided by the SCCs or the BCRs can be complied with in practice. If this is not the case, you should assess whether you can provide supplementary measures to ensure an essentially equivalent level of protection as provided in the EEA, and if the law or practice of the third country will not impinge on these supplementary measures so as to prevent their effectiveness.

2.5.3 Ad hoc contractual clauses (Art. 46.3(a) GDPR)

61. The reasoning put forward by the Schrems II judgment also applies to other transfer instruments pursuant to Article 46 (2) GDPR since all of these instruments are basically of contractual nature, so the guarantees foreseen and the commitments taken by the parties therein cannot bind third country public authorities.[64] The Schrems II judgement is therefore relevant for transfers of personal data on the basis of ad hoc contractual clauses, since third countries laws may affect the protection provided by such instruments. The precise impact of the Schrems II judgment on ad hoc clauses is still under discussion. The EDPB will provide more details as soon as possible.

2.6 STEP 6: RE-EVALUATE AT APPROPRIATE INTERVALS

62. You must monitor, on an ongoing basis, and where appropriate in collaboration with data importers, developments in the third country to which you have transferred personal data that could affect your initial assessment of the level of protection and the decisions you may have taken accordingly on your transfers. Accountability is a continuing obligation (Article 5(2) GDPR).

63. You should put sufficiently sound mechanisms in place to ensure that you promptly suspend or end transfers where:
–   the importer has breached or is unable to honour the commitments it has taken in the Article 46 GDPR transfer tool; or
–   the supplementary measures are no longer effective in that third country.

NOTES

19   See EDPB Guidelines 3/2018 on the territorial scope of the GDPR (Article 3) https://edpb.europa.eu/our-work-tools/our-documents/guidelines/guidelines-32018-territorial-scope-gdpr-article-3-version_en

20   EDPB Guidelines 2/2020 on Articles 46 (2)(a) and 46 (3)(b) of Regulation 2016/679 for transfers of personal data between EEA and non-EEA public authorities and bodies; see https://edpb.europa.eu/our-work-tools/public-consultations-art-704/2020/guidelines-22020-articles-46-2-and-46-3-b_en

21   Article 5(2) GDPR and Article 24 (1) GDPR.

22   Please note that remote access by an entity from a third country to data located in the EEA is also considered a transfer.

23   See Article 30 GDPR and in particular paragraphs 1.e and 2.c. Moreover, your records of processing should contain a description of your processing activities (including, but not limited to, the categories of data subjects, the categories of personal data and purposes of the processing and specific information about data transfers. Some controllers and processors are exempt from the obligation to keep records of processing (Article 30.5 GDPR). For guidance on this exemption, see Article 29 Working Party, Position Paper on the derogations from the obligation to maintain records of processing activities pursuant to Article 30.5 GDPR (endorsed by the EDPB on 25 May 2018).

24   Under GDPR transparency rules, you must inform data subjects about transfers of personal data to third countries (Articles 13.1.f and 14.1.f GDPR). In particular, you must inform them of the existence or absence of an adequacy decision by the European Commission, or in the case of transfers referred to in Articles 46 or 47 GDPR, or the second subparagraph of Article 49.1 GDPR, refer to the appropriate or suitable safeguards and the means by which to obtain a copy of them or where they have been made available. The information provided to the data subject must be correct and current, especially in light of the Court's case law concerning transfers.

25 Where the controller has granted its prior specific or general written authorisation in accordance with Article 28.2 GDPR.

26 Article 5.1.c GDPR.

27 See FAQ nr. 11 "*it should be borne in mind that even providing access to data from a third country, for instance for administration purposes, also amounts to a transfer*", EDPB Frequently Asked Questions on the judgment of the Court of Justice of the European Union in Case C-311/18 - Data Protection Commissioner v Facebook Ireland Ltd and Maximillian Schrems, 23 July 2020.

28 The European Commission has the power to determine, on the basis of Article 45 GDPR whether a country outside the EU offers an adequate level of data protection. Likewise the European Commission has the power to determine that an international organisation offers an adequate level of protection.

29 Article 45.1 GDPR.

30 https://ec.europa.eu/info/law/law-topic/data-protection/international-dimension-data-protection/adequacy-decisions_en

31 Provided you and data importer have implemented measures to comply with the other obligations under the GDPR; otherwise implement those measures.

32 The European Commission must review periodically all adequacy decisions and monitor if the third countries benefitting from adequacy decisions continue to ensure an adequate level of protection (see Art. 45.3 and 45.4 GDPR). Also, the CJEU may invalidate adequacy decisions (see its judgments on the cases C-362/14 (Schrems I) and C-311/18 (Schrems II)).

33 C-311/18 (Schrems II), paragraphs 118 - 120. Supervisory authorities may not disregard the adequacy decision and suspend or prohibit transfers of personal data to such countries citing only the inadequacy of the level of protection. They may only exercise their power to suspend or prohibit transfers of personal data to that third country on other grounds (e.g. insufficient security measures in violation of Article 32 GDPR, no legal basis validly underpins the data processing as such in violation of Article 6 GDPR). Supervisory authorities may examine, with complete independence, whether the transfer of that data complies with the requirements laid down by the GDPR and, where relevant, bring an action before the national courts in order for them, if they have doubts as to the validity of the Commission adequacy decision, to make a reference for a preliminary ruling before the European Court of Justice for the purposes of examining its validity.

34 Case C-362/14 (Schrems I).

35 C-311/18 (Schrems II), paragraphs 130 and 133. See also point 2.3 below.

36 For further guidance on this see https://edpb.europa.eu/our-work-tools/our-documents/guidelines/guidelines-22018-derogations-article-49-under-regulation_en.

37 Article 44 GDPR.

38 C-311/18 (Schrems II), paragraphs 105 and second finding.

39 See also paragraph 43 here below.

40 Some third countries do not permit encrypted data to be imported.

41 Where the controller has granted its prior specific or general written authorisation in accordance with Article 28.2 GDPR.

42 See Articles 47 and 52 of the EU Charter of Fundamental Rights, Article 23.1 GDPR, and EDPB Recommendations 02/2020 on the European Essential Guarantees for surveillance measures, 10 November 2020, https://edpb.europa.eu/our-work-tools/our-documents/recommendations/edpb-recommendations-022020-european-essential_en.

43 C-311/18 (Schrems II), paragraph 104.

44 For instance: Convention 108 (Convention for the Protection of Individuals with regard to Automatic Processing of Personal Data, ETS no. 108) or Convention 108+ (Modernised Convention for the Protection of Individuals with Regard to the Processing of Personal Data, CETS no 223) provide enforceable, international legal remedies in case of data protection violations and contribute to provide a minimum level of protection of personal data and respect for private life.

45 See paragraph 43 here below as well as Annex 3.

46 Art. 5(2) GDPR.

47 See also Annex 3.

48 CJEU C-311/18 (Schrems II), paragraph 134-135.

49 FISA 702 is applicable if the data is obtained "from or with the assistance of an electronic communication service provider" (Section 702 FISA = 50 USC § 1881a, under (h)(2)(A)(vi)), which in turn is defined in 50 USC § 1881b)(4) as

> "(A) a telecommunications carrier, as that term is defined in section 153 of title 47;
> (B) a provider of electronic communication service, as that term is defined in section 2510 of title 18;
> (C) a provider of a remote computing service, as that term is defined in section 2711 of title 18;
> (D) any other communication service provider who has access to wire or electronic communications either as such communications are transmitted or as such communications are stored; or
> (E) an officer, employee, or agent of an entity described in subparagraph (A), (B), (C), or (D)."

50 C-311/18 (Schrems II), paragraph 96.

51 Recital 109 of the GDPR and C-311/18 (Schrems II), paragraph 133.

52 Where such access goes beyond what is necessary and proportionate in a democratic society; see Articles 47 and 52 of the EU Charter of Fundamental Rights, Article 23.1 GDPR, and EDPB Recommendations 02/2020 on the European Essential Guarantees for surveillance measures, 10 November 2020, https://edpb.europa.eu/our-work-tools/our-documents/recommendations/edpb-recommendations-022020-european-essential_en.

53 The GDPR assigns distinct obligations to controllers and processors. Transfers can be controller-to-controller, between joint controllers, controller-to-processor, and, subject to the authorisation of the controller, processor-to-controller or processor-to-processor.

54 See footnote 25.

55 Where such access goes beyond what is necessary and proportionate in a democratic society; see Articles 47 and 52 of the EU Charter of Fundamental Rights, Article 23.1 GDPR, and EDPB Recommendations 02/2020 on the European Essential Guarantees for surveillance measures, 10 November 2020, https://edpb.europa.eu/our-work-tools/our-documents/recommendations/edpb-recommendations-022020-european-essential_en.

56 C-311/18 (Schrems II), paragraph 135.

57 See Clause 12 in the annex to the SCC Decision 87/2010; see the (optional) Extra termination clause in Annex B SCC 2004/915/EC.

58   See EDPB Frequently Asked Questions on the judgment of the Court of Justice of the European Union in Case C-311/18 - Data Protection Commissioner v Facebook Ireland Ltd and Maximillian Schrems adopted 23 July 2020 and in particular FAQ 5, 6 and 9. See also Clause 4(g) Commission Decision 2010/87/EU; Clause 5(a) Commission Decision 2001/497/EC and Annex 'Set II' clause II (c) of Commission Decision 2004/915/EC.

59   C-311/18 (Schrems II), paragraphs 113 and 121.

60   Recital 109 of the GDPR states: "The possibility for the controller or processor to use standard data-protection clauses adopted by the Commission or by a supervisory authority should prevent controllers or processors neither from including the standard data-protection clauses in a wider contract, such as a contract between the processor and another processor, nor from adding other clauses or additional safeguards provided that they do not contradict, directly or indirectly, the standard contractual clauses adopted by the Commission or by a supervisory authority or prejudice the fundamental rights or freedoms of the data subjects." Similar provisions are provided in sets of SCCs adopted by the European Commission under Directive 95/45/EC.

61   See by analogy, the EDPB Opinion 17/2020 on the draft Standard Contractual Clauses submitted by the Slovenian SA (Article 28(8) GDPR) on Art. 28 SCC already adopted which contains a similar provision ("In addition, the Board recalls that the possibility to use Standard Contractual Clauses adopted by a supervisory authority does not prevent the parties from adding other clauses or additional safeguards provided that they do not contradict, directly or indirectly, the adopted standard contractual clauses or prejudice the fundamental rights or freedoms of the data subjects. Furthermore, where the standard data protection clauses are modified, the parties will no longer be deemed to have implemented adopted standard contractual clauses"), https://edpb.europa.eu/sites/edpb/files/files/file1/edpb_opinion_202017_art28sccs_si_en.pdf.

62   CJEU, C-311/18 (Schrems II), paragraph 132.

63   Article 29 Working Party, Working Document setting up a table with the elements and principles to be found in Binding Corporate Rules, as last revised and adopted on 6 February 2018, WP 256 rev.01; Article 29 Working Party, Working Document setting up a table with the elements and principles to be found in Binding Corporate Rules, as last revised and adopted on 6 February 2018, WP 257 rev.01.

64   CJEU, C-311/18 (Schrems II), paragraph 132.

3 CONCLUSION

[2.389]

64. The GDPR lays down rules on processing personal data in the EEA and in doing so allows for free movement of personal data within the EEA. Chapter V of the GDPR governs transfers of personal data to third countries and sets a high bar: the transfer must not undermine the level of protection of natural persons guaranteed by the GDPR (Article 44 GDPR). The CJEU C-311/18 (Schrems II) judgement underscores the need to ensure the continuity of the level of protection afforded under the GDPR to personal data transferred to a third country.[65]

65. To ensure an essentially equivalent level of protection of your data, you must first and foremost know thoroughly your transfers. You must also check that the data you transfer is adequate, relevant and limited to what is necessary in relation to the purposes for which it is transferred to and processed in the third country.

66. You must also identify the transfer tool you are relying on for your transfers. If the transfer tool is not an adequacy decision, you must verify on a case-by-case basis whether (or not) the law or practice of the third country of destination undermines the safeguards contained in the Article 46 GDPR transfer tool in the context of your transfers. Where the Article 46 GDPR transfer tool alone fails to achieve for the personal data you transfer a level of protection essentially equivalent, supplementary measures may fill the gap.

67. Where you are not able to find or implement effective supplementary measures that ensure that the transferred personal data enjoys an essentially equivalent level of protection, you must not start transferring personal data to the third country concerned on the basis of your chosen transfer tool. If you are already conducting transfers, you are required to promptly suspend or end the transfer of personal data.

68. The competent supervisory authority has the power to suspend or end transfers of personal data to the third country if the protection of the data transferred that EU law requires, in particular Articles 45 and 46 GDPR and the Charter of Fundamental Rights, is not ensured.

For the European Data Protection Board

The Chair

(Andrea Jelinek)

NOTES

65   C-311/18 (Schrems II), paragraph 93.

ANNEX 1: DEFINITIONS

[2.390]

. . .

- "Third country" means any country that is not a Member State of the EEA.
- "EEA" means the European Economic Area and it includes the Member States of the European Union and Iceland, Norway and Liechtenstein. The GDPR applies to the latter by virtue of the EEA Agreement, in particular its Annex XI and Protocol 37.
- "GDPR" refers to Regulation (EU) 2016/679 of the European Parliament and of the Council of 27 April 2016 on the protection of natural persons with regard to the processing of personal data and on the free movement of such data, and repealing Directive 95/46/EC (General Data Protection Regulation).

- "The Charter" refers to the Charter of Fundamental Rights of the European Union, OJ C 326, 26.10.2012, p. 391–407.
- "CJEU" or "the Court" refer to the Court of Justice of the European Union. It constitutes the judicial authority of the European Union and, in cooperation with the courts and tribunals of the Member States, it ensures the uniform application and interpretation of EU law.
- "Data exporter" means the controller or processor within the EEA who transfers personal data to a controller or processor in a third country.
- "Data importer" means the controller or processor in a third country who receives or gets access to personal data transferred from the EEA.
- "Article 46 GDPR transfer tool": refers to the appropriate safeguards under Article 46 GDPR that data exporters shall put in place when transferring personal data to a third country, in the absence of an adequacy decision pursuant to Article 45(3) GDPR. Article 46(2) and (3) of the GDPR contains the list of Article 46 GDPR transfer tools that controllers and processors may use.
- "SCCs" means standard data protection clauses (or "standard contractual clauses") adopted by the European Commission for personal data transfers between controllers or processors in the EEA and controllers or processors outside the EEA. Standard contractual clauses adopted by the European Commission are a transfer tool under the GDPR, as per Article 46(2)(c) and (5) GDPR.

ANNEX 2: EXAMPLES OF SUPPLEMENTARY MEASURES

[2.391]
69. The following measures are examples of supplementary measures you could consider when you reach Step 4 "Adopt supplementary measures". This list is not exhaustive. Selecting and implementing one or several of these measures will not necessarily and systematically ensure that your transfer meets the essential equivalence standard that EU law requires. You should select those supplementary measures that can effectively guarantee this level of protection for your transfers.

70. Any supplementary measure may only be deemed effective in the meaning of the CJEU judgment "Schrems II" if and to the extent that it addresses the specific deficiencies identified in your assessment of the legal situation in the third country. If, ultimately, you cannot ensure an essentially equivalent level of protection, you must not transfer the personal data.

71. As a controller or processor, you may already be required to implement some of the measures described in this annex, even if your data importer is covered by an adequacy decision, just as you may be required to implement them when you process data within the EEA.[66]

TECHNICAL MEASURES

72. This section describes in a non-exhaustive manner examples of technical measures, which may supplement safeguards found in Article 46 GDPR transfer tools to ensure compliance with the level of protection required under EU law in the context of a transfer of personal data to a third country. These measures will be especially needed where the law of that country imposes on the data importer obligations which are contrary to the safeguards of Article 46 GDPR transfer tools and are, in particular, capable of impinging on the contractual guarantee of an essentially equivalent level of protection against access by the public authorities of that third country to that data[67].

73. For further clarity, this section specifies first the technical measures that could potentially be effective in certain scenarios/use-cases to ensure an essentially equivalent level of protection. The section continues with some scenarios/use cases in which no technical measures could be found to ensure this level of protection.

Scenarios for which *effective* measures could be found

74. The measures listed below are intended to ensure that access to the transferred data by public authorities in third countries does not impinge on the effectiveness of the appropriate safeguards contained in the Article 46 GDPR transfer tools. These measures apply even if the public authorities' access complies with the law of the importer's country, where such access goes beyond what is necessary and proportionate in a democratic society[68]. These measures aim to preclude potentially infringing access by preventing the authorities from identifying the data subjects, inferring information about them, singling them out in another context, or associating the transferred data with other datasets they may possess that may contain, among other data, online identifiers provided by the devices, applications, tools and protocols used by data subjects in other contexts.

75. Public authorities in third countries may endeavour to access transferred data
(a) In transit by accessing the lines of communication used to convey the data to the recipient country. This access may be passive in which case the contents of the communication, possibly after a selection process, are simply copied. The access may, however, also be active in the sense that the public authorities interpose themselves into the communication process by not only reading the content, but also manipulating or suppressing parts of it.
(b) While in custody by an intended recipient of the data by either accessing the processing facilities themselves, or by requiring a recipient of the data to locate, and extract data of interest and turn it over to the authorities.

76. This section considers scenarios where measures are applied that are effective in both cases. Different supplementary measures may apply and be sufficient in the given circumstance of a concrete transfer if only one type of access is foreseen by the law of the recipient country. It is therefore necessary for the data exporter to carefully analyse, with the support of the data importer, the obligations laid upon the latter.

> As an example, US data importers that fall under 50 USC § 1881a (FISA 702) are under a direct obligation to grant access to or turn over imported personal data that are in their possession, custody or control. This may extend to any cryptographic keys necessary to render the data intelligible.

77. The scenarios describe specific circumstances, and measures taken. Any changes to the scenarios may give rise to different conclusions.

78. Controllers may have to apply some or all of the measures described here irrespective of the level of protection provided for by the laws applicable to the data importer because they are needed to comply with Articles 25 and 32 GDPR in the concrete circumstances of the transfer. In other words, exporters may be required to implement the measures described in this paper even if their data importers are covered by an adequacy decision, just as controllers and processors may be required to implement them when data is processed within the EEA.

Use Case 1: Data storage for backup and other purposes that do not require access to data in the clear

79. A data exporter uses a hosting service provider in a third country to store personal data, e.g., for backup purposes.

If

(1)   the personal data is processed using strong encryption before transmission,

(2)   the encryption algorithm and its parameterization (e.g., key length, operating mode, if applicable) conform to the state-of-the-art and can be considered robust against cryptanalysis performed by the public authorities in the recipient country taking into account the resources and technical capabilities (e.g., computing power for brute-force attacks) available to them,

(3)   the strength of the encryption takes into account the specific time period during which the confidentiality of the encrypted personal data must be preserved,

(4)   the encryption algorithm is flawlessly implemented by properly maintained software the conformity of which to the specification of the algorithm chosen has been verified, e.g., by certification,

(5)   the keys are reliably managed (generated, administered, stored, if relevant, linked to the identity of an intended recipient, and revoked), and

6. the keys are retained solely under the control of the data exporter, or other entities entrusted with this task which reside in the EEA or a third country, territory or one or more specified sectors within a third country, or at an international organisation for which the Commission has established in accordance with Article 45 GDPR that an adequate level of protection is ensured,

then the EDPB considers that the encryption performed provides an effective supplementary measure.

Use Case 2: Transfer of pseudonymised Data

80. A data exporter first pseudonymises data it holds, and then transfers it to a third country for analysis, e.g., for purposes of research.

If

(1)   a data exporter transfers personal data processed in such a manner that the personal data can no longer be attributed to a specific data subject, nor be used to single out the data subject in a larger group, without the use of additional information[69],

(2)   that additional information is held exclusively by the data exporter and kept separately in a Member State or in a third country, territory or one or more specified sectors within a third country, or at an international organisation for which the Commission has established in accordance with Article 45 GDPR that an adequate level of protection is ensured,

(3)   disclosure or unauthorised use of that additional information is prevented by appropriate technical and organisational safeguards, it is ensured that the data exporter retains sole control of the algorithm or repository that enables re-identification using the additional information, and

(4)   the controller has established by means of a thorough analysis of the data in question taking into account any information that the public authorities of the recipient country may possess that the pseudonymised personal data cannot be attributed to an identified or identifiable natural person even if cross-referenced with such information,

then the EDPB considers that the pseudonymisation performed provides an effective supplementary measure.

81. Note that in many situations, factors specific to the physical, physiological, genetic, mental, economic, cultural or social identity of a natural person, their physical location or their interaction with an internet based service at specific points in time[70] may allow the identification of that person even if their name, address or other plain identifiers are omitted.

82. This is particularly true whenever the data concern the use of information services (time of access, sequence of features accessed, characteristics of the device used etc.). These services might well be, as for the importer of personal data, under the obligation to grant access to the same public authorities in their jurisdiction, which will then likely possess data about the use of those information services by the person(s) they target.

83. Moreover, given the use of some information services is public by nature, or their exploitability by parties with substantial resources, controllers will have to take extra care considering that public authorities in their jurisdiction likely possess data about the use of information services by a person they target.

Use Case 3: Encrypted data merely transiting third countries

84. A data exporter wishes to transfer data to a destination recognised as offering adequate protection in accordance with Article 45 GDPR. The data is routed via a third country.

If

(1)   a data exporter transfers personal data to a data importer in a jurisdiction ensuring adequate protection, the data is transported over the internet, and the data may be geographically routed through a third country not providing an essentially equivalent level of protection,

(2)   transport encryption is used for which it is ensured that the encryption protocols employed are state-of-the-art and provide effective protection against active and passive attacks with resources known to be available to the public authorities of the third country,

(3)   decryption is only possible outside the third country in question,

(4)   the parties involved in the communication agree on a trustworthy public-key certification authority or infrastructure,

(5)   specific protective and state-of-the-art measures are used against active and passive attacks on transport-encrypted,

(6)   in case the transport encryption does not provide appropriate security by itself due to experience with vulnerabilities of the infrastructure or the software used, personal data is also encrypted end-to-end on the application layer using state-of-the-art encryption methods,

(7)   the encryption algorithm and its parameterization (e.g., key length, operating mode, if applicable) conform to the state-of-the-art and can be considered robust against cryptanalysis performed by the public authorities in the transiting country taking into account the resources and technical capabilities (e.g., computing power for brute-force attacks) available to them,

(8)   the strength of the encryption takes into account the specific time period during which the confidentiality of the encrypted personal data must be preserved,

(9)   the encryption algorithm is flawlessly implemented by properly maintained software the conformity of which to the specification of the algorithm chosen has been verified, e.g., by certification,

(10)   the existence of backdoors (in hardware or software) has been ruled out,

(11)   the keys are reliably managed (generated, administered, stored, if relevant, linked to the identity of the intended recipient, and revoked), by the exporter or by an entity trusted by the exporter under a jurisdiction offering an essentially equivalent level of protection,

then the EDPB considers that transport encryption, if needed in combination with end-to-end content encryption, provides an effective supplementary measure.

Use Case 4: Protected recipient

85. A data exporter transfers personal data to a data importer in a third country specifically protected by that country's law, e.g., for the purpose to jointly provide medical treatment for a patient, or legal services to a client.

If

(1)   the law of a third country exempts a resident data importer from potentially infringing access to data held by that recipient for the given purpose, e.g. by virtue of a duty to professional secrecy applying to the data importer,

(2)   that exemption extends to all information in the possession of the data importer that may be used to circumvent the protection of privileged information (cryptographic keys, passwords, other credentials, etc.),

(3)   the data importer does not employ the services of a processor in a way that allows the public authorities to access the data while held by the processor, nor does the data importer forward the data to another entity that is not protected, on the basis of Article 46 GDPR transfer tools,

(4)   the personal data is encrypted before it is transmitted with a method conforming to the state of the art guaranteeing that decryption will not be possible without knowledge of the decryption key (end-to-end encryption) for the whole length of time the data needs to be protected,

(5)   the decryption key is in the sole custody of the protected data importer, and appropriately secured against unauthorised use or disclosure by technical and organisational measures conforming to the state of the art, and

(6)   the data exporter has reliably established that the encryption key it intends to use corresponds to the decryption key held by the recipient,

then the EDPB considers that the transport encryption performed provides an effective supplementary measure.

Use Case 5: Split or multi-party processing

86. The data exporter wishes personal data to be processed jointly by two or more independent processors located in different jurisdictions without disclosing the content of the data to them. Prior to transmission, it splits the data in such a way that no part an individual processor receives suffices to reconstruct the personal data in whole or in part. The data exporter receives the result of the processing from each of the processors independently, and merges the pieces received to arrive at the final result which may constitute personal or aggregated data.

If

(1)   a data exporter processes personal data in such a manner that it is split into two or more parts each of which can no longer be interpreted or attributed to a specific data subject without the use of additional information,

(2)   each of the pieces is transferred to a separate processor located in a different jurisdiction,

(3)   the processors optionally process the data jointly, e.g. using secure multi-party computation, in a way that no information is revealed to any of them that they do not possess prior to the computation,

(4)   the algorithm used for the shared computation is secure against active adversaries,

(5)   there is no evidence of collaboration between the public authorities located in the respective jurisdictions where each of the processors are located, which would allow them access to all sets of personal data held by the processors and enable them to reconstitute and exploit the content of the personal data in a clear form in circumstances where such exploitation would not respect the essence of the fundamental rights and freedoms of the data subjects. Similarly, public authorities of either country should not have the authority to access personal data held by processors in all jurisdictions concerned.

(6)   the controller has established by means of a thorough analysis of the data in question, taking into account any information that the public authorities of the recipient countries may possess, that the pieces of personal data it transmits to the processors cannot be attributed to an identified or identifiable natural person even if cross-referenced with such information,

then the EDPB considers that the split processing performed provides an effective supplementary measure.

Scenarios in which *no effective* measures could be found

87.   The measures described below under certain scenarios would not be effective in ensuring an essentially equivalent level of protection for the data transferred to the third country. Therefore, they would not qualify as supplementary measures.

Use Case 6: Transfer to cloud services providers or other processors which require access to data in the clear

88.   A data exporter uses a cloud service provider or other processor to have personal data processed according to its instructions in a third country.

If

(1)   a controller transfers data to a cloud service provider or other processor,

(2)   the cloud service provider or other processor needs access to the data in the clear in order to execute the task assigned, and

(3)   the power granted to public authorities of the recipient country to access the transferred data goes beyond what is necessary and proportionate in a democratic society,[71]

then the EDPB is, considering the current state of the art, incapable of envisioning an effective technical measure to prevent that access from infringing on data subject rights. The EDPB does not rule out that further technological development may offer measures that achieve the intended business purposes, without requiring access in the clear.

89.   In the given scenarios, where unencrypted personal data is technically necessary for the provision of the service by the processor, transport encryption and data-at-rest encryption even taken together, do not constitute a supplementary measure that ensures an essentially equivalent level of protection if the data importer is in possession of the cryptographic keys.

Use Case 7: Remote access to data for business purposes

90.   A data exporter makes personal data available to entities in a third country to be used for shared business purposes. A typical constellation may consist of a controller or processor established on the territory of a Member State transferring personal data to a controller or processor in a third country belonging to the same group of undertakings, or group of enterprises engaged in a joint economic activity. The data importer may, for example, use the data it receives to provide personnel services for the data exporter for which it needs human resources data, or to communicate with customers of the data exporter who live in the European Union by phone or email.

If

(1)   a data exporter transfers personal data to a data importer in a third country by making it available in a commonly used information system in a way that allows the importer direct access of data of its own choice, or by transferring it directly, individually or in bulk, through use of a communication service,

(2)   the importer uses the data in the clear for its own purposes,

(3)   the power granted to public authorities of the recipient country to access the transferred data goes beyond what is necessary and proportionate in a democratic society,

then the EDPB is incapable of envisioning an effective technical measure to prevent that access from infringing on data subject rights.

91.   In the given scenarios, where unencrypted personal data is technically necessary for the provision of the service by the processor, transport encryption and data-at-rest encryption even taken together, do not constitute a supplementary measure that ensures an essentially equivalent level of protection if the data importer is in possession of the cryptographic keys.

ADDITIONAL CONTRACTUAL MEASURES

92. These measures will generally consist of unilateral, bilateral or multilateral[72] contractual commitments.[73] If an Article 46 GDPR transfer tool is used, it will in most cases already contain a number of (mostly contractual) commitments by the data exporter and the data importer aimed at serving as safeguards for the personal data.[74]

93. In some situations, these measures may complement and reinforce the safeguards the transfer tool and relevant legislation of the third country may provide, when, taking into account the circumstances of the transfer, these do not meet all the conditions required to ensure a level of protection essentially equivalent to that guaranteed within the EU. Provided the nature of contractual measures, generally not capable of binding the authorities of that third country, when they are not party to the contract[75], these measures should be combined with other technical and organisational measures to provide the level of data protection required. Selecting and implementing one or several of these measures will not necessarily and systematically ensure that your transfer meets the essential equivalence standard that EU law requires.

94. Depending on what contractual measures are already included in the Article 46 GDPR transfer tool that is relied on, additional contractual measures may also be helpful to allow EEA-based data exporters to become aware of new developments affecting the protection of the data transferred to third countries.

95. As said, contractual measures will not be able to rule out the application of the legislation of a third country which does not meet the EDPB European Essential Guarantees standard in those cases in which the legislation obliges importers to comply with the orders to disclose data they receive from public authorities.[76]

96. Some examples of these potential contractual measures are listed below and classified in accordance with their nature:

Providing for the contractual obligation to use specific technical measures

97. *Depending on the specific circumstances of the transfers, the contract may need to provide that for transfers to take place, specific technical measures would have to be put in place (see supra the technical measures suggested).*

98. *Conditions for effectiveness:*
–   This clause could be effective in those situations where the need for technical measures has been identified by the exporter. It would then have to be provided in a legal form to ensure that the importer also commits to put in place the necessary technical measures if need be.

Transparency obligations:

99. *The exporter could add annexes to the contract with information that the importer would provide, based on its best efforts, on the access to data by public authorities, including in the field of intelligence provided the legislation complies with the EDPB European Essential Guarantees, in the destination country. This might help the data exporter to meet its obligation to document its assessment of the level of protection in the third country.*

100. The importer could be for instance required to:
(1)   enumerate the laws and regulations in the destination country applicable to the importer or its (sub) processors that would permit access by public authorities to the personal data that are subject to the transfer, in particular in the areas of intelligence, law enforcement, administrative and regulatory supervision applicable to the transferred data;
(2)   in the absence of laws governing the public authorities' access to data provide information and statistics based on the importer's experience or reports from various sources (e.g. partners, open sources, national case law and decisions from oversight bodies) on access by public authorities to personal data in situations of the kind of the data transfer at hand (i.e. in the specific regulatory area; regarding the type of entities to which the data importer belongs; . . .)
(3)   indicate which measures are taken to prevent the access to transferred data (if any);
(4)   provide sufficiently detailed information on all requests of access to personal data by public authorities which the importer has received over a specified period of time,[77] in particular in the areas mentioned under (1) above and comprising information about the requests received, the data requested, the requesting body and the legal basis for disclosure and to what extent the importer has disclosed the data request;[78]
(5)   specify whether and to what extent the importer is legally prohibited to provide the information mentioned under (1) – (5) above.

101. This information could be provided by way of structured questionnaires that the importer would fill in and sign and compounded by the importer's contractual obligation to declare within a set period of time any potential change to this information, as is current practice for due diligence processes.

102. *Conditions for effectiveness:*
–   The importer must be able to provide the exporter with these types of information to the best of its knowledge and after having used its best efforts to obtain it.[79]
–   This obligation imposed on the importer is a means to ensure that the exporter becomes and remains aware of the risks attached to the transfer of data to a third country. It will thus enable the exporter to desist from concluding the contract, or if the information changes following its conclusion, to fulfil its obligation to suspend the transfer and/or terminate the contract if the law

of the third country, the safeguards contained in the Article 46 GDPR transfer tool used and any additional safeguards it may have adopted can no longer ensure a level of protection essentially equivalent to that in the EU. This obligation can however neither justify the importer's disclosure of personal data nor give rise to the expectation that there will be no further access requests.

***

103. *The exporter could also add clauses whereby the importer certifies that (1) it has not purposefully created back doors or similar programming that could be used to access the system and/or personal data (2) it has not purposefully created or changed its business processes in a manner that facilitates access to personal data or systems, and (3) that national law or government policy does not require the importer to create or maintain back doors or to facilitate access to personal data or systems or for the importer to be in possession or to hand over the encryption key.*[80]

104. *Conditions for effectiveness:*
–   The existence of legislation or government policies preventing importers from disclosing this information may render this clause ineffective. The importer will thus not be able to enter into the contract or will need to notify to the exporter of its inability to continue complying with its contractual commitments.[81]
–   The contract must include penalties and/or the exporter's ability to terminate the contract on short notice in those cases in which the importer does not reveal the existence of a back door or similar programming or manipulated business processes or any requirement to implement any of these or fails to promptly inform the exporter once their existence comes to its knowledge.

***

105. *The exporter could reinforce its power to conduct audits*[82] *or inspections of the data processing facilities of the importer, on-site and/or remotely, to verify if data was disclosed to public authorities and under which conditions (access not beyond what is necessary and proportionate in a democratic society), for instance by providing for a short notice and mechanisms ensuring the rapid intervention of inspection bodies and reinforcing the autonomy of the exporter in selecting the inspection bodies.*

106. *Conditions for effectiveness:*
–   The scope of the audit should legally and technically cover any processing by the importer's processors or sub-processors of the personal data transmitted in the third country to be fully effective.
–   Access logs and other similar trails should be tamper proof so that the auditors can find evidence of disclosure. Access logs and other similar trails should also distinguish between accesses due to regular business operations and accesses due to orders or requests for access.

***

107. *Where the law and practice of the third country of the importer was initially assessed and deemed to provide an essentially equivalent level of protection as provided in the EU for data transferred by the exporter, the exporter could still strengthen the obligation of the data importer to inform promptly the data exporter of its inability to comply with the contractual commitments and as a result with the required standard of "essentially equivalent level of data protection".*[83].

108. This inability to comply may result from changes in the third country's legislation or practice.[84] The clauses could set specific and strict time limits and procedures for the swift suspension of the transfer of data and/or the termination of the contract and the importer's return or deletion of the data received. Keeping track of the requests received, their scope, and the effectiveness of the measures adopted to counter them, should provide the exporter with sufficient indications to exercise its duty to suspend or end the transfer and/or terminate the contract.

109. *Conditions for effectiveness:*
–   The notification needs to take place before access is granted to the data. Otherwise, by the time the exporter receives the notification, the rights of the individual may have already been violated if the request is based on laws of that third country that exceed what the level of data protection afforded under EU law permits. The notification may still serve to prevent future violations and to allow the exporter to fulfil its duty to suspend the transfer of personal data to the third country and/or terminate the contract.
–   The data importer must monitor any legal or policy developments that might lead to its inability to comply with its obligations, and promptly inform the data exporter of any such changes and developments, and if possible ahead of their implementation to enable the data exporter to recover the data from the data importer.
–   The clauses should provide for a quick mechanism whereby the data exporter authorises the data importer to promptly secure or return the data to the data exporter, or if this is not feasible, delete or securely encrypt the data without necessarily waiting for the exporter's instructions, if a specific threshold to be agreed between the data exporter and the data importer is met. The importer should implement this mechanism from the beginning of the data transfer and test it regularly to ensure that it can be applied on short notice.
–   Other clauses could enable the exporter to monitor the importer's compliance with these obligations via audits, inspections and other verification measures and to enforce them with penalties on the importer and/or the exporter's capacity to suspend the transfer and/or terminate immediately the contract.

***

110. *Insofar as allowed by national law in the third country, the contract could reinforce the transparency obligations of the importer by providing for a "Warrant Canary" method, whereby the importer commits to regularly publish (e.g. at least every 24 hours) a cryptographically signed message informing the exporter that as of a certain date and time it has received no order to disclose personal data or the like. The absence of an update of this notification will indicate to the exporter that the importer may have received an order.*

111. *Conditions for effectiveness:*
–   The regulations of the third country must permit the data importer to issue this form of passive notification to the exporter.
–   The data exporter must automatically monitor the warrant canary notifications.
–   The data importer must ensure that its private key for signing the Warrant Canary is kept safe and that it cannot be forced to issue false Warrant Canaries by the regulations of the third country. To this end, it might be of use if several signatures by different persons are needed and/or the Warrant Canary is issued by a person outside the third country's jurisdiction.

Obligations to take specific actions

112. *The importer could commit to reviewing, under the law of the country of destination, the legality of any order to disclose data, notably whether it remains within the powers granted to the requesting public authority, and to challenge the order if, after a careful assessment, it concludes that there are grounds under the law of the country of destination to do so. When challenging an order, the data importer should seek interim measures to suspend the effects of the order until the court has decided on the merits. The importer would have the obligation not to disclose the personal data requested until required to do so under the applicable procedural rules. The data importer would also commit to providing the minimum amount of information permissible when responding to the order, based on a reasonable interpretation of the order.*

113. *Conditions for effectiveness:*
–   The legal order of the third country must offer effective legal avenues to challenge orders to disclose data.
–   This clause will always offer a very limited additional protection as an order to disclose data may be lawful under the legal order of the third country, but this legal order may not meet EU standards. This contractual measure will necessarily need to be complementary to other supplementary measures.
–   The challenges to the orders must have a suspensive effect under the law of the third country. Otherwise, public authorities would still have access to the individuals' data and any ensuing action in favor of the individual would have the limited effect of allowing him/her to claim damages for negative consequences resulting from the data disclosure.
–   The importer will need to be able to document and demonstrate to the exporter the actions it has taken, exercising its best efforts, to fulfill this commitment.

114. *In the same situation as described above, the the importer could commit to inform the requesting public authority of the incompatibility of the order with the safeguards contained in the Article 46 GDPR transfer tool[85] and the resulting conflict of obligations for the importer. The importer would notify simultaneously and as soon as possible the exporter and/or the competent supervisory authority from the EEA, insofar as possible under the third country legal order.*

115. *Conditions for effectiveness:*
–   Such information on the protection conferred by EU law and the conflict of obligations should have some legal effect in the legal order of the third country, such as a judicial or administrative review of the order or request for access, the requirement of a judicial warrant, and/or a temporary suspension of the order to add some protection to the data.
–   The legal system of the country must not prevent the importer from notifying the exporter or at least the competent supervisory authority from the EEA of the order or request for access received.
–   The importer will need to be able to document and demonstrate to the exporter the actions it has taken, exercising its best efforts, to fulfill this commitment.

Empowering data subjects to exercise their rights

116. *The contract could provide that personal data transmitted in plain text in the normal course of business (including in support cases) may only be accessed with the express or implied consent of the exporter and/or the data subject.*

117. *Conditions for effectiveness:*
–   This clause could be effective in those situations in which importers receive requests from public authorities to cooperate on a voluntary basis, as opposed to e.g. data access by public authorities that occurs without the data importer's knowledge or against its will.
–   In some situations the data subject may not be in a position to oppose the access or to give a consent that meets all the conditions set out under EU law (freely given, specific, informed, and unambiguous) (e.g in the case of employees[86].
–   National regulations or policies compelling the importer not to disclose the order for access may render this clause ineffective, unless it can be backed with technical methods requiring the exporter's or the data subject's intervention for the data in plant text to be accessible. Such technical measures to restrict access may be envisaged in particular if access is only granted in specific support or service cases, but the data itself is stored in the EEA.

118. *The contract could oblige the importer and/or the exporter to notify promptly the data subject of the request or order received from the public authorities of the third country, or of the importer's inability to comply with the contractual commitments, to enable the data subject to seek information and an effective redress (e.g. by lodging a claim with his/her competent supervisory authority and/or judicial authority and demonstrate his/her standing in the courts of the third country).*

119. *Conditions for effectiveness:*
–   This notification could alert the data subject to potential accesses by public authorities in third countries to his/her data. It could thus enable the data subject to seek additional information with the exporters and to lodge a claim with his/her competent supervisory authority. This clause could also address some of the difficulties an individual may face in demonstrating his/her standing (locus standi) before third country courts to challenge the public authorities' access to his/her data.
–   National regulations and policies may prevent this notification to the data subject. The exporter and importer could nonetheless commit to informing the data subject as soon as the restrictions on the disclosure of data are lifted and to make its best efforts to obtain the waiver of the prohibition to disclose. At a minimum, the exporter or the competent supervisory authority could notify the data subject of the suspension or termination of the transfer of his/her personal data due to the importer's inability to comply with its contractual commitments as a result of its receipt of a request for access.

***

120. *The contract could commit the exporter and importer to assist the data subject in exercising his/her rights in the third country jurisdiction through ad hoc redress mechanisms and legal counselling.*

121. *Conditions for effectiveness*
–   National regulations and policies may impose conditions that may undermine the effectiveness of the ad hoc redress mechanisms provided for.
–   Legal counselling could be helpful for the data subject, especially considering how complex and costly it can be for a data subject to understand a third country's legal system and to exercise legal actions from abroad, potentially in a foreign language. However, this clause will always offer a limited additional protection, as providing assistance and legal counselling to data subjects cannot in itself remedy a third country's legal order failure to provide for a level of protection essentially equivalent to that guaranteed within the EU. This contractual measure will necessarily need to be complementary to other supplementary measures.

This supplementary measure would only be effective provided that the law of the third country provides for redress before its national courts or that an ad hoc redress mechanism exist. In any case, this would however not be an efficient supplementary measure against surveillance measures if no redress mechanism exists.

ORGANISATIONAL MEASURES

122.   Additional organisational measures may consist of internal policies, organisational methods, and standards controllers and processors could apply to themselves and impose on the importers of data in third countries. They may contribute to ensuring consistency in the protection of personal data during the full cycle of the processing. Organisational measures may also improve the exporters' awareness of risk of and attempts to gain access to the data in third countries, and their capacity to react to them. Selecting and implementing one or several of these measures will not necessarily and systematically ensure that your transfer meets the essential equivalence standard that EU law requires. Depending on the specific circumstances of the transfer and the assessment performed on the legislation of the third country, organisational measures are needed to complement contractual and/or technical measures, in order to ensure a level of protection of the personal data essentially equivalent to that guaranteed within the EU.

123.   The assessment of the most suitable measures has to be done on a case by cases basis keeping in mind the need for controllers and processors to respect the accountability principle. Below, the EDPB lists some examples of organisational measures that exporters can implement, albeit the list is not exhaustive and other measures may also be appropriate :

Internal policies for governance of transfers especially with groups of enterprises

124.   *Adoption of adequate internal policies with clear allocation of responsibilities for data transfers, reporting channels and standard operating procedures for cases of covert or official requests from public authorities to access the data. Especially in case of transfers among groups of enterprises, these policies may include, among others, the appointment of a specific team, which should be based within the EEA, composed by experts on IT, data protection and privacy laws, to deal with requests that involve personal data transferred from the EU; the notification to the senior legal and corporate management and to the data exporter upon receipt of such requests; the procedural steps to challenge disproportionate or unlawful requests and the provision of transparent information to data subjects.*

125.   Development of specific training procedures for personnel in charge of managing requests for access to personal data from public authorities, which should be periodically updated to reflect new legislative and jurisprudential developments in the third country and in the EEA. The training procedures should include the requirements of EU law as to access by public authorities to personal data, in particular as following from Article 52 (1) of the Charter of Fundamental Rights. Awareness of personnel should be raised in particular by means of assessment of practical examples of public authorities' data access requests and by applying the standard following from Article 52(1) of the Charter of Fundamental Rights to such practical examples. Such training should take into account the particular situation of the data importer, e.g. legislation and regulations of the third country to which the data importer is subject to, and should be developed where possible in cooperation with the data exporter.

126. *Conditions for effectiveness:*
– These policies may only be envisaged for those cases where the request from public authorities in the third country is compatible with EU law.[87] When the request is incompatible, these policies would not suffice to ensure an equivalent level of protection of the personal data and, as said above, transfers must be stopped or appropriate supplementary measures to avoid the access must be put in place.

Transparency and accountability measures

127. *Document and record the requests for access received from public authorities and the response provided, alongside the legal reasoning and the actors involved (e.g. if the exporter has been notified and its reply, the assessment of the team in charge of dealing with such requests, etc.). These records should be made available to the data exporter, who should in turn provide them to the data subjects concerned where required.*

128. *Conditions for effectiveness:*
– National legislation in the third country may prevent disclosure of the requests or substantial information thereof and therefore render this practice ineffective. The data importer should inform the exporter of its inability to provide such documents and records, thus offering the exporter the option to suspend the transfers if such inability would lead to a decrease of the level of protection.

***

129. *Regular publication of transparency reports or summaries regarding governmental requests for access to data and the kind of reply provided, insofar publication is allowed by local law.*

130. *Conditions for effectiveness:*
– The information provided should be relevant, clear and as detailed as possible. National legislation in the third country may prevent disclosure of detailed information. In those cases, the data importer should employ its best efforts to publish statistical information or similar type of aggregated information.

Organisation methods and data minimisation measures

131. *Already existing organisational requirements under the accountability principle, such as the adoption of strict and granular data access and confidentiality policies and best practices, based on a strict need-to-know principle, monitored with regular audits and enforced through disciplinary measures may also be useful measures in a transfer context. Data minimisation should be considered in this regard, in order to limit the exposure of personal data to unauthorised access. For example, in some cases it might not be necessary to transfer certain data (e.g. in case of remote access to EEA data, such as in support cases, when restricted access is granted instead of full access; or when the provision of a service only requires the transfer of a limited set of data, and not an entire database).*

132. *Conditions for effectiveness:*
– Regular audits and strong disciplinary measures should be in place in order to monitor and enforce compliance with the data minimisation measures also in the transfer context.
– The data exporter shall perform an assessment of the personal data in its possession before the transfer takes place, in order to identify those sets of data that are not necessary for the purposes of the transfer and, therefore, won't be shared with the data importer.
– Data minimisation measures should be accompanied with technical measures as to ensure that data are not subject to unauthorised access. For example, the implementation of secure multiparty computation mechanisms and the spread of encrypted datasets among different trusted entities can prevent by design that any unilateral access lead to the disclosure of identifiable data.

***

133. *Development of best practices to appropriately and timely involve and provide access to information to the data protection officer, if existent, and to the legal and internal auditing services on matters related to international transfers of personal data transfers.*

134. *Conditions for effectiveness:*
– The data protection officer, if existent, and the legal and internal auditing team shall be provided with all the relevant information prior to the transfer, and shall be consulted on the necessity of the transfer and the additional safeguards, if any.
– Relevant information should include, for example, the assessment on the necessity of the transfer of the specific personal data, an overview of the laws of the third country applicable and the safeguards the importer committed to implement.

Adoption of standards and best practices

135. *Adoption of strict data security and data privacy policies, based on EU certification or codes of conducts or on international standards (e.g. ISO norms) and best practices (e.g. ENISA) with due regard to the state of the art, in accordance with the risk of the categories of data processed and the likelihood of attempts from public authorities to access it.*

Others

136. *Adoption and regular review of internal policies to assess the suitability of the implemented complementary measures and identify and implement additional or alternative solutions when necessary, to ensure that an equivalent level of protection to that guaranteed within the EU of the personal data transferred is maintained.*

***

137. *Commitments from the data importer to not engage in any onward transfer of the personal data within the same or other third countries, or suspend ongoing transfers, when an equivalent level of protection of the personal data to that afforded within the EU cannot be guaranteed in the third country.*[88]

NOTES

[66]   Article 5.2 GDPR, Article 32 GDPR.

[67]   C-311/18 (Schrems II), paragraph 135.

[68]   See Articles 47 and 52 of the EU Charter of Fundamental Rights, Article 23.1 GDPR, and EDPB Recommendations on the European Essential Guarantees for Surveillance Measures.

[69]   In line with Article 4(5) GDPR: "'pseudonymisation' means the processing of personal data in such a manner that the personal data can no longer be attributed to a specific data subject without the use of additional information, provided that such additional information is kept separately and is subject to technical and organisational measures to ensure that the personal data are not attributed to an identified or identifiable natural person;".

[70]   Art. 4(1) GDPR: "'personal data' means any information relating to an identified or identifiable natural person ('data subject'); an identifiable natural person is one who can be identified, directly or indirectly, in particular by reference to an identifier such as a name, an identification number, location data, an online identifier or to one or more factors specific to the physical, physiological, genetic, mental, economic, cultural or social identity of that natural person;".

[71]   See Articles 47 and 52 of the EU Charter of Fundamental Rights, Article 23.1 GDPR, and EDPB Recommendations on the European Essential Guarantees for Surveillance Measures.

[72]   E.g. within BCRs which should in any case regulate some of the measures listed below.

[73]   They will have a private nature and not be considered as international agreements under public international law. Accordingly, they will normally fail to bind the third country's public authority as non-parties to the contract when concluded with private bodies in third countries, as the Court underlined in its judgment C-311/18 (Schrems II), paragraph 125.

[74]   See judgment C-311/18 (Schrems II), paragraph 137 where the Court as a result recognised that the SCC contain « *effective mechanisms that make it possible, in practice, to ensure compliance with the level of protection required by EU law and that transfers of personal data pursuant to the clauses of such a decision are suspended or prohibited in the event of the breach of such clauses or it being impossible to honour them* » see also paragraph 148).

[75]   C-311/18 (Schrems II), paragraph 125.

[76]   CJEU judgment C-311/18 (Schrems II), paragraph 132.

[77]   The length of period should depend on the risk for the rights and freedoms of the data subjects whose data are subject to the transfer at stake – e.g. the last year before closure of the data export instrument with the data exporter

[78]   Complying with this duty does not as such amount to providing for an appropriate level of protection. At the same time any inappropriate disclosure that has actually happened leads to the necessity of implementing supplementary measures.

[79]   See paragraph 32.5 above.

[80]   This clause is important to guarantee an adequate level of protection of the personal data transferred and should usually be required.

[81]   See paragraph 32.5 above.

[82]   See for instance Clause 5.f of SCCs between controllers and processors Decision 2010/87/EU, the audits could also be provided within a code of conduct or through certification.

[83]   Clause 5.a and d.i of SCCs Decision 2010/87/EU.

[84]   See C-311/18 (Schrems II), paragraph 139 in which the Court asserts that "*although Clause 5(d)(i) allows a recipient of personal data not to notify a controller established in the European Union of a legally binding request for disclosure of the personal data by a law enforcement authority, in the event of legislation prohibiting that recipient from doing so, such as a prohibition under criminal law the aim of which is to preserve the confidentiality of a law enforcement investigation, the recipient is nevertheless required, pursuant to Clause 5(a) in the annex to the SCC Decision, to inform the controller of his or her inability to comply with the standard data protection clauses.*"

[85]   For instance, the SCCs provide that the processing of data, including the transfer thereof, has been and will continue to be carried out in accordance with "*the applicable data protection law*". This law is defined as "*the legislation protecting the fundamental rights and freedoms of individuals and, in particular, their right to privacy with respect to the processing of personal data applicable to a data controller in the Member State in which the data exporter is established*". The CJEU confirms that the provisions of the GDPR, read in light of the EU Charter of Fundamental rights, form part of that legislation, see CJEU C-311/18 (Schrems II), paragraph 138.

[86]   Article 4(11) GDPR.

[87]   See Case C-362/14 (« Schrems I »), par. 94; C-311/18 (Schrems II), paragraphs 168, 174, 175 and 176.

[88]   C-311/18 (Schrems II), paragraphs 135 and 137.

ANNEX 3: POSSIBLE SOURCES OF INFORMATION TO ASSESS A THIRD COUNTRY

[2.392]
138.   Your data importer should be in a position to provide you with relevant sources and information relating to the third country in which it is established and the laws applicable to it. You may also refer to several sources of information, such as the ones listed below non-exhaustively:
−   Case-law of the Court of Justice of the European Union (CJEU) and of the European Court of Human Rights (ECtHR)[89] as referred to in the European Essential Guarantees recommendations;[90]

–   Adequacy decisions in the country of destination if the transfer relies on a different legal basis;[91]
–   Resolutions and reports from intergovernmental organisations, such as the Council of Europe,[92] other regional bodies[93]; and UN bodies and agencies (e.g. UN Human Rights Council,[94] Human Rights Committee[95]);
–   National case-law or decisions taken by independent judicial or administrative authorities competent on data privacy and data protection of third countries;
–   Reports from academic institutions, and civil society organizations (e.g. NGOs and trade associations).

NOTES

[89]   See factsheet of the ECtHR jurisprudence on mass surveillance: https://www.echr.coe.int/Documents/FS_Mass_surveillance_ENG.pdf

[90]   https://www.coe.int/en/web/data-protection/reports-studies-and-opinions

[91]   C-311/18 (Schrems II), paragraph 141; see adequacy decisions in https://ec.europa.eu/info/law/law-topic/data-protection/international-dimension-data-protection/adequacy-decisions_en

[92]   https://www.coe.int/en/web/data-protection/reports-studies-and-opinions

[93]   See for instance country reports of the Inter-American Commission on Human Rights (IACHR), https://www.oas.org/en/iachr/reports/country.asp.

[94]   See https://www.ohchr.org/EN/HRBodies/UPR/Pages/Documentation.aspx

[95]   see: https://tbinternet.ohchr.org/_layouts/15/treatybodyexternal/TBSearch.aspx?Lang=en&TreatyID=8&DocTypeID=5

EUROPEAN DATA PROTECTION BOARD: RECOMMENDATIONS 2/2020 ON THE EUROPEAN ESSENTIAL GUARANTEES FOR SURVEILLANCE MEASURES

Adopted on 10 November 2020

[2.393]

NOTES
© European Data Protection Board.

TABLE OF CONTENTS

THE EUROPEAN DATA PROTECTION BOARD

Having regard to Article 70(1)(e) of the Regulation 2016/679/EU of the European Parliament and of the Council of 27 April 2016 on the protection of natural persons with regard to the processing of personal data and on the free movement of such data, and repealing Directive 95/46/EC, (hereinafter "GDPR"),[1]

Having regard to the EEA Agreement and in particular to Annex XI and Protocol 37 thereof, as amended by the Decision of the EEA joint Committee No 154/2018 of 6 July 2018[2],

Having regard to Article 12 and Article 22 of its Rules of Procedure,

Having regard to the Article 29 Working Party working document on the justification of interferences with the fundamental rights to privacy and data protection through surveillance measures when transferring personal data (European Essential Guarantees hereinafter "EEG"), WP237,

HAS ADOPTED THE FOLLOWING RECOMMENDATIONS

NOTES

[1]   This paper does not address situations of transfers or onward sharing falling under the scope of the Law Enforcement Directive (Directive (EU) 2016/680).

[2]   References to "Member States" made throughout this document should be understood as references to "EEA Member States".

1. INTRODUCTION

[2.394]
1.   Following the Schrems I judgment, EU Data Protection Authorities assembled in the Working Party 29 drew upon the jurisprudence to identify the European Essential Guarantees, which need to be

respected to make sure interferences with the rights to privacy and the protection of personal data, through surveillance measures, when transferring personal data, do not go beyond what is necessary and proportionate in a democratic society.

2. The EDPB would like to stress that the European Essential Guarantees are based on the jurisprudence of the Court of Justice of the European Union (hereinafter: CJEU) related to Articles 7, 8, 47 and 52 of the Charter of Fundamental Rights of the EU (hereinafter: the Charter) and, as the case may be, on the jurisprudence of the European Court of Human Rights (hereinafter: ECtHR) related to Article 8 of the European Convention on Human Rights (hereinafter: ECHR) dealing with surveillance issues in States party to the ECHR.[3]

3. The update of this paper is meant to further develop the European Essential Guarantees, originally drafted in response to the Schrems I judgment[4] by reflecting the clarifications provided by the CJEU (and by the ECtHR) since it was first published, in particular in its landmark Schrems II judgment.[5].

4. In its Schrems II judgment, the CJEU stated that the examination of the Commission Decision 2010/87/EU on standard contractual clauses for the transfer of personal data to processors established in third countries, in the light of Articles 7, 8 and 47 of the Charter, has disclosed nothing to affect the validity of that decision, but invalidated the Privacy Shield Decision. The CJEU held that the Privacy Shield Decision was incompatible with Article 45 (1) GDPR, in the light of Articles 7, 8, and 47 of the Charter. The judgment can thus serve as an example where surveillance measures in a third country (in this case the U.S. with Section 702 FISA and Executive Order 12 333) are neither sufficiently limited nor object of an effective redress available to data subjects to enforce their rights, as required under EU law in order to consider the level of protection in a third country to be "essentially equivalent" to that guaranteed within the European Union within the meaning of Article 45 (1) of the GDPR.

5. The reasons for the invalidation of the Privacy Shield also have consequences on other transfer tools.[6] Even though the Court interpreted Article 46(1) GDPR in the context of the validity of the Standard Contractual Clauses (hereinafter: SCCs), its interpretation applies to any transfer to third countries relying on any of the tools referred to in Article 46 GDPR[7].

6. It is ultimately for the CJEU to judge whether interferences with a fundamental right can be justified. However, in absence of such a judgment and in application of the standing jurisprudence, data protection authorities are required to assess individual cases, either ex officio or following a complaint, and to either refer the case to a national Court if they suspect that the transfer does not comply with Article 45 where there is an adequacy decision, or to suspend or prohibit the transfer if they find Article 46 GDPR cannot be complied with and the protection of the data transferred required by EU law cannot be ensured by other means.

7. The aim of the updated European Essential Guarantees is to provide elements to examine, whether surveillance measures allowing access to personal data by public authorities in a third country, being national security agencies or law enforcement authorities, can be regarded as a justifiable interference or not.

8. Indeed, the European Essential Guarantees form part of the assessment to conduct in order to determine whether a third country provides a level of protection essentially equivalent to that guaranteed within the EU but do not aim on their own at defining all the elements which are necessary to consider that a third country provides such a level of protection in accordance with Article 45 of the GDPR. Likewise, they do not aim on their own at defining all the elements that might be necessary to consider when assessing whether the legal regime of a third country prevents the data exporter and data importer from ensuring appropriate safeguards in accordance with Article 46 of the GDPR.

9. Therefore, the elements provided in this paper should be seen as the essential guarantees to be found in the third country when assessing the interference, entailed by a third country surveillance measures, with the rights to privacy and to data protection, rather than a list of elements to demonstrate that the legal regime of a third country as a whole is providing an essentially equivalent level of protection.

10. Article 6(3) of the Treaty on European Union establishes that the fundamental rights enshrined in the ECHR constitute general principles of EU law. However, as the CJEU recalls in its jurisprudence, the latter does not constitute, as long as the European Union has not acceded to it, a legal instrument which has been formally incorporated into EU law.[8] Thus, the level of protection of fundamental rights required by Article 46(1) of the GDPR must be determined on the basis of the provisions of that regulation, read in the light of the fundamental rights enshrined in the Charter. This being said, according to Article 52(3) of the Charter the rights contained therein which correspond to rights guaranteed by the ECHR are to have the same meaning and scope as those laid down by that Convention, and consequently, as recalled by the CJEU, the jurisprudence of the ECtHR concerning rights which are also foreseen in the Charter of Fundamental Rights of the EU must be taken into account, as a minimum threshold of protection to interpret corresponding rights in the Charter.[9] According to the last sentence of Article 52(3) of the Charter, however, "[t]his provision shall not prevent Union law providing more extensive protection."

11. Therefore, the substance of the Essential Guarantees will continue to be partly based on the jurisprudence of the ECtHR, to the extent that the Charter as interpreted by the CJEU does not provide for a higher level of protection which prescribes other requirements than the ECtHR case law.

12. This paper explains the background and further details the four European Essential Guarantees.

NOTES

[3] In these Recommendations, the term "fundamental rights" is derived from the EU Charter of Fundamental Rights of the EU. However, it is used to also cover the "human rights" as included in the European Convention on Human Rights.

[4] CJEU judgment of 6 October 2015, Maximillian Schrems v Data Protection Commissioner, Case C-362/14, EU:C:2015:650 (hereinafter: Schrems I).

⁵ CJEU judgment of 16 July 2020, Data Protection Commissioner v Facebook Ireland Ltd, Maximillian Schrems, case C-311/18, ECLI:EU:C:2020:559 (hereinafter: Schrems II).
⁶ See §105 of Schrems II.
⁷ See §92 of Schrems II.
⁸ See § 98 of Schrems II.
⁹ See § 124 of joined cases C-511/18, C-512/18 and C-520/18, La Quadrature du Net and others (hereinafter: La Quadrature du Net and others).

2. INTERFERENCES WITH FUNDAMENTAL RIGHTS

[2.395]

13. The fundamental rights to respect for private and family life, including communications, and to the protection of personal data are laid down in Articles 7 and 8 of the Charter and apply to everyone. Article 8 furthermore sets conditions for the processing of personal data to be lawful and recognizes the right of access and rectification, as well as imposes that these rules are subject to the control of an independent authority.

14. "(T)he operation of having personal data transferred from a Member State to a third country constitutes, in itself, processing of personal data".[10] Thus, Articles 7 and 8 of the Charter apply to this specific operation and their protection extend to the data transferred, which is why data subjects whose personal data are transferred to a third country must be afforded a level of protection essentially equivalent to that which is guaranteed within the European Union.[11]

15. According to the CJEU, when the fundamental right to respect for private life enshrined in Article 7 of the Charter is affected, by means of processing an individual's personal data, the right to data protection is also affected, as such processing falls within the scope of Article 8 of the Charter, and, accordingly, must necessarily satisfy the data protection requirement laid down in that article.[12]

16. Therefore, as regards possible interference with fundamental rights under the EU law, the obligation imposed on providers of electronic communications services (. . .) to retain traffic data for the purpose of making it available, if necessary, to the competent national authorities, raises issues relating to compatibility with Articles 7 and 8 of the Charter.[13] The same applies to other types of data processing, such as the transmission of data to persons other than users or access to that data with a view to its use[14], which, thus, entails an interference with those fundamental rights. Moreover, access to the data by a public authority constitutes a further interference, according to settled case-law.[15]

17. In order to find an interference, it does not matter "whether the information in question relating to private life is sensitive or whether the persons concerned have been inconvenienced in any way on account of that interference."[16] The CJEU also stressed that whether or not the retained data has been subsequently used is irrelevant.[17]

18. However, Articles 7 and 8 of the Charter are not absolute rights, but must be considered in relation to their function in society.[18]

19. The Charter includes a necessity and proportionality test to frame limitations to the rights it protects. Article 52(1) of the Charter specifies the scope of possible limitations to Articles 7 and 8 by stating that "any limitation on the exercise of the rights and freedoms recognised by this Charter must be provided for by law and respect the essence of those rights and freedoms. Subject to the principle of proportionality, limitations may be made only if they are necessary and genuinely meet objectives of general interest recognised by the Union or the need to protect the rights and freedoms of others".

20. The CJEU reiterated that EU legislation involving interference with the fundamental rights guaranteed by Articles 7 and 8 of the Charter "must lay down clear and precise rules governing the scope and application of the measure and imposing minimum safeguards, so that the persons whose personal data is affected have sufficient guarantees that data will be effectively protected against the risk of abuse", in particular where personal data is subjected to automatic processing and "where there is a significant risk of unlawful access to that data".[19]

21. According to the CJEU, the protection of the right to privacy requires that derogations from and restrictions to the right to data protection "must apply in so far as is strictly necessary". Furthermore, an objective of general interest must be reconciled with the fundamental rights affected by the measure, "by properly balancing" such objective against the rights at issue.[20]

22. Consequently, access, retention and further use of personal data by public authorities within the remit of surveillance measures must not exceed the limits of what is strictly necessary, assessed in the light of the Charter, otherwise it "cannot be considered to be justified, within a democratic society".[21]

23. The four European Essential Guarantees, as they are developed in the next chapter, intend to further specify how to assess the level of interference with the fundamental rights to privacy and to data protection in the context of surveillance measures by public authorities in a third country, when transferring personal data, and what legal requirements must consequently apply in order to evaluate whether such interferences would be acceptable under the Charter.

NOTES

10 CJEU, Schrems II, § 83.
11 CJEU, Schrems II, § 96.
12 CJEU, Schrems II, §§ 170-171.
13 CJEU, case C-623/17, Privacy International (hereinafter: Privacy International), § 60.
14 CJEU, Privacy International, § 61.

15   ECtHR, Leander, §48; ECtHR, Rotaru §46; CJEU, Digital Rights Ireland, §35.
16   CJEU, Schrems II, § 171, including cited jurisprudence.
17   CJEU, Schrems II, §171, including cited jurisprudence.
18   CJEU, Privacy International, §63.
19   CJEU, Privacy International, §68 and jurisprudence referred therein.
20   CJEU, Privacy International, §68 and jurisprudence referred therein.
21   CJEU, Privacy International, §81.

3. THE EUROPEAN ESSENTIAL GUARANTEES

[2.396]

24. Following the analysis of the jurisprudence, the EDPB considers that the applicable legal requirements to make the limitations to the data protection and privacy rights recognised by the Charter justifiable can be summarised in four European Essential Guarantees:

(A)   Processing should be based on clear, precise and accessible rules
(B)   Necessity and proportionality with regard to the legitimate objectives pursued need to be demonstrated
(C)   An independent oversight mechanism should exist
(D)   Effective remedies need to be available to the individual

25. The Guarantees are based on the fundamental rights to privacy and data protection that apply to everyone, irrespective of their nationality.

GUARANTEE A - PROCESSING SHOULD BE BASED ON CLEAR, PRECISE AND ACCESSIBLE RULES

26. Under Article 8(2) of the Charter, personal data should inter alia, be processed "for specified purposes and on the basis of the consent of the person concerned or some other legitimate basis laid down by law",[22] as the CJEU recalled in the Schrems II ruling. Furthermore, under Article 52(1) of the Charter, any limitation on the exercise of the rights and freedoms recognised by the Charter within the EU must be provided for by law. Thus, a justifiable interference needs to be in accordance with the law.

27. This legal basis should lay down clear and precise rules governing the scope and application of the measure in question and imposing minimum safeguards.[23] In addition, the Court recalled that "legislation must be legally binding under domestic law".[24] In this regard, the CJEU clarified that the assessment of the applicable third country law should focus on whether it can be invoked and relied on by individuals before a court.[25] The Court therefore indicates that the rights granted to data subjects shall be actionable; where individuals are not provided with enforceable rights against public authorities, the level of protection granted cannot be considered as essentially equivalent to that arising from the Charter, contrary to the requirement in Article 45(2)(a) of the GDPR.[26]

28. Furthermore, the Court stressed that the applicable law must indicate in what circumstances and under which conditions a measure providing for the processing of such data may be adopted[27] (see infra under Guarantee B the relation between these requirements and the principles of necessity and proportionality).

29. Moreover, the CJEU has also indicated that "the requirement that any limitation on the exercise of fundamental rights must be provided for by law implies that the legal basis which permits the interference with those rights must itself define the scope of the limitation on the exercise of the right concerned".[28]

30. Finally, the European Court of Human Rights "does not consider that there is any ground to apply different principles covering the accessibility and clarity of the rules governing the interception of individual communications, on the one hand, and more general programmes of surveillance".[29] The ECtHR as well has clarified that the legal basis should at least include a definition of the categories of people that might be subject to surveillance, a limit on the duration of the measure, the procedure to be followed for examining, using and storing the data obtained, and the precautions to be taken when communicating the data to other parties.[30]

31. Lastly, the interference must be foreseeable as to its effect for the individual in order to give him/her adequate and effective protection against arbitrary interference and the risk of abuse. As a result, the processing must be based on a precise, clear but also accessible (i.e. public) legal basis.[31] The ECtHR, concerning this question, recalled in the Zakharov case that "the reference to 'foreseeability' in the context of interception of communications cannot be the same as in many other fields". It specified that in the context of secret measures of surveillance, such as the interception of communications, "foreseeability cannot mean that an individual should be able to foresee when the authorities are likely to intercept his communications so that he can adapt his conduct accordingly". However, considering that in this kind of situation the risks of arbitrariness are evident "it is essential to have clear, detailed rules on interception of telephone conversations, especially as the technology available for use is continually becoming more sophisticated. The domestic law must be sufficiently clear to give citizens an adequate indication as to the circumstances in which and the conditions on which public authorities are empowered to resort to any such measures".[32]

GUARANTEE B - NECESSITY AND PROPORTIONALITY WITH REGARD TO THE LEGITIMATE OBJECTIVES PURSUED NEED TO BE DEMONSTRATED

32. In accordance with the first sentence of Article 52(1) of the Charter, any limitation on the exercise of the rights and freedoms recognised by the Charter must respect the essence of those rights and freedoms. Under the second sentence of Article 52(1) of the Charter, subject to the principle of proportionality, limitations may be made to those rights and freedoms only if they are necessary and genuinely meet objectives of general interest recognised by the Union or the need to protect the rights and freedoms of others.[33]

33. Regarding the principle of proportionality, the Court held, in relation to Member State laws, that the question as to whether a limitation on the rights to privacy and to data protection may be justified must be assessed, on the one hand, by measuring the seriousness of the interference entailed by such a limitation[34] and by verifying that the importance of the public interest objective pursued by that limitation is proportionate to that seriousness, on the other hand.[35]

34. In La Quadrature du net and others, it can be noted that the CJEU ruled, in relation to the law of a Member State and not to a third country law, that the objective of safeguarding national security is, due to its importance, capable of justifying measures entailing more serious interferences with fundamental rights, than those which might be justified by other objectives such as of combating crime. It found however that this is the case as long as there are sufficiently solid grounds for considering that the State concerned is confronted with a serious threat to national security that is shown to be genuine and present or foreseeable and subject to meeting the other requirements laid down in Article 52(1) of the Charter.[36]

35. In this regard, according to the settled case-law of the Court, derogations from and limitations on the protection of personal data must apply only in so far as is strictly necessary.[37] In order to satisfy this requirement, besides laying down clear and precise rules governing the scope and application of the measure in question, the legislation in question must impose minimum safeguards, so that the persons whose data have been transferred have sufficient guarantees to protect effectively their personal data against the risk of abuse. "It must, in particular, indicate in what circumstances and under which conditions a measure providing for the processing of such data may be adopted, thereby ensuring that the interference is limited to what is strictly necessary. The need for such safeguards is all the greater where personal data is subject to automated processing".[38]

36. In Schrems II, the CJEU has stressed that legislation of a third country which does not indicate any limitations on the power it confers to implement surveillance programmes for the purposes of foreign intelligence cannot ensure a level of protection essentially equivalent to that guaranteed by the Charter. Indeed, according to the case law, a legal basis which permits interference with fundamental rights must, in order to satisfy the requirements of the principle of proportionality, itself define the scope of the limitation on the exercise of the right concerned.[39]

37. Regarding the principle of necessity, the CJEU has made clear that legislations "authorising, on a generalised basis, storage of all the personal data of all the persons whose data has been transferred from the European Union (...) without any differentiation, limitation or exception being made in the light of the objective pursued and without an objective criterion being laid down by which to determine the limits of the access of the public authorities to the data and of its subsequent use, for purposes which are specific, strictly restricted and capable of justifying the interference which both access to the data and its use entail", do not comply with that principle.[40] In particular, laws permitting public authorities to have access on a generalised basis to the content of electronic communications must be regarded as compromising the essence of the fundamental right to respect for private life, as guaranteed by Article 7 of the Charter.[41]

38. Likewise, however this time when assessing a Member State law and not a third country law, the CJEU held in La Quadrature du Net and others, that "legislation requiring the retention of personal data must always meet objective criteria that establish a connection between the data retained and the objective pursued".[42] In the same context, in Privacy International, it also held that the legislator "must rely on objective criteria in order to define the circumstances and conditions under which the competent national authorities are to be granted access to the data at issue".[43]

GUARANTEE C - INDEPENDENT OVERSIGHT MECHANISM

39. The EDPB recalls that an interference takes place at the time of collection of the data, but also at the time the data is accessed by a public authority for further processing. The ECtHR has specified multiple times that any interference with the right to privacy and data protection should be subject to an effective, independent and impartial oversight system that must be provided for either by a judge or by another independent body[44] (e.g. an administrative authority or a parliamentary body). The independent oversight over the implementation of surveillance measures was also taken into account by the CJEU in the Schrems II judgment.[45]

40. The ECtHR specifies that while prior (judicial) authorization of surveillance measures is an important safeguard against arbitrariness, regard must also be given to the actual operation of the system of interception, including the checks and balances on the exercise of power, and the existence or absence of actual abuse.[46] In the Schrems II case, the CJEU also took into account the scope of the supervisory role of the oversight mechanism, which did not cover the individual surveillance measures.[47].

41. With regard to Member States law, the CJEU identified a number of measures which are in compliance with EU law only if they are subject to effective review carried out by a court or an independent administrative authority whose decision is binding. The aim of that review is to verify that a situation justifying the measure exists and the conditions and safeguards that must be laid down are observed.[48] For real-time collection of traffic and location data, the review should allow to check ex ante, inter alia, whether it is authorised only within the limits of what is strictly necessary. In cases of duly justified urgency, the measures may take place without such prior review; however, the Court still requires that the subsequent review takes place within a short time.[49]

42. As to the independence of oversight mechanisms in relation to surveillance, the findings of the CJEU concerning the independence of a body in the context of redress could be taken into account (see infra under guarantee D). Furthermore, the case law of the ECtHR may offer additional elements. This Court has expressed its preference for a judge to be responsible to maintain oversight. However, it is not excluded that another body may be responsible, "as long as it is sufficiently independent from the executive"[50] and "of the authorities carrying out the surveillance, and [is] vested with sufficient powers and competence to exercise an effective and continuous control".[51] The ECtHR added that "the manner of appointment and the legal status of the members of the supervisory body"[52] need to be taken into account when assessing independence. This includes "persons qualified to hold judicial office, appointed either by parliament or by the Prime Minister. In contrast, a Minister of Internal Affairs – who not only was a political appointee and a member of the executive, but was directly involved in the commissioning of special means of surveillance – was found to be insufficiently independent."[53] The ECtHR also "notes that it is essential that the supervisory body has access to all relevant documents, including closed materials".[54] Finally, the ECtHR takes into account "whether the supervisory body's activities are open to public scrutiny".[55]

GUARANTEE D - EFFECTIVE REMEDIES NEED TO BE AVAILABLE TO THE INDIVIDUAL

43. The final European Essential Guarantee is related to the redress rights of the individual. (S)he must have an effective remedy to satisfy his/her rights when (s)he considers that they are not or have not been respected. The CJEU explained in Schrems I that "legislation not providing for any possibility for an individual to pursue legal remedies in order to have access to personal data relating to him, or to obtain the rectification or erasure of such data, does not respect the essence of the fundamental right to effective judicial protection, as enshrined in Article 47 of the Charter. The first paragraph of Article 47 of the Charter requires everyone whose rights and freedoms guaranteed by the law of the European Union are violated to have the right to an effective remedy before a tribunal in compliance with the conditions laid down in that article."[56]

44. When assessing a Member State law allowing real time collection of traffic and location data, the Court considered that notification is necessary "to enable the persons affected to exercise their rights under Articles 7 and 8 of the Charter to request access to their personal data that has been the subject of those measures and, where appropriate, to have the latter rectified or erased, as well as to avail themselves, in accordance with the first paragraph of Article 47 of the Charter, of an effective remedy before a tribunal".[57] Nevertheless, it also recognized that the notification of persons whose data has been collected or analysed must occur only to the extent that and as soon as the notification no longer jeopardizes the tasks for which those authorities are responsible.[58]

45. For the ECtHR, as well, the question of an effective remedy is inextricably linked to the notification of a surveillance measure to the individual once the surveillance is over. In particular, the Court found that "there is in principle little scope for recourse to the courts by the individual concerned unless the latter is advised of the measures taken without his or her knowledge and thus able to challenge their legality retrospectively or, in the alternative, unless any person who suspects that his or her communications are being or have been intercepted can apply to courts, so that the courts' jurisdiction does not depend on notification to the interception subject that there has been an interception of his communications".[59] The ECtHR thus acknowledged that in some cases there might be no notification, however an effective remedy must be provided. In this case, this Court has made clear, for instance in the Kennedy case, that a court offers sufficient redress possibilities, if it meets a series of criteria, i.e. an independent and impartial body, which has adopted its own rules of procedure, consisting of members that must hold or have held high judicial office or be experienced lawyers and that there is no evidential burden to be overcome in order to lodge an application with it.[60] In undertaking its examination of complaints by individuals, the court should have access to all relevant information,[61] including closed materials. Finally, it should have the powers to remedy non-compliance.[62]

46. Article 47 of the Charter refers to a tribunal, even though in language versions other than English the preference is given to the word "court",[63] while the ECHR only obliges Members States to ensure that "everyone whose rights and freedoms are violated shall have an effective remedy before a national authority",[64] which does not necessarily need to be a judicial authority.[65]

47. The CJEU, in the context of the Schrems II judgment when assessing the adequacy of the level of protection of a third country, has reiterated that "data subjects must have the possibility of bringing legal action before an independent and impartial court in order to have access to their personal data, or to obtain the rectification or erasure of such data".[66] In the same context, the CJEU considers that an effective judicial protection against such interferences can be ensured not only by a court, but also by a body[67] which offers guarantees essentially equivalent to those required by Article 47 of the Charter. In its Schrems II ruling, the CJEU both underlined that the independence of the court or body has to be ensured, especially from the executive, with all necessary guarantees, including with regards to its conditions of dismissal or revocation of the appointment,[68] and that the powers which should be granted to a court have to be compliant with the requirements of Article 47 of the Charter. In this regard, the body[69] shall be granted the power to adopt decisions that are binding on the intelligence services, in accordance with legal safeguards on which data subjects could rely.[70]

NOTES

[22]   See §173 Schrems II.

[23]   See §175 and §180 Schrems II and Opinion 1/15 (EU-Canada PNR Agreement) of 26 July 2017, § 139 and the case-law cited.

[24]   See § 68 Privacy International – It should also be clear that in the French version of the judgment the Court uses the word "réglementation" which is broader than only acts of Parliament.

[25] See § 181 Schrems II, in this paragraph the CJEU refers to the US Presidential Policy Directive 28.

[26] See § 181 Schrems II.

[27] See § 68 of Privacy International, in relation to Member State law.

[28] See Schrems II, § 175 and the case-law cited, as well as Privacy International, § 65.

[29] ECtHR, Liberty, §63.

[30] ECtHR, Weber and Saravia, §95.

[31] ECtHR, Malone, §§65, 66.

[32] ECtHR, Zakharov, §229.

[33] Schrems II, § 174.

[34] In this context, the court noted for instance that "the interference constituted by the real-time collection of data that allows terminal equipment to be located appears particularly serious, since that data provides the competent national authorities with a means of accurately and permanently tracking the movements of users of mobile telephones (. . .)" (La Quadrature du Net and others, § 187, including cited jurisprudence).

[35] La Quadrature du Net and others, § 131.

[36] §§136 and 137. See also Privacy International, as the Court specified, such threats can be distinguished, by their nature and particular seriousness, from the general risk that tensions or disturbances, even of a serious nature, affecting public security will arise. § 75. For instance, in La Quadrature du Net and others, the Court noted that the automated analysis of traffic and location data covering generally and indiscriminately the data of persons using electronic communications systems constitutes an interference particularly serious so that, such measure can meet the requirement of proportionality only in situations in which the Member State concerned is facing a serious threat to national security which is shown to be genuine and present or foreseeable, and, among other conditions, provided that the duration of the retention is limited to what is strictly necessary (§§174-177).

[37] Schrems II, §176, including cited jurisprudence.

[38] Schrems II, § 175.

[39] Schrems II, § 180.

[40] Schrems I, § 93 with further references. See, however this time in relation to a Member State law and not a third country law, Privacy International, § 71, including cited jurisprudence. In this case, the Court stated that a Member State legislation requiring providers of electronic communications services to disclose traffic data and location data to the security and intelligence agencies by means of general and indiscriminate transmission exceeds the limits of what is strictly necessary and cannot be considered to be justified, within a democratic society, as required by the Directive on privacy and electronic communication, read in light of the Charter (§81).

[41] Schrems I, §94.

[42] La Quadrature du Net and others, § 133. In this context, the Court confirmed that legislative measures which provide, as a preventive measure, for the general and indiscriminate retention of traffic and location data, are precluded by the Directive on privacy and electronic communication, read in light of the Charter. By contrast, the Court ruled that, in situations of a serious threat to national security that is shown to be genuine and present or foreseeable, the legislator may allow, for safeguarding national security, recourse to an instruction requiring providers of electronic communications services to retain, generally and indiscriminately, traffic and location data. Such measure must however meet specific conditions. In particular, the instruction may be given only for a period that is limited in time to what is strictly necessary, which may be extended if that threat persists (§168).

[43] Privacy International, § 78, including cited jurisprudence. In Privacy International, as regards an authority's access to personal data provided under a Member State law, the Court ruled that "general access to all retained data, regardless of whether there is any link, at least indirect, with the aim pursued, cannot be regarded as being limited to what is strictly necessary" (§77 -78).

[44] ECtHR, Klass, §§17, 51.

[45] Schrems II, §§ 179, 183.

[46] ECtHR, Big Brother Watch under appeal §§319-320.

[47] Schrems II, § 179.

[48] CJEU, La Quadrature du Net and others, §§ 168, 189.

[49] CJEU, La Quadrature du Net and others, § 189.

[50] ECtHR, Zakharov, §258, Iordachi and Others v. Moldova, §§ 40 and §§ 51 and Dumitru Popescu v. Romania, §§ 70¬73.

[51] ECtHR, Klass §56 and Big Brother Watch under appeal §318

[52] ECtHR, Zakharov, §278.

[53] ECtHR, Zakharov, §278.

[54] ECtHR, Zakharov, §281.

[55] ECtHR, Zakharov, §283.

[56] CJEU, Schrems I, §95.

[57] See § 190 of La Quadrature du Net and others and CJEU, Opinion 1/15, §220.

[58] See § 191 of La Quadrature du Net and others.

[59] ECtHR, Zakharov, §234.

[60] ECtHR, Kennedy, § 190.

[61] The EDPB notes that the Council of Europe Commissioner for Human Rights considers that the so-called "third parties" rule – under which intelligence agencies in one country that provide data to intelligence agencies in another country can impose a duty on the receiving agencies to not disclose the transferred data to any third party – should not apply to oversight bodies in order not to undermine the possibility of an effective remedy (Issue Paper on Democratic and effective oversight of national security services).

[62] ECtHR, Kennedy §167.

[63] The word tribunal is for example translated as "Gericht" in German and "gerecht" in Dutch.

[64] Article 13 ECHR.

[65] ECtHR, Klass §67.

[66] See § 194 Schrems II.

[67] See §197 Schrems II in which the Court expressly uses this word.

68   See § 195 Schrems II.
69   See §197 Schrems II in which the Court expressly uses this word.
70   See § 196 Schrems II.

4. FINAL REMARKS

[2.397]
48.   The four European Essential Guarantees are to be seen as core elements to be found when assessing the level of interference with the fundamental rights to privacy and data protection. They should not be assessed independently, as they are closely interlinked, but on an overall basis, reviewing the relevant legislation in relation to surveillance measures, the minimum level of safeguards for the protection of the rights of the data subjects and the remedies provided under the national law of the third country.

49.   These guarantees require a certain degree of interpretation, especially since the third country legislation does not have to be identical to the EU legal framework.

50.   As the ECtHR stated in Kennedy, an "assessment depends on all the circumstances of the case, such as the nature, scope and duration of the possible measures, the grounds required for ordering them, the authorities competent to authorise, carry out and supervise them, and the kind of remedy provided by national law".[71]

51.   Consequently, the assessment of the third country surveillance measures against the EEG may lead to two conclusions:
- The third country legislation at issue does not ensure the EEG requirements: in this case, the third country legislation would not offer a level of protection essentially equivalent to that guaranteed within the EU.
- The third country legislation at issue satisfies the EEG.

52.   When assessing the adequacy of the level of protection, pursuant to Article 45 GDPR, the Commission will have to evaluate whether the EEG are satisfied as part of the elements to be considered to guarantee that the third country legislation as a whole offers a level of protection essentially equivalent to that guaranteed within the EU.

53.   When data exporters rely, along with the data importers, on appropriate safeguards under Article 46 of the GDPR, given the requirements of the third country legislation specifically applicable to the data transferred, they would need to ensure that an essentially equivalent level of protection is effectively achieved. In particular, where the law of the third country does not comply with the EEG requirements, this would imply to ensure that the law at stake will not impinge on the guarantees and safeguards surrounding the transfer, in order for a level of protection essentially equivalent to that guaranteed within the EU to be still provided.

54.   The EDPB has issued further guidelines and recommendations to be taken into account to proceed with the assessment, depending on the transfer tool to be used and on the necessity to provide appropriate safeguards, including as the case may be, supplementary measures.[72]

55.   Furthermore, it should be noted that the European Essential Guarantees are based on what is required by the law. The EDPB underlines that the European Essential Guarantees are based on the fundamental rights that apply to everyone, irrespective of their nationality.

56.   The EDPB reiterates that the European Essential Guarantees are a referential standard when assessing the interference, entailed by third country surveillance measures, in the context of international data transfers. These standards stem from EU law and the jurisprudence of the CJEU and the ECtHR, which is binding on Member States.

NOTES
71   ECtHR, Kennedy §153.
72   Adequacy Referential WP 254 rev.01, Revised and Adopted 6 February 2018; EDPB Recommendations 01/2020 on measures that supplement transfer tools to ensure compliance with the EU level of protection of personal data, 10 November 2020.

EUROPEAN DATA PROTECTION BOARD: GUIDELINES 10/2020 ON RESTRICTIONS UNDER ARTICLE 23 GDPR: VERSION FOR PUBLIC CONSULTATION
Version 1.0
Adopted on 15 December 2020

[2.398]

TABLE OF CONTENTS

THE EUROPEAN DATA PROTECTION BOARD

Having regard to Article 70 (1)(e) of the Regulation 2016/679/EU of the European Parliament and of the Council of 27 April 2016 on the protection of natural persons with regard to the processing of personal data and on the free movement of such data, and repealing Directive 95/46/EC, (hereinafter "GDPR"),

Having regard to the EEA Agreement and in particular to Annex XI and Protocol 37 thereof, as amended by the Decision of the EEA joint Committee No 154/2018 of 6 July 2018[1],

Having regard to Article 12 and Article 22 of its Rules of Procedure,

HAS ADOPTED THE FOLLOWING GUIDELINES

1 INTRODUCTION

[2.399]
1.   This document seeks to provide guidance as to the application of Article 23 GDPR. These Guidelines provide a thorough analysis of the criteria to apply restrictions, the assessments that need to be observed, how data subjects can exercise their rights once the restriction is lifted and the consequences for infringements of Article 23 GDPR.

2.   The protection of natural persons in relation to the processing of personal data is a fundamental right. Article 16(2) TFEU mandates the European Parliament and the Council to lay down the rules in relation to the protection of personal data and the rules relating to the free movement of personal data. The GDPR protects the rights and freedoms of natural persons and in particular their right to data protection. Data protection cannot be ensured without adhering to the rights and principles set out in the GDPR (Articles 12 to 22 and Article 34, as well as Article 5 in so far as its provisions correspond to the rights and obligations provided in Articles 12 to 22 GDPR). All these rights and obligations are at the core of the fundamental right to data protection and their application should be the general rule. In particular, any limitation to the fundamental right to data protection needs to observe Article 52 of the Charter of fundamental rights of the European Union ("the Charter").

3.   It is against this background that Article 23 GDPR should be read and interpreted. This provision is entitled 'restrictions' and it provides that, under Union or Member State law, the application of certain provisions of the Regulation, mainly relating to the rights of the data subjects and controllers' obligations, may be restricted in the situations therein listed. Restrictions should be seen as exceptions to the general rule of allowing the exercise of rights and observing the obligations enshrined in the GDPR[2]. As such, restrictions should be interpreted narrowly, only be applied in specifically provided circumstances and only when certain conditions are met.

4.   Even in exceptional situations, the protection of personal data cannot be restricted in its entirety. It must be upheld in all emergency measures, as per Article 23 GDPR thus contributing to the respect of the overarching values of democracy, rule of law and fundamental rights on which the Union is founded: any measure taken by Member States shall respect the general principles of law, the essence of the fundamental rights and freedoms and shall not be irreversible and data controllers and processors shall continue to comply with data protection rules.

5.   In all cases, where Union or Member State law allows restrictions to data subjects' rights or to the obligations of the controllers (including joint controllers[3]) and processors[4], it should be noted that the accountability principle, as laid down in Art. 5(2) GDPR, is still applicable. This means that the controller is responsible for, and shall be able to demonstrate to the data subjects his or her compliance with the EU data protection framework, including the principles relating to the processing of their data.

6.   When the EU or national legislator lays down restrictions based on Art. 23 GDPR, it shall ensure that it meets the requirements set out in Art. 52(1) of Charter, and in particular conduct a proportionality assessment so that restrictions are limited to what is strictly necessary.

[1]   References to "Member States" made throughout this document should be understood as references to "EEA Member States".

[2]   These situations do not include the scenarios where the Law Enforcement Directive applies.

[3]   In case of joint controllership, especially in case where controllers are from different Member states, restrictions applicable in accordance with Article 23 should be considered and taken into account so that joint controllers clarify in the arrangement their respective roles.

[4]   Although from now on the guidelines will refer to "controllers" only, the recommendations are addressed, where applicable, also to processors.

2 THE MEANING OF RESTRICTIONS

[2.400]
7. The term restrictions is not defined in the GDPR. Article 23 and Recital 73 GDPR only list the conditions under which restrictions can be applied.

8. In these guidelines, the term restrictions will be defined as any limitation of scope of the obligations and rights provided for in Articles 12 to 22 and 34 GDPR as well as corresponding provisions of Article 5 in accordance with Article 23 GDPR. A restriction to an individual right has to safeguard important objectives, for instance, the protection of rights and freedoms of others or important objectives of general public interest of the Union or of a Member State which are listed in Article 23(1) GDPR. Therefore, restrictions of data subjects' rights can only occur when the listed interests are at stake[5] and these restrictions aim at safeguarding such interests.

9. Consequently, the grounds for the restriction need to be clear. To be lawful, restrictions shall be provided for in a legislative measure, concern a limited number of rights of data subjects and/or controller's obligations which are listed in Article 23 GDPR[6], respect the essence of the fundamental rights and freedoms at issue, be a necessary and proportionate measure in a democratic society and safeguard one of the grounds set out in Article 23(1) GDPR as described below.

10. In addition, as mentioned in Recital 73 GDPR, restrictions should be in accordance with the requirements set out in the Charter and the European Convention for the Protection of Human Rights and Fundamental Freedoms.

11. In addition to restrictions referred to in Article 23, the GDPR also lays down provision relating to specific processing situations as per Chapter IX, where Member States may provide by law specific measures impacting data subjects' rights, such as exemptions or derogations (for instance, Articles 85 or 89 GDPR). However these guidelines do not address those cases.

12. Restricting the scope of the obligations and rights provided for in Article 12 to 22 and Article 34 may take different forms but never reaching the point of a general suspension of all rights. Legislative measures laying down the provisions for the application of restrictions under Article 23 GDPR may also foresee that the exercise of a right is delayed in time, that a right is exercised partially or circumscribed to certain categories of data or that a right can be exercised indirectly through an independent supervisory authority.

NOTES
5   These interests are exhaustively listed in Article 23 (1) GDPR.
6   There are certain rights which cannot be restricted under Article 23 GDPR, such as the right to submit a complaint to the supervisory authority (Article 77 GDPR).

3 REQUIREMENTS OF ARTICLE 23(1) GDPR

[2.401]
13. Article 23(1) GDPR lists a number of requirements, which will be detailed below. All those requirements need to be met in order for a measure to be lawfully relied upon.

3.1 RESPECT OF THE ESSENCE OF THE FUNDAMENTAL RIGHTS AND FREEDOMS

14. One of the main objectives of data protection law is to enhance data subjects' control over personal data concerning them. Any restriction shall respect the essence of the right that is being restricted. This means that restrictions that are extensive and intrusive to the extent that they void a fundamental right of its basic content, cannot be justified. In any case, a general exclusion of all data subjects' rights with regard to all data processing operations as well as a general limitation of the rights mentioned in Article 23 GDPR of all data subjects for specific data processing operations or with regard to specific controllers would not respect the essence of the fundamental right to the protection of personal data, as enshrined in the Charter. If the essence of the right is compromised, the restriction shall be considered unlawful, without the need to further assess whether it serves an objective of general interest or satisfies the necessity and proportionality criteria.

15. In order to guarantee this control, data subjects have a number of rights within the right to data protection and the controller has a number of obligations vis a vis the data subject, set out under Articles 12 to 22 and Article 34 GDPR, as well as Article 5 in so far as its provisions correspond to the rights and obligations provided for in Articles 12 to 22 GDPR. It is against this background that Article 23 GDPR should be read and interpreted.

3.2 LEGISLATIVE MEASURES LAYING DOWN RESTRICTIONS AND THE NEED TO BE FORESEEABLE (REC. 41 AND CJEU CASE LAW)

16. The requirement of a legislative measure entails that controllers can only rely on a restriction provided for by Article 23 GDPR to the extent that this restriction has been specified in Union or Member state law. Without the corresponding legislative measure, controllers cannot rely directly on the grounds listed in Article 23(1) GDPR. Recital 41 GDPR states that "[w]here this Regulation refers to a legal basis or a legislative measure, this does not necessarily require a legislative act adopted by a parliament, without prejudice to requirements pursuant to the constitutional order of the Member State concerned. However, such a legal basis or legislative measure should be clear and precise and its application should be foreseeable to persons subject to it, in accordance with the case-law of the Court of Justice of the European Union [. . .] and the European Court of Human Rights"[7].

17.   According to Article 52(1) of the Charter, any limitation on the exercise of the rights and freedoms recognised by the Charter shall be 'provided for by law'. This echoes the expression 'in accordance with the law' in Article 8(2) of the European Convention of Human Rights[8], which means not only compliance with domestic law, but also relates to the quality of that law without prejudice to the nature of the act, requiring it to be compatible with the rule of law. In particular, the domestic law must be **sufficiently clear in its terms to give citizens an adequate indication of the circumstances in and conditions under which controllers are empowered to resort to any such restrictions**. The same strict standard should be applied for any restrictions that could be imposed by Member States. In line with the GDPR and the case law of the Court of Justice of the European Union (CJEU) and of the European Court of Human Rights (ECtHR), it is indeed essential that legislative measures, which seek to restrict the scope of data subject rights or of controller's obligations, are foreseeable for the data subjects.

18.   While any legislative measure must in any case be adapted to the objective pursued and meet the foreseeability criterion, a legislative measure laying down the provisions for the application of restrictions under Article 23 GDPR does not always have to be limited in time or linked to a specific period.

(a)   In some cases, the restriction is not specifically linked to a timeframe because the ground for the restriction to be safeguarded by the legislative measure is not in itself limited in time. In light of the principle of necessity and proportionality, it is necessary to ensure that such legislative measures relate to a ground for restriction to be safeguarded on an ongoing basis, or permanently, in a democratic society. For instance, a legislative measure restricting the scope of the obligations and rights provided for in Article 12 to 22 and Article 34, for safeguarding the protection of judicial independence and judicial proceedings may for example be considered as fulfilling a continuing objective in a democratic society and therefore may not be limited in time.

(b)   In other cases, the ground for the restriction to be safeguarded is in itself limited in time and therefore the legislative measure should provide a limitation in time in order to meet the foreseeability criterion. For example, where restrictions are adopted in the context of a state of emergency to safeguard public health, the EDPB considers that restrictions, imposed for a duration not precisely limited in time, do not meet the foreseeability criterion, including when such restriction apply retroactively or are subject to undefined conditions.

19.   This link between the foreseen restrictions and the objective pursued should be clearly established and demonstrated in the concerned legislative measure or additional supplementary documents. For instance, the mere existence of a pandemic alone is not a sufficient reason to provide for any kind of restriction on the rights of data subjects; rather, any restriction shall clearly contribute to the safeguard of an important objective of general public interest of the Union or of a Member State.

3.3 GROUNDS FOR THE RESTRICTIONS

20.   In order to adopt a legislative measure for restrictions and to apply a restriction in a concrete case, one or several of the following conditions stated in Article 23(1) GDPR need to be met. This list is exhaustive, meaning restrictions cannot be carried out under any other conditions than the ones listed below.

21.   The link between the foreseen restrictions and the objective pursued should be clearly stated in the legislative measure.

3.3.1 National security, defence and public security

22.   A restriction to data subject rights can have national or public security and/or defence of the Member States as an objective to be safeguarded, as stated in Article 23(1)(a), (b) and (c) GDPR.

23.   Moreover, public security includes protection of human life, especially in response to natural or manmade disasters.

3.3.2 Prevention, investigation, detection and prosecution of criminal offences or the execution of criminal penalties including the safeguarding against and the prevention of threats to public security

24.   In certain cases, providing information to the data subjects who are under investigation might jeopardise the success of that investigation. Therefore, the restriction of the right to information or other data subject's rights may be necessary, under Article 23(1)(d) GDPR. This is relevant for instance in the framework of anti-money laundering or the activities of forensic laboratories[9]

25.   Nonetheless, the omitted information shall, in accordance with the case law of the CJEU, be provided once and if it is no longer possible for it to jeopardise the investigation being carried out[10]. This means that a specific (tailor-made) data protection notice should be given to the data subject as soon as possible, stating the different rights such as access, rectification etc.

26.   Also, the objective of safeguarding public security includes the protection of human life especially in response to natural or manmade disasters[11].

3.3.3 Other important objectives of general public interest

27.   Article 23(1)(e) GDPR mentions as other important objectives of general public interest of the Union or of a Member-State important economic or financial interest, including monetary, budgetary and taxation matters, public health and social security. It may concern for instance the keeping of public registers kept for reasons of general public interest or the further processing of archived personal data to provide specific information related to the political behaviour under former totalitarian state regimes[12]. On the other hand, the costs incurred as a consequence of providing information and thus the financial burden on public budgets are not sufficient to justify a public interest in restricting the rights of the data subjects.

3.3.4 Protection of judicial independence and judicial proceedings

28.   Article 23(1)(f) GDPR also foresees the need to restrict certain data subjects' rights or controller's obligations, in order to protect judicial independence and judicial proceedings.

29.   The scope of these restrictions should be aligned with national legislation regulating these matters.

3.3.5 Prevention, investigation, detection and prosecution of breaches of ethics for regulated professions

30.   Article 23(1)(g) GDPR mentions breaches of ethics for regulated professions, such as medical doctors and lawyers.

31.   These are cases in which an investigation does not relate in principle with criminal offences as, where the investigation concerns a criminal offence, the ground set out under point 3.3.2 would be applicable.

3.3.6 Monitoring, inspection or regulatory function connected to the exercise of official authority in the cases referred to in points (a) to (e) and (g) of Article 23 GDPR

The ground for restriction mentioned in Article 23(2)(h) GDPR refers to a potential limitation when there is an inspection or a monitoring exercise or a regulatory function connected, even if only occasionally, to the exercise of official authority in the cases referred to in points 3.3.1 to 3.3.3 and 3.3.5.

3.3.7 Protection of the data subject or the rights and freedoms of others

32.   Article 23(1)(i) GDPR refers to a ground for restriction that aims to protect the data subject or the rights and freedoms of other persons.

33.   One can illustrate a restriction to protect the rights and freedoms of others with an example of an investigation where the identity of an alleged victim, witnesses or whistle-blower cannot be disclosed in order to protect them from retaliations.

3.3.8 Enforcement of civil law claims

34.   Article 23(1)(j) GDPR also includes the enforcement of civil law claims as a ground for restrictions. While Article 23(1)(j) GDPR allows limitations to protect the individual interests of a (potential) litigant, Article 23(1)(f) GDPR allows limitations to protect the court proceedings themselves as well as the applicable procedural rules.

3.4 Data subjects' rights and controller's obligations which may be restricted

35.   In accordance with Article 23 GDPR, only Article 5 as far as its provisions correspond to the rights and obligations provided for in Article 12 to 22, Articles 12 to 22 and 34 GDPR can be restricted. The restrictions to obligations regard restrictions to the principles relating to the processing of personal data as far as its provisions correspond to the rights and obligations provided in Article 12 to 22 GDPR and to the communication of a personal data breach to the data subjects . Article 5 GDPR, which establishes the principles relating to the processing of personal data, is one of the most important articles in the GDPR. Restrictions to the data protection principles need to be duly justified by an exceptional situation, respecting the essence of the fundamental rights and freedoms at issue and following a necessity and proportionality test. It should be noted that Article 5 GDPR can be only restricted in so far as its provisions correspond to the rights and obligations provided in Articles 12 to 22 GDPR.

36.   The restrictions to rights concern the right to transparent information (Article 12 GDPR), right to information (Articles 13 and 14 GDPR), right of access (Article 15 GDPR), right to rectification (Article 16 GDPR), right to erasure (Article 17 GDPR), right to restriction of processing (Article 18 GDPR), notification obligation regarding rectification or erasure of personal data or restriction of processing (Article 19 GDPR), right to data portability (Article 20 GDPR), right to object (Article 21 GDPR), right not to be subject to an automated individual decision making (Article 22 GDPR).

37.   This means that any other data subjects' rights - such as the right to lodge a complaint to the supervisory authority (Article 77GDPR) - or other controllers' obligations cannot be restricted.

3.5 NECESSITY AND PROPORTIONALITY TEST

38.   Restrictions are only lawful when they are a necessary and proportionate measure in a democratic society, as stated in Article 23(1) GDPR. This means that restrictions need to pass a necessity and proportionality test in order to be compliant with the GDPR[13].

39.   The objective of general interest provides the background against which the necessity of the measure may be assessed. It is therefore important to identify the objective of general interest in sufficient detail so as to allow the assessment on whether the measure is necessary. For example, if in administrative proceedings it is necessary to restrict part of the investigation, but some information can already be disclosed to the data subjects concerned, then that information should be provided to the person. The case law of the CJEU applies a strict necessity test for any limitations on the exercise of the rights to personal data protection and respect for private life with regard to the processing of personal data: 'derogations and limitations in relation to the protection of personal data (. . .) must apply only insofar as is strictly necessary'[14]. The ECtHR applies a test of strict necessity depending on the context and all circumstances at hand, such as with regard to secret surveillance measures[15].

40. If this test is satisfied, the proportionality of the envisaged measure will be assessed. Should the draft measure not pass the necessity test, there is no need to examine its proportionality. A measure which is not proved to be necessary should not be proposed unless and until it has been modified to meet the requirement of necessity.

41. The necessity and proportionality test will typically imply assessing the risks to the rights and freedoms of the data subjects. The risks to the rights and freedoms of data subjects will be detailed in point 4.7 of this guidelines.

42. According to the proportionality principle, the content of the legislative measure cannot exceed what is strictly necessary to safeguard the objectives listed in Article 23(1)(a) to (j) GDPR. The general public interest of the restriction must therefore be appropriate for attaining the legitimate objectives pursued by the legislation at issue and not exceed the limits of what is appropriate and necessary in order to achieve those objectives. According to the CJEU case law, Article 23 GDPR cannot be interpreted as being capable of conferring on Member States the power to undermine respect for private life, disregarding Article 7 of the Charter, or any of the other guarantees enshrined therein. In particular, the power conferred on Member States by Article 23(1) GDPR may be exercised only in accordance with the requirement of proportionality, according to which derogations and limitations in relation to the protection of personal data must apply only in so far as is strictly necessary[16].

43. A proposed restriction measure should be supported by evidence describing the problem to be addressed by that measure, how it will be addressed by it, and why existing or less intrusive measures cannot sufficiently address it. There is also a requirement to demonstrate how any proposed interference or restriction genuinely meet objectives of general interest of the State and EU or the need to protect the rights and freedoms of others. The restriction of data protection rights will need to focus on specific risks.

44. For example, if restrictions contribute to safeguarding public health in a state of emergency, the EDPB considers that the restrictions must be strictly limited in scope (e.g. as to the purpose, data subject rights concerned or the categories of controllers concerned) and in time. In particular, it must be limited to the emergency state period. Data subject rights can be restricted but not denied.

NOTES

[7] The type of legislative measures considered has to be in line with EU law or with the national law. Depending on the degree of interference of the restriction, a particular legislative measure, taking into account the level of norm, could be required at national level.

[8] See in particular, European Court of Human Rights, 14 September 2010, Sanoma Uitgevers B.V. v. The Netherlands, EC:ECHR:2010:0914JUD003822403, paragraph 83: "Further, as regards the words "in accordance with the law" and "prescribed by law" which appear in Articles 8 to 11 of the Convention, the Court observes that it has always understood the term "law" in its "substantive" sense, not its "formal" one; it has included both "written law", encompassing enactments of lower ranking statutes and regulatory measures taken by professional regulatory bodies under independent rule-making powers delegated to them by Parliament, and unwritten law. "Law" must be understood to include both statutory law and judge-made "law". In sum, the "law" is the provision in force as the competent courts have interpreted it". On the notion of 'provided for by law', the criteria developed by the European Court of Human Rights should be used as suggested in CJEU Advocates General opinions in joined cases C 203/15 and C 698/15, Tele2 Sverige AB, ECLI:EU:C:2016:572, paragraphs 137- 154 or in case C-70/10, Scarlet Extended, ECLI:EU:C:2011:255, paragraph 99.

[9] Recital 19 GDPR.

[10] Opinion 1/15 of the CJEU (Grand Chamber) on the Draft PNR Agreement between Canada and the European Union, 26 July 2017, ECLI:EU:C:2017:592.

[11] Recital 73 GDPR.

[12] Recital 73 GDPR.

[13] Within the mission of the supervisory authorities and in order to ensure legal certainty it is advisable that the proportionality and necessity test is documented. Supervisory authorities may request additional documentation.

[14] See CJEU, judgment of 16 December 2008, case C-73/07, Tietosuojavaltuutettu v. Satakunnan Markkinapörssi Oy and Satamedia Oy, ECLI:EU:C:2008:727, paragraph 56.

[15] See ECtHR, Szabo and Vissy v. Hungary, 12 January 2016, paragraph 73.

[16] CJEU, judgment of 6 October 2020, La Quadrature du net and others joined cases C-511/18, C-512/18 and C-520/18, ECLI:EU:C:2020:791, paragraph 210. For example, in relation to data retention by online public communication services and hosting services providers, the CJEU concluded, paragraph 212, that "Article 23(1) (GDPR), read in the light of Articles 7, 8 and 11 and Article 52(1) of the Charter, must be interpreted as precluding national legislation which requires that providers of access to online public communication services and hosting service providers retain, generally and indiscriminately, inter alia, personal data relating to those services".

---

4 REQUIREMENTS OF ARTICLE 23 (2) GDPR

[2.402]
45. According to the CJEU case law, any legislative measure adopted on the basis of Article 23(1) GDPR must, in particular, comply with the specific requirements set out in Article 23(2) of the GDPR.[17] Article 23(2) GDPR states that the legislative measures imposing restrictions to the rights of data subjects and the controllers' obligations shall contain, where relevant, specific provisions about several criteria outlined below. As a rule, all the requirements detailed below should be included in the legislative measure imposing restrictions under Article 23 GDPR.

46. Exceptions to this rule, based on the fact that one or more provisions in Article 23(2) GDPR are not relevant regarding the legislative measure foreseeing the restriction of data subjects' rights, need to be duly justified by the legislator. The EDPB's interpretation of the expression "where relevant" in Article 23 (2) GDPR is linked to the circumstances.

47. Article 23(2)(a) GDPR mentions the purposes of the processing or categories of processing as one of the specific provisions that shall be mentioned in any legislative measures restricting the rights of data subjects or controllers' obligations. As per Recital 8 GDPR, the reason for the restriction should be comprehensible to persons to whom it applies. This also involves a clear understanding of how and when the restriction may apply.

48. For example, national legislation on prevention and investigation of breaches of ethics for regulated professions might state that if the disclosure of the fact that a person is under investigation for a serious breach may be prejudicial to the purpose of the investigation, the information may not be disclosed to the data subject for a limited time.

49. The possible purposes of the processing need to be linked to the grounds of the restrictions mentioned in point 3.3 of these guidelines.

50. It should be said that sometimes the exercise of data subjects' rights helps the controllers performing their function. For example, the right to rectification can contribute to the quality of the data.

4.1 CATEGORIES OF PERSONAL DATA

51. Article 23(2)(b) GDPR states that the categories of personal data involved in restrictions are to be indicated in the legislative measure foreseeing those restrictions[18].

52. In the same vein, restrictions entailing special categories of personal data may have a bigger impact on the data subjects and, therefore, the legislative measure setting such a restriction should mention the special categories therein involved.

4.2 SCOPE OF THE RESTRICTIONS

53. Article 23(2)(c) GDPR prescribes that the scope of the restrictions shall also be specified, i.e. which rights are concerned and how far they are going to be limited, for instance, that a restriction only concerns the right to restriction of processing (Article 18 GDPR), or that it may concern access, rectification and confidentiality of communication.

4.3 SAFEGUARDS TO PREVENT ABUSE OR UNLAWFUL ACCESS OR TRANSFER

54. Article 23(2)(d) GDPR states that the legislative measure shall include safeguards to prevent abuse or unlawful access or transfer. This refers in particular to organisational and/or technical measures[19] which are necessary in order to avoid breaches or unlawful transfers such as the storage in a safe way of physical documents. For example, in some Member States the exercise of rights in respect of processing carried out in specific sectors can be exercised through the mediation of the national SA.

55. The legislative measure may also concern periodic measures to review a given decision on restrictions. The legislator may propose that each restriction implemented by the controller should be reviewed periodically to ensure that the justification for it is still valid.

4.4 SPECIFICATION OF THE CONTROLLER

56. Article 23(2)(e) GDPR requires that the legislative measure specifies who the controller is or who the categories of the controller are. This appointment of the controllers in the legislative measure not only favours legal certainty regarding the responsibility for the processing operations in relation to the restrictions, but also will allow data subjects to know whom to address when exercising their rights, once the restriction is lifted.

4.5 STORAGE PERIODS

57. Article 23(2)(f) GDPR establishes that the legislative measure must include a specific provision regarding the storage periods and applicable safeguards taking into account the nature, scope and purposes of the processing/categories of processing. For instance, the retention period could be calculated as the duration of the processing operation plus additional time for potential litigation.

4.6 RISKS TO DATA SUBJECTS' RIGHTS AND FREEDOMS

58. Article 23(2)(g) GDPR requires that the legislative measure include the risks to data subject's rights and freedoms entailed by the restrictions. This is a very important step, which helps in the necessity and proportionality test of the restrictions.

59. The goal of this assessment of the risks to data subjects' rights and freedoms is twofold. On the one hand, it provides an overview of the potential impact of restrictions on data subjects. On the other hand, it provides elements for the necessity and proportionality test of the restrictions. In this regard and if applicable, a data protection impact assessment should be considered.

60. The legislator should assess the risks to data subject's rights and freedoms from the perspective of the data subjects. It is not always mandatory to perform a DPIA, but concrete risks to data subjects - such as erroneous profiling leading to discrimination, reduced human dignity[20], freedom of speech, the right to privacy and data protection[21], a bigger impact on vulnerable groups (such as children or persons with disability), to mention a few - may be stated in the legislative measure, if applicable.

61. When such assessment is provided, the EDPB considers necessary to include it in the recitals or explanatory memorandum of the legislation or in the impact assessment[22].

4.7 RIGHT TO BE INFORMED ABOUT THE RESTRICTION, UNLESS PREJUDICIAL TO THE PURPOSE OF THE RESTRICTION

62. Article 23(2)(h) GDPR states that, unless it may be prejudicial to the purpose of the restriction, data subjects shall be informed of the restriction. This means that data subjects should be informed about the restriction to their right to information as a rule. To that purpose, a general data protection notice may be sufficient.

63. For example, where a data subject specifically asks to exercise a particular right at a very delicate moment of a given administrative investigation, the data subject should, if possible, be informed of the reasons for the restriction. However, if informing the data subject of the reasons for the restriction would result in cancelling the effect of the restriction (i.e. would hamper the preliminary effects of the investigation), that information may not be disclosed. Restrictions may be adopted to protect investigations. In this case, restrictions must remain necessary and proportionate and to do so an assessment should be performed by the controller to check whether informing the data subject of the restriction is prejudicial to the purpose of the restriction.

64. In other words, in extraordinary circumstances, for instance in the very preliminary stages of an investigation, if the data subject requests information if he or she is being investigated, the controller could decide not to grant that information at that moment - if this restriction is lawful and strictly necessary in the specific case it where prejudicial to the purpose of the restriction.

65. At a later stage, such as after the preliminary phase of the investigation or inquiry is completed, data subjects should receive a (specific) data protection notice. It is still possible at this stage that certain rights continue to be restricted, such as the right of access to the information about the opening an investigation, or to the allegations of potential victims of harassment[23]. This fact should be indicated in the data protection notice along with an indication of a period in which the rights will be fully restored, if possible.

NOTES

17 CJEU, judgment of 6 October 2020, La Quadrature du Net and others joined cases C-511/18, C-512/18 and C-520/18, ECLI:EU:C:2020:791, paragraph 209.

18 Where possible, the controller can go further and list the specific data items to which the restriction of rights may apply, such as the preliminary results of an investigation, a decision opening an inquiry, etc.

19 See EDPB Guidelines 4/2019 on Article 25 data protection by design and by default, available at: https://edpb.europa.eu/sites/edpb/files/consultation/edpb_guidelines_201904_dataprotection_by_design_an d_by_default.pdf

20 Human dignity is a right protected by Article 1 of the Charter.

21 Articles 7 and 8 of the Charter.

22 See Article 35 (10) GDPR.

23 For further information, see CJEU, judgment of 17 July 2014, YS v Minister voor Immigratie, Integratie en Asiel and Minister voor Immigratie, Integratie en Asiel v M and S, cases C-141/12 and C-372/12, ECLI:EU:C:2014:2081, paragraphs 45 and 46 and judgment of 20 December 2017, Novak, case C-434/16, ECLI:EU:C:2017:994, paragraph 56.

24 CJEU, judgment 4 December 2018, Case C-378/17, ECLI:EU:C:2018:979, paragraph 38.

5 ACCOUNTABILITY PRINCIPLE

[2.403]
66. In light of the accountability principle (Article 5(2) GDPR), the controller should document the application of restrictions on concrete cases by keeping a record of their application. This record should include the applicable reasons for the restrictions, which grounds among those listed in Article 23(1) GDPR apply (where the legislative measure allows for restrictions on different grounds), its timing and the outcome of the necessity and proportionality test. The records should be made available on request to the data protection supervisory authority (SA).

67. In case the controller has a data protection officer (DPO), the DPO should be informed without undue delay whenever data subject rights are restricted in accordance with the legislative measure. The DPO should be given access to the associated records and any documents concerning the factual or legal context in which the restriction takes place. The involvement of the DPO in the application of restrictions should also be documented.

6 CONSULTATION WITH THE SAS (ARTICLES 36(4) AND 57(1)(C) GDPR)

[2.404]
68. In accordance with Article 36(4) GDPR, where restrictions are adopted at the level of the Member States, SAs shall be consulted before the adoption of the legislative measure to be adopted by a national parliament, or of a regulatory measure based on such a legislative measure envisaging the restriction of data subjects' rights under Article 23 GDPR.

69. Also, it is within the tasks of the SAs to provide advice on legislative measures relating to the protection of individuals' rights and freedoms regarding their personal data processing, in accordance with Article 57(1)(c) GDPR.

70. If SAs are not duly consulted, they can issue under Article 58(3)(b) GDPR on their own initiative opinions to the national parliament, the Member State government or, in accordance with Member State law, to other institutions or bodies as well as to the public on any issue related to the protection of personal data.

71.   At that stage and if applicable, the SAs may ask for a data protection impact assessment (DPIA) under Article 35 GDPR. That assessment will be helpful in the description of the risks to the data subjects' rights mentioned above in point 4.6.

72.   In addition, data protection legislation at national level may set out specific procedures regarding the adoption of legislative measures that aim at restricting the rights afforded by Articles 12 to 22 and Article 34 GDPR, in line with Article 23 GDPR. This could be the case only if in line with the GDPR.

7 EXERCISE OF DATA SUBJECTS' RIGHTS AFTER THE LIFTING OF THE RESTRICTION

[2.405]
73.   The controller should lift the restrictions as soon as the circumstances that justify them no longer apply. If the data subjects have not yet been informed of the restrictions before that moment, they should be at the latest when the restriction if lifted.

74.   During the application of a restriction, data subjects may be allowed to exercise certain rights, if not all their rights need to be restricted. In order to assess when the restriction can be partially or integrally lifted, a necessity and proportionality test may be performed several times during the application of a restriction.

75.   When the restriction is lifted - which should be documented in the record mentioned in point 5 -, data subjects can exercise all their rights.

76.   If the controller does not allow data subjects to exercise their rights after the restriction has been lifted, the data subject can submit a complaint to the SA against the controller, in accordance with Article 57(1)(f) GDPR.

8 INFRINGEMENTS OF ARTICLE 23 GDPR

8.1 NON-OBSERVATION OF ARTICLE 23 GDPR REQUIREMENTS BY A MEMBER STATE

[2.406]
77.   The European Commission, as Guardian of the Treaties, has the duty to monitor the application of EU primary and secondary law and to ensure its uniform application throughout the EU, including by taking actions where national measures would fail to comply with EU law.

78.   Furthermore, where the legislatives measures imposing restrictions under Article 23 GDPR do not comply with the GDPR, in accordance with Article 58(5) GDPR and where appropriate, SAs shall have the power to bring infringements of this Regulation to the attention of the judicial authorities to commence or engage otherwise in legal proceedings, in order to enforce the provisions of the GDPR.

79.   According to the principle of supremacy of EU law, the "duty to disapply national legislation that is contrary to EU law is owed not only by national courts, but also by all organs of the State – including administrative authorities – called upon, within the exercise of their respective powers, to apply EU law"[24].

8.2 NON-OBSERVATION OF A LEGISLATIVE MEASURE IMPOSING SUCH RESTRICTIONS BY A CONTROLLER

80.   Where the legislative measures imposing restrictions under Article 23 GDPR comply with the GDPR but are infringed by a controller, SAs can make use of their advisory, investigative, corrective and powers against it, as in any other case of non-observation of GDPR rules.

81.   In accordance with the powers foreseen in Article 58(1) GDPR, the SAs have the following investigative powers:
- order the controller and the processor, and, where applicable, the controller's or processor's representative to provide any information it requires for the performance of its tasks;
- carry out investigations in the form of data protection audits;
- notify the controller or the processor of an alleged infringement of the GDPR;
- obtain, from the controller and the processor, access to all personal data and to all information necessary for the performance of its tasks;
- obtain access to any premises of the controller and the processor, including to any data processing equipment and means, in accordance with Union or Member State procedural law.

82.   If corrective measures need to be applied, the SAs can in accordance with Article 58 (2) GDPR:
- **issue warnings** to a controller or processor that intended processing operations are likely to infringe provisions of this Regulation;
- **issue reprimands** to a controller or a processor where processing operations have infringed provisions of the GDPR;
- **order** the controller or the processor **to comply** with the data subject's requests to exercise his or her rights pursuant to the GDPR;
- **order** the controller or processor **to bring processing operations into compliance** with the provisions of the GDPR, where appropriate, in a specified manner and within a specified period;
- **order** the controller **to communicate a personal data breach to the data subject**;
- **impose** a temporary or definitive limitation including **a ban** on processing;
- **order** the rectification or erasure of personal data or restriction of processing pursuant to Articles 16, 17 and 18 GDPR and the notification of such actions to recipients to whom the personal data have been disclosed pursuant to Article 17(2) and Article 19 GDPR;

- **impose an administrative fine** pursuant to Article 83, in addition to, or instead of measures referred to in Article 58(2) GDPR, depending on the circumstances of each individual case;
- **order** the suspension of data flows to a recipient in a third country or to an international organisation.

83. Regarding the SAs advisory powers foreseen in Article 58(3) GDPR, they can:
- advice the controllers in accordance with the prior consultation procedure referred to in Article 36(1) and (5) GDPR;
- authorise processing referred to in Article 36(5) GDPR, if the law of the Member State requires such prior authorisation.

9 CONCLUSIONS

[2.407]

84. Article 23 GDPR allows under specific conditions, a national or Union legislator to restrict, by way of a legislative measure, the scope of the obligations and rights provided for in Articles 12 to 22 and Article 34, as well as Article 5 GDPR in so far as its provisions correspond to the rights and obligations provided for in Articles 12 to 22, when such a restriction respects the essence of the fundamental rights and freedoms and is a necessary and proportionate measure in a democratic society to safeguard, inter alia, important objectives of general public interest of the Union or of a Member State.

85. Restrictions of data subjects' rights need to observe the requirements stated in Article 23 GDPR. The Member States or the Union issuing the legislative measures setting those restrictions and the controllers applying them should be aware of the exceptional nature of these restrictions.

86. The proportionality test should be carried out before the decision-making of applying a restriction by the legislator.

87. SAs should be consulted before the adoption of the legislative measures setting the restrictions and have the powers to enforce its compliance with the GDPR.

88. Once restrictions are lifted, data subjects must be allowed to exercise their rights by the controller.

10 ANNEX: CHECK-LISTS – ARTICLE 23 GDPR IN A NUTSHELL

10.1 REQUIREMENTS UNDER ARTICLE 23(1) GDPR

[2.408]
—

(i)   *Respect of the essence of the fundamental rights and freedoms*
(ii)   *Proportionality and necessity test*
(iii) *Legislative measures laying down restrictions and the need to be foreseeable (Rec. 41 and CJEU case law)*
(iv)   *Data subjects' rights and controller's obligations which may be restricted*
    (a)   the right to transparent information (Article 12 GDPR),
    (b)   right to information (Articles 13 and 14 GDPR),
    (c)   right of access (Article 15 GDPR),
    (d)   right to rectification (Article 16 GDPR),
    (e)   right to erasure (Article 17 GDPR),
    (f)   right to restriction of processing (Article 18 GDPR),
    (g)   notification obligation regarding rectification or erasure of personal data or restriction of processing (Article 19 GDPR),
    (h)   right to data portability (Article 20 GDPR),
    (i)   right to object (Article 21 GDPR),
    (j)   right not to be subject to an automated individual decision making (Article 22 GDPR)
    (k)   obligations provided in Article 12 to 22 GDPR (Article 5 GDPR) and
    (l)   the communication of a personal data breach to the data subjects (Article 34 GDPR)
(v)   Grounds for the restrictions
    (a)   national security;
    (b)   defence;
    (c)   public security;
    (d)   the prevention, investigation, detection or prosecution of criminal offences or the execution of criminal penalties, including the safeguarding against and the prevention of threats to public security;
    (e)   other important objectives of general public interest of the Union or of a Member State, in particular an important economic or financial interest of the Union or of a Member State, including monetary, budgetary and taxation a matters, public health and social security;
    (f)   the protection of judicial independence and judicial proceedings;
    (g)   the prevention, investigation, detection and prosecution of breaches of ethics for regulated professions;
    (h)   a monitoring, inspection or regulatory function connected, even occasionally, to the exercise of official authority in the cases referred to in points (a) to (e) and (g);
    (i)   the protection of the data subject or the rights and freedoms of others;
    (j)   the enforcement of civil law claims.

10.2 REQUIREMENTS UNDER ARTICLE 23(2) GDPR

(i)   the purposes of the processing or categories of processing;

(ii)   the categories of personal data;

(iii)   the scope of the restrictions introduced;

(iv)   the safeguards to prevent abuse or unlawful access or transfer;

(v)   the specification of the controller or categories of controllers;

(vi)   the storage periods and the applicable safeguards taking into account the nature, scope and purposes of the processing or categories of processing;

(vii)   the risks to the rights and freedoms of data subjects; and

(viii)   the right of data subjects to be informed about the restriction, unless that may be prejudicial to the purpose of the restriction.

EUROPEAN DATA PROTECTION BOARD: GUIDELINES 1/2021 ON EXAMPLES REGARDING DATA BREACH NOTIFICATION: VERSION FOR PUBLIC CONSULTATION
Version 1.0

Adopted on 14 January 2021

[2.409]

NOTES

    This document has been published for public consultation. A subsequent version of this document is expected to be adopted by the EDPB following publication of this book

    © European Data Protection Board.

TABLE OF CONTENTS

THE EUROPEAN DATA PROTECTION BOARD

Having regard to Article 70(1e) of the Regulation 2016/679/EU of the European Parliament and of the Council of 27 April 2016 on the protection of natural persons with regard to the processing of personal data and on the free movement of such data, and repealing Directive 95/46/EC, (hereinafter "GDPR"),

Having regard to the EEA Agreement and in particular to Annex XI and Protocol 37 thereof, as amended by the Decision of the EEA joint Committee No 154/2018 of 6 July 2018[1],

Having regard to Article 12 and Article 22 of its Rules of Procedure,

Having regard to the Communication from the Commission to the European Parliament and the Council titled Data protection as a pillar of citizens' empowerment and the EU's approach to the digital transition - two years of application of the General Data Protection Regulation[2],

HAS ADOPTED THE FOLLOWING GUIDELINES

[1]   References to "Member States" made throughout this document should be understood as references to "EEA Member States".

[2]   COM(2020) 264 final, 24 June 2020.

1 INTRODUCTION

[2.410]

1.   The GDPR introduces the requirement for a personal data breach to be notified to the competent national supervisory authority (hereinafter "SA") and, in certain cases, to communicate the breach to the individuals whose personal data have been affected by the breach (Articles 33 and 34).

2.   The Article 29 Working Party already produced a *general* guidance on data breach notification in October 2017, analysing the relevant Sections of the GDPR (Guidelines on Personal data breach notification under Regulation 2016/679, WP 250) (hereinafter "Guidelines WP250)[3]. However, due to its nature and timing, this guideline did not address all practical issues in sufficient detail. Therefore, the need has arisen for a *practice-oriented, case-based* guidance that utilizes the experiences gained by SAs since the GDPR is applicable.

3. This document is intended to complement the Guidelines WP 250 and it reflects the common experiences of the SAs of the EEA since the GDPR became applicable. Its aim is to help data controllers in deciding how to handle data breaches and what factors to consider during risk assessment.

4. As part of any attempt to address a breach the controller should first be able to recognize one. The GDPR defines a "personal data breach" in Article 4(12) as "a breach of security leading to the accidental or unlawful destruction, loss, alteration, unauthorised disclosure of, or access to, personal data transmitted, stored or otherwise processed".

5. In its Opinion 03/2014 on breach notification[4] and in its Guidelines WP 250, WP29 explained that breaches can be categorised according to the following three well-known information security principles:
- "Confidentiality breach" - where there is an unauthorised or accidental disclosure of, or access to, personal data.
- "Integrity breach" - where there is an unauthorised or accidental alteration of personal data.
- "Availability breach" - where there is an accidental or unauthorised loss of access to, or destruction of, personal data[5].

6. A breach can potentially have a range of significant adverse effects on individuals, which can result in physical, material, or non-material damage. The GDPR explains that this can include loss of control over their personal data, limitation of their rights, discrimination, identity theft or fraud, financial loss, unauthorised reversal of pseudonymization, damage to reputation, and loss of confidentiality of personal data protected by professional secrecy. It can also include any other significant economic or social disadvantage to those individuals. One of the most important obligation of the data controller is to evaluate these risks to the rights and freedoms of data subjects and to implement appropriate technical and organizational measures to address them.

7. Accordingly, the GDPR requires the controller to:
- document any personal data breaches, comprising the facts relating to the personal data breach, its effects and the remedial action taken[6];
- notify the personal data breach to the supervisory authority, unless the data breach is unlikely to result in a risk to the rights and freedoms of natural persons[7];
- communicate the personal data breach to the data subject when the personal data breach is likely to result in a high risk to the rights and freedoms of natural persons[8].

8. Data breaches are problems in and of themselves, but they are also symptoms of a vulnerable, possibly outdated data security regime, thus indicate system weaknesses to be addressed. As a general truth, it is always better to prevent data breaches by preparing in advance, since several consequences of them are by nature irreversible. Before a controller can *fully* assess the risk arising from a breach caused by some form of attack, the root cause of the issue should be identified, in order to identify whether any vulnerabilities that gave rise to the incident are still present, and are still therefore exploitable. In many cases the controller is able to identify that the incident is likely to result in a risk, and is therefore to be notified. In other cases the notification does not need to be postponed until the risk and impact surrounding the breach has been fully assessed, since the full risk assessment can happen in parallel to notification, and the information thus gained may be provided to the SA in phases without undue further delay[9].

9. The breach should be notified when the controller is of the opinion that it is likely to result in a risk to the rights and freedoms of the data subject. Controllers should make this assessment at the time they become aware of the breach. The controller should not wait for a detailed forensic examination and (early) mitigation steps before assessing whether or not the data breach is likely to result in a risk and thus should be notified.

10. If a controller self-assesses the risk to be unlikely, but it turns out that the risk materializes, the relevant SA can use its corrective powers and may resolve to sanctions.

11. Every controller should have plans, procedures in place for handling eventual data breaches. Organisations should have clear reporting lines and persons responsible for certain aspects of the recovery process.

12. Training and awareness on data protection issues of the staff of the controller focusing on personal data breach management (identification of a personal data breach incident and further actions to be taken, etc.) is also essential for the controllers. This training should be regularly repeated, depending on the type of the processing activity and size of the controller, addressing latest trends and alerts coming from cyberattacks or other security incidents.

13. The principle of accountability and the concept of data protection by design could incorporate analysis that feeds into a data controller's own "Handbook on Handling Personal Data Breach" that aims to establish facts for each facet of the processing at each major stage of the operation. Such a handbook prepared in advance would provide a much quicker source of information to allow data controllers to mitigate the risks and meet the obligations without undue delay. This would ensure that if a personal data breach was to occur, people in the organisation would know what to do, and the incident would more than likely be handled quicker than if there were no mitigations or plan in place.

14. Though the cases presented below are fictitious, they are based on typical cases from the SA's collective experience with data breach notifications. The analyses offered relate explicitly to the cases under scrutiny, but with the goal to provide assistance for data controllers in assessing their own data breaches. Any modification in the circumstances of the cases described below may result in different or more significant levels of risk, thus requiring different or additional measures. These guidelines structure the cases according to certain categories of breaches (e.g. ransomware attacks). Certain mitigating measures are called for in each case when dealing with a certain category of breaches. These measures are not necessarily repeated in each case analysis belonging to the same category of breaches. For the cases belonging to the same category only the differences are laid out. Therefore, the reader should read all cases relevant to relevant category of a breach to identify and distinguish all the correct measures to be taken.

15. The internal documentation of a breach is an obligation independent of the risks pertaining to the breach, and must be performed in each and every case. The cases presented below try to shed some light on whether or not to notify the breach to the SA and communicate it to the data subjects affected.

NOTES

3   G29 WP250 rev.1, 6 February 2018, Guidelines on Personal data breach notification under Regulation 2016/679 - endorsed by the EDPB, https://ec.europa.eu/newsroom/article29/item-detail.cfm?item_id=612052.

4   G29 WP213, 25 March 2014, Opinion 03/2014 on Personal Data Breach Notification, p. 5, https://ec.europa.eu/justice/article-29/documentation/opinionrecommendation/index_en.htm#maincontentSec4.

5   See Guidelines WP 250, p. 7.

6   GDPR Article 33(5).

7   GDPR Article 33(1).

8   GDPR Article 34(1).

9   GDPR Article 33(4).

2 RANSOMWARE

[2.411]

16. A frequent cause for a data breach notification is a ransomware attack suffered by the data controller. In these cases a malicious code encrypts the personal data, and subsequently the attacker asks the controller for a ransom in exchange for the decryption code. This kind of attack can usually be classified as a breach of availability, but often also a breach of confidentiality could occur.

2.1 CASE NO. 01: RANSOMWARE WITH PROPER BACKUP AND WITHOUT EXFILTRATION

Computer systems of a small manufacturing company were exposed to a ransomware attack, and data stored in those systems was encrypted. The data controller used encryption at rest, so all data accessed by the ransomware was stored in encrypted form using a state-of-the-art encryption algorithm. The decryption key was not compromised in the attack, i.e. the attacker could neither access it nor use it indirectly. In consequence, the attacker only had access to encrypted personal data. In particular, neither the email system of the company, nor any client systems used to access it were affected. The company is using the expertise of an external cybersecurity company to investigate the incident. Logs tracing all data flows leaving the company (including outbound email) are available. After analysing the logs and the data collected by the detection systems the company has deployed, an internal investigation supported by the external cybersecurity company determined *with certainty* that the perpetrator only encrypted data, without exfiltrating it. The logs show no outward data flow in the timeframe of the attack. The personal data affected by the breach relates to clients and employees of the company, a few dozen individuals altogether. A backup was readily available, and the data was restored a few hours after the attack took place. The breach did not result in any consequences on the day-to-day operation of the controller. There was no delay in employee payments or handling client requests.

17. In this case the following elements were realized from the definition of a "personal data breach": a breach of security led to unlawful alteration and unauthorized access to personal data stored.

2.1.1 CASE No. 01 – Prior measures and risk assessment

18. As with all risks posed by external actors, the likelihood that a ransomware attack is successful can be drastically reduced by tightening the security of the data controlling environment. The majority of these breaches can be prevented by ensuring that appropriate organizational, physical and technological security measures have been taken. Examples of such measures are proper patch management and the use of an appropriate anti-malware detection system. Having a proper and separate backup will help to mitigate the consequences of a successful attack should it occur. Moreover, an employee security education, training, and awareness (SETA) program, will help to prevent and recognise this kind of attack. (A list of advisable measures can be found in section 2.5) Among those measures, a proper patch management that ensures that the systems are up to date and all known vulnerabilities of the deployed systems are fixed is one of the most important since most of the ransomware attacks exploit well-known vulnerabilities.

19. When assessing the risks, the controller should investigate the breach and identify the type of the malicious code to understand the possible consequences of the attack. Among those risks to be considered is the risk that data was exfiltrated without leaving a trace in the logs of the systems.

20. In this example, the attacker had access to personal data and the confidentiality of cipher text containing personal data in encrypted form was compromised. However, any data that might have been exfiltrated cannot be read or used by the perpetrator, at least for the time being. The encryption technique used by the data controller conforms to the state-of-the-art. The decryption key was not compromised and presumably could also not be determined by other means. In consequence, the confidentiality risks to the rights and freedoms of natural persons are reduced to a minimum barring cryptanalytic progress that renders the encrypted data intelligible in the future.

21. The data controller should consider the impact and severity of the breach. In this case, it appears the risks to the rights and freedoms of data subjects result from the lack of availability of the personal data, and the confidentiality of the personal data is not compromised[10]. In this example, the adverse effects of the breach were mitigated fairly soon after the breach occurred. Having a proper backup regime[11] makes the effects of the breach less severe and here the controller was able to effectively make use of it.

22.   On the severity of the consequences for the data subjects, only minor consequences could be identified since the affected data was restored in a few hours, the breach did not result in any consequences on the day-to-day operation of the controller and had no significant effect on the data subjects (e.g. employee payments or handling client requests).

2.1.2 CASE No. 01 – Mitigation and obligations

23.   Without a backup few measures to remediate the loss of personal data can be undertaken by the controller, and the data has to be collected again. In this particular case however, the impacts of the attack could effectively be contained by resetting all compromised systems to a clean state known to be free of malicious code, fixing the vulnerabilities and restoring the affected data soon after the attack.

Without a backup, data is lost and the severity may increase because risks or impacts to individuals may also do so.

24.   The timeliness of an effective data restoration from the readily available backup is a key variable when analysing the breach. Specifying an appropriate timeframe to restore the compromised data depends on the unique circumstances of the breach at hand. The GDPR states that a personal data breach shall be notified without undue delay and, where feasible, not later than after 72 hours. Therefore, it could be determined that exceeding the 72-hour time limit is unadvisable in any case, but when dealing with high risk level cases, even complying with this deadline can be viewed as unsatisfactory.

25.   In this case, following a detailed impact assessment and incident response process, the controller determined that the breach was unlikely to result in a risk to the rights and freedoms of natural persons, hence no communication to the data subjects is necessary, nor does the breach require a notification to the SA. However, as all data breaches, it should be documented in accordance with Article 33 (5). The organisation may also need (or later be required by the SA) to update and remediate its organizational and technical personal data security handling and risk mitigation measures and procedures.

Actions necessary based on the identified risks		
No risk (internal register)	Risk (notify SA)	High Risk (communicate to data subjects)
√	X	X

2.2 CASE NO. 02: RANSOMWARE WITHOUT PROPER BACKUP

One of the computers used by an agricultural company was exposed to a ransomware attack and its data was encrypted by the attacker. The company is using the expertise of an external cybersecurity company to monitor their network. Logs tracing all data flows leaving the company (including outbound email) are available. After analysing the logs and the data the other detection systems have collected the internal investigation aided by the cybersecurity company determined that the perpetrator only encrypted the data, without exfiltrating it. The logs show no outward data flow in the timeframe of the attack. The personal data affected by the breach relates to the employees and clients of the company, a few dozen individuals altogether. No special categories of data were affected. No backup was available in an electronic form. Most of the data was restored from paper backups. The restoration of the data took 5 working days and led to minor delays in the delivery of orders to customers.

2.2.1 CASE No. 02 – Prior measures and risk assessment

26.   The data controller should have adopted the same prior measures as mentioned in part 2.1. and in section 2.9. The major difference to the previous case is the lack of an electronic backup and the lack of encryption at rest. This leads to critical differences in the following steps.

27.   When assessing the risks, the controller should investigate the method of infiltration and identify the type of the malicious code to understand the possible consequences of the attack. In this example the ransomware encrypted the personal data without exfiltrating it. As a result, it appears the risks to the rights and freedoms of data subjects result from the lack of availability of the personal data, and the confidentiality of the personal data is not compromised. A thorough examination of the firewall logs and its implications is essential in determining the risk. The data controller should present the factual findings of these investigations upon request.

28.   The data controller needs to keep in mind that if the attack is more sophisticated the malware has the functionality to edit log files and remove the trace. So - given that logs are not forwarded or replicated to a central log server - even after a thorough investigation that determined that the personal data was not exfiltrated by the attacker, the data controller cannot state that the absence of a log entry proves the absence of exfiltration, therefore the likelihood of a confidentiality breach cannot be entirely dismissed.

29.   The data controller should assess the risks of this breach if the data was accessed by the attacker. During the risk assessment, the data controller should also take into consideration the nature, the sensitivity, the volume, and the context of personal data affected in the breach. In this case no special categories of personal data are affected, and the quantity of breached data and the number of affected data subjects is low.

30. Gathering exact information on the unauthorized access is key for determining the risk level and preventing a new or continued attack. If the data had been copied from the database, it would obviously have been a risk-increasing factor. When uncertain about the specifics of the illegitimate access, the worse scenario should be considered and the risk should be assessed accordingly.

31. The absence of a backup database can be considered a risk enhancing factor depending on the severity of consequences for the data subjects resulting from the lack of availability of the data.

2.2.2 CASE No. 02 – Mitigation and obligations

32. Without a backup few measures to remediate the loss of personal data can be undertaken by the controller, and the data has to be collected again, unless some other source is available (e.g. order confirmation e-mails). Without a backup, data may be lost and the severity will depend on the impact for the individuals.

33. The restoration of the data should not prove to be overly problematic[12] if the data is still available on paper, but given the lack of an electronic backup database, a notification to the SA is considered necessary, as the restoration of the data took some time and could cause some delays in the orders' delivery to customers and a considerable amount of meta-data (e.g. logs, time stamps) might not be retrievable.

34. Informing the data subjects about the breach may also depend on the length of time the personal data is unavailable and the difficulties it might cause in the operation of the controller as a result (e.g. delays in transferring employee's payments). As these delays in payments and deliveries may lead to financial loss for the individuals whose data has been compromised, one could also argue the breach is likely to result in a high risk. Also, it might not be possible to avoid informing the data subjects if their contribution is needed for restoring the encrypted data.

35. This case serves as an example for a ransomware attack with risk to the rights and freedoms of the data subjects, but not reaching high risk. It should be documented in accordance with Article 33 (5) and notified to the SA in accordance with Article 33 (1). The organisation may also need (or be required by the SA) to update and remediate its organizational and technical personal data security handling and risk mitigation measures and procedures.

Actions necessary based on the identified risks		
No risk (internal register)	Risk (notify SA)	High Risk (communicate to data subjects)
√	√	X

2.3 CASE NO. 03: RANSOMWARE WITH BACKUP AND WITHOUT EXFILTRATION IN A HOSPITAL

The information system of a hospital / healthcare centre was exposed to a ransomware attack and a significant proportion of its data was encrypted by the attacker. The company is using the expertise of an external cybersecurity company to monitor their network. Logs tracing all data flows leaving the company (including outbound email) are available. After analysing the logs and the data the other detection systems have collected the internal investigation aided by the cybersecurity company determined that the perpetrator only encrypted the data without exfiltrating it. The logs show no outward data flow in the timeframe of the attack. The personal data affected by the breach relates to the employees and patients, which represented thousands of individuals. Backups were available in an electronic form. Most of the data was restored but this operation lasted 2 working days and led to major delays in treating the patients with surgery cancelled / postponed, and to a lowering the level of service due to the unavailability of the systems.

2.3.1 CASE No. 03 – Prior measures and risk assessment

36. The data controller should have adopted the same prior measures as mentioned in part 2.1. and in section 2.5. The major difference to the previous case is the high severity of consequences for a substantial part of the data subjects.

37. The quantity of breached data and the number of affected data subjects are high, because hospitals usually process large quantities of data. The unavailability of the data has a high impact on a substantial part of the data subjects. Moreover, there is a residual risk of high severity to the confidentiality of the patient data.

38. The type of the breach, nature, sensitivity, and volume of personal data affected in the breach are important. Even though a backup for the data existed and it could be restored in a few days, a high risk still exists due to the severity of consequences for the data subjects resulting from the lack of availability of the data at the moment of the attack and the following days.

2.3.2 CASE No. 03 – Mitigation and obligations

39. A notification to the SA is considered necessary, as special categories of personal data are involved and the restoration of the data could take a long time, resulting in major delays in patient care. Informing the data subjects about the breach is necessary due to the impact for the patients, even after restoring the encrypted data. While data relating to all patients treated in the hospital during the last years have been encrypted, only those patients who were scheduled to be treated in the hospital during the time the computer system was unavailable were impacted. The controller should communicate the data breach to those patients directly. Direct communication to the other patients some of which may not have been in the hospital for more than twenty years may not be required due to the exception in Article 34 (3) c). In such a case, there shall instead be a public communication or similar measure whereby the data subjects are informed in an equally effective manner. In this case, the hospital should make the ransomware attack and its effects public.

40. This case serves as an example for a ransomware attack with high risk to the rights and freedoms of the data subjects. It should be documented in accordance with Article 33 (5), notified to the SA in accordance with Article 33 (1) and communicated to the data subjects in accordance with Article 34 (1). The organisation also needs to update and remediate its organizational and technical personal data security handling and risk mitigation measures and procedures.

Actions necessary based on the identified risks		
No risk (internal register)	Risk (notify SA)	High Risk (communicate to data subjects)
√	√	√

2.4 CASE NO. 04: RANSOMWARE WITHOUT BACKUP AND WITH EXFILTRATION

The server of a public transportation company was exposed to a ransomware attack and its data was encrypted. According to the findings of the internal investigation the perpetrator not only encrypted the data, but also exfiltrated it. The type of breached data was the personal data of clients and employees, and of the several thousand people using the services of the company (e.g. buying tickets online). Beyond basic identity data, identity card numbers and financial data such as credit card details are involved in the breach. A backup database existed, but it was also encrypted by the attacker.

2.4.1 CASE No. 04 – Prior measures and risk assessment

41. The data controller should have adopted the same prior measures as mentioned in part 2.1. and in section 2.5. Though backup was in place, it was also affected by the attack. This arrangement alone raises questions about the quality of the controller's prior IT security measures and should be further scrutinised during the investigation, since in a well-designed backup regime the backup has to be securely stored without access from the main system, otherwise it could be compromised in the same attack.

42. This breach concerns not only data availability, but confidentiality as well, since the attacker may have modified and / or copied data from the server. Therefore, the type of the breach results in high risk.

43. The nature, sensitivity, and volume of personal data increases the risks further, because the number of individuals affected is high, as is the overall quantity of affected personal data. Beyond basic identity data, identity documents and financial data such as credit card details are involved too. A data breach concerning these types of data presents high risk in and of themselves, and if processed together, they could be used for – among others - identity theft or fraud.

44. Due to either faulty server logic or organizational controls, the backup files were affected by the ransomware, preventing the restore of data and enhancing the risk.

45. This data breach presents a high risk to the rights and freedoms of individuals, because it could likely lead to both material (e.g. financial loss since credit card details were affected) and non-material damage (e.g. identity theft or fraud since identity card details were affected).

2.4.2 CASE No. 04 – Mitigation and obligations

46. Communication to the data subjects is essential, so they can make the necessary steps to avoid material damage (e.g. block their credit cards).

47. Aside from documenting the breach in accordance with Article 33 (5), a notification to the SA is also mandatory in this case (Article 33 (1)) and the controller is also obliged to communicate the breach to the data subjects (Article 34 (1)). The latter could be undertaken on a person-by-person basis, but for individuals where contact data is not available the controller should do so publicly, e.g. by way of a notification on its website. In the latter case a precise and clear communication is required, in plain sight on the homepage of the controller, with exact references of the relevant GDPR provisions. The organisation may also need to update and remediate its organizational and technical personal data security handling and risk mitigation measures and procedures.

Actions necessary based on the identified risks		
Internal documentation	Notification to SA	Communication to data subjects
√	√	√

2.5 ORGANIZATIONAL AND TECHNICAL MEASURES FOR PREVENTING / MITIGATING THE IMPACTS OF RANSOMWARE ATTACKS

48. The fact that a ransomware attack could have taken place is usually a sign of one or more vulnerabilities in the controller's system. This also applies in ransomware cases in which the personal data has been encrypted, but has not been exfiltrated. Regardless of the outcome and the consequences of the attack, the importance of an all-encompassing evaluation of the data security system - with particular emphasis on IT security - cannot be stressed enough. The identified weaknesses and security holes are to be documented and addressed without delay.

49. Advisable measures:

(The list of the following measures is by no means exclusive or comprehensive. Rather, the goal is to provide prevention ideas and possible solutions. Every processing activity is different, hence the controller should make the decision on which measures fit the given situation the most.)

- Keeping the firmware, operating system and application software on the servers, client machines, active network components, and any other machines on the same LAN (including Wi-Fi devices) up to date. Ensuring that all reasonable IT security measures are in place, making sure they are effective and keeping them regularly updated when processing or circumstances change or evolve. This includes keeping detailed logs of which patches are applied at which timestamp.
- Designing and organising processing systems and infrastructure to segment or isolate data systems and networks to avoid propagation of malware within the organisation and to external systems.
- The existence of an up-to-date, secure and tested backup procedure. Media for medium- and long-term back-up should be kept separate from operational data storage and out of reach of third parties even in case of a successful attack (such as daily incremental backup and weekly full backup).
- Having / obtaining an appropriate, up-to-date, effective and integrated anti-malware software.
- Having an appropriate, up-to-date, effective and integrated firewall and intrusion detection and prevention system. Directing network traffic through the firewall/intrusion detection, even in the case of home office or mobile work (e.g. by using VPN connections to organizational security mechanisms when accessing the internet)
- Training employees on the methods of recognising and preventing IT attacks. The controller should provide means to establish whether emails and messages obtained by other means of communication are authentic and trustworthy. Employees should be trained to recognize when such an attack has realized, how to take the endpoint out of the network and their obligation to immediately report it to the security officer.
- Emphasize the need of identifying the type of the malicious code to see the consequences of the attack and be able to find the right measures to mitigate the risk. In case a ransomware attack has succeeded and there is no back-up available, tools available such as the ones by the "no more ransom" (nomoreransom.org) project may be applied to retrieve data. However, in case a safe backup is available, restoring the data from it is advisable.
- Forwarding or replication all logs to a central log server (possibly including the signing or cryptographic time-stamping of log entries).
- Strong encryption and authentication, in particular for administrative access to IT systems (2FA), appropriate key and password management.
- Vulnerability and penetration testing on a regular basis.
- Establish a Computer Security Incident Response Team (CSIRT) or Computer Emergency Response Team (CERT) within the organization, or join a collective CSIRT/CERT. Create an Incident Response Plan, Disaster Recovery Plan and a Business Continuity Plan, and make sure that these are thoroughly tested.
- When assessing countermeasures – risk analysis should be reviewed.

NOTES

[10] Technically, encryption of data will involve "access" to original data, and in the case of ransomware, the deletion of the original – the data needs to be accessed by ransomware code to encrypt it, and to remove the original data. An attacker may take a copy of the original before deletion, but personal data will not always be extracted. As a data controller's investigation progresses, new information may come to light to make this assessment change. Access that results in unlawful destruction, loss, alteration, unauthorised disclosure of the personal data, or to a security risk to a data subject, even without interpretation of the data may be as severe as access with interpretation of the personal data.

[11] Backup procedures should be structured, consistent and repeatable. Examples of back up procedures are the 3-2-1 method and the grandfather-father-son method. Any method should always be tested for effectiveness in coverage and when data is to be restored. Testing should also be repeated at intervals and especially when changes occur in the processing operation or its circumstances to ensure the integrity of the system.

[12] This will depend on the complexity and structure of the personal data. In the most complex scenarios, re-establishing data integrity, consistency with metadata, ensuring the correct relationships within data structures and checking data accuracy may take significant resources and effort.

3 DATA EXFILTRATION ATTACKS

[2.412]
50. Attacks that exploit vulnerabilities in services offered by the controller to third parties over the internet, e.g. committed by way of injection attacks (e.g. SQL injection, path traversal), website compromising and similar methods, may resemble ransomware attacks in that the risk emanates from the action of an unauthorized third party, but those attacks typically aim at copying, exfiltrating and abusing personal data for some malicious end. Hence, they are mainly breaches of confidentiality and, possibly, also data integrity. At the same time, if the controller is aware of the characteristics of this kind of breaches, there are many measures available to controllers that can substantially reduce the risk of a successful execution of an attack.

3.1 CASE NO. 05: EXFILTRATION OF JOB APPLICATION DATA FROM A WEBSITE

An employment agency was the victim of a cyber-attack, which placed a malicious code on its website. This malicious code made personal information submitted through online job application forms and stored on the webserver accessible to unauthorized person(s). 213 such forms are possibly affected, after analysing the affected data it was determined that no special categories of data were affected in the breach. The particular malware toolkit installed had functionalities that allowed the attacker to remove any history of exfiltration and also allowed processing on the server to be monitored and to have personal data captured. The toolkit was discovered only a month after its installation.

3.1.1 CASE No. 05 – Prior measures and risk assessment

51. The security of the data controller's environment is extremely important, as the majority of these breaches can be prevented by ensuring that all systems are constantly updated, sensitive data is encrypted and applications are developed according to high security standards like strong authentication, measures against brute force, attacks, "escaping" or "sanitising"[13] user inputs, etc. Periodic IT security audits, vulnerability assessments and penetration tests are also required in order to detect these kinds of vulnerabilities in advance and fix them. In this particular case, file integrity monitoring tools in production environment might have helped to detect the code injection. (A list of advisable measures is to be found in section 3.7).

52. The controller should always start to investigate the breach by identifying the type of the attack and its methods, in order to assess what measures are to be taken. To make it fast and efficient, the data controller should have an incident response plan in place which specifies the swift and necessary steps to take control over the incident. In this particular case, the type of the breach was a risk enhancing factor since not only was data confidentiality curtailed, the infiltrator also had the means to establish changes in the system, so data integrity also became questionable.

53. The nature, sensitivity and volume of personal data affected in the breach should be assessed to determine to what extent the breach affected the data subjects. Though no special categories of personal data were affected, the accessed data contains considerable information about the individuals from the online forms, and such data could be misused in a number of ways (targeting with unsolicited marketing, identity theft, etc.), so the severity of the consequences should increase the risk to the right and freedoms of the data subjects.

3.1.2 CASE No. 05 – Mitigation and obligations

54. If possible, after solving the problem, the database should be compared with the one stored in a secure backup. The experiences drawn from the breach should be utilized in updating the IT infrastructure. The data controller should return all affected IT systems to a known clean state, remedy the vulnerability and implement new security measures to avoid similar data breaches in the future, e.g. file integrity checks and security audits. If personal data was not only exfiltrated, but also deleted, the controller has to take systematic action to recover the personal data in the state it was in before the breach. It may be necessary to apply full backups, incremental changes and then possibly rerun the processing since the last incremental backup – which requires that the controller is able to replicate the changes made since the last backup. This could require that the controller has the system designed to retain the daily input files in case they need to be processed again and requires a robust method of storage and a suitable retention policy.

55. In light of the above, as the breach is likely to result in a high risk to the rights and freedoms of natural persons, the data subjects should definitely be informed about it (Article 34(1)), which of course means that the relevant SA(s) should also be involved in the form of a data breach notification. Documenting the breach is obligatory according to Article 33 (5) GDPR and makes the assessment of the situation easier.

Actions necessary based on the identified risks		
Internal documentation	Notification to SA	Communication to data subjects
√	√	√

3.2 CASE NO. 06: EXFILTRATION OF HASHED PASSWORD FROM A WEBSITE

An SQL Injection vulnerability was exploited to gain access to a database of the server of a cooking website. Users were only allowed to choose arbitrary pseudonyms as usernames. The use of email addresses for this purpose was discouraged. Passwords stored in the database were hashed with a strong algorithm and the salt was not compromised. Affected data: hashed passwords of 1.200 users. For safety's sake, the controller informed the data subjects about the breach via e-mail and asked them to change their passwords, especially if the same password was used for other services.

3.2.1 CASE No. 06 – Prior measures and risk assessment

56. In this particular case data confidentiality is compromised, but the passwords in the database were hashed with an up-to-date method, which would decrease the risk regarding the nature, sensitivity, and volume of personal data. This case presents no risks to the rights and freedoms of the data subjects.

57. Furthermore, no contact information (e.g. e-mail addresses or phone numbers) of data subjects was compromised, which means there is no significant risk for the data subjects of being targeted by fraud attempts (e.g. receiving phishing e-mails or fraudulent text messages and phone calls). No special categories of personal data were involved.

58. Some user names could be regarded as personal data, but the subject of the website does not allow for negative connotations. Although it has to be noted that the risk assessment may change, if the type of the website and the data accessed could reveal special categories of personal data (e. g. website of a political party or trade union). Using state of the art encryption could mitigate the adverse effects of the breach. Assuring that a limited number of attempts to login is allowed will prevent brute force login attacks to be successful, thus reducing largely the risks imposed by attackers already knowing the usernames.

3.2.2 CASE No. 06 – Mitigation and obligations

59. The communication to the data subjects in some cases could be considered a mitigating factor, since the data subjects are also in a position to make the necessary steps to avoid further damages from the breach, for example by changing their password. In this case, notification was not mandatory, but in many cases it can be considered a good practice.

60. The data controller should correct the vulnerability and implement new security measures to avoid similar data breaches in the future like, for example, systematic security audits to the website.

61. The breach should be documented in accordance with Article 33 (5) but no notification or communication needed.

62. Also, it is strongly advisable to communicate a breach involving passwords to data subjects in any case even when the passwords were stored using a salted hash with an algorithm conforming to the state-of- the-art. The use of authentication methods obviating the need to process passwords on the server side is preferable. Data subjects should be given the choice to take appropriate measures regarding their own passwords.

Actions necessary based on the identified risks		
Internal documentation	Notification to SA	Communication to data subjects
√	X	X

3.3 CASE NO. 07: CREDENTIAL STUFFING ATTACK ON A BANKING WEBSITE

A bank suffered a cyber-attack against one of its online banking websites. The attack aimed to enumerate all possible login user IDs using a fixed trivial password. The passwords consist of 8 digits. Due to a vulnerability of the website, in some cases information regarding data subjects (name, surname, gender, date and place of birth, fiscal code, user identification codes) were leaked to the attacker, even if the used password was not correct or the bank account not active anymore. This affected around 100.000 data subjects. Out of these, the attacker successfully logged into around 2.000 accounts which were using the trivial password tried by the attacker. After the fact, the controller was able to identify all illegitimate log-on attempts. The data controller could confirm that, according to antifraud checks, no transactions were performed by these accounts during the attack. The bank was aware of the data breach because its security operations centre detected a high number of login requests directed toward the website. In response, the controller disabled the possibility to log in to the website by switching it off and forced password resets of the compromised accounts. The controller communicated the breach only to the users with the compromised accounts, i.e. to users whose passwords were compromised or whose data was disclosed.

3.3.1 CASE No. 07 – Prior measures and risk assessment

63. It is important to mention that controllers handling sensitive data, financial information, etc. have a larger responsibility in terms of providing adequate data security, e.g. having a security operation's centre and other incident prevention, detection and response measures. Not meeting these higher standards will certainly result in more serious measures during an SA's investigation.

64. The breach concerns financial data beyond the identity and user ID information, making it particularly severe. The number of individuals affected is high.

65. The fact that a breach could happen in such a sensitive environment points to significant data security holes in the controller's system, and may be an indicator of a time when the review and update of affected measures is "necessary" in line with Articles 24 (1), 25 (1), and 32 (1) of the GDPR. The breached data permits the unique identification of data subjects and contains other information about them (including gender, date and place of birth), furthermore it can be used by the attacker to guess the customers' passwords or to run a spear phishing campaign directed at the bank customers.

66. For these reasons, the data breach was deemed likely to result in a high risk to the rights and freedoms of all the data subjects concerned. Therefore, the occurrence of material (e.g. financial loss) and non- material damage (e.g. identity theft or fraud) is a conceivable outcome.

3.3.2 CASE No. 07 – Mitigation and obligations

67. The controller's measures mentioned in the case description are adequate. In the wake of the breach it also corrected the vulnerability of the website and took other steps to prevent similar future data breaches, such as adding two-factor authentication to the concerned website and moving up to a strong customer authentication.

68. Documenting the breach according to Article 33 (5) GDPR and notifying the SA about it are not optional in this scenario. Furthermore, the controller should notify all 100.000 data subjects (including the data subjects whose accounts were not compromised) in accordance with Article 34 GDPR.

Actions necessary based on the identified risks		
Internal documentation	Notification to SA	Communication to data subjects
√	√	√

3.4 ORGANIZATIONAL AND TECHNICAL MEASURES FOR PREVENTING / MITIGATING THE IMPACTS OF HACKER ATTACKS

69. Just as in case of ransomware attacks, regardless of the outcome and the consequences of the attack, re-evaluating IT security is compulsory for controllers in similar cases.

70. Advisable measures:[14]

(The list of the following measures is by no means exclusive or comprehensive. Rather, the goal is to provide prevention ideas and possible solutions. Every processing activity is different, hence the controller should make the decision on which measures fit the given situation the most.)

- State-of-the-art encryption and key management, especially when passwords, sensitive or financial data are being processed. Cryptographic hashing and salting for secret information (passwords) is always preferred over encryption of passwords. The use of authentication methods obviating the need to process passwords on the server side is preferable.
- Keeping the system up to date (software and firmware). Ensuring that all IT security measures are in place, making sure they are effective and keeping them regularly updated when processing or circumstances change or evolve. In order to be able to demonstrate compliance with Article 5(1)(f) in accordance with Article 5 (2) GDPR the controller should maintain a record of all updates performed, including also the time when they were applied.
- Use of strong authentication methods like two-factor authentication and authentication servers, complemented by an up-to-date password policy.
- Secure development standards include the filtering of user input (using white listing as far as practicable), escaping user inputs and brute force prevention measures (such as limiting the maximum amount of retries). "Web Application Firewalls" may assist in the effective use of this technique.
- Strong user privileges and access control management policy in place.
- Use of appropriate, up-to-date, effective and integrated firewall, intrusion detection and other perimeter defence systems.
- Systematic IT security audits and vulnerability assessments (penetration testing).
- Regular reviews and testing to ensure that backups can be used to restore any data whose integrity or availability was affected.
- No session ID in URL in plain text.

NOTES

13   Escaping or sanitizing user inputs is a form of input validation, which ensures that only properly formatted data is entered into an information system.

14   For secure web application development see also: https://www.owasp.org/index.php/Main_Page

4 INTERNAL HUMAN RISK SOURCE

[2.413]
71. The role of human error in personal data breaches has to be highlighted, due to its common appearance. Since these types of breaches can be both intentional and unintentional, it is very hard for the data controllers to identify the vulnerabilities and adopt measures to avoid them. The International Conference of Data Protection and Privacy Commissioners recognized the importance of addressing such human factors and adopted the resolution to address the role of human error in personal data breaches in October 2019[15]. This resolution stresses that appropriate safeguarding measures should be taken to prevent human errors and provides a non-exhaustive list of such safeguards and approaches.

4.1 CASE NO. 08: EXFILTRATION OF BUSINESS DATA BY A FORMER EMPLOYEE

During his period of notice, the employee of a company copies business data from the company's database he is authorized to access, and needs to fulfil his job. Months later, after quitting the job, he uses the data thus gained (mainly basic contact data) to contact the clients of the company to entice them to his new business.

4.1.1 CASE No. 08 – Prior measures and risk assessment

72. In this particular case no prior measures were taken to prevent the employee from copying contact information of the company's clientele, since he needed – and had – legitimate access to this information. Since fulfilling most customer relation jobs require some kind of employee access to personal data, these data breaches may be the most difficult to prevent. Limitations to the scope of access may limit the work the given employee is able to do. However, well thought out access policies and constant control can help prevent such breaches.

73. As usual, during risk assessment the type of the breach and the nature, sensitivity, and volume of personal data affected are to be taken into consideration. These kinds of breaches are typically breaches of confidentiality, since the database is usually left intact, its content "merely" copied for further use. The quantity of data affected is usually also low or medium. In this particular case no special categories of personal data were affected, the employee only needed the contact information of clients to enable him to get in touch with them after leaving the company. Therefore, the data concerned is not sensitive.

74.   Although the only goal of the ex-employee that maliciously copied the data may be limited to gaining the contact information of the company's clientele for his own commercial purposes, the controller is not in a position to consider the risk for the affected data subjects to be low, since the controller does not have any kind of reassurance on the intentions of the employee. Thus, while the consequences of the breach might be limited to the exposure to uncalled-for self-marketing of the ex-employee, further and more grave abuse of the stolen data is not ruled out.

4.1.2 CASE No. 08 – Mitigation and obligations

75.   The mitigation of the adverse effects of the breach in the above case is difficult. It might need to involve immediate legal action to prevent the former employee from abusing and disseminating the data any further. As a next step, the avoidance of similar future situations should be the goal. The controller might try to order the ex-employee to stop using the data, but the success of this action is dubious at best.

76.   There is no "one-size fits-all" solution to these kinds of cases, but a systematic approach may help to prevent them. For example, the company may consider – when possible - withdrawing certain forms of access from employees who have signalled their intention to quit or implementing access logs so that unwanted access can be logged and flagged. The contract signed with employees should include clauses that prohibit such actions.

77.   All in all, as the given breach will not result in a high risk to the rights and freedoms of natural persons, a notification to the SA will suffice. However, the information to the data subjects might be beneficial for the data controller too, since it might be better that they hear from the company about the data leak rather than from the ex-employee who tries to contact them. Data breach documentation in accordance with Article 33 (5) is a legal obligation.

Actions necessary based on the identified risks		
Internal documentation	Notification to SA	Communication to data subjects
√	√	X

4.2 CASE NO. 09: ACCIDENTAL TRANSMISSION OF DATA TO A TRUSTED THIRD PARTY

An insurance agent noticed that – made possible by the faulty settings of an Excel file received by e-mail – he was able to access information related to two dozen customers not belonging to his scope. He is bound by professional secrecy and was the sole recipient of the e-mail. The arrangement between the data controller and the insurance agent obliges the agent to signal a personal data breach without undue delay to the data controller. Therefore, the agent instantly signalled the mistake to the controller, who corrected the file and sent it out again, asking the agent to delete the former message. According to the above-mentioned arrangement the agent has to confirm the deletion in a written statement, which he did. The information gained includes no special categories of personal data, only contact data and data about the insurance itself (insurance type, amount). After analysing the personal data affected by the breach the data controller did not identify any special characteristics on the side of the individuals or the data controller that may affect the level of impact of the breach.

4.2.1 CASE No. 09 – Prior measures and risk assessment

78.   Unlike the previous case, here the breach does not derive from a deliberate action of an employee, but from an unintentional human error caused by inattentiveness. These kinds of breaches may be avoided by a) enforcing training, education and awareness programs where employees gain a better understanding of the importance of personal data protection, b) reducing file exchange through e-mail, instead using dedicated systems for processing customer data for example, c) double checking files before sending, d) separating the creation and sending of files.

79.   This data breach concerns only the confidentiality of the data, and the integrity and the accessibility thereof are left intact. The data breach only concerned about two dozen costumers, hence the quantity of data affected can be considered as low. Furthermore, the personal data affected does not contain any sensitive data. The fact that the data processor immediately contacted the data controller after becoming aware of the data breach can be considered a risk mitigating factor. (The possibility of data having been sent to other insurance agents should also be evaluated and, if confirmed, proper measures should be taken.) Due to the appropriate steps taken after the data breach, it will probably not have any impact on the data subjects' rights and freedoms.

80.   The combination of the low number of individuals affected, the immediate detection of the breach and the measures taken to have its effects minimized make this particular case no risk.

4.2.2 CASE No. 09 – Mitigation and obligations

81.   Moreover, other risk mitigating circumstances are at play as well: the agent is bound by professional secrecy; he himself reported the problem to the controller; and he deleted the file upon request. Raising awareness and possibly including additional steps in checking documents involving personal data will probably help avoid similar cases in the future.

82.   Besides documenting the breach in accordance with Article 33 (5), there is no need for any other action.

Actions necessary based on the identified risks		
Internal documentation	Notification to SA	Communication to data subjects
√	X	X

4.3 ORGANIZATIONAL AND TECHNICAL MEASURES FOR PREVENTING / MITIGATING THE IMPACTS OF INTERNAL HUMAN RISK SOURCES

83. A combination of the below mentioned measures – applied depending on the unique features of the case – should help to lower the chance of a similar breach reoccurring.

84. Advisable measures:

(The list of the following measures is by no means exclusive or comprehensive. Rather, the goal is to provide prevention ideas and possible solutions. Every processing activity is different, hence the controller should make the decision on which measures fit the given situation the most.)

- Periodic implementation of training, education and awareness programs for employees on their privacy and security obligations and the detection and reporting of threats to the security of personal data[16]. Develop an awareness program to remind employees of the most commons errors leading to personal data breaches and how to avoid them.
- Establishment of robust and effective data protection and privacy practices, procedures and systems[17].
- Evaluation of privacy practices, procedures and systems to ensure continued effectiveness[18].
- Making proper access control policies and forcing users to follow the rules.
- Implementing techniques to force user authentication when accessing sensitive personal data.
- Disabling the company related account of the user as soon as the person leaves the company.
- Checking unusual dataflow between the file server and employee workstations.
- Setting up I/O interface security in the BIOS or through the use of software controlling the use of computer interfaces (lock or unlock e. g. USB/CD/DVD etc.).
- Reviewing employees' access policy (e.g. logging access to sensitive data and requiring the user to input a business reason, so that this is available for audits).
- Disabling open cloud services.
- Forbidding and preventing access to known open mail services.
- Disabling print screen function in OS.
- Enforcing a clean desk policy.
- Automated locking all computers after a certain amount of time of inactivity.
- Use mechanisms (e.g. (wireless) token to log on/open locked accounts) for fast user switches in shared environments.
- Use of dedicated systems for managing personal data that apply appropriate access control mechanisms and that prevent human mistake, such as sending of communications to the wrong subject. The use of spreadsheets and other office documents is not an appropriate means to manage client data.

NOTES

[15] The International Conference of Data Protection and Privacy Commissioners, Resolution to address the role of human error in personal data breaches, October 2019, http://globalprivacyassembly.org/wpcontent/uploads/2019/10/AOIC-Resolution-FINAL-ADOPTED.pdf

[16] Section 2) subsection (i) of the Resolution to address the role of human error in personal data breaches.

[17] Section 2) subsection (ii) of the Resolution to address the role of human error in personal data breaches.

[18] Section 2) subsection (iii) of the Resolution to address the role of human error in personal data breaches.

5 LOST OR STOLEN DEVICES AND PAPER DOCUMENTS

[2.414]

85. A frequent type of case is the loss or theft of portable devices. In these cases, the controller has to take into consideration the circumstances of the processing operation, such as the type of data stored on the device, as well as the supporting assets, and the measures taken prior to the breach to ensure an appropriate level of security. All of these elements affect the potential impacts of the data breach. The risk assessment might be difficult, as the device is no longer available.

86. These kinds of breaches can be always classified as breaches of confidentiality. However, if there is no backup for the stolen database, then the breach type can also be breach of availability and breach of integrity.

87. The scenarios bellow demonstrate how the above mentioned circumstances influence the likelihood and severity of the data breach.

5.1 CASE NO. 10: STOLEN MATERIAL STORING ENCRYPTED PERSONAL DATA

During a break-in into a children's day-care centre, two tablets were stolen. The tablets contained an app which held personal data about the children attending the day-care centre. Name, date of birth, personal data about the education of the children were concerned. Both the encrypted tablets which were turned off at the time of the break-in, and the app were protected by a strong password. Back-up data was effectively and readily available to the controller. After becoming aware of the break-in, the day-care remotely issued a command to wipe the tablets shortly after the discovery of the break-in.

5.1.1 CASE No. 10 – Prior measures and risk assessment

88. In this particular case the data controller took adequate measures to prevent and mitigate the impacts of a potential data breach by using device encryption, introducing adequate password protection and securing back-up of the data stored on the tablets. (A list of advisable measures is to be found in section 5.7).

89. After becoming aware of a breach, the data controller should assess the risk source, the systems supporting the data processing, the type of personal data involved and the potential impacts of the data breach on the concerned individuals. The data breach described above would have concerned confidentiality, availability and integrity of the concerned data, however due to the appropriate proceedings of the data controller prior and after the data breach none of these occurred.

5.1.2 CASE No. 10 – Mitigation and obligations

90. The confidentiality of the personal data on the devices was not compromised due to the strong password protection on both the tablets and the apps. The tablets were set up in such a way that setting a password also means that the data on the device is encrypted. This was further enhanced by the controller's action to attempt to remotely wipe everything from the stolen devices.

91. Due to the measures taken, the confidentiality of the data was kept intact too. Furthermore, the backup ensured the continuous availability of the personal data, hence no potential negative impact could have occurred.

92. Due to these facts, the above described data breach was unlikely to result in a risk to the rights and freedoms of the data subjects, hence no notification to the SA or the concerned data subjects was necessary. However, this data breach must also be documented in accordance with Article 33 (5).

Actions necessary based on the identified risks		
Internal documentation	Notification to SA	Communication to data subjects
√	X	X

5.2 CASE NO. 11: STOLEN MATERIAL STORING NON-ENCRYPTED PERSONAL DATA

The electronic notebook device of an employee of a service provider company was stolen. The stolen notebook contained names, surnames, sex, addresses and date of births of more than 100000 customers. Due to the unavailability of the stolen device it was not possible to identify if other categories of personal data were also affected. The access to the notebook's hard drive was not protected by any password. Personal data could be restored from daily backups available.

5.2.1 CASE No. 11 – Prior measures and risk assessment

93. No prior safety measures were taken by the data controller, hence the personal data stored on the stolen notebook was easily accessible for the thief or any other person coming into possession of the device thereafter.

94. This data breach concerns the confidentiality of the data stored on the stolen device.

95. The notebook containing the personal data was vulnerable in this case because it did not possess any password protection or encryption. The lack of basic security measures enhances the risk level for the affected data subjects. Furthermore, the identification of the concerned data subjects is also problematic, which also increases the severity of the breach. The considerable number of concerned individuals increases the risk, nevertheless, no special categories of personal data were concerned in the data breach.

96. During the risk assessment the controller should take into consideration the potential consequences and adverse effects of the confidentiality breach. As a result of the breach the concerned data subjects may suffer identity fraud relying on the data available on the stolen device, so risk is considered to be high.

5.2.2 CASE No. 11 – Mitigation and obligations

97. Turning on device encryption and the use of strong password protection of the stored database could have prevented the data breach to result in a risk to the rights and freedoms of the data subjects.

98. Due to these circumstances the notification of the SA is required, the notification of the concerned data subjects is also necessary.

Actions necessary based on the identified risks		
Internal documentation	Notification to SA	Communication to data subjects
√	√	√

Part 2   Data Protection: EU Law etc

5.3 CASE NO. 12: STOLEN PAPER FILES WITH SENSITIVE DATA

A paper log book was stolen from a drug addiction rehab facility. The book contained basic identity and health data of the patients admitted to the rehab facility. The data was only stored on paper and no backup was available to the doctors treating the patients. The book was not stored in a locked drawer or a room, the data controller had neither an access control regime nor any other safeguarding measure for the paper documentation.

5.3.1 CASE No. 12 – Prior measures and risk assessment

99. No prior safety measures were taken by the data controller, hence the personal data stored in this book was easily accessible for the person who found it. Moreover, the nature of the personal data stored in the book makes the lack of backup data a very serious risk factor.

100. This case serves as an example for a high-risk data breach. Due to the failure of appropriate safety precautions, sensitive health data pursuant to Article 9 (1) GDPR was lost. Since in this case a special category of personal data was concerned, the potential risks to the concerned data subjects was increased, which should be also taken into consideration by the controller assessing the risk.

101. This breach concerns the confidentiality, availability and integrity of the concerned personal data. As a result of the breach, medical secrecy is broken and unauthorized third parties may gain access to the patients' private medical information, what may have severe impact on the patient's personal life. The availability breach may also disturb the continuity of the patients' treatment. Since the modification/deletion of parts of the book's content may not be excluded, the integrity of the personal data is also compromised.

5.3.2 CASE No. 12 – Mitigation and obligations

102. During the assessment of the safeguarding measures the type of the supporting asset should be considered as well. Since the patient log book was a physical document, its safeguarding should have been organized differently than that of an electronic device. The pseudonymisation of the patients' names, the storage of the book in a safeguarded premises and in a locked drawer or a room, and proper access control with authentication when accessing it could have prevented the data breach.

103. The above described data breach may severely impact the concerned data subjects; hence the notification of the SA and communication of the breach to the concerned data subjects is mandatory.

Actions necessary based on the identified risks		
Internal documentation	Notification to SA	Communication to data subjects
√	√	√

5.4 ORGANIZATIONAL AND TECHNICAL MEASURES FOR PREVENTING / MITIGATING THE IMPACTS OF LOSS OR THEFT OF DEVICES

104. A combination of the below mentioned measures – applied depending on the unique features of the case – should help to lower the chance of a similar breach reoccurring.

105. Advisable measures:

(The list of the following measures is by no means exclusive or comprehensive. Rather, the goal is to provide prevention ideas and possible solutions. Every processing activity is different, hence the controller should make the decision on which measures fit the given situation the most.)

- Turn on device's encryption (such as Bitlocker, Veracrypt or DM-Crypt).
- Use passcode/password on all devices. Encrypt all mobile electronic devices in a way that requires the input of a complex password for decryption.
- Use multi-factor authentication.
- Turn on the functionalities of highly mobile devices that allow them to be located in case of loss or misplacement.
- Use MDM (Mobile Devices Management) software/app and localization. Use anti-glare filters. Close down any unattended devices.
- If possible and appropriate to the data processing in question, save personal data not on a mobile device, but on a central back-end server.
- If the workstation is connected to the corporate LAN, do an automatic backup from the work folders provided it is unavoidable that personal data is stored there
- Use a secure VPN (e.g. which requires a separate second factor authentication key for the establishment of a secure connection) to connect mobile devices to back-end servers.
- Provide physical locks to employees in order to enable them to physically secure mobile devices they use while they remain unattended.
- Proper regulation of device usage outside the company.
- Proper regulation of device usage inside the company.
- Use MDM (Mobile Devices Management) software/app and enable the remote wipe function.
- Use centralised device management with minimum rights for the end users to install software.
- Install physical access controls.
- Avoid storing sensitive information in mobile devices or hard drives. If there is need to access the company's internal system, secure channels should be used such as previously stated.

6 MISPOSTAL

[2.415]
106. The risk source is an internal human error in this case as well, but here no malicious action led to the breach. It is the result of inattentiveness. Little can be undertaken by the controller after it happened, so prevention is even more important in these cases than in other breach types.

6.1 CASE NO. 13: SNAIL MAIL MISTAKE

> Two orders for shoes were packed by a retail company. Due to human error two packing bills were mixed up with the result that both products and the relevant packing bills were sent to the wrong person. This means that the two customers got each other's orders, including the packing bills containing the personal data. After becoming aware of the breach the data controller recalled the orders and sent them to the right recipients.

6.1.1 CASE No. 13 – Prior measures and risk assessment

107. The bills contained the personal data required for a successful delivery (name, address, plus the item purchased and its price). It is important to identify how the human error could have happened in the first place, and if in any way, it could have been prevented. In the particular case describe the risk is low, since no special categories of personal data or other data whose abuse might lead to substantial negative effects were involved, the breach is not a result of a systemic error on the controller's part and only two individuals are concerned. No negative effect on the individuals could be identified.

6.1.2 CASE No. 13 – Mitigation and obligations

108. The controller should provide for a free return of the items and the accompanying bills, and it also should request the wrong recipients to destroy / delete all eventual copies of the bills containing the other person's personal data.

109. Even if the breach itself does not pose a high risk to rights and freedoms of the affected individuals, and thus communication to the data subjects is not mandated by Article 34 GDPR, communication of the breach to them cannot be avoided, as their cooperation is needed to mitigate the risk.

Actions necessary based on the identified risks		
Internal documentation	Notification to SA	Communication to data subjects
√	X	X

6.2 CASE NO. 14: SENSITIVE PERSONAL DATA SENT BY MAIL BY MISTAKE

> The employment department of a public administration office sent an e-mail message – about upcoming trainings - to the individuals registered in its system as jobseekers. By mistake, a document containing all these jobseekers' personal data (name, e-mail address, postal address, social security number) was attached to this e-mail. The number of affected individuals is more than 60000. Subsequently the office contacted all the recipients and asked them to delete the previous message and not to use the information contained in it.

6.2.1 CASE No. 14 – Prior measures and risk assessment

110. Stricter rules should have been implemented for sending such messages. The introduction of additional control mechanisms need to be considered.

111. The number of affected individuals is considerable, and the involvement of their social security number, along with other, more basic personal data, further increases the risk, which can be identified as high. The eventual distribution of the data by any of the recipients cannot be contained by the controller.

6.2.2 CASE No. 14 – Mitigation and obligations

112. As mentioned earlier, the means to effectively mitigate the risks of a similar breach, are limited. Though the controller asked for the deletion of the message, it cannot force the recipients to do so, and as a consequence, nor can it be certain that they comply with the request.

113. The execution of all three below indicated actions should be self-evident in a case like this.

Actions necessary based on the identified risks		
Internal documentation	Notification to SA	Communication to data subjects
√	√	√

6.3 CASE NO. 15: PERSONAL DATA SENT BY MAIL BY MISTAKE

> A list of participants on a course in Legal English which takes place in a hotel for 5 days is by mistake sent to 15 former participants of the course instead of the hotel. The list contains names, e-mail addresses and food preferences of the 15 participants. Only two participants have filled in their food preferences, stating that they are lactose intolerant. None of the participants have a protected identity. The controller discovers the mistake immediately after sending the list and informs the recipients of the mistake and asks them to delete the list.

Part 2   Data Protection: EU Law etc

6.3.1 CASE No. 15 - Prior measures and risk assessment

114. Stricter rules should have been implemented for sending of such messages. The introduction of additional control mechanisms need to be considered.

115. The risks deriving from the nature, the sensitivity, the volume and the context of the personal data are low. The personal data includes sensitive data on food preferences of two of the participants. Even if the information that someone is lactose intolerant is health data, the risk that this data will be used in a detrimental way should be considered relatively low. While in the case of data concerning health it is usually assumed that the breach is likely to result in a high risk for the data subject[19], at the same time in this particular case no risk can be identified that the breach will lead to physical, material or non-material damages of the data subject due to the unauthorised disclosure of lactose intolerance information. Contrary to some other food preferences, lactose intolerance can normally not be linked to any religious or philosophical beliefs. The quantity of the breached data and the number of affected data subjects is very low as well.

6.3.2 CASE No. 15 – Mitigation and obligations

116. In summary, it can be stated that the breach had no significant effect on the data subjects. The fact that the controller immediately contacted the recipients after becoming aware of the mistake can be considered as a mitigating factor.

117. If an email is sent to an incorrect/unauthorised recipient, it is recommended that the data controller should Bcc a follow up email to the unintended recipients apologising, instructing that the offending email should be deleted, and advising recipients that they do not have the right to further use the email addresses identified to them.

118. Due to these facts this data breach was unlikely to result in a risk to the rights and freedoms of the data subjects, hence no notification to the SA or the concerned data subjects was necessary. However, this data breach must also be documented in accordance with Article 33 (5).

Actions necessary based on the identified risks		
Internal documentation	Notification to SA	Communication to data subjects
√	X	X

6.4 CASE NO. 16: SNAIL MAIL MISTAKE

An insurance group offers car insurances. To do this, it sends out regularly adjusted contribution policies by snail mail. In addition to the name and address of the policyholder, the letter contains the vehicle registration number, the insurance rates of the current and next insurance year, the approximate annual mileage and the policyholder's date of birth. Health data according to Article 9 GDPR, payment data (bank details), economic and financial data are not included.   Letters are packed by automated enveloping machines. Due to a mechanical error, two letters for different policyholders are inserted into one envelope and sent to one policyholder by letter post. The policyholder opens the letter at home and takes a look at his correctly delivered letter as well as at the incorrectly delivered letter from another policyholder.

6.4.1 CASE No. 16 - Prior measures and risk assessment

119. The incorrectly delivered letter contains the name, address, date of birth, license plate number and the classification of the insurance rate of the current and the next year. If the insurance rate increases in the following year, this indicates a motor vehicle claim submitted to the insurance company. The effects on the affected person are to be regarded as medium, since information not publicly available such as the date of birth or vehicle registration numbers, and if the insurance rate increases, a not insignificant claim, which could also have been an accident, was disclosed to the unauthorized recipient. The probability of misuse of this data is assessed to be between low and medium. However, while many recipients will probably dispose of the wrongly received letter in the garbage, in individual cases it cannot be completely ruled out that the letter will be posted in social networks or that the policyholder will be contacted.

6.4.2 CASE No. 16 – Mitigation and obligations

120. The controller should have the original document returned at its own expense. The wrong recipient should also be informed that he/she may not misuse the information read.

121. It will probably never be possible to completely prevent a postal delivery error in a mass mailing using fully automated machines. However, in the event of an increased frequency, it is necessary to check whether the enveloping machines are set and maintained correctly enough, or if some other systemic issue leads to such a breach.

Actions necessary based on the identified risks		
Internal documentation	Notification to SA	Communication to data subjects
√	√	X

6.5 ORGANIZATIONAL AND TECHNICAL MEASURES FOR PREVENTING / MITIGATING THE IMPACTS OF MISPOSTAL

122. A combination of the below mentioned measures – applied depending on the unique features of the case - should help to lower the chance of a similar breach reoccurring.

123. Advisable measures:

(The list of the following measures is by no means exclusive or comprehensive. Rather, the goal is to provide prevention ideas and possible solutions. Every processing activity is different, hence the controller should make the decision on which measures fit the given situation the most.)
- Setting exact standards – with no room for interpretation - for sending letters / e-mails.
- Adequate training for personnel on how to send letters / e-mails.
- When sending e-mails to multiple recipients, they are listed in the 'bcc' field by default.
- Extra confirmation is required when sending e-mails to multiple recipients, and they are not listed in the 'bcc' field.
- Application of the four-eyes principle.
- Automatic addressing instead of manual, with data extracted from an available and up-to- date database; the automatic addressing system should be regularly reviewed to check for hidden errors and incorrect settings.
- Application of message delay (e.g. the message can be deleted / edited within a certain time period after clicking the press button).
- Disabling autocomplete when typing in e-mail addresses.
- Awareness sessions on most common mistakes leading to a personal data breach.
- Training sessions and manuals on how to handle incidents leading to a personal data breach and who to inform (involve DPO).

NOTES
[19] See Guidelines WP 250, p. 23.

7 OTHER CASES – SOCIAL ENGINEERING

7.1 CASE NO. 17: IDENTITY THEFT

[2.416]

> The contact centre of a telecommunication company receives a telephone call from someone that poses as a client. The supposed client demands the company to change the email address to which the billing information should be sent from there on. The worker of the contact centre validates the client's identity by asking for certain personal data, as defined by the procedures of the company. The caller correctly indicates the requested client's fiscal number and postal address (because he had access to these elements). After the validation, the operator makes the requested change and, from there on, the billing information is sent to the new email address. The procedure does not foresee any notification to the former email contact. The following month the legitimate client contacts the company, inquiring why he is not receiving billing to his email address, and denies any call from him demanding the change of the email contact. Later, the company realizes that the information has been sent to an illegitimate user and reverts the change.

7.1.1 CASE No. 17 - Risk assessment, mitigation and obligations

124. This case serves as an example on the importance of prior measures. The breach, from a risk aspect, presents a high level of risk, as billing data can give information about the data subject's private life (e.g. habits, contacts) and could lead to material damage (e.g. stalking, risk to physical integrity). The personal data obtained during this attack can also be used in order to facilitate account takeover in this organisation or exploit further authentication measures in other organisations. Considering these risks, the "appropriate" authentication measure should meet a high bar, depending on what personal data can be processed as a result of authentication.

125. As a result, both a notification to the SA and a communication to the data subject are needed from the controller.

126. The prior client validation process is clearly to be refined in light of this case. The methods used for authentication were not sufficient. The malicious party was able to pretend to be the intended user by the use of publicly available information and information that they otherwise had access to.

127. The use of this type of static knowledge-based authentication (where the answer does not change, and where the information is not "secret" such as would be the case with a password) is not recommended.

128. Instead, the organisation should use a form of authentication which would result in a high degree of confidence that the authenticated user is the intended person, and not anyone else. The introduction of an out-of-band multi-factor authentication method would solve the problem, e.g. to verify the change demand, by sending a confirmation request to the former contact; or adding extra questions and requiring information only visible on the previous bills. It is the controller's responsibility to decide which measures to introduce, as it knows the details and requirements of its internal operation the best.

Actions necessary based on the identified risks		
Internal documentation	Notification to SA	Communication to data subjects

(Right margin, vertical text): Part 2   Data Protection: EU Law etc

Actions necessary based on the identified risks		
√	√	√

7.2 CASE NO. 18: EMAIL EXFILTRATION

A hypermarket chain detected, 3 months after its configuration, that some email accounts had been altered and rules created so that every email containing certain expressions (e.g. "invoice", "payment", "bank wiring", "credit card authentication", "bank account details") would be moved to an unused folder and also forwarded to an external email address. Also, by that time, a social engineering attack had already been performed, i.e., the attacker, posing as a supplier, had had that supplier bank account details altered into his own. Finally, by that time, several fake invoices had been sent that included the new bank account detail. The monitoring system of the email platform ended up giving an alert regarding the folders. The company was unable to detect how the attacker was able to gain access to the email accounts to begin with, but it supposed that an infected email was to blame for giving access to the group of users in charge of the payments.

Due to the keyword-based forwarding of emails, the attacker received information on 99 employees: name and wage of a particular month regarding 89 data subjects; name, civil status, number of children, wage, work hours and remainder information on the salary receipt of 10 employees whose contracts were ended. The controller only notified the 10 employees belonging to the latter group.

7.2.1 CASE No. 18 - Risk assessment, mitigation and obligations

129. Even if the attacker was probably not aiming at collecting personal data, since the breach could lead to both material (e.g. financial loss) and non-material damage (e.g. identity theft or fraud), or the data could be used to facilitate other attacks (e.g. phishing), the personal data breach is likely to result in a high risk to the rights and freedoms of natural persons. Therefore the breach should be communicated to all 99 employees and not only to the 10 employees whose salary information was leaked.

130. After becoming aware of the breach, the controller forced a password change for the compromised accounts, blocked sending emails to the attacker's email account, notified the service provider of the email used by the attacker regarding his or her actions, removed the rules set by the attacker and refined the alerts of the monitoring system in order to give an alert as soon as an automatic rule is created. Alternatively, the controller could remove the right for users to set forwarding rules, needing the IT service team to do it only on request or it could introduce a policy that users should check and report on the rules set on their accounts once per week or more often, in areas handling financial data.

131. The fact that a breach could happen and go undetected for so long and the fact that, in a longer time, social engineering could have been used for altering more data, highlighted significant problems in the controller's IT security system. These should be addressed without delay, like emphasizing automation reviews and change controls, incident detection and response measures. Controllers handling sensitive data, financial information, etc. have a larger responsibility in terms of providing adequate data security.

Actions necessary based on the identified risks		
Internal documentation	Notification to SA	Communication to data subjects
√	√	√

EUROPEAN DATA PROTECTION BOARD: GUIDELINES 2/2021 ON VIRTUAL VOICE ASSISTANTS: VERSION FOR PUBLIC CONSULTATION
Version 1.0
Adopted on 9 March 2021

[2.417]

NOTES

This document has been published for public consultation. A subsequent version of this document is expected to be adopted by the EDPB following publication of this book

TABLE OF CONTENTS

EXECUTIVE SUMMARY

[2.418]

A virtual voice assistant (VVA) is a service that understands voice commands and executes them or mediates with other IT systems if needed. VVAs are currently available on most smartphones and tablets, traditional computers, and, in the recent years, even standalone devices like smart speakers.

VVAs act as interface between users and their computing devices and online services such as search engines or online shops. Due to their role, VVAs have access to a huge amount of personal data including all users' commands (e.g. browsing or search history) and answers (e.g. appointments in the agenda).

The vast majority of VVA services have been designed by few VVA designers. However, VVAs can work jointly with applications programmed by third parties (VVA application developers) to provide more sophisticated commands.

To run properly, a VVA needs a terminal device provided with microphones and speakers. The device stores voice and other data that current VVAs transfer to remote VVA servers.

Data controllers providing VVA services and their processors have therefore to consider both the GDPR[1] and the e-Privacy Directive[2].

These guidelines identify some of the most relevant compliance challenges and provide recommendations to relevant stakeholders on how to address them.

Data controllers providing VVA services through screenless terminal devices must still inform users according to the GDPR when setting up the VVA or installing, or using a VVA app for the first time. Consequently, we recommend to VVA providers/designers and developers to develop voice-based interfaces to facilitate the mandatory information.

Currently, all VVAs require at least one user to register in the service. Following the obligation of data protection by design and by default, VVA providers/designers and developers should consider the necessity of having a registered user for each of their functionalities.

The user account employed by many VVA designers bundle the VVA service with other services such as email or video streaming. The EDPB considers that data controllers should refrain from such practices as they involve the use of lengthy and complex privacy policies that would not comply with the GDPR's transparency principle.

The guidelines consider four of the most common purposes for which VVAs process personal data: executing requests, improving the VVA machine learning model, biometric identification and profiling for personalized content or advertising.

Insofar the VVA data is processed in order to execute the user's requests, i.e. as strictly necessary in order to provide a service requested by the user, data controllers are exempted from the requirement of prior consent under Article 5(3) e-Privacy Directive. Conversely, such consent as required by Article 5(3) e-Privacy Directive would be necessary for the storing or gaining of access to information for any purpose other than executing users' request.

Some VVA services retain personal data until their users require their deletion. This is not in line with the storage limitation principle. VVAs should store data for no longer than is necessary for the purposes for which the personal data are processed.

If a data controller becomes aware (e.g. due to quality review processes) of the accidental collection of personal data, they should verify that there is a valid legal basis for each purpose of processing of such data. Otherwise, the accidentally collected data should be deleted.

VVAs may process data of multiple data subjects. VVA providers/designers should therefore implement access control mechanisms to ensure personal data confidentiality, integrity and availability. However, some traditional access control mechanisms such as passwords are not fit for the VVA context since they would have to by spoken aloud. The guidelines provide some considerations in this regard, including a section specific to the processing special categories of data for biometric identification.

VVA providers/designers should consider that when collecting user's voice, the recording might contain other individuals' voice or data such as background noise that is not necessary for the service. VVA designers should therefore consider technologies filtering the unnecessary data and ensuring that only the user's voice is recorded.

When evaluating the need for a Data Protection Impact Assessment (DPIA), the EDPB considers that it is very likely that VVA services fall into the categories and conditions identified as requiring a DPIA.

Data controllers providing VVA services should ensure users can exercise their data subject rights using easy-to-follow voice commands. VVA providers/designers, as well as app developers should at the end of the process inform users that their rights have been duly factored, by voice or by providing a writing notification to the user's mobile, account or any other mean chosen by the user.

NOTES

[1]   Regulation 2016/679/EU of the European Parliament and of the Council of 27 April 2016 on the protection of natural persons with regard to the processing of personal data and on the free movement of such data, and repealing Directive 95/46/EC], (hereinafter "GDPR")

[2]   Directive 2002/58/EC of the European Parliament and of the Council of 12 July 2002 concerning the processing of personal data and the protection of privacy in the electronic communications sector (Directive on privacy and electronic

communications) as amended by Directive 2006/24/EC and Directive 2009/136/EC (hereinafter "e-Privacy Directive").

The European Data Protection Board

Having regard to [Article 70 (1j) and (1e) of the Regulation 2016/679/EU of the European Parliament and of the Council of 27 April 2016 on the protection of natural persons with regard to the processing of personal data and on the free movement of such data, and repealing Directive 95/46/EC], (hereinafter "GDPR"),

Having regard to the EEA Agreement and in particular to Annex XI and Protocol 37 thereof, as amended by the Decision of the EEA joint Committee No 154/2018 of 6 July 2018[3],

Having regard to Article 12 and Article 22 of its Rules of Procedure,

HAS ADOPTED THE FOLLOWING GUIDELINES

1 GENERAL

[2.419]

1. Recent technological advances have greatly increased the accuracy and popularity of virtual voice assistants (VVA). Among other devices, VVAs have been integrated in smartphones, connected vehicles, smart speakers and smart TVs. This integration has given the VVAs access to information of an intimate nature that could, if not properly managed, harm the individuals' rights to data protection and privacy. Consequently, VVAs and the devices integrating them have been under the scrutiny of different data protection authorities.

2. There are several advantages to using speech-based interactions such as: the naturalness of the interaction which does not involve specific learning from the users, the speed of execution of the command and the extension of the field of action which can allow faster access to information. However, relying on speech also brings in difficulties in interpreting the message correctly: variability of the audio signal between different speakers, acoustic environment, ambiguity of the language, etc.

3. In practice, the fluidity or simplification of tasks remains the primary motivation for equipping oneself with VVAs. This may involve, for example, placing/answering a call, setting a timer, etc., especially when the users have their hands unavailable. Home automation is the major application put forward by the designers of VVAs. By proposing to simplify the execution of tasks (turning on the light, adjusting the heating, lowering the shutters, etc.) and to centralize them through a single tool that can be easily activated remotely, they fit into the discourse as a domestic facilitator. In addition to personal or domestic use, voice commands can be of interest in professional environments where it is difficult to handle computer tools and use written commands (e.g. manufacturing work).

4. In theory, the main beneficiaries of the voice interface could be people with disabilities or dependency for whom the use of traditional interfaces is problematic. Virtual voice assistance can provide easier access to information and computer resources and thus promote inclusive logics as the use of the voice makes it possible to overcome the difficulties associated with the written word, which can be found among certain classes of users.

5. Finally, health is also an area where there are many cases of use for conversational agents, vocal or not. For instance, during the Covid-19 pandemic, various callbots were deployed to offer a pre-diagnosis to calling users. In the long term some anticipate that the entire patient care process could be impacted by human/assistant interactions: not only for wellbeing and prevention, but also for treatment and support.

6. There are currently more than 3 billion smartphones and all of them have integrated VVAs, most of them switched on by default. Some of the most widespread operating systems in personal computers and laptops also integrate VVAs. The recent rise of smart speakers (147 million were sold in 2019[4]) is bringing VVAs to millions of homes and offices. However, current VVA designs do not offer by default authentication or access control mechanisms.

7. This document seeks to provide guidance as to the application of the GDPR in the context of the VVAs.

NOTES
  [3] References to "Member States" made throughout this document should be understood as references to "EEA Member States".

2 TECHNOLOGY BACKGROUND

2.1 BASIC CHARACTERISTICS OF VIRTUAL VOICE ASSISTANTS

[2.420]

8. A VVA can be defined as a software application that provides capabilities for oral dialogue with a user in natural language.

9. Natural language has a semantics specific to human language. Depending on the characteristics of the language and the diversity of the lexicon, the same instruction can be formulated in multiple ways, whereas some commands may seem similar but relate to two different objects. Inference mechanisms are then frequently used to resolve these ambiguities, for example, depending on what has been said previously, the time when the instruction was given, the place, the person's interests, etc.

10.   A VVA can be broken down into modules allowing to perform different tasks: sound capture and restitution, automatic speech transcription (speech to text), automatic language processing, dialogue strategies, access to ontologies (data sets and structured concepts related to a given domain) and external knowledge sources, language generation, voice synthesis (text to speech), etc. Concretely, the assistant should allow interaction in order to perform actions (e.g. "turn on the radio", "turn off the light") or to access knowledge (e.g. "what will the weather be like tomorrow?", "is the 7:43 a.m. train running?"). It thus plays the role of intermediary and orchestrator who is supposed to facilitate the accomplishment of the user's tasks.

11.   In practice, a VVA is not a smart speaker but a smart speaker can be equipped with a voice assistant. It is common to confuse both of them, however, the latter is only a material incarnation of the former. A VVA can be deployed in a smartphone, a smart speaker, a connected watch, a vehicle, a household appliance, etc.

12.   The organization of the underlying data processing may involve multiple information flow patterns. It is possible to isolate three main entities:

The physical instance: the hardware element in which the assistant is embodied (smartphone, speaker, smart TV, etc.) and which carries microphones, speakers and network and computing capacities (more or less developed depending on the case).

The software instance: the part implementing the human-machine interaction strictly speaking and which integrates the modules for automatic speech recognition, natural language processing, dialogue and speech synthesis. This can be operated directly within the physical equipment, but in many cases is performed remotely.

The resources: external data such as content databases, ontologies or business applications that provide knowledge (e.g. "tell the time on the West Coast of the United States", "read my emails") or enable the requested action to be carried out in a concrete way (e.g. "increase the temperature by 1.5°C").

13.   VVAs allow the installation of third party components or apps that expand their core functionalities. Each VVA name the components differently but all involve the exchange of users' personal data between the VVA designer and the app developer.

14.   Although most VVAs do not share the voice snippet with the app developers, these actors still process personal data. Moreover, depending on the nature of the functionality provided, the app developer receives intentions and slots which could include sensitive information like health data.

2.2 ACTORS IN THE VVA ECOSYSTEM

15.   A VVA may involve a great number of actors and intermediaries throughout the execution chain. In practice, up to five different actors can be identified. Depending on business models and technological choices, some actors may however take on several combinations of roles, for example, designer and integrator or designer and application developer:

(a)   **The VVA provider (or designer):** responsible for the development of the VVA, designs and defines its possibilities and default functionalities: activation modalities, choice of architecture, data access, record management, hardware specifications, etc.

(b)   **The VVA application developer:** as for mobile applications, creates applications extending the VVA's default functionalities. To do this, it is necessary to respect the development constraints imposed by the designer.

(c)   **The integrator:** manufacturer of connected objects, who wishes to equip them with a VVA. It should respect the requirements defined by the designer.

(d)   **The owner:** in charge of physical spaces receiving people (accommodation places, professional environments, rental vehicles, etc.) he/she wishes to provide a VVA to his/her audience (possibly with dedicated applications).

(e)   **The user:** final link in the VVA value chain, who can use it on various devices (speaker, TV, smartphone, watch, etc.) depending on how and where the VVA has been deployed and set up.

2.3 STEP-BY-STEP DESCRIPTION

16.   In order for a VVA to carry out an action or to access information, a succession of tasks is carried out:

(1)   Deployed within a piece of equipment (smartphone, loudspeaker, vehicle), the VVA is on standby. To be precise, it is constantly listening. However, until a specific wake-up expression has been detected no audio is transmitted out of the device receiving the voice and no other operation than wake-up expression detection is performed. For this purpose a buffer of a few seconds is used (see following section for more details).

(2)   The user says the wake-up expression and the VVA locally compares the audio with the wake-up expression. If they match, the VVA opens a listening channel and the audio content is immediately transmitted.

(3)   In many cases, if the processing of the command is done remotely, a second check of the keyword pronunciation is done on the server side to limit unwanted activations.

(4)   The user states his request that is transmitted on the fly to the VVA provider. The sequence of speech spoken is then automatically transcribed (speech to text).

(5)   Using natural language processing (NLP) technologies, the command is interpreted. The intentions of the message are extracted and information variables (slots) are identified. A dialogue manager is then used to specify the interaction scenario to be implemented with the user by providing the appropriate response scheme.

Part 2   Data Protection: EU Law etc

(6)   If the command involves a functionality provided by a third party app (skill, action, shortcut, etc.), the VVA provider sends to the app developer the intentions and information variables (slots) of the message.

(7)   A response adapted to the user's request is identified – at least supposedly, the answer "I don't have the answer to your question" being an adapted response in the case the VVA was not able to correctly interpret the request. If necessary, remote resources are used: publicly accessible knowledge databases (online encyclopaedia, etc.) or by authentication (bank account, music application, customer account for online purchase, etc.) and the information variables (slots) are filled with the recovered knowledge.

(8)   An answer phrase is created and/or an action is identified (lowering the blinds, raising the temperature, playing a piece of music, answering a question, etc.). The sentence is synthesized (text to speech) and/or the action to be performed is sent to the equipment executed.

(9)   The VVA returns to standby.

Please note that while currently most voice related processing is performed in remote servers, some VVA providers are developing systems that could perform part of this processing locally[5].

2.4 WAKE-UP EXPRESSIONS

17.   In order to be used, a VVA should be "awake". This means that the assistant switches to an active listening mode in order to receive orders and commands from its user. While this wake-up can also sometimes be achieved by a physical action (e.g. by pressing a button, pressing the smart speaker, etc.), almost all VVAs on the market are based on the detection of a wake-up expression or word to switch to active listening mode (also known as activation word or wake-up word / hot word).

18.   To do this, the assistant relies on the use of the microphone and slight computational capabilities to detect whether the keyword has been spoken. This analysis, which takes place continuously from the moment the VVA is on, is carried out exclusively locally. Only when the keyword has been recognised are the audio recordings processed for interpretation and execution of the command, which in many cases means sending them to remote servers via the Internet. Keyword detection is based on machine learning techniques. The major challenge in using such methods is that the detection is probabilistic. Thus, for each word or expression pronounced, the system provides a confidence score as to whether the keyword has actually been pronounced. If this score turns out to be higher than a predefined threshold value, this is considered to be the case. Such a system is therefore not free of errors: in some cases activation may not be detected even though the keyword has been said (false rejection) and in other cases activation may be detected even though the user has not said the keyword (false acceptance).

19.   In practice, an acceptable compromise should be found between these two types of errors to define the threshold value. However, since the consequence of a false detection of the keyword might be the sending of audio recordings, unexpected and unwanted transmissions of data are likely to occur. Very often, VVA providers implementing remote processing use a two-pass mechanism for this detection: a first pass embedded locally at the equipment level and a second one performed on remote servers where the next data processing are taking place. In this case, developers tend to set up a relatively low threshold in order to enhance the user experience and ensure that when the user says the keyword, it is almost always recognized – even if this means "over-detecting" it – and then implement a second detection pass on the server side, which is more restrictive.

2.5 VOICE SNIPPETS AND MACHINE LEARNING

20.   VVAs rely on machine learning methods to perform a wide range of tasks (keyword detection, automatic speech recognition, natural language processing, speech synthesis, etc.) and thus necessitate large datasets to be collected, selected, labelled, etc.

21.   The over- or under-representations of certain statistical characteristics can influence the development of machine learning-based tasks and subsequently reflect it in its calculations, and thus in its way of functioning. Thus, just as much as its quantity, the quality of the data plays a major role in the finesse and accuracy of the learning process.

22.   In order to increase the quality of the VVA and improve the machine learning methods deployed, VVA designers might wish to have access to data relating to the use of the device in real conditions – i.e. voice snippets – in order to work on its improvement.

23.   Whether it is to qualify the learning database or to correct errors made when the algorithm is deployed, learning and training of artificial intelligence systems necessarily require human intervention. This part of the work, known as digital labor, raises questions about both working conditions and safety. In this context, news media have also reported data transfers between VVA designers and subcontractors allegedly without the necessary privacy protection guarantees.

NOTES
4   For example, see a press release of 1 August 2019 by the Hamburg Data Protection and Information authority: https://datenschutz-hamburg.de/pressemitteilungen/2019/08/2019-08-01-google-assistant
5   This has been reported, for example, here: https://www.amazon.science/blog/alexas-new-speech-recognition-abilities-showcased-at-interspeech.

3 ELEMENTS OF DATA PROTECTION

3.1 LEGAL FRAMEWORK

[2.421]
24.   The relevant EU legal framework for VVAs is in the first instance the GDPR, as processing of

personal data belongs to the core function of the VVAs. In addition to the GDPR, the e-Privacy Directive[6] sets a specific standard for all actors who wish to store or access information stored in the terminal equipment of a subscriber or user in the EEA.

25. In accordance with the definition of "*terminal equipment*"[7], smartphones, smart TVs and similar IoT devices are examples for terminal equipment. **Consequently, VVAs should be considered as "terminal equipment" and the provisions of Article 5(3) e-Privacy Directive apply whenever information in the VVA is stored or accessed.**[8]

26. Any processing operations of personal data following the aforementioned processing operations, including processing personal data obtained by accessing information in the terminal equipment, must also have a legal basis under Article 6 GDPR in order to be lawful.[9]

27. Since the controller, when seeking consent for storing or gaining of access to information pursuant to Article 5(3) e-Privacy Directive, will have to inform the data subject about all the purposes of the processing (meaning the "subsequent processing") – including any processing following the aforementioned operations – consent under Article 6 GDPR will generally be the most adequate legal basis to cover the subsequent processing of the personal data. Hence, consent will likely constitute the legal basis both for the storing and gaining of access to information already stored and the processing of personal data following the aforementioned processing operations. Indeed, when assessing compliance with Article 6 GDPR, one should take into account that the processing as a whole involves specific activities for which the EU legislature has sought to provide additional protection.[10] Moreover, controllers must take into account the impact on data subjects' rights when identifying the appropriate lawful basis in order to respect the principle of fairness.[11] The bottom line is that Article 6 GDPR cannot be relied upon by controllers in order to lower the additional protection provided by Article 5(3) e-Privacy Directive.

28. As shown in section 2.3 (steps 2 and 3), current VVAs require access to the voice data stored by the VVA device.[12] Therefore, Article 5(3) e-Privacy Directive applies. The applicability of Article 5(3) e-Privacy Directive means that the storing of information as well as the accessing to information already stored in a VVA requires, as a rule, end-user's prior consent[13] but allows for two exceptions: first, carrying out or facilitating the transmission of a communication over an electronic communications network, or, second, as strictly necessary in order to provide an information society service explicitly requested by the subscriber or user.

29. The second exception ("strictly necessary in order to provide an information society service explicitly requested by the subscriber or user") would allow a VVA service provider to process users' data to execute users' requests (see par. 72 in section 3.4.1) without the consent foreseen in Article 5(3) e-Privacy Directive. Conversely, such **consent as required by Article 5(3) e-Privacy Directive would be necessary for** the storing or gaining of access to information for **any purpose other than executing users' request** (e.g. user profiling). Data controllers would need to attribute consent to specific users. Consequently, data controllers should only process non-registered users data to execute their requests.

30. VVAs can accidentally capture audio of individuals who did not intend to use a VVA service. First, to a certain extent and depending on the VVAs, the wake-up expression can be changed. Individuals who are not aware of this change could accidentally use the updated wake-up expression. Second, VVAs can detect the wake-up expression by mistake or by error. It is highly unlikely that either of the exceptions foreseen in Article 5(3) e-Privacy Directive are applicable in the event of an accidental activation. Furthermore, consent as defined in the GDPR must be the "unambiguous indication of the data subject's wishes". Thus, it is highly unlikely that an accidental activation could be interpreted as a valid consent. If data controllers become aware (e.g. through automated or human review) that the VVA service has accidentally processed personal data, they should verify that there is a valid legal basis for each purpose of processing of such data. Otherwise, the accidentally collected data should be deleted.

31. Moreover, it should be noted that the personal data processed by VVAs may be highly sensitive in nature. It may carry personal data both in its content (meaning of the spoken text) and its meta-information (sex or age of the speaker etc.). The EDPB recalls that voice data is inherently biometric personal data.[14] As a result, when such data is processed for the purpose of uniquely identifying a natural person or is inherently or determined to be special category personal data, the processing must have a valid legal basis in Article 6 and be accompanied by a derogation from Article 9 GDPR (see section 3.8 below).

3.2 IDENTIFICATION OF DATA PROCESSING AND STAKEHOLDERS

32. Considering the multiple possibilities of assistance that a VVA can provide in so many different environments of a data subject's daily life,[15] it is worth noting that careful consideration should be taken with the processing of personal data, which can also be impacted by different stakeholders.

3.2.1 Processing of personal data

33. From a personal data protection perspective, several constants can be observed irrespective of the VVA type (i.e. type of device, functionalities, services or combination of them) that can be used by a data subject. Such constants relate to the plurality of personal data, data subjects and data processing at stake.

Plurality of personal data types

34. The definition of personal data under Article 4(1) GDPR includes a wide variety of different data and applies in a technologically neutral context to any information that relates "to an identified or identifiable natural person".[16] Any interaction of a data subject with a VVA can fall under the scope of this definition. Once the interaction takes place, diverse range of personal data may be processed throughout the operation of the VVA as described in section 2.4.

35. From the initial request to the related answer, action or follow-up (e.g. setting up a weekly alert), the first personal data input will therefore generate subsequent personal data. This includes primary data (e.g. account data, voice recordings, requests history), observed data (e.g. device data that relates to a data subject, activity logs, online activities), as well as inferred or derived data (e.g. user profiling). VVAs use speech to mediate between users and all the connected services (e.g. a search engine, an online shop or a music streaming service) but unlike other intermediaries, VVAs may have full access to the requests' content and consequently provide the VVA designer with a wide variety of personal data depending on the purposes of the processing.

36. The plurality of personal data processed when using a VVA, also refers to a plurality of personal data categories for which attention should be paid (see below section 3.8). The EDPB recalls that when special categories of data[17] are processed, Article 9 GDPR requires the controller to identify a valid exemption from the prohibition to processing in Article 9(1) and a valid legal basis under Article 6(1), using an appropriate means identified under Article 9(2). Explicit consent may be one of the appropriate derogations where consent is the legal basis relied on under Article 6(1). Article 9 also notes (in detail) that the Member States may introduce further conditions to processing of biometric or other special categories data.

Plurality of data subjects

37. When using a VVA, personal data are processed from the first interaction with the VVA. For some data subjects this refers to the purchase of a VVA and/or the configuration of a user account (i.e. registered users). For other data subjects it refers to the first time they knowingly interact with the VVA of another data subject who purchased and/or configured this VVA (i.e. non-registered users). Besides these two categories of data subjects, there is a third one: accidental users who, registered or not, unknowingly make requests to the VVA (e.g. saying the correct wake-up expression without knowing the VVA is active, or saying other words that are mistakenly identified by the VVA as the wake-up expression).

38. The term plurality of data subjects also refers to multiple users for one VVA (e.g. device shared between registered and non-registered users, between colleagues, in a family, at school) and different types of users based on their condition (e.g. an adult, a child, an elder or a disable person). While a VVA can offer easier interaction with a digital tool and many benefits for some categories of data subjects, it is important to take into consideration the specificities of each category of data subjects and the context of use of the VVA.

Plurality of data processing

39. The technologies used to provide a VVA also have an impact on the amount of the processed data and the types of processing. The more a VVA provides services or features and is connected to other devices or services managed by other parties, the more the amount of personal data being processed and repurposing processing increases. This results in a plurality of processing carried out by automated means as described in section 2. Besides automated means, some processing may also involve human means. This is the case for example, when the implemented technology involves human intervention, such as the review of transcription of voices into texts, or the provision of annotations on personal data that can be used to insert new models in a machine-learning technology. This is also the case when humans analyse personal data (e.g. metadata) in order to improve the service provided by a VVA.

3.2.2 Processing by data controllers and processors

40. Data subjects should be in a position to understand and identify the roles at stake and should be able to contact or act with each stakeholder as required under the GDPR. The distribution of roles should not be to the detriment of the data subjects, even though scenarios can be complicated or evolving. In order to assess their roles, stakeholders are referred to the EDPB Guidelines 7/2020 on the concepts of controller and processor in the GDPR.[18]

41. As indicated in paragraph 16, the main stakeholders can be identified under the role of a provider or designer, an application developer, an integrator, an owner, or a combination of them. Different scenarios are possible, depending on who is doing what in the stakeholders' business relationship, on the user's request, the personal data, the data processing activities and their purposes. They should clearly decide and inform data subjects on the conditions under which each of them will act and comply with the resulting roles of controllers, joint-controllers or processors as provided for by the GDPR.[19] Each of them may take on one or several roles, as they may be a unique data controller, a joint controller, or a data processor for one data processing whereas carrying out another role for another data processing.

42. From a high-level perspective, the designer may act as a data controller when determining the purposes and means of a processing, but may intervene as a data processor when processing personal data on behalf of other parties, such as an application developer. The VVA user would therefore be subject to several data controllers: the application developer and the designer. It is also possible that the designer, the integrator and the developer are grouped into a single body acting as a unique data controller. In any case, the applicable qualifications have to be established on a case-by-case analysis.

Example 1:
The designer of the VVA processes user data for many purposes, including improving the VVA voice comprehension skills and respond accurately to requests. Therefore, and although this purpose may lead to the processing of data resulting from the use of applications provided by third parties, there is only one data controller: the designer of the VVA, on whose behalf and for whose purposes the processing is performed.

> **Example 2**:
> A bank offers to its customers an application that can be directly queried via the VVA in order to manage their accounts.
> Two actors are involved in the processing of personal data: the designer of the VVA and the developer of the banking application.
> In the scenario presented, the bank is the data controller for the provision of the service since it determines the purposes and essential means of processing related to the application allowing interaction with the assistant. Indeed, it offers a dedicated application that allows the user, a customer of the bank, to manage his/her accounts remotely. In addition, it decides on the means of processing by choosing appropriate processor, which is the designer of the VVA and can play an important role in assisting with its expertise to determining these means (for example, it can operate the development platform that allows third-party applications to be integrated into the VVA and, therefore, sets the framework and conditions to be respected by application developers).

43. On the data subject side, it is worth noting that several stakeholders may process the same personal data, even if the data subject does not really expect other parties than the VVA provider to be involved in the processing chain. So when a data subject acts with the VVA provider in relation to his/her personal data (e.g. exercise of data subject's rights), this does not automatically mean that this action will apply to the same personal data that is processed by another stakeholder. When these stakeholders are independent controllers, it is important that a clear information notice is given to the data subjects, explaining the various stages and actors of the processing. Moreover, in cases of joint controllership, it should be made clear if every controller is competent to comply with all data subject's rights or which controller is competent for which right.[20]

> **Example 3**:
> In this scenario, the designer of the VVA wishes to use the data collected and processed for the service provided by the bank in order to improve its voice recognition system. The designer of the VVA, who processes the data for its own purposes, will then have the status of controller for this specific processing.

44. As many stakeholders may be involved in the processing chain, and respectively many staff, risky situations may occur if no appropriate measures and safeguards are in place. Controllers are accountable for them and therefore should focus on protecting personal data, notably by choosing appropriate business partners and data processors, applying privacy by default and by design principles,[21] implementing adequate security and other GDPR tools such as audits and legal agreements (e.g. Article 26 for joint controllers or Article 28 GDPR for processors).

45. VVA ecosystem is a complex one, where potentially many actors could exchange and process personal data as data controllers or processors. It is of utmost importance to clarify the role of each actor in respect of each processing and to follow the data minimisation principle also in respect of the data exchange.

46. In addition, controllers should be vigilant on personal data transfers and guarantee the required level of protection throughout the processing chain, in particular when they use services located outside of the EEA.

3.3 TRANSPARENCY

47. Since VVAs process personal data (e.g. users' voice, location or the content of the communication), they must comply with the transparency requirements of the GDPR as regulated in Article 5(1)(a) as well as Article 12 and Article 13 (enlightened by Recital 58). Data controllers are obliged to inform users of the processing of their personal data in a concise, transparent, intelligible form, and in an easily accessible way.

48. Failure to provide necessary information is a breach of obligations that may affect the legitimacy of the data processing. Complying with the transparency requirement is an imperative, since it serves as a control mechanism over the data processing and allows users to exercise their rights. Informing users properly on how their personal data is being used makes more difficult for data controllers to misuse the VVA for purposes that go far beyond user expectations. For example, patented technologies aim to infer health status and emotional states from a user's voice and adapt the services provided accordingly.

49. Complying with the transparency requirements can be particularly difficult for the VVA service provider or any other entity acting as data controller. Given the specific nature of VVAs, data controllers face several obstacles to comply with the GDPR's transparency requirements:

- **Multiple users**: data controllers should inform all users (registered, non-registered and accidental users), not only the user setting up the VVA.
- **Ecosystem complexity**: as explained in the technology background section, the identities and roles of those processing personal data when using a VVA is far from evident for the users.
- **Specificities of the vocal interface**: digital systems are not yet fit for voice-only interactions as the almost systemic use of a companion screen proves. However, adapting to the vocal interface and being able to inform the user clearly and correctly through this means is a necessity.

50. VVAs can be regarded as finite states machines going through a number of states during their ordinary functioning. They can be listening locally for the detection of wake-up expressions, or interacting with a remote server to resolve a command, but they can assume many other states depending on the context (e.g. if there is background environmental sound) or the user talking to them (e.g. they may talk to an identified or unknown user). Unfortunately, these situations take place in a substantial asymmetry of information with the user, who is hardly aware if the device is listening, and even less on the status in which it lies.

51. It is highly recommended that VVA designers and developers take adequate steps to fill those asymmetries, making the functioning of VVAs more interactive. Users should be informed of the status in which the device currently lies. This enhancement in transparency can be achieved both making the dialogue man-machine more interactive (e.g. the device might acknowledge in some way the reception of a vocal command), or broadcasting the status of the machine with specific signals. There are many options that can be explored in this regard, ranging from the use of specific vocal acknowledgements and visible icons or lights, or the use of displays on the device.

52. These issues are especially relevant considering the plurality of users and the presence among them of vulnerable categories of individuals, such as children, elderly people or users with audio-visual disabilities.

53. Two important questions become evident from the issues above: what is it the most feasible way to inform users and when is the appropriate time to inform them? These issues should be further examined in two different situations, depending on whether the VVA has only one user (such as a personal smart phone) or potentially multiple users (e.g. smart home device). Using the VVA technology, a subversion of these two basic settings could also occur, e.g. when a user has a personal smart phone and connects this to a car. The VVA of the smart phone, which could reasonably be expected to be used by that user only, is now "extended" to the others in the car.

54. Currently, all VVAs are connected to a user account and/or are set up by an application that requires one. The question of how data controllers could consider informing these users about the privacy policy while setting up the VVA should be addressed as described in the Article 29 Working Party Guidelines on transparency. Apps should make the necessary information available in an online store prior to download[22]. This way the information is given the earliest time possible and at the latest, at the time the personal data is obtained. Some VVA providers include third-party apps in the VVA default setup so these apps can execute those apps by using specific wake up expressions. VVAs using this third-party app deployment strategy should ensure that users get the necessary information also on the third-party processing.

55. However, many VVA designers require VVA user accounts that bundle the VVA service with multiple other services like email, video streaming or purchases to name a few. The decision by the VVA designer of linking the account to many different services has the effect of requiring very lengthy and complex privacy policies. The length and complexity of such privacy policies greatly hinder fulfilling the transparency principle.

Example 4:

A VVA designer requires its users to have an account to access the VVA service. This user account is not specific to the VVA service and can be used for other services offered by the VVA designer such as email, cloud storage and social media. To create the account, users have to read and accept a 30 pages long privacy policy. The policy includes information on the processing of personal data by all the services that could be linked with the account.

The information provided by the VVA designer in this case should not be deemed as concise and its complexity reduces the required transparency. Therefore, the VVA designer would not be complying with the transparency requirements as set out in Articles 12 and 13 GDPR.

---

56. Although the most common way to provide necessary information is in writing, the GDPR allows "other means" as well. Recital 58 explicitly states that the information can be given in electronic form, e.g. through a website. In addition, when choosing the appropriate method to inform the data subjects, account should be taken to the specific circumstances, such as the manner the data controller and the data subject otherwise interact with each other.[23] An option for devices without a screen could be to provide a link which is easy to understand, either directly or in an e-mail. Already existing solutions could serve as example for the information, e.g. call centres' practices of notifying the caller about a phone call being recorded and directing them to their privacy policies. The constraints of screen less VVA does not exempt the data controller from providing the necessary information according to the GDPR when setting up the VVA or installing or using a VVA app. VVA providers and developers should develop voice-based interfaces to facilitate the mandatory information.

57. VVAs could be of great interest for users with impaired vision since they provide an alternative interaction means with the IT services that traditionally rely on visual information. According to Article 12 (1) GDPR providing the necessary information orally is possible exclusively if requested so by the data subject, but not as the default method. However, the constraints of screen less VVAs would require automated oral information means that could be augmented by written means. When using audio to inform data subjects, data controllers should provide the necessary information in a way that is concise and clear. Furthermore, data subjects should be able to re-listen[24].

58. Taking the appropriate measures to comply with GDPR transparency requirements is more complex when there are multiple users of the VVA other than the owner of the device. VVA designers must consider how to properly inform non-registered and accidental users when their personal data is processed. When consent is the legal basis for processing users' data, users must be properly informed for the consent to be valid[25].

59. In order to comply with the GDPR, data controllers should find a way to inform not only registered users, but also non-registered users and accidental VVA users. These users should be informed at the earliest time possible **and at the latest, at the time of** the processing. This condition could be especially difficult to fulfil in practice.

60. Certain corporate specificities should also not be detrimental to the data subjects. As many stakeholders are global companies or are well known for a specific business activity (e.g. telecommunication, e-commerce, information technologies, web activities), the way they provide a VVA service should be clear. Adequate information should make the data subjects understand whether or not their use of the VVA will be linked to other processing activities managed by the VVA service provider (e.g. telecommunication, e-commerce, information technologies or web activities) apart from the strict use of the VVA.

Example 5:
To use its assistant, a VVA designer which also provides a social media platform and a search engine, requires the user to link his/her account to the assistant. By linking his/her account to the use of the VVA, the designer can thus enhance the profile of its users through the use of the assistant, the applications (or skills) that are installed, the orders placed, etc. Hence assistant interactions are a new source of information attached to a user. VVA designer should provide users' with clear information as to how their data will be processed for each service and with controls allowing the user to choose if the data will be used or not for profiling.

Recommendations

61. When users are informed about the VVA processing of personal data using a user account's privacy policy and the account is linked to other independent services (e.g. email or online purchases), the EDPB recommends the privacy policy to have a clearly separated section regarding the VVA processing of personal data.

62. The information provided to the user should match the exact collection and processing that is carried out. While some meta-information is contained in a voice sample (e.g. stress level of the speaker), it is not automatically clear, whether such analysis is performed. It is crucial that controllers are transparent on what specific aspects of the raw data they process.

63. Furthermore it should at all times be apparent which state the VVA is in. Users should be able to determine whether a VVA is currently listening on its closed-loop circuit and especially whether it is streaming information to its back-end. This information should also be accessible for people with disabilities such as colour blindness (daltonism), deafness (anaccousia). Specific care should be given to the fact that VVAs suggest a usage scenario where eye-contact to the device is not necessary. So, all user feedback, including state changes should be available in visual and acoustic form at least.

64. Particular consideration should be applied if devices allow adding third party functionality ("apps" for VVAs). While some general information can be given to the user when they are the ones adding such functionality (given that it is the user's choice), during normal use of the device, the boundaries between the various controllers involved can be much less clear, i.e. the user might be not sufficiently informed how and by whom their data is processed (and to which extent) in a specific query.

65. All information about processing based on data collected and derived from the processing of recorded voice should also be available to users according to Article 12 GDPR.

66. VVA controllers should make transparent what kind of information a VVA can derive about its surroundings, such as but not limited to other people in the room, music running in the background, any processing of the voice for medical or marketing other reasons, pets, etc.

3.4 PURPOSE LIMITATION AND LEGAL BASIS

67. The processing of voice requests by VVAs has an evident purpose, the execution of the request. However, there often are additional purposes which are not so evident, like the improvement of the VVA natural language understanding capacities by training VVA model with machine learning techniques. Among the most common purposes for processing personal data by VVAs we find:
- Execute users' requests
- VVA improvement by training of the machine learning model and human review and labelling of voice transcriptions
- User identification (using voice data)
- User profiling for personalized content or advertising

68. Due to their role as intermediaries and the way they are designed, VVAs process a wide variety of personal and non-personal data. This allows processing personal data for many purposes that go beyond answering the users' requests and that could go totally unnoticed. By analysing data collected via VVAs, it is possible to know or infer user interests, schedules, driving routes or habits. This could enable personal data processing for unforeseen purposes (e.g. sentiment analysis or health condition assessment[26]), which would be far beyond the reasonable user expectations.

69. Data controllers should clearly specify their purpose(s) in relation to the context in which the VVA is used, so that they are clearly understood by the data subjects (e.g. presenting purposes in categories). In line with Article 5(1) GDPR, the personal data should be collected for specific, explicit and legitimate purposes and not further processed in a manner that is incompatible with these purposes.

3.4.1 Execute users' requests

70. The main use for a VVA is to issue voice commands that need to be executed by the VVA

or an associated app or service (e.g. a music streaming service, a mapping service or an electronic lock). The user's voice and potentially other data (e.g. the user's position when requesting a route for a certain destination) might therefore be processed.

> **Example 6:**
> The passenger of a smart car including a VVA requests a route to the closest gas station. The VVA processes the user voice to understand the command and the car's position to find the route and sends it to the smart component to show it in the car's screen.

71. Insofar as the processing of voice commands involves the storage or access to information stored in the terminal devices of the end-user, Article 5(3) of the e-Privacy Directive must be complied with. While Article 5(3) includes the general principle that such storage or access requires the prior consent of the end-user, it also provides for an exemption to the consent requirement where it is "strictly necessary in order for the provider of an information society service explicitly requested by the subscriber or user to provide the service". Insofar as the voice data is processed in order to execute the user's requests, it is exempted from the requirement of prior consent.

72. As indicated earlier, any processing operations of personal data subsequent to the storage or access to information in the terminal device of end-users must have a legal basis under Article 6 GDPR to be lawful.

73. There are two consecutive processing operations taking place on the VVA. As mentioned above the first one requires access to the VVA (and therefore the conditions of Article 5(3) e-Privacy Directive must be met). In addition to the conditions of Article 5(3) e-Privacy Directive, this second step also requires a legal basis under Article 6 GDPR.

74. When an individual takes the decision to use a VVA, this action generally implies that the initial user first needs to register an account to activate the VVA. In other words, this situation refers to a contractual relationship[27] between the registered user and the VVA controller. In view of its substance and fundamental objective, the core purpose of this contract is to use the VVA in order to execute the user's request of assistance.

75. Any personal data processing that is necessary to execute the user's request can therefore rely on the legal basis of the performance of the contract[28]. Such processing notably includes the capture of the user's voice request, its transcription to text, its interpretation, the information exchanged with knowledge sources to prepare the reply and then, the transcription to a vocal final reply that ends the user's request.

76. Performance of a contract can be a legal basis for processing personal data using machine learning (ML) when it is necessary for the provision of the service. Processing personal data using ML for other purposes which are not necessary such as service improvement should not rely on that legal basis.

77. Last but not least, the legal bases of the performance of the contract and consent under the GDPR should not be confused. The consent provided for entering into, i. e. agreeing to the contract is part of the validity of this contract and does not refer to the specific meaning of the consent under the GDPR[29].

78. When using a VVA does not require to previously configure a user account to the VVA, consent could be a possible legal basis.

3.4.2 Improve the VVA by training the ML systems and manually reviewing of the voice and transcripts

79. The accents and variations of human speech are vast. While all VVAs are functional once out of the box, their performance can improve by adjusting them to the specific characteristics of users' speech. As mentioned in section 2.6, this adjustment process relies on machine learning methods and consists of two processes: adding to the VVA training dataset new data collected from its users and the human review of the data processed for the execution of a fraction of the requests.

> **Example 7:**
> A VVA user has to issue three times the same voice command due to the VVA not understanding it. The three voice commands and the associated transcriptions are passed to human reviewers to review and correct the transcriptions. The voice commands and reviewed transcriptions are added to the VVA training dataset to improve its performance.

80. The processing activities described in the example should not be considered as (strictly) "necessary for the performance of a contract" within the meaning of Article 6(1)(b) GDPR, and therefore require another legal basis from Article 6 GDPR. The main reason being that VVAs are already functional when they come out of the box and can already perform as (strictly) necessary for the performance of the contract. The EDPB does not consider that Article 6(1)(b) would generally be an appropriate lawful basis for processing for the purposes of improving a service or developing new functions within an existing service. In most cases, a user enters into a contract to avail of an existing service. While the possibility of improvements and modifications to a service may routinely be included in contractual terms, such processing usually cannot be regarded as being objectively necessary for the performance of the contract with the user.

3.4.3 User identification[30] (using voice data)

81. The use of voice data for user identification implies the processing of biometric data as defined in Article 4.14 of the GDPR. Consequently, the data controller will need to identify an exemption under Article 9 of the GDPR in addition to the identification of a legal basis under Article 6 of the GDPR[31].

82. Of the exemptions listed in Article 9 of the GDPR, only data subjects' explicit consent seems applicable for this specific purpose.

83. However, since this purpose requires to apply the specific legal regime of Article 9 of the GDPR further details follow in the section 3.8, related to the processing of special categories of data.

3.4.4 User profiling for personalized content or advertising

84. As mentioned above, VVAs have access to the content of all voice commands even when they are aimed at services provided by third parties. This access would enable the VVA designer to construct very accurate user profiles that could be used to offer personalized services or advertisements.

> **Example 8:**
> Each time a VVA user makes an Internet search, the VVA adds labels signalling topics of interest to the user profile. The results for each new search are presented to the user ordered taking into account those labels.
>
> **Example 9:**
> Each time a VVA user makes a purchase from an e-commerce service, the VVA stores a record of the purchase order. The VVA provider enables third parties to target the VVA user with targeted advertisements on the basis of past purchases.

85. Personalisation of content may (but does not always) constitute an intrinsic and expected element of a VVA. Whether such processing can be regarded as an intrinsic aspect of the VVA service will depend on the precise nature of the service provided, the expectations of the average data subject in light not only of the terms of service but also the way the service is promoted to users, and whether the service can be provided without personalisation.[32]

86. Where personalisation takes place in the context of a contractual relationship and as part of a service explicitly request by the end-user (and the processing is limited to what is strictly necessary to provide this service), such processing may be based on article 6(1)(b) of the GDPR.

87. If processing is not strictly "necessary for the performance of a contract" within the meaning of Article 6(1)(b) GDPR, the VVA provider must, in principle, seek the consent of the data subject. Indeed, because consent will be required under Article 5(3) of the e-Privacy directive for the storing or gaining of access to information (see paragraphs 29-30 above), consent under Article 6(1)(a) GDPR will also, in principle, be the appropriate legal basis for the processing of personal data following those operations as reliance on legitimate interest could, in certain cases, risk undermining the additional level of protection provided by Article 5(3) of the e-Privacy directive.

88. Regarding user profiling for advertisement, it should be noted that this purpose is never considered as a service explicitly requested by the end-user. Thus, in case of processing for this purpose users' consent should be systematically collected.

Recommendations

89. Users should be informed of the purpose of processing personal data and that purpose should accord with their expectations of the device they purchase. In case of a VVA, that purpose – from a user's point of view – clearly is the processing of their voice for the sole purpose of interpreting their query and provide meaningful responses (be that answers to a query or other reactions like remote-controlling a light switch).

90. When the processing of personal data is based on consent, such consent "should be given in relation to *one or more specific* purposes and that a data subject has a choice in relation to each of them". Moreover, "a controller that seeks consent for various different purposes should provide a separate opt-in for each purpose, to allow users to give specific consent for specific purposes"[33]. For example, users should be able to separately consent or not for the manual review and labelling of voice transcriptions or the use of their voice data for user identification/authentication (see section 3.8).

3.5 PROCESSING OF CHILDREN'S DATA

91. Children can also interact with the VVAs or can create their own profiles connected to the ones of the adults. Some VVAs are embedded in devices which are specifically aimed at children.

92. When the legal basis for the processing is the performance of a contract, the conditions for processing children data will depend on national contract laws.

93. When the legal basis for the processing is consent and according to Article 8(1) GDPR, processing of children's data is only lawful *"where the child is at least 16 years old. Where the child is below the age of 16 years, such processing should be lawful only if and to the extent that consent is given or authorized by the holder of parental responsibility over the child"*. Consequently, to comply with the GDPR, when consent is the legal basis, explicit permission should be sought from parents or guardians to collect, process, and store children's data (voice, transcripts, etc.).

94. Parental controls are available to a certain degree but in their current form they are not user friendly (e.g. it is necessary to sign in a new service) or have limited capacities. Data controllers should invest in developing means for parents or guardians to control children use of VVAs.

3.6 DATA RETENTION

95. VVAs process and generate a wide variety of personal data like voice, transcriptions of voice, metadata or system logs. These types of data could be processed for a wide range of purposes like provision of a service, NLP improvement, personalization or scientific research. Following the GDPR data storage limitation principle, VVAs should store data for no longer than is necessary for the purposes for which the personal data are processed. Therefore, the data retention periods should be tied to different processing purposes. VVA service providers or third-parties providing services through VVAs should assess the maximum retention period for each data set and purpose.

96. The data minimization principle is closely related to the data storage limitation principle. Not only do data controllers need to limit the data storage period, but also the type and quantity of data.

97. Data controllers should ask themselves, among others the following questions: Is it necessary to store all voice recordings or all transcriptions to achieve the purpose X? Is it necessary to store the voice data once the transcription has been stored? In that case, for what purpose? How long is voice or transcription data necessary for each purpose? The answer to these and other similar questions will define the retention periods that should be part of the information available to the data subjects.

98. Some VVA store by default personal data like voice snippets or transcriptions for an undefined period while providing users means to delete such data. Retaining personal data indefinitely goes against the storage limitation principle. Providing data subjects with means to delete their personal data does not remove the data controller's responsibility of defining and enforcing a data retention policy.

99. VVA design needs to take into account users' controls to delete their personal data in their devices and in all remote storage systems. These controls may be required to resolve different kind of users' requests, for example, a request of erasure or the withdrawal of previously given consent. The design of some VVAs did not take into account this requirement.[34]

100. As in other contexts, data controllers may need to retain personal data as evidence of a service provided to a user to comply with a legal obligation. The data controller may retain personal data based on that basis. However, the data retained should remain the minimum necessary to comply with such a legal obligation and for the minimum amount of time. Of course, the data retained for the purpose of complying with a legal obligation should not be used for any other purposes without a legal basis under Article 6 GDPR.

> **Example 10:**
> A user purchases a TV in an e-commerce service using a voice command issued to a VVA. Even if the user requests afterwards the deletion of their data, the VVA provider or developer could still retain some data on the grounds of their legal obligation set by tax regulation to keep purchase evidence. However, the data stored for this purpose should not exceed the minimum necessary to comply with the legal obligation and could not be processed for any other purposes without a legal basis under Article 6 GDPR.

101. As mentioned in section 2, VVAs voice recognition capacity improves by training machine learning systems with users' data. If users do not consent or withdraw their consent to the use of their data for such purpose, their data could not be lawfully used to train any more model and should be deleted by the data controller, assuming that there is no other purpose justifying the continued retention. However, there is evidence that there may be risks of re-identification in some machine learning models.[35]

102. Data controllers and processors should use models which do not restrict their ability to stop processing if an individual revokes their consent, nor should they use models which restrict their ability to facilitate data subject rights. Controllers and processors should apply mitigation measures to reduce the re-identification risk to an acceptable threshold.

103. In the event that the user withdraws his or her consent, the data collected from the user can no longer be used for further training of the model. Nevertheless, the model previously trained using this data does not have to be deleted. The EDPB however highlights that there is evidence that there may be risks of personal data leaking in some machine learning models In particular, numerous studies showed that reconstruction as well as membership inference attacks can be performed, allowing attackers to retrieve information about individuals.[36] Data controllers and processors should therefore apply mitigation measures to reduce the re-identification risk to an acceptable threshold to make sure they use models which do not contain personal data.

104. Data subjects should not be nudged to keep their data indefinitely. While deleting stored voice data or transcriptions might have an impact on the service performance, such impact should be explained to users in a clear and measurable way. VVA service providers should avoid making general statements on the degradation of the service after personal data is deleted.

105. Anonymizing voice recordings is specially challenging, as it is possible to identify users through the content of the message itself and the characteristics of voice itself. Nevertheless, some research[37] is being conducted on techniques that could allow to remove situational information like background noises and anonymize the voice.

Recommendations

106. From a user's perspective, the main purpose of processing their data is querying and receiving responses and/or triggering actions like playing music or turning on or off lights. After a query has been answered or a command executed, the personal data should be deleted unless the VVA designer or developer has a valid legal basis to retain them for a specific purpose.

107. Before considering anonymization as means for fulfilling the data storage limitation principle, VVA providers and developers should check the anonymization process renders the voice unidentifiable.

108. Configuration defaults should reflect these requirements by defaulting to an absolute minimum of stored user information. If these options are presented as part of a setup wizard, the default setting should reflect this, and all options should be presented as equal possibilities without visual discrimination.

109. When during the review process the VVA provider or developer detects a recording originated on a mistaken activation, the recording and all the associated data should be immediately deleted and not used for any purpose.

3.7 SECURITY

110. To securely process personal data, VVAs should protect their confidentiality, integrity and availability. Apart from risks stemming from elements on the VVA ecosystem, using voice as communication means creates a new set of security risks.

111. VVAs are multiuser. They may allow for more than one registered user and anyone on their surroundings can issue commands and use their services. Any VVA service requiring confidentiality will involve some access control mechanism and user authentication. Without access control, anyone able to issue voice commands to the VVA could access, modify or delete any users' personal data it (e.g. ask for received messages, user's address or calendar events). Issuing voice commands to the VVA does not require being physically close to it since they can be manipulated, for example, via signal broadcasting[38] (e.g. radio or TV). Some of the known methods to remotely issue commands to VVAs like laser[39] or ultrasonic (inaudible) waves[40] are not even detectable by human senses.

112. User authentication can rely on one or more of the following factors: something you know (such as a password), something you have (such as a smart card) or something you are (such as a voice fingerprint). A closer look at these authentication factors in the VVA context shows that:
- Authentication using something the user knows is problematic. The secret that would allow users to prove their identity should be spoken aloud, exposing it to anyone in the surroundings. VVAs communication channel is the surrounding air, a channel type that cannot be fortified in the way traditional channels are (e.g. by limiting the access to the channel or encrypting its content).
- Authentication using something the user has would require the VVA service providers to create, distribute and manage "tokens" that could be used as proof of identity.
- Authentication using something the user is implies the use of biometric data for the purpose of uniquely identifying a natural person (see section 3.8 below).

113. VVA user accounts are associated to the devices in which the service is provided. Often the same account used to manage the VVA is used to manage other services. For example, owners of an Android mobile phone and a Google Home speaker can and most likely associate their Google account to both devices. Most VVAs do not require or offer an identification or authentication mechanism when a device providing a VVA service has just one user account.

114. When there is more than one user account associated with the device, some VVAs offer an optional basic access control in the form of PIN number with no real user authentication. Some other VVAs have the option to use voice fingerprint recognition as identification mechanism.

115. Although user identification or authentication might not be necessary to access all VVA services, it will definitely be for some. Without an identification or authentication mechanism, anyone could access other users' data and modify or erase them at will. For example, anyone close to a smart speaker could delete other users' playlists from the music streaming service, commands from the command history or contacts from the contact list.

116. Most VVAs blindly trust their local networks. Any compromised device in the same network could change the settings of the smart speaker or allow the installation of malware or to associate fake apps/skills to it without the user's knowledge or agreement.[41]

117. VVAs, like any other software, are subject to software vulnerabilities. However, due to the VVA market concentration[42] any vulnerability could affect millions of VVA users. If working as currently designed, VVAs do not send any information to the speech recognition cloud service until the wake-up expression is detected. However, software vulnerabilities could allow an attacker to bypass the VVA set-up and security measures. It could then be possible for example to get a copy of all data sent to the VVA cloud and forward it to a server controlled by the attacker.

118. Data lawfully processed or derived by VVAs allow building a fairly accurate profile of their users as VVA know or can infer the location, the relations and the interests of their users. VVAs are increasingly present in users' homes and smartphones. This circumstance increases the risk of mass surveillance and mass profiling. Consequently, the security measures to protect the data both in transit and at rest, in the devices and in the Cloud, should match those risks.

119. The increasing use of VVA in conjunction with not adequately balanced access rights by law enforcement authorities could induce a chilling effect that would undermine fundamental rights like freedom of speech.

120. Law enforcement authorities, both in[43] and out[44] of the EU, have already expressed their interest in accessing the voice snippets captured by VVAs. Access to data processed or derived by VVAs in the EU should comply with the existing EU data protection and privacy regulation framework. In case some Member States consider issuing specific legislation restricting the fundamental rights to privacy and data protection, such restrictions should always comply with the requirement set out in Article 23 of the GDPR[45].

121. The human review of voice recordings and associated data to improve VVA service quality is a common practice among VVA providers. Due to the sensitive nature of the data that is processed by this human reviewers and the fact that this process is often subcontracted to a processors, it is of utmost relevance that adequate security measures are put in place.

Recommendations

122. VVA designers and application developers should provide secure state-of-the-art authentication procedures to users.

123. Human reviewers should always receive the strictly necessary pseudonymised data. The legal agreements governing the review should expressly forbid any processing that could lead to the identification of the data subject.

124. If emergency calling is provided as a service through the VVA, a stable uptime[46] should be guaranteed.

3.8 PROCESSING OF SPECIAL CATEGORIES OF DATA

125. As previously mentioned, VVAs have access to information of an intimate nature which can be protected under Article 9 of the GDPR (see section 3.8.1), such as biometric data (see section 3.8.2). Therefore, VVA designers and developers must carefully identify in which cases the processing implies special categories of data.

3.8.1 General considerations when processing special categories of data

126. VVAs may process special categories of data in different circumstances:
- As part of their own services, for example when managing medical appointments in users' agendas.
- When acting as interface for third-party services, VVA providers process the content of the commands. Depending on the type of service requested by the user, VVA providers could process special categories of data. An example could be when a user issues commands to a VVA to use a third-party app used to keep track of her ovulation.[47]
- When voice data is used for the purpose of uniquely identify the user, as developed below.

3.8.2 Specific considerations when processing biometric data

127. Some VVA have the capability of uniquely identifying their users merely based on their voice. This process is known as voice template recognition. During the enrolment phase of voice recognition, the VVA processes a user's voice to create a voice template (or voiceprint). During its regular use, the VVA can calculate the voice template of any users and compare it to the enrolled templates to uniquely identify the user who executed a command.

> **Example 11:**
> A group of users set up a VVA to use voice template recognition. After doing so, each of them enrol their voice templates.
> Later, a user requests the VVA access to the meetings in his or her agenda. Since access to the agenda requires user identification, the VVA extracts the template from the request's voice, calculates its voice template and checks if it matches an enrolled user and if that specific user has access to the agenda.

128. In the example above, the recognition of a the user's voice on the basis of a voice template amounts to the processing of special categories of personal data within the meaning of Article 9 GDPR (processing of biometric data for the purpose of uniquely identifying a natural person).[48] The processing of biometric data for the purpose of user identification as required in the example will require the explicit consent of the data subject(s) concerned (Article 9(2)(a) GDPR). Therefore, when obtaining users' consent, data controllers must comply with the conditions of Article 7 and recital 32 of the GDPR and should offer an alternative identification method to biometrics, with regard to the free nature of consent.

129. When using voice data for biometric identification or authentication, data controllers are required to make transparent where biometric identification is used and how voiceprints (biometric templates) are stored and propagated across devices. To fulfil this transparency requirement, the EDPB recommends to provide the answers to the following questions:
- Does the activation of voice identification on one device automatically activate this feature on all other devices running with the same account?
- Does the activation of voice identification propagate through the VVA controller's infrastructure to devices owned by other users?
- Where are biometric templates generated, stored and matched?
- Are biometric templates accessible to VVA providers, developers or others?

130. When the registered user configures the VVAs to identify the voice of its users, the voice of non-registered and accidental users will also be processed for the purpose of uniquely identifying them.

131. Indeed, detecting the voice of the right speaker also involves comparing it with that of other people in the assistant's vicinity. In other words, the speaker recognition functionality implemented in voice assistants may require the voice biometrics of people speaking in the household to be recorded, to allow the user's voice characteristics to be distinguished from those of the person who wishes to be recognised. Biometric identification may therefore have the consequence of subjecting uninformed persons to biometric processing, by registering their template and comparing it with that of the user wishing to be recognised.

132. In order to avoid such collection of biometric data without the knowledge of the data subjects while allowing a user to be recognized by the assistant, solutions based on the user's data alone should be given priority. In concrete terms, this means that biometric recognition is only activated at each use at the user's initiative, and not by a permanent analysis of the voices heard by the assistant. For instance, a specific keyword or question to the persons present could be provided in order to obtain their consent to trigger biometric processing. For example, the user can say "identification" or the assistant can ask "do you wish to be identified" and wait for a positive response to activate biometric processing.

Example 12:
If the user wishes to set up biometric authentication for access to certain protected data such as his/her bank account, the voice assistant could activate speaker verification, when he/she launches the application only, and verify his/her identity in this way.

Recommendations

133. Voice templates should be generated, stored and matched exclusively on the local device, not in remote servers.

134. Due to the sensitiveness of the voiceprints, standards such as ISO/IEC 24745 and techniques of biometric template protection[49] should be thoroughly applied.

135. If a VVA uses voice based biometric identification VVA providers should:
•   Ensure that the identification is accurate enough to reliably associate personal data to the right data subjects.
•   Ensure that the accuracy is similar for all user groups by checking that there is no substantial bias towards different demographic groups.

3.9 DATA MINIMIZATION

136. Controllers should minimize the amount of data that is collected directly or indirectly and obtained by processing and analysis, e.g. not perform any analysis on the user's voice or other audible information to derive information about their mental state, possible disease or circumstances of their life.

137. Roll out settings by default that limit any data collecting and/or processing to a minimum required amount needed to provide the service.

138. Depending on the location, use context and microphone sensitivity, VVA could collect third parties' voice data as part of the background noise when collecting the users' voice. Even if background noise does not include voice data, it can still include situational data that could be processed to derive information about the subject (e.g. location).

Recommendations

139. In order to avoid recording background voices and situational information, VVA service providers should apply automated background-noise filtering.

140. VVA designers should consider technologies deleting the background noise and conversations ensuring that only the user voice is recorded.[50]

3.10 ACCOUNTABILITY

141. For any processing that is based on consent, controllers are obliged to be able to prove the consent of data subjects according to Article 7 (1) GDPR. Voice data can be used for accountability (e.g. to prove consent). The retention obligation for such voice data would then be dictated by the accountability requirements of the relevant specific legislation.

142. When evaluating the need for a Data Protection Impact Assessment (DPIA), the EDPB set out criteria[51] to be used by data protection authorities in creating lists of processing operations that require a mandatory DPIA and provide examples of processing that are likely to require a DPIA. It is very likely that VVA services fall into the categories and conditions identified as needing a DPIA. This includes considering if the device may be observing monitoring or controlling data subjects or systematically monitoring at large scale as per Article 35(3)(c), use of "new technology", or the processing of sensitive data and data concerning vulnerable data subjects.

143. All data collection and processing activities must be documented in accordance with Article 30 GDPR. That includes all processing involving voice data.

Recommendations

144. If voice messages are to be used to inform users according to Article 13, the data controllers should publish such messages on their website so they are accessible to the users and the data protection authorities.

3.11 DATA PROTECTION BY DESIGN AND BY DEFAULT

145. VVA providers and developers should consider the necessity of having a registered user for each of their functionalities. While it is clear that it is necessary to have a registered user to manage an agenda or an address book, it is not so clear that making a phone call or an Internet search requires the VVA to have a registered user.

146. By default, services which do not require an identified user should not associate any of the VVA identified users to the commands. A privacy and data protection friendly default VVA would only process users' data for executing users' requests and would store neither voice data nor a register of executed commands.

147. While some devices can only run one VVA, others can choose among different VVAs. VVA providers should develop industry standards enabling data portability in accordance with Article 20 of the GDPR.

148. Some VVA providers alleged their VVAs could not delete all users' data even when requested by the data subject. VVA providers should ensure that all users' data can be erased at the user's request in accordance with Article 17 of the GDPR.

NOTES

6   Directive 2002/58/EC of the European Parliament and of the Council of 12 July 2002 concerning the processing of personal data and the protection of privacy in the electronic communications sector (Directive on privacy and electronic communications) as amended by Directive 2006/24/EC and Directive 2009/136/EC (hereinafter "e-Privacy Directive").

7   Article 1 of Commission Directive 2008/63/EC of 20 June 2008 on competition in the markets in telecommunications terminal equipment, defines *"terminal equipment"* as (a) an *"equipment directly or indirectly connected to the interface of a public telecommunications network to send, process or receive information; in either case (direct or indirect), the connection may be made by wire, optical fibre or electromagnetically; a connection is indirect if equipment is placed between the terminal and the interface of the network; (b) satellite earth station equipment"*;

8   See EDPB Guidelines 1/2020 paragraph 12 for similar reasoning regarding connected vehicles (hereinafter "EDPB Guidelines 1/2020"). See also EDPB, Opinion 5/2019 on the interplay between the e-Privacy Directive and the GDPR, in particular regarding to competence, tasks and powers of data protection authorities.

9   Opinion 5/2019, paragraph 41.

10 Opinion 5/2019, paragraph 41.

11 EDPB Guidelines 2/2019 on the processing of personal data under Article 6(1)(b) GDPR in the context of the provision of online services to data subjects, Version 2.0, 8 October 2019, paragraph 1.

12 It is possible that future VVA devices will adopt the edge computing paradigm and be capable of providing some service locally. In such event, it will be necessary to reassess the applicability of the e-Privacy Directive.

13 See also EDPB Guidelines 1/2020, paragraph 14.

14 Article 4(14) GDPR defines biometric data as 'personal data resulting from specific technical processing relating to the physical, physiological or behavioural characteristics of a natural person, which allow or confirm the unique identification of that natural person, such as facial images or dactyloscopic data'

15 For example: at home, in a vehicle, in the street, at work or in any other private, public or professional spaces or a combination of these spaces.

16 Article 4(1) GDPR also specifies that *"an identifiable natural person is one who can be identified, directly or indirectly, in particular by reference to an identifier such as a name, an identification number, location data, an online identifier or to one or more factors specific to the physical, physiological, genetic, mental, economic, cultural or social identity of that natural person"*.

17 Article 9(1) GDPR defines special categories of personal as *"personal data revealing racial or ethnic origin, political opinions, religious or philosophical beliefs, or trade union membership, and the processing of genetic data, biometric data for the purpose of uniquely identifying a natural person, data concerning health or data concerning a natural person's sex life or sexual orientation shall be prohibited."*

18 EDPB Guidelines 07/2020 on the concepts of controller and processor in the GDPR, V1.0, adopted on 2 September 2020.

19 GDPR, Articles 12-14, Article 26.

20 EDPB Guidelines 07/2020 on the concepts of controller and processor in the GDPR, V1.0, adopted on 2 September 2020, par. 162 (hereinafter "Guidelines 7/2020").

21 See EDPB 4/2019 Guidelines on Article 25 Data Protection by Design and by Default, Version 2.0, adopted on 20 October 2020.

22 Guidelines on transparency under Regulation 2016/679, WP260 rev. 01, endorsed by EDPB (hereinafter "WP29 Guidelines WP260"), paragraph 11.

23 WP29 Guidelines WP260, paragraph 19.

24 WP29 Guidelines WP260, paragraph 21.

25 GDPR, Article 4 (11).

26 Eoghan Furey, Juanita Blue, "Alexa, Emotion, Privacy and GDPR", Conference paper, Human Computer Interaction Conference, July [2018].

27 Provided that *"the contract is valid pursuant to applicable national contract laws"*, extract from Guidelines 2/2019 on the processing of personal data under Article 6(1)(b) GDPR in the context of the provision of online services to data subjects ("Guidelines 2/2019"), §26.

28 In accordance with the Guidelines 2/2019, which moreover states that the Opinion 06/2014 remains relevant to Article 6(1)(b) and the GDPR (see in particular pages 11, 16, 17, 18 and 55 in this Opinion 06/2014).

29 See Guidelines 2/2019, respectively §18, §19, §20, §21 and §27.

30 Technically, the notion of identification has to be distinguished from verification (authentication). Identification is a one-to-many (1: N) search and comparison and requires in principle a database in which several individuals are listed. Differently, the processing for verification purposes is a one-to-one (1:1) comparison and is used to verify and to confirm by a biometric comparison whether an individual is the same person as the one from whom the biometric data originates. To the knowledge of the EDPB, VVA on the market rely on the sole use of speaker identification technologies.

31 GDPR considers that the mere nature of data is not always sufficient to determine if it qualifies as special categories of data since "the processing of photographs [. . .] are covered by the definition of biometric data only when processed through a specific technical means allowing the unique identification or authentication of a natural person." (recital 51) The same reasoning applies to voice.

32 See also Guidelines 2/2019 on the processing of personal data under Article 6(1)(b) GDPR in the context of the provision of online services to data subjects Version 2.0 8 October 2019, paragraph 57.

33 See Guidelines on consent under Regulation 2016/679, section 3.2.

34 See Amazon's letter of 28 June 2019 in response to US Senator Christopher Coons: https://www.coons.senate.gov/imo/media/doc/Amazon%20Senator%20Coons__Response%20Letter__6.28.19[3].pdf.

35 Veale Michael, Binns Reuben and Edwards Lilian 2018 "Algorithms that remember: model inversion attacks and data

protection law" Phil. Trans. R. Soc. A.37620180083, doi: 10.1098/rsta.2018.0083.

36   N. Carlini et al, "Extracting Training Data from Large Language Models", December 2020.

37   J. Qian, H. Du, J. Hou, L. Chen, T. Jung and X. Li, "Speech Sanitizer: Speech Content Desensitization and Voice Ano-nymization," in *IEEE Transactions on Dependable and Secure Computing*, doi: 10.1109/TDSC.2019.2960239. A. Cohen-Hadria, M. Cartwright, B. McFee and J. P. Bello, "Voice Anonymization in Urban Sound Recordings," *2019 IEEE 29th International Workshop on Machine Learning for Signal Processing (MLSP)*, Pittsburgh, PA, USA, 2019, pp. 1-6, doi: 10.1109/MLSP.2019.8918913. See, for example, VoicePrivacy (https://www.voiceprivacychallenge.org), an initiative to develop privacy preservation solutions for speech technology.

38   X. Yuan et al., "All Your Alexa Are Belong to Us: A Remote Voice Control Attack against Echo" 2018 IEEE Global Com-munications Conference (GLOBECOM), Abu Dhabi, United Arab Emirates, 2018, pp. 1-6, doi: 10.1109/GLOCOM.2018.8647762.

39   See, for example, https://lightcommands.com.

40   See, for example, https://surfingattack.github.io.

41   See, for example, Deepak Kumar et al., *Skill Squatting Attacks on Amazon Alexa*, USENIX Security Symposium, August 2018, https://www.usenix.org/conference/usenixsecurity18/presentation/kumar Security Research Labs, *Smart Spies: Al-exa and Google Home expose users to vishing and* eavesdropping, November 2019, https://srlabs.de/bites/smart-spies

42   The VVA market is currently shared among less than a dozen service providers.

43   See, for example, https://www.ft.com/content/ad765972-87a2-11e9-a028-86cea8523dc2

44   See, for example, https://cdt.org/insights/alexa-is-law-enforcement-listening

45   See also EDPB, Guidelines 10/2020 on restrictions under Article 23 GDPR.

46   The time a device or a service can be left unattended without crashing, or needing to be rebooted for administrative or maintenance purposes.

47   See for example, a product available here: https://www.amazon.com/Ethan-Fan-Ovulation-Period-Tracker/dp/B07CRLSHKY

49   See, for example: Jain, Anil & Nandakumar, Karthik & Nagar, Abhishek. (2008). "*Biometric Template Security*". EUR-ASIP Journal on Advances in Signal Processing. 2008. 10.1155/2008/579416. S. K. Jami, S. R. Chalamala and A. Y. Jindal, "*Biometric Template Protection Through Adversarial Learning*" 2019 IEEE International Conference on Consumer Elec-tronics (ICCE), Las Vegas, NV, USA, 2019, pp. 1-6, doi: 10.1109/ICCE.2019.8661905.

50   J. Qian, H. Du, J. Hou, L. Chen, T. Jung and X. Li, "Speech Sanitizer: Speech Content Desensitization and Voice Ano-nymization," in *IEEE Transactions on Dependable and Secure Computing*, doi: 10.1109/TDSC.2019.2960239.

51   Article 29 Working Party, Guidelines on Data Protection Impact Assessment (DPIA), wp248, rev.01, endorsed by EDPB.

4 MECHANISMS TO EXERCISE DATA SUBJECT RIGHTS

[2.422]

149.   In compliance with the GDPR, data controllers providing VVA services must allow all users, registered and non-registered, to exercise their data subject rights.

150.   VVA providers and developers should facilitate data subjects' control over their data during the entire processing period, in particular ease their right of access, rectification, erasure, their right to restrict the processing and, depending on the legal basis of the processing, their right to data portability and their right to object.

151.   The data controller should provide information on the data subject's rights at the time when data subjects switch on a VVA and at the latest, at the time when the first user's voice request is processed.

152.   Given that the main interaction means for VVAs is voice, VVA designers should ensure that users, registered or not, can exercise any data subject rights, using easy-to-follow voice commands. VVA designers, as well as app developers in case they are part of the solution, should at the end of the exercise process inform the user that his/her rights have been duly factored, by voice or by providing a writing notification to the user's mobile, account or any other mean chosen by the user.

153.   At least, VVA designers and app developers, notably, should implement specific tools providing an effective and efficient way to exercise such rights. They should therefore propose for their devices, a way to exercise data subjects' rights as by providing the data subject with self-service tools, as a profile management system[52]. This could facilitate an efficient and timely handling of data subject's rights and will enable the data controller to include the identification mechanism in the self-service tool.

154.   In regards of the exercise of data subjects rights in case of multiple users, when a user, registered or not, exercises one of his or her rights, he or she should do so without prejudice to any other users' rights. All the users, registered and non-registered can exercise their rights as long as the data controller is still processing the data. Data controller should set up a process ensuring that data subject rights are exercised.

4.1 RIGHT TO ACCESS

155.   According to Article 12(1) GDPR, communication under Article 15 should be provided in writing, or by other means, including, where appropriate, by electronic means. As regards access to the personal data undergoing processing, Article 15(3) states that where the data subject makes the request by electronic means, and unless otherwise requested by the data subjects, the information should be provided in a commonly used electronic form. What could be considered as a commonly used electronic form should be based upon the reasonable expectations of the data subjects and not upon what format the data controller uses in its daily operations. The data subject should not be obliged to buy specific software or hardware in order to get access to the information.

156.   On demand, data controllers should therefore send a copy of personal data, and audio data (including voice recordings and transcriptions) in particular, in a common format readable by the data subject.

157. When deciding about the type of format the information under Article 15 GDPR should be provided in, the data controller needs to keep in mind that the format should enable the information to be presented in a way that is both intelligible and easy accessible. Data controllers should also tailor the information to the specific situation of the data subject making the request.

Example 13:

A data controller providing a VVA service receives, from a user, both a request of access and a request for data portability. The data controller decides to provide the information under both Article 15 and Article 20 in a PDF file. In such a case, the data controller should not be considered to handle both requests in a correct manner. A PDF file technically fulfils the obligations on the data controller under Article 15, but does not fulfil the obligations on the data controller under Article 20.[53]

It should be noted that simply referring users to a history of their interactions with the voice assistant does not appear to enable the data controller to meet all its obligations under the right of access, as the accessible data generally represents only part of the information processed in the context of providing the service.

---

158. The right of access should not be used to counter / to get around the principles of minimisation and data retention.

4.2 RIGHT TO RECTIFICATION

159. To facilitate data rectification, users, registered or not, should be able to manage and update, at any time, their data by voice directly from the VVA device, as described above. Furthermore self-service tool should be implemented inside the device or an application in order to help them to rectify easily their personal data. Users should be notified by voice, or by writing of the update.

160. More generally, the right to rectification applies to any opinions and inferences[54] of the data controller, including profiling, and should consider the vast majority of data is highly subjective.[55]

4.3 RIGHT TO ERASURE

161. Users, registered or not, should be able, at any time, by voice from the VVA device, or from a self-service tool integrated into any device associated to the VVA, to delete data concerning them. In this respect, the personal data can be deleted by a data subject as easily as it is submitted. Due to the inherent difficulties of anonymising voice data and the wide variety of personal data collected from, observed and inferred about the data subject,[56] in this context the right to erasure could be hardly accommodated by anonymising personal datasets. As the GDPR is technology neutral and technology evolves rapidly, it will nevertheless not be excluded that right to erasure may be made effective through anonymization.

162. In some cases, without a third party screen or the possibility of displaying data stored (e.g. a mobile application or a tabular device), it is difficult to have a preview of the recorded tracks, to judge the relevance of the suggestions. A dashboard (or an application) widely accessible to users in order to ease its use should be supplied with the voice assistant to delete the history of the requests asked and customize the tool according to user's needs.[57]

163. For any data processing and, in particular, when registered data subjects consent to the voice recordings to be transcribed and used by the provider for the improvement of its services, VVA providers should, on demand of the user, be able to delete the initial voice recording as well as any related transcription of the personal data.

164. The data controller should ensure that no more processing may occur, after the exercise of the right of erasure. In regards to previous actions, the right to erasure may meet some legal and technical limits, notably.

Example 14:

If prior to the deletion request, a user made an online purchase by means of his/her VVA, the VVA provider may delete the voice recording relating to the online purchase and ensure no more future further use. However, the purchase will still be effective as well as the vocal order or the written transcription processed by the e-commerce website (here the exemption is based of legal obligation of the e-commerce website).

In the same vein, if prior to the deletion request, the user added a specific song to his/her playlist, by means of his/her VVA, the VVA providers will be able to delete the oral request, but not the past consequences of such request (the erasure will not impact the user's playlist).

---

165. Based on the above, in case the same personal data is processed for different processing purposes, data controllers should interpret erasure requests as a clear signal to stop processing of the data for all purposes that are not legally exempted.

166. In accordance with the conditions set out in Article 21(1) GDPR, data processed on the basis of legitimate interests of the VVA providers should not be an exemption to the right of erasure, in particular, because data subjects do not reasonably expect further processing of their personal data.

4.4 RIGHT TO DATA PORTABILITY

167. The data processing made by the VVA providers falls under the scope of data portability, as processing operations are mainly based, on the data subject's consent (under Article 6(1)(a), or under Article 9(2)(a) when it comes to special categories of personal data) or, on a contract to which the data subject is a party under Article 6(1)(b).

168. In practice, the right to data portability should facilitate switching between different VVA providers. VVAs operating in a digital environment in particular and data subject's voice being recorded in an application or a platform, the right to data portability should be granted for all personal data provided by the data subject. Furthermore, the data controller should offer users the possibility of directly retrieving their personal data from their user area, as a self-service tool. The users should also be able to exercise this right through voice command.

169. VVA providers and developers should give to the data subjects an extensive control over the personal data concerning him or her, in order to allow them to transfer personal data from a VVA provider to another. Data subjects should, therefore, receive his/her personal data provided to the data controller, in a structured, commonly used and machine-readable format as well as from means[58] that contribute to answer data portability requests (such as download tools and Application Programming Interfaces)[59]. As stated in the Guidelines on the right to data portability, in case of large or complex personal data collection, that could be the case here, the data controller should provide an overview "in a concise, transparent, intelligible and easily accessible form, using clear and plain language" (see Article 12(1) GDPR) in such a way that data subjects should always have clear information of what data to download or transmit to another data controller in relation to a given purpose. For example, data subjects should be in a position to use software applications to easily identify, recognize and process specific data from it.

170. This right should allow the user to retrieve for his/her personal use, the data that he/she has communicated by means of his/her voice (e.g. the history of voice interactions) and within the framework of the creation of his/her user account (e.g.: name and first name), notably.

171. For the full application of this data subjects' right in a context of one digital single market, VVA designers and app developers, notably, should develop common machine-readable formats that ease interoperability of the data format between VVA systems[60], including the standard formats for voice data. Technologies should be structured in order to ensure that personal data, including voice data, processed are easily and fully reusable by the new controller[61].

172. In regards to the format, VVA providers should provide personal data using commonly used open formats (e.g. mp3, wav, csv, gsm, etc.) along with suitable metadata used in order to accurately describe the meaning of exchanged information.[62]

NOTES

[52]   Profile management system is understood as a place within the VVA system, where users may, anytime, store its preferences, set modification and change easily his/her privacy settings.

[53]   WP29 Guidelines on the right to data portability – endorsed by the EDPB, p. 18.

[54]   The fact that opinions and inferences can qualify as personal data has been confirmed by the CJEU, which noted that the term 'any information' in the definition of personal data includes information that is 'not only objective but also subjective, in the form of opinions and assessments, provided that it 'relates' to the data subject' – Case C-434/16 *Peter Nowak v Data Protection Commissioner* ECLI:EU:C:2017:994 [34].

[55]   Getting Data Subject Rights Right, A submission to the EDPB from data protection academics, November 2019.

[56]   Article 29 Working Party Opinion 05/2014 on Anonymisation Techniques, adopted on 10 April 2014.

[57]   "Assistants vocaux et enceintes connectées, l'impact de la voix sur l'offre et les usages culturels et médias", the French "Conseil Supérieur de l'Audiovisuel", May 2019.

[58]   See as an illustration, the reasoning of the Article 29 Working Party in the Guidelines on the right to data portability – endorsed by the EDPB, p. 16:

"On a technical level, data controllers should explore and assess two different and complimentary paths for making portable data available to the data subjects or to other data controllers:

–   a direct transmission of the overall dataset of portable data (or several extracts of parts of the global dataset);
–   an automated tool that allows extraction of relevant data.

The second way may be preferred by data controllers in cases involving of complex and large data sets, as it allows for the extraction of any part of the data-set that is relevant for the data subject in the context of his or her request, may help minimizing risk, and possibly allows for use of data synchronization mechanisms (e.g. in the context of a regular communication between data controllers). It may be a better way to ensure compliance for the "new" data controller, and would constitute good practice in the reduction of privacy risks on the part of the initial data controller".

[59]   In this respect: Article 29 Working Party Guidelines on the right to data portability – endorsed by the EDPB, p. 1.

[60]   In this respect: recital 68 of the GDPR; WP29 Guidelines on the right to data portability – endorsed by the EDPB, p. 17.

[61]   "In this respect, recital 68 encourages data controllers to develop interoperable formats that enable data portability but without creating an obligation for controllers to adopt or maintain processing systems which are technically compatible. The GDPR does, however, prohibit controllers from establishing barriers to the transmission" – WP29 Guidelines on the right to data portability – endorsed by the EDPB, p. 5.

5 ANNEX:
AUTOMATIC SPEECH RECOGNITION, SPEECH SYNTHESIS AND NATURAL LANGUAGE PROCESSING

[2.423]
173. Following the theoretical foundations of signal processing, notably Claude Shannon's information and sampling theories, automatic speech processing has become a fundamental component of engineering sciences. At the crossroads of physics (acoustics, wave propagation), applied mathematics (modelling, statistics), computer science (algorithms, learning techniques) and human sciences (perception, reasoning), speech processing has rapidly been broken down into numerous subjects of study: speaker identification and verification, automatic speech recognition, voice synthesis, emotion detection, etc. Over the last fifteen years or so, the discipline as a whole has made very significant progress, with various factors contributing to this: improved methods, a significant increase in computing capacities and greater volumes of data available.

5.1 AUTOMATIC SPEECH RECOGNITION (ASR)

174. The automatic speech recognition (also known as speech to text) used to involve three distinct stages aimed at: 1) determine which phonemes were said using an acoustic model; 2) determine which words were said using a phonetic dictionary; 3) transcribe the sequence of words (sentence) most likely to have been said using a language model. Today, with the progress made possible by deep learning (a machine learning technique), many systems offer "end to end" automatic speech recognition. This avoids the need to go through the complex training of three different models while offering better performance in terms of results and processing time. Almost all major digital players now offer their own ASR implementations that can be easily used by API systems, but open source systems also exist (for example, DeepSpeech[63] or Kaldi[64]).

5.2 NATURAL LANGUAGE PROCESSING (NLP)

175. Natural Language Processing is a multidisciplinary field involving linguistics, computer science and artificial intelligence, which aims to create natural language processing tools for a variety of applications. The fields of research and applications are numerous: syntactic analysis, machine translation, automatic text generation and summarization, spell checking, question answering systems, text mining, named entity recognition, sentiment analysis, etc. Concretely, NLP's goal is to give computers the ability to read, understand and derive meaning from human languages. The development of NLP applications is challenging because computer tools traditionally require humans to interact with them in a programming language that is formal, meaning precise, unambiguous and highly structured. Human speech, however, is not always precise. It is often ambiguous and the linguistic structure can depend on many complex variables, including slang, regional dialects and social context.

176. Syntax and semantic analysis are two main techniques used with NLP. Syntax is the arrangement of words in a sentence to make grammatical sense. NLP uses syntax to assess meaning from a language based on grammatical rules. Syntax techniques used include parsing (grammatical analysis for a sentence), word segmentation (which divides a large piece of text to units), sentence breaking (which places sentence boundaries in large texts), morphological segmentation (which divides words into groups) and stemming (which divides words with inflection in them to root forms). Semantics involves the use and meaning behind words. NLP applies algorithms to understand the meaning and structure of sentences. Techniques that NLP uses with semantics include word sense disambiguation (which derives meaning of a word based on context), named entity recognition (which determines words that can be categorized into groups), and natural language generation (which will use a database to determine semantics behind words). While earlier approaches to NLP involved rules-based approaches, where simple machine learning algorithms were told what words and phrases to look for in text and given specific responses when those phrases appeared, current approaches to NLP are based on deep learning, a type of AI that examines and uses patterns in data to improve a program's understanding.

5.3 SPEECH SYNTHESIS

177. Speech synthesis is the artificial production of human speech. Speech synthesis has mainly been implemented by concatenation of vocal units that are stored in a database. This technique consists in selecting, from all the recordings of an actor previously transcribed into phonemes, syllables and words, the bricks of sound that correspond to the words that one wishes to have pronounced by the VVA and to assemble them one after the other to form an intelligible sentence with natural diction. Alternatively, a speech synthesizer can incorporate a model of the vocal tract and other human voice characteristics in order to model the parameters of a voice such as intonation, rhythm, and timbre, by generative statistical models (such as WaveNet[65], Tacotron[66] or DeepVoice[67]) and to create a completely synthetic voice output.

NOTES

[62]   EDPB strongly encourages cooperation between industry stakeholders and trade associations to work together on a common set of interoperable standards and formats to deliver the requirements of the right to data portability.

[63]   https://github.com/mozilla/DeepSpeech

[64]   https://github.com/kaldi-asr/kaldi

[65]   Aäron van den Oord et Sander Dieleman, *WaveNet: A generative model for raw audio*, Deepmind blog, September 2016, https://deepmind.com/blog/article/wavenet-generative-model-raw-audio.

[66]   Yuxuan Wang, *Expressive Speech Synthesis with Tacotron*, Google AI blog, March 2018, https://ai.googleblog.com/2018/03/expressive-speech-synthesis-with.html.

[67]   *Deep Voice 3: 2000-Speaker Neural Text-to-Speech*, Baidu Research blog, October 2017 http://research.baidu.com/Blog/index-view?id=91.

EUROPEAN DATA PROTECTION BOARD: GUIDELINES 3/2021 ON THE APPLICATION OF ARTICLE 65(1)(A) GDPR: VERSION FOR PUBLIC CONSULTATION

Adopted on 13 April 2021

[2.424]

NOTES

This document has been published for public consultation. A subsequent version of this document is expected to be adopted by the EDPB following publication of this book

© European Data Protection Board.

TABLE OF CONTENTS

1 INTRODUCTION AND SCOPE

[2.425]
1.   Article 65(1)(a) GDPR requires the EDPB to issue a legally binding decision whenever a Lead Supervisory Authority (LSA) issues a draft decision within the meaning of Article 60(3) GDPR and decides not to follow a relevant and reasoned objection expressed by a Concerned Supervisory Authority (CSA) or is of the opinion that the objection is not relevant or reasoned[1].

2.   Article 65(1)(a) GDPR is a **dispute resolution** mechanism meant to ensure the correct and consistent application of the GDPR in cases involving cross-border processing of personal data[2]. It aims to resolve conflicting views among the LSA(s) and CSA(s) on the merits of the case, in particular whether there is an infringement of the GDPR or not, in order to ensure the correct and consistent application of the GDPR in individual cases[3].

3.   Under the so-called 'one-stop-shop mechanism', which applies to cross-border processing of personal data, the LSA acts as the sole interlocutor for the controller or processor for the processing at issue[4]. The LSA is responsible for carrying out the necessary investigations, communicating the relevant information to all CSAs and preparing a draft decision[5]. Prior to the adoption of the draft decision, the LSA is required to cooperate with the CSAs in an endeavour to reach consensus and the LSA and CSAs to exchange all relevant information[6].

4.   Once a draft decision has been prepared, the LSA shall submit this draft decision to all CSAs for their opinion and take due account of their views[7]. Within four weeks after having been consulted, a CSA can express a "relevant and reasoned objection" to the draft decision[8]. When no CSA objects, the LSA may proceed to adopt the decision. If any CSA expresses an objection, the LSA must decide whether it will follow the relevant and reasoned objection or is of the opinion that the objection is not relevant or reasoned. If the LSA does not intend to follow the objection(s) or considers the objection(s) are not relevant and reasoned, the LSA is obliged to refer the case to the EDPB for dispute resolution[9].

5.   The EDPB will then act as a dispute resolution body and adopt a **legally binding decision**. The LSA, and in some situations the CSA with which the complaint was lodged[10], must adopt its final decision on the basis of the EDPB decision. The final decision of the competent supervisory authority will be addressed to the controller or processor and, where relevant, to the complainant.

6.   These Guidelines clarify the application of Article 65(1)(a) GDPR. In particular, they clarify the application of the relevant provisions of the GDPR and Rules of Procedure, delineate the **main stages** of the procedure and clarify the **competence of the EDPB** when adopting a legally binding decision on the basis of Article 65(1)(a) GDPR. The Guidelines also include a description of the applicable **procedural safeguards and remedies**.

7.   The present Guidelines do not concern dispute resolution by the EDPB in cases where:
•   there are conflicting views on which of the supervisory authorities concerned is competent for the main establishment (Article 65(1)(b) GDPR);
•   a competent supervisory authority does not request the opinion of the Board in the cases referred to in Article 64(1), or does not follow the opinion of the Board issued under Article 64 (Article 65(1)(c) GDPR).

NOTES
[1]   On the concept of relevant an reasoned objection see European Data Protection Board, Guidelines 9/2020 on relevant and reasoned objection under Regulation 2016/679, Version 2.0, 9 March 2021 (hereafter, "RRO Guidelines"), https://edpb.europa.eu/sites/edpb/files/files/file1/edpb_guidelines_202009_rro_final_en.pdf.

2   The cooperation and consistency mechanism is applicable to 'individual cases' regardless of whether the case concerns a complaint or ex officio inquiry/investigation.

3   Recital (136) and Article 65(1)(a) GDPR.

4   Article 56(6) GDPR. In cases involving data subject complaint(s), each CSA acts as the main point of contact for the data subject(s) in the territory of its Member State. See Article 60(7)-(9), Article 65(6) and article 77(2) GDPR. See also Recitals (130) and (141) GDPR.

5   See Article 60(3) GDPR. In accordance with Article 60(2) GDPR, the LSA may request at any time the other CSA to provide mutual assistance pursuant to Article 61 and may conduct joint operations pursuant to Article 62 GDPR.

6   This duty of cooperation applies to every stage of the procedure, starting with the inception of the case and extending to the whole decision-making process, see Article 60(1) GDPR and RRO Guidelines, paragraph 1. As part of the cooperation procedure, the LSA and CSAs are also required to exchange all relevant information with each other (Article 60(1) GDPR).

7   Article 60(3) GDPR.

8   Article 60(4) GDPR.

9   Articles 60(4), 63 and 65(1)(a) GDPR. If the LSA intends to follow the objection(s) that are deemed relevant and reasoned, it shall submit a revised draft decision to all the CSAs. The CSAs then have a period of two weeks during which they can express their relevant and reasoned objections to the revised draft decision (Article 60(5) GDPR). See also RRO GLS, paragraphs 2-3.

10 This will apply in particular if the complaint is totally or partially dismissed (Article 60 (8)-(9) GDPR). See further at paragraph 51 and following.

2 LEGAL FRAMEWORK AND RULES OF PROCEDURE

2.1 RIGHT TO GOOD ADMINISTRATION

[2.426]
8.   The EDPB is subject to the Charter of fundamental rights of the European Union (CFEU), including Article 41 (right to good administration). This is also reflected in Article 11(1) EDPB Rules of Procedure[11], which confirms that the EDPB must respect the right to good administration as set out by Article 41 CFEU.

9.   Article 41 CFEU grants every person the right to have his or her affairs handled **impartially, fairly and within a reasonable time** by the institutions, bodies, offices and agencies of the Union. This includes the right of every person:
*   **to be heard** before any individual measure, which would affect him or her adversely is taken; and
*   **to have access** to his or her file, while respecting the legitimate interests of confidentiality and of professional and business secrecy.

The right to good administration also includes the obligation of the administration to give reasons for its decisions.

2.2 GDPR

10.   Article 65(1) GDPR identifies three different situations in which the EDPB acts as a dispute resolution body. The main rules applicable to the dispute resolution procedures are set out in Article 65(2)-(6) GDPR.

11.   In case of a dispute resolution on the basis of Article 65(1)(a) GDPR, regard must also be given to Article 60 GDPR, which applies to the cooperation between the LSA and CSA in individual cases involving cross-border processing and specifies in which cases the LSA submit the matter to the EDPB for dispute resolution. While these Guidelines focus primarily on the application of Article 65(1)(a) GDPR, reference will also be made to the provisions of Article 60 GDPR insofar as they are relevant to clarify the main stages of the procedure and competence of the EDPB under Article 65(1)(a) GDPR.

2.3 EDPB RULES OF PROCEDURE (ROP)

12.   Article 11 RoP further clarifies the rules applicable in cases where the EDPB is called upon to take a binding decision, including in the context of the dispute resolution procedure. Article 11(2) RoP contains rules that apply specifically to the dispute resolution procedure of Article 65(1)(a) GDPR.

13.   While not the focus of these Guidelines, regard will also be had to Article 22 (Voting), Article 32 (Access to documents), Article 33 (Confidentiality of discussions) and Article 40 (Calculation of time limits) of the RoP, as appropriate.

NOTES
11   EDPB Rules of Procedure, adopted on 25 May 2018, as last modified and adopted on 8 October 2020, available at https://edpb.europa.eu/sites/edpb/files/files/file1/edpb_rop_version_7_adopted_20201008_en.pdf (hereafter 'RoP').

3 MAIN STAGES OF THE PROCEDURE (OVERVIEW)

3.1 CONDITIONS FOR ADOPTING A BINDING DECISION

[2.427]
14.   The general conditions for the adoption of a binding decision by the EDPB are set forth in Article 60(4)-(5) and Article 65(1)(a) GDPR.

15.   The EDPB shall be competent to issue binding decisions on the basis of Article 65(1)(a) GDPR when the following conditions are met:

- the submission of a draft decision within the meaning of Article 60(3) by the LSA to the CSAs;
- at least one CSA has raised (one or more) objection(s) to the (revised) draft decision of the LSA within the deadline provided by Article 60(4)-(5) GDPR; and
- the LSA has decided to not follow the objection(s) on the draft decision or rejected it (them) as not relevant or reasoned.

16. When these conditions are met, the EDPB shall be competent to adopt a binding decision on the basis of Article 65(1)(a) GDPR, which shall concern all the matters which are the subject of the relevant and reasoned objection(s), in particular whether there is an infringement of the GDPR[12].

17. A mere "comment" expressed by a CSA in relation to a draft decision does not amount to an objection within the meaning of Article 4(24) GDPR. The existence of comments shall therefore not give rise to the obligation to trigger the Article 65(1)(a) procedure if the LSA decides not to give any effect to the comment. Moreover, any comment expressed does not constitute as such a matter to be decided by the EDPB as part of its binding decision. The LSA is required, however, to take due account of the views expressed by all CSAs[13] and, in cases where the conditions of Article 56(2) are met, take utmost account of the views expressed by the CSA with whom the complaint has been lodged when preparing the draft decision and take due account of the views expressed by all CSAs[14].

3.2 ASSESSMENT OF THE COMPLETENESS OF THE FILE

18. Article 11(2) RoP provides that the Chair and the LSA are responsible for deciding whether the file is complete[15]. The assessment of the completeness of the file is an important step in the procedure, designed to ensure that all conditions for adopting a binding decision are met and that the EDPB has all the information necessary for doing so[16]. The assessment of completeness of the file also serves as the starting point for the legal deadlines mentioned in Article 65(2)-(3) GDPR[17]. Finally, the assessment of completeness of the file also seeks to ensure compliance with the right to be heard contained in Article 41 CFEU.

19. When submitting the matter to the EDPB for dispute resolution, the LSA shall include:
(a)   the **draft decision or revised draft decision** subject to the objection(s);
(b)   a **summary** of the relevant facts and grounds;
(c)   the **objection(s) made** by the supervisory authority(/-ies) concerned in accordance with Article 6(4) (and where relevant Article 60(5) GDPR);
(d)   an **indication** as to whether the LSA **does not follow** the relevant and reasoned objection or is of the opinion that the objection is **not relevant or reasoned**;
(e)   **documentation proving the timing and format of the provision of the (revised) draft decision and of the objection(s)** by the concerned supervisory authority (/-ies)[18]; and
(f)   in accordance with Article 41 of the European Charter on Fundamental Rights, the **written observations the LSA collected from the persons that might be adversely affected by the Boards** decision, together with confirmation and evidence of which documents submitted to the Board were provided to them when they were invited to **exercise their right to be heard** or a clear identification of the elements for which it is not the case[19].

20. The wording of Article 60(4) GDPR and Article 11(2) RoP makes clear that the LSA is responsible for ensuring that the file is complete and submitting all relevant information to the EDPB. Where necessary, however, the Secretariat may request from the LSA and/or CSAs additional information within a specific timeframe[20]. The ability to request additional information should be interpreted in light of the objective of ensuring that the EDPB is provided with all information necessary to take a binding decision concerning all the matters which are the subject of the relevant and reasoned objection(s), in particular whether there is an infringement of the GDPR.

> **Example 1:**
> A draft decision includes several references to internal documentation of the controller. Even though the LSA's (disputed) finding of an infringement is evidenced in its draft decision with reference to the contents of this documentation, the LSA does not include a copy thereof when submitting the matter to the EDPB for dispute resolution. The Secretariat may request the LSA to provide a copy of the documentation that is referenced within a specific timeframe if needed to help decide the subject matter of the relevant and reasoned objection(s).

The ability to request additional information at a later stage does not diminish the responsibility of the LSA to provide all relevant information from the outset when submitting the matter to the EDPB. As the responsibility for ensuring that the file is complete lies with the LSA, the requesting of additional information from the LSA and/or CSA should in principle only be necessary in exceptional circumstances. Moreover, as the LSA and CSA are obliged to exchange all relevant information in the course of the cooperation procedure, the relevant information should already have been provided to CSAs prior to launching the dispute resolution procedure. If all information necessary to take a binding decision on the objections raised is also transmitted by the LSA when referring the subject matter to the EDPB, it will not be necessary for the Secretariat to request additional information before declaring the file complete.

21. It should be noted that a request for additional information merely seeks to ensure the completeness of the file. It does not imply any judgement regarding the merit of the objections raised, nor does it alter in any way the subject matter referred to the EDPB. Once the file is deemed complete and the subject matter is referred to the EDPB, in exceptional circumstances, additional information may also be requested at a later stage in the procedure (i.e. once the subject matter has been referred to the Board) if necessary to remedy any omissions. This will be subject to a decision by the EDPB[21].

22. When necessary, the documents submitted by the LSA and/or CSA will be translated into English by the Secretariat[22]. The translation may also be limited to the specific parts which are likely to be relevant to help decide the subject matter of the relevant and reasoned objection(s). The LSA and/or CSA will have to agree on the translation[23].

Example 2:
In its draft decision, the LSA concludes that only one of the infringements of the GDPR alleged by the complainant materialised. The CSA considers in its relevant and reasoned objection that the other infringements alleged by the complainant were also committed while the draft decision does not fully explain the factual elements necessary to conclude the infringements did not occur. Therefore, the Secretariat requests the LSA to provide a copy of the necessary parts of the investigation report within a specific timeframe[24]. If the translation of these parts is necessary, it will be translated into English by the Secretariat and the LSA will have to agree on the translation.

---

23. Once the Chair and the LSA have decided that the file is complete (and the competent supervisory authority agreed on any required English translations), the Secretariat on behalf of the Chair will refer the subject-matter to the members of the EDPB without undue delay[25].

24. If the LSA fails to provide the information listed above within the set timeframe[26], the Chair will ask the Secretariat to refer the subject-matter to the EDPB. The EDPB will then assess, on a case-by-case basis, whether it can proceed to adopt its decision on the basis of the information already provided, or whether it is necessary to first obtain the information requested (e.g., confirmation and evidence of which documents submitted to the Board were provided to them when they were invited to exercise their right to be heard or a clear identification of the elements for which it is not the case) before adopting a decision.

Relationship with the right to be heard

25. The assessment of completeness of the file also seeks to ensure compliance with the right to be heard contained in Article 41 CFEU. Article 11(2) RoP provides that the EDPB shall take into account only the documents which were provided by the LSA and the other CSA(s) before the matter is referred to the Board. Any person who might be adversely affected should therefore in principle already have been invited to exercise their right to be heard[27]. Where necessary, the Board will take further actions ensuring the right to be heard of the affected persons in relation to the elements within the documents that are part of the file that will be considered by the EDPB in making its decision[28].

26. Once the file has been declared complete, LSA and CSA(s) are in principle not able to submit any additional information concerning the subject matter of the dispute (unless requested by the Secretariat with a view of remedying an omission in accordance with Article 11(2) RoP[29]). Only in exceptional circumstances can the Board decide to consider further documents that it deems necessary. For example, the LSA cannot introduce new elements of fact supporting its decision not to follow one or more objections which were not previously communicated before the matter was referred to the EDPB[30]. Moreover, all information relevant to the assessment of the objections raised should already be exchanged between the LSA and CSA prior to the initiation of the Article 65(1)(a) procedure in an endeavour to reach consensus (as in doing so it may also help avoid the need for trigger the dispute resolution mechanism).

27. Once the file has been declared complete and the subject matter has been referred to the EDPB, the EDPB must issue a binding decision in relation to each objection raised, unless the CSA who raised a particular objection decides to withdraw it. As the withdrawal of the objection signifies the end of the dispute between the LSA and CSA, it is no longer necessary for the EDPB to resolve the matter[31]. Similarly, the LSA may be able to withdraw a referral to the EDPB on the basis of Article 60(4) GDPR in cases where it later decides that it would like to follow each of the objections raised. The withdrawal of either an objection or referral should occur only in very exceptional cases, however, as the obligation for LSA and CSAs to seek consensus under Article 60 GDPR requires that the dispute resolution mechanism will only be triggered in cases of persistent disagreement and where reaching consensus was not possible.

3.3 ESTABLISHMENT OF DEADLINE(S)

28. The default legal deadline for the EDPB to adopt a binding decision is one month after the Chair and the competent supervisory authority have decided that the file is complete[32]. The deadline may be extended by a further month on account of the complexity of the subject-matter[33]. If the EDPB has not been able to adopt a decision, upon expiry of such an extension, it shall do so within two weeks following the expiration of the extension[34].

3.3.1 Calculation

29. The calculation of the deadline for the adoption of the binding decision must be done on the basis of Regulation 1182/71[35]. According to Article 3(2)(c) of Regulation 1182/71,

> "*a period expressed in weeks, months or years shall start at the beginning of the first hour of the first day of the period, and shall end with the expiry of the last hour of whichever day in the last week, month or year is the same day of the week, or falls on the same date, as the day from which the period runs*".

The Court of Justice has confirmed that, for instance, if an event which is the point from which a period of a week starts to run happens on a Monday, the period will end on the following Monday, which will be the dies ad quem (deadline expiration date).[36] Likewise, if the time limit is expressed in months and the triggering event occurs on the 20th March, the period will end on the 20th April.

30.   The start date (*'dies a quo'*) in the application of Article 65(1)(a) GDPR consists of the day when the Chair and the competent supervisory authority have decided that the file is complete and the subject matter is referred to the EDPB by the Secretariat via the information and communication system mentioned in Article 17 of the EDPB Rules of Procedure.

31.   Since the GDPR does not express periods in working days, the time limits concerned include public holidays, Sundays and Saturdays[37]. However, when the last day of a period is a public holiday, Sunday or Saturday, the period shall end with the expiry of the last hour of the following working day[38], thus the deadline expiration date (*'dies ad quem'*) shall be the following working day.

3.3.2 Decision to extend by one month

32.   Article 65(2) GDPR allows the first one-month deadline to be extended by a further month, taking into account the complexity of the subject-matter. The extension needs to be decided by the Chair of the EDPB, either on its own initiative or at the request of at least one third of the members of the EDPB[39]. The extension decision must be taken prior to the expiration of the one month deadline.

3.3.3 Extension by two weeks

33.   The binding decision must in principle be adopted by two-thirds majority at the latest two months after the file has been considered complete and the subject-matter has been referred to the EDPB. However, if the EDPB has not been able to adopt a decision within the extended timeframe because the required majority is not reached, the EDPB shall then adopt the decision within two weeks following the expiration of the second month by simple majority of its members[40].

34.   During the two additional weeks, modifications can be made to the draft binding decision that was previously submitted for adoption by two-thirds majority if necessary to achieve the simple majority. In other words, the draft binding decision may be adapted and adjusted in case the two-thirds majority is not reached.

3.4 PREPARATION OF THE DRAFT EDPB BINDING DECISION

35.   According to Article 11(5) RoP, the binding decisions *"shall be prepared and drafted by the secretariat and, upon decision of the Chair, together with a rapporteur and expert subgroups members"*[41]. Therefore, the EDPB Secretariat should act as lead rapporteur and the Chair should decide on the involvement of an expert subgroup and of co-rapporteurs.

36.   As soon as the LSA has submitted the matter to the EDPB for dispute resolution, the Secretariat should start the assessment of the completeness of the file. During this assessment, the Chair is invited to decide on the possible involvement of co-rapporteurs and will invite EDPB members to express an interest to become co-rapporteurs (unless the Chair decides not to involve co-rapporteurs for this case)[42]. In order to ensure fairness and impartiality, the (group of) co-rapporteur(s) should not include delegations from either the LSA or CSAs that submitted objections in relation to the draft decision[43].

37.   Finally, it should be noted that the Chair may also decide to involve the members of one or more other expert subgroups, depending on the needs of the case.

38.   As indicated earlier, Article 11(2) RoP states that the EDPB shall take into account only the documents which were provided by the LSA and the other CSA(s) once the matter is referred to the EDPB. This means that the LSA or CSA(s) cannot during the drafting stage introduce new elements of fact supporting their respective positions.

39.   In accordance with Article 76(1) GDPR, discussions of the Board and of expert subgroups shall be confidential when they concern the consistency mechanism[44]. Moreover, an obligation of professional secrecy is also imposed on the staff of all EEA national supervisory authorities[45], the EDPS and the EDPB Secretariat[46]. This means that the duty of confidentiality and professional secrecy, which is of paramount importance, shall be respected by the EDPB and its members also in relation to Article 65(1)(a) dispute resolution cases. This concerns both the discussions and the documents exchanged.

3.5 ADOPTION OF THE EDPB BINDING DECISION

40.   All majorities referred to by the GDPR (or by the RoP) refer to the total number of members of the EDPB entitled to vote, regardless of whether they are present or not[47].

41.   While not having the right to vote, EFTA EEA supervisory authorities (i.e. Iceland, Liechtenstein and Norway) shall have the right to express their positions on all items discussed and/or voted[48].

42.   In accordance with Article 68(6) GDPR, the EDPS shall have voting rights only on decisions which concern principles and rules applicable to the Union institutions, bodies, offices and agencies which correspond in substance to those of the GDPR. Where that is the case, the EDPS is entitled to vote on the decision as a whole.

43.   Every EDPB member entitled to vote who is not represented at a plenary meeting can delegate its voting rights to another member of the Board entitled to vote and attending the plenary meeting[49].

44.   The majority required for the adoption of a binding decision under Article 65(1)(a) GDPR is two-thirds of the EDPB members entitled to vote[50]. Where the EDPB has been unable to adopt a decision by two- thirds majority, the EDPB shall adopt its decision within the following two weeks by simple majority. Where the members of the Board are split, the decision shall by adopted by the vote of the Chair[51].

3.6 NOTIFICATION TO THE SUPERVISORY AUTHORITIES CONCERNED

45. Once the EDPB has adopted its binding decision, the Chair of the EDPB shall notify the decision to all the supervisory authorities concerned without undue delay[52]. Therefore, all the CSAs in the case need to be notified of the draft decision.

46. The notification will be performed by the Secretariat on behalf of the Chair via the information and communication system mentioned in Article 17 RoP.

3.7 FINAL DECISION OF THE SUPERVISORY AUTHORITY(IES)

47. Within one month after the notification of the EDPB decision to the supervisory authorities, the LSA and/or CSA (as the case may be[53]) must adopt a final decision[54]. Each final decision must be adopted "on the basis of" the decision of the EDPB. Moreover, the final decision(s) must refer to the decision by the EDPB and must specify that this decision will be published on the EDPB website. The final decision(s) of the LSA and/or CSA shall also "attach" the decision of the EDPB[55].

3.7.1 "On the basis of"

48. The requirement of adopting a final decision "on the basis of" the EDPB decision reflects the fact that the EDPB's decision is legally binding upon the LSA (and/or eventually the CSA(s) in case of need to adopt a final decision toward the data subjects[56]) as addressee(s) of the decision[57].

49. The aim of the binding decision is to resolve conflicting views among the LSA(s) and CSA(s) on the merits of the case, in particular whether there is an infringement of the GDPR, in order to ensure the correct and consistent application of the GDPR in individual cases[58].

50. The final decision must be adopted on the basis of the EDPB's decision and must, therefore, give full effect to the binding direction(s) as set out in the EDPB's decision. For example, if the EDPB has determined that there has indeed been an infringement of the GDPR, the LSA or CSA may not determine otherwise. In the same vein, if the EDPB has determined that envisaged action in relation to the controller or processor does not comply with the GDPR, the LSA or CSA must adapt their course of action accordingly[59].

3.7.2 Decision(s) by LSA and/or CSA

51. The final decision of the LSA and, as the case may be, the CSA with whom the complaint has been lodged, shall be adopted under the terms of Article 60(7), (8) and (9) GDPR[60].

52. The point of departure is that the LSA will be required to adopt and notify its final decision to the main establishment or single establishment of the controller or processor and inform the other supervisory authorities concerned as well as the EDPB of its final decision (including a summary of the relevant facts and grounds)[61]. One important derogation to this requirement concerns the situation where a complaint has been dismissed or rejected.

53. In cases where a complaint has been dismissed or rejected, the supervisory authority with which the complaint was lodged shall adopt the decision and notify it to the complainant and shall inform the controller thereof[62].

54. In case of need to take a decision to only partially dismiss a complaint, the LSA shall adopt the decision for the part concerning actions in relation to the controller or the processor, shall notify it to the main establishment or single establishment of the controller or processor on the territory of its Member State and shall inform the complainant thereof, while the supervisory authority of the complainant shall adopt the decision for the part concerning dismissal or rejection of that complaint, and shall notify it to that complainant and shall inform the controller or processor thereof[63].

55. Each natural or legal person has the right to an effective judicial remedy before the competent national court against a decision of a supervisory authority which produces legal effects concerning that person, in line with Article 78 GDPR[64].

3.7.3 Notification of the EDPB

56. The LSA or, as the case may be, the CSA with which the complaint has been lodged, is required to inform the EDPB of the date when its final decision is notified respectively to the controller or the processor and to the data subject[65].

3.8 PUBLICATION OF THE EDPB BINDING DECISION

57. In accordance with Article 65(5) GDPR, the publication of the EDPB binding decision on the website of the Board shall occur "without undue delay" after the LSA has notified the final national decision to the controller/processor and/or the CSA has notified the data subject (in case of a dismissal of a complaint). Whenever possible, "without undue delay" should be interpreted as suggesting that the publication of the EDPB binding decision should happen on the same day where the final national decision is notified to the controller/processor/complainant.

58. In order to allow the EDPB to publish its binding decision "without undue delay" after the notification of the final national decision, Article 65(6) GDPR requires the competent supervisory authority to inform the Board of the date when its final decision is notified respectively to the controller or processor and to the data subject. To avoid undue delays, each competent supervisory authority should inform the Secretariat of the date on which notification of the national decision is expected to take place, preferably at least one day in advance.

59. Article 339 TFEU requires the members and staff of the EU institutions not to disclose information of the kind covered by the obligation of professional secrecy, in particular information about undertakings, their business relations or their cost components[66]. As a consequence, some portions of the EDPB binding decision may need to be redacted in order to avoid disclosure of information covered by professional secrecy. The Secretariat will evaluate the need to redact such elements on the basis of EU law and the case law of the CJEU[67].

60. The EDPB will also publish the final national decision(s) in its register[68], taking into consideration possible restrictions under national law of the competent supervisory authority concerning the publication of its decisions. Where such restrictions apply, the SAs should inform the Secretariat of any such restrictions.

NOTES

[12]   See Section 4 for further details concerning the competence of the EDPB in accordance with Article 65(1)(a) GDPR.

[13]   Article 60(3) GDPR.

[14]   Article 56(4) and Article 60(1) GDPR.

[15]   The Secretariat carries out the analysis on the completeness of the file on behalf of the Chair.

[16]   When necessary, the documents submitted by the competent authority will be translated into English by the EDPB Secretariat.

[17]   See Article 11(4) RoP and see further Section 3.3.

[18]   The aim of providing this information is to allow the Secretariat to verify the objection has been provided in writing and within the legal deadline. The timing and format of the provision of the (revised) draft decision and of the objection(s) can be proven, for example, via the relevant and reasoned objections report from the information and communication system mentioned in Article 17 of the RoP.

[19]   Article 11(2) RoP. See also section 5.

[20]   Article 11(2) RoP.

[21]   Article 11(2) RoP provides that in exceptional circumstances, the EDPB can decide to consider further documents it deems necessary. As a result, the additional information may be requested by the Secretariat/Chair but the EDPB will have to decide if it will consider or not the additional info received.

[22]   The competent authority must express its agreement with the translation provided (Article 11(2) RoP).

[23]   Article 11(2) RoP.

[24]   Article 11(2) RoP.

[25]   Article 11(2) RoP.

[26]   Such a time-frame should be decided on a case-by-case basis, taking into account the nature and volume of the documents requested. The Secretariat should consult with the LSA (or where applicable, CSA) to seek their views as to what constitutes an appropriate timeframe.

[27]   See in particular Article 11(2) RoP: "[...] *together with confirmation and evidence of which documents submitted to the Board were provided to them when they were invited to exercise their right to be heard or a clear identification of the elements for which it is not the case.*"

[28]   See Section 5 for additional information regarding the exercise of the right to be heard.

[29]   See paragraph 20 above.

[30]   Indeed, the wording of Article 11(2)d RoP confirms that when launching the procedure, the LSA should give an "indication" as to whether it does not follow the relevant and reasoned objection or is of the opinion that the objection is not relevant or reasoned (i.e. simply an indication as to whether it follows or not the objections). As a result, no new elements may be submitted going beyond those of which the CSAs were informed prior to the submission to the Board.

[31]   In cases where the withdrawal concerns the only objection which the LSA has decided not to follow or considered as not relevant and reasoned, the EDPB shall no longer be required to issue a binding decision in accordance with Article 65(1)(a) GDPR.

[32]   Article 65(2) GDPR in conjunction with Article 11(4) RoP.

[33]   Article 65(2) GDPR.

[34]   Article 65(3) GDPR. See also paragraph 32.

[35]   Regulation (EEC, Euratom) No 1182/71 of the Council of 3 June 1971 determining the rules applicable to periods, dates and time limits, O.J. 8.6.197, L 124/1. Article 40 RoP confirms that "*In order to calculate the periods and time limits expressed in the GDPR and in these Rules of Procedure, Regulation 1182/71 of the Council of 3 June 1971 determining the rules applicable to periods, dates and time limits shall apply*".

[36]   See the Judgment in *Maatschap Toeters, MC Verberk v. Productschap Vee en Vlees*, C-171/03, ECLI::EU:C:2004:714, paragraph 33.

[37]   Article 3(3) of Regulation 1182/71.

[38]   Article 3(4) of Regulation 1182/71.

[39]   Article 11(4) RoP.

[40]   See Article 65(3) GDPR. Regarding the calculation of the majority and voting rights of EDPB members see further Section 3.5 (Adoption of the EDPB binding decision).

[41]   See also Article 75(6)(g) GDPR, which provides that the Secretariat shall be responsible in particular for the preparation, drafting and publication of decisions on the settlement of disputes between supervisory authorities.

[42]   If the call for expression of interests to serve as co-rapporteur is made prior to the assessment that the file is complete, care should be taken not to disclose any elements of the file until after the assessment has been made and the subject matter has been referred to the EDPB.

[43]   See also the Judgment in *Dr. August Wolff GmbH & Co. KG Arzneimittel*, Case C-680/16 P, 27 March 2019, ECLI:EU:C:2019:257, paragraphs 29-41.

[44]   Article 33 RoP.

[45]   Article 54 (2) GDPR.

[46]   Article 56 of Regulation (EU) 2018/1725.

[47]   Article 22(3) RoP.

[48] See the Decision of the EEA joint Committee No 154/2018 of 6 July 2018 amending Annex XI (Electronic communication, audiovisual services and information society) and Protocol 37 (containing the list provided for in Article 101) to the EEA Agreement [2018/1022], See also Recital (7) and Article 4(1) RoP.

[49] The Chair and the secretariat shall be notified of any delegation of voting rights. Article 22(5)5 RoP.

[50] Article 65(2) GDPR in conjunction with Article 22(3) RoP.

[51] Article 65(3) GDPR.

[52] Article 65(5) GDPR.

[53] In case of partial or complete dismissal of a complaint, see Article 60(8) and (9) GDPR.

[54] Article 65(6) GDPR.

[55] The requirement that the final decision « attach » the EDPB decision does not mean that the EDPB decision must be annexed to the final decision within a single document (it is sufficient that the EDPB decision is communicated to the controller or processor together with the final decision).

[56] See Article 60(8) and (9) GDPR.

[57] Recital (136) and (143) GDPR.

[58] Recital (136) and Article 65(1)(a) GDPR.

[59] See Section 4 (Competence of the EDPB), in particular section 4.2 (Matters subject of the relevant and reasoned objection).

[60] Article 65(6) GDPR.

[61] Article 60(7) GDPR.

[62] Article 60(8) GDPR.

[63] Article 60(8) GDPR.

[64] See also Recital (143) GDPR. See further Section 8 (Judicial remedies).

[65] Article 65(6) GDPR.

[66] An obligation of professional secrecy is also imposed on the staff of the EU institutions by the Staff Regulations and on the staff of the EDPS, including the EDPB Secretariat, also by Article 56 of Regulation (EU) 2018/1725. An obligation of professional secrecy is also imposed by Article 54 (2) GDPR on the members and staff of each supervisory authority.

[67] See, for instance, Judgments in *Bank Austria Creditanstalt*, T-198/03, 30 May 2006, ECLI:EU:T:2006:136; in *Evonik Degussa*, T-341/12, 28 January 2015, ECLI:EU:T:2015:51; in *Akzo Nobel* NV, T-345/12, 28 January 2015, ECLI:EU:T:2015:50; in *MasterCard, Inc.*, T-516/11, 9 September 2014, EU:T:2014:759; in *Stichting Greenpeace Nederland*, T-545/11 RENV, 21 November 2018, ECLI:EU:T:2018:817; in *Amicus Therapeutics UK Ltd*, T-33/17, 25 September 2018, ECLI:EU:T:2018:595; in *Pergan Hilfsstoffe für industrielle Prozesse GmbH*, Case T-474/04 , 12 October 2007, [2007] ECR II-4225.

[68] Article 70(1)(y) GDPR requires the EDPB to maintain a publicly accessible electronic register of decisions taken by supervisory authorities and courts on issues handled in the consistency mechanism. See https://edpb.europa.eu/our-work-tools/consistency-findings/register-for-decisions.

4 COMPETENCE OF THE EDPB

[2.428]

61. The aim of the consistency mechanism, including Article 65(1)(a) GDPR, is to contribute to the **consistent application** of the GDPR throughout the Union. Recital (136) clearly indicates that the competence of the EDPB to issue a binding decision in case of conflicting views among LSA and CSAs in the context of the cooperation mechanism relates to the **merits of the case**, in particular whether there is an infringement of the GDPR[69].

62. According to Article 65(1)(a) GDPR, the EDPB binding decision shall concern **all the matters which are the subject of the relevant and reasoned objection**. Therefore, the EDPB will assess **only** issues included in the objections that have been raised in relation to the draft or revised draft decision of the LSA. The EDPB will not reassess the whole case nor will it address issues that might be raised in the course of the Article 65 procedure but were not the subject of the reasoned and relevant objections submitted prior to the submission of the dispute to the EDPB.

63. The dispute between the LSA and the CSA(s) may concern either the fact that the LSA does not follow one or more relevant and reasoned objections or that the LSA is of the opinion that one or more objections is not relevant or reasoned. The EDPB will assess, in relation to each objection raised, whether the objection meets the requirements of Article 4(24) GDPR and, if so, address the merits of the objection in the binding decision.

4.1 ASSESSMENT OF WHETHER THE OBJECTIONS ARE RELEVANT AND REASONED

64. In its Guidelines on relevant and reasoned objections, the EDPB has clarified the conditions that must be met in order for an objection to be considered "relevant and reasoned" within the meaning of Article 4(24) GDPR[70].

65. When a LSA refers a dispute to the EDPB for resolution in accordance with Article 60(4) and 63 GDPR, the EDPB must first assess whether the objection(s) raised in fact meet the conditions of being relevant and reasoned[71].

66. The EDPB recalls that in order for an objection to be considered as "relevant", there must be a direct connection between the objection and the substance of the draft decision at issue. More specifically, the objection needs to concern either whether there is an infringement of the GDPR or whether the envisaged action in relation to the controller or processor complies with the GDPR[72].

67. In order for an objection to be "reasoned", it should be coherent, clear, precise and detailed in explaining the reasons for the objection. It should set forth, clearly and precisely, the essential elements on which the CSA based its assessment, and the link between the envisaged consequences of the draft decision (if it was to be issued as it is) and the significance of the anticipated risks for data subjects' fundamental rights and freedoms and, where applicable, for the free flow of personal data within the Union[73].

68.   When assessing whether the objections in fact meet the conditions of being relevant and reasoned, the assessment carried out by the EDPB will be both **substantial and formal**. In other words, the EDPB will take into account the specific wording used by the CSA within each of the objections raised and whether each element of Article 4(24) GDPR is explicitly mentioned in relation to each specific objection; thus requiring an explicit reference to the risks posed by the draft decision as regards the fundamental rights and freedoms of data subjects[74].

69.   In its binding decision, the EDPB will not take any position on the merits of any substantial issues raised by objections that do not meet the conditions of Article 4(24) GDPR. If an objection does not meet the conditions of Article 4(24) GDPR, the binding decision of the EDPB remains without any prejudice to any assessments the EDPB may be called upon to make in other cases, including with the same parties, taking into account the contents of the relevant draft decision and the objections raised by the CSAs.

4.2 MATTERS SUBJECT OF THE RELEVANT AND REASONED OBJECTION

70.   In its Guidelines on relevant and reasoned objections, the EDPB also clarified the possible subject matter (substance) of a relevant and reasoned objection[75]. Those Guidelines describe a number of examples of objections that may meet the requirements of Article 4(24) GDPR. These examples relate to possible disagreements between the LSA and CSA on the following matters:
(1)   the existence of a given infringement of the GDPR;
(2)   the existence of additional or alternative infringements of the GDPR;
(3)   gaps in the draft decision justifying the need for further investigation;
(4)   insufficient factual information or reasoning;
(5)   procedural aspects; and
(6)   the specific action envisaged by the draft decision.

4.2.1 Existence of a given infringement of the GDPR

71.   A first example of a possible relevant and reasoned objection involves the disagreement between the LSA and CSA as to whether or not a given provision of the GDPR has been infringed[76]. Such a disagreement may arise where the draft decision adopted by the LSA either:
•   explicitly confirms the existence of an infringement of a specific article of the GDPR, but the CSA considers that this article of the GDPR has not been infringed[77];
•   explicitly confirms that a particular article of the GDPR has not been infringed, whereas the CSA considers that the article in question has been infringed.

72.   In accordance with Article 65(1)(a) GDPR, the EDPB shall take a binding decision concerning all the matters which are the subject of the relevant and reasoned objections, "*in particular whether there is an infringement of the GDPR*". The EDPB must make a binding decision which shall whenever possible, taking into account the elements of the file and the right to be heard, provide a final conclusion on the application of the GDPR in relation to the case at hand. In other words, the EDPB shall assess the merits of the arguments raised by the CSA in the objection against those of the LSA and make a final determination as to whether or not the given infringement of the GDPR took place or not. The EDPB will instruct the LSA to alter a finding of an infringement or to include one whenever necessary. In such cases, the LSA will then be obliged to implement the change in its final decision, taking into account the binding decision of the EDPB in relation to the objection raised.

4.2.2 Additional or alternative infringements of the GDPR

73.   A second example of a possible relevant and reasoned objection involves disagreement between the LSA and CSA as to the conclusions to be drawn from the findings of the investigation. For instance, the objection may state that the findings amount to the infringement of a provision of the GDPR other than (and/or in addition to) those already analysed by the draft decision[78].

74.   As previously indicated, the EDPB must make a binding decision which shall whenever possible, taking into account the elements of the file and the respondent's right to be heard, provide a final conclusion on the application of the GDPR in relation to the case at hand. This can potentially include a determination of the existence of additional (or alternative) infringements, provided that the file contains sufficient factual elements to substantiate the alleged infringement and the persons who would be adversely affected have been or can be heard in relation to the objections alleging the existence of an additional or alternative infringement[79].

Example 3:
The draft decision of a LSA states that the controller failed to comply with the duty to inform pursuant to Article 14 GDPR (information to be provided where personal data have not been obtained from the data subject). The draft decision states that the controller should have provided the information in paragraphs 14(1) and 14(2)(a) and (e) GDPR and finds no other infringements of Article 14. One of the CSAs considers that the controller should have provided all the information referred to in Article 14(2)(b) and (f) GDPR, as the default position is that all such information set out in that subarticle should be provided to the data subject unless one or more categories of the information does not exist or is not applicable.[80] Provided the objection raised by the CSA meets the requirements of Article 4(24), and taking into account the elements of the file and the right to be heard, the EDPB will decide whether or not the controller additionally infringed Article 14(2)(b) and (f) GDPR, in addition to Article 14(1) and Art. 14(2)(a) and (e) GDPR.

---

75. If the EDPB determines, following a relevant and reasoned objection to this effect, that additional and/or alternative provisions of the GDPR have been infringed, the LSA will be obliged to reflect this in its final decision, taking into account the binding decision of the EDPB in relation to the objection raised.

76. It may be possible, in exceptional cases, that the file submitted to the EDPB does not contain sufficient factual elements to allow the EDPB to make a final conclusion regarding the existence of the infringement identified by the relevant and reasoned objection. In most cases, however, the information exchanged during the cooperation procedure should be sufficient to enable the CSA to substantiate its objection in such a way that the EDPB shall be able make a final determination whether or not there has been an infringement of the GDPR[81]. Furthermore, when the LSA submits the matter to the Secretariat to obtain a binding decision on the basis of Article 65(1)(a) GDPR, the Secretariat may also request the LSA and/or CSA to provide additional information that is necessary to ensure the file is complete[82].

4.2.3 Gaps in the draft decision justifying the need for further investigation by the LSA

77. A third example of a possible relevant and reasoned objection involves disagreement between the LSA and CSA as to whether the draft decision has sufficiently investigated the relevant infringements of the GDPR[83].

Example 4:
The LSA, upon receiving a complaint, considers that not all of the allegations of infringements contained in the complaint merit investigation. In its draft decision, the LSA only addresses those aspects of the complaint which it decided to investigate without any statement regarding the other alleged infringements of the GDPR. The CSA considers that the LSA in its investigation unjustifiably failed to address a number of alleged infringements raised by the complainant and submits a relevant and reasoned objection based on the failure of the LSA to properly handle the complaint to safeguard the rights of the data subject.

---

78. Article 57(1)(f) GDPR imposes a duty upon supervisory authorities to handle each and every complaint submitted to them and to investigate the subject matter of the complaint "to the extent appropriate". The term "to the extent appropriate" provides the competent supervisory authority with a margin of discretion as regards the extent or depth of the investigation needed. However, this discretionary power must be exercised with all due diligence[84] and in accordance with the relevant provisions of the GDPR implying mutual cooperation.

79. If the EDPB, on the basis of a relevant and reasoned objection, determines that the LSA has unjustifiably failed to investigate or in any other way address some of the issues raised by the complaint, the EDPB can issue a binding decision specifying the need for LSA to handle the matter further and to investigate – to the extent appropriate – the remaining subject matter of the complaint. To the extent that the draft decision allows it, the LSA should in principle first seek to finalise its draft decision as regards those matters that do not require further investigation within the deadline specified by Article 65(6).

80. For those matters requiring further investigation, it may be necessary for the LSA to open a new case file. In case a new case file is opened to address the remaining issues, the LSA is required to comply with all cooperation provisions under the GDPR. This may lead to submitting a new draft decision in accordance with A60(3) GDPR which addresses the outstanding alleged infringement. In situations where it is not possible for the LSA to follow this course of action (e.g., when there is inextricable link between the matter requiring further investigation and the other parts of the LSA's draft decision that are to be finalised), it may be necessary for the LSA to first investigate the matter further and prepare an updated draft decision.

81. In any event, the LSA shall be required to further address the matter and keep the members of the EDPB informed of the steps taken. Moreover, the CSAs can seek to use the cooperation and consistency mechanisms provided for in the GDPR in case the LSA does not fulfil its obligations flowing from the Article 65 decision (i.e addressing the remaining issues to be resolved)[85].

4.2.4 Insufficient factual information or reasoning

82. A fourth example of a possible relevant and reasoned objection involves disagreement between the LSA and CSA as to whether sufficient factual elements and/or reasoning have been included in the draft decision[86]. For instance, a CSA might consider that the conclusion by the LSA included the draft decision is not adequately supported by the assessment carried out and the evidence presented[87]. In such a case the EDPB shall also be competent to issue a binding decision, provided the objection raised meets the whole threshold of Article 4(24) GDPR, including a link between the allegedly insufficient analysis and the existence of an infringement or the envisaged action[88].

83. In a situation where the draft decision of the LSA contains insufficient factual elements or reasoning, there are essentially two possible scenarios.

84. In the first scenario, the file on the basis of which the EDPB shall make its decision already contains sufficient information that would allow to address the lack of sufficient factual elements or reasoning in the draft decision. In such cases, the EDPB shall, within the scope of the relevant and reasoned objection, determine to what extent the LSA should amend its draft decision in order to remedy the insufficiency of reasoning, by making reference to the relevant elements included in the file.

> **Example 5:**
> The draft decision of the LSA establishes an infringement of the GDPR based on findings of fact supported by documentary evidence which were provided in the file to the EDPB. A number of CSAs submit relevant and reasoned objections outlining that the link between the documentary evidence and the finding of infringement is not sufficiently reasoned in the draft decision. The EDPB decision finds that the objection(s) are relevant and reasoned and indicates the correct legal interpretation and reasoning that the LSA should incorporate in its final decision.

85. In the second scenario, the file on the basis of which the EDPB shall make its decision does not contain sufficient factual elements to address the insufficiency of factual elements or reasoning.

> **Example 6:**
> The draft decision of the LSA finds that there is no infringement of Article 6(1)(a) GDPR and that the processing in question is lawful on the basis of the data subject's consent. However, neither the draft decision nor any other document in the file provides any further materials or analysis as to whether the conditions of Article 7 GDPR have been met. The draft decision simply states that the processing has been lawfully based on consent, without providing further reasoning or evidence. A CSA raises an objection against this lack of reasoning, arguing that the absence of this analysis gives rise to uncertainty surrounding the finding of no infringement in this case.

If the EDPB determines that the file on the basis of which the EDPB shall make its decision does not contain sufficient factual elements that would allow to remedy the insufficiency of reasoning, the EDPB can issue a binding decision specifying the need for LSA to investigate or address the matter further with a view of obtaining sufficient factual information, in line with what is specified in paragraphs 79-81 above.

4.2.5 Procedural aspects

86. A fifth example of a possible relevant and reasoned objection involves a disagreement between the LSA and CSA as to whether the procedural requirements imposed by the GDPR have been properly respected and this affects the conclusion reached in the draft decision[89].

87. The EDPB recalls that the aim of the dispute resolution mechanism of Article 65(1)(a) GDPR is to resolve conflicting views on the merits of the case[90]. It is not intended to resolve possible disputes regarding procedural requirements or duties of cooperation[91].

88. An objection involving a disagreement concerning procedural requirements will only be considered relevant and reasoned if the objection also puts forward arguments clarifying the different conclusion that the LSA should have reached in its draft decision. In its decision, the EDPB will resolve the dispute surrounding the conclusions reached in the draft decision.

89. If the procedural deficiencies leave the EDPB unable to resolve the dispute surrounding the conclusions reached by the draft decision (e.g. due to a lack of sufficient factual elements), the EDPB will recall the importance of the duty of cooperation and issue a binding decision specifying the need for LSA to investigate or address the matter further, in line with what is specified in paragraphs 79-81 above and ensuring full compliance with the procedural requirements in the GDPR which were not met.

4.2.6 Action envisaged

90. A sixth example of a possible relevant and reasoned objection involves disagreement between the LSA and CSA as to whether the envisaged action in relation to the controller or processor complies with the GDPR[92].

91. The EDPB recalls that Recital (150) GDPR states that the consistency mechanism may also be used to promote a consistent application of administrative fines. As a result, if the assessment of the EDPB within this context identifies shortcomings in the reasoning leading to the imposition of the fine at stake, the LSA will be instructed to re-assess the fine and remedy the identified shortcomings[93].

92. Fines are by no means the only action a supervisory authority can envisage. A relevant and reasoned objection may therefore also relate to other envisaged actions, taking into account the range of powers listed in Article 58(2) GDPR. Each envisaged measure should be appropriate, necessary and proportionate in view of ensuring compliance with this Regulation, taking into account the circumstances of each individual case[94]. In this context, it should be recalled that the decision to reject or dismiss a complaint, in whole or in part, also constitutes an envisaged action capable of being subject of a relevant and reasoned objection.

93. If the EDPB, on the basis of a relevant and reasoned objection, determines that the envisaged action included in the draft decision does not comply with the GDPR, it shall instruct the LSA to re-assess the envisaged action and change the draft decision in accordance with the binding decision of the EDPB.

NOTES

[69] Recital (136) stipulates that "*[...] The Board should also be empowered to adopt legally binding decisions where there are disputes between supervisory authorities. For that purpose, it should issue, in principle by a two-thirds majority of its members, legally binding decisions in clearly specified cases where there are conflicting views among supervisory authorities, in particular in the cooperation mechanism between the lead supervisory authority and supervisory authorities concerned on the merits of the case, in particular whether there is an infringement of this Regulation.*"

[70] RRO GLS, paragraphs 12-21.

71   As clarified earlier, the LSA shall submit the matter to the EDPB either if it does not follow the relevant and reasoned objection or if it is of the opinion that the objection is not relevant or reasoned. See section 3.1 above.

72   RRO GLS, paragraph 12. An objection raised fulfils the criterion of being "relevant" when, if followed, it would entail a change leading to a different conclusion as to whether there is an infringement of the GDPR or as to whether the envisaged action in relation to the controller or processor, as proposed by the LSA, complies with the GDPR. RRO GLS, paragraph 13.

73   RRO GLS, paragraph 19. See also RRO GLS, paragraph 16. (*"In order for the objection to be "reasoned", it needs to include clarifications and arguments as to why an amendment of the decision is proposed (i.e. the legal / factual mistakes of the LSA's draft decision). It also needs to demonstrate how the change would lead to a different conclusion as to whether there is an infringement of the GDPR or whether the envisaged action in relation to the controller or processor complies with the GDPR."*).

74   See also RRO GLS, paragraphs 7 and 37.

75   RRO GLS, paragraphs 22-48.

76   RRO GLS, paragraphs 24-25.

77   The RRO GLS include the following example : The CSA argues that LSA did not take into consideration the fact that the household exemption is not applicable to some of the processing operations conducted by a controller and involving the use of CCTV, hence that there is no infringement of the GDPR.

78   RRO GLS, paragraph 26.

79   See section 5 regarding the right to be heard.

80   See also Article 29 Working Party Guidelines on transparency under Regulation 2016/679, 29 November 2017, WP260 rev.01, 11 April 2018, paragraph 46.

81   Where appropriate, the CSA and LSA can make use of Article 61 and 62 GDPR with a view of obtaining the necessary information prior to the issuance of the draft decision.

82   See section 3.2 above.

83   RRO GLS, paragraph 27.

84   Judgment in *Schrems*, C-362/14, 6 October 2015, ECLI:EU:C:2015:650, paragraph 63.

85   The EDPB recalls the possibility for CSAs make use, where appropriate, of the ability to request mutual assistance pursuant to Article 61 GDPR (which also allow CSAs, in case the LSA fails to comply, to adopt a provisional measure in accordance with Article 66) or requests for an opinion pursuant to Article 64(2) GDPR (which is explicitly deemed by the legislator as particularly appropriate where a SA does not comply with its obligations for mutual assistance under Article 61 GDPR). The latter procedure may, eventually, produce a binding decision of the EDPB in accordance with Article 65(1)(c) GDPR. See also Advocate General Bobek, Opinion in *Facebook Ireland Limited*, C-645/19, ECLI:EU:C:2021:5, paragraphs 115-121. Additionally, the EDPB may also, in its binding decision under Article 65(1)(a) GDPR, invite the CSA to request the LSA to further investigate via an Article 61 Mutual Assistance request.

86   RRO GLS, paragraph 29.

87   *Ibid.*

88   RRO GLS, paragraph 29.

89   RRO GLS, paragraph 30.

90   See above at paragraph 61.

91   In this regard, the EDPB recalls Articles 61, 64(2), 65(1)(c) and 66 of the GDPR.

92   See also RRO GLS, paragraphs 32 et seq.

93   RRO GLS, paragraph 34.

94   Recital (129) GDPR.

5 THE RIGHT TO BE HEARD

5.1 Applicability

[2.429]
94.   The right to be heard before an administration takes a measure that would adversely affect a person is enshrined in Article 41 CFEU and has long been recognised as a general principle of EU law[95]. The right to be heard is also included in Article 16 of the European Code of Good Administrative Behaviour and reflected in Article 11 RoP.

95.   Article 41 CFEU is addressed not to the Member States but solely to the institutions, bodies, offices and agencies of the European Union[96]. Nevertheless, the right to be heard has also been recognised as *"inherent in respect for the rights of the defence, which is a **general principle of EU law**"*[97] *and therefore also applies when Member States adopt decisions which come within the scope of EU law*[98].

96.   The right to be heard applies to administrative proceedings of which the outcome is likely to affect the (legal or natural) person's interests. It also applies in situations where the administration of EU law is divided or shared between EU and the Member States (so-called "composite procedures"[99]). Article 41(2)(a) CFEU is framed in terms of individual measures that would adversely affect the person, with no specific requirement that the contested measure should be initiated against that person[100].

97.   Article 65(2) GDPR provides that the EDPB's decision *"shall be [...] addressed to the lead supervisory authority and all the supervisory authorities concerned and binding on them"*. Article 65(2) GDPR reflects the fact that the binding decision of the EDPB aims to resolve a dispute that has emerged among two or more national supervisory authorities. In accordance with the procedure under Article 60 GDPR, LSA will have shared its legal analysis in the draft decision and in relation to the objections raised during the cooperation procedure. The CSA(s) likewise will have shared its (their) objection(s) in relation to the draft decision, including any materials to substantiate their objection. In addition, both the LSA and CSAs can share their views in the course of the preparation and adoption of the EDPB decision[101].

98. Article 65(2) GDPR also confirms that the EDPB decision does not address directly any party other than the LSA and CSAs. Nevertheless, the decision adopted by the EDPB at European level shall be binding on the LSA or, as the case may be, the CSA with which the complaint has been lodged and is therefore decisive for the outcome of the procedure at national level. It therefore also may affect the interests of persons who were part of the procedure that gave rise to the draft decision.

99. As a result, any of these persons which would be adversely affected by the decision, in particular the controller(s) and/or processor(s) who are addressed by the draft decision of the LSA, as well as any other person which would be adversely affected by the decision, must be afforded the right to be heard in relation to the subject matter which is brought before the EDPB pursuant to Articles 60(4), 63 and 65(1)(a) GDPR.

5.2 PURPOSE

100. The right to be heard is described by the Court as guaranteeing *"every person the opportunity to make known his views effectively during an administrative procedure and before the adoption of any decision liable to affect his interests adversely"*[102]. As clarified by the CJEU, the purpose of the rule, that the addressee of an adverse decision must be placed in a position to submit his observations before that decision is taken, is to put the competent authority in a position effectively to take all relevant information into account. In order to ensure that the person concerned is in fact protected, the purpose of that rule is, inter alia, to enable that person to correct an error or submit such information relating to his or her personal circumstances as will argue in favour of the adoption or non-adoption of the decision, or in favour of it having a specific content[103].

101. The right to respond is also part of the right to be heard since an *"administrative procedure requires that the person concerned should be able [...] to put his own case and properly make his views known on the relevant circumstances and, where necessary, on the documents taken into account by the Community institutions"*[104]. Except in cases where legislation expressly provides for the possibility of an oral hearing, such as in the competition proceedings, the right to be heard does not necessarily require an oral hearing[105].

5.3 TIMING

5.3.1 At national level and prior to referral to the EDPB

102. Before the EDPB is given the task of issuing a binding decision, every supervisory authority is under and obligation to respect the right to be heard in the context of its national procedure, as a general principle of EU law[106]. Indeed, every supervisory authority needs to *"respect the right of every person to be heard before any individual measure which would affect him or her adversely is taken"*[107]. The right to be heard applies regardless of whether the case is cross-border in nature or not.

103. Even in the absence of specific provisions under national law, the LSA should, in advance of triggering Article 65(1)(a) GDPR, ensure that procedure conducted at national level takes into account the requirements of the right to be heard as a general principle of EU law.

5.3.2 During the assessment of completeness of the file

104. When the LSA submits the matter to the Secretariat with a view of obtaining a binding decision of the EDPB under Article 65(1)(a) GDPR, the Secretariat should assess which persons would possibly be adversely affected by the EDPB decision in the sense of Article 41 of the Charter. It should also assess whether each of those persons was offered the opportunity to exercise its right to be heard.

105. It is not sufficient that the LSA has heard the persons who might be adversely affected in the course of the national procedure prior to the adoption of its draft decision within the meaning of Article 60(3) GDPR. Before the EDPB will be in a position to resolve the dispute, the right to be heard must also be afforded in relation to any objections raised in relation to the draft decision, in particular where the LSA chooses not to follow the objection (or considers it as not being relevant reasoned).

106. When submitting the matter to the Secretariat, the LSA is expected to demonstrate how the right to be heard has been afforded to persons benefitting from this right in the course of the national procedure leading to the draft decision. As regards the documents shared when submitting the matter to the Secretariat, the LSA should specifically mention whether or not these documents (or the relevant contents thereof[108]) were subject to the right to be heard and with regard to which persons[109]. Replies or summaries of the hearing(s) should be provided as well.

107. The accommodation of the right to be heard is an essential element of the procedure, in the absence of which the subject matter of the dispute cannot be settled by the EDPB. As a result, the gathering and verification of the relevant information is carried out in the context of the check on the completeness of the file, before the subject matter is referred to the EDPB. Only after all the relevant verifications have been made by the Secretariat, the Chair shall be in the position to declare the file complete[110].

108. If there are relevant documents or information that have not been subject to the right to be heard, the Chair may instruct the Secretariat to ask the supervisory authorities (LSA / CSA) to take the necessary actions to enable any party that could be affected to be heard. If necessary, the Chair may instruct the Secretariat to take measures to directly ensure the right to be heard at the EDPB level. In both instances, the persons who would be adversely affected shall be invited to exercise the right to be heard on the relevant documents or information within a specific timeframe, taking into account the complexity of the subject matter (as well as possible needs for translation).

NOTES
95 See e.g. Judgment in *France v. Commission*, C-301/87, 14 February 1980, paragraph 29.
96 See e.g. Judgment in *Cicala*, C-482/10, 21 December 2011, ECLI:EU:C:2011:868, paragraph 28.
97 See e.g. Judgment in *Mukarubega*, C-166/13, 5 November 2014, ECLI:EU:C:2014:2336, paragraph 45.
98 *Ibid.*, paragraph 46. See also Judgments in *Glencore Agriculture Hungary Kft.*, C-189/18, 16 October 2019, ECLI:EU:C:2019:861, paragraph 39 ("*[. . . .] The authorities of the Member States are subject to that obligation when they take decisions which come within the scope of EU law, even though the EU law applicable does not expressly provide for such a procedural requirement*") and in *Teodor Ispas*, Case C-298/16, 9 November 2017, ECLI:EU:C:2017:843, paragraph 26. See also the Opinion of Advocate General Bobek in *Teodor Ispas*, Case C-298/16, 7 September 2017, ECLI:EU:C:2017:650, paragraphs 35-69.
99 Regarding composite administrative procedures, see e.g. the Opinion of Advocate General Compos Sánchez-Bordana in *Silvio Berlusconi*, Case C-219/17, 27 June 2018, ECLI:EU:C:2018:502, paragraphs 57-79. See also F. Brito Bastos, "Beyond Executive Federalism. The Judicial Crafting of the Law of Composite Administrative Decision-Making", Thesis submitted for assessment with a view to obtaining the degree of Doctor of Laws of the European University Institute, Florence, 13 June 2018, in particular at p. 120-163.
100 P. Craig, "Article 41 - Right to Good Administration", in *EU Charter of Fundamental Rights : A Commentary*, edited by Steve Peers, et al., Bloomsbury Publishing, 2014, p. 1079.
101 However, according to the RoP, in exceptional circumstances, the EDPB can decide to consider further documents (Article 11(2) in fine RoP).
102 See e.g. Judgments in *M.M.*, C-277/11, 22 November 2012, EU:C:2012:744, paragraph 87; *Mukarubega*, paragraph 46; *Glencore Agriculture Hungary*, paragraph 39 and the case law cited therein.
103 Judgment in *Glencore*, paragraph 41 and 52.
104 See e.g. the Judgment in *Technische Universität Munchen*, C-269/90, 21 November 1991, paragraph 25.
105 See Article 12 of Regulation 773/2004 (O.J 27 April 2004, L 123, p. 18). See also the Opinion of Advocate General Wahl in *SKW Stahl-Metallurgie GmbH and Holding AG v European Commission*, C-154/14, 3 September 2015, ECLI:EU:C:2015:543, paragraphs 45-47.
106 See paragraphs 95 above.
107 Recital (129) GDPR.
108 For purposes of the procedure under Article 65(1)(a) GDPR, the scope of which is limited resolving disputes concerning the objections raised, the right to be heard does not need to extend to elements beyond the subject matter of the dispute.
109 See Article 11(2)(f) RoP, which specifies that the LSA when submitting the matter to the Secretariat should include, *inter alia*, ""*in accordance with Article 41 of the European Charter on Fundamental Rights, the written observations the LSA collected from the persons that might be adversely affected by the Board's decision, together with confirmation and evidence of which documents submitted to the Board were provided to them when they were invited to exercise their right to be heard or a clear identification of the elements for which it is not the case*".
110 See also section 3.2 above.

6 ACCESS TO THE FILE

[2.430]
109. The right to good administration includes the right of every person to have access to the file, while respecting the legitimate interests of confidentiality and of professional and business secrecy[111].

110. Access to the documents and information that form the basis of an administrative decision is closely connected with the right to be heard[112]. In accordance with that principle, 'the addressees of decisions which significantly affect their interests must be placed in a position in which they can effectively make known their views as regards the *information on which the authorities intend to base their decision*'[113].

111. The right of access to the file of the EDPB as part of the right to good administration is distinct from the general right of access to documents held by the European institutions, bodies, offices and agencies pursuant to Regulation (EC) No 1049/2001[114], Article 15(3) TFEU or Article 42 of the Charter[115]. The right of access to the file and the right of access to documents are subject to different criteria and exceptions and pursue different purposes.

112. The right of access to the file extends to the documents shared with the EDPB to resolve the dispute in accordance with Article 65(1)(a) procedure, save where they involve business secrets of other undertakings, confidential information, as assessed by the EDPB on a case by case basis.

113. The right of access to the file shall not extend to confidential information and internal documents of the EDPB or the SAs (e.g. email correspondence or preparatory documents). In particular, the right of access shall not extend to exchanges between the EDPB and its members once the procedure has been launched[116].

NOTES
111 Article 41(2)b CFEU. The SA acting on behalf of the EDPB cannot make a general reference to confidentiality to justify a total refusal to disclose documents in its file to persons adversely affected, nor can it give blank pages on the ground that they contained business secrets without providing a more comprehensible non-confidential version, or a summary of the documents.
112 Opinion of Advocate General Bobek in *Teodor Ispas*, Case C-298/16, 7 September 2017, ECLI:EU:C:2017:650, paragraphs 117 and following.
113 Opinion of Advocate General Bobek in *Teodor Ispas*, Case C-298/16, 7 September 2017, ECLI:EU:C:2017:650, paragraphs 117 and following. See in the same vein also Opinion of Advocate General Bobek in *Glencore Agriculture Hungary Kft.*, C-189/18, 16 October 2019, ECLI:EU:C:2019:861, paragraph 51
114 Regulation (EC) No 1049/2001 of the European Parliament and of the Council of 30 May 2001 regarding public access

to European Parliament, Council and Commission documents (OJ L 145, 31.5.2001, p. 43). Article 2(1) of Regulation (EC) No 1049/2001 sets out that any citizen of the EU, and any natural or legal person residing or having its registered office in a Member State, has a right of access to documents of the EU institutions, subject to the principles, conditions and limits defined in that Regulation.
[115]   Article 32 RoP.
[116]   See also Article 33 RoP.

7 THE DUTY TO GIVE REASONS

[2.431]
114.   The right to good administration contained in Article 41 CFEU also includes the obligation of the administration to give reasons for its decisions[117].

115.   The duty to give reasons entails informing the addressee of the decision of the **factual and legal grounds** on which it is based, thereby enabling the person to decide whether to seek judicial review and facilitate the exercise of that review by the courts[118].

116.   The EDPB must articulate, in a clear and unequivocal fashion the reasoning underlying in its decision in such a way as to enable the persons affected to ascertain the reasons for its decision. While the EDPB does not need to state *all* legal and factual reasons leading to its decision, it must explain those which were of *decisive* importance[119]. In the same vein, the EDPB is also not obliged to adopt an explicit position on all the arguments raised. It is sufficient for the decision to set out, in a clear and unambiguous manner, the principal issues of law and of fact upon which it is based and which are necessary in order that the reasoning which has led the EDPB to its decision may be understood. What ultimately matters is that the statement of reasons by the EDPB enables all persons affected by the decision to ascertain whether the relevant provisions have been applied correctly.

117.   The EDPB must in its statement of reasons set out all the relevant grounds and motives for the adoption of its decision – including those that originate from the national level. This means that insofar as the facts set out in the draft decision or related documents are decisive for the decision of the EDPB, then the EDPB should include them in its statement of reasons[120].

118.   In relation to objections where the EDPB simply agrees with the reasons contained in the draft decision by the LSA or the decision of the LSA not to follow the relevant and reasoned objection (or to consider them not relevant or reasoned), the EDPB may fulfil its duty to state reasons by simply referring back to the position of the LSA, provided the affected persons were informed of those positions of the LSA and given the opportunity to be heard in relating to those positions[121].

119.   In light of the aforementioned considerations, the binding decision adopted by the EDPB on the basis of Article 65(1)(a) GDPR should in principle include a summary of dispute as well as an assessment of whether the conditions for adopting a binding decision are met. For each objection raised, the EDPB will then in principle[122]:
- summarise main elements of the draft decision which are related to the subject matter of the objection;
- summarise the main elements of the objection raised;
- summarise the position of the LSA or CSA in relation to the objection raised; and
- summarise the position of the persons who may be adversely affected in relation to the objection.

Once the relevant elements have been set out, the EDPB will assess, in relation to each objection raised, whether the EDPB meets requirements of Article (24) GDPR and, if so, address the merits of the objection in the binding decision[123].

120.   The operative parts of the decision should be clearly identified as such and included at the end of the decision, rendering explicit to what extent the competent authority is required/not required to amend its draft decision before finalisation.

NOTES
[117]   Article 41(2)c CFEU.
[118]   See e.g., Judgment in *Métropole Télévision SA*, T-206/99, 21 March 2011, paragraph 44. See also P. Craig, "Article 41 - Right to Good Administration", in *EU Charter of Fundamental Rights: A Commentary*, edited by Steve Peers, et al., Bloomsbury Publishing, 2014, p. 1085.
[119]   See e.g. Judgments of the General Court in *L'Air liquide*, Cases T-185/06, 16 June 2011, EU:T:2011:275, paragraph 64; in *Ryanair Ltd*, T-123/09, 28 March 2012, EU:T:2012:164, paragraph 178-179; and in *FIH Holding A/S*, T-386/14, 15 September 2016, EU:T:2016:474, paragraph 94.
[120]   Based on F. Brito Bastos, "Beyond Executive Federalism. The Judicial Crafting of the Law of Composite Administrative Decision-Making", Thesis submitted for assessment with a view to obtaining the degree of Doctor of Laws of the European University Institute, Florence, 13 June 2018, p. 176 and following.
[121]   *Ibid.*
[122]   The draft binding decision of the EDPB should in principle synthesize the main elements of facts preceding the dispute, together with a summary of the main arguments put forth, unless the specific wording used is essential for a proper discussion/understanding of the issue at stake.
[123]   It should be noted that the EDPB does not take any position on the merit of any substantial issues raised by objections deemed not to meet the requirements stipulated by Article 4(24) GDPR. Where that is the case, the decision of the EDPB is without any prejudice to any assessments the EDPB may be called upon to make in other cases, including with the same parties, taking into account the contents of the relevant draft decision and the objections raised by the CSAs.

8 JUDICIAL REMEDIES

[2.432]
121.   Article 47 of the Charter guarantees the right to an effective remedy and to a fair trial. This is

linked to the need to ensure the compatibility of the acts of the EU institutions with the European Union legal order, which is a task generally entrusted to the Court of Justice and to the courts of the European Union.

122. Good administrative behaviour entails informing persons affected by the measure of the available appeal mechanism[124]. The EDPB decision will refer to the possibilities open to appeal it (i.e. to seek annulment), whereas the competent supervisory authority will refer to the appeal mechanisms available at national level. The competent supervisory authority may in its final decision also choose make reference to the possibilities to seek annulment of the decision of the EDPB on the basis of which the final decision was adopted, as clarified by Recital (143) GDPR (in addition to providing information regarding possible appeal mechanisms at national level in relation to its final decision).

123. While Recital (143) refers to the possibility of persons directly and individually concerned by a decision of the EDPB bringing an action for annulment before the CJEU, the position on standing will ultimately be assessed by the CJEU in light of the conditions provided for in Article 263 TFEU.

124. An action for annulment before the Court of Justice does not suspend the effects of the decision of the EDPB[125]. The competent SAs will therefore still have to comply with the decision of the EDPB adopted on the basis of Article 65(1)(a) GDPR, notwithstanding the appeal. This is without prejudice to the right to effective judicial remedy by the controller or processor at national level in accordance with Article 78 GDPR.

8.1 SUPERVISORY AUTHORITIES

125. Article 65(2) GDPR makes clear that decisions adopted by the EDPB on the basis of Article 65(1)(a) GDPR are binding upon the lead supervisory authority and all the concerned supervisory authorities. National SAs must adopt their final decision on the basis of the EDPB decision. Article 65(2) also makes clear the decision is an act "addressed to" the LSA and the CSAs - it does not directly address any third parties[126].

126. According to Recital (143) GDPR, as addressees of the decisions of the Board, the concerned supervisory authorities which wish to challenge them have to bring action within two months of being notified of them, in accordance with Article 263 TFEU. This means, inter alia, that the supervisory authorities acting before the Court of Justice against a binding decision of the EDPB would need to do so relying on one of the listed grounds for annulment contained in Article 263 TFEU.

127. Although only the LSA and some CSAs (pursuant to Article 60(8) and (9) GDPR) shall adopt their national decision on the basis of the EDPB binding decision, the decision is addressed to all the CSAs involved in the cross-border case. Article 65(2) GDPR mentions all the CSAs as addressees of the decision and the final national decision is the product of a co-decision making process which is strongly affected by the decision of the EDPB. As a consequence, all the supervisory authorities that are concerned in a given cross-border case (see Article 4(22) GDPR) are "addressed" by the decision and therefore entitled to bring action for annulment of the EDPB decision.

128. Although the supervisory authorities concerned, as Members of the EDPB, gain knowledge of the content of the EDPB binding decision in the occasion of its adoption pursuant to Article 65(2) GDPR, the time limitation for them to bring action will start when the decision is notified to them by the EDPB Secretariat, acting on behalf of the Chair[127] and using the internal information and communication system[128].

8.2 CONTROLLER, PROCESSOR, COMPLAINANT, OR OTHER ENTITY

129. Entities other than the addressees may be entitled to act before the Court of Justice for the annulment of the EDPB binding decision if the decision is of direct and individual concern to them[129].

130. Recital (143) explicitly mentions that controllers, processors, or complainants may be directly and individually concerned by an EDPB binding decision. These requirements are, however, interpreted restrictively by the Court of Justice and therefore a case-by-case analysis is necessary[130].

131. The action for annulment by a controller, processor or complainant, needs to be brought within two months of the publication of the EDPB binding decision on the website of the Board[131]. As indicated earlier, the publication of the EDPB's decision on its website occurs without delay after the final national decision is notified to the controller, processor and/or data subject[132].

132. Since the national decision needs to attach the EDPB decision, the person who receives notification of the national decision will at the same time receive the Article 65(1)(a) decision. However, this does not amount to "notification" of the EDPB decision in the sense of the Treaties as interpreted by the CJEU[133]. Additionally, according to Article 263 TFEU and the CJEU case law, the criterion of the day on which a measure comes to the knowledge of the applicant is a subsidiary one, i.e. it is only relevant where the act is neither published nor notified to the applicant[134]. Consequently, the two-month period starts when the decision is published on the website of the Board.

133. Without prejudice to this right under Article 263 TFEU, each natural or legal person also has an effective judicial remedy before the competent national court against those final decisions taken by supervisory authorities, which produces legal effects concerning that person[135]. This right has to be exercised in accordance with the applicable national legislation. Article 78(4) GDPR specifies that where proceedings are brought against a decision of a supervisory authority which was preceded by an opinion or decision of the Board in the consistency mechanism, the supervisory authority shall forward that opinion or decision to the court.

134. Where a decision of a supervisory authority implementing an Article 65 GDPR decision of the EDPB is challenged before a national court and the validity of the decision of the EDPB is at issue, the national court does not have the power to declare the EDPB's Article 65 GDPR decision invalid. Where it considers the decision invalid, it must refer the question of validity to the Court of Justice in accordance with Article 267 TFEU[136].

135. However, a national court may not refer a question on the validity of a decision of the EDPB when the requesting natural or legal person was under the legal conditions to bring an action for annulment of that decision before the CJEU (in particular if it was directly and individually concerned), but had not done so within the two-month period laid down in Article 263 TFEU. Therefore, when the directly and individually concerned persons decide to not bring an action for annulment of the EDPB binding decision, this will prevent them from challenging the validity of the EDPB binding decision in front of national courts.

NOTES

[124]   See also Commission 'Code of Good administrative behaviour', Point 3, third indent: 'Where Community law so provides, measures notified to an interested party should clearly state that an appeal is possible and describe how to submit it, (the name and office address of the person or department with whom the appeal must be lodged and the deadline for lodging it).Where appropriate, decisions should refer to the possibility of starting judicial proceedings and/or of lodging a complaint with the European Ombudsman in accordance with Article 230 or 195 of the Treaty establishing the European Community.' European Ombudsman 'Code of Good administrative behaviour', Article 19 - indication of the possibilities of appeal: 'A decision of the Institution which may adversely affect the rights or interests of a private person shall contain an indication of the appeal possibilities available for challenging the decision. It shall in particular indicate the nature of the remedies, the bodies before which they can be exercised, as well as the time limits for exercising them. Decisions shall in particular refer to the possibility of judicial proceedings and complaints to the European Ombudsman under the conditions specified in, respectively, Articles [263] and Articles [228 TFEU].'

[125]   Article 278 TFEU (ex Article 242 TEC): *"Actions brought before the Court of Justice of the European Union shall not have suspensory effect. The Court may, however, if it considers that circumstances so require, order that application of the contested act be suspended."*

[126]   See also paragraph 98 above.

[127]   See, e.g. Judgment of the General Court in *Access Info Europe v Council*, T-233/09, ECLI:EU:T:2011:105, paragraph 28 (*"Where the addressee has been notified, it is the date of notification which is to be taken into consideration for the purposes of calculating the time allowed [...] for bringing proceedings, not the date on which cognisance was taken, which comes into play only as an alternative in cases where there is no notification"*).

[128]   See Article 17 EDPB RoP.

[129]   Recital (143) GDPR.

[130]   See also the Opinion of Advocate General Bobek in *Facebook Ireland Limited*, C-645/19, ECLI:EU:C:2021:5, footnote 52.

[131]   Recital 143 GDPR.

[132]   Article 65 (5) GDPR.

[133]   According to the CJEU case law, *"notification is the operation by which the author of a decision of individual relevance communicates the latter to the addressees and thus puts them in a position to take cognisance of it"* (Judgment of the Court of First Instance in *Olsen v Commission*, T-17/02, ECLI:EU:T:2005:218, paragraph 74).

[134]   Judgment of the Court of First Instance in Olsen v Commission, T-17/02, ECLI:EU:T:2005:218, paragraphs 73 and 81 (specifying that *"the criterion of the day on which a measure came to the knowledge of an applicant, as the starting point of the period prescribed for instituting proceedings, is subsidiary to the criteria of publication or notification of the measure"*, and therefore where there is publication *"it is of little importance whether the applicant had sufficient knowledge of the contested decision [earlier]"* since that *"issue is not relevant for determining the starting point of the period for bringing an action because it is not appropriate to apply [...] the criterion of the day on which a measure came to the knowledge of an applicant, which is provided for in the alternative"* in Article 263 TFEU).

[135]   Recital (143) GDPR. This includes the exercise of investigative, corrective, and authorisation powers, or the dismissal or rejection of complaints, but not including non-legally binding measures.

[136]   Recital (143) GDPR.

PART 3
DATA PROTECTION – INTERNATIONAL TREATIES

CONVENTION FOR THE PROTECTION OF INDIVIDUALS WITH REGARD TO AUTOMATIC PROCESSING OF PERSONAL DATA

Strasbourg, 28.1.1981

[3.1]

NOTES

© Council of Europe (Text including amendments approved by the Committee of Ministers, in Strasbourg, on 15 June 1999)
For the text of this Convention as it will be amended by its Protocol CETS No 223, see **[3.31]**. Protocol CETS No 223 and the accompanying explanatory report are reproduced at **[3.29]**, **[3.30]** respectively.

PREAMBLE

The member States of the Council of Europe, signatory hereto,

Considering that the aim of the Council of Europe is to achieve greater unity between its members, based in particular on respect for the rule of law, as well as human rights and fundamental freedoms;

Considering that it is desirable to extend the safeguards for everyone's rights and fundamental freedoms, and in particular the right to the respect for privacy, taking account of the increasing flow across frontiers of personal data undergoing automatic processing;

Reaffirming at the same time their commitment to freedom of information regardless of frontiers;

Recognising that it is necessary to reconcile the fundamental values of the respect for privacy and the free flow of information between peoples,

Have agreed as follows:

CHAPTER I
GENERAL PROVISIONS

ARTICLE 1   OBJECT AND PURPOSE

[3.2]
The purpose of this Convention is to secure in the territory of each Party for every individual, whatever his nationality or residence, respect for his rights and fundamental freedoms, and in particular his right to privacy, with regard to automatic processing of personal data relating to him ("data protection").

ARTICLE 2   DEFINITIONS

[3.3]
For the purposes of this Convention:
(a)   "personal data" means any information relating to an identified or identifiable individual ("data subject");
(b)   "automated data file" means any set of data undergoing automatic processing;
(c)   "automatic processing" includes the following operations if carried out in whole or in part by automated means: storage of data, carrying out of logical and/or arithmetical operations on those data, their alteration, erasure, retrieval or dissemination;
(d)   "controller of the file" means the natural or legal person, public authority, agency or any other body who is competent according to the national law to decide what should be the purpose of the automated data file, which categories of personal data should be stored and which operations should be applied to them.

ARTICLE 3   SCOPE

[3.4]
(1) The Parties undertake to apply this Convention to automated personal data files and automatic processing of personal data in the public and private sectors.

(2) Any State or the European Communities may, at the time of signature or when depositing their instrument of ratification, acceptance, approval or accession, or at any later time, give notice by a declaration addressed to the Secretary General of the Council of Europe:
(a)   that they will not apply this Convention to certain categories of automated personal data files, a list of which will be deposited. In this list they shall not include, however, categories of automated data files subject under their domestic law to data protection provisions. Consequently, they shall amend this list by a new declaration whenever additional categories of automated personal data files are subjected to data protection provisions under their domestic law;
(b)   that they will also apply this Convention to information relating to groups of persons, associations, foundations, companies, corporations and any other bodies consisting directly or indirectly of individuals, whether or not such bodies possess legal personality;
(c)   that they will also apply this Convention to personal data files which are not processed automatically.

(3) Any State or the European Communities which have extended the scope of this Convention by any of the declarations provided for in sub-paragraph 2.b or c above may give notice in the said declaration that such extensions shall apply only to certain categories of personal data files, a list of which will be deposited.

(4) Any Party which has excluded certain categories of automated personal data files by a declaration provided for in sub-paragraph 2.a above may not claim the application of this Convention to such categories by a Party which has not excluded them.

(5) Likewise, a Party which has not made one or other of the extensions provided for in subparagraphs 2.b and c above may not claim the application of this Convention on these points with respect to a Party which has made such extensions.

(6) The declarations provided for in paragraph 2 above shall take effect from the moment of the entry into force of the Convention with regard to the State or the European Communities which have made them if they have been made at the time of signature or deposit of their instrument of ratification, acceptance, approval or accession, or three months after their receipt by the Secretary General of the Council of Europe if they have been made at any later time. These declarations may be withdrawn, in whole or in part, by a notification addressed to the Secretary General of the Council of Europe. Such withdrawals shall take effect three months after the date of receipt of such notification.

CHAPTER II
BASIC PRINCIPLES FOR DATA PROTECTION

ARTICLE 4   DUTIES OF THE PARTIES

[3.5]
(1) Each Party shall take the necessary measures in its domestic law to give effect to the basic principles for data protection set out in this chapter.

(2) These measures shall be taken at the latest at the time of entry into force of this Convention in respect of that Party.

ARTICLE 5   QUALITY OF DATA

[3.6]
Personal data undergoing automatic processing shall be:
(a)   obtained and processed fairly and lawfully;
(b)   stored for specified and legitimate purposes and not used in a way incompatible with those purposes;
(c)   adequate, relevant and not excessive in relation to the purposes for which they are stored;
(d)   accurate and, where necessary, kept up to date;
(e)   preserved in a form which permits identification of the data subjects for no longer than is required for the purpose for which those data are stored.

ARTICLE 6   SPECIAL CATEGORIES OF DATA

[3.7]
Personal data revealing racial origin, political opinions or religious or other beliefs, as well as personal data concerning health or sexual life, may not be processed automatically unless domestic law provides appropriate safeguards. The same shall apply to personal data relating to criminal convictions.

ARTICLE 7   DATA SECURITY

[3.8]
Appropriate security measures shall be taken for the protection of personal data stored in automated data files against accidental or unauthorised destruction or accidental loss as well as against unauthorised access, alteration or dissemination.

ARTICLE 8   ADDITIONAL SAFEGUARDS FOR THE DATA SUBJECT

[3.9]
Any person shall be enabled:
(a)   to establish the existence of an automated personal data file, its main purposes, as well as the identity and habitual residence or principal place of business of the controller of the file;
(b)   to obtain at reasonable intervals and without excessive delay or expense confirmation of whether personal data relating to him are stored in the automated data file as well as communication to him of such data in an intelligible form;
(c)   to obtain, as the case may be, rectification or erasure of such data if these have been processed contrary to the provisions of domestic law giving effect to the basic principles set out in Articles 5 and 6 of this Convention;
(d)   to have a remedy if a request for confirmation or, as the case may be, communication, rectification or erasure as referred to in paragraphs b and c of this article is not complied with.

ARTICLE 9   EXCEPTIONS AND RESTRICTIONS

[3.10]
(1) No exception to the provisions of Articles 5, 6 and 8 of this Convention shall be allowed except within the limits defined in this article.

(2) Derogation from the provisions of Articles 5, 6 and 8 of this Convention shall be allowed when such derogation is provided for by the law of the Party and constitutes a necessary measure in a democratic society in the interests of:

(a)   protecting State security, public safety, the monetary interests of the State or the suppression of criminal offences;

(b)   protecting the data subject or the rights and freedoms of others.

(3) Restrictions on the exercise of the rights specified in Article 8, paragraphs b, c and d, may be provided by law with respect to automated personal data files used for statistics or for scientific research purposes when there is obviously no risk of an infringement of the privacy of the data subjects.

ARTICLE 10   SANCTIONS AND REMEDIES

[3.11]
Each Party undertakes to establish appropriate sanctions and remedies for violations of provisions of domestic law giving effect to the basic principles for data protection set out in this chapter.

ARTICLE 11   EXTENDED PROTECTION

[3.12]
None of the provisions of this chapter shall be interpreted as limiting or otherwise affecting the possibility for a Party to grant data subjects a wider measure of protection than that stipulated in this Convention.

CHAPTER III
TRANSBORDER DATA FLOWS

ARTICLE 12   TRANSBORDER FLOWS OF PERSONAL DATA AND DOMESTIC LAW

[3.13]
(1) The following provisions shall apply to the transfer across national borders, by whatever medium, of personal data undergoing automatic processing or collected with a view to their being automatically processed.

(2) A Party shall not, for the sole purpose of the protection of privacy, prohibit or subject to special authorisation transborder flows of personal data going to the territory of another Party.

(3) Nevertheless, each Party shall be entitled to derogate from the provisions of paragraph 2:

(a)   insofar as its legislation includes specific regulations for certain categories of personal data or of automated personal data files, because of the nature of those data or those files, except where the regulations of the other Party provide an equivalent protection;

(b)   when the transfer is made from its territory to the territory of a non-Contracting State through the intermediary of the territory of another Party, in order to avoid such transfers resulting in circumvention of the legislation of the Party referred to at the beginning of this paragraph.

CHAPTER IV
MUTUAL ASSISTANCE

ARTICLE 13   CO-OPERATION BETWEEN PARTIES

[3.14]
(1) The Parties agree to render each other mutual assistance in order to implement this Convention.

(2) For that purpose:

(a)   each Party shall designate one or more authorities, the name and address of each of which it shall communicate to the Secretary General of the Council of Europe;

(b)   each Party which has designated more than one authority shall specify in its communication referred to in the previous sub-paragraph the competence of each authority.

(3) An authority designated by a Party shall at the request of an authority designated by another Party:

(a)   furnish information on its law and administrative practice in the field of data protection;

(b)   take, in conformity with its domestic law and for the sole purpose of protection of privacy, all appropriate measures for furnishing factual information relating to specific automatic processing carried out in its territory, with the exception however of the personal data being processed.

ARTICLE 14   ASSISTANCE TO DATA SUBJECTS RESIDENT ABROAD

[3.15]
(1) Each Party shall assist any person resident abroad to exercise the rights conferred by its domestic law giving effect to the principles set out in Article 8 of this Convention.

(2) When such a person resides in the territory of another Party he shall be given the option of submitting his request through the intermediary of the authority designated by that Party.

(3) The request for assistance shall contain all the necessary particulars, relating inter alia to:

(a)   the name, address and any other relevant particulars identifying the person making the request;

(b)   the automated personal data file to which the request pertains, or its controller;

(c)   the purpose of the request.

ARTICLE 15   SAFEGUARDS CONCERNING ASSISTANCE RENDERED BY DESIGNATED AUTHORITIES

[3.16]
(1) An authority designated by a Party which has received information from an authority designated by

another Party either accompanying a request for assistance or in reply to its own request for assistance shall not use that information for purposes other than those specified in the request for assistance.

(2) Each Party shall see to it that the persons belonging to or acting on behalf of the designated authority shall be bound by appropriate obligations of secrecy or confidentiality with regard to that information.

(3) In no case may a designated authority be allowed to make under Article 14, paragraph 2, a request for assistance on behalf of a data subject resident abroad, of its own accord and without the express consent of the person concerned.

ARTICLE 16   REFUSAL OF REQUESTS FOR ASSISTANCE

[3.17]
A designated authority to which a request for assistance is addressed under Articles 13 or 14 of this Convention may not refuse to comply with it unless:
(a)   the request is not compatible with the powers in the field of data protection of the authorities responsible for replying;
(b)   the request does not comply with the provisions of this Convention;
(c)   compliance with the request would be incompatible with the sovereignty, security or public policy (*ordre public*) of the Party by which it was designated, or with the rights and fundamental freedoms of persons under the jurisdiction of that Party.

ARTICLE 17   COSTS AND PROCEDURES OF ASSISTANCE

[3.18]
(1) Mutual assistance which the Parties render each other under Article 13 and assistance they render to data subjects abroad under Article 14 shall not give rise to the payment of any costs or fees other than those incurred for experts and interpreters. The latter costs or fees shall be borne by the Party which has designated the authority making the request for assistance.

(2) The data subject may not be charged costs or fees in connection with the steps taken on his behalf in the territory of another Party other than those lawfully payable by residents of that Party.

(3) Other details concerning the assistance relating in particular to the forms and procedures and the languages to be used, shall be established directly between the Parties concerned.

CHAPTER V
CONSULTATIVE COMMITTEE

ARTICLE 18   COMPOSITION OF THE COMMITTEE

[3.19]
(1) A Consultative Committee shall be set up after the entry into force of this Convention.

(2) Each Party shall appoint a representative to the committee and a deputy representative. Any member State of the Council of Europe which is not a Party to the Convention shall have the right to be represented on the committee by an observer.

(3) The Consultative Committee may, by unanimous decision, invite any non-member State of the Council of Europe which is not a Party to the Convention to be represented by an observer at a given meeting.

ARTICLE 19   FUNCTIONS OF THE COMMITTEE

[3.20]
The Consultative Committee:
(a)   may make proposals with a view to facilitating or improving the application of the Convention;
(b)   may make proposals for amendment of this Convention in accordance with Article 21;
(c)   shall formulate its opinion on any proposal for amendment of this Convention which is referred to it in accordance with Article 21, paragraph 3;
(d)   may, at the request of a Party, express an opinion on any question concerning the application of this Convention.

ARTICLE 20   PROCEDURE

[3.21]
(1) The Consultative Committee shall be convened by the Secretary General of the Council of Europe. Its first meeting shall be held within twelve months of the entry into force of this Convention. It shall subsequently meet at least once every two years and in any case when one-third of the representatives of the Parties request its convocation.

(2) A majority of representatives of the Parties shall constitute a quorum for a meeting of the Consultative Committee.

(3) Every Party has a right to vote. Each State which is a Party to the Convention shall have one vote. Concerning questions within their competence, the European Communities exercise their right to vote and cast a number of votes equal to the number of Member States that are Parties to the Convention and have transferred their competencies to the European Communities in the field concerned. In this case,

those member States of the Communities do not vote, and the other member States may vote. The European Communities do not vote when a question which does not fall within their competence is concerned.

(4) After each of its meetings, the Consultative Committee shall submit to the Committee of Ministers of the Council of Europe a report on its work and on the functioning of the Convention.

(5) Subject to the provisions of this convention, the Consultative Committee shall draw up its own Rules of Procedure.

CHAPTER VI
AMENDMENTS

ARTICLE 21   AMENDMENTS

[3.22]
(1) Amendments to this Convention may be proposed by a Party, the Committee of Ministers of the Council of Europe or the Consultative Committee.

(2) Any proposal for amendment shall be communicated by the Secretary General of the Council of Europe to the member States of the Council of Europe, to the European Communities, and to every non-member State which has acceded to or has been invited to accede to this Convention in accordance with the provisions of Article 23.

(3) Moreover, any amendment proposed by a Party or the Committee of Ministers shall be communicated to the Consultative Committee, which shall submit to the Committee of Ministers its opinion on that proposed amendment.

(4) The Committee of Ministers shall consider the proposed amendment and any opinion submitted by the Consultative Committee and may approve the amendment.

(5) The text of any amendment approved by the Committee of Ministers in accordance with paragraph 4 of this article shall be forwarded to the Parties for acceptance.

(6) Any amendment approved in accordance with paragraph 4 of this article shall come into force on the thirtieth day after all Parties have informed the Secretary General of their acceptance thereof.

CHAPTER VII
FINAL CLAUSES

ARTICLE 22   ENTRY INTO FORCE

[3.23]
(1) This Convention shall be open for signature by the member States of the Council of Europe. It is subject to ratification, acceptance or approval. Instruments of ratification, acceptance or approval shall be deposited with the Secretary General of the Council of Europe.

(2) This Convention shall enter into force on the first day of the month following the expiration of a period of three months after the date on which five member States of the Council of Europe have expressed their consent to be bound by the Convention in accordance with the provisions of the preceding paragraph.

(3) In respect of any member State which subsequently expresses its consent to be bound by it, the Convention shall enter into force on the first day of the month following the expiration of a period of three months after the date of deposit of the instrument of ratification, acceptance or approval.

ARTICLE 23   ACCESSION BY NON-MEMBER STATES OR THE EUROPEAN COMMUNITIES

[3.24]
(1) After the entry into force of this Convention, the Committee of Ministers of the Council of Europe may invite any non member State of the Council of Europe to accede to this Convention by a decision taken by the majority provided for in Article 20.d of the Statute of the Council of Europe and by the unanimous vote of the representatives of the Contracting States entitled to sit on the committee.

(2) The European Communities may accede to the Convention.

(3) In respect of any acceding State, or of the European Communities on accession, the Convention shall enter into force on the first day of the month following the expiration of a period of three months after the date of deposit of the instrument of accession with the Secretary General of the Council of Europe.

ARTICLE 24   TERRITORIAL CLAUSE

[3.25]
(1) Any State or the European Communities may at the time of signature of when depositing their instrument of ratification, acceptance, approval or accession, specify the territory or territories to which this Convention shall apply.

(2) Any State or the European Communities may at any later date, by a declaration addressed to the Secretary General of the Council of Europe, extend the application of this Convention to any other

territory specified in the declaration. In respect of such territory the Convention shall enter into force on the first day of the month following the expiration of a period of three months after the date of receipt of such declaration by the Secretary General.

ARTICLE 25   RESERVATIONS

[3.26]
No reservation may be made in respect of the provisions of this Convention.

ARTICLE 26   DENUNCIATION

[3.27]
(1) Any Party may at any time denounce this Convention by means of a notification addressed to the Secretary General of the Council of Europe.

(2) Such denunciation shall become effective on the first day of the month following the expiration of a period of six months after the date of receipt of the notification by the Secretary General.

ARTICLE 27   NOTIFICATIONS

[3.28]
The Secretary General of the Council of Europe shall notify the member States of the Council of Europe, the European Communities, and any State which has acceded to this Convention of:
(a)   any signature;
(b)   the deposit of any instrument of ratification, acceptance, approval or accession;
(c)   any date of entry into force of this Convention in accordance with Articles 22, 23 and 24;
(d)   any other act, notification or communication relating to this Convention.

In witness whereof the undersigned, being duly authorised thereto, have signed this Convention.

Done at Strasbourg, the 28th day of January 1981, in English and in French, both texts being equally authoritative, in a single copy which shall remain deposited in the archives of the Council of Europe. The Secretary General of the Council of Europe shall transmit certified copies to each member State of the Council of Europe and to any State invited to accede to this Convention.

PROTOCOL AMENDING THE CONVENTION FOR THE PROTECTION OF INDIVIDUALS WITH REGARD TO AUTOMATIC PROCESSING OF PERSONAL DATA
[Strasbourg, 25.VI.2018]

[3.29]

NOTES
 © Council of Europe.

PREAMBLE

The member States of the Council of Europe and the other Parties to the Convention for the Protection of Individuals with regard to Automatic Processing of Personal Data (ETS No. 108), opened for signature in Strasbourg on 28 January 1981 (hereinafter referred to as "the Convention"),

Having regard to Resolution No. 3 on data protection and privacy in the third millennium adopted at the 30th Council of Europe Conference of Ministers of Justice (Istanbul, Turkey, 24-26 November 2010);

Having regard to the Parliamentary Assembly of the Council of Europe's Resolution 1843 (2011) on the protection of privacy and personal data on the Internet and online media and Resolution 1986 (2014) on improving user protection and security in cyberspace;

Having regard to Opinion 296 (2017) on the draft protocol amending the Convention for the Protection of Individuals with regard to Automatic Processing of Personal Data (ETS No. 108) and its explanatory memorandum, adopted by the Standing Committee on behalf of the Parliamentary Assembly of the Council of Europe on 24 November 2017;

Considering that new challenges to the protection of individuals with regard to the processing of personal data have emerged since the Convention was adopted;

Considering the need to ensure that the Convention continues to play its pre-eminent role in protecting individuals with regard to the processing of personal data, and more generally in protecting human rights and fundamental freedoms,

Have agreed as follows:

ARTICLE 1

1   The first recital of the preamble of the Convention shall be replaced by the following:

"The member States of the Council of Europe, and the other signatories hereto,"

2   The third recital of the preamble of the Convention shall be replaced by the following:

"Considering that it is necessary to secure the human dignity and protection of the human rights and fundamental freedoms of every individual and, given the diversification, intensification and globalisation of data processing and personal data flows, personal autonomy based on a person's right to control his or her personal data and the processing of such data;"

3 The fourth recital of the preamble of the Convention shall be replaced by the following:

"Recalling that the right to protection of personal data is to be considered in respect of its role in society and that it has to be reconciled with other human rights and fundamental freedoms, including freedom of expression;"

4 The following recital shall be added after the fourth recital of the preamble of the Convention:

"Considering that this Convention permits account to be taken, in the implementation of the rules laid down therein, of the principle of the right of access to official documents;"

5 The fifth recital of the preamble of the Convention shall be deleted. New fifth and sixth recitals shall be added, which read as follows:

"Recognising that it is necessary to promote at the global level the fundamental values of respect for privacy and protection of personal data, thereby contributing to the free flow of information between people;"

"Recognising the interest of a reinforcement of international co-operation between the Parties to the Convention,"

ARTICLE 2

The text of Article 1 of the Convention shall be replaced by the following:

"The purpose of this Convention is to protect every individual, whatever his or her nationality or residence, with regard to the processing of their personal data, thereby contributing to respect for his or her human rights and fundamental freedoms, and in particular the right to privacy."

ARTICLE 3

1 *Littera* b of Article 2 of the Convention shall be replaced by the following:

"b   'data processing' means any operation or set of operations performed on personal data, such as the collection, storage, preservation, alteration, retrieval, disclosure, making available, erasure, or destruction of, or the carrying out of logical and/or arithmetical operations on such data;"

2 *Littera* c of Article 2 of the Convention shall be replaced by the following:

"c   where automated processing is not used, 'data processing' means an operation or set of operations performed upon personal data within a structured set of such data which are accessible or retrievable according to specific criteria;"

3 *Littera* d of Article 2 of the Convention shall be replaced by the following:

"d   'controller' means the natural or legal person, public authority, service, agency or any other body which, alone or jointly with others, has decision-making power with respect to data processing;"

4 The following new *litterae* shall be added after *littera* d of Article 2 of the Convention:

"e   'recipient' means a natural or legal person, public authority, service, agency or any other body to whom data are disclosed or made available;

f   'processor' means a natural or legal person, public authority, service, agency or any other body which processes personal data on behalf of the controller."

ARTICLE 4

1 Paragraph 1 of Article 3 of the Convention shall be replaced by the following:

"1   Each Party undertakes to apply this Convention to data processing subject to its jurisdiction in the public and private sectors, thereby securing every individual's right to protection of his or her personal data."

2 Paragraph 2 of Article 3 of the Convention shall be replaced by the following:

"2   This Convention shall not apply to data processing carried out by an individual in the course of purely personal or household activities."

3 Paragraphs 3 to 6 of Article 3 of the Convention shall be deleted.

ARTICLE 5

The title of Chapter II of the Convention shall be replaced by the following:

"Chapter II – Basic principles for the protection of personal data".

ARTICLE 6

1 Paragraph 1 of Article 4 of the Convention shall be replaced by the following:

"1   Each Party shall take the necessary measures in its law to give effect to the provisions of this Convention and secure their effective application."

2 Paragraph 2 of Article 4 of the Convention shall be replaced by the following:

"2   These measures shall be taken by each Party and shall have come into force by the time of ratification or of accession to this Convention."

3 A new paragraph shall be added after paragraph 2 of Article 4 of the Convention:

"3   Each Party undertakes:

a   to allow the Convention Committee provided for in Chapter VI to evaluate the effectiveness of the measures it has taken in its law to give effect to the provisions of this Convention; and

b   to contribute actively to this evaluation process."

ARTICLE 7

1 The title of Article 5 shall be replaced by the following:

"**Article 5 – Legitimacy of data processing and quality of data**".

2 The text of Article 5 of the Convention shall be replaced by the following:

"1   Data processing shall be proportionate in relation to the legitimate purpose pursued and reflect at all stages of the processing a fair balance between all interests concerned, whether public or private, and the rights and freedoms at stake.

2   Each Party shall provide that data processing can be carried out on the basis of the free, specific, informed and unambiguous consent of the data subject or of some other legitimate basis laid down by law.

3   Personal data undergoing processing shall be processed lawfully.

4   Personal data undergoing processing shall be:

a   processed fairly and in a transparent manner;

b   collected for explicit, specified and legitimate purposes and not processed in a way incompatible with those purposes; further processing for archiving purposes in the public interest, scientific or historical research purposes or statistical purposes is, subject to appropriate safeguards, compatible with those purposes;

c   adequate, relevant and not excessive in relation to the purposes for which they are processed;

d   accurate and, where necessary, kept up to date;

e   preserved in a form which permits identification of the data subjects for no longer than is necessary for the purposes for which those data are processed."

ARTICLE 8

The text of Article 6 of the Convention shall be replaced by the following:

"1   The processing of:

–   genetic data;

–   personal data relating to offences, criminal proceedings and convictions, and related security measures;

–   biometric data uniquely identifying a person;

–   personal data for the information they reveal relating to racial or ethnic origin, political opinions, trade-union membership, religious or other beliefs, health or sexual life,

shall only be allowed where appropriate safeguards are enshrined in law, complementing those of this Convention.

2   Such safeguards shall guard against the risks that the processing of sensitive data may present for the interests, rights and fundamental freedoms of the data subject, notably a risk of discrimination."

ARTICLE 9

The text of Article 7 of the Convention shall be replaced by the following:

"1   Each Party shall provide that the controller, and where applicable the processor, takes appropriate security measures against risks such as accidental or unauthorised access to, destruction, loss, use, modification or disclosure of personal data.

2   Each Party shall provide that the controller notifies, without delay, at least the competent supervisory authority within the meaning of Article 15 of this Convention, of those data breaches which may seriously interfere with the rights and fundamental freedoms of data subjects."

ARTICLE 10

A new Article 8 shall be added after Article 7 of the Convention as follows:

"**Article 8 – Transparency of processing**

1   Each Party shall provide that the controller informs the data subjects of:

    a   his or her identity and habitual residence or establishment;
    b   the legal basis and the purposes of the intended processing;
    c   the categories of personal data processed;
    d   the recipients or categories of recipients of the personal data, if any; and
    e   the means of exercising the rights set out in Article 9,
as well as any necessary additional information in order to ensure fair and transparent processing of the personal data.

2   Paragraph 1 shall not apply where the data subject already has the relevant information.

3   Where the personal data are not collected from the data subjects, the controller shall not be required to provide such information where the processing is expressly prescribed by law or this proves to be impossible or involves disproportionate efforts."

ARTICLE 11

1   The former Article 8 of the Convention shall be renumbered Article 9 and the title shall be replaced by the following:

"Article 9 – Rights of the data subject".

2   The text of Article 8 of the Convention (new Article 9) shall be replaced by the following:

   "1   Every individual shall have a right:
    a   not to be subject to a decision significantly affecting him or her based solely on an automated processing of data without having his or her views taken into consideration;
    b   to obtain, on request, at reasonable intervals and without excessive delay or expense, confirmation of the processing of personal data relating to him or her, the communication in an intelligible form of the data processed, all available information on their origin, on the preservation period as well as any other information that the controller is required to provide in order to ensure the transparency of processing in accordance with Article 8, paragraph 1;
    c   to obtain, on request, knowledge of the reasoning underlying data processing where the results of such processing are applied to him or her;
    d   to object at any time, on grounds relating to his or her situation, to the processing of personal data concerning him or her unless the controller demonstrates legitimate grounds for the processing which override his or her interests or rights and fundamental freedoms;
    e   to obtain, on request, free of charge and without excessive delay, rectification or erasure, as the case may be, of such data if these are being, or have been, processed contrary to the provisions of this Convention;
    f   to have a remedy under Article 12 where his or her rights under this Convention have been violated;
    g   to benefit, whatever his or her nationality or residence, from the assistance of a supervisory authority within the meaning of Article 15, in exercising his or her rights under this Convention.
   2   Paragraph 1.a shall not apply if the decision is authorised by a law to which the controller is subject and which also lays down suitable measures to safeguard the data subject's rights, freedoms and legitimate interests."

ARTICLE 12

A new Article 10 shall be added after the new Article 9 of the Convention as follows:

"Article 10 – Additional obligations

   1   Each Party shall provide that controllers and, where applicable, processors, take all appropriate measures to comply with the obligations of this Convention and be able to demonstrate, subject to the domestic legislation adopted in accordance with Article , paragraph 3, in particular to the competent supervisory authority provided for in Article 5, that the data processing under their control is in compliance with the provisions of this Convention.

   2   Each Party shall provide that controllers and, where applicable, processors, examine the likely impact of intended data processing on the rights and fundamental freedoms of data subjects prior to the commencement of such processing, and shall design the data processing in such a manner as to prevent or minimise the risk of interference with those rights and fundamental freedoms.

   3   Each Party shall provide that controllers, and, where applicable, processors, implement technical and organisational measures which take into account the implications of the right to the protection of personal data at all stages of the data processing.

   4   Each Party may, having regard to the risks arising for the interests, rights and fundamental freedoms of the data subjects, adapt the application of the provisions of paragraphs 1, 2 and 3 in the law giving effect to the provisions of this Convention, according to the nature and volume of the data, the nature, scope and purpose of the processing and, where appropriate, the size of the controller or processor."

ARTICLE 13

The former Articles 9 to 12 of the Convention shall become Articles 11 to 14 of the Convention.

ARTICLE 14

The text of Article 9 of the Convention (new Article 11) shall be replaced by the following:

"1   No exception to the provisions set out in this chapter shall be allowed except to the provisions of Article 5, paragraph 4, Article 7, paragraph 2, Article 8, paragraph 1, and Article 9, when such an exception is provided for by law, respects the essence of the fundamental rights and freedoms and constitutes a necessary and proportionate measure in a democratic society for:

    a   the protection of national security, defence, public safety, important economic and financial interests of the State, the impartiality and independence of the judiciary or the prevention, investigation and prosecution of criminal offences and the execution of criminal penalties, and other essential objectives of general public interest;

    b   the protection of the data subject or the rights and fundamental freedoms of others, notably freedom of expression.

2   Restrictions on the exercise of the provisions specified in Articles 8 and 9 may be provided for by law with respect to data processing for archiving purposes in the public interest, scientific or historical research purposes or statistical purposes when there is no recognisable risk of infringement of the rights and fundamental freedoms of data subjects.

3   In addition to the exceptions allowed for in paragraph 1 of this article, with reference to processing activities for national security and defence purposes, each Party may provide, by law and only to the extent that it constitutes a necessary and proportionate measure in a democratic society to fulfil such an aim, exceptions to Article 4, paragraph , Article 14, paragraphs 5 and 6, and Article 15, paragraph 2, *litterae* a, b, c and d.

This is without prejudice to the requirement that processing activities for national security and defence purposes are subject to independent and effective review and supervision under the domestic legislation of the respective Party."

ARTICLE 15

The text of Article 10 of the Convention (new Article 12) shall be replaced by the following:

"Each Party undertakes to establish appropriate judicial and non-judicial sanctions and remedies for violations of the provisions of this Convention."

ARTICLE 16

The title of Chapter III shall be replaced by the following:

"Chapter III – Transborder flows of personal data".

ARTICLE 17

1   The title of Article 2 of the Convention (new Article 4) shall be replaced by the following:

"Article 14 – Transborder flows of personal data".

2   The text of Article 1 of the Convention (new Article 14) shall be replaced by the following:

"1   A Party shall not, for the sole purpose of the protection of personal data, prohibit or subject to special authorisation the transfer of such data to a recipient who is subject to the jurisdiction of another Party to the Convention. Such a Party may, however, do so if there is a real and serious risk that the transfer to another Party, or from that other Party to a non-Party, would lead to circumventing the provisions of the Convention. A Party may also do so if bound by harmonised rules of protection shared by States belonging to a regional international organisation.

2   When the recipient is subject to the jurisdiction of a State or international organisation which is not Party to this Convention, the transfer of personal data may only take place where an appropriate level of protection based on the provisions of this Convention is secured.

3   An appropriate level of protection can be secured by:

    a   the law of that State or international organisation, including the applicable international treaties or agreements; or

    b   *ad hoc* or approved standardised safeguards provided by legally-binding and enforceable instruments adopted and implemented by the persons involved in the transfer and further processing.

4   Notwithstanding the provisions of the previous paragraphs, each Party may provide that the transfer of personal data may take place if:

    a   the data subject has given explicit, specific and free consent, after being informed of risks arising in the absence of appropriate safeguards; or

    b   the specific interests of the data subject require it in the particular case; or

    c   prevailing legitimate interests, in particular important public interests, are provided for by law and such transfer constitutes a necessary and proportionate measure in a democratic society; or d   it constitutes a necessary and proportionate measure in a democratic society for freedom of expression.

5   Each Party shall provide that the competent supervisory authority, within the meaning of Article 1 of this Convention, is provided with all relevant information concerning the transfers of data referred to in paragraph 3, *littera* b and, upon request, paragraph 4, *litterae* b and c.

6   Each Party shall also provide that the supervisory authority is entitled to request that the person who transfers data demonstrates the effectiveness of the safeguards or the existence of prevailing legitimate interests and that the supervisory authority may, in order to protect the rights and fundamental freedoms of data subjects, prohibit such transfers, suspend them or subject them to conditions."

3   The text of Article 12 of the Convention (new Article 14) includes the provisions of Article 2 of the Additional Protocol of 2001 regarding supervisory authorities and transborder data flows (ETS No. 181) on transborder flows of personal data to a recipient which is not subject to the jurisdiction of a Party to the Convention.

ARTICLE 18

A new Chapter IV shall be added after Chapter III of the Convention, as follows:

"**Chapter IV – Supervisory authorities**".

ARTICLE 19

A new Article 15 includes the provisions of Article 1 of the Additional Protocol of 2001 (ETS No.181) and reads as follows:

"**Article 15 – Supervisory authorities**

1   Each Party shall provide for one or more authorities to be responsible for ensuring compliance with the provisions of this Convention.

2   To this end, such authorities:

    a   shall have powers of investigation and intervention;

    b   shall perform the functions relating to transfers of data provided for under Article 14, notably the approval of standardised safeguards;

    c   shall have powers to issue decisions with respect to violations of the provisions of this Convention and may, in particular, impose administrative sanctions;

    d   shall have the power to engage in legal proceedings or to bring to the attention of the competent judicial authorities violations of the provisions of this Convention;

    e   shall promote:

        i   public awareness of their functions and powers, as well as their activities;

        ii   public awareness of the rights of data subjects and the exercise of such rights;

        iii   awareness of controllers and processors of their responsibilities under this Convention;

        specific attention shall be given to the data protection rights of children and other vulnerable individuals.

3   The competent supervisory authorities shall be consulted on proposals for any legislative or administrative measures which provide for the processing of personal data.

4   Each competent supervisory authority shall deal with requests and complaints lodged by data subjects concerning their data protection rights and shall keep data subjects informed of progress.

5   The supervisory authorities shall act with complete independence and impartiality in performing their duties and exercising their powers and in doing so shall neither seek nor accept instructions.

6   Each Party shall ensure that the supervisory authorities are provided with the resources necessary for the effective performance of their functions and exercise of their powers.

7   Each supervisory authority shall prepare and publish a periodical report outlining its activities.

8   Members and staff of the supervisory authorities shall be bound by obligations of confidentiality with regard to confidential information to which they have access, or have had access to, in the performance of their duties and exercise of their powers.

9   Decisions of the supervisory authorities may be subject to appeal through the courts.

10   The supervisory authorities shall not be competent with respect to processing carried out by bodies when acting in their judicial capacity."

ARTICLE 20

1   Chapters IV to VII of the Convention shall be renumbered to Chapters V to VIII of the Convention.

2   The title of Chapter V shall be replaced by "**Chapter V – Co-operation and mutual assistance**".

3   A new Article 17 shall be added, and former Articles 1 to 27 of the Convention shall become Articles 16 to 1 of the Convention.

Part 3   International Treaties

ARTICLE 21

1 The title of Article 3 of the Convention (new Article 6) shall be replaced by the following:

"**Article 16 – Designation of supervisory authorities**".

2 Paragraph 1 of Article 13 of the Convention (new Article 16) shall be replaced by the following:

"1 The Parties agree to co-operate and render each other mutual assistance in order to implement this Convention."

3 Paragraph 2 of Article 1 of the Convention (new Article 16) shall be replaced by the following:

"2 For that purpose:
a each Party shall designate one or more supervisory authorities within the meaning of Article 15 of this Convention, the name and address of each of which it shall communicate to the Secretary General of the Council of Europe;
b each Party which has designated more than one supervisory authority shall specify the competence of each authority in its communication referred to in the previous *littera*."

4 Paragraph 3 of Article 13 of the Convention (new Article 16) shall be deleted.

ARTICLE 22

A new Article 17 shall be added after the new Article 16 of the Convention as follows:

"**Article 17 – Forms of co-operation**
1 The supervisory authorities shall co-operate with one another to the extent necessary for the performance of their duties and exercise of their powers, in particular by:
a providing mutual assistance by exchanging relevant and useful information and co-operating with each other under the condition that, as regards the protection of personal data, all the rules and safeguards of this Convention are complied with;
b co-ordinating their investigations or interventions, or conducting joint actions;
c providing information and documentation on their law and administrative practice relating to data protection.
2 The information referred to in paragraph 1 shall not include personal data undergoing processing unless such data are essential for co-operation, or where the data subject concerned has given explicit, specific, free and informed consent to its provision.
3 In order to organise their co-operation and to perform the duties set out in the preceding paragraphs, the supervisory authorities of the Parties shall form a network."

ARTICLE 23

1 The title of Article 4 of the Convention (new Article 8) shall be replaced by the following:

"**Article 18 – Assistance to data subjects**".

2 The text of Article 14 of the Convention (new Article 18) shall be replaced by the following:

"1 Each Party shall assist any data subject, whatever his or her nationality or residence, to exercise his or her rights under Article 9 of this Convention.
2 Where a data subject resides on the territory of another Party, he or she shall be given the option of submitting the request through the intermediary of the supervisory authority designated by that Party.
3 The request for assistance shall contain all the necessary particulars, relating *inter alia* to:
a the name, address and any other relevant particulars identifying the data subject making the request;
b the processing to which the request pertains, or its controller;
c the purpose of the request."

ARTICLE 24

1 The title of Article 5 of the Convention (new Article 9) shall be replaced by the following:

"**Article 19 – Safeguards**".

2 The text of Article 15 of the Convention (new Article 19) shall be replaced by the following:

"1 A supervisory authority which has received information from another supervisory authority, either accompanying a request or in reply to its own request, shall not use that information for purposes other than those specified in the request.
2 In no case may a supervisory authority be allowed to make a request on behalf of a data subject of its own accord and without the express approval of the data subject concerned."

ARTICLE 25

1 The title of Article 6 of the Convention (new Article 20) shall be replaced by the following:

"**Article 20 – Refusal of requests**".

2 The recital of Article 16 of the Convention (new Article 0) shall be replaced by the following:

"A supervisory authority to which a request is addressed under Article 17 of this Convention may not refuse to comply with it unless:"

3 *Littera* a of Article 16 of the Convention (new Article 20) shall be replaced by the following:

"a	the request is not compatible with its powers."

4 *Littera* c of Article 16 of the Convention (new Article 20) shall be replaced by the following:

"c	compliance with the request would be incompatible with the sovereignty, national security or public order of the Party by which it was designated, or with the rights and fundamental freedoms of individuals under the jurisdiction of that Party."

ARTICLE 26

1 The title of Article 7 of the Convention (new Article 2) shall be replaced by the following:

"Article 21 – Costs and procedures".

2 Paragraph 1 of Article 17 of the Convention (new Article 1) shall be replaced by the following:

"1	Co-operation and mutual assistance which the Parties render each other under Article 17 and assistance they render to data subjects under Articles 9 and 18 shall not give rise to the payment of any costs or fees other than those incurred for experts and interpreters. The latter costs or fees shall be borne by the Party making the request."

3 The terms "his or her" shall replace "his" in paragraph 2 of Article 17 of the Convention (new Article 21).

ARTICLE 27

The title of Chapter V of the Convention (new Chapter VI) shall be replaced by the following:

"Chapter VI – Convention Committee".

ARTICLE 28

1 The terms "Consultative Committee" in paragraph 1 of Article 8 of the Convention (new Article 22) shall be replaced by "Convention Committee".

2 Paragraph 3 of Article 18 of the Convention (new Article) shall be replaced by the following:

"3	The Convention Committee may, by a decision taken by a majority of two-thirds of the representatives of the Parties, invite an observer to be represented at its meetings."

3 A new paragraph 4 shall be added after paragraph 3 of Article 18 of the Convention (new Article 22):

"4	Any Party which is not a member of the Council of Europe shall contribute to the funding of the activities of the Convention Committee according to the modalities established by the Committee of Ministers in agreement with that Party."

ARTICLE 29

1 The terms "Consultative Committee" in the recital of Article 9 of the Convention (new Article 23) shall be replaced by "Convention Committee".

2 The term "proposals" in *littera* a of Article 19 of the Convention (new Article 3) shall be replaced with the term "recommendations".

3 References to "Article 21" in *littera* b and "Article 21 paragraph " in *littera* c of Article 19 of the Convention (new Article 2) shall be replaced respectively by references to "Article 25" and "Article 25, paragraph ".

4 *Littera* d of Article 19 of the Convention (new Article 23) shall be replaced by the following:

"d	may express an opinion on any question concerning the interpretation or application of this Convention;".

5 The following additional *litterae* shall be added following *littera* d of Article 19 of the Convention (new Article 23):

"e	shall prepare, before any new accession to the Convention, an opinion for the Committee of Ministers relating to the level of personal data protection of the candidate for accession and, where necessary, recommend measures to take to reach compliance with the provisions of this Convention;

f	may, at the request of a State or an international organisation, evaluate whether the level of personal data protection the former provides is in compliance with the provisions of this Convention and, where necessary, recommend measures to be taken in order to reach such compliance;

g	may develop or approve models of standardised safeguards referred to in Article 14;

h	shall review the implementation of this Convention by the Parties and recommend measures to be taken in the case where a Party is not in compliance with this Convention;

i	shall facilitate, where necessary, the friendly settlement of all difficulties related to the application of this Convention."

ARTICLE 30

The text of Article 20 of the Convention (new Article 24) shall be replaced by the following:

Part 3	International Treaties

"1   The Convention Committee shall be convened by the Secretary General of the Council of Europe. Its first meeting shall be held within twelve months of the entry into force of this Convention. It shall subsequently meet at least once a year, and in any case when one-third of the representatives of the Parties request its convocation.

2   After each of its meetings, the Convention Committee shall submit to the Committee of Ministers of the Council of Europe a report on its work and on the functioning of this Convention.

3   The voting arrangements in the Convention Committee are laid down in the elements for the rules of procedure appended to Protocol CETS No. [22].

4   The Convention Committee shall draw up the other elements of its rules of procedure and establish, in particular, the procedures for evaluation and review referred to in Article , paragraph 3, and Article 23, *litterae* e, f and h on the basis of objective criteria."

ARTICLE 31

1 Paragraphs 1 to 4 of Article 2 of the Convention (new Article 25) shall be replaced by the following:

"1   Amendments to this Convention may be proposed by a Party, the Committee of Ministers of the Council of Europe or the Convention Committee.

2   Any proposal for amendment shall be communicated by the Secretary General of the Council of Europe to the Parties to this Convention, to the other member States of the Council of Europe, to the European Union and to every non-member State or international organisation which has been invited to accede to this Convention in accordance with the provisions of Article 8.

3   Moreover, any amendment proposed by a Party or the Committee of Ministers shall be communicated to the Convention Committee, which shall submit to the Committee of Ministers its opinion on that proposed amendment.

4   The Committee of Ministers shall consider the proposed amendment and any opinion submitted by the Convention Committee, and may approve the amendment."

2 An additional paragraph 7 shall be added after paragraph 6 of Article 1 of the Convention (new Article 5) as follows:

"7   Moreover, the Committee of Ministers may, after consulting the Convention Committee, unanimously decide that a particular amendment shall enter into force at the expiration of a period of three years from the date on which it has been opened to acceptance, unless a Party notifies the Secretary General of the Council of Europe of an objection to its entry into force. If such an objection is notified, the amendment shall enter into force on the first day of the month following the date on which the Party to this Convention which has notified the objection has deposited its instrument of acceptance with the Secretary General of the Council of Europe."

ARTICLE 32

1 Paragraph 1 of Article 22 of the Convention (new Article 26) shall be replaced by the following:

"1   This Convention shall be open for signature by the member States of the Council of Europe and by the European Union. It is subject to ratification, acceptance or approval. Instruments of ratification, acceptance or approval shall be deposited with the Secretary General of the Council of Europe."

2 The terms "member State" in paragraph 3 of Article 22 of the Convention (new Article 6) shall be replaced by "Party".

ARTICLE 33

The title and the text of Article 23 of the Convention (new Article 27) shall be replaced as follows:

"Article 27 – Accession by non-member States or international organisations

1   After the entry into force of this Convention, the Committee of Ministers of the Council of Europe may, after consulting the Parties to this Convention and obtaining their unanimous agreement, and in light of the opinion prepared by the Convention Committee in accordance with Article 23.e, invite any State not a member of the Council of Europe or an international organisation to accede to this Convention by a decision taken by the majority provided for in Article 20.d of the Statute of the Council of Europe and by the unanimous vote of the representatives of the Contracting States entitled to sit on the Committee of Ministers.

2   In respect of any State or international organisation acceding to this Convention according to paragraph 1 above, the Convention shall enter into force on the first day of the month following the expiration of a period of three months after the date of deposit of the instrument of accession with the Secretary General of the Council of Europe."

ARTICLE 34

Paragraphs 1 and 2 of Article 24 of the Convention (new Article 28) shall be replaced by the following:

"1   Any State, the European Union or other international organisation may, at the time of signature or when depositing its instrument of ratification, acceptance, approval or accession, specify the territory or territories to which this Convention shall apply.

2   Any State, the European Union or other international organisation may, at any later date, by a declaration addressed to the Secretary General of the Council of Europe, extend the application of this Convention to any other territory specified in the declaration. In respect of such territory the Convention shall enter into force on the first day of the month following the expiration of a period of three months after the date of receipt of such declaration by the Secretary General."

ARTICLE 35

1   The term "State" in the recital of Article 27 of the Convention (new Article 3) shall be replaced by "Party".

2   References to "Articles , 3 and 4" in *littera* c shall be replaced by references to "Articles 6, 7 and 8".

ARTICLE 36 – SIGNATURE, RATIFICATION AND ACCESSION

1   This Protocol shall be open for signature by Contracting States to the Convention. It shall be subject to ratification, acceptance or approval. Instruments of ratification, acceptance or approval shall be deposited with the Secretary General of the Council of Europe.

2   After the opening for signature of this Protocol and before its entry into force, any other State shall express its consent to be bound by this Protocol by accession. It may not become a Party to the Convention without acceding simultaneously to this Protocol.

ARTICLE 37 – ENTRY INTO FORCE

1   This Protocol shall enter into force on the first day of the month following the expiration of a period of three months after the date on which all Parties to the Convention have expressed their consent to be bound by the Protocol, in accordance with the provisions of paragraph 1 of Article 36.

2   In the event this Protocol has not entered into force in accordance with paragraph 1, following the expiry of a period of five years after the date on which it has been opened for signature, the Protocol shall enter into force in respect of those States which have expressed their consent to be bound by it in accordance with paragraph 1, provided that the Protocol has at least thirty-eight Parties. As between the Parties to the Protocol, all provisions of the amended Convention shall have effect immediately upon entry into force.

3   Pending the entry into force of this Protocol and without prejudice to the provisions regarding the entry into force and the accession by non-member States or international organisations, a Party to the Convention may, at the time of signature of this Protocol or at any later moment, declare that it will apply the provisions of this Protocol on a provisional basis. In such cases, the provisions of this Protocol shall apply only with respect to the other Parties to the Convention which have made a declaration to the same effect. Such a declaration shall take effect on the first day of the third month following the date of its receipt by the Secretary General of the Council of Europe.

4   From the date of entry into force of this Protocol, the Additional Protocol to the Convention for the Protection of Individuals with regard to Automatic Processing of Personal Data, regarding supervisory authorities and transborder data flows (ETS No. 181) shall be repealed.

5   From the date of the entry into force of this Protocol, the amendments to the Convention for the Protection of Individuals with regard to Automatic Processing of Personal Data, approved by the Committee of Ministers, in Strasbourg, on 1 June 1999, have lost their purpose.

ARTICLE 38 – DECLARATIONS RELATED TO THE CONVENTION

From the date of entry into force of this Protocol, with respect to a Party having entered one or more declarations in pursuance of Article 3 of the Convention, such declaration(s) will lapse.

ARTICLE 39 – RESERVATIONS

No reservation may be made to the provisions of this Protocol.

ARTICLE 40 – NOTIFICATIONS

The Secretary General of the Council of Europe shall notify the member States of the Council of Europe and any other Party to the Convention of:

(a)   any signature;
(b)   the deposit of any instrument of ratification, acceptance, approval or accession;
(c)   the date of entry into force of this Protocol in accordance with Article 37;
(d)   any other act, notification or communication relating to this Protocol.

In witness whereof the undersigned, being duly authorised thereto, have signed this Protocol.

Done at [Strasbourg], this [25th day of June 2018], in English and in French, both texts being equally authentic, in a single copy which shall be deposited in the archives of the Council of Europe. The Secretary General of the Council of Europe shall transmit certified copies to each member State of the Council of Europe, to other Parties to the Convention and any State invited to accede to the Convention.

APPENDIX TO THE PROTOCOL: ELEMENTS FOR THE RULES OF PROCEDURE OF THE CONVENTION COMMITTEE

1   Each Party has a right to vote and shall have one vote.

2 A two-thirds majority of representatives of the Parties shall constitute a quorum for the meetings of the Convention Committee. In case the amending Protocol to the Convention enters into force in accordance with its Article 37 () before its entry into force in respect of all Contracting States to the Convention, the quorum for the meetings of the Convention Committee shall be no less than 34 Parties to the Protocol.

3 The decisions under Article 2 shall be taken by a four-fifths majority. The decisions pursuant to Article 2, *littera* h, shall be taken by a four-fifths majority, including a majority of the votes of States Parties not members of a regional integration organisation that is a Party to the Convention.

4 Where the Convention Committee takes decisions pursuant to Article 23, *littera* h, the Party concerned by the review shall not vote. Whenever such a decision concerns a matter falling within the competence of a regional integration organisation, neither the organisation nor its member States shall vote.

5 Decisions concerning procedural issues shall be taken by a simple majority.

6 Regional integration organisations, in matters within their competence, may exercise their right to vote in the Convention Committee, with a number of votes equal to the number of their member States that are Parties to the Convention. Such an organisation shall not exercise its right to vote if any of its member States exercises its right.

7 In case of vote, all Parties must be informed of the subject and time for the vote, as well as whether the vote will be exercised by the Parties individually or by a regional integration organisation on behalf of its member States.

8 The Convention Committee may further amend its rules of procedure by a two-thirds majority, except for the voting arrangements which may only be amended by unanimous vote of the Parties and to which Article 25 of the Convention applies.

EXPLANATORY REPORT
TO THE PROTOCOL AMENDING THE CONVENTION FOR THE PROTECTION OF INDIVIDUALS WITH REGARD TO AUTOMATIC PROCESSING OF PERSONAL DATA[*]

[Strasbourg, 25.VI.2018]

[3.30]

NOTES

© Council of Europe.

[*] This document will become the Explanatory Report of Convention 108 as modified by the amending Protocol.

I. Introduction

1. In the 35 years that have elapsed since the Convention for the Protection of Individuals with regard to Automated Processing of Personal Data, also known as Convention 108 (hereafter also referred to as "the Convention") was opened for signature, the Convention has served as the foundation for international data protection law in over 40 European countries. It has also influenced policy and legislation far beyond Europe's shores. With new challenges to human rights and fundamental freedoms, notably to the right to private life, arising every day, it appeared clear that the Convention should be modernised in order to better address emerging privacy challenges resulting from the increasing use of new information and communication technologies (IT), the globalisation of processing operations and the ever greater flows of personal data, and, at the same time, to strengthen the Convention's evaluation and follow-up mechanism.

2. A broad consensus on the following aspects of the modernisation process emerged: the general and technologically neutral nature of the Convention's provisions must be maintained; the Convention's coherence and compatibility with other legal frameworks must be preserved; and the Convention's open character, which gives it a unique potential as a universal standard, must be reaffirmed. The text of the Convention is of a general nature and can be supplemented with more detailed soft-law sectoral texts in the form notably of Committee of Ministers' recommendations elaborated with the participation of interested stakeholders.

3. The modernisation work was carried out in the broader context of various parallel reforms of international data protection instruments and taking due account of the 1980 (revised in 2013) Guidelines on the Protection of Privacy and Transborder Flows of Personal Data of the Organisation for Economic Co-operation and Development (OECD), the 1990 United Nations Guidelines for the Regulation of Computerized Personal Data Files, the European Union's (EU) framework[1] since 1995, the Asia-Pacific Economic Cooperation Privacy framework (2004) and the 2009 "International Standards on the Protection of Privacy with regard to the processing of Personal Data".[2] With regard to the EU data protection reform package in particular, the works ran in parallel and utmost care was taken to ensure consistency between both legal frameworks. The EU data protection framework gives substance and amplifies the principles of Convention 108 and takes into account accession to Convention 108, notably with regard to international transfers.[3]

4. The Consultative Committee set up by Article 18 of the Convention prepared draft modernisation proposals which were adopted at its 29th Plenary meeting (27-30 November 2012) and submitted to the Committee of Ministers. The Committee of Ministers subsequently entrusted the ad hoc Committee on data protection (CAHDATA) with the task of finalising the modernisation proposals. This was completed on the occasion of the 3rd meeting of the

CAHDATA (1-3 December 2014). Further to the finalisation of the EU data protection framework, another CAHDATA was established with a view to examine outstanding issues. The last CAHDATA meeting (15-16 June 2016) finalised its proposals and transmitted them to the Committee of Ministers for consideration and adoption.

5. The text of this explanatory report is intended to guide and assist the application of the provisions of the Convention and provides an indication as to how the drafters envisaged the operation of the Convention.

6. The Committee of Ministers has endorsed the explanatory report. In this respect, the explanatory report forms part of the context in which the meaning of certain terms used in the Convention is to be ascertained (note: ref. Article 31, paragraphs 1 and 2 of the United Nations Vienna Convention on the Law of Treaties).

The Protocol was adopted by the Committee of Ministers on 18 May 2018. The appendix to the Protocol forms an integral part of the Protocol and has the same legal value as the other provisions of the Protocol.

This Protocol was opened for signature in Strasbourg, on 25 June 2018.

II. Commentaries

7. The purpose of this Protocol is to modernise the Council of Europe Convention for the Protection of Individuals with regard to Automatic Processing of Personal Data (ETS No.108) and its Additional Protocol regarding supervisory authorities and transborder flows (ETS No. 181), and to strengthen their application. From its entry into force, the Additional Protocol shall be considered an integral part of the Convention as amended.

8. The explanatory reports to Convention 108 and to its additional protocol remain relevant in so far as they provide historical context and describe the evolution of both instruments, and they can be read in conjunction with the present document for those purposes.

Preamble

9. The preamble reaffirms the commitment of the signatory States to human rights and fundamental freedoms.

10. A major objective of the Convention is to put individuals in a position to know about, to understand and to control the processing of their personal data by others. Accordingly, the preamble expressly refers to the right to personal autonomy and the right to control one's personal data, which stems in particular from the right to privacy, as well as to the dignity of individuals. Human dignity requires that safeguards be put in place when processing personal data, in order for individuals not to be treated as mere objects.

11. Taking into account the role of the right to protection of personal data in society, the preamble underlines the principle that the interests, rights and fundamental freedoms of individuals have, where necessary, to be reconciled with each other. It is in order to maintain a careful balance between the different interests, rights and fundamental freedoms that the Convention lays down certain conditions and restrictions with regard to the processing of information and the protection of personal data. The right to data protection is for instance to be considered alongside the right to 'freedom of expression' as laid down in Article 10 of the European Convention on Human Rights (ETS No. 5), which includes the freedom to hold opinions and to receive and impart information. Furthermore, the Convention confirms that the exercise of the right to data protection, which is not absolute, should notably not be used as a general means to prevent public access to official documents.[4]

12. Convention 108, through the principles it lays down and the values it enshrines, protects the individual while providing a framework for international data flows. This is important as global information flows play an increasingly significant role in modern society, enabling the exercise of fundamental rights and freedoms while triggering innovation and fostering social and economic progress, while also playing a vital role in ensuring public safety. The flow of personal data in an information and communication society must respect the fundamental rights and freedoms of individuals. Furthermore, the development and use of innovative technologies should also respect those rights. This will help to build trust in innovation and new technologies and further enable their development.

13. As international co-operation between supervisory authorities is a key element for effective protection of individuals, the Convention aims to reinforce such co-operation, notably by requiring Parties to render mutual assistance, and providing the appropriate legal basis for a framework of co-operation and exchange of information for investigations and enforcement.

CHAPTER I – GENERAL PROVISIONS

Article 1 – Object and purpose

14. The first article describes the Convention's object and purpose. This article focuses on the subject of protection: individuals are to be protected when their personal data is processed.[5] More recently, data protection has been included as a fundamental right in Article 8 of the Charter of Fundamental Rights of the EU as well as in the constitutions of several Parties to the Convention.

15. The guarantees set out in the Convention are extended to every individual regardless of nationality or residence. No discrimination between citizens and third country nationals in the application of these guarantees is allowed.[6] Clauses restricting data protection to a State's own nationals or legally resident foreign nationals would be incompatible with the Convention.

Article 2 – Definitions

16. The definitions used in this Convention are meant to ensure the uniform application of terms to express certain fundamental concepts in national legislation.

LITT. A. – "PERSONAL DATA"

17. "Identifiable individual" means a person who can be directly or indirectly identified. An individual is not considered "identifiable" if his or her identification would require unreasonable time, effort or resources. Such is the case, for example, when identifying a data subject would require excessively complex, long and costly operations. The

issue of what constitutes "unreasonable time, efforts or resources" should be assessed on a case-by-case basis. For example, consideration could be given to the purpose of the processing and taking into account objective criteria such as the cost, the benefits of such an identification, the type of controller, the technology used, etc. Furthermore, technological and other developments may change what constitutes "unreasonable time, effort or other resources".

18. The notion of "identifiable" refers not only to the individual's civil or legal identity as such, but also to what may allow to "individualise" or single out (and thus allow to treat differently) one person from others. This "individualisation" could be done, for instance, by referring to him or her specifically, or to a device or a combination of devices (computer, mobile phone, camera, gaming devices, etc.) on the basis of an identification number, a pseudonym, biometric or genetic data, location data, an IP address, or other identifier. The use of a pseudonym or of any digital identifier/digital identity does not lead to anonymisation of the data as the data subject can still be identifiable or individualised. Pseudonymous data is thus to be considered as personal data and is covered by the provisions of the Convention. The quality of the pseudonymisation techniques applied should be duly taken into account when assessing the appropriateness of safeguards implemented to mitigate the risks to data subjects.

19. Data is to be considered as anonymous only as long as it is impossible to re-identify the data subject or if such re-identification would require unreasonable time, effort or resources, taking into consideration the available technology at the time of the processing and technological developments. Data that appears to be anonymous because it is not accompanied by any obvious identifying element may, nevertheless in particular cases (not requiring unreasonable time, effort or resources), permit the identification of an individual. This is the case, for example, where it is possible for the controller or any person to identify the individual through the combination of different types of data, such as physical, physiological, genetic, economic, or social data (combination of data on the age, sex, occupation, geolocation, family status, etc.). Where this is the case, the data may not be considered anonymous and is covered by the provisions of the Convention.

20. When data is made anonymous, appropriate means should be put in place to avoid re- identification of data subjects, in particular, all technical means should be implemented in order to guarantee that the individual is not, or is no longer, identifiable. They should be regularly re-evaluated in light of the fast pace of technological development.

LITT. B. AND C. – "DATA PROCESSING"

21. "Data processing" starts from the collection of personal data and covers all operations performed on personal data, whether partially or totally automated. Where automated processing is not used, data processing means an operation or set of operations performed upon personal data within a structured set of such data which are accessible or retrievable according to specific criteria, allowing the controller or any other person to search, combine or correlate the data related to a specific data subject.

LITT. D. –"CONTROLLER"

22. "Controller" refers to the person or body having decision-making power concerning the purposes and means of the processing, whether this power derives from a legal designation or factual circumstances that are to be assessed on a case-by-case basis. In some cases, there may be multiple controllers or co-controllers (jointly responsible for a processing and possibly responsible for different aspects of that processing). When assessing whether the person or body is a controller, special account should be taken of whether that person or body determines the reasons justifying the processing, in other terms its purposes and the means used for it. Further relevant factors for this assessment include whether the person or body has control over the processing methods, the choice of data to be processed and who is allowed to access it. Those who are not directly subject to the controller and carry out the processing on the controller's behalf, and solely according to the controller's instructions, are to be considered processors. The controller remains responsible for the processing also where a processor is processing the data on his or her behalf.

LITT. E. – "RECIPIENT"

23. "Recipient" is an individual or an entity who receives personal data or to whom personal data is made available. Depending on the circumstances, the recipient may be a controller or a processor. For example, an enterprise can send certain data of employees to a government department that will process it as a controller for tax purposes. It may send it to a company offering storage services and acting as a processor. The recipient can be a public authority or an entity that has been granted the right to exercise a public function but where the data received by the authority or entity is processed in the framework of a particular inquiry in accordance with the applicable law, that public authority or entity shall not be regarded as a recipient. Requests for disclosure from public authorities should always be in writing, reasoned and occasional and should not concern the entirety of a filing system or lead to the interconnection of filing systems. The processing of personal data by those public authorities should comply with the applicable data protection rules according to the purposes of the processing.

LITT. F. – "PROCESSOR"

24. "Processor" is any natural or legal person (other than an employee of the data controller) who processes data on behalf of the controller and according to the controller's instructions. The instructions given by the controller establish the limit of what the processor is allowed to do with the personal data.

ARTICLE 3 – SCOPE

25. According to paragraph 1, each Party should apply the Convention to all processing, whether within the public or private sector, subject to its jurisdiction.

26. Making the scope of the protection dependent on the notion of "jurisdiction" of the Parties, is justified by the objective of better standing the test of time and accommodating continual technological developments.

27. Paragraph 2 excludes processing carried out for purely personal or household activities from the scope of the Convention. This exclusion aims at avoiding the imposition of unreasonable obligations on data processing carried out by individuals in their private sphere for activities relating to the exercise of their private life. Personal or household activities are activities which are closely and objectively linked to the private life of an individual and which do not significantly impinge upon the personal sphere of others. These activities have no professional or commercial aspects and relate exclusively to personal or household activities such as storing family or private pictures on a computer, creating a list of the contact details of friends and family members, correspondence, etc. The sharing of data within the private sphere encompasses notably the sharing between a family, a restricted circle of friends or a circle which is limited in its size and based on a personal relationship or a particular relation of trust.

28. Whether activities are "purely personal or household activities" will depend on the circumstances. For example, when personal data is made available to a large number of persons or to persons obviously external to the private sphere, such as a public website on the internet, the exemption will not apply. Likewise, the operation of a camera system, as a result of which a video recording of people is stored on a continuous recording device such as a hard disk drive, installed by an individual in his or her family home for the purposes of protecting the property, health and life of the home owners, but which covers, even partially, a public space and is accordingly directed outwards from the private setting of the person processing the data in that manner, cannot be regarded as an activity which is a purely "personal or household" activity.[7]

29. The Convention nonetheless applies to data processing carried out by providers of the means for processing personal data for such personal or household activities.

30. While the Convention concerns data processing relating to individuals, the Parties may extend the protection in their domestic law to data relating to legal persons in order to protect their legitimate interests. The Convention applies to living individuals: it is not meant to apply to personal data relating to deceased persons. However, this does not prevent Parties from extending the protection to deceased persons.

CHAPTER II – BASIC PRINCIPLES OF DATA PROTECTION

Article 4 – Duties of the Parties
31. As this article indicates, the Convention obliges Parties to incorporate its provisions into their law and secure their effective application in practice; how this is done depends on the applicable legal system and the approach taken regarding the incorporation of international treaties.

32. The term "law of the Parties" denotes, according to the legal and constitutional system of the particular country, all enforceable rules, whether of statute law or case law. It must meet the qualitative requirements of accessibility and previsibility (or "foreseeability"). This implies that the law should be sufficiently clear to allow individuals and other entities to regulate their own behaviour in light of the expected legal consequences of their actions, and that the persons who are likely to be affected by this law should have access to it. It encompasses rules that place obligations or confer rights on persons (whether natural or legal) or which govern the organisation, powers and responsibilities of public authorities or lay down procedure. In particular, it includes States' constitutions and all written acts of legislative authorities (laws in the formal sense) as well as all regulatory measures (decrees, regulations, orders and administrative directives) based on such laws. It also covers international conventions applicable in domestic law, including EU law. Furthermore, it includes all other statutes of a general nature, whether of public or private law (including the law of contracts), together with court decisions in common law countries, or in all countries, established case law interpreting a written law. In addition, it includes any act of a professional body under powers delegated by the legislator and in accordance with its independent rule-making powers.

33. Such a "law of the Parties" may be usefully reinforced by voluntary regulation measures in the field of data protection, such as codes of good practice or codes for professional conduct. However, such voluntary measures are not by themselves sufficient to ensure full compliance with the Convention.

34. Where international organisations are concerned,[8] in some situations, the law of such international organisations may be applied directly at the national level of the member States of such organisations depending on each national legal system.

35. The effectiveness of the application of the measures giving effect to the provisions of the Convention is of crucial importance. The role of the supervisory authority (or authorities), together with any remedies that are available to data subjects, should be considered in the overall assessment of the effectiveness of a Party's implementation of the Convention's provisions.

36. It is further stipulated in paragraph 2 that the measures giving effect to the Convention shall be taken by the Parties concerned and shall have come into force by the time of ratification or accession, that is when a Party becomes legally bound by the Convention. This provision aims to enable the Convention Committee to verify whether all "necessary measures" have been taken, to ensure that the Parties to the Convention observe their commitments and provide the expected level of data protection in their national law. The process and criteria used for this verification are to be clearly defined in the Convention Committee's rules of procedure.

37. Parties commit in paragraph 3 to contribute actively to the evaluation of their compliance with their commitments, with a view to ensuring regular assessment of the implementation of the principles of the Convention (including its effectiveness). Submission of reports by the Parties on the application of their data protection law could be one possible element of this active contribution.

38. In exercising its powers under paragraph 3, the Convention Committee shall not evaluate whether a Party has taken effective measures, to the extent it has made use of exceptions and restrictions in accordance with the provisions of this Convention. It follows that under Article 11 paragraph 3 a Party shall not be required to provide classified information to the Convention Committee.

39. The evaluation of a Party's compliance will be carried out by the Convention Committee on the basis of an objective, fair and transparent procedure established by the Convention Committee and fully described in its rules of procedure.

Article 5 – Legitimacy of data processing and quality of data

40. Paragraph 1 provides that data processing must be proportionate, that is, appropriate in relation to the legitimate purpose pursued and having regard to the interests, rights and freedoms of the data subject or the public interest. Such data processing should not lead to a disproportionate interference with these interests, rights and freedoms. The principle of proportionality is to be respected at all stages of processing, including at the initial stage, i.e. when deciding whether or not to carry out the processing.

41. Paragraph 2 prescribes two alternate essential pre-requisites for a lawful processing: the individual's consent or a legitimate basis prescribed by law. Paragraphs 1, 2, 3 and 4 of Article 5 are cumulative and must be respected in order to ensure the legitimacy of the data processing.

42. The data subject's consent must be freely given, specific, informed and unambiguous. Such consent must represent the free expression of an intentional choice, given either by a statement (which can be written, including by electronic means, or oral) or by a clear affirmative action and which clearly indicates in this specific context the acceptance of the proposed processing of personal data. Mere silence, inactivity or pre-validated forms or boxes should not, therefore, constitute consent. Consent should cover all processing activities carried out for the same purpose or purposes (in the case of multiple purposes, consent should be given for each different purpose). There may be cases with different consent decisions (e.g. where the nature of the data is different even if the purpose is the same – such as health data versus location data: in such cases the data subject may consent to the processing of his or her location data but not to the processing of the health data). The data subject must be informed of the implications of his or her decision (what the fact of consenting entails and the extent to which consent is given). No undue influence or pressure (which can be of an economic or other nature) whether direct or indirect, may be exercised on the data subject and consent should not be regarded as freely given where the data subject has no genuine or free choice or is unable to refuse or withdraw consent without prejudice.

43. In the context of scientific research it is often not possible to fully identify the purpose of personal data processing for scientific research purposes at the time of data collection. Therefore, data subjects should be allowed to give their consent to certain areas of scientific research in keeping with recognised ethical standards for scientific research. Data subjects should have the opportunity to give their consent only to certain areas of research or parts of research projects to the extent allowed by the intended purpose.

44. An expression of consent does not waive the need to respect the basic principles for the protection of personal data set out in Chapter II of the Convention and the proportionality of the processing, for instance, still has to be considered.

45. The data subject has the right to withdraw the consent he or she gave at any time (which is to be distinguished from the separate right to object to processing). This will not affect the lawfulness of the data processing that occurred before the data controller has received his or her withdrawal of consent but does not allow continued processing of data, unless justified by some other legitimate basis laid down by law.

46. The notion of "legitimate basis laid down by law", referred to in paragraph 2, encompasses, *inter alia*, data processing necessary for the fulfilment of a contract (or pre- contractual measures at the request of the data subject) to which the data subject is party; data processing necessary for the protection of the vital interests of the data subject or of another person; data processing necessary for compliance with a legal obligation to which the controller is subject; and data processing carried out on the basis of grounds of public interest or for overriding legitimate interests of the controller or of a third party.

47. Data processing carried out on grounds of public interest should be provided for by law, *inter alia*, for monetary, budgetary and taxation matters, public health and social security, the prevention, investigation, detection and prosecution of criminal offences and the execution of criminal penalties, the protection of national security, defence, the prevention, investigation, detection and prosecution of breaches of ethics for regulated professions, the enforcement of civil law claims and the protection of judicial independence and judicial proceedings. Data processing may serve both a ground of public interest and the vital interests of the data subject as, for instance, in the case of data processed for humanitarian purposes including monitoring a life-threatening epidemic and its spread or in humanitarian emergencies. The latter may occur in situations of natural disasters where processing of personal data of missing persons may be necessary for a limited time for purposes related to the emergency context – which is to be evaluated on a case-by-case basis. It can also occur in situations of armed conflicts or other violence.[9] The processing of personal data by official authorities for the purpose of achieving the aims, laid down by constitutional law or by international public law, of officially recognised religious associations can also be considered as being carried out on grounds of public interest.

48. The conditions for legitimate processing are set out in paragraphs 3 and 4. Personal data should be processed lawfully, fairly and in a transparent manner. Personal data must also have been collected for explicit, specified and legitimate purposes, and the processing of that particular data must serve those purposes, or at least not be incompatible with them. The reference to specified "purposes" indicates that it is not permitted to process data for undefined, imprecise or vague purposes. What is considered a legitimate purpose depends on the circumstances as the objective is to ensure that a balancing of all rights, freedoms and interests at stake is made in each instance; the right to the protection of personal data on the one hand, and the protection of other rights on the other hand, as, for example, between the interests of the data subject and the interests of the controller or of society.

49. The concept of compatible use should not hamper the transparency, legal certainty, predictability or fairness of the processing. Personal data should not be further processed in a way that the data subject might consider unexpected, inappropriate or otherwise objectionable. In order to ascertain whether a purpose of further processing is compatible with the purpose for which the personal data is initially collected, the controller, after having met all the requirements for the lawfulness of the original processing, should take into account, inter alia, any link between those purposes and the purposes of the intended further processing; the context in which the personal data has been collected, in particular the reasonable expectations of data subjects based on their relationship with the controller as to its further use; the nature of the personal data; the consequences of the intended further processing for data subjects; and the existence of appropriate safeguards in both the original and intended further processing operations.

50. The further processing of personal data, referred to in paragraph 4,b. for archiving purposes in the public interest, scientific or historical research purposes or statistical purposes is a priori considered as compatible provided that other safeguards exist (such as, for instance, anonymisation of data or data pseudonymisation, except if retention of the identifiable form is necessary; rules of professional secrecy; provisions governing restricted access and communication of data for the above-mentioned purposes, notably in relation to statistics and public archives; and other technical and organisational data-security measures) and that the operations, in principle, exclude any use of the information obtained for decisions or measures concerning a particular individual. "Statistical purposes" refers to the elaboration of statistical surveys or the production of statistical, aggregated results. Statistics aim at analysing and characterising mass or collective phenomena in a considered population.[10] Statistical purposes can be pursued either by the public or the private sector. Processing of data for "scientific research purposes" aims at providing researchers with information contributing to an understanding of phenomena in varied scientific fields (epidemiology, psychology, economics, sociology, linguistics, political science, criminology, etc.) with a view to establishing permanent principles, laws of behaviour or patterns of causality which transcend all the individuals to whom they apply.[11] "Historical research purposes" includes genealogical research. "Archiving purposes in the public interest" can also include archives originating from private entities, where a public interest is involved.

51. Personal data undergoing processing should be adequate, relevant and not excessive. Furthermore, the data should be accurate and, where necessary, regularly kept up to date.

52. The requirement of paragraph 4,c. that data be "not excessive" first requires that data processing should be limited to what is necessary for the purpose for which it is processed. It should only be processed if, and as long as, the purposes cannot reasonably be fulfilled by processing information that does not involve personal data. Furthermore, this requirement not only refers to the quantity, but also to the quality of personal data. Personal data which is adequate and relevant but would entail a disproportionate interference in the fundamental rights and freedoms at stake should be considered as excessive and not be processed.

53. The requirement of paragraph 4,e. concerning the time-limits for the storage of personal data means that data should be deleted once the purpose for which it was processed has been achieved, or that it should only be kept in a form that prevents any direct or indirect identification of the data subject.

54. Limited exceptions to Article 5 paragraph 4 are permitted under the conditions specified in Article 11 paragraph 1.

Article 6 – Special categories of data

55. Processing of certain types of data, or processing of certain data for the sensitive information it reveals, may lead to encroachments on interests, rights and freedoms. This can for instance be the case where there is a potential risk of discrimination or injury to an individual's dignity or physical integrity, where the data subject's most intimate sphere, such as his or her sex life or sexual orientation, is being affected, or where processing of data could affect the presumption of innocence. It should only be permitted where appropriate safeguards, which complement the other protective provisions of the Convention, are provided for by law. The requirement of appropriate safeguards, complementing the provisions of the Convention, does not exclude the possibility provided under Article 11 to allow exceptions and restrictions to the rights of data subjects granted under Article 9.

56. In order to prevent adverse effects for the data subject, processing of sensitive data for legitimate purposes needs to be accompanied by appropriate safeguards (which are adapted to the risks at stake and the interests, rights and freedoms to be protected), such as for instance, alone or cumulatively; the data subject's explicit consent; a law covering the intended purpose and means of the processing or indicating the exceptional cases where processing such data would be permitted; a professional secrecy obligation; measures following a risk analysis; a particular and qualified organisational or technical security measure (data encryption, for example).

57. Specific types of data processing may entail a particular risk for data subjects independently of the context of the processing. This is, for instance, the case with the processing of genetic data, which can be left by individuals and can reveal information on the health or filiation of the person, as well as of third parties. Genetic data are all data relating to the genetic characteristics of an individual which have been either inherited or acquired during early prenatal development, as they result from an analysis of a biological sample from the individual concerned: chromosomal, DNA or RNA analysis or analysis of any other element enabling equivalent information to be obtained. Similar risks occur with the processing of data related to criminal offences (which includes suspected offences), criminal convictions (based on criminal law and in the framework of criminal proceedings) and related security measures (involving deprivation of liberty for instance) which require the provision of appropriate safeguards for the rights and freedoms of data subjects.

58. Processing of biometric data, that is data resulting from a specific technical processing of data concerning the physical, biological or physiological characteristics of an individual which allows the unique identification or authentication of the individual, is also considered sensitive when it is precisely used to uniquely identify the data subject.

59. The context of the processing of images is relevant to the determination of the sensitive nature of the data. The processing of images will not generally involve processing of sensitive data as the images will only be covered by the definition of biometric data when being processed through a specific technical mean which permits the unique identification or authentication of an individual. Furthermore, where processing of images is intended to reveal racial, ethnic or health information (see the following point), such processing will be considered as processing of sensitive data. On the contrary, images processed by a video surveillance system solely for security reasons in a shopping area will not generally be considered as processing of sensitive data.

60. Processing of sensitive data has the potential to adversely affect data subjects' rights when it is processed for specific information it reveals. While the processing of family names can in many circumstances be void of any risk for individuals (e.g. common payroll purposes), such processing could in some cases involve sensitive data, for example when the purpose is to reveal the ethnic origin or religious beliefs of the individuals based on the linguistic origin of their names. Information concerning health includes information concerning the past, present and future,

Part 3   International Treaties

physical or mental health of an individual, and which may refer to a person who is sick or healthy. Processing images of persons with thick glasses, a broken leg, burnt skin or any other visible characteristics related to a person's health can only be considered as processing sensitive data when the processing is based on the health information that can be extracted from the pictures.

61. Where sensitive data has to be processed for a statistical purpose it should be collected in such a way that the data subject is not identifiable. Collection of sensitive data without identification data is a safeguard within the meaning of Article 6. Where there is a legitimate need to collect sensitive data for statistical purposes in identifiable form (so that a repeat or longitudinal survey can be carried out, for example), appropriate safeguards should be put in place.[12]

Article 7 – Data security

62. The controller and, where applicable the processor, should take specific security measures, both of technical and organisational nature, for each processing, taking into account: the potential adverse consequences for the individual, the nature of the personal data, the volume of personal data processed, the degree of vulnerability of the technical architecture used for the processing, the need to restrict access to the data, requirements concerning long-term storage, and so forth.

63. Security measures should take into account the current state of the art of data-security methods and techniques in the field of data processing. Their cost should be commensurate with the seriousness and probability of the potential risks. Security measures should be kept under review and updated where necessary.

64. While security measures are aimed at preventing a number of risks, paragraph 2 contains a specific obligation in cases where a data breach has nevertheless occurred that may seriously interfere with the fundamental rights and freedoms of the individual. For instance, the disclosure of data covered by professional confidentiality, or which may result in financial, reputational, or physical harm or humiliation, could be deemed to constitute a "serious" interference.

65. Where such a data breach has occurred, the controller is required to notify the relevant supervisory authorities of the incident, subject to the exception permitted under Article 11 paragraph 1. This is the minimum requirement. The controller should also notify the supervisory authorities of any measures taken and/or proposed to address the breach and its potential consequences.

66. The notification made by the controller to the supervisory authorities does not preclude other complementary notifications. For instance, the controller may also recognise the need to notify the data subjects in particular when the data breach is likely to result in a significant risk for the rights and freedoms of individuals, such as discrimination, identity theft or fraud, financial loss, damage to reputation, loss of confidentiality of data protected by professional secrecy or any other significant economic or social disadvantage, and to provide them with adequate and meaningful information on, notably, the contact points and possible measures that they could take to mitigate the adverse effects of the breach. In cases where the controller does not spontaneously inform the data subject of the data breach, the supervisory authority, having considered the likely adverse effects of the breach, should be allowed to require the controller to do so. Notification to other relevant authorities such as those in charge of computer systems security may also be desirable.

Article 8 – Transparency of processing

67. The controller is required to act transparently when processing data in order to ensure fair processing and to enable data subjects to understand and thus fully exercise their rights in the context of such data processing.

68. Certain essential information has to be compulsorily provided in a proactive manner by the controller to the data subjects when directly or indirectly (not through the data subject but through a third-party) collecting their data, subject to the possibility to provide for exceptions in line with Article 11 paragraph 1. Information on the name and address of the controller (or co-controllers), the legal basis and the purposes of the data processing, the categories of data processed and recipients, as well as the means of exercising the rights can be provided in any appropriate format (either through a website, technological tools on personal devices, etc.) as long as the information is fairly and effectively presented to the data subject. The information presented should be easily accessible, legible, understandable and adapted to the relevant data subjects (for example, in a child friendly language where necessary). Any additional information that is necessary to ensure fair data processing or that is useful for such purposes, such as the preservation period, the knowledge of the reasoning underlying the data processing, or information on data transfers to a recipient in another Party or non- Party (including whether that particular non-Party provides an appropriate level of data protection, or the measures taken by the controller to guarantee such an appropriate level of data protection) is also to be provided.

69. The controller is not required to provide this information where the data subject has already received it, or in the case of an indirect collection of data through third parties where the processing is expressly prescribed by law, or where this proves to be impossible or it involves disproportionate efforts because the data subject is not directly identifiable or the controller has no way to contact the data subject. Such impossibility can be both of a legal nature (in the context of a criminal investigation for instance) or of a practical nature (for instance when a controller is only processing pictures and does not know the names and contact details of the data subjects).

70. The data controller may use any available, reasonable and affordable means to inform data subjects collectively (through a website or public notice) or individually. If it is impossible to do so when commencing the processing, it can be done at a later stage, for instance when the controller is put in contact with the data subject for any new reason.

Article 9 – Rights of the data subject

71. This article lists the rights that every individual should be able to exercise concerning the processing of personal data relating to him or her. Each Party shall ensure, within its legal order, that all those rights are available for every data subject together with the necessary legal and practical, adequate and effective means to exercise them.

72. These rights include the following:

- the right of everyone not to be subject to a purely automated decision significantly affecting them without having their views taken into consideration (littera a.) ;
- the right of everyone to request confirmation of a processing of data relating to them and to access the data at reasonable intervals and without excessive delay or expense (littera b.);
- the right of everyone to be provided, on request, with knowledge of the reasoning underlying data processing where the results of such processing are applied to them (littera c.);
- the right of everyone to object on grounds relating to their situation, to a processing of personal data relating to them, unless the controller demonstrates legitimate grounds for the processing which override their interests or rights and fundamental freedoms (littera d.);
- the right of everyone to rectification or erasure of inaccurate, false, or unlawfully processed data (littera e.);
- the right of everyone to a remedy if any of the previous rights is not respected (littera f.);
- the right of everyone to obtain assistance from a supervisory authority (littera g.).

73. These rights may have to be reconciled with other rights and legitimate interests. They can, in accordance with Article 11, be limited only where this is provided for by law and constitutes a necessary and proportionate measure in a democratic society. For instance, the right to erasure of personal data may be restricted to the extent that processing is necessary for compliance with a legal obligation which requires processing by law to which the controller is subject or for the performance of a task carried out in the public interest or in the exercise of official authority vested in the controller.

74. While the Convention does not specify from whom a data subject may obtain confirmation, communication, rectification, and so on, or to whom to object or express his or her views, in most cases, this will be the controller, or the processor on his or her behalf. In exceptional cases, the means to exercise the rights to access, rectification and erasure may involve the intermediary of the supervisory authority. Concerning health data, rights may also be exercised in a different manner than through direct access. They may be exercised, for instance, with the assistance of a health professional when it is in the interest of the data subject, notably to help him/her understand the data or ensure that the data subject's psychological state is appropriately considered when imparting information – in line, of course, with deontological principles.

75. Littera a. It is essential that an individual who may be subject to a purely automated decision has the right to challenge such a decision by putting forward, in a meaningful manner, his or her point of view and arguments. In particular, the data subject should have the opportunity to substantiate the possible inaccuracy of the personal data before it is used, the irrelevance of the profile to be applied to his or her particular situation, or other factors that will have an impact on the result of the automated decision. This is notably the case where individuals are stigmatised by application of algorithmic reasoning resulting in limitation of a right or refusal of a social benefit or where they see their credit capacity evaluated by a software only. However, an individual cannot exercise this right if the automated decision is authorised by a law to which the controller is subject and which also lays down suitable measures to safeguard the data subject's rights and freedoms and legitimate interests.

76. Littera b. Data subjects should be entitled to know about the processing of their personal data. The right of access should, in principle, be free of charge. However, the wording of littera b. is intended to allow the controller in certain specific conditions to charge a reasonable fee where the requests are excessive and to cover various approaches that could be adopted by a Party for appropriate cases. Such a fee should be exceptional and in any case reasonable, and not prevent or dissuade data subjects from exercising their rights. The controller or processor could also refuse to respond to manifestly unfounded or excessive requests, in particular because of their repetitive character. The controller should in all cases justify such a refusal. To ensure a fair exercise of the right of access, the communication "in an intelligible form" applies to the content as well as to the form of a standardised digital communication.

77. Littera c. Data subjects should be entitled to know the reasoning underlying the processing of data, including the consequences of such a reasoning, which led to any resulting conclusions, in particular in cases involving the use of algorithms for automated- decision making including profiling. For instance in the case of credit scoring, they should be entitled to know the logic underpinning the processing of their data and resulting in a "yes" or "no" decision, and not simply information on the decision itself. Having an understanding of these elements contributes to the effective exercise of other essential safeguards such as the right to object and the right to complain to a competent authority.

78. Littera d. As regards the right to object, the controller may have a legitimate ground for data processing, which overrides the interests or rights and freedoms of the data subject. For example, the establishment, exercise or defence of legal claims or reasons of public safety could be considered as overriding legitimate grounds justifying the continuation of the processing. This will have to be demonstrated on a case-by-case basis and failure to demonstrate such compelling legitimate grounds while pursuing the processing could be considered as unlawful. The right to object operates in a distinct and separate manner from the right to obtain rectification or erasure (littera e.).

79. Objection to data processing for marketing purposes should lead to unconditional erasing or removing of the personal data covered by the objection.

80. The right to object may be limited by virtue of a law, for example, for the purpose of the investigation or prosecution of criminal offences. In this case, the data subject can, as the case may be, challenge the lawfulness of the processing on which it is based. When data processing is based on valid consent given by the data subject, the right to withdraw consent can be exercised instead of the right to object. A data subject may withdraw his or her consent and subsequently have to assume the consequences possibly deriving from other legal texts such as the obligation to compensate the controller. Likewise where data processing is based on a contract, the data subject can take the necessary steps to revoke the contract.

81. Littera e. The rectification or erasure, if justified, must be free of charge. In the case of rectifications and erasures obtained in conformity with the principle set out in littera e., those rectifications and erasures should, where possible, be brought to the attention of the recipients of the original information, unless this proves to be impossible or involves disproportionate efforts.

82. Littera g. aims at ensuring effective protection of data subjects by providing them the right to an assistance of a supervisory authority in exercising the rights provided by the Convention. When the data subject resides in the territory of another Party, he or she can submit the request through the intermediary of the authority designated by that

Party. The request for assistance should contain sufficient information to permit identification of the data processing in question. This right can be limited according to Article 11 or adapted in order to safeguard the interests of a pending judicial procedure.

83. Limited exceptions to Article 9 are permitted under the conditions specified in Article 11, paragraph 1.

Article 10 - Additional obligations

84. In order to ensure that the right to the protection of personal data is effective, additional obligations are imposed on the controller as well as, where applicable, the processor(s).

85. According to paragraph 1, the obligation on the controller to ensure adequate data protection is linked to the responsibility to verify and be in a position to demonstrate that data processing is in compliance with the applicable law. The data protection principles set out in the Convention, which are to be applied at all stages of processing, including the design phase, aim at protecting data subjects and are also a mechanism for enhancing their trust. Appropriate measures that the controller and processor may have to take to ensure compliance include: training employees; setting up appropriate notification procedures (for instance to indicate when data have to be deleted from the system); establishing specific contractual provisions where the processing is delegated in order to give effect to the Convention; as well as setting up internal procedures to enable the verification and demonstration of compliance.

86. If, in accordance with Article 11, paragraph 3, a Party choses to limit the powers of a supervisory authority within the meaning of Article 15 with reference to processing activities for national security and defence purposes, the controller has no obligation to demonstrate to such a supervisory authority compliance with data protection requirements for activities falling within the scope of the aforementioned exception.

87. A possible measure that could be taken by the controller to facilitate such a verification and demonstration of compliance would be the designation of a "data protection officer" entrusted with the means necessary to fulfil his or her mandate. Such a data protection officer, whose designation should be notified to the supervisory authority, could be internal or external to the controller.

88. Paragraph 2 clarifies that before carrying out a data processing activity, the controller will have to examine its potential impact on the rights and fundamental freedoms of the data subjects. This examination can be done without excessive formalities. It will also have to consider respect for the proportionality principle on the basis of a comprehensive overview of the intended processing. In some circumstances, where a processor is involved in addition to the controller, the processor will also have to examine the risks. IT systems developers, including security professionals, or designers, together with users and legal experts could assist in examining the risks.

89. Paragraph 3 specifies that in order to better guarantee an effective level of protection, controllers, and, where applicable, processors, should ensure that data protection requirements are integrated as early as possible, that is, ideally at the stage of architecture and system design, in data processing operations through technical and organisational measures (data protection by design). This implementation of data protection requirements should be achieved not only as regards the technology used for processing the data, but also the related work and management processes. Easy-to-use functionalities that facilitate compliance with applicable law should be put in place. For example, secure online access to one's own data should be offered to data subjects where possible and relevant. There should also be easy-to-use tools to enable data subjects to take their data to another provider of their choice or keep the data themselves (data portability tools). When setting up the technical requirements for default settings, controllers and processors should choose privacy-friendly standard configurations so that the usage of applications and software does not infringe the rights of the data subjects (data protection by default), notably to avoid processing more data than necessary to achieve the legitimate purpose. For example, social networks should be configured by default so as to share posts or pictures only with restricted and chosen circles and not with the whole internet.

90. Paragraph 4 allows Parties to adapt the additional obligations listed in paragraphs 1 to 3 taking into consideration the risks at stake for the interests, rights and fundamental freedoms of the data subjects. Such adaptation should be done considering the nature and volume of data processed, the nature, scope and purposes of the data processing and, in certain cases, the size of the processing entity. The obligations could be adapted, for example, so as not to entail excessive costs for small and medium-sized enterprises (SMEs) processing only non- sensitive personal data received from customers in the framework of commercial activities and not re-using it for other purposes. Certain categories of data processing, such as processing which does not entail any risk for data subjects, may even be exempt from some of the additional obligations prescribed in this article.

Article 11 - Exceptions and restrictions

91. No exceptions to the provisions of Chapter II are allowed except for a limited number of provisions (Article 5 paragraph 4, Article 7 paragraph 2, Article 8 paragraph 1 and Article 9) on condition that such exceptions are provided for by law, that they respect the essence of the fundamental rights and freedoms, and are necessary in a democratic society for the grounds listed in litterae a. and b. of the first paragraph of Article 11. A measure which is "necessary in a democratic society" must pursue a legitimate aim and thus meet a pressing social need which cannot be achieved by less intrusive means. Such a measure should, furthermore, be proportionate to the legitimate aim being pursued and the reasons adduced by the national authorities to justify it should be relevant and adequate. Such a measure must be prescribed by an accessible and foreseeable law, which must be sufficiently detailed.

92. All processing of personal data must be lawful, fair and transparent in relation to the data subjects, and only processed for specific purposes. This does not in itself prevent the law enforcement authorities from carrying out activities such as covert investigations or video surveillance. Such activities can be done for the purposes of the prevention, investigation, detection or prosecution of criminal offences and the execution of criminal penalties, including the safeguarding against and the prevention of threats to national security and public safety, as long as they are laid down by law and constitute a necessary and proportionate measure in a democratic society with due regard for the legitimate interests of the data subjects.

93. The necessity of such exceptions needs to be examined on a case-by-case basis and in light of the essential objectives of general public interest, as is detailed in litterae a. and b. of the first paragraph. Littera a. lists some objectives of general public interest of the State or of the international organisation which may require exceptions.

94. The notion of "national security" should be interpreted on the basis of the relevant case law of the European Court of Human Rights.[13]

95. The term "important economic and financial interests" covers, in particular, tax collection requirements and exchange control. The term "prevention, investigation and prosecution of criminal offences and the execution of criminal penalties" in this littera includes the prosecution of criminal offences and the application of sanctions related thereto. The term "other essential objectives of general public interest" covers inter alia, the prevention, investigation, detection and prosecution of breaches of ethics for regulated professions and the enforcement of civil law claims.

96. Littera b. concerns the rights and fundamental freedoms of private parties, such as those of the data subject himself or herself (for example when a data subject's vital interests are threatened because he or she is missing) or of third parties, such as freedom of expression, including freedom of journalistic, academic, artistic or literary expression, and the right to receive and impart information, confidentiality of correspondence and communications, or business or commercial secrecy and other legally protected secrets. This should apply in particular to processing of personal data in the audio-visual field and in news archives and press libraries. In order to take account of the importance of the right to freedom of expression in every democratic society, it is necessary to interpret notions relating to that freedom, such as journalism, broadly.

97. The second paragraph leaves open the possibility of restricting the provisions set out in Articles 8 and 9 with regard to certain data processing carried out for archiving purposes in the public interest, scientific or historical research purposes, or statistical purposes which pose no recognisable risk of infringement to the rights and fundamental freedoms of data subjects. For instance, this could be the case with the use of data for statistical work, in the public and private fields alike, in so far as this data is published in aggregate form and provided that appropriate data protection safeguards are in place (see paragraph 50).

98. The additional exceptions allowed to Article 4 paragraph 3, Article 14 paragraphs 5 and 6, and Article 15 paragraph 2, litterae a., b., c., and d., in respect of processing activities for national security and defence purposes are without prejudice to applicable requirements in relation to the independence and effectiveness of review and supervision mechanisms.[14]

Article 12 – Sanctions and remedies

99. In order for the Convention to guarantee an effective level of data protection, the duties of the controller and processor and the rights of data subjects should be reflected in the Parties' legislation with corresponding sanctions and remedies.

100. It is left to each Party to determine the nature (civil, administrative, criminal) of these judicial as well as non-judicial sanctions. These sanctions have to be effective, proportionate and dissuasive. The same goes for remedies: data subjects must have the possibility to judicially challenge a decision or practice, the definition of the modalities to do so being left with the Parties. Non-judicial remedies also have to be made available to data subjects. Financial compensation for material and non-material damages where applicable, caused by the processing and collective actions could also be considered.

Article 13 – Extended protection

101. This article is based on a similar provision, Article 53 of the European Convention on Human Rights. The Convention confirms the principles of data protection law which all Parties are ready to adopt. The text emphasises that these principles constitute only a basis on which Parties may build a more advanced system of protection. The expression "wider measure of protection" therefore refers to a standard of protection which is higher, not lower, than that already required by the Convention.

CHAPTER III – TRANSBORDER FLOWS OF PERSONAL DATA[15]

Article 14 – Transborder flows of personal data

102. The aim of this article is to facilitate the free flow of information regardless of frontiers (recalled in the preamble), while ensuring an appropriate protection of individuals with regard to the processing of personal data. A transborder data transfer occurs when personal data is disclosed or made available to a recipient subject to the jurisdiction of another State or international organisation.

103. The purpose of the transborder flow regime is to ensure that personal data originally processed within the jurisdiction of a Party (data collected or stored there, for instance), which is subsequently under the jurisdiction of a State which is not Party to the Convention, continues to be processed with appropriate safeguards. What is important is that data processed within the jurisdiction of a Party always remains protected by the relevant data protection principles of the Convention. While there may be a wide variety of systems of protection, protection afforded has to be of such quality as to ensure that human rights are not affected by globalisation and transborder data flows.

104. Article 14 applies only to the outflow of data, not to its inflow, since the latter are covered by the data protection regime of the recipient Party.

105. Paragraph 1 applies to data flows between Parties to the Convention. Data flows cannot be prohibited or subjected to special authorisation "for the sole purpose of the protection of personal data." However, the Convention does not restrict the freedom of a Party to limit the transfer of personal data to another Party for other purposes, including for instance national security, defence, public safety, or other important public interests (including protection of state secrecy).

106. The rationale of the provision in paragraph 1 is that all Parties, having subscribed to the common core of data protection provisions set out in the Convention, are expected to offer a level of protection that is considered appropriate and therefore in principle allows data to circulate freely. There might, however, be exceptional cases where there is a real and serious risk that this free circulation of personal data will lead to the circumvention of the provisions of the Convention. As an exception, this provision has to be interpreted restrictively and Parties cannot rely on it in cases where the risk is either hypothetical or minor. Therefore, a Party may only invoke the exception in a specific case when it has clear and reliable evidence that transferring the data to another Party could significantly

undermine the protections afforded to that data under the Convention, and that the likelihood of this happening is high. This might be the case, for instance, when certain protections afforded under the Convention are no longer guaranteed by the other Party (for instance because its supervisory authority is no longer able to effectively exercise its functions) or when data transferred to another Party is likely to be further transferred (onward transfer) without an appropriate level of protection being ensured. A further exception recognised in international law exists where Parties are bound by harmonised rules of protection shared by States belonging to regional (economic) organisations that seek a deeper level of integration.

107. Among others, this applies to the member States of the EU. However, as explicitly stated in the General Data Protection Regulation (EU) 2016/679, a third country's accession to Convention 108 and its implementation will be an important factor when applying the EU's international transfer regime, in particular when assessing whether the third country offers an adequate level of protection (which in turn allows the free flow of personal data).

108. Paragraph 2 provides for an obligation to ensure, in principle, that "an appropriate level of protection based on the provisions of the Convention is secured". At the same time, according to paragraph 4, Parties may transfer data even in the absence of an appropriate level of protection where this is justified, among others, by "prevailing legitimate interests, in particular important public interests" to the extent these are provided for by law and such transfers constitute a necessary and proportionate measure in a democratic society (littera c.). Personal data may thus be transferred on grounds that are similar to those listed in Article 11, paragraphs 1 and 3. In all cases, Parties remain free under the Convention to restrict data transfers to non-Parties, be it for the purpose of data protection or for other reasons.

109. Paragraph 2 refers to transborder flows of personal data to a recipient that is not subject to the jurisdiction of a Party. As for any personal data flowing outside national frontiers, an appropriate level of protection is to be guaranteed. In cases where the recipient is not a Party to the Convention, the Convention establishes two mechanisms to ensure that the level of data protection is indeed appropriate: either by law, or by *ad hoc* or approved standardised safeguards that are legally binding and enforceable, as well as duly implemented.

110. Paragraphs 2 and 3 apply to all forms of appropriate protection, whether provided by law or by standardised safeguards. The law must include the relevant elements of data protection as set out in this Convention. The level of protection should be assessed for each transfer or category of transfers. Various elements of the transfer should be examined such as: the type of data; the purposes and duration of processing for which the data are transferred; the respect of the rule of law by the country of final destination; the general and sectoral legal rules applicable in the State or organisation in question; and the professional and security rules which apply there.

111. The content of the *ad hoc* or standardised safeguards must include the relevant elements of data protection. Moreover, the contractual terms could be such, for example, that the data subject is provided with a contact person on the staff of the person responsible for the data transfers, whose responsibility it is to ensure compliance with the substantive standards of protection. The data subject would be free to contact this person at any time and at no cost in relation to the data processing or transfers and, where applicable, obtain assistance in exercising his or her rights.

112. The assessment as to whether the level of protection is appropriate must take into account the principles of the Convention, the extent to which they are met in the recipient State or organisation – in so far as they are relevant for the specific case of transfer – and how the data subject is able to defend his or her interests where there is non-compliance. The enforceability of data subjects' rights and the provision of effective administrative and judicial redress for the data subjects whose personal data are being transferred should be taken into consideration in the assessment. Similarly, the assessment can be made for a whole State or organisation thereby permitting all data transfers to such a destination.

113. Paragraph 4 enables Parties to derogate from the principle of requiring an appropriate level of protection and to allow a transfer to a recipient which does not ensure such protection. Such derogations are permitted in limited situations only: with the data subject's consent or specific interest and/or where there are prevailing legitimate interests provided by law and/or the transfer constitutes a necessary and proportionate measure in a democratic society for freedom of expression. Such derogations should respect the principles of necessity and proportionality.

114. Paragraph 5 makes provision for a complementary safeguard: namely that the competent supervisory authority be provided with all relevant information concerning the transfers of data referred to in paragraphs 3.b, and, upon request 4.b and 4.c. The authority should be entitled to request relevant information about the circumstances and justification of these transfers. Under the conditions laid down in Article 11, paragraph 3, exceptions to Article 14, paragraph 5 are permissible.

115. According to paragraph 6, the supervisory authority should be entitled to request that the effectiveness of the measures taken or the existence of prevailing legitimate interests be demonstrated, and to prohibit, suspend or impose conditions on the transfer if this proves necessary to protect the rights and fundamental freedoms of the data subjects. Under the conditions laid down in Article 11, paragraph 3 exceptions to Article 14, paragraph 6 are permissible.

116. Ever increasing data flows and the related need to increase the protection of personal data also require an increase in international enforcement co-operation among competent supervisory authorities.

CHAPTER IV – SUPERVISORY AUTHORITIES[16]

Article 15 – Supervisory authorities

117. This article aims at ensuring the effective protection of individuals by requiring the Parties to provide for one or more independent and impartial public supervisory authorities that contribute to the protection of the individuals' rights and freedoms with regard to the processing of their personal data. Such authorities may be a single commissioner or a collegiate body. In order for data protection supervisory authorities to be able to provide for an appropriate remedy, they need to have effective powers and functions and enjoy genuine independence in the fulfilment of their duties. They are an essential component of the data protection supervisory system in a democratic society. In so far as Article 11, paragraph 3, applies, other appropriate mechanisms for independent and effective review and supervision of processing activities for national security and defence purposes may be provided for by the Parties.

118. Paragraph 1 clarifies that more than one authority might be needed to meet the particular circumstances of different legal systems (e.g. federal States). Specific supervisory authorities whose activity is limited to a specific sector (electronic communications sector, health sector, public sector, etc.) may also be put in place. This also applies to the processing of personal data for journalistic purposes if it is necessary to reconcile the right to the protection of personal data with the right to freedom of expression. The supervisory authorities should have the necessary infrastructure and financial, technical and human resources (lawyers, IT specialists) to take prompt and effective action. The adequacy of resources should be kept under review. Article 11, paragraph 3 allows for exceptions to the powers of supervisory authorities with reference to processing activities for national security and defence purposes (where such exceptions apply, other paragraphs of this article may as a consequence not be applicable or relevant). This is however without prejudice to applicable requirements in relation to the independence and effectiveness of review and supervision mechanisms.[17]

119. Parties have a certain amount of discretion as to how to set up the authorities for enabling them to carry out their task. According to paragraph 2, however, they must have, subject to the possibility to provide for exceptions in line with Article 11, paragraph 3, at least the powers of investigation and intervention and the powers to issue decisions with respect to violations of the provisions of the Convention. The latter may involve the imposition of administrative sanctions, including fines. Where the legal system of the Party does not provide for administrative sanctions, paragraph 2 may be applied in such a manner that the sanction is proposed by the competent supervisory authority and imposed by the competent national courts. In any event, any sanctions imposed need to be effective, proportionate and dissuasive.

120. The authority shall be endowed with powers of investigation, subject to the possibility to provide for exceptions in line with Article 11, paragraph 3, such as the possibility to ask the controller and processor for information concerning the processing of personal data and to obtain it. By virtue of Article 15, such information should be made available, in particular, when the supervisory authority is approached by a data subject wishing to exercise the rights provided for in Article 9. The latter is subject to exceptions of Article 11, paragraph 1.

121. The supervisory authority's power of intervention, provided for in paragraph 1, may take various forms in the Parties' law. For example, the authority could be empowered to oblige the controller to rectify, delete or destroy inaccurate or illegally processed data on its own account or if the data subject is not able to exercise these rights personally. The power to take action against controllers who are unwilling to communicate the required information within a reasonable time would also be a particularly effective demonstration of the power of intervention. This power could also include the possibility to issue opinions prior to the implementation of data processing operations (where processing presents particular risks to the rights and fundamental freedoms, the supervisory authority should be consulted by controllers from the earliest stage of design of the processes), or to refer cases, where appropriate, to relevant competent authorities.

122. Moreover, according to paragraph 4 every data subject should have the possibility to request the supervisory authority to investigate a claim concerning his or her rights and liberties in respect of personal data processing. This helps to guarantee the right to an appropriate remedy, in keeping with Articles 9 and 12. The necessary resources to fulfil this duty should be provided. According to their available resources, the supervisory authorities should be given the possibility to define priorities to deal with the requests and complaints lodged by data subjects.

123. The Parties should give the supervisory authority the power either to engage in legal proceedings or to bring any violations of data protection rules to the attention of the judicial authorities, subject to the possibility to provide for exceptions in line with Article 11 paragraph 3. This power derives from the power to carry out investigations, which may lead the authority to discover an infringement of an individual's right to protection. The Parties may fulfil the obligation to grant this power to the authority by enabling it to make decisions.

124. Where an administrative decision produces legal effects, every affected person has the right to have an effective judicial remedy in accordance with the applicable national law.

125. Paragraph 2,e. deals with the awareness raising role of the supervisory authorities. In this context, it seems particularly important that the supervisory authority proactively ensures the visibility of its activities, functions and powers. To this end, the supervisory authority must inform the public through periodical reports (see paragraph 131). It may also publish opinions, issue general recommendations concerning the correct implementation of data protection rules or use any other means of communication. Moreover, it must provide information to individuals and to data controllers and processors about their rights and obligations concerning data protection. While raising awareness on data protection issues, the authorities have to be attentive to specifically address children and vulnerable categories of persons through adapted ways and languages.

126. As provided for under paragraph 3, supervisory authorities are, in accordance with the applicable national law, entitled to give opinions on any legislative or administrative measures which provide for the processing of personal data. Only general measures are meant to be covered by this consultative power, not individual measures.

127. In addition to this consultation foreseen under paragraph 3, the authority could also be asked to give its opinion when other measures concerning personal data processing are in preparation, such as for instance codes of conduct or technical norms.

128. Article 15 does not prevent the allocation of other powers to the supervisory authorities.

129. Paragraph 5 clarifies that supervisory authorities cannot effectively safeguard individual rights and freedoms unless they exercise their functions in complete independence. A number of elements contribute to safeguarding the independence of the supervisory authority in the exercise of its functions, including the composition of the authority; the method for appointing its members; the duration of exercise and conditions of cessation of their functions; the possibility for them to participate in relevant meetings without undue restrictions; the option to consult technical or other experts or to hold external consultations; the availability of sufficient resources to the authority; the possibility to hire its own staff; or the adoption of decisions without being subject to external interference, whether direct or indirect.

130. The prohibition on seeking or accepting instructions covers the performance of the duties as a supervisory authority. This does not prevent supervisory authorities from seeking specialised advice where it is deemed necessary as long as the supervisory authorities exercise their own independent judgment.

131. Transparency on the work and activities of the supervisory authorities is required under paragraph 7 through, for instance, the publication of annual activity reports comprising inter alia information related to their enforcement actions.

132. Notwithstanding this independence, it must be possible to appeal against the decisions of the supervisory authorities through the courts in accordance with the principle of the rule of law, as provided for under paragraph 9.

133. Moreover, while supervisory authorities should have the legal capacity to act in court and seek enforcement, the intervention (or lack of) of a supervisory authority should not prevent an affected individual from seeking a judicial remedy (see paragraph 124).

134. Paragraph 10 of Article 15 states that supervisory authorities shall not be competent with respect to processing carried out by independent bodies when acting in their judicial capacity. Such exemption from supervisory powers should be strictly limited to genuine judicial activities, in accordance with national law.

CHAPTER V – CO-OPERATION AND MUTUAL ASSISTANCE

Article 16 – Designation of supervisory authorities

135. Chapter V (Articles 16 to 21) forms a set of provisions on co-operation and mutual assistance between Parties, through their various authorities, in giving effect to the data protection laws implemented pursuant to the Convention. These provisions are obligatory except in cases referred to in Article 20. Under Article 16, the Parties shall designate one or more authorities and communicate their contact details, as well as their substantive and territorial competences, if applicable, to the Secretary General of the Council of Europe. Subsequent articles provide for a detailed framework for co-operation and mutual assistance.

136. While the co-operation between Parties will generally be carried out by the supervisory authorities established under Article 15, it cannot be excluded that a Party designates another authority to give effect to the provisions of Article 16.

137. The co-operation and general assistance is relevant for controls a priori as well as for controls aposteriori (for example to verify the activities of a specific data controller). The information exchanged may be of a legal or factual character.

Article 17 – Forms of co-operation

138. According to Article 17, supervisory authorities within the meaning of Article 15 shall co- operate with one another to the extent necessary for the performance of their duties and the exercise of their powers. Given that Article 17 circumscribes the co-operation of supervisory authorities to what is necessary "for the performance of their duties and exercise of their powers" and the fact that the ability of a supervisory authority to co-operate relies on the extent of its powers, the provision does not apply to the extent that a Party makes use of Article 11, paragraph 3, entailing a limitation of the powers of supervisory authorities pursuant to Article 15, paragraph 2, litterae a. to d.

139. Co-operation may take various forms, some "hard" forms, such as enforcement of data protection laws through mutual assistance, in which the legality of action of each supervisory authority is indispensable, to some "soft" forms, such as awareness-raising, training, staff exchange.

140. The catalogue of possible co-operation activities is not exhaustive. In the first place, supervisory authorities shall provide each other with mutual assistance, especially by sharing any relevant and useful information. This information could be of a two-fold nature: "information and documentation on their law and administrative practice relating to data protection" (which normally does not raise any issues, such information could be exchanged freely and made publicly available) as well as confidential information, including personal data.

141. As far as personal data is concerned, such data can be exchanged only if it is essential for the co-operation, that is, if without its provision the co-operation would be rendered ineffective, or if the "data subject concerned has given explicit, specific, free and informed consent". In any case, the transfer of personal data must comply with the provisions of the Convention, and in particular Chapter II (see also Article 20 providing for the grounds for refusal).

142. Further to the provision of relevant and useful information, the goals of co-operation can be achieved by co-ordinated investigations or interventions as well as joint actions. For the applicable procedures, supervisory authorities shall refer to the applicable domestic legislation such as codes of administrative, civil or criminal procedure, or supra or international commitments by which their jurisdictions are bound, for example, mutual legal assistance treaties, having assessed their legal capacity to enter into a co-operation of that type.

143. Paragraph 3 refers to a network of supervisory authorities, as a means to contribute to the rationalisation of the co-operation process and thus to the efficiency of the protection of personal data. It is important to note that the Convention refers to "a network" in singular form. This does not prohibit supervisory authorities originating from the Parties to take part in other relevant networks.

Article 18 – Assistance to data subjects

144. Paragraph 1 ensures that data subjects, whether in a Party to the Convention or in a third country will be enabled to exercise their rights recognised in Article 9 regardless of their place of residence or their nationality.

145. According to paragraph 2, where the data subject resides in another Party he or she is given the option to pursue his or her rights either directly in the country where information relating to the data subject concerned is processed, or indirectly, through the intermediary of the designated authority.

146. Moreover, data subjects residing abroad may also have the opportunity to pursue their rights with the assistance of the diplomatic or consular agents of their own country.

147. Paragraph 3 specifies that requests be as specific as possible in order to expedite the procedure.

Article 19 – Safeguards

148. This article ensures that supervisory authorities shall be bound by the same obligation to observe discretion and confidentiality towards data protection authorities of other Parties and data subjects residing abroad.

149. Assistance from a supervisory authority on behalf of a data subject may only be given in response to a request from this data subject. The authority must have received a mandate from the data subject and may not act autonomously in his or her name. This provision is of fundamental importance for mutual trust, on which mutual assistance is based.

Article 20 – Refusal of requests

150. This article states that Parties are bound to comply with requests for co-operation and mutual assistance. The grounds for refusal to comply are enumerated exhaustively.

151. The term "compliance" which is used in littera c. should be understood in the broader sense as covering not only the reply to the request, but also the action preceding it. For example, a requested authority might refuse action not only if transmission to the requesting authority of the information asked for might be harmful for the rights and fundamental freedoms of an individual, but also if the very fact of seeking the information might prejudice his or her rights and fundamental freedoms. Furthermore, a requested authority may be required by applicable national law to ensure that other public order interests are protected (e.g. ensuring the confidentiality of a police investigation). To this end a supervisory authority may be obliged to omit certain information or documents in its response to a request.

Article 21 – Costs and procedures

152. The provisions of this article are analogous to those found in other international instruments.

153. With a view to not burdening the Convention with a mass of implementing details, paragraph 3 of this article provides that procedure, forms and language to be used can be agreed between the Parties concerned. The text of this paragraph does not require any formal procedures, but allows for administrative arrangements, which may even be confined to specific cases. Moreover, it is advisable that Parties leave to the competent supervisory authorities the power to conclude such arrangements. The forms of co-operation and assistance may also vary from case to case. It is obvious that the transmission of a request for access to sensitive medical information will have requirements which differ from routine inquiries about entries in a population record.

CHAPTER VI – CONVENTION COMMITTEE

154. The purpose of Articles 22, 23 and 24 is to facilitate the effective application of the Convention and, where necessary, to perfect it. The Convention Committee constitutes another means of co-operation of the Parties in giving effect to the data protection laws implemented pursuant to the Convention.

155. A Convention Committee is composed of representatives of all Parties, from the national supervisory authorities or from the government.

156. The nature of the Convention Committee and the likely procedure followed could be similar to those set up under the terms of other conventions concluded in the framework of the Council of Europe.

157. Since the Convention addresses a constantly evolving subject, it can be expected that questions will arise both with regard to the practical application of the Convention (Article 23, littera a.) and with regard to its meaning (same article, littera d.).

158. The Rules of Procedure of the Convention Committee contain provisions regarding the right to vote of the Parties and the modalities of the exercise of this right, and are appended to the amending Protocol.

159. Any amendment to the Rules of Procedure is subject to a two-thirds majority, with the exception of amendments to the provisions on the right to vote and corresponding modalities, to which Article 25 of the Convention applies.

160. Upon accession, the EU shall make a statement clarifying the distribution of competences between the EU and its member States as regards the protection of personal data under the Convention. Subsequently, the EU will inform the Secretary General of any substantial modification in the distribution of competences.

161. According to Article 25, the Convention Committee is entitled to propose amendments to the Convention and examine other proposals for amendment formulated by a Party or the Committee of Ministers (Article 23 litterae b. and c.).

162. In order to guarantee the implementation of the data protection principles set by the Convention, the Convention Committee will have a key role in assessing compliance with the Convention, either when preparing an assessment of the level of data protection provided by a candidate for accession (Article 23 littera e.) or when periodically reviewing the implementation of the Convention by the Parties (Article 23 littera h.). The Convention Committee will also have the power to assess the compliance of the data protection system of a State or international organisation with the Convention if the State or organisation requires the Committee to do so (Article 23 littera f.).

163. In providing such opinions on the level of compliance with the Convention, the Convention Committee will work on the basis of a fair, transparent and public procedure detailed in its Rules of Procedure.

164. Furthermore, the Convention Committee may approve models of standardised safeguards for data transfers (Article 23 littera g.).

165. Finally, the Convention Committee may help to solve difficulties arising between Parties (Article 23 littera i.). Where disputes are concerned, the Convention Committee will seek a settlement through negotiation or any other amicable means.

CHAPTER VII – AMENDMENTS

Article 25 – Amendments

166. The Committee of Ministers, which adopted the original text of this Convention, is also competent to approve any amendments.

167. In accordance with paragraph 1, the initiative for amendments may be taken by the Committee of Ministers itself, by the Convention Committee or by a Party (whether a member State of the Council of Europe or not).

168. Any proposal for amendment that has not originated with the Convention Committee should be submitted to it, in accordance with paragraph 3, for an opinion.

169. In principle, any amendment shall enter into force on the thirtieth day after all the Parties have informed the Secretary General of the Council of Europe of their acceptance thereof. However, the Committee of Ministers may unanimously decide in certain circumstances, after consulting the Convention Committee, that such amendments shall enter into force following the expiry of a three-year time lapse, unless a Party notifies the Secretary General of an objection. This procedure, the purpose of which is to speed up the entry into force of amendments while preserving the principle of the consent of all the Parties, is intended to apply to minor and technical amendments.

CHAPTER VIII – FINAL CLAUSES

Article 26 – Entry into force
170. Since for the effectiveness of the Convention a wide geographic scope is considered essential, paragraph 2 sets at five the number of ratifications by member States of the Council of Europe necessary for the entry into force.

171. The Convention is open for signature by the European Union.[18]

Article 27 – Accession by non-member States and international organisations
172. The Convention, which was originally developed in close co-operation with the OECD and several non-European States, is open to any State around the globe complying with its provisions. The Convention Committee is entrusted with the task of assessing such compliance and preparing an opinion for the Committee of Ministers relating to the level of data protection of the candidate for accession.

173. Considering the frontierless nature of data flows, accession by countries and international organisations from all over the world is sought. International organisations that can accede to the Convention are solely international organisations which are defined as organisations governed by public international law.

Article 28 – Territorial clause
174. The application of the Convention to remote territories under the jurisdiction of Parties or on whose behalf a Party can make undertakings is of practical importance in view of the use that is made of distant countries for data processing operations either for reasons of cost and manpower or in view of the utilisation of alternating night and daytime data processing capability.

Article 29 – Reservations
175. The rules contained in this Convention constitute the most basic and essential elements for effective data protection. For this reason, the Convention allows no reservations to its provisions, which are, moreover, reasonably flexible, having regard to the exceptions and restrictions permitted under certain articles.

Article 30 – Denunciation
176. Any Party is allowed to denounce the Convention at any time.

Article 31 – Notifications
177. These provisions are in conformity with the customary final clauses contained in other conventions of the Council of Europe.

NOTES

1   General Data Protection Regulation (EU) 2016/679 ("GDPR") and Data Protection Directive for Police and Criminal Justice Authorities (EU) 2016/680 ("Police Directive").

2   Welcomed by the 31st International Conference of Data Protection and Privacy Commissioners, held in Madrid 4-6 November 2009.

3   See in particular Recital 105 of the GDPR.

4   See the Council of Europe Convention on Access to Official Documents (CETS No. 205).

5   "the protection of personal data is of fundamental importance to a person's enjoyment of his or her right to respect for private and family life as guaranteed by Article 8" - *ECtHR MS v. Sweden*, (Application No. 20837/92),1997, paragraph 41.

6   See Council of Europe Commissioner on Human Rights, The rule of law on the Internet and in the wider digital world, Issue Paper, CommDH/IssuePaper(2014)1, 8 December 2014, p. 48, point 3.3 'Everyone' without discrimination.

7   See Court of Justice of the EU, *František Ryneš v. Úřad*, 11 December 2014, C-212/13k.

8   International organisations are defined as organisations governed by public international law.

9   Where the four Geneva Conventions of 1949, the Additional Protocols thereto of 1977, and the Statutes of the International Red Cross and Red Crescent Movement apply.

10   Recommendation No. R (97) 18 of the Committee of Ministers to member States, concerning the protection of personal data collected and processed for statistical purposes, Appendix, point 1, 30 September 1997.

11   Explanatory Memorandum to Recommendation No. R (97) 18 of the Committee of Ministers to member States, concerning the protection of personal data collected and processed for statistical purposes, paragraphs 11 and 14.

12   See Recommendation Rec No. (97)18 of the Committee of Ministers, op cit.

13   The relevant case law includes in particular the protection of state security and constitutional democracy from, *inter alia*, espionage, terrorism, support for terrorism and separatism. Where national security is at stake, safeguards against unfettered power must be provided. Relevant decisions of the European Court of Human Rights can be found at the Court's website (hudoc.echr.coe.int).

[14] For Parties that are Council of Europe member States, such requirements have been developed by the case law of the European Court of Human Rights under Article 8 of the ECHR (see in particular ECtHR, Roman Zakharov v. Russia (Application No. 47143/06), 4 December 2015, paragraph 233; Szabó and Vissy v. Hungary (Application No. 37138/14), 12 January 2016, paragraphs 75 et seq.).

[15] From the entry into force of the Amending Protocol, the Additional Protocol regarding supervisory authorities and transborder flows (ETS No. 181) shall be considered an integral part of the Convention as amended.

[16] From the entry into force of the Amending Protocol, the Additional Protocol regarding supervisory authorities and transborder flows (ETS No. 181) shall be considered an integral part of the Convention as amended.

[17] See footnote 14.

[18] The amendments to the Convention approved by the Committee of Ministers on 15 June 1999 lose their purpose from the entry into force of the Protocol.

CONVENTION FOR THE PROTECTION OF INDIVIDUALS WITH REGARD TO AUTOMATIC PROCESSING OF PERSONAL DATA – AS IT WILL BE AMENDED BY ITS PROTOCOL CETS 223

[3.31]

NOTES
© Council of Europe.

PREAMBLE

The member States of the Council of Europe, and the other signatories hereto,

Considering that the aim of the Council of Europe is to achieve greater unity between its members, based in particular on respect for the rule of law, as well as human rights and fundamental freedoms;

Considering that it is necessary to secure the human dignity and protection of the human rights and fundamental freedoms of every individual and, given the diversification, intensification and globalisation of data processing and personal data flows, personal autonomy based on a person's right to control of his or her personal data and the processing of such data;

Recalling that the right to protection of personal data is to be considered in respect of its role in society and that it has to be reconciled with other human rights and fundamental freedoms, including freedom of expression;

Considering that this Convention permits account to be taken, in the implementation of the rules laid down therein, of the principle of the right of access to official documents;

Recognising that it is necessary to promote at the global level the fundamental values of respect for privacy and protection of personal data, thereby contributing to the free flow of information between people;

Recognising the interest of a reinforcement of international co-operation between the Parties to the Convention,

Have agreed as follows:

CHAPTER I – GENERAL PROVISIONS

ARTICLE 1 – OBJECT AND PURPOSE

[3.32]
The purpose of this Convention is to protect every individual, whatever his or her nationality or residence, with regard to the processing of their personal data, thereby contributing to respect for his or her human rights and fundamental freedoms, and in particular the right to privacy.

ARTICLE 2 – DEFINITIONS

[3.33]
For the purposes of this Convention:
(a)   "personal data" means any information relating to an identified or identifiable individual ("data subject");
(b)   "data processing" means any operation or set of operations performed on personal data, such as the collection, storage, preservation, alteration, retrieval, disclosure, making available, erasure, or destruction of, or the carrying out of logical and/or arithmetical operations on such data;
(c)   Where automated processing is not used, "data processing" means an operation or set of operations performed upon personal data within a structured set of such data which are accessible or retrievable according to specific criteria;
(d)   "controller" means the natural or legal person, public authority, service, agency or any other body which, alone or jointly with others, has decision-making power with respect to data processing;
(e)   "recipient" means a natural or legal person, public authority, service, agency or any other body to whom data are disclosed or made available;
(f)   "processor" means a natural or legal person, public authority, service, agency or any other body which processes personal data on behalf of the controller.

ARTICLE 3 – SCOPE

[3.34]
1. Each Party undertakes to apply this Convention to data processing subject to its jurisdiction in the public and private sectors, thereby securing every individual's right to protection of his or her personal data.

2. This Convention shall not apply to data processing carried out by an individual in the course of purely personal or household activities.

CHAPTER II – BASIC PRINCIPLES FOR THE PROTECTION OF PERSONAL DATA

ARTICLE 4 – DUTIES OF THE PARTIES

[3.35]
1. Each Party shall take the necessary measures in its law to give effect to the provisions of this Convention and secure their effective application.

2. These measures shall be taken by each Party and shall have come into force by the time of ratification or of accession to this Convention.

3. Each Party undertakes:
(a)   to allow the Convention Committee provided for in Chapter VI to evaluate the effectiveness of the measures it has taken in its law to give effect to the provisions of this Convention; and
(b)   to contribute actively to this evaluation process.

ARTICLE 5 – LEGITIMACY OF DATA PROCESSING AND QUALITY OF DATA

[3.36]
1. Data processing shall be proportionate in relation to the legitimate purpose pursued and reflect at all stages of the processing a fair balance between all interests concerned, whether public or private, and the rights and freedoms at stake.

2. Each Party shall provide that data processing can be carried out on the basis of the free, specific, informed and unambiguous consent of the data subject or of some other legitimate basis laid down by law.

3. Personal data undergoing processing shall be processed lawfully.

4. Personal data undergoing processing shall be:
(a)   processed fairly and in a transparent manner; b. collected for explicit, specified and legitimate purposes and not processed in a way
(b)   collected for explicit, specified and legitimate purposes and not processed in a way incompatible with those purposes; further processing for archiving purposes in the public interest, scientific or historical research purposes or statistical purposes is, subject to appropriate safeguards, compatible with those purposes;
(c)   adequate, relevant and not excessive in relation to the purposes for which they are processed;
(d)   accurate and, where necessary, kept up to date;
(e)   preserved in a form which permits identification of data subjects for no longer than is necessary for the purposes for which those data are processed.

ARTICLE 6 – SPECIAL CATEGORIES OF DATA

[3.37]
1. The processing of:
–   genetic data;
–   personal data relating to offences, criminal proceedings and convictions, and related security measures;
–   biometric data uniquely identifying a person;
–   personal data for the information they reveal relating to racial or ethnic origin, political opinions, trade-union membership, religious or other beliefs, health or sexual life,

shall only be allowed where appropriate safeguards are enshrined in law, complementing those of this Convention.

2. Such safeguards shall guard against the risks that the processing of sensitive data may present for the interests, rights and fundamental freedoms of the data subject, notably a risk of discrimination.

ARTICLE 7 – DATA SECURITY

[3.38]
1. Each Party shall provide that the controller, and, where applicable the processor, takes appropriate security measures against risks such as accidental or unauthorised access to, destruction, loss, use, modification or disclosure of personal data.

2. Each Party shall provide that the controller notifies, without delay, at least the competent supervisory authority within the meaning of Article 15 of this Convention, of those data breaches which may seriously interfere with the rights and fundamental freedoms of data subjects.

ARTICLE 8 – TRANSPARENCY OF PROCESSING

[3.39]
1. Each Party shall provide that the controller informs the data subjects of:

(a)   his or her identity and habitual residence or establishment;
(b)   the legal basis and the purposes of the intended processing;
(c)   the categories of personal data processed;
(d)   the recipients or categories of recipients of the personal data, if any; and
(e)   the means of exercising the rights set out in Article 9,

as well as any necessary additional information in order to ensure fair and transparent processing of the personal data.

2.   Paragraph 1 shall not apply where the data subject already has the relevant information.

3.   Where the personal data are not collected from the data subjects, the controller shall not be required to provide such information where the processing is expressly prescribed by law or this proves to be impossible or involves disproportionate efforts.

ARTICLE 9 – RIGHTS OF THE DATA SUBJECT

[3.40]
1.   Every individual shall have a right:
(a)   not to be subject to a decision significantly affecting him or her based solely on an automated processing of data without having his or her views taken into consideration;
(b)   to obtain, on request, at reasonable intervals and without excessive delay or expense, confirmation of the processing of personal data relating to him or her, the communication in an intelligible form of the data processed, all available information on their origin, on the preservation period as well as any other information that the controller is required to provide in order to ensure the transparency of processing in accordance with Article 8, paragraph 1;
(c)   to obtain, on request, knowledge of the reasoning underlying data processing where the results of such processing are applied to him or her;
(d)   to object at any time, on grounds relating to his or her situation, to the processing of personal data concerning him or her unless the controller demonstrates legitimate grounds for the processing which override his or her interests or rights and fundamental freedoms;
(e)   to obtain, on request, free of charge and without excessive delay, rectification or erasure, as the case may be, of such data if these are being, or have been, processed contrary to the provisions of this Convention;
(f)   to have a remedy under Article 12 where his or her rights under this Convention have been violated;
(g)   to benefit, whatever his or her nationality or residence, from the assistance of a supervisory authority within the meaning of Article 15, in exercising his or her rights under this Convention.

2.   Paragraph 1.a shall not apply if the decision is authorised by a law to which the controller is subject and which also lays down suitable measures to safeguard the data subject's rights, freedoms and legitimate interests.

ARTICLE 10 – ADDITIONAL OBLIGATIONS

[3.41]
1.   Each Party shall provide that controllers and, where applicable, processors, take all appropriate measures to comply with the obligations of this Convention and be able to demonstrate, subject to the domestic legislation adopted in accordance with Article 11, paragraph 3, in particular to the competent supervisory authority provided for in Article 15, that the data processing under their control is in compliance with the provisions of this Convention.

2.   Each Party shall provide that controllers and, where applicable, processors, examine the likely impact of intended data processing on the rights and fundamental freedoms of data subjects prior to the commencement of such processing, and shall design the data processing in such a manner as to prevent or minimise the risk of interference with those rights and fundamental freedoms.

3.   Each Party shall provide that controllers, and, where applicable, processors, implement technical and organisational measures which take into account the implications of the right to the protection of personal data at all stages of the data processing.

4.   Each Party may, having regard to the risks arising for the interests, rights and fundamental freedoms of the data subjects, adapt the application of the provisions of paragraphs 1, 2 and 3 in the law giving effect to the provisions of this Convention, according to the nature and volume of the data, the nature, scope and purpose of the processing and, where appropriate, the size of the controller or processor.

ARTICLE 11 – EXCEPTIONS AND RESTRICTIONS

[3.42]
1.   No exception to the provisions set out in this Chapter shall be allowed except to the provisions of Article 5 paragraph 4, Article 7 paragraph 2, Article 8 paragraph 1 and Article 9, when such an exception is provided for by law, respects the essence of the fundamental rights and freedoms and constitutes a necessary and proportionate measure in a democratic society for:
(a)   the protection of national security, defense, public safety, important economic and financial interests of the State, the impartiality and independence of the judiciary or the prevention, investigation and prosecution of criminal offences and the execution of criminal penalties, and other essential objectives of general public interest;
(b)   the protection of the data subject or the rights and fundamental freedoms of others, notably freedom of expression.

2. Restrictions on the exercise of the provisions specified in Articles 8 and 9 may be provided for by law with respect to data processing for archiving purposes in the public interest, scientific or historical research purposes or statistical purposes when there is no recognisable risk of infringement of the rights and fundamental freedoms of data subjects.

3. In addition to the exceptions allowed for in paragraph 1 of this article, with reference to processing activities for national security and defense purposes, each Party may provide, by law and only to the extent that it constitutes a necessary and proportionate measure in a democratic society to fulfill such aim, exceptions to Article 4 paragraph 3, Article 14 paragraphs 5 and 6 and Article 15, paragraph 2, litterae a, b, c and d.

This is without prejudice to the requirement that processing activities for national security and defense purposes are subject to independent and effective review and supervision under the domestic legislation of the respective Party.

ARTICLE 12 – SANCTIONS AND REMEDIES

[3.43]
Each Party undertakes to establish appropriate judicial and non-judicial sanctions and remedies for violations of the provisions of this Convention.

ARTICLE 13 – EXTENDED PROTECTION

[3.44]
None of the provisions of this chapter shall be interpreted as limiting or otherwise affecting the possibility for a Party to grant data subjects a wider measure of protection than that stipulated in this Convention.

CHAPTER III – TRANSBORDER FLOWS OF PERSONAL DATA

ARTICLE 14 – TRANSBORDER FLOWS OF PERSONAL DATA

[3.45]
1. A Party shall not, for the sole purpose of the protection of personal data, prohibit or subject to special authorisation the transfer of such data to a recipient who is subject to the jurisdiction of another Party to the Convention. Such a Party may, however, do so if there is a real and serious risk that the transfer to another Party, or from that other Party to a non-Party, would lead to circumventing the provisions of the Convention. A Party may also do so, if bound by harmonised rules of protection shared by States belonging to a regional international organisation.

2. When the recipient is subject to the jurisdiction of a State or international organisation which is not Party to this Convention, the transfer of personal data may only take place where an appropriate level of protection based on the provisions of this Convention is secured.

3. An appropriate level of protection can be secured by:
(a)   the law of that State or international organisation, including the applicable international treaties or agreements; or
(b)   ad hoc or approved standardised safeguards provided by legally-binding and enforceable instruments adopted and implemented by the persons involved in the transfer and further processing.

4. Notwithstanding the provisions of the previous paragraphs, each Party may provide that the transfer of personal data may take place if:
(a)   the data subject has given explicit, specific and free consent, after being informed of risks arising in the absence of appropriate safeguards; or
(b)   the specific interests of the data subject require it in the particular case; or
(c)   prevailing legitimate interests, in particular important public interests, are provided for by law and such transfer constitutes a necessary and proportionate measure in a democratic society; or
(d)   it constitutes a necessary and proportionate measure in a democratic society for freedom of expression.

5. Each Party shall provide that the competent supervisory authority, within the meaning of Article 15 of this Convention, is provided with all relevant information concerning the transfers of data referred to in paragraph 3, littera b and, upon request, paragraph 4, litterae b and c.

6. Each Party shall also provide that the supervisory authority is entitled to request that the person who transfers data demonstrates the effectiveness of the safeguards or the existence of prevailing legitimate interests and that the supervisory authority may, in order to protect the rights and fundamental freedoms of data subjects, prohibit such transfers, suspend them or subject them to condition.

CHAPTER IV – SUPERVISORY AUTHORITIES

ARTICLE 15 – SUPERVISORY AUTHORITIES

[3.46]
1 Each Party shall provide for one or more authorities to be responsible for ensuring compliance with the provisions of this Convention.

2 To this end, such authorities:
(a)   shall have powers of investigation and intervention;

(b)   shall perform the functions relating to transfers of data provided for under Article 14, notably the approval of standardised safeguards;
(c)   shall have powers to issue decisions with respect to violations of the provisions of this Convention and may, in particular, impose administrative sanctions;
(d)   shall promote:
  (i)   public awareness of their functions and powers as well as their activities;
  (ii)   public awareness of the rights of data subjects and the exercise of such rights;
  (iii)   awareness of controllers and processors of their responsibilities under this

Convention;

specific attention shall be given to the data protection rights of children and other vulnerable individuals.

3.   The competent supervisory authorities shall be consulted on proposals for any legislative or administrative measures which provide for the processing of personal data.

4.   Each competent supervisory authority shall deal with requests and complaints lodged by data subjects concerning their data protection rights and shall keep data subjects informed of progress.

5.   The supervisory authorities shall act with complete independence and impartiality in performing their duties and exercising their powers and in doing so shall neither seek nor accept instructions.

6.   Each Party shall ensure that the supervisory authorities are provided with the resources necessary for the effective performance of their functions and exercise of their powers.

7.   Each supervisory authority shall prepare and publish a periodical report outlining its activities.

8.   Members and staff of the supervisory authorities shall be bound by obligations of confidentiality with regard to confidential information to which they have access, or have had access to, in the performance of their duties and exercise of their powers.

9.   Decisions of the supervisory authorities may be subject to appeal through the courts.

10.   The supervisory authorities shall not be competent with respect to processing carried out by bodies when acting in their judicial capacity.

CHAPTER V – CO-OPERATION AND MUTUAL ASSISTANCE

ARTICLE 16 – DESIGNATION OF SUPERVISORY AUTHORITIES

[3.47]
1.   The Parties agree to co-operate and render each other mutual assistance in order to implement this Convention.

2.   For that purpose:
(a)   each Party shall designate one or more supervisory authorities within the meaning of Article 15 of this Convention, the name and address of each of which it shall communicate to the Secretary General of the Council of Europe;
(b)   each Party which has designated more than one supervisory authority shall specify the competence of each authority in its communication referred to in the previous *littera*.

ARTICLE 17 – FORMS OF CO-OPERATION

[3.48]
1.   The supervisory authorities shall co-operate with one another to the extent necessary for the performance of their duties and exercise of their powers, in particular by:
(a)   providing mutual assistance by exchanging relevant and useful information and co-operating with each other under the condition that, as regards the protection of personal data, all the rules and safeguards of this Convention are complied with;
(b)   co-ordinating their investigations or interventions, or conducting joint actions;
(c)   providing information and documentation on their law and administrative practice relating to data protection.

2.   The information referred to in paragraph 1 shall not include personal data undergoing processing unless such data are essential for co-operation, or where the data subject concerned has given explicit, specific, free and informed consent to its provision.

3.   In order to organise their co-operation and to perform the duties set out in the preceding paragraphs, the supervisory authorities of the Parties shall form a network.

ARTICLE 18 – ASSISTANCE TO DATA SUBJECTS

[3.49]
1.   Each Party shall assist any data subject, whatever his or her nationality or residence, to exercise his or her rights under Article 9 of this Convention.

2.   Where a data subject resides on the territory of another Party, he or she shall be given the option of submitting the request through the intermediary of the supervisory authority designated by that Party.

3.   The request for assistance shall contain all the necessary particulars, relating *inter alia* to:
(a)   the name, address and any other relevant particulars identifying the data subject making the request;

Part 3   International Treaties

(b)   the processing to which the request pertains, or its controller;
(c)   the purpose of the request.

ARTICLE 19 – SAFEGUARDS

[3.50]
1. A supervisory authority which has received information from another supervisory authority, either accompanying a request or in reply to its own request, shall not use that information for purposes other than those specified in the request.

2. In no case may a supervisory authority be allowed to make a request on behalf of a data subject of its own accord and without the express approval of the data subject concerned.

ARTICLE 20 – REFUSAL OF REQUESTS

[3.51]
A supervisory authority to which a request is addressed under Article 17 of this Convention may not refuse to comply with it unless:
(a)   the request is not compatible with its powers;
(b)   the request does not comply with the provisions of this Convention; c. compliance with the request would be incompatible with the sovereignty, national
(c)   compliance with the request would be incompatible with the sovereignty, national security or public order of the Party by which it was designated, or with the rights and fundamental freedoms of individuals under the jurisdiction of that Party.

ARTICLE 21 – COSTS AND PROCEDURES

[3.52]
1. Co-operation and mutual assistance which the Parties render each other under Article 17 and assistance they render to data subjects under Articles 9 and 18 shall not give rise to the payment of any costs or fees other than those incurred for experts and interpreters. The latter costs or fees shall be borne by the Party making the request.

2. The data subject may not be charged costs or fees in connection with the steps taken on his or her behalf in the territory of another Party other than those lawfully payable by residents of that Party.

3. Other details concerning the co-operation and assistance, relating in particular to the forms and procedures and the languages to be used, shall be established directly between the Parties concerned.

CHAPTER VI – CONVENTION COMMITTEE

ARTICLE 22 – COMPOSITION OF THE COMMITTEE

[3.53]
1. A Convention Committee shall be set up after the entry into force of this Convention.

2. Each Party shall appoint a representative to the committee and a deputy representative. Any member State of the Council of Europe which is not a Party to the Convention shall have the right to be represented on the committee by an observer.

3. The Convention Committee may, by a decision taken by a majority of two-thirds of the representatives of the Parties, invite an observer to be represented at its meetings.

4. Any Party which is not a member of the Council of Europe shall contribute to the funding of the activities of the Convention Committee according to the modalities established by the Committee of Ministers in agreement with that Party.

ARTICLE 23 – FUNCTIONS OF THE COMMITTEE

[3.54]
The Convention Committee:
(a)   may make recommendations with a view to facilitating or improving the application of the Convention;
(b)   may make proposals for amendment of this Convention in accordance with Article 25;
(c)   shall formulate its opinion on any proposal for amendment of this Convention which is referred to it in accordance with Article 25, paragraph 3;
(d)   may express an opinion on any question concerning the interpretation or application of this Convention;
(e)   shall prepare, before any new accession to the Convention, an opinion for the Committee of Ministers relating to the level of personal data protection of the candidate for accession and, where necessary, recommend measures to take to reach compliance with the provisions of this Convention;
(f)   may, at the request of a State or an international organisation, evaluate whether the level of personal data protection the former provides is in compliance with the provisions of this Convention and, where necessary, recommend measures to be taken to reach such compliance;
(g)   may develop or approve models of standardised safeguards referred to in Article 14;
(h)   shall review the implementation of this Convention by the Parties and recommend measures to be taken in the case where a Party is not in compliance with this Convention;

(i)   shall facilitate, where necessary, the friendly settlement of all difficulties related to the application of this Convention.

ARTICLE 24 – PROCEDURE

[3.55]
1.   The Convention Committee shall be convened by the Secretary General of the Council of Europe. Its first meeting shall be held within twelve months of the entry into force of this Convention. It shall subsequently meet at least once a year, and in any case when one-third of the representatives of the Parties request its convocation.

2.   After each of its meetings, the Convention Committee shall submit to the Committee of Ministers of the Council of Europe a report on its work and on the functioning of this Convention.

3.   The voting arrangements in the Convention Committee are laid down in the elements for the Rules of Procedure appended to Protocol CETS No. [223].

4.   The Convention Committee shall draw up the other elements of its Rules of Procedure and establish, in particular, the procedures for evaluation and review referred to in Article 4, paragraph 3, and Article 23, litterae e, f and h on the basis of objective criteria.

CHAPTER VII – AMENDMENTS

ARTICLE 25 – AMENDMENTS

[3.56]
1.   Amendments to this Convention may be proposed by a Party, the Committee of Ministers of the Council of Europe or the Convention Committee.

2.   Any proposal for amendment shall be communicated by the Secretary General of the Council of Europe to the Parties to this Convention, to the other member States of the Council of Europe, to the European Union and to every non-member State or international organisation which has been invited to accede to this Convention in accordance with the provisions of Article 28.

3.   Moreover, any amendment proposed by a Party or the Committee of Ministers shall be communicated to the Convention Committee, which shall submit to the Committee of Ministers its opinion on that proposed amendment.

4.   The Committee of Ministers shall consider the proposed amendment and any opinion submitted by the Convention Committee and may approve the amendment.

5.   The text of any amendment approved by the Committee of Ministers in accordance with paragraph 4 of this article shall be forwarded to the Parties for acceptance.

6.   Any amendment approved in accordance with paragraph 4 of this article shall come into force on the thirtieth day after all Parties have informed the Secretary General of their acceptance thereof.

7.   Moreover, the Committee of Ministers may, after consulting the Convention Committee, decide unanimously that a particular amendment shall enter into force at the expiration of a period of three years from the date on which it has been opened to acceptance, unless a Party notifies the Secretary General of the Council of Europe of an objection to its entry into force. If such an objection is notified, the amendment shall enter into force on the first day of the month following the date on which the Party to this Convention which has notified the objection has deposited its instrument of acceptance with the Secretary General of the Council of Europe.

CHAPTER VIII – FINAL CLAUSES

ARTICLE 26 – ENTRY INTO FORCE

[3.57]
1.   This Convention shall be open for signature by the member States of the Council of Europe and by the European Union. It is subject to ratification, acceptance or approval. Instruments of ratification, acceptance or approval shall be deposited with the Secretary General of the Council of Europe.

2.   This Convention shall enter into force on the first day of the month following the expiration of a period of three months after the date on which five member States of the Council of Europe have expressed their consent to be bound by the Convention in accordance with the provisions of the preceding paragraph.

3.   In respect of any Party which subsequently expresses its consent to be bound by it, the Convention shall enter into force on the first day of the month following the expiration of a period of three months after the date of deposit of the instrument of ratification, acceptance or approval.

ARTICLE 27 – ACCESSION BY NON-MEMBER STATES OR INTERNATIONAL ORGANISATIONS

[3.58]
1.   After the entry into force of this Convention, the Committee of Ministers of the Council of Europe may, after consulting the Parties to this Convention and obtaining their unanimous agreement, and in light of the opinion prepared by the Convention Committee in accordance with Article 23.e, invite any State not a member of the Council of Europe or an international organisation to accede to

this Convention by a decision taken by the majority provided for in Article 20.d of the Statute of the Council of Europe and by the unanimous vote of the representatives of the Contracting States entitled to sit on the Committee of Ministers.

2. In respect of any State or international organisation acceding to this Convention according to paragraph 1 above, the Convention shall enter into force on the first day of the month following the expiration of a period of three months after the date of deposit of the instrument of accession with the Secretary General of the Council of Europe.

ARTICLE 28 – TERRITORIAL CLAUSE

[3.59]
1. Any State, the European Union or other international organisation may, at the time of signature or when depositing its instrument of ratification, acceptance, approval or accession, specify the territory or territories to which this Convention shall apply.

2. Any State, the European Union or other international organisation may, at any later date, by a declaration addressed to the Secretary General of the Council of Europe, extend the application of this Convention to any other territory specified in the declaration. In respect of such territory the Convention shall enter into force on the first day of the month following the expiration of a period of three months after the date of receipt of such declaration by the Secretary General.

3. Any declaration made under the two preceding paragraphs may, in respect of any territory specified in such declaration, be withdrawn by a notification addressed to the Secretary General. The withdrawal shall become effective on the first day of the month following the expiration of a period of six months after the date of receipt of such notification by the Secretary General.

ARTICLE 29 – RESERVATIONS

[3.60]
No reservation may be made in respect of the provisions of this Convention.

ARTICLE 30 – DENUNCIATION

[3.61]
1. Any Party may at any time denounce this Convention by means of a notification addressed to the Secretary General of the Council of Europe.

2. Such denunciation shall become effective on the first day of the month following the expiration of a period of six months after the date of receipt of the notification by the Secretary General.

ARTICLE 31 – NOTIFICATIONS

[3.62]
The Secretary General of the Council of Europe shall notify the member States of the Council and any Party to this Convention of:
(a)   any signature;
(b)   the deposit of any instrument of ratification, acceptance, approval or accession;
(c)   any date of entry into force of this Convention in accordance with Articles 26, 27 and 28;
(d)   any other act, notification or communication relating to this Convention.

PART 4
EPRIVACY – UK LAW

PRIVACY AND ELECTRONIC COMMUNICATIONS (EC DIRECTIVE) REGULATIONS 2003

(SI 2003/2426)

NOTES

Made: 18 September 2003.
Authority: European Communities Act 1972, s 2(2).
Commencement: 11 December 2003.

ARRANGEMENT OF REGULATIONS

SCHEDULES

[4.1]
1 Citation and commencement

These Regulations may be cited as the Privacy and Electronic Communications (EC Directive) Regulations 2003 and shall come into force on 11th December 2003.

[4.2]
2 Interpretation

(1) In these Regulations—

"bill" includes an invoice, account, statement or other document of similar character and "billing" shall be construed accordingly;

"call" means a connection established by means of a telephone service available to the public allowing two-way communication in real time;

"communication" means any information exchanged or conveyed between a finite number of parties by means of a public electronic communications service, but does not include information conveyed as part of a programme service, except to the extent that such information can be related to the identifiable subscriber or user receiving the information;

"communications provider" has the meaning given by section 405 of the Communications Act 2003;

["consent" by a user or subscriber corresponds to the data subject's consent in the GDPR (as defined in section 3(10) of the Data Protection Act 2018);]

"corporate subscriber" means a subscriber who is—

(a)   a company within the meaning of section 735(1) of the Companies Act 1985;

(b)   a company incorporated in pursuance of a royal charter or letters patent;

(c)   a partnership in Scotland;

(d)   a corporation sole; or

(e)   any other body corporate or entity which is a legal person distinct from its members;

"the Directive" means Directive 2002/58/EC of the European Parliament and of the Council of 12 July 2002 concerning the processing of personal data and the protection of privacy in the electronic communications sector (Directive on privacy and electronic communications);

"electronic communications network" has the meaning given by section 32 of the Communications Act 2003;

"electronic communications service" has the meaning given by section 32 of the Communications Act 2003;

"electronic mail" means any text, voice, sound or image message sent over a public electronic communications network which can be stored in the network or in the recipient's terminal equipment until it is collected by the recipient and includes messages sent using a short message service;

"enactment" includes an enactment comprised in, or in an instrument made under, an Act of the Scottish Parliament;

"individual" means a living individual and includes an unincorporated body of such individuals;

"the Information Commissioner" and "the Commissioner" both mean the Commissioner appointed under [the Data Protection Act 2018];

"information society service" has the meaning given in regulation 2(1) of the Electronic Commerce (EC Directive) Regulations 2002;

"location data" means any data processed in an electronic communications network [or by an electronic communications service] indicating the geographical position of the terminal equipment of a user of a public electronic communications service, including data relating to—

(f)   the latitude, longitude or altitude of the terminal equipment;

(g)   the direction of travel of the user; or

(h)   the time the location information was recorded;

"OFCOM" means the Office of Communications as established by section 1 of the Office of Communications Act 2002;

["personal data breach" means a breach of security leading to the accidental or unlawful destruction, loss, alteration, unauthorised disclosure of, or access to, personal data transmitted, stored or otherwise processed in connection with the provision of a public electronic communications service;]

"programme service" has the meaning given in section 201 of the Broadcasting Act 1990;

"public communications provider" means a provider of a public electronic communications network or a public electronic communications service;

"public electronic communications network" has the meaning given in section 151 of the Communications Act 2003;

"public electronic communications service" has the meaning given in section 151 of the Communications Act 2003;

"subscriber" means a person who is a party to a contract with a provider of public electronic communications services for the supply of such services;

"traffic data" means any data processed for the purpose of the conveyance of a communication on an electronic communications network or for the billing in respect of that communication and includes data relating to the routing, duration or time of a communication;

"user" means any individual using a public electronic communications service; and

"value added service" means any service which requires the processing of traffic data or location data beyond that which is necessary for the transmission of a communication or the billing in respect of that communication.

(2) Expressions used in these Regulations that are not defined in paragraph (1) and are defined in the Data Protection Act 1998 shall have the same meaning as in that Act.

(3)   . . .

(4) Any reference in these Regulations to a line shall, without prejudice to paragraph (3), be construed as including a reference to anything that performs the function of a line, and "connected", in relation to a line, is to be construed accordingly.

NOTES

Para (1): definition "consent" inserted by the Data Protection, Privacy and Electronic Communications (Amendments etc) (EU Exit) Regulations 2019, SI 2019/419, reg 8(1), (2); words in square brackets in definition "the Information Commissioner" substituted by the Data Protection Act 2018, s 211(1)(b), Sch 19, Pt 2, paras 291, 292; in definition "location data" words in square brackets inserted and definition "personal data breach" inserted by the Privacy and Electronic Communications (EC Directive) (Amendment) Regulations 2011, SI 2011/1208, regs 2, 3.

Para (3): revoked by SI 2019/419, reg 8(1), (3).

3 *(Revokes the Telecommunications (Data Protection and Privacy) Regulations 1999, SI 1999/2093, together with the amending SI 2000/157.)*

[4.3]
4   Relationship between these Regulations and [the data protection legislation]

[(1)] Nothing in these Regulations shall relieve a person of his obligations under [the data protection legislation] in relation to the processing of personal data.

[(2) In this regulation—
  "the data protection legislation" has the same meaning as in the Data Protection Act 2018 (see section 3 of that Act);
  "personal data" and "processing" have the same meaning as in Parts 5 to 7 of that Act (see section 3(2), (4) and (14) of that Act).

(3) Regulation 2(2) and (3) (meaning of certain expressions) do not apply for the purposes of this regulation.]

NOTES

Words in square brackets in heading substituted, original text renumbered as para (1), words in square brackets in para (1) substituted and paras (2), (3) added, by the Data Protection Act 2018, s 211(1)(b), Sch 19, Pt 2, paras 291, 293.

[4.4]
5   Security of public electronic communications services

(1) Subject to paragraph (2), a provider of a public electronic communications service ("the service provider") shall take appropriate technical and organisational measures to safeguard the security of that service.

[(1A) The measures referred to in paragraph (1) shall at least—
  (a) ensure that personal data can be accessed only by authorised personnel for legally authorised purposes;
  (b) protect personal data stored or transmitted against accidental or unlawful destruction, accidental loss or alteration, and unauthorised or unlawful storage, processing, access or disclosure; and
  (c) ensure the implementation of a security policy with respect to the processing of personal data.]

(2) If necessary, the measures required by paragraph (1) may be taken by the service provider in conjunction with the provider of the electronic communications network by means of which the service is provided, and that network provider shall comply with any reasonable requests made by the service provider for these purposes.

(3) Where, notwithstanding the taking of measures as required by paragraph (1), there remains a significant risk to the security of the public electronic communications service, the service provider shall inform the subscribers concerned of—
  (a) the nature of that risk;
  (b) any appropriate measures that the subscriber may take to safeguard against that risk; and
  (c) the likely costs to the subscriber involved in the taking of such measures.

(4) For the purposes of paragraph (1), a measure shall only be taken to be appropriate if, having regard to—
  (a) the state of technological developments, and
  (b) the cost of implementing it,
it is proportionate to the risks against which it would safeguard.

(5) Information provided for the purposes of paragraph (3) shall be provided to the subscriber free of any charge other than the cost to the subscriber of receiving or collecting the information.

[(6) The Information Commissioner may audit the measures taken by a provider of a public electronic communications service to safeguard the security of that service.]

NOTES

Paras (1A), (6): inserted by the Privacy and Electronic Communications (EC Directive) (Amendment) Regulations 2011, SI 2011/1208, regs 2, 4.

[4.5]
[5A   Personal data breach

(1) In this regulation and in regulations 5B and 5C, "service provider" has the meaning given in regulation 5(1).

(2) If a personal data breach occurs, the service provider shall, without undue delay, notify that breach to the Information Commissioner.

(3) Subject to paragraph (6), if a personal data breach is likely to adversely affect the personal data or privacy of a subscriber or user, the service provider shall also, without undue delay, notify that breach to the subscriber or user concerned.

(4) The notification referred to in paragraph (2) shall contain at least a description of—
  (a) the nature of the breach;

(b)   the consequences of the breach; and

(c)   the measures taken or proposed to be taken by the provider to address the breach.

(5) The notification referred to the paragraph (3) shall contain at least—

(a)   a description of the nature of the breach;

(b)   information about contact points within the service provider's organisation from which more information may be obtained; and

(c)   recommendations of measures to allow the subscriber to mitigate the possible adverse impacts of the breach.

(6) The notification referred to in paragraph (3) is not required if the service provider has demonstrated, to the satisfaction of the Information Commissioner that—

(a)   it has implemented appropriate technological protection measures which render the data unintelligible to any person who is not authorised to access it, and

(b)   that those measures were applied to the data concerned in that breach.

(7) If the service provider has not notified the subscriber or user in compliance with paragraph (3), the Information Commissioner may, having considered the likely adverse effects of the breach, require it to do so.

(8) Service providers shall maintain an inventory of personal data breaches comprising—

(a)   the facts surrounding the breach,

(b)   the effects of that breach, and

(c)   remedial action taken

which shall be sufficient to enable the Information Commissioner to verify compliance with the provisions of this regulation. The inventory shall only include information necessary for this purpose.

[(9) This regulation does not apply in relation to any personal data breach which is to be notified to the Investigatory Powers Commissioner in accordance with a code of practice made under the Investigatory Powers Act 2016.]]

NOTES

Inserted by the Privacy and Electronic Communications (EC Directive) (Amendment) Regulations 2011, SI 2011/1208, regs 2, 5.

Para (9): added by the Investigatory Powers Act 2016, s 271(1), Sch 10, Pt 1, para 14.

[4.6]
[5B   Personal data breach: audit

The Information Commissioner may audit the compliance of service providers with the provisions of regulation 5A.]

NOTES

Inserted by the Privacy and Electronic Communications (EC Directive) (Amendment) Regulations 2011, SI 2011/1208, regs 2, 5.

[4.7]
[5C   Personal data breach: enforcement

(1) If a service provider fails to comply with the notification requirements of regulation 5A, the Information Commissioner may issue a fixed monetary penalty notice in respect of that failure.

(2) The amount of a fixed monetary penalty under this regulation shall be £1,000.

(3) Before serving such a notice, the Information Commissioner must serve the service provider with a notice of intent.

(4) The notice of intent must—

(a)   state the name and address of the service provider;

(b)   state the nature of the breach;

(c)   indicate the amount of the fixed monetary penalty;

(d)   include a statement informing the service provider of the opportunity to discharge liability for the fixed monetary penalty;

(e)   indicate the date on which the Information Commissioner proposes to serve the fixed monetary penalty notice; and

(f)   inform the service provider that he may make written representations in relation to the proposal to serve a fixed monetary penalty notice within the period of 21 days from the service of the notice of intent.

(5) A service provider may discharge liability for the fixed monetary penalty if he pays to the Information Commissioner the amount of £800 within 21 days of receipt of the notice of intent.

(6) The Information Commissioner may not serve a fixed monetary penalty notice until the time within which representations may be made has expired.

(7) The fixed monetary penalty notice must state—

(a)   the name and address of the service provider;

(b)   details of the notice of intent served on the service provider;

(c)   whether there have been any written representations;

(d)   details of any early payment discounts;

(e)   the grounds on which the Information Commissioner imposes the fixed monetary penalty;

(f)   the date by which the fixed monetary penalty is to be paid; and

(g)   details of, including the time limit for, the service provider's right of appeal against the imposition of the fixed monetary penalty.

(8) A service provider on whom a fixed monetary penalty is served may appeal to the Tribunal against the issue of the fixed monetary penalty notice.

(9) Any sum received by the Information Commissioner by virtue of this regulation must be paid into the Consolidated Fund.

(10) In England and Wales and Northern Ireland, the penalty is recoverable—
- (a) if a county court so orders, as if it were payable under an order of that court;
- (b) if the High Court so orders, as if it were payable under an order of that court.

(11) In Scotland, the penalty may be enforced in the same manner as an extract registered decree arbitral bearing a warrant for execution issued by the sheriff court of any sheriffdom in Scotland.]

NOTES

Inserted by the Privacy and Electronic Communications (EC Directive) (Amendment) Regulations 2011, SI 2011/1208, regs 2, 5.

[4.8]
6 Confidentiality of communications

(1) Subject to paragraph (4), a person shall not [store or] gain access to information stored, in the terminal equipment of a subscriber or user unless the requirements of paragraph (2) are met.

(2) The requirements are that the subscriber or user of that terminal equipment—
- (a) is provided with clear and comprehensive information about the purposes of the storage of, or access to, that information; and
- [(b) has given his or her consent].

(3) Where an electronic communications network is used by the same person to store or access information in the terminal equipment of a subscriber or user on more than one occasion, it is sufficient for the purposes of this regulation that the requirements of paragraph (2) are met in respect of the initial use.

[(3A) For the purposes of paragraph (2), consent may be signified by a subscriber who amends or sets controls on the internet browser which the subscriber uses or by using another application or programme to signify consent.]

(4) Paragraph (1) shall not apply to the technical storage of, or access to, information—
- (a) for the sole purpose of carrying out . . . the transmission of a communication over an electronic communications network; or
- (b) where such storage or access is strictly necessary for the provision of an information society service requested by the subscriber or user.

NOTES

Para (1): words "store or" in square brackets substituted by the Privacy and Electronic Communications (EC Directive) (Amendment) Regulations 2011, SI 2011/1208, regs 2, 6(1), (2).

Para (2): sub-para (b) substituted by SI 2011/1208, regs 2, 6(1), (3).

Para (3A): inserted by SI 2011/1208, regs 2, 6(1), (4).

Para (4): in sub-para (a) words omitted revoked by SI 2011/1208, regs 2, 6(1), (5).

[4.9]
7 Restrictions on the processing of certain traffic data

(1) Subject to paragraphs (2) and (3), traffic data relating to subscribers or users which are processed and stored by a public communications provider shall, when no longer required for the purpose of the transmission of a communication, be—
- (a) erased;
- (b) in the case of an individual, modified so that they cease to constitute personal data of that subscriber or user; or
- (c) in the case of a corporate subscriber, modified so that they cease to be data that would be personal data if that subscriber was an individual.

(2) Traffic data held by a public communications provider for purposes connected with the payment of charges by a subscriber or in respect of interconnection payments may be processed and stored by that provider until the time specified in paragraph (5).

(3) Traffic data relating to a subscriber or user may be processed and stored by a provider of a public electronic communications service if—
- (a) such processing and storage are for the purpose of marketing electronic communications services, or for the provision of value added services to that subscriber or user; and
- (b) the subscriber or user to whom the traffic data relate has [previously notified the provider that he consents] to such processing or storage; and
- (c) such processing and storage are undertaken only for the duration necessary for the purposes specified in subparagraph (a).

(4) Where a user or subscriber has given his consent in accordance with paragraph (3), he shall be able to withdraw it at any time.

(5) The time referred to in paragraph (2) is the end of the period during which legal proceedings may be brought in respect of payments due or alleged to be due or, where such proceedings are brought within that period, the time when those proceedings are finally determined.

(6) Legal proceedings shall not be taken to be finally determined—
- (a) until the conclusion of the ordinary period during which an appeal may be brought by either party (excluding any possibility of an extension of that period, whether by order of a court or otherwise), if no appeal is brought within that period; or
- (b) if an appeal is brought, until the conclusion of that appeal.

(7) References in paragraph (6) to an appeal include references to an application for permission to appeal.

Part 4   ePrivacy: UK law

NOTES

Para (3): in sub-para (b) words in square brackets substituted by the Privacy and Electronic Communications (EC Directive) (Amendment) Regulations 2011, SI 2011/1208, regs 2, 7.

[4.10]

8 Further provisions relating to the processing of traffic data under regulation 7

(1) Processing of traffic data in accordance with regulation 7(2) or (3) shall not be undertaken by a public communications provider unless the subscriber or user to whom the data relate has been provided with information regarding the types of traffic data which are to be processed and the duration of such processing and, in the case of processing in accordance with regulation 7(3), he has been provided with that information before his consent has been obtained.

(2) Processing of traffic data in accordance with regulation 7 shall be restricted to what is required for the purposes of one or more of the activities listed in paragraph (3) and shall be carried out only by the public communications provider or by a person acting under his authority.

(3) The activities referred to in paragraph (2) are activities relating to—
   (a) the management of billing or traffic;
   (b) customer enquiries;
   (c) the prevention or detection of fraud;
   (d) the marketing of electronic communications services; or
   (e) the provision of a value added service.

(4) Nothing in these Regulations shall prevent the furnishing of traffic data to a person who is a competent authority for the purposes of any provision relating to the settling of disputes (by way of legal proceedings or otherwise) which is contained in, or made by virtue of, any enactment.

[4.11]

9 Itemised billing and privacy

(1) At the request of a subscriber, a provider of a public electronic communications service shall provide that subscriber with bills that are not itemised.

(2) OFCOM shall have a duty, when exercising their functions under Chapter 1 of Part 2 of the Communications Act 2003, to have regard to the need to reconcile the rights of subscribers receiving itemised bills with the rights to privacy of calling users and called subscribers, including the need for sufficient alternative privacy-enhancing methods of communications or payments to be available to such users and subscribers.

[4.12]

10 Prevention of calling line identification—outgoing calls

(1) This regulation applies, subject to regulations 15 and 16, to outgoing calls where a facility enabling the presentation of calling line identification is available.

(2) The provider of a public electronic communications service shall provide users originating a call by means of that service with a simple means to prevent presentation of the identity of the calling line on the connected line as respects that call.

(3) The provider of a public electronic communications service shall provide subscribers to the service, as respects their line and all calls originating from that line, with a simple means of preventing presentation of the identity of that subscriber's line on any connected line.

(4) The measures to be provided under paragraphs (2) and (3) shall be provided free of charge.

[4.13]

11 Prevention of calling or connected line identification—incoming calls

(1) This regulation applies to incoming calls.

(2) Where a facility enabling the presentation of calling line identification is available, the provider of a public electronic communications service shall provide the called subscriber with a simple means to prevent, free of charge for reasonable use of the facility, presentation of the identity of the calling line on the connected line.

(3) Where a facility enabling the presentation of calling line identification prior to the call being established is available, the provider of a public electronic communications service shall provide the called subscriber with a simple means of rejecting incoming calls where the presentation of the calling line identification has been prevented by the calling user or subscriber.

(4) Where a facility enabling the presentation of connected line identification is available, the provider of a public electronic communications service shall provide the called subscriber with a simple means to prevent, without charge, presentation of the identity of the connected line on any calling line.

(5) In this regulation "called subscriber" means the subscriber receiving a call by means of the service in question whose line is the called line (whether or not it is also the connected line).

[4.14]

12 Publication of information for the purposes of regulations 10 and 11

Where a provider of a public electronic communications service provides facilities for calling or connected line identification, he shall provide information to the public regarding the availability of such facilities, including information regarding the options to be made available for the purposes of regulations 10 and 11.

[4.15]
13   Co-operation of communications providers for the purposes of regulations 10 and 11

For the purposes of regulations 10 and 11, a communications provider shall comply with any reasonable requests made by the provider of the public electronic communications service by means of which facilities for calling or connected line identification are provided.

[4.16]
14   Restrictions on the processing of location data

(1) This regulation shall not apply to the processing of traffic data.

(2) Location data relating to a user or subscriber of a public electronic communications network or a public electronic communications service may only be processed—
  (a)   where that user or subscriber cannot be identified from such data; or
  (b)   where necessary for the provision of a value added service, with the consent of that user or subscriber.

(3) Prior to obtaining the consent of the user or subscriber under paragraph (2)(b), the public communications provider in question must provide the following information to the user or subscriber to whom the data relate—
  (a)   the types of location data that will be processed;
  (b)   the purposes and duration of the processing of those data; and
  (c)   whether the data will be transmitted to a third party for the purpose of providing the value added service.

(4) A user or subscriber who has given his consent to the processing of data under paragraph (2)(b) shall—
  (a)   be able to withdraw such consent at any time, and
  (b)   in respect of each connection to the public electronic communications network in question or each transmission of a communication, be given the opportunity to withdraw such consent, using a simple means and free of charge.

(5) Processing of location data in accordance with this regulation shall—
  (a)   only be carried out by
      (i)   the public communications provider in question;
      (ii)   the third party providing the value added service in question; or
      (iii) a person acting under the authority of a person falling within (i) or (ii); and
  (b)   where the processing is carried out for the purposes of the provision of a value added service, be restricted to what is necessary for those purposes.

[4.17]
15   Tracing of malicious or nuisance calls

(1) A communications provider may override anything done to prevent the presentation of the identity of a calling line where—
  (a)   a subscriber has requested the tracing of malicious or nuisance calls received on his line; and
  (b)   the provider is satisfied that such action is necessary and expedient for the purposes of tracing such calls.

(2) Any term of a contract for the provision of public electronic communications services which relates to such prevention shall have effect subject to the provisions of paragraph (1).

(3) Nothing in these Regulations shall prevent a communications provider, for the purposes of any action relating to the tracing of malicious or nuisance calls, from storing and making available to a person with a legitimate interest data containing the identity of a calling subscriber which were obtained while paragraph (1) applied.

[4.18]
16   Emergency calls

(1) For the purposes of this regulation, "emergency calls" means calls to either the national emergency call number 999 or the single European emergency call number 112.

(2) In order to facilitate responses to emergency calls—
  (a)   all such calls shall be excluded from the requirements of regulation 10;
  (b)   no person shall be entitled to prevent the presentation on the connected line of the identity of the calling line; and
  (c)   the restriction on the processing of location data under regulation 14(2) shall be disregarded.

[4.19]
[16A   Emergency alerts

(1) A relevant public communications provider (P) may, for the purpose of providing an emergency alert service, disregard the restrictions on the processing of data relating to users or subscribers set out in paragraph (2) if the conditions set out in paragraph (3) are met.

(2) The restrictions are—
  (a)   the restrictions on the processing of traffic data under regulations 7(1) and 8(2); and
  (b)   the restrictions on the processing of location data under regulations 14(2) and 14(5).

(3) The conditions are—
  (a)   P is notified by a relevant public authority that—
      (i)   an emergency within the meaning of section 1(1) of the Civil Contingencies Act 2004 has occurred, is occurring or is about to occur; and
      (ii)   it is expedient to use an emergency alert service;
  (b)   P is directed by the relevant public authority to convey a specified communication over a specified time period to users or subscribers of P's public electronic communications network whom P considers—
      (i)   are in one or more specified places in the United Kingdom which is or may be affected by the emergency; or

      (ii)   have been in a specified place affected by the emergency since the emergency occurred but are no longer in the place; and

  (c) P complies with that direction.

(4) P may, for the purpose of testing an emergency alert service, disregard the restrictions on the processing of data relating to users or subscribers set out in paragraph (2) if the conditions set out in paragraph (5) are met.

(5) The conditions are—

  (a) P is notified by a Minister of the Crown that, in the Minister's opinion, it is necessary to test an emergency alert service for the purpose of ensuring that the service is maintained in good working order and is an effective means of communicating with users and subscribers in an emergency;

  (b) the Minister gives directions as to how the test is to be conducted; and

  (c) P complies with the directions in sub-paragraph (b).

(6) Traffic data or location data which relate to users or subscribers of a public electronic communications network and are processed in accordance with this regulation must, within 7 days of the expiry of the time period specified by the relevant public authority pursuant to paragraph (3)(b) or, as the case may be, within 48 hours of receipt of the Minister's directions pursuant to paragraph (5)(b), be—

  (a) erased; or

  (b)

      (i)   in the case of an individual, modified so that they cease to constitute personal data of that user or subscriber; or

      (ii)   in the case of a corporate subscriber, modified so that they cease to be data that would be personal data if that user or subscriber was an individual.

(7) The processing of traffic data or location data in accordance with this regulation shall be carried out only by P or by a person acting under P's authority.

(8) For the purposes of this regulation—

  (a) "emergency alert service" means a service comprising one or more communications to mobile telecommunications devices over a public electronic communications network to warn, advise or inform users or subscribers in relation to an aspect or effect of an emergency which may affect or have affected them by reason of their location;

  (b) "relevant public authority" means—

      (i)   a Minister of the Crown;

      (ii)   the Scottish Ministers;

      (iii) the Welsh Ministers;

      (iv) a Northern Ireland department;

      (v)   a chief officer of police within the meaning of section 101(1) of the Police Act 1996;

      (vi) the chief constable of the Police Service of Scotland;

      (vii) the chief constable of the Police Service of Northern Ireland;

      (viii) the chief constable of the British Transport Police Force;

      (ix) the Environment Agency;

      (x)   the Scottish Environment Protection Agency;

      (xi) the Natural Resources Body for Wales;

  (c) "relevant public communications provider" means a person who—

      (i)   provides a public electronic communications network;

      (ii)   provides cellular mobile electronic communications services; and

      (iii) holds a wireless telegraphy licence granted under section 8 of the Wireless Telegraphy Act 2006.]

NOTES

Inserted by the Privacy and Electronic Communications (EC Directive) (Amendment) Regulations 2015, SI 2015/355, reg 2(1), (2).

[4.20]

17 Termination of automatic call forwarding

(1) Where—

  (a) calls originally directed to another line are being automatically forwarded to a subscriber's line as a result of action taken by a third party, and

  (b) the subscriber requests his provider of electronic communications services ("the subscriber's provider") to stop the forwarding of those calls,

the subscriber's provider shall ensure, free of charge, that the forwarding is stopped without any avoidable delay.

(2) For the purposes of paragraph (1), every other communications provider shall comply with any reasonable requests made by the subscriber's provider to assist in the prevention of that forwarding.

[4.21]

18 Directories of subscribers

(1) This regulation applies in relation to a directory of subscribers, whether in printed or electronic form, which is made available to members of the public or a section of the public, including by means of a directory enquiry service.

(2) The personal data of an individual subscriber shall not be included in a directory unless that subscriber has, free of charge, been—

  (a) informed by the collector of the personal data of the purposes of the directory in which his personal data are to be included, and

  (b) given the opportunity to determine whether such of his personal data as are considered relevant by the producer of the directory should be included in the directory.

(3) Where personal data of an individual subscriber are to be included in a directory with facilities which enable users of that directory to obtain access to that data solely on the basis of a telephone number—
    (a)   the information to be provided under paragraph (2)(a) shall include information about those facilities; and
    (b)   for the purposes of paragraph (2)(b), the express consent of the subscriber to the inclusion of his data in a directory with such facilities must be obtained.

(4) Data relating to a corporate subscriber shall not be included in a directory where that subscriber has advised the producer of the directory that it does not want its data to be included in that directory.

(5) Where the data of an individual subscriber have been included in a directory, that subscriber shall, without charge, be able to verify, correct or withdraw those data at any time.

(6) Where a request has been made under paragraph (5) for data to be withdrawn from or corrected in a directory, that request shall be treated as having no application in relation to an edition of a directory that was produced before the producer of the directory received the request.

(7) For the purposes of paragraph (6), an edition of a directory which is revised after it was first produced shall be treated as a new edition.

(8) In this regulation, "telephone number" has the same meaning as in section 56(5) of the Communications Act 2003 but does not include any number which is used as an internet domain name, an internet address or an address or identifier incorporating either an internet domain name or an internet address, including an electronic mail address.

[4.22]
19   Use of automated calling systems
(1) A person shall neither transmit, nor instigate the transmission of, communications comprising recorded matter for direct marketing purposes by means of an automated calling [or communication] system except in the circumstances referred to in paragraph (2).

[(2) Those circumstances are where—
    (a)   the called line is that of a subscriber who has previously notified the caller that for the time being he consents to such communications being sent by, or at the instigation of, the caller on that line, and
    (b)   the person transmitting, or instigating the transmission of, such communications—
        (i)   does not prevent presentation of the identity of the calling line on the called line; or
        (ii)   presents the identity of a line on which he can be contacted.]

(3) A subscriber shall not permit his line to be used in contravention of paragraph (1).

(4) For the purposes of this regulation, an automated calling system is a system which is capable of—
    (a)   automatically initiating a sequence of calls to more than one destination in accordance with instructions stored in that system; and
    (b)   transmitting sounds which are not live speech for reception by persons at some or all of the destinations so called.

NOTES
    Para (1): words in square brackets inserted by the Privacy and Electronic Communications (EC Directive) (Amendment) Regulations 2011, SI 2011/1208, regs 2, 8.
    Para (2): substituted by the Privacy and Electronic Communications (EC Directive) (Amendment) Regulations 2016, SI 2016/524, reg 2(1), (2).

[4.23]
20   Use of facsimile machines for direct marketing purposes
(1) A person shall neither transmit, nor instigate the transmission of, unsolicited communications for direct marketing purposes by means of a facsimile machine where the called line is that of—
    (a)   an individual subscriber, except in the circumstances referred to in paragraph (2);
    (b)   a corporate subscriber who has previously notified the caller that such communications should not be sent on that line; or
    (c)   a subscriber and the number allocated to that line is listed in the register kept under regulation 25.

(2) The circumstances referred to in paragraph (1)(a) are that the individual subscriber has previously notified the caller that he consents for the time being to such communications being sent by, or at the instigation of, the caller.

(3) A subscriber shall not permit his line to be used in contravention of paragraph (1).

(4) A person shall not be held to have contravened paragraph (1)(c) where the number allocated to the called line has been listed on the register for less than 28 days preceding that on which the communication is made.

(5) Where a subscriber who has caused a number allocated to a line of his to be listed in the register kept under regulation 25 has notified a caller that he does not, for the time being, object to such communications being sent on that line by that caller, such communications may be sent by that caller on that line, notwithstanding that the number allocated to that line is listed in the said register.

(6) Where a subscriber has given a caller notification pursuant to paragraph (5) in relation to a line of his—
    (a)   the subscriber shall be free to withdraw that notification at any time, and
    (b)   where such notification is withdrawn, the caller shall not send such communications on that line.

(7) The provisions of this regulation are without prejudice to the provisions of regulation 19.

[4.24]
21   [Calls for direct marketing purposes]
[(A1) A person shall neither use, nor instigate the use of, a public electronic communications service for the purposes of making calls (whether solicited or unsolicited) for direct marketing purposes except where that person—
    (a)   does not prevent presentation of the identity of the calling line on the called line; or
    (b)   presents the identity of a line on which he can be contacted.]

(1) A person shall neither use, nor instigate the use of, a public electronic communications service for the purposes of making unsolicited calls for direct marketing purposes where—

    (a) the called line is that of a subscriber who has previously notified the caller that such calls should not for the time being be made on that line; or

    (b) the number allocated to a subscriber in respect of the called line is one listed in the register kept under regulation 26.

(2) A subscriber shall not permit his line to be used in contravention of [paragraphs (A1) or (1)].

(3) A person shall not be held to have contravened paragraph (1)(b) where the number allocated to the called line has been listed on the register for less than 28 days preceding that on which the call is made.

(4) Where a subscriber who has caused a number allocated to a line of his to be listed in the register kept under regulation 26 has notified a caller that he does not, for the time being, object to such calls being made on that line by that caller, such calls may be made by that caller on that line, notwithstanding that the number allocated to that line is listed in the said register.

(5) Where a subscriber has given a caller notification pursuant to paragraph (4) in relation to a line of his—

    (a) the subscriber shall be free to withdraw that notification at any time, and

    (b) where such notification is withdrawn, the caller shall not make such calls on that line.

[(6) Paragraph (1) does not apply to a case falling within regulation 21A [or 21B].]

NOTES

Provision heading: words in square brackets substituted by the Privacy and Electronic Communications (EC Directive) (Amendment) Regulations 2016, SI 2016/524, reg 2(1), (3)(c).

Para (A1): inserted by SI 2016/524, reg 2(1), (3)(a).

Para (2): words in square brackets substituted by SI 2016/524, reg 2(1), (3)(b).

Para (6): added by the Financial Guidance and Claims Act 2018, s 35(1), (2); words in square brackets inserted by the Privacy and Electronic Communications (Amendment) (No 2) Regulations 2018, SI 2018/1396, reg 2(1), (2).

[4.25]
[21A Calls for direct marketing of claims management services

(1) A person must not use, or instigate the use of, a public electronic communications service to make unsolicited calls for the purposes of direct marketing in relation to claims management services except in the circumstances referred to in paragraph (2).

(2) Those circumstances are where the called line is that of a subscriber who has previously notified the caller that for the time being the subscriber consents to such calls being made by, or at the instigation of, the caller on that line.

(3) A subscriber must not permit the subscriber's line to be used in contravention of paragraph (1).

(4) In this regulation, "claims management services" means the following services in relation to the making of a claim—

    (a) advice;

    (b) financial services or assistance;

    (c) acting on behalf of, or representing, a person;

    (d) the referral or introduction of one person to another;

    (e) the making of inquiries.

(5) In paragraph (4), "claim" means a claim for compensation, restitution, repayment or any other remedy or relief in respect of loss or damage or in respect of an obligation, whether the claim is made or could be made—

    (a) by way of legal proceedings,

    (b) in accordance with a scheme of regulation (whether voluntary or compulsory), or

    (c) in pursuance of a voluntary undertaking.]

NOTES

Commencement: 8 September 2018.

Inserted by the Financial Guidance and Claims Act 2018, s 35(1), (3).

[4.26]
[21B Calls for direct marketing in relation to pension schemes

(1) A person must not use, or instigate the use of, a public electronic communications service to make unsolicited calls to an individual for the purpose of direct marketing in relation to occupational pension schemes or personal pension schemes, except where paragraph (2) or (3) applies.

(2) This paragraph applies where—

    (a) the caller is an authorised person or a person who is the trustee or manager of an occupational pension scheme or a personal pension scheme; and

    (b) the called line is that of an individual who has previously notified the caller that for the time being the individual consents to such calls being made by the caller on that line.

(3) This paragraph applies where—

    (a) the caller is an authorised person or a person who is the trustee or manager of an occupational pension scheme or a personal pension scheme;

    (b) the recipient of the call has an existing client relationship with the caller on the line and the relationship is such that the recipient might reasonably envisage receiving unsolicited calls for the purpose of direct marketing in relation to occupational pension schemes or personal pension schemes; and

(c)   the recipient of the call has been given a simple means of refusing (free of charge except for the costs of the transmission of the refusal) the use of the recipient's contact details for the purpose of such direct marketing, at the time that the details were initially collected and, where the recipient did not initially refuse the use of the details, at the time of each subsequent communication.

(4) A subscriber must not permit the subscriber's line to be used in contravention of paragraph (1).

(5) In this regulation—

(a)   "authorised person" has the meaning given in section 31 of the Financial Services and Markets Act 2000;

(b)   "direct marketing in relation to occupational pension schemes or personal pension schemes" includes—

    (i)   the marketing of a product or service to be acquired using funds held, or previously held, in an occupational pension scheme or a personal pension scheme,

    (ii)   the offer of any advice or other service that promotes, or promotes the consideration of, the withdrawal or transfer of funds from an occupational pension scheme or a personal pension scheme, and

    (iii)   the offer of any advice or other service to enable the assessment of the performance of an occupational pension scheme or a personal pension scheme (including its performance in comparison with other forms of investment);

(c)   "existing client relationship" does not include a relationship established at the instigation of the caller primarily for the purpose of avoiding the restriction in paragraph (1); and

(d)   "occupational pension scheme" and "personal pension scheme" have the meanings given in section 1(1) of the Pension Schemes Act 1993.]

NOTES

Commencement: 9 January 2019.

Inserted by the Privacy and Electronic Communications (Amendment) (No 2) Regulations 2018, SI 2018/1396, reg 2(1), (3).

[4.27]

22   Use of electronic mail for direct marketing purposes

(1) This regulation applies to the transmission of unsolicited communications by means of electronic mail to individual subscribers.

(2) Except in the circumstances referred to in paragraph (3), a person shall neither transmit, nor instigate the transmission of, unsolicited communications for the purposes of direct marketing by means of electronic mail unless the recipient of the electronic mail has previously notified the sender that he consents for the time being to such communications being sent by, or at the instigation of, the sender.

(3) A person may send or instigate the sending of electronic mail for the purposes of direct marketing where—

(a)   that person has obtained the contact details of the recipient of that electronic mail in the course of the sale or negotiations for the sale of a product or service to that recipient;

(b)   the direct marketing is in respect of that person's similar products and services only; and

(c)   the recipient has been given a simple means of refusing (free of charge except for the costs of the transmission of the refusal) the use of his contact details for the purposes of such direct marketing, at the time that the details were initially collected, and, where he did not initially refuse the use of the details, at the time of each subsequent communication.

(4) A subscriber shall not permit his line to be used in contravention of paragraph (2).

[4.28]

23   Use of electronic mail for direct marketing purposes where the identity or address of the sender is concealed

A person shall neither transmit, nor instigate the transmission of, a communication for the purposes of direct marketing by means of electronic mail—

(a)   where the identity of the person on whose behalf the communication has been sent has been disguised or concealed; . . .

(b)   where a valid address to which the recipient of the communication may send a request that such communications cease has not been provided;

[(c)   where that electronic mail would contravene regulation 7 of the Electronic Commerce (EC Directive) Regulations 2002; or

(d)   where that electronic mail encourages recipients to visit websites which contravene that regulation].

NOTES

Word omitted from para (a) revoked and paras (c), (d) inserted, by the Privacy and Electronic Communications (EC Directive) (Amendment) Regulations 2011, SI 2011/1208, regs 2, 9.

[4.29]

24   Information to be provided for the purposes of regulations 19 [to 21A]

(1) Where a public electronic communications service is used for the transmission of a communication for direct marketing purposes the person using, or instigating the use of, the service shall ensure that the following information is provided with that communication—

(a)   in relation to a communication to which regulations 19 (automated calling systems) and 20 (facsimile machines) apply, the particulars mentioned in paragraph (2)(a) and (b);

(b)   in relation to a communication to which regulation 21 [or 21A] (telephone calls) applies, the particulars mentioned in paragraph (2)(a) and, if the recipient of the call so requests, those mentioned in paragraph (2)(b).

(2) The particulars referred to in paragraph (1) are—

(a)   the name of the person;

(b) either the address of the person or a telephone number on which he can be reached free of charge.

NOTES

Provision heading: words in square brackets substituted by the Financial Guidance and Claims Act 2018, s 35(1), (4)(a).

Para (1): in sub-para (b) words in square brackets inserted by the Financial Guidance and Claims Act 2018, s 35(1), (4)(b).

[4.30]

25 Register to be kept for the purposes of regulation 20

(1) For the purposes of regulation 20 [the Commissioner] shall maintain and keep up-to-date, in printed or electronic form, a register of the numbers allocated to subscribers, in respect of particular lines, who have notified [the Commissioner or, prior to 30th December 2016, OFCOM] (notwithstanding, in the case of individual subscribers, that they enjoy the benefit of regulation 20(1)(a) and (2)) that they do not for the time being wish to receive unsolicited communications for direct marketing purposes by means of facsimile machine on the lines in question.

(2) [The Commissioner] shall remove a number from the register maintained under paragraph (1) where [the Commissioner has] reason to believe that it has ceased to be allocated to the subscriber by whom [the Commissioner was or, prior to 30th December 2016, OFCOM were] notified pursuant to paragraph (1).

(3) On the request of—
   (a) a person wishing to send, or instigate the sending of, such communications as are mentioned in paragraph (1), or
   (b) a subscriber wishing to permit the use of his line for the sending of such communications,
for information derived from the register kept under paragraph (1), [the Commissioner] shall, unless it is not reasonably practicable so to do, on the payment to [the Commissioner] of such fee as is, subject to paragraph (4), required by [the Commissioner], make the information requested available to that person or that subscriber.

(4) For the purposes of paragraph (3) [the Commissioner] may require different fees—
   (a) for making available information derived from the register in different forms or manners, or
   (b) for making available information derived from the whole or from different parts of the register,
but the fees required by [the Commissioner] shall be ones in relation to which the Secretary of State has notified [the Commissioner] that he is satisfied that they are designed to secure, as nearly as may be and taking one year with another, that the aggregate fees received, or reasonably expected to be received, equal the costs incurred, or reasonably expected to be incurred, by [the Commissioner] in discharging [the Commissioner's] duties under paragraphs (1), (2) and (3).

(5) The functions of [the Commissioner] under paragraphs (1), (2) and (3), other than the function of determining the fees to be required for the purposes of paragraph (3), may be discharged on [the Commissioner's] behalf by some other person in pursuance of arrangements made by [the Commissioner] with that other person.

NOTES

Paras (1)–(5): words in square brackets in each place substituted by the Privacy and Electronic Communications (EC Directive) (Amendment) (No 2) Regulations 2016, SI 2016/1177, reg 2.

[4.31]

26 Register to be kept for the purposes of regulation 21

(1) For the purposes of regulation 21 [the Commissioner] shall maintain and keep up-to-date, in printed or electronic form, a register of the numbers allocated to . . . subscribers, in respect of particular lines, who have notified [the Commissioner or, prior to 30th December 2016, OFCOM] that they do not for the time being wish to receive unsolicited calls for direct marketing purposes on the lines in question.

[(1A) Notifications to [the Commissioner] made for the purposes of paragraph (1) by corporate subscribers shall be in writing.]

(2) [The Commissioner] shall remove a number from the register maintained under paragraph (1) where [the Commissioner has] reason to believe that it has ceased to be allocated to the subscriber by whom [the Commissioner was or, prior to 30th December 2016, OFCOM were] notified pursuant to paragraph (1).

[(2A) Where a number allocated to a corporate subscriber is listed in the register maintained under paragraph (1), [the Commissioner] shall, within the period of 28 days following each anniversary of the date of that number being first listed in the register, send to the subscriber a written reminder that the number is listed in the register.]

(3) On the request of—
   (a) a person wishing to make, or instigate the making of, such calls as are mentioned in paragraph (1), or
   (b) a subscriber wishing to permit the use of his line for the making of such calls,
for information derived from the register kept under paragraph (1), [the Commissioner] shall, unless it is not reasonably practicable so to do, on the payment to [the Commissioner] of such fee as is, subject to paragraph (4), required by [the Commissioner], make the information requested available to that person or that subscriber.

(4) For the purposes of paragraph (3) [the Commissioner] may require different fees—
   (a) for making available information derived from the register in different forms or manners, or
   (b) for making available information derived from the whole or from different parts of the register,
but the fees required by [the Commissioner] shall be ones in relation to which the Secretary of State has notified [the Commissioner] that he is satisfied that they are designed to secure, as nearly as may be and taking one year with another, that the aggregate fees received, or reasonably expected to be received, equal the costs incurred, or reasonably expected to be incurred, by [the Commissioner] in discharging [the Commissioner's] duties under paragraphs (1), (2) and (3).

(5) The functions of [the Commissioner] under paragraphs (1), (2)[, (2A)] and (3), other than the function of determining the fees to be required for the purposes of paragraph (3), may be discharged on [the Commissioner's] behalf by some other person in pursuance of arrangements made by [the Commissioner] with that other person.

NOTES

Para (1): words in square brackets substituted by the Privacy and Electronic Communications (EC Directive) (Amendment) (No 2) Regulations 2016, SI 2016/1177, reg 2; word omitted revoked by the Privacy and Electronic Communications (EC Directive) (Amendment) Regulations 2004, SI 2004/1039, reg 2(1), (2).

Para (1A): inserted by SI 2004/1039, reg 2(1), (3); words in square brackets substituted by SI 2016/1177, reg 2.

Para (2): words in square brackets substituted by SI 2016/1177, reg 2.

Para (2A): inserted by SI 2004/1039, reg 2(1), (4); words in square brackets substituted by SI 2016/1177, reg 2.

Paras (3), (4): words in square brackets substituted by SI 2016/1177, reg 2.

Para (5): words in square brackets substituted by SI 2016/1177, reg 2; reference to ", (2A)" in square brackets inserted by SI 2004/1039, reg 2(1), (5).

[4.32]
27 Modification of contracts

To the extent that any term in a contract between a subscriber to and the provider of a public electronic communications service or such a provider and the provider of an electronic communications network would be inconsistent with a requirement of these Regulations, that term shall be void.

[4.33]
28 National security

(1) Nothing in these Regulations shall require a communications provider to do, or refrain from doing, anything (including the processing of data) if exemption from the requirement in question is required for the purpose of safeguarding national security.

(2) Subject to paragraph (4), a certificate signed by a Minister of the Crown certifying that exemption from any requirement of these Regulations is or at any time was required for the purpose of safeguarding national security shall be conclusive evidence of that fact.

(3) A certificate under paragraph (2) may identify the circumstances in which it applies by means of a general description and may be expressed to have prospective effect.

(4) Any person directly affected by the issuing of a certificate under paragraph (2) may appeal to the Tribunal against the issuing of the certificate.

(5) If, on an appeal under paragraph (4), the Tribunal finds that, applying the principles applied by a court on an application for judicial review, the Minister did not have reasonable grounds for issuing the certificate, the Tribunal may allow the appeal and quash the certificate.

(6) Where, in any proceedings under or by virtue of these Regulations, it is claimed by a communications provider that a certificate under paragraph (2) which identifies the circumstances in which it applies by means of a general description applies in the circumstances in question, any other party to the proceedings may appeal to the Tribunal on the ground that the certificate does not apply in those circumstances and, subject to any determination under paragraph (7), the certificate shall be conclusively presumed so to apply.

(7) On any appeal under paragraph (6), the Tribunal may determine that the certificate does not so apply.

(8) In this regulation—
  [(a) "the Tribunal", in relation to any appeal under this regulation, means—
      (i)   the Upper Tribunal, in any case where it is determined by or under Tribunal Procedure Rules that the Upper Tribunal is to hear the appeal; or
      (ii)   the First-tier Tribunal, in any other case;]
  (b) Subsections (8), (9), (10) and (12) of section 28 of and Schedule 6 to that Act apply for the purposes of this regulation as they apply for the purposes of section 28;
  (c) section 58 of that Act shall apply for the purposes of this regulation as if the reference in that section to the functions of the Tribunal under that Act included a reference to the functions of the Tribunal under paragraphs (4) to (7) of this regulation; and
  (d) subsections (1), (2) and (5)(f) of section 67 of that Act shall apply in respect of the making of rules relating to the functions of the Tribunal under this regulation.

NOTES

Para (8): sub-para (a) substituted by the Transfer of Tribunal Functions Order 2010, SI 2010/22, art 5(2), Sch 3, para 40.

[4.34]
29 Legal requirements, law enforcement etc

(1) Nothing in these Regulations shall require a communications provider to do, or refrain from doing, anything (including the processing of data)—
  (a) if compliance with the requirement in question—
      (i)   would be inconsistent with any requirement imposed by or under an enactment or by a court order; or
      (ii)   would be likely to prejudice the prevention or detection of crime or the apprehension or prosecution of offenders; or
  (b) if exemption from the requirement in question—
      (i)   is required for the purposes of, or in connection with, any legal proceedings (including prospective legal proceedings);
      (ii)   is necessary for the purposes of obtaining legal advice; or
      (iii) is otherwise necessary for the purposes of establishing, exercising or defending legal rights.

[4.35]
[29A

(1) Where regulations 28 and 29 apply, communications providers must establish and maintain internal procedures for responding to requests for access to users' personal data.

(2) Communications providers shall on demand provide the Information Commissioner with information about—
  (a) those procedures;
  (b) the number of requests received;
  (c) the legal justification for the request; and
  (d) the communications provider's response.]

NOTES
  Inserted by the Privacy and Electronic Communications (EC Directive) (Amendment) Regulations 2011, SI 2011/1208, regs 2, 10.

[4.36]
30 Proceedings for compensation for failure to comply with requirements of the Regulations

(1) A person who suffers damage by reason of any contravention of any of the requirements of these Regulations by any other person shall be entitled to bring proceedings for compensation from that other person for that damage.

(2) In proceedings brought against a person by virtue of this regulation it shall be a defence to prove that he had taken such care as in all the circumstances was reasonably required to comply with the relevant requirement.

(3) The provisions of this regulation are without prejudice to those of regulation 31.

[4.37]
31 Enforcement—extension of Part V of the Data Protection Act 1998

(1) The provisions of Part V [and sections 55A to 55E] of the Data Protection Act 1998 and of Schedules 6 and 9 to that Act are extended for the purposes of these Regulations and, for those purposes, shall have effect subject to the modifications set out in Schedule 1.

(2) In regulations 32 and 33, "enforcement functions" means the functions of the Information Commissioner under the provisions referred to in paragraph (1) as extended by that paragraph [and the functions set out in regulations 31A and 31B].

(3) The provisions of this regulation are without prejudice to those of regulation 30.

NOTES
  Paras (1), (2): words in square brackets inserted by the Privacy and Electronic Communications (EC Directive) (Amendment) Regulations 2011, SI 2011/1208, regs 2, 11.

[4.38]
[31A Enforcement: third party information notices

(1) The Information Commissioner may require a communications provider (A) to provide information to the Information Commissioner by serving on A a notice ("a third party information notice").

(2) The third party information notice may require A to release information held by A about another person's use of an electronic communications network or an electronic communications service where the Information Commissioner believes that the information requested is relevant information.

(3) Relevant information is information which the Information Commissioner considers is necessary to investigate the compliance of any person with these Regulations.

(4) The notice shall set out—
  (a) the information requested,
  (b) the form in which the information must be provided;
  (c) the time limit within which the information must be provided; and
  (d) information about the rights of appeal conferred by these Regulations.

(5) The time limit referred to in paragraph (4)(c) shall not expire before the end of the period in which an appeal may be brought. If an appeal is brought, the information requested need not be provided pending the determination or withdrawal of the appeal.

(6) In an urgent case, the Commissioner may include in the notice—
  (a) a statement that the case is urgent; and
  (b) a statement of his reasons for reaching that conclusion,
in which case paragraph (5) shall not apply.

(7) Where paragraph (6) applies, the communications provider shall have a minimum of 7 days (beginning on the day on which the notice is served) to provide the information requested.

(8) A person shall not be required by virtue of this regulation to disclose any information in respect of—
  (a) any communication between a professional legal adviser and the adviser's client in connection with the giving of legal advice with respect to the client's obligations, liabilities or rights under these Regulations, or
  (b) any communication between a professional legal adviser and the adviser's client, or between such an adviser or the adviser's client and any other person, made in connection with or in contemplation of proceedings under or arising out of these Regulations (including proceedings before the Tribunal) and for the purposes of such proceedings.]

NOTES
  Inserted by the Privacy and Electronic Communications (EC Directive) (Amendment) Regulations 2011, SI 2011/1208, regs 2, 12.

[4.39]
[31B   Enforcement: appeals

(1) A communications provider on whom a third party information notice has been served may appeal to the Tribunal against the notice.

(2) Appeals shall be determined in accordance with section 49 of and Schedule 6 to the Data Protection Act 1998 as modified by Schedule 1 to these Regulations.]

NOTES

Inserted by the Privacy and Electronic Communications (EC Directive) (Amendment) Regulations 2011, SI 2011/1208, regs 2, 12.

[4.40]
32   Request that the Commissioner exercise his enforcement functions

Where it is alleged that there has been a contravention of any of the requirements of these Regulations either OFCOM or a person aggrieved by the alleged contravention may request the Commissioner to exercise his enforcement functions in respect of that contravention, but those functions shall be exercisable by the Commissioner whether or not he has been so requested.

[4.41]
33   Technical advice to the Commissioner

OFCOM shall comply with any reasonable request made by the Commissioner, in connection with his enforcement functions, for advice on technical and similar matters relating to electronic communications.

34, 35   *(Regs 34, 35 amend SI 2000/2699, SI 2003/1094 (both outside the scope of this work).)*

[4.42]
36   Transitional provisions

The provisions in Schedule 2 shall have effect.

[4.43]
[37   Review of implementation

(1) Before the end of each review period, the Secretary of State must—
   (a)   carry out a review of the [implementing provisions];
   (b)   set out the conclusions of the review in a report; and
   (c)   publish the report.

[(1A) "The implementing provisions" means the provisions contained in or made under an Act that were relied on by the United Kingdom immediately before exit day to implement the Directive, so far as those provisions remain in force.]

(2)   . . .

(3) The report must in particular—
   (a)   set out the objectives intended to be achieved by the [implementing provisions];
   (b)   assess the extent to which those objectives are achieved; and
   (c)   assess whether those objectives remain appropriate and, if so, the extent to which they could be achieved with a system that imposes less regulation.

(4) "Review period" means—
   (a)   the period of five years beginning with the 26th May 2011; and
   (b)   subject to paragraph (5), each successive period of 5 years.

(5) If a report under this regulation is published before the last day of the review period to which it relates, the following review period is to being with the day on which that report is published.]

NOTES

Inserted by the Privacy and Electronic Communications (EC Directive) (Amendment) Regulations 2011, SI 2011/1208, regs 2, 13.

Paras (1), (3): words in square brackets substituted by the Electronic Communications (Amendment etc.) (EU Exit) Regulations 2019, SI 2019/919, reg 3(1), (2), (5).

Para (1A): inserted by SI 2019/919, reg 3(1), (3).

Para (2): revoked by SI 2019/919, reg 3(1), (4).

SCHEDULES

SCHEDULE 1
MODIFICATIONS FOR THE PURPOSES OF THESE REGULATIONS TO PART V [AND SECTIONS 55A TO 55E] OF THE DATA PROTECTION ACT 1998 AND SCHEDULES 6 AND 9 TO THAT ACT AS EXTENDED BY REGULATION 31

NOTES

Schedule heading: words in square brackets inserted by the Privacy and Electronic Communications (EC Directive) (Amendment) Regulations 2011, SI 2011/1208, regs 2, 14(a).

Regulation 31

[Modifications of the Data Protection Act 1998]

[4.44]
1 In section 40—

(a) in subsection (1), for the words "data controller" there shall be substituted the word "person", for the words "data protection principles" there shall be substituted the words "requirements of the Privacy and Electronic Communications (EC Directive) Regulations 2003 (in this Part referred to as "the relevant requirements")" and for the words "principle or principles" there shall be substituted the words "requirement or requirements";

(b) in subsection (2), the words "or distress" shall be omitted;

(c) subsections (3), (4), (5), (9) and (10) shall be omitted; and

(d) in subsection (6)(a), for the words "data protection principle or principles" there shall be substituted the words "relevant requirement or requirements."

2 In section 41(1) and (2), for the words "data protection principle or principles", in both places where they occur, there shall be substituted the words "relevant requirement or requirements".

[2A Sections 41A to 41C shall be omitted.]

3 Section 42 shall be omitted.

4 In section 43—

(a) for subsections (1) and (2) there shall be substituted the following provisions—

"(1) If the Commissioner reasonably requires any information for the purpose of determining whether a person has complied or is complying with the relevant requirements, he may serve that person with a notice (in this Act referred to as "an information notice") requiring him, within such time as is specified in the notice, to furnish the Commissioner, in such form as may be so specified, with such information relating to compliance with the relevant requirements as is so specified.

(2) An information notice must contain a statement that the Commissioner regards the specified information as relevant for the purpose of determining whether the person has complied or is complying with the relevant requirements and his reason for regarding it as relevant for that purpose."

(b) in subsection (6)(a), after the word "under" there shall be inserted the words "the Privacy and Electronic Communications (EC Directive) Regulations 2003 or";

(c) in subsection (6)(b), after the words "arising out of" there shall be inserted the words "the said Regulations or"; and

[(d) in subsection (8), for "under this Act" there shall be substituted "under the Privacy and Electronic Communications (EC Directive) Regulations 2003";

(e) in subsection (8B), for "under this Act (other than an offence under section 47)" there shall be substituted "under the Privacy and Electronic Communications (EC Directive) Regulations 2003"; and

(f) subsection (10) shall be omitted].

5 Sections 44, 45 and 46 shall be omitted.

[6 In section 47—

(a) in subsection (1), "special information notice" there shall be substituted "third party information notice"; and

(b) in subsection (2), for "special information notice" there shall be substituted "third party information notice".]

7 In section 48—

(a) in subsections (1) and (3), for the words "an information notice or a special information notice", in both places where they occur, there shall be substituted the words "or an information notice";

(b) in subsection (3) for the words "43(5) or 44(6)" there shall be substituted the words "or 43(5)"; and

(c) subsection (4) shall be omitted.

8 In section 49 subsection (5) shall be omitted.

[8A [Except where paragraph 8AA applies, in section 55A—]

(a) in subsection (1)—

    (i) for "data controller" there shall be substituted "person", and

    (ii) for "of section 4(4) by the data controller" there shall be substituted "of the requirements of the Privacy and Electronic Communications (EC Directive) Regulations 2003";

(b) in subsection (3), for "data controller" there shall be substituted "person";

(c) subsection (3A) shall be omitted;

(d) in subsection (4), for "data controller" there shall be substituted "person";

(e) in subsection (9), the definition of "data controller" shall be omitted.

[8AA In section 55A, when applied to regulations 19 to 24 of these Regulations—

(a) in subsection (1)—

    (i) for "data controller" there shall be substituted "person";

    (ii) in paragraph (a), for "of section 4(4) by the data controller" there shall be substituted "of the requirements of the Privacy and Electronic Communications (EC Directive) Regulations 2003, and"; and

    (iii) for paragraphs (b) and (c) there shall be substituted—

        "(b) subsection (2) or (3) applies.";

(b) in subsection (3)—

    (i) for "data controller" there shall be substituted "person"; and

    (ii) for paragraph (a) substitute—

        "(a) knew or ought to have known that there was a risk that the contravention would occur, but";

(c) subsection (3A) shall be omitted;

[(ca) before subsection (4) there shall be inserted the following subsections—

"(3B)   If a monetary penalty notice has been served under this section on a body, the Commissioner may also serve a monetary penalty notice on an officer of the body if the Commissioner is satisfied that the contravention in respect of which the monetary penalty notice was served on the body—
> (a)   took place with the consent or connivance of the officer, or
> (b)   was attributable to any neglect on the part of the officer.

(3C)   In subsection (3B)—
> "body" means a body corporate or a Scottish partnership;
> "officer" in relation to a body means—
> > (a)   in relation to a body corporate—
> > > (i)   a director, manager, secretary or other similar officer of the body or any person purporting to act in such capacity, or
> > > (ii)   where the affairs of the body are managed by its members, a member; or
> > (b)   in relation to a Scottish partnership, a partner or any person purporting to act as a partner.".]

(d)   in subsection (4), for "data controller" there shall be substituted "person [on whom it is served]"; and
(e)   in subsection (9), the definition of "data controller" shall be omitted.]

8B   In section 55B, for the words "data controller" (in subsections (1), (3) and (4)), there shall be substituted the word "person".]

[8C   In section 55E, for the words "data controller" in subsection (2), there shall be substituted the word "person".]

9   In paragraph 4(1) of [Schedule 6], for the words " (2) or (4)" there shall be substituted the words "or (2)".

10   In paragraph 1 of Schedule 9—
(a)   for subparagraph (1)(a) there shall be substituted the following provision—

> "(a)   that a person has contravened or is contravening any of the requirements of the Privacy and Electronic Communications (EC Directive) Regulations 2003 (in this Schedule referred to as "the 2003 Regulations") or" . . .

[(b)   in subparagraph (1A) for "data controller" there shall be substituted "person", and for "requirement imposed by an assessment notice" there shall be substituted "the audit provisions in regulations 5 and 5B of the 2003 Regulations";
(c)   in subparagraph (1B)—
> (i)   for "data controller" there shall be substituted "person";
> (ii)   for "data protection principles" there shall be substituted "the requirements of the 2003 Regulations";
> (iii)   for "assessment notice" there shall be substituted "audit notice"; and
> (iv)   the words "subparagraph (2) and" shall be omitted;
(d)   subparagraph (2) shall be omitted;
(e)   in subparagraphs (3)(d)(ii) and (3)(f) for the words "data controller" there shall be substituted "person", and for the words "the data protection principles" there shall be substituted "the requirements of the 2003 Regulations].

[10A   In paragraph 2(1A) of Schedule 9 for "assessment notice" there shall be substituted "audit notice".]

11   In paragraph 9 of Schedule 9—
(a)   in subparagraph (1)(a) after the words "rights under" there shall be inserted the words "the 2003 Regulations or"; and
(b)   in subparagraph (1)(b) after the words "arising out of" there shall be inserted the words "the 2003 Regulations or".

[Modifications of Secondary Legislation

12   Modification of the Data Protection (Monetary Penalties) (Maximum Penalty and Notices) Regulations 2010

(1)   The Data Protection (Monetary Penalties) (Maximum Penalty and Notices) Regulations 2010 are extended for the purposes of these Regulations and have effect subject to the following modifications.

(2)   Regulation 1 applies as if in paragraph (2), at the end, there were inserted "as modified by regulation 31(1) of, and Schedule 1 to, the Privacy and Electronic Communications (EC Directive) Regulations 2003".

(3)   Regulation 3 (notices of intent) applies as if—
(a)   in paragraph (a) for "data controller" there were substituted "person";
(b)   paragraph (b)(i) were omitted;
(c)   for paragraph (b)(ii) there were substituted—

> "(ii)   the nature of the contravention of the Privacy and Electronic Communications (EC Directive) Regulations 2003,"; and

(d)   in a case where paragraph 8AA of Schedule 1 to the Privacy and Electronic Communications (EC Directive) Regulations 2003 applies—
> (i)   paragraph (b)(iv) were omitted, and
> (ii)   after paragraph (v) there were inserted—

> > "(vi)   if the notice is served on an officer of a body, the reason the Commissioner considers that the officer has responsibility for the contravention.".

(4)   Regulation 4 (monetary penalty notices) applies as if—

(a) in paragraphs (a), (b) and (g) for "data controller" there were substituted "person";

(b) paragraph (d)(i) were omitted;

(c) for paragraph (d)(ii) there were substituted—

"(ii)   the nature of the contravention of the Privacy and Electronic Communications (EC Directive) Regulations 2003,"; and

(d) in a case where paragraph 8AA of Schedule 1 to the Privacy and Electronic Communications Regulations 2003 applies—

(i)   paragraph (d)(iv) were omitted, and

(ii)   after paragraph (d)(v) there were inserted—

"(vi)   if the notice is served on an officer of a body, the reason the Commissioner considers that the officer has responsibility for the contravention;".

13   Modification of the Data Protection (Monetary Penalties) Order 2010

(1) The Data Protection (Monetary Penalties) Order 2010 is extended and has effect for the purposes of these Regulations subject to the following modifications.

(2) Article 1(2) (interpretation) applies as if at the end there were inserted "as modified by regulation 31(1) of, and Schedule 1 to, the Privacy and Electronic Communications (EC Directive) Regulations 2003".

(3) Article 5(2) (monetary penalty notices: cancellation) applies as if after "take any further action" there were inserted "against the person on whom that notice was served".

(4) Article 6(c) (monetary penalty notices: enforcement) applies as if for "data controller" there were substituted "person on whom the notice is served".]

NOTES

Heading preceding para 1: inserted by the Privacy and Electronic Communications (Amendment) Regulations 2018, SI 2018/1189, reg 2(1), (2).

Para 2A: inserted by the Privacy and Electronic Communications (EC Directive) (Amendment) Regulations 2011, SI 2011/1208, regs 2, 14(b).

Para 4: sub-paras (d)–(f) substituted, for sub-para (d) as originally enacted, by SI 2011/1208, reg s 2, 14(c).

Para 6: substituted by SI 2011/1208, regs 2, 14(d).

Para 8A: inserted by SI 2011/1208, regs 2, 14(e); words in square brackets substituted by the Privacy and Electronic Communications (EC Directive) (Amendment) Regulations 2015, SI 2015/355, reg 2(1), (3).

Para 8AA: inserted by SI 2015/355, reg 2(1), (4); sub-para (ca) and words in square brackets in sub-para (d) inserted, by SI 2018/1189, reg 2(1), (3).

Para 8B: inserted by SI 2011/1208, regs 2, 14(e).

Para 8C: inserted by SI 2015/355, reg 2(1), (5).

Para 9: words in square brackets substituted by SI 2011/1208, regs 2, 14(f).

Para 10: word omitted from sub-para (a) revoked and sub-paras (b)–(e) substituted, for sub-para (b) as originally enacted, by SI 2011/1208, regs 2, 14(g).

Para 10A: inserted by SI 2011/1208, regs 2, 14(h).

Paras 12, 13: added, together with preceding heading, by SI 2018/1189, reg 2(1), (4).

SCHEDULE 2
TRANSITIONAL PROVISIONS

Regulation 36

Interpretation

[4.45]

1 In this Schedule "the 1999 Regulations" means the Telecommunications (Data Protection and Privacy) Regulations 1999 and "caller" has the same meaning as in regulation 21 of the 1999 Regulations.

Directories

2 (1) Regulation 18 of these Regulations shall not apply in relation to editions of directories first published before 11th December 2003.

(2) Where the personal data of a subscriber have been included in a directory in accordance with Part IV of the 1999 Regulations, the personal data of that subscriber may remain included in that directory provided that the subscriber—

(a) has been provided with information in accordance with regulation 18 of these Regulations; and

(b) has not requested that his data be withdrawn from that directory.

(3) Where a request has been made under subparagraph (2) for data to be withdrawn from a directory, that request shall be treated as having no application in relation to an edition of a directory that was produced before the producer of the directory received the request.

(4) For the purposes of subparagraph (3), an edition of a directory, which is revised after it was first produced, shall be treated as a new edition.

Notifications

3 (1) A notification of consent given to a caller by a subscriber for the purposes of regulation 22(2) of the 1999 Regulations is to have effect on and after 11th December 2003 as a notification given by that subscriber for the purposes of regulation 19(2) of these Regulations.

(2) A notification given to a caller by a corporate subscriber for the purposes of regulation 23(2)(a) of the 1999 Regulations is to have effect on and after 11th December 2003 as a notification given by that subscriber for the purposes of regulation 20(1)(b) of these Regulations.

(3) A notification of consent given to a caller by an individual subscriber for the purposes of regulation 24(2) of the 1999 Regulations is to have effect on and after 11th December 2003 as a notification given by that subscriber for the purposes of regulation 20(2) of these Regulations.

(4) A notification given to a caller by an individual subscriber for the purposes of regulation 25(2)(a) of the 1999 Regulations is to have effect on and after the 11th December 2003 as a notification given by that subscriber for the purposes of regulation 21(1) of these Regulations.

Registers Kept Under Regulations 25 and 26

4 (1) A notification given by a subscriber pursuant to regulation 23(4)(a) of the 1999 Regulations to the Director General of Telecommunications (or to such other person as is discharging his functions under regulation 23(4) of the 1999 Regulations on his behalf by virtue of an arrangement made under regulation 23(6) of those Regulations) is to have effect on or after 11th December 2003 as a notification given pursuant to regulation 25(1) of these Regulations.

(2) A notification given by a subscriber who is an individual pursuant to regulation 25(4)(a) of the 1999 Regulations to the Director General of Telecommunications (or to such other person as is discharging his functions under regulation 25(4) of the 1999 Regulations on his behalf by virtue of an arrangement made under regulation 25(6) of those Regulations) is to have effect on or after 11th December 2003 as a notification given pursuant to regulation 26(1) of these Regulations.

References in these Regulations to OFCOM

5 In relation to times before an order made under section 411 of the Communications Act 2003 brings any of the provisions of Part 2 of Chapter 1 of that Act into force for the purpose of conferring on OFCOM the functions contained in those provisions, references to OFCOM in these Regulations are to be treated as references to the Director General of Telecommunications.

PART 5
EPRIVACY – EU LAW

DIRECTIVE OF THE EUROPEAN PARLIAMENT AND OF THE COUNCIL

(2002/58/EC)

of 12 July 2002

concerning the processing of personal data and the protection of privacy in the electronic communications sector (Directive on privacy and electronic communications)

[5.1]

NOTES

Date of publication in OJ: OJ L201, 31.7.2002, p 37.
© European Union, 1998–2021.

THE EUROPEAN PARLIAMENT AND THE COUNCIL OF THE EUROPEAN UNION,

Having regard to the Treaty establishing the European Community, and in particular Article 95 thereof,

Having regard to the proposal from the Commission,[1]

Having regard to the opinion of the Economic and Social Committee,[2]

Having consulted the Committee of the Regions,

Acting in accordance with the procedure laid down in Article 251 of the Treaty,[3]

Whereas:

(1) Directive 95/46/EC of the European Parliament and of the Council of 24 October 1995 on the protection of individuals with regard to the processing of personal data and on the free movement of such data[4] requires Member States to ensure the rights and freedoms of natural persons with regard to the processing of personal data, and in particular their right to privacy, in order to ensure the free flow of personal data in the Community.

(2) This Directive seeks to respect the fundamental rights and observes the principles recognised in particular by the Charter of fundamental rights of the European Union. In particular, this Directive seeks to ensure full respect for the rights set out in Articles 7 and 8 of that Charter.

(3) Confidentiality of communications is guaranteed in accordance with the international instruments relating to human rights, in particular the European Convention for the Protection of Human Rights and Fundamental Freedoms, and the constitutions of the Member States.

(4) Directive 97/66/EC of the European Parliament and of the Council of 15 December 1997 concerning the processing of personal data and the protection of privacy in the telecommunications sector[5] translated the principles set out in Directive 95/46/EC into specific rules for the telecommunications sector. Directive 97/66/EC has to be adapted to developments in the markets and technologies for electronic communications services in order to provide an equal level of protection of personal data and privacy for users of publicly available electronic communications services, regardless of the technologies used. That Directive should therefore be repealed and replaced by this Directive.

(5) New advanced digital technologies are currently being introduced in public communications networks in the Community, which give rise to specific requirements concerning the protection of personal data and privacy of the user. The development of the information society is characterised by the introduction of new electronic communications services. Access to digital mobile networks has become available and affordable for a large public. These digital networks have large capacities and possibilities for processing personal data. The successful cross-border development of these services is partly dependent on the confidence of users that their privacy will not be at risk.

(6) The Internet is overturning traditional market structures by providing a common, global infrastructure for the delivery of a wide range of electronic communications services. Publicly available electronic communications services over the Internet open new possibilities for users but also new risks for their personal data and privacy.

(7) In the case of public communications networks, specific legal, regulatory and technical provisions should be made in order to protect fundamental rights and freedoms of natural persons and legitimate interests of legal persons, in particular with regard to the increasing capacity for automated storage and processing of data relating to subscribers and users.

(8) Legal, regulatory and technical provisions adopted by the Member States concerning the protection of personal data, privacy and the legitimate interest of legal persons, in the electronic communication sector, should be harmonised in order to avoid obstacles to the internal market for electronic communication in accordance with Article 14 of the Treaty. Harmonisation should be limited to requirements necessary to guarantee that the promotion and development of new electronic communications services and networks between Member States are not hindered.

(9) The Member States, providers and users concerned, together with the competent Community bodies, should cooperate in introducing and developing the relevant technologies where this is necessary to apply the guarantees provided for by this Directive and taking particular account of the objectives of minimising the processing of personal data and of using anonymous or pseudonymous data where possible.

(10) In the electronic communications sector, Directive 95/46/EC applies in particular to all matters concerning protection of fundamental rights and freedoms, which are not specifically covered by the provisions of this Directive, including the obligations on the controller and the rights of individuals. Directive 95/46/EC applies to non-public communications services.

(11) Like Directive 95/46/EC, this Directive does not address issues of protection of fundamental rights and freedoms related to activities which are not governed by Community law. Therefore it does not alter the existing balance between the individual's right to privacy and the possibility for Member States to take the measures referred to in Article 15(1) of this Directive, necessary for the protection of public security, defence, State security (including the economic well-being of the State when the activities relate to State security matters) and the enforcement of

criminal law. Consequently, this Directive does not affect the ability of Member States to carry out lawful interception of electronic communications, or take other measures, if necessary for any of these purposes and in accordance with the European Convention for the Protection of Human Rights and Fundamental Freedoms, as interpreted by the rulings of the European Court of Human Rights. Such measures must be appropriate, strictly proportionate to the intended purpose and necessary within a democratic society and should be subject to adequate safeguards in accordance with the European Convention for the Protection of Human Rights and Fundamental Freedoms.

(12)   Subscribers to a publicly available electronic communications service may be natural or legal persons. By supplementing Directive 95/46/EC, this Directive is aimed at protecting the fundamental rights of natural persons and particularly their right to privacy, as well as the legitimate interests of legal persons. This Directive does not entail an obligation for Member States to extend the application of Directive 95/46/EC to the protection of the legitimate interests of legal persons, which is ensured within the framework of the applicable Community and national legislation.

(13)   The contractual relation between a subscriber and a service provider may entail a periodic or a one-off payment for the service provided or to be provided. Prepaid cards are also considered as a contract.

(14)   Location data may refer to the latitude, longitude and altitude of the user's terminal equipment, to the direction of travel, to the level of accuracy of the location information, to the identification of the network cell in which the terminal equipment is located at a certain point in time and to the time the location information was recorded.

(15)   A communication may include any naming, numbering or addressing information provided by the sender of a communication or the user of a connection to carry out the communication. Traffic data may include any translation of this information by the network over which the communication is transmitted for the purpose of carrying out the transmission. Traffic data may, *inter alia*, consist of data referring to the routing, duration, time or volume of a communication, to the protocol used, to the location of the terminal equipment of the sender or recipient, to the network on which the communication originates or terminates, to the beginning, end or duration of a connection. They may also consist of the format in which the communication is conveyed by the network.

(16)   Information that is part of a broadcasting service provided over a public communications network is intended for a potentially unlimited audience and does not constitute a communication in the sense of this Directive. However, in cases where the individual subscriber or user receiving such information can be identified, for example with video-on-demand services, the information conveyed is covered within the meaning of a communication for the purposes of this Directive.

(17)   For the purposes of this Directive, consent of a user or subscriber, regardless of whether the latter is a natural or a legal person, should have the same meaning as the data subject's consent as defined and further specified in Directive 95/46/EC. Consent may be given by any appropriate method enabling a freely given specific and informed indication of the user's wishes, including by ticking a box when visiting an Internet website.

(18)   Value added services may, for example, consist of advice on least expensive tariff packages, route guidance, traffic information, weather forecasts and tourist information.

(19)   The application of certain requirements relating to presentation and restriction of calling and connected line identification and to automatic call forwarding to subscriber lines connected to analogue exchanges should not be made mandatory in specific cases where such application would prove to be technically impossible or would require a disproportionate economic effort. It is important for interested parties to be informed of such cases and the Member States should therefore notify them to the Commission.

(20)   Service providers should take appropriate measures to safeguard the security of their services, if necessary in conjunction with the provider of the network, and inform subscribers of any special risks of a breach of the security of the network. Such risks may especially occur for electronic communications services over an open network such as the Internet or analogue mobile telephony. It is particularly important for subscribers and users of such services to be fully informed by their service provider of the existing security risks which lie outside the scope of possible remedies by the service provider. Service providers who offer publicly available electronic communications services over the Internet should inform users and subscribers of measures they can take to protect the security of their communications for instance by using specific types of software or encryption technologies. The requirement to inform subscribers of particular security risks does not discharge a service provider from the obligation to take, at its own costs, appropriate and immediate measures to remedy any new, unforeseen security risks and restore the normal security level of the service. The provision of information about security risks to the subscriber should be free of charge except for any nominal costs which the subscriber may incur while receiving or collecting the information, for instance by downloading an electronic mail message. Security is appraised in the light of Article 17 of Directive 95/46/EC.

(21)   Measures should be taken to prevent unauthorised access to communications in order to protect the confidentiality of communications, including both the contents and any data related to such communications, by means of public communications networks and publicly available electronic communications services. National legislation in some Member States only prohibits intentional unauthorised access to communications.

(22)   The prohibition of storage of communications and the related traffic data by persons other than the users or without their consent is not intended to prohibit any automatic, intermediate and transient storage of this information in so far as this takes place for the sole purpose of carrying out the transmission in the electronic communications network and provided that the information is not stored for any period longer than is necessary for the transmission and for traffic management purposes, and that during the period of storage the confidentiality remains guaranteed. Where this is necessary for making more efficient the onward transmission of any publicly accessible information to other recipients of the service upon their request, this Directive should not prevent such information from being further stored, provided that this information would in any case be accessible to the public without restriction and that any data referring to the individual subscribers or users requesting such information are erased.

(23)   Confidentiality of communications should also be ensured in the course of lawful business practice. Where necessary and legally authorised, communications can be recorded for the purpose of providing evidence of a commercial transaction. Directive 95/46/EC applies to such processing. Parties to the communications should be informed prior to the recording about the recording, its purpose and the duration of its storage. The recorded

communication should be erased as soon as possible and in any case at the latest by the end of the period during which the transaction can be lawfully challenged.

(24)   Terminal equipment of users of electronic communications networks and any information stored on such equipment are part of the private sphere of the users requiring protection under the European Convention for the Protection of Human Rights and Fundamental Freedoms. So-called spyware, web bugs, hidden identifiers and other similar devices can enter the user's terminal without their knowledge in order to gain access to information, to store hidden information or to trace the activities of the user and may seriously intrude upon the privacy of these users. The use of such devices should be allowed only for legitimate purposes, with the knowledge of the users concerned.

(25)   However, such devices, for instance so-called 'cookies', can be a legitimate and useful tool, for example, in analysing the effectiveness of website design and advertising, and in verifying the identity of users engaged in on-line transactions. Where such devices, for instance cookies, are intended for a legitimate purpose, such as to facilitate the provision of information society services, their use should be allowed on condition that users are provided with clear and precise information in accordance with Directive 95/46/EC about the purposes of cookies or similar devices so as to ensure that users are made aware of information being placed on the terminal equipment they are using. Users should have the opportunity to refuse to have a cookie or similar device stored on their terminal equipment. This is particularly important where users other than the original user have access to the terminal equipment and thereby to any data containing privacy-sensitive information stored on such equipment. Information and the right to refuse may be offered once for the use of various devices to be installed on the user's terminal equipment during the same connection and also covering any further use that may be made of those devices during subsequent connections. The methods for giving information, offering a right to refuse or requesting consent should be made as user-friendly as possible. Access to specific website content may still be made conditional on the well-informed acceptance of a cookie or similar device, if it is used for a legitimate purpose.

(26)   The data relating to subscribers processed within electronic communications networks to establish connections and to transmit information contain information on the private life of natural persons and concern the right to respect for their correspondence or concern the legitimate interests of legal persons. Such data may only be stored to the extent that is necessary for the provision of the service, for the purpose of billing and for interconnection payments, and for a limited time. Any further processing of such data which the provider of the publicly available electronic communications services may want to perform, for the marketing of electronic communications services or for the provision of value added services, may only be allowed if the subscriber has agreed to this on the basis of accurate and full information given by the provider of the publicly available electronic communications services about the types of further processing it intends to perform and about the subscriber's right not to give or to withdraw his/her consent to such processing. Traffic data used for marketing communications services or for the provision of value added services should also be erased or made anonymous after the provision of the service. Service providers should always keep subscribers informed of the types of data they are processing and the purposes and duration for which this is done.

(27)   The exact moment of the completion of the transmission of a communication, after which traffic data should be erased except for billing purposes, may depend on the type of electronic communications service that is provided. For instance for a voice telephony call the transmission will be completed as soon as either of the users terminates the connection. For electronic mail the transmission is completed as soon as the addressee collects the message, typically from the server of his service provider.

(28)   The obligation to erase traffic data or to make such data anonymous when it is no longer needed for the purpose of the transmission of a communication does not conflict with such procedures on the Internet as the caching in the domain name system of IP addresses or the caching of IP addresses to physical address bindings or the use of log-in information to control the right of access to networks or services.

(29)   The service provider may process traffic data relating to subscribers and users where necessary in individual cases in order to detect technical failure or errors in the transmission of communications. Traffic data necessary for billing purposes may also be processed by the provider in order to detect and stop fraud consisting of unpaid use of the electronic communications service.

(30)   Systems for the provision of electronic communications networks and services should be designed to limit the amount of personal data necessary to a strict minimum. Any activities related to the provision of the electronic communications service that go beyond the transmission of a communication and the billing thereof should be based on aggregated, traffic data that cannot be related to subscribers or users. Where such activities cannot be based on aggregated data, they should be considered as value added services for which the consent of the subscriber is required.

(31)   Whether the consent to be obtained for the processing of personal data with a view to providing a particular value added service should be that of the user or of the subscriber, will depend on the data to be processed and on the type of service to be provided and on whether it is technically, procedurally and contractually possible to distinguish the individual using an electronic communications service from the legal or natural person having subscribed to it.

(32)   Where the provider of an electronic communications service or of a value added service subcontracts the processing of personal data necessary for the provision of these services to another entity, such subcontracting and subsequent data processing should be in full compliance with the requirements regarding controllers and processors of personal data as set out in Directive 95/46/ EC. Where the provision of a value added service requires that traffic or location data are forwarded from an electronic communications service provider to a provider of value added services, the subscribers or users to whom the data are related should also be fully informed of this forwarding before giving their consent for the processing of the data.

(33)   The introduction of itemised bills has improved the possibilities for the subscriber to check the accuracy of the fees charged by the service provider but, at the same time, it may jeopardise the privacy of the users of publicly available electronic communications services. Therefore, in order to preserve the privacy of the user, Member States should encourage the development of electronic communication service options such as alter-native payment facilities which allow anonymous or strictly private access to publicly available electronic communications services, for example calling cards and facilities for payment by credit card. To the same end, Member States may ask the operators to offer their subscribers a different type of detailed bill in which a certain number of digits of the called number have been deleted.

(34)   It is necessary, as regards calling line identification, to protect the right of the calling party to withhold the presentation of the identification of the line from which the call is being made and the right of the called party to reject calls from unidentified lines. There is justification for overriding the elimination of calling line identification presentation in specific cases. Certain subscribers, in particular help lines and similar organisations, have an interest in guaranteeing the anonymity of their callers. It is necessary, as regards connected line identification, to protect the right and the legitimate interest of the called party to withhold the presentation of the identification of the line to which the calling party is actually connected, in particular in the case of forwarded calls. The providers of publicly available electronic communications services should inform their subscribers of the existence of calling and connected line identification in the network and of all services which are offered on the basis of calling and connected line identification as well as the privacy options which are available. This will allow the subscribers to make an informed choice about the privacy facilities they may want to use. The privacy options which are offered on a per-line basis do not necessarily have to be available as an automatic network service but may be obtainable through a simple request to the provider of the publicly available electronic communications service.

(35)   In digital mobile networks, location data giving the geographic position of the terminal equipment of the mobile user are processed to enable the transmission of communications. Such data are traffic data covered by Article 6 of this Directive. However, in addition, digital mobile networks may have the capacity to process location data which are more precise than is necessary for the transmission of communications and which are used for the provision of value added services such as services providing individualised traffic information and guidance to drivers. The processing of such data for value added services should only be allowed where subscribers have given their consent. Even in cases where subscribers have given their consent, they should have a simple means to temporarily deny the processing of location data, free of charge.

(36)   Member States may restrict the users' and subscribers' rights to privacy with regard to calling line identification where this is necessary to trace nuisance calls and with regard to calling line identification and location data where this is necessary to allow emergency services to carry out their tasks as effectively as possible. For these purposes, Member States may adopt specific provisions to entitle providers of electronic communications services to provide access to calling line identification and location data without the prior consent of the users or subscribers concerned.

(37)   Safeguards should be provided for subscribers against the nuisance which may be caused by automatic call forwarding by others. Moreover, in such cases, it must be possible for subscribers to stop the forwarded calls being passed on to their terminals by simple request to the provider of the publicly available electronic communications service.

(38)   Directories of subscribers to electronic communications services are widely distributed and public. The right to privacy of natural persons and the legitimate interest of legal persons require that subscribers are able to determine whether their personal data are published in a directory and if so, which. Providers of public directories should inform the subscribers to be included in such directories of the purposes of the directory and of any particular usage which may be made of electronic versions of public directories especially through search functions embedded in the software, such as reverse search functions enabling users of the directory to discover the name and address of the subscriber on the basis of a telephone number only.

(39)   The obligation to inform subscribers of the purpose(s) of public directories in which their personal data are to be included should be imposed on the party collecting the data for such inclusion. Where the data may be transmitted to one or more third parties, the subscriber should be informed of this possibility and of the recipient or the categories of possible recipients. Any transmission should be subject to the condition that the data may not be used for other purposes than those for which they were collected. If the party collecting the data from the subscriber or any third party to whom the data have been transmitted wishes to use the data for an additional purpose, the renewed consent of the subscriber is to be obtained either by the initial party collecting the data or by the third party to whom the data have been transmitted.

(40)   Safeguards should be provided for subscribers against intrusion of their privacy by unsolicited communications for direct marketing purposes in particular by means of automated calling machines, telefaxes, and e-mails, including SMS messages. These forms of unsolicited commercial communications may on the one hand be relatively easy and cheap to send and on the other may impose a burden and/or cost on the recipient. Moreover, in some cases their volume may also cause difficulties for electronic communications networks and terminal equipment. For such forms of unsolicited communications for direct marketing, it is justified to require that prior explicit consent of the recipients is obtained before such communications are addressed to them. The single market requires a harmonised approach to ensure simple, Community-wide rules for businesses and users.

(41)   Within the context of an existing customer relationship, it is reasonable to allow the use of electronic contact details for the offering of similar products or services, but only by the same company that has obtained the electronic contact details in accordance with Directive 95/46/EC. When electronic contact details are obtained, the customer should be informed about their further use for direct marketing in a clear and distinct manner, and be given the opportunity to refuse such usage. This opportunity should continue to be offered with each subsequent direct marketing message, free of charge, except for any costs for the transmission of this refusal.

(42)   Other forms of direct marketing that are more costly for the sender and impose no financial costs on subscribers and users, such as person-to-person voice telephony calls, may justify the maintenance of a system giving subscribers or users the possibility to indicate that they do not want to receive such calls. Nevertheless, in order not to decrease existing levels of privacy protection, Member States should be entitled to uphold national systems, only allowing such calls to subscribers and users who have given their prior consent.

(43)   To facilitate effective enforcement of Community rules on unsolicited messages for direct marketing, it is necessary to prohibit the use of false identities or false return addresses or numbers while sending unsolicited messages for direct marketing purposes.

(44)   Certain electronic mail systems allow subscribers to view the sender and subject line of an electronic mail, and also to delete the message, without having to download the rest of the electronic mail's content or any attachments, thereby reducing costs which could arise from downloading unsolicited electronic mails or attachments. These

arrangements may continue to be useful in certain cases as an additional tool to the general obligations established in this Directive.

(45)   This Directive is without prejudice to the arrangements which Member States make to protect the legitimate interests of legal persons with regard to unsolicited communications for direct marketing purposes. Where Member States establish an opt-out register for such communications to legal persons, mostly business users, the provisions of Article 7 of Directive 2000/31/EC of the European Parliament and of the Council of 8 June 2000 on certain legal aspects of information society services, in particular electronic commerce, in the internal market (Directive on electronic commerce)[6] are fully applicable.

(46)   The functionalities for the provision of electronic communications services may be integrated in the network or in any part of the terminal equipment of the user, including the software. The protection of the personal data and the privacy of the user of publicly available electronic communications services should be independent of the configuration of the various components necessary to provide the service and of the distribution of the necessary functionalities between these components. Directive 95/46/EC covers any form of processing of personal data regardless of the technology used. The existence of specific rules for electronic communications services alongside general rules for other components necessary for the provision of such services may not facilitate the protection of personal data and privacy in a technologically neutral way. It may therefore be necessary to adopt measures requiring manufacturers of certain types of equipment used for electronic communications services to construct their product in such a way as to incorporate safeguards to ensure that the personal data and privacy of the user and subscriber are protected. The adoption of such measures in accordance with Directive 1999/5/EC of the European Parliament and of the Council of 9 March 1999 on radio equipment and telecommunications terminal equipment and the mutual recognition of their conformity[7] will ensure that the introduction of technical features of electronic communication equipment including software for data protection purposes is harmonised in order to be compatible with the implementation of the internal market.

(47)   Where the rights of the users and subscribers are not respected, national legislation should provide for judicial remedies. Penalties should be imposed on any person, whether governed by private or public law, who fails to comply with the national measures taken under this Directive.

(48)   It is useful, in the field of application of this Directive, to draw on the experience of the Working Party on the Protection of Individuals with regard to the Processing of Personal Data composed of representatives of the supervisory authorities of the Member States, set up by Article 29 of Directive 95/46/EC.

(49)   To facilitate compliance with the provisions of this Directive, certain specific arrangements are needed for processing of data already under way on the date that national implementing legislation pursuant to this Directive enters into force,

NOTES

[1]   OJ C365 E, 19.12.2000, p 223.

[2]   OJ C123, 25.4.2001, p 53.

[3]   Opinion of the European Parliament of 13 November 2001 (not yet published in the Official Journal), Council Common Position of 28 January 2002 (OJ C113 E, 14.5.2002, p 39) and Decision of the European Parliament of 30 May 2002 (not yet published in the Official Journal). Council Decision of 25 June 2002.

[4]   OJ L281, 23.11.1995, p 31.

[5]   OJ L24, 30.1.1998, p 1.

[6]   OJ L178, 17.7.2000, p 1.

[7]   OJ L91, 7.4.1999, p 10.

HAVE ADOPTED THIS DIRECTIVE:

[5.2]
Article 1   Scope and aim
[1. This Directive provides for the harmonisation of the national provisions required to ensure an equivalent level of protection of fundamental rights and freedoms, and in particular the right to privacy and confidentiality, with respect to the processing of personal data in the electronic communication sector and to ensure the free movement of such data and of electronic communication equipment and services in the Community.]
2. The provisions of this Directive particularise and complement Directive 95/46/EC for the purposes mentioned in paragraph 1. Moreover, they provide for protection of the legitimate interests of subscribers who are legal persons.
3. This Directive shall not apply to activities which fall outside the scope of the Treaty establishing the European Community, such as those covered by Titles V and VI of the Treaty on European Union, and in any case to activities concerning public security, defence, State security (including the economic well-being of the State when the activities relate to State security matters) and the activities of the State in areas of criminal law.

NOTES

Para 1: substituted by European Parliament and Council Directive 2009/136/EC, Art 2(1).

[1]   OJ L91, 7.4.1999, p 10.

[5.3]
Article 2   Definitions
Save as otherwise provided, the definitions in Directive 95/46/ EC and in Directive 2002/21/EC of the European Parliament and of the Council of 7 March 2002 on a common regulatory framework for electronic communications networks and services (Framework Directive)[1] shall apply.
The following definitions shall also apply:
    (a)   'user' means any natural person using a publicly available electronic communications service, for private or business purposes, without necessarily having subscribed to this service;
    (b)   'traffic data' means any data processed for the purpose of the conveyance of a communication on an electronic communications network or for the billing thereof;

[(c) 'location data' means any data processed in an electronic communications network or by an electronic communications service, indicating the geographic position of the terminal equipment of a user of a publicly available electronic communications service;]

(d) 'communication' means any information exchanged or conveyed between a finite number of parties by means of a publicly available electronic communications service. This does not include any information conveyed as part of a broadcasting service to the public over an electronic communications network except to the extent that the information can be related to the identifiable subscriber or user receiving the information;

(e) . . .

(f) 'consent' by a user or subscriber corresponds to the data subject's consent in Directive 95/46/EC;

(g) 'value added service' means any service which requires the processing of traffic data or location data other than traffic data beyond what is necessary for the transmission of a communication or the billing thereof;

(h) 'electronic mail' means any text, voice, sound or image message sent over a public communications network which can be stored in the network or in the recipient's terminal equipment until it is collected by the recipient;

[(i) 'personal data breach' means a breach of security leading to the accidental or unlawful destruction, loss, alteration, unauthorised disclosure of, or access to, personal data transmitted, stored or otherwise processed in connection with the provision of a publicly available electronic communications service in the Community.]

NOTES

Point (c) substituted, point (e) repealed and point (i) added by European Parliament and Council Directive 2009/136/EC, Art 2(2).

¹   OJ L108, 24.4.2002, p 33.

[5.4]
[Article 3   Services concerned
This Directive shall apply to the processing of personal data in connection with the provision of publicly available electronic communications services in public communications networks in the Community, including public communications networks supporting data collection and identification devices.]

NOTES

Substituted by European Parliament and Council Directive 2009/136/EC, Art 2(3).

[5.5]
Article 4   [Security of processing]
1. The provider of a publicly available electronic communications service must take appropriate technical and organisational measures to safeguard security of its services, if necessary in conjunction with the provider of the public communications network with respect to network security. Having regard to the state of the art and the cost of their implementation, these measures shall ensure a level of security appropriate to the risk presented.
[1a. Without prejudice to Directive 95/46/EC, the measures referred to in paragraph 1 shall at least:
— ensure that personal data can be accessed only by authorised personnel for legally authorised purposes,
— protect personal data stored or transmitted against accidental or unlawful destruction, accidental loss or alteration, and unauthorised or unlawful storage, processing, access or disclosure, and,
— ensure the implementation of a security policy with respect to the processing of personal data,
Relevant national authorities shall be able to audit the measures taken by providers of publicly available electronic communication services and to issue recommendations about best practices concerning the level of security which those measures should achieve.]
2. In case of a particular risk of a breach of the security of the network, the provider of a publicly available electronic communications service must inform the subscribers concerning such risk and, where the risk lies outside the scope of the measures to be taken by the service provider, of any possible remedies, including an indication of the likely costs involved.
[3. In the case of a personal data breach, the provider of publicly available electronic communications services shall, without undue delay, notify the personal data breach to the competent national authority.

When the personal data breach is likely to adversely affect the personal data or privacy of a subscriber or individual, the provider shall also notify the subscriber or individual of the breach without undue delay.

Notification of a personal data breach to a subscriber or individual concerned shall not be required if the provider has demonstrated to the satisfaction of the competent authority that it has implemented appropriate technological protection measures, and that those measures were applied to the data concerned by the security breach. Such technological protection measures shall render the data unintelligible to any person who is not authorised to access it.

Without prejudice to the provider's obligation to notify subscribers and individuals concerned, if the provider has not already notified the subscriber or individual of the personal data breach, the competent national authority, having considered the likely adverse effects of the breach, may require it to do so.

The notification to the subscriber or individual shall at least describe the nature of the personal data breach and the contact points where more information can be obtained, and shall recommend measures to mitigate the possible adverse effects of the personal data breach. The notification to the competent national authority shall, in addition, describe the consequences of, and the measures proposed or taken by the provider to address, the personal data breach.
4. Subject to any technical implementing measures adopted under paragraph 5, the competent national authorities may adopt guidelines and, where necessary, issue instructions concerning the circumstances in which providers are required to notify personal data breaches, the format of such notification and the manner in which the notification is to be made. They shall also be able to audit whether providers have complied with their notification obligations under this paragraph, and shall impose appropriate sanctions in the event of a failure to do so.

Providers shall maintain an inventory of personal data breaches comprising the facts surrounding the breach, its effects and the remedial action taken which shall be sufficient to enable the competent national authorities to verify compliance with the provisions of paragraph 3. The inventory shall only include the information necessary for this purpose.

5. In order to ensure consistency in implementation of the measures referred to in paragraphs 2, 3 and 4, the Commission may, following consultation with the European Network and Information Security Agency (ENISA), the Working Party on the Protection of Individuals with regard to the Processing of Personal Data established by Article 29 of Directive 95/46/EC and the European Data Protection Supervisor, adopt technical implementing measures concerning the circumstances, format and procedures applicable to the information and notification requirements referred to in this Article. When adopting such measures, the Commission shall involve all relevant stakeholders particularly in order to be informed of the best available technical and economic means of implementation of this Article.

Those measures, designed to amend non-essential elements of this Directive by supplementing it, shall be adopted in accordance with the regulatory procedure with scrutiny referred to in Article 14a(2).]

NOTES

Article heading: substituted by European Parliament and Council Directive 2009/136/EC, Art 2(4)(a).
Para 1a: inserted by European Parliament and Council Directive 2009/136/EC, Art 2(4)(b).
Paras 3–5: inserted by European Parliament and Council Directive 2009/136/EC, Art 2(4)(c).

[5.6]
Article 5   Confidentiality of the communications

1. Member States shall ensure the confidentiality of communications and the related traffic data by means of a public communications network and publicly available electronic communications services, through national legislation. In particular, they shall prohibit listening, tapping, storage or other kinds of interception or surveillance of communications and the related traffic data by persons other than users, without the consent of the users concerned, except when legally authorised to do so in accordance with Article 15(1). This paragraph shall not prevent technical storage which is necessary for the conveyance of a communication without prejudice to the principle of confidentiality.

2. Paragraph 1 shall not affect any legally authorised recording of communications and the related traffic data when carried out in the course of lawful business practice for the purpose of providing evidence of a commercial transaction or of any other business communication.

[3. Member States shall ensure that the storing of information, or the gaining of access to information already stored, in the terminal equipment of a subscriber or user is only allowed on condition that the subscriber or user concerned has given his or her consent, having been provided with clear and comprehensive information, in accordance with Directive 95/46/EC, inter alia, about the purposes of the processing. This shall not prevent any technical storage or access for the sole purpose of carrying out the transmission of a communication over an electronic communications network, or as strictly necessary in order for the provider of an information society service explicitly requested by the subscriber or user to provide the service.]

NOTES

Para 3: substituted by European Parliament and Council Directive 2009/136/EC, Art 2(5).

[5.7]
Article 6   Traffic data

1. Traffic data relating to subscribers and users processed and stored by the provider of a public communications network or publicly available electronic communications service must be erased or made anonymous when it is no longer needed for the purpose of the transmission of a communication without prejudice to paragraphs 2, 3 and 5 of this Article and Article 15(1).

2. Traffic data necessary for the purposes of subscriber billing and interconnection payments may be processed. Such processing is permissible only up to the end of the period during which the bill may lawfully be challenged or payment pursued.

[3. For the purpose of marketing electronic communications services or for the provision of value added services, the provider of a publicly available electronic communications service may process the data referred to in paragraph 1 to the extent and for the duration necessary for such services or marketing, if the subscriber or user to whom the data relate has given his or her prior consent. Users or subscribers shall be given the possibility to withdraw their consent for the processing of traffic data at any time.]

4. The service provider must inform the subscriber or user of the types of traffic data which are processed and of the duration of such processing for the purposes mentioned in paragraph 2 and, prior to obtaining consent, for the purposes mentioned in paragraph 3.

5. Processing of traffic data, in accordance with paragraphs 1, 2, 3 and 4, must be restricted to persons acting under the authority of providers of the public communications networks and publicly available electronic communications services handling billing or traffic management, customer enquiries, fraud detection, marketing electronic communications services or providing a value added service, and must be restricted to what is necessary for the purposes of such activities.

6. Paragraphs 1, 2, 3 and 5 shall apply without prejudice to the possibility for competent bodies to be informed of traffic data in conformity with applicable legislation with a view to settling disputes, in particular interconnection or billing disputes.

NOTES

Para 3: substituted by European Parliament and Council Directive 2009/136/EC, Art 2(6).

[5.8]
Article 7   Itemised billing
1. Subscribers shall have the right to receive non-itemised bills.
2. Member States shall apply national provisions in order to reconcile the rights of subscribers receiving itemised bills with the right to privacy of calling users and called subscribers, for example by ensuring that sufficient alternative privacy enhancing methods of communications or payments are available to such users and subscribers.

[5.9]
Article 8   Presentation and restriction of calling and connected line identification
1. Where presentation of calling line identification is offered, the service provider must offer the calling user the possibility, using a simple means and free of charge, of preventing the presentation of the calling line identification on a per-call basis. The calling subscriber must have this possibility on a per-line basis.
2. Where presentation of calling line identification is offered, the service provider must offer the called subscriber the possibility, using a simple means and free of charge for reasonable use of this function, of preventing the presentation of the calling line identification of incoming calls.
3. Where presentation of calling line identification is offered and where the calling line identification is presented prior to the call being established, the service provider must offer the called subscriber the possibility, using a simple means, of rejecting incoming calls where the presentation of the calling line identification has been prevented by the calling user or subscriber.
4. Where presentation of connected line identification is offered, the service provider must offer the called subscriber the possibility, using a simple means and free of charge, of preventing the presentation of the connected line identification to the calling user.
5. Paragraph 1 shall also apply with regard to calls to third countries originating in the Community. Paragraphs 2, 3 and 4 shall also apply to incoming calls originating in third countries.
6. Member States shall ensure that where presentation of calling and/or connected line identification is offered, the providers of publicly available electronic communications services inform the public thereof and of the possibilities set out in paragraphs 1, 2, 3 and 4.

[5.10]
Article 9   Location data other than traffic data
1. Where location data other than traffic data, relating to users or subscribers of public communications networks or publicly available electronic communications services, can be processed, such data may only be processed when they are made anonymous, or with the consent of the users or subscribers to the extent and for the duration necessary for the provision of a value added service. The service provider must inform the users or subscribers, prior to obtaining their consent, of the type of location data other than traffic data which will be processed, of the purposes and duration of the processing and whether the data will be transmitted to a third party for the purpose of providing the value added service. Users or subscribers shall be given the possibility to withdraw their consent for the processing of location data other than traffic data at any time.
2. Where consent of the users or subscribers has been obtained for the processing of location data other than traffic data, the user or subscriber must continue to have the possibility, using a simple means and free of charge, of temporarily refusing the processing of such data for each connection to the network or for each transmission of a communication.
3. Processing of location data other than traffic data in accordance with paragraphs 1 and 2 must be restricted to persons acting under the authority of the provider of the public communications network or publicly available communications service or of the third party providing the value added service, and must be restricted to what is necessary for the purposes of providing the value added service.

[5.11]
Article 10   Exceptions
Member States shall ensure that there are transparent procedures governing the way in which a provider of a public communications network and/or a publicly available electronic communications service may override:
   (a)   the elimination of the presentation of calling line identification, on a temporary basis, upon application of a subscriber requesting the tracing of malicious or nuisance calls. In this case, in accordance with national law, the data containing the identification of the calling subscriber will be stored and be made available by the provider of a public communications network and/or publicly available electronic communications service;
   (b)   the elimination of the presentation of calling line identification and the temporary denial or absence of consent of a subscriber or user for the processing of location data, on a per-line basis for organisations dealing with emergency calls and recognised as such by a Member State, including law enforcement agencies, ambulance services and fire brigades, for the purpose of responding to such calls.

[5.12]
Article 11   Automatic call forwarding
Member States shall ensure that any subscriber has the possibility, using a simple means and free of charge, of stopping automatic call forwarding by a third party to the subscriber's terminal.

[5.13]
Article 12   Directories of subscribers
1. Member States shall ensure that subscribers are informed, free of charge and before they are included in the directory, about the purpose(s) of a printed or electronic directory of subscribers available to the public or obtainable through directory enquiry services, in which their personal data can be included and of any further usage possibilities based on search functions embedded in electronic versions of the directory.

2. Member States shall ensure that subscribers are given the opportunity to determine whether their personal data are included in a public directory, and if so, which, to the extent that such data are relevant for the purpose of the directory as determined by the provider of the directory, and to verify, correct or withdraw such data. Not being included in a public subscriber directory, verifying, correcting or withdrawing personal data from it shall be free of charge.

3. Member States may require that for any purpose of a public directory other than the search of contact details of persons on the basis of their name and, where necessary, a minimum of other identifiers, additional consent be asked of the subscribers.

4. Paragraphs 1 and 2 shall apply to subscribers who are natural persons. Member States shall also ensure, in the framework of Community law and applicable national legislation, that the legitimate interests of subscribers other than natural persons with regard to their entry in public directories are sufficiently protected.

[5.14]
[Article 13   Unsolicited communications

1. The use of automated calling and communication systems without human intervention (automatic calling machines), facsimile machines (fax) or electronic mail for the purposes of direct marketing may be allowed only in respect of subscribers or users who have given their prior consent.

2. Notwithstanding paragraph 1, where a natural or legal person obtains from its customers their electronic contact details for electronic mail, in the context of the sale of a product or a service, in accordance with Directive 95/46/EC, the same natural or legal person may use these electronic contact details for direct marketing of its own similar products or services provided that customers clearly and distinctly are given the opportunity to object, free of charge and in an easy manner, to such use of electronic contact details at the time of their collection and on the occasion of each message in case the customer has not initially refused such use.

3. Member States shall take appropriate measures to ensure that unsolicited communications for the purposes of direct marketing, in cases other than those referred to in paragraphs 1 and 2, are not allowed either without the consent of the subscribers or users concerned or in respect of subscribers or users who do not wish to receive these communications, the choice between these options to be determined by national legislation, taking into account that both options must be free of charge for the subscriber or user.

4. In any event, the practice of sending electronic mail for the purposes of direct marketing which disguise or conceal the identity of the sender on whose behalf the communication is made, which contravene Article 6 of Directive 2000/31/EC, which do not have a valid address to which the recipient may send a request that such communications cease or which encourage recipients to visit websites that contravene that Article shall be prohibited.

5. Paragraphs 1 and 3 shall apply to subscribers who are natural persons. Member States shall also ensure, in the framework of Community law and applicable national legislation, that the legitimate interests of subscribers other than natural persons with regard to unsolicited communications are sufficiently protected.

6. Without prejudice to any administrative remedy for which provision may be made, inter alia, under Article 15a(2), Member States shall ensure that any natural or legal person adversely affected by infringements of national provisions adopted pursuant to this Article and therefore having a legitimate interest in the cessation or prohibition of such infringements, including an electronic communications service provider protecting its legitimate business interests, may bring legal proceedings in respect of such infringements. Member States may also lay down specific rules on penalties applicable to providers of electronic communications services which by their negligence contribute to infringements of national provisions adopted pursuant to this Article.]

NOTES

Art 13 substituted by European Parliament and Council Directive 2009/136/EC, Art 2(7).

[5.15]
Article 14   Technical features and standardisation

1. In implementing the provisions of this Directive, Member States shall ensure, subject to paragraphs 2 and 3, that no mandatory requirements for specific technical features are imposed on terminal or other electronic communication equipment which could impede the placing of equipment on the market and the free circulation of such equipment in and between Member States.

2. Where provisions of this Directive can be implemented only by requiring specific technical features in electronic communications networks, Member States shall inform the Commission in accordance with the procedure provided for by Directive 98/34/EC of the European Parliament and of the Council of 22 June 1998 laying down a procedure for the provision of information in the field of technical standards and regulations and of rules on information society services.[1]

3. Where required, measures may be adopted to ensure that terminal equipment is constructed in a way that is compatible with the right of users to protect and control the use of their personal data, in accordance with Directive 1999/5/EC and Council Decision 87/95/EEC of 22 December 1986 on standardisation in the field of information technology and communications[2].

NOTES

[1]   OJ L204, 21.7.1998, p 37. Directive as amended by Directive 98/ 48/EC (OJ L217, 5.8.1998, p 18).
[2]   OJ L36, 7.2.1987, p 31. Decision as last amended by the 1994 Act of Accession.

[5.16]
[Article 14a   Committee procedure

1. The Commission shall be assisted by the Communications Committee established by Article 22 of Directive 2002/21/EC (Framework Directive).

2. Where reference is made to this paragraph, Article 5a(1) to (4) and Article 7 of Decision 1999/468/EC shall apply, having regard to the provisions of Article 8 thereof.

3. Where reference is made to this paragraph, Article 5a(1), (2), (4) and (6) and Article 7 of Decision 1999/468/EC shall apply, having regard to the provisions of Article 8 thereof.]

NOTES
Art 14a inserted by European Parliament and Council Directive 2009/136/EC, Art 2(8).

[5.17]
Article 15   Application of certain provisions of Directive 95/46/EC
1. Member States may adopt legislative measures to restrict the scope of the rights and obligations provided for in Article 5, Article 6, Article 8(1), (2), (3) and (4), and Article 9 of this Directive when such restriction constitutes a necessary, appropriate and proportionate measure within a democratic society to safeguard national security (i.e. State security), defence, public security, and the prevention, investigation, detection and prosecution of criminal offences or of unauthorised use of the electronic communication system, as referred to in Article 13(1) of Directive 95/46/EC. To this end, Member States may, *inter alia*, adopt legislative measures providing for the retention of data for a limited period justified on the grounds laid down in this paragraph. All the measures referred to in this paragraph shall be in accordance with the general principles of Community law, including those referred to in Article 6(1) and (2) of the Treaty on European Union.
[1a. Paragraph 1 shall not apply to data specifically required by Directive 2006/24/EC of the European Parliament and of the Council of 15 March 2006 on the retention of data generated or processed in connection with the provision of publicly available electronic communications services or of public communications networks[1] to be retained for the purposes referred to in Article 1(1) of that Directive.]
[1b. Providers shall establish internal procedures for responding to requests for access to users' personal data based on national provisions adopted pursuant to paragraph 1. They shall provide the competent national authority, on demand, with information about those procedures, the number of requests received, the legal justification invoked and their response.]
2. The provisions of Chapter III on judicial remedies, liability and sanctions of Directive 95/46/EC shall apply with regard to national provisions adopted pursuant to this Directive and with regard to the individual rights derived from this Directive.
3. The Working Party on the Protection of Individuals with regard to the Processing of Personal Data instituted by Article 29 of Directive 95/46/EC shall also carry out the tasks laid down in Article 30 of that Directive with regard to matters covered by this Directive, namely the protection of fundamental rights and freedoms and of legitimate interests in the electronic communications sector.

NOTES
Para 1a: inserted by European Parliament and Council Directive 2006/24/EC, Art 11.
Para 1b: inserted by European Parliament and Council Directive 2009/136/EC, Art 2(9).
[1]   OJ L105, 13.4.2006, p 54.

[5.18]
[Article 15a   Implementation and enforcement
1. Member States shall lay down the rules on penalties, including criminal sanctions where appropriate, applicable to infringements of the national provisions adopted pursuant to this Directive and shall take all measures necessary to ensure that they are implemented. The penalties provided for must be effective, proportionate and dissuasive and may be applied to cover the period of any breach, even where the breach has subsequently been rectified. The Member States shall notify those provisions to the Commission by 25 May 2011, and shall notify it without delay of any subsequent amendment affecting them.
2. Without prejudice to any judicial remedy which might be available, Member States shall ensure that the competent national authority and, where relevant, other national bodies have the power to order the cessation of the infringements referred to in paragraph 1.
3. Member States shall ensure that the competent national authority and, where relevant, other national bodies have the necessary investigative powers and resources, including the power to obtain any relevant information they might need to monitor and enforce national provisions adopted pursuant to this Directive.
4. The relevant national regulatory authorities may adopt measures to ensure effective cross-border cooperation in the enforcement of the national laws adopted pursuant to this Directive and to create harmonised conditions for the provision of services involving cross-border data flows.
    The national regulatory authorities shall provide the Commission, in good time before adopting any such measures, with a summary of the grounds for action, the envisaged measures and the proposed course of action. The Commission may, having examined such information and consulted ENISA and the Working Party on the Protection of Individuals with regard to the Processing of Personal Data established by Article 29 of Directive 95/46/EC, make comments or recommendations thereupon, in particular to ensure that the envisaged measures do not adversely affect the functioning of the internal market. National regulatory authorities shall take the utmost account of the Commission's comments or recommendations when deciding on the measures.]

NOTES
Art 15a inserted by European Parliament and Council Directive 2009/136/EC, Art 2(10).

[5.19]
Article 16   Transitional arrangements
1. Article 12 shall not apply to editions of directories already produced or placed on the market in printed or off-line electronic form before the national provisions adopted pursuant to this Directive enter into force.
2. Where the personal data of subscribers to fixed or mobile public voice telephony services have been included in a public subscriber directory in conformity with the provisions of Directive 95/46/EC and of Article 11 of Directive 97/66/EC before the national provisions adopted in pursuance of this Directive enter into force, the personal data of

such subscribers may remain included in this public directory in its printed or electronic versions, including versions with reverse search functions, unless subscribers indicate otherwise, after having received complete information about purposes and options in accordance with Article 12 of this Directive.

[5.20]
Article 17   Transposition
1. Before 31 October 2003 Member States shall bring into force the provisions necessary to comply with this Directive. They shall forthwith inform the Commission thereof.
When Member States adopt those provisions, they shall contain a reference to this Directive or be accompanied by such a reference on the occasion of their official publication. The methods of making such reference shall be laid down by the Member States.
2. Member States shall communicate to the Commission the text of the provisions of national law which they adopt in the field governed by this Directive and of any subsequent amendments to those provisions.

[5.21]
Article 18   Review
The Commission shall submit to the European Parliament and the Council, not later than three years after the date referred to in Article 17(1), a report on the application of this Directive and its impact on economic operators and consumers, in particular as regards the provisions on unsolicited communications, taking into account the international environment. For this purpose, the Commission may request information from the Member States, which shall be supplied without undue delay. Where appropriate, the Commission shall submit proposals to amend this Directive, taking account of the results of that report, any changes in the sector and any other proposal it may deem necessary in order to improve the effectiveness of this Directive.

[5.22]
Article 19   Repeal
Directive 97/66/EC is hereby repealed with effect from the date referred to in Article 17(1).
References made to the repealed Directive shall be construed as being made to this Directive.

[5.23]
Article 20   Entry into force
This Directive shall enter into force on the day of its publication in the *Official Journal of the European Communities*.

[5.24]
Article 21   Addressees
This Directive is addressed to the Member States.
Done at Brussels, 12 July 2002.

PART 6
HUMAN RIGHTS

HUMAN RIGHTS ACT 1998

(1998 c 42)

An Act to give further effect to rights and freedoms guaranteed under the European Convention on Human Rights; to make provision with respect to holders of certain judicial offices who become judges of the European Court of Human Rights; and for connected purposes.

[9 November 1998]

ARRANGEMENT OF SECTIONS

Introduction

[6.1]

1 The Convention Rights

(1) In this Act "the Convention rights" means the rights and fundamental freedoms set out in—

   (a) Articles 2 to 12 and 14 of the Convention,

   (b) Articles 1 to 3 of the First Protocol, and

   (c) [Article 1 of the Thirteenth Protocol],

as read with Articles 16 to 18 of the Convention.

(2) Those Articles are to have effect for the purposes of this Act subject to any designated derogation or reservation (as to which see sections 14 and 15).

(3) The Articles are set out in Schedule 1.

(4) The [Secretary of State] may by order make such amendments to this Act as he considers appropriate to reflect the effect, in relation to the United Kingdom, of a protocol.

(5) In subsection (4) "protocol" means a protocol to the Convention—

    (a) which the United Kingdom has ratified; or

    (b) which the United Kingdom has signed with a view to ratification.

(6) No amendment may be made by an order under subsection (4) so as to come into force before the protocol concerned is in force in relation to the United Kingdom.

NOTES

Sub-s (1): in para (c) words in square brackets substituted by the Human Rights Act 1998 (Amendment) Order 2004, SI 2004/1574, art 2(1).

Sub-s (4): words in square brackets substituted by the Secretary of State for Constitutional Affairs Order 2003, SI 2003/1887, art 9, Sch 2, para 10(1).

[6.2]

2 Interpretation of Convention rights

(1) A court or tribunal determining a question which has arisen in connection with a Convention right must take into account any—

    (a) judgment, decision, declaration or advisory opinion of the European Court of Human Rights,

    (b) opinion of the Commission given in a report adopted under Article 31 of the Convention,

    (c) decision of the Commission in connection with Article 26 or 27(2) of the Convention, or

    (d) decision of the Committee of Ministers taken under Article 46 of the Convention,

whenever made or given, so far as, in the opinion of the court or tribunal, it is relevant to the proceedings in which that question has arisen.

(2) Evidence of any judgment, decision, declaration or opinion of which account may have to be taken under this section is to be given in proceedings before any court or tribunal in such manner as may be provided by rules.

(3) In this section "rules" means rules of court or, in the case of proceedings before a tribunal, rules made for the purposes of this section—

    (a) by . . . [the Lord Chancellor or] the Secretary of State, in relation to any proceedings outside Scotland;

    (b) by the Secretary of State, in relation to proceedings in Scotland; or

    (c) by a Northern Ireland department, in relation to proceedings before a tribunal in Northern Ireland—

        (i) which deals with transferred matters; and

        (ii) for which no rules made under paragraph (a) are in force.

NOTES

Sub-s (3): in para (a) words omitted were repealed by the Secretary of State for Constitutional Affairs Order 2003, SI 2003/1887, art 9, Sch 2, para 10(2) and words in square brackets were inserted by the Transfer of Functions (Lord Chancellor and Secretary of State) Order 2005, SI 2005/3429, art 8, Schedule, para 3.

Legislation

[6.3]

3 Interpretation of legislation

(1) So far as it is possible to do so, primary legislation and subordinate legislation must be read and given effect in a way which is compatible with the Convention rights.

(2) This section—

    (a) applies to primary legislation and subordinate legislation whenever enacted;

    (b) does not affect the validity, continuing operation or enforcement of any incompatible primary legislation; and

    (c) does not affect the validity, continuing operation or enforcement of any incompatible subordinate legislation if (disregarding any possibility of revocation) primary legislation prevents removal of the incompatibility.

[6.4]

4 Declaration of incompatibility

(1) Subsection (2) applies in any proceedings in which a court determines whether a provision of primary legislation is compatible with a Convention right.

(2) If the court is satisfied that the provision is incompatible with a Convention right, it may make a declaration of that incompatibility.

(3) Subsection (4) applies in any proceedings in which a court determines whether a provision of subordinate legislation, made in the exercise of a power conferred by primary legislation, is compatible with a Convention right.

(4) If the court is satisfied—

    (a) that the provision is incompatible with a Convention right, and

    (b) that (disregarding any possibility of revocation) the primary legislation concerned prevents removal of the incompatibility,

it may make a declaration of that incompatibility.

(5) In this section "court" means—

    [(a) the Supreme Court;]

    (b) the Judicial Committee of the Privy Council;

    (c) the [Court Martial Appeal Court];

    (d) in Scotland, the High Court of Justiciary sitting otherwise than as a trial court or the Court of Session;

    (e) in England and Wales or Northern Ireland, the High Court or the Court of Appeal;

    [(f) the Court of Protection, in any matter being dealt with by the President of the Family Division, the [Chancellor of the High Court] or a puisne judge of the High Court].

(6) A declaration under this section ("a declaration of incompatibility")—
    (a) does not affect the validity, continuing operation or enforcement of the provision in respect of which it is given; and
    (b) is not binding on the parties to the proceedings in which it is made.

NOTES
Sub-s (5): para (a) substituted by the Constitutional Reform Act 2005, s 40(4), Sch 9, Pt 1, para 66(1), (2); in para (c) words in square brackets substituted by the Armed Forces Act 2006, s 378(1), Sch 16, para 156; para (f) inserted by the Mental Capacity Act 2005, s 67(1), Sch 6, para 43 and words in square brackets in para (f) substituted by the Crime and Courts Act 2013, s 21(4), Sch 14, Pt 3, para 5(5).

[6.5]
5 Right of Crown to intervene
(1) Where a court is considering whether to make a declaration of incompatibility, the Crown is entitled to notice in accordance with rules of court.
(2) In any case to which subsection (1) applies—
    (a) a Minister of the Crown (or a person nominated by him),
    (b) a member of the Scottish Executive,
    (c) a Northern Ireland Minister,
    (d) a Northern Ireland department,
is entitled, on giving notice in accordance with rules of court, to be joined as a party to the proceedings.
(3) Notice under subsection (2) may be given at any time during the proceedings.
(4) A person who has been made a party to criminal proceedings (other than in Scotland) as the result of a notice under subsection (2) may, with leave, appeal to the [Supreme Court] against any declaration of incompatibility made in the proceedings.
(5) In subsection (4)—
    "criminal proceedings" includes all proceedings before the [Court Martial Appeal Court]; and
    "leave" means leave granted by the court making the declaration of incompatibility or by the [Supreme Court].

NOTES
Sub-s (4): words in square brackets substituted by the Constitutional Reform Act 2005, s 40(4), Sch 9, Pt 1, para 66(1), (3).
Sub-s (5): in definition "criminal proceedings" words in square brackets substituted by the Armed Forces Act 2006, s 378(1), Sch 16, para 157; in definition "leave" words in square brackets substituted by the Constitutional Reform Act 2005, s 40(4), Sch 9, Pt 1, para 66(1), (3).

Public authorities

[6.6]
6 Acts of public authorities
(1) It is unlawful for a public authority to act in a way which is incompatible with a Convention right.
(2) Subsection (1) does not apply to an act if—
    (a) as the result of one or more provisions of primary legislation, the authority could not have acted differently; or
    (b) in the case of one or more provisions of, or made under, primary legislation which cannot be read or given effect in a way which is compatible with the Convention rights, the authority was acting so as to give effect to or enforce those provisions.
(3) In this section "public authority" includes—
    (a) a court or tribunal, and
    (b) any person certain of whose functions are functions of a public nature,
but does not include either House of Parliament or a person exercising functions in connection with proceedings in Parliament.
(4) . . .
(5) In relation to a particular act, a person is not a public authority by virtue only of subsection (3)(b) if the nature of the act is private.
(6) "An act" includes a failure to act but does not include a failure to—
    (a) introduce in, or lay before, Parliament a proposal for legislation; or
    (b) make any primary legislation or remedial order.

NOTES
Sub-s (4): repealed by the Constitutional Reform Act 2005, ss 40(4), 146, Sch 9, Pt 1, para 66(1), (4), Sch 18, Pt 5.

[6.7]
7 Proceedings
(1) A person who claims that a public authority has acted (or proposes to act) in a way which is made unlawful by section 6(1) may—
    (a) bring proceedings against the authority under this Act in the appropriate court or tribunal, or
    (b) rely on the Convention right or rights concerned in any legal proceedings,
but only if he is (or would be) a victim of the unlawful act.
(2) In subsection (1)(a) "appropriate court or tribunal" means such court or tribunal as may be determined in accordance with rules; and proceedings against an authority include a counterclaim or similar proceeding.
(3) If the proceedings are brought on an application for judicial review, the applicant is to be taken to have a sufficient interest in relation to the unlawful act only if he is, or would be, a victim of that act.
(4) If the proceedings are made by way of a petition for judicial review in Scotland, the applicant shall be taken to have title and interest to sue in relation to the unlawful act only if he is, or would be, a victim of that act.
(5) Proceedings under subsection (1)(a) must be brought before the end of—

(a)   the period of one year beginning with the date on which the act complained of took place; or

(b)   such longer period as the court or tribunal considers equitable having regard to all the circumstances,

but that is subject to any rule imposing a stricter time limit in relation to the procedure in question.

(6)   In subsection (1)(b) "legal proceedings" includes—

(a)   proceedings brought by or at the instigation of a public authority; and

(b)   an appeal against the decision of a court or tribunal.

(7)   For the purposes of this section, a person is a victim of an unlawful act only if he would be a victim for the purposes of Article 34 of the Convention if proceedings were brought in the European Court of Human Rights in respect of that act.

(8)   Nothing in this Act creates a criminal offence.

(9)   In this section "rules" means—

(a)   in relation to proceedings before a court or tribunal outside Scotland, rules made by . . . [the Lord Chancellor or] the Secretary of State for the purposes of this section or rules of court,

(b)   in relation to proceedings before a court or tribunal in Scotland, rules made by the Secretary of State for those purposes,

(c)   in relation to proceedings before a tribunal in Northern Ireland—

(i)   which deals with transferred matters; and

(ii)   for which no rules made under paragraph (a) are in force,

rules made by a Northern Ireland department for those purposes,

and includes provision made by order under section 1 of the Courts and Legal Services Act 1990.

(10)   In making rules, regard must be had to section 9.

(11)   The Minister who has power to make rules in relation to a particular tribunal may, to the extent he considers it necessary to ensure that the tribunal can provide an appropriate remedy in relation to an act (or proposed act) of a public authority which is (or would be) unlawful as a result of section 6(1), by order add to—

(a)   the relief or remedies which the tribunal may grant; or

(b)   the grounds on which it may grant any of them.

(12)   An order made under subsection (11) may contain such incidental, supplemental, consequential or transitional provision as the Minister making it considers appropriate.

(13)   "The Minister" includes the Northern Ireland department concerned.

NOTES

Sub-s (9): in para (a) words omitted repealed by the Secretary of State for Constitutional Affairs Order 2003, SI 2003/1887, art 9, Sch 2, para 10(2) and words in square brackets inserted by the Transfer of Functions (Lord Chancellor and Secretary of State) Order 2005, SI 2005/3429, art 8, Schedule, para 3.

Rules: the Proscribed Organisations Appeal Commission (Human Rights Act 1998 Proceedings) Rules 2006, SI 2006/2290; the Human Rights Act 1998 (Jurisdiction) (Scotland) Rules 2000, SSI 2000/301.

[6.8]
8   Judicial remedies

(1)   In relation to any act (or proposed act) of a public authority which the court finds is (or would be) unlawful, it may grant such relief or remedy, or make such order, within its powers as it considers just and appropriate.

(2)   But damages may be awarded only by a court which has power to award damages, or to order the payment of compensation, in civil proceedings.

(3)   No award of damages is to be made unless, taking account of all the circumstances of the case, including—

(a)   any other relief or remedy granted, or order made, in relation to the act in question (by that or any other court), and

(b)   the consequences of any decision (of that or any other court) in respect of that act,

the court is satisfied that the award is necessary to afford just satisfaction to the person in whose favour it is made.

(4)   In determining—

(a)   whether to award damages, or

(b)   the amount of an award,

the court must take into account the principles applied by the European Court of Human Rights in relation to the award of compensation under Article 41 of the Convention.

(5)   A public authority against which damages are awarded is to be treated—

(a)   in Scotland, for the purposes of section 3 of the Law Reform (Miscellaneous Provisions) (Scotland) Act 1940 as if the award were made in an action of damages in which the authority has been found liable in respect of loss or damage to the person to whom the award is made;

(b)   for the purposes of the Civil Liability (Contribution) Act 1978 as liable in respect of damage suffered by the person to whom the award is made.

(6)   In this section—

"court" includes a tribunal;

"damages" means damages for an unlawful act of a public authority; and

"unlawful" means unlawful under section 6(1).

[6.9]
9   Judicial acts

(1)   Proceedings under section 7(1)(a) in respect of a judicial act may be brought only—

(a)   by exercising a right of appeal;

(b)   on an application (in Scotland a petition) for judicial review; or

(c)   in such other forum as may be prescribed by rules.

(2)   That does not affect any rule of law which prevents a court from being the subject of judicial review.

[(3)   In proceedings under this Act in respect of a judicial act done in good faith, damages may not be awarded otherwise than—

(a) to compensate a person to the extent required by Article 5(5) of the Convention, or

(b) to compensate a person for a judicial act that is incompatible with Article 6 of the Convention in circumstances where the person is detained and, but for the incompatibility, the person would not have been detained or would not have been detained for so long.]

(4) An award of damages permitted by subsection (3) is to be made against the Crown; but no award may be made unless the appropriate person, if not a party to the proceedings, is joined.

(5) In this section—

"appropriate person" means the Minister responsible for the court concerned, or a person or government department nominated by him;

"court" includes a tribunal;

"judge" includes a member of a tribunal, a justice of the peace [(or, in Northern Ireland, a lay magistrate)] and a clerk or other officer entitled to exercise the jurisdiction of a court;

"judicial act" means a judicial act of a court and includes an act done on the instructions, or on behalf, of a judge; and

"rules" has the same meaning as in section 7(9).

NOTES

Sub-s (3) substituted by Human Rights Act 1998 (Remedial) Order 2020, SI 2020/1160, art 2(1).

Sub-s (5): in definition "judge" words in square brackets inserted by the Justice (Northern Ireland) Act 2002, s 10(6), Sch 4, para 39.

Rules: the Human Rights Act 1998 (Jurisdiction) (Scotland) Rules 2000, SSI 2000/301.

Remedial action

[6.10]

10 Power to take remedial action

(1) This section applies if—

(a) a provision of legislation has been declared under section 4 to be incompatible with a Convention right and, if an appeal lies—

(i) all persons who may appeal have stated in writing that they do not intend to do so;

(ii) the time for bringing an appeal has expired and no appeal has been brought within that time; or

(iii) an appeal brought within that time has been determined or abandoned; or

(b) it appears to a Minister of the Crown or Her Majesty in Council that, having regard to a finding of the European Court of Human Rights made after the coming into force of this section in proceedings against the United Kingdom, a provision of legislation is incompatible with an obligation of the United Kingdom arising from the Convention.

(2) If a Minister of the Crown considers that there are compelling reasons for proceeding under this section, he may by order make such amendments to the legislation as he considers necessary to remove the incompatibility.

(3) If, in the case of subordinate legislation, a Minister of the Crown considers—

(a) that it is necessary to amend the primary legislation under which the subordinate legislation in question was made, in order to enable the incompatibility to be removed, and

(b) that there are compelling reasons for proceeding under this section,

he may by order make such amendments to the primary legislation as he considers necessary.

(4) This section also applies where the provision in question is in subordinate legislation and has been quashed, or declared invalid, by reason of incompatibility with a Convention right and the Minister proposes to proceed under paragraph 2(b) of Schedule 2.

(5) If the legislation is an Order in Council, the power conferred by subsection (2) or (3) is exercisable by Her Majesty in Council.

(6) In this section "legislation" does not include a Measure of the Church Assembly or of the General Synod of the Church of England.

(7) Schedule 2 makes further provision about remedial orders.

NOTES

Orders: the Marriage Act 1949 (Remedial) Order 2007, SI 2007/438; the Asylum and Immigration (Treatment of Claimants, etc) Act 2004 (Remedial) Order 2011, SI 2011/1158; the Sexual Offences Act 2003 (Remedial) Order 2012, SI 2012/1883; Human Fertilisation and Embryology Act 2008 (Remedial) Order 2018, SI 2018/1413; British Nationality Act 1981 (Remedial) Order 2019, SI 2019/1164; Human Rights Act 1998 (Remedial) Order 2020, SI 2020/1160.

Other rights and proceedings

[6.11]

11 Safeguard for existing human rights

A person's reliance on a Convention right does not restrict—

(a) any other right or freedom conferred on him by or under any law having effect in any part of the United Kingdom; or

(b) his right to make any claim or bring any proceedings which he could make or bring apart from sections 7 to 9.

[6.12]

12 Freedom of expression

(1) This section applies if a court is considering whether to grant any relief which, if granted, might affect the exercise of the Convention right to freedom of expression.

(2) If the person against whom the application for relief is made ("the respondent") is neither present nor represented, no such relief is to be granted unless the court is satisfied—

(a) that the applicant has taken all practicable steps to notify the respondent; or

(b) that there are compelling reasons why the respondent should not be notified.

(3) No such relief is to be granted so as to restrain publication before trial unless the court is satisfied that the applicant is likely to establish that publication should not be allowed.

(4) The court must have particular regard to the importance of the Convention right to freedom of expression and, where the proceedings relate to material which the respondent claims, or which appears to the court, to be journalistic, literary or artistic material (or to conduct connected with such material), to—

    (a)   the extent to which—

          (i)   the material has, or is about to, become available to the public; or

          (ii)   it is, or would be, in the public interest for the material to be published;

    (b)   any relevant privacy code.

(5) In this section—

    "court" includes a tribunal; and

    "relief" includes any remedy or order (other than in criminal proceedings).

[6.13]
13   Freedom of thought, conscience and religion

(1) If a court's determination of any question arising under this Act might affect the exercise by a religious organisation (itself or its members collectively) of the Convention right to freedom of thought, conscience and religion, it must have particular regard to the importance of that right.

(2) In this section "court" includes a tribunal.

Derogations and reservations

[6.14]
14   Derogations

(1) In this Act "designated derogation" means . . . any derogation by the United Kingdom from an Article of the Convention, or of any protocol to the Convention, which is designated for the purposes of this Act in an order made by the [Secretary of State].

(2) . . .

(3) If a designated derogation is amended or replaced it ceases to be a designated derogation.

(4) But subsection (3) does not prevent the [Secretary of State] from exercising his power under subsection (1) . . . to make a fresh designation order in respect of the Article concerned.

(5) The [Secretary of State] must by order make such amendments to Schedule 3 as he considers appropriate to reflect—

    (a)   any designation order; or

    (b)   the effect of subsection (3).

(6) A designation order may be made in anticipation of the making by the United Kingdom of a proposed derogation.

NOTES

Sub-s (1): words omitted repealed by the Human Rights Act (Amendment) Order 2001, SI 2001/1216, art 2(a); words in square brackets substituted by the Secretary of State for Constitutional Affairs Order 2003, SI 2003/1887, art 9, Sch 2, para 10(1).

Sub-s (2): repealed by SI 2001/1216, art 2(b).

Sub-s (4): words in square brackets substituted by SI 2003/1887, art 9, Sch 2, para 10(1); reference omitted repealed by SI 2001/1216, art 2(c).

Sub-s (5): words in square brackets substituted by SI 2003/1887, art 9, Sch 2, para 10(1).

Orders: the Human Rights Act 1998 (Designated Derogation) Order 2001, SI 2001/3644; Human Rights Act 1998 (Amendment No 2) Order 2001, SI 2001/4032.

[6.15]
15   Reservations

(1) In this Act "designated reservation" means—

    (a)   the United Kingdom's reservation to Article 2 of the First Protocol to the Convention; and

    (b)   any other reservation by the United Kingdom to an Article of the Convention, or of any protocol to the Convention, which is designated for the purposes of this Act in an order made by the [Secretary of State].

(2) The text of the reservation referred to in subsection (1)(a) is set out in Part II of Schedule 3.

(3) If a designated reservation is withdrawn wholly or in part it ceases to be a designated reservation.

(4) But subsection (3) does not prevent the [Secretary of State] from exercising his power under subsection (1)(b) to make a fresh designation order in respect of the Article concerned.

(5) The [Secretary of State] must by order make such amendments to this Act as he considers appropriate to reflect—

    (a)   any designation order; or

    (b)   the effect of subsection (3).

NOTES

Sub-ss (1), (4), (5): words in square brackets substituted by the Secretary of State for Constitutional Affairs Order 2003, SI 2003/1887, art 9, Sch 2, para 10(1).

[6.16]
16   Period for which designated derogations have effect

(1) If it has not already been withdrawn by the United Kingdom, a designated derogation ceases to have effect for the purposes of this Act . . . at the end of the period of five years beginning with the date on which the order designating it was made.

(2) At any time before the period—

    (a)   fixed by subsection (1) . . . , or

    (b)   extended by an order under this subsection,

comes to an end, the [Secretary of State] may by order extend it by a further period of five years.

(3) An order under section 14(1) . . . ceases to have effect at the end of the period for consideration, unless a resolution has been passed by each House approving the order.

(4) Subsection (3) does not affect—

    (a) anything done in reliance on the order; or

    (b) the power to make a fresh order under section 14(1) . . .

(5) In subsection (3) "period for consideration" means the period of forty days beginning with the day on which the order was made.

(6) In calculating the period for consideration, no account is to be taken of any time during which—

    (a) Parliament is dissolved or prorogued; or

    (b) both Houses are adjourned for more than four days.

(7) If a designated derogation is withdrawn by the United Kingdom, the [Secretary of State] must by order make such amendments to this Act as he considers are required to reflect that withdrawal.

NOTES

    Sub-s (1): words omitted repealed by the Human Rights Act (Amendment) Order 2001, SI 2001/1216, art 3(a).

    Sub-s (2): in para (b) words omitted repealed by SI 2001/1216, art 3(b); words in square brackets substituted by the Secretary of State for Constitutional Affairs Order 2003, SI 2003/1887, art 9, Sch 2, para 10(1).

    Sub-s (3): reference omitted repealed by SI 2001/1216, art 3(c).

    Sub-s (4): in para (b) reference omitted repealed by SI 2001/1216, art 3(d).

    Sub-s (7): words in square brackets substituted by SI 2003/1887, art 9, Sch 2, para 10(1).

    Orders: Human Rights Act (Amendment) Order 2001, 2001/1216; Human Rights Act 1998 (Amendment) Order 2005, SI 2005/1071.

[6.17]
17   Periodic review of designated reservations

(1) The appropriate Minister must review the designated reservation referred to in section 15(1)(a)—

    (a) before the end of the period of five years beginning with the date on which section 1(2) came into force; and

    (b) if that designation is still in force, before the end of the period of five years beginning with the date on which the last report relating to it was laid under subsection (3).

(2) The appropriate Minister must review each of the other designated reservations (if any)—

    (a) before the end of the period of five years beginning with the date on which the order designating the reservation first came into force; and

    (b) if the designation is still in force, before the end of the period of five years beginning with the date on which the last report relating to it was laid under subsection (3).

(3) The Minister conducting a review under this section must prepare a report on the result of the review and lay a copy of it before each House of Parliament.

Judges of the European Court of Human Rights

[6.18]
18   Appointment to European Court of Human Rights

(1) In this section "judicial office" means the office of—

    (a) Lord Justice of Appeal, Justice of the High Court or Circuit judge, in England and Wales;

    (b) judge of the Court of Session or sheriff, in Scotland;

    (c) Lord Justice of Appeal, judge of the High Court or county court judge, in Northern Ireland.

(2) The holder of a judicial office may become a judge of the European Court of Human Rights ("the Court") without being required to relinquish his office.

(3) But he is not required to perform the duties of his judicial office while he is a judge of the Court.

(4) In respect of any period during which he is a judge of the Court—

    (a) a Lord Justice of Appeal or Justice of the High Court is not to count as a judge of the relevant court for the purposes of section 2(1) or 4(1) of the [Senior Courts Act 1981] (maximum number of judges) nor as a judge of the [Senior Courts] for the purposes of section 12(1) to (6) of that Act (salaries etc);

    (b) a judge of the Court of Session is not to count as a judge of that court for the purposes of section 1(1) of the Court of Session Act 1988 (maximum number of judges) or of section 9(1)(c) of the Administration of Justice Act 1973 ("the 1973 Act") (salaries etc);

    (c) a Lord Justice of Appeal or judge of the High Court in Northern Ireland is not to count as a judge of the relevant court for the purposes of section 2(1) or 3(1) of the Judicature (Northern Ireland) Act 1978 (maximum number of judges) nor as a judge of the [Court of Judicature] of Northern Ireland for the purposes of section 9(1)(d) of the 1973 Act (salaries etc);

    (d) a Circuit judge is not to count as such for the purposes of section 18 of the Courts Act 1971 (salaries etc);

    (e) a sheriff is not to count as such for the purposes of section 14 of the Sheriff Courts (Scotland) Act 1907 (salaries etc);

    (f) a county court judge of Northern Ireland is not to count as such for the purposes of section 106 of the County Courts Act (Northern Ireland) 1959 (salaries etc).

(5) If a sheriff principal is appointed a judge of the Court, section 11(1) of the Sheriff Courts (Scotland) Act 1971 (temporary appointment of sheriff principal) applies, while he holds that appointment, as if his office is vacant.

(6) Schedule 4 makes provision about judicial pensions in relation to the holder of a judicial office who serves as a judge of the Court.

(7) The Lord Chancellor or the Secretary of State may by order make such transitional provision (including, in particular, provision for a temporary increase in the maximum number of judges) as he considers appropriate in relation to any holder of a judicial office who has completed his service as a judge of the Court.

[(7A) The following paragraphs apply to the making of an order under subsection (7) in relation to any holder of a judicial office listed in subsection (1)(a)—

(a) before deciding what transitional provision it is appropriate to make, the person making the order must consult the Lord Chief Justice of England and Wales;

(b) before making the order, that person must consult the Lord Chief Justice of England and Wales.

(7B) The following paragraphs apply to the making of an order under subsection (7) in relation to any holder of a judicial office listed in subsection (1)(c)—

(a) before deciding what transitional provision it is appropriate to make, the person making the order must consult the Lord Chief Justice of Northern Ireland;

(b) before making the order, that person must consult the Lord Chief Justice of Northern Ireland.

(7C) The Lord Chief Justice of England and Wales may nominate a judicial office holder (within the meaning of section 109(4) of the Constitutional Reform Act 2005) to exercise his functions under this section.

(7D) The Lord Chief Justice of Northern Ireland may nominate any of the following to exercise his functions under this section—

(a) the holder of one of the offices listed in Schedule 1 to the Justice (Northern Ireland) Act 2002;

(b) a Lord Justice of Appeal (as defined in section 88 of that Act).]

NOTES

Sub-s (4): words in square brackets substituted by the Constitutional Reform Act 2005, s 59(5), Sch 11, Pt 1, para 1(2), Pt 2, para 4(1), (3), Pt 3, para 6(1), (3).

Sub-ss (7A)–(7D): inserted by the Constitutional Reform Act 2005, s 15(1), Sch 4, Pt 1, para 278.

Orders: the Judicial Pensions (European Court of Human Rights) Order 1998, SI 1998/2768; the Judicial Pensions (European Court of Human Rights) (Amendment) Order 2012, SI 2012/489.

Parliamentary procedure

[6.19]

19 Statements of compatibility

(1) A Minister of the Crown in charge of a Bill in either House of Parliament must, before Second Reading of the Bill—

(a) make a statement to the effect that in his view the provisions of the Bill are compatible with the Convention rights ("a statement of compatibility"); or

(b) make a statement to the effect that although he is unable to make a statement of compatibility the government nevertheless wishes the House to proceed with the Bill.

(2) The statement must be in writing and be published in such manner as the Minister making it considers appropriate.

Supplemental

[6.20]

20 Orders etc under this Act

(1) Any power of a Minister of the Crown to make an order under this Act is exercisable by statutory instrument.

(2) The power of . . . [the Lord Chancellor or] the Secretary of State to make rules (other than rules of court) under section 2(3) or 7(9) is exercisable by statutory instrument.

(3) Any statutory instrument made under section 14, 15 or 16(7) must be laid before Parliament.

(4) No order may be made by . . . [the Lord Chancellor or] the Secretary of State under section 1(4), 7(11) or 16(2) unless a draft of the order has been laid before, and approved by, each House of Parliament.

(5) Any statutory instrument made under section 18(7) or Schedule 4, or to which subsection (2) applies, shall be subject to annulment in pursuance of a resolution of either House of Parliament.

(6) The power of a Northern Ireland department to make—

(a) rules under section 2(3)(c) or 7(9)(c), or

(b) an order under section 7(11),

is exercisable by statutory rule for the purposes of the Statutory Rules (Northern Ireland) Order 1979.

(7) Any rules made under section 2(3)(c) or 7(9)(c) shall be subject to negative resolution; and section 41(6) of the Interpretation Act (Northern Ireland) 1954 (meaning of "subject to negative resolution") shall apply as if the power to make the rules were conferred by an Act of the Northern Ireland Assembly.

(8) No order may be made by a Northern Ireland department under section 7(11) unless a draft of the order has been laid before, and approved by, the Northern Ireland Assembly.

NOTES

Sub-ss (2), (4): words omitted repealed by SI 2003/1887, art 9, Sch 2, para 10(2); words in square brackets inserted by the Transfer of Functions (Lord Chancellor and Secretary of State) Order 2005, SI 2005/3429, art 8, Schedule, para 3.

[6.21]

21 Interpretation, etc

(1) In this Act—

"amend" includes repeal and apply (with or without modifications);

"the appropriate Minister" means the Minister of the Crown having charge of the appropriate authorised government department (within the meaning of the Crown Proceedings Act 1947);

"the Commission" means the European Commission of Human Rights;

"the Convention" means the Convention for the Protection of Human Rights and Fundamental Freedoms, agreed by the Council of Europe at Rome on 4th November 1950 as it has effect for the time being in relation to the United Kingdom;

"declaration of incompatibility" means a declaration under section 4;

"Minister of the Crown" has the same meaning as in the Ministers of the Crown Act 1975;

"Northern Ireland Minister" includes the First Minister and the deputy First Minister in Northern Ireland;

"primary legislation" means any—

(a) public general Act;

    (b)   local and personal Act;

    (c)   private Act;

    (d)   Measure of the Church Assembly;

    (e)   Measure of the General Synod of the Church of England;

    (f)   Order in Council—

        (i)   made in exercise of Her Majesty's Royal Prerogative;

        (ii)   made under section 38(1)(a) of the Northern Ireland Constitution Act 1973 or the corresponding provision of the Northern Ireland Act 1998; or

        (iii)   amending an Act of a kind mentioned in paragraph (a), (b) or (c);

and includes an order or other instrument made under primary legislation (otherwise than by the [Welsh Ministers, the First Minister for Wales, the Counsel General to the Welsh Assembly Government], a member of the Scottish Executive, a Northern Ireland Minister or a Northern Ireland department) to the extent to which it operates to bring one or more provisions of that legislation into force or amends any primary legislation;

"the First Protocol" means the protocol to the Convention agreed at Paris on 20th March 1952;

   . . .

"the Eleventh Protocol" means the protocol to the Convention (restructuring the control machinery established by the Convention) agreed at Strasbourg on 11th May 1994;

["the Thirteenth Protocol" means the protocol to the Convention (concerning the abolition of the death penalty in all circumstances) agreed at Vilnius on 3rd May 2002;]

"remedial order" means an order under section 10;

"subordinate legislation" means any—

    (a)   Order in Council other than one—

        (i)   made in exercise of Her Majesty's Royal Prerogative;

        (ii)   made under section 38(1)(a) of the Northern Ireland Constitution Act 1973 or the corresponding provision of the Northern Ireland Act 1998; or

        (iii)   amending an Act of a kind mentioned in the definition of primary legislation;

    (b)   Act of the Scottish Parliament;

    [(ba)   Measure of the National Assembly for Wales;

    (bb)   Act of the National Assembly for Wales;]

    (c)   Act of the Parliament of Northern Ireland;

    (d)   Measure of the Assembly established under section 1 of the Northern Ireland Assembly Act 1973;

    (e)   Act of the Northern Ireland Assembly;

    (f)   order, rules, regulations, scheme, warrant, byelaw or other instrument made under primary legislation (except to the extent to which it operates to bring one or more provisions of that legislation into force or amends any primary legislation);

    (g)   order, rules, regulations, scheme, warrant, byelaw or other instrument made under legislation mentioned in paragraph (b), (c), (d) or (e) or made under an Order in Council applying only to Northern Ireland;

    (h)   order, rules, regulations, scheme, warrant, byelaw or other instrument made by a member of the Scottish Executive[, Welsh Ministers, the First Minister for Wales, the Counsel General to the Welsh Assembly Government], a Northern Ireland Minister or a Northern Ireland department in exercise of prerogative or other executive functions of Her Majesty which are exercisable by such a person on behalf of Her Majesty;

"transferred matters" has the same meaning as in the Northern Ireland Act 1998; and

"tribunal" means any tribunal in which legal proceedings may be brought.

(2) The references in paragraphs (b) and (c) of section 2(1) to Articles are to Articles of the Convention as they had effect immediately before the coming into force of the Eleventh Protocol.

(3) The reference in paragraph (d) of section 2(1) to Article 46 includes a reference to Articles 32 and 54 of the Convention as they had effect immediately before the coming into force of the Eleventh Protocol.

(4) The references in section 2(1) to a report or decision of the Commission or a decision of the Committee of Ministers include references to a report or decision made as provided by paragraphs 3, 4 and 6 of Article 5 of the Eleventh Protocol (transitional provisions).

(5) . . .

NOTES

Sub-s (1): in definition "primary legislation" words in square brackets substituted by the Government of Wales Act 2006, s 160(1), Sch 10, para 56(1), (2); definition "the Sixth Protocol" (omitted) repealed by the Human Rights Act 1998 (Amendment) Order 2004, SI 2004/1574, art 2(2); definition "the Thirteenth Protocol" inserted by SI 2004/1574, art 2(2); in definition "subordinate legislation" paras (ba), (bb) and words in square brackets in para (h) inserted by the Government of Wales Act 2006, s 160(1), Sch 10, para 56(1), (3), (4).

Sub-s (5): repealed by the Armed Forces Act 2006, s 378(2), Sch 17.

National Assembly for Wales: see further, in relation to the renaming of the National Assembly for Wales as the Senedd Cymru or the Welsh Parliament, the Senedd and Elections (Wales) Act 2020, s 2 (with effect from 6 May 2020). See also ss 3–9 of the 2020 Act in relation to the renaming of Acts of the National Assembly for Wales, Members of the National Assembly for Wales, etc.

[6.22]

22 Short title, commencement, application and extent

(1) This Act may be cited as the Human Rights Act 1998.

(2) Sections 18, 20 and 21(5) and this section come into force on the passing of this Act.

(3) The other provisions of this Act come into force on such day as the Secretary of State may by order appoint; and different days may be appointed for different purposes.

(4) Paragraph (b) of subsection (1) of section 7 applies to proceedings brought by or at the instigation of a public authority whenever the act in question took place; but otherwise that subsection does not apply to an act taking place before the coming into force of that section.

(5) This Act binds the Crown.

(6) This Act extends to Northern Ireland.

(7) . . .

NOTES

Sub-s (7): repealed by the Armed Forces Act 2006, s 378(2), Sch 17.

Orders: the Human Rights Act 1998 (Commencement) Order 1998, SI 1998/2882; the Human Rights Act 1998 (Commencement No 2) Order 2000, SI 2000/1851.

SCHEDULE 1
THE ARTICLES

Section 1(3)

PART I THE CONVENTION

RIGHTS AND FREEDOMS

Article 2
Right to life

[6.23]

1 Everyone's right to life shall be protected by law. No one shall be deprived of his life intentionally save in the execution of a sentence of a court following his conviction of a crime for which this penalty is provided by law.

2 Deprivation of life shall not be regarded as inflicted in contravention of this Article when it results from the use of force which is no more than absolutely necessary:

    (a) in defence of any person from unlawful violence;

    (b) in order to effect a lawful arrest or to prevent the escape of a person lawfully detained;

    (c) in action lawfully taken for the purpose of quelling a riot or insurrection.

Article 3
Prohibition of torture

No one shall be subjected to torture or to inhuman or degrading treatment or punishment.

Article 4
Prohibition of slavery and forced labour

1 No one shall be held in slavery or servitude.

2 No one shall be required to perform forced or compulsory labour.

3 For the purpose of this Article the term "forced or compulsory labour" shall not include:

    (a) any work required to be done in the ordinary course of detention imposed according to the provisions of Article 5 of this Convention or during conditional release from such detention;

    (b) any service of a military character or, in case of conscientious objectors in countries where they are recognised, service exacted instead of compulsory military service;

    (c) any service exacted in case of an emergency or calamity threatening the life or well-being of the community;

    (d) any work or service which forms part of normal civic obligations.

Article 5
Right to liberty and security

1 Everyone has the right to liberty and security of person. No one shall be deprived of his liberty save in the following cases and in accordance with a procedure prescribed by law:

    (a) the lawful detention of a person after conviction by a competent court;

    (b) the lawful arrest or detention of a person for non-compliance with the lawful order of a court or in order to secure the fulfilment of any obligation prescribed by law;

    (c) the lawful arrest or detention of a person effected for the purpose of bringing him before the competent legal authority on reasonable suspicion of having committed an offence or when it is reasonably considered necessary to prevent his committing an offence or fleeing after having done so;

    (d) the detention of a minor by lawful order for the purpose of educational supervision or his lawful detention for the purpose of bringing him before the competent legal authority;

    (e) the lawful detention of persons for the prevention of the spreading of infectious diseases, of persons of unsound mind, alcoholics or drug addicts or vagrants;

    (f) the lawful arrest or detention of a person to prevent his effecting an unauthorised entry into the country or of a person against whom action is being taken with a view to deportation or extradition.

2 Everyone who is arrested shall be informed promptly, in a language which he understands, of the reasons for his arrest and of any charge against him.

3 Everyone arrested or detained in accordance with the provisions of paragraph 1(c) of this Article shall be brought promptly before a judge or other officer authorised by law to exercise judicial power and shall be entitled to trial within a reasonable time or to release pending trial. Release may be conditioned by guarantees to appear for trial.

4 Everyone who is deprived of his liberty by arrest or detention shall be entitled to take proceedings by which the lawfulness of his detention shall be decided speedily by a court and his release ordered if the detention is not lawful.

5 Everyone who has been the victim of arrest or detention in contravention of the provisions of this Article shall have an enforceable right to compensation.

Article 6
Right to a fair trial

1 In the determination of his civil rights and obligations or of any criminal charge against him, everyone is entitled to a fair and public hearing within a reasonable time by an independent and impartial tribunal established by law. Judgment shall be pronounced publicly but the press and public may be excluded from all or part of the trial in the interest of morals, public order or national security in a democratic society, where the interests of juveniles or the protection of the private life of the parties so require, or to the extent strictly necessary in the opinion of the court in special circumstances where publicity would prejudice the interests of justice.

2 Everyone charged with a criminal offence shall be presumed innocent until proved guilty according to law.

3 Everyone charged with a criminal offence has the following minimum rights:
(a) to be informed promptly, in a language which he understands and in detail, of the nature and cause of the accusation against him;
(b) to have adequate time and facilities for the preparation of his defence;
(c) to defend himself in person or through legal assistance of his own choosing or, if he has not sufficient means to pay for legal assistance, to be given it free when the interests of justice so require;
(d) to examine or have examined witnesses against him and to obtain the attendance and examination of witnesses on his behalf under the same conditions as witnesses against him;
(e) to have the free assistance of an interpreter if he cannot understand or speak the language used in court.

Article 7
No punishment without law

1 No one shall be held guilty of any criminal offence on account of any act or omission which did not constitute a criminal offence under national or international law at the time when it was committed. Nor shall a heavier penalty be imposed than the one that was applicable at the time the criminal offence was committed.

2 This Article shall not prejudice the trial and punishment of any person for any act or omission which, at the time when it was committed, was criminal according to the general principles of law recognised by civilised nations.

Article 8
Right to respect for private and family life

1 Everyone has the right to respect for his private and family life, his home and his correspondence.

2 There shall be no interference by a public authority with the exercise of this right except such as is in accordance with the law and is necessary in a democratic society in the interests of national security, public safety or the economic well-being of the country, for the prevention of disorder or crime, for the protection of health or morals, or for the protection of the rights and freedoms of others.

Article 9
Freedom of thought, conscience and religion

1 Everyone has the right to freedom of thought, conscience and religion; this right includes freedom to change his religion or belief and freedom, either alone or in community with others and in public or private, to manifest his religion or belief, in worship, teaching, practice and observance.

2 Freedom to manifest one's religion or beliefs shall be subject only to such limitations as are prescribed by law and are necessary in a democratic society in the interests of public safety, for the protection of public order, health or morals, or for the protection of the rights and freedoms of others.

Article 10
Freedom of expression

1 Everyone has the right to freedom of expression. This right shall include freedom to hold opinions and to receive and impart information and ideas without interference by public authority and regardless of frontiers. This Article shall not prevent States from requiring the licensing of broadcasting, television or cinema enterprises.

2 The exercise of these freedoms, since it carries with it duties and responsibilities, may be subject to such formalities, conditions, restrictions or penalties as are prescribed by law and are necessary in a democratic society, in the interests of national security, territorial integrity or public safety, for the prevention of disorder or crime, for the protection of health or morals, for the protection of the reputation or rights of others, for preventing the disclosure of information received in confidence, or for maintaining the authority and impartiality of the judiciary.

Article 11
Freedom of assembly and association

1 Everyone has the right to freedom of peaceful assembly and to freedom of association with others, including the right to form and to join trade unions for the protection of his interests.

2 No restrictions shall be placed on the exercise of these rights other than such as are prescribed by law and are necessary in a democratic society in the interests of national security or public safety, for the prevention of disorder or crime, for the protection of health or morals or for the protection of the rights and freedoms of others. This Article shall not prevent the imposition of lawful restrictions on the exercise of these rights by members of the armed forces, of the police or of the administration of the State.

Article 12
Right to marry

Men and women of marriageable age have the right to marry and to found a family, according to the national laws governing the exercise of this right.

Article 14
Prohibition of discrimination

The enjoyment of the rights and freedoms set forth in this Convention shall be secured without discrimination on any ground such as sex, race, colour, language, religion, political or other opinion, national or social origin, association with a national minority, property, birth or other status.

Article 16
Restrictions on political activity of aliens

Nothing in Articles 10, 11 and 14 shall be regarded as preventing the High Contracting Parties from imposing restrictions on the political activity of aliens.

Article 17
Prohibition of abuse of rights

Nothing in this Convention may be interpreted as implying for any State, group or person any right to engage in any activity or perform any act aimed at the destruction of any of the rights and freedoms set forth herein or at their limitation to a greater extent than is provided for in the Convention.

Article 18
Limitation on use of restrictions on rights

The restrictions permitted under this Convention to the said rights and freedoms shall not be applied for any purpose other than those for which they have been prescribed.

PART II THE FIRST PROTOCOL

Article 1
Protection of property

[6.24]

Every natural or legal person is entitled to the peaceful enjoyment of his possessions. No one shall be deprived of his possessions except in the public interest and subject to the conditions provided for by law and by the general principles of international law.

The preceding provisions shall not, however, in any way impair the right of a State to enforce such laws as it deems necessary to control the use of property in accordance with the general interest or to secure the payment of taxes or other contributions or penalties.

Article 2
Right to education

No person shall be denied the right to education. In the exercise of any functions which it assumes in relation to education and to teaching, the State shall respect the right of parents to ensure such education and teaching in conformity with their own religious and philosophical convictions.

Article 3
Right to free elections

The High Contracting Parties undertake to hold free elections at reasonable intervals by secret ballot, under conditions which will ensure the free expression of the opinion of the people in the choice of the legislature.

[PART III ARTICLE 1 OF THE THIRTEENTH PROTOCOL
Abolition of the Death Penalty

[6.25]

The death penalty shall be abolished. No one shall be condemned to such penalty or executed.]

NOTES

Pt III substituted by the Human Rights Act 1998 (Amendment) Order 2004, SI 2004/1574, art 2(3).

SCHEDULE 2
REMEDIAL ORDERS

Section 10

Orders

[6.26]

1 (1) A remedial order may—

(a) contain such incidental, supplemental, consequential or transitional provision as the person making it considers appropriate;

(b) be made so as to have effect from a date earlier than that on which it is made;

(c) make provision for the delegation of specific functions;

(d) make different provision for different cases.

(2) The power conferred by sub-paragraph (1)(a) includes—

(a) power to amend primary legislation (including primary legislation other than that which contains the incompatible provision); and

(b) power to amend or revoke subordinate legislation (including subordinate legislation other than that which contains the incompatible provision).

(3) A remedial order may be made so as to have the same extent as the legislation which it affects.

(4) No person is to be guilty of an offence solely as a result of the retrospective effect of a remedial order.

Procedure

2 No remedial order may be made unless—

(a) a draft of the order has been approved by a resolution of each House of Parliament made after the end of the period of 60 days beginning with the day on which the draft was laid; or

(b) it is declared in the order that it appears to the person making it that, because of the urgency of the matter, it is necessary to make the order without a draft being so approved.

Orders laid in draft

3 (1) No draft may be laid under paragraph 2(a) unless—

(a) the person proposing to make the order has laid before Parliament a document which contains a draft of the proposed order and the required information; and

(b) the period of 60 days, beginning with the day on which the document required by this sub-paragraph was laid, has ended.

(2) If representations have been made during that period, the draft laid under paragraph 2(a) must be accompanied by a statement containing—

(a) a summary of the representations; and

(b) if, as a result of the representations, the proposed order has been changed, details of the changes.

Urgent cases

4 (1) If a remedial order ("the original order") is made without being approved in draft, the person making it must lay it before Parliament, accompanied by the required information, after it is made.

(2) If representations have been made during the period of 60 days beginning with the day on which the original order was made, the person making it must (after the end of that period) lay before Parliament a statement containing—

(a) a summary of the representations; and

(b) if, as a result of the representations, he considers it appropriate to make changes to the original order, details of the changes.

(3) If sub-paragraph (2)(b) applies, the person making the statement must—

(a) make a further remedial order replacing the original order; and

(b) lay the replacement order before Parliament.

(4) If, at the end of the period of 120 days beginning with the day on which the original order was made, a resolution has not been passed by each House approving the original or replacement order, the order ceases to have effect (but without that affecting anything previously done under either order or the power to make a fresh remedial order).

Definitions

5 In this Schedule—

"representations" means representations about a remedial order (or proposed remedial order) made to the person making (or proposing to make) it and includes any relevant Parliamentary report or resolution; and

"required information" means—

(a) an explanation of the incompatibility which the order (or proposed order) seeks to remove, including particulars of the relevant declaration, finding or order; and

(b) a statement of the reasons for proceeding under section 10 and for making an order in those terms.

Calculating periods

6 In calculating any period for the purposes of this Schedule, no account is to be taken of any time during which—

(a) Parliament is dissolved or prorogued; or

(b) both Houses are adjourned for more than four days.

[7 (1) This paragraph applies in relation to—

(a) any remedial order made, and any draft of such an order proposed to be made,—
    (i) by the Scottish Ministers; or
    (ii) within devolved competence (within the meaning of the Scotland Act 1998) by Her Majesty in Council; and
(b) any document or statement to be laid in connection with such an order (or proposed order).

(2) This Schedule has effect in relation to any such order (or proposed order), document or statement subject to the following modifications.

(3) Any reference to Parliament, each House of Parliament or both Houses of Parliament shall be construed as a reference to the Scottish Parliament.

(4) Paragraph 6 does not apply and instead, in calculating any period for the purposes of this Schedule, no account is to be taken of any time during which the Scottish Parliament is dissolved or is in recess for more than four days.]

NOTES

Para 7: inserted by SI 2000/2040, art 2(1), Schedule, Pt I, para 21.
Orders: the Marriage Act 1949 (Remedial) Order 2007, SI 2007/438; the Asylum and Immigration (Treatment of Claimants, etc) Act 2004 (Remedial) Order 2011, SI 2011/1158; the Sexual Offences Act 2003 (Remedial) Order 2012, SI 2012/1883; Human Fertilisation and Embryology Act 2008 (Remedial) Order 2018, SI 2018/1413; British Nationality Act 1981 (Remedial) Order 2019, SI 2019/1164; Human Rights Act 1998 (Remedial) Order 2020, SI 2020/1160.

SCHEDULE 3
DEROGATION AND RESERVATION

Sections 14 and 15

(Original Pt I repealed by the Human Rights Act (Amendment) Order 2001, SI 2001/1216, art 4. New Pt I inserted by the Human Rights Act 1998 (Amendment No 2) Order 2001, SI 2001/4032, art 2, Schedule and subsequently repealed by the Human Rights Act 1998 (Amendment) Order 2005, SI 2005/1071, art 2.)

PART II RESERVATION

[6.27]
At the time of signing the present (First) Protocol, I declare that, in view of certain provisions of the Education Acts in the United Kingdom, the principle affirmed in the second sentence of Article 2 is accepted by the United Kingdom only so far as it is compatible with the provision of efficient instruction and training, and the avoidance of unreasonable public expenditure.
Dated 20 March 1952. Made by the United Kingdom Permanent Representative to the Council of Europe.

SCHEDULE 4
JUDICIAL PENSIONS

Section 18(6)

Duty to make orders about pensions

[6.28]
1 (1) The appropriate Minister must by order make provision with respect to pensions payable to or in respect of any holder of a judicial office who serves as an ECHR judge.

(2) A pensions order must include such provision as the Minister making it considers is necessary to secure that—
(a) an ECHR judge who was, immediately before his appointment as an ECHR judge, a member of a judicial pension scheme is entitled to remain as a member of that scheme;
(b) the terms on which he remains a member of the scheme are those which would have been applicable had he not been appointed as an ECHR judge; and
(c) entitlement to benefits payable in accordance with the scheme continues to be determined as if, while serving as an ECHR judge, his salary was that which would (but for section 18(4)) have been payable to him in respect of his continuing service as the holder of his judicial office.

Contributions

2 A pensions order may, in particular, make provision—
(a) for any contributions which are payable by a person who remains a member of a scheme as a result of the order, and which would otherwise be payable by deduction from his salary, to be made otherwise than by deduction from his salary as an ECHR judge; and
(b) for such contributions to be collected in such manner as may be determined by the administrators of the scheme.

Amendments of other enactments

3 A pensions order may amend any provision of, or made under, a pensions Act in such manner and to such extent as the Minister making the order considers necessary or expedient to ensure the proper administration of any scheme to which it relates.

Definitions

4 In this Schedule—
"appropriate Minister" means—
    (a) in relation to any judicial office whose jurisdiction is exercisable exclusively in relation to Scotland, the Secretary of State; and
    (b) otherwise, the Lord Chancellor;
"ECHR judge" means the holder of a judicial office who is serving as a judge of the Court;
"judicial pension scheme" means a scheme established by and in accordance with a pensions Act;

"pensions Act" means—
  (a)   the County Courts Act (Northern Ireland) 1959;
  (b)   the Sheriffs' Pensions (Scotland) Act 1961;
  (c)   the Judicial Pensions Act 1981; or
  (d)   the Judicial Pensions and Retirement Act 1993;
  [(e)   the Public Service Pensions Act 2013;] and
"pensions order" means an order made under paragraph 1.

NOTES

Para 4: in definition "pensions Act" para (e) inserted by the Public Service Pensions Act 2013, s 27, Sch 8, para 26.
Orders: the Judicial Pensions (European Court of Human Rights) Order 1998, SI 1998/2768.

UNITED NATIONS: UNIVERSAL DECLARATION OF HUMAN RIGHTS (1948)

[6.29]

NOTES

© 2021 United Nations. Reprinted with the permission of the United Nations.
The Universal Declaration of Human Rights was proclaimed by the United Nations General Assembly in Paris on 10 December 1948 (General Assembly resolution 217 A) as a common standard of achievements for all peoples and all nations.

PREAMBLE

Whereas recognition of the inherent dignity and of the equal and inalienable rights of all members of the human family is the foundation of freedom, justice and peace in the world,

Whereas disregard and contempt for human rights have resulted in barbarous acts which have outraged the conscience of mankind, and the advent of a world in which human beings shall enjoy freedom of speech and belief and freedom from fear and want has been proclaimed as the highest aspiration of the common people,

Whereas it is essential, if man is not to be compelled to have recourse, as a last resort, to rebellion against tyranny and oppression, that human rights should be protected by the rule of law,

Whereas it is essential to promote the development of friendly relations between nations,

Whereas the peoples of the United Nations have in the Charter reaffirmed their faith in fundamental human rights, in the dignity and worth of the human person and in the equal rights of men and women and have determined to promote social progress and better standards of life in larger freedom,

Whereas Member States have pledged themselves to achieve, in cooperation with the United Nations, the promotion of universal respect for and observance of human rights and fundamental freedoms,

Whereas a common understanding of these rights and freedoms is of the greatest importance for the full realization of this pledge,

Now, therefore,

The General Assembly,

Proclaims this Universal Declaration of Human Rights as a common standard of achievement for all peoples and all nations, to the end that every individual and every organ of society, keeping this Declaration constantly in mind, shall strive by teaching and education to promote respect for these rights and freedoms and by progressive measures, national and international, to secure their universal and effective recognition and observance, both among the peoples of Member States themselves and among the peoples of territories under their jurisdiction.

ARTICLE 1

All human beings are born free and equal in dignity and rights. They are endowed with reason and conscience and should act towards one another in a spirit of brotherhood.

ARTICLE 2

Everyone is entitled to all the rights and freedoms set forth in this Declaration, without distinction of any kind, such as race, colour, sex, language, religion, political or other opinion, national or social origin, property, birth or other status.

Furthermore, no distinction shall be made on the basis of the political, jurisdictional or international status of the country or territory to which a person belongs, whether it be independent, trust, non-self-governing or under any other limitation of sovereignty.

ARTICLE 3

Everyone has the right to life, liberty and security of person.

ARTICLE 4

No one shall be held in slavery or servitude; slavery and the slave trade shall be prohibited in all their forms.

ARTICLE 5

No one shall be subjected to torture or to cruel, inhuman or degrading treatment or punishment.

ARTICLE 6

Everyone has the right to recognition everywhere as a person before the law.

ARTICLE 7

All are equal before the law and are entitled without any discrimination to equal protection of the law. All are entitled to equal protection against any discrimination in violation of this Declaration and against any incitement to such discrimination.

ARTICLE 8

Everyone has the right to an effective remedy by the competent national tribunals for acts violating the fundamental rights granted him by the constitution or by law.

ARTICLE 9

No one shall be subjected to arbitrary arrest, detention or exile.

ARTICLE 10

Everyone is entitled in full equality to a fair and public hearing by an independent and impartial tribunal, in the determination of his rights and obligations and of any criminal charge against him.

ARTICLE 11

(1)   Everyone charged with a penal offence has the right to be presumed innocent until proved guilty according to law in a public trial at which he has had all the guarantees necessary for his defence.

(2)   No one shall be held guilty of any penal offence on account of any act or omission which did not constitute a penal offence, under national or international law, at the time when it was committed. Nor shall a heavier penalty be imposed than the one that was applicable at the time the penal offence was committed.

ARTICLE 12

No one shall be subjected to arbitrary interference with his privacy, family, home or correspondence, nor to attacks upon his honour and reputation. Everyone has the right to the protection of the law against such interference or attacks.

ARTICLE 13

(1)   Everyone has the right to freedom of movement and residence within the borders of each State.

(2)   Everyone has the right to leave any country, including his own, and to return to his country.

ARTICLE 14

(1)   Everyone has the right to seek and to enjoy in other countries asylum from persecution.

(2)   This right may not be invoked in the case of prosecutions genuinely arising from non-political crimes or from acts contrary to the purposes and principles of the United Nations.

ARTICLE 15

(1)   Everyone has the right to a nationality.

(2)   No one shall be arbitrarily deprived of his nationality nor denied the right to change his nationality.

ARTICLE 16

(1)   Men and women of full age, without any limitation due to race, nationality or religion, have the right to marry and to found a family. They are entitled to equal rights as to marriage, during marriage and at its dissolution.

(2)   Marriage shall be entered into only with the free and full consent of the intending spouses.

(3)   The family is the natural and fundamental group unit of society and is entitled to protection by society and the State.

ARTICLE 17

(1)   Everyone has the right to own property alone as well as in association with others.

(2)   No one shall be arbitrarily deprived of his property.

ARTICLE 18

Everyone has the right to freedom of thought, conscience and religion; this right includes freedom to change his religion or belief, and freedom, either alone or in community with others and in public or private, to manifest his religion or belief in teaching, practice, worship and observance.

ARTICLE 19

Everyone has the right to freedom of opinion and expression; this right includes freedom to hold opinions without interference and to seek, receive and impart information and ideas through any media and regardless of frontiers.

ARTICLE 20

(1)   Everyone has the right to freedom of peaceful assembly and association.
(2)   No one may be compelled to belong to an association.

ARTICLE 21

(1)   Everyone has the right to take part in the government of his country, directly or through freely chosen representatives.
(2)   Everyone has the right to equal access to public service in his country.
(3)   The will of the people shall be the basis of the authority of government; this will shall be expressed in periodic and genuine elections which shall be by universal and equal suffrage and shall be held by secret vote or by equivalent free voting procedures.

ARTICLE 22

Everyone, as a member of society, has the right to social security and is entitled to realization, through national effort and international co-operation and in accordance with the organization and resources of each State, of the economic, social and cultural rights indispensable for his dignity and the free development of his personality.

ARTICLE 23

(1)   Everyone has the right to work, to free choice of employment, to just and favourable conditions of work and to protection against unemployment.
(2)   Everyone, without any discrimination, has the right to equal pay for equal work.
(3)   Everyone who works has the right to just and favourable remuneration ensuring for himself and his family an existence worthy of human dignity, and supplemented, if necessary, by other means of social protection.
(4)   Everyone has the right to form and to join trade unions for the protection of his interests.

ARTICLE 24

Everyone has the right to rest and leisure, including reasonable limitation of working hours and periodic holidays with pay.

ARTICLE 25

(1)   Everyone has the right to a standard of living adequate for the health and well-being of himself and of his family, including food, clothing, housing and medical care and necessary social services, and the right to security in the event of unemployment, sickness, disability, widowhood, old age or other lack of livelihood in circumstances beyond his control.
(2)   Motherhood and childhood are entitled to special care and assistance. All children, whether born in or out of wedlock, shall enjoy the same social protection.

ARTICLE 26

(1)   Everyone has the right to education. Education shall be free, at least in the elementary and fundamental stages. Elementary education shall be compulsory. Technical and professional education shall be made generally available and higher education shall be equally accessible to all on the basis of merit.
(2)   Education shall be directed to the full development of the human personality and to the strengthening of respect for human rights and fundamental freedoms. It shall promote understanding, tolerance and friendship among all nations, racial or religious groups, and shall further the activities of the United Nations for the maintenance of peace.
(3)   Parents have a prior right to choose the kind of education that shall be given to their children.

ARTICLE 27

(1)   Everyone has the right freely to participate in the cultural life of the community, to enjoy the arts and to share in scientific advancement and its benefits.
(2)   Everyone has the right to the protection of the moral and material interests resulting from any scientific, literary or artistic production of which he is the author.

ARTICLE 28

Everyone is entitled to a social and international order in which the rights and freedoms set forth in this Declaration can be fully realized.

ARTICLE 29

(1)   Everyone has duties to the community in which alone the free and full development of his personality is possible.
(2)   In the exercise of his rights and freedoms, everyone shall be subject only to such limitations as are determined by law solely for the purpose of securing due recognition and respect for the rights and freedoms of others and of meeting the just requirements of morality, public order and the general welfare in a democratic society.
(3)   These rights and freedoms may in no case be exercised contrary to the purposes and principles of the United Nations.

Part 6   Human Rights

ARTICLE 30

Nothing in this Declaration may be interpreted as implying for any State, group or person any right to engage in any activity or to perform any act aimed at the destruction of any of the rights and freedoms set forth herein.

CONVENTION FOR THE PROTECTION OF HUMAN RIGHTS AND FUNDAMENTAL FREEDOMS
Rome, 4.XI.1950

[6.30]

NOTES

© Council of Europe.

The text of the Convention is presented as amended by the provisions of Protocol No 14 (CETS 194) as from its entry into force on 1 June 2010. The text of the Convention had previously been amended according to the provisions of Protocol No 3 (ETS 45), which entered into force on 21 September 1970, of Protocol No 5 (ETS 55), which entered into force on 20 December 1971, and of Protocol No 8 (ETS 118), which entered into force on 1 January 1990, and comprised also the text of Protocol No 2 (ETS 44) which, in accordance with Article 5 thereof, had been an integral part of the Convention since its entry into force on 21 September 1970. All provisions which had been amended or added by these Protocols were replaced by Protocol No 11 (ETS 155), as from the date of its entry into force on 1 November 1998. As from that date, Protocol No 9 (ETS 140), which entered into force on 1 October 1994, was repealed and Protocol No 10 (ETS 146) lost its purpose.

The current state of signatures and ratifications of the Convention and its Protocols as well as the complete list of declarations and reservations are available at www.conventions.coe.int.

The Governments signatory hereto, being members of the Council of Europe,

Considering the Universal Declaration of Human Rights proclaimed by the General Assembly of the United Nations on 10th December 1948;

Considering that this Declaration aims at securing the universal and effective recognition and observance of the Rights therein declared;

Considering that the aim of the Council of Europe is the achievement of greater unity between its members and that one of the methods by which that aim is to be pursued is the maintenance and further realisation of Human Rights and Fundamental Freedoms;

Reaffirming their profound belief in those fundamental freedoms which are the foundation of justice and peace in the world and are best maintained on the one hand by an effective political democracy and on the other by a common understanding and observance of the Human Rights upon which they depend;

Being resolved, as the governments of European countries which are like-minded and have a common heritage of political traditions, ideals, freedom and the rule of law, to take the first steps for the collective enforcement of certain of the rights stated in the Universal Declaration,

Have agreed as follows:

ARTICLE 1   OBLIGATION TO RESPECT HUMAN RIGHTS

[6.31]

The High Contracting Parties shall secure to everyone within their jurisdiction the rights and freedoms defined in Section I of this Convention.Section I

RIGHTS AND FREEDOMS

ARTICLE 2   RIGHT TO LIFE

[6.32]

1. Everyone's right to life shall be protected by law. No one shall be deprived of his life intentionally save in the execution of a sentence of a court following his conviction of a crime for which this penalty is provided by law.

2. Deprivation of life shall not be regarded as inflicted in contravention of this Article when it results from the use of force which is no more than absolutely necessary:
(a)   in defence of any person from unlawful violence;
(b)   in order to effect a lawful arrest or to prevent the escape of a person lawfully detained;
(c)   in action lawfully taken for the purpose of quelling a riot or insurrection.

ARTICLE 3   PROHIBITION OF TORTURE

No one shall be subjected to torture or to inhuman or degrading treatment or punishment.

ARTICLE 4   PROHIBITION OF SLAVERY AND FORCED LABOUR

1. No one shall be held in slavery or servitude.

2. No one shall be required to perform forced or compulsory labour.

3. For the purpose of this Article the term "forced or compulsory labour" shall not include:

(a)   any work required to be done in the ordinary course of detention imposed according to the provisions of Article 5 of this Convention or during conditional release from such detention;

(b)   any service of a military character or, in case of conscientious objectors in countries where they are recognised, service exacted instead of compulsory military service;

(c)   any service exacted in case of an emergency or calamity threatening the life or well-being of the community;

(d)   any work or service which forms part of normal civic obligations.

ARTICLE 5   RIGHT TO LIBERTY AND SECURITY

1. Everyone has the right to liberty and security of person. No one shall be deprived of his liberty save in the following cases and in accordance with a procedure prescribed by law:

(a)   the lawful detention of a person after conviction by a competent court;

(b)   the lawful arrest or detention of a person for non-compliance with the lawful order of a court or in order to secure the fulfilment of any obligation prescribed by law;

(c)   the lawful arrest or detention of a person effected for the purpose of bringing him before the competent legal authority on reasonable suspicion of having committed an offence or when it is reasonably considered necessary to prevent his committing an offence or fleeing after having done so;

(d)   the detention of a minor by lawful order for the purpose of educational supervision or his lawful detention for the purpose of bringing him before the competent legal authority;

(e)   the lawful detention of persons for the prevention of the spreading of infectious diseases, of persons of unsound mind, alcoholics or drug addicts or vagrants;

(f)   the lawful arrest or detention of a person to prevent his effecting an unauthorised entry into the country or of a person against whom action is being taken with a view to deportation or extradition

2. Everyone who is arrested shall be informed promptly, in a language which he understands, of the reasons for his arrest and of any charge against him.

3. Everyone arrested or detained in accordance with the provisions of paragraph 1 (c) of this Article shall be brought promptly before a judge or other officer authorised by law to exercise judicial power and shall be entitled to trial within a reasonable time or to release pending trial. Release may be conditioned by guarantees to appear for trial.

4. Everyone who is deprived of his liberty by arrest or detention shall be entitled to take proceedings by which the lawfulness of his detention shall be decided speedily by a court and his release ordered if the detention is not lawful.

5. Everyone who has been the victim of arrest or detention in contravention of the provisions of this Article shall have an enforceable right to compensation.

ARTICLE 6   RIGHT TO A FAIR TRIAL

1. In the determination of his civil rights and obligations or of any criminal charge against him, everyone is entitled to a fair and public hearing within a reasonable time by an independent and impartial tribunal established by law. Judgment shall be pronounced publicly but the press and public may be excluded from all or part of the trial in the interests of morals, public order or national security in a democratic society, where the interests of juveniles or the protection of the private life of the parties so require, or to the extent strictly necessary in the opinion of the court in special circumstances where publicity would prejudice the interests of justice.

2. Everyone charged with a criminal offence shall be presumed innocent until proved guilty according to law.

3. Everyone charged with a criminal offence has the following minimum rights:

(a)   to be informed promptly, in a language which he understands and in detail, of the nature and cause of the accusation against him;

(b)   to have adequate time and facilities for the preparation of his defence;

(c)   to defend himself in person or through legal assistance of his own choosing or, if he has not sufficient means to pay for legal assistance, to be given it free when the interests of justice so require;

(d)   to examine or have examined witnesses against him and to obtain the attendance and examination of witnesses on his behalf under the same conditions as witnesses against him;

(e)   to have the free assistance of an interpreter if he cannot understand or speak the language used in court.

ARTICLE 7   NO PUNISHMENT WITHOUT LAW

1. No one shall be held guilty of any criminal offence on account of any act or omission which did not constitute a criminal offence under national or international law at the time when it was committed. Nor shall a heavier penalty be imposed than the one that was applicable at the time the criminal offence was committed.

2. This Article shall not prejudice the trial and punishment of any person for any act or omission which, at the time when it was committed, was criminal according to the general principles of law recognised by civilised nations.

ARTICLE 8   RIGHT TO RESPECT FOR PRIVATE AND FAMILY LIFE

1.   Everyone has the right to respect for his private and family life, his home and his correspondence.

2.   There shall be no interference by a public authority with the exercise of this right except such as is in accordance with the law and is necessary in a democratic society in the interests of national security, public safety or the economic well-being of the country, for the prevention of disorder or crime, for the protection of health or morals, or for the protection of the rights and freedoms of others.

ARTICLE 9   FREEDOM OF THOUGHT, CONSCIENCE AND RELIGION

1.   Everyone has the right to freedom of thought, conscience and religion; this right includes freedom to change his religion or belief and freedom, either alone or in community with others and in public or private, to manifest his religion or belief, in worship, teaching, practice and observance.

2.   Freedom to manifest one's religion or beliefs shall be subject only to such limitations as are prescribed by law and are necessary in a democratic society in the interests of public safety, for the protection of public order, health or morals, or for the protection of the rights and freedoms of others.

ARTICLE 10   FREEDOM OF EXPRESSION

1.   Everyone has the right to freedom of expression. This right shall include freedom to hold opinions and to receive and impart information and ideas without interference by public authority and regardless of frontiers. This Article shall not prevent States from requiring the licensing of broadcasting, television or cinema enterprises.

2.   The exercise of these freedoms, since it carries with it duties and responsibilities, may be subject to such formalities, conditions, restrictions or penalties as are prescribed by law and are necessary in a democratic society, in the interests of national security, territorial integrity or public safety, for the prevention of disorder or crime, for the protection of health or morals, for the protection of the reputation or rights of others, for preventing the disclosure of information received in confidence, or for maintaining the authority and impartiality of the judiciary.

ARTICLE 11   FREEDOM OF ASSEMBLY AND ASSOCIATION

1.   Everyone has the right to freedom of peaceful assembly and to freedom of association with others, including the right to form and to join trade unions for the protection of his interests.

2.   No restrictions shall be placed on the exercise of these rights other than such as are prescribed by law and are necessary in a democratic society in the interests of national security or public safety, for the prevention of disorder or crime, for the protection of health or morals or for the protection of the rights and freedoms of others. This Article shall not prevent the imposition of lawful restrictions on the exercise of these rights by members of the armed forces, of the police or of the administration of the State.

ARTICLE 12   RIGHT TO MARRY

Men and women of marriageable age have the right to marry and to found a family, according to the national laws governing the exercise of this right.

ARTICLE 13   RIGHT TO AN EFFECTIVE REMEDY

Everyone whose rights and freedoms as set forth in this Convention are violated shall have an effective remedy before a national authority notwithstanding that the violation has been committed by persons acting in an official capacity.

ARTICLE 14   PROHIBITION OF DISCRIMINATION

The enjoyment of the rights and freedoms set forth in this Convention shall be secured without discrimination on any ground such as sex, race, colour, language, religion, political or other opinion, national or social origin, association with a national minority, property, birth or other status.

ARTICLE 15   DEROGATION IN TIME OF EMERGENCY

1.   In time of war or other public emergency threatening the life of the nation any High Contracting Party may take measures derogating from its obligations under this Convention to the extent strictly required by the exigencies of the situation, provided that such measures are not inconsistent with its other obligations under international law.

2.   No derogation from Article 2, except in respect of deaths resulting from lawful acts of war, or from Articles 3, 4 (paragraph 1) and 7 shall be made under this provision.

3.   Any High Contracting Party availing itself of this right of derogation shall keep the Secretary General of the Council of Europe fully informed of the measures which it has taken and the reasons therefor. It shall also inform the Secretary General of the Council of Europe when such measures have ceased to operate and the provisions of the Convention are again being fully executed.

ARTICLE 16   RESTRICTIONS ON POLITICAL ACTIVITY OF ALIENS

Nothing in Articles 10, 11 and 14 shall be regarded as preventing the High Contracting Parties from imposing restrictions on the political activity of aliens.

ARTICLE 17　PROHIBITION OF ABUSE OF RIGHTS

Nothing in this Convention may be interpreted as implying for any State, group or person any right to engage in any activity or perform any act aimed at the destruction of any of the rights and freedoms set forth herein or at their limitation to a greater extent than is provided for in the Convention.

ARTICLE 18　LIMITATION ON USE OF RESTRICTIONS ON RIGHTS

The restrictions permitted under this Convention to the said rights and freedoms shall not be applied for any purpose other than those for which they have been prescribed.Section II

EUROPEAN COURT OF HUMAN RIGHTS

ARTICLE 19　ESTABLISHMENT OF THE COURT

[6.33]
To ensure the observance of the engagements undertaken by the High Contracting Parties in the Convention and the Protocols thereto, there shall be set up a European Court of Human Rights, hereinafter referred to as "the Court". It shall function on a permanent basis.

ARTICLE 20　NUMBER OF JUDGES

The Court shall consist of a number of judges equal to that of the High Contracting Parties.

ARTICLE 21　CRITERIA FOR OFFICE

1.　The judges shall be of high moral character and must either possess the qualifications required for appointment to high judicial office or be jurisconsults of recognised competence.

2.　The judges shall sit on the Court in their individual capacity.

3.　During their term of office the judges shall not engage in any activity which is incompatible with their independence, impartiality or with the demands of a full-time office; all questions arising from the application of this paragraph shall be decided by the Court.

ARTICLE 22　ELECTION OF JUDGES

The judges shall be elected by the Parliamentary Assembly with respect to each High Contracting Party by a majority of votes cast from a list of three candidates nominated by the High Contracting Party.

ARTICLE 23　TERMS OF OFFICE AND DISMISSAL

1.　The judges shall be elected for a period of nine years. They may not be re-elected.

2.　The terms of office of judges shall expire when they reach the age of 70.

3.　The judges shall hold office until replaced. They shall, however, continue to deal with such cases as they already have under consideration.

4.　No judge may be dismissed from office unless the other judges decide by a majority of two-thirds that that judge has ceased to fulfil the required conditions.

ARTICLE 24　REGISTRY AND RAPPORTEURS

1.　The Court shall have a Registry, the functions and organisation of which shall be laid down in the rules of the Court.

2.　When sitting in a single-judge formation, the Court shall be assisted by rapporteurs who shall function under the authority of the President of the Court. They shall form part of the Court's Registry.

ARTICLE 25　PLENARY COURT

The plenary Court shall
(a)　elect its President and one or two Vice-Presidents for a period of three years; they may be re-elected;
(b)　set up Chambers, constituted for a fixed period of time;
(c)　elect the Presidents of the Chambers of the Court; they may be re-elected;
(d)　adopt the rules of the Court;
(e)　elect the Registrar and one or more Deputy Registrars;
(f)　make any request under Article 26, paragraph 2.

ARTICLE 26　SINGLE-JUDGE FORMATION, COMMITTEES, CHAMBERS AND GRAND CHAMBER

1.　To consider cases brought before it, the Court shall sit in a single-judge formation, in committees of three judges, in

Chambers of seven judges and in a Grand Chamber of seventeen judges. The Court's Chambers shall set up committees for a fixed period of time.

2.　At the request of the plenary Court, the Committee of Ministers may, by a unanimous decision and for a fixed period, reduce to five the number of judges of the Chambers.

3.   When sitting as a single judge, a judge shall not examine any application against the High Contracting Party in respect of which that judge has been elected.

4.   There shall sit as an *ex officio* member of the Chamber and the Grand Chamber the judge elected in respect of the High Contracting Party concerned. If there is none or if that judge is unable to sit, a person chosen by the President of the Court from a list submitted in advance by that Party shall sit in the capacity of judge.

5.   The Grand Chamber shall also include the President of the Court, the Vice-Presidents, the Presidents of the Chambers and other judges chosen in accordance with the rules of the Court. When a case is referred to the Grand Chamber under Article 43, no judge from the Chamber which rendered the judgment shall sit in the Grand Chamber, with the exception of the President of the Chamber and the judge who sat in respect of the High Contracting Party concerned.

ARTICLE 27   COMPETENCE OF SINGLE JUDGES

1.   A single judge may declare inadmissible or strike out of the Court's list of cases an application submitted under Article 34, where such a decision can be taken without further examination.

2.   The decision shall be final.

3.   If the single judge does not declare an application inadmissible or strike it out, that judge shall forward it to a committee or to a Chamber for further examination.

ARTICLE 28   COMPETENCE OF COMMITTEES

1.   In respect of an application submitted under Article 34, a committee may, by a unanimous vote,
(a)   declare it inadmissible or strike it out of its list of cases, where such decision can be taken without further examination; or
(b)   declare it admissible and render at the same time a judgment on the merits, if the underlying question in the case, concerning the interpretation or the application of the Convention or the Protocols thereto, is already the subject of well-established case-law of the Court.

2.   Decisions and judgments under paragraph 1 shall be final.

3.   If the judge elected in respect of the High Contracting Party concerned is not a member of the committee, the committee may at any stage of the proceedings invite that judge to take the place of one of the members of the committee, having regard to all relevant factors, including whether that Party has contested the application of the procedure under paragraph 1.(b).

ARTICLE 29   DECISIONS BY CHAMBERS ON ADMISSIBILITY AND MERITS

1.   If no decision is taken under Article 27 or 28, or no judgment rendered under Article 28, a Chamber shall decide on the admissibility and merits of individual applications submitted under Article 34. The decision on admissibility may be taken separately.

2.   A Chamber shall decide on the admissibility and merits of inter-State applications submitted under Article 33. The decision on admissibility shall be taken separately unless the Court, in exceptional cases, decides otherwise.

ARTICLE 30   RELINQUISHMENT OF JURISDICTION TO THE GRAND CHAMBER

Where a case pending before a Chamber raises a serious question affecting the interpretation of the Convention or the Protocols thereto, or where the resolution of a question before the Chamber might have a result inconsistent with a judgment previously delivered by the Court, the Chamber may, at any time before it has rendered its judgment, relinquish jurisdiction in favour of the Grand Chamber, unless one of the parties to the case objects.

ARTICLE 31   POWERS OF THE GRAND CHAMBER

The Grand Chamber shall
(a)   determine applications submitted either under Article 33 or Article 34 when a Chamber has relinquished jurisdiction under Article 30 or when the case has been referred to it under Article 43;
(b)   decide on issues referred to the Court by the Committee of Ministers in accordance with Article 46, paragraph 4; and
(c)   consider requests for advisory opinions submitted under Article 47.

ARTICLE 32   JURISDICTION OF THE COURT

1.   The jurisdiction of the Court shall extend to all matters concerning the interpretation and application of the Convention and the Protocols thereto which are referred to it as provided in Articles 33, 34, 46 and 47.

2.   In the event of dispute as to whether the Court has jurisdiction, the Court shall decide.

ARTICLE 33   INTER-STATE CASES

Any High Contracting Party may refer to the Court any alleged breach of the provisions of the Convention and the Protocols thereto by another High Contracting Party.

ARTICLE 34　INDIVIDUAL APPLICATIONS

The Court may receive applications from any person, non-governmental organisation or group of individuals claiming to be the victim of a violation by one of the High Contracting Parties of the rights set forth in the Convention or the Protocols thereto. The High Contracting Parties undertake not to hinder in any way the effective exercise of this right.

ARTICLE 35　ADMISSIBILITY CRITERIA

1.　The Court may only deal with the matter after all domestic remedies have been exhausted, according to the generally recognised rules of international law, and within a period of six months from the date on which the final decision was taken.

2.　The Court shall not deal with any application submitted under Article 34 that
(a)　is anonymous; or
(b)　is substantially the same as a matter that has already been examined by the Court or has already been submitted to another procedure of international investigation or settlement and contains no relevant new information.

3.　The Court shall declare inadmissible any individual application submitted under Article 34 if it considers that:
(a)　the application is incompatible with the provisions of the Convention or the Protocols thereto, manifestly ill-founded, or an abuse of the right of individual application; or
(b)　the applicant has not suffered a significant disadvantage, unless respect for human rights as defined in the Convention and the Protocols thereto requires an examination of the application on the merits and provided that no case may be rejected on this ground which has not been duly considered by a domestic tribunal.

4.　The Court shall reject any application which it considers inadmissible under this Article. It may do so at any stage of the proceedings.

ARTICLE 36　THIRD PARTY INTERVENTION

1.　In all cases before a Chamber or the Grand Chamber, a High Contracting Party one of whose nationals is an applicant shall have the right to submit written comments and to take part in hearings.

2.　The President of the Court may, in the interest of the proper administration of justice, invite any High Contracting Party which is not a party to the proceedings or any person concerned who is not the applicant to submit written comments or take part in hearings.

3.　In all cases before a Chamber or the Grand Chamber, the Council of Europe Commissioner for Human Rights may submit written comments and take part in hearings.

ARTICLE 37　STRIKING OUT APPLICATIONS

1.　The Court may at any stage of the proceedings decide to strike an application out of its list of cases where the circumstances lead to the conclusion that
(a)　the applicant does not intend to pursue his application; or
(b)　the matter has been resolved; or
(c)　for any other reason established by the Court, it is no longer justified to continue the examination of the application.

However, the Court shall continue the examination of the application if respect for human rights as defined in the Convention and the Protocols thereto so requires.

2.　The Court may decide to restore an application to its list of cases if it considers that the circumstances justify such a course.

ARTICLE 38　EXAMINATION OF THE CASE

The Court shall examine the case together with the representatives of the parties and, if need be, undertake an investigation, for the effective conduct of which the High Contracting Parties concerned shall furnish all necessary facilities.

ARTICLE 39　FRIENDLY SETTLEMENTS

1.　At any stage of the proceedings, the Court may place itself at the disposal of the parties concerned with a view to securing a friendly settlement of the matter on the basis of respect for human rights as defined in the Convention and the Protocols thereto.

2.　Proceedings conducted under paragraph 1 shall be confidential.

3.　If a friendly settlement is effected, the Court shall strike the case out of its list by means of a decision which shall be confined to a brief statement of the facts and of the solution reached.

4.　This decision shall be transmitted to the Committee of Ministers, which shall supervise the execution of the terms of the friendly settlement as set out in the decision.

ARTICLE 40　PUBLIC HEARINGS AND ACCESS TO DOCUMENTS

1.　Hearings shall be in public unless the Court in exceptional circumstances decides otherwise.

2. Documents deposited with the Registrar shall be accessible to the public unless the President of the Court decides otherwise.

ARTICLE 41   JUST SATISFACTION

If the Court finds that there has been a violation of the Convention or the Protocols thereto, and if the internal law of the High Contracting Party concerned allows only partial reparation to be made, the Court shall, if necessary, afford just satisfaction to the injured party.

ARTICLE 42   JUDGMENTS OF CHAMBERS

Judgments of Chambers shall become final in accordance with the provisions of Article 44, paragraph 2.

ARTICLE 43   REFERRAL TO THE GRAND CHAMBER

1. Within a period of three months from the date of the judgment of the Chamber, any party to the case may, in exceptional cases, request that the case be referred to the Grand Chamber.

2. A panel of five judges of the Grand Chamber shall accept the request if the case raises a serious question affecting the interpretation or application of the Convention or the Protocols thereto, or a serious issue of general importance.

3. If the panel accepts the request, the Grand Chamber shall decide the case by means of a judgment.

ARTICLE 44   FINAL JUDGMENTS

1. The judgment of the Grand Chamber shall be final.

2. The judgment of a Chamber shall become final
(a)   when the parties declare that they will not request that the case be referred to the Grand Chamber; or
(b)   three months after the date of the judgment, if reference of the case to the Grand Chamber has not been requested; or
(c)   when the panel of the Grand Chamber rejects the request to refer under Article 43.

3. The final judgment shall be published.

ARTICLE 45   REASONS FOR JUDGMENTS AND DECISIONS

1. Reasons shall be given for judgments as well as for decisions declaring applications admissible or inadmissible.

2. If a judgment does not represent, in whole or in part, the unanimous opinion of the judges, any judge shall be entitled to deliver a separate opinion.

ARTICLE 46   BINDING FORCE AND EXECUTION OF JUDGMENTS

1. The High Contracting Parties undertake to abide by the final judgment of the Court in any case to which they are parties.

2. The final judgment of the Court shall be transmitted to the Committee of Ministers, which shall supervise its execution.

3. If the Committee of Ministers considers that the supervision of the execution of a final judgment is hindered by a problem of interpretation of the judgment, it may refer the matter to the Court for a ruling on the question of interpretation. A referral decision shall require a majority vote of two-thirds of the representatives entitled to sit on the committee.

4. If the Committee of Ministers considers that a High Contracting Party refuses to abide by a final judgment in a case to which it is a party, it may, after serving formal notice on that Party and by decision adopted by a majority vote of two-thirds of the representatives entitled to sit on the committee, refer to the Court the question whether that Party has failed to fulfil its obligation under paragraph 1.

5. If the Court finds a violation of paragraph 1, it shall refer the case to the Committee of Ministers for consideration of the measures to be taken. If the Court finds no violation of paragraph 1, it shall refer the case to the Committee of Ministers, which shall close its examination of the case.

ARTICLE 47   ADVISORY OPINIONS

1. The Court may, at the request of the Committee of Ministers, give advisory opinions on legal questions concerning the interpretation of the Convention and the Protocols thereto.

2. Such opinions shall not deal with any question relating to the content or scope of the rights or freedoms defined in Section I of the Convention and the Protocols thereto, or with any other question which the Court or the Committee of Ministers might have to consider in consequence of any such proceedings as could be instituted in accordance with the Convention.

3. Decisions of the Committee of Ministers to request an advisory opinion of the Court shall require a majority vote of the representatives entitled to sit on the committee.

ARTICLE 48   ADVISORY JURISDICTION OF THE COURT

The Court shall decide whether a request for an advisory opinion submitted by the Committee of Ministers is within its competence as defined in Article 47.

ARTICLE 49   REASONS FOR ADVISORY OPINIONS

1. Reasons shall be given for advisory opinions of the Court.

2. If the advisory opinion does not represent, in whole or in part, the unanimous opinion of the judges, any judge shall be entitled to deliver a separate opinion.

3. Advisory opinions of the Court shall be communicated to the Committee of Ministers.

ARTICLE 50   EXPENDITURE ON THE COURT

The expenditure on the Court shall be borne by the Council of Europe.

ARTICLE 51   PRIVILEGES AND IMMUNITIES OF JUDGES

The judges shall be entitled, during the exercise of their functions, to the privileges and immunities provided for in Article 40 of the Statute of the Council of Europe and in the agreements made thereunder.Section III

MISCELLANEOUS PROVISIONS

ARTICLE 52   INQUIRIES BY THE SECRETARY GENERAL

[6.34]
On receipt of a request from the Secretary General of the Council of Europe any High Contracting Party shall furnish an explanation of the manner in which its internal law ensures the effective implementation of any of the provisions of the Convention.

ARTICLE 53   SAFEGUARD FOR EXISTING HUMAN RIGHTS

Nothing in this Convention shall be construed as limiting or derogating from any of the human rights and fundamental freedoms which may be ensured under the laws of any High Contracting Party or under any other agreement to which it is a party.

ARTICLE 54   POWERS OF THE COMMITTEE OF MINISTERS

Nothing in this Convention shall prejudice the powers conferred on the Committee of Ministers by the Statute of the Council of Europe.

ARTICLE 55   EXCLUSION OF OTHER MEANS OF DISPUTE SETTLEMENT

The High Contracting Parties agree that, except by special agreement, they will not avail themselves of treaties, conventions or declarations in force between them for the purpose of submitting, by way of petition, a dispute arising out of the interpretation or application of this Convention to a means of settlement other than those provided for in this Convention.

ARTICLE 56   TERRITORIAL APPLICATION

1. Any State may at the time of its ratification or at any time thereafter declare by notification addressed to the Secretary General of the Council of Europe that the present Convention shall, subject to paragraph 4 of this Article, extend to all or any of the territories for whose international relations it is responsible.

2. The Convention shall extend to the territory or territories named in the notification as from the thirtieth day after the receipt of this notification by the Secretary General of the Council of Europe.

3. The provisions of this Convention shall be applied in such territories with due regard, however, to local requirements.

4. Any State which has made a declaration in accordance with paragraph 1 of this Article may at any time thereafter declare on behalf of one or more of the territories to which the declaration relates that it accepts the competence of the Court to receive applications from individuals, non-governmental organisations or groups of individuals as provided by Article 34 of the Convention.

ARTICLE 57   RESERVATIONS

1. Any State may, when signing this Convention or when depositing its instrument of ratification, make a reservation in respect of any particular provision of the Convention to the extent that any law then in force in its territory is not in conformity with the provision. Reservations of a general character shall not be permitted under this Article.

2. Any reservation made under this Article shall contain a brief statement of the law concerned.

ARTICLE 58   DENUNCIATION

1. A High Contracting Party may denounce the present Convention only after the expiry of five years from the date on which it became a party to it and after six months' notice contained in a notification addressed to the Secretary General of the Council of Europe, who shall inform the other High Contracting Parties.

2. Such a denunciation shall not have the effect of releasing the High Contracting Party concerned from its obligations under this Convention in respect of any act which, being capable of constituting a violation of such obligations, may have been performed by it before the date at which the denunciation became effective.

Part 6   Human Rights

3. Any High Contracting Party which shall cease to be a member of the Council of Europe shall cease to be a Party to this Convention under the same conditions.

4. The Convention may be denounced in accordance with the provisions of the preceding paragraphs in respect of any territory to which it has been declared to extend under the terms of Article 56.

ARTICLE 59   SIGNATURE AND RATIFICATION

1. This Convention shall be open to the signature of the members of the Council of Europe. It shall be ratified. Ratifications shall be deposited with the Secretary General of the Council of Europe.

2. The European Union may accede to this Convention.

3. The present Convention shall come into force after the deposit of ten instruments of ratification.

4. As regards any signatory ratifying subsequently, the Convention shall come into force at the date of the deposit of its instrument of ratification.

5. The Secretary General of the Council of Europe shall notify all the members of the Council of Europe of the entry into force of the Convention, the names of the High Contracting Parties who have ratified it, and the deposit of all instruments of ratification which may be effected subsequently.

Done at Rome this 4th day of November 1950, in English and French, both texts being equally authentic, in a single copy which shall remain deposited in the archives of the Council of Europe. The Secretary General shall transmit certified copies to each of the signatories.

CHARTER OF FUNDAMENTAL RIGHTS OF THE EUROPEAN UNION

NOTES
Date of publication in OJ: OJ C326, 26.10.2012, p 391.
© European Union, 1998–2021.

PREAMBLE

[6.35]
The peoples of Europe, in creating an ever closer union among them, are resolved to share a peaceful future based on common values.

Conscious of its spiritual and moral heritage, the Union is founded on the indivisible, universal values of human dignity, freedom, equality and solidarity; it is based on the principles of democracy and the rule of law. It places the individual at the heart of its activities, by establishing the citizenship of the Union and by creating an area of freedom, security and justice.

The Union contributes to the preservation and to the development of these common values while respecting the diversity of the cultures and traditions of the peoples of Europe as well as the national identities of the Member States and the organisation of their public authorities at national, regional and local levels; it seeks to promote balanced and sustainable development and ensures free movement of persons, services, goods and capital, and the freedom of establishment.

To this end, it is necessary to strengthen the protection of fundamental rights in the light of changes in society, social progress and scientific and technological developments by making those rights more visible in a Charter.

This Charter reaffirms, with due regard for the powers and tasks of the Union and for the principle of subsidiarity, the rights as they result, in particular, from the constitutional traditions and international obligations common to the Member States, the European Convention for the Protection of Human Rights and Fundamental Freedoms, the Social Charters adopted by the Union and by the Council of Europe and the case-law of the Court of Justice of the European Union and of the European Court of Human Rights. In this context the Charter will be interpreted by the courts of the Union and the Member States with due regard to the explanations prepared under the authority of the Praesidium of the Convention which drafted the Charter and updated under the responsibility of the Praesidium of the European Convention.

Enjoyment of these rights entails responsibilities and duties with regard to other persons, to the human community and to future generations.

The Union therefore recognises the rights, freedoms and principles set out hereafter.

TITLE I   DIGNITY

Article 1 Human dignity

[6.36]
Human dignity is inviolable. It must be respected and protected.

Article 2 Right to life

1. Everyone has the right to life.

2. No one shall be condemned to the death penalty, or executed.

Article 3 Right to the integrity of the person

1.	Everyone has the right to respect for his or her physical and mental integrity.

2.	In the fields of medicine and biology, the following must be respected in particular:

(a)	the free and informed consent of the person concerned, according to the procedures laid down by law;

(b)	the prohibition of eugenic practices, in particular those aiming at the selection of persons;

(c)	the prohibition on making the human body and its parts as such a source of financial gain;

(d)	the prohibition of the reproductive cloning of human beings.

Article 4 Prohibition of torture and inhuman or degrading treatment or punishment

No one shall be subjected to torture or to inhuman or degrading treatment or punishment.

Article 5 Prohibition of slavery and forced labour

1.	No one shall be held in slavery or servitude.

2.	No one shall be required to perform forced or compulsory labour.

3.	Trafficking in human beings is prohibited.

TITLE II FREEDOMS

Article 6 Right to liberty and security

[6.37]
Everyone has the right to liberty and security of person.

Article 7 Respect for private and family life

Everyone has the right to respect for his or her private and family life, home and communications.

Article 8 Protection of personal data

1.	Everyone has the right to the protection of personal data concerning him or her.

2.	Such data must be processed fairly for specified purposes and on the basis of the consent of the person concerned or some other legitimate basis laid down by law. Everyone has the right of access to data which has been collected concerning him or her, and the right to have it rectified.

3.	Compliance with these rules shall be subject to control by an independent authority.

Article 9 Right to marry and right to found a family

The right to marry and the right to found a family shall be guaranteed in accordance with the national laws governing the exercise of these rights.

Article 10 Freedom of thought, conscience and religion

1.	Everyone has the right to freedom of thought, conscience and religion. This right includes freedom to change religion or belief and freedom, either alone or in community with others and in public or in private, to manifest religion or belief, in worship, teaching, practice and observance.

2.	The right to conscientious objection is recognised, in accordance with the national laws governing the exercise of this right.

Article 11 Freedom of expression and information

1.	Everyone has the right to freedom of expression. This right shall include freedom to hold opinions and to receive and impart information and ideas without interference by public authority and regardless of frontiers.

2.	The freedom and pluralism of the media shall be respected.

Article 12 Freedom of assembly and of association

1.	Everyone has the right to freedom of peaceful assembly and to freedom of association at all levels, in particular in political, trade union and civic matters, which implies the right of everyone to form and to join trade unions for the protection of his or her interests.

2.	Political parties at Union level contribute to expressing the political will of the citizens of the Union.

Article 13 Freedom of the arts and sciences

The arts and scientific research shall be free of constraint. Academic freedom shall be respected.

Article 14 Right to education

1.	Everyone has the right to education and to have access to vocational and continuing training.

2.	This right includes the possibility to receive free compulsory education.

3.   The freedom to found educational establishments with due respect for democratic principles and the right of parents to ensure the education and teaching of their children in conformity with their religious, philosophical and pedagogical convictions shall be respected, in accordance with the national laws governing the exercise of such freedom and right.

Article 15 Freedom to choose an occupation and right to engage in work

1.   Everyone has the right to engage in work and to pursue a freely chosen or accepted occupation.

2.   Every citizen of the Union has the freedom to seek employment, to work, to exercise the right of establishment and to provide services in any Member State.

3.   Nationals of third countries who are authorised to work in the territories of the Member States are entitled to working conditions equivalent to those of citizens of the Union.

Article 16 Freedom to conduct a business

The freedom to conduct a business in accordance with Union law and national laws and practices is recognised.

Article 17 Right to property

1.   Everyone has the right to own, use, dispose of and bequeath his or her lawfully acquired possessions. No one may be deprived of his or her possessions, except in the public interest and in the cases and under the conditions provided for by law, subject to fair compensation being paid in good time for their loss. The use of property may be regulated by law in so far as is necessary for the general interest.

2.   Intellectual property shall be protected.

Article 18 Right to asylum

The right to asylum shall be guaranteed with due respect for the rules of the Geneva Convention of 28 July 1951 and the Protocol of 31 January 1967 relating to the status of refugees and in accordance with the Treaty on European Union and the Treaty on the Functioning of the European Union (hereinafter referred to as 'the Treaties').

Article 19 Protection in the event of removal, expulsion or extradition

1.   Collective expulsions are prohibited.

2.   No one may be removed, expelled or extradited to a State where there is a serious risk that he or she would be subjected to the death penalty, torture or other inhuman or degrading treatment or punishment.

TITLE III EQUALITY

Article 20 Equality before the law

[6.38]
Everyone is equal before the law.

Article 21 Non-discrimination

1.   Any discrimination based on any ground such as sex, race, colour, ethnic or social origin, genetic features, language, religion or belief, political or any other opinion, membership of a national minority, property, birth, disability, age or sexual orientation shall be prohibited.

2.   Within the scope of application of the Treaties and without prejudice to any of their specific provisions, any discrimination on grounds of nationality shall be prohibited.

Article 22 Cultural, religious and linguistic diversity

The Union shall respect cultural, religious and linguistic diversity.

Article 23 Equality between women and men

Equality between women and men must be ensured in all areas, including employment, work and pay.

The principle of equality shall not prevent the maintenance or adoption of measures providing for specific advantages in favour of the under-represented sex.

Article 24 The rights of the child

1.   Children shall have the right to such protection and care as is necessary for their well-being. They may express their views freely. Such views shall be taken into consideration on matters which concern them in accordance with their age and maturity.

2.   In all actions relating to children, whether taken by public authorities or private institutions, the child's best interests must be a primary consideration.

3.   Every child shall have the right to maintain on a regular basis a personal relationship and direct contact with both his or her parents, unless that is contrary to his or her interests.

Article 25 The rights of the elderly

The Union recognises and respects the rights of the elderly to lead a life of dignity and independence and to participate in social and cultural life.

Article 26 Integration of persons with disabilities

The Union recognises and respects the right of persons with disabilities to benefit from measures designed to ensure their independence, social and occupational integration and participation in the life of the community.

TITLE IV   SOLIDARITY

Article 27 Workers' right to information and consultation within the undertaking

[6.39]
Workers or their representatives must, at the appropriate levels, be guaranteed information and consultation in good time in the cases and under the conditions provided for by Union law and national laws and practices.

Article 28 Right of collective bargaining and action

Workers and employers, or their respective organisations, have, in accordance with Union law and national laws and practices, the right to negotiate and conclude collective agreements at the appropriate levels and, in cases of conflicts of interest, to take collective action to defend their interests, including strike action.

Article 29 Right of access to placement services

Everyone has the right of access to a free placement service.

Article 30 Protection in the event of unjustified dismissal

Every worker has the right to protection against unjustified dismissal, in accordance with Union law and national laws and practices.

Article 31 Fair and just working conditions

1. Every worker has the right to working conditions which respect his or her health, safety and dignity.

2. Every worker has the right to limitation of maximum working hours, to daily and weekly rest periods and to an annual period of paid leave.

Article 32 Prohibition of child labour and protection of young people at work

The employment of children is prohibited. The minimum age of admission to employment may not be lower than the minimum school-leaving age, without prejudice to such rules as may be more favourable to young people and except for limited derogations.

Young people admitted to work must have working conditions appropriate to their age and be protected against economic exploitation and any work likely to harm their safety, health or physical, mental, moral or social development or to interfere with their education.

Article 33 Family and professional life

1. The family shall enjoy legal, economic and social protection.

2. To reconcile family and professional life, everyone shall have the right to protection from dismissal for a reason connected with maternity and the right to paid maternity leave and to parental leave following the birth or adoption of a child.

Article 34 Social security and social assistance

1. The Union recognises and respects the entitlement to social security benefits and social services providing protection in cases such as maternity, illness, industrial accidents, dependency or old age, and in the case of loss of employment, in accordance with the rules laid down by Union law and national laws and practices.

2. Everyone residing and moving legally within the European Union is entitled to social security benefits and social advantages in accordance with Union law and national laws and practices.

3. In order to combat social exclusion and poverty, the Union recognises and respects the right to social and housing assistance so as to ensure a decent existence for all those who lack sufficient resources, in accordance with the rules laid down by Union law and national laws and practices.

Article 35 Health care

Everyone has the right of access to preventive health care and the right to benefit from medical treatment under the conditions established by national laws and practices. A high level of human health protection shall be ensured in the definition and implementation of all the Union's policies and activities.

Article 36 Access to services of general economic interest

The Union recognises and respects access to services of general economic interest as provided for in national laws and practices, in accordance with the Treaties, in order to promote the social and territorial cohesion of the Union.

Article 37 Environmental protection

A high level of environmental protection and the improvement of the quality of the environment must be integrated into the policies of the Union and ensured in accordance with the principle of sustainable development.

Article 38 Consumer protection

Union policies shall ensure a high level of consumer protection.

TITLE V   CITIZENS' RIGHTS

Article 39 Right to vote and to stand as a candidate at elections to the European Parliament

[6.40]

1. Every citizen of the Union has the right to vote and to stand as a candidate at elections to the European Parliament in the Member State in which he or she resides, under the same conditions as nationals of that State.

2. Members of the European Parliament shall be elected by direct universal suffrage in a free and secret ballot.

Article 40 Right to vote and to stand as a candidate at municipal elections

Every citizen of the Union has the right to vote and to stand as a candidate at municipal elections in the Member State in which he or she resides under the same conditions as nationals of that State.

Article 41 Right to good administration

1. Every person has the right to have his or her affairs handled impartially, fairly and within a reasonable time by the institutions, bodies, offices and agencies of the Union.

2. This right includes:

(a)   the right of every person to be heard, before any individual measure which would affect him or her adversely is taken;

(b)   the right of every person to have access to his or her file, while respecting the legitimate interests of confidentiality and of professional and business secrecy;

(c)   the obligation of the administration to give reasons for its decisions.

3. Every person has the right to have the Union make good any damage caused by its institutions or by its servants in the performance of their duties, in accordance with the general principles common to the laws of the Member States.

4. Every person may write to the institutions of the Union in one of the languages of the Treaties and must have an answer in the same language.

Article 42 Right of access to documents

Any citizen of the Union, and any natural or legal person residing or having its registered office in a Member State, has a right of access to documents of the institutions, bodies, offices and agencies of the Union, whatever their medium.

Article 43 European Ombudsman

Any citizen of the Union and any natural or legal person residing or having its registered office in a Member State has the right to refer to the European Ombudsman cases of maladministration in the activities of the institutions, bodies, offices or agencies of the Union, with the exception of the Court of Justice of the European Union acting in its judicial role.

Article 44 Right to petition

Any citizen of the Union and any natural or legal person residing or having its registered office in a Member State has the right to petition the European Parliament.

Article 45 Freedom of movement and of residence

1. Every citizen of the Union has the right to move and reside freely within the territory of the Member States.

2. Freedom of movement and residence may be granted, in accordance with the Treaties, to nationals of third countries legally resident in the territory of a Member State.

Article 46 Diplomatic and consular protection

Every citizen of the Union shall, in the territory of a third country in which the Member State of which he or she is a national is not represented, be entitled to protection by the diplomatic or consular authorities of any Member State, on the same conditions as the nationals of that Member State.

TITLE VI   JUSTICE

Article 47 Right to an effective remedy and to a fair trial

[6.41]
Everyone whose rights and freedoms guaranteed by the law of the Union are violated has the right to an effective remedy before a tribunal in compliance with the conditions laid down in this Article.

Everyone is entitled to a fair and public hearing within a reasonable time by an independent and impartial tribunal previously established by law. Everyone shall have the possibility of being advised, defended and represented.

Legal aid shall be made available to those who lack sufficient resources in so far as such aid is necessary to ensure effective access to justice.

Article 48 Presumption of innocence and right of defence

1. Everyone who has been charged shall be presumed innocent until proved guilty according to law.

2. Respect for the rights of the defence of anyone who has been charged shall be guaranteed.

Article 49 Principles of legality and proportionality of criminal offences and penalties

1. No one shall be held guilty of any criminal offence on account of any act or omission which did not constitute a criminal offence under national law or international law at the time when it was committed. Nor shall a heavier penalty be imposed than the one that was applicable at the time the criminal offence was committed. If, subsequent to the commission of a criminal offence, the law provides for a lighter penalty, that penalty shall be applicable.

2. This Article shall not prejudice the trial and punishment of any person for any act or omission which, at the time when it was committed, was criminal according to the general principles recognised by the community of nations.

3. The severity of penalties must not be disproportionate to the criminal offence.

Article 50 Right not to be tried or punished twice in criminal proceedings for the same criminal offence

No one shall be liable to be tried or punished again in criminal proceedings for an offence for which he or she has already been finally acquitted or convicted within the Union in accordance with the law.

TITLE VII   GENERAL PROVISIONS GOVERNING THE INTERPRETATION AND APPLICATION OF THE CHARTER

Article 51 Field of application

[6.42]
1. The provisions of this Charter are addressed to the institutions, bodies, offices and agencies of the Union with due regard for the principle of subsidiarity and to the Member States only when they are implementing Union law. They shall therefore respect the rights, observe the principles and promote the application thereof in accordance with their respective powers and respecting the limits of the powers of the Union as conferred on it in the Treaties.

2. The Charter does not extend the field of application of Union law beyond the powers of the Union or establish any new power or task for the Union, or modify powers and tasks as defined in the Treaties.

Article 52 Scope and interpretation of rights and principles

1. Any limitation on the exercise of the rights and freedoms recognised by this Charter must be provided for by law and respect the essence of those rights and freedoms. Subject to the principle of proportionality, limitations may be made only if they are necessary and genuinely meet objectives of general interest recognised by the Union or the need to protect the rights and freedoms of others.

2. Rights recognised by this Charter for which provision is made in the Treaties shall be exercised under the conditions and within the limits defined by those Treaties.

3. In so far as this Charter contains rights which correspond to rights guaranteed by the Convention for the Protection of Human Rights and Fundamental Freedoms, the meaning and scope of those rights shall be the same as those laid down by the said Convention. This provision shall not prevent Union law providing more extensive protection.

4. In so far as this Charter recognises fundamental rights as they result from the constitutional traditions common to the Member States, those rights shall be interpreted in harmony with those traditions.

5. The provisions of this Charter which contain principles may be implemented by legislative and executive acts taken by institutions, bodies, offices and agencies of the Union, and by acts of Member States when they are implementing Union law, in the exercise of their respective powers. They shall be judicially cognisable only in the interpretation of such acts and in the ruling on their legality.

6. Full account shall be taken of national laws and practices as specified in this Charter.

7.   The explanations drawn up as a way of providing guidance in the interpretation of this Charter shall be given due regard by the courts of the Union and of the Member States.

Article 53 Level of protection

Nothing in this Charter shall be interpreted as restricting or adversely affecting human rights and fundamental freedoms as recognised, in their respective fields of application, by Union law and international law and by international agreements to which the Union or all the Member States are party, including the European Convention for the Protection of Human Rights and Fundamental Freedoms, and by the Member States' constitutions.

Article 54 Prohibition of abuse of rights

Nothing in this Charter shall be interpreted as implying any right to engage in any activity or to perform any act aimed at the destruction of any of the rights and freedoms recognised in this Charter or at their limitation to a greater extent than is provided for herein.

PART 7
KEY BREXIT TREATIES AND RELATED UK LEGISLATION

EUROPEAN UNION (WITHDRAWAL) ACT 2018

(2018 c 16)

NOTES

Editorial note: only certain key provisions of the Act which are relevant to data protection law are reproduced here. Provisions not reproduced are not annotated.

Note (interpretation of terms used in notes below): as to the meaning of "exit day" and "IP completion day", see s 20 of this Act at **[7.18]**, and the European Union (Withdrawal Agreement) Act 2020, s 39 respectively. Note that s 39(5) of the 2020 Act provides that IP completion day means 31 December 2020 at 11.00pm.

ARRANGEMENT OF SECTIONS

SCHEDULES

An Act to repeal the European Communities Act 1972 and make other provision in connection with the withdrawal of the United Kingdom from the EU.

[26 June 2018]

Repeal of the ECA

[7.1]
1   Repeal of the European Communities Act 1972
The European Communities Act 1972 is repealed on exit day.

NOTES
Commencement: 17 August 2019.

[Savings for implementation period

[7.2]
1A   Saving for ECA for implementation period
(1)–(4)   . . .
(5)   Subsections (1) to (4) are repealed on IP completion day.
(6)   In this Act—

Part 7   Key Brexit Materials

"the implementation period" means the transition or implementation period provided for by Part 4 of the withdrawal agreement and beginning with exit day and ending on IP completion day;

"IP completion day" (and related expressions) have the same meaning as in the European Union (Withdrawal Agreement) Act 2020 (see section 39(1) to (5) of that Act);

"withdrawal agreement" has the same meaning as in that Act (see section 39(1) and (6) of that Act).

(7) In this Act—

(a) references to the European Communities Act 1972 are to be read, so far as the context permits or requires, as being or (as the case may be) including references to that Act as it continues to have effect by virtue of subsections (2) to (4) above, and

(b) references to any Part of the withdrawal agreement or the EEA EFTA separation agreement include references to any other provisions of that agreement so far as applying to that Part.]

NOTES

Commencement: exit day.

Inserted, together with the previous heading, by the European Union (Withdrawal Agreement) Act 2020, s 1.

Sub-ss (1)–(4) were repealed by subsection (5) above.

[7.3]

[1B Saving for EU-derived domestic legislation for implementation period

(1)–(5) . . .

(6) Subsections (1) to (5) are repealed on IP completion day.

(7) In this Act "EU-derived domestic legislation" means any enactment so far as—

(a) made under section 2(2) of, or paragraph 1A of Schedule 2 to, the European Communities Act 1972,

(b) passed or made, or operating, for a purpose mentioned in section 2(2)(a) or (b) of that Act,

(c) relating to—

(i) anything which falls within paragraph (a) or (b), or

(ii) any rights, powers, liabilities, obligations, restrictions, remedies or procedures which are recognised and available in domestic law by virtue of section 2(1) of the European Communities Act 1972, or

(d) relating otherwise to the EU or the EEA,

but does not include any enactment contained in the European Communities Act 1972 or any enactment contained in this Act or the European Union (Withdrawal Agreement) Act 2020 or in regulations made under this Act or the Act of 2020.]

NOTES

Commencement: exit day.

Inserted by the European Union (Withdrawal Agreement) Act 2020, s 2.

Sub-ss (1)–(5): repealed by subsection (6) above.

Retention of [saved EU law at end of implementation period]

NOTES

Words in square brackets in the above heading substituted by the European Union (Withdrawal Agreement) Act 2020, s 41(4), Sch 5, Pt 2, paras 38, 39.

[7.4]

2 Saving for EU-derived domestic legislation

(1) EU-derived domestic legislation, as it has effect in domestic law immediately before [IP completion day], continues to have effect in domestic law on and after [IP completion day].

(2) . . .

(3) This section is subject to section 5 and Schedule 1 (exceptions to savings and incorporation) [and section 5A (savings and incorporation: supplementary)].

NOTES

Commencement: IP completion day.

Words in square brackets in sub-s (1) substituted, sub-s (2) repealed, and words in square brackets in sub-s (3) inserted, by the European Union (Withdrawal Agreement) Act 2020, s 25(1).

[7.5]

3 Incorporation of direct EU legislation

(1) Direct EU legislation, so far as operative immediately before [IP completion day], forms part of domestic law on and after [IP completion day].

(2) In this Act "direct EU legislation" means—

(a) any EU regulation, EU decision or EU tertiary legislation, as it has effect in EU law immediately before [IP completion day] and so far as—

[(ai) it is applicable to and in the United Kingdom by virtue of Part 4 of the withdrawal agreement,

(bi) it neither has effect nor is to have effect by virtue of section 7A or 7B,]

(i) it is not an exempt EU instrument (for which see section 20(1) and Schedule 6), [and]

(ii) . . .

(iii) its effect is not reproduced in an enactment to which section 2(1) applies,

(b) any Annex to the EEA agreement, as it has effect in EU law immediately before [IP completion day] and so far as—

[(ai) it is applicable to and in the United Kingdom by virtue of Part 4 of the withdrawal agreement,

(bi) it neither has effect nor is to have effect by virtue of section 7A or 7B,]

(i) it refers to, or contains adaptations of, anything falling within paragraph (a), and

(ii) its effect is not reproduced in an enactment to which section 2(1) applies, or

(c)	Protocol 1 to the EEA agreement (which contains horizontal adaptations that apply in relation to EU instruments referred to in the Annexes to that agreement), as it has effect in EU law immediately before [IP completion day and so far as—
	(i)	it is applicable to and in the United Kingdom by virtue of Part 4 of the withdrawal agreement, and
	(ii)	it neither has effect nor is to have effect by virtue of section 7A or 7B,]

(3)	For the purposes of this Act, any direct EU legislation is operative immediately before [IP completion day] if—
	(a)	in the case of anything which comes into force at a particular time and is stated to apply from a later time, it is in force and applies immediately before [IP completion day],
	(b)	in the case of a decision which specifies to whom it is addressed, it has been notified to that person before [IP completion day], and
	(c)	in any other case, it is in force immediately before [IP completion day].

(4)	This section—
	(a)	brings into domestic law any direct EU legislation only in the form of the English language version of that legislation, and
	(b)	does not apply to any such legislation for which there is no such version,
but paragraph (a) does not affect the use of the other language versions of that legislation for the purposes of interpreting it.

(5)	This section is subject to section 5 and Schedule 1 (exceptions to savings and incorporation) [and section 5A (savings and incorporation: supplementary)].

NOTES

Commencement: IP completion day.

All amendments to this section were made by the European Union (Withdrawal Agreement) Act 2020, s 25(2).

[7.6]
**4	Saving for rights etc under section 2(1) of the ECA**

(1)	Any rights, powers, liabilities, obligations, restrictions, remedies and procedures which, immediately before [IP completion day]—
	(a)	are recognised and available in domestic law by virtue of section 2(1) of the European Communities Act 1972, and
	(b)	are enforced, allowed and followed accordingly,
continue on and after [IP completion day] to be recognised and available in domestic law (and to be enforced, allowed and followed accordingly).

(2)	Subsection (1) does not apply to any rights, powers, liabilities, obligations, restrictions, remedies or procedures so far as they—
	(a)	form part of domestic law by virtue of section 3,
	[(aa)	are, or are to be, recognised and available in domestic law (and enforced, allowed and followed accordingly) by virtue of section 7A or 7B,] or
	(b)	arise under an EU directive (including as applied by the EEA agreement) and are not of a kind recognised by the European Court or any court or tribunal in the United Kingdom in a case decided before [IP completion day] (whether or not as an essential part of the decision in the case).

(3)	This section is subject to section 5 and Schedule 1 (exceptions to savings and incorporation) [and section 5A (savings and incorporation: supplementary)].

NOTES

Commencement: IP completion day.

All amendments to this section were made by the European Union (Withdrawal Agreement) Act 2020, s 25(3).

See further: the Private International Law (Implementation of Agreements) Act 2020, s 1(4), Sch 5, Pt 1.

[7.7]
**5	Exceptions to savings and incorporation**

(1)	The principle of the supremacy of EU law does not apply to any enactment or rule of law passed or made on or after [IP completion day].

(2)	Accordingly, the principle of the supremacy of EU law continues to apply on or after [IP completion day] so far as relevant to the interpretation, disapplication or quashing of any enactment or rule of law passed or made before [IP completion day].

(3)	Subsection (1) does not prevent the principle of the supremacy of EU law from applying to a modification made on or after [IP completion day] of any enactment or rule of law passed or made before [IP completion day] if the application of the principle is consistent with the intention of the modification.

(4)	The Charter of Fundamental Rights is not part of domestic law on or after [IP completion day].

(5)	Subsection (4) does not affect the retention in domestic law on or after [IP completion day] in accordance with this Act of any fundamental rights or principles which exist irrespective of the Charter (and references to the Charter in any case law are, so far as necessary for this purpose, to be read as if they were references to any corresponding retained fundamental rights or principles).

(6)	Schedule 1 (which makes further provision about exceptions to savings and incorporation) has effect.

[(7)	Subsections (1) to (6) and Schedule 1 are subject to relevant separation agreement law (for which see section 7C.)]

NOTES

Commencement: 4 July 2018 (sub-s (6) certain purposes); IP completion day (otherwise).

Sub-ss (1)–(5): words in square brackets substituted by the European Union (Withdrawal Agreement) Act 2020, s 25(4)(a).

Sub-s (7): added by the European Union (Withdrawal Agreement) Act 2020, s 25(4)(b).

Part 7   Key Brexit Materials

[7.8]
[5A Savings and incorporation: supplementary
The fact that anything which continues to be, or forms part of, domestic law on or after IP completion day by virtue of section 2, 3 or 4 has an effect immediately before IP completion day which is time-limited by reference to the implementation period does not prevent it from having an indefinite effect on and after IP completion day by virtue of section 2, 3 or 4.]

NOTES
Commencement: IP completion day.
Inserted by the European Union (Withdrawal Agreement) Act 2020, s 25(5).
Transitional provisions: nothing in this section prevents the modification on or after IP completion day of Retained EU law by an enactment passed or made before IP completion day and coming into force or otherwise having effect on or after IP completion day (whether or not that enactment is itself retained EU law). See the European Union (Withdrawal) Act 2018 and European Union (Withdrawal Agreement) Act 2020 (Commencement, Transitional and Savings Provisions) Regulations 2020, SI 2020/1622, reg 17.

[7.9]
6 Interpretation of retained EU law
(1) A court or tribunal—
    (a) is not bound by any principles laid down, or any decisions made, on or after [IP completion day] by the European Court, and
    (b) cannot refer any matter to the European Court on or after [IP completion day].
(2) Subject to this and subsections (3) to (6), a court or tribunal may have regard to anything done on or after [IP completion day] by the European Court, another EU entity or the EU so far as it is relevant to any matter before the court or tribunal.
(3) Any question as to the validity, meaning or effect of any retained EU law is to be decided, so far as that law is unmodified on or after [IP completion day] and so far as they are relevant to it—
    (a) in accordance with any retained case law and any retained general principles of EU law, and
    (b) having regard (among other things) to the limits, immediately before [IP completion day], of EU competences.
(4) But—
    (a) the Supreme Court is not bound by any retained EU case law,
    (b) the High Court of Justiciary is not bound by any retained EU case law when—
        (i) sitting as a court of appeal otherwise than in relation to a compatibility issue (within the meaning given by section 288ZA(2) of the Criminal Procedure (Scotland) Act 1995) or a devolution issue (within the meaning given by paragraph 1 of Schedule 6 to the Scotland Act 1998), or
        (ii) sitting on a reference under section 123(1) of the Criminal Procedure (Scotland) Act 1995,
    [(ba) a relevant court or relevant tribunal is not bound by any retained EU case law so far as is provided for by regulations under subsection (5A),] and
    (c) no court or tribunal is bound by any retained domestic case law that it would not otherwise be bound by.
(5) In deciding whether to depart from any retained EU case law [by virtue of subsection (4)(a) or (b)], the Supreme Court or the High Court of Justiciary must apply the same test as it would apply in deciding whether to depart from its own case law.
[(5A) A Minister of the Crown may by regulations provide for—
    (a) a court or tribunal to be a relevant court or (as the case may be) a relevant tribunal for the purposes of this section,
    (b) the extent to which, or circumstances in which, a relevant court or relevant tribunal is not to be bound by retained EU case law,
    (c) the test which a relevant court or relevant tribunal must apply in deciding whether to depart from any retained EU case law, or
    (d) considerations which are to be relevant to—
        (i) the Supreme Court or the High Court of Justiciary in applying the test mentioned in subsection (5), or
        (ii) a relevant court or relevant tribunal in applying any test provided for by virtue of paragraph (c) above.
(5B) Regulations under subsection (5A) may (among other things) provide for—
    (a) the High Court of Justiciary to be a relevant court when sitting otherwise than as mentioned in subsection (4)(b)(i) and (ii),
    (b) the extent to which, or circumstances in which, a relevant court or relevant tribunal not being bound by retained EU case law includes (or does not include) that court or tribunal not being bound by retained domestic case law which relates to retained EU case law,
    (c) other matters arising in relation to retained domestic case law which relates to retained EU case law (including by making provision of a kind which could be made in relation to retained EU case law), or
    (d) the test mentioned in paragraph (c) of subsection (5A) or the considerations mentioned in paragraph (d) of that subsection to be determined (whether with or without the consent of a Minister of the Crown) by a person mentioned in subsection (5C)(a) to (e) or by more than one of those persons acting jointly.
(5C) Before making regulations under subsection (5A), a Minister of the Crown must consult—
    (a) the President of the Supreme Court,
    (b) the Lord Chief Justice of England and Wales,
    (c) the Lord President of the Court of Session,
    (d) the Lord Chief Justice of Northern Ireland,
    (e) the Senior President of Tribunals, and
    (f) such other persons as the Minister of the Crown considers appropriate.
(5D) No regulations may be made under subsection (5A) after IP completion day.]

(6) Subsection (3) does not prevent the validity, meaning or effect of any retained EU law which has been modified on or after [IP completion day] from being decided as provided for in that subsection if doing so is consistent with the intention of the modifications.

[(6A) Subsections (1) to (6) are subject to relevant separation agreement law (for which see section 7C).]

(7) In this Act—

"retained case law" means—

     (a)   retained domestic case law, and

     (b)   retained EU case law;

"retained domestic case law" means any principles laid down by, and any decisions of, a court or tribunal in the United Kingdom, as they have effect immediately before [IP completion day] and so far as they—

     (a)   relate to anything to which section 2, 3 or 4 applies, and

     (b)   are not excluded by section 5 or Schedule 1,

     (as those principles and decisions are modified by or under this Act or by other domestic law from time to time);

"retained EU case law" means any principles laid down by, and any decisions of, the European Court, as they have effect in EU law immediately before [IP completion day] and so far as they—

     (a)   relate to anything to which section 2, 3 or 4 applies, and

     (b)   are not excluded by section 5 or Schedule 1,

     (as those principles and decisions are modified by or under this Act or by other domestic law from time to time);

"retained EU law" means anything which, on or after [IP completion day], continues to be, or forms part of, domestic law by virtue of section 2, 3 or 4 or subsection (3) or (6) above (as that body of law is added to or otherwise modified by or under this Act or by other domestic law from time to time);

"retained general principles of EU law" means the general principles of EU law, as they have effect in EU law immediately before [IP completion day] and so far as they—

     (a)   relate to anything to which section 2, 3 or 4 applies, and

     (b)   are not excluded by section 5 or Schedule 1,

     (as those principles are modified by or under this Act or by other domestic law from time to time).

NOTES

Commencement: 4 July 2018 (sub-s (7)); IP completion day (otherwise).

The words "IP completion day" in square brackets were substituted, sub-s (4)(ba) was inserted, the words "by virtue of subsection (4)(a) or (b)" in square brackets in sub-s (5) were inserted, and sub-s (6A) was inserted, by the European Union (Withdrawal Agreement) Act 2020, s 26(1)(a)–(c), (e).

Sub-ss (5A)–(5D) were inserted by the European Union (Withdrawal Agreement) Act 2020, s 26(1)(d).

The words "IP completion day" in square brackets in sub-s (7) (in each place that they occur) were substituted by the European Union (Withdrawal Agreement) Act 2020, s 26(1)(a).

[7.10]

7   Status of retained EU law

(1) Anything which—

     (a)   was, immediately before exit day, primary legislation of a particular kind, subordinate legislation of a particular kind or another enactment of a particular kind, and

     (b)   continues to be domestic law on and after exit day by virtue of [section 1A(2) or 1B(2)],

continues to be domestic law as an enactment of the same kind.

[(1A) Anything which—

     (a)   was, immediately before IP completion day, primary legislation of a particular kind, subordinate legislation of a particular kind or another enactment of a particular kind, and

     (b)   continues to be domestic law on and after IP completion day by virtue of section 2,

continues to be domestic law as an enactment of the same kind.]

(2) Retained direct principal EU legislation cannot be modified by any primary or subordinate legislation other than—

     (a)   an Act of Parliament,

     (b)   any other primary legislation (so far as it has the power to make such a modification), or

     (c)   any subordinate legislation so far as it is made under a power which permits such a modification by virtue of—

         (i)   paragraph 3, 5(3)(a) or (4)(a), 8(3), 10(3)(a) or (4)(a), 11(2)(a) or 12(3) of Schedule 8,

         (ii)   any other provision made by or under this Act,

         (iii)   any provision made by or under an Act of Parliament passed before, and in the same Session as, this Act, or

         (iv)   any provision made on or after the passing of this Act by or under primary legislation.

(3) Retained direct minor EU legislation cannot be modified by any primary or subordinate legislation other than—

     (a)   an Act of Parliament,

     (b)   any other primary legislation (so far as it has the power to make such a modification), or

     (c)   any subordinate legislation so far as it is made under a power which permits such a modification by virtue of—

         (i)   paragraph 3, 5(2) or (4)(a), 8(3), 10(2) or (4)(a) or 12(3) of Schedule 8,

         (ii)   any other provision made by or under this Act,

         (iii)   any provision made by or under an Act of Parliament passed before, and in the same Session as, this Act, or

         (iv)   any provision made on or after the passing of this Act by or under primary legislation.

(4) Anything which is retained EU law by virtue of section 4 cannot be modified by any primary or subordinate legislation other than—

     (a)   an Act of Parliament,

    (b)   any other primary legislation (so far as it has the power to make such a modification), or

    (c)   any subordinate legislation so far as it is made under a power which permits such a modification by virtue of—

        (i)   paragraph 3, 5(3)(b) or (4)(b), 8(3), 10(3)(b) or (4)(b), 11(2)(b) or 12(3) of Schedule 8,

        (ii)   any other provision made by or under this Act,

        (iii)   any provision made by or under an Act of Parliament passed before, and in the same Session as, this Act, or

        (iv)   any provision made on or after the passing of this Act by or under primary legislation.

(5) For other provisions about the status of retained EU law, see—

    (a)   section 5(1) to (3) [and (7)] (status of retained EU law in relation to other enactments or rules of law),

    (b)   section 6 (status of retained case law and retained general principles of EU law),

  [(ba) section 7C (status of case law of European Court etc in relation to retained EU law which is relevant separation agreement law),]

    (c)   section 15(2) and Part 2 of Schedule 5 (status of retained EU law for the purposes of the rules of evidence),

    (d)   paragraphs 13 to 16 of Schedule 8 (affirmative and enhanced scrutiny procedure for, and information about, instruments which amend or revoke subordinate legislation under section 2(2) of the European Communities Act 1972 including subordinate legislation implementing EU directives),

    (e)   paragraphs 19 and 20 of that Schedule (status of certain retained direct EU legislation for the purposes of the Interpretation Act 1978), and

    (f)   paragraph 30 of that Schedule (status of retained direct EU legislation for the purposes of the Human Rights Act 1998).

(6) In this Act—

    "retained direct minor EU legislation" means any retained direct EU legislation which is not retained direct principal EU legislation;

    "retained direct principal EU legislation" means—

        (a)   any EU regulation so far as it—

            (i)   forms part of domestic law on and after [IP completion day] by virtue of section 3, and

            (ii)   was not EU tertiary legislation immediately before [IP completion day], or

        (b)   any Annex to the EEA agreement so far as it—

        (as modified by or under this Act or by other domestic law from time to time).

            (i)   forms part of domestic law on and after [IP completion day] by virtue of section 3, and

            (ii)   refers to, or contains adaptations of, any EU regulation so far as it falls within paragraph (a),

NOTES

Commencement: exit day (sub-ss (1) and (6)); IP completion day (otherwise).

Sub-s (1): words in square brackets substituted by the European Union (Withdrawal Agreement) Act 2020, s 41(4), Sch 5, Pt 2, paras 38, 40(1), (2).

Sub-s (1A): inserted by the European Union (Withdrawal Agreement) Act 2020, s 41(4), Sch 5, Pt 2, paras 38, 40(1), (3).

Sub-s (5): words in square brackets inserted by the European Union (Withdrawal Agreement) Act 2020, s 41(4), Sch 5, Pt 2, paras 38, 40(1), (4).

Sub-s (6): words in square brackets substituted by the European Union (Withdrawal Agreement) Act 2020, s 41(4), Sch 5, Pt 2, paras 38, 40(1), (5).

[Further aspects of withdrawal

[7.11]

7A General implementation of remainder of withdrawal agreement

(1) Subsection (2) applies to—

    (a)   all such rights, powers, liabilities, obligations and restrictions from time to time created or arising by or under the withdrawal agreement, and

    (b)   all such remedies and procedures from time to time provided for by or under the withdrawal agreement,

as in accordance with the withdrawal agreement are without further enactment to be given legal effect or used in the United Kingdom.

(2) The rights, powers, liabilities, obligations, restrictions, remedies and procedures concerned are to be—

    (a)   recognised and available in domestic law, and

    (b)   enforced, allowed and followed accordingly.

(3) Every enactment (including an enactment contained in this Act) is to be read and has effect subject to subsection (2).

(4) This section does not apply in relation to Part 4 of the withdrawal agreement so far as section 2(1) of the European Communities Act 1972 applies in relation to that Part.

(5) See also (among other things)—

    (a)   Part 3 of the European Union (Withdrawal Agreement) Act 2020 (further provision about citizens' rights),

    (b)   section 20 of that Act (financial provision),

    (c)   section 7C of this Act (interpretation of law relating to withdrawal agreement etc),

    (d)   section 8B of this Act (power in connection with certain other separation issues),

    (e)   section 8C of this Act (power in connection with the Protocol on Ireland/Northern Ireland in withdrawal agreement), and

    (f)   Parts 1B and 1C of Schedule 2 to this Act (powers involving devolved authorities in connection with certain other separation issues and the Ireland/Northern Ireland Protocol).]

NOTES

Commencement: exit day.

Inserted by the European Union (Withdrawal Agreement) Act 2020, s 5.

[7.12]
[7B   General implementation of EEA EFTA and Swiss agreements
(1) Subsection (2) applies to all such rights, powers, liabilities, obligations, restrictions, remedies and procedures as—
    (a)   would from time to time be created or arise, or (in the case of remedies or procedures) be provided for, by or under the EEA EFTA separation agreement or the Swiss citizens' rights agreement, and
    (b)   would, in accordance with Article 4(1) of the withdrawal agreement, be required to be given legal effect or used in the United Kingdom without further enactment,
if that Article were to apply in relation to the EEA EFTA separation agreement and the Swiss citizens' rights agreement, those agreements were part of EU law and the relevant EEA states and Switzerland were member States.
(2) The rights, powers, liabilities, obligations, restrictions, remedies and procedures concerned are to be—
    (a)   recognised and available in domestic law, and
    (b)   enforced, allowed and followed accordingly.
(3) Every enactment (other than section 7A but otherwise including an enactment contained in this Act) is to be read and has effect subject to subsection (2).
(4) See also (among other things)—
    (a)   Part 3 of the European Union (Withdrawal Agreement) Act 2020 (further provision about citizens' rights),
    (b)   section 7C of this Act (interpretation of law relating to the EEA EFTA separation agreement and the Swiss citizens' rights agreement etc),
    (c)   section 8B of this Act (power in connection with certain other separation issues), and
    (d)   Part 1B of Schedule 2 to this Act (powers involving devolved authorities in connection with certain other separation issues).
(5) In this section "the relevant EEA states" means Norway, Iceland and Liechtenstein.
(6) In this Act "EEA EFTA separation agreement" and "Swiss citizens' rights agreement" have the same meanings as in the European Union (Withdrawal Agreement) Act 2020 (see section 39(1) of that Act).]

NOTES
Commencement: exit day.
Inserted by the European Union (Withdrawal Agreement) Act 2020, s 5.

[7.13]
[7C   Interpretation of relevant separation agreement law
(1) Any question as to the validity, meaning or effect of any relevant separation agreement law is to be decided, so far as they are applicable—
    (a)   in accordance with the withdrawal agreement, the EEA EFTA separation agreement and the Swiss citizens' rights agreement, and
    (b)   having regard (among other things) to the desirability of ensuring that, where one of those agreements makes provision which corresponds to provision made by another of those agreements, the effect of relevant separation agreement law in relation to the matters dealt with by the corresponding provision in each agreement is consistent.
(2) See (among other things)—
    (a)   Article 4 of the withdrawal agreement (methods and principles relating to the effect, the implementation and the application of the agreement),
    (b)   Articles 158 and 160 of the withdrawal agreement (jurisdiction of the European Court in relation to Part 2 and certain provisions of Part 5 of the agreement),
    (c)   Articles 12 and 13 of the Protocol on Ireland/Northern Ireland in the withdrawal agreement (implementation, application, supervision and enforcement of the Protocol and common provisions),
    (d)   Article 4 of the EEA EFTA separation agreement (methods and principles relating to the effect, the implementation and the application of the agreement), and
    (e)   Article 4 of the Swiss citizens' rights agreement (methods and principles relating to the effect, the implementation and the application of the agreement).
(3) In this Act "relevant separation agreement law" means—
    (a)   any of the following provisions or anything which is domestic law by virtue of any of them—
        (i)   section 7A, 7B, 8B or 8C or Part 1B or 1C of Schedule 2 or this section, or
        (ii)   Part 3, or section 20, of the European Union (Withdrawal Agreement) Act 2020 (citizens' rights and financial provision), or
    (b)   anything not falling within paragraph (a) so far as it is domestic law for the purposes of, or otherwise within the scope of—
        (i)   the withdrawal agreement (other than Part 4 of that agreement),
        (ii)   the EEA EFTA separation agreement, or
        (iii)   the Swiss citizens' rights agreement,
as that body of law is added to or otherwise modified by or under this Act or by other domestic law from time to time.]

NOTES
Commencement: exit day.
Inserted by the European Union (Withdrawal Agreement) Act 2020, s 26(2).

Main powers in connection with withdrawal

[7.14]
8   Dealing with deficiencies arising from withdrawal
(1) A Minister of the Crown may by regulations make such provision as the Minister considers appropriate to prevent, remedy or mitigate—
    (a)   any failure of retained EU law to operate effectively, or

Part 7   Key Brexit Materials

(b) any other deficiency in retained EU law,

arising from the withdrawal of the United Kingdom from the EU.

(2) Deficiencies in retained EU law are where the Minister considers that retained EU law—

(a) contains anything which has no practical application in relation to the United Kingdom or any part of it or is otherwise redundant or substantially redundant,

(b) confers functions on, or in relation to, EU entities which no longer have functions in that respect under EU law in relation to the United Kingdom or any part of it,

(c) makes provision for, or in connection with, reciprocal arrangements between—

    (i) the United Kingdom or any part of it or a public authority in the United Kingdom, and

    (ii) the EU, an EU entity, a member State or a public authority in a member State,

which no longer exist or are no longer appropriate,

(d) makes provision for, or in connection with, other arrangements which—

    (i) involve the EU, an EU entity, a member State or a public authority in a member State, or

    (ii) are otherwise dependent upon the United Kingdom's membership of the EU [or Part 4 of the withdrawal agreement],

and which no longer exist or are no longer appropriate,

(e) makes provision for, or in connection with, any reciprocal or other arrangements not falling within paragraph (c) or (d) which no longer exist, or are no longer appropriate, as a result of the United Kingdom ceasing to be a party to any of the EU Treaties [or as a result of either the end of the implementation period or any other effect of the withdrawal agreement],

[(ea) is not clear in its effect as a result of the operation of any provision of sections 2 to 6 or Schedule 1,]

(f) does not contain any functions or restrictions which—

    (i) were in an EU directive and in force immediately before [IP completion day] (including any power to make EU tertiary legislation), and

    (ii) it is appropriate to retain, or

(g) contains EU references which are no longer appropriate.

(3) There is also a deficiency in retained EU law where the Minister considers that there is—

(a) anything in retained EU law which is of a similar kind to any deficiency which falls within subsection (2), or

(b) a deficiency in retained EU law of a kind described, or provided for, in regulations made by a Minister of the Crown.

(4) But retained EU law is not deficient merely because it does not contain any modification of EU law which is adopted or notified, comes into force or only applies on or after [IP completion day].

(5) Regulations under subsection (1) may make any provision that could be made by an Act of Parliament.

(6) Regulations under subsection (1) may (among other things) provide for functions of EU entities or public authorities in member States (including making an instrument of a legislative character or providing funding) to be—

(a) exercisable instead by a public authority (whether or not established for the purpose) in the United Kingdom, or

(b) replaced, abolished or otherwise modified.

(7) But regulations under subsection (1) may not—

(a) impose or increase taxation or fees,

(b) make retrospective provision,

(c) create a relevant criminal offence,

(d) establish a public authority,

(e) . . .

(f) amend, repeal or revoke the Human Rights Act 1998 or any subordinate legislation made under it, or

(g) amend or repeal the Scotland Act 1998, the Government of Wales Act 2006 or the Northern Ireland Act 1998 (unless the regulations are made by virtue of paragraph 21(b) of Schedule 7 to this Act or are amending or repealing any provision of those Acts which modifies another enactment).

(8) No regulations may be made under this section after the end of the period of two years beginning with [IP completion day].

(9) The reference in subsection (1) to a failure or other deficiency arising from the withdrawal of the United Kingdom from the EU includes a reference to any failure or other deficiency arising from[—

(a) any aspect of that withdrawal, including (among other things)—

    (i) the end of the implementation period, or

    (ii) any other effect of the withdrawal agreement, or

(b) that withdrawal, or any such aspect of it, taken together] with the operation of any provision, or the interaction between any provisions, made by or under this Act [or the European Union (Withdrawal Agreement) Act 2020].

NOTES

Commencement: 26 June 2018.

All amendments to this section were made by the European Union (Withdrawal Agreement) Act 2020, s 27(1).

Regulations: many Regulations have been made under this section, most of which are outside the scope of this work and have, therefore, not been listed. The ones of most relevance to this Handbook are the following: the Electronic Identification and Trust Services for Electronic Transactions (Amendment etc) (EU Exit) Regulations 2019, SI 2019/89; the Electronic Communications and Wireless Telegraphy (Amendment etc) (EU Exit) Regulations 2019, SI 2019/246; the Data Protection, Privacy and Electronic Communications (Amendments etc) (EU Exit) Regulations 2019, SI 2019/419; the European Union (Withdrawal) Act 2018 (Consequential Modifications and Repeals and Revocations) (EU Exit) Regulations 2019, SI 2019/628; the Network and Information Systems (Amendment etc) (EU Exit) Regulations 2019, SI 2019/653; the Geo-Blocking Regulation (Revocation) (EU Exit) Regulations 2019, SI 2019/880; the Electronic Communications (Amendment etc) (EU Exit) Regulations 2019, SI 2019/919; the Network and Information Systems (Amendment etc) (EU Exit) (No 2) Regulations 2019, SI 2019/1444; the Electronic Communications and Wireless Telegraphy (Amendment) (European Electronic Communications Code and EU Exit) Regulations 2020, SI 2020/1419; the Data Protection, Privacy and

Electronic Communications (Amendments etc) (EU Exit) Regulations 2020, SI 2020/1586; the Framework for the Free Flow of Non-Personal Data (Revocation) (EU Exit) Regulations 2021, SI 2021/83.

[7.15]
[8A   Supplementary power in connection with implementation period
(1) A Minister of the Crown may by regulations—
   (a)   provide for other modifications for the purposes of section 1B(3)(f)(i) (whether applying in all cases or particular cases or descriptions of case),
   (b)   provide for subsection (3) or (4) of section 1B not to apply to any extent in particular cases or descriptions of case,
   (c)   make different provision in particular cases or descriptions of case to that made by subsection (3) or (4) of that section,
   (d)   modify any enactment contained in this Act in consequence of any repeal made by section 1A(5) or 1B(6), or
   (e)   make such provision not falling within paragraph (a), (b), (c) or (d) as the Minister considers appropriate for any purpose of, or otherwise in connection with, Part 4 of the withdrawal agreement.
(2) The power to make regulations under subsection (1) may (among other things) be exercised by modifying any provision made by or under an enactment.
(3) In subsection (2) "enactment" does not include primary legislation passed or made after IP completion day.
(4) No regulations may be made under subsection (1) after the end of the period of two years beginning with IP completion day.]

NOTES
   Commencement: 23 January 2020.
   Inserted by the European Union (Withdrawal Agreement) Act 2020, s 3.

[7.16]
[8B   Power in connection with certain other separation issues
(1) A Minister of the Crown may by regulations make such provision as the Minister considers appropriate—
   (a)   to implement Part 3 of the withdrawal agreement (separation provisions),
   (b)   to supplement the effect of section 7A in relation to that Part, or
   (c)   otherwise for the purposes of dealing with matters arising out of, or related to, that Part (including matters arising by virtue of section 7A and that Part).
(2) A Minister of the Crown may by regulations make such provision as the Minister considers appropriate—
   (a)   to implement Part 3 of the EEA EFTA separation agreement (separation provisions),
   (b)   to supplement the effect of section 7B in relation to that Part, or
   (c)   otherwise for the purposes of dealing with matters arising out of, or related to, that Part (including matters arising by virtue of section 7B and that Part).
(3) Regulations under this section may make any provision that could be made by an Act of Parliament.
(4) Regulations under this section may (among other things) restate, for the purposes of making the law clearer or more accessible, anything that forms part of domestic law by virtue of—
   (a)   section 7A above and Part 3 of the withdrawal agreement, or
   (b)   section 7B above and Part 3 of the EEA EFTA separation agreement.
(5) But regulations under this section may not—
   (a)   impose or increase taxation or fees,
   (b)   make retrospective provision,
   (c)   create a relevant criminal offence,
   (d)   establish a public authority,
   (e)   amend, repeal or revoke the Human Rights Act 1998 or any subordinate legislation made under it, or
   (f)   amend or repeal the Scotland Act 1998, the Government of Wales Act 2006 or the Northern Ireland Act 1998 (unless the regulations are made by virtue of paragraph 21(b) of Schedule 7 to this Act or are amending or repealing any provision of those Acts which modifies another enactment).
(6) In this section references to Part 3 of the withdrawal agreement or of the EEA EFTA separation agreement include references to any provision of EU law which is applied by, or referred to in, that Part (to the extent of the application or reference).]

NOTES
   Commencement: 19 May 2020.
   Inserted by the European Union (Withdrawal Agreement) Act 2020, s 18.
   Regulations: Regulations made under this section are considered to be outside the scope of this work.

[7.17]
[8C   Power in connection with Ireland/Northern Ireland Protocol in withdrawal agreement
(1) A Minister of the Crown may by regulations make such provision as the Minister considers appropriate—
   (a)   to implement the Protocol on Ireland/Northern Ireland in the withdrawal agreement,
   (b)   to supplement the effect of section 7A in relation to the Protocol, or
   (c)   otherwise for the purposes of dealing with matters arising out of, or related to, the Protocol (including matters arising by virtue of section 7A and the Protocol).
(2) Regulations under subsection (1) may make any provision that could be made by an Act of Parliament (including modifying this Act).
(3) Regulations under subsection (1) may (among other things) make provision facilitating the access to the market within Great Britain of qualifying Northern Ireland goods.
(4) Such provision may (among other things) include provision about the recognition within Great Britain of technical regulations, assessments, registrations, certificates, approvals and authorisations issued by—

(a) the authorities of a member State, or

(b) bodies established in a member State,

in respect of qualifying Northern Ireland goods.

(5) Regulations under subsection (1) may (among other things) restate, for the purposes of making the law clearer or more accessible, anything that forms part of domestic law by virtue of section 7A and the Protocol.

[(5A) Regulations under subsection (1) may not amend, repeal or otherwise modify the operation of section 47 of the United Kingdom Internal Market Act 2020 ("the 2020 Act"), except by making—

(a) provision of the sort that is contemplated by section 47(2) of the 2020 Act (permitted checks);

(b) provision under subsection (6);

(c) provision of the sort described in paragraph 21(b) of Schedule 7 (supplementary and transitional provision etc) in connection with—

(i) provision within either of the preceding paragraphs;

(ii) Articles 5 to 10 of the Northern Ireland Protocol ceasing to apply (and the resulting operation of section 55(1) of the 2020 Act).]

(6) A Minister of the Crown may by regulations define "qualifying Northern Ireland goods" for the purposes of this Act.

(7) In this section any reference to the Protocol on Ireland/Northern Ireland includes a reference to—

(a) any other provision of the withdrawal agreement so far as applying to the Protocol, and

(b) any provision of EU law which is applied by, or referred to in, the Protocol (to the extent of the application or reference),

but does not include the second sentence of Article 11(1) of the Protocol (which provides that the United Kingdom and the Republic of Ireland may continue to make new arrangements that build on the provisions of the Belfast Agreement in other areas of North-South cooperation on the island of Ireland).]

NOTES

Commencement: 19 May 2020.

Inserted by the European Union (Withdrawal Agreement) Act 2020, s 21.

Sub-s (5A): inserted by the United Kingdom Internal Market Act 2020, s 55(3). See also s 55(1) which provides that this subsection ceases to have effect when Articles 5 to 10 of the Northern Ireland Protocol cease to apply.

Regulations: Regulations made under this section are considered to be outside the scope of this work.

General and final provision

[7.18]

20 Interpretation

(1) In this Act—

"Charter of Fundamental Rights" means the Charter of Fundamental Rights of the European Union of 7 December 2000, as adapted at Strasbourg on 12 December 2007;

["Commons sitting day" means a day on which the House of Commons is sitting (and a day is only a day on which the House of Commons is sitting if the House begins to sit on that day);"]

"devolved authority" means—

(a) the Scottish Ministers,

(b) the Welsh Ministers, or

(c) a Northern Ireland department;

"domestic law" means—

(a) in [sections 3, 7A and 7B], the law of England and Wales, Scotland and Northern Ireland, and

(b) in any other case, the law of England and Wales, Scotland or Northern Ireland;

"the EEA" means the European Economic Area;

"enactment" means an enactment whenever passed or made and includes—

(a) an enactment contained in any Order in Council, order, rules, regulations, scheme, warrant, byelaw or other instrument made under an Act,

(b) an enactment contained in any Order in Council made in exercise of Her Majesty's Prerogative,

(c) an enactment contained in, or in an instrument made under, an Act of the Scottish Parliament,

(d) an enactment contained in, or in an instrument made under, a Measure or Act of the National Assembly for Wales,

(e) an enactment contained in, or in an instrument made under, Northern Ireland legislation,

(f) an enactment contained in any instrument made by a member of the Scottish Government, the Welsh Ministers, the First Minister for Wales, the Counsel General to the Welsh Government, a Northern Ireland Minister, the First Minister in Northern Ireland, the deputy First Minister in Northern Ireland or a Northern Ireland department in exercise of prerogative or other executive functions of Her Majesty which are exercisable by such a person on behalf of Her Majesty,

(g) an enactment contained in, or in an instrument made under, a Measure of the Church Assembly or of the General Synod of the Church of England, and

(h) except in sections [1B] and 7 or where there is otherwise a contrary intention, any retained direct EU legislation;

"EU decision" means—

(a) a decision within the meaning of Article 288 of the Treaty on the Functioning of the European Union, or

(b) a decision under former Article 34(2)(c) of the Treaty on European Union;

"EU directive" means a directive within the meaning of Article 288 of the Treaty on the Functioning of the European Union;

"EU entity" means an EU institution or any office, body or agency of the EU;

"EU reference" means—

(a) any reference to the EU, an EU entity or a member State,

      (b)   any reference to an EU directive or any other EU law, or

      (c)   any other reference which relates to the EU;

"EU regulation" means a regulation within the meaning of Article 288 of the Treaty on the Functioning of the European Union;

"EU tertiary legislation" means—

      (a)   any provision made under—

           (i)   an EU regulation,

           (ii)   a decision within the meaning of Article 288 of the Treaty on the Functioning of the European Union, or

          (iii)   an EU directive,

               by virtue of Article 290 or 291(2) of the Treaty on the Functioning of the European Union or former Article 202 of the Treaty establishing the European Community, or

      (b)   any measure adopted in accordance with former Article 34(2)(c) of the Treaty on European Union to implement decisions under former Article 34(2)(c),

          but does not include any such provision or measure which is an EU directive;

"exempt EU instrument" means anything which is an exempt EU instrument by virtue of Schedule 6;

"exit day" [means [31 January 2020] at 11.00 pm (and) see subsections (2) to (5));

["future relationship agreement" has the same meaning as in the European Union (Future Relationship) Act 2020 (see section 37 of that Act);]

["Joint Committee" means the Joint Committee established by Article 164(1) of the withdrawal agreement;]

["Lords sitting day" means a day on which the House of Lords is sitting (and a day is only a day on which the House of Lords is sitting if the House begins to sit on that day);]

"member State" (except in the definitions of "direct EU legislation" and "EU reference") does not include the United Kingdom;

"Minister of the Crown" has the same meaning as in the Ministers of the Crown Act 1975 and also includes the Commissioners for Her Majesty's Revenue and Customs;

"modify" includes amend, repeal or revoke (and related expressions are to be read accordingly);

"Northern Ireland devolved authority" means the First Minister and deputy First Minister in Northern Ireland acting jointly, a Northern Ireland Minister or a Northern Ireland department;

"primary legislation" means—

      (a)   an Act of Parliament,

      (b)   an Act of the Scottish Parliament,

      (c)   a Measure or Act of the National Assembly for Wales, or

      (d)   Northern Ireland legislation;

"public authority" means a public authority within the meaning of section 6 of the Human Rights Act 1998;

["ratify", whether in relation to the withdrawal agreement or otherwise, has the same meaning as it does for the purposes of Part 2 of the Constitutional Reform and Governance Act 2010 in relation to a treaty (see section 25 of that Act);]

"relevant criminal offence" means an offence for which an individual who has reached the age of 18 (or, in relation to Scotland or Northern Ireland, 21) is capable of being sentenced to imprisonment for a term of more than 2 years (ignoring any enactment prohibiting or restricting the imprisonment of individuals who have no previous convictions);

"retained direct EU legislation" means any direct EU legislation which forms part of domestic law by virtue of section 3 (as modified by or under this Act or by other domestic law from time to time, and including any instruments made under it on or after [IP completion day]);

"retrospective provision", in relation to provision made by regulations, means provision taking effect from a date earlier than the date on which the regulations are made;

"subordinate legislation" means—

      (a)   any Order in Council, order, rules, regulations, scheme, warrant, byelaw or other instrument made under any Act, or

      (b)   any instrument made under an Act of the Scottish Parliament, Northern Ireland legislation or a Measure or Act of the National Assembly for Wales,

          and (except in section 7 or Schedule 2 or where there is a contrary intention) includes any Order in Council, order, rules, regulations, scheme, warrant, byelaw or other instrument made on or after [IP completion day] under any retained direct EU legislation;

"tribunal" means any tribunal in which legal proceedings may be brought;

"Wales" and "Welsh zone" have the same meaning as in the Government of Wales Act 2006 (see section 158 of that Act);

. . .

(2) In this [Act references to before, after or on exit day, or to beginning with exit day, are to be read as references to before, after or at 11.00 pm on [31 January 2020] or (as the case may be) to beginning with 11.00 pm on that day].

(3) Subsection (4) applies if the day or time on or at which the Treaties are to cease to apply to the United Kingdom in accordance with Article 50(3) of the Treaty on European Union is different from that specified in the definition of "exit day" in subsection (1).

(4) A Minister of the Crown [must] by regulations—

      (a)   amend the definition of "exit day" in subsection (1) to ensure that the day and time specified in the definition are the day and time that the Treaties are to cease to apply to the United Kingdom, and

      (b)   amend subsection (2) in consequence of any such amendment.

(5) In subsections (3) and (4) "the Treaties" means the Treaty on European Union and the Treaty on the Functioning of the European Union.

[(5A) In this Act references to anything which continues to be domestic law by virtue of section 1B(2) include—

(a) references to anything to which section 1B(2) applies which continues to be domestic law on or after exit day (whether or not it would have done so irrespective of that provision), and

(b) references to anything which continues to be domestic law on or after exit day by virtue of section 1B(2) (as that body of law is added to or otherwise modified by or under this Act or by other domestic law from time to time).]

(6) In this Act references to anything which continues to be domestic law by virtue of section 2 include references to anything to which subsection (1) of that section applies which continues to be domestic law on or after [IP completion day] (whether or not it would have done so irrespective of that section).

(7) In this Act references to anything which is retained EU law by virtue of section 4 include references to any modifications, made by or under this Act or by other domestic law from time to time, of the rights, powers, liabilities, obligations, restrictions, remedies or procedures concerned.

(8) References in this Act (however expressed) to a public authority in the United Kingdom include references to a public authority in any part of the United Kingdom.

(9) References in this Act to former Article 34(2)(c) of the Treaty on European Union are references to that Article as it had effect at any time before the coming into force of the Treaty of Lisbon.

(10) Any other reference in this Act to—

(a) an Article of the Treaty on European Union or the Treaty on the Functioning of the European Union, or

(b) Article 10 of Title VII of Protocol 36 to those treaties,

includes a reference to that Article as applied by Article 106a of the Euratom Treaty.

NOTES

Commencement: 26 June 2018.

Sub-s (1) was amended as follows:

Definition "Commons sitting day" inserted by the European Union (Withdrawal Agreement) Act 2020, s 41(4), Sch 5, Pt 2, paras 38, 44(1), (2)(a).

Words in square brackets in the definition "domestic law" substituted by the European Union (Withdrawal Agreement) Act 2020, s 41(4), Sch 5, Pt 2, paras 38, 44(1), (2)(b).

Figure in square brackets in the para (h) of the definition "enactment" substituted by the European Union (Withdrawal Agreement) Act 2020, s 41(4), Sch 5, Pt 2, paras 38, 44(1), (2)(c).

Words in first (outer) pair of square brackets in the definition "exit day" substituted by the European Union (Withdrawal) Act 2018 (Exit Day) (Amendment) (No 2) Regulations 2019, SI 2019/859, reg 2(1), (2). Words "31 January 2020" in square brackets substituted by the European Union (Withdrawal) Act 2018 (Exit Day) (Amendment) (No 3) Regulations 2019, SI 2019/1423, reg 2(1), (2).

Definition "future relationship agreement" inserted by the European Union (Future Relationship) Act 2020, s 39(3), (5), Sch 6, Pt 1, para 6.

Definitions "Joint Committee", "Lords sitting day" and "ratify" inserted by the European Union (Withdrawal Agreement) Act 2020, s 41(4), Sch 5, Pt 2, paras 38, 44(1), (2)(d), (e).

Words in square brackets in the definitions "retained direct EU legislation" and "subordinate legislation" substituted by the European Union (Withdrawal Agreement) Act 2020, s 41(4), Sch 5, Pt 2, paras 38, 44(1), (2)(f), (g).

Definition "withdrawal agreement" (omitted) repealed by the European Union (Withdrawal Agreement) Act 2020, s 41(4), Sch 5, Pt 2, paras 38, 44(1), (2)(h).

Sub-s (2): words first (outer) pair of in square brackets substituted by SI 2019/859, reg 2(1), (3). Words "31 January 2020" in square brackets substituted by SI 2019/1423, reg 2(1), (3).

Sub-s (4): word in square brackets substituted the European Union (Withdrawal) (No 2) Act 2019, s 4(1).

Sub-s (5A): inserted by the European Union (Withdrawal Agreement) Act 2020, s 41(4), Sch 5, Pt 2, paras 38, 44(1), (3).

Sub-s (6): words in square brackets substituted by the European Union (Withdrawal Agreement) Act 2020, s 41(4), Sch 5, Pt 2, paras 38, 44(1), (4).

National Assembly for Wales: see further, in relation to the renaming of the National Assembly for Wales as the Senedd Cymru or the Welsh Parliament, the Senedd and Elections (Wales) Act 2020, s 2 (with effect from 6 May 2020). See also ss 3–9 of the 2020 Act in relation to the renaming of Acts of the National Assembly for Wales, Members of the National Assembly for Wales, etc.

Regulations: the European Union (Withdrawal) Act 2018 (Exit Day) (Amendment) Regulations 2019, SI 2019/718; the European Union (Withdrawal) Act 2018 (Exit Day) (Amendment) (No 2) Regulations 2019, SI 2019/859; the European Union (Withdrawal) Act 2018 (Exit Day) (Amendment) (No 3) Regulations 2019, SI 2019/1423. Note that the amendments made by the European Union (Withdrawal) Act 2018 (Exit Day) (Amendment) (No 2) Regulations 2019 supersede the amendments made by the European Union (Withdrawal) Act 2018 (Exit Day) (Amendment) Regulations 2019, SI 2019/718.

[7.19]
21 Index of defined expressions

(1) In this Act, the expressions listed in the left-hand column have the meaning given by, or are to be interpreted in accordance with, the provisions listed in the right-hand column.

Expression	*Provision*
[Anything which continues to be domestic law by virtue of section 1B(2)	Section 20(5A)]
Anything which continues to be domestic law by virtue of section 2	Section 20(6)
Anything which is retained EU law by virtue of section 4	Section 20(7)
Article (in relation to the Treaty on European Union or the Treaty on the Functioning of the European Union)	Section 20(10)
Charter of Fundamental Rights	Section 20(1)
[Commons sitting day	Section 20(1)]

Expression	*Provision*
Devolved authority	Section 20(1)
Direct EU legislation	Section 3(2)
Domestic law	Section 20(1)
The EEA	Section 20(1)
EEA agreement	Schedule 1 to the Interpretation Act 1978
[EEA EFTA separation agreement	Section 7B(6)]
Enactment	Section 20(1)
The EU	Schedule 1 to the Interpretation Act 1978
EU decision	Section 20(1)
[EU-derived domestic legislation	Section 1B(7)]
EU directive	Section 20(1)
EU entity	Section 20(1)
EU institution	Schedule 1 to the Interpretation Act 1978
EU instrument	Schedule 1 to the Interpretation Act 1978
Euratom Treaty	Schedule 1 to the Interpretation Act 1978
EU reference	Section 20(1)
EU regulation	Section 20(1)
[European Communities Act 1972	Section 1A(7)(a)]
European Court	Schedule 1 to the Interpretation Act 1978
EU tertiary legislation	Section 20(1)
EU Treaties	Schedule 1 to the Interpretation Act 1978
Exempt EU instrument	Section 20(1)
Exit day (and related expressions)	Section 20(1) to (5)
Former Article 34(2)(c) of Treaty on European Union	Section 20(9)
[Future relationship agreement	Section 20(1)]
[Implementation period	Section 1A(6)]
[IP completion day (and related expressions)	Section 1A(6)]
[Joint Committee	Section 20(1)]
[Lords sitting day	Section 20(1)]
Member State	Section 20(1) and Schedule 1 to the Interpretation Act 1978
Minister of the Crown	Section 20(1)
Modify (and related expressions)	Section 20(1)
Northern Ireland devolved authority	Section 20(1)
Operative (in relation to direct EU legislation)	Section 3(3)
[Part (of withdrawal agreement or EEA EFTA separation agreement)	Section 1A(7)(b)]
Primary legislation	Section 20(1)
Public authority	Section 20(1)
Public authority in the United Kingdom (however expressed)	Section 20(8)
[Qualifying Northern Ireland goods	Section 8C(6)]
[Ratify	Section 20(1)]
Relevant criminal offence	Section 20(1) (and paragraph 44 of Schedule 8)
[Relevant separation agreement law	Section 7C(3)]
Retained case law	Section 6(7)
Retained direct EU legislation	Section 20(1)
Retained direct minor EU legislation	Section 7(6)
Retained direct principal EU legislation	Section 7(6)
Retained domestic case law	Section 6(7)
Retained EU case law	Section 6(7)
Retained EU law	Section 6(7)
Retained general principles of EU law	Section 6(7)

Expression	Provision
Retrospective provision	Section 20(1)
Subordinate legislation	Section 20(1)
[Swiss citizens' rights agreement	Section 7B(6)]
Tribunal	Section 20(1)
Wales	Section 20(1)
Welsh zone	Section 20(1)
Withdrawal agreement	[Section 1A(6)]

(2) See paragraph 22 of Schedule 8 for amendments made by this Act to Schedule 1 to the Interpretation Act 1978.

NOTES
Commencement: 26 June 2018.
Entry "Future relationship agreement" inserted by the European Union (Future Relationship) Act 2020, s 39(3), (5), Sch 6, Pt 1, para 7.
All other amendments to this section were made by the European Union (Withdrawal Agreement) Act 2020, s 41(4), Sch 5, Pt 2, paras 38, 45.

[7.20]
22 Regulations
Schedule 7 (which makes provision about the scrutiny by Parliament and the devolved legislatures of regulations under this Act and contains other general provision about such regulations) has effect.

NOTES
Commencement: 26 June 2018.

[7.21]
23 Consequential and transitional provision
(1) A Minister of the Crown may by regulations make such provision as the Minister considers appropriate in consequence of this Act.
(2) The power to make regulations under subsection (1) may (among other things) be exercised by modifying any provision made by or under an enactment.
(3) In subsection (2) "enactment" does not include primary legislation passed or made after [IP completion day].
(4) No regulations may be made under subsection (1) after the end of the period of 10 years beginning with [IP completion day].
(5) Parts 1 and 2 of Schedule 8 (which contain consequential provision) have effect.
(6) A Minister of the Crown may by regulations make such transitional, transitory or saving provision as the Minister considers appropriate in connection with the coming into force of any provision of this Act (including its operation in connection with exit day [or IP completion day]).
(7) Parts 3 and 4 of Schedule 8 (which contain transitional, transitory and saving provision) have effect.
(8) The enactments mentioned in Schedule 9 (which contains repeals not made elsewhere in this Act) are repealed to the extent specified.

NOTES
Commencement: 26 June 2018 (sub-ss (1)–(4), (6), and sub-s (7) for certain purposes); 4 July 2018 (sub-ss (5), (7), (8) for certain purposes); 1 March 2019 (sub-s (7) for certain purposes); exit day (sub-s (5) for certain purposes); 31 December 2020 (sub-s (8) for certain purposes); IP completion day (sub-ss (5), (7), and sub-s (8) for certain purposes); to be appointed (otherwise).
All amendments to this section were made by the European Union (Withdrawal Agreement) Act 2020, s 41(4), Sch 5, Pt 2, paras 38, 46.
Regulations: the European Union (Withdrawal) Act 2018 (Commencement and Transitional Provisions) Regulations 2018, SI 2018/808; the European Communities (Designation Orders) (Revocation) (EU Exit) Regulations 2018, SI 2018/1011; the European Union (Definition of Treaties Orders) (Revocation) (EU Exit) Regulations 2018, SI 2018/1012; the Data Protection, Privacy and Electronic Communications (Amendments, etc) (EU Exist) Regulations 2019, SI 2019/419; the European Union (Withdrawal) Act 2018 (Commencement No 5, Transitional Provisions and Amendment) Regulations 2020, SI 2020/74; the European Union (Withdrawal) Act 2018 and European Union (Withdrawal Agreement) Act 2020 (Commencement, Transitional and Savings Provisions) Regulations 2020, SI 2020/1622. Other Regulations made under this section are not listed as they are outside the scope of this work.

[7.22]
24 Extent
(1) Subject to subsections (2) and (3), this Act extends to England and Wales, Scotland and Northern Ireland.
(2) Any provision of this Act which amends or repeals an enactment has the same extent as the enactment amended or repealed.
(3) Regulations under section 8(1) or 23 may make provision which extends to Gibraltar—
  (a) modifying any enactment which—
    (i) extends to Gibraltar and relates to European Parliamentary elections, or
    (ii) extends to Gibraltar for any purpose which is connected with Gibraltar forming part of an electoral region, under the European Parliamentary Elections Act 2002, for the purposes of such elections, or
  (b) which is supplementary, incidental, consequential, transitional, transitory or saving provision in connection with a modification within paragraph (a).

NOTES
Commencement: 26 June 2018.
Regulations: made under this section are considered to be outside the scope of this work.

[7.23]
25 Commencement and short title
(1) The following provisions—
   (a)   sections 8 to 11 (including Schedule 2),
   (b)   paragraphs 4, 5, 21(2)(b), 48(b), 51(2)(c) and (d) and (4) of Schedule 3 (and section 12(8) and (12) so far as relating to those paragraphs),
   (c)   sections 13 and 14 (including Schedule 4),
   (d)   sections 16 to 18,
   (e)   sections 20 to 22 (including Schedules 6 and 7),
   (f)   section 23(1) to (4) and (6),
   (g)   paragraph 41(10), 43 and 44 of Schedule 8 (and section 23(7) so far as relating to those paragraphs),
   (h)   section 24, and
   (i)   this section,
come into force on the day on which this Act is passed.
(2) In section 12—
   (a)   subsection (2) comes into force on the day on which this Act is passed for the purposes of making regulations under section 30A of the Scotland Act 1998,
   (b)   subsection (4) comes into force on that day for the purposes of making regulations under section 109A of the Government of Wales Act 2006, and
   (c)   subsection (6) comes into force on that day for the purposes of making regulations under section 6A of the Northern Ireland Act 1998.
(3) In Schedule 3—
   (a)   paragraph 1(b) comes into force on the day on which this Act is passed for the purposes of making regulations under section 57(4) of the Scotland Act 1998,
   (b)   paragraph 2 comes into force on that day for the purposes of making regulations under section 80(8) of the Government of Wales Act 2006,
   (c)   paragraph 3(b) comes into force on that day for the purposes of making regulations under section 24(3) of the Northern Ireland Act 1998,
   (d)   paragraph 24(2) comes into force on that day for the purposes of making regulations under section 30A of the Scotland Act 1998,
   (e)   paragraph 24(3) comes into force on that day for the purposes of making regulations under section 57(4) of the Scotland Act 1998,
   (f)   paragraph 25 comes into force on that day for the purposes of making regulations under section 30A or 57(4) of the Scotland Act 1998,
   (g)   paragraph 43 comes into force on that day for the purposes of making regulations under section 80(8) or 109A of the Government of Wales Act 2006, and
   (h)   paragraphs 57 and 58 come into force on that day for the purposes of making regulations under section 6A or 24(3) of the Northern Ireland Act 1998;
and section 12(7) and (12), so far as relating to each of those paragraphs, comes into force on that day for the purposes of making the regulations mentioned above in relation to that paragraph.
(4) The provisions of this Act, so far as they are not brought into force by subsections (1) to (3), come into force on such day as a Minister of the Crown may by regulations appoint; and different days may be appointed for different purposes.
(5) This Act may be cited as the European Union (Withdrawal) Act 2018.

NOTES
Commencement: 26 June 2018.
Regulations: the European Union (Withdrawal) Act 2018 (Commencement and Transitional Provisions) Regulations 2018, SI 2018/808; the European Union (Withdrawal) Act 2018 (Commencement No 2) Regulations 2019, SI 2019/399; the European Union (Withdrawal) Act 2018 (Commencement No 3) Regulations 2019, SI 2019/1077; the European Union (Withdrawal) Act 2018 (Commencement No 4) Regulations 2019, SI 2019/1198; the European Union (Withdrawal) Act 2018 (Commencement No 5, Transitional Provisions and Amendment) Regulations 2020, SI 2020/74; the European Union (Withdrawal) Act 2018 and European Union (Withdrawal Agreement) Act 2020 (Commencement, Transitional and Savings Provisions) Regulations 2020, SI 2020/1622.

Part 7   Key Brexit Materials

SCHEDULES

SCHEDULE 1
FURTHER PROVISION ABOUT EXCEPTIONS TO SAVINGS AND INCORPORATION
Section 5(6)

Challenges to validity of retained EU law

[7.24]
1. (1) There is no right in domestic law on or after [IP completion day] to challenge any retained EU law on the basis that, immediately before [IP completion day], an EU instrument was invalid.
(2) Sub-paragraph (1) does not apply so far as—
   (a)   the European Court has decided before [IP completion day] that the instrument is invalid, or
   (b)   the challenge is of a kind described, or provided for, in regulations made by a Minister of the Crown.

(3) Regulations under sub-paragraph (2)(b) may (among other things) provide for a challenge which would otherwise have been against an EU institution to be against a public authority in the United Kingdom.

General principles of EU law

2. No general principle of EU law is part of domestic law on or after [IP completion day] if it was not recognised as a general principle of EU law by the European Court in a case decided before [IP completion day] (whether or not as an essential part of the decision in the case).

3. (1) There is no right of action in domestic law on or after [IP completion day] based on a failure to comply with any of the general principles of EU law.

(2) No court or tribunal or other public authority may, on or after [IP completion day]—

    (a)   disapply or quash any enactment or other rule of law, or

    (b)   quash any conduct or otherwise decide that it is unlawful,

because it is incompatible with any of the general principles of EU law.

Rule in Francovich

4. There is no right in domestic law on or after [IP completion day] to damages in accordance with the rule in *Francovich*.

Interpretation

5. (1) References in section 5 and this Schedule to the principle of the supremacy of EU law, the Charter of Fundamental Rights, any general principle of EU law or the rule in *Francovich* are to be read as references to that principle, Charter or rule so far as it would otherwise continue to be, or form part of, domestic law on or after [IP completion day] [by virtue of section 2, 3, 4 or 6(3) or (6) and otherwise in accordance with this Act].

(2) Accordingly (among other things) the references to the principle of the supremacy of EU law in section 5(2) and (3) do not include anything which would bring into domestic law any modification of EU law which is adopted or notified, comes into force or only applies on or after [IP completion day].

NOTES

Commencement: 4 July 2018 (para 1(2)(b) for the purpose of making regulations, and para 1(3)); IP completion day (otherwise).

The words "IP completion day" in square brackets were substituted by the European Union (Withdrawal Agreement) Act 2020, s 25(6)(a).

The words "by virtue of section 2, 3, 4 or 6(3) or (6) and otherwise in accordance with this Act" in square brackets were substituted by the European Union (Withdrawal Agreement) Act 2020, s 25(6)(b).

Regulations: the Challenges to Validity of EU Instruments (EU Exit) Regulations 2019, SI 2019/673. These Regulations make provision about the exceptions to the saving and incorporation of EU law set out in paragraph 1, which provides that, on or after IP completion day, no challenge can be brought in the UK courts to retained EU law on the basis that immediately before IP completion day, an EU instrument was invalid. Regulations 1 and 2 provide for citation, commencement and interpretation. Regulation 3 provides that this exception for claims in respect of validity will not apply in respect of a certain class of claims. They must be based on whether an EU instrument was invalid immediately before IP completion day under the grounds in Article 263 TFEU and relate to proceedings which have begun before IP completion day but are not yet decided. Regulation 4 gives jurisdiction to courts and tribunals in the UK to declare an EU instrument invalid in these cases. Regulation 5 makes provision for notice to be given to a Minister of the Crown or the devolved administrations about any proceedings under these Regulations. Regulation 6 allows for a Minister of the Crown or the devolved administrations to be able to intervene in proceedings under these Regulations.

EUROPEAN UNION (FUTURE RELATIONSHIP) ACT 2020

(2020 c 29)

An Act to make provision to implement, and make other provision in connection with, the Trade and Cooperation Agreement; to make further provision in connection with the United Kingdom's future relationship with the EU and its member States; to make related provision about passenger name record data, customs and privileges and immunities; and for connected purposes.

[31 December 2020]

NOTES

Commencement: the commencement of this Act is provided for by s 40 at **[7.55]**; subsections (6), (7) of that section provide that certain provisions of this Act come into force on the day on which this Act is passed (31 December 2020). The European Union (Future Relationship) Act 2020 (Commencement No 1) Regulations 2020 (SI 2020/1662) provides for ss 21, 27 and 34 to come into force 1 March 2021 and the remaining sections to come into force on 31 December 2020 (see reg 2(a)).

ARRANGEMENT OF SECTIONS

PART 1
SECURITY

Criminal records

PART 2
TRADE AND OTHER MATTERS

PART 3
GENERAL IMPLEMENTATION

PART 4
SUPPLEMENTARY AND FINAL PROVISION

SCHEDULES

PART 1 SECURITY
Criminal records

[7.25]
1 Duty to notify member States of convictions
(1) This section applies where—
  (a) an individual who is a national of a member State has been convicted by or before a court in a part of the United Kingdom, and
  (b) the conviction is recorded in the criminal records database for that part.
(2) This section also applies where—
  (a) an individual who is a national of a member State has been convicted in UK service disciplinary proceedings (whether or not in a part of the United Kingdom), and
  (b) the conviction is recorded in the criminal records database for any part of the United Kingdom.
(3) The designated UK authority must notify the central authority of the member State of the conviction.
(4) If the individual is a national of more than one member State, the designated UK authority must notify the central authority of each of those member States of the conviction.
(5) Notification under this section must be given before the end of the period of 28 days beginning with the day on which the conviction is recorded in the criminal records database.
(6) A notification under this section—
  (a) must include the information listed in Schedule 1, and
  (b) may include any other information that the designated UK authority considers appropriate.
(7) If the record of the conviction is amended so as to alter or delete any of the information mentioned in paragraph 13, 14, 16, 17, 19 or 20 of Schedule 1 (information about the conviction), subsections (3) to (6) apply in relation to the amendment as they apply in relation to the conviction.
(8) Nothing in this section requires the designated UK authority to disclose any information if the disclosure would contravene the data protection legislation (but, in determining whether the disclosure would contravene that legislation, the duties imposed by this section are to be taken into account).
(9) For the purposes of this section it does not matter if the individual is a national of the United Kingdom as well as a national of a member State.

NOTES
Commencement: 31 December 2020.

[7.26]
2 Retention of information received from member States
(1) This section applies where—
  (a) an individual who is a UK national has been convicted under the law of a member State, and
  (b) the central authority of the member State notifies the designated UK authority of the conviction.
(2) The designated UK authority must retain a record of—
  (a) the conviction, and
  (b) any other information listed in Schedule 1 that is included in the notification.
(3) The record may be retained in whatever way the designated UK authority considers appropriate.
(4) If the designated UK authority is notified by the central authority of any amendment or deletion relating to the information contained in the record, the designated UK authority must amend the record accordingly.
(5) Nothing in this section requires the designated UK authority to retain any information if the retention would contravene the data protection legislation (but, in determining whether the retention would contravene that legislation, the duty imposed by subsection (2) is to be taken into account).

NOTES
Commencement: 31 December 2020.

[7.27]
3 Transfers to third countries of personal data notified under section 2
(1) Personal data notified to the designated UK authority as mentioned in section 2 may not be transferred to a third country unless conditions A and B are met.
(2) Condition A is that the transfer—
  (a) is based on adequacy regulations, or
  (b) is based on there being appropriate safeguards.
(3) For the purposes of subsection (2)—
  (a) the reference to a transfer being based on adequacy regulations has the same meaning as it has for the purposes of Part 3 of the Data Protection Act 2018;
  (b) the reference to a transfer being based on there being appropriate safeguards is to be read in accordance with section 75 of that Act.
(4) Condition B is that the intended recipient has functions relating to the prevention, investigation, detection or prosecution of criminal offences or the execution of criminal penalties, including the safeguarding against and the prevention of threats to public security.
(5) See also section 73 of the Data Protection Act 2018 for additional conditions that must be met before personal data may be transferred to a third country (in particular, that the transfer must be necessary for any of the law enforcement purposes).

(6) Where personal data within subsection (1) is transferred to a third country, the person making the transfer must make it a condition of the transfer that the data may be used only for the purpose for which it is being transferred.

(7) In this section—

"personal data" has the same meaning as in the Data Protection Act 2018 (see section 3(2) of that Act);

"third country" means a country or territory other than—

(a)   the United Kingdom, or

(b)   a member State.

NOTES

Commencement: 31 December 2020.

[7.28]

4   Requests for information from member States

(1) The designated UK authority may, for any of the law enforcement purposes, make a request to the central authority of a member State for information relating to any overseas convictions of an individual recorded in a criminal records database of the member State.

(2) If an individual who is a national of a member State makes a request to the designated UK authority for information relating to the individual's overseas convictions, the designated UK authority must make a request to the central authority of that member State for information relating to any overseas convictions of the individual recorded in a criminal records database of the member State.

(3) If the individual is a national of more than one member State, the designated UK authority must make a request to the central authority of each of those member States for the information.

(4) Any information provided to the designated UK authority in response to a request made under this section may be used only—

(a)   for the purpose or purposes for which it was requested, and

(b)   in accordance with any restrictions specified by the central authority that provided it.

(5) But subsection (4) does not prohibit the use of such information for the purpose of preventing an immediate and serious threat to public security.

(6) In this section "overseas conviction" means a conviction under the law of a country or territory outside the United Kingdom.

NOTES

Commencement: 31 December 2020.

[7.29]

5   Requests for information made by member States

(1) If—

(a)   the central authority of a member State makes a request to the designated UK authority for information relating to an individual's convictions, and

(b)   conditions A and B are met,

the designated UK authority must, as soon as practicable before the end of the relevant period, provide the information to the central authority (but see subsection (5)).

(2) Condition A is that the request is made—

(a)   for any of the law enforcement purposes, or

(b)   for the purposes of enabling the central authority to comply with a request made by an individual who is a UK national for information relating to the individual's convictions.

(3) Condition B is that the information—

(a)   is recorded in the criminal records database for a part of the United Kingdom, or

(b)   is retained in accordance with section 2.

(4) "The relevant period" means the period of 20 working days beginning with the day on which the designated UK authority receives the request.

(5) Subsection (1) does not require the designated UK authority to provide any information relating to a conviction that is spent unless—

(a)   the request has been made for the purposes of any criminal investigation or criminal proceedings, or

(b)   subsection (6) applies.

(6) If the request has been made for the purposes of determining the suitability of an individual to work with children, the information to be provided under subsection (1) must include any information relating to any conviction of the individual for a child sexual offence (whether or not spent).

(7) Nothing in this section requires the designated UK authority to disclose any information if the disclosure would contravene the data protection legislation (but, in determining whether the disclosure would contravene that legislation, the duties imposed by this section are to be taken into account).

(8) In this section—

"ancillary offence" means—

(a)   an offence of attempting or conspiring to commit a child sexual offence,

(b)   an offence under Part 2 of the Serious Crime Act 2007 in relation to a child sexual offence,

(c)   an offence of inciting a person to commit a child sexual offence,

(d)   an offence of aiding, abetting, counselling or procuring the commission of a child sexual offence, or

(e)   an offence of being involved art and part in the commission of a child sexual offence;

"child" means an individual under the age of 18;

"child sexual offence" means—

(a)   an offence consisting of—

(i)   the sexual abuse or sexual exploitation of a child, or

(ii)   conduct relating to such abuse or exploitation,

Part 7   Key Brexit Materials

(b)   an offence relating to indecent images of a child,

(c)   an offence consisting of any other behaviour carried out in relation to a child that is of a sexual nature or carried out for sexual purposes, or

(d)   an ancillary offence;

and for these purposes "offence" includes an offence under a law that is no longer in force;

"conviction" means—

(a)   a conviction by or before a court in a part of the United Kingdom,

(b)   a conviction in UK service disciplinary proceedings (whether or not in a part of the United Kingdom), or

(c)   a conviction under the law of a country or territory outside the United Kingdom;

"criminal proceedings" means—

(a)   proceedings before a court for dealing with an individual accused of an offence, or

(b)   proceedings before a court for dealing with an individual convicted of an offence, including proceedings in respect of a sentence or order;

"working day" means any day other than—

(a)   Saturday or Sunday,

(b)   Christmas Day,

(c)   Good Friday, and

(d)   any day which is a bank holiday in England and Wales under the Banking and Financial Dealings Act 1971.

(9) For the purposes of this section a conviction is "spent" if—

(a) in the case of a conviction in Northern Ireland, it is a spent conviction for the purposes of the Rehabilitation of Offenders (Northern Ireland) Order 1978 (SI 1978/1908 (NI 27));

(b) in any other case, it is a spent conviction for the purposes of the Rehabilitation of Offenders Act 1974.

NOTES

Commencement: 31 December 2020.

[7.30]
6 Interpretation of the criminal records provisions

(1) In the criminal records provisions—

"central authority", in relation to a member State, means an authority designated by the government of that member State as the appropriate authority for requesting, receiving or providing information relating to convictions;

"conviction", in relation to UK service disciplinary proceedings—

(a)   in the case of proceedings in respect of a service offence, includes anything that under section 376(1) and (2) of the Armed Forces Act 2006 (which relates to summary hearings and the Summary Appeal Court) is to be treated as a conviction for the purposes of that Act;

(b)   in the case of any other UK service disciplinary proceedings, includes a finding of guilt in those proceedings;

and "convicted", in relation to UK service disciplinary proceedings, is to be read accordingly;

"criminal records database" means—

(a)   in relation to England and Wales, the names database held by the Secretary of State for the use of constables;

(b)   in relation to Scotland, the criminal history database of the Police Service of Scotland held for the use of police forces generally;

(c)   in relation to Northern Ireland, the names database maintained by the Department of Justice in Northern Ireland for the purpose of recording convictions and cautions;

(d)   in relation to a member State, any database maintained in respect of the member State that corresponds to the criminal records database for England and Wales;

"the criminal records provisions" means sections 1 to 5, this section and Schedule 1;

"designated UK authority" means a person designated for the purposes of the criminal records provisions by a direction given by the Secretary of State;

"the law enforcement purposes" means the purposes of the prevention, investigation, detection or prosecution of criminal offences or the execution of criminal penalties, including the safeguarding against and the prevention of threats to public security;

"service offence" means—

(a)   a service offence within the meaning of the Armed Forces Act 2006, or

(b)   an SDA offence within the meaning of the Armed Forces Act 2006 (Transitional Provisions etc) Order 2009 (SI 2009/1059);

"UK national" means an individual who is—

(a)   a British citizen, a British overseas territories citizen, a British National (Overseas) or a British Overseas citizen,

(b)   a person who under the British Nationality Act 1981 is a British subject, or

(c)   a British protected person within the meaning of that Act;

"UK service disciplinary proceedings" means—

(a)   any proceedings (whether or not before a court) in respect of a service offence (except proceedings before a civilian court within the meaning of the Armed Forces Act 2006);

(b)   any proceedings under the Army Act 1955, the Air Force Act 1955, or the Naval Discipline Act 1957 (whether before a court-martial or before any other court or person authorised under any of those Acts to award a punishment in respect of an offence);

(c)   any proceedings before a Standing Civilian Court established under the Armed Forces Act 1976.

(2) The following provisions (which deem a conviction of a person discharged not to be a conviction) do not apply for the purposes of the criminal records provisions to a conviction of an individual for an offence in respect of which an order has been made discharging the individual absolutely or conditionally—

(a) section 247 of the Criminal Procedure (Scotland) Act 1995;

(b) Article 6 of the Criminal Justice (Northern Ireland) Order 1996 (SI 1996/3160 (NI 24));

(c) section 14 of the Powers of Criminal Courts (Sentencing) Act 2000;

(d) section 82 of the Sentencing Code;

(e) section 187 of the Armed Forces Act 2006 or any corresponding earlier enactment.

(3) The appropriate national authority may by regulations amend this section so as to change the meaning of "criminal records database" in relation to a part of the United Kingdom.

(4) For the purposes of subsection (3) the "appropriate national authority" is—

(a) in relation to England and Wales, the Secretary of State;

(b) in relation to Scotland, the Scottish Ministers;

(c) in relation to Northern Ireland, the Department of Justice in Northern Ireland.

NOTES

Commencement: 31 December 2020.

Passenger and vehicle registration data

[7.31]

7 Passenger name record data

In Schedule 2—

(a) Part 1 amends the Passenger Name Record Data and Miscellaneous Amendments Regulations 2018 (SI 2018/598) (the "PNR regulations");

(b) Part 2 makes provision for an interim period;

(c) Part 3 confers power to modify the PNR regulations to apply to sea and rail travel.

NOTES

Commencement: 31 December 2020.

[7.32]

8 Disclosure of vehicle registration data

(1) The Secretary of State may disclose vehicle registration data in accordance with—

(a) Article LAW.PRUM.15 of the Trade and Cooperation Agreement (automated searching of vehicle registration data), and

(b) Chapter 3 of Annex LAW-1 to that agreement (exchange of vehicle registration data).

(2) A disclosure under this section does not breach—

(a) any obligation of confidence owed by the Secretary of State, or

(b) any other restriction on the disclosure of data (however imposed).

(3) Nothing in this section authorises the making of a disclosure which contravenes the data protection legislation (save that the power conferred by this section is to be taken into account in determining whether any disclosure contravenes that legislation).

(4) Nothing in this section limits the circumstances in which data may be disclosed under any other enactment or rule of law.

(5) "Vehicle registration data" has the meaning given by Article LAW.PRUM.6 of the Trade and Cooperation Agreement (definitions).

NOTES

Commencement: to be appointed.

Evidence

[7.33]

9 Mutual assistance in criminal matters

Schedule 3 contains provision about mutual assistance in criminal matters.

NOTES

Commencement: 31 December 2020.

---

10   *(S 10 amends the Accreditation of Forensic Service Providers Regulations 2018 (SI 2018/1276), regs 2, 4.)*

Extradition

11–13   *(S 11 amends the Extradition Act 2003 (Designation of Part 1 Territories) Order 2003, SI 2003/3333 and the Extradition Act 2003 (Designation of Part 2 Territories) Order 2003, SI 2003/3334 (outside the scope of this work). Ss 12, 13 amend the Extradition Act 2003 (outside the scope of this work).)*

PART 2 TRADE AND OTHER MATTERS

Information about non-food product safety

[7.34]

14 Disclosure of non-food product safety information within UK

(1) This section applies to information which relates to the safety of non-food products and is supplied by the European Commission, or such person as the Commission may specify by written notice to the Secretary of State, to a relevant authority for the purpose of giving effect to a provision of—

(a) Article TBT.9 of the Trade and Cooperation Agreement (including any annex to that Article), or

(b) a non-food product safety annex.

(2) A relevant authority may disclose that information for a permitted purpose.

(3) The following are the "permitted purposes" for the purpose of subsection (2)—

    (a)   to ensure health and safety,

    (b)   to ensure the protection of consumers, and

    (c)   to ensure the protection of the environment.

(4) A person who receives information as a result of subsection (2) may not—

    (a)   use the information for a purpose other than a permitted purpose, or

    (b)   further disclose that information except with the consent of the relevant authority who disclosed the information.

NOTES

Commencement: 31 December 2020.

[7.35]

15   Disclosure of non-food product safety information to Commission

(1) This section applies to information held by a relevant authority which relates to the safety of non-food products.

(2) A relevant authority may disclose information to the European Commission, or such person as the Commission may specify by written notice to the Secretary of State, for the purpose of giving effect to a provision of—

    (a)   Article TBT.9 of the Trade and Cooperation Agreement (including any annex to that Article), or

    (b)   a non-food product safety annex.

NOTES

Commencement: 31 December 2020.

[7.36]

16   Offence relating to disclosure under section 14(4)(b)

(1) A person commits an offence if the person, in contravention of section 14(4)(b), discloses information which relates to a person whose identity—

    (a)   is specified in the disclosure, or

    (b)   can be deduced from it.

(2) It is a defence for a person charged with an offence under this section to prove that the person reasonably believed—

    (a)   that the disclosure was lawful, or

    (b)   that the information had already lawfully been made available to the public.

(3) A prosecution for an offence under this section—

    (a)   may be brought in England and Wales only with the consent of the Director of Public Prosecutions;

    (b)   may be brought in Northern Ireland only with the consent of the Director of Public Prosecutions for Northern Ireland.

(4) A person guilty of an offence under this section is liable—

    (a)   on conviction on indictment, to imprisonment for a term not exceeding two years, to a fine or to both, or

    (b)   on summary conviction—

        (i)   in England and Wales, to imprisonment for a term not exceeding 12 months, to a fine or to both;

        (ii)   in Scotland, to imprisonment for a term not exceeding 12 months, to a fine not exceeding the statutory maximum or to both;

        (iii)   in Northern Ireland, to imprisonment for a term not exceeding 6 months, to a fine not exceeding the statutory maximum or to both.

(5) In relation to an offence committed before the commencement of paragraph 24(2) of Schedule 22 to the Sentencing Act 2020, the reference in subsection (4)(b)(i) to 12 months is to be read as a reference to 6 months.

NOTES

Commencement: 31 December 2020.

[7.37]

17   General provisions about disclosure of non-food product safety information

(1) Nothing in section 14 or 15 limits the circumstances in which information may be disclosed under any other enactment or rule of law.

(2) A disclosure under section 14 or 15 does not breach—

    (a)   any obligation of confidence owed by the relevant authority, or

    (b)   any other restriction on the disclosure of information (however imposed).

(3) Nothing in this section, or in section 14 or 15, authorises a disclosure of information if the disclosure would contravene the data protection legislation (but in determining whether a disclosure would do so, the powers conferred by sections 14(2) and 15(2) are to be taken into account).

NOTES

Commencement: 31 December 2020.

[7.38]

18   Interpretation of sections 14 to 17

(1) In sections 14 to 17 and this section—

    "market surveillance" means any activity conducted or measure taken for the purpose of ensuring that a product complies with relevant legal requirements;

    "market surveillance authority" means—

        (a)   a person in the United Kingdom with any function of carrying out market surveillance that is conferred by an enactment or rule of law, and

(b)   a person in any other country or territory with any corresponding function;

"non-food product safety annex" means one of the following annexes to the Trade and Cooperation Agreement—

(a)   TBT-1: Motor vehicles and equipment and parts thereof, or

(b)   TBT-3: Chemicals;

"permitted purpose" has the meaning given by section 14(3);

"relevant authority" means—

(a)   a Minister of the Crown, or

(b)   the Health and Safety Executive;

"relevant legal requirements" means such requirements of the law relating to a product as apply in the territory in which the product is made available on the market, put into service or put into use.

(2) For the purposes of sections 14 and 15 and this section, information which relates to the safety of non-food products includes—

(a)   information about whether, and the extent to which, a non-food product complies, or may comply, with any—

(i)   relevant legal requirement, or

(ii)   other assessment that relates to product safety,

(b)   information about developments, or potential developments, in the field of safety of non-food products, and

(c)   the exercise of functions by market surveillance authorities in relation to non-food products.

NOTES

Commencement: 31 December 2020.

Use of relevant international standards

[7.39]

19   Use of relevant international standards

Schedule 4 contains amendments about the use of international standards.

NOTES

Commencement: 31 December 2020.

Customs and tax

20, 21   (*Amend the Customs and Excise Management Act 1979 and the Taxation (Cross-border Trade) Act 2018 (outside the scope of this work).*)

[7.40]

22   Administrative co-operation on VAT and mutual assistance on tax debts

(1) The arrangements contained in the Protocol have effect (and do so in spite of anything in any enactment).

(2) The Commissioners for Her Majesty's Revenue and Customs are the competent authority in the United Kingdom responsible for the application of the Protocol.

(3) A reference in any enactment to arrangements having effect by virtue of, or by virtue of an Order in Council under, section 173 of the Finance Act 2006 (international tax enforcement arrangements) includes a reference to arrangements having effect by virtue of this section.

(4) In this section "the Protocol" means—

(a)   the protocol, contained in the Trade and Cooperation Agreement, on administrative co-operation and combating fraud in the field of Value Added Tax and on mutual assistance for the recovery of claims relating to taxes and duties, and

(b)   any decision or recommendation adopted by the Specialised Committee in accordance with that protocol.

(5) In subsection (4)—

(a)   a reference to the Trade and Cooperation Agreement or to any provision of it is to that agreement or provision as it has effect at the relevant time;

(b)   a reference to a decision or recommendation adopted by the Specialised Committee in accordance with any provision is to a decision or recommendation so adopted at or before the relevant time.

(6) In subsection (5) "the relevant time" means the time at which the protocol mentioned in subsection (4)(a) comes into effect (or, if it comes into effect at different times for different purposes, the earliest such time).

(7) The Commissioners for Her Majesty's Revenue and Customs may by regulations amend subsection (6) so as to substitute a later time for that for the time being specified there.

NOTES

Commencement: 31 December 2020.

Transport

[7.41]

23   Licences for access to the international road haulage market

In Regulation (EC) No 1072/2009 of the European Parliament and of the Council of 21 October 2009 on common rules for access to the international road haulage market, for the model licence set out in Annex 2 (UK licence for the Community model) substitute the model licence set out in Part B of Appendix Road.A.1.3 to Annex Road-1 to the Trade and Cooperation Agreement.

NOTES

Commencement: 31 December 2020.

24   (*Amends European Parliament and Council Regulation 1072/2009/EU on the common rules for access to the international road haulage market (outside the scope of this work).*)

[7.42]
25 Disclosure of data relating to drivers' cards for tachographs
(1) The Secretary of State may disclose data from the GB electronic register in accordance with—
  (a) Article 13(2) of Section 2 of Appendix Road.C 1.1 to the Trade and Cooperation Agreement (interconnection and accessibility of electronic registers of data relating to drivers' cards for tachographs), or
  (b) Article 13(4) of Section 2 of Appendix Road.C 1.1 to the Trade and Cooperation Agreement (access for control officers to electronic registers of data relating to drivers' cards for tachographs).
(2) The Department for Infrastructure may disclose data from the NI electronic register in accordance with—
  (a) Article 13(2) of Section 2 of Appendix Road.C 1.1 to the Trade and Cooperation Agreement (interconnection and accessibility of electronic registers of data relating to drivers' cards for tachographs), or
  (b) Article 13(4) of Section 2 of Appendix Road.C 1.1 to the Trade and Cooperation Agreement (access for control officers to electronic registers of data relating to drivers' cards for tachographs).
(3) A disclosure under this section does not breach—
  (a) any obligation of confidence owed by the Secretary of State or the Department for Infrastructure, or
  (b) any other restriction on the disclosure of data (however imposed).
(4) Nothing in this section authorises the making of a disclosure which contravenes the data protection legislation (save that the power conferred by this section is to be taken into account in determining whether any disclosure contravenes that legislation).
(5) Nothing in this section limits the circumstances in which data may be disclosed under any other enactment or rule of law.
(6) In this section—
  "GB electronic register" means any electronic register maintained by the Secretary of State in accordance with Article 13(1) of Section 2 of Appendix Road.C 1.1 to the Trade and Cooperation Agreement (maintenance of electronic registers of data relating to drivers' cards for tachographs);
  "NI electronic register" means any electronic register maintained by the Department for Infrastructure in accordance with Article 13(1) of Section 2 of Appendix Road.C 1.1 to the Trade and Cooperation Agreement (maintenance of electronic registers of data relating to drivers' cards for tachographs).

NOTES
Commencement: 31 December 2020.

Social security

[7.43]
26 Social security co-ordination
(1) The following provisions of the Trade and Cooperation Agreement, in its English language version, form part of domestic law on and after the relevant day—
  (a) the SSC Protocol;
  (b) Title I of Heading 4 of Part 2 (Trade);
  (c) Articles COMPROV.17 and FINPROV.2, so far as applying to the SSC Protocol.
(2) Any enactment has effect on and after the relevant day with such modifications as—
  (a) are required in consequence of subsection (1) or otherwise for the purposes of implementing the provisions mentioned in that subsection, and
  (b) are capable of being ascertained from those provisions or otherwise from the Trade and Cooperation Agreement.
(3) Subsections (1) and (2)—
  (a) are subject to any equivalent or other provision—
    (i) which (whether before, on or after the relevant day) is made by or under this Act or any other enactment or otherwise forms part of domestic law, and
    (ii) which is for the purposes of (or has the effect of) implementing to any extent the Trade and Cooperation Agreement or any other future relationship agreement, and
  (b) do not limit the scope of any power which is capable of being exercised to make any such provision.
(4) The references to the Trade and Cooperation Agreement in—
  (a) subsections (1) and (2), and
  (b) the definition of "the SSC Protocol" in subsection (5),
are (except as provided in that definition) references to the agreement as it has effect on the relevant day.
(5) In this section—
  "domestic law" means—
    (a) in subsection (1), the law of England and Wales, Scotland and Northern Ireland, and
    (b) in subsection (3)(a)(i), the law of England and Wales, Scotland or Northern Ireland;
  "relevant day", in relation to any provision mentioned in subsection (1) or any aspect of it, means—
    (a) so far as the provision or aspect concerned is provisionally applied before it comes into force, the time and day from which the provisional application applies, and
    (b) so far as the provision or aspect concerned is not provisionally applied before it comes into force, the time and day when it comes into force;
  "the SSC Protocol" means the Protocol on Social Security Coordination contained in the Trade and Cooperation Agreement, as that protocol is modified or supplemented from time to time in accordance with Article SSC 11(6), Article SSC 11(8) or Article SSC 68 of that protocol;
and references to the purposes of (or having the effect of) implementing an agreement (or any provision of an agreement) include references to the purposes of (or having the effect of) making provision consequential on any such implementation.

NOTES
Commencement: 31 December 2020.

Privileges and immunities

27   (*Amends the International Organisations Act 1968 (outside the scope of this work).*)

Energy

28   (*Amends the Nuclear Safeguards (Fissionable Material and Relevant International Agreements) (EU Exit) Regulations 2019, SI 2019/195, and the Nuclear Safeguards (EU Exit) Regulations 2019, SI 2019/196 (outside the scope of this work).*)

PART 3 GENERAL IMPLEMENTATION

General implementation of agreements

[7.44]
29   General implementation of agreements
(1) Existing domestic law has effect on and after the relevant day with such modifications as are required for the purposes of implementing in that law the Trade and Cooperation Agreement or the Security of Classified Information Agreement so far as the agreement concerned is not otherwise so implemented and so far as such implementation is necessary for the purposes of complying with the international obligations of the United Kingdom under the agreement.
(2) Subsection (1)—
    (a)   is subject to any equivalent or other provision—
        (i)   which (whether before, on or after the relevant day) is made by or under this Act or any other enactment or otherwise forms part of domestic law, and
        (ii)   which is for the purposes of (or has the effect of) implementing to any extent the Trade and Cooperation Agreement, the Security of Classified Information Agreement or any other future relationship agreement, and
    (b)   does not limit the scope of any power which is capable of being exercised to make any such provision.
(3) The references in subsection (1) to the Trade and Cooperation Agreement or the Security of Classified Information Agreement are references to the agreement concerned as it has effect on the relevant day.
(4) In this section—
    "domestic law" means the law of England and Wales, Scotland or Northern Ireland;
    "existing domestic law" means—
        (a)   an existing enactment, or
        (b)   any other domestic law as it has effect on the relevant day;
    "existing enactment" means an enactment passed or made before the relevant day;
    "modifications" does not include any modifications of the kind which would result in a public bill in Parliament containing them being treated as a hybrid bill;
    "relevant day", in relation to the Trade and Cooperation Agreement or the Security of Classified Information Agreement or any aspect of either agreement, means—
        (a)   so far as the agreement or aspect concerned is provisionally applied before it comes into force, the time and day from which the provisional application applies, and
        (b)   so far as the agreement or aspect concerned is not provisionally applied before it comes into force, the time and day when it comes into force;
and references to the purposes of (or having the effect of) implementing an agreement include references to the purposes of (or having the effect of) making provision consequential on any such implementation.

NOTES
Commencement: 31 December 2020.

[7.45]
30   Interpretation of agreements
A court or tribunal must have regard to Article COMPROV.13 of the Trade and Cooperation Agreement (public international law) when interpreting that agreement or any supplementing agreement.

NOTES
Commencement: 31 December 2020.

Powers

[7.46]
31   Implementation power
(1) A relevant national authority may by regulations make such provision as the relevant national authority considers appropriate—
    (a)   to implement the Trade and Cooperation Agreement, the Nuclear Cooperation Agreement, the Security of Classified Information Agreement or any relevant agreement, or
    (b)   otherwise for the purposes of dealing with matters arising out of, or related to, the Trade and Cooperation Agreement, the Nuclear Cooperation Agreement, the Security of Classified Information Agreement or any relevant agreement.
(2) Regulations under this section may make any provision that could be made by an Act of Parliament (including modifying this Act).
(3) Regulations under this section may (among other things and whether with the same or a different effect) re-implement any aspect of—
    (a)   the Trade and Cooperation Agreement,
    (b)   the Nuclear Cooperation Agreement,
    (c)   the Security of Classified Information Agreement, or

(d) any relevant agreement,

which has already been implemented (whether by virtue of this Act or otherwise).

(4) But regulations under this section may not—

(a) impose or increase taxation or fees,

(b) make retrospective provision,

(c) create a relevant criminal offence,

(d) amend, repeal or revoke the Human Rights Act 1998 or any subordinate legislation made under it, or

(e) amend or repeal the Scotland Act 1998, the Government of Wales Act 2006 or the Northern Ireland Act 1998 (unless the regulations are made by virtue of paragraph 27(b) of Schedule 5 to this Act or are amending or repealing any provision of those Acts which modifies another enactment).

(5) Subsection (4)(b) does not apply in relation to any regulations under this section which are for the purposes of replacing or otherwise modifying, or of otherwise making provision in connection with, the provision made by section 37(4) and (5).

(6) See also Part 2 of Schedule 5 (general restrictions on certain powers of devolved authorities: devolved competence etc).

(7) In this section "relevant agreement" means—

(a) any future relationship agreement which is not the Trade and Cooperation Agreement, the Nuclear Cooperation Agreement or the Security of Classified Information Agreement, or

(b) any agreement which falls within Article 2.4.4 of Chapter 2 of Title XI of Heading 1 of Part 2 of the Trade and Cooperation Agreement (competition co-operation agreement) (including any agreement which so falls as modified or supplemented from time to time in accordance with any provision of it or of any future relationship agreement).

NOTES

Commencement: 31 December 2020.

[7.47]

32 Powers relating to the start of agreements

(1) A relevant national authority may by regulations make such provision as the relevant national authority considers appropriate in connection with—

(a) the Trade and Cooperation Agreement, the Nuclear Cooperation Agreement or the Security of Classified Information Agreement (to any extent) coming into force, or becoming provisionally applied, later than IP completion day and after a period of time during which the agreement concerned was (to that extent) neither in force nor provisionally applied, or

(b) the ending, suspension or resumption of any provisional application of the Trade and Cooperation Agreement, the Nuclear Cooperation Agreement or the Security of Classified Information Agreement.

(2) Regulations under this section may make any provision that could be made by an Act of Parliament (including modifying this Act).

(3) Regulations under this section may not—

(a) create a relevant criminal offence,

(b) amend, repeal or revoke the Human Rights Act 1998 or any subordinate legislation made under it, or

(c) amend or repeal the Scotland Act 1998, the Government of Wales Act 2006 or the Northern Ireland Act 1998 (unless the regulations are made by virtue of paragraph 27(b) of Schedule 5 to this Act or are amending or repealing any provision of those Acts which modifies another enactment).

(4) See also Part 2 of Schedule 5 (general restrictions on certain powers of devolved authorities: devolved competence etc).

NOTES

Commencement: 31 December 2020.

[7.48]

33 Powers relating to the functioning of agreements

(1) A relevant national authority may by regulations make such provision as the relevant national authority considers appropriate for the purposes of, or otherwise in connection with, the suspension, resumption or termination of—

(a) the Trade and Cooperation Agreement,

(b) the Security of Classified Information Agreement, or

(c) any other future relationship agreement,

in accordance with the terms applicable to the agreement.

(2) A relevant national authority may by regulations make such provision as the relevant national authority considers appropriate—

(a) to implement or remove any relevant remedial measures which the United Kingdom has decided to take under the Trade and Cooperation Agreement or any other future relationship agreement, or

(b) otherwise for the purposes of, or otherwise in connection with, the taking of any relevant remedial measures by the United Kingdom or another party to the Trade and Cooperation Agreement or any other future relationship agreement.

(3) A relevant national authority may by regulations make such provision as the relevant national authority considers appropriate—

(a) to implement any agreed resolution of a dispute between the United Kingdom and another party under the Trade and Cooperation Agreement, the Security of Classified Information Agreement or any other future relationship agreement, or

(b) for the purposes of, or otherwise in connection with, any other decision of the United Kingdom in connection with any such dispute (other than a decision to suspend, resume, terminate or take relevant remedial measures).

(4) Regulations under this section may make any provision that could be made by an Act of Parliament (including modifying this Act).

(5) But regulations under this section may not—

   (a) make retrospective provision,

   (b) create a relevant criminal offence,

   (c) confer a power to legislate,

   (d) implement a ruling of an arbitration tribunal under the Trade and Cooperation Agreement or any other future relationship agreement,

   (e) amend, repeal or revoke the Human Rights Act 1998 or any subordinate legislation made under it, or

   (f) amend or repeal the Scotland Act 1998, the Government of Wales Act 2006 or the Northern Ireland Act 1998 (unless the regulations are made by virtue of paragraph 27(b) of Schedule 5 to this Act or are amending or repealing any provision of those Acts which modifies another enactment).

(6) Subsection (5)(c) does not prevent—

   (a) the modification of a power to legislate, or

   (b) the extension of such a power for similar purposes to those for which it was conferred.

(7) See also Part 2 of Schedule 5 (general restrictions on certain powers of devolved authorities: devolved competence etc).

(8) References in this section to the suspension, resumption or termination of a future relationship agreement include references to—

   (a) its suspension, resumption or termination in whole or in part or for a particular purpose or purposes, and

   (b) anything equivalent in effect to a suspension, resumption or termination (however expressed).

(9) In this section "relevant remedial measures" means—

   (a) any safeguard measures, or re-balancing measures, which any party to the Trade and Cooperation Agreement or any supplementing agreement is entitled to take under Article INST.36 of the Trade and Cooperation Agreement (including that Article as it has effect in relation to any supplementing agreement),

   (b) any other safeguard measures or re-balancing measures, or

   (c) any other remedial measures which any party to a future relationship agreement is entitled to take under that agreement or any other future relationship agreement,

and includes any interim or temporary measures which fall within paragraph (a), (b) or (c) but does not include any suspension, resumption or termination which falls within subsection (1).

NOTES

Commencement: 31 December 2020.

Financial provision

[7.49]

34   Funding of PEACE PLUS programme

(1) There may be paid out of money provided by Parliament any expenditure which the Secretary of State may incur in making payments to the EU or an EU entity to support the PEACE PLUS programme and any successor programmes.

(2) In subsection (1)—

   "EU entity" means an EU institution or any office, body or agency of the EU;

   "the PEACE PLUS programme" means the programme of the EU which is the successor to the programme known as PEACE IV (Ireland-United Kingdom).

NOTES

Commencement: 1 March 2021.

[7.50]

35   General financial provision

(1) There may be paid out of money provided by Parliament any expenditure incurred by a Minister of the Crown, government department or other public authority by virtue of any future relationship agreement.

(2) A Minister of the Crown, government department or devolved authority may incur expenditure, for the purpose of, or in connection with, preparing for anything about which provision may be made under a power to make subordinate legislation conferred or modified by or under this Act, before any such provision is made.

(3) There is to be paid out of money provided by Parliament—

   (a) any expenditure incurred by a Minister of the Crown, government department or other public authority by virtue of this Act, and

   (b) any increase attributable to this Act in the sums payable by virtue of any other Act out of money so provided.

(4) Subsection (3) is subject to any other provision made by or under this Act or any other enactment.

(5) In this section "government department" means any department of the Government of the United Kingdom.

NOTES

Commencement: 31 December 2020.

Parliamentary scrutiny

[7.51]

36   Requirements in Part 2 of CRAGA

Section 20 of the Constitutional Reform and Governance Act 2010 (treaties to be laid before Parliament before ratification) does not apply in relation to the Trade and Cooperation Agreement, the Nuclear Cooperation Agreement or the Security of Classified Information Agreement (but this does not affect whether that section applies in relation to any treaty which modifies or supplements the agreement concerned).

NOTES
Commencement: 31 December 2020.

PART 4 SUPPLEMENTARY AND FINAL PROVISION
Supplementary

[7.52]
37 Interpretation
(1) In this Act—

"the data protection legislation" has the same meaning as in the Data Protection Act 2018 (see section 3 of that Act);

"devolved authority" means—
   (a)   the Scottish Ministers,
   (b)   the Welsh Ministers, or
   (c)   a Northern Ireland department;

"enactment" means an enactment whenever passed or made and includes—
   (a)   an enactment contained in any Order in Council, order, rules, regulations, scheme, warrant, byelaw or other instrument made under an Act of Parliament,
   (b)   an enactment contained in any Order in Council made in exercise of Her Majesty's Prerogative,
   (c)   an enactment contained in, or in an instrument made under, an Act of the Scottish Parliament,
   (d)   an enactment contained in, or in an instrument made under, a Measure or Act of Senedd Cymru,
   (e)   an enactment contained in, or in an instrument made under, Northern Ireland legislation,
   (f)   an enactment contained in any instrument made by a member of the Scottish Government, the Welsh Ministers, the First Minister for Wales, the Counsel General to the Welsh Government, a Northern Ireland Minister, the First Minister in Northern Ireland, the deputy First Minister in Northern Ireland or a Northern Ireland department in exercise of prerogative or other executive functions of Her Majesty which are exercisable by such a person on behalf of Her Majesty,
   (g)   an enactment contained in, or in an instrument made under, a Measure of the Church Assembly or of the General Synod of the Church of England, and
   (h)   any retained direct EU legislation;

"future relationship agreement" means—
   (a)   the Trade and Cooperation Agreement,
   (b)   the Nuclear Cooperation Agreement,
   (c)   the Security of Classified Information Agreement, or
   (d)   any of the following so far as it is not a treaty to which section 20 of the Constitutional Reform and Governance Act 2010 applies (ignoring section 22 of that Act) (treaties to be laid before Parliament before ratification)—
      (i)   a supplementing agreement, or
      (ii)   an agreement under, or otherwise envisaged (whether as part of particular arrangements or otherwise) by, an agreement falling within paragraph (a), (b) or (c) or sub-paragraph (i),
            (as the agreement concerned is modified or supplemented from time to time in accordance with any provision of it or of any other agreement falling within paragraph (a), (b) or (c) or this paragraph);

"member State" does not include the United Kingdom;

"Minister of the Crown" has the same meaning as in the Ministers of the Crown Act 1975 and also includes the Commissioners for Her Majesty's Revenue and Customs;

"modify" includes amend, repeal or revoke (and related expressions are to be read accordingly);

"Northern Ireland devolved authority" means the First Minister and deputy First Minister in Northern Ireland acting jointly, a Northern Ireland Minister or a Northern Ireland department;

"the Nuclear Cooperation Agreement" means the Agreement between the Government of the United Kingdom of Great Britain and Northern Ireland and the European Atomic Energy Community for cooperation on the safe and peaceful uses of nuclear energy (as that agreement is modified or supplemented from time to time in accordance with any provision of it or of any other future relationship agreement);

"PNR regulations" has the meaning given by section 7(a);

"power to legislate" does not include a power—
   (a)   to make rules of procedure for any court or tribunal, or
   (b)   to give directions as to matters of administration;

"primary legislation" means—
   (a)   an Act of Parliament,
   (b)   an Act of the Scottish Parliament,
   (c)   a Measure or Act of Senedd Cymru, or
   (d)   Northern Ireland legislation;

"relevant criminal offence" means an offence for which an individual who has reached the age of 18 (or, in relation to Scotland or Northern Ireland, 21) is capable of being sentenced to imprisonment for a term of more than 2 years (ignoring any enactment prohibiting or restricting the imprisonment of individuals who have no previous convictions);

"relevant national authority" means—
   (a)   a Minister of the Crown,
   (b)   a devolved authority, or
   (c)   a Minister of the Crown acting jointly with one or more devolved authorities;

"retained direct EU CAP legislation" has the same meaning as in the Direct Payments to Farmers (Legislative Continuity) Act 2020 (see section 2(10) of that Act);

"retrospective provision", in relation to provision made by regulations, means provision taking effect from a date earlier than the date on which the regulations are made;

"the Security of Classified Information Agreement" means the Agreement between the European Union and the United Kingdom of Great Britain and Northern Ireland concerning security procedures for exchanging and protecting classified information (as that agreement is modified or supplemented from time to time in accordance with any provision of it or of any other future relationship agreement);

"subordinate legislation" means any Order in Council, order, rules, regulations, scheme, warrant, byelaw or other instrument made under any primary legislation; and (except in Part 2 of Schedule 5) includes any Order in Council, order, rules, regulations, scheme, warrant, byelaw or other instrument made on or after IP completion day (or, in the case of any retained direct EU CAP legislation, on or after exit day) under any retained direct EU legislation;

"supplementing agreement" means an agreement which constitutes a supplementing agreement by virtue of Article COMPROV.2 of the Trade and Cooperation Agreement;

"the Trade and Cooperation Agreement" means the Trade and Cooperation Agreement between the European Union and the European Atomic Energy Community, of the one part, and the United Kingdom of Great Britain and Northern Ireland, of the other part (as that agreement is modified or supplemented from time to time in accordance with any provision of it or of any other future relationship agreement);

"treaty" has the same meaning as in Part 2 of the Constitutional Reform and Governance Act 2010 (see section 25 of that Act);

"tribunal" means any tribunal in which legal proceedings may be brought.

(2) For the purposes of this Act, examples of where an agreement or part of an agreement is modified or supplemented in accordance with any provision of the agreement or of any other future relationship agreement include where it is modified or supplemented as a result of—

    (a) a decision or other act of any council, committee, sub-committee or other body of persons established by virtue of the agreement or another future relationship agreement, or

    (b) any arrangements provided for by virtue of the agreement or another future relationship agreement.

(3) References in this Act to the Trade and Cooperation Agreement, the Nuclear Cooperation Agreement or the Security of Classified Information Agreement also include references to the agreement concerned—

    (a) as provisionally applied, and

    (b) as modified or supplemented from time to time on or before its coming into force and otherwise than in accordance with any provision of it or of any other future relationship agreement.

(4) Subsection (5) applies if, in accordance with any provision of the Trade and Cooperation Agreement, the Nuclear Cooperation Agreement or the Security of Classified Information Agreement, any version of the agreement concerned which results from a process of final legal revision replaces from the beginning the signed version of the agreement and is established as authentic and definitive.

(5) References in this Act or any other enactment to the Trade and Cooperation Agreement, the Nuclear Cooperation Agreement or (as the case may be) the Security of Classified Information Agreement, or to any provision or collection of provisions of the agreement concerned, are to be read as modified accordingly.

NOTES

Commencement: 31 December 2020.

National Assembly for Wales: see further, in relation to the renaming of the National Assembly for Wales as the Senedd Cymru or the Welsh Parliament, the Senedd and Elections (Wales) Act 2020, s 2 (with effect from 6 May 2020). See also ss 3–9 of the 2020 Act in relation to the renaming of Acts of the National Assembly for Wales, Members of the National Assembly for Wales, etc.

[7.53]
38 Regulations

Schedule 5 contains provision about regulations under this Act (including provision about procedure).

NOTES

Commencement: 31 December 2020.

[7.54]
39 Consequential and transitional provision etc

(1) A Minister of the Crown may by regulations make such provision as the Minister considers appropriate in consequence of this Act.

(2) The power to make regulations under subsection (1) may (among other things) be exercised by modifying any provision made by or under an enactment.

(3) Part 1 of Schedule 6 contains consequential provision.

(4) A Minister of the Crown may by regulations make such transitional, transitory or saving provision as the Minister considers appropriate in connection with the coming into force of any provision of this Act.

(5) Part 2 of Schedule 6 contains transitional, transitory and saving provision.

NOTES

Commencement: 31 December 2020.

Final

[7.55]
40 Extent, commencement and short title

(1) Subject to subsections (2) to (5), this Act extends to England and Wales, Scotland and Northern Ireland.

(2) Section 25(1) extends to England and Wales and Scotland only.

(3) Section 25(2) extends to Northern Ireland only.

(4) Paragraph 2 of Schedule 4 extends to England and Wales and Scotland only.

(5) Subject to subsection (4), any provision of this Act which amends or repeals an enactment has the same extent as the enactment amended or repealed.

(6) The following provisions—

(a) section 6(1) for the purposes of the Secretary of State giving a direction as provided for in the definition of "designated UK authority",

(b) paragraph 4 of Schedule 2 for the purposes of the Secretary of State giving a direction under regulation 4A(1) of the PNR regulations and any other provision of that Schedule so far as necessary for those purposes (and section 7 so far as relating to those provisions),

(c) paragraph 2(1) to (5) of Schedule 3 (and section 9 so far as relating to those provisions),

(d) sections 30 to 33,

(e) sections 35 to 38 (including Schedule 5),

(f) section 39(1), (2) and (4),

(g) paragraphs 4 and 11 to 13 of Schedule 6 (and section 39(3) and (5) so far as relating to those paragraphs), and

(h) this section,

come into force on the day on which this Act is passed.

(7) The provisions of this Act, so far as they are not brought into force by subsection (6), come into force on such day as a Minister of the Crown may by regulations appoint; and different days may be appointed for different purposes.

(8) This Act may be cited as the European Union (Future Relationship) Act 2020.

NOTES

Commencement: 31 December 2020.

Regulations: the European Union (Future Relationship) Act 2020 (Commencement No 1) Regulations 2020, SI 2020/1662.

SCHEDULES

SCHEDULE 1
INFORMATION TO BE INCLUDED IN NOTIFICATION OF CONVICTION

Section 1(6)

Introductory

[7.56]

1 (1) This Schedule sets out the information that is required by section 1 to be included in a notification of an individual's conviction.

(2) The information mentioned in paragraphs 4, 8 to 12, 15 and 18 is required to be included only if it is recorded in the criminal records database referred to in subsection (1) or (as the case may be) subsection (2) of that section.

Information about the individual

2 The individual's name.

3 Any previous name of the individual.

4 Any other name used by the individual.

5 The individual's gender.

6 The individual's date and place of birth.

7 The individual's nationality or nationalities.

8 The names of the individual's parents.

9 The number of any passport held by the individual.

10 The issue number (if any) and description of any other identity document (within the meaning of section 7 of the Identity Documents Act 2010) held by the individual.

11 The individual's fingerprints.

12 A photograph or other image of the individual's face.

Information about the conviction

13 The date of the conviction.

14 (1) In the case of a conviction by or before a court, the court by or before which the individual was convicted.

(2) In any other case, the person or description of person by or before which the individual was convicted.

15 The reference number of the conviction.

16 The offence of which the individual was convicted.

17 The date on which the offence was committed (or, if the offence was committed over a period of time, that period).

18 The place where the offence was committed.

19 Any sentence imposed in respect of the offence.

In this paragraph "sentence" includes anything that under section 376(1) and (3) of the Armed Forces Act 2006 (punishments awarded by officers etc) is to be treated as a sentence for the purposes of that Act.

20 Any other order made in respect of the offence.

NOTES

Commencement: 31 December 2020.

SCHEDULE 2
PASSENGER NAME RECORD DATA

Section 7

PART 1 AMENDMENTS TO THE PNR REGULATIONS

(Amends the Passenger Name Record Data and Miscellaneous Amendments Regulations 2018, SI 2018/598, regs 2, 3, 5, 6, 7, 11, 12, 13, 14, 16 and insert regs 4A, 10, 11A, 11B, 13A, 13B.)

PART 2 INTERIM PERIOD: MODIFICATIONS FOR RESTRICTED EU PNR DATA THAT IS SUBJECT TO DELETION

[7.57]

17 (1) Until the commencement of paragraph 14, the PNR regulations have effect—

  (a) as if the regulation 13AA set out in sub-paragraph (2) were inserted before regulation 14, and

  (b) with the modifications set out in sub-paragraphs (3) to (5).

(2) The regulation is—

"13AA Retention and deletion of EU PNR data by the PIU: interim period

(1) For the purposes of this regulation, EU PNR data is "restricted EU PNR data" if it relates to a person arriving in the United Kingdom who—

    (a)   is not a UK national, and

    (b)   resides outside the United Kingdom.

(2) For the purposes of this regulation, restricted EU PNR data relating to a person is subject to deletion if—

    (a)   the PIU, acting as such, knows that the person has left the United Kingdom, or

    (b)   the period for which the person is permitted to stay in the United Kingdom has expired.

(3) But restricted EU PNR data is not subject to deletion—

    (a)   if, on the basis of a risk assessment based on objectively established criteria, the PIU considers that retention of the restricted EU PNR data is necessary for the purpose described in regulation 6(3)(a), or

    (b)   where the restricted EU PNR data is used in the context of specific cases for a purpose described in regulation 6(3).

(4) The PIU must secure that restricted EU PNR data that is subject to deletion—

    (a)   is accessible only by authorised persons, and

    (b)   is accessed by them only for the purpose of determining whether it is subject to deletion.

(5) Where restricted EU PNR data is subject to deletion—

    (a)   the PIU must permanently delete it as soon as possible, using best efforts, taking into account the special circumstances referred to in Article LAW.PNR.28(10) of the Agreement, and

    (b)   an authorised person must record the date and time of deletion.

(6) Paragraphs (7) to (9) apply where the PIU receives a request for restricted EU PNR data.

(7) If the record mentioned in paragraph (9)(b)(iii) indicates that a previous request relating to that data has been refused under paragraph (9)(a), the PIU must refuse the request as a result of that record (and without further accessing the data).

(8) In any other case, the PIU must refuse the request unless an authorised person has—

    (a)   made a determination as to whether the data is subject to deletion, and

    (b)   as a result has determined that it is not subject to deletion.

(9) If the authorised person determines under paragraph (8)(a) that the restricted EU PNR data is subject to deletion, the PIU must—

    (a)   refuse the request, and

    (b)   record—

        (i)   the request;

        (ii)   the date and time that the restricted EU PNR data was accessed under paragraph (8)(a);

        (iii)   that the request was refused on the ground that the restricted EU PNR data was subject to deletion;

        (iv)   the date and time of the refusal.

(10) In this regulation, "authorised person" means a person specifically authorised by the PIU to access restricted EU PNR data.

(11) The PIU must limit the number of authorised persons to the minimum number practicable.

(12) In this regulation, "UK national" means—

    (a)   a British citizen,

    (b)   a person who is a British subject by virtue of Part 4 of the British Nationality Act 1981 and who has a right of abode in the United Kingdom, or

    (c)   a person who is a British overseas territories citizen by virtue of a connection to Gibraltar.

(13) Nothing in this regulation is to be taken to affect the generality of regulation 14."

(3) Regulation 4A has effect as if—

  (a) in paragraphs (5) and (6) the references to the functions of the designated independent authority under the PNR regulations included references to that authority's functions under Article LAW.PNR.28(12) of the Agreement, and

(b) paragraph (5) also required the PIU to make the records mentioned in regulation 13AA(5)(b) and (9)(b) available to the designated independent authority for the purposes of the authority's functions under that provision of the Agreement.

For this purpose, "the Agreement", "designated independent authority" and "the PIU" have the same meanings as in the PNR regulations.

(4) Regulations 11A and 11B each have effect as if the following were inserted at the end—

"(3) This regulation does not apply to restricted EU PNR data that is subject to deletion (within the meaning of regulation 13AA), or to the results of processing that data or analytical information containing that data."

(5) Regulation 13(1A) has effect as if the reference to regulation 13B were a reference to regulation 13AA.

NOTES
Commencement: 31 December 2020.

PART 3 SEA AND RAIL TRAVEL: POWER TO MODIFY PNR REGULATIONS ETC

[7.58]

18 (1) This paragraph applies if an agreement (a "new agreement") is made between the United Kingdom and the EU or one or more member States which (whether with or without variation)—
  (a) applies the provisions of Title III of Part 3 of the Trade and Cooperation Agreement to sea or rail travel as they apply to air travel, or
  (b) makes provision about sea or rail travel corresponding to those provisions of that Agreement.

(2) The Secretary of State may by regulations make such provision as the Secretary of State considers appropriate—
  (a) to implement the new agreement, or
  (b) otherwise for the purposes of dealing with matters arising out of, or related to, the new agreement.

(3) Regulations under sub-paragraph (2) may modify the PNR regulations (as they have effect for the time being).

(4) Paragraph 15 of Schedule 8 to the European Union (Withdrawal) Act 2018 (explanatory statements for instruments amending or revoking regulations etc under section 2(2) of the European Communities Act 1972) does not apply in relation to any modification by virtue of sub-paragraph (3).

NOTES
Commencement: 31 December 2020.

SCHEDULE 3
MUTUAL ASSISTANCE IN CRIMINAL MATTERS

(Amends the Law Enforcement and Security (Amendment) (EU Exit) Regulations 2019, SI 2019/742, the Crime (International Co-operation) Act 2003;, the Proceeds of Crime Act 2002 (External Investigations) Order 2013, SI 2013/2605, the Proceeds of Crime Act 2002 (External Investigations) (Scotland) Order 2015, SI 2015/206 (outside the scope of this work).)

SCHEDULE 4
TECHNICAL BARRIERS TO TRADE: USE OF RELEVANT INTERNATIONAL STANDARDS

(Amends the Medical Devices Regulations 2002, SI 2002/618, the General Product Safety Regulations 2005, SI 2005/1803, the Supply of Machinery (Safety) Regulations 2008, SI 2008/1597, the Ecodesign for Energy-Related Products Regulations 2010, SI 2010/2617, the Toys (Safety) Regulations 2011, SI 2011/1881, the Restriction of the Use of Certain Hazardous Substances in Electrical and Electronic Equipment Regulations 2012, SI 2012/3032, the Explosives Regulations 2014, SI 2014/1638, the Pyrotechnic Articles (Safety) Regulations 2015, SI 2015/1553, the Electromagnetic Compatibility Regulations 2016, SI 2016/1091, the Simple Pressure Vessels (Safety) Regulations 2016, SI 2016/1092, the Lifts Regulations 2016, SI 2016/1093, the Electrical Equipment (Safety) Regulations 2016, SI 2016/1101, the Pressure Equipment (Safety) Regulations 2016, SI 2016/1105, the Equipment and Protective Systems Intended for Use in Potentially Explosive Atmospheres Regulations 2016, SI 2016/1107, the Non-automatic Weighing Instruments Regulations 2016, SI 2016/1152, the Measuring Instruments Regulations 2016, SI 2016/1153, the Recreational Craft Regulations 2017, SI 2017/737, the Radio Equipment Regulations 2017, SI 2017/1206, Regulation 1223/2009/EC, Regulation 305/2011/EU, Commission Implementing Regulation 402/2013/EU, Regulation 2016/424/EU, Regulation 2016/425/EU, Regulation 2016/426/EU (outside the scope of this work).)

SCHEDULE 5
REGULATIONS UNDER THIS ACT

Section 38

PART 1 PROCEDURE
Criminal records

[7.59]

1 (1) A statutory instrument containing regulations under section 6(3) of the Secretary of State is subject to annulment in pursuance of a resolution of either House of Parliament.

(2) Regulations under section 6(3) of the Scottish Ministers are subject to the negative procedure (see section 28 of the Interpretation and Legislative Reform (Scotland) Act 2010 (asp 10)).

(3) Regulations under section 6(3) of the Department of Justice in Northern Ireland are subject to negative resolution within the meaning of section 41(6) of the Interpretation Act (Northern Ireland) 1954 as if they were a statutory instrument within the meaning of that Act.

Passenger name record data

2 A statutory instrument containing regulations under paragraph 18 of Schedule 2 may not be made unless a draft of the instrument has been laid before, and approved by a resolution of, each House of Parliament.

Administrative co-operation on VAT and mutual assistance on tax debts

3 A statutory instrument containing regulations under section 22(7) may not be made unless a draft of the instrument has been laid before, and approved by a resolution of, the House of Commons.

Implementation power: before IP completion day

4 (1) A statutory instrument which—
    (a) contains regulations under section 31 of a Minister of the Crown acting alone, and
    (b) is to be made before IP completion day,
may not be made unless a draft of the instrument has been laid before, and approved by a resolution of, each House of Parliament.

(2) Regulations which are to be made—
    (a) under section 31 by the Scottish Ministers acting alone, and
    (b) before IP completion day,
are subject to the affirmative procedure (see section 29 of the Interpretation and Legislative Reform (Scotland) Act 2010 (asp 10)).

(3) A statutory instrument which—
    (a) contains regulations under section 31 of the Welsh Ministers acting alone, and
    (b) is to be made before IP completion day,
may not be made unless a draft of the instrument has been laid before, and approved by a resolution of, Senedd Cymru.

(4) Regulations which are to be made—
    (a) under section 31 by a Northern Ireland department acting alone, and
    (b) before IP completion day,
may not be made unless a draft of the regulations has been laid before, and approved by a resolution of, the Northern Ireland Assembly.

(5) This paragraph is subject to paragraphs 14 to 17 (urgency procedures for regulations to which this paragraph applies).

5 (1) This paragraph applies to regulations under section 31 of a Minister of the Crown acting jointly with a devolved authority which are to be made before IP completion day.

(2) The procedure provided for by sub-paragraph (3) applies in relation to regulations to which this paragraph applies as well as any other procedure provided for by this paragraph which is applicable in relation to the regulations concerned.

(3) A statutory instrument containing regulations to which this paragraph applies may not be made unless a draft of the instrument has been laid before, and approved by a resolution of, each House of Parliament.

(4) Regulations to which this paragraph applies which are made jointly with the Scottish Ministers are subject to the affirmative procedure.

(5) Section 29 of the Interpretation and Legislative Reform (Scotland) Act 2010 (affirmative procedure) applies in relation to regulations to which sub-paragraph (4) applies as it applies in relation to devolved subordinate legislation (within the meaning of Part 2 of that Act) which is subject to the affirmative procedure (but as if references to a Scottish statutory instrument were references to a statutory instrument).

(6) Section 32 of the Interpretation and Legislative Reform (Scotland) Act 2010 (laying) applies in relation to the laying before the Scottish Parliament of a statutory instrument containing regulations to which sub-paragraph (4) applies as it applies in relation to the laying before that Parliament of a Scottish statutory instrument (within the meaning of Part 2 of that Act).

(7) A statutory instrument containing regulations to which this paragraph applies which are made jointly with the Welsh Ministers may not be made unless a draft of the instrument has been laid before, and approved by a resolution of, Senedd Cymru.

(8) Regulations to which this paragraph applies which are made jointly with a Northern Ireland department may not be made unless a draft of the regulations has been laid before, and approved by a resolution of, the Northern Ireland Assembly.

Implementation power: on or after IP completion day

6 (1) A statutory instrument which—
    (a) contains regulations under section 31 of a Minister of the Crown acting alone which contain provision falling within sub-paragraph (2), and
    (b) is to be made on or after IP completion day,
may not be made unless a draft of the instrument has been laid before, and approved by a resolution of, each House of Parliament.

(2) Provision falls within this sub-paragraph if it—
    (a) amends, repeals or revokes primary legislation or retained direct principal EU legislation, or
    (b) creates a power to legislate.

(3) Any other statutory instrument which—

(a) contains regulations under section 31 of a Minister of the Crown acting alone, and

(b) is made on or after IP completion day,

is (if a draft of the instrument has not been laid before, and approved by a resolution of, each House of Parliament) subject to annulment in pursuance of a resolution of either House of Parliament.

(4) See paragraph 8 for certain restrictions on the choice of procedure under sub-paragraph (3).

(5) Regulations under section 31 of the Scottish Ministers acting alone which—

(a) contain provision falling within sub-paragraph (2), and

(b) are to be made on or after IP completion day,

are subject to the affirmative procedure (see section 29 of the Interpretation and Legislative Reform (Scotland) Act 2010 (asp 10)).

(6) Any other regulations under section 31 of the Scottish Ministers acting alone which are made on or after IP completion day are (if they have not been subject to the affirmative procedure) subject to the negative procedure (see section 28 of the Interpretation and Legislative Reform (Scotland) Act 2010).

(7) A statutory instrument which—

(a) contains regulations under section 31 of the Welsh Ministers acting alone which contain provision falling within sub-paragraph (2), and

(b) is to be made on or after IP completion day,

may not be made unless a draft of the instrument has been laid before, and approved by a resolution of, Senedd Cymru.

(8) Any other statutory instrument which—

(a) contains regulations under section 31 of the Welsh Ministers acting alone, and

(b) is made on or after IP completion day,

is (if a draft of the instrument has not been laid before, and approved by a resolution of, Senedd Cymru) subject to annulment in pursuance of a resolution of Senedd Cymru.

(9) See paragraph 9 for certain restrictions on the choice of procedure under sub-paragraph (8).

(10) Regulations under section 31 of a Northern Ireland department acting alone which—

(a) contain provision falling within sub-paragraph (2), and

(b) are to be made on or after IP completion day,

may not be made unless a draft of the regulations has been laid before, and approved by a resolution of, the Northern Ireland Assembly.

(11) Any other regulations under section 31 of a Northern Ireland department acting alone which are made on or after IP completion day are (if a draft of the regulations has not been laid before, and approved by a resolution of, the Northern Ireland Assembly) subject to negative resolution within the meaning of section 41(6) of the Interpretation Act (Northern Ireland) 1954 as if they were a statutory instrument within the meaning of that Act.

(12) This paragraph is subject to paragraphs 14 to 17 (urgency procedures for regulations to which this paragraph applies).

7 (1) This paragraph applies to regulations under section 31 of a Minister of the Crown acting jointly with a devolved authority which are made, or (as the case may be) are to be made, on or after IP completion day.

(2) The procedure provided for by sub-paragraph (3) or (4) applies in relation to regulations to which this paragraph applies as well as any other procedure provided for by this paragraph which is applicable in relation to the regulations concerned.

(3) A statutory instrument containing regulations to which this paragraph applies which contain provision falling within paragraph 6(2) may not be made unless a draft of the instrument has been laid before, and approved by a resolution of, each House of Parliament.

(4) Any other statutory instrument containing regulations to which this paragraph applies is (if a draft of the instrument has not been laid before, and approved by a resolution of, each House of Parliament) subject to annulment in pursuance of a resolution of either House of Parliament.

(5) Regulations to which this paragraph applies which are made jointly with the Scottish Ministers and contain provision falling within paragraph 6(2) are subject to the affirmative procedure.

(6) Any other regulations to which this paragraph applies which are made jointly with the Scottish Ministers are (if they have not been subject to the affirmative procedure) subject to the negative procedure.

(7) Section 29 of the Interpretation and Legislative Reform (Scotland) Act 2010 (affirmative procedure) applies in relation to regulations to which sub-paragraph (5) or (6) applies and which are subject to the affirmative procedure as it applies in relation to devolved subordinate legislation (within the meaning of Part 2 of that Act) which is subject to the affirmative procedure (but as if references to a Scottish statutory instrument were references to a statutory instrument).

(8) Sections 28(2), (3) and (8) and 31 of the Interpretation and Legislative Reform (Scotland) Act 2010 (negative procedure etc) apply in relation to regulations to which sub-paragraph (6) applies and which are subject to the negative procedure as they apply in relation to devolved subordinate legislation (within the meaning of Part 2 of that Act) which is subject to the negative procedure (but as if references to a Scottish statutory instrument were references to a statutory instrument).

(9) Section 32 of the Interpretation and Legislative Reform (Scotland) Act 2010 (laying) applies in relation to the laying before the Scottish Parliament of a statutory instrument containing regulations to which sub-paragraph (5) or (6) applies as it applies in relation to the laying before that Parliament of a Scottish statutory instrument (within the meaning of Part 2 of that Act).

(10) A statutory instrument containing regulations to which this paragraph applies which are made jointly with the Welsh Ministers and contain provision falling within paragraph 6(2) may not be made unless a draft of the instrument has been laid before, and approved by a resolution of, Senedd Cymru.

(11) Any other statutory instrument containing regulations to which this paragraph applies which are made jointly with the Welsh Ministers is (if a draft of the instrument has not been laid before, and approved by a resolution of, Senedd Cymru) subject to annulment in pursuance of a resolution of Senedd Cymru.

(12) Regulations to which this paragraph applies which are made jointly with a Northern Ireland department and contain provision falling within paragraph 6(2) may not be made unless a draft of the regulations has been laid before, and approved by a resolution of, the Northern Ireland Assembly.

(13) Any other regulations to which this paragraph applies which are made jointly with a Northern Ireland department are (if a draft of the regulations has not been laid before, and approved by a resolution of, the Northern Ireland Assembly) subject to negative resolution within the meaning of section 41(6) of the Interpretation Act (Northern Ireland) 1954 as if they were a statutory instrument within the meaning of that Act.

(14) If in accordance with sub-paragraph (4),(6), (11) or (13)—
　(a)　either House of Parliament resolves that an address be presented to Her Majesty praying that an instrument be annulled, or
　(b)　a relevant devolved legislature resolves that an instrument be annulled,
nothing further is to be done under the instrument after the date of the resolution and Her Majesty may by Order in Council revoke the instrument.

(15) In sub-paragraph (14) "relevant devolved legislature" means—
　(a)　in the case of regulations made jointly with the Scottish Ministers, the Scottish Parliament,
　(b)　in the case of regulations made jointly with the Welsh Ministers, Senedd Cymru, and
　(c)　in the case of regulations made jointly with a Northern Ireland department, the Northern Ireland Assembly.

(16) Sub-paragraph (14) does not affect the validity of anything previously done under the instrument or prevent the making of a new instrument.

(17) Sub-paragraphs (14) to (16) apply in place of provision made by any other enactment about the effect of such a resolution.

8　(1) Sub-paragraph (2) applies if a Minister of the Crown, who is to make within the period of two years beginning with IP completion day a statutory instrument to which paragraph 6(3) applies, is of the opinion that the appropriate procedure for the instrument is for it to be subject to annulment in pursuance of a resolution of either House of Parliament.

(2) The Minister may not make the instrument so that it is subject to that procedure unless—
　(a)　condition 1 is met, and
　(b)　either condition 2 or 3 is met.

(3) Condition 1 is that a Minister of the Crown—
　(a)　has made a statement in writing to the effect that in the Minister's opinion the instrument should be subject to annulment in pursuance of a resolution of either House of Parliament, and
　(b)　has laid before each House of Parliament—
　　(i)　a draft of the instrument, and
　　(ii)　a memorandum setting out the statement and the reasons for the Minister's opinion.

(4) Condition 2 is that a committee of the House of Commons charged with doing so and a committee of the House of Lords charged with doing so have, within the relevant period, each made a recommendation as to the appropriate procedure for the instrument.

(5) Condition 3 is that the relevant period has ended without condition 2 being met.

(6) Sub-paragraph (7) applies if—
　(a)　a committee makes a recommendation as mentioned in sub-paragraph (4) within the relevant period,
　(b)　the recommendation is that the appropriate procedure for the instrument is for a draft of it to be laid before, and approved by a resolution of, each House of Parliament before it is made, and
　(c)　the Minister who is to make the instrument is nevertheless of the opinion that the appropriate procedure for the instrument is for it to be subject to annulment in pursuance of a resolution of either House of Parliament.

(7) Before the instrument is made, the Minister must make a statement explaining why the Minister does not agree with the recommendation of the committee.

(8) If the Minister fails to make a statement required by sub-paragraph (7) before the instrument is made, a Minister of the Crown must make a statement explaining why the Minister has failed to do so.

(9) A statement under sub-paragraph (7) or (8) must be made in writing and be published in such manner as the Minister making it considers appropriate.

(10) In this paragraph "the relevant period" means the period—
　(a)　beginning with the first day on which both Houses of Parliament are sitting after the day on which the draft instrument was laid before each House as mentioned in sub-paragraph (3)(b)(i), and
　(b)　ending with whichever of the following is the later—
　　(i)　the end of the period of 10 Commons sitting days beginning with that first day, and
　　(ii)　the end of the period of 10 Lords sitting days beginning with that first day.

(11) For the purposes of sub-paragraph (10)—
　(a)　where a draft of an instrument is laid before each House of Parliament on different days, the later day is to be taken as the day on which it is laid before both Houses,
　(b)　"Commons sitting day" means a day on which the House of Commons is sitting, and
　(c)　"Lords sitting day" means a day on which the House of Lords is sitting,
and, for the purposes of sub-paragraph (10) and this sub-paragraph, a day is only a day on which the House of Commons or the House of Lords is sitting if the House concerned begins to sit on that day.

(12) Nothing in this paragraph prevents a Minister of the Crown from deciding at any time before a statutory instrument to which paragraph 6(3) applies is made that another procedure should apply in relation to the instrument (whether under paragraph 6(3) or 14).

(13) Section 6(1) of the Statutory Instruments Act 1946 (alternative procedure for certain instruments laid in draft before Parliament) does not apply in relation to any statutory instrument to which this paragraph applies.

9 (1) Sub-paragraph (2) applies if the Welsh Ministers are to make within the period of two years beginning with IP completion day a statutory instrument to which paragraph 6(8) applies and are of the opinion that the appropriate procedure for the instrument is for it to be subject to annulment in pursuance of a resolution of Senedd Cymru.

(2) The Welsh Ministers may not make the instrument so that it is subject to that procedure unless—
  (a) condition 1 is met, and
  (b) either condition 2 or 3 is met.

(3) Condition 1 is that the Welsh Ministers—
  (a) have made a statement in writing to the effect that in their opinion the instrument should be subject to annulment in pursuance of a resolution of Senedd Cymru, and
  (b) have laid before Senedd Cymru—
      (i) a draft of the instrument, and
      (ii) a memorandum setting out the statement and the reasons for the Welsh Ministers' opinion.

(4) Condition 2 is that a committee of Senedd Cymru charged with doing so has made a recommendation as to the appropriate procedure for the instrument.

(5) Condition 3 is that the period of 14 days beginning with the first day after the day on which the draft instrument was laid before Senedd Cymru as mentioned in sub-paragraph (3)(b)(i) has ended without any recommendation being made as mentioned in sub-paragraph (4).

(6) In calculating the period of 14 days, no account is to be taken of any time during which Senedd Cymru is—
  (a) dissolved, or
  (b) in recess for more than four days.

(7) Nothing in this paragraph prevents the Welsh Ministers from deciding at any time before a statutory instrument to which paragraph 6(8) applies is made that another procedure should apply to the instrument (whether under paragraph 6(8) or 16).

(8) Section 6(1) of the Statutory Instruments Act 1946 as applied by section 11A of that Act (alternative procedure for certain instruments laid in draft before Senedd Cymru) does not apply in relation to any statutory instrument to which this paragraph applies.

Powers relating to the start of agreements

10 (1) A statutory instrument containing regulations under section 32 of a Minister of the Crown acting alone may not be made unless a draft of the instrument has been laid before, and approved by a resolution of, each House of Parliament.

(2) Regulations under section 32 of the Scottish Ministers acting alone are subject to the affirmative procedure (see section 29 of the Interpretation and Legislative Reform (Scotland) Act 2010 (asp 10)).

(3) A statutory instrument containing regulations under section 32 of the Welsh Ministers acting alone may not be made unless a draft of the instrument has been laid before, and approved by a resolution of, Senedd Cymru.

(4) Regulations under section 32 of a Northern Ireland department acting alone may not be made unless a draft of the regulations has been laid before, and approved by a resolution of, the Northern Ireland Assembly.

(5) This paragraph is subject to paragraphs 14 to 17 (urgency procedures for regulations to which this paragraph applies).

11 (1) This paragraph applies to regulations under section 32 of a Minister of the Crown acting jointly with a devolved authority.

(2) The procedure provided for by sub-paragraph (3) applies in relation to regulations to which this paragraph applies as well as any other procedure provided for by this paragraph which is applicable in relation to the regulations concerned.

(3) A statutory instrument containing regulations to which this paragraph applies may not be made unless a draft of the instrument has been laid before, and approved by a resolution of, each House of Parliament.

(4) Regulations to which this paragraph applies which are made jointly with the Scottish Ministers are subject to the affirmative procedure.

(5) Section 29 of the Interpretation and Legislative Reform (Scotland) Act 2010 (affirmative procedure) applies in relation to regulations to which sub-paragraph (4) applies as it applies in relation to devolved subordinate legislation (within the meaning of Part 2 of that Act) which is subject to the affirmative procedure (but as if references to a Scottish statutory instrument were references to a statutory instrument).

(6) Section 32 of the Interpretation and Legislative Reform (Scotland) Act 2010 (laying) applies in relation to the laying before the Scottish Parliament of a statutory instrument containing regulations to which sub-paragraph (4) applies as it applies in relation to the laying before that Parliament of a Scottish statutory instrument (within the meaning of Part 2 of that Act).

(7) A statutory instrument containing regulations to which this paragraph applies which are made jointly with the Welsh Ministers may not be made unless a draft of the instrument has been laid before, and approved by a resolution of, Senedd Cymru.

(8) Regulations to which this paragraph applies which are made jointly with a Northern Ireland department may not be made unless a draft of the regulations has been laid before, and approved by a resolution of, the Northern Ireland Assembly.

Powers relating to the functioning of agreements

12 (1) A statutory instrument containing regulations under section 33 of a Minister of the Crown acting alone which contain provision falling within sub-paragraph (2) may not be made unless a draft of the instrument has been laid before, and approved by a resolution of, each House of Parliament.

(2) Provision falls within this sub-paragraph if it amends, repeals or revokes—
  (a) primary legislation, or
  (b) retained direct principal EU legislation.

(3) Any other statutory instrument containing regulations under section 33 of a Minister of the Crown acting alone is subject to annulment in pursuance of a resolution of either House of Parliament.

(4) Regulations under section 33 of the Scottish Ministers acting alone which contain provision falling within sub-paragraph (2) are subject to the affirmative procedure (see section 29 of the Interpretation and Legislative Reform (Scotland) Act 2010 (asp 10)).

(5) Any other regulations under section 33 of the Scottish Ministers acting alone are subject to the negative procedure (see section 28 of the Interpretation and Legislative Reform (Scotland) Act 2010).

(6) A statutory instrument containing regulations under section 33 of the Welsh Ministers acting alone which contain provision falling within sub-paragraph (2) may not be made unless a draft of the instrument has been laid before, and approved by a resolution of, Senedd Cymru.

(7) Any other statutory instrument containing regulations under section 33 of the Welsh Ministers acting alone is subject to annulment in pursuance of a resolution of Senedd Cymru.

(8) Regulations under section 33 of a Northern Ireland department acting alone which contain provision falling within sub-paragraph (2) may not be made unless a draft of the regulations has been laid before, and approved by a resolution of, the Northern Ireland Assembly.

(9) Any other regulations under section 33 of a Northern Ireland department acting alone are subject to negative resolution within the meaning of section 41(6) of the Interpretation Act (Northern Ireland) 1954 as if they were a statutory instrument within the meaning of that Act.

(10) This paragraph is subject to paragraphs 14 to 17 (urgency procedures for regulations to which this paragraph applies).

13 (1) This paragraph applies to regulations under section 33 of a Minister of the Crown acting jointly with a devolved authority.

(2) The procedure provided for by sub-paragraph (3) or (4) applies in relation to regulations to which this paragraph applies as well as any other procedure provided for by this paragraph which is applicable in relation to the regulations concerned.

(3) A statutory instrument containing regulations to which this paragraph applies which contain provision falling within paragraph 12(2) may not be made unless a draft of the instrument has been laid before, and approved by a resolution of, each House of Parliament.

(4) Any other statutory instrument containing regulations to which this paragraph applies is subject to annulment in pursuance of a resolution of either House of Parliament.

(5) Regulations to which this paragraph applies which are made jointly with the Scottish Ministers and contain provision falling within paragraph 12(2) are subject to the affirmative procedure.

(6) Any other regulations to which this paragraph applies which are made jointly with the Scottish Ministers are subject to the negative procedure.

(7) Section 29 of the Interpretation and Legislative Reform (Scotland) Act 2010 (affirmative procedure) applies in relation to regulations to which sub-paragraph (5) applies as it applies in relation to devolved subordinate legislation (within the meaning of Part 2 of that Act) which is subject to the affirmative procedure (but as if references to a Scottish statutory instrument were references to a statutory instrument).

(8) Sections 28(2), (3) and (8) and 31 of the Interpretation and Legislative Reform (Scotland) Act 2010 (negative procedure etc) apply in relation to regulations to which sub-paragraph (6) applies as they apply in relation to devolved subordinate legislation (within the meaning of Part 2 of that Act) which is subject to the negative procedure (but as if references to a Scottish statutory instrument were references to a statutory instrument).

(9) Section 32 of the Interpretation and Legislative Reform (Scotland) Act 2010 (laying) applies in relation to the laying before the Scottish Parliament of a statutory instrument containing regulations to which sub-paragraph (5) or (6) applies as it applies in relation to the laying before that Parliament of a Scottish statutory instrument (within the meaning of Part 2 of that Act).

(10) A statutory instrument containing regulations to which this paragraph applies which are made jointly with the Welsh Ministers and contain provision falling within paragraph 12(2) may not be made unless a draft of the instrument has been laid before, and approved by a resolution of, Senedd Cymru.

(11) Any other statutory instrument containing regulations to which this paragraph applies which are made jointly with the Welsh Ministers is subject to annulment in pursuance of a resolution of Senedd Cymru.

(12) Regulations to which this paragraph applies which are made jointly with a Northern Ireland department and contain provision falling within paragraph 12(2) may not be made unless a draft of the regulations has been laid before, and approved by a resolution of, the Northern Ireland Assembly.

(13) Any other regulations to which this paragraph applies which are made jointly with a Northern Ireland department are subject to negative resolution within the meaning of section 41(6) of the Interpretation Act (Northern Ireland) 1954 as if they were a statutory instrument within the meaning of that Act.

(14) If in accordance with sub-paragraph (4),(6), (11) or (13)—

(a) either House of Parliament resolves that an address be presented to Her Majesty praying that an instrument be annulled, or

(b) a relevant devolved legislature resolves that an instrument be annulled,

nothing further is to be done under the instrument after the date of the resolution and Her Majesty may by Order in Council revoke the instrument.

(15) In sub-paragraph (14) "relevant devolved legislature" means—

(a) in the case of regulations made jointly with the Scottish Ministers, the Scottish Parliament,

(b) in the case of regulations made jointly with the Welsh Ministers, Senedd Cymru, and

(c) in the case of regulations made jointly with a Northern Ireland department, the Northern Ireland Assembly.

(16) Sub-paragraph (14) does not affect the validity of anything previously done under the instrument or prevent the making of a new instrument.

(17) Sub-paragraphs (14) to (16) apply in place of provision made by any other enactment about the effect of such a resolution.

Implementation and other powers: certain urgent cases

14 (1) Sub-paragraph (2) applies to—

(a) a statutory instrument to which paragraph 4(1) or 6(1) applies,

(b) a statutory instrument to which paragraph 6(3) applies which would not otherwise be made without a draft of the instrument being laid before, and approved by a resolution of, each House of Parliament, or

(c) a statutory instrument to which paragraph 10(1) or 12(1) applies.

(2) The instrument may be made without a draft of the instrument being laid before, and approved by a resolution of, each House of Parliament if it contains a declaration that the Minister of the Crown concerned is of the opinion that, by reason of urgency, it is necessary to make the regulations without a draft being so laid and approved.

(3) After an instrument is made in accordance with sub-paragraph (2), it must be laid before each House of Parliament.

(4) Regulations contained in an instrument made in accordance with sub-paragraph (2) cease to have effect at the end of the period of 28 days beginning with the day on which the instrument is made unless, during that period, the instrument is approved by a resolution of each House of Parliament.

(5) In calculating the period of 28 days, no account is to be taken of any time during which—

(a) Parliament is dissolved or prorogued, or

(b) either House of Parliament is adjourned for more than four days.

(6) If regulations cease to have effect as a result of sub-paragraph (4), that does not—

(a) affect the validity of anything previously done under the regulations, or

(b) prevent the making of new regulations.

(7) Sub-paragraph (8) applies to a statutory instrument to which paragraph 6(3) applies where the Minister of the Crown who is to make the instrument is of the opinion that the appropriate procedure for the instrument is for it to be subject to annulment in pursuance of a resolution of either House of Parliament.

(8) Paragraph 8 does not apply in relation to the instrument if the instrument contains a declaration that the Minister is of the opinion that, by reason of urgency, it is necessary to make the regulations without meeting the requirements of that paragraph.

15 (1) Sub-paragraph (2) applies to—

(a) regulations to which paragraph 4(2) or 6(5) applies,

(b) regulations to which paragraph 6(6) applies which would not otherwise be made without being subject to the affirmative procedure, or

(c) regulations to which paragraph 10(2) or 12(4) applies.

(2) The regulations may be made without being subject to the affirmative procedure if the regulations contain a declaration that the Scottish Ministers are of the opinion that, by reason of urgency, it is necessary to make the regulations without them being subject to that procedure.

(3) After regulations are made in accordance with sub-paragraph (2), they must be laid before the Scottish Parliament.

(4) Regulations made in accordance with sub-paragraph (2) cease to have effect at the end of the period of 28 days beginning with the day on which they are made unless, during that period, the regulations are approved by resolution of the Scottish Parliament.

(5) In calculating the period of 28 days, no account is to be taken of any time during which the Scottish Parliament is—

(a) dissolved, or

(b) in recess for more than four days.

(6) If regulations cease to have effect as a result of sub-paragraph (4), that does not—

(a) affect the validity of anything previously done under the regulations, or

(b) prevent the making of new regulations.

16 (1) Sub-paragraph (2) applies to—

(a) a statutory instrument to which paragraph 4(3) or 6(7) applies,

(b) a statutory instrument to which paragraph 6(8) applies which would not otherwise be made without a draft of the instrument being laid before, and approved by a resolution of, Senedd Cymru, or

(c) a statutory instrument to which paragraph 10(3) or 12(6) applies.

(2) The instrument may be made without a draft of the instrument being laid before, and approved by a resolution of, Senedd Cymru if it contains a declaration that the Welsh Ministers are of the opinion that, by reason of urgency, it is necessary to make the regulations without a draft being so laid and approved.

(3) After an instrument is made in accordance with sub-paragraph (2), it must be laid before Senedd Cymru.

(4) Regulations contained in an instrument made in accordance with sub-paragraph (2) cease to have effect at the end of the period of 28 days beginning with the day on which the instrument is made unless, during that period, the instrument is approved by a resolution of Senedd Cymru.

(5) In calculating the period of 28 days, no account is to be taken of any time during which Senedd Cymru is—
   (a) dissolved, or
   (b) in recess for more than four days.

(6) If regulations cease to have effect as a result of sub-paragraph (4), that does not—
   (a) affect the validity of anything previously done under the regulations, or
   (b) prevent the making of new regulations.

(7) Sub-paragraph (8) applies to a statutory instrument to which paragraph 6(8) applies where the Welsh Ministers are of the opinion that the appropriate procedure for the instrument is for it to be subject to annulment in pursuance of a resolution of Senedd Cymru.

(8) Paragraph 9 does not apply in relation to the instrument if the instrument contains a declaration that the Welsh Ministers are of the opinion that, by reason of urgency, it is necessary to make the regulations without meeting the requirements of that paragraph.

17 (1) Sub-paragraph (2) applies to—
   (a) regulations to which paragraph 4(4) or 6(10) applies,
   (b) regulations to which paragraph 6(11) applies which would not otherwise be made without a draft of the regulations being laid before, and approved by a resolution of, the Northern Ireland Assembly, or
   (c) regulations to which paragraph 10(4) or 12(8) applies.

(2) The regulations may be made without a draft of the regulations being laid before, and approved by a resolution of, the Northern Ireland Assembly if they contain a declaration that the Northern Ireland department concerned is of the opinion that, by reason of urgency, it is necessary to make the regulations without a draft being so laid and approved.

(3) After regulations are made in accordance with sub-paragraph (2), they must be laid before the Northern Ireland Assembly.

(4) Regulations made in accordance with sub-paragraph (2) cease to have effect at the end of the period of 28 days beginning with the day on which they are made unless, during that period, the regulations are approved by a resolution of the Northern Ireland Assembly.

(5) In calculating the period of 28 days, no account is to be taken of any time during which the Northern Ireland Assembly is—
   (a) dissolved,
   (b) in recess for more than four days, or
   (c) adjourned for more than six days.

(6) If regulations cease to have effect as a result of sub-paragraph (4), that does not—
   (a) affect the validity of anything previously done under the regulations, or
   (b) prevent the making of new regulations.

Consequential provision

18 A statutory instrument containing regulations under section 39(1) is subject to annulment in pursuance of a resolution of either House of Parliament.

NOTES

Commencement: 31 December 2020.

PART 2 GENERAL RESTRICTIONS ON CERTAIN POWERS OF DEVOLVED AUTHORITIES

No power to make provision outside devolved competence

[7.60]

19 (1) No provision may be made by a devolved authority acting alone in regulations under section 31, 32 or 33 unless the provision is within the devolved competence of the devolved authority.

(2) See paragraphs 23 to 25 for the meaning of "devolved competence" for the purposes of this Part.

Requirement for consent where it would otherwise be required

20 (1) The consent of a Minister of the Crown is required before any provision is made by the Welsh Ministers acting alone in regulations under section 31, 32 or 33 so far as that provision, if contained in an Act of Senedd Cymru, would require the consent of a Minister of the Crown.

(2) The consent of the Secretary of State is required before any provision is made by a Northern Ireland department acting alone in regulations under section 31, 32 or 33 so far as that provision, if contained in an Act of the Northern Ireland Assembly, would require the consent of the Secretary of State.

(3) Sub-paragraph (1) or (2) does not apply if—
   (a) the provision could be contained in subordinate legislation made otherwise than under this Act by the Welsh Ministers acting alone or (as the case may be) a Northern Ireland devolved authority acting alone, and
   (b) no such consent would be required in that case.

(4) The consent of a Minister of the Crown is required before any provision is made by a devolved authority acting alone in regulations under section 31, 32 or 33 so far as that provision, if contained in—
   (a) subordinate legislation made otherwise than under this Act by the devolved authority, or

(b) subordinate legislation not falling within paragraph (a) and made otherwise than under this Act by (in the case of Scotland) the First Minister or Lord Advocate acting alone or (in the case of Northern Ireland) a Northern Ireland devolved authority acting alone,

would require the consent of a Minister of the Crown.

(5) Sub-paragraph (4) does not apply if—
   (a) the provision could be contained in—
      (i)   an Act of the Scottish Parliament, an Act of Senedd Cymru or (as the case may be) an Act of the Northern Ireland Assembly, or
      (ii)   different subordinate legislation of the kind mentioned in sub-paragraph (4)(a) or (b) and of a devolved authority acting alone or (as the case may be) other person acting alone, and
   (b) no such consent would be required in that case.

Requirement for joint exercise where it would otherwise be required

21 (1) No regulations may be made under section 31, 32 or 33 by the Scottish Ministers, so far as they contain provision which relates to a matter in respect of which a power to make subordinate legislation otherwise than under this Act is exercisable by—
   (a) the Scottish Ministers acting jointly with a Minister of the Crown, or
   (b) the First Minister or Lord Advocate acting jointly with a Minister of the Crown,
unless the regulations are, to that extent, made jointly with the Minister of the Crown.

(2) No regulations may be made under section 31, 32 or 33 by the Welsh Ministers, so far as they contain provision which relates to a matter in respect of which a power to make subordinate legislation otherwise than under this Act is exercisable by the Welsh Ministers acting jointly with a Minister of the Crown, unless the regulations are, to that extent, made jointly with the Minister of the Crown.

(3) No regulations may be made under section 31, 32 or 33 by a Northern Ireland department, so far as they contain provision which relates to a matter in respect of which a power to make subordinate legislation otherwise than under this Act is exercisable by—
   (a) a Northern Ireland department acting jointly with a Minister of the Crown, or
   (b) another Northern Ireland devolved authority acting jointly with a Minister of the Crown,
unless the regulations are, to that extent, made jointly with the Minister of the Crown.

(4) Sub-paragraph (1), (2) or (3) does not apply if the provision could be contained in—
   (a) an Act of the Scottish Parliament, an Act of Senedd Cymru or (as the case may be) an Act of the Northern Ireland Assembly without the need for the consent of a Minister of the Crown, or
   (b) different subordinate legislation made otherwise than under this Act by—
      (i)   the Scottish Ministers, the First Minister or the Lord Advocate acting alone,
      (ii)   the Welsh Ministers acting alone, or
      (iii)   (as the case may be), a Northern Ireland devolved authority acting alone.

Requirement for consultation where it would otherwise be required

22 (1) No regulations may be made under section 31, 32 or 33 by the Welsh Ministers acting alone, so far as they contain provision which, if contained in an Act of Senedd Cymru, would require consultation with a Minister of the Crown, unless the regulations are, to that extent, made after consulting with the Minister of the Crown.

(2) No regulations may be made under section 31, 32 or 33 by the Scottish Ministers acting alone, so far as they contain provision which relates to a matter in respect of which a power to make subordinate legislation otherwise than under this Act is exercisable by the Scottish Ministers, the First Minister or the Lord Advocate after consulting with a Minister of the Crown, unless the regulations are, to that extent, made after consulting with the Minister of the Crown.

(3) No regulations may be made under section 31, 32 or 33 by the Welsh Ministers acting alone, so far as they contain provision which relates to a matter in respect of which a power to make subordinate legislation otherwise than under this Act is exercisable by the Welsh Ministers after consulting with a Minister of the Crown, unless the regulations are, to that extent, made after consulting with the Minister of the Crown.

(4) No regulations may be made under section 31, 32 or 33 by a Northern Ireland department acting alone, so far as they contain provision which relates to a matter in respect of which a power to make subordinate legislation otherwise than under this Act is exercisable by a Northern Ireland department after consulting with a Minister of the Crown, unless the regulations are, to that extent, made after consulting with the Minister of the Crown.

(5) Sub-paragraph (2), (3) or (4) does not apply if—
   (a) the provision could be contained in an Act of the Scottish Parliament, an Act of Senedd Cymru or (as the case may be) an Act of the Northern Ireland Assembly, and
   (b) there would be no requirement for the consent of a Minister of the Crown, or for consultation with a Minister of the Crown, in that case.

(6) Sub-paragraph (2), (3) or (4) does not apply if—
   (a) the provision could be contained in different subordinate legislation made otherwise than under this Act by—
      (i)   the Scottish Ministers, the First Minister or the Lord Advocate acting alone,
      (ii)   the Welsh Ministers acting alone, or
      (iii)   (as the case may be) a Northern Ireland devolved authority acting alone, and
   (b) there would be no requirement for the consent of a Minister of the Crown, or for consultation with a Minister of the Crown, in that case.

Meaning of devolved competence

23 A provision is within the devolved competence of the Scottish Ministers for the purposes of this Part if—

(a)   it would be within the legislative competence of the Scottish Parliament if it were contained in an Act of that Parliament (ignoring section 29(2)(d) of the Scotland Act 1998 so far as relating to EU law and retained EU law), or

(b)   it is provision which could be made in other subordinate legislation by the Scottish Ministers, the First Minister or the Lord Advocate acting alone (ignoring section 57(2) of the Scotland Act 1998 so far as relating to EU law and section 57(4) of that Act).

24 A provision is within the devolved competence of the Welsh Ministers for the purposes of this Part if—

(a)   it would be within the legislative competence of Senedd Cymru if it were contained in an Act of Senedd Cymru (ignoring section 108A(2)(e) of the Government of Wales Act 2006 so far as relating to EU law and retained EU law but including any provision that could be made only with the consent of a Minister of the Crown), or

(b)   it is provision which could be made in other subordinate legislation by the Welsh Ministers acting alone (ignoring section 80(8) of the Government of Wales Act 2006).

25 A provision is within the devolved competence of a Northern Ireland department for the purposes of this Part if—

(a)   the provision, if it were contained in an Act of the Northern Ireland Assembly—

    (i)   would be within the legislative competence of the Assembly (ignoring section 6(2)(d) of the Northern Ireland Act 1998), and

    (ii)   would not require the consent of the Secretary of State,

(b)   the provision—

    (i)   amends or repeals Northern Ireland legislation, and

    (ii)   would, if it were contained in an Act of the Northern Ireland Assembly, be within the legislative competence of the Assembly (ignoring section 6(2)(d) of the Northern Ireland Act 1998) and require the consent of the Secretary of State, or

(c)   the provision is provision which could be made in other subordinate legislation by any Northern Ireland devolved authority acting alone (ignoring section 24(1)(b) and (3) of the Northern Ireland Act 1998).

NOTES

Commencement: 31 December 2020.

PART 3   GENERAL PROVISION ABOUT POWERS UNDER ACT

Scope and nature of powers: general

[7.61]

26 (1)   Any power to make regulations under this Act—

(a)   so far as exercisable by a Minister of the Crown or by a Minister of the Crown acting jointly with a devolved authority, is exercisable by statutory instrument,

(b)   so far as exercisable by the Welsh Ministers or by the Welsh Ministers acting jointly with a Minister of the Crown, is exercisable by statutory instrument, and

(c)   so far as exercisable by a Northern Ireland department (other than when acting jointly with a Minister of the Crown), is exercisable by statutory rule for the purposes of the Statutory Rules (Northern Ireland) Order 1979 (SI 1979/1573 (NI 12)) (and not by statutory instrument).

(2)   For regulations made under this Act by the Scottish Ministers, see also section 27 of the Interpretation and Legislative Reform (Scotland) Act 2010 (asp 10) (Scottish statutory instruments).

27 Any power to make regulations under this Act—

(a)   may be exercised so as to make different provision for different cases or descriptions of case, different circumstances, different purposes or different areas, and

(b)   includes power to make supplementary, incidental, consequential, transitional, transitory or saving provision.

28 The fact that a power to make regulations is conferred by this Act does not affect the extent of any other power to make subordinate legislation under this Act or any other enactment.

Anticipatory exercise of powers in relation to future relationship agreements etc

29 Any power to make regulations under this Act in relation to a future relationship agreement or an agreement falling within section 31(7)(b) is also capable of being exercised before the agreement concerned is signed, provisionally applied or ratified or before it comes into force.

Scope of appointed day power

30 The power of a Minister of the Crown under section 40(7) to appoint a day includes a power to appoint a time on that day if the Minister considers it appropriate to do so.

Disapplication of certain review provisions

31 Section 28 of the Small Business, Enterprise and Employment Act 2015 (duty to review regulatory provisions in secondary legislation) does not apply in relation to any power to make regulations under this Act.

Hybrid instruments

32 If an instrument, or a draft of an instrument, containing regulations under this Act would, apart from this paragraph, be treated as a hybrid instrument for the purposes of the standing orders of either House of Parliament, it is to proceed in that House as if it were not a hybrid instrument.

Procedure on re-exercise of certain powers

33 A power to make regulations which, under this Schedule, is capable of being exercised subject to different procedures may (in spite of section 14 of the Interpretation Act 1978) be exercised, when revoking, amending or re-enacting an instrument made under the power, subject to a different procedure from the procedure to which the instrument was subject.

Combinations of instruments

34 (1) Sub-paragraph (2) applies to a statutory instrument containing regulations under this Act which is subject to a procedure before Parliament for the approval of the instrument in draft before it is made or its approval after it is made.

(2) The statutory instrument may also include regulations under this Act or another enactment which are made by statutory instrument which is subject to a procedure before Parliament that provides for the annulment of the instrument after it has been made.

(3) Where regulations are included as mentioned in sub-paragraph (2), the procedure applicable to the statutory instrument is the procedure mentioned in sub-paragraph (1) and not the procedure mentioned in sub-paragraph (2).

(4) Sub-paragraphs (1) to (3) apply in relation to a statutory instrument containing regulations under this Act which is subject to a procedure before Senedd Cymru as they apply in relation to a statutory instrument containing regulations under this Act which is subject to a procedure before Parliament but as if the references to Parliament were references to Senedd Cymru.

(5) Sub-paragraphs (1) to (3) apply in relation to a statutory rule as they apply in relation to a statutory instrument but as if the references to Parliament were references to the Northern Ireland Assembly.

(6) Sub-paragraphs (1) to (3) apply in relation to a statutory instrument containing regulations under this Act which is subject to a procedure before the Scottish Parliament, Senedd Cymru or the Northern Ireland Assembly as well as a procedure before Parliament as they apply to a statutory instrument containing regulations under this Act which is subject to a procedure before Parliament but as if the references to Parliament were references to Parliament and the Scottish Parliament, Senedd Cymru or (as the case may be) the Northern Ireland Assembly.

(7) This paragraph does not prevent the inclusion of other regulations in a statutory instrument or statutory rule which contains regulations under this Act (and, accordingly, references in this Schedule to an instrument containing regulations are to be read as references to an instrument containing (whether alone or with other provision) regulations).

NOTES
Commencement: 31 December 2020.

SCHEDULE 6
CONSEQUENTIAL AND TRANSITIONAL PROVISION ETC

Section 39(3) and (5)

PART 1 CONSEQUENTIAL PROVISION

(Part 1 of this Schedule contains amendments to primary legislation. In so far as relevant to this work, they have been incorporated at the appropriate place.)

PART 2 TRANSITIONAL, TRANSITORY AND SAVING PROVISION
Passenger name record data

[7.62]
9 The amendments made by Schedule 2 do not have effect in relation to—
  (a) any request to which regulation 106A of the Law Enforcement and Security (Amendment) (EU Exit) Regulations 2019 (SI 2019/742) applies, or
  (b) any PNR data, or the result of processing such data, in relation to which regulation 106B(2) of those regulations has effect.

Extradition

10 The amendments made by section 12 do not apply for the purpose of deciding whether the offence specified in a Part 1 warrant is an extradition offence if the person in respect of whom the warrant is issued is arrested under the warrant, or under section 5 of the Extradition Act 2003 on the basis of a belief related to the warrant, before IP completion day.

"relevant criminal offence"

11 (1) The definition of "relevant criminal offence" in section 37(1) is to be read, until the appointed day, as if for the words "the age of 18 (or, in relation to Scotland or Northern Ireland, 21)" there were substituted "the age of 21".

(2) In sub-paragraph (1), "the appointed day" means the day on which the amendment made to section 81(3)(a) of the Regulation of Investigatory Powers Act 2000 by paragraph 211 of Schedule 7 to the Criminal Justice and Court Services Act 2000 comes into force.

Powers of devolved authorities in relation to EU law

12 Section 57(2) of the Scotland Act 1998, section 80(8) of the Government of Wales Act 2006 and section 24(1)(b) of the Northern Ireland Act 1998, so far as relating to EU law, do not apply to the making of regulations under section 31, 32 or 33.

Modifications of subordinate legislation

13 The fact that a modification of subordinate legislation has been made by this Act does not of itself prevent the subordinate legislation as modified from being further modified under the power under which it was made or by other subordinate legislation.

NOTES
Commencement: 31 December 2020.

AGREEMENT ON THE WITHDRAWAL OF THE UNITED KINGDOM OF GREAT BRITAIN AND NORTHERN IRELAND FROM THE EUROPEAN UNION AND THE EUROPEAN ATOMIC ENERGY COMMUNITY

[7.63]

NOTES
    Editorial note: only certain key provisions of this Agreement which are relevant to data protection law are reproduced here. Provisions not reproduced are not annotated.
    Date of publication in OJ: OJ L29, 31.1.2020, p 7.
© European Union, 1998–2021.

PREAMBLE

THE EUROPEAN UNION AND THE EUROPEAN ATOMIC ENERGY COMMUNITY

AND

THE UNITED KINGDOM OF GREAT BRITAIN AND NORTHERN IRELAND,

CONSIDERING that on 29 March 2017 the United Kingdom of Great Britain and Northern Ireland ("United Kingdom"), following the outcome of a referendum held in the United Kingdom and its sovereign decision to leave the European Union, notified its intention to withdraw from the European Union ("Union") and the European Atomic Energy Community ("Euratom") in accordance with Article 50 of the Treaty on European Union ("TEU"), which applies to Euratom by virtue of Article 106a of the Treaty establishing the European Atomic Energy Community ("Euratom Treaty"),

WISHING to set out the arrangements for the withdrawal of the United Kingdom from the Union and Euratom, taking account of the framework for their future relationship,

NOTING the guidelines of 29 April and 15 December 2017 and of 23 March 2018 provided by the European Council in the light of which the Union is to conclude the Agreement setting out the arrangements for the withdrawal of the United Kingdom from the Union and Euratom,

RECALLING that, pursuant to Article 50 TEU, in conjunction with Article 106a of the Euratom Treaty, and subject to the arrangements laid down in this Agreement, the law of the Union and of Euratom in its entirety ceases to apply to the United Kingdom from the date of entry into force of this Agreement,

STRESSING that the objective of this Agreement is to ensure an orderly withdrawal of the United Kingdom from the Union and Euratom,

RECOGNISING that it is necessary to provide reciprocal protection for Union citizens and for United Kingdom nationals, as well as their respective family members, where they have exercised free movement rights before a date set in this Agreement, and to ensure that their rights under this Agreement are enforceable and based on the principle of non-discrimination; recognising also that rights deriving from periods of social security insurance should be protected,

RESOLVED to ensure an orderly withdrawal through various separation provisions aiming to prevent disruption and to provide legal certainty to citizens and economic operators as well as to judicial and administrative authorities in the Union and in the United Kingdom, while not excluding the possibility of relevant separation provisions being superseded by the agreement(s) on the future relationship,

CONSIDERING that it is in the interest of both the Union and the United Kingdom to determine a transition or implementation period during which – notwithstanding all consequences of the United Kingdom's withdrawal from the Union as regards the United Kingdom's participation in the institutions, bodies, offices and agencies of the Union, in particular the end, on the date of entry into force of this Agreement, of the mandates of all members of institutions, bodies and agencies of the Union nominated, appointed or elected in relation to the United Kingdom's membership of the Union – Union law , including international agreements, should be applicable to and in the United Kingdom, and, as a general rule, with the same effect as regards the Member States, in order to avoid disruption in the period during which the agreement(s) on the future relationship will be negotiated,

RECOGNISING that, even if Union law will be applicable to and in the United Kingdom during the transition period, the specificities of the United Kingdom as a State having withdrawn from the Union mean that it will be important for the United Kingdom to be able to take steps to prepare and establish new international arrangements of its own, including in areas of Union exclusive competence, provided such agreements do not enter into force or apply during that period, unless so authorised by the Union,

RECALLING that the Union and the United Kingdom have agreed to honour the mutual commitments undertaken while the United Kingdom was a member of the Union through a single financial settlement,

CONSIDERING that in order to guarantee the correct interpretation and application of this Agreement and compliance with the obligations under this Agreement, it is essential to establish provisions ensuring overall governance, in particular binding dispute-settlement and enforcement rules that fully respect the autonomy of the respective legal orders of the Union and of the United Kingdom as well as the United Kingdom's status as a third country,

ACKNOWLEDGING that, for an orderly withdrawal of the United Kingdom from the Union, it is also necessary to establish, in separate protocols to this Agreement, durable arrangements addressing the very specific situations relating to Ireland/Northern Ireland and to the Sovereign Base Areas in Cyprus,

ACKNOWLEDGING further that, for an orderly withdrawal of the United Kingdom from the Union, it is also necessary to establish, in a separate protocol to this Agreement, the specific arrangements in respect of Gibraltar applicable in particular during the transition period,

UNDERLINING that this Agreement is founded on an overall balance of benefits, rights and obligations for the Union and the United Kingdom,

NOTING that in parallel with this Agreement, the Parties have made a Political Declaration setting out the framework for the future relationship between the European Union and the United Kingdom of Great Britain and Northern Ireland,

CONSIDERING that there is a need for both the United Kingdom and the Union to take all necessary steps to begin as soon as possible from the date of entry into force of this Agreement, the formal negotiations of one or several agreements governing their future relationship with a view to ensuring that, to the extent possible, those agreements apply from the end of the transition period,

HAVE AGREED AS FOLLOWS:

PART ONE
COMMON PROVISIONS

ARTICLE 1   OBJECTIVE

[7.64]
This Agreement sets out the arrangements for the withdrawal of the United Kingdom of Great Britain and Northern Ireland ("United Kingdom") from the European Union ("Union") and from the European Atomic Energy Community ("Euratom").

ARTICLE 2   DEFINITIONS

[7.65]
For the purposes of this Agreement, the following definitions shall apply:
(a)   "Union law" means:
    (i)   the Treaty on European Union ("TEU"), the Treaty on the Functioning of the European Union ("TFEU") and the Treaty establishing the European Atomic Energy Community ("Euratom Treaty"), as amended or supplemented, as well as the Treaties of Accession and the Charter of Fundamental Rights of the European Union, together referred to as "the Treaties";
    (ii)   the general principles of the Union's law;
    (iii) the acts adopted by the institutions, bodies, offices or agencies of the Union;
    (iv)   the international agreements to which the Union is party and the international agreements concluded by the Member States acting on behalf of the Union;
    (v)   the agreements between Member States entered into in their capacity as Member States of the Union;
    (vi)   acts of the Representatives of the Governments of the Member States meeting within the European Council or the Council of the European Union ("Council");
    (vii) the declarations made in the context of intergovernmental conferences which adopted the Treaties;
(b)   "Member States" means the Kingdom of Belgium, the Republic of Bulgaria, the Czech Republic, the Kingdom of Denmark, the Federal Republic of Germany, the Republic of Estonia, Ireland, the Hellenic Republic, the Kingdom of Spain, the French Republic, the Republic of Croatia, the Italian Republic, the Republic of Cyprus, the Republic of Latvia, the Republic of Lithuania, the Grand Duchy of Luxembourg, Hungary, the Republic of Malta, the Kingdom of the Netherlands, the Republic of Austria, the Republic of Poland, the Portuguese Republic, Romania, the Republic of Slovenia, the Slovak Republic, the Republic of Finland and the Kingdom of Sweden;
(c)   "Union citizen" means any person holding the nationality of a Member State;
(d)   "United Kingdom national" means a national of the United Kingdom, as defined in the New Declaration by the Government of the United Kingdom of Great Britain and Northern Ireland of 31 December 1982 on the definition of the term "nationals"[1] together with Declaration No 63 annexed to the Final Act of the intergovernmental conference which adopted the Treaty of Lisbon[2];
(e)   "transition period" means the period provided in Article 126;
(f)   "day" means a calendar day, unless otherwise provided in this Agreement or in provisions of Union law made applicable by this Agreement .

NOTES
[1]   OJ C23, 28.1.1983, p 1.
[2]   OJ C306, 17.12.2007, p 270.

ARTICLE 3 TERRITORIAL SCOPE

[7.66]
1. Unless otherwise provided in this Agreement or in Union law made applicable by this Agreement, any reference in this Agreement to the United Kingdom or its territory shall be understood as referring to:
(a) the United Kingdom;
(b) Gibraltar, to the extent that Union law was applicable to it before the date of entry into force of this Agreement;
(c) the Channel Islands and the Isle of Man, to the extent that Union law was applicable to them before the date of entry into force of this Agreement;
(d) the Sovereign Base Areas of Akrotiri and Dhekelia in Cyprus, to the extent necessary to ensure the implementation of the arrangements set out in the Protocol on the Sovereign Base Areas of the United Kingdom of Great Britain and Northern Ireland in Cyprus annexed to the Act concerning the conditions of accession of the Czech Republic, the Republic of Estonia, the Republic of Cyprus, the Republic of Latvia, the Republic of Lithuania, the Republic of Hungary, the Republic of Malta, the Republic of Poland, the Republic of Slovenia and the Slovak Republic to the European Union;
(e) the overseas countries and territories listed in Annex II to the TFEU having special relations with the United Kingdom[1], where the provisions of this Agreement relate to the special arrangements for the association of the overseas countries and territories with the Union.

2. Unless otherwise provided in this Agreement or in Union law made applicable by this Agreement, any reference in this Agreement to Member States, or their territory, shall be understood as covering the territories of the Member States to which the Treaties apply as provided in Article 355 TFEU.

NOTES
[1] Anguilla, Bermuda, British Antarctic Territory, British Indian Ocean Territory, British Virgin Islands, Cayman Islands, Falkland Islands, Montserrat, Pitcairn, Saint Helena, Ascension and Tristan da Cunha, South Georgia and the South Sandwich Islands, and Turks and Caicos Islands.

ARTICLE 4 METHODS AND PRINCIPLES RELATING TO THE EFFECT, THE IMPLEMENTATION AND THE APPLICATION OF THIS AGREEMENT

[7.67]
1. The provisions of this Agreement and the provisions of Union law made applicable by this Agreement shall produce in respect of and in the United Kingdom the same legal effects as those which they produce within the Union and its Member States.

Accordingly, legal or natural persons shall in particular be able to rely directly on the provisions contained or referred to in this Agreement which meet the conditions for direct effect under Union law.

2. The United Kingdom shall ensure compliance with paragraph 1, including as regards the required powers of its judicial and administrative authorities to disapply inconsistent or incompatible domestic provisions, through domestic primary legislation.

3. The provisions of this Agreement referring to Union law or to concepts or provisions thereof shall be interpreted and applied in accordance with the methods and general principles of Union law.

4. The provisions of this Agreement referring to Union law or to concepts or provisions thereof shall in their implementation and application be interpreted in conformity with the relevant case law of the Court of Justice of the European Union handed down before the end of the transition period.

5. In the interpretation and application of this Agreement, the United Kingdom's judicial and administrative authorities shall have due regard to relevant case law of the Court of Justice of the European Union handed down after the end of the transition period.

ARTICLE 5 GOOD FAITH

[7.68]
The Union and the United Kingdom shall, in full mutual respect and good faith, assist each other in carrying out tasks which flow from this Agreement.

They shall take all appropriate measures, whether general or particular, to ensure fulfilment of the obligations arising from this Agreement and shall refrain from any measures which could jeopardise the attainment of the objectives of this Agreement.

This Article is without prejudice to the application of Union law pursuant to this Agreement, in particular the principle of sincere cooperation.

ARTICLE 6 REFERENCES TO UNION LAW

[7.69]
1. With the exception of Parts Four and Five, unless otherwise provided in this Agreement all references in this Agreement to Union law shall be understood as references to Union law, including as amended or replaced, as applicable on the last day of the transition period.

2. Where in this Agreement reference is made to Union acts or provisions thereof, such reference shall, where relevant, be understood to include a reference to Union law or provisions thereof that, although replaced or superseded by the act referred to, continue to apply in accordance with that act.

Part 7   Key Brexit Materials

3. For the purposes of this Agreement, references to provisions of Union law made applicable by this Agreement shall be understood to include references to the relevant Union acts supplementing or implementing those provisions.

ARTICLE 7   REFERENCES TO THE UNION AND TO MEMBER STATES

[7.70]

1. For the purposes of this Agreement, all references to Member States and competent authorities of Member States in provisions of Union law made applicable by this Agreement shall be understood as including the United Kingdom and its competent authorities, except as regards:

(a)   the nomination, appointment or election of members of the institutions, bodies, offices and agencies of the Union, as well as the participation in the decision-making and the attendance in the meetings of the institutions;

(b)   the participation in the decision-making and governance of the bodies, offices and agencies of the Union;

(c)   the attendance in the meetings of the committees referred to in Article 3(2) of Regulation (EU) No 182/2011 of the European Parliament and of the Council,[1] of Commission expert groups or of other similar entities, or in the meetings of expert groups or similar entities of bodies, offices and agencies of the Union, unless otherwise provided in this Agreement.

2. Unless otherwise provided in this Agreement, any reference to the Union shall be understood as including Euratom.

NOTES

[1]   Regulation (EU) No 182/2011 of the European Parliament and of the Council of 16 February 2011 laying down the rules and general principles concerning mechanisms for control by Member States of the Commission's exercise of implementing powers (OJ L55, 28.2.2011, p 13).

ARTICLE 8   ACCESS TO NETWORKS, INFORMATION SYSTEMS AND DATABASES

[7.71]

Unless otherwise provided in this Agreement, at the end of the transition period the United Kingdom shall cease to be entitled to access any network, any information system and any database established on the basis of Union law. The United Kingdom shall take appropriate measures to ensure that it does not access a network, information system or database which it is no longer entitled to access.

PART THREE
SEPARATION PROVISIONS
TITLE VII
DATA AND INFORMATION PROCESSED OR OBTAINED BEFORE THE END OF THE TRANSITION PERIOD, OR ON THE BASIS OF THIS AGREEMENT

ARTICLE 70   DEFINITION

[7.72]

For the purposes of this Title, "Union law on the protection of personal data" means:

(a)   Regulation (EU) 2016/679, with the exception of Chapter VII thereof;

(b)   Directive (EU) 2016/680 of the European Parliament and of the Council[1];

(c)   Directive 2002/58/EC of the European Parliament and of the Council[2];

(d)   any other provisions of Union law governing the protection of personal data.

NOTES

[1]   Directive (EU) 2016/680 of the European Parliament and of the Council of 27 April 2016 on the protection of natural persons with regard to the processing of personal data by competent authorities for the purposes of the prevention, investigation, detection or prosecution of criminal offences or the execution of criminal penalties, and on the free movement of such data, and repealing Council Framework Decision 2008/977/JHA (OJ L119, 4.5.2016, p 89).

[2]   Directive 2002/58/EC of the European Parliament and of the Council of 12 July 2002 concerning the processing of personal data and the protection of privacy in the electronic communications sector (Directive on privacy and electronic communications) (OJ L201, 31.7.2002, p 37).

ARTICLE 71   PROTECTION OF PERSONAL DATA

[7.73]

1. Union law on the protection of personal data shall apply in the United Kingdom in respect of the processing of personal data of data subjects outside the United Kingdom, provided that the personal data:

(a)   were processed under Union law in the United Kingdom before the end of the transition period; or

(b)   are processed in the United Kingdom after the end of the transition period on the basis of this Agreement.

2. Paragraph 1 shall not apply to the extent the processing of the personal data referred to therein is subject to an adequate level of protection as established in applicable decisions under Article 45(3) of Regulation (EU) 2016/679 or Article 36(3) of Directive (EU) 2016/680.

3. To the extent that a decision referred to in paragraph 2 has ceased to be applicable, the United Kingdom shall ensure a level of protection of personal data essentially equivalent to that under Union law on the protection of personal data in respect of the processing of personal data of data subjects referred to in paragraph 1.

ARTICLE 72   CONFIDENTIAL TREATMENT AND RESTRICTED USE OF DATA AND INFORMATION IN THE UNITED KINGDOM

[7.74]
Without prejudice to Article 71, in addition to Union law on the protection of personal data, the provisions of Union law on confidential treatment, restriction of use, storage limitation and requirement to erase data and information shall apply in respect of data and information obtained by authorities or official bodies of or in the United Kingdom or by contracting entities, as defined in Article 4 of Directive 2014/25/EU of the European Parliament and of the Council,[1] that are of or in the United Kingdom:
(a)   before the end of the transition period; or
(b)   on the basis of this Agreement.

NOTES

[1]   Directive 2014/25/EU of the European Parliament and of the Council of 26 February 2014 on procurement by entities operating in the water, energy, transport and postal services sectors and repealing Directive 2004/17/EC, OJ L94, 28.3.2014, p 243.

ARTICLE 73   TREATMENT OF DATA AND INFORMATION OBTAINED FROM THE UNITED KINGDOM

[7.75]
The Union shall not treat data and information obtained from the United Kingdom before the end of the transition period, or obtained after the end of the transition period on the basis of this Agreement, differently from data and information obtained from a Member State, on the sole ground of the United Kingdom having withdrawn from the Union.

ARTICLE 74   INFORMATION SECURITY

[7.76]
1.   The provisions of Union law on the protection of EU classified information and Euratom classified information shall apply in respect of classified information that was obtained by the United Kingdom either before the end of the transition period or on the basis of this Agreement or that was obtained from the United Kingdom by the Union or a Member State either before the end of the transition period or on the basis of this Agreement.

2.   The obligations resulting from Union law regarding industrial security shall apply to the United Kingdom in cases where the tendering, contracting or grant award procedure for the classified contract, classified subcontract or classified grant agreement was launched before the end of the transition period.

3.   The United Kingdom shall ensure that cryptographic products that use classified cryptographic algorithms developed under the control of, and evaluated and approved by the Crypto Approval Authority of a Member State or of the United Kingdom, which have been approved by the Union by the end of the transition period and that are present in the United Kingdom, are not transferred to a third country.

4.   Any requirements, limitations and conditions set out in the Union approval of cryptographic products shall apply to those products.

PART FOUR
TRANSITION

ARTICLE 126   TRANSITION PERIOD

[7.77]
There shall be a transition or implementation period, which shall start on the date of entry into force of this Agreement and end on 31 December 2020.

ARTICLE 127   SCOPE OF THE TRANSITION

[7.78]
1.   Unless otherwise provided in this Agreement, Union law shall be applicable to and in the United Kingdom during the transition period.

However, the following provisions of the Treaties, and acts adopted by the institutions, bodies, offices or agencies of the Union, shall not be applicable to and in the United Kingdom during the transition period:
(a)   provisions of the Treaties and acts which, pursuant to Protocol (No 15) on certain provisions relating to the United Kingdom of Great Britain and Northern Ireland, Protocol (No 19) on the Schengen *acquis* integrated into the framework of the European Union or Protocol (No 21) on the position of the United Kingdom and Ireland in respect of the area of freedom, security and justice, or pursuant to the provisions of the Treaties on enhanced cooperation, were not binding upon and in the United Kingdom before the date of entry into force of this Agreement as well as acts amending such acts;
(b)   Article 11(4) TEU, point (b) of Article 20(2), Article 22 and the first paragraph of Article 24 TFEU, Articles 39 and 40 of the Charter of Fundamental Rights of the European Union, and the acts adopted on the basis of those provisions.

2.   In the event that the Union and the United Kingdom reach an agreement governing their future relationship in the areas of the Common Foreign and Security Policy and the Common Security and

Defence Policy which becomes applicable during the transition period, Chapter 2 of Title V of the TEU and the acts adopted on the basis of those provisions shall cease to apply to the United Kingdom from the date of application of that agreement.

3. During the transition period, the Union law applicable pursuant to paragraph 1 shall produce in respect of and in the United Kingdom the same legal effects as those which it produces within the Union and its Member States, and shall be interpreted and applied in accordance with the same methods and general principles as those applicable within the Union.

4. The United Kingdom shall not participate in any enhanced cooperation:
(a)   in relation to which authorisation was granted after the date of entry into force of this Agreement; or
(b)   within the framework of which no acts were adopted before the date of entry into force of this Agreement.

5. During the transition period, in relation to measures which amend, build upon or replace an existing measure adopted pursuant to Title V of Part Three of the TFEU by which the United Kingdom is bound before the date of entry into force of this Agreement, Article 5 of Protocol (No 19) on the Schengen *acquis* integrated into the framework of the European Union and Article 4a of Protocol (No 21) on the position of the United Kingdom and Ireland in respect of the area of freedom, security and justice shall continue to apply *mutatis mutandis*. The United Kingdom shall not, however, have the right to notify its wish to take part in the application of new measures pursuant to Title V of Part Three of the TFEU other than those measures referred to in Article 4a of Protocol No 21.

In order to support continuing cooperation between the Union and the United Kingdom, under the conditions set out for cooperation with third countries in the relevant measures, the Union may invite the United Kingdom to cooperate in relation to new measures adopted under Title V of Part III TFEU.

6. Unless otherwise provided in this Agreement, during the transition period, any reference to Member States in the Union law applicable pursuant to paragraph 1, including as implemented and applied by Member States, shall be understood as including the United Kingdom.

7. By way of derogation from paragraph 6:
(a)   for the purposes of Article 42(6) and Article 46 TEU and of Protocol (No 10) on permanent structured cooperation established by Article 42 TEU, any references to Member States shall be understood as not including the United Kingdom. This shall not preclude the possibility for the United Kingdom to be invited to participate as a third country in individual projects under the conditions set out in Council Decision (CFSP) 2017/2315[1] on an exceptional basis, or in any other form of cooperation to the extent allowed and under the conditions set out by future Union acts adopted on the basis of Article 42(6) and Article 46 TEU;
(b)   where acts of the Union provide for the participation of Member States, nationals of Member States or natural or legal persons residing or established in a Member State in an information exchange, procedure or programme which continues to be implemented or which starts after the end of the transition period, and where such participation would grant access to security-related sensitive information that only Member States, nationals of Member States, or natural or legal persons residing or established in a Member State, are to have knowledge of, in such exceptional circumstances the references to Member States in such Union acts shall be understood as not including the United Kingdom. The Union shall notify the United Kingdom of the application of this derogation;
(c)   for the purposes of the recruitment of officials and other servants of the institutions, bodies, offices or agencies of the Union, any references to Member States in Articles 27 and 28(a) of the Staff Regulations and in Article 1 of Annex X thereto and in Articles 12, 82 and 128 of the Conditions of Employment of Other Servants of the European Union, or in the relevant provisions of other staff rules applicable to those institutions, bodies, offices or agencies, shall be understood as not including the United Kingdom.

NOTES

[1]   Council Decision (CFSP) 2017/2315 of 11 December 2017 establishing permanent structured cooperation (PESCO) and determining the list of participating Member States (OJ L331, 14.12.2017, p 57).

ARTICLE 128   INSTITUTIONAL ARRANGEMENTS

[7.79]
1. Notwithstanding Article 127, during the transition period Article 7 shall apply.

2. For the purposes of the Treaties, during the transition period, the parliament of the United Kingdom shall not be considered to be a national parliament of a Member State, except as regards Article 1 of Protocol (No 1) on the role of national parliaments in the European Union and, in respect of proposals which are in the public domain, Article 2 of that Protocol.

3. During the transition period, provisions of the Treaties which grant institutional rights to Member States enabling them to submit proposals, initiatives or requests to the institutions shall be understood as not including the United Kingdom[1].

4. For the purposes of participation in the institutional arrangements laid down in Articles 282 and 283 TFEU and in Protocol (No 4) on the Statute of the European system of central banks and of the European Central Bank, with the exception of Article 21(2) of that Protocol, during the transition period, the Bank of England shall not be considered to be a national central bank of a Member State.

5. By way of derogation from paragraph 1 of this Article and from Article 7, during the transition period, representatives or experts of the United Kingdom, or experts designated by the United Kingdom, may, upon invitation, exceptionally attend meetings or parts of meetings of the committees referred to in Article 3(2) of Regulation (EU) No 182/2011, meetings or parts of meetings of Commission expert groups, meetings or parts of meetings of other similar entities, and meetings or parts of meetings of bodies, offices or agencies, where and when representatives or experts of the Member States or experts designated by Member States take part, provided that one of the following conditions is fulfilled:

(a)   the discussion concerns individual acts to be addressed during the transition period to the United Kingdom or to natural or legal persons residing or established in the United Kingdom;

(b)   the presence of the United Kingdom is necessary and in the interest of the Union, in particular for the effective implementation of Union law during the transition period.

During such meetings or parts of meetings, the representatives or experts of the United Kingdom or experts designated by the United Kingdom shall have no voting rights and their presence shall be limited to the specific agenda items that fulfil the conditions set out in point (a) or (b).

6. During the transition period, the United Kingdom shall not act as leading authority for risk assessments, examinations, approvals or authorisations at the level of the Union or at the level of Member States acting jointly as referred to in the acts and provisions listed in Annex VII.

7. During the transition period, where draft Union acts identify or refer directly to specific Member State authorities, procedures, or documents, the United Kingdom shall be consulted by the Union on such drafts, with a view to ensuring the proper implementation and application of those acts by and in the United Kingdom.

NOTES

1   This should in particular concern Articles 7, 30, 42(4), 48(2)–(6) and 49 TEU and Articles 25, 76(b), 82(3), 83(3), 86(1), 87(3), 135, 218(8), 223(1), 262, 311 and 341 TFEU.

ARTICLE 129   SPECIFIC ARRANGEMENTS RELATING TO THE
UNION'S EXTERNAL ACTION

[7.80]

1. Without prejudice to Article 127(2), during the transition period, the United Kingdom shall be bound by the obligations stemming from the international agreements concluded by the Union, by Member States acting on its behalf, or by the Union and its Member States acting jointly, as referred to in point (a)(iv) of Article 2.[1]

2. During the transition period, representatives of the United Kingdom shall not participate in the work of any bodies set up by international agreements concluded by the Union, or by Member States acting on its behalf, or by the Union and its Member States acting jointly, unless:

(a)   the United Kingdom participates in its own right; or

(b)   the Union exceptionally invites the United Kingdom to attend, as part of the Union's delegation, meetings or parts of meetings of such bodies, where the Union considers that the presence of the United Kingdom is necessary and in the interest of the Union, in particular for the effective implementation of those agreements during the transition period; such presence shall only be allowed where Member States participation is permitted under the applicable agreements.

3. In accordance with the principle of sincere cooperation, the United Kingdom shall refrain, during the transition period, from any action or initiative which is likely to be prejudicial to the Union's interests, in particular in the framework of any international organisation, agency, conference or forum of which the United Kingdom is a party in its own right.

4. Notwithstanding paragraph 3, during the transition period, the United Kingdom may negotiate, sign and ratify international agreements entered into in its own capacity in the areas of exclusive competence of the Union, provided those agreements do not enter into force or apply during the transition period, unless so authorised by the Union.

5. Without prejudice to Article 127(2), whenever there is a need for coordination, the United Kingdom may be consulted, on a case-by-case basis.

6. Following a decision of the Council falling under Chapter 2 of Title V TEU, the United Kingdom may make a formal declaration to the High Representative of the Union for Foreign Affairs and Security Policy, indicating that, for vital and stated reasons of national policy, in those exceptional cases it will not apply the decision. In a spirit of mutual solidarity, the United Kingdom shall refrain from any action likely to conflict with or impede Union action based on that decision, and the Member States shall respect the position of the United Kingdom.

7. During the transition period, the United Kingdom shall not provide commanders of civilian operations, heads of mission, operation commanders or force commanders for missions or operations conducted under Articles 42, 43 and 44 TEU, nor shall it provide the operational headquarters for such missions or operations, or serve as framework nation for Union battlegroups. During the transition period, the United Kingdom shall not provide the head of any operational actions under Article 28 TEU.

NOTES

1   The Union will notify the other parties to these agreements that during the transition period the United Kingdom is to be treated as a Member State for the purposes of these agreements.

ARTICLE 130   SPECIFIC ARRANGEMENTS RELATING TO FISHING OPPORTUNITIES

[7.81]

1. As regards the fixing of fishing opportunities within the meaning of Article 43(3) TFEU for any period falling within the transition period, the United Kingdom shall be consulted in respect of the fishing opportunities related to the United Kingdom, including in the context of the preparation of relevant international consultations and negotiations.

2.   For the purposes of paragraph 1, the Union shall offer the opportunity to the United Kingdom to provide comments on the Annual Communication from the European Commission on fishing opportunities, the scientific advice from the relevant scientific bodies and the proposals from the European Commission for fishing opportunities for any period falling within the transition period.

3.   Notwithstanding point (b) of Article 129(2), with a view to allowing the United Kingdom to prepare its future membership in relevant international fora, the Union may exceptionally invite the United Kingdom to attend, as part of the Union's delegation, international consultations and negotiations referred to in paragraph 1 of this Article, to the extent allowed for Member States and permitted by the specific forum.

4.   Without prejudice to Article 127(1), the relative stability keys for the allocation of fishing opportunities referred to in paragraph 1 of this Article shall be maintained.

ARTICLE 131   SUPERVISION AND ENFORCEMENT

[7.82]
During the transition period, the institutions, bodies, offices and agencies of the Union shall have the powers conferred upon them by Union law in relation to the United Kingdom and to natural and legal persons residing or established in the United Kingdom. In particular, the Court of Justice of the European Union shall have jurisdiction as provided for in the Treaties.

The first paragraph shall also apply during the transition period as regards the interpretation and application of this Agreement.

ARTICLE 132   EXTENSION OF THE TRANSITION PERIOD

[7.83]
1.   Notwithstanding Article 126, the Joint Committee may, before 1 July 2020, adopt a single decision extending the transition period for up to 1 or 2 years.[1]

2.   In the event that the Joint Committee adopts a decision under paragraph 1, the following shall apply:
(a)   by way of derogation from Article 127(6), the United Kingdom shall be considered as a third country for the purposes of the implementation of the Union programmes and activities committed under the multiannual financial framework applying as from the year 2021;
(b)   by way of derogation from Article 127(1) and without prejudice to Part Five of this Agreement, the applicable Union law concerning the Union's own resources relating to the financial years covered by the extension of the transition period shall not apply to the United Kingdom after 31 December 2020;
(c)   by way of derogation from Article 127 (1) of this Agreement, Articles 107, 108 and 109 TFEU shall not apply to measures of the United Kingdom authorities, including on rural development, supporting the production of and trade in agricultural products in the United Kingdom up to an annual level of support which shall not be more than the total amount of expenditure incurred in the United Kingdom under the Common Agricultural Policy in 2019, and provided that a minimum percentage of that exempted support complies with the provisions of Annex 2 to the WTO Agreement on Agriculture. Such minimum percentage shall be determined on the basis of the last available percentage by which the overall expenditure under the Common Agricultural Policy in the Union complied with the provisions of Annex 2 to the WTO Agreement on Agriculture. In the event that the period by which the transition period is extended is not a multiple of 12 months, the maximum annual level of exempted support in the year for which the extended transition period covers less than 12 months shall be reduced pro rata;
(d)   for the period from 1 January 2021 to the end of the transition period, the United Kingdom shall make a contribution to the Union budget, as determined in accordance with paragraph 3;
(e)   subject to point (d) of paragraph 3, Part Five of this Agreement shall not be affected.

3.   A decision of the Joint Committee under paragraph 1 shall:
(a)   establish the appropriate amount of the contribution of the United Kingdom to the Union budget for the period from 1 January 2021 to the end of the transition period, taking into account the status of the United Kingdom during that period, as well as the modalities of payment of that amount;
(b)   specify the maximum level of exempted support, as well as the minimum percentage thereof that shall comply with the provisions of Annex 2 to the WTO Agreement on Agriculture, as referred to in point (c) of paragraph 2;
(c)   lay down any other measure necessary for the implementation of paragraph 2;
(d)   adapt the dates or periods referred to in Articles 51, 62, 63, 84, 96, 125, 141, 156, 157 and Annexes IV and V to reflect the extension of the transition period.

NOTES
[1]   In case of extension, the Union will notify other parties to international agreements thereof.

TRADE AND COOPERATION AGREEMENT BETWEEN THE EUROPEAN UNION AND THE EUROPEAN ATOMIC ENERGY COMMUNITY, OF THE ONE PART, AND THE UNITED KINGDOM OF GREAT BRITAIN AND NORTHERN IRELAND, OF THE OTHER PART

[7.84]

NOTES
    Editorial note: only certain key provisions of this Agreement which are relevant to data protection law are reproduced here. Provisions not reproduced are not annotated.
    Date of publication in OJ: OJ L444, 31.12.2020, p 14.
© European Union, 1998–2021.

CONTENTS

[7.85]

THE EUROPEAN UNION AND THE EUROPEAN ATOMIC ENERGY COMMUNITY AND THE UNITED KINGDOM OF GREAT BRITAIN AND NORTHERN IRELAND,

    REAFFIRMING their commitment to democratic principles, to the rule of law, to human rights, to countering proliferation of weapons of mass destruction and to the fight against climate change, which constitute essential elements of this and supplementing agreements,

    RECOGNISING the importance of global cooperation to address issues of shared interest,

    RECOGNISING the importance of transparency in international trade and investment to the benefit of all stakeholders,

    SEEKING to establish clear and mutually advantageous rules governing trade and investment between the Parties,

    CONSIDERING that in order to guarantee the efficient management and correct interpretation and application of this Agreement and any supplementing agreement as well as compliance with the obligations under those agreements, it is essential to establish provisions ensuring overall governance, in particular dispute settlement and enforcement rules that fully respect the autonomy of the respective legal orders of the Union and of the United Kingdom, as well as the United Kingdom's status as a country outside the European Union,

    BUILDING upon their respective rights and obligations under the Marrakesh Agreement Establishing the World Trade Organization, done on 15 April 1994, and other multilateral and bilateral instruments of cooperation,

    RECOGNISING the Parties' respective autonomy and rights to regulate within their territories in order to achieve legitimate public policy objectives such as the protection and promotion of public health, social services, public

education, safety, the environment including climate change, public morals, social or consumer protection, animal welfare, privacy and data protection and the promotion and protection of cultural diversity, while striving to improve their respective high levels of protection,

BELIEVING in the benefits of a predictable commercial environment that fosters trade and investment between them and prevents distortion of trade and unfair competitive advantages, in a manner conducive to sustainable development in its economic, social and environmental dimensions,

RECOGNISING the need for an ambitious, wide-ranging and balanced economic partnership to be underpinned by a level playing field for open and fair competition and sustainable development, through effective and robust frameworks for subsidies and competition and a commitment to uphold their respective high levels of protection in the areas of labour and social standards, environment, the fight against climate change, and taxation,

RECOGNISING the need to ensure an open and secure market for businesses, including medium-sized enterprises, and their goods and services through addressing unjustified barriers to trade and investment,

NOTING the importance of facilitating new opportunities for businesses and consumers through digital trade, and addressing unjustified barriers to data flows and trade enabled by electronic means, whilst respecting the Parties' personal data protection rules,

DESIRING that this Agreement contributes to consumer welfare through policies ensuring a high level of consumer protection and economic well-being, as well as encouraging cooperation between relevant authorities,

CONSIDERING the importance of cross-border connectivity by air, by road and by sea, for passengers and for goods, and the need to ensure high standards in the provision of transportation services between the Parties,

RECOGNISING the benefits of trade and investment in energy and raw materials and the importance of supporting the delivery of cost efficient, clean and secure energy supplies to the Union and the United Kingdom,

NOTING the interest of the Parties in establishing a framework to facilitate technical cooperation and develop new trading arrangements for interconnectors which deliver robust and efficient outcomes for all timeframes,

NOTING that cooperation and trade between the Parties in these areas should be based on fair competition in energy markets and non-discriminatory access to networks,

RECOGNISING the benefits of sustainable energy, renewable energy, in particular offshore generation in the North Sea, and energy efficiency,

DESIRING to promote the peaceful use of the waters adjacent to their coasts and the optimum and equitable utilisation of the marine living resources in those waters including the continued sustainable management of the shared stocks,

NOTING that, the United Kingdom withdrew from the European Union and that with effect from 1 January 2021, the United Kingdom is an independent coastal State with corresponding rights and obligations under international law,

AFFIRMING that the sovereign rights of the coastal States exercised by the Parties for the purpose of exploring, exploiting, conserving and managing the living resources in their waters should be conducted pursuant to and in accordance with the principles of international law, including the United Nations Convention on the Law of the Sea of 10 December 1982,

RECOGNISING the importance of the coordination of social security rights enjoyed by persons moving between the Parties to work, to stay or to reside, as well as the rights enjoyed by their family members and survivors,

CONSIDERING that cooperation in areas of shared interest, such as science, research and innovation, nuclear research or space, in the form of the participation of the United Kingdom in the corresponding Union programmes under fair and appropriate conditions will benefit both Parties,

CONSIDERING that cooperation between the United Kingdom and the Union relating to the prevention, investigation, detection or prosecution of criminal offences and to the execution of criminal penalties, including the safeguarding against and prevention of threats to public security, will enable the security of the United Kingdom and the Union to be strengthened,

DESIRING that an agreement is concluded between the United Kingdom and the Union to provide a legal base for such cooperation,

ACKNOWLEDGING that the Parties may supplement this Agreement with other agreements forming an integral part of their overall bilateral relations as governed by this Agreement and that the Agreement on Security Procedures for Exchanging and Protecting Classified Information is concluded as such a supplementing agreement, and enables the exchange of classified information between the Parties under this Agreement or any other supplementing agreement,

HAVE AGREED AS FOLLOWS:

PART ONE:
COMMON AND INSTITUTIONAL PROVISIONS

TITLE I: GENERAL PROVISIONS

[7.86]
Article COMPROV.1: Purpose
This Agreement establishes the basis for a broad relationship between the Parties, within an area of prosperity and good neighbourliness characterised by close and peaceful relations based on cooperation, respectful of the Parties' autonomy and sovereignty.

Article COMPROV.2: Supplementing agreements
1. Where the Union and the United Kingdom conclude other bilateral agreements between them, such agreements shall constitute supplementing agreements to this Agreement, unless otherwise provided for in those agreements. Such supplementing agreements shall be an integral part of the overall bilateral relations as governed by this Agreement and shall form part of the overall framework.
2. Paragraph 1 also applies to:

(a) agreements between the Union and its Member States, of the one part, and the United Kingdom, of the other part; and

(b) agreements between Euratom, of the one part, and the United Kingdom, of the other part.

Article COMPROV.3: Good faith

1. The Parties shall, in full mutual respect and good faith, assist each other in carrying out tasks that flow from this Agreement and any supplementing agreement.

2. They shall take all appropriate measures, whether general or particular, to ensure the fulfilment of the obligations arising from this Agreement and from any supplementing agreement, and shall refrain from any measures which could jeopardise the attainment of the objectives of this Agreement or any supplementing agreement.

TITLE II: PRINCIPLES OF INTERPRETATION AND DEFINITIONS

[7.87]
Article COMPROV.13: Public international law

1. The provisions of this Agreement and any supplementing agreement shall be interpreted in good faith in accordance with their ordinary meaning in their context and in light of the object and purpose of the agreement in accordance with customary rules of interpretation of public international law, including those codified in the Vienna Convention on the Law of Treaties, done at Vienna on 23 May 1969.

2. For greater certainty, neither this Agreement nor any supplementing agreement establishes an obligation to interpret their provisions in accordance with the domestic law of either Party.

3. For greater certainty, an interpretation of this Agreement or any supplementing agreement given by the courts of either Party shall not be binding on the courts of the other Party.

Article COMPROV.16: Private rights

1. Without prejudice to Article MOBI.SSC.67 [Protection of individual rights] and with the exception, with regard to the Union, of Part Three [Law enforcement and judicial cooperation], nothing in this Agreement or any supplementing agreement shall be construed as conferring rights or imposing obligations on persons other than those created between the Parties under public international law, nor as permitting this Agreement or any supplementing agreement to be directly invoked in the domestic legal systems of the Parties.

2. A Party shall not provide for a right of action under its law against the other Party on the ground that the other Party has acted in breach of this Agreement or any supplementing agreement.

Article COMPROV.17: Definitions

1. For the purposes of this Agreement and any supplementing agreement, and unless otherwise specified, the following definitions apply:

(a) "data subject" means an identified or identifiable natural person; an identifiable person being a person who can be identified, directly or indirectly, in particular by reference to an identifier such as a name, an identification number, location data or an online identifier, or to one or more factors specific to the physical, physiological, genetic, mental, economic, cultural or social identity of that natural person;

(b) "day" means a calendar day;

(c) "Member State" means a Member State of the European Union;

(d) "personal data" means any information relating to a data subject;

(e) "State" means a Member State or the United Kingdom, as the context requires;

(f) "territory" of a Party means in respect of each Party the territories to which the Agreement applies in accordance with Article FINPROV.1 [Territorial scope];

(g) "the transition period" means the transition period provided for in Article 126 of the Withdrawal Agreement; and

(h) "Withdrawal Agreement" means the Agreement on the withdrawal of the United Kingdom of Great Britain and Northern Ireland from the European Union and the European Atomic Energy Community, including its Protocols.

2. Any reference to the "Union", "Party" or "Parties" in this Agreement or any supplementing agreement shall be understood as not including the European Atomic Energy Community, unless otherwise specified or where the context otherwise requires.

TITLE III: INSTITUTIONAL FRAMEWORK

[7.88]
Article INST.1: Partnership Council

1. A Partnership Council is hereby established. It shall comprise representatives of the Union and of the United Kingdom. The Partnership Council may meet in different configurations depending on the matters under discussion.

2. The Partnership Council shall be co-chaired by a Member of the European Commission and a representative of the Government of the United Kingdom at ministerial level. It shall meet at the request of the Union or the United Kingdom, and, in any event, at least once a year, and shall set its meeting schedule and its agenda by mutual consent.

3. The Partnership Council shall oversee the attainment of the objectives of this Agreement and any supplementing agreement. It shall supervise and facilitate the implementation and application of this Agreement and of any supplementing agreement. Each Party may refer to the Partnership Council any issue relating to the implementation, application and interpretation of this Agreement or of any supplementing agreement.

4. The Partnership Council shall have the power to:

(a) adopt decisions in respect of all matters where this Agreement or any supplementing agreement so provides;

(b) make recommendations to the Parties regarding the implementation and application of this Agreement or of any supplementing agreement;

(c) adopt, by decision, amendments to this Agreement or to any supplementing agreement in the cases provided for in this Agreement or in any supplementing agreement;

(d) except in relation to Title III [Institutional Framework] of Part One [Common and institutional provisions], until the end of the fourth year following the entry into force of this Agreement, adopt decisions amending this Agreement or any supplementing agreement, provided that such amendments are necessary to correct errors, or to address omissions or other deficiencies;

(e) discuss any matter related to the areas covered by this Agreement or by any supplementing agreement;

(f) delegate certain of its powers to the Trade Partnership Committee or to a Specialised Committee, except those powers and responsibilities referred to in point (g) of Article INST.1(4) [Partnership Council];

(g) by decision, establish Trade Specialised Committees and Specialised Committees, other than those referred to in Article INST.2(1) [Committees], dissolve any Trade Specialised Committee or Specialised Committee, or change the tasks assigned to them; and

(h) make recommendations to the Parties regarding the transfer of personal data in specific areas covered by this Agreement or any supplementing agreement.

5. The work of the Partnership Council shall be governed by the rules of procedure set out in ANNEX INST-1 [Rules of Procedure of the Partnership Council and Committees]. The Partnership Council may amend that Annex.

Article INST.2: Committees

1. The following Committees are hereby established:

(a) the Trade Partnership Committee, which addresses matters covered by Titles I to VII, Chapter 4 [Energy goods and raw materials] of Title VIII, Titles IX to XII of Heading One [Trade] of Part Two, Heading Six [Other provisions] of Part Two, and Annex ENER-2 [ENERGY AND ENVIRONMENTAL SUBSIDIES];

(b) the Trade Specialised Committee on Goods which addresses matters covered by Chapter 1 of Title I of Heading One of Part Two and Chapter four [Energy goods and raw materials] of Title VIII of Heading One of Part Two;

(c) the Trade Specialised Committee on Customs Cooperation and Rules of Origin, which addresses matters covered by Chapters 2 and 5 of Title I of Heading One of Part Two, the Protocol on mutual administrative assistance in customs matters and the provisions on customs enforcement of intellectual property rights, fees and charges, customs valuation and repaired goods;

(d) the Trade Specialised Committee on Sanitary and Phytosanitary Measures, which addresses matters covered by Chapter 3 of Title I of Heading One of Part Two;

(e) the Trade Specialised Committee on Technical Barriers to Trade, which addresses matters covered by Chapter 4 of Title I of Heading One of Part Two and Article ENER.25 [Cooperation on standards] of Title VIII [Energy] of Heading One of Part Two;

(f) the Trade Specialised Committee on Services, Investment and Digital Trade, which addresses matters covered by Titles II to IV of Heading One of Part Two and Chapter 4 [Energy Goods and Raw Materials] of Title VIII of Heading One of Part Two;

(g) the Trade Specialised Committee on Intellectual Property, which addresses matters covered by Title V of Heading One of Part Two;

(h) the Trade Specialised Committee on Public Procurement, which addresses matters covered by Title VI of Heading One of Part Two;

(i) the Trade Specialised Committee on Regulatory Cooperation, which addresses matters covered by Title X of Heading One of Part Two;

(j) the Trade Specialised Committee on Level Playing Field for Open and Fair Competition and Sustainable Development, which addresses matters covered by Title XI of Heading One of Part Two and Annex ENER-2 [ENERGY AND ENVIRONMENTAL SUBSIDIES];

(k) the Trade Specialised Committee on Administrative Cooperation in VAT and Recovery of Taxes and Duties, which addresses matters covered by the Protocol on administrative cooperation and combating fraud in the field of Value Added Tax and on mutual assistance for the recovery of claims relating to taxes and duties;]

(l) the Specialised Committee on Energy,

    (i) which addresses matters covered by Title VIII of Heading One of Part Two, with the exception of Chapter 4 [Energy Goods and Raw Materials], Article ENER.25 [Cooperation on Standards] and Annex ENER-2 [ENERGY AND ENVIRONMENTAL SUBSIDIES], and

    (ii) which can discuss and provide expertise to the relevant Trade Specialised Committee on matters pertaining to Chapter four [Energy Goods and Raw Materials] and Article ENER.25 [Cooperation on Standards] of Title VIII of Heading One of Part Two;

(m) the Specialised Committee on Air Transport, which addresses matters covered by Title I of Heading Two of Part Two;

(n) the Specialised Committee on Aviation Safety, which addresses matters covered by Title II of Heading Two of Part Two;

(o) the Specialised Committee on Road Transport, which addresses matters covered by Heading Three [Road Transport] of Part Two;

(p) the Specialised Committee on Social Security Coordination, which addresses matters covered by Heading Four of Part Two and the Protocol on Social Security Coordination;

(q) the Specialised Committee on Fisheries, which addresses matters covered by Heading Five [Fisheries] of Part Two;

(r) the Specialised Committee on Law Enforcement and Judicial Cooperation, which addresses matters covered by Part Three [Law enforcement and judicial cooperation in criminal matters]; and

(s) the Specialised Committee on Participation in Union Programmes, which addresses matters covered by Part Five [Union programmes].

2. With respect to issues related to Titles I to VII, Chapter 4 [Energy goods and raw materials] of Title VIII, Titles IX to XII of Heading One [Trade] of Part Two, Heading Six [Other provisions] of Part Two and Annex ENER-2 [ENERGY AND ENVIRONMENTAL SUBSIDIES], the Trade Partnership Committee referred to in paragraph 1 of this Article shall have the power to:

    (a) assist the Partnership Council in the performance of its tasks and, in particular, report to the Partnership Council and carry out any task assigned to it by the latter;

    (b) supervise the implementation of this Agreement or any supplementing agreement;

    (c) adopt decisions or make recommendations as provided for in this Agreement or any supplementing agreement or where such power has been delegated to it by the Partnership Council;

    (d) supervise the work of the Trade Specialised Committees referred to in paragraph 1 of this Article;

    (e) explore the most appropriate way to prevent or solve any difficulty that may arise in relation to the interpretation and application of this Agreement or any supplementing agreement, without prejudice to Title I [Dispute settlement] of Part Six ;

    (f) exercise the powers delegated to it by the Partnership Council pursuant to point (f) of Article INST.1(4) [Partnership Council];

    (g) establish, by decision, Trade Specialised Committees other than those referred to in paragraph 1 of this Article, dissolve any such Trade Specialised Committee, or change the tasks assigned to them; and

    (h) establish, supervise, coordinate and dissolve Working Groups, or delegate their supervision to a Trade Specialised Committee.

3. With respect to issues related to their area of competence, Trade Specialised Committees shall have the power to:

    (a) monitor and review the implementation and ensure the proper functioning of this Agreement or any supplementing agreement;

    (b) assist the Trade Partnership Committee in the performance of its tasks and, in particular, report to the Trade Partnership Committee and carry out any task assigned to them by it;

    (c) conduct the preparatory technical work necessary to support the functions of the Partnership Council and the Trade Partnership Committee, including when those bodies have to adopt decisions or recommendations,

    (d) adopt decisions in respect of all matters where this Agreement or any supplementing agreement so provides;

    (e) discuss technical issues arising from the implementation of this Agreement or of any supplementing agreement, without prejudice to Title I [Dispute Settlement] of Part Six; and

    (f) provide a forum for the Parties to exchange information, discuss best practices and share implementation experience.

4. With respect to issues related to their area of competence, Specialised Committees shall have the power to:

    (a) monitor and review the implementation and ensure the proper functioning of this Agreement or any supplementing agreement;

    (b) assist the Partnership Council in the performance of its tasks and, in particular, report to the Partnership Council and carry out any task assigned to them by it;

    (c) adopt decisions, including amendments, and recommendations in respect of all matters where this Agreement or any supplementing agreement so provides or for which the Partnership Council has delegated its powers to a Specialised Committee in accordance with point (f) of Article INST.1(4) [Partnership Council];

    (d) discuss technical issues arising from the implementation of this Agreement or any supplementing agreement;

    (e) provide a forum for the Parties to exchange information, discuss best practices and share implementation experience;

    (f) establish, supervise, coordinate and dissolve Working Groups; and

    (g) provide a forum for consultation pursuant to Article INST.13(7) [Consultations] of Title I [Dispute Settlement] of Part Six.

5. Committees shall comprise representatives of each Party. Each Party shall ensure that its representatives on the Committees have the appropriate expertise with respect to the issues under discussion.

6. The Trade Partnership Committee shall be co-chaired by a senior representative of the Union and a representative of the United Kingdom with responsibility for trade-related matters, or their designees. It shall meet at the request of the Union or the United Kingdom, and, in any event, at least once a year, and shall set its meeting schedule and its agenda by mutual consent.

7. The Trade Specialised Committees and the Specialised Committees shall be co-chaired by a representative of the Union and a representative of the United Kingdom. Unless otherwise provided for in this Agreement, or unless the co-chairs decide otherwise, they shall meet at least once a year.

8. Committees shall set their meeting schedule and agenda by mutual consent.

9. The work of the Committees shall be governed by the rules of procedure set out in ANNEX INST-X [Rules of Procedure of the Partnership Council and Committees].

10. By derogation from paragraph 9, a Committee may adopt and subsequently amend its own rules that shall govern its work.

Article INST.3: Working Groups

1. The following Working Groups are hereby established:

    (a) the Working Group on Organic Products, under the supervision of the Trade Specialised Committee on Technical Barriers to Trade;

    (b) the Working Group on Motor Vehicles and Parts, under the supervision of the Trade Specialised Committee on Technical Barriers to Trade;

    (c) the Working Group on Medicinal Products, under the supervision of the Trade Specialised Committee on Technical Barriers to Trade;

    (d) the Working Group on Social Security Coordination, under the supervision of the Specialised Committee on Social Security Coordination;

2. Working Groups shall, under the supervision of Committees, assist Committees in the performance of their tasks and, in particular, prepare the work of Committees and carry out any task assigned to them by the latter.

3. Working Groups shall comprise representatives of the Union and of the United Kingdom and shall be co-chaired by a representative of the Union and a representative of the United Kingdom.

4. Working Groups shall set their own rules of procedure, meeting schedule and agenda by mutual consent.

Article INST.4: Decisions and recommendations

1. The decisions adopted by the Partnership Council, or, as the case may be, by a Committee, shall be binding on the Parties and on all the bodies set up under this Agreement and under any supplementing agreement, including the arbitration tribunal referred to in Title I [Dispute settlement] of Part Six. Recommendations shall have no binding force.

2. The Partnership Council or, as the case may be, a Committee, shall adopt decisions and make recommendations by mutual consent.

Article INST.5: Parliamentary cooperation

1. The European Parliament and the Parliament of the United Kingdom may establish a Parliamentary Partnership Assembly consisting of Members of the European Parliament and of Members of the Parliament of the United Kingdom, as a forum to exchange views on the partnership.

2. Upon its establishment, the Parliamentary Partnership Assembly:
   (a) may request relevant information regarding the implementation of this Agreement and any supplementing agreement from the Partnership Council, which shall then supply that Assembly with the requested information;
   (b) shall be informed of the decisions and recommendations of the Partnership Council; and
   (c) may make recommendations to the Partnership Council.

Article INST.6: Participation of civil society

The Parties shall consult civil society on the implementation of this Agreement and any supplementing agreement, in particular through interaction with the domestic advisory groups and the Civil Society Forum referred to in Articles INST.7 [Domestic advisory groups] and INST.8 [Civil Society Forum].

Article INST.7: Domestic advisory groups

1. Each Party shall consult on issues covered by this Agreement and any supplementing agreement its newly created or existing domestic advisory group or groups comprising a representation of independent civil society organisations including non-governmental organisations, business and employers' organisations, as well as trade unions, active in economic, sustainable development, social, human rights, environmental and other matters. Each Party may convene its domestic advisory group or groups in different configurations to discuss the implementation of different provisions of this Agreement or of any supplementing agreement.

2. Each Party shall consider views or recommendations submitted by its domestic advisory group or groups. Representatives of each Party shall aim to consult with their respective domestic advisory group or groups at least once a year. Meetings may be held by virtual means.

3. In order to promote public awareness of the domestic advisory groups, each Party shall endeavour to publish the list of organisations participating in its domestic advisory group or groups as well as the contact point for that or those groups

4. The Parties shall promote interaction between their respective domestic advisory groups, including by exchanging where possible the contact details of members of their domestic advisory groups.

Article INST.8: Civil Society Forum

1. The Parties shall facilitate the organisation of a Civil Society Forum to conduct a dialogue on the implementation of Part Two of this Agreement. The Partnership Council shall adopt operational guidelines for the conduct of the Forum.

2. The Civil Society Forum shall meet at least once a year, unless otherwise agreed by the Parties. The Civil Society Forum may meet by virtual means.

3. The Civil Society Forum shall be open for the participation of independent civil society organisations established in the territories of the Parties, including members of the domestic advisory groups referred to in Article INST.7 [Domestic advisory groups]. Each Party shall promote a balanced representation, including non-governmental organisations, business and employers' organisations and trade unions, active in economic, sustainable development, social, human rights, environmental and other matters.

PART TWO:
TRADE, TRANSPORT, FISHERIES AND OTHER ARRANGEMENTS

TITLE III: DIGITAL TRADE

CHAPTER 1: GENERAL PROVISIONS

[7.89]
Article DIGIT.1 Objective

The objective of this Title is to facilitate digital trade, to address unjustified barriers to trade enabled by electronic means and to ensure an open, secure and trustworthy online environment for businesses and consumers.

Article DIGIT.2 Scope
1. This Title applies to measures of a Party affecting trade enabled by electronic means.
2. This Title does not apply to audio-visual services.

Article DIGIT.3 Right to regulate
The Parties reaffirm the right to regulate within their territories to achieve legitimate policy objectives, such as the protection of public health, social services, public education, safety, the environment including climate change, public morals, social or consumer protection, privacy and data protection, or the promotion and protection of cultural diversity.

Article DIGIT.4 Exceptions
For greater certainty, nothing in this Title prevents the Parties from adopting or maintaining measures in accordance with Article EXC.1 [General exceptions], Article EXC.4 [Security exceptions] and Article SERVIN.5.39 [Prudential carve-out] for the public interest reasons set out therein.

Article DIGIT.5 Definitions
1. The definitions in Article SERVIN.1.2 [Definitions] of Title II [Services and investment] of this Heading apply to this Title.
2. For the purposes of this Title:
   (a) "consumer" means any natural person using a public telecommunications service for other than professional purposes;
   (b) "direct marketing communication" means any form of commercial advertising by which a natural or legal person communicates marketing messages directly to a user via a public telecommunications service and covers at least electronic mail and text and multimedia messages (SMS and MMS);
   (c) "electronic authentication" means an electronic process that enables the confirmation of:
      (i) the electronic identification of a natural or legal person, or
      (ii) the origin and integrity of data in electronic form;
   (d) "electronic registered delivery service" means a service that makes it possible to transmit data between third parties by electronic means and provides evidence relating to the handling of the transmitted data, including proof of sending and receiving the data, and that protects transmitted data against the risk of loss, theft, damage or any unauthorised alterations;
   (e) "electronic seal" means data in electronic form used by a legal person which is attached to or logically associated with other data in electronic form to ensure the latter's origin and integrity;
   (f) "electronic signature" means data in electronic form which is attached to or logically associated with other data in electronic form that:
      (i) is used by a natural person to agree on the data in electronic form to which it relates; and
      (ii) is linked to the data in electronic form to which it relates in such a way that any subsequent alteration in the data is detectable;
   (g) "electronic time stamp" means data in electronic form which binds other data in electronic form to a particular time establishing evidence that the latter data existed at that time;
   (h) "electronic trust service" means an electronic service consisting of:
      (i) the creation, verification and validation of electronic signatures, electronic seals, electronic time stamps, electronic registered delivery services and certificates related to those services;
      (ii) the creation, verification and validation of certificates for website authentication; or
      (iii) the preservation of electronic signatures, seals or certificates related to those services;
   (i) "government data" means data owned or held by any level of government and by non-governmental bodies in the exercise of powers conferred on them by any level of government;
   (j) "public telecommunications service" means any telecommunications service that is offered to the public generally;
   (k) "user" means any natural or legal person using a public telecommunications service.

CHAPTER 2: DATA FLOWS AND PERSONAL DATA PROTECTION

Article DIGIT.6 Cross-border data flows
1. The Parties are committed to ensuring cross-border data flows to facilitate trade in the digital economy. To that end, cross-border data flows shall not be restricted between the Parties by a Party:
   (a) requiring the use of computing facilities or network elements in the Party's territory for processing, including by imposing the use of computing facilities or network elements that are certified or approved in the territory of a Party;
   (b) requiring the localisation of data in the Party's territory for storage or processing;
   (c) prohibiting the storage or processing in the territory of the other Party; or
   (d) making the cross-border transfer of data contingent upon use of computing facilities or network elements in the Parties' territory or upon localisation requirements in the Parties' territory.
2. The Parties shall keep the implementation of this provision under review and assess its functioning within three years of the date of entry into force of this Agreement. A Party may at any time propose to the other Party to review the list of restrictions listed in paragraph 1. Such a request shall be accorded sympathetic consideration.

Article DIGIT.7 Protection of personal data and privacy
1. Each Party recognises that individuals have a right to the protection of personal data and privacy and that high standards in this regard contribute to trust in the digital economy and to the development of trade.

2. Nothing in this Agreement shall prevent a Party from adopting or maintaining measures on the protection of personal data and privacy, including with respect to cross-border data transfers, provided that the law of the Party provides for instruments enabling transfers under conditions of general application[34] for the protection of the data transferred.

3. Each Party shall inform the other Party about any measure referred to in paragraph 2 that it adopts or maintains.

CHAPTER 3: SPECIFIC PROVISIONS

Article DIGIT.8 Customs duties on electronic transmissions

1. Electronic transmissions shall be considered as the supply of a service within the meaning of Title II [Services and investment] of this Heading.

2. The Parties shall not impose customs duties on electronic transmissions.

Article DIGIT.9 No prior authorisation

1. A Party shall not require prior authorisation of the provision of a service by electronic means solely on the ground that the service is provided online, and shall not adopt or maintain any other requirement having an equivalent effect. A service is provided online when it is provided by electronic means and without the parties being simultaneously present.

2. Paragraph 1 does not apply to telecommunications services, broadcasting services, gambling services, legal representation services or to the services of notaries or equivalent professions to the extent that they involve a direct and specific connection with the exercise of public authority.

Article DIGIT.10: Conclusion of contracts by electronic means

1. Each Party shall ensure that contracts may be concluded by electronic means and that its law neither creates obstacles for the use of electronic contracts nor results in contracts being deprived of legal effect and validity solely on the ground that the contract has been made by electronic means.

2. Paragraph 1 does not apply to the following:
   (a) broadcasting services;
   (b) gambling services;
   (c) legal representation services;
   (d) the services of notaries or equivalent professions involving a direct and specific connection with the exercise of public authority;
   (e) contracts that require witnessing in person;
   (f) contracts that establish or transfer rights in real estate;
   (g) contracts requiring by law the involvement of courts, public authorities or professions exercising public authority;
   (h) contracts of suretyship granted, collateral securities furnished by persons acting for purposes outside their trade, business or profession; or
   (i) contracts governed by family law or by the law of succession.

Article DIGIT.11 Electronic authentication and electronic trust services

1. A Party shall not deny the legal effect and admissibility as evidence in legal proceedings of an electronic document, an electronic signature, an electronic seal or an electronic time stamp, or of data sent and received using an electronic registered delivery service, solely on the ground that it is in electronic form.

2. A Party shall not adopt or maintain measures that would:
   (a) prohibit parties to an electronic transaction from mutually determining the appropriate electronic authentication methods for their transaction; or
   (b) prevent parties to an electronic transaction from being able to prove to judicial and administrative authorities that the use of electronic authentication or an electronic trust service in that transaction complies with the applicable legal requirements.

3. Notwithstanding paragraph 2, a Party may require that for a particular category of transactions, the method of electronic authentication or trust service is certified by an authority accredited in accordance with its law or meets certain performance standards which shall be objective, transparent and non-discriminatory and only relate to the specific characteristics of the category of transactions concerned.

Article DIGIT.12: Transfer of or access to source code

1. A Party shall not require the transfer of, or access to, the source code of software owned by a natural or legal person of the other Party.

2. For greater certainty:
   (a) the general exceptions, security exceptions and prudential carve-out referred to in Article DIGIT.4 [Exceptions] apply to measures of a Party adopted or maintained in the context of a certification procedure; and
   (b) paragraph 1 of this Article does not apply to the voluntary transfer of, or granting of access to, source code on a commercial basis by a natural or legal person of the other Party, such as in the context of a public procurement transaction or a freely negotiated contract.

3. Nothing in this Article shall affect:
   (a) a requirement by a court or administrative tribunal, or a requirement by a competition authority pursuant to a Party's competition law to prevent or remedy a restriction or a distortion of competition;
   (b) a requirement by a regulatory body pursuant to a Party's laws or regulations related to the protection of public safety with regard to users online, subject to safeguards against unauthorised disclosure;

    (c)   the protection and enforcement of intellectual property rights; and

    (d)   the right of a Party to take measures in accordance with Article III of the GPA as incorporated by Article PPROC.2 [Incorporation of certain provisions of the GPA and covered procurement] of Title VI [Public procurement] of this Heading.

Article DIGIT.13 Online consumer trust

1. Recognising the importance of enhancing consumer trust in digital trade, each Party shall adopt or maintain measures to ensure the effective protection of consumers engaging in electronic commerce transactions, including but not limited to measures that:

    (a)   proscribe fraudulent and deceptive commercial practices;

    (b)   require suppliers of goods and services to act in good faith and abide by fair commercial practices, including through the prohibition of charging consumers for unsolicited goods and services;

    (c)   require suppliers of goods or services to provide consumers with clear and thorough information, including when they act through intermediary service suppliers, regarding their identity and contact details, the transaction concerned, including the main characteristics of the goods or services and the full price inclusive of all applicable charges, and the applicable consumer rights (in the case of intermediary service suppliers, this includes enabling the provision of such information by the supplier of goods or services); and

    (d)   grant consumers access to redress for breaches of their rights, including a right to remedies if goods or services are paid for and are not delivered or provided as agreed.

2. The Parties recognise the importance of entrusting their consumer protection agencies or other relevant bodies with adequate enforcement powers and the importance of cooperation between these agencies in order to protect consumers and enhance online consumer trust.

Article DIGIT.14 Unsolicited direct marketing communications

1. Each Party shall ensure that users are effectively protected against unsolicited direct marketing communications.
2. Each Party shall ensure that direct marketing communications are not sent to users who are natural persons unless they have given their consent in accordance with each Party's laws to receiving such communications.
3. Notwithstanding paragraph 2, a Party shall allow natural or legal persons who have collected, in accordance with conditions laid down in the law of that Party, the contact details of a user in the context of the supply of goods or services, to send direct marketing communications to that user for their own similar goods or services.
4. Each Party shall ensure that direct marketing communications are clearly identifiable as such, clearly disclose on whose behalf they are made and contain the necessary information to enable users to request cessation free of charge and at any moment.
5. Each Party shall provide users with access to redress against suppliers of direct marketing communications that do not comply with the measures adopted or maintained pursuant to paragraphs 1 to 4.

Article DIGIT.15 Open government data

1. The Parties recognise that facilitating public access to, and use of, government data contributes to stimulating economic and social development, competitiveness, productivity and innovation.
2. To the extent that a Party chooses to make government data accessible to the public, it shall endeavour to ensure, to the extent practicable, that the data:

    (a)   is in a format that allows it to be easily searched, retrieved, used, reused, and redistributed;

    (b)   is in a machine-readable and spatially-enabled format;

    (c)   contains descriptive metadata, which is as standard as possible;

    (d)   is made available via reliable, user-friendly and freely available Application Programming Interfaces;

    (e)   is regularly updated;

    (f)   is not subject to use conditions that are discriminatory or that unnecessarily restrict re-use; and

    (g)   is made available for re-use in full compliance with the Parties' respective personal data protection rules.

3. The Parties shall endeavour to cooperate to identify ways in which each Party can expand access to, and use of, government data that the Party has made public, with a view to enhancing and generating business opportunities, beyond its use by the public sector.

Article DIGIT.16 Cooperation on regulatory issues with regard to digital trade

1. The Parties shall exchange information on regulatory matters in the context of digital trade, which shall address the following:

    (a)   the recognition and facilitation of interoperable electronic trust and authentication services;

    (b)   the treatment of direct marketing communications;

    (c)   the protection of consumers; and

    (d)   any other matter relevant for the development of digital trade, including emerging technologies.

2. Paragraph 1 shall not apply to a Party's rules and safeguards for the protection of personal data and privacy, including on cross-border transfers of personal data.

Article DIGIT.17 - Understanding on computer services

1. The Parties agree that, for the purpose of liberalising trade in services and investment in accordance with Title II [Services and Investment] of this Heading, the following services shall be considered as computer and related services, regardless of whether they are delivered via a network, including the Internet:

    (a)   consulting, adaptation, strategy, analysis, planning, specification, design, development, installation, implementation, integration, testing, debugging, updating, support, technical assistance or management of or for computers or computer systems;

(b) computer programmes defined as the sets of instructions required to make computers work and communicate (in and of themselves), as well as consulting, strategy, analysis, planning, specification, design, development, installation, implementation, integration, testing, debugging, updating, adaptation, maintenance, support, technical assistance, management or use of or for computer programmes;

(c) data processing, data storage, data hosting or database services;

(d) maintenance and repair services for office machinery and equipment, including computers; and

(e) training services for staff of clients, related to computer programmes, computers or computer systems, and not elsewhere classified.

For greater certainty, services enabled by computer and related services, other than those listed in paragraph 1, shall not be regarded as computer and related services in themselves.

NOTES

34 For greater certainty, "conditions of general application" refer to conditions formulated in objective terms that apply horizontally to an unidentified number of economic operators and thus cover a range of situations and cases.

PART THREE:
LAW ENFORCEMENT AND JUDICIAL COOPERATION IN CRIMINAL MATTERS

TITLE I: GENERAL PROVISIONS

[7.90]
Article LAW.GEN.1: Objective

1. The objective of this Part is to provide for law enforcement and judicial cooperation between the Member States and Union institutions, bodies, offices and agencies, on the one side, and the United Kingdom, on the other side, in relation to the prevention, investigation, detection and prosecution of criminal offences and the prevention of and fight against money laundering and financing of terrorism.

2. This Part only applies to law enforcement and judicial cooperation in criminal matters taking place exclusively between the United Kingdom, on the one side, and the Union and the Member States, on the other side. It does not apply to situations arising between the Member States, or between Member States and Union institutions, bodies, offices and agencies, nor does it apply to the activities of authorities with responsibilities for safeguarding national security when acting in that field.

Article LAW.GEN.2: Definitions

For the purposes of this Part, the following definitions apply:

(a) "third country" means a country other than a State;

(b) "special categories of personal data" means personal data revealing racial or ethnic origin, political opinions, religious or philosophical beliefs, or trade union membership, genetic data, biometric data processed for the purpose of uniquely identifying a natural person, data concerning health or data concerning a natural person's sex life or sexual orientation;

(c) "genetic data" means all personal data relating to the genetic characteristics of an individual that have been inherited or acquired, which give unique information about the physiology or the health of that individual, resulting in particular from an analysis of a biological sample from the individual in question;

(d) "biometric data" means personal data resulting from specific technical processing relating to the physical, physiological or behavioural characteristics of a natural person which allow or confirm the unique identification of that natural person, such as facial images or dactyloscopic data;

(e) "processing" means any operation or set of operations which is performed on personal data or on sets of personal data, whether or not by automated means, such as collection, recording, organisation, structuring, storage, adaptation or alteration, retrieval, consultation, use, disclosure by transmission, dissemination or otherwise making available, alignment or combination, restriction, erasure or destruction;

(f) "personal data breach" means a breach of security leading to the accidental or unlawful destruction, loss, alteration, unauthorised disclosure of, or access to, personal data transmitted, stored or otherwise processed;

(g) "filing system" means any structured set of personal data which are accessible according to specific criteria, whether centralised, decentralised or dispersed on a functional or geographical basis;

(h) "Specialised Committee on Law Enforcement and Judicial Cooperation" means the Committee by that name established by Article INST.2 [Committees].

Article LAW.GEN.3: Protection of human rights and fundamental freedoms

1. The cooperation provided for in this Part is based on the Parties' and Member States' long-standing respect for democracy, the rule of law and the protection of fundamental rights and freedoms of individuals, including as set out in the Universal Declaration of Human Rights and in the European Convention on Human Rights, and on the importance of giving effect to the rights and freedoms in that Convention domestically.

2. Nothing in this Part modifies the obligation to respect fundamental rights and legal principles as reflected, in particular, in the European Convention on Human Rights and, in the case of the Union and its Member States, in the Charter of Fundamental Rights of the European Union.

Article LAW.GEN.4: Protection of personal data

8. The cooperation provided for in this Part is based on the Parties' long-standing commitment to ensuring a high level of protection of personal data.

9. To reflect that high level of protection, the Parties shall ensure that personal data processed under this Part is subject to effective safeguards in the Parties' respective data protection regimes, including that:

   (a) personal data is processed lawfully and fairly in compliance with the principles of data minimisation, purpose limitation, accuracy and storage limitation;

   (b) processing of special categories of personal data is only permitted to the extent necessary and subject to appropriate safeguards adapted to the specific risks of the processing;

   (c) a level of security appropriate to the risk of the processing is ensured through relevant technical and organisational measures, in particular as regards the processing of special categories of personal data;

   (d) data subjects are granted enforceable rights of access, rectification and erasure, subject to possible restrictions provided for by law which constitute necessary and proportionate measures in a democratic society to protect important objectives of public interest;

   (e) in the event of a data breach creating a risk to the rights and freedoms of natural persons, the competent supervisory authority is notified without undue delay of the breach; where the breach is likely to result in a high risk to the rights and freedoms of natural persons, the data subjects are also notified, subject to possible restrictions provided for by law which constitute necessary and proportionate measures in a democratic society to protect important objectives of public interest;

   (f) onward transfers to a third country are allowed only subject to conditions and safeguards appropriate to the transfer ensuring that the level of protection is not undermined;

   (g) the supervision of compliance with data protection safeguards and the enforcement of data protection safeguards are ensured by independent authorities; and

   (h) data subjects are granted enforceable rights to effective administrative and judicial redress in the event that data protection safeguards have been violated.

10. The United Kingdom, on the one side, and the Union, also on behalf of any of its Member States, on the other side, shall notify the Specialised Committee on Law Enforcement and Judicial Cooperation of the supervisory authorities responsible for overseeing the implementation of, and ensuring compliance with, data protection rules applicable to cooperation under this Part. The supervisory authorities shall cooperate to ensure compliance with this Part.

11. The provisions on the protection of personal data set out in this Part apply to the processing of personal data wholly or partly by automated means, and to the processing other than by automated means of personal data which form part of a filing system or are intended to form part of a filing system.

12. This Article is without prejudice to the application of any specific provisions in this Part relating to the processing of personal data.

Article LAW.GEN.5: Scope of cooperation where a Member State no longer participates in analogous measures under Union law

1. This Article applies if a Member State ceases to participate in, or enjoy rights under, provisions of Union law relating to law enforcement and judicial cooperation in criminal matters analogous to any of the relevant provisions of this Part.

2. The United Kingdom may notify the Union in writing of its intention to cease to operate the relevant provisions of this Part in relation to that Member State.

3. A notification given under paragraph 2 takes effect on the date specified therein, which shall be no earlier than the date on which the Member State ceases to participate in, or to enjoy rights under, the provisions of Union law referred to in paragraph 1.

4. If the United Kingdom gives notification under this Article of its intention to cease to apply the relevant provisions of this Part, the Specialised Committee on Law Enforcement and Judicial Cooperation shall meet to decide what measures are needed to ensure that any cooperation initiated under this Part that is affected by the cessation is concluded in an appropriate manner. In any event, with regard to all personal data obtained through cooperation under the relevant provisions of this Part before they cease to be applied, the Parties shall ensure that the level of protection under which the personal data were transferred is maintained after the cessation takes effect.

5. The Union shall notify the United Kingdom in writing, through diplomatic channels, of the date on which the Member State is to resume its participation in, or the enjoyment of rights under, the provisions of Union law in question. The application of the relevant provisions of this Part shall be reinstated on that date or, if later, on the first day of the month following the day on which that notification has been given.

6. To facilitate the application of this Article, the Union shall inform the United Kingdom when a Member State ceases to participate in, or enjoy rights under, provisions of Union law relating to law enforcement and judicial cooperation in criminal matters analogous to the relevant provisions of this Part.

TITLE II: EXCHANGES OF DNA, FINGERPRINTS AND VEHICLE REGISTRATION DATA

[7.91]
Article LAW.PRUM.5: Objective
The objective of this Title is to establish reciprocal cooperation between the competent law enforcement authorities of the United Kingdom, on the one side, and the Member States, on the other side, on the automated transfer of DNA profiles, dactyloscopic data and certain domestic vehicle registration data.

Article LAW.PRUM.6: Definitions
For the purposes of this Title, the following definitions apply:

   (a) "competent law enforcement authority" means a domestic police, customs or other authority that is authorised by domestic law to detect, prevent and investigate offences or criminal activities and to exercise authority and take coercive measures in the context of such activities; agencies, bodies or other units dealing especially with national security issues are not competent law enforcement authorities for the purposes of this Title;

   (b) "search" and "comparison", as referred to in Articles LAW.PRUM.8 [Automated searching of DNA profiles], LAW.PRUM.9 [Automated comparison of DNA profiles], LAW.PRUM.12 [Automated searching of dactyloscopic data], and LAW.PRUM.17 [Implementing measures] mean the procedures by which it is established whether there is a match between, respectively, DNA data or dactyloscopic data which have been communicated by one State and DNA data or dactyloscopic data stored in the databases of one, several, or all of the other States;

(c) "automated searching", as referred to in Article LAW.PRUM.15 [Automated searching of vehicle registration data], means an online access procedure for consulting the databases of one, several, or all of the other States;

(d) "non-coding part of DNA" means chromosome regions not genetically expressed, i.e. not known to provide for any functional properties of an organism;

(e) "DNA profile" means a letter or numeric code which represents a set of identification characteristics of the non-coding part of an analysed human DNA sample, i.e. the particular molecular structure at the various DNA locations (loci);

(f) "DNA reference data" means DNA profile and reference number; DNA reference data shall only include DNA profiles established from the non-coding part of DNA and a reference number; DNA reference data shall not contain any data from which the data subject can be directly identified; DNA reference data which is not attributed to any natural person (unidentified DNA profiles) shall be recognisable as such;

(g) "reference DNA profile" means the DNA profile of an identified person;

(h) "unidentified DNA profile" means the DNA profile obtained from traces collected during the investigation of criminal offences and belonging to a person not yet identified;

(i) "note" means a State's marking on a DNA profile in its domestic database indicating that there has already been a match for that DNA profile on another State's search or comparison;

(j) "dactyloscopic data" means fingerprint images, images of fingerprint latents, palm prints, palm print latents and templates of such images (coded minutiae), when they are stored and dealt with in an automated database;

(k) "dactyloscopic reference data" means dactyloscopic data and reference number; dactyloscopic reference data shall not contain any data from which the data subject can be directly identified; dactyloscopic reference data which is not attributed to any natural person (unidentified dactyloscopic data) shall be recognisable as such;

(l) "vehicle registration data" means the data-set as specified in Chapter 3 of ANNEX LAW-1;

(m) "individual case", as referred to in Article LAW.PRUM.8(1) [Automated searching of DNA profiles], second sentence, Article LAW.PRUM.12(1) [Automated searching of dactyloscopic data], second sentence and Article LAW.PRUM.15(1) [Automated searching of vehicle registration data], means a single investigation or prosecution file; if such a file contains more than one DNA profile, or one piece of dactyloscopic data or vehicle registration data, they may be transmitted together as one request;

(n) "laboratory activity" means any measure taken in a laboratory when locating and recovering traces on items, as well as developing, analysing and interpreting forensic evidence regarding DNA profiles and dactyloscopic data, with a view to providing expert opinions or exchanging forensic evidence;

(o) "results of laboratory activities" means any analytical outputs and directly associated interpretation;

(p) "forensic service provider" means any organisation, public or private, that carries out laboratory activities at the request of competent law enforcement or judicial authorities;

(q) "domestic accreditation body" means the sole body in a State that performs accreditation with authority derived from the State.

Article LAW.PRUM.7: Establishment of domestic DNA analysis files
1. The States shall open and keep domestic DNA analysis files for the investigation of criminal offences.
2. For the purpose of implementing this Title, the States shall ensure the availability of DNA reference data from their domestic DNA analysis files as referred to in paragraph 1.
3. The States shall declare the domestic DNA analysis files to which Articles LAW.PRUM.7 [Establishment of domestic DNA analysis files] to LAW.PRUM.10 [Collection of cellular material and supply of DNA profiles] and Articles LAW.PRUM.13 [National contact points], LAW.PRUM.14 [Supply of further personal data and other information] and LAW.PRUM. 17 [Implementing measures] apply and the conditions for automated searching as referred to in Article LAW.PRUM.8(1) [Automated searching of DNA profiles].

Article LAW.PRUM.8: Automated searching of DNA profiles
1. For the investigation of criminal offences, States shall allow other States' national contact points as referred to in Article LAW.PRUM.13 [National contact points] access to the DNA reference data in their DNA analysis files, with the power to conduct automated searches by comparing DNA profiles. Searches may be conducted only in individual cases and in compliance with the requesting State's domestic law.
2. If an automated search shows that a DNA profile supplied matches DNA profiles entered in the requested State's searched file, the requested State shall send to the national contact point of the requesting State in an automated way the DNA reference data with which a match has been found. If no match can be found, this shall be notified automatically.

Article LAW.PRUM.9: Automated comparison of DNA profiles
1. For the investigation of criminal offences, the States, via their national contact points, shall compare the DNA profiles of their unidentified DNA profiles with all DNA profiles from other domestic DNA analysis files' reference data in accordance with mutually accepted practical arrangements between the States concerned. DNA profiles shall be supplied and compared in automated form. Unidentified DNA profiles shall be supplied for comparison only where provided for under the requesting State's domestic law.
2. If a State, as a result of the comparison referred to in paragraph 1, finds that any DNA profiles supplied by another State match any of those in its DNA analysis files, it shall supply that other State's national contact point with the DNA reference data with which a match has been found without delay.

Article LAW.PRUM.10: Collection of cellular material and supply of DNA profiles
Where, in ongoing investigations or criminal proceedings, there is no DNA profile available for a particular individual present within a requested State's territory, the requested State shall provide legal assistance by collecting and examining cellular material from that individual and by supplying the DNA profile obtained to the requesting State, if:
    (a) the requesting State specifies the purpose for which it is required;
    (b) the requesting State produces an investigation warrant or statement issued by the competent authority, as required under that State's domestic law, showing that the requirements for collecting and examining cellular material would be fulfilled if the individual concerned were present within the requesting State's territory; and
    (c) under the requested State's law, the requirements for collecting and examining cellular material and for supplying the DNA profile obtained are fulfilled.

Article LAW.PRUM.11: Dactyloscopic data
For the purpose of implementing this Title, the States shall ensure the availability of dactyloscopic reference data from the file for the domestic automated fingerprint identification systems established for the prevention and investigation of criminal offences.

Article LAW.PRUM.12: Automated searching of dactyloscopic data
1. For the prevention and investigation of criminal offences, States shall allow other States' national contact points, as referred to in Article LAW.PRUM.13 [National contact points], access to the reference data in the automated fingerprint identification systems which they have established for that purpose, with the power to conduct automated searches by comparing dactyloscopic data. Searches may be conducted only in individual cases and in compliance with the requesting State's domestic law.
2. The confirmation of a match of dactyloscopic data with reference data held by the requested State shall be carried out by the national contact point of the requesting State by means of the automated supply of the reference data required for a clear match.

Article LAW.PRUM.13: National contact points
1. For the purposes of the supply of data as referred to in Articles LAW.PRUM.8 [Automated searching of DNA profiles], LAW.PRUM.9 [Automated comparison of DNA profiles] and LAW.PRUM.12 [Automated searching of dactyloscopic data], the States shall designate national contact points.
2. In respect of the Member States, national contact points designated for an analogous exchange of data within the Union shall be considered as national contact points for the purpose of this Title.
3. The powers of the national contact points shall be governed by the applicable domestic law.

Article LAW.PRUM.14: Supply of further personal data and other information
If the procedure referred to in Articles LAW.PRUM.8 [Automated searching of DNA profiles], LAW.PRUM.9 [Automated comparison of DNA profiles] and LAW.PRUM.12 [Automated searching of dactyloscopic data] show a match between DNA profiles or dactyloscopic data, the supply of further available personal data and other information relating to the reference data shall be governed by the domestic law, including the legal assistance rules, of the requested State, without prejudice to Article LAW.PRUM.17(1) [Implementing measures].

Article LAW.PRUM.15: Automated searching of vehicle registration data
1. For the prevention and investigation of criminal offences and in dealing with other offences within the jurisdiction of the courts or a public prosecutor in the requesting State, as well as in maintaining public security, States shall allow other States' national contact points, as referred to in paragraph 2, access to the following domestic vehicle registration data, with the power to conduct automated searches in individual cases:
    (a) data relating to owners or operators; and
    (b) data relating to vehicles.
2. Searches may be conducted under paragraph 1 only with a full chassis number or a full registration number and in compliance with the requesting State's domestic law.
3. For the purposes of the supply of data as referred to in paragraph 1, the States shall designate a national contact point for incoming requests from other States. The powers of the national contact points shall be governed by the applicable domestic law.

Article LAW.PRUM.16: Accreditation of forensic service providers carrying out laboratory activities
1. The States shall ensure that their forensic service providers carrying out laboratory activities are accredited by a domestic accreditation body as complying with EN ISO/IEC 17025.
2. Each State shall ensure that the results of accredited forensic service providers carrying out laboratory activities in other States are recognised by its authorities responsible for the prevention, detection, and investigation of criminal offences as being equally reliable as the results of domestic forensic service providers carrying out laboratory activities accredited to EN ISO/IEC 17025.
3. The competent law enforcement authorities of the United Kingdom shall not carry out searches and automated comparison in accordance with Articles LAW.PRUM.8 [Automated searching of DNA profiles], LAW.PRUM.9 [Automated comparison of DNA profiles] and LAW.PRUM.12 [Automated searching of dactyloscopic data] before the United Kingdom has implemented and applied the measures referred to in paragraph 1 of this Article.
4. Paragraphs 1 and 2 do not affect domestic rules on the judicial assessment of evidence.
5. The United Kingdom shall communicate to the Specialised Committee on Law Enforcement and Judicial Cooperation the text of the main provisions adopted to implement and apply the provisions of this Article.

Part 7   Key Brexit Materials

Article LAW.PRUM.17: Implementing measures
1. For the purposes of this Title, States shall make all categories of data available for searching and comparison to the competent law enforcement authorities of other States under conditions equal to those under which they are available for searching and comparison by domestic competent law enforcement authorities. States shall supply further available personal data and other information relating to the reference data as referred to in Article LAW.PRUM.14 [Supply of further personal data and other information] to the competent law enforcement authorities of other States for the purposes of this Title under conditions equal to those under which they would be supplied to domestic authorities.
2. For the purpose of implementing the procedures referred to in Articles LAW.PRUM.8 [Automated searching of DNA profiles], LAW.PRUM.9 [Automated comparison of DNA profiles], LAW.PRUM.12 [Automated searching of dactyloscopic data] and LAW.PRUM.15 [Automated searching of vehicle registration data], technical and procedural specifications are laid down in ANNEX LAW-1.
3. The declarations made by Member States in accordance with Council Decisions 2008/615/JHA[77] and 2008/616/JHA[78] shall also apply in their relations with the United Kingdom.

Article LAW.PRUM.18: Ex ante evaluation
1. In order to verify whether the United Kingdom has fulfilled the conditions set out in Article LAW.PRUM.17 [Implementing measures] and ANNEX LAW-1, an evaluation visit and a pilot run, to the extent required by ANNEX LAW-1, shall be carried out in respect of, and under conditions and arrangements acceptable to, the United Kingdom. In any event, a pilot run shall be carried out in relation to the searching of data under Article LAW.PRUM.15 [Automated searching of vehicle registration data].
2. On the basis of an overall evaluation report on the evaluation visit and, where applicable, the pilot run, as referred to in paragraph 1, the Union shall determine the date or dates from which personal data may be supplied by Member States to the United Kingdom pursuant to this Title.
3. Pending the outcome of the evaluation referred to in paragraph 1, from the date of the entry into force of this Agreement, Member States may supply to the United Kingdom personal data as referred to in Articles LAW.PRUM.8 [Automated searching of DNA profiles], LAW.PRUM.9 [Automated comparison of DNA profiles], LAW.PRUM.12 [Automated searching of dactyloscopic data] and LAW.PRUM.14 [Supply of further personal data and other information] until the date or dates determined by the Union in accordance with paragraph 2 of this Article, but not longer than nine months after the entry into force of this Agreement. The Specialised Committee on Law Enforcement and Judicial Cooperation may extend this period once by a maximum of nine months.

Article LAW.PRUM.19: Suspension and disapplication
1. In the event that the Union considers it necessary to amend this Title because Union law relating to the subject matter governed by this Title is amended substantially, or is in the process of being amended substantially, it may notify the United Kingdom accordingly with a view to agreeing on a formal amendment of this Agreement in relation to this Title. Following such notification, the Parties shall engage in consultations.
2. Where within nine months of that notification the Parties have not reached an agreement amending this Title, the Union may decide to suspend the application of this Title or any provisions of this Title for a period of up to nine months. Before the end of that period, the Parties may agree on an extension of the suspension for an additional period of up to nine months. If by the end of the suspension period the Parties have not reached an agreement amending this Title, the suspended provisions shall cease to apply on the first day of the month following the expiry of the suspension period, unless the Union informs the United Kingdom that it no longer seeks any amendment to this Title. In that case, the suspended provisions of this Title shall be reinstated.
3. If any of the provisions of this Title are suspended under this Article, the Specialised Committee on Law Enforcement and Judicial Cooperation shall meet to decide what steps are needed to ensure that any cooperation initiated under this Title and affected by the suspension is concluded in an appropriate manner. In any event, with regard to all personal data obtained through cooperation under this Title before the provisions concerned by the suspension provisionally cease to apply, the Parties shall ensure that the level of protection under which the personal data were transferred is maintained after the suspension takes effect.

TITLE III: TRANSFER AND PROCESSING OF PASSENGER NAME RECORD DATA

[7.92]
Article LAW.PNR.18: Scope
1. This Title lays down rules under which passenger name record data may be transferred to, processed and used by the United Kingdom competent authority for flights between the Union and the United Kingdom, and establishes specific safeguards in that regard.
2. This Title applies to air carriers operating passenger flights between the Union and the United Kingdom.
3. This Title also applies to air carriers incorporated, or storing data, in the Union and operating passenger flights to or from the United Kingdom.
4. This Title also provides for police and judicial cooperation in criminal matters between the United Kingdom and the Union in respect of PNR data.

Article LAW.PNR.19: Definitions
For the purposes of this Title, the following definitions apply:
  (a) "air carrier" means an air transport undertaking with a valid operating licence or equivalent permitting it to carry out carriage of passengers by air between the United Kingdom and the Union;
  (b) "passenger name record" ("PNR") means a record of each passenger's travel requirements which contains information necessary to enable reservations to be processed and controlled by the booking and participating

air carriers for each journey booked by or on behalf of any person, whether it is contained in reservation systems, departure control systems used to check passengers into flights, or equivalent systems providing the same functionalities; specifically, as used in this Title, PNR data consists of the elements set out in ANNEX LAW-2;

(c) "United Kingdom competent authority" means the United Kingdom authority responsible for receiving and processing PNR data under this Agreement; if the United Kingdom has more than one competent authority it shall provide a passenger data single window facility that allows air carriers to transfer PNR data to a single data transmission entry point and shall designate a single point of contact for the purpose of receiving and making requests under Article LAW.PNR.22 [Police and judicial Cooperation];

(d) "Passenger Information Units" ("PIUs") means the Units established or designated by Member States that are responsible for receiving and processing PNR data;

(e) "terrorism" means any offence listed in ANNEX LAW-7;

(f) "serious crime" means any offence punishable by a custodial sentence or detention order for a maximum period of at least three years under the domestic law of the United Kingdom.

Article LAW.PNR.20: Purposes of the use of PNR data

1. The United Kingdom shall ensure that PNR data received pursuant to this Title is processed strictly for the purposes of preventing, detecting, investigating or prosecuting terrorism or serious crime and for the purposes of overseeing the processing of PNR data within the terms set out in this Agreement.

2. In exceptional cases, the United Kingdom competent authority may process PNR data where necessary to protect the vital interests of any natural person, such as:

(a) a risk of death or serious injury; or

(b) a significant public health risk, in particular as identified under internationally recognised standards.

3. The United Kingdom competent authority may also process PNR data on a case-by-case basis where the disclosure of relevant PNR data is compelled by a United Kingdom court or administrative tribunal in a proceeding directly related to any of the purposes referred to in paragraph 1.

Article LAW.PNR.21: Ensuring PNR data is provided

1. The Union shall ensure that air carriers are not prevented from transferring PNR data to the United Kingdom competent authority pursuant to this Title.

2. The Union shall ensure that air carriers may transfer PNR data to the United Kingdom competent authority through authorised agents, who act on behalf of and under the responsibility of an air carrier, pursuant to this Title.

3. The United Kingdom shall not require an air carrier to provide elements of PNR data which are not already collected or held by the air carrier for reservation purposes.

4. The United Kingdom shall delete any data transferred to it by an air carrier pursuant to this Title upon receipt of that data, if that data element is not listed in ANNEX LAW-2.

Article LAW.PNR.22: Police and judicial cooperation

1. The United Kingdom competent authority shall share with Europol or Eurojust, within the scope of their respective mandates, or with the PIUs of the Member States all relevant and appropriate analytical information containing PNR data as soon as possible in specific cases where necessary to prevent, detect, investigate, or prosecute terrorism or serious crime.

2. At the request of Europol or Eurojust, within the scope of their respective mandates, or of the PIU of a Member State, the United Kingdom competent authority shall share PNR data, the results of processing those data, or analytical information containing PNR data, in specific cases where necessary to prevent, detect, investigate, or prosecute terrorism or serious crime.

3. The PIUs of the Member States shall share with the United Kingdom competent authority all relevant and appropriate analytical information containing PNR data as soon as possible in specific cases where necessary to prevent, detect, investigate, or prosecute terrorism or serious crime.

4. At the request of the United Kingdom competent authority, the PIUs of the Member States shall share PNR data, the results of processing those data, or analytical information containing PNR data, in specific cases where necessary to prevent, detect, investigate, or prosecute terrorism or serious crime.

5. The Parties shall ensure that the information referred to in paragraphs 1 to 4 is shared in accordance with agreements and arrangements on law enforcement or information sharing between the United Kingdom and Europol, Eurojust, or the relevant Member State. In particular, the exchange of information with Europol under this Article shall take place through the secure communication line established for the exchange of information through Europol.

6. The United Kingdom competent authority and the PIUs of the Member States shall ensure that only the minimum amount of PNR data necessary is shared under paragraphs 1 to 4.

Article LAW.PNR.23: Non-discrimination

The United Kingdom shall ensure that the safeguards applicable to the processing of PNR data apply to all natural persons on an equal basis without unlawful discrimination.

Article LAW.PNR.24: Use of special categories of personal data

Any processing of special categories of personal data shall be prohibited under this Title. To the extent that any PNR data which is transferred to the United Kingdom competent authority includes special categories of personal data, the United Kingdom competent authority shall delete such data.

Article LAW.PNR.25: Data security and integrity
1. The United Kingdom shall implement regulatory, procedural or technical measures to protect PNR data against accidental, unlawful or unauthorised access, processing or loss.
2. The United Kingdom shall ensure compliance verification and the protection, security, confidentiality, and integrity of the data. In that regard, the United Kingdom shall:
   (a) apply encryption, authorisation, and documentation procedures to the PNR data;
   (b) limit access to PNR data to authorised officials;
   (c) hold PNR data in a secure physical environment that is protected with access controls; and
   (d) establish a mechanism that ensures that PNR data queries are conducted in a manner consistent with Article LAW.PNR.20 [Purposes of the use of PNR data].
3. If a natural person's PNR data is accessed or disclosed without authorisation, the United Kingdom shall take measures to notify that natural person, to mitigate the risk of harm, and to take remedial action.
4. The United Kingdom competent authority shall promptly inform the Specialised Committee on Law Enforcement and Judicial Cooperation of any significant incident of accidental, unlawful or unauthorised access, processing or loss of PNR data.
5. The United Kingdom shall ensure that any breach of data security, in particular any breach leading to accidental or unlawful destruction or accidental loss, alteration, unauthorised disclosure or access, or any unlawful forms of processing, are subject to effective and dissuasive corrective measures which may include sanctions.

Article LAW.PNR.26: Transparency and notification of passengers
1. The United Kingdom competent authority shall make the following available on its website:
   (a) a list of the legislation authorising the collection of PNR data;
   (b) the purposes for the collection of PNR data;
   (c) the manner of protecting PNR data;
   (d) the manner and extent to which PNR data may be disclosed;
   (e) information regarding the rights of access, correction, notation and redress; and
   (f) contact information for inquiries.
2. The Parties shall work with interested third parties, such as the aviation and air travel industry, to promote transparency at the time of booking regarding the purpose of the collection, processing and use of PNR data, and regarding how to request access, correction and redress. Air carriers shall provide passengers with clear and meaningful information in relation to the transfer of PNR data under this Title, including the details of the recipient authority, the purpose of the transfer and the right to request from the recipient authority, access to and correction of the personal data of the passenger that has been transferred.
3. Where PNR data retained in accordance with Article LAW.PNR.28 [Retention of PNR data] has been used subject to the conditions set out in Article LAW.PNR.29 [Conditions for the use of PNR data] or has been disclosed in accordance with Article LAW.PNR.31 [Disclosure within the United Kingdom] or Article LAW.PNR.32 [Disclosure outside the United Kingdom], the United Kingdom shall notify the passengers concerned in writing, individually and within a reasonable time once such notification is no longer liable to jeopardise the investigations by the public authorities concerned to the extent that the relevant contact information of the passengers is available or can be retrieved, taking into account reasonable efforts. The notification shall include information on how the natural person concerned can seek administrative or judicial redress.

Article LAW.PNR.27: Automated processing of PNR data
1. The United Kingdom competent authority shall ensure that any automated processing of PNR data is based on non-discriminatory, specific and reliable pre-established models and criteria to enable it to:
   (a) arrive at results targeting natural persons who might be under a reasonable suspicion of involvement or participation in terrorism or serious crime; or
   (b) in exceptional circumstances, protect the vital interests of any natural person as set out in Article LAW.PNR.20(2) [Purposes of the use of PNR data].
2. The United Kingdom competent authority shall ensure that the databases against which PNR data are compared are reliable, up to date and limited to those databases it uses in relation to the purposes set out in Article LAW.PNR.20 [Purposes of the use of PNR data].
3. The United Kingdom shall not take any decision adversely affecting a natural person in a significant manner solely on the basis of automated processing of PNR data.

Article LAW.PNR.28: Retention of PNR data
1. The United Kingdom shall not retain PNR data for more than five years from the date that it receives the PNR data.
2. No later than six months after the transfer of the PNR data referred to in paragraph 1, all PNR data shall be depersonalised by masking out the following data elements which could serve to identify directly the passenger to whom the PNR data relate or any other natural person:
   (a) names, including the names of other passengers on the PNR and number of passengers on the PNR travelling together;
   (b) addresses, telephone numbers and electronic contact information of the passenger, the persons who made the flight reservation for the passenger, persons through whom the air passenger may be contacted and persons who are to be informed in the event of an emergency;
   (c) all available payment and billing information, to the extent that it contains any information which could serve to identify a natural person;
   (d) frequent flyer information;

(e)   other supplementary information (OSI), special service information (SSI) and special service request (SSR) information, to the extent that they contain any information which could serve to identify a natural person; and

(f)   any advance passenger information (API) data that have been collected.

3. The United Kingdom competent authority may unmask PNR data only if it is necessary to carry out investigations for the purposes set out in Article LAW.PNR.20 [Purposes of the use of PNR data]. Such unmasked PNR data shall be accessible only to a limited number of specifically authorised officials.

4. Notwithstanding paragraph 1, the United Kingdom shall delete the PNR data of passengers after their departure from the country unless a risk assessment indicates the need to retain such PNR data. In order to establish that need, the United Kingdom shall identify objective evidence from which it may be inferred that certain passengers present the existence of a risk in terms of the fight against terrorism and serious crime.

5. For the purposes of paragraph 4, unless information is available on the exact date of departure, the date of departure should be considered as the last day of the period of maximum lawful stay in the United Kingdom of the passenger concerned.

6. The use of the data retained under this Article is subject to the conditions laid down in Article LAW.PNR.29 [Conditions for the use of PNR].

7. An independent administrative body in the United Kingdom shall assess on a yearly basis the approach applied by the United Kingdom competent authority as regards the need to retain PNR data pursuant to paragraph 4.

8. Notwithstanding paragraphs 1, 2 and 4, the United Kingdom may retain PNR data required for any specific action, review, investigation, enforcement action, judicial proceeding, prosecution, or enforcement of penalties, until concluded.

9. The United Kingdom shall delete the PNR data at the end of the PNR data retention period.

10. Paragraph 11 applies due to the special circumstances that prevent the United Kingdom from making the technical adjustments necessary to transform the PNR processing systems which the United Kingdom operated whilst Union law applied to it into systems which would enable PNR data to be deleted in accordance with paragraph 4.

11. The United Kingdom may derogate from paragraph 4 on a temporary basis for an interim period, the duration of which is provided for in paragraph 13, pending the implementation by the United Kingdom of technical adjustments as soon as possible. During the interim period, the United Kingdom competent authority shall prevent the use of the PNR data that is to be deleted in accordance with paragraph 4 by applying the following additional safeguards to that PNR data:

(a)   the PNR data shall be accessible only to a limited number of authorised officials and only where necessary to determine whether the PNR data should be deleted in accordance with paragraph 4;

(b)   the request to use the PNR data shall be refused in cases where the data is to be deleted in accordance with paragraph 4, and no further access shall be granted to that data where the documentation referred to in point (d) of this paragraph indicates that an earlier request for use has been refused;

(c)   deletion of the PNR data shall be ensured as soon as possible using best efforts, taking into account the special circumstances referred to in paragraph 10; and

(d)   the following shall be documented in accordance with Article LAW.PNR.30 [Logging and documenting of PNR data processing], and such documentation shall be made available to the independent administrative body referred to in paragraph 7 of this Article:

     (i)   any requests to use the PNR data;

     (ii)   the date and time of the access to the PNR data for the purpose of assessing whether deletion of the PNR data was required;

     (iii)   that the request to use the PNR data was refused on the basis that the PNR data should have been deleted under paragraph 4, including the date and time of the refusal; and

     (iv)   the date and time of the deletion of the PNR data in accordance with point (c) of this paragraph.

12. The United Kingdom shall provide to the Specialised Committee on Law Enforcement and Judicial Cooperation, nine months after the entry into force of this Agreement and again a year later if the interim period is extended for a further year:

(a)   a report from the independent administrative body referred to in paragraph 7 of this Article, which shall include the opinion of the United Kingdom supervisory authority referred to in Article LAW.GEN.4(3) [Protection of personal data] as to whether the safeguards provided for in paragraph 11 of this Article have been effectively applied; and

(b)   the assessment of the United Kingdom of whether the special circumstances referred to in paragraph 10 of this Article persist, together with a description of the efforts made to transform the PNR processing systems of the United Kingdom into systems which would enable PNR data to be deleted in accordance with paragraph 4 of this Article.

13. The Specialised Committee on Law Enforcement and Judicial Cooperation shall meet within one year of the entry into force of this Agreement to consider the report and assessment provided under paragraph 12. Where the special circumstances referred to in paragraph 10 persist, the Partnership Council shall extend the interim period referred to in paragraph 11 for one year. The Partnership Council shall extend the interim period for one further final year, under the same conditions and following the same procedure as for the first extension where, in addition, substantial progress has been made, although it has not yet been possible to transform the United Kingdom PNR processing systems into systems which would enable PNR data to be deleted in accordance with paragraph 4.

14. If the United Kingdom considers that a refusal by the Partnership Council to grant either of those extensions was not justified, it may suspend this Title with one month's notice.

15. On the third anniversary of the date of entry into force of this Agreement, paragraphs 10 to 14 shall cease to apply.

Article LAW.PNR.29: Conditions for the use of PNR data

1. The United Kingdom competent authority may use PNR data retained in accordance with Article LAW.PNR.28 [Retention of PNR data] for purposes other than security and border control checks, including any disclosure under Article LAW.PNR.31 [Disclosure within the United Kingdom] and Article LAW.PNR.32 [Disclosure outside the United Kingdom], only where new circumstances based on objective grounds indicate that the PNR data of one or more passengers might make an effective contribution to the attainment of the purposes set out in Article LAW.PNR.20 [Purposes of the use of PNR data].

2. Use of PNR data by the United Kingdom competent authority in accordance with paragraph 1 shall be subject to prior review by a court or by an independent administrative body in the United Kingdom based on a reasoned request by the United Kingdom competent authority submitted within the domestic legal framework of procedures for the prevention, detection or prosecution of crime, except:

(a) in cases of validly established urgency; or

(b) for the purpose of verifying the reliability and currency of the pre-established models and criteria on which the automated processing of PNR data is based, or of defining new models and criteria for such processing.

Article LAW.PNR.30: Logging and documenting of PNR data processing

The United Kingdom competent authority shall log and document all processing of PNR data. It shall only use such logging or documentation to:

(a) self-monitor and to verify the lawfulness of data processing;

(b) ensure proper data integrity;

(c) ensure the security of data processing; and

(d) ensure oversight.

Article LAW.PNR.31: Disclosure within the United Kingdom

1. The United Kingdom competent authority shall not disclose PNR data to other public authorities in the United Kingdom unless the following conditions are met:

(a) the PNR data is disclosed to public authorities whose functions are directly related to the purposes set out in Article LAW.PNR.20 [Purposes of the use of PNR data];

(b) the PNR data is disclosed only on a case-by-case basis;

(c) the disclosure is necessary, in the particular circumstances, for the purposes set out in Article LAW.PNR.20 [Purposes of the use of PNR data];

(d) only the minimum amount of PNR data necessary is disclosed;

(e) the receiving public authority affords protection equivalent to the safeguards described in this Title; and

(f) the receiving public authority does not disclose the PNR data to another entity unless the disclosure is authorised by the United Kingdom competent authority in accordance with the conditions laid down in this paragraph.

2. When transferring analytical information containing PNR data obtained under this Title, the safeguards set out in this Article shall apply.

Article LAW.PNR.32: Disclosure outside the United Kingdom

1. The United Kingdom shall ensure that the United Kingdom competent authority does not disclose PNR data to public authorities in third countries unless all the following conditions are met:

(a) the PNR data is disclosed to public authorities whose functions are directly related to the purposes set out in Article LAW.PNR.20 [Purposes of the use of PNR data];

(b) the PNR data is disclosed only on a case-by-case basis;

(c) the PNR data is disclosed only if necessary for the purposes set out in Article LAW.PNR.20 [Purposes of the use of PNR data];

(d) only the minimum amount of PNR data necessary is disclosed; and

(e) the third country to which the PNR data is disclosed has either concluded an agreement with the Union that provides for the protection of personal data comparable to this Agreement or is subject to a decision of the European Commission pursuant to Union law that finds that the third country ensures an adequate level of data protection within the meaning of Union law.

2. As an exception to point (e) of paragraph 1, the United Kingdom competent authority may transfer PNR data to a third country if:

(a) the head of that authority, or a senior official specifically mandated by the head, considers that the disclosure is necessary for the prevention and investigation of a serious and imminent threat to public security or to protect the vital interests of any natural person; and

(b) the third country provides a written assurance, pursuant to an arrangement, agreement or otherwise, that the information shall be protected in line with the safeguards applicable under United Kingdom law to the processing of PNR data received from the Union, including those set out in this Title.

3. A transfer in accordance with paragraph 2 of this Article shall be documented. Such documentation shall be made available to the supervisory authority referred to in Article LAW.GEN.4(3) [Protection of personal data] on request, including the date and time of the transfer, information about the receiving authority, the justification for the transfer and the PNR data transferred.

4. If, in accordance with paragraph 1 or 2, the United Kingdom competent authority discloses PNR data collected under this Title that originates in a Member State, the United Kingdom competent authority shall notify the authorities of that Member State of the disclosure at the earliest appropriate opportunity. The United Kingdom shall make that notification in accordance with agreements or arrangements on law enforcement or information sharing between the United Kingdom and that Member State.

5. When transferring analytical information containing PNR data obtained under this Title, the safeguards set out in this Article shall apply.

Article LAW.PNR.33: Method of transfer

Air carriers shall transfer PNR data to the United Kingdom competent authority exclusively on the basis of the 'push method', a method by which air carriers transfer PNR data into the database of the United Kingdom competent authority, and in accordance with the following procedures to be observed by air carriers, by which they:

(a) transfer PNR data by electronic means in compliance with the technical requirements of the United Kingdom competent authority or, in the case of a technical failure, by any other appropriate means ensuring an appropriate level of data security;

(b) transfer PNR data using a mutually accepted messaging format; and

(c) transfer PNR data in a secure manner using common protocols as required by the United Kingdom competent authority.

Article LAW.PNR.34: Frequency of transfer

1. The United Kingdom competent authority shall require air carriers to transfer the PNR data:

(a) initially from no earlier than 96 hours before the scheduled flight service departure time; and

(b) a maximum number of five times as specified by the United Kingdom competent authority.

2. The United Kingdom competent authority shall permit air carriers to limit the transfer referred to in point (b) of paragraph 1 to updates of the PNR data transferred as referred to in point (a) of that paragraph.

3. The United Kingdom competent authority shall inform air carriers of the specified times for the transfers.

4. In specific cases where there is an indication that additional access to PNR data is necessary to respond to a specific threat related to the purposes set out in Article LAW.PNR.20 [Purposes of the use of PNR data], the United Kingdom competent authority may require an air carrier to provide PNR data prior to, between or after the scheduled transfers. In exercising that discretion, the United Kingdom competent authority shall act judiciously and proportionately, and shall use the method of transfer described in Article LAW.PNR.33 [Method of transfer].

Article LAW.PNR.35: Cooperation

The United Kingdom competent authority and the PIUs of the Member States shall cooperate to pursue the coherence of their PNR data processing regimes in a manner that further enhances the security of individuals in the United Kingdom, the Union and elsewhere.

Article LAW.PNR.36: Non-derogation

This Title shall not be construed as derogating from any obligation between the United Kingdom and Member States or third countries to make or respond to a request under a mutual assistance instrument.

Article LAW.PNR.37: Consultation and review

1. The Parties shall advise each other of any measure that is to be enacted that may affect this Title.

2. When carrying out joint reviews of this Title as referred to in Article LAW.OTHER.135(1) [Review and evaluation], the Parties shall pay particular attention to the necessity and proportionality of processing and retaining PNR data for each of the purposes set out in Article LAW.PNR.20 [Purposes of the use of PNR data]. The joint reviews shall also include an examination of how the United Kingdom competent authority has ensured that the pre-established models, criteria and databases referred to in Article LAW.PNR.27 [Automated processing of PNR data] are reliable, relevant and current, taking into account statistical data.

Article LAW.PNR 38: Suspension of cooperation under this Title

1. In the event that either Party considers that the continued operation of this Title is no longer appropriate, it may notify the other Party accordingly of its intention to suspend the application of this Title. Following such notification, the Parties shall engage in consultations.

2. Where within 6 months of that notification the Parties have not reached a resolution, either Party may decide to suspend the application of this Title for a period of up to 6 months. Before the end of that period, the Parties may agree an extension of the suspension for an additional period of up to 6 months. If by the end of the suspension period the Parties have not reached a resolution with respect to this Title, this Title shall cease to apply on the first day of the month following the expiry of the suspension period, unless the notifying Party informs the other Party that it wishes to withdraw the notification. In that case, the provisions of this Title shall be reinstated.

3. If this Title is suspended under this Article, the Specialised Committee on Law Enforcement and Judicial Cooperation shall meet to decide what steps are needed to ensure that any cooperation initiated under this Title that is affected by the suspension is concluded in an appropriate manner. In any event, with regard to all personal data obtained through cooperation under this Title before the provisions concerned by the suspension provisionally cease to apply, the Parties shall ensure that the level of protection under which the personal data were transferred is maintained after the suspension takes effect.

TITLE IV: COOPERATION ON OPERATIONAL INFORMATION

[7.93]

Article LAW.OPCO.1: Cooperation on Operational Information

1. The objective of this Title is for the Parties to ensure that the competent authorities of the United Kingdom and of the Member States are able to, subject to the conditions of their domestic law and within the scope of their powers, and to the extent that this is not provided for in other Titles of this Part, assist each other through the provision of relevant information for the purposes of:

(a) the prevention, investigation, detection or prosecution of criminal offences;
(b) the execution of criminal penalties;
(c) safeguarding against, and the prevention of, threats to public safety; and
(d) the prevention and combating of money laundering and the financing of terrorism.

2. For the purposes of this Title, a "competent authority" means a domestic police, customs or other authority that is competent under domestic law to undertake activities for the purposes set out in paragraph 1.

3. Information, including information on wanted and missing persons as well as objects, may be requested by a competent authority of the United Kingdom or of a Member State, or provided spontaneously to a competent authority of the United Kingdom or of a Member State. Information may be provided in response to a request or spontaneously, subject to the conditions of the domestic law which applies to the providing competent authority and within the scope of its powers.

4. Information may be requested and provided to the extent that the conditions of the domestic law which applies to the requesting or providing competent authority do not stipulate that the request or provision of information has to be made or channelled via judicial authorities.

5. In urgent cases, the providing competent authority shall respond to a request, or provide information spontaneously, as soon as possible.

6. A competent authority of the requesting State may, in accordance with relevant domestic law, at the time of making the request or at a later point in time, seek consent from the providing State for the information to be used for evidential purposes in proceedings before a judicial authority. The providing State may, subject to the conditions set out in Title VIII [Mutual Legal Assistance] and the conditions of the domestic law which applies to it, consent to the information being used for evidential purposes before a judicial authority in the requesting State. Equally, where information is provided spontaneously, the providing State may consent to the information being used for evidential purposes in proceedings before a judicial authority in the receiving State. Where consent is not given under this paragraph, the information received shall not be used for evidential purposes in proceedings before a judicial authority.

7. The providing competent authority may, under relevant domestic law, impose conditions on the use of the information provided.

8. A competent authority may provide under this Title any type of information which it holds, subject to the conditions of the domestic law which applies to it and within the scope of its powers. This may include information from other sources, only if onward transfer of that information is permitted in the framework under which it was obtained by the providing competent authority.

9. Information may be provided under this Title via any appropriate communication channel, including the secure communication line for the purpose of provision of information through Europol.

10. This Article shall not affect the operation or conclusion of bilateral agreements between the United Kingdom and Member States, provided that the Member States act in compliance with Union law. It shall also not affect any other powers which are available to the competent authorities of the United Kingdom or of the Member States under applicable domestic or international law to provide assistance through the sharing of information for the purposes set out in paragraph 1.

TITLE V: COOPERATION WITH EUROPOL

[7.94]
Article LAW.EUROPOL.46: Objective
The objective of this Title is to establish cooperative relations between Europol and the competent authorities of the United Kingdom in order to support and strengthen the action by the Member States and the United Kingdom, as well as their mutual cooperation in preventing and combating serious crime, terrorism and forms of crime which affect a common interest covered by a Union policy, as referred to in Article LAW.EUROPOL.48 [Forms of crime].

Article LAW.EUROPOL.47: Definitions
For the purposes of this Title, the following definitions apply:
(a) "Europol" means the European Union Agency for Law Enforcement Cooperation, set up under Regulation (EU) 2016/794[79] (the "Europol Regulation");
(b) "competent authority" means, for the Union, Europol and, for the United Kingdom, a domestic law enforcement authority responsible under domestic law for preventing and combating criminal offences;

Article LAW.EUROPOL.48: Forms of crime
1. The cooperation established under this Title relates to the forms of crime within Europol's competence, as listed in ANNEX LAW-3, including related criminal offences.
2. Related criminal offences are criminal offences committed in order to procure the means of committing the forms of crime referred to in paragraph 1, criminal offences committed in order to facilitate or carry out such crimes, and criminal offences committed to ensure impunity for such crimes.
3. Where the list of forms of crime for which Europol is competent under Union law is changed, the Specialised Committee on Law Enforcement and Judicial Cooperation may, upon a proposal from the Union, amend ANNEX LAW-3 accordingly from the date when the change to Europol's competence enters into effect.

Article LAW.EUROPOL.49: Scope of cooperation
The cooperation may, in addition to the exchange of personal data under the conditions laid down in this Title and in accordance with the tasks of Europol as outlined in the Europol Regulation, in particular include:
(a) the exchange of information such as specialist knowledge;
(b) general situation reports;
(c) results of strategic analysis;

(d) information on criminal investigation procedures;
(e) information on crime prevention methods;
(f) participation in training activities; and
(g) the provision of advice and support in individual criminal investigations as well as operational cooperation.

Article LAW.EUROPOL.50: National contact point and liaison officers

1. The United Kingdom shall designate a national contact point to act as the central point of contact between Europol and the competent authorities of the United Kingdom.
2. The exchange of information between Europol and the competent authorities of the United Kingdom shall take place between Europol and the national contact point referred to in paragraph 1. This does not preclude, however, direct exchanges of information between Europol and the competent authorities of the United Kingdom, if considered appropriate by both Europol and the relevant competent authorities.
3. The national contact point shall also be the central point of contact in respect of review, correction and deletion of personal data.
4. To facilitate the cooperation established under this Title, the United Kingdom shall second one or more liaison officers to Europol. Europol may second one or more liaison officers to the United Kingdom.
5. The United Kingdom shall ensure that its liaison officers have speedy and, where technically possible, direct access to the relevant domestic databases of the United Kingdom that are necessary for them to fulfil their tasks.
6. The number of liaison officers, the details of their tasks, their rights and obligations and the costs involved shall be governed by working arrangements concluded between Europol and the competent authorities of the United Kingdom as referred to in Article LAW.EUROPOL.59 [Working and administrative arrangements].
7. Liaison officers from the United Kingdom and representatives of the competent authorities of the United Kingdom may be invited to operational meetings. Member State liaison officers and third-country liaison officers, representatives of competent authorities from the Member States and third countries, Europol staff and other stakeholders may attend meetings organised by the liaison officers or the competent authorities of the United Kingdom.

Article LAW.EUROPOL.51: Exchanges of information

1. Exchanges of information between the competent authorities shall comply with the objective and provisions of this Title. Personal data shall be processed only for the specific purposes referred to in paragraph 2.
2. The competent authorities shall clearly indicate, at the latest at the moment of transferring personal data, the specific purpose or purposes for which the personal data are being transferred. For transfers to Europol, the purpose or purposes of such transfer shall be specified in line with the specific purposes of processing set out in the Europol Regulation. If the transferring competent authority has not done so, the receiving competent authority, in agreement with the transferring authority, shall process the personal data in order to determine their relevance as well as the purpose or purposes for which it is to be further processed. The competent authorities may process personal data for a purpose other than the purpose for which they have been provided only if authorised to do so by the transferring competent authority.
3. The competent authorities receiving the personal data shall give an undertaking stating that such data will be processed only for the purpose for which they were transferred. The personal data shall be deleted as soon as they are no longer necessary for the purpose for which they were transferred.
4. Europol and the competent authorities of the United Kingdom shall determine without undue delay, and in any event no later than six months after receipt of the personal data, if and to what extent those personal data are necessary for the purpose for which they were transferred and inform the transferring authority accordingly.

Article LAW.EUROPOL.52: Restrictions on access to and further use of transferred personal data

1. The transferring competent authority may indicate, at the moment of transferring personal data, any restriction on access thereto or the use to be made thereof, in general or specific terms, including as regards its onward transfer, erasure or destruction after a certain period of time, or its further processing. Where the need for such restrictions becomes apparent after the personal data have been transferred, the transferring competent authority shall inform the receiving competent authority accordingly.
2. The receiving competent authority shall comply with any restriction on access or further use of the personal data indicated by the transferring competent authority as described in paragraph 1.
3. Each Party shall ensure that information transferred under this Title was collected, stored and transferred in accordance with its respective legal framework. Each Party shall ensure, as far as possible, that such information has not been obtained in violation of human rights. Nor shall such information be transferred if, to the extent reasonably foreseeable, it could be used to request, hand down or execute a death penalty or any form of cruel or inhuman treatment.

Article LAW.EUROPOL.53: Different categories of data subjects

1. The transfer of personal data in respect of victims of a criminal offence, witnesses or other persons who can provide information concerning criminal offences, or in respect of persons under the age of 18, shall be prohibited unless such transfer is strictly necessary and proportionate in individual cases for preventing or combating a criminal offence.
2. The United Kingdom and Europol shall each ensure that the processing of personal data under paragraph 1 is subject to additional safeguards, including restrictions on access, additional security measures and limitations on onward transfers.

Article LAW.EUROPOL.54: Facilitation of flow of personal data between the United Kingdom and Europol
In the interest of mutual operational benefits, the Parties shall endeavour to cooperate in the future with a view to ensuring that data exchanges between Europol and the competent authorities of the United Kingdom can take place as quickly as possible, and to consider the incorporation of any new processes and technical developments which might assist with that objective, while taking account of the fact that the United Kingdom is not a Member State.

Article LAW.EUROPOL.55: Assessment of reliability of the source and accuracy of information
1. The competent authorities shall indicate as far as possible, at the latest at the moment of transferring the information, the reliability of the source of the information on the basis of the following criteria:
   (a) where there is no doubt as to the authenticity, trustworthiness and competence of the source, or if the information is provided by a source which has proved to be reliable in all instances;
   (b) where the information is provided by a source which has in most instances proved to be reliable;
   (c) where the information is provided by a source which has in most instances proved to be unreliable;
   (d) where the reliability of the source cannot be assessed.
2. The competent authorities shall indicate as far as possible, at the latest at the moment of transferring the information, the accuracy of the information on the basis of the following criteria:
   (a) information the accuracy of which is not in doubt;
   (b) information known personally to the source but not known personally to the official passing it on;
   (c) information not known personally to the source but corroborated by other information already recorded;
   (d) information not known personally to the source and which cannot be corroborated.
3. Where the receiving competent authority, on the basis of information already in its possession, comes to the conclusion that the assessment of information or of its source supplied by the transferring competent authority in accordance with paragraphs 1 and 2 needs correction, it shall inform that competent authority and shall attempt to agree on an amendment to the assessment. The receiving competent authority shall not change the assessment of information received or of its source without such agreement.
4. If a competent authority receives information without an assessment, it shall attempt as far as possible and where possible in agreement with the transferring competent authority to assess the reliability of the source or the accuracy of the information on the basis of information already in its possession.
5. If no reliable assessment can be made, the information shall be evaluated as provided for in point (d) of paragraph 1 and point (d) of paragraph 2.

Article LAW.EUROPOL.56: Security of the information exchange
1. The technical and organisational measures put in place to ensure the security of the information exchange under this Title shall be laid down in administrative arrangements between Europol and the competent authorities of the United Kingdom as referred to in Article LAW.EUROPOL.59 [Working and administrative arrangements].
2. The Parties agree on the establishment, implementation and operation of a secure communication line for the purpose of the exchange of information between Europol and the competent authorities of the United Kingdom.
3. Administrative arrangements between Europol and the competent authorities of the United Kingdom as referred to in Article LAW.EUROPOL.58 [Exchange of classified and sensitive non-classified information] shall regulate the secure communication line's terms and conditions of use.

Article LAW.EUROPOL.57: Liability for unauthorised or incorrect personal data processing
1. The competent authorities shall be liable, in accordance with their respective legal frameworks, for any damage caused to an individual as a result of legal or factual errors in information exchanged. In order to avoid liability under their respective legal frameworks vis-à-vis an injured party, neither Europol nor the competent authorities of the United Kingdom may plead that the other competent authority had transferred inaccurate information.
2. If damages are awarded either against Europol or against the competent authorities of the United Kingdom because of the use by either of them of information which was erroneously communicated by the other, or communicated as a result of a failure on the part of the other to comply with their obligations, the amount paid as compensation under paragraph 1 either by Europol or by the competent authorities of the United Kingdom shall be repaid by the other, unless the information was used in breach of this Title.
3. Europol and the competent authorities of the United Kingdom shall not require each other to pay for punitive or non-compensatory damages under paragraphs 1 and 2.

Article LAW.EUROPOL.58: Exchange of classified and sensitive non-classified information
The exchange and protection of classified and sensitive non-classified information, if necessary under this Title, shall be regulated in working and administrative arrangements as referred to in Article LAW.EUROPOL.59 [Working and administrative arrangements] between Europol and the competent authorities of the United Kingdom.

Article LAW.EUROPOL.59: Working and administrative arrangements
1. The details of cooperation between the United Kingdom and Europol, as appropriate to complement and implement the provisions of this Title, shall be the subject of working arrangements in accordance with Article 23(4) of the Europol Regulation and administrative arrangements in accordance with Article 25(1) of the Europol Regulation concluded between Europol and the competent authorities of the United Kingdom.
2. Without prejudice to any provision in this Title and while reflecting the status of the United Kingdom as not being a Member State, Europol and the competent authorities of the United Kingdom shall, subject to a decision by Europol's Management Board, include, in working arrangements or administrative arrangements, as the case may be, provisions complementing or implementing this Title, in particular allowing for:

(a) consultations between Europol and one or more representatives of the national contact point of the United Kingdom on policy issues and matters of common interest for the purpose of realising their objectives and coordinating their respective activities, and of furthering cooperation between Europol and the competent authorities of the United Kingdom;

(b) the participation of one or more representatives of the United Kingdom as observer or observers in specific meetings of the Europol Heads of Unit meetings in line with the rules of proceedings of such meetings;

(c) the association of one or more representatives of the United Kingdom to operational analysis projects, in accordance with the rules set out by the appropriate Europol governance bodies;

(d) the specification of liaison officers' tasks, their rights and obligations and the costs involved; or

(e) cooperation between the competent authorities of the United Kingdom and Europol in the event of privacy or security breaches.

3. The substance of working and administrative arrangements may be set out together in one document.

Article LAW.EUROPOL.60: Notification of implementation

1. The United Kingdom and Europol shall each make publicly available a document setting out in an intelligible form the provisions regarding the processing of personal data transferred under this Title including the means available for the exercise of the rights of data subjects, and shall each ensure that a copy of that document be provided to the other.

2. Where not already in place, the United Kingdom and Europol shall adopt rules specifying how compliance with the provisions regarding the processing of personal data will be enforced in practice. The United Kingdom and Europol shall each send a copy of those rules to the other and to the respective supervisory authorities.

Article LAW.EUROPOL.61: Powers of Europol

Nothing in this Title shall be construed as creating an obligation on Europol to cooperate with the competent authorities of the United Kingdom beyond Europol's competence as set out in the relevant Union law.

TITLE VI: COOPERATION WITH EUROJUST

[7.95]
Article LAW.EUROJUST.61: Objective

The objective of this Title is to establish cooperation between Eurojust and the competent authorities of the United Kingdom in combating serious crimes as referred to in Article LAW.EUROJUST.63 [Forms of crime].

Article LAW.EUROJUST.62: Definitions

For the purposes of this Title, the following definitions apply:

(a) "Eurojust" means the European Union Agency for Criminal Justice Cooperation, set up under Regulation (EU) 2018/1727[80] (the "Eurojust Regulation");

(b) "competent authority" means, for the Union, Eurojust, represented by the College or a National Member and, for the United Kingdom, a domestic authority with responsibilities under domestic law relating to the investigation and prosecution of criminal offences;

(c) "College" means the College of Eurojust, as referred to in the Eurojust Regulation;

(d) "National Member" means the National Member seconded to Eurojust by each Member State, as referred to in the Eurojust Regulation;

(e) "Assistant" means a person who may assist a National Member and the National Member's Deputy, or the Liaison Prosecutor, as referred to in the Eurojust Regulation and in Article LAW.EUROJUST.66(3) [Liaison Prosecutor] respectively;

(f) "Liaison Prosecutor" means a public prosecutor seconded by the United Kingdom to Eurojust and subject to the domestic law of the United Kingdom as regards the public prosecutor's status;

(g) "Liaison Magistrate" means a magistrate posted by Eurojust to the United Kingdom in accordance with Article LAW.EUROJUST.67 [Liaison Magistrate];

(h) "Domestic Correspondent for Terrorism Matters" means the contact point designated by the United Kingdom in accordance with Article LAW.EUROJUST.65 [Contact points to Eurojust], responsible for handling correspondence related to terrorism matters.

Article LAW.EUROJUST.63: Forms of crime

1. The cooperation established under this Title relates to the forms of serious crime within the competence of Eurojust, as listed in ANNEX LAW-4, including related criminal offences.

2. Related criminal offences are the criminal offences committed in order to procure the means of committing forms of serious crime referred to in paragraph 1, criminal offences committed in order to facilitate or commit such serious crimes, and criminal offences committed to ensure impunity for such serious crimes.

3. Where the list of forms of serious crime for which Eurojust is competent under Union law is changed, the Specialised Committee on Law Enforcement and Judicial Cooperation may, upon a proposal from the Union, amend ANNEX LAW-4 accordingly from the date when the change to Eurojust's competence enters into effect.

Article LAW.EUROJUST.64: Scope of cooperation

The Parties shall ensure that Eurojust and the competent authorities of the United Kingdom cooperate in the fields of activity set out in Articles 2 and 54 of the Eurojust Regulation and in this Title.

Article LAW.EUROJUST.65: Contact points to Eurojust

1. The United Kingdom shall put in place or appoint at least one contact point to Eurojust within the competent authorities of the United Kingdom.

2. The United Kingdom shall designate one of its contact points as the United Kingdom Domestic Correspondent for Terrorism Matters.

Article LAW.EUROJUST.66: Liaison Prosecutor

1. To facilitate the cooperation established under this Title, the United Kingdom shall second a Liaison Prosecutor to Eurojust.
2. The mandate and the duration of the secondment shall be determined by the United Kingdom.
3. The Liaison Prosecutor may be assisted by up to five Assistants, reflecting the volume of cooperation. When necessary, Assistants may replace the Liaison Prosecutor or act on the Liaison Prosecutor's behalf.
4. The United Kingdom shall inform Eurojust of the nature and extent of the judicial powers of the Liaison Prosecutor and the Liaison Prosecutor's Assistants within the United Kingdom to accomplish their tasks in accordance with this Title. The United Kingdom shall establish the competence of its Liaison Prosecutor and the Liaison Prosecutor's Assistants to act in relation to foreign judicial authorities.
5. The Liaison Prosecutor and the Liaison Prosecutor's Assistants shall have access to the information contained in the domestic criminal record, or in any other register of the United Kingdom, in accordance with domestic law in the case of a prosecutor or person of equivalent competence.
6. The Liaison Prosecutor and the Liaison Prosecutor's Assistants shall have the power to contact the competent authorities of the United Kingdom directly.
7. The number of Assistants referred to in paragraph 3 of this Article, the details of the tasks of the Liaison Prosecutor and the Liaison Prosecutor's Assistants, their rights and obligations and the costs involved shall be governed by a working arrangement concluded between Eurojust and the competent authorities of the United Kingdom as referred to in Article LAW.EUROJUST.75 [Working arrangement].
8. The working documents of the Liaison Prosecutor and the Liaison Prosecutor's Assistants shall be held inviolable by Eurojust.

Article LAW.EUROJUST.67: Liaison Magistrate

1. For the purpose of facilitating judicial cooperation with the United Kingdom in cases in which Eurojust provides assistance, Eurojust may post a Liaison Magistrate to the United Kingdom, in accordance with Article 53 of the Eurojust Regulation.
2. The details of the Liaison Magistrate's tasks referred to in paragraph 1 of this Article, the Liaison Magistrate's rights and obligations and the costs involved, shall be governed by a working arrangement concluded between Eurojust and the competent authorities of the United Kingdom as referred to in Article LAW.EUROJUST.75 [Working arrangement].

Article LAW.EUROJUST.68: Operational and strategic meetings

1. The Liaison Prosecutor, the Liaison Prosecutor's Assistants, and representatives of other competent authorities of the United Kingdom, including the contact point to Eurojust, may participate in meetings with regard to strategic matters at the invitation of the President of Eurojust and in meetings with regard to operational matters with the approval of the National Members concerned.
2. National Members, their Deputies and Assistants, the Administrative Director of Eurojust and Eurojust staff may attend meetings organised by the Liaison Prosecutor, the Liaison Prosecutor's Assistants, or other competent authorities of the United Kingdom, including the contact point to Eurojust.

Article LAW.EUROJUST.69: Exchange of non-personal data

Eurojust and the competent authorities of the United Kingdom may exchange any non-personal data in so far as those data are relevant for the cooperation under this Title, and subject to any restrictions pursuant to Article LAW.EUROJUST.74 [Exchange of classified and sensitive non-classified information].

Article LAW.EUROJUST.70: Exchange of personal data

1. Personal data requested and received by competent authorities under this Title shall be processed by them only for the objectives set out in Article LAW.EUROJUST.61 [Objective], for the specific purposes referred to in paragraph 2 of this Article and subject to the restrictions on access or further use referred to in paragraph 3 of this Article.
2. The transferring competent authority shall clearly indicate, at the latest at the moment of transferring personal data, the specific purpose or purposes for which the data are being transferred.
3. The transferring competent authority may indicate, at the moment of transferring personal data, any restriction on access thereto or the use to be made thereof, in general or specific terms, including as regards its onward transfer, erasure or destruction after a certain period of time, or its further processing. Where the need for such restrictions becomes apparent after the personal data have been provided, the transferring authority shall inform the receiving authority accordingly.
4. The receiving competent authority shall comply with any restriction on access or further use of the personal data indicated by the transferring competent authority as provided for in paragraph 3.

Article LAW.EUROJUST.71: Channels of transmission

1. Information shall be exchanged:
    (a) either between the Liaison Prosecutor or the Liaison Prosecutor's Assistants or, if none is appointed or otherwise available, the United Kingdom's contact point to Eurojust and the National Members concerned or the College;

   (b)   if Eurojust has posted a Liaison Magistrate to the United Kingdom, between the Liaison Magistrate and any competent authority of the United Kingdom; in that event, the Liaison Prosecutor shall be informed of any such information exchanges; or

   (c)   directly between a competent authority in the United Kingdom and the National Members concerned or the College; in that event, the Liaison Prosecutor and, if applicable, the Liaison Magistrate shall be informed of any such information exchanges.

2. Eurojust and the competent authorities of the United Kingdom may agree to use other channels for the exchange of information in particular cases.

3. Eurojust and the competent authorities of the United Kingdom shall each ensure that their respective representatives are authorised to exchange information at the appropriate level and in accordance with United Kingdom law and the Eurojust Regulation respectively, and are adequately screened.

Article LAW.EUROJUST.72: Onward transfers

The competent authorities of the United Kingdom and Eurojust shall not communicate any information provided by the other to any third country or international organisation without the consent of whichever of the competent authorities of the United Kingdom or Eurojust provided the information and without appropriate safeguards regarding the protection of personal data.

Article LAW.EUROJUST.73: Liability for unauthorised or incorrect personal data processing

1. The competent authorities shall be liable, in accordance with their respective legal frameworks, for any damage caused to an individual as a result of legal or factual errors in information exchanged. In order to avoid liability under their respective legal frameworks vis-à-vis an injured party, neither Eurojust nor the competent authorities of the United Kingdom may plead that the other competent authority had transferred inaccurate information.

2. If damages are awarded against any competent authority because of its use of information which was erroneously communicated by the other, or communicated as a result of a failure on the part of the other to comply with their obligations, the amount paid as compensation under paragraph 1 by the competent authority shall be repaid by the other, unless the information was used in breach of this Title.

3. Eurojust and the competent authorities of the United Kingdom shall not require each other to pay for punitive or non-compensatory damages under paragraphs 1 and 2.

Article LAW.EUROJUST.74: Exchange of classified and sensitive non-classified information

The exchange and protection of classified and sensitive non-classified information, if necessary under this Title, shall be regulated by a working arrangement as referred to in Article LAW.EUROJUST.75 [Working arrangement] concluded between Eurojust and the competent authorities of the United Kingdom.

Article LAW.EUROJUST.75: Working arrangement

The modalities of cooperation between the Parties as appropriate to implement this Title shall be the subject of a working arrangement concluded between Eurojust and the competent authorities of the United Kingdom in accordance with Articles 47(3) and 56(3) of the Eurojust Regulation.

Article LAW.EUROJUST.76: Powers of Eurojust

Nothing in this Title shall be construed as creating an obligation on Eurojust to cooperate with the competent authorities of the United Kingdom beyond Eurojust's competence as set out in the relevant Union law.

TITLE VII: SURRENDER

[7.96]
Article LAW.SURR.76: Objective

The objective of this Title is to ensure that the extradition system between the Member States, on the one side, and the United Kingdom, on the other side, is based on a mechanism of surrender pursuant to an arrest warrant in accordance with the terms of this Title.

Article LAW.SURR.77: Principle of proportionality

Cooperation through the arrest warrant shall be necessary and proportionate, taking into account the rights of the requested person and the interests of the victims, and having regard to the seriousness of the act, the likely penalty that would be imposed and the possibility of a State taking measures less coercive than the surrender of the requested person particularly with a view to avoiding unnecessarily long periods of pre-trial detention.

Article LAW.SURR.78: Definitions

For the purposes of this Title, the following definitions apply:

   (a)   "arrest warrant" means a judicial decision issued by a State with a view to the arrest and surrender by another State of a requested person, for the purposes of conducting a criminal prosecution or executing a custodial sentence or detention order;

   (b)   "judicial authority" means an authority that is, under domestic law, a judge, a court or a public prosecutor. A public prosecutor is considered a judicial authority only to the extent that domestic law so provides;

   (c)   "executing judicial authority" means the judicial authority of the executing State which is competent to execute the arrest warrant by virtue of the domestic law of that State;

   (d)   "issuing judicial authority" means the judicial authority of the issuing State which is competent to issue an arrest warrant by virtue of the domestic law of that State.

Article LAW.SURR.79: Scope

1. An arrest warrant may be issued for acts punishable by the law of the issuing State by a custodial sentence or a detention order for a maximum period of at least 12 months or, where a sentence has been passed or a detention order has been made, for sentences or detention orders of at least four months.

2. Without prejudice to paragraphs 3 and 4, surrender is subject to the condition that the acts for which the arrest warrant has been issued constitute an offence under the law of the executing State, whatever the constituent elements or however it is described.

3. Subject to Article LAW.SURR.80 [Grounds for mandatory non-execution of the arrest warrant], points (b) to (h) of Article LAW.SURR.81(1) [Other grounds for non-execution of the arrest warrant], Article LAW.SURR.82 [Political offence exception], Article LAW.SURR.83 [Nationality exception] and Article LAW.SURR.84 [Guarantees to be given by the issuing State in particular cases], a State shall not refuse to execute an arrest warrant issued in relation to the following behaviour where such behaviour is punishable by deprivation of liberty or a detention order of a maximum period of at least 12 months:

    (a) the behaviour of any person who contributes to the commission by a group of persons acting with a common purpose of one or more offences in the field of terrorism referred to in Articles 1 and 2 of the European Convention on the Suppression of Terrorism, done at Strasbourg on 27 January 1977, or in relation to illicit trafficking in narcotic drugs and psychotropic substances, or murder, grievous bodily injury, kidnapping, illegal restraint, hostage-taking or rape, even where that person does not take part in the actual execution of the offence or offences concerned; such contribution must be intentional and made with the knowledge that the participation will contribute to the achievement of the group's criminal activities; or

    (b) terrorism as defined in ANNEX LAW-7.

4. The United Kingdom and the Union, acting on behalf of any of its Member States, may each notify the Specialised Committee on Law Enforcement and Judicial Cooperation that, on the basis of reciprocity, the condition of double criminality referred to in paragraph 2 will not be applied, provided that the offence on which the warrant is based is:

    (a) one of the offences listed in paragraph 5, as defined by the law of the issuing State; and

    (b) punishable in the issuing State by a custodial sentence or a detention order for a maximum period of at least three years.

5. The offences referred to in paragraph 4 are:

- participation in a criminal organisation;
- terrorism as defined in ANNEX LAW-7;
- trafficking in human beings;
- sexual exploitation of children and child pornography;
- illicit trafficking in narcotic drugs and psychotropic substances;
- illicit trafficking in weapons, munitions and explosives;
- corruption, including bribery;
- fraud, including that affecting the financial interests of the United Kingdom, a Member State or the Union;
- laundering of the proceeds of crime;
- counterfeiting currency;
- computer-related crime;
- environmental crime, including illicit trafficking in endangered animal species and endangered plant species and varieties;
- facilitation of unauthorised entry and residence;
- murder;
- grievous bodily injury;
- illicit trade in human organs and tissue;
- kidnapping, illegal restraint and hostage-taking;
- racism and xenophobia;
- organised or armed robbery;
- illicit trafficking in cultural goods, including antiques and works of art;
- swindling;
- racketeering and extortion;
- counterfeiting and piracy of products;
- forgery of administrative documents and trafficking therein;
- forgery of means of payment;
- illicit trafficking in hormonal substances and other growth promoters;
- illicit trafficking in nuclear or radioactive materials;
- trafficking in stolen vehicles;
- rape;
- arson;
- crimes within the jurisdiction of the International Criminal Court;
- unlawful seizure of aircraft, ships or spacecraft; and
- sabotage.

Article LAW.SURR.80: Grounds for mandatory non-execution of the arrest warrant

The execution of the arrest warrant shall be refused:

    (a) if the offence on which the arrest warrant is based is covered by an amnesty in the executing State, where that State had jurisdiction to prosecute the offence under its own criminal law;

    (b) if the executing judicial authority is informed that the requested person has been finally judged by a State in respect of the same acts, provided that, if a penalty has been imposed, it has been enforced, is in the process of being enforced or can no longer be enforced under the law of the sentencing State; or

(c)   if the person who is the subject of the arrest warrant may not, owing to the person's age, be held criminally responsible for the acts on which the arrest warrant is based under the law of the executing State.

Article LAW.SURR.81: Other grounds for non-execution of the arrest warrant

1. The execution of the arrest warrant may be refused:

(a)   if, in one of the cases referred to in Article LAW.SURR.79(2) [Scope], the act on which the arrest warrant is based does not constitute an offence under the law of the executing State; however, in relation to taxes or duties, customs and exchange, the execution of the arrest warrant shall not be refused on the grounds that the law of the executing State does not impose the same kind of tax or duty or does not contain the same type of rules as regards taxes or duties, customs and exchange regulations as the law of the issuing State;

(b)   if the person who is the subject of the arrest warrant is being prosecuted in the executing State for the same act as that on which the arrest warrant is based;

(c)   if the judicial authorities of the executing State have decided either not to prosecute for the offence on which the arrest warrant is based or to halt proceedings, or if a final judgment which prevents further proceedings has been passed upon the requested person in a State in respect of the same acts;

(d)   if the criminal prosecution or punishment of the requested person is statute-barred under the law of the executing State and the acts fall within the jurisdiction of that State under its own criminal law;

(e)   if the executing judicial authority is informed that the requested person has been finally judged by a third country in respect of the same acts provided that, if a penalty has been imposed, it has been enforced, is in the process of being enforced or can no longer be enforced under the law of the sentencing country;

(f)   if the arrest warrant has been issued for the purposes of execution of a custodial sentence or detention order and the requested person is staying in, or is a national or a resident of the executing State and that State undertakes to execute the sentence or detention order in accordance with its domestic law; if consent of the requested person to the transfer of the sentence or detention order to the executing State is required, the executing State may refuse to execute the arrest warrant only after the requested person consents to the transfer of the sentence or detention order;

(g)   if the arrest warrant relates to offences which:

     (i)   are regarded by the law of the executing State as having been committed in whole or in part in the territory of the executing State or in a place treated as such or

     (ii)   have been committed outside the territory of the issuing State, and the law of the executing State does not allow prosecution for the same offences if committed outside its territory;

(h)   if there are reasons to believe on the basis of objective elements that the arrest warrant has been issued for the purpose of prosecuting or punishing a person on the grounds the person's sex, race, religion, ethnic origin, nationality, language, political opinions or sexual orientation, or that that person's position may be prejudiced for any of those reasons;

(i)   if the arrest warrant has been issued for the purpose of executing a custodial sentence or a detention order and the requested person did not appear in person at the trial resulting in the decision, unless the arrest warrant states that the person, in accordance with further procedural requirements defined in the domestic law of the issuing State:

     (i)   in due time:

         (A)   either was summoned in person and thereby informed of the scheduled date and place of the trial which resulted in the decision, or by other means actually received official information of the scheduled date and place of that trial in such a manner that it was unequivocally established that the person was aware of the date and place of the scheduled trial;

         and

         (B)   was informed that a decision may be handed down if that person did not appear for the trial;

         or

     (ii)   being aware of the date and place of the scheduled trial, had given a mandate to a lawyer, who was either appointed by the person concerned or by the State, to defend him or her at the trial, and was indeed defended by that lawyer at the trial;

         or

     (iii)   after being served with the decision and being expressly informed about the right to a retrial or appeal in which the person has the right to participate and which allows the merits of the case, including fresh evidence, to be re-examined, and which may lead to the original decision being reversed:

         (A)   expressly stated that the person did not contest the decision;

         or

         (B)   did not request a retrial or appeal within the applicable time frame;

         or

     (iv)   was not personally served with the decision but:

         (A)   will be personally served with it without delay after the surrender and will be expressly informed of the right to a retrial or appeal in which the person has the right to participate and which allows the merits of the case, including fresh evidence, to be re-examined, and which may lead to the original decision being reversed;

         and

         (B)   will be informed of the time frame within which the person has to request such a retrial or appeal, as mentioned in the relevant arrest warrant.

2. Where the arrest warrant is issued for the purpose of executing a custodial sentence or detention order under the conditions in point (i) (iv) of paragraph 1 and the person concerned has not previously received any official information about the existence of the criminal proceedings against him or her, that person may, when being informed about the content of the arrest warrant, request to receive a copy of the judgment before being surrendered. Immediately after having been informed about the request, the issuing authority shall provide the copy of the judgment via the executing authority to the person concerned. The request of the person concerned shall neither delay the surrender procedure nor delay the decision to execute the arrest warrant. The provision of the judgment to the person concerned shall be for information purposes only; it shall not be regarded as a formal service of the judgment nor actuate any time limits applicable for requesting a retrial or appeal.

3. Where a person is surrendered under the conditions in point (i) (iv) of paragraph 1 and that person has requested a retrial or appeal, until those proceedings are finalised the detention of that person awaiting such retrial or appeal shall be reviewed in accordance with the domestic law of the issuing State, either on a regular basis or upon request of the person concerned. Such a review shall in particular include the possibility of suspension or interruption of the detention. The retrial or appeal shall begin within due time after the surrender.

Article LAW.SURR.82: Political offence exception

1. The execution of an arrest warrant may not be refused on the grounds that the offence may be regarded by the executing State as a political offence, as an offence connected with a political offence or as an offence inspired by political motives.

2. However, the United Kingdom and the Union, acting on behalf of any of its Member States, may each notify the Specialised Committee on Law Enforcement and Judicial Cooperation that paragraph 1 will be applied only in relation to:

    (a) the offences referred to in Articles 1 and 2 of the European Convention on the Suppression of Terrorism;

    (b) offences of conspiracy or association to commit one or more of the offences referred to in Articles 1 and 2 of the European Convention on the Suppression of Terrorism, if those offences of conspiracy or association correspond to the description of behaviour referred to in Article LAW.SURR.79(3) [Scope] of this Agreement; and

    (c) terrorism as defined in ANNEX LAW-7 to this Agreement.

3. Where an arrest warrant has been issued by a State having made a notification as referred to in paragraph 2 or by a State on behalf of which such a notification has been made, the State executing the arrest warrant may apply reciprocity.

Article LAW.SURR.83: Nationality exception

1. The execution of an arrest warrant may not be refused on the grounds that the requested person is a national of the executing State.

2. The United Kingdom, and the Union, acting on behalf of any of its Member States, may each notify the Specialised Committee on Law Enforcement and Judicial Cooperation that that State's own nationals will not be surrendered or that the surrender of their own nationals will be authorised only under certain specified conditions. The notification shall be based on reasons related to the fundamental principles or practice of the domestic legal order of the United Kingdom or the State on behalf of which a notification was made. In such a case, the Union, on behalf of any of its Member States or the United Kingdom, as the case may be, may notify the Specialised Committee on Law Enforcement and Judicial Cooperation within a reasonable time after the receipt of the other Party's notification that the executing judicial authorities of the Member State or the United Kingdom, as the case may be, may refuse to surrender its nationals to that State or that surrender shall be authorised only under certain specified conditions.

3. In circumstances where a State has refused to execute an arrest warrant on the basis that, in the case of the United Kingdom, it has made a notification or, in the case of a Member State, the Union has made a notification on its behalf, as referred to in paragraph 2, that State shall consider instituting proceedings against its own national which are commensurate with the subject matter of the arrest warrant, having taken into account the views of the issuing State. In circumstances where a judicial authority decides not to institute such proceedings, the victim of the offence on which the arrest warrant is based shall be able to receive information on the decision in accordance with the applicable domestic law.

4. Where a State's competent authorities institute proceedings against its own national in accordance with paragraph 3, that State shall ensure that its competent authorities are able to take appropriate measures to assist the victims and witnesses in circumstances where they are residents of another State, particularly with regard to the way in which the proceedings are conducted.

Article LAW.SURR.84: Guarantees to be given by the issuing State in particular cases

The execution of the arrest warrant by the executing judicial authority may be subject to the following guarantees:

    (a) if the offence on which the arrest warrant is based is punishable by a custodial life sentence or a lifetime detention order in the issuing State, the executing State may make the execution of the arrest warrant subject to the condition that the issuing State gives a guarantee deemed sufficient by the executing State that the issuing State will review the penalty or measure imposed, on request or at the latest after 20 years, or will encourage the application of measures of clemency for which the person is entitled to apply under the law or practice of the issuing State, aiming at the non-execution of such penalty or measure;

    (b) if a person who is the subject of an arrest warrant for the purposes of prosecution is a national or resident of the executing State, the surrender of that person may be subject to the condition that the person, after being heard, is returned to the executing State in order to serve there the custodial sentence or detention order passed against him or her in the issuing State; if the consent of the requested person to the transfer of the sentence or detention order to the executing State is required, the guarantee that the person be returned to the executing State to serve the person's sentence is subject to the condition that the requested person, after being heard, consents to be returned to the executing State;

(c) if there are substantial grounds for believing that there is a real risk to the protection of the fundamental rights of the requested person, the executing judicial authority may require, as appropriate, additional guarantees as to the treatment of the requested person after the person's surrender before it decides whether to execute the arrest warrant.

Article LAW.SURR.85: Recourse to the central authority

1. The United Kingdom and the Union, acting on behalf of any of its Member States, may each notify the Specialised Committee on Law Enforcement and Judicial Cooperation of, in the case of the United Kingdom, the its central authority and, in the case of the Union, the central authority for each State, having designated such an authority, or, if the legal system of the relevant State so provides, of more than one central authority to assist the competent judicial authorities.

2. When notifying the Specialised Committee on Law Enforcement and Judicial Cooperation under paragraph 1, the United Kingdom and the Union, acting on behalf of any of its Member States, may each indicate that, as a result of the organisation of the internal judicial system of the relevant States, the central authority or central authorities are responsible for the administrative transmission and receipt of arrest warrants as well as for all other official correspondence relating to the administrative transmission and receipt of arrest warrants. Such indication shall be binding upon all the authorities of the issuing State.

Article LAW.SURR.86: Content and form of the arrest warrant

1. The arrest warrant shall contain the following information set out in accordance with the form contained in ANNEX LAW-5:

(a) the identity and nationality of the requested person;
(b) the name, address, telephone and fax numbers and e-mail address of the issuing judicial authority;
(c) evidence of an enforceable judgment, an arrest warrant or any other enforceable judicial decision having the same effect that fall within the scope of Article LAW.SURR.79 [Scope];
(d) the nature and legal classification of the offence, particularly in respect of Article LAW.SURR.79 [Scope];
(e) a description of the circumstances in which the offence was committed, including the time, place and degree of participation in the offence by the requested person;
(f) the penalty imposed, if there is a final judgment, or the prescribed scale of penalties for the offence under the law of the issuing State; and
(g) if possible, other consequences of the offence.

2. The arrest warrant shall be translated into the official language or one of the official languages of the executing State. The United Kingdom and the Union, acting on behalf of any of its Member States, may each notify the Specialised Committee on Law Enforcement and Judicial Cooperation that a translation in one or more other official languages of a State will be accepted.

Article LAW.SURR.87: Transmission of an arrest warrant

If the location of the requested person is known, the issuing judicial authority may transmit the arrest warrant directly to the executing judicial authority.

Article LAW.SURR.88: Detailed procedures for transmitting an arrest warrant

1. If the issuing judicial authority does not know which authority is the competent executing judicial authority, it shall make the requisite enquiries, in order to obtain that information from the executing State.

2. The issuing judicial authority may request the International Criminal Police Organisation ("Interpol") to transmit an arrest warrant.

3. The issuing judicial authority may transmit the arrest warrant by any secure means capable of producing written records under conditions allowing the executing State to establish the authenticity of the arrest warrant.

4. All difficulties concerning the transmission or the authenticity of any document needed for the execution of the arrest warrant shall be dealt with by direct contacts between the judicial authorities involved, or, where appropriate, with the involvement of the central authorities of the States.

5. If the authority which receives an arrest warrant is not competent to act upon it, it shall automatically forward the arrest warrant to the competent authority in its State and shall inform the issuing judicial authority accordingly.

Article LAW.SURR.89: Rights of a requested person

1. If a requested person is arrested for the purpose of the execution of an arrest warrant, the executing judicial authority, in accordance with its domestic law, shall inform that person of the arrest warrant and of its contents, and also of the possibility of consenting to surrender to the issuing State.

2. A requested person who is arrested for the purpose of the execution of an arrest warrant and who does not speak or understand the language of the arrest warrant proceedings shall have the right to be assisted by an interpreter and to be provided with a written translation in the native language of the requested person or in any other language which that person speaks or understands, in accordance with the domestic law of the executing State.

3. A requested person shall have the right to be assisted by a lawyer in accordance with the domestic law of the executing State upon arrest.

4. The requested person shall be informed of the person's right to appoint a lawyer in the issuing State for the purpose of assisting the lawyer in the executing State in the arrest warrant proceedings. This paragraph is without prejudice to the time limits set out in Article LAW.SURR.101 [Time limits for surrender of the person].

5. A requested person who is arrested shall have the right to have the consular authorities of that person's State of nationality, or if that person is stateless, the consular authorities of the State where that person usually resides, informed of the arrest without undue delay and to communicate with those authorities, if that person so wishes.

Article LAW.SURR.90: Keeping the person in detention

When a person is arrested on the basis of an arrest warrant, the executing judicial authority shall take a decision on whether the requested person should remain in detention, in accordance with the law of the executing State. The person may be released provisionally at any time in accordance with the domestic law of the executing State, provided that the competent authority of that State takes all the measures it deems necessary to prevent the person from absconding.

Article LAW.SURR.91: Consent to surrender

1. If the arrested person indicates that he or she consents to surrender, that consent and, if appropriate, the express renunciation of entitlement to the speciality rule referred to in Article LAW.SURR.105(2) [Possible prosecution for other offences] must be given before the executing judicial authority, in accordance with the domestic law of the executing State.
2. Each State shall adopt the measures necessary to ensure that the consent and, where appropriate, the renunciation referred to in paragraph 1 are established in such a way as to show that the person concerned has expressed them voluntarily and in full awareness of the consequences. To that end, the requested person shall have the right to a lawyer.
3. The consent and, where appropriate, the renunciation referred to in paragraph 1 shall be formally recorded in accordance with the procedure laid down by the domestic law of the executing State.
4. In principle, consent may not be revoked. Each State may provide that the consent and, if appropriate, the renunciation referred to in paragraph 1 of this Article may be revoked in accordance with the rules applicable under its domestic law. In such a case, the period between the date of the consent and that of its revocation shall not be taken into consideration in establishing the time limits laid down in Article LAW.SURR.101 [Time limits for surrender of the person]. The United Kingdom and the Union, acting on behalf of any of its Member States, may each notify the Specialised Committee on Law Enforcement and Judicial Cooperation that it wishes to have recourse to this possibility, specifying the procedures whereby revocation of the consent is possible and any amendments to those procedures.

Article LAW.SURR.92: Hearing of the requested person

Where the arrested person does not consent to surrender as referred to in Article LAW.SURR.91 [Consent to surrender], that person shall be entitled to be heard by the executing judicial authority, in accordance with the law of the executing State.

Article LAW.SURR.93: Surrender decision

1. The executing judicial authority shall decide whether the person is to be surrendered within the time limits and in accordance with the conditions defined in this Title, in particular the principle of proportionality as set out in Article LAW.SURR.77 [Principle of proportionality].
2. If the executing judicial authority finds the information communicated by the issuing State to be insufficient to allow it to decide on surrender, it shall request that the necessary supplementary information, in particular with respect to Article LAW.SURR. 77 [Principle of proportionality], Articles LAW.SURR.80 [Grounds for mandatory non-execution of the arrest warrant] to LAW.SURR.82 [Political offence exception], Article LAW.SURR.84 [Guarantees to be given by the issuing State in particular cases] and Article LAW.SURR.86 [Content and form of the arrest warrant], be furnished as a matter of urgency and may fix a time limit for the receipt thereof, taking into account the need to observe the time limits provided for in Article LAW.SURR.95 [Time limits and procedures for the decision to execute the arrest warrant].
3. The issuing judicial authority may forward any additional useful information to the executing judicial authority at any time.

Article LAW.SURR.94: Decision in the event of multiple requests

1. If two or more States have issued a European arrest warrant or an arrest warrant for the same person, the decision as to which of those arrest warrants is to be executed shall be taken by the executing judicial authority, with due consideration of all the circumstances, especially the relative seriousness of the offences and place of the offences, the respective dates of the arrest warrants or European arrest warrants and whether they have been issued for the purposes of prosecution or for the execution of a custodial sentence or detention order, and of legal obligations of Member States deriving from Union law regarding, in particular, the principles of freedom of movement and non-discrimination on grounds of nationality.
2. The executing judicial authority of a Member State may seek the advice of Eurojust when making the choice referred to in paragraph 1.
3. In the event of a conflict between an arrest warrant and a request for extradition presented by a third country, the decision as to whether the arrest warrant or the extradition request takes precedence shall be taken by the competent authority of the executing State with due consideration of all the circumstances, in particular those referred to in paragraph 1 and those mentioned in the applicable convention.
4. This Article is without prejudice to the States' obligations under the Statute of the International Criminal Court.

Article LAW.SURR.95: Time limits and procedures for the decision to execute the arrest warrant

1. An arrest warrant shall be dealt with and executed as a matter of urgency.

2. In cases where the requested person consents to surrender, the final decision on the execution of the arrest warrant shall be taken within ten days after the consent was given.

3. In other cases, the final decision on the execution of the arrest warrant shall be taken within 60 days after the arrest of the requested person.

4. Where in specific cases the arrest warrant cannot be executed within the time limits laid down in paragraphs 2 or 3, the executing judicial authority shall immediately inform the issuing judicial authority of that fact, giving the reasons for the delay. In such cases, the time limits may be extended by a further 30 days.

5. As long as the executing judicial authority has not taken a final decision on the arrest warrant, it shall ensure that the material conditions necessary for the effective surrender of the person remain fulfilled.

6. Reasons must be given for any refusal to execute an arrest warrant.

Article LAW.SURR.96: Situation pending the decision

1. Where the arrest warrant has been issued for the purpose of conducting a criminal prosecution, the executing judicial authority shall either:
   (a) agree that the requested person should be heard according to Article LAW.SURR.97 [Hearing the person pending the decision]; or
   (b) agree to the temporary transfer of the requested person.

2. The conditions and the duration of the temporary transfer shall be determined by mutual agreement between the issuing and executing judicial authorities.

3. In the case of temporary transfer, the person must be able to return to the executing State to attend hearings which concern that person as part of the surrender procedure.

Article LAW.SURR.97: Hearing the person pending the decision

1. The requested person shall be heard by a judicial authority. To that end, the requested person shall be assisted by a lawyer designated in accordance with the law of the issuing State.

2. The requested person shall be heard in accordance with the law of the executing State and with the conditions determined by mutual agreement between the issuing and executing judicial authorities.

3. The competent executing judicial authority may assign another judicial authority of its State to take part in the hearing of the requested person in order to ensure the proper application of this Article.

Article LAW.SURR.98: Privileges and immunities

1. Where the requested person enjoys a privilege or immunity regarding jurisdiction or execution in the executing State, the time limits referred to in Article LAW.SURR.95 [Time limits and procedures for the decision to execute the arrest warrant] only start running when, or if, the executing judicial authority is informed of the fact that the privilege or immunity has been waived.

2. The executing State shall ensure that the material conditions necessary for effective surrender are fulfilled when the person no longer enjoys such privilege or immunity.

3. Where power to waive the privilege or immunity lies with an authority of the executing State, the executing judicial authority shall request that authority to exercise that power without delay. Where power to waive the privilege or immunity lies with an authority of another State, third country or international organisation, the issuing judicial authority shall request that authority to exercise that power.

Article LAW.SURR.99: Competing international obligations

1. This Agreement does not prejudice the obligations of the executing State where the requested person has been extradited to that State from a third country and where that person is protected by provisions of the arrangement under which that person was extradited concerning the speciality rule. The executing State shall take all necessary measures for requesting without delay the consent of the third country from which the requested person was extradited so that the requested person can be surrendered to the State which issued the arrest warrant. The time limits referred to in Article LAW.SURR.95 [Time limits and procedures for the decision to execute the arrest warrant] do not start running until the day on which the speciality rule ceases to apply.

2. Pending the decision of the third country from which the requested person was extradited, the executing State shall ensure that the material conditions necessary for effective surrender remain fulfilled.

Article LAW.SURR.100: Notification of the decision

The executing judicial authority shall notify the issuing judicial authority immediately of the decision on the action to be taken on the arrest warrant.

Article LAW.SURR.101: Time limits for surrender of the person

1. The requested person shall be surrendered as soon as possible on a date agreed between the authorities concerned.

2. The requested person shall be surrendered no later than ten days after the final decision on the execution of the arrest warrant.

3. If the surrender of the requested person within the time limit in paragraph 2 is prevented by circumstances beyond the control of any of the States, the executing and issuing judicial authorities shall immediately contact each other and agree on a new surrender date. In that event, the surrender shall take place within ten days of the new date thus agreed.

4. The surrender may exceptionally be temporarily postponed for serious humanitarian reasons, for example if there are substantial grounds for believing that the surrender would manifestly endanger the requested person's life or health. The execution of the arrest warrant shall take place as soon as those grounds have ceased to exist. The executing judicial authority shall immediately inform the issuing judicial authority and agree on a new surrender date. In that event, the surrender shall take place within ten days of the new date - agreed.

Part 7   Key Brexit Materials

5. Upon the expiry of the time limits referred to in paragraphs 2 to 4, if the requested person is still being held in custody, that person shall be released. The executing and issuing judicial authorities shall contact each other as soon as it appears that a person is to be released under this paragraph and agree the arrangements for the surrender of that person.

Article LAW.SURR.102: Postponed or conditional surrender

1. After deciding to execute the arrest warrant, the executing judicial authority may postpone the surrender of the requested person so that the requested person may be prosecuted in the executing State or, if the requested person has already been sentenced, so that the requested person may serve, a sentence passed for an act other than that referred to in the arrest warrant in the territory of the executing State.
2. Instead of postponing the surrender, the executing judicial authority may temporarily surrender the requested person to the issuing State under conditions to be determined by mutual agreement between the executing and the issuing judicial authorities. The agreement shall be made in writing and the conditions shall be binding on all the authorities in the issuing State.

Article LAW.SURR.103: Transit

1. Each State shall permit the transit through its territory of a requested person who is being surrendered provided that it has been given information on:
   (a) the identity and nationality of the person subject to the arrest warrant;
   (b) the existence of an arrest warrant;
   (c) the nature and legal classification of the offence; and
   (d) the description of the circumstances of the offence, including the date and place.
2. The State, on behalf of which a notification has been made in accordance with Article LAW.SURR.83(2) [Nationality exception] to the effect that its own nationals will not be surrendered or that surrender will be authorised only under certain specified conditions, may refuse the transit of its own nationals through its territory under the same terms or submit it to the same conditions.
3. The States shall designate an authority responsible for receiving transit requests and the necessary documents, as well as any other official correspondence relating to transit requests.
4. The transit request and the information referred to in paragraph 1 may be addressed to the authority designated pursuant to paragraph 3 by any means capable of producing a written record. The State of transit shall notify its decision by the same procedure.
5. This Article does not apply in the case of transport by air without a scheduled stopover. However, if an unscheduled landing occurs, the issuing State shall provide the authority designated pursuant to paragraph 3 with the information referred to in paragraph 1.
6. Where a transit concerns a person who is to be extradited from a third country to a State, this Article applies *mutatis mutandis*. In particular, references to an "arrest warrant" shall be treated as references to an "extradition request".

Article LAW.SURR.104: Deduction of the period of detention served in the executing State

1. The issuing State shall deduct all periods of detention arising from the execution of an arrest warrant from the total period of detention to be served in the issuing State as a result of a custodial sentence or detention order being passed.
2. All information concerning the duration of the detention of the requested person on the basis of the arrest warrant shall be transmitted by the executing judicial authority or the central authority designated under Article LAW.SURR.85 [Recourse to the central authority] to the issuing judicial authority at the time of the surrender.

Article LAW.SURR.105: Possible prosecution for other offences

1. The United Kingdom and the Union, acting on behalf of any of its Member States, may each notify the Specialised Committee on Law Enforcement and Judicial Cooperation that, in relations with other States to which the same notification applies, consent is presumed to have been given for the prosecution, sentencing or detention of a person with a view to the carrying out of a custodial sentence or detention order for an offence committed prior to the person's surrender, other than that for which that person was surrendered, unless in a particular case the executing judicial authority states otherwise in its decision on surrender.
2. Except in the cases referred to in paragraphs 1 and 3, a person surrendered may not be prosecuted, sentenced or otherwise deprived of liberty for an offence committed prior to that person's surrender other than that for which the person was surrendered.
3. Paragraph 2 of this Article does not apply in the following cases:
   (a) the person, having had an opportunity to leave the territory of the State to which that person has been surrendered, has not done so within 45 days of that person's final discharge or has returned to that territory after leaving it;
   (b) the offence is not punishable by a custodial sentence or detention order;
   (c) the criminal proceedings do not give rise to the application of a measure restricting personal liberty;
   (d) the person could be liable to a penalty or a measure not involving the deprivation of liberty, in particular a financial penalty or a measure in lieu of a financial penalty, even if the penalty or measure may give rise to a restriction of the person's personal liberty;
   (e) the person consented to be surrendered, where appropriate at the same time as the person renounced the speciality rule, in accordance with Article LAW.SURR.91 [Consent to surrender];
   (f) the person, after the person's surrender, has expressly renounced entitlement to the speciality rule with regard to specific offences preceding the person's surrender; renunciation must be given before the competent judicial

authority of the issuing State and be recorded in accordance with that State's domestic law; the renunciation must be drawn up in such a way as to make clear that the person concerned has given it voluntarily and in full awareness of the consequences; to that end, the person shall have the right to a lawyer; and

(g)   the executing judicial authority which surrendered the person gives its consent in accordance with paragraph 4 of this Article.

4. A request for consent shall be submitted to the executing judicial authority, accompanied by the information referred to in Article LAW.SURR.86(1) [Content and form of the arrest warrant] and a translation as referred to in Article LAW.SURR.86(2) [Content and form of the arrest warrant]. Consent shall be given where the offence for which it is requested is itself subject to surrender in accordance with the provisions of this Title. Consent shall be refused on the grounds referred to in Article LAW.SURR.80 [Grounds for mandatory non-execution of the arrest warrant] and otherwise may be refused only on the grounds referred to in Article LAW.SURR.81 [Other grounds for non-execution of the arrest warrant], or Article LAW.SURR.82(2) [Political offence exception] and Article LAW.SURR.83(2) [Nationality exception]. The decision shall be taken no later than 30 days after receipt of the request. For the situations laid down in Article LAW.SURR.84 [Guarantees to be given by the issuing State in particular cases] the issuing State must give the guarantees provided for therein.

Article LAW.SURR.106: Surrender or subsequent extradition

1. The United Kingdom and the Union, acting on behalf of any of its Member States, may each notify the Specialised Committee on Law Enforcement and Judicial Cooperation that, in relations with other States to which the same notification applies, the consent for the surrender of a person to a State other than the executing State pursuant to an arrest warrant or European arrest warrant issued for an offence committed prior to that person's surrender is presumed to have been given, unless in a particular case the executing judicial authority states otherwise in its decision on surrender.

2. In any case, a person who has been surrendered to the issuing State pursuant to an arrest warrant or European arrest warrant may be surrendered to a State other than the executing State pursuant to an arrest warrant or European arrest warrant issued for any offence committed prior to the person's surrender without the consent of the executing State in the following cases:

(a)   the requested person, having had an opportunity to leave the territory of the State to which that person has been surrendered, has not done so within 45 days of that person's final discharge, or has returned to that territory after leaving it;

(b)   the requested person consents to be surrendered to a State other than the executing State pursuant to an arrest warrant or European arrest warrant; consent must be given before the competent judicial authorities of the issuing State and be recorded in accordance with that State's domestic law; it must be drawn up in such a way as to make clear that the person concerned has given it voluntarily and in full awareness of the consequences; to that end, the requested person shall have the right to a lawyer; and

(c)   the requested person is not subject to the speciality rule, in accordance with points (a), (e), (f) or (g) of Article LAW.SURR.105(3) [Possible prosecution for other offences].

3. The executing judicial authority shall consent to the surrender to another State in accordance with the following rules:

(a)   the request for consent shall be submitted in accordance with Article LAW.SURR.87 [Transmission of an arrest warrant], accompanied by the information set out in Article LAW.SURR.86(1) [Content and form of the arrest warrant] and a translation as referred to in Article LAW.SURR.86(2) [Content and form of the arrest warrant];

(b)   consent shall be given where the offence for which it is requested is itself subject to surrender in accordance with the provisions of this Agreement;

(c)   the decision shall be taken no later than 30 days after receipt of the request; and

(d)   consent shall be refused on the grounds referred to in Article LAW.SURR.80 [Grounds for mandatory non-execution of the arrest warrant] and otherwise may be refused only on the grounds referred to in Article LAW.SURR.81 [Other grounds for non-execution of the arrest warrant], Article LAW.SURR.82(2) [Political offence exception] and Article LAW.SURR.83(2) [Nationality exception].

4. For the situations referred to in Article LAW.SURR.84 [Guarantees to be given by the issuing State in particular cases], the issuing State shall give the guarantees provided for therein.

5. Notwithstanding paragraph 1, a person who has been surrendered pursuant to an arrest warrant shall not be extradited to a third country without the consent of the competent authority of the State which surrendered the person. Such consent shall be given in accordance with the Conventions by which that State is bound, as well as with its domestic law.

Article LAW.SURR.107: Handing over of property

1. At the request of the issuing judicial authority or on its own initiative, the executing judicial authority shall, in accordance with its domestic law, seize and hand over property which:

(a)   may be required as evidence; or

(b)   has been acquired by the requested person as a result of the offence.

2. The property referred to in paragraph 1 shall be handed over even if the arrest warrant cannot be carried out owing to the death or escape of the requested person.

3. If the property referred to in paragraph 1 is liable to seizure or confiscation in the territory of the executing State, that State may, if the property is needed in connection with pending criminal proceedings, temporarily retain it or hand it over to the issuing State on condition that it is returned.

4. Any rights which the executing State or third parties may have acquired in the property referred to in paragraph 1 shall be preserved. Where such rights exist, the issuing State shall return the property without charge to the executing State as soon as the criminal proceedings have been terminated.

Part 7   Key Brexit Materials

Article LAW.SURR.108: Expenses
1. Expenses incurred in the territory of the executing State for the execution of an arrest warrant shall be borne by that State.
2. All other expenses shall be borne by the issuing State.

Article LAW.SURR.109: Relation to other legal instruments
1. Without prejudice to their application in relations between States and third countries, this Title, from the date of entry into force of this Agreement, replaces the corresponding provisions of the following conventions applicable in the field of extradition in relations between the United Kingdom, on the one side, and Member States, on the other side:
   (a) the European Convention on Extradition, done at Paris on 13 December 1957, and its additional protocols; and
   (b) the European Convention on the Suppression of Terrorism, as far as extradition is concerned.
2. Where the Conventions referred to in paragraph 1 apply to the territories of States or to territories for whose external relations a State is responsible to which this Title does not apply, those Conventions continue to govern the relations existing between those territories and the other States.

Article LAW.SURR.110: Review of notifications
When carrying out the joint review of this Title as referred to in Article LAW.OTHER.135(1) [Review and evaluation], the Parties shall consider the need to maintain the notifications made under Article LAW.SURR.79(4) [Scope], Article LAW.SURR.82(2) [Political offence exception] and Article LAW.SURR.83(2) [Nationality exception]. If the notifications referred to in Article LAW.SURR.83(2) [Nationality exception] are not renewed, they shall expire five years after the date of entry into force of this Agreement. Notifications as referred to in Article LAW.SURR.83(2) [Nationality exception] may only be renewed or newly made during the three months prior to the fifth anniversary of the entry into force of this Agreement and, subsequently, every five years thereafter, provided that the conditions set out in Article LAW.SURR.83(2) [Nationality exception] are met at that time.

Article LAW.SURR.111: Ongoing arrest warrants in case of disapplication
Notwithstanding Article LAW.GEN.5 [Scope of cooperation where a Member State no longer participates in analogous measure under Union law]; Article.LAW.OTHER.136 [Termination] and Article LAW.OTHER.137 [Suspension], the provisions of this Title apply in respect of arrest warrants where the requested person was arrested before the disapplication of this Title for the purposes of the execution of an arrest warrant, irrespective of the decision of the executing judicial authority as to whether the requested person is to remain in detention or be provisionally released.

Article LAW.SURR.112: Application to existing European arrest warrants
This Title shall apply in respect of European arrest warrants issued in accordance with Council Framework Decision 2002/584/JHA[81] by a State before the end of the transition period where the requested person has not been arrested for the purpose of its execution before the end of the transition period.

TITLE VIII: MUTUAL ASSISTANCE

[7.97]
Article LAW.MUTAS.113: Objective
1. The objective of this Title is to supplement the provisions, and facilitate the application between Member States, on the one side, and the United Kingdom, on the other side, of:
   (a) the European Convention on Mutual Assistance in Criminal Matters, done at Strasbourg on 20 April 1959 (the "European Mutual Assistance Convention");
   (b) the Additional Protocol to the European Mutual Assistance Convention, done at Strasbourg on 17 March 1978; and
   (c) the Second Additional Protocol to the European Mutual Assistance Convention, done at Strasbourg on 8 November 2001.
2. This Title is without prejudice to the provisions of Title IX [Exchange of information extracted from the criminal record], which takes precedence over this Title.

Article LAW.MUTAS.114: Definition of competent authority
For the purposes of this Title, "competent authority" means any authority which is competent to send or receive requests for mutual assistance in accordance with the provisions of the European Mutual Assistance Convention and its Protocols and as defined by States in their respective declarations addressed to the Secretary General of the Council of Europe. "Competent authority" also includes Union bodies notified in accordance with point (c) of Article LAW.OTHER.134(7) [Notifications]; with regard to such Union bodies, the provisions of this Title apply accordingly.

Article LAW.MUTAS.115: Form for a request for mutual assistance
1. The Specialised Committee on Law Enforcement and Judicial Cooperation shall undertake to establish a standard form for requests for mutual assistance by adopting an annex to this Agreement.
2. If the Specialised Committee on Law Enforcement and Judicial Cooperation has adopted a decision in accordance with paragraph 1, requests for mutual assistance shall be made using the standard form.
3. The Specialised Committee on Law Enforcement and Judicial Cooperation may amend the standard form for requests for mutual assistance as may be necessary.

Article LAW.MUTAS.116 Conditions for a request for mutual assistance

1. The competent authority of the requesting State may only make a request for mutual assistance if it is satisfied that the following conditions are met:

(a)   the request is necessary and proportionate for the purpose of the proceedings, taking into account the rights of the suspected or accused person; and

(b)   the investigative measure or investigative measures indicated in the request could have been ordered under the same conditions in a similar domestic case.

2. The requested State may consult the requesting State if the competent authority of the requested State is of the view that the conditions in paragraph 1 are not met. After the consultation, the competent authority of the requesting State may decide to withdraw the request for mutual assistance.

Article LAW.MUTAS.117: Recourse to a different type of investigative measure

1. Wherever possible, the competent authority of the requested State shall consider recourse to an investigative measure other than the measure indicated in the request for mutual assistance if:

(a)   the investigative measure indicated in the request does not exist under the law of the requested State; or

(b)   the investigative measure indicated in the request would not be available in a similar domestic case.

2. Without prejudice to the grounds for refusal available under the European Mutual Assistance Convention and its Protocols and under Article LAW.MUTAS.119 [*Ne bis in idem*], paragraph 1 of this Article does not apply to the following investigative measures, which shall always be available under the law of the requested State:

(a)   the obtaining of information contained in databases held by police or judicial authorities that is directly accessible by the competent authority of the requested State in the framework of criminal proceedings;

(b)   the hearing of a witness, expert, victim, suspected or accused person or third party in the territory of the requested State;

(c)   any non-coercive investigative measure as defined under the law of the requested State; and

(d)   the identification of persons holding a subscription to a specified phone number or IP address.

3. The competent authority of the requested State may also have recourse to an investigative measure other than the measure indicated in the request for mutual assistance if the investigative measure selected by the competent authority of the requested State would achieve the same result by less intrusive means than the investigative measure indicated in the request.

4. If the competent authority of the requested State decides to have recourse to a measure other than that indicated in the request for mutual assistance as referred to in paragraphs 1 or 3, it shall first inform the competent authority of the requesting State, which may decide to withdraw or supplement the request.

5. If the investigative measure indicated in the request does not exist under the law of the requested State or would not be available in a similar domestic case, and there is no other investigative measure which would have the same result as the investigative measure requested, the competent authority of the requested State shall inform the competent authority of the requesting State that it is not possible to provide the assistance requested.

Article LAW.MUTAS.118: Obligation to inform

The competent authority of the requested State shall inform the competent authority of the requesting State by any means and without undue delay if:

(a)   it is impossible to execute the request for mutual assistance due to the fact that the request is incomplete or manifestly incorrect; or

(b)   the competent authority of the requested State, in the course of the execution of the request for mutual assistance, considers without further enquiries that it may be appropriate to carry out investigative measures not initially foreseen, or which could not be specified when the request for mutual assistance was made, in order to enable the competent authority of the requesting State to take further action in the specific case.

Article LAW.MUTAS.119: *Ne bis in idem*

Mutual assistance may be refused, in addition to the grounds for refusal provided for under the European Mutual Assistance Convention and its Protocols, on the ground that the person in respect of whom the assistance is requested and who is subject to criminal investigations, prosecutions or other proceedings, including judicial proceedings, in the requesting State, has been finally judged by another State in respect of the same acts, provided that, if a penalty has been imposed, it has been enforced, is in the process of being enforced or can no longer be enforced under the law of the sentencing State.

Article LAW.MUTAS.120: Time limits

1. The requested State shall decide whether to execute the request for mutual assistance as soon as possible and in any event no later than 45 days after the receipt of the request and shall inform the requesting State of its decision.

2. A request for mutual assistance shall be executed as soon as possible and in any event no later than 90 days after the decision referred to in paragraph 1 of this Article or after the consultation referred to in Article LAW.MUTAS.116(2) [Conditions for a request for mutual assistance] has taken place.

3. If it is indicated in the request for mutual assistance that, due to procedural deadlines, the seriousness of the offence or other particularly urgent circumstances, a shorter time limit than that provided for in paragraph 1 or 2 is necessary, or if it is indicated in the request that a measure for mutual assistance is to be carried out on a specific date, the requested State shall take as full account as possible of that requirement.

4. If a request for mutual assistance is made to take provisional measures pursuant to Article 24 of the Second Additional Protocol to the European Mutual Assistance Convention, the competent authority of the requested State shall decide on the provisional measure, and shall communicate that decision to the competent authority of the

requesting State, as soon as possible after the receipt of the request. Before lifting any provisional measure taken pursuant to this Article, the competent authority of the requested State, wherever possible, shall give the competent authority of the requesting State an opportunity to present its reasons in favour of continuing the measure.

5. If in a specific case, the time limit provided for in paragraph 1 or 2, or the time limit or specific date referred to in paragraph 3 cannot be met, or the decision on taking provisional measures in accordance with paragraph 4 is delayed, the competent authority of the requested State shall, without delay, inform the competent authority of the requesting State by any means, giving the reasons for the delay, and shall consult with the competent authority of the requesting State on the appropriate timing to execute the request for mutual assistance.

6. The time limits referred to in this Article do not apply if the request for mutual assistance is made in relation to any of the following offences and infringements that fall within scope of the European Mutual Assistance Convention and its Protocols, as defined in the law of the requesting State:

(a) speeding, if no injury or death was caused to another person and if the excess speed was not significant;
(b) failure to wear a seatbelt;
(c) failure to stop at a red light or other mandatory stop signal;
(d) failure to wear a safety helmet; or
(e) using a forbidden lane (such as the forbidden use of an emergency lane, a lane reserved for public transport, or a lane closed down for road works).

7. The Specialised Committee on Law Enforcement and Judicial Cooperation shall keep the operation of paragraph 6 under review. It shall undertake to set time limits for the requests to which paragraph 6 applies within three years of the entry into force of this Agreement, taking into account the volume of requests. It may also decide that paragraph 6 shall no longer apply.

Article LAW.MUTAS.121: Transmission of requests for mutual assistance

1. In addition to the channels of communication provided for under the European Mutual Assistance Convention and its Protocols, if direct transmission is provided for under their respective provisions, requests for mutual assistance may also be transmitted directly by public prosecutors in the United Kingdom to competent authorities of the Member States.

2. In addition to the channels of communication provided for under the European Mutual Assistance Convention and its Protocols, in urgent cases, any request for mutual assistance, as well as spontaneous information, may be transmitted via Europol or Eurojust, in line with the provisions in the respective Titles of this Agreement.

Article LAW.MUTAS.122: Joint Investigation Teams

If the competent authorities of States set up a Joint Investigation Team, the relationship between Member States within the Joint Investigation Team shall be governed by Union law, notwithstanding the legal basis referred to in the Agreement on the setting up of the Joint Investigation Team.

TITLE IX: EXCHANGE OF CRIMINAL RECORD INFORMATION

[7.98]
Article LAW.EXINF.120: Objective

1. The objective of this Title is to enable the exchange between the Members States, on the one side, and the United Kingdom, on the other side, of information extracted from the criminal record.

2. In the relations between the United Kingdom and the Member States, the provisions of this Title:

(a) supplement Articles 13 and 22(2) of the European Convention on Mutual Assistance in Criminal Matters and its Additional Protocols of 17 March 1978 and 8 November 2001; and
(b) replace Article 22(1) of the European Convention on Mutual Assistance in Criminal Matters, as supplemented by Article 4 of its Additional Protocol of 17 March 1978.

3. In the relations between a Member State, on the one side, and the United Kingdom, on the other side, each shall waive the right to rely on its reservations to Article 13 of the European Convention on Mutual Assistance in Criminal Matters and to Article 4 of its Additional Protocol of 17 March 1978.

Article LAW.EXINF.121: Definitions

For the purposes of this Title, the following definitions apply:

(a) "conviction" means any final decision of a criminal court against a natural person in respect of a criminal offence, to the extent that the decision is entered in the criminal record of the convicting State;
(b) "criminal proceedings" means the pre-trial stage, the trial stage and the execution of a conviction;
(c) "criminal record" means the domestic register or registers recording convictions in accordance with domestic law.

Article LAW.EXINF.122: Central authorities

Each State shall designate one or more central authorities that shall be competent for the exchange of information extracted from the criminal record pursuant to this Title and for the exchanges referred to in Article 22(2) of the European Convention on Mutual Assistance in Criminal Matters.

Article LAW.EXINF.123: Notifications

1. Each State shall take the necessary measures to ensure that all convictions handed down within its territory are accompanied, when provided to its criminal record, by information on the nationality or nationalities of the convicted person if that person is a national of another State.

2. The central authority of each State shall inform the central authority of any other State of all criminal convictions handed down within its territory in respect of nationals of the latter State, as well as of any subsequent alterations or deletions of information contained in the criminal record, as entered in the criminal record. The central authorities of the States shall communicate such information to each other at least once per month.

3. If the central authority of a State becomes aware of the fact that a convicted person is a national of two or more other States, it shall transmit the relevant information to each of those States, even if the convicted person is a national of the State within whose territory that person was convicted.

Article LAW.EXINF.124: Storage of convictions

1. The central authority of each State shall store all information notified under Article LAW.EXINF.123 [Notifications].

2. The central authority of each State shall ensure that if a subsequent alteration or deletion is notified under Article LAW.EXINF.123(2) [Notifications], an identical alteration or deletion is made to the information stored in accordance with paragraph 1 of this Article.

3. The central authority of each State shall ensure that only information which has been updated in accordance with paragraph 2 of this Article is provided when replying to requests made under Article LAW.EXINF.125 [Requests for information].

Article LAW.EXINF.125: Requests for information

1. If information from the criminal record of a State is requested at domestic level for the purposes of criminal proceedings against a person or for any purposes other than that of criminal proceedings, the central authority of that State may, in accordance with its domestic law, submit a request to the central authority of another State for information and related data to be extracted from the criminal record.

2. If a person asks the central authority of a State other than the State of the person's nationality for information on the person's own criminal record, that central authority shall submit a request to the central authority of the State of the person's nationality for information and related data to be extracted from the criminal record in order to be able to include that information and related data in the extract to be provided to the person concerned.

Article LAW.EXINF.126: Replies to requests

1. Replies to requests for information shall be transmitted by the central authority of the requested State to the central authority of the requesting State as soon as possible and in any event within 20 working days from the date the request was received.

2. The central authority of each State shall reply to requests made for purposes other than that of criminal proceedings in accordance with its domestic law.

3. Notwithstanding paragraph 2, when replying to requests made for the purposes of recruitment for professional or organised voluntary activities involving direct and regular contacts with children, the States shall include information on the existence of criminal convictions for offences related to sexual abuse or sexual exploitation of children, child pornography, solicitation of children for sexual purposes, including inciting, aiding and abetting or attempting to commit any of those offences, as well as information on the existence of any disqualification from exercising activities involving direct and regular contacts with children arising from those criminal convictions.

Article LAW.EXINF.127: Channel of communication

The exchange between States of information extracted from the criminal record shall take place electronically in accordance with the technical and procedural specifications laid down in ANNEX LAW-6.

Article LAW.EXINF.128: Conditions for the use of personal data

1. Each State may use personal data received in reply to its request under Article LAW.EXINF.126 [Replies to requests] only for the purposes for which they were requested.

2. If the information was requested for any purposes other than that of criminal proceedings, personal data received under Article LAW.EXINF.126 [Replies to requests] may be used by the requesting State in accordance with its domestic law only within the limits specified by the requested State in the form set out in Chapter 2 of ANNEX LAW-6.

3. Notwithstanding paragraphs 1 and 2 of this Article, personal data provided by a State in reply to a request under Article LAW.EXINF.126 [Replies to requests] may be used by the requesting State to prevent an immediate and serious threat to public security.

4. Each State shall ensure that their central authorities do not disclose personal data notified under Article LAW.EXINF.123 [Notifications] to authorities in third countries unless the following conditions are met:

    (a) the personal data are disclosed only on a case-by-case basis;

    (b) the personal data are disclosed to authorities whose functions are directly related to the purposes for which the personal data are disclosed under point (c) of this paragraph;

    (c) the personal data are disclosed only if necessary:

        (i) for the purposes of criminal proceedings;

        (ii) for any purposes other than that of criminal proceedings; or

        (iii) to prevent an immediate and serious threat to public security;

    (d) the personal data may be used by the requesting third country only for the purposes for which the information was requested and within the limits specified by the State that notified the personal data under Article LAW.EXINF.123 [Notifications]; and

(e) the personal data are disclosed only if the central authority, having assessed all the circumstances surrounding the transfer of the personal data to the third country, concludes that appropriate safeguards exist to protect the personal data.

5. This Article does not apply to personal data obtained by a State under this Title and originating from that State.

TITLE X: ANTI-MONEY LAUNDERING AND COUNTER TERRORIST FINANCING

[7.99]
Article LAW.AML.127: Objective
The objective of this Title is to support and strengthen action by the Union and the United Kingdom to prevent and combat money laundering and terrorist financing.

Article LAW.AML.128: Measures to prevent and combat money laundering and terrorist financing
1. The Parties agree to support international efforts to prevent and combat money laundering and terrorist financing. The Parties recognise the need to cooperate in preventing the use of their financial systems to launder the proceeds of all criminal activity, including drug trafficking and corruption, and to combat terrorist financing.
2. The Parties shall exchange relevant information, as appropriate within their respective legal frameworks.
3. The Parties shall each maintain a comprehensive regime to combat money laundering and terrorist financing, and regularly review the need to enhance that regime, taking account of the principles and objectives of the Financial Action Task Force Recommendations.

Article LAW.AML.129 Beneficial ownership transparency for corporate and other legal entities
1. For the purposes of this Article, the following definitions apply:
    (a) "beneficial owner" means any individual in respect of a corporate entity who, in accordance with the Party's laws and regulations:
        (i)   exercises or has the right to exercise ultimate control over the management of the entity;
        (ii)   ultimately owns or controls directly or indirectly more than 25% of the voting rights or shares or other ownership interests in the entity, without prejudice to each Party's right to define a lower percentage; or
        (iii) otherwise controls or has the right to control the entity;
    In respect of legal entities such as foundations, Anstalt and limited liability partnerships, each Party has the right to determine similar criteria for identifying the beneficial owner, or, if they choose, to apply the definition set out in point (a) of Article AML.130(1) [Beneficial Ownership transparency of legal arrangements], having regard to the form and structure of such entities.
    In respect of other legal entities not mentioned above, each Party shall take into account the different forms and structures of such entities and the levels of money laundering and terrorist financing risks associated with such entities, with a view to deciding the appropriate levels of beneficial ownership transparency.
    (b) "basic information about a beneficial owner" means the beneficial owner's name, month and year of birth, country of residence and nationality, as well as the nature and extent of the interest held, or control exercised, over the entity by the beneficial owner;
    (c) "competent authorities" means:
        (i)   public authorities, including Financial Intelligence Units, that have designated responsibilities for combating money laundering or terrorist financing;
        (ii)   public authorities that have the function of investigating or prosecuting money laundering, associated predicate offences or terrorist financing, or that have the function of tracing, seizing or freezing and confiscating criminal assets;
        (iii) public authorities that have supervisory or monitoring responsibilities aimed at ensuring compliance with anti-money laundering or counter terrorist financing requirements.
    This definition is without prejudice to each Party's right to identify additional competent authorities that can access information about beneficial owners.
2. Each Party shall ensure that legal entities in its territory maintain adequate, accurate and up-to-date information about beneficial owners. Each Party shall put in place mechanisms to ensure that their competent authorities have timely access to such information.
3. Each Party shall establish or maintain a central register holding adequate, up-to-date and accurate information about beneficial owners. In the case of the Union, the central registers shall be set up at the level of the Member States. This obligation shall not apply in respect of legal entities listed on a stock exchange that are subject to disclosure requirements regarding an adequate level of transparency. Where no beneficial owner is identified in respect of an entity, the register shall hold alternative information, such as a statement that no beneficial owner has been identified or details of the natural person or persons who hold the position of senior managing official in the legal entity.
4. Each Party shall ensure that the information held in its central register or registers is made available to its competent authorities without restriction and in a timely manner.
5. Each Party shall ensure that basic information about beneficial owners is made available to any member of the public. Limited exceptions may be made to the public availability of information under this paragraph in cases where public access would expose the beneficial owner to disproportionate risks, such as risks of fraud, kidnapping, blackmail, extortion, harassment, violence or intimidation, or where the beneficial owner is a minor or otherwise legally incapable.
6. Each Party shall ensure that there are effective, proportionate and dissuasive sanctions against legal or natural persons who fail to comply with requirements imposed on them in connection with the matters referred to in this Article.

7. Each Party shall ensure that its competent authorities are able to provide the information referred to in paragraphs 2 and 3 to the competent authorities of the other Party in a timely and effective manner and free of charge. To that end, the Parties shall consider ways to ensure the secure exchange of information.

Article LAW.AML.130 Beneficial ownership transparency of legal arrangements

1. For the purposes of this Article, the following definitions apply:
   - (a) "beneficial owner" means the settlor, the protector (if any), trustees, the beneficiary or class of beneficiaries, any person holding an equivalent position in relation to a legal arrangement with a structure or function similar to an express trust, and any other natural person exercising ultimate effective control over a trust or a similar legal arrangement;
   - (b) "competent authorities" means:
     - (i) public authorities, including Financial Intelligence Units, that have designated responsibilities for combating money laundering or terrorist financing;
     - (ii) public authorities that have the function of investigating or prosecuting money laundering, associated predicate offences or terrorist financing or the function of tracing, seizing or freezing and confiscating criminal assets;
     - (iii) public authorities that have supervisory or monitoring responsibilities aimed at ensuring compliance with anti-money laundering or counter terrorist financing requirements.

This definition is without prejudice to each Party's right to identify additional competent authorities that can access information about beneficial owners.

2. Each Party shall ensure that trustees of express trusts maintain adequate, accurate and up-to-date information about beneficial owners. These measures shall also apply to other legal arrangements identified by each Party as having a structure or function similar to trusts.

3. Each Party shall put in place mechanisms to ensure that its competent authorities have timely access to adequate, accurate and up-to-date information about beneficial owners of express trusts and other legal arrangements with a structure or function similar to trusts in its territory.

4. If the beneficial ownership information about trusts or similar legal arrangements is held in a central register, the State concerned shall ensure that the information is adequate, accurate and up-to-date, and that competent authorities have timely and unrestricted access to such information. The Parties shall endeavour to consider ways to provide access to beneficial ownership information about trusts and similar legal arrangements to individuals or organisations who can demonstrate a legitimate interest in seeing such information.

5. Each Party shall ensure that there are effective, proportionate and dissuasive sanctions against legal or natural persons who fail to comply with requirements imposed on them in connection with the matters referred to in this Article.

6. Each Party shall ensure that its competent authorities are able to provide the information referred to in paragraph 3 to the competent authorities of the other Party in a timely and effective manner and free of charge. To that end, the Parties shall consider ways to ensure the secure exchange of information.

TITLE XI: FREEZING AND CONFISCATION

[7.100]

Article LAW.CONFISC.1: Objective and principles of cooperation

1. The objective of this Title is to provide for cooperation between the United Kingdom, on the one side, and the Member States, on the other side, to the widest extent possible for the purposes of investigations and proceedings aimed at the freezing of property with a view to subsequent confiscation thereof and investigations and proceedings aimed at the confiscation of property within the framework of proceedings in criminal matters. This does not preclude other cooperation pursuant to Article LAW.CONFISC.10(5) and (6) [Obligation to confiscate]. This Title also provides for cooperation with Union bodies designated by the Union for the purposes of this Title.

2. Each State shall comply, under the conditions provided for in this Title, with requests from another State:
   - (a) for the confiscation of specific items of property, as well as for the confiscation of proceeds consisting in a requirement to pay a sum of money corresponding to the value of proceeds;
   - (b) for investigative assistance and provisional measures with a view to either form of confiscation referred to in point (a).

3. Investigative assistance and provisional measures sought under point (b) of paragraph 2 shall be carried out as permitted by and in accordance with the domestic law of the requested State. Where the request concerning one of these measures specifies formalities or procedures which are necessary under the domestic law of the requesting State, even if unfamiliar to the requested State, the latter shall comply with such requests to the extent that the action sought is not contrary to the fundamental principles of its domestic law.

4. The requested State shall ensure that the requests coming from another State to identify, trace, freeze or seize the proceeds and instrumentalities, receive the same priority as those made in the framework of domestic procedures.

5. When requesting confiscation, investigative assistance and provisional measures for the purposes of confiscation, the requesting State shall ensure that the principles of necessity and proportionality are respected.

6. The provisions of this Title apply in place of the "international cooperation" Chapters of the Council of Europe Convention on Laundering, Search, Seizure and Confiscation of the Proceeds from Crime and on the Financing of Terrorism, done at Warsaw on 16 May 2005 ("the 2005 Convention") and the Convention on Laundering, Search, Seizure and Confiscation of the Proceeds from Crime, done at Strasbourg on 8 November 1990 ("the 1990 Convention"). Article LAW.CONFISC.2 [Definitions] of this Agreement replaces the corresponding definitions in Article 1 of the 2005 Convention and Article 1 of the 1990 Convention. The provisions of this Title do not affect the States' obligations under the other provisions of the 2005 Convention and the 1990 Convention.

Article LAW.CONFISC.2: Definitions

For the purposes of this Title, the following definitions apply:

(a) "confiscation" means a penalty or a measure ordered by a court following proceedings in relation to a criminal offence or criminal offences, resulting in the final deprivation of property;

(b) "freezing" or "seizure" means temporarily prohibiting the transfer, destruction, conversion, disposition or movement of property or temporarily assuming custody or control of property on the basis of an order issued by a court or other competent authority;

(c) "instrumentalities" means any property used or intended to be used, in any manner, wholly or in part, to commit a criminal offence or criminal offences;

(d) "judicial authority" means an authority that is, under domestic law, a judge, a court or a public prosecutor; a public prosecutor is considered a judicial authority only to the extent that domestic law so provides;

(e) "proceeds" means any economic benefit, derived from or obtained, directly or indirectly, from criminal offences, or an amount of money equivalent to that economic benefit; it may consist of any property as defined in this Article;

(f) "property" includes property of any description, whether corporeal or incorporeal, movable or immovable, and legal documents or instruments evidencing title or interest in such property, which the requesting State considers to be:

(i) the proceeds of a criminal offence, or its equivalent, whether the full amount of the value of such proceeds or only part of the value of such proceeds;

(ii) the instrumentalities of a criminal offence, or the value of such instrumentalities;

(iii) subject to confiscation under any other provisions relating to powers of confiscation under the law of the requesting State, following proceedings in relation to a criminal offence, including third party confiscation, extended confiscation and confiscation without final conviction.

Article LAW.CONFISC.3: Obligation to assist

The States shall afford each other, upon request, the widest possible measure of assistance in the identification and tracing of instrumentalities, proceeds and other property liable to confiscation. Such assistance shall include any measure providing and securing evidence as to the existence, location or movement, nature, legal status or value of those instrumentalities, proceeds or other property.

Article LAW.CONFISC.4: Requests for information on bank accounts and safe deposit boxes

1. The requested State shall, under the conditions set out in this Article, take the measures necessary to determine, in answer to a request sent by another State, whether a natural or legal person that is the subject of a criminal investigation holds or controls one or more accounts, of whatever nature, in any bank located in its territory and, if so, provide the details of the identified accounts. These details shall in particular include the name of the customer account holder and the IBAN number, and, in the case of safe deposit boxes, the name of the lessee or a unique identification number.

2. The obligation set out in paragraph 1 applies only to the extent that the information is in the possession of the bank keeping the account.

3. In addition to the requirements of Article LAW.CONFISC.25 [Content of request], the requesting State shall, in the request:

(a) indicate why it considers that the requested information is likely to be of substantial value for the purposes of the criminal investigation into the offence;

(b) state on what grounds it presumes that banks in the requested State hold the account and specify, to the widest extent possible, which banks and accounts may be involved; and

(c) include any additional information available which may facilitate the execution of the request.

4. The United Kingdom and the Union, acting on behalf of any of its Member States, may each notify the Specialised Committee on Law Enforcement and Judicial Cooperation that this Article will be extended to accounts held in non-bank financial institutions. Such notifications may be made subject to the principle of reciprocity.

Article LAW.CONFISC.5: Requests for information on banking transactions

1. On request by another State, the requested State shall provide the particulars of specified bank accounts and of banking operations which have been carried out during a specified period through one or more accounts specified in the request, including the particulars of any sending or recipient account.

2. The obligation set out in paragraph 1 applies only to the extent that the information is in the possession of the bank keeping the account.

3. In addition to the requirements of Article LAW.CONFISC.25 [Content of request], the requesting State shall indicate in its request why it considers the requested information relevant for the purposes of the criminal investigation into the offence.

4. The requested State may make the execution of such a request dependent on the same conditions as it applies in respect of requests for search and seizure.

5. The United Kingdom and the Union, acting on behalf of any of its Member States, may each notify the Specialised Committee on Law Enforcement and Judicial Cooperation that this Article will be extended to accounts held in non-bank financial institutions. Such notifications may be made subject to the principle of reciprocity.

Article LAW.CONFISC.6: Requests for the monitoring of banking transactions

1. The requested State shall ensure that, at the request of another State, it is able to monitor, during a specified period, the banking operations that are being carried out through one or more accounts specified in the request and to communicate the results of the monitoring to the requesting State.

2. In addition to the requirements of Article LAW.CONFISC.25 [Content of request], the requesting State shall indicate in its request why it considers the requested information relevant for the purposes of the criminal investigation into the offence.

3. The decision to monitor shall be taken in each individual case by the competent authorities of the requested State, in accordance with its domestic law.

4. The practical details regarding the monitoring shall be agreed between the competent authorities of the requesting and requested States.

5. The United Kingdom and the Union, acting on behalf of any of its Member States, may each notify the Specialised Committee on Law Enforcement and Judicial Cooperation that this Article will be extended to accounts held in non-bank financial institutions. Such notifications may be made subject to the principle of reciprocity.

Article LAW.CONFISC.7: Spontaneous information

Without prejudice to its own investigations or proceedings, a State may without prior request forward to another State information on instrumentalities, proceeds and other property liable to confiscation, where it considers that the disclosure of such information might assist the receiving State in initiating or carrying out investigations or proceedings or might lead to a request by that State under this Title.

Article LAW.CONFISC.8: Obligation to take provisional measures

1. At the request of another State which has instituted a criminal investigation or proceedings, or an investigation or proceedings for the purposes of confiscation, the requested State shall take the necessary provisional measures, such as freezing or seizing, to prevent any dealing in, transfer or disposal of property which, at a later stage, may be the subject of a request for confiscation or which might satisfy the request.

2. A State which has received a request for confiscation pursuant to Article LAW.CONFISC.10 [Obligation to confiscate] shall, if so requested, take the measures referred to in paragraph 1 of this Article in respect of any property which is the subject of the request or which might satisfy the request.

3. Where a request is received under this Article, the requested State shall take all necessary measures to comply with the request without delay and with the same speed and priority as for a similar domestic case and send confirmation without delay and by any means of producing a written record to the requesting State.

4. Where the requesting State states that immediate freezing is necessary since there are legitimate grounds to believe that the property in question will immediately be removed or destroyed, the requested State shall take all necessary measures to comply with the request within 96 hours of receiving the request and send confirmation to the requesting State by any means of producing a written record and without delay.

5. Where the requested State is unable to comply with the time limits under paragraph 4, the requested State shall immediately inform the requesting State, and consult with the requesting State on the appropriate next steps.

6. Any expiration of the time limits under paragraph 4 does not extinguish the requirements placed on the requested State by this Article.

Article LAW.CONFISC.9: Execution of provisional measures

1. After the execution of the provisional measures requested in conformity with Article LAW.CONFISC.8(1) [Obligation to take provisional measures], the requesting State shall provide spontaneously and as soon as possible to the requested State all information which may question or modify the extent of those measures. The requesting State shall also provide without delay all complementary information required by the requested State and which is necessary for the implementation of and the follow-up to the provisional measures.

2. Before lifting any provisional measure taken pursuant to Article LAW.CONFISC.8 [Obligation to take provisional measures], the requested State shall, wherever possible, give the requesting State an opportunity to present its reasons in favour of continuing the measure.

Article LAW.CONFISC.10: Obligation to confiscate

1. The State which has received a request for confiscation of property situated in its territory shall:
   (a) enforce a confiscation order made by a court of the requesting State in relation to such property; or
   (b) submit the request to its competent authorities for the purpose of obtaining an order of confiscation and, if such an order is granted, enforce it.

2. For the purposes of point (b) of paragraph 1, the States shall, whenever necessary, have competence to institute confiscation proceedings under their own domestic law.

3. Paragraph 1 also applies to confiscation consisting in a requirement to pay a sum of money corresponding to the value of proceeds, if property against which the confiscation can be enforced is located in the requested State. In such cases, when enforcing confiscation pursuant to paragraph 1, the requested State shall, if payment is not obtained, realise the claim on any property available for that purpose.

4. If a request for confiscation concerns a specific item of property, the requesting State and requested State may agree that the requested State may enforce the confiscation in the form of a requirement to pay a sum of money corresponding to the value of the property.

5. A State shall cooperate to the widest extent possible under its domestic law with a State requesting the execution of measures equivalent to confiscation of property, where the request has not been issued in the framework of proceedings in criminal matters, in so far as such measures are ordered by a judicial authority of the requesting State in relation to a criminal offence, provided that it has been established that the property constitutes proceeds or:
   (a) other property into which the proceeds have been transformed or converted; or
   (b) property acquired from legitimate sources, if proceeds have been intermingled, in whole or in part, with such property, up to the assessed value of the intermingled proceeds; or

(c)   income or other benefit derived from the proceeds, from property into which proceeds of crime have been transformed or converted or from property with which the proceeds of crime have been intermingled, up to the assessed value of the intermingled proceeds, in the same manner and to the same extent as proceeds.

6. The measures referred to in paragraph 5 include measures which allow the seizure, detention and forfeiture of property and assets by means of applications to civil courts.

7. The requested State shall take the decision on the execution of the confiscation order without delay, and, without prejudice to paragraph 8 of this Article, no later than 45 days after receiving the request. The requested State shall send confirmation to the requesting State by any means of producing a written record and without delay. Unless grounds for postponement under Article LAW.CONFISC.17 [Postponement] exist, the requested State shall take the concrete measures necessary to execute the confiscation order without delay and, at least, with the same speed and priority as for a similar domestic case.

8. Where the requested State is unable to comply with the time limit under paragraph 7, the requested State shall immediately inform the requesting State, and consult with the requesting State on the appropriate next steps.

9. Any expiration of the time limit under paragraph 7 does not extinguish the requirements placed on the requested State by this Article.

Article LAW.CONFISC.11: Execution of confiscation

1. The procedures for obtaining and enforcing the confiscation under Article LAW.CONFISC.10 [Obligation to confiscate] shall be governed by the domestic law of the requested State.

2. The requested State shall be bound by the findings as to the facts in so far as they are stated in a conviction or judicial decision issued by a court of the requesting State or in so far as such conviction or judicial decision is implicitly based on them.

3. If the confiscation consists in the requirement to pay a sum of money, the competent authority of the requested State shall convert the amount thereof into the currency of that State at the rate of exchange applicable at the time when the decision to enforce the confiscation is taken.

Article LAW.CONFISC.12: Confiscated property

1. Subject to paragraphs 2 and 3 of this Article, property confiscated pursuant to Articles LAW.CONFISC.10 [Obligation to confiscate] and LAW.CONFISC.11 [Execution of confiscation] shall be disposed of by the requested State in accordance with its domestic law and administrative procedures.

2. When acting on the request made by another State pursuant to Article LAW.CONFISC.10 [Obligation to confiscate], the requested State shall, to the extent permitted by its domestic law and if so requested, give priority consideration to returning the confiscated property to the requesting State so that it can give compensation to the victims of the crime or return such property to their legitimate owners.

3. Where acting on the request made by another State in accordance with Article LAW.CONFISC.10 [Obligation to confiscate], and after having taken into account the right of a victim to restitution or compensation of property pursuant to paragraph 2 of this Article, the requested State shall dispose of the money obtained as a result of the execution of a confiscation order as follows:

(a)   if the amount is equal to or less than EUR 10 000, the amount shall accrue to the requested State; or

(b)   if the amount is greater than EUR 10 000, the requested State shall transfer 50 % of the amount recovered to the requesting State.

4. Notwithstanding paragraph 3, the requesting State and requested State may, on a case-by-case basis, give special consideration to concluding other such agreements or arrangements on disposal of property as they deem appropriate.

Article LAW.CONFISC.13: Right of enforcement and maximum amount of confiscation

1. A request for confiscation made under Article LAW.CONFISC.10 [Obligation to confiscate] does not affect the right of the requesting State to enforce the confiscation order itself.

2. Nothing in this Title shall be interpreted as permitting the total value of the confiscation to exceed the amount of the sum of money specified in the confiscation order. If a State finds that this might occur, the States concerned shall enter into consultations to avoid such an effect.

Article LAW.CONFISC.14: Imprisonment in default

The requested State shall not impose imprisonment in default or any other measure restricting the liberty of a person as a result of a request under Article LAW.CONFISC.10 [Obligation to confiscate] without the consent of the requesting State.

Article LAW.CONFISC.15: Grounds for refusal

1. Cooperation under this Title may be refused if:

(a)   the requested State considers that executing the request would be contrary to the principle of *ne bis in idem*; or

(b)   the offence to which the request relates does not constitute an offence under the domestic law of the requested State if committed within its jurisdiction; however, this ground for refusal applies to cooperation under Articles LAW.CONFISC.3 [Obligation to assist] to LAW.CONFISC.7 [Spontaneous information] only in so far as the assistance sought involves coercive action.

2. The United Kingdom and the Union, acting on behalf of any of its Member States, may each notify the Specialised Committee on Law Enforcement and Judicial Cooperation that, on the basis of reciprocity, the condition of double criminality referred to in point (b) of paragraph 1 of this Article will not be applied provided that the offence giving rise to the request is:

(a) one of the offences listed in Article LAW.SURR.79(4) [Scope], as defined by the law of the requesting State; and

(b) punishable by the requesting State by a custodial sentence or a detention order for a maximum period of at least three years.

3. Cooperation under Articles LAW.CONFISC.3 [Obligation to assist] to LAW.CONFISC.7 [Spontaneous information], in so far as the assistance sought involves coercive action, and under Articles LAW.CONFISC.8 [Obligation to take provisional measures] and LAW.CONFISC.9 [Execution of provisional measures] may also be refused if the measures sought could not be taken under the domestic law of the requested State for the purposes of investigations or proceedings in a similar domestic case.

4. Where the domestic law of the requested State so requires, cooperation under Articles LAW.CONFISC.3 [Obligation to assist] to LAW.CONFISC.7 [Spontaneous information], in so far as the assistance sought involves coercive action, and under Articles LAW.CONFISC.8 [Obligation to take provisional measures] and LAW.CONFISC.9 [Execution of provisional measures] may also be refused if the measures sought or any other measures having similar effects would not be permitted under the domestic law of the requesting State, or, as regards the competent authorities of the requesting State, if the request is not authorised by a judicial authority acting in relation to criminal offences.

5. Cooperation under Articles LAW.CONFISC.10 [Obligation to confiscate] to LAW.CONFISC.14 [Imprisonment in default] may also be refused if:

(a) under the domestic law of the requested State, confiscation is not provided for in respect of the type of offence to which the request relates;

(b) without prejudice to the obligation pursuant to Article LAW.CONFISC.10(3) [Obligation to confiscate], it would be contrary to the principles of the domestic law of the requested State concerning the limits of confiscation in respect of the relationship between an offence and:

    (i) an economic advantage that might be qualified as its proceeds; or

    (ii) property that might be qualified as its instrumentalities;

(c) under the domestic law of the requested State, confiscation may no longer be imposed or enforced because of the lapse of time;

(d) without prejudice to Article LAW.CONFISC.10 (5) and (6) [Obligation to confiscate], the request does not relate to a previous conviction, or a decision of a judicial nature or a statement in such a decision that an offence or several offences have been committed, on the basis of which the confiscation has been ordered or is sought;

(e) confiscation is either not enforceable in the requesting State, or it is still subject to ordinary means of appeal; or

(f) the request relates to a confiscation order resulting from a decision rendered in absentia of the person against whom the order was issued and, in the opinion of the requested State, the proceedings conducted by the requesting State leading to such decision did not satisfy the minimum rights of defence recognised as due to everyone against whom a criminal charge is made.

6. For the purposes of point (f) of paragraph 5 a decision is not considered to have been rendered in absentia if:

(a) it has been confirmed or pronounced after opposition by the person concerned; or

(b) it has been rendered on appeal, provided that the appeal was lodged by the person concerned.

7. When considering, for the purposes of point (f) of paragraph 5, whether the minimum rights of defence have been satisfied, the requested State shall take into account the fact that the person concerned has deliberately sought to evade justice or the fact that that person, having had the possibility of lodging a legal remedy against the decision made in absentia, elected not to do so. The same applies where the person concerned, having been duly served with the summons to appear, elected not to do so nor to ask for adjournment.

8. The States shall not invoke bank secrecy as a ground to refuse any cooperation under this Title. Where its domestic law so requires, a requested State may require that a request for cooperation which would involve the lifting of bank secrecy be authorised by a judicial authority acting in relation to criminal offences.

9. The requested State shall not invoke the fact that:

(a) the person under investigation or subject to a confiscation order by the authorities of the requesting State is a legal person as an obstacle to affording any cooperation under this Title;

(b) the natural person against whom an order of confiscation of proceeds has been issued has died or a legal person against whom an order of confiscation of proceeds has been issued has subsequently been dissolved as an obstacle to affording assistance in accordance with point (a) of Article LAW.CONFISC.10(1) [Obligation to confiscate]; or

(c) the person under investigation or subject to a confiscation order by the authorities of the requesting State is mentioned in the request both as the author of the underlying criminal offence and of the offence of money laundering as an obstacle to affording any cooperation under this Title.

Article LAW.CONFISC.16: Consultation and information

Where there are substantial grounds for believing that the execution of a freezing or confiscation order would entail a real risk for the protection of fundamental rights, the requested State shall, before it decides on the execution of the freezing or confiscation order, consult the requesting State and may require any necessary information to be provided.

Article LAW.CONFISC.17: Postponement

The requested State may postpone action on a request if such action would prejudice investigations or proceedings by its authorities.

Article LAW.CONFISC.18: Partial or conditional granting of a request

Before refusing or postponing cooperation under this Title, the requested State shall, where appropriate after having consulted the requesting State, consider whether the request may be granted partially or subject to such conditions as it deems necessary.

Article LAW.CONFISC.19: Notification of documents

1. The States shall afford each other the widest measure of mutual assistance in the serving of judicial documents to persons affected by provisional measures and confiscation.
2. Nothing in this Article is intended to interfere with:
   (a) the possibility of sending judicial documents, by postal channels, directly to persons abroad; and
   (b) the possibility for judicial officers, officials or other competent authorities of the State of origin to effect service of judicial documents directly through the consular authorities of that State or through the judicial authorities, including judicial officers and officials, or other competent authorities of the State of destination.
3. When serving judicial documents to persons abroad affected by provisional measures or confiscation orders issued in the sending State, that State shall indicate what legal remedies are available under its domestic law to such persons.

Article LAW.CONFISC.20: Recognition of foreign decisions

1. When dealing with a request for cooperation under Articles LAW.CONFISC.8 [Obligation to take provisional measures] to LAW.CONFISC.14 [Imprisonment in default] the requested State shall recognise any decision issued by a judicial authority taken in the requesting State regarding rights claimed by third parties.
2. Recognition may be refused if:
   (a) third parties did not have adequate opportunity to assert their rights;
   (b) the decision is incompatible with a decision already taken in the requested State on the same matter;
   (c) it is incompatible with the *ordre public* of the requested State; or
   (d) the decision was taken contrary to provisions on exclusive jurisdiction provided for by the domestic law of the requested State.

Article LAW.CONFISC.21: Authorities

1. Each State shall designate a central authority to be responsible for sending and answering requests made under this Title, the execution of such requests or their transmission to the authorities competent for their execution.
2. The Union may designate a Union body which may, in addition to the competent authorities of the Member States, make and, if appropriate, execute requests under this Title. Any such request is to be treated for the purposes of this Title as a request by a Member State. The Union may also designate that Union body as the central authority responsible for the purpose of sending and answering requests made under this Title by, or to, that body.

Article LAW.CONFISC.22: Direct communication

1. The central authorities shall communicate directly with one another.
2. In urgent cases, requests or communications under this Title may be sent directly by the judicial authorities of the requesting State to judicial authorities of the requested State. In such cases, a copy shall be sent at the same time to the central authority of the requested State through the central authority of the requesting State.
3. Where a request is made pursuant to paragraph 2 and the authority is not competent to deal with the request, it shall refer the request to the competent national authority and shall directly inform the requesting State that it has done so.
4. Requests or communications under Articles LAW.CONFISC.3 [Obligation to assist] to LAW.CONFISC.7 [Spontaneous information], which do not involve coercive action, may be directly transmitted by the competent authorities of the requesting State to the competent authorities of the requested State.
5. Draft requests or communications under this Title may be sent directly by the judicial authorities of the requesting State to the judicial authorities of the requested State prior to a formal request to ensure that the formal request can be dealt with efficiently upon receipt and that it contains sufficient information and supporting documentation for it to meet the requirements of the law of the requested State.

Article LAW.CONFISC.23: Form of request and languages

1. All requests under this Title shall be made in writing. They may be transmitted electronically, or by any other means of telecommunication, provided that the requesting State is prepared, upon request, to produce a written record of such communication and the original at any time.
2. Requests under paragraph 1 shall be made in one of the official languages of the requested State or in any other language notified by or on behalf of the requested State in accordance with paragraph 3.
3. The United Kingdom and the Union, acting on behalf of any of its Member States, may each notify the Specialised Committee on Law Enforcement and Judicial Cooperation of the language or languages which, in addition to the official language or languages of that State, may be used for making requests under this Title.
4. Requests under Article LAW.CONFISC.8 [Obligation to take provisional measures] for provisional measures shall be made using the prescribed form at ANNEX LAW-8.
5. Requests under Article LAW.CONFISC.10 [Obligation to confiscate] for confiscation shall be made using the prescribed form at ANNEX LAW-8.
6. The Specialised Committee on Law Enforcement and Judicial Cooperation may amend the forms referred to in paragraphs 4 and 5 as may be necessary.
7. The United Kingdom and the Union, acting on behalf of any of its Member States may each notify the Specialised Committee on Law Enforcement and Judicial Cooperation that it requires the translation of any supporting documents into one of the official languages of the requested State or any other language indicated in accordance with

paragraph 3 of this Article. In the case of requests pursuant to Article LAW.CONFISC.8(4) [Obligation to take provisional measures], such translation of supporting documents may be provided to the requested State within 48 hours after transmitting the request, without prejudice to the time limits provided for in Article LAW.CONFISC.8(4) [Obligation to take provisional measures].

Article LAW.CONFISC.24: Legalisation
Documents transmitted in application of this Title shall be exempt from all legalisation formalities.

Article LAW.CONFISC.25: Content of request
1. Any request for cooperation under this Title shall specify:
   (a) the authority making the request and the authority carrying out the investigations or proceedings;
   (b) the object of and the reason for the request;
   (c) the matters, including the relevant facts (such as date, place and circumstances of the offence) to which the investigations or proceedings relate, except in the case of a request for notification;
   (d) insofar as the cooperation involves coercive action:
       (i) the text of the statutory provisions or, where that is not possible, a statement of the relevant applicable law; and
       (ii) an indication that the measure sought or any other measures having similar effects could be taken in the territory of the requesting State under its own domestic law;
   (e) where necessary and in so far as possible:
       (i) details of the person or persons concerned, including name, date and place of birth, nationality and location, and, in the case of a legal person, its seat; and
       (ii) the property in relation to which cooperation is sought, its location, its connection with the person or persons concerned, any connection with the offence, as well as any available information about other persons, interests in the property; and
   (f) any particular procedure the requesting State wishes to be followed.
2. A request for provisional measures under Article LAW.CONFISC.8 [Obligation to take provisional measures] in relation to seizure of property on which a confiscation order consisting of the requirement to pay a sum of money may be realised shall also indicate a maximum amount for which recovery is sought in that property.
3. In addition to the information referred to in paragraph 1 of this Article, any request under Article LAW.CONFISC.10 [Obligation to confiscate] shall contain:
   (a) in the case of point (a) of Article LAW.CONFISC.10(1) [Obligation to confiscate]:
       (i) a certified true copy of the confiscation order made by the court in the requesting State and a statement of the grounds on the basis of which the order was made, if they are not indicated in the order itself;
       (ii) an attestation by the competent authority of the requesting State that the confiscation order is enforceable and not subject to ordinary means of appeal;
       (iii) information as to the extent to which the enforcement of the order is requested; and
       (iv) information as to the necessity of taking any provisional measures;
   (b) in the case of point (b) of Article LAW.CONFISC.10(1) [Obligation to confiscate], a statement of the facts relied upon by the requesting State sufficient to enable the requested State to seek the order under its domestic law;
   (c) where third parties have had the opportunity to claim rights, documents demonstrating that this has been the case.

Article LAW.CONFISC.26: Defective requests
1. If a request does not comply with the provisions of this Title or the information supplied is not sufficient to enable the requested State to deal with the request, that State may ask the requesting State to amend the request or to complete it with additional information.
2. The requested State may set a time limit for the receipt of such amendments or information.
3. Pending receipt of the requested amendments or information in relation to a request under Article LAW.CONFISC.10 [Obligation to confiscate], the requested State may take any of the measures referred to in Articles LAW.CONFISC.3 [Obligation to assist] to LAW.CONFISC.9 [Execution of provisional measures].

Article LAW.CONFISC.27: Plurality of requests
1. Where the requested State receives more than one request under Article LAW.CONFISC.8 [Obligation to take provisional measures] or Article LAW.CONFISC.10 [Obligation to confiscate] in respect of the same person or property, the plurality of requests shall not prevent that State from dealing with the requests involving the taking of provisional measures.
2. In the case of a plurality of requests under Article LAW.CONFISC.10 [Obligation to confiscate], the requested State shall consider consulting the requesting States.

Article LAW.CONFISC.28: Obligation to give reasons
The requested State shall give reasons for any decision to refuse, postpone or make conditional any cooperation under this Title.

Article LAW.CONFISC.29: Information
1. The requested State shall promptly inform the requesting State of:
   (a) the action initiated on the basis of a request under this Title;

(b) the final result of the action carried out on the basis of a request under this Title;

(c) a decision to refuse, postpone or make conditional, in whole or in part, any cooperation under this Title;

(d) any circumstances which render impossible the carrying out of the action sought or are likely to delay it significantly; and

(e) in the event of provisional measures taken pursuant to a request under Articles LAW.CONFISC.3 [Obligation to assist] to Article LAW.CONFISC.8 [Obligation to take provisional measures], such provisions of its domestic law as would automatically lead to the lifting of the provisional measure.

2. The requesting State shall promptly inform the requested State of:

(a) any review, decision or any other fact by reason of which the confiscation order ceases to be wholly or partially enforceable; and

(b) any development, factual or legal, by reason of which any action under this Title is no longer justified.

3. Where a State, on the basis of the same confiscation order, requests confiscation in more than one State, it shall inform all States which are affected by the enforcement of the order about the request.

Article LAW.CONFISC.30: Restriction of use

1. The requested State may make the execution of a request dependent on the condition that the information or evidence obtained is not, without its prior consent, to be used or transmitted by the authorities of the requesting State for investigations or proceedings other than those specified in the request.

2. Without the prior consent of the requested State, information or evidence provided by it under this Title shall not be used or transmitted by the authorities of the requesting State in investigations or proceedings other than those specified in the request.

3. Personal data communicated under this Title may be used by the State to which they have been transferred:

(a) for the purposes of proceedings to which this Title applies;

(b) for other judicial and administrative proceedings directly related to proceedings referred to under point (a);

(c) for preventing an immediate and serious threat to public security; or

(d) for any other purpose, only with the prior consent of the communicating State, unless the State concerned has obtained the consent of the data subject.

4. This Article shall also apply to personal data not communicated but obtained otherwise under this Title.

5. This Article does not apply to personal data obtained by the United Kingdom or a Member State under this Title and originating from that State.

Article LAW.CONFISC.31: Confidentiality

1. The requesting State may require that the requested State keep confidential the facts and substance of the request, except to the extent necessary to execute the request. If the requested State cannot comply with the requirement of confidentiality, it shall promptly inform the requesting State.

2. The requesting State shall, if not contrary to basic principles of its domestic law and if so requested, keep confidential any evidence and information provided by the requested State, except to the extent that its disclosure is necessary for the investigations or proceedings described in the request.

3. Subject to the provisions of its domestic law, a State which has received spontaneous information under Article LAW.CONFISC.7 [Spontaneous information] shall comply with any requirement of confidentiality as required by the State which supplies the information. If the receiving State cannot comply with such a requirement, it shall promptly inform the transmitting State.

Article LAW.CONFISC.32: Costs

The ordinary costs of complying with a request shall be borne by the requested State. Where costs of a substantial or extraordinary nature are necessary to comply with a request, the requesting and requested States shall consult in order to agree the conditions on which the request is to be executed and how the costs will be borne.

Article LAW.CONFISC.33: Damages

1. Where legal action on liability for damages resulting from an act or omission in relation to cooperation under this Title has been initiated by a person, the States concerned shall consider consulting each other, where appropriate, to determine how to apportion any sum of damages due.

2. A State which has become the subject of litigation for damages shall endeavour to inform the other State of such litigation if that State might have an interest in the case.

Article LAW.CONFISC.34: Legal remedies

1. Each State shall ensure that persons affected by measures under Articles LAW.CONFISC.8 [Obligation to take provisional measures] to LAW.CONFISC.11 [Execution of confiscation] have effective legal remedies in order to preserve their rights.

2. The substantive reasons for requested measures under Articles LAW.CONFISC.8 [Obligation to take provisional measures] to LAW.CONFISC.11 [Execution of confiscation] shall not be challenged before a court in the requested State.

TITLE XII: OTHER PROVISIONS

[7.101]
Article LAW.OTHER.134: Notifications
1. By the date of entry into force of this Agreement, the Union and the United Kingdom shall make any of the notifications provided for in Article LAW.SURR.82(2) [Political offence exception], Article LAW.SURR.83(2) [Nationality exception], and Article LAW.SURR.91(4) [Consent to surrender] and shall, to the extent it is possible to do so, indicate whether no such notification is to be made.

To the extent that such a notification or indication has not been made in relation to a State, at the point in time referred to in the first subparagraph, notifications may be made in relation to that State as soon as possible and at the latest two months after the entry into force of this Agreement.

During that interim period, any State in relation to which no notification provided for in Article LAW.SURR.82(2) [Political offence exception], Article LAW.SURR.83(2) [Nationality exception], or Article LAW.SURR.91(4) [Consent to surrender] has been made, and which has not been the subject of an indication that no such notification is to be made, may avail itself of the possibilities provided for in that Article as if such a notification had been made in respect of that State. In the case of Article LAW.SURR.83(2) [Nationality exception], a State may only avail itself of the possibilities provided for in that Article to the extent that to do so is compatible with the criteria for making a notification.

2. The notifications referred to in Article LAW.SURR.79(4) [Scope], Article LAW.SURR.85(1) [Recourse to the central authority], Article LAW.SURR.86(2) [Content and form of the arrest warrant], Article LAW.SURR.105(1) [Possible prosecution for other offences], Article LAW.SURR.106(1) [Surrender or subsequent extradition], Article LAW.CONFISC.4(4) [Requests for information on bank accounts and safe deposit boxes], Article LAW.CONFISC.5(5) [Requests for information on banking transactions], Article LAW.CONFISC.6(5) [Requests for the monitoring of banking transactions], Article LAW.CONFISC.15(2) [Grounds for refusal], and Article LAW.CONFISC.23(3) and (7) [Form of request and languages] may be made at any time.

3. The notifications referred to in Article LAW.SURR.85(1) [Recourse to the central authority], Article LAW.SURR.86(2) [Content and form of the arrest warrant] and Article LAW.CONFISC.23(3) and (7) [Form of request and languages] may be modified at any time.

4. The notifications referred to in Article LAW.SURR.82(2) [Political offence exception], Article LAW.SURR.83(2) [Nationality exception], Article LAW.SURR.85(1) [Recourse to the central authority], Article LAW.SURR.91(4) [Consent to surrender], Article LAW.CONFISC.4(4) [Requests for information on bank accounts and safe deposit boxes], Article LAW.CONFISC.5(5) [Requests for information on banking transactions], and Article LAW.CONFISC.6(5) [Requests for the monitoring of banking transactions] may be withdrawn at any time.

5. The Union shall publish information on notifications of the United Kingdom referred to in Article LAW.SURR.85(1) [Recourse to the central authority] in the Official Journal of the European Union.

6. By the date of entry into force of this Agreement, the United Kingdom shall notify the Union of the identity of the following authorities:
- (a) the authority responsible for receiving and processing PNR data under Title III [Transfer and processing of passenger name record data (PNR)];
- (b) the authority considered as the competent law enforcement authority for the purposes of Title V [Cooperation with Europol] and a short description of its competences;
- (c) the national contact point designated under Article LAW.EUROPOL.50(1) [National contact point and liaison officers];
- (d) the authority considered as the competent authority for the purposes of Title VI [Cooperation with Eurojust] and a short description of its competences;
- (e) the contact point designated under Article LAW.EUROJUST.65(1) [Contact points to Eurojust];
- (f) the United Kingdom Domestic Correspondent for Terrorism Matters designated under Article LAW.EUROJUST.65(2) [Contact points to Eurojust];
- (g) the authority competent by virtue of domestic law of the United Kingdom to execute an arrest warrant, as referred to in point (c) of Article LAW.SURR.78 [Definitions], and the authority competent by virtue of the domestic law of the United Kingdom to issue an arrest warrant, as referred to in point (d) of Article LAW.SURR.78 [Definitions];
- (h) the authority designated by the United Kingdom under Article LAW.SURR.103(3) [Transit];
- (i) the central authority designated by the United Kingdom under Article LAW.EXINF.122 [Central authorities];
- (j) the central authority designated by the United Kingdom under Article LAW.CONFISC.21(1) [Authorities].

The Union shall publish information about the authorities referred to in the first subparagraph in the Official Journal of the European Union.

7. By the date of entry into force of this Agreement, the Union shall, on its behalf or on behalf of its Member States as the case may be, notify the United Kingdom, of the identity of the following authorities:
- (a) the Passenger Information Units established or designated by each Member State for the purposes of receiving and processing PNR data under Title III [Transfer and processing of passenger name record data (PNR)];
- (b) the authority competent by virtue of the domestic law of each Member State to execute an arrest warrant, as referred to in point (c) of Article LAW.SURR.78 [Definitions], and the authority competent by virtue of the domestic law of each Member State to issue an arrest warrant, as referred to in point (d) of Article LAW.SURR.78 [Definitions];
- (c) the authority designated for each Member State under Article LAW.SURR.103(3) [Transit];
- (d) the Union body referred to in Article LAW.MUTAS.114 [Definition of competent authority];
- (e) the central authority designated by each Member State under Article LAW.EXINF.122 [Central authorities];
- (f) the central authority designated by each Member State under Article LAW.CONFISC.21(1) [Authorities];
- (g) any Union body designated under the first sentence of Article LAW.CONFISC.21(2) [Authorities] and whether it is also designated as a central authority under the last sentence of that paragraph.

8. The notifications made under paragraph 6 or 7 may be modified at any time. Such modifications shall be notified to the Specialised Committee on Law Enforcement and Judicial Cooperation.

9. The United Kingdom and the Union may notify more than one authority with respect to points (a), (b), (d), (e), (g), (h), (i) and (j) of paragraph 6 and with respect to paragraph 7 respectively and may limit such notifications for particular purposes only.

10. Where the Union makes the notifications referred to in this Article, it shall indicate to which of its Member States the notification applies or whether it is making the notification on its own behalf.

Article LAW.OTHER.135: Review and evaluation

1. This Part shall be jointly reviewed in accordance with Article FINPROV.3 [Review] or at the request of either Party where jointly agreed.

2. The Parties shall decide in advance on how the review is to be conducted and shall communicate to each other the composition of their respective review teams. The review teams shall include persons with appropriate expertise with respect to the issues under review. Subject to applicable laws, all participants in a review shall be required to respect the confidentiality of the discussions and to have appropriate security clearances. For the purposes of such reviews, the United Kingdom and the Union shall make arrangements for appropriate access to relevant documentation, systems and personnel.

3. Without prejudice to paragraph 2, the review shall in particular address the practical implementation, interpretation and development of this Part.

Article LAW.OTHER.136: Termination

1. Without prejudice to Article FINPROV.8 [Termination], each Party may at any moment terminate this Part by written notification through diplomatic channels. In that event, this Part shall cease to be in force on the first day of the ninth month following the date of notification.

2. However, if this Part is terminated on account of the United Kingdom or a Member State having denounced the European Convention on Human Rights or Protocols 1, 6 or 13 thereto, this Part shall cease to be in force as of the date that such denunciation becomes effective or, if the notification of its termination is made after that date, on the fifteenth day following such notification.

3. If either Party gives notice of termination under this Article, the Specialised Committee on Law Enforcement and Judicial Cooperation shall meet to decide what measures are needed to ensure that any cooperation initiated under this Part is concluded in an appropriate manner. In any event, with regard to all personal data obtained through cooperation under this Part before it ceases to be in force, the Parties shall ensure that the level of protection under which the personal data were transferred is maintained after the termination takes effect.

Article LAW.OTHER.137: Suspension

1. In the event of serious and systemic deficiencies within one Party as regards the protection of fundamental rights or the principle of the rule of law, the other Party may suspend this Part or Titles thereof, by written notification through diplomatic channels. Such notification shall specify the serious and systemic deficiencies on which the suspension is based.

2. In the event of serious and systemic deficiencies within one Party as regards the protection of personal data, including where those deficiencies have led to a relevant adequacy decision ceasing to apply, the other Party may suspend this Part or Titles thereof, by written notification through diplomatic channels. Such notification shall specify the serious and systemic deficiencies on which the suspension is based.

3. For the purposes of paragraph 2, "relevant adequacy decision" means:
   (a) in relation to the United Kingdom, a decision adopted by the European Commission, in accordance with Article 36 of Directive (EU) 2016/680[82] or analogous successor legislation, attesting to the adequate level of protection;
   (b) in relation to the Union, a decision adopted by the United Kingdom attesting to the adequate level of protection for the purposes of transfers falling within the scope of Part 3 of the Data Protection Act 2018[83] or analogous successor legislation.

4. In relation to the suspension of Title III [Transfer and processing of passenger name record data (PNR)] or Title X [Anti-money laundering and counter terrorist financing], references to a "relevant adequacy decision" also include:
   (a) in relation to the United Kingdom, a decision adopted by the European Commission, in accordance with Article 45 of the General Data Protection Regulation (EU) 2016/679[84] or analogous successor legislation attesting to the adequate level of protection;
   (b) in relation to the Union, a decision adopted by the United Kingdom attesting to the adequate level of protection for the purposes of transfers falling within the scope of Part 2 of the Data Protection Act 2018 or analogous successor legislation.

5. The Titles concerned by the suspension shall provisionally cease to apply on the first day of the third month following the date of the notification referred to in paragraph 1 or 2, unless, no later than two weeks before the expiry of that period, as extended, as the case may be, in accordance with point (d) of paragraph 7, the Party which notified the suspension gives written notification to the other Party, through diplomatic channels, of its withdrawal of the first notification or of a reduction in scope of the suspension. In the latter case, only the Titles referred to in the second notification shall provisionally cease to apply.

6. If one Party notifies the suspension of one or several Titles of this Part pursuant to paragraph 1 or 2, the other Party may suspend all of the remaining Titles, by written notification through diplomatic channels, with three months' notice.

7. Upon the notification of a suspension pursuant to paragraph 1 or 2, the Partnership Council shall immediately be seized of the matter. The Partnership Council shall explore possible ways of allowing the Party that notified the suspension to postpone its entry into effect, to reduce its scope or to withdraw it. To that end, upon a recommendation of the Specialised Committee on Law Enforcement and Judicial Cooperation, the Partnership Council may:

(a) agree on joint interpretations of provisions of this Part;

(b) recommend any appropriate action to the Parties;

(c) adopt appropriate adaptations to this Part which are necessary to address the reasons underlying the suspension, with a maximum validity of 12 months; and

(d) extend the period referred to in paragraph 5 by up to three months.

8. If either Party gives notification of suspension under this Article, the Specialised Committee on Law Enforcement and Judicial Cooperation shall meet to decide what measures are needed to ensure that any cooperation initiated under this Part and affected by the notification is concluded in an appropriate manner. In any event, with regard to all personal data obtained through cooperation under this Part before the Titles concerned by the suspension provisionally cease to apply, the Parties shall ensure that the level of protection under which the personal data were transferred is maintained after the suspension takes effect.

9. The suspended Titles shall be reinstated on the first day of the month following the day on which the Party having notified the suspension pursuant to paragraph 1 or 2 has given written notification to the other Party, through diplomatic channels, of its intention to reinstate the suspended Titles. The Party having notified the suspension pursuant to paragraph 1 or 2 shall do so immediately after the serious and systemic deficiencies on the part of the other Party on which the suspension was based have ceased to exist.

10. Upon the notification of the intention to reinstate the suspended Titles in accordance with paragraph 9, the remaining Titles suspended pursuant to paragraph 6 shall be reinstated at the same time as the Titles suspended pursuant to paragraph 1 or 2.

Article LAW.OTHER.138: Expenses

The Parties and the Member States, including institutions, bodies, offices and agencies of the Parties or the Member States, shall bear their own expenses which arise in the course of implementation of this Part, unless otherwise provided for in this Agreement.

TITLE XIII: DISPUTE SETTLEMENT

[7.102]

Article LAW.DS.1: Objective

The objective of this Title is to establish a swift, effective and efficient mechanism for avoiding and settling disputes between the Parties concerning this Part, including disputes concerning this Part when applied to situations governed by other provisions of this Agreement, with a view to reaching a mutually agreed solution, where possible.

Article LAW.DS.2: Scope

1. This Title applies to disputes between the Parties concerning this Part (the "covered provisions").

2. The covered provisions shall include all provisions of this Part, with the exception of:

(a) Article LAW.GEN.5 [Scope for cooperation where a Member State no longer participates in analogous measures under Union law];

(b) Article LAW.PRUM.19 [Suspension and disapplication];

(c) Article LAW.PNR.28(14) [Retention of PNR data];

(d) Article LAW.PNR.38 [Suspension of cooperation under this Title];

(e) Article LAW.OTHER.136 [Termination];

(f) Article LAW.OTHER.137 [Suspension]; and

(g) Article LAW.DS.6 [Suspension].

Article LAW.DS.3: Exclusivity

The Parties undertake not to submit a dispute between them regarding this Part to a mechanism of settlement other than that provided for in this Title.

Article LAW.DS.4: Consultations

1. If a Party ("the complaining Party") considers that the other Party ("the responding Party") has breached an obligation under this Part, the Parties shall endeavour to resolve the matter by entering into consultations in good faith, with the aim of reaching a mutually agreed solution.

2. The complaining Party may seek consultations by means of a written request delivered to the responding Party. The complaining Party shall specify in its written request the reasons for the request, including identification of the acts or omissions that the complaining Party considers as giving rise to the breach of an obligation by the responding Party, specifying the covered provisions it considers applicable.

3. The responding Party shall reply to the request promptly, and no later than two weeks after the date of its delivery. Consultations shall be held regularly within a period of three months following the date of delivery of the request in person or by any other means of communication agreed by the Parties.

4. The consultations shall be concluded within three months of the date of delivery of the request, unless the Parties agree to continue the consultations.

5. The complaining Party may request that the consultations be held in the framework of the Specialised Committee on Law Enforcement and Judicial Cooperation or in the framework of the Partnership Council. The first meeting shall take place within one month of the request for consultations referred to in paragraph 2 of this Article. The Specialised Committee on Law Enforcement and Judicial Cooperation may at any time decide to refer the matter to

the Partnership Council. The Partnership Council may also seize itself of the matter. The Specialised Committee on Law Enforcement and Judicial Cooperation, or as the case may be, the Partnership Council, may resolve the dispute by a decision. Such a decision shall be considered a mutually agreed solution within the meaning of Article LAW.DS.5 [Mutually agreed solution].

6. The complaining Party may at any time unilaterally withdraw its request for consultations. In such a case, the consultations shall be terminated immediately.

7. Consultations, and in particular all information designated as confidential and positions taken by the Parties during consultations, shall be confidential.

Article LAW.DS.5: Mutually agreed solution

1. The Parties may at any time reach a mutually agreed solution with respect to any dispute referred to in Article LAW.DS.2 [Scope].

2. The mutually agreed solution may be adopted by means of a decision of the Specialised Committee on Law Enforcement and Judicial Cooperation or the Partnership Council. Where the mutually agreed solution consists of an agreement on joint interpretations of provisions of this Part by the Parties, that mutually agreed solution shall be adopted by means of a decision of the Partnership Council.

3. Each Party shall take the measures necessary to implement the mutually agreed solution within the agreed time period.

4. No later than the date of expiry of the agreed time period, the implementing Party shall inform the other Party in writing of any measures taken to implement the mutually agreed solution.

Article LAW.DS.6: Suspension

1. Where consultations under Article LAW.DS.4 [Consultations] have not led to a mutually agreed solution within the meaning of Article LAW.DS.5 [Mutually agreed solution], provided that the complaining Party has not withdrawn its request for consultations in accordance with Article LAW.DS.4(6) [Consultations], and where it considers that the respondent Party is in serious breach of its obligations under the covered provisions referred to in Article LAW.DS.4(2) [Consultations], the complaining Party may suspend the Titles of this Part to which the serious breach pertains, by written notification through diplomatic channels. Such notification shall specify the serious breach of obligations by the responding Party on which the suspension is based.

2. The Titles concerned by the suspension shall provisionally cease to apply on the first day of the third month following the date of the notification referred to in paragraph 1 or any other date mutually agreed by the Parties, unless, no later than two weeks before the expiry of that period, the complaining Party gives written notification to the responding Party, through diplomatic channels, of its withdrawal of the first notification or of a reduction in scope of the suspension. In the latter case, only the Titles referred to in the second notification shall provisionally cease to apply.

3. If the complaining Party notifies the suspension of one or several Titles of this Part pursuant to paragraph 1, the respondent Party may suspend all of the remaining Titles, by written notification through diplomatic channels, with three months' notice.

4. If a notification of suspension is given under this Article, the Specialised Committee on Law Enforcement and Judicial Cooperation shall meet to decide what measures are needed to ensure that any cooperation initiated under this Part and affected by the notification is concluded in an appropriate manner. In any event, with regard to all personal data obtained through cooperation under this Part before the Titles concerned by the suspension provisionally cease to apply, the Parties shall ensure that the level of protection under which the personal data were transferred is maintained after the suspension takes effect.

5. The suspended Titles shall be reinstated on the first day of the month following the date on which the complaining Party has given written notification to the respondent Party, through diplomatic channels, of its intention to reinstate the suspended Titles. The complaining Party shall do so immediately when it considers that the serious breach of the obligations on which the suspension was based has ceased to exist.

6. Upon notification by the complaining Party of its intention to reinstate the suspended Titles in accordance with paragraph 5, the remaining Titles suspended by the respondent Party pursuant to paragraph 3 shall be reinstated at the same time as the Titles suspended by the complaining Party pursuant to paragraph 1.

Article LAW.DS.7: Time Periods

1. All time periods laid down in this Title shall be counted in weeks or months, as the case may be, from the day following the act to which they refer.

2. Any time period referred to in this Title may be modified by mutual agreement of the Parties.

NOTES

[77] Council Decision 2008/615/JHA of 23 June 2008 on the stepping up of cross-border cooperation, particularly in combating terrorism and cross-border crime (OJ EU L 210, 6.8.2008, p. 1).

[78] Council Decision 2008/616/JHA of 23 June 2008 on the implementation of Decision 2008/615/JHA on the stepping up of cross-border cooperation, particularly in combating terrorism and cross-border crime (OJ EU L 210, 6.8.2008, p. 12).

[79] Regulation (EU) 2016/794 of the European Parliament and of the Council of 11 May 2016 on the European Union Agency for Law Enforcement Cooperation (Europol) and replacing and repealing Council Decisions 2009/371/JHA, 2009/934/JHA, 2009/935/JHA, 2009/936/JHA and 2009/968/JHA (OJ EU L 135, 24.5.2016, p. 53).

[80] Regulation (EU) 2018/1727 of the European Parliament and of the Council of 14 November 2018 on the European Union Agency for Criminal Justice Cooperation (Eurojust), and replacing and repealing Council Decision 2002/187/JHA (OJ EU L 295, 21.11.2018, p. 138)

[81] Council Framework Decision 2002/584/JHA of 13 June 2002 on the European arrest warrant and the surrender procedures between Member States (OJ EU L 190, 18.7.2002, p. 1).

[82] Directive (EU) 2016/680 of the European Parliament and of the Council of 27 April 2016 on the protection of natural

persons with regard to the processing of personal data by competent authorities for the purposes of the prevention, investigation, detection or prosecution of criminal offences or the execution of criminal penalties, and on the free movement of such data, and repealing Council Framework Decision 2008/977/JHA (OJ EU L 119, 4.5.2016, p. 89).

83 2018 chapter 12.

84 Regulation (EU) 2016/679 of the European Parliament and of the Council of 27 April 2016 on the protection of natural persons with regard to the processing of personal data and on the free movement of such data, and repealing Directive 95/46/EC (General Data Protection Regulation) (Text with EEA relevance) (OJ EU L 119, 4.5.2016, p. 1).

PART FOUR:
THEMATIC COOPERATION

TITLE II: CYBER SECURITY

[7.103]
Article CYB.1: Dialogue on cyber issues
The Parties shall endeavour to establish a regular dialogue in order to exchange information about relevant policy developments, including in relation to international security, security of emerging technologies, internet governance, cybersecurity, cyber defence and cybercrime.

Article CYB.2: Cooperation on cyber issues
1. Where in their mutual interest, the Parties shall cooperate in the field of cyber issues by sharing best practices and through cooperative practical actions aimed at promoting and protecting an open, free, stable, peaceful and secure cyberspace based on the application of existing international law and norms for responsible State behaviour and regional cyber confidence-building measures.
2. The Parties shall also endeavour to cooperate in relevant international bodies and forums, and endeavour to strengthen global cyber resilience and enhance the ability of third countries to fight cybercrime effectively.

Article CYB.3: Cooperation with the Computer Emergency Response Team – European Union
Subject to prior approval by the Steering Board of the Computer Emergency Response Team – European Union (CERT-EU), CERT-EU and the national UK computer emergency response team shall cooperate on a voluntary, timely and reciprocal basis to exchange information on tools and methods, such as techniques, tactics, procedures and best practices, and on general threats and vulnerabilities.

Article CYB.4: Participation in specific activities of the Cooperation Group established pursuant to Directive (EU) 2016/1148
1. With a view to promoting cooperation on cyber security while ensuring the autonomy of the Union decision-making process, the relevant national authorities of the United Kingdom may participate at the invitation, which the United Kingdom may also request, of the Chair of the Cooperation Group in consultation with the Commission, in the following activities of the Cooperation Group:
    (a) exchanging best practices in building capacity to ensure the security of network and information systems;
    (b) exchanging information with regard to exercises relating to the security of network and information systems;
    (c) exchanging information, experiences and best practices on risks and incidents;
    (d) exchanging information and best practices on awareness-raising, education programmes and training; and
    (e) exchanging information and best practices on research and development relating to the security of network and information systems.
2. Any exchange of information, experiences or best practices between the Cooperation Group and the relevant national authorities of the United Kingdom shall be voluntary and, where appropriate, reciprocal.

Article CYB.5: Cooperation with the EU Agency for Cybersecurity (ENISA)
1. With a view to promoting cooperation on cyber security while ensuring the autonomy of the Union decision-making process, the United Kingdom may participate at the invitation, which the United Kingdom may also request, of the Management Board of the EU Cybersecurity Agency (ENISA), in the following activities carried out by ENISA:
    (a) capacity building;
    (b) knowledge and information; and
    (c) awareness raising and education.
2. The conditions for the participation of the United Kingdom in ENISA's activities referred to in paragraph 1, including an appropriate financial contribution, shall be set out in working arrangements adopted by the Management Board of ENISA subject to prior approval by the Commission and agreed with the United Kingdom.
3. The exchange of information, experiences and best practices between ENISA and the United Kingdom shall be voluntary and, where appropriate, reciprocal.

Part 7 Key Brexit Materials

PART SIX:
DISPUTE SETTLEMENT AND HORIZONTAL PROVISIONS

TITLE I: DISPUTE SETTLEMENT

CHAPTER 1: GENERAL PROVISIONS

[7.104]
Article INST.9: Objective
The objective of this Title is to establish an effective and efficient mechanism for avoiding and settling disputes between the Parties concerning the interpretation and application of this Agreement and supplementing agreements, with a view to reaching, where possible, a mutually agreed solution.

Article INST.10: Scope
1. This Title applies, subject to paragraphs 2, 3, 4 and 5, to disputes between the Parties concerning the interpretation and application of the provisions of this Agreement or of any supplementing agreement ("covered provisions").
2. The covered provisions shall include all provisions of this Agreement and of any supplementing agreement with the exception of:
   (a) paragraphs 1 to 6 of Article GOODS.17 [Trade remedies] and Article GOODS.21 [Cultural property] of Title I of Heading One Part Two;
   (b) Annex TBT-X [Medicinal products];
   (c) Title VII [Small and medium sized enterprises] of Heading one of Part Two;
   (d) Title X [Good regulatory practices and regulatory cooperation] of Heading One of Part Two;
   (e) paragraphs 1, 2 and 4 of Article LPFS.1.1 [Principles and objectives] and paragraphs 1 and 3 of Article LPFS.1.2 [Right to regulate, precautionary approach and scientific and technical information] of Chapter 1 [General provisions], Chapter 2 [Competition policy], Articles LPFS.3.9 [Independent authority or body and cooperation] and LPFS.3.10 [Courts and tribunals] of Chapter 2 [Subsidy control]; and Chapter 5 [Taxation] of Title XI [Level playing field for open and fair competition and sustainable development] of Heading One of Part Two, and paragraphs 4 to 9 of Article LPFS.9.4 [Rebalancing] of Chapter 9 [Horizontal and institutional provisions] of Title XI [Level playing field for open and fair competition and sustainable development] of Heading One of Part Two;
   (f) Part Three [Law enforcement and judicial cooperation in criminal matters], including when applying in relation to situations governed by other provisions of this Agreement;
   (g) Part Four [Thematic cooperation];
   (h) Title II [Basis for cooperation] of Part Six [Dispute settlement and horizontal provisions];
   (i) Article FINPROV.10A [Interim provision for transmission of personal data to the United Kingdom] of Part Seven; and
   (j) the Agreement on security procedures for exchanging and protecting classified information;
3. The Partnership Council may be seized by a Party with a view to resolving a dispute with respect to obligations arising from the provisions referred to in paragraph 2.
4. Article INST.11 [Exclusivity] shall apply to the provisions referred to in paragraph 2.
5. Notwithstanding paragraphs 1 and 2, this Title shall not apply with respect to disputes concerning the interpretation and application of the provisions of the Protocol on Social Security Coordination or its annexes in individual cases.

Article INST.11: Exclusivity
The Parties undertake not to submit a dispute between them regarding the interpretation or application of provisions of this Agreement or of any supplementing agreement to a mechanism of settlement other than those provided for in this Agreement.

Article INST.12: Choice of forum in case of a substantially equivalent obligation under another international agreement
1. If a dispute arises regarding a measure allegedly in breach of an obligation under this Agreement or any supplementing agreement and of a substantially equivalent obligation under another international agreement to which both Parties are party, including the WTO Agreement, the Party seeking redress shall select the forum in which to settle the dispute.
2. Once a Party has selected the forum and initiated dispute settlement procedures either under this Title or under another international agreement, that Party shall not initiate such procedures under the other international agreement with respect to the particular measure referred to in paragraph 1, unless the forum selected first fails to make findings for procedural or jurisdictional reasons.
3. For the purposes of this Article:
   (a) dispute settlement procedures under this Title are deemed to be initiated by a Party's request for the establishment of an arbitration tribunal under Article INST.14 [Arbitration procedures];
   (b) dispute settlement procedures under the WTO Agreement are deemed to be initiated by a Party's request for the establishment of a panel under Article 6 of the Understanding on Rules and Procedure Governing the Settlement of Disputes of the WTO; and
   (c) dispute settlement procedures under any other agreement are deemed to be initiated if they are initiated in accordance with the relevant provisions of that agreement.

4. Without prejudice to paragraph 2, nothing in this Agreement or any supplementing agreement shall preclude a Party from suspending obligations authorised by the Dispute Settlement Body of the WTO or authorised under the dispute settlement procedures of another international agreement to which the Parties are party. The WTO Agreement or any other international agreement between the Parties shall not be invoked to preclude a Party from suspending obligations under this Title.

CHAPTER 2: PROCEDURE

Article INST.13: Consultations

1. If a Party ("the complaining Party") considers that the other Party ("the respondent Party") has breached an obligation under this Agreement or under any supplementing agreement, the Parties shall endeavour to resolve the matter by entering into consultations in good faith, with the aim of reaching a mutually agreed solution.

2. The complaining Party may seek consultations by means of a written request delivered to the respondent Party. The complaining Party shall specify in its written request the reasons for the request, including the identification of the measures at issue and the legal basis for the request, and the covered provisions it considers applicable.

3. The respondent Party shall reply to the request promptly, and in any case no later than 10 days after the date of its delivery. Consultations shall be held within 30 days of the date of delivery of the request in person or by any other means of communication agreed by the Parties. If held in person, consultations shall take place in the territory of the respondent Party, unless the Parties agree otherwise.

4. The consultations shall be deemed concluded within 30 days of the date of delivery of the request, unless the Parties agree to continue consultations.

5. Consultations on matters of urgency, including those regarding perishable goods or seasonal goods or services, shall be held within 20 days of the date of delivery of the request. The consultations shall be deemed concluded within those 20 days unless the Parties agree to continue consultations.

6. Each Party shall provide sufficient factual information to allow a complete examination of the measure at issue, including an examination of how that measure could affect the application of this Agreement or any supplementing agreement. Each Party shall endeavour to ensure the participation of personnel of their competent authorities who have expertise in the matter subject to the consultations.

7. For any dispute concerning an area other than Titles I to VII, Chapter four [Energy and raw materials] of Title VIII, Titles IX to XII of Heading One or Heading Six of Part Two, at the request of the complaining Party, the consultations referred to in paragraph 3 of this Article shall be held in the framework of a Specialised Committee or of the Partnership Council. The Specialised Committee may at any time decide to refer the matter to the Partnership Council. The Partnership Council may also seize itself of the matter. The Specialised Committee, or, as the case may be, the Partnership Council, may resolve the dispute by a decision. The time periods referred to in paragraph 3 of this Article shall apply. The venue of meetings shall be governed by the rules of procedure of the Specialised Committee or, as the case may be, the Partnership Council.

8. Consultations, and in particular all information designated as confidential and positions taken by the Parties during consultations, shall be confidential, and shall be without prejudice to the rights of either Party in any further proceedings.

Article INST.14: Arbitration procedure

1. The complaining Party may request the establishment of an arbitration tribunal if:
   (a) the respondent Party does not respond to the request for consultations within 10 days of the date of its delivery;
   (b) consultations are not held within the time periods referred to in Article INST.13(3), (4) or (5) [Consultations];
   (c) the Parties agree not to have consultations; or
   (d) consultations have been concluded without a mutually agreed solution having been reached.

2. The request for the establishment of the arbitration tribunal shall be made by means of a written request delivered to the respondent Party. In its request, the complaining Party shall explicitly identify the measure at issue and explain how that measure constitutes a breach of the covered provisions in a manner sufficient to present the legal basis for the complaint clearly.

Article INST.15: Establishment of an arbitration tribunal

1. An arbitration tribunal shall be composed of three arbitrators.

2. No later than 10 days after the date of delivery of the request for the establishment of an arbitration tribunal, the Parties shall consult with a view to agreeing on the composition of the arbitration tribunal.

3. If the Parties do not agree on the composition of the arbitration tribunal within the time period provided for in paragraph 2, each Party shall appoint an arbitrator from the sub-list for that Party established pursuant to Article INST.27 [Lists of arbitrators] no later than five days after the expiry of the time period provided for in paragraph 2 of this Article. If a Party fails to appoint an arbitrator from its sub-list within that time period, the co-chair of the Partnership Council from the complaining Party shall select, no later than five days after the expiry of that time period, an arbitrator by lot from the sub-list of the Party that has failed to appoint an arbitrator. The co-chair of the Partnership Council from the complaining Party may delegate such selection by lot of the arbitrator.

4. If the Parties do not agree on the chairperson of the arbitration tribunal within the time period provided for in paragraph 2 of this Article, the co-chair of the Partnership Council from the complaining Party shall select, no later than five days after the expiry of that time period, the chairperson of the arbitration tribunal by lot from the sub-list of chairpersons established pursuant to Article INST.27 [Lists of arbitrators]. The co-chair of the Partnership Council from the complaining Party may delegate such selection by lot of the chairperson of the arbitration tribunal.

5. Should any of the lists provided for in Article INST.27 [Lists of arbitrators] not be established or not contain sufficient names at the time a selection is made pursuant to paragraphs 3 or 4 of this Article, the arbitrators shall be selected by lot from the individuals who have been formally proposed by one Party or both Parties in accordance with Annex INST-X [Rules of procedure].

6. The date of establishment of the arbitration tribunal shall be the date on which the last of the three arbitrators has notified to the Parties the acceptance of his or her appointment in accordance with Annex INST-X [Rules of procedure].

Article INST.16: Requirements for arbitrators

1. All arbitrators shall:
   (a) have demonstrated expertise in law and international trade, including on specific matters covered by Titles I to VII, Chapter four [Energy and raw materials] of Title VIII, Titles IX to XII of Heading One [Trade] of Part Two or Heading Six [Other provisions] of Part Two, or in law and any other matter covered by this Agreement or by any supplementing agreement and, in the case of a chairperson, also have experience in dispute settlement procedures;
   (b) not be affiliated with or take instructions from either Party;
   (c) serve in their individual capacities and not take instructions from any organisation or government with regard to matters related to the dispute; and
   (d) comply with Annex INST-X [Code of Conduct].]

2. All arbitrators shall be persons whose independence is beyond doubt, who possess the qualifications required for appointment to high judicial office in their respective countries or who are jurisconsults of recognised competence.

3. In view of the subject-matter of a particular dispute, the Parties may agree to derogate from the requirements listed in point (a) of paragraph 1.

Article INST.17: Functions of the arbitration tribunal

The arbitration tribunal:
   (a) shall make an objective assessment of the matter before it, including an objective assessment of the facts of the case and the applicability of, and conformity of the measures at issue with, the covered provisions;
   (b) shall set out, in its decisions and rulings, the findings of facts and law and the rationale behind any findings that it makes; and
   (c) should consult regularly with the Parties and provide adequate opportunities for the development of a mutually agreed solution.

Article INST.18: Terms of reference

1. Unless the Parties agree otherwise no later than five days after the date of the establishment of the arbitration tribunal, the terms of reference of the arbitration tribunal shall be:
   "*to examine, in the light of the relevant covered provisions of this Agreement or of a supplementing agreement, the matter referred to in the request for the establishment of the arbitration tribunal, to decide on the conformity of the measure at issue with the provisions referred to in Article INST.10 [Scope] and to issue a ruling in accordance with Article INST.20 [Ruling of the arbitration tribunal]*".

2. If the Parties agree on terms of reference other than those referred to in paragraph 1, they shall notify the agreed terms of reference to the arbitration tribunal within the time period referred to in paragraph 1.

Article INST.19: Urgent proceedings

1. If a Party so requests, the arbitration tribunal shall decide, no later than 10 days after the date of its establishment, whether the case concerns matters of urgency.

2. In cases of urgency, the applicable time periods set out in Article INST.20 [Ruling of the Arbitration Tribunal] shall be half the time prescribed therein.

Article INST.20: Ruling of the arbitration tribunal

1. The arbitration tribunal shall deliver an interim report to the Parties within 100 days after the date of establishment of the arbitration tribunal. If the arbitration tribunal considers that this deadline cannot be met, the chairperson of the arbitration tribunal shall notify the Parties in writing, stating the reasons for the delay and the date on which the arbitration tribunal plans to deliver its interim report. The arbitration tribunal shall not deliver its interim report later than 130 days after the date of establishment of the arbitration tribunal under any circumstances.

2. Each Party may deliver to the arbitration tribunal a written request to review precise aspects of the interim report within 14 days of its delivery. A Party may comment on the other Party's request within six days of the delivery of the request.

3. If no written request to review precise aspects of the interim report is delivered within the time period referred to in paragraph 2, the interim report shall become the ruling of the arbitration tribunal.

4. The arbitration tribunal shall deliver its ruling to the Parties within 130 days of the date of establishment of the arbitration tribunal. When the arbitration tribunal considers that that deadline cannot be met, its chairperson shall notify the Parties in writing, stating the reasons for the delay and the date on which the arbitration tribunal plans to deliver its ruling. The arbitration tribunal shall not deliver its ruling later than 160 days after the date of establishment of the arbitration tribunal under any circumstances.

5. The ruling shall include a discussion of any written request by the Parties on the interim report and clearly address the comments of the Parties.

6. For greater certainty, a 'ruling' or 'rulings' as referred to in Articles INST.17 [Functions of the arbitration tribunal], INST.18 [Terms of reference], INST.28 [Replacement of arbitrators] and Article INST.29(1), (3), (4) and (6) [Arbitration tribunal rulings and decisions] shall be understood to refer also to the interim report of the arbitration tribunal.

CHAPTER 3: COMPLIANCE

Article INST.21: Compliance measures
1. If, in its ruling referred to in Article INST.20(1) [Ruling of the arbitration tribunal], the arbitration tribunal finds that the respondent Party has breached an obligation under this Agreement or under any supplementing agreement, that Party shall take the necessary measures to comply immediately with the ruling of the arbitration tribunal in order to bring itself in compliance with the covered provisions.
2. The respondent Party, no later than 30 days after delivery of the ruling, shall deliver a notification to the complaining Party of the measures which it has taken or which it envisages to take in order to comply.

Article INST.22: Reasonable Period of Time
1. If immediate compliance is not possible, the respondent Party, no later than 30 days after delivery of the ruling referred to in Article INST.20(1) [Ruling of the arbitration tribunal], shall deliver a notification to the complaining Party of the length of the reasonable period of time it will require for compliance with the ruling referred to in Article INST.20(1) [Ruling of the arbitration tribunal]. The Parties shall endeavour to agree on the length of the reasonable period of time to comply.
2. If the Parties have not agreed on the length of the reasonable period of time, the complaining Party may, at the earliest 20 days after the delivery of the notification referred to in paragraph 1, request in writing that the original arbitration tribunal determines the length of the reasonable period of time. The arbitration tribunal shall deliver its decision to the Parties within 20 days of the date of delivery of the request.
3. The respondent Party shall deliver a written notification of its progress in complying with the ruling referred to in Article INST.20(1) [Ruling of the arbitration tribunal] to the complaining Party at least one month before the expiry of the reasonable period of time.
4. The Parties may agree to extend the reasonable period of time.

Article INST.23: Compliance Review
1. The respondent Party shall, no later than the date of expiry of the reasonable period of time, deliver a notification to the complaining Party of any measure that it has taken to comply with the ruling referred to in Article INST.20(1) [Ruling of the arbitration tribunal].
2. When the Parties disagree on the existence of, or the consistency with the covered provisions of, any measure taken to comply, the complaining Party may deliver a request, which shall be in writing, to the original arbitration tribunal to decide on the matter. The request shall identify any measure at issue and explain how that measure constitutes a breach of the covered provisions in a manner sufficient to present the legal basis for the complaint clearly. The arbitration tribunal shall deliver its decision to the Parties within 45 days of the date of delivery of the request.

Article INST.24: Temporary Remedies
1. The respondent Party shall, at the request of and after consultations with the complaining Party, present an offer for temporary compensation if:
  (a) the respondent Party delivers a notification to the complaining Party that it is not possible to comply with the ruling referred to in Article INST.20(1) [Ruling of the arbitration tribunal]; or
  (b) the respondent Party fails to deliver a notification of any measure taken to comply within the deadline referred to in Article INST.21 [Compliance Measures] or before the date of expiry of the reasonable period of time; or
  (c) the arbitration tribunal finds that no measure taken to comply exists or that the measure taken to comply is inconsistent with the covered provisions.
2. In any of the conditions referred to in points (a), (b) and (c) of paragraph 1, the complaining Party may deliver a written notification to the respondent Party that it intends to suspend the application of obligations under the covered provisions if:
  (a) the complaining Party decides not to make a request under paragraph 1; or
  (b) the Parties do not agree on the temporary compensation within 20 days after the expiry of the reasonable period of time or the delivery of the arbitration tribunal decision under Article INST.23 [Compliance Review] if a request under paragraph 1 is made.
The notification shall specify the level of intended suspension of obligations.
3. Suspension of obligations shall be subject to the following conditions:
  (a) Obligations under Heading Four [Social security coordination and visas for short-term visits] of Part Two, the Protocol on Social Security Coordination or its annexes or Part Five [Union programmes] may not be suspended under this Article;
  (b) By derogation from point (a), obligations under Part Five [Union programmes] may be suspended only where the ruling referred to in Article INST.20(1) [Ruling of the arbitration tribunal] concerns the interpretation and implementation of Part Five [Union programmes];
  (c) Obligations outside Part Five [Union programmes] may not be suspended where the ruling referred to in Article INST.20(1) [Ruling of the arbitration tribunal] concerns the interpretation and implementation of Part Five [Union programmes]; and

(d) Obligations under Title II [Services and Investment] of Heading One of Part Two in respect of financial services may not be suspended under this Article, unless the ruling referred to in Article INST.20(1) [Ruling of the arbitration tribunal] concerns the interpretation and application of obligations under Title II [Services and Investment] of Heading One of Part Two in respect of financial services.

4. Where a Party persists in not complying with a ruling of an arbitration panel established under an earlier agreement concluded between the Parties, the other Party may suspend obligations under the covered provisions referred to in Article INST.10 [Scope]. With the exception of the rule in point (a) of paragraph 3, all rules relating to temporary remedies in case of non-compliance and to review of any such measures shall be governed by the earlier agreement.

5. The suspension of obligations shall not exceed the level equivalent to the nullification or impairment caused by the violation.

6. If the arbitration tribunal has found the violation in Heading One [Trade] or Heading Three [Road] of Part Two, the suspension may be applied in another Title of the same Heading as that in
which the tribunal has found the violation, in particular if the complaining party is of the view that such suspension is effective in inducing compliance.

7. If the arbitration tribunal has found the violation in Heading Two [Aviation]:
   (a) the complaining party should first seek to suspend obligations in the same Title as that in which the arbitration tribunal has found the violation;
   (b) if the complaining party considers that it is not practicable or effective to suspend obligations with respect to the same Title as that in which the tribunal has found the violation, it may seek to suspend obligations in the other Title under the same Heading.

8. If the arbitration tribunal has found the violation in Heading One [Trade], Heading Two [Aviation], Heading Three [Road] or Heading Five [Fisheries] of Part Two, and if the complaining party considers that it is not practicable or effective to suspend obligations within the same Heading as that in which the arbitration tribunal has found the violation, and that the circumstances are serious enough, it may seek to suspend obligations under other covered provisions.

9. In the case of point (b) of paragraph 7 and paragraph 8, the complaining Party shall state the reasons for its decision.

10. The complaining Party may suspend the obligations 10 days after the date of delivery of the notification referred to in paragraph 2 unless the respondent Party made a request under paragraph 11.

11. If the respondent Party considers that the notified level of suspension of obligations exceeds the level equivalent to the nullification or impairment caused by the violation or that the principles and procedures set forth in point (b) of paragraph 7, paragraph 8 or paragraph 9 have not been followed, it may deliver a written request to the original arbitration tribunal before the expiry of the 10 day period set out in paragraph 10 to decide on the matter. The arbitration tribunal shall deliver its decision on the level of the suspension of obligations to the Parties within 30 days of the date of the request. Obligations shall not be suspended until the arbitration tribunal has delivered its decision. The suspension of obligations shall be consistent with that decision.

12. The arbitration tribunal acting pursuant to paragraph 11 shall not examine the nature of the obligations to be suspended but shall determine whether the level of such suspension exceeds the level equivalent to the nullification or impairment caused by the violation. However, if the matter referred to arbitration includes a claim that the principles and procedures set forth in point (b) of paragraph 7, paragraph 8 or paragraph 9 have not been followed, the arbitration tribunal shall examine that claim. In the event the arbitration tribunal determines that those principles and procedures have not been followed, the complaining party shall apply them consistently with point (b) of paragraph 7, paragraph 8 and paragraph 9. The parties shall accept the arbitration tribunal's decision as final and shall not seek a second arbitration procedure. This paragraph shall under no circumstances delay the date as of which the complaining Party is entitled to suspend obligations under this Article.

13. The suspension of obligations or the compensation referred to in this Article shall be temporary and shall not be applied after:
   (a) the Parties have reached a mutually agreed solution pursuant to Article INST.31 [Mutually agreed solution];
   (b) the Parties have agreed that the measure taken to comply brings the respondent Party into compliance with the covered provisions; or
   (c) any measure taken to comply which the arbitration tribunal has found to be inconsistent with the covered provisions has been withdrawn or amended so as to bring the respondent Party into compliance with those covered provisions.

Article INST.25: Review of any measure taken to comply after the adoption of temporary remedies

1. The respondent Party shall deliver a notification to the complaining Party of any measure it has taken to comply following the suspension of obligations or following the application of temporary compensation, as the case may be. With the exception of cases under paragraph 2, the complaining Party shall terminate the suspension of obligations within 30 days from the delivery of the notification. In cases where compensation has been applied, with the exception of cases under paragraph 2, the respondent Party may terminate the application of such compensation within 30 days from the delivery of its notification that it has complied.

2. If the Parties do not reach an agreement on whether the notified measure brings the respondent Party into compliance with the covered provisions within 30 days of the date of delivery of the notification, the complaining Party shall deliver a written request to the original arbitration tribunal to decide on the matter. The arbitration tribunal shall deliver its decision to the Parties within 46 days of the date of the delivery of the request. If the arbitration tribunal finds that the measure taken to comply is in conformity with the covered provisions, the suspension of obligations or compensation, as the case may be, shall be terminated. When relevant, the level of suspension of obligations or of compensation shall be adjusted in light of the arbitration tribunal decision.

CHAPTER 4: COMMON PROCEDURAL PROVISIONS

Article INST.26: Receipt of information

1. On request of a Party, or on its own initiative, the arbitration tribunal may seek from the Parties relevant information it considers necessary and appropriate. The Parties shall respond promptly and fully to any request by the arbitration tribunal for such information.

2. On request of a Party, or on its own initiative, the arbitration tribunal may seek from any source any information it considers appropriate. The arbitration tribunal may also seek the opinion of experts as it considers appropriate and subject to any terms and conditions agreed by the Parties, where applicable.

3. The arbitration tribunal shall consider amicus curiae submissions from natural persons of a Party or legal persons established in a Party in accordance with Annex INST-X [Rules of Procedure].

4. Any information obtained by the arbitration tribunal under this Article shall be made available to the Parties and the Parties may submit comments on that information to the arbitration tribunal.

Article INST.27: Lists of arbitrators

1. The Partnership Council shall, no later than 180 days after the date of entry into force of this Agreement, establish a list of individuals with expertise in specific sectors covered by this Agreement or its supplementing agreements who are willing and able to serve as members of an arbitration tribunal. The list shall comprise at least 15 persons and shall be composed of three sub-lists:

   (a) one sub-list of individuals established on the basis of proposals by the Union;

   (b) one sub-list of individuals established on the basis of proposals by the United Kingdom; and

   (c) one sub-list of individuals who are not nationals of either Party who shall serve as chairperson to the arbitration tribunal.

Each sub-list shall include at least five individuals. The Partnership Council shall ensure that the list is always maintained at this minimum number of individuals.

2. The Partnership Council may establish additional lists of individuals with expertise in specific sectors covered by this Agreement or by any supplementing agreement. Subject to the agreement of the Parties, such additional lists may be used to compose the arbitration tribunal in accordance with the procedure set out in Article INST.15(3) and (5) [Establishment of an arbitration tribunal]. Additional lists shall be composed of two sub-lists:

   (a) one sub-list of individuals established on the basis of proposals by the Union; and

   (b) one sub-list of individuals established on the basis of proposals by the United Kingdom.

3. The lists referred to in paragraphs 1 and 2 shall not comprise persons who are members, officials or other servants of the Union institutions, of the Government of a Member State, or of the Government of the United Kingdom.

Article INST.28: Replacement of arbitrators

If during dispute settlement procedures under this Title, an arbitrator is unable to participate, withdraws, or needs to be replaced because that arbitrator does not comply with the requirements of the Code of Conduct, the procedure set out in Article INST.15 [Establishment of the arbitration tribunal] shall apply. The time period for the delivery of the ruling or decision shall be extended for the time necessary for the appointment of the new arbitrator.

Article INST.29: Arbitration tribunal decisions and rulings

1. The deliberations of the arbitration tribunal shall be kept confidential. The arbitration tribunal shall make every effort to draft rulings and take decisions by consensus. If this is not possible, the arbitration tribunal shall decide the matter by majority vote. In no case shall separate opinions of arbitrators be disclosed.

2. The decisions and rulings of the arbitration tribunal shall be binding on the Union and on the United Kingdom. They shall not create any rights or obligations with respect to natural or legal persons.

3. Decisions and rulings of the arbitration tribunal cannot add to or diminish the rights and obligations of the Parties under this Agreement or under any supplementing agreement.

4. For greater certainty, the arbitration tribunal shall have no jurisdiction to determine the legality of a measure alleged to constitute a breach of this Agreement or of any supplementing agreement, under the domestic law of a Party. No finding made by the arbitration tribunal when ruling on a dispute between the Parties shall bind the domestic courts or tribunals of either Party as to the meaning to be given to the domestic law of that Party.

4A. For greater certainty, the courts of each Party shall have no jurisdiction in the resolution of disputes between the Parties under this Agreement.

5. Each Party shall make the rulings and decisions of the arbitration tribunal publicly available, subject to the protection of confidential information.

6. The information submitted by the Parties to the arbitration tribunal shall be treated in accordance with the confidentiality rules laid down in ANNEX-INST-X [Rules of procedure].

Article INST.30: Suspension and termination of the arbitration proceedings

At the request of both Parties, the arbitration tribunal shall suspend its work at any time for a period agreed by the Parties and not exceeding 12 consecutive months. The arbitration tribunal shall resume its work before the end of the suspension period at the written request of both Parties, or at the end of the suspension period at the written request of either Party. The requesting Party shall deliver a notification to the other Party accordingly. If a Party does not request the resumption of the arbitration tribunal's work at the expiry of the suspension period, the authority of the arbitration tribunal shall lapse and the dispute settlement procedure shall be terminated. In the event of a suspension of the work of the arbitration tribunal, the relevant time periods shall be extended by the same time period for which the work of the arbitration tribunal was suspended.

Article INST.31: Mutually agreed solution
5. The Parties may at any time reach a mutually agreed solution with respect to any dispute referred to in Article INST.10 [Scope].
6. If a mutually agreed solution is reached during panel proceedings, the Parties shall jointly notify the agreed solution to the chairperson of the arbitration tribunal. Upon such notification, the arbitration proceedings shall be terminated.
7. The solution may be adopted by means of a decision of the Partnership Council. Mutually agreed solutions shall be made publicly available. The version disclosed to the public shall not contain any information either Party has designated as confidential.
8. Each Party shall take the measures necessary to implement the mutually agreed solution within the agreed time period.
9. No later than the date of expiry of the agreed time period, the implementing Party shall inform the other Party in writing of any measures thus taken to implement the mutually agreed solution.

Article INST.32: Time Periods
1. All time periods laid down in this Title shall be counted in days from the day following the act to which they refer.
2. Any time period referred to in this Title may be modified by mutual agreement of the Parties.
3. The arbitration tribunal may at any time propose to the Parties to modify any time period referred to in this Title, stating the reasons for the proposal.

Article INST.34: Costs
1. Each Party shall bear its own expenses derived from the participation in the arbitration tribunal procedure.
2. The Parties shall share jointly and equally the expenses derived from organisational matters, including the remuneration and expenses of the members of the arbitration tribunal. The remuneration of the arbitrators shall be in accordance with INST-ANNEX-X [Rules of procedure].

Article INST.34A: Annexes
1. Dispute settlement procedures set out in this Title shall be governed by the rules of procedure set out in ANNEX INST-X [Rules of Procedure] and conducted in accordance with the ANNEX INST-X [Code of Conduct].
2. The Partnership Council may amend the ANNEXES INST-X [Rules of procedure] and INST-X [Code of conduct].

CHAPTER 5: SPECIFIC ARRANGEMENTS FOR UNILATERAL MEASURES

Article INST.34B: Special procedures for remedial measures and rebalancing
1. For the purposes of Article 3.12 [Remedial measures] of Chapter 3 [Subsidy control] and Article 9.4(2) and (3) [Rebalancing] of Chapter 9 [Institutional provisions] of Title XI [Level playing field for open and fair competition and sustainable development] of Heading One of Part Two, this Title applies with the modifications set out in this Article.
2. By derogation from Article INST.15 [Establishment of an arbitration tribunal] and Annex INST-X [Rules of procedure for dispute settlement], if the Parties do not agree on the composition of the arbitration tribunal within two days, the co-chair of the Partnership Council from the complaining Party shall select, no later than one day after the expiry of the two-day time period, an arbitrator by lot from the sub-list of each Party and the chairperson of the arbitration tribunal by lot from the sub-list of chairpersons established pursuant to Article INST.27 [Lists of arbitrators]. The co-chair of the Partnership Council from the complaining Party may delegate such selection by lot of the arbitrator or chairperson. Each individual shall confirm his or her availability to both Parties within two days from the date on which he or she was informed of his or her appointment. The organisational meeting referred to in Rule 10 of Annex INST-X [Rules of procedure for dispute settlement] shall take place within 2 days from the establishment of the arbitration tribunal.
3. By derogation from Rule 11 of Annex INST-X [Rules of procedure for dispute settlement] the complaining Party shall deliver its written submission no later than seven days after the date of establishment of the arbitration tribunal. The respondent Party shall deliver its written submission no later than seven days after the date of delivery of the written submission of the complaining Party. The arbitration tribunal shall adjust any other relevant time periods of the dispute settlement procedure as necessary to ensure the timely delivery of the report.
4. Article INST.20 [Ruling of the arbitration tribunal] does not apply and references to the ruling in this Title shall be read as references to the ruling referred to in
  (a) paragraph 10 of Article 3.12 [Remedial measures] of Chapter 3 [Subsidy control] of Title XI [Level playing field for open and fair competition and sustainable development]; or
  (b) point (c) of Article 9.4(3) [Rebalancing].
5. By derogation from Article INST.23(2) [Compliance review], the arbitration tribunal shall deliver its decision to the Parties within 30 days from the date of delivery of the request.

Article INST.34C: Suspension of obligations for the purposes of Article LPFS.3.12(12), Article FISH.9(5) and Article FISH.14(7)
1. The level of suspension of obligations shall not exceed the level equivalent to the nullification or impairment of benefits under this Agreement or under a supplementing agreement that is directly caused by the remedial measures from the date the remedial measures enter into effect until the date of the delivery of the arbitration ruling.
2. The level of suspension of obligations requested by the complaining Party and the determination of the level of suspension of obligations by the arbitration tribunal shall be based on facts demonstrating that the nullification or impairment arises directly from the application of the remedial measure and affects specific goods, service suppliers, investors or other economic actors and not merely on allegation, conjecture or remote possibility.

3. The level of nullified or impaired benefits requested by the complaining Party or determined by the arbitration tribunal:

   (a)   shall not include punitive damages, interest or hypothetical losses of profits or business opportunities;

   (b)   shall be reduced by any prior refunds of duties, indemnification of damages or other forms of compensation already received by the concerned operators or the concerned Party; and

   (c)   shall not include the contribution to the nullification or impairment by wilful or negligent action or omission of the concerned Party or any person or entity in relation to whom remedies are sought pursuant to the intended suspension of obligations.

Article INST.34D: Conditions for rebalancing, remedial, compensatory and safeguard measures

Where a Party takes a measure under Article 3.12 [Remedial measures] of Chapter three [Subsidy control] or Article 9.4 [Rebalancing] of Chapter nine [Institutional provisions] of Title XI [Level playing field for open and fair competition and sustainable development] of Heading One [Trade], Article ROAD.11 [Remedial measures] of Heading Three [Road transport], Article FISH.9 [Compensatory measures in case of withdrawal or reduction of access] or Article FISH.14 [Remedial measures and

dispute resolution] of Heading Five of Part Two or Article INST.36 [Safeguards] of Title III of Part Six, that measure shall only be applied in respect of covered provisions within the meaning of Article INST.10 [Scope] and shall comply, mutatis mutandis, with the conditions set out in Article INST.24(3) [Temporary remedies].

TITLE II: BASIS FOR COOPERATION

[7.105]

Article COMPROV.4: Democracy, rule of law and human rights

1. The Parties shall continue to uphold the shared values and principles of democracy, the rule of law, and respect for human rights, which underpin their domestic and international policies. In that regard, the Parties reaffirm their respect for the Universal Declaration of Human Rights and the international human rights treaties to which they are parties.

2. The Parties shall promote ough shared values and principles in international forums. The Parties shall cooperate in promoting those values and principles, including with or in third countries.

Article COMPROV.5: Fight against climate change

1. The Parties consider that climate change represents an existential threat to humanity and reiterate their commitment to strengthening the global response to this threat. The fight against human-caused climate change as elaborated in the United Nations Framework Convention on Climate Change (UNFCCC) process, and in particular in the Paris Agreement adopted by the Conference of the Parties to the United Nations Framework Convention on Climate Change at its 21st session (the "Paris Agreement"), inspires the domestic and external policies of the Union and the United Kingdom. Accordingly, each Party shall respect the Paris Agreement and the process set up by the UNFCCC and refrain from acts or omissions that would materially defeat the object and purpose of the Paris Agreement.

2. The Parties shall advocate the fight against climate change in international forums, including by engaging with other countries and regions to increase their level of ambition in the reduction of greenhouse emissions.

Article COMPROV.6: Countering proliferation of weapons of mass destruction

1. The Parties consider that the proliferation of weapons of mass destruction (WMD) and their means of delivery, to both state and non-state actors, represents one of the most serious threats to international stability and security. The Parties therefore agree to cooperate and to contribute to countering the proliferation of weapons of mass destruction and their means of delivery through full compliance with and national implementation of existing obligations under international disarmament and non-proliferation treaties and agreements and other relevant international obligations.

2. The Parties, furthermore, agree to cooperate on and to contribute to countering the proliferation of weapons of mass destruction and their means of delivery by:

   (a)   taking steps to sign, ratify, or accede to, as appropriate, and fully implement all other relevant international instruments; and

   (b)   establishing an effective system of national export controls, controlling the export as well as transit of WMD-related goods, including a WMD end-use control on dual use technologies and containing effective sanctions for breaches of export controls.

3. The Parties agree to establish a regular dialogue on those matters.

Article COMPROV.7: Small arms and light weapons and other conventional weapons

1. The Parties recognise that the illicit manufacture, transfer and circulation of small arms and light weapons (SALW), including their ammunition, their excessive accumulation, their poor management, inadequately secured stockpiles and their uncontrolled spread continue to pose a serious threat to peace and international security.

2. The Parties agree to observe and fully implement their respective obligations to deal with the illicit trade in SALW, including their ammunition, under existing international agreements and UN Security Council resolutions, as well as their respective commitments within the framework of other international instruments applicable in this area, such as the UN Programme of Action to prevent, combat and eradicate the illicit trade in SALW in all its aspects.

3. The Parties recognise the importance of domestic control systems for the transfer of conventional arms in line with existing international standards. The Parties recognise the importance of applying such controls in a responsible manner, as a contribution to international and regional peace, security and stability, and to the reduction of human suffering, as well as to the prevention of diversion of conventional weapons.

4. The Parties undertake, in that regard, to fully implement the Arms Trade Treaty and to cooperate with each other within the framework of that Treaty, including in promoting the universalisation and full implementation of that Treaty by all UN member states.

Part 7   Key Brexit Materials

5. The Parties therefore undertake to cooperate in their efforts to regulate or improve the regulation of international trade in conventional arms and to prevent, combat and eradicate the illicit trade in arms.

6. The Parties agree to establish a regular dialogue on those matters.

Article COMPROV.8: The most serious crimes of concern to the international community

1. The Parties reaffirm that the most serious crimes of concern to the international community as a whole must not go unpunished and that their effective prosecution must be ensured by taking measures at the national level and by enhancing international cooperation, including with the International Criminal Court. The Parties agree to fully support the universality and integrity of the Rome Statute of the International Criminal Court and related instruments.

2. The Parties agree to establish a regular dialogue on those matters.

Article COMPROV.9: Counter-terrorism

1. The Parties shall cooperate at the bilateral, regional and international levels to prevent and combat acts of terrorism in all its forms and manifestations in accordance with international law, including, where applicable, international counterterrorism-related agreements, international humanitarian law and international human rights law, as well as in accordance with the principles of the Charter of the United Nations.

2. The Parties shall enhance cooperation on counter-terrorism, including preventing and countering violent extremism and the financing of terrorism, with the aim of advancing their common security interests, taking into account the United Nations Global Counter-Terrorism Strategy and relevant United Nations Security Council resolutions, without prejudice to law enforcement and judicial cooperation in criminal matters and intelligence exchanges.

3. The Parties agree to establish a regular dialogue on those matters. This dialogue will, *inter alia*, aim to promote and facilitate:

    (a) the sharing of assessments on the terrorist threat;

    (b) the exchange of best practices and expertise on counter terrorism;

    (c) operational cooperation and exchange of information; and

    (d) exchanges on cooperation in the framework of multilateral organisations.

Article COMPROV.10: Personal data protection

1. The Parties affirm their commitment to ensuring a high level of personal data protection. They shall endeavour to work together to promote high international standards.

2. The Parties recognise that individuals have a right to the protection of personal data and privacy and that high standards in this regard contribute to trust in the digital economy and to the development of trade, and are a key enabler for effective law enforcement cooperation. To that end, the Parties shall undertake to respect, each in the framework of their respective laws and regulations, the commitments they have made in this Agreement in connection with that right.

3. The Parties shall cooperate at bilateral and multilateral levels, while respecting their respective laws and regulations. Such cooperation may include dialogue, exchanges of expertise, and cooperation on enforcement, as appropriate, with respect to personal data protection.

4. Where this Agreement or any supplementing agreement provide for the transfer of personal data, such transfer shall take place in accordance with the transferring Party's rules on international transfers of personal data. For greater certainty, this paragraph is without prejudice to the application of any specific provisions in this Agreement relating to the transfer of personal data, in particular Article DIGIT.7 [Protection of personal data and privacy] and Article LAWGEN.4 [Protection of personal data], and to Title I of Part Six [Dispute Settlement]. Where needed, each Party will make best efforts, while respecting its rules on international transfers of personal data, to establish safeguards necessary for the transfer of personal data, taking into account any recommendations of the Partnership Council under point (h) of Article INST.1(4) [Partnership Council].

Article COMPROV.11: Global cooperation on issues of shared economic, environmental and social interest

1. The Parties recognise the importance of global cooperation to address issues of shared economic, environmental and social interest. Where it is in their mutual interest, they shall promote multilateral solutions to common problems.

2. While preserving their decision-making autonomy, and without prejudice to other provisions of this Agreement or any supplementing agreement, the Parties shall endeavour to cooperate on current and emerging global issues of common interest such as peace and security, climate change, sustainable development, cross-border pollution, environmental protection, digitalisation, public health and consumer protection, taxation, financial stability, and free and fair trade and investment. To that end, they shall endeavour to maintain a constant and effective dialogue and to coordinate their positions in multilateral organisations and forums in which the Parties participate, such as the United Nations, the Group of Seven (G-7) and the Group of Twenty (G-20), the Organisation for Economic Co-operation and Development, the International Monetary Fund, the World Bank and the World Trade Organization.

Article COMPROV.12: Essential elements

Article COMPROV.4(1) [Democracy, rule of law and human rights], Article COMPROV.5(1) [Fight against climate change] and Article COMPROV.6(1) [Countering proliferation of weapons of mass destruction] constitute essential elements of the partnership established by this Agreement and any supplementing agreement.

TITLE III: FULFILLMENT OF OBLIGATIONS AND SAFEGUARD MEASURES

[7.106]
Article INST.35: Fulfilment of obligations described as essential elements
1. If either Party considers that there has been a serious and substantial failure by the other Party to fulfil any of the obligations that are described as essential elements in Article COMPROV.12 [Essential elements], it may decide to terminate or suspend the operation of this Agreement or any supplementing agreement in whole or in part.
2. Before doing so, the Party invoking the application of this Article shall request that the Partnership Council meet immediately, with a view to seeking a timely and mutually agreeable solution. If no mutually agreeable solution is found within 30 days from the date of the request to the Partnership Council, the Party may take the measures referred to in paragraph 1.
3. The measures referred to in paragraph 1 shall be in full respect of international law and shall be proportionate. Priority shall be given to the measures which least disturb the functioning of this Agreement and of any supplementing agreements.
4. The Parties consider that, for a situation to constitute a serious and substantial failure to fulfil any of the obligations described as essential elements in Article COMPROV.12 [Essential Elements], its gravity and nature would have to be of an exceptional sort that threatens peace and security or that has international repercussions. For greater certainty, an act or omission which materially defeats the object and purpose of the Paris Agreement shall always be considered as a serious and substantial failure for the purposes of this Article.

Article INST.36: Safeguard measures
1. If serious economic, societal or environmental difficulties of a sectorial or regional nature, including in relation to fishing activities and their dependent communities, that are liable to persist arise, the Party concerned may unilaterally take appropriate safeguard measures. Such safeguard measures shall be restricted with regard to their scope and duration to what is strictly necessary in order to remedy the situation. Priority shall be given to those measures which will least disturb the functioning of this Agreement.
2. The Party concerned shall, without delay, notify the other Party through the Partnership Council and shall provide all relevant information. The Parties shall immediately enter into consultations in the Partnership Council with a view to finding a mutually agreeable solution.
3. The Party concerned may not take safeguard measures until one month has elapsed after the date of notification referred to in paragraph 2, unless the consultation procedure pursuant to paragraph 2 has been jointly concluded before the expiration of the stated time limit. When exceptional circumstances requiring immediate action exclude prior examination, the Party concerned may apply forthwith the safeguard measures strictly necessary to remedy the situation.
The Party concerned shall, without delay, notify the measures taken to the Partnership Council and shall provide all relevant information.
4. If a safeguard measure taken by the Party concerned creates an imbalance between the rights and obligations under this Agreement or under any supplementing agreement, the other Party may take such proportionate rebalancing measures as are strictly necessary to remedy the imbalance. Priority shall be given to those measures which will least disturb the functioning of this Agreement. Paragraphs 2 to 4 shall apply *mutatis mutandis* to such rebalancing measures.
5. Either Party may, without having prior recourse to consultations pursuant to Article INST.13 [Consultations], initiate the arbitration procedure referred to in Article INST.14 [Arbitration procedure] to challenge a measure taken by the other Party in application of paragraphs 1 to 5 of this Article.
6. The safeguard measures referred to in paragraph 1 and the rebalancing measures referred to in paragraph 5 may also be taken in relation to a supplementing agreement, unless otherwise provided therein.

PART SEVEN:
FINAL PROVISIONS

[7.107]
Article FINPROV.1: Territorial scope
1. This Agreement applies to:
    (a) the territories to which the Treaty on European Union and the Treaty on the Functioning of the European Union and the Treaty establishing the European Atomic Energy Community are applicable, and under the conditions laid down in those Treaties; and
    (b) the territory of the United Kingdom.
2. This Agreement also applies to the Bailiwick of Guernsey, the Bailiwick of Jersey and the Isle of Man to the extent set out in Heading Five [Fisheries] and Article OTH.9 [Geographical application] of Heading Six [Other provisions] of Part Two of this Agreement.
3. This Agreement shall neither apply to Gibraltar nor have any effects in that territory.
4. This Agreement does not apply to the overseas territories having special relations with the United Kingdom: Anguilla; Bermuda; British Antarctic Territory; British Indian Ocean Territory; British Virgin Islands; Cayman Islands; Falkland Islands; Montserrat; Pitcairn, Henderson, Ducie and Oeno Islands; Saint Helena, Ascension and Tristan da Cunha; South Georgia and the South Sandwich Islands; and Turks and Caicos Islands.

Article FINPROV.2: Relationship with other agreements
This Agreement and any supplementing agreement apply without prejudice to any earlier bilateral agreement between the United Kingdom of the one part and the Union and the European Atomic Energy Community of the other part. The Parties reaffirm their obligations to implement any such Agreement.

Part 7   Key Brexit Materials

Article FINPROV.3: Review
The Parties shall jointly review the implementation of this Agreement and supplementing agreements and any matters related thereto five years after the entry into force of this Agreement and every five years thereafter.

Article FINPROV.6: Classified information and sensitive non-classified information
Nothing in this Agreement or in any supplementing agreement shall be construed as requiring a Party to make available classified information.

Classified information or material provided by or exchanged between the Parties under this Agreement or any supplementing agreement shall be handled and protected in compliance with the Agreement on security procedures for exchanging and protecting classified information and any implementing arrangement concluded under it.

The Parties shall agree upon handling instructions to ensure the protection of sensitive non-classified information exchanged between them.

Article FINPROV.7: Integral parts of this Agreement
1. The Protocols, Annexes, Appendices and footnotes to this Agreement shall form an integral part of this Agreement.
2. Each of the Annexes to this Agreement, including its appendices, shall form an integral part of the Section, Chapter, Title, Heading or Protocol that refers to that Annex or to which reference is made in that Annex. For greater certainty:
   (a) Annex INST-X [RULES OF PROCEDURE OF THE PARTNERSHIP COUNCIL AND COMMITTEES] forms an integral part of Title III [Institutional provisions] of Part One;
   (b) Annexes ORIG-1 [INTRODUCTORY NOTES TO PRODUCT SPECIFIC RULES OF ORIGIN], ORIG-2 [PRODUCT SPECIFIC RULES OF ORIGIN], ORIG-2A [ORIGIN QUOTAS AND ALTERNATIVES TO THE PRODUCT-SPECIFIC RULES OF ORIGIN IN ANNEX ORIG-2], ORIG-2B [TRANSITIONAL PRODUCT-SPECIFIC RULES FOR ELECTRIC ACCUMULATORS AND ELECTRIFIED VEHICLES], ORIG-3 [SUPPLIER's DECLARATION], ORIG-4 [TEXT OF THE STATEMENT OF ORIGIN], ORIG-5 [JOINT DECLARATION CONCERNING THE PRINCIPALITY OF ANDORRA] and ORIG-6 [JOINT DECLARATION CONCERNING THE REPUBLIC OF SAN MARINO] form an integral part of Chapter two [Rules of Origin] of Title I of Heading One of Part Two;
   (c) Annex SPS-1 [CRITERIA REFERRED TO IN ARTICLE SPS.19(d)] forms an integral part of Chapter Three [Sanitary and Phytosanitary Measures] of Title I of Heading One of Part Two;
   (d) Annex TBT-XX [ARRANGEMENT REFERRED TO IN ARTICLE TBT.9(4) FOR THE REGULAR EXCHANGE OF INFORMATION IN RELATION TO THE SAFETY OF NON-FOOD PRODUCTS AND RELATED PREVENTIVE, RESTRICTIVE AND CORRECTIVE MEASURES], Annex TBT-ZZ [ARRANGEMENT REFERRED TO IN ARTICLE TBT.9(5) FOR THE REGULATORY EXCHANGE OF INFORMATION REGARDING MEASURES TAKEN ON NON-COMPLIANT NON-FOOD PRODUCTS, OTHER THAN THOSE COVERED BY ARTICLE TBT.9(4), Annex TBT-1 [MOTOR VEHICLES AND EQUIPMENT AND PARTS THEREOF], Annex TBT-2 [MEDICINAL PRODUCTS], Annex TBT-3 [CHEMICALS], Annex TBT-4 [ORGANIC PRODUCTS] and Annex TBT-5 [TRADE IN WINE] form an integral part of Chapter Four [Technical Barriers to Trade] of Title I of Heading One of Part Two;
   (e) Annex CUSTMS-1 [AUTHORISED ECONOMIC OPERATORS] forms an integral part of Chapter Five [Customs and trade facilitation] of Title I of Heading One of Part Two;
   (f) Annexes SERVIN-1 [EXISTING MEASURES], SERVIN-2 [FUTURE MEASURES], SERVIN-3 [BUSINESS VISITORS FOR ESTABLISHMENT PURPOSES, INTRA-CORPORATE TRANSFEREES AND SHORT-TERM BUSINESS VISITORS], SERVIN-4 [CONTRACTUAL SERVICE SUPPLIERS AND INDEPENDENT PROFESSIONALS], SERVIN-5 [MOVEMENT OF NATURAL PERSONS] and SERVIN-6 [GUIDELINES FOR ARRANGEMENTS ON THE RECOGNITION OF PROFESSIONAL QUALIFICATIONS] form an integral part of Title II [Services and Investment] of Heading One of Part Two;
   (g) Annex PPROC-1 [PUBLIC PROCUREMENT] forms an integral part of Title VI [Public procurement] of Heading One of Part Two;
   (h) Annexes ENER-1 [LISTS OF ENERGY GOODS, HYDROCARBONS AND RAW MATERIALS], ENER-2 [ENERGY AND ENVIRONMENTAL SUBSIDIES], ENER-3 [NON-APPLICATION OF THIRD-PARTY ACCESS AND OWNERSHIP UNBUNDLING TO INFRASTRUCTURE] and ENER-4 [ALLOCATION OF ELECTRICITY INTERCONNECTOR CAPACITY AT THE DAY-AHEAD MARKET TIMEFRAME] form an integral part of Title VIII [Energy] of Heading One of Part Two;
   (i) Annex ENER-2 [ENERGY AND ENVIRONMENTAL SUBSIDIES] forms an integral part of Title XI [LPFOFCSD] of Heading One of Part Two;
   (j) Annex AVSAF-1 [AIRWORTHINESS AND ENVIRONMENT CERTIFICATION] and any annex adopted in accordance with Article AVSAF.12 [Adoption and amendments of Annexes to this Title] form an integral part of Title Two [Aviation safety] of Heading Two of Part Two;
   (k) Annex ROAD-1 [TRANSPORT OF GOODS BY ROAD] forms an integral part of Title I [Transport of goods by road] of Heading Three of Part Two;
   (l) Annexes ROAD-2 [MODEL OF AUTHORISATION FOR AN INTERNATIONAL REGULAR AND SPECIAL REGULAR SERVICE], ROAD-3 [MODEL OF APPLICATION FOR AN AUTHORISATION FOR AN INTERNATIONAL REGULAR AND SPECIAL REGULAR SERVICE] and ROAD-4 [MODEL OF JOURNEY FORM FOR OCCASIONAL SERVICES] form an integral part of Title II [Transport of passengers by road] of Heading Three of Part Two;
   (m) [Annexes FISH.1, FISH.2, FISH.3 and FISH.4 [PROTOCOL ON ACCESS TO WATERS] form an integral part of Heading Five [Fisheries] of Part Two]];
   (n) Annex LAW-1 [EXCHANGES OF DNA, FINGERPRINTS AND VEHICLE REGISTRATION DATA] forms an integral part of Title II [Exchanges of DNA, fingerprints and vehicle registration data] of Part Three;

(o) Annex LAW-2 [PASSENGER NAME RECORD DATA] forms an integral part of Title III [Transfer and processing of passenger name record data] of Part Three;

(p) Annex LAW-3 [FORMS OF CRIME FOR WHICH EUROPOL IS COMPETENT] forms an integral part of Title V [Cooperation with Europol] of Part Three;

(q) Annex LAW-4 [FORMS OF SERIOUS CRIME FOR WHICH EUROJUST IS COMPETENT] forms an integral part of Title VI [Cooperation with Eurojust] of Part Three;

(r) Annex LAW-5 [ARREST WARRANT] forms an integral part of Title VII [Surrender] of Part Three;

(s) Annex LAW-6 [EXCHANGE OF CRIMINAL RECORD INFORMATION – TECHNICAL AND PROCEDURAL SPECIFICATIONS] forms an integral part of Title IX [Exchange of criminal record information] of Part Three;

(t) Annex LAW-7 [DEFINITION OF TERRORISM] forms an integral part of Title III [Transfer and processing of passenger name record data], Title VII [Surrender] and Title XI [Freezing and confiscation] of Part Three;

(u) Annex LAW-8 [FREEZING AND CONFISCATION] forms an integral part of Title XI [Freezing and confiscation] of Part Three;

(v) Annex UNPRO-1 [IMPLEMENTATION OF THE FINANCIAL CONDITIONS [Article UNPRO.2.1.11]] forms an integral part of Section 2 [Rules for financing the participation in Union programmes and activities] of Chapter one of Part Five [Participation in Union programmes, sound financial management and financial provisions];

(w) Annex INST-X [RULES OF PROCEDURE FOR DISPUTE SETTLEMENT] and Annex INST-X [CODE OF CONDUCT FOR ARBITRATORS] form an integral part of Title I [Dispute Settlement] of Part Six;

(x) the ANNEX TO THE PROTOCOL ON ADMINISTRATIVE COOPERATION AND COMBATING FRAUD IN THE FIELD OF VALUE ADDED TAX AND ON MUTUAL ASSISTANCE FOR THE RECOVERY OF CLAIMS RELATING TO TAXES AND DUTIES forms an integral part of the Protocol on administrative cooperation and combating fraud in the field of value added tax and on mutual assistance for the recovery of claims relating to taxes and duties;

(y) Annexes SSC-1 [CERTAIN BENEFITS IN CASH TO WHICH THE PROTOCOL SHALL NOT APPLY], SSC-2 [RESTRICTION OF RIGHTS TO BENEFITS IN KIND FOR MEMBERS OF THE FAMILY OF A FRONTIER WORKER], SSC-3 [MORE RIGHTS FOR PENSIONERS RETURNING TO THE COMPETENT STATE], SSC-4 [CASES IN WHICH THE PRO RATA CALCULATION SHALL BE WAIVED OR SHALL NOT APPLY], SSC-5 [BENEFITS AND AGREEMENTS WHICH ALLOW THE APPLICATION OF ARTICLE SSC.49 [Overlapping of benefits of the same kind]], SSC-6 [SPECIAL PROVISIONS FOR THE APPLICATION OF THE LEGISLATION OF THE MEMBER STATES AND OF THE UNITED KINGDOM], SSC-7 [IMPLEMENTING PART] and SSC-8 [TRANSITIONAL PROVISIONS REGARDING THE APPLICATION OF ARTICLE SSC.11 [DETACHED WORKERS]] and their Appendices form an integral part of the Protocol on Social Security Coordination.

Article FINPROV.8: Termination

Either Party may terminate this Agreement by written notification through diplomatic channels. This Agreement and any supplementing agreement shall cease to be in force on the first day of the twelfth month following the date of notification.

Article FINPROV.9: Authentic texts

This Agreement shall be drawn up in duplicate in the Bulgarian, Croatian, Czech, Danish, Dutch, English, Estonian, Finnish, French, German, Greek, Hungarian, Irish, Italian, Latvian, Lithuanian, Maltese, Polish, Portuguese, Romanian, Slovak, Slovenian, Spanish and Swedish languages. By 30 April 2021, all language versions of the Agreement shall be subject to a process of final legal revision. Notwithstanding the previous sentence, the process of final legal revision for the English version of the Agreement shall be finalised at the latest by the day referred to in Article FINPROV.11(1) [Entry into force and provisional application] if that day is earlier than 30 April 2021.

The language versions resulting from the above process of final legal revision shall replace ab initio the signed versions of the Agreement and shall be established as authentic and definitive by exchange of diplomatic notes between the Parties.

Article FINPROV.10: Future accessions to the Union

1. The Union shall notify the United Kingdom of any new request for accession of a third country to the Union. 2. During the negotiations between the Union and a third country regarding the accession of that country to the Union[86], the Union shall endeavour to: (a) on request of the United Kingdom and, to the extent possible, provide any information regarding any matter covered by this Agreement and any supplementing agreement; and

(b) take into account any concerns expressed by the United Kingdom. 3. The Partnership Council shall examine any effects of accession of a third country to the Union on this Agreement and any supplementing agreement sufficiently in advance of the date of such accession. 4. To the extent necessary, the United Kingdom and the Union shall, before the entry into force of the agreement on the accession of a third country to the Union: (a) amend this Agreement or any supplementing agreement, (b) put in place by decision of the Partnership Council any other necessary adjustments or transitional arrangements regarding this Agreement or any supplementing agreement;

(c) decide within the Partnership Council whether:
    (i) to apply Article VSTV.1 [Visas for short visits] to the nationals of that third country; or
    (ii) to establish transitional arrangements as regards Article VSTV.1 [Visas for short visits] in relation to that third country and its nationals once it accedes to the Union.

5. In the absence of a decision under point (c)(i) or (ii) of paragraph 4 by the entry into force of the agreement on the accession of the relevant third country to the Union, Article VSTV.1 [Visas for short visits] shall not apply to nationals of that third country.

6. In the event that the Partnership Council establishes transitional arrangements as referred to in point (c)(ii) of paragraph 4, it shall specify their duration. The Partnership Council may extend the duration of those transitional arrangements.

7. Before the expiry of the transitional arrangements referred to in point (c)(ii) of paragraph 4, the Partnership Council shall decide whether to apply Article VSTV.1 [Visas for short visits] to the nationals of that third country from the end of the transitional arrangements. In the absence of such a decision Article VSTV.1 [Visas for short visits] shall not apply in relation to the nationals of that third country from the end of the transitional arrangements.

8. Point (c) of paragraph 4, and paragraphs 5 to 7 are without prejudice to the Union's prerogatives under its domestic legislation.

9. For greater certainty, without prejudice to point (c) of paragraph 4 and paragraphs 5 to 7, this Agreement shall apply in relation to a new Member State of the Union from the date of accession of that new Member State to the Union.

Article FINPROV.10A: Interim provision for transmission of personal data to the United Kingdom

1. For the duration of the specified period, transmission of personal data from the Union to the United Kingdom shall not be considered as transfer to a third country under Union law, provided that the data protection legislation of the United Kingdom on 31 December 2020, as it is saved and incorporated into United Kingdom law by the European Union (Withdrawal) Act 2018 and as

modified by the Data Protection, Privacy and Electronic Communications (Amendments etc) (EU Exit) Regulations 2019[87] ("the applicable data protection regime"), applies and provided that the United Kingdom does not exercise the designated powers without the agreement of the Union within the Partnership Council.

2. Subject to paragraphs 3 to 11, paragraph 1 shall also apply in respect of transfers of personal data from Iceland, the Principality of Liechtenstein and the Kingdom of Norway to the United Kingdom during the specified period made under Union law as applied in those states by the Agreement on the European Economic Area done at Porto on 2 May 1992, for so long as paragraph 1 applies to transfers of personal data from the Union to the United Kingdom, provided that those states notify both Parties in writing of their express acceptance to apply this provision.

3. In this Article, the "designated powers" means the powers:
   (a) to make regulations pursuant to sections 17A, 17C and 74A of the UK Data Protection Act 2018;
   (b) to issue a new document specifying standard data protection clauses pursuant to section 119A of the UK Data Protection Act 2018;
   (c) to approve a new draft code of conduct pursuant to Article 40(5) of the UK GDPR, other than a code of conduct which cannot be relied on to provide appropriate safeguards for transfers of personal data to a third country under Article 46(2)(e) of the UK GDPR;
   (d) to approve new certification mechanisms pursuant to Article 42(5) of the UK GDPR, other than certification mechanisms which cannot be relied on to provide appropriate safeguards for transfers of personal data to a third country under Article 46(2)(f) of the UK GDPR;
   (e) to approve new binding corporate rules pursuant to Article 47 of the UK GDPR;
   (f) to authorise new contractual clauses referred to in Article 46(3)(a) of the UK GDPR; or
   (g) to authorise new administrative arrangements referred to in Article 46(3)(b) of the UK GDPR.

4. The "specified period" begins on the date of entry into force of this Agreement and, subject to paragraph 5, ends:
   (a) on the date on which adequacy decisions in relation to the UK are adopted by the European Commission under Article 36(3) of Directive (EU) 2016/680 and under Article 45(3) of Regulation (EU) 2016/679, or
   (b) on the date four months after the specified period begins, which period shall be extended by two further months unless one of the Parties objects;
whichever is earlier.

5. Subject to paragraphs 6 and 7, if, during the specified period, the United Kingdom amends the applicable data protection regime or exercises the designated powers without the agreement of the Union within the Partnership Council, the specified period shall end on the date on which the powers are exercised or the amendment comes into force.

6. The references to exercising the designated powers in paragraphs 1 and 5 do not include the exercise of such powers the effect of which is limited to alignment with the relevant Union data protection law.

7. Anything that would otherwise be an amendment to the applicable data protection regime which is:
   (a) made with the agreement of the Union within the Partnership Council; or
   (b) limited to alignment with the relevant Union data protection law;
shall not be treated as an amendment to the applicable data protection regime for the purposes of paragraph 5 and instead should be treated as being part of the applicable data protection regime for the purposes of paragraph 1.

8. For the purposes of paragraphs 1, 5 and 7, "the agreement of the Union within the Partnership Council" means:
   (a) a decision of the Partnership Council as described in paragraph 11; or
   (b) deemed agreement as described in paragraph 10.

9. Where the United Kingdom notifies the Union that it proposes to exercise the designated powers or proposes to amend the applicable data protection regime, either party may request, within five working days, a meeting of the Partnership Council which must take place within two weeks of such request.

10. If no such meeting is requested, the Union is deemed to have given agreement to such exercise or amendment during the specified period.

11. If such a meeting is requested, at that meeting the Partnership Council shall consider the proposed exercise or amendment and may adopt a decision stating that it agrees to the exercise or amendment during the specified period.

12. The United Kingdom shall, as far as is reasonably possible, notify the Union when, during the specified period, it enters into a new instrument which can be relied on to transfer personal data to a third country under Article 46(2)(a) of the UK GDPR or section 75(1)(a) of the UK Data Protection Act 2018 during the specified period. Following a notification by the United Kingdom under this paragraph, the Union may request a meeting of the Partnership Council to discuss the relevant instrument.

13. Title I [Dispute Settlement] of Part Six does not apply in respect of disputes regarding the interpretation and application of this Article.

Article FINPROV.11: Entry into force and provisional application

1. This Agreement shall enter into force on the first day of the month following that in which both Parties have notified each other that they have completed their respective internal requirements and procedures for establishing their consent to be bound.

2. The Parties agree to provisionally apply this Agreement from 1 January 2021 provided that prior to that date they have notified each other that their respective internal requirements and procedures necessary for provisional application have been completed. Provisional application shall cease on one of the following dates, whichever is the earliest:

   (a)   28 February 2021 or another date as decided by the Partnership Council; or

   (b)   the day referred to in paragraph 1.

3. As from the date from which this Agreement is provisionally applied, the Parties shall understand references in this Agreement to "the date of entry into force of this Agreement" or to "the entry into force of this Agreement" as references to the date from which this Agreement is provisionally applied.

NOTES

  86   For greater certainty, paragraphs 2 to 9 apply in respect of negotiations between the Union and a third country for accession to the Union taking place after the entry into force of this Agreement, notwithstanding the fact a request for accession took place before the entry into force of this Agreement.

  87   As amended by the Data Protection, Privacy and Electronic Communications (Amendments etc) (EU Exit) Regulations 2020.

DECLARATIONS REFERRED TO IN THE COUNCIL DECISION ON THE SIGNING ON BEHALF OF THE UNION, AND ON A PROVISIONAL APPLICATION OF THE TRADE AND COOPERATION AGREEMENT AND OF THE AGREEMENT CONCERNING SECURITY PROCEDURES FOR EXCHANGING AND PROTECTING CLASSIFIED INFORMATION

[7.108]

NOTES

Date of publication in OJ: OJ L444, 31.12.2020, p 1475. Only the Declaration in relation to data protection is relevant to this Handbook; and the other Declarations have been omitted. The full document is also available at: EU-UK_Declarations_24.12.2020. pdf (publishing.service.gov.uk).

© European Union, 1998–2021.

DECLARATION ON THE ADOPTION OF ADEQUACY DECISIONS WITH RESPECT TO THE UNITED KINGDOM

The Parties take note of the European Commission's intention to promptly launch the procedure for the adoption of adequacy decisions with respect to the UK under the General Data Protection Regulation and the Law Enforcement Directive, and its intention to work closely to that end with the other bodies and institutions involved in the relevant decision-making procedure.